THE FOUR-STAR ENCYCLOPEDIA OF WHO'S WHO IN HOLLYWOOD . . . FROM THE SILENT ERA TO THE PRESENT

"The perfect book for settling those 'wasn't he also in . . . ?' and 'didn't she also do . . . ?' conversations." —*Roanoke Times & World News*

"A volume that all film buffs will enjoy owning." —*Classic Images*

Leonard Maltin's Movie Encyclopedia constitutes a veritable who's who of film history. With more than 2,000 entries, it covers all of Hollywood's most beloved and most famous stars and hundreds of lesser-known actors, plus directors, writers, composers, cinematographers, and others in behind-the-scenes roles.

Whether you're interested in the cinema history of Meryl Streep or Bette Davis, Roy Rogers or Jean Gabin, D. W. Griffith or C. B. DeMille, Richard Widmark or Denzel Washington, all the information is here, including date and place of birth, names and dates of key films, outstanding parts, notable TV and stage appearances, nominations and awards, marriages and divorces, and when applicable, time and cause of death.

Thorough, informative, and entertaining to read, *Leonard Maltin's Movie Encyclopedia* is the perfect complement to his bestselling, annually updated *Movie & Video Guide*.

LEONARD MALTIN'S MOVIE ENCYCLOPEDIA

LEONARD MALTIN is one of America's foremost film historians. After establishing himself with a series of definitive books (on topics ranging from Hollywood cameramen to the history of cartoons), he has become known to an even wider audience as the film critic and resident film buff on television's popular syndicated program *Entertainment Tonight*. He also hosts a daily radio program, *Leonard Maltin on Video*. Besides his *Movie & Video Guide*, which celebrated its twenty-fifth anniversary in print in 1994, his titles include *Of Mice and Magic: A History of American Animated Cartoons, The Great Movie Comedians, The Disney Films, The Art of the Cinematographer, Movie Comedy Teams, Selected Short Subjects (The Great Movie Shorts), The Whole Film Sourcebook,* and (as co-author) *The Little Rascals: The Life and Times of Our Gang.* He is a member of the Authors Guild, and serves on the Advisory Board of the Hollywood Entertainment Museum. Mr. Maltin lives, writes, and watches movies in Los Angeles, California.

EDITED BY LEONARD MALTIN

LEONARD
MALTIN'S
MOVIE
ENCYCLOPEDIA

Co-Editors
SPENCER GREEN • LUKE SADER

Research Editor
CATHLEEN ANDERSON

Research Associates
BEN HERNDON • DOUGLAS TODD

Contributing Editors
ED HULSE • BILL WARREN
ROB EDELMAN

Contributors
ROBERT S. BIRCHARD • DOUG BROD
RON GOLDBERG • GLENN KENNY
MICHAEL SCHLESINGER

A PLUME BOOK

PLUME

Published by the Penguin Group
Penguin Books USA Inc., 375 Hudson Street,
New York, New York 10014, U.S.A.
Penguin Books Ltd, 27 Wrights Lane,
London W8 5TZ, England
Penguin Books Australia Ltd, Ringwood,
Victoria, Australia
Penguin Books Canada Ltd, 10 Alcorn Avenue,
Toronto, Ontario, Canada M4V 3B2
Penguin Books (N.Z.) Ltd, 182–190 Wairau Road,
Auckland 10, New Zealand

Penguin Books Ltd, Registered Offices:
Harmondsworth, Middlesex, England

Published by Plume, an imprint of Dutton Signet,
a division of Penguin Books USA Inc.
Previously published in a Dutton edition.

First Plume Printing, November, 1995
10 9 8 7 6 5 4 3 2 1

Printed in the United States of America
Original hardcover design by Steven N. Stathakis

FOREWORD

I don't know how many claims I can make for the uniqueness of this volume, but it may well be the first reference book to have acquired information outside a bathroom.

One day this past spring, my wife, emerging from the ladies' room at our local movie theater, said jokingly, "If you have any questions for Kim Darby, I just ran into her."

"I *do* have a question for her!" I exclaimed—and waited so I could ask why some filmographies listed her as being in *Red Sky at Morning* (1970) when I could find no trace of her in the cast listing. (This dilemma had reared its head just two days earlier.) The friendly Miss Darby smiled and explained that she was under contract to Hal Wallis at the time and had been scheduled to make *Red Sky* but got out of her commitment in order to appear in *The Grissom Gang* for Robert Aldrich instead. Apparently one reference book cited her credit from an early cast announcement, and others repeated the error.

Until now! How many generations of film researchers will thank me for this, I do not know. But I *do* know that a reference book is made up of thousands upon thousands of such facts; some of them may seem unimportant in the greater scheme of things, but in truth, each one bears equal weight. The goal is simple: getting it right—all of it, if possible.

Why even attempt an encyclopedia of this kind? One motivation, I must admit, was a dissatisfaction with some similar books on the market: In this computer-driven age of information, techies believe that credit-sorting is a science. That's how one book folded credits for producer Bernard Schwartz into the films of Tony Curtis, who was born with that same name. Similarly, screenwriting credits for Arthur Marx turned up in the filmography of his uncle Harpo.

Another reason was to update and amplify the work of such yeomanly researchers as the late Ephraim Katz and Leslie Halliwell. No one who compiles this kind of book can fail to be in their debt.

My challenge was to produce an original work that would have a contemporary edge, without ignoring the past. Achieving that balance was difficult, I'll admit, given a finite page count, but I think my colleagues and I have managed to strike a fairly happy medium. John Singleton and Tilda Swinton are here, but so are Busby Berkeley and ZaSu Pitts. The emphasis is on the American mainstream, but we tried to include representative figures from the world of independent and documentary film—as well as key names from B movies of the past. I'm sorry we couldn't have included even more, in every field.

This book is intended as a film reference, but it seemed foolish to exclude a subject's major accomplishments in theater and television. I particularly wanted to acknowledge the huge arena of made-for-TV movies, which has been ignored in many reference books. In addition, a number of major directors have made music videos, which I thought worth mentioning, along with actors' credits for feature films released direct to home video.

I also felt it was important to add perspective to our write-ups so that they would offer more than a mere laundry list of credits. That's why so many actors' roles are described, and why significant achievements in every career are singled out.

Finally, I wanted to add sidelights and footnotes wherever possible to flesh out our entries. It's interesting to know that one of composer John Williams' early credits was playing piano on Henry Mancini's recording of the "Peter Gunn" theme; and that a theater in Southern California bears the name of actor Richard Basehart. While stopping this side of "trivia," I think these nuggets of information are both useful and fun.

Ah, but verifying all this information—that's another matter. Some facts are easy to find or double-check; others come out of left field. While I was waiting to interview Dorothy Lamour several years ago, the actress' assistant said to me, "You know, almost every reference book has her real name wrong." I asked how that was, and she explained that Lamour's first husband was a bandleader who used the stage name Herbie Kaye. His real name was

Kaumeyer, and somewhere along the line someone printed this as Lamour's maiden name. In fact, she was born Slaton. Only a chance conversation enabled me to avoid the error in this volume.

A similar bit of serendipity allowed me to learn that the late writer-director Richard Brooks had invented his own name. A colleague attended his memorial service, where this fact was publicly revealed for the first time; as a result, I believe I am the first to publish his given name, Ruben Sax.

Some errors are inevitable, it seems, in a work of this size and scope, but birth dates and birthplaces are a particular minefield. Look up a birth date for an actor in more than one sourcebook, and chances are you'll find at least one discrepancy—maybe two or three. We made literally hundreds of telephone calls all over the world to find, confirm, and reconfirm this information: to unions, agents, managers, publicists, parents, halls of records, and even the individuals themselves. (Sometimes, we caught people red-handed fibbing about their birth dates.)

While we're on the subject of dates, please note that for movies we cite the year of release in their country of origin, which may differ from their U.S. release dates. This is consistent with the method we use in the *Movie and Video Guide*.

To accumulate a thousand pages of verified information is no easy task, and I couldn't have accomplished it alone. No one person knows everything about every subject, and it was vital to have a broad base of input, as well as a system of cross-checks. I was lucky to call on a stalwart support team of film buffs and writers, many of whom also work with me on my *Movie and Video Guide*. Luke Sader's watchful eye, Cathleen Anderson's willingness to learn more than she ever wanted to know about who was born where and when, Ben Herndon's diligence, Bill Warren's search for *"le mot juste"* in every instance, all combined to strengthen the material in these pages. Without the erudite and fact-focused Spencer Green, however, this book might not exist at all; his willingness to devote himself to the project at a crucial moment made all the difference in the world. I can never thank him enough.

After the initial preparation and writing on this volume came what we laughingly referred to as the "finishing" stage. For the better part of a year, my life was not my own. I have a lot of catching up to do with my wife, Alice, and daughter, Jessie, but I know they share my pride in having completed the book you hold in your hands.

A procedural note: This book was completed during the latter part of 1993 and the first half of 1994. Every effort was made to keep our entries as current as possible, but for the most part we chose to leave out work in progress because so much can happen in a film's lifetime: people quit, people die, titles change, and so on. Every day I'd see items in *Daily Variety* and *The Hollywood Reporter* and want to add to our write-ups; after a while, I thought of the process as writing in quicksand. We did manage to incorporate a lot of up-to-date material, however, and I think this will help to make our book both vital and informative.

Thank you for joining us on our maiden voyage.

—LEONARD MALTIN
June 1994

LEONARD
MALTIN'S
M O V I E
ENCYCLOPEDIA

ABBOTT AND COSTELLO. Actors. (**Bud Abbott**—b. Oct. 2, 1895, Asbury Park, N.J., as William A. Abbott; d. Apr. 24, 1974. **Lou Costello**—b. Mar. 6, 1906, Paterson, N.J., as Louis Francis Cristillo; d. Mar. 3, 1959.) The most successful comedy team of the 1940s, Abbott and Costello consistently made the yearly list of filmdom's top 10 moneymakers, and while their popularity among moviegoers waned during the 1950s, the boys won over new generations of fans with a TV series and endless re-runs of their old movies.

Abbott—the tall, jowly, fast-talking straight man—was born to circus perform-ers but didn't have much success breaking into show business himself until 1931 when, as a Brooklyn theater cashier, he filled in for Costello's usual straight man. The short, chubby Costello—a former newsboy, soda jerk, and salesman whose brief, late 1920s fling in Hollywood only got him some stunt and extra work (in, among others, the 1927 Laurel & Hardy comedy *The Battle of the Century)*—developed an instant rapport with Abbott. They subsequently worked together in burlesque, vaudeville, on Broadway, and on radio, polishing their act to a high gloss, before getting their first joint Holly-wood opportunity in Universal's *One Night in the Tropics* (1940). Although they were only supporting players, they stole the show with their rapid-fire cross-talk routines (including the classic "Who's on First?").

Universal starred the team in a low-budget 1941 comedy, *Buck Privates;* its enormous (and unexpected) success con-vinced the studio they were bona-fide stars. *In the Navy, Hold That Ghost, Keep 'Em Flying* (also 1941), *Ride 'Em Cow-boy, Pardon My Sarong, Who Done It?* (all 1942), *It Ain't Hay, Hit the Ice* (both 1943), *In Society* (1944), and *Here Come the Co-eds* (1945) followed. The films were short on characterization, but long on slapstick (mostly featuring the agile Costello) and beautifully timed patter rou-tines (many of which were cleaned-up burlesque skits written or polished by their personal writer John Grant). MGM borrowed the team several times, for *Rio Rita* (1942, which saw the boys in roles taken by Wheeler & Woolsey in the 1929 original), *Lost in a Harem* (1944) and *Bud Abbott and Lou Costello in Hollywood* (1945), none of which achieved the suc-cess of the Universal efforts despite sig-nificantly higher production expenditures.

A restless Costello prodded Universal to break their formula, and the studio started experimenting with *The Naughty Nineties* (1945), a period piece that included a re-prise of "Who's on First?" *Little Giant* and the more successful *The Time of Their Lives* (both 1946) had Bud and Lou work-ing independently of each other. Subse-quent films were hit-and-miss: *The Wistful Widow of Wagon Gap, Buck Privates Come Home* (both 1947), a sequel to their first hit, *The Noose Hangs High* (1948), released by Eagle-Lion but produced at Universal (and a remake of a little-known studio B picture from 1939, *For Love or Money).* Then someone concocted *Abbott and Costello Meet Frankenstein* (1948). The blend of comedy and horror (with Frankenstein, Dracula, and The Wolf Man on hand) was just right, and the film pro-pelled Bud and Lou back to the top of the box-office heap. *Abbott and Costello Meet the Killer, Boris Karloff* (1949), *Abbott and Costello Meet the Invisible Man* (1951), *Abbott and Costello Meet Dr. Jekyll and Mr. Hyde* (1953, also costarring Karloff), and *Abbott and Costello Meet the Mummy* (1955) utilized the same format, albeit with progressively diminishing results.

None of the team's other starring vehicles—which included *Mexican Hay-ride* (1948, a curiously disemboweled ver-sion of a hit play with Cole Porter music), *Africa Screams* (1949), *Abbott and Costello in the Foreign Legion* (1950), *Comin' Round the Mountain* (1951), the kiddie-oriented *Jack and the Beanstalk, Lost in Alaska, Abbott and Costello Meet Captain Kidd* (all 1952), *Abbott and Costello Go to Mars* (1953), *Abbott and Costello Meet the Keystone Kops* (1955), and *Dance With Me, Henry* (1956)—was particularly noteworthy. By this time their popularity had been eclipsed by the youn-ger, wilder team of Martin and Lewis.

They still proved potent on TV, how-ever, on "The Colgate Comedy Hour" (1951–54) and "The Abbott and Costello Show" (1952–54), in the latter performing many of the routines originally written for their films. The team split up in 1956 and Lou, who reportedly harbored solo star-ring ambitions for years, top-lined the me-diocre *The 30-Foot Bride of Candy Rock* just before his death in 1959. Abbott, a lifelong epileptic whose steadily deteriorating health finally sent him to a nursing home, was reduced to poverty after the IRS nailed him for back taxes. He loaned his voice to a 1966 series of Abbott and Costello animated cartoons.

ABEL, WALTER. Actor. *(b. June 6, 1898, St. Paul, Minn.; d. March 26, 1987.)* "I'm not happy. I'm not happy at all." It was a catchphrase for a short time in the 1940s, and the man who spoke it—in the 1940 romance *Arise, My Love*—was this slender, dapper actor, who'd had a lengthy stage career going back to the late teens. Abel's first film appearance of note was in *Liliom* (1930), but his casting (some might say miscasting) as D'Artagnan in the 1935 version of *The Three Musketeers* brought him to Hollywood to stay. One of the most versatile screen actors of his day, Abel could play any role, comedic or dramatic, but seemed most effective in roles that called for him to be perplexed, jittery, or just downright distraught; in *Two in the Dark* (1936, one of his few starring vehicles), he's an amnesiac who thinks he may have committed a murder. Abel worked steadily through the post–World War 2 era, appearing in such films as *Fury* (1936), *Wise Girl* (1937), *Dance Girl Dance* (1940), *Hold Back the Dawn* (1941), *Star Spangled Rhythm* (as the studio chief at Paramount Pictures), *Holiday Inn* (both 1942), *Mr. Skeffington* (1944), *Kiss and Tell* (1945, as Shirley Temple's dad), *The Kid From Brooklyn* (1946), and *That Lady in Ermine* (1948). His later screen work includes stints in *Night People* (1954), *Raintree County* (1957), and *Mirage* (1965), as well as an occasional TV movie. He remained active into the 1980s, appearing with Katharine Hepburn in *The Ultimate Solution of Grace Quigley* (1984). He also hosted a weekly anthology series, "Suspicion" (1957–59).

ABRAHAM, F. MURRAY. Actor. *(b. Oct. 24, 1940, Pittsburgh, Pa.)* Tall, balding character actor of Arabic descent and intense presence. Originally a stage star, his movie career seems decidedly secondary, though he is always compelling, whether as the Abbie Hoffman–like fugitive in *The Big Fix* (1978), the Bolivian drug lord in *Scarface* (1983), or the frustrated composer Salieri (his Oscar-winning tour de force) in *Amadeus* (1984). Abraham demonstrated his comic ability with a hilarious turn as a gay bathhouse denizen in *The Ritz* (1976), his icy determination as an inquisitor in *The Name of the Rose* (1986), a convict in *An Innocent Man* (1989), and his prescience in working without billing in *The Bonfire of the Vanities* (1991), as the paranoid New York district attorney running for mayor. In 1993 he turned up in two spoofs, *National Lampoon's Loaded Weapon 1* and *Last Action Hero*, in which heavy-handed comic reference was made to his role as Salieri.

ABRAHAMS, JIM. Director, writer. *(b. May 10, 1944, Shorewood, Wis.)* As one-third of the "ZAZ" filmmaking triumverate (along with brothers David and Jerry Zucker), Abrahams can lay credit to cocreating some of the 1980s' best movie comedies. An improvisational comic like his partners, Abrahams entered the film business in 1977, when Hollywood beckoned ZAZ and the team wrote *The Kentucky Fried Movie* (which was directed by John Landis), a collection of sketches lampooning venerable pop-culture institutions. *Airplane!* (1980), *Top Secret!* (1984), *Ruthless People* (1986), and *The Naked Gun* (1988) followed, with the three partners sharing writing, producing, and directing chores. Abrahams struck out on his own with a Bette Midler-Lily Tomlin comedy, *Big Business* (1988), a conventional mistaken-identity farce. His *Welcome Home, Roxy Carmichael* (1990) failed to excite critics or customers, but he returned to form with *Hot Shots!* (1991), a *Top Gun* sendup very much in the old ZAZ tradition, and its 1993 sequel, *Hot Shots! Part Deux.*

ACKLAND, JOSS. Actor. *(b. Feb. 29, 1928, London.)* Jowly, unctuous British character actor, a stage veteran of nearly 50 years and a prolific screen actor since 1969, who only recently attracted attention from American critics and audiences. Ackland's performances as the decadent aristocrat in *White Mischief* (1987) and a corrupt South African official in *Lethal Weapon 2* (1989) made him, if not exactly a household name, a recognizable face to stateside moviegoers. Although his stage work includes Shakespeare and musical

comedy, film audiences seem to prefer him as a smug, stuffy, and generally villainous type.
OTHER FILMS INCLUDE: 1969: *Crescendo;* 1973: *England Made Me;* 1974: *The Black Windmill;* 1979: *Saint Jack;* 1987: *The Sicilian;* 1990: *The Hunt for Red October;* 1991: *The Object of Beauty;* 1992: *The Mighty Ducks;* 1993: *Nowhere to Run;* 1994: *Mother's Boys.*

ADAM, KEN. Production designer, art director. *(b. Feb. 5, 1921, Berlin.)* Wizardly designer who has added style and imagination to period pieces, futuristic films, realistic dramas, and even musicals. After studying architecture at London University, he worked as a draftsman on films like *The Brass Monkey* and *The Queen of Spades* (both 1948) and gradually assumed art direction chores on films including *Around the World in 80 Days* (1956, for which he received his first Oscar nomination), *The Angry Hills* (1959), and *The Trials of Oscar Wilde* (1960). He began his long association with the James Bond films on the very first one, *Dr. No* (1962), and as the series' budgets increased, Adam constructed more elaborate, spectacular sets for *Thunderball* (1965), *You Only Live Twice* (1967), *Diamonds Are Forever* (1971), *The Spy Who Loved Me* (1977, another Oscar nomination), and *Moonraker* (1979). He was also the production designer on the Harry Palmer spy films *The Ipcress File* (1965) and *Funeral in Berlin* (1966), as well as *Goodbye, Mr. Chips* (1969), *The Seven Percent Solution* (1976), *Agnes of God* (1985), *Crimes of the Heart* (1986), and *The Freshman* (1990). Some of Adam's most impressive work includes the expressionistic War Room from *Dr. Strangelove* (1964), the meticulously recreated 18th-century architecture of *Barry Lyndon* (1975, which won him the Oscar), the brilliantly stylized Edward Hopperesque settings of *Pennies From Heaven* (1981), and the witty, Oscar-nominated sets for *Addams Family Values* (1993). He received a second Oscar for *The Madness of King George* (1994).

ADAMS, BROOKE. Actress. *(b. Feb. 8, 1949, New York City.)* Dark-haired, girlish-looking leading lady whose career failed to develop as predicted by enthusiastic pundits. A child actress and ballet student, she debuted in a forgettable 1975 horror film, *Shock Waves,* but registered well as the lead in *Invasion of the Body Snatchers* and *Days of Heaven* (both 1978). Adams, who resembles Genevieve Bujold, was expected to go places, but most of her subsequent screen work has been insignificant, with the exception of *Key Exchange* (1985), in which she reprised her well-received stage role.
OTHER FILMS INCLUDE: 1979: *Cuba;* 1983: *The Dead Zone;* 1985: *The Stuff;* 1991: *The Unborn;* 1992: *Gas, Food Lodging.*

ADAMS, JULIE. Actress. *(b. Oct. 17, 1926, Waterloo, Iowa, as Betty May Adams.)* One wouldn't think to look to *Creature from the Black Lagoon* (1954) for lyrical moments, but the underwater pas de deux between the killer amphibian and this statuesque heroine is still a milestone of subtle eroticism. Adams, a former secretary, broke into films in the late 1940s, originally appearing under her given first name before changing it to Julia, then finally Julie. She was leading lady to sagebrush stars James Ellison and Russell Hayden in a series of six ultra-cheap Westerns, shot back to back over a four-week period in 1950. She was signed by Universal, where she remained confined to the range, putting her in both A and B oaters, among them *The Dalton Gang* (1949), *Bend of the River, Horizons West, The Lawless Breed* (all 1952), *Mississippi Gambler,* and *The Man From the Alamo* (both 1953); other roles in this period include small ones in *Red Hot and Blue* (1949) and *Hollywood Story* (1951). After *Creature,* she had more varied parts (including female leads) in the likes of *The Private War of Major Benson* (1955), *Slaughter on Tenth Avenue* (1957), *The Underwater City* (1962), *Tickle Me* (1965), *The Last Movie* (1971), *McQ* (1973), *The Wild McCulloughs* (1975), and *The Killer Inside Me* (1976). Her TV series include "Yancy Derringer" (1958–59), "The Jimmy Stewart Show" (1971–72, as his wife), and "Code Red" (1981–82). Adams continued to work on TV in the 1980s and had a recurring role on "Murder, She Wrote" in the early 1990s. She was married at one time to Ray Danton.

ADAMS, NICK. Actor. *(b. July 16, 1931, Nanticoke, Pa., as Nicholas Adamshock; d. Feb. 7, 1968.)* The poor man's James Dean (one of them, anyway), Adams appeared with that actor in *Rebel Without a Cause* (1955), and also played in *Picnic* and *Mister Roberts* that same year in small but noticeable supporting roles. A callow-looking actor whose stabs at "intensity" of performance usually came off as petulance, he did manage to snag an Oscar nomination for his role in *Twilight of Honor* (1963), and was popular as the star of TV's "The Rebel" (1959–62). By the mid 1960s he was reduced to leads in shabby horror and sci-fi films—including *Frankenstein Conquers the World* and *Monster Zero* (both 1966)—and his fatal overdose on prescription drugs was widely considered to be suicide.
OTHER FILMS INCLUDE: 1952: *Somebody Loves Me* (his first); 1956: *Our Miss Brooks;* 1958: *No Time for Sergeants;* 1959: *The FBI Story, Pillow Talk;* 1962: *The Interns;* 1963: *The Hook;* 1965: *Young Dillinger;* 1968: *Mission Mars* (his last).

ADJANI, ISABELLE. Actress. *(b. June 27, 1955, Paris.)* Dark French beauty whose early film appearances inspired critics on both sides of the Atlantic to hail her as "the next Jeanne Moreau." After making several TV commercials and feature films as a schoolgirl, Adjani joined the prestigious Comédie-Française in the early 1970s and attracted the attention of director François Truffaut, who cast her in the lead for 1975's *The Story of Adele H.* Oscar-nominated for that mature, intense performance, Adjani went on to star in several movies, including *The Tenant* (1976), *Nosferatu the Vampire,* and *The Brontë Sisters* (both 1979). Her two American-made films—*The Driver* (1978) and *Ishtar* (1988)—were memorable duds; these and other lackluster vehicles tarnished Adjani's reputation, but she restored its luster with a brilliant, Oscar-nominated performance in *Camille Claudel* (1989). She has a child with actor Daniel Day-Lewis.
OTHER FILMS INCLUDE: 1969: *Le Petit Bougnat* (her first); 1974: *The Slap;* 1981: *Possession, Quartet;* 1983: *One Deadly Summer;* 1985: *Subway;* 1993: *Toxic Affair;* 1994: *Queen Margot.*

ADLON, PERCY. Director, screenwriter. *(b. June 1, 1935, Munich.)* After studying art and theater history, Adlon worked in state-run theatres, in radio, and then television, for which he made documentaries. He directed the successful TV film *The Guardian and the Poet* (1979) and graduated to feature films with *Celeste* (1981, an account of the relationship between Marcel Proust and his housekeeper) and *Five Last Days* (1982). *The Swing* (1983), adapted from memoirs of a family in Bavaria, marked a more playful tone for Adlon, which was heightened in *Sugarbaby* (1985), a delightfully offbeat tale of a mortuary attendant (played by Marianne Sagebrecht) who tries to seduce a subway conductor. This was the first Adlon film to win attention in the U.S., and he earned critical praise for his off-center sensibilities, as well as his singular use of colors and unusual camera angles (and for the casting of the obese Sagebrecht in the starring role). Sagebrecht became, in fact, the central figure in his next two films as well, first as a stranger who is stuck at a California roadside diner in *Bagdad Cafe* (1988) and then as a spending-obsessed housewife in *Rosalie Goes Shopping* (1989). His latest, *Younger and Younger* (1993), is a typically unusual mix of drama, comedy, and fantasy set at a storage facility.

ADRIAN, IRIS. Actress. *(b. May 29, 1913, Los Angeles, as Iris Adrian Hostetter; d. Sept. 21, 1994.)* "Do ya think I got off the bus from Stupidsville last night?" With her peroxide-blond hair, shopworn looks, and nasal bray, this brassy, in-your-face comic actress could never be confused with Garbo or Dietrich. Which actually worked out just fine: She was one of the screen's most distinctive character actresses. A former beauty contest winner and Ziegfeld dancer, Adrian arrived in Hollywood at the dawn of the talkie era, and kept the sound engineers' ears ringing with her high-decibel renderings of strippers, molls, waitresses, and floozies. You couldn't miss her, but she's most noticeable in *Paramount on Parade* (1929), *Rumba* (1935), *Our Relations, Gold Diggers of 1937* (both 1936), *Go West* (1940), *Road to Zanzibar* (1941), *Roxie Hart* (as murderess Two Gun Gert), *Orchestra Wives* (both 1942), *Lady of Burlesque, His*

Butler's Sister (as one of the Sunshine Twins), *Action in the North Atlantic* (all 1943), *The Woman in the Window* (1944), *The Paleface* (1948), *My Favorite Spy* (1951), *The Fast and the Furious* (1954), *The Buccaneer* (1958), *Blue Hawaii, The Errand Boy* (both 1961), and *The Odd Couple* (1968). In later years, she became a staple in Disney pictures, notably *That Darn Cat* (1965), *The Love Bug* (1969), *Scandalous John* (1971), *The Apple Dumpling Gang* (1975), *The Shaggy D.A.* (1976), and *Freaky Friday* (1977). She was also a regular on "The Ted Knight Show" (1978).

AGAR, JOHN. Actor. *(b. Jan. 31, 1921, Chicago.)* Handsome, all-American leading man, mostly of inexpensive genre films of the 1950s. A World War 2 veteran, he won worldwide notoriety when he married Shirley Temple in 1946, and when John Ford cast her in *Fort Apache* (1948) he decided to use Agar as well. The following year he reteamed with Temple in *Adventure in Baltimore* and with John Wayne in Ford's *She Wore a Yellow Ribbon* and *Sands of Iwo Jima,* but his career stalled shortly thereafter. An acrimonious divorce and well-publicized bouts with booze relegated Agar to bland leading roles in B horror pictures such as *Tarantula* (1955), *The Mole People* (1956), and *The Brain From Planet Arous* (1958); his outrageous overacting in the latter film has made it something of a cult classic. He appeared with John Wayne in *Chisum* (1970) and *Big Jake* (1971) before taking minor roles in TV shows and doing promotional chores for Brunswick's Senior Bowling program. Young, TV-influenced directors of sci-fi epics have cast Agar—mostly for nostalgia appeal—in such films as *Miracle Mile* (1989) and *Nightbreed* (1990), among others.

AGUTTER, JENNY. Actress. *(b. Dec. 20, 1952, Taunton, England.)* Perennially cast in roles that exploit her understated sensuality, the wholesomely pretty Agutter began her film career at age 12 in *East of Sudan* (1964). Trained as a ballet dancer, she appeared in several inconsequential British productions before making her Hollywood debut in *Star!* (1968). Agutter was not yet 20 when she starred in Nicolas Roeg's controversial *Walkabout* (1971), playing a teenaged girl stranded in the Australian outback with an Aboriginal boy. Despite having won critical acclaim for her performance, Agutter didn't appear in significant mainstream films until resurfacing in *Logan's Run* (1976) and *The Eagle Has Landed* (1977). She was widely feted for her performance in *Equus* (1977), but her subsequent movie work has been sporadic. OTHER FILMS INCLUDE: 1981: *The Survivor, An American Werewolf in London;* 1984: *Secret Places;* 1987: *Dark Tower;* 1990: *King of the Wind, Child's Play 2;* 1992: *Freddie as F.R.O.7* (voice only).

AHERNE, BRIAN. Actor. *(b. May 2, 1902, King's Norton, England; d. Feb. 10, 1986.)* Traditionally handsome, urbane British leading man whose film career included silent films from 1924 (beginning with *The Eleventh Commandment)* in his native land, but who worked most frequently in Hollywood after 1933. Like fellow Brits Patric Knowles and Ian Hunter (all three were interchangeable, in the minds of American audiences), Aherne was consistent in the quality of his performances, always convincing but seldom inspiring. (He did, though, snare an Oscar nomination for a supporting role in 1939's *Juarez.*). He published a witty autobiography, "A Proper Job," in 1969, and then wrote an intimate biography of his friend George Sanders, "A Dreadful Man" in 1979. OTHER FILMS INCLUDE: 1933: *Song of Songs;* 1937: *The Great Garrick;* 1940: *The Lady in Question, Vigil in the Night;* 1942: *My Sister Eileen;* 1946: *The Locket;* 1954: *Prince Valiant;* 1961: *Susan Slade;* 1967: *Rosie.*

AIELLO, DANNY. Actor. *(b. June 20, 1935, New York City.)* One of the screen's most compulsively watchable players, Aiello has virtually cornered the market on tough, urban ethnic types, playing cops, hoods, and working-class Italian patriarchs. This accomplished stage veteran was in his late 30s when he made his screen debut in *Bang the Drum Slowly* (1973), but he has worked steadily in films since. Although his characters are often crass, vulgar, and violent, Aiello has also portrayed sensitive, kindly men—

with an earthy sense of humor. His films include *The Godfather, Part II* (1974), *The Front* (1976), *Bloodbrothers* (1978), *Fort Apache, The Bronx* (1981), *Once Upon a Time in America* (1984), *The Purple Rose of Cairo, The Stuff* (both 1985), *Radio Days,* and *The Pick-Up Artist* (both 1987). Aiello's career shifted into high gear following his well-received turn as Cher's mama's-boy suitor in *Moonstruck* (1987). He was Oscar-nominated for his portrayal of Sal, the pizzeria proprietor in Spike Lee's *Do the Right Thing* (1989, for which Lee allowed him to write much of his dialogue). Eddie Murphy used him in *Harlem Nights* (1989), and he appeared in *Jacob's Ladder* and *The Closer* (both 1990) before startling moviegoers with his singing voice in *Once Around* (1991, playing Holly Hunter's father) and *Hudson Hawk* (1991, as Bruce Willis' sidekick). By 1992 Aiello had seemingly demonstrated his ability to carry a movie, but his starring vehicle *Ruby* (1992) flopped at the box office and disappeared almost instantly. Since then he has appeared in *Mistress* (1992), *The Pickle* (1993, in the leading role, as a desperate moviemaker), *The Cemetery Club* (1993, as Ellen Burstyn's love interest), *Me and the Kid* (1993), *Ready to Wear/Prêt-à-Porter,* and *The Professional* (both 1994).

AIMÉE, ANOUK. Actress. *(b. Apr. 27, 1932, Paris, as Francoise Sorya Dreyfus.)* Regal, intelligent but enigmatic beauty who, in films since 1947's *La Maison sous la mer* (billed as "Anouk"). She has given effective performances as a jaded socialite (in Fellini's *La Dolce Vita,* 1960), as a carefree cabaret dancer (in Jacques Demy's *Lola,* 1961), and a somewhat mousy, neglected wife (in Fellini's *8½,* 1963). Aimée received a Best Actress Academy Award nomination for her role in *A Man and a Woman,* the international success that made her a top star. She costarred with Omar Sharif in *The Appointment* (1969), but has for the most part remained in Europe to act in foreign-language films. She also starred in the "20 Years Later" sequel to *A Man and a Woman* (1986), and for the last decade has appeared in one film per year. Her latest is *Dr. Bethune* (1990). She was once married to British actor Albert Finney.

ALBERT, EDDIE. Actor. *(b. Apr. 22, 1908, Rock Island, Ill., as Edward Albert Heimberger.)* Best known as the constantly flabbergasted Oliver Douglas in the surreal TV sitcom "Green Acres" (1965–71), the seemingly ageless, all-American Albert flew on the circus trapeze and gave song recitals, before settling on acting as a career. Debuting in the military-academy comedy *Brother Rat* (1938), he immediately won attention with his pleasant manner and effortless comic touch. Under contract to Warner Bros. he costarred in *Brother Rat and a Baby, Four Wives* (both 1939), *A Dispatch From Reuters* (1940), *Four Mothers,* and *The Wagons Roll at Night* (both 1941). After wartime duty, his career was slow to restart, but in the 1950s he found a niche in second leads that enabled him to shift from affable comedic types to heavies and back again. He even snared an Oscar nomination for his supporting role in William Wyler's *Roman Holiday* (1953). And he was especially effective as the cowardly Army officer in *Attack!* (1956). Other major credits in that fruitful decade: *Carrie* (1952), *Oklahoma!* (as Ali Hakim), *I'll Cry Tomorrow* (both 1955), *The Teahouse of the August Moon* (1956), and *The Sun Also Rises* (1957). Albert's latter-day film roles emphasized his menacing, waspish (and WASP-ish) side, as seen in his memorable performances in *The Heartbreak Kid* (1972, picking up his second Oscar nomination as Cybill Shepherd's father) and *The Longest Yard* (1974, as a ruthless prison warden). He's also appeared in his share of exploitation quickies, including *The Devil's Rain* (1975), a horror flick much beloved of so-bad-it's-good cultists. His latest is *The Girl From Mars* (1991). In 1990 he reunited with Eva Gabor for an unmemorable TV reunion movie, *Return to Green Acres.* In the 1950s he was involved in the production of nontheatrical films, and has long been an active crusader for environmental causes. Albert married exotically beautiful actress Margo *(Lost Horizon, The Leopard Man)* in 1945; their son Edward Albert (born 1951), a promising leading man in the early 1970s who debuted opposite Goldie Hawn in *Butterflies Are Free* (1972), still acts in films and on TV.

ALBERTSON, FRANK. Actor. *(b. Feb. 2, 1909, Fergus Falls, Minn.; d. Feb. 29, 1964.)* He's the one who *didn't* marry Donna Reed in *It's a Wonderful Life* (1946). One of Hollywood's perennial juveniles, Albertson appeared in dozens of films and plays during his 35-year tenure in show business. He began as a prop boy in the silent-film era; in his first major role, a young naval cadet in John Ford's *Salute* (1929), he displayed the youthful exuberance that would characterize most of his subsequent screen work. Perhaps best remembered as the naive young playwright ("Hail and farewell!") in *Room Service* (1938), although his later work included plum roles in *Psycho* (1960, as the boorish tycoon) and *Bye Bye Birdie* (1963, as the blustery mayor).
OTHER FILMS INCLUDE: 1930: *Born Reckless;* 1931: *A Connecticut Yankee;* 1935: *Alice Adams;* 1936: *The Plainsman;* 1939: *Bachelor Mother;* 1942: *Wake Island;* 1947: *The Hucksters;* 1958: *The Last Hurrah.*

ALBERTSON, JACK. Actor. *(b. June 16, 1907, Lynn, Mass.; d. Nov. 25, 1981.)* Nondescript-looking character actor, a veteran of vaudeville, burlesque, and legitimate stage, who came to movies in 1954, recreating his stage role in *Top Banana* (which was, in fact, actually filmed on stage at New York's Winter Garden theater). He played a wide variety of roles thereafter, but seemed most comfortable in comedic parts. He also worked extensively on TV, costarring in the "Chico and the Man" sitcom (1974–79).
OTHER FILMS INCLUDE: 1956: *The Harder They Fall;* 1962: *Days of Wine and Roses;* 1968: *The Subject Was Roses* (for which he won an Oscar as Best Supporting Actor); 1971: *Willy Wonka and the Chocolate Factory* (a highlight); 1972: *The Poseidon Adventure;* 1981: *Dead and Buried.*

ALDA, ALAN. Actor, writer, director. *(b. Jan. 28, 1936, New York City.)* Good-natured leading man who in the late 1970s was everyone's ideal of the "sensitive male." The son of actor Robert Alda, his early work was primarily on stage, with occasional forays into TV, notably as a semi-regular on "That Was the Week That Was" (1964–65). His first noteworthy film role was as author George Plimpton in *Pa-*

per Lion (1968), and he was a surprisingly credible hillbilly in 1970's *The Moonshine War.* Then in 1972, he was cast as Hawkeye in the TV series version of "M*A*S*H," and though it was almost canceled that first season, it went on for 11 years, and won Alda four Emmys in the process: two for acting, one each for writing and directing. His total involvement in the show left little time for outside work, but he was effective as Caryl Chessman in the TV movie *Kill Me If You Can,* and in 1978 appeared in two films based on hit Broadway comedies, *California Suite* and *Same Time, Next Year.*
In 1979, Alda wrote and starred (opposite a young Meryl Streep) in a political drama, *The Seduction of Joe Tynan,* and two years later donned the director's cap as well with *The Four Seasons,* a bittersweet romantic comedy that spun off a brief TV series. His later films, which continued his often-glib exploration of human nature, were *Sweet Liberty* (1986), a Hollywood satire; *A New Life* (1988), about middle-age divorcées, and *Betsy's Wedding* (1990), a genial cousin to *Father of the Bride.* Cast against type, he was deliciously sleazy as an egotistical filmmaker in Woody Allen's *Crimes and Misdemeanors* (1989). Allen used him again to good effect in *Manhattan Murder Mystery* (1993), and, perhaps taking a cue from Woody's casting idea, he was hired to play an egocentric doctor in the AIDS telefeature *And the Band Played On* (1993). Alda has also been active on stage in recent years, in London and on Broadway, in a revival of "Our Town" and in Neil Simon's "Jake's Women."

ALDA, ROBERT. Actor. *(b. Feb. 26, 1914, New York City, as Alphonse Giuseppe Giovanni Roberto D'Abruzzo; d. May 3, 1986.)* Handsome vaudevillian-turned-screen-actor who debuted as composer George Gershwin in *Rhapsody in Blue* (1945). Alda, the son of an immigrant barber, had the potential of a classic leading man, but after only a few more prestige films (1946's *Cloak and Dagger* and 1947's *Nora Prentiss*), he was reduced to the likes of *Tarzan and the Slave Girl* (1950) and *Two Gals and a Guy* (1951). Stage work offered Alda more rewarding opportunities; he starred on Broadway in "Guys and Dolls" and "What Makes

Sammy Run?" After moving to Rome in 1960, he appeared in many European coproductions, and in the 1970s and 1980s delighted fans with his guest appearances on American TV—including two on "M*A*S*H" with his son Alan Alda.

ALDRICH, ROBERT. Director. *(b. Aug. 9, 1918, Cranston, R.I.; d. Dec. 5, 1983.)* Flamboyant producer/director who has earned a sizable cult for his distinctive collection of over-the-top melodramas with a perversely comic edge. After a long stint as an assistant director to Chaplin and Renoir, among others, he branched into feature-film directing in the 1950s with such tough, gritty films as *Kiss Me Deadly* (still considered the definitive Mike Hammer movie), *The Big Knife* (both 1955), and *Attack!* (1956). But his more colorful side soon asserted itself with such crowd-pleasers as *What Ever Happened to Baby Jane?* (1962), which kicked off an entire cycle of aging female stars in horror movies, *The Dirty Dozen* (1967), and *The Longest Yard* (1974). The profits from *Dozen* allowed him to buy an entire studio, which he dubbed Associates & Aldrich, but he was unable to make a go of it.
OTHER FILMS INCLUDE: 1953: *The Big Leaguer;* 1954: *Apache, Vera Cruz;* 1956: *Autumn Leaves;* 1961: *The Last Sunset;* 1963: *Hush ... Hush, Sweet Charlotte;* 1966: *The Flight of the Phoenix;* 1968: *The Legend of Lylah Clare, The Killing of Sister George;* 1970: *Too Late the Hero;* 1971: *The Grissom Gang;* 1972: *Ulzana's Raid;* 1973: *Emperor of the North;* 1977: *Twilight's Last Gleaming, The Choirboys;* 1979: *The Frisco Kid.*

ALEXANDER, JANE. Actress. *(b. Oct. 28, 1939, Boston, as Jane Quigley.)* Perhaps one of the finest actresses working in America today (in *any* medium), this proudly unglamorous actress is noted for her finely delineated characterizations, both in supporting performances and starring turns. After studying at Sarah Lawrence College and at the University of Edinburgh, Alexander joined Washington's Arena Stage in 1966, playing 15 different roles over the next three seasons. She made her Broadway debut in 1969's "The Great White Hope," playing the doomed lover of prizefighter Jack Jefferson; it was a Tony-winning portrayal she reprised in the 1970 film version, snagging an Oscar nomination in the process. She subsequently picked up two other nominations, as a reluctant informant in *All the President's Men* (1976) and as Dustin Hoffman's steadfast friend in *Kramer vs. Kramer* (1979). Alexander appeared to good advantage in several prestigious TV movies as well, playing Eleanor Roosevelt in two Emmy-winning dramas, *Eleanor and Franklin* (1976) and *Eleanor and Franklin: The White House Years* (1977). She won unanimously excellent notices and another Oscar nomination for her role as the indomitable mother in *Testament,* a 1983 film chronicling the aftermath of a nuclear attack. Most of her best opportunities have come in made-for-TV movies: *Playing for Time* (1980, which won her an Emmy), *Calamity Jane* (playing the title role), *Malice in Wonderland,* as legendary gossip columnist Hedda Hopper (both 1984), *Blood & Orchids* (1986), *In Love and War* (1987), and *Daughter of the Streets* (1990).
Like other actresses of her caliber who have been frustrated by the paucity of well-written, suitable female roles, Alexander turned to producing with *Square Dance* (1987), a charming if not altogether effective coming-of-age story in which she played Winona Ryder's saucy mother. She also appeared, uncredited, as Matthew Broderick's mother in *Glory* (1989). More recently, she played on Broadway in "The Sisters Rosensweig," and in 1993 was named by President Clinton to head the National Endowment for the Arts.
OTHER FILMS INCLUDE: 1971: *A Gunfight;* 1972: *The New Centurions;* 1978: *The Betsy;* 1980: *Brubaker;* 1984: *City Heat.*

ALLEN, DEDE. Editor. *(b. Dec. 3, 1925, Cleveland, Ohio.)* Brilliant film editor who has worked on some of the best American films of the 1960s and 1970s, becoming a trusted collaborator of such directors as Arthur Penn, Sidney Lumet, and Warren Beatty. She began her career in the mail room at Columbia in 1943 and got her first chance as a sound cutter because so many men were off at war. She struggled to establish herself, first in Hollywood, then in New York, cutting the low-budget *Terror From the Year 5000* (1958) before winning a major assignment, editing *Odds Against Tomorrow* (1959) for director (and former film editor) Robert Wise. She brought a virtuoso sense of rhythm to Robert Rossen's stylistic landmark *The Hustler* (1961) and Elia Kazan's *America, America* (1963), and was indispensable to the artistic success of *Bonnie and Clyde* (1967), *Rachel, Rachel* (1968), *Alice's Restaurant* (1969), *Little Big Man* (1970), *Slaughterhouse-Five* (1972), *Serpico* (1973), *Dog Day Afternoon* and *Night Moves* (both 1975). More recently, she co-edited (and executive-produced) the epic *Reds* (1981), and edited *Mike's Murder* (1984), *The Breakfast Club* (1985), *The Milagro Beanfield War* (1988) and *Henry & June* (1990). In his review of *Serpico*, John Simon wrote, "Miss Allen has an almost uncanny knack for sensing the right moment at which to cut off a shot . . . She lets it speak to us, as it were, subliminally, and the eruption of joy with which we realize that we have worked out its meaning is the very energy that carries us forward to the next scene." She earned two Oscar nominations, for *Dog Day Afternoon* and for co-editing *Reds*.

ALLEN, IRWIN. Producer, director. *(b. June 12, 1916, New York City; d. Nov. 2, 1991.)* The C. B. DeMille of the grand-scale "disaster" picture turned to film production after first enjoying a substantial career in the publishing industry as a writer, editor, and literary agent. Allen's first taste of celluloid success came in the form of an Oscar for his tyro documentary *The Sea Around Us* (1953). His penchant for grandiose subject matter was realized in films such as *The Animal World* (1956), *The Story of Mankind* (1957), *The Big Circus* (1959), and *The Lost World* (1960) before he achieved commercial success with *Voyage to the Bottom of the Sea* (1961), a well-remembered sci-fi extravaganza. Its all-star cast, elaborate special effects, and apocalyptic menace foreshadowed the producer's later works. He adapted the film into a weekly TV series that ran from 1964 through 1967; during the same period he also produced "Lost in Space" and "Land of the Giants." Returning to feature-film production, Allen hit the box-office jackpot with *The Poseidon Adventure* (1972), which singlehandedly spawned the popular disaster genre of the

1970s. His special-effects crews also had a field day with the Oscar-nominated *The Towering Inferno* (1974), but by the end of the decade, tired rehashes like *The Swarm* (1978) and the inevitable *Beyond the Poseidon Adventure* (1979) were no longer attracting big audiences. One of Allen's final forays into the disaster genre was appropriately titled *When Time Ran Out . . .* (1980). His wife Sheila had small roles in a number of his films.

ALLEN, JAY PRESSON. Screenwriter, producer. *(b. Mar. 3, 1922, Fort Worth, as Jacqueline Presson.)* Allen has divided her time among Broadway, film, and television projects, achieving great success in all three media. She wrote for "Philco TV Playhouse" during the 1950s and gained fame adapting the Muriel Spark novella "The Prime of Miss Jean Brodie" for the Broadway and London stage; she later adapted the screenplay, as well, for the 1969 film which won Maggie Smith a Best Actress Oscar. Her first screenplay was the dense and complex *Marnie* (1964) for Alfred Hitchcock. She later earned an Oscar nomination for adapting the classic musical *Cabaret* (1972) for Bob Fosse, and also cowrote *Travels With My Aunt* (1972, directed by George Cukor and also starring Smith) and *Funny Lady* (1975). She began a fruitful collaboration with director Sidney Lumet with the comedy *Just Tell Me What You Want* (1980, adapted from her own novel), followed by *Prince of the City* (1981, cowritten with Lumet and earning another Oscar nomination) and an adaptation of Ira Levin's *Deathtrap* (1982). She also produced or executive-produced the last three films. Allen has written the acclaimed plays "The First Wife," "Forty Carats" (based on a French original), and "Tru," but arguably her most widely known (and widely seen) work was the acclaimed dramatic TV series "Family" (1976–80), which she created. She and producer/husband Lewis Allen prepared and wrote the 1990 remake of *Lord of the Flies*, but later disowned it.

ALLEN, KAREN. Actress. *(b. Oct. 5, 1951, Carrollton, Ill.)* After "overnight" stardom in a megahit like *Raiders of the Lost Ark*, most actresses would try to cash in, and campaign to appear in the sequel. Allen did neither, after making a major impression as tough-talking Marion Ravenwood opposite Harrison Ford, preferring to focus on stage work and choose her film roles carefully. Her first movie, *The Whidjitmaker* (1976), went totally unnoticed—as did she. Two years later, she played a likable coed and the voice of reason in the rowdy-frat-boy epic, *National Lampoon's Animal House* (1978), which won her a small but loyal following. Her best screen opportunities have come in *The Wanderers* (1979), *Cruising* (1980), and particularly *Starman*, though her own starring vehicle *Until September* (both 1984) was a disappointment. She had a small role as a social worker in *Malcolm X* (1992). An actress who projects intelligence and warmth, Allen was costar of the 1994 series "The Road Home."

OTHER FILMS INCLUDE: 1982: *Shoot the Moon, Split Image;* 1987: *Backfire, The Glass Menagerie;* 1988: *Scrooged;* 1991: *Sweet Talker;* 1993: *The Sandlot, King of the Hill, Ghost in the Machine.*

ALLEN, NANCY. Actress. *(b. June 24, 1950, New York City.)* As the sexy blond high-school heartbreaker in *Carrie* (1976), Allen attracted attention not only from fans but from the film's director, Brian De Palma, who married her. He later showcased her comic talents in his *Home Movies* (1979), subjected her to a slasher in *Dressed to Kill* (1980), and entangled her in mayhem for *Blow Out* (1981). Allen, who started out in TV commercials, got her first break in *The Last Detail* (1973), and after *Carrie* landed lively roles in *I Wanna Hold Your Hand* (1978) and Steven Spielberg's *1941* (1979). But her divorce from De Palma seems to have also separated her from good movies, and her lackluster performances have belied the promise she showed early on.

OTHER FILMS INCLUDE: 1983: *Strange Invaders;* 1984: *Not for Publication, The Philadelphia Experiment;* 1987: *RoboCop;* 1988: *Poltergeist III;* 1990: *RoboCop 2;* 1993: *RoboCop 3.*

ALLEN, REX. Actor. *(b. Dec. 31, 1922, Wilcox, Ariz.)* This lanky, sandy-haired, velvety-voiced veteran of radio and rodeo engagements, billed as "The Arizona Cowboy," was the last of Hollywood's singing cowboy stars. He worked for Republic, the studio that had previously made stars of Gene Autry and Roy Rogers; unfortunately, the B Western was already facing stiff competition from TV by the time Allen debuted in 1949's *The Arizona Cowboy.* Nonetheless, he made nearly 20 films for the studio, supported by such sidekicks as Buddy Ebsen and Slim Pickens. Allen, whose other starring vehicles included *Under Mexicali Stars* (1950), *The Old Overland Trail* (1952), and *Down Laredo Way* (1953), moved over to the small screen as the star of "Frontier Doctor" (1958), and subsequently appeared on many TV variety shows. His voice became familiar to millions when he narrated a series of Walt Disney wildlife films during the 1960s; he performed a similar task for the 1973 animated feature film, *Charlotte's Web,* and was extremely successful doing radio and TV commercial voice-overs until his retirement.

ALLEN, WOODY. Actor, director, screenwriter. *(b. Dec. 1, 1935, Brooklyn, N.Y., as Allen Stewart Konigsberg.)* The odyssey of this artist, who from beginnings as a cerebral-schlemiel stand-up comic has become one of the leading luminaries in American film, is unique in cinema history. Nobody has tried so doggedly to break free of the constraints of a tried-and-true comic persona as Allen. And nobody has chalked up such a wildly mixed track record doing so. After years writing material for other comics, Allen began performing in 1961, turning his natural shyness into a comic device, delivering devastating one-liners in a sad deadpan and often punctuating his jokes with a little gulp that suggested he was about to vomit. His first movie job, as screenwriter and actor in 1965's *What's New, Pussycat?,* instantly made him a demi-icon of the swinging sixties. In 1966's ingenious *What's Up, Tiger Lily?,* Allen and several character actors (including his then-wife Louise Lasser) dubbed ridiculous dialogue onto an already silly-looking Japanese spy thriller. When making his first film as a director, the crime-documentary parody *Take the Money and Run* (1969), Allen had to be convinced to squelch a doomy, portentous side to which he gave free rein in later works: *Money*'s editor, Ralph Rosenblum, recalled that its first cut ended with Allen being slaughtered, à la Bonnie and Clyde, in a scene completely at odds with the rest of the movie.

After *Money* came a series of dazzling comedies—*Bananas* (1971), *Everything You Always Wanted to Know About Sex* (*but were afraid to ask)* (1972), *Sleeper* (1973), *Love and Death* (1975)—in which Allen honed his Manhattan schlemiel persona to a fine edge while reveling in absurdist gags, outlandish situations, and pointed social satire. 1977's *Annie Hall* was a breakthrough movie; while very funny, it was also a serious and often moving look at modern urban romance, and it won Allen a Best Director Oscar (he shared the Academy's Best Screenplay Oscar with cowriter Marshall Brickman, and was also nominated for Best Actor). From that point on, Allen's films became more serious, starting with *Interiors* (1978), a heavy, Bergman-influenced drama which he wrote and directed but did not star in. The film, replete with self-conscious, straight-out-of-film-school visual compositions, was neither an artistic nor commercial success (although it received several Oscar nominations including Best Director and Screenplay), but seemed to provide Allen with the tools needed to blend comedy and drama. He's done that with varying degrees of success in all his subsequent films, which he makes at the steady rate of one a year.

Manhattan (1979), a bittersweet romantic comedy that painted New York City in nostalgic black-and-white and underscored its scenes with Gershwin music, was critically and commercially successful, and snagged him another Academy Award nomination for Best Screenplay. In the acerbic and candid self-portrait *Stardust Memories* (1980) he poked fun at those who yearned for his "earlier, funnier" films, then responded with *A Midsummer Night's Sex Comedy* (1982) and the ingenious *Zelig* (1983) in which he played a human chameleon (thanks to some delicious cinematic sleight-of-hand). *Broadway Danny Rose* (1984), *The Purple Rose of Cairo* (1985), and *Radio Days* (1987) garnered him more Oscar nominations for screenwriting. He nailed one for *Hannah and Her Sisters* (1986), one of his most mature films, and one of his biggest box-office successes. His dramatic efforts from this period, *September* (1987) and *Another Woman* (1988), were marred by the same heavy-handedness he'd displayed in *Interiors,* and were not well received. 1989's *Crimes and Misdemeanors,* however, showed him back in form, albeit with a curious, existentialist opus that dispelled the notion that evil deeds never remain unpunished; it was a startling concept that he made not only convincing but, at times, uproariously funny. *Alice* (1990), a starring vehicle for his former love, Mia Farrow, had moments of brilliance but was on the whole very ordinary. *Shadows and Fog* (1992), another downbeat, leaden drama, found critics impatient with Allen's relentless efforts to recast himself as an American Bergman; it won the director some of his most uncomplimentary reviews.

Allen was married to Louise Lasser, who appeared in several of his earlier films, and then had long-term relationships with leading lady Diane Keaton and with Mia Farrow, who appeared in almost all of his 1980s pictures. Farrow and Allen had one son together, but became international gossip fodder in 1992 when he was forced to admit a romantic liaison with her adopted daughter Soon-Yi Previn; she subsequently accused him of sexually molesting their child. This unprecedented publicity brouhaha (for two extremely private people) gave unexpected notoriety to Allen's concurrently released *Husbands and Wives* (1992), an excellent film that nonetheless caused snickering at many showings because of "leading" dialogue between Allen and Farrow. He then called on Diane Keaton to replace Farrow in *Manhattan Murder Mystery* (1993), his lightest comedy in years, and earned Oscar nominations for directing and cowriting *Bullets Over Broadway* (1994), the wryly comic tale of a young playwright at odds with the New York theatre world in the 1920s. He then turned to TV, directing, writing and starring in an adaptation of his play *Don't Drink the Water* (1994), and then acting opposite Peter Falk in an updated version of Neil Simon's *The Sunshine Boys* (1995).

Back in 1967 he costarred in the all-star James Bond spoof *Casino Royale,* as "Jimmy" Bond, but in the intervening years he has rarely appeared in films he hasn't also written and directed himself. There have been a few notable exceptions:

Play It Again, Sam (1972), adapted from his delightful hit Broadway play, which he performed many times on stage; *The Front* (1976), in which he was ideally cast as a nebbish who fronts for blacklisted writers during the McCarthy era; and Paul Mazursky's *Scenes from a Mall* (1991), in which he was amusingly and improbably cast as an I-live-in-L.A.-and-like-it lawyer (complete with pony tail!) opposite Bette Midler. It was an endearing and accomplished performance which, unfortunately, was not supported by an equally accomplished script. He also appeared briefly in Jean-Luc Godard's odd, experimental *King Lear* (1987).

ALLEY, KIRSTIE. Actress. *(b. Jan. 12, 1955, Wichita, Tex.)* Quirky, striking, brunette actress with throaty voice who seemed to have scored an immediate hit in *Star Trek II: The Wrath of Khan* (1982), her first movie. Alley's career stalled almost immediately, largely due to personal problems, but she rebounded after replacing Shelley Long on the "Cheers" TV show from 1987 to 1993. (She subsequently won an Emmy for her performance.) Her newly discovered flair for comedy translated to the big screen only fitfully in comedies such as *Summer School* (1987), *Look Who's Talking* (1989), *Madhouse, Sibling Rivalry,* and *Look Who's Talking Too* (all 1990), along with *Look Who's Talking Now* (1993). Married to actor Parker Stevenson.

ALLYSON, JUNE. Actress. *(b. Oct. 7, 1917, Bronx, N.Y., as Ella Geisman.)* The movies' perennial girl-next-door began her career in a chorus line on Broadway. By the late 1930s, though, the movie bug had bitten, and Allyson was appearing in two-reel shorts such as *Dime a Dance* (1937) for Educational Pictures, and other mini-musicals for Warner Bros., all filmed in New York. But the pert, diminutive dancer attracted little attention until being featured in the 1941 Broadway show "Best Foot Forward." She was signed by MGM to repeat her stage role in the 1943 film version, and was groomed for stardom.

Bright-eyed and bouncy, Allyson became popular in a series of peppy musicals—*Thousands Cheer, Girl Crazy*

(both 1943), *Two Girls and a Sailor* (1944), *Two Sisters From Boston* (1946), and *Good News* (1947) among them—that exploited her terp talent and husky voice without making great demands on her limited acting ability. The year 1948 marked a change in direction for Allyson's career: Although she'd worked in a few nonmusical films, she was cast in several "straight" movies, including *The Three Musketeers* (1948) and *Little Women* (1949). *The Stratton Story* (1949) offered Allyson the first of three costarring roles with James Stewart—*The Glenn Miller Story* (1954) and *Strategic Air Command* (1955) were the others—and solidified her screen image as the kind of girl men like to marry. (In real life she was married to screen crooner/tough guy Dick Powell.)

With solid dramatic credentials behind her, Allyson got some good roles in the 1950s—in *The Shrike* (1955) with Jose Ferrer, for instance—but, overall, her output in the 1950s was largely confined to dismal vehicles, including ill-advised remakes of two classic screwball comedies, *You Can't Run Away From It* [*It Happened One Night*] (1956), and *My Man Godfrey* (1957). Allyson's big-screen appearances have been rare since 1960, but her wholesome image remains fixed in the American consciousness. She can even make incontinence seem socially acceptable, as she has proved in her long-running series of TV spots for Depends.

ALMENDROS, NESTOR. Cinematographer. *(b. Oct. 30, 1930, Barcelona; d. Mar. 4, 1992.)* Top-rank cinematographer whose work found favor with leading directors on both sides of the Atlantic. Raised and educated in Cuba, Almendros first achieved recognition in France, where he worked with both François Truffaut, on *The Wild Child* (1969) and *The Story of Adele H* (1975), and Eric Rohmer, for whom he photographed *Claire's Knee* (1971) and *Chloe in the Afternoon* (1972), among others. These pictures brought his work to the attention of Hollywood's then-burgeoning fraternity of neorealist directors. Almendros' first American film was Terrence Malick's *Days of Heaven* (1978), which won him an Oscar for best cinematography. Thereafter he earned nominations for *Kramer vs. Kramer* (1979), *The Blue Lagoon*

(1980), and *Sophie's Choice* (1982). He also photographed *Places in the Heart* (1984), *Heartburn* (1986), and *New York Stories* (1989, the Martin Scorsese segment). Almendros also produced several scathing documentaries on the social injustices perpetrated by the Castro regime, and wrote a number of eloquent articles about the art of cinematography, as well as an autobiographical career study, "A Man With a Camera" (1980).

ALMODOVAR, PEDRO. Director, writer. *(b. Sept. 25, 1951, Calzoda de Calatrava, Spain.)* One of the most original writer-directors to emerge during the 1980s, Almodovar has been called "Godard with a human face—a happy face." While working for Madrid's National Telephone Company in the 1970s, he become a member of the city's pop subculture, making raunchy 8mm films, acting in avant-garde theater groups, and performing in drag in a punk-rock band. His first features—*Pepi, Luci, Bom and Other Girls On The Heap* (1980), and *Labyrinth of Passions* (1981) were extensions of his underground tastes and became cult hits, but *Dark Habits* (1984), about an order of delinquent nuns, gained serious international attention. Almodovar's popularity increased with *What Have I Done to Deserve This?* (1985), *Matador* (1986), and *Law of Desire* (1987), which established his style of melodrama, comedy, and kitsch that frequently flouted conventions of taste. *Women on the Verge of a Nervous Breakdown* (1988), a more subdued and conventional but still distinctive comedy, became a worldwide hit and was nominated for a Best Foreign Film Oscar. The controversial *Tie Me Up! Tie Me Down!* (1990), *High Heels* (1991), and *Kika* (1993) show Almodovar's creative energy running full speed.

ALONSO, MARIA CONCHITA. Actress, singer. *(b. June 29, 1957, Cuba.)* This Latin beauty was already a star before she ever set foot in the U.S.—a recording star in South America. (She'd also won the title Miss Teenager of the World in 1971.) Her Hollywood career started out on a high note with an engaging performance opposite Robin Williams in *Moscow on the Hudson* (1984). But such are the lim-

ited opportunities available to women, let alone ethnic women, in American films, that nowadays she's better known for hissing profanities in megabudget shoot-em-ups such as *The Running Man* (1987) and *Predator 2* (1990). Her best dramatic opportunity to date came, quixotically, in *Colors* (1988), playing a superfluous role in an unnecessary subplot.
OTHER FILMS INCLUDE: 1986: *A Fine Mess, Touch and Go;* 1987: *Extreme Prejudice;* 1989: *Vampire's Kiss;* 1991: *McBain;* 1993: *The House of the Spirits.*

ALONZO, JOHN A. Cinematographer. *(b. June 12, 1934, Dallas.)* One of the top cameramen in Hollywood today, Alonzo has shot many of the top critical and commercial hit films of the last 20 years, including *Harold and Maude* (1971), *Chinatown* (1974, for which he was Oscar-nominated), *Close Encounters of the Third Kind* (1977), *Norma Rae* (1978), *Scarface* (1983), *Steel Magnolias* (1989), *Internal Affairs* (1990), and *HouseSitter* (1992). His malleable style enables him to adapt to any visual design; his extensive use of amber hues and subtle lighting in *Chinatown*, for example, has become de rigueur for cinematographers trying to recreate a 1930s-style urban milieu. He also directed the comedy *FM* (1978).

ALTMAN, ROBERT. Director, producer, screenwriter. *(b. Feb. 20, 1925, Kansas City, Mo.)* Irreverent, iconoclastic director whose films have won kudos from critics and film buffs for decades, though his box-office hits have been few and far between. His career has had more than its share of ups and downs, but Altman has never "sold out," remaining a maverick at every turn. After serving in World War 2 as a pilot, Altman wrote magazine stories and radio scripts (and even had one story turned into a movie, 1948's *Bodyguard*) before signing on with a small Kansas City company that made industrial films. He spent nearly a decade there before entering the theatrical arena with a low-budget epic called *The Delinquents* (1957, which he produced and wrote as well as directed). He followed it with a documentary, *The James Dean Story,* that same year, which gave him an entree to television, where he became a prolific director of series episodes. Over the next decade he helmed installments of "Alfred Hitchcock Presents," "Combat," and "Bonanza," among others.

Altman's next feature films, *Countdown* (1968) and *That Cold Day in the Park* (1969), elicited some raised-eyebrow comments from critics, but it was *MASH* (1970), a black comedy about a Korean War medical unit, that cemented his reputation. An irreverent and original film, it solidified techniques he'd experimented with in his earlier work, and also solidified his relationship with a handful of actors who became part of his unofficial stock company. The film earned him an Oscar nomination, and made him bankable in Hollywood, at least temporarily. His revisionist genre pieces *McCabe and Mrs. Miller* (a 1971 Western) and *The Long Goodbye* (a 1973 Philip Marlowe whodunit) added to Altman's rapidly expanding prestige, and the underrated *Images* (1972), *Thieves Like Us,* and *California Split* (both 1974) reaffirmed his individualistic approach to narrative filmmaking.

Nashville (1975), a brilliant mosaic of American life set in the country music capital, brought Altman another Academy Award nomination and showed him at the peak of his powers. (Plans to show a much longer version of the film in miniseries form on TV sadly never came to fruition.) It proved a tough act to follow. His subsequent films became increasingly odd and remote. *Buffalo Bill and the Indians, or Sitting Bull's History Lesson* (1976), the fascinating *3 Women* (1977), *A Wedding* (1978), the charming *A Perfect Couple, Quintet,* and *H.E.A.L.T.H.* (all 1979) had flashes of brilliance but seemed to reflect an artist who'd gone astray. Altman's attempt to return to the commercial mainstream resulted in the spectacularly awful *Popeye* (1980).

The director retreated and retrenched, directing for the stage and returning to film with an occasional offbeat project: *Come Back to the Five and Dime, Jimmy Dean, Jimmy Dean* (1982), *Streamers,* (1983), *Secret Honor* (1984), *Fool for Love, O.C. and Stiggs* (both 1985), *Beyond Therapy* (1987, stupefyingly bad), *Aria* (1988, an omnibus film in which he directed one segment), and *Vincent & Theo* (1990). Television proved a more fruitful medium for him during the 1980s.

Altman directed a handful of plays and small-scale films, as well as the highly praised cinema-verité election campaign parody, *Tanner* (a 1988 cable series that won him an Emmy) on which he collaborated with cartoonist Garry Trudeau. He also directed a first-rate TV production of *The Caine Mutiny Court-Martial* (1988).

Then, in 1992, Altman brought Michael Tolkin's sardonic satire of Hollywood dealmaking to life for the big screen. *The Player* (1992) restored the director to favor and earned him another Oscar nomination. More important, it reminded longtime fans of the Altman of yore: a challenging and creative filmmaker in full command of his craft. He took time off from films to direct an opera production of "McTeague" before persuading another all-star cast of actors to appear in his three-hour mosaic of Raymond Carver stories, *Short Cuts* (1993), which earned him an Oscar nomination. He then relocated to Paris to film the dismal fashion world satire *Ready to Wear/Prêt-à-Porter* (1994).

Altman has influenced many filmmakers, especially his former assistant and protégé Alan Rudolph, for whom he produced *Welcome to L.A.* (1977) and *Mrs. Parker and the Vicious Circle* (1994).

ALTON, JOHN. Cinematographer. *(b. Oct. 5, 1901, Hungary.)* Brilliant cinematographer whose mastery of chiaroscuro and deep-focus photographic techniques helped define the film noir look of the 1940s and 1950s. A former lab man who shot several films while traveling throughout Europe and South America, Alton perfected his visual style shooting B pictures for Republic in the early 1940s. His photographic manual, "Painting with Light," is still studied by budding cinematographers. After many years out of the limelight, the 92-year-old cinematographer was honored at the 1993 Telluride Film Festival. FILMS INCLUDE: 1942: *The Affairs of Jimmy Valentine;* 1947: *Bury Me Dead, T-Men;* 1948: *He Walked By Night;* 1951: *An American in Paris;* 1953: *I, the Jury;* 1955: *The Big Combo;* 1960: *Elmer Gantry.*

ALVARADO, TRINI. Actress. *(b. Jan. 10, 1967, New York City.)* After appearing in movies for more than a decade, this appealing, doe-eyed young actress landed

what should have been a career-making plum role, that of Bette Midler's illegitimate daughter in *Stella* (1990), Midler's remake of a classic soap opera. But the movie flopped, leaving the engaging Alvarado still in search of That Good Part. Actually, she'd had a pretty good one in *Sweet Lorraine* (1987), a low-budget tale of a Catskills summer not unlike *Dirty Dancing* (but without the music), but the film wasn't widely seen.
OTHER FILMS INCLUDE: 1979: *Rich Kids;* 1980: *Times Square;* 1984: *Mrs. Soffel;* 1988: *Satisfaction;* 1989: *The Chair;* 1992: *The Babe;* 1993: *American Friends;* 1994: *Little Women.*

AMECHE, DON. Actor. *(b. May 31, 1908, Kenosha, Wis., as Dominic Amici; d. Dec. 6, 1993.)* Few people from any walk of life, much less actors, live to see their names become part of the language, but this charming, mustached leading man was so memorable in *The Story of Alexander Graham Bell* (1939) that for years afterward a telephone was known as an "ameche." A veteran of dramatic radio (like his brother Jim), Ameche debuted on-screen in a 1933 Chicago-made short subject, *Beauty at the World's Fair,* and settled in Hollywood after winning a bit in *Clive of India* (1935) that earned him a long-term contract at 20th Century-Fox. He spent many years playing straight-arrow types, second bananas and, finally, leads in such light fare as *One in a Million* (1936), *Alexander's Ragtime Band, In Old Chicago* (both 1938), *The Three Musketeers, Midnight* (both 1939), *Down Argentine Way* (1940), *Moon Over Miami* (1941), *Heaven Can Wait* (1943, a rare and delicious turn as a not-so-nice-guy), and *Wing and a Prayer* (1944). Many of the Fox films made use of his fine singing voice, as well.

Ameche was as active on network radio as he was on-screen, but as his film career waned, he found newfound success on the airwaves with Frances Langford as The Bickersons, whose hilarious battles continued on record albums and commercials for decades to come. From the 1950s through the 1970s, he worked only sporadically, most notably as the emcee on the TV circus program "International Showtime." Then he was plucked out of semiretirement to play one of the wealthy, miserly brothers in *Trading Places* (1983,

with Ralph Bellamy as his selfish sibling), and suddenly he was "hot" again. His exuberant performance as one of the rejuvenated old men in *Cocoon* (1985) earned him a Best Supporting Actor Oscar and brought full circle one of the great comeback stories of recent Hollywood history.

Aside from the inevitable *Cocoon: The Return* (1988), later roles included *Harry and the Hendersons* (1987), a bravura turn as a timid bootblack in *Things Change* (1988), a costarring turn in the little-seen *Oddball Hall* (1990), a farcical role as Tom Selleck's forgetful father in *Folks!* (1992), and cameos in *Coming to America* (1988) and *Oscar* (1991), both directed by the man responsible for putting Ameche's career back on track, John Landis. His unmistakable voice was put to excellent use in the live-action Disney animal saga *Homeward Bound: The Incredible Journey* (1993). He completed his scenes in *Corrina, Corrina* (1994) just days before his death.

AMES, LEON. Actor. *(b. Jan. 20, 1903, Portland, Ind., as Leon Waycoff; d. Oct. 12, 1993.)* Why couldn't all fathers be as warm and understanding as Leon Ames? Though he started out as a conventional leading man (and, by the mid-1930s, a character player), this tall, suave, and usually mustachioed actor became one of the great dads of film and television back in the days when father really did know best. His first role of note was that of the hero in *Murders in the Rue Morgue* (1932), billed under his real name (he changed it in 1935). He followed it with parts in *Parachute Jumper* (1933), *The Count of Monte Cristo* (1934), *Reckless* (1935), *Stowaway* (1936), and *Suez* (1938), to name a very few. He also appeared in numerous detective films, among them *Charlie Chan on Broadway* (1937), *Mysterious Mr. Moto* (1938), *Ellery Queen and the Murder Ring* (1941), and *Crime Doctor* (1943); he was one of the best "red herrings" in the business. When MGM cast Ames as the head of the household in *Meet Me in St. Louis* (1944), he registered strongly (though it turns out that wasn't him singing with Mary Astor—he was dubbed by producer Arthur Freed); subsequently, the studio kept him busy in such films as *Thirty Seconds Over Tokyo* (also 1944), *Son of Lassie, Weekend* *at the Waldorf* (both 1945), *Yolanda and the Thief, The Postman Always Rings Twice* (both 1946), *Song of the Thin Man* (1947), *A Date With Judy* (1948), *Little Women, Battleground* (both 1949), *Crisis* (1950), and *It's a Big Country* (1951).

Ames' later features included *Peyton Place* (1957), *From the Terrace* (1960), *The Absent-Minded Professor* (1961), *The Monkey's Uncle* (1965), *On a Clear Day You Can See Forever, Tora! Tora! Tora!* (both 1970), *Hammersmith Is Out* (1972), *Just You and Me, Kid* (1979), *Testament* (1983), and *Peggy Sue Got Married* (1986). On TV, he followed in the footsteps of such notable screen dads as William Powell and Spencer Tracy in the series versions of "Life With Father" (1953–55) and "Father of the Bride" (1961–62), and played The Next-Door Neighbor in the final two seasons of "Mr. Ed" (1963–65).

AMIS, SUZY. Actress. *(b. Jan. 5, 1961, Oklahoma City.)* An exception to the rule that models don't become good actresses, Amis has impressed critics in a variety of roles, mostly in unsuccessful movies. After modeling in Europe for several years, she returned to the U.S. and won the role of Michael Caine's nubile daughter in the sex comedy *Blame It On Rio* (1984), but bowed out when she learned topless scenes were involved. (The part later went to Demi Moore.) She debuted in *Fandango* (1985) instead, and made a strong impression in the play "Fresh Horses" before doing *The Big Town* (1987), *Rocket Gibraltar* (1988), *Twister* (1988) and *Where The Heart Is* (1990). After some time off, she returned to the screen with strong roles in 1993's *Watch It* and *Rich in Love*, and gave an excellent lead performance—her first—in *The Ballad of Little Jo* (also 1993), as a 19th-century woman who moved to the West and lived on the frontier disguised as a man. Her real-life husband, Sam Robards, played a society photographer who seduces her.

ANDERSON, GILBERT M. Actor, producer. *(b. March 21, 1882, Little Rock, Ark., as Max Aronson; d. Jan. 20, 1971.)* This beefy, stolid actor wouldn't even be a footnote in most reference books if he

hadn't been in the right place at the right time. Noting the amazing success of Thomas Edison's *The Great Train Robbery* (1903), in which he played several bit parts, Anderson produced, directed, and starred in dozens of Western shorts (most of them lost) throughout the movies' early years. He created and played the screen's first cowboy hero, Bronco Billy, in 1909; he also cofounded (with George K. Spoor) the Essanay film studio. By the mid 1920s, both Essanay and Anderson were washed up, victims of a rapidly maturing industry. He made a cameo appearance, his last before the cameras, in 1965's *The Bounty Hunter.*

ANDERSON, JUDITH (DAME). Actress. *(b. Feb. 10, 1898, Adelaide, Australia, as Frances Margaret Anderson; d. Jan. 3, 1992.)* Exceptional actress who failed to replicate her stage success in Hollywood, despite a few memorable roles, notably her Oscar-nominated turn as the housekeeper Mrs. Danvers in Alfred Hitchcock's *Rebecca* (1940). Making her stage debut in her native Australia, Anderson came to America in 1918, earning a reputation as one of the New York theater's finest actresses; her Lady Macbeth (in 1937 and 1941 productions) is nearly legendary. A striking woman who lacked the conventional beauty of most successful female stars, Anderson was tagged as a character actress from the start. In 1984 she began a three-year stint on the TV soap "Santa Barbara." She was named Dame Commander of the British Empire in 1960.
OTHER FILMS INCLUDE: 1933: *Blood Money* (her first, playing a hard-boiled nightclub owner); 1940: *Forty Little Mothers;* 1941: *Lady Scarface* (second-billed as a female gangster); 1942: *All Through the Night, Kings Row;* 1943: *Edge of Darkness, Stage Door Canteen;* 1944: *Laura;* 1945: *And Then There Were None;* 1946: *Diary of a Chambermaid, The Strange Love of Martha Ivers, Specter of the Rose;* 1947: *Pursued, Tycoon;* 1950: *The Furies;* 1953: *Salome;* 1956: *The Ten Commandments;* 1958: *Cat on a Hot Tin Roof;* 1960: *Cinderfella;* 1961: *Don't Bother to Knock;* 1963: *Macbeth* (reprising her Lady Macbeth in this telefilm); 1970: *A Man Called Horse;* 1974: *Inn of the Damned;* 1984: *Star Trek III: The Search for Spock;* 1986: *Impure Thoughts.*

ANDERSON, KEVIN. Actor. *(b. Jan. 13, 1960, Waukeegan, Ill.)* Versatile up-and-coming actor who caught critics' attention with his performance as the shy Phillip in *Orphans* (1987), a role he originated on stage with Chicago's Steppenwolf Company, and then played on New York's Theatre Row. Following this, Anderson appeared in several little-seen movies like *A Walk on the Moon* (1987), *Miles From Home* (1988, directed by the Steppenwolf Company's Gary Sinise), and *In Country* (1989) before attaining box-office success as the college drama professor who falls for Julia Roberts in *Sleeping With the Enemy* (1991). He has also starred in Mike Figgis' *Liebestraum* (1991), *Hoffa* (1992, as Robert F. Kennedy), *The Night We Never Met* (1993), and has many stage credits, including the Broadway (and later TV) production of "Orpheus Descending" opposite Vanessa Redgrave. In 1993 he won the William Holden part in the London stage production of Andrew Lloyd Webber's musical version of "Sunset Boulevard."

ANDERSON, LINDSAY. Director. *(b. Apr. 17, 1923, Bangalore, India; d. Aug. 30, 1994.)* Born to a Scottish major-general stationed in Raj-era India, Anderson was educated at Oxford before cofounding (along with future directors Karel Reisz and Tony Richardson) "Sequence," a highly influential film magazine. In his essays for "Sequence," "Sight and Sound," and "The London Times," Anderson advocated a greater emphasis on social consciousness in filmmaking. His writings along these lines contributed greatly to the "Free Cinema" movement of the 1950s, which favored universalist subject matter and exhibited general disdain for Hollywood-type commercial product (though one of his heroes was director John Ford, about whom he wrote a 1981 book). Beginning his directing career in 1948 with small-scale, personal, non-narrative films such as *Meet the Pioneers,* Anderson won an Oscar in 1953 for *Thursday's Children,* a touching documentary about deaf children. His first feature film, *This Sporting Life* (1963), told the story of a disturbed rugby champion with low-key dramatics. Anderson is best known to American film buffs for his trenchant trilogy starring Malcolm

McDowell as Mick Travis, a British "everyman" who survives the public school system in *if.* . . . (1968), the media in *O Lucky Man!* (1973), and the medical establishment in *Britannia Hospital* (1982). His trademark outrage at social inequities was muted in the elegiac *The Whales of August* (1987), but he returned somewhat to form with the bitterly funny made-for-cable *Glory! Glory!* (1989), a satire on televangelism. Also active as a stage director in London. He took occasional acting roles, most notably in *Chariots of Fire* (1981), and in 1992 adapted his book on John Ford into a television documentary which he hosted on-camera.

ANDERSSON, BIBI. Actress. *(b. Nov. 11, 1935, Stockholm.)* One of the brightest performers in Ingmar Bergman's famed "repertory company," Andersson was a 17-year-old drama student appearing on stage when Bergman cast her in a soap commercial. She later received a small role in his film *Smiles of a Summer Night* (1955), and then gained greater prominence in *The Seventh Seal* (1956), *Wild Strawberries* (1957, doing double duty as a student and as Victor Sjostrom's childhood sweetheart), and *Brink of Life* (1958), for which she won the Best Actress Award at Cannes. Her later films for Bergman included *The Touch* (1971), *Scenes From a Marriage* (1973), and two of his most complex works, *Persona* (1966) and *The Passion of Anna* (1969), both of which showcase her abilities to the fullest as she runs through the gamut of psychological traumas. Andersson's work in the U.S. has ranged from roles in solid entertainments—*Duel at Diablo* (1966) and *I Never Promised You a Rose Garden* (1977)—to vehicles unworthy of her talents, such as *The Kremlin Letter* (1970), *Airport '79—The Concorde* (1979), and *Exposed* (1983).

ANDRESS, URSULA. Actress. *(b. Mar. 19, 1936, Bern, Switzerland.)* Her emergence from the sea, bikini-clad, in the first James Bond film, *Dr. No* (1962), provided the swinging sixties with its splashy equivalent of the Birth of Venus; none of her subsequent, multifarious film appearances has been nearly as memorable. She had appeared in several racy-for-their-time

Italian pictures beginning with 1954's *The Loves of Casanova,* and has not shown terrific discrimination or talent since. Her stoic beauty—and the Bond notoriety—propelled her career in the 1960s, with such credits as *4 for Texas, Fun in Acapulco* (both 1963, the latter with Elvis Presley), *She, What's New, Pussycat?, The Tenth Victim* (all 1965), *The Blue Max* (1966), and *Casino Royale* (1967), but by the 1970s she had exhausted her appeal and showed little but her epidermis in *The Sensuous Nurse* (1976) and *Slaves of the Cannibal God* (1978). Once married to actor John Derek (with whom she costarred in 1965's *Nightmare in the Sun),* she met much younger hunk Harry Hamlin on the set of *Clash of the Titans* (1981) and later bore his child.

ANDREWS, ANTHONY. Actor. *(b. Jan. 12, 1948, London.)* Blond British heartthrob who conquered America via TV, notably with the miniseries "Upstairs, Downstairs" and "Brideshead Revisited," but has yet to translate that success to feature films. His first movie roles were bits in *Take Me High* (1974) and *Percy's Progress* (also 1974, aka *It's Not the Size That Counts),* followed by somewhat larger roles in *Operation Daybreak* (1976), *Under the Volcano* (1984), *The Holcroft Covenant* (1985), *The Lighthorsemen* (1987), and *Hanna's War* (1988). But the "telly" remains his real home; in addition to the series "Danger UXB," he has appeared in such TV movies as *A War of Children, QB VII, Ivanhoe* (as Wilfred), *The Scarlet Pimpernel* (in the title role), *Agatha Christie's "Sparkling Cyanide,"* *Suspicion,* and *The Woman He Loved* (as Edward VIII).

ANDREWS, DANA. Actor. *(b. Jan. 1, 1912, Collins, Mo., as Carver Andrews; d. Dec. 17, 1992.)* If you ever get on a plane and find Dana Andrews is the pilot, *get off!* He played ill-fated captains in three airborne disaster dramas: *Zero Hour!* (1957, which was spoofed accurately in *Airplane!), The Crowded Sky* (1960), and *Airport '75* (1974). It's a rare quirk in the career of a sturdy, dependable leading man who was so good at playing ordinary guys, be they gangsters or family men, that it somewhat limited his stardom

(though he never wanted for work). He kept busy both at Goldwyn and 20th Century-Fox—they shared his contract—in the 1940s, starring or costarring in such films as *The Westerner* (1940), *Ball of Fire, Swamp Water, Belle Starr, Tobacco Road* (all 1941), *The Ox-Bow Incident, Crash Dive* (1943), *Up in Arms, Wing and a Prayer* (both 1944), *State Fair, A Walk in the Sun* (both 1945), *Boomerang, Daisy Kenyon* (both 1947), and *Where the Sidewalk Ends* (1950).

Andrews' first great starring role, though, was that of the hard-boiled police detective drawn inexorably into the world (and under the spell) of a beautiful murder victim in the classic whodunit *Laura* (1944). His other personal milestone was as the bomber pilot who cannot adjust to civilian life in *The Best Years of Our Lives* (1946), a role that showed more emotional depth than most of the conventional leading-man assignments that followed. Though probably 10 years too old for the character as written, he pulled it off beautifully.

Among Andrews' more notable titles in the 1950s and beyond were *Elephant Walk* (1954), *Beyond a Reasonable Doubt, While the City Sleeps* (both 1956), *Curse of the Demon* (1958), *Battle of the Bulge, Crack in the World, The Satan Bug, In Harm's Way, The Loved One* (all 1965), *Hot Rods to Hell* (1967, reunited with *State Fair* costar Jeanne Crain), *Innocent Bystanders* (1972), and *The Last Tycoon* (1976). He starred on TV as a college president in the daytime drama "Bright Promise" (1969–72), and was notable as General George C. Marshall in the miniseries "Ike" (1979).

ANDREWS, JULIE. Actress. *(b. Oct. 1, 1935, Walton-on-Thames, England, as Julia Elizabeth Wells.)* For millions around the world, she'll always be Mary Poppins, or Maria, the governess to the Von Trapp family. Those indelible performances in *Mary Poppins* (1964) and *The Sound of Music* (1965) earned her an Oscar and an Oscar nomination, respectively—a great way to start any film career, having swept Broadway off its feet for a decade. Though it's little remembered, Andrews costarred with Bing Crosby in what is sometimes called the first made-for-TV movie, the musical *High Tor* (1956). But after Poppins and Maria, her image as a goody two-shoes was cemented, despite creditable work in *The Americanization of Emily* (1964) and *Hawaii* (1966). She starred in a promising but problematic Hitchcock movie, *Torn Curtain* (1966), and two musical flops in a row, *Star!* (1968, as Gertrude Lawrence) and *Darling Lili* (1970, her first collaboration with husband Blake Edwards). She's since worked mostly for her husband, who plotted to torpedo her Poppins image once and for all by having her bare her breasts in his satiric Hollywood tale *S.O.B.* (1981). Other credits: *Thoroughly Modern Millie* (1967), *The Tamarind Seed* (1974), *10* (1979), *Little Miss Marker* (1980), *Victor/Victoria* (1982, Oscar nomination), *The Man Who Loved Women* (1983), *Duet for One,* and *That's Life!* (both 1986). (A gag appearance with Peter Sellers in one of Edwards' Pink Panther farces wound up on the cutting-room floor, alas.) An ill-fated 1992 TV sitcom ("Julie") was followed by an equally star-crossed feature-film return opposite Marcello Mastroianni (*A Fine Romance,* 1992). Andrews found solace in a national concert tour, and then took New York by storm when she joined the ensemble cast of an off-Broadway Stephen Sondheim revue, "Putting It Together" in 1993. Surely someone in the film industry can find suitable work for such a talented woman.

ANGELI, PIER. Actress. *(b. June 19, 1932, Cagliaru, Sardinia, as Anna Maria Pierangeli; d. Sept. 10, 1971.)* After being discovered by director Leonide Moguy, who cast her as a sensitive teenager (which she was) in *Tomorrow Is Too Late* (1950), this petite, delicate actress was signed by MGM. Like her sister, actress Marisa Pavan, Angeli never quite seemed at home in Hollywood productions—although she was usually cast in roles tailored for her gentle, soulful nature. The breakup of her five-year marriage to singer Vic Damone and the lackluster nature of her Hollywood vehicles drove Angeli back to Europe, where she languished in mediocre, exploitative potboilers. She died of a drug overdose shortly after the release of *In the Folds of the Flesh* (1971).
OTHER FILMS INCLUDE: 1951: *Teresa;* 1953: *Sombrero;* 1955: *The Silver Cha-*

lice; 1956: *Somebody Up There Likes Me;* 1958: *Merry Andrew;* 1962: *Sodom and Gomorrah.*

ANHALT, EDWARD. Screenwriter. *(b. Mar. 28, 1914, New York City.)* Veteran screenwriter who has long been admired for his craftsmanship and versatility. He began making short educational films before joining Pathé News and then CBS, where he served on early television dramas and documentaries. While serving in the army during World War 2, Anhalt and his wife Edna jointly worked on pulp magazine stories which they sold to publications like "Amazing Stories," "Argosy," and "Detective Story." After the war, they collaborated on the scripts for such films as *Bulldog Drummond Strikes Back* (1947) and *The Crime Doctor's Diary* (1949) and won an Oscar for the story of Elia Kazan's tense plague drama *Panic in the Streets* (1950). They earned an Oscar nomination for the story of a fine, understated, chiller, *The Sniper* (1952, the first of four films for Stanley Kramer), and collaborated on the adaptation of *The Member of the Wedding* (1952), *Not as a Stranger* (1955) and *The Pride and the Passion* (1957). The couple divorced and Edward went solo on a number of very different projects, including the WW2 films *In Love and War* and *The Young Lions* (both 1958), the melodramas *The Restless Years* (1959) and *The Sins of Rachel Cade* (1960), adaptations of *Wives and Lovers* (1963) and the historical drama *Becket* (1964, which won him another Oscar), the Jerry Lewis comedy *Boeing Boeing* (1965), the post–OK Corral Western *Hour of the Gun* (1967), and the documentary-like *The Boston Strangler* (1968). He also adapted *The Madwoman of Chaillot* (1969), *Luther* (1974), and *The Man in the Glass Booth* (1975) and cowrote *Girls, Girls, Girls* (1962), *The Satan Bug* (1965), *Jeremiah Johnson* (1972), *Escape to Athena* (1979), *Green Ice* (1981), and *The Holcroft Covenant* (1985).

ANKERS, EVELYN. Actress. *(b. Aug. 17, 1918, Valparaiso, Chile; d. Aug. 28, 1985.)* If Fay Wray was the "Scream Queen" of the 1930s, then this handsome, auburn-haired leading lady surely held that title in the

1940s. Of British parentage, she embarked on her film career in the U.K., appearing in such films as *Rembrandt* (1936), *Fire Over England, Knight Without Armour, Wings of the Morning* (all 1937), *The Villiers Diamond* (her first lead), and *Murder in the Family* (both 1938, opposite an equally youthful Jessica Tandy). She came to Hollywood after Britain had been attacked by the Nazis, and was contracted by Universal in 1941. Her first break came in the Abbott and Costello starrer *Hold That Ghost* (1941); immediately after, she costarred opposite Lon Chaney, Jr., in the smash hit *The Wolf Man.* That pretty much sealed her fate, and for the next few years she exercised her larynx in *Ghost of Frankenstein, Sherlock Holmes and the Voice of Terror* (both 1942), *Son of Dracula, Captive Wild Woman, The Mad Ghoul* (all 1943), *The Invisible Man's Revenge, Jungle Woman* (both 1944), and *The Frozen Ghost* (1945). She occasionally got to play a villainess, as in 1944's *Weird Woman* and the Sherlock Holmes entry *The Pearl of Death.* And to be fair, there *were* some nonhorror films among Ankers' Universal output, too, among them *His Butler's Sister* (1943), *Ladies Courageous,* and *Pardon My Rhythm* (both 1944).

Ankers worked less frequently on-screen after leaving Universal in 1946, turning up in *Queen of Burlesque, The French Key* (both 1946), *The Lone Wolf in London* (1947), *Tarzan's Magic Fountain* (1949), and *The Texan and Calamity Jane* (1950, as Jane). Her only noteworthy appearance thereafter was in a 1960 religious film, *No Greater Love.* She was married to actor Richard Denning, and they eventually retired to Hawaii, where she was content to stay out of camera range for the remainder of her life.

ANNAKIN, KEN. Director, producer, screenwriter. *(b. Aug. 10, 1914, Beverley, East Yorkshire, England.)* British director who cut his teeth making documentaries in the early 1940s and moved on to fictional features like *Holiday Camp* (1947), *Miranda* (1949), *Hotel Sahara* (1951), and excellent episodes of the Somerset Maugham omnibus films *Quartet* (1948, "The Colonel's Lady"), and *Trio* (1950, "The Verger"). Then Walt Disney, seeking a British director to make costume films for him in the U.K., hired Annakin for *The Story of Robin Hood and his Merrie Men* (1952). The results were so good that Disney hired him to make *The Sword and the Rose* (1953), the exciting mountain-climbing saga *Third Man on the Mountain* (1959), and escapist *Swiss Family Robinson* (1960), which collectively stand as some of his best work. He was one of three directors on *The Longest Day* (1962), but his biggest post-Disney success was undoubtedly *Those Magnificent Men in Their Flying Machines* (1965), for which he shared an Oscar nomination for Best Screenplay.

OTHER FILMS INCLUDE: 1955: *Value for Money;* 1957: *Across the Bridge;* 1965: *The Battle of the Bulge;* 1969: *Those Daring Young Men in Their Jaunty Jalopies;* 1975: *Paper Tiger;* 1979: *The Fifth Musketeer;* 1982: *The Pirate Movie;* 1988: *The New Adventures of Pippi Longstocking.*

ANNAUD, JEAN-JACQUES. Director, screenwriter. *(b. Oct. 1, 1943, Draveil, France.)* Internationally acclaimed filmmaker who began his career directing hundreds of television commercials during the late 1960s and early 1970s. He wrote and directed his first film, *Black and White in Color* (1976), influenced by his own experiences in military service in Cameroon, Africa. It made little money in his native country, but went on to win an Oscar as Best Foreign Film. Annaud's follow-up, *Hot Head* (1979), established his reputation in France, and his next film *Quest for Fire* (1981), a unique story of primitive man set 80,000 years ago, won French Cesar Awards for Best Picture and Best Director. It firmly established Annaud as a director of uncategorizable films who shies away from anything that could be described as formulaic. He directed Sean Connery in an adaptation of Umberto Eco's challenging novel *The Name of the Rose* (1986), set in the 13th century, and then made international stars out of a bear cub and a nine-foot two-inch Kodiak in *The Bear* (1989), which related the friendship of the two animals with virtually no dialogue. Annaud's most recent film, *The Lover* (1992), caused an uproar with its provocative—and sexually explicit—depiction of a romance between a French girl and a wealthy Chinese man in 1920s French Indochina.

ANN-MARGRET. Actress, singer, dancer. *(b. Apr. 28, 1941, Valsjobyn, Sweden, as Ann Margret Olsson.)* A musical appearance on an Oscar broadcast (singing the title song from *Bachelor in Paradise*) made Hollywood sit up and take notice of this Illinois-raised Swedish beauty. Her combination of squeaky-clean, all-American looks and uninhibited dancing led to a spate of fluffy roles, but she eventually matured into a talented dramatic actress as well. She first appeared on film in *Pocketful of Miracles* (1961) and *State Fair* (1962) in vapid but appealing ingenue roles. Her movie career picked up once she established her vibrant, youthful screen persona with the tuneful *Bye Bye Birdie* (1963) and *Viva Las Vegas* (1964, with Elvis Presley). She also achieved a kind of immortality in an animated guest appearance as "Ann-Margrock" on an episode of "The Flintstones." But with musicals already out, she floundered in various floozy roles throughout the 1960s, reaching a nadir of sorts in the campus-rebellion drama *R.P.M.* (1970). Daringly cast in Mike Nichols' frank drama *Carnal Knowledge* (1971), she sparkled as a pathetically needy sexpot and received an Academy Award nomination. (She was nominated again in 1975 for her role in the rock opera *Tommy.*)

A 22-foot fall from a platform in 1972 nearly ended her career *and* her life, but she made a near-miraculous recovery. In 1978 she gave a mature, perfectly realized performance in *Magic,* a psychothriller costarring Anthony Hopkins. Since then, she's settled into lusty-older-woman roles in middling-to-bad movies such as *Lookin' to Get Out* (1982), *Twice in a Lifetime* (1985), *A Tiger's Tale* (1987), *A New Life* (1988), *Newsies* (1992), and *Grumpy Old Men* (1993). She has had more success on the small screen, with fine work in TV movies like *Who Will Love My Children?* (1983) and *A Streetcar Named Desire* (1984) and the miniseries "The Two Mrs. Grenvilles" (1987), "Alex Haley's Queen" (1993) and "Scarlett" (1994, as Belle Watling). She published her autobiography in 1994.

ANSPACH, SUSAN. Actress. *(b. Nov. 23, 1945, New York City.)* Her offbeat good looks, tousled blond hair and aura of uninhibited curiosity made her a natural in supporting roles in "with-it" 1970s pictures like *The Landlord* (1970), *Play It Again, Sam* (1972, hilariously deadpan as Woody Allen's free-spirited ex-wife), and *Blume in Love* (1973, this time as George Segal's ex-wife). Her best role, though, was one of her first, a music teacher who falls for Jack Nicholson in *Five Easy Pieces* (1970). An Actors' Studio alumnus whose stage experience included plays with Dustin Hoffman, Robert Duvall, and Al Pacino, Anspach never found a niche in mainstream films. After *The Big Fix* (1978) and *Running* (1979), she experienced her last cinematic blaze of glory as a repressed housewife in Dusan Makavejev's subversive *Montenegro* (1981); since then she's been seen mainly in B pictures such as *Into the Fire* (1988) and *Killer Instinct* (1990).

ANTONELLI, LAURA. Actress. *(b. Nov. 28, 1941, Pola, Italy.)* She had the face of an angel and the body of a . . . well, you know the rest. And that was precisely Antonelli's appeal during her heyday in the 1970s, when the screen had liberalized its portrayal of sexual mores. The voluptuous brunette might have been another Bardot; unfortunately a string of fairly unmemorable pictures and a lack of Bardot's *je ne sais quoi* kept her from advancing beyond sex-symbol status. Her most popular pictures stateside include *The Divine Nymph* (1971), *Till Marriage Do Us Part, Malicious* (both 1974), *The Innocent* (1978, one of her best, the last film of director Luchino Visconti), and *Wifemistress* (1977). Last seen here opposite Tony Musante in 1989's *Collector's Item.* Antonelli was once linked romatically with French star Jean-Paul Belmondo.

ANTONIONI, MICHELANGELO. Director. *(b. Sept. 29, 1912, Ferrara, Italy.)* Although he came from a different generation than the French and Italian filmmakers who created such a stir on the international scene in the late 1950s and early 1960s, Antonioni was often grouped with them anyway, mainly because his breakthrough picture, *L'Avventura* (1960), was released at the height of the cinematic New Wave. Unlike novice auteurs of the time such as Pasolini, Godard, and Truffaut, Antonioni was already a seasoned director with several documentary shorts and fairly conventional (albeit cerebral) features to his credit when he made *L'Avventura*. This enigmatic and sometimes eerie character study, with its architectural rigor employed in the service of a plot that Antonioni refused to resolve (at least in any commonly accepted narrative fashion), created an immediate critical furor and forever attached to its creator's name the term "modern alienation." The director's work deals with a lot more than that, but the inability of his characters to communicate with each other is a constant in almost all of his films. *La Notte* (1961) and *L'Eclisse* (1962) followed, completing a trilogy on the alienation theme.

Antonioni showed particular sympathy to his female characters in the films that followed; his first color picture, *The Red Desert* (1964), which starred then-lover Monica Vitti (who had shared in the sensation created by *L'Avventura)*, can easily be read as a feminist film. Antonioni's second breakthrough picture was *Blowup* (1966), his first English-language film, which earned Oscar nominations for Best Director and Screenplay. A dazzling riddle on perception versus reality, it first captured audiences with its more superficial aspects, being in part a hip, up-to-the-minute depiction of swinging London that contained a sexual frankness heretofore unseen in commercial cinema (it was the first major studio release to feature full frontal nudity—about a half-second's worth, but enough to get noticed).

The success of *Blowup* brought Antonioni to America, where in 1970 he made the disastrous *Zabriskie Point*, a very misguided attempt to portray the student radical movement of the era. (In a disquieting case of life imitating bad art, the film's lead, Mark Frechette, was convicted after an SLA-style bank robbery and was killed in prison.) Taking a hiatus from commercial filmmaking (during which time he directed a documentary), Antonioni returned in 1975 with the breathtaking *The Passenger.* Featuring one of Jack Nicholson's most finely modulated performances, and some of the most beautiful imagery Antonioni ever captured on film, the movie was widely misunderstood on release. After a number of abortive attempts to get another project entitled *Suffer or Die* off the ground (both Debra Winger and Mick Jagger were approached to star) Antonioni returned to Italy, where he continued directing sporadically (including *Il Misterio di Oberwald*, a shot-on-video work featuring Vitti). His work no longer commands the international audience it once did, and his last few pictures did not get U.S. releases. *The Crew,* a project he was set to direct for Martin Scorsese's production company, has been put on indefinite hold. In 1995 he received an honorary Academy Award.

ANWAR, GABRIELLE. Actress. *(b. Feb. 4, 1970, Laleham, England.)* Attractive actress who charmed moviegoers as Al Pacino's tango partner in 1992's *Scent of a Woman*. Trained at a London drama and dance school, Anwar appeared in many BBC-TV productions before making her film debut in the U.S.-Yugoslavian production *Manifesto* (1988). She followed with *If Looks Could Kill* (1991) before making a splash (literally) as real-life "diving girl" on horseback Sonora Webster in the sincere and underrated Disney picture *Wild Hearts Can't Be Broken* (1991). Had the film been a hit, it could have been a star-making vehicle for the radiant Anwar (who also managed to suppress her British accent for this American role). Since the success of *Scent of a Woman*, she has starred as Michael J. Fox's love interest in *For Love or Money* (1993) and as the heroine in Abel Ferrara's gruesome *Body Snatchers* (1994).

APTED, MICHAEL. Director, producer. *(b. Feb. 19, 1941, Aylesbury, Buckinghamshire, England.)* Talented filmmaker whose sensitivity to characters and their environments is evident in both his fiction films and documentaries. Apted studied law and history at Cambridge University, then worked at Granada Television as a researcher. Within a few years, he became a prominent and versatile TV director, winning several British Emmys for his work and compiling scores of credits. He made his feature debut with *Triple Echo* (1973) and scored a hit with *Stardust* (1975), which chronicled—with uncanny believability—the rise of a Beatles-like music group. After *The Squeeze* (1977) and the intriguing *Agatha* (1979), Apted had his first international hit with *Coal Miner's Daughter* (1980), the biography of country singer Loretta Lynn, which won Sissy Spacek a Best Actress Oscar. Since then Apted has tackled a variety of films, but tries to alternate Hollywood movies with smaller, more personal projects and documentaries. His credits include *Continental Divide* (1981), *Kipperbang* (1982), *Gorky Park* (1983), *Firstborn* (1984), *Bring on the Night* (1985), *Critical Condition* (1987), *Gorillas in the Mist* (1988), *Class Action* (1991), *Thunderheart,* and its documentary companion piece, *Incident at Oglala* (both 1992), and *Nell* (1994). But Apted's most remarkable achievement remains his unique series of documentaries—*7 Up, 7 Plus 7, 21, 28 Up,* and *35 Up*—which have followed the lives of 14 Britons since the age of seven—in seven-year increments.

ARAU, ALFONSO. Actor, director. *(b. Jan. 11, 1932, Mexico City.)* Familiar to American audiences for his character performances—usually as evil bandits—Arau is also a talented filmmaker and one of Mexico's top actors and directors. Extensively trained in theatre, vaudeville, and television, Arau began acting in Mexican films in the late 1960s and made his American debut in the Sam Peckinpah classic *The Wild Bunch* (1969), as Herrera. Since then, he has appeared in the cult favorite *El Topo, Scandalous John* (both 1971), *Posse* (1975), *Used Cars* (1980), *Romancing the Stone* (1984) and *¡Three Amigos!* (1986, in a near-parody of his *Wild Bunch* role). He has won awards for his Mexican films *The Barefoot Eagle* and *Calzonzin Inspector* and received international acclaim for directing *Like Water for Chocolate* (1992), the story of a young woman who expresses her emotions through cooking, which became one of the most successful foreign-language films ever released in the U.S. It was based on a best-selling novel written by his wife, Laura Esquivel.

ARBUCKLE, ROSCOE "FATTY." Actor, producer, director. *(b. Mar. 24, 1887, Smith Center, Kans., as Roscoe Conkling Arbuckle; d. June 29, 1933.)* It's a shame that this rotund, jolly-faced actor—one of the silent screen's biggest stars and major talents—is mainly remembered for his role in one of Hollywood's most notorious scandals. A Kansas youth who entered show business as a carnival performer, Arbuckle got into movies in 1908, his pudgy but expressive face and corpulent figure making him a natural for slapstick comedy. Signing with producer Mack Sennett in 1913, he made dozens of short subjects with Keystone Kops, bathing beauties, and popular leading lady Mabel Normand. Arbuckle, who wrote and directed films as early as 1915, launched his own production company (for which he hired another talented comic named Buster Keaton) in 1917. His subsequent films, including *Out West* (1918), *Back Stage* (1919), *The Roundup* (1920), and *Brewster's Millions* (1921) among them, were extremely successful. The humor, especially in the Keaton-Arbuckle collaborations (with Al St. John as the third member of the triumverate) are particularly raucous slapstick sessions, and often very funny.

In 1921, following a notorious "wild party" in which actress Virginia Rappe suffered a ruptured bladder (allegedly sustained as a result of Arbuckle's amorous advances), the comedian was accused of manslaughter and tried three times before being acquitted in 1923. By then, however, he had been blacklisted by Hollywood; his starring films were withdrawn from circulation and he could only secure pseudonymous work (billed as "William B. Goodrich") as a director. Mostly behind the megaphone until he died, Arbuckle's directorial efforts included an early Eddie Cantor feature, *Special Delivery* (1927) and a short subject, *Windy Riley Goes Hollywood* (1931), starring Louise Brooks.

He finally got a chance to work on-screen again in a series of two-reel short subjects for Warner-Vitaphone in the early 1930s; though the quality varied (the best one is 1933's *Buzzin' Around),* the most remarkable aspect of these knockabout comedies is how Arbuckle—after all he'd been through—was able to recapture the wide-eyed innocence of his original screen personality. Unfortunately, the comeback was short-lived; he died in mid-1933, with several of those short subjects yet to be released.

ARCHER, ANNE. Actress. *(b. Aug. 25, 1947, Los Angeles.)* A striking, silky-voiced brunette probably best remembered as the "perfect" wife in Adrian Lyne's 1987 megahit *Fatal Attraction,* Archer was born into a show-business family: Her father, John Archer, was an actor, and her mother, Marjorie Lord, starred opposite Danny Thomas in the popular TV series "Make Room for Daddy." She studied theater arts at Claremont College before landing her first film assignment opposite Jon Voight in *The All-American Boy* (1970). Archer worked in *Cancel My Reservation* (1972) with Bob Hope, enjoyed plum roles in the made-for-TV movies *The Blue Knight* (1973) and *The Mark of Zorro* (1974), played Sam Elliott's old flame in *Lifeguard* (1976), and was Chuck Norris' first leading lady in *Good Guys Wear Black* (1977). Roles in *Paradise Alley* (1978), *Hero at Large* (1980), and *Green Ice* (1981) did little to advance her career, which finally got a well-deserved boost from her work in the 1981 off-Broadway success, "A Coupla White Chicks Sitting Around Talking." With husband Terry Jastrow, she wrote, produced, and starred in *Waltz Across Texas* (1982), a pleasant if unspectacular modern romance. She tackled her first mother part in *The Check Is in the Mail* (1986), before being cast as Michael Douglas' spouse in *Fatal Attraction,* which won her critical acclaim and an Oscar nomination. *Love at Large, Narrow Margin* (both 1990), and *Eminent Domain* (1991) gave her meaty parts, but *Patriot Games,* in which she played Harrison Ford's wife, finally brought her another hit. Recent credits include *Body of Evidence, Short Cuts* (both 1993) and *Clear and Present Danger* (1994).

ARDANT, FANNY. Actress. *(b. Mar. 22, 1949, Monte Carlo.)* Tall, leggy, long-faced but quite striking actress; François Truffaut's protégée and lover, she appeared in two of his last pictures, *The Woman Next Door* (1981) and *Confidentally Yours* (1983). Infrequently seen here, she impressed American audiences in *Swann in Love* (1984, costarring Jeremy Irons), and Alain Resnais's peculiar, deliberately stagey *Mèlo* (1986). She also appeared to good advantage in Ettore Scola's *The Family* (1987).

ARDEN, EVE. Actress. *(b. Apr. 30, 1912, Mill Valley, Calif., as Eunice Quedens; d. Nov. 12, 1990.)* If this tall, attractive blonde didn't exactly invent the character of the leading lady's sardonic, wise-cracking—and usually dateless—best friend, she certainly set the standard for all the others. She'd been on stage since her teens, and even had bits in a couple of early musicals, *The Song of Love* (1929) and *Dancing Lady* (1933), for which production records list her under her real name. In 1934, she returned to New York and became a Ziegfeld girl, but three years later she was back on the Coast, and almost immediately molded her screen persona as a cynical would-be actress in *Stage Door* (1937). She worked virtually nonstop thereafter, most notably in *Having Wonderful Time, Letter of Introduction* (both 1938), *At the Circus* (1939, as perhaps the only woman to get the best of Groucho), *Slightly Honorable, Comrade X* (both 1940), *Ziegfeld Girl, Whistling in the Dark, Manpower* (all 1941), *Let's Face It* (1943), *Cover Girl* (1944), *Mildred Pierce* (1945, with a dazzling performance that earned her an Oscar nomination), *Night and Day, The Kid From Brooklyn* (both 1946), *The Unfaithful, Voice of the Turtle* (both 1947), *One Touch of Venus* (1948), *Tea for Two, Paid in Full* (both 1950), and *We're Not Married* (1952).

That same year marked a turning point in Arden's career: She'd been playing Connie Brooks, the utterly sane (but still sharp-tongued) schoolteacher in a well-liked radio sitcom, "Our Miss Brooks," since 1948, but in 1952 the show moved to TV and became an instant smash. It ran four years, earning her an Emmy in 1953, and even spinning off a feature version in 1956. She concentrated on TV thereafter, including two more sitcoms, "The Eve Arden Show" (1957–58) and "The Mothers-In-Law" (1967–69), and such TV movies as *All My Darling Daughters* (1972). Arden also returned to the stage during this period. But she still made occasional film appearances, notably in *Anatomy of a Murder* (1959), *The Dark at the Top of the Stairs* (1960), *Sergeant*

Deadhead (1965), *Under the Rainbow* (1981), and the *Grease* movies (1978 and 1982). Hers was a unique comic talent, and the screen is much poorer for her absence. Her autobiography, "Three Phases of Eve," was published in 1985.

ARGENTO, DARIO. Director. *(b. Sept. 7, 1943, Italy.)* Horror-film director and cult favorite credited as influencing most latter-day "splatter" films. He entered the business as a screenwriter, collaborating with Bernardo Bertolucci on the script for *Once Upon a Time in the West* (1969). Argento's first directorial efforts, *The Bird With the Crystal Plumage* (1969) and *Cat o' Nine Tails* (1971), combined the plot devices of an old penny dreadful with Hitchcockian cinematic flair. *Deep Red* (1975), *Suspiria* (1977), and *Inferno* (1980) found Argento incorporating the influence of Italian horror-movie maestro Mario Bava into his already ornate visual style, which celebrated striking imagery and idiosyncratic use of color over plot and structure. *Creepers* (1985) and *Opera* (1987), made a decade later, reveal a mastery of visual technique, although Argento's disturbing visions and sadistic flirtations make these works tough going for mainstream viewers. He turned to producing, overseeing *Dawn of the Dead* (1978) and *Demons* (1986), among others. Argento and friend/partner George Romero codirected *Two Evil Eyes* (1991), a long-shelved horror anthology that failed to generate any excitement—even among Argento cultists—when it was finally released. In 1993 Argento returned to the U.S. to make another English-language film (with a prominent American cast), *Trauma.*

ARKIN, ALAN. Actor. *(b. Mar. 26, 1934, New York City.)* Talented actor whose distinctive style of wry, deadpan dialogue delivery and mastery of dialect has made his diverse screen performances a delight, beginning with an Oscar-nominated turn in *The Russians Are Coming, The Russians Are Coming* (1966), in which he played an abandoned Russian sailor. Again nominated for an Academy Award as the deaf-mute in *The Heart Is a Lonely Hunter* (1968), Arkin has successfully alternated dramatic and comedic roles. He briefly

supplanted Peter Sellers as *Inspector Clouseau* (1968), played a 1930s movie director in *Hearts of the West* (1975), interpreted Freud in *The Seven Percent Solution* (1976), donned superhero togs in *The Return of Captain Invincible* (1982), and, more recently, played a gentle but bored suburbanite in *Edward Scissorhands* (1990) and an eccentric mechanic in *The Rocketeer* (1991). He is frequently better than his material, as proved by his superior comic turns in *The In-Laws* (1979), *Improper Channels* (1979), and *Simon* (1980), to name a few. Arkin took stabs at directing in 1971, adapting Jules Feiffer's play *Little Murders* to the screen, and in 1977, helming the truly wretched *Fire Sale.* More recently, he held his own in the all-star *Glengarry Glen Ross* (1992) and gave a warm-hearted performance as the aging camp director in the nostalgic *Indian Summer* (1993). He also contributed an amusing cameo (without billing) as a mild-mannered police chief in 1993's *So I Married an Axe Murderer.* His son Adam Arkin has become a familiar face in films and especially on television, as a regular cast member of several series including "Northern Exposure," 1993's "Big Wave Dave's," in which he had the starring role, and "Chicago Hope" (1994–).

ARLEN, RICHARD. Actor. *(b. Sept. 1, 1899, Charlottesville, Va., as Richard Cornelius van Mattimore; d. Mar. 28, 1976.)* You'd think any actor who could be a silent-screen idol and *still* be starring in movies a full four decades later ought to be better known than this ruggedly handsome, good-humored leading man is today. A former journalist and pilot, the scion of the van Mattimores broke into the movies in the early 1920s—in the 1923 *Vengeance of the Deep,* he's billed under his real name—and eventually became a contract player at Paramount, popping up in such films as *Behind the Front, You'd Be Surprised* (both 1926), and *Rolled Stockings* (1927), before the studio put him in a leading role in its World War 1 epic *Wings* (1927). It made Arlen an instant star, and he was immediately working nonstop in such varied fare as *Beggars of Life* (1928), *The Four Feathers, The Virginian* (both 1929), *The Border Legion* (1930), *Touchdown!* (1931), *Tiger Shark* (on loan to

Warner Bros.), *Island of Lost Souls* (both 1932), *College Humor, Alice in Wonderland* (as the Cheshire Cat), *Three-Cornered Moon* (all 1933), and *Come On, Marines!* (1934). His star on the wane, he was dropped by Paramount in 1935 and almost immediately became mired in a string of unimportant programmers. He still managed to appear in occasional A films, such as *Let 'Em Have It* (1935) and *Artists and Models* (1937), but the die was cast.

In 1939 Universal teamed Arlen with Andy Devine; as the "Aces of Action," they roared through 14 B films, including *Mutiny on the Blackhawk* (1939), *Hot Steel* (1940), and *Raiders of the Desert* (1941). He then starred in another series of grade-B actioners for the Pine-Thomas unit at Paramount, usually teamed with Chester Morris; titles include *Power Dive* (1941), *Flying Blind,* and *The Wrecking Crew* (both 1942). Arlen worked sporadically thereafter, occasionally snagging a juicy lead such as his mad scientist in *The Lady and the Monster* (1944, the first film version of the classic sci-fi story, "Donovan's Brain"). His later films include *When My Baby Smiles at Me* (1948), *Hurricane Smith* (1952), *Warlock* (1959), *The Best Man* (1964), and *The Human Duplicators* (1965).

When Arlen's longtime friend A. C. Lyles produced a series of budget Westerns at Paramount in the mid-1960s, the star returned to his old studio for *Law of the Lawless* (1964), *Town Tamer* (1965), and *Buckskin* (1968), among others. Paramount also gave Arlen his last screen role, in the 1976 spoof *Won Ton Ton, the Dog Who Saved Hollywood,* more than half a century after he'd first strolled onto the lot. His first wife was silent-film leading lady Jobyna Ralston.

ARLISS, GEORGE. Actor. (b. Apr. 10, 1868, London, as George Augustus Andrews; d. Feb. 5, 1946.) Monocle firmly in place, finger raised defiantly in the air, stately oratory grandly filling the room—if people remember this leonine, cultured actor at all, it is for the distinguished historical figures he played on-screen during the 1920s and 1930s. But that's only half the story: Arliss was also a splendid light comedy actor who made numerous charming domestic frou-frous as well, often ap-

pearing opposite his wife, Florence Montgomery. Originally a stage star (and one trained in the grand manner), the slight but imposing Arliss came to America around the turn of the century and pretty much settled here for the next three decades. He made quite a few silent films— *The Devil, Disraeli* (both 1921), *The Ruling Passion, The Man Who Played God* (both 1922), *The Green Goddess* (1923), and *$20 a Week* (1924) among them—but he wasn't thrilled with the medium. Talkies, of course, were different; here, truly, such a dynamic actor could dominate the screen. His first sound film, a remake of *Disraeli* (1929), earned Arliss a Best Actor Oscar, and he immediately settled in as Warner Bros.' "prestige" star, appearing in such further dramatic pieces as *The Green Goddess* (1930), *Alexander Hamilton* (for which he also provided the story), *The Millionaire* (both 1931), *The Man Who Played God* (1932), and *Voltaire* (1933). Interspersed with these were the comedies: *Old English* (1930), *A Successful Calamity* (1932), *The Working Man* (a remake of *$20 a Week*), and *The King's Vacation* (both 1933).

When Warners' production chief Darryl Zanuck left in 1933 to start his own company, Twentieth Century Pictures, Arliss went with him and made *House of Rothschild* (a dual role as father and son), *The Last Gentleman* (both 1934), and *Cardinal Richelieu* (1935). He then returned to England and made a few more films, notably *Transatlantic Tunnel* (1935), *East Meets West* (1936), and *Dr. Syn* (1937), then retired to take care of Florence, who had become blind. In all of Arliss' performances, his plummy voice, bemused expression, and absolute command of audience attention mark him as a very special performer in sore need of rediscovery. Their son, Leslie Arliss, became a writer/director whose credits include *The Night Has Eyes* (1942), *The Wicked Lady* (1945, and cowriter of the 1983 remake), *Idol of Paris* (1948), and *See How They Run* (1952). Arliss published two volumes of autobiography: "Up the Years from Bloomsbury" (1927) and "My Ten Years in the Studios" (1940).

ARMENDARIZ, PEDRO. Actor. (b. May 9, 1912, Churubusco, Mexico; d. June 18, 1963.) At one time Mexico's most popular male star (working often with director Emilio Fernandez and costar Dolores Del Rio, in films like 1943's *Maria Candelaria),* Armendariz made his American film debut for director John Ford in *The Fugitive* (1947), and subsequently appeared in the director's *Fort Apache* and *3 Godfathers* (both 1948), in which he costarred. Educated in Texas and California, Armendariz began acting in Mexican movies in 1935; only one of them, *The Pearl* (1945, based on the John Steinbeck novella), received wide distribution in the U.S., but it left a lasting impression. Other films include *The Torch* (1950), *El Bruto* (1952, for director Luis Buñuel), *The Littlest Outlaw* (1955, for Disney), *The Conqueror* (1956), *The Big Boodle* (1957), *Francis of Assisi* (1961), *Captain Sinbad,* and his last, *From Russia, With Love* (both 1963). During the filming of that movie, Armendariz learned he had cancer, and committed suicide. His son, Pedro Armendariz, Jr., has been active in films since the 1970s.

ARMETTA, HENRY. Actor. *(b. July 4, 1888, Palermo, Italy; d. Oct. 21, 1945.)* When people refer to the stereotyped movie Italian of years past, they're usually referring to the endearing Armetta, a short, stocky, moon-faced fellow who spoke in a comic broken English and listed to one side as he walked. He came to this country as a stowaway in his teens; while pressing pants at the famous Lambs Club in New York City, he met a prominent producer who got him a bit part in a play, which led to a long stage career. He went to Hollywood in 1923, eventually appearing in over 120 movies, nearly always as a waiter, organ grinder, or tailor. Among his more prominent credits: D. W. Griffith's *Lady of the Pavements* (1929), *Scarface* (1932), *Poor Little Rich Girl* (1936) with Shirley Temple, and The Marx Brothers' *The Big Store* (1941). As good-natured Poppa Gambini, he was the unofficial star of a series of Fox B pictures including *Speed to Burn* (1938) and *Winner Take All* (1939). One of movies' most familiar players, he was even caricatured in several 1930s cartoons.

ARMSTRONG, GILLIAN. Director. *(b. Dec. 18, 1950, Melbourne, Australia.)* "At

her best," Molly Haskell has written, ". . . Gillian Armstrong cuts closer to the core of women's divided yearnings than any other director." In the early 1970s, she began working as an editor for a commercial house that made educational and industrial films, then won a scholarship to the Australian Film and Television School. She went on to direct several prize-winning documentary and short films. She made an auspicious feature directing debut with *My Brilliant Career* (1979), about a woman determined to be a writer in 1890s Australia. The film received international acclaim, won seven Australian Film Institute Awards—including Best Film and Best Direction—and made a star out of its leading lady, Judy Davis. Armstrong followed with the clever musical *Starstruck* (1982), then succumbed to the lure of Hollywood. Her first film was the moody *Mrs. Soffel* (1984), which starred Diane Keaton as a prison warden's wife who falls in love with convicted murderer Mel Gibson. It was not a success, and she returned to Australia, where she was reunited with Judy Davis for *High Tide* (1987), the story of a woman who rediscovers the daughter she had abandoned years earlier. Again Armstrong agreed to try an American project, but later described the (little-seen) political love story *Fires Within* (1991) as the worst experience of her life, because the film was taken away from her during postproduction. Armstrong retrenched in her native country, and earned worldwide acclaim for *The Last Days of Chez Nous* (1993), a brittle portrait of a love triangle involving a writer, her husband, and her younger sister. She returned to Hollywood to direct a marvelous adaptation of *Little Women* (1994).

ARMSTRONG, ROBERT. Actor. *(b. Nov. 20, 1890, Saginaw, Mich., as Donald Smith; d. Apr. 20, 1973.)* In the immortal "It was beauty killed the beast," this slick-haired, doughy-faced character actor got one of the most famous exit lines in movie history, uttered in *King Kong* (1933) by his character, adventurous filmmaker Carl Denham, a role he repeated in the same-year sequel, *The Son of Kong.* He worked on stage and in vaudeville prior to his first screen role in *The Main Event* (1927), and had his first big success the next year in Howard Hawks' *A Girl in Every Port.* Armstrong played a variety of tough guys on both sides of the law in such films as *The Cop* (1928), *Big Money, Paid* (both 1930), *Iron Man* (1931), *Panama Flo,* and *The Lost Squadron* (both 1932); that same year, while *Kong* was still in production, he played the effete drunk in *The Most Dangerous Game,* partially shot at night on vacant *Kong* sets. His other films include *"G" Men* (1935), *Public Enemy's Wife* (1936), *Three Legionnaires* (1937), *The Night Hawk* (1938), *Man of Conquest* (1939, as Jim Bowie), *Dive Bomber* (1941), *My Favorite Spy* (1942), *The Mad Ghoul* (1943), *Blood on the Sun* (1945, as a Japanese villain!), *The Sea of Grass, The Fugitive* (both 1947), *The Paleface* (1948), and *Mighty Joe Young* (1949, another giant-ape tale, in which he virtually reprised his *Kong* role). He also appeared in several serials, most notably *Gang Busters* (1942).

From the 1950s on, Armstrong concentrated on TV guest shots, though he still did an occasional feature, like *Johnny Cool* (1963) and *For Those Who Think Young* (1964). But it's *Kong* that will always be his calling card; indeed, its hold on him continued even to the obituary page: he and the film's coproducer, Merian C. Cooper, died within 24 hours of each other.

ARNOLD, EDWARD. Actor. *(b. Feb. 18, 1890, New York City, as Guenther Schneider; d. Apr. 26, 1956.)* He was Diamond Jim Brady and Johann Sutter, Daniel Webster and Nero Wolfe. Few character actors achieved the particular kind of stardom that came to Edward Arnold in the 1930s, playing historical figures and dynamic, larger-than-life characters. Burly and round-faced, with piercing eyes and sharp nose, Arnold was a commanding presence. A child of New York's Lower East Side tenements, Arnold appeared in an amateur production of "The Merchant of Venice" while still in his teens. He worked in several Broadway shows and briefly flirted with movie stardom in 1915 as the lead in several dozen Chicago-made films, returning to the stage during the 1920s. Arnold's trip to Hollywood in 1932 began his most productive period. He played Diamond Jim Brady in *Diamond Jim* (1935) and *Lillian Russell* (1940), Daniel Webster in

All That Money Can Buy (1941, aka *The Devil and Daniel Webster),* tycoon Jim Fisk in *The Toast of New York* (1937), and Johann Sutter in *Sutter's Gold* (1936). He's also seen at his best in *Meet Nero Wolfe* (1935), *Come and Get It* (1936), *You Can't Take It With You* (1938), *Mr. Smith Goes to Washington* (1939), *Johnny Apollo* (1940), *Meet John Doe* (1941, a particularly juicy role as a would-be Fascist power broker), *Eyes in the Night* (1942) and *The Hidden Eye* (1945, a pair of films that starred him as blind detective Duncan McClain), *The Hucksters* (1947), *Command Decision* (1948), *Annie Get Your Gun* (1950), *Living It Up* (1954), and *Miami Expose* (1956), to name a few. He continued acting in prominent supporting roles up until his death. His autobiography, "Lorenzo Goes to Hollywood," was published in 1940.

ARQUETTE, ROSANNA. Actress. *(b. Aug. 10, 1959, New York City.)* This pouty, slender actress frequently plays fragile, misunderstood, and sometimes neurotic women, and while her star never ascended to the heights predicted for her, Arquette has enjoyed considerable success as an offbeat leading lady. Out of an acting family, she was bitten by the bug while in grade school, and left home at age 15, trading the lights of New York for the hills of Hollywood. She played small roles in several films—including *Zuma Beach* (1978 telefilm), *More American Graffiti* (1979), *Gorp* (1980), and *S.O.B.* (1981), before achieving recognition in 1982 as the killer's girlfriend in the widely seen made-for-TV movie *The Executioner's Song,* and in the title role in *Johnny Belinda,* an above-average TV-movie remake. Writer-director John Sayles starred her in his quirky, low-budgeted *Baby, It's You* (1983), but her breakout role was that of the bored housewife in *Desperately Seeking Susan* (1985), anchoring what had been touted as a low-budget vehicle for pop singer Madonna.

A supporting turn in *Silverado* (1985) didn't offer Arquette much opportunity, but she was a memorable suicide victim in *After Hours* (1985), Martin Scorsese's Yuppie-in-wonderland black comedy. *8 Million Ways to Die, Nobody's Fool* (both 1986), *Amazon Women on the Moon* (1987), *The Big Blue* (1988), *New York*

Stories (1989), *Sweet Revenge* (1990), *Flight of the Intruder, Black Rainbow* (both 1991), *Nowhere to Run,* and the telefilm *The Wrong Man* (both 1993) have kept her in the public eye, but that's about all. Arquette still displays the same appeal that first captivated viewers, but the breaks haven't come her way.

Her sister Patricia Arquette has enjoyed a rapid rise to success, with starring roles in a handful of 1993 releases: *Ethan Frome, Trouble Bound, Inside Monkey Zetterland,* and *True Romance.*

ARTHUR, JEAN. Actress. *(b. Oct. 17, 1905, New York City, as Gladys Georgianna Greene; d. June 19, 1991.)* One of the screen's most popular players—and Frank Capra's favorite actress—was a high-school dropout, beginning her career as a model and turning to acting while still in her teens. In 1923 she won a small role in John Ford's *Cameo Kirby,* which launched her in movies. She quickly drifted into in-genue roles in innumerable low-budget Westerns starring Wally Wales, Buddy Roosevelt, and others, and even starred in a serial, *The Masked Menace* (1927). By 1929, though, she'd landed at Paramount (as a rather lackluster starlet, it should be noted), playing opposite William Powell in two Philo Vance mysteries, *The Canary Murder Case* and *The Greene Murder Case,* and opposite Warner Oland in two dismal adaptations of Sax Rohmer stories, *The Mysterious Dr. Fu Manchu* and *The Return of Dr. Fu Manchu* (all 1929).

Signed by Columbia in 1933, she played second fiddle to action hero Jack Holt (in 1934's *Whirlpool* and *The Defense Rests)* before John Ford (on loan to the studio) cast her in *The Whole Town's Talking* (1935), a brilliant comedy-drama that al-lowed the actress to demonstrate her here-tofore unsuspected comic ability. Frank Capra built on the Arthur image estab-lished in Ford's film by featuring her in *Mr. Deeds Goes to Town* (1936), *You Can't Take It With You* (1938), and *Mr. Smith Goes to Washington* (1939), in roles that combined no-nonsense pragmatism with romantic vulnerability. Arthur also played Calamity Jane for Cecil B. DeMille in *The Plainsman* (1936), and quickly became a favorite of Hollywood's leading directors in such prime 1930s films as *Easy Living, History Is Made at Night* (both 1937), and *Only Angels Have Wings* (1938).

The early 1940s offered Arthur two comic gems for director George Stevens: In *The Talk of the Town* (1942) and *The More the Merrier* (1943, for which she re-ceived an Oscar nomination), she gave seemingly effortless, hilarious perfor-mances. Extremely likeable and piquantly sexy, with one of the most distinctive voices in Hollywood history, she com-pletely erased the memory of the bland in-genue of the late 1920s and early 1930s. (Her face looked best from the right side, and once a star, she insisted she be photo-graphed that way.)

A dispute with Columbia Pictures head Harry Cohn drove Arthur from movies in 1944, though her reputation for being "difficult" followed her to New York, where she deserted the stage production of "Born Yesterday," leaving the role open for newcomer Judy Holliday. (She re-turned to Broadway in 1950 to play Peter Pan.) She made only two more films: *A Foreign Affair* (1948), for director Billy Wilder, in which, as a prim congress-woman from the Corn Belt, she gets de-lightfully drunk and sings the Iowa State Song; and *Shane* (1953), again with George Stevens, in a decidedly unglamo-rous role as the frontier housewife whose love for rancher Van Heflin is challenged by deep stirrings aroused by visiting gun-fighter Alan Ladd.

She made occasional stage appearances and taught drama, then in 1966 she starred as an attorney in a CBS sitcom, "The Jean Arthur Show." Jerome Lawrence and Rob-ert E. Lee wrote the play "First Monday in October" for Arthur. It offered a meaty role about the then-imaginary first female Supreme Court Justice, but she walked out mid-rehearsal, and retreated to her Carmel home. Her second husband (1932–49) was Frank Ross, who produced or coproduced several of her pictures, including *The Devil and Miss Jones* (1941), a screwball comedy not to be confused with the simi-larly titled porno flick of the 1970s. Ar-thur lived out her later years as a recluse, but came to enjoy some of the latter-day recognition she received for her outstand-ing work on-screen.

ARZNER, DOROTHY. Director. *(b. Jan. 3, 1900, San Francisco; d. Oct. 1, 1979.)*

Once lionized as the "only" female director of her time, Arzner may not be the pioneer she was painted to be (since research has documented a number of women who directed in the silent era), but she was certainly the most prominent female director to function in the studio system of the 1920s and 1930s. Though many have struggled to find gender significance in all her work, there is no question she brought a distinctive point of view to a number of films about strong-willed, independent women. A former waitress, ambulance driver, and stenographer, she performed the latter task in the script department of Famous Players in 1919. Promoted to script girl (now known as continuity director), then film editor, Arzner showed a natural aptitude for motion pictures (especially in her cutting of 1922's *Blood and Sand* and 1923's *The Covered Wagon).* She spent some time writing scenarios (including the 1926 hit *Old Ironsides,* which she cowrote with director James Cruze), and finally got a chance to direct with *Fashions for Women* (1927). She went on to direct Clara Bow, Paramount's resident sex symbol, in *Get Your Man* (1927) and *The Wild Party* (1929).

Arzner's talkies include *Paramount on Parade* (1930, selected sequences), *Working Girls* (1931), *Merrily We Go to Hell* (1932), *Christopher Strong* (1933, an early triumph for Katharine Hepburn), *Nana* (1934), *Craig's Wife* (1936, arguably her best film, and Rosalind Russell's big break), *Dance, Girl, Dance* (1940), and *First Comes Courage* (1943). During World War 2 she directed training films for WACs, and after the war became involved in the new medium of television, eventually getting involved in the production of commercials. In later years she taught filmmaking at UCLA; one of her students was Francis Ford Coppola.

ASHBY, HAL. Director. *(b. 1929, Ogden, Utah; d. Dec. 27, 1988.)* Noted throughout his career as a director with whom actors loved to work, Ashby inauspiciously started in the movie business as an office clerk at Universal Studios. Working his way up to assistant editor by the 1960s, Ashby became a full-fledged editor on Tony Richardson's *The Loved One* (1965). He cut some of the decade's biggest hits,

chalking up an Oscar nomination for his scissoring of *The Russians Are Coming! The Russians Are Coming!* (1966) and winning an Academy Award for his editorial work on Norman Jewison's *In the Heat of the Night* (1967). Ashby's relationship with the director paid off three years later, when Jewison removed himself from the helm of *The Landlord* (1970), paving the way for Ashby's directorial debut. Commercial and critical acclaim followed for such pictures as the cult classic *Harold and Maude* (1971), *The Last Detail* (1973) and *Shampoo* (1975); Ashby's first and only Oscar nomination for Best Director came in 1978 for the poignant *Coming Home.* His *Bound for Glory* (1976), a biopic on folk singer Woody Guthrie, didn't achieve much box-office success but was one of the director's finest outings. Unfortunately, after achieving his last commercial success with *Being There* (1979), Ashby directed a series of uninspired flops—including *Second-Hand Hearts* (1981), *Lookin' to Get Out* (1982), *The Slugger's Wife* (1985), and *8 Million Ways to Die* (1986)—before his untimely death in 1988.

ASHCROFT, PEGGY (DAME). Actress. *(b. Dec. 22, 1907, London; d. June 14, 1991.)* One of the world's most highly respected Shakespearean actresses, Peggy Ashcroft was one of the few women to be granted the title of Dame Commander of the Order of the British Empire (in 1956) for her stunning achievements in the theater. She amassed a prolific theatrical repertoire following her 1926 stage debut, and even served for a time as director of the Royal Shakespeare Company. She's probably best known to American audiences for her Oscar-winning portrayal of Mrs. Moore in *A Passage to India* (1984). OTHER FILMS INCLUDE: 1935: *The 39 Steps;* 1941: *Quiet Wedding;* 1959: *The Nun's Story;* 1968: *Secret Ceremony;* 1971: *Sunday, Bloody Sunday;* 1974: *The Pedestrian;* 1980: *Caught on a Train;* 1986: *When the Wind Blows;* 1988: *Madame Sousatzka;* 1989: *She's Been Away.*

ASHLEY, ELIZABETH. Actress. *(b. Aug. 30, 1939, Ocala, Fla.)* Intense, talented actress who specializes in playing harsh, catty females. She came to Hollywood after achieving great success on the stage. Ashley's first Broadway characterization, in 1961's "Take Her, She's Mine," won her a Tony Award, and she followed that with another well-received portrayal in Neil Simon's "Barefoot in the Park" in 1963. The raven-tressed, sloe-eyed Ashley made her film debut in *The Carpetbaggers* (1964), playing the disturbed ex-wife of George Peppard (whom she married offscreen as well). She provided expert supporting performances in *Ship of Fools* and *The Third Day* (both 1965), among others, before abandoning the screen for personal reasons. She returned in the early 1970s, subsequently appearing in *The Marriage of a Young Stockbroker* (1971), *Golden Needles, Rancho Deluxe* (both 1974), *92 in the Shade* (1975), *Coma* (1978), *Paternity* (1981), *Split Image* (1982), *Dragnet* (1987), *Dangerous Curves* (1988), and *Vampire's Kiss* (1989), among others. Ashley also starred in a well-received stage revival of "Cat on a Hot Tin Roof," and enjoyed a plum supporting role in the TV series "Evening Shade" (1990–94).

ASSANTE, ARMAND. Actor. *(b. Oct. 4, 1949, New York City.)* This dark, soberfaced actor with hooded eyes has turned in many fine performances since first attracting attention as Sylvester Stallone's brother in *Paradise Alley* (1978). He has showed a surprising flair for comedy in *Private Benjamin* (1980), *Unfaithfully Yours* (1984), and *The Marrying Man* (1991), although it must be noted that in those films other characters got most of the laughs. Assante was a petulant Mike Hammer in *I, the Jury* (1982), but made a chilling drug lord in *Q&A* (1990). Genuine screen stardom seems to have eluded him, but in recent years Assante has racked up some impressive performances in both starring and supporting roles, including *The Mambo Kings, 1492: Conquest of Paradise,* and *Hoffa* (all 1992), the comic parody *Fatal Instinct* (1993), and *Judge Dredd* (1995).

ASTAIRE, FRED. Actor, dancer. *(b. May 10, 1899, Omaha, Nebr.; d. June 22, 1987.)* "Can't sing. Can't act. Slightly balding. Can dance a little." Fittingly, the studio toad who wrote that screen-test ev-

aluation is long forgotten, but the greatest dancer in movie history is not. With his sister Adele, he danced his way from vaudeville to Broadway, where they starred in hit musicals for nearly 15 years (and reportedly appeared in a 1915 Mary Pickford movie, *Fanchon the Cricket*). He played himself in *Dancing Lady* (1933), his first film; later that year, he was teamed with Ginger Rogers as the second leads in *Flying Down to Rio*, where their footwork in "The Carioca" stole the show.

RKO quickly realized it had a potential gold mine, and over the next six years Astaire and Rogers made eight more films together, all of them a blend of astonishing choreography (usually in concert with Hermes Pan), brilliant songs by the likes of Irving Berlin, Cole Porter, and Jerome Kern, eye-popping sets, and vintage comedy plots propelled by vintage comedy actors. Buffs all have their favorites, but *Top Hat* (1935) and *Swing Time* (1936) are generally considered the best of the lot. (The others: *The Gay Divorcee,* 1934; *Roberta,* 1935; *Follow the Fleet,* 1936; *Shall We Dance?,* 1937; *Carefree,* 1938; *The Story of Vernon and Irene Castle,* 1939) Though worshipped as a dancer, in these and other films Astaire winningly introduced more enduring song hits than any other performer of his generation.

After Rogers broke up the team to concentrate on her acting, Astaire embarked on his "solo" career, giving full vent to his imaginative terpsichorean ideas, and dancing opposite—among others—Eleanor Powell in *Broadway Melody of 1940,* Rita Hayworth in 1941's *You'll Never Get Rich* and *You Were Never Lovelier,* Bing Crosby in 1942's *Holiday Inn* and 1946's *Blue Skies,* Gene Kelly in 1946's *Ziegfeld Follies,* Judy Garland in 1948's *Easter Parade,* Jane Powell in 1951's *Royal Wedding,* Cyd Charisse in 1953's *The Band Wagon* and 1957's *Silk Stockings,* and Audrey Hepburn in 1957's *Funny Face,* as well as reuniting with Rogers in *The Barkleys of Broadway* (1949).

With the passing of the studio musical, he produced and starred in three TV specials that remain landmarks of the medium. He also took a few straight acting roles in such films as *On the Beach* (1959), *The Pleasure of His Company* (1960), *The Notorious Landlady* (1962), *The Towering Inferno* (1974, which inexplicably earned him an Oscar nomination), and *Ghost Story* (1981), made one final musical, *Finian's Rainbow* (1968), and cohosted the two *That's Entertainment!* compilations (1974 and 1976), the second of which featured his last dancing on film—alongside compatriot Gene Kelly. Having won two Emmys for his musical specials, he added another for acting in the TV movie *A Family Upside Down* (1978). In any medium, he epitomized elegance and style. He never won an Academy Award for a specific performance, but did receive a special Oscar in 1949.

ASTOR, MARY. Actress. *(b. May 3, 1906, Quincy, Ill., as Lucille Vasconcellos Langhanke; d. Sept. 25, 1987.)* "You're good . . . you're very good," Humphrey Bogart's Sam Spade told her in *The Maltese Falcon* (1941). And he was right: Astor's Brigid O'Shaughnessy—cool, ruthless, beautiful— to this day retains her reputation as one of the screen's greatest femme fatales. Off- screen, this sophisticated, versatile lead- ing lady led a private life more vivid and eventful than any screenwriter could con- coct. A beauty-prize winner while still in her teens, Astor came to Hollywood dur- ing the silent era, landing extra work and bit roles before becoming John Barrymore's leading lady in *Beau Brummel* (1924). Astor's elegance and delicate beauty made her one of the most desired women in Hollywood; though only 18 years old, she was a magnet for Barrymore, who courted her right in front of the camera—with her unsuspecting mother watching from the sidelines.

Astor appeared in many costume dramas and swashbucklers throughout the 1920s, including *Don Q, Son of Zorro* (1925, with Douglas Fairbanks) and *Don Juan* (1926, with Barrymore again). Talkies found her briefly at RKO—in *Runaway Bride* (1930), *Behind Office Doors* (1931), and *The Lost Squadron*—and at MGM, with Clark Gable and Jean Harlow in the torrid *Red Dust* (both 1932), before re- turning to her home studio, Warner Bros., where she costarred in *Convention City, The Little Giant, The Kennel Murder Case* (all 1933), *The Case of the Howling Dog* (the first Perry Mason mystery), *Upper- world, The Man With Two Faces* (all 1934), to name just a few.

Astor was in the process of a divorce and custody battle with her physician hus- band in 1936 when her diary, which she had faithfully kept for years, was intro- duced to the court as evidence. Revelation of the frank descriptions of her affairs, es- pecially with playwright George S. Kaufman, made Astor a notorious figure. But that same year she scored a personal triumph as the lonely American expatriate who fell for Walter Huston in *Dodsworth,* revitalizing her career. Astor assumed character roles beginning in the late 1930s, appearing to good advantage in *The Prisoner of Zenda, The Hurricane* (both 1937), *Midnight* (1939), and *Turn- about* (1940), before reaching her career high-water mark in 1941 with her *Falcon* characterization and her Academy Award- winning supporting role in *The Great Lie.* She was delightful as a scatterbrained heiress in *The Palm Beach Story* (1942), and shortly thereafter settled into mother roles, in the likes of *Thousands Cheer* (1943), *Meet Me in St. Louis* (1944), *Des- ert Fury* (1947), *Little Women* (1949), and, most strikingly, in *A Kiss Before Dying* (1956). Her final films were *Youngblood Hawke* (1964) and *Hush . . . Hush, Sweet Charlotte* (1965). As acting opportunities dwindled she turned to writing, turning out five novels, an autobiography (1959's "My Story"), and one of the best accounts of working in Hollywood, "A Life on Film" (1967). Astor spent her last years alone in the Motion Picture Country Home.

ATHERTON, WILLIAM. Actor. *(b. July 30, 1947, Orange, Conn.)* A lean, hand- some WASP whose early portrayals typed him as high-strung, sensitive, and often troubled, Atherton started acting on stage while still in high school. He studied with the famous Pasadena Playhouse company and at Carnegie Tech before making his film debut in *The New Centurions* (1972). Juicy supporting roles in *Class of '44* (1973), *The Sugarland Express* (1974, as Goldie Hawn's husband), and *The Hin- denburg* (1975) saw Atherton tagged as someone to watch, and his complex, care- fully realized character performances in *The Day of the Locust* (1975) and *Looking for Mr. Goodbar* (1977) bore that out. Since that time, however, he has spent most of his time on-screen playing pomp- ous and presumptuous prigs in such movies as *Ghostbusters* (1984), *Real Genius* (1985), *Die Hard* (1988, as the self-important TV reporter, a role he repeated in the 1990 sequel), and *Oscar* (1991). He did fare well in a 1990 made-for-TV horror movie, *Buried Alive,* but his feature-film career seems stuck in a rut.

ATTENBOROUGH, RICHARD (LORD). Actor, director, producer. *(b. Aug. 29, 1923, Cambridge, England.)* Making his screen acting debut in Noël Coward's 1942 war drama *In Which We Serve,* Attenborough apotheosized the English wimp, and continued doing so in many of his roles throughout the 1940s and 1950s. He never projected strength or confidence, and often played cowardly, untrustworthy worms. He was memorable as the extremely subservient husband of unhinged medium Kim Stanley in *Seance on a Wet Afternoon* (1964), which he coproduced with director Bryan Forbes. In later years he played steely intellectual types, such as the prisoner mastermind who stages *The Great Escape* (1963). Attenborough turned to directing in the late 1960s, beginning with the well-received antiwar satire *Oh, What a Lovely War!* (1969). Following *Young Winston* (1972) and *A Bridge Too Far* (1977), he achieved great success with *Gandhi* (1982) and won an Oscar as Best Director, but his followup, *A Chorus Line* (1985) was a misfire. He returned to historical drama with 1987's anti-apartheid tale *Cry Freedom,* and finally fulfilled a long-held ambition to bring to film the life of Charlie Chaplin in 1992. *Chaplin* was an ambitious and well-intentioned film, but failed at the box-office. Ironically, Attenborough's next film became the biggest box-office hit of all time: Steven Spielberg's *Jurassic Park* (1993), in which he accepted his first acting role in years. He then directed Anthony Hopkins (for the fifth time) in *Shadowlands* (1993), before returning to the screen as Kris Kringle in the remake of *Miracle on 34th Street* (1994).

ATWILL, LIONEL. Actor. *(b. Mar. 1, 1885, Croydon, England; d. Apr. 22, 1946.)* A master of suave screen villainy, Atwill initially intended to be an architect. The theater beckoned, however, and he made his stage debut in 1905. Stocky but sinister, and capable of projecting great cruelty, Atwill came to Hollywood in 1932 and was immediately thrust into a series of horror films—*Dr. X, Mystery of the Wax Museum, The Vampire Bat, The Sphinx, Secret of the Blue Room,* and *Murders in the Zoo* among them—all filmed in a two-year period. He played important supporting roles in major films, as well, notably *The Devil Is a Woman* (1935, opposite Marlene Dietrich), *Captain Blood* (1935), *Till We Meet Again* (1936), *The Road Back* (1937), *Three Comrades* (1938), *The Three Musketeers* (1939, as de Rochefort), *Boom Town* (1940), and *To Be or Not to Be* (1942). But Atwill is perhaps best known for his horror-film appearances. Especially memorable as the monocled, one-armed police inspector in *Son of Frankenstein* (1939), he also costarred in *Man-Made Monster* (1941, in an archetypal mad-scientist portrayal), *The Ghost of Frankenstein* (1942), *Frankenstein Meets the Wolf Man* (1943), *House of Frankenstein* (1944), and *House of Dracula* (1945), among others. He made a perfect suspect in *Charlie Chan in Panama* and *Charlie Chan's Murder Cruise* (both 1940) and brought his gleeful villainy to a pair of Sherlock Holmes films *(The Hound of the Baskervilles,* 1939, and *Sherlock Holmes and the Secret Weapon,* 1942, with a florid performance as Prof. Moriarty). He died, quite suddenly, while making a serial, *Lost City of the Jungle;* the script was rewritten in mid-production to downplay his absence.

AUBERJONOIS, RENE. Actor. *(b. June 1, 1940, New York City.)* Slight, edgy character actor of French-Canadian descent best known as a member of Robert Altman's informal acting company, as part of which, along with Michael Murphy, Bud Cort, and John Schuck, he contributed to some of the 1970s' most offbeat films, including *MASH* (as Father Mulcahy), *Brewster McCloud* (both 1970), *McCabe & Mrs. Miller* (1971), and *Images* (1972). (His first film was 1964's *Lilith.*) Since then he has appeared sporadically, turning in effective performances in such otherwise forgettable pictures as *The Big Bus, King Kong* (both 1976), *The Eyes of Laura Mars* (1978), and *Where the Buf-*

falo Roam (1980). Auberjonois, a likable performer, has also played countless comic heavies in episodic TV and in made-fors. He may be best known for his roles on the TV sitcom "Benson" (1980–86) and the science-fiction series "Star Trek: Deep Space Nine" (1993–, as the shape-shifter Odo), though Broadway audiences may remember him better for such plays as the musical "Coco," for which he won a Tony Award, and "Big River." He was also seen in the 1992 BBC-TV production of "Ashenden." Auberjonois has lent voices to such animated features as *The Little Mermaid* (1989) and *Little Nemo: Adventures in Slumberland* (1992), and took a small but significant character part in the independent feature *The Ballad of Little Jo* (1993).

AUDRAN, STEPHANE. Actress. *(b. Nov. 2, 1932, Versailles, France, as Collette Suzanne Dacheville.)* Aristocratic, coolly beautiful French blonde best known for her work in the films of ex-husband Claude Chabrol, starting with a small role in *The Cousins* (1959). She was Ginette, the shopgirl who wanted success on the stage in *Les Bonnes Femmes* (1960), the mistress of the killer Landru in *Bluebeard* (1962), and also appeared in *Les Godelureaux* (1960), *The Tiger Likes Fresh Blood* (1964), *Marie-Chantal contre le docteur Kha* (1965) and *La Ligne de Demarcation* (1966). It was her performance in *Les Biches* (1968) as a rich lesbian who becomes involved in a ménage à trois that first gained her real critical notice, and the fire that burned underneath her exquisitely serene surface was fully developed in *La Femme infidele* (1968), *Le Boucher* (1969, marvelous as a schoolteacher who falls in love with a murdering butcher), *Just Before Nightfall* (1971) and the very sensual *Wedding in Blood* (1973). Her work for others includes Buñuel's Academy Award–winning masterpiece, *The Discreet Charm of the Bourgeoisie* (1972), *Vincent, Francois, Paul and the Others* (1974), the British remake of *Ten Little Indians* (1975), *The Silver Bears* (1978), Bertrand Tavernier's *Coup de torchon* (1981), and most impressively, her performance as the mysterious cook in the Danish Oscar-winner *Babette's Feast* (1987). Audran continued to work with Chabrol in *Violette* (1978), *Cop au vin* (1984), *Quiet Days in Clichy* (1990) and most recently, *Betty* (1993). She was also briefly married to actor Jean-Louis Trintignant.

AUER, MISCHA. Actor. *(b. Nov. 17, 1905, St. Petersburg, Russia, as Mischa Ounskowski; d. March 5, 1967.)* Taking his stage name from his famous grandfather— violin virtuoso Leopold Auer—this pop-eyed, glum-looking actor began his long career with stage work during the 1920s. He made his film debut in *Something Always Happens* (1928), and appeared in a variety of minor parts, including sinister swamis and boisterous Bolsheviks, for a number of years (in films like *Viva Villa!* and *Lives of a Bengal Lancer*). Following his hilarious, Oscar-nominated turn as a freeloading, ersatz nobleman (who can imitate a monkey) in *My Man Godfrey* (1936), however, Auer was signed to a long-term contract by Universal and cast more frequently in broad comedic roles. He's at his zaniest in *100 Men and a Girl* (1937), *You Can't Take It With You* (1938), *Destry Rides Again* (1939), *Spring Parade* (1940), *Hellzapoppin* (1941), *Cracked Nuts* (1941, in the lead), and *Lady in the Dark* (1944). He's also part of the ensemble in *And Then There Were None* (1945). In his later years Auer acted in many European films; his last screen credit was *Arrivederci, Baby* (1966).

AUGUST, BILLE. Director, screenwriter, cinematographer. *(b. Nov. 9, 1948, Copenhagen.)* After studying photography, August worked as a cinematographer on several Swedish films before making his directorial debut, *In My Life* (1978). He followed with a variety of TV projects and the feature film *Zappa* (1983) and the coming-of-age saga *Twist and Shout* (1985) before winning the Cannes Film Festival's Palme D'Or and the Best Foreign Language Film Oscar for *Pelle the Conqueror* (1988), a beautifully crafted, engrossing story of Swedish immigrant laborers in late 19th-century Denmark that starred Max von Sydow. *Pelle* also impressed Ingmar Bergman, who asked August to direct his epic script *The Best Intentions* (1992). He then tackled the all-star South American saga *The House of the Spirits* (1993). He also earned an Emmy nomination for an episode of George Lucas' TV series "The Young Indiana Jones Chronicles."

AUMONT, JEAN-PIERRE. Actor. *(b. Jan. 5, 1909, Paris, as Jean-Pierre Salomons.)* Continental leading man with talent to go along with his charm. Aumont began his career on the stage in Paris, where his popularity in the 1930s led to many film assignments, including *Jean de la lune* (1931), *Maria Chapdelaine* (1934), *Tarass Boulba* (1936), *Drole de drame* (1937, also known as *Bizarre, Bizarre)*, and *La Belle Etoile* (1938). After serving with distinction in the early days of World War 2 (earning both the Croix de Guerre and the Legion of Honor) he emigrated to the U.S. and was signed by MGM to appear in the wartime dramas *Assignment in Brittany* (1943, billed as Pierre Aumont) and *The Cross of Lorraine* (also 1943). He became a familiar presence in Hollywood movies, playing opposite such leading ladies as Ginger Rogers *(Heartbeat,* 1946), Yvonne De Carlo *(Song of Scheherazade,* 1947, as Rimski-Korsakov), and Jean Simmons *(Hilda Crane,* 1956). He married Maria Montez, with whom he starred in *Siren of Atlantis* (1948); she died in 1951. (Their daughter, Tina Aumont, later became an actress.)

After the war, Aumont divided his time between the U.S. and Europe, and worked on stage and television as well as films. Other feature credits include *Lili* (1953), *Royal Affairs in Versailles* (1954), *John Paul Jones* (1959), *The Devil at 4 O'Clock* (1961), *Castle Keep* (1969), *The Happy Hooker, Mahogany, Catherine & Co.* (all 1975), *Blackout* (1978), *Something Short of Paradise* (1979), and *Sweet Country* (1986), but his best latter-day opportunity came when François Truffaut gave him a key role in his valentine to moviemaking, *Day for Night* (1973). His third wife is actress Marisa Pavan. His autobiography, "Sun and Shadow," was published in 1976.

AUTRY, GENE. Actor. *(b. Sept. 29, 1907, Tioga, Tex.)* When Western singer Gene Autry went to Hollywood in 1934, he couldn't act, he couldn't ride, he couldn't rope, and he couldn't shoot. But that didn't prevent him from becoming the screen's most popular cowboy star within just a few years, revitalizing the whole genre and paving the way for Roy Rogers, Tex Ritter, and other Western warblers. Eventually, Autry's saddle skills increased dramatically (and his horse, Champion, eventually acquired costar billing), but he was never much of an actor, though that didn't bother his fans.

Autry's personal success built the fortune of his home studio, Republic, which purchased many hit songs for him to yodel in such films as *Round-Up Time in Texas* (1937), *South of the Border, In Old Monterey, Mexicali Rose* (all 1939), and *Back in the Saddle* (1941, introducing his theme song). After his wartime service, Autry returned briefly to Republic but in 1947 set up shop on the Columbia lot, where he made several dozen musical Westerns before turning to TV in the early 1950s. In addition to his own series, his Flying A Productions also produced such early TV westerns as "The Range Rider" and "Annie Oakley." He also enjoyed long-running success on the radio with his weekly "Melody Ranch" series, and sold millions of records over the years, including his unlikeliest (but most enduring) hit, "Rudolph the Red-Nosed Reindeer." A shrewd businessman from the start, Autry invested wisely and retired from performing in the late 1950s, a multimillionaire.

In the 1980s he and his second wife, Jackie, determined to build a museum derived in part from his personal collection of authentic Western memorabilia, and in 1988 The Gene Autry Western Heritage Museum opened its doors. His autobiography, bearing the name of his signature song, "Back in the Saddle Again," was published in 1978.

AVALON, FRANKIE. Actor, singer. *(b. Sept. 18, 1939, Philadelphia.)* One of many Philly-born pop singers to emerge in the immediate post-Elvis era, Avalon acquitted himself ably on screen in such films as *The Alamo* (1960) and *Voyage to the Bottom of the Sea* (1961). But he earned enduring fame opposite Annette Funicello in a series of teen-oriented musical comedies beginning with *Beach Party* (1963), the success of which led to several sequels, including *Muscle Beach Party* (1964), *Bikini Beach* (also 1964, in which he had a dual role), and *Beach Blanket Bingo* (1965). As a symbol of his era, Avalon ap-

peared in the 1950s-themed musical
Grease (1978), singing "Beauty School
Drop-out." The still-youthful-looking Avalon was reteamed with Funicello in 1987's
Back to the Beach, a harmless but lame
throwback that failed to inspire 1980s audiences. Avalon and Funicello still perform together at "nostalgia" shows around
the country.

AVERY, TEX. Animation director. *(b.
Feb. 26, 1908, Dallas, as Frederick Bean
Avery; d. Aug. 26, 1980.)* One of the primary innovators in American cartoon history, he helped forge the wacky "house
style" that came to be associated with
Warner Bros. A youthful cartoonist, he
drifted to California and the animation
business, and having worked for Walter
Lantz for several years, passed himself off
as an experienced director when Warners'
producer Leon Schlesinger was hiring. In
1935 he was given his own unit, and with
such other "young turks" as Chuck Jones
and Bob Clampett, began accelerating the
pace and sharpening the gags in their cartoons (including a great many jokes referring to the cartoons themselves!). Avery
was instrumental in developing the Porky
Pig and Daffy Duck characters, but is
credited more strongly for solidifying
Bugs Bunny, and defining his relationship
to Elmer Fudd, in his 1940 cartoon *A Wild
Hare.* (He also provided the hilariously
hearty laugh voiced by various characters
in his films.)

In 1941 Avery left Warners, helped devise the *Speaking of Animals* series, and
then found a new home at MGM. Here his
talent reached full flower, and his cartoons
became more manic than ever. Among his
masterpieces: *Red Hot Riding Hood*
(1943, with a libidinous wolf and sexy-
babe Riding Hood who appeared in a
handful of other shorts), *Bad Luck Blackie*
(1949), and perhaps best of all, *King Size
Canary* (1947), in which a product called
Jumbo-Gro gives new dimension (literally) to the archetypal cartoon chase between a cat and a bird.

Avery also introduced the understated
character of Droopy, and the overstated,
anarchic (and short-lived) Screwball
Squirrel. He left MGM in the mid-1950s,
and worked for a short time for Walter
Lantz, where he directed the penguin
character Chilly Willy (in *I'm Cold* and

The Legend of Rockabye Point). Thereafter he directed TV commercials, including
a long-running series for Raid, and even
directed Bugs Bunny in a TV spot for
Kool-Aid. Toward the end of his life he
joined his MGM colleagues Bill Hanna
and Joe Barbera at their studio to super-
vise a series of TV cartoons. They were
thrilled to have him, because they knew
what everyone else in the animation business knew: Tex Avery was one of a kind.

AVILDSEN, JOHN G. Director. *(b.
Dec. 21, 1935, Chicago.)* Cinematic jack-of-
all-trades whose filmmaking experience
included stints as a cinematographer, editor, assistant director, and production manager before he wielded the megaphone for
the first time on *Okay Bill* (1968).
Avildsen's early films—crude and unpo-
lished, looking more like student films
than professional movies—included *Guess
What We Learned in School Today?*
(1970) and *Cry Uncle!* (1971). His modestly budgeted *Joe* (1970) was a surprise
(if limited) hit, and he garnered excellent
reviews for *Save the Tiger* (1973). Avildsen won a Best Director Oscar for *Rocky*
(1976), but his next few efforts fizzled,
and he didn't regain audience favor until
The Karate Kid (1984), which he followed
up with two sequels. He also directed the
gritty *Lean on Me* (1989), the *Rocky*esque
movie about apartheid, *The Power of One*
(1992), and *8 Seconds* (1994).

AXELROD, GEORGE. Director, screenwriter, producer. *(b. June 9, 1922, New York
City.)* Talented screenwriter, whose best
films had fun with the conventions of sex
and morality and the men and women
trapped within these boundaries. After an
early career as an actor and stage manager, Axelrod wrote hundreds of scripts
for radio and TV and achieved success in
the 1950s with his Broadway plays "The
Seven Year Itch" and "Will Success Spoil
Rock Hunter?" Hollywood beckoned and
he wrote his first screenplay, *Phffft!*
(1954), a raucous comedy with Jack
Lemmon and Judy Holliday. He adapted
his play for the 1955 film of *The Seven
Year Itch* (directed by Billy Wilder) and
also adapted *Bus Stop* (1956); they both
provided Marilyn Monroe with roles that
would come to typify her persona as a

woman who innocently dazzles men with
her sexuality. Axelrod earned an Oscar
nomination for adapting Truman Capote's
Breakfast at Tiffany's (1961), then wrote
and coproduced a film unlike anything he'd tried before: the brilliant Cold
War thriller *The Manchurian Candidate*
(1962). He wrote and produced two sex
comedies, both directed by Richard
Quine—*Paris When It Sizzles* (1964) and
How to Murder Your Wife (1965)—before
making his directing debut with *Lord Love
a Duck* (1966, which he also wrote and
produced), an outrageous satire that takes
aim at almost every conceivable aspect of
American culture, and for the most part,
hits. He also wrote and directed the disappointing *The Secret Life of an American
Wife* (1968). Since then he has worked
only sporadically, on the poorly executed
remake of *The Lady Vanishes* (1979) and
the thrillers *The Holcroft Covenant* (1985)
and *The Fourth Protocol* (1987).

AYKROYD, DAN. Actor, screenwriter,
producer. *(b. July 1, 1952, Ottawa.)* A
former criminology student who came to
prominence first with Toronto's Second
City comedy troupe, and later as one of
the original cast members of "Saturday
Night Live," the multitalented Aykroyd
has been wasted in more atrocious films
than almost any screen contemporary of
his skill and stature. He appeared with
SNL partner and friend John Belushi in
1941 (1979), *The Blues Brothers* (1980),
and *Neighbors* (1981), and with Eddie
Murphy in *Trading Places* (1983), which
may be his best film. He's been well utilized in *Ghostbusters* (1984, which he
cowrote) and its 1989 sequel, and his Jack
Webb takeoff in *Dragnet* (1987) brightened an otherwise dismal film. Cast
against type as Jessica Tandy's son in
Driving Miss Daisy (1989), Aykroyd was
surprisingly effective, and was Oscar-
nominated for his role. Terrible comedies
like *Loose Cannons* (1989) and *Nothing
but Trouble* (1991), which he wrote,
directed, and starred in, were wastes of
time for both him and his fans. He redeemed himself with ingratiating performances in *Sneakers* (1992), *Chaplin* (1992,
improbably but well cast as Mack
Sennett) and *Coneheads* (1993), an expansion of the 1970s "Saturday Night Live"

skit, which he cowrote. It was his gentlest
and most satisfying comedy in years.

AYRES, LEW. Actor. *(b. Dec. 28, 1908,
Minneapolis.)* This boyishly handsome,
soft-spoken actor reached his career pinnacle early on, playing a patriotic young
German soldier in Lewis Milestone's antiwar epic *All Quiet on the Western Front*
(1930). It was a role that had profound
resonance for the actor in real life. Ayres
was a dance-band musician not yet out of
his teens when, spotted by Hollywood talent scouts, he made his film debut in
1929's *The Sophomore* and appeared opposite Greta Garbo in *The Kiss* that same
year. Under contract to Universal, Ayres
starred in such films as *Iron Man, Spirit of
Notre Dame* (both 1931), *The Impatient
Maiden, Night World, Okay America!* (all
1932), and *Don't Bet on Love* (1933, opposite soon-to-be wife Ginger Rogers);
unfortunately, none of them rose above
programmer level.
   Ayres' career fared no better when he
decided to freelance. With the exception
of *State Fair* (1933, a Will Rogers vehicle), he worked mainly in undistinguished
B pictures like *She Learned About Sailors*
(1934), *Silk Hat Kid* (1935), *Murder With
Pictures* (1936), *Lady Be Careful*, and
Scandal Street (both 1937). In 1936 he
starred in an above-average Republic programmer, *The Leathernecks Have Landed*,
in return for the opportunity to direct
Hearts in Bondage, a modestly budgeted
but eminently respectable account of the
Civil War battle between the *Monitor* and
the *Merrimac*.
   In 1938, after earning kudos as
Katharine Hepburn's spoiled younger
brother in *Holiday*, Ayres went to MGM
to play an idealistic intern in *Young Dr.
Kildare*, the success of which launched a
long and profitable series. Teamed with
Lionel Barrymore (as his crusty mentor)
and Laraine Day (as the nurse who loves
him), Ayres finally found a role that suited
his thoughtful, quiet nature. He appeared
in eight subsequent Kildare entries—along
with other MGM pictures such as *Spring
Madness* (1938), *These Glamour Girls*
(1939), *Maisie Was a Lady* (1941), and
Fingers at the Window (1942)—before being dropped by the studio when he announced himself to be a conscientious objector, an act tantamount to treason during

World War 2. In fact, he served with the Army as a medical orderly, distinguishing himself on the front lines. His religious beliefs, not an aversion to danger, had compelled him to shun combat.

After the war, Ayres regained public favor in several fine films, including *The Dark Mirror* (1946), *The Unfaithful* (1947), and, especially, *Johnny Belinda* (1948), for which he was Oscar-nominated as a kindly small-town doctor. (He also reprised the part of Kildare for a radio series with Lionel Barrymore.) His movie appearances during the 1950s were spotty, although he did well as the unfortunate scientist who unleashed the monstrous power of *Donovan's Brain* (1953) in that sci-fi favorite. He later appeared in *Advise and Consent* (1962), *The Carpetbaggers* (1964), *The Man, The Biscuit Eater* (both 1972), *Battle for the Planet of the Apes* (1973), *Damien—Omen II* (1978), and *Battlestar Galactica* (1979), in addition to a slew of telefilms, including *The Questor Tapes* (1973), *Of Mice and Men* (1981), and *Cast the First Stone* (1989).

Ayres' lifelong interest in religion led him to almost singlehandedly make *Altars of the East* (1955) and *Altars of the World* (1976), documentaries based on his own research and written works.

AZNAVOUR, CHARLES. Actor, songwriter, singer. (b. May 22, 1924, Paris, as Shahnour Varenagh Aznavourian.) Small, dark, sad-eyed performer whose natural acting ability made him an effective, engaging lead in Truffaut's *Shoot the Piano Player* (1960), and an always-welcome supporting player in many international productions. Round-shouldered and worldweary, he often suggests an adult Charlie Brown. His other films include *The Testament of Orpheus* (1960), *Paris in the Month of August* (1966), *Candy* (1968), *Ten Little Indians* (1975), *The Tin Drum* (1979) and, of all things, *The Yiddish Connection* (1986). Away from films, however, Aznavour is still best known as a balladeer who regularly packs concert halls around the world.

BACALL, LAUREN. Actress. (b. Sept. 16, 1924, as Betty Joan Persky, New York City.) Her unforgettable instruction on whistling in her first film, 1944's *To Have and Have Not,* is the thinking woman's variation on Mae West's "come up and see me some time," and that distinction provides a valuable clue to Bacall's uniqueness. Although the beautiful, lithe ex-model was dubbed "The Look" upon arriving in Hollywood, it was more than the raised eyebrow that made her irresistible when she finally got before the camera. It was the way she delivered a line—worldly but never jaded, slyly cynical but never sour—that cinched her appeal. Bacall broke into pictures courtesy of the then Mrs. Howard Hawks, who showed a "Harper's Bazaar" cover shot of Bacall to her producer/director husband. He had Bacall flown in from the East Coast almost instantly and cast her opposite Humphrey Bogart in *To Have and Have Not.* The 19-year-old ingenue and 45-year-old screen star fell in love on the set, and married in 1945. They appeared together in three other films: In *The Big Sleep* (1946, also directed by Hawks), their uncanny chemistry rescued that picture from its impenetrable plot. While 1947's *Dark Passage* was the least interesting of their films together, 1948's classic *Key Largo* exploited their chemistry in a darker, more mature context.

Few of Bacall's other films were memorable; among her costarring vehicles were *Confidential Agent* (1945), *Young Man With a Horn* (1950), the very enjoyable *How to Marry a Millionaire* (1953), *Woman's World* (1954), *The Cobweb, Blood Alley* (both 1955), soap opera supreme, *Written on the Wind* (1956), *The Gift of Love* (1958), and *Flame Over India* (1959). She spent much of the 1950s caring for her ailing husband, until his death from cancer in 1957. In 1961 Bacall married actor Jason Robards, Jr. (they divorced in 1969). Her film appearances in the 1960s and 1970s were sporadic; indeed, she took eight years off from the screen between 1966 and 1974, coming back in Sidney Lumet's all-star adaptation of Agatha Christie's *Murder on the Orient Express.* During her hiatus from Hollywood she worked on the stage, garnering kudos for her work in Broadway's "Applause." In 1981 she played a star terrorized by a crazed admirer in *The Fan*—touching a raw nerve in that era of John Hinckley and Mark Chapman—and since then has taken occasional supporting roles in telefilms and features, including that of James

Caan's agent in *Misery* (1990), a costarring part opposite Anthony Quinn in the unreleased *A Star for Two*, and the hostess (originally played by Billie Burke) in the TV remake of *Dinner at Eight* (1989). In 1993 she reunited with Gregory Peck (her costar in 1957's romantic comedy *Designing Woman)* for the enjoyable TV movie *The Portrait*, and costarred in *A Foreign Field* with Alec Guinness. Her distinctive voice has also been heard with growing frequency on TV commercials.

BACKUS, JIM. Actor. *(b. Mar. 25, 1913, Cleveland; d. July 3, 1989.)* Pugnacious comedy actor who earned immortality in the 1950s as the voice of cartoon curmudgeon Mr. Magoo, and again a decade later as the oblivious millionaire on TV's "Gilligan's Island" (1964–67). His movie characterizations and other TV roles were mostly cut from the same cloth: the boozy pilot in *It's a Mad Mad Mad Mad Mad World* (1963), the conniving stockbroker in *The Wheeler Dealers* (1964), and Mr. Dithers in a 1968 revival of "Blondie." Backus also had several memorable dramatic roles earlier in his career, though, including that of James Dean's father in *Rebel Without a Cause* (1955) and the brutal sheriff in *Macabre* (1958).

BACON, KEVIN. Actor. *(b. July 8, 1958, Philadelphia.)* No Brat-Packer he, Bacon emerged at the same time as many other youthful performers, but has shown himself to be an actor with serious ambitions—and the talent to back it up. After working on the daytime soaps "The Guiding Light" and "Search for Tomorrow," this slender, boyish actor with impish grin and engaging demeanor appeared in a string of hit movies, including *National Lampoon's Animal House* (1978, debuting as a slimy ROTC student), *Friday the 13th* (1980), and Barry Levinson's 1982 comic sleeper, *Diner,* in which he sparkled amid a uniformly excellent ensemble cast. Bacon, who studied at the Manning St. Actor's Theatre and was an apprentice at Circle-in-the-Square in New York, made his off-Broadway debut in "Getting Out," and won an Obie for his performance in "Forty Deuce," playing a teenage hustler (a role he repeated in a lackluster 1982 film adaptation).

A starring role in the 1984 film *Footloose* brought Bacon box-office notoriety (if not critical acclaim), but also marked the beginning of what would become a somewhat uneven adult film career. He went on to star in such oddities as *Quicksilver* (1986), *White Water Summer,* *End of the Line* (both 1987), and *She's Having a Baby* (1988)—none of them particularly successful. (He also made an amusing cameo appearance in John Hughes' *Planes, Trains & Automobiles* in 1987.)

Bacon had choice parts in two 1989 films, *Criminal Law* (as a psychopathic, wealthy killer) and *The Big Picture* (as an award-winning film student sucked into the Hollywood maw), which were little seen in theaters but achieved some success in the home video market. He also raised eyebrows with a finely tuned performance in PBS's "Lemon Sky," for the American Playhouse series, which also introduced him to future wife Kyra Sedgwick (with whom he starred in 1990's abysmal *Pyrates).*

OTHER FILMS INCLUDE: 1990: *Flatliners, Tremors;* 1991: *Queens Logic, He Said, She Said, JFK;* 1992: *A Few Good Men;* 1994: *The River Wild;* 1995: *Murder in the First, Apollo 13.*

BADHAM, JOHN. Director. *(b. Aug. 25, 1939, Luton, England.)* A seasoned veteran of TV direction when he turned to feature films in 1976 (with *The Bingo Long Traveling All-Stars & Motor Kings),* Badham achieved success with *Saturday Night Fever* (1977), capitalizing on two then-current crazes: disco dancing and John Travolta. His subsequent output has been uneven, ranging from *Dracula* (1979) to *Whose Life Is It Anyway?* (1981), but Badham's strong suit seems to be slick, commercial entertainment, as evidenced by *Blue Thunder* (1983), *WarGames* (1983), *Short Circuit* (1986), *Stakeout* (1987), *Bird on a Wire* (1990), *The Hard Way* (1991), *Point of No Return* (1993), and *Another Stakeout* (1993). His sister, Mary Badham, is well remembered by movie buffs for her Oscar-nominated performance as Scout in *To Kill a Mockingbird* (1962).

BAINTER, FAY. Actress. *(b. Dec. 7, 1892, Los Angeles; d. Apr. 16, 1968.)* Fay

Bainter was already middle-aged by the time she made her first movie (1934's *This Side of Heaven*), but the actress' career actually began at age six, when she appeared with a southern California stock company. In 1938 she was nominated for two Academy Awards, the first actor ever to be simultaneously named in both lead and supporting categories; she won Best Supporting Actress for her portrayal of Aunt Belle in *Jezebel* (and lost as Best Actress in *White Banners*). Frequently cast as an understanding mother or faithful spouse, befitting her gentle manner and appearance.
OTHER FILMS INCLUDE: 1937: *Quality Street, Make Way for Tomorrow;* 1940: *Young Tom Edison, Our Town;* 1943: *The Human Comedy;* 1945: *State Fair;* 1947: *The Secret Life of Walter Mitty;* 1953: *The President's Lady;* 1962: *The Children's Hour* (for which she was again Oscar-nominated).

BAKER, CARROLL. Actress. *(b. May 28, 1931, Johnstown, Pa.)* This beautiful blonde never quite attained the stardom once predicted for her, despite having achieved considerable notoriety as the thumb-sucking, infantile bride in Elia Kazan's adaptation of Tennessee Williams' *Baby Doll* (1956), a performance that earned her an Oscar nomination and the promise of great success. She got hooked on show business while still a young girl, first as a member of a dance company, then as a magician's assistant. Her classical beauty helped Baker land roles in TV commercials and a walk-on in a Broadway show; her progress convinced her to enroll at Lee Strasberg's Actors' Studio. Several TV dramas and a productive stint in the play "All Summer Long" followed, and Baker got her first notable screen role opposite James Dean in *Giant* (1956). Prominent parts in *The Big Country* (1958), *But Not for Me* (1959, opposite Clark Gable), *Something Wild* (1961, directed by then-husband Jack Garfein), *How the West Was Won* (1962), and *Cheyenne Autumn* (1964) followed. She played a hedonistic movie star patterned on Jean Harlow in *The Carpetbaggers* (1964), and played the platinum blonde herself in *Harlow* (1965), a poor biopic. As her Hollywood standing dissipated, Baker went to Europe, where she starred in exploitative fare such as *The Sweet Body of Deborah* (1969) and

Bloody Mary (1972). She stayed there for many years, working steadily, before returning to America in the late 1970s. In recent years she has contributed striking character performances to a handful of films. Her autobiography, "Baby Doll," was published in 1983.
OTHER FILMS INCLUDE: 1980: *The Watcher in the Woods;* 1983: *Star 80;* 1986: *Native Son;* 1987: *Ironweed;* 1990: *Kindergarten Cop.*

BAKER, JOE DON. Actor. *(b. Feb. 12, 1936, Groesbeck, Tex.)* One of the most pleasant surprises in Martin Scorsese's 1991 *Cape Fear* was Joe Don Baker, likable and convincing as a seasoned, no-nonsense private investigator; his perfectly wrought characterization reminded both critics and audiences that he was capable of stellar performances—something that, alas, most of us had forgotten. As a tall, rugged leading man, Baker enjoyed his greatest popularity in the mid 1970s, following his star-making performance as two-fisted sheriff Buford Pusser in *Walking Tall* (1973). By that time he'd already been in movies for several years, typed in "bubba" roles by his physical appearance and Texas drawl. His star shone brightly for a short while, in escapist action fare such as *Golden Needles* (1974), *Framed,* and *Mitchell* (both 1975), but as he got older and put on weight he slid into character parts, often playing heavies. Other credits include *The Natural* (1984, as the Babe Ruth–inspired character The Whammer, an inspired piece of casting), *Fletch* (1985), and *The Living Daylights* (1987). He has appeared in many made-for-TV movies. His latter-day films include *Criminal Law* (1988), *The Children* (1990), the telefilm *Citizen Cohn* (1992, as Sen. Joseph McCarthy), and *The Distinguished Gentleman* (also 1992).

BAKER, KATHY. Actress. *(b. June 8, 1950, Midland, Tex.)* This enormously talented actress, very appealing but not conventionally beautiful, hasn't been assigned typical leading-lady parts in movies, enabling her to create a gallery of diverse characterizations in films of uneven merit. She initially studied drama at the California Institute of the Arts, but abandoned the program when she went to Paris, staying there several years. Upon returning to America, she worked on stage and screen, winning an Obie in 1983 for her performance in "Fool for Love" and registering well in *The Right Stuff* that same year. She's played a hooker in *Street Smart* (1987), a substance abuser in *Clean and Sober* (1988), a shy schoolteacher in *Jacknife* (1989), and a lusty suburbanite in *Edward Scissorhands* (1990). Recent credits include *Jennifer 8* (1992), *Mad Dog and Glory* (1993), and the critically acclaimed TV series "Picket Fences" (1992–) in which she stars with Tom Skerritt, for which she won an Emmy.

BAKER, RICK. Makeup artist. *(b. Dec. 8, 1950, Binghamton, N.Y.)* A fan of horror movies as a child, he experimented with movie makeup effects at a young age and even worked as a lab assistant for legendary makeup artist Dick Smith; now Rick Baker, too, is widely acknowledged as one of the best in the field. He graduated from designing puppets to working on low-budget films like *The Thing With Two Heads* (1972), *Schlock* (1973), and *It's Alive!* (1974) and hit the big time designing the costume for (and playing) *King Kong* in 1976. After more chores on *The Incredible Melting Man, It Lives Again* (both 1978), and *The Howling* (1980), Baker won the first Academy Award ever given in the category of "Best Makeup Design" for the stunning full-body werewolf transformations in his pal John Landis' *An American Werewolf in London* (1981). He won another Oscar for designing the endearing Sasquatch Harry in *Harry and the Hendersons* (1987) and nominations for the elaborate gorilla costumes in *Greystoke: The Legend of Tarzan, Lord of the Apes* (1984) and Eddie Murphy's and Arsenio Hall's multiple disguises in *Coming to America* (1987). Baker has also worked on *The Funhouse* (1981), *Gorillas in the Mist* (1988), *Gremlins 2: The New Batch* (1990, which he also coproduced), and *Wolf* (1994), and earned a third Oscar for designing and creating the astounding Bela Lugosi makeup for Martin Landau in *Ed Wood* (also 1994). He also created makeup effects for the Michael Jackson video "Thriller" as well as his full-length video "Moonwalk" (1988) and shared an Emmy (with Stan Winston) for the marvelous ag-

ing transformation of Cicely Tyson in 1974's TV movie *The Autobiography of Miss Jane Pittman.*

BAKER, STANLEY (SIR). Actor, producer. *(b. Feb. 8, 1927, Ferndale, Wales; d. June 28, 1976.)* Virile Welsh actor noted for his hard-boiled characterizations in British thrillers and action films of varying quality and effectiveness. Baker started acting while still in his teens, making his movie debut in *Undercover* (1943), but acquiring considerable stage experience before seriously pursuing film work in the early 1950s. Baker, who produced some of his later films, was knighted in 1976, just a few months before his death from lung cancer.
OTHER FILMS INCLUDE: 1953: *The Cruel Sea* (his first major screen success); 1954: *Hell Below Zero;* 1959: *The Angry Hills;* 1961: *The Guns of Navarone;* 1963: *Zulu* (a standout); 1967: *Robbery;* 1972: *Innocent Bystanders;* 1975: *Zorro.*

BAKSHI, RALPH. Animator, director. *(b. Oct. 26, 1938, Haifa, Palestine.)* Two-fisted animation director and filmmaker who was raised on the streets of Brooklyn and brought that street sensibility to his best films. A talented cartoonist, he was hired by the Terrytoons studio at the age of 18 as a paint opaquer, gradually became an animator, and in his early 20s was a full-fledged director, piloting episodes of such made-for-TV cartoons as "Deputy Dawg" and last-gasp theatrical shorts like *James Hound.* In 1966 he was appointed supervising director of the studio and created an imaginative TV series, "The Mighty Heroes." Shortly thereafter, he left to run Paramount's New York–based cartoon studio, which was still producing animated shorts for theatrical release. Before the year was out, however, the company's new owner, Gulf + Western, decided to shut down the operation. Bakshi and producer Steve Krantz then put together a low-budget feature film, *Fritz the Cat* (1972). Touted as "the first X-rated animated cartoon," it made waves as well as money; sexy, violent, topical, satirical, it was a groundbreaking effort, and immediately established Bakshi as a major talent. *Heavy Traffic* (1973) was even more impressive: an explosive, violent, semiautobiographical street saga. Bakshi's third feature, *Coonskin* (1975), an often-ingenious satire of *Song of the South*, proved too controversial, however, and was shelved by Paramount after igniting a firestorm of protest at its first showings. Bakshi then turned to the safer territory of science fiction for *Wizards* (1977) and attempted to film at least part of Tolkien's *Lord of the Rings* (1978), but animation fans were distressed to see that he had rotoscoped (traced) the animated movements from live-action figures. The energy and originality of his earlier work were missing. Bakshi's career moved in fits and starts after that, with box-office failures impeding some of his more ambitious plans. He spent most of his time painting, then resurfaced in 1987 as producer of a new Mighty Mouse series for TV, returning to his Terrytoons roots but with a hip new slant; the actual directing of the show was left to his protégé John Kricfalusi. (The two also made an animated music video for Mick Jagger, "Harlem Shuffle.") Having blended animation and live-action before, Bakshi revived the idea for 1992's *Cool World*, his first feature film in many years, but the result was poorly conceived and executed. Young moviegoers lured by the titillation of its sexy female star (voiced and acted in the "live" sequences by Kim Basinger) probably had no idea that Bakshi had gone much further—much more successfully—20 years earlier. Other films include *American Pop* (1981), *Hey, Good Lookin'* (1982), *Fire and Ice* (1983).

BALABAN, BOB. Actor, director. *(b. Aug. 16, 1945, Chicago.)* During the late 1970s and 1980s, producers looking for physically unprepossessing, soft-spoken intellectual types rarely got past the letter B in their casting directories. No one surpassed Balaban in those roles—and the more dispassionate or loathsome the character, the better he was. He first attracted attention in *Close Encounters of the Third Kind* (1977), playing a cartographer drafted to be François Truffaut's interpreter. (He later wrote a book on the making of the film.) He also appeared in *Altered States* (1980), *Absence of Malice, Whose Life Is It, Anyway?* (both 1981), *Dead-Bang* (1989), *Amos & Andrew* (1993), and *Greedy* (1994), to name just a few. Balaban made his directorial debut

with the black comedy *Parents* (1989) and then helmed *My Boyfriend's Back* (1993).

BALCON, MICHAEL. Producer, distributor. *(b. May 19, 1896, Birmingham, England; d. Oct. 16, 1977.)* More than any other man, Michael Balcon is responsible for the growth and maturation of the British film industry. He founded Gainsborough Studios in 1928, and over the next two decades assumed stewardship of Gaumont-British, Ealing, and MGM-British studios. His personal film output, which included *Man of Aran* (1934), *The 39 Steps* (1935), *Sabotage* (1936), *A Yank at Oxford* (1938), *Dead of Night* (1945), *Nicholas Nickleby* (1947), *Kind Hearts and Coronets* (1949), and *The Man in the White Suit* (1951) among others, boasted superior production values and top creative personnel. He took a chance on young Alfred Hitchcock, hiring him as director of *The Pleasure Garden* (1925), and developed musical performer Jessie Matthews into an international star during the 1930s. Balcon's grandson is actor Daniel Day-Lewis.

BALDWIN, ALEC. Actor. *(b. Apr. 3, 1958, Amityville, N.Y.)* One of the more impressive young actors to hit Broadway in the 1980s, this dark-haired, blue-eyed heartthrob attained screen stardom late in the decade, alternating leading-man assignments with spicy character roles. After apprenticing on soap operas and in such TV movies as *Sweet Revenge* and *Dress Gray,* Baldwin made his feature debut in the barely released mystery *Forever, Lulu* (1987). His breakthrough year, 1988, saw him appearing in an amazing five films, showing a formidable range: as Kevin Bacon's not-to-be-trusted friend in *She's Having a Baby,* the benign and bewildered ghost husband in *Beetlejuice,* a swaggering mafioso in *Married to the Mob,* a slick producer in *Talk Radio,* and a lower-class clod in *Working Girl.*

Baldwin played Jimmy Swaggart in *Great Balls of Fire!* (1989), followed by a psychotic killer in *Miami Blues,* the heroic Jack Ryan in *The Hunt for Red October,* and a ghostly lover in *Alice* (all 1990). Then came the Neil Simon "comedy" *The Marrying Man* (1991); his romance with costar Kim Basinger (whom he subsequently married) and their alleged behavior during production seriously tarnished his clean-cut image (it didn't help that the picture itself was a dog). He was replaced by Harrison Ford on the *Red October* sequel, *Patriot Games,* after a well-publicized disagreement with Paramount. Since then he has recreated his off-Broadway performance in the film version of *Prelude to a Kiss* (1992) and galvanized the screen in a brief but unforgettable appearance as a profane, bullying sales executive in *Glengarry Glen Ross* (1992, in a role especially written by David Mamet for the film adaptation of his play). He returned to Broadway in a much-publicized revival of "A Streetcar Named Desire," then returned to Hollywood to play a cocky but gifted surgeon in *Malice* (1993), a career criminal opposite Basinger in *The Getaway* (1994), and the mysterious Lamont Cranston in a film version of *The Shadow* (also 1994).

Three of Baldwin's brothers are also actors: William costarred in *Internal Affairs* and *Flatliners* (both 1990), and starred in *Backdraft* (1991), *Sliver* and *Three of Hearts* (both 1993); Stephen appeared in *The Beast* (1988), *Born on the Fourth of July* (1989), *Crossing the Bridge* (1992), and *Posse* (1993), in addition to costarring on the TV series "The Young Riders"; and Daniel played the barfly Cheesy on the Valcrie Bertinelli sitcom "Sydney" and later costarred in the series "Homicide: Life on the Streets" (1993–).

BALL, LUCILLE. Actress, producer. (b. Aug. 6, 1911, Ceeron, N.Y.; d. Apr. 26, 1989.) Though she is unquestionably the most beloved comedienne of her time, that success came to Lucille Ball after 20 years of largely unrewarding work in Hollywood—and it came not in movies, but on TV. She started out as a Goldwyn Girl, visible in the chorus of such Eddie Cantor films as *Roman Scandals* (1933) and *Kid Millions* (1934), and worked her way up to bits in everything from *Top Hat* (1935) to a Three Stooges short, *Three Little Pigskins* (also 1935). She raised eyebrows as one of the wisecracking actresses in *Stage Door* (1937), and RKO, by then her home studio, promoted her to starring parts in a variety of comedies and dramas over the next five years. Most were grade-B potboilers like *The Affairs of Annabel, Next Time I Marry, Annabel Takes a Tour* (all 1938), *Beauty for the Asking, Panama Lady* (1939), and *You Can't Fool Your Wife* (1940).

Ball often played quick-witted, sharp-tongued characters in this period; she was sufficiently beautiful to be a leading lady but could just as easily be cast as a scheming harpy. She had a thankless role in The Marx Brothers' *Room Service* (1938), but fared better in the exceptional adventure yarn *Five Came Back* (1939), as a burlesque star in *Dance, Girl, Dance* (1940), in the Broadway musical adaptation *Too Many Girls* (also 1940), where she met a conga player named Desi Arnaz, and in the melodramatic leading role of *The Big Street* (1942).

She then moved to MGM and decorated such musicals and comedies as *Du Barry Was a Lady, Best Foot Forward* (both 1943), *Without Love* (1945), *Easy to Wed,* and *Ziegfeld Follies* (both 1946). But her best opportunities came elsewhere, in such late 1940s dramas as *The Dark Corner* (1946), *Lured* (1947), and *Easy Living* (1949), and in the comedies *Sorrowful Jones, Miss Grant Takes Richmond* (both 1949), *Fancy Pants,* and *The Fuller Brush Girl* (both 1950), which anticipated her slapstick antics on TV.

In 1951, she and Arnaz formed a production company, Desilu, to produce their own starring TV series, "I Love Lucy." Lucy revealed to an astonished Hollywood—and a huge viewing audience—her heretofore overlooked gifts as a physical comedienne. Ball won two Emmys and captivated the nation as the wacky housewife desperate to enter show business. During its run, she and Arnaz also starred in two tailor-made features, *The Long, Long Trailer* (1954) and *Forever Darling* (1956). Desilu also became a major supplier of TV programs; in 1957 the company bought the defunct RKO studios, where Lucy had toiled for so many years. When she and Arnaz divorced in 1960, she ran the studio herself until selling it to Paramount in 1968, and kept busy with her own sitcom, which in various forms ran another 12 years and earned her another two Emmys.

In the early 1960s she starred with Bob Hope in two films, the "adult" comedies *The Facts of Life* (1960) and *Critic's Choice* (1963). She later took a cameo in *A Guide for the Married Man* (1967), but starred in only two more movies, the agreeable family comedy *Yours, Mine and Ours* (1968) and the ill-advised musical *Mame* (1974), for which she was, sadly, too old by then. Her two children by Arnaz, Lucie and Desi Jr., both appeared on her later sitcom and went on to their own careers, he as a rock star and sometime actor, she in such Broadway musical hits as "They're Playing Our Song."

BALLARD, CARROLL. Director. *(b. Oct. 14, 1937, Lake Tahoe, Cal.)* Talented director whose best films examine the relationship between man and nature in spectacular visual terms. A graduate of the UCLA Film School, Ballard first gained notice for the documentaries he made for the U.S. Information Agency, *Beyond This Winter's Wheat* (1965) and *Harvest* (1966), which was nominated for an Oscar. More documentaries followed—*The Perils of Priscilla* (1969), about a lost cat told from its point of view, and *Rodeo* (1970), about bull rider Larry Mahan—before UCLA classmate Francis Ford Coppola offered him the job of directing *The Black Stallion* (1979). Ballard turned this adaptation of the Walter Farley novel into a moving and almost dreamlike visual experience. His next project was *Never Cry Wolf* (1983), based on Farley Mowat's experiences studying wolves in the Arctic, starring Charles Martin Smith. Since then, he has directed *Nutcracker, the Motion Picture* (1986) and *Wind* (1992), in which characters and story paled next to the awesome sailing sequences. Pauline Kael wrote, "The visual imagination Ballard brings to the natural landscape is so intense that his imagery makes you feel like a pagan—as if you were touching when you're only looking."

BALLARD, LUCIEN. Cinematographer. *(b. May 6, 1908, Miami, Okla.; d. Oct. 1, 1988.)* This college-educated young man liked to say that the turning-point in his life was being invited to a wild party by Clara Bow, which convinced him he belonged in show business. After working in a variety of jobs at Paramount and becoming an assistant cameraman, he apprenticed with Josef von Sternberg on such Marlene Dietrich films as *Morocco* (1930) and the sumptuous *The Devil Is a*

Woman (1935), learning more than any school could possibly teach him about lighting in the process. Von Sternberg even gave him cinematographer's credit on his Columbia film *Crime and Punishment* (1935), but his tenure at that studio was mostly undistinguished (although he did photograph some Three Stooges shorts!). He fared better at 20th-Century-Fox in the 1940s, where he shot such films as *Orchestra Wives* (1942), *Tonight We Raid Calais* (1943) and *The Lodger* (1944), on which he met and married Merle Oberon. He went on to photograph her in *Temptation* (1946), *Night Song* (1947), and *Berlin Express* (1948) before their divorce in 1949.

His gritty treatment of Stanley Kubrick's *The Killing* (1956) was much noticed, and along with his standard studio assignments, which were always well shot, he worked with some of the period's more adventurous directors, including Budd Boetticher (1955's *The Magnificent Matador,* 1956's *The Killer Is Loose,* 1958's *Buchanan Rides Alone,* 1960's *The Rise and Fall of Legs Diamond,* and the documentary *Arruza)* and Sam Peckinpah (1962's *Ride the High Country,* 1969's *The Wild Bunch,* 1970's *The Ballad of Cable Hogue,* 1972's *Junior Bonner* and *The Getaway),* as well as the reliable journeyman Henry Hathaway, for whom he shot many films including *True Grit* (1969). His other credits ranged from *Inferno* (1953, in 3D) to Walt Disney's *The Parent Trap* (1961) to Blake Edwards' *The Party* (1968), as well as *The Caretakers* (1963), which got him his only Oscar nomination among more than a hundred feature films. Ballard once said, "I want to contribute to a picture, not just work on it. I'm their man if they want more than a cameraman." Many top producers and directors did; that's why he was always in demand.

BALLHAUS, MICHAEL. Cinematographer. *(b. Aug. 5, 1935, Berlin.)* It was while watching the legendary Max Ophuls—a relative—filming *Lola Montes* that Ballhaus knew what he wanted to do with his life. A renowned cinematographer in Europe (he shot 15 of Rainer Werner Fassbinder's films), he moved to the United States in 1982 and, after making his American debut lensing John Sayles' *Baby, It's You* (1983), became one of the most sought-after cinematographers in the business, known for his rich, voluptuous colors and sculpted images. He has worked with director Martin Scorsese, himself a creator of memorable images, most dazzlingly on *The Color of Money* (1986) and *GoodFellas* (1990). In 1992 he shot Francis Ford Coppola's lush *Bram Stoker's Dracula,* and reunited with Scorsese for the visually sumptuous *The Age of Innocence* (1993). It was followed by James L. Brooks' *I'll Do Anything* (1994). He has been Oscar-nominated for *Broadcast News* (1987) and *The Fabulous Baker Boys* (1989), which critic Pauline Kael described as having "a funky languor."

BALSAM, MARTIN. Actor. *(b. Nov. 4, 1919, Bronx, N.Y.)* We all knew that Balsam, playing the cynical, skeptical private detective Arbogast in Hitchcock's *Psycho* (1960), never had a chance against Anthony Perkins' Norman Bates—but we all jumped out of our seats when he was knifed to death at the top of a staircase. A veteran of the New York stage and an alumnus of the famous Actors' Studio, Balsam has appeared in dozens of movies since debuting in 1954's *On the Waterfront.* He turned in an excellent performance, in an "everyman" character type, as the jury foreman in *12 Angry Men* (1957). Sometimes cranky, sometimes comical, sometimes both, he always makes his presence felt, even in marginal roles. He's particularly good in ensemble-cast pictures such as *Seven Days in May* (1964), *Tora! Tora! Tora!* (1970), *Murder on the Orient Express, The Taking of Pelham One Two Three* (both 1974), and *All the President's Men* (1976). He received an Oscar for his supporting role as Jason Robards' sensible brother in *A Thousand Clowns* (1965). From 1979 to 1981 he joined the cast of TV's "Archie Bunker's Place," as Carroll O'Connor's business partner. In 1991 Balsam cameoed as a judge in Martin Scorsese's remake of *Cape Fear,* a nod to the fact that he appeared in the 1962 original.

BANCROFT, ANNE. Actress. *(b. Sept. 17, 1931, Bronx, N.Y., as Anna Maria Louisa Italiano.)* As young Hollywood contract player Anna Marno, this sharp-featured, witty, and versatile actress appeared in such deathless 1950s classics as *Don't Bother to Knock* (1952), *Demetrius and the Gladiators,* and *Gorilla at Large* (both 1954). In search of better roles, she headed back to New York and the stage, and there met with great success opposite Henry Fonda in the 1958 production of *Two for the Seesaw* (for which she won a Tony) and with what was to become the first of her signature roles as Annie Sullivan in *The Miracle Worker,* which in 1959 brought her another Tony as well as a New York Drama Critics Award. The stage was set for a triumphant return to Hollywood, and sure enough she received a Best Actress Academy Award for her reprisal of the Sullivan role in the 1962 film version of the play. She followed with an Oscar-nominated performance in the British-made *The Pumpkin Eater* (1964), a bleak tale of marital strife scripted by celebrated playwright Harold Pinter. She also appeared in John Ford's final feature, *7 Women* (1966). The second of her signature roles was as Mrs. Robinson, the sexually frustrated upper-middle-class wife who icily seduces Dustin Hoffman in 1967's *The Graduate.* (The role brought her another Oscar nomination).

She appeared in roles both comic and dramatic throughout the 1970s and 1980s, including an unbilled cameo in her husband Mel Brooks' *Silent Movie* (1976) and a full lead opposite him in a 1983 remake of Lubitsch's *To Be or Not to Be.* She also appeared in several pictures made by Brooks' production company Brooksfilms, including David Lynch's *The Elephant Man* (1980) and the 1987 sleeper *84 Charing Cross Road.* Her directing and screenwriting debut, 1979's *Fatso,* received mixed notices. Along the way she earned yet another Best Actress nomination, for her role opposite Shirley MacLaine in the battle-of-the-bitchy-ex-ballet-dancers melodrama *The Turning Point* (1977), and one more as the Mother Superior, opposite Jane Fonda, in *Agnes of God* (1985).

Most recently, Bancroft has been taking interesting character/cameo roles, in such films as *Love Potion No. 9* (1992), *Honeymoon in Vegas* (1992, as Nicolas Cage's dying mother), *Point of No Return* (1993, in the part played by Jeanne Moreau in *La Femme Nikita*), *Malice* (1993), and *Mr. Jones* (1993).

BANCROFT, GEORGE. Actor. *(b. Sept. 30, 1882, Philadelphia; d. Oct. 2, 1956.)* Annapolis graduate, theater owner, and erstwhile minstrel man who—while not a classic matinee idol type—became one of the 1920s' top screen stars. Powerfully built, with rugged features, he first attracted attention in *Pony Express* (1925), and starred the following year in another historical epic, *Old Ironsides* (1926). His two best silent movies were both gritty melodramas directed by Josef von Sternberg, *Underworld* (1927) and *Docks of New York* (1928). Bancroft seemed to weather the transition to sound with no problem; his robust baritone and gruff manner complemented his appearance. But his thunder was stolen by a newer, younger crop of movie tough-guys, and by 1934 he was reduced to supporting roles (albeit good ones) in films such as *Mr. Deeds Goes to Town* (1936), *Angels With Dirty Faces* (1938), *Each Dawn I Die* (1939), and, memorably, as the sheriff in *Stagecoach* (1939). He appeared in *Young Tom Edison, Northwest Mounted Police* (both 1940), and a number of other films before leaving Hollywood in 1942 to begin a new career as a rancher.

BAND, CHARLES. Producer, director. *(b. Dec. 27, 1951, Los Angeles.)* Filmmaker best known for an apparently endless series of low-budget science-fiction and horror movies. The son of director Albert Band *(I Bury the Living),* Charles grew up on a diet of comic books and genre thrillers while living in Rome, where his father was working. His first films were experimental shorts; he produced his first feature film *(Mansion of the Doomed,* 1977) when he was still in his 20s. A visionary of B budgets, he founded Media Home Entertainment and was a pioneer in the home-video field, producing films like *Crash!* (1977) and *Laserblast* (1978) that had some theatrical release but were designed to be video fodder.

Eventually he sold Media and returned to directing with a 3-D genre picture, *Metalstorm: The Destruction of Jared-Syn* (1983). That same year he founded Empire Entertainment and produced a series of medium- to low-budget films, often shot in Italy: *The Dungeonmaster* (1985), *Eliminators, Ghost Warrior* (aka *Swordkill), Zone Troopers,* and the Stuart

Gordon films *From Beyond* and *Dolls* (all 1986). His Empire empire collapsed in the late 1980s, but he bounced back with a new company called Full Moon Entertainment, which produces a steady stream of home-video product for Paramount. The films rarely employ name actors or directors, concentrating instead on a crisp, big-budget "look" (thanks to expert cinematographers); most of them are aimed at the teenage-to-early-20's market. Band has created series from some of his more successful films, including *Trancers* (1985, aka *Future Cop), Puppetmaster* (1989), *Dollman* (1991), and *Subspecies* (1991). (Several of these films feature tiny, doll-sized menaces, apparently one of Band's pet subjects.) He occasionally directs, sometimes in collaboration with his father, as on *Dr. Mordrid* (1992). A master marketer who modeled himself on Marvel Comics maestro Stan Lee, Band also started including on each Full Moon cassette "Videozone" behind-the-scenes shorts on the making of the films just screened, often introducing them himself. The movies themselves are generally mediocre, but that doesn't seem to matter to the legion of Full Moon fans.

BANKHEAD, TALLULAH. Actress. *(b. Jan. 31, 1903, Huntsville, Ala.; d. Dec. 12, 1968.)* Few who saw her in her prime would have guessed that Tallulah Bankhead, the toast of Broadway and one of New York's most flamboyant characters, was born in Alabama and educated in a convent school. A teenage beauty-contest winner, she moved to New York and played minor roles on stage and in silent films (1918's *Thirty a Week* and *When Men Betray)* before moving to London, where she established herself as a talented dramatic actress. Resuming her American stage career in 1930, she alternately delighted and outraged audiences with her performances, both on stage and off. At the dawn of the talking-picture era she signed with Paramount, making routine programmers such as *My Sin* (1931), *Faithless,* and *Thunder Below* (both 1932) but never achieving the prominence she enjoyed on Broadway. Alfred Hitchcock gave Bankhead her best film role as one of the castaways in *Lifeboat* (1944); after that award-winning performance, however, she appeared only sporadically in movies. Her last film was the undistinguished *Die! Die! My Darling!* (1965), although she did voice-over narration for *The Daydreamer* (1966).

BANKS, LESLIE. Actor. *(b. June 9, 1890, West Derby, England; d. Apr. 21, 1952.)* Debonair British actor who, despite his prominence in the theater, didn't make his screen debut until 1932, and only then in the American-made *The Most Dangerous Game*, playing the suave, sadistic Count Zaroff and neatly stealing the show from nominal stars Joel McCrea and Robert Armstrong. Banks, who owed his scarred face and frozen expression to a paralyzing injury suffered during World War 1, also appeared in Hitchcock's 1934 version of *The Man Who Knew Too Much, Sanders of the River* (1935, a seldom-seen but fascinating African adventure also starring Paul Robeson), *Fire Over England* (1937), *Jamaica Inn* (1939), *Henry V* (1945), and *The Small Back Room* (1949), to name a few.

BARA, THEDA. Actress. *(b. July 29, 1890, Cincinnati, as Theodosia Goodman; d. Apr. 13, 1955.)* The screen's first sex symbol, albeit an unlikely one: Bara's unspectacular but admittedly exotic features and her ample figure, observed today, reminds one just how radically ideals of feminine allure have changed over the years. She was one of Hollywood's first "manufactured" stars; an army of publicity men labored mightily to create a phony past for her, and ascribed to her supernatural powers and abilities that only the most gullible fans could have believed. A tailor's daughter, Bara worked as an extra in films before playing a memorable femme fatale in *A Fool There Was* (1915, uttering the famous line, "Kiss me, my fool!"). She appeared in dozens of silent films from 1914 to 1919, playing famous vamps of fact and fiction such as Cleopatra, Salome, Carmen, and Madame Du Barry. She starred on Broadway during the 1920s, and attempted a screen comeback in 1926 for comedy producer Hal Roach, only to find that increasingly sophisticated movie audiences snickered at her anachronistic acting style.

Bara quit the screen cold; little was heard from her until her death from cancer in 1955. She was married to director Charles Brabin.
OTHER FILMS INCLUDE: 1915: *The Two Orphans;* 1916: *East Lynne, Romeo and Juliet;* 1917: *Heart and Soul;* 1918: *The She Devil;* 1919: *Kathleen Mavourneen;* 1921: *The Price of Silence;* 1925: *The Unchastened Woman;* 1926: *The Dancer of Paris.*

BARDOT, BRIGITTE. Actress. *(b. Sept. 28, 1934, Paris, as Camille Javal.)* This blond siren trumpeted one of the first blasts of the sexual revolution by baring her beauteous body in then-husband Roger Vadim's . . . *And God Created Woman* (1956). She came to personify a kind of "French naughtiness" and frank sexuality to more straitlaced—and censorship-bound—Americans. She worked with Jean-Luc Godard, most memorably as the female lead in his international coproduction *Contempt* (1963), in which her character went by Bardot's own real name, Camille. By the 1960s she was able to poke fun at her own sexy image, teamed with French beauty Jeanne Moreau in Louis Malle's lighthearted *Viva Maria!* (1965), and playing herself, the object of young Billy Mumy's affection in the Hollywood concoction *Dear Brigitte* (1965). Bardot retired from films in 1974 and has become a champion of animal rights; every couple of years or so she makes news with some kind of bizarre action or pronouncement, usually related to her pet cause. Her son Nicholas Charrier is also an actor.
OTHER FILMS INCLUDE: 1952: *Les Dents longues* (her first); 1955: *Helen of Troy;* 1958: *The Night Heaven Fell;* 1968: *Spirits of the Dead;* 1973: *Don Juan.*

BARI, LYNN. Actress. *(b. Dec. 18, 1913, Roanoke, Va. as Marjorie Fisher; d. Nov. 20, 1989.)* "Claudette Colbert with biceps" is how one critic described this trim, attractive brunette, who played "the other woman" so often that she and Ralph Bellamy could've formed a club. She began in films as a chorus girl, and can be glimpsed in that capacity as early as *Dancing Lady* (1933). In 1934 Fox signed Bari to a long-term contract, and put her to work playing a succession of telephone operators, secretaries, and dancing girls in the likes of *Stand Up and Cheer* (1934),

Thanks a Million (1935), *Pigskin Parade* (1936), *Wee Willie Winkie* (1937), and others. By 1938 she had graduated to strong supporting roles in A pictures and leading-lady chores in B's. In fact, she was the queen "B" of the lot, appearing in *Mr. Moto's Gamble* (1938), *Return of the Cisco Kid,* and *Charlie Chan in City in Darkness* (both 1939), to name a few, in between notable stints in *Hollywood Cavalcade* (1939), *Kit Carson* (1940, on loan to independent producer Edward Small), *Earthbound* (1940), *Blood and Sand* (1941), *The Magnificent Dope* (1942), and *Hello Frisco, Hello* (1943, one of her best "other woman" turns), among others.

Although dubbed, Bari "introduced" two fine songs in films with the Glenn Miller Orchestra, "I Know Why and So Do You" in *Sun Valley Serenade* (1941), and "At Last" in *Orchestra Wives* (1942). Bari's later films include *The Bridge of San Luis Rey* (1944), *Nocturne, Margie* (both 1946), *The Kid From Cleveland* (1949), *I'd Climb the Highest Mountain* (1951), *Has Anybody Seen My Gal?* (1952), *Francis Joins the Navy* (1954), *Abbott and Costello Meet the Keystone Kops* (1955), *Damn Citizen* (1958), *Trauma* (1962), and *Young Runaways* (1968). She also worked extensively in early TV, mostly in live drama, and even starred in two early sitcoms, "Boss" and "Detective's Wife." In retrospect, she impresses as one of a legion of talented, personable performers who, for a variety of reasons, never reached the top rank of Hollywood stars.

BARKER, LEX. Actor. *(b. May 8, 1919, Rye, N.Y., as Alexander Crichlow Barker, Jr.; d. May 11, 1973.)* The tenth actor to play Tarzan on the silver screen, he donned the ape-man's loincloth in five films, beginning with *Tarzan's Magic Garden* (1949) and ending with *Tarzan and the She-Devil* (1953). It was an incongruous assignment for the handsome, rugged actor, who'd come to movies from a society background, debuting in *Doll Face* (1946). Barker's most distinguished screen credit came when Federico Fellini cast him as a hard-drinking American muscleman actor—not exactly a stretch—in *La Dolce Vita* (1960), punching out Marcello Mastroianni for getting too cozy with wife Anita Ekberg. As work in Hollywood dried up, Barker spent most of the 1960s in Germany, where he enjoyed much popularity and made a great many films. His last major picture was *Woman Times Seven* (1967), also featuring Ekberg. Barker, who was once married to actresses Arlene Dahl and Lana Turner, died of a heart attack.

BARKIN, ELLEN. Actress. *(b. Apr. 16, 1954, Bronx, N.Y.)* Offbeat leading lady with looks to match her choice of roles: Short and slender (but curvy), with narrow eyes, bent nose, and crooked mouth, Barkin is anything but beautiful judged in the "traditional" Hollywood manner. But she exudes sensuality and passion, which accounts in large degree for the success she's achieved in a wide variety of films released during the last decade. Barkin first gained attention as a neglected young wife in *Diner* (1982), following that performance with similarly fine turns in *Tender Mercies, Daniel,* and *Eddie and the Cruisers* (all 1983). She was a delightfully oddball female lead in the loopy *The Adventures of Buckaroo Banzai Across the Eighth Dimension* (1984), and raised eyebrows with her steamy stint as a feisty prosecutor in *The Big Easy* (1987). Since then, Barkin has essayed several roles calling for frank sexuality, in the hopelessly muddled *Siesta* (1987, with then-husband Gabriel Byrne), the gritty thriller *Sea of Love* (1989), and the smarmy sex-change comedy *Switch* (1991). A teaming with Jack Nicholson promised much but delivered the misfire *Man Trouble* (1992) instead. She was outstanding as the errant mother in search of a perfect husband in *This Boy's Life* (1993), appeared with Byrne in *Into the West* (also 1993), and starred in *Bad Company* (1995) and *Wild Bill* (also 1995, as Calamity Jane).

BARNES, BINNIE. Actress. *(b. Mar. 25, 1905, London, as Gertrude Maude Barnes.)* Former chorus girl and dance-hall hostess who broke into films in her native country in 1929, impressed moviegoers as Catherine Howard in *The Private Life of Henry VIII* (1933), and came to Hollywood in 1934, where she played occasional leads but achieved considerable success as an "other woman" type and comedic character actress. Especially memorable as Lillian Russell in *Diamond Jim* (1935)

and villainous Milady De Winter in *The Three Musketeers* (1939). Long married to producer Mike Frankovich.
OTHER FILMS INCLUDE: 1934: *The Private Life of Don Juan;* 1936: *Sutter's Gold, The Last of the Mohicans* (in the female leads), *Three Smart Girls;* 1938: *Broadway Melody of 1938, The Divorce of Lady X;* 1939: *Man About Town, Frontier Marshal;* 1941: *Tight Shoes;* 1942: *In Old California, I Married an Angel;* 1944: *Up in Mabel's Room;* 1945: *The Spanish Main, It's in the Bag;* 1946: *The Time of Their Lives;* 1948: *If Winter Comes;* 1953: *Decameron Nights;* 1966: *The Trouble With Angels;* 1973: *40 Carats.*

BARRIE, WENDY. Actress. *(b. Apr. 18, 1912, Hong Kong, as Wendy Jenkins; d. May 8, 1978.)* Pert British actress who was unable to capitalize on her initial screen success in *The Private Life of Henry VIII* (1933) as the less-than-proper Jane Seymour, a high-visibility role that should have been a better career springboard for her. Originally a stage performer, Barrie had previously appeared in a couple of minor films: *It's a Boy* and *Wedding Rehearsal* (both 1932), but the success of *Henry* led her to Hollywood, where she tried hard to carve out a career, but ultimately was not successful and gave up after a decade. Among the more notable films she appeared in are *The Big Broadcast of 1936* (1935), *Dead End, A Girl With Ideas* (both 1937), *I Am the Law* (1938), *The Hound of the Baskervilles, Five Came Back* (both 1939), *The Saint Takes Over* (1940), *The Gay Falcon* (1941), and the all-star British-emigré epic *Forever and a Day* (1943). She then found greater success as a radio and (later) TV hostess, appearing in her own talk show (her sign-off was "be a good bunny"), a children's show called "The Adventures of Oky Doky," and "Picture This," a weekly NBC game show that only ran 10 minutes! Her last film appearance was a cameo in *It Should Happen to You* (1954), about a frustrated actress doing anything to get publicity. Wendy Barrie probably could have written it.

BARRY, JOHN. Composer, songwriter. *(b. Nov. 3, 1933, York, England.)* Prolific and extraordinarily successful musician who is probably best known for composing the scores for most of the James Bond movies. While serving in the British Army during the early 1950s, he took a correspondence course with bandleader Stan Kenton and worked in the military band. Out of the service, Barry and some of his Army friends formed the John Barry Seven, which gained fame for its jazzy, electric sounds, and Barry himself went on to produce and arrange music for other artists. His first film score was for *Beat Girl* (1958) but Barry gained international movie fame when he was asked to quickly redo the theme for the first James Bond film, *Dr. No* (1962). Since then, he has scored *From Russia With Love* (1963), *Goldfinger* (1964), *You Only Live Twice* (1967), *On Her Majesty's Secret Service* (1969), *Diamonds Are Forever* (1971), *The Man With the Golden Gun* (1974), *Moonraker* (1979), *Octopussy* (1983), *A View to a Kill* (1985), and *The Living Daylights* (1987). Barry's lush scores have often added immeasurably to the appeal and popularity of many films, and have often yielded hit songs as well. He won Oscars for *Born Free* (1966, as well as for Best Song), *The Lion in Winter* (1968), *Out of Africa* (1985), and *Dances With Wolves* (1990).
OTHER FILMS INCLUDE: 1969: *Midnight Cowboy;* 1975: *The Day of the Locust;* 1976: *Robin and Marian;* 1981: *Body Heat;* 1985: *Jagged Edge;* 1986: *Peggy Sue Got Married;* 1992: *Chaplin;* 1993: *Indecent Proposal, Deception.*

BARRYMORE, DREW. Actress. *(b. Feb. 22, 1975, Los Angeles.)* Scion of the legendary acting family, at the age of five this once-precocious cherub landed a small part as William Hurt's daughter in *Altered States* and a larger one in *E.T. The Extra-Terrestrial* two years later. She played major roles in other films— including *Irreconcilable Differences* (1984) and two Stephen King adaptations, *Firestarter* (1984) and *Cat's Eye* (1985)—but her career was overshadowed in the late 1980s by her highly publicized bouts with alcohol and drugs (and a resulting suicide attempt), an eerie echo of her family's troubled history. 1989 saw the release of *Far From Home,* her first adolescent movie role. In 1990 she coauthored a book about her substance dependencies and subsequent rehabilitation, and in 1992 she made further news by posing nude for a national magazine to promote her sexually charged movie *Poison Ivy* (1992). That same year she had a provocative (but brief) part as a murder witness in *The Sketch Artist,* co-starred in the well-received independent feature *Guncrazy* (1992), and was one of three actresses to play the headline-making "Long Island Lolita" in the telefilm *The Amy Fisher Story* (1993). She then appeared in a provocative series of print ads for Guess Jeans. She had a sexy cameo in *Wayne's World 2* (1993), then costarred in the distaff Western *Bad Girls* (1994). Her star rose dramatically in 1995 with the release of *Boys on the Side, Mad Love,* and *Batman Forever.*

BARRYMORE, ETHEL. Actress. *(b. Aug. 15, 1879, Philadelphia, as Edith Blythe; d. June 18, 1959.)* Distaff member of the famous acting family, a turn-of-the-century Broadway star who was known as "the first lady of the American stage." She toyed with silent-film acting in the teens, beginning with *The Nightingale* (1914), but abandoned it during the 1920s. She joined brothers John and Lionel at MGM for 1932's *Rasputin and the Empress,* playing the Czarina; it was her talkie debut and their only film together. Appearing on-screen periodically thereafter, she won an Oscar for her supporting role in *None But the Lonely Heart* (1944, opposite Cary Grant), and received nominations for her roles in *The Spiral Staircase* (1946), *The Paradine Case* (1947), and *Pinky* (1949). Her last film was *Johnny Trouble* (1957).

BARRYMORE, JOHN. Actor. *(b. Feb. 15, 1882, Philadelphia, as John Blythe; d. May 29, 1942.)* One of the screen's legendary stars, this former matinee idol—known as "The Great Profile"—scaled the heights of his profession while still a comparatively young man, yet he gleaned little satisfaction from his success and spent much of his life in hedonistic pursuits, eventually squandering both his fortune and his talent. The youngest of the "Fabulous Barrymores" (behind Ethel and Lionel), he parlayed his considerable artistic abilities into a job as a New York-based newspaper cartoonist before succumbing to the lure of the footlights shortly after the turn

of the century. (He came by it naturally; his parents were stage stars Maurice Barrymore and Georgiana Drew.) Barrymore, like his siblings, became a distinguished thespian; his interpretations of Shakespeare's Richard III and Hamlet were spoken of with awe and reverence decades after his appearances in the roles.

Unlike some stage performers who scoffed at acting in "the flickers," Barrymore gravitated to the motion picture medium early on, making his screen debut in *An American Citizen* (1914). His bravura acting style seemed perfectly suited to silent-film trouping, and he quickly carved a niche for himself in both romantic leads and colorful character roles. His most memorable silent films include *Raffles* (1917), *Dr. Jekyll and Mr. Hyde* (1920, in which his portrayal of the unrepressed Hyde suggested an unnerving affinity for characters with unleashed libidos), *Sherlock Holmes* (1922, in the title role), *Beau Brummel* (1924, again in the title role), *The Sea Beast* (in this *Moby Dick* adaptation as Captain Ahab, a role he'd repeat in the 1930 talkie remake), *Don Juan* (both 1926, in the title role of this, the first movie to utilize the Vitaphone recording system for music and synchronized sound effects), and *The Beloved Rogue* (1927, as Francois Villon). His romantic prowess was legend; he wooed young Mary Astor during their scenes in *Beau Brummel,* right under her watchful mother's eyes!

Needless to say, the advent of talkies proved a boon to Barrymore's career, enabling moviegoers to hear his matchless voice, a privilege heretofore reserved for patrons of the stage. He delivered a Shakespearean soliloquy in Warner Bros.' all-star revue, *The Show of Shows* (1929), then starred for the studio in *General Crack, The Man From Blankley's, Moby Dick* (all 1930), *Svengali,* and *The Mad Genius* (both 1931), in the latter two films indulging his penchant for playing eccentric, amoral characters (and donning makeup that buried his handsome features).

He was lured to MGM, home studio of his brother, Lionel, in 1932, costarring with his elder sibling in *Arsene Lupin* (playing the title role) and with an all-star cast headed by Greta Garbo in the Oscar-winning *Grand Hotel.* That same year he also starred in two well-received films for

RKO, *State's Attorney* (loosely based on the life story of criminal lawyer William Fallon, written by Barrymore crony Gene Fowler) and *A Bill of Divorcement* (delivering an admirably restrained performance as the long-lost father of Katharine Hepburn, in her film debut). He shared top billing with Lionel and Ethel in *Rasputin and the Empress* (their only film together), and distinguished the all-star casts of *Dinner at Eight* (memorable for his chilling, wordless depiction of a suicide's final moments) and *Night Flight* (both 1933). He then scored a triumph—even though he was seemingly miscast—as the driven, betrayed Jewish lawyer of *Counsellor-at-Law,* William Wyler's flawless adaptation of an Elmer Rice play. The following year, he threw restraint to the winds and tore through *Twentieth Century* (a delicious comedy in which he played an egotistical theatrical producer pursuing his temperamental star, played with equal abandon by Carole Lombard) like a hurricane.

But Barrymore's freewheeling lifestyle began to affect his work; one scene in *Counsellor-at-Law* took him dozens of takes to master, and succeeding assignments found him increasingly dependent on the use of cue cards placed just outside camera range. Moreover, years of drinking and debauchery began to show on his face and figure.

Barrymore credibly played Mercutio in MGM's opulent production of *Romeo and Juliet* (1936, earning an Oscar nomination), but almost immediately thereafter began his descent into B-movie hell. He got top billing for a supporting role in *Bulldog Drummond Comes Back* (1937, the first of three series entries in which he played Scotland Yard's Colonel Nielsen to John Howard's Drummond), but he clearly chafed beneath the melodramatic constraints of the thick-ear material given him. He played an ingenious wife-killer in *Night Club Scandal* (also 1937), scowling his way through a mediocre assignment with ill-disguised disdain, and lent weight to a solid costarring role with Jeanette MacDonald and Nelson Eddy in *Maytime* that same year. His breezy, if overripe comic performances in *True Confessions* (1937), *Hold That Co-Ed* (1938), *The Great Man Votes,* and *Midnight* (both 1939) were fun to watch, but by 1940 he was parodying himself, on Rudy Vallee's

radio show and in such second-rate films as *The Great Profile* (1940), *World Premiere,* and *Playmates* (both 1941). Even though he distinguished the last-named film—a Kay Kyser vehicle—with the famous soliloquy from "Hamlet," Barrymore had become a bloated buffoon who mugged shamelessly for the cameras. It was almost fortunate that he died when he did, as his career degradation would undoubtedly have led him to studios such as Monogram or PRC.

Barrymore was married to poetess Michael Strange, actress Dolores Costello, and model Elaine Barrie, and his affairs were almost too numerous to count. He wrote an autobiography, "Confessions of an Actor," in 1926, and was the subject of a worshipful biography, "Good Night, Sweet Prince," written by cohort Gene Fowler in 1944. His daughter Diana, herself an actress cursed with self-destructive impulses, offered another view of him in her 1957 autobiography, "Too Much, Too Soon." His son, John Barrymore, Jr., had an erratic career in films, but John Jr.'s daughter, Drew Barrymore, has restored the family name to prominence in recent years.

BARRYMORE, LIONEL. Actor, director. *(b. April 28, 1878, Philadelphia, as Lionel Blythe; d. Nov. 15, 1954.)* The brother of John and Ethel Barrymore, Lionel had the most enduring film career of the trio. He made scores of films—from 1909 nearly up to the time of his death, with only occasional forays to the stage in between—but is perhaps best remembered as curmudgeonly Dr. Gillespie, the wheelchair-bound surgeon who dispensed advice to young Doctor Kildare in a long-running MGM series. Lionel was an actor in the grand manner, and his performances could be wildly inconsistent. He was affecting in *Christopher Bean* (1933), and his over-the-top portrayal of Billy Bones in *Treasure Island* (1934) was appropriate, but he often descended to the level of self-parody, as a misguided and bellicose father figure in pictures such as *Sweepings* (1933) and *Duel in the Sun* (1946). Frank Capra used this aspect of Barrymore's talent in casting the actor as the mean Mr. Potter in *It's a Wonderful Life* (also 1946), though the director also thought of him eight years earlier to play the genial patriarch in *You Can't Take It With You* (1938). Nonetheless, the old ham could be very effective, even if he did have a tendency to chew scenery, and he won an Oscar for his performance in *A Free Soul* (1931).

He appeared with his brother John in the MGM films *Grand Hotel, Arsene Lupin* (both 1932), and *Dinner at Eight* (1933, though they have no scenes together); they were joined by sister Ethel for the only all-Barrymore endeavor, *Rasputin and the Empress* (1932), with Lionel winning the showiest part as the fabled mad monk.

Lionel was a man of many talents. He was an acclaimed artist (especially for his etchings of seaside scenes) and he composed a number of concert pieces. In the late 1920s he tried his hand at film directing, but for all his talent as an actor, he proved to be absolutely inept behind a megaphone. *Madame X* and *His Glorious Night* (both 1929) have to be numbered among the worst films ever made. Although Barrymore originated the role of Judge Hardy in *A Family Affair* (1937), the film that kicked off the Andy Hardy series, Lewis Stone took over the role in subsequent entries. Barrymore did play the continuing role of Dr. Gillespie in the long-running Dr. Kildare series, beginning with *Young Dr. Kildare* (1938). In fact, when Lew Ayres left the series in 1942, it was revamped to make Barrymore the star, with young contract actors (including Van Johnson) assigned to play Kildare-like interns.

Barrymore was a favorite of MGM head Louis B. Mayer, and even though wheelchair-bound with severe arthritis from the late 1930s on, he stayed on the payroll, with parts written to accommodate his infirmity. Even in later years he gave commanding, often affecting, performances in such films as *Key Largo* (1948), *Down to the Sea in Ships* (1949), and *Lone Star* (1952). Barrymore wrote two books, a novel, "Mr. Cantowine," and a family biography, "We Barrymores." He was married to actresses Doris Rankin (1904–23) and Irene Fenwick (1923–36). OTHER FILMS INCLUDE: 1924: *America;* 1928: *Sadie Thompson;* 1932: *Mata Hari;* 1935: *Ah, Wilderness!;* 1936: *The Devil-Doll;* 1937: *Camille;* 1944: *Since You Went Away.*

BARTEL, PAUL. Actor, director. *(b. Aug. 6, 1938, Brooklyn, N.Y.)* Balding and portly, with a red, beaver-like beard, Bartel excels at the portrayal of pompous eccentrics, but has another career behind the camera. His directorial debut, the peculiar and disturbing *Private Parts* (1972), flopped miserably, and Bartel cast his lot with independent producer Roger Corman, for whom he acted, shot second unit (on 1974's *Big Bad Mama),* and eventually directed *Death Race 2000* (1975) and *Cannonball* (1976). His pet project, the hilarious black comedy *Eating Raoul* (1982), saw director Bartel starring as well, teamed with frequent collaborator Mary Woronov. *Raoul* was surprisingly successful, for such an offbeat subject, and led to talk of a yet-unrealized sequel to be titled *Bland Ambition.* But Bartel's subsequent films, as director, haven't been nearly as profitable (or well-received): *Not for Publication* (1984), *Lust in the Dust* (1985), *The Longshot* (1986). (He also directed an episode of Steven Spielberg's TV anthology "Amazing Stories.")

The relatively lavish *Scenes From the Class Struggle in Beverly Hills* (1989), while far from a box-office hit, was deemed something of a comeback for the quirky director. His next film as actor-director was 1993's *Shelf Life.*
OTHER FILMS (AS ACTOR) INCLUDE: 1970: *Hi, Mom!;* 1976: *Eat My Dust, Hollywood Boulevard;* 1978: *Piranha;* 1979: *Rock 'n' Roll High School;* 1982: *White Dog;* 1983: *Heart Like a Wheel;* 1985: *Into the Night, National Lampoon's European Vacation, Chopping Mall* (with Raoul's Mary Woronov); 1987: *Amazon Women on the Moon;* 1990: *Gremlins 2: The New Batch;* 1991: *The Pope Must Die(t);* 1993: *Posse.*

BARTHELMESS, RICHARD. Actor. *(b. May 9, 1895, New York City; d. Aug. 17, 1963.)* Dark-haired, handsome, soulful leading man—once described by Lillian Gish as possessing "the most beautiful face of any man who ever went before the camera"—and one of the silent era's greatest stars. Active in college dramatics, Barthelmess went into films immediately after graduating, thanks in part to his family's friendship with famed actress Alla Nazimova. He debuted in *War Brides* (1916), and was best used by D. W. Griffith in *Broken Blossoms* (1919), which cast him as a young Chinaman in love with Limehouse waif Lillian Gish, and *Way Down East* (1920), playing Gish's champion once again in this rural romance, climaxed by his breathtaking race across the ice floes to rescue her. By now a firmly entrenched star, Barthelmess formed his own production company, Inspiration Pictures, getting off to an impressive start with *Tol'able David* (1921), another rural drama, directed by Henry King. Such popular films as *The Enchanted Cottage* (1924), *The Patent Leather Kid* (1927), and *The Noose* (1928) kept him on top of the Hollywood heap; he was even Oscar-nominated for his work in the latter two pictures.

Barthelmess was under contract to Warner Bros., home of the Vitaphone process, when sound revolutionized moviemaking, and he maintained his popularity in the sound films *The Dawn Patrol, Son of the Gods,* and *The Lash* (all 1930). But he seemed somewhat ill at ease before the microphone, delivering dialogue in clipped tones between tight lips. Even so, he commanded the respect of the Warner brass—including studio chief Darryl Zanuck—and chose many of the properties adapted for his starring vehicles. Barthelmess' talkies gravitated increasingly toward social issues: *The Last Flight* (1931) cast him as a former WW1 aviator, one of the "lost generation" of disaffected American expatriates in Europe during the 1920s; *The Cabin in the Cotton* (1932) had him playing a poor sharecropper; *Heroes for Sale* (1933) found him in the role of a WW1 veteran-turned-hobo during the Depression; *Massacre* somewhat improbably featured him as an educated Indian battling crooked government officials; and *A Modern Hero* (both 1934) offered him as an avaricious circus performer whose burgeoning fortune is wiped out by a stock-market crash. Interesting though they were, Barthelmess' social consciousness films weren't profitable for the studio, and he was released in 1934.

After starring in a conventional but well-done thriller for Paramount, *Four Hours to Kill* (1935), Barthelmess went abroad for an extended trip. He appeared with Dolly Haas (who, coincidentally, played the Lillian Gish part in a British remake of *Broken Blossoms)* in *Spy of Napoleon* (1936). Upon returning to America, he took character roles in *Only Angels Have Wings* (1939, as a disgraced flyer who redeems himself during a time of crisis), *The Man Who Talked Too Much* (1940), *The Spoilers,* and *The Mayor of 44th Street* (both 1942), before retiring from the screen. He joined the Naval Reserve during World War 2, and thereafter lived in comfortable retirement until dying of cancer in 1963.

BARTHOLOMEW, FREDDIE. Actor. *(b. Mar. 28, 1924, London, as Frederick Llewellyn; d. Jan. 23, 1992.)* This very popular child star of the 1930s, with his curly hair and almost girlishly pretty face, was for a brief time one of the top box-office draws. The London-born lad, on stage from the age of three, won the plum role of *David Copperfield* (1935) while reportedly "visiting" Hollywood with his aunt (from whom his natural parents tried to wrest the boy they had given up, after he became a star). Soft-spoken and mild-mannered, he appeared to best advantage in period dramas such as *Little Lord Fauntleroy* (1936), *Captains Courageous* (1937), *Kidnapped* (1938), and *The Swiss Family Robinson* (1940). Bartholomew's appeal diminished as he got older; he made few films in the 1940s, and only *St. Benny the Dip* in 1951 before abandoning acting. He hosted old movies on New York television in the early 1950s, and then moved behind the camera, eventually becoming an executive with an advertising agency that produced leading soap operas for TV. Bitter about his earlier stardom, he shunned interviews for decades, and finally broke his silence in 1992, shortly before his death, to appear in the documentary "MGM: When The Lion Roars."

BARTY, BILLY. Actor. *(b. Oct. 25, 1924, Millsboro, Pa., as William John Bertanzetti.)* This fair-haired midget, whose movie career dates back to "Mickey McGuire" silent comedies of the late 1920s, is still fondly remembered as a mischievous little tyke in 1930s films such as *Alice in Wonderland* (1933) and *A Midsummer Night's Dream* (1935), in addition to Busby Berkeley musical extravaganzas in *Footlight Parade, Gold Diggers of 1933,* and *Roman Scandals* (all 1933). Barty has worked consistently since then, prolifically on television, and memorably in *The Day of the Locust* (1975), *The Lord of the Rings* (1978), *Under the Rainbow* (1981), *Willow* (1988), and *Life Stinks* (1991). As an adult, he's a real ham, glowering at fellow cast members and often snarling lines in his gravelly voice, and functions best in absurdly comic roles.

BARYSHNIKOV, MIKHAIL. Actor, dancer. *(b. Jan. 27, 1947, Riga, Latvia.)* Accepted by the prestigious Kirov Ballet at the age of 15, Baryshnikov performed with the troupe from 1966 to 1974, when he defected to Canada. He joined the American Ballet Theatre later that year, and solidified his reputation as one of the world's most celebrated dancers. Turning to film work in 1977, he won an Oscar nomination for his film-debut role as a self-absorbed ballet star in *The Turning Point.* Since that time he has occasionally dabbled in screen acting. *White Nights* (1985) was concocted as a vehicle for him and tap dancer Gregory Hines, and *Dancers* (1987) was another hand-tailored script about an amorous ballet star. But Baryshnikov has never achieved real screen stardom to match his stature in the world of dance. Other films: *That's Dancing!* (1985, as one of the on-camera hosts), *The Cabinet of Dr. Ramirez,* and *Company Business,* a spy thriller (both 1991). The bedroom-eyed Baryshnikov is also well known for his much-publicized romantic liaisons, including one with actress Jessica Lange, with whom he fathered a daughter, Alexandra.

BASEHART, RICHARD. Actor. *(b. Aug. 31, 1914, Zanesville, Ohio; d. Sept. 17, 1984.)* Square-jawed, talented, but humorless actor, primarily in strong supporting roles, who worked as a reporter and a radio announcer before succumbing to the lure of the greasepaint in the late 1930s. Made an impressive movie debut in *Repeat Performance* (1947) and roused critical praise in *He Walked by Night* (1948). Basehart's other memorable films include *Fourteen Hours* (1951), in which he played a would-be suicide; *La Strada* (1954), playing The Fool; *Moby Dick* (1956), as Ishmael; *The Brothers Karamazov* (1958), as Ivan; and *Hitler* (1962), in the title role. Basehart also

starred in the TV series "Voyage to the Bottom of the Sea" in the early 1960s; unfortunately, his subsequent films—with the exception of *Being There* (1979)—were unequal to his ability. At one time he was married to actress Valentina Cortese. A theater in Woodland Hills, California, is named for him.

BASINGER, KIM. Actress. *(b. Dec. 8, 1953, Athens, Ga.)* Leggy, full-lipped blonde whose sultry screen presence—the camera really loves her—was honed by years of experience as a top fashion model. Basinger left the cover-girl life for acting in the early 1980s, after testing the waters in the made-for-TV *Katie: Portrait of a Centerfold* in 1978. She made her film debut in 1981's *Hard Country,* but wasn't really noticed until she became a "Bond girl" in *Never Say Never Again* (1983), and promoted the film with a nude layout in "Playboy." Routinely cast as a sex object, Basinger gamely stumbled through *The Natural* (1984) and Robert Altman's *Fool for Love* (1985) before landing the starring role in the 1986 pulp hit *Nine½ Weeks.* Afterward, she branched out into comedy, starring in several regrettable flops including *Nadine, Blind Date* (both 1987) and *My Stepmother Is an Alien* (1988). She played reporter Vicki Vale in *Batman* (1989), the phenomenal success of which boosted her standing as a bankable star. She behaved accordingly, reportedly hampering (with costar and later husband Alec Baldwin) completion of *The Marrying Man* (1991).

Critics generally haven't been kind to Basinger, to say the least, but she occasionally surprises—and confounds—her detractors. She showed promise in a reasonably complex role as a seductive schemer in *Final Analysis* (1992). When all's said and done, though, she owes her success more to the raw, animal sexuality she so ably projects, rather than to whatever acting ability she's demonstrated to date. Early in 1993 she garnered headlines for a film she *didn't* make: The producers of the black comedy *Boxing Helena* won a multimillion-dollar judgment against her after she allegedly reneged on her agreement to star. (The verdict was later overturned.) Other recent credits include *Cool World* (1992, as the voice and model for sexy animated character Holli Wood), *The*

Real McCoy (1993), *Wayne's World 2* (also 1993, parodying her own sexy screen image as Honey Hornée), *The Getaway* (1994, opposite Baldwin), and *Ready to Wear/Prêt-à-Porter* (also 1994).

BASS, SAUL. Graphic designer, director. *(b. May 8, 1920, New York City.)* Directors from Alfred Hitchcock to Martin Scorsese have turned to this brilliant graphic designer to fashion main titles which will set the mood for their films. He first worked with Otto Preminger on *Carmen Jones* (1954), but it was his design concept for *The Man With the Golden Arm* (1955) that really caught people's attention. Thereafter, he created posters and logos for all of Preminger's films, among them *Bonjour Tristesse* (1958), *Anatomy of a Murder* (1959), *Exodus* (1960), and *Advise and Consent* (1962). He also brought his design expertise and sense of humor to the main titles of *Around the World in 80 Days* (1956). After making an arresting title sequence for Hitchcock's *Vertigo* (1958), the director hired him to not only make titles, but also act as visual consultant on *North by Northwest* (1959) and *Psycho* (1960). For the latter film, Bass actually laid out a blueprint for the bravura shower murder sequence. He later designed the elaborate epilogue title sequence for *West Side Story* (1961), filmed an eerie cat "walking the line" for *Walk on the Wild Side* (1962), and conceived the racing sequences for *Grand Prix* (1966). In the mid 1960s, Bass grew tired of being an appendage to other people's films, and started making his own very personal short subjects *(The Searching Eye, The Solar Film, Notes on the Popular Arts),* several of which were nominated for Academy Awards; *Why Man Creates* (1968) in fact won an Oscar as Best Live-Action Short Subject. In 1974 he made his feature-film directing debut with the science fiction story *Phase IV,* but the picture was not a success. After filming an elaborate and amusing title sequence for *That's Entertainment, Part 2* (1976), he returned to the world of graphic design, where he created logos for corporations and products ranging from United Air Lines to Lawry's seasonings. After a long hiatus from film titles, he started accepting assignments again in the 1980s, working with his wife Elaine. They started simply, with designs for films like *Broadcast News* (1987) and Martin Scorsese's *GoodFellas* (1990), before diving into more ambitious and elaborate work. Their moody design for Scorsese's *Cape Fear* (1991) was topped by their brilliant evocation of *The Age of Innocence* (1993). Like all great Bass titles, this one set the stage for the film that followed and offered moviegoers a miniature film within a film.

BASSETT, ANGELA. Actress. *(b. Aug. 16, 1958, New York City.)* After working her way up from bits to supporting roles in films, Bassett landed the lead as soul singer Tina Turner in the biopic *What's Love Got to Do With It* (1993), and scored a knockout with her electric, and totally credible, performance. A graduate of the Yale School of Drama, Bassett worked on Broadway and put in her time on a TV soap opera before winning small parts in films like *F/X* (1986), *Kindergarten Cop* (1990), and the John Sayles films *City of Hope* (1991) and *Passion Fish* (1992). Meatier roles finally came her way in *Boyz N the Hood* (1991, opposite her *What's Love Got to Do With It* costar Laurence Fishburne) and *Malcolm X* (1992, as Betty Shabazz, the black leader's wife). She also impressed as Michael Jackson's mom Katherine in the TV miniseries "The Jacksons: An American Dream" (1992), but it was the Tina Turner movie that propelled Bassett to the brink of stardom and an Oscar nomination.

BATES, ALAN. Actor. *(b. Feb. 17, 1934, Derbyshire, England.)* A burly, thoroughly masculine actor who came to prominence during the "angry young man" phase of British screen drama, he's best known in America for playing director Paul Mazursky's Ideal Male in 1978's *An Unmarried Woman.* While he generally plays solid, decent types, he's been quite effective in menacing roles too, as evidenced by his work in *The Shout* (1978). Bates played uncle to Mel Gibson's Hamlet in Franco Zeffirelli's 1990 film of Shakespeare's play. Bates was nominated for a Best Actor Academy Award for his work in *The Fixer* (1968), but he's probably still best known for his nude wrestling match

with Oliver Reed in *Women in Love* (1969).
OTHER FILMS INCLUDE: 1960: *The Entertainer;* 1961: *Whistle Down the Wind;* 1964: *The Guest/The Caretaker, Nothing but the Best, Zorba the Greek;* 1966: *Georgy Girl, King of Hearts;* 1967: *Far from the Madding Crowd;* 1971: *The Go-Between;* 1974: *Butley;* 1975: *In Celebration, Royal Flash;* 1979: *The Rose,* 1981: *Quartet, Return of the Soldier;* 1982: *Britannia Hospital;* 1984: *An Englishman Abroad* (telefilm), *A Voyage Round My Father* (telefilm); 1986: *Duet for One;* 1987: *A Prayer for the Dying;* 1989: *Club Extinction* (also known as *Dr. M*); 1992: *Secret Friends;* 1994: *Silent Tongue.*

BATES, KATHY. Actress. *(b. June 18, 1948, Memphis, Tenn.)* Revenge can be very sweet: The role of the plain, dumpy waitress in the play "Frankie and Johnny in the Clair de Lune" was written specifically for this pleasantly plain-looking, slightly dumpy actress, who played it to perfection. But when it came time to do the movie, Bates was passed over for the glamorous Michelle Pfeiffer. So, instead, she played the psychotic nurse in *Misery* (1990) and won a Best Actress Oscar, while *Frankie and Johnny* crashed and burned at the box office. Though primarily a stage actress, Bates has made film appearances since the 1970s, with small roles in such pictures as *Straight Time* (1978), *Come Back to the Five and Dime, Jimmy Dean, Jimmy Dean* (1982), *Summer Heat* (1987), *Arthur 2: On the Rocks* (1988), *Men Don't Leave, Dick Tracy,* and *White Palace* (all 1990). In 1991 she snagged two plum roles: that of the fanatical Christian fundamentalist stuck in the Amazon in *At Play in the Fields of the Lord,* and the downtrodden Southern housewife who enjoys a special relationship with an older woman (Jessica Tandy) in *Fried Green Tomatoes.* In 1992 she joined Tandy again, along with superstars Shirley MacLaine and Marcello Mastroianni, in *Used People.* Bates, like many of her contemporaries, affects a natural acting style, never allowing artifice to get in the way of emotional honesty.
OTHER FILMS INCLUDE: 1992: *Prelude to a Kiss;* 1993: *Hostages* (telefilm), *A Home of Our Own;* 1994: *North,* "The Stand" (TV miniseries, unbilled cameo); 1995: *Dolores Claiborne.*

BAVA, MARIO. Director, cinematographer. *(b. July 14, 1914, San Remo, Italy; d. Apr. 27, 1980.)* The acknowledged master of the continental horror film, a veteran cinematographer whose brilliantly conceived compositions, camera movements, and atmospheric trappings influenced directors Dario Argento and Martin Scorsese, among others. Bava, one of Italy's top cinematographers, made his directorial debut with *Black Sunday* (1961)—which, among other things, spotlighted darkly beautiful Barbara Steele, the dream date for a whole generation of horror-movie mavens and misfits. His subsequent films, idiosyncratic and always placing imagery above content, include *Hercules in the Haunted World* (1961), *Black Sabbath* (1963), *Planet of the Vampires* (1965), *Twitch of the Death Nerve* (1971, a precursor to American-made "slasher" movies of the 1970s and 1980s), and *Lisa and the Devil* (1975). Bava's son Lamberto has followed in the family footsteps; his own films include the popular *Demons* (1986) and *Demons 2* (1987).

BAXTER, ANNE. Actress. *(b. May 7, 1923, Michigan City, Ind.; d. Dec. 12, 1985.)* This positively radiant actress, who'll always be best remembered for her Oscar-nominated performance as the scheming ingenue in *All About Eve* (1950), was once described by critic Andrew Sarris as one of the women who "shine with special brilliance from midnight to five o'clock in the morning of the soul." She began acting lessons under Russian emigre actress Maria Ouspenskaya at the age of 11 and made her Broadway debut at 13. Called to Hollywood in 1940, Baxter debuted on-screen in *20 Mule Team.* A Fox contract didn't keep director Orson Welles from casting her in *The Magnificent Ambersons,* in which she showed the potential she wouldn't fully realize for several more years. Baxter's bright, wholesome good looks made her a natural for sympathetic roles, and she won a Best Supporting Actress Oscar for playing a rescued bad girl in *The Razor's Edge* (1946). But she is best known for her work in *Eve,* as the conniving parasite who shrewdly attaches herself to established actress Margo Channing (played by Bette Davis) and eventually upends her.

(Years later Baxter took the Margo role in "Applause," a stage musical based on *Eve.*) Her other films of the 1950s were uneven, although she vamped quite successfully as the Pharaoh's Moses-smitten wife in DeMille's 1956 remake of *The Ten Commandments.*

In 1961 Baxter and second husband Randolph Galt (her first was actor John Hodiak) left Hollywood to live on a cattle station in the Australian Outback; she chronicled the arduous experience in a well-received book, 1976's "Intermission: A True Story." Her final narrative feature film was *Jane Austen in Manhattan;* in 1983 she participated in a documentary about her grandfather, architect Frank Lloyd Wright. Baxter was a regular on the TV series "Hotel" before succumbing to cancer in 1985.

BAXTER, WARNER. Actor. *(b. Mar. 29, 1891, Columbus, Ohio; d. May 7, 1951.)* This generally stolid leading man surprised critics and audiences alike with his flashy portrayal of O. Henry's "Cisco Kid" in the 1929 *In Old Arizona* (one of the first all-talking Westerns), for which he won a Best Actor Academy Award. (He reprised the role officially twice, for 1931's *The Cisco Kid* and 1939's *The Return of the Cisco Kid,* and unofficially in several other Westerns like 1930's *The Arizona Kid.*) A former salesman who learned acting in stock touring companies, he first broke into films in 1914's *Her Own Money.* Solidly built, with keen eyes and a pencil mustache, Baxter appeared (mostly in leading roles) in many silent films, including *The Awful Truth* (1925), *The Great Gatsby* (1926, in the title role), and *West of Zanzibar* (1928). Following his triumph as Cisco, he starred in many major-studio productions (mostly for Fox) throughout the 1930s. As he got older and his popularity waned, Baxter starred as "The Crime Doctor" in a series of 10 B mysteries for Columbia, beginning with *Crime Doctor* (1943) and ending with *Crime Doctor's Diary* (1949). He may be best remembered as the ailing but vociferous stage director Julian Marsh in *42nd Street* (1933).
OTHER FILMS INCLUDE: 1930: *Happy Days;* 1931: *Daddy Long Legs;* 1932: *Six Hours to Live* (an offbeat, little-known melodrama with fantasy/sci-fi elements); 1933:

Penthouse; 1934: *Stand Up and Cheer, Broadway Bill* (for director Frank Capra); 1935: *King of Burlesque* (in which he sings with Alice Faye); 1936: *The Prisoner of Shark Island* (as the doctor who treated Lincoln assassin John Wilkes Booth, for director John Ford), *Robin Hood of El Dorado* (as Joaquin Murietta), *Road to Glory;* 1938: *Kidnapped;* 1940: *Earthbound;* 1944: *Lady in the Dark;* 1950: *State Penitentiary* (his last).

BAYE, NATHALIE. Actress. *(b. July 6, 1948, Mainneville, France.)* Attractive, sensual French actress and former dancer who studied at the Paris Conservatoire before making her film debut in Truffaut's *Day for Night* (1973). Lithe and expressive, Baye took to screen acting immediately and quickly became a favorite, faring best in *A Week's Vacation* (1980), *The Return of Martin Guerre* (1982), *Beethoven's Nephew, Detective* (both 1985), and *The Man Inside* (1990).

BEAL, JOHN. Actor. *(b. Aug. 13, 1909, Joplin, Mo., as John Bliedung.)* Though his film career was never anything to shout about, this youthful, handsome supporting player and occasional leading man did earn a footnote in the trivia books as the star of the very first TV show to win an Emmy: "The Necklace," an episode of a dramatic anthology series called "Your Star Time." Otherwise, Beal's career consisted of a succession of nondescript starring roles in B pictures and supporting roles in A pictures, and he kept busy on the stage when movie roles weren't coming his way. Something about his face suggested petulance and duplicity, and he was expert at delineating weakling young men. He lacked the virility (or, rather, the ability to project it) that might have won him more interesting leading roles. He was married to actress Helen Craig.
FILMS INCLUDE: 1933: *Another Language;* 1934: *The Little Minister* (a promising role opposite Katharine Hepburn); 1935: *Break of Hearts* (also with Hepburn), *Les Miserables;* 1937: *Double Wedding, Madame X;* 1938: *Port of Seven Seas;* 1939: *The Cat and the Canary* (one of his best character parts); 1942: *The Great Commandment;* 1943: *Edge of Darkness;* 1947: *Key Witness;* 1952: *My Six Convicts;* 1957: *The Vampire* (title role); 1959: *The Sound and the Fury;*

1960: *Ten Who Dared;* 1974: *The House That Cried Murder;* 1993: *The Firm.*

BEALS, JENNIFER. Actress. *(b. Dec. 19, 1963, Chicago.)* Intelligent, dark, doe-eyed actress whose career seemed destined for "Most Likely to Become a Trivia Question" status. In 1983, as a fresh-faced, energetic young performer, she was touted as having the makings of a great new star, based on the mega-success of her first film, *Flashdance.* Her improbable steelworker-by-day-dancer-by-night characterization catapulted her into the international limelight; her ensemble of tattered jeans and oversized, off-the-shoulder sweatshirt sparked a fashion trend for a generation of adolescents. Her star quickly waned, though, once reports surfaced that stand-ins had actually performed her dance numbers. Beals played the eponymous female lead in *The Bride* (1985), a pop remake of the classic *Bride of Frankenstein* that sank like a stone, taking with it most of the residual momentum from her fledgling career. She appeared on-screen infrequently after that, concentrating on drama lessons and her education, but came back with effective character performances in *In the Soup* (1992) and *Mrs. Parker and the Vicious Circle* (1994) and roles in *Devil in a Blue Dress* and *Four Rooms* (both 1995). Beals also starred in several made-for-cable movies and the 1992 TV series "2000 Malibu Road."
OTHER FILMS INCLUDE: 1988: *Split Decisions, Vampire's Kiss* (as a sexy bloodsucker); 1990: *Docteur M;* 1991: *Blood and Concrete.*

BÉART, EMMANUELLE. Actress. *(b. Aug. 14, 1965, Gassin, France.)* The rapturously beautiful Béart was an au pair living in Montreal when she met director Robert Altman, who encouraged her to become an actress. She subsequently went to drama school and, proving Altman's hunch correct, has become one of France's leading stars. After a small role in *Premiers Desirs* (1983), she caught French critics' attention in *Un Amour interdit* (1985) and *L'Amour en douce* (1986, as a call girl) and won a Cesar Award as Best Actress for her performance as the ethereal title character in Claude Berri's *Manon of the Spring* (1987). That same

year, she made her American debut in the instantly forgettable *Date With an Angel* (1987). Since then, she has demonstrated an impressive range, with stunning performances as an artist's model in *La Belle Noiseuse* (1991) and, especially, as a violinist in *Un Coeur en hiver* (1992), for which she studied over the course of a year in order to convincingly play a world-class musician. The film also reunited her on-screen with real-life companion Daniel Auteuil, whom she met while making *Manon.*

THE BEATLES. Musicians, actors. *(George Harrison—b. Feb. 25, 1943, Liverpool, England. John Lennon—b. Oct. 9, 1940, Liverpool, England; d. Dec. 8, 1980. Paul McCartney—b. June 18, 1942, Liverpool, England. Ringo Starr—b. June 7, 1940, Dingle, England, as Richard Starkey.)* In 1955, young Paul McCartney joined a music group called The Quarrymen led by a rebellious teen named John Lennon. Paul's friend George Harrison joined as guitarist and the group evolved into The Beatles (named in tribute to Buddy Holly's Crickets), playing in local clubs and gaining notoriety in Hamburg, Germany, for their anti-authority attitudes and hardrocking music. By the time Ringo Starr became the group's permanent drummer, Beatlemania was on the rise in Britain and, eventually, the U.S. The Fab Four went on to change the sound of popular music, and along the way, made some enduring contributions to the movies as well. Their debut film, *A Hard Day's Night* (1964), was a low-budget project intended to capitalize on the quartet's early fame, nothing more. The final product stunned critics as much as it delighted audiences: a pseudofictional look at a day in the Beatles' lives, which wonderfully captured their irreverent, anarchic energy (thanks to the Beatles' on-camera presence, Alun Owen's Oscar-nominated script, and Richard Lester's direction). *Help!* (1965, also directed by Lester) was not quite as well received, but was still a madcap, colorful romp. The lads directed and produced their next project, *Magical Mystery Tour* (1967), a made-for-TV movie that was mostly improvised—and savaged by critics. Their next "appearance" was much more successful, in the imaginative, psychedelically designed animated feature *Yellow Submarine* (1968). (The Beatles did not participate in the film's production—except for an appearance at the end—and the voices for their animated characters were spoken by actors.) Their last film together was the documentary *Let It Be* (1970), a painful look at the group's disintegration as they worked in the studio; the film's music won an Oscar for Original Song Score.

Individually, the Beatles pursued widely varying careers. Lennon was the first to appear in a movie without the other three—in Richard Lester's dark comedy *How I Won the War* (1967). He and wife Yoko Ono worked together on many experimental films including *Bottoms* (1967, a pastiche of various human derrieres), *Number 5* (1968, a slow-motion record of Lennon's facial expressions), and *Fly* (1971, an examination of a nude woman from a fly's point of view). Ono later provided some of this material for inclusion in the documentary *Imagine: John Lennon* (1988).

Ringo, hailed as the "natural" of the group, enjoyed some fame as an actor, with appearances in *Candy* (1968), *The Magic Christian* (1969), *200 Motels* (1971), *Son of Dracula* (1974), Ken Russell's *Lisztomania* (1975, as the Pope), and proved himself an engaging leading man in the prehistoric comedy *Caveman* (1981).

Paul McCartney scored *The Family Way* (1966), earned an Oscar nomination (with wife Linda) for writing the title song of the James Bond movie *Live and Let Die* (1973), which they performed on the soundtrack, and starred in *Give My Regards to Broad Street* (1984), an excuse to showcase a series of musical numbers and some Beatles songs. In 1991 he asked director Richard Lester to direct a documentary of his current group's tour, which was released as *Get Back*.

Surprisingly, it was George Harrison, the "quiet" Beatle, who made the biggest splash in the film world. His production company, HandMade Films, was originally founded to enable the Monty Python movie *Life of Brian* (1979) to secure a release. Since then, Harrison has served as executive producer, along with partner Denis O'Brien, on a number of unusual and eclectic films, including *Time Bandits* (1981), *The Missionary* (1982), *A Private Function* (1985), *Mona Lisa* and *Shanghai*

Surprise (both 1986), *Withnail & I* (1987), *How to Get Ahead in Advertising* and *Track 29* (both 1988). He has also made cameos in some of the aforementioned films and contributed songs to their soundtracks. In 1978 Harrison made a cameo appearance in the uproarious made-for-TV satire *The Rutles: All You Need Is Cash*, proving that his sense of humor extended to the subject of The Beatles.

BEATTY, NED. Actor. *(b. July 6, 1937, Louisville, Ky.)* This portly character player gave one of the 1970s' most courageous and harrowing performances as the brutalized rafter in *Deliverance* (1972, his film debut), forever etching his ruddy, round face in the minds of moviegoers everywhere. Since then, this stage veteran has exhibited tremendous range, playing all kinds of roles in all kinds of pictures. His turn as a monolithic broadcasting executive in *Network* (1976) earned Beatty an Academy Award nomination for Best Supporting Actor, and his appearances in popular 1970s films—among them *Nashville* (1975), *All the President's Men*, *Silver Streak* (both 1976), and *Superman* (1978)—made him an iconic presence during that decade. His TV work included the highly lauded telefeature *Friendly Fire* (1979) with Carol Burnett. The 1980s found his career somewhat in decline, although his work maintained the same high level of quality, in *Back to School* (1986), *The Big Easy* (1987), and *Switching Channels* (1988). Actor-writer Adrian Dunbar and director Peter Chelsom tailored the role of Irish singer Josef Locke specifically for him, and he played it for all it was worth in the 1991 sleeper *Hear My Song*. His recent credits include *Prelude to a Kiss* (1992) and *Rudy* (1993), and he starred in the TV series "Homicide: Life on the Streets" (1993–) and had a recurring role as John Goodman's father on "Roseanne."

BEATTY, WARREN. Actor, director, producer. *(b. Mar. 30, 1937, Richmond, Va., as Warren Beaty.)* One of the screen's most charismatic leading men, Beatty belied his "pretty boy" status by producing, directing, and occasionally cowriting a handful of challenging and even noncommercial films. The younger brother of actress Shirley MacLaine, he participated in amateur theatrics while just a young boy. Beatty attended college for a year before dropping out to study acting with Stella Adler. He appeared on stage and in TV productions (including a recurring role on "The Many Loves of Dobie Gillis" in 1959–60) before making his feature-film debut in *Splendor in the Grass* (1961). His dark, brooding good looks and elusive manner made him particularly effective as a cynical opportunist. After working in *The Roman Spring of Mrs. Stone* (also 1961), *All Fall Down* (1962), *Lilith* (1964), *Mickey One* (1965), *Promise Her Anything,* and *Kaleidoscope* (both 1966), Beatty hit paydirt with his performance as Depression-era bank robber Clyde Barrow in the ground-breaking gangster saga *Bonnie and Clyde* (1967, with Faye Dunaway in the distaff lead), which he also produced. Beatty's antihero spin on the sociopathic Barrow helped endear the film to youthful, rebellious, anti-authoritarian audiences of the turbulent late 1960s; the movie was an enormous success, and secured Beatty Oscar nominations for Best Actor and Best Picture.

Offscreen for several years, Beatty returned to star in *The Only Game in Town* (1970, a flop), Robert Altman's *McCabe and Mrs. Miller* (1971), *$* (aka *Dollars,* 1972), *The Parallax View* (1974), and the uncharacteristic comedy *The Fortune* (1975) before tackling another "personal" production, *Shampoo* (also 1975), the story of an amoral Southern California hairdresser, which he also produced and cowrote; it was a big box-office hit and earned him an Oscar nomination for his and Robert Towne's screenplay). Beatty, who by this time had established a reputation as a slow, deliberate worker and perfectionist, took three years to fashion his next starring vehicle, *Heaven Can Wait* (1978), an updated remake of 1941's *Here Comes Mr. Jordan* that he produced, starred in, cowrote with Elaine May and codirected with Buck Henry. *Heaven,* his third movie costarring Julie Christie, snagged Academy Award nominations for Beatty in all four capacities.

Beatty's next film was his most unusual: *Reds* (1981), an epic, romantic drama of the Russian Revolution, costarred him as real-life American journalist/idealist John Reed, opposite Diane Keaton (with whom he was then linked offscreen). It again earned him Oscar nominations for Best Picture, Best Screenplay, Best Actor, and Best Director; he won in the latter category. He subsequently took another long sabbatical, returning to the screen in the ill-fated (and ill-advised) comedy *Ishtar* (1987), costarring with old friend Dustin Hoffman for director Elaine May, another old friend. A bomb of legendary proportions, it drew critical fire, but otherwise had little effect on Beatty, who executive-produced *The Pick-up Artist* that same year for writer-director James Toback.

Beatty raised eyebrows by purchasing screen rights to the "Dick Tracy" comic strip, which he brought to the screen in 1990. *Dick Tracy* was a highly stylized but ultimately (and perhaps deliberately) two-dimensional adventure that costarred Beatty with pop singer Madonna. Its success reestablished his box-office potency, and his rumored romance with Madonna reconfirmed his appeal to tabloid journalists. (He was also seen, briefly and uncomfortably, in her 1991 documentary *Truth or Dare.*) But some critics felt that for all his versatility behind the camera, Beatty's performances had become monotonous; his John Reed was not much different from his Dick Tracy. The actor finally broke the mold with *Bugsy* (1991), a Toback-written biopic of gangster Bugsy Siegel that featured his most forceful and effective screen performance to date. Perhaps, relieved of having to write or direct, he could concentrate solely on his work in front of the camera; the result was an Academy Award nomination. His fiery scenes with leading lady Annette Bening were apparently not entirely the result of great acting, however; she soon announced that she was pregnant, and Beatty, Hollywood's most notorious bachelor, married her. They subsequently starred in a remake of *Love Affair* (1994).

BEAVERS, LOUISE. Actress. (b. Mar. 8, 1902, Cincinnati; d. Oct. 26, 1962.) Like many black performers of her era, Beavers was typecast in thankless servant roles—and, in fact, she *had* been a servant, to silent star Leatrice Joy. Making her film debut in *Uncle Tom's Cabin* (1927), Beavers continued in films for several years before snaring her greatest part, that of the reluctant entrepreneur and heartsick mother in 1934's *Imitation of Life,* virtually

costarring with Claudette Colbert. Giving
a moving and restrained performance, she
won substantial critical acclaim. But opportunities for black performers were limited in those days, and Beavers returned to
rubber-stamp roles. Still, this must be
said: she was always good. And sometimes, when the dialogue was sharp, she
was delightful. She later starred in the
"Beulah" TV series.
OTHER FILMS INCLUDE: 1932: *She Done
Him Wrong;* 1933: *Bombshell;* 1934: *Dr.
Monica;* 1935: *General Spanky;* 1936: *Bullets
or Ballots;* 1938: *Brother Rat;* 1939: *Made for
Each Other* (with a great speech about spitting out the seeds in the watermelon of
life); 1941: *Belle Starr;* 1942: *Holiday Inn;*
1948: *Mr. Blandings Builds His Dream House;*
1957: *Tammy and the Bachelor;* 1960: *The
Facts of Life.*

BEDELIA, BONNIE. Actress. *(b. Mar. 25,
1952, New York City.)* Attractive, independent actress who entered movies and TV in
the late 1960s after appearing as a dancer
on Broadway and in the New York City
Ballet. Making a good impression in *They
Shoot Horses, Don't They?* (1969) and
Lovers and Other Strangers (1970),
Bedelia was widely touted as an exciting
new talent, but she became exceptionally
picky about accepting conventional movie
roles and, consequently, worked infrequently throughout the 1970s. She
achieved something of a "comeback" with
her extraordinary performance as race
driver Shirley Muldowney in *Heart Like a
Wheel* (1983). She was similarly impressive in minor films such as *The Boy Who
Could Fly* and *Violets Are Blue* (both
1986), displaying grace, intelligence, and
strength. Most recently she has achieved
popular success as Bruce Willis' gutsy
wife in *Die Hard* (1988) and *Die Hard 2*
(1990), and as Harrison Ford's spouse in
Presumed Innocent (also 1990). She has
been active in telefilms and miniseries (including 1993's "The Fire Next Time") and
costarred in the Stephen King feature
Needful Things (also 1993).

BEERY, NOAH. Actor. *(b. Jan. 17, 1884,
Kansas City, Mo.; d. Apr. 1, 1946.)* The older
brother of Wallace Beery began his film
career in 1917, after nearly 20 years on
the stage, and was almost from the first

typed as a screen heavy. His craggy features and broad, swaggering manner made
him a perfect bad guy in *The Mark of
Zorro, The Sea Wolf* (both 1920), *Wild
Horse Mesa, The Coming of Amos* (both
1925), *Beau Geste* (1926, as Lejaune), and
Noah's Ark (1929), to name a very few.
The advent of talking pictures added another dimension to Beery's screen perfidy;
his rich, booming bass voice barked orders at cowering henchmen, snarled
threats at intrepid heroes, chortled lascivi-
ously at captured heroines. He occasionally worked for major studios, but the
bulk of his sound films were B Westerns,
serials, and thrillers produced by the independent companies. Beery's notable talkies include *Riders of the Purple Sage*
(1931), *To the Last Man* (1933), *David
Harum* (1934), *Bad Man of Brimstone*
(1938), *Mexicali Rose* (1939), *The Tulsa
Kid* (1940, as a William S. Hart-styled
"good bad man"), and *Outlaws of Pine
Ridge* (1942).

BEERY, NOAH, JR. Actor. *(b. Aug. 10,
1913, New York City; d. Nov. 1, 1994.)*
Though a generation of baby boomers
probably first encountered him as the
kindly clown Joey on the popular TV series "Circus Boy," and a later generation
discovered him as James Garner's dad
Rocky on "The Rockford Files," this son
of a great actor (and nephew of another,
Wallace) had a career almost as long as
Hollywood cinema itself. After appearing
with his father in *The Mark of Zorro*
(1920), followed by another role in
Penrod (1922), Noah, Jr., went to military
school, resuming his acting career at the
end of the decade. Almost always appearing as the easygoing, good-natured sidekick, he was a dependable, even reassur-
ing presence in zillions of pictures. A
small sampling: *Heroes of the West* (1932,
a lead of sorts in this Western serial), *The
Call of the Savage* (1935, a Tarzan clone
in this serial), *Ace Drummond* (1936), *The
Road Back* (1937), *Only Angels Have
Wings, Of Mice and Men* (both 1939), *Sergeant York, Riders of Death Valley* (both
1941, the latter being Universal's
"Million-Dollar Serial"), *Gung Ho* (1943),
The Daltons Ride Again (1945), *The Cat
Creeps* (1946, top-billed, but actually the
hero's sidekick once again), *Red River*
(1948), *Destination Moon* (1950), *The*

Texas Rangers (1951), *The Story of Will Rogers* (1952), *Jubal* (1956), *The Spirit of St. Louis* (1957), *Inherit the Wind* (1960, in a show-stopping bit role as Farmer Stebbins), *7 Faces of Dr. Lao* (1964), *Heaven With a Gun* (1969), *Little Fauss and Big Halsy* (1970, as Michael J. Pollard's father!), *Walking Tall* (1973 and a 1975 sequel), and *The Spikes Gang* (1974).

As a fresh-faced young leading man at Universal, Beery achieved some success in several outdoor dramas costarring him with horses and dogs, including *Stormy* (1935), *The Mighty Treve* (1937), and *Forbidden Valley* (1938). His numerous other TV series include "Hondo," "Doc Elliott," "Riverboat," "The Yellow Rose," and "The Quest," as well as countless guest shots. He appeared once with his father, in a cameo in *Show Girl in Hollywood* (1930), and once with his uncle, in *20 Mule Team* (1940, becoming "the only juvenile to ever get a close-up in a Wallace Beery movie").

BEERY, WALLACE. Actor. *(b. Apr. 1, 1885, Kansas City, Mo.; d. Apr. 15, 1949.)* The sound-era ascent to stardom of this ungainly, gravel-voiced, rubber-faced character actor still baffles a later generation of film aficionados, who see him primarily as a blustery old ham who'd chew any scenery he couldn't blow down. The younger brother of Noah Beery, a successful character player and heavy, Wallace broke into show business by joining a circus while still a teenager. He later played stock and even sang in Broadway revues before entering films in 1913 as the star of a series of comedy shorts produced by Essanay, in which he played a blowsy woman named "Swedie." This led him to Mack Sennett's studio in California, where he met petite Gloria Swanson, to whom he was married from 1916 to 1918. He graduated from Sennett's to feature films in Mary Pickford's *The Little American* (1917) and *Joanna Enlists* (1918), and soon proved his versatility in character parts—especially heavies.

Beery's silent films include *The Last of the Mohicans* (1920, as the villainous Magua), *The Four Horsemen of the Apocalypse* (1921), *Robin Hood* (1922, playing King Richard the Lion-Hearted, a role he reprised in a 1923 starrer), *The Spanish Dancer* (1923), *The Sea Hawk* (1924), *The Lost World* (as the intrepid Professor Challenger), *The Wanderer, Pony Express* (all 1925), *Behind the Front* (1926, the first of several broad service comedies in which he was teamed with Raymond Hatton), *Old Ironsides* (also 1926), *Beggars of Life* (1928), and *Stairs of Sand* (1929).

In 1930 Beery wound up at MGM, where his felicitous teaming with Marie Dressler in the heart-tugging *Min and Bill* (1930) began his unlikely ascent to stardom. He landed an Oscar nomination that year for his portrayal of a convict in *The Big House,* then played Western lawman Pat Garrett in *Billy the Kid.* But his greatest plum was the role of a washed-up boxer inspired by the love of his small son (Jackie Cooper) in *The Champ* (1931); this performance won him a Best Actor Oscar. He reteamed with Marie Dressler for *Tugboat Annie* and with Jackie Cooper in *The Bowery* (both 1933), *Treasure Island* (1934, as Long John Silver), and *O'Shaughnessy's Boy* (1935). His Pancho Villa in *Viva Villa!* (also 1934) was more Beery than bandit, but satisfied his fans. Metro also took great pains to include roles for Beery in their all-star films such as *Grand Hotel* (1932), *Dinner at Eight* (1933), and *China Seas* (1935). One of his best films of the period, on loan to 20th Century-Fox, was the colorful adventure yarn *A Message to Garcia* (1936).

By 1938, Beery had settled into the characterization of blustery, good-natured rogue, a role he played with little variation in most of his subsequent films, all of them made by Metro. He continued to get top billing and star treatment, even though his late 1930s and 1940s vehicles were little more than handsome B pictures. Beery's later films include *The Bad Man of Brimstone* (1937), *Port of Seven Seas* (1938), *Sergeant Madden* (1939), *20 Mule Team* (1940, with his nephew Noah, Jr., as juvenile lead), *Barnacle Bill* (1941), *Jackass Mail* (1942), *Salute to the Marines* (1943, costarring brother Noah), *Barbary Coast Gent* (1944, again with Noah), *Bad Bascomb* (1946), *The Mighty McGurk* (1946), *A Date With Judy* (1948, in a supporting role that even had him sing one chorus of a song), and *Big Jack* (1949). In several of those films he was teamed with character actress Marjorie Main, in an effort to rekindle the Beery-Dressler spark, and it worked. Predictable as his performances may have become, Beery always satisfied his fans.

BEGLEY, ED. Actor. *(b. Mar. 25, 1901, Hartford, Conn.; d. Apr. 28, 1970.)* The son of Irish immigrants, Begley began performing while still a young boy; he appeared in minstrel shows as well as community productions, before joining the local radio station, performing on dramatic shows and even announcing for programs. He eventually became a professional radio actor, and made his Broadway debut in 1943. Four years later he won his first film role in *Boomerang!* and immediately became a busy supporting player, in such films as *Sitting Pretty, Deep Waters, The Street With No Name* (all 1948), *Dark City* (1950), *On Dangerous Ground* (1951), and *Lone Star* (1952). In the 1950s his roles got bigger and juicier. He recreated his bravura small-screen performance in the film version of Rod Serling's TV play *Patterns* (1956), and sparkled as Juror Number Ten in *12 Angry Men* (1957), another TV adaptation. He won a Best Supporting Actor Oscar as the rapacious Boss Finley in *Sweet Bird of Youth* (1962), and played a more endearing patriarch in *The Unsinkable Molly Brown* (1964). By now a specialist in the portrayal of cantankerous old men, he was particularly effective in 1968's counterculture saga *Wild in the Streets*. His son is actor Ed Begley, Jr.

BEGLEY, ED, JR. Actor. *(b. Sept. 16, 1949, Los Angeles.)* Tall, blond-haired character actor and occasional leading man; more handsome than his father, but not exactly what you'd call a matinee idol. Born and raised in Hollywood, he got into the family business right out of college, debuting in *Now You See Him, Now You Don't* (1972). He had supporting roles in such varied films as *The In-Laws* (1979), *Cat People* (1982), *This Is Spinal Tap* (1984), *Amazon Women on the Moon* (1987), and *The Accidental Tourist* (1988), and is still basically considered a second-stringer, but he snagged male leads in *She-Devil* (1989) and *Meet the Applegates* (1991), which exercised his comedic skills. Also known for his Emmy-nominated performance as Dr. Ehrlich on the "St. Elsewhere" TV series (1982–88), he starred in 1994's "Winnetka Road."

Recent films include *Greedy* and *Even Cowgirls Get the Blues* (both 1994).

BEL GEDDES, BARBARA. Actress. *(b. Oct. 31, 1922, New York City.)* A much-praised stage actress (and daughter of noted stage designer Norman Bel Geddes) before making her film debut in 1947's *The Long Night,* Bel Geddes earned an Oscar nomination the following year for her appealing performance as the aspiring authoress whose first-person narration frames *I Remember Mama* (1948). But she preferred the stage to films, and appeared in only a handful over the next few decades, though most were for leading directors, including *Blood on the Moon* (1948), *Caught* (1949), *Panic in the Streets* (1950), *Fourteen Hours* (1951), *Vertigo* (1958, arguably her most memorable screen role), *The Five Pennies, Five Branded Women* (both 1959), *By Love Possessed* (1961), and *Summertree* (1971). In the 1970s and 1980s she played Miss Ellie, one of the few decent characters in the wildly popular prime-time soap "Dallas."

BELLAMY, RALPH. Actor. *(b. June 17, 1904, Chicago; d. Nov. 29, 1991.)* Prolific actor of stage, screen, radio, and TV, with over 100 feature films to his credit. Often a leading man, Bellamy achieved greater success in supporting roles as "the other man," in which capacity he earned an Oscar nomination as Cary Grant's rival for Irene Dunne in *The Awful Truth* (1937), and even parodied himself in the brilliant comedy *His Girl Friday* (1940). He also achieved fame as former U.S. President Franklin Delano Roosevelt in *Sunrise at Campobello* (1960), reprising the role he'd played on Broadway. Bellamy started his show-business career right out of high school, apprenticing with several stock companies in various jobs and even running his own before making his Broadway debut in 1929.

Making his film debut in the gangster film *The Secret Six* (1931), Bellamy spent most of the next 15 years in movies, frequently playing principled but dull suitors invariably rejected by lively leading ladies, but also essaying heroic roles as well. He starred in numerous whodunits, first as Inspector Trent (in four 1933–34 programmers beginning with *Before Midnight)* and then as super-sleuth Ellery Queen (in four terrible 1940–41 B's beginning with *Ellery Queen, Master Detective).* After 1945 he made only sporadic film appearances, concentrating his energies on stage and in TV (where he starred in the series "Man Against Crime" from 1949 to 1954 and was a regular on "The Eleventh Hour," "The Survivors," "The Most Deadly Game," and "Christine Cromwell"). Director John Landis gave Bellamy's film career a big boost by casting him in *Trading Places* (1983, as a ruthless Wall Street manipulator and brother to Don Ameche), *Amazon Women on the Moon* (1987), and *Coming to America* (1988, a cameo).

Bellamy, whose accolades included New York Drama Critics and Tony awards, was also one of the founding members of the Screen Actors Guild and a four-term president of Actors' Equity. He received an honorary Oscar in 1986. His autobiography, "When the Smoke Hit the Fan," was published in 1979.

OTHER FILMS INCLUDE: 1931: *Surrender;* 1932: *Air Mail;* 1933: *Below the Sea, The Picture Snatcher;* 1934: *Spitfire, Woman in the Dark;* 1935: *Air Hawks, Eight Bells, Hands Across the Table;* 1936: *The Man Who Lived Twice* (a much-underrated B with Bellamy starring), *Wild Brian Kent* (with Bellamy as a Western lead); 1938: *Boy Meets Girl, Carefree;* 1939: *Blind Alley, Let Us Live;* 1940: *Brother Orchid;* 1941: *Affectionately Yours, Dive Bomber, Footsteps in the Dark, The Wolf Man;* 1942: *The Great Impersonation* (in a dual role), *The Ghost of Frankenstein;* 1943: *Stage Door Canteen;* 1944: *Guest in the House;* 1945: *Lady on a Train;* 1955: *The Court-Martial of Billy Mitchell;* 1966: *The Professionals;* 1968: *Rosemary's Baby* (chilling in a sinister supporting role); 1970: *Doctors' Wives;* 1972: *Cancel My Reservation;* 1977: *Oh, God!;* 1987: *Disorderlies;* 1988: *The Good Mother;* 1990: *Pretty Woman* (his last).

BELMONDO, JEAN-PAUL. Actor. *(b. Apr. 9, 1933, Neuilly-sur-Seine, France.)* This charismatic French star—the logical successor to Jean Gabin—galvanized international film audiences as the Bogart-worshiping thug in *Breathless* (1959), his first starring vehicle and the directorial debut of Jean-Luc Godard. With his thick lips, bumpy nose, and tousled hair, Belmondo neatly upended the conception of "movie-star looks." A sculptor's son, he performed in small provincial theaters in France before breaking into films in 1958. Following his triumphant appearance in *Breathless,* Belmondo became the New Wave's principal star attraction, effortlessly carrying more than a dozen films before redefining his persona in *That Man From Rio* (1965), playing an ultra-suave, totally unflappable secret agent à la James Bond. He brightened the all-star casts of several international productions, including *Is Paris Burning?* (1966) and *Casino Royale* (1967). *Mississippi Mermaid* (1968), *Borsalino* (1970), *The Burglars* (1971), *Stavisky* (1974), *L'animal* (1977), *Le Professionnel* (1981), and *Happy Easter* (1984) are among his other starring vehicles.

Belmondo, like the greatest Hollywood stars who toiled under the homogenized studio system, drew moviegoers to even the shabbiest productions; part of his charm derived from his seeming disregard for whatever absurdities might be taking place on-screen. His laid-back style consistently captivated audiences, and although his youthful rebelliousness and ebullience are long gone, he has aged gracefully into more distinguished roles, including Cyrano de Bergerac.

BELUSHI, JAMES (JIM). Actor. *(b. June 15, 1954, Chicago.)* Stocky comedy actor who, like his older brother John, started on stage with the Second City comedy troupe and graduated to TV and movies. (He can be glimpsed early in 1978's *The Fury.)* After costarring with then-unknown Michael Keaton in the sitcom "Working Stiffs" (1979), Belushi made his *real* feature-film debut in *Thief* (1981). A stint on "Saturday Night Live" was followed by breakthrough roles in *About Last Night* and *Salvador* (both 1986); he portrayed foul-mouthed louts—a Belushi specialty—in both films. He was teamed to good effect with Arnold Schwarzenegger in *Red Heat* (1988, as a renegade cop), but his subsequent starring vehicles—including *K-9* (1989), *Mr. Destiny,* and *Taking Care of Business* (both 1990)—have been negligible at best. Recent credits include *Traces of Red* (1992), *Last Action Hero* (1993, a cameo appearance), and the notorious TV miniseries "Wild Palms" (1993).

BELUSHI, JOHN. Actor. *(b. Jan. 24, 1949, Chicago; d. Mar. 5, 1982.)* Rotund, expressive, and volatile comedian who, after apprenticeships with the Second City comedy troupe and the National Lampoon radio show during the early 1970s, won fame as a gifted comic actor with a gallery of memorable characters created for the first four years of "Saturday Night Live." He debuted on theater screens in the Jack Nicholson-directed *Goin' South* (1978), then scored big as Bluto in *National Lampoon's Animal House* (1978), and joined fellow SNL alumnus Dan Aykroyd for *1941* (1979), *The Blues Brothers* (1980, based on their TV characters) and *Neighbors* (1981). Belushi took a stab at a more conventional lead role in *Continental Divide* (1981, with Blair Brown), playing a gruff newspaper columnist. His soaring drug consumption hampered his work, however, and several scheduled film projects were aborted before his tragic drug-induced death in 1982.

BENDIX, WILLIAM. Actor. *(b. Jan. 4, 1906, New York City; d. Dec. 14, 1964.)* This beefy, genially homely character actor and occasional leading man usually played affable, dimwitted tough guys (usually with Brooklyn accents) on-screen, but he was capable of much more—and never failed to prove it, when given the opportunity. Born into a cultured family—his father was a conductor with the New York Metropolitan Opera Orchestra—Bendix played minor-league baseball for several years before turning to acting in local theaters around the New York–New Jersey area. He made his Broadway reputation in the role of an Irish cop in William Saroyan's "The Time of Your Life" (1939), and also played a policeman in a Vitaphone short subject called *No Parking,* made that same year. He went to Hollywood in 1942, making his film debut in *Woman of the Year.* Bendix immediately won star billing (albeit in a minor Hal Roach comedy, *Brooklyn Orchid)* and was Oscar-nominated for his effective supporting performance in *Wake Island* (1942). That same, busy year, he also contributed a memorable portrayal of a sadis-

tic hoodlum who beats up Alan Ladd in *The Glass Key.* He was brilliant in *The Hairy Ape* (1944), playing the brutish ship stoker in that Eugene O'Neill adaptation. Alfred Hitchcock used him effectively in *Lifeboat* that same year.

Bendix also appeared in *A Bell for Adano* (1945), *The Blue Dahlia, The Dark Corner* (both 1946), *Calcutta, The Web* (both 1947), *The Babe Ruth Story* (1948, in the title role, putting his ball-playing skills to work), *A Connecticut Yankee in King Arthur's Court,* and *Streets of Laredo* (both 1949), among others, before turning his attention to the small screen—where, as good-hearted everyman Chester A. Riley, he enjoyed several years of stardom in "The Life of Riley" (1953–58). Bendix continued to work in movies during the 1950s—he was teamed with Groucho Marx in 1952's *A Girl in Every Port,* for example—but he directed more of his energies to TV, in episodic drama as well as on "Riley," as the decade wore on. His last few films were undistinguished Westerns: *Law of the Lawless* (1964) and *Young Fury* (1965, released posthumously).

BENIGNI, ROBERTO. Actor, director, screenwriter. *(b. Oct. 27, 1952, Tuscany, Italy.)* Talented comic actor whose enormous popularity in his native Italy is spreading quickly across international waters. He learned the Italian tradition of improvised song and poetry while still in his teens and became part of Rome's underground theater in the late 1960s. One of the monologues he performed, "Cioni Mario," was adapted into the little-seen film *Berlinguer ti volgio (I Love You, Berlinguer).* Soon after, Benigni starred in his own TV series and appeared in Marco Ferreri's *Chiedo Asilo* (1979) and Bertolucci's *Luna* (1979). He starred in and directed *Tu mi turbi* (1983) and achieved great success with his second directing effort, *Non ci resta che piangere* (1985), as well as *Tuttobenigni* (1985), adapted from his smash one-man stage show. He also wrote, starred in, and directed *Little Devils* (1988) with Walter Matthau, and *Johnny Stecchino* (1992), a comedy about a bus driver who is mistaken for a Mafioso, which became the highest-grossing film in Italian history. Benigni was featured in Fellini's *The Voice of the Moon*

(1990), but is probably best known to American audiences for his work in the Jim Jarmusch films *Down by Law* (1986) and *Night on Earth* (1992, as the Roman taxi driver who confesses his sex life to a priest). Blake Edwards then selected him to star in *Son of the Pink Panther* (1993), a failed attempt to revive the slapstick series.

BENING, ANNETTE. Actress. *(b. May 5, 1958, Topeka, Kans.)* At the moment in her career when her name was becoming established with critics and audiences alike, Bening achieved her greatest notoriety by putting her work on hold to have Warren Beatty's baby. After working in regional theater and on the New York stage (and receiving a Tony nomination for "Coastal Disturbances") she debuted on film as Dan Aykroyd's wife in *The Great Outdoors* (1988). She appeared in the lavish costume drama *Valmont* (1989), and in a small but telling role in *Postcards From the Edge,* but really sparkled in her Oscar-nominated role as the sexy con artist Myra in *The Grifters* (both 1990). She shifted gears to play wifely second fiddle to Robert De Niro in *Guilty by Suspicion* and Harrison Ford in *Regarding Henry* (both 1991), but commanded the screen as tart-tongued starlet Virginia Hill opposite Warren Beatty's Bugsy Siegel in *Bugsy* (also 1991). Their offscreen relationship led to Bening's pregnancy (which cost her the role of Catwoman in 1992's *Batman Returns),* and enabled her to snare a more impressive—and, over the years, hotly desired—role: Beatty's wife. She then costarred with him in a remake of *Love Affair* (1994).

BENJAMIN, RICHARD. Actor, director. *(b. May 22, 1938, New York City.)* Diffident, lethargic-seeming leading man adept at playing gentle comic heroes, often assimilated Jews. He worked initially on stage, then achieved national attention as costar (with his wife, Paula Prentiss) on the TV series "He and She" in the mid 1960s. Benjamin's carefully wrought portrayal of romantic frustration in *Goodbye, Columbus* (1969), his first feature film, led to a spate of similar parts. He excelled at depicting people driven to the brink—comedically in *Love at First Bite*

(1979) and dramatically in *Westworld* (1973)—and won a Golden Globe award for his role as Walter Matthau's beleaguered nephew in *The Sunshine Boys* (1975). Other notable performances include *Diary of a Mad Housewife* (1970), *Portnoy's Complaint* (1972), *The Last of Sheila* (1973), and *House Calls* (1978). In 1982 he turned to directing with the well-received *My Favorite Year* and has since remained behind the camera.
OTHER FILMS (AS DIRECTOR) INCLUDE: 1984: *Racing with the Moon, City Heat;* 1988: *Little Nikita;* 1990: *Downtown, Mermaids;* 1993: *Made in America;* 1994: *Milk Money.*

BENNETT, BRUCE. Actor. *(b. May 19, 1909, Tacoma, Wash., as Herman Brix.)* Was there an athlete in the 1932 Olympics who *didn't* play Tarzan? Champion shot-putter Herman Brix, a tall, superbly muscled youth with ruggedly handsome features and a low growl of a voice, was handpicked by the Ape Man's creator, Edgar Rice Burroughs, to star in the 1935 Burroughs-financed serial, *The New Adventures of Tarzan,* following in the footsteps of fellow Olympic stars Johnny Weissmuller and Buster Crabbe. (He'd previously played bits in such films as 1934's *Riptide* and *Student Tour.)* The Brix vehicle, shot on location in the wilds of Guatemala, was more faithful to Burroughs' character than the Weissmuller films, but its chances were sabotaged by MGM—dashing Brix's hopes for stardom. He toiled in other serials—including *Shadow of Chinatown* (1936), *Hawk of the Wilderness, The Lone Ranger, The Fighting Devil Dogs* (all 1938), and *Daredevils of the Red Circle* (1939)—and a series of cheap adventure flicks for producer Sam Katzman before signing with Columbia in 1940. Trying to leave his athletic reputation behind, he changed his name to Bruce Bennett, and learned his chosen craft from the ground up, apprenticing in bit parts in Three Stooges shorts, B Westerns, and low-budget crime films, even starring in some, such as *The Secret Seven* (1940) and *Underground Agent* (1942).

As the years passed, Bennett got better and so did the pictures: *The Man With Nine Lives, Before I Hang* (both 1940), *The More the Merrier,* and *Sahara* (both 1943). Bennett got his best breaks at Warner Bros. (though mainly in meaty supporting roles) in such films as *Mildred Pierce* (1945), *A Stolen Life* (1946), *The Man I Love* (1947, a decent leading role), *Nora Prentiss, Dark Passage* (both 1947), *Treasure of the Sierra Madre* (1948, playing the ill-fated American who attempts to join Humphrey Bogart's expedition for gold), *Silver River* (1948), and *Task Force* (1949), among others. *Angels in the Outfield* (1951), *Sudden Fear* (1952), *Dream Wife* (1953), *Strategic Air Command* (1955), and *Love Me Tender* (1956) showed an aging Bennett in a variety of character parts. By the time he made the ultra-cheap genre films *The Alligator People* (1959) and *The Fiend of Dope Island* (1961), though, he recognized that he'd come full circle and, except for an occasional TV appearance (and a role in the legendary, unreleased *Deadhead Miles,* made in 1972), retired from acting.

BENNETT, CONSTANCE. Actress. *(b. Oct. 22, 1904, New York City; d. July 24, 1965.)* High-spirited blond actress who, though little remembered today, was at one time (in the early 1930s) one of the most popular (and highly paid) stars on screen. Born to matinee idol Richard Bennett, she received a first-class education before eloping at age 16 (the marriage was annulled) and making her screen debut at age 17 (in *Reckless Youth,* although as a young girl she'd had a bit in 1916's *The Valley of Decision*). Supporting roles and occasional leads followed, including a little-known serial appearance in 1924's *Into the Net;* a Zane Grey Western, 1925's *Code of the West;* and such popular fare as *Sally, Irene and Mary* (also 1925). She dropped acting in 1926 for the life of a newly married sophisticate. Following her 1929 divorce, she took a stab at talkies and rebuilt her career; such melodramas and soapers as *Three Faces East* (as an elegant spy), *Sin Takes a Holiday, Common Clay* (all 1930), *The Easiest Way, Born to Love, Bought* (all 1931), *Lady With a Past,* and *Rockabye* (both 1932) made Bennett a major star, and she surprised everyone with a finely tuned performance as the fledgling star in *What Price Hollywood?* (1932), the earliest screen version of *A Star Is Born.*

Bennett showed her versatility in the likes of *Our Betters* (1933), *Moulin Rouge, The Affairs of Cellini* (both 1934),

After Office Hours (1935), *Ladies in Love* (1936), *Topper* (1937, in a career standout as ghostess-with-the-mostest Marian Kirby, a role she repeated in the 1939 sequel, *Topper Takes a Trip), Merrily We Live* (1938), *Tail Spin* (1939), and *Two-Faced Woman* (1941, in a hilarious performance supporting Greta Garbo). In the 1940s Bennett's star faded somewhat, and she descended to B-movie limbo with *Wild Bill Hickok Rides, Sin Town,* and *Madame Spy* (all 1942). Supporting roles in *Centennial Summer* (1946) and *The Unsuspected* (1947) were high points in a waning career, and by the early 1950s she all but abandoned the screen in favor of stage work. Bennett, a legendary clotheshorse and fashion plate, founded her own cosmetics company in the 1950s. She died shortly after completing her scenes for *Madame X* (1966), still looking chic while playing Lana Turner's mother. Her sisters Joan and (to a lesser extent) Barbara were also actresses.

BENNETT, JOAN. Actress. *(b. Feb. 27, 1910, Palisades, N.J.; d. Dec. 7, 1990.)* Undeniably beautiful but frequently vapid leading lady of the 1930s who blossomed into a more interesting actress during the 1940s. The daughter of actor Richard Bennett and younger sister of actress Constance, she attended expensive boarding schools before taking up acting in 1928 (she had, as a small child in 1916, appeared on-screen in her father's *The Valley of Decision*). Samuel Goldwyn cast her as a youthful damsel-in-distress opposite Ronald Colman in the wildly successful *Bulldog Drummond* (1929), a star-making role that led her first to Warner Bros.—where she appeared opposite the studio's top male stars, George Arliss (in 1929's *Disraeli)* and John Barrymore (in 1930's *Moby Dick)*—and then to Fox. She stayed at the latter studio for several years, starring in many handsomely made but unimportant programmers, such as *Scotland Yard* (1930), *Hush Money* (1931), *She Wanted a Millionaire, Careless Lady, The Trial of Vivienne Ware, Weekends Only, Wild Girl* (all 1932, the last named a tongue-in-cheek adaptation of Bret Harte's "Salomy Jane's Kiss," and one of her most charming vehicles), and *Arizona to Broadway* (1933).

Bennett freelanced for a time, playing

Amy in RKO's *Little Women* (1933) and assuming leading-lady chores in *The Man Who Reclaimed His Head* and *The Pursuit of Happiness* (both 1934) before settling at Paramount, where she appeared in *Private Worlds, Mississippi* (opposite Bing Crosby and W. C. Fields), *Two for Tonight, She Couldn't Take It* (all 1935), *Big Brown Eyes, 13 Hours by Air, Two in a Crowd, Wedding Present* (all 1936), *The Texans,* and *Artists and Models Abroad* (both 1938). During this period she was loaned to costar with Colman in *The Man Who Broke the Bank at Monte Carlo* (1935) and Warner Baxter ("He wore three-inch heels," was all the taciturn Bennett would ever say about this leading man) in *Vogues of 1938* (1937).

Independent producer Walter Wanger hired Bennett to costar in *Trade Winds,* a 1938 romantic drama released by United Artists, in which she dyed her hair black to help disguise herself. She kept it black offscreen as well, and for the rest of her life. Oddly enough, the change in hair color seemed to bring with it a new vitality in her performances. She played spirited queens in two swashbucklers, *The Man in the Iron Mask* (1939) and *The Son of Monte Cristo* (1940), and struggled gamely with a Cockney accent in Fritz Lang's *Man Hunt* (1941). Bennett was decorative at best in *Confirm or Deny* (1941), *Twin Beds* (1942), *Margin for Error* (1943), and others before again starring for Lang as a scheming femme fatale in *The Woman in the Window* (1944), turning in her best work to date. Lang used her again—with equal success—in *Scarlet Street* (1945) and *The Secret Beyond the Door* (1948). Director Max Ophuls did fairly well with her in *The Reckless Moment* (1949), in which she played a murderer pursued by blackmailer James Mason.

Bennett made a glamorous mother (to Elizabeth Taylor) in *Father of the Bride* (1950, costarring with Spencer Tracy), a role she reprised in *Father's Little Dividend* (1951). But the balance of her screen output was sparse, perhaps owing to the scandal resulting from the 1952 shooting of her agent, Jennings Lang, by an insanely jealous Wanger (who'd married her in 1940). Her subsequent films include *Highway Dragnet* (1954), *We're No Angels* (1955), *There's Always Tomorrow* (1956), *Desire in the Dust* (1960), *House of Dark Shadows* (1970,

playing the role she'd originated on TV in the popular Gothic soap opera), *Inn of the Damned* (1974), and *Suspiria* (1977). After making a few minor telefilms, Bennett retired to her fourth husband, writer David Wilde, who remained devoted to her until her death in 1990. She became active in the cosmetics business, and published her autobiography (which also chronicled her colorful family), "The Bennett Playbill," in 1970.

BENNY, JACK. Actor. *(b. Feb. 14, 1894, Waukegan, Ill., as Benjamin Kubelsky; d. Dec. 26, 1974.)* This beloved radio and TV comedian joked for nearly 30 years about his notorious movie flop, *The Horn Blows at Midnight.* That it wasn't such a bad film was beside the point; its box-office failure gave Benny a goldmine of material, and as always, he was more than willing to make himself the brunt of the jokes.

A former vaudevillian (and yes, violin player), he hit the boards, initially billed as Ben K. Benny, after serving in the Navy during World War 1. After appearing in a few short subjects, he made his feature-film debut in MGM's *The Hollywood Revue of 1929* and starred for the first time in *The Medicine Man* (1930). But Benny wasn't cut out to be a movie star; he fared much better on radio, where he established his persona as a wisecracking tightwad.

He appeared in a number of 1930s musicals and comedies, including *Transatlantic Merry-Go-Round* (1934), *Broadway Melody of 1936, It's in the Air* (both 1935), *The Big Broadcast of 1937, College Holiday* (both 1936), *Artists and Models* (1937), and *Artists and Models Abroad* (1938). *Man About Town* (1939) brought his radio sidekicks Eddie "Rochester" Anderson and Phil Harris along for laughs; they were reunited in *Buck Benny Rides Again* (1940), this time in their familiar broadcast characterizations. *Love Thy Neighbor* (also 1940) was a disappointing effort to bring the phony feud between Benny and fellow funster Fred Allen to the screen, but Benny's next two starring vehicles, *Charley's Aunt* (1941) and *To Be or Not to Be* (1942), were probably his best films. Ernst Lubitsch directed the latter, with Benny as "that great, *great* actor, Joseph Tura," whose

Polish theater group bravely stands up to the Nazis. It was his finest hour on screen.

He also brightened *George Washington Slept Here* (also 1942), *The Meanest Man in the World* (1943, again featuring Rochester), *Hollywood Canteen* (1944), *The Horn Blows at Midnight* (1945), *It's in the Bag* (also 1945, in a guest appearance in this Fred Allen vehicle), and numerous later films in which he took small supporting roles and unbilled cameos, including *It's a Mad Mad Mad Mad World* (1963) and *A Guide for the Married Man* (1967). "The Jack Benny Show" was a TV staple from 1950 to 1965, and he also appeared in innumerable specials and guest shots. Benny, who in later years always gave his age as 39, married Sadye Marks in 1927; as Mary Livingstone, she costarred with him on radio and TV, and authored a memoir about him in 1978.

BENSON, ROBBY. Actor, director, screenwriter, producer. *(b. Jan. 21, 1956, Dallas, as Robert Segal.)* The son of a writer father and actress mother, this dark-haired youth enjoyed success in the mid 1970s as a teen actor in coming-of-age movies: 1972's *Jory* (his big-screen debut), 1973's *Jeremy,* 1975's *Ode to Billy Joe,* and 1977's *One on One* (which he also cowrote), to name a few. He smoothed over rough relationships with screen dads Jack Lemmon in *Tribute* (1980) and Paul Newman in *Harry and Son* (1984). Still boyish-looking, Benson spends much of his time these days behind the camera. His 1988 motion-picture directorial debut, *White Hot,* was also the first American movie shot in the high-definition television system. His 1990 domestic comedy, *Modern Love,* was a family affair in that it costarred his wife, singer-actress Karla DeVito, and their children. The 1992 direct-to-video *Invasion of Privacy,* a psychological thriller, cast him as an ex-con with a fixation on glamorous Jennifer O'Neill, and he was properly bloodcurdling. But his greatest triumph was as the (unrecognizable) voice of the Beast in Disney's animated *Beauty and the Beast* (1991), which has led to other cartoon assignments (including TV's "Exo-Squad") calling on his heretofore unsuspected vocal abilities.

BENTON, ROBERT. Screenwriter, director. *(b. Sept. 29, 1932, Waxahachie, Tex.)* Benton and David Newman were "Esquire" editors when they collaborated on the script for *Bonnie and Clyde* (1967); their screenwriting debut brought them instant notoriety and an Oscar nomination. Their subsequent credits include *There Was a Crooked Man . . .* (1970) and *Superman* (1978). Benton started directing with the offbeat Western *Bad Company* (1972), and his output since has been sparse but select. His *The Late Show* (1977) was an offbeat thriller praised for the rapport of its lead characters, portrayed by Art Carney and Lily Tomlin. *Kramer vs. Kramer* (1979), starring Dustin Hoffman and then-newcomer Meryl Streep, *wasn't* offbeat, but *was* a subtle and moving domestic drama that won Benton Academy Awards for Best Director and Best Adapted Screenplay. He tripped up trying to emulate Hitchcock with *Still of the Night* (1982), but bounced back with his contribution to the popular "we're-gonna-lose-the-farm" genre, *Places in the Heart* (1984), for which he won a Best Screenplay Oscar. *Nadine* (1987) was a misfire, but he then reunited with Hoffman for the adaptation of E. L. Doctorow's novel *Billy Bathgate* (1991). *Nobody's Fool* (1994), with Paul Newman as a small-town loser, was Benton's best film in years and earned him an Oscar nomination for Adapted Screenplay.

BERENGER, TOM. Actor. *(b. May 31, 1950, Chicago.)* For all his intensity and versatility, this sleepy-eyed, thick-lipped leading man has managed to fall short of real stardom—though he continues to deliver first-rate performances year after year. The former journalism student took up acting in his early 20s and did considerable stage work (as well as a stint on "One Life to Live") before making his movie debut as one of Diane Keaton's pickups in *Looking for Mr. Goodbar* (1977). His feature-film assignments over the next few years were varied: a Hungarian stud in *In Praise of Older Women* (1978), the young Butch in *Butch and Sundance: The Early Days* (1979), Billy Fallon in the TV movie *Flesh and Blood* (1979), a mercenary in *The Dogs of War* (1980), an engineer in *Beyond the Door*

(1982), and one of the members of *Eddie and the Cruisers* (1983).

Also in 1983, Berenger turned heads as the self-doubting TV star in *The Big Chill,* although it took another three years for him to get a similar showcase role, as the tough but hateful sergeant in *Platoon* (1986, an Oscar-nominated performance). Berenger has also impersonated a singing cowboy in the spoof *Rustlers' Rhapsody* (1985), a cop who falls for his charge in *Someone to Watch Over Me* (1987), the beleaguered mountain guide in *Shoot to Kill,* a Klansman in *Betrayed* (both 1988), a cynical baseball player in *Major League* (1989 and 1994's *Major League II),* a comically deadpan detective in *Love at Large,* a land speculator in Ireland in *The Field* (both 1990), an amnesia victim in *Shattered,* and the half-Indian who returns to his roots in *At Play in the Fields of the Lord* (both 1991). In 1993 he top-lined *Sniper,* a dismal drama about U.S. assassins in the jungle, costarred in *Sliver* and *Gettysburg,* and made a memorable appearance in the closing episodes of "Cheers" as Kirstie Alley's love interest. His talent is undeniable, yet he seems destined to be the Lloyd Nolan of the baby-boom generation.

BERENSON, MARISA. Actress. *(b. Feb. 15, 1947, New York City.)* Perhaps better known as an international jet-setter than an actress, Berenson entered motion pictures following an illustrious modeling career. Her first break came from Luchino Visconti, who cast her in *Death in Venice* (1971); her work came to the attention of Bob Fosse, who found a supporting role for her in *Cabaret* (1972). Stanley Kubrick subsequently cast her as the heroine in his 1975 epic *Barry Lyndon,* but in its wake, Berenson's career started to dwindle; she made some European pictures such as *Casanova & Co.* (1976) and *Flagrant Desire* (1986) before appearing in *White Hunter, Black Heart* (1990). These days, Berenson's face is more likely to appear in the society pages than in the entertainment section.

BERESFORD, BRUCE. Director, screenwriter, producer. *(b. Aug. 16, 1940, Sydney, Australia.)* Australian director who, more than any other, fostered his country's film renaissance in the 1970s, his greatest achievement being the internationally acclaimed *Breaker Morant* (1979, which earned him an Oscar nomination for Best Screenplay), a splendid drama built around a true incident during the Boer War. Its worldwide success brought Beresford offers from Hollywood, where he chose to make the intimate drama *Tender Mercies* (1983), for which he was Oscar-nominated. His American directorial career has been uneven, ranging from the universally disliked *King David* (1985) to the Oscar-winning *Driving Miss Daisy* (1989). *Her Alibi* (also 1989) was a slick but passionless Hollywood product, but his return to more personal and provocative material has not been noteworthy either; neither the ambitious ethnographic *Black Robe* nor the South African-based *Mister Johnson* (both 1991) achieved any real success. OTHER FILMS INCLUDE: 1972: *The Adventures of Barry McKenzie;* 1975: *Side by Side;* 1976: *Don's Party;* 1978: *Money Movers;* 1981: *Puberty Blues;* 1986: *The Fringe Dwellers* (also wrote and produced); *Crimes of the Heart;* 1987: *Aria* (wrote and directed "Die Tote Stadt"); 1993: *Rich in Love;* 1994: *A Good Man in Africa.*

BERGEN, CANDICE. Actress. *(b. May 8, 1946, Beverly Hills.)* The daughter of ventriloquist/comedian Edgar Bergen first appeared on-screen at the age of 11, telling Groucho Marx on an episode of "You Bet Your Life" that she wanted to be a dress designer when she grew up. When she began acting some years later, it looked as though she *should* have. Critics tore her apart for her blond, patrician good looks and stiff acting, and her choice of film projects—including *The Group* (1966), *Getting Straight* (1970), and *The Hunting Party* (1971), among others—didn't exactly inspire moviegoers either. Bergen subsequently turned in fine portrayals in *T. R. Baskin* and *Carnal Knowledge* (both 1971), suggesting that she had greater potential than previously suspected, but she seemed more interested in photojournalism (for which she showed surprising aptitude) and didn't gain widespread acceptance as a screen actress until winning an Oscar nomination for her turn as Burt Reynolds' ex-wife in *Starting Over* (1979). She has since gone on to greater popularity as the star of the criti-

cally acclaimed "Murphy Brown" TV show, for which she has received four Emmy Awards. Bergen is married to director Louis Malle. Her mother, Frances Bergen, has resumed an acting career in recent years, appearing in such films as *Eating* (1990) and *Made in America* (1993). Candice published an autobiography, "Knock Wood," in 1984.
OTHER FILMS INCLUDE: 1967: *Live For Life;* 1974: *11 Harrowhouse;* 1975: *The Wind and the Lion;* 1978: *A Night Full of Rain;* 1981: *Rich and Famous;* 1985: *Stick.*

BERGER, HELMUT. Actor. *(b. May 29, 1944, Salzburg, as Helmut Steinberger.)* This unmistakably Aryan actor has been typecast as a Nazi pervert ever since doing a drag Dietrich in Luchino Visconti's *The Damned* (1969). Well, not always a *Nazi* pervert: He played the title role in 1970's *Dorian Gray,* which laid a heavy layer of kink on Oscar Wilde's story. He made a specialty of tormented characters, but nonetheless achieved a high level of international popularity. His other films include *Ludwig* (1973), *The Romantic Englishwoman* (1975), *Eroina* (1980), *Tunnel* (1983), *Code Name: Emerald* (1985) and, more recently, *Nie im Leben* (1990).

BERGIN, PATRICK. Actor. *(b. Feb. 4, 1951, Dublin.)* Handsome Irish actor who made a big impression on American audiences as Julia Roberts' obsessive husband in *Sleeping With the Enemy* (1991). The son of a theater owner and brother of an actor, Bergin moved to London when he was 17 and set up an experimental theater group of his own. He landed roles on English TV and in the films *The Courier* and *Taffin* (both 1988) before receiving critical acclaim as explorer Sir Richard Burton in the historical epic *Mountains of the Moon* (1990). Seemingly in position to play heroic figures in the grand tradition, Bergin instead found a niche in Hollywood playing slimy villains, as in *Sleeping, Love Crimes* (as a sex criminal), and *Patriot Games,* as an IRA terrorist (both 1992). He *did* get to play Robin Hood in the 1991 TV movie of the same name, and in a 1993 cable-TV film he was cast as Dr. Frankenstein. He also costarred in *The Hummingbird Tree* (1992 telefilm made

for the BBC) and in 1993's *Map of the Human Heart.*

BERGMAN, ANDREW. Writer, director, producer. *(b. Feb. 20, 1945, Queens, N.Y.)* Since his first film credit, as one of the writers of Mel Brooks' *Blazing Saddles* (1974), Andrew Bergman has emerged as one of today's most original comedy filmmakers. He first gained some measure of prominence when his doctoral dissertation on Depression movies called "We're in the Money" was published as a book; he then wrote a pair of well-received comic novels, "The Big Kissoff of 1944" and "Hollywood Le Vine," featuring New York detective Jack Le Vine. Bergman's first solo screenplay was the Alan Arkin–Peter Falk cult classic *The In-Laws* (1979); he then wrote and directed *So Fine* (1981), a little-seen comedy that parodied the fashion industry. An attempt to rekindle the comic spirit of *The In-Laws* with several of the same principals failed so miserably that *Big Trouble* was barely released in 1985, and Bergman had his name removed from the film. Bergman wrote or cowrote the screenplays for such comedies as *Oh, God! You Devil* (1984), *Fletch* (1985), and *Soapdish* (1991), but won his best reviews for writing and directing *The Freshman* (1990), which featured Marlon Brando as a Mafia don (in a marvelous parody of his own *Godfather* performance). He followed up with the equally bright and quirky *Honeymoon in Vegas* (1992) and *It Could Happen to You* (1994).

BERGMAN, INGMAR. Director, screenwriter. *(b. July 14, 1918, Uppsala, Sweden.)* One of the most important figures of the modern cinema, this phenomenally talented artist, through a series of films dating back to the 1940s, practically created and defined his own genre. Noted for pictures that probe the inner reaches of human emotion, Bergman has served as a model for generations of filmmakers around the world. His primary concerns are spiritual conflict and the fragility of the psyche; within these frameworks, he has crafted a body of work celebrated for its technical and textual innovation. Bergman's interest in life's enduring questions was undoubtedly fueled by a strict Lutheran upbringing (his father was chaplain to the Swedish royal family). As a child, Bergman displayed an active imagination and a love for the theater, which was also manifested during his training as an actor and director at the University of Stockholm.

Entering the Swedish film industry as a script assistant, Bergman first tasted screen success as the writer of Alf Sjoberg's *Torment* in 1944. He made his directorial debut one year later, with 1945's *Kris*, but the prototypical Bergman picture, filled with the thematic and stylistic aspects that were to become the director's trademark, would not appear until 1949, beginning with *The Devil's Wanton.* This otherwise minor work touched on many of Bergman's continuing concerns: God, the Devil, spiritual torment, and mortality. It was followed by a series of pictures which marked Bergman's maturation as an artist—*Summer With Monika,* the circus allegory *Sawdust and Tinsel* (both 1953), and *Smiles of a Summer Night* (1955), a romantic comedy of manners set in the country, which nonetheless has many fierce, pointed attitudes about love (and which also inspired the Broadway musical "A Little Night Music" by Stephen Sondheim and Woody Allen's *A Midsummer Night's Sex Comedy* in 1982.) *Smiles of a Summer Night* also presaged Bergman's magnum opus, *The Seventh Seal* (1957). That tale (set in medieval times) of man's search for meaning—and his chess game with Death—not only became an art-house staple but, along with the same year's *Wild Strawberries* (starring the great Swedish director Victor Sjostrom as a professor looking back at his life), established a Bergman stock company, consisting of actors Gunnar Bjornstrand, Erland Josephson, Max von Sydow, Ingrid Thulin, Harriet Andersson, and Bibi Andersson, and cinematographer Gunnar Fischer; Liv Ullmann and cinematographer Sven Nykvist would later join the illustrious group.

Bergman continued to strike out into new narrative and thematic areas with *The Magician* (1958), an examination of the role of the artist; *The Virgin Spring* (1959), another medieval morality play, but much more stark, with a father avenging his daughter's rape and murder; *The Devil's Eye* (1960), a slight, amusing diversion with the Devil trying to corrupt a pure woman; and the disturbing "trilogy" of *Through a Glass, Darkly, Winter Light* (both 1962), and *The Silence* (1963), which probes loneliness and the loss of faith. *All These Women* (1964) was a minor comedic jibe at critics, notable only as Bergman's first color film. It did not prepare audiences or critics for *Persona* (1966), a masterpiece exploring the nature of art and identity through the relationship between a nurse (Bibi Andersson) and a withdrawn actress (Ullmann, her first for Bergman). Another extraordinary series of "chamber" films followed, examining war (*Shame,* 1968), madness (*Hour of the Wolf,* 1968), and isolation (*The Passion of Anna,* 1969).

After a disappointing English-language debut, *The Touch* (1971, starring Elliott Gould), Bergman had his biggest U.S. success with *Cries and Whispers* (1972), an unrelenting look at a family awaiting death that marked the peak of his visual mastery (invaluably aided by Nykvist, who won an Oscar for his cinematography on this film). He went on to the disintegration of a marriage in *Scenes From a Marriage* (1973, originally made in long form for Swedish television), a marvelous adaptation of Mozart's *The Magic Flute* (1975), and a psychiatrist's nervous breakdown in *Face to Face* (1976, also made for Swedish television, and featuring a staggering Ullmann performance) before he was arrested in his home country for tax evasion. Supported by German backers, he made *The Serpent's Egg* (1978, dealing with the roots of Fascism in 1920s Berlin), the story of a mother-daughter conflict, *Autumn Sonata* (1978, starring Ingrid Bergman in her last film performance), and *From the Life of the Marionettes* (1980). *Fanny and Alexander* (1983), a family saga set in turn-of-the-century Sweden, was a beautiful, charming, and surprisingly joyful summation of his life and most of the themes in his films. It was warmly greeted on both sides of the Atlantic. It was announced as the director's final film, but his made-for-television *After the Rehearsal* (1984) followed it in U.S. theaters. Since the mid 1980s Bergman has concentrated on directing for the theater. His script for *The Best Intentions* (1992), depicting the courtship of his parents, was directed by Bille August. His subsequent screenplay,

Sunday's Children (1993), was directed by his son, Daniel Bergman.

Bergman was nominated five times for Best Screenplay Oscars (*Wild Strawberries, Through a Glass, Darkly, Cries and Whispers, Autumn Sonata, Fanny and Alexander*) and three times as Best Director (*Cries and Whispers, Face to Face, Fanny and Alexander*). *Cries and Whispers* was nominated for Best Picture and the films *The Virgin Spring, Through a Glass, Darkly,* and *Fanny and Alexander* won the awards for Best Foreign Language Film. He personally won the Academy's prestigious Irving Thalberg Memorial award in 1970. His autobiography, "The Magic Lantern," was published in 1987.

BERGMAN, INGRID. Actress. *(b. Aug. 29, 1913, Stockholm; d. Aug. 29, 1982.)* Radiant, almost ethereally beautiful Swedish actress, forever immortalized as Ilsa Lund, the star-crossed heroine of *Casablanca* (1942), to whom Humphrey Bogart's Rick utters the deathless line, "Here's looking at you, kid." A former student at Stockholm's Royal Dramatic Theater School, she became a leading lady immediately upon entering Sweden's film industry in 1934. Her costarring turn in *Intermezzo* (1936), later brought to the attention of producer David O. Selznick, inspired him to remake the film in Hollywood with Bergman reprising her role opposite Leslie Howard. The film's critical and commercial success instantly established Bergman as a star, and she appeared in *Adam Had Four Sons, Rage in Heaven,* and *Dr. Jekyll and Mr. Hyde* (all 1941, improbably but successfully cast as "bad girl" Ivy in the last-named film) before going to Warner Bros. to costar with Bogie in *Casablanca,* the making of which was fraught with so many problems (including daily script rewrites) that the players were convinced it would be a failure. No one was more surprised than Bergman when it became a hit *twice*—both upon initial release and, in the 1960s, as the cornerstone of a Bogart cult.

For the next few years it seemed as though Bergman was incapable of a career misstep. She was widely praised for her turns in *For Whom the Bell Tolls* (1943, nominated for an Academy Award), *Gaslight* (1944, winning an Oscar for her harrowing characterization of Charles Boy-

er's persecuted wife), *Spellbound* (for Alfred Hitchcock), *Saratoga Trunk, The Bells of St. Mary's* (all 1945, particularly well received—and Oscar-nominated—as a nun in the last-named film), *Notorious* (1946, also for Hitchcock), and *Joan of Arc* (1948, a little old for, but effective in, the title role, snagging yet another Oscar nomination). But her squeaky-clean image was sullied when she deserted her husband and daughter to become the live-in lover of Italian director Roberto Rossellini. Bergman appeared for Rossellini in several European films, beginning with *Stromboli* (1949), but her movies were virtually banned from American screens owing to vitriolic attacks on her character from a wide range of civic groups.

Bergman's career wasn't "rehabilitated" until 1956, when director Anatole Litvak cast her as an amnesiac coaxed into impersonating the daughter of a Russian czar in *Anastasia* (1956), a performance that won her a second Oscar and reopened Hollywood doors for her. Having married Rossellini in 1950, Bergman was by this time raising three children (one of whom would later become an actress herself) and had no great desire to return to Tinseltown, although she starred in American-financed films shot in Europe, including *Indiscreet, The Inn of the Sixth Happiness* (both 1958), *Goodbye Again* (1961), *The Visit,* and *The Yellow Rolls-Royce* (both 1964). She finally returned to Hollywood for *Cactus Flower* (1969), in which she was poorly cast as a prim nurse to dentist Walter Matthau. She won her third Oscar as a standout in the all-star cast of *Murder on the Orient Express* (1974), first of the lavish Agatha Christie whodunits of the 1970s and 1980s. She went back to Europe and was importuned by Vincente Minnelli to support his daughter Liza in *A Matter of Time* (1976), a perfectly dreadful affair. Bergman finished her career working for countryman Ingmar Bergman in *Autumn Sonata* (1978), earning an Oscar nomination as a concert pianist who locks horns with her daughter, Liv Ullmann. Her swan song— equally notable—was an Emmy-winning performance as Israeli prime minister Golda Meir in the TV miniseries "A Woman Called Golda" (1982). Her daughters are TV personality Pia Lindstrom and actress Isabella Rossellini. Her autobiography, "Ingrid Bergman: My Story," was published in 1972.

BERKELEY, BUSBY. Director, choreographer. *(b. Nov. 29, 1895, Los Angeles, as William Berkeley Enos; d. Mar. 14, 1976.)* The name of this film innovator will forever evoke the image of geometrical patterns of showgirls in synchronized motion. More than a mere choreographer for the popular Warner Bros. musicals of the 1930s, Berkeley was a cinematic innovator whose audacious use of gigantic sets and unusual camera angles forever changed the way musical entertainment was presented on-screen. Berkeley came from a theatrical family; he made his own stage debut at the age of five, and after serving in World War 1 returned to acting, then garnered an excellent reputation as a Broadway director before going to Hollywood in 1930 at the behest of producer Samuel Goldwyn. His first Hollywood assignments included Goldwyn's lavish Eddie Cantor musicomedies, among them *Whoopee!* (1930), *Palmy Days* (1931), *The Kid From Spain* (1932), and *Roman Scandals* (1933). But he really came into his own at Warners, beginning in 1933, which saw the release of *42nd Street, Gold Diggers of 1933,* and *Footlight Parade,* on which he was credited as director of musical sequences (and this was truly the case; the nominal directors of those films had nothing to do with the production numbers).

Such memorable numbers as "42nd Street," "We're in the Money," "My Forgotten Man," "Pettin' in the Park," "Honeymoon Hotel," "Shanghai Lil," and "By a Waterfall" distinguished the Warners musicals, and several Berkeley concoctions immediately entered the film vocabulary. The overhead shot he used to best show off his kaleidoscopic choreography became known as the "Berkeley top shot," and his often outrageous use of dancers to create lavish tableaux was as controversial as it was popular. His well of ideas seemed inexhaustible, and they came to fruition in hit after hit: *Dames, Fashions of 1934, Wonder Bar* (all 1934), *Go Into Your Dance, In Caliente* (both 1935), *Gold Diggers of 1937* (1936), and *Varsity Show* (1937). Among his most talked-about sequences was the incredibly melancholic, expressionistic "Lullaby of Broad-

way," from *Gold Diggers of 1935,* which climaxed when its party-girl principal plunged to her death in a skyscraper fall.

Although Berkeley stayed primarily within the musical genre once becoming a full-fledged director (beginning with *Gold Diggers of 1935),* he occasionally tried his hand at other genres, including the 1939 crime melodrama *They Made Me a Criminal.* His elaborate brand of musical spectacle went out of fashion as the 1930s waned, and his directorial vehicles of the 1940s—including *Strike Up the Band, Forty Little Mothers* (both 1940), *Babes on Broadway* (1941), *For Me and My Gal* (1942), *The Gang's All Here* (1943, his first film in Technicolor, with which he achieved positively psychedelic results), *Cinderella Jones* (1946), and *Take Me Out to the Ball Game* (1949)—were an uneven lot.

He supervised musical numbers in other films on a sporadic basis, and in 1970 returned to Broadway, directing "No, No Nanette" for fellow Warners alumnus Ruby Keeler. He staged musical sequences for *Broadway Serenade* (1939), *Lady Be Good, Ziegfeld Girl, Born to Sing* (all 1941), *Girl Crazy* (1943), *Call Me Mister* (1951), *Million Dollar Mermaid* (1952), *Small Town Girl* (1953), *Rose Marie* (1954), and *Billy Rose's Jumbo* (1962).

BERLE, MILTON. Actor. *(b. July 12, 1908, New York City, as Milton Berlinger.)* Best known and much beloved for his groundbreaking work on "the tube" (where his pioneering success in the late 1940s and early 1950s earned him the nickname "Mr. Television"), this shamelessly broad comedian actually has had an interesting film career. A child actor who worked in vaudeville and the "flickers" (reportedly he's in 1914's *Tillie's Punctured Romance* and *The Perils of Pauline),* Berle enjoyed considerable success on the legitimate stage—including a stint in the Ziegfeld Follies—before making his "adult" film debut in 1937's *New Faces of 1937* (featuring a hilarious sketch with Richard Lane as his straight man). In the 1940s Berle was cast in a number of films as the kind of brash, wisecracking character he developed on stage; later in the 1960s, he got to play dramatic parts as well.
OTHER FILMS INCLUDE: 1920: *Humoresque, The Mark of Zorro;* 1926: *Sparrows*

(with Mary Pickford); 1941: *Tall, Dark and Handsome, Sun Valley Serenade, Rise and Shine;* 1942: *Whispering Ghosts* (in the lead); 1943: *Over My Dead Body, Margin for Error* (the latter his best film vehicle); 1949: *Always Leave Them Laughing* (the story of a Berle-like comedian who hits it big on TV); 1960: *The Bellboy, Let's Make Love* (both in cameos as himself); 1963: *It's a Mad Mad Mad Mad World;* 1965: *The Loved One;* 1966: *The Oscar;* 1967: *Who's Minding the Mint?;* 1969: *The April Fools;* 1974: *Lepke;* 1976: *Won Ton Ton, the Dog Who Saved Hollywood;* 1979: *The Muppet Movie;* 1983: *Smorgasbord;* 1991: *Autobahn.*

BERNHARD, SANDRA. Actress, co-medienne. *(b. June 6, 1955, Flint, Mich.)* Completely original performer whose in-your-face approach to comedy is off-putting but frequently rewarding. Gap-toothed, with frizzy hair, the striking but unattractive Bernhard won't be tapped to play conventional leads, it's safe to say. She worked as a Beverly Hills manicurist in the 1970s to supplant her budding career as a stand-up comic, and, following a less-than-memorable debut in *Cheech & Chong's Nice Dreams* (1981), stunned moviegoers with a riveting performance as a psychotic fan in *The King of Comedy* (1983). She has since appeared in *Follow That Bird* (1985), *Track 29* (1988), and the critically acclaimed *Without You I'm Nothing* (1990), a film version of her thought-provoking, one-woman show about modern pop culture. She was one of the few bright spots in *Hudson Hawk* (1991), playing the wacky wife of equally amusing Richard E. Grant. She has a recurring role as an openly gay character on TV's "Roseanne," and appeared in *Inside Monkey Zetterland* (1993). She has also written two books featuring her distinctive humor.

BERNSTEIN, ELMER. Composer. *(b. Apr. 14, 1922, New York City.)* No relation to conductor Leonard, this Bernstein has written a formidable number of major movie scores, including some of the most identifiable of all time—the pulsating jazz accompaniment for *The Man With the Golden Arm* (1955), the majestic treatment for C. B. DeMille's *The Ten Commandments* (1956), the cool, bluesy theme for *Walk on the Wild Side* (1961), and the definitive Western anthem for *The Magnificent Seven* (1960), which gained enduring fame in a long-running series of Marlboro cigarette commercials. In spite of his association with "serious" movies, he was tapped by John Landis to score *National Lampoon's Animal House* (1978) and subsequently became the composer of choice for a raft of contemporary comedies including *Meatballs* (1979), *Airplane!, The Blues Brothers* (both 1980), and *Ghostbusters* (1984). Bernstein impressed critics and fans alike with the lyrical Irish score he composed for *My Left Foot* (1989) and won kudos for his work on *The Grifters* (1990), reestablishing himself as one of the finest of contemporary film composers. Long devoted to the history and scholarship of film music, he has conducted many albums of great movie scores, and was asked by director Martin Scorsese to adapt Bernard Herrmann's score for the 1962 *Cape Fear* for the 1991 remake. Scorsese then had him score *The Age of Innocence* (1993) which earned an Oscar nomination.

BERNSTEIN, WALTER. Screenwriter, director. *(b. Aug. 20, 1919, Brooklyn, N.Y.)* A veteran of the G.I. magazine "Yank" during World War II, Bernstein later became a staff writer for "The New Yorker" and wrote TV plays for numerous shows like "Studio One," "Philco Playhouse," and "Robert Montgomery Presents." He cowrote his first screenplay, the Burt Lancaster thriller *Kiss the Blood off My Hands,* in 1948, but his budding film career was cut short by the Hollywood blacklist of the 1950s. It was not until 1959 that he received his next credit, on the Sidney Lumet–directed *That Kind of Woman.* He cowrote the screenplays for *Heller in Pink Tights* (1960), *Paris Blues* (1961), and the outstanding WW2 picture *The Train* (1965), and adapted the white knuckle Cold War drama *Fail-Safe* (1964) and *The Money Trap* (1966). He collaborated with director Martin Ritt on *The Molly Maguires* (1970, which he also coproduced) and his most memorable work, *The Front* (1976), a tough, serio-comic look at the McCarthy era, which starred Woody Allen as a man who "fronts" for blacklisted writers. The screenplay paralleled Bernstein's own years of dealing with "fronts," and it earned him an Oscar nomination. He went on to adapt *Semi-Tough* (1977) and *The Betsy* (1978) and co-wrote *An Almost Perfect Affair* and *Yanks* (both 1979) before writing and directing a very tame remake of *Little Miss Marker* (1980). Since then, he has written *The House on Carroll Street* (1988, a thriller set during the McCarthy era) and "Return to Kansas City," one segment of the made-for-cable movie *Men and Women 2* (1991).

BERTOLUCCI, BERNARDO. Director. *(b. May 16, 1940, Parma, Italy.)* Bertolucci grew up with two passions: cinema and poetry. He showed proficiency at both while still in his teens. He won a prize for his book of poems, "In Search of Mystery," while studying at Rome University, then dropped out of college after landing the position of assistant director on Pier Paolo Pasolini's *Accatone.* Pasolini, also a poet (and novelist), became something of an artistic mentor for Bertolucci. In 1962 he directed his first feature, *The Grim Reaper;* as heavy-handed as its title, it failed critically and commercially. He spent the next two years putting together *Before the Revolution* (1964), a haunting, multifaceted tale of a love affair between a confused postadolescent and his beautiful, unconventional, and deeply troubled aunt. During the mid 1960s he worked on some documentaries for Shell Oil.

In 1968 Bertolucci made *Partner,* a reworking of Poe's "William Wilson." *The Conformist* (1971), a study of the seductive elements of fascism, helped solidify his reputation as a filmmaker of international importance and earned him an Oscar nomination for Adapted Screenplay. With 1973's *Last Tango in Paris,* a still-shocking, frank look at despair and sexuality (which gained much of its power from the mere presence of Marlon Brando, who gave his most spiritually naked performance), he was hailed by some as the most important director in film, period (and received a Best Director Oscar nomination). Others denounced *Last Tango* as obscene. The director now admits to having been emotionally unprepared for the extreme reactions to the film.

The original cut of Bertolucci's *1900* (1977, described by the director as "a so-cialist *Gone With the Wind"),* which starred Gerard Depardieu and Robert De Niro and spanned some 40 years of Italian history, came in at over five hours. When producer Alberto Grimaldi threatened to hack it to three, Bertolucci himself reluctantly provided Paramount—which was prepared to take Grimaldi's cut—with a version that clocked in at a little over four hours. (Paramount restored the original version in 1991, which Bertolucci found pleasing but ironic.)

After the critical and commercial failure of the American-financed *Luna* (1979, starring Jill Clayburgh), Bertolucci returned to the Italian scene. *The Tragedy of a Ridiculous Man* (1981) was done on a more modest scale than any of his 1970s films, but was little noticed. A collaboration with British producer Jeremy Thomas brought him back to "the big picture," as it were. *The Last Emperor* (1987), shot on location in mainland China, instantly restored Bertolucci's international stature and, in fact, enhanced it; the film won Oscars for both Best Picture and Best Director. Accepting his statuette, Bertolucci amusingly referred to Hollywood as "the big nipple." His next film, a distressingly lumbering adaptation of Paul Bowles' novel *The Sheltering Sky* (1990), starred John Malkovich and Debra Winger. His long-planned epic *Little Buddha* finally arrived in theaters in 1994.

BEY, TURHAN. Actor. *(b. Mar. 30, 1919, Vienna.)* Handsome, exotic leading man and character actor. Born to a Turkish father and Czechoslovakian mother, Bey coveted a motion picture career while still a student. He won bit parts in two Warner Bros. movies before signing with Universal in 1941. Appearing initially as a supporting player in *Raiders of the Desert, Burma Convoy* (both 1941), *Bombay Clipper* (1942), and other B films, Bey finally got a chance to strut his stuff in the big-budget Technicolor epic *Arabian Nights* (1942), alongside stars Jon Hall and Maria Montez. He was reteamed with them in *White Savage* (1943), *Ali Baba and the Forty Thieves* (1944), and *Sudan* (1945, winning costar billing above Hall). Bey delivered an excellent performance in *Dragon Seed* (1944) on loan to MGM, and left Universal in 1946, hoping for better parts. As a freelance he starred in *Out* *of the Blue* (1947), *Adventures of Casanova,* and *The Amazing Mr. X* (both 1948) before retiring from the screen in 1953. He eventually moved to Europe but returned to Hollywood in the 1990s, ready to work again. In 1993, after forty years away from acting, Bey took a character role in the independent feature *Healer,* and did a guest shot on the TV series "Sea Quest."

BIBERMAN, HERBERT J. Director, producer, screenwriter. *(b. Mar. 4, 1900, Philadelphia; d. June 30, 1971.)* Although he owes most of his notoriety to the dubious distinction of being one of the "Hollywood Ten," convicted of contempt of Congress during the House Un-American Activities Committee hearings (an offense that sent him to jail for six months), Biberman was a talented, stylish filmmaker with one bona fide masterpiece to his credit: the still-impressive *Salt of the Earth* (1954), a taut story about striking New Mexico miners. (Financed by the miners' union, it received little distribution or exhibition until later years.) An alumnus of the Theater Guild, he came to Hollywood in 1935 and spent the next several years directing and writing conventional Hollywood fare—although his modest efforts, such as 1935's *One Way Ticket,* 1936's *Meet Nero Wolfe, The Master Race,* and *Action in Arabia* (both 1944)—were a cut above the general run of program pictures. Biberman's last film, *Slaves* (1969), was indifferently received, effectively ending his career. His wife, actress Gale Sondergaard, was also blacklisted.

BICKFORD, CHARLES. Actor. *(b. Jan. 1, 1889, Cambridge, Mass.; d. Nov. 9, 1967.)* A solid character actor with bushy hair and a "don't tread on me" look in his eyes, the gruff, burly Bickford lent authority to every role he played. He'd already been a sailor and an engineer by the time he started acting (in burlesque) in 1914. He came to films in 1929 after enjoying 10 years on the Broadway stage. His first two movies premiered within days of each other: *South Sea Rose* was a Fox film, and *Dynamite* (both 1929) was a Cecil B. DeMille production for MGM. DeMille would give the actor some of his best

roles: Cash Hawkins in the 1931 remake of *The Squaw Man;* Garrett, the hard-boiled gangster in *This Day and Age* (1933); gunrunner John Latimer in *The Plainsman* (1936); and the captain's mate in *Reap the Wild Wind* (1942). Bickford was also excellent in the big-city fairy tale *Little Miss Marker* (1934), playing a variation of his *This Day and Age* character, but for most of his career he alternated between supporting roles in A pictures and leads in B's.

His reputation reached its peak in the 1940s, although by that time he was exclusively playing supporting roles. He received Oscar nominations for his work in *The Song of Bernadette* (1943), *The Farmer's Daughter* (1947), and *Johnny Belinda* (1948), and narrowly missed out on one for his work in the all-star war drama *Command Decision* (1948). By the 1950s Bickford was usually called upon to play dependable elder-statesmen types in such pictures as *A Star Is Born* (1954), *The Court-Martial of Billy Mitchell* (1955), and *You Can't Run Away From It* (1956). In the mid 1960s Bickford replaced Lee J. Cobb as the owner of Shiloh Ranch in the NBC TV series "The Virginian" (1966-67). His autobiography, "Bulls, Balls, Bicycles and Actors," was published in 1965.

BIEHN, MICHAEL. Actor. *(b. July 31, 1956, Anniston, Ala.)* Intense actor who has played heroes and villains in a number of enormously popular action-adventure films—and revealed greater range than one might expect from a performer with his pretty-boy looks. He debuted as the title character in *The Fan* (1981), as the psychotic admirer of Lauren Bacall, then portrayed a member of a secret racist society in *The Lords of Discipline* (1983). He hit the big time in his next role as Kyle Reese, a soldier from the future sent to stop Arnold Schwarzenegger in James Cameron's classic *The Terminator* (1984). Biehn starred in Cameron's next two films, the Oscar-winning *Aliens* (1986) and *The Abyss* (1989, a standout performance as the unbalanced naval officer), as well as the supernatural thriller *The Seventh Sign* (1988) and *Navy SEALS* (1990). He reteamed with *Lords of Discipline* director Franc Roddam for the mountain-climbing drama *K-2* (1992). Other credits include *Rampage* (1992) and *Deadfall* (1993).

BIKEL, THEODORE. Actor, singer. *(b. May 24, 1924, Vienna.)* Versatile character actor, usually seen in ethnic roles, who has carved a parallel career of even greater note as an international troubadour and folk singer. Raised in Palestine, he studied at the Royal Academy of Dramatic Art in London, and performed on both the London and New York stage. He made an auspicious screen debut in *The African Queen* (1951) as a German naval officer, and ironically (considering his longtime activism on behalf of Israel) was frequently cast as a German. He was a submarine commander in *The Enemy Below* (1957), "that dreadful Hungarian" in *My Fair Lady* (1964), and a bemused host in Frank Zappa's *200 Motels* (1971). Bikel received a Supporting Oscar nomination for *The Defiant Ones* (1958), as the sheriff who pursues Tony Curtis and Sidney Poitier. He also created the role of Capt. Von Trapp in the original Broadway cast of Rodgers and Hammerstein's "The Sound of Music." Bikel remains active in political causes around the world; he had a recurring role on the TV drama "Falcon Crest" and appears in many miniseries and made-for-TV movies like *The Final Days* (1989, as Henry Kissinger).
OTHER FILMS INCLUDE: 1952: *Melba;* 1953: *The Little Kidnappers;* 1955: *The Colditz Story;* 1957: *The Pride and the Passion;* 1958: *Fräulein, I Want to Live!* 1959: *The Angry Hills, The Blue Angel;* 1960: *A Dog of Flanders;* 1966: *The Russians Are Coming! The Russians Are Coming!* 1968: *Sweet November;* 1969: *My Side of the Mountain;* 1984: *Prince Jack;* 1986: *Very Close Quarters;* 1987: *Dark Tower;* 1989: *See You in the Morning;* 1991: *Shattered;* 1993: *Benefit of the Doubt.*

BINOCHE, JULIETTE. Actress. *(b. Mar. 9, 1964, Paris.)* Lovely, delicate-looking actress who has made an impact in many French and international films. After supporting roles in films like *La Vie de famille/Family Life* (1984) and Jean-Luc Godard's *Hail Mary* (1985), she gained attention in leading roles in the melodrama *Rendez-vous* (1985) and *Bad Blood* (1986). She made a memorable English-language debut as a sexually free-spirited woman in Philip Kaufman's dazzling adaptation of *The Unbearable Lightness of Being* (1988) and starred as a one-eyed, gun-carrying painter in *Les Amants du Pont Neuf* (1990). Since then, she has portrayed Cathy in *Wuthering Heights* (not released in the U.S.) and gave a darkly ambiguous performance as a woman who seduces Jeremy Irons in Louis Malle's *Damage* (both 1992). In 1993 she won a Best Actress Award at the Venice Film Festival for *Blue.*

BIRKIN, JANE. Actress, writer. *(b. Dec. 14, 1947, London.)* During the 1960s, Birkin was renowned as a symbol of swinging London and is remembered fondly as a "legendary waif." She began acting on stage, then made her film debut in Richard Lester's *The Knack, and How to Get It* (1965). She was next seen as one of the models who romp nude with David Hemmings in Antonioni's controversial classic *Blowup* (1966), then gained international fame with such roles as a drug-addict hippie in *Les Chemins de Katmandu,* Brigitte Bardot's lover in *Don Juan 73* (1973), an androgynous bartender in *Je t'aime moi non plus,* and two Agatha Christie films: *Death on the Nile* (1978) and *Evil Under the Sun* (1982). Most recently, she wrote and starred in *Kung Fu Master* (1987, directed by Agnes Varda), and played Dirk Bogarde's daughter in *Daddy Nostalgia* (1991) and Michel Piccoli's wife in *La Belle Noiseuse* (1991).

BISSET, JACQUELINE. Actress. *(b. Sept. 13, 1944, Weybridge, England, as Jacqueline Fraser.)* This quiet brunette beauty went from bit parts to full-fledged stardom over a decade's time—but got more attention from her exposure in bikinis and wet T-shirts than she ever did for her performances. The former model started her movie career in minor roles in *The Knack, and How to Get It* (1965), Roman Polanski's *Cul-de-Sac* (1966), and *Casino Royale* (1967). She made more of an impact on audiences when she lost her bikini top during a surfside romp in *The Sweet Ride* (1968), and pictures of Bisset sans halter surfaced in just about every magazine shortly thereafter. Suddenly a hot commodity, Bisset toiled in many movies of varying quality, including

Bullitt, The Detective (both 1968), *Airport,* and *The Grasshopper* (both 1970). Her striking good looks and sophisticated manner occasionally landed her more significant parts, notably as the female lead in François Truffaut's Oscar-winning *Day for Night* (1973), playing an actress recovering from a nervous breakdown.

Bisset appeared in *The Life and Times of Judge Roy Bean* (1972) and *Murder on the Orient Express* (1974) before making a splash, so to speak, as the wet-T-shirted heroine of *The Deep* (1977). She deserved better; although she had by this time become a capable actress, she was mired in unfortunate pictures such as *The Greek Tycoon* (her character modeled after Jackie O.), *Who Is Killing the Great Chefs of Europe?* (both 1978), and *Inchon* (1982). Like many other actresses, she finally decided to try producing her own vehicles, and succeeded with *Rich and Famous* (1981).

Bisset's subsequent films include *Class* (1983) and John Huston's *Under the Volcano* (1984). Since then she has appeared on-screen sporadically, trying her hand at comedy (in 1989's *Scenes From the Class Struggle in Beverly Hills)* in addition to appearing in the quasi-exploitational *Wild Orchid* (1990). True to form (and all too typically) her performance as Josephine in a Napoleonic TV miniseries got more attention for her cleavage than for anything else. A 1990 Bisset film, *The Maid,* was scarcely released.

BLACK, KAREN. Actress. *(b. July 1, 1942, Park Ridge, Ill., as Karen Blanche Ziegler.)* Although she has played leads (very well, in most cases), this versatile actress has enjoyed some of her greatest successes in character roles that made use of her offbeat looks and chameleonic talents. While working as a waitress in New York during the early 1960s, Black attended the Lee Strasberg Institute, toiled in minor stage roles, and eventually landed a part in the Broadway production of "The Playroom" in 1965. Critically acclaimed for her stage work, Black headed west, debuting on-screen in *You're a Big Boy Now* (1967) before raising eyebrows as a drugged-out prostitute in the 1969 smash *Easy Rider.*

The following year, Black earned an Oscar nomination for her supporting per-

formance as a working-class waitress in *Five Easy Pieces;* this led to choice roles in *Drive, He Said, Born to Win* (both 1971), *Portnoy's Complaint* (1972), *The Pyx* (1973), *The Great Gatsby* (1974), *Burnt Offerings* (1976), and *In Praise of Older Women* (1977), among others, making her one of the most prolific screen stars of the 1970s. Her most noteworthy characterizations of that decade included a would-be ingenue in *The Day of the Locust* (1975), a country/western star in *Nashville* (1975), and a small-time criminal in Alfred Hitchcock's final picture, *Family Plot* (1976). A 1975 TV movie, *Trilogy of Terror,* provided Black the opportunity for a real tour de force, playing four roles in three separate stories.

By the 1980s, though, Black found herself working in less challenging (and less meritorious) movies, such as *The Squeeze* (1980), *Can She Bake a Cherry Pie?* (1983), *Cut and Run, Invaders From Mars* (both 1986), and *Homer & Eddie* (1989). The early 1990s saw her talents squandered in cheap, witless genre films such as *Twisted Justice, Zapped Again* (both 1990), *Chained Heat II* (1991), and *Evil Spirits* (1992). It seems inexplicable that an actress of her obvious talents could be so thoroughly wasted.

BLACKMER, SIDNEY. Actor. *(b. July 13, 1895, Salisbury, N.C.; d. Oct. 5, 1973.)* Handsome, suave heavy and supporting player, also known for his numerous stage and screen stints as Teddy Roosevelt. Blackmer started his movie career in the early silent days, but upon establishing himself on Broadway, he eschewed film work until the advent of talkies. He played some romantic leads in the early 1930s, notably in *Deluge* (1933), but soon drifted into character roles, usually playing smooth, sinister opportunists in such movies as *The Count of Monte Cristo, The President Vanishes, Transatlantic Merry-Go-Round* (all 1934), *The Little Colonel* (1935), *Thank You, Mr. Moto* (1937), *In Old Chicago* (1938), and many others. Blackmer played Roosevelt some 14 times over the years, in such films as *This Is My Affair* (1937), *In Old Oklahoma* (1943), *Buffalo Bill* (1944), and *My Girl Tisa* (1948). He later returned to Broadway, where he won a Tony for his performance in "Come Back, Little Sheba," and created the part of Boss Finley in "Sweet Bird of Youth." Later film credits include *The High and the Mighty* (1954), *High Society* (1956), *How to Murder Your Wife* (1965) and, most notably, *Rosemary's Baby* (1968), as Ruth Gordon's husband. Blackmer also worked frequently in TV, right up to the time of his death.

BLADES, RUBEN. Actor, singer. *(b. July 16, 1948, Panama City.)* We can safely say that Blades is the only Panamanian pop star included in this book. Having already helped popularize salsa music, he began acting in small films produced during the early 1980s (often writing the music as well) and proved to be a natural. He first attracted attention as an egocentric salsa singer in *Crossover Dreams* (1985, which he cowrote), and eventually found roles in mainstream Hollywood fare, notably as a shrewd orderly in *Critical Condition,* a cop in both *Fatal Beauty* (both 1987) and *Predator 2* (1990), a level-headed sheriff in *The Milagro Beanfield War* (1988), a bumbling crook in *Disorganized Crime* (1989), a bookie in *Mo' Better Blues,* and a shady club owner in *The Two Jakes* (both 1990). A graduate of Harvard Law School, he is also a political activist and has considered running for president of Panama. Incidentally, his name is properly pronounced *"Blah*-des," but he has resigned himself to "Blaidz."

BLAINE, VIVIAN. Actress. *(b. Nov. 21, 1921, Newark, N.J., as Vivienne Stapleton.)* Talented actress and singer whose work in films paled alongside her showstopping work on Broadway. She was already an accomplished nightclub performer and band singer by the time 20th Century-Fox signed her to a contract in 1942. Her early film work—in 1942's *Thru Different Eyes* and *Girl Trouble*—showed little promise, although she brightened up with Laurel and Hardy in *Jitterbugs* (1943) and got an opportunity to strut her stuff in the Technicolored escapism of *Greenwich Village* (1944) and *State Fair* (1945, featuring the only original film score written by Rodgers and Hammerstein), even though it was Jeanne Crain who got that film's best song. *Doll Face, If I'm Lucky,* and *Three Little Girls in Blue* (all 1946) followed in rapid succession, after which

Blaine returned to the stage, where in 1950 she created the role of ditzy night-club star Adelaide in the musical hit "Guys and Dolls." It was a once-in-a-lifetime opportunity, and fortunately Samuel Goldwyn and Joseph L. Mankiewicz had her repeat the characterization for their 1955 film version. She has appeared on screen intermittently since then, in *Public Pigeon No. One* (1957), *Richard* (1972), *The Dark* (1978), *Parasite* (1982), and *I'm Going to Be Famous* (1983), among others.

BLAIR, JANET. Actress. *(b. Apr. 23, 1921, Altoona, Pa., as Martha Lafferty.)* It's a cruel bit of fate that this petite, lovely singer/actress' best-known performance (in the title role of 1942's *My Sister Eileen*) has since been eclipsed by the one in the 1955 remake—ironically, by another Janet (Leigh). A former band singer, she signed a contract with Columbia in 1941, and went to work immediately in projects ranging from that year's *Three Girls About Town* to *Blondie Goes to College* (1942). That same year, she was loaned to Universal for an impressive dramatic performance in *Broadway.* Other features include *Something to Shout About* (1943), *Once Upon a Time* (1944), *Tonight and Every Night* (1945, in which she held her own teamed with Rita Hayworth), *Tars and Spars* (1946), *The Fabulous Dorseys* (1947), and *The Fuller Brush Man* (1948). She worked frequently in television, especially variety shows, and was a regular on "Caesar's Hour," where she showed an adeptness at comedy that Hollywood never took advantage of. Her later films include *Public Pigeon No. One* (1957), *Burn, Witch, Burn!* (1962, impressive in the title role), *Boys' Night Out* (1962), and *The One and Only, Genuine, Original Family Band* (1968). In 1971 she was cast as Henry Fonda's wife in the short-lived TV series "The Smith Family."

BLAIR, LINDA. Actress. *(b. Jan. 22, 1959, St. Louis, Mo.)* She probably figures that no one in America will ever be able to look at her without thinking of the little girl whose head spun like a top in *The Exorcist* (1973), and she's probably right. This preternaturally chubby-faced former child model made her motion picture debut in 1970's *The Way We Live Now,* and appeared in several other TV shows and movies before taking the role of the possessed teen, for which she was Oscar-nominated as Best Supporting Actress. Between reprising the role in the 1977 sequel and parodying it in the 1990 comedy *Repossessed,* Blair has appeared in *Airport 1975, Sara T.—Portrait of a Teenage Alcoholic* (a 1975 telefilm), *Hell Night* (1981), and, playing an adult, in *Chained Heat* (1983), *Savage Streets* (1984), *Grotesque, Witchery* (both 1988), *Up Your Alley, The Chilling* (both 1989), *House 5* (1990), and *Fatal Bond* (1991). Some of her early 1980s films were heavy-duty exploitation items in which Blair suffered frequent indignities (including nude and rape scenes); happily, her recent outings have been slightly tamer.

BLAKE, ROBERT. Actor. *(b. Sept. 18, 1933, Nutley, N.J., as Michael Gubitosi.)* He was the tousle-haired Mexican boy who sold Humphrey Bogart the winning lottery ticket in *The Treasure of the Sierra Madre* (1948), but for many Blake is best remembered as undercover cop Tony Baretta on the popular TV crime series "Baretta" (1975–78). Actually, this short, dark, solidly built Emmy winner began his acting career four decades earlier: In the late 1930s he was the cute (if often whiny) Mickey in MGM's "Our Gang" shorts, using his real name of Mickey Gubitosi. He also gained youthful fame as the young Indian sidekick Little Beaver in 23 "Red Ryder" Westerns made between 1944 and 1947. The rebellious Blake worked frequently in the late 1940s and 1950s (in films like *Pork Chop Hill*) before a stint in the military. In the late 1960s, Blake relaunched his career in the plum role of a psychotic murderer in *In Cold Blood* (1967), followed by the equally meaty part of an Indian fugitive in *Tell Them Willie Boy Is Here* (1969). ("Introduced" to audiences at this time, his publicity made no mention of any earlier screen work!) He was particularly effective as an obnoxious motorcycle cop in *Electra Glide in Blue* (1973), but his outspokenness and blunt manner didn't endear him to Hollywood establishment. "Banished" to TV, Blake forged himself a successful career and was, for a time, the darling of

the chat-show circuit. He produced and starred in a TV remake of *Of Mice and Men* (1981) and won raves as the late Teamsters boss Jimmy Hoffa in the telefilm *Blood Feud* (1983). More recently he earned an Emmy nomination for *Judgment Day: The John List Story* (1993).

BLANC, MEL. Voice artist, actor. *(b. May 30, 1908, San Francisco; d. July 10, 1989)* Supremely talented voice artist and comic actor who gained immortality as the voice of the Warner Bros. cartoon characters, including Bugs Bunny, Daffy Duck, Porky Pig, Tweety and Sylvester, Yosemite Sam, Foghorn Leghorn, and Pepe Le Pew. (The only major speaking character he didn't do was Elmer Fudd, whose voice was provided by radio actor Arthur Q. Bryan.) Blanc joined the studio in 1937, and replaced the previous Porky, who hadn't been able to turn a stutter into a humorous device. Before Warners signed him to a contract in the 1940s, Blanc also performed voices for MGM, Columbia, and other cartoon studios; in fact, he was the original voice of Woody Woodpecker. In later years he was equally busy on TV, as Barney Rubble in "The Flintstones" and as the title character in "Heathcliff," to name just two. He was also associated for decades with Jack Benny, on both radio and TV. His on-screen appearances were few and far between, but he had amusing moments in *Neptune's Daughter* (1949), *Champagne for Caesar* (1950), and *Kiss Me, Stupid* (1964); he also provided off-screen voices for *Strange Brew* (1983). His autobiography, "That's *Not* All, Folks!" was published in 1988.

BLIER, BERTRAND. Director. *(b. Mar. 14, 1939, Paris.)* Cynical black-humor specialist whose films never cease to offend. Blier began his film career in Paris as an assistant to American expatriate filmmaker John Berry. After making a series of cinema-verité documentaries, Blier graduated to features in 1967 with *Breakdown,* and hit the international spotlight with *Going Places* (1974). This violent, hedonistic (often misogynistic) but mesmerizing film not only launched Blier's career, but brought international acclaim to then-unknowns Gerard Depardieu and Patrick Dewaere. Blier also starred Depardieu and

Deware in *Get Out Your Handkerchiefs* (1978), a relatively lighthearted tale of a twisted ménage à trois, which won that year's Academy Award for Best Foreign Language Film. Since then, Blier has applied his controversial talents toward such subjects as incest *(Beau Pere,* 1981) and sexual objectification *(Too Beautiful for You,* 1989, also starring Depardieu). His 1993 film *Un, Deux, Trois Soleil* won Marcello Mastroianni a Supporting Actor award at the Venice Film Festival. He is the son of actor Bernard Blier.

BLONDELL, JOAN. Actress. *(b. Aug. 30, 1909, New York City; d. Dec. 25, 1979.)* Fans of Warner Bros. movies of the 1930s don't have to go very far to find Blondell. The saucer-eyed, brassy blonde starred in more of the studio's movies during that decade than any other actress. A trouper since childhood, who toured around the world with her parents, Blondell settled in Texas when she was a teenager, winning a beauty contest in Dallas and using that title to get stage work in New York. She and James Cagney appeared on Broadway in "Penny Arcade," and were both signed by Warner Bros., where they repeated their roles in the movie version of the play, *Sinner's Holiday* (1930).

The voluptuous actress was often cast as a sexually uninhibited woman (and frequently seen in flimsy negligees); her way with a wisecrack won her fans right from the start in such films as *Night Nurse, The Public Enemy, Blonde Crazy* (her first lead, opposite Cagney), *Big Business Girl* (all 1931), *Union Depot, Miss Pinkerton, Three on a Match, Lawyer Man, The Greeks Had a Word for Them, Make Me a Star* (all 1932), *Blondie Johnson, Gold Diggers of 1933* (in which she sang "Remember My Forgotten Man"), *Convention City* (a notorious sex comedy said to have precipitated drafting of the Production Code), *Footlight Parade* (again opposite Cagney), *Havana Widows* (first of a series that teamed her with Glenda Farrell and cast them as wisecracking gold diggers), *Goodbye Again* (all 1933), *Dames, He Was Her Man* (both 1934), *Traveling Saleslady, We're in the Money* (both 1935), *Colleen, Bullets or Ballots, Three Men on a Horse, Gold Diggers of 1937* (all 1936), *The King and the Chorus Girl* (1937), and many more (whew!). Her

post-Warners films include *East Side of Heaven* (1939), *Topper Returns, Three Girls About Town* (both 1941), *Cry Havoc* (1943), *A Tree Grows in Brooklyn* (1945, giving one of her best performances as the colorful Aunt Sissy), *Christmas Eve* (1946), *The Corpse Came C.O.D.* and *Nightmare Alley* (both 1947).

Although Blondell earned an Oscar nomination for her turn in *The Blue Veil* (1951, supporting Jane Wyman), her 1950s output was sparse. She became a blowsy broad (with a sharp tongue) on-screen in *The Opposite Sex* (the 1956 remake of *The Women), Desk Set* (1957, supporting Spencer Tracy and Katharine Hepburn), *Will Success Spoil Rock Hunter?* (also 1957), *Angel Baby* (1960), *Advance to the Rear* (1964), *The Cincinnati Kid* (1965), *Stay Away, Joe* (1968), *Support Your Local Gunfighter* (1971), John Cassavetes' *Opening Night* (1977), *Grease* (1978), and *The Woman Inside* (1981, her last). She also appeared on the TV series "Here Comes the Brides" (1968-70). Her novel about vaudeville life, "Center Door Fancy," published in 1972, was autobiographical. Blondell was married to cameraman George Barnes, actor Dick Powell, and producer Mike Todd.

BLOOM, CLAIRE. Actress. *(b. Feb. 15, 1931, London.)* Beautiful, dark-haired, refined English actress with Shakespearean training whose second film appearance, as the ingenue in Charlie Chaplin's *Limelight* (1952), thrust her into the international spotlight. Never a top star in the commercial sense, she has distinguished herself since then with a series of outstanding performances. In 1990 she married novelist Philip Roth. She published an autobiography, "Limelight and After," in 1987. OTHER FILMS INCLUDE: 1948: *The Blind Goddess* (her first); 1953: *Innocents in Paris;* 1955: *Richard III* (opposite Laurence Olivier); 1956: *Alexander the Great;* 1958: *The Brothers Karamazov, The Buccaneer;* 1959: *Look Back in Anger* (a standout); 1962: *The Chapman Report;* 1963: *The Haunting* (a marvelous, understated chiller that remains one of her best-remembered films); 1964: *The Outrage* (a Western version of the Japanese film *Rashomon);* 1965: *The Spy Who Came in From the Cold;* 1968: *Charly;* 1969: *The Illustrated Man* (opposite Rod Steiger, from whom she would shortly be divorced after ten years of marriage); 1970: *A Severed Head*; 1973. *A Doll's House*; 1977: *Islands in the Stream*; 1981: *Clash of the Titans*; 1987: *Sammy and Rosie Get Laid*; 1989: *Crimes and Misdemeanors*.

Jim; 1938: *Swiss Miss*; 1940: *The Boys From Syracuse*; 1941: *Road to Zanzibar*; 1942: *The Moon and Sixpence*; 1946: *Two Sisters From Boston*; 1950: *Fancy Pants*; 1954: *Bowery to Bagdad*.

BLOOM, VERNA. Actress. *(b. Aug. 7, 1939, Lynn, Mass.)* Most moviegoers will think of her as the college dean's dipsomaniac wife who gets seduced by one of the frat-house rowdies in *National Lampoon's Animal House* (1978). The raucous role doesn't do justice to Bloom's ability, though; she's a seasoned stage performer whose infrequent film work has always been of high caliber. Her best role, arguably, came in Haskell Wexler's electrifying *Medium Cool* (1969); she also starred with Peter Fonda in his fledgling directorial effort, *The Hired Hand* (1971), and worked twice for Clint Eastwood, in *High Plains Drifter* (1973) and *Honkytonk Man* (1982). She is married to *Time* critic Jay Cocks, and has appeared in two films directed by Cocks' friend Martin Scorsese: 1985's *After Hours* and 1988's *The Last Temptation of Christ,* in which she played Mary; Cocks, uncredited, collaborated with Scorsese on the script's final draft.

BLORE, ERIC. Actor. *(b. Dec. 23, 1887, London; d. Mar. 1, 1959.)* One of the screen's most memorable supporting players, Blore established himself in Hollywood with a string of appearances in Fred Astaire–Ginger Rogers musicals: *Flying Down to Rio* (1933), *The Gay Divorcee* (1934), *Top Hat* (1935), *Swing Time* (1936), and *Shall We Dance* (1937). Generally cast as an acerbic butler, valet, or waiter, Blore occasionally stepped out of character with hilarious results; he's particularly funny as the social-climbing cardsharp in *The Lady Eve* (1941). Blore abandoned the insurance business as a young man to take up acting, and had considerable stage experience before coming to Hollywood. His often outrageous mugging, with pouty expressions, upturned nose, and arched eyebrows usually provoked smiles, and he was consistently better than his material, as proven by his several appearances in Columbia's "Lone Wolf" series of B thrillers.
OTHER FILMS INCLUDE: 1935: *Diamond*

BLYTH, ANN. Actress. *(b. Aug. 16, 1928, Mt. Kisco, N.Y.)* She'll always be remembered as the Daughter from Hell in *Mildred Pierce* (1945), a performance that earned her an Oscar nomination, but this tiny, fresh-faced brunette was singing at the age of five and was an operatic soprano and a Broadway actress before she'd barely completed puberty. She came to Hollywood and Universal Pictures at 15, and appeared in four 1944 musicals—*Chip Off the Old Block, Babes on Swing Street, The Merry Monahans,* and *Bowery to Broadway*—before being cast in the Joan Crawford classic, on loan-out from her home studio. She kept busy for the next decade in a variety of parts, notably in *Brute Force* (1947), *Mr. Peabody and the Mermaid* (1948, as the mermaid), *Another Part of the Forest* (1948), *Top o' the Morning* (1949), *The Great Caruso, The Golden Horde* (both 1951), *All The Brothers Were Valiant* (1953), *Rose Marie* (in the title role), *The Student Prince* (both 1954), *Kismet* (1955), and two 1957 biopics: *The Helen Morgan Story,* in the title role opposite Paul Newman, and *The Buster Keaton Story,* opposite former teenage dancing partner Donald O'Connor.

Blyth returned to musical theater and the concert stage thereafter, but made occasional TV appearances, including a long-running series of commercials for Hostess Cupcakes—which would suggest that not too many American mothers remembered *Mildred Pierce.* In the early 1990s Blyth was still performing in regional theater and summer stock.

BOETTICHER, BUDD. Director, writer. *(b. July 29, 1916, Chicago; as Oscar Boetticher.)* No-nonsense director, primarily of Westerns and action-adventure movies, whose forceful, uncluttered style and preferred subject matter (uncompromising men of action pitted against each other and/or against the world) pigeonholed him as a less-than-meets-the-eye filmmaker. An athletic youth who was a professional matador in Mexico during the 1930s,

Boetticher worked for Fox as a technical adviser on the bullfighting epic *Blood and Sand* (1941). He spent several years as an assistant director before wielding the megaphone on several Columbia B's in the mid 1940s, beginning with *The Missing Juror* (1944). He covered his favorite subject in *The Bullfighter and the Lady* (1951, earning an Academy Award nomination for Best Story), and ramrodded several well-wrought, medium-budgeted Westerns starring Randolph Scott, including *Seven Men From Now* (1956), *Decision at Sundown, The Tall T* (both 1957), and *Buchanan Rides Alone* (1958).

In 1960, after completing a minor but compelling gangster drama, *The Rise and Fall of Legs Diamond,* Boetticher began a seven-year odyssey that was to have culminated in a documentary on famed matador Carlos Arruza; the failed project bankrupted him, cost him his marriage, and nearly killed him before Arruza died in a car crash. Boetticher's efforts to reinstate himself in Hollywood were unsuccessful, and his career has been moribund since the early 1970s. He appeared as an actor in *Tequila Sunrise* (1988). He published his autobiography, "When in Disgrace . . ." in 1989.
OTHER FILMS INCLUDE: 1945: *Escape in the Fog;* 1948: *Behind Locked Doors;* 1949: *The Wolf Hunters;* 1952: *Horizons West;* 1953: *City Beneath the Sea, The Man From the Alamo, Wings of the Hawk;* 1955: *The Magnificent Matador;* 1971: *Arruza, A Time for Dying.*

BOGARDE, DIRK (SIR). Actor. *(b. Mar. 28, 1921, London, as Derek Niven van den Bogaerde.)* You could call him effete, but that wouldn't capture the essence of his persona. You could call him handsome, but that wouldn't describe his features or physicality. Dirk Bogarde is one of the British cinema's greatest stars, a distinguished actor whose films were consistently among the best the British film industry offered for many years. A prolific performer whose screen career dates back to an extra job in *Come on George* (1939), Bogarde was one of the first actors to portray a homosexual without making the character a "type," in 1961's *Victim,* as a gay lawyer going up against a gang of blackmailers. This brought him the credibility as a "serious" actor that had eluded

him as the popular star of minor comedies and dramas released during the 1940s and 1950s. He is especially well remembered in the "Doctor" series, including *Doctor in the House* (1954), *Doctor at Large* (1957), and *Doctor in Distress* (1963).

During the 1960s Bogarde appeared in a number of films directed in England by expatriate U.S. director Joseph Losey, including the chilling classic *The Servant* (1963), written by Harold Pinter. He was one of the male leads in *Darling* (1965), another quintessential 1960s British film. Never content to play the "stock" Englishman, Bogarde consistently took risks, some perhaps ill-advised—for example, playing a former concentration camp guard in the distasteful *The Night Porter* (1974)—but many of them paid off, such as his turn in Alain Resnais's diverting, cerebral *Providence* (1977). Bogarde retired from the screen after working on German director Rainer Werner Fassbinder's adaptation of Nabokov's *Despair* (1979), and turned to writing, his first love. He's now written several books, including some well-received volumes of memoirs (notably 1978's "Snakes and Ladders"), before returning to film work with a canny performance in Bertrand Tavernier's *Daddy Nostalgia* (1990).
OTHER FILMS INCLUDE: 1948: *Quartet;* 1950: *The Blue Lamp, So Long at the Fair;* 1953: *Appointment in London, Desperate Moment;* 1954: *The Sleeping Tiger, The Sea Shall Not Have Them;* 1955: *Simba, Cast a Dark Shadow;* 1957: *Night Ambush* (original title, *Ill Met by Moonlight*); 1958: *A Tale of Two Cities;* 1959: *Libel;* 1960: *Song Without End, The Angel Wore Red;* 1962: *Damn the Defiant!;* 1963: *I Could Go On Singing;* 1964: *Agent 8¾* (original title, *Hot Enough for June,*) *King and Country;* 1966: *Modesty Blaise;* 1967: *Accident;* 1969: *Oh! What A Lovely War, Justine, The Damned;* 1971: *Death in Venice;* 1977: *A Bridge Too Far;* 1981: *The Patricia Neal Story* (telefilm).

BOGART, HUMPHREY. Actor. *(b. Jan. 23, 1899, New York City; d. Jan. 14, 1957.)* One of the screen's most legendary figures was a pop-culture icon to generations of movie watchers unborn when he enjoyed his initial successes. Bogart was also an extremely unlikely bet for stardom: His slight stature, weatherbeaten features, scarred lip, and withering snarl hardly qualified him in Hollywood's glamour-obsessed Golden Age. Fortunately for this talented tough guy, he was in the right place (Warner Bros.) at the right time (the onset of World War 2) to win audience approval in the rugged thrillers and action films in which that studio specialized.

Bogart, the son of a distinguished surgeon, actually studied medicine himself for a time before enlisting in the Navy during World War 1. Caught in a blast aboard ship, he sustained facial wounds that scarred and partially paralyzed his upper lip, accounting for one of his distinctive screen trademarks. A talented (and, according to silent-screen star Louise Brooks, sensitive) stage actor during the 1920s, Bogart made his screen debut in a 1930 short subject, *Broadway's Like That,* and alternated stints in theater and film for the next few years. His career ratcheted upward when he played vicious killer Duke Mantee in "The Petrified Forest" on Broadway; costar Leslie Howard insisted he recreate the role in the 1936 film adaptation, which won him a Warners contract.

Although Bogart scored in *Forest* and, on loan to Goldwyn, in *Dead End* (1937, again playing a killer), his home studio mired him in B pictures (1936's *Isle of Fury,* for example) and secondary roles in bigger-budgeted fare (supporting Bette Davis in 1937's *Marked Woman* and 1939's *Dark Victory).* He was solid playing gangsters in 1938's *Angels with Dirty Faces* and 1939's *The Roaring Twenties* (both opposite Cagney), but was ludicrous as a zombie in 1939's *The Return of Dr. X* and a Mexican bandit in the 1940 Errol Flynn Western *Virginia City.*

Bogart owes his stardom to George Raft, who turned down the two 1941 roles that boosted him to the top: "Mad Dog" Earle in *High Sierra* and Sam Spade in *The Maltese Falcon.* As his box-office standing improved, Warners designed vehicles that would enable him to retain his tough-guy persona while playing sympathetic characters. Beginning with his "Rick" in *Casablanca* (1942), the single role for which he is best remembered (and which earned him his first Oscar nomination), Bogart etched memorable portraits as another Rick-type in *To Have and Have Not* (1944, during the production of which he met and married Lauren Bacall, his fourth and final wife), private eye Philip

Marlowe in *The Big Sleep* (1946), a reformed crook in *Key Largo* (1948), the greed-crazed Fred C. Dobbs in *The Treasure of the Sierra Madre* (also 1948), a Hollywood burnout in *In a Lonely Place* (1950), the unstable Captain Queeg in *The Caine Mutiny* (1954, Oscar-nominated), an escaped killer in *The Desperate Hours* (1955), and a weary sportswriter in *The Harder They Fall* (1956, his last film).

While never noted as a comedian, Bogart was supremely funny in *All Through the Night* (1942), *Sabrina* (1954), and *We're No Angels* (1955), as well as *The African Queen* (1951, opposite Katharine Hepburn), in his Oscar-winning performance as boozy riverboat skipper Charlie Allnut. A lifelong smoker, he succumbed to throat cancer in 1957. Though well respected in his lifetime, Bogart didn't attain cult status until his films were rediscovered by younger viewers in the late 1960s: His blunt, no-nonsense, cynical and world-weary manner translated into a pop-culture existentialism that spoke volumes to the alienated youth of that turbulent era, and though the antiestablishment fervor has cooled, he remains arguably the most popular male star of Hollywood's Golden Age.

BOGDANOVICH, PETER. Writer, producer, director. *(b. July 30, 1939, Kingston, N.Y.)* Many French cineasts and film critics went on to become major filmmakers, but in America only one such scholar made that transition: Peter Bogdanovich. This lifelong film buff wrote dozens of articles, books, and program notes about Hollywood before settling there in the mid 1960s. He fell in with producer Roger Corman, becoming a jack-of-all-trades on *The Wild Angels* (1966) and reworking a Russian sci-fi epic into *Voyage to the Planet of Prehistoric Women* (1967). Bogdanovich's first real film was the suspenseful *Targets* (1968), which he directed, produced, and cowrote with then-wife Polly Platt. After making a documentary, *Directed by John Ford* (1971), he directed the melancholy Larry McMurtry story *The Last Picture Show* (1971), which became a major critical and commercial hit. It won Oscars for veterans Ben Johnson and Cloris Leachman (as well as nominations for Director and Screenplay, which Bogdanovich cowrote with McMurtry), and made stars of its younger actors, notably Cybill Shepherd, with whom the director began a lengthy relationship.

Celebrated as Hollywood's latest wunderkind, he made two more big hits: the screwball farce *What's Up, Doc?* (1972) and another period piece, *Paper Moon* (1973), which brought an Oscar to debuting Tatum O'Neal. Both films were very much dependent on references to earlier films and directors, but there was no denying his superb craftsmanship and assured handling of actors. But it was perceived that his relationship with Cybill Shepherd led to his undoing. Two Shepherd vehicles—*Daisy Miller* (1974) and *At Long Last Love* (1975)—were major stiffs, and the well-intentioned *Nickelodeon* (1976) was pronounced D.O.A. at the box office. After a return to the Corman fold for the low-budget *Saint Jack* (1979), he made a colorful romantic comedy, *They All Laughed* (1981), which ultimately devastated him both emotionally and financially. By the time the film was released, costar Dorothy Stratten, who'd become his companion, was murdered; Bogdanovich then went bankrupt trying to regain the rights to the film from its original distributor. After a period of self-imposed exile, he began to work again, though his output has been small: the excellent *Mask* (1985), a comedy misfire, *Illegally Yours* (1988), a *Picture Show* sequel, *Texasville* (1990), the all-star farce *Noises Off* (1992), and the Nashville-based *The Thing Called Love* (1993). In 1991 Bogdanovich reedited *The Last Picture Show* for video release, and participated in a fascinating documentary, *Picture This: The Times of Peter Bogdanovich in Archer City, Texas* (released in 1992) about the making of *Picture Show* and its sequel 20 years later.

BOLGER, RAY. Actor, dancer. *(b. Jan. 10, 1904, Dorchester, Mass.; d. Jan. 15, 1987.)* This rubber-faced (and -limbed) dancer/ singer/comedian has become so widely identified as the Scarecrow in *The Wizard of Oz* (1939) that the role has almost obliterated the rest of his considerable career. Not surprisingly, he came from vaudeville, as half of "Sanford and Bolger," and appeared in George White's Scandals as well as numerous Broadway shows. A featured

spot in 1936's *The Great Ziegfeld* launched him in film, and he assumed comedy-relief chores in *Rosalie* (1937) and *Sweethearts* (1938) before his most famous role. *Wizard* apart, Bolger never found a perfect niche on-screen, as he did on Broadway. Fortunately, he got to recreate his great stage success in the film version of *Where's Charley?* (1952), preserving what became his signature song, "Once in Love with Amy." His other films are *Sunny* (1941), *Four Jacks and a Jill* (1942), *Stage Door Canteen* (1943), *The Harvey Girls* (1946, reunited with Judy Garland), *Look for the Silver Lining, Make Mine Laughs* (both 1949), *April in Paris* (1952), and *Babes in Toyland* (1961, as the "evil" Barnaby).

Bolger also lent his voice to *The Daydreamer* (1966), made cameo appearances in two 1979 films, *Just You and Me, Kid* and *The Runner Stumbles,* and was one of the hosts of *That's Dancing!* (1985). He was also a familiar face on TV, including all the popular variety shows (especially Judy Garland's 1963 series), and a sitcom, "Where's Raymond?," which later became simply "The Ray Bolger Show."

BOLOGNA, JOSEPH. Actor, screenwriter. *(b. Dec. 30, 1938, Brooklyn, N.Y.)* Versatile character actor known for his toughguy supporting roles as well as his comedic work on stage and screen with wife Renee Taylor. After marrying in 1965, Bologna and Taylor cowrote the Broadway hit comedy "Lovers and Other Strangers," and received Oscar nominations for writing the 1970 film adaptation. They wrote and costarred in the romantic comedy *Made for Each Other* (1971) and won Emmys for writing the 1973 TV special "Acts of Love and Other Comedies." Bologna went on to featured roles in *Cops and Robbers* (1973), *The Big Bus* (1976), and *Chapter Two* (1979), and gave perhaps his best performance as the swaggering 1950s TV star King Kaiser (based somewhat on Sid Caesar) in *My Favorite Year* (1982). He has since appeared in *Blame It on Rio, The Woman in Red* (both 1984), *Transylvania 6-5000* (1985), and *Coupe de Ville* (1990), and was featured as Walter Winchell in the made-for-cable movie *Citizen Cohn* (1992). He and Taylor codirected and costarred in the film *It*

Had to Be You (1989), adapted from their play.

BOLT, ROBERT. Writer, director. *(b. Aug. 25, 1924, Sale, England; d. Feb. 20, 1995.)* Bolt gained his international reputation for depicting history through the lives of heroic figures with his play about Sir Thomas More, "A Man for All Seasons," and won an Oscar for scripting its 1966 film adaptation. He earned an Academy Award nomination for his very first screenplay, *Lawrence of Arabia* (1962), for David Lean, and then continued collaborating with the director on *Doctor Zhivago* (1965, netting Bolt his first Oscar) and *Ryan's Daughter* (1970). He directed his own screenplay of *Lady Caroline Lamb* (1972), which starred his wife Sarah Miles. A later stroke partially paralyzed him, but he continued to work; his screenplay for *The Bounty* (1984) was condensed from two scripts he had originally written for Lean to direct, and he was working on an adaptation of Joseph Conrad's "Nostromo" at the time of Lean's death in 1991. He also wrote the telefilm *Without Warning: The James Brady Story* (1991).

BOND, WARD. Actor. *(b. Apr. 9, 1903, Denver, Colo.; d. Nov. 5, 1960.)* It was oddly ironic that when he was cast in his last feature, *Rio Bravo* (1959), Bond was better known as a TV star—for his long-running hit series "Wagon Train"—than for the countless films in which he'd appeared over the preceding three decades. Even more amazingly, the star of that film—John Wayne—had appeared alongside him in his first, 1929's *Salute,* when both were still playing on the USC football team and were hired as extras by director John Ford. It was the start of an extraordinary director/actor relationship that lasted almost the length of Bond's life. A tall, sturdy actor with a gruff voice and no-nonsense manner, he could play pretty much anything—and did. He seems to have been in half the movies made in the 1930s, appearing in small roles in, among many others, *The Big Trail* (1930), *Wild Boys of the Road* (in a chilling bit as a rapist), *Heroes for Sale* (both 1933), *It Happened One Night, Broadway Bill,* in a small part he later repeated for director Frank Capra in his 1950 remake *Riding High* (both 1934), *Black Fury, She Gets Her Man* (both 1935), *Conflict, The Leathernecks Have Landed* (both 1936), *Dead End, Night Key, You Only Live Once* (all 1937), *Bringing Up Baby, The Amazing Dr. Clitterhouse, The Law West of Tombstone, Professor Beware* (all 1938), and a blizzard of 1939 classics: *Gone With the Wind, Dodge City, The Oklahoma Kid, They Made Me a Criminal, Made for Each Other, Frontier Marshal,* including two by Ford: *Young Mr. Lincoln* and *Drums Along the Mohawk.* The next year saw a similarly nonstop pace, with two more Fords—*The Long Voyage Home* and *The Grapes of Wrath*—as well as *Buck Benny Rides Again, The Mortal Storm,* and *Santa Fe Trail.*

Though the size of Bond's roles increased, his pace didn't slow down, and he kept busy thereafter in *The Maltese Falcon* (as one of the cops), *Manpower, Swamp Water, Sergeant York, Tobacco Road* (all 1941), *Gentleman Jim* (1942), *The Falcon Takes Over* (a 1942 B film adapted from Raymond Chandler's "Farewell, My Lovely," with Bond as the murderous Moose Malloy, one of his best characterizations), *A Guy Named Joe, Hello Frisco, Hello* (1943), *The Sullivans, Tall in the Saddle* (both 1944), *They Were Expendable* (1945), *It's a Wonderful Life* (1946, as Bert the cop), *My Darling Clementine* (1946), *The Fugitive, Unconquered* (both 1947), *Fort Apache, Tap Roots, Joan of Arc, 3 Godfathers* (all 1948), *Kiss Tomorrow Goodbye, Wagon Master* (both 1950), *The Great Missouri Raid, On Dangerous Ground* (both 1951), *The Quiet Man* (1952, as the priest/narrator), *Hondo* (1953), *Gypsy Colt, Johnny Guitar* (both 1954), *The Long Gray Line, Mister Roberts* (both 1955), *The Searchers* (1956), *The Wings of Eagles* (1957, as movie director "John Dodge," parodying Ford), and a gag cameo in *Alias Jesse James* (1959) as Major Seth Adams, his "Wagon Train" character. By the way, although the series was based on *Wagon Master,* in that Ford feature he'd played a religious fanatic, not the lead. He died at the height of the show's—and his—popularity, leaving behind generations of fans to whom he was like a favorite uncle. However, in sharp contrast to his latter-day screen image, Bond made many enemies during the

1950s, as a rabid anticommunist in Hollywood.

BONDI, BEULAH. Actress. *(b. May 3, 1892, Chicago; d. Jan. 11, 1981.)* Bondi played her first grandmother at the age of 20, foreshadowing much of her later screen work. She made her film debut in *Street Scene* (1931, recreating her stage characterization), won other roles in *Arrowsmith* (1931) and *Rain* (1932), and soon developed a reputation as one of the movie colony's finest character actresses. A small, pleasantly homely woman, Bondi infused many of her roles with great spirit and determination. She'd made her stage debut at the age of seven, and spent several decades on stage, in stock, and repertory theater, before moving to Broadway. Often cast as mothers, grandmothers, and hardy pioneer women—both sweet and vicious—she snagged Oscar nominations for her performances in *The Gorgeous Hussy* (1936) and *Of Human Hearts* (1938), but she was equally impressive in *Trail of the Lonesome Pine* (1936), *Mr. Smith Goes to Washington* (1939), *Remember the Night, Our Town* (both 1940), *Penny Serenade, The Shepherd of the Hills* (both 1941), *Watch on the Rhine* (1943), *The Southerner* (1945), *It's a Wonderful Life* (1946, as Ma Bailey), *The Snake Pit* (1948), *So Dear to My Heart* (1948), *Back From Eternity* (1956), *A Summer Place* (1959), and many others. Arguably her greatest film vehicle was Leo McCarey's *Make Way for Tomorrow* (1937), in which she and Victor Moore movingly played an elderly couple shunned by their children. Bondi played James Stewart's mother four times on film, and again on television in later years. Her guest shot on a two-part episode of "The Waltons" in 1976 earned her an Emmy—at the age of 85.

BONHAM CARTER, HELENA. Actress. *(b. May 26, 1966, London.)* You'd never suspect this tiny, pale, frail-looking British actress of the strength and passion she has exhibited in high-profile period pieces such as the 19th-century *A Room With a View* (1985), the Tudor *Lady Jane* (1986), and Franco Zeffirelli's *Hamlet* (1990, as Ophelia). One of Bonham Carter's few modern roles was that of a flamboyant, high-energy woman pursuing a 32-year-old virgin in 1989's *Getting It Right*. Her latest costume parts were in E. M. Forster adaptations: *Where Angels Fear to Tread* (1991) and the near-perfect *Howards End* (1992). She played the title role in the 1993 telefilm *Fatal Deception: Mrs. Lee Harvey Oswald*, then returned to period clothes for *Mary Shelley's Frankenstein* (1994).

BOORMAN, JOHN. Director. *(b. Jan. 18, 1933, Shepperton, England.)* Cerebral, ambitious director who joined the BBC in 1955 as an assistant editor after having written film reviews for magazines and BBC radio. A series of innovative documentaries for that network preceded his first feature in 1965, the spirited *Having a Wild Weekend*, which starred the Dave Clark Five in an obvious effort to emulate the previous year's Beatles hit, *A Hard Day's Night*. Although the picture was only modestly successful, it brought Boorman to Hollywood, where he directed the Lee Marvin actioner *Point Blank* (1967) and the intriguing two-character drama *Hell in the Pacific* (1968). Right in tune with the 1960s' innovative movie-making techniques, Boorman subsequently helmed mature pictures marked by superb visual sense and (usually) complex narrative structure. The terrifying backwoods odyssey *Deliverance* (1972) earned him an Oscar nomination for Best Director (and as its producer, for Best Picture), and *Zardoz* (1974) has garnered a latter-day following for its intelligent science fiction. Boorman's fanciful side got the better of him in the ill-advised *Exorcist II: The Heretic* (1977), but he returned to form with the gloriously pictorial Arthurian epic *Excalibur* (1981). He starred son Charley in *The Emerald Forest* (1985), a heartfelt story of Amazon tribes in the rapidly vanishing rain forests. *Hope and Glory* (1987), a semiautobiographical look at London during the Blitz, garnered Oscar nominations for Best Picture, Best Screenplay, and Best Director. *Where the Heart Is* (1990) disappointed critics and audiences alike, and seemed very much unlike one of his films—though it bore comparison to his offbeat British picture, *Leo the Last*

(1970). He next directed *Beyond Rangoon* (1995).

BOOTH, JAMES. Actor. *(b. Dec. 19, 1930, Croydon, England.)* Shifty-looking, slightly rumpled British character actor and occasional lead, a veteran of London's Theatre Workshop and the Old Vic. He's particularly adept at limning smooth-talking rakes such as the seducer of Shirley MacLaine in *The Bliss of Mrs. Blossom* (1968). Booth, who made his film debut in 1959's *Jazzboat,* is another of those talented actors who's nearly always better than his material. Regrettably, his later work has been done in films very much beneath his ability. He was briefly a regular on the "Twin Peaks" TV show, very much in his element as a lugubrious phony.
OTHER FILMS INCLUDE: .1960: *The Trials of Oscar Wilde;* 1961: *In the Doghouse;* 1964: *Zulu* (a standout as a reluctant hero); 1965: *The Secret of My Success;* 1970: *Darker Than Amber, Macho Callahan;* 1971: *Revenge* (aka *Inn of the Frightened People,* contributing the only skillful performance in that sordid little thriller); 1974: *That'll Be the Day;* 1975: *Brannigan;* 1980: *The Jazz Singer;* 1981: *Zorro, the Gay Blade;* 1985: *Pray for Death;* 1987: *Avenging Force, Moon in Scorpio;* 1989: *Deep Space;* 1991: *American Ninja 4: The Annihilation.*

BOOTH, MARGARET. Editor. *(b. Jan. 16, 1898.)* Top film editor who got her cutting-room start in 1921, working as an assistant for the Louis B. Mayer studio at a time when women actually dominated the craft. She coedited *Why Men Leave Home* (1924), *Fine Clothes* (1925), *In Old Kentucky* (1927), and several others before becoming a full-fledged editor with what was by now MGM. She cut some of that studio's best films of the 1930s, including *Susan Lenox: Her Fall and Rise* (1931), *Strange Interlude* (1932), *Bombshell, Dancing Lady* (both 1933), *The Barretts of Wimpole Street* (1934), *Reckless, Mutiny on the Bounty* (both 1935), *Romeo and Juliet* (1936), *Camille* (1937), and *A Yank at Oxford* (1938). In 1939 she became the studio's supervising film editor, a post she held for nearly 30 years. She was then hired by producer Ray Stark, and supervised such films as *The*

Way We Were (1973), *The Black Bird* (1975), and *Murder by Death* (1976), among others. She won an honorary Oscar in 1977 for her cumulative accomplishments in her field.

BOOTH, SHIRLEY. Actress. *(b. Aug. 30, 1907, New York City, as Thelma Booth Ford; d. Sept. 16, 1992.)* Dumpy, frumpy stage star who achieved considerable impact as a screen actress despite the fact that she only made five films. She'd been acting on Broadway since the mid 1920s, in such hits as "Three Men on a Horse" and "My Sister Eileen," before winning a Tony in 1950 for her role as the hapless woman married to a younger man in "Come Back, Little Sheba." She recreated the role in the 1952 film version, and won an Oscar for that as well. Her other films were *Main Street to Broadway* (1953), *About Mrs. Leslie* (1954), *Hot Spell,* and *The Matchmaker* (both 1958), the latter from the Thornton Wilder play that was the basis for *Hello, Dolly!* In 1961, she began the long-running sitcom "Hazel," based on the popular comic strip about a sassy housemaid, and won two Emmys and even greater stardom. (An earlier generation enjoyed *listening* to her as Miss Duffy on the popular radio comedy "Duffy's Tavern," created by her then-husband Ed Gardner.) She also starred in a later, short-lived sitcom, "A Touch of Grace," and a TV-movie, *The Smugglers.* But the stage was her home, so for most people her best work is an ever-fading memory.

BORG, VEDA ANN. Actress. *(b. Jan. 11, 1915, Roxbury, Mass.; d. Aug. 16, 1973.)* Former New York fashion model brought to Hollywood in 1936. First signed by Paramount and later by Warners, she played bits in many B movies—almost always as a wisecracking gun moll or chorus girl—before being sidelined in 1939 after a near-fatal car crash. Plastic surgery restored her severely injured face, and she returned to the screen in 1940. Although she played occasional leads, she specialized in character parts calling for brassy dames. Borg was featured in dozens of low-budget potboilers, including *Duke of the Navy* (1941), *Two Yanks in Trinidad* (1942), *Revenge of the Zombies* (1943), *Detective Kitty O'Day,* and *The Falcon in*

Hollywood (both 1944). Her memorable later roles included a tough-talking showgirl in *Guys and Dolls* (1955) and Mrs. Dickinson in *The Alamo* (1960).

BORGNINE, ERNEST. Actor. *(b. Jan. 24, 1917, Hamden, Conn.)* Burly, gap-toothed, frog-voiced (with a face to match) supporting player and infrequent lead who was the 1950s' nonpareil movie heavy, particularly memorable as the brutal sergeant in *From Here to Eternity* (1953), the hot-tempered gunslinger in *Johnny Guitar* (1954), the goon who underestimates Spencer Tracy in *Bad Day at Black Rock* (1955), and the ruthless rancher in *Jubal* (1956). But it was his turn as the mild-mannered, shy butcher *Marty* (1955) that earned Borgnine an Oscar—and a broader range of roles. He's been busy ever since, racking up superb performances as the wily general in *The Dirty Dozen* (1967), one of the "honorable" members of *The Wild Bunch* (1969), the sadistic train conductor in *Emperor of the North Pole* (1973) and, on TV, football coach Vince Lombardi. Ironically, Borgnine owes his fame with baby boomers to his starring stint as the long-suffering skipper on the sitcom "McHale's Navy" (1962–66), as well as a 1964 feature film of the same name. He later costarred on "Airwolf" (1984–86), and has appeared in numerous TV movies, including a trio of "Dirty Dozen" sequels. Sadly, many of his more recent films—*Skeleton Coast* (1988), *Turnaround* (1989), and *Moving Target* (1990), for example—haven't been worthy of his talent. Borgnine's marriage to Ethel Merman was one of Hollywood's legendary fiascoes, lasting barely a month; his present wife, Tova, is a cosmetics entrepreneur.
OTHER FILMS INCLUDE: 1956: *The Catered Affair, The Best Things in Life Are Free* (as songwriter Lew Brown); 1958: *The Vikings, The Badlanders;* 1960: *Man on a String* (as real-life spy Boris Morros); 1962: *Barabbas;* 1965: *The Flight of the Phoenix;* 1966: *The Oscar;* 1968: *Ice Station Zebra;* 1968: *The Legend of Lylah Clare;* 1971: *Willard;* 1972: *Bunny O'Hare, Hannie Caulder, The Poseidon Adventure;* 1974: *Law and Disorder;* 1975: *The Devil's Rain, Hustle;* 1978: *Crossed Swords, Convoy;* 1979: *The Black Hole, All Quiet on the Western Front* (telefilm, for which he was Emmy-nominated in the role

originated by Louis Wolheim in 1930); 1981: *Escape From New York;* 1983: *The Warriors;* 1988: *Spike of Bensonhurst;* 1992: *Mistress* (a cameo as himself).

BORZAGE, FRANK. Director, actor. *(b. Apr. 23, 1893, Salt Lake City; d. June 19, 1962.)* Sensitive . . . delicate . . . romantic. All words associated with this distinguished director, unknown to the public at large but a sentimental favorite with film buffs everywhere. Borzage (pronounced "Bor-ZAY-ghee") chiefly worked in the arena of romantic melodrama, and at his peak in the late 1920s, his soft-focus (in more ways than one) style was much admired and imitated. He began in show business as an actor at the age of 13, mostly in touring stock companies. In 1912 he arrived in Hollywood and hooked up with Thomas Ince's company, and appeared in numerous Westerns before moving over to Mutual in 1916, where he began directing as well as acting in two-reelers with titles like *That Gal of Burke's* and *The Silken Spider.* That same year, he directed and starred in five short features, including *Immediate Lee* and *Enchantment.* In 1917 he signed with Triangle and, with Allan Dwan as producer, helmed numerous melodramas over the next two years, including *Until They Get Me* (1917) and *The Ghost Flower* (1918). He freelanced thereafter, scoring his first big hit at Paramount with the sentimental Jewish drama *Humoresque* (1920).

Borzage alternated Westerns with melodrama for the next few years, among them *The Duke of Chimney Butte* (1921), *The Good Provider* (1922), and *Secrets* (1924). He concentrated for a time on comedy: the Buck Jones vehicle *Lazybones,* Somerset Maugham's *The Circle* (both 1925), and such marital spoofs as 1926's *Early to Wed, Marriage License?,* and *The First Year.* Then, at Fox in 1927, he teamed Janet Gaynor and Charles Farrell in the tender love story *Seventh Heaven,* which was a box-office sensation; both he and Gaynor collected Oscar statuettes for their contributions to the picture. They all reteamed for two more such films—*Street Angel* (1928) and *Lucky Star* (1929) —before sound came in. Borzage's first talkie was a Will Rogers comedy, *They Had to See Paris* (1929), and he continued apace with such films as *Liliom*

(1930), *Bad Girl* (1931, which won him a second Oscar), and *Young America* (1932). Returning to freelancing, he directed such diverse films (many with underlying pacifist sentiments) as *A Farewell to Arms* (1932), *Secrets* (a remake of his 1924 film, and Mary Pickford's last movie), *Man's Castle* (both 1933), *Little Man, What Now?, No Greater Glory, Flirtation Walk* (all 1934), *Shipmates Forever* (1935), *Desire, Hearts Divided* (both 1936), *History Is Made at Night, The Big City, Mannequin* (all 1937), *Three Comrades* (1938), *Strange Cargo, The Mortal Storm* (both 1940), *Smilin' Through* (1941), *Stage Door Canteen* (1943), *Till We Meet Again* (1944), *The Spanish Main* (1945), and the low-budget psychological thriller *Moonrise* (1948), one of his least typical films. That was his last film for a decade; he made only two more, *China Doll* (1958) and the epic *The Big Fisherman* (1959), before retiring.

In a world too often coarse and heartless, his films were very civilized entertainments, and if they sometimes veered toward sappiness—*Lucky Star* ends with the crippled hero rising out of his wheelchair and dragging himself through miles of snow-covered fields to save the woman he loves—it was little enough to endure for the pleasure of inhabiting his idealized world for just a little while.

BOSCO, PHILIP. Actor. (b. Sept. 26, 1930, Jersey City, N.J.) Stocky, balding supporting actor, primarily on Broadway (he won a Tony in 1990 for his role in the hit farce "Lend Me a Tenor"), who almost always plays pompous, overbearing characters. Bosco's tyro screen appearance, in a small role in *Requiem for a Heavyweight* (1962), failed to inspire him to "go Hollywood," and he didn't really pursue movie work in earnest until the mid 1980s. A devoted New Yorker, he appears mostly in films shot in or near the Big Apple. His noteworthy roles include an obnoxious contractor in *The Money Pit*, a concerned schoolmaster in *Children of a Lesser God* (both 1986), a business tycoon in *Working Girl* (1988), a fastidious bus driver in *Quick Change* (1990), and a crooked police officer in *F/X2* (1991). He also played Geena Davis's father in *Angie* and a judge in *Nobody's Fool* (both 1994).

BOTTOMS, TIMOTHY. Actor. (b. Aug. 30, 1951, Santa Barbara, Calif.) The oldest and arguably most talented of the three acting Bottoms brothers (Joseph and Sam are the others), Timothy got off to an impressive start in films in 1971, debuting as a teen who has an affair with a considerably older woman in *The Last Picture Show*, and following up that performance with a thoughtful, heart-rending turn as a mangled WW1 vet in the overwrought *Johnny Got His Gun*. This winning streak continued with insightful roles in the acclaimed productions *The Paper Chase* (1973, as a first-year law student) and *The White Dawn* (1974), but subsequent appearances in mostly action or genre fare have not made good use of his talents. Other films include *The Crazy World of Julius Vrooder* (1974), *Rollercoaster* (1977), *In the Shadow of Kilimanjaro* (1986), *Invaders from Mars* (1986), *The Drifter* (1988), *Return to the River Kwai* (1989), and *Texasville* (1990), in which he reprised his role from *The Last Picture Show*. He also executive produced a documentary about the making of both films, *Picture This: The Times of Peter Bogdanovich*, in which he confessed his intense infatuation with costar Cybill Shepherd! Brother Joseph (born April 22, 1954) made his film debut in the adventure film *The Dove* (1974). Sam (born October 17, 1955) is best known as a grunt in *Apocalypse Now* (1979).

BOW, CLARA. Actress. (b. Aug. 25, 1905, Brooklyn, N.Y.; d. Sept. 27, 1965.) The very embodiment of the Jazz Age, the vivacious "It" girl led a stormy life that rivaled that of her on-screen characters in its emotional turbulence, lack of pretense and sexual inhibition, and ultimate tragedy. A beauty contest winner who longed to escape from her abusive father and insane mother, Bow came to Hollywood in her teens, and found work in independent pictures, at first in kid-sister roles. Her early films include *Beyond the Rainbow, Down to the Sea in Ships* (both 1922, "discovered" in the latter film by director Elmer Clifton), *Maytime* (1923), *Black Oxen, Daughters of Pleasure, Empty Hearts* (all 1924), *The Adventurous Sex, Capital Punishment, Free to Love, Kiss Me Again, The Plastic Age,* and *The Primrose Path* (all 1925). When B. P. Schulberg, her producer and mentor, went to Paramount in 1925 he brought Bow with him, and at that point she started getting the star buildup she deserved. Flapper-era audiences were delighted by her frisky nature and undisguised sexual openness, and her Paramount pictures, including *Mantrap, Kid Boots, Fascinating Youth* (all 1926), *Children of Divorce, Hula,* and *Get Your Man* (all 1927), skillfully exploited those qualities.

Off camera, Bow presented more of a problem; her footloose behavior, along with the antics of her father (who'd come west to "manage" his daughter's career), resulted in several scandals and caused the studio no little inconvenience. Her sexual liaisons were legion, and she had a torrid affair with Victor Fleming, who directed her in *Mantrap* and *Hula.* In 1927 she also starred in *It,* which dramatized authoress Elinor Glyn's theory that certain women possessed a certain indefinable, irresistible magic, to which she referred as "It," a quality that Bow had in spades. Her success in the picture gave her her famous nickname. (A young Gary Cooper, another of Bow's beaux, had a bit part in the picture.) She ended 1927, her peak year, as the nominal female lead in the first Oscar-winning Best Picture, *Wings,* still her most widely seen film, if hardly the most typical. More hits followed, including *The Fleet's In, Red Hair, Ladies of the Mob* (all 1928).

Bow, who'd always been plagued by insecurity, was terrorized by the coming of sound and embarrassed by her pronounced Brooklyn accent. She developed a world-class case of mike fright, frequently going into hysterics while trying to shoot a simple dialogue scene. Paramount did its best to promote her ("You've Had an Eyeful of 'It,' Now Get an Earful!" ran one ad for 1929's *The Wild Party),* but she was obviously ill at ease in talkies, and audiences sensed it. *Dangerous Curves* and *The Saturday Night Kid* (also 1929) performed respectably at box offices, but Bow's heyday was clearly past. Her extremely public private life kept her in the headlines (no one has ever disproved the widely circulated tale that she once "entertained" the entire USC football team one night), but it was publicity Paramount didn't welcome. She became increasingly difficult, put on weight and, continually depressed, lost much of the effervescence that had endeared her to moviegoers. Declining grosses for *True to the Navy, Her Wedding Night, Love Among the Millionaires* (all 1930), *No Limit* and *Kick In* (both 1931) finally convinced Paramount to drop her, and Schulberg was only too happy to distance himself from his former protégée.

Bow married cowboy star Rex Bell in 1931, and for a time enjoyed a measure of personal stability. She lost weight, moved over to Fox, and gave extremely good performances in two starring vehicles, *Call Her Savage* (1932) and *Hoopla* (1933), which turned out to be her best sound films. But the sad fact was that the "It Girl" era had passed, and Depression audiences had no use for the Roaring Twenties—or its icons—in the 1930s. With few regrets, she retired from the screen, and lived a fitfully harmonious life with Bell and her sons. While no full-scale Bow revival has been forthcoming, she has remained a cult figure to those who regard the Flapper Age as something unique, and her special brand of sexual chemistry still occasionally impresses film buffs who discover her today.

BOWIE, DAVID. Actor, singer. *(b. Jan. 8, 1947, London, as David Jones.)* Known in rock 'n' roll circles as "The Thin White Duke" for his slender, delicately handsome appearance, this blond, androgynous performer also possesses an unusual physical trait: two different colored eyes. This no doubt has added to his chameleonlike persona, which he has parlayed into a fairly successful big-screen side-career playing mysterious characters of often exotic origin. He made his feature debut in a small role in the British comedy-drama *The Virgin Soldiers* (1969), and was perfectly cast as the titular protagonist of the spacey cult hit *The Man Who Fell to Earth* (1976). He also won kudos for his early 1980s Broadway starring role as the deformed John Merrick in *The Elephant Man,* which he performed sans special makeup. As suits his odd good looks, Bowie's roles tend toward the fantastic, though he has been effective in the more dramatic *Merry Christmas, Mr. Lawrence* (1983) and *The Last Temptation of Christ* (1988, as Pontius Pilate).
OTHER FILMS INCLUDE: 1973: *Ziggy Stardust and the Spiders From Mars* (Bowie in concert performance); 1979: *Just a Gigolo;*

1981. *Christiane F,* 1983. *The Hunger;* 1985: *Into the Night;* 1986: *Absolute Beginners, Labyrinth;* 1992: *The Linguini Incident, Twin Peaks: Fire Walk With Me.*

BOYD, STEPHEN. Actor. *(b. July 4, 1928, Belfast; d. June 2, 1977.)* Handsome leading man best known for his roles in several historical epics, including *The Fall of the Roman Empire* (1964), *The Bible* (1966) and, of course, *Ben-Hur* (1959), in which, as the villainous Massala, he gave a virile, memorable performance, and went up against Charlton Heston (and lost, naturally) in the famous chariot-race sequence. The dimpled, often wooden Boyd is also assured a place in movie history as the star of the mega-awful inside-Hollywood drama *The Oscar* (1966). Played in various B-grade foreign productions throughout the 1970s.
OTHER FILMS INCLUDE: 1955: *An Alligator Named Daisy* (his debut); 1957: *Abandon Ship;* 1958: *The Bravados;* 1959: *Woman Obsessed, The Best of Everything;* 1962: *Billy Rose's Jumbo;* 1964: *Genghis Khan;* 1966: *Fantastic Voyage;* 1969: *Slaves.*

BOYD, WILLIAM. Actor, producer. *(b. June 5, 1895, Cambridge, Ohio; d. Sept. 12, 1972.)* William Boyd is inextricably linked with the character he most frequently played on-screen, two-fisted western hero Hopalong Cassidy. (So much so, in fact, that his widow, actress Grace Bradley, often still refers to him as "Hoppy.") Born in Ohio, he moved with his family to Oklahoma when still quite young, picking up a regional accent. Working his way across the country to Hollywood with a succession of transient jobs, he landed extra work for Cecil B. DeMille in 1919's *Why Change Your Wife?* and soon became a DeMille favorite, appearing in many of his films, including *The Volga Boatman* (1926), *King of Kings* (1927, as Simon of Cyrene), and the DeMille-produced *Road to Yesterday* (1925), *The Last Frontier,* and *The Yankee Clipper* (both 1926), among others. His career was nearly halted by reports of scandalous behavior actually committed by another actor named William Boyd, forcing the DeMille player to become "Bill" and the errant character actor to call himself William "Stage" Boyd.

Boyd appeared in modest programmers for Pathe and RKO, including *The Painted Desert* (1931, a precursor to his successful Westerns), *Carnival Boat* (1932), *Lucky Devils* (1933), and *Flaming Gold* (1934). Initially contracted to play the heavy in *Hop-A-Long Cassidy* (1935), first in a proposed series based on the novels of Clarence E. Mulford, Boyd wound up playing the title role (much rewritten for him) when first choice James Gleason (an apt choice to play the wiry, wizened little Irishman created by Mulford) nixed the project. It was well received, as were the followups *The Eagle's Brood, Bar 20 Rides Train* (both 1935), *Call of the Prairie, Three on the Trail,* and *Heart of the West* (all 1936). Boyd, flanked by sidekicks Jimmy Ellison and George (later "Gabby") Hayes, took audiences completely by surprise in his new incarnation. He went on to make a total of 66 Cassidy Westerns; among the best were *Hopalong Cassidy Returns* (1936), *Texas Trail* (1937), *In Old Mexico* (1938), *Three Men from Texas* (1940), and *Hoppy Serves a Writ* (1943).

Fortified with a UA distribution deal, Boyd bought the rights to the character in 1946, but his dozen self-produced pictures weren't very good, and the series petered out. Then Boyd acquired the older pictures from Paramount, and sold them all to TV in 1949. Thus began the Hoppy craze; the 55-year-old actor became an "overnight" sensation, thanks to the films' constant TV exposure. Boyd also produced a half-hour series featuring Hoppy, and shrewdly licensed the character (and his image) for a myriad of products, making himself a multimillionaire. He played Hoppy in a cameo for his old boss, Cecil B. DeMille, in *The Greatest Show on Earth* (1952), and made dozens of appearances in character at circuses and rodeos. When, in later years, his appearance altered drastically due to health problems (and surgeries), Boyd became a recluse, preferring his fans to remember Hoppy the way he'd been. He contracted Parkinson's disease, and was cared for by Grace, whom he'd married in 1937, for the remainder of his days.

BOYER, CHARLES. Actor. *(b. Aug. 28, 1897, Figeac, France; d. Aug. 26, 1978.)* Although he never really said "Come with me to the Casbah," that line has always evoked the image of this suave, debonair French actor (the way the similarly mythical "Play it again, Sam," evokes Bogart). He did movie work in both France and Germany from 1920 to 1930, making his U.S. film debut in *The Magnificent Lie* (1931), and found work in French-language versions of Hollywood movies before finally establishing himself as a leading man in American pictures. Bouncing between Hollywood and France throughout the 1930s, he enjoyed tremendous popularity in both countries, especially with feminine audiences (for obvious reasons). He cultivated an image as a great lover in *The Garden of Allah* (1936) and *History Is Made at Night* (1937) before playing the dashing thief Pepe le Moko in *Algiers* (1938), the picture set in large part in the Casbah.

Not content to coast on a reputation as a matinee idol, Boyer fought for meatier roles, and in the 1940s produced several of the films in which he appeared, including *Tales of Manhattan* (1942) and *Flesh and Fantasy* (1943). He was surprisingly effective as a villain in *Gaslight* (1944), probably the best of his 1940s films. He grew gracefully into more mature character parts in the 1950s and 1960s, and made TV history by teaming with Dick Powell to launch Four Star Productions (being one of the stars of its self-named weekly anthology show). To the end of his durable and distinguished career, he represented the quintessential Frenchman to most American moviegoers. Boyer reacted to the death of his wife, 1930s actress Pat Paterson, by taking his own life just two days before his 81st birthday. OTHER FILMS INCLUDE: 1934: *Caravan;* 1935: *Private Worlds;* 1936: *Mayerling;* 1937: *Conquest;* 1939: *Love Affair;* 1940: *All This, and Heaven Too;* 1941: *Back Street, Hold Back the Dawn;* 1946: *Cluny Brown;* 1948: *Arch of Triumph;* 1952: *The Happy Time, The Earrings of Madame de …;* 1955: *The Cobweb;* 1961: *Fanny;* 1966: *How to Steal a Million;* 1967: *Barefoot in the Park;* 1969: *The Madwoman of Chaillot;* 1973: *Lost Horizon;* 1974: *Stavisky;* 1976: *A Matter of Time* (his last).

BOYLE, PETER. Actor. *(b. Oct. 18, 1933, Philadelphia.)* Large, sad-eyed actor best known for his sharp and often endearing

portrayals of eccentric characters. Once a monk in the Christian Brothers order, Boyle decided to pursue acting as his calling and moved to New York, where he studied with Uta Hagen, appeared off-Broadway, did a tour of "The Odd Couple," and later worked in Chicago's Second City troupe. He made early film appearances in *The Virgin President* (1968), *Medium Cool* (1969), and *Diary of a Mad Housewife* (1970), but it was his performance as the title hardhat bigot in the sleeper *Joe* (1970) that first brought him fame. He followed in a variety of different movies, including *T.R. Baskin* (1971), *The Candidate* (1972, as Robert Redford's mysterious campaign manager, Luke), *Crazy Joe* (in the title role, as racketeer Joey Gallo), *The Friends of Eddie Coyle, Kid Blue, Slither* and *Steelyard Blues* (all 1973, the last being one of his favorite roles as the nutty Eagle). He scored a comic bull's-eye as the misunderstood monster in Mel Brooks' *Young Frankenstein* (1974) and continued to win sizable supporting roles throughout the 1970s in *Taxi Driver* (1976), *The Brink's Job, F.I.S.T.* (both 1978) and *Hardcore* (1979). He stole *Where the Buffalo Roam* (1980) from Bill Murray and had notable turns in *Outland* (1981) and *Hammett* (1982), but he seemed to drift into lackluster films that tarnished his reputation somewhat: *Yellowbeard* (1983), *Johnny Dangerously* (1984), *Turk 182!* (1985), *Surrender* (1987), *Walker* and *Red Heat* (both 1988). He had his best comic opportunity in years as an escaped mental patient in *The Dream Team* (1989) and has since appeared in *Speed Zone* (1989), *Men of Respect* (1990), *Kickboxer II* (1991), *Honeymoon in Vegas* (1992), *Malcolm X* (1992, a cameo), *Born to Be Wild,* and *Bulletproof Heart* (both 1995). On TV, he won raves playing Senator Joseph McCarthy in *Tail Gunner Joe* (1977) and had his own short-lived series, "Joe Bash" (1986).

BRACCO, LORRAINE. Actress. *(b. 1950, Brooklyn, N.Y.)* Former model who could be one of the premier leading ladies of the 1990s, especially if she gets scripts tailored to her distinctive *Noo Yawk* persona. Tall, sharp-featured, and harsh-voiced (with a pronounced Brooklyn accent), Bracco is particularly effective as strong-willed, sassy urban types. She made her screen debut in the French-made *Duos sur Canape* (1979, when she was working for Radio Luxembourg) and appeared in a couple of other European productions. American audiences first noticed her as the beleagured wife of middle-class cop Tom Berenger in *Someone to Watch Over Me* (1987). Roles in *The Pick-up Artist* (1987), *The Dream Team,* and *Sing* (both 1989) gave Bracco additional screen experience but little else. Her brilliant portrayal of Mafia wife Karen Hill in Martin Scorsese's *GoodFellas* (1990), a characterization for which her New Yorker's aggressiveness and accent were perfectly suited, elevated Bracco to the upper ranks of movie actresses (and earned her an Oscar nomination). Subsequent assignments in *Switch, Talent for the Game* (both 1991), and three 1992 releases—*Radio Flyer, Medicine Man,* and the steamy *Traces of Red*—didn't utilize her talents nearly as well. Formerly married to actor Harvey Keitel.

BRACKEN, EDDIE. Actor. *(b. Feb. 7, 1920, Astoria, Queens, N.Y.)* For a few years in the 1940s this talented actor was immensely popular, owing to a series of lighthearted, escapist comedies and musicals in which he appeared for Paramount. His comic persona—perpetually nervous, bewildered, lovably helpless—was developed in such films as *Brother Rat* (1938, his film debut), *Too Many Girls* (1940), *Life With Henry* (as Henry Aldrich's best friend), *Caught in the Draft* (both 1941), *The Fleet's In, Sweater Girl, Star Spangled Rhythm* (all 1942), and *Young and Willing* (1943). The brilliant writer-director Preston Sturges saw in Bracken a perfect protagonist, and cast him as Norval Jones, the pleasantly befuddled 4-F who'll do almost anything for Betty Hutton in the hilarious and still astounding *The Miracle of Morgan's Creek* (completed 1942, released 1944). He was even better in a more complex variation of the same character, a Marine washout who returns to his hometown pretending to have seen action, in *Hail the Conquering Hero* (also 1944). The two Sturges films represented Bracken's career high point; the good-natured foolishness of *Rainbow Island* (1944), *Bring on the Girls, Hold That Blonde* (both 1945), *Ladies' Man*

(1947), and *The Girl From Jones Beach* (1949) kept him in the public eye but found him running in place.

Bracken had solid supporting roles in *Summer Stock* (1950), *About Face* (a remake of *Brother Rat),* and *We're Not Married* (both 1952), but retired from films to pursue stage and TV work and, later, business ventures (including the establishment of a small theater chain, the failure of which nearly bankrupted him). Bracken appears in films sporadically, but usually to good effect, as witness his character parts in *National Lampoon's Vacation* (1983, as Wally of Wally World) and *Oscar* (1991, especially likable as a stuttering stool pigeon). Most recently he's had good, colorful supporting roles in *Home Alone 2: Lost in New York* (1992), *Rookie of the Year* (1993), and *Arthur Miller's The American Clock* (1993 telefilm).

BRACKETT, CHARLES. Writer, producer. *(b. Nov. 26, 1892, Saratoga Springs, N.Y.; d. Mar. 9, 1969.)* Brilliant screenwriter, originally a novelist and drama critic, who rose to fame when he teamed with Billy Wilder in the late 1930s on several outstanding scripts, including *Ninotchka* (1939), *Arise, My Love* (1940), *Hold Back the Dawn, Ball of Fire* (both 1941), *The Major and the Minor* (1942), and *Five Graves to Cairo* (1943), the last two of which were directed by Wilder. Beginning with the Oscar-winning *The Lost Weekend* (1945), Brackett turned producer as well. The pair split up following the classic *Sunset Blvd.* (1950), and Brackett moved to 20th Century-Fox, where he wrote and/or produced *Niagara* (1953), *The King and I* (1956), and *State Fair* (1962, his last), among others.

BRADY, ALICE. Actress. *(b. Nov. 2, 1892, New York City; d. Oct. 28, 1939.)* Born into a prominent show-business family (her father was famous stage producer William Brady), Alice Brady began performing in operettas, then branched out into Broadway plays and silent films, where she became a major star in such films as *La Boheme* (1916) and *Betsy Ross* (1917). A lovely and popular leading lady on stage, she reentered films in the 1930s as a character actress, competing with Billie Burke (her contemporary, with a career not unlike her own) for all the scatterbrained socialite roles in Hollywood. She was especially memorable playing flighty matrons in *The Gay Divorcee* (1934), *My Man Godfrey* (1936), and *One Hundred Men and a Girl* (1937), but she won an Academy Award for her dramatic portrayal of Mrs. O'Leary in 1938's *In Old Chicago.* Her last film was *Young Mr. Lincoln* (1939); she died of cancer before it was released.

BRAGA, SONIA. Actress. *(b. June 8, 1950, Maringa, Parana, Brazil.)* Sexy, smoldering actress who rose to stardom in her native country through work on a series of lavish soap operas for the Brazilian network TV Globo. She was featured in the films *A Moreninha* (1969), *Captain Bandiera vs. Dr. Moura Brasil* (1970) and *The Couple* (1974), but it wasn't until her role as a woman with two lovers—her husband, who is alive, and her ex-husband, who is a ghost—in *Dona Flor and Her Two Husbands* (1978), that she gained international attention. Braga was the main attraction in *Lady on the Bus* (1978), *I Love You* (1981) and *Gabriela* (1983, a remake of one of the soaps in which she performed) and she made her English-language debut in *Kiss of the Spider Woman* (1985) playing three roles: Raul Julia's girlfriend, a French chanteuse, and the title character. Her subsequent American efforts—*The Milagro Beanfield War, Moon Over Parador* (both 1988), and *The Rookie* (1990)—have not come close to unleashing the sensuality she has demonstrated, clothed and unclothed, in her previous work. Most recently, she appeared in *Roosters* (1995) with Edward James Olmos.

BRANAGH, KENNETH. Actor, director. *(b. Dec. 1, 1960, Belfast.)* It's got to be tough when you're still in your 20s and responsible critics are hailing you as "the new Olivier," but this dashing actor-director seems to be managing quite handily. A graduate of the Royal Academy of Dramatic Arts, he won immediate acclaim for his stage work; eventually he joined the Royal Shakespeare Company, but soon left to cofound the Renaissance Theatre Company, which toured the world performing the classics. Branagh made his feature-film debut in 1987 with perfor-

mances as an inept agent in *High Season* and a tortured war veteran in *A Month in the Country.* He then took the Olivier myth head-on by starring in and directing a vibrant remake of *Henry V* (1989), earning Oscar nominations for both chores. Branagh stormed Hollywood to do the stylish mystery *Dead Again* (1991), directing and playing two roles: a fast-talking L.A. detective and (in flashbacks) a suave German conductor. His wife, Emma Thompson, costarred opposite him in *Henry V* and *Dead Again.*

His next directorial effort, made on home turf, was the appealing contemporary comedy-drama *Peter's Friends* (1992), in which he also played the long-suffering husband of obnoxious TV star Rita Rudner. In 1993 he tackled Shakespeare once more in an exuberant rendering of *Much Ado About Nothing,* showing tremendous command as actor, director, and adaptor. In these films his talents have been matched by the performances of his brilliant and versatile wife. (They also costarred in a 1993 television production of "Look Back in Anger.") He appeared (without billing) as a Nazi in the poorly received *Swing Kids* (also 1993).

With money he received as a prize for *Henry V* Branagh directed a short subject based on a Chekhov playlet, *Swan Song* (1992), starring John Gielgud and Richard Briers, which was nominated for an Academy Award. Following these very personal projects he directed and starred as the good Doctor in a poorly received version of *Mary Shelley's Frankenstein* (1994) for producer Francis Ford Coppola. He wrote an autobiography, "Beginning," in 1989 (at the age of 28) in order to raise money for the second season of his Renaissance Theatre Company.

BRAND, NEVILLE. Actor. *(b. Aug. 13, 1921, Kewanee, Ill.; d. Apr. 16, 1992.)* Craggy-faced, gravel-voiced character actor and veteran screen heavy. A headline-making World War 2 hero, Brand studied drama in New York but quickly decided he preferred movie work to stage acting. The sinister cast of his features qualified him for villain parts, and he worked steadily after making his film debut in *D.O.A.* (1950). He played mobster Al Capone in both the pilot film for TV's "The Untouchables" (released theatrically in 1962

as *The Scarface Mob)* and *The George Raft Story* (1961). He worked infrequently in the 1980s.
OTHER FILMS INCLUDE: 1953: *Stalag 17;* 1954: *Riot in Cell Block 11* (in the lead); 1957: *The Tin Star;* 1962: *Birdman of Alcatraz;* 1969: *The Desperados;* 1973: *Scalawag;* 1976: *Eaten Alive;* 1980: *Without Warning.*

BRANDAUER, KLAUS MARIA. Actor. *(b. June 22, 1944, Alt Aussee, Austria.)* Devilish-looking international star who plays villains and sympathetic characters with equal ease; he's a talented and skillful performer, but the duality in his screen persona keeps him away from traditional leading-man roles. The stage-trained Brandauer made his film debut in *The Salzburg Connection* (1972), but was so displeased with his work that he returned to the theater, where he'd begun in the early 1960s, and became a leading actor of Austria's National Theatre. He was lured back to the screen with the lead in Istvan Szabo's *Mephisto* (1981), which won a Best Foreign Film Oscar and gained Brandauer international recognition. He worked again with Szabo in *Colonel Redl* (1985) and *Hanussen* (1988), and built a following with American audiences as James Bond's nemesis in *Never Say Never Again* (1983), the boxing champion in *Streets of Gold* (1986), and the Soviet scientist in *The Russia House* (1990). In *Out of Africa* (1985), the American film for which he's best remembered, Brandauer received a Best Supporting Actor nomination for his sly portrayal of Baron Bror Blixen.
OTHER FILMS INCLUDE: 1985: *The Lightship,* 1991: *White Fang,* 1992: *Becoming Colette.*

BRANDO, MARLON. Actor. *(b. Apr. 3, 1924, Omaha, Nebr.)* An enigmatic superstar widely regarded as America's greatest actor, Marlon Brando has been a Hollywood icon since the early 1950s. His unmistakable, naturalistic "method" acting style made him one of the most influential figures in cinema, paving the way for such latter-day disciples as James Dean, Paul Newman, and Robert De Niro. Brando was by all accounts "difficult" even as a youngster, having been expelled from several schools, including a military academy. Upon being prodded by his father to find some direction for himself, he chose to follow his muse to New York. There he studied Stanislavsky's acting techniques at the New School before enrolling at the Actors' Studio to work with Lee Strasberg and Stella Adler. Brando applied his "method" training to summer-stock roles, in which he scored enough rave reviews to merit his first shot at Broadway in "I Remember Mama" (1944). Several acclaimed theatrical performances followed, including his landmark interpretation of the loutish Stanley Kowalski in Tennessee Williams' "A Streetcar Named Desire" (1947).

Brando made his screen debut in *The Men* (1950), studying for his part as an embittered paraplegic by lying in bed for a month at a veterans' hospital. The following year Brando reprised his Stanley Kowalski characterization for Elia Kazan's film adaptation of *Streetcar,* earning the first of four consecutive Academy Award nominations for Best Actor (the others were for 1952's *Viva Zapata!* 1953's *Julius Caesar,* and 1954's *On the Waterfront).* Although not nominated for his indelible (and enduring) performance as the misunderstood rebel in *The Wild One* (also 1954), Brando finally struck Oscar gold that year for his work in Kazan's *Waterfront.* His complex portrayal of Terry Malloy, a washed-up boxer turned mob stooge and informant, became a landmark of American cinema.

In typical fashion, Brando followed his *Waterfront* success with a series of roles in which he played against type. In *Guys and Dolls* (1955), he tried his hand at musicals in the singing role of Sky Masterson; in *The Teahouse of the August Moon* (1956), he made the daring move of playing a Japanese interpreter who is vaguely homosexual. Another Oscar nomination came in 1957 for *Sayonara. The Young Lions* (1958) cast him as a Nazi officer during World War 2, and he played a wandering tramp in *The Fugitive Kind* (1959), another Tennessee Williams adaptation.

Brando made his directorial debut with *One-Eyed Jacks* (1961), an ambitious if confused anti-Western. His reputation began to suffer following release of the bloated 1962 remake of *Mutiny on the*

Bounty (with Brando in the Clark Gable role of Fletcher Christian), which came in grotesquely over budget, thanks in part to his capricious penchant for "inspired" improvisation and painstaking attempts to achieve the "perfect mood." The actor's few forays in screen comedy, including *Bedtime Story* (1964) and Charlie Chaplin's ill-fated *A Countess From Hong Kong* (1967), nearly sank his career; indeed, by the end of the decade, Brando was nearly a forgotten figure. Such odd and unusual films as *Reflections in a Golden Eye* (1967) and *Burn!* (1969) put Brando outside the mainstream—to the extent that he had to test for the role of mob boss Vito Corleone. That remarkable performance in *The Godfather* (1972) not only netted Brando his second Oscar, but restored the luster to his tarnished reputation. Brando amplified his renewed notoriety by sending a young woman in Indian costume to refuse the award, based on the actor's outrage over the plight of Native Americans. He snagged yet another Oscar nomination for his work in *Last Tango in Paris* (1973), playing a middle-aged man carnally involved with a young stranger.

Since delivering those two milestone performances, Brando has worked less frequently, appearing both in brilliant movies *(Apocalypse Now,* 1979) and silly ones *(Superman,* 1978; *The Formula,* 1980), based exclusively on a producer's willingness to pay his exorbitant fee. He was again Oscar-nominated in 1989 for *A Dry White Season,* and has been seen in *The Freshman* (1990, in a comic takeoff of his Vito Corleone characterization), *Christopher Columbus: The Discovery* (1992, as Torquemada), and *Don Juan DeMarco* (1995). For all his eccentricities, Brando remains one of the most powerful, arresting, and unpredictable actors in film history.

BRENNAN, EILEEN. Actress. *(b. Sept. 3, 1937, Los Angeles.)* This striking character player made her feature-film debut in *Divorce American Style* (1967), and subsequently became one of the screen's most prominent supporting actresses. In *The Last Picture Show* (1971), *Scarecrow, The Sting* (both 1973), *Daisy Miller* (1974), and *FM* (1978), Brennan played a succession of saucy, earthy, sometimes vulgar but usually sympathetic women. A favorite of director Peter Bogdanovich, he was the only one to ever make use of her musical talents, which had first gained her prominence off-Broadway; alas, those talents were squandered in the director's musical flop *At Long Last Love* (1975). In *Private Benjamin* (1980) she had the Oscar-nominated role of Goldie Hawn's mean commanding officer, Captain Doreen Lewis, and later reprised the part in a TV-series spinoff (1981–83), for which she earned an Emmy. Seriously injured in a 1984 auto accident, she returned to work three years later.

OTHER FILMS INCLUDE: 1985: *Clue* (filmed before her accident); 1988: *Rented Lips, Sticky Fingers;* 1990: *Stella, Texasville, White Palace.*

BRENNAN, WALTER. Actor. *(b. July 25, 1894, Swampscott, Mass.; d. Sept. 21, 1974.)* Walter Brennan was still in his 30s when he began playing crotchety old men onscreen, and he did it better than just about anyone else. At that time his wiry frame, thinning hair, lost teeth, and weary expression made him look much older than he really was, which may have hurt his vanity but stood him in good stead with movie producers. While studying engineering in college, Brennan caught the acting bug and toured with small vaudeville troupes prior to serving a hitch in the armed services during World War 1. He went to Hollywood in the mid-1920s and entered pictures as an extra; within a few years he was playing bits (in films like 1930's *The King of Jazz,* 1935's *The Bride of Frankenstein,* and even The Three Stooges' 1934 short-subject *Woman Haters),* but he eventually graduated to supporting roles. The first actor to win three Academy Awards—for *Come and Get It* (1936), *Kentucky* (1938), and *The Westerner* (1940, in a particularly vivid performance as mercurial Judge Roy Bean)—Brennan displayed his range in dozens of roles, most effectively in Westerns. He supported John Wayne in *Red River* (1948) and *Rio Bravo* (1959), and made a memorable Ike Clanton in *My Darling Clementine* (1946). Among his more than 100 feature films: *The Adventures of Tom Sawyer* (1938), *The Story of Vernon and Irene Castle* (1939), *Sergeant York* (1941, another Oscar nomination),

Meet John Doe (1941), *The Pride of the Yankees* (1942), *To Have and Have Not* (1944), *Task Force* (1949), *Bad Day at Black Rock* (1955), *Come Next Spring* (1956), *How the West Was Won* (1962), *Those Calloways* (1965), and *The Gnome-Mobile* (1967). With an impressive body of film work behind him, Brennan starred in three TV series, "The Real McCoys" (which ran six seasons), "Tycoon," and "The Guns of Will Sonnett." He even had a hit record in later years, the spoken/sung "Old Rivers," which led to several albums of similar material.

BRENT, GEORGE. Actor. *(b. March 15, 1904, Shannonsbridge, Ireland, as George Nolan; d. May 26, 1979.)* With such flamboyant performers as Cagney, Robinson, and Bogart on the Warner lot, this tall, urbane actor stood out just by being wooden! A former member of the Abbey Theatre (though only in small parts), he eventually made his way to the U.S. and Broadway, and came to Hollywood when sound opened up the door for stage actors, making an inauspicious starring debut opposite Rin-Tin-Tin in a 1931 Mascot serial, *The Lightning Warrior.* He was signed by Warner Bros. in 1932 and spent the next 20 years being outacted by many of the movies' top leading ladies, notably Bette Davis. Among his prominent films are *Under Suspicion, Charlie Chan Carries On* (both 1931), *So Big, The Purchase Price* (both 1932), *42nd Street, Baby Face* (both 1933), *The Painted Veil* (1934), *Front Page Woman* (1935), *The Golden Arrow* (1936), *Submarine D-1* (1937), *Gold Is Where You Find It, Jezebel* (both 1938), *Dark Victory* (as the doctor), *The Old Maid, The Rains Came* (all 1939), *The Fighting 69th* (1940), *The Great Lie* (1941), *In This Our Life, Silver Queen* (both 1942), *The Spiral Staircase* (1946), *The Corpse Came C.O.D.* (1947), *The Kid From Cleveland* (1949), *Montana Belle* (1952), *Mexican Manhunt* (1953), and *Death of a Scoundrel* (1956).

After some TV work, including a regular stint on "Fireside Theatre" and a starring role on "Wire Service," Brent retired to his ranch, reemerging just before his death to play Judge Uerhard Gesell in the Watergate-gets-religion epic *Born Again* (1978). Brent was married to fellow Warner Bros. contractee Ruth Chatterton from 1932 to 1934; they costarred in that studio's *The Crash* (1932), *Female,* and *Lilly Turner* (both 1933), three of Chatterton's best Warners vehicles. Brent was also briefly married to actresses Constance Worth and Ann Sheridan.

BRESSON, ROBERT. Director. *(b. Sept. 25, 1907, Bromont-Lamothe, France.)* One of the most rigorously ascetic directors in film history, Bresson eschewed any overt stylistic flourishes whatsoever, employing wooden but distinctive-looking nonactors to perform lead roles, and telling extremely simple, often pointedly despairing tales detailing the ruination of pure souls in a cruel world. Trained as a painter, he entered the film industry in 1933 as a screenwriter. Bresson made his directorial debut in 1943 with *Ladies of the Street.* His early films were his most conventional, but by *Diary of a Country Priest* (1950), unusually restive for a tale of "spiritual redemption," his style had matured. Unlike many French directors rendered irrelevant by the New Wavers of the 1950s and 1960s, Bresson turned out some of his finest work in the late 1960s, including *Au Hasard Balthazar* (1966), *Mouchette* (1967), and *Une Femme Douce* (1969). His nihilistic, unsparing, and surprisingly bloody *L'Argent* (1983) was a prize-winning Cannes Film Festival entry and proved that, well into his 70s, Bresson could still make provocative films; it will likely stand as his last, though.
OTHER FILMS INCLUDE: 1956: *A Man Escaped;* 1959: *Pickpocket;* 1962: *The Trial of Joan of Arc;* 1971: *Four Nights of a Dreamer;* 1974: *Lancelot du Lac.*

BREST, MARTIN. Director, screenwriter, producer. *(b. Aug. 8, 1951, Bronx, N.Y.).* As a film student at New York University in the early 1970s, Brest first won attention with his award-winning short subject *Hot Dogs for Gauguin* (which starred a then-unknown Danny DeVito). He then wrote and directed his first feature, *Hot Tomorrows* (1977), while part of a fellowship program at the American Film Institute. Two years later he was directing a major Hollywood feature film with George Burns, Art Carney, and Lee Strasberg. *Going in Style* (1979) was as self-assured as his student films had been, and held great promise for the young filmmaker. But false starts and disappointments stalled his momentum until he was called in to direct Eddie Murphy in *Beverly Hills Cop* (1984), a cannily well-made film, and a commercial smash. Brest continues to pick and choose his projects carefully. In 1988 he directed Robert De Niro in an atypical comic role (opposite Charles Grodin) in *Midnight Run;* in 1992 he steered Al Pacino to an Academy Award in *Scent of a Woman.* (He was nominated for Best Director and the film, which he produced, as Best Picture.) Brest has also taken bit parts in *Fast Times at Ridgemont High* (1982) and *Spies Like Us* (1985).

BRICKMAN, MARSHALL. Director, screenwriter. *(b. Aug. 25, 1941, Rio de Janeiro.)* Brickman began his career as a musician, playing with the folk group The Tarriers (with future actor Alan Arkin; the group even appeared in a 1957 movie, *Calypso Heat Wave)* and then with The Journeymen (alongside pre–Mamas and Papas John and Michelle Phillips). He turned to writing for television and worked on "Candid Camera," "The Tonight Show," and "The Dick Cavett Show" (as writer and then producer), before collaborating with fellow comedy-writing graduate Woody Allen (whom he had known since the early 1960s) on the screenplay for the wonderful sci-fi slapstick outing *Sleeper* (1973). They shared Oscars for writing the classic *Annie Hall* (1977), which was named Best Picture that year (rare for a comedy), then were nominated again for *Manhattan* (1979). At that point, Brickman earned the clout to direct his own scripts, but his solo films—the very slight *Simon* (1980, starring Alan Arkin), the low-key romantic comedy *Lovesick* (1983), and the muddle-headed nuclear war fable *The Manhattan Project* (1986)—were undistinguished at best. Brickman also cowrote *For the Boys* (1991) and received "consultant" credit on *The Cemetery Club* (1993) before reteaming with Woody for the lighthearted *Manhattan Murder Mystery* (1993), a return to the "early, funny" mood of the *Sleeper* years. He also appeared on-screen with old friend Cavett in *Funny* (1989), a film which consists of people telling their favorite jokes.

BRICKMAN, PAUL. Director, screenwriter. *(b. Apr. 23, 1949, Chicago.)* Following work as a camera assistant and a story analyst for several studios, Brickman had two screenplays produced in 1977: the formula sequel *The Bad News Bears in Breaking Training* and *Handle With Care* (aka *Citizens Band),* a loose, charming collection of vignettes about truckers and their CBs, which marked him as a name to watch (and helped establish its director, Jonathan Demme). He hit the jackpot as a director with *Risky Business* (1983), a sleeper hit about a teenager (Tom Cruise, in a star-making role) who turns his parents' home into a bordello. Brickman also wrote the poorly received international arms comedy *Deal of the Century* (1983) and wrote and directed *Men Don't Leave* (1990), a sadly neglected film with Jessica Lange (never better) as a widowed mother looking for a new life.

BRIDGES, BEAU. Actor, director. *(b. Dec. 9, 1941, Los Angeles, as Lloyd Vernet Bridges III.)* Though he lacks his brother Jeff's good looks and sex appeal, the oldest son of actor Lloyd Bridges has nonetheless forged himself a durable screen career as a likable, now-pudgy mensch. He first appeared on-screen at age 7 in the film noir classic *Force of Evil* (1948) and worked in several subsequent movies as a child actor; as a young man, when his dreams of becoming a basketball player fizzled, he took up acting full-time. He starred in such interesting (if not overwhelmingly successful) films as *Gaily, Gaily* (1969), *The Landlord* (1970), *Lovin' Molly* (1974), and *Greased Lightning* (1977), but earned the best notices of his career playing a low-rent nightclub pianist opposite his brother in *The Fabulous Baker Boys* (1989). On TV he won an Emmy playing former Reagan press secretary James Brady in *Without Warning* (1991). He directed (and appeared with) both his dad and his son in the 1986 TV movie *The Thanksgiving Promise.* He is also the director of two violent, low-budget action films, in which he starred: *The Wild Pair* (1987) and *Seven Hours to Judgment* (1988), and has piloted several gentler, kinder films for TV. In 1993 he costarred with his father in the TV series "Harts of the West," which he also executive produced.

OTHER FILMS INCLUDE: 1949: *The Red Pony;* 1965: *Village of the Giants;* 1972: *Hammersmith Is Out;* 1975: *The Other Side of the Mountain;* 1979: *Norma Rae;* 1984: *The Hotel New Hampshire;* 1987: *The Killing Time;* 1990: *Daddy's Dyin' ... Who's Got the Will?;* 1993: *Married to It, Sidekicks, The Positively True Adventures of the Alleged Texas Cheerleader-Murdering Mom* (telefilm), *Elvis and the Colonel: The Untold Story* (telefilm, as Col. Tom Parker).

BRIDGES, JAMES. Writer, director. *(b. Feb. 3, 1936, Paris, Ark.; d. June 6, 1993.)* Intelligent filmmaker whose best movies deal with less-than-clear-cut predicaments faced by intelligent people: the barren couple in *The Baby Maker* (1970), the pressured Harvard law students in *The Paper Chase* (1973), the nuclear-plant workers in *The China Syndrome* (1979). (Bridges earned Oscar nominations for the screenplays of the last two). Beginning his show-business career as an actor who worked considerably in early TV, Bridges wrote scripts for "Alfred Hitchcock Presents" and other shows before graduating to the big screen. *September 30, 1955* (1978) was typical of Bridges' originality as a writer and director, and rejected Hollywood's penchant for superficial treatment of the 1950s. That he could steer Hollywood heartthrob John Travolta into a thoughtful film like *Urban Cowboy* (1980) led admirers to expect more of the same, but his subsequent films, the obscure *Mike's Murder* (1984), the embarrassing *Perfect* (1985) and the disappointing *Bright Lights, Big City* (1988) did not fulfill that promise.

BRIDGES, JEFF. Actor. *(b. Dec. 4, 1949, Los Angeles.)* The son of actor Lloyd Bridges (and brother of Beau, also an actor), this boyishly handsome leading man of the 1970s has matured into one of the finest actors in films. He made his debut as an infant, cuddled by Jane Greer in *The Company She Keeps* (1950), but first gained prominence with performances in the TV movie *Silent Night, Lonely Night* (1969) and the feature film *Halls of Anger* (1970). Peter Bogdanovich's Texas-set drama *The Last Picture Show* (1971) established him as an up-and-coming leading man; he earned his first Oscar nomination as a young citizen of a small Texas town. Bridges subsequently played a number of disaffected, fatalistic young men, some of them sympathetic, others not. He also revealed his fondness for interesting and offbeat characters, and his willingness to play them even in patently uncommercial films. *Fat City* (1972, as a boxer's young protégé), *Bad Company* (also 1972), *The Iceman Cometh, The Last American Hero* (as a race-car driver), *Lolly Madonna XXX* (all 1973), *Thunderbolt and Lightfoot* (1974, stealing this Clint Eastwood picture with his Oscar-nominated turn as a clever drifter), *Rancho Deluxe,* and *Hearts of the West* (both 1975) kept Bridges in the limelight.

The failures of *King Kong* (1976), *Somebody Killed Her Husband* (1978), *Winter Kills, The American Success Company* (both 1979), *Heaven's Gate* (1980), *Cutter's Way* (1981), *Kiss Me Goodbye,* and *Tron* (both 1982)—none of which, it should be noted, could be traced to Bridges' door—seriously impeded his career. But two 1984 films, *Against All Odds* and *Starman,* got him back on track. The first, a remake of the 1947 film noir *Out of the Past,* teamed him with Rachel Ward and hit moviegoers just right; the second, in which he played an alien who lands on Earth and assumes human form, brought him another Academy Award nomination. The hugely successful *Jagged Edge* (1985) teamed him with Glenn Close in an illogical but suspenseful courtroom drama, *8 Million Ways to Die* (1986) cast him as an alcoholic ex-cop turned detective, *The Morning After* (also 1986) saw him come to the aid of a booze-soaked movie star played by Jane Fonda. *Nadine* (1987) paired Bridges with up-and-coming Kim Basinger to negligible effect.

Tucker: The Man and His Dream (1988) gave Bridges his best role in years as the naive but visionary car manufacturer beset by the big automakers and corrupt Congressmen. He followed it with *The Fabulous Baker Boys* (1989), cast opposite brother Beau in an uneven drama about sibling performers whose lounge act is endangered by their female vocalist, Michelle Pfeiffer. *Texasville* (1990), Bogdanovich's 20-years-later sequel to *The Last Picture Show,* was mildly diverting but no match for the original film. He rebounded in Terry Gilliam's *The Fisher*

King (1991), as a talk-radio host devastated by an emotional crisis but rehabilitated by his association with a street person played by Robin Williams. It was a brilliant and cathartic performance. He followed it by commissioning Martin Bell, the director of the harrowing documentary *Streetwise,* to direct a fictional feature in which he would star. *American Heart,* boasting another superb performance, made its way to theaters in 1993. Other recent films include *The Vanishing, Fearless* (both 1993), *Blown Away* (1994), and *Wild Bill* (1995).

BRIDGES, LLOYD. Actor. *(b. Jan. 15, 1913, San Leandro, Calif.)* This virile, blond, squinty-eyed actor established himself as the swimming star of TV's "Sea Hunt" (1957–61), but his small-screen success is only part of a lengthy career. As a young man the California-born Bridges worked his way across country playing stock, making a Broadway debut in a 1939 production of "Othello." He came to Hollywood in 1941 as a Columbia contract player; like all others who labored at that studio during the 1940s he appeared in B Westerns, serials, and comedy shorts (including some with The Three Stooges). Bridges won his first leading role in the routine *She's a Soldier Too* (1944), and took the lead in *Secret Agent X-9* (1945), a Universal serial. Still not a top star, he did at least get bigger pictures: *A Walk in the Sun* (1945), *Canyon Passage* (1946), *Unconquered* (1947), *Moonrise* (1948), and *Home of the Brave* (1949), among others. He played the hero in an aquatic adventure, *16 Fathoms Deep* (1948), but lost top-billing to heavy Lon Chaney, Jr. *Rocket Ship X-M* (1950) saw Bridges in number-one position on the credits, although he still played supporting roles— most memorably as a traitorous deputy sheriff to Gary Cooper in *High Noon* (1952).

Although Bridges admitted he'd once been a member of the Communist Party during the House Un-American Activities Committee hearings, he wasn't blacklisted outright, and continued to work (albeit in minor movies) throughout the 1950s. "Sea Hunt" and "The Lloyd Bridges Show" (1962–63) made him familiar to TV audiences, and while he continued to appear in films, it took a wild and woolly role in the smash comedy *Airplane!* (1980), and its 1982 sequel, to revitalize his career. Since then he's appeared in *Weekend Warriors* (1986), *Tucker: The Man and His Dream* (in an unbilled cameo supporting son Jeff), *Cousins* (both 1989, playing a lusty senior), *Joe Versus the Volcano* (1990), *Hot Shots!* (1991, in an *Airplane*-type role as a dotty Naval commander), *Honey, I Blew Up the Kid* (1992), and *Hot Shots! Part Deux* (1993).

A prolific TV actor, Bridges has done many made-fors and episodic work, and has starred or costarred in a number of short-lived series, including "The Loner" (1965–66), "San Francisco International Airport" (1970–71), "Joe Forrester" (1975–76), "Paper Dolls" (1984), and "Capital News" (1990). His sons Jeff and Beau are both accomplished actors. In 1993 he accepted a costarring role with Beau in the TV series "Harts of the West."

OTHER FILMS INCLUDE: 1941: *The Lone Wolf Takes a Chance, Here Comes Mr. Jordan;* 1942: *Alias Boston Blackie, The Commandos Strike at Dawn, Shut My Big Mouth;* 1943: *The Heat's On, The Crime Doctor's Strangest Case, Sahara;* 1944: *The Master Race, Saddle Leather Law;* 1947: *Ramrod;* 1950: *Colt .45;* 1951: *The Whistle at Eaton Falls;* 1953: *The Tall Texan;* 1956: *The Rainmaker;* 1958: *The Goddess;* 1966: *Around the World Under the Sea;* 1969: *The Happy Ending;* 1972: *To Find a Man;* 1979: *The Fifth Musketeer.*

BRIMLEY, WILFORD. Actor. *(b. Sept. 27, 1934, Salt Lake City.)* Corpulent, rumpled-looking character actor, most frequently seen in glasses and bushy mustache, who startled moviegoers with his deceptively simple portrayal of a hapless nuke-plant employee in *The China Syndrome* (1979). He's been busy ever since, promising to become the screen's foremost delineator of lovable curmudgeons, notably in *Cocoon* (1985) and *Cocoon: The Return* (1988), and in a long-running series of Quaker Oats commercials. He occasionally essays sharper characters, such as the show-stopping lawyer in *Absence of Malice* (1981), but is most effective in softer characterizations. He starred in the family-oriented TV series "Our House" (1986–88) and was also memorable in *The Electric Horseman* (1979), *The Thing*

(1982), *Tender Mercies* (1983), *Country, The Natural, The Stone Boy* (all 1984), and *End of the Line* (1987, a leading role). More recently he's had juicy supporting roles in *The Firm* and *Hard Target* (both 1993).

BRODERICK, MATTHEW. Actor. *(b. Aug. 21, 1962, New York City.)* Lip-synching to "Twist and Shout" in the streets of Chicago, this boyishly handsome leading man delighted audiences with his portrayal of a happy-go-lucky truant in John Hughes' comedy *Ferris Bueller's Day Off* (1986). It was a star-making performance for the son of actor James Broderick, who'd followed in his father's footsteps while still in his teens, taking to the stage and winning a Tony Award for his performance in Neil Simon's "Brighton Beach Memoirs" (1983). A year earlier Broderick had made his film debut in a supporting role in the Simon-written *Max Dugan Returns* (1983). But it was his role as a computer hacker in the popular high-tech thriller *WarGames* (1983) that really alerted moviegoers to a bright new talent.

Broderick's contemporary demeanor seemed out of place in the medieval costume fantasy *Ladyhawke* (1985) and he couldn't salvage the science-run-amok thriller *Project X* (1987). But his career was jeopardized by negative publicity surrounding a tragic accident in which the car he was driving (while vacationing in Ireland with then-girlfriend Jennifer Grey) struck another vehicle and killed two people. The following year he was back onscreen, however, winning strong reviews as a wisecracking WW2-era draftee in another Neil Simon adaptation, *Biloxi Blues* (1988), followed by a likable, sympathetic performance as Harvey Fierstein's murdered gay lover in *Torch Song Trilogy* the same year.

Family Business (1989) cast Broderick as a third-generation burglar, encouraged by granddad Sean Connery but restrained by father Dustin Hoffman. He was quite funny as a college student mixed up with the mob (chiefly, Marlon Brando) in *The Freshman* (1990), and outstanding in one of his most ambitious parts: a young Union officer commanding an all-black infantry regiment during the Civil War in *Glory* (1989). Recent films include *Out on a Limb* (1992), *The Night We Never Met*

(1993), and *The Road to Wellville* (1994). He appeared in the 1994 Broadway revival of the musical "How to Succeed in Business Without Really Trying," winning a Tony for his performance in 1995.

BROMBERG, J. EDWARD. Actor. *(b. Dec. 25, 1903, Temesvar, Hungary; d. Dec. 6, 1951.)* Short, dark, and stocky supporting player who worked as a salesman and laundryman before taking up acting in his mid 20s. First appeared in 1926 at New York's Greenwich Village Playhouse, and spent the next 10 years on stage. Signed by Fox in 1936, Bromberg played a series of character roles in *The Crime of Dr. Forbes, Under Two Flags* (both 1936), *Hollywood Cavalcade* (1939, as fictitious movie mogul Dave Spingold), *Jesse James* (1939), *The Return of Frank James, The Mark of Zorro* (both 1940), *The Phantom of the Opera, Son of Dracula* (both 1943), and others. He played father figures, villains, and ethnic types and though he wasn't cut out for romantic leads, he did star in 1937's *Fair Warning,* as a mild-mannered detective. An early victim of the Communist witch hunts, Bromberg died of a heart attack while appearing in a Dalton Trumbo play in London.

BRONSON, CHARLES. Actor. *(b. Nov. 3, 1921, Ehrenfield, Penn., as Charles Buchinsky.)* He once said, "I guess I look like a rock quarry that someone has dynamited," but despite his craggy, unconventional features and taciturn manner, Charles Bronson became an international star relatively late in his career, depicting men of action who were not afraid to use violence to get a job done. Bronson was one of fifteen children born to Lithuanian immigrant parents, and though he was the only member of the family to complete high school, he joined his brothers working in the coal mines to support the family. He served during World War 2 as a tailgunner, then used his G.I. Bill rights to study art in Philadelphia and, intrigued by acting, enrolled at California's Pasadena Playhouse. An instructor there recommended him to director Henry Hathaway for a movie role and the result was Buchinsky's debut in *You're in the Navy Now* (1951). He secured more bit parts—

mostly as tough-looking window dressing—in films like *The People Against O'Hara, The Mob* (both 1951) and *Red Skies of Montana* (1952) and graduated to more substantial roles in *Pat and Mike* (1952, where he is beaten up by Katharine Hepburn!) and *House of Wax* (1953, as Vincent Price's mute assistant, Igor).

He began playing Indians in 1954's *Apache* and received good notices as Captain Jack in *Drum Beat* (also 1954, and the film in which he was first credited as Charles Bronson). He alternated features like *Vera Cruz* (1954) with television work, and won larger roles in B movies like *Big House, U.S.A.* and *Target Zero* (both 1955). Good supporting roles continued in big features like *Jubal* (1956) and *Run of the Arrow* (1957, as Chief Blue Buffalo), but his leads were confined to a string of B's like *Gang War, Showdown at Boot Hill, Machine Gun Kelly,* and *When Hell Broke Loose* (all 1958). Following his own TV series, "Man With a Camera" (1958–60, as photographer Mike Kovac), Bronson had his first taste of film stardom as Bernardo, one of the *The Magnificent Seven* (1960). *Master of the World, A Thunder of Drums* (both 1961), *X-15,* and *Kid Galahad* (both 1962), were followed with a solid role in *The Great Escape* (1963), as the claustrophobic tunnel-digger Danny Velinski. He had more good parts in *4 for Texas* (1963), *The Sandpiper* (1965), and the smash *The Dirty Dozen* (1967) before heading to Europe, where he spent the next few years. He appeared in *Guns for San Sebastian* and *Villa Rides* (both 1968), and then teamed with Alain Delon for *Adieu l'ami* (1968), which was a smash in France, before starring in the classic *Once Upon a Time in the West* (1968), directed by Sergio Leone (who had originally offered him the role in *A Fistful of Dollars* that made Clint Eastwood a star).

These films established Bronson as a top box-office draw in Europe, and the stylish *Rider on the Rain, The Family* (both 1970), *Cold Sweat* (1971), and *Red Sun* (1972) raised him to the ranks of the most popular stars worldwide. Duplicating that success in the U.S. came slowly with *Chato's Land, The Mechanic, The Valachi Papers* (all 1972), and *Mr. Majestyk* (1974), until Bronson's frequent collaborator Michael Winner directed him in

Death Wish (1974), a revenge fantasy about an architect who turns vigilante when his wife and daughter are raped. The movie was both controversial and extremely popular (and spawned four inferior sequels in 1982, 1985, 1987, and 1994). It also established Bronson as a star in his own country and set the tough, cold, violent persona he would project from that time on. There were some exceptions along the way, most notably the excellent *Hard Times* (1975, as a 1930s streetfighter), the offbeat black comedy *From Noon Till Three* (1976, the best of many teamings with his wife, Jill Ireland), and *The White Buffalo* (1977, as Wild Bill Hickok). However, Bronson stuck with action-thrillers like *Breakout* (1975), *Telefon* (1977), and *Love and Bullets* (1979) and spent the 1980s in gory fodder like *Ten to Midnight* (1983), *The Evil That Men Do* (1984), *Murphy's Law* (1986), and *Kinjite: Forbidden Subjects* (1989), exterminating a variety of pimps and psychos. Bronson did some of his most interesting work in TV movies, including *Raid on Entebbe* (1977), *Act of Vengeance* (1986, as United Mine Workers official Jack Yablonski), and in the title role of *The Sea Wolf* (1993), although his role as a stern father in Sean Penn's *The Indian Runner* (1991) proved he could become a character actor if he chose to. He was married to actress Jill Ireland from 1968 until her death in 1990.

BROOK, CLIVE. Actor. (b. June 1, 1887, London, as Clifford Brook; d. Nov. 17, 1974.) The screen epitome of British stiff-upper-lip reserve and stoicism, this classically handsome performer dabbled in journalism and insurance before turning to acting. Following a successful stage debut in 1918, Brook established a name for himself and in 1920 made his starring screen debut in *Trent's Last Case.* He came to America in the mid 1920s under contract to Paramount, and appeared in many Hollywood silents, including *Underworld, Hula, Barbed Wire* (all 1927), and *The Four Feathers* (1929). He made his talkie debut playing the title role in *The Return of Sherlock Holmes* (1929), and played the part again in *Sherlock Holmes,* a 1932 Fox adaptation of the venerable William Gillette play. Brook, whose perfect diction and suave, unflappable manner perfectly complemented his flawless appearance, was memorable opposite Marlene Dietrich in von Sternberg's *Shanghai Express* (1932) and in the all-British cast of the Oscar-winning *Cavalcade* (1933).

Back in England, Brook appeared in *Love in Exile* (1936), *Action for Slander* (1938), *The Ware Case, Return to Yesterday,* one of his most charming portrayals, as a noted actor who briefly returns to an earlier, uncomplicated existence in local theater (both 1939), *Convoy* (1940), *Breach of Promise* (1942), and *Shipbuilders* (1944). His proudest achievement was cowriting, coproducing, and directing *On Approval* (1944), in which he also starred. Brook then retired from films, although he continued to act on stage and made occasional TV appearances. He returned to the screen just once, playing a supporting role in *The List of Adrian Messenger* (1963), still ramrod-straight with perfect poise and diction.

BROOKS, ALBERT. Actor, director, writer. (b. July 22, 1947, as Albert Einstein, Los Angeles.) It's not entirely surprising that a comedian's son named Albert Einstein would grow up to be both cerebral and funny. (His father was radio comedian Parkyakarkus.) Brooks got his show-biz start as a variety show writer and performer, and always displayed a unique sensibility—appearing on "The Tonight Show" as a talking mime, for instance. He also recorded several outstanding comedy albums. His first film, a short subject called *The Famous Comedians School,* was aired on the early 1970s PBS series "The Great American Dream Machine." Brooks refined his deadpan style of faux-cinema-verité in a series of shorts for TV's "Saturday Night Live," and then expanded the notion for *Real Life* (1979), a feature-length spoof of the PBS series "An American Family," which he directed, cowrote, and starred in. (He also filmed a sidesplitting coming-attractions trailer for the film, promoting it in a bogus 3-D format.) It won excellent reviews but did little business, a pattern sustained by Brooks' subsequent features, the angst-ridden comedy *Modern Romance* (1981), the yuppies-as-Easy-Rider *Lost in America* (1985), and the afterlife romp *Defending Your Life* (1991). His films never quite hit a comic bull's-eye, but they are invariably filled with clever ideas and memorable moments.

He has also acted in other people's films, playing a starchy political campaigner in *Taxi Driver* (1976), Goldie Hawn's ill-fated husband in *Private Benjamin* (1980), Dan Aykroyd's car-mate in *Twilight Zone—The Movie* (1983), an unsuspecting manager in *Unfaithfully Yours* (1984), and, in an Oscar-nominated performance, the TV reporter-who-would-be-anchorman in *Broadcast News* (1987). He reunited with that film's writer-director, James L. Brooks, for *I'll Do Anything* (1994). His brother, Bob Einstein, is familiar to TV viewers as Officer Judy (from "The Smothers Brothers Comedy Hour"), and more recently as the ersatz stuntman "Super Dave" Osborne.

BROOKS, JAMES L. Director, screenwriter, producer. (b. May 9, 1940, North Bergen, N.J.) The creator (or cocreator) of hit TV shows "Room 222" (1969–74), "The Mary Tyler Moore Show" (1970–77), and "Taxi" (1978–83), the multitalented Brooks made his feature-film debut writing, producing, and directing *Terms of Endearment* (1983), which won Academy Awards for Best Picture, Best Director, and Best Screenplay—not a bad way to start a film career. His long suit is character delineation (possibly a byproduct of his extensive work in episodic TV), which was amply demonstrated in his handling of the three principal, sympathetic but not totally likable characters of *Broadcast News* (1987), Oscar-nominated for Best Picture and Best Screenplay. It wasn't until 1994 that he wrote and directed another feature, the near-musical *I'll Do Anything.* Not that he hasn't been busy; his company produced "The Tracey Ullman Show" and its wildly successful animated spinoff, "The Simpsons," among others. Brooks produced *Big* (1988), *Say Anything,* and *The War of the Roses* (both 1989), and acted in *Real Life* (1979) and *Modern Romance* (1981).

BROOKS, LOUISE. Actress. (b. Nov. 14, 1906, Cherryvale, Kans.; d. Aug 8, 1985.) For an actress who was barely a second-tier star during her Hollywood career, this beautiful actress with the black, bobbed hair certainly has achieved an immortality that none of her contemporaries (and, for that matter, Brooks herself) would ever have predicted. Smart, sassy, and sensual, she ranks today as one of the silent screen's greatest stars, yet her career was hardly as spectacular as her adoring acolytes would have one believe. Brooks trained as a dancer from childhood, began as a showgirl in the "flapper" era, and worked in the 1924 "George White's Scandals" and the 1925 "Ziegfeld Follies" before signing with Paramount to appear in films. Her early movies—*The Street of Forgotten Women, The American Venus* (both 1925), *Love 'Em and Leave 'Em* (1926), *It's the Old Army Game* (also 1926, with W. C. Fields), and *Beggars of Life* (1928) among them—showed Brooks to be a pleasant but unimpressive screen personality.

A high-living, sexually insatiable woman who called her own shots, regardless of the consequences, Brooks elected to leave Hollywood in 1928 rather than shoot new sound scenes for the silent *The Canary Murder Case* (1929), a whodunit begun before the transition to talking pictures. Sailing to Europe, she found her interest in film acting rekindled by German director G. W. Pabst, who convinced her to star in his *Pandora's Box* (1928). He saw in Brooks the perfect persona for the nymphomaniac Lulu in his gritty tale of amorality, and her characterization is currently ranked among the great silent-screen performances. The following year, Brooks appeared in Pabst's equally powerful *Diary of a Lost Girl,* rendering another remarkably sensitive, sensual portrayal. Nonetheless, upon her return to Hollywood Brooks found herself persona non grata. Her long, slow slide into cinematic obscurity culminated with her appearances in two humble B Westerns, *Empty Saddles* (1936, with Buck Jones) and *Overland Stage Raiders* (1938, with John Wayne), in which this once-vibrant screen personality seems as pale and vapid as any other horse-opera ingenue. She returned to New York, working briefly as a nightclub performer.

Brooks was "rediscovered" by the French film theorists of the 1950s; by then, she was living more or less as a recluse in Rochester, New York, frequently studying films held at the George Eastman House film archive. Her sudden notoriety sparked her interest in writing, and with the help of such individuals as William Paley and Kenneth Tynan, Brooks became a respected essayist on film. A collection of her writings, called "Lulu in Hollywood," was published in 1982. By that time, wracked with pain and suffering from emphysema, she was completely bedridden. Formerly married to top director Eddie Sutherland, and at various times the mistress to wealthy and famous men, Brooks died alone in 1985.

BROOKS, MEL. Director, producer, screenwriter, actor. *(b. June 28, 1926, Brooklyn, N.Y., as Melvin Kaminsky.)* Comedy writer-director whose satiric touch and farcical stylings are influenced both by vaudeville and Borscht Belt shtick. Brooks started his career as a stand-up comic in the 1940s, heavily influenced by Harry Ritz of The Ritz Brothers. While working the Catskills, he met Sid Caesar, who later hired him as one of the writers for his fledgling TV series. "Your Show of Shows" and its follow-up, "Caesar's Hour," boasted such other writers as Woody Allen, Neil Simon, and costar Carl Reiner.

After years of writing sketches for TV and Broadway revues (one of which, *New Faces,* was filmed in 1954), Brooks made his first mark on film by creating, with Ernie Pintoff, a hilarious Oscar-winning animated short, *The Critic* (1963). He scored a hit on TV by cocreating "Get Smart" (1965–69), and this won him the backing, from Joseph E. Levine, for his first feature film, *The Producers* (1968), which he wrote and directed. Dismissed by some as "too Jewish," disliked by others as "too manic," it nonetheless became a success, and won Brooks an Oscar for Best Screenplay. He followed it with another independently made feature, *The Twelve Chairs* (1970), in which he also costarred. As *The Producers* was inspired by old show-biz jokes and lore about making money on a flop show, this was based on a famous Russian folk tale that had been filmed several times before. Both were clearly "personal" projects that bore Brooks' unmistakable stamp.

Warner Bros. bankrolled his next film, and while the fears of "inside" material, and too-Jewish humor remained, the cowboy-movie spoof *Blazing Saddles* (1973) pulverized audiences, and pointed Brooks in a new direction: parody. It also established his "stock company" of actors, and had him working for the first time with cowriters. (Richard Pryor was one of the screenwriters of *Blazing Saddles.*) Gene Wilder cowrote Brooks' next great success, *Young Frankenstein* (1974), a hilarious horror spoof. Future filmmaker Barry Levinson joined his writing team for subsequent features. But Brooks' efforts became more scattershot, and predictable, in *Silent Movie* (1976), the Hitchcock parody *High Anxiety* (1977), the historical epic sendup *History of the World—Part I* (1981) and the space-opera spoof *Spaceballs* (1987). Brooks also moved in front of the camera; content to play supporting or cameo roles at first, he took the leads in *Silent Movie, High Anxiety,* and *History of the World—Part I.* Manic and irrepressible, he carried the films on his hunched shoulders, slamming over corny jokes, puerile double entendres, and silly sight-gags with gusto. He and wife Anne Bancroft even took the Jack Benny and Carole Lombard parts in a middling remake of Lubitsch's *To Be or Not to Be* (1983).

During the 1980s his production company Brooksfilm produced some uncharacteristically serious films, including David Lynch's first commercial feature *(The Elephant Man,* 1980), David Cronenberg's first Hollywood shot *(The Fly,* 1986), *The Doctor and the Devils* (1985), *84 Charing Cross Road* (1987, a vehicle for Bancroft), and *Solarbabies* (1986), among others. As an actor, Brooks has appeared in *The Muppet Movie* (1979), and *Sunset People* (1984), and lent his voice to *Look Who's Talking Too* (1990).

After a four-year hiatus, Brooks returned to movies with *Life Stinks* (1991), in which he starred as a tycoon who spent a month living with the homeless in order to win a bet. The very subject matter of his lackluster comedy made audiences uneasy. Brooks learned his lesson, and returned to parody for his next film, *Robin Hood: Men in Tights* (1993).

BROOKS, RICHARD. Writer, producer, director. *(b. May 18, 1912, Philadelphia, as Ruben Sax; d. Mar. 11, 1992.)* Dynamic, rugged filmmaker who was not afraid to tackle sensitive subjects, and was a leader in forcing Hollywood to "grow up." He began his screenwriting career, amusingly,

with a couple of Maria Montez epics, *White Savage* (1943) and *Cobra Woman* (1944), but quickly moved up to more challenging ideas in *Brute Force* (1947) and *Key Largo* (1948). With the support of Cary Grant, he made his directorial debut in 1950 with the medical thriller *Crisis,* but his subsequent films were variable until *Blackboard Jungle* (1955), a landmark drama that electrified the country in its unvarnished look at juvenile delinquency. He followed it with an extraordinary string of literary and theatrical adaptations—*The Catered Affair* (1956), *Something of Value* (1957), *The Brothers Karamazov, Cat on a Hot Tin Roof* (both 1958), *Elmer Gantry* (1960), which won him a screenplay Oscar, *Sweet Bird of Youth* (1962), *Lord Jim* (1965), and *In Cold Blood* (1967)—all of which proved that adult, issue-oriented storytelling could still succeed as mass-market entertainment. (Even his 1966 *The Professionals,* ostensibly a broad-appeal Western, tackled several serious issues in between explosions.)

Brooks' work mellowed somewhat, but he could still deliver a knockout punch, be it a large-scale adventure like *Bite the Bullet* (1975), or an intimate shocker like *Looking for Mr. Goodbar* (1977). His last few films were major disappointments, including *Wrong Is Right* (1982) and *Fever Pitch* (1985). He was Oscar-nominated for writing *Blackboard Jungle,* and for writing and directing *Cat on a Hot Tin Roof, In Cold Blood,* and *The Professionals.*

BROPHY, EDWARD. Actor. *(b. Feb. 27, 1895, New York City; d. May 27, 1960.)* Short, round, and balding, with bushy eyebrows and pliable features, the well-educated Brophy nearly always played "dese-dem-dose" characters in movies, more often than not wearing a derby. His first screen credit was 1919's *Yes or No,* with Norma Talmadge, but in the late 1920s he wound up at MGM, working behind the scenes until Buster Keaton recruited him for a part in *The Cameraman* (1928). He subsequently appeared in several other Keaton films, and soon became a regular fixture on-screen.

His typical parts included gangsters, fight managers, dumb cops, and stooges. Brophy is memorable as a nervous hood

in *The Thin Man* (1934), an executed murderer in *Mad Love*, a dumb cop in *Remember Last Night* (both 1935), and a dull-witted, anachronistic ward heeler in *The Last Hurrah* (1958, his last film). He also appeared as reformed hood Goldie Locke in several "Falcon" movies starring Tom Conway, and achieved a kind of screen immortality as the voice of Timothy the Mouse in Walt Disney's *Dumbo* (1941).
OTHER FILMS INCLUDE: 1931: *The Champ;* 1932: *Freaks;* 1935: *China Seas;* 1938: *A Slight Case of Murder, You Can't Cheat an Honest Man;* 1942: *All Through the Night;* 1944: *Cover Girl.*

BROWN, BLAIR. Actress. *(b. Apr. 23, 1947, Washington, D.C.)* Red-haired, attractive leading lady who specializes in intelligent-but-flawed or insecure women, best exemplified by her starring role in the TV series "The Days and Nights of Molly Dodd" (1987–91). Primarily a stage actress, Brown was not exactly catapulted to stardom by her film debut, a supporting part in *The Choirboys* (1977). In fact, her film appearances have been relatively sparse since her first lead, in 1980's *Altered States.* Brown has acted opposite a singularly atypical roster of male costars: Paul Simon in *One-Trick Pony* (1980), John Belushi in *Continental Divide* (1981), then-husband Richard Jordan in *A Flash of Green* (1984), Bruno Ganz in *Strapless* (1989), and Bob Hoskins in *Passed Away* (1992).

BROWN, BRYAN. Actor. *(b. June 23, 1947, Sydney, Australia.)* Ruggedly handsome Australian leading man who began acting in Britain in the mid 1970s and turned heads in one of his earliest movie roles, as one of the accused soldiers in Bruce Beresford's Boer War drama *Breaker Morant* (1979). Best known in the U.S. as the special-effects whiz in the colorful *F/X* (1986) and in its 1991 sequel, *F/X2*, Brown won high-profile roles as Tom Cruise's suicidal mentor in *Cocktail* (1988) and as Sigourney Weaver's love interest in *Gorillas in the Mist* (1988). Although he usually plays intense, stoic characters, Brown also projects a likability that, to date, hasn't been sufficiently tapped. (Recognizing this, he produced his

own romantic comedy vehicle, *Sweet Talker,* in 1990.) He is married to actress Rachel Ward, with whom he costarred in the popular TV miniseries "The Thorn Birds" (1983) and *The Good Wife* (1986).
OTHER FILMS INCLUDE: 1977: *The Love Letters From Teralba Road* (his first); 1978: *The Chant of Jimmie Blacksmith, Newsfront;* 1981: *The Winter of Our Dreams;* 1984: *Give My Regards to Broad Street;* 1985: *Rebel;* 1986: *Tai-Pan;* 1991: *Prisoners of the Sun;* 1993: *The Last Hit* (telefilm).

BROWN, CLARENCE. Director. *(b. May 10, 1890, Clinton, Mass.; d. Aug. 17, 1987.)* Although auteurists sneer at any attempt to include Brown in the pantheon of pictorial stylists, this workmanlike director turned out a large number of handsome motion pictures during his lengthy career, and was Oscar-nominated six times. As a young man, Brown entered the film business as an assistant to famed director Maurice Tourneur, whose masterful visual sense distinguished many films of the silent era. (Brown reportedly finished directing Tourneur's 1920 version of *The Last of the Mohicans* after the director was taken ill.) He directed many of what have come to be regarded as classic silent films, including *The Eagle, Smouldering Fires* (both 1925), *Kiki* (1926), *Flesh and the Devil* (1927, the first of his seven films starring Greta Garbo, whose favorite director he was), *The Trail of '98,* and *A Woman of Affairs* (both 1928, the latter another smash for Garbo).

Brown's talkies, which include *Anna Christie* (for which he got an Oscar nod), *Romance* (both 1930, another Oscar nod), *A Free Soul* (1931, still another Oscar nod), *Emma* (1932), *Night Flight* (1933), *Sadie McKee* (1934), *Anna Karenina, Ah, Wilderness* (both 1935), *Wife vs. Secretary, The Gorgeous Hussy* (both 1936), *Conquest* (1937), *Idiot's Delight* (1939), *Edison the Man* (1940), *The Human Comedy* (1943, his fourth Oscar nomination), *The White Cliffs of Dover, National Velvet* (both 1944, another nomination), and *The Yearling* (1946, his final Oscar nomination), are all extremely well handled, but bear the MGM studio stamp, and lack the individual point of view, or flamboyance, that might have earned him a greater reputation. His finest film, though, was a singularly straightforward one, made relatively late in his career: the 1949 adaptation of William Faulkner's *Intruder in the Dust*, the story of a poor black man unjustly accused of murder, which combined an engaging murder-mystery with an eloquent plea for racial tolerance. It was the last great picture he made. Brown spent three decades at MGM, an impressive record for longevity.

BROWN, JIM. Actor. *(b. Feb. 17, 1935, St. Simons Island, Ga.)* One of the greatest football players who ever lived (fullback with the Cleveland Browns for a decade, from 1957 to 1967), this good-looking athlete was drafted by Hollywood and lent his imposing presence to a number of high-profile movies in the 1960s, and starred in "blaxploitation" films in the 1970s. He also served as president of Richard Pryor's production company for a time. After a long absence from mainstream movies, he took a role in Arnold Schwarzenegger's *The Running Man* (1987) and then spoofed his own image in *I'm Gonna Git You Sucka* (1988).
OTHER FILMS INCLUDE: 1964: *Rio Conchos;* 1967: *The Dirty Dozen;* 1968: *Dark of the Sun, The Split, Ice Station Zebra;* 1970: *... tick ... tick ... tick ..., El Condor, The Grasshopper;* 1972: *Slaughter, Black Gunn;* 1973: *Slaughter's Big Rip-off, I Escaped From Devil's Island, The Slams;* 1974: *Three the Hard Way;* 1975: *Take a Hard Ride;* 1978: *Fingers.*

BROWN, JOE E. Actor. *(b. July 28, 1892, Holgate, Ohio; d. July 6, 1973.)* Rubberfaced, cavern-mouthed comic actor whose screen star shone brightly during the early 1930s. Brown, a former circus clown, vaudevillian, and stage star (who also briefly played semi-pro baseball), made his film debut in 1928's *Crooks Can't Win,* and subsequently appeared in several shorts and feature films, including the lead in *Painted Faces* (1929). But it was at Warner Bros. that he achieved real stardom; after supporting roles in *Sally, On With the Show* (both 1929), *Hold Everything,* and *Top Speed* (both 1930), Brown was given the chance to carry films on his own. He alternated playing loudmouthed, egotistical rubes with soft-spoken, Milquetoasty naifs. But his surefire laughgetters—the broadmouthed bellow, the slow double-take, the breathtaking pratfalls—were always included. His star vehicles include *Local Boy Makes Good, The Tenderfoot, You Said a Mouthful* (all 1932), *Son of a Sailor* (1933), *A Very Honorable Guy, Six Day Bike Rider* (both 1934), *Bright Lights* (1935), *Polo Joe,* and *Earthworm Tractors* (1936); his baseballthemed farces, *Elmer the Great* (1933) and *Alibi Ike* (1935), were especially popular. He also played Flute in Warners' allstar production of Shakespeare's *A Midsummer Night's Dream* (1935).

Diminishing returns on Brown's pictures forced him into independent productions, of which *Fit for a King* (1937) and *The Gladiator* (1938, a comic retelling of the same Philip Wylie story that inspired "Superman" creators Jerry Siegel and Joe Shuster) were the best. His starring career ended with a series of low-budget Columbia comedies, including *Beware, Spooks!* (1939), *So You Won't Talk* (1940), and *Shut My Big Mouth* (1942), and one Republic vehicle, *Chatterbox* (1943). He spent considerable time entertaining U.S. troops during World War 2, and revived his screen career with *The Tender Years* (1947, in a rare but effective dramatic turn). Brown, whose acrobatic dancing had always been a highlight in his earlier films, was perfectly cast as Captain Andy in *Show Boat* (1951), and popped up in the all-star casts of *Around the World in 80 Days* (1956) and *It's a Mad Mad Mad Mad World* (1963). But by far the best role of his latter-day screen career was that of the dotty millionaire in *Some Like It Hot* (1959), delivering the now-famous last line: "Nobody's perfect." His final film was *The Comedy of Terrors* (1964). His 1959 autobiography was titled "Laughter Is a Wonderful Thing."

BROWN, JOHNNY MACK. Actor. *(b. Sept. 1, 1904, Dothan, Ala.; d. Nov. 14, 1974.)* It's more than a little amazing to consider that this beloved cowboy star, who made more than 100 starring B Westerns, also once played leading man to Greta Garbo and Joan Crawford. An All-American halfback (and Rose Bowl star) from the University of Alabama, the husky, wavy-haired Brown nixed offers from professional football teams to act in movies instead. Making his debut in 1926's *The Bugle Call,* Brown signed with

MGM in 1927, and appeared opposite the studio's top leading ladies: Garbo in *The Divine Woman, A Woman of Affairs* (both 1928), and *The Single Standard* (1929); Crawford in *Our Dancing Daughters* (1928) and *Montana Moon* (1930); and Norma Shearer in *A Lady of Chance* (1928). But his casting in the title role of King Vidor's lavish wide-screen Western *Billy the Kid* in 1930 (and his sho-nuff Alabama accent) sealed his doom as a romantic leading man at MGM. After completing the gangster film *The Secret Six* (1931), Brown freelanced for several years, appearing in *The Last Flight* (1931), *Female* (1933), and *Belle of the Nineties* (1934, opposite Mae West), among others, before signing with Supreme Pictures to become a series Western star in 1935.

Brown top-lined over two dozen B oaters for Supreme, ranging from very good (*Between Men,* his first) to very bad (1937's *Bar Z Bad Men*). Although Brown was a capable actor, it was his athletic abilities that made him a Saturday-matinee favorite; stuntmen agreed that he "threw the best punch in pictures," and he never failed to bring down the house with his frequent displays of expert gun twirling. He went to Universal in 1939 and, beginning with *Desperate Trails,* starred in nearly 20 action-packed horse operas on his own, then teamed with singing cowboy Tex Ritter for seven more in 1942–43. (Brown also starred in four Universal serials, of which the first, 1935's *Rustlers of Red Dog,* was by far the best.) Dissatisfied with the joint billing at Universal, Brown signed with Monogram in 1943; beginning with *The Ghost Rider,* he rode the range for that small studio in 66 Westerns over the next nine years. By then a middle-aged cowpoke with graying hair and rapidly expanding waistline, he retired from the screen. In his later years the ever courteous, always smiling Brown managed and served as host for a popular Hollywood restaurant. Mainly for the fun of it, he played cameos in several 1960s Westerns: *The Bounty Killer, Requiem for a Gunfighter* (both 1965), and *Apache Uprising* (1966, his last film).

BROWNE, ROSCOE LEE. Actor. *(b. May 2, 1925, Woodbury, N.J.)* Bald, black character actor with considerable stage ex-perience; his cultured voice and bearing make him a natural in haughty roles, even when playing a butler (as in the TV series "Soap"). He has interpreted assorted scientists, officials, and government types both comic and serious in such varied films as *The Comedians* (1967), *Topaz* (1969), *Uptown Saturday Night* (1974), *Logan's Run* (1976), *Twilight's Last Gleaming* (1977), *Legal Eagles,* and *Jumpin' Jack Flash* (both 1986), and appeared in a number of "blaxploitation" flicks as well. He has been a regular on several TV series, including "Falcon Crest," and may probably be best remembered as the sympathetic cook in *The Cowboys* (1972). He remains active on stage and earned a 1992 Tony award nomination for "Two Trains Running."

BROWNING, TOD. Director. *(b. July 12, 1880, Louisville, Ky.; d. Oct. 6, 1962.)* The man who made *Dracula* (1931), Browning was once dubbed "the Edgar Allan Poe of the cinema." He ran away from home at age 16 to join the circus, which later served to provide background for *The Show, The Unknown* (both 1927), and *Freaks* (1932). Browning drifted into motion pictures, appearing in and assisting D. W. Griffith on *Intolerance* (1916). He became a director in 1917, helming many nondescript pictures before being teamed with silent star Lon Chaney at MGM. Their nine films included *The Unholy Three* (1925), *The Black Bird* (1926), *The Road to Mandalay* (1927), and *West of Zanzibar* (1928). Promoted in their day as macabre thrillers, they turned out to be routine and repetitive melodramas, and deflate the reputation Browning enjoyed years ago when movie history relied more heavily on recollection than on firsthand screenings.

Chaney was actually set to star in Browning's screen adaptation of Bram Stoker's "Dracula" before the actor's untimely death in 1930. As a replacement, Browning chose Hungarian actor Bela Lugosi, who had starred in the Broadway stage production—and the rest is history. Virtually all Browning's talents and shortcomings as a director are to be found in this 1931 classic. The atmospheric opening scenes are still creepy and evocative, but once the action shifts to England, the film becomes a stilted exercise in canned theater, carried mainly by Lugosi's archetypal performance. *Dracula*'s success kicked off the talkies' first horror cycle, and Browning followed it with the astonishing *Freaks* (1932, drawing on his circus days), *Mark of the Vampire* (1935, again with Lugosi, a remake of *London After Midnight*), and *The Devil Doll* (1936). By this time he was no longer considered an "A" director and had little clout to make films the way he wanted at MGM. He retired after directing *Miracles for Sale* (1939), a routine whodunit with supernatural trappings.

BRUCE, NIGEL. Actor. *(b. Sept. 4, 1895, Ensenada, Mexico; d. Oct. 8, 1953.)* Best known as Dr. Watson to Basil Rathbone's Sherlock Holmes in 14 movies and scores of radio programs, Bruce had a long stage career in England before coming to Hollywood and becoming a staunch (and much loved) member of the town's British colony. He had already mastered the technique of playing ineffectual, blustery, upper-class Brits, and repeated that characterization in most of his American screen roles. His pre-Holmes films include *Treasure Island* (1934), *Becky Sharp*, *She* (both 1935), *Trail of the Lonesome Pine*, and *The Charge of the Light Brigade* (both 1936). He first played Dr. Watson in 1939's *The Hound of the Baskervilles,* and last appeared as the character in 1946's *Dressed to Kill;* the portrayal has endeared him to generations of fans.
OTHER FILMS INCLUDE: 1940: *Rebecca, The Blue Bird;* 1941: *Suspicion* (as Beaky); 1942: *Roxie Hart;* 1945: *Son of Lassie;* 1947: *The Two Mrs. Carrolls;* 1948: *Julia Misbehaves;* 1952: *Limelight.*

BRYNNER, YUL. Actor. *(b. July 12, 1915, in Sakhalin, Russia; d. Oct. 10, 1985.)* Rarely has an actor been so identified with one role as Brynner with the King of Siam. His unforgettable performance as the imperious monarch in the 1951 Broadway musical "The King and I" made him a star, and fortunately, he got to recreate his Tony Award winning role in the 1956 film version (which earned him an Oscar).
Brynner was a larger-than-life character whose gypsy ancestry and colorful background (including a stint with a circus and study at the Sorbonne) led him to Amer-

ica, the stage, and then to television, in its earliest years, where he established himself as a director. An audition for Rodgers and Hammerstein changed the course of his life. Although other parts came his way after *The King and I,* and he gave fine performances in films ranging from *Anastasia* (1956) and *The Ten Commandments* (also 1956, as the Pharaoh Rameses) to *The Magnificent Seven* (1960) and *Westworld* (1973, in which he was amusingly cast as a steely-eyed gunslinger who just happened to be a robot), he turned again and again to the role of the King, in several stage revivals and in a short-lived 1972 TV series, "Anna and the King." He died of lung cancer and, knowing of his ailment, taped antismoking commercials that aired after his death. Incidentally, in his 1949 film debut, *Port of New York,* he had hair. He was married for many years to actress Virginia Gilmore.
OTHER FILMS INCLUDE: 1958: *The Brothers Karamazov, The Buccaneer;* 1959: *The Journey, The Sound and the Fury, Solomon and Sheba;* 1960: *Once More, with Feeling, Surprise Package;* 1962: *Escape From Zahrain, Taras Bulba;* 1963: *Kings of the Sun;* 1964: *Flight From Ashiya, Invitation to a Gunfighter;* 1965: *Saboteur: Code Name Morituri;* 1966: *Cast a Giant Shadow, Return of the Seven, Triple Cross;* 1967: *The Double Man, The Long Duel;* 1968: *Villa Rides;* 1969: *The Madwoman of Chaillot, The Magic Christian* (cameo); 1970: *The Battle of Neretva;* 1971: *Adios Sabata, Catlow, The Light at the Edge of the World, Romance of a Horsethief;* 1972: *Fuzz;* 1973: *The Serpent;* 1976: *Futureworld* (a sequel to *Westworld* in which he reprised his robot role).

BUCHANAN, EDGAR. Actor. *(b. Mar. 21, 1903, Humansville, Mo.; d. Apr. 4, 1979.)* Former dentist Buchanan took up acting at age 36, joining the famous Pasadena Playhouse theater group. He started in films in 1939, appearing in Westerns such as *When the Daltons Rode, Arizona* (both 1940), and *Texas* (1941), quickly establishing a reputation as a major character player. He delivered dialogue, generally from one side of his mouth, with a gravelly voice, peering suspiciously with squinty eyes. He had solid parts in *Penny Serenade* (1941), *Buffalo Bill* (1944), *The Sea of Grass* (1947), *The Black Arrow* (1948), *Cheaper by the Dozen* (1950), *Hu-*

man Desire (1954), *Come Next Spring* (1956), *Move Over, Darling* (1963), and *Benji* (1974). Adept at playing cowardly, corrupt officials and vicious bandits, he worked in more than 100 Westerns alone, and was particularly good in *The Man From Colorado* (1948), *The Great Missouri Raid* (1950), and *Shane* (1953), not to mention his scene-stealing performance as a drunken judge in *Ride the High Country* (1962). In later years, he costarred with William Boyd in the "Hopalong Cassidy" TV series. Baby boomers best remember him as Uncle Joe on "Petticoat Junction" (1963–70). His friend and frequent costar Glenn Ford brought him back to costar in his TV series "Cade's County" in the early 1970s.

BUCHANAN, JACK. Actor, producer, director. (*b. Apr. 2, 1891, Glasgow; d. Oct. 20, 1957.*) The very embodiment of "debonair," this nasal yet suave British singer-dancer-comedian seemed to have been born in top hat, white tie, and tails; indeed, if he is remembered at all in this country, it is for his side-splitting performance as the egotistical theatrical genius opposite Mr. Top Hat himself, Fred Astaire, in *The Band Wagon* (1953). He was working on both the stage and in silent films from the teens, notably in *Auld Lang Syne* (1917), *Bulldog Drummond's Third Round* (1925), and *Confetti* (1927). At the dawn of sound, he made two films in the United States: *Paris* (1929) and *Monte Carlo* (1930, an early Lubitsch talkie), but soon returned to the U.K. and kept busy producing as well as acting. He even directed one film, *That's a Good Girl* (1935). He also starred in Preston Sturges' last film, the ill-fated *Les Carnets du Major Thompson* (1956, aka *The French, They Are a Funny Race).*
OTHER FILMS INCLUDE: 1931: *Man of Mayfair;* 1932: *Goodnight Vienna;* 1935: *Brewster's Millions;* 1937: *The Sky's the Limit* (also produced); 1938: *Break the News* (also produced); 1940: *Bulldog Sees It Through.*

BUCHHOLZ, HORST. Actor. (*b. Dec. 4, 1932, Berlin.*) Dark-haired, handsome if petulant-looking actor who played tempestuous young men with considerable skill early in his career—notably as the quick-tempered gunfighter-wannabe in *The*

Magnificent Seven (1960) and as Pamela Tiffin's anticapitalist beau in *One, Two, Three* (1961). He had debuted in *Marianna* (1955) and won a Cannes Film Festival award for his turn in *Sky Without Stars* that same year. He played Marco Polo in *Marco the Magnificent* (1965) and Johann Strauss, Jr., in *The Great Waltz* (1972) but otherwise hasn't had much luck in sustaining his appeal on these shores.
OTHER FILMS INCLUDE: 1959: *Tiger Bay;* 1961: *Fanny;* 1963: *Nine Hours to Rama, The Empty Canvas;* 1979: *Avalanche Express;* 1984: *Sahara;* 1985: *Code Name: Emerald;* 1992: *Aces: Iron Eagle III;* 1993: *Faraway, So Close!*

BUJOLD, GENEVIEVE. Actress. (*b. July 1, 1942, Montreal.*) Intelligent, underused French-Canadian actress who has weathered more than her share of career ups and downs, alternating Hollywood assignments with films in her native country. The convent-educated Bujold studied drama at the Quebec Conservatory and subsequently acted in French-Canadian theater. A trip to Europe brought the dark, petite, soulful actress to the attention of French director Alain Resnais, who cast her opposite Yves Montand in *La Guerre Est Finie* (1966). Philippe De Broca's cult hit *King of Hearts* (1966) proved to be an admirable showcase for Bujold, but her startling performance in *Anne of the Thousand Days* (1969) earned Bujold an Oscar nomination and made her a recognizable if lower-tier star. In 1967 she'd married director Paul Almond, who featured her in some of his unusual, offbeat films (*Act of the Heart, Isabel)* before their divorce in 1973.
   A string of mostly forgettable American pictures followed, though she was impressive in a dual mother-daughter role in Brian De Palma's *Obsession* (1976) and as a doomed prostitute in *Murder by Decree* (1979). She was an unlikely leading lady to action star Clint Eastwood in the psycho-thriller *Tightrope* (1984), and contributed intriguing performances to several Alan Rudolph films, *Choose Me* (1984), *Trouble in Mind* (1985), and *The Moderns* (1988). In David Cronenberg's *Dead Ringers* (1988), she was a confused love interest to identical twins played by

Jeremy Irons. Her latest credit is *An Ambush of Ghosts* (1993).

BUÑUEL, LUIS. Director. *(b. Feb. 22, 1900, Aragon, Spain; d. July 29, 1983.)* One of the screen's greatest artists, a director whose unerring instincts and assured grasp of cinematic technique enabled him to create some of film's most memorable images. Buñuel met painter Salvador Dali while studying at the University of Madrid in the late teens. They later found themselves in Paris at the height of the surrealist movement, where they pooled their considerable talents and made the eyebrow-raising short *Un Chien andalou* (1928), replete with disturbing and sometimes disgusting images (including a slit eyeball). The film inspired riots at the time, which seemed to please its two anarchic, antibourgeois creators; its follow-up, the featurette *L'Age d'or* (1930), is more Buñuel's than Dali's, combining dreamlike imagery and anarchic energy with a genuinely hilarious comedic sensibility. After the sardonic documentary *Las Hurdes* in 1932, Buñuel took a 15-year layoff from directing. During a stay in the U.S. he worked for the Museum of Modern Art, preparing documentaries for export to foreign countries, and as a dubbing supervisor of Spanish films at Warners. He was considered as director for *The Beast With Five Fingers* (1946), and did some preproduction work on it, but the job went to Robert Florey (Buñuel later used a disembodied hand—*Beast*'s central shock image—in a dream sequence for his 1962 feature *The Exterminating Angel).*

His directing career began again in Mexico in the late 1940s; many of his films from this period, mostly assignment jobs, are undistinguished but bear interesting touches. Some, however, are genuinely excellent; the best remembered are *Los Olvidados* (1950), an unflinching look at Mexican poverty and juvenile delinquency, and *Nazarin* (1958), the story of a humble priest that was one of Buñuel's harshest critiques of Christianity. Buñuel's real renaissance as a filmmaker began in 1960, when he returned to his native Spain to direct *Viridiana,* the deceptively simple tale of a novitiate pulled from the convent to tend to a family tragedy, unprepared for the corruption of the outside world she meets. The Franco regime in Spain banned it on release. Buñuel followed with one great work after another, attacking the most sacred of cows—particularly the Catholic church and the complacency of society—with remarkable energy and little mercy: *The Exterminating Angel* (1962), a savage assault on the bourgeois mentality, with guests trapped at a dinner party; *Diary of a Chambermaid* (1964), a costume picture updated to encompass the rise of fascism in the 1930s; the short religious parable *Simon of the Desert* (1965); a full flowering of surrealism in *Belle de jour* (1967), with Catherine Deneuve as a respectable wife who enjoys working at a whorehouse; *The Milky Way* (1969), a viciously funny, intricate trip through Catholic dogma; and *Tristana* (1970), with favorite Buñuel actor Fernando Rey as the guardian of Deneuve, and their—to put it mildly—odd relationship. When *Tristana* was nominated for a Best Foreign Language Film Oscar, the great anarchist, typically, commented, "Nothing would disgust me more, morally, than receiving an Oscar." His next film, *The Discreet Charm of the Bourgeoisie* (1972), a marvelous, surrealistic odyssey about a group of dinner guests unable to finish a meal, *did* win the Oscar. Buñuel's reaction is unknown. He followed it with the equally bizarre, if less well-received, *The Phantom of Liberty* (1974).

Buñuel also had a good deal of fun with erotic obsession; his last film, the hysterical *That Obscure Object of Desire* (1977), chortles mightily at an old patrician's love for a frustratingly virginal beauty (played by two different actresses). While Buñuel is categorized as a surrealist, he is in fact one of the least overtly "visual" directors. In fact, it's the offhandedness in the telling of so many of his movies that makes them so great. His always-light touch never tips off the viewer that there's an emotional bomb about to blow soon. The director made two English-language films: 1952's excellent, unusual *Adventures of Robinson Crusoe* (with Dan O'Herlihy) and *The Young One* (1960). His autobiography, "My Last Sigh," was published posthumously in 1983.

BURKE, BILLIE. Actress. *(b. Aug. 7, 1885, Washington, D.C., as Mary William Ethelbert Appleton Burke; d. May 14, 1970.)*

"Are you a good witch?" With that helium voice and cheery, dimpled smile, she was inspired casting as Glinda in *The Wizard of Oz* (1939), but in fact that was only one highlight in the life and career of this light-haired, lighthearted actress who had the odd distinction of seeing herself played on-screen by Myrna Loy when her own career had barely reached the halfway point (she was the widow of Florenz Ziegfeld; the film was the Oscar-winning *The Great Ziegfeld* [1936], for which Burke coached Loy). The daughter of a great circus clown—which perhaps explains her real name—she made her debut on the London stage while still in her teens, and eventually came to Broadway, where she became a huge star and inevitably drew Ziegfeld's attention. From 1916 to 1921, she starred in silent films, such as *Gloria's Romance* (1916, at that time the most expensive—and classiest—movie serial ever made, but a box-office bomb), *Peggy* (1916), *Arms and the Girl* (1917), *The Make-Believe Wife* (1918), and *The Education of Elizabeth* (1921) before returning to Broadway.

When Burke's husband was wiped out in the Wall Street crash, she went back to Hollywood, and all but patented the role of the ditsy, fluttery, upper-class matron. Among her numerous sound films are *A Bill of Divorcement* (1932), *Dinner at Eight* (as the hostess), *Christopher Strong* (both 1933), *We're Rich Again* (1934), *Becky Sharp, Doubting Thomas* (both 1935), *Craig's Wife* (1936), *Topper* (1937, as Mrs. Topper), *Parnell* (1937), *Merrily We Live* (1938), *Topper Takes a Trip, Zenobia* (both 1939), *Irene* (1940), *Topper Returns, The Man Who Came to Dinner* (both 1941), *In This Our Life* (1942), *The Cheaters* (1945), *The Barkleys of Broadway* (1949), *Father of the Bride* (1950), *Father's Little Dividend* (1951), *Small Town Girl* (1953), *The Young Philadelphians* (1959), *Sergeant Rutledge,* and *Pepe* (both 1960). When her career was at a low ebb in the late 1940s, she even starred in a couple of two-reel comedies for Columbia. She also worked often in early TV, and costarred in the notoriously short-lived sitcom "Doc Corkle" (1952). She wrote two autobiographies, "With a Feather on My Nose" in 1949 and "With Powder on My Nose" in 1959.

BURNS AND ALLEN. Actors. (*George Burns*—b. Jan. 20, 1896, New York City, as Nathan Birnbaum. *Gracie Allen*—b. July 26, 1902, San Francisco; d. Aug. 27, 1964.) Both performing vaudevillians from childhood, neither achieved particular distinction in their overcrowded field until teaming in 1922. The mentally nimble Burns initially fired off all the jokes, but as the act evolved it became apparent that Allen's scatterbrained magpie antics got better laughs, so Burns wisely adopted the pose of straight man. Like many vaudeville stalwarts, they broke into movies with the coming of sound, recreating their popular stage routines in short subjects (notably 1929's *Lamb Chops*). After several such efforts, Burns and Allen were signed by Paramount to play comedy support in many of the studio's musicals and comedies, beginning with *The Big Broadcast* (1932) and including *International House, College Humor* (both 1933), *We're Not Dressing, Six of a Kind, Many Happy Returns* (all 1934), *Love in Bloom, The Big Broadcast of 1936* (1935), *College Holiday, The Big Broadcast of 1937* (1936), and *College Swing* (1938). Their best screen moments came at RKO, getting to sing and dance—charmingly—with Fred Astaire in *A Damsel in Distress* (1937). At MGM they backed up Eleanor Powell in *Honolulu* (1939).

Gracie appeared without George in *The Gracie Allen Murder Case* (1939, with Warren William as detective Philo Vance), *Mr. and Mrs. North* (1941, perfectly cast as the charming madcap of Frances and Richard Lockridge's murder mystery), and *Two Girls and a Sailor* (1944). They continued to work together on radio and TV. "The George Burns and Gracie Allen Show" enjoyed an eight-year run (1950–58) on CBS, after which time Gracie retired and George continued solo for another season. She died from cancer six years later. The still vital Burns subsequently starred in the TV series "Wendy and Me" (1964–65) and "George Burns Comedy Week" (1985). Off the big screen for many years, Burns made a triumphant return in *The Sunshine Boys* (1975), winning a Best Supporting Actor Oscar for his portrayal of a crotchety vaudeville star reunited with his slightly addled partner Walter Matthau. He followed this triumph with an even more endearing performance, as the Deity Himself (albeit a cigar-

smoking, golf-hatted one) in *Oh, God!*
(1977), along with its less enchanting sequels, *Oh God! Book II* (1980), and *Oh,
God! You Devil* (1984). He has also appeared in *Sgt. Pepper's Lonely Hearts
Club Band, Movie Movie* (both 1978), *Just
You and Me, Kid* (1979), *Going in Style*
(also 1979, a standout as one of three elderly New Yorkers who rob a bank to re-
lieve their boredom), and *18 Again!*
(1988). He has written a handful of books
reminiscing about his life with Gracie and
his adventures in show business. The
ever-youthful comedian is booked to play
the London Palladium on his 100th birthday.

BURR, RAYMOND. Actor. *(b. May 21,
1917, New Westminster, B.C.; d. Sept. 12,
1993.)* As TV's "Perry Mason," Burr
worked on the right side of the law from
1957 on, but longtime moviegoers (and
late-show devotees) also know him as the
dark, bulky, saturnine heavy of many
films made during the 1940s and 1950s.
He began acting on the stage and drifted
into radio work, where his rich, ominous
voice stood the Canadian-born Burr in
good stead. (He worked often with Jack
Webb, and starred in his own short-lived
radio series, "Fort Laramie," in 1956.)
San Quentin (1946), his first film, set the
pattern for most of Burr's big-screen characterizations; he played more than his
share of cold-blooded, sadistic killers. His
films include *Desperate* (1947), *Ruthless,
Raw Deal* (in which he meets a particularly grisly end), *Walk a Crooked Mile,
The Pitfall, Adventures of Don Juan* (all
1948), *Black Magic, Abandoned* (both
1949), *Love Happy* (also 1949, chasing
the Marx Brothers!), *A Place in the Sun*
(1951, as the *prosecuting* attorney), *Mara
Maru, Meet Danny Wilson* (both 1952),
*The Blue Gardenia, Tarzan and the She-
Devil* (both 1953), *Gorilla at Large* (1954,
a 3-D murder mystery), *Rear Window*
(also 1954, with his hair dyed white for
director Alfred Hitchcock), *A Man Alone*
(1955), *Godzilla* (1956, with Burr starring
in the English-language version of this
seminal Japanese monster movie), *Affair
in Havana* (1957), *Desire in the Dust*
(1960), *P.J.* (1968), and *Tomorrow Never
Comes* (1977). In recent years he enjoyed tongue-in-cheek casting in *Airplane
II: The Sequel* (1982), *Godzilla 1985,* and

Delirious (1991). Burr played wheelchair-
bound cop "Ironside" in a 1967–75 TV
series, and made innumerable "Perry Mason" made-for-TV movies from 1985 to
the time of his death.

BURSTYN, ELLEN. Actress. *(b. Dec. 7,
1932, Detroit, as Edna Rae Gillooly.)* Earthy,
appealing star of the 1970s who acted
under several names (most often Edna
Rae) on stage and in TV shows during the
late 1950s and early 1960s. A student of
Lee Strasberg at the Actors' Studio, she
debuted on-screen in 1964's *For Those
Who Think Young,* billed as Ellen McRae.
Later adopting her (then third) married
name, Burstyn, she appeared in several
other nondescript pictures throughout the
1960s, hitting the jackpot with 1971's *The
Last Picture Show.* Burstyn's role as a
free-spirited woman in a dying Texas
town brought her the New York Film Critics' and National Film Critics' awards for
Best Supporting Actress, although she lost
the Best Supporting Actress Oscar to her
costar, Cloris Leachman. The critical kudos enabled Burstyn to exercise greater
control over her roles; already in middle
age, she found herself in the enviable position of having movies written and developed with her in mind. Her two biggest
successes were *The Exorcist* (1973), for
which she snagged another Oscar nomination as Linda Blair's worried mother, and
Alice Doesn't Live Here Anymore (1974),
a project she packaged and sold to Warner
Bros. herself. Good move: she finally won
an Academy Award as the single mother
struggling to get along. Among her other
films are *Tropic of Cancer, Alex in Wonderland* (both 1970), *The King of Marvin
Gardens* (1972, in a moving performance
as an aging chippie), *Harry and Tonto*
(1974, as Art Carney's daughter), and
Providence (1977). She earned additional
Oscar nominations for her role as an adulterous wife in *Same Time, Next Year*
(1978, recreating her Tony Award-winning
stage performance) and as a faith healer in
the underrated *Resurrection* (1980). She
found more opportunitites on TV than in
features during the 1980s, and starred in
the high-profile telefilms *The People vs.
Jean Harris* (1981, as murderess Harris),
Pack of Lies (1987), and *Mrs. Lambert
Remembers Love* (1991). Her other more
recent films include *Twice in a Lifetime*

(1985), *Hanna's War* (1988), *Dying Young* (1991), and *The Cemetery Club* (1993, in a most welcome leading role).

BURTON, RICHARD. Actor. *(b. Nov. 10, 1925, Pontrhydfen, South Wales, as Richard Walter Jenkins, Jr.; d. Aug. 5, 1984.)* A Welsh miner's son who never forgot his roots, Richard Burton gained a reputation as one of the world's finest actors, and then was criticized for placing fame and money above art and dedication to his craft. Through the help of his schoolmaster, Philip Burton, young Richard Jenkins received a scholarship to Oxford University (later taking Burton's name as his own), and studied acting; along the way he developed a distinctive and beautiful speaking voice. He made his first stage appearance in 1943, but his career did not begin in earnest until after he left the British Navy in 1947.

The Last Days of Dolwyn (1948) provided young Burton his film debut, and he made a striking impression in a stage revival of "The Lady's Not for Burning" in 1949. When Burton came with the play to Broadway the following year, he registered solidly with American producers, and was chosen to play the male lead in *My Cousin Rachel* (1952), a Daphne du Maurier mystery. His success in that film led to a flurry of Hollywood activity in such pictures as *The Robe* (1953), *The Rains of Ranchipur,* and *Prince of Players* (both 1955), but he did not set the box office on fire and subsequently spent much of his time on the stage both in Britain and in the U.S.

Burton starred in several respectable British films in the late 1950s, including *Look Back in Anger* (1959), but his elevation to superstardom began with his casting as King Arthur in the Broadway musical "Camelot" in 1960 (which won him a Tony Award), and his role as Marc Antony in the 1963 film version of *Cleopatra.* A star-crossed production, it was begun and halted several times in several different countries with several different directors. During the making of the film, Burton and his costar Elizabeth Taylor carried on an affair, which led both to divorce their current mates—and become headline fodder around the world.

The Burton-Taylor team became hot box office, and although he played "Hamlet"

on stage (which was also photographed for showing in movie theaters) and *Becket* in the movies (both 1964), he commanded the most audience attention in slick entertainments with his wife, such as *The V.I.P.s* (1963) and *The Sandpiper* (1965). Art and commerce found a common ground in the couple's *Who's Afraid of Virginia Woolf?* (1966) and *The Taming of the Shrew* (1967), but audiences grew restive with both his on-again, off-again relationship with Taylor, and the later films they did together: *The Comedians* (1967), *Dr. Faustus, Boom!* (both 1968), *Hammersmith Is Out* (1972), and the TV movie *Divorce His—Divorce Hers* (1973).

In fact, Burton became notorious for appearing in films—always for the money, which he never denied—that wasted his considerable talents, including *Bluebeard* (1972), *The Voyage* (1973), *The Klansman* (1974), *Exorcist II: The Heretic* (1977), *The Medusa Touch* (1978), *Lovespell* (1979), *Absolution* (1981, filmed in 1978), and *Wagner* (1983). Burton was honored seven times with Oscar nominations, as Best Supporting Actor for *My Cousin Rachel* (odd, since he was the male lead) and as best actor for *The Robe, Becket, The Spy Who Came in From the Cold* (1965), *Who's Afraid of Virginia Woolf?, Anne of the Thousand Days* (1969), and *Equus* (1977), but he never won the gold statue.

His final work was in a well-received 1984 miniseries, "Ellis Island" (which featured his daughter, actress Kate Burton) and the impressive remake of *1984* (1984). He wrote of his relationship with Taylor in the slim but charming volume "Meeting Mrs. Jenkins" (1966).

OTHER FILMS INCLUDE: 1951: *Green Grow the Rushes;* 1956: *Alexander the Great;* 1959: *Bitter Victory;* 1962: *The Longest Day;* 1964: *The Night of the Iguana;* 1968: *Candy;* 1969: *Where Eagles Dare;* 1971: *Raid on Rommel;* 1973: *Massacre in Rome;* 1978: *The Wild Geese;* 1980: *Circle of Two.*

BURTON, TIM. Director. *(b. Aug. 25, 1958, Burbank, Calif.)* Unique, original filmmaker whose creative visual style and dark sense of humor stem, in part, from the horror films he loved (and identified with) as a child. He studied animation at the California Institute of the Arts and then worked at Walt Disney Studios, where he made two shorts that crystallized many themes in his later work: *Vincent* (1982), a stop-motion animation salute to Vincent Price (one of Burton's heroes, who narrates the short), and *Frankenweenie* (1984), a live-action reinterpretation of the horror classic, with a young boy who brings his dead dog back to life. The Disney studios didn't quite know what to do with either film (neither one went into national release), but *Frankenweenie* caught the attention of Paul Reubens, who hired Burton to direct his alter-ego Pee-wee Herman in *Pee-wee's Big Adventure* (1985), a stylized, inventive, and surprisingly charming comedy that works because of Burton's affection for comic strip irreverence.

Burton's next film, *Beetlejuice* (1988), the story of a dead couple trying to deal with the afterlife, retained that irreverence (mostly in Michael Keaton's wonderfully over-the-top performance as a daffy demonic spirit) but showcased a much more sophisticated visual sense. (Increasingly bigger budgets allowed him to let his imagination run wild.) Burton then directed *Batman* (1989), a brooding, revisionist take on the character which quickly became one of the biggest moneymakers in box office history. His new-found clout enabled him to make the decidedly less commercial *Edward Scissorhands* (1990), a fable of an artificial boy set in a hyperrealistic suburbia that is probably Burton's most personal work, dealing with the plight of the outcast in a forbidding world. It was based on a character he'd developed in his boyhood; the film also featured Vincent Price as Edward Scissorhands' creator. Burton directed the mean-spirited sequel *Batman Returns* (1992) before returning to his roots, producing *The Nightmare Before Christmas* (1993), a dazzling display of stop-motion animation; though directed by Henry Selick, it was based on Burton's designs and story. It was complemented by the music of Burton's longtime composer-collaborator, Danny Elfman. He followed it with *Ed Wood* (1994).

BUSCEMI, STEVE. Actor. *(b. Dec. 13, 1957, Brooklyn, N.Y.)* Talented actor who made his first big impression on film as Nick, the pop songwriter dying of AIDS in *Parting Glances* (1986). A veteran of stand-up comedy, experimental theater, and even a stint as a fire fighter, Buscemi has appeared in such diverse films as *Vibes* (1988), the "Life Lessons" segment of *New York Stories* (as a performance artist), *Mystery Train, Slaves of New York* (all 1989), *Miller's Crossing* (1990), *Billy Bathgate* (1991) and *Barton Fink* (1991, as . . . Chet). Almost all of these parts were small; some were fleeting. His performance as Mr. Pink in the acclaimed *Reservoir Dogs* (1992) raised moviegoers' (and critics') awareness of him; he went on to star as a hapless filmmaker trying to finance his 500-page script in the low-budget comedy *In the Soup* (1992). Recent credits include *Rising Sun, Twenty Bucks* (both 1993), *Even Cowgirls Get the Blues,* and *The Hudsucker Proxy* (both 1994).

BUSEY, GARY. Actor. *(b. June 29, 1944, Goose Creek, Tex.)* Nearly a star on more than one occasion, this actor's career has had more than its share of ups and downs. The once-lanky Busey worked as a drummer with Leon Russell, Kris Kristofferson, and Willie Nelson before turning to acting. The son of a Native American father and an Irish mother, Busey was raised in Oklahoma, where he worked on a ranch and rode bulls. His movie career started with 1971's biker epic *Angels Hard as They Come* (and almost ended in a tragic real-life motorcycle accident in December 1988). He moved up to chunky supporting roles in *A Star Is Born* (1976) and *Straight Time* (1978) before strapping on a guitar to play the title role (and actually perform his own songs) in *The Buddy Holly Story* (1978), for which he earned an Oscar nomination. Other prime roles came in *Big Wednesday* (1978), *Foolin' Around* (1980), *Barbarosa* (1982), *D.C. Cab* (1983), *The Bear* (1984, as Coach "Bear" Bryant), *Insignificance* (as a Joe DiMaggio prototype), *Silver Bullet* (both 1985), and *Eye of the Tiger* (1986). Once a protagonist, he more recently has found his juiciest opportunities in sinister supporting roles in *Lethal Weapon* (1987), *Predator 2* (1990), *Hider in the House* (1991), and *Under Siege* (1992). 1993 offered him two unusually good supporting roles: as a freewheeling private eye in *The Firm,* and as a down-on-his-luck pitcher who befriends the *Rookie of the Year.* He continues to star in low-grade features and higher-profile cable TV movies.

BUTTERWORTH, CHARLES. Actor. *(b. July 26, 1896, South Bend, Ind.; d. June 13, 1946.)* Slender, wide-eyed Butterworth was a popular Milquetoast type: slightly addled, he delivered non sequitur dialogue with great comic expertise. He graduated from Notre Dame with a degree in law, drifted into journalism, and finally took up acting in the late 1920s. After appearing in several big Broadway musical comedies, he made his film debut in 1930's *The Life of the Party.* Probably his best role is that of Algy Longworth, befuddled friend of Ronald Colman's Drummond in *Bulldog Drummond Strikes Back* (1934). MGM even tried starring him in his own comedy vehicle, *Baby Face Harrington* (1935, in a dual role). Also memorably funny in *The Mad Genius* (1931), *Love Me Tonight* (1932), *Penthouse* (1933), *Hollywood Party* (1934), *Magnificent Obsession* (1935), *Every Day's a Holiday* (1937), and *The Boys From Syracuse* (1940), among others. Sadly, Butterworth wound up his career in bargain-basement B pictures. He died in an automobile accident.

BUTTONS, RED. Actor. *(b. Feb. 5, 1919, New York City, as Aaron Chwatt.)* Lots of clowns want to play Hamlet, but this compact, red-haired comedian not only got the chance to do heavy drama, he won an Oscar for it: as the star-crossed sergeant in *Sayonara* (1957). He got his comic training in burlesque and in the resorts of the Catskills. (Believe it or not, he took his stage name not from his hair, but from the uniform he wore as a bellboy!) He eventually moved to Broadway, and made his film debut in 1944 recreating his stage role in *Winged Victory.* In 1952, he headlined a TV variety series, and became an instant star, with his "Strange things are happening" briefly becoming a national catch-phrase, though the show only lasted three years. *Sayonara* didn't exactly restore him to prominence, but he did keep reasonably busy, appearing in *Imitation General* (1958), *The Big Circus* (1959), *One, Two, Three* (1961, in a gag cameo), *Hatari!, Five Weeks in a Balloon, The Longest Day* (all 1962), *Gay Purr-ee*

(1963, voice only), *A Ticklish Affair* (1963), *Your Cheatin' Heart* (1964), *Harlow* (1965, the Carroll Baker version), *Stagecoach* (1966), *They Shoot Horses, Don't They?* (1969), *Who Killed Mary What's'ername?* (1971, a rare lead as a boxer-turned-detective), *The Poseidon Adventure* (1972), *Gable and Lombard* (1976), *Viva Knievel!, Pete's Dragon* (both 1977), *Movie Movie* (1978), and *When Time Ran Out . . .* (1980).

Buttons also worked often in TV, starring in a short-lived sitcom, "The Double Life of Henry Phyfe" (1966), and even spending a season on "Knots Landing" (1987). And, of course, he made countless appearances on the Dean Martin roasts, where his "Never Got a Dinner" routine (cleaned up from the versions he performs at Hollywood functions) never wore out its welcome.

BYINGTON, SPRING. Actress. *(b. Oct. 17, 1893, Colorado Springs; d. Sept. 7, 1971.)* Although she often played scatterbrained wives and society matrons of the Mary Boland/Alice Brady type, she was more delicate and birdlike, and enjoyed a lengthy career in motherly (and grandmotherly) roles. Byington started performing at the age of 14 in a Denver stock company, and eventually came to Broadway under the auspices of George S. Kaufman. Her first motion picture was 1933's *Little Women* (as Marmee), which set the tone for the rest of her career. She was Oscar-nominated for her work in *You Can't Take It With You* (1938); also very effective in *Mutiny on the Bounty, Way Down East* (both 1935), *Dodsworth, The Charge of the Light Brigade* (both 1936), *The Adventures of Tom Sawyer* (1938), *The Story of Alexander Graham Bell* (1939), *The Devil and Miss Jones, Meet John Doe* (both 1941), *Roxie Hart* (1942), *Heaven Can Wait* (1943), *I'll Be Seeing You, The Enchanted Cottage* (both 1945), *In the Good Old Summertime* (1949), *Louisa* (1950), and *Please Don't Eat the Daisies* (1960). She also starred in Fox's popular B-movie series "The Jones Family" in the 1930s, and gained latter-day recognition as the star of TV's "December Bride" (1954–61). She also had a featured role on "Laramie" (1961–63).

BYRNE, GABRIEL. Actor. *(b. May 12, 1950, Dublin.)* This handsome, brooding actor originally considered becoming a missionary when he was just a boy, but after some time in a seminary he was thrown out for smoking. He later studied archeology and languages and held a number of jobs before becoming involved in theater and gaining success in Ireland on the popular TV drama series "Bracken." After small roles in the films *On a Paving Stone* (1978) and *The Outsider* (1979), he was cast as the father of King Arthur in John Boorman's *Excalibur* (1981) and won larger parts in *Hanna K* and *The Keep* (both 1983). He finally scored leads as an academic trying to finish a project in *Reflections* and a determined journalist in the excellent thriller *Defence of the Realm* (both 1985). A mixed bag of projects followed: Ken Russell's *Gothic* (1986), the inept comedy *Hello Again,* the bizarre *Julia and Julia* (both 1987), the historical picture *Lionheart* (1987, as The Black Prince), the surrealistic *Siesta* (also 1987, on which he met his wife-to-be, Ellen Barkin), the WW2 drama *A Soldier's Tale* (1988), and *Dark Obsession* (1989). It wasn't until the Coen brothers' gangster saga *Miller's Crossing* (1990) that an American director effectively used his dark, implosive energy. He has since appeared in *Shipwrecked* (1990), the wretched *Cool World* (1992), *Point of No Return, A Dangerous Woman,* and the dour Irish fable *Into the West* (all 1993, the last featuring Barkin; he also associate-produced). He also co-produced *In the Name of the Father* (1993) with director-writer Jim Sheridan, a friend from his Irish theater days.

CAAN, JAMES. Actor. *(b. Mar. 26, 1939, Queens. N.Y.)* Caan has turned in a number of varied, excellent performances over the years, but his career has had more than its share of ups and downs. He studied at Sanford Meisner's Neighborhood Playhouse and then with acting coach Wynn Handman. Numerous stage and TV appearances followed, along with a bit in Billy Wilder's *Irma la Douce* (1963) and his first major role as one of Olivia de Havilland's tormentors in *Lady in a Cage* (1964). He impressed as a stock-car racer in *Red Line 7000* (1965) and a gambler who can't shoot in *El Dorado* (1967, both

directed by Howard Hawks) and had leading roles in *Games* (1967), *Submarine X-1, Countdown* (directed by Robert Altman), and *Journey to Shiloh* (all 1968). He showed great sensitivity as a brain-damaged football hero in Francis Ford Coppola's early film *The Rain People* (1969) and continued to display versatility in *Rabbit, Run* (1970) and *T. R. Baskin* (1971).

A one-two combination finally shot him to stardom: as the doomed football player Brian Piccolo in the hugely popular TV movie *Brian's Song* (1970) and a hot-headed Sonny Corleone in Coppola's epic gangster saga *The Godfather* (1972, a role he briefly reprised in the 1974 sequel). Caan earned a Supporting Actor Oscar nomination for *The Godfather* and then starred in a number of very different projects: *Slither, Cinderella Liberty* (both 1973), *Freebie and the Bean* (1974), and *The Gambler* (1974, one of his best performances), *Funny Lady* (as producer/songwriter Billy Rose), *The Killer Elite,* and *Rollerball* (all 1975). He even parodied himself in Mel Brooks' *Silent Movie* (1976).

Unfortunately, Caan was in a few too many misfires: *Harry and Walter Go to New York* (1976), *A Bridge Too Far,* Claude Lelouch's *Another Man, Another Chance* (both 1977), *Comes a Horseman* (1978) and *Chapter Two* (1979). He made an impressive directorial debut with *Hide in Plain Sight* (1980), a drama—in which he also starred—about the witness protection program, but almost no one saw it. He then had one of his best roles in years as a master burglar in *Thief* (1981), but neither this nor the romantic fantasy *Kiss Me Goodbye* (1982) put him back on the A-list. He was sidelined by personal problems, and walked off the movie *The Holcroft Covenant* (1985). When he returned to films, after five years, as a tough Army sergeant in Coppola's Vietnam War–era *Gardens of Stone* (1987), Caan received some of the best reviews of his career. He was well cast as a cop in *Alien Nation* (1988), but his big break came when Warren Beatty dropped out of a project called *Misery* (1990). Caan stepped in, playing an author held hostage by a psycho fan. The movie was a hit, and though Kathy Bates' Oscar-winning performance got most of the attention, it was Caan's subtle work (confined to a bed and wheelchair for most of the proceedings) that made the movie work. Back in top form, Caan contributed a cameo to *Dick Tracy* (1990), played an egotistical show-biz star opposite Bette Midler in *For the Boys* (1991), a gangster who sets his sights on Sarah Jessica Parker (and won't take no for an answer) in *Honeymoon in Vegas* (1992), and a college football coach in *The Program* (1993). He also played Dennis Quaid's vicious father in *Flesh and Bone* (1993).

CABOT, BRUCE. Actor. *(b. Apr. 20, 1904, Carlsbad, N.M. as Jacques Etienne de Bujac; d. May 3, 1972.)* He was the coura-geous Jack Driscoll, who saved Ann Darrow (Fay Wray) from the clutches of her simian suitor in *King Kong* (1933), and the characterization dogged him throughout a lengthy screen career. Cabot, the scion of a family of diplomats, report-edly wangled a screen test out of RKO producer David O. Selznick after meeting him at a 1932 Hollywood party. He played bits and second leads in a number of RKO films over the next two years, including *What Price Hollywood?, The Roadhouse Murder* (both 1932), *Lucky Devils, Ann Vickers, The Great Jasper, Flying Devils, Finishing School,* and *Murder on the Blackboard,* in addition to *Kong.* (He was also announced to play Count Zaroff in 1932's *The Most Dangerous Game,* a part that ultimately went to Leslie Banks.) Tall and handsome, Cabot had a vaguely sinis-ter, cold-blooded quality about him (as well as a harsh, metallic voice) that suited him for heavies as well as heroes. He played gangsters in *Let 'Em Have It* (1935) and *Show Them No Mercy* (1936), and was a chilling Magua in *The Last of the Mohicans* (1936).

Cabot alternated good-guy and bad-guy roles throughout his career, although he generally played heroes in B pictures. A longtime drinking buddy of John Wayne, he spent his later years working almost exclusively in the Duke's starring vehi-cles, such as *The Comancheros* (1961), *Hatari!* (1962), *McLintock!* (1963), *The War Wagon* (1967), *The Green Berets* (1968), *Hellfighters* (1969), *Chisum* (1970), and *Big Jake* (1971).
OTHER FILMS INCLUDE: 1936: *Legion of Terror, Robin Hood of El Dorado;* 1937: *Bad Guy;* 1938: *Sinners in Paradise;* 1939: *Bad Man of Brimstone, Dodge City;* 1940: *Susan and God, Captain Caution;* 1941: *Sundown, Wild Bill Hickok Rides;* 1945: *Fallen Angel;* 1947: *Angel and the Badman;* 1949: *Sorrow-ful Jones;* 1951: *Best of the Badmen;* 1956: *The Red Cloak;* 1958: *The Quiet American;* 1965: *Black Spurs, In Harm's Way, Cat Ballou;* 1966: *The Chase;* 1971: *Diamonds Are Forever.*

CAESAR, SID. Actor. *(b. Sept. 8, 1922, Yonkers, N.Y.)* If "Uncle Miltie" was TV's first king, then Sid Caesar was surely its crown prince. A burly, forceful comedian with an astonishing array of dialects, a ge-nius for pantomime, and an amazing phys-ical grace, he spent much of World War 2 performing with the Tars and Spars ser-vicemen's troupe; those antics were filmed and released to theaters as *Tars and Spars* in 1946. In 1949 Caesar and Imogene Coca headlined a short-lived TV variety series called "Admiral Broadway Revue." The following year they were starring in the far more successful "Your Show of Shows," a weekly live revue that earned him an Emmy and kept theaters empty on Saturday nights. (Some of the series' best sketches were compiled for a 1973 theatri-cal feature, *Ten From Your Show of Shows.*) It was followed by the similar "Caesar's Hour," which won him a second Emmy. His first major movie role was the long-suffering dentist in *It's a Mad Mad Mad Mad World* (1963), followed by leads in a pair of William Castle comedies, *The Busy Body* and *The Spirit Is Willing* (both 1967). Other hilarious turns include a hap-less studio chief in Mel Brooks' *Silent Movie* (1976), a deranged veteran in *Fire Sale* (1977), a senile millionaire in *The Cheap Detective* (1978), and a bumbling caveman in *History of the World—Part I* (1981, again directed by Brooks, who'd been one of the "Your Show of Shows" scribes), as well as amusing cameos in *A Guide for the Married Man* (1967), *Air-port '75* (1974), *Grease* (1978 and a 1982 sequel), *Over the Brooklyn Bridge* (1984), and *Stoogemania* (1985).

CAGE, NICOLAS. Actor. *(b. Jan. 7, 1964, Long Beach, Calif.)* Nicolas Coppola, the nephew of director Francis Ford Coppola, changed his name to avoid coasting on his famous uncle's coattails.

Tall, with thick eyebrows and an ever-present hangdog countenance, Cage was one of the 1980s' least-likely stars, making his film debut in *Fast Times at Ridgemont High* (1982), then landing a leading role in the independent hit *Valley Girl* (1983). He subsequently appeared in *Rumble Fish* (1983), *Racing With the Moon, The Cotton Club, Birdy* (all 1984), *The Boy in Blue* (1986), and *Peggy Sue Got Married* (also 1986, as Kathleen Turner's boyfriend and husband), directed by his uncle. Two 1987 performances, as the hapless, good-hearted bandit in *Raising Arizona* and Cher's reluctant beau in *Moonstruck*, solidified Cage's box-office standing. He briefly turned action hero in the war drama *Fire Birds* (1990), but was much more comfortable as the Elvis-like drifter in *Wild at Heart* (1990), a sex-crazed creep in *Zandalee* (1991), and a farcically put-upon bridegroom-to-be in *Honeymoon in Vegas* (1992). Recent films include *Amos & Andrew, Deadfall* (both 1993, the latter directed by his brother Christopher Coppola), *Guarding Tess, Red Rock West, Trapped in Paradise* (all 1994), and the remake of *Kiss of Death* (1995, in the Richard Widmark role). Cage seems more interested in pursuing offbeat, even eccentric projects than in attaining superstardom; any man who would eat a live cockroach on camera (as he did in 1989's *Vampire's Kiss*) is clearly ready to give his all for his art.

CAGNEY, JAMES. Actor. (b. July 17, 1899, New York City; d. Mar. 30, 1986.) The words used to describe him are often the same: "cocky," "pugnacious," "jaunty," "energetic." In truth, though, this unique movie star possessed an appeal that's not easy to identify. Cagney's surface gestures and mannerisms—many of them adopted from people he knew in the streets of New York's Lower East Side—are easy to catalog: the clipped speech, the hitching up of trousers, the aggressive body language. But his peculiar level of intensity, his capacity for introspection (which prompted longtime pal Pat O'Brien to nickname him "the faraway fella"), his ability to draw on previously unseen reservoirs of emotion . . . these all mark him as a very special screen personality.

A "street kid" born into a lower-class family, Cagney earned his keep by work-ing in restaurants and poolrooms before taking up performing on a full-time basis (initially as a female impersonator!) in the post-WW1 years. He married while still a young man, and with his wife Frances toured in vaudeville before securing parts in Broadway shows during the late 1920s. It was his stint as a small-time grifter in "Sinner's Holiday" that won him (as well as fellow cast member Joan Blondell) a ticket to Hollywood to appear in the 1930 film version produced by Warner Bros. Signed to a term contract, Cagney was assigned supporting roles in *Doorway to Hell, Other Men's Women* (both 1930), *The Millionaire,* and *Smart Money* (both 1931) before getting his big break as bootlegger Tom Powers in *The Public Enemy* (also 1931), William Wellman's spectacular entry in Warners' series of gritty gangster films. Cagney's dynamic performance (including the famous scene in which he shoved a half-grapefruit into actress Mae Clarke's face), supplemented by excellent supporting players, incisive direction, and savage action, made the film a tremendous hit and rocketed him to stardom.

Of course, it took some time for that to sink in. The custom at Warners was to keep contract players busy, and Cagney was rushed into back-to-back star vehicles tailored for his tough-guy image—but often leavened with humor: *Taxi!* (in which he showed off his fluency in Yiddish), *The Crowd Roars, Winner Take All* (all 1932), *Hard to Handle, Picture Snatcher, The Mayor of Hell,* and *Lady Killer* (all 1933) among them. He took a brief respite from the beer-and-bullets milieu to show off his terpsichorean talents as the theatrical producer turned performer in *Footlight Parade* (also 1933), in which he danced with top studio hoofer Ruby Keeler in the "Shanghai Lil" production number.

By 1935 several things had happened. Cagney wearied of his cookie-cutter tough-guy assignments, and lobbied for more money and better parts. (Always politically active—a troublemaker, in the eyes of Jack Warner—he was one of the founders of the Screen Actors Guild.) At the same time, the end of Prohibition signaled a change, with gangster pictures supplanted by crime dramas that glorified the good guys instead of the bad guys. Cagney was in the forefront of the new trend, playing a two-fisted FBI agent in "*G" Men* (1935). That year he also played devil-may-care aviators in *Ceiling Zero* and *Devil Dogs of the Air* (teamed with Pat O'Brien in both), and was most improbably cast as Bottom in Warners' all-star version of Shakespeare's *A Midsummer Night's Dream.* By year's end, though, he'd ankled Warners in the middle of his contract.

Along with brother William (a sometime actor himself), Cagney set up his own production company at the independent distributing company Grand National Pictures. The ostensible aim was to personally develop and produce the kinds of pictures he couldn't get at Warners—and net him a piece of the action besides. But his first Grand National offering, *Great Guy* (1936), was distressingly similar to the Warners products he claimed to be tired of; aside from reuniting him with Mae Clarke, it added nothing to either his reputation or his bank account. A lavish (by Grand National standards) musical, *Something to Sing About* (1937), was more to Cagney's liking but went way over budget and failed to recoup its costs. With a third property tucked under his arm, Cagney slunk back to Warners with his tail between his legs.

Angels With Dirty Faces (1938), developed for Cagney's Grand National unit by Rowland Brown, was given top production mounting by Warners and catapulted its star back into the limelight (earning him an Oscar nomination as well). Over the next few years, he was still assigned tough-guy material—such as *The Roaring Twenties* (1939), *Each Dawn I Die,* and *City for Conquest* (both 1940)—but also got starring roles in Westerns (1939's *The Oklahoma Kid*), lighthearted adventure films (1940's *Torrid Zone),* war films (1940's *The Fighting 69th* and 1942's *Captains of the Clouds),* and comedies (1941's *The Strawberry Blonde* and *The Bride Came C.O.D.).* Cagney climaxed his Warners stint with his favorite role, that of pioneering Broadway showman George M. Cohan, in the Michael Curtiz-directed biopic, *Yankee Doodle Dandy* (1942), which not only gave him plenty of opportunities to sing and dance, but also was designed to be a patriotic morale booster for war-weary audiences. It was a rousing success on both counts, and earned Cagney his only Academy Award.

Cagney still yearned for his independence, however. He left Warners again in 1943, and starred in only four movies over the next five years: *Johnny Come Lately* (1943), an evocative story about the travails of a small-town newspaper, which in one scene revealed his skills as a sketch artist; *Blood on the Sun* (1945), which featured Cagney as an American reporter stationed in Japan before Pearl Harbor; *13 Rue Madeleine* (1946), a documentary-style story about O.S.S. agents in war-torn Europe; and *The Time of Your Life* (1948), a tepid adaptation of the William Saroyan play about colorful characters in a waterfront dive. He went back to Warners for an Indian Summer gangster picture, *White Heat* (1949), a commercial success that, among other things, put the line "Top o'the world, Ma!" into our pop-culture lexicon, and showed that he was still as vigorous as ever.

Cagney's 1950s pictures were a mixed bag, beginning with 1950's *Kiss Tomorrow Goodbye* and *West Point Story.* There were many bright spots: In 1955 he played gangster Martin "the Gimp" Snyder to Doris Day's Ruth Etting in *Love Me or Leave Me* (picking up another Oscar nomination), the hilariously odious ship's captain in *Mister Roberts,* and a happily hoofing George M. Cohan for one delightful scene in *The Seven Little Foys,* Bob Hope's biopic of stage star Eddie Foy. He directed one film, 1956's *Short Cut to Hell,* a remake of Alan Ladd's *This Gun for Hire* produced by his good friend A. C. Lyles, but that single experience sated his curiosity about wielding the megaphone. He played silent-screen great Lon Chaney in a fanciful but well-made biopic, *Man of a Thousand Faces* (1957), and appeared in the musical *Never Steal Anything Small,* the potent Irish terrorist drama *Shake Hands With the Devil* (both 1959), and *The Gallant Hours* (1960, as Admiral Bull Halsey). At this point, he became more vocal about retiring, and went out in fine style as the frazzled Coca-Cola executive stationed in West Berlin for Billy Wilder's marvelous comedy *One, Two, Three* (1961). It was a uniquely dynamic performance, and his last screen appearance for 20 years.

Content to sit in his Martha's Vineyard home and paint, Cagney came out of retirement in 1981, claiming that his doctor had ordered him to do *something* to stay active. Obviously ill, puffy, and fatigued, Cagney nonetheless delivered a serviceable performance as a crusty police commissioner in Milos Forman's *Ragtime* (1981). He appeared before the cameras only once more, in the teary telefilm *Terrible Joe Moran* (1984). In 1974 the American Film Institute gave him its Life Achievement Award in a nationally broadcast ceremony; he was chipper and charming, and even danced up the steps to the podium to receive his award. The following year, he wrote an autobiography, "Cagney by Cagney."

CAINE, MICHAEL. Actor. *(b. Mar. 14, 1933, London, as Maurice Mickelwhite, Jr.)* How does one evaluate the oeuvre of an actor who frankly admits that he chooses his film projects (a) for the locations on which they're to be shot, and (b) on the amount of money he's to be paid? (He's certainly honest, if nothing else.) It would be difficult in most cases, but a prodigiously talented actor such as Caine makes it even more so. He's frequently far better than the films in which he appears: He's given stellar performances in the likes of Woody Allen's *Hannah and Her Sisters* (1986, winning a Best Supporting Actor Oscar in the bargain), *Alfie* (1966), *Sleuth* (1972), and *Educating Rita* (1983)—Oscar nominees all. But these outstanding credits must be lumped in with his appearances in such lesser films as *Beyond the Poseidon Adventure* (1979), *Blame It on Rio* (1984), and *Sweet Liberty* (1986, in which Caine's performance was pronounced the "only redeeming feature" by some critics).

Born to a poor Depression-era London family, Caine spent his early childhood years in a two-room Camberwell flat without electricity. During World War 2, he and his mother and brother were assigned to an evacuee home in rural Norfolk. At 16, the rebellious lad quit school and eventually went on to serve as a private in the British army, being posted abroad during the Korean War. Back in London, facing bleak job prospects, he answered an ad in "The Stage" and joined the Horsham Repertory Company in Sussex as assistant stage manager. He graduated to acting via bit parts, which led to bigger roles, and at the end of the season, Caine (now Michael Scott) joined the Lowestoft Theatre in Suffolk, where he met his future wife, actress Patricia

Haines. A movie marquee for *The Caine Mutiny* inspired his new name—and, seemingly, brought him better luck: By the late 1960s, Caine had appeared in more than 100 TV shows and films such as *A Hill in Korea* (1956, his first movie), *How to Murder a Rich Uncle* (1957), *The Day the Earth Caught Fire, The Wrong Arm of the Law* (both 1962), *Zulu* (1964, in a standout role as an insouciant army officer), *The Ipcress File* (1965, the first of three appearances as master spy Harry Palmer), *Funeral in Berlin, The Wrong Box* (both 1966), *Hurry Sundown, Woman Times Seven* (both 1967), *The Magus* (1968), and *The Battle of Britain* (1969).

The success of *Alfie* and the Harry Palmer movies made Caine an international star, but he squandered his standing by accepting roles in a string of undistinguished 1970s efforts, including *Get Carter* (1971), *X, Y, and Zee, Pulp* (both 1972), *The Black Windmill* (1974), *Harry and Walter Go to New York* (1976), and *The Swarm* (1978), to name a few. But he frequently got choice roles in better films as well, making the most of his opportunities in *Sleuth* (1972, opposite Laurence Olivier in a lighthearted tour de force), *The Man Who Would Be King* (1975, opposite Sean Connery in a rugged adventure story), and *California Suite* (1978, delivering a deft comic performance).

The 1980s found Caine continuing the same trend; how to reconcile the abovementioned *Hannah and Her Sisters, Educating Rita,* Brian DePalma's stylish thriller *Dressed to Kill* (1980), *The Whistle Blower* (1986) with the likes of *The Hand* (1981), *Water* (1985), and *Jaws the Revenge* (1987)? Toward the decade's end, Caine got two bright comic roles: as a sophisticated con man in competition with Steve Martin in *Dirty Rotten Scoundrels,* and as a bungling Sherlock Holmes perpetually "rescued" by the brilliant Doctor Watson (Ben Kingsley) in *Without a Clue* (both 1988). In his finest performance in years, Caine played a chillingly ruthless, beleaguered businessman who casually eliminates his wife, boss, and business rival in *A Shock to the System* (1990), a delicious black comedy that enjoyed only limited box-office success. He was also good in *Noises Off* (1992) and the cable telefilm *Blue Ice* (1993), and played an unsubtle villain in *On Deadly Ground* (1994).

Aside from his remarkably prolific and consistent acting career, Caine has also dabbled in the restaurant business, as part owner of London's Langan's Brasserie. He has written two books, "Michael Caine's Moving Picture Show" (1988), a collection of anecdotes, and his autobiography "What's It All About?" (1993). In addition, his master class, Acting on Film, was turned into a successful videotape and book.

CALHERN, LOUIS. Actor. *(b. Feb. 16, 1895, New York City; d. May 12, 1956.)* Tall, hawk-nosed actor with cultured voice and dignified bearing. A seasoned stage actor, he played some leads in silent films of the 1920s (including Lois Weber's *The Blot*), but by the 1930s was in demand as a character actor in Hollywood. (He continued to play leading roles on the stage.) Calhern is well remembered today as conniving Ambassador Trentino in the 1933 Marx Brothers film *Duck Soup* (and confirmed his sense of humor in Wheeler and Woolsey's equally nonsensical *Diplomaniacs* that same year). He reached his peak in the 1950s playing a master criminal in *The Asphalt Jungle* (1950), Oliver Wendell Holmes in *The Magnificent Yankee* (also 1950, for which he was Oscar-nominated), the title role of *Julius Caesar* (1953), and a cynical teacher in *Blackboard Jungle* (1955). Calhern married four times (to actresses), and died while filming *The Teahouse of the August Moon* (1956).
OTHER FILMS INCLUDE: 1932: *Night After Night;* 1933: *20,000 Years in Sing Sing;* 1934: *The Count of Monte Cristo;* 1935: *The Last Days of Pompeii;* 1937: *The Life of Emile Zola;* 1939: *Juarez;* 1943: *Heaven Can Wait;* 1944: *Up in Arms;* 1946: *Notorious;* 1949: *The Red Pony;* 1950: *Annie Get Your Gun* (as a singing Buffalo Bill); 1952: *The Prisoner of Zenda, We're Not Married;* 1954: *Executive Suite;* 1956: *High Society.*

CALHOUN, RORY. Actor. *(b. Aug. 8, 1922, Los Angeles, as Francis Durgin.)* Stalwart, craggy-faced actor who achieved his greatest fame, as so many others did, in a western TV series in the late 1950s, in this case "The Texan." His film career actually dates back to the mid 1940s, when he had a bit in *Something for the Boys*

(1944). He went on to play a succession of tough guys—some good, some bad—in a variety of films, including *The Great John L.* (1945), *The Red House* (1947), *Sand* (1949), *A Ticket to Tomahawk* (1950), *I'd Climb the Highest Mountain* (1951), *With a Song in My Heart* (1952), *How to Marry a Millionaire* (1953), *River of No Return* (1954), *The Spoilers* (1956), *The Hired Gun* (1957), *The Colossus of Rhodes* (1961), *Marco Polo* (1962, title role), *Requiem for a Heavyweight* (1962), *Black Spurs* (1965), *Dayton's Devils* (1968), *Night of the Lepus* (1972), and *Love and the Midnight Auto Supply* (1977). Calhoun turned up in *Pure Country* (1992), looking a little older but no less virile.

CALLEIA, JOSEPH. Actor. *(b. Aug. 14, 1897, Malta, as Joseph Spurin-Calleja; d. Oct. 31, 1975.)* This former European concert singer and Broadway actor made his film debut in 1935. His dark, sinister looks made him an ideal heavy, beginning with *Public Hero No. 1* (1935). But he occasionally played sympathetic roles as well, such as the sly police inspector in *Algiers* (1938) and Orson Welles' devoted sidekick in *Touch of Evil* (1958). Once, in 1937's *Man of the People,* he even got the girl—and top billing besides. Calleia had other memorable roles in *Marie Antoinette* (1938), *Juarez, Golden Boy* (both 1939), *My Little Chickadee* (1940), *The Jungle Book* (1942), *For Whom the Bell Tolls* (1943), *Gilda* (1946), and *The Alamo* (1960).

CAMERON, JAMES. Director, screenwriter, producer. *(b. Aug. 16, 1954, Kapuskasing, Ontario.)* Specialist in muscular, special-effects-heavy movies, and signatory to one of the most expensive "sweetheart" deals in Hollywood history (a five-picture pact with Fox inked in 1992). Cameron was a set designer for Roger Corman's New World Pictures before graduating to directing with *Piranha II: The Spawning* (1981), a negligible assignment. He hit pay dirt with his next feature, *The Terminator* (1984), a remarkably well-crafted action thriller whose sleeper success made Cameron a "hot property" overnight. His subsequent films—1986's *Aliens,* 1989's *The Abyss,* 1991's *Terminator 2: Judgment Day,* and

1994's *True Lies,* all of which he wrote and directed—have been big, long, expensive, effects-laden projects with wide audience appeal (though *The Abyss* missed the mark, and like *Aliens,* had to be considerably trimmed just before release to conform to the studio's demands for reasonable running time). Despite his having cowritten the reactionary *Rambo: First Blood Part II,* his own pictures, including *Aliens* and *The Abyss,* tend to espouse liberal ideas. Cameron is deeply involved in cutting-edge technology, and has also paid more attention to the release of his films on laserdisc than any other director in Hollywood. Both *Aliens* and *The Abyss* were released in special editions which not only restored footage cut from theatrical release, but took advantage of the filmmaker's use of the Super 35 format, allowing him to create a full-frame image instead of panning-and-scanning his widescreen releases.

CAMERON, ROD. Actor. *(b. Dec. 7, 1910, Calgary, Alberta, as Nathan Cox; d. Dec. 21, 1983.)* Although everyone knows Harrison Ford as Indiana Jones, not many people know the real prototype of that character: this virile, squinty-eyed, granite-jawed action hero, who starred in the 1943 serial *Secret Service in Darkest Africa*—the inspiration for *Raiders of the Lost Ark.* The brawny Cameron began his screen career as a stand-in (for Fred MacMurray) and stuntman, then got his first real acting job in *The Old Maid* (1939)—only to see it end up on the cutting-room floor. He went on to find steady work thereafter, swinging between small roles in A pictures to leads in serials and B films. He starred in the TV series "City Detective" (1953), "State Trooper" (1957–59), and "Coronado 9" (1959–60) and made headlines in 1960 by marrying his ex-mother-in-law.
OTHER FILMS INCLUDE: 1940: *Christmas in July, Northwest Mounted Police;* 1941: *The Monster and the Girl, Nothing But the Truth;* 1942: *Wake Island, The Remarkable Andrew* (as Jesse James), *The Fleet's In;* 1943: *G-Men vs. the Black Dragon* (his first starring serial), *Gung Ho!;* 1944: *Mrs. Parkington;* 1945: *Salome, Where She Danced;* 1946: *The Runaround;* 1948: *Belle Starr's Daughter;* 1950: *Dakota Lil;* 1951: *Oh! Susanna;* 1952: *Ride the Man Down;* 1954: *Southwest Passage;*

1956: *Yaqui Drums;* 1958: *The Man Who Died Twice;* 1965: *The Bounty Killer, Requiem for a Gunfighter;* 1971: *The Last Movie;* 1972: *Evel Knievel;* 1975: *Psychic Killer;* 1977: *Love and the Midnight Auto Supply.*

CAMPION, JANE. Director, writer. *(b. Apr. 30, 1954, Waikanae, New Zealand.)* Acclaimed filmmaker whose unusual examinations of female "outsiders" have made her one of cinema's most interesting new voices. After studying at the Australian Film and Television School, she made short films which played to great acclaim at the Cannes Film Festival in the 1980s; *Peel* won the Palme D'Or for Best Short Film. Her 1985 TV movie *2 Friends* won awards for Best Director and Best TV Film from the Australian Film Institute. In 1989 she wrote and directed her first feature, *Sweetie* (1989), a darkly humorous account of an eccentric woman and her relationship with her family. It established Campion on the international film scene, but her reputation was cemented by *An Angel at My Table* (1990), a brilliant, empathetic study of New Zealand writer Janet Frame running nearly three hours. (It was shown on television in Australia, and theatrically around the world.) She moved up another notch in prestige and bankability for her next project. Her dense and mystical story *The Piano* (1993), set in 1850s New Zealand, chronicled a most unusual love triangle. It won Campion worldwide acclaim and an Oscar for Best Screenplay (plus nominations for Best Director and Best Picture).

CANDY, JOHN. Actor. *(b. Oct. 31, 1950, Toronto; d. Mar. 6, 1994.)* This rotund, talented, and immensely likable comic actor spent too much time in substandard movies—even after achieving stardom—but his personal appeal remained intact. Candy established several comic personas with Toronto's Second City comedy troupe and on the "SCTV" show in the late 1970s and early 1980s. He worked in several Canadian-made films—1975's *It Seemed Like a Good Idea at the Time,* 1976's *Find the Lady,* and 1978's *The Silent Partner* among them—before breaking into Hollywood movies (thanks to the American popularity of the syndicated "SCTV") with small parts in *Lost and*

Found, 1941 (both 1979), *The Blues Brothers* (1980), and *Stripes* (1981), which all showed him to be very much at home on the big screen. Candy fared best in strong supporting roles and cameos (1983's *National Lampoon's Vacation,* 1984's *Splash!,* and *Nothing Lasts Forever,* 1985's *Volunteers,* and 1986's *Little Shop of Horrors,* for example). *Summer Rental* (1985) was the first starring vehicle to allow him to play a human being, not a caricature, but this pleasant film was not well received; poor material sabotaged many of his other starring vehicles, such as *Armed and Dangerous* (1986), *The Great Outdoors* (1988), *Who's Harry Crumb?* (1989), and *Delirious* (1991).

Writer-producer-director John Hughes used Candy to best advantage and featured him in *Planes, Trains & Automobiles* (1987) and *Uncle Buck* (1989); Candy returned the favor by contributing cameo appearances to Hughes' productions *Home Alone* (1990), and *Career Opportunities* (1991). The comic actor added pathos to his repertoire as the lonely mother-dominated cop in *Only the Lonely* (1991). He had a surprisingly effective cameo in Oliver Stone's *JFK* (1991) and appeared without billing as a Chicago sportscaster in *Rookie of the Year* (1993). He also costarred in 1993's *Cool Runnings* as a former Olympic athlete who's persuaded to coach the Jamaican bobsled team. The part required acting, not comic shtick, and again Candy proved to be a natural. In 1994, he completed *Canadian Bacon,* and directed a TV movie, *Hostage for a Day,* before succumbing to a heart attack on location for *Wagons East,* robbing the world of a great talent and warm screen presence.

CANNON, DYAN. Actress, producer, director. *(b. Jan. 4, 1937, Tacoma, Wash., as Samille Diane Freisen.)* Lusty actress whose naturalistic, uninhibited acting style made her one of the screen's most desirable leading ladies. Cannon began her performing career as a singer in her mother's synagogue; she subsequently moved to Los Angeles, where she worked as a model. Billed as Diane Cannon, she made her movie debut in the forgettable *This Rebel Breed* (1959), and was seen in *The Rise and Fall of Legs Diamond* (1960). In 1961 she met Cary Grant and allowed her

career to languish while she concentrated on their relationship; they lived together for three years before getting married in 1965. The union lasted only a few years, ending in an acrimonious divorce proceeding. (Although it produced Grant's—and Cannon's—only child, daughter Jennifer.)

Cannon resumed her acting career in 1969, winning almost overnight stardom as the prudish wife in *Bob & Carol & Ted & Alice,* for which she was Oscar-nominated as Best Supporting Actress. The 1970s were good years for Cannon, who appeared in *The Love Machine, Such Good Friends* (both 1971), *The Anderson Tapes, The Burglars* (both 1972), *Shamus, The Last of Sheila* (both 1973), *The Virginia Hill Story* (a 1974 TV movie in which she played the same character portrayed by Annette Bening in 1991's *Bugsy*), *Heaven Can Wait* (earning a second Oscar nomination), and *Revenge of the Pink Panther* (both 1978).

Eager to learn about filmmaking, she enrolled in an AFI workshop, and in 1976 she produced a short about preadolescent sexual curiosity called *Number One,* which received an Oscar nomination for Best Live-Action Short Subject. She followed this with an ambitious feature (in which she also starred), *For the First Time* (1979). After making *Coast to Coast, Honeysuckle Rose* (both 1980), *Deathtrap,* and *Author! Author!* (both 1982), Cannon became less active on-screen, turning up more often in made-for-TV movies and miniseries. She spent several years making (and trying to finance) an autobiographical feature, *The End of Innocence,* which finally saw release in 1991. But at least in the TV arena, she remains a viable leading lady, still vibrant (and sexy) in her 50s. Arnold Schwarzenegger directed her in his cable-TV movie *Christmas in Connecticut* (1992). She also costarred in *The Pickle* (1993).

CANOVA, JUDY. Actress. *(b. Nov. 20, 1916, Jacksonville, Fla., as Juliet Canova; d. Aug. 5, 1983.)* Long before "Hee-Haw" there was Judy Canova, a slender, horse-faced woman who was Hollywood's hottest hillbilly. She entered show business as part of her parents' vaudeville act, and later worked in radio as well, singing hillbilly songs and establishing a comic persona. She was featured on Broadway, and made her film debut in 1935's *In Caliente,* singing a countrified chorus of "The Lady in Red." In 1937 Paramount built an entire film around her *(Thrill of a Lifetime)* but decided not to give her a long-term contract. Republic signed her in 1940, and she starred in a successful series of cornpone comedies for the studio, the best of which were *Scatterbrain* (1940) and *Chatterbox* (1943, with Joe E. Brown). She also appeared in *The Adventures of Huckleberry Finn* (1960) and *Cannonball* (1976). A broad, toothy grin and ear-splitting yodel were her trademarks, and although she was never a top-rank star, Judy Canova is still fondly remembered. Her daughter is Diana Canova.

OTHER FILMS INCLUDE: 1941: *Sis Hopkins;* 1942: *Sleepytime Gal, Joan of Ozark;* 1944: *Louisiana Hayride;* 1951: *Honeychile;* 1955: *Carolina Cannonball.*

CANTOR, EDDIE. Actor. *(b. Jan. 31, 1892, New York City, as Edward Israel Iskowitz; d. Oct. 10, 1964.)* One of the true show-business legends, this banjo-eyed entertainer did it all: vaudeville, stage, radio, movies, TV, nightclubs . . . he was even a singing waiter. The "Ziegfeld Follies" star made his film debut in the New York-produced film version of his stage hit, *Kid Boots* (1926), which he followed up with *Special Delivery* (1927); while solidly entertaining, it took talkies to make him a bona fide movie star. Cantor's energetic singing and his unique dialogue delivery made him a hit in a series of lavish escapist musicals produced by Samuel Goldwyn, beginning with a Technicolor adaptation of the Ziegfeld-produced Cantor stage success, *Whoopee!* (1930), which set the pattern for the star's subsequent vehicles: a silly love story with good-looking juveniles, lavish production numbers staged by Busby Berkeley and featuring the gorgeous Goldwyn Girls (who included Betty Grable, Paulette Goddard, Virginia Bruce, and Lucille Ball), and plenty of cornball, sometimes risqué one-liners delivered by Cantor with his trademark eyeball-rolling punctuation. Many of his highlight numbers also featured him in blackface. *Palmy Days* (1931), *The Kid From Spain* (1932), *Roman Scandals* (1933), *Kid Millions* (1934, with a Technicolor number for the finale), and *Strike Me Pink* (1936) were virtually interchangeable save for casts, character names, and story locations.

Cantor, whose weekly radio show was a mainstay during this time, appeared sporadically in films after that: *Ali Baba Goes to Town* (1937), a tuneful, topical musical comedy, was followed by the snappy *Forty Little Mothers* (1940), *Thank Your Lucky Stars* (1943), *Hollywood Canteen, Show Business* (both 1944), *If You Knew Susie* (1948), and *The Story of Will Rogers* (1952, playing himself in a cameo). Cantor received a special Oscar in 1956 for his numerous humanitarian efforts over the years. He also wrote four volumes of memoirs: "My Life Is in Your Hands" (1928), "Take My Life" (1957), "The Way I See It" (1959), and "As I Remember Them" (1962).

CANUTT, YAKIMA. Actor, stuntman, director. *(b. Nov. 29, 1895, Colfax, Wash., as Enos Edward Canutt; d. May 24, 1986.)* The ne plus ultra of movie stuntmen, this former rodeo champion set the standard for achievement within that select group of thrill-makers, not only performing some of the screen's most incredible feats of daring, but actually inventing many of the safety devices still used by stunt daredevils today. At age 17 Canutt was riding in Wild West shows in the Northwest (he got his nickname as one of Washington State's "Yakima Riders"), and a few years later he was named World's Champion Rodeo Rider. In 1924 he started working in films, playing bits, stunting, and finally starring (albeit in incredibly cheap independent oaters such as 1927's *The Iron Rider*). Talkies weren't kind to Yak; his weak, oddly pitched voice didn't register well, so he confined himself to playing heavies, Indians, and doing stunts. He worked in dozens of Westerns and serials during the 1930s, at one time or another doubling nearly every cowboy star, and concentrating offscreen on developing mechanical devices that would take some of the risk out of stuntwork. In 1939 he astounded mainstream (read: adult) audiences with his daring feats for *Stagecoach,* although his off-the-horses-and-under-the-coach stunt had been in his "repertoire" since 1931's *The Lightning Warrior.* Yak also stunted for Clark Gable in *Gone With the Wind* (1939), driving a carriage through the Atlanta fire, and played a bit as a Reconstruction-days renegade.

Canutt continued to do some stunts and play supporting roles in the early 1940s at his home studio, Republic, but gradually worked his way behind the camera, becoming a second-unit director (one who specializes in action or location scenes shot without the principal players) and, with 1945's *Sheriff of Cimarron,* a full-fledged director. Canutt worked at major studios as well, doing spectacular second-unit work for *Ivanhoe* (1952), *Knights of the Round Table* (1953), *Helen of Troy* (1955), *Zarak* (1956), *Spartacus* (1960), *El Cid* (1961), *How the West Was Won* (1962), *Cat Ballou* (1965), *Khartoum* (1966), *Rio Lobo* (1970), and *Breakheart Pass* (1976), among others. His finest work, though, was his staging of the famous chariot race in William Wyler's 1959 remake of *Ben-Hur;* his own son Joe doubled for Charlton Heston in the long shots. Canutt won a special Oscar in 1966 for his contribution to the art of stuntwork. His autobiography, "Stunt Man," was published in 1979.

CAPRA, FRANK. Writer, producer, director. *(b. May 18, 1897, Bisaquino, Sicily; d. Sept. 3, 1991.)* So many people think of Capra only in terms of his "Little Guy" films that they'd be shocked to realize those movies constituted only a portion of a remarkable career that spanned nearly half a century. He began as a gag writer for silent comedy kings Hal Roach and Mack Sennett, eventually working for comic actor Harry Langdon as a writer and later director. After the egocentric star decided to direct himself, Capra went to Columbia—then a minor studio—and began an amazing affiliation that, through his efforts, brought the company "major" status. He did everything from tearjerkers to adventures to comedies to whodunits, and tackled such dicey issues as Jewish assimilation in *The Younger Generation* (1929), evangelism in *The Miracle Woman* (1931), miscegenation in *The Bitter Tea of General Yen,* and bank fraud in *American Madness* (both 1932).

Capra's successful, sentimental comedy *Lady for a Day* (1933) brought him to the top rank of directors, and *It Happened One Night* (1934) cemented his reputation by becoming the first film to win all five

top Oscars. Within four years, he would win two more Best Director trophies, for *Mr. Deeds Goes to Town* (1936), and *You Can't Take It With You* (1938), his second Best Picture winner. This incredible winning streak was the result of a felicitous collaboration with screenwriter Robert Riskin, who with Capra developed the little-guy-bucks-the-system theme that was eventually dubbed "Capra-corn." Capra's peerless handling of actors resulted in many star-making performances, and some of the best opportunities that Hollywood's character players ever had.

After a lavish adaptation of *Lost Horizon* (1937) and his masterpiece *Mr. Smith Goes to Washington* (1939), Capra left Columbia for Warners, where he made two films in 1941—*Meet John Doe,* certainly the darkest of the "little guy" dramas, which flirted with the danger of fascism in prewar America, and the black comedy *Arsenic and Old Lace* (not released until 1944)—before World War 2 beckoned, resulting in several outstanding documentaries in the "Why We Fight" series. After the war, he formed Liberty Pictures with George Stevens and William Wyler, but *It's a Wonderful Life* (1946) and *State of the Union* (1948) were box-office flops, and the unit eventually dissolved. He coasted through two Bing Crosby vehicles, *Riding High* (1950, an exact remake—complete with stock footage—of his 1934 *Broadway Bill*) and *Here Comes the Groom* (1951), then retreated from Hollywood, though he did make several marvelous educational TV programs for Bell Telephone. When he did attempt a comeback, the films (1959's *A Hole in the Head* and 1961's *Pocketful of Miracles,* a remake of his *Lady for a Day*) only served to underscore how wonderful (and effortless) his earlier films had been.

Capra's 1971 autobiography, "The Name Above the Title," is one of the most entertaining books ever written about the movie industry—compulsively readable though, as it turns out, fanciful. (In 1992 Joseph McBride effectively rebutted that book with an exhaustively detailed biography, "Frank Capra: The Catastrophe of Success.") He lived long enough to see a new generation rediscover his work, but it was a bittersweet irony that America fell in love with *It's a Wonderful Life* because the film fell into the public domain, running on TV during the Christmas holidays. It brought him no income, and was colorized against his wishes. Capra himself had finally become The Little Guy— and, sadly, he could not prevail.

CAPSHAW, KATE. Actress. *(b. Nov. 3, 1953, Fort Worth, Tex.)* Earthy, vivacious leading lady who made a capital debut as the megatolerant wife in *A Little Sex* (1982) and was equally fine in the lost-youth comedy/drama *Windy City* (1984). But her over-the-top performance in *Indiana Jones and the Temple of Doom* (1984) was savaged by critics, sending her career into a tailspin. More recently, she has come back in smaller, quieter roles in *Black Rain* (1989), *Love at Large* (1990), and *My Heroes Have Always Been Cowboys* (1991). She also starred in the short-lived TV parody series "Black Tie Affair" (1993). She is married to her *Indiana Jones* director, Steven Spielberg.
OTHER FILMS INCLUDE: 1984: *Dreamscape, Best Defense;* 1986: *Power, SpaceCamp.*

CARDINALE, CLAUDIA. Actress. *(b. Apr. 15, 1939, Tunis.)* Beautiful, curvaceous, husky-voiced Italian actress groomed to be her country's successor to sex symbols Sophia Loren and Gina Lollobrigida, but who failed to reach the pinnacle attained by her predecessors. A teenaged beauty-contest winner who took acting lessons in Rome, she debuted in 1958's *Les Noces Venetienne,* but made a much bigger impression in the international success *Big Deal on Madonna Street* later that year. Her career was orchestrated by producer Franco Cristaldi, who later married her (just as Carlo Ponti had groomed, then wed Loren). A prolific screen player, Cardinale starred or costarred in dozens of films—including some of the most distinguished Italian productions of the 1960s, such as *Rocco and His Brothers* (1960), *The Leopard, 8½* (both 1963), *Cartouche* (1964), and, after her American sojourn, *Once Upon a Time in the West* (1968).

Cardinale never mastered the English language to the degree that Loren did, which may account for her inability to make the same impression on U.S. audiences. Her American-made (or American-financed) films include *The Pink Panther, Circus World* (both 1964), *Blindfold, Lost Command, The Professionals* (all 1966), *Don't Make Waves* (1967), *The Hell With Heroes* (1968), and *A Fine Pair* (1969). Unlike many European sexpots of the 1960s, Cardinale remained active throughout the 1970s and 1980s, evolving gracefully into character roles. Her later films include *The Red Tent* (1971), *Conversation Piece* (1975), *Escape to Athena* (1979), *The Gift* (1982), *Fitzcarraldo* (also 1982, and one of her best, as the woman who never gives up on the dreamer played by Klaus Kinski), *Henry IV* (1984), *History* (1986), *A Man in Love* (1987, as Greta Scacchi's mother), and, almost thirty years after her appearance in the original, *Son of the Pink Panther* (1993).

CAREY, HARRY. Actor. *(b. Jan. 16, 1878, New York City; d. Sept. 21, 1947.)* One of the screen's earliest superstars, Carey tried several professions before turning to the theater, where he wrote and occasionally directed in addition to acting. He joined the film industry in 1909, working with pioneer director D. W. Griffith on Biograph shorts. Carey's relationship with another pioneer—John Ford—was even more fruitful. Ford cut his teeth directing Carey, and together they made several well-received Westerns (including 1917's *Straight Shooting*), inventing plot devices that would see reuse in hundreds of horse operas. Carey's star waned in the late 1920s, although he gave one of his best performances as a heavy in *Trail of '98* (1929). He made a comeback playing the title role in MGM's jungle spectacular *Trader Horn* (1931), but when he rose to leading lady Edwina Booth's defense when she sued the studio, Metro boss Louis B. Mayer reportedly had him blackballed. His subsequent leads were mostly restricted to quickie Westerns and serials. Following his starring turn in *The Last Outlaw* (1936), a charming modern-day Western (based on a story by Ford), Carey forged a new career playing supporting roles, which he did superbly in *Sutter's Gold* (1936), *Kid Galahad* (1937), *Mr. Smith Goes to Washington* (1939, for which he snagged an Oscar nomination), *Shepherd of the Hills* (1941), *The Spoilers* (1942), *Duel in the Sun* (1946), and *Angel and the Badman* (1947), to name a few.

Carey's appeal rested on his ability to show inner warmth leaking through a tough-as-nails exterior, expressed with facial gestures and eloquent body language (which John Wayne later said he emulated). The actor met his wife, Olive Carey, on a film set in the teens, and after his death she became part of John Ford's stock company of players. Ford opened his 1948 film *3 Godfathers* with an eloquent tribute to Carey, "bright star of the early Western sky," and hired his son, Harry Carey, Jr., to costar in the film.

CAREY, HARRY, JR. Actor. *(b. May 16, 1921, Saugus, Calif.)* Son of the beloved character actor and Western star, Harry Jr. (nicknamed Dobe as a child) served in the Navy during World War 2, then decided to pursue an acting career. His father, although estranged from his early partner and friend John Ford, told Dobe that when he died "the old man" would look after him. Sure enough, when Carey Sr. died Ford gave Jr. a showy costarring role in *3 Godfathers* (1948, which Ford dedicated to Sr.) and made him part of his stock company, featuring him in *She Wore a Yellow Ribbon* (1949), *Wagon Master* (1950, another costarring role), *Rio Grande* (1950), *The Long Gray Line, Mister Roberts* (1955), *The Searchers* (1956), and *Cheyenne Autumn* (1964). By this time he was an established character player, closely associated with Westerns, and he kept busy in scores of TV episodes, a running role on the "Spin and Marty" segment of "The Mickey Mouse Club," and numerous feature films, including three for Howard Hawks (who'd featured him in 1948's *Red River*)—*Monkey Business* (1952), *Gentlemen Prefer Blondes* (1953), and *Rio Bravo* (1959)—and a handful of films with John Wayne (with whom he'd starred in *3 Godfathers*): *The Comancheros* (1961), *The Undefeated* (1969), *Big Jake* (1971), and *Cahill—United States Marshal* (1973). Contemporary directors like Peter Bogdanovich and Joe Dante who revere that period—and directors like Ford and Hawks—have gone out of their way to put Carey in their films, like *Nickelodeon* (1976), *Gremlins* (1984), and *Illegally Yours* (1988), while Ford scholar Lindsay Anderson gave Carey not only his best role in years (as a New England handyman) but the chance to make movie

history: In *The Whales of August* (1987) Carey costarred with Lillian Gish, as his father had exactly seventy-five years earlier! Most recently, Carey has been featured in such latter-day Westerns as *Back to the Future Part III* (1990) and *Tombstone* (1993). His autobiography, "Company of Heroes," was published in 1994.

CAREY, MACDONALD. Actor. *(b. Mar. 15, 1913, Sioux City, Iowa; d. Mar. 21, 1994.)* A most unlikely leading man, even in his earliest films, Carey surely owed what screen success he enjoyed to some mysterious "everyman" appeal that overshadowed his vapid appearance and seemingly diffident manner. Certainly no one could have thought of his early film performances, as a mild-mannered medico in *Dr. Broadway* (1942, his film debut) or a love-smitten cop in *Shadow of a Doubt* (1943) as "dynamic" or "riveting." A successful radio actor and stage performer whose credits included the hit Broadway show "Lady in the Dark," Carey joined the Marines in 1943, staying in uniform for four years. He returned to Paramount in 1947, subsequently appearing—with competence, certainly, but little distinction—in *Suddenly, It's Spring* (1947), *Dream Girl* (1948), *Bride of Vengeance* (1949, as Cesare Borgia), and *The Great Gatsby* (1949, as Nick Carraway), among others. Carey also worked in many Westerns, among them *Streets of Laredo, Comanche Territory, Copper Canyon* (all 1949), *The Great Missouri Raid* (1950), *Outlaw Territory* (1953), and the unheralded sleeper *Stranger at My Door* (1956).

Carey played patriot Patrick Henry in *John Paul Jones* (1959), having by that time settled comfortably into character roles. He also appeared in *Blue Denim* (1959), *The Damned* (1962), *Tammy and the Doctor* (1963), and *End of the World* (1977). A veteran of daytime TV, he played patriarch Tom Horton in the soap opera "Days of Our Lives" for more than 25 years. Carey wrote several books of poetry and a 1991 autobiography, "The Days of My Life."

CAREY, PHILIP. Actor. *(b. July 15, 1925, Hackensack, N.J.)* How many actors can say they worked for John Ford, Russ Meyer, and Jonathan Demme in the course of a long and varied career? This granite-jawed, stolid second lead played Raymond Chandler's famous detective Philip Marlowe on early TV, for which he deserves some measure of fame, but he also brought a rare sense of humor to action roles he essayed on the big screen. Carey broke into movies in 1951, and kept busy for the next 25 years in such films as *Operation Pacific* (1951), *Springfield Rifle* (1952), *Calamity Jane, Gun Fury* (both 1953), *Pushover* (1954), *Mister Roberts, The Long Gray Line* (both 1955), *Wicked as They Come* (1957), *The Screaming Mimi* (1958, opposite Anita Ekberg in a rare lead), *Tonka* (1958), *Dead Ringer, The Time Travelers* (both 1964), *The Great Sioux Massacre* (1965, as Custer), *Once You Kiss a Stranger* (1969), *The Seven Minutes* (1971), and *Fighting Mad* (1976).

In addition to the "Philip Marlowe" series, Carey also starred on TV in "Tales of the 77th Bengal Lancers" (1956–57) and narrated "Untamed World" (1968–75), but he is best known as the long-suffering Captain Parmalee on the comic Western "Laredo" (1965–67), episodes of which were edited into two ersatz theatrical features, *Three Guns for Texas* (1968) and *Backtrack* (1969). Also the stone-faced spokesman for Granny Goose Potato Chips in a long-running series of commercials, Carey has achieved latter-day success as Asa Buchanan, the slick Simon Legree of the daytime soap opera "One Life to Live" (since 1979).

CAREY, TIMOTHY. Actor. *(b. Mar. 11, 1929, Brooklyn, N.Y.; d. May 11, 1994.)* Tall, deep-voiced, and creepy-looking, this eccentric character actor played minor but important roles in several major films of the 1950s, including *East of Eden* (1955), *The Killing* (1956, as a hired gunman), and *Paths of Glory* (1957, as one of the doomed soldiers). By the mid-1960s, however, he was essaying standard-issue heavy parts in B films and TV shows. (He appeared in two 1960s favorites, however: 1965's *Beach Blanket Bingo* and 1968's *Head.*) John Cassavetes used Carey in a couple of his films, *Minnie and Moskowitz* (1971), and, given second-billing, *The Killing of a Chinese Bookie* (1976). In later years, perhaps influenced by cult interest in him, Carey cast himself as an al-most mythical figure, deliberately obscuring his background.

CARLINO, LEWIS JOHN. Screenwriter, director. *(b. Jan. 1, 1932, New York City.)* After establishing himself as an up-and-coming playwright—with the acclaimed "Cages," "Telemachus Clay," and "Double Talk" produced off-Broadway—Carlino wrote his first screenplay, *Seconds* (1966), an ingenious (and well-regarded) adaptation of David Ely's novel about a middle-aged businessman who is given a completely new life. He went on to cowrite *The Fox* (1968) and *A Reflection of Fear* (1973) and penned screenplays for *The Brotherhood* (1968, a powerful look at the Mafia), *The Mechanic* (1972, starring Charles Bronson as an assassin), and *Crazy Joe* (1973, starring Peter Boyle as real-life racketeer Joe Gallo).

He made his directorial debut with the sensual, highly provocative *The Sailor Who Fell From Grace With the Sea* (1976, which he also adapted) and earned an Oscar nomination for cowriting *I Never Promised You a Rose Garden* (1977), an intelligent, sympathetic account of a real-life case of schizophrenia. Carlino probably had his greatest success directing and writing *The Great Santini* (1979, from Pat Conroy's novel), a blistering look at a strained father-son relationship. He also wrote the fine (but little-seen) spiritual drama *Resurrection* (1980) and *Haunted Summer* (1988) and a took a wildly divergent turn as a director with the smarmy sex comedy *Class* (1983).

CARLSON, RICHARD. Actor, director. *(b. Apr. 29, 1912, Albert Lea, Minn.; d. Nov. 25, 1977.)* One of the real problems with most 1950s sci-fi movies is that it's almost impossible to remember if the leading man is Richard Carlson or Hugh Marlowe. The best way: if it's in 3-D, it's Carlson; he starred in three depthies—*It Came From Outer Space, The Maze* (both 1953), and his most famous film, *Creature From the Black Lagoon* (1954). A former stage actor and director, he broke into movies in 1938, mainly in juvenile and light hero roles; among his more prominent credits are *The Young in Heart* (1938), *Dancing Co-Ed* (1939), *The Ghost Breakers, The Howards of Virginia, Too*

Many Girls (all 1940), *The Little Foxes, Hold That Ghost, Back Street* (all 1941), *Fly by Night, White Cargo* (both 1942), *Presenting Lily Mars* (1943), *So Well Remembered* (1947), *Behind Locked Doors* (1948), *King Solomon's Mines* (1950), *The Blue Veil* (1951), *Retreat, Hell!* (1952), *Magnetic Monster, Seminole,* and *All I Desire* (all 1953).

In 1954, Carlson directed his first film, *Riders to the Stars,* which he also starred in, followed by three more he directed only: *Four Guns to the Border* (also 1954), *Appointment With a Shadow,* and *The Saga of Hemp Brown* (both 1958), and the acting-and-directing *Kid Rodelo* (1966). Later acting-only titles include *Bengazi* (1955), *The Helen Morgan Story* (1957), *Tormented* (1960), *The Power* (1968), *Valley of Gwangi,* and *Change of Habit* (both 1969). He also worked frequently in early TV, including starring roles in "MacKenzie's Raiders" and the notorious "I Led Three Lives," in which, as double agent Herbert Philbrick, he really did find Communists under everyone's bed. Carlson also starred in Frank Capra's Bell Science films "Hemo the Magnificent" (1957) and "The Unchained Goddess" (1958), and directed the latter under Capra's supervision.

CARMICHAEL, IAN. Actor. *(b. June 20, 1920, Hull, England.)* Buoyant, affable British actor, specializing in blandly good-looking, generally incompetent but likable public-school twits of the type perfectly embodied by P. G. Wodehouse's Bertie Wooster (whom Carmichael has played on British TV). It's a screen persona he has mastered with seeming effortlessness. A stage performer since 1939, he also toiled in music halls during the 1940s, learning to get laughs the hard way. Carmichael made his screen debut in *Bond Street* (1948), and subsequently appeared in *Meet Mr. Lucifer* (1953), *Betrayed, The Colditz Story* (both 1954), *Storm Over the Nile* (1955), *Private's Progress* (1956, one of his best roles, as a military misfit), *The Brothers in Law* (1957), *I'm All Right Jack* (1959), *School for Scoundrels* (1960), *Heavens Above* (1963), *Hide and Seek* (1964), *Seven Magnificent Deadly Sins* (1971), *From Beyond the Grave* (1975), and *The Lady Vanishes* (1979), among others. American audiences may know him best for his delightful characterization of master sleuth Lord Peter Wimsey in televised adaptations (extraordinarily faithful ones, at that) of Dorothy L. Sayers' classic mystery novels.

CARNEY, ART. Actor. *(b. Nov. 4, 1918, Mt. Vernon, N.Y.)* It may not seem like much of an achievement to be the world's most famous sewer worker, but Ed Norton occupies a very special place in American hearts, due chiefly to his impeccable portrayal by this dextrous, supple-voiced actor. Prior to "The Honeymooners," which earned Carney five of his seven Emmys, he primarily worked on stage (where he created the role of fussy Felix Unger in the original production of "The Odd Couple") and in other early live TV shows. Though he'd made sporadic film appearances, it was his first leading role, as an old man hitting the road with his cat in *Harry and Tonto* (1974), that won him an Oscar and reaffirmed his extraordinary talent. He followed it with other offbeat parts: a fundamentalist preacher turned lawman in *W.W. and the Dixie Dancekings* (1975), an aging private eye in *The Late Show* (1977), a senile surgeon in *House Calls* (1978), a pair of bad-news doctors in *Movie Movie* (also 1978), and one of a trio of elderly stick-up artists in *Going in Style* (1979). He played a police detective in the TV series "Lanigan's Rabbi," and appeared in the telefilms *Terrible Joe Moran* (an Emmy-winning part) and *Izzy and Moe* (reuniting him with "Honeymooners" costar Jackie Gleason).
OTHER FILMS INCLUDE: 1965: *The Yellow Rolls-Royce;* 1967: *A Guide for the Married Man;* 1979: *Sunburn, Roadie;* 1981: *Take This Job and Shove It;* 1984: *Firestarter, The Muppets Take Manhattan;* 1985: *The Naked Face;* 1993: *Last Action Hero.*

CARON, LESLIE. Actress, dancer. *(b. July 1, 1931, Boulogne-Billancourt, France.)* The beautiful Caron, a dancer from age 10, was dancing in the Ballets des Champs-Elysées when she was spotted by Gene Kelly, then scouting Paris for a leading lady to appear opposite him in his paean to George Gershwin, *An American in Paris* (1951). She got the job, making a spectacular film debut, entrancing audiences with a warm, natural performance, and winning an MGM contract in the bargain. Lithe, charming Caron—whose pouty lips and (occasionally) imperious facial expressions immediately tip her nationality—toiled in dramas as well as musicals while at Metro. Her films include *The Man With a Cloak* (1951), *Glory Alley* (1952), *The Story of Three Loves* (1953), *Lili* (also 1953, one of Caron's best, earning her a Best Actress Oscar nomination), *The Glass Slipper, Daddy Long Legs* (1955, opposite Fred Astaire, made on loan to Fox), *Gaby* (1956), and *Gigi* (1958, another triumph for MGM).

Caron expanded her repertoire with solid work in a serious drama, *The L-Shaped Room* (1963), proving she didn't need to wear dancing shoes to keep moviegoers riveted and earning another Oscar nomination. Alas, many of her subsequent films—foreign-made efforts alternating with Hollywood productions—weren't particularly memorable: *Father Goose* (1964, with Cary Grant), *Is Paris Burning?* (1966), *Madron* (1970), *Chandler* (1971), *The Man Who Loved Women* (the 1977 French version), *Goldengirl* (1979), *Chanel Solitaire* (1981), *Dangerous Moves* (1985), *The Sealed Train* (1987), *Dirty Night* (1990), *Damage* (1992), and *Funny Bones* (1995).

CARPENTER, JOHN. Writer, director. *(b. Jan. 16, 1948, Carthage, N.Y.)* This talented and prolific filmmaker was a movie buff at an early age, forming his own production company while still in his teens. While attending the University of Southern California's film school, he began work on *Dark Star,* a sci-fi comedy short that was later expanded to feature length (on a paltry $60,000 budget) and released theatrically in 1974. His second feature, *Assault on Precinct 13* (1976), was an homage to his idol, Howard Hawks, and basically updated that director's *Rio Bravo* in an urban setting. Carpenter's breakthrough film was the stylish and very scary *Halloween* (1978), the seminal "slasher" film; made for $300,000, it was the most profitable independent movie of its day, and to date has spawned four sequels. A fecund directorial period followed, including the higher-budgeted, higher-profiled *The Fog* (1980), *Escape From New York* (1981), *The Thing* (1982,

a Hawks remake), *Christine* (1983), *Starman* (1984), and *Big Trouble in Little China* (1986), many of which he also scripted and scored.

Angry at major-studio inefficiency, Carpenter determined to make modest films again, and retain a greater degree of control. His track record so far has been spotty: *Prince of Darkness* (1987), *They Live* (1988), *Memoirs of an Invisible Man* (1991), *In the Mouth of Madness* and *Village of the Damned* (both 1995)—none of them hits. He also cowrote *Eyes of Laura Mars* (1978) and wrote and directed such TV movies as *Someone's Watching Me!* (1978) and *Elvis* (1979), which starred his frequent collaborator Kurt Russell. In 1993 he produced the cable-TV series "John Carpenter's Body Bags," in which he also appears. Carpenter was briefly married to his sometime leading lady, Adrienne Barbeau.

CARRADINE, DAVID. Actor, director. *(b. Dec. 8, 1936, Hollywood, as John Arthur Carradine.)* This oldest son of character actor John Carradine seems to be playing catch-up with his legendarily prolific father (who appeared in more than 500 films) by starring in countless low-rung action and sci-fi vehicles. Dark, thick-lipped, and sinewy, the brooding Carradine apprenticed in inconsequential Westerns of the 1960s such as *Taggart* (1964, his first movie). He hit his stride a decade later in a string of superior action quickies for producer Roger Corman, including Martin Scorsese's *Boxcar Bertha* (1972, costarring with his then-wife Barbara Hershey) and Paul Bartel's *Death Race 2000* (1975). A student of the martial arts, he put his training to good use as the existential drifter Kane in the TV series "Kung Fu" (1972–74), and in such films as *Circle of Iron* (1978). He gave what is certainly his best performance in *Bound for Glory* (1976), playing folk singer Woody Guthrie. Then, in true Hollywood-maverick style, he directed the little-seen *You and Me* (1977, again with Hershey) and directed, edited, produced, acted in, and provided the music for *Americana* (1981).

Carradine even costarred in an Ingmar Bergman film, *The Serpent's Egg* (1978), but the prestige accruing from that assignment was short-lived; he now only infrequently snags supporting roles in high-profile productions, of which the Mel Gibson–Goldie Hawn vehicle *Bird on a Wire* (1990) is a good example. He costarred with half-brothers Keith and Robert in Walter Hill's fraternal Western *The Long Riders* (1980), and later appeared with them and their dad in an episode of TV's "The Fall Guy." In 1986 he starred in the telefilm *Kung Fu: The Movie*, then reprised his 20-year-old character in the TV series "Kung Fu: The Legend Continues" (1993–).

OTHER FILMS INCLUDE: 1970: *Macho Callahan;* 1973: *Mean Streets;* 1976: *Cannonball;* 1978: *Deathsport;* 1982: *Q;* 1983: *Lone Wolf McQuade;* 1986: *Armed Response;* 1989: *Future Force, Sundown, The Vampire in Retreat;* 1990: *Sonny Boy;* 1991: *Dune Warriors;* 1992: *Roadside Prophets.*

CARRADINE, JOHN. Actor. *(b. Feb. 5, 1906, New York City; d. Nov. 27, 1988.)* This gaunt, deep-voiced Shakespearean actor would be a safe choice to win any competition for Most Movies Ever Made. A classically trained stage actor of the bravura school, he relished showy character parts, no matter how minor the footage; he can truly be said to have believed the old adage, "There are no small roles, only small actors." Carradine wasn't above chewing a little scenery here and there, and left unrestrained he frequently could be seen going over the top. But when handled by a great director—say, John Ford, for whom Carradine was extremely effective—he delivered brilliant performances. He can be glimpsed in bit roles in the early 1930s, in everything from *The Sign of the Cross* (1932) to such Universal horror classics as *The Black Cat* (1934) and *Bride of Frankenstein* (1935).

In the late 1930s, Carradine worked virtually nonstop in dozens of films, including such John Ford landmarks as *Stagecoach, Drums Along the Mohawk* (both 1939), and *The Grapes of Wrath* (1940), as well as *Captains Courageous* (1937), *Jesse James, The Hound of the Baskervilles* (both 1939), and *Blood and Sand* (1941). In the 1940s, he renewed his association with Universal horror films, playing Dracula in *House of Frankenstein* (1944) and *House of Dracula* (1945), as well as starring in *Captive Wild Woman* (1943), *The Mummy's Ghost,* and *The In-visible Man's Revenge* (both 1944); he also gave one of his best performances, oddly, in the title role of *Bluebeard* (1944) over at the tiny PRC studio.

After the war, Carradine found himself mostly limited to smaller roles, playing everything from a handyman in *Johnny Guitar* (1954) to Moses' brother in *The Ten Commandments* (1956), and began an association with the cheap, independent horror film that lasted until his death; among the relatively more amusing were *The Incredible Petrified World* (1958), *Billy the Kid vs. Dracula* (1966, as Dracula), *Hillbillys in a Haunted House* (1967), *Terror in the Wax Museum* (1973), *Satan's Cheerleaders* (1977), and *The Monster Club* (1980). Carradine's more distinguished later films include *The Last Hurrah* (1958), *Cheyenne Autumn* (1964), *The Last Tycoon, The Shootist* (both 1976), *The Howling* (1981), and *Peggy Sue Got Married* (1986), and he provided a voice for *The Secret of NIMH* (1982). Three of his sons—David, Keith, and Robert—have followed in his footsteps.

CARRADINE, KEITH. Actor, singer, songwriter. *(b. Aug. 8, 1950, San Mateo, Calif.)* Earning a Best Song Oscar for "I'm Easy" (which he composed and performed) in Robert Altman's sprawling drama *Nashville* (1975) put this slim, lanky, blond leading man on the show-biz map. He pursued an acting career in the late 1960s after dropping out of college, winding up on Broadway in the counterculture musical "Hair." Carradine made his first film, the Kirk Douglas–Johnny Cash Western *A Gunfight* (1971), the same year he was featured in *McCabe and Mrs. Miller,* the picture that introduced him to Robert Altman, who also used him in *Thieves Like Us* in 1974. Altman protégé Alan Rudolph later directed Carradine in a series of small-scale, offbeat features: *Welcome to L.A.* (1977), *Choose Me* (1984), *Trouble in Mind* (1985), and *The Moderns* (1988). He also appeared as a director in the much-seen music video of Madonna's "Material Girl." Carradine is the son of actor John Carradine, brother of actor Robert, and half-brother of actor David; the actress Martha Plimpton is his daughter. In 1991 he returned to Broadway and enjoyed a

smash success in the title role of the musical "The Will Rogers Follies."
OTHER FILMS INCLUDE: 1977: *The Duellists;* 1978: *Old Boyfriends, Pretty Baby;* 1980: *The Long Riders* (with his brothers); 1981: *Southern Comfort;* 1989: *Cold Feet;* 1990: *Daddy's Dyin' ... Who's Got the Will?;* 1991: *The Ballad of the Sad Cafe, Alone Together.*

CARRADINE, ROBERT. Actor. *(b. Mar. 24, 1954, Los Angeles.)* In *Massacre at Central High* (1976), this youngest son of actor John Carradine played a high school student. At the age of 30, in 1984's *Revenge of the Nerds,* he was just entering college. While his career has often been overshadowed by his more famous brother Keith and half-brother David, the youngest Carradine displays an ingenuousness that makes even his lesser films (and there are plenty of them) worth watching. He made his film debut in the John Wayne Western *The Cowboys* (1972), later appearing in the short-lived 1974 TV show based on the film.
OTHER FILMS INCLUDE: 1973: *Mean Streets;* 1976: *The Pom-Pom Girls;* 1978: *Coming Home;* 1980: *The Big Red One* (in a well-delineated dramatic role—perhaps his best); 1982: *Tag: The Assassination Game;* 1987: *Revenge of the Nerds II: Nerds in Paradise;* 1989: *Rude Awakening;* 1992: *Revenge of the Nerds III: The Next Generation* (telefilm).

CARRERA, BARBARA. Actress. *(b. Dec. 31, 1945, Managua, Nicaragua.)* Feline, olive-skinned, and almond-eyed ex-model whose cool dark looks make her ideally suited to play seductive villainesses or exotic damsels. She made her feature-film debut in *Puzzle of a Downfall Child* (1970), but is probably best-known as sexy Fatima Blush in Sean Connery's 007 comeback film, *Never Say Never Again* (1983). As befits her limited acting ability, Carrera has been featured in mostly ornamental roles in such action or genre fare as *The Master Gunfighter* (1975), *Embryo* (1976), *The Island of Dr. Moreau* (1977), *Condorman* (1981), *I, the Jury* (1982), *Lone Wolf McQuade* (1983), *Wild Geese II* (1985), and *Wicked Stepmother* (1989).

CARREY, JIM. Actor. *(b. Jan. 17, 1962, Newmarket, Ontario.)* Rubber-faced comic actor whose manic energy and general goofiness have evoked comparisons to Jerry Lewis and made him one of the hottest stars in films today.' After years of standup comedy performances on the comedy club circuit, and a very short-lived sitcom, "The Duck Factory" (1984), Carrey won featured roles in *Once Bitten* (1985), *Peggy Sue Got Married* (1986, as a loudmouthed classmate of Kathleen Turner's), *The Dead Pool* (1988), and *Earth Girls Are Easy* (1989) before attracting major attention for his strange characterizations on TV's "In Living Color" (1990–94), on which he was "the white guy." The surprise success of his debut starring vehicle, *Ace Ventura: Pet Detective* (1994), made him an overnight sensation and made moviegoers eager to see his subsequent 1994 releases, *The Mask,* in which he became a human cartoon, and *Dumb and Dumber,* which cast him as a lovable imbecile opposite Jeff Daniels. (The extraordinary success of these films inspired a video company to release a shelved 1991 comedy, *High Strung,* in which he had a small, unbilled part.) He then played The Riddler in *Batman Forever* (1995). The 1992 TV movie *Doing Time on Maple Drive,* which cast Carrey as an alcoholic, shows he could expand his range if he wanted to—and if his fans would permit.

CARRILLO, LEO. Actor. *(b. Aug. 6, 1880, Los Angeles; d. Sept. 10, 1961.)* Leo Carrillo's enduring fame derives from his characterization of Pancho on the "Cisco Kid" TV show, but there was much more to his show-business career. A former newspaper cartoonist, Carrillo first attracted attention as a dialect comedian in vaudeville. He broke into movies in the late 1920s, just as sound was coming in, and most often played a malapropistic Latin character. He was sometimes a heavy, as in *Girl of the Rio* (1932), but more often played the fool. His particular brand of buffoonery must be seen to be appreciated in *Moonlight and Pretzels* (1933), *Viva Villa!* (1934), *Love Me Forever, In Caliente* (both 1935), *History Is Made at Night* (1937), *Manhattan Merry-Go-Round, Girl of the Golden West, Too Hot to Handle* (all 1938), *Lillian Russell*

(1940, as Tony Pastor), *American Empire* (1942), *Ghost Catchers* (1944), and *The Fugitive* (1947), among others. He first played Pancho to Duncan Renaldo's Cisco in a 1950 series of B Westerns, before achieving latter-day celebrity in the long-running television show. Proud of his Californian heritage, he wrote a book, *The California I Love*, in 1961.

CARROLL, LEO G. Actor. *(b. Oct. 25, 1892, Weedon, England; d. Oct. 16, 1972.)* Eminent interpreter of British characters, equally facile with sympathetic and unsympathetic roles. He appeared both on London and Broadway stages between 1912 and 1934, when he went to Hollywood. Carroll made lasting impressions in two late 1930s films, *A Christmas Carol* (1938, as Marley's Ghost) and *Wuthering Heights* (1939). He was a favorite of Alfred Hitchcock, who featured him in *Rebecca* (1940), *Suspicion* (1941), *Spellbound* (1945, his juiciest part), *The Paradine Case* (1947), *Strangers on a Train* (1951), and *North by Northwest* (1959). Carroll was also popular on TV as the befuddled banker "Topper" (1953–56) and later as spy-network chief Alexander Waverly on "The Man From U.N.C.L.E." (1964–68).
OTHER FILMS INCLUDE: 1935: *Clive of India;* 1939: *The Private Lives of Elizabeth and Essex, Tower of London;* 1945: *The House on 92nd St.;* 1947: *Forever Amber;* 1950: *Father of the Bride;* 1952: *The Bad and the Beautiful;* 1955: *We're No Angels;* 1963: *The Prize.*

CARROLL, MADELEINE. Actress. *(b. Feb. 26, 1906, West Bromwich, England; d. Oct. 2, 1987.)* Classically cool, beautiful British blonde who first attracted the attention of American audiences as the heroine of two imported thrillers directed by Alfred Hitchcock: *The 39 Steps* (1935) and *Secret Agent* (1936). Carroll had been acting in British films since 1928 (in *The Guns of Loos*), having abandoned both teaching and modeling for an acting career in 1927. She came to Hollywood in 1936, achieving immediate prominence in *The General Died at Dawn* (opposite Gary Cooper), *Lloyd's of London* (opposite Tyrone Power), and *The Case Against Mrs. Ames*. Her function in American

movies was largely decorative, although she made a spirited Princess Flavia in *The Prisoner of Zenda* (1937, costarring with Ronald Colman) and a convincing snobbish heiress in *On the Avenue* (1937, costarring with Dick Powell and Alice Faye). Her other Hollywood films—including five light comedies opposite Fred MacMurray—included *Blockade* (1938), *Cafe Society, Honeymoon in Bali* (both 1939), *Safari, Northwest Mounted Police* (both 1940), *Virginia, One Night in Lisbon* (both 1941), *Bahama Passage* (opposite then-husband Sterling Hayden), *My Favorite Blonde* (both 1942, opposite Bob Hope in the latter), *Don't Trust Your Husband* (1948), and *The Fan* (1949, her last film). Carroll became an American citizen in 1943, but returned to England during World War 2 to work in the relief effort.

CARROLL, NANCY. Actress. *(b. Nov. 19, 1904, New York City, as Ann Veronica La Hiff; d. Aug. 6, 1965.)* Bubbly, button-cute redhead who juggled dramatic roles with musical-comedy turns during her all-too-brief stardom in the early sound era. Although the former chorus girl had been in movies since 1927 (her first film was *Ladies Must Dress*), it took roles in a few pioneering talkies (including 1929's *The Dance of Life*) to showcase her properly. Carroll shifted from the demands of a heavy melodrama like 1930's *Dangerous Paradise* to song-and-dance work in a frothy musical like *Follow Thru* (1930, which, shot in Technicolor, showed off her bright red hair, baby-blue eyes, and peaches-and-cream complexion) without missing a beat.
   Carroll, who was Oscar-nominated for her performance in *Devil's Holiday* (1930), retired from the screen in 1938. She toured in stage vehicles for many years to come, admitting in retrospect that her hot temper and uncooperative attitude cost her her star berth in Hollywood.
OTHER FILMS INCLUDE: 1928: *Abie's Irish Rose;* 1929: *The Shopworn Angel, Close Harmony, Sweetie;* 1930: *Honey, Paramount on Parade;* 1931: *Stolen Heaven, The Night Angel;* 1932: *Hot Saturday* (which gave her two top leading men—Cary Grant and Randolph Scott), *The Man I Killed, Scarlet Dawn, Child of Manhattan;* 1933: *The Woman Accused, The Kiss Before the Mirror;*

1934: *Transatlantic Merry-Go-Round, Jealousy;* 1935: *Atlantic Adventure* (her last starring vehicle); 1938: *There Goes My Heart, That Certain Age* (as Deanna Durbin's mother).

CARSON, JACK. Actor. *(b. Oct. 27, 1910, Carmen, Manitoba; d. Jan. 2, 1963.)* Describing most of the characters Jack Carson played on-screen as "big, lumbering dopes" might not be very elegant (nor, possibly, entirely fair to this talented performer), but it would be pretty accurate. In fact, the Canadian-born Carson had few equals in the portrayal of obstreperous, obnoxious, often dull-witted lunkheads. Beginning in films as a contract player for RKO—where his films included *Stage Door* (1937), *Bringing Up Baby, Carefree* (both 1938), and *Lucky Partners* (1940)—the bulky, dark-haired actor frequently registered with audiences even in the tiniest of parts. He appeared in *Mr. Smith Goes to Washington, Destry Rides Again* (both 1939), and *I Take This Woman* (1940), among others, before signing a long-term contract with Warner Bros. in 1941. He stayed there for the rest of the decade, ensconced as a versatile utility actor; he appeared in *The Strawberry Blonde, Navy Blues* (both 1941), *The Male Animal, Gentleman Jim, Larceny, Inc.* (all 1942), *The Hard Way, Thank Your Lucky Stars* (both 1943), *Arsenic and Old Lace* (1944, hilarious as a cop/playwright), *Mildred Pierce* (1945), and *One More Tomorrow* (1946), among others.

Beginning with *Two Guys From Milwaukee* (1946), Carson was elevated to costar status with handsome Dennis Morgan; Warners hoped they would be the studio's answer to Hope and Crosby, and while they made several reasonably entertaining films—including *Two Guys From Texas* (1948) and *It's a Great Feeling* (1949, a funny Hollywood spoof)—Jack and Dennis were never any threat to Bob and Bing. Although thought of principally as a comic actor, Carson got a wider variety of roles in the 1950s, and was seen to good advantage in *The Good Humor Man* (1950, in the lead), *A Star Is Born* (1954, as the cynical publicity director), *The Bottom of the Bottle* (1956), *Cat on a Hot Tin Roof, Rally 'Round the Flag, Boys!* (both 1958), and *The Bramble Bush* (1960). His last film was *King of the Roaring Twenties* (1961); he died of stomach cancer. He was once married to actress Lola Albright.

CARTWRIGHT, VERONICA. Actress. *(b. Apr. 20, 1949, Bristol, England.)* Talented character actress who began her career as a child, playing Robert Wagner's younger sister in the film *In Love and War* (1958). She had parts in *The Children's Hour* (1962) and Hitchcock's *The Birds* (1963), and recurring roles on TV shows like "Leave It to Beaver" and "Daniel Boone" (as Fess Parker's daughter). As Cartwright reached adolescence, parts became scarce and she moved to England, returning to films (and to Hollywood) with an acclaimed performance as the stage actress Harlene in *Inserts* (1976). She followed with a series of terrific performances in *Goin' South,* the remake of *Invasion of the Body Snatchers* (both 1978), *Alien* (1979, as the navigator, Lambert), and *The Right Stuff* (1983, as Gus Grissom's distraught wife). She has since appeared in *My Man Adam* (1985), *Flight of the Navigator* (1986), *Valentino Returns* (1989), and *Man Trouble* (1992), and was amusingly hysterical as Felicia, the suspicious wife in *The Witches of Eastwick* (1987).

CASEY, BERNIE. Actor. *(b. June 8, 1939, Wyco, Wyo.)* Unlike many of his colleagues, this tall, muscular, former pro footballer moved from 1970s "blaxploitation" pics (such as 1973's *Cleopatra Jones* and 1976's *Dr. Black, Mr. Hyde*) to supporting roles in more mainstream fare (1976's *The Man Who Fell to Earth,* 1981's *Sharky's Machine,* 1983's *Never Say Never Again,* and 1984's *Revenge of the Nerds*). The hard-bitten, taciturn Casey made his movie debut in 1969's *Guns of the Magnificent Seven.* In 1988, he parodied his action hero status in the sendup *I'm Gonna Git You Sucka.*
OTHER FILMS INCLUDE: 1988: *Rent-a-Cop;* 1989: *Bill and Ted's Excellent Adventure;* 1990: *Another 48 HRS, Chains of Gold;* 1993: *The Cemetery Club, Street Knight.*

CASSAVETES, JOHN. Actor, director, screenwriter, producer. *(b. Dec. 9, 1929, New York City; d. Feb. 3, 1989.)* One of the most unique characters in the annals of Hollywood, Cassavetes was both an accomplished actor and an innovative film-maker whose experimental, inexpensive features were American counterparts to the films that were the product of France's New Wave. His acting career began during the halcyon days of TV drama, when he not only honed his acting craft, but learned the limitations of time and budgetary constraints that would serve him well as an independent filmmaker. As an actor, Cassavetes often tried too hard; smoldering intensity was, admittedly, in vogue during the Brando-and-Dean-inspired 1950s, but he frequently overdid it. His early films included *14 Hours* (1951, from which he was cut completely), *Taxi* (1953, his "proper" film debut), *Crime in the Streets* (1956), and *Edge of the City* (1957).

Cassavetes' first directorial attempt, the 16mm feature film *Shadows* (1960), dealt with an interracial relationship, which was heady subject matter for the times. The film was considered a watershed in the birth of American independent cinema. He championed an improvisational approach to filmmaking, often developing his screenplays out of improvised monologues by his actors. *Too Late Blues* (1962) and *A Child Is Waiting* (1963) were essentially mainstream in nature, and showed Cassavetes capable of handling major productions with taste and sensitivity. His acting successes often financed his directorial endeavors; proceeds from his Oscar-nominated performance in *The Dirty Dozen* (1967) and the 1968 smash *Rosemary's Baby* provided much of the budget for *Faces* (1968), a harrowing treatise on the disintegration of a marriage that netted him an Oscar nomination for Best Original Screenplay.

Husbands (1970), *Minnie and Moskowitz* (1971), and *A Woman Under the Influence* (1974, which earned Cassavetes a third Oscar nomination, this time as Best Director) were all modest, gritty little dramas that featured his own stock company, which included wife Gena Rowlands and personal friends Ben Gazzara and Seymour Cassel. He also wrote and directed *The Killing of a Chinese Bookie* (1976), *Opening Night* (1977), *Gloria* (1980), *Love Streams* (1984), and directed *Big Trouble* (1985). He starred in some of his films (*Husbands, Love Streams*) and appeared in several others. As an actor, he also appeared in *Capone* (1975), *Mikey*

and Nicky (1976), *The Fury* (1978, a memorable, hissable heavy), *Incubus, Whose Life Is It Anyway?* (both 1981), *Tempest* (1982), and *Marvin and Tige* (1984).

CASSEL, SEYMOUR. Actor. *(b. Jan. 22, 1935, Detroit.)* As Sam Catchem, loyal sidekick to supercop Dick Tracy, this venerable supporting player had one of his choicest parts in recent memory in Warren Beatty's lavish 1990 comic-strip caper . . . though it wasn't a very prestigious assignment for an actor of Cassel's credentials. Trained at New York City's American Theater Wing and the Actors' Studio, this crusty blond supporting actor appeared in many of buddy John Cassavetes' films, including *Too Late Blues* (1962), *Faces* (1968), which earned him a Best Supporting Actor Oscar nomination, and *Minnie and Moskowitz* (1971), which gave him a bona fide leading role opposite Cassavetes' wife, Gena Rowlands. He also helped produce *Shadows* (1960). In recent years he's been more visible than ever, often in smallish but colorful supporting roles. In 1993 alone he appeared in *Boiling Point, Indecent Proposal* (as Robert Redford's chauffeur), and *Chain of Desire;* 1992's *In the Soup* gave him a costarring part.

OTHER FILMS INCLUDE: 1968: *The Sweet Ride;* 1976: *The Last Tycoon;* 1978: *Convoy;* 1987: *Tin Men;* 1988: *Colors;* 1991: *White Fang;* 1992: *Honeymoon in Vegas.*

CASSIDY, JOANNA. Actress. *(b. Aug. 2, 1944, Camden, N.J.)* Vigorous, raw-boned, red-haired actress whose combination of brains and strength have yet to make her the major star she ought to be, despite critical plaudits as the gutsy reporter in *Under Fire* (1983) and the world-weary barmaid in *Who Framed Roger Rabbit* (1988). Cassidy's other films include *The Stepford Wives* (1975), *The Late Show* (1977), *Stay Hungry* (1976), *Club Paradise* (1986), and *The Package* (1989); she's fondly remembered as the snake-charming stripper in *Blade Runner* (1982). The actress has also been a regular on several TV series, most effectively as Dabney Coleman's long-suffering girlfriend on "Buffalo Bill" (1983–84; ironically, in 1990 she played his wife in

Where the Heart Is). She got one of her best latter-day parts as the wife of American Express honcho James Robinson (played by Fred Dalton Thompson) in *Barbarians at the Gate* (1993 telefilm).

CASTLE, WILLIAM. Producer, director, actor. *(b. Apr. 24, 1914, New York City; d. May 31, 1977.)* Low-budget filmmaker whose promotional artistry generally overshadowed the (limited) merits of the movies themselves. Castle began his show-biz career while in his teens, having conned his way into a Broadway show by lying about his age. He made his way to Hollywood in 1937, landing work as a dialogue director and learning the ropes before making his directorial debut with a Boston Blackie thriller, *The Chance of a Lifetime,* in 1943. He toiled in Columbia's B-movie vineyards for many years, churning out low-budget mysteries in the "Whistler" and "Crime Doctor" series, although he directed a shoestring classic, *When Strangers Marry* (1944, starring Dean Jagger, Kim Hunter and, in his first memorable role, Robert Mitchum), for the King brothers, independent producers releasing through Monogram. In the late 1940s he took up producing as well; he was associate producer on Orson Welles' *The Lady From Shanghai* (1948). Castle directed low- and medium-budgeted Westerns almost exclusively during the early and mid 1950s, and finally turned to the horror film—his true métier—late in the decade.

A great believer in hype, Castle pioneered the use of outrageous gimmickry to sell tickets. For his 1958 film *Macabre,* he took out insurance policies for audience members who might die of fright during the film. For exhibition of *House on Haunted Hill,* a 1958 cult favorite, Castle rigged plastic skeletons in the theaters, which whizzed over viewers' heads at a key point in the action; this was touted to audiences as "Emergo." For *The Tingler* (1959), he went so far as to wire selected seats in theaters with buzzers to literally shock audiences. *13 Ghosts* (1960) went to theaters with optical effects necessitating use of special glasses. *Homicidal, Mr. Sardonicus* (both 1961), *The Old Dark House* (1963), *Strait-Jacket* (1964), *I Saw What You Did* (1965), *The Busy Body* (1967), and *Project X* (1968) were among his later schlock . . . er,

*shock*ers. Castle also participated in more dignified fare, producing *Rosemary's Baby* (1968) and acting in *The Day of the Locust* (1975). Joe Dante's 1993 movie *Matinee* paid homage to Castle in the character of "Lawrence Woolsey," played by John Goodman. Castle published his autobiography, "Step Right Up! I'm Gonna Scare the Pants Off America," in 1976.

CATES, PHOEBE. Actress. *(b. July 16, 1963, New York City.)* Attractive, dark-haired, bright-eyed, and girlish lead who enjoyed teen-model stardom in the 1970s and a middling career in features since the early 1980s. Having made an initial impact in sexy roles in the teen flicks *Fast Times at Ridgemont High* and the *Blue Lagoon* knock-off *Paradise* (both 1982), she later enjoyed success as Zach Galligan's fresh-scrubbed girlfriend in *Gremlins* (1984) and its sequel *Gremlins 2: The New Batch* (1990). Cates, whose other movies include *Bright Lights, Big City, Shag* (both 1988), *Heart of Dixie* (1989), *Drop Dead Fred* (1991), *Bodies, Rest & Motion* (1993), and *My Life's in Turnaround* (1994), is an earnest performer in drama but is much more appealing in lighthearted roles. Her father is producer-director Joseph Cates and her uncle, director Gilbert Cates. She is married to actor Kevin Kline, in whose film *I Love You to Death* (1990) she made an amusing unbilled cameo as one of his one-night stands. She had one of her best roles as the mysterious *Princess Caraboo* (1994).

CATON-JONES, MICHAEL. Director. *(b. Oct. 15, 1957, Broxburn, Scotland.)* After gaining attention at Britain's National Film School for his shorts *Liebe Mutter* and *The Riveter,* Caton-Jones directed projects for BBC-TV and won international acclaim for his feature debut, *Scandal* (1989), a compelling look at Britain's Profumo–Keeler sex scandal of the early 1960s. The film won him attention from Hollywood, and various assignments followed: the cliché-ridden *Memphis Belle* (1990), the pleasant Michael J. Fox vehicle *Doc Hollywood* (1991), the unflinching, powerful adaptation of Tobias Wolff's *This Boy's Life* (1993), starring Robert De

Niro—the director's finest work to date—
and *Rob Roy* (1995).

CATTRALL, KIM. Actress. *(b. Aug. 21,
1956, Liverpool.)* If all gym teachers displayed as much, uh, enthusiasm as the
sexually voracious instructor Cattrall
played in *Porky's* (1981), maybe our nation's youth would be in better shape. Actually, the notoriety she achieved in that
trashy role doesn't do justice to this
charming, offbeat leading lady. Educated
in Canada, London, and New York,
Cattrall first attracted attention as a brainwashed cultist in *Ticket to Heaven* (1981),
which was followed by the *Porky's* breakthrough. She's been poorly utilized since,
often in such frivolous comedies as *Police
Academy* (1984), *Mannequin* (1987), and
Honeymoon Academy (1990), but occasionally gets meatier roles such as the
adulterous wife in *Masquerade* (1988).
She costarred in the 1993 miniseries
"Wild Palms" and the TV series "Angel
Falls" (1993).
OTHER FILMS INCLUDE: 1975: *Rosebud* (her
debut); 1980: *Tribute*; 1985: *Turk 182!*; 1986:
Big Trouble in Little China; 1990: *The Bonfire of
the Vanities*; 1991: *Star Trek VI: The Undis-
covered Country* (as a treacherous Vulcan).

CAZALE, JOHN. Actor. *(b. Aug. 12,
1935, Boston; d. Mar. 12, 1978.)* Slight,
sad-looking character actor whose short
film career included some of the best
American films of the 1970s. After award-
winning work on the stage, Cazale debuted in Francis Ford Coppola's Oscar-
winning *The Godfather* (1972) as Fredo,
the weak-willed son of Don Corleone
(Marlon Brando), a role he reprised in *The
Godfather, Part II* (1974). He also appeared as Gene Hackman's assistant in
The Conversation (1974) and Al Pacino's
crime partner Sal in *Dog Day Afternoon*
(1975). His last film was another Oscar-
winner, *The Deer Hunter* (1978, opposite
his then-fiancée Meryl Streep), which was
released after his death from cancer.

CHABROL, CLAUDE. Director,
screenwriter. *(b. June 24, 1930, Paris.)* One
of the most celebrated of France's New
Wave of directors, Chabrol has maintained a remarkable and sustained body of
work over the years, with penetrating and
often unforgettable studies of murder, obsession, adultery, and the facades of human relationships. He originally studied
pharmacy, but became interested in films
writing for "Cahiers du Cinema" and, in
1957, co-authoring (with Eric Rohmer) an
extensive study of Alfred Hitchcock. Using money inherited by his first wife,
Chabrol funded his feature debut, *Le Beau
Serge* (1958), considered the breakthrough
film of the young New Wave directors.
His style matured with *The Cousins*
(1959), which was succesful enough to let
him form a production company. (The
film also featured Stephane Audran in her
first film role; she would marry Chabrol
in 1964 and appear in almost twenty of
his films.) *Les Bonnes Femmes* (1960), a
brilliant study of four working-class Parisian shopgirls, was not a success with
critics who were put off by the harsh elements of murder and ironic detachment,
which would become hallmarks of
Chabrol's style. (It's now considered a
masterwork of the New Wave.) As Andrew Sarris wrote in 1966, when the film
was finally released in the U.S., "Never
has there been such an uneasy alliance of
realism and romanticism, and yet never
has so much beauty flowed out of so
much baseness."
Les Godelureaux (1960) and *Ophelia*
(1962, a modern variation on "Hamlet")
were also coolly received, and along with
Landru/Bluebeard (1962), the true-life
story of a "Bluebeard" who murdered
women in the 1920s, were box office failures. Unable to fund his own projects,
Chabrol turned to commercial avenues,
directing the slight but stylish *The Tiger
Likes Fresh Blood* (1964) and *An Orchid
for the Tiger* (1965, both with Roger
Hanin as "The Tiger," a security agent in
the James Bond mold), the spy thriller
Marie-Chantal contre le docteur Kha
(1965) and the popular WW2 saga *La
Ligne de demarcation* (1966). He returned
to more serious themes in *Les Biches*
(1968), a complex ménage à trois set in
St. Tropez. *La Femme infidele* (1968),
about a man who murders his wife's lover,
was the first of a series of films that subtly and exquisitely probed the placidity of
marriage and bourgeois respectability.
These included *Le Boucher* (1969), where
a schoolteacher falls for a butcher who is
also a killer; *This Man Must Die* (1970),

with a distraught man methodically seeking the killer of his son; *Just Before Nightfall* (1971), in which a husband kills his mistress and admits his crime—but no one particularly cares; and *Wedding in Blood* (1973), with married Audran and Michel Piccoli having a torrid affair. Such subject matter often earned Chabrol the title of "the French Hitchcock," but his style is more objective and cool, and—despite the savage satire employed—not without compassion and understanding.

Chabrol's subsequent output was mixed, from the odd mystery-thriller *Ten Days Wonder* (1972) to the dour *Une Partie de Plasir (Pleasure Party)*, 1975, starring Chabrol's frequent screenwriter/collaborator Paul GeGauff) to *The Twist* (1976), a dull look at upper-class infidelity. He returned to a real-life murder case in the well received *Violette* (1978, with Isabelle Huppert giving a Cannes Festival Award–winning performance as a woman who poisons her parents), then studied village life in Brittany in *The Proud Ones* (1980). He followed with fine thrillers *Cop au vin* (1984), *Inspector Lavardin* (1986, both featuring Jean Poiret as the wily inspector), and *Masques* (1987). *The Story of Women* (1988), with Huppert as another real-life woman, who performed abortions in Vichy France during World War 2, was Chabrol at his best; *Quiet Days in Clichy* (1990) with Andrew McCarthy was not. Unpredictable as ever, Chabrol made a very cold adaptation of *Madame Bovary* (1991) and then returned to the theme of infidelity with *Betty* (1993). Chabrol also contributed segments to the omnibus films *The Seven Deadly Sins* (1962) and *Six in Paris* (1965, in which he and Audran portrayed battling spouses) and appeared in several of his own films as well as those by fellow countrymen.

CHAN, JACKIE. Actor, writer, producer, director. *(b. Apr. 7, 1954, Hong Kong.)* He's the biggest non-Hollywood movie star in the world. More a kindred spirit to Buster Keaton than Bruce Lee, this broad-nosed, Beatle-haircutted whirligig has been captivating audiences around the world for more than a decade, though he has yet to rise above cult status in America. Chan first worked in the burgeoning kung fu movie industry as a stuntman, becoming a second-unit director before he turned 20.

Initially groomed as a new Bruce Lee, he didn't click with audiences until he started playing for laughs. Chan's most popular films, many of which he also wrote, produced, and directed, include *Project A* (1983 and a 1987 sequel), *Wheels on Wheels* (1984), the Indiana Jones-ish *Armor of God* (1986 and a 1991 sequel), *Police Story* (1987 and a 1989 sequel), *Dragons Forever* (1988), a change-of-pace comedy-drama *Miracles* (1990), and *Twin Dragons* (1992). More recent credits include *Police Story 3—Supercop* (1992) and *Crime Story* (1993). His first attempts to crack Hollywood resulted in the less than exciting *The Big Brawl* (1980), *Cannonball Run* (1981 and a 1984 sequel), and *The Protector* (1985).

CHANDLER, JEFF. Actor. *(b. Dec. 15, 1918, Brooklyn, N.Y., as Ira Grossel; d. June 17, 1961.)* Rugged, virile leading man of Westerns, action dramas, and occasional soap operas of the 1950s, easily identifiable by his silvery hair, dimpled chin, muscular physique, and distinctive voice. A successful radio actor under his real name (who costarred with Eve Arden in "Our Miss Brooks"), Chandler made his screen debut in *Johnny O'Clock* (1947), in a supporting role, then got the star buildup (and a new name) while under contract to Universal. He was surprisingly effective in *Broken Arrow* (1950) as Indian chief Cochise (even earning an Oscar nomination for his performance), a role he played again in *The Battle at Apache Pass* (1952) and, briefly, in *Taza, Son of Cochise* (1954). Chandler died, tragically, of blood poisoning sustained during back surgery.
OTHER FILMS INCLUDE: 1949: *Abandoned, Sword in the Desert;* 1950: *Two Flags West;* 1951: *Flame of Araby, The Iron Man, Smuggler's Island;* 1952: *Because of You, Red Ball Express, Yankee Buccaneer;* 1953: *East of Sumatra, The Great Sioux Uprising;* 1954: *Sign of the Pagan, Yankee Pasha;* 1955: *Female on the Beach, Foxfire* (for which he sang the title song), *The Spoilers;* 1956: *Away All Boats, Toy Tiger;* 1957: *Jeanne Eagels, The Lady Takes a Flyer, The Tattered Dress;* 1958: *Raw Wind in Eden;* 1959: *The Jayhawkers, Thunder in the Sun;* 1960: *The Plunderers;* 1961: *Return to Peyton Place;* 1962: *Merrill's Marauders* (his last).

CHANEY, LON. Actor. *(b. Apr. 1, 1883, Colorado Springs, as Alonzo Chaney; d. Aug. 26, 1930.)* The movies' "Man of a Thousand Faces" is still a legendary figure, and although the relatively recent rediscovery of many of his starring films—previously thought lost—has somewhat deflated his reputation, there's no denying that he was one of the foremost talents of the silent screen. Born to deaf-mute parents, he honed his ability to communicate via pantomime at an early age. Eager to escape the obvious limitations of his home life, the young Chaney worked at the local opera house, painting flats, collecting props, and learning how to apply makeup. He left home at 17 to tour as an actor, traveling across the country before settling in Hollywood in 1912 to begin his film career. (His first film appearance is credited to 1913's *Poor Jake's Demise,* although he may have worked as an extra before that.)

Chaney's features—craggy and severe—disqualified him from romantic leads, but he quickly became a versatile supporting player. He became proficient in creating elaborate makeups and prosthetic devices, and frequently withstood pain or discomfort to create an illusion. One such characterization, that of a phony cripple in *The Miracle Man* (1919), won him special notice. The following year, he played a legless master criminal in *The Penalty* (1920), the first of many starring vehicles tailored to his peculiar talents. He fashioned a 20-pound harness to simulate a hump for his role as Quasimodo, *The Hunchback of Notre Dame* (1923). Chaney's genius lay not only in the creation of such bizarre and grotesque disguises, but his ability to project his emotions through the heaviest makeups. His Quasimodo is one such example of that ability, and *Hunchback* became his biggest hit to date. For the same studio, Universal, he starred as *The Phantom of the Opera* (1925), designing an even more horrific countenance to shock movie audiences that came to this lavishly produced thriller about the ghost of the Paris Opera House. *Phantom,* which many contemporary critics thought too repugnant for 1920s moviegoers, went on to become Chaney's most popular film (and the most frequently revived).

For many years, Chaney's reputation depended to a great extent upon his work for director Tod Browning at MGM. Based upon Browning's surviving horror films, including *Dracula* (1931) and *Mark of the Vampire* (1935), the silent Chaney vehicles he directed were presumed to have the same value. As these films resurfaced, one by one, in the late 1960s and 1970s, they were reevaluated and, in many cases, found lacking. While some of them—*He Who Gets Slapped* (1924), *The Road to Mandalay* (1926), *Mr. Wu* (1927), and *West of Zanzibar* (1928)—did indeed feature Chaney in impressive makeups, they proved to be rather conventional melodramas. On the plus side, rediscovered MGMs such as *Tell It to the Marines* (1926) and *While the City Sleeps* (1928), which offered the star "straight" roles, showed him to possess considerable personality and charm not readily apparent in his "character" parts.

Chaney, initially fearful of sound films, made his first talkie, *The Unholy Three* (a remake of his 1925 hit) in 1930. It was an overnight success, and Tod Browning immediately announced that Chaney would play the title role in his upcoming production of *Dracula*. But the Man of a Thousand Faces died of throat cancer just one month later. His son Creighton had a long film career, billed for most of it as Lon Chaney, Jr.

OTHER FILMS INCLUDE: 1919: *False Faces, Victory;* 1920: *Treasure Island* (as Blind Pew); 1922: *Shadows, Oliver Twist* (in the latter as Fagin); 1923: *All the Brothers Were Valiant;* 1925: *The Monster;* 1926: *The Black Bird;* 1927: *The Unknown, Mockery;* 1928: *The Big City, Laugh, Clown, Laugh;* 1929: *Where East Is East.*

CHANEY, LON, JR. Actor. *(b. Feb. 10, 1906, Oklahoma City, as Creighton Chaney; d. July 12, 1973.)* Proving that the apple doesn't fall far from the tree, Chaney, Jr., thrilled and chilled moviegoers with his portrayals of famous movie monsters, but never achieved his father's status in the film industry. He always harbored a desire to emulate his dad, and finally entered films in 1932, starring in a lackluster serial titled *The Last Frontier* and also playing bits and second leads, billed as Creighton Chaney. He became "Lon Jr." in 1936, hoping the name change would boost his career. Fairly trim and handsome in his youth, Chaney gained weight rapidly in the late 1930s; his bulky physique and fleshy face disqualified him from consideration for romantic leads. As a 20th Century-Fox contractee, he had walk-ons and small roles in *Charlie Chan on Broadway* (1937), *Alexander's Ragtime Band* (1938), and *Jesse James* (1939), to name a few. On the strength of his powerful performance as the half-witted Lenny in *Of Mice and Men* (1939, an unusual A-movie assignment for the actor), however, Universal signed Chaney with the intention of making him a horror-movie star. He achieved special billing as tortured lycanthrope Larry Talbot in *The Wolf Man* (1941), reprising the role in several subsequent films (including 1948's *Abbott and Costello Meet Frankenstein*). Chaney also starred in *The Ghost of Frankenstein, The Mummy's Tomb* (both 1942), *Son of Dracula* (1943), *The Mummy's Ghost* (1944), and *The Mummy's Curse* (1945), and in Universal's "Inner Sanctum" series of the mid 1940s. When the studio's horror-film cycle died out, so did his starring career; by decade's end he was playing character roles. His last worthwhile part was as the retired sheriff in *High Noon* (1952). From the late 1950s on, beset with personal problems and in failing health, he accepted parts in a succession of cheap, shoddy films, ending his career in *Dracula vs. Frankenstein* (1971).

CHANNING, STOCKARD. Actress. *(b. Feb. 13, 1944, New York City.)* Intense actress whose offbeat looks and formidable range made her a real casting challenge. She first gained notice as the chameleonlike murderer in a 1973 TV movie, *The Girl Most Likely To . . . ,* and followed that highly praised performance with such diverse big-screen characters as the daffy heiress in *The Fortune* (1975), the lucky hostess on *The Big Bus,* the crafty car thief in *Dandy, the All-American Girl* (both 1976), and the astrologist in *The Fish That Saved Pittsburgh* (1980)—none of them exactly box-office champs. (She did have supporting roles in two 1978 hits, *The Cheap Detective* and *Grease.*) After two valiant but failed attempts at sitcoms, she moved on to Broadway and achieved genuine stardom there, winning a Tony award. She played a Brazilian rain-forest insect (!) in *Meet the Applegates* (1991), and was Oscar-nominated for re-creating her Broadway role in *Six Degrees of Separation* (1993). OTHER FILMS INCLUDE: 1983: *Without a Trace;* 1986: *Heartburn;* 1993: *Married to It;* 1995: *Smoke.*

CHAPLIN, CHARLES (SIR). Actor, director, producer, screenwriter, composer. *(b. Apr. 16, 1889, London; d. Dec. 25, 1977.)* He has been called the single most influential artist in the history of motion pictures; certainly no other movie star enjoyed the international, iconographic status he attained early in the silent era and maintained well past the coming of sound. And certainly no other creative talent did as much as he to elevate screen comedy to a high art. Perhaps most significant, though, is the fact that he helped make the motion picture a medium of emotional expression, taking it forever out of the category of a mere flickering novelty.

Charles Spencer Chaplin was born to British music-hall entertainers who had skirted around the edges of prosperity without ever achieving it. His parents separated when he was only a year old, and he stayed with his mother, whose stage career dissipated as he got older. Chaplin's father died a hopeless alcoholic, and his mother's increasingly fragile health and tenuous mental state forced him and older half-brother Sydney to work for their suppers. Already steeped in show-business traditions, he did some childhood hoofing and occasionally acted on the legitimate stage. At the age of 17 he joined the music hall troupe of impresario Fred Karno, with whom he honed his pantomimic skills.

While touring with Karno in America in 1912, Chaplin—whose comic drunk was the highlight of the troupe's show—was seen by Mack Sennett, the godfather of movie comedy, who hired him away to appear in moving pictures. He debuted on screen in *Making a Living* (1914), all but unrecognizable in top hat, frock coat, and mustache. *Kid Auto Races at Venice* (also 1914) saw him wearing a derby hat and droopy trousers, and brandishing a cane; it was the first appearance of what would come to be known as "the Little Tramp," a character Chaplin continued to refine in his short-subject appearances during a year-long tenure with Sennett's Keystone company.

He began directing with his 13th film,

Caught in the Rain (also 1914), and gradually moved away from the simple slapstick frenetics of the Keystones. Already a familiar face to moviegoers, and an increasingly valuable property to Sennett, Chaplin felt he was worth more than the $175 a week he was getting paid, and in 1915 signed with Essanay (another pioneering film company) for $1,250 a week with bonuses. He maintained complete creative control over his short subjects, and during the Essanay period evolved the Tramp character further, adding the little subtleties and the touch of pathos for which he became famous worldwide. The Tramp was truly an Everyman for international audiences, all of whom could easily identify with the downtrodden little fellow whose eternal optimism in the face of adversity inspired them all. It was *The Tramp* (1915) that gave audiences their first glimpse of a Chaplin trademark: the final shot of the little fellow, alone, shuffling away from the camera down a long, barren stretch of road.

In 1916 Chaplin moved operations to Mutual. By now he commanded a weekly salary of $10,000 (with bonuses adding up to $150,000), enjoyed creative autonomy, and was given a month to produce each of his two-reel comedies—in an era when most were cranked out in a few days. With his characterization set, he applied himself to crafting his films with painstaking precision, often improvising and rehearsing for days to get a sequence that might last only a minute or less. His skill at pantomime and his athletic flair for expressive physical comedy manifested themselves in set pieces that were choreographed like dance routines with splitsecond timing. *Easy Street, The Rink, The Cure,* and *The Immigrant* are just a few of the brilliant comedies Chaplin made during his stay at Mutual in 1916–17.

First National beckoned him with a million-dollar contract in 1918, demanding only a minimal output (initially eight two-reelers per year) but anticipating the same huge worldwide profits that had come to be expected of his films. *A Dog's Life, Shoulder Arms* (both 1918), and *The Kid* (1921, his first feature film) are among his best efforts for First National. As well compensated as he was, though, Chaplin longed for the total freedom and security of his own company. In 1919 he cofounded, along with Douglas Fairbanks,

Mary Pickford, and D. W. Griffith, the United Artists Corporation, through which the four cinematic giants would release their subsequent product. When Chaplin's contract with First National ran out, he made films exclusively for UA distribution, never again returning to the shackles of a studio contract.

He directed his first United Artists release, the sophisticated *A Woman of Paris* (1923), which starred his former leading lady Edna Purviance and Adolphe Menjou; Chaplin himself took only a brief cameo. The film flopped badly, and a chastened Chaplin returned to the security of his Little Tramp for *The Gold Rush* (1925), one of his enduring masterpieces, still an often-revived favorite from the silent era. It exuded the great attention to detail, both in setting and performance, that would become a Chaplin hallmark even as it reduced his output. Fully three years elapsed between it and *The Circus* (1928), another fine comedy, for which he was awarded a special Oscar at the first Academy Awards ceremony in 1928.

Chaplin had by this time already been the recipient of unwanted controversy. Although he campaigned vigorously for the sale of U.S. War Bonds during World War 1, he was castigated for not returning to his homeland to join the Armed Forces (actually, a medical problem kept him out of uniform). His penchant for younger women found him marrying two 16-year-olds, Mildred Harris (an actress from whom he was divorced after two years) and Lita Grey (who bore him two sons and won a million-dollar divorce settlement after three years), a 19-year-old starlet, Paulette Goddard (from whom he was divorced in 1942), and finally, 18-year-old Oona O'Neill (the daughter of playwright Eugene O'Neill). All these liaisons generated reams of unwelcome publicity.

In 1928, the talking-picture revolution threw the entire movie industry into turmoil, but Chaplin dealt with sound in his own unique way: He simply ignored it. He reckoned, correctly, that sound would ruin the simple appeal of his Tramp character, and hurl the pathetic little figure into a world more real (and certainly more coarse) than the stylized fantasy milieu he then inhabited. *City Lights* (1931), his next and arguably greatest picture, made certain concessions: It sported a fully orchestrated musical score—composed, for the most part, by Chaplin himself—and used sound effects sparingly, and to clever effect. The story itself concerned the Tramp's efforts to help the blind girl he loved hopelessly, and the final scene—in which, having had her sight restored through his efforts, the girl first sees that her benefactor is a shabby little wretch—still brings sobs to the throats of audiences with its exquisite poignancy.

Modern Times (1936) saw Chaplin flouting convention yet again by delivering to moviegoers another silent film. Another masterwork, it costarred Paulette Goddard, the former chorus girl whom he married in 1933. A brilliant commentary on the insanity of a rapid-paced, highly industrialized (and, in Chaplin's view, dehumanized) society, it delighted audiences with richly orchestrated comic set pieces. Unfortunately, its apparent anticapitalist overtones would come back to haunt the filmmaker years later.

The Great Dictator (1940) earned Chaplin several Oscar nominations—for his acting, the script, and Best Picture—and saw him tackle dialogue for the first time. It offered a relentlessly ridiculous caricature of Hitler and Nazism, and gave movie fans their last look at the Little Tramp, incarnated for this picture only as a Jewish barber whose resemblance to a fascist dictator gets him into trouble.

Chaplin was off the screen for seven years, during which time the motion picture matured to the point where his next contribution didn't seem nearly as important as his previous efforts. *Monsieur Verdoux* (1947), a bitter, cynical black comedy, cast him as a murderous Bluebeard, a characterization not appreciated by film fans of the day. (It did, however, get nominated for a Best Screenplay Oscar.) The story's pacifist leanings ran him afoul of political conservatives in America, then marshaling their forces for the Cold War against Communism. They pointed to *Verdoux*, and also to *Modern Times* and its implied distaste for capitalism, and set Chaplin up to be knocked down by the House Un-American Activities Committee, which suspected him of being a Communist. He denied the charges while testifying before the committee, but public outcry for his deportation continued.

Chaplin, for all his years in America, never bothered to become a citizen, and when he went to London in 1952 with fourth wife Oona, he was informed that he would not get a reentry visa to America. Ironically, he was on his way to the British premiere of *Limelight,* his nostalgic tale of a once-great music-hall performer fallen on hard times. Although the film had several wonderful sequences—including one that teamed him with another legendary film comic, Buster Keaton—it impressed many as overlong and indulgent. With the U.S., his most important market, sour on him, Chaplin found himself the producer of another flop. (Because it was never "officially" released in Los Angeles in 1952, *Limelight* was eligible for an Academy Award twenty years later, and in fact won one, for Best Score, in 1972!)

A profoundly bitter Chaplin resolved never to return to America. He settled in Switzerland with Oona and their children (one of whom, Geraldine, became an actress in film), lampooning with considerable bitterness American manners and mores in *A King in New York* (1957, unreleased in the U.S. until 1976), and gamely attempting a directorial comeback with *A Countess From Hong Kong* (1967), a totally anachronistic, poorly realized romantic comedy starring Marlon Brando and Sophia Loren.

In 1972 Chaplin consented to return to America for the Academy Awards ceremony, where he was presented a special Oscar for career achievement to a tumultuous ovation from the assembled crowd of Hollywood dignitaries. He was similarly feted later at New York's Philharmonic Hall, and was knighted by the Queen in 1975. His "My Autobiography" was published in 1964. A biographical film, *Chaplin,* was released in 1992.

CHAPLIN, GERALDINE. Actress. *(b. July 31, 1944, Santa Monica, Calif.)* Thin, delicate-featured actress, the daughter of film legend Charlie Chaplin and granddaughter of playwright Eugene O'Neill, who made her movie debut as a street urchin in her father's *Limelight* (1952). The sensitive, fragile Chaplin made her first major "adult" appearance in David Lean's epic *Doctor Zhivago* (1965) and, not thinking of herself as a leading-lady type, subsequently specialized in colorful and sometimes eccentric character roles. She has been featured in *The Hawaiians*

(1970), *The Four Musketeers* (1975, as Anne of Austria), *Roseland* (1977), and *White Mischief* (1987), but is probably best known for her work in the Robert Altman films *Nashville* (1975, as the annoying BBC reporter), *Buffalo Bill and the Indians* (1976, as Annie Oakley), and *A Wedding* (1978), as well as the films of Altman protégé Alan Rudolph, *Welcome to L.A.* (1977), *Remember My Name* (1978), and *The Moderns* (1987). In 1992 she was cast, somewhat eerily, as her own grandmother in *Chaplin,* and gave an affecting performance as Charlie's mother, whose life was cursed by madness. In 1993 she appeared in *The Age of Innocence* and *A Foreign Field.*

CHAPMAN, MICHAEL. Cinematographer, director. *(b. Nov. 21, 1935, Boston.)* One of America's top cinematographers, Chapman began his career as a camera operator for the great Gordon Willis on films like *Loving* (1970), *Klute* (1971), *The Godfather,* and *Bad Company* (both 1972). He graduated to cinematographer on a number of impressive projects including *The Last Detail* (1973), *Taxi Driver, The Front* (both 1976), *Personal Best* (1982), *Shoot to Kill* (1988), *Ghostbusters II* (1989), *The Fugitive* (1993, Oscar-nominated), and the Philip Kaufman films *The White Dawn* (1974), *Invasion of the Body Snatchers* (1978), *The Wanderers* (1979), and *Rising Sun* (1993). His most unusual achievement may be the black-and-white photography he delivered for *Dead Men Don't Wear Plaid* (1982), which had to match the look of various old movies that were spliced into new footage with Steve Martin. His finest work, arguably, was Martin Scorsese's *Raging Bull* (1980), which earned Chapman an Oscar nomination. Chapman also directed the Tom Cruise vehicle *All the Right Moves* (1983) and the ill-received *The Clan of the Cave Bear* (1986). He has appeared in some of the films he's photographed, including *The Last Detail* and *Doc Hollywood* (1991).

CHARISSE, CYD. Actress, dancer. *(b. Mar. 8, 1922, Amarillo, Tex., as Tula Ellice Finklea.)* The gorgeous gal with the legs that just go on forever, musical star Charisse owes much of her fame to those glamorous gams. A ballet prodigy from childhood, she was featured in the Ballet Russe at age 13. She married her dance teacher, Nico Charisse, when she was just 18, and made her film debut with him in a handful of "Soundies" musical shorts in 1941. She was billed as Lily Norwood for her feature debut in *Something to Shout About* (1943), and subsequently played a few bit roles under that name. Signed by MGM in 1946 and renamed Cyd Charisse, she was carefully spotted in that studio's prestigious musicals, where the producers saw to it that she made the maximum impact in the minimal amount of screen time, in *The Harvey Girls, Ziegfeld Follies, Three Wise Fools, Till the Clouds Roll By* (all 1946), *Fiesta, The Unfinished Dance* (both 1947), *Words and Music* (1948), *The Kissing Bandit* (1949), and others—always in support. Her striking appearance opposite Gene Kelly in the sensational "Broadway Ballet" of *Singin' in the Rain* (1952) was the turning point in her career. The following year, she costarred with Fred Astaire in *The Band Wagon* (1953), and their dance numbers together were, for lack of a better word, heavenly. She also had memorable dance numbers in the otherwise unseen *Sombrero* (1953) and *Deep in My Heart* (1954).

The mid 1950s saw MGM's musical cycle just about played out, but Charisse rode out the last wave in *Brigadoon* (1954), *It's Always Fair Weather* (1955), *Invitation to the Dance* (1957), and *Silk Stockings* (1957), the musical remake of Garbo's *Ninotchka* that reteamed her with Astaire. She'd become a passably good actress by now, but without dance numbers (and costumes) she was just another Hollywood beauty. Dramatic turns in *Twilight of the Gods* and *Party Girl* (both 1958) were followed by appearances in foreign-made productions the likes of *Five Golden Hours* (1961), *Two Weeks in Another Town* (1962), *Assassination in Rome* (1963), *Maroc 7* (1967), and *Warlords of Atlantis* (1978). She did get to costar in a British-made ballet feature, *Black Tights* (1960), and performed an elegant striptease in the campy spy thriller *The Silencers* (1966), but has since worked sporadically in Hollywood, mostly in TV, often accompanied by her second husband, singer-actor Tony Martin. Their joint autobiography, "The Two of Us," was published in 1976. In 1992 she made her Broadway debut in the musical "Grand Hotel," and released an exercise video.

CHASE, CHARLEY. Actor, director. *(b. Oct. 20, 1893, Baltimore, as Charles Parrott; d. June 20, 1940.)* One of movie comedy's unsung heroes, Charley (not Charlie) Chase was a great talent, and a popular star whose work has yet to be fully appreciated. He got his start, like so many others, with Mack Sennett, in the early teens, and can be seen in such early Charlie Chaplin films as *The Knockouts, The Masquerader,* and *Dough and Dynamite* (all 1914); he also had a minor role in the early Sennett feature *Tillie's Punctured Romance* (1914). Within a year he was also working behind the camera, at first as codirector with Roscoe "Fatty" Arbuckle and Ford Sterling, then working solo with such stars as Wallace Beery and Gloria Swanson. Chase moved on from Sennett to direct comedies at a variety of other studios in the late teens and early 1920s.

In 1921 he was signed by producer Hal Roach, who also hired his brother James. James worked briefly on camera, billed as Jimmy—then Paul—Parrott, but found greater success behind the scenes (later directing Laurel and Hardy and Our Gang). Charley, on the other hand, was hired to direct such stars as Snub Pollard, but wound up in front of the camera instead. By the mid 1920s, working in collaboration with director Leo McCarey, he was headlining the most consistently clever series of two-reel comedies of their time. Among the titles: *Crazy Like a Fox, Bad Boy, His Wooden Wedding, Mighty Like a Moose, Dog Shy.*

Chase survived the transition to talkies, and now had the chance to sing in his films, as well. In 1929 he starred—and sang—in a 1929 Universal feature, *Modern Love.* Charley alternated between playing a young man-about-town (as in his best talkie short, 1931's *The Pip From Pittsburgh,* with Thelma Todd) and domestic comedies in which he was often a henpecked husband. His costarring stint in Laurel and Hardy's feature *Sons of the Desert* (1933) proved that he could play a different kind of role just as well: that of an obnoxious lout. But when Hal Roach tried to phase out short subjects, Chase's test feature *Bank Night* wasn't well received, and was cut back to two reels for release as *Neighborhood House* in 1936; his supporting part in Patsy Kelly's *Kelly the Second* (1936) could have led to a new career in character parts, but that too did not come to pass. So Chase wound up at Columbia Pictures, starring in yet another series of funny two-reelers, and directing such other comedy stars as Andy Clyde and The Three Stooges. One of his best starring comedies, *The Heckler* (1940), was also one of his last. Charley Chase drank himself to an early grave, but is still celebrated by comedy buffs around the world, and leaves behind an enormous volume of work waiting to be rediscovered.

CHASE, CHEVY. Actor. *(b. Oct. 8, 1944, New York City.)* "Good evening, I'm Chevy Chase and you're not." With those words, a star was born in 1975. Originally hired by "Saturday Night Live" as a writer, he ended up on camera in the weekly news segment, "Weekend Update," and became the show's first breakout star, winning Emmy awards for his acting and writing. After a season and a half, he heeded the siren call of Hollywood and after nearly two years, starred opposite Goldie Hawn in 1978's *Foul Play.* (He'd already appeared on theater screens in 1974's skit-comedy patchwork *The Groove Tube* and 1976's *Tunnelvision,* but without achieving any recognition.) *Foul Play*'s success led to *Caddyshack* (1980), another hit, but then came an extraordinary run of turkeys: *Oh, Heavenly Dog!, Seems Like Old Times* (both 1980), *Modern Problems, Under the Rainbow* (both 1981), and *Deal of the Century* (1983). Chase's breezy comic style and expressive face, it developed, might save a poorly written TV skit, but not a full-length feature.

Ironically, for someone who rose to fame as a smart-ass, it was as a bumbling middle-class father that he scored his biggest movie hit: *National Lampoon's Vacation* (1983), which so far has spawned two vacation sequels: *European* (1985) and *Christmas* (1989). Next came *Fletch* (1985), generally considered his best film to date, in which his wisecracking persona perfectly defined Gregory MacDonald's reporter-cum-detective; it too led to a sequel, *Fletch Lives* (1989). But so many of his subsequent films, often teaming him with other SNL alumni, have been less than hilarious—*Spies Like Us* (1985), *¡Three Amigos!* (1986), *Caddyshack II, Funny Farm* (both 1988), *Nothing but Trouble* (1991), and *Memoirs of an Invisible Man* (1991)—it's baffling that someone who began as such a brilliantly funny writer could be such a poor judge of scripts. In 1993 he launched a (disastrous) nightly TV talk show, made a cameo appearance in *Last Action Hero,* and then starred in *Cops and Robbersons* (1994).

CHATTERTON, RUTH. Actress. *(b. Dec. 24, 1893, New York City; d. Nov. 24, 1961.)* She had the role of a lifetime in Fran Dodsworth, the snobbish, self-absorbed wife of retired industrialist Walter Huston in the film adaptation of Sinclair Lewis's *Dodsworth* (1936), and she did it proud. Amazingly, though, it was her final role in Hollywood. This intelligent, cultured-sounding actress, the daughter of a well-known New York architect, was the toast of Broadway at age 20, thanks to her star turn in "Daddy Long Legs." She came to movies at the dawn of the talkie era, first impressing audiences in a series of overwrought but entertaining soap operas including *Sins of the Fathers* (1928), *Charming Sinners* (1929), Madame X (also 1929, which earned her an Oscar nomination), *Anybody's Woman, Sarah and Son* (both 1930, the latter garnering her another Academy Award nomination), *Unfaithful,* and *The Magnificent Lie* (both 1931). She often essayed the fallen woman, but a natural aggressiveness shone through her performances, and she wasn't always sympathetic. (In real life, Chatterton was no shrinking violet, either; in addition to her other talents she was an accomplished aviatrix.)

Chatterton moved to Warner Bros. in 1932 and enjoyed more robust fare, including *The Crash* (1932, the first of three films in which she starred opposite then-husband George Brent), *Female* (a particularly fervent role-reversal vehicle about a female business tycoon), *Lilly Turner,* and *Frisco Jenny* (all 1933). *Lady of Secrets* (1936), a Columbia-made throwback to her earlier vehicles, fizzled at the box office. Sensing that there was no imminent encore to the triumph of *Dodsworth* (and perhaps unwilling to play in support), she

left Hollywood for England in 1936, where she later made two films, 1938's *The Rat* and *A Royal Divorce,* before retiring from the screen altogether; she continued to work on the stage. Chatterton was also an accomplished authoress, having penned a successful play, "Monsieur Brotonneau," in 1930, and several novels in the 1950s.

CHAYEFSKY, PADDY. Screenwriter. *(b. Jan. 29, 1923, Bronx, N.Y.; d. Aug. 1, 1981.)* One of Hollywood's most respected and celebrated authors, Chayefsky began his literary career as a playwright, concentrating on small, intimate stories of the kind he may have actually experienced as an apprentice in his uncle's print shop. He eventually made a name for himself writing radio and teleplays, one of which became 1955's *Marty,* a touching tale of a homely butcher and lonely schoolteacher that won Chayefsky his first Oscar. (His first credit was 1951's *As Young As You Feel,* which was adapted from his story.) Dividing his work between Hollywood and Broadway over the next two decades, Chayefsky penned a series of acerbic works that were often heavy on social commentary, like *The Bachelor Party* (1957), the Marilyn Monroe-inspired *The Goddess* (1958), *The Hospital* (1971), which won him his second Oscar, and *Network* (1976), which brought in a third. He also adapted such films as *The Americanization of Emily* (1964) and *Paint Your Wagon* (1969). Chayefsky's last film was the Ken Russell extravaganza *Altered States* (1980). The director's decision to have the actors deliver Chayefsky's dialogue in breathless, rapid-fire manner so infuriated the author that he had his name withdrawn from the credits.

CHAYKIN, MAURY. Actor. *(b. July 27, 1949.)* You could wrack your brain for hours trying to put a name to this character actor's pudgy face, so we'll help you out: He played the nutty, suicidal Major Fambrough, the Union officer who wanted to know why Kevin Costner wanted an assignment on the frontier in *Dances With Wolves* (1990). This corpulent supporting player also had a small but memorable role as the psychotic father who imprisoned a young salesman as a birthday gift

to his teenage daughter in *Cold Comfort* (1988), a Canadian suspense thriller.
OTHER FILMS INCLUDE: 1983: *War-Games;* 1984: *Harry and Son, The Vindicator, Def-Con 4;* 1987: *Wild Thing;* 1988: *Iron Eagle II;* 1989: *Breaking In;* 1990: *Where the Heart Is, Mr. Destiny;* 1992: *Leaving Normal, Hero;* 1993: *Sommersby, Josh and S.A.M., Money for Nothing;* 1994: *Whale Music.*

CHEECH AND CHONG. Actors, writers, directors. *(Richard "Cheech" Marin*—b. July 13, 1946, Los Angeles. *Thomas Chong*—b. May 24, 1938, Edmonton, Alberta.) Once-popular comedy team, a casualty of the "just say no" era, who dabbled in films, almost always playing perpetually stoned hippies. The two first teamed in Vancouver, where they honed their comedic personas in improvisational theater. In the early 1970s, they released a series of comedy albums that found much favor with surreptitious members of the drug counterculture. *Up in Smoke* (1978), which brought them to the silver screen, became one of the highest (sic) grossing films of that year. Several quasi-sequels followed: *Cheech & Chong's Next Movie* (1980), *Cheech & Chong's Nice Dreams* (1981), *Cheech & Chong's Still Smokin'* (1983), *Cheech & Chong's The Corsican Brothers* (1984). They also appeared in *It Came From Hollywood* (1982), *Yellowbeard* (1983), and *After Hours* (1985). The two broke up the act in 1985, with Chong keeping a low profile, starring in and directing *Far Out Man* (1990) and Marin moving on to write and direct *Born in East L.A.* (1987), in which he starred as well. He has also appeared in *Ghostbusters II, Rude Awakening* (a C&C-type throwback), *Troop Beverly Hills* (all 1989), and *The Shrimp on the Barbie* (1990). Marin has also appeared on the TV series "Golden Palace" (1992–93). Chong is the father of actress Rae Dawn Chong.

CHER. Actress, singer. *(b. May 20, 1946, El Centro, Calif., as Cherilyn Sarkisian La Piere.)* Her Top 40 hits and TV series with then-husband Sonny Bono in the 1960s and 1970s made Cher a pop culture icon before she ever hit the silver screen. Her struggle to be taken seriously as an actress while not sacrificing any of the campy

flamboyance she displayed in her singing career has provided consistent fodder for the entertainment media. She first surprised doubters with a credible turn in a "small" picture, Robert Altman's *Come Back to the 5 and Dime, Jimmy Dean, Jimmy Dean* (1982). She had appeared in three films before that, including the William Friedkin-directed *Good Times* (1967, with Sonny). She was nominated for a Best Supporting Actress Academy Award for a strong performance as title character Meryl Streep's unglamorous, hardheaded lesbian roommate in *Silkwood* (1983), her first prestige production. Cher's clashes with director Peter Bogdanovich on the set of her next picture, the I-was-a-teenage-Elephant-Man tearjerker *Mask* (1985, which earned her a shared Best Actress award at Cannes), along with her general outspokenness, penchant for tattoos, and exhibitionistic fashion sense ignited a media myth she appeared to resent even as she stoked its fires.

The Oscar that she coveted did not elude her for long; she won the 1987 Best Actress Academy Award for her performance in *Moonstruck,* a romantic comedy centering around some eccentric Brooklyn Italians. She was also featured with two other major female stars, Susan Sarandon and Michelle Pfeiffer, in 1987's desultory *The Witches of Eastwick;* after taking time from films to pick up the slack of her increasingly irrelevant but still fairly lucrative singing career, she made *Mermaids* (1990), during the shooting of which her displeasure with original director Frank Oz led to his being replaced by Richard Benjamin. Cher was inactive on screen for several years, focusing instead on hugely successful exercise videos and infomercials. After cameos (as herself) in the Robert Altman films *The Player* (1992) and *Ready to Wear/Prêt-à-Porter* (1994), she returned as a hit man's target in *Faithful* (1995).

CHEVALIER, MAURICE. Actor, singer. *(b. Sept. 12, 1888, Paris; d. Jan. 1, 1972.)* The epitome of French charm and sophistication, this legendary performer—instantly recognizable by his dancing eyes, slick hair, and thick lower lip—had the good fortune to be in America at the dawn of the talkie age, and helped revolutionize movie musicals by freeing them from the constraints of corny backstage plots and settings. Chevalier, an acrobat who turned to singing after being sidelined in a severe accident, made several short films in France (beginning with 1908's *Trop credule*). He served in the French army during World War 1, was wounded, captured, and imprisoned by the Germans. (He learned English from a fellow prisoner.) After the war, he returned to entertaining and became the toast of Parisian music halls. Chevalier came to America in 1928, and after making a short subject *(Bonjour New York!)* on the East Coast he went to Hollywood. He worked for Paramount, which designed airy, sophisticated (and often naughty) vehicles that would emphasize his continental charm. *The Love Parade* (1929) teamed him with debuting Jeanette MacDonald in a suave musical directed by Ernst Lubitsch; Chevalier was Oscar-nominated for his performance. (He also starred in the foreign-language version of this and several subsequent films as well.) He sang a couple of songs in the all-star revue *Paramount on Parade* (1930), and went to the company's Astoria, Long Island, studio that same year to make *The Big Pond*, which earned him another Oscar nomination.

Chevalier's insouciant manner and blithe delivery of juicy dialogue (often of the double entendre variety) endeared him to sophisticated audiences, although theaters in rural areas eventually rebelled against the Lubitsch–Chevalier type of picture, complaining that they were too continental for their audiences. *The Smiling Lieutenant* (1931) and *One Hour With You* (1932) were both delightful, but Chevalier's collaboration with director Rouben Mamoulian, 1932's *Love Me Tonight,* was even more effective. Supported by Jeanette MacDonald and Myrna Loy, blessed with some of the best songs written by Rodgers and Hart, Chevalier delivered one of his finest performances as a tailor mistaken for royalty. It was the high point of his screen career and, in fact, marked a turning point for the singer. His later vehicles, including *A Bedtime Story, The Way to Love* (both 1933), *The Merry Widow* (1934), and *Folies Bergère* (1935) all had their points, but didn't reach, much less surpass, the plateau reached by *Love Me Tonight*. Then, too, the Production Code had defanged the kind of tart scripts

he'd been given, and American musicals had become more sophisticated.

Returning to Europe, Chevalier starred or costarred in several English and French films during the late 1930s, including *The Beloved Vagabond* (1936), *Man of the Hour* (1937), and *Break the News* (1938, with another veteran song-and-dance man, Jack Buchanan). World War 2 interrupted Chevalier's film career, and he was accused—but later vindicated—of being a Nazi collaborator. He went to Hollywood in the mid 1950s just in time for the waning years of the American movie musical's golden age. Now gray-haired and jowly, but still a twinkly-eyed rake, he appeared in *Love in the Afternoon* (1957, wittily cast by Billy Wilder as a dour private eye), *Gigi* (1958, which gave him several new signature songs, "I Remember It Well" and "Thank Heaven for Little Girls"), *Count Your Blessings* (1959), *Can-Can* (1960), *Fanny* (1961), *In Search of the Castaways* (1962), *I'd Rather Be Rich* (1964), *Monkeys, Go Home!* (1967), and *The Aristocats* (1970, singing the title song). He won a special Oscar in 1958.

CHRISTIE, JULIE. Actress. *(b. Apr. 14, 1941, Chukua, Assam, India.)* British actress whose trim, blond beauty and forthright acting style was right in step with the mod 1960s. Stage-trained at London's Central School of Music and Drama, Christie worked in repertory theater in the late 1950s and early 1960s, polishing her technique before making her tyro screen appearance in 1962's *Crooks Anonymous*. She earned the attention of critics and public alike as the girlfriend of *Billy Liar* (1963), then won a Best Actress Oscar as the free-thinking social climber in *Darling* (1965, a role written with her in mind). That same year, she played Lara in *Doctor Zhivago,* and Sean O'Casey's lover in *Young Cassidy.*

After starring in a pair of lavish literary adaptations, *Fahrenheit 451* (1967) and *Far From the Madding Crowd* (1967), Christie came to America to play the unhinged title character in *Petulia* (1968). She made a pair of arty dramas, *In Search of Gregory* (1970) and *The Go-Between* (1971), in England before returning to the States to costar with Warren Beatty in *McCabe and Mrs. Miller* (1971, for which she was Oscar-nominated); they began a lengthy affair that encompassed several years, reams of publicity, and two more films: the satiric *Shampoo* (1975) and the comic fantasy *Heaven Can Wait* (1978). She also starred in the cult movie *Don't Look Now* (1973), had a cameo (as herself) in *Nashville* (1975), and was raped by a computer in *Demon Seed* (1977).

Christie's output in recent years has been erratic, with only four films—*The Return of the Soldier* (1981), *Heat and Dust* (1983), *Power* (1986), and *Fools of Fortune* (1990)—receiving any meaningful theatrical distribution in America. She reteamed with *Don't Look Now*'s Donald Sutherland for the cable-TV movie *The Railway Station Man* (1992).

CHRISTOPHER, DENNIS. Actor. *(b. Dec. 2, 1955, Philadelphia.)* Thin, boyish-looking actor who gained wide acclaim as Dave, the romantic Bloomington, Indiana, bicyclist in the sleeper hit *Breaking Away* (1979). Before this, he had worked on the New York stage and had small roles in *Fellini's Roma* (1972), *September 30, 1955* (1978), and the Robert Altman films *3 Women* (1977) and *A Wedding* (1978). Following the success of *Breaking Away,* Christopher gave a flamboyant performance as a cinema-loving killer in *Fade to Black* (1980), played an American Olympic runner in the Oscar-winning *Chariots of Fire* (1981), and a soldier who helps operate an orphanage in *Don't Cry, It's Only Thunder* (1982). Since then, he has concentrated on stage work and turned up in small films like *Jake Speed* (1986), *A Sinful Life* (1989), and *Circuitry Man* (1990).

CIANNELLI, EDUARDO. Actor. *(b. Aug. 30, 1889, Italy; d. Oct. 8, 1969.)* Sinister supporting player with saturnine features and richly accented voice, specializing in the portrayal of cold-blooded heavies—but equally capable of playing light and comic parts. Recipient of a degree in medicine from the University of Naples and former grand opera singer, Ciannelli came to the United States in the 1920s, and performed in the original companies of famous plays including *The Front Page, Reunion in Vienna,* and *Winterset.* (He recreated his stage roles in film versions of the latter two.) Outstand-

ing as the white-slaver in *Marked Woman* (1937) and the high-priest of Kali in *Gunga Din* (1939). Also prominent in *Foreign Correspondent* (1940), *Kitty Foyle* (1940, as a sympathetic restaurateur), *Paris Calling* (1941), *Cairo* (1942), *For Whom the Bell Tolls, They Got Me Covered* (both 1943), *The Mask of Dimitrios, Passage to Marseille* (both 1944), *A Bell for Adano* (1945), *Dillinger* (1945), and *The Creeper* (1948), among others. He even "starred" in a 1940 Republic serial, *Mysterious Dr. Satan* (billed as he was for the duration of World War 2, as "Edward"). Later films include *The Chase* (1966), *The Brotherhood* (1968), *Mackenna's Gold,* and *The Secret of Santa Vittoria* (both 1969). His last film, *Boot Hill* (1970), was released after his death.

CIMINO, MICHAEL. Director. *(b. Feb. 3, 1939, New York City.)* Only in Hollywood could a director with such a taste for excess coast on the success of one picture. This onetime protégé of Clint Eastwood, who cowrote *Magnum Force* (1973) and wrote and directed *Thunderbolt and Lightfoot* (1974) for the star, was much lauded for his wrenching drama *The Deer Hunter* (1978, Oscars for Best Picture, Best Director, and Best Supporting Actor, nomination for Best Screenplay). Given a blank check by United Artists, he produced the bloated, empty, financially disastrous *Heaven's Gate* (1980), the failure of which virtually bankrupted the troubled company. None of his subsequent films, including *Year of the Dragon* (1985), *The Sicilian* (1987), and *Desperate Hours* (1990), have been box-office successes. While not without talent, Cimino seems unwilling and unable to curb his tendencies toward wretched excess.

CLAIR, RENÉ. Director, screenwriter. *(b. Nov. 11, 1898, Paris, as René-Lucien Chomette; d. Mar. 15, 1981.)* An early exponent of French film comedy who took a stab at Hollywood filmmaking with passably good results, Clair is fondly remembered today for his stylishly witty and charming satires, whimsical fantasies, and surrealistic romps. He worked as a journalist for a short time before acting in the films of Louis Feuillade, from whose works he learned the art of cinematic storytelling. Abandoning the life of a performer, he studied filmmaking technique under director Jacques de Barnocelli and made his directing debut with *Paris qui dort* (*The Crazy Ray,* 1924), a sprightly comic fantasy laced with socially conscious satire. With his second film, *Entr'acte,* Clair established himself as a talent that would bear watching.

Clair's subsequent films received exposure in American art houses, and by the time he came to Hollywood in 1941, his charming and ingenious comic films *The Italian Straw Hat* (1927), the early talkie *Under the Roofs of Paris* (1930), *Le Million* (1931), *À nous la liberté* (1932, which was said to have influenced Chaplin's *Modern Times*), the British-made *The Ghost Goes West* (1935), and *Break the News* (1938) had acquired solid reputations. His American films, including *The Flame of New Orleans* (1941), *I Married a Witch* (1942), *It Happened Tomorrow* (1944), and *And Then There Were None* (1945), were somewhat more conventional in treatment than his early triumphs, but were successful on their own terms, especially the latter, one of the most visually stylish Agatha Christie thrillers ever filmed.

Returning to his homeland after it was liberated from the Nazis, Clair tackled more challenging subjects with less success: *Man About Town* (1947), *Beauty and the Devil* (1950, a Faustian fable), *Beauties of the Night* (1954), *The Grand Maneuver* (1956), and *Love and the Frenchwoman* (1961) were all deemed to be below his pre-war standard. Ironically (and Clair certainly appreciated irony), he was increasingly revered for his pioneering contributions to film, even as his commercial stock was plummeting. His last film was *Les Fêtes galantes* (1965).

CLAMPETT, BOB. Animation director. (b. May 8, 1913, San Diego; d. May 2, 1984.) One of the innovative talents who helped shape the Warner Bros. cartoon department in the 1930s and 1940s. Like his colleague Tex Avery, Clampett's sense of humor was direct and "in your face." His characters would distort themselves in astonishing ways for the sake of a laugh, and that gave Clampett's cartoons a distinctive look that separated them from those of his peers.

He started with the Warner Bros. cartoon studio in the early 1930s, when Hugh Harman and Rudolf Ising were in charge, and worked his way up to a position as full-fledged animator by the middle of the decade. When Avery was given his own unit—and the freedom to reshape the "cute" cartoons they were making into more daring and funny films—Clampett was one of his avid converts. Several years later he was given the chance to direct films himself, and spurred on by Avery's innovations, forged his own brand of comedy within the Warners house style. Piloting the Porky Pig series in the late 1930s, he came up with one funny idea after another, reaching his peak with the startlingly surreal *Porky in Wackyland* (1938). He also developed the character of Daffy Duck, giving him his initial lunatic personality.

Clampett's full-throttle cartoons include such gems as *The Daffy Doc* (1938), *A Coy Decoy, Wabbit Twouble* (1941, in which he's billed as Wobert Cwampett—and all the credits are written in Elmer Fudd-ese), *Horton Hatches the Egg, A Tale of Two Kitties* (with a prototype of Tweety Bird), and the notorious *Coal Black and de Sebben Dwarfs* (all 1942), *Tin Pan Alley Cats, Tortoise Wins by a Hare,* and the *Fantasia* spoof *Corny Concerto* (all 1943), *What's Cookin', Doc?* (1944, with Bugs Bunny disrupting the Academy Awards), *The Old Grey Hare* (1944), *Draftee Daffy* (1945), *The Great Piggy Bank Robbery, Book Revue,* and *Kitty Cornered* (all 1946).

Clampett left the studio in 1946, worked briefly for Columbia, and then made an even bigger name for himself in the earliest days of TV as the producer of the hugely popular, award-winning puppet show "Time for Beany." Years later he revived his characters in a popular half-hour animated series, "Beany and Cecil." Clampett was also a famous pack rat, saving original animation art years before anyone ever thought it would have value.

CLARK, BOB. Director. (b. Aug. 5, 1941, New Orleans.) After working on a few obscure movie projects, Clark directed a $50,000 sendup of *Night of the Living Dead* called *Children Shouldn't Play With Dead Things* (1972). His collaborator was fellow University of Miami student Alan Ormsby, with whom Clark made two other horror movies—*Deathdream* (1972, as producer and director) and *Deranged* (1974, as uncredited producer)—before moving to Canada. There Clark cranked out several thrillers—most notably *Breaking Point* (1976) and *Murder by Decree* (1979, a Sherlock Holmes-vs.-Jack the Ripper tale)—before hitting paydirt with the immensely popular (if tasteless) *Porky's* (1981). His subsequent films, most of them major studio productions such as *Tribute* (1980), *Rhinestone* (1984), *From the Hip* (1987), and *Loose Cannons* (1990), have been uneven in quality (and box-office success), but Clark's oeuvre also includes the highly regarded *A Christmas Story* (1983), which has become a holiday perennial à la *It's a Wonderful Life.* Plans for a sequel with collaborator Jean Shepherd have been brewing ever since the original's success; *It Runs in My Family* was finally released in 1994. For cable TV he directed *Arthur Miller's The American Clock* (1993).

CLARK, CANDY. Actress. *(b. June 20, 1947, Norman, Okla.)* No one was surprised when this offbeat, attractive former model was nominated for a Best Supporting Actress Oscar for her role in *American Graffiti* (1973). Her performance as a good-time girl was one of the picture's biggest assets, and with peroxide-blond hair she bore an uncanny resemblance to the young Stella Stevens, who could just as easily have been cast in the role had the picture been made a few years earlier. What *was* surprising to many was that Clark's career never amounted to much after that early recognition. She'd debuted in *Fat City* (1972), and appeared to advantage in *The Man Who Fell to Earth* (1976) and *Handle With Care* (1977), but a few years later she was toiling in the likes of *Amityville 3-D* (1983), *The Blob* (1988), and *Original Intent* (1991), and alongside rap star Vanilla Ice in his vanity movie *Cool as Ice* (1991). She also appeared in *Buffy the Vampire Slayer* (1992).

CLARK, DANE. Actor. *(b. Feb. 18, 1913, Brooklyn, N.Y., as Bernard Zanville.)* Smooth, short, dark-featured leading man and char-

acter actor who limned good guys and villains with equal authority, combining qualities of both types in his finest performance, playing a tormented killer on the run in the 1948 thriller *Moonrise.* A former athlete (who also had a law degree from St. John's and once worked on a road gang), he was on stage from the mid 1930s, and made his first few movies—including *Sunday Punch, The Pride of the Yankees, Wake Island, The Glass Key* (all 1942), and *Action in the North Atlantic* (1943)—billed under his real name. Signed by Warner Bros. in a clear attempt to make him the new John Garfield, he was rechristened Dane Clark, and went on to appear in such films as *Destination Tokyo, Hollywood Canteen* (both 1944), *God Is My Co-Pilot, Pride of the Marines* (both 1945), *A Stolen Life* (1946), *That Way With Women* (1947), *Whiplash* (1948), *Barricade* (1950), *Fort Defiance* (1951), *Go, Man, Go!* (1954, which he also coproduced), *Massacre* (1956), and *The McMasters* (1970). From the 1950s on, he worked extensively in TV, appearing on most of the early dramatic anthologies, and starring in two series, "Bold Venture" and "Wire Service," as well as regular roles on "The Untouchables" and "The New Perry Mason" (as Lt. Tragg). His more noteworthy TV movies include *Say Goodbye, Maggie Cole, James Dean* (as James Whitmore), *Once an Eagle,* and *The French Atlantic Affair.*

CLARKE, MAE. Actress. *(b. Aug. 16, 1907, Philadelphia, as Mary Klotz; d. Apr. 29, 1992.)* She'll always be remembered as the girl on the receiving end of James Cagney's grapefruit in *The Public Enemy* (1931), but Mae Clarke was more than just a target. The nightclub dancer turned actress shone as one of the bright lights of the early talkie era. Attractive but just short of beautiful, Clarke developed her own naturalistic acting style, eliciting raves from critics for her costarring performances in three other 1931 releases, *Waterloo Bridge, Frankenstein,* and *The Front Page.* Bad luck and personal problems drove her out of the limelight, though, and by the mid 1930s she was playing leads in unimportant B pictures such as *The House of a Thousand Candles* and *Wild Brian Kent* (both 1936). She reteamed with Cagney in *Great Guy*

(1936), and her onetime leading man Lew Ayres cast her in his only directorial effort, *Hearts in Bondage* (1936), but these opportunities failed to rekindle her career. A few years later she was doing bits, and she appeared only sporadically throughout the 1940s, 1950s, and 1960s. Her last leading role came in the Republic serial *King of the Rocket Men* (1949).

CLAVELL, JAMES. Novelist, director, screenwriter, producer. *(b. Oct. 10, 1924, Sydney; d. Sept. 7, 1994.)* Although most Americans instantly know Clavell as the author of such historically based bestsellers as "Tai-Pan" and "Shogun," few realize that he was a filmmaker before he was a novelist. The son of a British Royal Navy Captain, Clavell served in the Royal Artillery during World War 2 and was a P.O.W. for three years in Singapore. After the war—and an accident which ended his military career—he became interested in films and eventually emigrated to the U.S. in 1953. His early credits as screenwriter include the sci-fi classic *The Fly* (1958) and the *King Solomon's Mines* sequel *Watusi* (1959). He later cowrote *The Great Escape* (1963), *633 Squadron* (1964), and the fine thriller *The Satan Bug* (1965). Clavell made his debut as director-writer-producer with the negligible *Five Gates to Hell* (1959). He showed more promise as a triple-hyphenate on the unusual Western *Walk Like a Dragon* (1960) and achieved enduring fame for the irresistible *To Sir With Love* (1967), with Sidney Poitier as a teacher winning over students in a rough East End London school. He also directed *Where's Jack?* (1969, about British highwayman Jack Sheppard) and the epic *The Last Valley* (1971, which he also wrote and produced). His first novel, "King Rat"—written during a Hollywood writers' strike—was published in 1962 and made into a film three years later by Bryan Forbes. "Tai-Pan" was filmed in 1986, while "Shogun" and "Noble House" became successful TV miniseries in 1980 and 1988, respectively.

CLAYBURGH, JILL. Actress. *(b. Apr. 30, 1944, New York City.)* Tall, patrician Broadway actress who moved over to film and was the very model of the 1970s modern, liberated woman, as best exemplified by her well-received star turn in *An Unmarried Woman* (1978), which brought her an Oscar nomination here and the Best Actress Award at the Cannes Film Festival. Almost unnoticed in her tyro screen appearance in 1969's *The Wedding Party,* she worked mostly on stage and in TV before landing small roles in such films as *Portnoy's Complaint* (1972) and *The Thief Who Came to Dinner* (1973).

Clayburgh accumulated more movie work and in 1976 managed both to hit the top, as Gene Wilder's love interest in the smash *Silver Streak,* and scrape the bottom, as the distaff half of *Gable and Lombard,* a legendary fiasco. She displayed considerable comedic prowess in *Semi-Tough* (1977), *Starting Over* (1979, another Oscar nomination), *It's My Turn* (1980), and *First Monday in October* (1981), in which she prophetically played a conservative Supreme Court justice just before Sandra Day O'Connor did it for real. In fact, she owed much of her success to roles that cast her as sensitive, pragmatic, independent women; moviegoers (especially feminine ones) associated her with the burgeoning feminist movement and changing attitudes about women's roles in society.

Clayburgh also played a doomed opera diva in *Luna* (1979) and a pill-popping director in *I'm Dancing as Fast as I Can* (1982), the latter scripted by playwright-husband David Rabe. She sparkled in such TV-movies as *Hustling* (1975, as a hooker) and *Griffin and Phoenix* (1976, as one of two terminally ill lovers). Relatively inactive in films lately, she was excellent, however, as a distraught mother in *Where Are the Children?* (1986) and a photojournalist in *Shy People* (1987). Foresaking a full-time career to raise a family, Clayburgh was little-seen for several years, but has recently become more visible, in telefilms and such features as *Whispers in the Dark* (1992), *Rich in Love* (1993), and *Naked in New York* (1994).

CLAYTON, JACK. Director. *(b. Mar. 1, 1921, Brighton, England; d. Feb. 2, 1995.)* Notable British director who brought many interesting literary works to the screen. When he was a teenager, Clayton worked for Alexander Korda's Denham Studios and rose from tea boy to assistant director to film editor. After serving with the RAF during World War 2, he became an associate producer on many of Korda's films, then directed the Oscar-winning short *The Bespoke Overcoat* (1956). His first feature was the internationally acclaimed *Room at the Top* (1959), a harsh indictment of the British class system, which won two Oscars, earned Clayton a Best Director nomination, and was credited with spearheading Britain's movement toward realism in films. Clayton followed with the classic ghost story *The Innocents* (1961, based on Henry James' "Turn of the Screw"), then laid back for several years, establishing a pattern he followed thereafter. He directed *The Pumpkin Eater* in 1964, *Our Mother's House* in 1967, and then, seven years later, the high-profile American production of F. Scott Fitzgerald's *The Great Gatsby* (1974). Perhaps in response to its failure, he didn't take another assignment for nine years; it was the Disney studio production of Ray Bradbury's *Something Wicked This Way Comes* (1983), another disappointment. His last feature film, the British-made *The Lonely Passion of Judith Hearne* (1987), featured a superb performance by Maggie Smith as a spinster who struggles with the emptiness of her life; it won Clayton critical plaudits for the first time in many years. He reteamed with Smith in 1992 for a telefilm, *Memento Mori,* which he also cowrote.

CLIFT, MONTGOMERY. Actor. *(b. Oct. 17, 1920, Omaha, Nebr., as Edward Montgomery Clift; d. July 23, 1966.)* Handsome, soft-spoken, introspective leading man who exuded star quality in—and earned an Oscar nomination for—his first released film, *The Search* (1948), and went on to become one of the brightest talents of the 1950s and 1960s. An actor from age 12, he made his Broadway debut two years later. He matured into a formidable talent, appearing opposite Tallulah Bankhead in "The Skin of Our Teeth," opposite Alfred Lunt and Lynn Fontanne in "There Shall Be No Night," and in the 1944 revival of Thornton Wilder's "Our Town." Clift's boyish appearance belied the brooding, psychologically complex characterizations of which he was capable. Lured by Hollywood in 1946, he was signed to play John Wayne's rebellious son in *Red River,* the release of which was delayed until after *The Search* had already played in theaters. His striking and believable performances in both films established him as an overnight star.

Already a hot property, Clift found himself much in demand. He appeared in *The Heiress* (1949), perfectly cast as the young man who woos spinster Olivia de Havilland, and *The Big Lift* (1950) before costarring with Elizabeth Taylor in George Stevens' *A Place in the Sun* (1951), a brilliant remake of Dreiser's "An American Tragedy." His moving and credible portrayal of the social inferior who murders pregnant factory girl Shelley Winters to clear the path for his romance with socialite Taylor earned Clift his second Oscar nod. His third came for his turn as a sensitive soldier in pre-WW2 Hawaii in *From Here to Eternity* (1953). That same year he played a priest who hears a murderer's confession in Alfred Hitchcock's *I Confess* and a willing participant in an adulterous romance with Jennifer Jones in *Indiscretion of an American Wife.*

In 1957, while filming the Civil War drama *Raintree County* (which again costarred him with Elizabeth Taylor), Clift was badly injured in a car crash that permanently scarred his matinee-idol face and obliterated his self-confidence. He was never the same afterward, although some speculate that his inner turmoil—complicated by drug and alcohol abuse—lent an added dimension, certainly an edge, to his subsequent performances. He was really on his toes opposite Marlon Brando in the excellent WW2 drama *The Young Lions* (1958), and was reunited with Taylor for the film version of Tennessee Williams' *Suddenly, Last Summer* (1959). While Taylor and Katharine Hepburn had most of the juicy scenes, Clift more than held his own as the understanding brain surgeon. *Judgment at Nuremberg* (1961) gave him another plum role, as an unbalanced victim of Nazi atrocities, for which he received his fourth and final Academy Award nomination.

Clift took third billing to Clark Gable and Marilyn Monroe for John Huston's troubled production of *The Misfits* (1961), an Arthur Miller drama about contemporary cowboys. He appeared to have his personal demons under control, as he did playing the title role in *Freud* (1962), but he subsequently spent several years offscreen, returning only once, in the wholly embarrassing *The Defector* (1966). He died shortly after completing the film.

CLIVE, COLIN. Actor. *(b. Jan. 20, 1898, St-Malo, France, as Clive Greig; d. June 25, 1937.)* Eccentric, mannered actor whose place in movie history is assured for his performances as Dr. Henry Frankenstein in *Frankenstein* (1931) and *Bride of Frankenstein* (1935). (Who can ever forget his cries of "It's alive! It's alive!"?) Son of a British colonel, he left the military for a stage career. Handsome in a brooding, sensitive way, with slick, dark hair, he often played tortured, introspective characters. Clive entered films by repeating one of his stage successes in the movie version of *Journey's End* (1930) for director James Whale, who then cast him in *Frankenstein.*
OTHER FILMS INCLUDE: 1933: *Christopher Strong;* 1934: *Jane Eyre* (as Rochester); 1935: *Mad Love, Clive of India, The Man Who Broke the Bank at Monte Carlo;* 1937: *History Is Made at Night.*

CLOSE, GLENN. Actress. *(b. Mar. 19, 1947, Greenwich, Conn.)* She earned an Academy Award nomination in her first feature-film role, as Robin Williams' free-spirited, nonconformist mother in *The World According to Garp* (1982), then shocked moviegoers who knew her only in this middle-aged role by playing a contemporary yuppie in *The Big Chill* (1983, getting another nomination). She has since snagged three additional Oscar nods while establishing herself as one of the screen's most talented and interesting female stars. The striking, aristocratic blond actress played on the New York stage for several years, and even did a few TV movies (including 1979's *Too Far to Go* and *Orphan Train*), before being chosen for *Garp* by director George Roy Hill while appearing on Broadway in "Barnum."

Close has displayed admirable versatility in her film assignments, bringing distinction to thoughtful projects, such as 1988's *Dangerous Liaisons,* in which she played a manipulative sexual opportunist, and 1990's *Reversal of Fortune,* which cast her as real-life comatose heiress Sunny Von Bulow, and lending a touch of class

to more dubious fare, such as 1985's *Jagged Edge,* the prototype for a whole slew of "erotic thrillers," and 1987's *Fatal Attraction,* the controversially smarmy melodrama that cast her as the psychotic mistress of Michael Douglas. She hasn't had much success with comedy, however, as *Maxie* (1985), her lone comedy vehicle, will attest (though the fault wasn't hers).

Close served as executive producer (and starred in) the well-received TV movie *Sarah, Plain and Tall* (1991) and its sequel *Skylark* (1992). She returned to Broadway in "Death and the Maiden" in 1992 and won her second Tony Award for her performance (her first was for "The Real Thing"); then in 1993 she agreed to tackle the demanding role of Norma Desmond in the musical version of *Sunset Blvd.* She won a Tony in 1995 for her performance.
OTHER FILMS INCLUDE: 1984: *The Stone Boy, Greystoke: The Legend of Tarzan, Lord of the Apes* (providing uncredited dubbing for female lead Andie MacDowell), *The Natural, Something About Amelia* (a TV movie that earned her an Emmy nomination); 1988: *Light Years* (voice only); 1989: *Immediate Family;* 1990: *Hamlet* (as Gertrude); 1991: *Meeting Venus, Hook* (in an unbilled cameo); 1993: *The House of the Spirits;* 1994: *The Paper;* 1995: *Serving in Silence: The Margarethe Cammermeyer Story* (TV movie), *Mary Reilly.*

CLYDE, ANDY. Actor. *(b. Mar. 25, 1892, Blairgowrie, Scotland; d. May 18, 1967.)* A wiry Scot with walrus mustache and a great double-take, Clyde was born into a theatrical family, and emigrated to America in the mid 1920s. He became one of Mack Sennett's all-purpose comics (often teamed with Billy Bevan) and continued starring in Sennett two-reelers right into the sound era. In 1935 he moved to Columbia and continued making two-reel comedies for that studio until the division shut down in 1959. He alternated between bumpkin characters and confused, henpecked husbands. His Scottish burr was apparent but not overpowering in talkies like *Million Dollar Legs* (1932), *The Little Minister* (1934), and *Annie Oakley* (1935), in which he had small but amusing parts. During the late 1930s, Clyde made a curious transition, playing Western sidekicks and rustic characters. He was California

Carlson in dozens of "Hopalong Cassidy" Westerns from 1940 to 1948 (reprising the role on the Hoppy radio show) and supported Whip Wilson from 1948 to 1950. In later years he guest-starred on several TV shows, and was a semiregular on "The Real McCoys" (1957–63) and "No Time for Sergeants" (1964–65). His brother David and sister Jean were also active in films.

COBB, LEE J. Actor. *(b. Dec. 8, 1911, New York City, as Leo Jacob; d. Feb. 11, 1976.)* Although Cobb reached his career summit with his portrayal of Willy Loman in the original 1949 stage production of "Death of a Salesman," he was also well known for a long string of successful character roles in motion pictures. Cobb was a child prodigy on the violin, but a broken wrist dashed his hopes for musical greatness and he became an actor instead. He joined the famous Group Theatre, and appeared in Clifford Odets' "Waiting for Lefty" and "Golden Boy." His first film, in which he played the lead villain, was *North of the Rio Grande* (1937), a "Hopalong Cassidy" Western. He returned to Hollywood in 1939 to reprise his stage role as the Italian papa in *Golden Boy.*

Cobb worked in B movies through the mid 1940s, graduating to meaty supporting roles in major productions such as *The Song of Bernadette* (1943), *Anna and the King of Siam* (1946), *Boomerang!, Captain From Castile* (both 1947), *Call Northside 777,* and *The Dark Past* (both 1948). He made a convincing heavy, with his bulky frame, cruel mouth, and piercing eyes. He was Oscar-nominated for his performances in *On the Waterfront* (1954, as labor kingpin Johnny Friendly) and *The Brothers Karamazov* (1958, as Feodor).

When parts were scarce, in the late 1960s and early 1970s, Cobb worked in Europe in low-grade features. He was a regular on "The Virginian" TV series (1962–66), as Judge Garth, and reprised his Willy Loman characterization for a 1966 TV version of "Salesman." He returned to series television for "The Young Lawyers" (1970–71).
OTHER FILMS INCLUDE: 1956: *The Man in the Gray Flannel Suit;* 1957: *12 Angry Men, The Three Faces of Eve;* 1958: *Man of the West;* 1960: *Exodus;* 1962: *How the West Was Won;* 1966: *Our Man Flint;* 1967: *In Like Flint;* 1968: *Coogan's Bluff;* 1969: *Mackenna's Gold;* 1973: *The Exorcist.*

COBURN, CHARLES. Actor. *(b. June 19, 1877, Savannah, Ga.; d. Aug. 30, 1961.)* Aristocratic Southern gentleman, very much at home wearing high collars and smoking big cigars. He played many gruff but lovable types in secondary roles and for a time became a top-billed character star. A former theater manager who at one time ran his own acting troupe, he entered films in 1938, already an elderly man. Coburn's best remembered characters include the card sharp in *The Lady Eve* (1941), the matchmaker in *The More the Merrier* (1943, for which he won an Oscar for Best Supporting Actor), and in a change of pace, the vengeful doctor who amputates Ronald Reagan's legs in *Kings Row* (1942). At the age of 80 he starred in *How to Murder a Rich Uncle* (1957), and two years later he was cast as Benjamin Franklin in *John Paul Jones* (1959).
OTHER FILMS INCLUDE: 1939: *Stanley and Livingstone;* 1941: *The Devil and Miss Jones;* 1943: *Heaven Can Wait;* 1944: *Knickerbocker Holiday, Wilson;* 1946: *The Green Years;* 1948: *The Paradine Case;* 1950: *Louisa;* 1952: *Monkey Business* (as Marilyn Monroe's boss); 1953: *Gentlemen Prefer Blondes* (as Marilyn Monroe's suitor).

COBURN, JAMES. Actor. *(b. Aug. 31, 1928, Laurel, Nebr.)* Lean, athletic actor who gained fame for his suave characterizations and action leads, but never quite made it to the front rank of stars. After army service, Coburn studied acting in California and New York and worked on stage and live television before making his film debut as an outlaw in the Randolph Scott Western *Ride Lonesome* (1959). Another Western role came in *Face of a Fugitive* (1959), but it was his performance as the knife-throwing Britt in *The Magnificent Seven* (1960)—surrounded by other "macho" actors—that put him on the map. He didn't have many lines, but his physical presence spoke volumes. Soon he was featured in *Hell Is For Heroes* (1962), *Charade* (1963), and *The Great Escape* (1963, as the Australian Sedgwick). More supporting roles followed in *The Americanization of Emily* (1964), *Major Dundee* (1965, directed by

Sam Peckinpah), and then, finally, a lead in the crime drama *Dead Heat on a Merry-Go-Round* (1966), before he achieved his greatest success as super agent Derek Flint (a role that fit him like a glove) in the James Bond spoof *Our Man Flint* (1966) and the sequel *In Like Flint* (1967). One of his best performances was as the title character of *The President's Analyst* (1967, which he also produced), a wicked (and neglected) satire about what happens to the nation's number one shrink when he quits. *Candy* (1968), *Duffy* (1969), and *Last of the Mobile Hot-Shots* (1970) were poor, but many 1970s films offered him interesting opportunities in roles such as an aging rodeo rider in *The Honkers* (1971), an explosives expert in Sergio Leone's *Duck, You Sucker* (1972), a producer in the ingenious mystery *The Last of Sheila* (1973), a participant in a 600-mile horse race in *Bite the Bullet* (1975), a fight promoter in *Hard Times* (also 1975), and in the leading roles of two more Peckinpah films: 1973's *Pat Garrett and Billy the Kid* (as the reluctant lawman Garrett) and 1977's *Cross of Iron* (as a WW2 corporal).

More formula pictures followed, like *Firepower* (1979), *The Baltimore Bullet* (1980), *High Risk,* and *Looker* (both 1981), but by this time Coburn was suffering from rheumatoid arthritis which severely weakened him. He appeared sporadically, mostly in little-seen films like *Martin's Day* (1984), *Death of a Soldier* (1986), and *Walking After Midnight* (1988). His voice remained familiar to audiences on a flock of TV commercials, while he concentrated on diet, physical therapy, and exercise. He was back in good form in *Young Guns II* (1990, in a role harkening back to his *Pat Garrett* days, as an enemy of Billy the Kid) and played a CIA agent in *Hudson Hawk* (1991), a film that unsuccessfully tried to duplicate the flip-hip attitude of Coburn's own Flint films. Recently, he's been busy again in *Sister Act 2, Deadfall* (1993), and the film version of *Maverick* (1994). He also cowrote the story (with his friend Bruce Lee) of an odd movie called *The Silent Flute* which was released in 1978.

COCHRAN, STEVE. Actor. *(b. May 25, 1917, Eureka, Calif.; d. June 15, 1965.)* You know you've swung from one extreme to the other when, in the course of three years, you go from making love to Mae West in a Broadway revival of "Diamond Lil" to beating up Doris Day on-screen in *Storm Warning* (1951). The burly, dark, good-looking Cochran usually played heavies on film, but he handled occasional sympathetic parts with equal aplomb. A one-time cowpuncher, he developed his acting skills in local theater, eventually went to Broadway, and broke into film by menacing Danny Kaye in 1945's *Wonder Man* and 1946's *The Kid From Brooklyn.* That same year, he also appeared in *The Best Years of Our Lives,* followed by *Copacabana* (1947), *A Song Is Born* (1948), *White Heat* (1949), *The Damned Don't Cry* (1950), *Jim Thorpe— All American* (1951), *Operation Secret* (1952), *She's Back on Broadway, The Desert Song* (both 1953), *Private Hell 36, Carnival Story* (both 1954), and *Come Next Spring* (1956, excellent as a peripatetic farmer in a much-underrated movie). The next year, he went to Italy to star as an emotionally troubled man in Antonioni's *Il Grido,* a partially successful film. Returning to the U.S. and less arty fare, he appeared in *I, Mobster* (1958), *The Beat Generation* (1959), *Deadly Companions* (1961), *Of Love and Desire* (1963), and *Mozambique* (1965). Just before his death, Cochran wrote, produced, directed, and starred in *Tell Me in the Sunlight,* which after two years received a token release in 1967.

COCTEAU, JEAN. Director, screenwriter, playwright. *(b. July 5, 1889, Maisons-Lafitte, France; d. Oct. 11, 1963.)* A Renaissance man in the term's truest sense, Cocteau made memorable contributions to the international cinema but was equally well known for his efforts as a playwright, novelist, poet, actor, painter, and sculptor. His first film, the memorable *The Blood of a Poet* (made 1930, released 1932), synthesized many of the surrealist cinema's conceits and added to them Cocteau's own vision and expert handling of sound, then still a novelty in French films. He penned dialogue and adapted several stories for the screen over the next 15 years, then wrote and directed *La Belle et la bête (Beauty and the Beast)* (1946), a more conventional but no less artistic film that starred his friend (and favorite actor) Jean Marais. A significant critical success, the film won its brilliant auteur a following in America, where it became an art-house staple.

The subsequent Cocteau–Marais collaborations are numbered among the best works of both men: *The Eagle With Two Heads, The Storm Within* (both 1948, both adapted by Cocteau from his own plays), and especially *Orpheus* (1950), which cast Marais as a feckless young poet who follows the spirit of his dead wife to Hell, where he is judged by the netherworld's denizens. Stylized and self-conscious, *Orpheus* nonetheless features some of Cocteau's most striking images.

Throughout the 1950s Cocteau contributed dialogue, narration, and occasionally full screenplays to the films of others, making only one more significant feature of his own—1959's *The Testament of Orpheus,* a fascinating if self-absorbed retelling of the Orpheus legend that was privately financed and released. The director's perceptive examination of the medium, "Cocteau on the Film," was published in 1952.

COEN, ETHAN. Producer, writer. *(b. Sept. 21, 1957, St. Louis Park, Minn.)* **COEN, JOEL.** Director, writer. *(b. Nov. 29, 1954, St. Louis Park, Minn.)* These quiet, well-educated brothers—Ethan a graduate of Princeton University, Joel a New York University grad—work in tandem as one of the most acclaimed contemporary moviemaking teams. Lifelong film buffs, their own movies are loaded with references to classic cinema—yet the Coens infuse their movies with a highly distinctive style and an individualistic, slightly skewed worldview. Their debut film, the Texas-based noir *Blood Simple* (1984), made them overnight sensations with critics (though the film was not a box-office success). It set a pattern for their subsequent work, both in its preference for style over substance, and its aloofness, which has kept the Coen movies from appealing to a wide, mainstream audience. Their hyperkinetic 1987 screwball comedy, *Raising Arizona,* costarring Nicolas Cage and Holly Hunter, and featuring the innovative camera work of Barry Sonnenfeld, won the brothers their best reviews (and biggest audience) to date. The elegiac gang-

ster drama *Miller's Crossing* (1990), which "borrowed" liberally from Dashiell Hammett's novel "The Glass Key," and *Barton Fink* (1991), a wickedly funny, surrealistic fable of Hollywood in the early 1940s (that earned unprecedented awards at Cannes for Best Picture, Director, and Actor), reasserted the duo's mastery of visual detail and almost operatic stylization—but, like their earlier films, failed to connect with moviegoers on an emotional level. The same might be said of their even more ambitious *The Hudsucker Proxy* (1994).

COHEN, LARRY. Director, writer. *(b. July 15, 1941, New York City.)* Low-budget auteur whose exploitative pictures are a notch above the typical genre fare. Growing up in New York City, Cohen learned rudimentary filmmaking techniques at the City College Film Institute. He broke into the movie business as a screenwriter, first on TV Westerns and later on the likes of *I Deal in Danger* (1966) and *Daddy's Gone A-Hunting* (1969). In the early 1970s, he took up directing, cranking out pictures that were heavy on social consciousness and laced with irony. His *Black Caesar* (1973) was one of the most successful "blaxploitation" films; the same year's *Bone* examined racial attitudes and stereotyping among middle-class whites. Cohen turned his attention to the horror genre with *It's Alive!* (1974), a story about a monsterish mutant baby deformed by environmental pollution. This loopy picture was successful enough to spawn two sequels, *It Lives Again* (1978) and *It's Alive III: Island of the Alive* (1987). Cohen's work, not always easy to classify in spite of recognizable genre trappings, is characterized by taut action and ambitious philosophical concerns. For example, his *Demon* (aka *God Told Me To,* 1977) dealt with nothing less than a possible Messiah from outer space, while *The Stuff* (1985) was as much a critique of unbridled consumerism as horror picture. He also had the distinction of directing Bette Davis in her final film, on which she worked just one week, *Wicked Stepmother* (1989). Cohen's screenwriting talents and budgetary efficiency have brought him work on larger-scale studio projects, notably *I, the Jury* (1982, on which he was replaced as director), *Best Seller* (1987), and *Maniac*

Cop (1988). He wrote the screenplay for 1993's mainstream thriller *Guilty as Sin.*

COLBERT, CLAUDETTE. Actress. *(b. Sept. 13, 1905, Paris, as Claudette Lily Chauchoin.)* Although Colbert began her film career in 1927, she was a rather nondescript leading lady until 1932, when Cecil B. DeMille approached her with the offer: "Claudette, how would you like to play the wickedest woman in the world?" She jumped at the chance to play Poppea in *The Sign of the Cross,* and DeMille brought out the haughty sensuality and earthy humor that finally set her apart from the crowd of die-cut screen ingenues. (The film also gave her one of her all-time sexiest roles, with a now-famous nude milk bath among its highlights.) She originally came to America in 1911 dreaming of a career in fashion design, but was persuaded to go on stage in 1923, and soon became a reliable Broadway leading lady. Colbert made her first film, the undistinguished *For the Love of Mike* (1927) for director Frank Capra, and signed with Paramount at the dawn of the sound era. Her first talkie, *The Hole in the Wall* (1929), was based on a 1920 play about a fake spiritualist and costarred Edward G. Robinson. She worked with Maurice Chevalier in *The Big Pond* (1930) and *The Smiling Lieutenant* (1931), and appeared with legendary stage star George M. Cohan in *The Phantom President* (1932), but failed to generate much excitement among movie fans. After *Sign,* she took the lead in the seminal screwball comedy, *Three-Cornered Moon* (1933), which boosted her stock and gave audiences their first real taste of her comic skill.

Following her appearance in DeMille's social comedy *Four Frightened People* (1934, as a plain Jane who gets more glamorous with each successive scene), Colbert was loaned to Columbia for Capra's *It Happened One Night* (also 1934), and won an unexpected Oscar for her canny, untheatrical comic performance as a spoiled rich kid on the run. Her famous "hitchhiking" scene (in which she exposed a shapely leg to stop a passing motorist), along with costar Clark Gable's reluctance to wear undershirts, made the Oscar-winning screwball comedy the talk of the nation. Her stardom cemented, Colbert

played another classic femme fatale in DeMille's *Cleopatra* (1934). She snared an Oscar nomination for her tempered dramatic performance in the psychiatric drama *Private Worlds* (1935), but it was in comedy that Colbert found her most appreciative audiences. Vehicles like *She Married Her Boss, The Gilded Lily, The Bride Comes Home* (all 1935), *Bluebeard's Eighth Wife* (1938), *It's a Wonderful World,* and the delicious *Midnight* (both 1939) showed time and time again that she was one of the screen's leading light comediennes. Writer-director Preston Sturges took full advantage of that talent when he handed her the leading role in his deliriously funny *The Palm Beach Story* (1942). But Colbert managed to escape pigeonholing in Hollywood by taking on a variety of parts in dramatic films as well, from the costume dramas *Maid of Salem* (1937) and John Ford's *Drums Along the Mohawk* (1939, which cast her as a frontier wife), to such high-grade weepers as *Arise, My Love* (1940, reportedly the actress' favorite film) and *Remember the Day* (1941).

During World War 2, Colbert continued to make light comedies (1943's *No Time for Love* and 1945's *Guest Wife,* for example) but also starred in patriotic exercises such as *So Proudly We Hail* (1943) and *Since You Went Away* (1944, for which she received her third Best Actress nomination as a courageous matriarch). After the war, she scored in two side-splitting comedies: Mervyn LeRoy's *Without Reservations* (1946), as an authoress in search of a "perfect man," and Chester Erskine's *The Egg and I* (1947), as an urban sophisticate plopped down in the middle of a chicken farm. Though she continued to give solid dramatic performances, in the psychological drama *The Secret Heart* (1946), the thriller *Sleep, My Love* (1948), and especially *Three Came Home* (1950), in which she movingly portrayed a prisoner of war, her vehicles became less interesting in the early 1950s, and her starring career petered out. (Her last starring film was 1955's *Texas Lady,* and her last major appearance was as Troy Donahue's mother in 1961's *Parrish.*)

Colbert found ample opportunities on the stage instead. She earned a 1959 Tony nomination for her work on Broadway in "The Marriage-Go-Round," and continued to tour in elegant stage vehicles right through the 1980s, working several times with Rex Harrison. In 1987 Colbert appeared with Ann-Margret in a two-part CBS TV miniseries, "The Two Mrs. Grenvilles," dazzling viewers with her ageless appearance and panache. After nearly 70 years as a performer, she announced her formal retirement in 1992. Her first husband was actor-director Norman Foster. They divorced in 1935, and she subsequently wed Dr. Joel Pressman, who died in 1968.

COLEMAN, DABNEY. Actor. *(b. Jan. 3, 1932, Austin, Tex.)* Shifty-eyed, mustachioed, nervous-looking actor who has raised the portrayal of comic jerks and loudmouths to an art form, particularly in the TV shows "Buffalo Bill" and "The Slap Maxwell Story." Coleman enacted small roles in TV shows and movies dating back to the 1960s, including a wacky neighbor on "That Girl," and can be seen in *The Slender Thread* (1965), *Downhill Racer* (1969), *Bite the Bullet* (1975), and *North Dallas Forty* (1979), to name just a few. Coleman's breakthrough role, though, was that of the callous employer in *9 to 5* (1980). He *did* get a shot at a rare sympathetic role in *On Golden Pond* (1981, as Jane Fonda's new boyfriend), but reverted to type in *Tootsie* (1982), and *WarGames* (1983), by which time his reputation as a first-rate screen lout was cemented. His starring vehicles—*Short Time* and *Where the Heart Is* (both 1990)—have been uneven, but Coleman continues to do fine work in supporting roles, such as his lisping porno king in *Dragnet* (1987) and the drag-queen insect in *Meet the Applegates* (1991). Recent films include *There Goes the Neighborhood* (1992), *Amos & Andrew, The Beverly Hillbillies* (both 1993), and *Clifford* (1994).

COLLINS, JOAN. Actress. *(b. May 23, 1933, London.)* Beautiful brunette who's had a roller-coaster career. She made her feature debut as a beauty contest entrant in *Lady Godiva Rides Again* (1951) and appeared in a handful of other British films before gaining international attention as the femme fatale in Howard Hawks' sprawling epic of ancient Egypt, *Land of the Pharaohs* (1955).

Brought to Hollywood with great fan-

fare, Collins established herself in *The Virgin Queen* (1955), *The Girl in the Red Velvet Swing* (1955, as notorious showgirl Evelyn Nesbit), *The Opposite Sex* (1956, in the role played by Joan Crawford in the original, *The Women*), *The Bravados* (1958), *Rally 'Round the Flag, Boys!* (1958, trying to seduce Paul Newman), *Seven Thieves, Esther and the King* (both 1960), and *The Road to Hong Kong* (1962).

Collins worked infrequently during her 1963–71 marriage to songwriter/performer Anthony Newley, although she starred opposite him in his notorious sex comedy *Can Hieronymus Merkin Ever Forget Mercy Humppe and Find True Happiness?* (1969). When she returned to films fulltime, it was in shoddy thrillers and horror/sci-fi fare, including *Inn of the Frightened People* (1971), *Tales From the Crypt* (1972), *Tales That Witness Madness* (1973), and *Empire of the Ants* (1977), as well as *The Big Sleep* (1978). She also appeared on episodic TV, including a memorable "Star Trek" episode, "City on the Edge of Forever."

By the late 1970s she was starring in tawdry sexploitation films like *The Stud* (1978) and *The Bitch* (1979), both based on novels written by her sister Jackie. Then she landed the role of super-bitch Alexis Carrington in the prime-time TV soap "Dynasty" (1981–89) and soared to the top of the show-biz heap, achieving greater worldwide fame and recognition than she'd ever enjoyed before. She even posed for a nude layout in "Playboy" magazine. (She also made one forgettable film, *Homework,* in 1982.) Since then she's appeared in (and produced) TV movies and miniseries, acted on stage, and written several steamy novels (like her successful sister). Her kiss-and-tell autobiography "Past Imperfect" was published in 1978 and updated in 1984.

COLLINS, RAY. Actor. *(b. Dec. 10, 1888, Sacramento, Calif.; d. July 11, 1965.)* Collins, best known as Lt. Tragg on the "Perry Mason" TV show (where he appeared 1957–64), started acting as a child, and worked extensively in stock companies. He came to Broadway in the 1920s, began working in the newly developing medium of dramatic radio, and became a charter member of Orson Welles' Mercury Theater group. Collins made his film debut as Boss Jim Geddys in Welles' *Citizen Kane* (1941), and followed that with an excellent portrayal of Jack Amberson in *The Magnificent Ambersons* (1942), another Welles production. Short and dour, he played many character roles, mainly heavies, before abandoning the big screen for relative security on episodic TV.

OTHER FILMS INCLUDE: 1942: *The Big Street;* 1943: *The Human Comedy;* 1944: *The Seventh Cross;* 1946: *The Best Years of Our Lives;* 1947: *The Bachelor and the Bobby-Soxer;* 1948: *Command Decision;* 1949: *The Fountainhead, The Heiress;* 1950: *Summer Stock;* 1955: *The Desperate Hours;* 1956: *The Solid Gold Cadillac;* 1958: *Touch of Evil* (again for Welles).

COLMAN, RONALD. Actor. *(b. Feb. 9, 1891, Richmond, England; d. May 19, 1958.)* The very model of British charm and culture, this impeccable leading man also possessed one of the most beautiful voices ever heard. A former office boy who dabbled in amateur theatricals before enlisting in Her Majesty's Army during World War 1, he returned to England after being wounded in 1916. He appeared both on stage and screen as a juvenile leading man, making his film debut in a short subject called *The Live Wire* (1917), and emigrating to the United States a short time later. He appeared on stage and in a few minor film roles before being spotted by Lillian Gish, who selected him as her leading man in *The White Sister* (1923) and, the following year, in *Romola*. Robust heroics were not in the Colman repertoire, but he made a handsome and convincing romantic lead in *$20 a Week, Her Night of Romance* (both 1924), *His Supreme Moment, The Sporting Venus, Her Sister From Paris, The Dark Angel, Stella Dallas, Lady Windermere's Fan* (all 1925), and *Kiki* (1926) before adding derring-do to his image as the dashing Foreign Legionnaire in *Beau Geste* (also 1926).

Following the success of that lavish adventure film, Colman enjoyed a period of popularity as one of the screen's top stars; under contract to Samuel Goldwyn (and frequently teamed with beautiful Vilma Banky) he top-lined such films as *The Winning of Barbara Worth* (1926, in which he was nearly upstaged by newcomer Gary Cooper), *The Night of Love,*

The Magic Flame (both 1927), *Two Lovers* (1928), and *The Rescue* (1929). The advent of talking pictures aided Colman's career immeasurably; his cultured, mellifluous voice perfectly complemented his appearance. He was Oscar-nominated for his tongue-in-cheek portrayal of a reckless adventurer in *Bulldog Drummond* (1929), a joyously entertaining comedy-melodrama; he repeated the role five years later in *Bulldog Drummond Strikes Back,* one of those rare sequels that is superior to the original.

Following that auspicious debut, Colman starred in a string of generally well-received (if occasionally stodgy) early talkies, including *Condemned* (1929, another Oscar-nominated performance), *Raffles* (in the title role), *The Devil to Pay* (both 1930), *Arrowsmith* (one of his best parts, in this Sinclair Lewis adaptation), *The Unholy Garden* (both 1931), *Cynara* (1932), and *The Masquerader* (1933). Signing with Darryl F. Zanuck's 20th Century Pictures to do the Drummond sequel, he remained for *Clive of India* and *The Man Who Broke the Bank at Monte Carlo* (both 1935). Then, as a freelancer, he embarked upon a series of remarkable roles that essentially defined the Colman screen persona most people remember.

At MGM he played the role of Sydney Carton (sans mustache) in the lavish adaptation of Dickens' *A Tale of Two Cities,* and was identified ever after with its memorable finale (" 'Tis a far, far better thing that I do . . ."). He then returned to the Foreign Legion in *Under Two Flags* (1936), in which both Claudette Colbert and Rosalind Russell vied for his attentions. Frank Capra's *Lost Horizon* (1937) gave Colman the role he was born to play, that of soldier-statesman Robert Conway, the intended leader of the Tibetan paradise known as Shangri-la. It was another role, like Sydney Carton, that he personalized and made his own. He played a dual role in *The Prisoner of Zenda* (1937, for producer David O. Selznick), and was equally convincing as the weak-willed King Rudolf V and the daring Rudolph Rassendyl who would save his throne; he and Madeleine Carroll made a particularly striking couple. He then became the fourth (and most successful) actor to tackle the role of French poet Francois Villon in *If I Were King* (1938), effortlessly reciting the title poem (which became part of every nightclub mimic's routine when impersonating him), and went on to play an artist gradually losing his sight in *The Light That Failed* (1939).

Following two frivolous star vehicles (1940's *Lucky Partners*, with Ginger Rogers and 1941's *My Life With Caroline*, with Anna Lee), he returned to peak form in *The Talk of the Town* (1942), a brilliant comedy-drama directed by George Stevens, in which he played a Supreme Court justice-elect locked in philosophical debate with fugitive Cary Grant. A novel by the author of "Lost Horizon," James Hilton, gave him another plum role: *Random Harvest* (1942) cast him as a post–WW1 amnesiac taken under the wing of music-hall star Greer Garson; it netted Colman his third Academy Award nomination. In *Kismet* (1944) he played a wily Arabian Nights magician, which offered a change of pace but little else.

It was becoming increasingly difficult for the middle-aged actor to find suitable starring roles. When Colman returned to the screen in 1946, it was in a character lead as a stuffy Boston patriarch in the witty film version of John P. Marquand's *The Late George Apley*. He followed it with a chillingly effective performance as an actor who finds it increasingly difficult to separate his stage work from reality in the backstage melodrama *A Double Life* (1947, written by Garson Kanin and Ruth Gordon), a tour de force for which he finally won a Best Actor Oscar. He made only a few more film appearances after that, most notably as the game-show contestant in the comic *Champagne for Caesar* (1950). He finished up his film career lending a touch of class to the juvenile Irwin Allen "spectacle" modestly called *The Story of Mankind* (1957). When film work became scarce, Colman busied himself on radio—a perfect medium for an actor with his wonderful voice. He hosted and guest-starred on scores of shows, and he and his wife, actress Benita Hume, were recurring guests on "The Jack Benny Show." A radio series was created especially for them in the late 1940s: in "The Halls of Ivy," Colman played college president William Todhunter Hall, and the popular show later had a brief TV run in 1954–55. It was a perfect vehicle for this most perfect gentleman. Colman is buried in Montecito, California, near the fashionable San Ysidro Ranch, which he owned and operated for many years.

COLTRANE, ROBBIE. Actor. *(b. Mar. 30, 1950, Ruthergien, Scotland.)* He's not black and he doesn't play the tenor sax. But he *is* an uninhibited, tubby comedy actor who's been brightening British cinema for more than a decade, providing expert comic relief in such films as *Flash Gordon* (1980), *Britannia Hospital* (1982), *Krull* (1983), *Absolute Beginners* (1986), and *Henry V* (1989, as Falstaff). Coltrane limned a serious role as a mechanic in *Mona Lisa* (1986), and came to America to play the awestruck racetrack teller in *Let It Ride* (1989). But he gained major recognition on both sides of the Atlantic for his starring roles in religious garb, playing a small-time crook in drag in *Nuns on the Run* (1990), and the erroneously chosen Pope Dave in *The Pope Must Die(t)* (1991).
OTHER FILMS INCLUDE: 1985: *Revolution, Defence of the Realm;* 1986: *Caravaggio;* 1989: *Bert Rigby, You're a Fool;* 1993: *The Adventures of Huck Finn.*

COLUMBUS, CHRIS. Director, screenwriter. *(b. Sept. 10, 1958, Spangler, Pa.)* This still youthful writer-director can boast of having concocted several of the biggest moneymaking movies of all time. Caught up in horror movies and comic books as a boy, he started making 8mm movies in junior high school, and later attended film school at New York University. He was working in a comic book shop when Steven Spielberg bought his script for *Gremlins* (1984), and brought him to Hollywood, where he went on to write *Reckless* (1984) and two more Spielberg productions, *The Goonies* and *Young Sherlock Holmes* (both 1985). He got his first chance to direct with 1987's *Adventures in Babysitting*, then wrote and directed *Heartbreak Hotel* (1990); neither was terribly well received. Then in 1990 John Hughes offered him the chance to direct his script of *Home Alone*, which stunned Hollywood by becoming the most successful movie comedy ever made. Naturally, Columbus also made the 1992 sequel. But as a reward, Hughes agreed to produce *Only the Lonely* (1991), Columbus' more personal project, a bittersweet comedy about a shy man trying to shed his mother's apron strings. The writer-director considers it his best film. His latest credits: *Home Alone 2: Lost in New York* (1992), *Mrs. Doubtfire* (1993, also cowrote), and *Nine Months* (1995, also wrote).

COMDEN AND GREEN. Writers, lyricists, actors. (**Betty Comden**—b. May 3, 1919, Brooklyn N.Y. **Adolph Green**—b. Dec. 2, 1918, Bronx, N.Y.) As members of the performing troupe known as The Revuers, Comden and Green made their screen debut with fellow player Judy Holliday in *Greenwich Village* (1944)—but their material was cut from the film! Instead, they made their mark on Broadway as the librettists, lyricists, and stars of the musical hit "On the Town," on which they collaborated with two other young talents: composer Leonard Bernstein and choreographer Jerome Robbins. Their talent was as obvious as their ebullience, and MGM musical producer Arthur Freed brought them to Hollywood, where they wrote *Good News* (1947, screenplay and the song "The French Lesson"), *Take Me Out to the Ball Game* (1949, songs only), and *The Barkleys of Broadway* (1949, screenplay), but their egos suffered a bruising when they learned they would not appear on-screen in the film version of their own show *On the Town* (1949). They struck out again when they fashioned supporting parts for themselves in *The Band Wagon* (1953, an Oscar-nominated screenplay) but lost out to Nanette Fabray and Oscar Levant. Their consolation was a lifetime of acclaim for those films and the one often cited as the greatest musical ever made, *Singin' in the Rain* (1952, screenplay), which they concocted from Freed's instruction to create a showcase for his and Nacio Herb Brown's old songs. (They also wrote a new one, "Make 'Em Laugh," with Freed.) Other screenplays include *It's Always Fair Weather* (1955, an Oscar-nominated sequel to *On the Town*), *Auntie Mame* (1958, adaptation), *Bells Are Ringing* (1960, from their Broadway play), and *What a Way to Go!* (1964). Active on Broadway, both as writers and performers, through the 1990s (winning Tony Awards for such shows as "On the Twentieth Century" and "The Will Rogers Follies"), they

contributed one song to *The Addams Family* (1991). In recent years Green has taken acting roles in *Simon* (1979), *My Favorite Year* (1982), and Alain Resnais's *I Want to Go Home* (1989). Comden had a notable bit part in *Garbo Talks* (1984) as Greta Garbo, whom she resembles.

COMPTON, JOYCE. Actress. (b. Jan. 27, 1907, Lexington, Ky., as Eleanor Hunt.) Stealing a scene from Cary Grant and Irene Dunne is no small feat, but this pretty comedienne with the pale blond hair and magnolia-drenched accent managed to do just that: In *The Awful Truth* (1937), as Grant's floozy date, she sang "Gone With the Wind" while an air jet blew up her skirt. That willingness to be a good sport paid off in all sorts of roles, but the giddy, good-natured airhead remained a Compton specialty. A former beauty contest winner, she entered films in 1925 and kept plenty busy for the next 25 years. When she became too old to play ditzy blondes, she took up nursing.
OTHER FILMS INCLUDE: 1925: *What Fools Men;* 1926: *Syncopating Sue;* 1929: *Wild Party, Salute;* 1930: *High Society Blues;* 1931: *Up Pops the Devil;* 1932: *Afraid to Talk;* 1933: *Only Yesterday;* 1934: *Imitation of Life;* 1935: *Go Into Your Dance, Magnificent Obsession, Rustlers of Red Dog* (playing a "straight" ingenue role in this Johnny Mack Brown serial); 1936: *Love Before Breakfast;* 1937: *Kid Galahad, The Toast of New York;* 1938: *Trade Winds, Artists and Models Abroad;* 1939: *Balalaika, Rose of Washington Square;* 1940: *City for Conquest;* 1941: *Blues in the Night, Manpower;* 1943: *Let's Face It;* 1945: *Roughly Speaking, Mildred Pierce, Pillow to Post;* 1946: *The Best Years of Our Lives, Night and Day;* 1947: *Scared to Death;* 1948: *Sorry, Wrong Number, A Southern Yankee;* 1949: *Mighty Joe Young;* 1950: *Jet Pilot* (released 1957); 1951: *Grand Canyon;* 1958: *Girl in the Woods.*

CONNELLY, JENNIFER. Actress. (b. Dec. 12, 1970, New York City.) Who'd ever have dreamed that the spindly little girl who danced so enchantingly in *Once Upon a Time in America* (1984) would grow up to become a pneumatic dream girl of the 1990s? After other juvenile roles in the Italian shocker *Creepers* (1985), the fantasy *Labyrinth,* and the romantic comedy *Seven Nights in Heaven* (both 1986), the pretty, blue-eyed Connelly took some time off from film work, reappearing as a gorgeous teenager in the offbeat comedy *Some Girls* (1989). Still angelic-looking, but having matured into a voluptuous young woman, Connelly stunned audiences as a small-town "nice girl" (who appeared in an eye-popping nude scene) in *The Hot Spot* (1990), and as a spoiled heiress in the teen comedy *Career Opportunities* (1991), though neither clicked at the box office. She then played the wholesome girlfriend/aspiring actress in *The Rocketeer* (also 1991), and went on to appear in *The Heart of Justice* (1993 telefilm), and John Singleton's *Higher Learning* (1995).

CONNERY, SEAN. Actor. *(b. Aug. 25, 1930, Edinburgh, Scotland, as Thomas Connery.)* "The name's Bond. James Bond." And try as he might, Sean Connery's never going to totally escape his identification as that debonair secret agent with the license to kill. To his credit, though, he's been able to supplant his Agent 007 image with a wide range of impressive performances since abandoning the Bond role. After a three-year stint in the British navy, Connery toiled in a series of odd jobs—milkman, bricklayer, lifeguard—before his weight-lifting hobby enabled him to represent Scotland in the 1950 Mr. Universe contest. He eventually approached acting as a lark, an understandable decision for one of working-class origins, and debuted on-screen in *Lilacs in the Spring* (1954).

American audiences first noticed Connery as a heavy in *Tarzan's Greatest Adventure,* and then as a personable romantic lead in *Darby O'Gill and the Little People* (both 1959). He was lost in the huge all-star cast of the WW2 epic *The Longest Day* (1962), but stardom was just around the corner. His polished demeanor and ultra-masculine appeal was noticed by producer Harry Saltzman, who cast him as James Bond in the first big-screen 007 adventure, *Dr. No* (1962). (The character had appeared on U.S. TV in 1954, played by Barry Nelson in an adaptation of *Casino Royale*.)

The first Bond film was so popular that it spawned its own genre, and Connery reprised the role in *From Russia, With Love* (1963), *Goldfinger* (1964), *Thunderball* (1965), *You Only Live Twice* (1967), and *Diamonds Are Forever* (1971), before wearying of the role—and its straitjacketing of his career. He'd traded on his newfound stardom to win leading roles in Hitchcock's *Marnie* (1964), *A Fine Madness* (1966), *Shalako* (1968), *The Molly Maguires* (1970), and *The Anderson Tapes* (1972)—but none of them were blockbuster hits, and Connery publicly despaired of ever shaking the 007 image. It took a while, but slick performances in such diverse vehicles as *Zardoz, Murder on the Orient Express* (both 1974), *The Man Who Would Be King, The Wind and the Lion* (both 1975), *Robin and Marian* (1976), *Cuba* (1979), and *Outland* (1981) did the trick.

Then, amazingly, Connery returned to his star-making role in 1983's prophetically titled *Never Say Never Again,* in a good-humored performance as a more "mature" Bond. Connery's popularity actually increased as his years advanced; balding, gray-bearded, and considerably thicker around the middle, he's still considered one of the sexiest men alive. He's played a medieval detective in *The Name of the Rose* (1986), an alien gladiator in two *Highlander* films (also 1986, and 1991), a tough Irish cop in *The Untouchables* (1987, for which he won a Best Supporting Actor Academy Award), a stiff-necked soldier in *The Presidio* (1988), a good-natured thief in *Family Business,* a dotty archaeologist in *Indiana Jones and the Last Crusade* (both 1989), a Russian sub commander in *The Hunt for Red October,* a boozy publisher in *The Russia House* (both 1990), King Richard the Lion Hearted in *Robin Hood: Prince of Thieves* (1991), an iconoclastic scientist in *Medicine Man* (1992), and an expert in Japanese relations in *Rising Sun* (1993). He also executive produced the last two films. As Connery has reached senior-citizenship, his international popularity shows no signs of abating, as witness his roles in *Just Cause* (1995) and *First Knight* (also 1995, as King Arthur).

CONNOLLY, WALTER. Actor. *(b. Apr. 8, 1887, Cincinnati; d. May 28, 1940.)* Connolly was already a top stage actor when he made his movie debut in *Washington Merry-Go-Round* (1932). A little shorter than average, heavyset and mustached, he was almost unparalleled at depicting apoplexy on screen, something he did quite frequently in supporting roles. As a Columbia contract player, he appeared in many of that studio's best films of the 1930s, including *Twentieth Century* (1934) and four for director Frank Capra: *Lady for a Day, The Bitter Tea of General Yen* (both 1933), *It Happened One Night* (1934, as Claudette Colbert's father), and *Broadway Bill* (also 1934). He occasionally played leads at Columbia, and was spectacularly miscast as super sleuth Nero Wolfe in *The League of Frightened Men* (1937). He was also cast as a Chinese uncle in *The Good Earth* (1937), and had the title role in 1939's *The Great Victor Herbert*. He is best remembered by many as newspaper editor Oliver Stone (!) in *Nothing Sacred* (1937), in which he tells reporter Fredric March he's going to "take his heart out and stuff it—like an olive."

CONRAD, WILLIAM. Actor, director, producer. *(b. Sept. 27, 1920, Louisville, Ky.; d. Feb. 11, 1994.)* Thick-set, scowling, tight-lipped, rumbling-voiced character actor —a veteran of dramatic radio—who turned to motion pictures in 1946 (making a memorable debut as one of *The Killers*) and TV much later. A natural screen heavy, Conrad actually represented both sides of the law on big screens and small; he played detectives in three TV series, the long-running "Cannon" (1971–76), the short-lived "Nero Wolfe" (1981), and "Jake and the Fatman" (1987–91), though radio fans know him best for his 10-year run as Matt Dillon on "Gunsmoke," a role he lost to James Arness on TV. He also reached unsuspected comic heights as narrator of the "Rocky and Bullwinkle" TV cartoons. His films as actor include *Body and Soul* (1947), *Sorry, Wrong Number, Joan of Arc* (both 1948), *Any Number Can Play, East Side, West Side* (both 1949), *One Way Street* (1950), *Cry Danger* (1951), *Lone Star* (1952), *Cry of the Hunted* (1953), *The Naked Jungle* (1954), *Five Against the House* (1955), *Johnny Concho* (1956), *-30-* (1959, as the ultimate sarcastic newspaper managing editor), *Moonshine County Express* (1977), and *Killing Cars* (1986). He also worked as a TV and movie producer, and directed such

films as *Two on a Guillotine, My Blood Runs Cold,* and *Brainstorm* (all 1965).

CONRIED, HANS. Actor. *(b. Apr. 15, 1917, Baltimore; d. Jan. 5, 1982.)* Master dialectician with great comedic talent, sometimes mired in thankless dramatic roles (especially early in his career, when he was several times cast as a Nazi). Conried's appearance—he was tall, slender, with thick, wavy hair—and his sometimes imperious manner led him to be cast as ascetics and absentminded eccentrics. He worked on radio before breaking into movies in 1939 (and remained one of the busiest actors in radio history). Conried's most memorable performance is as the demonic piano teacher in *The 5,000 Fingers of Dr. T* (1953), one of two leading roles in his film career (the other was in Arch Oboler's *The Twonky* that same year). He had a 13-year run as Uncle Tonoose on the "Make Room for Daddy" TV show from 1958 to 1971, hosted "Fractured Flickers" and was the voice of Snidely Whiplash in Dudley Do-Right cartoons on "Rocky and Bullwinkle."
OTHER FILMS INCLUDE: 1938: *Dramatic School;* 1942: *Once Upon a Honeymoon, Journey Into Fear;* 1943: *Hitler's Children;* 1947: *The Senator Was Indiscreet;* 1950: *Summer Stock;* 1956: *Bus Stop;* 1964: *The Patsy.*

CONTE, RICHARD. Actor. *(b. Mar. 24, 1914, Jersey City, N.J., as Nicholas Peter Conte; d. Apr. 15, 1975.)* Dimpled, dark-haired actor whose unmistakable Italian ancestry typed him in gangster roles; he frequently played bitter scions of immigrant families as well. Making his film debut in a small role in 20th Century-Fox's *Heaven With a Barbed Wire Fence* (a 1939 B in which he was billed under his real name), Conte scored his first meaty role in the studio's all-star war drama, 1943's *Guadalcanal Diary,* and appeared in several similar films—including *The Purple Heart* (1944), *A Bell for Adano,* and *A Walk in the Sun* (both 1945)—before settling into gritty, naturalistic noirs and melodramas such as *13 Rue Madeleine* (1946), *Call Northside 777, Cry of the City* (both 1948), *House of Strangers* (a standout performance as Edward G. Robinson's wayward son),

Whirlpool, Thieves' Highway (all 1949), *The Sleeping City* (1950), *Hollywood Story, The Raging Tide* (both 1951), *The Fighter* (1952), *The Blue Gardenia* (1953), *Highway Dragnet* (1954), *The Big Combo, The Big Tip-Off, I'll Cry Tomorrow, New York Confidential* (all 1955), and *The Brothers Rico* (1957).

Conte slipped into supporting roles in the late 1950s and early 1960s; his dark, brooding good looks gave way to an increasingly craggy face with a sinister cast. He appeared in *They Came to Cordura* (1959), *Ocean's Eleven* (1960), *The Eyes of Annie Jones* (1963), *Circus World* (1964), *The Greatest Story Ever Told* (1965, as Barabbas), *Assault on a Queen* (1966), *Hotel, Tony Rome* (both 1967), *Lady in Cement* (1968), and *Operation Cross Eagles* (1969) before assuming his best-remembered latter-day role, that of the treacherous Don Barzini in *The Godfather* (1972). It was also his last Hollywood film: Conte finished his career in minor Italian-made crime and action movies, working steadily until his death in 1975.

CONTI, BILL. Composer. *(b. Apr. 13, 1943, Providence, R.I.)* Popular composer whose signature composition is the theme for 1976's Oscar winner *Rocky* (and its four sequels). A Juilliard graduate, Conti was in Italy orchestrating for film composers and songwriters when he was hired as musical supervisor on Paul Mazursky's *Blume in Love* (1973). He subsequently began his career as a composer, writing scores for films like Mazursky's *Harry and Tonto* (1974), *Handle With Care* (1977), *An Unmarried Woman* (1978, again for Mazursky), *Gloria, Private Benjamin* (both 1980), *That Championship Season* (1982), *The Karate Kid* (1984, and its 1986 and 1989 sequels), *F/X* (1986), *Baby Boom, Broadcast News* (both 1987), *Lean on Me* (1989), *Bound by Honor* and *The Adventures of Huck Finn* (both 1993). Conti was Oscar-nominated for the song "Gonna Fly Now" from *Rocky* and the title song from the James Bond picture *For Your Eyes Only* (1981) and won the prize for his rousing score for *The Right Stuff* (1983). He has also composed numerous TV themes including "Dynasty," "Falcon Crest," and "Lifestyles of the Rich and Famous" and served as musical director for The Academy Awards ceremonies for many years.

CONTI, TOM. Actor. *(b. Nov. 22, 1941, Paisley, Scotland.)* Lively, talented character lead and supporting player, always a pleasure to watch, who has failed to achieve significant commercial success. Conti, a skilled dialectician equally adept at comedy and drama, delivers consistently outstanding performances but, alas, has little or no box-office "pull." Primarily a stage actor (he won a Tony in 1979 for "Whose Life Is It, Anyway?"), his film activity was limited until the early 1980s, when he played the titular POW in *Merry Christmas, Mr. Lawrence* (1983), the boozy, womanizing poet in *Reuben, Reuben* (also 1983, Oscar-nominated as Best Actor), and the hilariously rattled "partner" of would-be spy JoBeth Williams in *American Dreamer* (1984). More recently seen as the lusty Greek restaurateur in *Shirley Valentine* (1989), Conti has also appeared in several quirky little films that had little theatrical exposure, such as *Miracles* (1984) and *Saving Grace* (1986).

CONWAY, TIM. Actor. *(b. Dec. 15, 1933, Willoughby, Ohio.)* Balding, chunky comic actor who originally endeared himself to TV audiences as the bumbling ensign in the 1960s sitcom "McHale's Navy" (which also spawned two feature films, 1964's *McHale's Navy* and 1965's *McHale's Navy Joins the Air Force*). Conway toiled in several other series—all flops—before appearing in a string of slapsticky family films, some of them for Disney (often teamed with Don Knotts), among them *The World's Greatest Athlete* (1973), *The Apple Dumpling Gang* (1975), *Gus* (1976), *The Billion Dollar Hobo* (1978), *The Apple Dumpling Gang Rides Again* (1979), *The Prize Fighter* (1979), and *Private Eyes* (1980). Paul Bartel directed him in the racetrack comedy *The Longshot* (1986), his last starring vehicle to date. He's best remembered for his hilarious antics on "The Carol Burnett Show," which earned him three Emmy Awards; he has recently starred in several video productions as Dorf, a comedic dwarf.

CONWAY, TOM. Actor. *(b. Sept. 15, 1904, St. Petersburg, Russia, as Thomas Charles Sanders; d. Apr. 22, 1967.)* The brother of actor George Sanders, Conway hit Hollywood in 1940, hoping to emulate his sibling's success. In fact, he had little luck until Sanders tired of his Raffles-like character in RKO's "Falcon" series and convinced the studio to replace him with his brother. Well built and handsome, Conway sported a pencil mustache and played The Falcon with an insouciance nearly equal to that of his brother. He made 13 films in the series, including *The Falcon Strikes Back* (1943), *The Falcon in Mexico* (1945), and *The Falcon's Alibi* (1946). He also appeared in *Tarzan's Secret Treasure* (1941), *Rio Rita* (1942), *The Seventh Victim, I Walked With a Zombie* (both 1943), and *Voodoo Woman* (1957), among others, but his career is best described as undistinguished.

COOGAN, JACKIE. Actor. *(b. Oct. 24, 1914, Los Angeles; d. Mar. 1, 1984.)* As a tattered, runny-nosed little waif, this accomplished young actor—the movies' first real child star—earned more than $4 million in a few short years. But although he eventually sued his family to get the money, Coogan found himself broke: his parents had spent all but $250,000 of it by 1938. Four-year-old Coogan was working in an outdoor revue with swimming star Annette Kellerman when he was seen by Charlie Chaplin, who used him first in the 1919 short *A Day's Pleasure,* then in the feature film he inspired, *The Kid* (1921). It was that film, with its skillful blending of comedy and pathos, that established Chaplin as an artist and Coogan as a star in his own right. A natural actor with enormous appeal, he starred in *Peck's Bad Boy* (1921), *Oliver Twist* (1922), *Daddy, Long Live the King* (both 1923), *Little Robinson Crusoe* (1924), *Old Clothes* (1925), *Buttons* (1926), and several others before reaching puberty and seeing his popularity decline.

Leading roles in the talkies *Tom Sawyer* (1930) and *Huckleberry Finn* (1931) didn't help his career any; the public, ever fickle, turned to other younger and cuter child stars (including his own brother Robert, who costarred with Jackie Cooper in *Skippy* and *Sooky* in the early 1930s). Offscreen for several years, Coogan reap-

peared with then-wife Betty Grable in *College Swing* (1938), the year he sued his mother and stepfather. He got half of the remaining quarter-million, and his case led to passage of the Child Actors Bill, also known as the Coogan Act, which has effectively curtailed similar abuses.

After divorcing Grable in 1939, Coogan dropped out of movies, returning only occasionally. After *Kilroy Was Here* (1947) and *French Leave* (1948), he was relegated to character roles—often heavies—in *Outlaw Women* (1952), *The Proud Ones* (1956), *The Joker Is Wild, The Buster Keaton Story* (both 1957), *High School Confidential!* (1958), *Sex Kittens Go to College* (1960), *John Goldfarb, Please Come Home* (1964), *A Fine Madness* (1966), *Marlowe* (1969), *Cahill—U.S. Marshal* (1973), and *Human Experiments* (1979). Coogan did achieve latter-day stardom, of a sort, as bald-headed Uncle Fester on the "Addams Family" TV series (1964–66, 1973–74). Earlier, he'd costarred with Russell Hayden in the syndicated "Cowboy G-Men" (1952).

COOK, ELISHA, JR. Actor. *(b. Dec. 26, 1903, San Francisco; d. May 18, 1995.)* Slightly built, jittery, pop-eyed character actor whose delineations of small-time hoods, cowardly grifters, and neurotic stool pigeons are second to none in all movie history. Unforgettable as Wilmer, the psychotic "gunsel" of Sydney Greenstreet in *The Maltese Falcon* (1941), Cook was one of the screen's most recognizable supporting players. He was acting before he was shaving, trouping in stock, vaudeville, and on Broadway before making his film debut in *Her Unborn Child* (1929). Cook worked on stage for several more years before coming to Hollywood and establishing himself. His memorable roles include that of a cagey songwriter in *Tin Pan Alley* (1940), a quietly sinister hotel clerk in *I Wake Up Screaming* (1941), a hopped-up drummer in *Phantom Lady* (1944), a hapless would-be tough guy in *The Big Sleep* (1946), and a feisty, tough-talking homesteader in *Shane* (1953). OTHER FILMS INCLUDE: 1936: *Pigskin Parade;* 1937: *They Won't Forget;* 1940: *The Stranger on the Third Floor;* 1944: *Up in Arms;* 1945: *Dillinger;* 1947: *Born to Kill;* 1949:

Flaxy Martin; 1953: *I, the Jury;* 1956: *The Killing* (another outstanding performance); 1961: *One-Eyed Jacks;* 1963: *Johnny Cool;* 1968: *Rosemary's Baby;* 1970: *El Condor;* 1973: *Emperor of the North Pole;* 1975: *The Black Bird* (a *Maltese Falcon* spoof); 1979: *The Champ;* 1982: *Hammett, National Lampoon Goes to the Movies.*

COOLIDGE, MARTHA. Director. *(b. Aug. 17, 1946, New Haven, Conn.)* One of the more prominent female directors working in Hollywood, Coolidge is known for films dealing with the problems and pains of sexuality. She received extensive training at the Rhode Island School of Design, New York's School of Visual Arts, and the New York University Institute of Film and Television graduate school; during that period she made many prize-winning films and documentaries. Her first directorial job was a short film, *Not a Pretty Picture* (1975), examining a high school date rape. It won acclaim and attention, as did her feature-length *City Girl* (1983), which led to a job directing the modest commercial feature comedy *Valley Girl* (1983), with Nicolas Cage in his first starring role. This film's unexpectedly positive reviews won Coolidge major studio assignments, but *Joy of Sex* (1984) was barely released, and *Real Genius* (1985) and *Plain Clothes* (1988) were disappointing at best. Coolidge found more satisfying work in television, and finally scored a bull's-eye with the theatrical feature *Rambling Rose* (1991), the story of a free-spirited young woman in a small Southern town, which earned Oscar nominations for its stars Laura Dern and Diane Ladd. Recent credits include *Crazy in Love* (1992 telefilm), *Lost in Yonkers* (1993), and *Angie* (1994).

COOPER, GARY. Actor. *(b. May 7, 1901, Helena, Mont., as Frank James Cooper; d. May 13, 1961.)* The movies' archetypal "strong, silent type," this tall, laconic leading man defined Hollywood heroism in a way most other actors never could. Many of his characters, whether by choice or design, were cut from distinctly American cloth: slow to anger, predisposed to peaceful solutions, but unafraid to use force rooted in justice. Although the softspoken Cooper was a college graduate

(and briefly, a newspaper cartoonist), his saddle skills—hard won in his Montana youth—actually got him into movies, first as an extra in numerous Hollywood Westerns, then as an eleventh-hour replacement for the second male lead in Henry King's *The Winning of Barbara Worth* (1926), in which the lanky young man managed to steal many of the scenes he shared with matinee idol Ronald Colman—a not-inconsiderable feat that led Paramount Pictures to sign him.

Initially he supported the studio's top stars—Clara Bow in *It* (1927) and *Children of Divorce* (1927), Bow, Richard Arlen, and Buddy Rogers in the Oscar-winning *Wings* (1927)—but made his own mark as a top-billed star of Paramount's program Westerns, including 1927's *Arizona Bound, Nevada,* and *The Last Outlaw.* He was paired with Colleen Moore in *Lilac Time* and Nancy Carroll in *Shopworn Angel,* two successful 1929 dramas set during World War 1. Talkies found Cooper refining his naturally taciturn Western character; in *The Virginian* (1929), he rarely spoke unless he had something to say, including the famous line, "When you call me that, *smile,*" delivered to swearing badman Walter Huston. In 1930 he starred in *The Texan* and *A Man From Wyoming* (as well as taking a cameo in the all-star *Paramount on Parade*) before being teamed with exotic Marlene Dietrich in *Morocco,* a scorching desert romance that found him in Legionnaire's garb, and led him away from Westerns. Although Cooper frequently essayed roles that called for him to be shy or reticent, his offscreen conduct vitiated that image; his affairs with Bow, Lupe Velez, and others were both numerous and well known.

Cooper played a hard-boiled gunman in *City Streets* (1931), a gangster story written by Dashiell Hammett; his performance suggests that he'd have been right at home playing one of Hammett's pulp-fiction detectives. *I Take This Woman, His Women* (both 1931), *The Devil and the Deep,* and *A Farewell to Arms* (both 1932, the last-named a Hemingway adaptation costarring Helen Hayes) refined and reinforced his new image as a romantic leading man. And, while ostensibly miscast as an artist in Ben Hecht's spicy adaptation of Noël Coward's witty *Design for Living* (1933, directed by Ernst Lubitsch), Coop acquitted himself admirably. It's unfortunate that he didn't choose to appear in more comedies, because he certainly had the knack. He continued to top-line some of Paramount's most successful films of the 1930s, including *The Lives of a Bengal Lancer* (1935), *Desire,* and *The General Died at Dawn* (both 1936), before going to Columbia to star as small-town sage Longfellow Deeds in *Mr. Deeds Goes to Town* (1936), one of Frank Capra's best populist comedies and one of Cooper's signature roles; it earned him his first Oscar nomination.

Back at Paramount he played a romanticized Wild Bill Hickok in Cecil B. DeMille's *The Plainsman* (1936) and starred in *Souls at Sea* (1937) before tackling (most improbably) the title character in *The Adventures of Marco Polo* (1938), continuing a working relationship with producer Sam Goldwyn begun with *The Wedding Night* (1935). He lapsed back into "shucks, ma'am" mode for Goldwyn's formula comedy *The Cowboy and the Lady,* pleasantly paired with Merle Oberon. It fared better than *Bluebeard's Eighth Wife* (1938), a rare misfire for Lubitsch (working from a Billy Wilder–Charles Brackett script, no less). *Beau Geste* (1939) saw him back in form; although hardly the type to play an aristocratic young Englishman who joins the Foreign Legion to save his family from disgrace, Cooper cut a dashing figure in the distinctive Legionnaire uniform, and the surefire remake of the 1926 film was a solid hit. Two more Goldwyn-produced efforts, *The Real Glory* (1939) and *The Westerner* (1940, in which he matched wits with Walter Brennan's Judge Roy Bean), preceded Cooper's return to DeMille for *Northwest Mounted Police* (1940), a robust if somewhat silly Technicolor actioner.

Cooper's next four films set a high-water mark in screen acting—and sheer starpower—seldom (if ever) equaled since. He played an idealistic hobo turned media hero in Frank Capra's bittersweet *Meet John Doe* (1941), then portrayed real-life pacifist-turned-WW1 hero Alvin York in *Sergeant York* later that year, winning the Best Actor Oscar for his performance. *Ball of Fire* (also 1941, a Goldwyn picture directed by Howard Hawks) showed he hadn't forgotten how to play comedy; as one of the prissy pro-

fessors who enlists wisecracking burlesque dancer Barbara Stanwyck to help them with a slang encyclopedia, Cooper showed himself to be a terrific straight man. And *The Pride of the Yankees* (1942, also for Goldwyn), featured him as baseball great Lou Gehrig (then recently deceased) in a touching, warm biopic that yielded another Oscar nomination.

He earned another Oscar nod for his hardbitten performance in *For Whom the Bell Tolls* (1943), based on the novel by his friend Ernest Hemingway, but his next few vehicles, while certainly pleasant, suggested that he might be marking time: *The Story of Dr. Wassell, Casanova Brown* (both 1944, the former directed by Cecil B. DeMille), *Along Came Jones* (1945, which he also produced), *Saratoga Trunk* (1945), *Cloak and Dagger* (1946), *Unconquered* (1947), and *Good Sam* (1948). Cooper was riveting as the iconoclastic architect in *The Fountainhead* (1949), an ambitious but middling Ayn Rand adaptation. More routine films followed—*Task Force* (1949), *Bright Leaf, Dallas* (both 1950), and *You're in the Navy Now* (1951) among them—before an aging, weary-looking Cooper assumed what may be his greatest role, that of the embattled marshal abandoned by the townspeople he spent years protecting, in *High Noon* (1952), a controversial film that was at once both the epitome and the antithesis of the "traditional" Western. The Academy presented him with another Oscar for his sterling performance.

In the Indian Summer of his career, Cooper starred in a number of meritorious productions that used his age as an asset—including *The Court-Martial of Billy Mitchell* (1955), *Friendly Persuasion* (1956), *Love in the Afternoon* (1957, paired romantically with Audrey Hepburn and directed by Billy Wilder), *Man of the West* (1958), and *The Hanging Tree* (1959)—but his energies seemed to wane with each passing film. *The Naked Edge* (1961), a routine thriller shot in England, showed a listless Cooper just going through the motions; it proved to be his last film. In April 1961 he won a special, career-achievement Academy Award, which was accepted by his friend James Stewart. By that time a cancer-riddled Cooper was too ill to accept it. A month later he was dead.

COOPER, GLADYS (DAME). Actress. *(b. Dec. 18, 1888, Lewisham, England; d. Nov. 17, 1971.)* One of the stage's great beauties during Edwardian days, she occasionally graced British films in the. teens and early 1920s, but the body of her screen work was done in Hollywood after 1940, where she was invariably cast as an upper-class matron, usually with a cool, cynical edge. She appeared in *Rebecca, Kitty Foyle* (both 1940), and *That Hamilton Woman* (1941), and was Oscar-nominated for her work in *Now, Voyager* (1942) and *The Song of Bernadette* (1943). She snared a third nomination, toward the end of her career, for her performance as Henry Higgins' mother in *My Fair Lady* (1964). She also appeared in "The Rogues" TV series in that year.
OTHER FILMS INCLUDE: 1935: *The Iron Duke;* 1943: *Forever and a Day, Mr. Lucky;* 1944: *The White Cliffs of Dover;* 1946: *The Green Years;* 1947: *The Bishop's Wife;* 1948: *The Pirate;* 1949: *Madame Bovary;* 1958: *Separate Tables;* 1963: *The List of Adrian Messenger;* 1967: *The Happiest Millionaire* (in which she sings).

COOPER, JACKIE. Actor, director. *(b. Sept. 15, 1921, Los Angeles.)* As a pug-nosed blond with pouting mouth and the ability to shed tears in buckets, Jackie Cooper was one of Hollywood's top child stars in the 1930s. He broke into movies as a tiny player in comedy shorts, appearing in 15 "Our Gang" episodes between 1929 and 1931. His uncle, director Norman Taurog, put Cooper into the title role of *Skippy* (1931), a successful film based on a popular comic strip, which earned the youngster a Best Actor Oscar nomination (making him the youngest actor to receive that honor, a record he still holds) and catapulted him into the upper echelons of MGM's star roster. He appeared opposite blustery Wallace Beery in *The Champ* (1931), *The Bowery* (1933), *Treasure Island* (1934), and *O'Shaughnessy's Boy* (1935), and copped star billing in *Sooky* (also 1931), *When a Feller Needs a Friend* (1932), and *Peck's Bad Boy* (1934), among others. Like most child stars, Cooper found his popularity waning as he reached adolescence, and weathered a turbulent period in his personal life while looking for a new direction in his professional life.

Cooper played Dead End–like tough kids in *The Devil Is a Sissy* (1936) for Metro and *Boy of the Streets* (1937) for Monogram, where he starred in several other, less gritty dramas, including *Gangster's Boy* (1938) and *Streets of New York* (1939). He starred in a serial, 1939's *Scouts to the Rescue,* and played the screen's first Henry Aldrich in *What a Life!* that same year. Straight dramatic roles in *The Return of Frank James* (1940) and *Ziegfeld Girl* (1941), among others, gave him an opportunity to demonstrate his not inconsiderable acting ability, but World War 2 intervened and he went into the service. Upon leaving he found movie roles few and far between; *Stork Bites Man, Kilroy Was Here* (both 1947), and *French Leave* (1948), execrable low-budgeters, convinced him to get out of Hollywood for a while. He toured with stock companies for years, and even landed on Broadway, before launching a second successful career, this time on TV. He worked in live television, starred in two popular filmed series, "The People's Choice" (1955–58) and "Hennesey" (1959–62), and eventually focused his talents behind the camera as a director and producer. (At one point he was the executive in charge of production for Screen Gems, the Columbia TV subsidiary.)
Cooper helmed the feature film *Stand Up and Be Counted* (1972) in addition to dozens of TV series episodes and telefilms (including 1978's *Rainbow,* a biopic of his good friend Judy Garland). He won Emmys for directing episodes of "M*A*S*H" and "The White Shadow." He still found time to act, appearing in many TV guest spots and playing "Daily Planet" editor Perry White in the *Superman* movies starring Christopher Reeve (1978, 1981, 1983, and 1987); he also appeared in *Surrender* (1987). His autobiography, "Please Don't Shoot My Dog," was published in 1981. No less an authority than Roddy McDowall, himself an "ex-moppet," cites Cooper as the most gifted child star in movie history.

COOPER, MERIAN C. Producer, director. *(b. Oct. 24, 1893, Jacksonville, Fla.; d. Apr. 21, 1973.)* With partner Ernest B. Schoedsack, this former lieutenant colonel and globe-trotting adventurer gave movie audiences some of the most breathtaking films, fiction and nonfiction, of the 1920s and 1930s, most notably *King Kong* (1933). Cooper and Schoedsack shared producing, directing, photographic, and editorial chores on their exotic documentaries—including *Grass* (1925), *Chang* (1927), and *Gow the Head Hunter* (1928)—before signing with Paramount to provide the spectacular Sudan-shot footage interpolated into *The Four Feathers* (1929), the team's first fictional film. (They were *all* fictional to some degree, though; neither man was averse to staging events used in their documentaries.) Cooper joined RKO in 1932 as a producer and shortly thereafter became head of production, a post he held for several years. During that time, he either personally produced or "green-lighted" some of RKO's most famous films: *The Most Dangerous Game, The Phantom of Crestwood* (both 1932), *King Kong, Son of Kong, Morning Glory, Little Women, Flying Down to Rio* (all 1933), *The Lost Patrol* (1934), *She,* and *The Last Days of Pompeii* (both 1935). He worked as vice president of Selznick International Pictures for several years, and joined the Army Air Corps during World War 2.

In 1947 Cooper and director John Ford formed Argosy Productions as an independent unit; together they brought *The Fugitive* (1947), *3 Godfathers, Fort Apache* (both 1948), *She Wore a Yellow Ribbon, Mighty Joe Young* (both 1949), *Wagon Master, Rio Grande* (both 1950), *The Quiet Man* (1952, the only movie on which Cooper worked to be Oscar-nominated for Best Picture), *The Sun Shines Bright* (1953), and *The Searchers* (1956) to the screen. Cooper also produced *This Is Cinerama* (1952), the first film to utilize that wide-screen process. In 1952 he received a special Oscar for his "many innovations and contributions to the art of motion pictures." Toward the end of his life Cooper, once one of the most distinguished men in Hollywood, was managing a small motel in Southern California.

COPPOLA, FRANCIS (FORD). Director, producer, screenwriter. *(b. Apr. 7, 1939, Detroit.)* Talented, controversial director whose towering achievements have been mirrored by a series of critical and box-office disasters. The son of a composer father and an actress mother, Coppola was among the first of the new breed of directors in the 1960s who came to the industry via film school, rather than studio service or Hollywood connections. He initially studied theater at Hofstra University, and then attended UCLA to learn more about film. His more practical schooling came during an apprenticeship with Roger Corman, toiling as a script doctor, sound dubber, and film editor. Coppola's first directing assignment for Corman, *Dementia 13* (1963), was filmed in three days while summering in Ireland. His "thesis" film for UCLA, the sporadically funny *You're a Big Boy Now* (1966), was acquired by Warner Bros., whose execs were sufficiently impressed to hand him the directorial reins on a big-budget musical, *Finian's Rainbow* (1968)—which became his first great flop.

Coppola rebounded with a less expensive, more personal feature, *The Rain People* (1969). (He also labored as a screenwriter during this period, working on nearly a dozen scripts, including 1966's *Is Paris Burning?* and 1970's *Patton,* for which he shared a Best Screenplay Oscar.) He then ascended from the ranks of promising new directors to the head of the A-list by making *The Godfather* (1972), a brilliantly crafted gangster saga that became the biggest box-office hit in movie history. Winning a second Oscar for Best Screenplay and a first nomination for Best Director, Coppola saw his star on the rise once again.

After the dual successes of 1974's *The Godfather, Part II* and *The Conversation*—both were nominated for Best Screenplay (the former won); both were nominated for Best Picture (again, going to *Godfather II*)—Coppola was hailed as one of the most powerful directors in Hollywood. Unfortunately, his next major project, the mammoth *Apocalypse Now* (1979) nearly broke Coppola, financially and spiritually. Less a Vietnam picture than existentialist parable, the horrifyingly expensive film was an artistic triumph (Oscar-nominated for Best Picture) but a lukewarm box-office draw; Coppola's Zoetrope Studios, which he had lovingly fashioned as a state-of-the-art production facility, was barely rescued from bankruptcy.

The director, anxious to salvage both his reputation and his financial stability, followed *Apocalypse Now* with a series of commercially oriented pictures. Some, like *The Black Stallion* (1979, which he executive-produced), were successful; others, like his adaptations of S. E. Hinton's teen gothics *The Outsiders* and *Rumble Fish* (both 1983), weren't. Two heavily touted "comeback" vehicles, the elephantine *One From the Heart* (1982) and the scandal-plagued *The Cotton Club* (1984), showed Coppola's mastery of motion-picture technique but failed to recoup their costs upon initial theatrical release. A favorite subject of movie gossip, Coppola was said to have "lost it."

Since then, Coppola's output has been uneven, ranging from the exceptional (*Peggy Sue Got Married,* 1986) to the forgettable (*Gardens of Stone,* 1987). His attempt at an old-fashioned, inspirational Hollywood biopic, *Tucker: The Man and His Dream* (1988), was seen by some as an autobiographical parable, the director identifying himself with the brashly idealistic 1940s car designer. His episode of the omnibus film *New York Stories* (1989), "Life Without Zoe," was an embarrassing, self-indulgent exercise in home-movie-as-mass-entertainment folderol.

Finally, he succumbed to commercial pressure and agreed to make *The Godfather, Part III* (1990), which showed flashes of directorial brilliance (and earned him Oscar nominations for Best Picture and Director), and was unquestionably the most interesting Coppola film in years. Like his other recent films, it was not a megahit—but then, Coppola had given himself an almost impossible act to follow. He decided to take on an entirely different kind of project with *Bram Stoker's Dracula* (1992), a film in which every artifice known to contemporary filmmakers was employed for maximum visual impact. Its success has led him to produce a followup, *Mary Shelley's Frankenstein* (1994), directed by Kenneth Branagh. He also executive-produced *Wind* (1992) and *The Secret Garden* (1993).

Significantly, Coppola has been helpful in assisting foreign directors, notably Wim Wenders and Akira Kurosawa, to secure American release of their films, and he was instrumental in bringing the restored version of Abel Gance's silent masterpiece *Napoleon* (1927) to American audiences.

CORDAY, MARA. Actress. *(b. Jan. 3, 1932, Santa Monica, Calif., as Marilyn Watts.)* Dark-haired, statuesque actress and 1950s cult figure who had more acting ability than she was permitted to exhibit in such potboilers as *Francis Joins the Wacs* (1954) or *The Giant Claw* (1957). A former chorus girl and photographer's model (she was a mainstay of 1950s men's magazines, including "Playboy"), she made her film debut in *Two Tickets to Broadway* (1951). As a freelance performer, she played both ingenues and tarts with equal relish in such films as *Tarzan's Savage Fury, Sea Tiger* (both 1952), *The Lady Wants Mink, Sweethearts on Parade* (both 1953), *Playgirl* (1954, opposite future husband Richard Long), before being signed to a contract at Universal-International in 1954. In her leading-lady chores for that studio, Corday sometimes went "over the top," but nonetheless made a sultry female lead in *The Man From Bitter Ridge, Tarantula* (both 1955), *Naked Gun, Francis in the Haunted House, Raw Edge, A Day of Fury, The Quiet Gun* (all 1956), *Girl in Death Row, The Black Scorpion* (both 1957), and *Girls on the Loose* (1958). She also appeared in support in *So This Is Paris* (1954) and *Man Without a Star* (1955). Corday took a lengthy hiatus from the screen, but returned to acting after Long's untimely death. She's since appeared in *The Gauntlet* (1977), *Sudden Impact* (1983), *Pink Cadillac* (1989), and *The Rookie* (1990), all for her fellow 1950s U-I contract player Clint Eastwood, in addition to TV shows and made-fors.

COREY, WENDELL. Actor. *(b. Mar. 20, 1914, Dracut, Mass.; d. Nov. 8, 1968.)* A minister's son who turned to life upon the wicked stage in 1934, the poker-faced Corey made his way to Broadway in the early 1940s, appearing in several prominent shows before being signed to a movie contract by producer Hal Wallis in 1946. He made his film debut in a strong supporting role in *Desert Fury* (1947), and went on to meaty roles in *I Walk Alone, The Search, Sorry, Wrong Number* (all 1948), *The Accused, Any Number Can Play, Holiday Affair, The File on Thelma Jordon* (all 1949), *The Furies, Harriet Craig* (all 1950), *The Wild Blue Yonder* (1951), *Carbine Williams* (1952), and many others. A reasonably good actor, Corey lacked the charisma to make him a star; his few leading-man turns are bland at best. But he ably projected menace when called upon to do so, and few could rival his cynical delivery of tart dialogue. His later films include *Rear Window* (1954), *The Big Knife* (1955), *The Killer Is Loose, The Rainmaker* (both 1956), *Loving You* (1957), *Alias Jesse James* (1956, as Jesse), *Blood on the Arrow* (1964), *Agent for H.A.R.M., Picture Mommy Dead, Women of the Prehistoric Planet, Cyborg 2087* (all 1966), *Astro-Zombies* (1968, his career low-point). A onetime president of the Academy of Motion Picture Arts and Sciences and the Screen Actors Guild, he made a brief but unsuccessful stab at politics in 1966. Corey died of a liver ailment brought on by alcoholism.

CORMAN, ROGER. Producer, director. *(b. Apr. 5, 1926, Los Angeles.)* A virtual one-man American Film Institute, this former King of the Drive-Ins merits our esteem both for his own body of work and for giving first opportunities to much of the top talent in Hollywood today. In 1954 he hooked up with producers James Nicholson and Samuel Arkoff, and directed *The Monster From the Ocean Floor* for $10,000. The company, called American-International, was off and running, as Corman produced and directed an amazing number of films, usually in 10 days (and even less), using a repertory corps of actors (who often doubled as the production crew), and injecting his thread-bare Westerns, rock-'n'-roll dramas, horror movies, and sci-fi with healthy doses of humor and social comment. The more memorable include *Attack of the Crab Monsters, Not of This Earth, Rock All Night* (all 1957), *Cry Baby Killer* (1958, Jack Nicholson's first film), *A Bucket of Blood* (1959), *The Last Woman on Earth* (Robert Towne's first script), and *The Little Shop of Horrors* (both 1960). *Shop,* which developed an enduring cult following, eventually inspired a hit stage musical (itself filmed in 1986).

In 1960 Corman discovered Edgar Allan Poe, and *House of Usher* launched a series of eight colorful but inexpensively made chillers, all but one starring Vincent Price;

The Masque of the Red Death (1964) is widely considered the best. He also directed a young William Shatner in the antiracism story *The Intruder* (1961), his first box-office flop, and gave Francis Coppola his first real directing job with *Dementia 13* (1963). After the Poe cycle ran its course, he tapped into the burgeoning counterculture market with the hugely successful *The Wild Angels* (1966), and *The Trip,* and made his first big studio film at Fox, *The St. Valentine's Day Massacre* (both 1967).

In 1970 Corman stopped directing to form his own company, New World, and produced a long string of successful drive-in fare, written and/or directed by such neophytes as Jonathan Demme, Jonathan Kaplan, Joe Dante, Allan Arkush, James Cameron, Paul Bartel, John Sayles, and Ron Howard; he also gave Peter Bogdanovich and Martin Scorsese their studio directing debuts. At New World Pictures he also, incongruously, distributed to American audiences such distinguished fare as Ingmar Bergman's *Cries and Whispers* (1972) and Federico Fellini's *Amarcord* (1974).

After selling his interest in New World, he launched Concorde Pictures, which specialized in the kind of low-budget product with which he began his career. In 1990 he finally returned to directing with *Frankenstein Unbound,* and has expressed a desire to do more. In his own way, he is as influential as any filmmaker who ever lived, and several of his "graduates" have acknowledged their debt by giving him cameo roles in such films as *The Godfather, Part II* (1974), *The Howling* (1980), *Swing Shift* (1984), *The Silence of the Lambs* (1991), and *Philadelphia* (1993). He published his autobiography, "How I Made A Hundred Movies in Hollywood and Never Lost a Dime," in 1990.

CORRIGAN, RAY "CRASH." Actor. *(b. Feb. 14, 1907, Milwaukee, as Ray Bernard; d. Aug. 10, 1976.)* Muscular physical-culture instructor turned action star and, so help us, professional ape impersonator. He entered films as a stuntman and bit player in the early 1930s (he claimed to have doubled Johnny Weissmuller in 1932's *Tarzan, the Ape Man*). As Ray "Crash" Corrigan, he starred in the sci-fi serial *Undersea King-*

dom (for which, contrary to other reports, he was billed as "Crash" so his name would sound like "Flash Gordon"), and played "Tucson" Smith in the first 24 of the "Three Mesquiteers" Westerns, beginning with *The Three Mesquiteers* (1936) and ending with *New Frontier* (1939). During this period he bought a large tract of land in California's San Fernando Valley, and rented the picturesque location to movie producers.

Corrigan and fellow "Mesquiteer" alumnus Max Terhune joined John "Dusty" King to become "The Range Busters" in 24 Monogram Westerns—many of them shot at "Corriganville"—from 1940 to 1943. Corrigan also made his own ape suit and farmed himself out to cheapie producers of threadbare jungle epics like *Zamba* (1949) and *Killer Ape* (1953). The zenith (or perhaps nadir) of this work ethic was reached in *The White Gorilla* (1945), in which Corrigan played the male lead and *two* gorillas. He wore *another* monster suit as the creature in *It! The Terror From Beyond Space* (1958). Corrigan ran a Wild West show at Corriganville until the early 1960s, when he sold his property to Bob Hope for a reported $3 million.

CORT, BUD. Actor. *(b. Mar. 29, 1950, New Rochelle, N.Y., as Walter Edward Cox.)* Idiosyncratic, youthful character actor, best known for his work in 1970s cult items. He made his film debut as a flower child in *Sweet Charity* (1969), and made five films the following year, including the groundbreaking black comedy *MASH*. The film's director, Robert Altman, then cast him in the leading role of his very strange *Brewster McCloud* (1970), as a misfit who wants to fly in the Houston Astrodome. Already a counterculture icon, Cort achieved his greatest success in 1972 as Ruth Gordon's teenage love interest in *Harold and Maude*. He worked less frequently during the 1980s, and when he did turn up it was usually in modest, unexciting films such as *Die Laughing* (1980), *Love Letters* (1983), and *Maria's Lovers* (1984). He also provided the voice of a computer in *Electric Dreams* (1984). More recently, he's turned up as quirky, oddball types in low-budget affairs like 1988's *The Chocolate War* and 1990's *Brain Dead*. In 1992 he made his screen

directing debut with the (predictably) oddball *Ted and Venus*.

CORTEZ, STANLEY. Cinematographer. *(b. Nov. 4, 1908, New York City, as Stanley Krantz.)* First-call cinematographer since the 1940s and brother to actor Ricardo Cortez, he worked as a portrait photographer in New York before becoming an assistant cameraman on *The Green Archer* (1925). After serving apprenticeships with Pathé and Paramount, he became a full-fledged director of photography on *Four Days Wonder* in 1937. His Oscar-nominated collaboration with Gregg Toland on *The Magnificent Ambersons* (1942) solidified Cortez' reputation as a masterful black-and-white cinematographer (even his humble B movies, such as 1938's *The Black Doll* and *The Lady in the Morgue*, reveal an amazing grasp of lighting technique), and his versatile photographic stylings became much in demand for more than three decades, ranging from the surrealism of *The Night of the Hunter* (1955) to the stark realism of *The Three Faces of Eve* (1957) and on through film noir in *Shock Corridor* (1963). Also Oscar-nominated for his dreamy imagery in *Since You Went Away* (1944), Cortez spent the last few years of his career shooting miniatures. *When Time Ran Out . . .* (1980) was the last feature film on which he worked.

COSTA-GAVRAS. Director. *(b. Feb. 12, 1933, Athens, as Constantin Costa-Gavras.)* Arguably filmdom's premier political polemicist, Costa-Gavras studied film in France and made his first feature film—*The Sleeping Car Murder* (1965), a solid albeit conventional thriller—in that country. In *Z* (1969), he used thriller techniques to tell an explicitly political tale condemning the Greek junta system, thus making his mark on the international filmmaking community. The picture won an Oscar as Best Foreign Language Film and earned Costa-Gavras nominations as director and cowriter. He bounced around the world, setting movies against the backdrops of repressive regimes; his Uruguayan study, *State of Siege* (1973), was denounced here for its anti-Americanism and seeming endorsement of political terrorism. In his first "Hollywood" film,

Missing (1982), Costa-Gavras continued to court controversy, now with the aid of top U.S. stars Jack Lemmon and Sissy Spacek, and won an Oscar for cowriting the screenplay. His *Hanna K.* (1983) infuriated many with its pro-Palestinian stance. The director's subsequent pictures, including *Betrayed* (1988) and *Music Box* (1990), continued to deal with hot issues but were not as powerful or passionate as previous works. He acted in *Madame Rosa* (1977), an Oscar-winning foreign film starring Simone Signoret. In 1993 he directed and cowrote *The Little Apocalypse*.

COSTNER, KEVIN. Actor, director. (b. Jan. 18, 1955, Los Angeles.) It seems fitting somehow that one of the stars who defined American film in the 1980s graduated from college with a degree in marketing. Making his screen bow in *Sizzle Beach, U.S.A.* (1981), Costner spent the next few years puttering around Hollywood, doing bits in *Night Shift* (1982) and *Table for Five* (1983). His big break seemed to arrive when Lawrence Kasdan tapped him to play Alex, the charismatic friend whose suicide reunites a group of former 1960s rebels in *The Big Chill* (1983), but Kasdan decided the flashback material featuring Costner didn't fit in with the rest of the film, and audiences only caught fleeting glimpses of him as a corpse. Kasdan made amends later by costarring Costner as a reckless young shootist in the so-so *nouveau* Western *Silverado* (1985). Costner's all-American-boy good looks and earnest manner won him the role of righteous Prohibition-era gangbuster Eliot Ness in Brian De Palma's loose adaptation of *The Untouchables* (1987), much revamped from both Ness' memoirs and the TV series. In fact, his boy-next-door appeal was such that the surprise ending of 1987's *No Way Out,* revealing him as the secret heavy after he'd been so sexy and earnest for the previous two hours, was widely denounced by critics and moviegoers, who nonetheless flocked to see the twisty thriller.

1988's bullpen comedy *Bull Durham* (in which he played a straight role while costar Tim Robbins got to goof around) and 1989's baseball-as-metaphor fantasy *Field of Dreams* solidified Costner's standing as the preeminent male screen star of the moment, and he used his clout to produce, direct, and star in *Dances With Wolves* (1990) for Orion. Based on a novel by Costner's friend Michael Blake, the film—about a Civil War soldier who finds fulfillment living among the Lakota Sioux—was a source of great apprehension to Orion, but it turned out to be the surprise smash of 1990, winning Costner a Best Director Academy Award. It was by any measure a triumph. Costner then took a fair amount of heat for playing the avenger of Sherwood Forest with a British accent that ranged from fair to nonexistent in *Robin Hood: Prince of Thieves* (1991). But a star is a star, which the box-office success of the film proved anew.

The actor then brought his considerable clout to Oliver Stone's highly charged *JFK* (1991), in the role of New Orleans D.A. Jim Garrison, and helped to make a "political movie" a hit. Functioning as producer, he persuaded pop music diva Whitney Houston to join him in an old-fashioned Star Vehicle, *The Bodyguard* (1992), based on a Kasdan script that was originally intended for Steve McQueen. He then gave a forceful performance as an escaped convict who kidnaps a little boy in *A Perfect World* (1993), with Clint Eastwood as his costar and director. As a still-youthful star and fledgling director, he could ask for no better role model. In fact, he followed Eastwood into Western territory with *Wyatt Earp* (1994). His next project was *Waterworld* (1995), reportedly the most expensive film ever made.

COTTEN, JOSEPH. Actor. (b. May 15, 1905, Petersburg, Va.; d. Feb. 6, 1994.) This former stage and radio actor, whose distinctive voice served him well during his tenure as one of Orson Welles' Mercury Players, followed his mentor to Hollywood and made his film debut in Welles' classic *Citizen Kane* (1941), playing the Great Man's friend and drama critic Jed Leland. (The actor himself had earlier worked in the same capacity.) After appearing in *Lydia* that same year, Cotten rejoined Welles for *The Magnificent Ambersons* and *Journey Into Fear* (both 1942). Neither film turned out as Welles envisioned, but Cotten, now firmly established, eased into a prolific career as leading man, starring as the charming, quietly sinister wife-killer in Alfred Hitchcock's

Shadow of a Doubt (1943), then playing Deanna Durbin's beau in *Hers to Hold* that same year. He supported Ingrid Bergman and Charles Boyer in the Victorian-era chiller *Gaslight* (1944), then joined the excellent all-star cast of John Cromwell's touching WW2 domestic drama *Since You Went Away* (also 1944), the first film to pair him with frequent co-star Jennifer Jones, with whom he made *Love Letters* (1945), *Duel in the Sun* (1946, losing her to Gregory Peck), and *Portrait of Jennie* (1948).

Cotten frequently played male leads but usually took second billing to his female costars: Jones, Ginger Rogers (in 1944's *I'll Be Seeing You),* Loretta Young (in 1947's *The Farmer's Daughter* and 1951's *Half Angel),* Bette Davis (in 1949's *Beyond the Forest),* Ingrid Bergman (in Hitchcock's *Under Capricorn,* also 1949), and Barbara Stanwyck (in 1951's *The Man With a Cloak).* He also played second fiddle to Welles again in Carol Reed's marvelous thriller, *The Third Man* (1949), cast as the American writer who finds his old friend masterminding a black-market operation in postwar Vienna. (He later made an unbilled appearance in Welles' 1958 melodrama, *Touch of Evil,* playing a cockeyed coroner.)

By the early 1950s Cotten's peak period was behind him; he began to alternate leading roles with supporting parts, and eventually drifted into foreign-made crime dramas, horror movies, and Hollywood-produced telefilms. In the early 1960s he hosted and narrated the well-remembered TV series "Hollywood and the Stars." Cotten married actress Patricia Medina in 1960. His autobiography, "Vanity Will Get You Somewhere," was published in 1987.

OTHER FILMS INCLUDE: 1951: *Peking Express;* 1952: *The Steel Trap;* 1953: *Niagara* (second-billed to Marilyn Monroe); 1955: *Special Delivery;* 1956: *The Bottom of the Bottle;* 1957: *The Halliday Brand;* 1958: *From the Earth to the Moon;* 1960: *The Angel Wore Red;* 1961: *The Last Sunset;* 1965: *Hush ... Hush, Sweet Charlotte;* 1966: *The Oscar, The Money Trap;* 1967: *Jack of Diamonds;* 1968: *Petulia;* 1969: *Latitude Zero;* 1970: *The Grasshopper, Tora! Tora! Tora!;* 1971: *The Abominable Dr. Phibes;* 1972: *Baron Blood;* 1973: *Soylent Green;* 1977: *Twilight's Last Gleaming, Airport '77;* 1978: *The Wild Geese;* 1980: *The Hearse, Heaven's Gate.*

COURTENAY, TOM. Actor. *(b. Feb. 25, 1937, Yorkshire, England.)* Sad-looking, soft-spoken British actor (mostly known for his stage work), who has made his best impressions as fatalistic, sometimes rebellious working-class protagonists struggling against the injustices of his country's socioeconomic system. Courtenay first captured moviegoers' attention in his debut leading role in *The Loneliness of the Long Distance Runner* (1962). He was later Oscar-nominated for his supporting performance as Pasha in *Doctor Zhivago* (1965). Eighteen years later, with too few films in between, he scored another triumph in the title role of *The Dresser* (1983), recreating his acclaimed stage performance, and was nominated for the Oscar once more. In 1991's *Let Him Have It* he gave a heart-rending performance as the working-class father of a youth convicted of murder.

OTHER FILMS INCLUDE: 1962: *Private Potter;* 1963: *Billy Liar;* 1964: *King and Country;* 1965: *King Rat;* 1966: *The Night of the Generals;* 1967: *The Day the Fish Came Out;* 1968: *A Dandy in Aspic, Otley;* 1971: *One Day in the Life of Ivan Denisovich;* 1987: *Happy New Year, Leonard Part 6;* 1990: *The Last Butterfly.*

COWAN, JEROME. Actor. *(b. Oct. 6, 1897, New York City; d. Jan. 24, 1972.)* Already well established on Broadway before making his film debut in 1936's *Beloved Enemy,* Cowan carved a niche for himself as one of Hollywood's most urbane character actors. He tossed off even the most banal B-movie dialogue with panache, and although frequently cast as a jaded lounge lizard or rejected suitor, he often outclassed his leading men. Cowan was extremely effective as Miles Archer in *The Maltese Falcon* (1941); as a Warner Bros. contract player he worked in countless other studio films, including *Castle on the Hudson, Torrid Zone* (both 1940), *The Great Lie, High Sierra* (both 1941), *Mission to Moscow* (1943), as well as *The Kid From Brooklyn* (1946), *Miracle on 34th Street* (1947), *The Fountainhead* (1949), *Visit to a Small Planet* (1960), *Pocketful of Miracles* (1961), *The*

Patsy (1964), *The Gnome-Mobile* (1967), and *The Comic* (1969), to name just a few. He replaced Jonathan Hale as Dagwood Bumstead's boss in the "Blondie" series in the 1940s. His sardonic manner made him a fairly convincing private eye in two starring vehicles, *Find the Blackmailer* (1943) and *Crime By Night* (1944). He later appeared on the TV series "Tycoon" (1964–65).

COX, ALEX. Director, screenwriter. *(b. Dec. 15, 1954, Liverpool.)* While studying law at Oxford, Cox became interested in drama and eventually went to film school at Bristol University and UCLA. After years of writing screenplays that remained unproduced, he got the chance to write and direct *Repo Man* (1984), a wild journey through urban chaos, with touches of black comedy, science fiction, and social satire that became a cult hit. Even more impressive was his next picture, *Sid and Nancy* (1986), a stunning look at the relationship of punk rocker Sid Vicious and groupie Nancy Spungen (brilliantly played by Gary Oldman and Chloe Webb), which promised great things for Cox. Unfortunately, his follow-up, *Straight to Hell* (1987), a spaghetti-Western spoof, was a mess, and *Walker* (1988), a ham-fisted "history" of 19th-century adventurer William Walker (played by Ed Harris), was no better, stressing parallels to present-day foreign policy issues. Cox returned to the screen in 1992 with the Mexican-made *Highway Patrolman,* then agreed to direct a film adaptation of Ian McKellen's 20th-century stage version of *Richard III,* calling on his heretofore unsuspected love for Shakespeare.

COX, PAUL. Director, screenwriter. *(b. Apr. 16, 1940, Velo, Netherlands.)* Australian cinema chronicler Brian MacFarlane has written, "More than any other Australian filmmaker [Paul Cox] has been insistently concerned with relationships, between men and women, parents and children; and he is clearly interested in the erotic and its power to disturb orderly, cultured surfaces." Dutch-born Cox, an Australian since the 1960s, started making films in the mid-1970s, winning attention on his home turf with *Kostas* (1979) and international acclaim with his charming and off-

beat romantic comedy *Lonely Hearts* two years later. Cox's emotional, highly personal films as writer-director—including *Lonely Hearts, Man of Flowers* (1983), and *My First Wife* (1984)—established him as an original. He temporarily abandoned fictional filmmaking to make *Vincent—The Life and Death of Vincent Van Gogh* (1987), an imaginative documentary based on Van Gogh's letters which Cox wrote, directed, photographed, and edited. He acted in Werner Herzog's *Where the Green Ants Dream* (1984), and Herzog returned the favor, playing briefly in *Man of Flowers.* Cox's other films include *Death and Destiny* (1985), *Island* (1989), *The Golden Braid* (1990), and the remarkable *A Woman's Tale* (1991), the story of a woman dying of cancer (played by an actress, Sheila Florance, who was actually facing the ordeal).

COX, RONNY. Actor. *(b. Aug. 23, 1938, Cloudcroft, N. Mex.)* Rangy, sandy-haired actor who spent much of his early career playing nice, decent men in such films as *Deliverance* (1972), *Bound for Glory* (1976), *Harper Valley P.T.A.* (1978), and countless TV movies, including *The Jesse Owens Story.* But since portraying the hard-nosed police captain in *Beverly Hills Cop* (1984, and in its 1987 sequel), Cox has won tougher roles, most effectively playing coldhearted, corporate villains in *Robocop* (1987), *Total Recall* (1990), and on TV's "St. Elsewhere" (1987–88).

COYOTE, PETER. Actor. *(b. Oct. 10, 1942, New York City, as Peter Cohon.)* Tall, dark, saturnine actor equally at home in sinister or sympathetic roles. A veteran of San Francisco's local theater scene, he began his movie career in 1980's *Die Laughing,* allegedly choosing his screen name after a healing spiritual encounter with . . . you guessed it, a coyote. He snagged supporting roles in *Tell Me a Riddle* (1980), *The Pursuit of D. B. Cooper,* and *Southern Comfort* (both 1981) before playing the mysterious scientist billed as "Keys" in *E.T. The Extra-Terrestrial* (1982). It was hardly a star-making characterization, and Coyote continued his screen career in low key. But his obvious ability (and the duality of his screen presence) eventually won him a number of interesting roles—some leads, some supporting parts. Coyote's no rubber-stamp leading man, and one always suspects that his next film will be the one that makes everybody sit up and take notice of him. Coyote has also appeared in many made-for-TV movies and miniseries and does commercial voice-overs.

OTHER FILMS INCLUDE: 1984: *Cross Creek*; 1985: *Jagged Edge* (very impressive as a ruthless prosecutor); 1987: *Outrageous Fortune, A Man in Love*; 1989: *Heart of Midnight*; 1991: *Crooked Hearts*; 1992: *Bitter Moon*; 1993: *Kika*.

CRABBE, LARRY "BUSTER." Actor. *(b. Feb. 17, 1907, Oakland, Calif., as Clarence Linden Crabbe; d. Apr. 23, 1983.)* Right up to the day he died—literally—Buster Crabbe was still getting fan mail from all over the world, most of it commenting on his portrayal of interplanetary adventurer Flash Gordon, the comic-strip crusader he brought to life in three memorable movie serials: *Flash Gordon* (1936), *Flash Gordon's Trip to Mars* (1938), and *Flash Gordon Conquers the Universe* (1940). Born in California but raised in Hawaii, Crabbe became a top swimmer and even won a gold medal in the 1932 Los Angeles Olympics. He initially worked in movies as a stunt double (swimming for Joel McCrea in 1932's *The Most Dangerous Game*, to begin with) and was signed by Paramount the following year. Top-billed in *King of the Jungle* (1933) as an imitation Tarzan—he played the Ape Man himself later that year, on loan to indie producer Sol Lesser, in the serial *Tarzan the Fearless*—Crabbe gave a good accounting of himself but was sent to the B-picture units for seasoning. Over the next six years he played in Westerns (1933's *To the Last Man*, 1935's *Nevada*, 1936's *Arizona Raiders*), comedies (1934's *You're Telling Me*, with W. C. Fields), crime dramas (1937's *King of Gamblers*, 1938's *Tip-Off Girls*), and collegiate yarns (1935's *Hold 'Em Yale*, 1936's *Rose Bowl*, 1939's *Million Dollar Legs*). He was loaned to Universal for the first two Flash Gordon serials and two other chapterplays, *Red Barry* (1938) and *Buck Rogers* (1939).

The handsome, brawny Crabbe spent most of the 1940s at the PRC studios, churning out dozens of ultra-cheap Westerns (playing an overage Billy the Kid in 1941–43 oaters) and occasional B's, such as *Jungle Man* (1941) and *Queen of Broadway* (1942). Leaving PRC in 1946, Crabbe played heavies in various low-budgeters, including *Swamp Fire* (1946, opposite fellow Olympic swimming star and former Tarzan Johnny Weissmuller), *Last of the Redmen* (1947, as Magua in this "Last of the Mohicans" remake), and *Caged Fury* (1948). At Columbia he starred in three serials: *The Sea Hound* (1947), *Pirates of the High Seas* (1950), and *King of the Congo* (1952).

No stranger to the small screen, Crabbe hosted an early 1950s kiddie show, "Buster's Buddies," and starred in the 1955–57 series "Captain Gallant of the French Foreign Legion," which was filmed in and around Morocco. Back in the States, he made a few more movies—including *Badman's Country* (1958), *Gunfighters of Abilene* (1960), and *The Bounty Killer* (1965)—before getting involved in the swimming-pool business and taking a post as athletic director at a New York summer resort hotel. He was surprisingly effective—and even touching—in a low-budget improvisational comedy, *The Comeback Trail* (made 1971, but never officially released), playing a former Western star persuaded to come out of retirement by unscrupulous producers who insure him heavily and then try to kill him during shooting of a new film.

In later years Crabbe made frequent appearances at nostalgia-oriented film festivals. As a lark he took a supporting role in a 1979 episode of the "Buck Rogers" TV series, and appeared in *The Alien Dead* (made 1981, released 1985), directed by a longtime fan.

CRAIN, JEANNE. Actress. *(b. May 25, 1925, Barstow, Calif.)* Could there be a male moviegoer whose heart didn't beat just a little faster at the sight of this winsome, auburn-haired beauty dreamily singing (dubbed, of course) "It Might as Well be Spring" in *State Fair* (1945)? With her vibrant green eyes, dimpled smile, and wholesome sexuality, the former beauty-contest winner (Miss Long Beach of 1941) made an altogether adorable girl-next-door in her 1940s films for 20th

Century-Fox, then snared an Academy Award nomination as a young, light-skinned black woman passing for white in Elia Kazan's *Pinky* (1949). Outgrowing her bobby-soxer image in the 1950s, Crain attempted more demanding roles and mature characterizations, but her "glamour-girl" phase yielded few memorable turns. She more or less "retired" in 1962, returning to the screen only a few times.
OTHER FILMS INCLUDE: 1943: *The Gang's All Here* (her first, in a one-line bit part); 1944: *Home in Indiana, In the Meantime, Darling, Winged Victory;* 1945: *Leave Her to Heaven;* 1946: *Centennial Summer, Margie* (a Roaring Twenties tunefest that's one of her most satisfying star vehicles); 1948: *Apartment for Peggy;* 1949: *A Letter to Three Wives, The Fan;* 1950: *Cheaper by the Dozen, I'll Get By;* 1951: *The Model and the Marriage Broker, People Will Talk, Take Care of My Little Girl;* 1952: *Belles on Their Toes, O'Henry's Full House;* 1953: *Dangerous Crossing, Vicki;* 1954: *Duel in the Jungle;* 1955: *Man Without a Star, Gentlemen Marry Brunettes, The Second Greatest Sex;* 1956: *The Fastest Gun Alive;* 1957: *The Joker Is Wild, The Tattered Dress;* 1960: *Guns of the Timberland;* 1961: *Twenty Plus Two;* 1962: *Madison Avenue, Nefertiti, Queen of the Nile;* 1967: *Hot Rods to Hell;* 1972: *Skyjacked;* 1974: *The Night God Screamed.*

CRAVEN, FRANK. Actor, screenwriter. *(b. Aug. 24, 1875, Boston; d. Sept. 1, 1945.)* As one of Broadway's émigrés to Hollywood after the coming of sound, this veteran playwright and actor initially made his mark as a script doctor (and even directed one minor film, *That's Gratitude,* in 1934), but by the mid-1930s he had returned to acting. A smallish man with wispy hair and rumpled face (often seen smoking a pipe), he played many kindly father figures, usually in rural settings. Perhaps best remembered as the Stage Manager in Thornton Wilder's Pulitzer Prize–winning play "Our Town," and the 1940 screen adaptation as well.
FILMS INCLUDE: 1933: *State Fair;* 1935: *Barbary Coast;* 1937: *Penrod and Sam;* 1939: *Our Neighbors, The Carters* (in the lead); 1940: *City for Conquest;* 1942: *Pittsburgh, Keeper of the Flame;* 1943: *Son of Dracula, The Human Comedy;* 1944: *Destiny.*

CRAVEN, WES. Director. *(b. Aug. 2, 1939, Cleveland.)* Genteel, literate director who has turned out some of the most relentless horror films ever made. Craven studied philosophy and literature at Wheaton College and Johns Hopkins, and had actually become a professor of literature before joining up with Sean *(Friday the 13th)* Cunningham as a film editor. He caused a stir with his first directorial outing, *Last House on the Left* (1972), a shockingly violent tale of senseless mayhem and revenge reportedly adapted from Ingmar Bergman's *The Virgin Spring.* Craven more or less disappeared for five years before returning to the big screen with *The Hills Have Eyes* (1977), which brought him enough critical and commercial attention to precipitate a constant flow of horror vehicles, some successful (1981's *Deadly Blessing)* and some not (1982's *Swamp Thing).* Craven's most popular movie, from a box-office standpoint, was *A Nightmare on Elm Street* (1984), which introduced child-killer Freddy Krueger to the moviegoing public and spawned six sequels (the last of which, 1994's *Wes Craven's New Nightmare,* was the only one he directed) that made its studio—New Line—one of the most successful independents in the business. *The Hills Have Eyes Part II* (1985) didn't enjoy its predecessor's success, nor did *Deadly Friend* (1986). He created a fanciful TV sitcom called "The People Next Door," which lasted just one month in 1989, and executive produced "Nightmare Cafe" (1992), which starred *Elm Street*'s Robert Englund. He bounced back, with a vengeance, in 1991, when his *The People Under the Stairs* garnered many excellent reviews and turned a respectable profit.

CRAWFORD, BRODERICK. Actor. *(b. Dec. 9, 1911, Philadelphia; d. Apr. 26, 1986.)* One of the toughest-talking actors ever to fill a movie screen, the gruff, imposing Crawford actually got his seasoning in vaudeville, where his parents, Lester Crawford and Helen Broderick, were stars. (His mother later became a major Broadway comedienne, and is well remembered for her supporting role in the Fred Astaire–Ginger Rogers movie musical *Swing Time.*) Crawford made his name on Broadway in the 1937 production of

John Steinbeck's *Of Mice and Men,* giving a powerful performance as the dim-witted Lennie, but he was passed over for the 1939 film version (in which Lon Chaney, Jr., played the part). Instead, he landed supporting and costarring roles in a slew of Hollywood pictures, including *Woman Chases Man* (1937), *Beau Geste, The Real Story* (both 1939), *When the Daltons Rode, Seven Sinners* (both 1940). He made a name for himself, and even got leading roles in a handful of comedies and gangster yarns like Damon Runyon's *Tight Shoes* (1941), and *Butch Minds the Baby* (1942).

The turning point in Crawford's career was his casting as Willy Stark, the Huey Long–inspired character in Robert Rossen's Oscar-winning Best Picture *All the King's Men* (1949, based on the Robert Penn Warren novel). His forceful performance earned him an Academy Award and made him an instant star; the following year he scored another bull's-eye as blustery business tycoon Harry Brock in *Born Yesterday* (1950). But it soon became apparent that parts as good as these were hard to come by for a nontraditional leading man like the stocky Crawford (especially with Paul Douglas, who created the role of Brock on Broadway, in vogue in Hollywood at the exact same time), and the quality of his vehicles eroded. He even returned to Damon Runyon territory, after a decade, to star in *Stop, You're Killing Me* (1952).

Crawford's legendary drinking, no secret in Hollywood, may have contributed to his career's steady slide. After giving a charming performance in Federico Fellini's *Il bidone* (1955) he agreed to star in a TV cop series, "Highway Patrol," and dominated the airwaves for the next four years growling "10-4, 10-4" into a walkie-talkie. (He later starred in two more short-lived series, "King of Diamonds" in 1961, and "The Interns" in 1970–71.) In the 1960s, Crawford worked mostly in tacky European-made films, but in the late 1970s he had memorable moments in two mainstream movies, Larry Cohen's outrageous *The Private Files of J. Edgar Hoover* (1977, in the title role) and in a hilarious cameo as himself in *A Little Romance* (1979).

OTHER FILMS INCLUDE: 1942: *Larceny, Inc., Broadway;* 1948: *The Time of Your Life;* 1949: *Anna Lucasta;* 1951: *The Mob;* 1952: *Scandal Sheet;* 1954: *Night People, Human Desire, Down Three Dark Streets;* 1955: *New York Confidential, Big House, U.S.A., Not as a Stranger;* 1956: *Between Heaven and Hell;* 1958: *The Decks Ran Red;* 1964: *A House Is Not a Home;* 1966: *Kid Rodelo, The Oscar;* 1970: *Hell's Bloody Devils;* 1973: *Terror in the Wax Museum.*

CRAWFORD, JOAN. Actress. *(b. Mar. 23, 1904, San Antonio, Tex., as Lucille Le Sueur; d. May 10, 1977.)* It's one of Hollywood's fey jokes that one of the most dominant of female stars is probably best known to a whole generation of moviegoers as the wire hanger–wielding Mother From Hell, but that does an injustice to this amazing performer. In her youth a saucer-eyed, curvaceous beauty, Crawford underwent a remarkable metamorphosis as she got older; her hardened features, including flashing eyes and a cruel mouth, perfectly suited the manipulative, catty, unscrupulous women she later played. In truth, she clung to leading-lady status longer than she should have, but it was a hard-won status and one she was loathe to abandon. (And it can be legitimately maintained that, unlike many actresses who clawed their way to the top, she was as talented as she was ambitious.) A backstage child—her stepfather was a vaudeville theater manager—she took up dancing and by age 16 was working both in a Broadway chorus and an after-hours nightclub when MGM executive Harry Rapf spotted her and signed her to a studio contract. She debuted—under her real name—in 1925's *Pretty Ladies,* then became Joan Crawford in *Old Clothes* that same year. More substantial roles followed in *Sally, Irene and Mary* (also 1925, as Irene), and *The Boob* (1926, as a Prohibition agent!), before she was loaned to First National to star opposite Harry Langdon in *Tramp, Tramp, Tramp* (also 1926).

She returned to MGM and costarred in numerous melodramas, among them *Taxi Dancer, The Unknown* (opposite Lon Chaney), *Winners of the Wilderness* (all 1927), and *Four Walls* (1928); her roles were largely decorative, and contemporary reviewers didn't indicate any special confidence in her ability. But then came *Our Dancing Daughters,* in which she performed a spirited Charleston atop a table, literally dancing her way into the memories of moviegoers. The picture's surprise success made Crawford an "instant" star, and she worked hard to convince both her bosses and her newly won fans that she had the right stuff. (She later top-lined in two follow-ups to *Daughters,* 1929's *Our Modern Maidens* and 1930's *Our Blushing Brides.)* More romances followed: *Dream of Love* (also 1928), *The Duke Steps Out, Untamed* (both 1929, the latter her first talkie). Crawford demonstrated her hoofing abilities once again in a vigorous novelty number in *The Hollywood Revue of 1929.* She bulldozed her way into Hollywood's royal family by marrying Douglas Fairbanks, Jr., that same year; they divorced in 1933.

Crawford was an MGM stalwart for more than a decade, generally playing tough, independent-minded women—often poor shop girls or secretaries striving for success against formidable odds—in the likes of *Paid* (1930), *Dance, Fools, Dance, Possessed* (both 1931), *Grand Hotel* (1932, as the secretary), *Rain* (also 1932, out of character but very convincing as South Seas trollop Sadie Thompson), *Today We Live* (1933, opposite Franchot Tone, whom she wed in 1935), *Dancing Lady* (also 1933, singing and dancing opposite Fred Astaire in his screen debut), *Sadie McKee, Chained* (both 1934), *The Gorgeous Hussy* (1936), *The Last of Mrs. Cheyney* (1937), *Mannequin* (1938), *Ice Follies of 1939, The Women* (both 1939), *Strange Cargo, Susan and God* (both 1940), and *A Woman's Face* (1941). But her star went into decline (she'd been labeled "box-office poison" by a movie-industry trade paper in 1938), and after completing *Above Suspicion* (1943), MGM prexy Louis B. Mayer showed her the door.

Crawford did not work on-screen for two years except for a guest shot in *Hollywood Canteen* (1944). She persuaded Warner Bros. to cast her in the title role in *Mildred Pierce* (1945), and her Oscar-winning turn as a sacrificing mother put her back on top. It was a gamble for the actress, who didn't relish playing mother parts and feared she'd be typecast in them. Crawford remained at Warners in such films as *Humoresque* (1946), *Possessed* (1947, which earned her another Oscar nomination), and *Flamingo Road* (1949), and rebuilt her reputation as a top

screen star. Her later work was somewhat erratic, but her more memorable characterizations of the period include the definitive horror-housewife in *Harriet Craig* (1950), the terrorized playwright in *Sudden Fear* (1952, an Oscar-nominated performance), a bitchy Broadway star in *Torch Song* (1953, back at MGM), the tough saloon-keeper in *Johnny Guitar* (1954, to this day a favorite cult Western), frustrated women in *Female on The Beach* (1955) and *Autumn Leaves* (1956), and a nasty magazine editor in *The Best of Everything* (1959).

In 1955 she married Pepsi-Cola chairman Alfred Steele; he died four years later, and she remained on the board of directors. In her 50s, she seemed to be at career's end, but in 1962 director Robert Aldrich teamed her with Bette Davis (not exactly a harmonious pairing) in *What Ever Happened to Baby Jane?,* a critical and commercial smash that revitalized both women's careers and kicked off an entire cycle of horror movies featuring older women. She dropped out of the follow-up, *Hush . . . Hush, Sweet Charlotte,* but did make two for horrormeister William Castle, *Strait-Jacket* (1964) and *I Saw What You Did* (1965), as well as *Berserk* (1967) and *Trog* (1970, her final film) for English directors. Crawford's last nonhorror role was that of a venal nurse in *The Caretakers* (1963). In 1969 she starred in a telefilm that served as the pilot for a series called "Night Gallery." In it she played a wealthy woman who will stop at nothing to find a donor for her eye transplant operation. One of her last performances, it was also one of her best; her director was a newcomer named Steven Spielberg.

She had been dead barely a year when her adopted daughter, Christina, wrote "Mommie Dearest," chronicling her traumatic experiences in Crawford's tyrannical household. It sparked endless talk and seriously damaged the actress' public image. The book was filmed in 1981, with Faye Dunaway as Crawford, but it was done in a campy style that further chipped away at her legend. It was an ignoble footnote to a distinctive and fascinating career.

CREGAR, LAIRD. Actor. *(b. July 28, 1916, Philadelphia, as Samuel Laird Cregar; d.*

Dec. 9, 1944.) Hulking, brutish character actor whose heavy-lidded gaze and coldly sinister voice made him an ideal movie heavy in the early 1940s. Three inches over six feet tall, he made an ideal bouncer before taking up acting in the late 1930s. An alumnus of the Pasadena Playhouse, Cregar broke into films in 1940 with a bit part in *Granny Get Your Gun,* an undistinguished Warners B picture. Signed by Fox later that year, he immediately was promoted to colorful supporting roles in *Hudson's Bay* (1940), *Blood and Sand,* and *Charley's Aunt* (both 1941), before chilling moviegoers as the sadistic detective of *I Wake Up Screaming* (also 1941). Fox used Cregar in a variety of roles in *Rings on Her Fingers, Ten Gentlemen From West Point, The Black Swan* (all 1942), *Heaven Can Wait* (as a dress-suited Lucifer), *Hello Frisco, Hello* (playing a comic panhandler), and *Holy Matrimony* (both 1943). But it was in his quietly sinister turns in the Victorian-era shudder shows *The Lodger* (1944) and the posthumously released *Hangover Square* (1945) that Cregar made his most memorable impressions. Ironically, the burly actor longed to play leading-man types and suffered a heart attack while crash-dieting. He was just 28 years old.

CRENNA, RICHARD. Actor. *(b. Nov. 30, 1927, Los Angeles.)* So many people associate this solid actor with his work in TV (beginning with two classic 1950s sitcoms, as squeaky-voiced student Walter Denton in "Our Miss Brooks" and as the hard-working Luke in "The Real McCoys") that they probably aren't aware of Crenna's fairly substantial feature-film credits. His first movie was Irene Dunne's last, the comic fantasy *It Grows on Trees* (1952), and he toiled in *Our Miss Brooks* (1955) and *Over-Exposed* (1956) in between small-screen stints. It wasn't until his third series, "Slattery's People," went off the air in 1965 that Crenna pursued movie work in earnest, with roles in such popular films as *The Sand Pebbles* (1966), *Wait Until Dark* (1967), *Marooned* (1969), and *Doctors' Wives* (1971). He spent the 1970s mostly slaving in B movies, making a comeback of sorts as the murder victim in *Body Heat* (1981). He assumed the role of Sylvester Stallone's commanding officer in *First Blood* (1982) after both Kirk

Douglas and William Devane abandoned it, reprising the characterization in the 1985 and 1988 *Rambo* sequels. (He later parodied the part in 1993's *Hot Shots! Part Deux.)* Crenna also scored as the nouveau riche father in *The Flamingo Kid* (1984), and played a similar, though nastier, character in the following year's *Summer Rental.* He continues to work in TV, ranging from such short-lived sitcoms as "It Takes Two" and "All's Fair" to such movies as *The Rape of Richard Beck,* for which he won an Emmy; his sharp portrayal of a police detective in *Doubletake* led to several sequels.

CRICHTON, CHARLES. Director, producer. *(b. Aug. 6, 1910, Cheshire, England.)* This Oxford-educated director, a veteran of the British film industry from 1935, made his mark on cinema history as the leading exponent of a comedic style brought to fruition in the many films he made for the Ealing Studios during the late 1940s and 1950s. He started, as did so many great directors, in the cutting room, editing *Sanders of the River* (1935), *Things to Come* (1936), *Elephant Boy* (1937), *The Thief of Bagdad* (1940), and several other Korda productions. Crichton's first shot behind the megaphone, *For Those in Peril* (1944), led to an assignment on the brilliant supernatural omnibus *Dead of Night* (1945). *Hue and Cry* (1947) found him collaborating with Alastair Sim in the first of Crichton's high-profile films. *The Lavender Hill Mob* (1951), *The Titfield Thunderbolt* (1953), *The Divided Heart* (1954), *Law and Disorder* (1956), *The Battle of the Sexes* (1959), *The Boy Who Stole a Million* (1960), and *He Who Rides a Tiger* (1965) are among the director's films. He didn't always score a hit, but on the whole his average was very good. And he showed everyone he hadn't lost his comedic touch by directing *A Fish Called Wanda* (1988), written by and starring John Cleese; it netted Crichton his first Oscar nomination.

CRICHTON, MICHAEL. Novelist, director, screenwriter. *(b. Oct. 23, 1942, Chicago.)* Phenomenally successful writer who has carved out an enviable niche in Hollywood, with adaptations of his own books and a number of original screenplays.

While studying at Harvard Medical School, Crichton began writing novels (under pseudonyms) to pay the bills, and one, "A Case of Need," won an Edgar Award from the Mystery Writers of America. (It was later adapted into the 1972 film *The Carey Treatment.*) His novel "The Andromeda Strain," written under his own name in 1969, became his first best-seller; it also became a film, as did his subsequent novels "Dealing: Or the Berkeley-to-Boston Forty Brick Lost-Bag-Blues" (written with his brother Douglas) and "The Terminal Man." His track record enabled Crichton to win the chance to direct an original screenplay, *Westworld* (1973), a minor science-fiction classic about a futuristic resort populated by robots that, inevitably, run amok. He followed with the popular thriller *Coma* (1978), which featured Genevieve Bujold as an unusually tough heroine, and then helmed the lighthearted adaptation of his own novel *The Great Train Robbery* (1979). Less successful high-tech thrillers followed—*Looker* (1981) and *Runaway* (1984). *Physical Evidence* (1988, which he directed but did not write) did not turn the tide. His stock soared in 1993 when two of his most popular novels were brought to the screen back to back; he cowrote the screenplays for the controversial *Rising Sun* (1993) and *Jurassic Park* (also 1993), a story of modern-day dinosaurs that quickly became the most popular movie in history. In 1994, Crichton created the hit medical drama "E.R." and coproduced the film adaptation of his novel *Disclosure.* He scored again in 1995, with *Congo.*

CRISP, DONALD. Actor, director. *(b. July 27, 1880, Aberfeldy, Scotland; d. May 25, 1974.)* Oxford-educated Crisp is one of the movie industry's true pioneers, active on both sides of the camera. He acted in Biograph films beginning in 1908, worked with D. W. Griffith in *The Birth of a Nation* (1915, as General Grant) and, memorably, in *Broken Blossoms* (1919, as Lillian Gish's brutish father). He directed and codirected classic silent films including *The Navigator* (1924, with Buster Keaton) and *Don Q, Son of Zorro* (1925). He returned to acting exclusively with the advent of talkies, always cutting an impressive figure with his military bearing

and stern visage. Crisp sometimes did play sympathetic roles, such as the Welsh patriarch in *How Green Was My Valley* (1941), for which he won an Academy Award. He's also in *Red Dust* (1932), *The Little Minister* (1934), *Mutiny on the Bounty* (1935), *The Charge of the Light Brigade* (1936), *The Life of Emile Zola, The White Angel* (both 1937), *Jezebel, The Dawn Patrol* (both 1938), *Juarez, Daughters Courageous, Wuthering Heights* (all 1939), *The Sea Hawk* (1940), *Lassie Come Home* (1943), *The Uninvited* (1944), *National Velvet* (1944, as Elizabeth Taylor's father), *Prince Valiant* (1954), and *The Long Gray Line* (1955). At 75, he was still impressive as the ruthless cattle baron in *The Man From Laramie* (1955), and went on to deliver equally forceful performances in *The Last Hurrah* (1958), *Pollyanna* (1960), *Greyfriars Bobby* (1961), and *Spencer's Mountain* (1963). His wife was screenwriter Jane Murfin.

CROMWELL, JOHN. Director, actor. *(b. Dec. 23, 1888, Toledo, Ohio; d. Sept. 26, 1979.)* A longtime stage performer who had already produced and directed many plays by the time he got to Hollywood in 1929, Cromwell made his movie debut as an actor in that year's *The Dummy.* He shared directorial responsibilities with Edward Sutherland on *Close Harmony* and *The Dance of Life* (also 1929), learning the mechanics of film directing before striking out on his own. For the most part Cromwell eschewed flashy camera moves or other stylistic flourishes that might, in his view, distract from the story or the performances. Late in life he appeared in front of the cameras again, playing bit parts for Robert Altman in *3 Women* (1977) and *A Wedding* (1978, with his wife, actress Ruth Nelson). Married four times to actresses, one of whom, Kay Johnson, appeared in several of his 1930s films.

OTHER FILMS INCLUDE: 1930: *Street of Chance;* 1931: *Scandal Sheet;* 1933: *Sweepings, Ann Vickers;* 1934: *Spitfire, Of Human Bondage;* 1936: *Little Lord Fauntleroy;* 1937: *The Prisoner of Zenda;* 1938: *Algiers* (a remake of the French *Pepe le Moko);* 1939: *Made for Each Other;* 1940: *Abe Lincoln in Illinois;* 1942: *Son of Fury;* 1944: *Since You Went Away;* 1945: *The Enchanted Cottage;*

1946: *Anna and the King of Siam;* 1947: *Dead Reckoning;* 1950: *Caged;* 1951: *The Racket;* 1958: *The Goddess;* 1960: *A Matter of Morals.*

CRONENBERG, DAVID. Director. *(b. Mar. 15, 1943, Toronto.)* Highly influential horror director whose works are often metaphors for larger social questions. Cronenberg began directing films at the University of Toronto, where his experimental shorts *Stereo* (1969) and *Crimes of the Future* (1970) received much critical acclaim. His first feature, *They Came From Within* (1975) was partially financed by the CBC, which may have regretted supporting this lurid tale of parasites that induce uncontrollable sexual desire in their victims. This theme of released repression surfaced again in *Rabid* (1977), which starred former porn queen Marilyn Chambers as an unwitting sexual vampire. Cronenberg's fascination with "horror from within" continued with *The Brood* (1979), in which children are literally born from hatred, and *Videodrome* (1983), a sci-fi tour de force in which TV viewers are controlled by electronic signals embedded behind violent pornography. Cronenberg's successes with these independent productions led him to Hollywood, where he directed the big-budget, mainstream genre offerings *The Dead Zone* (1983) and *The Fly* (1986, also appearing on-screen as an obstetrician). He then helmed one of his most sophisticated films, *Dead Ringers* (1988), a chilling tale that starred Jeremy Irons (in a brilliant pair of performances) as twin gynecologists. Never one to shirk a challenge, Cronenberg proceeded to film the "unfilmable" William Burroughs novel *Naked Lunch* (1991). Then in 1993 he brought the challenging Broadway play *M. Butterfly* to the screen. The slender, bespectacled director again appeared on-screen as a convincing heavy in Clive Barker's *Nightbreed* (1990).

CRONYN, HUME. Actor, screenwriter. *(b. July 18, 1911, London, Ontario.)* Bookish character actor equally masterful in writing and performing. As a drama student at McGill University, the slight-statured Cronyn also excelled in the manly arts, and was actually nominated for the Canadian Olympic Boxing team in the 1930s. He appeared in Canadian stage productions while still a student, and made his way down to Broadway later in the decade, not only acting but writing and directing as well. Cronyn's Hollywood career began with a small but showy role as a whodunit addict in Alfred Hitchcock's *Shadow of a Doubt* (1943); he played a radio operator in the same director's *Lifeboat* (1944), and later cowrote screenplays for Hitchcock's *Rope* (1948) and *Under Capricorn* (1949).

Cronyn essayed a wide variety of character roles in films throughout the 1940s, most notably in *The Seventh Cross* (1944, Oscar-nominated in this drama of concentration-camp escapees), *The Postman Always Rings Twice* (1946, as a lawyer), and *Brute Force* (1947, as a sadistic prison warden). He even costarred with Fanny Brice in a vaudeville sketch as part of *Ziegfeld Follies* (1946). His Hollywood work dropped off in the 1950s and 1960s while he returned to the stage, often teaming with wife Jessica Tandy, whom he'd met and married in 1942. (They appeared as *father and daughter* in the 1946 drama *The Green Years.*) They played together on Broadway in "The Four Poster" (1951), and appeared in tandem many times thereafter, notably in the Pulitzer Prize–winning "The Gin Game" (1978) and, on-screen, in the hit *Cocoon* (1985) and its 1988 sequel. They also worked together in **batteries not included* (1987). Cronyn has appeared in such TV productions as *Foxfire* (1987, with Tandy, from the play he cowrote), *Day One* (1989), and *Broadway Bound* (1992, which won him an Emmy). He published his autobiography, "A Terrible Liar," in 1992. OTHER FILMS INCLUDE: 1951: *People Will Talk;* 1960: *Sunrise at Campobello* (as a Roosevelt confidant); 1963: *Cleopatra* (as Sosigenes); 1964: *Hamlet;* 1969: *The Arrangement;* 1970: *There Was a Crooked Man ...;* 1974: *The Parallax View, Conrack;* 1981: *Honky Tonk Freeway;* 1982: *The World According to Garp* (with Tandy); 1984: *Impulse;* 1993: *The Pelican Brief.*

CROSBY, BING. Actor, singer, producer. *(b. May 2, 1901, Tacoma, Wash., as Harry Lillis Crosby; d. Oct. 14, 1977.)* With his relaxed jazz phrasing and intelligent interpretation of song lyrics, Bing Crosby revolutionized popular vocal styles in the late 1920s and early 1930s, and pioneered the crossover success of pop singers on movie screens. While attending Gonzaga University, Crosby joined forces with Al Rinker and Harry Barris to form a vocal trio. "The Rhythm Boys" became a featured specialty with the Paul Whiteman band, with whom they made their film debut in the 1930 Technicolor revue *The King of Jazz.* Crosby decided to leave the group, and was championed by Mary Pickford. He sang to America's Sweetheart in several publicity shorts and made a brief appearance singing "There's No Low-Down Lower Than That" in Douglas Fairbanks' 1931 version of *Reaching for the Moon.* A 15-minute CBS radio show made Crosby a household name, and Mack Sennett signed the crooner for a half dozen two-reelers. Although the shorts were not particularly funny, Crosby proved to be a winning screen personality with a breezy, offhand style. In other words, a natural. (Although initially someone decided his prominent ears should be taped back for the cameras.)

Crosby signed with Paramount in 1932 and became a major screen star with his first starring feature, *The Big Broadcast.* In the 1930s he appeared in sparkling, sometimes surreal entertainments like *Going Hollywood* (1933, on loan to MGM), *We're Not Dressing* (1934), *Mississippi* (1935), and *Anything Goes* (1936), introducing a raft of song standards along the way. *Rhythm on the Range* (1936, featuring "I'm an Old Cowhand") and *Waikiki Wedding* (1937, spotlighting the Oscar-winning "Sweet Leilani") continued his winning streak, but in the late 1930s Crosby's solo vehicles (like *Paris Honeymoon* and *The Star Maker)* became more ponderous and somewhat less entertaining. Then in 1940 he was teamed with comedian and off-camera buddy Bob Hope in *The Road to Singapore.* The picture offered a winning combination of songs, romance, in-jokes, and burlesque shtick. Over the next 20 years, the team went on the *Road to Zanzibar* (1941), . . . *Morocco* (1942), . . . *Utopia* (1945), . . . *Rio* (1947), . . . *Bali* (1952), and . . . *Hong Kong* (1962), exchanging snappy patter, kidding each other's public personas, and generally seeming to have a good time.

Holiday Inn (1942) paired the singer with Fred Astaire; Crosby's rendition of Irving Berlin's "White Christmas" went on to become the biggest-selling record of all time. He and Astaire later reteamed for Berlin's *Blue Skies* (1946). In 1944 he was tapped by director Leo McCarey to play Father O'Malley in the sentimental comedy-drama *Going My Way,* proving himself to be a fine, understated dramatic actor. (The movie also gave him an Oscar-winning song, "Swinging on a Star.") The performance earned him an Oscar; one year later, he got another nomination for McCarey's sequel *The Bells of St. Mary's* (1945, which costarred Ingrid Bergman). Around this time Crosby tested—in full makeup—to play Will Rogers in a proposed screen biography that never came to fruition. But it was getting harder to create fresh movie ideas for a middle-aged crooner, as witness *The Emperor Waltz* (1948), *Mr. Music* (1950), *Riding High* (1950), and *Here Comes the Groom* (1951).

Crosby took another chance, and received critical plaudits (plus an Oscar nomination) for his most dramatic work to date, as an alcoholic singer in *The Country Girl* (1954). His remaining musicals were mediocre at best (though 1954's *White Christmas* was a box-office smash), but *High Society* (1956) offered a last hurrah, as this *Philadelphia Story* remake gave him a tailor-made role, a chance to work with Frank Sinatra and Louis Armstrong at the peak of their powers, and a beautiful duet, crooning "True Love" with leading lady Grace Kelly. Crosby kept busy on-screen through the mid 1960s, in mostly undistinguished fare; his last musical was the Sinatra "rat pack" saga *Robin and the Seven Hoods* (1964), and his final dramatic role was in the 1966 remake of *Stagecoach.*

Throughout his film career, Crosby remained active (and hugely successful) in records, radio, and television. In addition to many guest appearances, he was a frequent host of ABC's "Hollywood Palace" (1964–70), and also starred in a half-hour sitcom, "The Bing Crosby Show," in the 1964–65 season. His last dramatic work, in fact, was in a made-for-TV movie, *Dr. Cook's Garden* (1970). His Bing Crosby Productions was an active TV supplier, but his greatest contribution to the medium was the financing of research and development for videotape. He was married first to Fox starlet Dixie Lee from

1930 until her death in 1952, and married actress Kathryn Grant in 1957. Crosby published his autobiography, "Call Me Lucky," in 1953.

CROTHERS, BENJAMIN SCATMAN. Actor. *(b. May 23, 1910, Terre Haute, Ind., as Benjamin Crothers; d. Nov. 26, 1986.)* Though primarily a musical performer, the ebullient Crothers (whose nickname Scatman came from the scat singing he did early in his career) emerged as a lively, distinctive character actor in the last decade of his life. He taught himself to play drums and guitar as a youth, and formed a band that traveled throughout the Midwest during the 1930s. Crothers came to L.A. in 1948 with the band, and made his film debut in *Meet Me at the Fair* (1953). He worked in TV during the 1950s and 1960s, but later found himself in great demand in films, and worked constantly until his death. Crothers' bald pate and wrinkled face made him instantly recognizable to moviegoers who were usually delighted to see him on screen. He appeared in four movies with Jack Nicholson: *The King of Marvin Gardens* (1972), *The Fortune* (1975), *One Flew Over the Cuckoo's Nest* (1975), and, most memorably, *The Shining* (1980, playing a psychic hotel chef). He is also remembered as Louie the Garbage Man from the TV sitcom "Chico and the Man" (1974–78).
OTHER FILMS INCLUDE: 1961: *The Sins of Rachel Cade;* 1964: *Lady in a Cage, The Patsy;* 1969: *Hello, Dolly!;* 1970: *The Great White Hope;* 1972: *Lady Sings the Blues;* 1974: *Truck Turner;* 1976: *The Shootist;* 1978: *Mean Dog Blues, The Cheap Detective;* 1980: *Bronco Billy;* 1983: *Twilight Zone—The Movie.*

CROUSE, LINDSAY. Actress. *(b. May 12, 1948, New York City.)* Capable supporting actress and occasional leading lady, in films since the 1970s, and most effective as aloof, no-nonsense, brainy types. Nominated for a Best Supporting Actress Oscar for *Places in the Heart* (1984), Crouse was perfect as the tense psychiatrist involved in a labyrinthine con game in *House of Games* (1987), which gave her a rare leading role; it was scripted and directed by her then-husband, David Mamet. Incidentally, her full name, Lindsay Ann Crouse, is a pun; her father, Russel Crouse, was half of the enormously successful Broadway writing/producing team of (Howard) Lindsay and Crouse.
OTHER FILMS INCLUDE: 1976: *All the President's Men;* 1977: *Slap Shot;* 1981: *Prince of the City;* 1982: *The Verdict;* 1983: *Daniel;* 1984: *Iceman;* 1989: *Communion;* 1990: *Desperate Hours;* 1993: *Chantilly Lace* (telefilm); 1994: *Being Human.*

CRUISE, TOM. Actor. *(b. July 3, 1962, Syracuse, N.Y., as Thomas Cruise Mapother IV.)* One of the top box-office stars of the 1980s and 1990s, Cruise effortlessly projects youthful sex appeal, but has put his name (and growing reputation) on the line more than once to prove himself an actor as well. Overcoming a difficult childhood—during which his family moved at least a dozen times, his parents divorced, and his father died of cancer—the young, dyslexic Cruise spent a year at a Franciscan monastery before deciding that acting was his true calling. By the age of 18 he had landed his first movie part, in *Endless Love* (1981). Following roles of increasing importance in *Taps* (1981), *Losin' It,* and *The Outsiders* (both 1983), Cruise achieved true notoriety in 1983 following his engaging lead performances in *Risky Business* and *All the Right Moves.* The sword-and-sorcery opus *Legend* (1985) saw him marking time, but he achieved superstar status after appearing as the cocky young fighter pilot in the hugely popular *Top Gun* (1986), and subsequently attracted favorable notices for his work in *The Color of Money* (1986, well paired with Paul Newman) and *Rain Man* (1988, holding his own opposite Dustin Hoffman), shedding the "pretty boy" and "beefcake" rep he'd been saddled with. *Cocktail* (1988) may have been a misstep, but he shook off criticism and jumped into his next project with characteristic determination.

Described by fellow actors as dedicated and absorbed in his craft, the magnetic, handsome young star with the devastating smile received the nation's attention (and an Academy Award nomination for Best Actor) for his portrayal of paralyzed Vietnam vet Ron Kovic in *Born on the Fourth of July* (1989). The environmentally conscious Cruise serves—along with ex-wife Mimi Rogers—on the board of the Earth Communications Office. Australian actress Nicole Kidman, Cruise's costar in *Days of Thunder* (1990), became the charismatic young star's second wife on Christmas Eve, 1990. They appeared together in the much heralded *Far and Away* (1992), which turned out to be little more than a vehicle for the extraordinarily good-looking couple. He then worked opposite a more challenging costar, Jack Nicholson, in *A Few Good Men* (1992), and toplined the legal thriller *The Firm* (1993). Cruise has matured as an actor, while retaining the appeal that made him popular in the first place; what's more, he's used the clout of stardom to help get some worthwhile films made. In 1993 he made his debut behind the camera, directing an episode of "Fallen Angels" for TV and in 1994 starred in *Interview With the Vampire*, amidst cries of miscasting from devotees of Anne Rice's book.

CRYER, JON. Actor. *(b. Apr. 16, 1965, New York City.)* The son of actor David Cryer and songwriter-actress Gretchen Cryer, this young, dark-haired actor specializes in overeager and pouty youths. He made his tyro screen appearance in a showy part opposite Demi Moore in *No Small Affair* (1984), and aroused further interest as the troubled outcast in *Pretty in Pink* (1986). Starring roles in *Hiding Out* (1987) and *Morgan Stewart's Coming Home* (1987, a monumental turkey clearly intended to do for Cryer what *Ferris Bueller* had done for Matthew Broderick) failed to generate any excitement in him as a leading man. Cryer did earn good notices for his 1990 TV sitcom "The Famous Teddy Z." Back in supporting roles, he milked his part as a goofball pilot in the *Airplane*-style *Hot Shots!* (1991) for plenty of laughs.

CRYSTAL, BILLY. Actor, writer, producer. *(b. Mar. 14, 1947, Long Beach, N.Y.)* Bright, likable, curly-haired comedian, one of the few who's successfully made the transition from stand-up comic to movie star. He first won over TV audiences as the acerbic gay stepson on "Soap" (1977–81), following that with a short-lived variety show (on which he introduced his infamous Fernando Lamas impression) and several cable specials. Crystal made his feature starring debut as the world's first pregnant man in the indifferently received *Rabbit Test* (1978), written and directed by Joan Rivers. But it was the 1984–85 season of "Saturday Night Live" that made him a star and Fernando's "You look mahhhhvelous!" a hot catchphrase. He returned to movie leading roles as a wise-cracking cop in *Running Scared* (1986), a tormented writing teacher in *Throw Momma From the Train* (1987), a long-suffering son in *Memories of Me* (1988, which he also wrote and coproduced), a male chauvinist in *When Harry Met Sally . . .* (1989), and an ad-man suffering his midlife crisis in *City Slickers* (1991, which he also produced). *Mr. Saturday Night* (1992) drew on Crystal's fascination with the peccadilloes of show business, and inspired him to direct for the first time. (He'd already created and produced an exceptionally intelligent comedy series about a man in therapy, "Sessions," for cable TV in 1992.) Succumbing to the lure of success, he made a standard sequel *City Slickers II: The Legend of Curly's Gold* (1994) before cowriting and directing himself and Debra Winger in *Forget Paris* (1995). He has also won plaudits, and three Emmys, as the quick-witted host of the Academy Awards (1990–93). In 1986 he published a possibly premature autobiography, "Absolutely Mahvelous."

CUKOR, GEORGE. Director. *(b. July 7, 1899, New York City; d. Jan. 24, 1983.)* His unfair designation as a "woman's director" was Hollywood shorthand for the fact that Cukor was gay; in reality, he was a splendid director of both male and female actors, far more comfortable with pace and performance than visual technique, and his obvious skill and taste made him one of the aces of Hollywood's Golden Age. A distinguished theatrical director in the 1920s (who worked with Ethel Barrymore and Jeanne Eagels, among others), he migrated to Hollywood in 1929 with the first wave of Broadway talent "imported" during the early years of talkies. He was a dialogue director on *All Quiet on the Western Front* (1930), a job he also held on several early Paramount talkies before becoming a solo director with *Tarnished Lady* (1931). Shortly thereafter, Cukor met legendary producer David O. Selznick, then production chief for RKO; their professional association began with *A Bill of Divorcement* (the 1932 drama that introduced Katharine Hepburn to the screen), and continued when Selznick moved to MGM, where Cukor directed *Dinner at Eight* (1933) and *David Copperfield* (1935) for the producer, and also helmed the classics *Romeo and Juliet* (1936), *Camille* (1937, starring Greta Garbo), and *Holiday* (1938, again with Hepburn, and Cary Grant as well), before being assigned by Selznick to *Gone With the Wind* (1939). He was fired 10 days after the start of production—on some accounts due to star Clark Gable's resentment of having to work with a director who, aside from being homosexual, lavished most of his attention on female lead Vivien Leigh.

While the dismissal apparently remained a thorn in his side for the rest of his life, it didn't diminish Cukor's reputation or ability to make sparkling comedies and dramas. *The Women* (1939), with its all-star female cast headed by Norma Shearer and Joan Crawford, and *The Philadelphia Story* (1940), which reteamed him with Hepburn and Grant, proved that. He had several unfortunate assignments during the 1940s, including the 1941 Garbo fiasco *Two-Faced Woman.* But Cukor's bounce back, beginning in the late years of the decade, was strong indeed; he helmed two of the finest Spencer Tracy–Katharine Hepburn vehicles, *Adam's Rib* (1949) and *Pat and Mike* (1952), both cowritten by Garson Kanin and Ruth Gordon. Other highlights from Cukor's later years include *Born Yesterday* (1950, the last great screwball comedy, starring Judy Holliday) and *A Star Is Born* (1954, remaking a 1937 Selznick production, with Judy Garland).

Cukor received his only Best Director Oscar for *My Fair Lady* (1964). That film aside, he seemed at sea for much of the decade, witness such misfires as the "frank" sex drama *The Chapman Report* (1962) and a faux-erotic adaptation of Lawrence Durrell's *Justine* (1969). His last big-screen effort, *Rich and Famous* (1981), was an ill-advised attempt to graft *The Women*'s elegant bitchiness to a contemporary setting; the only thing critics praised was Cukor's stamina, since he made it at the ripe age of 82.

OTHER FILMS INCLUDE: 1931: *Girls About Town;* 1932: *What Price Hollywood?;* 1935: *Sylvia Scarlett;* 1941: *A Woman's Face;* 1942: *Her Cardboard Lover, Keeper of the Flame;* 1944: *Gaslight;* 1947: *A Double Life;* 1952: *The Marrying Kind;* 1953: *The Actress;* 1957: *Les Girls;* 1960: *Let's Make Love;* 1976: *The Blue Bird.*

CULKIN, MACAULAY. Actor. *(b. Aug. 26, 1980, New York City.)* This sweet-faced young boy became the movies' most unexpected superstar when *Home Alone* (1990), the comic story of an eight-year-old forced to fend for himself, became a runaway smash. He had already appeared in *Rocket Gibraltar* (1987), *Uncle Buck* (1989), *See You in the Morning* (1989), and *Jacob's Ladder* (1990), and after *Home Alone* appeared in *My Girl* (1991). He received an estimated $5 million for *Home Alone 2: Lost in New York* (1992), and "starred" in the TV cartoon series "Wish Kid." In 1993 he took a dramatic turn—and a marketing challenge—by playing an evil child in *The Good Son,* and lent both his name and presence to the ballet movie *The Nutcracker.* The next year he took leads in *Getting Even With Dad, The Pagemaster,* and *Ri¢hie Ri¢h* (all 1994). His father Kit was also a child actor, and his younger brother Kieran has appeared in several films, including the remake of *Father of the Bride* (1991) and *Nowhere to Run* (1993).

CUMMINGS, CONSTANCE. Actress. *(b. May 15, 1910, Seattle, as Constance Halverstadt.)* This charming, attractive brunette is often thought to be British (having married English playwright Benn Levy and spent much of her career in England), but she's actually the daughter of a prominent Washington state lawyer. Bitten by the acting bug in her teens, Cummings worked in stock and appeared on the New York stage in the late 1920s. She made her film debut in *The Criminal Code* (1931), and then seldom stopped to take a breath, appearing as the ingenue in *Movie Crazy* (opposite Harold Lloyd), *Behind the Mask, Night After Night* (all 1932), *Broadway Thru a Keyhole* (1933, in which she sings with Russ Columbo), *This Man Is Mine* (1934, one of her best parts, as a catty socialite who steals Ralph Bellamy from Irene Dunne), and *Remember Last Night?* (1935), among others. After marrying Levy, she made occasional movies in England, including *Seven Sinners* (1936), *Haunted Honeymoon* (1940, playing Harriet to Robert Montgomery's Lord Peter Wimsey), *The Foreman Went to France* (1941), *Finger of Guilt* (1956), *The Battle of the Sexes* (1960), *A Boy Ten Feet Tall* (1963), and *Jane Eyre* (1971). She's exceptional in Noël Coward's *Blithe Spirit* (1945) as Rex Harrison's new wife. Cummings has made few film appearances since the late 1950s, but she has been very active on stage on both sides of the Atlantic.

CUMMINGS, ROBERT. Actor. *(b. June 9, 1908, Joplin, Mo., as Clarence R. Cummings; d. Dec. 1, 1990.)* He once pretended to be an aristocrat named Blade Stanhope Conway, but this eternally buoyant leading man brought a down-to-earth talent to every role he played (attributing his lasting youthfulness to a rigid health-food diet) during a lengthy career in film and on TV. Cummings worked extensively in the 1930s, first as an extra (his earliest known credit is the 1933 Laurel and Hardy comedy *Sons of the Desert),* then as a Paramount and Universal contract player with supporting roles and secondary leads in such films as *Hollywood Boulevard* (1936), *Wells Fargo, The Last Train From Madrid* (both 1937), *College Swing* (1938), *The Under-Pup* (1939), and *One Night in the Tropics* (1940).

Cummings achieved star status opposite Deanna Durbin in *Three Smart Girls Grow Up* (1939), *Spring Parade* (1940), and *It Started With Eve* (1941), and he continued to delight audiences in such comedies as *The Devil and Miss Jones, Moon Over Miami* (both 1941), *Princess O'Rourke* (1943), *Tell It to the Judge* (1949), *The First Time* (1952), *How to Be Very, Very Popular* (1955), *My Geisha* (1962), *Beach Party* (1963), and *What a Way to Go!* (1964). Cummings also gave solid dramatic performances in *Kings Row* (1942), *Flesh and Fantasy* (1943), *The Lost Moment* (1947), *Paid in Full* (1950), a pair of Hitchcock thrillers, *Saboteur* (1942) and *Dial M for Murder* (1954), and the original live TV presentation of "Twelve Angry Men," for which he won an Emmy. He'll always be remembered for his

long-running "The Bob Cummings Show" (1955–59; aka "Love That Bob"), in which his skirt-chasing photographer was an amazing departure from the nuclear-family-obsessed world of 1950s sitcoms. He was also the show's principal director. In 1960 Cummings authored a health-and-positive-thinking book called "Stay Young and Vital."

CUMMINS, PEGGY. Actress. *(b. Dec. 18, 1925, Prestatyn, North Wales.)* Pert, pretty British actress celebrated by cultists for her eye-opening portrayal of the femme fatale in the film noir classic *Gun Crazy* (1949), also as the female lead in the literate horror film *Curse of the Demon* (1958). An accomplished stage performer while still in her teens, Cummins debuted on screen in 1940's *Dr. Dowd,* and made several other films in England before coming to Hollywood—amid great fanfare—to star in *Forever Amber.* Production was suspended after one month, however, when it was decided the script needed work—and Cummins wasn't worldly enough for the leading role; she was replaced by Linda Darnell. Subsequent films, on both sides of the Atlantic, include *The Late George Apley* (1947), *Escape* (1948), *If This Be Sin* (1949), *Always a Bride* (1953), *The Love Lottery* (1954), *Carry on Admiral* (1957), *Dentist in the Chair* (1960), and *In the Doghouse* (1961).

CURRIE, FINLAY. Actor. *(b. Jan. 20, 1878, Edinburgh; d. May 9, 1968.)* An imposing presence on-screen well into his 80s, this former choirmaster took up acting in 1898, and first appeared on film in 1932 after many years on stage. He was a white-haired, burly man with bushy eyebrows, regularly seen in authoritative parts, strong-willed and stern. At his best as the convict Magwitch in *Great Expectations* (1946), for which he is best remembered.
OTHER FILMS INCLUDE: 1933: *The Good Companions;* 1941: *49th Parallel;* 1945: *I Know Where I'm Going!;* 1950: *Treasure Island;* 1951: *Quo Vadis?* (as the apostle Peter); 1952: *Ivanhoe;* 1957: *Saint Joan;* 1959: *Ben-Hur, Solomon and Sheba* (as King David); 1960: *Kidnapped, The Adventures of Huckleberry Finn;* 1961: *Francis of Assisi* (as Pope

Innocent III); 1963: *Cleopatra, Billy Liar;* 1964: *The Three Lives of Thomasina, The Fall of the Roman Empire;* 1965: *Bunny Lake Is Missing.*

CURRY, TIM. Actor. *(b. Apr. 19, 1946, Cheshire, England.)* He's already attained inclusion in the pantheon of cult-movie personalities for his portrayal of Dr. Frank N. Furter in the amiable horror-film parody (and perennial midnight-movie favorite) *The Rocky Horror Picture Show* (1975), but there's much more to this talented actor than lipstick and net stockings. Curry studied drama at Birmingham University, where he received a thorough grounding in Shakespeare and modern theater. But it took the lead in the London stage production of "Rocky Horror" in 1973 to make him a star. Curry is a natural comedy player, as he's demonstrated in *Annie* (1982), *Clue* (1985), *Pass the Ammo* (1988), *Oscar* (1991, hysterically funny as a priggish speech instructor), *Passed Away,* and *Home Alone 2* (both 1992), but he's also been effective in dramatic roles in such productions as *The Shout* (1978), *The Ploughman's Lunch* (1983), and *The Hunt for Red October* (1990). His sonorous voice made him a perfect choice to play a hypnotically hideous demon in *Legend* (1985), and has since served him well in the field of animation (he was Captain Hook on the TV series "Peter Pan and the Pirates," for instance, which won him an Emmy). He divides his time between the theater, TV, and movie work. Recent films include *National Lampoon's Loaded Weapon 1* and *The Three Musketeers* (both 1993, in the latter as Cardinal Richelieu) and the hit *Congo* (1995).

CURTIS, JAMIE LEE. Actress. *(b. Nov. 22, 1958, Los Angeles.)* A consistently engaging performer, Curtis managed to escape typecasting in teen slasher movies to carve a reputation as a first-class comedienne. Neither as pretty nor as voluptuous as her mom, actress Janet Leigh, the attractive, intelligent Curtis has also shown considerable range and technical skill as a dramatic actress, particularly in some of her 1980s films. She first attracted attention in the cast of the TV sitcom "Operation Petticoat" (1977–78), based on the 1959 movie that starred her father, Tony Curtis,

but she came to prominence in a string of low- and medium-budget horror films, beginning with John Carpenter's *Halloween* (1978) and followed by *Prom Night, Terror Train, The Fog* (all 1980), and *Halloween II* (1981). She showed promise in a more demanding role, that of doomed Playboy model Dorothy Stratten in the made-for-TV *Death of a Centerfold: The Dorothy Stratten Story* (1981).

Curtis' "breakout" film, and first comedy success, was the Dan Aykroyd–Eddie Murphy starrer *Trading Places* (1983); her turn as a good-natured prostitute raised eyebrows and won her leading-lady status. Roles in the modest *Love Letters* (1983) and *Grandview, U.S.A.* (1984) boosted her stock, although the box-office fizzle of *Perfect* (1985), in which she played an aerobics instructor to John Travolta's investigative reporter, was a temporary setback. *A Man in Love* (1987) gave Curtis a plum part as the wife of Peter Coyote thrown over for glamorous Greta Scacchi, but it was her starring role in *A Fish Called Wanda* (1988) that cemented her reputation as a gifted comic actress. She worked hard, to little avail, in the silly cop thriller *Blue Steel* (1990), and was positively ubiquitous in 1991, appearing in *Queens Logic, Dreamland, My Girl,* and *Criminals* on the big screen, and costarring in the comedy series "Anything But Love" (1989–92). She also wrote a children's book. 1994 films include *My Girl 2, Mother's Boys* (as a psycho!), and *True Lies.* She is married to Christopher Guest.

CURTIS, TONY. Actor. *(b. June 3, 1925, New York City, as Bernard Schwartz.)* A product of the "star is made" studio system, the energetic, good-looking Curtis has been consistently taken for granted, in spite of many first-rate performances. The son of a Hungarian immigrant (who had been an amateur actor in Budapest), Curtis was involved with street gangs as a child, but eventually joined the Navy during World War 2. He turned to acting in the late 1940s and studied at New York's Dramatic Workshop. While playing the lead in a production of "Golden Boy," a Universal talent scout spotted him and Bernie Schwartz was signed to a seven-year contract (starting at $100 a week). His name was changed to "Anthony Curtis."

He was put through the usual barrage of drama, voice, fencing, and horse riding lessons before landing his first role in *Criss Cross* (1949), where he briefly danced with Yvonne De Carlo; he also appeared in *City Across the River, The Lady Gambles,* and *Francis* (all 1949) and more prominently in *Johnny Stool Pigeon* (also 1949), *I Was a Shoplifter,* and *Kansas Raiders* (both 1950). Bolstered by the Universal publicity mill and growing fan support, Curtis got his first lead in *The Prince Who Was a Thief* (1951, opposite another Universal contract player, Piper Laurie). His accent was all too apparent, though the legend that he said "Yonda lies da castle of my fodda" is simply untrue. The film turned to out be a box-office success, and Curtis soon toplined another costumer, *Son of Ali Baba* (1952). He got to stretch as a deaf mute boxer in *Flesh and Fury* (also 1952) and starred with his wife Janet Leigh in the fanciful biopic *Houdini* (1953), but returned to formula in *The All-American, Forbidden* (both also 1953), *The Black Shield of Falworth* (1954), *The Purple Mask,* and *The Square Jungle* (both 1955). By now he was a box-office star, and he and Leigh were fan-magazine fodder as Hollywood's ideal couple.

Trapeze (1956), a big-budget box-office smash about a love triangle set against the big top, marked a turning point for Curtis; for the first time, critics paid attention to his work, not just his looks. He followed with a string of films that offered him the best roles of his career: *Sweet Smell of Success* (1957, as a boot-licking press agent to Burt Lancaster's Walter Winchell–like columnist), *The Defiant Ones* (1958, earning an Oscar nomination as an escaped convict chained to Sidney Poitier), *Some Like It Hot* (1959, partnered with Jack Lemmon, as a cross-dressing musician, who tries to woo Marilyn Monroe), and *Operation Petticoat* (1959, opposite his long time idol Cary Grant, whom he parodied in *Some Like It Hot* and many other films). At the outset of the 1960s, Curtis appeared in the epic *Spartacus* (1960) and impressed in *The Great Impostor* (1960) and especially *The Outsider* (1961, as Native American war hero Ira Hayes), but except for a diversion like *Taras Bulba* (1962), he confined himself to lightweight comedies like *Forty Pounds of Trouble* (1963), *Goodbye Char-lie, Sex and the Single Girl* (both 1964), *The Great Race* (1965), *Boeing Boeing* (also 1965, teamed with a restrained Jerry Lewis), and the box-office duds *Not With My Wife You Don't!* (1966), *Don't Make Waves* (1967), and *The Chastity Belt* (1968).

Eager to try something meaty once more, Curtis lobbied hard to play mass murderer Albert De Salvo in *The Boston Strangler* (1968), and gave a powerful, complex performance. The film, however, did not rejuvenate his career, and he followed with the indifferently received *Those Daring Young Men in Their Jaunty Jalopies* (1969), *Suppose They Gave a War and Nobody Came?,* and *You Can't Win 'Em All* (both 1970, the latter with Charles Bronson). He was quite effective as a gangster in *Lepke* (1975) and received his best reviews in years as a fading, impotent star in *The Last Tycoon* (1976), but again wound up in nondescript efforts like *The Bad News Bears Go to Japan* (1978), *Little Miss Marker, The Mirror Crack'd* (both 1980), and such outright embarrassments as *Sextette* and *The Manitou* (both 1978).

More recent credits include such oddities as *Othello—The Black Commando* (1982), *Where Is Parsifal?* (1984), and *Midnight* (1989). He took a recurring role in the TV series "Vegas" (1978–81) and played Sam Giancana in the telefeature *Mafia Princess* (1986). Curtis' marvelous work in the TV movie *The Scarlett O'Hara War* (1980, as David O. Selznick) and in Nicolas Roeg's *Insignificance* (1985, as a Joe McCarthy–like senator) only remind you how good he can be. In recent years he has also achieved some prominence as an artist, with his paintings featured in several high-profile galleries. Formerly married to Leigh and actress Christine Kaufmann, with whom he starred in *Wild and Wonderful* (1964). His daughters, Jamie Lee Curtis and Kelly Curtis, are both actresses. He wrote one novel, and he published an autobiography, "Tony Curtis: The Autobiography," in 1993.

CURTIZ, MICHAEL. Director. *(b. Dec. 24, 1888, Budapest, as Mihaly Kertesz; d. April 11, 1962.)* The director of the legendary *Casablanca* (1942) had almost as prolific a career in his native Hungary and other European countries as he did in Hollywood. First working in movies as an actor (debuting in 1912), Curtiz helmed approximately 60 films before coming to America (where he made more than 100 movies) in 1926. An efficient craftsman generally disliked by both casts and crews, he was a film "commandant" in the mold of other dictatorial Prussian types such as Otto Preminger and Erich von Stroheim. But Curtiz seemed not to have the artistic ambitions of those masters; he rarely initiated his own projects, doing whatever Warner Bros. (where he spent most of his American career) assigned him. Which isn't to say that he didn't impart his own style to the pictures; an astute practitioner of the German Expressionist tradition in filmmaking, he brought a keen visual sense to his movies right from the beginning of his Hollywood tenure, imbuing routine melodramas such as *The Third Degree* (1927, his first American film) with eye-popping camera angles and compositions.

When talkies came in, Curtiz worked in a wider number of genres than other directors with more "personal" styles; he did horror films (1932's *Doctor X, The Mystery of the Wax Museum* of 1933, 1936's *The Walking Dead*), crime dramas (*Angels With Dirty Faces* of 1938), prison pictures (1933's *20,000 Years in Sing Sing*), whodunits (1935's *The Case of the Curious Bride*), tearjerkers, and domestic dramas (1938's *Four Daughters*, 1939's *Daughters Courageous*), Westerns (1939's *Dodge City*, 1940's *Virginia City*), historical action pictures (1935's *Captain Blood*, 1936's *The Charge of the Light Brigade*, 1938's *The Adventures of Robin Hood*, 1940's *The Sea Hawk*), Biblical spectacles (1929's *Noah's Ark*, 1954's *The Egyptian*), war films (1941's *Dive Bomber*, 1942's *Captains of the Clouds*), musicals (1930's *Mammy*, 1942's *Yankee Doodle Dandy*, 1943's *This Is the Army*, 1946's *Night and Day*, 1954's *White Christmas*), and straight melodramas (1930's *The Mad Genius*, 1945's *Mildred Pierce*, 1947's *The Unsuspected*).

His superior skills, and the conviction he managed to bring to even the silliest scenarios, made Curtiz more than just a studio hack, and most of his films continue to hold up as models of cinematic storytelling, although "auteur" theorists refuse to take him seriously because his work isn't confined to one genre or imbued with a consistent "worldview." Often a bridesmaid, he earned Oscar nominations for *Four Daughters, Angels with Dirty Faces,* and *Yankee Doodle Dandy*. Amazingly, Curtiz won his only Oscar for *Casablanca,* a troubled production that had been written off by its cast and chaotically shot with almost daily script revisions. As the studio system of filmmaking waned in the 1950s, so did Curtiz' career. He directed one of Elvis Presley's most credible films, *King Creole* (1958), and made his cinematic swan song, *The Comancheros,* in 1961.

CUSACK, JOAN. Actress. *(b. Oct. 11, 1962, Evanston, Ill.)* Quirky comic actress with offbeat looks; older sister of John. She made her film debut at 16 in *My Bodyguard* (1980), appearing with her brother a few years later in *Class* (1983) and *Sixteen Candles* (1984). As an English major at the University of Wisconsin at Madison, she spent most of her time with a local improvisational comedy group at the Ark Theater, where she returned in 1987 to direct "Death of an Anarchist." Cusack (who, despite the kooky characters she's often played, is described as serious and thoughtful when offstage) joined the cast of TV's "Saturday Night Live" for the 1985–86 season. Roles in such hit films as *Broadcast News* (1987, as a TV station intern), *Married to the Mob* (1988), *Working Girl* (also 1988, which earned her an Academy Award nomination for Best Supporting Actress), *Say Anything . . .* (1989, with brother John, playing his sister), and *Men Don't Leave* (1990) brought Joan well into the cinema limelight. She finally got a bona fide leading role in *My Blue Heaven* (1990), playing a dedicated, overzealous prosecutor. Her performances on stage (including her role in the off-Broadway plays "Brilliant Traces" and Shakespeare's "Cymbeline") earned rhapsodic reviews and gave her credence as a serious actress. Recent films include *Hero* (1992, as Dustin Hoffman's ex-wife), *Toys* (also 1992, as Robin Williams' spacy sister), and *Addams Family Values* (1993, as a lethal nanny).

CUSACK, JOHN. Actor. *(b. June 28, 1966, Evanston, Ill.)* This dark-haired, sly, and brashly appealing young actor has managed to transcend his Brat Pack origins with a number of well-rounded, finely delineated performances. A natural performer and high school dramatist, Cusack first reached the screen in youth-oriented movies such as *Class* (1983, with Rob Lowe and Andrew McCarthy) and *Sixteen Candles* (1984, with Molly Ringwald and Anthony Michael Hall), but in short order he established himself as a genuine talent standing out from a group of intermittently interesting personalities. He was a wry sad sack in two relatively innovative teen comedies, 1985's *Better Off Dead* and 1986's *One Crazy Summer*, and genuinely impressive in Rob Reiner's 1985 *The Sure Thing*. His mother forbade him from participating in the arduous Philippines shoot of *Platoon* (1986), but Cusack subsequently went after juicy parts in smaller, less ambitious projects, including John Sayles' drama of the 1919 White Sox scandal, *Eight Men Out* (1988) and the music video satire *Tapeheads* (also 1988, with his friend Tim Robbins, for whom he did a cameo in the latter's directorial debut film, *Bob Roberts*). In 1990 Cusack enjoyed significant success in an "adult" role as a small-time con artist in Stephen Frears' chilly neo-noir thriller *The Grifters*, coming into his own as an adult actor. He confirmed this promise with leading roles in Woody Allen's delightful *Bullets Over Broadway* (1994) and the political drama *City Hall* (1995). OTHER FILMS INCLUDE: 1989: *Fat Man and Little Boy*; 1992: *Shadows and Fog*; 1993: *Money for Nothing*.

CUSHING, PETER. Actor. *(b. May 26, 1913, Surrey, England; d. Aug. 11, 1994.)* Best known to the world as the prototypical embodiment of the "mad scientist," Cushing learned his craft at the Guildhall School of Music and Drama. Ironically, his first roles were in America, where he appeared on Broadway and in supporting roles, like *The Man in the Iron Mask* (1939) and the Laurel and Hardy feature *A Chump at Oxford* (1940). Returning to England, Cushing's first British film was Olivier's adaptation of *Hamlet* (1948). Offers brought him back to Hollywood, where he began a career in the horror/sci-fi genre which would last for more than three decades. *The Curse of Franken-*

stein (1957) paired Cushing's Dr. Frankenstein with Christopher Lee as the monster; the two would then work together on countless low-budget horror pictures, forging a genre that would become known as the Hammer Film, after the releasing studio. The two also appeared in the studio's production of *The Hound of the Baskervilles* (1959), with Cushing well cast as Sherlock Holmes. Curiously, Cushing's cool intelligence and clipped manner rarely found expression in more substantial cinematic vehicles, 1977's *Star Wars* being a noteworthy exception. In 1986 he published "Peter Cushing: An Autobiography."

OTHER FILMS INCLUDE: 1940: *Vigil in the Night*; 1952: *Moulin Rouge*; 1954: *The Black Knight*; 1956: *Magic Fire, Alexander the Great*; 1957: *The Abominable Snowman*; 1958: *Horror of Dracula, The Revenge of Frankenstein*; 1959: *John Paul Jones*; 1960: *The Brides of Dracula*; 1962: *Night Creatures*; 1964: *The Evil of Frankenstein, The Gorgon, Dr. Terror's House of Horrors*; 1965: *She, The Skull*; 1966: *Daleks—Invasion Earth 2150 A.D.*; 1967: *Frankenstein Created Woman, Torture Garden*; 1970: *Frankenstein Must Be Destroyed!, The Vampire Lovers*; 1971: *The House That Dripped Blood, I, Monster, Twins of Evil*; 1972: *Fear in the Night, Asylum, Dracula A.D. 1972, Tales From the Crypt, Horror Express*; 1973: *The Creeping Flesh, Count Dracula and His Vampire Bride, And Now the Screaming Starts, From Beyond the Grave*; 1974: *Frankenstein and the Monster From Hell, The Beast Must Die, Madhouse*; 1975: *Legend of the Werewolf, The Ghoul*; 1976: *Land of the Minotaur, At the Earth's Core*; 1979: *Arabian Adventure*; 1981: *Monster Island*; 1983: *House of the Long Shadows*; 1984: *Top Secret!*; 1986: *Biggles: Adventures in Time*.

DAFOE, WILLEM. Actor. *(b. July 22, 1955, Appleton, Wis., as William Dafoe.)* A lean, sharp-featured actor with a seductive, serpentine smile, Dafoe finds himself in the unusual (but enviable) position of bouncing back and forth between leads and showy character parts—and he's equally effective in either. Following an inauspicious movie debut in *Heaven's Gate* (1980), the stage-seasoned Dafoe toiled in several minor films, usually as sadistic villains, before his turn in William

Friedkin's *To Live and Die in L.A.* (1985) set the mold for the postmodern heavy and, in so doing, elevated him to a higher rank of player. For 1986's *Platoon,* director Oliver Stone cast him against type as a Christ-like soldier; in 1988 Martin Scorsese went all the way and made Dafoe the lead in *The Last Temptation of Christ. (Platoon* earned him an Oscar nomination.) Since then he's been playing mainly heroic roles—an FBI agent in *Mississippi Burning* (1988), a boxer imprisoned by Nazis in *Triumph of the Spirit* (1989), a daring pilot in *Flight of the Intruder* (1991), a small-town cop working undercover in *White Sands* (1992)— although he did revert to his initial type in John Waters' *Cry-Baby* (1990), with a cameo as a bullying reformatory guard, and in *Wild at Heart* (1990), playing a lascivious bandit in bad need of an orthodontist. He's also been in *Light Sleeper* (1992), *Faraway, So Close!* (1993), the notorious *Body of Evidence* (also 1993, as the lawyer led astray by kinky client Madonna), and *Tom & Viv* (1994, as T. S. Eliot).

DAILEY, DAN. Actor. *(b. Dec. 14, 1914, New York City; d. Oct. 16, 1978.)* A tall, solidly built actor, with fair hair and complexion, blue eyes, and a mischevous grin, this popular musical star moved with more style and grace than one would normally expect from a man of his size. First appearing on stage as a child in a minstrel show (!), Dailey also sang and danced in vaudeville, burlesque, and stock before reaching Broadway in 1937, cast in the original production of "Babes in Arms." MGM snatched him up in 1940; the first role they gave this song-and-dance man was as a Nazi in *The Mortal Storm* (1940)! Soon he was back in his element (billed as Dan Dailey, Jr.) in *Ziegfeld Girl, Lady Be Good* (both 1941), *Panama Hattie* (1942), and others. Dailey entered the Army during World War 2 and rose to the rank of lieutenant. Afterward, he poked around Hollywood for work and was cast opposite Betty Grable in *Mother Wore Tights* (1947), acquitting himself well and securing a Fox contract. Grable liked Dailey immensely, and they became a popular musical-comedy team in *When My Baby Smiles at Me* (1948, which net-

ted him a Best Actor Oscar nomination), *My Blue Heaven* (1950), and *Call Me Mister* (1951).

Dailey starred in musicals until the genre petered out in the mid 1950s, then continued on screen in both comic and dramatic roles. Though seldom praised for his thespic talents, he was a natural. The high point of his musical career came in 1955 when he worked alongside Gene Kelly and Michael Kidd in *It's Always Fair Weather,* holding his own in that formidable company. He also worked on stage and in nightclubs, as well as in the TV series "Four Just Men" (1959), "The Governor and J.J." (1969–70), and "Faraday and Company" (1973–74), and frequent series guest shots and telefilms. Throughout his moderately successful career, Dailey frequently said he never forgot that he was basically "just a song and dance man." He was married and divorced three times.

OTHER FILMS INCLUDE: 1948: *Give My Regards to Broadway, Chicken Every Sunday;* 1949: *You're My Everything;* 1950: *When Willie Comes Marching Home, A Ticket to Tomahawk, I'll Get By;* 1951: *I Can Get It for You Wholesale;* 1952: *What Price Glory?, Meet Me at the Fair;* 1953: *The Girl Next Door, Taxi;* 1954: *There's No Business Like Show Business;* 1956: *Meet Me in Las Vegas, The Best Things in Life Are Free* (in the latter as songwriter Ray Henderson); 1957: *The Wings of Eagles;* 1958: *Underwater Warrior;* 1960: *Pepe;* 1962: *Hemingway's Adventures of a Young Man;* 1977: *The Private Files of J. Edgar Hoover.*

DALL, JOHN. Actor. *(b. 1918, New York City, as John Jenner Thompson; d. Jan. 15, 1971.)* Tall slender actor whose screen career failed to ignite despite three prominent roles early on: in support of Bette Davis in *The Corn Is Green* (1945), for which he was Oscar-nominated; as one of the sophisticated, coolly sadistic thrill-killers in Alfred Hitchcock's *Rope* (1948); and as the titular terror in *Gun Crazy* (1949). (In fact, the actor's apparent lack of warmth may have inhibited his career.) Dall, a Columbia graduate and alumnus of the Pasadena Playhouse, worked on Broadway in bit parts from 1941 and won a lead role in the 1944 comedy hit "Dear Ruth."

OTHER FILMS INCLUDE: 1947: *Something in the Wind;* 1948: *Another Part of the Forest;* 1951: *The Man Who Created Himself;* 1960: *Spartacus;* 1961: *Atlantis, the Lost Continent.*

DALLESANDRO, JOE. Actor. *(b. Dec. 31, 1948, Pensacola, Fla.)* Handsome, androgynous, thoroughly amateurish leading man in some of Andy Warhol's more popular movies directed by Paul Morrissey. He starred in the "acclaimed" trilogy comprised of *Flesh* (1968), *Trash* (1970), and *Heat* (1972). He also starred in the lavish productions of *Andy Warhol's Frankenstein* and *Andy Warhol's Dracula* (both 1974), which were released here in 3-D. Bit parts in mainstream features in the 1980s, such as *The Cotton Club* (1984), *Critical Condition* (1987), *Sunset* (1988), and *Cry-Baby* (1990), haven't done much to advance his post-Warhol career. His incredibly stilted line-readings and zombielike reactions may be at least partly to blame.

DALTON, TIMOTHY. Actor. *(b. Mar. 21, 1944, Colwyn Bay, Wales.)* Highly regarded for rescuing the character of James Bond from the depths of self-parody, this darkly handsome leading man—who, with mustache, bears a resemblance to swashbuckling star Errol Flynn—began as a stage actor, graduating to film work in the late 1960s. He initially appeared in large-scale costume dramas such as *The Lion in Winter* (1968), *Wuthering Heights* (1970, as Heathcliff), and *Mary, Queen of Scots* (1971). He spent much of the 1970s working almost exclusively on stage, but returned to film work late in the decade. Dalton's spot in camp history is assured by his participation in *Sextette* (1978, playing Mae West's love interest), *Flash Gordon* (1980, as Prince Barin), and *Brenda Starr* (1989, released 1992, as Brooke Shields' mystery man). He first tackled Ian Fleming's Secret Agent 007 in *The Living Daylights* (1987), and followed that with *Licence to Kill* (1989). But he never cut up as Bond, the way he did as an Errol Flynn–ish movie star in *The Rocketeer* (1991). In 1994 Dalton inherited Clark Gable's role of Rhett Butler in the miniseries "Scarlett."

DANCE, CHARLES. Actor. *(b. Oct. 19, 1946, Plymouth, England.)* Talented British actor who spent five years with The Royal Shakespeare Company before gaining fame here and abroad as Sergeant Guy Perron in the TV miniseries "The Jewel in the Crown" (1983). He had debuted in the small role of a gunman in the James Bond film *For Your Eyes Only* (1981), but made a striking impact as Meryl Streep's patient diplomat husband in *Plenty* (1985). He played sinister villains in *The Golden Child* (1986) and *Last Action Hero* (1993), but had more impressive parts in *The McGuffin* (1985), *Good Morning, Babylon* (1987, memorable as D. W. Griffith), *White Mischief* (also 1987), *Pascali's Island* (1988) and *Alien³* (1992). He has also appeared in the TV movies *Out on a Limb* (1987, opposite Shirley MacLaine) and *The Phantom of the Opera* (1990, in the title role).

DANDRIDGE, DOROTHY. Actress, singer. *(b. Nov. 9, 1923, Cleveland; d. Sept. 8, 1965.)* Beautiful, vibrant, talented and, ultimately, tragic black actress who starred in two memorable musicals, *Carmen Jones* (1954, for which she was Oscar-nominated) and *Porgy and Bess* (1959). A former child performer who had a bit in the 1937 Marx Brothers vehicle *A Day at the Races* and worked in numerous musical "soundies" in the early 1940s (including The Mills Brothers' *Paper Doll,* in the title role, and a sexy *Cow Cow Boogie),* Dandridge won fame as a nightclub entertainer later in the decade. She flirted with stardom throughout the 1950s, but a paucity of good roles for black performers stymied her efforts to attain real success in film. Dandridge, who declared bankruptcy in 1962, died after overdosing on booze and pills. An autobiography, "Everything and Nothing," was published posthumously in 1970.
OTHER FILMS INCLUDE: 1941: *Bahama Passage, The Lady From Louisiana, Sun Valley Serenade* (dancing to "Chattanooga Choo Choo" with the Nicholas Brothers), *Sundown;* 1942: *Drums of the Congo;* 1944: *Hit Parade of 1943, Atlantic City, Since You Went Away;* 1951: *The Harlem Globetrotters, Tarzan's Peril;* 1953: *Bright Road, Remains to Be Seen;* 1957: *Island in the Sun, Tamango;* 1958:

The Decks Ran Red; 1960: Moment of Danger; 1961: The Murder Men.

D'ANGELO, BEVERLY. Actress. *(b. Nov. 15, 1954, Columbus, Ohio.)* There were some who thought that this actress's remarkable turn as country singer Patsy Cline, in the Loretta Lynn biopic *Coal Miner's Daughter* (1980), would usher in a fecund creative period for the former rock singer, artist, and stage performer; alas, it never really materialized, and D'Angelo remains mired in silly comedies (such as *National Lampoon's Vacation* and its sequels) and occasional dramas (such as 1991's *The Miracle).* Nonetheless, the talented and attractive blonde—easily identifiable by her pale blue eyes, marked overbite, and overripe figure—perseveres. D'Angelo, who once worked for the Hanna-Barbera animation studio, played on Broadway in the 1970s before making her film debut in a minuscule part in Woody Allen's *Annie Hall* (1977). She moved on to slightly larger roles in that year's *First Love* and *The Sentinel,* then *Every Which Way but Loose* (1978), and *Hair* (1979), in which she finally got a chance to strut her stuff. Post–*Coal Miner's Daughter,* she worked in *Honky Tonk Freeway, Paternity* (both 1981), *National Lampoon's Vacation* (1983), *Finders Keepers* (1984), *Big Trouble, National Lampoon's European Vacation* (both 1985), *In the Mood, Maid to Order* (all 1987, in the last as Ally Sheedy's hip fairy godmother), *Aria, High Spirits, Trading Hearts* (all 1988), *Cold Front, National Lampoon's Christmas Vacation* (both 1989), *Daddy's Dyin' . . . Who's Got the Will?, Pacific Heights* (both 1990, unbilled in the latter), *The Pope Must Die(t), Lonely Hearts* (both 1991), and *Man Trouble* (1992). She has also been active in made-for-TV movies.

DANGERFIELD, RODNEY. Actor. *(b. Nov. 22, 1921, Babylon, N.Y., as Jack Cohen.)* Though he claims to never have gotten respect, this bug-eyed, tie-tugging comedian certainly enjoys considerable popularity. Having worked nightclubs in the 1940s under the stage name Jack Roy, Dangerfield was a businessman throughout the 1950s, and returned to stand-up comedy in the 1960s, opening his namesake comedy club in New York in 1969. He first appeared on-screen in the low-budget, barely released comedy *The Projectionist* (1971), and landed a regular spot on TV's "The Dean Martin Show" (1972–73). By the next decade, as an established, constantly touring headliner, he was ready for another shot at screen stardom, and got it as a rich but vulgar slob in the hit comedy *Caddyshack* (1980). His subsequent starring vehicles *Easy Money* (1983) and *Back to School* (1986) gave Dangerfield watchers more of the same, and were also successful. But his is essentially a one-joke character, and several starring films seem to have milked his persona for all it's worth, as proved by the dismal *Ladybugs* (1992). The summer of 1991 saw the release of *Rover Dangerfield,* a feature-length animated film in which his voice was used for a canine version of his character.

DANIELL, HENRY. Actor. *(b. Mar. 5, 1894, London; d. Oct. 31, 1963.)* Saturnine interpreter of predominantly villainous roles, a classically trained actor who came to America in the 1920s to appear opposite Ethel Barrymore on stage. Suavely malevolent, he tormented Greta Garbo in *Camille* (1937), traded insults (and swords) with Errol Flynn in *The Private Lives of Elizabeth and Essex* (1939) and *The Sea Hawk* (1940), and played cold-blooded Nazis in *Mission to Moscow, Watch on the Rhine* (both 1943), and for comic effect in Charlie Chaplin's *The Great Dictator* (1940, as Garbitsch). He's also unforgettable as the cadaver-coveting doctor in *The Body Snatcher,* and as Sherlock Holmes' arch-enemy, Professor Moriarty, in *The Woman in Green* (both 1945). He was a favorite of director George Cukor, for whom he made *Camille, Holiday* (1938), *The Philadelphia Story* (1940), *A Woman's Face* (1941), and *The Chapman Report* (1962); he died shortly after finishing his scenes in Cukor's *My Fair Lady* (1964). When fashioning his villainous role in *The Princess Bride* (1987), actor/mimic Christopher Guest patterned his performance after Daniell's in *The Sea Hawk*—and reproduced his voice precisely.
OTHER FILMS INCLUDE: 1937: *Madame X;* 1938: *Marie Antoinette;* 1947: *Song of Love* (as Franz Liszt); 1954: *The Egyptian;*

1956: *The Man in the Gray Flannel Suit, Lust for Life;* 1957: *The Sun Also Rises, Witness for the Prosecution;* 1959: *The Four Skulls of Jonathan Drake* (in the lead); 1962: *The Notorious Landlady.*

DANIELS, BEBE. Actress. *(b. Jan. 14, 1901, Dallas, as Phyllis Daniels; d. March 16, 1971.)* If you've seen *42nd Street* (1933), you know her as Dorothy Brock, the tempestuous stage star whose last-minute sprained ankle gives understudy Peggy Sawyer (Ruby Keeler) her big break. That performance, along with her outstanding turn as John Barrymore's long-suffering secretary in the same year's *Counsellor-at-Law,* tagged Daniels as a masterful dramatic actress. But few realize that she was one of the silent screen's ablest light comediennes, having costarred with Harold Lloyd in dozens of short comedies from 1916 to 1919. Signed by Paramount, she appeared in several Cecil B. DeMille films—including *Male and Female* (1919), *Why Change Your Wife?* (1920), and *The Affairs of Anatol* (1921)—and later starred in a whole series of fast and funny programmers for the studio, including *Miss Bluebeard* (1924), *Miss Brewster's Millions* (1926), *She's a Sheik* (1927), and *Feel My Pulse* (1928). She possessed a keen sense of comedic timing and could match double takes and pratfalls with the best of them.

In 1929, dropped by Paramount, Daniels went to the newly formed RKO and starred in the super-musical *Rio Rita,* which was a huge hit and revitalized her career. She costarred with Douglas Fairbanks in *Reaching for the Moon* (1930), played the Brigid O'Shaunessey role in the original *The Maltese Falcon* (1931, shown on TV as *Dangerous Female),* and even took a turn as Edward G. Robinson's mistress in *Silver Dollar* (1932). By 1935, however, Daniels' popularity had diminished significantly; ironically, in that year's *Music Is Magic,* she played an aging movie star forced to compete with newer, younger personalities. It was her last American film. Daniels and husband Ben Lyon (a former favorite whose career was also fading) went to England in 1936, playing the London Palladium, teaming on radio (in "Life with the Lyons"), and appearing in several movies, including two based on the radio show:

Life With the Lyons (1953) and *The Lyons in Paris* (1955), her last.

DANIELS, JEFF. Actor. *(b. Feb. 19, 1955, Athens, Ga.)* Low-key leading man whose WASPish good looks and reserved manner make him an appealing performer if not a dynamic screen presence. Educated at Central Michigan University, Daniels harbored ambitions of acting and made his way to New York, where he eventually achieved some prominence in the theater, winning a 1982 Obie Award for his one-man performance in a revival of Dalton Trumbo's "Johnny Got His Gun." Although by then he had already made his screen debut in *Ragtime* (1981), Daniels' theatrical success led to his being cast in a meaty role in *Terms of Endearment* (1983), as the philandering husband of cancer-stricken Debra Winger. Woody Allen made use of Daniels' restrained persona and clean-cut good looks by casting him as the movie star who steps out of the screen to help lonely Mia Farrow in *The Purple Rose of Cairo* (1985); it was a breakthrough part for Daniels (who actually replaced Michael Keaton after production had begun). He followed it with a turn as a smug yuppie, a "rebel who's only channeled his rebellion into the mainstream," in 1986's *Something Wild.*
OTHER FILMS INCLUDE: 1987: *Radio Days;* 1988: *Checking Out, The House on Carroll Street* (as an FBI agent during the blacklist days), *Sweet Hearts Dance* (as the reluctant suitor of Elizabeth Perkins); 1990: *Arachnophobia* (as the beleaguered homeowner), *Love Hurts, Welcome Home, Roxy Carmichael;* 1991: *The Butcher's Wife* (as a comically overwrought psychiatrist); 1992: *Pay Dirt, Rain Without Thunder, There Goes the Neighborhood;* 1993: *Gettysburg;* 1994: *Dumb and Dumber.*

DANIELS, WILLIAM H. Cinematographer. *(b. Dec. 1, 1895, Cleveland; d. June 14, 1970.)* Distinguished first-call cameraman equally proficient at black-and-white and color cinematography, and a master lighting stylist best known as Greta Garbo's personal lensman. Educated at USC, he broke into movies as an assistant operator for Triangle in 1917; two years later he was a full-fledged director of photogra-

phy. Daniels frequently worked with director Erich von Stroheim, and he deserves much of the credit for the naturalistic look of *Greed* (1925).
OTHER FILMS INCLUDE: 1919: *Blind Husbands;* 1922: *Foolish Wives;* 1925: *The Torrent;* 1926: *The Temptress;* 1927: *Flesh and the Devil;* 1928: *A Woman of Affairs;* 1932: *Mata Hari, Grand Hotel;* 1933: *Dinner at Eight, Queen Christina;* 1936: *Romeo and Juliet;* 1939: *Ninotchka;* 1941: *Back Street;* 1943: *Girl Crazy;* 1947: *Brute Force;* 1948: *The Naked City* (a decidedly unglamorous, documentary-style urban thriller for which he won his only Oscar); 1952: *Pat and Mike;* 1958: *Cat on a Hot Tin Roof;* 1960: *Can-Can;* 1962: *How the West Was Won;* 1963: *The Prize;* 1967: *In Like Flint;* 1970: *Move.*

DANNER, BLYTHE. Actress. *(b. Feb. 3, 1944, Philadelphia.)* Attractive, wholesome-looking, husky-voiced stage actress who has made occasional screen appearances. Despite having leading roles in such films as *Lovin' Molly* (1974) and *Futureworld* (1976), Danner has usually been relegated to standard supporting roles to which she brings considerable skill and charm. The patient, long-suffering wife is a Danner specialty, and two of her best roles along this line came in adaptations of Pat Conroy novels, *The Great Santini* (1979) and *The Prince of Tides* (1991). She costarred with fellow *1776* player Ken Howard in the 1973 TV series "Adam's Rib," and also appeared in the later series "Tattinger's" (1988) and "Nick and Hillary" (1989). She played the troubled Zelda Fitzgerald in a 1974 telefilm, *F. Scott Fitzgerald and "The Last of the Belles."* Danner's husband is TV producer Bruce Paltrow; their daughter Gwyneth is an actress whose credits include *Flesh and Bone* (1993), *Mrs. Parker and the Vicious Circle* (1994), and *Seven* (1995).
OTHER FILMS INCLUDE: 1972: *1776* (as Martha Jefferson); 1975: *Hearts of the West;* 1986: *Brighton Beach Memoirs;* 1988: *Another Woman;* 1990: *Alice, Mr. & Mrs. Bridge;* 1992: *Husbands and Wives.*

DANO, ROYAL. Actor. *(b. Nov. 16, 1922, New York City; d. May 15, 1994.)* You'd never peg this big, roughhewn character actor for a native New Yorker based on the roles he's played in movies. Beginning with 1950's *Undercover Girl,* Dano worked in dozens of movies, almost always playing Western heavies or menacing rural types. He enjoyed *some* parts outside the outdoor-action arena, appearing in *Moby Dick* (1956), *King of Kings* (1961, as Peter), *Big Bad Mama* (1974), *The Right Stuff* (1983), and *Teachers* (1984). Later he became a staple of low-budget genre efforts, of which 1988's *Killer Klowns From Outer Space* and 1990's *Spaced Invaders* are, sadly, all too typical. In his last years, Dano eschewed most of the sinister parts and played crotchety old-timers.
OTHER FILMS INCLUDE: 1951: *The Red Badge of Courage;* 1952: *Bend of the River;* 1954: *Johnny Guitar;* 1958: *Man of the West;* 1966: *Gunpoint;* 1968: *Day of the Evil Gun;* 1993: *The Dark Half.*

DANSON, TED. Actor. *(b. Dec. 29, 1947, Flagstaff, Ariz.)* Best known for his role as brash, womanizing Sam Malone on TV's "Cheers" (which won him an Emmy Award for the 1989–90 season, and another for 1992–93), this imposing actor worked hard in his movie career to overcome his TV typecasting as a callous hunk. The son of an archaeologist, Danson spent two years at Stanford University, where he "drifted into acting." Moving to New York City, he found work in commercials and soap operas, and met future wife Casey, at an EST seminar. Danson made his New York stage debut in 1972's "The Real Inspector Hound." His first film role, in *The Onion Field,* came in 1979—the same year his wife suffered a paralyzing stroke while giving birth to their daughter, Kate. Three years of caring for wife and child put Danson's career on hold, but in 1981, after Casey's recovery, he appeared as a District Attorney in Lawrence Kasdan's steamy thriller *Body Heat,* just before landing the part of Sam on "Cheers."
Danson also portrayed an incestuous father in the 1984 TV drama *Something About Amelia,* and went on to appear in such films as *3 Men and a Baby* (1987, as one of three bachelors entrusted with an infant, based on a French farce), *Cousins* (1989, an enjoyable, Americanized version of the French hit *Cousin, Cousine),*

Dad (1989, as a preoccupied yuppie who rehabilitates himself while caring for ailing father Jack Lemmon), and *3 Men and a Little Lady* (1990's sequel to his 1987 hit). He's also appeared in *Creepshow* (1982), *Little Treasure* (1985), and the abysmal alleged comedy *A Fine Mess* (1986), redeeming himself with an expert, moving performance in *Just Between Friends* (1986). Most recently he starred with Whoopi Goldberg in the dopey comedy *Made in America* (1993). An active environmentalist, Danson founded the American Ocean's Campaign in 1987.

DANTE, JOE. Director. *(b. Nov. 28, 1946, Morristown, N.J.)* A lifelong movie buff who turned his love into his career, Dante first displayed his encyclopedic knowledge of movies (especially horror/fantasy/sci-fi movies) in the 1960s publication "Castle of Frankenstein." When his boyhood friend Jon Davison got a job with producer Roger Corman in the 1970s, he sent for Dante and had him hired as New World Pictures' principal editor of preview trailers. (Along with the typical New World exploitation fodder, Dante also cut trailers for the likes of Fellini's *Amarcord.* He also got to edit an occasional feature, including 1977's *Grand Theft Auto,* which marked Ron Howard's directing debut.) When Davison bet Corman that he could produce a New World film in one week for $50,000, it was up to Dante and Allan Arkush to direct it. The result was *Hollywood Boulevard* (1976), which gave Dante his baptism of fire behind the camera.

In 1978 he directed his first feature, *Piranha,* an effective, tongue-in-cheek, low-budget thriller about killer fish written by John Sayles. He followed it with the more ambitious *The Howling* (1981), a vivid werewolf tale cowritten by Sayles. This brought him to the attention of Steven Spielberg, who hired both Dante and Jon Davison to work on one segment of *Twilight Zone—The Movie* (1983). Theirs was a bizarre story about a boy who holds his family prisoner in a cartoonlike house.

Dante's career then took a giant leap as Spielberg hired him to direct his big-budget scare movie *Gremlins* (1984). His career has moved in fits and starts since then, with hits and misses along the way,

including *Explorers* (1985), *Amazon Women on the Moon* (1987, some sequences only), *Innerspace* (1987), *The 'burbs* (1989), *Gremlins 2: The New Batch* (1990), and *Matinee* (1993).

At his best, Dante manages to capture in his work the wonder—and humor—of 1950s and 1960s movies that first turned him on; his films are overflowing with in-jokes for like-minded movie buffs. He remains loyal to many actors of that period (and the sci-fi/fantasy genre) and uses them in his films as often as possible. He also indulges his love for cartoons, having given famed animation director Chuck Jones a cameo in *Gremlins* and hired him to create animated gags for the closing credits of *Gremlins 2.*

DANTINE, HELMUT. Actor. *(b. Oct. 7, 1917, Vienna; d. May 3, 1982.)* One of the screen's most prominent portrayers of Nazi swine during the WW2 years, this darkly handsome supporting player and occasional lead fled his native country in the late 1930s, emigrating to California and beginning his U.S. acting career at the Pasadena Playhouse, where he was spotted by a talent scout and signed to a Warner Bros. contract. Although he was loaned out for *To Be or Not to Be* and *Mrs. Miniver* (both 1942, the latter giving him an attention-grabbing role as the downed German flier who confronts Greer Garson), Dantine spent the war years at Warners, beginning with *International Squadron* (1941), *Casablanca* (1942, in a sympathetic role as the careless newlywed who gambles away his visa money), *Edge of Darkness, Mission to Moscow, Northern Pursuit* (all 1943), *Passage to Marseille, The Mask of Dimitrios* (both 1944), *Hotel Berlin,* and *Escape in the Desert* (both 1945).

Dantine directed one lackluster war film, the 1958 *Thundering Jets.* Around that time he married Niki Schenck, daughter of film mogul Nicholas M. Schenck, and in 1959 went to work at Schenck Enterprises, spending most of the remainder of his career in production and distribution. His last screen appearances were in a pair of films he executive produced, *Bring Me the Head of Alfredo Garcia* (1974), and *The Killer Elite* (1975), both directed by Sam Peckinpah.

OTHER FILMS INCLUDE: 1948: *The Whis-pering City;* 1953: *Call Me Madam;* 1956: *War and Peace;* 1958: *Tempest;* 1965: *Operation Crossbow.*

DANTON, RAY. Actor, director. *(b. Sept. 19, 1931, New York City; d. Feb. 11, 1992.)* This handsome, dark-haired, cleft-chinned leading man was one of the screen's busiest B-movie leads during the 1950s and 1960s. A veteran of radio plays and summer stock, Danton made his initial impact in two 1955 actioners, *The Looters* and *Chief Crazy Horse.* In 1959 he played a young rapist in the sensationalistic *The Beat Generation.* But Danton found his metier in the gangster film: He played the titular tough guys in *The George Raft Story* (1960) and *The Rise and Fall of Legs Diamond* (1961). Unable to crack Hollywood's caste system (it was difficult for B-movie stars to graduate to big-budget fare), Danton eventually tried his hand at directing in the 1970s, churning out scores of TV episodes (he was the principal director of "Cagney and Lacey") and a few lurid low-budget horror efforts, including 1972's *Crypt of the Living Dead,* 1973's *Deathmaster,* and 1975's *Psychic Killer,* the last of which featured his wife, actress Julie Adams.

DARBY, KIM. Actress. *(b. July 8, 1948, Hollywood, as Deborah Zerby.)* Best remembered as the stubborn, spunky frontier girl who hired boozy marshal John Wayne to track down her father's killers in *True Grit* (1969), Darby never again got as interesting a character as that one. The daughter of veteran musical performers, she sang and danced professionally at an early age, and appeared as a teenager in episodic TV before making her feature-film debut in *Bye Bye Birdie* (1963, as an extra). After *True Grit* she won fair-to-middling roles in *Norwood, The Strawberry Statement* (both 1970), and *The Grissom Gang* (1971), then drifted into telefilm work and appeared in theatrical movies only sporadically thereafter.
OTHER FILMS INCLUDE: 1965: *The Restless Ones, Bus Riley's Back in Town;* 1969: *Generation;* 1978: *The One and Only;* 1985: *Better Off Dead;* 1987: *Teen Wolf Too;* 1989: *Deadly Embrace.*

DARNELL, LINDA. Actress. *(b. Oct. 16, 1921, Dallas, as Monetta Eloyse Darnell; d. Apr. 10, 1965.)* Linda Darnell was one of the most beautiful women on the screen in the 1940s, and she projected a likable screen personality, but she could never be considered a great actress. Often, as in John Ford's *My Darling Clementine* (1946) or Preston Sturges' *Unfaithfully Yours* (1948), Darnell was the one false note in otherwise outstanding productions. Darnell's mother pushed her young daughter into a show biz career: dancing lessons at 5, modeling at 14, "Gateway to Hollywood" contest winner at 16. She had a 1937 screen test to RKO and made the rounds without much success until signing with 20th Century-Fox in 1939. After making her debut in *Hotel for Women,* Darnell appeared in some of the studio's most prestigious films. She was costarred with Tyrone Power in *Brigham Young—Frontiersman* (1940) and in remakes of classic silents—*The Mark of Zorro* (1940) and *Blood and Sand* (1941).

A favorite of Fox studio head Darryl Zanuck, Darnell worked in a number of popular and successful films, among them *The Song of Bernadette* (1943, unbilled as The Virgin Mary), *It Happened Tomorrow, Buffalo Bill* (both 1944), *Hangover Square* (1945), and *Anna and the King of Siam* (1946), but she remained little more than a highly decorative leading lady. Her one full-fledged star turn came with *Forever Amber* (1947), a troubled production, playing a fiery leading role for which she had not been first choice. She simply couldn't carry a dramatic vehicle on her own. Her best opportunity came in Joseph L. Mankiewicz's *A Letter to Three Wives* (1949), but there was no encore.

Darnell's career sputtered in the 1950s with pictures like *Blackbeard, the Pirate, Island of Desire* (both 1952), and a handful of Italian and Spanish potboilers. Although she did some stage and TV work, she virtually disappeared from the big screen after 1957. Her last film, *Black Spurs* (1965), was completed just before her death. While visiting her former secretary in Chicago, Darnell was burned to death in a house fire, reportedly while watching a TV rerun of her 1940 girl-makes-good Hollywood fantasy, *Star Dust.*

DARWELL, JANE. Actress. *(b. Oct. 15, 1879, Palmyra, Mo.; d. Aug. 13, 1967.)* "Needless to say," opined Darwell upon winning an Oscar for her performance as Ma Joad in *The Grapes of Wrath* (1940), "this is my favorite role." It was the crowning achievement of a 50-year screen career during which she appeared in more than 200 movies. Well-educated, she had a solid background in dramatics, and was featured with the famous Henry Duffy stock company before making her Broadway debut. Plump and dowdy, but with kindly eyes and rosy cheeks, she was usually cast in mother parts in stories with bucolic settings—though she also played prison matrons, midwives, and even (in one instance) a nurse-cum-detective, top-billed in *The Great Hospital Mystery* (1937). She appeared in several silent films before beginning her Hollywood career in earnest with *Huckleberry Finn* (1931), graduating from bit parts to featured roles. Infirm and living in retirement at the Motion Picture Country Home and Hospital, she was courted by Walt Disney personally to play the small but important role of The Bird Woman in *Mary Poppins* (1964).

OTHER FILMS INCLUDE: 1933: *Only Yesterday, Design for Living;* 1934: *David Harum;* 1936: *Captain January, Poor Little Rich Girl;* 1939: *Jesse James, Gone With the Wind* (as Dolly Merriwether); 1940: *Brigham Young—Frontiersman;* 1943: *The Ox-Bow Incident;* 1946: *My Darling Clementine;* 1948: *3 Godfathers;* 1950: *Wagon Master, Caged;* 1952: *We're Not Married;* 1956: *There's Always Tomorrow;* 1958: *The Last Hurrah.*

DASSIN, JULES. Director, screenwriter, actor. *(b. Dec. 18, 1911, Middletown, Conn.)* This versatile director came up through the Hollywood studio system, made his mark there, then went on to even greater success abroad. He studied drama in Europe and acted in New York's Yiddish theater in the late 1930s before writing for radio and directing on the stage. He went to Hollywood in 1940 and worked as an assistant on films for Garson Kanin and Alfred Hitchcock, later being signed by MGM. There he "apprenticed" as a director of short subjects, graduating to grade-B feature films with 1942's *Nazi Agent.* He followed with a number of forgettable romances and comedies like *The Affairs of Martha, Reunion in France* (both also 1942), *A Letter for Evie* (1945), and *Two Smart People* (1946). (An exception was the amusing comedy-fantasy *The Canterville Ghost,* in 1944, with Charles Laughton and Margaret O'Brien.) It wasn't until the late 1940s that Dassin commanded attention with a series of tough, gritty films, starting with *Brute Force* (1947), a classic prison thriller written by Richard Brooks. The stark murder yarn *Naked City* (1948) won praise for its authentic use of New York locations, and *Thieves' Highway* (1949) was an exciting, realistic story about California truckers and the mob.

The taint of Hollywood's blacklist forced Dassin to England where he made *Night and the City* (1950), an archetypal film noir with Richard Widmark. Dassin made his next film in France: *Rififi* (1954) is one of the best heist movies ever made, with a justifiably famous half-hour sequence in which four thieves break into a jewelry store in complete silence. The film earned Dassin a Best Director award at Cannes.

After the Christ allegory *He Who Must Die* (1957) and the all-star *Where the Hot Wind Blows!* (1958, which featured Dassin's future wife, Melina Mercouri), the director scraped together a meager budget to make *Never on Sunday* (1960), which starred Mercouri as a life-long prostitute and Dassin himself as her leading man. (He couldn't afford an established American leading man.) The ribald comedy, considered shocking in its day, turned out to be an international smash; it earned Mercouri a Best Actress award at Cannes and Dassin two Oscar nominations, for Best Director and Best Screenplay. The director made *Phaedra* (1962) with Mercouri, and returned to the caper film with the highly enjoyable *Topkapi* (1964, which won Peter Ustinov an Oscar), but none of his films since then has achieved similar critical or commercial success. Titles include *10:30 Summer* (1966, cowritten with Marguerite Duras), *Up Tight* (1968, a Black remake of *The Informer*), *Promise at Dawn* (1970), *A Dream of Passion* (1978), and *Circle of Two* (1980). In the late 1960s he adapted *Never on Sunday* into a Broadway musical, "Illya, Darling," for Mercouri. He also appeared as an actor in *Rififi* and *Promise at Dawn*, billed in both as Perlo Vita.

DAVENPORT, NIGEL. Actor. *(b. May 23, 1928, Cambridge, England.)* Talented if unspectacular British supporting player and occasional character lead with extensive stage, TV, and film credits. The Oxford graduate, who began acting in the early 1950s, made his film debut in 1959's *Look Back in Anger.*
OTHER FILMS INCLUDE: 1960: *Peeping Tom;* 1963: *In the Cool of the Day;* 1965: *Sands of the Kalahari;* 1966: *A Man for All Seasons* (a meaty role as the Duke of Norfolk); 1968: *The Strange Affair;* 1969: *The Virgin Soldiers;* 1971: *Mary, Queen of Scots, Living Free;* 1974: *Phase IV;* 1977: *The Island of Dr. Moreau;* 1979: *Zulu Dawn;* 1981: *Chariots of Fire;* 1984: *Greystoke: The Legend of Tarzan, Lord of the Apes;* 1986: *Caravaggio;* 1988: *Without a Clue.*

DAVES, DELMER. Director, screenwriter, producer. *(b. July 24, 1904, San Francisco; d. Aug 17, 1977.)* Straightforward, unpretentious director of Hollywood melodramas, Westerns, and war films. A Stanford University law student, he was bitten by the movie bug in 1923, landing a job as prop boy on *The Covered Wagon;* he then acted in several late silents and early talkies, and wrote screenplays for a number of 1930s pictures, including *Dames, Flirtation Walk* (both 1934), *The Petrified Forest* (1936), and *Love Affair* (1939). Daves' directorial debut was *Destination Tokyo* (1943), which he helped script. That became the pattern on most of his subsequent films, including *Hollywood Canteen* (1944), *Pride of the Marines* (1945), *Dark Passage* (1947), *Task Force* (1949), *Bird of Paradise* (1951), *Drum Beat* (1954), *Jubal* (1956), *A Summer Place* (1959), *Susan Slade* (1961), *Spencer's Mountain* (1963), and *Youngblood Hawke* (1964). Although Daves had a strong visual sense, and knew how and where to place the camera for best effect, he never forgot that he was a storyteller first, and all his films have direct, uncomplicated narratives.

DAVI, ROBERT. Actor. *(b. June 26, 1954, Astoria, N.Y.)* Crater-faced, seemingly emotionless character actor and occasional lead, best as cold-blooded heavies but equally facile as hard-boiled cops. Educated at Long Island's Hofstra University and The Actors' Studio, Davi started acting on stage but worked movies into his schedule beginning in 1984. He's appeared in *City Heat* (1984), *The Goonies* (1985), *Raw Deal* (1986), *Wild Thing* (1987), *Die Hard* (1988, as Special Agent Johnson), and *Maniac Cop 2* (1990). Davi's high-profile gig as James Bond's arch-foe in 1989's *Licence to Kill* should have been a breakthrough role, but to date he still labors in supporting parts and as an occasional lead in direct-to-video movies. Recent credits include *Christopher Columbus: The Discovery* (1992), *Son of the Pink Panther* (1993), and *Cops and Robbersons* (1994).

DAVIDOVICH, LOLITA. Actress. *(b. July 15, 1961, Toronto.)* In her first major film role, as stripper Blaze Starr in *Blaze* (1989), this leggy young actress more than held her own opposite veteran Paul Newman. A relative newcomer to the screen, she'd had small roles in *The Big Town* and *Adventures in Babysitting* (both 1987), billed as Lolita David, before snaring the part of the lusty redhead who seduced a Louisiana governor. She played Andie MacDowell's friend in *The Object of Beauty* (1991) and that same year appeared as an impoverished Russian wife in *The Inner Circle.* She tried her hand at Hitchcockian thrillers in Brian De Palma's *Raising Cain* (1992), and was extremely winning as a small-town waitress in *Leap of Faith* the same year. A warm, appealing personality, Davidovich should be wary of being typecast in best-friend or floozy-with-heart-of-gold roles; she can do that easily if the right scripts come her way. Recent credits include *Keep the Change* (1992 telefilm), *Boiling Point* (1993), *Intersection,* and *Cobb* (both 1994).

DAVIES, MARION. Actress. *(b. Jan. 3, 1897, Brooklyn, N.Y., as Marion Cecilia Douras; d. Sept. 22, 1961.)* Her long-running relationship with newspaper tycoon William Randolph Hearst (and its prolonging effect on her career) and the fascinating stories generated by it have, sadly, obscured the very genuine talents of this delightful comedienne. A former chorus girl and

Ziegfeld Follies player, she made her film debut in 1917's *Runaway Romany*. From the first, this moon-faced blonde with the twinkling blue eyes displayed the right stuff for silent movies. Her pantomimic skills were considerable and, although very pretty, she was unafraid to make herself look ridiculous in exaggerated comic situations. Hearst met her soon after she'd started working in movies, and formed Cosmopolitan Pictures solely to produce starring vehicles for her. Cosmopolitan lavished enormous sums of money on Davies' pictures, and although they received thousands of dollars in free publicity (and uniformly good reviews) from the Hearst-owned papers nationwide, they never recouped their costs.

Nonetheless, Davies proved herself a talented screen personality in *The Belle of New York* (1919), *The Restless Sex* (1920), *Enchantment* (1921), *When Knighthood Was in Flower* (1922), *Little Old New York* (1923), and many others. Hearst loved seeing her in expensive costume pictures such as *Janice Meredith* (1924) and *Quality Street* (1937), but in retrospect she seems to have fared just as well, if not better, in contemporary comedies like *Tillie the Toiler, The Fair Co-Ed* (both 1927), and especially two directed by King Vidor, *The Patsy* (in which she performs devastating visual impressions of silent-film stars like Lillian Gish and Gloria Swanson) and the delightful backstage-in-Hollywood saga *Show People* (both 1928). Unfortunately, Hearst's relentless efforts to, in essence, shove her down the public's throat eventually had just the opposite effect. But he persisted, making Cosmopolitan's distribution deals first with Paramount, then Goldwyn, and then MGM. Studio executives feared Hearst and the power he wielded, and acquiesced to his demands concerning Davies' pictures.

The coming of sound terrified Davies, who had never completely overcome a childhood stutter. That deficiency, coupled with rising production costs (some of which MGM had assumed to placate Hearst) and declining audience interest, kept her in the background of the early talkie era. *Not So Dumb, The Floradora Girl* (both 1930), *The Bachelor Father, Five and Ten* (both 1931), *Polly of the Circus, Blondie of the Follies* (both 1932), *Peg o' My Heart,* and *Going Hollywood* (both 1933), starring vehicles all, often

saw Davies overshadowed by costars, including Clark Gable, Bing Crosby, and Billie Dove. Hearst left MGM in 1934 after quarreling over the types of roles Davies was getting. He set up shop at Warner Bros., but stayed only a few years. Davies' films there, including *Page Miss Glory* (1935), *Hearts Divided, Cain and Mabel* (both 1936), and *Ever Since Eve* (1937), were pleasant enough but not sufficiently strong to warrant continued investment in her career. A financially ailing Hearst dissolved Cosmopolitan in 1937, and Davies retired to his several homes, including the lavish castle in San Simeon, where she was known as a gracious hostess to Hollywood royalty. The greatest disservice to her reputation was done by Orson Welles' *Citizen Kane,* which led people to believe that Davies was a no-talent like Susan Alexander in the fictionalized saga. Fortunately, her best films refute that. She went into business after Hearst's death, making quite a name for herself without anyone's help.

DAVIES, TERENCE. Director, screenwriter. *(b. Nov. 10, 1945, Liverpool, England.)* Deeply personal filmmaker, whose autobiographically influenced work began with the short films "Children," "Madonna and Child," and "Death and Transfiguration," charting the life of a character named Robert Walker from childhood to death and examining how he copes with family, religion, and his own homosexuality. Davies' first feature, *Distant Voices, Still Lives* (1988) paralleled his own family's harsh life in working-class Liverpool during the 1940s and 1950s and won international acclaim for its unique structure, poetic images, and stunning use of music. *The Long Day Closes* (1992) is a happier examination of postwar Liverpool and cemented Davies' growing reputation.

DAVIS, ANDREW. Director, cinematographer. *(b. Nov. 21, 1946, Chicago.)* Action director whose former experience as a cameraman has enlivened many genre pictures. He worked as a journalist, TV cameraman, and photographer before serving as a cameraman on Haskell Wexler's landmark feature, *Medium Cool* (1969). He then earned cinematographer's credits on several low-budget pictures before producing, directing, and cowriting the independent film *Stony Island* (1978), about a group of young rhythm and blues performers. Davis went on to direct the low-budget *The Final Terror* (1981) and photographed such films as *Over the Edge* (1979) and *Angel* (1984) before he found his niche, as director of *Code of Silence* (1985), a cop picture that is considered the best of the Chuck Norris vehicles. Davis cowrote and directed Steven Seagal's successful debut *Above the Law* (1988), and also directed Gene Hackman in *The Package* (1989). Most recently, he teamed up again with Seagal for the blockbuster action hit *Under Siege* (1992), and directed the crackerjack big-screen adaptation of the 1960s TV show *The Fugitive* (1993), with Harrison Ford in the title role.

DAVIS, BETTE. Actress. *(b. Apr. 5, 1908, Lowell, Mass., as Ruth Elizabeth Davis; d. Oct. 6, 1989.)* Most budding screen actresses might have thrown in the towel if they had been appraised, like Davis was, as having "about as much sex appeal as Slim Summerville." (That from Universal president Carl Laemmle, after seeing her debut performance in 1930's *Bad Sister.)* But this feisty, unique star defied her studio critics repeatedly and fooled them all by achieving ever greater success; by the time she died Davis had won a status enjoyed by no other Hollywood actress, and if her struggles took a heavy toll on her personal life, we can at least be grateful that they gave us so many memorable movie moments.

Davis decided that she wanted to be an actress while in high school, and worked in student productions and regional theater. Famed acting teacher Eva Le Gallienne rejected Davis' application to study with her, so the young hopeful went instead to John Murphy Anderson's school. Her early professional career in stock was undistinguished to say the least; director George Cukor fired her from a show in upstate New York. She made her Broadway debut in 1929's "Broken Dishes," and the following year was rebuffed in her first attempt to crash the movies when she got a thumbs-down after screen-testing for Samuel Goldwyn. She was signed by Universal later that year, but her tenure there was brief, with supporting stints in only a few movies, including *Waterloo Bridge* (1931).

Davis freelanced briefly (making, among several lackluster movies, a ludicrous 1932 thriller, *The Menace,* for Columbia) before securing a berth at Warner Bros., where she first showed her ability in a meaty supporting role in the George Arliss vehicle *The Man Who Played God* (1932). Although the studio didn't quite know how to exploit her, she was at least kept busy in a string of program pictures that included *Cabin in the Cotton* (also 1932, in which, as a spoiled Southern belle, she uttered the immortal line, "Ah'd like ta kiss ya, but ah jest washed mah hay-yah!"), *The Dark Horse, Three on a Match* (both also 1932), *20,000 Years in Sing Sing* (with Spencer Tracy), *Ex-Lady, The Working Man, Parachute Jumper, Bureau of Missing Persons* (all 1933), *Fashions of 1934* (a reasonably big musical, albeit one with a thankless part for Davis), *The Big Shakedown, Fog Over Frisco,* and *Jimmy the Gent* (all 1934, in the last-named with James Cagney).

After being loaned out to RKO to play the conniving waitress in John Cromwell's *Of Human Bondage* (a role for which she actively lobbied), and scoring her first major triumph in the part, Davis intensified her efforts to secure better roles in Warners pictures. Initially she was put off, but finally got a meaty character as the former star rehabilitated by Franchot Tone in *Dangerous* (1935), which earned Davis her first Academy Award. The studio brass, as much to humble the increasingly difficult star as for any other reason, continued to put her in lame programmers for a time, but eventually bestowed upon her the quality vehicles she richly deserved. (Not, however, before being sued—unsuccessfully—by Davis in an attempt to break her contract.)

She snagged Best Actress Oscar nominations five years in a row—for *Jezebel* (1938, which she won), *Dark Victory* (1939), *The Letter* (1940), *The Little Foxes* (1941), and *Now, Voyager* (1942)—then earned another in 1944 for *Mr. Skeffington.* She played in both period pictures and contemporary dramas, bringing her own unique passion and charisma to each role while debunking the conventional wisdom that ceded superstar status to more "glamorous" female stars. Her other Warners films included *The Petrified*

Forest (1936), *Kid Galahad, Marked Woman, That Certain Woman* (all 1937), *The Sisters* (1938), *Juarez, The Old Maid, The Private Lives of Elizabeth and Essex* (all 1939), *All This, and Heaven Too* (1940), *The Great Lie, The Bride Came C.O.D., The Man Who Came to Dinner* (all 1941, taking a supporting role—at her own request—in the last-named, a terrific adaptation of the hilarious George S. Kaufman–Moss Hart play), *In This Our Life* (1942), *Watch on the Rhine, Thank Your Lucky Stars, Old Acquaintance* (all 1943), *Hollywood Canteen* (1944), *The Corn Is Green* (1945), *Deception, A Stolen Life* (both 1946), *June Bride* (1948), and *Beyond the Forest* (1949, contributing another memorable movie line when, upon entering a shabby house, she says, "What a dump!").

Finally freed from her Warners contract, but with her star somewhat diminished by weaker pictures of the late 1940s, Davis bounced back with the stunning, Oscar-nominated characterization of aging actress Margo Channing (who, in a Davis moment that almost descends to self-caricature, utters the unforgettable "Fasten your selt belts . . . it's going to be a bumpy night!") in *All About Eve* (1950). She played another actress, and received another Oscar nod, in *The Star* (1952), but her other, relatively few 1950s films—with the exception of *The Virgin Queen* (1955) and *Storm Center* (1956)—were largely undistinguished. In 1961 Frank Capra gave her a scene-stealing character, Apple Annie, in *Pocketful of Miracles,* and she received her last Academy Award nomination as a demented former child star in *What Ever Happened to Baby Jane?* (1962, costarring another legendary Hollywood bitch, Joan Crawford, with whom Davis didn't get along—to put it mildly).

Davis' other 1960s vehicles included *The Empty Canvas* (1963), *Dead Ringer, Where Love Has Gone* (both 1964), *Hush . . . Hush, Sweet Charlotte, The Nanny* (both 1965), *The Anniversary* (1968), and *Connecting Rooms* (1969)—an uninspiring lot, to say the least. While she appeared in *Bunny O'Hare* (1971), *Burnt Offerings* (1976), *Return From Witch Mountain, Death on the Nile* (both 1978), and *The Watcher in the Woods* (1980), Davis spent most of the remainder of her career on the small screen, working in TV movies of varying quality. She did return to the big screen in Lindsay Anderson's elegiac *The Whales of August* (1987), which costarred her with another legendary star, Lillian Gish. Davis walked off the set of *Wicked Stepmother* (1990), a cheesy little horror comedy, but since she had already shot a number of scenes, director Larry Cohen elected to keep her in the final cut. She died shortly after working on the awful film.

Davis' stormy personal life included four unsuccessful marriages, the last to actor Gary Merrill (1950–60), with whom she appeared in *All About Eve.* In 1977, she was the first female recipient of the American Film Institute's Life Achievement Award.

DAVIS, BRAD. Actor. *(b. Nov. 6, 1949, Tallahassee, Fla.; d. Sept. 8, 1991.)* Intense actor who is best remembered for his film debut as Billy Hayes, the American incarcerated for drug smuggling in Alan Parker's harrowing *Midnight Express* (1978). He followed as a 1960s Harvard student in the weak *A Small Circle of Friends* (1980), a small role as an Olympic runner in the Oscar-winning *Chariots of Fire* (1981), and as a gay sailor in Fassbinder's last film, *Querelle* (1982), but never achieved the success his impressive debut seemed to promise. His later credits include *Cold Steel, Heart* (both 1987), the very amusing *Rosalie Goes Shopping* (1989), and *Hangfire* (1991), as well as the TV miniseries "Robert Kennedy and His Times" (1985), and the telefilms *Sybil* (1976), *A Rumor of War* (1980), Robert Altman's production *The Caine Mutiny Court-Martial* (1988, as Queeg), and *The Habitation of Dragons* (1992), his last work before his death of complications of AIDS. Before he died, Davis wrote a book proposal (later published) that attacked the Hollywood community for its attitude in dealing with AIDS victims.

DAVIS, GEENA. Actress. *(b. Jan. 21, 1957, Wareham, Mass., as Virginia Davis.)* This leggy, square-jawed ex-model made her feature debut as a lingerie-clad soap star in *Tootsie* (1982), displaying the coltish sexiness that, along with her natural warmth and good humor, has infused her later characterizations. Her facility for comedy, aptly demonstrated in *Beetlejuice* (1988) and *Quick Change* (1990), was recognized by her peers when they voted her a Best Supporting Actress Oscar for her turn as a slightly batty, exuberant dog trainer in *The Accidental Tourist* (1988). (She deliberately lost weight to play the role, remembering author Anne Tyler's description of her character as chicken-legged.) Davis's ripe, earthy performance as a fugitive housewife turned bandit in *Thelma & Louise* (1991, with Susan Sarandon) earned her a Best Actress Oscar nomination. She headed a marvelous ensemble cast in Penny Marshall's *A League of Their Own* (1992, about an all-girl baseball team in the 1940s) and costarred with Dustin Hoffman and Andy Garcia in *Hero* that same year. She then affected a New York accent and persona for *Angie* (1994). She is divorced from actor Jeff Goldblum, with whom she starred in *Transylvania 6-5000* (1985), *The Fly* (1986), and *Earth Girls Are Easy* (1989). She also appeared on the TV sitcoms "Buffalo Bill" (1983–84) and "Sara" (1985, in the leading role). She married director Renny Harlin in 1993; they jointly produced her movie *Speechless* (1994), and he directed her in the pirate adventure *Cutthroat Island* (1995).

DAVIS, JOAN. Actress. *(b. June 29, 1907, St. Paul Minn., as Madonna Josephine Davis; d. May 23, 1961.)* Long-limbed, rubber-faced, but not unattractive comedienne who, after years of movie work, became a top TV star in the early 1950s. One of the few female clowns in pictures, she performed knockabout comedy with all the energy and aplomb of an old vaude-villian—which she was (teamed with husband Si Wills). After debuting in a 1935 Mack Sennett two-reeler, *Way Up Thar,* she signed with 20th Century-Fox in 1937, appearing in *The Holy Terror, On the Avenue, Wake Up and Live* (doing her patented comedic dance routine, pratfalls and all), *Love and Hisses, Angel's Holiday,* and *Life Begins in College* (her first meaty role)—all that same year. She stayed at Fox until 1941, brightening, among others, *Sally, Irene and Mary, Hold That Co-ed* (both 1938), *Tail Spin, Day-time Wife* (both 1939), *Free, Blonde and 21* (1940), and *Sun Valley Serenade* (1941).

As a freelancer, Davis worked at nearly every studio in town, as a perfect comic foil for Lou Costello in 1941's *Hold That Ghost,* as the star of such grade-B vehicles as *Beautiful but Broke, Kansas City Kitty* (both 1944), and *She Wrote the Book* (1945, well teamed with rubber-legged Leon Errol), and as Eddie Cantor's vis-à-vis in *Show Business* (1944) and *George White's Scandals* (1945), to name a few. Davis excelled at physical comedy, but she took a backseat to no one when it came to delivering wry dialogue, and she milked laughs from even the most puerile material. Her last film was *Harem Girl* (1952). Her TV series, "I Married Joan," played the NBC network from 1952 to 1955, and was syndicated for many years thereafter. Her daughter, Beverly Wills, also pursued an acting career.

DAVIS, JUDY. Actress. *(b. Apr. 23, 1955, Perth, Australia.)* She may not have Julia Roberts' pull at the box office, but Judy Davis has established herself as one of the best actresses working today, with stellar turns in a variety of unusual roles. After attending a convent school, the rebellious Davis left home and sang with a band that toured Taiwan and Japan. After three months of this, she returned home and studied at Australia's National Institute of Dramatic Art. (Mel Gibson was one of her classmates.) She made her film debut with *High Rolling* (1977), but caught everyone's attention as Sybylla Melvyn, the determined, free-thinking writer in Gillian Armstrong's *My Brilliant Career* (1979). The performance won Davis Best Actress awards in Australia and Britain and set the tone for her own career, in which she's repeatedly played strong-willed, sometimes eccentric heroines who are frequently at odds with society at large. She starred in films by other rising Aussies—John Duigan's *The Winter of Our Dreams* (1981) and Phillip Noyce's *Heatwave* (1983)—and made one bomb (1982's political thriller *The Final Option,* as a terrorist) before being chosen by David Lean to star in *A Passage to India* (1984). She received an Academy Award nomination for her subtle work as the repressed Adela Quested, although she and Lean apparently did not get along and had differing views of how the role should be played. Davis next did *Kangaroo* (1986, opposite husband Colin Friels) and reunited with director Gillian Armstrong for *High Tide* (1987, also featuring Friels), one of her best performances, as a woman who encounters the daughter she had abandoned years earlier. After *Georgia* (1988) and a brief role in Woody Allen's *Alice* (1990), she dazzled moviegoers with four quite different and startlingly delineated performances in 1991: as George Sand in *Impromptu*, the doomed secretary/mistress in *Barton Fink*, the disapproving Harriet in *Where Angels Fear to Tread*, and the dual role based on Joan Burroughs and Jane Bowles in *Naked Lunch*. She scored another Oscar nomination (as Supporting Actress) for her brilliant work as an uptight New Yorker in Woody Allen's *Husbands and Wives* (1992). Recent films include *The Ref* and *The New Age* (both 1994). She has also appeared in the TV miniseries "A Woman Called Golda" (1982, as the young Golda Meir) and the acclaimed TV movie *One Against the Wind* (1991, as a WW2 heroine).

DAVIS, OSSIE. Actor, director, screenwriter. *(b. Dec. 18, 1917, Cogdell, Ga.)* Physically imposing, passionate black actor of stage and screen, also known for his writing and directing ability. Although he was a college graduate, Davis labored in many menial jobs (and served a stint in the Army during World War 2) before making his Broadway debut in 1946. He first appeared on-screen in *No Way Out* (1950), supporting Sidney Poitier (also making his film debut) and appearing with Ruby Dee, who became his wife. It was another 13 years before Davis reached the screen again, then in *Gone Are the Days* (1963), an adaptation of his own play "Purlie Victorious." He acted in *The Cardinal* (1963), *Shock Treatment* (1964), *The Hill* (1965), *A Man Called Adam* (1966), *The Scalphunters* (1968), *Sam Whiskey,* and *Slaves* (both 1969) before becoming the director of *Cotton Comes to Harlem* (1970, which he cowrote), a fast-moving crime drama about two unorthodox black cops. Davis has also directed *Black Girl* (1972), *Gordon's War* (1973), and *Countdown at Kusini* (1976). Still busy (with a supporting role on "Evening Shade," 1990–94), he has had a particularly fruitful association with filmmaker Spike Lee, appearing in *School Daze* (1988), *Do the*

Right Thing (1989), and *Jungle Fever* (1991). In Lee's *Malcolm X* (1992) he reads the eulogy he'd delivered in real life at the black leader's funeral, which he also reads on the soundtrack of the 1972 documentary *Malcolm X.*
OTHER FILMS INCLUDE: 1979: *Hot Stuff;* 1985: *Avenging Angel;* 1989: *Route One/U.S.A.;* 1990: *Joe Versus the Volcano;* 1992: *Gladiator;* 1993: *Grumpy Old Men.*

DAVIS, SAMMY, JR. Singer, dancer, actor. *(b. Dec. 28, 1925, New York City; d. May 16, 1990.)* Most of Davis' screen appearances depict him squandering his many talents. His Broadway and movie debuts were both in 1956, with "Mr. Wonderful" on stage and *The Benny Goodman Story* on-screen; shortly after that, he fell in with Frank Sinatra, Dean Martin, and their Vegas-crazy Rat Pack, which defined his screen persona for the next several years. He appeared with various Pack members in mediocre show-biz time capsules like *Ocean's Eleven* (1960) and *Robin and the Seven Hoods* (1964). In 1968 he made one half of a comedy/thriller buddy team with Peter Lawford in the cleverly titled *Salt and Pepper;* Jerry Lewis directed them in 1970's even lamer *One More Time,* the only Lewis-helmed picture in which Jerry doesn't appear. Davis' work in 1969's *Sweet Charity* demonstrates his undeniable stamina and showmanship, and he gave a performance of savvy and dignity as an over-the-hill song and dance man who's got a few tricks left in 1989's *Tap,* his final feature. Throughout his career he excited some genuine controversy—with his marriage to white actress Mai Britt and conversion to Judaism in the 1960s—and then some kinky intrigue, detailing a penchant for pornography in his second autobiography, "Hollywood in a Suitcase." A lifelong smoker, he died of throat cancer, leaving an estate more than $5 million in debt.

DAVISON, BRUCE. Actor. *(b. June 28, 1946, Philadelphia.)* As Willard in the 1971 horror thriller of the same name, this blond, wide-eyed actor played a disturbed outcast who dispatched an army of rats to devour his enemies. Almost 20 years later he was Oscar-nominated for his sensitive portrayal of a man caring for his dying,

AIDS-infected lover in *Longtime Companion.* A respected actor on stage and television (and a tyro director who cut his teeth on the "Harry and the Hendersons" series in which he starred), he's certainly come a long way since debuting on the big screen in 1969's coming-of-age drama *Last Summer.* His performance as a child molester in the chilling prison drama *Short Eyes* (1977) is a particular highlight on his résumé.

OTHER FILMS INCLUDE: 1970: *The Strawberry Statement;* 1974: *Mame;* 1984: *Crimes of Passion;* 1985: *Spies Like Us;* 1986: *The Ladies Club;* 1990: *Steel and Lace;* 1991: *Oscar;* 1993: *Short Cuts, Six Degrees of Separation.*

DAVIS-VOSS, SAMMI. Actress. *(b. June 21, 1964, Worcester, England.)* Girlish, blond British actress of considerable talent who has been lucky enough to work with first-rate talents. She won kudos for her performance as a heroin addict in Neil Jordan's *Mona Lisa* (1986), then got similarly enthusiastic notices for her work in John Boorman's WW2 reminiscence, *Hope and Glory* (1987). The iconoclastic Ken Russell gave her a rather insipid part in his horror-film sendup *The Lair of the White Worm* (1988), but made up for it with the lead in his 1989 adaptation of D. H. Lawrence's *The Rainbow,* her best role to that date. Davis has talent to spare and will bear watching in the 1990s. She landed a plum TV role in the WW2-era U.S. series "Homefront" (1991–93).

OTHER FILMS INCLUDE: 1987: *Lionheart, A Prayer for the Dying;* 1988: *Consuming Passions;* 1990: *The Horseplayer, Shadow of China.*

DAY, DORIS. Actress, singer. *(b. Apr. 3, 1924, Cincinnati, as Doris von Kappelhoff.)* At one time the country's top female movie star and a best-selling recording star, this vivacious blonde has always made what she does look easy. First a fresh-faced leading lady in Hollywood musicals, then the distaff star in candy-coated sex farces (most often opposite Rock Hudson), she also proved herself a capable dramatic actress in such films as *Young Man With a Horn* (a thinly disguised 1950 biopic of jazz great Bix Biederbecke), *Storm Warning* (a 1951 melodrama), *Love Me or Leave Me* (a 1955 biopic of troubled

songbird Ruth Etting), *The Man Who Knew Too Much* (a 1956 Hitchcock thriller in which she introduced the Oscar-winning song "Que Sera Sera"), and *Midnight Lace* (a 1960 thriller that had her targeted for murder).

A band singer and recording star who performed on stage and radio with the Bob Crosby and Les Brown orchestras, Day appeared with Brown in a pair of 1941 "soundies" shorts, but didn't make her first feature until 1948, signing with Warner Bros. and debuting in *Romance on the High Seas.* She subsequently appeared in many tune-filled frolics for that studio, including *It's a Great Feeling, My Dream Is Yours* (both 1949), *Tea for Two, The West Point Story* (both 1950), *Lullaby of Broadway, On Moonlight Bay* (both 1951), *April in Paris, I'll See You in My Dreams* (both 1952), *By the Light of the Silvery Moon* (1953), *Lucky Me* (1954), and *Young at Heart* (1955), among others. *Calamity Jane* (1953) broke the mold with a feisty, original script, casting Day as the Wild West's leading tomboy (who introduced the Oscar-winning hit song "Secret Love"); it remains her favorite part. *The Pajama Game* (1957) gave her another plum, the lead in a vibrant adaptation of the Broadway hit, brimming with great songs.

After a pair of enjoyable comedies, *Teacher's Pet* and *Tunnel of Love* (both 1958), Day's film career shifted gears with *Pillow Talk* (1959), the first of her fast-moving sex comedies with Rock Hudson. Handsomely produced and cleverly written, it offered audiences plenty of wit and a smidgen of suggestiveness; Day earned an Oscar nomination for her performance, and the film steered her career in a new direction with even greater success. In the 1960s she reigned as America's top box-office attraction, in a series of saucy comedies: *Please Don't Eat the Daisies* (1960), *Lover Come Back, That Touch of Mink* (both 1962), *Move Over, Darling, The Thrill of It All* (both 1963), *Send Me No Flowers* (1964), *Do Not Disturb* (1965), and *The Glass Bottom Boat* (1966). (Her lone musical during this period was the ill-fated 1962 *Billy Rose's Jumbo.*) This winning streak was broken by *The Ballad of Josie, Caprice* (both 1967), *Where Were You When the Lights Went Out?* and *With Six You Get Eggroll* (both 1968); these clumsy vehicles seemed out of fashion, and Day fared much better on television, starring in "The Doris Day Show" (1968–73).

The star's 1975 autobiography, "Doris Day: Her Own Story," described a troubled life much at variance with the cheery image she presented on-screen. Among other things, she reported that longtime husband Martin Melcher, who died in 1968 shortly after committing her to the TV series without consulting her, had wiped out her personal fortune. (She later regained much of it by suing her former lawyer, who had colluded in the mismanagement, for damages.) An indefatigable animal-rights activist, Day has concentrated her efforts in that arena for many years now, and has resisted offers to return to performing.

DAY, LARAINE. Actress. *(b. Oct. 13, 1917, Roosevelt, Utah, as Laraine Johnson.)* Even as the button-cute ingenue of *Border G-Men* and *The Painted Desert*, two 1938 George O'Brien B Westerns made for RKO, this demure actress showed great promise. The daughter of a prominent Mormon businessman, she'd taken up acting with the Long Beach Players stock company and won a bit role in the classic weepie *Stella Dallas* (1937). Immediately following her Western chores, she was signed to a contract by MGM, which changed her surname to Day and placed her in *Sergeant Madden* and *Tarzan Finds a Son* (both 1939) before adding her to the *Dr. Kildare* series as love interest for Lew Ayres. Cast as Nurse Mary Lamont, she made seven films in the series, beginning with *Calling Dr. Kildare* (1939) and ending with *Dr. Kildare's Wedding Day* (1941, in which her character was killed off, a rare occurrence in movie series). Alfred Hitchcock borrowed her to be leading lady in his *Foreign Correspondent* (1940), and after the Kildares, MGM (and then RKO) promoted her to starring roles in popular audience fare.

Day's major films include *Mr. Lucky* (a big hit that paired her with Cary Grant), *Journey for Margaret* (both 1943), *Bride by Mistake* (1944), *Those Endearing Young Charms, Keep Your Powder Dry* (both 1945), *The Locket* (1946, an effective performance as a psychopath), *Tycoon* (1947), *My Dear Secretary* (1948), and *Woman on Pier 13* (1949). She worked less frequently during the 1950s (although she was memorable as part of the ensemble cast of 1954's *The High and the Mighty),* partially because, as the wife of baseball manager Leo Durocher, she became active in the game, earning the sobriquet "First Lady of Baseball." Her last feature film was *House of Dracula's Daughter* (1972). She has written two books: "Day With Giants" and "The America We Love."

DAY-LEWIS, DANIEL. Actor. *(b. Apr. 29, 1957, London.)* Some call him the British De Niro, and this darkly handsome leading man certainly qualifies for the title. Like his American counterpart, Day-Lewis immerses himself in his characters, sometimes affecting physical changes to make his performances more truthful. For *The Last of the Mohicans* (1992), he engaged in rigorous bodybuilding to make credible his portrayal of an 18th-century outdoorsman raised by Indians. The grandson of British film producer Sir Michael Balcon and the son of poet laureate Cecil Day-Lewis, he studied drama at the Bristol Arts Centre. His first film was *Sunday, Bloody Sunday* (1971). After minor roles in *Gandhi* (1982) and *The Bounty* (1984), Day-Lewis startled moviegoers as a homosexual tough boy (with multicolored hair) in Stephen Frears' *My Beautiful Laundrette* (1985). That caught the attention of the Merchant/Ivory production team, which cast him as an upperclass twit in *A Room With a View* (1985). Americans who saw that film and *Laundrette* within the same year were more keenly aware that a major new talent was on the scene. (Unfortunately, his first American-made film, 1988's *Stars and Bars,* was simply dreadful.) In keeping with his habit of extensive preparation, Day-Lewis studied the Czechoslovakian language and adopted a Czech accent as Tomas in Philip Kaufman's adaptation of Milan Kundera's *The Unbearable Lightness of Being* (1988), and lived in a wheelchair for weeks to create his Oscar-winning characterization of quadriplegic Irish writer Christy Brown in *My Left Foot* (1989). It is not known what steps he took to prepare for Martin Scorsese's *The Age of Innocence* (1993, as Edith Wharton's repressed hero) and *In the Name of the Father* (also 1993, Oscar-nominated as an Irish man falsely convicted as a terrorist).

___

DEAD END KIDS, THE. Actors. *(Leo Gorcey—b. June 3, 1917, New York City; d. June 2, 1969. Huntz Hall—b. Aug. 15, 1919, New York City, as Henry Richard Hall. Gabriel Dell—b. Oct. 4, 1919, Brooklyn, N.Y., as Gabriel DelVecchio; d. July 3, 1988. Billy Halop—b. May 11, 1920, Brooklyn, N.Y.; d. Nov. 9, 1976. Bobby Jordan—b. Apr. 1, 1923, New York City; d. Sept. 10, 1965. Bernard Punsly—b. July 11, 1922, New York City.)* Little did anyone know when the hit Broadway play "Dead End" was filmed in 1937 that it was planting the seeds for the most complicated family tree in movie history, spanning four groups with overlapping members, who turned out a total of 89 features and serials over a 21-year period. Producer Samuel Goldwyn signed the six members listed above to two-year contracts when he brought them out to Hollywood to recreate, in his movie *Dead End,* their stage roles as slum skids who worshipped gangster Humphrey Bogart. However, their offscreen antics (Gorcey alone got four traffic tickets in less than three weeks) drove the producer crazy, so he sold their contracts to Warner Bros., which immediately put them into a programmer called *Crime School* (1938). Warners shortly thereafter loaned Halop, Hall, Punsly, and Dell to Universal for a modest B picture, *Little Tough Guy* (also 1938), which performed surprisingly well at the box-office.

After *Crime School* became a hit, Warners reunited the Kids in *Angels With Dirty Faces* (also 1938), which reworked the *Dead End* theme with gangster James Cagney as the object of their idolatry. *Hell's Kitchen, They Made Me a Criminal,* and *Angels Wash Their Faces* (all 1939) followed, none of them up to the level of *Dirty Faces,* and all six boys were dropped by Warners.

At that point the Kids more or less split up, with Halop, Hall, Punsly, and Dell returning to Universal—where, in various combinations with such new faces as David Gorcey (Leo's brother), Billy Benedict, and Hally Chester, they were billed as "The Dead End Kids and Little Tough Guys" and appeared in eight B pictures and three serials between 1940 and 1943.

Leo Gorcey and Jordan went to Monogram and quickie producer Sam Katzman, who started his own concurrent series, "The East Side Kids," in 1940. Stanley Clements, Bennie Bartlett, Donald Haines, and former "Our Gang" kid Ernie "Sunshine Sammy" Morrison initially filled out the new group; Hall joined the ranks in 1941 and Dell came back the following year, usually playing a heavy.

The Monograms weren't better than the Universals, but some of them have achieved lasting pop-culture status, notably a pair that costar Bela Lugosi, *Spooks Run Wild* (1941) and *Ghosts on the Loose* (1943). Gorcey and Hall more or less assumed leadership of this motley group, consolidating the dumb-guy-and-dumberguy relationship that persisted until the end of their joint careers. Katzman, already known as one of Hollywood's most pecunious producers, allotted minuscule budgets to the series, and when the boys ad-libbed (which was most of the time), their spontaneous ripostes more often than not survived in the finished films, lending an unanticipated measure of low-rent charm. Among the better efforts in this series are *Bowery Blitzkrieg* (1941), *Let's Get Tough* (1942, in which they take on Japanese saboteurs), *Kid Dynamite* (1943), *Bowery Champs* (1944), and *Docks of New York* (1945).

In 1946 Gorcey's agent, Jan Grippo, started a new Monogram series to replace the Katzman offerings. Briefly partnered with studio workhorse Lindsley Parsons, he reconfigured the group and renamed it "The Bowery Boys." Gorcey and Hall—now playing Terence Aloysius Mahoney, aka "Slip," and Horace Debussy Jones, aka "Sach," respectively—became front-and-center stars, with the others (generally Benedict, Dell, and David Gorcey, with Bobby Jordan in the earlier entries) generally shunted to the background. The most important addition to the group was Gorcey *pere,* Bernard; after playing a bit in the first effort, *Live Wires* (1946), he was cast as the diminutive Louie Dumbrowski, owner of the sweet shop that was the gang's favorite hangout, who acted as foil for the boys until his death in 1956.

Early "Bowery Boys" installments, directed by such B-movie notables as Phil Karlson, Del Lord, and William Beaudine, still tried to keep a serious side, but increasingly slapstick and farce dominated the series. Veteran players such as Betty Compson, Frankie Darro, Sheldon Leonard, Donald MacBride, Russell Simpson, Ellen Corby, Byron Foulger, Lucien Littlefield, and Dan Seymour popped up in supporting roles, always victimized by the boys' ad-libbing and scene-stealing antics. Among the better "Bowery Boys" comedies are *Live Wires* (actually a remake of a story Monogram had filmed three times before with different casts and titles), *Bowery Bombshell, Spook Busters* (both 1946), *Hard Boiled Mahoney* (a weird excursion into film noir territory), *Bowery Buckaroos* (both 1947), *Jinx Money* (1948), *Master Minds* (1949), *Let's Go Navy* (1951), and *No Holds Barred* (1952).

In 1953 Monogram became Allied Artists, a new producer—Ben Schwalb—took over the series, and the last vestige of drama was erased in such juvenile entries as *Loose in London, Clipped Wings* (both 1953), *The Bowery Boys Meet the Monsters* (1954, the series' top grosser and, to many, its high point), *High Society, Spy Chasers* (both 1955), and *Dig That Uranium* (1956). Then Bernard Gorcey died; a distraught Leo increased his already prodigious alcohol intake, and quit the series after one more film, *Crashing Las Vegas* (1956). Hall won top billing, and former East Sider Stanley Clements joined the series as Stanislaus Coveleske, aka "Duke." The Bowery Boys limped through seven more films before finally throwing in the towel after *In the Money* (1958).

Most of the Kids continued to act, albeit much less frequently and in small roles. Gorcey took occasional bits, memorably as a befuddled cabbie in *It's a Mad Mad Mad Mad World* (1963). In 1967 he published his autobiography, via a vanity press; it was titled "An Original Dead End Kid Presents: Dead End Yells, Wedding Bells, Cockle Shells, and Dizzy Spells." Hall kept busy on stage and in TV (where he appeared in a short-lived 1971 sitcom, "The Chicago Teddy Bears"), and acted in several features, among them *Herbie Rides Again* (1974), *Valentino* (1977, cast, incredibly, as movie pioneer Jesse L. Lasky), *The Escape Artist* (1982), and *Cyclone* (1987). Dell also worked on stage, was a regular on the late 1950s TV incarnation of "The Steve Allen Show," and had bits in such features as *Earthquake* (1974), *Framed* (1975),

and *The Escape Artist* (1982). Halop (who'd had the most extensive show-biz career of all the Kids, dating back to his radio stardom in the mid-1930s) is best remembered, post–*Dead End,* as cabbie Bert Munson from the "All in the Family" TV show; he also played a studio projectionist in the Hollywood-themed series "Bracken's World." His later film appearances include *For Love or Money* (1963), *A Global Affair* (1964), *Mister Buddwing* (1965), and *Fitzwilly* (1967). Jordan's subsequent show-biz career was negligible and he died tragically young. Punsly retired from acting in 1943 and used his earnings to put himself through medical school; he later became a successful physician.

DEAN, JAMES. Actor. *(b. Feb. 8, 1931, Marion, Ind.; d. Sept. 30, 1955.)* A fallen American icon in the tradition of Elvis, Marilyn, and fewer than a handful of others, Dean's enormous cultural resonance exists in inverse proportion to his actual body of work. He had starring roles in only three films. His appeal combined a reticent ruggedness with an air of painful introspection; his outburst of "You're tearin' me apart!" in *Rebel Without a Cause* (1955) was the closest he came to explicitly stating an emotional dilemma. How much of Dean's character was an expression of his "true self" as opposed to a creation of Method acting will never really be known, and to a certain extent it's the blurring of such boundaries that makes Dean such an enduring figure—fans from every generation can easily believe the actor was the thing he embodied.

Dean worked in theater and had a couple of movie bits (including one in Samuel Fuller's 1951 Korean war drama *Fixed Bayonets)* before moving to New York where he did stage and TV work. A Broadway appearance in an adaptation of André Gide's "The Immoralist" attracted the attention of Hollywood producers; he tested for Warner Bros. and was subsequently cast as one of the rival brothers in Elia Kazan's 1955 film of John Steinbeck's novel, *East of Eden.* His performance in that film created a sensation; without consciously trying, he became a symbol of the increasingly alienated youth of the post-WW2 era. His next role, as a confused teen in Nicholas Ray's *Rebel*

Without a Cause, had an even more explicit appeal to young moviegoers.

Dean had completed work on George Stevens' *Giant* (1956) when he was killed in a crash while speeding his Porsche Spider to Salinas, California, to participate in an auto race. His cult was such that Stevens received letters from Dean fans threatening to kill the director should he cut a single frame of Dean's performance. He received a posthumous Best Actor Oscar nomination for *Giant,* just as he did the year before for *East of Eden.* Dean's short life and career has been dissected and chronicled in a large number of books, documentaries, and reminiscences, and legions of fans still flock to his Indiana grave each year.

DECAMP, ROSEMARY. Actress. *(b. Nov. 14, 1911, Prescott, Ariz.)* Attractive and talented actress who settled almost immediately into supporting roles and became one of the busiest players in Hollywood. After an inauspicious debut in *Cheers for Miss Bishop* (1941), she won plum roles in 1942's *Jungle Book* (as Sabu's mother) and *Yankee Doodle Dandy* (as James Cagney's mother), which established her with audiences (as well as producers). A radio veteran who spent seventeen years playing Nurse Judy on "Dr. Christian," she went on to become an especially familiar face on TV in "The Life of Riley" (1949, in its first incarnation, as the wife of Jackie Gleason), "The Bob Cummings Show" (1955–59), and "That Girl" (1966–70). In 1991 her memoir, "Stories from Hollywood," was published as an audio book.
OTHER FILMS INCLUDE: 1941: *Hold Back the Dawn;* 1943: *This Is the Army* (as Ronald Reagan's mother!); 1944: *The Merry Monahans, Bowery to Broadway;* 1945: *Rhapsody in Blue, Pride of the Marines;* 1947: *Nora Prentiss;* 1949: *Look for the Silver Lining;* 1950: *The Big Hangover;* 1951: *On Moonlight Bay;* 1953: *By the Light of the Silvery Moon, So This Is Love;* 1955: *Strategic Air Command;* 1960: *13 Ghosts.*

DE CARLO, YVONNE. Actress. *(b. Sept. 1, 1922, Vancouver, B.C., as Peggy Yvonne Middleton.)* This former dancer broke into films in 1942, working as an extra and graduating to bit parts in short

subjects, soundies musicals, and such feature films as *This Gun for Hire* (as a showgirl) and *The Road to Morocco* (as a harem girl), but not achieving stardom until she was cast in exotic adventure films and clad (or rather, *un*clad) in harem garb. And when she wasn't cavorting with sheiks or viziers, she was kicking up her heels in Wild West saloons. De Carlo's starring roles, beginning with *Salome, Where She Danced* (1945), didn't usually require much in the way of emoting, but she gamely rose to the occasion when something more than looking beautiful was required.

De Carlo enjoyed a personal triumph in the original cast of Stephen Sondheim's 1971 Broadway musical "Follies," introducing the song "I'm Still Here." The TV generation knows her as Lily Munster, a role she played on "The Munsters" TV series (1964–66) and in a 1966 feature film, *Munster, Go Home.* The cast reunited for 1981's TV movie *The Munsters' Revenge.* Her autobiography, "Yvonne," was published in 1987.
OTHER FILMS INCLUDE: 1942: *Harvard, Here I Come* (her debut); 1943: *For Whom the Bell Tolls, So Proudly We Hail;* 1944: *Kismet;* 1945: *Frontier Gal;* 1947: *Song of Scheherazade, Brute Force;* 1948: *Black Bart* (as Lola Montez), *Casbah;* 1949: *Criss Cross, Calamity Jane and Sam Bass;* 1950: *The Desert Hawk* (as Scheherazade again); 1951: *Hotel Sahara, Silver City;* 1954: *Tonight's the Night;* 1956: *Flame of the Islands, Death of a Scoundrel, The Ten Commandments;* 1957: *Band of Angels* (opposite Clark Gable); 1963: *McLintock!;* 1966: *Hostile Guns;* 1971: *The Seven Minutes;* 1975: *Blazing Stewardesses;* 1978: *Nocturna;* 1987: *American Gothic;* 1991: *Oscar.*

DEE, FRANCES. Actress. *(b. Nov. 26, 1907, Los Angeles, as Jean Dee.)* Lissome, beautiful actress whose many competent performances failed to win her a spot in Hollywood's top ranks, although she did win one of her leading men, Joel McCrea, to whom she was married for nearly 60 years. Born in California but raised in Chicago, where she attended college, Dee spent a summer vacation visiting relatives near Hollywood. She worked as an extra, mostly as a lark, until being "discovered" by Maurice Chevalier, who insisted over his director's objections that she be cast in his *The Playboy of Paris* (1930). Paramount signed her to a contract, and she duly appeared in many of the studio's programmers, most notably the 1931 version of Dreiser's *An American Tragedy*, playing the society girl portrayed by Elizabeth Taylor in the better-known 1951 remake.

Dee went to RKO for *The Silver Cord* (1933), delivering a first-rate performance as a sensitive, lovesick girl dominated by her possessive mother. She fell in love with leading man McCrea, whom she married later that year. Dee had another memorable role in 1933, that of a frankly nymphomaniacal heiress in *Blood Money*. It was a standout among the many insipid ingenue roles she was handed during that period. (She also played spirited young women in 1934's *Finishing School* and 1935's *Becky Sharp*, to excellent effect.) *Wells Fargo* (1937) reunited her with McCrea on-screen; in real life she was already a mother, as well as partner in McCrea's sprawling San Fernando Valley ranch. Although she continued to delight audiences with her screen work—especially opposite Ronald Colman in *If I Were King* (1938)—Dee spent most of her time raising her family. But even in her last screen appearances, such as *Mr. Scoutmaster* (1953) and *Gypsy Colt* (1954), she was startlingly beautiful. Although her marriage to McCrea had its ups and downs, she remained devoted to him until his death in 1990. Her son Jody McCrea had a short-term acting career in the 1960s.

OTHER FILMS INCLUDE: 1930: *Along Came Youth;* 1931: *June Moon;* 1932: *Love Is a Racket, If I Had a Million;* 1933: *King of the Jungle, One Man's Journey, Little Women* (in the last-named as Meg); 1934: *Coming-Out Party, Of Human Bondage;* 1937: *Souls at Sea;* 1941: *A Man Betrayed;* 1943: *I Walked With a Zombie;* 1947: *The Private Affairs of Bel Ami;* 1948: *Four Faces West* (with McCrea); 1952: *Because of You.*

DEE, RUBY. Actress. *(b. Oct. 27, 1924, Cleveland, as Ruby Ann Wallace.)* Intelligent, empathic actress who got most of the few really good parts written for black women in the 1950s and 1960s. Harlem-raised, she began performing with the American Negro Theatre in the mid 1940s and made a smashing debut on Broadway in "Anna Lucasta" (1946). Her first film was *No*

Way Out (1950), a violent tale of race hatred that paired her with Sidney Poitier (also debuting), whose wife she later played in the gritty *Edge of the City* (1957). *(No Way Out* also featured her future husband, Ossie Davis.) In *The Jackie Robinson Story* (1950), Dee portrayed the great ballplayer's wife; 40 years later, she played his mother in a telepic, *The Court-Martial of Jackie Robinson.* Spike Lee cast her in colorful supporting roles for his *Do the Right Thing* (1989) and *Jungle Fever* (1991, both of which also featured Davis). Dee has worked diligently with Davis on behalf of many civil rights groups.

OTHER FILMS INCLUDE: 1954: *Go, Man, Go!;* 1958: *St. Louis Blues;* 1960: *Virgin Island;* 1961: *A Raisin in the Sun* (a career high point); 1963: *The Balcony;* 1967: *The Incident;* 1972: *Buck and the Preacher;* 1976: *Countdown at Kusini;* 1982: *Cat People;* 1990: *Love at Large;* 1993: *Cop. and a Half.*

DEE, SANDRA. Actress. *(b. Apr. 23, 1942, Bayonne, N.J., as Alexandra Zuck.)* She was Gidget, and she was Tammy, and for a time she was young America's ideal. A child actress and model, Dee worked in TV and movies while still a highschooler; her first film was *Until They Sail* (1957). In 1959 she gave a mature, accomplished performance as Lana Turner's daughter in the three-handkerchief weepie *Imitation of Life*, was paired romantically with Troy Donahue in *A Summer Place*, and appeared as the original screen *Gidget*. The triple parlay made her a star. *Tammy Tell Me True* (1961) and *Tammy and the Doctor* (1963) reinforced her teen-goddess status, and her seemingly picture-perfect marriage to music star Bobby Darin made them fan-magazine favorites. (They costarred on-screen in 1961's *Come September,* 1962's *If a Man Answers,* and 1965's *That Funny Feeling,* and their names were even mentioned in special-material lyrics for "Chop Suey" in Rodgers and Hammerstein's *Flower Drum Song* in 1961.) But once the swinging sixties, with its attendant drug culture and sexual revolution, swept American pop culture, her career petered out. During the 1970s she worked on TV in a few made-fors and series, and gradually faded from view.

OTHER FILMS INCLUDE: 1960: *A Portrait*

in Black; 1963: *Take Her, She's Mine;* 1964: *I'd Rather Be Rich* (playing a role taken by Deanna Durbin in a 1941 version of the same story); 1966: *A Man Could Get Killed;* 1968: *Rosie!;* 1970: *The Dunwich Horror.*

DE HAVEN, GLORIA. Actress. *(b. July 23, 1924, Los Angeles.)* Vivacious leading lady who never rose to the top ranks of musical stardom—though she seemed to have the requisite talent. Born to veteran vaudevillians Carter De Haven and Flora Parker (known professionally as Mr. and Mrs. Carter De Haven), she got her first experience before the camera as an extra in Charlie Chaplin's *Modern Times* (1936). (Her father was by then an associate of Chaplin's.) She played bits in other films (1940's *Susan and God,* 1941's *The Penalty)* and sang with the Bob Crosby and Jan Savitt bands before becoming an MGM contractee while still in her teens. She won featured roles in *Best Foot Forward, Thousands Cheer* (both 1943), *Broadway Rhythm, Two Girls and a Sailor* (which cemented her girl-next-door image), *The Thin Man Goes Home, Step Lively* (all 1944, the last at RKO, in which she gave Frank Sinatra his first screen kiss), *Between Two Women* (1945), and *Summer Holiday* (1946, released 1948).

MGM continued to feature her in both musical and nonmusical films (she starred opposite Red Skelton in *The Yellow Cab Man,* and played her mother, Mrs. Carter De Haven, in *Three Little Words,* both in 1950) but real stardom proved elusive. Nevertheless, she kept working, on stage and TV and in occasional films; in the late 1960s she hosted a popular morning movie program on New York TV. She still appears in nightclubs, as appealing and talented as ever. Her first husband was actor John Payne.

OTHER FILMS INCLUDE: 1949: *Scene of the Crime, Yes, Sir, That's My Baby;* 1950: *Summer Stock, I'll Get By;* 1951: *Two Tickets to Broadway;* 1953: *Down Among the Sheltering Palms;* 1954: *So This Is Paris;* 1955: *The Girl Rush;* 1976: *Won Ton Ton, the Dog Who Saved Hollywood;* 1979: *Bog.*

DE HAVILLAND, OLIVIA. Actress. *(b. July 1, 1916, Tokyo.)* One of the sweetest ingenues on screen during the 1930s, this delicately beautiful leading lady graduated to more demanding roles during the 1940s, coming into her own late in the decade with a handful of top-caliber performances, two of which earned her Academy Awards. The older sister of actress Joan Fontaine, the convent-educated de Havilland cut her acting teeth in college shows, and was seen in one of them by famous impresario Max Reinhardt, then casting his highly touted film production of *A Midsummer Night's Dream* (1935) for Warner Bros. He cast the 19-year-old as Hermia, and she was signed to a contract by the studio. At first just another contract player at Warners, her charming presence opposite another relative newcomer, Errol Flynn, in *Captain Blood* (1935) set the course of her career at the studio. She and Flynn were teamed 10 times, and in fact she seemed ideally suited to lavish costume pictures like *The Charge of the Light Brigade, Anthony Adverse* (both 1936), *The Adventures of Robin Hood* (1938, as Maid Marian, one of her most winning characterizations), *Dodge City,* and *The Private Lives of Elizabeth and Essex* (both 1939).

Warners loaned de Havilland to David O. Selznick, who cleverly cast her against type as the long-suffering Melanie in *Gone With the Wind* (1939), for which she earned a Best Supporting Actress Academy Award nomination, and screen immortality. Returning to her home studio, de Havilland appeared in *Santa Fe Trail* (1940), *The Strawberry Blonde* (a cunning comic part), *They Died With Their Boots On* (both 1941), *The Male Animal* (1942), and *Princess O'Rourke* (1943). During this period, her only outstanding dramatic opportunity came, as before, on loanout— this time to Paramount, where she played a spinsterish schoolteacher wooed by Charles Boyer in *Hold Back the Dawn* (1941). Nominated for her first Best Actress Oscar, she ironically lost to sister Fontaine.

By 1943, chafing against her treatment at Warners, she insisted on getting better roles and was suspended for six months. That extended the duration of her seven-year term, according to Warners, but de Havilland sued the studio and eventually won her freedom as well as the suit. (It is still known in law books as "the de Havilland case.")

Immediately, she sought out roles commensurate with the dramatic talent she'd previously displayed—and got them. She played twins, one of them evil, in *The Dark Mirror* (1946), and later that year delivered her first Oscar-winning performance, as an unwed mother who gives up her baby in *To Each His Own*. *The Snake Pit* (1948) gave her one of her juiciest opportunities as a mental patient (earning her an Oscar nomination), and *The Heiress* (1949) starred her as another spinster, this time wooed by fortune-hunter Montgomery Clift in an impeccable adaptation of the Henry James novel; her performance earned her another Academy Award.

Following that triumph, she left the screen to tackle Broadway, achieving some success there and only sporadically returning to movie work. Her later films, in more mature roles, include *My Cousin Rachel* (1952), *That Lady* (1955), *Not as a Stranger* (1955), *The Ambassador's Daughter* (1956), *The Proud Rebel* (1958), *Libel* (1959), *Lady in a Cage* (1964, her best latter-day lead), *Hush . . . Hush, Sweet Charlotte* (1965, opposite a scenery-chewing Bette Davis), *The Adventurers* (1970), *Pope Joan* (1972), *Airport '77* (1977), *The Swarm* (1978), and *The Fifth Musketeer* (1979). De Havilland has also appeared in a handful of telefilms, including *Murder Is Easy* (1982), *The Royal Romance of Charles and Diana* (1982, as the Queen Mother), and *The Woman He Loved* (1988). She married French editor Pierre Galante and moved to Paris; in 1962 she wrote a book, "Every Frenchman Has One," about her experiences there.

DEKKER, ALBERT. Actor. *(b. Dec. 20, 1904, Brooklyn, N.Y., as Albert van Dekker; d. May 5, 1968.)* As the sinister *Dr. Cyclops* (1940), tall, hulking, and (for this role, anyway) bald and bespectacled, this dependable character actor scared the bejesus out of many theatergoers—so much so, according to contemporary sources, that it's amazing he wasn't permanently typed as a horror-movie menace. That would have been an injustice: the stage-trained Dekker, a Broadway regular throughout the 1930s before making his Hollywood debut in *The Great Garrick* (1937), could play any kind of part. He was a convincing Louis XIII in *The Man in the Iron Mask* (1939), a shifty

legionnaire in *Beau Geste* (1939), a madman and his saintly twin brother in *Among the Living* (1941), Western lawman Bat Masterson in *The Woman of the Town* (1943), and reluctant detective Johnny Fletcher in *The French Key* (1946, one of his personal favorites), among others. His death by strangulation was declared accidental, although many believed it to be a suicide.

OTHER FILMS INCLUDE: 1942: *Once Upon a Honeymoon;* 1943: *In Old Oklahoma;* 1946: *The Killers;* 1947: *Gentleman's Agreement;* 1950: *The Furies;* 1951: *As Young As You Feel* (as Marilyn Monroe's boss); 1954: *The Silver Chalice;* 1955: *East of Eden, Kiss Me Deadly;* 1959: *Middle of the Night, Suddenly, Last Summer;* 1967: *Come Spy With Me;* 1969: *The Wild Bunch.*

DELANY, DANA. Actress. *(b. March 13, 1956, New York City.)* Attractive actress best known as U.S. Army nurse Colleen McMurphy on the acclaimed TV series "China Beach" (a role that earned her two Emmy Awards). She appeared in Broadway and off-Broadway shows as well as the soap operas "Love of Life" and "As the World Turns" before gaining recognition on prime-time shows and supporting roles in *Almost You* (1984) and *Where the River Runs Black* (1986). She was featured in *Masquerade, Moon Over Parador* (both 1988), and *Patty Hearst* (also 1988, as one of the Symbionese Liberation Army members). In 1992 she displayed her versatility in the light comedy *HouseSitter* and in the drama *Light Sleeper* as an ex-drug addict. She also appeared in *Tombstone,* the miniseries "Wild Palms," and lent her voice to *Batman: Mask of the Phantasm* (all 1993). In 1994 she starred in *Exit to Eden.*

DELERUE, GEORGES. Composer. *(b. Mar. 12, 1925, Roubaix, France; d. Mar. 20, 1992.)* Internationally renowned composer who first gained fame for the scores of many of France's New Wave of filmmakers in the early 1960s. Delerue won a scholarship to the Paris Conservatory and worked as an orchestra leader on French television before scoring short films and several documentaries for Alain Resnais. Following his contribution to Resnais's *Hiroshima, Mon Amour* (1959),

Delerue composed scores for François Truffaut: *Shoot the Piano Player* (1960), *Jules and Jim* (1962); Phillipe De Broca: *Five-Day Lover* (1961), *Cartouche* (1962), *King of Hearts* (1966); Jean-Luc Godard: *Contempt* (1963); and Louis Malle: *Viva Maria!* (1965). The rise of these French directors boosted Delerue's stature and soon he was composing for a wide range of directors and projects, including *A Man for All Seasons* (1966), *Women in Love* (1969), *The Conformist* (1970), *The Day of the Jackal* (1973), *Get Out Your Handkerchiefs* (1978), and in Hollywood, *Silkwood* (1983), *Platoon* (1986), *Biloxi Blues* (1988), *Steel Magnolias* (1989), *Mister Johnson* (1991), and *Rich in Love* (1993). He continued his association with Truffaut through the years, working on *Two English Girls* (1971), *Such a Gorgeous Kid Like Me* (1972), *Day for Night* (1973), *Love on the Run* (1979), *The Last Metro* (1980), and *Confidentially Yours* (1983). Delerue was Oscar-nominated for *Anne of the Thousand Days* (1969), *The Day of the Dolphin* (1973), *Julia* (1977), and *Agnes of God* (1985), and won for *A Little Romance* (1979).

DEL RIO, DOLORES. Actress. *(b. Aug. 3, 1905, Durango, Mexico, as Lolita Dolores Martinez Asunsolo Lopez Negrette; d. Apr. 11, 1983.)* Exotic, enigmatically beautiful Mexican actress whose lovely face and figure made her one of the screen's most eminently watchable stars. In the silent era she played many ethnic types—most notably the French girl Charmaine in *What Price Glory?* (1926)—but her unmistakable accent limited her casting after the coming of sound. The convent-educated banker's daughter, a cousin to Hollywood film star Ramon Novarro, made her movie debut in *Joanna* (1925); she was billed as Del Rio, her married name, and continued to use it after her husband died in 1928. She was most effective, not surprisingly, as sultry, spirited Latin women, but she memorably played a dewy-eyed Polynesian native in *Bird of Paradise* (1932, perhaps her best-remembered starring vehicle) and a French trollop in *Madame DuBarry* (1934). She was also the top-billed star of *Flying Down to Rio* (1933), an RKO musical stolen by the dancing debut of Fred Astaire and Ginger Rogers.

Her Hollywood career largely behind her by 1942, Del Rio moved back to Mexico and became that country's preeminent movie star, working with its leading filmmaker, Emilio Fernandez, and leading man Pedro Armendariz in such films as *Maria Candelaria* (1943), *Bugambilia,* and *Los Abandonadas* (both 1944). She also appeared in the Mexican theater, and as late as the 1970s was starring on stage as Camille. She periodically returned to Hollywood to play supporting roles, and looked breathtakingly beautiful to the end of her life. In the 1930s she was married to art director Cedric Gibbons.

OTHER FILMS INCLUDE: 1927: *The Loves of Carmen;* 1928: *Ramona;* 1929: *The Trail of '98;* 1932: *Girl of the Rio;* 1934: *Wonder Bar;* 1935: *In Caliente;* 1937: *Lancer Spy, The Devil's Playground;* 1938: *International Settlement;* 1942: *Journey Into Fear;* 1947: *The Fugitive;* 1960: *Flaming Star* (as Elvis Presley's mother); 1964: *Cheyenne Autumn;* 1967: *More Than a Miracle;* 1978: *The Children of Sanchez.*

DEL RUTH, ROY. Director. *(b. Oct. 18, 1895, Philadelphia; d. Apr. 27, 1961.)* Though mostly a footnote to all but the most dedicated movie buffs, this talented, versatile director, a veteran of the silent era, accounted for an extraordinary string of Warner Bros. films of the early 1930s, virtually defining that studio's style in the pre-Production Code era. His films of this period include *The Maltese Falcon* (1931, the first of three versions), *Taxi, Blessed Event* (both 1932), *Employees' Entrance, The Mind Reader, Lady Killer,* and *Little Giant* (all 1933). Leaving Warners in 1934 to freelance, Del Ruth helmed a series of major musicals and comedies, including *Kid Millions* (1934), *Broadway Melody of 1936* (1935), *Born to Dance* (1936), *On the Avenue, Broadway Melody of 1938* (both 1937), *Topper Returns* (1941), and *DuBarry Was a Lady* (1943). Prolific and able, Del Ruth was a directorial chameleon, a journeyman helmer easily adaptable to any studio's style. Among his later (and weaker) films are *About Face* (1952), *The Phantom of the Rue Morgue* (1954), and *The Alligator People* (1959). He also worked in episodic TV throughout the 1950s. He was married to actress Winnie Lightner.

DELON, ALAIN. Actor. *(b. Nov. 8, 1935, Seaux, France.)* Unlike his contemporary, Jean-Paul Belmondo, Delon epitomized the popular image of a continental movie star; he was almost perfectly handsome by Gallic standards, with dark hair, straight nose, strong chin, and expressive eyes. A former French marine (and earlier, a knockabout with a shady background), Delon drifted into movie acting in the late 1950s, working with many prominent New Wave directors and appearing in many international productions, including a handful of Hollywood movies.

While not a classically trained actor, Delon mastered the art of performing before a camera, relying on his good looks and enigmatic persona to carry him. A frequent delineator of screen gangsters, his involvement in a notorious murder scandal in the late 1960s intrigued the public and actually boosted his stock among continental filmgoers. He also produced, wrote, starred in, and composed a song for *Parole de Flic* (1985). Delon is now, like Belmondo, something of an institution; hence Jean-Luc Godard's comment, apropos their work together on *Nouvelle Vague* (1990): "I shot him as if he were a tree."
OTHER FILMS INCLUDE: 1958: *Christine;* 1960: *Rocco and His Brothers;* 1963: *The Leopard;* 1965: *The Yellow Rolls-Royce, Once a Thief;* 1966: *Is Paris Burning?, Texas Across the River;* 1968: *Spirits of the Dead;* 1970: *Borsalino;* 1971: *Red Sun;* 1972: *The Assassination of Trotsky;* 1975: *Zorro;* 1977: *Le Gang;* 1979: *The Concorde—Airport '79;* 1983: *Swann in Love.*

DELUISE, DOM. Actor, director. *(b. Aug. 1, 1931, Brooklyn, N.Y.)* Rotund comic whose raspy, effeminate voice has also graced several animated features, including 1982's *The Secret of NIMH,* 1986's *An American Tail,* 1989's *All Dogs Go to Heaven,* and 1991's *An American Tail: Fievel Goes West.* DeLuise's screen appearances date back to *Fail-Safe* (1964), although he did the bulk of his movie work in the 1970s and 1980s. He's in Brooks' *The 12 Chairs* (1970), *Blazing Saddles* (1974), *Silent Movie* (1976), and *History of the World—Part I* (1981). Longtime pal Burt Reynolds made DeLuise a sidekick in *The Cannonball Run* (1980) and *The Best Little Whorehouse in Texas* (1982). Mel Brooks' wife

Anne Bancroft directed him in his only starring screen vehicle to date, *Fatso* (1980). In 1993 he contributed one of the funniest scenes to Brooks' *Robin Hood: Men in Tights,* doing a parody of Marlon Brando's godfather role. He directed *Hot Stuff* (1979). His sons Peter and Michael are also actors.

DEMAREST, WILLIAM. Actor. *(b. Feb. 27, 1892, St. Paul, Minn.; d. Dec. 28, 1983.)* One of Hollywood's most durable character players, the crusty but lovable Demarest, like many of his contemporaries, came from a varied show-business background that included carnival, vaudeville, stock, and Broadway work; he was even a professional boxer. In movies from 1927 (debuting in the landmark *The Jazz Singer*), he played cops, pugs, reporters, promoters, and other Brooklynese types. Writer-director Preston Sturges exploited Demarest's baleful qualities—and his ability to do breathtaking pratfalls—in a string of hilarious characterizations, including the crooked politician in *The Great McGinty* (1940), the suspicious valet in *The Lady Eve* (1941), the hardboiled Marine sergeant in *Hail the Conquering Hero* (1944), and Betty Hutton's dyspeptic dad in *The Miracle of Morgan's Creek* (1944). He joined the cast of the TV series "My Three Sons" in 1965 as Uncle Charley after William Frawley died, and stayed until 1972. An avid golfer, he was still playing in his 80s, and appearing in celebrity tournaments.
OTHER FILMS INCLUDE: 1929: *The Broadway Melody;* 1935: *Diamond Jim, The Good Fairy;* 1937: *Easy Living;* 1938: *Rebecca of Sunnybrook Farm;* 1939: *Mr. Smith Goes to Washington;* 1942: *Pardon My Sarong;* 1946: *The Jolson Story* (earning an Oscar nomination); 1947: *The Perils of Pauline;* 1948: *The Night Has a Thousand Eyes;* 1949: *Jolson Sings Again, Sorrowful Jones;* 1952: *What Price Glory?;* 1963: *It's a Mad Mad Mad Mad World;* 1965: *That Darn Cat.*

DEMILLE, CECIL B. Director, producer. *(b. Aug. 12, 1881, Ashfield, Mass.; d. Jan. 21, 1959.)* To a generation of moviegoers, Cecil B. DeMille was the very image of a Hollywood producer-director. With his theatrical voice and manner, and his penchant for puttees, megaphones, and other such accoutrements, he fit the role to a tee, and perpetuated that image through appearances—as himself—in short subjects (like *Hollywood Extra Girl*), feature films (like *Sunset Blvd.*), his own preview trailers, and on radio's popular weekly series "Lux Radio Theatre," which he hosted from 1936 to 1945.

DeMille was, first and foremost, a showman; he was also a superb storyteller. He was sometimes accused of being simplistic, but that approach suited mass audiences just fine, and in the 1990s his 1956 production of *The Ten Commandments* still draws a formidable audience for its annual television broadcasts.

He came from a theatrical family; his father, a clergyman, also wrote plays, and his mother had a touring theatrical troupe. When his older brother William enrolled in the Academy of Dramatic Arts in New York City, he followed suit, learning his trade as an actor, then stage manager, and then playwright (with his brother) under the tutelage of famed impresario David Belasco in the early part of the 20th century. In 1913 he joined Jesse Lasky and Samuel Goldfish (later Goldwyn) to form the Jesse L. Lasky Feature Play Co. (the foundation of Paramount Pictures) and make a feature-length version of a play, "The Squaw Man." (1914). *The Squaw Man* has often been referred to as the first feature-length film and the first film to be made in Hollywood; neither statement is true. DeMille didn't even direct it himself; he collaborated with Oscar Apfel. But the film was indeed a great success, and helped put all three of its creators on their feet in the movie business.

DeMille began blowing his own horn right from the start: he appeared on screen in prologues or curtain-raising sequences of some of his earliest films, establishing himself with audiences. In collaboration with art director Wilfred Buckland and cameraman Alvin Wyckoff, DeMille learned to tell his stories in cinematic terms, some of them quite bold and inventive for their time. Early features like *The Warrens of Virginia, The Cheat* (both 1915), *Maria Rosa* (1916), *Joan the Woman, The Little American* (both 1917), and *The Whispering Chorus* (1918) are still impressive today.

In 1919 DeMille moved into the realm of social comedy with *Don't Change Your Husband* and *Male and Female*. The latter film included a now notorious scene of Gloria Swanson preparing for her bath and discreetly disrobing before the camera, with the help of a servant. The scene caused a sensation, and the canny DeMille followed up with a series of similar pictures, including *Why Change Your Wife?* (1920), *The Affairs of Anatol* (1921), and *Saturday Night* (1922).

Gloria Swanson was one of many actors to benefit from exposure in DeMille films. He was responsible for making opera singer Geraldine Farrar, light comedienne Bebe Daniels, and leading men Wallace Reid and William Boyd first-rank stars, and while DeMille didn't discover Claudette Colbert or Charlton Heston, it was their work in his movies that solidified their stardom.

A series of scandals rocked Hollywood in the early 1920s, and forced the industry to defend itself against accusations of being a modern-day Gomorrah. DeMille responded by making the cautionary melodrama *Manslaughter* (1922), and then *The Ten Commandments* (1923), which offered a modern-day morality tale with an elaborate Biblical flashback. He followed it, several years later, with a reverent production of *The King of Kings* (1927). To a publicly pious DeMille, there was no contradiction in having made saucy sex comedies just a few years earlier.

In the mid-1920s he launched his own production company, for which he supervised a slate of films, and directed *The Road to Yesterday* (1925, featuring the first of many DeMille train wrecks), *The Volga Boatman* (1926), and other "run of the DeMille" pictures. With the coming of sound, he moved to MGM for the grandiose, high-camp *Madam Satan* (1930) and a surprisingly low-key, effective remake of *The Squaw Man* (1931). (He had already remade his cornerstone movie in 1918!)

DeMille hit his stride once more when he returned to Paramount, where he would remain for the rest of his career. He drew on prior experience to mix historical drama with sex in *The Sign of the Cross* (1932) and *Cleopatra* (1934), as well as the somewhat tamer *The Crusades* (1935), and ventured into offbeat territory for the chilling vigilante tale *This Day and Age* (1933) and the endearingly silly romantic adventure yarn *Four Frightened People* (1934).

For the most part, however, DeMille

made nothing but "big" movies from that point on: big Westerns like *The Plainsman* (1936) and *Union Pacific* (1939), big costume adventures like *The Buccaneer* (1938) and *Reap the Wild Wind* (1942). With advancing age, he took more time on each new project, and his final films— *Samson and Delilah* (1949), the circus saga *The Greatest Show on Earth* (1952, winner of the Best Picture Oscar), and *The Ten Commandments* (1956)—were, progressively, the biggest he'd ever tackled. (He produced a lavish remake of *The Buccaneer* in 1958, but gave his son-in-law Anthony Quinn the opportunity to direct.)

DeMille became a hated figure to many in Hollywood through his heavyhanded wielding of power for political purposes, especially during the McCarthy era, but even his worst enemies admitted that as a showman he was unsurpassed. When he died in 1959 it was truly the end of an epoch in the Hollywood he helped to create. His memoir, "The Autobiography of Cecil B. DeMille" was published posthumously in 1959. His daughter Katherine DeMille had a minor acting career, starting in her father's films in the 1930s.

DEMME, JONATHAN. Director, writer, producer. *(b. Feb. 22, 1944, Baldwin, N.Y.)* Quirky, engaging filmmaker who looks at genre films from a skewed perspective. A former critic and publicist, he got his start, as did so many others, with prolific producer Roger Corman, writing and/or producing such epics as *Angels Hard as They Come* (1971) and *Black Mama, White Mama* (1972). He directed three films for Corman: *Caged Heat* (1974, which he also wrote), *Crazy Mama* (1975), and *Fighting Mad* (1976, which he also wrote), all sex-and-violence mellers, but leavened with an offbeat sense of humor. His first film on his own was *Citizens' Band* (1977), a piquant study of CB radio operators. Despite rave reviews, it did no business at all (one New York theater ran it for free and still nobody came), even after its title was changed to *Handle With Care.* After a superb Hitchcock-style thriller, *Last Embrace* (1979), came *Melvin and Howard* (1980), a fantasia on the life of would-be Howard Hughes beneficiary Melvin Dummar. Despite more glowing notices and two Oscars, it too was a complete bust.

Demme's first brush with Big Hollywood Stars, the Goldie Hawn vehicle *Swing Shift* (1984) was a career low point, but he bounced back with the extraordinary Talking Heads concert film, *Stop Making Sense* (also 1984). His reputation (and the grosses) grew with the unhinged comedy-thrillers *Something Wild* (1986) and *Married to the Mob* (1988), as well as *Miami Blues* (1990), which he produced. (He also directed another performance film, Spalding Gray's *Swimming to Cambodia* in 1987.) His commercial breakthrough finally came with the outstanding nail-biter *The Silence of the Lambs* (1991), which earned him an Oscar as Best Director. Typical of Demme's generosity toward young filmmakers, he spoke of exciting new talent in the directing ranks while giving his thank-you speech. Since then he's directed an extremely personal documentary about a most unusual member of his family, *Cousin Bobby* (1992), executive produced *Household Saints* (1993), and tackled the difficult subject of AIDS in *Philadelphia* (1993).

DE MORNAY, REBECCA. Actress. *(b. Aug. 29, 1961, Los Angeles.)* Attractive blond leading lady who has eschewed typical ingenue roles in favor of more colorful—and sometimes provocative— characters. Unfortunately, the finished films don't always justify her choice of parts, though her second-billed role in the 1992 hit *The Hand That Rocks the Cradle,* in which she played a psychotic nanny, gave her stock a definite boost. California-born but educated in Europe, De Mornay studied acting at Lee Strasberg's Actors' Studio before making her film debut with a bit part in Francis Ford Coppola's *One From the Heart* (1982). She first raised eyebrows as the feisty hooker in *Risky Business* (1983), then won good reviews for a completely different characterization in *The Trip to Bountiful* (1985). Her sexually charged performance in Roger Vadim's 1987 Americanized remake of his own *And God Created Woman* went for naught; the highly touted film bombed. Nonetheless, she deserves credit for sticking to her avowed policy of playing "interesting" modern women.

Pleased with her success in *The Hand That Rocks the Cradle,* Touchstone Pictures top-lined her opposite Don Johnson in a 1993 thriller, *Guilty as Sin*. She was also chosen to play Milady de Winter in *The Three Musketeers* (1993).

OTHER FILMS INCLUDE: 1983: *Testament;* 1985: *The Slugger's Wife, Runaway Train;* 1986: *The Murders in the Rue Morgue* (a telefilm); 1987: *Crack, Beauty and the Beast* (the latter a made-for-video production); 1988: *Feds;* 1989: *Dealers;* 1990: *By Dawn's Early Light, Grand Tour* (both telefilms); 1991: *Backdraft.*

DEMPSEY, PATRICK. Actor. *(b. Jan. 13, 1966, Lewiston, Me.)* Curly-haired, personable leading man of youth-oriented features, generally cast as lighthearted, often bashful, characters. Although busy, Dempsey has yet to win box-office stature, possibly because so many of his vehicles have been misfires: *Can't Buy Me Love* (1987), *In the Mood* (also 1987, the best of the lot and a much underrated film, with Dempsey as real-life "woo woo kid" Sonny Wisecarver), *Some Girls* (1988), *Happy Together,* and *Loverboy* (both 1989). Dempsey showed his dramatic mettle as a young Meyer Lansky in *Mobsters* (1991) and in the title role of the miniseries "JFK: Reckless Youth" (1993). OTHER FILMS INCLUDE: 1985: *Heaven Help Us;* 1987: *Meatballs III;* 1988: *In a Shallow Grave;* 1990: *Coupe de Ville;* 1991: *Run.*

DEMY, JACQUES. Director, screenwriter. *(b. June 5, 1931, Pont-Château, France; d. Oct. 27, 1990.)* "Of all the New Wave directors who once professed their joy in cinema," David Thomson wrote, "Demy has remained the most faithful to the delights of sight and sound and to the romance of movie iconography." After studying art and film, Demy worked with animator Paul Grimault and filmmaker Georges Rouquier before making several short films of his own. These paved the way for his first feature, *Lola* (1961), starring Anouk Aimée as a cabaret singer who must choose among several lovers. The film's stylish camerawork (influenced by Max Ophuls, to whom it was dedicated) and buoyant romantic flavor would characterize much of Demy's work. Next came the dazzling *Bay of Angels* (1962), with Jeanne Moreau as a compulsive gambler, but it was *The Umbrellas of Cherbourg* (1964), a romance between a garage mechanic and a shopgirl, that melted audiences' hearts. All of the actors' dialogue was sung, and the lavish photography and sets reflected Demy's fondness for the Hollywood musical; the film won the Grand Prix at Cannes and earned Oscar nominations for Demy's screenplay and the beautiful score by Demy and Michel Legrand. Demy attempted to recapture the *Umbrellas* magic in *The Young Girls of Rochefort* (1968), and though its deliberate artifice was unusual to watch (and listen to), it was not successful, despite the presence of Gene Kelly in the cast. Anouk Aimée returned as Lola in *Model Shop* (1969), Demy's first film made in America, and *Donkey Skin* (1971) was a charming adaptation of the Charles Perrault fairy tale. After a surprisingly grim version of *The Pied Piper* (1972), Demy's work became less interesting, with the obvious comedy *The Slightly Pregnant Man* (1973) and *Lady Oscar* (1979). His next films—*A Room in Town* (1982), *Parking* (1985), and *Three Places for the 26th* (1988)—were all musicals, but failed to rekindle the spirit of his earlier works. Demy was married to filmmaker Agnes Varda from 1962 until his death. Her loving tribute film, *Jacquot* (original title, *Jacquot de Nantes;* released in U.S. 1993)—filmed while he was still alive—celebrates his childhood and how it influenced his later work on the screen.

DENEUVE, CATHERINE. Actress. *(b. Oct. 22, 1943, Paris, as Catherine Dorleac.)* Breathtakingly beautiful blond actress who for many years was France's top female screen star. Her icy manner was skillfully exploited by directors Roman Polanski (in 1965's *Repulsion)* and Luis Buñuel (in 1967's *Belle de Jour* and 1970's *Tristana),* among others. She was equally effective in a pair of François Truffaut films, *The Mississippi Mermaid* (1968) and *The Last Metro* (1980). Deneuve also delivers lighter, more accessible performances as well: she was utterly charming, for example, in *The Umbrellas of Cherbourg* (1964), the film that brought her international recognition following several years of desultory screen appearances. Still a ravishing beauty, Deneuve has unfortunately limited her U.S. exposure in recent years to TV commercials and occasional films such as *The*

Hunger (1983, in a surprisingly erotic role as a vampire) and *Scene of the Crime* (1986, a muddled psychological thriller). She earned her first Oscar nomination for *Indochine* (1992).

A free-spirited nonconformist, Deneuve has given birth out of wedlock to children fathered by former lovers Roger Vadim and Marcello Mastroianni. Her sister, Françoise Dorleac, was herself a talented actress whose career was cut short by a tragic car accident in 1967; they costarred in Jacques Demy's *The Young Girls of Rochefort* (1968).
OTHER FILMS INCLUDE: 1956: *Les Collegiennes;* 1960: *Les Parisiennes;* 1968: *Mayerling;* 1969: *The April Fools;* 1970: *Donkey Skin;* 1972: *Dirty Money;* 1975: *Hustle;* 1981: *Choice of Arms;* 1984: *Love Songs;* 1993: *My Favorite Season.*

DE NIRO, ROBERT. Actor. *(b. Aug. 17, 1943, New York City.)* Arguably the most impressive actor working in films today, De Niro has managed to limn a whole gallery of fascinating, fully developed characters while exposing very little of himself. His willingness to submerge himself totally in any part—even to the point of physical metamorphosis—accounts for much of his success, but De Niro's passion, intensity, and animal magnetism come through in every film assignment he's undertaken, giving his screen performances a welcome consistency regardless of the role he's playing.

The son of New York artists, De Niro studied acting with Lee Strasberg and Stella Adler and toiled, like many of their students, in off-Broadway theatrical productions. He made early screen appearances in *Greetings* (1968) and *The Wedding Party* (1969, but made in 1963), low-budget films directed by Brian De Palma, and took roles in *Hi, Mom!, Bloody Mama* (both 1970), *Jennifer on My Mind, Born to Win,* and *The Gang That Couldn't Shoot Straight* (all 1971) before getting plum roles in 1973's *Bang the Drum Slowly* (as a mentally deficient, terminally ill ballplayer) and *Mean Streets* (as an irresponsible street tough in his first film for director Martin Scorsese).

De Niro's breakthrough role was that of the young Vito Corleone in the flashback sequences of *The Godfather, Part II* (1974), which won him a Best Supporting Actor Academy Award and brought him to the attention of moviegoers, who were captivated by his mature, subtly nuanced performance. He carried a major film for the first time as charismatic movie producer Monroe Stahr in *The Last Tycoon* (1976), Elia Kazan's adaptation of an F. Scott Fitzgerald novel, and riveted audiences as a borderline-psychotic cabbie with a messianic complex in Scorsese's harrowing *Taxi Driver* that same year, earning his first Best Actor nomination.

New York, New York (1977), Scorsese's uneven attempt to make a glamorous Hollywood musical (albeit one invested with his own contemporary sensibilities), paired De Niro with Liza Minnelli but just didn't come off. *The Deer Hunter* (1978), however, gave him a great (if somewhat enigmatic) character in the Pennsylvania steelworker who joins the Green Berets during the Vietnam War; his outstanding performance earned him critical raves and another Oscar nod.

Raging Bull (1980) reunited him with Scorsese. Cast as prizefighter Jake La Motta, De Niro threw himself into role preparation with his customary vigor, bulking up not only for the fight scenes, but gaining a full 40 pounds to play the middle-aged, out-of-shape La Motta as a cabaret owner. A masterpiece of naturalistic screen acting, his portrayal won him a Best Actor Oscar.

Even given the success he's achieved on his own, De Niro is at his best when teamed with Scorsese, who has a gift for eliciting jaw-dropping performances from his star, as witness *The King of Comedy* (1983, as wannabe comic Rupert Pupkin), *GoodFellas* (1990, as coldblooded gangster Jimmy Conway), and *Cape Fear* (1991, Oscar-nominated again as sadistic ex-con Max Cady).

De Niro eschews the conventional in his choice of roles; even in a buddy movie like *Midnight Run* (1988), he brings an added dimension to his parts. He's certainly not afraid to go over the top, as he did with tongue-in-cheek playing the sinister Louis Cyphre in Alan Parker's *Angel Heart* (1987) and as Chicago mob kingpin Al Capone in De Palma's *The Untouchables* (1987). And no one on the screen today can match him for depicting inner conflict, as he did so well in *Jacknife* (1989), playing a Vietnam vet whose eccentricity and corny humor mask a seri-

ously wounded psyche. It's precisely those traits that make him the most compulsively watchable male star currently working. After delivering a harrowing performance as a small-minded bully in *This Boy's Life* (1993), De Niro took the plunge and directed his first feature film (in which he also costarred), the well-received *A Bronx Tale* (also 1993). He then played the Creature in *Mary Shelley's Frankenstein* (1994) and reteamed with Scorsese—the eighth time—for *Casino* (1995).
OTHER FILMS INCLUDE: 1981: *True Confessions*; 1984: *Once Upon a Time in America*, *Falling in Love*; 1985: *Brazil*; 1986: *The Mission*; 1989: *We're No Angels* (also executive produced); 1990: *Stanley & Iris*, *Awakenings* (Oscar-nominated); 1991: *Guilty by Suspicion*, *Backdraft*; 1992: *Mistress* (also coproduced), *Night and the City*; 1993: *Mad Dog and Glory*.

DENNEHY, BRIAN. Actor. *(b. July 9, 1939, Bridgeport. Conn.)* Burly, light-haired supporting player and occasional leading man whose Irish charm and engaging grin made him a popular second-tier star in the 1980s. After numerous TV movies, including *Pearl*, *Dummy*, *Skokie*, and *A Real American Hero* (a *Walking Tall* spinoff in which he played the lead), Dennehy captured attention with small but showy portrayals in such films as *Semi-Tough* (1977) and *Foul Play* (1978), leading to stronger assignments in *10* (1979, as the philosophical bartender), *First Blood* (1982, as the sheriff hunting Rambo), *Cocoon* (1985 and its 1988 sequel, as the friendly alien leader), and *Silverado* (also 1985, as a Western heavy), among others. Elevated to costar and leading-man status, Dennehy frequently plays tough, no-nonsense cops, as in *F/X* (1986 and its 1991 sequel), *Best Seller* (1987), and *The Last of the Finest* (1990). Also impressive as a smarmy district attorney in *Presumed Innocent* (1990). Most recently, Dennehy has been busy in TV movies and miniseries, including *Deadly Matrimony*, *Teamster Boss: The Jackie Presser Story* (both 1992), "Murder in the Heartland" (1993), and *Foreign Affairs* (also 1993), opposite Joanne Woodward. After the failed TV drama "Birdland" (1994), Dennehy appeared in *Tommy Boy* (1995).

DENNING, RICHARD. Actor. *(b. Mar. 27, 1914, Poughkeepsie, N.Y., as Louis Denninger.)* Blonde, tan, and muscular, this generally competent if uninspired actor seemed destined, from his debut in a supporting role in 1937's *Hold 'Em Navy*, for a lengthy career as a B-movie lead—and, with few exceptions, that's exactly what he became. As a Paramount contractee, he appeared in *Her Jungle Love* (1937), *The Buccaneer*, *King of Alcatraz* (both 1938), *Union Pacific*, *Million Dollar Legs* (both 1939), *Parole Fixer*, *Northwest Mounted Police* (both 1940), *Beyond the Blue Horizon*, and *The Glass Key* (both 1942), mostly in supporting roles, before leaving the studio to play a hard-boiled detective in *Quiet Please, Murder* (1942). Thereafter he bounced around from studio to studio, essaying leads and character roles in second-string pictures—many of them sci-fi cheapies—such as *Unknown Island* (1948), *Double Deal* (1950), *The 49th Man* (1953), *Creature From the Black Lagoon* (1954, one of his better films), *Creature With the Atom Brain* (1955), *The Day the World Ended* (1956), *An Affair to Remember* (1957, a lonely A picture amid a swarm of Bs), *Twice-Told Tales* (1963), and the unforgettable *I Sailed to Tahiti with an All Girl Crew* (1968).
Denning, who married 1940s "scream queen" Evelyn Ankers, moved to Hawaii in the late 1960s, and played the state governor in the TV series "Hawaii Five-O" (1968–80). Earlier, he'd starred on the small screen in "Mr. and Mrs. North" (1952–54) and "Michael Shayne" (1960–61).

DENNIS, SANDY. Actress. *(b. Apr. 27, 1937, Hastings, Nebr.; d. Mar. 1, 1992.)* Blond, toothy Broadway actress who pretty much peaked on screen in the late 1960s, though she never really considered movie work a priority. With her whiny voice and sharp features, Dennis seemed unusually suited to play neurotic victims, and indeed won an Oscar as the hapless Honey in *Who's Afraid of Virginia Woolf?* (1966). She quickly followed it as a frustrated teacher in *Up the Down Staircase* (1967), a tentative lesbian in *The Fox*, a terminally ill romantic in *Sweet November* (both 1968), a lonely spinster in *That Cold*

Day in the Park (1969), and a terrorized New York tourist in the comic *The Out-of-Towners* (1970). Her film work thereafter was sporadic, but she was a dead ringer for John Dean in the Watergate satire *Nasty Habits* (1976), and etched colorful performances in *Demon* (aka *God Told Me To*, 1977), *The Four Seasons* (1981), *Come Back to the 5 and Dime, Jimmy Dean, Jimmy Dean* (1982), *Another Woman* (1988), *Parents* (1989), and *The Indian Runner* (1991). She was also something of an iconoclast in real life: long believed married to jazz great Gerry Mulligan, she eventually acknowledged that they never made it official.

DENNY, REGINALD. Actor. *(b. Nov. 20, 1891, Richmond, Surrey, England, as Reginald Leigh Daymore; d. June 16, 1967.)* Remembered by many as one of the screen's typical "silly-ass" Englishmen—a characterization Denny popularized as Algy in Paramount's "Bulldog Drummond" movies—he was also a top silent star, equally at home with drawing-room comedy and action-packed melodrama. Handsome and athletic, with expressive, pale eyes and a square jaw, Denny achieved stardom as a boxer in Universal's "Leather Pushers" series during the 1920s, and made more than a dozen light domestic comedies, including *Skinner's Dress Suit* (1925), before American moviegoers had any idea he came from England. In the sound era, his cultured voice and British accent limited his choice of roles, but he continued to deliver fine performances, often as stuffy Brits. Kids who grew up in Hollywood in decades past know him more as the owner of Reginald Denny's Hobby Shop, an extremely popular Hollywood Boulevard store for model kits and the like.

OTHER FILMS INCLUDE: 1930: *Madam Satan*; 1931: *Private Lives*; 1934: *The Lost Patrol*; 1935: *Anna Karenina*; 1936: *Romeo and Juliet*; 1937: *Bulldog Drummond Comes Back* (first in a series of eight titles); 1940: *Rebecca*; 1942: *Sherlock Holmes and the Voice of Terror*; 1947: *The Secret Life of Walter Mitty, My Favorite Brunette*; 1948: *Mr. Blandings Builds His Dream House*; 1953: *Abbott and Costello Meet Dr. Jekyll and Mr. Hyde*; 1965: *Cat Ballou*; 1966: *Batman*.

DE PALMA, BRIAN. Director, screenwriter, producer. *(b. Sept. 11, 1940, Newark, N.J.)* Once touted as "the American Hitchcock," De Palma remains one of the most controversial filmmakers on the contemporary screen; the merits of his work are violently debated by critics and scholars, some of whom believe him a talented craftsman who has successfully synthesized the styles of earlier directors, some of whom believe him a manipulative misogynist whose go-for-the-gut style sacrifices the intellectual for the visceral. He was educated at Sarah Lawrence College, where theatrical director Wilford Leach was his mentor. De Palma's early features were 1960s satires; *The Wedding Party*, filmed in 1963, got fitful release in 1969—its only distinction was the casting of young Robert De Niro and Jill Clayburgh in leading roles; while *Greetings* (1968) has dated badly (although it does afford viewers the opportunity to see De Niro cavorting in Central Park), his follow-up, *Hi, Mom!* (1970), still has some punch. The hallucinogenic, cutting *Sisters* (1973) set the tone for De Palma's subsequent features; his Hitchcock homages culminated with *Obsession* (1976), virtually an uncredited remake of *Vertigo* that reportedly did not please the then-living Master of Suspense one whit. (His 1974 *Phantom of the Paradise* had taken its grand guignol less seriously.)

De Palma invented the telekinetic-teen horror genre with 1976's *Carrie*, which contains both genuine shocks and clever humor. *The Fury* (1978) takes the premise to the point of ridiculousness but contains some impressive cinematic and special-effects pyrotechnics. In 1979 he took a break from high-profile Hollywood filmmaking to teach a master class at his alma mater, Sarah Lawrence, which wound up as a feature film—albeit a threadbare one—called *Home Movies;* it starred his then-wife Nancy Allen and Kirk Douglas. 1980's *Dressed to Kill*, De Palma's take on *Psycho*, was jolting for both its violence and sexual content. The extreme critical reaction to it convinced him to keep pushing the envelope further, resulting in the paranoid conspiracy shocker *Blow Out* (1981) and *Body Double* (1984), a thriller set in the porn industry, featuring a scene in which a woman is drilled into the floor. He also updated the 1930s gangster classic *Scarface* (1983) to contemporary Miami, with Al Pacino as a profane, drug-crazed Cuban hero. But a gangster comedy, *Wise Guys* (1986), was an even worse financial failure.

Just as his career seemed commercially irredeemable, he directed the popular hit *The Untouchables* (1987) from a script by playwright David Mamet. This Prohibition-era morality tale also catapulted lead Kevin Costner to superstardom. De Palma then made the wrenching Vietnam war drama *Casualties of War* (1989), a box-office flop, and a painfully heavy-handed adaptation of Tom Wolfe's popular novel, *The Bonfire of the Vanities* (1990), which left him in dire need of another hit. He returned to familiar territory (with John Lithgow, who'd worked with him twice before) for the shocker *Raising Cain* (1992), and then took on a more ambitious project, with Al Pacino, *Carlito's Way* (1993).

DEPARDIEU, GERARD. Actor. *(b. Dec. 27, 1948, Chateauroux, France.)* Perhaps filmdom's most ungainly sex symbol, this popular and prolific leading man is equally comfortable as a lumbering, lovable lug, a menacing hulk, or a classical hero. Introduced to American audiences as a wandering, nasty ne'er-do-well in *Going Places* (1974), Depardieu also impressed moviegoers in *1900* (1977), *Get Out Your Handkerchiefs* (1978), *The Last Metro* (1980), *The Return of Martin Guerre* (1982), *Jean de Florette* (1986), and *The Possessed* (1987). In 1984 he wrote and directed an adaptation of *Tartuffe*. His American film debut, opposite Andie MacDowell in the romantic comedy *Green Card* (1990), failed to catapult him to stateside stardom. In his native France, however, his star still shines bright, especially following his acclaimed performance in *Cyrano de Bergerac* (1990, which earned an Oscar nomination and a Best Actor award at Cannes), and he continues to work in English-language productions such as *1492* (1992), in which he played Christopher Columbus. He appeared with his son Guillame in *Tous les matins du monde* (1992), and then worked for Jean-Luc Godard in *Hélas pour moi (Oh, Woe Is Me,* 1993).
OTHER FILMS INCLUDE: 1973: *Stavisky;* 1974: *Vincent, Francois, Paul ... and the Others;* 1975: *Maîtresse;* 1976: *The Last Woman;*
1978: *Les Chiens;* 1979: *Buffet froid, Mon oncle d'Amerique;* 1981: *Choice of Arms, The Woman Next Door;* 1982: *Danton;* 1983: *Les Comperes, The Moon in the Gutter;* 1985: *One Woman or Two;* 1989: *Henry V, Too Beautiful for You;* 1990: *Uranus;* 1994: *Germinal, My Father, the Hero, Colonel Chabert, A Pure Formality.*

DEPP, JOHNNY. Actor. *(b. June 9, 1963, Owensboro, Ky.)* Former teen heartthrob who gained popularity in the TV series "21 Jump Street," but has matured into a genuinely gifted actor. His big-screen debut came in the original *A Nightmare on Elm Street* (1984), and he appeared in *Platoon* (1986) as well, but it was his tongue-in-cheek portrayal of the title character in John Waters' *Cry-Baby* (1989) that really opened eyes to Depp's ability. He demonstrated remarkable ability in bringing to life the title character in Tim Burton's whimsical paean to outsiders, *Edward Scissorhands* (1990), delivering a touching and inventive performance. In *Benny & Joon* (1993) he delivered on that promise with another endearing performance, in which he incorporated the manner (and in some cases actual routines) of silent-screen greats Charlie Chaplin and Buster Keaton. Other recent credits include *What's Eating Gilbert Grape* (also 1993), the title role in Tim Burton's *Ed Wood* (1994), *Arizona Dream* (1995, filmed in 1991), and *Don Juan DeMarco* (also 1995).

DEREK, BO. Actress, producer. *(b. Nov. 20, 1956, Long Beach, Calif., as Mary Cathleen Collins.)* TV host and comedian David Letterman once introduced a sanded plank of cedarwood as Bo Derek's acting coach. Few, if any, critics have disagreed on the quality of her performances, but the greater problem (adding insult to injury) has been the quality of her films. This blond, pale-eyed sex symbol shot to stardom (and made cornrows fashionable) in the title role of Blake Edwards' *10* (1979), as the "perfect" beauty who's the focus of Dudley Moore's comic obsession. Years earlier, an agent had brought the teenaged girl to actor/director John Derek's attention. He immediately put her in his film *Fantasies* (shot in 1973), which was not released until the actress—now Mrs. John

Derek—was a star, in 1981. (She'd also had a small part in 1977's *Orca.*) With the exception of *A Change of Seasons* (1980), which opened with footage of the well-endowed beauty bouncing up and down in a hot tub, most of her remaining films have been directed by her husband—*Tarzan, the Ape Man* (1981), *Bolero* (1984), and *Ghosts Can't Do It* (1990)—and all have been virtually unwatchable. Recent non-John films include *Hot Chocolate* (1992), the telefilm *Shattered Image, Woman of Desire* (both 1994), and *Tommy Boy* (1995).

DEREK, JOHN. Actor, director, producer, cinematographer. (b. Aug. 12, 1926, Hollywood, Calif.) The son of director Lawson Harris and actress Dolores Johnson, it was only natural that the matinee idol–handsome Derek would gravitate toward acting. He had small roles in *Since You Went Away* (his debut) and *I'll Be Seeing You* (both 1944); then, after the war, he was "introduced" in *Knock On Any Door* (1949), as a juvenile delinquent defended on a murder charge by Humphrey Bogart, followed by the Oscar-winning *All the King's Men* (also 1949, as Broderick Crawford's football-playing son). It was an auspicious start for the intense young actor. A series of costume epics and B's followed, including *Rogues of Sherwood Forest* (1950, as Robin Hood's son), *The Mask of the Avenger* (1951), *Scandal Sheet* (1952), *Thunderbirds, Ambush at Tomahawk Gap* (both 1953), *The Adventures of Hajji Baba* (1954), *The Ten Commandments* (1956, as Joshua), and *Fury at Showdown* (1957). After *Exodus* (1960), Derek took up photography; while making *Nightmare in the Sun* (1964, which he also produced) he shot nude pictures of the film's star, his then-wife Ursula Andress, which later appeared in *Playboy* magazine. He also directed her in *Once Before I Die* (1965). He later married Linda Evans, whom he directed in *Childish Things* (1969); while they were still married, he discovered a 16-year-old California girl named Mary Cathleen Collins whom he starred in his 1973 film *Fantasies* (released in 1981). He later married her; when, as Bo Derek, she became a sensation in Blake Edwards' comedy *10* (1979), he made her the main attraction, frequently unclothed, in a number of wretched films which he directed and photographed: *Tarzan, the Ape Man* (1981), *Bolero* (1984), and *Ghosts Can't Do It* (1990).

DERN, BRUCE. Actor. (b. June 4, 1936, Winnetka, Ill.) Although he's played some likable characters in his lengthy career, Dern is still remembered as an intense, tightly wound character player whose quiet, outwardly placid demeanor frequently seems to mask explosive, violent emotions seething beneath the surface. His tyro screen appearance, in a bit part in Elia Kazan's *Wild River* (1960), didn't reveal a particularly brilliant performer, but Dern worked incessantly through the 1960s, both in films and in episodic TV, honing his talents. He played in such thrillers as *Marnie* (1964) and *Hush . . . Hush, Sweet Charlotte* (1965), and in such Westerns as *The War Wagon* (1967), *Will Penny* (1968), and *The Cowboys* (1972), nearly always cast as a heavy. He was a regular in the Roger Corman troupe, playing assorted drug-crazed psychotics in the likes of *The Wild Angels* (1966), *The Trip* (1967), and *Psych-Out* (1968).

Dern's trademarked over-the-top outbursts, while never failing to amuse moviegoers, threatened to typecast the wild-eyed actor, but he enjoyed more challenging assignments in *They Shoot Horses, Don't They?* (1969), *Drive, He Said* (1971), *Silent Running* (1971, in the lead), *The Great Gatsby* (1974), *Smile* (1975, one of his all-time best), and *Family Plot* (1976, Hitchcock's last film, in the lead). He even earned an Oscar nomination for Best Supporting Actor as Jane Fonda's troubled husband (another unbalanced character, come to think of it) in Hal Ashby's *Coming Home* (1978).

Alternating psycho parts with more conventional characterizations (and occasional leads), Dern continued to work in films throughout the 1980s, albeit at a more relaxed pace; his films during that decade include *Tattoo* (1981, a tawdry drama that aroused controversy when Dern claimed that his spicy love scenes with costar Maud Adams were the real thing), *That Championship Season* (1982), *On the Edge* (1985), *The Big Town* (1987), *World Gone Wild* (1988), and *The 'burbs* (1989). He earned some of his best notices in years playing a sleazy con man in the noir thriller *After Dark, My Sweet* (1990), and had another juicy role as a town boss in *Diggstown* (1992). Formerly married to actress Diane Ladd; their daughter is actress Laura Dern.

DERN, LAURA. Actress. *(b. Feb. 10, 1967, Santa Monica, Calif.)* This willowy blonde has managed thus far to avoid typecasting in wide-eyed, virginal ingenue parts, although she's clearly suited to such roles and has played them skillfully in the past. The daughter of actor Bruce Dern and actress Diane Ladd, she appeared with mom in *White Lightning* (1973) and *Alice Doesn't Live Here Anymore* (1974) before making her official screen debut in Adrian Lyne's *Foxes* (1980). Her turn as a blind camper who befriends freakish Eric Stoltz in *Mask* (1985) was all innocence and vulnerability, and her leading performance as a confused, coltish girl at the point of womanhood in *Smooth Talk* (1985) demonstrated her versatility. As if to emphasize the point, Dern appeared as a girl-next-door type in David Lynch's *Blue Velvet* (1986), and played an extremely uninhibited white-trash character in the same director's *Wild at Heart* (1990). She portrayed Claire Clairmont in *Haunted Summer* (1988), and costarred in *Fat Man and Little Boy* (1989). In 1991 Dern enchanted audiences with her most mature, accomplished performance to date, playing a love-starved, promiscuous but gentle orphan in *Rambling Rose* (1991). By this time, her mom was supporting *her* on screen; they became the first mother and daughter to earn simultaneous Oscar nominations. Dern was excellent in the 1992 cable-TV movie *Afterburn*. She then costarred in two high-profile 1993 films: *Jurassic Park* and *A Perfect World*.

DESCHANEL, CALEB. Cinematographer, director. *(b. Sept. 21, 1941, Philadelphia.)* After making two short noncommercial films of his own, Deschanel—with the help of former USC classmate George Lucas—met Francis Ford Coppola and did second-unit photography on *Apocalypse Now* (1979). That same year, elevated to director of photography, he stunned moviegoers with his cinematography for the Coppola-produced *The Black Stallion* and *Being There*. Deschanel was characterized by one critic as having achieved a "cleanness of image and a brilliant luminosity."

He received Oscar nominations for his camerawork on *The Right Stuff* (1983) and *The Natural* (1984), and has directed the films *The Escape Artist* (1982) and *Crusoe* (1988). He also helmed several episodes of the David Lynch–produced TV series "Twin Peaks." His wife, actress Mary Jo Deschanel, played one of the astronauts' wives in *The Right Stuff*, and also appeared on "Twin Peaks."

DE SICA, VITTORIO. Actor, director. *(b. July 7, 1902, Sora, Italy; d. Nov. 13, 1974.)* One of the creators of the postwar Italian neorealist school of filmmaking, De Sica has been honored the world over for his work. He began his career as a stage actor and made his film debut as a child in *The Clemenceau Affair* (1918). From the early 1920s to the end of his life he remained a popular Italian film star, appearing in such international successes as *The Earrings of Madame de . . .* (1953), *A Farewell to Arms* (1957, for which he received a Best Supporting Actor Oscar nomination), *General della Rovere* (1959), and *The Amorous Adventures of Moll Flanders* (1965). He even appeared in *Andy Warhol's Dracula* (1974)!

From the early 1940s on De Sica also directed films; his first effort was *Rose, Scarlatte* (1940), in which he also acted. None of his early films attracted much attention because of World War 2, but *The Children Are Watching Us* (1943), which he cowrote with Cesare Zavattini, won its fair share of kudos. Two of his postwar films, the emotionally powerful *Shoeshine* (1946) and *The Bicycle Thief* (1947), established his reputation worldwide and gave life to the neorealist movement with their seamless blend of straightforward storytelling and naturalistic mise-en-scène. In the years before a Foreign-Film category existed, the Academy of Motion Picture Arts and Sciences' Board of Directors voted *Shoeshine* a special Oscar, stating: "The high quality of this motion picture, brought to eloquent life in a country scarred by war, is proof to the world that the creative spirit can triumph over adversity." In 1949 the Academy voted *The Bicycle Thief* the most outstanding foreign-language film released in the U.S. *Miracle in Milan* (1951) and *Umberto D* (1952) also received international acclaim.

For four years De Sica concentrated on

acting to the exclusion of directorial assignments, but in 1961 he made *Two Women*, a return to peak form for which Sophia Loren won a Best Actress Oscar. He remained active through the decade, turning out entertainments like *Marriage, Italian Style* and *Yesterday, Today, and Tomorrow* (both 1964), winning another Oscar for the latter. *The Garden of the Finzi-Continis* (1971) brought him a fourth gold statuette from the Academy. De Sica was separated from his first wife and lived with Spanish actress Maria Mercader from 1942. They were married in 1968 when De Sica became a French citizen and was finally able to obtain a divorce. He died after an operation for the removal of a tumor from his lungs.

DE TOTH, ANDRE. Director, producer, screenwriter. *(b. May 15, 1913, Mako, Hungary, as Andreas Toth.)* This colorful director is best remembered for making the popular 3-D movie *House of Wax* (1953), despite the fact that he is blind in one eye! Anyone familiar with this indomitable personality would agree that nothing as trivial as that would stop him. He began his career in Hungary in the early 1930s and rose to the position of director before fleeing on the eve of World War 2. In England, his countryman Alexander Korda gave him work as a second-unit director on his spectacular production of *The Thief of Bagdad* (1940). Then he moved to Hollywood and worked again for Korda shooting second-unit for *Jungle Book* (1942) before earning his director's stripes on a series of B movies like *Passport to Suez* (1943) and *None Shall Escape* (1944).

He made a name for himself directing film noir tales and tough-minded Westerns, including *Ramrod* (1947, with his then-wife Veronica Lake), *The Pitfall* (1948), *Slattery's Hurricane* (1949, again with Lake), *Man in the Saddle* (1951), *Springfield Rifle* (1952), *The Stranger Wore a Gun* (1953), *The Bounty Hunter* (1954), and *The Indian Fighter* (1955). He also shared an Oscar nomination for cowriting the story of the notable anti-Western *The Gunfighter* (1950).

In later years, the resourceful De Toth worked mostly in Europe, producing such films as *Billion Dollar Brain* (1967), *Play Dirty* (1968), and *El Condor* (1970). He returned to Hollywood in the 1980s and has kept busy with a variety of projects, including a small acting role in Tobe Hooper's *Spontaneous Combustion* (1990), and teaching a film class at USC.

DEVINE, ANDY. Actor. *(b. Oct. 7, 1905, Flagstaff, Ariz., as Jeremiah Schwartz; d. Feb. 18, 1977.)* This rotund, scratchy-voiced actor broke into films in 1926 after attending several colleges and, briefly, studying to be a Catholic priest. Initially working as an extra (alongside another hopeful named Walter Brennan), he soon graduated to character parts in such films as *The Spirit of Notre Dame* (1931), *Law and Order* (1932), *The President Vanishes* (1934), *Romeo and Juliet* (1936, a unique change of pace, as Peter), *A Star Is Born* (1937), and *In Old Chicago* (1938). He usually played comic relief, although he was equally effective in occasional straight roles. Moviegoers came to recognize him by his high-pitched chuckle, curly hair, and ample girth. Following his part in *Stagecoach* (1939, as the stage driver), Devine won costar billing with former matinee idol Richard Arlen in a series of B melodramas produced by Universal, including *Mutiny on the Blackhawk* (1939) and *Raiders of the Desert* (1941). He also played Roy Rogers' sidekick, Cookie Bullfincher, in a handful of 1947–48 horse operas. In the 1950s, most of his work was confined to TV, both as Jingles, sidekick to Guy Madison's "Wild Bill Hickok," and as the jovial host of "Andy's Gang," a kiddie show. In a "Twilight Zone" episode called "Hocus-Pocus and Frisby," Devine was well cast as tale-spinning Mr. Frisby, who to his surprise is visited by real-life aliens. He served for many years as honorary mayor of Van Nuys, California, and was a favorite son of Kingman, Arizona, where "Andy Devine Days" are still celebrated—and a local museum honors his life and career. OTHER FILMS INCLUDE: 1940: *Buck Benny Rides Again* (reprising his ongoing part from Jack Benny's radio show), *When the Daltons Rode;* 1941: *The Flame of New Orleans;* 1942: *Arabian Nights;* 1944: *Ali Baba and the Forty Thieves;* 1946: *Canyon Passage* (along with his sons); 1951: *The Red Badge of Courage;* 1955: *Pete Kelly's Blues;* 1960: *The Adventures of Huckleberry Finn;* 1962: *The Man Who Shot Liberty Valance, How the West Was Won;* 1963: *It's a*

Mad Mad Mad Mad World; 1968: *The Ballad of Josie;* 1970: *Myra Breckinridge.*

DEVITO, DANNY. Actor, director. *(b. Nov. 17, 1944, Asbury Park, N.J.)* Who would ever have guessed that this short, frazzle-haired actor—best known to TV lovers as the cheerfully malevolent troll Louie De Palma on "Taxi" (1978–83)—would become not only a big-screen star in his own right but a respected director as well? It seemed unlikely, but this dynamic, homuncular talent has done so (even if his 1992 biopic *Hoffa* was both a critical and commercial disappointment). A student at New York's American Academy of Dramatic Arts, DeVito in his salad days acted anywhere he could, even taking a part in what became an award-winning NYU student film, *Hot Dogs for Gauguin,* directed by future Hollywood filmmaker Martin Brest. He made his "mainstream" film debut with a small part in the 1972 Sophia Loren starrer *Lady Liberty,* and appeared in *Scalawag* and *Hurry Up, or I'll Be 30* (both 1973) before joining the talented ensemble cast of *One Flew Over the Cuckoo's Nest* (1975), registering strongly as one of Jack Nicholson's fellow mental patients.

DeVito subsequently worked in *The Van* (1976), *The World's Greatest Lover* (1977), *Goin' South* (1978, again with Nicholson), *Going Ape!* (1981, an inept comedy starring "Taxi" costar Tony Danza), and *Terms of Endearment* (1983) before really tickling moviegoers with a scene-stealing supporting role in the Michael Douglas–Kathleen Turner romp, *Romancing the Stone* (1984). That same year, he made his directorial debut with the TV movie *The Ratings Game,* in which he also starred with his actress wife, Rhea Perlman. After finishing *Johnny Dangerously* (1984), he was reunited with Douglas and Turner for a *Stone* sequel, *Jewel of the Nile* (1985). DeVito brought his trademark lunacy to *Head Office* and *Ruthless People* (both 1986), then directed his first theatrical feature, *Throw Momma From the Train* (1987), in which he played the childish, murder-minded son of a domineering mother. It was an auspicious big-screen effort with a distinctive visual style. He played an amoral salesman in *Tin Men* (also 1987) and the libidinous brother of Arnold Schwarzenegger in *Twins* (1988) before wielding the megaphone again, this time on *The War of the Roses* (1989), a devilishly funny (and often tasteless) black comedy about a divorcing couple played by old friends Douglas and Turner.

On familiar histrionic turf as a ruthless Wall Street predator, DeVito starred in *Other People's Money* (1991) before appearing—in grotesque makeup—as the villainous Penguin in *Batman Returns* (1992). DeVito and Jack Nicholson teamed once again for *Hoffa* (also 1992), a lavish, fanciful biopic that generated more ink than coin. This time, the visual flamboyance that had served him well in *Throw Momma From the Train* and *The War of the Roses* seemed overbearing, particularly in light of an underwritten script. An avid laser-disc fan, DeVito prepared his own "special edition" of *Roses* and planned ahead of time for similar treatment of *Hoffa.* DeVito also starred in *Jack the Bear* (1993), *Junior* (reteamed with Arnold Schwarzenegger) and *Renaissance Man* (both 1994); in addition, through his production company, Jersey Films, DeVito executive-produced *Pulp Fiction* (1994) and coproduced *Reality Bites* (1994) and *Get Shorty* (1995, in which he also acted).

DEWHURST, COLLEEN. Actress. *(b. June 3, 1926, Montreal; d. Aug. 22, 1991.)* Legendary, husky-voiced actress, famous for her performances in Eugene O'Neill plays, whose strong presence graced far too few movies. She played supporting roles in *The Nun's Story* (1959), *A Fine Madness* (1966), *The Cowboys* (1972, as a madam), *McQ* (1974, as John Wayne's love interest), *Ice Castles* (1979), *The Dead Zone* (1983), and *The Boy Who Could Fly* (1986), and cut an imposing figure as Diane Keaton's ultra-WASP mother in *Annie Hall* (1977). Revered on Broadway, she achieved greater audience recognition toward the end of her career for her TV work, in the acclaimed miniseries "Anne of Green Gables" and its offshoots, and as Candice Bergen's tough-talking mother on the TV sitcom "Murphy Brown," which earned her two Emmy Awards. In 1991 she appeared onscreen with her son (by actor George C. Scott) Campbell Scott in *Dying Young.* The Canadian-made *Termini Station,* filmed in 1989, was released in the U.S.

after her death in 1991; so was *Bed and Breakfast* (1992), filmed in 1989.

DE WILDE, BRANDON. Actor. *(b. Apr. 9, 1942, Brooklyn, N.Y.; d. July 6, 1972.)* He was the homely, freckle-faced youngster who wailed, "Shane! Come back! Come back, Shane!" in the classic 1953 Western titled . . . *Shane.* His scenes opened and closed the movie, which would've made a spectacular screen debut (in fact, he was Oscar-nominated for it)—if he hadn't already amazed audiences the year before with his first movie performance in the Carson McCullers drama *The Member of the Wedding,* reprising a role he'd done on Broadway nearly 500 times! Born into a show-biz family, de Wilde starred in a 1953–54 TV series, "Jamie," and subsequently appeared in *Night Passage* (1957), *Blue Denim* (1959), *All Fall Down* (1962), *Hud* (1963), *In Harm's Way* (1965), *The Deserter* (1971), and *Black Jack* (1972), among others. He died after being critically injured in a car crash.

DE YOUNG, CLIFF. Actor. *(b. Feb. 12, 1945, Inglewood, Calif.)* This youthful leading man of TV first achieved recognition as a young father in the telefilms *Sunshine* (1973) and *Sunshine Christmas* (1977), and in the related 1975 sitcom. His work in features has been relatively minor, including a supporting role in the hip vampire tale *The Hunger* (1983) and leads in low-budget, video-oriented fare such as *Fear* (1988). Something about De Young's pleasant features suggests lack of character, and he is particularly suited to play treacherous yuppie careerists. He was an ambitious young sheriff in *Flashback* (1989), typical of his unsympathetic roles. De Young has been outstanding in the telefilm *The Lindbergh Kidnapping Case* (1976) and the miniseries "Robert Kennedy and His Times" (1985).

DIAMOND, I. A. L. Writer. *(b. June 27, 1920, Ungeny, Rumania; d. Apr. 21, 1988.)* Veteran skilled comedy writer who worked on numerous Hollywood films of the 1940s and 1950s—including *Two Guys From Milwaukee* (1946), *Texas* (1948), *Love Nest* (1951), *Monkey Busi-*

ness (1952), and *That Certain Feeling* (1956)—before being tapped by Billy Wilder to cowrite *Love in the Afternoon* (1957), launching a creative partnership that resulted in a series of movie classics. The pair collaborated on *Some Like It Hot* (1959), *The Apartment* (1960, for which they shared a Best Screenplay Oscar), *One, Two, Three* (1961), *Irma la Douce* (1963), *The Fortune Cookie* (1966, Oscar-nominated), and *The Private Life of Sherlock Holmes* (1970). Diamond soloed on *Cactus Flower* (1969). The *I* in his name stands for Isadore; he claimed to have added the *A* and *L* because "they look interesting after *I.*"

DICKINSON, ANGIE. Actress. *(b. Sept. 30, 1931, Kulm, N.D., as Angeline Brown.)* This ex-beauty queen was already a well-known (and middle-aged albeit glamorous) movie actress when she gained notoriety in 1974 for appearing nude in producer Roger Corman's exploitative *Big Bad Mama.* She also stirred up controversy six years later for her sexy scenes in Brian De Palma's *Dressed to Kill,* which were skillfully augmented with help from an obvious body double. This pretty, sharp-faced performer made her tyro screen appearance in a bit part in the musical *Lucky Me* (1954), and toiled in numerous low-budget genre films (including Sam Fuller's 1957 *China Gate)* before snagging the femme lead in Howard Hawks' *Rio Bravo* (1959), her first major movie. Plum roles in *Ocean's Eleven* (1960), *The Sins of Rachel Cade* (1961), and *Point Blank* (1967), among others, failed to secure stardom for Dickinson. She did, however, enjoy a long run on TV as an undercover cop in the series "Police Woman" (1974–78), and has maintained a high profile as star of numerous made-for-TV movies and miniseries, including 1993's notorious "Wild Palms." She is divorced from composer Burt Bacharach.
OTHER FILMS INCLUDE: 1964: *The Killers;* 1969: *Sam Whiskey;* 1971: *Pretty Maids All in a Row, The Resurrection of Zachary Wheeler;* 1981: *Death Hunt;* 1987: *Big Bad Mama II;* 1994: *Even Cowgirls Get the Blues.*

DIETERLE, WILLIAM. Director, actor. *(b. July 15, 1893, Rheinpfalz, Germany, as*

Wilhelm Dieterle; d. Dec. 9, 1972.) Dieterle appeared as an actor in many German silent classics—most notably Murnau's *Faust* (1926)—while directing and often playing the lead in a number of somber melodramas (he gave Marlene Dietrich her first lead role, opposite him, in 1923's *Der Mensch am Wave).* He went to Hollywood in 1930 and worked mainly for Warner Bros., where he turned out thrillers (including 1936's *Satan Met a Lady,* second of the studio's three versions of Dashiell Hammett's "The Maltese Falcon"), melodramas (1934's *Fog Over Frisco),* comedies (1933's *Grand Slam),* and many reverent and prestigious biopics, most notably *The Story of Louis Pasteur* (1936), *The White Angel* (also 1936, the Florence Nightingale story), and *The Life of Emile Zola* (1937, his only Oscar nomination). Dieterle also codirected the opulent *A Midsummer Night's Dream* (1935) with famed German impresario Max Reinhardt, for whom he had worked as an actor in the 1920s.

He was responsible for a good many meritorious films that have yet to receive the praise they're due, among them his poignant yet melodramatic "lost generation" saga *The Last Flight* (1931), the sparkling, Lubitsch-like romantic comedy *Jewel Robbery* (1932), his masterful production of *The Hunchback of Notre Dame* (1939), and especially the dazzling *All That Money Can Buy* (1941), based on Benet's "The Devil and Daniel Webster," in which he brought the stylistic flourishes of Murnau and strains of other 1920s German fantasies to bear on a quintessentially American story. Producer David O. Selznick was the first to recognize Dieterle's affinity for lush, romantic dramas, which was borne out by the success of *I'll Be Seeing You* (1944), *Love Letters* (1945), *Portrait of Jennie* (1948), and *September Affair* (1950).

Dieterle returned to Europe in the late 1950s and directed one film in Italy and two in Germany before retiring. Everyone who worked with Dieterle remembers his one absolute distinction among Hollywood directors: he always wore white gloves.

OTHER FILMS INCLUDE: 1932: *Man Wanted, Six Hours to Love* (a striking mixture of romance, melodrama, sci-fi, and fantasy, steeped in the European filmmaking tradition), *Lawyer Man;* 1933: *Female;* 1934:

Fashions of 1934, Madame du Barry; 1935: *Dr. Socrates;* 1939: *Juarez;* 1940: *Dr. Ehrlich's Magic Bullet;* 1942: *Tennessee Johnson;* 1944: *Kismet* (which reunited him with Dietrich); 1948: *The Accused;* 1950: *Dark City;* 1952: *The Turning Point;* 1953: *Salome;* 1954: *Elephant Walk;* 1957: *Omar Khayyam;* 1960: *Mistress of the World* (an anachronistic feature-film remake of a 1920 German serial); 1964: *Quick, Let's Get Married* (a dreadful cheapie that reunited him with Ray Milland and Ginger Rogers; also known as *Seven Different Ways).*

DIETRICH, MARLENE. Actress. *(b. Dec. 27, 1901, Berlin, as Maria Dietrich; d. May 6, 1992.)* She entranced moviegoers for more than three decades, and was every bit as enigmatic offscreen as the leggy femmes fatales she essayed on-screen. She had a carefully developed skill for anticipating how her every move would photograph, and she took great pains not only with her makeup and costuming, but also with her lighting and the staging of her scenes. Her numerous affairs with both men and women were ill-kept secrets, yet she managed to avoid scandal with more success than most, and was content to have her private persona shaped by her public one. A gifted child whose talent with the violin was rendered useless by a wrist injury, she studied acting with the distinguished stage impresario Max Reinhardt. In 1923 she landed her first screen role, as a maid, in *The Little Napoleon* (aka *Men Are Like This).* She next played the monocled mistress of Emil Jannings in *Tragedy of Love* (also 1923), striking a defiant note already. Over the next few years she worked in both plays and films; among the latter were *The Joyless Street, Manon Lescaut* (both 1926), *A Modern Du Barry, The Imaginary Baron* (both 1927), *Cafe Electric* and *I Kiss Your Hand, Madame* (both 1928), and *The Ship of Lost Souls* (1929). Then Jannings, who had returned to Germany from a sojourn in Hollywood, convinced director Josef von Sternberg (himself a Hollywood émigré) to make another film with him. The director saw Dietrich on-stage and was entranced; he subsequently cast her as Lola-Lola, the seductive singer who brings ruin to an aging teacher (Jannings) in *The Blue Angel* (1930)—which, filmed in both German- and English-language versions, was an international smash. Her husky-voiced rendition of the song "Falling in Love Again" became a Dietrich trademark.

When von Sternberg returned to Paramount later that year he brought Dietrich with him; they collaborated on six more films that virtually defined exotic romanticism on-screen: *Morocco* (1930) *Dishonored* (1931), *Shanghai Express, Blonde Venus* (both 1932), *The Scarlet Empress* (1934), and *The Devil Is a Woman* (1935). Mysterious and alluring, Dietrich mesmerized audiences even as she shocked them by wearing men's clothing, doing nude swimming scenes, performing in a gorilla suit (in the "Hot Voodoo" number in *Blonde Venus,* a Dietrich classic), and suggesting various and sundry sexual excesses. (During this time she also appeared in 1933's *Song of Songs,* directed by Rouben Mamoulian, which featured a rather detailed nude statue of the actress.) Eventually the von Sternberg–Dietrich relationship ran its course, both personally and professionally, but she continued to play exotic roles in *Desire, The Garden of Allah* (both 1936), *Angel,* and *Knight Without Armour* (both 1937), albeit to diminishing returns. She made a "comeback" of sorts in a comedic Western, *Destry Rides Again* (1939), in which, playing the saloon girl Frenchy, she successfully kidded her own image (and made a hit out of the song "See What the Boys in the Back Room Will Have").

Dietrich made several costume and action films over the next few years, occasionally opposite John Wayne, with whom she was once linked; among them were *Seven Sinners* (1940), *The Flame of New Orleans, Manpower* (both 1941), *The Spoilers, Pittsburgh* (both 1942, both costarring her with Wayne and Randolph Scott), and *Kismet* (1944, in the latter performing a seductive dance in harem garb and gold paint). When Hitler importuned her to come back to Germany and make pro-Nazi films, she not only refused but went back to Europe, entertaining American troops with the USO! Her postwar work was sporadic, but its high points included a gypsy in *Golden Earrings* (1947), an ex-Nazi entertainer in *A Foreign Affair* (1948), aging stars in *Stage Fright* (1950, in which she sang "La Vie en Rose") and *No Highway in the Sky* (1951), another saloon singer in *Rancho*

Notorious (1952, the performance later spoofed by Madeline Kahn in *Blazing Saddles),* the wife of a murder suspect in *Witness for the Prosecution* (1957), a gypsy fortune-teller in *Touch of Evil* (1958), and a German aristocrat in *Judgment at Nuremberg* (1961). During this time, conscious about her advancing age, Dietrich was more prominent as a cabaret entertainer, often performing songs in an unusual spoken/singing style. Her final film appearances were cameos in *Paris When It Sizzles* (1964) and *Just a Gigolo* (1979).

In 1984 her old friend Maximilian Schell made a superb documentary of her life, *Marlene;* she agreed to provide commentary but refused to appear on camera. She spent the last years of her life in Paris; when she died, her request to be buried in her native Germany was resisted by huffy bureaucrats who'd never forgiven her anti-Nazi stance, but they eventually relented. Even in death, Dietrich ruffled feathers as almost no other movie personality could. Almost immediately following her death several biographers prepared lengthy, revealing portraits of this fascinating woman; perhaps the definitive (and most shocking) was the one written by her daughter, Maria Riva. Her son, incidentally, is production designer J. Michael Riva.

DIFFRING, ANTON. Actor. *(b. Oct. 20, 1918, Koblenz, Germany; d. May 20, 1989.)* One of the screen's premier villains, this German-born actor's appearance—fair hair and complexion, cruel mouth, steely eyes—made him a perfect screen Nazi, and he was teutonically typed for many years. He studied at Berlin's Academy of Drama and made his way to Canada during World War 2, performing on stage for several years before making his first film, *State Secret,* in 1950. Although he'd proved himself a capable and earnest performer, Diffring's physiognomy and cool, clipped speech confined him to primarily unsympathetic roles.

OTHER FILMS INCLUDE: 1951: *Hotel Sahara;* 1954: *Betrayed;* 1955: *I Am a Camera;* 1959: *The Man Who Could Cheat Death* (a memorable lead role in a stylish horror film); 1960: *Circus of Horrors;* 1966: *The Blue Max, Fahrenheit 451;* 1969: *Where Eagles Dare;* 1971: *Zeppelin;* 1974: *The Beast Must*

Die; 1977: *Valentino;* 1978: *Hitler's Son;* 1981: *Victory;* 1985: *Marie Ward;* 1986: *Operation Dead End;* 1988: *Faceless.*

DILLMAN, BRADFORD. Actor. *(b. Apr. 14, 1930, San Francisco.)* This Yale-educated leading man debuted on Broadway in 1953, landed his first starring role on TV on "Kraft Television Theatre" in 1954, and made his movie bow four years later in *A Certain Smile.* A handsome, if somewhat colorless character player, Dillman startled moviegoers (and won a Cannes Film Festival acting award to boot) as one of the youthful killers in *Compulsion* (1959), based on the famous Leopold-Loeb murder case. Since then he has played other smiling, mild-mannered psychopaths, as well as white-collar crooks, weakling husbands, and even a leading man (mainly in low-budget genre films). A highpoint: his portrayal of Willie Oban in the 1973 filming of *The Iceman Cometh.*
OTHER FILMS INCLUDE: 1960: *Crack in the Mirror;* 1961: *Sanctuary;* 1966: *The Plainsman;* 1968: *Sergeant Ryker, Jigsaw;* 1970: *The Mephisto Waltz;* 1973: *The Way We Were;* 1974: *Chosen Survivors;* 1975: *Bug;* 1976: *Mastermind;* 1978: *Piranha, The Swarm;* 1979: *Love and Bullets;* 1983: *Sudden Impact;* 1987: *Hot Pursuit, Man Outside;* 1989: *Lords of the Deep.*

DILLON, MATT. Actor. *(b. Feb. 18, 1964, New Rochelle, N.Y.)* As the junkie-thief in *Drugstore Cowboy* (1989), Gus Van Sant's slice of contemporary (low) life, this square-jawed, fair-skinned, dark-browed young actor finally impressed critics. His nuanced performance came as a shock to those who had written him off from the beginning for his glowering, simian-like performances as tough teens in *Over the Edge* (1979, his debut), *Little Darlings,* and *My Bodyguard* (both 1980). As a teen heartthrob, Dillon perfectly portrayed alienated young men in Tim Hunter's *Tex* (1982) and two adaptations of S. E. Hinton novels for Francis Ford Coppola, *Rumble Fish* and *The Outsiders* (both 1983).
A light, witty role as the cabana boy with stars in his eyes in Garry Marshall's nostalgic *The Flamingo Kid* (1984) proved to be the turning point in Dillon's career,

though his films since then have not always lived up to expectations, as witness *Target* (1985) and *Native Son* (1986). He was excellent in the otherwise lackluster gambling drama *The Big Town* (1987) and in *Kansas* (1988); both films cast him in unsympathetic but well-rounded roles. The possibility of playing a bad guy was further exploited in *A Kiss Before Dying* (1991), in which he was an ambitious psychopath. Recent credits include *Singles* (1992), *Mr. Wonderful, The Saint of Fort Washington* (both 1993), and *Golden Gate* (1994). Younger brother Kevin Dillon has appeared in *Heaven Help Us* (1985), *Platoon* (1986), *The Blob* (1988), *Immediate Family* (1989), and *The Doors* (1991).

DILLON, MELINDA. Actress. *(b. Oct. 13, 1939, Hope, Ariz.)* Slender, soft-spoken blond character actress and occasional lead best seen in characterizations calling for sensitivity and emotional fragility. A successful stage actress who appeared in the original Broadway production of "Who's Afraid of Virginia Woolf?," Dillon broke into movies with a small role in *The April Fools* (1969). She's best remembered for her two Oscar-nominated performances, as the worried mother in *Close Encounters of the Third Kind* (1977) and the disturbed libel victim in *Absence of Malice* (1981). In a lighter vein, she contributed a delightfully dotty characterization of a Depression-era Midwest mom in *A Christmas Story* (1983).
OTHER FILMS INCLUDE: 1976: *Bound for Glory;* 1977: *Slap Shot;* 1978: *F.I.S.T.;* 1984: *Songwriter;* 1987: *Harry and the Hendersons;* 1989: *Spontaneous Combustion, Staying Together;* 1991: *The Prince of Tides;* 1992: *Captain America;* 1993: *Demolition Man.*

DINEHART, ALAN. Actor. *(b. Oct. 3, 1889, St. Paul; d. July 17, 1944.)* Veteran screen villain who was tall, dark, and jowly with narrow, slitted eyes and a cruel mouth. Dinehart made the portrayal of suave heavies a specialty, playing ruthless businessmen, corrupt politicos, and cold-blooded gangsters with equal relish. His characters often had designs on the leading ladies—who, rather foolishly, frequently looked up to him until the last reel, when his perfidy was invariably exposed.

OTHER FILMS INCLUDE: 1931: *The Brat;* 1932: *Street of Women* (an atypical sympathetic role), *Washington Merry-Go-Round* (first of his slimy powerbroker characterizations); 1934: *Jimmy the Gent, The Cat's Paw;* 1935: *Dante's Inferno, Thanks a Million;* 1936: *Charlie Chan at the Race Track;* 1937: *Ali Baba Goes to Town;* 1938: *Rebecca of Sunnybrook Farm;* 1939: *Second Fiddle;* 1940: *Slightly Honorable* (outstanding as a dimwitted, crooked district attorney); 1942: *Girl Trouble;* 1944: *The Whistler, Oh, What a Night.*

DISNEY, WALT. Producer. *(b. Dec. 5, 1901, Chicago; d. Dec. 15, 1966.)* The most successful and influential producer in the history of moviemaking, Walt Disney started as a cartoonist, became an animator, virtually reinvented the medium of animated cartoons, moved on to live-action fantasy, and then found other worlds to conquer. The company that bears his name still trades on the goodwill he developed during his lifetime.

In his early teens he studied at the Kansas City Art Institute, which enabled him to find work as a commercial artist later on. In the early 1920s he and a young friend, Ub Iwerks, had their first brush with animation at the Kansas City Film Ad Company, where they worked on commercials for local merchants which appeared in the city's theaters. Disney decided to strike out on his own, with Iwerks at his side. Their "Newman's Laugh-O-Grams" cartoons appeared onscreen at the Newman's Theatre; a subsequent series of ambitious fairy-tale parodies marked their first attempt to make full-fledged films on their own. But Disney spent more on the films than he made, and quickly went broke.

In 1923 he set out for Hollywood, retrenched, with the help of his brother Roy (his lifelong business partner), and sent for Iwerks and other Kansas City colleagues to make a new series of "Alice" films with a live-action girl cavorting in a cartoon world. (It was a switch on Max Fleischer's successful "Out of the Inkwell" series, which had a cartoon Koko in a live-action setting.) The series was modestly successful, enough so to launch Disney's career and enable him and Roy to settle comfortably in Los Angeles.

Their subsequent series, "Oswald the Lucky Rabbit," was launched in 1927, and saw the studio's animation growing more fluid and imaginative. But when Disney's distributor snatched Oswald—and most of his staff—from under his nose during a bitter contract negotiation, Disney had to start from scratch. It was then that Mickey Mouse was born, sketched by Ub Iwerks and patterned closely after the rubbery-limbed Oswald. Disney determined to retain control of the films—and the character—himself, so he made his first two Mickey Mouse cartoons "on spec," before realizing that adding sound would give him a leg up on his competition. The third Mickey short, *Steamboat Willie* (1928), was made with a synchronized soundtrack, and when Disney managed to get it into theaters, it was a sensation. He and his mouse were "overnight" successes.

Within a few short years Mickey Mouse was one of the biggest stars in movies and Walt Disney was being hailed as a genius. He launched the "Silly Symphonies" series, and developed supporting characters like Pluto, Goofy, and eventually Donald Duck in the ongoing Mickey cartoons. He experimented with color in the 1932 *Flowers and Trees,* and as he had with sound, forced his competitors to follow suit. (In return for trying out the new three-strip Technicolor, however, he won exclusive use of its brilliant color system for three years.)

Disney was always trying to push animation forward; he had his staff take art classes to improve their drawing, and eventually established a school on the studio premises. By the mid 1930s he was talking seriously about making a feature-length cartoon. This was considered madness; no one, he was told, would sit through such a film, and what's more, it would hurt people's eyes. But Disney worked toward that goal, increasing his staff and improving their skills to get them ready for the challenge. When *Snow White and the Seven Dwarfs* (1937) opened, Disney had the last laugh. It was a milestone, both artistically and financially. It also solidified the importance of music in Disney's work, producing a handful of songs that led the hit parade and went on to become standards.

Rather than repeat himself, which would have been the conventional wisdom after such a success, Disney followed other paths. *Pinocchio* (1940) was another sensation, more sophisticated than *Snow White* in its techniques and in its storytelling. But *Fantasia* (also 1940) was even more daring, a bold experiment combining music and art that many consider the pinnacle of Disney's career. It was destined never to be a commercial success, but in fact it nearly bankrupted the visionary producer. With the coming of World War 2, and his heavy involvement in training and morale-building films, it took many years for Disney to get back on his feet, financially. A bitter 1941 strike disrupted his staff, and left him further embittered about his dreams for a bright new future in animation.

But Disney had an uncanny way of rebounding from every setback. *Dumbo* (1941) and *Bambi* (1942) showed the studio in full command of its powers, while *The Reluctant Dragon* (1941) offered moviegoers a look behind the scenes at Disney's. The wartime *Victory Through Air Power* (1943) explored the dramatic power of animation for propagandistic purposes, as did such popular wartime shorts as *Der Fuehrer's Face* (1942). A government-sponsored tour of South America, promoting our wartime "Good Neighbor Policy," led to the delightful features *Saludos Amigos* (1943) and *The Three Caballeros* (1945).

Those South American films also experimented with the blending of live-action and animation, several leaps beyond what Disney had done with his "Alice" series of the 1920s. The process was further refined in *Song of the South* (1946), in which the interaction between live and animated characters was positively astounding. From here it was only a short step to branching out into full-time production of live-action movies, which Disney did in earnest in the 1950s. A chance meeting with nature photographers Alfred and Elma Milotte led to his bankrolling a series of "true-life" films which wound up winning multiple Academy Awards—for a series of short subjects and the feature films *The Living Desert* (1953) and *The Vanishing Prairie* (1954). Heading off in another unexpected direction, he took advantage of frozen funds in England to make colorful period adventures and swashbucklers like *Treasure Island* (1950), *The Story of Robin Hood* (1952), and *The Sword and the Rose* (1953) there,

before embarking on his most expensive home-grown project, *20,000 Leagues Under the Sea* (1954).

Moving into TV production, and consumed by the opening of his amusement park Disneyland, Disney let his live-action slate languish in the mid-1950s. The surprise success of a simple slapstick comedy with fantasy overtones, *The Shaggy Dog* (1959), led him into a new and highly profitable arena, followed in earnest by *The Absent Minded Professor* (1961) and then bled dry in a series of increasingly formulaic feature comedies in the 1960s and 1970s. The box-office success of *Pollyanna* (1960) showed that Disney also had a corner on Americana in Hollywood, and this too became a studio stock in trade. (It also marked him as a star-maker, for bringing Hayley Mills to Hollywood.)

Disney had never abandoned animation during this time. There was always an animated feature in the works, each one taking several years to complete, and drawing on the talents of the same solid staff that had been with him since *Snow White*. (A regular slate of cartoon shorts continued along, as well.) *Cinderella* (1950), *Alice in Wonderland* (1951), *Lady and the Tramp* (1955), the groundbreakingly expensive *Sleeping Beauty* (1959), *One Hundred and One Dalmatians* (1961), and *The Sword in the Stone* (1963) all bore the unmistakable Disney stamp.

But in 1964 Disney produced a film that topped everything he'd done before. The magical *Mary Poppins* drew on every Disney resource to create a masterpiece of fantasy, storytelling, music, and animation. It marked the culmination of his career.

A lifelong smoker, Disney succumbed to lung cancer in December 1966. He had been working on a live-action musical, *The Happiest Millionaire,* and an animated feature, *The Jungle Book,* at the time of his death; both were released posthumously in 1967. His studio continued to function on sheer inertia for a number of years, but everyone knew that the magic ingredient was missing. Walt Disney was irreplaceable.

DIVINE. Actor. *(b. Oct. 19, 1945, Baltimore as Harris Glenn Milstead; d. Mar. 7, 1988.)* Cinema's most famous 300-pound female impersonator, Divine achieved cult notoriety in a series of films directed by friend and Baltimore native John Waters. They met in high school, drawn together by their similar taste for the bizarre and tacky, and Waters began casting him in his early movies like *Roman Candles* (1966), *Eat Your Makeup* (1968, as Jackie Kennedy), *Mondo Trasho* (1970), and *Multiple Maniacs* (1971). *Pink Flamingos* (1972) was probably their most infamous achievement, and a scene in which Divine eats dog feces became a turning point in their careers, not to mention in cult movies. Divine followed in Waters' *Female Trouble* (1974) and began to achieve wider success in more accessible movies like the "Odorama" sensation *Polyester* (1981, with Tab Hunter), *Lust in the Dust* (1985, directed by Paul Bartel), and his and Waters' biggest success, *Hairspray* (1988), a funny, campy tribute to the early 1960s which opened a week and a half before his death. Divine had two convincing male roles in Alan Rudolph's *Trouble in Mind* (1985, as crime kingpin Hilly Blue) and *Out of the Dark* (1988). He also performed onstage in the plays "Women Behind Bars" and "The Neon Woman" and recorded many disco songs that were international successes.

DIX, RICHARD. Actor. *(b. July 18, 1894, St. Paul, Minn., as Ernest Carlton Brimmer; d. Sept. 20, 1949.)* To many film buffs, the image of this steely-eyed, square-jawed, solidly built leading man conjures up memories of heroes such as Yancey Cravat, the indomitable frontiersman of the Oscar-winning *Cimarron* (1931, for which he was nominated as well). But Dix first made his mark as one of the screen's most personable light comedians in such silent films as *The Lucky Devil, Womanhandled, Too Many Kisses* (all 1925), *The Quarterback* (1926), *The Gay Defender* (1927), and *Easy Come, Easy Go* (1928).

A former medical student who abandoned his studies to act in stock just before serving in World War 1, Dix first appeared on Broadway in 1919 and made his movie debut in that year's *One of the Finest.* He initially made his mark as a leading man in features for Goldwyn, including *Not Guilty* (1921, playing twins), *The Glorious Fool* (1922), and *Souls for Sale* (1923). His early successes at Paramount included Cecil B. DeMille's *The Ten Commandments* (1923, in the "modern" portion of the story) and *The Vanishing American* (1925, a spectacular Zane Grey Western that cast him as a noble Indian warrior). Although Dix frequently clashed with studio management, Paramount regarded him highly: by 1928 he was making $4,500 a week.

Lured to the newly formed RKO in 1929, Dix first starred in George M. Cohan's venerable comedy-thriller, *Seven Keys to Baldpate* (1929), and followed it up with several breezy comedies. After his success as an action star in the sprawling *Cimarron*, he more frequently played virile, two-fisted characters, in films like *Hell's Highway, The Lost Squadron, The Conquerors* (all 1932), and *Ace of Aces* (1933). But the quality of his vehicles started to slip after just a few years, and by the end of the decade he was making B pictures. He played Sam Houston in Republic's first A movie, *Man of Conquest* (1939), then starred in a series of B+ Westerns for producer Harry Sherman, including *Cherokee Strip* (1940), *Tombstone—The Town Too Tough to Die, American Empire* (both 1942), and *The Kansan* (1943).

After returning briefly to RKO for the Val Lewton–produced chiller *The Ghost Ship* (1943)—in which, as the quietly insane sea captain, Dix delivered one of his best 1940s performances—he inked a deal with Columbia to star in a series based on the popular radio show "The Whistler." These modestly budgeted thrillers, each of which starred Dix in different roles, not all of them sympathetic, kept him busy from 1944 to 1947; after completing his seventh series stanza, *The 13th Hour,* Dix retired from the screen. He died of a heart attack two years later.

OTHER FILMS INCLUDE: 1923: *The Christian, To the Last Man;* 1929: *Redskin;* 1931: *The Public Defender;* 1934: *Stingaree;* 1935: *Transatlantic Tunnel;* 1936: *Yellow Dust;* 1937: *It Happened in Hollywood;* 1938: *Blind Alibi.*

DMYTRYK, EDWARD. Director. *(b. Dec. 4, 1908, British Columbia.)* Although Dmytryk's career as a filmmaker spanned four decades, he is perhaps best remembered as a victim of the House Un-American Activities Committee (HUAC) witchhunts of the 1950s. Born to Ukrainian immigrants, Dmytryk was raised in

Los Angeles, where he worked a series of studio odd jobs as a teenager. He became a cutter at Paramount, directing one independently made B Western, *Trail of the Hawk* (1935), before being called in at the eleventh hour to salvage the Betty Grable vehicle *Million Dollar Legs* (1939), for which he remained uncredited. His rescue work didn't escape notice, though, and soon he signed to direct at Columbia, where he initially toiled on unrewarding B pictures such as *The Confessions of Boston Blackie* and *Secrets of the Lone Wolf* (both 1941). In 1942 he went to RKO, where the success of his low-budget, high-quality programmer *Hitler's Children* (1943) won him more prestigious projects. Dmytryk soon found his artistic niche, directing a string of popular favorites: *Murder, My Sweet* (1944, one of the best Philip Marlowe mysteries), *Back to Bataan, Cornered* (both 1945), *Till the End of Time* (1946), and *Crossfire* (1947), one of the first Hollywood pictures to decry anti-Semitism, for which he earned an Oscar nomination as Best Director. Unfortunately, that same year would prove a disastrous one for Dmytryk. His "foreign"-sounding name, Ukrainian roots, and left-liberal views were enough to attract suspicion in an age of unparalleled political paranoia, and he was called to testify before HUAC regarding possible involvement with the Communist party. Dmytryk refused to answer the committee, and became a member of the blacklisted "Hollywood Ten."

Fired by RKO, Dmytryk went into self-exile in England, where he directed several minor pictures. When he returned to the U.S. to renew his passport, he was arrested and spent six months in jail. Upon his release, Dmytryk recanted his previous uncooperative stance and, in the best Stalinist tradition, agreed to name names. This released him from the blacklist, and he returned to filmmaking. In 1979 Dmytryk wrote an autobiography, "It's a Hell of a Life but Not a Bad Living," and has since authored several books on filmmaking, including "On Directing" and "Cinema: Concept and Practice." He also taught for a number of years at the University of Southern California and the University of Texas at Austin. He is married to former actress Jean Porter, who appeared in *Till the End of Time*.

OTHER FILMS INCLUDE: 1953: *The Juggler;* 1954: *The Caine Mutiny;* 1955: *The Left Hand of God;* 1957: *Raintree County;* 1958: *The Young Lions;* 1959: *The Blue Angel;* 1962: *Walk on the Wild Side;* 1964: *The Carpetbaggers;* 1966: *Alvarez Kelly;* 1972: *Bluebeard;* 1975: *The Human Factor;* 1976: *He Is My Brother.*

DONAHUE, TROY. Actor. (b. Jan. 27, 1937, New York City, as Merle Johnson, Jr.) This tall, blond, baby-faced pin-up king, who sent hearts aflutter as Sandra Dee's young lover in 1959's *A Summer Place,* studied journalism at Columbia University before trying his hand at acting. Shortly after breaking into summer stock, Donahue appeared in *Man Afraid* (1957), which launched his film career. He signed with Warner Bros. in 1959 and was a teen heartthrob for several years in the likes of *Parrish* (1961), *Rome Adventure* (1962), and *My Blood Runs Cold* (1964). Moving over to TV, he enjoyed some success on "Surfside 6" (1960–62) and "Hawaiian Eye" (1962–63). After being dropped by Warners in 1966 his career floundered. In 1974 he appeared in a bit part in *The Godfather, Part II,* as a playboy named, appropriately enough, Merle Johnson. He kept a low profile after that, and was reportedly homeless and living in New York's Central Park during the early 1980s. (Although he can be spotted in a supporting role in 1984's *Grandview, U.S.A.,* indicating a fairly rapid change in fortune.) By the latter half of the decade he was appearing in self-explanatory cheapies like *Assault of the Party Nerds* (1989). Director John Waters, a big fan, cast Donahue in *Cry-Baby* (1990), and the former teen idol seems to be making a living in low-budget, direct-to-video epics.

DONAT, ROBERT. Actor. (b. Mar. 18, 1905, Manchester, England; d. June 9, 1958.) One of the finest actors ever to appear on screen, Robert Donat owed much of his success to his fine speaking voice, which he trained from childhood (initially to overcome a stutter). After spending several years in local theater, playing the classics, Donat made his London stage debut in 1930 and started acting in films two years later (in 1932's *Men of Tomorrow*). His accomplished performance as the juvenile lead of *The Private Life of Henry*

VIII (1933) established Donat as a comer, and Hollywood drafted him for the title role in *The Count of Monte Cristo* (1934), a lavish if stately adaptation of the classic adventure novel. Donat didn't take to Tinseltown, however, and returned to England (despite Warner Bros.' desire for him to star as *Captain Blood*).

Over the next several years he starred in a number of high-profile films, including Hitchcock's *The 39 Steps* (1935, in a delicious performance opposite Madeleine Carroll), Rene Clair's *The Ghost Goes West* (1936), *Knight Without Armour* (1937, opposite Marlene Dietrich), and King Vidor's *The Citadel* (1938, Oscar-nominated as an idealistic young doctor), but it was the movie adaptation of James Hilton's *Goodbye, Mr. Chips* (1939) that gave the actor his bid for screen immortality. His warmhearted performance, as a dedicated teacher who devotes his life to his students, won him an Academy Award, but the actor's persistent self-doubts (as well as a debilitating asthma condition) kept him from pursuing a more active screen career.

He directed and produced one film, *The Cure for Love,* in 1949. In 1953 he married actress Renee Asherson.
OTHER FILMS INCLUDE: 1942: *The Young Mr. Pitt* (as William Pitt); 1943: *Adventures of Tartu;* 1945: *Vacation From Marriage;* 1947: *Captain Boycott* (a cameo as Charles Parnell); 1948: *The Winslow Boy;* 1951: *The Magic Box* (in which he played motion-picture pioneer William Friese-Greene); 1954: *Lease of Life;* 1958: *The Inn of the Sixth Happiness* (his last).

DONEN, STANLEY. Producer, director. *(b. Apr. 13, 1924, Columbia, S.C.)* With the possible exception of Vincente Minnelli, no other director has made as many classic musicals. A former choreographer, he met Gene Kelly on Broadway and eventually followed him to Hollywood, where they codirected three masterpieces at MGM: *On the Town* (1949), its semi-sequel *It's Always Fair Weather* (1955), and what may be the most popular of all movie musicals, *Singin' in the Rain* (1952). On his own, he did such other memorable tuners as *Take Me Out to the Ball Game* (1949), *Royal Wedding* (1951), *Give a Girl a Break* (1953), *Seven Brides for Seven Brothers* (1954), and *Funny*

Face (1957). He also coproduced and codirected two classic Warner musicals with George Abbott: *The Pajama Game* (1957) and *Damn Yankees* (1958). All of these are marked by infectious high spirits, innovative choreography (e.g., Fred Astaire's dance on the ceiling in *Royal Wedding,* Kelly dancing on roller skates in *Fair Weather*), and a thorough command of the medium (he was the first musical director to effectively exploit Cinema-Scope).

When studio musicals went out of fashion, Donen turned to sophisticated romantic comedy, producing and directing such charmers as *Indiscreet* (1958), *The Grass Is Greener, Surprise Package* (both 1960), and the definitive Hitchcock pastiche, *Charade* (1963). He found it increasingly difficult to find material worthy of his taste and stylishness, and experienced ups and downs with his later output, including the cult Faust spoof *Bedazzled,* a perceptive romantic drama, *Two for the Road* (both 1967), a homosexual comedy, *Staircase* (1969), Lerner and Loewe's last musical, *The Little Prince* (1974), a bloated Roaring 20s action-comedy, *Lucky Lady* (1975), a clever parody of 1930s Warner Bros. films, *Movie Movie* (1978), and even an outer space thriller, *Saturn 3* (1980). Donen's last film to date is the sex farce *Blame It On Rio* (1984), but his is a talent too lively and distinctive to remain idle for long. In 1993 he made his Broadway directing debut with the short-lived "The Red Shoes."

DONLEVY, BRIAN. Actor. *(b. Feb. 9, 1899, Portadown, Ireland; d. Apr. 5, 1972.)* He was an unlikely leading man. Short (he wore platform shoes), stocky (he wore a girdle), with wavy brown hair (he wore a toupee), flashing smile (he wore false teeth), and piercing blue eyes (*those* were real), Donlevy had already carved a niche for himself as one of Hollywood's most dependable heavies when he was assigned to star as the corrupt politician in Preston Sturges' directorial debut, *The Great McGinty* (1940). That movie's surprise success boosted both its director and him into the upper brackets.

The Irish-born Donlevy was apparently every bit as tough as he looked. In America from childhood, he lied about his age to join the U.S. Army's 1916 pursuit of Mexican revolutionary Pancho Villa, then joined the Lafayette Escadrille as a pilot during World War 1. He took up acting in the early 1920s, appeared on Broadway in small roles, and played bits in a few New York–made silent films, including *Monsieur Beaucaire* (1924), *School for Wives* (1925), and *Mother's Boy* (1928). Donlevy eventually won larger roles on stage, and came to Hollywood in 1935 to play the first of many gangster roles in *Another Face.* He appeared in such films as *Barbary Coast* (1935),•*Strike Me Pink, Thirteen Hours by Air* (1936), and *Crack-Up* (1937) before getting his first sympathetic lead in 1937's *Born Reckless.*

Donlevy made a memorably sadistic Sergeant Markoff in the 1939 version of P. C. Wren's Foreign Legion adventure, *Beau Geste,* and successfully plied his villainous trade in *Jesse James, Union Pacific,* and *Destry Rides Again* (all 1939) before assuming the role of crooked politico McGinty (which he reprised in Sturges' 1944 comedy hit *The Miracle of Morgan's Creek*). Donlevy worked steadily throughout the 1940s on both sides of the law, in *Brigham Young—Frontiersman* (1940), *I Wanted Wings, Billy the Kid* (both 1941), *The Remarkable Andrew* (physically miscast but delightful nonetheless as the ghost of Andrew Jackson), *The Glass Key* (as a memorably shady politician), *Wake Island* (all 1942), *Hangmen Also Die* (1943), *An American Romance* (1944), *The Virginian, Canyon Passage, Two Years Before the Mast* (all 1946), *The Beginning or the End, Kiss of Death, Killer McCoy* (all 1947), *A Southern Yankee, Command Decision* (both 1948), *The Lucky Stiff,* and *Impact* (both 1949).

His screen output dwindled in the 1950s, partially due to TV work (including a lead in the 1951–52 series, "Dangerous Assignment," and a whole slew of anthology-show appearances) and partially due to his heavy drinking. He seemed to age about 20 years during that decade, as was evident in *Hoodlum Empire* (1951), *Ride the Man Down* (1952), *The Big Combo* (1955, as a memorable mob boss with a hearing-aid), *The Creeping Unknown* (a 1956 British sci-fi opus, aka *The Quatermass Experiment,* that gave him his last significant starring role), *Enemy From Space* (1957, a *Quatermass* sequel), *Escape From Red Rock* (1958), *Juke Box Rhythm,* and *Never So Few* (both 1959). He worked during the 1960s in undistin-guished drive-in fodder such as *Girl in Room 13* (1961), *The Curse of the Fly* (1965), *Gammera, The Invincible, How to Stuff a Wild Bikini* (both 1965), *Waco* (1966), *Hostile Guns* (1967), and *Pit Stop* (1969).

DONNER, RICHARD. Director, producer. *(b. Apr. 24, 1930, New York City.)* A competent mainstream director with an uncanny middlebrow empathy and little by way of personal signature, Donner in all likelihood would have been a favorite of moguls in the studio era. In today's Hollywood, he functions almost as a one-man studio of his own, initiating, producing, and directing highly commercial projects. Originally an actor, he broke into directing via television, helming episodes of "The Twilight Zone" and "The Fugitive." His first feature was the quasi sci-fi thriller *X-15* (1961); his second, the post–Rat Pack "comedy" *Salt and Pepper* (1968), which starred Sammy Davis, Jr. and Peter Lawford. He achieved his first major commercial success with the 1976 Satanic thriller, *The Omen,* and cemented his reputation with *Superman* (1978).

Most of Donner's subsequent films have been action-based and/or fantasy-tinged; a rare exception was the low-key *Inside Moves* (1980), an interesting little drama about handicapped misfits. Its indifferent reception sent Donner scurrying back to the safe haven of common-denominator star vehicles. He hit paydirt with *Lethal Weapon* (1987), the megahit cop thriller starring Mel Gibson and Danny Glover, and has since produced and directed two equally successful sequels (1989 and 1992); a third one is promised. He also executive produced *The Final Conflict* (1981), *The Lost Boys* (1987), and *Free Willy* (1993). He took over the reins of the abused-child drama *Radio Flyer* (1992) after his wife, producer Lauren Shuler-Donner, fired its first-time director, but the ambitious production failed just the same. He was also the model for Gene Hackman's portrayal of a director in *Postcards From the Edge,* according to the actor, who worked for him in *Superman.*
OTHER FILMS INCLUDE: 1982: *The Toy;* 1985: *Ladyhawke, The Goonies;* 1988: *Scrooged;* 1994: *Maverick.*

D'ONOFRIO, VINCENT. Actor. *(b. June 30, 1959, Brooklyn, N.Y.)* This young actor pulled a De Niro to perform the role of a boot-camp underachiever turned full-blown psycho in Kubrick's Vietnam movie *Full Metal Jacket* (1987), adding many pounds to his normally slender frame. Because he was a complete unknown at the time, audiences couldn't appreciate the extent of his physical transformation but were impressed by his uncanny, terrifying performance. Since returning to his normal dimensions, D'Onofrio hasn't snagged a role as memorable, but has, been reasonably good in *Adventures in Babysitting* (1987), *Mystic Pizza* (1988), and *Dying Young* (1991). In 1991 he played an Argentinian pimp with peculiar ideas about propriety in Leonard Schrader's peculiar *Naked Tango.* Recent credits include *Fires Within* (1991, with his then-wife Greta Scacchi), *The Player* (1992), *Household Saints* (1993), *Being Human,* and *Ed Wood* (both 1994).

DONOHOE, AMANDA. Actress. *(b. June 29, 1962, London.)* Silky-seductive, coolly attractive British actress who often plays sexually provocative characters. She's best known to big-screen audiences as a delightfully campy snake goddess in Ken Russell's *The Lair of the White Worm* (1988), and as Sammi Davis' lesbian lover in *The Rainbow* (1989), another Russell-directed opus. Donohoe first impressed moviegoers as the free-spirited sensualist in Nicolas Roeg's *Castaway* (1986), an awful film but a stunning showcase for her. She joined the cast of TV's "L.A. Law," again cast as a lesbian, in 1990, and stayed for two seasons.
OTHER FILMS INCLUDE: 1988: *Foreign Body;* 1989: *Diamond Skulls, Tank Malling, Dark Obsession* (released in U.S. in 1991); 1990: *Paper Mask.*

DOOLEY, PAUL. Actor, writer. *(b. Feb. 22, 1928, Parkersburg, W.Va.)* Droopy-faced character actor, who began his career with the Second City comedy troupe and cocreated the acclaimed children's TV series "The Electric Company." Dooley has appeared in many films by director Robert Altman, starting with *A Wedding* (1978), and including *A Perfect Couple* (1979), *Popeye* (1980, as Wimpy), and *O.C. &*

Stiggs (1987), but he's probably best remembered for his portrayals of comically beleaguered fathers in *Breaking Away* (1979, to Dennis Christopher) and *Sixteen Candles* (1983, to Molly Ringwald). He's also done many radio and TV commercials and series appearances, plying his trade with distinctive, rubber-faced aplomb. In 1988 he costarred with Phyllis Newman in the short-lived series "Coming of Age." Recent credits include *Cooperstown* (telefilm), *My Boyfriend's Back,* and *A Dangerous Woman* (all 1993).

DORS, DIANA. Actress. *(b. Oct. 23, 1931, Swindon, England, as Diana Fluck; d. May 4, 1984.)* The quintessential 1950s blonde bombshell, English style. In her own words: "The only sex symbol England produced since Lady Godiva." First displaying her charms to moviegoers in *The Shop at Sly Corner* (1946), Dors worked tirelessly throughout the 1950s, mostly in potboilers but in one excellent, noirish thriller: *Yield to the Night* (1956), which won the buxom blonde rave reviews for her turn as a convicted murderess reflecting on her crime. She continued working long after her sex-symbol appeal waned, in such films as *Deep End* (1970) and the campy horror comedy *Theatre of Blood* (1973). Growing increasingly obese as she got older, she soon provided a Brit correlative to Shelley Winters. In later years she appeared in several rock videos for glamour-worshipping singer Adam Ant; her last film appearance was in Joseph Losey's *Steaming* (1985), which was also that director's final film. She published two autobiographical books, "For Adults Only" (1978) and "Behind Closed Doors" (1979).

DOUGLAS, KIRK. Actor, producer, director. *(b. Dec. 9, 1916, Amsterdam, N.Y., as Issur Danielovitch.)* His ready grin, granite-chisled features, cleft chin, and an approach to acting that made him equally convincing in both sympathetic and unsympathetic roles made Kirk Douglas one of the brightest stars of post-WW 2 Hollywood (and, later, the international arena as well). Born into immigrant poverty, he saw an acting scholarship as his ticket out of the ghetto. He secured small roles on Broadway before entering the Navy in

World War 2, and afterward resumed his stage career. His old classmate Lauren Bacall suggested that producer Hal Wallis test him, resulting in his being cast in the lead role in *The Strange Love of Martha Ivers* (1946). Douglas won excellent reviews, which encouraged him to remain in Hollywood, and in 1947 he made the classic noir *Out of the Past,* the film adaptation of Eugene O'Neill's *Mourning Becomes Electra* (as Peter), and the undernourished drama *I Walk Alone* (the first of several films with close friend Burt Lancaster). Douglas also had a key role in the multi-Oscared *A Letter to Three Wives* (1949), then scored a knockout as the venal boxer Midge Kelly in that year's *Champion,* a classic prizefighting drama that cemented his stardom and earned him his first Oscar nomination as Best Actor.

Now acknowledged to be a top leading man, Douglas played a thinly disguised Bix Beiderbecke in *Young Man With a Horn,* the "gentleman caller" in Tennessee Williams' *The Glass Menagerie* (both 1950), a heartlessly ambitious reporter in *Ace in the Hole* (aka *The Big Carnival*), a two-fisted cop in *Detective Story* (both 1951), a frontiersman in *The Big Sky,* a ruthless movie producer in *The Bad and the Beautiful* (both 1952, the latter Oscar-nominated), an intrepid seaman in *20,000 Leagues Under the Sea* (1954, in which he sang "A Whale of a Tale"), the title role in *Ulysses* (1955), a sharp-tongued cowpoke in *Man Without a Star* (1955), artist Vincent van Gogh in *Lust for Life* (1956, again, Oscar-nominated), gambler/gunfighter Doc Holliday in *Gunfight at the O.K. Corral,* and a war-sickened colonel in *Paths of Glory* (both 1957). Douglas infused every role with passion, and his performances were often multilayered ones; he could bring sinister traits to sympathetic characters, and vice versa. Something in his eyes, in his voice, behind that toothy grin, suggested lurking menace in some characters and suppressed mirth in others. But in all cases he kept audiences glued to their seats. He formed his own production company, Bryna, in 1958; its initial venture was a big-scale adventure film, *The Vikings* (1958), followed by *The Devil's Disciple* (1959), which was a coproduction with Lancaster's company, and the sexy melodrama *Strangers When We Meet* (1960). That same year also saw the release of Douglas' most ambitious film, the epic drama of Roman Empire days, *Spartacus;* as its producer, he broke a long-standing Hollywood blacklist by insisting that scripter Dalton Trumbo (a member of the "Hollywood Ten") get proper screen credit for his contribution.

Douglas remained busy throughout the 1960s and 1970s, with a decided emphasis on Westerns and war films; among the more notable were *Town Without Pity, The Last Sunset* (both 1961), the cult "modern" Western *Lonely Are the Brave, Two Weeks in Another Town* (both 1962, the latter a semi-sequel to *The Bad and the Beautiful*), *The List of Adrian Messenger* (1963), *Seven Days in May* (1964), *In Harm's Way* (1965), *Cast a Giant Shadow* (1966), *The War Wagon* (1967), *The Brotherhood* (1968), *The Arrangement* (1969), *There Was a Crooked Man . . .* (1970), *A Gunfight* (1971), and two that he directed: *Scalawag* (1973) and *Posse* (1975). Thereafter he concentrated on character roles in such varied fare as *Once Is Not Enough* (also 1975), *The Fury* (1978), *Home Movies* (a hilarious turn as an egocentric star), *The Villain* (bravely mocking movie-Western villainy in a ham-fisted, cartoonish parody, both 1979), *The Final Countdown* (1980), *The Man From Snowy River* (1982, in a dual role for this Down-Under "Western"), and *Tough Guys* (1986, his last film with Lancaster). And though he abandoned the first Rambo film, *First Blood,* early in its production, he eventually worked with star Sylvester Stallone in *Oscar* (1991). More recently he was cast as Michael J. Fox's crafty uncle in *Greedy* (1994).

His autobiography, "The Ragman's Son" (1988), was a best-seller, and in recent years he has expanded his literary career to writing novels as well, most notably "The Gift." Though he has never won an Oscar, Douglas did receive the American Film Institute's Life Achievement Award in 1991. His four sons all followed him into show business: actor Eric, producers Joel and Peter, and actor/producer Michael. Incidentally, it was Michael who pulled off Kirk's greatest dream: making Ken Kesey's novel *One Flew Over the Cuckoo's Nest* into a film. Kirk had played the lead role on stage and hoped to reprise it on screen, but in the years it took to launch the project he outgrew the role and surrendered it to Jack Nicholson.

DOUGLAS, MELVYN. Actor. *(b. Apr. 5, 1901, Macon Ga., as Melvyn Edouard Hesselberg; d. Aug. 4, 1981.)* He was the guy who made Garbo laugh in *Ninotchka* (1939), but that was only one of the many achievements of this charming, debonair leading man. In his youth one of Hollywood's most accomplished farceurs, in old age one of its finest character actors, Douglas deserves to have his film work more widely celebrated. He took up acting after serving in World War 1, touring in various stock companies before reaching Broadway in 1928. His delightful turn in the play "Tonight or Never" won Douglas an opportunity in Hollywood, reprising the role in a 1931 movie adaptation starring Gloria Swanson.

Initially, Douglas essayed conventional roles, many of them secondary leads. He was insouciant in *The Old Dark House* (1932), intrepid in *The Vampire Bat,* and dour in *Counsellor-at-Law* (both 1933). It wasn't until 1935 and *She Married Her Boss* that the essential Douglas crystallized: dapper, sophisticated, with a wry sense of humor and a flippant manner of dialogue delivery (which included cracking his voice for comic punctuation). In *The Lone Wolf Returns* (1935), *And So They Were Married, Theodora Goes Wild* (both 1936), *Angel, I Met Him in Paris,* and *I'll Take Romance* (all 1937), among others, Douglas established himself as a dependable if minor star. The late 1930s saw him playing police detectives or amateur sleuths in a spate of comedy-mysteries, among them *Arsene Lupin Returns, Fast Company* (with Florence Rice in MGM's second-string effort to spawn a "Thin Man"–like series), *There's Always a Woman* (all 1938), and *The Amazing Mr. Williams* (1939).

The suave, lighthearted Douglas made an ideal counterpart to Greta Garbo in Ernst Lubitsch's hilarious *Ninotchka,* and he costarred with her again in her final film vehicle, *Two-Faced Woman* (1941). (They had been paired earlier, in 1932's *As You Desire Me.)* In the interim he brightened many a mediocre comedy script, including *Good Girls Go to Paris* (1939), *Too Many Husbands, He Stayed for Breakfast, Third Finger, Left Hand* (all 1940), and *This Thing Called Love* (1941), as well as Lubitsch's *That Uncertain Feeling* and *A Woman's Face* (both 1941). After completing *They All Kissed the Bride*

(1942), he joined the war effort, first as a director of the Office of Civilian Defense, then as an army officer.

Unfortunately, the intervening years had seen the demise of the sort of romantic comedy in which Douglas flourished. For the next few years he alternated leads with supporting roles in *The Sea of Grass, The Guilt of Janet Ames* (both 1947), *Mr. Blandings Builds His Dream House* (1948, a felicitous return to comedy with a tailor-made part), *A Woman's Secret, The Great Sinner* (both 1949), and *My Forbidden Past* (1951) before abandoning Hollywood for more satisfying assignments on Broadway. He was offscreen for a full decade, distinguishing himself on the stage and making occasional TV appearances, before returning in *Billy Budd* (1962).

No longer young and dashing, Melvyn Douglas returned to movies as a character actor of substance. He won a Best Supporting Actor Oscar for his performance as Paul Newman's highly ethical, uncompromising father in *Hud* (1963), and that success propelled him into a lengthy second career on screen, in such films as *Advance to the Rear, The Americanization of Emily* (both 1964), *Rapture* (1965), *Hotel* (1967), *I Never Sang for My Father* (1970, Oscar-nominated for his honest performance as Gene Hackman's elderly, difficult parent), *One Is a Lonely Number, The Candidate* (both 1972), *The Tenant* (1976), *Twilight's Last Gleaming* (1977), *Being There* (1979, winning another Oscar for his role as a political kingmaker), *The Changeling* (1979), *Ghost Story,* and *The Hot Touch* (both 1981). He added stature to every one of those films. Politically active in private life, he was married for nearly 50 years to actress-turned-politician Helen Gahagan. His autobiography, "See You at the Movies," was published posthumously in 1986.

DOUGLAS, MICHAEL. Actor, producer. *(b. Sept. 25, 1944, New Brunswick, N.J.)* He delivered one of the 1980s' most memorable lines of dialogue—"Greed is good"—as ruthless arbitrageur Gordon Gekko in *Wall Street* (1987), winning himself an Academy Award in the process. It was a fitting tribute to a superb actor whose multifaceted talents have made him one of the movie industry's most formidable figures. The son of Kirk Douglas, this rugged actor has a slightly less pronounced version of his dad's legendary cleft chin (and occasionally affects the elder Douglas's clench-toothed dialogue delivery). Making his film debut in *Hail, Hero!* (1969), Douglas first gained public attention as detective Karl Malden's young, hot-headed partner on the early 1970s TV series "The Streets of San Francisco." He spent several years trying to launch the screen version of Ken Kesey's novel "One Flew Over the Cuckoo's Nest" (his father had acted in a stage version of the piece), which became an award-winning sensation in 1975; coproducer Douglas did not act in the film, but did take home one of its Best Picture Oscars. He played ruggedly masculine but enlightened characters in the late 1970s and early 1980s, including a news cameraman in the 1979 anti-nuke drama *The China Syndrome*, which he also produced.

Douglas has been teamed most felicitously with Kathleen Turner, first in the quirky romantic adventure *Romancing the Stone* (1984), its sequel, *The Jewel of the Nile* (1985) and in *The War of the Roses* (1989), a vicious black comedy in which both stars die at the fade-out. In recent years he's been playing a number of edgier roles as well, including the aforementioned Wall Street tycoon and a family man who's too easily led astray by a sexy Glenn Close in the hugely popular (and, some said, cautionary) thriller *Fatal Attraction* (1987). He was a frankly dislikable cop in *Black Rain* (1989), and then he played another cop in *Basic Instinct* (1992), this one dumb enough to fall in love with a lethal Sharon Stone. His presence in *Shining Through* (1992), as Melanie Griffith's boss and protector, seemed perfunctory. He then delivered forceful performances in *Falling Down* (1993) and *Disclosure* (1994).
OTHER FILMS INCLUDE: 1970: *Adam at 6 A.M.;* 1971: *Summertree;* 1972: *Napoleon and Samantha;* 1979: *Running* (also executive produced); 1980: *It's My Turn;* 1983: *The Star Chamber;* 1984: *Starman* (producer only); 1985: *A Chorus Line.*

DOUGLAS, PAUL. Actor. *(b. Nov. 4, 1907, Philadelphia; d. Sept. 11, 1959.)* Burly, lantern-jawed leading man and character actor who enjoyed considerable popularity during the 1950s. He generally played gruff, lovable (and sometimes dull-witted), bearish types, most successfully in comedies and light dramas. A Yale graduate who enjoyed a successful career as a radio announcer and sportscaster before turning to acting, Douglas played the boorish scrap-iron king in Garson Kanin's Broadway production of "Born Yesterday," which led to his signing with 20th Century-Fox. He made his screen debut in a tailor-made role in *A Letter to Three Wives* (1949), and followed it with a string of successful films that offered him equally compatible parts: *It Happens Every Spring, Everybody Does It* (both 1949), *The Big Lift, Love That Brute, Panic in the Streets* (all 1950), *14 Hours, The Guy Who Came Back, Rhubarb* (all 1951, with an unbilled cameo in the latter), *When in Rome, Clash by Night, We're Not Married* (all 1952, with Marilyn Monroe in the latter two), *Forever Female* (1953), *Executive Suite, High and Dry, Green Fire* (all 1954), *Joe Macbeth* (a curious modern-day version of Shakespeare's "Macbeth" set in the underworld), *The Leather Saint, The Solid Gold Cadillac* (all 1956, reunited in the last with his "Born Yesterday" Broadway costar, Judy Holliday), *This Could Be the Night, Beau James* (both 1957), and *The Mating Game* (1959), among others. On TV he appeared in a 1959 version of "Judgment at Nuremberg." Douglas was married five times; his last two wives were actresses Virginia Field and Jan Sterling.

DOURIF, BRAD. Actor. *(b. Mar. 18, 1950, Huntington, W.Va.)* This frail-looking, rabbity actor delivered a standout performance as the gentle, stuttering mental patient Billy Bibbit in *One Flew Over the Cuckoo's Nest* (1975)—no small accomplishment, given that film's expert ensemble cast, led by Jack Nicholson. But despite having snagged an Oscar nomination for the role, and not counting his eye-opening stint as an obsessed preacher in John Huston's *Wise Blood* (1979), Dourif hasn't really enjoyed the success he richly deserves. The impact he's made in plum roles in such quality films as *Eyes of Laura Mars* (1978), *Ragtime* (1981), *Blue Velvet* (1986), and *Mississippi Burning* (1988) has been offset by his frequent forays in the horror/sci-fi genre, including *Dune* (1984), *Child's Play* (1988; as the voice of "Chucky," the demon doll, also in the 1990 and 1991 sequels), *Spontaneous Combustion, The Exorcist III,* and *Stephen King's Graveyard Shift* (all 1990). Dourif's other 1990 films, *Sonny Boy* and *Hidden Agenda,* at least constituted a departure from such fare. Recent credits include *Amos & Andrew* and the TV miniseries "Wild Palms" (both 1993).

DOWN, LESLEY-ANNE. Actress. *(b. Mar. 17, 1954, London.)* Stunning British actress who began modeling for commercials when she was 10 and was voted "Britain's Most Beautiful Teenager" a few years later. Soon after, she appeared in films like *School for Unclaimed Girls* (1969), *Countess Dracula* (1970), *Pope Joan* (1972), and *Scalawag* (1973), but the blossoming beauty caught the attention of American audiences as Georgina in the acclaimed TV series "Upstairs, Downstairs." That show's success put her in hot demand as a romantic—and often, simply decorative—lead in *The Pink Panther Strikes Again* (1976), *A Little Night Music* (1977), *The Betsy* (1978), *The Great Train Robbery, Hanover Street* (both 1979), *Rough Cut* (1980), and *Sphinx* (1981). Since then, Down has appeared mostly in TV movies and miniseries like "The Hunchback of Notre Dame" and "North and South," and its sequels, with only occasional films like *Nomads* (1986) and *Death Wish V* (1994) in between.

DOWNEY, ROBERT, JR. Actor. *(b. Apr. 4, 1965, New York City.)* The son of once-celebrated independent movie director Robert Downey—and a dead ringer for his father's younger self—this brash young actor debuted on-screen as a puppy in his father's satire *Pound* (1970). He won small roles in such films as *Firstborn* (1984), *Weird Science* (1985), and *Back to School* (1986). A quick-witted performer with a ready smirk, he outpaced his fellow Brat Packers with performances that stood out in, but didn't quite redeem, spotty-at-best films such as *Less Than Zero* (1987), *The Pick-up Artist* (1987), and *Johnny Be Good* (1988). Following a strong supporting role as a young, idealistic lawyer and foil to James Woods' jaded ex-activist

in *True Believer* (1989), he displayed both charm and comic prowess in the comedy-fantasy *Chances Are* (1989), and got to play buddies with Mel Gibson in the flop *Air America* (1990). He seemed ill at ease (and badly miscast) as a slimy soap-opera producer in the ensemble comedy *Soapdish* (1991), and didn't fare much better in his father's comedy *Too Much Sun* (also 1991).

He then devoted himself to learning everything he could learn—or absorb in some way—about Charlie Chaplin, in order to play the movies' supreme genius both in both onscreen and offscreen guise, from youth to old age. His performance in *Chaplin* (1992) was nothing short of astonishing, and it earned him an Academy Award nomination. That's a tough act to follow, but he did, by delivering an assured comic performance in the sentimental fantasy *Heart and Souls* (1993). He participated in the freeform documentary *The Last Party* (also 1993), set at the 1992 Democratic National Convention; his father appears in the film as well. Recent credits include *Short Cuts* (1993), *Natural Born Killers,* and *Only You* (both 1994).

DRESSLER, MARIE. Actress. *(b. Nov. 9, 1869, Coburg, Canada, as Leila Marie Koerber; d. July 28, 1934.)* Seldom has there been a more unlikely Hollywood star, or one whose appeal is more difficult to describe: "Homely" is too kind a word for her looks; "ungainly" doesn't do her figure justice; "gruff" can't begin to explain her screen persona. Nonetheless, she enjoyed several years of enormous popularity just before her death in the early 1930s, and she did perform the greatest double take in movie history (responding to Jean Harlow's "I was reading a book the other day. . . ," setting up the closing line in 1933's *Dinner at Eight*). A lifelong performer with experience in light opera as well as vaudeville and the legitimate stage, she was lucky enough to costar opposite Charlie Chaplin for her film debut in *Tillie's Punctured Romance* (1914). Several sequels followed, but Dressler spent much of the silent era offscreen. Signed by MGM in 1927, she quickly reestablished herself as a top supporting comedienne in *The Callahans and the Murphys* (1927), *The Patsy,* and *Bringing Up Father* (both 1928), among others. But her showy role as the waterfront hag in Greta Garbo's *Anna Christie* (1930) made her a sensation, and her heart-tugging performance opposite Wallace Beery in *Min and Bill* the same year won her an Academy Award.

Overnight, the has-been of the mid 1920s was the number-one box-office star in America. She costarred with Polly Moran in a series of slapstick comedy features, including *Caught Short* (1930), *Reducing, Politics* (both 1931), and *Prosperity* (1932), and alternated those lightweight films with more substantial starring vehicles like *Emma* (1932, which got her another Oscar nod), *Tugboat Annie* (reteamed with Beery), the aforementioned *Dinner at Eight,* and *Christopher Bean* (all 1933), her last film. Her autobiography, "My Story," was published in 1933.

DREYER, CARL THEODOR. Director. *(b. Feb. 3, 1898, Copenhagen; d. Mar. 20, 1968.)* A brilliant director whose two certifiable masterpieces, the highly expressive silent *The Passion of Joan of Arc* (1928) and the incredibly eerie sound film *Vampyr* (1932), vouchsafe his reputation as one of the all-time greats, erstwhile screenwriter Dreyer began his directing career in 1912 aping D. W. Griffith. By the late 1920s he had developed a pure visual style of such depth and breadth that the few intertitles in his movies seem superfluous (the same goes for the sparse dialogue heard in *Vampyr*). His perfectionism and refusal to compromise insured a limited output over the years; he made only 15 features in a career spanning four decades. Dreyer's movies after *Vampyr* are not widely seen here; of these, 1943's witchhunt drama *Day of Wrath,* 1955's *Ordet,* and 1964's *Gertrud* are the most renowned.

DREYFUSS, RICHARD. Actor. *(b. Oct. 29, 1947, Brooklyn, N.Y.).* Whether he's playing with his mashed potatoes (1977's *Close Encounters of the Third Kind*), scheming to sell aluminum siding (1987's *Tin Men*), or trying to murder one of his patients (1991's *What About Bob?*), this compulsively likable, extraordinarily talented actor brings to his roles a coiled-spring intensity matched by few other contemporary screen performers. After playing bit parts for several years beginning with *The Graduate* and *Valley of the Dolls* (both 1967), Dreyfuss earned kudos as a thoughtful teenager, bound for college but cruising his small town for one last night in *American Graffiti* (1973). His obvious intelligence enabled him to convincingly play two very different boy wonders in *The Apprenticeship of Duddy Kravitz* (1974) and *Inserts* (1976), before pulling a hat trick by appearing in three consecutive blockbusters: *Jaws* (1975, as a cocky shark expert), *Close Encounters of the Third Kind* (1977, as an obsessive UFO tracer), and *The Goodbye Girl* (also 1977, in an Oscar-winning performance as an arrogant actor). Dreyfuss next played a hip private eye in *The Big Fix* (1978), a piano whiz in *The Competition* (1980), and a quadriplegic in *Whose Life Is It, Anyway?* (1981), doing fine work in movies that failed to achieve the success of his earlier films.

The next five years Dreyfuss spent mostly on stage or wrestling with a well-publicized drug problem, making a movie comeback in *Down and Out in Beverly Hills* (1986). By then, his prematurely gray hair had aged him ever so slightly, enough to disqualify him from playing the sharp-tongued whiz kids he'd interpreted earlier. He's kept busy ever since in a wide variety of roles: a very patient attorney in *Nuts,* a lovesick cop in *Stakeout* (both in 1987), an actor impersonating a dictator in *Moon Over Parador* (1988), a ghost in *Always,* and a compulsive gambler in *Let It Ride* (both 1989). Dreyfuss had two other memorable roles in 1991, that of a glib, annoying entrepreneur in *Once Around* (romancing *Always* costar Holly Hunter) and a pompous, celebrity-obsessed shrink in *What About Bob?* He's also taken small but showy roles in *Postcards From the Edge* (1990, as a doctor) and *Rosencrantz and Guildenstern Are Dead* (1990, as a Shakespearean actor). His recent films reveal an actor who continues to develop, and who continues to surprise critics who'd written him off years ago. Recent credits include *Prisoner of Honor* (1991 telefilm, which he coproduced, about the Dreyfus affair), *Lost in Yonkers, Another Stakeout* (both 1993), and *Silent Fall* (1994).

DRU, JOANNE. Actress. (b. Jan. 31, 1923, Logan, W.Va., as Joanne La Coque.) Beautiful, vivacious actress best remembered for her no-nonsense, gutsy heroines in the post-WW2 Western classics *Red River* (1948), *She Wore a Yellow Ribbon* (1949), and *Wagon Master* (1950). No shrinking violet, she; Dru seemed very much at home in horse operas, and made quite a few during the 1950s. A former show girl, she made a less than spectacular film debut in the excruciating *Abie's Irish Rose* (1946), but was effective in *All the King's Men* (1949), *711 Ocean Drive* (1950), *The Pride of St. Louis* (1952), *Outlaw Territory* (1953), *Forbidden* (1954), *Sincerely Yours* (1955), *Hell on Frisco Bay* (1956), *The Light in the Forest* (1958), *September Storm* (1960), and *Sylvia* (1965). Her "comeback" appearance, in 1981's *Super Fuzz,* was ill advised, to say the least. The sister of game-show host Peter Marshall, she was previously married to Dick Haymes and John Ireland (who directed and costarred with her in his 3-D Western *Hannah Lee/Outlaw Territory* in 1953).

DUFF, HOWARD. Actor. (b. Nov. 24, 1917, Bremerton, Wash.; d. July 8, 1990.) Once he hit the screen in 1947, this burly leading man's gruff voice was instantly recognizable: He'd spent several years playing private eye Sam Spade on a hit radio show. With acting experience dating back to pre-WW2 stage work in his native Washington, Duff made a solid impression with moviegoers portraying tough guys in Westerns and crime dramas. After an auspicious start in *Brute Force* (1947) and *The Naked City* (1948), however, he was relegated to second-tier films by the taint of left-wing affiliations during the Hollywood witch-hunt era—which also cost him his radio gig as Sam Spade. He reemerged in the 1960s as a solid character actor in leading films.

Duff was married to actress-director Ida Lupino, with whom he appeared in *Women's Prison* (1955) and the TV series "Mr. Adams and Eve" (1957–58). In addition to working in numerous made-fors throughout the 1970s and 1980s, he was a regular on the prime-time soaps "Flamingo Road" (1981–82), "Knots Landing" (1984–85), and "Dallas" (1988–89).
OTHER FILMS INCLUDE: 1949: *Calamity Jane and Sam Bass;* 1950: *Spy Hunt;* 1953: *Roar of the Crowd;* 1954: *Tanganyika;* 1955: *Flame of the Islands;* 1956: *While the City Sleeps;* 1962: *Boys' Night Out;* 1968: *Panic in the City;* 1977: *The Late Show;* 1978: *A Wedding;* 1979: *Kramer vs. Kramer;* 1980: *Oh God! Book II;* 1987: *No Way Out.*

DUIGAN, JOHN. Director, screenwriter. (b. June 19, 1949, Hartney Witney, Hampshire, England.) One of the "new wave" of Australian filmmakers, Duigan has turned out a number of diverse, interesting films, many of them dealing with the pains of young adulthood. He originally planned to act and write, and worked in experimental theater groups after leaving the University of Melbourne. With a government grant, he directed low-budget films like *The Firm Man* (1974) and *Trespassers* (1976). The features *Mouth to Mouth* (1978), about teenage couples stealing to survive, and *The Winter of Our Dreams* (1981), with Judy Davis as a prostitute involved with married Bryan Brown, put Duigan on the map and established him as a director with a subtle eye for cultural and political details. He is probably best known for the charming, award-winning films *The Year My Voice Broke* (1987) and *Flirting* (1990), two parts of a proposed trilogy which has so far followed young Danny Embling from lovesick adolescence in the early 1960s through life at a boarding school in 1965 and his relationship with a Ugandan girl. Duigan has directed one American film, *Romero* (1989), with Raul Julia as El Salvador's Archbishop Oscar Romero, and most recently directed and cowrote the erotic *Wide Sargasso Sea* (1993) and directed and wrote *Sirens* (1994).

DUKAKIS, OLYMPIA. Actress. (b. June 20, 1931, Lowell, Mass.) Like her famous cousin, presidential candidate Michael, this Dukakis made a lot of noise in 1988, but has only been heard from sporadically since. The daughter of Greek immigrant parents, and a former physical therapist, Dukakis began her theatrical career in summer stock after taking adult-education acting classes at Boston University. She first appeared on stage as a sexagenarian; her next role was that of a

100-year-old woman. The movies beckoned in 1964, and she debuted on film in *Lilith*. She alternated film and stage work throughout the 1960s and 1970s, appearing without much notice in *Twice a Man* (1964), *John and Mary* (1969, as Dustin Hoffman's mother), *Made for Each Other* (1971), *Death Wish* (1974), *The Wanderers* (1979), and others. By 1988, already typed in parts calling for older, ethnic women, Dukakis had earned two Obies for off-Broadway performances and won an Academy Award for her vivid portrayal of Cher's Italian mother in *Moonstruck* (1987). The feisty, outspoken actress subsequently costarred in *Working Girl* (1988), *Steel Magnolias, Dad* (both 1989), *Look Who's Talking* (also 1989, and its 1990 sequel), and *In the Spirit* (1990), to name a few. Dukakis teaches drama at New York University and runs a small theater company in New Jersey with her husband, actor Louis Zorich. Recent credits include *Over the Hill* (1992), "Sinatra" (the 1992 miniseries in which she played Frankie's mother), *The Cemetery Club*, and *Look Who's Talking Now* (both 1993).

DUKE, BILL. Director, actor. *(b. Feb. 26, 1943, Poughkeepsie, N.Y.)* Imposing black actor who has recently made an impressive transition to directing features. Originally interested in studying medicine, Duke turned to drama instead and received kudos for his short film *The Hero*, made while studying at the American Film Institute. This led to television assignments, and before long he was turning out episodes of "Hill Street Blues," "Cagney & Lacey," and "Dallas," and won acclaim with an American Playhouse presentation of "The Killing Floor" (1984), which dealt with unions in turn-of-the-century Chicago stockyards. Duke built up a considerable acting resume, too, beginning with *Car Wash* (1976), *American Gigolo* (1980), *Commando* (1985), *Predator* (1987), and *Bird on a Wire* (1990), before directing his first theatrical feature, *A Rage in Harlem* (1991), an adaptation of Chester Himes' crime novel. He followed with *Deep Cover* (1992), which starred Laurence Fishburne as an undercover narc, then switched gears with the comedies *The Cemetery Club* (1993) and *Sister Act 2: Back in the Habit*

(1993). He made a cameo as a dogged detective in *Menace II Society* (1993).

DUKE, PATTY. Actress. *(b. Dec. 14, 1946, New York City, as Anna Marie Duke.)* At the time, the youngest actress to win an Academy Award, for *The Miracle Worker* (1962), Duke was honored for recreating the role of blind, deaf Helen Keller that made her a Broadway star. Ironically, the actress is better remembered today for her TV comedy series, "The Patty Duke Show" (1963–66), in which she played identical cousins. Hollywood never quite knew what to do with her, as her starring vehicles *Billie* (1965) and *Me, Natalie* (1969) confirmed. (She'd made her official screen debut in 1958's *The Goddess*.) Duke shocked fans by agreeing to costar in the "scandalous" *Valley of the Dolls* (1967), but it didn't open doors either. She found better opportunities on TV, in the acclaimed telefeature *My Sweet Charlie* (1970), which won her the first of three Emmys; the others were awarded for the miniseries "Captains and the Kings" (1976) and a remake of *The Miracle Worker* (1979) in which she took the adult role of Annie Sullivan, opposite Melissa Gilbert. She remains active in made-for-TV movies, and wrote an autobiography, "Call Me Anna," (1987) which described her harrowing childhood; she coproduced and starred in a TV adaptation of the book in 1990. She served for several years as president of the Screen Actors Guild, the first female to hold that post. She was married to actor John Astin (and for a time billed herself as Patty Duke Astin); their son Sean Astin has become a successful actor, with starring roles in *Staying Together* (1989), *Toy Soldiers* (1991), and *Rudy* (1993), while his brother Mackenzie Astin was featured in the TV sitcom "The Facts of Life."

DULLEA, KEIR. Actor. *(b. May 30, 1936, Cleveland.)* . . . gone tomorrow. Blank-looking Dullea made a vivid impression in the early 1960s, first in *The Hoodlum Priest* (1961), then as a disturbed youth in Frank Perry's *David and Lisa* (1963, the role that many believed would catapult him to stardom), and as the creepy brother in Otto Preminger's *Bunny Lake Is Missing* (1965). He is probably best known, however, for his role as astronaut Dave Bowman in Kubrick's *2001: A Space Odyssey* (1968), wherein the director took full advantage of the actor's tabula rasa qualities. Dullea next took the title role in the tepid, embarrassing *De Sade* (1969). Appeared mostly in Canadian productions and B thrillers since that time, although he did reprise the Bowman role in the everything's-going-to-be-all-right *2001* sequel, *2010* (1984), of which Kubrick had no part.

DUMBRILLE, DOUGLASS. Actor. *(b. Oct. 13, 1890, Hamilton, Ontario; d. Apr. 2, 1974.)* Venerable screen heavy who plied his trade in more than 200 films. The Canadian-born Dumbrille was a bank clerk and onion farmer before taking up acting. With his dark, thin mustache, penetrating eyes, and hawk nose, the deep-voiced Dumbrille naturally gravitated to unsympathetic roles on stage and screen. He debuted opposite Claudette Colbert in *His Woman* (1930), and went on to appear in *King of the Jungle* (1933), *The Lives of a Bengal Lancer* (1935, as Mohammed Khan), *Cardinal Richelieu, The Lone Wolf Returns* (both 1935), *Mr. Deeds Goes to Town* (1936), *A Day at the Races, Ali Baba Goes to Town* (both 1937), *Charlie Chan at Treasure Island* (1939), *The Three Musketeers* (1939, as Athos), *Virginia City* (1940), *Road to Utopia* (1945), *The Cat Creeps* (1946), *Son of Paleface* (1952), *The Ten Commandments* (1956), and *Shock Treatment* (1964), among many others. He played the same role in Frank Capra's *Broadway Bill* (1934) and its remake, *Riding High* (1950), and also appeared in both versions of *The Buccaneer* (1938 and 1958). He had a top-billed role just once, in 1938, as the hero of a Zane Grey Western, *The Mysterious Rider.* Late in life, he married the young daughter of his friend and fellow actor Alan Mowbray. Dumbrille remained active in television through the 1960s.

DUMONT, MARGARET. Actress. *(b. Oct. 20, 1889, Brooklyn, N.Y., as Margaret Baker; d. Mar. 6, 1965.)* "Remember," says Groucho Marx in *Duck Soup,* "we're fighting for this woman's honor—which is probably more than she ever did." Insults like that built the foundation of Groucho's relationship on stage and screen with the stately Margaret Dumont. Although she played in nearly 30 films, usually cast as a haughty, aristocratic dowager, she's most closely associated with The Marx Brothers, with whom she appeared in seven films: *The Cocoanuts* (1929), *Animal Crackers* (1930), *Duck Soup* (1933), *A Night at the Opera* (1935), *A Day at the Races* (1937), *At the Circus* (1939), and *The Big Store* (1941). A veteran of the Broadway stage since before World War 1 (who also did some minor work in silent films), Dumont followed the Marxes to Hollywood, where her regal bearing made her a perfect comic foil for screen funnymen W. C. Fields in *Never Give a Sucker an Even Break* (1941, as Mrs. Hemoglobin), Laurel and Hardy in *The Dancing Masters* (1943), Jack Benny in *The Horn Blows at Midnight* (1945), Danny Kaye in *Up in Arms* (1944), and Abbott and Costello in *Little Giant* (1946). As late as 1962 she was playing the same\kind of role (and getting a cake in the face) in *Zotz!*

DUNAWAY, FAYE. Actress. *(b. Jan. 14, 1941, Bascom, Fla.)* A beautiful Southern blonde with real, old-fashioned movie-star appeal, Dunaway reached her highest level of popularity in an era when leading men were showing more "realistic" traits. Subsequently, her glamour rubbed off on considerably less elegant types such as Dustin Hoffman and Jack Nicholson. But Dunaway is an extremely skilled actress who was every bit as capable as any of her costars, so there was never any incongruity in even the least likely pairings. A theater arts major from Boston University's School of Fine and Applied Arts, Dunaway made her screen debut in *The Happening,* and quickly followed with Otto Preminger's *Hurry Sundown* (both 1967), immediately drawing attention to herself. But she made the biggest impression (and got an Academy Award nomination) in another film that year, *Bonnie and Clyde,* paired with Warren Beatty in a crime film that romanticized its bankrobber protagonists and then annihilated them in an unprecedented on-screen massacre that galvanized audiences.

Most of her subsequent 1960s roles were successful but unspectacular; she played a savvy investigator opposite jaded millionaire Steve McQueen in *The Thomas Crown Affair* (1968), and the young love interest of Kirk Douglas' adman-gone-goofy in Elia Kazan's leaden *The Arrangement* (1969). The 1970s brought her a number of meaty roles, including a turn opposite Dustin Hoffman in 1970's *Little Big Man,* and the tragic female lead of *Chinatown* (1974) opposite Jack Nicholson. Her on-set clashes with director Roman Polanski became the stuff of Hollywood legend. Her work in the film netted her a second Academy Award nomination. Two years later she actually won a Best Actress Oscar for her portrayal of a ruthless network-TV executive in the outrageous satire *Network* (1976). She also appeared in *The Three Musketeers* (1974) and *The Four Musketeers* (1975) as villainous Milady de Winter; in *Three Days of the Condor* (1975), sheltering hunted man Robert Redford; and in *Eyes of Laura Mars* (1978), as a high-fashion photographer.

Then, somehow, her career lost momentum. The quality of her performances hadn't declined, but the quality of her *parts* had. The 1980s found her laboring in the likes of *The First Deadly Sin* (1980), *The Wicked Lady* (1983), *Supergirl,* (1984, a super turkey), *Ordeal by Innocence* (1984), *Burning Secret, Midnight Crossing* (both 1988), and *Wait Until Spring, Bandini* (1989). The decade was redeemed—partially—by two outstanding performances: Dunaway camped it up playing movie star and abusive mom Joan Crawford in *Mommie Dearest* (1981), and took an uncharacteristically gritty turn as an alcoholic lowlife in *Barfly* (1987, opposite Mickey Rourke), winning serious critical attention again. She has worked steadily, generally in supporting roles, since that time. She did enjoy a well-written lead opposite Richard Widmark in a made-for-TV movie, *Cold Sassy Tree* (1989), and was properly chilling as the sexless wife of Robert Duvall in *The Handmaid's Tale* (1990). Recent credits include *Double Edge* (1992), *The Temp* (1993), *Arizona Dream* (1995, filmed in 1991), and *Don Juan DeMarco* (1995). In the fall of 1993 she made her TV sitcom debut as the star of the short-lived "It Had to Be You."

DUNN, JAMES. Actor. *(b. Nov. 2, 1901, New York City; d. Sept. 1, 1967.)* Breezy, brash, good-looking Irishman whose film roles mainly consisted of . . . breezy, brash, good-looking Irishmen. He might be forgotten today, if he hadn't costarred with Shirley Temple in three 1934 hits *(Stand Up and Cheer, Baby Take a Bow,* and *Bright Eyes)* and, relatively late in his career, won an Oscar for his touching performance as the ne'er-do-well father in *A Tree Grows in Brooklyn* (1945). Dunn worked on stage before hitting Hollywood in 1931, where he was paired with ingenue Sally Eilers in *Bad Girl,* a surprise hit that got them reunited for *Over the Hill* (1931), *Dance Team* (1932), and *Sailor's Luck* (1933). He seemed a natural for musical comedy, and Fox spotted him opposite Alice Faye (1934's *365 Nights in Hollywood,* 1935's *George White's Scandals)* and Shirley Temple before putting him in a few lackluster B's and sending him on his way. In the late 1930s he was still playing the same youthful character he'd patented at Fox, only now in minor-league films—and he'd outgrown the part. Dunn had been offscreen for several years before taking the role of Jimmy Nolan in *Tree,* and surprisingly, the Oscar win didn't do much for his career. His later films include *The Golden Gloves Story* (1950), *The Bramble Bush* (1960), *Hemingway's Adventures of a Young Man* (1962), and *The Oscar* (1966). In the late 1930s Dunn was married to beautiful starlet Frances Gifford, with whom he costarred in two Poverty Row potboilers, *Hold That Woman* and *Mercy Plane* (both 1940). He costarred in a 1954–56 TV sitcom, "It's a Great Life."

DUNNE, GRIFFIN. Actor, producer. *(b. June 8, 1955, New York City.)* Unprepossessing, dark-haired actor who was stomach-churningly memorable as a steadily decomposing lycanthrope victim in the horror comedy *An American Werewolf in London* (1981); since then, his on-screen persona has been that of an irritating, self-absorbed yuppie. Dunne has been involved in the production end of moviemaking since 1979, when he coproduced and appeared in *Head Over Heels.* (His partner in production is former actress Amy Robinson; the two sometimes work in tandem with *Animal House*

ROTC commander Mark Metcalf.) Generally working on smaller, independent
films, Dunne and colleagues produced
Scorsese's *After Hours* (1985, a well-
received yuppie black comedy reminiscent
of *Alice in Wonderland* in which Dunne
played the lead), and they have recently
worked on bigger studio productions, including the Susan Sarandon starrer *White
Palace* (1990) and the Richard Dreyfuss–
Holly Hunter romantic comedy *Once
Around* (1991; Dunne played a predictably
obnoxious boyfriend). He had a small but
important role in *My Girl* (1991) and took
the lead in *Search and Destroy* (1995).
Formerly married to model/actress Carey
Lowell.

DUNNE, IRENE. Actress. *(b. Dec. 20,
1898, Louisville, Ky.; d. Sept. 4, 1990.)* For all
the classic Hollywood films she made in
the 1930s and 1940s, Irene Dunne seemed
destined to be forgotten by the 1970s. No
star of her stature suffered from having
more films withdrawn from circulation
due to rights problems. The facts (and the
films) reveal that Dunne was one of the
most appealing, versatile, and popular
stars of the 1930s. An aspiring opera
singer who didn't make the cut at the
Metropolitan, Dunne ventured into musical comedy in the early 1920s. She made
her Broadway debut in "The Clinging
Vine" (1922), but her big break came
when she was cast as Magnolia Hawks in
the road company of "Show Boat." She
was signed by RKO in 1930 and made her
screen debut in the part-color, all-talking
musical *Leathernecking* with vaudeville
comics Ken Murray and Eddie Foy, Jr.
Dunne's second film was the big-scale
Western *Cimarron* (1931), the epic frame-
work of which allowed her to mature on-
screen from a young pioneer wife to an
indomitable, middle-aged woman. The
film won a Best Picture Oscar and Dunne
was nominated for her costarring role. She
then became one of the three-hanky brigade in such high-profile weepies as *Back
Street* (1932) and *Magnificent Obsession*
(1935). All three of these pictures were
later remade, and Dunne's versions remained virtually unseen after their original
release. The same fate befell *Roberta*
(1935, remade as *Lovely to Look At*), a famous Jerome Kern musical brought to
RKO as a Dunne vehicle but stolen by the

increasingly popular team of Fred Astaire
and Ginger Rogers.

But Dunne really had a chance to show
what she could do when she was cast in
the second film version of *Show Boat*
(1936). The role of Magnolia, which she
knew so well, offered the star an opportunity to play on the lighter side as well as
the dramatic—although, at 38, she
strained credulity in the early scenes
showing Magnolia as a teenager. (The picture was withdrawn when MGM brought
out its 1951 version.) Her performance as
a prim and proper small-town girl who
writes a scandalous novel under a phony
name in *Theodora Goes Wild* (1936)
earned Dunne her second Oscar nomination and made her Hollywood's first
choice as a screwball comedienne. (Despite its reputation, though, *Theodora*
didn't make it to TV until the mid 1970s.)

Through the early 1940s Dunne had a
nearly unbroken string of comedy hits,
with only an occasional return to soap
opera; even mild amusements like *High,
Wide, and Handsome* (1937) and *Joy of
Living* (1938) were brightened by her
presence. *The Awful Truth* (1937) was actually the third screen version of Arthur
Richman's play, but the others were
quickly forgotten amid the perfect chemistry between Dunne and costar Cary Grant.
Dunne received her third Oscar nomination for the picture, but again Oscar was
elusive. She was reteamed with Grant for
My Favorite Wife (1940) and *Penny Serenade* (1941). The Academy nominated
Dunne a fourth time for *Love Affair*
(1939, opposite Charles Boyer), a skillful
blend of romance, light comedy, and soap
opera. Again the Oscar was denied, and
again the film disappeared when it was remade as *An Affair to Remember* (1957).

During World War 2, Dunne starred in
the fantasy melodrama *A Guy Named Joe*
(1943, remade by Steven Spielberg as *Always* in 1989), and this led to a series of
dramatic portrayals in such handsome productions as *The White Cliffs of Dover*
(1944) and *Anna and the King of Siam*
(1946). She also starred in the film versions of two classic American plays, *Life
With Father* (1947) and *I Remember
Mama* (1948, for which she earned a fifth
Oscar nomination). After the pale comedy
It Grows on Trees (1952), Dunne retired
from the screen and turned to politics and
business. She was appointed an alternate

delegate to the United Nations by President Eisenhower, and later served on the board of directors of Technicolor with fellow screen actor George Murphy. Dunne was rescued from relative obscurity in the 1970s when the American Film Institute and the Los Angeles County Art Museum began to screen her long-unseen best work, and as a result, the films finally were cleared for TV reissue. The long-unsung actress was too ill to accept her Kennedy Center Honors in 1985, but longtime fans saw the ceremony as vindication—and a reminder of her great talent.

DUNNOCK, MILDRED. Actress. *(b. Jan. 25, 1906, Baltimore; d. July 5, 1991.)* Well-respected character actress who came to Broadway after a teaching career, and made her stage debut as a Welsh schoolteacher in "The Corn Is Green," a role she reprised in the 1945 movie version. Dunnock made her most vivid film impressions as the wheelchair-bound woman pushed down a flight of stairs by Richard Widmark in *Kiss of Death* (1947), and as Linda Loman, the long-suffering wife in *Death of a Salesman* (1951), the latter another role she immortalized on film after playing it in the landmark Broadway production. She received a Best Supporting Actress Oscar nomination for her work in *Salesman* and another for her role as the crazed aunt in Elia Kazan's film of Tennessee Williams' *Baby Doll* (1956). Dunnock also appeared in *Peyton Place* (1957), *The Nun's Story* (1959), *Sweet Bird of Youth* (1962), *7 Women* (1966), *The Spiral Staircase* (1975), and *The Pick-up Artist* (1987). Kazan once noted that she was "a superb actress who didn't find nearly the roles she deserved."

DURANTE, JIMMY. Actor. *(b. Feb. 10, 1893, New York City; d. Jan. 28, 1980.)* The old "schnozzola" was the living embodiment of the term "beloved entertainer": Everyone adored him, but no one could ever really figure out just what it was he did. He sang, he danced, he played the piano and, of course, he clowned—but he wasn't really great at any of these tasks. Mostly, it was the sheer force of his overbearing personality that won viewers over. He began in vaudeville and nightclubs as one-third of Clayton, Jackson, and Durante, appearing in Ziegfeld's 1929 production "Show Girl," and making his film debut (solo) in *Roadhouse Nights* (1930). MGM signed him up in 1931 and teamed him with the fading Buster Keaton, reasonably assuming his blustery character would perfectly complement the Great Stone Face. It was fine in theory but rotten in execution, as *The Passionate Plumber, Speak Easily* (both 1932), and *What! No Beer?* (1933) proved.

Durante was more successful opposite George M. Cohan in *The Phantom President* (1932), and provided deft comic relief in a pair of heavy dramas, *The Wet Parade* (1932, as a prohibition agent!) and *Hell Below* (1933). He played manager Knobby Walsh in *Joe Palooka* (1934), in which he also introduced (on film) his signature tune, "Inka Dinka Doo." Other memorable turns followed in *Hollywood Party, Strictly Dynamite* (both 1934), *Start Cheering, Little Miss Broadway* (both 1938), *Melody Ranch* (1940, opposite Gene Autry and Ann Miller), *You're in the Army Now,* and *The Man Who Came to Dinner* (both 1941, in the latter as Banjo, a character modeled on Harpo Marx).

It was an older, mellow Durante who really lit up the screen in his featured numbers in such films as *Music for Millions* (1944, in which he sings "Umbriago"), *Two Sisters From Boston* (1946), *It Happened in Brooklyn* (1947), and *On an Island With You* (1948). He also headlined George Pal's modest novelty-comedy *The Great Rupert* (1950), and had a scene-stealing costarring role in *Billy Rose's Jumbo* (1962), based on a Rodgers and Hart Broadway show in which he'd starred almost 30 years earlier. Durante's last screen role was a fitting one: Smiler Grogan, the crook who kicked the bucket—literally—in *It's a Mad Mad Mad Mad World* (1963). He was also a fixture in the early days of TV variety shows, headlining his own series as well as others like "The Colgate Comedy Hour," and winning an Emmy in the process. Durante's fame was rekindled posthumously when his recordings of "As Time Goes By" and "Make Someone Happy" were used on the soundtrack of the smash hit *Sleepless in Seattle* (1993); the accompanying album was a similar success, putting Durante "on the charts" in the 1990s.

DURAS, MARGUERITE. Director, screenwriter, novelist. *(b. Apr. 14, 1914, Indochina, as Marguerite Donnadieu.)* Multitalented artist who achieved fame in the 1940s as a novelist and playwright and turned to film in 1959. She scripted Alain Resnais's *Hiroshima, Mon Amour,* a seminal New Wave effort (which earned her an Academy Award nomination), and wrote and/or directed nearly 20 movies, many of them based on her novels and plays. To Duras, plot and narrative structure always take a back seat to exploration of interpersonal relationships, and most of her films are quirky, to say the least. In *The Truck* (1977), for example, Duras plays herself, chatting with Gerard Depardieu about their proposed film *The Truck.* Duras's *India Song* (1975), however, is a nakedly sensual drama every bit as engrossing as the screen's greatest romantic dramas. More recently, *The Lover* (1992), based on her autobiographical novel, scored an international success.

DURBIN, DEANNA. Actress, singer. *(b. Dec. 4, 1921, Winnipeg, as Edna Mae Durbin.)* She's almost forgotten today, her films seldom revived, but at her peak, as a wholesome, effervescent, teenaged singing star, she enjoyed tremendous popularity, and for several years was the top money-making attraction of Universal Pictures. A naturally gifted singer who undertook vigorous training as a small child, Durbin made her film debut with another talented youngster, Judy Garland, in a 1935 MGM short subject called *Every Sunday* that was intended to serve as a tryout for both girls (and saw Durbin referred to on-screen by her real name, Edna). Metro signed the dynamic Garland to a long-term contract immediately afterward but failed to act as promptly in Durbin's case. She then contracted with Universal, at that time undergoing a wrenching transitional period following the departure of founder Carl Laemmle, and was "introduced" with special screen billing as one of the *Three Smart Girls* (1936).

The prim teenager of *Every Sunday* was gone, and in her place was an irresistible, fresh-faced youngster who exuded personality—and sang like an angel. Durbin's instant bonding with movie audiences made her the de facto star of *Three Smart Girls,* which became Universal's highest-grossing film of that year. Producer Joe Pasternak was entrusted with the responsibility of developing starring vehicles for Deanna (who achieved greater recognition by singing on Eddie Cantor's radio show). Successive Durbin films deviated little from the winning formula of her initial effort: Her high-octane exuberance and precociousness frequently led her into mischief, but her schemes were usually well intentioned, and she invariably triumphed over adversity with twinkling eyes, cheery smile, and sunny song. *One Hundred Men and a Girl* (1937, featuring Leopold Stokowski), *Mad About Music, That Certain Age* (both 1938), *Three Smart Girls Grow Up, First Love* (both 1939), *Spring Parade,* and *It's a Date* (both 1940) almost slavishly adhered to the formula, with amazingly durable results. But much as Universal would have liked to prevent it, Durbin matured, blossoming into a lovely young woman. *It Started with Eve* (1941) was the first of her starring vehicles to acknowledge the fact, although she'd gotten her first screen kiss back in *First Love* (from Robert Stack, making his film debut).

Durbin retained her personal popularity, but her studio demonstrated uncertainty in developing a new format in which she could thrive. *Hers to Hold* (1943), a *Three Smart Girls* sequel, was so far removed from the original concept that the connection was useless. *The Amazing Mrs. Holliday* (also 1943), with Deanna playing mother hen to war refugees, seemed as though it had been developed for another star altogether. And the inaptly titled *Christmas Holiday* (1944), which had her married to killer-on-the-run Gene Kelly (!) ended tragically, befuddling and irritating both critics and audiences. *Lady on a Train* (1945), a lighthearted whodunit, saw Durbin as a vivacious blonde (she was naturally auburn-haired) whose insatiable curiosity embroils her in a murder plot; it was the most successful attempt to adapt her earlier persona to a grown-up Deanna.

Slowly, inexorably, Durbin lost her hold on audiences, as proved by diminishing returns reported for *I'll Be Yours* (1946), *Something in the Wind* (1947), *Up in Central Park,* and *For the Love of Mary* (both 1948). After the last-named film she retired abruptly. For many years she has lived in France and Switzerland with her third husband, director Charles David, and resisted all offers to be interviewed, or to return to the U.S. for appearances of any kind. She has reported, however, that she is perfectly content—and yes, she still sings. Durbin received a special Academy Award in 1938.

DURNING, CHARLES. Actor. (b. Feb. 28, 1923, Highland Falls, N.Y.)

One of the screen's most familiar faces, Durning is the epitome of a character actor, demonstrating versatility and excellence from role to role and often outshining many of the stars he nominally "supports." After service in World War 2, he worked at numerous jobs, including a ballroom dancing instructor, before theatrical producer Joseph Papp saw him onstage and hired him for the New York Shakespeare Festival. Durning performed in over thirty plays—as well as early films like *Harvey Middleman, Fireman* (1965), *Hi, Mom!*, and *I Walk the Line* (both 1970)—before his breakthrough stage performance in the Tony Award–winning drama "That Championship Season" and a role as a crooked cop in the Oscar-winning smash hit *The Sting* (1973). Since then, he has worked practically nonstop; among his more memorable parts: a policeman trying to negotiate with Al Pacino in *Dog Day Afternoon* (1975), the President in *Twilight's Last Gleaming* (1977), Burt Reynolds' brother in *Starting Over* (1979), a shady businessman in *True Confessions* (1981), Jessica Lange's father who courts Dustin Hoffman in *Tootsie* (1982), a singing, dancing governor of Texas in *The Best Little Whorehouse in Texas* (1982, an Oscar-nominated turn), a Nazi in *To Be or Not to Be* (1983, another Oscar nomination), and an imposing monsignor in *Mass Appeal* (1984). He won a Tony Award as Big Daddy in the 1989 Broadway revival of *Cat on a Hot Tin Roof,* and his TV credits include the marvelous *Queen of the Stardust Ballroom* (1975), *Death of a Salesman* (1985, recreating his role from the Broadway revival with Dustin Hoffman), the short-lived series "The Cop and the Kid" (1975), and Burt Reynolds' "Evening Shade" (1990–94).
OTHER FILMS INCLUDE: 1973: *Sisters;* 1974: *The Front Page;* 1975: *The Hindenburg;* 1977: *The Choirboys;* 1978: *The Fury;* 1979: *The Muppet Movie, North Dallas Forty;* 1980: *The Final Countdown;* 1981: *Sharky's Ma-*

chine; 1985: *Big Trouble, The Man With One Red Shoe;* 1986: *Tough Guys, Where the River Runs Black;* 1987: *Happy New Year, The Rosary Murders, Cop;* 1988: *Far North;* 1990: *Dick Tracy;* 1991: *V.I. Warshawski;* 1993: *The Music of Chance;* 1994: *The Hudsucker Proxy.*

DURYEA, DAN. Actor. (b. Jan. 23, 1907, White Plains, N.Y.; d. June 7, 1968.)

He was one of filmdom's oddest stars, and certainly one of its strangest leading men. On-screen, Duryea exhibited every human weakness: He was mean-spirited, cowardly, selfish, weak—and yet, somehow, strangely compelling if not totally endearing. A Cornell graduate and former advertising executive, he worked on stage for six years before making his screen debut for Samuel Goldwyn in *The Little Foxes* (1941), reprising his Broadway role as the weakling nephew of Regina Giddins (played by Bette Davis). His most memorable films include *The Woman in the Window, Ministry of Fear* (both 1944), and *Scarlet Street* (1945) for director Fritz Lang. His first notable "good guy" role was played in the Deanna Durbin whodunit *Lady on a Train* (1945). He was memorably nasty opposite James Stewart in Anthony Mann's *Winchester '73* (1950), but many of his subsequent assignments were routine crime melodramas and Westerns. Duryea never lacked for work and moved freely between big screen and TV jobs. He starred in the 1952 syndicated series "China Smith" and had a featured role in "Peyton Place."
OTHER FILMS INCLUDE: 1941: *Ball of Fire;* 1945: *Along Came Jones;* 1946: *Black Angel;* 1949: *Criss Cross;* 1951: *Chicago Calling;* 1953: *Thunder Bay;* 1955: *The Marauders;* 1957: *The Burglar, Slaughter on Tenth Avenue;* 1960: *Platinum High School;* 1962: *Six Black Horses;* 1964: *Taggart;* 1965: *The Bounty Killer;* 1966: *Flight of the Phoenix, Incident at Phantom Hill;* 1968: *The Bamboo Saucer.*

DUTTON, CHARLES S. Actor. (b. Jan. 30, 1951, Baltimore.)

This actor's true-life story is as amazing as anything ever depicted on screen: Dutton quit school, spent time in reform schools, and then went to jail at the age of 17 for killing a man in a street fight. He spent some eight years in and out of prison and gradually

developed an interest in theater, acting
with other inmates in a drama group.
When he was released in 1976, Dutton
studied theater and was later accepted at
the Yale School of Drama. There he met
director Lloyd Richards who chose Dutton
to star in August Wilson's "Ma Rainey's
Black Bottom" on Broadway; the performance earned Dutton a Tony nomination. He had similar Broadway triumphs
in Wilson's "Joe Turner's Come and
Gone" and "The Piano Lesson" and,
around that time, began appearing in films
like *No Mercy* (1986), *"Crocodile" Dundee II* (1988), *Jacknife* (1989), and *Q & A*
(1990). He has been busier than ever, with
strong supporting roles in *Alien³* (1992, as
a hard-headed inmate in a prison of the future), *Mississippi Masala* (1992), *The Distinguished Gentleman* (1992), *Menace II
Society* (1993), and *Rudy* (1993). He is
also familiar to TV audiences as the title
character of the TV series "Roc," a name
taken from his former street nickname.

DUVALL, ROBERT. Actor. *(b. Jan. 5,
1931, San Diego.)* A striking, intense-
looking man with a face that wouldn't
look out of place on Mount Rushmore,
Duvall is one of the most gifted actors to
grace the screen. Despite his commanding
presence, Duvall doesn't enjoy the star
status shared by many of his contemporaries. In his 30-year movie career he has
deftly mixed lead roles with character portrayals, and while many of his films have
been less than perfect, few would claim
that he has given a bad performance in
any of them. Working in stock and off-
Broadway in the late 1950s and early
1960s, he also appeared on TV before
making his film debut as the retarded Boo
Radley in *To Kill a Mockingbird* (1962).
Although his tight-lipped, taciturn manner
suggested him for heavy parts, he has displayed wide range in a diverse array of
roles, including two for burgeoning director Robert Altman: *Countdown* (1968) and
MASH (1970, as Frank Burns).

Duvall's solid, assured performance in
The Rain People (1969) marked the beginning of a lengthy association with director Francis Ford Coppola, for whom he
played cool Mafia mouthpiece Tom Hagen
in both *The Godfather* (1972, earning an
Oscar nomination) and *The Godfather,
Part II* (1974), and a crazed colonel ("I

love the smell of napalm in the
morning . . .") in the Vietnam-based epic
Apocalypse Now (1979, getting another
Oscar nod).

Other memorable roles include that of a
TV executive in *Network* (1976) and a
domineering father in *The Great Santini*
(1979, which got him a Best Actor Oscar
nomination). Many critics felt that
Duvall's finest part was that of a
washed-up country singer in *Tender Mercies* (1983, for which he wrote and performed his own songs); members of the
Motion Picture Academy agreed, and finally voted him a Best Actor Oscar for his
performance. In recent years he has
costarred with Robert Redford in *The Natural* (1984), with Sean Penn in *Colors*
(1988, as a streetwise L.A. cop), with
Natasha Richardson and Faye Dunaway in
The Handmaid's Tale (1990), and with
Tom Cruise in *Days of Thunder* (1990).
He was especially memorable as the dour
but kindhearted Southern patriarch in
Rambling Rose (1991), as a nasty newspaper publisher in *Newsies* (1992), and as a
middle-aged, highly intuitive L.A. police
detective in *Falling Down* (1993). Other
recent credits include *The Plague* (1992),
Geronimo, Wrestling Ernest Hemingway
(both 1993), *The Paper* (1994), and *The
Scarlet Letter* (1995).

Throughout his career he has opted for
interesting parts, not blockbuster hits, and
his filmography is dotted with good "little"
films like *Tomorrow* (1972) and *The Stone
Boy* (1984). In recent years he found two
of his best opportunities in TV miniseries:
the outstanding Western saga "Lonesome
Dove" (1989), in which he played a salty
former Texas Ranger, and *Stalin* (1992) in
which he took the title role, under an elaborate makeup. Duvall has directed two
movies, *We're Not the Jet Set* (1974) and
Angelo, My Love (1983).

DUVALL, SHELLEY. Actress, producer.
(b. July 7, 1949, Fort Worth.) "Duvall may
be the closest thing we've ever come to a
female Buster Keaton," Pauline Kael
wrote. "Her eccentric grace is like his—it
seems to come from the inside out." Director Robert Altman "discovered" Duvall
in Houston where he was shooting *Brewster McCloud* (1970) and gave her a small
role as an Astrodome tour guide. She
worked with him again in *McCabe and*

Mrs. Miller (1971) and in a costarring role in *Thieves Like Us* (1974), where she caught critics' attention as the bride of escaped convict Keith Carradine and demonstrated her appealing, goofy, airy naturalness. She appeared in a 1975 PBS adaptation of F. Scott Fitzgerald's "Bernice Bobs Her Hair," and returned to character parts for Altman in *Nashville* (1975) and *Buffalo Bill and the Indians* (1976), also appearing fleetingly in *Annie Hall* (1977) as one of Woody Allen's dates.

Altman's *3 Women* (1977) gave Duvall her greatest role as a pathetic spa physiotherapist; the director encouraged her to invent much of her own dialogue, and the performance earned her a Best Actress Award at Cannes. Two more memorable roles followed—as the terrified wife in Stanley Kubrick's *The Shining* and as Olive Oyl in Altman's *Popeye* (both 1980)—but since then, she has appeared only occasionally, in *Time Bandits* (1981), *Roxanne* (1987), and *Suburban Commando* (1991). She has concentrated instead on a producing career, committing herself to the creation of high-quality children's entertainment for cable TV and home video. She has used her show-business connections to persuade top stars to appear in these productions, and has won praise and numerous awards for such series as "Faerie Tale Theatre," "Shelley Duvall's Tall Tales," and "Shelley Duvall's Bedtime Stories" and the special "Mother Goose Rock 'n' Rhyme," produced through her own companies Platypus Productions and Think Entertainment. She played Darlin' Clementine in one of her own "Tall Tales" episodes. Duvall also executive-produced the cable-TV remake of *Dinner at Eight* (1989).

DVORAK, ANN. Actress, dancer. *(b. Aug. 2, 1912, New York City, as Ann McKim; d. Dec. 10, 1979.)* Slender, leggy ingenue and secondary female lead of many early 1930s movies, mostly at Warner Bros. This olive-skinned, brown-eyed actress, a former dance instructor and occasional chorus girl, broke into films as a bit player in such musicals as *The Hollywood Revue of 1929* and *Free and Easy* (1930). Under the guidance of Howard Hughes, in 1932 she won dramatic parts in *Sky Devils*, opposite Spencer Tracy, and *Scarface*,

in which she is the object of unrequited incestuous desires (understated, of course) of her gangster brother, played by Paul Muni. As a Warners contractee, Dvorak fit right into the urban milieu frequently utilized in most of the studio's films. She appeared in Warners' *Three on a Match, Love Is a Racket, The Strange Case of Molly Louvain* (all 1932), *College Coach* (1933), *Massacre, Murder in the Clouds* (both 1934), *"G"-Men, Bright Lights, Sweet Music* (giving her a rare opportunity to dance on-screen), and *Dr. Socrates* (all 1935), among others. Warners certainly didn't use Dvorak to best advantage, but she didn't fare much better as a freelance player, to which viewers of *Racing Lady* (1937), *Manhattan Merry-Go-Round, Gangs of New York* (both 1938), *Cafe Hostess*, and *Girls of the Road* (both 1940) can attest.

Accompanied by then-husband Leslie Fenton, she made a couple of pictures in England during the WW 2 years, and even drove an ambulance there to aid the war effort. Returning to Hollywood in 1945, she found starring roles few and far between. OTHER FILMS INCLUDE: 1945: *Flame of the Barbary Coast;* 1946: *Abilene Town;* 1947: *The Long Night, Out of the Blue;* 1950: *Our Very Own, The Return of Jesse James;* 1951: *I Was an American Spy, The Secret of Convict Lake* (after which she retired).

DWAN, ALLAN. Director. *(b. Apr. 3, 1885, Toronto, Canada, as Joseph Aloysius Dwan; d. Dec. 2, 1981.)* Although he was one of the movie industry's true pioneers, this prolific journeyman broke into show business in a most prosaic fashion. After graduating from Notre Dame University, Dwan joined the staff of the Cooper-Hewitt Electric Company, where he hoped to become an electrical engineer. While installing mercury vapor lamps in the Chicago Post Office in 1909, George K. Spoor of the Essanay Company asked Dwan if the lights would be suitable for film production, and hired him to bring his talents to the movies. Dwan sold Spoor some stories he had written in college and became Essanay's scenario editor. The following year he was lured away by a rival Chicago producer, the American Film Manufacturing Company, popularly known as the Flying "A." Sent to San Juan Capistrano to check up on the Flying

"A" Western unit, Dwan found the director off on a binge. He advised abandoning the unit, but the Chicago office ordered him to take over as director.

Dwan's first film, *Brandishing a Bad Man* (1911), was completed in a few hours, and over the next two years he turned out better than one film a week for the Flying "A." A dispute with star J. Warren Kerrigan got Dwan fired, and he went to Universal with a recommendation from Marshall Neilan, his former chauffeur, assistant, and codirector at American. By 1915 he was working with D. W. Griffith as one of the directors on the Triangle–Fine Arts lot. Dwan made several of Douglas Fairbanks' early films, including *A Modern Musketeer* (1917), and is credited with developing the perambulating camera tower that Griffith used to photograph the great hall of Babylon for *Intolerance* (1916).

By the early 1920s, Dwan had become one of Hollywood's most respected directors. He rejoined his old associate Douglas Fairbanks for *Robin Hood* (1922) and made some of Gloria Swanson's best pictures, including *Zaza* (1923), *Manhandled* (1924), and *Stage Struck* (1925). Those who knew him in the 1920s remembered that his great success made him rather arrogant, but after turning out first-class entertainments like *The Iron Mask, Tide of Empire* (both 1929), *What a Widow!* (1930), and *While Paris Sleeps* (1931), he went to Britain to make some (forgettable) pictures.

When Dwan returned to Hollywood two years later, he was a forgotten man and was forced to take a "salvage job" on *Hollywood Party* (1934). At Fox he decided to "keep my head down" and join the legion of B picture directors, though he was occasionally rewarded with major assignments like the Shirley Temple vehicles *Heidi* (1937) and *Rebecca of Sunnybrook Farm,* and *Suez* (both 1938). He managed to give panache to the Ritz Brothers' *The Three Musketeers,* and his *Frontier Marshal* (both 1939) was one of the best A Westerns made during the 1930s. At Universal, he directed a deliciously tongue-in-cheek Western, *Trail of the Vigilantes* (1940), and in the mid 1940s he turned out a series of popular farces for producer Edward Small, including *Abroad With Two Yanks* (1944), *Brewster's Millions,* and *Getting Gertie's Gar-*

ter (both 1945). He also piloted the hugely popular *Sands of Iwo Jima* (1949) during a spell at Republic Pictures.

Through the 1950s Dwan continued to turn out interesting pictures like *Silver Lode, Cattle Queen of Montana* (both 1954), and *The Restless Breed* (1957), most of which refused to take themselves too seriously and were better than their budgets and schedules would normally permit. Director Peter Bogdanovich conducted an extended oral history with Dwan that was published as "Allan Dwan: The Last Pioneer" in 1971.

DZUNDZA, GEORGE. Actor. *(b. July 19, 1945, Rosenheim, Germany.)* A Brian Dennehy without the sex appeal, this genial, roly-poly character player takes a nononsense, street-smart approach to his acting. His movie credits date back to 1978 and *The Deer Hunter,* but it's only been within the last few years that Dzundza has really started to establish himself. Usually seen in blue-collar roles or as cops, he did a standout job in Sondra Locke's crime-drama *Impulse* (1990), and garnered good reviews for his work in the TV series "Law and Order" (1990–91). His other films include *Best Defense* (1984), *No Mercy* (1986), *The Beast* (1988), and *White Hunter, Black Heart* (1990, as a Sam Spiegel–inspired movie producer, complete with dialect). Dzundza scored big as the lovesick meat-cutter in *The Butcher's Wife* (1991), and again just a few months later as Michael Douglas' cop partner in *Basic Instinct* (1992).

EASTWOOD, CLINT. Actor, producer, director. *(b. May 31, 1930, San Francisco.)* How many would ever have thought that a tall, laconic, squinty star of spaghetti Westerns and cop thrillers would end up directing art movies? Not many, we'd guess. In truth, though, that's been just another phase, just a natural extension of a career that has consistently confounded expectations. Reportedly an easygoing but shiftless young man who'd already worked in a variety of dead-end menial jobs (such as gas-station attendant) before reaching Hollywood in 1955, Eastwood wangled a contract at Universal thanks to director Arthur Lubin, and played bit parts that year in *Francis in the Navy, Tarantula,* and *Revenge of the Creature.*

Universal subsequently dropped Eastwood, but in 1959 he signed to star in the TV series "Rawhide," which kept him busy for the next six years. During the 1964 hiatus, he flew to Italy to star in a Western quickie, and thought no more of it until he found out that *A Fistful of Dollars* was a titanic success. He went back the next summer and again donned his flat-brimmed sombrero and ragged poncho in a sequel, *For a Few Dollars More,* and again for *The Good, the Bad, and the Ugly* (both 1966). That year, all three were finally released in the U.S., and "The Man With No Name" (as his character was billed) suddenly found himself atop the box-office charts. His icy, tight-lipped, implacable character—a trigger-happy gunman with his own moral code—struck just the right chord with 1960s audiences, who were just discovering in Humphrey Bogart a Hollywood relic with similar existential appeal. (It hardly mattered that Eastwood's character parodied the traditional Western-movie hero.)

Finally a star in his own country, Eastwood thereafter wisely varied his roles—though singing in the ambitious Western musical *Paint Your Wagon* (1969) may have stretched things a bit too far—and began a fruitful collaboration with director Don Siegel that resulted in such excellent and distinctive films as *Coogan's Bluff* (1968), *Two Mules for Sister Sara* (1970), *The Beguiled,* and of course, *Dirty Harry* (both 1971), which spawned four sequels, virtually invented the loose-cannon cop genre, and gave him the screen character for which he will always be remembered. (Ironically, he only took the role after Frank Sinatra dropped out at the last minute.)

In 1971, Eastwood made his directorial debut with the chiller *Play Misty for Me,* and continued to wield the megaphone frequently thereafter. Eastwood also set up his own production company, Malpaso, and for the next 15 years churned out hit after hit, alternating action films with off-beat comedies; notable in this period were *High Plains Drifter* (1973), *The Outlaw—Josey Wales* (1976), *The Gauntlet* (1977), *Every Which Way But Loose* (1978), *Escape From Alcatraz* (1979, directed by Siegel), *Tightrope* (1984), *Pale Rider* (1985, a return to Westerns and a thinly

disguised reworking of *Shane*), and *Heartbreak Ridge* (1986).

As Eastwood neared 60, his star began to dim, but he continued to surprise. He directed *Bird* (1988), a critically acclaimed biography of jazz great Charlie Parker; starred in and directed *White Hunter, Black Heart* (1990, playing a film director modeled after John Huston); and assumed the same chores on *The Rookie* (1991, with Charlie Sheen). Extremely canny about alternating mass-audience movies with more personal, limited-appeal projects, Eastwood managed to combine both types of films with *Unforgiven* (1992), a revisionist Western that won rave reviews—as well as Academy Awards for Best Picture and Best Director—and did extremely well at the box office. Following this personal triumph, he agreed to act in someone else's movie for the first time in years and delivered one of the best performances of his career as an aging Secret Service man (who just happens to play jazz piano) in *In the Line of Fire* (1993). Definitely on a winning streak, he then teamed up with Kevin Costner to costar in and direct *A Perfect World* (also 1993). In 1995, Eastwood won the Academy's Irving Thalberg award, then directed and acted opposite Meryl Streep in *The Bridges of Madison County* (1995). He has also served as mayor of his hometown of Carmel, California. It may be revealing that this superstar of shoot-'em-ups both urban and Western has said for years that his own favorite of his films is the cerebral and highly stylized *The Beguiled.*

EBSEN, BUDDY. Actor; dancer. *(b. Apr. 2, 1908, Belleville, Ill., as Christian Rudolph Ebsen.)* While he's familiar to TV fans as cornpone millionaire Jed Clampett on the sitcom "The Beverly Hillbillies" (1962–71) and as the soft-spoken P.I. "Barnaby Jones" (1973–80)—and to an earlier generation as Fess Parker's sidekick in Disney's "Davy Crockett" shows in the 1950s—this tall, lanky actor actually began his show-biz career decades earlier, performing in theater and vaudeville (with his sister as dancing partner) before entering motion pictures. He showed off his loose-limbed hoofing style in *Broadway Melody of 1936* (1935), *Captain January* (1936), and *Broadway Mel-*

ody of 1938 (1937), and generally played mild-mannered, bucolic types. His subsequent films, with the exception of two features compiled from the "Davy Crockett" episodes (one from 1955, the other from 1956) and *Breakfast at Tiffany's* (1961), for the most part have been insubstantial. They include *Parachute Battalion* (1941), *Red Garters* (1954), and *The One and Only, Genuine, Original Family Band* (1968). In 1993 he revisited his past, appearing as Barnaby Jones in a cameo for the slicked-up movie version of *The Beverly Hillbillies*!

EDDY, NELSON. Actor, singer. *(b. June 29, 1901, Providence, R.I.; d. Mar. 6, 1967.)* This stolid, blond baritone was, as half of the most successful singing team in 1930s movies, one of Hollywood's top stars. Yet the source of his appeal escapes today's viewers, who see in him a personable but essentially humorless performer. A one-time newspaper reporter who parlayed a lifelong passion for singing into a successful career in opera (first with the Philadelphia Civic Opera, later with New York's Metropolitan), he was signed by MGM in 1933. He sang with little discernible impact in *Dancing Lady, Broadway to Hollywood* (both 1933), and *Student Tour* (1934). Then he was teamed with popular musical star Jeanette MacDonald in the Victor Herbert operetta *Naughty Marietta* (1935).

The unexplained success of *Naughty Marietta*—at a time when backstage musicals of the Busby Berkeley variety held sway over the nation's box-offices—transformed him overnight into a major star. He and Jeanette were ideally mated on-screen, and their chaste version of romantic love had wide appeal (that endures to this day, as a legion of "MacEddy" fans will attest). He and MacDonald were profitably reteamed in *Rose Marie* (1936), *Maytime* (1937), *Girl of the Golden West, Sweethearts* (both 1938), *New Moon, Bitter Sweet* (both 1940), and the ill-conceived modern-day musical fantasy *I Married an Angel* (1942).

Eddy occasionally appeared minus MacDonald: with Eleanor Powell in *Rosalie* (1937), Ilona Massey in *Balalaika*, Virginia Bruce in *Let Freedom Ring* (both 1939), and Risë Stevens in *The Chocolate Soldier* (1941). Released by Metro, he went to Universal for its lavish Technicolor remake of *The Phantom of the Opera* (1943), in which he cut a dashing figure and sang with his accustomed gusto, but was completely overshadowed by the exploits of titular terror Claude Rains. After *Knickerbocker Holiday* (1944) and *Northwest Outpost* (1947, a dismal Rudolf Friml operetta that reunited him with Massey), he abandoned acting for concert appearances, nightclub performances, and recordings. One unheralded highlight of his screen career came in Walt Disney's 1946 animated feature *Make Mine Music*. Eddy narrated and provided all the voices for a delightful comic tale called "The Whale Who Wanted to Sing at the Met" (aka "Willie the Operatic Whale"), revealing colors, and a sense of humor—even about himself—that seldom crept into his other performances.

EDEN, BARBARA. Actress. *(b. Aug. 23, 1934, Tucson, Ariz., as Barbara Huffman.)* This fresh-faced curvaceous, all-American former cheerleader made her film debut in a bit part in the plane-crash drama *Back From Eternity* (1956), and appeared in her first major TV role that same year on "West Point." Two years later she starred in the TV sitcom "How to Marry a Millionaire," but shortly thereafter returned to feature-film work (although she picked up many guest spots in episodic TV for several years thereafter). She was competent but largely decorative in such films as *Flaming Star* (1960), *Voyage to the Bottom of the Sea* (1961), *The Interns* (1962), and *7 Faces of Dr. Lao* (1964) before becoming a familiar face—and midriff—as the bottle-inhabiting blonde on the hit TV sitcom "I Dream of Jeannie" (1965–70). Subsequently, she has started a cottage industry of sorts, playing upbeat suburban housewives—and an occasional femme fatale—in innumerable TV movies. After starring in the feature-film comedy *Harper Valley P.T.A.* (1978), she was tapped for a short-lived TV series spawned by the movie's impressive ratings when it was first broadcast on television. Still popping up frequently on TV, she also tours the country in revivals of major plays. 1985 and 1991 saw her reuniting with "Jeannie" costar Bill Daily (but not lead Larry Hagman) for reunion telefilms. Eden was married to actor Michael Ansara from 1958 to 1973.

EDWARDS, ANTHONY. Actor. *(b. July 19, 1963, Santa Barbara, Calif.)* From the minute you saw him in *Top Gun* (1986), playing the straight-arrow pal to reckless test pilot Tom Cruise, you knew he wouldn't make it past the fourth reel. And he didn't. The second-banana role fit Edwards like a glove, but this tall, open-faced, likable young actor also has plenty of leading roles under his tightly notched belt. In TV commercials since he was 16, Edwards attended London's Royal Academy of Dramatic Art and USC before making his tyro film appearance in 1982's *Fast Times at Ridgemont High.* He made a very convincing nerd in *Revenge of the Nerds* (1984), a lowbrow comedy hit that spawned a 1987 sequel (in which, wisely, he restricted his role to a cameo appearance). 1985's *Gotcha!* and *The Sure Thing* moved his career along, although the ponderous *Summer Heat* (1987) and the ridiculous *Miracle Mile* (1989) didn't do him any good. Edwards received his most favorable notices in the title role of *Mr. North* (1988), playing the forthright, ingenious young man who electrifies a Prohibition-era community. Although still young-looking enough to play a student, he actually played a college counselor in *How I Got Into College* (1989), and a naive suburban cop transferred to the funky part of town with world-weary Forest Whitaker in *Downtown* (1990). He had a recurring role on TV's "Northern Exposure" (1992–93) and joined the cast of "E.R." (1994–). Edwards wasn't the first in his family to be involved in the industry: His grandfather designed Walt Disney Studios in the 1930s.

EDWARDS, BLAKE. Producer, director, screenwriter. *(b. July 26, 1922, Tulsa, Okla., as William Blake McEdwards.)* In the 1960s, Andrew Sarris wrote that Edwards "is one writer-director who has got some of his biggest laughs out of jokes that are too gruesome for most horror films." Today, Edwards is still mining the pain from slapstick, and though his track record is erratic, the style is uniquely his own. His stepfather, Jack McEdwards, a production manager, often used him as a movie extra,

and Edwards got his first speaking role in *Ten Gentlemen From West Point* (1942). After some minor roles, he and a friend wrote and produced the low-budget Western *Panhandle* (1948), which also gave Edwards his first—and last—starring role. He decided to stick to writing and created the successful radio show "Richard Diamond: Private Detective" for Dick Powell. This led to Hollywood attention, and he wrote several musical scripts with actor turned director Richard Quine—*Rainbow 'Round My Shoulder, Sound Off* (both 1952), and *All Ashore* (1953). He also cocreated a TV sitcom for Mickey Rooney, "Hey Mulligan" (aka "The Mickey Rooney Show," 1954–55), before winning the opportunity to direct his own script for the Frankie Laine vehicle *Bring Your Smile Along* (1955). He followed this mild musical comedy with a number of different projects that showcased impressive versatility and energy: the Prohibition spoof *He Laughed Last* (1956, which he also wrote), the hit submarine comedy caper *Operation Petticoat* (1959), the charming adaptation of *Breakfast at Tiffany's* (1961, which won the Oscar for its unforgettable theme, "Moon River"), the thriller *Experiment in Terror* (1962), and the bleak, harrowing *Days of Wine and Roses* (1962), with Jack Lemmon and Lee Remick as alcoholics.

On a roll, Edwards created one of film comedy's great characters, the accident-prone Inspector Clouseau, brilliantly played by Peter Sellers in *The Pink Panther* (1964) and the even better *A Shot in the Dark* (1964). This established Edwards as a modern-day master of sight gags and slapstick comedy, though his efforts in this field over the years have been extremely hit-and-miss, even in his gargantuan silent-comedy homage, *The Great Race* (1965, which Edwards dedicated on-screen to "Mr. Laurel and Mr. Hardy"), with its huge but not terribly funny pie-throwing melee. *What Did You Do in the War, Daddy?* (1966) and the slapstick set-piece *The Party* (1968, with Peter Sellers) met with varying degrees of success from critics and the public, but *Darling Lili* (1970), a romantic spoof with Edwards' wife Julie Andrews as a WWI spy, was a notorious flop, which Edwards attributed to Paramount's insistence on adding musical numbers and aerial combat sequences. His next films, *Wild Rovers* (1971) and

The Carey Treatment (1972), were recut by MGM head James Aubrey and also bombed. (Many years later, Edwards got to recut *Lili* and *Rovers,* and the results were reevaluated much more favorably.)

Depressed, Edwards retreated to Switzerland for some time, then teamed up with Sellers again for *The Return of the Pink Panther* (1975), which prompted the lively if formulaic followups *The Pink Panther Strikes Back* (1976) and *Revenge of the Pink Panther* (1978). With his commercial standing restored, he wrote, directed and produced three of his best films: *10* (1979), a comic study of male menopause that made stars out of Dudley Moore and Bo Derek; *S.O.B.* (1981), a stinging Hollywood satire in which Andrews buried her "Mary Poppins" image forever by bearing her breasts; and *Victor/ Victoria* (1982), a stylish and delightful comedy (arguably, Edwards' finest film) with Andrews as a singer who becomes a hit in 1930s Paris disguised as a man. Since then, Edwards' nonstop output has been mixed, ranging from silly but winning farce (*Micki + Maude,* 1984; *Skin Deep,* 1989) to the more introspective (*The Man Who Loved Women,* 1983; *That's Life!,* 1986—both co-authored by Edwards and his analyst, Dr. Milton Wexler) to stale retreads of old formulas (*A Fine Mess,* 1986; *Blind Date,* 1987; *Switch,* 1991). There have also been the ill-advised attempts to keep the Panther series going, long after Sellers' death in 1980, with *Trail of the Pink Panther* (1982), *Curse of the Pink Panther* (1983), and most recently, *Son of the Pink Panther* (1993), with Italian comic actor Roberto Benigni.

In addition to the films that have featured his wife, such as *The Tamarind Seed* (1974), *10,* and *Victor/Victoria,* Edwards has featured his daughter Jennifer in *S.O.B., The Man Who Loved Women,* and *Son of the Pink Panther,* and enabled his son Geoffrey to apprentice as an editor on many of his projects; he even filmed most of *That's Life!* at his Malibu home. Edwards also created the stylish TV detective series "Peter Gunn" (1958–61) and "Mr. Lucky" (1959–60), which launched his hugely successful and enduring relationship with composer Henry Mancini. (He later revived Peter Gunn in the 1967 theatrical movie *Gunn* and a 1989 telefeature, *Peter Gunn.*) His attempt at a situation-comedy vehicle for Andrews, "Julie," lasted only a few episodes in 1992.

EGAN, RICHARD. Actor. *(b. July 29, 1921, San Francisco; d. July 20, 1987.)* Well-educated (with a master's degree from Stanford), beefy, handsome leading man of 1950s action-adventure films. A passable actor, he was too stolid and humorless to be credible in anything else, especially comedies or musicals. Following his service stint in World War 2, Egan was a teacher for several years before going to Hollywood, where his brawny physique and rugged manner suited him for vigorous heroics. He died from prostate cancer. FILMS INCLUDE: 1950: *The Damned Don't Cry;* 1951: *Hollywood Story;* 1953: *Split Second;* 1954: *Demetrius and the Gladiators;* 1955: *Untamed, Violent Saturday, Underwater!* (the last opposite Jane Russell—it was a toss-up as to who had the bigger chest); 1956: *The Revolt of Mamie Stover, Love Me Tender* (the latter with Elvis Presley in his first screen role); 1959: *A Summer Place;* 1960: *Esther and the King;* 1967: *Valley of Mystery;* 1969: *The Big Cube;* 1979: *The Sweet Creek County War.*

EGGAR, SAMANTHA. Actress. *(b. Mar. 5, 1939, Hampstead, London.)* Attractive British actress, probably best remembered as the art student held captive by Terence Stamp in *The Collector* (1965), a performance that earned a Best Acting prize at Cannes, as well as an Oscar nomination. Before this, she had acted with several Shakespeare repertory companies and went on to appear in the films *The Wild and the Willing* (1959), *Doctor in Distress* (1963), and *Psyche '59* (1964). After the success of *The Collector,* she costarred in *Return From the Ashes* (1965), *Walk, Don't Run* (1966), *Doctor Dolittle* (1967), *The Molly Maguires, The Lady in the Car With Glasses and a Gun, The Walking Stick* (all 1970), and *The Light at the Edge of the World* (1971). Since then, her credits—with the exceptions of *The Seven Percent Solution* (1976, as Mary Watson) and *Why Shoot the Teacher?* (1977)—have been mostly undistinguished projects, or worse, like *The Dead Are Alive* (1972), *The Brood* (1979, directed by David Cronenberg), *The Ex-*

terminator (1980), *Demonoid, Messenger of Death* (1981), *Curtains* (1982), and *Round Numbers* (1992). She also works regularly in television and costarred with Yul Brynner in the short-lived "Anna and the King" series in 1972. In 1993 she costarred in the TV miniseries "The Secret of Lake Success."

EGOYAN, ATOM. Director, writer. *(b. July 19, 1960, Cairo.)* Raised in Victoria, British Columbia, Egoyan was an honors student at the University of Toronto, where he began making short films. From his debut feature, *Next of Kin* (1984), he has been concerned with the power of imagery in contemporary society, and the manner in which individuals have become isolated and alienated in an increasingly voyeuristic and technology-fixated world. *The Adjuster* (1991), his best film to date, is a highly provocative account of an insurance adjuster who peeks in on the lives of his clients, while his wife, a censor, secretly tapes the pornographic material she is classifying. The talent displayed in his first features got him assignments directing episodes of the new "Twilight Zone" and "Alfred Hitchcock Presents" TV series. His other features, which have won him growing acclaim throughout the film community, include *Family Viewing* (1987), *Speaking Parts* (1989), *Montreal vu par* (1991, as codirector), *Gross Misconduct* (1992 telefeature), *Calendar* (1993), and *Exotica* (1994).

EICHHORN, LISA. Actress. *(b. Feb. 4, 1952, Reading, Pa.)* Reliable actress whose initial shot at stardom didn't pan out. American-born Eichhorn attended the Royal Academy of Dramatic Art in London and shortly after graduating got her first movie job, opposite Richard Gere in *Yanks* (1979). Unfortunately, the film was a notorious flop, and neither Merchant and Ivory's *The Europeans* (also 1979) nor the barely released *Why Would I Lie?* (1980) did much to establish her with audiences, though *Cutter's Way* (1981) won critical plaudits and a fervent following. She has spent considerable time on stage in London, New York, and Los Angeles, and worked in television both in the U.S. and abroad. Her film work has been sporadic, with such varied credits as *Wildrose*

(1984, as a female iron worker), and *Opposing Force* (1986), *Grim Prairie Tales* (1990) and the TV miniseries "A Woman Named Jackie" (1991). She registered strongly in two 1993 films, *The Vanishing* (as Jeff Bridges' wife) and *King of the Hill* (as the young protagonist's consumptive mother).

EISENSTEIN, SERGEI. Director, theoretician. *(b. Jan. 29, 1898, Riga, Latvia; d. Feb. 10, 1948.)* Perhaps best identified as the Soviet Union's D. W. Griffith, this cinematic pioneer is remembered for his classic depictions of events leading up to the 1917 Russian Revolution; these include the silent films *Strike* (1924), *Battleship Potemkin* (1925), and *October* (aka *Ten Days That Shook the World*, 1928). In these and other films Eisenstein refined the practice of cinematic montage—the use of quick cutting to manipulate cinematic time and/or convey a certain meaning—although today many of his cinematic juxtapositions, like cutting from a shot of the head of the pre-Bolshevik provisional government to one of a preening peacock, come off as hopelessly obvious. In other cases, like the still unmatched Odessa Steps sequence in *Potemkin,* his work is masterful. His burgeoning international reputation brought him to America in the early 1930s; after several abortive attempts at mounting a production here, including a disastrous foray to Mexico to make a documentary, *Que Viva Mexico* (the footage from which was subsequently assembled several different ways by people claiming to know what the director's true intentions were), Eisenstein returned to Russia. He was subjected to increasing harassment by Stalin's regime, leading to many never-completed projects and work delays.

Under watchful eyes, he turned out the rousing *Alexander Nevsky* (1938) for the government propaganda machine; this story of a 13th-century Russian military triumph was meant to inspire the populace for the coming battle with Nazi Germany. His last project was a projected three-part biography, *Ivan the Terrible;* only two magnificent-looking but dramatically florid parts were completed before Eisenstein's death from a heart attack.

EKBERG, ANITA. Actress. *(b. Sept. 29, 1931, Malmö, Sweden.)* A woman whose pneumatic aspect was so extreme as to be caricaturish, this former Miss Sweden made an inauspicious Hollywood debut as a Venusian maiden in *Abbott and Costello Go to Mars* (1953). The statuesque, imposing Ekberg, difficult to cast, turned up in Jayne Mansfield–like roles in Frank Tashlin's comedies *Artists and Models* (1955) and *Hollywood or Bust* (1956), both starring Dean Martin and Jerry Lewis, and *Back from Eternity* (1956). She was serviceable in Gerd Oswald's thriller *Screaming Mimi* (1958), but really hit her stride playing a bombshell actress in Fellini's *La Dolce Vita* (1960). The Italian director also cast her in his contribution to the 1962 omnibus film *Boccaccio '70.* She had practically disappeared from American screens by the early 1970s, and made only periodic appearances in European films. She resurfaced in Hollywood, considerably overweight, to appear in embarrassing trifles such as *Gold of the Amazon Women* (1979) and *Daisy Chain* (1981). Fellini featured the now alarmingly bloated Ekberg in his 1987 *Intervista.*

ELAM, JACK. Actor. *(b. Nov. 13, 1916, Miami, Ariz.)* Wild-eyed, croaky-voiced character actor second to none in the ancient and venerable art of scene-stealing. His career falls into three distinct phases: In the 1950s and 1960s, he was a matchless thug in *High Noon, Rancho Notorious* (both 1952), *Kiss Me Deadly* (1955), *Gunfight at the O.K. Corral* (1957), *Baby Face Nelson* (1958), and *The Comancheros* (1961). In the late 1960s he drifted into comedic portrayals, mostly in Westerns, often playing a self-parodying Western heavy, as in *Once Upon a Time in the West* (1968), *Support Your Local Sheriff!* (1969), *Rio Lobo* (1970), and *Support Your Local Gunfighter* (1971). By the mid 1970s, Elam had essayed dozens of such roles; gradually, over the next few years—upon becoming "too old and too fat to jump on a horse," as he puts it—Elam grew a long beard and settled into lovable-old-coot characterizations. Much of his work in the last decade has been confined to TV movies *(Once Upon a Texas Train* and *Where the Hell's That Gold?!!?,* both 1988) and independent,

modestly budgeted theatrical movies such as *Aurora Encounter* (1986), *The Giant of Thunder Mountain* (1991), and *Suburban Commando* (1991). Elam has also been featured in the sitcoms "Struck by Lightning" (1979) and "Easy Street" (1986–87).

ELFMAN, DANNY. Composer. *(b. May 29, 1953, Los Angeles.)* Elfman leads a double life: as one of the most successful and sought-after film composers in Hollywood, and as a charter member of the cult rock group Oingo Boingo (along with brother Richard Elfman). His first assignment was providing music for his brother's bizarre feature film *Forbidden Zone* (1980), but it was his circusy, cartoonish score for *Pee-wee's Big Adventure* (1985) that made people sit up and take notice. That was director Tim Burton's first feature, and they've worked together since then on *Beetlejuice* (1988), *Batman* (1989), *Edward Scissorhands* (1990) and *Batman Returns* (1992). Elfman has also scored such diverse films as *Back to School* (1986), *Midnight Run, Big Top Pee-wee* (both 1988), *Dick Tracy,* and *Darkman* (both 1990). Initially typecast for his *Pee-wee*–type music, then associated with the rich textures of the symphonic *Batman* score, Elfman has continued to defy those who would pigeonhole him, as his excellent (and atypical) work on *Sommersby* (1993) and *Black Beauty* (1994) confirms. He also composed the theme music for TV's "The Simpsons" and provided a song score for Tim Burton's *Nightmare Before Christmas* (1993), as well as singing the voice of lead character Jack Skellington.

ELIZONDO, HECTOR. Actor. *(b. Dec. 12, 1936, New York City.)* Even people who hated *Pretty Woman* (1990) had to concede that Elizondo's warm, knowing performance as the fatherly hotel manager was an absolute gem of screen acting. It was just one highlight in the career of this bald, gap-toothed, usually mustachioed character actor who has played a Mexican bandit in *Valdez Is Coming* (1971), a psychopathic killer in *The Taking of Pelham One Two Three* (1974), a dogged detective in *The Fan* (1981), a middle-class family man in *The Flamingo Kid* (1984), and an incorruptible football coach in *Necessary Roughness* (1991), to name a few. Garry Marshall considers Elizondo a good-luck charm, casting him in every film he's directed, most recently as a Greek coffee shop owner in *Frankie and Johnny* (1991). Among his extensive TV credits, the high point would be his avuncular D.A. on "Foley Square" (1985–86), with the low being Captain Renault in the David Soul version of "Casablanca" (1983). He copped a rare starring role in the 1992 miniseries "The Burden of Proof."

ELLIOTT, DENHOLM. Actor. *(b. May 31, 1922, London; d. Oct. 6, 1992.)* "I'm often given parts that aren't as big as they are colorful, but people remember them," Elliott once said. "When it's a minor or supporting role, you learn to make the most of what you're given. I can make two lines seem like Hamlet."

Like many career character actors, Elliott gained disproportionate fame in the last years of his life by appearing in a handful of wildly popular films—as Dan Aykroyd's valet, who now must serve Eddie Murphy, in *Trading Places* (1983), and as Harrison Ford's professional colleague Marcus Brody in *Raiders of the Lost Ark* (1981) and *Indiana Jones and the Last Crusade* (1989).

Elliott pursued a stage career after spending three years in a prisoner-of-war camp during World War 2. He made his London stage debut in 1946, his film debut in 1949 *(Dear Mr. Prohack)*, and his Broadway debut one year after that. Always reliable, often inspired, Elliott came into his own (at least in movies) during the 1970s and 1980s with a series of plum parts, the best of which was arguably the drunken, dissolute filmmaker who fashions an "artistic" Bar Mitzvah movie in *The Apprenticeship of Duddy Kravitz* (1974). He earned an Academy Award nomination for his performance as Mr. Emerson in *A Room With a View* (1985). He also worked occasionally in television, and in 1991 he inherited the role of John Le Carré's fabled spy George Smiley from Alec Guinness for the TV movie *A Murder of Quality*. He died one year later from AIDS-related tuberculosis. He was once married to actress Virginia McKenna.

OTHER FILMS INCLUDE: 1952: *Breaking the Sound Barrier, The Holly and the Ivy;* 1953: *The Cruel Sea;* 1955: *The Night My Number Came Up;* 1964: *Nothing But the Best;* 1965: *King Rat;* 1966: *Alfie;* 1968: *The Night They Raided Minsky's, The Sea Gull;* 1973: *A Doll's House* (Claire Bloom version); 1976: *Robin and Marian* (as Will Scarlett), *Voyage of the Damned;* 1978: *The Boys From Brazil, Watership Down* (voice); 1979: *Cuba, Saint Jack, Zulu Dawn;* 1980: *Bad Timing: A Sensual Obsession;* 1982: *The Missionary, Brimstone and Treacle;* 1983: *The Hound of the Baskervilles* (made for TV); 1984: *The Razor's Edge;* 1985: *A Private Function;* 1985: *Defence of the Realm;* 1987: *Maurice, September;* 1991: *Toy Soldiers;* 1992: *Noises Off.*

ELLIOTT, SAM. Actor. *(b. Aug. 9, 1944, Sacramento, Calif.)* This rail-thin, rough-hewn leading man and character player has played so many laconic loners that you'd just like to reach into the movie screen, grab him by the shoulders, and shake him up a little bit. He's been acting for a good many years, especially in the Western genre, for which he's a natural. In fact, Elliott first met his significant other, actress Katharine Ross, on the set of his first movie, *Butch Cassidy and the Sundance Kid* (1969), in which he had a bit role as a card player. He first attracted attention as the aging title character in *Lifeguard* (1976), which teamed him with rising young female leads Anne Archer and Kathleen Quinlan. Perfect as a taciturn cowboy, he starred in the TV miniseries "The Sacketts" (1979) and "The Shadow Riders" (1982). Elliott's other films include *Mask* (1985), *Fatal Beauty* (1987) and *Roadhouse* (1989, playing an aging bouncer who's treated like a world-weary gunfighter). *Sibling Rivalry* (1990) offered Elliott a comic change of pace as Kirstie Alley's adulterous partner, who has a fatal heart attack while they're in bed together. In *Rush* (1991) he played a sympathetic police captain who tried to keep undercover narc Jennifer Jason Leigh from going over the edge. With Ross he coproduced and costarred in a made-for-cable adaptation of Louis L'Amour's low-key Western *Conagher* (1991), which garnered excellent reviews. Continuing in period roles (which seem to suit him), he also appeared in *Gettysburg* and *Tombstone* (both 1993, in the latter as Virgil Earp).

ELLIOTT, WILLIAM "WILD BILL."
Actor. *(b. Oct. 15, 1903, Pattonsburg, Mo., as Gordon Elliott; d. Nov. 26, 1965.)* "I'm a peaceable man," he'd say, and then—whammo!—down the heavies would go. It was the inevitable scene in this lanky, tight-lipped cowboy star's dozens of low-budget Westerns, and it never failed to get a whoop from Saturday-matinee audiences. Elliott, who made his film debut in a bit in *The Plastic Age* (1925), spent years lingering in backgrounds as a dress extra or "tennis, anyone?" type. He can be spotted in most of the Warner Bros. films of the early and mid-1930s, and in speaking roles from around 1934 on. Columbia, looking for a new Western star and seeing in the taciturn Elliott some of the qualities of a William S. Hart, starred him in a 1938 serial, *The Great Adventures of Wild Bill Hickok.* With that chapterplay's success, Gordon Elliott became "Wild Bill," and was launched in a series of B Westerns beginning with 1938's *In Early Arizona.*

By 1943, with his star on the rise, Elliott moved to Republic—a Western star's mecca—and the following year, he made *Tucson Raiders,* the first of 16 films as comic-strip cowboy sensation Red Ryder. He bore no resemblance to the printed-page character, but the action-packed oaters were enormously popular just the same. In 1946, Elliott got "kicked upstairs" to A Westerns like *Plainsman and the Lady* (1946), *The Fabulous Texan* (1947), and *Hellfire* (1949, a particularly good one). But adult audiences didn't take to him as the kids had, and by 1950 he was back in B Westerns, this time for Monogram. While lacking the Republic polish, Elliott's Monograms—especially *The Longhorn, The Showdown* (both 1950), *Waco* (1952), and *Bitter Creek* (1954)—were taut, well-made little films. When the B Western market died in the mid 1950s, Elliott shifted to detective dramas, such as *Sudden Danger* (1955) and *Footsteps in the Night* (1957, his last), which met with indifference at box offices. A lifelong smoker—and ad pitchman for cigarettes—he died of lung cancer.

ELWES, CARY. Actor. *(b. Oct. 26, 1962, London.)* Boyishly handsome actor who has established his versatility in a number of comedic and dramatic roles. Born into a family of painters, Elwes left England to attend Sarah Lawrence College in New York; after gaining stage experience in off-Broadway plays, he returned to England and made his film debut in *Another Country* (1984). Elwes costarred in the historical drama *Lady Jane* (1985), and then made his first big impression playing for laughs as the farm boy Westley in the hit *The Princess Bride* (1987). Since then, he has been seen as Tom Cruise's racing competitor in *Days of Thunder* (1990), Matthew Broderick's gallant second-in-command in *Glory* (1989), the absurdly ego-ridden fighter pilot in *Hot Shots!* (1991), and the helpless fiancé of ill-fated Lucy (Sadie Frost) in *Bram Stoker's Dracula* (1992). He starred opposite Bridget Fonda in *Leather Jackets,* a modern-day Romeo and Juliet story set amid warring street gangs; made in 1992, it bypassed U.S. theatrical release and went straight to home video. He costarred in *The Crush* (1993) and served Mel Brooks well as the convincing—and authentically British—hero of *Robin Hood: Men in Tights* (also 1993).

ENGLUND, ROBERT. Actor. *(b. June 6, 1949, Los Angeles.)* It's got to be a little daunting for an actor to realize that his most famous, career-making characterization is one that smothers his face under heavy makeup—and casts him as a child molester and murderer. But that may be this boyish, curly-haired actor's lot in life, to be remembered as the blood-curdling Freddy Krueger, "star" of the *Nightmare on Elm Street* movies. Possibly the most unlikely horror star since mild-mannered, soft-spoken Boris Karloff, Englund studied acting at UCLA before landing his first feature-film role as a backwoods lover in *Buster and Billie* (1974), a hayseed Romeo and Juliet story. A series of inconsequential roles followed—including *Hustle* (1975), *St. Ives, A Star Is Born, Stay Hungry* (all 1976), *Big Wednesday* (1978), *The Fifth Floor* (1980), *Dead and Buried,* and *Galaxy of Terror* (both 1981)—before director Wes Craven tapped him to play the nocturnal nemesis of the original *A Nightmare on Elm Street* (1984). Through the success of that picture and its six sequels, Englund has become something of a cult figure; with his newly earned clout he landed a directorial opportunity in 1988 with *976-EVIL* (which, unfortunately, wasn't successful). Despite efforts to branch into mainstream movies, Englund's post-Freddy roles haven't exactly been challenging ones: He played the titular terror in the minor remake of *The Phantom of the Opera* (1989), and appeared as a comic heavy in the Andrew Dice Clay vehicle, *The Adventures of Ford Fairlane* (1990). He also starred in the TV series "Nightmare Cafe" (1992), executive produced by Wes Craven, and *The Mangler* (1995).

EPHRON, NORA. Screenwriter, director. (b. May 19, 1941, New York City.) Witty, erudite writer and essayist who has become a leading screenwriter and, more recently, a director. She first made her name writing caustic comic pieces for "Esquire" and other publications; her collection "Crazy Salad" made the best-seller lists. Her parents, Phoebe and Henry Ephron, were leading Hollywood screenwriters for many years; in fact, teenaged Nora was reportedly the inspiration for *Take Her, She's Mine* (1963), in which "she" was played by Sandra Dee. She followed their roman à clef example by chronicling her failed marriage to writer Carl Bernstein in a novel called "Heartburn," which she adapted for the screen in 1986; "she" was played in that film by Meryl Streep. She got an Oscar nomination for her first screenwriting effort (with frequent partner Alice Arlen), *Silkwood* (1983). Other writing credits include *Cookie* (1989, also executive produced), *When Harry Met Sally* (1989, another Oscar nomination; she also associate produced), and *My Blue Heaven* (1990, also executive produced). She made her directing debut with 1992's *This Is My Life*, which she cowrote with her sister Delia. It was critically well received, but financially disappointing; she made up for that with her next film as cowriter-director, *Sleepless in Seattle* (1993), an unqualified smash hit. *Mixed Nuts* (1994) did not repeat that success.

EPSTEIN, PHILIP and JULIUS. Screenwriters. (b. Aug. 22, 1909, New York City; **Philip Epstein**—d. Feb. 7, 1952.) These twin brothers were among the most reliable screenwriters of the sound era;

they collaborated on a large number of projects, generally comedies and melodramas, many adapted from the stage. The stage adaptation that ensured them screen immortality was from an unproduced play called "Everybody Comes to Rick's," a wartime romance that was retitled *Casablanca* for Hollywood and won the brothers a Best Screenplay Academy Award for 1943. (Although a handful of writers worked on the screenplay, latter-day scholarship has determined that most of the film's wit can be attributed to the Epsteins' efforts.) Julius remained active in screenwriting after his brother's premature death, and received Academy Award nominations in 1972 (for writing *Pete 'n' Tillie*) and 1983 (for his particularly witty adaptation of Peter DeVries' wry novel *Reuben, Reuben*).

OTHER FILMS INCLUDE: 1934: *Living on Velvet* (their first); 1938: *Four Daughters* (for which Julius was Oscar-nominated); 1941: *The Man Who Came to Dinner; The Strawberry Blonde;* 1942: *Yankee Doodle Dandy;* 1944: *Arsenic and Old Lace;* 1948: *Romance on the High Seas.*

ERICKSON, LEIF. Actor. (b. Oct. 27, 1911, Alameda, Calif., as William Anderson; d. Jan. 29, 1986.) Tall, beefy, deep-voiced character actor who'd been a band singer and trombone player before getting into movies in 1935. An inauspicious debut (as a corpse) in the Zane Grey Western *Wanderer of the Wasteland* (1935) was Erickson's first assignment under a Paramount contract; he was initially billed as "Glenn" Erickson. He was under contract to Universal during the early 1940s before entering the Armed Forces, and was twice wounded during World War 2. A pleasant personality translated indifferently onscreen and he never really hit it big. Erickson, who was once married to actress Frances Farmer, also appeared on stage and in many TV shows, including "The High Chaparral" (1967–71).

OTHER FILMS INCLUDE: 1935: *Nevada;* 1936: *College Holiday* (as the juvenile lead); 1937: *Waikiki Wedding, Conquest;* 1938: *The Big Broadcast of 1938, Ride a Crooked Mile;* 1939: *One Third of a Nation;* 1941: *Nothing but the Truth;* 1942: *The Fleet's In, Eagle Squadron, Pardon My Sarong, Night Monster;* 1947: *The Gangster;* 1948: *Sorry, Wrong Number, The Snake Pit;* 1950: *Stella, Three*

Secrets; 1951: *Show Boat;* 1952: *Sailor Be-ware, Carbine Williams;* 1953: *Invaders From Mars;* 1954: *On the Waterfront* (as Glover); 1956: *Tea and Sympathy;* 1958: *The Young Lions, Twilight of the Gods;* 1964: *Strait-Jacket, The Carpetbaggers;* 1965: *Mirage;* 1972: *Man and Boy;* 1975: *Winter Hawk;* 1977: *Twilight's Last Gleaming.*

ERMEY, R[ONALD] LEE. Actor. *(b. Mar. 24, 1944, Emporia, Kans.)* If Ermey's riveting performance as drill instructor Gunnery Sergeant Hartman in Stanley Kubrick's *Full Metal Jacket* (1987) seemed genuine, that's because Ermey was in fact a Marine who served during the Vietnam War. After retiring on full medical disability pay, Ermey got a part as a chopper pilot in *Apocalypse Now* (1979) and served as technical advisor on two other Vietnam-based movies, *The Boys in Company C* (1978) and *Purple Hearts* (1984), in which he played small parts. His portrayal of Hartman was hailed by critics, and since then he has played a variety of supporting roles in such films as *Fletch Lives, Mississippi Burning* (both 1988), *Demonstone* (1990), *Sommersby, Hexed* (both 1993), and *Body Snatchers* (1994).

ERROL, LEON. Actor. *(b. July 3, 1881, Sydney, Australia; d. Oct. 12, 1951.)* Popular character actor in features and star of more than 100 two-reel comedy shorts. Short and balding, with pinched features and a raspy voice, Errol convulsed stage and screen audiences with his rubber-legged drunk routine, a sketch he developed in vaudeville and burlesque before taking it to the Ziegfeld Follies in 1911. Errol made his film debut in *Yolanda* (1924), and subsequently appeared in *Sally, Clothes Make the Pirate* (both 1925), *Lunatic at Large* (1927), and other silent films, but he found his greatest screen success during the talkie era. Errol played support in *Finn and Hattie, Her Majesty, Love* (both 1931), *Alice in Wonderland* (1933), *We're Not Dressing* (1934), *Coronado* (1935), and others throughout the decade. In 1933 he began his long-running series of starring shorts for RKO, most of which featured him as a sputtering, henpecked husband with a wandering eye.

Errol joined RKO's "Mexican Spitfire"

series with *The Girl From Mexico* (1939), and played the dual role of kindly Uncle Matt and eccentric Lord Epping in several follow-ups made between 1940 and 1942, including *Mexican Spitfire* (1940), *Mexican Spitfire's Blessed Event* (1941), and *Mexican Spitfire at Sea* (1942). He also appeared in many Universal B pictures during the 1940s, as well as *Never Give a Sucker an Even Break* (1941, with W. C. Fields), *The Invisible Man's Revenge* (1944), *She Gets Her Man* (1945, with Joan Davis), and *The Noose Hangs High* (1948, with Abbott and Costello). He also played manager Knobby Walsh in a series of Joe Palooka films in the 1940s.

ERWIN, STUART. Actor. *(b. Feb. 14, 1902, Squaw Valley, Calif.; d. Dec. 21, 1967.)* Bitten by the acting bug while still in college, Erwin played on stage throughout the mid and late 1920s before making his screen debut in 1928. Husky and plain-looking, he had leads in several early talkies but achieved greater success in secondary roles. He specialized in playing slow-witted but amiable hayseeds, and even picked up an Oscar nomination playing one in *Pigskin Parade* (1936). Erwin was the first of several actors to play comic-strip slugger Joe Palooka, in *Palooka* (1934), and he replaced Lee Tracy as the American reporter in *Viva Villa!* that same year. He's also excellent in *Make Me a Star* (1932), *The Stranger's Return, International House* (both 1933), *Ceiling Zero* (1935), *Three Blind Mice* (1938), *Hollywood Cavalcade* (1939), *Our Town* (1940, as the milkman), *The Bride Came C.O.D.* (1941), and *The Great Mike* (1944). In 1950 Erwin revitalized his career by starring in the early TV sitcom "The Trouble With Father" (1950–55; originally titled "Life With the Erwins," then later "The Stu Erwin Show"), as the archetypal Bumbling Father. The show costarred his wife June Collyer, with whom he costarred in the 1931 movie *Dude Ranch.* In later years he took supporting roles in the Disney comedies *Son of Flubber* (1963) and *The Misadventures of Merlin Jones* (1964).

ESPOSITO, GIANCARLO. Actor. *(b. Apr. 26, 1958, Copenhagen.)* This extremely versatile actor has been practically unrecognizable in each of the Spike Lee movies he's appeared in, from a manipulative frat leader in *School Daze* (1988) to a hysterical neighborhood would-be activist in *Do the Right Thing* (1989) to a dandy, pliable pianist in *Mo' Better Blues* (1990). Other credits include *Bob Roberts* (1992, as the radical journalist), *Amos & Andrew* (1993, as an activist), and *Beverly Hills Cop 3* (1994). He costarred in a 1993 series, "Bakersfield P.D."

ESTEVEZ, EMILIO. Actor. *(b. May 12, 1962, New York City.)* As a wide-eyed, mercurial, quick-triggered Billy the Kid in *Young Guns* (1988) and its 1990 sequel, this sandy-haired former Brat Packer finally found a colorful character and latched on to commercially successful starring vehicles—but it remains to be seen if he can parlay that success into more prestigious films. One of the several acting offspring of Martin Sheen, Estevez (who uses his real surname) began performing in TV movies as a teenager. The 1982 Disney drama *Tex* afforded him his first feature-film credit, which he followed in quick succession with Francis Coppola's *The Outsiders* and the horror anthology *Nightmares* (both 1983). One year later he made his first real impact as a comically disaffected punker in the loopy cult hit *Repo Man* (1984). He also contributed fine ensemble work in two films of the so-called Brat Pack of young actors, *The Breakfast Club* and *St. Elmo's Fire* (both 1985). Not content with staying in front of the camera, the ambitious Estevez began flexing other creative muscles by writing and starring in the contemporary teen-angst drama *That Was Then, This Is Now* (1985), adding directing to his palette with the poorly received *Wisdom* (1986) and *Men at Work* (1990, which costarred brother Charlie). In between these two personal failures, he offered a winning comic performance in the action comedy *Stakeout* (1987). In 1992 he starred with Mick Jagger and Anthony Hopkins in the sci-fi thriller *Freejack*. Recent credits include *The Mighty Ducks* (1992), *National Lampoon's Loaded Weapon 1, Judgment Night, Another Stakeout* (all 1993), and *D2: The Mighty Ducks* (1994). He was married to pop star Paula Abdul.

ESZTERHAS, JOE. Screenwriter, producer. *(b. Nov. 23, 1944, Csakanydoroszlo, Hungary.)* Perhaps the highest-paid writer in Hollywood, Eszterhas began his career as a newspaper reporter, then gained fame for his "gonzo"-type stories for "Rolling Stone" magazine. His book "Charlie Simpson's Apocalypse" caught the attention of a studio executive who asked him to try his hand at screenwriting. His first effort was *F.I.S.T.* (1978), cowritten with Sylvester Stallone, but he caught fire with the unexpected hit *Flashdance* (1983, cowritten with Tom Hedley) and the sleek courtroom thriller *Jagged Edge* (1985). He went on to write low-profile films like *Big Shots* (1987) and *Checking Out* (1989) as well as major dramas like *Betrayed* (1988) and *Music Box* (1989), both of which he also co-executive produced. Eszterhas is well known for the slick, sexy commercial thrillers *Basic Instinct* (1992) and *Sliver* (1993)—which each netted him some $3 million—and is even more well known for a power struggle with super agent Michael Ovitz when Eszterhas left Ovitz's Creative Artists Agency for International Creative Management. In a letter that became national news, Eszterhas quoted Ovitz as saying "foot soldiers" would "blow his brains out." So far, Eszterhas—who sold a four-page screenplay treatment to New Line for $4 million—is very much alive. He cowrote the Van Damme action vehicle *Nowhere to Run* (1993) and also wrote *Showgirls* and *Jade* (both 1995).

EVANS, EDITH (DAME). Actress. *(b. Feb. 8, 1888, London; d. Oct. 14, 1976.)* Masterful, legendary British stage star, renowned for her performances in theater classics, who brought her art to the screen in a series of memorable character roles in films of the 1940s through the 1970s. (She appeared in a brace of silent films, 1915's *A Welsh Singer* and 1916's *East Is East,* but remained primarily a stage star until the 1940s.) Her portrayal of Lady Bracknell in *The Importance of Being Earnest* (1952) showed that Evans, while definitely an actress in the "grand manner," could deliver subtle screen performances as well. Arguably her best film role was that of the old woman who suspects she's being spied on in *The Whis-*

perers (1966); it earned her an Oscar nomination. She was also nominated for *Tom Jones* (1963). Bryan Forbes, who directed her in *Whisperers* and *The Slipper and the Rose* (1976), later wrote a biography of the actress.
OTHER FILMS INCLUDE: 1959: *The Nun's Story;* 1964: *The Chalk Garden;* 1965: *Young Cassidy;* 1967: *Fitzwilly;* 1969: *The Madwoman of Chaillot, Crooks and Coronets;* 1970: *Scrooge, David Copperfield;* 1973: *A Doll's House;* 1977: *Nasty Habits.*

EVANS, GENE. Actor. *(b. July 11, 1922, Holbrook, Ariz.)* "Don't tell me about it—write it!" As the crusading, cigar-chomping editor in Sam Fuller's *Park Row* (1952), Gene Evans displayed the kind of talent and screen presence that would, in other players, be key requisites for stardom. But as a burly, harsh-voiced, not particularly handsome man, Evans settled for a career as a very busy character actor. Fuller gave him his other notable lead—the brutish sergeant in *The Steel Helmet* (1951)—as well as roles in *Fixed Bayonets* (1952), *Hell and High Water* (1954), and *Shock Corridor* (1963), the latter featuring him as a loony nuclear scientist. Sci-fi fans know him as the boozy but loyal surgeon pal in *Donovan's Brain* (1953) and as the hero of *The Giant Behemoth* (1959). Evans also appeared in numerous Westerns, from *Cattle Queen of Montana* (1954) to *Pat Garrett and Billy the Kid* (1973), and occasionally even comedies, including *Operation Petticoat* (1959) and *Support Your Local Sheriff!* (1969). His numerous TV movies include *The Shadow Riders, The Rhinemann Exchange,* and *The Sacketts.* An earlier generation will remember him as the father on "My Friend Flicka" (1956–57). He recently retired to become a gentleman farmer in Tennessee.

EVANS, MADGE. Actress. *(b. July 1, 1909, New York City; d. Apr. 26, 1981.)* Beautiful, charming, talented actress who nonetheless failed to achieve stardom. A child model and performer, she made her screen debut in 1914's *The Sign of the Cross,* and worked steadily until the mid 1920s, then concentrated on the stage. Evans returned to the screen in 1931 as a contract player at MGM and became one of the studio's busiest ingenues. Having matured into lovely young womanhood, she played mostly sweet, vapid types in such films as *Son of India, Sporting Blood, Heartbreak* (all 1931), *Huddle, Fast Life,* and *Lovers Courageous* (all 1932) before getting better parts in *The Greeks Had a Word for Them* (1932, as a gold digger), *Hell Below* (1932), *Hallelujah, I'm a Bum, The Mayor of Hell* (opposite James Cagney), *Dinner at Eight* (as John Barrymore's paramour), *Beauty for Sale* (all 1933), *Fugitive Lovers, Stand Up and Cheer* (both 1934), *David Copperfield* (1935, as Agnes), *Transatlantic Tunnel, Pennies From Heaven* (both 1936), and *The Thirteenth Chair* (1937).
Apparently puzzled by Evans' evident inability to enthrall audiences, MGM in the mid 1930s loaned her out frequently and assigned her to increasingly cheap, dismal programmers. Following *Army Girl* (1938), which she made for Republic (at that time a sure sign of decline for a former major-studio player) Evans retired from the screen. She married playwright Sidney Kingsley and continued to perform on stage through 1943, at that point abandoning her career for a happy marriage. Kingsley once said Evans collaborated on several of his plays over the years.

EWELL, TOM. Actor. *(b. Apr. 29, 1909, Owensboro, Ky., as Yewell Tompkins; d. Sept. 12, 1994.)* He's frozen in time, a bemused grin on his rough-hewn face, hands stuffed in the pockets of his rumpled suit, watching Marilyn Monroe's skirt billowing up in that classic moment from *The Seven Year Itch* (1955). It's a scene that's been endlessly reprinted and rescreened, and the single one that guarantees this talented player cinematic immortality. Ewell, a popular comic actor of the 1950s and 1960s, came to Hollywood from the stage, debuting on the big screen in 1940's *They Knew What They Wanted.* He first enjoyed real screen success as the wandering rake in *Adam's Rib* (1949). While hardly a leading-man type, he proved an ace comic foil opposite some of the 1950s' top screen sexpots—Sheree North in *The Lieutenant Wore Skirts* (1955) and Jayne Mansfield in *The Girl Can't Help It* (1956), besides Monroe—and was one of the better things about the lackluster 1962 remake of *State Fair.* He's probably best remembered by younger viewers as Robert Blake's boozing buddy on the 1970s TV series "Baretta." His last feature film was 1983's *Easy Money.*

FAIRBANKS, DOUGLAS. Actor, producer. *(b. May 23, 1883, Denver, as Douglas Elton Ulman; d. Dec. 12, 1939.)* The screen's first great swashbuckling hero, Douglas Fairbanks began his film career as the prototype of the All-American Boy. Energetic, athletic, and exuberant, he was an early proponent of vigorous exercise and a positive attitude, to ensure good health and physical well-being. His buoyant manner and broad pantomimical style hardly qualified Doug for acting honors, but during his heyday he became an idol to millions of boys. Growing up in the West, Fairbanks appeared in local theatricals from the age of 12 and attended the Colorado School of Mines. Moving to New York in the early 1900s, he later went to Harvard and dabbled at various odd jobs before resuming his love affair with the theater. He landed on Broadway in 1902 in "Her Lord and Master," but once again gave up the stage to marry Anna Beth Sully in 1907 and join a Wall Street brokerage firm in search of "security." His son, Douglas Fairbanks, Jr., was born in 1909.

Lured once again to the stage, Fairbanks reestablished himself in short order and became a Broadway favorite in such plays as "The New Henrietta" and "Officer 666." He was nearly signed for films by the Lasky Feature Play Company in 1914, but ultimately made his film debut in *The Lamb* for Triangle–Fine Arts in 1915. Pictures like *The Habit of Happiness* (1915), *The Americano,* and *American Aristocracy* (both 1916) quickly established the Fairbanks persona: good-natured, chivalrous, supremely self-confident—in short, a go-getter. His athletic ability was regularly put to use, and nearly every one of his films sported elaborate, exuberant stunt sequences in which he bounded all over the screen, cheerfully vanquishing his enemies and always getting the girl.

Fairbanks signed with Artcraft in 1917, becoming his own producer and appearing in *Reaching for the Moon* (1917), *He Comes Up Smiling,* and *Say! Young Fellow* (both 1918), as well as the Westerns *Wild and Woolly, The Man From Painted*

Post (both 1917), and *Arizona* (1918). He romanced (and reportedly lived with) the also-married Mary Pickford in the late teens, but they sidestepped potential scandal by divorcing their respective spouses and marrying in 1920, after which they were hailed around the world as the virtual king and queen of Hollywood. Their palatial residence in Beverly Hills was dubbed Pickfair, and it became the unofficial social capital of movieland.

With Pickford, Charlie Chaplin, and D. W. Griffith, Fairbanks founded United Artists Corporation in 1919, and his own *His Majesty, the American* was the company's first release. But Fairbanks' popularity was slipping due to the sameness of his vehicles. In 1920 he experimented with a period swashbuckler, *The Mark of Zorro,* which essentially grafted the Fairbanks persona onto a romantic adventure story with delightful results. It was a tremendous hit. After one more modern picture, *The Nut* (1921), confirmed the declining appeal of his modern-dress comedies, Fairbanks devoted the remainder of his silent-screen career to lavish costume pictures. He immersed himself in the crafting of these films, writing many of them himself, and supervising production of sets and design of costumes. *The Three Musketeers* (1921) was a lavish adaptation of the Dumas classic, while *Robin Hood* (1922) nearly dwarfed the lively star with its gigantic sets and ornate production values.

The actor-producer's greatest achievement was probably *The Thief of Bagdad* (1924), a high point of Hollywood production style in the silent era. *Don Q, Son of Zorro* (1925), a sequel to his 1920 hit, wasn't nearly as remarkable as its predecessor. *The Black Pirate* (1926), however, was a deft swashbuckler enhanced by the pastel hues of two-color Technicolor, and enlivened by some of Fairbanks' most famous stunts, including a spectacular slide down the huge sail of a massive ship. *The Gaucho* (1927), an odd blend of spectacle and religious mysticism, seemed to be a misstep for Fairbanks, but he was back in form with *The Iron Mask* (1929), a sequel to *The Three Musketeers* that sported two brief "talkie" scenes.

The all-talking *The Taming of the Shrew* (1929) costarred Fairbanks with Pickford in a Shakespearean romp, but the superstar combination didn't click at box offices, and Fairbanks, already unnerved by the burgeoning success of talkies, again shifted gears, returning to more modest, contemporary comedies. *Reaching for the Moon* (1931), *Mr. Robinson Crusoe,* and a home-movie-like travelogue, *Around the World in 80 Minutes* (1932), all had their moments but clearly showed the star in decline, as 1930s audiences found new heroes to worship. Fairbanks retired from the screen on a grace note, appearing as the aging lover in Alexander Korda's British production of *The Private Life of Don Juan* (1934). In the late 1930s, he and his son discussed the possibility of a joint screen vehicle that never came to fruition. Ever restless in his later years, Fairbanks was divorced by Pickford in 1936 and married Lady Sylvia Ashley, a chorus girl by training and a lady by marriage. He died in his sleep of a heart attack at age 56.

FAIRBANKS, DOUGLAS, JR. Actor. *(b. Dec. 9, 1909, New York City.)* Although he never quite reached the pinnacle of screen success and industry importance that his famous father attained, Doug Jr. did all right for himself, carving his own niche in movie history. The product of his father's first marriage, young Doug was an overweight, overly sensitive child who, as he later admitted, had serious self-esteem problems before losing weight and following in the family footsteps, beginning with a starring role in *Stephen Steps Out* (1923). Tall and slender, with an easily recognizable family resemblance but a decidedly more serious mien, he appeared in many silent films—including *Stella Dallas, Wild Horse Mesa* (both 1925), *Broken Hearts of Hollywood* (1926), *Is Zat So?* (1927), *A Woman of Affairs,* and *The Barker* (both 1928)—often cast as a spoiled, reckless youth. Doug Jr. got little encouragement from his famous father; indeed, their relationship during this period was little more than cordial.

Gradually, Fairbanks earned respect for his efforts. He impressed moviegoers as the brash reporter in Frank Capra's *The Power of the Press* (1928) and as the leading man in Joan Crawford's last silent film, *Our Modern Maidens* (1929). Doug Jr. got the girl both on- and off-screen; he and Crawford were married shortly after the completion of filming.

The early talkie years found Doug Jr. at Warner Bros.–First National, at first in such trifles as *Forward Pass* (1929) and *Loose Ankles* (1930), but soon in highly dramatic roles in *The Dawn Patrol, Outward Bound, Little Caesar* (all 1930), and *Chances* (1931) that finally took him out of the "callow youth" classification. Although he was never wholly convincing as a tough guy, Fairbanks played one in many hard-boiled Warners melodramas, some of which—*Union Depot, Love Is a Racket* (both 1932), and *The Life of Jimmy Dolan* (1933)—numbered among his best films of the 1930s. In fact, the more one sees of his work from this period (in films like 1932's *It's Tough to Be Famous* and 1933's *The Narrow Corner*) the more obvious it becomes that Fairbanks was a real unsung talent. He left Warners in 1934 to freelance, making several pictures in England (the best of which were 1934's *Catherine the Great* and 1937's *Jump for Glory*) before scoring a triumph as likable blackguard Rupert of Hentzau in David O. Selznick's elaborate remake of *The Prisoner of Zenda* (1937), starring Ronald Colman. It was Fairbanks' first full-blooded swashbuckling role, and he reminded moviegoers of his famous father, clad in black clothes, sporting a dapper little mustache, and wielding a saber with panache. (He and his father drew close around this time, and even talked of making a film together before Senior's death in 1939.)

Doug Jr. made several delightful if unimportant romantic comedies—including *The Joy of Living, Having Wonderful Time, The Rage of Paris,* and *Young in Heart* (all 1938)—before returning to robust adventure films with *Gunga Din* (1939, as the daring Sergeant Ballantine in this rousing classic), *The Sun Never Sets* (also 1939, once again helping save the British Empire), *Safari, Green Hell* (both 1940), and *The Corsican Brothers* (1941, another swashbuckler, this time playing twins). He also produced and starred in Ben Hecht's bizarre black comedy, *Angels Over Broadway* (1940).

During World War 2 Fairbanks served with distinction as a lieutenant commander with the U.S. Navy. When he returned to movie work in 1947, it was in the title role of *Sinbad the Sailor* (1947), an eye-filling Arabian Nights adventure that saw him adopting some of his late father's larger-than-life gestures and mannerisms. He appeared opposite Betty Grable in *That Lady in Ermine* (1948), and then produced and cowrote two costume vehicles for himself: *The Exile* (1948) and *The Fighting O'Flynn* (1949) before starring in a taut, contemporary thriller, *State Secret* (1950), in England. Fairbanks, a lifelong Anglophile who numbered members of the royal family among his friends, moved to Britain in the early 1950s. His subsequent screen work was both spotty and undistinguished (although he personally fared better than did the films themselves): *Three's Company, The Triangle, The Genie* (all 1953), *Destination Milan, The Last Moment* (both 1954), *Red and Blue* (1967). He also produced several films, including *Another Man's Poison* (1952) and *Chase a Crooked Shadow* (1958), and hosted, produced, and often appeared in the anthology TV series "Douglas Fairbanks Presents" (1952–57). Returning to the U.S., he toured in a number of stage plays, made TV guest appearances, and appeared with several other Hollywood "legends"— Fred Astaire, Melvyn Douglas, and John Houseman—in *Ghost Story* (1981), his last feature film to date. His talent has never been fully appreciated. His first volume of autobiography, "The Salad Days," was published in 1988; the second, "A Hell of a War," in 1993.

Purple Reef; 1962: *Pressure Point;* 1963: *The Balcony, It's a Mad Mad Mad Mad World;* 1964: *Robin and the Seven Hoods;* 1965: *The Great Race* (a standout slapstick performance as the hapless henchman of comic villain Jack Lemmon); 1966: *Penelope;* 1967: *Luv;* 1968: *Anzio;* 1969: *Castle Keep;* 1970: *Husbands* (the first of several films he did for friend and actor-director John Cassavetes); 1974: *A Woman Under the Influence* (a striking Cassavetes project, as Gena Rowlands' husband); 1976: *Mikey and Nicky* (opposite Cassavetes in a quirky Elaine May film); *Murder by Death* (spoofing Humphrey Bogart in this Neil Simon parody); 1977: *Opening Night* (for Cassavetes); 1978: *The Brink's Job, The Cheap Detective;* 1979: *The In-Laws* (the latter two among his best starring assignments); 1981: … *All the Marbles;* 1985: *Big Trouble* (a misfired attempt to rekindle the success of *The In-Laws,* directed by Cassavetes); 1987: *Happy New Year* (offering him a plum comic part but almost totally unseen), *Wings of Desire* (an offbeat assignment—playing himself—in this art-house favorite directed by Wim Wenders), *The Princess Bride* (as the film's storyteller); 1988: *Vibes;* 1989: *Cookie;* 1990: *In the Spirit, Motion and Emotion, Tune In Tomorrow* … (very funny in the last-named as a screwy soap-opera writer); 1993: *Faraway, So Close!;* 1995: *Roommates.*

FALK, PETER. Actor. *(b. Sept. 16, 1927, New York City.)* When most people think of this short, dark-haired, gravelly voiced actor today, they call to mind the character of rumpled, eccentric detective Lieutenant Columbo, a character he's been playing on the small screen for more than a quarter-century (beginning with 1967's *Prescription: Murder,* and every three or four weeks from 1971 to 1977 on the "NBC Sunday Mystery Movie"). His feature-film career extends back to 1958's *Wind Across the Everglades,* and while he spent many years playing dese-dem-dose gangsters of both dramatic and comedic bent—earning Supporting Actor Oscar nominations for such characterizations in 1960's *Murder, Inc.* and 1961's *Pocketful of Miracles*— he's been infinitely more entertaining in recent years, showing his versatility in both leading and supporting roles.
OTHER FILMS INCLUDE: 1959: *The Bloody Brood;* 1960: *Pretty Boy Floyd, Secret of the*

FARMER, FRANCES. Actress. *(b. Sept. 19, 1913, Seattle, Wash.; d. Aug. 1, 1970.)* Beautiful, intelligent, talented leading lady of the 1930s and early 1940s, whose unfortunate life story has become the preeminent cautionary fable describing the bleak underside of Hollywood success. Farmer came to Hollywood as the well-educated daughter of a prominent lawyer; her talent for writing, in the form of a prize-winning essay submitted to a radical journal, actually won her a trip to the Soviet Union as a high school student. Signed by Paramount in 1936, she appeared that year in *Too Many Parents, Border Flight,* and *Rhythm on the Range* before being loaned to Goldwyn for *Come and Get It* (also 1936). In the best performance(s) of her career, Farmer played both a lusty saloon singer and her daughter. Established as a dramatic actress of great skill, she returned to Paramount for roles in *Ebb Tide, Exclusive* (both 1937), and *Ride a Crooked Mile* (1938). But she chafed against the "indignities" she felt she had to endure, and refused to play the Hollywood game, either professionally or socially. She claimed to hate Tinseltown—except for the money—and honed her acting skills in the Group Theatre (beginning in 1937), eventually embarking on an ill-fated affair with author Clifford Odets. Rebellious and contemptuous, she was eventually dropped by Paramount, and the quality of her vehicles diminished. *South of Pago Pago, Flowing Gold* (both 1940), *World Premiere, Among the Living, Badlands of Dakota* (all 1941), and *Son of Fury* (1942, in which she was demoted to supporting-player status) hardly challenged her abilities.

Her descent into hell began one night in 1942, with a traffic ticket for drunk driving. Not one to keep her mouth shut, Farmer allowed the incident to degenerate into a shoving match, which ended with her being dragged off to jail. Farmer continued her tirade at her hearing, whereupon she was sentenced to 180 days in jail. When she was refused a phone call upon leaving the court, she became hysterical, and after much punching and kicking, was sent to a cell in a straitjacket. In prison Farmer was no more cooperative with the law than she was on the outside, and soon her erratic behavior landed her in a sanitarium. She was legally declared mentally incompetent by none other than her own mother, and sentenced to an asylum in her home state of Washington. Drugged with insulin and brutally treated by the asylum guards, Farmer's "treatment" even included a partial lobotomy. She was deemed well enough to return to work (outside of Hollywood, of course) in the 1950s, and she briefly hosted a TV show based in Indianapolis. Her last film was the thoroughly wretched *The Party Crashers* (1958). Farmer died of cancer at the age of 56. Her autobiography, "Will There Really Be a Morning?," was adapted for TV in 1982, the same year that Jessica Lange starred in a theatrical biopic, *Frances.*

FARNSWORTH, RICHARD. Actor, stuntman. *(b. Sept. 1, 1920, Los Angeles.)* There are few people who have made a successful transition from stunt work to acting and even fewer who have made it at nearly 60 years of age. Richard Farnsworth has done both. After leaving school, he joined the rodeo circuit in the

1930s and did his first film work riding with hundreds of extras in *The Adventures of Marco Polo* (1938). Since then, he worked as a rider or stunt man on some 300 films and TV shows, doubling many of Hollywood's biggest stars, including Montgomery Clift (on 1948's *Red River*), Jerry Lewis (in 1956's *Pardners*), Guy Madison (for the run of his popular "Wild Bill Hickok" TV series), and Steve McQueen on the pilot of "Wanted Dead or Alive." Farnsworth began to get small speaking parts in *The Cowboys* (1972), *The Duchess and the Dirtwater Fox* (1976), and *Another Man, Another Chance* (1977) before director Alan J. Pakula (who had worked with him on 1969's *The Stalking Moon*) gave him a major supporting role as an aging ranch hand in *Comes a Horseman* (1978). The performance earned him an Oscar nomination and a whole new career opened up. After character parts in *Tom Horn* and *Resurrection* (both 1980), Farnsworth got his first starring role as the aging "Gentleman Bandit" Bill Miner in *The Grey Fox* (1983) and earned Canada's equivalent of an Oscar for Best Actor. Since that film, Farnsworth has lent his natural easygoing charm to *Independence Day* (1983), *The Natural* (1984), *Into the Night* (1985), *The Two Jakes, Havana* (both 1990), *Misery* (1991), and *The Getaway* (1994), among others. He appeared in 1992 on the short-lived TV series "The Boys of Twilight" with his friend and *Natural* costar Wilford Brimley, and was featured in the acclaimed 1986 miniseries "Anne of Green Gables," as Anne's adoptive father.

FARRELL, CHARLES. Actor. *(b. Aug. 9, 1901, Onset Bay, Mass.; d. May 6, 1990.)* This handsome leading man was one of the silent screen's great lovers, teamed with petite Janet Gaynor in a number of enormously popular (if syrupy) romances, most notably *Seventh Heaven* (1927), *Street Angel,* the recently rediscovered *Lucky Star* (both 1928), and *Sunny Side Up* (1929). Farrell started out as a stage performer, but made his film debut in *The Cheat* (1923) and remained on large screens and small for the remainder of his acting career. His gentle voice and polite Yankee demeanor ill suited him for virile roles, which may account for the somewhat rapid decline in popularity he suffered in the 1930s. He more or less retired from acting in 1941, and spent the remainder of the decade managing the Palm Springs Racquet Club, which he'd cofounded with Ralph Bellamy. (Farrell also served as mayor of Palm Springs for many years.) He played the perpetually exasperated father of Gale Storm in TV's "My Little Margie" (1952–55), and briefly starred in "The Charlie Farrell Show" (1956) before retiring altogether.

OTHER FILMS INCLUDE: 1925: *The Freshman;* 1926: *Old Ironsides;* 1928: *Fazil, The River;* 1930: *Happy Days, City Girl, Liliom;* 1931: *The Man Who Came Back, Body and Soul, Delicious;* 1932: *Tess of the Storm Country, Wild Girl;* 1934: *The Big Shakedown, Change of Heart;* 1935: *Forbidden Heaven;* 1938: *Flight to Fame;* 1939: *Tail Spin;* 1941: *The Deadly Game.*

FARRELL, GLENDA. Actress. *(b. June 30, 1904, Enid, Okla.; d. May 1, 1971.)* Glenda Farrell made a career of playing wisecracking dames with hearts of brass. Trained in stock, Farrell landed on Broadway in the late 1920s. Her hard-boiled style caught the tenor of the times, and after a bit in Tiffany's *Lucky Boy* (1929), she was signed by Warner Bros. A gangster's moll in *Little Caesar* (1930), an accommodating hooker in *I Am a Fugitive From a Chain Gang* (1932), Farrell was a bit too strident to be a romantic lead or a sob-sister. She was paired with other actresses (especially Joan Blondell) in countless variations on the gold-digger theme; the Blondell-Farrell vehicle *Havana Widows* (1933) shows both women at their naughty, pre-Code best. She played a tough city reporter in *The Mystery of the Wax Museum* (1933), which set the pattern for the rest of Farrell's career—character work in A pictures and leads in B's. She returned to the newsroom for the Torchy Blane series, beginning with *Smart Blonde* in 1936, based on stories by Frederick Nebel, with the reporter's gender changed to accommodate Farrell; she appeared in seven of the nine series entries over the next three years, costarred with Barton MacLane.

As the 1930s came to a close, Farrell's "type" was no longer in vogue and film roles began to dry up. She continued to work in occasional films (1942's *The Talk of the Town* and *Johnny Eager,* a handful

of B's for Columbia and PRC), in the theater and on television. She won a supporting actress Emmy for "A Cardinal Act of Mercy," a 1962 entry in the "Ben Casey" series. In 1964 she worked with Jerry Lewis in *The Disorderly Orderly,* and appeared as Elvis Presley's mother in *Kissin' Cousins.* In 1969, Farrell was appearing on Broadway in "40 Carats" when she learned she had lung cancer.

FARROW, MIA. Actress. *(b. Feb. 9, 1945, Hollywood, as Maria de Lourdes Villiers Farrow.)* She fell victim to devil worshippers who coveted her unborn child in *Rosemary's Baby* (1968), and Mia Farrow is still remembered for her performance in that screen chiller. The daughter of actress Maureen O'Sullivan and director John Farrow, this tiny, fragile, doelike actress made her screen bow in *John Paul Jones* (1959, directed by her father), spent two years playing Alison MacKenzie on the TV series "Peyton Place" (1964–66), and cultivated a wild-child image before achieving stardom as the besieged young mother in *Baby.* Lead roles throughout the 1970s, in such films as *The Great Gatsby* (1974) and *A Wedding* (1978), followed, but Farrow hit her creative stride as the star of more than 10 movies—including *Zelig* (1983), *Hannah and Her Sisters* (1986), and *Alice* (1990)—directed by former boyfriend Woody Allen, with whom she has a son. Fashioning roles with her in mind, Allen brought out qualities in Farrow moviegoers had never seen before, from the gum-chewing ex-gangster's moll in *Broadway Danny Rose* (1984) to the lovesick Hollywood movie fan in *The Purple Rose of Cairo* (1985) to the cigarette-girl-turned-gossip queen in *Radio Days* (1987) to a despairing psychiatric patient in *Another Woman* (1988). It is by any measure a remarkable gallery of performances. In 1992 she and Allen made headlines for months in a vituperative splitup which had unintended repercussions when audiences watched them as a disintegrating couple on-screen in the concurrently released *Husbands and Wives* (1992). She was replaced by Diane Keaton in Woody's next film, *Manhattan Murder Mystery* (1993). Previous marriages to show-business personalities Frank Sinatra and composer/conductor André Previn ended in divorce. Her sister

Tisa, also an actress, has starred in *Fingers* (1978), *The Grim Reaper* (1981), and many European-made movies of varying quality.
OTHER FILMS INCLUDE: 1968: *A Dandy in Aspic, Secret Ceremony*; 1969: *John and Mary*; 1971: *See No Evil* (as a terrorized blind woman); 1978: *Avalanche, Death on the Nile*; 1979: *Hurricane*; 1982: *A Midsummer Night's Sex Comedy*; 1984: *Supergirl*; 1987: *September*; 1989: *New York Stories, Crimes and Misdemeanors*; 1992: *Shadows and Fog*; 1994: *Widows' Peak.*

FASSBINDER, RAINER WERNER.
Director, actor. *(b. May 31, 1946, Bad Worishofen, Germany; d. June 10, 1982.)*
Prolific, brilliant, and controversial, Fassbinder was a prominent figure in the New German Cinema of the 1970s. His bitter, cynical, and sometimes wrenchingly emotional films often dealt with personal betrayal and political duplicity, unsparingly criticizing postwar German society. In the late 1960s he began filming performances by his Anti-Theater troupe, where he first met many of the actors who became part of his unofficial repertory company, most notably Hanna Schygulla, who played female leads in his best films. The portly, pockmarked, soft-spoken director sometimes acted in his own films; he also led an excessive lifestyle and was despised by many. Fassbinder's best films are remarkably varied, including *The Bitter Tears of Petra Von Kant* (1973), *Effi Briest* (1974), and *The Marriage of Maria Braun* (1979). His masterwork was a 14-episode TV adaptation of "Berlin Alexanderplatz" (1980), which examined life in Germany during the 1920s. Fassbinder died, having overdosed on alcohol and cocaine, shortly after completing *Querelle* (1982), his second English-language film.
OTHER FILMS INCLUDE: 1974: *Ali: Fear Eats the Soul*; 1975: *Mother Kusters Goes to Heaven*; 1977: *Despair*; 1978: *The Stationmaster's Wife*; 1981: *Lili Marleen, Lola*; 1982: *Veronika Voss.*

FAYE, ALICE. Actress, singer. *(b. May 5, 1912, New York City, as Alice Jeanne Leppert.)* She never won any Oscars for her acting, and the critics never treated her with much more than benign tolerance, but when Alice Faye appeared on-screen to sing "Goodnight My Love," "This Year's Kisses," or "You'll Never Know," in her throaty contralto, she warmed the hearts of a million movie fans (many of whom still nurture those feelings today). Born and raised in New York City's "Hell's Kitchen," Alice quit school to become a chorus girl at age 14, dancing in the famous "George White's Scandals" revues. Shortly afterward she was "discovered" by crooner Rudy Vallee, who engaged her to sing with his band.

Vallee went to Hollywood to star in Fox's 1934 film version of *George White's Scandals*, and Faye, originally slated to do one song, became leading lady when co-star Lilian Harvey walked off the picture. Her success in the film won Alice a Fox contract. Initially, the studio saw her as a Jean Harlow clone: Her honey-blond hair was dyed platinum, her eyebrows were plucked, and she was garbed to show off her ample figure. She also played "tough babies," in such films as *She Learned About Sailors, Now I'll Tell* (both 1934), *365 Nights in Hollywood, George White's Scandals of 1935, Every Night at Eight* (on loan to Paramount), *Music Is Music*, and *King of Burlesque* (all 1935).

In 1936, however, producer Darryl F. Zanuck decided to soften Faye's image. Beginning with *Sing, Baby, Sing* (1936), the public saw a more endearing Alice Faye, with her natural hair coloring and eyebrows. Topical entertainments such as *On the Avenue, You Can't Have Everything, You're a Sweetheart* (on loan to Universal), *Wake Up and Live* (all 1937), and *Sally, Irene and Mary* (1938), along with her appearances in two 1936 Shirley Temple pictures, *Poor Little Rich Girl* and *Stowaway*, firmly established Faye as one of the screen's top musical stars. She introduced many popular standards during this period; Irving Berlin, who composed the songs for *On the Avenue*, said he'd rather have his songs introduced by Alice than any other screen thrush.

Faye won her best dramatic role to date in the historical drama *In Old Chicago* (1938), after which she and costar Tyrone Power were reteamed for the Irving Berlin musical *Alexander's Ragtime Band* (1938) and *Rose of Washington Square* (1939, a thinly disguised retelling of the doomed romance between Fanny Brice and gambler Nicky Arnstein). In *Hollywood Cav-*

alcade (1939), with Don Ameche, she appeared in Technicolor for the first time—and, in another first, received a pie in the face from Buster Keaton. She also starred opposite Ameche in *Lillian Russell* (1940) and *That Night in Rio* (1941). Then John Payne appeared opposite Alice in *Tin Pan Alley* (1940, with Betty Grable playing her sister), *Weekend in Havana, The Great American Broadcast* (both 1941), and *Hello Frisco, Hello* (1943), a remake of *King of Burlesque* in which Alice introduced the Oscar-winning "You'll Never Know," the song most often identified with her.

Faye, who'd married singer-bandleader Phil Harris in 1941 (after divorcing singer Tony Martin), took time off to have her second child after completing Busby Berkeley's *The Gang's All Here* (1943). In late 1944 she returned to Fox and was assigned to *Fallen Angel* (1945), a heavy drama costarring Dana Andrews and Linda Darnell. Although the film was ostensibly a Faye vehicle, many of her scenes were left on the cutting-room floor to make room for Darnell, whom Zanuck was building up. After seeing the picture in a studio projection room, Faye drove off the lot and never came back; Zanuck had her blackballed for walking out on her contract.

Content to stay at home and raise her two daughters, Faye kept her hand in show business by costarring with Harris on a long-running weekly radio show. She also made occasional TV appearances before taking a "comeback" role as the mother in a mediocre 1962 remake of *State Fair.* She cameoed in *Won Ton Ton, the Dog Who Saved Hollywood* (1976), and played a kindly waitress in *The Magic of Lassie* (1978), before making a major return to the spotlight in a national tour (and Broadway run) of the musical play "Good News." During the 1980s she toured again, for the Pfizer pharmaceutical company, trumpeting the virtues of physical fitness for senior citizens, for which she was an ideal spokesperson and role model.

FAYLEN, FRANK. Actor. *(b. Dec. 8, 1907, St. Louis; d. Aug. 2, 1985.)* Red-haired, ruddy-faced character actor, one of the screen's most prolific, equally at home in comedic and serious roles. Like so many supporting players of his era, Faylen came from a family of performers; born to vaudevillians, he was a clown and a hoofer before making his film debut in *Bullets or Ballots* (1936). Amiable clowning was his forte, but he also excelled in the portrayal of icy, sadistic heavies. His two most famous roles were that of the nasty male nurse attending to a drunken Ray Milland in *The Lost Weekend* (1945) and as Ernie the cabdriver in Frank Capra's *It's a Wonderful Life* (1946).

Faylen also played the dyspeptic dad of Dobie Gillis in the 1959–63 TV series. His wife, Carol Hughes, was a Warner Bros. contract player in the mid 1930s, appearing in 1936's *Three Men on a Horse* and *Earthworm Tractors,* among others, and played Dale Arden in *Flash Gordon Conquers the Universe* (1940). OTHER FILMS INCLUDE: 1937: *Kid Galahad, They Won't Forget;* 1939: *Nick Carter, Master Detective;* 1940: *The Grapes of Wrath;* 1941: *Come Live With Me;* 1944: *Address Unknown, The Canterville Ghost;* 1946: *The Blue Dahlia;* 1947: *The Perils of Pauline, Road to Rio;* 1948: *Blood on the Moon;* 1950: *Francis;* 1951: *Detective Story;* 1952: *The Sniper;* 1955: *The McConnell Story;* 1957: *Gunfight at the O.K. Corral;* 1965: *The Monkey's Uncle;* 1968: *Funny Girl.*

FELD, FRITZ. Actor. *(b. Oct. 15, 1900, Berlin; d. Nov. 18, 1993.)* Short, excitable character actor whose distinctive trademark was the "pop" he made by bouncing a palm off his rounded lips. An easily recognizable player with more than 500 film and TV appearances, Feld also dabbled in screenwriting, producing, and teaching. A disciple of German impresario Max Reinhardt, Feld came to America in 1923 and worked in many silent films before becoming a (mostly comic) character actor in talkies. He was often cast as a maître d' but also played a number of eccentric artists, flamboyant directors, and quack psychiatrists. In later years he plied his trade quite often in Disney movies (like 1975's *The Strongest Man in the World* and 1980's *Herbie Goes Bananas*), and had a very small but touching part in *Barfly* (1987). He was married to actress Virginia Christine. OTHER FILMS INCLUDE: 1937: *True Confessions, Hollywood Hotel;* 1938: *Bringing Up Baby, Champagne Waltz, The Affairs of*

Annabel; 1941: *World Premiere;* 1943: *The Phantom of the Opera;* 1944: *Knickerbocker Holiday;* 1947: *The Secret Life of Walter Mitty;* 1953: *Call Me Madam;* 1961: *Pocketful of Miracles;* 1969: *Hello, Dolly!;* 1976: *Silent Movie.*

FELDMAN, COREY. Actor. *(b. July 16, 1971, Reseda, Calif.)* After winning hearts at 14 with a sensitive performance in Rob Reiner's charming, nostalgic ensemble piece *Stand by Me* (1986), Feldman applied his talents to a number of increasingly obnoxious vehicles, including *License to Drive* (1988) and *Dream a Little Dream* (1989), both costarring his frequent cohort Corey Haim. Concurrently, he was living out a hyped-up, 1980s version of a child star's crash-and-burn, highlights of which include comedian Sam Kinison boasting of changing Feldman's life by introducing him to porn star Amber Lynn, and Feldman's own arrest for heroin possession in 1990. Feldman, a veteran of movies since 1979's *Time After Time,* had specialized in playing cute-but-precocious kids in such films as Steven Spielberg's *Gremlins* (1984) and *The Goonies* (1985). Most of his recent films have not been deemed worthy of theatrical release, going direct to video instead, but he did provide the voice of Donatello, one of the *Teenage Mutant Ninja Turtles* (1990).

FELDMAN, MARTY. Actor, screenwriter, director. *(b. July 8, 1933, London; d. Dec. 2, 1982.)* This slight, bug-eyed comic actor, originally from the London stage, was first seen by American audiences on the summer replacement TV series "The Marty Feldman Comedy Machine" (1972), and then gained prominence in the films of Mel Brooks and Gene Wilder. A wily comic with a facility for physical comedy, he realized he looked distinctive, and wasn't afraid to use his unique appearance to best comic effect, mugging outrageously. (Seemingly born to be a visual comic, he got a chance to prove it in Mel Brooks' 1976 *Silent Comedy.*) He's particularly good as Gene Wilder's second banana in 1974's *Young Frankenstein* ("That's *eye*-gor . . .") and 1975's *The Adventure of Sherlock Holmes' Smarter Brother.* After first writing, then performing, for British television, Feldman

made his film debut in 1969's *The Bed Sitting Room.* Like other members of Mel Brooks' "company," he tried fashioning a film of his own, but his writing/directing/starring debut, *The Last Remake of Beau Geste* (1977), was disappointingly spotty. He subsequently helmed 1980's *In God We Trust,* and made his final acting appearances posthumously, in both *Yellowbeard* (1983) and *Slapstick of Another Kind* (1984).

FELLINI, FEDERICO. Director, producer, screenwriter. *(b. Jan. 20, 1920, Rimini, Italy; d. Oct. 31, 1993.)* So distinctive and original is the vision of this Italian filmmaker that the adjective "Felliniesque," used to describe bizarre, colorful personages and events, has become almost commonplace. Indeed, it's even used by people who haven't seen a single Fellini film. This vision began taking shape early in the director's life when, as a youngster, he ran away from boarding school to join a circus. While he was retrieved after only a few days, the experience marked him for life; many of his best, most carefully realized works have the superabundant aura of a circus about them, and in 1971 he paid tribute to the big top in *The Clowns.* In his youth he also worked as a cartoonist, and maintained an interest in comic books even when he had become one of the world's most respected film directors.

A friendship with Italian actor Aldo Fabrizi led Fellini into the theater, and during the 1940s (a records snafu kept him out of the military) he worked as a radio and film scriptwriter. In the latter capacity he collaborated with neorealist director Roberto Rossellini, earning an Oscar nomination as one of the writers of the seminal *Open City* (1945) and later working for the maestro as assistant director. Fellini codirected *Variety Lights* (1950) with Alberto Lattuda, beginning his association with life-as-performance themes, then took solo credit for *The White Sheik* (1951), a farce about *fumetti* actors (*fumetti* are comic books with real actors in still photographs rather than hand-drawn panels) and a honeymooning couple. His third feature, *I Vitelloni* (1953), about a group of young men coming to terms with the approaching end of their easy adolescent lives, was an inspiration for many films to come, including

Barry Levinson's *Diner*. It was also the first Fellini film scored by Nino Rota, who composed haunting and memorable music for every one of the director's films thereafter, until Rota's death in 1979.

La Strada (1954), with Anthony Quinn as a brutish strongman who takes simple-minded Giulietta Masina (offscreen Mrs. Fellini) with him around the countryside, is generally acknowledged to be Fellini's first great film, and it won him his first Oscar for Best Foreign Language Film. It was followed by *Il Bidone* (1955) and, later, *The Nights of Cabiria* (1957, his second Oscar), a prostitute-with-heart-of-gold story that provided the inspiration for the Broadway (and film) musical "Sweet Charity." While *La Strada* contained more than its fair share of symbolism, most of Fellini's other works of the 1950s emphasized gritty realism, albeit with more than a touch of compassion and empathy. *La Dolce Vita* (1960) didn't explicitly enter the realm of the fantastic, but it marked the beginning of a period wherein the director's skewed sensibilities would be fully realized. It also marked the beginning of his longtime association with actor Marcello Mastroianni, who played a shallow reporter bored with the superficialities of contemporary Rome.

8½ (1963, third Oscar), generally considered to be Fellini's masterpiece, presented a dizzying mix of memory, fantasy, and realism, and followed the travails of film director Guido (Mastroianni) as he attempted to get his latest movie off the ground. Widely regarded as autobiographical, it inspired imitations from directors as diverse as Paul Mazursky, Bob Fosse, and Woody Allen—none of whom, it must be added, have come close to duplicating the original's élan. Fellini's first color feature, *Juliet of the Spirits* (1965), did for leading character Masina, a bored, bourgeois housewife, what *8½* did for film director Guido: open the door to a phantasmagorical inner world. This movie united Fellini's critical coterie worldwide, although a few observers responded more skeptically: director Luis Buñuel, for example, dismissed it as an exercise in "technical trickery."

Fellini contributed the best sequence to *Spirits of the Dead* (1968), entitled "Never Bet the Devil Your Head," and then made his name part of the title for his next effort, *Fellini Satyricon* (1969), a rib-

ald look at ancient Rome that featured then-corpulent fitness guru Richard Simmons (who at the time was appearing in Italian TV commercials) in a small role. Indeed, Fellini's films became a haven for all sorts of peculiar types, who were central to his hyperbolic way of looking at things.

In the 1970s critics began to accuse Fellini of self-parody, and indeed some of his films seemed like pale imitations of earlier works, but his vivid and nostalgic reminiscence, *Amarcord* (1974), was a great success, and earned him his fourth Academy Award. *Fellini's Roma* (1972), *Fellini's Casanova* (1976), and *Orchestra Rehearsal* (1979) were released to diminished critical enthusiasm and declining audiences. *And the Ship Sails On* (1984) didn't enjoy any more success than the director's 1970s films, but did at least feature some striking images and a riveting opening sequence. By the time of *Ginger and Fred* (1986), most of the talk was about Ginger Rogers' threatened lawsuit against Fellini for unauthorized use of first names (nothing ever came of it), and Woody Allen's reported intervention on Fellini's behalf to try and convince Irving Berlin to allow some of his songs to be used in the picture, a rather limp satire of television.

Fellini's star in the U.S. dimmed to the extent that his last picture, 1990's cute but decidedly minor *La Voce de La Luna*, failed to secure U.S. distribution. His 1987 mock-documentary, *Intervista*, which includes recreations of earlier Fellini films, finally saw American release in 1992. He wrote an autobiography, "Fellini on Fellini," in 1976. The legendary director received a special Academy Award honoring the body of his work in 1993.

FENN, SHERILYN. Actress. *(b. Feb. 1, 1965, Detroit.)* The sultry, voluptuous Fenn first came to public attention as sexy Audrey Horne on the cult TV series "Twin Peaks" (1990–91), which put her in position to become America's newest sex symbol. Before this, she traveled for years with her mother, who played keyboards for rock bands, and worked as a bunny at the L.A. Playboy Club before appearing in grade-B films like *Just One of the Guys, Out of Control* (both 1985), *The Wraith*

(1986), *Meridian* (1990, aka *Kiss of the Beast)*, and the campy Southern sex-fest *Two-Moon Junction* (1988). In 1992 she proved her mettle as an actress with varied roles in *Diary of a Hitman, Ruby* (as stripper Candy Cane) and, especially, in the remake of *Of Mice and Men* (as Curley's wife). Her ties with David Lynch include taking a cameo in his *Wild at Heart* (1990), and costarring in the black comedy *Boxing Helena* (1993, taking the role after it was turned down by Kim Basinger), directed by Lynch's daughter Jennifer. She also starred in Carl Reiner's 1940s detective spoof *Fatal Instinct* (1993). In 1995, Fenn won the title role in the TV miniseries "Liz: The Elizabeth Taylor Story."

FERRARA, ABEL. Director, screenwriter, actor. *(b. July 19, 1951, Bronx, N.Y.)* Independent filmmaker whose reputation for powerfully intense and brutal portraits of New York's mean streets has been widening beyond a cult audience. Phoebe Hoban wrote of Ferrara, "He doesn't so much push the edges of the envelope as rip it to shreds." For years, Ferrara and a close group of friends (many of whom are still colleagues) made inexpensive movies in New York before he directed (and starred in) his first real commercial film, *Driller Killer* (1979), about a painter who goes on a killing spree. He caught critics' attention with *Ms. 45* (1981), which starred longtime associate Zoe Tamerlis as a mute woman who becomes a vigilante after being raped. His *Fear City* (1984) led to offers to direct episodes of TV's "Miami Vice" and "Crime Story," but his subsequent theatrical features were barely released: *China Girl* (1987), a violent romantic thriller, and a political thriller, *Cat Chaser* (1988), based on an Elmore Leonard novel. Ferrara finally broke through the "cult" barrier with *King of New York* (1990), a stylish drama with Christopher Walken as a drug kingpin with a moral code, and the critically acclaimed *Bad Lieutenant* (1992), a harrowing story of moral redemption with Harvey Keitel in a stunning performance as a depraved cop looking for salvation. Moving closer to the mainstream, Ferrara then directed two flops, *Dangerous Game* (1993), which teamed Harvey Keitel and Madonna, and

Body Snatchers (1994), the second remake of *Invasion of the Body Snatchers.*

FERRER, JOSE. Actor, director. *(b. Jan. 8, 1912, Santurce, Puerto Rico, as Jose Vincente Ferrer de Otero y Cintron; d. Jan. 26, 1992.)* A commanding actor with a rich, distinctive voice and a theatrical bearing. After winning an Academy Award for *Cyrano de Bergerac* (recreating his Tony award–winning stage performance as Rostand's famous long-nosed hero), Ferrer entered a fruitful and prolific period of film activity, but by the 1960s his "moment" was gone, and he retreated into character parts in often unworthy films, which he readily admitted he took just to make a living.

While attending Princeton University he was bitten by the acting bug and made his Broadway debut in 1935. His versatility was dazzling to critics and audiences alike; he tackled the farcical comedy of *Charley's Aunt* and the demanding role of Iago to Paul Robeson's *Othello* with equal aplomb. He began directing as well and soon was hailed as Broadway's renaissance man; in 1952 he won Tony awards for directing three plays during the same season ("The Shrike," "Stalag 17," "The Fourposter"), and earned another Tony for acting in "The Shrike."

Ferrer made his film debut as the Dauphin with Ingrid Bergman in *Joan of Arc* (1948), earning his first Oscar nomination as Best Supporting Actor. Two years later he took home an Academy Award for his vivid performance as Cyrano. Thus began his most impressive period in films: as diminutive Toulouse-Lautrec in John Huston's *Moulin Rouge* (1952, Oscar-nominated), as the fallen Rev. Davidson opposite Rita Hayworth in *Miss Sadie Thompson* (1953), as defense attorney Lt. Barney Greenwald in *The Caine Mutiny* (1954), and as operetta composer Sigmund Romberg in the MGM musical *Deep in My Heart* (1954, in which he performs a tour de force one-man musical play). Echoing his Broadway success, he then directed himself in *The Shrike* (1955), *The Cockleshell Heroes* (1956), *The Great Man* (also 1956, and perhaps his all-time best; he also coscripted), *I Accuse!* (1958, as Capt. Dreyfus), and *The High Cost of Loving* (1958). He also directed but did not appear in *Return to Peyton Place* (1961) and the ill-fated remake of *State Fair* (1962), which blemished his career behind the camera and was in fact the last film he directed.

Subsequent acting credits include *Lawrence of Arabia* (1962), *Nine Hours to Rama* (1963), *Cyrano et D'Artagnan* (1964). *The Greatest Story Ever Told, Ship of Fools* (both 1965), *Enter Laughing* (1967, very funny as a hammy director), *Voyage of the Damned* (1976), Billy Wilder's *Fedora* (1978), *The Fifth Musketeer* (1979, as Athos), Woody Allen's *A Midsummer Night's Sex Comedy* (1982), *To Be or Not to Be* (1983), *Dune* (1984), and *Old Explorers* (1990, in a costarring part with James Whitmore), along with a great many potboilers and outright dogs. He also appeared in such TV movies as *Gideon's Trumpet* (1980, as Abe Fortas) and *Blood & Orchids* (1986), and had a recurring role as Julia Duffy's wealthy father on the "Newhart" TV sitcom in the 1980s. He remained active in theater productions to the very end of his life. He was married to actress Uta Hagen, and then to singer Rosemary Clooney; in a 1982 TV movie *Rosie: The Rosemary Clooney Story* he was portrayed by Tony Orlando. Their son Miguel Ferrer is also an actor.

FERRER, MEL. Actor, director, producer. *(b. Aug. 25, 1917, Elberon, N.J., as Melchior Gaston Ferrer.)* This Princeton dropout worked in radio and on Broadway before becoming a movie director, his credits including *The Girl of the Limberlost* (1945, his debut), *Vendetta* (1950), and *Green Mansions,* a 1959 romance that starred his then-wife, Audrey Hepburn. Ten years earlier, Ferrer made his big-screen acting debut in *Lost Boundaries* (1949, as a black man passing for white), and he returned to work in front of the cameras throughout the 1950s and 1960s. Perhaps his most memorable role was the self-pitying puppeteer in *Lili* (1953). Despite important roles in such notable productions as *War and Peace* (1956 with Hepburn) and *The Sun Also Rises* (1957), the tall, aristocratic-looking performer has consistently failed to impress audiences and, therefore, has never been considered a big star. He spent much of the 1960s abroad, in European productions, usually of low quality, returning home to land supporting roles in such American exploitation items as *Eaten Alive* (1977) and *The*

Fifth Floor (1979). During the 1980s he worked mainly in made-for-TV movies such as *Outrage!* (1986) and *Wild Jack* (1988).

FERRER, MIGUEL. Actor. *(b. Feb. 4, 1954, Santa Monica, Calif.)* Quick: name another actor who appeared on three primetime TV series simultaneously. This balding, spirited character actor, the son of Jose Ferrer (whom he closely resembles) and Rosemary Clooney, is quickly carving out a niche in flamboyant villainy with a sense of humor, and figures to be a notable player in the 1990s. Movie audiences first noticed him as the coke-snorting corporate baddie in *RoboCop* (1987), which he followed with a bit as a sinister biker in *Valentino Returns* (1988), and then went delightfully over the top as the scientist who flips out in *Deep Star Six* (1989). In 1990 he did manage a couple of relatively normal roles: as Kevin Costner's sidekick in *Revenge* and as a neighbor friend in *The Guardian.* His TV hat trick consisted of a Cajun cop on "Broken Badges," a politically ambitious D.A. on "Shannon's Deal," and, his best-known role to date, the acerbic medical examiner on "Twin Peaks" (all 1990–91). Recent films include *Twin Peaks: Fire Walk with Me* (1992), *Point of No Return, Hot Shots! Part Deux, Another Stakeout* (all 1993), and *Blank Check* (1994).

FETCHIT, STEPIN. Actor. *(b. May 30, 1902, Key West, Fla., as Lincoln Theodore Monroe Andrew Perry; d. Nov. 19, 1985.)* A performer whose very name became synonymous with degrading portrayals of blacks on-screen, Fetchit (who reportedly took his stage name from a favorite racehorse) is a troubling figure. This vaudeville veteran played slow, dim-witted, foot-shuffling, bug-eyed types—but did so with superb timing and comic know-how. He was a star in his own right, who signed a lucrative contract with Fox Films that not only kept him busy but featured him prominently alongside such stars as Will Rogers. His only leading role for Fox was in the all-black *Hearts in Dixie* (1930), although that same year he was featured with the "Our Gang" kids in a short subject, *A Tough Winter.*

Fetchit enjoyed an extremely extravagant lifestyle during his heyday, at one point owning 16 cars, including a pink Rolls-Royce. (He declared bankruptcy in 1947, however.) Although his work is rarely seen today—his scenes are often edited out of TV prints, regardless of the effect on continuity—a viewer who can get past all the historical "baggage" can discern a highly competent and funny performer. He must have taken some pride in his work as well; even after converting to the Muslim religion in the 1960s, he defended his work after a fashion, suing CBS for defamation of character in 1970 after the network showed clips of his films "out of context."

OTHER FILMS INCLUDE: 1927: *In Old Kentucky;* 1929: *Salute;* 1934: *David Harum, Judge Priest;* 1935: *The County Chairman, Charlie Chan in Egypt;* 1936: *Dimples;* 1937: *On the Avenue;* 1949: *Miracle in Harlem;* 1952: *Bend of the River;* 1953: *The Sun Shines Bright* (John Ford's own remake of his *Judge Priest,* with Fetchit recreating his original role); 1974: *Amazing Grace.*

FIELD, BETTY. Actress. *(b. Feb. 8, 1918, Boston; d. Sept. 13, 1973.)* Few screen actresses of the 1940s came on as strong as Field did in her first few film outings, but in spite of her obvious talent, she never became a bona fide movie star. Having attended New York's American Academy of Dramatic Arts, she hit Broadway in the late 1930s and established herself as a bright ingenue, especially in "What a Life!" the 1939 film version of which brought her to Hollywood. Just 21, she limned a richly detailed, smoldering portrayal of the slatternly wife in *Of Mice and Men* (1939), fought for the affections of John Wayne in *The Shepherd of the Hills* (1941), and startled moviegoers as a tragic, insane resident of *Kings Row* (1942). Although she made the most of solidly written roles in *Flesh and Fantasy* (1943) and *The Southerner* (1945), Field worked in films infrequently after World War 2—although she did turn up in a number of prestige pictures, such as *Picnic* (1955), *Bus Stop* (1956), *Butterfield 8* (1960), and *Birdman of Alcatraz* (1962). Her last film was *Coogan's Bluff* (1968). Field was once married to playwright Elmer Rice, who penned several stage vehicles for her.

FIELD, SALLY. Actress. *(b. Nov. 6, 1946, Pasadena, Calif.)* This girlishly attractive actress—the daughter of actress Margaret Field—began her career as the impossibly perky TV "Gidget" in 1965, then went on to play the impossibly perky "The Flying Nun" from 1967 to 1970. Some limited fame and financial rewards accrued, but both roles proved formidable obstacles in Field's subsequent attempt to make it as a serious actress. Things began going her way in the mid 1970s: She played the female lead in the quirky 1976 bodybuilding drama *Stay Hungry,* and a woman with 17 distinct personalities in the compelling breakthrough TV movie *Sybil* (1976), for which she won an Emmy. A romantic liaison with Burt Reynolds led to their costarring in 1977's *Smokey and the Bandit* and 1978's *Hooper,* a lighthearted look at movie stuntmen (which echoed her life as the stepdaughter of stuntman extraordinaire Jock Mahoney).

In 1979 Field took on a challenging, serious role as a reluctant union organizer in the drama *Norma Rae,* for which she won a Best Actress Academy Award. Field did solid leading work throughout the 1980s, playing an ambitious reporter in 1981's controversial *Absence of Malice,* a haunted widow in *Kiss Me Goodbye* (1982), and a determined Texas mother in *Places in the Heart* (1984, one of the more distinguished pictures in that decade's losing-the-farm subgenre; she won another Best Actress Academy Award for that film, occasioning her notorious "You like me" acceptance speech).

Like other actresses, she began developing and producing her own film vehicles, leading to such worthwhile projects as *Murphy's Romance* (1985), *Punchline* (1988), and *Steel Magnolias* (1989). She also starred in the melodramatic *Not Without My Daughter* and the broadly comic *Soapdish* (both 1991). That same year she wore a producer's hat for the first time on a film in which she did not star: the Julia Roberts tearjerker *Dying Young.* More recently, she provided the voice of Sassy the cat in *Homeward Bound: The Incredible Journey* (1993), played Robin Williams' estranged wife in *Mrs. Doubtfire* (1993) and Tom Hanks' mom in *Forrest Gump* (1994). She returned to TV as star and executive producer of the miniseries "A Woman of Independent Means" (1995).

FIELD, SHIRLEY ANNE. Actress. *(b. June 27, 1938, London.)* Pretty, red-haired actress most notable for her performances in two key films of the early 1960s "British New Wave": *The Entertainer* (1960, opposite Laurence Olivier) and *Saturday Night and Sunday Morning* (1960, opposite Albert Finney). After *Alfie* (1966), she concentrated on television and theater, but has reemerged on the big screen as a supporting player, bringing her warm, welcome presence to *My Beautiful Laundrette* (1985, as the mistress of the Pakistani uncle), *Shag, Getting It Right* (both 1989), and—most notably—*Hear My Song* (1991, as the grown-up beauty queen once chosen Miss Dairy Goodness by tenor Josef Locke).
OTHER FILMS INCLUDE: 1960: *Peeping Tom;* 1961: *Man in the Moon;* 1962: *The War Lover, These Are the Damned.*

FIELDS, W. C. Actor, screenwriter. *(b. Feb. 10, 1879, Philadelphia, as William Claude Dukenfield; d. Dec. 25, 1946.)* One of the most imitated movie stars of all time, this unique comedian made relatively few films, but his snarling voice, bulbous nose, comical hats, and well-known penchant for liquid refreshment have made him one of the screen's true comedic icons. A top star in vaudeville, primarily as a comic juggler, he made numerous silent films, beginning in 1915 (though from this vantage point it seems useless to watch Fields without listening to his distinctive voice). The motion picture did not seem to be his métier, in spite of frequent forays into the medium (including two vehicles, 1925's *Sally of the Sawdust* and 1926's *That Royle Girl,* which were directed by none other than D. W. Griffith). A handful of silent pictures served him well, however, so much so that *It's the Old Army Game* (1927) was later remade as *It's a Gift* (1934), and *So's Your Old Man* (1926) served as the blueprint for *You're Telling Me* (also 1934). Even *Sally of the Sawdust* was revived as *Poppy* in 1936.

Even in his heyday, Fields was an acquired taste, and his acerbic humor was not universally appreciated. Mack Sennett liked him and hired him to make four now-classic two-reelers: *The Dentist* (1932), *The Barber Shop, The Pharmacist,* and *The Fatal Glass of Beer* (all 1933);

like his first sound short, *The Golf Specialist* (1930), these twenty-minute films distilled some of his best, time-tested routines, to which he would return again and again.

Fields' biggest fan was peripatetic studio executive William LeBaron, who signed him at Paramount in the 1930s. At first he won supporting or costarring roles in such films as the multi-episode *If I Had a Million* (1932, as the exterminator of road hogs), the nonsense classic *Million Dollar Legs* (1932, as the King of Klopstokia), the all-star *Alice in Wonderland* (1933, as Humpty Dumpty) and *International House* (also 1933). Then he hit his stride in a series of starring vehicles which represent him at the peak of his powers: *Tillie and Gus* (1933), *You're Telling Me* (1934), *The Old-Fashioned Way* (1934, which highlights his wonderful juggling routine), *It's a Gift* (1934, a comic masterpiece and arguably his best film), and *The Man on the Flying Trapeze* (1935). He also costarred with Burns and Allen, Charles Ruggles, Mary Boland, and frequent vis-à-vis Alison Skipworth in *Six of a Kind* (1934) and provided comedy relief for musical lead Bing Crosby in *Mississippi* (1935). Fields received story credit for most of his films, usually under one of his colorful pseudonyms: Charles Bogle, Mahatma Kane Jeeves, Otis Criblecosis.

His finest hour came when MGM and producer David O. Selznick decided that Charles Laughton wasn't giving them what they wanted in their production of *David Copperfield* (1935), and they replaced him with Fields in the role of the fastidious and impoverished Mr. Micawber. It was inspired casting indeed; Fields was Fields, but he also captured Dickens' character to a tee. (Metro later thought of him for the role of the Wizard in *The Wizard of Oz,* which would have been another bull's-eye if the idea had been followed through.)

Ill health restricted Fields' movie work in the late 1930s, and *The Big Broadcast of 1938* marked his swan song at Paramount. But renewed popularity on radio, as the nemesis of Edgar Bergen's wooden dummy Charlie McCarthy, led to a screen teaming in *You Can't Cheat an Honest Man* (1939), and with it a Fields renaissance at Universal studios. *My Little Chickadee* (1940) paired him with the screen's other great iconoclast, Mae West,

The Bank Dick (1940) gave him his best vehicle since *It's a Gift,* and *Never Give a Sucker an Even Break* (1941) came as close to comic anarchy as anything ever produced at a mainstream Hollywood studio.

Thereafter, audiences only saw the Great Man in brief but welcome guest appearances (1944's *Follow the Boys* and *Song of the Open Road,* 1945's *Sensations of 1945;* his sequence was cut from 1942's *Tales of Manhattan*). His health failed, and he passed away, ironically enough for the world's most famous curmudgeon, on Christmas Day. Rod Steiger played him in a 1976 biopic, *W. C. Fields and Me.* In 1974 the comedian's grandson Ronald J. Fields compiled a book called "W. C. Fields by Himself," which dispelled many colorful legends about the performer, many of which he had perpetuated during his lifetime.

FIGGIS, MIKE. Director, screenwriter, composer. *(b. Feb. 28, 1948, Kenya.)* Before making his mark as a filmmaker, Figgis studied music in London and performed with the R & B group The Gas Board. He was a member of the British experimental theatre group The People Show for many years, before plunging into theatrical productions and eventually directing "The House," an acclaimed TV production that led to his feature debut, *Stormy Monday* (1988), a very stylish film noir piece, which he also wrote. That impressive debut won him an offer from Hollywood, where he directed the overheated police yarn *Internal Affairs* (1990, which gave Richard Gere one of his best roles as a slimy cop) and the bizarre *Liebestraum* (1991), a convoluted tale which showed Figgis' expertise at creating mood, though sometimes at the expense of his story. His other films include *Mr. Jones* (1993), again with Richard Gere, and the remake of Terrence Rattigan's *The Browning Version* (1994). Figgis has not forgotten his musical roots and composed the scores for *Stormy Monday* and *Liebestraum,* as well as coscoring *Internal Affairs.*

FINCH, PETER. Actor. *(b. Sept. 28, 1916, London; d. Jan. 14, 1977.)* "I'm mad as hell," he roared, "and I'm not going to take it anymore!" That was the battle cry of the frazzled TV anchorman played by Finch in *Network* (1976), and his performance in that film remains the one best remembered by American audiences. A rich childhood took him from France to India and back to his parents' native Australia, where he drifted during the Depression years, finding work in legitimate theater in 1935. The rugged, good-looking actor launched his screen career after several years in Australian radio and vaudeville. Finch's screen debut in 1938's *Dave and Dad Come to Town* didn't exactly make him a top screen attraction, and he continued in radio, occasionally narrating British films on the side. He came to London at the behest of Laurence Olivier, who made him a protégé. Although he appeared in a few films during the war years, his movie career didn't begin in earnest until the late 1940s. He worked in the Hollywood-financed productions *The Miniver Story* (1950) and *Elephant Walk* (1954), and played the evil Sheriff of Nottingham in Walt Disney's *The Story of Robin Hood* (1952), getting good notices and winning himself some fans. Several years of supporting roles followed, and he won British Film Academy awards for his work in *A Town Like Alice* (1956) and *The Trials of Oscar Wilde* (1960).

As he matured, Finch retained his good looks, although the weight of years added a weatherbeaten, world-weary cast to his features. He scored big in *Far From the Madding Crowd* (1967), and was Oscar-nominated for his work in the British-U.S. production *Sunday, Bloody Sunday* (1971). His lead role in the highly touted but inept, elephantine remake of *Lost Horizon* (1973) aborted an attempt to transform him into a Hollywood leading man, but *Network* went a long way toward undoing the damage. Finch died of a stroke during a promotional tour for that film; the Motion Picture Academy awarded him a posthumous Best Actor Oscar for his riveting performance.

OTHER FILMS INCLUDE: 1953: *The Story of Gilbert and Sullivan, The Heart of the Matter;* 1954: *Father Brown;* 1955: *Simon and Laura;* 1957: *The Pursuit of the Graf Spee;* 1959: *The Nun's Story;* 1960: *Kidnapped;* 1963: *In the Cool of the Day;* 1964: *The Pumpkin Eater;* 1966: *The Flight of the Phoenix;* 1971: *The Red Tent;* 1972: *Something to*

Hide; 1973: *The Nelson Affair;* 1977: *Raid on Entebbe* (telefilm, shown posthumously).

FINNEY, ALBERT. Actor. *(b. May 9, 1936, Lancashire, England.)* This popular British actor got the best scene in *Miller's Crossing* (1990), hands down. Who could ever forget him, playing a Prohibition-era Irish gangster, purposefully marching down a dark street in a hail of bullets, calmly firing a smoking machine gun to the strains of "Danny Boy" on the soundtrack? Sure, it's pure pulp, but a wonderful moment in a screen career loaded with them. Finney began as an extremely handsome, tousled-haired leading man associated with some of the brightest lights of the British Free Cinema movement of the early 1960s, which combined the working-class ethos of England's "angry young man" writers with the cinema-agitating tendencies of the French "nouvelle vague" directors.

Finney's first film was 1960's *The Entertainer,* in which he shared screen time with the great Laurence Olivier; he quickly followed up with *Saturday Night and Sunday Morning* (1960), a "kitchen sink" drama about a dissolute factory worker, directed by Karel Reisz from Alan Sillitoe's novel. Originally tapped for the title role in *Lawrence of Arabia,* Finney balked at the film's monumental shooting schedule and opted instead to play the title role in Tony Richardson's freewheeling adaptation of Henry Fielding's novel *Tom Jones* (1963). The bawdy film won him his first Oscar nomination and made him an international star overnight, but rather than taking the Hollywood plunge, Finney continued his stage work full force and appeared in relatively few films (but successful ones) during the 1960s, including *Two for the Road* (1967, opposite Audrey Hepburn) and *Charlie Bubbles* (1968, his directorial debut as well).

In the 1970s he made a transition to character roles and quirky leads, often unrecognizable under a mound of makeup—as the title character in *Scrooge* (1970), or as the chunky, mustached, insufferable detective Hercule Poirot in *Murder on the Orient Express* (1974, an Oscar-nominated turn). In the 1980s he took on more "visible" but no less varied roles, from the addled actor (reportedly based on the very theatrical Donald

Wolfit) in *The Dresser* (1983, an Oscar nomination) to the title role in the 1984 TV movie *Pope John Paul II;* other made-for-TV projects include *The Image* and *The Green Man* (both 1990). Though the quality of his recent films may be uneven, his work remains consistently outstanding. OTHER FILMS INCLUDE: 1981: *Wolfen, Looker;* 1982: *Shoot the Moon;* 1982: *Annie* (as Daddy Warbucks); 1984: *Under the Volcano* (snagging his fourth Academy Award nomination as the alcoholic protagonist of John Huston's ambitious drama); 1987: *Orphans;* 1992: *The Playboys;* 1993: *Rich in Love;* 1994: *The Browning Version, A Man of No Importance.*

FIORENTINO, LINDA. Actress. *(b. Mar. 9, 1960, Philadelphia, as Clorinda Fiorentino.)* This attractive, knowing, husky-voiced young actress (and former political science major) demonstrated unusual poise and ability—along with an uncommonly natural acting style—during her first year in movies: as a restless young woman in *Vision Quest,* a too-cool young sculptress in Martin Scorsese's *After Hours,* and a convincing femme fatale in the otherwise abysmal *Gotcha!* (all 1985 releases). While her turn as a sophisticated art-lover in 1988's *The Moderns* brought Fiorentino additional acclaim, she went on to appear in such forgettable films as *Queens Logic* (1991) and *Chain of Desire* (1992). Fiorentino finally got the breakthrough role she deserved in *The Last Seduction* (1994), playing one of the most conniving, relentless femme fatales in screen history. In 1995 she appeared in *Jade* and *The Desperate Trail* (telefilm).

FIRTH, COLIN. Actor. *(b. Sept. 10, 1960, Hampshire, England.)* Handsome young British lead who, after making his London stage debut in the spy drama "Another Country," made his film debut in the 1984 movie version of that play. His obvious ability duly noted by receptive critics, Firth has yet to establish a screen persona or become a bankable star. OTHER FILMS INCLUDE: 1984: *A Month in the Country;* 1988: *Apartment Zero;* 1989: *Valmont* (the "other" version of *Dangerous Liaisons*); 1990: *Wings of Fame;* 1993: *Hostages* (made for TV).

FIRTH, PETER. Actor. *(b. Oct. 27, 1953, Hampshire, England.)* Gifted British actor, slender and plaintive looking, who had a few unimportant film roles before creating a sensation as the emotionally troubled youth in Peter Shaffer's play "Equus." He repeated his role in the 1977 movie version, earning an Academy Award nomination yet failing to glean much success from his triumph. Firth has appeared on-screen fairly regularly since then, most notably in the well-received but scarcely seen *Letter to Brezhnev* (1985) and the smash hit *The Hunt for Red October* (1990).
OTHER FILMS INCLUDE: 1973: *Brother Sun, Sister Moon;* 1976: *Aces High, Joseph Andrews;* 1979: *Tess, When You Comin' Back, Red Ryder?;* 1981: *Tristan and Isolde;* 1983: *The Aerodrome;* 1984: *White Elephant;* 1985: *Lifeforce;* 1986: *A State of Emergency;* 1987: *Born of Fire;* 1988: *Prisoner of Rio;* 1989: *Deadly Triangle, Tree of Hands;* 1990: *Burn Down;* 1991: *The Pleasure Principle, Prisoners of Honor;* 1993: *Shadowlands.*

FISHBURNE, LAURENCE (LARRY). Actor. *(b. July 30, 1961, Augusta, Ga.)* An excellent, underused actor who finally started getting good roles in the early 1990s, Fishburne caught the acting bug at age 10, and made his film debut in *Cornbread, Earl and Me* (1975). Four years later he appeared as "Clean," one of the PT-boat crew members accompanying Martin Sheen on his odyssey in Francis Coppola's epic Vietnam saga *Apocalypse Now* (1979), an experience that Fishburne says had a profound effect on him. He also worked in Coppola's *Rumble Fish* (1983) and *The Cotton Club* (1984), Steven Spielberg's *The Color Purple* (1985), and Spike Lee's *School Daze* (1986), among others, but started making an impact on audiences as a vice lord in *King of New York* (1990), Gene Hackman's legal assistant in *Class Action* (1991), and especially, as Furious Styles, the father (and soul) of John Singleton's *Boyz N the Hood* (1991). Fishburne finally achieved leading-man status as an under-cover narcotics agent in *Deep Cover* (1992), and received a Tony Award that same year for his Broadway debut in August Wilson's acclaimed play, "Two Trains Running." In 1993 Fishburne doffed the name "Larry" in favor of Laurence, and scored an Oscar-nominated knockout as selfish soul singer Ike Turner in *What's Love Got to Do With It,* then turned in a typically strong supporting performance in *Searching for Bobby Fischer.* That same year he won an Emmy for an episode of the short-lived TV series "Tribeca." Since then, he has appeared in *Bad Company, Higher Learning,* and *Just Cause* (all 1995). Fishburne is also known to many kids as Cowboy Curtis from the TV series "Pee-wee's Playhouse."

FISHER, CARRIE. Actress, screenwriter. *(b. Oct. 21, 1956, Los Angeles.)* This daughter of show-biz couple Debbie Reynolds and Eddie Fisher appeared in stage productions with her mother before landing her first film job, as Warren Beatty's young seductress, in Hal Ashby's *Shampoo* (1975). Two years later, she appeared in her most widely recognized role, that of the feisty, outspoken Princess Leia in *Star Wars,* a characterization she repeated in the sequels *The Empire Strikes Back* (1980) and *Return of the Jedi* (1983). Since then, she has survived drug and alcohol dependency, a troubled marriage to singer-actor Paul Simon, and such cinematic flotsam as *Under the Rainbow* (1981) and *Hollywood Vice Squad* (1986) to become a lively, refreshingly cynical supporting actress in such comedies as *The 'burbs, When Harry Met Sally . . .* (both 1989), *Sibling Rivalry* (1990), and *Soapdish* (1991). She then revealed a hitherto unsuspected writing talent as the author of the semiautobiographical novel "Postcards from the Edge." Director Mike Nichols had her write the script for the 1990 film adaptation (with Shirley MacLaine in the role based, at least in part, on Fisher's mother). She followed it with other novels, "Surrender the Pink" and "Delusions of Grandma."

FISHER, TERENCE. Director, editor. *(b. Feb. 23, 1904, London; d. June 18, 1980.)* This prolific director began his long movie career editing British potboilers such as *Falling for You* (1933) and *Mr. Satan* (1938). He was given his first directing assignment, *Colonel Bogey,* in 1942; 10 years and many quickies later, he hooked up with the legendary Hammer Studios, where he specialized in moody,

Gothic horror pictures, many of them remakes featuring the classic movie monsters made famous by Universal Studios in the 1930s. As director, his films include *The Curse of Frankenstein* (1957), *Horror of Dracula* (1958), *The Mummy* (1959), *The Phantom of the Opera* (1962), and *Frankenstein and the Monster From Hell* (1972). They're all marked by Fisher's visual touches, including his extensive coverage of atmospheric sets and liberal use of color (especially red) in creating mood. OTHER FILMS INCLUDE: 1949: *The Astonished Heart, So Long at the Fair* (both as codirector); 1953: *Four-Sided Triangle;* 1959: *The Hound of the Baskervilles, The Man Who Could Cheat Death;* 1960: *The Brides of Dracula, The Two Faces of Dr. Jekyll;* 1961: *The Curse of the Werewolf;* 1964: *The Earth Dies Screaming, The Gorgon;* 1965: *Dracula— Prince of Darkness;* 1967: *Frankenstein Created Woman;* 1968: *The Devil Rides Out;* 1969: *Frankenstein Must Be Destroyed!*

FITZGERALD, BARRY. Actor. *(b. Mar. 10, 1888, Dublin, as William Joseph Shields; d. Jan. 4, 1961.)* A former clerk who joined Dublin's famous Abbey Theatre group as a young man, Fitzgerald first came to America with the troupe in the late 1920s. He continued to appear in theaters on both sides of the Atlantic and made his screen debut in Alfred Hitchcock's *Juno and the Paycock* (1930). He came to Hollywood to reprise his stage role in John Ford's movie version of Sean O'Casey's *The Plough and the Stars* (1936), and became the archetypal movie Irishman: short and wiry, with a thick brogue, dancing eyes, and mischievous grin. (The brogue was so thick that directors and beleaguered sound men often asked him to do second and third takes to make his dialogue more understandable.) The huge success of *Going My Way* (1944), for which he won the Best Supporting Actor Oscar, made him a promotable name, if not quite a star, and he was featured in such films as *Duffy's Tavern* (1945), *Two Years Before the Mast* (1946), *Variety Girl* (1947), *Welcome Stranger* (1947, reunited with *Going My Way* costar Bing Crosby), *Miss Tatlock's Millions* (1948), and *Top o' the Morning* (1949). He played against type in *The Naked City* (1948), and returned to familiar turf for John Ford's *The Quiet Man* (1952). His

last film was the British-made *Broth of a Boy* (1959). His brother, Arthur Shields, also acted in films and played similar roles, but without Fitzgerald's success; they both appeared in *The Plough and the Stars* and *The Quiet Man.* OTHER FILMS INCLUDE: 1938: *The Dawn Patrol;* 1940: *The Long Voyage Home;* 1941: *How Green Was My Valley, Tarzan's Secret Treasure;* 1944: *None But the Lonely Heart;* 1945: *And Then There Were None.*

FITZGERALD, GERALDINE. Actress. *(b. Nov. 24, 1914, Dublin.)* This Irish beauty, who limned iron-willed and sometimes unbalanced women in films on both sides of the Atlantic, reached the pinnacle of her Hollywood success immediately upon arriving there in 1939. Her film debut, supporting Bette Davis in *Dark Victory,* was followed by her memorable portrayal of Isabella in *Wuthering Heights,* which earned her an Academy Award nomination. Fitzgerald had many fine roles ahead of her, mostly at Warner Bros. during the 1940s, but never scaled the heights of stardom as did her fellow countrywoman Maureen O'Hara. (Possibly her frequent rebellions at Warners, which kept her on suspension for lengthy periods, had something to do with it.)

She reemerged in later years as a fine character actress, in films like *The Pawnbroker* (1965), *Rachel, Rachel* (1968), *The Last American Hero* (1973), *Harry and Tonto* (1974), *Echoes of a Summer* (1976), *Arthur* (1981), *Easy Money* (1983), *Poltergeist II* (1986), and *Arthur 2: On the Rocks* (1988). Active on the stage and television, she won particular notice in the 1980s as a charming and delightful cabaret performer. Fitzgerald took up stage directing in later years as well. Her son is British film and TV director Michael Lindsay-Hogg ("Brideshead Revisited"). OTHER FILMS INCLUDE: 1934: *Open All Night* (her first); 1935: *Turn of the Tide;* 1936: *Cafe Mascot;* 1937: *The Mill on the Floss;* 1940: *'Til We Meet Again;* 1941: *Flight From Destiny, Shining Victory;* 1942: *The Gay Sisters;* 1943: *Watch on the Rhine;* 1944: *Ladies Courageous, Wilson;* 1945: *The Strange Affair of Uncle Harry;* 1946: *Nobody Lives Forever* (opposite John Garfield in this romantic film), *O.S.S., Three Strangers* (surprisingly but effectively teamed with rascally rogues Sydney Greenstreet and Peter Lorre); 1948: *So*

Evil My Love; 1951: *The Late Edwina Blake;*
1958: *Ten North Frederick;* 1961: *The Fiercest
Heart.*

FIX, PAUL. Actor. *(b. Mar. 13, 1901,
Dobbs Ferry, N.Y.; d. Oct. 14, 1983.)* Ferretlike character actor, one of the screen's
foremost practitioners of cowardice,
treachery, and duplicity—but, offscreen,
one of the nicest guys in Hollywood. Fix
acted in stock and toured with small theatrical companies throughout the 1920s,
working his way to Hollywood and settling into movie work late in the decade.
He appeared as a heavy in many Westerns, but also played sneering hoods and
sniveling stool pigeons in crime pictures;
on occasion he played sympathetic
characters—but, one suspected, never with
his heart in it. Fix befriended (and even
coached) John Wayne in the 1930s and
continued to appear in his films for decades to come. He appeared as Sheriff Mi-
cah on the TV series "The Rifleman"
(1958–63).
FILMS INCLUDE: 1926: *Hoodoo Ranch;*
1928: *Lucky Star;* 1930: *Ladies Love Brutes;*
1932: *The Last Mile, Back Street;* 1933: *Zoo
in Budapest* (in a role that actually emphasized his weasel-like qualities); 1935: *The Eagle's Brood;* 1936: *The Prisoner of Shark
Island;* 1937: *Souls at Sea;* 1939: *Behind
Prison Gates;* 1940: *Black Friday, The Ghost
Breakers;* 1942: *Pittsburgh;* 1943: *Hitler—
Dead or Alive;* 1944: *The Fighting Seabees,
Tall in the Saddle;* 1945: *Flame of the Barbary
Coast;* 1947: *Tycoon;* 1948: *Red River, Force of
Evil;* 1950: *Surrender;* 1953: *Hondo;* 1954:
Johnny Guitar, The High and the Mighty;
1955: *Blood Alley;* 1956: *Giant;* 1963: *To Kill
a Mockingbird;* 1965: *Shenandoah, The Sons
of Katie Elder;* 1966: *Nevada Smith;* 1967: *El
Dorado;* 1969: *The Undefeated;* 1970: *Dirty
Dingus Magee;* 1972: *Night of the Lepus;*
1973: *Pat Garrett and Billy the Kid;* 1978:
Grayeagle.

FLAHERTY, ROBERT J. Producer, director. *(b. Feb. 16, 1884, Iron Mountain,
Mich.; d. July 23, 1951.)* Sometimes called
"the father of the motion-picture documentary," this enterprising filmmaker was
at least as much showman as documentarian. Nonetheless, he deserves credit for his
pioneering; he was the first to bring movie
cameras to some of the world's most inac-

cessible places, at considerable risk to his
comfort and, sometimes, his health. Born
to a prospector, Flaherty spent much of
his youth in the American West in search
of gold. His youthful travels nurtured a
lifelong yearning for exploration and a
profound curiosity about other peoples
and civilizations.
While traipsing around the Hudson Bay
area of northern Canada in 1913, Flaherty
took moving pictures of the Eskimo natives, most of which were lost in a fire
later on. It took him several years to raise
the money, but in 1920 he persuaded
wealthy investors to back another expedition, this time with more sophisticated
camera equipment. He was able to persuade an Eskimo family to let him film
their daily routines, which were later
edited into *Nanook of the North* (1922), a
ground-breaking success both critically
and commercially. Even then, Flaherty
was stretching the truth: For one sequence
he constructed half of an igloo shell and
persuaded Nanook and his family to pantomime occurrences that had taken place
earlier in cramped surroundings into
which the director couldn't bring his camera. (Tragically, the film's Eskimo protagonist died of starvation shortly after the
film's release.)
Nanook's success prompted Paramount's
Jesse L. Lasky to finance a Flaherty expedition to the South Seas. After nearly 20
months, the documentarian came back
with miles of footage detailing Polynesian
island life. But *Moana* (1926) got into
trouble with critics and experts who realized that the filmmaker had tinkered with
reality just a little too much; although the
film contained many beautiful scenes, it
was judged to be inaccurate in many details. It also flopped at the box office,
ending Flaherty's autonomous filmmaking
career.
Nonetheless, Hollywood respected Flaherty's expertise and passion. He was
assigned by MGM to codirect *White Shadows of the South Seas* (1928) with studio
workhorse W. S. Van Dyke, but he fought
incessantly with his collaborator and quit
the production in midstream. His collaboration with F. W. Murnau ended similarly,
with the German director buying out
Flaherty's financial interest in *Tabu*
(1931), another South Seas story, prior to
release. *Man of Aran* (1934) covered the
life of an island fisherman off the coast of

Ireland, and restored Flaherty's reputation as a serious documentarian, but *Elephant Boy* (1937), which he codirected with Zoltan Korda, was out-and-out fiction, albeit with a keen sense of verisimilitude owing to extensive location shooting in India.

Flaherty's final film, *Louisiana Story* (1948, made for the Standard Oil Company), told the story of a poor bayou family radically affected by the arrival of an oil-drilling crew. Although it too featured much "reenactment," *Louisiana Story* remained accurate in its general depiction of time, place, and people. At the time of his death the filmmaker was preparing to shoot a State Department–financed documentary on Hawaii.

FLEISCHER, MAX. *(b. July 19, 1889, Vienna; d. Sept. 11, 1972.)* This self-effacing cartoonist and inventor was Walt Disney's only serious rival for many years. Like Disney, and many other pioneering animators, he started out as a newspaper cartoonist. A serious art student, he also had scientific knowledge and curiosity; while working as art director for *Popular Science Monthly* he devised the idea of creating animated cartoons by filming live-action footage first, then tracing those movements one frame at a time. His brother Dave Fleischer donned a clown's costume and posed for Max's camera, and thus became the model for Koko the Clown. Max was awarded a patent for his invention, called the rotoscope, but was unable to sell the idea as a practical means of making movies because the work was too time-consuming. Eventually he and Dave realized that they could use the rotoscope as a tool to enhance their freehand work, and began producing *Out of the Inkwell* cartoons featuring Koko, and some amazingly lifelike animation. What's more, they came up with the idea of having that clown cavort in a real world, combining live-action and animation together. The series caught on, and ran from 1919 to 1929. (The "special effects" of the constantly clever series were enhanced by Max's follow-up invention, the rotograph, which allowed live-action footage to be rear-projected onto a pane of glass one frame at a time—enabling both Koko and the footage around him to move simultaneously.)

In the mid 1920s, Max produced the first "talking" cartoons in collaboration with Dr. Lee De Forest, and created a device called the Bouncing Ball to encourage audiences to sing along with lyrics printed on the screen. Unfortunately, these films were regarded as a novelty, and nothing more, and Max's innovation was largely ignored.

When the industry as a whole adopted sound, Max brought his Bouncing Ball to a much larger audience. But it was another character, introduced in 1930's *Dizzy Dishes,* which brought him greater fame: the sexy flapper Betty Boop. She became a major cartoon star, and her saucy adventures were extremely popular. When the motion picture industry adopted its Production Code in 1934, however, much of the pizzazz of Betty's films was stripped away (no pun intended); her costume became more demure, and so did the racy humor. While Disney's staff was largely Midwestern, and his early films reflected a rural sensibility, Max and Dave were city boys, and so were most of their animators and gagmen; their films were urban and ethnic. They may not have had Disney's polish, but they had their own distinctive sense of humor. Dave, the studio's director-in-chief, was a superb gagman who inspired his animators to cram as many funny ideas as possible into every frame of film.

In 1933, Fleischer negotiated to bring Elzie Segar's "Thimble Theatre" comic strip character Popeye to the screen, and this became the studio's most enduring claim to fame. Beginning with *Popeye the Sailor* (in which he sang his now-familiar theme song), this foghorn-voiced, pipe-smoking sailor man became one of the screen's greatest stars—seriously rivaling Disney's Mickey Mouse. So great was his popularity that Fleischer featured him in a trio of two-reel Technicolor "specials," *Popeye the Sailor Meets Sinbad the Sailor* (1936), *Popeye Meets Ali Baba and His Forty Thieves* (1937), and *Popeye Meets Aladdin and His Wonderful Lamp* (1939). For these films, Fleischer perfected a process in which cartoon cels were suspended on the edge of a revolving turntable, on which miniature sets were built of cardboard and papier-mâché; the result was an amazing, three-dimensional look.

Following the success of Disney's *Snow White and the Seven Dwarfs,* Fleischer's distributor, Paramount Pictures, pressured him to make feature films as well. Neither *Gulliver's Travels* (1939) nor *Mr. Bug Goes to Town,* (aka *Hoppity Goes to Town)* (1942) gave Disney any serious competition, but they did drain the studio's resources. By this time, Fleischer had moved from New York to Florida and expanded his staff to accommodate feature production. He also took on the challenge of bringing Superman to the screen in an elaborate and expensive series of cartoons beginning in 1941. They were among his finest achievements, but sadly, they were among his last.

Paramount seized control of the studio from Max and Dave Fleischer, and kept most of their personnel. Dave moved to Hollywood and found work at Columbia and other studios in years to come. Max retreated from the spotlight, and spent his later years working with his old friend Jam Handy in Detroit, producing educational films. He never got the credit he deserved for his many inventions and innovations. His son is director Richard Fleischer.

FLEISCHER, RICHARD. Director. *(b. Dec. 8, 1916, Brooklyn, New York.)* This stalwart Hollywood director, the son of animation pioneer Max Fleischer, studied drama at Yale and joined New York's RKO-Pathé newsreel operation in 1942, where he wrote and directed for the "This Is America" series and wrote and produced "Flicker Flashbacks." His success there earned him a chance to move to the "real" RKO studio in Hollywood, where he proved his mettle on a series of suspenseful, noirish grade-B programmers like *Bodyguard* (1948, based on a story cowritten by Robert Altman!), *The Clay Pigeon* (1949), *Trapped* (1949), *Follow Me Quietly* (1949), and *Armored Car Robbery* (1950). *The Narrow Margin* (1952), a thriller set aboard a train, is considered a classic today and a model of B moviemaking. (He also coproduced the Oscar-winning 1947 documentary *Design for Death.*) After *The Happy Time,* a 1953 charmer, and the 3-D flop *Arena* (1953), Fleischer got his first major assignment from Walt Disney (his father's former archrival!) on the enormously successful *20,000 Leagues Under the Sea* (1954). He has helmed many other "big" movies

since then, some of them well-done—*The Vikings* (1958), *Barabbas* (1962), *Fantastic Voyage* (1966), *Tora! Tora! Tora!* (1970)—and some of them notorious flops—*Doctor Dolittle* (1967), *Che!* (1969), and *Mandingo* (1975). Fleischer directed all kinds of stories, from cop dramas *(The New Centurions,* 1972) to science fiction *(Soylent Green,* 1973), to biographies *(The Incredible Sarah,* 1976), to costume pieces *(Crossed Swords,* 1977) without evidence of any particular personal style, although more than one critic has noted his attraction to real-life murder cases in *The Girl in the Red Velvet Swing* (1955), the excellent documentary-style *The Boston Strangler* (1968), *10 Rillington Place* (1970), and *Compulsion* (1959), a retelling of the Leopold-Loeb case that is one of his best films. Unlike some of his contemporaries, Fleischer continued to work steadily in the 1980s, albeit on unredeemable projects like *The Jazz Singer* (1980), *Tough Enough* (1982), *Amityville 3-D* (1983), *Conan the Destroyer* (1984), *Red Sonja* (1985), and *Million Dollar Mystery* (1987), proving (if nothing else) that he is a Survivor, First Class. He is involved in merchandising his father's creation Betty Boop and was executive producer of the aborted 1994 Betty Boop animated feature. His memoir, "Just Tell Me When to Cry," was published in 1993.

FLEMING, RHONDA. Actress. *(b. Aug. 10, 1923, Los Angeles, as Marilyn Louis.)* This ravishing redhead, whose ascent to stardom was immeasurably boosted by frequent appearances in Technicolor movies (in which her titian tresses, green eyes, and creamy skin showed to great advantage), started working in films shortly after graduating from Beverly Hills High School. After a couple of years doing extra work, she graduated to bits and supporting roles, beginning with *In Old Oklahoma* (1943). Fleming appeared in *When Strangers Marry, Since You Went Away* (both 1944), *Spellbound, The Spiral Staircase* (both 1945), *Adventure Island,* and *Out of the Past* (both 1947), before getting her first big break: as leading lady opposite Bing Crosby in his musical *A Connecticut Yankee in King Arthur's Court* (1949), one of the few films to ever take advantage of her trained singing voice. Subsequently Fleming starred in mostly routine crime thrillers, Westerns, and costume dramas, most often playing typical female leads but occasionally landing meatier fallen-women roles, to which she cleverly applied her naturally silky, seductive voice. She made occasional TV appearances throughout the 1960s and 1970s, but has been little seen since. She did agree to appear in *The Nude Bomb* (1980), principally because it was executive-produced by her husband, movie theater magnate Ted Mann (current owner of Hollywood's famous Chinese Theatre).

OTHER FILMS INCLUDE: 1950: *The Eagle and the Hawk;* 1951: *Little Egypt, Cry Danger;* 1952: *Hong Kong, The Golden Hawk;* 1953: *Pony Express, Those Redheads from Seattle;* 1954: *Jivaro, Yankee Pasha;* 1955: *Tennessee's Partner, Queen of Babylon;* 1956: *The Killer Is Loose, Slightly Scarlet, While the City Sleeps;* 1957: *Gunfight at the O.K. Corral, The Buster Keaton Story;* 1958: *Home Before Dark;* 1959: *Alias Jesse James, The Big Circus;* 1960: *The Crowded Sky;* 1961: *Revolt of the Slaves;* 1969: *Backtrack.*

FLEMING, VICTOR. Director. *(b. Feb. 23, 1883, Pasadena, Calif.; d. Jan. 23, 1949.)* Though known primarily as an "action" director—and for taking the reins of two of history's most beloved films—Fleming was more versatile than film history would seem to indicate. He got into the film industry by accident (he'd been a race car driver, and in later years was a well-known motorcyclist and airplane pilot), and worked his way up through the ranks on film crews, eventually serving as cinematographer to Allan Dwan, D. W. Griffith, and Douglas Fairbanks, Sr. He made his feature debut as a codirector on Fairbanks' *When the Clouds Roll by* (1920) and then soloed on *The Mollycoddle* (1921). After such interesting projects as *Red Hot Romance* (1922, written by Anita Loos) and a 1925 version of *Lord Jim,* he worked at Paramount and was noted for the Clara Bow vehicles *Mantrap* (1926, one of her best performances) and *Hula* (1927), Emil Jannings' first Hollywood film, *The Way of All Flesh* (1927), and Westerns like *The Rough Riders* (1927) and *The Virginian* (1929, a film that helped ensure Gary Cooper's stardom).

He went to MGM in 1932 and helmed the Jean Harlow classics *Red Dust* (1932, with Clark Gable) and *Bombshell* (1933, a terrific satire of Hollywood), going on to prove himself in a variety of memorable comedies, dramas, biographies, and action films like *The White Sister* (1933), *Treasure Island* (1934), *Captains Courageous* (1937), and *Test Pilot* (1938). In 1939, Fleming lucked into two of the great directing coups of all times. First he was selected to take over directing chores on the musical fantasy *The Wizard of Oz;* next, he was asked by David O. Selznick and Clark Gable to replace George Cukor on the epic *Gone With the Wind,* over concerns that Cukor was paying far more attention to Vivien Leigh than the rest of the film. (Fleming, ironically, was later replaced by Sam Wood after suffering a nervous breakdown.) *GWTW* earned Fleming a Best Director Oscar (just one of the film's many accolades).

One of MGM's most reliable directors, he took on such varied assignments in the 1940s as *Dr. Jekyll and Mr. Hyde* (1941), *Tortilla Flat* (1942), *A Guy Named Joe* (1943), *Adventure* (1946) and *Joan of Arc* (1948). It's ironic that someone known so much as Mr. Macho would have directed some of Hollywood's most potent weepies, not to mention memorable performances by such female stars as Clara Bow, Jean Harlow, and Ingrid Bergman.

FLETCHER, LOUISE. Actress. *(b. July 24, 1934, Birmingham, Ala.)* She was nothing short of blood-curdling as the dispassionate, ruthless, and vaguely sadistic Nurse Ratched in *One Flew Over the Cuckoo's Nest* (1975), coolly manipulating her mental hospital patients and thwarting rebellious Jack Nicholson, frequently displaying a sly half-smile. The daughter of deaf parents, this supporting actress appeared on such TV series as "Wagon Train" and "The Untouchables" in the early 1960s before taking a decade-long hiatus from performing. After landing a small role in the big-screen *Thieves Like Us* (1974), Fletcher was cast in *Cuckoo's Nest* and snagged a Best Actress Oscar for her work. Strangely, her subsequent parts weren't nearly as meaty, and she often tended to lapse into her Ratched characterization. Fletcher became typed in horror/sci-fi films, appearing in such pictures as *Exorcist II: The Heretic* (1977), *Mama*

Dracula (1980), *Strange Invaders* (1983), *Firestarter* (1984), *Invaders from Mars* (1986) and, more recently, *Shadowzone* (1990). Her best part after *Cuckoo's Nest* was as the chain-smoking scientist in *Brainstorm* (1983).
OTHER FILMS INCLUDE: 1986: *Nobody's Fool;* 1987: *Flowers in the Attic;* 1988: *Two-Moon Junction;* 1993: "The Fire Next Time" (TV miniseries).

FLOREY, ROBERT. Director, writer. *(b. Sept. 14, 1900, Paris; d. May 16, 1979.)* Everybody thinks that Busby Berkeley invented all those overhead geometric dance routines so popular in 1930s movie musicals, but it was this distinctive filmmaker who was doing it in 1929's *The Cocoanuts,* The Marx Brothers' first feature film. It's just one highlight in the career of an often overlooked yet highly individual talent. After writing and directing several shorts in France in the teens, Florey came to Hollywood and worked as an assistant director, then later as an art director. He made his feature writing/directing debut with *That Model From Paris* (1926), but it was a short subject he made the following year, *The Life and Death of a Hollywood Extra,* that actually caused people to sit up and take notice. He continued to alternate between directing and set design for the next few years, helming *One Hour of Love* (1927), *The Battle of Paris,* and *The Hole in the Wall* (both 1929) among others. Originally slated to direct *Frankenstein* (1931, for which he actually shot tests with Bela Lugosi, not Boris Karloff, in the monster makeup), he was ignominiously dumped to make room for prestigious director James Whale, at that time Universal's hottest director. Florey was given the Lugosi starrer *Murders in the Rue Morgue* (1932) as a consolation; although strictly a B picture in concept and execution, it's stylish enough to keep horror-movie fans wondering how the genre would have evolved if Florey had done *Frankenstein.*

His continental, visually oriented directorial style was somewhat submerged in a three-year stint at Warner Bros., where he helmed *Ex-Lady, Girl Missing* (both 1933), *Bedside, Smarty* (both 1934), *Don't Bet on Blondes,* and *The Florentine Dagger* (both 1935), among others, in that studio's staccato house style. He moved to

Paramount in 1936, beginning his peak period; although he mostly worked on B thrillers with stereotypical scripts and contract-player casts, he infused them with a rich, almost Impressionistic look that belied their meager budgets. His better Paramounts include *Hollywood Boulevard, The Preview Murder Mystery* (both 1936), *Daughter of Shanghai, King of Gamblers* (both 1937), *King of Alcatraz, Dangerous to Know* (both 1938), *Hotel Imperial, The Magnificent Fraud* (both 1939), and *Women Without Names* (1940).

Florey chafed against his pigeonholing as a B director at Paramount and left to freelance; his early 1940s efforts still included some stylish low-budgeters—most notably *The Face Behind the Mask* and *Meet Boston Blackie* (both 1941, for Columbia)—but he sometimes got bigger pictures too: *The Desert Song* (1944), *God Is My Co-Pilot* (1945), *The Beast With Five Fingers* (1946, an underrated horror film), *Tarzan and the Mermaids* (1948), *Johnny One Eye* (1950), and *The Vicious Years* (1950). He also assisted Charlie Chaplin on the troubled set of *Monsieur Verdoux* (1947), and actually recorded a vitriolic, incoherent Chaplin outburst that showed the great filmmaker on the verge of a nervous breakdown.

Florey moved into television in the early 1950s, and directed episodes of "Wagon Train," "Four Star Playhouse," "Zane Grey Theater," "The Twilight Zone," "Thriller," "The Untouchables," "The Outer Limits," and especially "The Loretta Young Show" before retiring in the late 1960s. He wrote several books on film theory and history.

FLYNN, ERROL. Actor. *(b. June 20, 1909, Hobart, Tasmania; d. Oct. 14, 1959.)* The handsome, devil-may-care hero of Hollywood's most exciting swashbucklers, Flynn shot to overnight stardom when brought on as a last-minute replacement for Robert Donat to play the title role in Warner Bros.' pirate epic *Captain Blood* (1935). His flamboyant charm and dashing magnetism quickly established Flynn as the sound era's claimant to the Douglas Fairbanks swashbuckling crown as he effortlessly portrayed a legion of heroic characters.

A rebellious, adventurous, peripatetic youth who was expelled from several schools and held various jobs before turning to acting, Flynn made his film debut as Fletcher Christian in a small Australian film, *In the Wake of the Bounty* (1933). After appearing in an English-made quota quickie for Warner Bros., *Murder at Monte Carlo* (1935), Flynn was brought to the company's Hollywood studio, where he played the small roles of a corpse in *The Case of the Curious Bride* and a playboy in *Don't Bet on Blondes* (both 1935).

After the great success of *Captain Blood,* Warner Bros. put Flynn in everything from light comedies to Westerns, but it was his romantic adventure films that were most popular with the public. Olivia de Havilland, his *Captain Blood* leading lady, was again cast opposite him in *The Charge of the Light Brigade* (1936). Loosely based on Tennyson's immortal poem, this thundering spectacle was directed by hard-driving Michael Curtiz who, despite the personal animosity between himself and his star, made Flynn unforgettable leading the charge into the Valley of Death. Curtiz eventually directed 12 of Flynn's better films.

Again teamed with de Havilland (with whom he made eight films in all), Flynn had his best-remembered role, as the definitive "merrie rogue" of Sherwood Forest, in *The Adventures of Robin Hood* (1938). This was the part he was born to play; indeed, few of his peers could don ornate period costumes, speak flowery heroic dialogue, or swing a saber with such valiance or grace.

Flynn expanded his buccaneering in *The Sea Hawk* (1940, another of his biggest hits), and later played two larger-than-life historical figures: Cavalry General George Armstrong Custer in the sweeping Western *They Died With Their Boots On* (1941) and boxing champ James J. Corbett in the evocative period piece *Gentleman Jim* (1942). In the former, moviegoers readily accepted the Irish-accented Tasmanian in the lead role of this largely fictional retelling of the events leading to the Little Big Horn battle. In fact, he played Western heroes throughout his career, in such films as *Dodge City* (1939), *Santa Fe Trail, Virginia City* (both 1940), *San Antonio* (1945), *Rocky Mountain,* and *Montana* (both 1950).

Flynn was less successful in brief forays into light comedy; the public clearly favored him swinging sabers rather than serving as comedic foil in the likes of *Perfect Specimen* (1937) or *Four's a Crowd* (1938). He was more popular in war films, notably a 1938 remake of the WW1-set *The Dawn Patrol,* and the WW2 adventures *Dive Bomber* (1941), *Desperate Journey* (1942), and *Objective, Burma!* (1945).

Flynn's offscreen life was, incredibly, even more colorful than his movies. An unabashed hedonist and insatiable womanizer, he was notorious for his nonstop drinking, wenching, and general high-spirited bacchanalia. In 1942, at the height of his popularity, he was charged with (but later acquitted of) statutory rape. The ordeal of the trial and resultant publicity crushed Flynn's spirit. Never a person to take acting seriously, his on-screen energy ebbed and he slid into a gradual but steady decline in the postwar years. The best of his earlier Warner Bros. films saw Flynn in roles that exuded a lust for adventure and derring-do, but few of his later films had the same effect. Only when cleverly cast in the title role of the tongue-in-cheek *Adventures of Don Juan* (1949) did he show a final glimpse of the magic that had made him popular.

Flynn's health deteriorated as well; the years of hard drinking showed—harshly—in his later screen appearances. Several of his final films saw Flynn cast as an alcoholic; in the film adaptation of Hemingway's *The Sun Also Rises* (1957) he limned a drunken American expatriate of the "lost generation" with an accuracy born of experience and in *Too Much, Too Soon* (1958) he portrayed his old boozing crony and fellow actor John Barrymore.

The star's final years found him aboard his beloved yacht "Zaca," anchored in Port Antonio, Jamaica. Here in an island paradise he said reminded him of his boyhood wanderings in New Guinea, Flynn worked on his posthumously published autobiography, the slyly titled "My Wicked, Wicked Ways" (1959). Flynn starred in the title role of *William Tell,* a European production begun in 1954 but never finished.

OTHER FILMS INCLUDE: 1937: *The Prince and the Pauper, Another Dawn;* 1938: *The Sisters;* 1939: *The Private Lives of Elizabeth and Essex* (with Bette Davis); 1941: *Footsteps in the Dark* (his one attempt at a comedy-mystery, none too good); 1943: *Edge of Darkness;* 1944: *Uncertain Glory;* 1946: *Never*

Say Goodbye; 1947: *Cry Wolf, Escape Me Never;* 1949: *That Forsyte Woman;* 1951: *Kim, Adventures of Captain Fabian;* 1952: *Mara Maru, Against All Flags;* 1953: *Master of Ballantrae;* 1954: *Crossed Swords;* 1955: *The Warriors, King's Rhapsody;* 1956: *Istanbul;* 1957: *The Big Boodle;* 1958: *The Roots of Heaven;* 1959: *Cuban Rebel Girls.*

FOCH, NINA. Actress. *(b. Apr. 20, 1924, Leyden, Holland, as Nina Consuelo Maud Fock.)* Stylish, aloof blond player, unquestionably gifted but rarely affecting in her film work. The daughter of a composer and an actress, she spent her early years in New York City, where she studied at the American Academy of Dramatic Arts and flirted with a career as a concert pianist before turning to acting. Signed by Columbia in 1943, Foch was hurled headlong into a spate of low-budget thrillers, beginning with *The Return of the Vampire* (1943), that did nothing to challenge her—with the exception of *My Name Is Julia Ross* (1945), a taut little nail-biter that won favorable reviews and boosted Foch into a better class of melodrama: *Johnny O'Clock* (1947), *The Dark Past* (1948), *Undercover Man,* and *Johnny Allegro* (both 1949). Upon leaving Columbia, she got better roles (but seldom leads) in the likes of *An American in Paris* (1951), *Scaramouche* (1952), *Executive Suite* (1954, for which she snagged a Best Supporting Actress Oscar nomination), *The Ten Commandments* (1956), *Cash McCall,* and *Spartacus* (both 1960). She was off the screen for over a decade (although she did some TV work during that time), and returned in 1971's *Such Good Friends.* Aside from supporting roles in *Rich and Famous* (1981), *Dixie Lanes* (1987), *Skin Deep* (1989), and *Morning Glory* (1993), Foch has worked almost exclusively in TV since the early 1970s, and is a highly respected acting teacher in Hollywood.

FONDA, BRIDGET. Actress. *(b. Jan. 27, 1964, Los Angeles.)* One of the very few third-generation movie stars, this fresh-faced, appealing young actress certainly has some good genes going for her. The daughter of actor-director Peter Fonda, niece of actress/fitness guru Jane Fonda, and granddaughter of actor Henry Fonda, young Bridget spent her childhood years in Los Angeles and Montana. While studying theater at New York University, she starred in a graduate student film called *PPT,* and the workshop stage productions "Confession" and "Pastels." Following her first film roles in *Aria* (1988, which nobody should have to admit having debuted in) and *You Can't Hurry Love* (1988, another stinker, but a lead role for Fonda), the talented young actress made critics and audiences stand up and take notice of her portrayal of British call girl Mandy Rice-Davies in the 1989 steamer *Scandal,* for which she affected a very credible British accent. Fonda worked nonstop throughout 1989 and 1990, appearing in such films as *Shag* (as the guileless beauty pageant contestant), *Strapless, Frankenstein Unbound, Leather Jackets,* and *The Godfather, Part III.* 1991 saw her back in supporting roles in *Drop Dead Fred* and *Doc Hollywood,* neither of which used her to good advantage. Her breakthrough parts came in 1992 (with the shared lead in *Single White Female* and an appealing light comic role in the ensemble film *Singles*) and 1993 (as the deadhead-turned-assassin in *Point of No Return* and the young woman courted and pursued by Eric Stoltz—her real-life companion—in *Bodies, Rest & Motion*). She continues to alternate commercial projects with more idiosyncratic efforts, like *Little Buddha, It Could Happen to You, The Road to Wellville, Camilla* (all 1994), and *City Hall* (1995).

FONDA, HENRY. Actor. *(b. May 16, 1905, Grand Island, Nebr.; d. Aug. 12, 1982.)* The words one associates most often with Henry Fonda are "honesty" and "integrity." He projected those qualities in the characters he played, and audiences came to associate them with Fonda himself. Similarly, those words can be used to describe his approach to acting. You never saw the wheels turning; you simply believed him.

Raised in Omaha, the son of a printer, Fonda initially harbored ambitions of being a newspaperman and to that end became a journalism major at the University of Minnesota. He dropped out after two years to get a job, and shortly thereafter started dabbling in amateur theatrics. He eventually quit his office-boy job and worked full-time at the Omaha Community Playhouse. In 1928, while back East, he met several participants of the University Players group, and was persuaded to join them. The company included such future theatrical luminaries as Joshua Logan, Mildred Natwick, Margaret Sullavan, and later, James Stewart. He spent several years with the group, marrying Sullavan in 1931 and divorcing her two years later. (They made an unsuccessful screen test together for MGM in New York.) By 1934 he had reached Broadway and after scoring his first big hit as the rural Romeo in 1935's "The Farmer Takes a Wife," he was invited to Hollywood to reprise the role in a movie version opposite Janet Gaynor.

The lanky, soft-spoken Fonda hit a chord that resonated among picture-show audiences, especially those in America's heartland, where his down-home manner reminded them of . . . themselves. He played rural youths in several more films, including *Way Down East* (also 1935), *The Trail of the Lonesome Pine* (1936, third-billed but no less memorable in his first Technicolor film), and *Slim* (1937). But he wasn't anxious to be typecast as a country bumpkin, and eagerly accepted a variety of assignments. He was teamed with former wife Sullavan in *The Moon's Our Home* (1936), a lame screwball comedy; with Sylvia Sidney, his *Lonesome Pine* costar, in *You Only Live Once* (1937, directed by Fritz Lang), a Bonnie-and-Clyde-type thriller; with Madeleine Carroll in *Blockade* (1938), a politically minded romance set during the Spanish Civil War; with Barbara Stanwyck in *The Mad Miss Manton* (1938), a screwball comedy-mystery; and with Bette Davis in *Jezebel* (also 1938), a torrid drama of the Old South.

Fonda's career got a major boost from his two-year stint with 20th Century-Fox. During that time he was assigned supporting roles—backing up Tyrone Power in *Jesse James* (1939, playing brother Frank), Don Ameche in *The Story of Alexander Graham Bell* (also 1939), and Alice Faye in *Lillian Russell* (1940)—and leads alike. Director John Ford deserves credit for developing and exploiting Fonda's unique appeal as an American Everyman. He first starred the actor in a colorful, colonial-era drama, *Drums Along the Mohawk*, then cast him in the title role of *Young Mr. Lincoln* (both 1939, Fonda more than rising to the challenge of playing this almost mythical giant of American history in the latter), and finally gave him the plum role of Okie migrant Tom Joad in his sober but brilliant adaptation of John Steinbeck's *The Grapes of Wrath* (1940). It was in the latter characterization, perhaps more than any other, that Fonda, deliberately or not, defined the essential American character: strong but gentle, independent but communal, pragmatic but optimistic, with a firm grasp of reality but a keen appreciation of faith. He was Oscar-nominated for this stirring performance but, amazingly, lost out (to his best friend, no less—Jimmy Stewart, winning for *The Philadelphia Story*).

After starring in *The Return of Frank James* and *Chad Hanna* (both 1940), Fonda was loaned to Paramount, where he played the male lead in Preston Sturges' *The Lady Eve* (1941), proving that he could play deadpan comedy and do pratfalls with the best of 'em. He also played comedic roles in *The Male Animal* and *The Magnificent Dope* (both 1942), but it was a drama, *The Ox-Bow Incident* (1943), that gave him another of his signature roles, in this unforgettable lynch-mob story set in the Old West. He returned to that milieu in 1946, after serving with distinction (winning a Bronze Star and a Presidential citation) in the U.S. Navy during World War 2, to play frontier lawman Wyatt Earp in John Ford's *My Darling Clementine*. Ford, perhaps wisely, ignored the historic Earp and had Fonda limn a character much closer to the stoic Western heroes Ford popularized in the silent era; the result was a classic morality play that still ranks as one of the landmarks of the Western genre.

Fonda worked for Ford again in 1947's *The Fugitive*, a brooding drama set in Mexico, and in 1948's *Fort Apache*, a cavalry-vs.-Indians story that cast him as a mustached martinet. Other postwar film assignments, like 1947's *Daisy Kenyon* and *The Long Night*, were unexciting (though he and James Stewart had fun together in one segment of 1948's *On Our Merry Way*). Fonda found greater satisfaction on the stage, in a play he came to love, "Mister Roberts," which he later reprised on film in 1955 (though, to his dismay, the movie version injected a great deal of comic horseplay, which led to a bitter—and irrevocable—fight between him and director John Ford; Mervyn LeRoy completed the film). Like many of the men he played on stage and screen, naval officer Roberts was a man of absolute integrity; this was a quality audiences came to associate with Fonda for the rest of his life. It's no accident he played U.S. presidents so often.

Following his triumph in the film version of *Mister Roberts,* Fonda's film career took an upward turn. In 1957 alone, he played the voice of reason in the brilliant jury drama *12 Angry Men* (a personal project that he also coproduced), an unjustly accused robbery suspect in Alfred Hitchcock's *The Wrong Man,* and a frontier bounty hunter in *The Tin Star.* He then played one of his most sophisticated roles, as an amorous theatrical producer in *Stage Struck* (a 1958 remake of Katharine Hepburn's *Morning Glory).* There were still some good solid roles to come—in films like *The Best Man* and *Fail-Safe* (both 1964)—and opposite Lucille Ball in the engaging family comedy *Yours, Mine and Ours* (1968). But too many of Fonda's 1960s films offered him glorified cameo roles, or undistinguished leads: *Advise and Consent, How the West Was Won, The Longest Day* (all 1962), *Spencer's Mountain* (1963), *Sex and the Single Girl* (1964), *The Rounders, In Harm's Way, Battle of the Bulge* (all 1965), *A Big Hand for the Little Lady* (1966), *Welcome to Hard Times* (1967), *Madigan* (1968). He made no bones about taking most of these assignments for the money—and to keep busy.

For sheer novelty, nothing could top his icy-cold turn as a hired killer in Sergio Leone's *Once Upon a Time in the West* (1968). He appeared another couple of times in cowboy garb, for 1970's *There Was a Crooked Man . . .* and *The Cheyenne Social Club* (the latter with James Stewart), and thereafter resigned himself to undemanding guest shots in the likes of *Midway* (1976), *Tentacles, Rollercoaster* (both 1977), *The Swarm* (1978), *City on Fire, Meteor* (both 1979), and a passel of telefilms, the best of which were *The Red Pony* (1973) and *Gideon's Trumpet* (1980). His cinematic swan song, thankfully, was the genuinely moving *On Golden Pond* (1981), which daughter Jane produced so they could star together. His performance as a crotchety old man who

is unforgiving of his grownup daughter won him his only Oscar.

Fonda starred in the TV series "The Deputy" (1959–61) and "The Smith Family" (1971–72), and guested on dozens of other shows. His celebrated one-man show on famed trial lawyer Clarence Darrow was broadcast by NBC in 1974. He also narrated many films and TV programs, from *The Battle of Midway* (1942) to *America's Sweetheart: The Mary Pickford Story* (1981). His children include actor Peter and actress Jane. In 1978 he was given a Life Achievement Award by the American Film Institute. Friends and colleagues still speak of his work with reverence and respect; he achieved what so few of them ever could on screen—total believability in every performance. His autobiography, "Fonda: My Life" was published in 1981.

FONDA, JANE. Actress, producer. *(b. Dec. 21, 1937, New York City.)* Few actresses today have been through as many metamorphoses as this beautiful and intelligent leading lady. The daughter of Henry Fonda broke into movies in 1960 as a coed in *Tall Story,* and spent much of the decade appearing in other romantic comedies such as *Period of Adjustment* (1962), *Sunday in New York* (1963), *Any Wednesday* (1966), and *Barefoot in the Park* (1967), with an occasional detour into drama, notably *Walk on the Wild Side* (1962), *The Chase* (1966), and the overheated sexual melodrama *Hurry Sundown* (1967) as well as *Circle of Love* (1964) for Roger Vadim, whom she went on to marry. She scored her biggest hits of that era in the title roles of two genre parodies, the hilarious Western *Cat Ballou* (1965) and Roger Vadim's colorful but muddled sci-fi opus *Barbarella* (1968). (Vadim also directed her and her brother Peter in one segment of 1968's *Spirits of the Dead.)* Shortly thereafter, she met political activist Tom Hayden, whom she eventually wed, and became deeply involved in antiwar activities during the Vietnam era, to the extent that she was tagged "Hanoi Jane." A 1972 documentary, *F.T.A.,* chronicles the antiwar revue she and Donald Sutherland toured during the war. (Decades later, her name still raises the hackles of some Americans who consider her a traitor.) Ironically, it was during this period that she solidified her reputation as an actress, first in 1969's *They Shoot Horses, Don't They?*, which earned her a first Best Actress Oscar nomination, and then as a hooker in *Klute* (1971), for which she won her first Oscar. Political activities kept her busy—and made her a Hollywood hot potato—for several years. As she eased back into film work, no longer the 1960s sexpot, she sought challenge and variety, and found it playing Nora in a TV production of *A Doll's House* (1973), a suburban wife-turned-bank robber in *Fun With Dick and Jane* (1976), Lillian Hellman in *Julia* (1977, Oscar-nominated), a tough rancher in *Comes a Horseman* (1978), an uptight New Yorker parrying with her ex-husband in Neil Simon's comedy *California Suite* (1978), and a TV newswoman in *The Electric Horseman* (1979, which reunited her with Robert Redford, from *Barefoot in the Park*). She won a second Oscar as the wife of a Vietnam vet whose experiences radicalize her in *Coming Home* (1978).

She then formed her own production company, and starred in such intelligent and topical films as *The China Syndrome* (1979, Oscar-nominated), the comic *9 to 5* (1980), and *Rollover*, as well as the smash comedy-drama *On Golden Pond* (both 1981, the latter performance Oscar-nominated), which finally gave her a vehicle in which she could costar with her father. As memories of the "controversial" Fonda subsided in the 1980s, she embarked on another career (and created a whole new image) by producing and appearing in an enormously successful line of exercise videos. At a time when other actresses her age were complaining about a lack of parts, she continued to etch memorable characterizations as a backwoods woman with a natural talent in the TV drama *The Dollmaker* (1984, which won her an Emmy), an investigative reporter in *Agnes of God* (1985), a murder suspect in *The Morning After* (1986, Oscar-nominated), a spinsterish schoolteacher in *Old Gringo* (1989), and a small-town teacher in *Stanley & Iris* (1990). When she married media mogul Ted Turner in 1991 she announced that she was retiring from acting. We can only hope she will someday change her mind.

FONDA, PETER. Actor, director. (b. Feb. 23, 1939, New York City.) Blessed with the appealing, all-American looks of his father, Henry Fonda, Peter began his big-screen career playing romantic leads in teen-appeal vehicles like *Tammy and the Doctor* (1963) and *The Young Lovers* (1964). As the swinging Sixties progressed, Fonda abandoned the mainstream and created a sensation starring in the 1966 Roger Corman biker flick *The Wild Angels* (his costar was fellow celebrity progeny Nancy Sinatra). He also began experimenting with drugs—which inspired not only his 1967 film *The Trip* but also Beatle John Lennon, who shared an LSD experience with Fonda and immortalized some of his acid-addled pronouncements in the song "She Said She Said." In 1969 Fonda produced and costarred in the definitive 1960s anti-establishment statement, *Easy Rider*, for which he shared an Academy Award nomination for Best Original Screenplay. His Hollywood career since that time has been spotty; he's acted mainly in sub-A action pictures. In 1971, Fonda directed and starred in the critically acclaimed Western *The Hired Hand* and followed with the sci-fi oddity *Idaho Transfer* (1973), in which he did not appear, and *Wanda Nevada* (1979), playing a gambler who wins young Brooke Shields in a poker game; father Henry made a brief appearance in the picture, marking the only time father and son worked together. Popular in Japan, he made a sci-fi film called *Daijoobu, Mai Furendo (All Right, My Friend)* there in 1983. In recent years his own child, Bridget Fonda, has become a star and was recently directed by Peter's old crony Roger Corman in 1990's *Frankenstein Unbound*. Peter made an amusing (and fleeting) cameo appearance in his daughter's 1993 movie *Bodies, Rest & Motion*—as a biker. He then took a supporting role in *Deadfall* (also 1993).

FONTAINE, JOAN. Actress. (b. Oct. 22, 1917, Tokyo, as Joan de Beauvoir de Havilland.) The younger sister of actress Olivia de Havilland, this poised, forceful actress began her movie career playing delicate, insipid ingenues—a potential career drawback that she turned to her advantage in two surprising characterizations that launched her as a top-flight star.

Born, like Olivia, in Tokyo to British parents, she toured with regional theater groups under the name Joan Burfield before making her screen debut thusly billed in a 1935 Joan Crawford starrer, *No More Ladies.* After more stage work, she landed at RKO where, billed as Joan Fontaine, she gave Ginger Rogers a break by appearing opposite Fred Astaire in *A Damsel in Distress* and supporting Katharine Hepburn in *Quality Street* (both 1937). Studio brass felt she needed more "seasoning," and so she was put to work in RKO potboilers such as *You Can't Beat Love* (also 1937), *Blonde Cheat, Sky Giant, Maid's Night Out,* and *The Duke of West Point* (all 1938).

Fontaine's luck changed in 1939. Not only did she play the gushy ingenue in *Gunga Din,* a mammoth hit that won her more recognition than all her previous programmers combined, she landed good supporting roles as doe-eyed innocents in MGM's *The Women* and Republic's *Man of Conquest* (as first wife of Texas pioneer Sam Houston). Then she was picked by producer David O. Selznick and director Alfred Hitchcock to play the lead in *Rebecca* (1940), the lavish adaptation of Daphne du Maurier's best-selling gothic romance. Under Hitchcock's guidance, she delivered a masterful, Oscar-nominated performance as a naive and victimized wife that drew on her long experience playing fragile-young-things and sprang to vivid life. She went one better the next year, playing the delicate wife of sinister Cary Grant in Hitchcock's *Suspicion* (1941), a mostly faithful adaptation of Francis Iles' chilling "Before the Fact." Fontaine's superb performance won her a well-deserved Oscar.

After appearing opposite Tyrone Power in the stirring wartime romance *This Above All* (1942), Fontaine tackled the difficult role of a young Belgian gamine who falls in love with older man Charles Boyer in *The Constant Nymph* (1943), and was rewarded with an Oscar nomination. (It remains her favorite film.) The following year she played another innocent in the remake of *Jane Eyre,* a slow-moving, overheated, but handsomely produced Charlotte Brontë adaptation that paired her with Orson Welles. Within a few years, she'd left such virginal characters far behind; as the 1940s wore on, her roles became more full-blooded, and she cheer-

fully played scheming bitches whenever the opportunity presented itself. Although arguably beneath an Oscar-winning actress, *The Devil's Own* (1966) was a surprisingly literate Hammer horror film that gave Fontaine her last lead, as a schoolteacher confronted with evidence of voodoo in her community. She has appeared in only a handful of made-for-TV movies since then. She published her autobiography, "No Bed of Roses," in 1978.

OTHER FILMS INCLUDE: 1945: *The Affairs of Susan;* 1946: *From This Day Forward;* 1947: *Ivy;* 1948: *The Emperor Waltz, Kiss the Blood Off My Hands, Letter From an Unknown Woman* (as the hopelessly infatuated pursuer of musician Louis Jourdan in this Max Ophuls classic); 1950: *Born to Be Bad, September Affair;* 1952: *Ivanhoe* (as Lady Rowena); 1953: *Decameron Nights, The Bigamist;* 1954: *Casanova's Big Night* (a rare comedy part opposite Bob Hope); 1956: *Serenade, Beyond a Reasonable Doubt;* 1957: *Island in the Sun;* 1958: *A Certain Smile;* 1961: *Voyage to the Bottom of the Sea;* 1962: *Tender Is the Night.*

FOOTE, HORTON. Screenwriter. *(b. Mar. 14, 1916, Wharton, Tex.)* Renowned writer who has brought a distinctive and very personal vision of small-town American life—inspired by his own hometown—to his work for the stage, TV, and the movies. Foote left home at 16 to study acting, first in Dallas, then at California's Pasadena Playhouse, and eventually in New York. He began writing plays to provide himself with good parts, but his interest in writing gradually outweighed his ambitions as an actor. He first gained critical attention for such plays as "The Chase" (which was filmed many years later), "The Trip to Bountiful," and "The Traveling Lady" (filmed as *Baby the Rain Must Fall* in 1965), and for numerous live TV dramas in the medium's "Golden Age." His screenplays include *Storm Fear* (1962), a beautiful adaptation of Harper Lee's *To Kill a Mockingbird* (1962), which won him an Oscar, *Baby the Rain Must Fall* (1965), *Hurry Sundown* (1967), *Tomorrow* (1972, an adaptation of William Faulkner), *Tender Mercies* (1983, which won him a second Oscar), and the remake of John Steinbeck's *Of Mice and Men* (1992). But much of his energy since the mid 1980s has gone into adaptations of his own plays, including *The Trip to Bountiful, 1918* (both 1985), *On Valentine's Day* (1986), and *Convicts* (1991), all of which have been produced on modest budgets and maintained the author's integrity. Foote's children Hallie and Horton, Jr., both actors, are featured in *1918* and *On Valentine's Day,* with Hallie playing a character based on Foote's mother, also named Hallie.

FORAN, DICK. Actor. *(b. June 18, 1910, Flemington, N.J.; d. Aug. 10, 1979.)* The beefy, red-headed Foran, scion of a prominent New Jersey family (of which he was the black sheep for having entered show business), came within a few weeks of beating Gene Autry to the silver screen as the first singing cowboy: His *Moonlight on the Prairie* (1935), first of 12 B Westerns he made for Warner Bros. in the 1930s, followed Autry's first oater into the marketplace by about a month. His notable screen debut gave him a closeup and a major song ("We're Out of the Red") in Fox's anti-Depression musical *Stand Up and Cheer* (1934), in which he was billed as Nick Foran. A likable performer, albeit one of limited range, he parlayed his subsequent cowboy-hero status into strong supporting roles in big-budget Warners' pictures such as *The Petrified Forest* (1936), *Boy Meets Girl* (1938), and *Daughters Courageous* (1939), but the studio dropped him in 1939.

At Universal, Foran became an all-around utility player, starring in serials (1940's *Winners of the West,* 1941's *Riders of Death Valley),* thrillers (1940's *The Mummy's Hand,* 1941's *Horror Island*), and musicals (1942's *Private Buckaroo).* He also supported the studio's top comedy team, Abbott & Costello, in *In the Navy* (1941) and *Ride 'Em Cowboy* (1942, in the latter introducing the standard "I'll Remember April"). His starring career petered out in the mid 1940s, although he contributed memorable supporting turns in *Fort Apache* (1948, as one of cavalryman Victor McLaglen's drinking buddies), *Chicago Confidential* (1957), and *Donovan's Reef* (1963).

FORBES, BRYAN. Director, screenwriter, producer, actor. *(b. July 26, 1926, Stratford, England.)* Veteran British writer and director who first came to his country's attention at age 16, as the chairman of the BBC radio program "Junior Brains Trust." Forbes began acting in the 1948 films *The Small Back Room* and *All Over the Town* and appeared in scores more, including *Sea Devils* (1953), *Appointment in London* (1953), *The Creeping Unknown* (1956, aka *The Quatermass Experiment*), *The Key* (1958), *The Guns of Navarone* (1961), and *A Shot in the Dark* (1964). He also gained notice as a screenwriter during the 1950s, starting with *The Cockleshell Heroes* (1956) and including *Danger Within/Breakout* (1959), *The League of Gentlemen* (1960), and *The Angry Silence* (1960), a study of a wildcat strike (Oscar-nominated for Best Screenplay). By 1959, Forbes had formed a production company with actor Richard Attenborough that produced several of the latter's films, including *The Angry Silence.* Two years later, Forbes made an excellent directing debut with *Whistle Down the Wind* (1961), from his own screenplay about three children who discover a fugitive murderer and think he is Christ. Next, Forbes wrote and directed the equally rewarding psychological studies *The L-Shaped Room* (1963) and *Seance on a Wet Afternoon* (1964), the latter with Attenborough (who coproduced with Forbes) and Kim Stanley in a superb performance as a fake medium. He followed with the POW drama *King Rat* (1965), the black comedy *The Wrong Box* (1966), and *The Whisperers* (1967), a character study of an old woman brilliantly played by Dame Edith Evans. In 1969, Forbes became head of London's Elstree Studios but resigned two years later. Since that time, his work has been entertaining but less interesting: *Long Ago Tomorrow* (1970, aka *The Raging Moon*), *The Stepford Wives* (1975), the Cinderella musical *The Slipper and the Rose* (1976), and *International Velvet* (1978). More recent efforts like *Better Than Never* (1983) and *The Naked Face* (1985) have been even less interesting, although he did work on the screenplay for *Chaplin* (1992), directed by his friend Attenborough. Forbes has been married to actress Nanette Newman since 1954; she has appeared in many of his films, including *The L-Shaped Room, Long Ago Tomorrow,* and *The Stepford Wives.* He has also written many fiction and nonfiction books, and an amusing autobiography, "Notes for a Life," in 1974.

FORD, GLENN. Actor. *(b. May 1, 1916, Quebec, as Gwyllyn Samuel Newton Ford.)* A skilled actor equally at home in comedy and drama, this darkly handsome actor (who matured into a rugged, rumpled-looking leading man) brought brooding intensity and, occasionally, an aloofness to his characterizations, making him capable of limning cold-hearted villains as well as engaging heroes. Glenn Ford grew up in Southern California and got his early acting training in school and local theatrical productions. Signed by Columbia Pictures in 1939, he made his feature-film debut in *Heaven With a Barbed Wire Fence,* and played in pictures as diverse as *Babies for Sale* (1940), *Blondie Plays Cupid, Texas* (both 1941), *The Adventures of Martin Eden* (1942), *Destroyers,* and *Desperadoes* (both 1943) before serving as a Marine in World War 2.

Ford hit the bricks running after his return to civilian life, playing opposite popular leading ladies Rita Hayworth in *Gilda* and Bette Davis in *A Stolen Life* (both 1946), but most of his pictures were forgettable programmers, excepting *The Man From Colorado* (1948), *Undercover Man* (1949), *The Big Heat, The Man From the Alamo* (both 1953), and *Human Desire* (1954). (He and Hayworth, who had shown particular chemistry in *Gilda,* were reteamed in 1948's *The Loves of Carmen,* 1952's *Affair in Trinidad,* and 1966's *The Money Trap.*) His performance as a courageous teacher facing tough inner-city youths in *Blackboard Jungle* (1955) made Ford a top-ranking star, and over the next decade he appeared in many popular films, including *Trial* (1955), *Teahouse of the August Moon* (1956), *3:10 to Yuma, Don't Go Near the Water* (both 1957), *Imitation General, The Sheepman* (both 1958), *The Gazebo* (1960), and a trio of ill-fated remakes, *Pocketful of Miracles, Cimarron* (both 1961) and *The Four Horsemen of the Apocalypse* (1962).

Although Ford continued to give fine performances in films like *Experiment in Terror* (1962), *Advance to the Rear, The Courtship of Eddie's Father* (both 1963), *Fate Is the Hunter* (1964), and *The Rounders* (1965), his film projects became less interesting in the later 1960s and early 1970s. *Is Paris Burning?* (1966), *Midway* (1976), and *Superman* (1978, as Clark Kent's adoptive father) are among his better later films. On TV Ford starred for a season in "Cade's County" (1971–72) and returned in 1975 with "The Family Holvak." Ford was married to musical star Eleanor Powell from 1943 to 1959. His last feature was the unworthy *Border Shootout* (1990), in which he delivered his customary solid performance. He published a memoir, "Glenn Ford R.F.D. Beverly Hills," in 1970.

FORD, HARRISON. Actor. *(b. July 13, 1942, Chicago.)* Ruggedly handsome, tight-lipped leading man whose filmic output includes starring roles in four of the 10 highest-grossing films of all time: *Star Wars* (1977), *The Empire Strikes Back* (1980), *Raiders of the Lost Ark* (1981), and *Return of the Jedi* (1983). That he has attained this magnitude of stardom is more than a little ironic, inasmuch as at one point in his sagging career, Ford actually quit acting to become a carpenter. Born to a suburban Chicago family, Ford flunked out of a midwestern college before ending up in Hollywood, where he was fortunate enough to get a contract with Columbia. A series of inconsequential roles in inconsequential pictures, beginning with *Dead Heat on a Merry-Go-Round* (1966), did little to further his career, but his rugged face made him a natural for Westerns like *Journey to Shiloh* (1968), as well as occasional guest-star status on TV fare like "Gunsmoke" and "The Virginian." After playing a minor part in the Elliott Gould vehicle *Getting Straight* (1970), Ford took up carpentry, a trade in which he was quite content, until a relatively unknown young director named George Lucas cast him in a supporting role in 1973's *American Graffiti.* He was impressive as a young cruiser, but despite his good showing, and a supporting role in Francis Ford Coppola's acclaimed *The Conversation* the next year, Ford was fortunate to have his handyman sideline, because his acting career seemed to be going nowhere.

In 1977, however, Lucas chose him for the plum role of cynical space pilot Han Solo in *Star Wars,* the mega-success of which finally made Harrison Ford a household name. He followed that with a series of box-office duds, including *Force 10 From Navarone, Hanover Street* (both 1978), and *The Frisco Kid* (1979), and had cameos in Coppola's *Apocalypse Now* (as Col. Lucas) and *More American Graffiti* (both 1979). But he scored once again as intrepid adventurer Indiana Jones in Steven Spielberg's homage to the adventure serial, *Raiders of the Lost Ark* (1981). Between sequels to *Star Wars* (in 1980 and 1983) and *Raiders* (1984's *Indiana Jones and the Temple of Doom* and 1989's *Indiana Jones and the Last Crusade*), Ford has accepted assignments in films somewhat more substantive than the big-budget, live-action cartoons that made him famous.

A gritty performance as a cop in the nihilistic future L.A. of *Blade Runner* (1982) demonstrated that he could deliver more than popcorn heroics. Another cop role, in *Witness* (1985), had a warmer side and some (repressed) romantic sparks; his performance earned him his first Oscar nomination and cemented his stardom with "grown-up" audiences. He followed it with a daring portrayal as an eccentric, idealistic inventor in *The Mosquito Coast* (1986), and played a Hitchcock protagonist in *Frantic* (1988), before showing his flair for romantic comedy in *Working Girl* (1988). He played a rather dour, adulterous lawyer accused of murder in *Presumed Innocent* (1990), and in 1991's *Regarding Henry,* he played an arrogant yuppie transformed into a heartwarming simpleton by the simple expedient of a mugger's bullet.

He was back in top form as the heroic ex-CIA Agent Jack Ryan in *Patriot Games* (1992, taking over the role originated by Alec Baldwin in *The Hunt for Red October*), demonstrating the charisma that has made him one of Hollywood's preeminent stars. Never was that more apparent than in 1993's blockbuster hit *The Fugitive.* In 1993 he made a guest appearance as Indiana Jones in one episode of George Lucas' lovingly produced TV series "The Young Indiana Jones Chronicles," then reprised the role of Jack Ryan in *Clear and Present Danger* (1994). Next, he starred in the remake of *Sabrina* (1995, in the Humphrey Bogart role). Ford is married to screenwriter Melissa Mathison.

FORD, JOHN. Director, producer. *(b. Feb. 1, 1895, Cape Elizabeth, Me., as Sean Aloysius O'Fienne; d. Aug. 31, 1973.)* The most honored of all American movie directors, John Ford was lauded by critics for his poetic vision, but he always insisted he was simply "a hard-nosed director" and that filmmaking was just "a job of work" to him. In truth, Ford had a singular vision which he brought to a vast body of work; most of his films (excepting routine studio assignments) are immediately recognizable as his and his alone—a remarkable achievement in a time when most films conformed to a studio's "personality," not a director's. There is continuity in Ford's work, as well, not just in his use of a familiar stock company of actors, or in revisiting favorite locations like Utah's Monument Valley, but in recurring themes and a distinctive point of view. Few filmmakers in the history of the medium have left their mark so indelibly on so many outstanding films; and, to Ford buffs, even his minor films have much to offer.

His brother Francis took "Ford" as a stage name and entered pictures in 1907. Young Jack (as he came to be known) joined Francis and his costar/partner Grace Cunard at Universal in 1914, first working as a prop man, then as an actor in Francis' starring serials *The Broken Coin* (1915) and *The Purple Mask* (1916). Although Francis frequently quarreled with Universal executives and eventually left the studio, Jack remained; he directed his first two-reeler, *The Tornado,* in 1917, and his first feature, *Straight Shooting,* later that same year. Many of Ford's early films were Westerns, and most of them starred Harry Carey. His already apparent talent for pictorially striking compositions made Ford a natural for horse operas (with their outdoor action scenes, magnificent vistas, etc.), and he worked with top screen cowboys Hoot Gibson, Buck Jones, and Tom Mix at Universal and Fox.

Formalizing his screen billing to John Ford in 1923 (an allusion to the Elizabethan playwright of the same name), the director scored with his handling of the John Gilbert vehicle *Cameo Kirby* (1923), but really shot to the top rank with *The Iron Horse* (1924), an epic Western detailing the building of the transcontinental railroad, filmed on location under arduous conditions. Another large-scale Western,

Three Bad Men (1926), used the Oklahoma land rush as its backdrop; its somewhat lesser reputation stems mainly from
the fact that was out of circulation for
many years. Its story and characterizations
presaged Ford's 1948 production of *3
Godfathers.* Ford's late silents—especially
Four Sons (1928)—were influenced by
the Germanic style of filmmaking then
prevalent in Hollywood, but he soon abandoned that highly impressionistic (and to
many, highly pretentious) approach to
moviemaking. The early talkie days saw
Ford, like many other directors, groping
for a command of the new storytelling
techniques imposed by the addition of
sound. He reunited with George O'Brien,
the burly, brash young star of *Iron Horse*
and *Three Bad Men,* for *Salute* (1929) and
The Seas Beneath (1931); both films were
moderately successful, and Ford maintained his position as one of the top Hollywood directors.

The 1930s found Ford further developing a distinctive style, which he honed
both on commercial, work-for-hire movies
and on modest, more personal productions. Critics lauded *The Informer* (1935),
a highly stylized story of betrayal during
the Irish Revolution for which Ford won a
Best Director Oscar; in retrospect, though,
it may be that Ford's best work of the period is found in less pretentious efforts including his Will Rogers vehicles (1933's
Dr. Bull, 1934's *Judge Priest,* 1935's
Steamboat 'Round the Bend) and *The
Whole Town's Talking.* By this time he
was already one of Hollywood's most colorful and irascible filmmakers. Although
publicity shots often showed him clad in
tweed jacket, colorful ascot, and neatly
creased fedora, he was more comfortable
in untied sneakers, a khaki shirt, and a
baseball cap. Often when he was nervous,
or in deep concentration, Ford would
chew on a corner of his handkerchief and
let it hang from his mouth. He was contemptuous of authority, and could be vicious in his sarcasm to those he found
pretentious, but he was also intensely
loyal to his "stock company," and in turn
inspired loyalty from cast and crew.

The single most important year of Ford's
career was undoubtedly 1939, which saw
the release of *Drums Along the Mohawk*
(a stirring drama of colonial America starring Henry Fonda and Claudette Colbert),
Young Mr. Lincoln (an inspiring biopic

with Fonda as the beloved president), and
Stagecoach, the latter a milestone not only
because it made a star of John Wayne
(who'd been an extra for Ford in 1928's
Mother Macree, Hangman's House, and
Four Sons), but because it revitalized a
genre long since abandoned to the producers of low-budget, Saturday-matinee
"horse operas." *Stagecoach,* which netted
Ford another Oscar nomination, sparked
interest in big-budget, "adult" Westerns—to which the director would return
throughout the remainder of his career. He
won back-to-back Oscars for *The Grapes
of Wrath* (1940) and *How Green Was My
Valley* (1941), both of which centered on
tight-knit families surviving in the face of
adversity. Vastly different from his previous films, they showed a more mature talent at work behind the camera. World War
2 intervened and Ford, serving in the Field
Photographic Branch of the OSS, turned
out several documentaries; two of them,
The Battle of Midway (1942) and *December 7th* (1943), were awarded Oscars. After the war, Ford returned to Hollywood
and demonstrated that he hadn't forgotten
how to make compelling entertainments:
They Were Expendable (1945) vividly
chronicled the exploits of PT-boat crews
in the South Pacific, and *My Darling
Clementine* (1946), an elegiac Western
with some of the director's most memorable images, starring Henry Fonda as a
considerably whitewashed Wyatt Earp.

In the late 1940s Ford and producer
Merian C. Cooper formed Argosy Productions, a partnership that produced some of
his best (and most personal) pictures. *Fort
Apache* (1948), *She Wore a Yellow Ribbon*
(1949), and *Rio Grande* (1950) comprised
Ford's unofficial Cavalry trilogy; John
Wayne starred in all three, supported by
many Ford regulars including George
O'Brien, Victor McLaglen, and Ward
Bond. *Wagon Master* (1950) repackaged
elements from *My Darling Clementine*
and was more notable for its western characters and atmosphere than for its story or
action. *The Quiet Man* (1952), which
starred Wayne as an American of Irish ancestry who settles on the Emerald Isle,
gave Ford ample opportunities to trumpet
his own Irish heritage; this stirring, beautiful film (much of it shot on location) won
him an unprecedented fourth Oscar.

His other 1950s films vary in quality, although many film fans and critics single

out *The Searchers* (1956), starring Wayne as a single-minded zealot who spends years pursuing the Indians who killed his relatives and kidnapped their young daughter, as the definitive Ford film. Still contentious, Ford was replaced as director of *Mister Roberts* (1955) by Mervyn LeRoy, reportedly because he quarreled with star Henry Fonda (who'd played the role on Broadway). To many, Ford's later films—including *The Last Hurrah* (1958), *The Man Who Shot Liberty Valance* (1962), and *Cheyenne Autumn* (1964)—seemed increasingly sentimental and derivative of earlier, better films. His final feature film, *7 Women* (1966), was an odd and unsuccessful throwback to the 1930s both in story and in technique. Although the aging and ill Ford delivered a curmudgeonly "performance" in Peter Bogdanovich's 1971 documentary, *Directed by John Ford*, it is obvious even in his last years that the director's crusty exterior concealed a sentimental heart. Ford was the first recipient of the American Film Institute's Life Achievement Award.

OTHER FILMS INCLUDE: 1931: *Arrowsmith;* 1932: *Air Mail, Flesh;* 1933: *Pilgrimage;* 1934: *The Lost Patrol, The World Moves On;* 1936: *The Prisoner of Shark Island, Mary of Scotland, The Plough and the Stars;* 1937: *Wee Willie Winkie, The Hurricane;* 1938: *Four Men and a Prayer, Submarine Patrol;* 1940: *The Long Voyage Home;* 1941: *Tobacco Road;* 1947: *The Fugitive;* 1952: *What Price Glory?;* 1953: *The Sun Shines Bright, Mogambo;* 1955: *The Long Gray Line;* 1957: *The Wings of Eagles, The Rising of the Moon;* 1959: *Gideon of Scotland Yard, The Horse Soldiers;* 1960: *Sergeant Rutledge;* 1961: *Two Rode Together;* 1963: *Donovan's Reef.*

FORD, WALLACE. Actor. *(b. Feb. 12, 1898, Batton, England, as Samuel Jones Grundy; d. June 11, 1966.)* You'd never know it to listen to him, but this stocky, not particularly handsome supporting player and occasional lead was born in England and spent his early years in London orphanages and foster homes. A runaway who joined a touring vaudeville troupe, Ford made his way to America and appeared on the Broadway stage in the 1920s, wiping out whatever English accent he might have had. A breezy, energetic player with a slight tendency to overact, Ford won more leading roles than

one might expect from his appearance, and was a fixture of Hollywood films, particularly in the 1930s.

FILMS INCLUDE: 1930: *Swellhead;* 1932: *Beast of the City, Freaks, Central Park;* 1933: *Employees Entrance, Night of Terror, Three-Cornered Moon;* 1934: *The Lost Patrol, Men in White;* 1935: *Mysterious Mr. Wong, The Whole Town's Talking, The Informer* (as Irish rebel Frankie McPhilip, whose betrayal sets the story into motion), *Mary Burns—Fugitive;* 1937: *A Son Comes Home;* 1939: *Back Door to Heaven;* 1940: *The Mummy's Hand;* 1942: *All Through the Night, The Mummy's Tomb;* 1943: *Shadow of a Doubt, The Ape Man;* 1945: *Blood on the Sun, Spellbound;* 1946: *Black Angel;* 1947: *Dead Reckoning,* 1948: *T-Men;* 1949: *The Set-Up;* 1950: *The Breaking Point, Harvey;* 1952: *Flesh and Fury;* 1955: *The Man From Laramie, The Spoilers;* 1956: *The Rainmaker;* 1958: *The Last Hurrah;* 1965: *A Patch of Blue.*

FOREMAN, CARL. Screenwriter, director, producer. *(b. July 23, 1914, Chicago; d. June 26, 1984.)* The man who wrote *High Noon*—and fled the country before it was released—Foreman was a major casualty of Hollywood's anti-Communist purge. Before entering World War 2 with the Army Signal Corps, he'd labored on Monogram's low-budget "East Side Kids" series (penning 1941's *Spooks Run Wild*). After the war, he joined fledgling producer Stanley Kramer, and following *So This Is New York* (1948, which he cowrote) they made such prestigious and socially conscious films as *Home of the Brave, Champion* (both 1949, the latter an Oscar-nominated script), *Cyrano de Bergerac, The Men* (both 1950, the latter Oscar nod number two), and—the summit of his career—*High Noon* (1952, Oscar nod number three). His appearance as an unfriendly witness before the House Un-American Activities Committee got Foreman blacklisted for his past Communist ties; he subsequently went to England, working on scripts (including 1957's Academy Award–winning *The Bridge on the River Kwai*) anonymously. Foreman eventually started his own production company, releasing *The Guns of Navarone* (1961), which he wrote and produced. He directed his own script of *The Victors* (1963), an ambitious but only partially successful drama of the immediate post-WW2 period in Europe. Foreman remained active in the British film industry, producing many films during the 1960s and 1970s (and earning yet another Oscar nomination for his script to 1972's *Young Winston);* he finally returned to the U.S. in 1975, but his later output (1978's *Force 10 From Navarone* and 1980's *When Time Ran Out . . .)* was generally undistinguished.

FORMAN, MILOS. Director. *(b. Feb. 18, 1932, Caslav, Czechoslovakia.)* Urbane, literate director who is one of the few foreign filmmakers to enjoy Hollywood success. Forman was born outside of Prague, which was to be torn by war during his childhood. His parents were liquidated in Nazi concentration camps, and Forman and his brothers were raised by relatives. As a young man, he studied at the prestigious Prague Film Faculty, where he made his first feature, *Black Peter,* in 1963. Two years later, his *Loves of a Blonde* was nominated for a Best Foreign Film Oscar, and soon Forman was at the forefront of his country's film industry. After the Russian invasion in 1968, Forman's brand of satiric social commentary (as in 1968's *The Firemen's Ball*) was not met with enthusiasm by the new authorities, and he came to Hollywood some two years later. His first American film, the dryly funny *Taking Off* (1971), met with some critical success, but it was not until 1975 that Forman struck gold: His adaptation of Ken Kesey's antiauthoritarian novel "One Flew Over the Cuckoo's Nest" swept that year's Academy Awards. Since then, Forman has directed large-scale works such as *Hair* (1979), *Ragtime* (1981), and *Amadeus* (1984, for which he earned another Best Director Oscar). His *Valmont* (1989), released here following the successful playoff of *Dangerous Liaisons* (adapted from the same play), didn't engender the same box-office response but has many adherents. In 1986 he agreed to appear on-camera playing Catherine O'Hara's husband in the Mike Nichols film *Heartburn;* it was a minor part, but it did reunite him (on-screen, at least) with his *Cuckoo's Nest* star Jack Nicholson. In 1978 Forman joined Columbia University as a Professor of Film and Co-Chair of the Film Division of their School of the Arts, a position he has held (with sabbaticals

for filmmaking) since then. In 1994 he published his autobiography, "Turnaround."

FORREST, FREDERIC. Actor. *(b. Dec. 23, 1936, Waxahachie, Tex.)* He made a convincingly cynical Dashiell Hammett in *Hammett* (1982), an ambitious if only partially realized noir produced by Forrest's principal benefactor, Francis Ford Coppola. In fact, many of this sleepy-eyed actor's best roles have been assigned him by Coppola, in the likes of *The Conversation* (1974), *Apocalypse Now* (1979), *One from the Heart* (1982), and *Tucker: The Man and His Dream* (1988). One exception, of course, is *The Rose* (1979) the non-Coppola rock-star nightmare for which he was Oscar-nominated as Best Supporting Actor. From a key supporting role in *When the Legends Die* (1972), his first important movie, right up to *The Two Jakes* (1990) and *Falling Down* (1993), Forrest has bounced back and forth between star turns and meaty character parts. That he has achieved significant success in both offers ample testimony to his ability. Some of his best roles have been in ambitious made-for-TV productions, including "Lonesome Dove" (1989, offering a chilling performance as an evil-spirited Indian) and *Citizen Cohn* (1992, in which he again played Dashiell Hammett).

FORREST, STEVE. Actor. *(b. Sept. 29, 1924, Huntsville, Tex., as William Forrest Andrews.)* One of a number of seemingly interchangable leading men who worked in 1950s' and 1960s' films, this fair-haired, virile actor—the younger brother of Dana Andrews—played bit parts in the early 1940s (including 1943's *Crash Dive*—which featured Andrews—and *The Ghost Ship),* graduated to more prominent supporting roles later in the decade, and then to leads in the 1950s. Forrest was very active on TV in the 1970s and 1980s, notably as the star of "SWAT" (1975–76). OTHER FILMS INCLUDE: 1952: *The Bad and the Beautiful;* 1953: *Battle Circus;* 1954: *Phantom of the Rue Morgue* (his first substantial hero part), *Rogue Cop;* 1957: *The Living Idol;* 1960: *Heller in Pink Tights;* 1962: *The Longest Day;* 1979: *Rascal;* 1971: *The Wild Country;* 1979: *North Dallas Forty;*

1981: *Mommie Dearest;* 1985: *Spies Like Us;* 1987: *Amazon Women on the Moon* (spoofing his own image).

FORSTER, ROBERT. Actor. *(b. July 13, 1941, Rochester, N.Y., as Robert Foster, Jr.)* This gruff but likable actor graduated from the stage to supporting work in late 1960s films before starring in Haskell Wexler's brilliant, cinema-verité-style drama *Medium Cool* (1969), as a TV cameraman who's become an observer instead of a participant in life. (It also gave him a groundbreaking, full-frontal nude scene.) Earlier, he had attracted critical attention in *Reflections in a Golden Eye* (1967), a bewildering misfire costarring Marlon Brando and Elizabeth Taylor. Although he starred in two 1970s crime series on TV—"Nakia" and "Banyon"—and in the cult favorite *Alligator* (1980), the brooding, darkly handsome Forster failed to achieve feature-film success. In recent years he has become something of a favorite thanks to the burgeoning home-video market, appearing in *The Banker* (1989), *Satan's Princess* (1990), and *Committed* (1991), among others. He also had supporting roles in *Delta Force* (1986, as a Middle Eastern terrorist) and *29th Street* (1991). Forster made his directorial debut with 1985's *Hollywood Harry,* in which he also starred.

FORSYTH, BILL. Director, writer. *(b. July 29, 1947, Glasgow.)* Perhaps the most important figure ever in the Scottish film industry, Forsyth crafts movies that are determinedly small in scope but grand in charm and magic. He started making industrial and documentary films with partners in the 1970s, then directed his first feature, *That Sinking Feeling* (1979), in about three weeks. It was well received (though not released in England until 1981, and not in the U.S. until 1984), and enabled him to secure financing for *Gregory's Girl* (1982), a gently comic story of teen romance that won Forsyth a British Screenplay Oscar and critical kudos. More raves came for *Local Hero* (1983), starring U.S. actors Burt Lancaster and Peter Riegert, about an American oil company trying to buy a tract of Scottish seacoast. Its success established Forsyth's style of low-key, eccentric comedy, but

nothing he's done since has captured as wide an audience, nor won him as much acclaim. He followed with *Comfort and Joy* (1984), then wrote and directed his first American film, *Housekeeping* (1987). *Breaking In* (1989), a comic caper film starring Burt Reynolds as an aging thief trying to pass along "trade secrets" to young apprentice Casey Siemaszko, was the first he shot in the U.S., but the change in locale had no effect on his quiet, idiosyncratic approach to storytelling. His latest: *Being Human* (1994).

FORSYTHE, WILLIAM. Actor. *(b. June 7, 1955, Brooklyn, N.Y.)* Tubby, wall-eyed, gap-toothed character actor most often seen as over-the-top characters, both comic and serious, in such films as *Once Upon a Time in America, Cloak & Dagger* (both 1984), *Extreme Prejudice, Raising Arizona* (both 1987), *Dead-Bang* (1989, as a hilariously stiff-shirted FBI agent), *Dick Tracy* (1990, as Flattop), *Stone Cold, Career Opportunities,* and *Out for Justice* (all 1991). Forsythe's physical makeup mitigates against his being assigned lead roles, but he seems perfectly comfortable—and attracts plenty of attention—in the offbeat parts. The year 1992 saw him in his finest (and largest) film role to date, playing one of three wheelchair-bound leads in the comedy-drama *The Waterdance.* Later that year he debuted as Prohibition-era gangster Al Capone in a new TV series version of "The Untouchables."

FOSSE, BOB. Director, choreographer. *(b. June 23, 1927, Chicago; d. Sept. 23, 1987.)* Former dancer and stage choreographer who appeared as an actor/dancer in several Hollywood films—including 1953's *The Affairs of Dobie Gillis, Give a Girl a Break,* and *Kiss Me, Kate*—before becoming a choreographer for *My Sister Eileen* (1955) and the exuberant movie versions of hit Broadway shows *The Pajama Game* (1957), *Damn Yankees* (1958), and *How to Succeed in Business Without Really Trying* (1967). He also costarred in *My Sister Eileen,* and performed one memorable mambo number with his then-wife Gwen Verdon in *Damn Yankees.* The short, intense, workaholic Fosse became a film director with *Sweet Charity* (1969), a dynamic musical staged and shot with astounding energy and innovation. The Tony-winning director picked up an Oscar for *Cabaret* (1972, which accounted for eight of the gold statuettes that year), and was nominated for the nonmusical, freeform biopic *Lenny* (1974). *All That Jazz* (1979) found Fosse in Fellini territory, directing Roy Scheider (playing an overachieving Fosse clone) in a vibrant but sometimes grotesque semiautobiographical story; he was Oscar-nominated for his direction and for cowriting the screenplay. The *real* Fosse appeared onscreen, acting and dancing, in *The Little Prince* (1974), and took a small role in the forgettable *Thieves* (1977). His last film was *Star 80* (1983), a sordid chronicle of the doomed "Playboy" Playmate Dorothy Stratten. As fans of his choreography could recognize distinctive Fosse trademarks, fans of his films came to appreciate his enormous creativity. In both dramatic and musical films, Fosse eschewed anything "ordinary." His work had bite and bravado in roughly equal doses.

FOSTER, JODIE. Actress, director. *(b. Nov. 19, 1962, Los Angeles, as Alicia Foster.)* Intense, talented young woman whose determination and artistic daring have made her one of the top actresses in Hollywood. Foster's career began early; as a child model and performer, she was managed by her mother—who, among other accomplishments, got young Jodie a modeling job as one of the bare-bottomed tykes in the Coppertone ads. Her first film was *Napoleon and Samantha* (1972), a Disney outing that cast her as a runaway. By the time she was a teenager, Foster already had several Hollywood pictures to her credit, including *One Little Indian* (1973), *Tom Sawyer* (1973), *Alice's Adventures in Wonderland* (1975), and *Echoes of a Summer* (1976), in addition to three interesting films: an early Martin Scorsese picture, *Alice Doesn't Live Here Anymore* (1974), playing a tough tomboy; *Bugsy Malone* (1976), a gangster spoof cast entirely with children, in which she plays a tough dame who's pelted with whipped cream "bullets" in the finale; and *Freaky Friday* (1977), an amusing Disney comedy in which she switched identities with onscreen mom Barbara Harris. (She also costarred with Helen Hayes and David

Niven in another 1977 Disney comedy, *Candleshoe*.) Scorsese, impressed with Foster, cast her as a teenaged prostitute opposite Robert De Niro in *Taxi Driver* (1976). Foster's startling performance in that film brought her more attention than she ever could have imagined. In addition to earning an Oscar nomination for Best Supporting Actress, her portrayal made Foster the object of obsessive fixation for one John Hinckley, who attempted to assassinate President Reagan on her behalf. By then, Foster had enrolled at Yale University, where she studied literature (and not acting: Foster is an instinctual actress and has never received formal theatrical training). During school vacations, she managed to appear in several features, including *Carny* (1980), *Foxes* (1980), and *The Hotel New Hampshire* (1984), before graduating in 1985.

Already fascinated by behind-the-camera work, Foster coproduced one of her starring vehicles, 1986's *Mesmerized*. She delivered mature, accomplished performances in the little-seen *Siesta* (1987), *Five Corners,* and *Stealing Home* (both 1988). But it was as a lower-class rape victim defending her character in *The Accused* (1988) that Foster galvanized audiences and won herself a Best Actress Oscar—a feat she repeated in 1991 for her portrayal of federal agent Clarice Starling in the megahit thriller *The Silence of the Lambs,* making her one of Hollywood's hottest properties. Having made her directorial debut with an episode of TV's "Tales from the Darkside," she entered the feature-film arena with *Little Man Tate* (1991). As director and star, Foster turned in an exceptional job, telling the story of a child prodigy—a character with whom she could certainly empathize. Her cameo in Woody Allen's *Shadows and Fog* (1992) brought Foster back to a role she'd played at age 12½: a prostitute. She costarred with Richard Gere in *Sommersby,* (1993) giving another affecting performance, and appeared in 1994's *Maverick*. Foster scored another Best Actress nomination for her portrayal of a backwoodswoman in *Nell* (1994), the first film made by her own company, Egg Productions. She then directed *Home for the Holidays*.

FOSTER, MEG. Actress. *(b. May 10, 1948, Reading, Pa.)* Have there ever been paler, more hypnotic orbs: Indeed, they've caused this stunning, athletic actress to be cast as a blind woman so often (most in episodic TV and made-fors) that it almost seemed like a gag when she turned up as a sighted person in *Blind Fury* (1989). When not cast in sightless parts, she's playing such nifty villainesses as a Moonie-like cultist in *Ticket to Heaven* (1981), Evil-Lyn in *Masters of the Universe* (1987), an alien fifth columnist in *They Live* (1988), and a two-faced corporate weasel in *Leviathan* (1989). She had more conventional roles in *Carny* (1980), *The Osterman Weekend* (1983), *The Emerald Forest* (1985), and *Relentless* (1989), and was unforgettable as a lesbian who falls in love with her gay male roommate in *A Different Story* (1978). Her TV work includes *Guyana Tragedy,* "Washington: Behind Closed Doors," and the "Sunshine" movies and series. But her biggest shot at stardom was cruelly snatched away: after the first six episodes of "Cagney and Lacey," CBS insisted she be replaced by someone "more feminine"(!) Producer Barney Rosenzweig made partial restitution by giving her a recurring role as a D.A. in "The Trials of Rosie O'Neill" (1990–92). Recent credits include *The Stepfather II* (1989) and *Best of the Best 2* (1993).

FOSTER, NORMAN. Director, actor. *(b. Dec. 13, 1900, Richmond, Ind., as Norman Hoeffer; d. July 7, 1976.)* A former journalist and stock player, this blandly good-looking, leading man appeared in many 1930s movies before turning his attention behind the camera late in the decade. Not exactly the macho type, he sometimes played men of weak character redeemed by the love of strong women. Foster's films as actor include *Gentlemen of the Press* (1929, his first), *Young Man of Manhattan* (1930, opposite Claudette Colbert, to whom he was briefly married), *Up Pops the Devil* (1931), *Girl of the Rio, Play Girl, Weekend Marriage, Smilin' Through* (all 1932), *State Fair, Pilgrimage, Professional Sweetheart* (all 1933), *Orient Express, Strictly Dynamite* (both 1934), *Escape From Devil's Island* (1935), *Fatal Lady* (1936), and *I Cover Chinatown* (a 1937 independent feature, shot in San Francisco, which also served as Foster's directorial debut). He joined 20th

Century-Fox as a director in 1937, and spent several years turning out B mysteries and melodramas, many of which he wrote or cowrote as well. These include many of the best Charlie Chan and Mr. Moto pictures, such as *Think Fast, Mr. Moto* (1937), *Mr. Moto Takes a Chance, Mysterious Mr. Moto* (both 1938), *Charlie Chan in Reno, Charlie Chan at Treasure Island* (both 1939), and *Charlie Chan in Panama* (1940).

Foster and Orson Welles became good friends, and Welles asked him to direct a Mercury Production called *My Friend Bonito* in Mexico in the early 1940s, but that production was shut down midstream and Foster was assigned instead to Mercury's *Journey Into Fear* (1942), in which Welles costarred. It was later claimed that Foster took over for Welles, and that Welles "really" directed much of the film, both of which claims Welles hotly denied in later years. (Foster also appeared onscreen in Welles' notorious, and never-completed, *The Other Side of the Wind,* in the 1970s.) His later directorial efforts include *Rachel and the Stranger, Kiss the Blood Off My Hands* (both 1948), *Father Is a Bachelor* (1950), *Navajo* (1952, a documentary with an all-Indian cast), and several feature films edited together from Disney TV shows, such as *Davy Crockett, King of the Wild Frontier* (1955), *The Nine Lives of Elfego Baca* (1959), and *The Sign of Zorro* (1960). Foster's last film was *Brighty of the Grand Canyon* (1967). He and actress Sally Blane were married from 1939 until his death.

FOSTER, PRESTON. Actor. *(b. Aug. 24, 1900, Ocean City, N.J.; d. July 14, 1970.)* Rugged, husky, handsome lead in movies of the 1930s, and then supporting player (and frequent heavy) in films of the 1940s and beyond. Foster sang with the Pennsylvania Grand Opera Company for a time before moving to Broadway in the late 1920s. Although he played bits in movies from 1928, it wasn't until he won the role of Killer Mears in *The Last Mile* (1932) that Foster achieved real recognition. Signed by Warners, he appeared in *Doctor X* (as the mad inventor of "synthetic flesh"), *I Am a Fugitive From a Chain Gang* (both 1932), *Ladies They Talk About* (1933), *Heat Lightning* (1934), and several others before moving to RKO. Foster initially got better opportunities there, playing leads in *The Last Days of Pompeii, Annie Oakley, We're Only Human,* and *Muss 'Em Up*—and choice supporting roles in John Ford's *The Informer* and Charles Vidor's *The Arizonian*—in 1935 alone. But when the burly Irishman failed to attain the stardom for which RKO had hoped, he was demoted to B pictures such as *The Outcasts of Poker Flat* and *You Can't Beat Love* (both 1937).

As a freelance actor, Foster starred as detective Bill Crane in three well-received Universal "Crime Club" mysteries—*The Westland Case* (1937), *The Lady in the Morgue,* and *The Last Warning* (both 1938)—as well as *Missing Evidence* (1939), *Geronimo, Moon Over Burma* (both 1940), *A Night in New Orleans,* and *Little Tokyo U.S.A.* (both 1942). He could be riveting, but occasionally gave listless, lethargic performances as well, which may have contributed to his drifting into character roles, although he still played occasional leads (most notably in 1944's *Roger Touhy—Gangster*). He starred in the "Waterfront" TV series (1954–55), guest-starred in many other small-screen shows, and even sang in nightclubs. OTHER FILMS INCLUDE: 1932: *Two Seconds;* 1943: *My Friend Flicka, Guadalcanal Diary;* 1945: *Thunderhead, The Valley of Decision;* 1946: *The Harvey Girls;* 1947: *King of the Wild Horses;* 1949: *The Big Cat;* 1951: *The Big Night;* 1953: *I the Jury;* 1957: *Destination 60,000;* 1964: *The Time Travelers;* 1968: *Chubasco* (his last).

FOWLEY, DOUGLAS. Actor. (b. May 30, 1911, New York City, as Daniel Vincent Fowley.) Like many character actors of Hollywood's "golden age," Fowley had an extensive show-business background: In addition to acting on stage and screen, he worked in nightclubs (as a comic, singer, and dancer), carnivals (as a "barker"), and vaudeville. Born and raised in Manhattan, Fowley's New York accent served him well when he portrayed cold-blooded urban gangsters—which he did many times throughout the 1930s and 1940s, in *Charlie Chan on Broadway* (1937), *Mr. Moto's Gamble* (1938), *Street of Missing Men* (1939), and *Ellery Queen, Master Detective* (1940), to name a few. He sometimes played fast-talking reporters (1934's *I Hate Women,* 1939's *Charlie Chan at*

Treasure Island, 1940's *Slightly Honorable*) and, somewhat improbably, Western heavies (1939's *Dodge City,* 1945's *Don't Fence Me In,* 1948's *Coroner Creek*). He had a plum comic role as the flustered movie director in *Singin' in the Rain* (1952). In later years, craggy and minus some teeth, he played old codgers in movies (1969's *The Good Guys and the Bad Guys,* 1976's *From Noon Till Three* and 1977's *The White Buffalo*) and TV shows. He was a regular on TV's "The Life and Legend of Wyatt Earp," playing Doc Holliday from 1957 to 1961.

FOX, EDWARD. Actor. (b. Apr. 13, 1937, London.) Fair-haired, blue-eyed British character actor and occasional lead whose taciturn demeanor ideally suits him for sinister heavies and chilly aristocrats. Probably best remembered as the cold-blooded assassin of *The Day of the Jackal* (1973). OTHER FILMS INCLUDE: 1963: *The Mind Benders* (his first); 1967: *The Frozen Dead, I'll Never Forget What's 'is Name;* 1969: *Battle of Britain, Oh! What a Lovely War;* 1970: *Skullduggery;* 1971: *The Go-Between;* 1973: *A Doll's House;* 1974: *Galileo;* 1977: *A Bridge Too Far;* 1978: *The Big Sleep, Force 10 From Navarone;* 1979: *The Cat and the Canary;* 1980: *The Mirror Crack'd;* 1982: *Gandhi;* 1983: *The Dresser, Never Say Never Again;* 1984: *The Bounty, The Shooting Party;* 1985: *Wild Geese II;* 1989: *Return to the River Kwai;* 1990: *They Never Slept.*

Edward's younger brother James, who bears a remarkable resemblance to his older sibling but seems less grave, is also a talented actor. In 1970 he forsook acting for religion, pursuing missionary goals before returning to films more than a decade later. He also wrote a book about his experiences, "Comeback: An Actor's Direction," in 1983. FILMS INCLUDE: 1962: *The Loneliness of the Long Distance Runner;* 1963: *The Servant;* 1965: *King Rat;* 1966: *The Chase;* 1967: *Thoroughly Modern Millie;* 1970: *Performance;* 1978: *No Longer Alone;* 1983: *Runners;* 1984: *Greystoke: The Legend of Tarzan, Lord of the Apes, A Passage to India;* 1986: *Absolute Beginners;* 1987: *High Season, The Whistle Blower;* 1989: *Farewell to the King;* 1990: *The Russia House;* 1992: *Patriot Games;* 1993: *The Remains of the Day.*

FOX, MICHAEL J. Actor. *(b. June 9, 1961, Edmonton, Alberta.)* Who would have guessed that this wee sitcom star would replicate his TV success on the big screen, becoming such an engaging young leading man? Certainly the odds were against it: many TV personalities have failed to make the transition, and the brash, diminutive Fox could easily have been a washout. He'd appeared in films before achieving success on TV, first in the obscure *Midnight Madness* (1980, Disney's first PG-rated movie), and subsequently as the runty, bullied high-school student in the ultraviolent *Class of 1984* (1982). Cast as irrepressible yuppie-in-training Alex P. Keaton on the TV sitcom "Family Ties" (1982–89), though, Fox shot to immediate stardom and won three consecutive Emmy awards. Amazingly, this success transferred almost as quickly to film when he was selected to replace Eric Stoltz (midway into production) as time-traveler Marty McFly in the Steven Spielberg production *Back to the Future* (1985), reprising the role in two sequels (1989 and 1990, which were actually shot back-to-back). While he does possess a winning mix of subtle naiveté and wise-guy opportunism, his stabs at more serious fare— *Light of Day* (1987), *Bright Lights, Big City* (1988), and *Casualties of War* (1989)—have not met with critical or commercial success. Fox is married to actress Tracey Pollan who played his girlfriend on "Family Ties."
OTHER FILMS INCLUDE: 1985: *Teen Wolf;* 1991: *The Hard Way; Doc Hollywood;* 1993: *Homeward Bound: The Incredible Journey* (as the voice of Chance the dog), *Life With Mikey, For Love or Money;* 1994: *Greedy.*

FRAKER, WILLIAM A. Cinematographer, director. *(b. Sept. 29, 1923, Los Angeles.)* Veteran cameraman whom Todd McCarthy called "in many ways the Dean of the New Breed cinematographers." He studied at the USC Film School and began his career as a still photographer before working as an editor and then as an assistant cameraman. Fraker worked as a camera operator on films like *Father Goose* (1964) and *Morituri* (1965) and then on the TV series "Daktari" before becoming director of photography with the films *Games* and *The President's Analyst* (both

1967). He vaulted to the top of the field with stylish work on two of 1968's biggest hits, *Bullitt* and *Rosemary's Baby,* and went on to receive Oscar nominations for a variety of stylistically different films: the dark, gloomy *Looking for Mr. Goodbar* (1977), the soft-focused *Heaven Can Wait* (1978), *1941* (1979), *WarGames* (1983), and *Murphy's Romance* (1985). He also directed several films: the melancholy Western *Monte Walsh* (1970), *A Reflection of Fear* (1973), and the disastrous (if good-looking) *The Legend of the Lone Ranger* (1980), and served for several years as president of the American Society of Cinematographers.
OTHER FILMS INCLUDE: 1969: *Paint Your Wagon;* 1973: *The Day of the Dolphin;* 1975: *Rancho Deluxe;* 1978: *American Hot Wax;* 1980: *Divine Madness;* 1984: *Irreconcilable Differences;* 1987: *Baby Boom;* 1990: *The Freshman;* 1992: *Honeymoon in Vegas.*

FRANCIOSA, ANTHONY. Actor. *(b. Oct. 28, 1928, New York City, as Anthony Papaleo.)* Franciosa was once touted as a superstar in the making, a prediction that never quite came true. The handsome, cleft-chinned, dark-haired actor initially won raves for his performance on Broadway in *A Hatful of Rain* and was nominated for a Best Actor Oscar when he reprised the role two years later in the 1957 movie version. He'd previously made his movie debut in *This Could Be the Night* and also appeared in Elia Kazan's *A Face in the Crowd* (also 1957). With such an impressive first year in movies, the pundits said, Franciosa could turn into another Gable. Showy roles in *The Long Hot Summer* (1958), *Career, The Naked Maja* (both 1959), *Period of Adjustment* (1962, opposite Jane Fonda), *The Pleasure Seekers,* and *Rio Conchos* (both 1964), among others, followed before Franciosa found small-screen stardom on the TV series "Valentine's Day" (1964–65), "The Name of the Game," (1968–71), and "Matt Helm" (1975–76). His latter-day film roles have been mostly in action-oriented dramas, including *Across 110th Street* (1972), *Firepower* (1979), and *Death Wish II* (1981).
OTHER FILMS INCLUDE: 1973: *Ghost in the Noonday Sun;* 1976: *The Drowning Pool;*

1990: *Backstreet Dreams;* 1992: *Double Threat.*

FRANCIS, FREDDIE. Director, cinematographer, producer. *(b. Dec. 22, 1917, London.)* One of Britain's most respected cinematographers and directors had his humble beginnings in the movie business as a teenage clapper boy. He served as a director of photography during World War 2, and later, as a civilian, became a camera operator in British films. He made his directorial debut with *2 and 2 Make 6* (1962), and his subsequent directorial output consisted primarily of British horror pics, including *The Evil of Frankenstein* (1964), *Trog* (1970), *Tales From the Crypt* (1972), *Asylum* (1973), and *The Doctor and the Devils* (1985). An Oscar winner for his striking cinematography on *Sons and Lovers* (1960) and *Glory* (1989), he also shot two of director David Lynch's films, *The Elephant Man* (1980, in widescreen black and white!) and *Dune* (1984), as well as Martin Scorsese's remake of *Cape Fear* (1991). That some of today's most adventurous young directors seek out a septugenarian to shoot their films says something about this gifted craftsman.

FRANCIS, KAY. Actress. *(b. Jan. 13, 1903, Oklahoma City, as Katherine Edwina Gibbs; d. Aug. 26, 1968.)* Film buffs still revere her, but the public at large has forgotten Kay Francis, despite the fact that she was one of the top screen stars of the 1930s. Dark-haired and sad-eyed, with a slight but easily distinguishable lisp, she often played fallen women and fashionable society types. Francis, once a stenographer (whose mother founded the Katherine Gibbs secretarial school), acted in summer stock and on Broadway before making her film debut opposite Walter Huston in *Gentlemen of the Press* (1929). As a Paramount contractee, she played foil to The Marx Brothers in *The Cocoanuts* (also 1929), and starred or costarred in *Street of Chance, Paramount on Parade, For the Defense* (all 1930), *Ladies' Man, 24 Hours,* and *Girls About Town* (all 1931), among others. *Trouble in Paradise* (1932) gave Francis one of her best screen roles, as the potential victim of jewel thieves Herbert Marshall and Miriam

Hopkins, in a stylish comedy directed by Ernst Lubitsch.

She signed with Warner Bros. in 1932, almost immediately getting another career-boosting role as the doomed lover of William Powell in the popular *One-Way Passage.* Warners kept her busy over the next seven years in mostly tailor-made vehicles, but the ascendancy of Bette Davis in the decade's later years eventually cost Francis her standing as the studio's top female star. Her Warners films include *Street of Women, Jewel Robbery* (both 1932), *Mary Stevens, M.D., The House on 56th Street* (both 1933), *Mandalay, Wonder Bar* (opposite Al Jolson), *British Agent* (all 1934), *I Found Stella Parish* (1935), *The White Angel* (1936, playing Florence Nightingale), *Stolen Holiday, Confession* (both 1937), *My Bill, Secrets of an Actress* (both 1938), and *King of the Underworld* (1939).

She went on to play "the other woman" with Cary Grant and Carole Lombard in *In Name Only* (1939), and Deanna Durbin's mother in *It's a Date* (1940), but soon drifted into B movies. A notable exception: *Four Jills in a Jeep* (1944), in which she played herself, one of four Hollywood actresses who entertained troops during World War 2. She retired from the screen in 1946, returned to the stage, and then left show business for good. She died of cancer and left most of her still-considerable fortune to various charities.

FRANK, HARRIET, JR., and IRVING RAVETCH. Screenwriters. *(Frank—b. Mar. 3, 1918, Los Angeles. Ravetch—b. Nov. 14, 1920, Long Beach, Calif.)* One of Hollywood's most enduring husband and wife teams, Frank and Ravetch are best known for the eight intelligent, deeply humane screenplays they wrote for director Martin Ritt. Both Frank and Ravetch graduated from UCLA but didn't meet until they were in MGM's young writers program. They married and worked separately on screenplays—Frank on *Steel River* and *Whiplash* (both 1948), Ravetch on *The Outriders* (1950) and *Vengeance Valley* (1951)—before collaborating on the story for *Ten Wanted Men* (1955). Their first joint screenplay was the adaptation of William Faulkner's *The Long Hot Summer* (1958) which also marked their first collaboration with Ritt. The couple followed with a series of fine adaptations, also directed by Ritt: Faulkner's *The Sound and the Fury* (1959), the outstanding *Hud* (1963, an adaptation of Larry McMurtry's novel "Horseman, Pass By"; Oscar-nominated), *Hombre* (1967), the fine but little-seen *Conrack* (1974, Pat Conroy's autobiographical novel), the unionization story *Norma Rae* (1979, Oscar-nominated), the charming comedy *Murphy's Romance* (1985), and Ritt's last film, *Stanley & Iris* (1990). (Ravetch also coproduced *Hud* and *Hombre*.) In addition, Frank and Ravetch wrote the screenplays for *Home From the Hill* (1960), *The Dark at the Top of the Stairs* (1960), *The Reivers* (1969, another Faulkner adaptation, which Ravetch also produced), *The Cowboys* (1972), and *The Spikes Gang* (1974).

FRANK, MELVIN. Writer, director, producer. (b. Aug. 13, 1913, Chicago; d. Oct. 13, 1988.) A graduate of the Bob Hope "school" for comedy writers, Frank got his seasoning on Hope's radio show in the late 1930s and early 1940s, and with his partner Norman Panama was drafted by the comedian to write for his movie vehicles as well. This led to a variety of assignments at Paramount in the 1940s—including *Happy Go Lucky* (1943), *And the Angels Sing* (1944), *Duffy's Tavern* (1945), and *Our Hearts Were Growing Up* (1946), as well as the Hope movies *My Favorite Blonde* (1942, story only), *Monsieur Beaucaire* (1946), and *The Road to Utopia* (1946, Oscar-nominated for Best Screenplay). Panama and Frank then struck out on their own, producing and writing the clever comedy *Mr. Blandings Builds His Dream House* (1948). They proceeded to produce, direct, and write a series of mostly successful comedies through the early 1960s, occasionally veering into drama (as in 1952's *Above and Beyond*). They spoofed Hopalong Cassidy in *Callaway Went Thataway* (1951), remade Preston Struges' hit play and film *Strictly Dishonorable* (1951), provided the sappy script for the smash hit *White Christmas* (1954), concocted two of Danny Kaye's all-time best vehicles, *Knock on Wood* (1954, Oscar-nominated) and *The Court Jester* (1956), and adapted their own Broadway success *Li'l Abner* (1959). They also moved Bob Hope into more

mature comedies, such as *That Certain Feeling* (1956) and *The Facts of Life* (1960, Oscar-nominated and one of their best) before reverting to formula in the final road trip, *The Road to Hong Kong* (1962).

After amicably parting with Panama, Melvin Frank alternated between writing and directing chores on a string of comedies, most of which he also produced, including *Strange Bedfellows* (1965, writer-director), *A Funny Thing Happened on the Way to the Forum* (1966, coscreenwriter), *Not With My Wife You Don't!* (1966, story only), *Buono Sera, Mrs. Campbell* (1968, writer-director), the popular hit *A Touch of Class* (1973, writer-director, Oscar-nominated for Best Picture and Best Screenplay and an Oscar winner for Glenda Jackson), Neil Simon's *The Prisoner of Second Avenue* (1975, director), *The Duchess and the Dirtwater Fox* (1976, writer-director), and *Lost and Found* (1979, writer-director, an attempt to rekindle the sparks of *A Touch of Class*). Unfortunately, his final film as director, *Walk Like A Man* (1987), barely received theatrical release.

FRANKENHEIMER, JOHN. Director. (b. Feb. 19, 1930, Malba, N.Y.) One of a number of Hollywood directors who came to movies from TV, Frankenheimer learned his craft while making training films for the Air Force during his stint in the service. He directed several episodes of highly regarded TV series such as "You Are There" before taking his first feature-film assignment, *The Young Stranger* (1957), itself an adaptation of a Frankenheimer-directed TV show. He raised eyebrows with a gritty, taut urban melodrama called *The Young Savages* (1961), and followed it with several extremely powerful, mainstream films, including *Birdman of Alcatraz, The Manchurian Candidate* (both 1962), *Seven Days in May* (1964), *Grand Prix, Seconds* (both 1966) and *The Fixer* (1968). His 1970s output—including *I Walk the Line* (1970), *The Iceman Cometh* (1973), *99 and 44/100% Dead* (1974), *French Connection II* (1975), *Black Sunday* (1977), and *Prophecy* (1979)—was not nearly as impressive a body of work. Frankenheimer, a solid storyteller whose visual sense sometimes conceals the weaknesses in scripts he's given, worked less frequently in the 1980s, registering spotty successes with such efforts as *The Holcroft Covenant* (1985), *52 Pick-Up* (1986), *Dead-Bang* (1989), *The Fourth War* (1990), and *Year of the Gun* (1991). Ironically, when *Manchurian Candidate* was reissued in 1988 after a lengthy stay on the shelf, more than one observer found it vastly superior to most contemporary films, in both content and style. In 1993 Frankenheimer directed Elizabeth Taylor in a highly touted—and highly budgeted—perfume commercial. He won an Emmy for directing the telefilm *Against the Wall* (1994) and followed with another acclaimed telefilm, *The Burning Season* (also 1994).

FRANKLIN, PAMELA. Actress. *(b. Feb. 4, 1950, Tokyo.)* Attractive, hauntingly pretty child actress (she made her screen debut at 11 in 1961's *The Innocents*) equally adept as sweet young things and nasty nymphets. Already a smooth, natural performer by the time she reached her teens, Franklin impressed as a wide-eyed youngster in the creepy thriller *The Nanny* (1965); at 19 she was one of Maggie Smith's "girls" in the school drama *The Prime of Miss Jean Brodie* (1969). Her performance as a sexually repressed psychic in the horror film *The Legend of Hell House* (1973) lent realistic, chilling, erotic tension to that unusual film. She has only been seen on the big screen sporadically since then, and then in generally undistinguished productions, of which *Food of the Gods* (1976), is sadly representative. She's worked in TV on both sides of the Atlantic since the early 1970s.

FRAWLEY, WILLIAM. Actor. *(b. Feb. 26, 1887, Burlington, Iowa; d. Mar. 3, 1966.)* Burly, balding, and gravel-voiced, this one-time vaudevillian is best known for playing Fred Mertz, landlord to Lucille Ball and Desi Arnaz in the legendary 1950s sitcom "I Love Lucy," but he was also a prolific character actor who appeared in more than 150 feature films from 1931 through 1962, usually but not always in comedic roles. He went on to play the peculiar role of "Uncle Bub," houseboy to Fred MacMurray in the popular 1960s sitcom "My Three Sons," until his death.
FILMS INCLUDE: 1931: *Surrender;* 1934: *Bolero, The Lemon Drop Kid (1934 and 1951* versions); 1936: *The General Died at Dawn;* 1939: *Rose of Washington Square;* 1942: *Roxie Hart;* 1947: *Miracle on 34th Street;* 1950: *Kiss Tomorrow Goodbye;* 1952: *Rancho Notorious;* 1962: *Safe at Home.*

FRAZEE, JANE. Actress, singer. *(b. July 18, 1918, Duluth, Minn., as Mary Jane Freshe; d. Sept. 6, 1985.)* Delightful screen performer, pert and pretty, whose bright personality, natural acting ability, and obvious musical talent should have propelled her into stardom's upper ranks. A child performer, the younger half of a sister act, Frazee had already been trouping in vaudeville and nightclubs before making her screen debut (with her sister) in a 1936 short, *Study and Understudy.* She was a breezy lead in such minor Universal musicals as *Melody and Moonlight* (1940), *What's Cookin'?, Get Hep to Love,* and *Moonlight in Havana* (all 1942), and performed the nominal musical and romantic chores in Abbott & Costello's *Buck Privates* and Olsen and Johnson's *Hellzapoppin* (both 1941). She moved to Columbia and then Republic, where she starred as *Rosie the Riveter* (1944) and *Calendar Girl* (1947), and then appeared opposite Roy Rogers in a string of musical Westerns, including *On the Old Spanish Trail* (1947), *The Gay Ranchero,* and *Under California Stars* (both 1948). She left feature-film work following *Rhythm Inn* (1951), but spent several years playing the long-suffering wife of George O'Hanlon in Warner Bros.' popular "Joe McDoakes" short subjects—revealing a hitherto hidden comic savvy. A successful businesswoman in later years, Frazee was married to silent-screen star and producer Glenn Tryon.

FREARS, STEPHEN. Director. *(b. June 20, 1941, Leicester, England.)* One of the "new generation" of British filmmakers, Frears came to a movie career after having earned a Cambridge law degree. An interest in the stage took him to the Royal Court Theatre, where he eventually made the acquaintance of director Karel Reisz.

Reisz offered him an assistant director position on *Morgan* (1966), during the filming of which he also met Lindsay Anderson and Albert Finney. Anderson hired Frears as his assistant on *if . . .* (1968), and Finney starred in Frears' first solo directorial outing, 1971's satirical *Gumshoe*, a reasonable if unspectacular success. He would not helm another theatrical feature for 14 years, but he worked profitably and creatively in British TV, fashioning bold and eclectic films such as *Bloody Kids* (1979), *Loving Walter*, and *Saigon—Year of the Cat* (both 1983), which for the most part received no U.S. distribution.

In 1984 Frears won international recognition for his direction of *The Hit*, a gangster yarn set in Spain, and the following year he collaborated with Anglo-Pakistani author Hanif Kureishi on a 16mm feature called *My Beautiful Laundrette*, which was originally shot for TV but later distributed to theaters. Worldwide attention followed for both Frears and (then unknown) actor Daniel Day-Lewis; Frears followed up with 1987's *Sammy and Rosie Get Laid*, a scathing satire on the decline of British society, and *Prick Up Your Ears*, a homosexual love story based on the memoirs of playwright Joe Orton. Hollywood beckoned Frears with an offer to direct the film version of Choderlos de Laclos's "Les Liaisons Dangereuses," which had enjoyed success as a play on Broadway. Frears' version, *Dangerous Liaisons* (1988), established the director as a bankable commodity, as he had by this time demonstrated his ability to handle projects big and small with style and efficiency. He followed *Liaisons* with a gritty, neo-noir Jim Thompson story, *The Grifters* (1990), a tale of small-time hustlers that harkened back to his *Gumshoe*, and earned him an Oscar nomination as Best Director. Following the Hollywood misfire *Hero* (1992), Frears helmed a BBC production that took just six weeks to shoot: Roddy Doyle's *The Snapper* (1993), a modest story about how an Irish working-class family responds to a teenage daughter's pregnancy. There isn't a false note in the film . . . or in Frears' willingness to forsake a plum job in Hollywood in favor of a good script. He followed with *Mary Reilly* (1995), a variation on the Jekyll and Hyde story.

FREED, ARTHUR. Lyricist, producer. *(b. Sept. 9, 1894, Charleston, S.C., as Arthur Grossman; d. Apr. 12, 1973.)* When one talks about the classic MGM musicals, one is really talking about the films produced by the Arthur Freed unit at Metro. Pictures like *Cabin in the Sky* (1943), *Meet Me in St. Louis* (1944), *The Pirate* (1948), and *Singin' in the Rain* (1952) all bore the distinctive stamp of the songwriter turned producer, who distinguished himself by assembling and motivating the best available talent for each of his films, while retaining a degree of control matched by few producers. A former song plugger, he worked in vaudeville and after service in World War 1 he started writing songs, often with partner Nacio Herb Brown. Hired by MGM in 1929, he penned lyrics for such musicals as that year's *The Hollywood Revue* (which introduced "Singin' in the Rain"), *Going Hollywood* (1933), and *Broadway Melody of 1936*, among others. In 1939 Freed was given a trial as associate producer on *The Wizard of Oz*, and almost immediately was given his own unit.

Gene Kelly, Judy Garland, and Fred Astaire did some of their best screen work for Freed, who also gave Vincente Minnelli, Stanley Donen, and Kelly their first opportunities to direct. His genius as a producer was in assembling the finest teams—arrangers, designers, choreographers, and so on—then working on Hollywood musicals. Freed won Best Picture Oscars for *An American in Paris* (1951) and *Gigi* (1958), but for musical fans it's a toss-up as to which is the best Freed musical—after *Singin' in the Rain*, that is. That happiest of all movies was based on a blatant contrivance: to shoehorn as many Freed–Brown songs into a single movie as possible. Screenwriters Betty Comden and Adolph Green met the challenge, and helped create Freed's supreme achievement, also possibly the greatest movie musical ever made. *The Harvey Girls* (1946), *Easter Parade* (1948), *On the Town* (1949), and *The Band Wagon* (1953) all vie for the affections of aficionados, as do numerous others.

Freed's career went into eclipse with the demise of the screen musical in the late 1950s. After a tepid screen adaptation of Jack Kerouac's *The Subterraneans* (1960), Freed finished his career with *Light in the Piazza* (1962). A well-respected Hollywood figure, he won the Irving Thalberg Memorial Award at the 1951 Academy Awards ceremony; he also got an honorary Oscar in 1967.

FREEMAN, KATHLEEN. Actress. *(b. Feb. 17, 1919, Chicago.)* Versatile comedy actress best known for her eight appearances as slapstick foil to Jerry Lewis. Though Freeman's film career dates back to 1947's *Wild Harvest,* she really hit her stride in the 1950s, spending more than 20 years playing gossips, teachers, housekeepers, and kvetches in such films as *Bonzo Goes to College, Singin' in the Rain* (both 1952, as vocal coach Phoebe Dinsmore), *Artists and Models* (1955), *Houseboat* (1958), *The Errand Boy* (1961), *The Nutty Professor* (1963), and *Support Your Local Sheriff!* (1969). She did occasionally land roles in such dramatic fare as *Naked City* (1948), *A Place in the Sun* (1951), *The Fly* (1958), and *Point Blank* (1967). On TV she was a regular on "The Beverly Hillbillies," "Topper," and "It's About Time," in addition to guesting on many other shows. After a period of relative inactivity, she contributed hilarious cameos in films of the 1980s, appearing as an imperious nun in *The Blues Brothers* (1980), a foul-mouthed landlady in *Dragnet,* the "Dream Lady" in *Innerspace,* an eccentric boarding-house landlady in *In the Mood* (all 1987), a tipsy TV chef in *Gremlins 2: The New Batch* (1990), a Salem schoolteacher in *Hocus Pocus* (1993), and Fred Ward's toughtalking mom in *Naked Gun 33⅓: The Final Insult* (1994).

FREEMAN, MORGAN. Actor. *(b. June 1, 1937, Memphis, Tenn.)* This tall, mellowvoiced black actor, one of the contemporary screen's most accomplished supporting players and character leads, has brought dignity as well as talent to a wide array of movie roles. Long before moviegoers knew his face, children were watching him as Easy Reader on the popular PBS TV series "The Electric Company." After considerable stage and TV experience, Freeman stunned movie audiences (and earned a Best Supporting Actor Oscar nomination) as the suavely vicious pimp in *Street Smart* (1987). Prior to that, he'd had small parts in *Brubaker*

(1980), *Eyewitness* (1981), *Teachers* (1984), *Marie, a True Story,* and *That Was Then, This Is Now* (both 1985). Since attaining stardom, he has played a number of uplifting characters in *Clean and Sober* (1988), *The Bonfire of the Vanities* (1990), and *Robin Hood: Prince of Thieves* (1991). Freeman was tireless in 1989, playing a Civil War sergeant in *Glory,* a disciplineminded high school principal in *Lean on Me,* a gentle chauffeur in *Driving Miss Daisy* (Oscar nomination for Best Actor), and even squeezing in a change of pace as a nasty cop in *Johnny Handsome.* He continues to work on stage—he made a notable Petruchio in a 1991 production of "The Taming of the Shrew," opposite Tracey Ullman. He costarred with Clint Eastwood in *Unforgiven* (1992) before making his directing debut on the little-seen apartheid story *Bopha!* (1993). Freeman earned another Best Actor nomination for his portrayal of a prison lifer in *The Shawshank Redemption* (1994) and, most recently, has costarred in *Outbreak* and *Seven* (both 1995).

FRELENG, FRIZ. Animation director, producer. *(b. Aug. 21, 1906, Kansas City, as Isadore Freleng; d. May 26, 1995.)* One of the mainstays of the Warner Bros. cartoon department, Freleng lacked the flamboyance of Tex Avery, and the wittiness of Chuck Jones; he simply made good cartoons, and kept making them year after year. (He also earned his studio three Academy Awards, for 1947's *Tweetie Pie,* 1955's *Speedy Gonzales,* and 1957's *Birds Anonymous.*) He broke into animation working for fellow Kansas Cityite Walt Disney, and was among the group led by Hugh Harman and Rudolf Ising that struck out on its own in 1927 to make Oswald the Lucky Rabbit cartoons. When Harman and Ising were hired to make cartoons for Warner Bros., Freleng went along, and worked on the very first short the studio released; he was there more than 30 years later when the unit closed its doors. (There was one brief foray at MGM in the late 1930s, but Freleng was happy to return to Warners.) Freleng's forte was musical cartoons, his most famous being *Rhapsody in Rivets* (1941) in which a skyscraper is built to the strains of Liszt's Second Hungarian Rhapsody. But his real strength was his versatility; he worked well with every character in the Warners stable, though in later years he specialized in Tweety and Sylvester, Speedy Gonzales, and Yosemite Sam (whose creation was inspired, it was said, by the diminutive and sometimes hotheaded Freleng himself). One of his most popular shorts in recent years was just a lark for Freleng at the time: *You Ought to Be in Pictures* (1940), a delightful blend of live-action and animation in which Daffy Duck convinces Porky Pig to walk out on producer Leon Schlesinger and try his luck in feature films.

When Warners decided to shut down its cartoon department in 1963, Freleng and partner David H. DePatie tried to keep the unit intact in order to produce cartoons themselves—and wound up selling shorts back to Warner Bros. when the studio had a change of heart and decided it wanted more cartoons after all! Meanwhile, DePatie-Freleng was establishing itself as a major supplier of animation with its successful Pink Panther series (inspired by the main titles of Blake Edwards' 1964 feature film), and such offshoots as *The Inspector* and *The Ant and the Aardvark.*

A renaissance of interest in Warners cartoons in the 1980s led Freleng back to Warners to direct some new segments for TV, and the compilation feature film *The Looney Looney Looney Bugs Bunny Movie* (1981) and *Daffy Duck's Fantastic Island* (1983). He also produced *Bugs Bunny's 3rd Movie: 1001 Rabbit Tales* (1982).

FRICKER, BRENDA. Actress. *(b. Feb. 17, 1945, Dublin.)* A veteran of numerous stage productions in England and her native Ireland, this rock-solid character actress won international acclaim and a Best Supporting Actress Academy Award for her luminous performance as Christy Brown's mother in *My Left Foot* (1989). Her first film credit was 1964's *Of Human Bondage,* but she made no impact in movies until her Oscar-winning role. She has since appeared in *The Field* (1990), *Home Alone 2: Lost in New York* (1992, as the pigeon lady), *Utz* (1993), and *So I Married an Axe Murderer* (also 1993, as Mike Myers' Scottish mother).

FRIEDKIN, WILLIAM. Director, screenwriter, producer. *(b. Aug. 29, 1939, Chicago.)* The Oscar-winning director of *The French Connection* (1971)—and Oscar nominee for *The Exorcist* (1973)—was once expected to become Hollywood's preeminent director, but his subsequent sporadic output and high percentage of box-office flops seem to have dispelled that notion. Friedkin directed hundreds of TV shows broadcast out of his native Chicago before turning to feature films with the Sonny & Cher starring vehicle *Good Times* (1967). He helmed *The Birthday Party* and *The Night They Raided Minsky's* (both 1968) before making a name for himself with the well-acted adaptation of Mart Crowley's play *The Boys in the Band* (1970). *The French Connection,* with its gritty realism and justifiably famous car chase, boosted him into filmdom's top ranks. After *The Exorcist,* however, Friedkin lost ground: His next film, *Sorcerer* (1977, an expensive remake of the French suspense classic *Wages of Fear),* failed to excite audiences, and *The Brink's Job* (1978), *Cruising* (1980), *Deal of the Century* (1983), *To Live and Die in L.A.* (1985), *Stalking Danger* (1986), and *Rampage* (1987, release delayed until 1992) gave him a string of box-office losers. He also directed a pair of TV movies, *C.A.T. Squad* (1986) and *C.A.T. Squad: Python Wolf* (1988). *The Guardian* (1990) brought Friedkin back to supernatural suspense and *Blue Chips* (1994) put him back in the mainstream. He was married at one time to actress Jeanne Moreau, and is currently married to film executive Sherry Lansing.

FRIELS, COLIN. Actor. *(b. Sept. 25, 1952, Glasgow.)* He's already been in movies for more than a decade, but most American moviegoers don't have the slightest idea who Colin Friels is. Nonetheless, once recognized, this slick, good-looking Australian leading man bears watching: No one who saw him as the slow-witted young inventor in *Malcolm* (1986) is likely to forget him; indeed, he has gone on to star in several intriguing Australian films, including *Warm Nights on a Slow Moving Train, Ground Zero* (both 1987) and *Grievous Bodily Harm* (1988), that have achieved more success in video stores than in movie theaters in the U.S. After first appearing on-screen in *Monkey Grip* (1981), Friels worked steadily in Australian and European productions before coming to Hollywood where, being capable of a seamless American accent, he has been suitably snaky in *Darkman* (1990) and *Class Action* (1991). He is married to actress Judy Davis, with whom he appeared in *Kangaroo* (1986) and *High Tide* (1987).

FROBE, GERT. Actor. *(b. Dec. 25, 1912, Planitz, Zwickau, Germany, as Gert Frober; d. 1988.)* While he's best known in the U.S. as 007 nemesis Goldfinger from the 1964 film of the same name, this gruff, stocky ex-musician, who turned to an acting career in his late 20s, played dozens of character roles—mostly heavies, and brutish ones at that—in European productions (mostly unseen here) during the 1950s, 1960s, and 1970s. He was especially memorable as the master villain Bellamy in the 1961 German adaptation of Edgar Wallace's *The Green Archer,* for which he was top-billed (a rare occurrence). His English-language films include *The Berliner* (1948), *The Longest Day* (1962), *Is Paris Burning* (1966), *Chitty Chitty Bang Bang* (1968), *$* (1971), *Ten Little Indians* (1975), and *Bloodline* (1979).

FULLER, SAMUEL Director, screenwriter, actor. *(b. Aug. 12, 1911, Worcester, Mass.)* Brash writer-director whose oeuvre includes many inexpensively made genre films, held in much higher regard today than when originally released. Fuller's movie work encompasses most of his varied experiences: he rode the rails as a hobo, wrote pulp fiction, worked as a crime reporter, and fought in Europe and North Africa during World War 2. Although he worked sporadically in Hollywood since 1938, Fuller didn't hit his stride until 1949; his first directorial chore, *I Shot Jesse James,* proved that he could turn out reliable B films in short order. His early movies included a first-rate Korean War drama, *The Steel Helmet* (1951), and a picaresque newspaper story, *Park Row* (1952). Fuller's films, fashioned by the brutal economy of means, are usually steeped in melodrama, and his blunt worldview is easily discernible. Cultists favor two of his 1960s movies, *Shock Corridor* (1963, America allegorized as a lunatic asylum) and *The*

Naked Kiss (1964, small-town hypocrisy exposed by reformed prostitute).

When directorial work for him petered out in the late 1960s, Fuller moved to France, occasionally playing cameos in other directors' films, such as *1941* and *Salem's Lot* (both 1979). He also acted in *The Last Movie* (1971), *The American Friend* (1977), *Hammett,* and *The State of Things* (both 1982), among others. His "comeback" picture, a striking and personal war drama titled *The Big Red One* (1980), fizzled at the box office, and his career was sidetracked a few years later when controversy erupted over his production *White Dog* (1982), about a hound trained to attack black people. Again he went to Europe, where he continued to find backing for films, which have not been released in the U.S. In *Tigrero: A Film That Was Never Made* (1994), Fuller tells filmmaker Jim Jarmusch about his futile attempts to make an adventure film set in the jungles of Brazil.

OTHER FILMS INCLUDE: 1950: *The Baron of Arizona;* 1951: *Fixed Bayonets;* 1953: *Pickup on South Street* (one of his most "mainstream" movies, and one of his best); 1957: *China Gate, Run of the Arrow;* 1959: *The Crimson Kimono;* 1961: *Underworld U.S.A.;* 1969: *Shark, Dead Pigeon on Beethoven Street.*

GABIN, JEAN. Actor. *(b. May 17, 1904, Mereil, France, as Jean-Alexis Moncorge; d. Nov. 16, 1976.)* Ruggedly handsome French film star who specialized in playing tragic heroes of innate nobility. After working briefly as a laborer, the young Gabin danced in the Folies Bergère, graduating to stage acting and, in 1930, movies (beginning with *Chacun sa chance*). His breakthrough film, *Maria Chapdelaine* (1934), established him as a strong, stoic type. A natural, intuitive screen actor, Gabin essayed memorable roles in *Zouzou* (1934, opposite Josephine Baker), *The Lower Depths* (1936), *Pepe le Moko* (in the title role), *Grand Illusion* (both 1937), *La Bête Humaine* (1938), *Daybreak* (1939), *The Room Upstairs* (1946), *Le Plaisir* (1951), *French Can-Can, Napoleon* (both 1954), *Les Misérables* (1957, as Jean Valjean), *Inspector Maigret* (the first of a popular series, in the title role), *Crime and Punishment* (both 1958), *Any Number Can Win*

(1963), *The Sicilian Clan* (1969), and *L'Année Sainte* (1976, his last film).

Gabin had a brief sojourn in Hollywood during the 1940s, resulting in *Moontide* (1942) and *The Imposter* (1944). After years of playing strong-willed iconoclasts, antiheroes, and everyman characters, Gabin (like his American counterpart Spencer Tracy) gracefully aged into the very embodiment of self-assuredness and respectability—but always with a bit of his soul shining through.

GABLE, CLARK. Actor. *(b. Feb. 1, 1901, Cadiz, Ohio, as William Clark Gable; d. Nov. 16, 1960.)* Ironically, the role for which this still-popular star is best remembered—that of Rhett Butler in *Gone With the Wind* (1939)—was one he didn't want to play. In fact, the "King of Hollywood" initially passed on several of the assignments that ultimately won him fame, and accepted several that he should have refused. Born into a transient family (his father was a wildcat oil driller), Gable dropped out of school and worked with his dad in the Oklahoma oil fields for several years before joining a touring stock company to learn the acting business. Under the tutelage of actress Josephine Dillon (whom he married in 1924 even though she was 14 years older), the dark-haired, jug-eared Gable worked diligently. While the couple was in Hollywood he got extra work in *Forbidden Paradise* (1924), *The Merry Widow, The Plastic Age* (both 1925), and other silent films, but juicy opportunities weren't as plentiful as he'd initially hoped, and eventually he and Dillon split up.

Gable toured some more, even playing on Broadway, but then came back to Los Angeles and played the brutal Killer Mears in a stage production of "The Last Mile" (which, in its Broadway incarnation, had launched the starring career of Spencer Tracy). His critically acclaimed performance led to several screen tests, and while the major studios hesitated to hire him, he did finally snare a solid supporting role as a villain in *The Painted Desert* (1931), a Pathé Western starring Bill Boyd. He worked at Warner Bros. that same year, playing gangsters in *The Finger Points* and *Night Nurse* (drawing gasps from audiences when he socked Barbara Stanwyck on the chin in the lat-

ter). But it was at MGM, where he first appeared in the Joan Crawford vehicle *Dance, Fools, Dance* (1931, again as a gangster), that Gable would ultimately find success. *A Free Soul* (also 1931) saw him once again as a gangster, this time defended on a murder rap by free-wheeling attorney Lionel Barrymore and romanced by the lawyer's equally free-spirited daughter Norma Shearer. Barrymore won an Oscar for his performance, but Gable was tagged a comer.

Sporting Blood (also 1931) saw him top-billed for the first time. Metro soon tumbled to the fact that Gable, even though he played tough guys, appealed to women precisely because he was "dangerous." The studio labored mightily to keep him in films that would capitalize on that persona while expanding his range. During the next few years he worked opposite most of MGM's female stars: Garbo in *Susan Lenox: Her Fall and Rise* (1932), Joan Crawford in *Possessed* (1931) and *Dancing Lady* (1933), Norma Shearer in *Strange Interlude* (1932), Myrna Loy in *Men in White* and *Manhattan Melodrama* (both 1934), and especially, blond bombshell Jean Harlow in *Red Dust* (1932, probably the best of Gable's early starring vehicles, and a huge hit) and *Hold Your Man* (1933). His popularity grew by leaps and bounds; nobody complained anymore about the size of his ears. And they seemed to like him both with and without mustache.

But nothing boosted Gable's stock more than Frank Capra's *It Happened One Night* (1934). MGM honcho Louis B. Mayer loaned Gable to lowly Columbia Pictures to make this film as a means of disciplining the unruly star. Gable feared that his appearance in a substandard picture would cost him much of his hard-earned momentum. Capra, who'd landed Paramount's Claudette Colbert as well, convinced his players that they wouldn't be embarrassed. Indeed, Gable's insouciant performance as a wisecracking reporter (opposite Colbert, as a runaway heiress) helped define his ultimate screen persona. The film was a sensational hit, and swept the Academy Awards—with Gable himself collecting an Oscar for his work. (The only people who weren't happy with him were undershirt manufacturers; when Gable stripped off his shirt in one scene to reveal nothing underneath, sales of men's undershirts reportedly plummeted.)

Back at Metro, Gable starred in *Chained, Forsaking All Others* (both 1934), and *After Office Hours* (1935)—pleasant but humdrum offerings—before racking up a string of memorable hits later in 1935. Darryl F. Zanuck (who once screen-tested Gable and said he looked like an ape) borrowed him for *The Call of the Wild,* a popular remake of the Jack London story that teamed him with beautiful Loretta Young. Returning to his home studio, he top lined the atmospheric adventure *China Seas* and stayed afloat to play Fletcher Christian in *Mutiny on the Bounty,* one of MGM's biggest moneymakers and one of the handful of films for which Gable (who was Oscar-nominated for his work) is best remembered. And the hits kept on coming: *Wife vs. Secretary, San Francisco, Cain and Mabel* (all 1936), *Saratoga* (1937, again opposite Harlow, whose untimely death during production necessitated much juggling of scenes and reshooting with a double), *Too Hot to Handle, Test Pilot* (both 1938, both with Myrna Loy), and *Idiot's Delight* (1939, out of his element, but gamely playing a song-and-dance man performing "Puttin' on the Ritz"). His only flop during the period was *Parnell* (1937), a laborious biopic in which he was miscast as the popular Irish nationalist.

Millions of fans, as well as producer David O. Selznick and, reportedly, authoress Margaret Mitchell, saw Gable as the only man in Hollywood suited to play dashing Rhett Butler, the charismatic Southern gentleman of *Gone With the Wind.* Gable himself was less sanguine about the prospect, especially with director George Cukor at the helm. But the stakes were high: Selznick had guaranteed MGM full distribution rights and an unprecedented share of the profits for Gable's services. Needless to say, by the time the troubled production finally premiered and Gable had spoken his immortal last line to Vivien Leigh's Scarlett O'Hara—"Frankly, my dear, I don't give a damn"—everyone knew that it would be one of the most successful movies ever made. (Gable was again nominated for an Oscar.)

By this time Gable had married screen star Carole Lombard, whom he'd known since they worked together in a 1932 Paramount potboiler, *No Man of Her Own.*

They began seeing each other after her divorce from William Powell in 1933 and finally married during the production of *Wind.* With two wives behind him, Gable seemed content at last with his new spouse, and his popularity continued unabated. In *Strange Cargo, Boom Town* (reunited with Colbert), *Comrade X* (all 1940), *Honky Tonk, They Met in Bombay* (both 1941), *Somewhere I'll Find You* (1942)—Gable was in peak form. He could hardly make a false step.

Then tragedy intervened. Lombard, returning from a war bond drive in late 1942, died in a plane crash. A crushed Clark Gable, sobered by the war and devastated by the loss of his beloved wife, enlisted in the Air Corps. He served with distinction, participating in several bombing raids over Nazi Germany, achieving the rank of major, and ultimately receiving the Distinguished Flying Cross. He returned to Hollywood in 1945, making a rather lackluster screen comeback in *Adventure* (about which the ad line "Gable's Back and Garson's Got Him!" was the most memorable thing).

Gable never regained the box-office standing he'd enjoyed before the war. MGM still gave him top production mounting, the best directors, and the pick of the studio's extensive star roster—but it just wasn't the same. *The Hucksters* (1947), *Homecoming* (1948), *Any Number Can Play* (1949), *Key to the City* (1950), *Across the Wide Missouri* (1951), *Lone Star* (1952), *Never Let Me Go* (1953), and *Betrayed* (1954) all came and went without much discernible impact on Gable's career. Of his later Metro pictures, only *Command Decision* (1948), an all-star adaptation of a hit Broadway play, showed a vibrant Gable in full command of his art. *Mogambo* (1953) confirmed that he was still as macho—and desirable to women—as ever. After all, how many other men could star in a remake of their own 21-year-old movie (1932's *Red Dust*) and get away with it?

By the time he left Metro in 1954 to freelance, Gable looked every bit the tired, restless matinee idol suggested by the toll of advancing years and personal hardships. His fourth and fifth wives, Sylvia Ashley (formerly married to, and widowed by, Douglas Fairbanks) and Kay Spreckels, both bore resemblance to Lombard, for whom, it is said, Gable mourned the rest of his life. *Soldier of Fortune, The Tall Men* (both 1955), *The King and Four Queens* (1956), *Band of Angels* (1957), *Teacher's Pet* (a welcome change-of-pace comedy), *Run Silent, Run Deep* (both 1958), *But Not for Me* (1959), and *It Started in Naples* (1960) got by on the strength of his name and former popularity, but the King's reign was clearly drawing to a close. Director John Huston was able to channel Gable's weariness into what was his last performance, that of an aging, brooding horse wrangler in Arthur Miller's *The Misfits* (1961, opposite Marilyn Monroe and Montgomery Clift). It was a fine film, and demonstrated that the star—who performed most of his own stunts during the arduous production—could still deliver the goods, with the right motivation and guidance. Sadly, he never got another chance to do so: Clark Gable died of a heart attack shortly after completing *The Misfits.* He never saw it, nor the only child he fathered, John Clark Gable, who was born several weeks later. That son is today an actor.

GABOR, ZSA ZSA. Actress. *(b. Feb. 6, 1918, Budapest, as Sari Gabor.)* Blond, bejeweled, and extravagant: These three words are synonymous with this 1936 Miss Hungary beauty pageant winner, who despite a lackluster film career has managed to become one of Hollywood's most recognizable (and often ridiculed) figures. In the U.S. since the early 1940s, she began appearing in movies and on TV (as an omnipresent talk-show guest) in the 1950s. Her pictures include *Lovely to Look At, We're Not Married* (both 1952), *Moulin Rouge* (also 1952, her best part), *Lili* (1953), and *Touch of Evil* (1958), although she's most fondly remembered by camp devotees as the star (but *not* the title character) in the chintzy space opera *Queen of Outer Space* (1958). Her second career, as a much-married professional celebrity, has included appearances in the likes of *Won Ton Ton, The Dog Who Saved Hollywood* (1983) and *Frankenstein's Great Aunt Tillie* (1985). In 1990 she was convicted of slapping a police officer during a traffic dispute and spent several days in jail—leading to an amusing cameo in the main title sequence of *The Naked Gun 2½: The Smell of Fear* (1991). She made a cameo appearance as

herself in *The Beverly Hillbillies* (1993). Formerly married to George Sanders. Her autobiography is titled "One Lifetime Is Not Enough" (1992). Her sister Eva Gabor had even less of a movie career (highlighted by 1958's *Gigi),* but became a familiar face on TV and starred in the popular 1960s series "Green Acres."

GALLAGHER, PETER. Actor. *(b. Aug. 19, 1955, Armonk, N.Y.)* Handsome stage-trained actor who has begun to come into his own on film following his success as the slimy lawyer John Millaney in *sex, lies and videotape . . .* (1989). Gallagher made an auspicious debut as pop singer Caesare in *The Idolmaker* (1980), which failed miserably at the box office, and later appeared as part of the ménage à trois in *Summer Lovers* (1982), which again failed to click. He also appeared in *Dreamchild* (1985) and *High Spirits* (1988) before finally landing an ideal screen vehicle. Following *sex, lies and videotape. . . ,* he had a small role in *Late for Dinner* (1991), and was memorable as movie executive Larry Levy in *The Player* (1992), opposite Tim Robbins, for whom he also appeared as a bubbleheaded news anchor in *Bob Roberts* (1992). More recent credits include *Malice, Short Cuts* (both 1993), *The Hudsucker Proxy,* and *Mother's Boys* (both 1994). Gallagher's stage credits include the critically acclaimed Broadway revivals of "Long Day's Journey Into Night" (for which he received a 1986 Tony nomination) and "Guys and Dolls," as Sky Masterson, in 1992. His latest films are *While You Were Sleeping* and *The Underneath* (both 1995).

GANCE, ABEL. Director, screenwriter, actor. *(b. Oct. 25, 1889, Paris; d. Nov. 10, 1981.)* This French filmmaker, a former lawyer's clerk and stage actor, was among the handful of pioneers (including D. W. Griffith and Sergei Eisenstein) who developed cinematic grammar. He directed his first film, *La Digue,* in 1911, and during the next several years experimented tirelessly with photographic processes and editing techniques. Gance's antiwar epic *J'Accuse* (1919) won him many admirers on both sides of the Atlantic, and enabled him to indulge his creative impulses on *La*

Roue (1923), an emotional, often melodramatic study of railroad workers that took several years to complete. Gance's masterpiece, *Napoleon* (1927), utilized virtually every iota of cinematic technique developed up to that time—and then some. Gance's use of a "triptych" three screens wide, predating the Cinerama process, startled audiences (even in 1981, when Francis Ford Coppola released film historian Kevin Brownlow's restoration of the film). At the time, however, *Napoleon* received limited distribution, and the heavily truncated American version was poorly received. Most of Gance's subsequent films were competent but generally undistinguished mainstream offerings, with the notable exceptions of *The End of the World* (1931, an early disaster movie) and a 1938 remake of *J'Accuse*. His last movie was *Bonaparte et la Revolution* (1971), a reworking of his favorite project (and lifelong obsession). Gance died in 1981, after having had the satisfaction of seeing his masterpiece restored and reissued to appreciative audiences around the world.

GANZ, BRUNO. Actor. *(b. Mar. 22, 1941, Zurich.)* Sad-looking leading man of the "New German Wave" of films, known for doomed, self-tortured protagonists. After achieving success on the stage in Germany, he won a major film role in Eric Rohmer's *The Marquise of O* (1976), which was followed by Werner Herzog's atmospheric *Nosferatu the Vampire* (1979) and Volker Schlondorff's *Circle of Deceit* (1981). He has appeared in *The Boys From Brazil* (1978), *The Girl From Lorraine* (1980), and *Strapless* (1989), but may be best known for his films with Wim Wenders, *The American Friend* (1977) and—especially—*Wings of Desire* (1988), playing an angel who wants to be human again. Recent films include the provocative Australian drama *The Last Days of Chez Nous,* the Italian-made *Especially on Sunday* (in the title segment), and *Faraway, So Close!,* a "sequel" to *Wings of Desire,* all released in 1993.

GANZ AND MANDEL. Screenwriters. *(**Lowell Ganz**—b. Aug. 31, 1948, New York City. **Babaloo Mandel**—b. Oct. 13, 1949, New York City.)* Highly successful screenwriters who have penned some of the most popular comedies of the past decade. By the age of 23, Ganz was a staff writer on the TV sitcom "The Odd Couple"; he went on to produce "Happy Days" and cocreate "Laverne and Shirley." Mandel, who was selling jokes to comics to support his screenwriting career, met Ganz at the Hollywood Comedy Store and Ganz eventually brought him to work on "Happy Days" as a creative consultant. Producer Brian Grazer and "Happy Days" alum Ron Howard approached Ganz and Mandel with an idea for a film about morgue workers caught in a prostitution ring, which Howard would direct. The film was *Night Shift* (1982) and became a hit; Ganz and Mandel teamed up again with Howard for the charming mermaid fantasy *Splash* (1984), which not only made stars of Tom Hanks and Daryl Hannah but earned the writing team an Oscar nomination for Best Original Screenplay. Since then, Ganz and Mandel have had an almost nonstop string of successes (1988's *Vibes* is the one major exception) that include *Gung-Ho* (1986) and *Parenthood* (1989), both directed by Ron Howard, the popular Billy Crystal–starrer *City Slickers* (1991) and the not-so-popular *Mr. Saturday Night* (1992). Most recently, Ganz and Mandel had another major hit with *A League of Their Own* (1992), which dealt with the seemingly "uncommercial" subject of the women's baseball league of World War 2. (They executive produced the short-lived TV sitcom spinoff, "A League of Their Own," in 1993, and wrote several episodes.) They also wrote 1994's *Greedy,* and cowrote—with frequent collaborator Crystal—*City Slickers 2: The Legend of Curly's Gold* (also 1994) and *Forget Paris* (1995). Mandel's adoptive first name, by the way, comes from a character in Philip Roth's "Portnoy's Complaint." His given name is Mark.

GARBO, GRETA. Actress. *(b. Sept. 18, 1905, Stockholm, as Greta Louisa Gustafsson; d. Apr. 15, 1990.)* Few screen personalities have been totally successful in isolating their private lives from their public personas, but this enigmatic Swedish beauty certainly accomplished it. What's most amazing is that, in avoiding media scrutiny and public contact, she did so in a way that actually enhanced the mysterious allure that had been so vital an element in her success. Born into poverty, she worked as a shopgirl in a large department store and was chosen to appear in a short film promoting it. She made a few other such commercial appearances before deciding that acting might be her ticket out of the working class. Remarkably, she won a scholarship to the Royal Dramatic Theater acting school and, while doing some minor stage work, was spotted there by film director Mauritz Stiller. He tested her for and then signed her to play a role in *The Story of Gosta Berling* (1924).

Garbo's feature-film debut, while well-received, hardly made her an overnight sensation. But Stiller believed in the young actress, and took her under his wing. She played second female lead in G. W. Pabst's *The Joyless Street* (1924, which also included Marlene Dietrich as an extra) before going to America with Stiller, who had been offered a Hollywood contract by MGM's Louis B. Mayer. The highly regarded director used his influence to get Garbo signed as well, a move initially resisted by Mayer. She was assigned to play the female lead, a Spanish prima donna, in Monta Bell's *The Torrent* (1926), opposite Ricardo Cortez, and although studio brass at first had little faith in her, they were amazed by the quality of her work. Moreover, studio publicity men crafted hard-sell promotional materials that not only sold the film but launched the Garbo mystique, creating an air of mystery surrounding the naturally quiet, reticent woman.

As Garbo's star rose, however, Stiller's fell. Slated to direct her next film, *The Temptress,* he quarreled relentlessly with MGM management and was finally replaced with the prosaic Fred Niblo. Although the picture turned out to be a middling artistic success, Garbo's femme-fatale characterization attracted curious moviegoers and made it a commercial hit. For her next film, *Flesh and the Devil* (1927), she was teamed with John Gilbert, then MGM's reigning male star, with whom she carried on a torrid affair that, not surprisingly, spilled over into their cinematic lovemaking. The release of *Flesh,* her best film to date, saw Garbo a full-fledged superstar. Certainly there was no one else like her on American movie screens, although other studios rushed to import similarly exotic European beauties

and shroud them in synthetic cloaks of secrecy. *Love* (also 1927) reunited Garbo with Gilbert; she played Anna Karenina in this Tolstoy adaptation, and once again moviegoers were treated to the sight of real-life lovers playing out their passion on the big screen.

Away from the cameras, though, Garbo began to have second thoughts about Gilbert (for reasons that were never made clear). They planned to marry, but she literally left Gilbert standing at the altar, which devastated him. (By this time her mentor Stiller had returned to Sweden.) The iconoclastic Garbo resolutely clung to her individuality; she really did, as she famously said in *Grand Hotel,* want to be left alone. And that impenetrable aloofness became an integral part of her mystique.

She continued to make silent films, all successful. *The Divine Woman, The Mysterious Lady, A Woman of Affairs* (all 1928), *Wild Orchids, The Single Standard,* and *The Kiss* (all 1929) depended almost entirely upon her presence alone. Her characters could be pure or sullied, willing or restrained, remote or accessible—it didn't much matter. It was Garbo people wanted to see. And hear. When MGM's publicity machine cranked out promotional material for her first talkie, *Anna Christie* (a Eugene O'Neill play that, in retrospect, was an ambitious and risky choice for the foreign-born, thickly accented actress), the dominant message was: "Garbo *Talks!*" And she did, in a husky voice that, although incongruous with her physical appearance, somehow suited her perfectly.

In unexceptional films like *Romance* (1930), *Inspiration, Susan Lenox: Her Fall and Rise* (both 1931, in the latter opposite Clark Gable), *Mata Hari,* and *As You Desire Me* (both 1932) she rose above often mediocre material; her mere presence made the films worth seeing. In *Grand Hotel* (1932) she created an archetype for herself, as the fatalistic ballerina, and got to work opposite John Barrymore, whom she greatly admired. *Queen Christina* (1933), which, at her request, reunited her with Gilbert (whose career had taken a sudden and dramatic turn for the worse with the advent of sound) was perhaps her best sound film. It contained several memorable moments, including a wordless scene in which, one morning after a rapturously happy tryst with Gilbert, she lingers in the room, touching and feeling furniture and objects so as to indelibly etch every detail of the joyous experience in her memory. Who but Garbo could have made the gesture so affecting?

After finishing *The Painted Veil* (1934), Garbo took the title roles in *Anna Karenina* (1935, a remake of *Love)* and *Camille* (1937, as the doomed heroine, one of her best-remembered talkies), delivering two more memorable performances in great parts perfectly suited to her persona. After *Conquest* (1937), she was off the screen for nearly two years, and when she returned, it was to star in a comedy—something she'd never tried before. "Garbo Laughs!" the ads declared, and they were accurate. *Ninotchka* (1939), directed by Ernst Lubitsch from a Billy Wilder–Charles Brackett script, starred her as a Russian Communist functionary who, while visiting Paris, falls in love with gay blade Melvyn Douglas. Lubitsch was the perfect choice to guide her through this territory, and she was charming in her comedy debut.

Two more years passed before she made another movie. While willing to try another comedy, *Two-Faced Woman* (1941) was a poor choice. With European distribution curtailed during World War 2, MGM tried to Americanize and "humanize" the star, with disastrous results. Stinging from this failure, Garbo weighed other script offers carefully. Several projects were planned, then abandoned, during the 1940s, and in 1949 she even submitted to a screen test for the backers of a proposed film. But nothing came to fruition, and it was speculated that with each passing year, the idea of returning to the spotlight seemed less and less desirable to the erstwhile actress. For the remainder of her life she lived as a loner, vacationing in Switzerland, on the French Riviera, and in Italy but making home base her apartment on New York City's fashionable Upper East Side. Once in a while she would speak to passersby who saw her on the street, but by and large she avoided the public eye. The woman whose passionate love affairs once filled fan-magazine stories with speculation never married. In 1954 she received a special Oscar (amazingly, she'd never won any during her career, although she'd been nominated for *Anna Christie, Romance, Camille,* and *Ninotchka)* for "her unforgettable screen performances." Needless to say, she did not accept the statuette in person.

GARCIA, ANDY. Actor. *(b. Apr. 12, 1956, Havana.)* Earnest, handsome, Cuban-born actor who came into his own as a leading man in the early 1990s. Having emigrated to Florida, Garcia learned his craft by playing regional theater in that state. He specialized in hard-bitten urban types, and has been particularly successful in characterizations calling for quiet intensity and moral rigidity. He has, however, shown a disturbing inclination to overact (as witness his over-the-top cop in 1992's *Jennifer 8).* Garcia made his big-screen debut in *Blue Skies Again* (1983), and has since appeared in *The Mean Season* (1985), *8 Million Ways to Die* (1986), *The Untouchables* (1987, a breakout role as a crack shot working with Eliot Ness), *American Roulette, Stand and Deliver* (both 1988), *Black Rain* (1989, as the partner of American cop Michael Douglas, on assignment in Japan), *The Godfather, Part III* (1990, Oscar-nominated as the cold-blooded, illegitimate nephew of Al Pacino's Michael Corleone), *Internal Affairs* (his first starring role), *A Show of Force* (both 1990), and *Dead Again* (1991, doing some of his scenes in phony-looking old-age makeup). He costarred in *Hero* (1992) and opposite Meg Ryan in *When a Man Loves a Woman* (1994). He also directed a documentary, *Cachao: Rhythm Like Nobody Else* (1993) about Cuban composer-performer Israel "Cachao" Lopez. Garcia appears in the film as well.

GARDENIA, VINCENT. Actor. *(b. Jan. 7, 1922, Naples, Italy, as Vincente Scognamiglio; d. Dec. 9, 1992.)* Born in Italy, raised in New York, this character player was blessed (fortunately for his career) with a distinctive, jowly, hangdog expression that made him a natural in cantankerous comic roles. But he also tackled more demanding parts—cops, mobsters, businessmen, frustrated patriarchs—and always showed passion and conviction in straight dramatic characterizations. His early films included *Cop Hater* (1958), *Murder, Inc.* (1960), and *Mad Dog Coll* (1961), in which his ethnicity dictated his casting as gangsters.

A stage veteran and Tony winner for Broadway's "The Prisoner of Second Avenue," Gardenia received Academy Award nominations for his supporting performances in *Bang the Drum Slowly* (1973, as a baseball manager) and *Moonstruck* (1987, as Cher's father). He had recurring roles on the TV series "All in the Family" and, more recently, "L.A. Law" (as Susan Ruttan's father) and won an Emmy for his performance in the made-for-TV movie *Age-Old Friends* (1989) with Hume Cronyn.
OTHER FILMS INCLUDE: 1971: *Little Murders*; 1974: *Death Wish*; 1978: *Heaven Can Wait*; 1986: *Little Shop of Horrors*; 1989: *Skin Deep.*

GARDINER, REGINALD. Actor. *(b. Feb. 27, 1903, Wimbledon, England; d. July 7, 1980.)* Suave and cultured in the Noël Coward manner, the dark-haired, mustached Gardiner was a popular stage and screen star in England for years before making his Broadway debut in 1935. A handsome and personable leading-man type, Gardiner often played urbane and eccentric Brits in Hollywood. He was active through the mid 1960s.
OTHER FILMS INCLUDE: 1936: *Born to Dance*; 1937: *A Damsel in Distress*; 1939: *The Flying Deuces*; 1940: *The Great Dictator*; 1941: *Sundown, The Man Who Came to Dinner* (one of his best parts, a thinly disguised Noël Coward); 1943: *Claudia*; 1946: *Cluny Brown*; 1954: *Black Widow*; 1957: *The Story of Mankind* (as Shakespeare); 1958: *Rock-a-Bye Baby*; 1965: *Do Not Disturb.*

GARDNER, AVA. Actress. *(b. Jan. 24, 1922, Smithfield, N.C.; d. Jan. 25, 1990.)* One of Hollywood's legendary "love goddesses," this green-eyed brunette beauty combined feline grace with passionate intensity, and while she never claimed to be (nor was ever recognized as) a great actress, she held her own in a number of memorable films. Gardner was born into a poor family, and had no loftier ambition than to become a secretary in New York until her picture was seen by MGM's East Coast talent executive. A screen test was arranged (deliberately silent, because her Southern accent was so thick) and she was judged to have potential. She flew west to Hollywood and cheerfully signed a term contract with the studio, which promptly enrolled her in acting classes and took hundreds of publicity shots of her before she ever stepped on a movie set.

Gardner spent several years playing undemanding bit parts in MGM Bs such as *We Were Dancing, Joe Smith, American, Kid Glove Killer, Calling Dr. Gillespie* (all 1942), *Pilot No. 5, Hitler's Madman* (both 1943), *Swing Fever, Three Men in White, Maisie Goes to Reno* (all 1944), and *She Went to the Races* (1945). She even appeared briefly in an MGM "Our Gang" short, *Mighty Lak a Goat,* for which her scene was reportedly directed by then-husband Mickey Rooney. In 1943 she was loaned to lowly Monogram Pictures to play the ingenue in *Ghosts on the Loose;* aside from being mauled by the East Side Kids and ogled by Bela Lugosi, her responsibilities were minimal. It took another loan-out assignment, that of a femme fatale in Universal's Hemingway adaptation, *The Killers* (1946), to make audiences sit up and take notice. Her good reviews prompted MGM to try her opposite the King himself, Clark Gable, in *The Hucksters* (1947), in which she played a self-assured nightclub singer. Gardner acquitted herself nicely and was promoted to full-fledged stardom.

In most films, her presence was basically decorative, but she contributed memorable performances to *Show Boat* (1951, as Julie, the beautiful mulatto, for which she performed several Jerome Kern songs that made it to the soundtrack album but were redubbed for the film itself), *Mogambo* (1953, opposite Gable in this remake of his earlier success *Red Dust,* with Gardner snagging an Oscar nomination for her interpretation of the tart-tongued character played in the original by Jean Harlow), and Joseph L. Mankiewicz's *The Barefoot Contessa* (1954), in a part she seemed born to play, an earthy Spanish dancer who's transformed into a screen goddess—but destined never to find personal happiness.

In 1957, life imitated art once again. Gardner divorced singer Frank Sinatra that year (they had married in 1951 following a tempestuous courtship) and, after playing American expatriate Lady Brett Ashley in the film adaptation of *The Sun Also Rises,* adopted her character's lifestyle and moved to Spain, where she was surrounded by adoring European jet-setters and matadors. Years of these hedonistic pursuits took their toll on her beauty; by the time she'd turned 50 she looked at least 10 years older. But as a mature, worldly actress, she delivered several interesting, multilayered performances. Her other husbands were actor Mickey Rooney (whom she wed shortly after joining Metro) and bandleader Artie Shaw.

In later years Gardner lived in London, but spent one season as a cast member of the TV series "Falcon Crest" (1985) and shortly before her death completed an autobiography, "Ava," which was published posthumously in 1990. More than one obituary declared her the most beautiful woman who ever stepped in front of a camera, and she was once in fact "voted" The Most Beautiful Woman in the World. OTHER FILMS INCLUDE: 1947: *Singapore;* 1948: *One Touch of Venus;* 1949: *The Bribe, East Side, West Side, The Great Sinner;* 1951: *Pandora and the Flying Dutchman, My Forbidden Past;* 1952: *Lone Star, The Snows of Kilimanjaro;* 1953: *The Band Wagon* (in a cameo as herself); 1953: *Knights of the Round Table;* 1956: *Bhowani Junction;* 1957: *The Little Hut;* 1959: *The Naked Maja, On the Beach;* 1960: *The Angel Wore Red;* 1963: *55 Days at Peking;* 1964: *Seven Days in May, The Night of the Iguana;* 1966: *The Bible;* 1969: *Mayerling;* 1972: *The Devil's Widow, The Life and Times of Judge Roy Bean* (as Lillie Langtry); 1974: *Earthquake;* 1975: *Permission to Kill;* 1976: *The Blue Bird;* 1977: *The Cassandra Crossing;* 1979: *City on Fire;* 1980: *The Kidnapping of the President;* 1981: *Priest of Love;* 1985: *The Long Hot Summer* (telefilm); 1986: *Harem.*

GARFIELD, ALLEN. Actor. *(b. Nov. 22, 1939, Newark, N.J., as Allen Goorwitz.)* Stocky supporting player in such irreverent counterculture films as *Greetings* (1968) and *Putney Swope* (1969), cast often as pushy, antiestablishment ethnic Jewish types. He was a boxer and journalist before entering films. Trained at the Actors' Studio, he snagged a few leads in such low-budget movies as *Cry Uncle!* (1970) and *Skateboard* (1977), but he's best remembered for his standout support in *Nashville* (1975) as Ronee Blakley's husband and manager. Garfield was practically ubiquitous in the 1970s—*Bananas* (1971), *The Candidate* (1972), and *The*

Conversation (1974) are just a few of his films—but was seen less frequently in the 1980s. In the late 1970s he decided to be billed under his real name, Allen Goorwitz, but later had a change of heart. In 1993 he played the title role in the low-budget, independent effort *Jack and His Friends.*
OTHER FILMS INCLUDE: 1970: *The Owl and the Pussycat;* 1971: *You've Got to Walk It Like You Talk It or You'll Lose Your Beat, Taking Off;* 1972: *Get to Know Your Rabbit;* 1973: *Slither;* 1976: *Gable and Lombard* (as Louis B. Mayer); 1978: *The Brink's Job* (a hilarious supporting role); 1980: *The Stunt Man* (as the paranoid screenwriter); 1983: *Get Crazy;* 1984: *Teachers, The Cotton Club;* 1986: *Desert Bloom;* 1989: *Cry Devil;* 1990: *Dick Tracy;* 1991: *Until the End of the World;* 1993: *Family Prayers.*

GARFIELD, JOHN. Actor. *(b. Mar. 4, 1913, New York City, as Julius Garfinkle; d. May 21, 1952.)* This short, dark-haired, broodingly handsome actor often played rebellious, tough urban characters—which didn't require much of a stretch. Born on New York City's Lower East Side to immigrant Jews, Garfield grew up in the streets, frequently clashing with both the police and neighborhood gangs. Verbally as well as physically combative, he won a debating contest sponsored by "The New York Times" and used the scholarship funds to enroll in the (Maria) Ouspenskaya Drama School. During the Depression years he took a few odd jobs and spent long periods riding the rails as a hobo. (Film buffs still debate whether that's him, as a sailor with one quick closeup, in the "Shanghai Lil" number of 1933's *Footlight Parade.*) He came back to New York and joined the politically progressive Group Theatre, making a name for himself as a charismatic performer and eventually winding up on Broadway.

Hollywood beckoned in 1938. Warner Bros. saw in Garfield the same urban-spawned edginess, pugnaciousness, and cynicism that James Cagney had brought to the studio years earlier. Although his screen characters were sometimes too surly to be wholly sympathetic, Garfield established a following after appearing in *Four Daughters* (1938, with a great showcase role as a fatalistic musician, for which he snagged an Academy Award nomination), *They Made Me a Criminal, Daughters Courageous, Blackwell's Island, Dust Be My Destiny, Four Wives, Juarez* (all 1939), and *Castle on the Hudson* (1940). Several of these were remakes of earlier Warners successes, and capitalized on Garfield's flinty personality and big-city background. But the studio eventually broadened his range of roles, just as it had done for Cagney. *Flowing Gold* (1940), *The Sea Wolf, Out of the Fog* (both 1941), *Dangerously They Live, Tortilla Flat* (both 1942, on loan to MGM for the latter), *Air Force, Thank Your Lucky Stars* (both 1943), *Destination Tokyo, Between Two Worlds* (both 1944), and *Pride of the Marines* (1945) took Garfield out of the urban milieu, although he was always at his best playing disaffected loners. (In 1944's *Hollywood Canteen* he played himself, as the cofounder—with Bette Davis—of this haven for transient servicemen in L.A.)

Garfield was ideally suited to play the amoral drifter who seduces married woman Lana Turner in *The Postman Always Rings Twice* (1946), the somewhat glamorized, diluted adaptation of a tough-as-nails James M. Cain novel that could have been written with Garfield in mind. He hit his peak in that post-WW2 period, portraying an ambitious musician in *Humoresque* (1946), an unprincipled boxer in *Body and Soul* (1947, an Oscar-nominated performance), and a racketeer's lawyer in *Force of Evil* (1948), all of them characterizations he brought to life with great passion and skill. He took a supporting role in *Gentleman's Agreement* (1947) because he believed so strongly in the film's purpose—to expose anti-Semitism in this country.

Garfield starred in *We Were Strangers* (1949), *Under My Skin* (1950), *The Breaking Point* (also 1950, a remake of *To Have and Have Not,* with Garfield in the Humphrey Bogart role), and *He Ran All the Way* (1951) before running afoul of the House Un-American Activities Committee, which couldn't find enough evidence to accuse him of being a Communist but managed to taint him just enough to get him blacklisted. (His left-wing political sympathies, a holdover from his Group Theatre days, were sufficiently suspicious for Hollywood executives.) He died of a heart attack a year later. Though

he made many fine films, and never gave a bad performance, he has somehow escaped the latter-day fame and cult heroism that have been bestowed on fellow urban hero Bogart. Like Bogie, Garfield deserves to be lionized, and rediscovered. Both his son, John Jr., and his daughter, Julie, went into acting.

GARGAN, WILLIAM. Actor. *(b. July 17, 1905, Brooklyn; d. Feb. 17, 1979.)* In most of his screen appearances, Gargan basically played himself: a robust, handsome, high-spirited Irishman. Another Broadway performer who went Hollywood to recreate a stage triumph on film (in the 1932 movie version of Philip Barry's *The Animal Kingdom),* Gargan stayed for 30 years. His "serious" film work included noteworthy performances in *Rain* (1932), *The Story of Temple Drake* (1933), *Four Frightened People* (1934), *You Only Live Once* (1937), *They Knew What They Wanted* (1940, for which he earned an Oscar nomination), *I Wake Up Screaming* (1941), *Who Done It?* (1942), *The Canterville Ghost* (1944), and *The Bells of St. Mary's* (1945), but he was breezier, and more entertaining, in B films such as *Headline Shooters* (1933), *Man Hunt* (1936), *Wings Over Honolulu* (1937), and *Bombay Clipper* (1942). He played master detective Ellery Queen in three 1942 Columbia programmers and later returned to crime-fighting as TV's "Martin Kane, Private Eye" from 1949 to 1951. After an operation for throat cancer cost him his voice box, Gargan became an indefatigable campaigner against smoking for the American Cancer Society. His autobiography, "Why Me?" was published in 1969. Gargan's older, heavier, and less handsome brother, Edward, also worked in movies, usually cast as a dumb cop.

GARLAND, BEVERLY. Actress. *(b. Oct. 17, 1926, Santa Cruz, Cal., as Beverly Fessenden.)* In her peak year, 1956, this spunky B-movie ingenue starred in five movies for just one producer (Roger Corman): *It Conquered the World, Gunslinger, Not of This Earth, Swamp Women,* and *Naked Paradise.* None of them, we might add, were Oscar contenders, but they did showcase this dynamic blond actress at her low-budget best. Debuting in the 1949 thriller *D.O.A.* (billed as Beverly Campbell), the sultry Garland enjoyed a brief stint at MGM before winding up, alledgedly the victim of a studio blacklist, as a favorite ingenue of indie producers. She did have a small role in Paramount's *The Desperate Hours* (1955), but toiled on low-budgeters for most of the next 10 years. Significantly, in 1957 she landed the lead in "Decoy," playing TV's first distaff police officer in a brief but well-remembered series. She appeared more frequently on TV in the 1960s, playing Bing Crosby's wife on his 1964 series, and joining the cast of "My Three Sons" as Fred MacMurray's new wife in 1969. Her acting assignments of late, save for a supporting role on the TV series "Scarecrow and Mrs. King" (1983–1987), have been scarce. She is now a successful Southern California hotelier.

GARLAND, JUDY. Actress, singer. *(b. June 10, 1922, Grand Rapids, Mich., as Frances Gumm; d. June 22, 1969.)* A furious, excessive talent and a true "victim" (if ever there was one) of the Hollywood studio system, Garland began her performing career at the age of three. While she and two older sisters were performing as the "Gumm Sisters Kiddie Act," showman George Jessel suggested the change of stage name to Garland; a few years later MGM boss Louis B. Mayer signed her to a contract after a personal audition. Her ability to steal hearts was revealed in *Broadway Melody of 1938,* in which she trilled "You Made Me Love You" to a photo of Clark Gable. Her distinctive voice and disarming sincerity made a big impression, and a year later she starred in the classic-to-be *The Wizard of Oz,* for which she won a special juvenile Oscar.

Garland's initial teaming with fellow teen star Mickey Rooney was in *Thoroughbreds Don't Cry* (1937), and they went on to work together in a series of MGM musicals—including *Babes in Arms* (1939), *Strike Up the Band* (1940), *Babes on Broadway* (1941), and *Girl Crazy* (1943)—to which they both brought an ever-pleasing charm and perkiness. She starred in *For Me and My Gal* (1942), which introduced movie audiences to Gene Kelly. All was not sweetness and light behind the scenes, however; Garland, like so many child stars, did not enjoy good relations with her driven stage mother, and even worse, her grueling schedule at the studio led to a dependency on pep and sleeping pills that was to dog her for the rest of her life and eventually end it.

Over the course of 28 years she was married five times—in 1945 to director Vincente Minnelli, with whom she had daughter Liza in 1946—and was involved in many well-publicized lawsuits, breakdowns, and suicide attempts. But it took quite a while before her spectacular unhappiness actually showed itself onscreen. In such period musicals as *Meet Me in St. Louis* (1944) and *The Pirate* (1948)—both directed by Minnelli—and *Easter Parade* (1948), as well as dramas like Minnelli's *The Clock* (1945), she was never anything less than charming.

After hitting rock bottom in the early 1950s after *Summer Stock* (1950)—that year she was even replaced as the star of *Annie Get Your Gun*—Garland bounced back, all vibrant and vulnerable, as aspiring actress Vicki Lester in Cukor's 1954 remake of *A Star Is Born,* a hand-tailored comeback vehicle she produced with then-husband Sid Luft. It earned her an Oscar nomination, but sadly, there were no follow-ups. She was excellent in later straight dramatic roles in *Judgment at Nuremberg* (1961 also Oscar-nominated) and *A Child Is Waiting* (1963), but the singing sequences in her last film, *I Could Go On Singing* (also 1963), show the emotionally turbulent performing style she developed in her adult years, a style that apparently corresponded perfectly to her own state of inner turmoil. Garland's final years were spent going from disappointment to disappointment: losing film roles, helplessly turning in shoddy live performances, marrying one younger man and divorcing him six months later, and so on. A "comeback" TV variety show gave her one last burst of glory in 1963–64, but though she recorded tracks and filmed costume tests for *Valley of the Dolls,* she had to be replaced by Susan Hayward when shooting began. An accidental overdose of sleeping pills took her life in 1969; her *Wizard of Oz* costar Ray Bolger commented sadly: "She just plain wore out."

GARMES, LEE. Cinematographer. *(b. May 27, 1898, Peoria, Ill.; d. Aug. 31, 1978.)* He was among the handful of cinematographers who raised motion-picture photography to an art in the 1920s and 1930s, and his lighting techniques contributed tremendously to the appeal of such exotic films as *Morocco* (1930, for which Garmes earned his first Oscar nomination), *Dishonored* (1931), *Shanghai Express* (1932, an Oscar-winning lensing job), and *Zoo in Budapest* (1933). He broke into the business as a camera operator in 1918, and worked his way up to director of photography within a few short years. His list of films includes *The Garden of Allah* (1927), *Disraeli* (1929), *Whoopee!* (1930 in two-color Technicolor), *An American Tragedy, City Streets* (both 1931), *Scarface, Call Her Savage* (both 1932), *Gone With the Wind* (1939, uncredited), *The Jungle Book* (1942), *Stormy Weather* (1943), *Since You Went Away* (1944, for which he was again Oscar-nominated), *The Secret Life of Walter Mitty* (1947), *Detective Story* (1951), and *The Desperate Hours* (1955). Garmes also collaborated with writers Ben Hecht and Charles MacArthur on several of their 1930s films, essentially codirecting *Crime Without Passion* (1934) and *The Scoundrel* (1935), and officially codirecting Hecht's *Angels Over Broadway* (1940). (He later photographed Hecht's directorial efforts, *Specter of the Rose,* in 1946 and *Actors and Sin* in 1952.) Garmes received his last Oscar nod for his camera work on *The Big Fisherman* (1959). An open-minded, resourceful craftsman who maintained enthusiasm for his craft right up to his dying day, Garmes married actress Ruth Hall in 1933.

GARNER, JAMES. Actor. *(b. Apr. 7, 1928, Norman, Okla., as James Scott Baumgarner.)* With a handful of others, Garner has the uncanny knack of making it look easy—"it" in his case being the construction of a rugged, consistently likable, always credible persona, on both the movie and TV screen. Like many other screen naturals, Garner, a high school dropout and Korean War hero who won the Purple Heart, more or less stumbled into acting; his first stage appearance was a nonspeaking role in the 1954 Broadway production of "The Caine Mutiny Court-Martial," the producer of which was an old boyhood chum. The title role in the lighthearted western TV series "Maverick" (1957–62) made him a star, and throughout the 1960s was equally effective in contemporary dramas such as *Cash McCall* (1960) and *The Children's Hour* (1962), male ensemble action pictures *The Great Escape* (1963) and *Grand Prix* (1966), Westerns *Duel at Diablo* (1966) and *Hour of The Gun* (1967, playing Wyatt Earp), and comedies *The Thrill of It All* (1963) and *The Americanization of Emily* (1964). Garner's easy humor made him perfect for director Burt Kennedy's offbeat but action-packed Western spoofs *Support Your Local Sheriff!* (1969) and *Support Your Local Gunfighter* (1971). Many have observed that of all the actors who have played Raymond Chandler's legendary detective Philip Marlowe, Garner, who starred in 1969's *Marlowe,* comes closest to Chandler's physical description of the character.

Garner perhaps gained his biggest fame as constantly put-upon detective Jim Rockford in the extremely popular TV series "The Rockford Files" (1974–80). During the late 1970s and early 1980s Garner's big-screen efforts were hit and miss, although he did score big as a sexually befuddled Chicago gangster in Blake Edwards' gender-bending comedy *Victor/Victoria* (1982) and was nominated for a Best Actor Academy Award for his turn as a free-thinking small-town pharmacist in Martin Ritt's *Murphy's Romance* (1985). Garner has appeared in some exceptional made-for-TV movies, including *Heartsounds* (1984), *Promise* (1986), *My Name is Bill W.* (1989), and *Barbarians at the Gate* (1993), to name just a few. Recent film credits include a cameo in *The Distinguished Gentleman* (1992, as an adulterous senator) and *Fire in the Sky* (1993). He also costarred in the big-screen version of *Maverick* (1994).

GARNETT, TAY. Director, screenwriter. *(b. June 13, 1894, Los Angeles; d. Oct. 3, 1977.)* He never won any Oscars—never even got nominated, for that matter—and auteurists yawn at the mention of his name, but this mainstream Hollywood director was responsible for dozens of vastly entertaining films from the 1920s to the 1970s. Some of them—including *One*

Way Passage (1932), *China Seas* (1935), and *The Postman Always Rings Twice* (1946)—have achieved reputations far outstripping what their makers ever expected. Garnett, a former gag writer for comedy producers Mack Sennett and Hal Roach, first started directing for Pathé in 1928, beginning with *Celebrity* (which, like many of his films, he also cowrote). No great visual stylist, he concentrated on unfolding his narratives with pace and verve. Once married to actress Patsy Ruth Miller, Garnett wrote his autobiography, "Light Up Your Torches and Pull Up Your Tights," in 1973.

OTHER FILMS INCLUDE: 1930: *Her Man;* 1932: *Okay America;* 1933: *S.O.S. Iceberg;* 1935: *She Couldn't Take It;* 1936: *Professional Soldier;* 1937: *Stand-In;* 1939: *Trade Winds;* 1940: *Slightly Honorable, Seven Sinners;* 1941: *Cheers for Miss Bishop;* 1942: *My Favorite Spy;* 1943: *Bataan;* 1944: *Mrs. Parkington;* 1949: *A Connecticut Yankee in King Arthur's Court;* 1951: *Soldiers Three;* 1954: *The Black Knight;* 1960: *A Terrible Beauty;* 1963: *Cattle King;* 1970: *The Delta Factor;* 1973: *Timber Tramp.*

GARR, TERI. Actress. *(b. Dec. 11, 1944, Lakewood, Ohio.)* Attractive blond actress whose stock-in-trade is her infectious smile and unerring sense of comedic timing. Garr studied drama and dance at California State University at Northridge, eventually making her way to the Actors' Studio in New York. She first appeared on screen as a go-go dancer in Elvis Presley movies, including *Fun in Acapulco* (1963), *Kissin' Cousins* (1964), and *Viva Las Vegas* (1964). She had a small role in the Monkees' movie *Head* (1968), and a regular supporting spot in TV's "The Sonny and Cher Comedy Hour." Garr demonstrated her talent in two 1974 supporting roles, in Francis Ford Coppola's *The Conversation* and Mel Brooks' *Young Frankenstein;* her comedic abilities were brought to the fore by Brooks, but many of her subsequent roles were "straight" ones. She played Richard Dreyfuss' frustrated wife in *Close Encounters of the Third Kind* (1977), John Denver's wife in *Oh, God!* (1977), and young Kelly Reno's mother in *The Black Stallion* (1979). Coppola wasted her in his abortive *One From the Heart* (1982), but director Sydney Pollack cast her opposite Dustin Hoffman in *Tootsie* (1982), and her performance netted her an Oscar nomination for Best Supporting Actress.

In the 1980s Garr was active both on the big screen and the TV talk-show circuit, appearing in such pictures as *The Black Stallion Returns, Mr. Mom* (both 1983), *Firstborn* (1984), and *After Hours* (1985). Subsequent feature films, including *Miracles* (1986), *Full Moon in Blue Water, Out Cold* (both 1988), *Let It Ride* (1989), *Short Time, Waiting for the Light* (both 1990), and *Mom and Dad Save the World* (1992), have squandered her talent. She has fared better in TV movies—including 1986's *Intimate Strangers* and 1987's *Pack of Lies*—which have offered her meatier roles. She has costarred in two TV series, the short-lived "Good and Evil" (1991) and "Good Advice" (1993, with Shelley Long).

GARRETT, BETTY. Actress, singer, dancer. *(b. May 23, 1919, St. Joseph, Mo.)* Bubbly, wholesomely attractive trouper, with comedic talent to spare, whose promising career in MGM musicals was cut short by McCarthy-era blacklisting (her husband, actor-singer Larry Parks, had confessed to prior affiliation with the Communist party). Garrett, an alumnas of the Mercury Theater and a former dancer with the Martha Graham company, was a Broadway regular in the mid 1940s, winning a Donaldson Award for her work in "Call Me Mister." Signed by MGM, she appeared in *The Big City, Words and Music* (both 1948), *On the Town* (as Frank Sinatra's romantic interest), *Take Me Out to the Ball Game* (reunited with *Town* stars Sinatra and Gene Kelly), and *Neptune's Daughter* (singing "Baby, It's Cold Outside" with Red Skelton; all 1949). Garrett made a couple of token movie appearances in *My Sister Eileen* (1955) and *Shadow on the Window* (1957), but never regained the career momentum she'd had in the late 1940s. Her career got a second wind in the 1970s, on stage and on TV, where she was a regular on the sitcoms "All in the Family" (1973–75) and "Laverne and Shirley" (1976–81).

GARSON, GREER. Actress. *(b. Sept. 29, 1908, County Down, Ireland.)* Perhaps the epitome of the MGM star, this elegant, dignified red-headed actress played stiff-upper-lip types in numerous 1940s weepies. Attractive but reserved, she endowed her characters with warmth and poise. After much work on stage, Garson came to Hollywood after debuting in *Goodbye, Mr. Chips* (1939), and remained to star in such popular, big-budgeted fare as *Pride and Prejudice* (1940, as Elizabeth), *Blossoms in the Dust,* and *When Ladies Meet* (both 1941), before being cast as the indomitable British matriarch in *Mrs. Miniver* (1942), an Oscar-winning characterization she reprised in *The Miniver Story* (1950) with her frequent costar Walter Pidgeon. She scored another triumph, cast against type, as a lively music-hall entertainer who took amnesiac Ronald Colman under her wing in *Random Harvest* (also 1942).

Her subsequent films include *Madame Curie* (1943), *Mrs. Parkington* (1944), *Adventure* (which prompted the immortal ad line, "Gable's Back and Garson's Got Him!"), *The Valley of Decision* (both 1945), *Desire Me* (1947), *Julia Misbehaves* (1948, which gave her a rare slapstick turn), *That Forsyte Woman* (1949), and *Julius Caesar* (1953, as Calpurnia). In later years Garson appeared only occasionally on-screen, in such films as *Sunrise at Campobello* (1960, playing Eleanor Roosevelt), *The Singing Nun* (1966), and *The Happiest Millionaire* (1967), coming out of happy retirement only to make a very rare TV or documentary appearance. One example: 1978's TV remake of *Little Women.* She earned seven Oscar nominations in all—for *Mr. Chips, Blossoms, Madame Curie, Mrs. Parkington, Valley of Decision,* and *Campobello.*

GASSMAN, VITTORIO. Actor, screenwriter, director. *(b. Sept. 1, 1922, Genoa.)* One of Italy's most popular and enduring stage and screen stars, Gassman had originally planned to become a lawyer, but encouraged by his mother, he entered Rome's Accademia Nazionale di Arte Dramatica. He made his stage debut in Milan in 1943 and became a highly respected actor, with more than 40 plays to his credit when he made his first film *Preludio d'amore* (1946). Gassman won notice outside of Italy playing Silvana Mangano's lover in the international hit *Bitter Rice* (1948), and as the villain in *Anna* (1951). He came to the U.S. in 1952 to visit actress Shelley Winters, and eventually married her. He signed a contract with MGM and made several mediocre films like *The Glass Wall, Cry of the Hunted* (both 1953), *Mambo,* and *Rhapsody* (both 1954), which if nothing else helped establish his name in this country. Unhappy, he ended the contract (and his marriage to Winters) and returned to Italy where he regained his popularity on the stage and formed his own theater company.

Gassman began a new phase of his film career as a bumbling crook in the classic caper *Big Deal on Madonna Street* (1958), which revealed his previously unsuspected comic abilities. He cemented his appeal with more comedies like *The Easy Life, Love and Larceny* (both 1963), *Let's Talk About Women* (1964), and *The Tiger and the Pussycat* (1967), and proved he still had an impressive range as the blind, retired military man in *Profumo di donna/Scent of a Woman* (1974), for which he won the Best Actor Award at Cannes.

After the charming comedy-drama *We All Loved Each Other So Much* (1977), Gassman returned to American films as the groom's father in Robert Altman's *A Wedding* (1978) and also appeared in *Quintet* (1979), *Sharky's Machine* (1981), and *Tempest* (1982). He is still as popular as ever in Italian films like *Big Deal on Madonna Street . . . 20 Years Later* (1986), and commands the screen playing grand roles like the demanding patriarch in *The Family* (1987) and the outrageous title character in *The Sleazy Uncle* (1991). Gassman also codirected, cowrote, and starred in *Kean* (1957), the three-episode *L'Alibi* (1969), and *Senza famiglia nullatenenti cercano affetto* (1972).

GAVIN, JOHN. Actor. *(b. Apr. 8, 1928, Los Angeles.)* He lost on-screen lover Janet Leigh to a madman's knife in *Psycho* (1960), scarcely batting an eye upon hearing the news. And that was probably his *best* screen performance! A stoic, handsome but colorless leading man whose first film was *Behind the High Wall* (1956), Gavin served for a time as president of the Screen Actors Guild, one of his more noteworthy Hollywood roles. His first major lead, in the classic weepie *Imitation of Life* (1959), led to his appearances in *Psycho* and *Spartacus* the following year. In the wake of innumerable spy spoofs that appeared after the success of James Bond, he starred in the French-Italian coproduction *O.S.S. 117 Double Agent* (1967), and later in *Thoroughly Modern Millie* (1967), *Pussycat, Pussycat I Love You* (1970), and *Heidi* (1979). He also starred in two failed TV series, "Destry" (1964) and "Convoy" (1965), before leaving show business for politics; during the Reagan administration he served as the U.S. Ambassador to Mexico. He is married to actress Constance Towers.

GAYNOR, JANET. Actress. *(b. Oct. 6, 1906, Philadelphia, as Laura Gainor; d. Sept. 14, 1984.)* The winner of the first Best Actress Oscar for her cumulative work in *Sunrise, Seventh Heaven* (both 1927), and *Street Angel* (1928), Janet Gaynor attained stardom by virtue of her ability to project sweetness without becoming cloying. The petite, winsome actress was pretty but not beautiful, convincing but not charismatic, and dependable but not inspired. Growing up in San Francisco, she came to Hollywood after high school specifically to get into pictures. She took odd jobs and played bit parts in Hal Roach comedies and cheap Westerns, but her career finally took off when she was cast opposite George O'Brien in the spectacular *The Johnstown Flood* (1926). She found herself incorporated into the Fox Studio's "Irish Mafia," working with John Ford in *The Shamrock Handicap,* with Ford and O'Brien in *The Blue Eagle* (both 1926), and with Charles Farrell in the smash hit *Seventh Heaven,* movingly playing a Parisian waif.

Gaynor was also a favorite of German director F. W. Murnau, who cast the diminutive actress in *Sunrise* (1927, again with O'Brien in this timeless classic, arguably the apogee of silent-film art) and *Four Devils* (1928). But Gaynor was best known for her on-screen teaming with Farrell, with whom she costarred in 10 films, among them *Street Angel* (1928), the moving *Lucky Star* and the jaunty musical *Sunny Side Up* (both 1929). Her delicate voice perfectly matched her dainty appearance, and she made the transition to talking pictures without trouble, although her type of screen heroine became an endangered species in the early 1930s.

She was superb as the orphan in *Daddy Long Legs* (1931) and made a strong impression in the first screen version of *State Fair* (1933). Making two pictures a year through the mid 1930s, Gaynor was voted the movies' top box-office female star in 1934. After *Ladies in Love* (1936), Gaynor left Fox for freelance work. She received an Oscar nomination for *A Star Is Born* (1937), one of her most endearing and persuasive performances, but after appearing in *Three Loves Has Nancy* and *Young in Heart* (both 1938) she retired from the screen. She did make occasional radio and TV appearances, but returned to the big screen only once for a mother role in *Bernadine* (1957) at her old studio, 20th Century-Fox. Her second husband was designer Gilbert Adrian, and she later married producer Paul Gregory. Gaynor died following complications from a car crash that also injured actress Mary Martin.

GAYNOR, MITZI. Actress, dancer. *(b. Sept. 4, 1930, Chicago, as Franceska Mitzi Gerber.)* Vivacious, voluptuous dancer, a former child ballerina who performed with the Los Angeles Civic Light Opera. *My Blue Heaven* (1950), Gaynor's first film, revealed a prodigious talent and a pleasing personality that should have boosted her to stardom. Unfortunately, most of her subsequent vehicles were second-rate musicals at best: *Take Care of My Little Girl, Golden Girl* (both 1951), *Bloodhounds of Broadway* (1952), *The I Don't Care Girl* (1953), *There's No Business Like Show Business* (1954), and *Anything Goes* (1956). *The Birds and the Bees* (1956) offered a comedy lead, *Les Girls* (1957) a chance to costar with Gene Kelly, and *South Pacific* (1958) the incredible opportunity to star in a world-famous Rodgers and Hammerstein musical. But again, the results were somehow disappointing. Her last feature film to date has been *For Love or Money* (1963); she subsequently carved out a niche for herself in live performances, and has toured successfully in nightclubs and theaters for several decades, as well as starring in her own TV specials.

GAZZARA, BEN. Actor. *(b. Aug. 28, 1930, New York City, as Biagio Anthony Gazzara.)* Tough, intelligent actor from the streets of Manhattan's Lower East Side, who first studied acting at New York's

New School for Social Research before working at the Actors' Studio. Like other New York-based actors during the early 1950s, he toiled in off-Broadway plays and on TV before landing on Broadway. His dark, sinister looks enabled him to make an arresting film debut in 1957's *The Strange One*, playing a disturbed military student. Gazzara played tough guys in *Anatomy of a Murder* (1959) and *Convicts Four* (1962), but he's also noted for his naturalistic, more sympathetic performances in three films by John Cassavetes: *Husbands* (1970), *The Killing of a Chinese Bookie* (1976), and *Opening Night* (1977). He also appeared as a Charles Bukowski–like figure in the independent feature *Tales of Ordinary Madness* (1981). Curiously, most people recognize him as the star of the TV series "Run for Your Life" (1965–68). During the 1980s he worked extensively in Italian films, but late in the decade returned home to ham it up as a scurrilous crime lord in *Road House* (1989). *Beyond the Ocean* (1990), which he also wrote and directed, has yet to be released. Gazzara was once married to actress Janice Rule. OTHER FILMS INCLUDE: 1961: *The Young Doctors;* 1973: *The Neptune Factor;* 1975: *Capone* (in the title role); 1976: *Voyage of the Damned;* 1979: *Saint Jack, Bloodline;* 1981: *They All Laughed;* 1982: *Inchon;* 1994: *Parallel Lives* (telefilm).

GEESON, JUDY. Actress. *(b. Sept. 10, 1948, Arundel, England.)* Pretty, girlish British ingenue who began her career playing plucky nymphets. She made her film debut in 1967 as a schoolgirl in *To Sir With Love*, which she followed up with roles in the prominent British features *Prudence and the Pill* (1968) and *Three Into Two Won't Go* (1969). Geeson proved to be an appealing female lead, albeit one of limited ability. Much of her subsequent film work has been in low-rung horror efforts, including *Doomwatch* (1972) and *Horror Planet* (1982), the latter a career nadir in which she plays a woman raped by an alien creature. More recently she has been active on stage and television, both in England and the U.S.

GELBART, LARRY. Screenwriter, playwright. *(b. Feb. 25, 1925, Chicago.)* Brilliant comedy writer renowed for his intricate, dazzling wordplay, whom Mel Brooks has called "the fastest of the fast, the wittiest man in the business." At the age of 16, he began writing gags for Danny Thomas, then made his name on the staff of radio's "Duffy's Tavern," followed by Bob Hope's popular radio show, and later, TV's legendary "Your Show of Shows." In 1962, he cowrote the Tony Award–winning Broadway musical "A Funny Thing Happened on the Way to the Forum," and cowrote his first screenplay, *The Notorious Landlady.* His film work since then has been sporadic, with the ingenious black comedy *The Wrong Box* (1966), the warm-hearted fable *Oh, God!* (1977, his first solo screen credit; Oscar-nominated), and the delightful thirties movie parody *Movie Movie* (1978) among the best, and *The Chastity Belt* (1968) and *Neighbors* (1981) among the worst. Other credits include *Not With My Wife You Don't!* (1966, cowriter), *A Fine Pair* (1969, cowriter), *Rough Cut* (1980, from which he had his name removed), and *Blame It on Rio* (1984), but his highwater mark came with *Tootsie* (1982), which in spite of numerous rewrites and tinkerings emerged a smash hit and one of the smartest comedies of the 1980s. It earned Gelbart another Oscar nomination, as "official" cowriter. He has remained active in theater ("Sly Fox," "City of Angels," "Mastergate") and created the landmark TV adaptation of Robert Altman's *MASH* (1972–83), which he produced and wrote for its first four seasons. That earned him the clout to develop another series without network interference or input, but "United States" (1980) was a commercial dud. In 1993 he wrote the dazzling cable-TV movie *Barbarians at the Gate,* which managed to turn a serious book about big-business wheeling and dealing into the stuff of grand entertainment.

GENN, LEO. Actor. *(b. Aug. 9, 1905, London; d. Jan. 26, 1978.)* Dark, urbane, silky-voiced British supporting player and character lead, a former lawyer who exchanged one form of acting for another. Although he'd made several films before World War 2 (including 1935's *The Immortal Gentleman* and 1938's *Drums*), and actually appeared in several during

the war while on leave (most notably Olivier's 1944 *Henry V,* playing the Constable of France), Genn achieved his real success after the conflict. He invested most of his roles with quiet authority, and was a favorite both in England and the U.S. on stage and screen.
OTHER FILMS INCLUDE: 1946: *Green for Danger* (as a murder suspect in this classic whodunit); 1947: *Mourning Becomes Electra;* 1948: *The Snake Pit* (as a sympathetic psychiatrist); 1950: *The Miniver Story;* 1951: *The Magic Box, Quo Vadis?* (in an Oscar-nominated turn as Petronius); 1955: *Lady Chatterley's Lover;* 1956: *Moby Dick* (as Starbuck); 1960: *Too Hot to Handle;* 1962: *The Longest Day;* 1965: *Ten Little Indians;* 1967: *Psycho-Circus;* 1973: *Escape to Nowhere;* 1975: *The Martyr.*

GEORGE, GLADYS. Actress. *(b. Sept. 13, 1900, Patton, Maine, as Gladys Anna Clare; d. Dec. 8, 1954.)* Born into a family of actors, this blond beauty achieved stage stardom in the 1920s and worked in a few unimportant silent films. Her movie career really blossomed in the mid 1930s when, in spite of her comedic talents, her most memorable roles were in tearjerkers and melodramas. She played a few leads, but soon became typed as a supporting player. She was particularly touching as the dissipated nightclubber who delivered James Cagney's epitaph in the last line of *The Roaring Twenties:* "He used to be a tough guy." She died of throat cancer in 1954.
OTHER FILMS INCLUDE: 1936: *Valiant Is the Word for Carrie* (for which she was Oscar-nominated); 1937: *They Gave Him a Gun, Madame X* (in the title role); 1940: *The Way of All Flesh;* 1946: *The Best Years of Our Lives;* 1951: Lullaby of Broadway (as Doris Day's mother).

GEORGE, SUSAN. Actress, producer. *(b. July 26, 1950, Surbiton, Surrey, England.)* A blond, usually tanned, attractive leading lady with Keane-Kid eyes, George has worked in films from the age of four. She's best remembered for her effective performance as Dustin Hoffman's victimized wife in *Straw Dogs* (1971). George also starred in *Dirty Mary Crazy Larry,* a surprise, low-budget action hit of 1974. She recently went to work behind the cameras as executive producer of *Stealing*

Heaven (1988) and *That Summer of White Roses* (1989). George is married to actor Simon MacCorkindale.
OTHER FILMS INCLUDE: 1967: *Billion Dollar Brain;* 1975: *Mandingo;* 1977: *Tintorera;* 1981: *Venom;* 1984: *The Jigsaw Man.*

GERE, RICHARD. Actor. *(b. Aug. 29, 1949, Philadelphia.)* The prototypical, dark, handsome leading man, Gere has made a career out of contradiction, appearing in big-budget megahits and shoestring potboilers alike, playing sensitive, generous heroes and coldhearted, ruthless villains with equal aplomb. Born to an artistically inclined family, Gere grew up on a farm outside of Syracuse, New York, where he spent much time writing and playing music. He attended the University of Massachusetts, but dropped out to join a rock 'n' roll commune in Vermont in 1970. His interest in acting eventually led Gere to New York, and he appeared on Broadway in "Grease" before landing his first screen roles, in *Report to the Commissioner* (1975) and *Baby Blue Marine* (1976). Gere's stock rose considerably in 1977 based on his riveting supporting role as a violent hustler in *Looking for Mr. Goodbar.* The next year he landed his first starring role in Terrence Malick's elegiac *Days of Heaven,* a lavishly shot epic that earned significant critical praise. Gere then starred in a pair of box-office disappointments, *Yanks* (1979) and the pretentious *American Gigolo* (1980), before scoring a major hit opposite Debra Winger in *An Officer and a Gentleman* (1982). This should have led to superstardom, but instead he found himself in a string of bombs that nearly relegated his career to the scrap heap. The misunderstood (and critically savaged) *King David* (1985), the lackluster *No Mercy,* the sanctimonious *Power* (both 1986), and the ill-conceived *Miles From Home* (1988) severely diminished his stature.
Just when he was about to become a Trivial Pursuit question, Gere bounced back in 1990 with the sleeper *Internal Affairs,* in which he played a chillingly corrupt, amoral cop, and the year's biggest hit, *Pretty Woman.* As the wealthy Prince Charming who rescues prostitute Julia Roberts, Gere made feminine hearts pitter-patter and thus immediately shot back into the limelight. *Final Analysis* (1992), a

sleazy but high-profile thriller, cast him as a psychiatrist enmeshed in a murder plot. He then executive produced and starred in *Sommersby* (1993), as a mystery man returning to his supposed wife after the Civil War, and appeared in *Mr. Jones,* the TV movie *And the Band Played On* (both 1993), *Intersection* (1994), and *First Knight* (1995, as Lancelot). Gere has used his commercial visibility to promote a number of social causes, most notably the plight of the exiled Tibetan religious leader, the Dalai Lama. He was married to model Cindy Crawford.

GERTZ, JAMI. Actress. *(b. Oct. 28, 1965, Chicago.)* Raven-tressed young actress who won a nationwide talent search run by Norman Lear, and landed the part of the annoying preppie, Muffy, on the TV sitcom "Square Pegs." She made her film debut in the now legendary 1981 bomb *Endless Love* (starring Brooke Shields) and, as if to make amends, went on to study drama at New York University. She subsequently appeared in such films as *Sixteen Candles, Alphabet City* (both 1984), *Mischief* (1985), *Crossroads, Quicksilver, Solarbabies* (all 1986), and *The Lost Boys* (1987), always cast as a fresh-faced teenager but somehow escaping inclusion in the 1980s "Brat Pack" of young actors. *Less Than Zero* (1987), an annoying screen version of Bret Easton Ellis' briefly trendy novel, gave her a chance to stretch somewhat as one of the cocaine-era "lost generation" of spoiled, wealthy college kids in Beverly Hills. Other credits include *Listen to Me, Renegades* (both 1989), *Sibling Rivalry* (1990), and *Don't Tell Her It's Me* (1991), as well as the 1991 TV sitcom "Sibs," and the 1994 TV movie *This Can't Be Love.*

GIANNINI, GIANCARLO. Actor. *(b. Aug. 1, 1942, Spezia, Italy.)* It's a tribute to Giannini's personality and screen presence that he's best remembered for a series of starring roles (mostly for director Lina Wertmuller) that cast him as dull-witted, naive, pompous, and/or slovenly characters. This charming, expressive Italian performer first studied acting at the Academia Nazionale in Rome, and made his screen debut in a small part in *Fango sulla metropoli* (1965). His association with Wertmuller dates back to the early 1960s, when he acted in her play "Two and Two Are No Longer Four." He appeared in supporting roles in *Anzio* (1968) and *The Secret of Santa Vittoria* (1969), among others, before Wertmuller chose him for the lead in *Love and Anarchy* (1973). He also starred in her first internationally acclaimed feature, *The Seduction of Mimi* (1974), playing an innocent stooge duped into an assassination plot. Giannini, by now the recipient of worldwide recognition, continued with Wertmuller in *Swept Away* (1975, as a coarse sailor marooned on a desert island with haughty Mariangela Melato) and *Seven Beauties* (1976, as a penny-ante lothario). This last film earned Giannini an Oscar nomination for Best Actor.

Giannini was seen to advantage in Luchino Visconti's *The Innocent* (1976), opposite Jennifer O'Neill and Laura Antonelli, and in Rainer Werner Fassbinder's *Lili Marleen* (1981). He also starred with Candice Bergen in Wertmuller's (disappointing) first English-language feature, *A Night Full of Rain* (1978). Efforts to broaden his appeal to Anglo audiences resulted in a few turkeys, including *American Dreamer* (1984), *Fever Pitch* (1985), and *Blood Red* (1989). Giannini was back in form, though, as the hapless nephew of scheming Vittorio Gassman in *The Sleazy Uncle* (1991), and as a deadpan police inspector in *Once Upon a Crime* (1992). He was also charming in the otherwise forgettable Francis Ford Coppola–directed sequence of *New York Stories* (1989).

GIBSON, HOOT. Actor. *(b. Aug. 6, 1892, Takamah, Nebr., as Edmund Richard Gibson; d. Aug. 23, 1962.)* If Tom Mix was the silent-era King of the Cowboys, then Hoot Gibson surely was the Clown Prince. An expert rider, Gibson generally played an easygoing cowboy whose exploits provoked as many laughs as thrills. He's been frequently described as "genially homely," thanks to a doughy face and snub-nose, but ranks with the screen's top cowboy stars nonetheless. A former circus performer, working cowboy, and rodeo rider, he entered the film business as a wrangler for Universal, but shortly graduated to stunts and bit parts. He frequently supported Harry Carey in films directed by

John (then Jack) Ford, most notably *Straight Shooting* (1917). By 1919 he was starring in two-reel Westerns, and only a few years later was making features. Gibson was one of Universal's mainstays throughout the 1920s; his starring vehicles were marketed to exhibitors as A pictures, including such hits as *Hit and Run* (1924), *Calgary Stampede* (1925), *Flaming Frontier, Chip of the Flying U* (both 1926), *The Silent Rider* (1927), and *King of the Rodeo* (1929).

Although Hoot (so named, reportedly, for his owl-hunting prowess) made the transition to sound without much apparent difficulty—beginning with 1920's *The Long Long Trail*—he was dropped by Universal in 1930 when the studio suspended Western production. He signed with a succession of independent producers and made several series of progressively cheaper horse operas, including *Wild Horse* (1931), *The Boiling Point, The Cowboy Counsellor* (both 1932), *Sunset Range* (1935), and *The Riding Avenger* (1936). He was offscreen for several years before making a comeback of sorts, teamed with Ken Maynard in the ultracheap "Trail Blazers" series made for Monogram in 1943–44. *Wild Horse Stampede, Blazing Guns* (both 1943), and *Sonora Stagecoach* (1944) show a tired-looking, overweight, and lethargic Gibson just going through the motions. Hoot retired, returning to the screen intermittently thereafter (in 1947's *Flight to Nowhere* and 1953's *The Marshal's Daughter,* for example). His final film work, a supporting role in 1959's *The Horse Soldiers,* was undertaken for his old friend and mentor John Ford. Gibson, who offscreen was a fast-living, hard-drinking free spirit, was thrice married to actresses: Helen Wagner (who, as Helen Gibson, was a star of silent serials), Sally Eilers, and June Gale.

GIBSON, MEL. Actor. *(b. Jan. 3, 1956, Peekskill, N.Y.)* The not-very-obscure object of desire for countless female film fans, this Australian heartthrob was actually born in the U.S., emigrating Down Under at the age of 12. His grandmother was an Australian opera singer who had moved to the States, and when Gibson's father, a railroad brakeman, was injured on the job,

he used the settlement money to move Gibson and his 11 siblings back to the old country. Gibson studied at the National Institute of Dramatic Arts, where as a student he made his cinema debut in *Summer City* (1976). Three years later he was cast as a young retarded man in *Tim* (1979), which earned him Australia's equivalent of the Oscar. He then won the lead in a grade-B sci-fi film called *Mad Max,* and that film's improbable success (over \$100 million at the box office and two sequels) launched Gibson on the road to stardom. *Road Warrior* (1981) satisfied his *Mad Max* fans, but Gibson scored mainstream successes in starring roles in two pictures directed by fellow Aussie Peter Weir. In *Gallipoli* (1981) he played a young soldier unaware of impending massacre, and in *The Year of Living Dangerously* (1983), he portrayed an Australian journalist and sometime love interest of Sigourney Weaver. He costarred with Anthony Hopkins in *The Bounty* (1984), taking the Fletcher Christian role that was previously played by Clark Gable and Marlon Brando.

Gibson has worked hard to shed the image, in which he was typed early in his career, as a good-looking hunk with meager acting talents. In addition to bread-and-butter roles in such action pictures and thrillers as *Mad Max: Beyond Thunderdome* (1985) and *Tequila Sunrise* (1988), he has tackled more demanding roles, notably opposite Diane Keaton in *Mrs. Soffel* (1984) and playing the title role (surprisingly well) in *Hamlet* (1990). He's most popular in lighthearted fare, where he can superimpose his own boisterous humor on his characters: the *Lethal Weapon* trilogy (1987, 1989, 1992), *Bird on a Wire,* and *Air America* (both 1990). The father of six children, he has shown real interest in upbeat, heartwarming movie fare, as evidenced by the romantic drama *Forever Young* (1992) and the film he chose for his directing debut, *The Man Without a Face* (1993), in which he also starred. He returned to his métier for the movie version of *Maverick* (1994), then tackled the hugely ambitious epic *Braveheart* (1995) and did himself proud as actor, director, and producer. In 1995 he also provided the voice of Captain John Smith for Disney's animated *Pocahontas.* His film company, Icon Productions, made the

Beethoven biopic *Immortal Beloved* (1994).

GIELGUD, JOHN (SIR). Actor, director. (b. Apr. 14, 1904, London.) One of the greatest actors of the century, who has become one of the most prolific film stars in recent memory. He debuted on stage at the Old Vic in London in 1921, with one line in "Henry V" ("Here is the number of the slaughter's French"), and went on to become a virtuoso Shakespearean actor, noted for his supremely beautiful voice. He played Romeo, King Lear, Macbeth, Antony, and a young Hamlet in 1930 that was referred to as "the high-water mark of English Shakespearean acting in our time." He did comedy and directed as well, and toured with "Hamlet" and "Blithe Spirit" during World War 2. Though he had debuted in the film *Who Is the Man?* (1924) and had starred in Alfred Hitchcock's *Secret Agent* (1936) and *The Prime Minister* (1941), he did not take movie work seriously until the 1950s, when he appeared as Cassius in *Julius Caesar* (1953), and lent his expertise to the endeavor. His presence, according to film historian David Shipman, "set the tone of the production." That same year, he was knighted for his service to the arts in England.

While still performing and directing for the stage in England and the U.S. (winning a Tony Award for directing the play "Big Fish, Little Fish"), he was memorable on-screen in *Richard III* (1955, opposite Laurence Olivier and Ralph Richardson), *Becket* (1964, an Oscar-nominated turn as King Louis VII), *The Loved One* (1965, a delicious black-comedy performance), *Oh! What a Lovely War* (1969), and *Providence* (1977). But it was his Oscar-winning comic performance as Dudley Moore's acid-tongued manservant in *Arthur* (1981) that resulted in widespread recognition from the movie-going masses. He has since added his regal presence to such films as *Chariots of Fire* (1981), *Gandhi* (1982), *The Shooting Party, Plenty* (both 1985), *The Whistle Blower* (1987), the controversial *Prospero's Books* (1991), *Shining Through,* and *The Power of One* (both 1992). That same year he starred in a short subject for director Kenneth Branagh called *Swan Song,* based on a Chekhov playlet about an aged actor. He has also acted in many TV films and miniseries, most notably "Brideshead Revisited," "War and Remembrance," and "Summer's Lease," for which he won an Emmy. He has written several books, including the memoirs "Early Stages" (1939) and "An Actor and His Times" (1979).

GIFFORD, FRANCES. Actress. (b. Dec. 7, 1920, Long Beach, Calif., as Mary Frances Gifford; d. Jan. 22, 1994.) She had young boys' hearts a-thumpin' as the scantily clad Nyoka in a 1941 Republic serial, *Jungle Girl,* and although she's probably best remembered for that role, this brunette beauty might have achieved much more. Beginning her acting career right out of high school, Gifford played bits and did extra work in such films as *Stage Door* (1937) and *Mr. Smith Goes to Washington* (1939) before costarring with then-husband James Dunn in two PRC cheapies, *Mercy Plane* and *Hold That Woman* (both 1940). She was extremely winning as Robert Benchley's studio tour guide in Walt Disney's *The Reluctant Dragon* (1941), looking especially beautiful in Technicolor. That same year she was signed by Paramount, where she had both supporting parts (1942's *The Glass Key,* 1943's *Henry Aldrich Gets Glamour*) and leads (*Tombstone—the Town Too Tough to Die, American Empire,* both 1942). After playing another jungle girl in *Tarzan Triumphs* (1943), Gifford moved to MGM, where she was given better roles in bigger pictures and showed real promise in *Cry Havoc* (1943), *Marriage Is a Private Affair* (1944), *Our Vines Have Tender Grapes* (1945), *The Arnelo Affair* (1947), and *Luxury Liner* (1948).

Seriously injured in a 1948 car accident, Gifford never really regained her self-confidence, and after making two films— *Riding High* (1950) and *Sky Commando* (1953)—in a difficult state of mind, she retired from the screen. Gifford spent several years in a mental institution but finally defeated her personal demons and, as recently as the late 1980s, was doing volunteer work for charitable organizations in Southern California.

GILBERT, BILLY. Actor. (b. Sept. 12, 1894, Louisville, Ky., as William Gilbert

Baron; d. Sept. 23, 1971.) One of the screen's most beloved character actors, Billy Gilbert is remembered for two particular talents: his skill as a dialectician and his ability to stretch a simple sneeze into a hilarious routine. (He was, reportedly, the only actor considered for the voice of Sneezy in Disney's *Snow White and the Seven Dwarfs.*) He played in vaudeville and burlesque prior to going to Hollywood in the late 1920s. He trouped in dozens of comedy shorts during the 1930s, supporting Laurel and Hardy, Charley Chase, and the Our Gang kids, and sometimes starring for producer Hal Roach. The moon-faced, bearlike Gilbert also appeared in more than 200 feature films, sometimes in prominent support and sometimes in tiny, unbilled bits, sneaking in his sneezing routine as often as he could get away with it. He played Greeks, Italians, Spaniards, and Germans with equal facility. Films include *Million Dollar Legs* (1932), *A Night at the Opera* (1935, one of those tiny walk-ons), *Sutter's Gold* (1936), *On the Avenue, Captains Courageous, 100 Men and a Girl* (all 1937), *Block-Heads* (1938), *Destry Rides Again* (1939), *His Girl Friday* (1940, as Joe Pettibone), *The Great Dictator* (1940, as Herring), *Tin Pan Alley* (1940, as the Sheik of Araby), *Week-end in Havana* (1941), *Anchors Aweigh* (1945), *Down Among the Sheltering Palms* (1953), and *Five Weeks in a Balloon* (1962). He also endeared himself to a generation of kids on TV's "Andy's Gang."

GILBERT, JOHN. Actor. *(b. July 10, 1899, Logan, Utah, as John Pringle; d. Jan. 9, 1936.)* One of the great stars of the silent screen, John Gilbert saw his career plummet in talkies—but not for the reason that's usually cited. Deliberate sabotage, not a high-pitched voice, was the likely culprit. Born into a theatrical family, Gilbert was already a stage veteran when he joined the Ince-Triangle film forces in 1916, working at first in William S. Hart's *Hell's Hinges.* Graduating to starring roles within a few years, he worked with top leading ladies Colleen Moore and Mary Pickford before signing with Fox, where he starred in a lavish production of *Monte Cristo* (1922) and played *Cameo Kirby* (1923) for director John Ford. In 1924 he

joined producer Louis B. Mayer, who'd just merged with Metro and Goldwyn, and made *He Who Gets Slapped* (1924) with Swedish director Victor Seastrom, *The Merry Widow* (1925) for Erich von Stroheim, and *The Big Parade* (1925) with King Vidor. It's for his work in that picture, the biggest box-office success of the silent era, that Gilbert is primarily remembered; as the clean-cut, idealistic young soldier exposed to the horrors of war, only to find true love right in the midst of it, Gilbert was comical, courageous, and tragic. It was his finest hour.

He capitalized on his popularity with *La Boheme* (1926, opposite Lillian Gish) and three films with Greta Garbo, *Flesh and the Devil* (1926), *Love* (1927), and *A Woman of Affairs* (1928). (The Gilbert-Garbo romance was duplicated offscreen, but a planned marriage never took place, and when Mayer suggested that Gilbert shouldn't have bothered, the star punched him in the face.) Gilbert also starred in modest program pictures such as *The Show, Twelve Miles Out* (both 1927), *The Cossacks* (1928), and *Desert Nights* (1929).

Although he made a good impression in a cameo for *The Hollywood Revue of 1929,* Gilbert suffered in his first starring talkie, *His Glorious Night* (1929), from the inept direction of actor Lionel Barrymore, and it proved to be a notorious failure. The legend that Gilbert's voice did not record well, however, is just that. It's widely believed that Mayer deliberately sabotaged the picture, partly out of revenge for the slugging, and partially because Gilbert's lucrative financial arrangement made his pictures less profitable to the studio: His MGM contract called for a salary of $250,000 a picture, and as his popularity slipped, the studio cut back on money for stories and directors, exacerbating Gilbert's tailspin. *Downstairs* (1932), for example, was a good picture (which the star also cowrote) but audiences disliked seeing the romantic hero as a ruthless womanizer.

Alcoholism contributed to Gilbert's decline, but he returned to MGM in 1933 at Garbo's request to play in *Queen Christina* (1933), and gave a creditable performance in Lewis Milestone's *The Captain Hates the Sea* (1934). He was scheduled to appear opposite Marlene Dietrich in *The Garden of Allah* when he suffered a fatal heart attack. Three of his four wives were actresses: Leatrice Joy, Ina Claire, and Virginia Bruce. His daughter, Leatrice Gilbert Fountain, tried to set her father's story straight in the biography "Dark Star."

GILBERT, LEWIS. Director, screenwriter, producer. *(b. Mar. 6, 1920, London.)* Veteran British director who began his film career as a child actor in silent films. He abandoned performing after *The Divorce of Lady X* (1938) and moved behind the camera, working as an assistant director. He made documentaries for the Royal Air Force during World War 2, while serving with the U.S. Air Corps Film Unit. Afterwards, he made more documentaries and debuted as a feature director with *The Little Ballerina* (1947). He directed comedies like *Time Gentlemen Please* (1952) and thrillers like *The Good Die Young* (1954), but made his reputation with a series of popular, sentimental, and often exciting war films (which he also wrote, cowrote, and/or produced) that include *The Sea Shall Not Have Them* (1954), *Reach for the Sky* (1956), *Carve Her Name With Pride* (1958), *Sink the Bismarck!* (1960) and *Damn the Defiant!* (1962). He switched gears with *Loss of Innocence* (1961), a nicely handled coming-of-age story, and later struck a worldwide chord with the sleeper hit *Alfie* (1966), the then-scandalous account of a Cockney swinger which rocketed Michael Caine to stardom. Since then, Gilbert has tackled teen romance in the awful *Friends* (1971) and *Paul and Michelle* (1974), as well as action-oriented films like *The Adventurers* (1970), *Operation Daybreak* (1976) and the three James Bond outings *You Only Live Twice* (1967), *The Spy Who Loved Me* (1977, one of the best Roger Moore entries) and *Moonraker* (1979). Gilbert also enjoyed success with adaptations of Willy Russell's stage plays *Educating Rita* (1983, with Julie Walters and Michael Caine in one of his best performances) and *Shirley Valentine* (1989).

GILFORD, JACK. Actor. *(b. July 25, 1907, New York City, as Jacob Gellman; d. June 4, 1990.)* Most baby boomers draw a blank when you mention Jack Gilford's name—until he's identified as the principal player in the 1960s long-running TV commercial for Cracker Jack. The rubber-faced Gilford was also a former vaudeville performer who, following his 1944 screen debut in *Hey, Rookie,* alternated movie work with stage stints. In later years, he specialized in kindly-old-timer roles (generally in high-profile comedies), but snagged an Oscar nomination for a superbly limned, dramatic character portrayal in *Save the Tiger* (1973).
OTHER FILMS INCLUDE: 1966: *A Funny Thing Happened on the Way to the Forum* (a career high point); 1967: *Enter Laughing;* 1969: *Who's Minding the Mint?;* 1970: *Catch-22;* 1971: *They Might Be Giants;* 1985: *Cocoon;* 1988: *Arthur 2: On the Rocks, Cocoon: The Return.*

GILROY, FRANK D. Screenwriter, director, playwright. *(b. Oct. 13, 1925, New York City.)* Gilroy began as a TV writer in the 1950s for shows like "Playhouse 90," "Kraft Television Theatre," and "Studio One" and cowrote the screenplays for *The Fastest Gun Alive* (1956) and *The Gallant Hours* (1960). He won fame—and a 1965 Pulitzer Prize—for the Broadway play "The Subject Was Roses," a strong family drama that he later adapted for the 1968 film with Patricia Neal. He also adapted his play "The Only Game in Town" for Warren Beatty and Elizabeth Taylor (1970), before making his directing debut the next year with *Desperate Characters* (1971, which he also adapted), an acclaimed study of a couple living in Brooklyn that features one of Shirley MacLaine's best performances. Gilroy went on to write and direct a series of small, offbeat (and little-seen) projects: a wry comic vehicle for Charles Bronson and Jill Ireland, *From Noon Till Three* (1976), the charming comedy *Once in Paris . . .* (1978), the perceptive character study *The Gig* (1985), and the winning fable *The Luckiest Man in the World* (1989). He also cowrote the Bette Midler bomb *Jinxed!* (1982), under a pseudonym.

GISH, LILLIAN. Actress. *(b. Oct. 14, 1893, Springfield, Ohio; d. Feb. 27, 1993.)* How to describe this luminous actress, so fragile, almost waiflike in appearance (even well into maturity), but so strong, so passionate in performance? She was, quite simply, one of the greatest talents to emerge from motion pictures, and certainly the finest of the silent-screen actresses. On stage from the age of 5, Lillian Gish first worked in movies with her sister Dorothy in 1912. An introduction from their friend Mary Pickford brought them to director D. W. Griffith, who cast them as on-screen siblings in *An Unseen Enemy* (and even gave their mother a role in the picture). Lillian, whose soulful presence perfectly suited the "Griffith heroine," quickly became one of the director's leading actresses. Among her early films for the Biograph company were some of the era's most outstanding, including *The Musketeers of Pig Alley* (1912), *The Lady and the Mouse* (1913), and *The Battle at Elderbrush Gulch* (1914). When Griffith left Biograph that same year to join Reliance-Majestic, Gish followed and starred in *Home, Sweet Home* and *The Battle of the Sexes* for him, as well as a number of pictures for other directors. Her breakthrough film was *The Birth of a Nation* (1915), Griffith's epic tale of the Civil War and its aftermath, in which she plays the Southern sweetheart of "Little Colonel" Henry B. Walthall; their homecoming reunion is one of the greatest moments in all screen history.

In Griffith's *Intolerance* (1916), another masterpiece, Gish had the symbolic role of The Woman Who Rocks the Cradle, but through the rest of 1916 and into 1917 Gish worked for other filmmakers turning out modest films for the Triangle–Fine Arts program. She then reached her career summit with a succession of Griffith classics: *Hearts of the World* (1918), *True Heart Susie, Broken Blossoms* (both 1919), *Way Down East* (1920, with the still-astounding ice-floe sequence, a physically demanding one for Gish), and *Orphans of the Storm* (1922, in which she costarred with sister Dorothy). These movies showed Gish in full command of her art, displaying a wide range of emotion with great subtlety and surety. In 1923 she left Griffith and acted in two European-made films for director Henry King, with neophyte leading man Ronald Colman, *The White Sister* (1923) and *Romola* (1924); both pictures were notable for their lavish production values, but were dramatically undernourished, and are among her weakest vehicles.

Gish subsequently signed with MGM, securing a contract that gave her story and script approval. MGM initially did well by Gish, with *La Boheme* (1926), costarring John Gilbert and directed by King Vidor, and *The Scarlet Letter* (also 1926), directed by Victor Seastrom. *Annie Laurie* (1927) and *The Enemy* (1928) were star vehicles, pure and simple, that showcased Gish admirably but provided her scant opportunity to break new ground. Her final silent film, *The Wind* (also 1928, directed by Seastrom), proved to be one of the great classics of the silent screen. As a delicate flower plucked from her safe environment and planted by her new husband in a windswept desert, Gish turned in a magnificent performance. But the film was a box-office failure, and at a time when MGM was promoting the flapper image of Joan Crawford and the exotic sensuality of Greta Garbo, Gish no longer seemed to fit at the studio. After making her first talkie, *One Romantic Night* (1930), Gish returned to the stage, where she worked steadily (excepting a brief interlude to make an unmemorable 1933 film called *His Double Life)* in Broadway productions of "Uncle Vanya," "Hamlet" (as Ophelia to John Gielgud's great Dane), and "Camille."

Gish returned to Hollywood as a character actress during World War 2, playing support in *The Commandos Strike at Dawn* (1942) and *Top Man* (1943), but thereafter made only sporadic screen appearances in such pictures as *Miss Susie Slagle's, Duel in the Sun* (both 1946; for the latter she received her only Oscar nomination, as Best Supporting Actress), and *Portrait of Jennie* (1948). *The Cobweb* (1955) was a trifle, but *Night of the Hunter* (also 1955), Charles Laughton's surrealistic adaptation of Davis Grubb's rural gothic, offered Gish her best screen role since *The Wind,* playing the feisty, indomitable spinster who rescues two children from evil preacher Robert Mitchum. It was a characterization different from any she had attempted, and she rose to the challenge magnificently. *Orders to Kill* (1958) and *The Unforgiven* (1960) also gave her good opportunities. The Disney production *Follow Me, Boys!* (1966) was followed in quick succession by *Warning Shot* and *The Comedians* in 1967, after which Gish again departed the screen—until Robert Altman tapped her for a near-comatose cameo in *A Wedding* (1978).

Those who would write her off were proven wrong, as she appeared in the TV remake of *Hobson's Choice* (1983), starred in *Hambone and Hillie* (1984), and contributed a very amusing cameo to *Sweet Liberty* (1986) as Alan Alda's addled mother.

Gish made her final screen appearance in 1987, some 75 years after her screen debut, playing Bette Davis' feisty but protective sister in Lindsay Anderson's elegiac *The Whales of August*. In 1971 she was awarded a special Oscar for "superlative artistry and for distinguished contributions to the progress of motion pictures." Gish wrote two volumes of memoirs, "The Movies, Mr. Griffith, and Me" (1969) and "Dorothy and Lillian Gish" (1973).

GLEASON, JACKIE. Actor. *(b. Feb. 26, 1916, Brooklyn, as Herbert John Gleason; d. June 24, 1987.)* The man who would help define TV comedy in the 1950s toiled without distinction in Hollywood a decade earlier. Minor roles in films with major stars like Bogart and Grable *(All Through the Night, Springtime in the Rockies,* both 1942) led nowhere, and the comedy lead in a 1942 B picture called *Tramp, Tramp, Tramp* was likewise a dead end. Only after his tremendous success on TV, with his own variety show and the immortal "Honeymooners" skits and half-hour series, did Gleason return to the big screen—not in comedy roles, for the most part, but in dramatic characterizations that showed another facet of his great talent. His big-screen peak, reached in the early 1960s, included an Oscar-nominated supporting performance as billiard king Minnesota Fats in *The Hustler* (1961), and skillful starring turns in *Requiem for a Heavyweight, Gigot* (both 1962 the latter a Chaplinesque vehicle which he also cowrote), *Papa's Delicate Condition,* and *Soldier in the Rain* (both 1963). He also appeared in *Skidoo* (1965), *Don't Drink the Water* (based on a Woody Allen play), and *How to Commit Marriage* (both 1969; in the latter teamed with Bob Hope). Considerably slimmed down, he made a screen comeback in the late 1970s, scoring a commercial smash in *Smokey and the Bandit* (1977), as a caricatured redneck sheriff; he also appeared in the 1980 and 1983 sequels. Other late credits include *Mr. Bil-*

lion (1977), *The Sting II, The Toy* (both 1982), and *Nothing in Common* (1986), which gave him one of his all-time best roles, as Tom Hanks' aging and irascible father. He and "Honeymooners" costar Art Carney were reunited in the made-for-TV movie *Izzy and Moe* (1985).

GLEASON, JAMES. Actor, screenwriter. *(b. May 23, 1886, New York City; d. Apr. 12, 1959.)* This native New Yorker, born into a theatrical family, wrote and acted in many popular plays during the Roaring Twenties and went to Hollywood in 1928 as a script doctor (after Fox produced a movie version of his play "Is Zat So?"— later remade in 1935 as *Two Fisted*). He contributed dialogue to several movies (including the original *Broadway Melody*) before settling down to a lengthy career as a character actor. Short and wiry, he specialized in playing feisty, irascible Irish cops, reporters, promoters, and grifters. In the 1930s he starred in two series: as Inspector Piper in RKO's "Hildegarde Withers" whodunits, and harried husband Joe Higgins in Republic's "Higgins Family" comedies (in which he appeared with real-life wife Lucile and son Russell). Gleason is still fondly remembered as the nervous trainer in *Here Comes Mr. Jordan* (1941); it was an Oscar-nominated performance. OTHER FILMS INCLUDE: 1922: *Polly of the Follies;* 1930: *Her Man;* 1932: *Blondie of the Follies;* 1933: *Hoopla;* 1936: *The Ex-Mrs. Bradford;* 1941: *Meet John Doe;* 1942: *Tales of Manhattan;* 1944: *Once Upon a Time, Arsenic and Old Lace;* 1945: *A Tree Grows in Brooklyn, The Clock;* 1946: *Home Sweet Homicide;* 1947: *Down to Earth* (reprising his character from *Here Comes Mr. Jordan);* 1950: *The Yellow Cab Man, Riding High;* 1951: *Come Fill the Cup;* 1952: *What Price Glory?;* 1955: *Night of the Hunter;* 1958: *The Last Hurrah* (his last film.)

GLEASON, PAUL. Actor. *(b. May 4, 1944, Jersey City, N.J.)* Here's a man who's clearly got an attitude problem: Whether he's playing the FBI agent in *Trading Places* (1983), the teacher in *The Breakfast Club* (1985), or the police chief in *Die Hard* (1988), Paul Gleason always has a chip on his shoulder. Actually, this utility supporting player is at his best playing uptight, belligerent authority figures and white-collar sleazebags. A veteran of TV soaps such as "All My Children" and "Another Life," and Roger Corman quickies, including *Private Duty Nurses* (1971), he has also appeared in *The Pursuit of D. B. Cooper* (1981), *She's Having a Baby* (1988), *Miami Blues* (1990).

GLENN, SCOTT. Actor. *(b. Jan. 26, 1942, Pittsburgh, Pa.)* Hollywood doesn't crank out many Westerns these days—more's the pity for this muscular, craggy-featured actor (and ex-Marine), who's shown he's a natural in the saddle in such oaters as *Cattle Annie and Little Britches* (1981), *Silverado* (1985), and the rodeo drama *My Heroes Have Always Been Cowboys* (1991). Though active in the 1970s, with small parts in films ranging from *Nashville* (1975) and *Apocalypse Now* (1979) to *Angels Hard as They Come* (1971) and *Fighting Mad* (1976), Glenn made a major impression on viewers as the vicious barfly in *Urban Cowboy* (1980). (Months earlier, he'd impressed everybody else by rescuing three small children from drowning.) Since then, he's wisely varied his roles, appearing as a swordsman/boxer in *The Challenge*, a tough-but-fair track coach in *Personal Best* (both 1982), astronaut Alan Shepard in *The Right Stuff*, an alien manhunter in *The Keep* (both 1983), a sleazy land-grabber in *The River* (1984), an ailing ex-boyfriend in *Miss Firecracker* (1989), a determined sub captain in *The Hunt for Red October* (1990), a coolly efficient FBI agent in *The Silence of the Lambs*, and a bigoted firefighter in *Backdraft* (both 1991). More recently he appeared in *Tall Tale* (1995). Glenn's sober-sided screen persona may limit his choice of roles; he has been warm and casual, but you'd be hard pressed to see him in a performance described as "light" or "breezy." Nonetheless, he merits our continued attention and appreciation.

GLOVER, CRISPIN. Actor. *(b. Sept. 20, 1964, New York City.)* "Eccentric" might be the best way to describe this jerky youth, who has given a series of uniquely stylized performances in movies of the 1980s and 1990s. He broke into films with small parts in *Racing With the Moon* and *Teachers* (both 1984), and made a big impression as Michael J. Fox's nerdy father in *Back to the Future* (1985), which led one critic to declare, "I'm not sure what to make of the performance, but the movie would be considerably more innocuous without it." He followed with an unconventional leading performance as a disaffected young man in *River's Edge* (1987), and has since appeared in *Where the Heart Is, Wild at Heart* (both 1990; unforgettably weird in the latter as a young man who walks around with live bugs in his underwear), *The Doors* (1991, as Andy Warhol, in an inspired piece of casting), and *Little Noises* (1992). Recent credits include the David Lynch TV movie *Hotel Room, What's Eating Gilbert Grape* (both 1993), and *Even Cowgirls Get the Blues* (1994). Glover has also written several books (one of which is called "Ratcatching") and recorded an album ("The Big Problem = The Solution. The Solution = Let It Be").

GLOVER, DANNY. Actor. *(b. July 22, 1947, San Francisco.)* Towering, authoritative but immensely likable black leading man equally at home in big action spectacles and kitchen-sink dramas. An alumnus of the Black Actors' Workshop of the American Conservatory Theatre, and a prolific stage performer, Glover first appeared on film in a tiny role in *Escape From Alcatraz* (1979), and subsequently labored in the forgettable *Chu Chu and the Philly Flash* (1981) and *Out* (1982), among others. He first attracted notice as Sally Field's farmhand in *Places in the Heart* (1984), enlarging on that success the following year as a murderous cop in *Witness*, a surprisingly believable cowboy in *Silverado*, and the contemptible "Mister" in *The Color Purple*. The size of Glover's roles grew with his reputation, and he scored as Vietnam combatants in *BAT 21* (1988) and *Flight of the Intruder* (1991), a monster-fighting police officer in *Predator 2*, a superstitious mobster in *A Rage in Harlem* (both 1990), and a tow-truck driver with heart and soul in *Grand Canyon* (1991). He was also memorable in the superb TV miniseries "Lonesome Dove" (1989). For all his dramatic power, he is still best known as the long-suffering partner of wacky cop Mel Gibson in the *Lethal Weapon* series (1987, 1989, 1992). But the star clout he's developed in films like that has enabled him to participate in more intimate, personal projects like *To Sleep With Anger* (1990, which he coproduced) and *Bopha!* (1993). He also costarred in the TV miniseries "Alex Haley's Queen," *The Saint of Fort Washington* (both also 1993), and *Angels in the Outfield* (1994).

GLOVER, JOHN. Actor. *(b. Aug. 7, 1944, Salisbury, Md.)* Critic Pauline Kael called him the "prime rotter" of 1980s films, and without question Glover played more despicable (and believable) villains than any other actor in the business. A onetime chorus boy and veteran of Broadway and regional theater productions, the gaunt, wavy-haired, preppy-looking Glover had small roles in *Julia* and *Annie Hall* (both 1977), among others, before achieving success and audience recognition in such films as *52 Pick-Up* (1986), *Masquerade, Scrooged* (both 1988), *RoboCop 2* (1990), and in such high-profile TV movies as *An Early Frost* (1985) and *Nutcracker: Money, Murder and Madness* (1986), and the miniseries "The Two Mrs. Grenvilles" (1987). His most delightful characterization to date has been flamboyantly eccentric tycoon Daniel Clamp in *Gremlins 2: The New Batch* (1990). He won a Tony award in 1995 for his performances in the play "Love! Valor! Compassion!"

GODARD, JEAN-LUC. Director, screenwriter, critic. *(b. Dec. 3, 1930, Paris.)* Andrew Sarris once wrote that Godard was "the most disconcerting of all contemporary directors, a veritable paragon of pardoxes, violent and yet vulnerable, the most elegant stylist and the most vulgar polemicist, the man of the moment and the artist for the ages." After making several shorts in the 1950s, this Swiss-educated former film critic helmed his first feature, *Breathless* (1959), which galvanized the international film scene. An offhand tribute not only to the whole film noir tradition but also to more conventional Hollywood cinema (Godard remarked that Jean Seberg's character in the picture could just as well have been the woman she portrayed in Preminger's 1958 *Bonjour Tristesse),* its jump cuts and hand-held shots delighted some with their spontaneity while outraging others for whom seamless editing and an unshakable

camera are sacrosanct. (It also made lead actor Jean-Paul Belmondo a star.) From that point on, 1960s film seemed to belong to Godard; his films were incredibly varied (he would go from a low-budget black-and-white satire like *Les Carabiniers* to a lush, wide-screen color production with an international cast like *Contempt* within less than a year) and, while widely controversial, were always eagerly awaited and studied. These included *Le Petit Soldat (The Little Soldier;* 1960), banned by France's Ministry of Information because of its attitude towards the Algerian war; *A Woman Is a Woman* (1961), with Godard's then-wife Anna Karina as a stripper turning to two men for a baby; *My Life to Live* (1962), with Karina as a prostitute; *Band of Outsiders* (1964), an extremely enjoyable reinterpretation of American gangster films; *A Married Woman* (1964), again with Karina dallying amongst lovers; and *Alphaville* (1965), a fascinating combination of the science fiction and detective genres. By the time of *Pierrot le Fou* (1965), Godard was embracing a more politically committed cinema and continually striving to subvert, annihilate, and reinvent the narrative form. *Made in USA* (1966) was a pseudo-thriller awash in political and pop references; *Masculine-Feminine* (1966), a loose, fragmented look at "the children of Marx and Coca-Cola"; *La Chinoise* (1967), a dialogue of revolution among Parisian students; and *Weekend* (1968), a brilliant attack on violent, consumer culture that remains one of Godard's most dazzling achievements.

After the Paris student rebellion in May 1968, Godard's involvement with far left factions became all-consuming and he began a new phase of his career, creating—or trying to create—a new cinema from the bottom up (frequently with collaborator Jean-Pierre Gorin). Some of these pieces were successful, some were not, and some were just bewildering; none of them was widely seen. The first was *Le Gai Savoir* (1968), featuring a political discourse between two people that lasts the duration of the film. In *Pravda* (1969), voices discuss events after the 1968 Czech invasion while appropriate images are shown; in *Tout va bien* (1972), journalist Jane Fonda and filmmaker Yves Montand are "radicalized" by striking workers; in *A Letter to Jane* (1972), Godard and Gorin discuss the meaning of a photograph of Jane Fonda shown on screen for the film's length. After this period, Godard concentrated on experiments with video for several years before returning to "commercial" film with the acclaimed *Every Man for Himself* (1980), about dispirited people coping with their place (and status) in the world. Most interestingly, *Every Man* featured a character named Godard, a character who says, "I make movies to keep myself busy. If I had the strength, I'd do nothing." Such autobiographical, self-critical (and self-defeating) flourishes were also present in *Passion* (1982), *First Name: Carmen* (1983, with Godard himself playing a washed-up director) and *The Rise and Fall of a Little Film Company from a novel by James Hadley Chase* (1986, made for French TV), which confronts the impossibility of making a film with any significance in the modern era.

He achieved some of his greatest latter-day notoriety for *Hail Mary* (1985), a typically idiosyncratic and iconoclastic modern nativity story that was praised by some and denounced by many others (including Pope John Paul II).

An abortive collaboration with Norman Mailer eventually resulted in the absolutely wacko English-language *King Lear* (1987), featuring Mailer and his daughter, theatrical director Peter Sellars, Brat Packer Molly Ringwald, veteran actor Burgess Meredith, Woody Allen, and Godard himself. His excellent 1990 film, *Nouvelle Vague,* failed to get any U.S. distribution. More recently, he debuted *Hélas pour moi* (1993), *Germany Year 90 Nine Zero* and the pseudo-autobiographical *JLG by JLG* (both 1994).

GODDARD, PAULETTE. Actress. *(b. June 3, 1911, Great Neck, N.Y., as Marion Levy; d. Apr. 23, 1990.)* It could be said of this former Ziegfeld girl that she married (and divorced) well, and although that's certainly true, she accomplished much more than that. The young Goddard came to Hollywood in the early 1930s to become a star, worked in some Hal Roach comedy shorts, and became one of the Goldwyn Girls, appearing in the Busby Berkeley chorus of the Eddie Cantor musicals *The Kid From Spain* (1932) and *Roman Scandals* (1933), among others. She got her big break from Charlie Chaplin,

who fell in love with her, and cast her as the gamine in his *Modern Times* (1936). It was an extremely winning performance. They subsequently wed, though reportedly the absence of a traditional wedding certificate (as their nuptials took place on a ship) caused producer David O. Selznick to change his mind about casting her as Scarlett O'Hara in *Gone With the Wind,* fearing reprisals from civic and church groups.

Goddard owed her initial fame to Chaplin, but she found success on her own in such pictures as *Dramatic School* (1938), *The Women* and *The Cat and the Canary* (both 1939). Never an actress of great range, Goddard had an earthy, intelligent quality—and a natural vivacity—that made her a screen favorite throughout the 1940s in *The Great Dictator* (opposite Chaplin again), *Second Chorus* (dancing with Fred Astaire and playing opposite future husband Burgess Meredith), and, reunited with *Cat* costar Bob Hope, *The Ghost Breakers* (all 1940), *Hold Back the Dawn, Nothing but the Truth* (both 1941), *Reap the Wild Wind, The Lady Has Plans* (both 1942), *The Crystal Ball* (1943), *Standing Room Only* (1944), *Kitty* (1945, as an 18th-century guttersnipe transformed into a lady, one of her best star vehicles), *The Diary of a Chambermaid* (1946, with Meredith), *Unconquered* (1947), *An Ideal Husband* (1948), and the underrated *Bride of Vengeance* (1949).

Goddard received a 1943 Best Supporting Actress Oscar nomination for her work as one of the Pacific-stationed WW2 nurses in *So Proudly We Hail!* Her 1950s films—including *Babes in Bagdad* (1952) and *Sins of Jezebel* (1953)—were undistinguished to say the least, and she retired from the screen, although she made a brief 1964 comeback as Claudia Cardinale's mother in the Italian-French coproduction *A Time of Indifference.* Divorced from Chaplin in 1942, she was later married to actor Burgess Meredith, and still later to novelist Erich Maria Remarque. An extremely wealthy woman, toward the end of her life she gave generous endowments to the New York University School of the Arts. She was portrayed by Diane Lane in the 1992 movie *Chaplin.*

GOLDBERG, WHOOPI. Actress. *(b. Nov. 13, 1955, New York City, as Caryn John-*

son.) When this actress/comedienne stepped up to receive her Best Supporting Actress Academy Award in 1991 for her crowd-pleasing turn as the streetwise, reluctant medium in *Ghost* (1990), it marked a pinnacle in a screen career with more than its share of ups and downs. She began performing as an improvisational trouper, and gradually evolved to stand-up comedy as a monologist, developing a series of distinct characters who illustrated the foibles of contemporary life. Producer-director Mike Nichols spotted her in San Francisco and brought her one-woman show to Broadway in 1984. An enormous success, it brought Goldberg to the attention of Steven Spielberg, who cast her in the pivotal role of Celie in his film adaptation of Alice Walker's *The Color Purple* (1985). Although she won an Oscar nomination and "overnight" stardom, Goldberg failed to capitalize on her success, owing partially to bad choices. She had a moderate hit in *Jumpin' Jack Flash* (1986), but thereafter slid downhill in increasingly foolish action-comedies such as *Burglar* and *Fatal Beauty* (both 1987), and more serious misfires like *The Telephone* (1988) and *Homer and Eddie* (1990). She continued to perform live, and in 1988 joined the cast of "Star Trek: The Next Generation" as the wise old humanoid bartender Guinan.

In 1990 Goldberg scored a double triumph as the infinitely patient housekeeper in the critically acclaimed *The Long Walk Home,* and as the aforementioned phony psychic in *Ghost.* She describes herself as a "character actor," and has no qualms about taking supporting roles—a rare quality in movie stars these days. She played a soap-opera scribe in *Soapdish* (1991) and a homicide detective in *The Player* (1992) before taking on another starring role—her most popular to date—in *Sister Act* (1992), an old-fashioned formula comedy that hit the bull's-eye, with Whoopi as an eyewitness to murder who hides out in a convent. Since then she's appeared in *Sarafina!* (1992), *National Lampoon's Loaded Weapon 1, Made in America,* the inevitable *Sister Act 2: Back in the Habit* (all 1993), *Corrina, Corrina* (1994), *The Lion King* (also 1994, as the voice of the hyena Shenzi), and *Boys on the Side* (1995). In 1990, she costarred in a short-lived TV sitcom adapted from the 1988 movie *Bag-*

dad Cafe, and hosted a nightly talk show, which lasted just one season, 1992–93. In 1994 she hosted the Academy Awards.

GOLDBLUM, JEFF. Actor. *(b. Oct. 22, 1952, Pittsburgh.)* In his best performances, the quirky, lanky Goldblum combines relaxed, naturalistic dialogue delivery with impeccable comic timing. But he just as easily slips into excessively mannered characterizations that can be off-putting, which may explain why he's not considered "box office." Following a small but memorable part as a violent thug in the original *Death Wish* (1974), he won small but noticeable roles from Robert Altman in *California Split* (1974) and *Nashville* (1975). He had a showy bit part in *Annie Hall* (1977, uttering the memorable line, "I forgot my mantra"), and a strong supporting role in *Invasion of the Body Snatchers* (1978). He costarred with Ben Vereen in the well-received (but poorly rated) 1980 TV series created by Stephen J. Cannell, "Tenspeed and Brown Shoe." Audience recognition finally came with his performance as the "People" magazine reporter in Lawrence Kasdan's *The Big Chill* (1983). He costarred in the cult favorite *The Adventures of Buckaroo Banzai Across the Eighth Dimension* (1984) and had his first starring role (opposite Michelle Pfeiffer) in John Landis' *Into the Night* (1985). His casting in *The Fly* (1986) proved to be inspired, as his intensity perfectly suited the role of a scientist who goes too far in his experiments. His costar in the film was his then-wife, Geena Davis, with whom he also appeared in the disappointing *Transylvania 6-5000* (1985) and *Earth Girls Are Easy* (1989)—the couple has since divorced. Goldblum has recently been active abroad, in *The Mad Monkey, The Tall Guy* (both 1989), *Mister Frost* (1990), and *The Favor, The Watch, and the Very Big Fish* (1991). He returned to the mainstream as the wisecracking mathematician in the megahit *Jurassic Park* (1993) and followed in *Hideaway* and *Nine Months* (both 1995).

GOLDMAN, BO. Screenwriter. *(b. Sept. 10, 1932, New York City.)* Acclaimed screenwriter whose best work has dealt realistically and sensitively with characters who have a penchant for self-destruction.

A Princeton graduate, Goldman had his first musical ("First Impressions") produced on Broadway when he was in his mid 20s. After that he worked on TV shows like "Playhouse 90" while trying to mount another musical and spent many lean years before writing his first screenplay, *Shoot the Moon,* a tough look at a disintegrating marriage. The script did not sell, but it stirred interest in Hollywood and Goldman was hired by Milos Forman to rewrite the screenplay of *One Flew Over the Cuckoo's Nest* (1975). The film swept the Oscars and Goldman earned one as cowriter. He next cowrote *The Rose* (1979), and won another Oscar for his charming original screenplay *Melvin and Howard* (1980), directed by a then up-and-coming Jonathan Demme. *Shoot the Moon* was finally produced in 1981 and despite its success, Goldman spent most of the 1980s working as an uncredited script doctor on films like *The Flamingo Kid* and *Swing Shift* (both 1984). He cowrote the spy thriller *Little Nikita* (1988) and contributed to *Dick Tracy* (1990) but did not have another solo screen credit until *Scent of a Woman* (1992 Oscar nomination for Adapted Screenplay), which was based on an earlier Italian film. Goldman's goal from the start has been to direct his own work, which has yet to happen.

GOLDMAN, WILLIAM. Screenwriter, novelist, playwright. *(b. Aug. 12, 1931, Highland Park, Ill.)* Talented writer whose smart, pungent dialogue is the most recognizable element of his screenplays. A published novelist since 1957, Goldman began his film career by penning *Masquerade* (1965), and hit it big with his script for *Harper* (1966), a detective thriller starring Paul Newman. He won Academy Awards for the trend-setting *Butch Cassidy and the Sundance Kid* (1969) and *All the President's Men* (1976, adapted from the best-seller), and adapted *Marathon Man* (1976), *Magic* (1978), and *The Princess Bride* (1987) from his own novels. He also adapted *A Bridge Too Far* (1977) and *Misery* (1991), and wrote *Year of the Comet* (1992), his first original screenplay in nearly 25 years; he cowrote the *Chaplin* biopic as well that same year, and wrote the big-screen adaptation of *Maverick* (1994) with Mel Gibson in the title role.

(Goldman continues to work, as he has for years, as an uncredited script doctor; for instance, in 1993 he reportedly contributed to *Last Action Hero.*) Goldman has also written several well-received books about the entertainment industry, including "The Season: A Candid Look at Broadway" and "Adventures in the Screen Trade: A Personal View of Hollywood and Screenwriting" (the latter containing one of the most-quoted analyses of Hollywood: "Nobody Knows Anything.").

GOLDSMITH, JERRY. Composer. *(b. Feb. 10, 1929, Los Angeles.)* If you have been a regular moviegoer during the past 20 years, chances are that Goldsmith has composed the music for some of your favorite films. He began conducting and composing music for CBS radio and television, and made his first impact on moviegoers in 1962 with his subtle scores for *Lonely Are the Brave* and *Freud.* He has since worked virtually nonstop on pictures both big and small, and has experimented with many different musical stylings on such films as *Lilies of the Field* (1963), *A Patch of Blue* (1965), *Our Man Flint* (1966), *Planet of the Apes* (1968), *Patton* (1970), *Chinatown* (1974), *Star Trek: The Motion Picture* (1979), *Under Fire* (1983), *Gremlins* (1984, the first of many films for director Joe Dante), *Rambo: First Blood Part II* (1985), *Hoosiers* (1986), and *The Russia House* (1990). Goldsmith has been nominated 15 times for Academy Awards and took one home for his frightening score of *The Omen* (1976). TV buffs remember him for his trendy music for the popular TV series "The Man From U.N.C.L.E." Recent credits include *Forever Young* (1992), *Dennis the Menace, Matinee, Rudy,* and *Malice* (all 1993).

GOLDWYN, SAMUEL. Producer. *(b. Aug. 27, 1882, Warsaw, Poland, as Samuel Goldfish; d. Jan. 31, 1974.)* A glove salesman who was the brother-in-law of vaudeville producer Jesse L. Lasky, Sam Goldfish first became interested in movies in 1910 and tried to persuade Lasky to bankroll a film company with little success. Lasky finally relented in 1913, and with Goldfish and Cecil B. DeMille formed the Jesse L. Lasky Feature Play Company.

Goldfish took the responsibility for selling the company's first picture, *The Squaw Man* (1914), and his skill at marketing made the Lasky company a success and led to a distribution contract with the newly formed Paramount Pictures. In 1916 the Lasky Company merged with another Paramount producer, Adolph Zukor's Famous Players Film Company. Goldfish and Zukor did not get along, and Lasky sided with his new partner over his relative by marriage.

Goldfish joined forces with Edgar and Archibald Selwyn to form Goldwyn Pictures in 1917. Goldfish liked the name of the company so much he took it as his own. He produced a number of quality films, and hired a number of "eminent authors" to write stories for Goldwyn Pictures, but box-office success was elusive, and by 1922 Goldwyn was forced out of the company, which later merged with Metro Pictures and Louis B. Mayer Productions to become Metro-Goldwyn-Mayer. On his own again, Goldwyn became an independent producer, who retained his independence for decades to come—and acquired a prestigious reputation none of his competitors could match in the 1930s and 1940s.

Goldwyn nurtured such stars as Ronald Colman and Vilma Banky in the silent era, Eddie Cantor and Danny Kaye in the talkies. During the sound era, William Wyler was the director most associated with Goldwyn, and the producer owed much of his prestige to the tasteful, impeccably crafted films turned out by Wyler. Goldwyn received Best Picture Oscar nominations for *Arrowsmith* (1931), *Dodsworth* (1936), *Dead End* (1937), *Wuthering Heights* (1939), and *The Little Foxes* (1941). He won an Oscar for *The Best Years of Our Lives* (1946), received the Irving G. Thalberg memorial award that same year, and took home the Jean Hersholt Humanitarian Award in 1957.

Goldwyn slowed his production activities in the 1950s, concentrating on big-budget musicals like *Hans Christian Andersen* (1952), *Guys and Dolls* (1955), and his last, *Porgy and Bess* (1959). He was known for his cantankerous, independent nature and was also noted for his way with a word. "Goldwynisms" like, "If nobody wants to see your picture, there's nothing you can do to stop them" and "include me out" earned him an immortality of sorts that's wholly separate from his filmmaking achievements. After his divorce from Blanche Lasky in 1919, he married actress Frances Howard in 1925. Their son, Samuel Goldwyn, Jr., is also a noted producer and film distributor, and the Samuel Goldwyn Company remains active to this day. Grandson Tony Goldwyn has launched a successful acting career, with such films as *Ghost* (1990), *Traces of Red* (1992), and *The Pelican Brief* (1993) to his credit. In 1989 the Goldwyn family allowed author A. Scott Berg to write a thorough (and revealing) chronicle of their patriarch, "Goldwyn: A Biography."

GOLINO, VALERIA. Actress. *(b. Oct. 22, 1966, Naples.)* Significant American stardom may be in the future for this dark-haired beauty of Greek-Italian parentage. Golino was discovered by director Lina Wertmuller, who cast the teenaged musician in *A Joke of Destiny* (1983); she found acting appealing and worked in several Italian pictures over the next few years. She's best known here as Tom Cruise's sympathetic girlfriend in *Rain Man* (1988). (Her other leading man that year was Pee-wee Herman in *Big Top Pee-wee*.) Golino's recent films include *Torrents of Spring* (1989), *The King's Whore, Indian Runner, Hot Shots!* (in which she poked fun at herself, most endearingly), and *Year of the Gun* (all 1991; in the last she's memorable as an Italian terrorist). Since it worked the first time, she and Charlie Sheen performed even more movie parody scenes in the sequel *Hot Shots! Part Deux* (1993), and she also appeared in *Clean Slate* (1994).

GOMEZ, THOMAS. Actor. *(b. July 10, 1905, New York City; d. June 18, 1971.)* A dark, thickset actor who often played brooding, growling heavies, Gomez broke into acting under the tutelage of famous Shakespearean actor Walter Hampden. Following many years on stage, he was signed by Universal in 1942, where he appeared in many films both major and minor. He was memorable as a sinister cop in *Phantom Lady* (1944) and a boozy Mexican peasant in *Ride the Pink Horse* (1947, a performance that netted him an Oscar nomination).

OTHER FILMS INCLUDE: 1942: *Sherlock Holmes and the Voice of Terror* (cast as a Nazi in his debut film), *Arabian Nights, Pittsburgh;* 1943: *Crazy House, White Savage;* 1947: *Captain From Castile;* 1948: *Force of Evil, Key Largo* (one of his best parts, as Edward G. Robinson's oily henchman), *Casbah;* 1956: *Trapeze;* 1968: *Stay Away, Joe;* 1970: *Beneath the Planet of the Apes.*

GOODMAN, JOHN. Actor. *(b. June 20, 1952, St. Louis, Mo.)* Tubby, jovial actor who brings an unusual degree of intelligence to his roles, even when playing morons. Formally trained (one of his college acting classmates was Kathleen Turner), Goodman began his movie career ignobly with small roles in the likes of *C.H.U.D.* and *Revenge of the Nerds* (both 1984). He quickly graduated to better roles in better movies, portraying a hapless guy advertising for a wife in *True Stories* (1986), one of the lunatic prison escapees in *Raising Arizona* (1987), and the sad, aging ex-footballer in *Everybody's All-American* (1988). That same year, he hit the big time (on TV, anyway) as the good-natured husband/father in the hit sitcom "Roseanne." By now established as a top character actor, Goodman landed key costarring roles as Sally Field's husband in *Punchline* (1988), a sanguine New York cop in *Sea of Love* (1989), a wisecracking flight instructor in *Always* (also 1989), and a comically macho exterminator in *Arachnophobia* (1990).

Despite his bulk, and his skill at limning unsympathetic characters, Goodman seems to strike a responsive chord when cast as an amiable slob—although that didn't make a success of his first starring vehicle, the tailor-made comedy *King Ralph* (1991), and it didn't keep the Coen brothers from making him a homicidal salesman in *Barton Fink* (1991). Goodman tackled the mythic character of baseball great Babe Ruth in *The Babe* (1992), earning excellent notices even from critics who didn't like the film. Another actor might have played the lead in *Matinee* (1993), that of a flamboyant movie huckster/producer, as a caricature; Goodman gave him warmth and likability. He also reinterpreted Broderick Crawford's performance as a self-made Harry Brock in the 1993 remake of *Born Yesterday,* and contributed a voice to the animated *We're Back: A Dinosaur's Story* (also 1993). He was then cast—ideally, in most people's minds—as Fred Flintstone in the 1994 adaptation, *The Flintstones.* As a modern-day Everyman, Goodman has unlimited potential.

GOODRICH, FRANCES and HACKETT, ALBERT. Writers. *(Goodrich*—b. Dec. 21, 1890, Belleville, N.J.; d. Jan. 29, 1984. *Hackett*—b. Feb. 16, 1900, New York City.*)* Probably no other screenwriting team in Hollywood history has been so influential yet remains so unknown, but this husband and wife collaboration generated numerous American screen classics, including several legendary MGM musicals. Both actors who turned to writing in the late 1920s, they came to Hollywood to pen the screen adaptation of their play, "Up Pops the Devil," produced by Paramount in 1931. By 1933, ensconced at MGM, they started cranking out scripts for mainstream projects, laced with witty, urbane dialogue and peopled with insouciant, often eccentric characters. *Penthouse* (1933) and *Fugitive Lovers* (1934) were popular enough, but it was the team's Oscar-nominated script for *The Thin Man* (for which they were encouraged by director W. S. Van Dyke to disregard the Dashiell Hammett original and concentrate on playful repartee between Nick and Nora Charles) that "made" them. They also wrote *Ah, Wilderness, Naughty Marietta* (both 1935), *After the Thin Man* (earning another Oscar nod for this delightful sequel), *Rose Marie, Small Town Girl* (all 1936), *The Firefly* (1937), and *Another Thin Man* (1939), among others.

They left Metro in 1939 and freelanced on several plays and films, most notably the screen adaptation of Moss Hart's *Lady in the Dark* (1944) and Frank Capra's *It's a Wonderful Life* (1946, although many hands reworked their initial script). Back at MGM, they wrote the musicals *Easter Parade, The Pirate,* and *Summer Holiday* (a tuneful remake of their *Ah, Wilderness),* all in 1948. Their subsequent efforts include *In the Good Old Summertime* (1949), *Father of the Bride* (1950, which gave them a third Oscar nomination), *Father's Little Dividend* (1951, a well-received sequel), *Give a Girl a Break* (1953), *The Long, Long Trailer, Seven Brides for Seven Brothers* (both 1954, the latter script garnering a fourth Oscar nomination), and *Gaby* (1956). For the stage they wrote "The Diary of Anne Frank," a Pulitzer Prize–winning play they adapted to the screen for a 1959 Fox production directed by George Stevens. Their last film was the mediocre *Five Finger Exercise* (1962), a melancholy swan song for the prolific team. However, in an extraordinary tribute to the lasting quality of the Goodrich–Hackett work, when *Father of the Bride* was remade in 1991, the script reused so much of their original dialogue and situations that they were given co-screenplay credit!

GORDON, C. HENRY. Actor. *(b. June 17, 1883, New York City, as Henry Racke; d. Dec. 3, 1940.)* This swarthy, suave, and sardonic character actor was among Hollywood's most dependable villains during the 1930s. One of the screen's nastiest heavies, Gordon always gave the impression of reveling in his perfidy. He seldom attempted dialects but was nonetheless cast in many ethnic roles: as an Italian gangster in *Gabriel Over the White House* (1933), as a Mongol warlord in *Roar of the Dragon* (1932), as an Indian Khan in *The Charge of the Light Brigade* (1936), and as Mexican general Santa Anna in *Man of Conquest* (1939). He was a perennial suspect in Charlie Chan movies: *Charlie Chan Carries On, The Black Camel* (both 1931), *Charlie Chan at the Olympics* (1937), *Charlie Chan in City in Darkness* (1939), and *Charlie Chan at the Wax Museum* (1940). Gordon did get two good opportunities to play a good guy, first as the hard-boiled, incorruptible cop in *Scarface* (1932), and then as famous fictional detective Valcour in *Love Letters of a Star* (1936). He died following complications arising from a leg amputation.

GORDON, KEITH. Actor, director, screenwriter. *(b. Feb. 3, 1961, New York City.)* Since making a splash as the bookish teen who joins forces with a prostitute to trap his mother's killer in Brian De Palma's *Dressed to Kill* (1980), this young, sensitive lead expanded beyond acting to try his hand behind the camera with consistently offbeat and personal projects. He cowrote and starred in the quirky comedy drama *Static* (1985) and was the scenarist

and director of the well-received, if little-seen, *The Chocolate War* (1988), and *A Midnight Clear* (1992). His other acting stints include the young "Joe Gideon" in *All That Jazz* (1979), Brian De Palma's *Home Movies* (1979), leads in John Carpenter's *Christine* (1983) and in the TV movie *Kent State* (1981). He played Rodney Dangerfield's bashful son in *Back to School* (1986), and starred on stage in Woody Allen's play "The Floating Lightbulb."

GORDON, LEO. Actor, screenwriter. *(b. Dec. 2, 1922, New York City.)* Hulking, brutish-looking actor, one of the screen's nastiest heavies, who also writes screenplays. A student at the American Academy of Dramatic Arts, Gordon did some stage work before making his film debut in *China Venture* (1953). His other films (as actor) include *Hondo* (1953), *Seven Angry Men* (1955), *The Conqueror* (1956), *Baby Face Nelson* (1957, playing John Dillinger), *The Intruder, Tarzan Goes to India* (both 1962), *Night of the Grizzly, Beau Geste* (both 1966), *The St. Valentine's Day Massacre* (1967), *You Can't Win 'Em All* (1970), *My Name Is Nobody* (1974), *Nashville Girl* (1976), and *Bog* (1978). He has written or cowritten the screenplays for *Black Patch* (1957), *Hot Car Girl* (1958), *Tower of London* (1962), *The Bounty Killer* (1965), *Tobruk* (1966), and *You Can't Win 'Em All* (1970), among others.

GORDON, RUTH. Actress, screenwriter. *(b. Oct. 30, 1896, Wollaston, Mass.; d. Aug. 28, 1985.)* When Ruth Gordon, at the age of 72, won an Oscar for her delightfully sinister supporting performance in *Rosemary's Baby* (1968), she declared, "I can't tell you how encouraging a thing like this is." It nicely summed up the energy and optimism she displayed over a 70-year career, which began with a 1915 stage debut as Peter Pan and went on to include many now-classic dramatic and comedic stage roles in the likes of "The Country Wife" and "The Matchmaker." Though she had appeared onscreen in *Camille* (1915) and *The Whirl of Life* (1916), Gordon's film career began in earnest with roles in *Abe Lincoln in Illinois* (as Mary Todd), *Dr. Ehrlich's Magic Bul-*

let (both 1940), and *Two-Faced Woman* (1941). She married playwright Garson Kanin in 1942; together they wrote a series of acclaimed screenplays that George Cukor directed: *A Double Life* (1947) and the Spencer Tracy–Katharine Hepburn classics *Adam's Rib* (1949) and *Pat and Mike* (1952), all three Oscar-nominated, as well as *The Marrying Kind* (1952). Gordon also wrote *The Actress* (1953), an adaptation of her own autobiographical play "Years Ago," which starred Jean Simmons in the title role.

In the mid 1960s, Gordon took up screen acting once again and got her second wind in no time, picking up an Oscar nomination for her turn in *Inside Daisy Clover* (1965), and then becoming a sensation in *Rosemary's Baby*. She followed her Oscar-winning performance with hilarious work in *Where's Poppa?* (1970), and achieved bona fide "cult" status as Bud Cort's lover in the black comedy *Harold and Maude* (1971). Gordon worked constantly until her death, appearing in *Every Which Way But Loose* (1978), *Boardwalk* (1979), *My Bodyguard* (1980), and *Maxie* (1985). She also worked extensively on TV, including an Emmy-winning turn on an episode of "Taxi." She wrote two volumes of autiobiography, "Myself Among Others" (1971) and "My Side" (1976).

GORDON, STUART. Director, screenwriter. *(b. Aug. 11, 1947, Chicago.)* Cult filmmaker who first gained notoriety in his senior year at the University of Wisconsin for staging a nude, psychedelic version of "Peter Pan." (He left college a few months short of graduation.) Gordon went on to form the Organic Theatre in 1969, and oversaw dozens of unique plays, including David Mamet's "Sexual Perversity in Chicago." He left the theater in 1983 and made his film debut with *Re-Animator* (1985), a deliriously grotesque (but very funny) adaptation of six H. P. Lovecraft stories, which was a surprise commercial and critical hit. Gordon returned to Lovecraft again for *From Beyond* (1986), then tackled murderous dolls in *Dolls* (1987), post-apocalyptic fighting machines in *Robot Jox* (1990), a graphic retelling of *The Pit and the Pendulum* (1991), and a high-tech futuristic prison in *Fortress* (1993). Gordon also cowrote the story of *Honey, I Shrunk the Kids* (1989) and was coexecutive producer on its sequel, *Honey, I Blew Up the Kid* (1992).

GOSSETT, LOUIS, JR. Actor. *(b. May 27, 1936, Brooklyn, N.Y.)* Talented actor who has become one of the leading black voices in American cinema. Born to a porter and a maid, Gossett began acting at the age of 17 when a leg injury took him away from basketball, his first love. He scored an improbable triumph in 1953 by landing a plum role in the Broadway production of *Take a Giant Step;* for this he won a Donaldson Award for best newcomer of the year. In 1958 Gossett was actually drafted by the New York Knickerbockers pro basketball team but, by then, he was committed to acting. Despite his success in both stage and screen versions of *A Raisin in the Sun* (1961), years of minor theatrical and TV ("The Nurses," "East Side, West Side") roles followed until 1977, when Gossett won an Emmy for his supporting performance in the monumental miniseries "Roots." Subsequently he became a much more visible screen figure, and won a Best Supporting Actor Oscar for his work as the hard-assed drill sergeant in *An Officer and a Gentleman* (1982). In recent years he's capitalized on that characterization, appearing as tough guys in *Iron Eagle* (1986, and its 1988 and 1992 sequels), *The Punisher* (1989), and *Toy Soldiers* (1991), as well as warm-hearted characters with tough exteriors.
OTHER FILMS INCLUDE: 1971: *Skin Game;* 1972: *Travels With My Aunt;* 1973: *The Laughing Policeman;* 1975: *The River Niger;* 1977: *The Choirboys, The Deep;* 1983: *Jaws 3-D;* 1985: *Enemy Mine;* 1986: *Firewalker;* 1987: *The Principal;* 1992: *Diggstown;* 1994: *Blue Chips, A Good Man in Africa.*

GOUGH, MICHAEL. Actor. *(b. Nov. 23, 1917, Malaya.)* Urbane British character actor (pronounced "Goff") whose screen career has taken him from Tolstoy's *Anna Karenina* (1948) to *Dr. Terror's House of Horrors* (1965) to *Batman* (1989). Despite his Shakespearean training and extensive experience in the British theater, Gough can't seem to shake moviegoers' perceptions of him as the poor man's Vincent Price. The tall, gaunt actor appeared in top British films during the 1940s and 1950s, including *Blanche Fury* (1948), *The Man in the White Suit* (1951), and *Richard III* (1955), but he also slaved in horror movies such as *Horror of Dracula* (1958), *The Phantom of the Opera* (1962), *Black Zoo* (1963), *Berserk* (1967), *Horror Hospital* (1972) and in a series of mad-scientist roles, *Konga* (1961), *The Skull* (1965), and *They Came From Beyond Space* (1967). Not that he's renounced more serious endeavors; Gough has turned in expert performances in *Women in Love* (1969), *The Boys From Brazil* (1978), *The Dresser* (1983), *Out of Africa* (1985), *The Age of Innocence* (1993), and *Wittgenstein* (also 1993, as Bertrand Russell), to name just a few. Contemporary moviegoers may know him best, however, as Alfred the butler in *Batman* (1989), *Batman Returns* (1992), and *Batman Forever* (1995).

GOULD, ELLIOTT. Actor. *(b. Aug. 29, 1938, Brooklyn, N.Y., as Elliott Goldstein.)* Few screen actors during the 1960s and 1970s personified the changes in the American zeitgeist as did this curly-haired leading man, whose engaging portrayals of wry, cynical, and often confused characters made him a counterculture favorite. A stage performer (and Broadway chorus-line dancer) while still in his teens, Gould, like many of his contemporaries, had some lean years: he sold vacuum cleaners and operated elevators to supplement his acting income. His starring role in "I Can Get It for You Wholesale" (opposite Barbra Streisand, whom he married in 1963) made Gould a Broadway success, although his first film, *The Confession* (1964), didn't advance his career. It took an Oscar-nominated performance in *Bob & Carol & Ted & Alice* (1969), a sexual-revolution farrago, to bring Gould a measure of screen stardom. And once he'd played Trapper John in Robert Altman's anarchistic, antiwar *MASH* (1970), Gould was fixed in the minds of youthful moviegoers as a counterculture hero. *Getting Straight* (1970), *Move,* and *Little Murders* (both 1971) reinforced his image, and he made an antiheroic Philip Marlowe in *The Long Goodbye* (1973, again directed by Altman, for whom Gould appeared as himself in 1975's *Nashville).*

Slowly but surely, the quality of Gould's vehicles diminished. *S*P*Y*S* (1974) was an ill-fated attempt to recapture the magic of *MASH* with that film's costar Donald Sutherland, and *California Split* (also 1974) was a Robert Altman misfire. *Whiffs* (1975), *Harry and Walter Go to New York, Mean Johnny Barrows* (both 1976), *Matilda* (1978), *The Lady Vanishes* (1979, an ill-advised remake), and *The Devil and Max Devlin* (1981) could have killed anyone's career. Subsequent films such as *Over the Brooklyn Bridge* (1983), *The Naked Face* (1985), *Inside Out* (1986), *The Telephone* (1988), *The Lemon Sisters,* and *Dead Men Don't Die* (both 1990) barely saw theatrical release. But, given the right part, Gould can still deliver, as he proved on Billy Crystal's 1991 cable sitcom, "Sessions," and in a melancholy supporting role in *Bugsy* (1991). His son by Barbra Streisand, Jason Gould, is also an actor.

GRABLE, BETTY. Actress. *(b. Dec. 18, 1916, St. Louis, as Ruth Elizabeth Grable; d. July 2, 1973.)* This peaches-and-cream blonde with the world-famous legs was one of Hollywood's biggest stars in the 1940s. A talented, extroverted child, she was brought to Hollywood by her ambitious mother, and was dancing in movie-musical chorus lines at age 14! That's Betty singing the first line in the first scene of Eddie Cantor's musical *Whoopee!* (1930). Producer Samuel Goldwyn signed her to a contract, and featured her in that film as well as *Palmy Days* (1931), *The Greeks Had a Word for Them,* and *The Kid from Spain* (both 1932). Billed as Frances Dean, she toiled in low-budget short subjects for Educational Pictures and RKO. Under her own name, she won the ingenue lead in Wheeler and Woolsey's *Hold 'Em Jail,* but could only muster bit parts in *Probation, Child of Manhattan* (all 1932), *Cavalcade, The Sweetheart of Sigma Chi, Melody Cruise, What Price Innocence?* (all 1933), and *Student Tour* (1934). Finally, she won a featured spot in the Fred Astaire-Ginger Rogers musical *The Gay Divorcee* (1934), doing a delightful novelty number, "Let's K-nock K-nees," with Edward Everett Horton. RKO signed her, but she continued to seesaw between leads (opposite Wheeler and Woolsey in 1935's *The Nitwits)* and bit parts (in 1936's Astaire–Rogers musical *Follow the Fleet);*

she even got a dramatic role in *Don't Turn 'Em Loose* (1936).

The epitome of the wholesome, vivacious, all-American coed, Grable played that part in most of her subsequent 1930s films: *Old Man Rhythm, Collegiate* (both 1935), *Pigskin Parade* (1936), *College Swing, Campus Confessions* (both 1938), and *Million Dollar Legs* (1939). A brief marriage to former child star Jackie Coogan in the late 1930s brought some notoriety; they costarred in *College Swing* and *Million Dollar Legs,* but divorced after just a few years. A stint on Broadway in 1939's Cole Porter musical hit "DuBarry Was a Lady" netted her a *Life* magazine cover, and some real recognition at last.

In 1940 Grable was signed by 20th Century-Fox, where she got a career-making "big break": The studio's resident musical star, Alice Faye, was sidelined by appendicitis, and Grable was selected to fill her shoes in *Down Argentine Way.* She held her own in this cheerful musical comedy—and looked great in Technicolor. After being teamed with Faye in *Tin Pan Alley* (also 1940), she received a major buildup by Fox. Starring vehicles—most of them colorful, lighthearted musicals—followed in dizzying succession: *Moon Over Miami* (1941), *Footlight Serenade, Song of the Islands, Springtime in the Rockies* (all 1942), *Coney Island, Sweet Rosie O'Grady* (both 1943), *Pin Up Girl* (1944), *Billy Rose's Diamond Horseshoe,* and *The Dolly Sisters* (both 1945). She infrequently took starring roles in dramatic pictures, the best of which were 1941's *I Wake Up Screaming* and *A Yank in the R.A.F.*

Grable owed her phenomenal popularity during World War 2 to several things, the two most important being her gorgeous gams. A 1943 bathing-suit photo that showed her from behind, peering over her shoulder with a saucy smile, was the number one favorite pinup of Allied soldiers overseas. Fox insured her legs for a million dollars with Lloyd's of London, garnering reams of publicity. Grable herself, keenly aware of her limitations as an actress, insisted on wearing revealing, colorful costumes in her musicals, all of which were exercises in wartime escapism—and which catapulted her in 1943 to the number-one spot on the list of Hollywood's top-grossing stars.

Grable's career fell into gradual decline after the war. Changes in public taste forced her into different types of pictures, among them period dramas and comedies for which she was ill-suited: *Do You Love Me?* (1946), *The Shocking Miss Pilgrim* (1947), *That Lady in Ermine, When My Baby Smiles at Me* (both 1948), and *The Beautiful Blonde from Bashful Bend* (1949, a particular misfire that teamed her with writer-director Preston Sturges). The surprise success of 1947's *Mother Wore Tights,* another period piece that Grable herself feared would flop, did at least provide her with a compatible screen partner in Dan Dailey, who costarred in several subsequent musicals with her.

The 1950s saw an aging, slightly overweight Grable struggling to maintain her star status in the face of stiff competition from television and a new generation of screen personalities. *Wabash Avenue, My Blue Heaven* (both 1950), *Call Me Mister, Meet Me After the Show* (both 1951), *The Farmer Takes a Wife* (1953), and *Three for the Show* (1955) were progressively weaker vehicles for the leggy star. Two of her most successful films that decade—*How to Marry a Millionaire* (1953, a reworking of her 1941 hit *Moon Over Miami)* and *How to Be Very, Very Popular* (1955, her final film)—owed much of their success to younger costars: a spectacles-sporting Marilyn Monroe in *Millionaire,* and a vibrant Sheree North in *Popular.*

To her credit, Grable saw the handwriting on the wall and left movies to concentrate on stage and nightclub work, which she did for the rest of her life—including a notable tour in the Broadway musical "Hello, Dolly!" Once linked romantically with George Raft, Tyrone Power, and John Payne, Grable married bandleader Harry James in 1943; they had two children and were divorced in 1965. She died of cancer.

GRAHAME, GLORIA. Actress. *(b. Nov. 28, 1925, Los Angeles, as Gloria Grahame Hallward; d. Oct. 5, 1981.)* Sulky, seductive blond actress who was one of Hollywood's top temptresses: She played more shady women (and outright tramps) than any other female performer on-screen during the late 1940s and 1950s. Even when she portrayed *good* girls, Grahame often layered her characterizations with unsympathetic traits. A native Angeleno who went to Hollywood High and acted with the Pasadena Players, she snagged an MGM contract in 1943, appearing in *Cry Havoc* (1943), *Blonde Fever* (1944), and *Without Love* (1945), before getting her first high-profile "bad girl" part (on loan-out) in Frank Capra's *It's a Wonderful Life* (1946, as Violet). Grahame went on to star or play support in *Crossfire* (1947), *A Woman's Secret* (1949), *In a Lonely Place* (1950, opposite Humphrey Bogart in a memorable film noir), before enjoying her best year, 1952: She won a Best Supporting Actress Oscar for playing a trollop in Vincente Minnelli's Hollywood melodrama *The Bad and the Beautiful*, and also appeared to good advantage in Cecil B. DeMille's *The Greatest Show on Earth, Macao* and *Sudden Fear.*

For the next few years Grahame was almost ubiquitous, making a few turkeys along with many fine films. But by the end of the decade her career was virtually moribund, although she did make something of a comeback in the 1970s. Grahame was married four times, once to *In a Lonely Place* director Nicholas Ray, and later to his son (from a previous marriage) Anthony.
OTHER FILMS INCLUDE: 1953: *The Glass Wall, Man on a Tightrope* (directed by Flia Kazan), *The Big Heat* (directed by Fritz Lang, with a memorable scene in which Lee Marvin throws scalding coffee in her face); 1954: Lang's *Human Desire, Naked Alibi, The Good Die Young;* 1955: *Not as a Stranger, Oklahoma!* (especially memorable as Ado Annie, the girl who "cain't say no"); 1957: *Ride Out for Revenge;* 1959: *Odds Against Tomorrow;* 1966: *Ride Beyond Vengeance;* 1971: *Blood and Lace, Chandler;* 1972: *The Loners;* 1974: *Mama's Dirty Girls;* 1976: *Mansion of the Doomed;* 1979: *Chilly Scenes of Winter, A Nightingale Sang in Berkeley Square.*

GRANGER, FARLEY. Actor. *(b. July 1, 1925, San Jose, Calif.)* This boyish-looking actor spent most of his early years on-screen playing darkly handsome but emotionally unstable young men, and while he enjoyed considerable success in those characterizations, his career declined rapidly once he'd reached his 30s. Granger was barely out of high school—and acting in little theaters around Los Angeles—

when he was signed by Samuel Goldwyn. After debuting on-screen as a Russian boy in *The North Star* (1943), he went on to appear in *The Purple Heart* (1944), *They Live by Night* (1947), *Enchantment* (1948), *Side Street, Our Very Own* (both 1950), *Behave Yourself!* (1952), and other films in the early 1950s. Alfred Hitchcock recognized Granger's potential, and gave him plum roles in *Rope* (1948, as one of the unbalanced prep-school killers) and *Strangers on a Train* (1951, as the tennis pro drawn into Robert Walker's murder plot).

Granger's canny characterizations of personable youths with submerged neuroses made his early career an interesting one, but he matured into a somewhat colorless leading man, and he eventually drifted out of mainstream Hollywood features into stage and TV work (including the soap operas "As The World Turns" and "One Life to Live") and sleazy foreign films.
OTHER FILMS INCLUDE: 1953: *Small Town Girl;* 1954: *Senso;* 1956: *The Girl in the Red Velvet Swing;* 1967: *Rogue's Gallery;* 1970: *They Call Me Trinity;* 1972: *The Serpent;* 1973: *Arnold;* 1974: *The Slasher;* 1981: *The Prowler;* 1984: *Deathmask;* 1986: *The Imagemaker, The Whoopee Girls.*

GRANGER, STEWART. Actor. *(b. May 6, 1913, London, as James Stewart; d. Aug. 16, 1993.)* A suave, virile leading man not quite as smooth and insouciant as his contemporary Errol Flynn, Granger nonetheless made a positive impression in action and swashbuckling roles in the 1950s, while Flynn's star was waning. He started out in British films of the 1930s and 1940s, including *A Southern Maid* (1933), *So This Is London* (1939), *The Man in Grey* (1943), *Waterloo Road* (1944), *Caesar and Cleopatra* (1946), and *Captain Boycott* (1947) before coming to Hollywood and an MGM contract. Granger played lead in the 1950 remake of *King Solomon's Mines,* an adventure yarn that was one of the inspirations for the Indiana Jones series. He was more than serviceable in the period Technicolor frolic *Scaramouche* (1952), and he played the title roles in color remakes of such adventure standards *The Prisoner of Zenda* (1952) and *Beau Brummel* (1954). He worked extensively in European coproductions during the 1960s, his wavy hair now a silvery gray, including *Sodom and Gomorrah* (1962), *Frontier Hellcat* (1964), *Red Dragon* (1966), *The Last Safari, Requiem for a Secret Agent* (both 1967), and *The Wild Geese* (1978). He worked largely in TV movies during the 1970s and 1980s, playing Sherlock Holmes in a 1972 remake of *The Hound of the Baskervilles.* The recycled action roles that made his name did not please him; he was quoted to the effect that he'd never been in a film he'd been proud of. He remained active in the 1980s, appearing as Prince Philip in *The Royal Romance of Charles and Diana,* a 1982 TV movie, and making his Broadway debut in 1989 opposite Rex Harrison and Glynis Johns in "The Circle," and winning excellent reviews. His 1981 autobiography is titled "Sparks Fly Upward."

GRANT, CARY. Actor. *(b. Jan. 18, 1904, Bristol, England, as Archibald Alexander Leach; d. Nov. 29, 1986.)* As a teenage runaway, Archibald Leach began his lengthy show-business career as an acrobat, juggler, and song-and-dance man, touring with small troupes and playing music halls all over England. In 1920, as one of the Bob Pender comedy troupe, he came to America on a two-year tour and decided to stay. He took several other jobs (including that of lifeguard) to supplement his modest solo performing career. After several years Leach returned to the U.K., where he achieved considerable success as an engaging leading man in lighthearted stage plays. He returned to the United States late in the decade, eventually starring on Broadway and embarking on a successful tour across the country. In 1931 he made his film debut as a jaunty sailor in a Paramount short subject, *Singapore Sue.*

Upon reaching Hollywood in 1932 he was screen-tested at the behest of Paramount studio chief B. P. Schulberg, signed to a long-term contract, and rechristened Cary Grant. (The studio's first choice was Cary Lockwood.) He made his feature-film debut in *This Is the Night,* a charming, sophisticated comedy of the type that would make him a top star. The urbane, personable Grant appeared in a slew of 1932 Paramount pictures—among them *Sinners in the Sun, Merrily We Go to Hell,*

Blonde Venus (opposite the studio's top female star, Marlene Dietrich), *The Devil and the Deep, Hot Saturday,* and *Madame Butterfly*—before costarring with Mae West in *She Done Him Wrong* (1933), a ribald, wildly successful comedy in which West exhorted Grant to "come up some time an' see me."

Over the next few years Grant tackled a wide variety of starring roles in costume dramas, war films, adventure pictures, and topical comedies. He built, slowly and steadily, a reputation as one of Hollywood's most dependable leading men. His films during this period, most of them made for Paramount, included *The Eagle and the Hawk, I'm No Angel* (also opposite West), *Alice in Wonderland* (all 1933, in the last-named as the Mock Turtle), *Thirty-Day Princess, Ladies Should Listen, Kiss and Make Up, Born to Be Bad* (all 1934), *Enter Madame, Wings in the Dark, The Last Outpost, Sylvia Scarlett* (all 1935, on loan to RKO in the last-named, opposite Katharine Hepburn), *Suzy* (for MGM, paired with Jean Harlow), *Big Brown Eyes, Wedding Present, The Amazing Quest of Ernest Bliss* (all 1936, the last-named a British-made comedy), *The Toast of New York,* and *When You're in Love* (both 1937).

He hit his stride in a string of sophisticated screwball comedies—beginning with *Topper* (1937)—in which he evolved the debonair, witty, uninhibited screen persona that ultimately brought him superstardom. The next several years saw Grant at his peak, alternating classic comedies (such as 1937's *The Awful Truth,* 1938's *Holiday* and *Bringing Up Baby,* 1940's *His Girl Friday, The Philadelphia Story,* and *My Favorite Wife)* with similarly well-remembered dramas (1939's *In Name Only* and 1941's *Penny Serenade,* for which he was Oscar-nominated), adventure films (1939's *Gunga Din* and *Only Angels Have Wings),* and thrillers (1941's *Suspicion,* the first of his many films for director Alfred Hitchcock).

He managed to balance the same kind of mix throughout the 1940s, in the witty social comedy-drama *The Talk of the Town* (1942), the charming star vehicle *Mr. Lucky* (1943), the energetic farce *Arsenic and Old Lace* (1944; made in 1941), the atypically moody drama *None but the Lonely Heart* (1944, a personal favorite of Grant's, with his characterization as a

Cockney drifter earning another Oscar nomination), the wartime submarine drama *Destination Tokyo* (1944), the crackling romantic thriller *Notorious* (1946, again for Hitchcock), the musical biography *Night and Day* (1946, as Cole Porter), and such airy seemingly effortless comedies as *Once Upon a Time* (1944), *The Bachelor and the Bobby-Soxer, The Bishop's Wife* (both 1947, in the latter as an angel in a Brooks Brothers suit), *Mr. Blandings Builds His Dream House, Every Girl Should Be Married* (both 1948, the latter costarring then-wife Betsy Drake), and *I Was a Male War Bride* (1949).

The 1950s and 1960s offered much the same, as Grant continued to charm movie-goers with a suave screen persona apparently impervious to the ravages of age. *Crisis* (1950) cast him in an unusual political drama; *People Will Talk* (1951) offered an intellectual social comedy, while *Monkey Business* (1952) tried hard, perhaps too hard, to replicate the screwball comedies of the 1930s; *To Catch a Thief* (1955) and *North by Northwest* (1959), Hitchcock films both, were successful (almost archetypal) star-director collaborations; and *An Affair to Remember* (1957) was an uncasy mix of classy comedy and hoary soap-opera cliché—though extremely popular. His leading ladies in this period included Ginger Rogers, Deborah Kerr, Grace Kelly, Doris Day, Marilyn Monroe, Audrey Hepburn, and Sophia Loren.

After *Walk, Don't Run* (1966), a middling remake of George Stevens' 1943 hit *The More the Merrier,* Grant retired from the screen. He may have reasoned, correctly, that the demise of the studio system and changing audience tastes signaled the dawn of an era in which his kind of movie was passé. He contented himself with forays into the business world, most effectively for the Faberge cosmetics company. In 1970 Grant, who never won an Oscar in competition, received a special Academy Award in recognition of his extraordinary career. His wives included actresses Virginia Cherrill, Betsy Drake, and Dyan Cannon (who bore him his only child, daughter Jennifer, now a budding actress), and heiress Barbara Hutton. Long reticent about interviews, and unwilling to write an autobiography, he surprised many in his final years by touring the country giving informal lectures about his career, and answering questions from his many fans. He died on the eve of one such appearance in Davenport, Iowa.

OTHER FILMS INCLUDE: 1952: *Room for One More* (again with Drake); 1953: *Dream Wife;* 1957: *The Pride and the Passion* (a rare piece of miscasting in this period turkey); 1958: *Indiscreet, Houseboat;* 1959: *Operation Petticoat* (costarring Tony Curtis, who then imitated Grant, hilariously, in his subsequent *Some Like It Hot); 1962: *That Touch of Mink;* 1963: *Charade* (an elegantly witty comedy-mystery); 1964: *Father Goose.*

GRANT, LEE. Actress, director. *(b. Oct. 31, 1927, New York City, as Lyova Haskell Rosenthal.)* Juilliard-trained actress whose promising movie career—she earned an Academy Award nomination for her first film role, that of the young shoplifter in *Detective Story* (1951)—was stifled by her blacklisting during the McCarthy era. (A similar fate befell her playwright husband, Arnold Manoff.) Aside from supporting roles in *Storm Fear* (1955) and *Middle of the Night* (1959), Grant didn't appear on the big screen again until 1963, at which time things picked up considerably. Since then she has been Oscar-nominated three times, winning a Best Supporting Actress statuette for her work in *Shampoo* (1975). She began directing with 1980's *Tell Me a Riddle,* and her 1985 documentary, *Down and Out in America,* won the Oscar for its category. Her screen appearances have dwindled in recent years, although she was in top form as a prosecuting attorney in Albert Brooks' *Defending Your Life* (1991) and the made-for-TV *Citizen Cohn* (1992), ironically cast as Roy Cohn's mother. Her daughter is actress Dinah Manoff.

OTHER FILMS INCLUDE: 1963: *The Balcony;* 1965: *Terror in the City;* 1967: *Divorce American Style, Valley of the Dolls, In the Heat of the Night;* 1968: *Buona Sera, Mrs. Campbell;* 1969: *Marooned;* 1970: *The Landlord* (an Oscar-nominated turn); 1971: *Plaza Suite;* 1972: *Portnoy's Complaint;* 1976: *Voyage of the Damned* (another Oscar nod); 1978: *Airport '77, Damien: Omen II, The Swarm;* 1979: *When You Comin' Back, Red Ryder?;* 1980: *Little Miss Marker;* 1981: *Visiting Hours;* 1984: *Teachers;* 1986: *Arriving Tuesday;* 1987: *The Big Town;* 1988: *Calling the Shots;* 1989: *Staying Together* (director only).

GRANT, RICHARD E. Actor. (b. May 5, 1957, Mbabane, Swaziland.) Arresting British actor who has contributed strong comic and dramatic performances to a number of offbeat films. Grant moved to London in 1982 and worked in the theater and on British TV before receiving attention in a short film about advertising called *Honest, Decent and True*. This led to the leading role as an unemployed actor in writer-director Bruce Robinson's chamber comedy *Withnail and I* (1987) and also in Robinson's next film, *How to Get Ahead in Advertising* (1989), in which Grant starred as an ad executive who develops a talking boil on his shoulder. Grant was also prominently featured in *Mountains of the Moon* (1990), *Henry & June* (1990, as Anaïs Nin's husband), and *Warlock* (1991, as a heroic warrior). He was memorably paired with Sandra Bernhard in the megabomb *Hudson Hawk* (1991), and gave sly comic performances in *L.A. Story* (1991, as perhaps his most "normal" character to date) and Robert Altman's *The Player* (1992). He then won the meaty role of Dr. Seward in *Bram Stoker's Dracula* (1992) and played a society gadfly in *The Age of Innocence* (1993).

GRANVILLE, BONITA. Actress. (b. Feb. 2, 1923, Chicago; d. Oct. 11, 1988.) She played schoolgirl sleuth Nancy Drew in four 1938–39 Warner Bros. B mysteries *(Nancy Drew, Detective, Nancy Drew, Trouble Shooter, Nancy Drew, Reporter,* and *Nancy Drew and the Hidden Staircase),* but that's only one of this spirited actress' achievements. Born to show people, she appeared on stage while still a toddler and was acting in films by 1932 (debuting in *Westward Passage).* An energetic lass given to overacting, she generally played precocious, obnoxious brats, but gave a restrained, genuinely chilling performance as the mischievous Mary in *These Three* (1936, an adaptation of Lillian Hellman's "The Children's Hour" directed by William Wyler), for which she was Oscar-nominated.

As an attractive young woman, Granville played ingenues and supporting characters; by the late 1940s she was starring in medium-budget movies for Monogram. She moved behind the camera when husband Jack Wrather, a millionaire oilman,

bought the rights to both the Lassie and Lone Ranger characters in the early 1950s. She supervised the "Lassie" TV series for years, and made her last acting appearance in *The Lone Ranger* (1956), later doing a cameo in *The Legend of the Lone Ranger* (1981). She did some TV work during the 1950s and 1960s but spent most of her time working with Wrather in his various business enterprises.

OTHER FILMS INCLUDE: 1935: *Ah, Wilderness;* 1936: *The Plough and the Stars;* 1937: *Maid of Salem;* 1938: *Merrily We Live, The Beloved Brat;* 1939: *Angels Wash Their Faces;* 1940: *The Mortal Storm, Forty Little Mothers;* 1942: *Syncopation, The Glass Key, Now, Voyager;* 1943: *Hitler's Children* (a B "sleeper" for which she got good reviews); 1944: *Andy Hardy's Blonde Trouble;* 1946: *Breakfast in Hollywood, Suspense;* 1947: *The Guilty;* 1948: *Strike It Rich;* 1950: *Guilty of Treason.*

GRAY, COLEEN. Actress. (b. Oct. 23, 1922, Staplehurst, Nebr., as Doris Jensen.) If this petite actress had gotten more roles like the little carny temptress she played in *Nightmare Alley* (1947), she might have been more successful in movies. Although she was girl-next-door pretty, Gray in that performance suggested a mischievous, feline quality that should have been exploited by other producers. As it was, she worked frequently in minor pictures as a lead and in occasional A pictures in support.

OTHER FILMS INCLUDE: 1945: *State Fair;* 1947: *Kiss of Death;* 1948: *Red River;* 1950: *Riding High;* 1951: *Lucky Nick Cain;* 1952: *Kansas City Confidential;* 1954: *Arrow in the Dust;* 1955: *Las Vegas Shakedown;* 1956: *The Killing;* 1958: *Johnny Rocco;* 1960: *The Leech Woman* (a career low point); 1965: *Town Tamer;* 1971: *The Late Liz.*

GRAY, SPALDING. Actor. (b. June 5, 1941, Providence, R.I.) Dubbed "the WASP Woody Allen," Gray began his acting career in New York during the 1970s, and debuted as a monologist late in the decade, first performing the autobiographical work, "Sex and Death to the Age of 14," about growing up in Rhode Island. Later cast as the aide to an American ambassador in *The Killing Fields* (1984), Gray used the experience as material for his four-hour performance piece "Swimming to Cambodia," which was filmed in 1987 by Jonathan Demme and became an arthouse hit. As a result, Gray's stock has gone up, and he has appeared as a character actor in a number of films, including *True Stories* (1986), *Beaches, Clara's Heart* (both 1988), *Straight Talk* (1992), *The Pickle, King of the Hill, Twenty Bucks* (all 1993), *The Paper* (1994), *Bad Company,* and *Beyond Rangoon* (both 1995). He also appeared on Broadway as the Stage Manager in an acclaimed revival of Thornton Wilder's "Our Town" in the early 1990s. He came to the screen in another filmed monologue, *Monster in a Box,* in 1992. Gray, a cofounder of the experimental Wooster Theatre Group in the late 1970s, also took some unorthodox acting jobs in his salad days: He had a major role in a hard-core sex film, *The Farmer's Daughter;* he was billed under his own name and given extensive dialogue, making identification positive—even though he later denied having appeared in the film.

GRAYSON, KATHRYN. Actress, singer. *(b. Feb. 9, 1922, Winston-Salem, N.C., as Zelma Kathryn Hedrick.)* This pretty, petite (but curvy) brunette brightened some of MGM's top musicals of the 1940s and 1950s, getting her best screen opportunities fairly late in her career. A coloratura soprano whose heart-shaped face sported dancing eyes, an upturned nose, and a dazzling smile, she was singing on the radio when discovered by MGM talent scouts. Given the traditional contract player's buildup, she posed for countless publicity photos, took acting lessons, and got some before-the-camera seasoning as the ingenue in a B picture, *Andy Hardy's Private Secretary* (1941), before being spotlighted in *The Vanishing Virginian* (1942). She appeared opposite some of Metro's top musical stars—Gene Kelly, Frank Sinatra and, later, Mario Lanza—in a succession of popular songfests, many of them shot in Technicolor. She played the riverboat belle Magnolia in *Show Boat* (1951) and the tempestuous actress Katharine in *Kiss Me Kate* (1953), her two best pictures. Grayson left the screen after filming *The Vagabond King* (1956) for Paramount. She later worked on stage and in nightclubs, and has made infrequent public appearances since. Her husbands included actor John Shelton and singer-songwriter Johnny Johnston.

OTHER FILMS INCLUDE: 1942: *Rio Rita, Seven Sweethearts;* 1943: *Thousands Cheer;* 1945: *Anchors Aweigh;* 1946: *Two Sisters From Boston, Ziegfeld Follies, Till the Clouds Roll By* (in the last named—a Jerome Kern biopic—as Magnolia in the *Show Boat* sequence, a dry run for her later role); 1947: *It Happened in Brooklyn;* 1948: *The Kissing Bandit;* 1949: *That Midnight Kiss;* 1950: *The Toast of New Orleans, Grounds for Marriage;* 1952: *Lovely to Look At;* 1953: *So This Is Love* (as songbird Grace Moore).

GREENAWAY, PETER. Director, writer. *(b. Apr. 5, 1942, Newport, Wales.)* Among the most controversial filmmakers in recent memory, Greenaway has divided critics and repulsed, confused, and thrilled audiences with his movies' bold visuals and often savage social commentary. He edited films in the 1960s and 1970s for Britain's Central Office of Information and, during that time, used the Office's facilities to produce his own experimental shorts. By 1978 his short narrative films and documentaries had attracted international attention and won many prizes. Greenaway's first feature, *The Draughtsman's Contract* (1983), was a critically acclaimed debut, and he followed it with *A Zed and Two Noughts* (1985), *The Belly of an Architect* (1987), and *Drowning by Numbers* (1988). His next film, *The Cook, the Thief, His Wife & Her Lover* (1989), a viscerally overwhelming black comedy, was extremely controversial; though initially stamped with an X rating, it was Greenaway's biggest success in the U.S. *Prospero's Books* (1991), a visually fascinating adaptation of Shakespeare's play using the latest computer technology and high-definition TV, illustrated Greenaway's continued determination to expand the boundaries of the film medium. He flouts contemporary manners and mores in his films, often deliberately shocking his audiences (with graphic, uninhibited displays of violence and sexuality, among other things) to make a point.

GREENE, GRAHAM. Actor. *(b. June 22, 1952, Six Nations Reserve, Ontario.)* A member of the Oneida Tribe, Greene is best known for his Oscar-nominated supporting performance as the sage Kicking Bird in Kevin Costner's *Dances With Wolves* (1990). He worked as an audio technician for rock bands before getting involved in theater in Britain and Toronto, and scored supporting roles in *Running Brave* (1983), *Revolution* (1985), and *Powwow Highway* (1989). He added color as a sharp police officer helping to solve a murder in *Thunderheart* (1992), starred in *Clearcut* (also 1992) and *Benefit of the Doubt* (1993), and was featured in a comic role in *Maverick* (1994). He also appeared to good effect as the sole survivor of a pre-WW1 Indian tribe in the cable-TV movie *The Last of His Tribe* (1992), opposite Jon Voight, and had a recurring role in TV's "Northern Exposure."

GREENE, RICHARD. Actor. *(b. Aug. 25, 1918, Plymouth, England; d. June 1, 1985.)* Boyishly handsome, exuberant secondary lead (and occasional star) of 1930s and 1940s movies who achieved lasting recognition as the star of the British-made "The Adventures of Robin Hood" TV series (seen here from 1955–58). Born into a show-business family, Greene started acting in his teens and came to Hollywood in 1938, signed by 20th Century-Fox. He made his screen debut as one of the brothers in *Four Men and a Prayer* (1938), and subsequently acted in *My Lucky Star, Kentucky* (also 1938), *The Little Princess, The Hound of the Baskervilles, Stanley and Livingstone* (all 1939), *Little Old New York, I Was an Adventuress* (both 1940), and *Forever Amber* (1947), among others. No Olivier he, but Greene possessed a pleasing personality that registered well on-screen. Later on the dashing Britisher made an ideal swashbuckling hero in such costume dramas as *The Desert Hawk* (1950), *Lorna Doone* (1951), *Rogue's March* (1952), and *Captain Scarlett* (1953). As a still-handsome, confident leading man in middle age, he played intrepid Sir Nayland Smith in *The Blood of Fu Manchu* (1968) and *The Castle of Fu Manchu* (1972). His final film was *Special Effects* (1984). He was married at one time to actress Patricia Medina.

GREENSTREET, SYDNEY. Actor. *(b. Dec. 27, 1879, Sandwich, England; d. Jan. 18,* *1954.)* "I'll tell you right out—I'm a man who likes talking to a man who likes to talk." Few actors have ever made such an impressive film debut. Greenstreet, a versatile performer with 40 years' experience on the stage, had shunned Hollywood until John Huston offered him the role of Kasper Gutman, the loquacious, enigmatic villain of *The Maltese Falcon* (1941). Greenstreet was masterful in the part, delighting audiences, astounding critics, and securing an Oscar nomination. (He also helped promote the film with an unforgettable coming-attractions trailer, the success of which led to similar duties for many of his subsequent Warner Bros. films.) He was reunited with *Falcon* star Humphrey Bogart in several movies (including the classic *Casablanca*), but he seemed most at ease opposite wily, diminutive Peter Lorre. The screen's original Odd Couple, they were teamed to pleasing effect in *Casablanca* (1942), *The Mask of Dimitrios* (1944), *The Verdict*, and *Three Strangers* (both 1946); audiences thrived on watching these schemers try to outwit each other. Greenstreet also appeared in *Across the Pacific* (1942), *Christmas in Connecticut* (1945), *Devotion* (1946), *The Hucksters* (1947, as the despotic soap tycoon), *The Woman in White* (1948), *It's a Great Feeling* (1949, in an amusing cameo as himself), *Flamingo Road* (1949), and *Malaya* (1950), among others. His obesity contributed to persistent health problems (including diabetes), and he died at 75.

GREENWOOD, JOAN. Actress. *(b. Mar. 4, 1921, London; d. Feb. 28, 1987.)* Blond British actress with inimitable husky voice, frequently cast in bad-girl parts, memorable as Lady Caroline Lamb in *The Bad Lord Byron* (1948). Stage-trained at the Royal Academy of Dramatic Art, Greenwood made her debut in the unexciting-sounding *John Smith Wakes Up* (1940). An actress apparently incapable of giving a bad performance, she contributed to a number of Britain's most prominent films. Among her credits: *The Man Within, Bad Sister* (both 1947), *Whisky Galore, Kind Hearts and Coronets* (both 1949), *The Man in the White Suit* (1951), *The Importance of Being Earnest* (1952), *Father Brown/The Detective* (1954), *Moonfleet* (1955), *Stage Struck*

(1958), *The Mysterious Island* (1961), *Tom Jones* (1963), and *The Water Babies* (1978). Her last film, completed shortly before her death, was the sprawling adaptation of Dickens' *Little Dorrit* (1987).

GREER, JANE. Actress. *(b. Sept. 9, 1924, Washington, D.C., as Bettejane Greer.)* If she'd never made another movie, this angelic brunette would rate an entry in this book for her portrayal of the icy, manipulative temptress who makes chumps of both Robert Mitchum and Kirk Douglas in the film noir classic *Out of the Past* (1947). (She was almost equally good in similar parts in other 1940s' noirs.) A beauty-contest winner and professional model from her teens, Greer was spotted in 1943 by Howard Hughes, who signed her to a personal contract. (She married Rudy Vallee the same year; it was a short-lived union.) Hughes "leased" her to RKO, where she appeared in *George White's Scandals, Two O'Clock Courage, Dick Tracy* (all 1945); *The Falcon's Alibi* (1946), *Sinbad the Sailor, They Won't Believe Me* (both 1947), *Station West* (1948), and *The Big Steal* (1949), among others. Hughes stymied her career for a time, refusing to let her work; when she finally gained her independence, she appeared in *The Prisoner of Zenda* (1952), *The Clown* (1953), *Run for the Sun* (1956), *The Man of a Thousand Faces* (1957), *Where Love Has Gone* (1964), *The Outfit* (1973), *Just Between Friends* (1986 as Mary Tyler Moore's mother), and *Immediate Family* (1989). In 1984 she was cast in *Against All Odds,* a reworking of *Out of the Past,* and was just as icy and manipulative playing the mother of Rachel Ward (now cast in Greer's original role) as she'd been in the earlier film, much to the delight of buffs. She also participated in an *Out of the Past* parody on TV's "Saturday Night Live" with her original costar Robert Mitchum. Her son Lawrence Lasker has coproduced several films, including *WarGames* (1983) and *Sneakers* (1992).

GREY, JENNIFER. Actress. *(b. Mar. 26, 1960, New York City.)* This pert, curly-haired daughter of actor-singer-dancer Joel Grey opened moviegoers' eyes as the lovesick, ugly-duckling teenager who blossoms (under Patrick Swayze's able tutelage) in *Dirty Dancing* (1987), a box-office sleeper. Following in the family footsteps, Grey started acting in the early 1980s, landing supporting roles in *Reckless, The Cotton Club, Red Dawn* (all 1984), and *American Flyers* (1985), before making her mark in the teen comedy *Ferris Bueller's Day Off* (1986) as the put-upon sister of Matthew Broderick (with whom she was once linked romantically). The following year, *Dirty Dancing* was a tremendous hit, and suddenly everyone knew who Jennifer Grey was. Inexplicably, she seemed unable to capitalize on that success in subsequent films; she has since appeared on the big screen infrequently, in such misguided efforts as the barely released Runyonesque travesty, *Bloodhounds of Broadway* (1989) and the sailing saga *Wind* (1992).

GREY, JOEL. Actor, singer, dancer. *(b. Apr. 11, 1932, Cleveland, as Joel Katz.)* Impish, energetic musical performer best known for his stage work, but the recipient of a Best Supporting Actor Oscar for his characterization of the attention-grabbing emcee in *Cabaret* (1972). He evolved into a first-rate character actor, playing a psychic in *Man on a Swing* (1974), a man of mystery in *The Seven Percent Solution* (1976), a wise man (buried under Asian makeup) in *Remo Williams: The Adventure Begins* (1985), an officious pencil-pusher in *Kafka* (1991), and Charles Durning's calculating, poker-playing companion in *The Music of Chance* (1993). His daughter is actress Jennifer Grey.
OTHER FILMS INCLUDE: 1952: *About Face* (his first, a remake of *Brother Rat*); 1957: *Calypso Heat Wave;* 1961: *Come September;* 1976: *Buffalo Bill and the Indians, or Sitting Bull's History Lesson.*

GREY, VIRGINIA. Actress. *(b. Mar. 22, 1917, Los Angeles.)* Slender, radiantly beautiful ingenue who worked steadily in films throughout the 1930s, 1940s, 1950s, and 1960s. As the daughter of a director and a film editor, she virtually grew up in the movie business. She played Little Eva in the 1927 version of *Uncle Tom's Cabin* and appeared in several other late silent and early talkie films before "retiring" to finish her schooling. As an ingenue, be-

ginning with 1937's *Secret Valley,* the honey-blond, blue-eyed Grey appeared in several dozen films, mostly for MGM. She mainly played leads in B films and support in A's. Although still youthfully beautiful in the post-World War 2 years, Grey found leading-lady roles scarce, and segued into supporting parts. She couldn't be called a great actress by any means, but she displayed enough talent and presence to keep employed far longer than many of her counterparts.
OTHER FILMS INCLUDE: 1937: *Rosalie;* 1938: *Test Pilot, Dramatic School;* 1939: *Idiot's Delight* (in Clark Gable's dancing troupe), *The Women, Another Thin Man;* 1940: *Three Cheers for the Irish;* 1941: *The Big Store;* 1942: *Tarzan's New York Adventure;* 1943: *Idaho* (as Roy Rogers' leading lady); 1945: *Flame of the Barbary Coast;* 1946: *Swamp Fire;* 1947: *Unconquered;* 1948: *Jungle Jim, Mexican Hayride;* 1951: *Bullfighter and the Lady;* 1954: *Target Earth;* 1957: *Jeanne Eagels;* 1960: *Portrait in Black;* 1961: *Flower Drum Song, Back Street;* 1963: *Black Zoo;* 1964: *The Naked Kiss;* 1966: *Madame X;* 1967: *Rosie;* 1970: *Airport.*

GRIER, PAM. Actress. *(b. May 26, 1949, Winston-Salem, N.C.)* Tall and voluptuous, the 1970s' Queen of Blaxploitation brought a formidable presence to such formulaic crowd-pleasers as *Coffy* (1973), *Foxy Brown* (1974), *Sheba Baby* (1975), and others, most of them vengeance-is-mine tales loaded with graphic nudity and liberal bloodletting. The cousin of pro-footballer Roosevelt Grier, Pam actually got her start in babes-in-bonds exploitation epics churned out by Roger Corman's New World. She was launched in *The Big Doll House* (1971) and was felicitously squared off against the equally statuesque Margaret Markov in *Black Mama, White Mama* (1972, an outlandish female version of *The Defiant Ones),* and *The Arena* (1974), where they played gladiators in Ancient Rome. She also appeared to good advantage in *Scream Blacula Scream* (1973) and *Bucktown* (1975), and tried to broaden her appeal as the comic-strip character *Friday Foster* (also 1975). But when the blaxploitation genre went into eclipse, so did her career. Grier's performance as the pathetic junkie in *Fort Apache, The Bronx* (1981) heralded her new career as a character actress, and she

has since made impressive appearances portraying a witch in *Something Wicked This Way Comes* (1983), no-nonsense cops both serious (1988's *Above the Law)* and comic (1987's *The Allnighter),* and a beleaguered high school teacher in *Class of 1999* (1990).

GRIFFITH, D. W. Director, producer. *(b. Jan. 22, 1875, La Grange, Ky., as David Wark Griffith; d. July 23, 1948.)* Often called the father of the motion picture, he was the first director to fully realize the medium's potential. His contemporary Cecil B. DeMille once declared of Griffith: "He taught us how to photograph thought." Griffith came to the movies as an actor for the Edison Company in 1907 after a modest career on the stage and as a writer of poetry and plays. He joined the Biograph Company in 1908, and over the next four years his one-reel pictures made the words "Biograph Tonight" a welcome sign in front of nickelodeons throughout the land. Griffith explored technique in such pictures as *The Lonely Villa* (1909) and *A Girl and Her Trust* (1912), which developed the device of cross-cutting to heighten screen tension; but many of Griffith's Biograph films, including *Sorrows of the Unfaithful* (1910) and *The Painted Lady* (1912), were strong psychological dramas that eschewed technique for content.

At Biograph Griffith discovered or developed the talents of Florence Lawrence, Mary Pickford, Lillian and Dorothy Gish, Mae Marsh, Robert Harron, Arthur Johnson, and Henry B. Walthall, the screen's earliest stars. He also gave Mack Sennett his first opportunities both as an actor and as a director. Throughout his tenure at Biograph, Griffith was at odds with management, which refused to allow him to make longer pictures, or to give him (or the Biograph players for that matter) screen credit, and when the company finally moved into longer films it insulted Griffith by bringing in an army of "legitimate" stage directors to helm their prestigious, but ultimately dull, adaptations of Klaw and Erlanger plays. Biograph even withheld two of Griffith's best 1913 Biographs, *The Battle at Elderbrush Gulch* and *Judith of Bethulia* (both 1914) until after he left the studio to avoid paying the director his contractual profit participation.

Branching out on his own in late 1913, Griffith joined Harry Aitken's Reliance-Majestic Company, and completed several features for the company before embarking on his most ambitious film, a 12-reel adaptation of Thomas Dixon's barnstorming stage melodrama "The Clansman," which was retitled *The Birth of a Nation* when it was released in 1915. With its sweeping battle scenes, tender moments of human drama, and the skillful (if highly inflammatory) ride of the Ku Klux Klan for a rousing climax, the film was a sensation, and Griffith was hailed as the "Shakespeare of the screen." He followed the Civil War epic with another large-scale film, *Intolerance* (1916), which unfolded three historic narratives and a modern story simultaneously by intercutting the action at dramatic moments. The film was recognized as a masterpiece, but it met with some audience resistance. Although it cost half a million dollars (not the $2 million reported in the trade papers), and was only a modest box-office failure, Griffith retreated to making inexpensive but profitable program pictures like *True Heart Susie* for Artcraft in 1917.

Thereafter, Griffith divided his time between independence and servitude, turning out potboilers like *The Love Flower* (1920) and *One Exciting Night* (1922) to finance large-scale efforts such as *Hearts of the World* (1918) and *Orphans of the Storm* (1922, one of his best silents, a French Revolution saga starring Lillian and Dorothy Gish). Griffith became one of the founders of United Artists in 1919, and his *Broken Blossoms,* with Lillian Gish and Richard Barthelmess, was hailed as an artistic and commercial triumph. His biggest box-office success came with an adaptation of the old theatrical warhorse *Way Down East* (1920). The dated melodrama of false marriage and true love was transformed by Griffith into a loving portrait of rural America, with a riveting climax on the ice floes.

Leaving Hollywood for New York in the early 1920s, Griffith became detached from mainstream commercial considerations. *America* (1924), a tale of the American Revolution, was a box-office disappointment, and the tepid response to his haunting *Isn't Life Wonderful?* (also 1924), about refugees in postwar Germany, forced Griffith to abandon independence and return to harness, this time for Adolph Zukor at Paramount. *Sally of the Sawdust* (1925) and *That Royle Girl* (1926) offered feature-film stardom to Broadway comic W. C. Fields, but proved that Griffith was more at home with drama. *The Sorrows of Satan* (also 1926) featured some extraordinary imagery and fine performances, but sported a weak story and was poorly received.

By now Griffith's career was faltering, and alcoholism contributed to his rapid decline. Although no longer a principal partner, Griffith signed as a contract director with producer Joseph M. Schenck at United Artists. With *Drums of Love, The Battle of the Sexes* (both 1928), and *Lady of the Pavements* (1929), Griffith proved he was still capable of making creditable films, and *Abraham Lincoln* (1930), his first all-talkie, offered promise that Griffith would make the transition to sound with little difficulty. However, the filmmaker still longed for independence, and using a windfall income-tax refund, he returned to New York to produce *The Struggle* (1931). A tale of the evils of devil rum, Griffith's story took place in the pre-WW1 years, and he staged it like a Biograph one-reeler, an artistic conceit lost on audiences, who just thought it old-fashioned.

Except for some stillborn projects, notably an English remake of *Broken Blossoms* (1936) and *One Million B.C.* (1939), both ultimately directed by others, Griffith was out of the business. Successful investments kept him comfortably well off, but he was bitter about being forgotten by the industry he helped to create. Griffith did a radio show based on his (highly colored) reminiscences in 1933, and received a special Oscar for his contributions to the art of motion pictures in 1935. He was well portrayed by Charles Dance in the evocative Italian film *Good Morning, Babylon* (1987).

GRIFFITH, HUGH. Actor. *(b. May 30, 1912, Marian Glas, Anglesey, North Wales; d. May 14, 1980.)* This boisterous, bushy-eyed character actor actually worked as a bank clerk before getting the acting itch. Making a 1939 stage debut, Griffith appeared on-screen in 1940's *Neutral Port* before being hustled into Her Majesty's Army for a six-year stretch. Once he returned to the screen in 1947, though, he worked consistently for the next 30 years on both sides of the Atlantic. Griffith most often played dynamic, overbearing characters, but also delineated sensitive types as well. His better-known films include *Kind Hearts and Coronets* (1949), *The Beggar's Opera* (1953), *Exodus* (1960), *Oliver!* (1968), and *Start the Revolution Without Me* (1970). Griffith is probably best remembered as blustery Squire Weston in *Tom Jones* (1963) and as crafty Sheik IIderim in *Ben-Hur* (1959), a typically flamboyant performance for which he won a Best Supporting Actor Oscar.

GRIFFITH, MELANIE. Actress. *(b. Aug. 9, 1957, New York City.)* When the blond, bubbly Griffith made her acting debut in *Night Moves* (1975), she was already a divorcée (having been the teen bride of actor Don Johnson, whom she met in 1973 while he was costarring with her mother, actress Tippi Hedren, in *The Harrad Experiment).* Often cast as an airheaded, precocious nymphet, Griffith worked in *Smile* (1975), *The Drowning Pool* (1976), *One on One, Joyride* (both 1977), and *Roar* (1981, produced by and starring her mother), and struggled with substance-abuse problems before getting her career back on track in the 1980s. She began attracting critical notice as a porno actress in *Body Double* (1984), and enhanced her reputation with an eye-opening performance as a free spirit in *Something Wild* (1986). Soon writers were asking when the public was going to take notice of this burgeoning talent; it finally happened when she won the part of an ambitious secretary in 1988's endearing comedy *Working Girl,* which earned her an Oscar nomination, and bona fide stardom. She showed maturing talent in the little-seen *Stormy Monday* (1988) and *Pacific Heights* (1990) and was generally wasted in *The Bonfire of the Vanities* (also 1990). Griffith remarried Don Johnson in 1989, and appeared opposite him in *Paradise* (1991), a sensitive domestic drama that showed them both to good advantage. And she displayed her ability to carry an old-fashioned star vehicle with the WW2-era espionage-romance *Shining Through* and the cop thriller set in the world of Hasidic Jews, *A Stranger Among Us* (both

1992). With her distinctive little-girl voice, she seemed an ideal choice to take on Judy Holliday's star-making role in the remake of *Born Yesterday* (1993) with Johnson and John Goodman.

OTHER FILMS INCLUDE: 1984: *Fear City* (in which she played a stripper); 1986: *Cherry 2000* (a witless sci-fi opus); 1990: *In the Spirit;* 1994: *Nobody's Fool, Milk Money.*

GRIFFITH, RAYMOND. Actor, writer, producer. *(b. Jan. 23, 1890, Boston; d. Nov. 25, 1957.)* Probably no single performer in movie history is as deserving of a major rediscovery as this impeccable silent-screen comedy actor. Today's hardened, seen-it-all film buffs still gasp with delight at the invention and hilarity of his work, seen infrequently in limited revivals. Generally clad in top hat, white tie and tails, carrying a cane and sporting a dapper mustache and unflappable air (not unlike French comedian Max Linder, to whom he bore an amazing resemblance), Griffith created a unique and bold screen persona. Originally a stage performer, he refined his comedy craft at the Mack Sennett Studios, first as a performer, and then as a writer and director. In 1922, he left and resumed his acting career, and quickly established himself as a solid second banana in slapstick comedies and sophisticated farces alike. Two years later, he signed with Paramount, and immediately scored hits as a society gigolo in *Open All Night* and as a bewildered suitor in *Changing Husbands.* A string of exemplary starring vehicles followed: *The Night Club* (1925), *Paths to Paradise* (1925), and *Hands Up!* (1926), to name a few. Alas, many of his films from this era no longer exist, accounting for his subsequent obscurity.

When sound came in, Griffith's hoarse, whispery voice made performing in talkies unthinkable (though he did try, notably as the lead in 1930's *Trent's Last Case,* a comedy-mystery directed by Howard Hawks) and, following his poignant, non-speaking cameo role as a doomed French soldier in *All Quiet on the Western Front* (1930), he retired from acting. Griffith's old friend Darryl F. Zanuck hired him as a writer and producer, and he worked on many classic films before retiring in the 1940s.

GRODIN, CHARLES. Actor. *(b. Apr. 21, 1935, Pittsburgh.)* The movies' quintessential square, this low-key comic actor possesses the ability to wring laughs out of even banal dialogue, thanks to his wry delivery and understated facial reactions. A student of Lee Strasberg and Uta Hagen, Grodin made his Broadway debut in 1962 and debuted on film two years later in *Sex and the Single Girl* (1964). He was screen-tested for the lead in *The Graduate* (1967) but reportedly turned it down! He won small supporting roles in *Rosemary's Baby* (1968) and *Catch-22* (1970, as the navigator Aardvark), but got his breakthrough role in *The Heartbreak Kid* (1972), as a sporting goods salesman who leaves his wife—on their honeymoon—to woo Cybill Shepherd. He starred in (and adapted) the heist comedy *11 Harrowhouse* (1974) and followed with an odd mix of projects: *King Kong* (1976), *Heaven Can Wait* (1978, stealing most of his scenes), *Sunburn* (1979), and Albert Brooks' first feature *Real Life* (1979, as the put-upon patriarch of a family under a documentarian's observation). He worked steadily throughout the 1980s in *Seems Like Old Times* (1980), *The Great Muppet Caper* (1981, playing love scenes opposite Miss Piggy), *The Woman in Red* (1984), and *The Lonely Guy* (1984, unforgettable as Steve Martin's really, really lonely friend). In 1985, he wrote, coproduced and costarred in *Movers and Shakers,* a comedy about moviemaking which barely got released. After the infamous *Ishtar* (1987), Grodin enjoyed one of his most popular successes in *Midnight Run* (1988), as a droll embezzler escorted by bounty hunter Robert De Niro; theirs was an inspired pairing. His other credits include the minor comedies *The Couch Trip* (1988) and *Taking Care of Business* (1990), as well as supporting roles in *Dave, Heart and Souls,* and *So I Married an Axe Murderer* (all 1993), and the lead in the sleeper comedy *Beethoven* (1992) and its 1993 sequel, *Beethoven's 2nd.* He also appeared in *Clifford* and *It Runs in My Family* (both 1994). Grodin's numerous Broadway credits include directing "Lovers and Other Strangers" and starring in "Same Time, Next Year" opposite Ellen Burstyn. On television, he has directed "Acts of Love and Other Comedies," "The Simon and Garfunkel Special" and won an Emmy as one of the writers on "The Paul Simon Special." He has also written the show business memoir "It Would Be So Nice If You Weren't Here" (1988) and "How I Get Through Life: A Wise and Witty Guide" (1992).

GUEST, CHRISTOPHER. Actor, writer, director. *(b. Feb. 5, 1948, New York City.)* Actor best known as Nigel Tufnel of the rock group Spinal Tap—introduced in the mock-rockumentary *This Is Spinal Tap* (1984)—who is proud of his amp system that goes all the way to "eleven." A comedy writer and performer who shone on National Lampoon's 1970s radio series (and record albums), Guest has had too few opportunities since then to showcase his considerable talents. He has taken dramatic and comedic roles on TV and in films like *Death Wish* (1974, a bit part as a cop), *Girlfriends* (1978), *The Long Riders* (1980, with his brother Nicholas), *Little Shop of Horrors* (1986), *The Princess Bride* (1987, in which he patterned his elegant villainy—and voice—after character actor Henry Daniell), *Beyond Therapy* (1987), *Sticky Fingers* (1988), and *A Few Good Men* (1992), directed by longtime friend Rob Reiner, for whom he also worked behind the camera on the TV sitcom "Morton and Hayes" (1992). He starred for a season on "Saturday Night Live" (1984–85), cowrote and directed the Hollywood satire *The Big Picture* (1989), and directed the TV remake of *Attack of the 50 Ft. Woman* (1993). He is married to Jamie Lee Curtis.

GUINNESS, ALEC (SIR). Actor. *(b. Apr. 2, 1914, London, as A. Guinness de Cuffe.)* Sir Alec may be the only member of British acting royalty whose voice can be heard in video arcades. As space-age gladiator Obi-Wan Kenobi, guardian of "The Force" and mythic hero of George Lucas' Star Wars trilogy, he has become a familiar face (and voice) to the MTV generation. Others regard him as one of the finest actors of the century, who seems constitutionally incapable of giving a bad performance. Initially an ad copywriter, the young Guinness took up acting while still in his early 20s. He played in "the classics" at Britain's legendary Old Vic theater, and even made a brief appearance on-screen in 1934's *Evensong.* But World

War 2 interrupted his career, which didn't get back on track until 1946.

Guinness' first really notable movie work was done for director David Lean in two Dickens adaptations, *Great Expectations* (1947, as Herbert Pocket) and *Oliver Twist* (1948, as Fagin). Guinness, on a roll now, brightened a whole slew of classic comedies made at the Ealing studio: *Kind Hearts and Coronets* (1949, in an astonishing eight roles), *The Man in the White Suit* (1951), *The Lavender Hill Mob* (also 1951, Oscar nominated), and *The Ladykillers* (1955), as well as comedies and dramas as diverse as *The Captain's Paradise* (1953), *Father Brown* (1954, the title role, aka *The Detective), The Horse's Mouth* (1958) and *Our Man in Havana* (1959). His script for *The Horse's Mouth* earned him an Oscar nomination.

Although primarily a character lead, Guinness by this time was also an acknowledged international star, and he worked in multinationally financed films that were widely released. During this period he appeared in *The Scapegoat* (1959), *Tunes of Glory* (1960), *A Majority of One* (1961), *Damn the Defiant!* (1962), *The Fall of the Roman Empire* (1964), *The Quiller Memorandum* (1966), *The Comedians* (1967), *Scrooge* (as Marley), *Cromwell* (both 1970), *Hitler: The Last Ten Days* (as Adolf) *Brother Sun, Sister Moon* (both 1973), *Murder by Death* (1976), and *Lovesick* (1983, as the ghost of Freud). And of course, he always returned to Lean: *The Bridge on the River Kwai* (1957), which won him an Oscar as the military martinet he originally thought unplayable, *Lawrence of Arabia* (1962, as Prince Feisal), *Doctor Zhivago* (1965, as Zhivago's half-brother Yeugraf), and *A Passage to India* (1984, as the Hindu sage Godbole).

Guinness played John Le Carré's master spy George Smiley in a pair of acclaimed 1980s TV miniseries, "Tinker, Tailor, Soldier, Spy" and "Smiley's People," and tutored young Luke Skywalker (Mark Hamill) in the ways of "The Force" in *Star Wars* (1977), *The Empire Strikes Back* (1980), and *Return of the Jedi* (1983). He was Oscar-nominated for *Star Wars,* and in 1980 Guinness won a special Oscar for his entire career—one which, happily, was far from over. He gave a magnificent performance in the lengthy production of *Little Dorrit* (1988, Oscar-nominated), and also appeared in *A Hand-* *ful of Dust* (also 1988), *Kafka* (1991), and *A Foreign Field* (1993). His autobiography, "Blessings in Disguise," was published in 1985.

GUTTENBERG, STEVE. Actor. (b. Aug. 24, 1958, Brooklyn.) Although this youthful-looking "everyman" has appeared in some of the 1980s' most successful films, his own standing in the film industry hasn't significantly improved: When producers cast serious dramas or big-budget action flicks, Guttenberg's is a name that, apparently, never comes up. Early film appearances—in *The Chicken Chronicles* (1977) and *The Boys From Brazil* (1978)—indicated he had something on the ball, and he showed promise in his first major role, playing the sports fanatic in Barry Levinson's ensemble comedy *Diner* (1982). That potential went unrealized in a succession of movies in which his apparent overeagerness to please rendered his performances shrill and one-note. Despite having starred in a few clunkers of major proportions, including *Can't Stop the Music* (1980), *The Man Who Wasn't There* (1983), *High Spirits* (1987), and *Don't Tell Her It's Me* (1990), he has also top-lined the hits *Police Academy* (1984, and three of the five sequels), *Cocoon* (1985), *Cocoon 2: The Return* (1988), *Short Circuit* (1986), *The Bedroom Window, 3 Men and a Baby* (both 1987), and *3 Men and a Little Lady* (1990). Guttenberg also appeared on the TV series "Billy" (1979) and "No Soap, Radio" (1982).

GWENN, EDMUND. Actor. (b. Sept. 26, 1875, Glamorgan, Wales; d. Sept. 6, 1959.) He *was* Kris Kringle in the Christmas perennial *Miracle on 34th Street* (1947), and won an Oscar for his endearing performance. In most of his American films, Edmund Gwenn appeared as a small and mild-mannered man with the face of an aged cherub. In his youth, Gwenn was a protégé of George Bernard Shaw, achieving notoriety for his role in the original production of "Man and Superman." British film credits include *Be Mine Tonight* (1932), *The Good Companions, Friday the 13th* (both 1933), and Alfred Hitchcock's *The Skin Game* (1931), and *Waltzes From Vienna* (1934, as Johann Strauss). He arrived in Hollywood in 1935, already 60 years old, and delivered consistently fine performances in *Sylvia Scarlett* (1935), *Anthony Adverse* (1936), *Pride and Prejudice* (1940), *Foreign Correspondent* (1940, again for Hitchcock, as the soft-spoken little assassin), *The Devil and Miss Jones, Charley's Aunt* (both 1941), *Lassie Come Home, Forever and a Day* (both 1943), *Between Two Worlds* (1944), *Apartment for Peggy* (1948), *Mister 880* (1950, a plum role as a benign counterfeiter that earned him an Oscar nomination), *Les Miserables* (1952), *Them!* (1954), and many other films. Alfred Hitchcock showcased him as the star of his sly black comedy *The Trouble With Harry* (1955), and he pulled it off to perfection, capping off a distinguished career. Though his deathbed quote has often been mangled, he apparently told visitor George Seaton, commenting on how tough it was to be dying: "It's tough . . . but not as tough as comedy!"

HAAS, LUKAS. Actor. *(b. Apr. 16, 1976, West Hollywood.)* Moviegoers fell in love with this child actor when he played the cute, pensive Amish boy in *Witness* (1985). Previously he'd appeared as Jane Alexander's small son in the nuclear-holocaust drama *Testament* (1983). Haas appeared as one of the youthful ensemble players in *Solarbabies* (1986), and then scored in two skillfully realized leading roles, as a displaced youngster in *The Wizard of Loneliness* and as an inquisitive one in *Lady in White* (both 1988). Although he was still a slight, unimposing lad, the increasingly precocious Haas got his best opportunity to date in *Rambling Rose* (1991), playing an intelligent, manipulative, sexually curious but prepubescent Southern boy. Also seen in *Music Box* and *See You in the Morning* (both 1989), and *Leap of Faith* (1992).

HACKETT, JOAN. Actress. *(b. May 1, 1942, New York City; d. Oct. 8, 1983.)* Broadway-seasoned actress and former fashion model who made her film debut as one of *The Group* (1966). She generally played straightforward, strong women, and worked mainly on stage and on TV. But Hackett had some fine movie moments as well, especially as the no-nonsense frontier woman in *Will Penny* (1968). Oscar-nominated for her work in *Only When I Laugh* (1981), Hackett had a special quality—along the lines of a Jean Arthur or Margaret Sullavan—that was simultaneously truthful and enchanting. She was married to actor Richard Mulligan. Hackett died from cancer.
OTHER FILMS INCLUDE: 1968: *Assignment to Kill;* 1969: *Support Your Local Sheriff!* (a delicious comic performance); 1972: *Rivals;* 1973: *The Last of Sheila* (one of her better assignments); 1974: *The Terminal Man;* 1975: *Mackintosh and T.J.;* 1979: *Mr. Mike's Mondo Video;* 1980: *One-Trick Pony;* 1982: *The Escape Artist.*

HACKFORD, TAYLOR. Director, producer. *(b. Dec. 3, 1944, Santa Barbara, Calif.)* Renowned for his direction of sexy, high-energy films, Hackford began his career making documentaries for public television. After winning an Oscar for the short subject "Teenage Father" in 1978, he directed his first feature, *The Idolmaker* (1980), a small but well-received film about a 1950s music producer that reflected Hackford's love of rock and roll and his early work presenting it on TV. His next film, *An Officer and a Gentleman* (1982), an old-fashioned love story with up-to-date sex and language, became a blockbuster and made stars out of its leads, Debra Winger and Richard Gere. Hackford followed with *Against All Odds* (1984), a remake of the film noir classic *Out of the Past,* and *White Nights* (1985), which teamed dancers Mikhail Baryshnikov and Gregory Hines in a Cold War drama. Hackford returned to his roots with the documentary *Chuck Berry Hail! Hail! Rock 'n' Roll* (1987) and then directed *Everybody's All-American* (1988) with Jessica Lange and Dennis Quaid, the ambitious Chicano gang drama *Bound by Honor* (1993), and *Dolores Claiborne* (1995). Hackford is cofounder of New Visions Pictures, which has released the smaller-budget films *The Long Walk Home* (1990), *Queens Logic,* and *Mortal Thoughts* (both 1991). He has lived for some time with actress Helen Mirren.

HACKMAN, GENE. Actor. *(b. Jan. 30, 1930, San Bernardino, Calif., as Eugene Alden Hackman.)* The unprepossessing Hackman is universally recognized as one of America's most versatile and convincing actors. His tremendous ability with "ordinary guy" roles has been rightly praised, sometimes at the expense of his equally impressive comic timing and the undercurrent of eccentricity that sometimes floats to the surface of his straightest roles. After serving in the Marine Corps, Hackman briefly studied journalism and did numerous odd jobs before deciding, relatively late in life (at 30), to try his hand at acting. He studied at Pasadena Playhouse (where, according to legend, he and fellow student Dustin Hoffman were tagged "Least Likely to Succeed"), and after summer stock and small TV and stage roles, he landed a part on Broadway in the comedy "Any Wednesday." He made his film debut in *Mad Dog Coll* (1961), but it was his role in *Lilith* (1964) which its star, Warren Beatty, remembered when he was casting his next film, *Bonnie and Clyde* (1967). Hackman's performance as Clyde's brother Buck Barrow earned raves and a Best Supporting Actor Oscar nomination. Soon he was ubiquitous onscreen, in *Riot* (1968), *Marooned,* and *The Gypsy Moths* (both 1969) and had particularly impressive turns as a ski coach in *Downhill Racer* (1969) and as Melvyn Douglas' distant son in *I Never Sang for My Father* (1970, earning another Oscar nomination). He became a star—and won a Best Actor Oscar—playing edgy, tough-as-nails cop Popeye Doyle in the hit thriller *The French Connection* (1971), an affirmation of his extraordinary talent as well as the shift in Hollywood from glamor-boy stars to everyday Joes.

Hackman went on to starring roles in a wide range of films, from the disaster epic *The Poseidon Adventure* to the dark *Prime Cut* (both 1972) to the downbeat character study *Scarecrow* (1973, well teamed with Al Pacino) and surprised even his most ardent fans with his hilarious cameo as the blind hermit in Mel Brooks' *Young Frankenstein* (1974). He gave, arguably, his greatest performance (and one of his personal favorites) as surveillance expert Harry Caul in Francis Ford Coppola's paranoia classic *The Conversation* (1974), a brilliantly subtle portrait of obsession and a stunning example of the character actor's craft. Hackman returned to the role of Popeye Doyle in *French Connection II* and had impressive parts in the western

saga *Bite the Bullet* and the critical favorite *Night Moves* (all 1975), along with such critical and commercial flops as *The Hunting Party* (1971), *Lucky Lady* (1975), *The Domino Principle,* and *March or Die* (both 1977). He took another surprising turn by playing the broadly comic villain Lex Luthor in 1978's smash hit *Superman,* after which he took several years off. He returned as Luthor (most amusingly) in *Superman II* (1980) and proved he was as sharp as ever in the little-seen comedy *All Night Long* and a small but incisive role as a magazine editor in *Reds* (both 1981).

Working with renewed vigor, Hackman tackled both supporting roles and leads, and seemed incapable of giving anything less than an excellent performance, even in unworthy vehicles. He was wonderful as a war correspondent in *Under Fire* (1983), a middle-aged man who leaves his wife in *Twice in a Lifetime* (1985), an inspirational high-school basketball coach in *Hoosiers* (1986), and a treacherous Secretary of Defense in *No Way Out* (1987) and added weight and believability to formula films like *Uncommon Valor* (1983) and *Target* (1985). He was tireless in 1988, appearing in Woody Allen's *Another Woman, Bat*21,* and *Full Moon in Blue Water,* and he received a Best Actor nomination—his first in 17 years—for his superb performance as an FBI man in the controversial civil rights drama *Mississippi Burning.* Hackman's vehicles continue to vary in quality, but never his performances, as witness *The Package* (1989), *Loose Cannons* (also 1989, a misfired comic pairing with Dan Aykroyd), *Postcards From the Edge* (1990, a well-wrought cameo as a movie director he modeled on Richard Donner), and *Class Action* (1991). He won a second Oscar (for Supporting Actor) as the sadistic sheriff in Clint Eastwood's Western *Unforgiven* (1992). Hackman has considered retirement more than once, particularly after suffering a near heart attack and undergoing angioplasty surgery in 1990. Fortunately for us, his health has not kept him from continuing to work. His superb performance as Tom Cruise's amoral mentor in *The Firm* (1993) showed the actor at the peak of his powers. Critic David Denby spoke for many when he called Hackman "consistently the finest American screen actor over the past quarter-century."

OTHER FILMS INCLUDE: 1966: *Hawaii* (bit

part); 1967: *Banning, A Covenant With Death, First to Fight;* 1968: *The Split;* 1971: *Doctors' Wives, Cisco Pike;* 1974: *Zandy's Bride;* 1977: *A Bridge Too Far;* 1981: *Eureka;* 1983: *Two of a Kind* (as the voice of God); 1984: *Misunderstood;* 1986: *Power;* 1987: *Superman IV: The Quest for Peace;* 1988: *Split Decisions;* 1990: *Narrow Margin;* 1993: *Geronimo: An American Legend;* 1994: *Wyatt Earp;* 1995: *The Quick and the Dead, Crimson Tide, Get Shorty.*

HAGEN, JEAN. Actress. *(b. Aug. 3, 1923, Chicago, as Jean Shirley Verhagen; d. Aug. 29, 1977).* If she'd never played anyone other than squeaky-voiced Linda Lamont, the hopelessly vain silent-screen star of *Singin' in the Rain* (1952, for which she was Oscar-nominated), this attractive, talented blond actress would still rate a place in Hollywood history. A former drama major who worked as a theater usherette before getting acting jobs on radio and stage, she debuted on screen in *Adam's Rib* (1949, playing the femme fatale who disrupts Judy Holliday's marriage), and scored her first real triumph as the female lead in *The Asphalt Jungle* (1950). Unfortunately, neither MGM nor any of the other studios for which Hagen worked seemed able to provide her with roles and vehicles that might have made her a real star. She played Danny Thomas' wife in the "Make Room for Daddy" TV series (1953–57).
OTHER FILMS INCLUDE: 1950: *Ambush;* 1951: *Night Into Morning;* 1952: *Carbine Williams;* 1953: *Latin Lovers, Half a Hero;* 1955: *The Big Knife;* 1959: *The Shaggy Dog;* 1960: *Sunrise at Campobello* (as Missy Le Hand); 1962: *Panic in the Year Zero;* 1964: *Dead Ringer.*

HAGERTY, JULIE. Actress. *(b. June 15, 1955, Cincinnati.)* She was letter-perfect in the comedic role of the harried flight attendant in her first film, *Airplane!* (1980), a role she reprised in that movie's 1982 sequel. But there's more to this Juilliard-educated actress—whose wide-eyed, sharp-featured face and quavering voice particularly suit her to play fragile, eccentric innocents and put-upon women—than meets the eye. She was excellent in two mid-1980s features, *Lost in America* (1985, as Albert Brooks' dotty spouse) and *Goodbye, New York* (1986, as an American woman stranded without money on an Israeli kibbutz). In 1992 she costarred in a short-lived TV sitcom, "Princesses."
OTHER FILMS INCLUDE: 1982: *A Midsummer Night's Sex Comedy;* 1985: *Bad Medicine;* 1989: *Bloodhounds of Broadway, Rude Awakening;* 1991: *What About Bob?;* 1992: *Noises Off.*

HAIM, COREY. Actor. *(b. Dec. 23, 1972, Toronto.)* Puppy-dog cute, sad-eyed juvenile actor whose teen-heartthrob status has yet to completely recover from widespread reports of drug abuse and wild behavior. He started in TV commercials at 10, and made his film debut in the 1984 thriller *Firstborn.* One year later, he was featured in *Murphy's Romance* (1985) and a well-received TV tearjerker, *A Time to Live* (also 1985), as Liza Minnelli's dying son. Haim, already skilled at projecting vulnerability, played a lovesick high-school freshman in *Lucas* (1986), a modest little sleeper that enjoyed greater success in home video. He fought vampire teens in *The Lost Boys* (1987), went joyriding in *License to Drive* (1988), and played second-fiddle to off-screen pal Corey Feldman in *Dream a Little Dream* (1989). (Most of his subsequent teen-oriented films—and there have been many—have been released directly to video.) *Fast Getaway* (1991), if anything, demonstrated that Haim, while still youthful-looking, is rapidly outgrowing his cutesy-poo image.

HAINES, RANDA. Director. *(b. Feb. 20, 1945, Los Angeles.)* Talented director who briefly studied acting with Lee Strasberg, then worked as a script supervisor for a New York production company for ten years. A short film she made while studying at the American Film Institute led to directing stints on two PBS movies and the acclaimed *Something About Amelia* (1984), a TV movie that dealt frankly with incest and earned Haines an Emmy nomination. She made her feature debut with the sensitive adaptation of *Children of a Lesser God* (1986), which earned Marlee Matlin a Best Actress Oscar and made Haines the first American woman to be nominated for a Directors Guild of America award (although the Oscars ignored her). Haines teamed up again with *Children* star William Hurt for an inside look at modern medicine, *The Doctor* (1991), and then directed *Wrestling Ernest Hemingway* (1993).

HALE, ALAN. Actor. *(b. Feb. 10, 1892, Washington, D.C., as Rufus Alan McKahan; d. Jan. 22, 1950.)* This robust, genial character actor, aside from appearing in hundreds of films during his 40-year career, occupies a special place in motion-picture history as the inventor of the folding theater seat. (His other inventions ranged from hand fire extinguishers to greaseless potato chips.) He made his screen debut in 1911, and played both leading and supporting roles in the silent era, including *The Americano* (1916, with Douglas Fairbanks), *The Four Horsemen of the Apocalypse* (1921), *The Covered Wagon* (1923), and *The Spieler* (1928); he even directed a handful of silents. His voice complemented his appearance, and he easily adapted to talkies. It's a credit to Hale's ability that he could convincingly play a brutish heavy in one film, and a boisterous buffoon in the next. He was a ubiquitous presence in Warner Bros. films of the 1930s and 1940s, but worked for all the major studios. He played Little John in both the 1922 and 1938 screen versions of *Robin Hood,* and repeated the role in *Rogues of Sherwood Forest* (1950), his last film. His son, Alan Hale, Jr. (1918–89), started acting in his teens, and made a number of films in the 1940s and 1950s (playing roles similar to those offered his father in earlier years) but made his greatest impression on TV as the Skipper in "Gilligan's Island" (1964–67).

OTHER FILMS INCLUDE: 1931: *Susan Lennox: Her Fall and Rise;* 1932: *Union Depot;* 1934: *It Happened One Night* (as the obnoxious road thief), *Imitation of Life, Of Human Bondage, Fog Over Frisco;* 1935: *The Crusades, The Last Days of Pompeii;* 1936: *Our Relations;* 1937: *The Prince and the Pauper;* 1939: *Dodge City, The Fighting 69th;* 1940: *They Drive By Night, The Sea Hawk, Santa Fe Trail;* 1941: *The Strawberry Blonde, Manpower;* 1942: *Gentleman Jim;* 1944: *Destination Tokyo;* 1946: *Night and Day;* 1948: *Adventures of Don Juan.*

HALEY, JACK. Actor. *(b. Aug. 10, 1898, Boston; d. June 6, 1979.)* People who remember Jack Haley only as the Tin Man from *The Wizard of Oz* (1939) might be surprised if they could inspect his lengthy résumé. A light comedian, passable singer, and graceful hoofer, he enjoyed a long career in vaudeville, on stage, in the movies, and on radio. Haley's film roles usually called upon him to be a jittery, slow-witted, but amiable character; he frequently played second bananas but had some leading roles as well. Aside from his turn in *Wizard,* Haley got his best screen opportunity in *Wake Up and Live* (1937), playing a mike-shy crooner coaxed by Alice Faye to sing over the air as "The Phantom Troubadour" (although his voice was dubbed by popular singer Buddy Clark). His son is producer-director Jack Haley, Jr., for whom Senior cameoed in a 1970 directorial effort, *Norwood.*

OTHER FILMS INCLUDE: 1927: *Broadway Madness;* 1930: *Follow Thru;* 1933: *Sitting Pretty;* 1934: *Here Comes the Groom;* 1935: *Coronado;* 1936: *Poor Little Rich Girl* (one of his best movies, with Shirley Temple and Alice Faye), *Pigskin Parade, F-Man;* 1937: *Pick a Star, She Had to Eat, Danger—Love at Work;* 1938: *Rebecca of Sunnybrook Farm* (again with Temple), *Alexander's Ragtime Band, Hold That Co-ed, Thanks for Everything;* 1941: *Moon Over Miami, Navy Blues;* 1942: *Beyond the Blue Horizon;* 1943: *Higher and Higher;* 1944: *One Body Too Many;* 1945: *George White's Scandals;* 1946: *People Are Funny, Vacation in Reno;* 1949: *Make Mine Laughs.*

HALL, ANTHONY MICHAEL. Actor. *(b. Apr. 14, 1968, Boston.)* Hall made his mark on the silver screen as an engagingly gawky nerd in the movies of teen-angst auteur John Hughes, most notably *Sixteen Candles* (1984) and *The Breakfast Club* (1985). The young actor, whose first movie was the forgettable *Six Pack* (1982), and who played Chevy Chase's son in *National Lampoon's Vacation* (1983), displayed a skill far beyond his years in these efforts, but his post-Hughes output—which included a brief stint on TV's "Saturday Night Live" (1985–86)—has been disappointing. A poorly constructed thriller titled *Out of Bounds* (1986) did nothing for his career, and to anyone watching *Johnny Be Good*

(1988) it was obvious that Hall no longer belonged in such a vehicle. He resurfaced as a lunky, thuggish high-school jock in *Edward Scissorhands* (1990). Recent credits include *Into the Sun* (1992), *Six Degrees of Separation* (1993), and *Hail Caesar* (also 1993), which he also directed.

HALL, CONRAD. Cinematographer. *(b. June 21, 1926, Tahiti.)* Veteran cameraman whose frequently dazzling work has been a major asset to both low- and big-budget films. He and two USC classmates produced a project called "Sea Theme" and sold it to television; from there, Hall worked on industrial and TV films and commercials during the 1950s, and was a cinematographer on the series "Stoney Burke" and "The Outer Limits" in the 1960s. After working on low-budget films like *Edge of Fury* (1958) and *Incubus* (1965), Hall got his first credit as director of photography on *The Wild Seed* (1965) and received an Oscar nomination that same year for *Saboteur: Code Name Morituri*. He got subsequent nominations for *The Professionals* (1966), the austere black and white *In Cold Blood* (1967, a career highpoint), and won the Oscar for the golden, soft-toned *Butch Cassidy and the Sundance Kid* (1969). He also filmed *Tell Them Willie Boy Is Here* (1969), *Fat City* (1972), *The Day of the Locust* (1975, another nomination), and *Marathon Man* (1976) before taking a hiatus to run a commercial production company with fellow cinematographer Haskell Wexler. Hall returned to shoot the elegant film-noirish *Black Widow* (1987), *Class Action* (1991), and received yet another nomination for *Tequila Sunrise* (1988). Recent credits include *Jennifer 8* (1992), *Searching for Bobby Fischer* (1993, Oscar-nominated), and *Love Affair* (1994).

HALL, JON. Actor. *(b. Feb. 23, 1913, Fresno, Calif., as Charles Hall Locher; d. Dec. 13, 1979.)* Brawny, athletic leading man who was once crowned "the King of Technicolor" (his queen was Maria Montez), Hall started in films as a bit player billed under his own name. The dark-haired, handsome actor worked his way up to substantial roles in *Here's to Romance, Charlie Chan in Shanghai* (both

1935), *The Lion Man,* and *The Mysterious Avenger* (both 1936), among others, before being cast as Dorothy Lamour's sarong-clad native lover in John Ford's *The Hurricane* (1937), a huge success. As Jon Hall, he became a leading man, and freelanced for several studios, appearing in *South of Pago Pago, Kit Carson* (both 1940), *Aloma of the South Seas* (1941), and *Eagle Squadron* (1942), before being paired with exotic Maria Montez in a Technicolor spectacle for Universal, *Arabian Nights* (1942). Escape-hungry wartime audiences made it a big hit, and Universal kept the Hall-Montez team together in *White Savage* (1943), *Ali Baba and the Forty Thieves, Cobra Woman, Gypsy Wildcat* (all 1944), and *Sudan* (1945). When the formula finally petered out, Hall's star began to wane.

He made several Westerns, among them *The Vigilantes Return* (1947), *Deputy Marshal* (1949, costarring then-wife Frances Langford), and *When the Redskins Rode* (1951), before starring as "Ramar of the Jungle" in a 1952–54 syndicated TV series, some episodes of which were cut together and released as feature films. Overweight and lethargic, he never regained his box-office standing, although he did stay in the movie business by renting out some expensive photographic equipment he'd collected over the years. He also directed one film, *The Beachgirls and the Monster* (1965, aka *Monster from the Surf*). Hall married actress Raquel Torres in 1959, and shot himself to death after spending several months in bed following an operation for bladder cancer.

HALL, PORTER. Actor. *(b. Sept. 19, 1888, Cincinnati; d. Oct. 6, 1953.)* One of Hollywood's top character actors during the 1930s and 1940s, Hall most frequently played shifty-eyed, nervous, cowardly characters; he was equally comfortable in comedic or dramatic variations of the same "type." He attended the University of Cincinnati and worked in numerous places (including a steel mill) before catching footlight fever. Hall toured with many small companies over the years, frequently appearing in modest productions of Shakespeare, before making his screen debut in *The Thin Man* (1934). Although he worked for most of the big studios, he spent most of his Hollywood career at Paramount. Hall is particularly memorable in *The General Died at Dawn, The Plainsman* (both 1936, in the latter as Jack McCall, Wild Bill Hickok's assassin), *Mr. Smith Goes to Washington* (1939), *His Girl Friday* (1940), *Sullivan's Travels* (1941), *The Miracle of Morgan's Creek* (1944), *Murder, He Says* (1945), and *Intruder in the Dust* (1949).

OTHER FILMS INCLUDE: 1935: *The Case of the Lucky Legs;* 1936: *The Story of Louis Pasteur, The Princess Comes Across, The Petrified Forest;* 1937: *Bulldog Drummond Escapes, Souls at Sea, Make Way for Tomorrow, True Confession, Wild Money, This Way Please, Hotel Haywire, Wells Fargo;* 1938: *Dangerous to Know, King of Alcatraz, Men With Wings, Tom Sawyer, Detective;* 1939: *They Shall Have Music;* 1940: *Dark Command, Arizona, Trail of the Vigilantes;* 1941: *The Parson of Panamint, Mr. and Mrs. North;* 1942: *The Remarkable Andrew;* 1943: *Woman of the Town, The Desperadoes;* 1944: *Standing Room Only, Going My Way, Double Indemnity, The Great Moment;* 1945: *Blood on the Sun, Kiss and Tell, Weekend at the Waldorf;* 1947: *Unconquered, Miracle on 34th Street;* 1948: *You Gotta Stay Happy, That Wonderful Urge;* 1949: *The Beautiful Blonde From Bashful Bend;* 1951: *Ace in the Hole (aka The Big Carnival);* 1952: *The Half-Breed;* 1953: *Pony Express;* 1954: *Return to Treasure Island.*

HALLSTROM, LASSE. Director, writer. *(b. June 2, 1946, Stockholm.)* After almost two decades of making various TV and feature films in Sweden, Hallstrom finally attracted worldwide attention (and Oscar nominations for Best Director and Best Screenplay) for his adaptation of *My Life as a Dog* (1985), a warmhearted yet poignant look at the antics of a mischievous 12-year-old. His early films, including *A Lover and His Lass* (1974), *Father-To-Be* (1979), *The Rooster* (1981), and *Happy We* (1983), were never released in the U.S. After the success of *My Life as a Dog,* Hallstrom's American debut, *Once Around* (1991), revealed an impressive grasp of character if not a flair for strong narrative. An American production of *Peter Pan*—a pet project of Hallstrom's—didn't come to pass, 1991's *Hook* effectively co-opting it. His most recent films are *What's Eating Gilbert Grape* (1993),

with Johnny Depp, and *Something to Talk About* (1995).

HAMILL, MARK. Actor. *(b. Sept. 25, 1952, Oakland, Calif.)* Boyish-looking actor who created the character of Luke Skywalker in George Lucas' classic *Star Wars* series. Not a terribly versatile performer, he got across enough energy and postadolescent frustration in *Star Wars* (1977) to create considerable sympathy for his character. Before that film, he had appeared in TV movies and done voiceovers for cartoons. He was in a serious auto accident after completing shooting on *Star Wars,* and much of his face had to be completely reconstructed, accounting for his gaunt, hollow look in the first sequel, *The Empire Strikes Back* (1980). As the trilogy continued, Hamill stood still as an actor while costar Harrison Ford grew into a very credible action hero and romantic lead, and while Hamill remains the focal point of all the movies, much of the intrigue of their storylines was transferred to Ford and costar Carrie Fisher by the time of wrap-up *Return of the Jedi* (1983). Buoyed by his *Star Wars* fame, Hamill was starred in *Corvette Summer* (1978), and featured in Samuel Fuller's WW2 ensemble piece *The Big Red One* (1980) and *The Night the Lights Went Out in Georgia* (1981), but never established himself as a bona fide star. (He fared better on Broadway, where he played "The Elephant Man" and Mozart in "Amadeus," to good reviews.) A big-budget British science fiction film, *Slipstream* (1989), never even got U.S. theatrical release. Hamill now stars in such video releases as *Black Magic Woman* (1990) and *Wishman* (1991). He's also the voice of The Joker on the animated "Batman" TV series, and in the feature *Batman: Mask of the Phantasm* (1993).

HAMILTON, GEORGE. Actor. *(b. Aug. 12, 1939, Memphis.)* It's a tossup whether this handsome, urbane actor is better known for his histrionic accomplishments or his impossibly deep tan, the cultivation of which has prompted much humor at Hamilton's expense; fortunately, he's a good sport about it. A latter-day product of the studio system, Hamilton had a starring role in his first film, *Crime*

& *Punishment, USA* (1959), an updated version of the Dostoyevsky novel. He appeared to good advantage in a number of early 1960s films, including *Home From the Hill, Where the Boys Are, All the Fine Young Cannibals* (all 1960), *By Love Possessed, A Thunder of Drums* (both 1961), *The Light in the Piazza* (1962), *The Victors,* and *Act One* (both 1963, in the latter as playwright Moss Hart), *Your Cheating Heart* (1965, one of his best parts, as country music legend Hank Williams), *The Power* (1968), and *You've Got to Be Kidding* (1967).

Hamilton was off the screen for several years, returning as both star and executive producer of a ludicrous biopic, *Evel Knievel* (1972). After appearing in *The Man Who Loved Cat Dancing* (1973) and *Once Is Not Enough* (1975), he turned his attentions to TV, acting in series episodes and telefilms for the next several years. His movie career took a brief upswing with two well-mounted parodies—*Love at First Bite* (1979, as Count Dracula) and *Zorro, the Gay Blade* (1981, starring in a dual role)—in which he displayed a surprising flair for goofy, often self-deprecating humor. But when further starring vehicles failed to materialize, Hamilton retreated to the relative "safety" of the small screen, becoming less active into the 1980s. He made something of a comeback in 1990 with a mature, effective supporting role as Al Pacino's mouthpiece in *The Godfather, Part III,* but seems too content to maintain his amazing tan and act as escort to many of the world's most visible women: One of Hollywood's most eligible bachelors, he's been photographed squiring Lynda Bird Johnson, Elizabeth Taylor, and Imelda Marcos, to name a very few.

HAMILTON, LINDA. Actress. *(b. Sept. 26, 1957, Salisbury, Md.)* Shaggy, edgy leading lady who has created a niche for herself in Hollywood movies, playing characters that endure in spite of unusual hardships—most notably Arnold Schwarzenegger, whom she battled in *The Terminator.* Hamilton began her career as a child actress, working in local Maryland productions before moving on to the Strasberg Institute in New York, where she studied with director Nicholas Ray. After an appearance on the soap opera "Search for Tomorrow," Hamilton concluded that Hollywood was where she needed to be to further her career. She landed movie-of-the-week roles in such fare as *Secrets of a Mother and Daughter* (1983) and *Club Med* (1986) before earning a starring part in a modestly budgeted sci-fi actioner called *The Terminator* in 1984. That picture's surprise success landed Hamilton in other films of the sci-fi/horror genre, including *Children of the Corn* (1984), *Black Moon Rising,* and *King Kong Lives* (both 1986), and on the popular TV series "Beauty and the Beast" (1987–90) which was her best-known work prior to release of the 1991 *Terminator* sequel, *Terminator 2: Judgment Day.* In 1994 she costarred in *Silent Fall.*

HAMILTON, MARGARET. Actress. *(b. Dec. 9, 1902, Cleveland; d. May 16, 1985.)* The screen's immortal Wicked Witch, whose cackling laugh rings in our collective memory, Hamilton only won the plum role in *The Wizard of Oz* (1939) after Gale Sondergaard bowed out of the production! She enjoyed a lengthy show-business career that included Broadway, summer stock, community theater, radio, and TV in addition to her dozens of movie appearances. A small woman with sharp features, she portrayed many nosy spinsters and malicious gossips. Although she toiled in small parts as well as large ones, Hamilton never gave a bad performance. A former schoolteacher, she remained passionately interested in education and served on school boards and in children's therapy groups. In later years she was a familiar face on TV as "Cora," promoting Maxwell House coffee in a long-running series of commercials. She also provided the voice of Aunt Em in the animated *Journey Back to Oz* (1974).

OTHER FILMS INCLUDE: 1933: *Another Language* (her debut); 1934: *Broadway Bill* (and its 1950 remake, *Riding High);* 1936: *These Three;* 1937: *You Only Live Once, Nothing Sacred;* 1938: *The Adventures of Tom Sawyer;* 1940: *My Little Chickadee;* 1943: *Johnny Come Lately;* 1947: *Mad Wednesday;* 1948: *State of the Union;* 1949: *The Red Pony;* 1951: *People Will Talk;* 1960: *13 Ghosts;* 1961: *Paradise Alley;* 1970: *Brewster McCloud* (in which her demise recalls *The Wizard of Oz), The Anderson Tapes.*

HAMILTON, MURRAY. Actor. *(b. Mar. 24, 1923, Washington, D.C.; d. Sept. 1, 1986.)* Utility supporting player in films since the 1950s, who drew on his stage background to play every kind of character imaginable, from comic rednecks to steely-eyed villains. He gained screen immortality as Mr. Robinson in *The Graduate* (1967), and is also well remembered as the mayor of the beach town terrorized by a great white shark in *Jaws* (1975) and *Jaws 2* (1978). He was nominated for a Tony Award in 1964 for the Broadway play "Absence of the Cello."
OTHER FILMS INCLUDE: 1951: *Bright Victory;* 1958: *No Time for Sergeants;* 1959: *Anatomy of a Murder;* 1961: *The Hustler;* 1966: *Seconds;* 1968: *No Way to Treat a Lady;* 1973: *The Way We Were;* 1976: *The Drowning Pool;* 1979: *The Amityville Horror;* 1980: *Brubaker;* 1983: *Hysterical.*

HANKS, TOM. Actor. *(b. July 9, 1956, Concord, Calif.)* The success of this college dropout is based on his breezy, spontaneous acting style, best exemplified in his triumphant, Oscar-nominated performance as a man who behaves like a young boy in Penny Marshall's *Big* (1988). This thin, curly-haired brunet actually made his film debut in the slasher thriller *He Knows You're Alone* eight years earlier, but didn't hit the big time until he accepted the role of reluctant cross-dresser Kip Wilson in the TV sitcom "Bosom Buddies" (1980–82). The show's success led to his being cast in the raucous *Bachelor Party* (1984), a witless but lighthearted comedy that launched him as a screen star.

Hanks' choices of projects haven't always been wise ones, but he has established himself as one of the brightest and most likable personalities in contemporary movies. In such vehicles as *Splash* (1984), as a man who falls for a mermaid, and *Turner & Hooch* (1989), as a cop with a dog for a partner, he has proved to be a major box-office draw as well. He also starred as a harried homeowner in *The Money Pit* (1986), Jackie Gleason's long-suffering son in *Nothing in Common* (1986), a hip detective in *Dragnet* (1987), a failed stand-up comic in *Punchline* (1988), a nervous suburbanite in *The 'burbs* (1989), and a terminally ill human sacrifice in *Joe versus the Volcano* (1990).

Hanks was badly miscast as yuppie investment banker Sherman McCoy in the ill-fated adaptation of *The Bonfire of the Vanities* (1990), but he was hardly responsible for the mess. In 1992 he gained weight to take on an unlikely character part as a boozy baseball manager/has-been in *A League of Their Own* and scored a great success, which was topped by his endearing performance as a wistful widower in the smash hit *Sleepless in Seattle* (1993) and a daring change of pace as a lawyer afflicted with AIDS in *Philadelphia* (1993), which won him an Oscar. He also made his directing debut in 1993 with episodes of the film-noirish TV series "Fallen Angels" and "A League of Their Own." Hanks cemented his superstardom with a sly comic portrayal of a slow-witted but fast-running innocent in the blockbuster *Forrest Gump* (1994); it earned him a second Best Actor Oscar. He followed this with *Apollo 13* (1995, as astronaut Jim Lovell). His wife is actress Rita Wilson, with whom he starred in *Volunteers* (1985); she contributed a hilarious scene to *Sleepless in Seattle.*

HANNA-BARBERA. Animation directors, producers. *(**William Hanna**—b. July 14, 1910, Melrose, New Mex. **Joseph Barbera**—b. Mar. 24, 1911, New York City.)* This durable team comprises one of the few "brand names" in animated cartoons, though they have been both praised and reviled for their work in this field. Praise came when they created the cat-and-mouse duo Tom and Jerry at MGM in the early 1940s; their perfection of a comic formula for these stars, and their creative manipulation of that formula through scores of cartoon shorts earned them an amazing seven Academy Awards, and worldwide renown. When the MGM cartoon department shut its doors in 1956, and Hanna and Barbera formed their own studio to produce cartoons expressly for TV, they succeeded with a double-edged sword. On the one hand, they rescued the floundering animation industry, and offered more employment for artists, writers, and technicians than any other cartoon entity since Disney in the 1930s. But at the same time, bowing to TV's economic pressures, they stripped the medium of animation to its barest essentials, and removed most of the art—the very art they'd helped to develop—in the process.

Joseph Barbera was heading for a career in banking when he started selling magazine cartoons on the side, in the 1930s. He subsequently found employment at the New York-based Van Beuren cartoon studio, and moved from there to Terrytoons. One of his colleagues sent word back that MGM was expanding its cartoon department, and Barbera answered the call in 1937. William Hanna had already cut his teeth on cartoons on the West Coast; the former journalism and engineering student went to work for Harman and Ising in 1931, bursting with story ideas. By 1937 he was being given a trial run as director. Hanna and Barbera gravitated toward each other, and were soon working as a team under the supervision of MGM's Hugh Harman and Rudolf Ising.

They received screen credit for a few one-shot cartoons like *The Goose Goes South* and *Officer Pooch* (both 1941), but once Tom and Jerry were established, in *Puss Gets the Boot* (1940, credited onscreen to Ising) they concentrated on those characters for the next 15 years. Barbera's strength was in gags and story development, while Hanna saw himself more as a director, with a solid sense of timing; they complemented each other perfectly. Their Oscars were awarded for *Yankee Doodle Mouse* (1943), *Mouse Trouble* (1944), *Quiet Please* (1945), *The Cat Concerto* (1947), *Mouse Cleaning* (1948), *Two Mouseketeers* (1952), and *Johann Mouse* (1953).

Hanna and Barbera got a wonderful opportunity when Gene Kelly and director George Sidney approached them to help create a sequence with Kelly for their MGM feature *Anchors Aweigh* (1945). The finished sequence, crafted with trial and error, was a smash, and the team provided similar material for the later features *Holiday in Mexico* (1946), *Dangerous When Wet* (1953, with Esther Williams), and Kelly's *Invitation to the Dance* (1957).

Their initial TV venture was "Ruff 'n' Reddy" in 1957. But their breakthrough came with the hit half-hour show "Huckleberry Hound" in 1959; it was followed by "Yogi Bear," "Quick Draw McGraw," and endless others. Their prime-time, "adult" hit "The Flintstones" (1960–66) proved to be a longer-running success

than anyone could have imagined. Their TV success even led them back to theatrical cartoons: Columbia commissioned a series of shorts (featuring Loopy de Loop) in the early 1960s, and then bankrolled two features, *Hey There, It's Yogi Bear* (1964) and *A Man Called Flintstone* (1966). The studio flirted with theatricals from time to time after that, but neither *Charlotte's Web* (1973), the long-in-production *Heidi's Song* (1982), nor the undernourished *Jetsons: The Movie* (1990) gave Disney any competition in that arena. Their bread-and-butter was TV animation, produced by the carload.

Since selling their studio, both Hanna and Barbera have remained as active as ever in animation. Barbera helped bring an old-fashioned gusto to a "Tom and Jerry Kids" TV series in the late 1980s, and coproduced a less successful feature, *Tom and Jerry: The Movie* in 1992. Hanna coexecutive produced a 1993 theatrical feature, *Once Upon a Forest*.

HANNAH, DARYL. Actress. *(b. Dec. 3, 1960, Chicago.)* If this actress' range was as wide as her smile, she'd be one of today's top screen attractions; sadly, this is not the case, and the lithe, long-limbed Hannah continues to confound observers by delivering accomplished performances in some films and seeming like a rank amateur in others. Her first role was a bit part in Brian De Palma's *The Fury* (1978), filmed while she was still a high-school student. Theatrical studies at UCLA followed, as did eventual feature roles in *The Final Terror* (1981), *Summer Lovers,* and *Blade Runner* (both 1982). As a statuesque "replicant" in the latter film, Hannah turned heads and had audiences scanning the end credits for her name. Her beauty, tempered by a palpable innocence, made her an ideal choice to play the mermaid who falls in love with Tom Hanks in *Splash* (1984), her first big hit and one of her most endearing portrayals. She was a coed pursued by a teenage rebel in *Reckless,* Mickey Rourke's girlfriend in *The Pope of Greenwich Village* (both 1984), a prehistoric ingenue in *The Clan of the Cave Bear,* a performance artist in *Legal Eagles* (both 1986), a jet-set interior designer in *Wall Street* (1987), a lovelorn ghost in *High Spirits* (1988), a fragile mental patient in *Crazy People* (1990), a missionary's wife in *At Play in the Fields of the Lord,* and a befuddled love interest to Chevy Chase in *Memoirs of an Invisible Man* (both 1991). Her best opportunities since *Splash* have come in the title role of *Roxanne* (1987), in which she exuded intelligence as well as femininity, and *Steel Magnolias* (1989), in which she played a Southern hairdresser who gets religion. In 1993 she played Jack Lemmon's daughter in *Grumpy Old Men* and starred in a TV remake of *Attack of the 50 Ft. Woman.* She also made headlines for her romance with John F. Kennedy, Jr.

HARDING, ANN. Actress. *(b. Aug. 7, 1901, Fort Sam Houston, Tex, as Dorothy Walton Gatley; d. Sept. 1, 1981.)* All but forgotten today, this dignified, patrician blonde was one of the biggest stars of the early talkie era, specializing in drawing-room dramas about fallen women and long-suffering mothers of noble character. A former insurance-company secretary who freelanced as a scenario reader for Famous Players-Lasky's New York office, she took up acting in 1921, making her stage debut with Greenwich Village's Provincetown Players and achieving Broadway success shortly thereafter. As one of the first wave of stage performers to deluge Hollywood in the early days of sound, she was signed by Pathé in 1929, making her movie debut in *Paris Bound.*

When Pathé merged with the newly formed RKO in 1930, Harding went along as a top star. She earned an Oscar nomination for her starring role in *Holiday* (1930, the same part played by Katharine Hepburn in the 1938 version of Philip Barry's play) and subsequently top lined such films as *The Girl of the Golden West* (also 1930), *East Lynne, Devotion* (both 1931), *The Conquerors, The Animal Kingdom, Prestige, Westward Passage* (all 1932), *When Ladies Meet, The Right to Romance* (both 1933), *Gallant Lady, The Life of Vergie Winters, The Fountain* (all 1934), *Biography of a Bachelor Girl, Peter Ibbetson* (one of her best, a romantic, ethereal story costarring Gary Cooper), *Enchanted April* (all 1935), *The Lady Consents* (a rare comedy role), *The Witness Chair* (both 1936), and *Love From a Stranger* (1937, very effective in this thriller).

Harding invariably played sympathetic women, usually victimized by selfish if charismatic men, but audiences eventually wearied of watching her suffer in silence with only an occasional tear or quivering chin to betray her anguish. She left the screen in 1937, ostensibly retiring to marry symphony conductor Werner Janssen, but within five years she was back in films, now a character actress, still portraying quiet, dignified women. After completing a 1957 made-for-TV film, *Young Man From Kentucky,* she retired for good.

OTHER FILMS INCLUDE: 1942: *Eyes in the Night;* 1943: *Mission to Moscow, The North Star;* 1944: *Nine Girls* (in this comedy-mystery as a spinsterish sorority adviser who turns out to be the killer!); 1945: *Those Endearing Young Charms* (as Laraine Day's mother, another fine role); 1946: *Janie Gets Married;* 1947: *It Happened on 5th Avenue;* 1950: *Two Weeks With Love, The Magnificent Yankee;* 1956: *The Man in the Gray Flannel Suit, Strange Intruder.*

HARDWICKE, CEDRIC (SIR). Actor. *(b. Feb. 19, 1883, Lye, England; d. Aug. 6, 1964.)* Few screen careers can match Hardwicke's for length, diversity, or distinction. Distinguished looking but not especially handsome, this classically trained stage actor made his London debut in 1912, rising to stage prominence in the 1920s (through a fruitful association with George Bernard Shaw). When he was knighted in 1934 he was the youngest actor ever given that singular honor. Hardwicke dabbled in film acting early on, but his screen career didn't begin in earnest until 1931, with the title role in *The Dreyfus Case;* it was followed by *Rome Express* (1932), *The Ghoul* (1933), *Nell Gwyn* (1934, as Charles II), and *Jew Suss* (1934). Hardwicke brought strength and dignity to his characters: He was the prophetic scientist in H. G. Wells' *Things to Come* (1936), and many years later narrated another ominous Wells tale, *The War of the Worlds* (1953). Working both in England and in Hollywood, he played Allan Quatermain in *King Solomon's Mines* (1937), Dr. Livingstone in *Stanley and Livingstone* (1939), Mr. Brink—the personification of Death—in *On Borrowed Time* (1939), Frollo in *The Hunchback of Notre Dame* (1939), Henry Cabot Lodge in *Wilson* (1944), and King Arthur in *A*

Connecticut Yankee in King Arthur's Court (1949). He alternated stage work with his film appearances, and appeared frequently on television (including a costarring role with Gertrude Berg in 1961–62's "Mrs. G. Goes to College") until his death in 1964. His autobiography, "A Victorian in Orbit," was published in 1961. Hardwicke's son Edward is also an actor; he was Dr. Watson to Jeremy Brett's Sherlock Holmes on British TV and played Anthony Hopkins' brother in *Shadowlands* (1993).

OTHER FILMS INCLUDE: 1935: *Les Miserables, Becky Sharp;* 1940: *Tom Brown's School Days;* 1941: *Suspicion;* 1942: *The Ghost of Frankenstein* (as Dr. Frankenstein); 1943: *Forever and a Day;* 1944: *The Lodger, Keys of the Kingdom;* 1947: *Nicholas Nickleby;* 1948: *I Remember Mama, Rope;* 1951: *The Desert Fox;* 1955: *Richard III, The Ten Commandments;* 1957: *The Story of Mankind, Baby Face Nelson;* 1962: *Five Weeks in a Balloon;* 1964: *The Pumpkin Eater.*

HARE, DAVID. Playwright, director, screenwriter. *(b. June 5, 1947, Sussex, England.)* Respected playwright whose work, from his first produced play "Slag" in 1970 to "Knuckle," "Pravda," and "A Map of the World," has examined contemporary social and political problems and the difficulty of moral and emotional expression. He wrote and directed the acclaimed TV films *Licking Hitler* (1977) and *Dreams of Leaving* (1980) before adapting his play *Plenty* for the screen in 1985, with Fred Schepisi directing Meryl Streep in the leading role of a woman who finds fulfillment during World War 2—and never again. Very soon after, Hare wrote and directed *Wetherby* (1985), a bleak story with Vanessa Redgrave as a schoolteacher who witnesses a grad student's suicide. Since then, he has written and directed *Paris by Night* (1988) and *Strapless* (1989), and adapted *The Secret Rapture* (1993) from his play. He also directed an episode of TV's "The Young Indiana Jones Chronicles."

HARLIN, RENNY. Director, producer. *(b. Mar. 15, 1959, Riihimaki, Finland.)* Topnotch action director who started his own production company while still a student at the University of Helsinki and made numerous commercials, documentaries, and shorts. Stymied by his country's film industry, Harlin came to the U.S. in the mid 1980s and directed the low-budget films *Born American* (1986) and *Prison* (1988), before gaining attention with the popular *A Nightmare on Elm Street 4: The Dream Master* (1988), possibly the best of the "Freddy Krueger" films. Bigger assignments followed: one, the Andrew "Dice" Clay vehicle *The Adventures of Ford Fairlane* (1990) bombed; the other, *Die Hard 2* (1990) was a hit and proved Harlin could handle a blockbuster budget and deliver the goods. His next film, *Cliffhanger* (1993), a thrilling mountain-climbing adventure, was also a hit and helped revive Sylvester Stallone's box-office appeal. Harlin also produced the quiet, low-budget *Rambling Rose* (1991), which starred his then-girlfriend, Laura Dern. In 1993 he married actress Geena Davis. They jointly produced her movie *Speechless* (1994), and he directed her in the pirate adventure *Cutthroat Island* (1995).

HARLOW, JEAN. Actress. *(b. Mar. 3, 1911, Kansas City, Mo., as Harlean Carpenter; d. June 7, 1937.)* She was a star for less than a decade. She headlined fewer than 20 films. Yet she had an impact that transcends statistics. With her brilliant platinum blond hair, ravishing figure, easy sensuality, and ready sense of humor, Jean Harlow was the most dynamic sex symbol of her era and one of the 1930s' brightest stars.

She started in films as an extra, and gained particular notice in a 1929 Laurel and Hardy silent short, *Double Whoopee.* That same year she had a small role in *The Saturday Night Kid,* which starred the woman she more or less supplanted as the screen's most uninhibited sex star, Clara Bow. Her big break came in 1930, when Howard Hughes cast her as the leading lady in the epic WW1 aviation drama *Hell's Angels.* Although her acting skills were dubious at best, she looked smashing (and was even photographed in two-color Technicolor for one extended sequence), and her offhanded question to Ben Lyon, "Would you be shocked if I changed into something more comfortable?" was quoted—and misquoted—for years to come. Hughes sent her on personal appearance tours and loaned her out to other studios. In 1931 alone she appeared in *The Secret Six, The Iron Man, The Public Enemy* (opposite James Cagney), *Goldie,* and *Platinum Blonde* (playing the title characters in the last two); 1932 began with *Beast of the City* and *Three Wise Girls.*

Still, there seemed little more to Harlow than her looks. It was MGM producer Paul Bern who took an interest in her, and encouraged his studio to build her up and give her other opportunities. She made the most of *Red-Headed Woman* (1932), giving one of the sexiest performances ever put on film, but leavening it with humor— Harlow's heretofore unseen trump card. The promise she showed in that film came to fruition in *Red Dust* (1932) in which she played a tramp with a heart, opposite Clark Gable. Overnight, it seemed, Harlow was not only a bona fide star, but a hit with the critics as well, who had dismissed her just one year earlier.

MGM now developed films to fit her personality, like *Hold Your Man* (1933), and gave her an irresistible opportunity to poke fun at herself (and even her leeching family) in *Bombshell* (1933), a Hollywood satire about a put-upon movie star. Then in the all-star *Dinner at Eight* (1933) she held her own with such legendary scene-stealers as Wallace Beery and Marie Dressler. The imposition of Hollywood's Production Code forced MGM to tone down Harlow's brassy image (although 1934's *The Girl From Missouri* just squeaked by). The result was a string of more genteel movies including the ill-advised musical *Reckless* (1935, in which both Harlow's singing and dancing were doubled), *China Seas, Riffraff* (both 1935), *Wife vs. Secretary, Suzy* (both 1936), and *Personal Property* (1937). The standout among her later films was *Libeled Lady* (1936) in which she battled perennial fiancé Spencer Tracy; it was a delicious comic performance.

During the filming of *Saratoga* (1937) she fell ill, and was dead ten days later. The world was shocked that someone so young, beautiful, and seemingly healthy could die so suddenly. Various causes were cited, but it wasn't until 1993 that biographer David Stenn revealed, from long-suppressed doctor's records and other evidence, that Harlow had been suffering from kidney disease since her teens.

With no known cure at the time, she was doomed. Public demand caused MGM to complete *Saratoga* with stand-in Mary Dees substituting for Harlow in several shots.

Hers was a shocking, tragic end, though it seemed in character with other personal problems that had dogged her life: a suffocating mother and parasitic stepfather; the mysterious death of her second husband, Paul Bern; another short-lived marriage to cinematographer Harold Rosson; and a long engagement to MGM star William Powell that never quite culminated in marriage. Rumors and mistruths about all of that fueled two screen biographies in 1965, both called *Harlow;* one starred Carroll Baker, the other Carol Lynley. Neither one managed to capture the magic that made Jean Harlow a star.

HARPER, JESSICA. Actress. *(b. Oct. 10, 1949, Chicago.)* Talented, attractive actress who has appeared in a number of highly unusual roles. After studying voice and modern dance at Sarah Lawrence College, she debuted on Broadway in "Hair" and later scored her first major film role in Brian De Palma's rock opera *Phantom of the Paradise* (1974), as the singer Phoenix. Harper appeared in *Love and Death* (1975), *Inserts* (1976), and the horror films *Suspiria* (1977) and *The Evictors* (1979) before achieving acclaim in a number of diverse performances, as one of Woody Allen's girlfriends in *Stardust Memories* (1980), Janet in *Shock Treatment,* Steve Martin's repressed wife in *Pennies From Heaven* (both 1981), and the object of Mark Linn-Baker's affections in *My Favorite Year* (1982). Harper has since been featured only in a few barely released films like *The Imagemaker* (1986), *The Blue Iguana* (1988), and *Big Man on Campus* (1990), and turned up for a season on "It's Garry Shandling's Show" (1989–90) as Garry's girlfriend.

HARPER, TESS. Actress. *(b. Aug. 15, 1950, Mammoth Spring, Ark., as Tessie Jean Washam.)* Blond, petite actress with striking blue eyes who received raves for her film debut as Robert Duvall's wife Rosa Lee in Bruce Beresford's *Tender Mercies* (1983) but has had too few opportunities to shine since then. After roles in *Silkwood* (1983) and *Flashpoint* (1984), she got to show her comic flair as the MaGrath sisters' bitchy cousin in Beresford's film of *Crimes of the Heart* (1986) and received a Supporting Actress Oscar nomination. Since then, Harper has made brief appearances in *Ishtar* (1987) and *Criminal Law* (1989) and has confined her major work to small, idiosyncratic films like *Far North* (1988), *Daddy's Dyin' . . . Who's Got the Will?* (1990), *The Man in the Moon* (1991), *My Heroes Have Always Been Cowboys* (1991), and *My New Gun* (1992). In 1994 she costarred in the TV series "Christy."

HARRIS, ED. Actor. *(b. Nov. 28, 1950, Tenafly, N.J.)* It's a solid indicator of Ed Harris' range that within one year (1983) he could play the clean-cut astronaut John Glenn in *The Right Stuff* and a cold-hearted mercenary in *Under Fire*. But this short, powerful leading man, his blond hair usually buzz-cut, is nothing if not unpredictable. He was discovered by George Romero, who starred him as the King Arthur–like motorcyclist who attempts to recreate Camelot on wheels in *Knightriders* (1981), and also cast him as one of the grasping relatives in *Creepshow* (1982). Harris met, courted, and married actress Amy Madigan while working with her in *Places in the Heart* (1984, playing an adulterous brother-in-law) and as a bigoted Texan in *Alamo Bay* (1985). A perfect modern-day Everyman, Harris can carry a picture on his own, but he seems to gravitate toward strong supporting roles. He was a distraught Vietnam vet in *Jacknife*, the underwater hero of *The Abyss* (both 1989), an ice-blooded New York Irish mob leader in *State of Grace* (1990), and a beleaguered Southern attorney in *Paris Trout* (1991). In 1992 he riveted audiences with his spellbinding performance as one of the unscrupulous, desperate real-estate salesmen in the all-star screen adaptation of David Mamet's *Glengarry Glen Ross*. Recent credits include the TV movie *Running Mates* (1992, opposite Diane Keaton), *Needful Things* (1993, as a sheriff), *China Moon* (1994), *Just Cause,* and *Apollo 13* (both 1995).

HARRIS, JULIE. Actress. *(b. Dec. 2, 1925, Grosse Pointe, Mich.)* Physically unprepossessing but gifted actress, a stage favorite who periodically dabbled in screen roles. Harris was born into a wealthy community of finishing schools and debutante balls, to which she voiced her rebellion by taking up acting. She attended the drama school at Yale, and made her theatrical debut in "It's a Gift" (1945). Harris made her screen debut in 1952's *The Member of the Wedding,* reprising her Broadway characterization (and earning an Oscar nomination) as a young girl prodded into maturity by events at home. Since then Harris has won some 20 awards, including two Emmys and five Tonys, for her work on stage, screen, and TV. In 1981, she became a regular on the popular TV series "Knots Landing." Although Harris' film career has been sporadic, her credits are impressive.
OTHER FILMS INCLUDE: 1955: *East of Eden;* 1958: *The Truth About Women;* 1962: *Requiem for a Heavyweight;* 1963: *The Haunting;* 1967: *Reflections in a Golden Eye;* 1968: *The Split;* 1970: *The People Next Door;* 1975: *The Hiding Place;* 1976: *Voyage of the Damned;* 1979: *The Bell Jar;* 1983: *Brontë;* 1986: *Leaving Home;* 1988: *Gorillas in the Mist;* 1991: *Paris Trout;* 1992: *HouseSitter;* 1993: *The Dark Half.*

HARRIS, RICHARD. Actor. *(b. Oct. 1, 1932, Limerick, Ireland.)* This feisty Irishman, a tall, slender, fair-haired performer with thin, bony face and piercing blue eyes, became an unlikely star after stunning movie watchers with a high-octane performance in *This Sporting Life* (1963). For his interpretation of the bitter young coal miner who becomes a professional rugby star, Harris earned an Oscar nomination and leapfrogged to the top of the international cinema's A list of leading men. A graduate of the London Academy of Music and Dramatic Art, he spent several years on the stage in Britain before making his movie debut in *Alive and Kicking* (1958). He quickly earned a reputation as an interesting performer, a rep borne out by his skillful supporting turns in *Shake Hands With the Devil, The Wreck of the Mary Deare* (both 1959), *The Guns of Navarone, Jungle Fighters* (both 1961), and *Mutiny on the Bounty* (1962).

Following his star-making stint in *This Sporting Life*, Harris appeared in *Red Desert* (1964), *Major Dundee, The Heroes of Telemark* (both 1965), *The Bible* (as Cain), *Hawaii* (both 1966), and *Caprice* (1967) before starring as King Arthur in the disappointing screen adaptation of *Camelot* (also 1967). (He later played the part in stage revivals of this Lerner and Loewe musical, and despite his limitations as a singer, even had a hit record with "MacArthur Park.") A secondary lead in *The Molly Maguires* and a starring role in the turgid historical saga *Cromwell* (both 1970) seemed to indicate Harris' film career was headed for the dumper.

But along came *A Man Called Horse* (also 1970), a modestly budgeted Western that starred him as an English aristocrat captured and tortured by Sioux Indians. Genuinely suspenseful if tastelessly gory (by standards of the day), it nonetheless became a surprise hit and boosted Harris' stock once again. He did two sequels, *The Return of a Man Called Horse* (1976) and *Triumphs of a Man Called Horse* (1983), neither of which enjoyed the original's success. Harris' pivotal year, 1970, also saw the actor turning his attentions behind the camera: He cowrote the screenplay for *The Lady in the Car With Glasses and a Gun* (in which he did not appear) and directed as well as starred in *The Hero* (released 1972), playing an aging soccer star.

Harris, a notorious wild man offscreen, enjoyed the high life throughout the 1970s, even though most of his films during that decade didn't offer cause to celebrate: *Man in the Wilderness* (1971), *The Deadly Trackers* (1973), *99 and 44/100% Dead, Juggernaut* (both 1974), *Echoes of a Summer* (1976), *The Cassandra Crossing, Gulliver's Travels, Orca, Golden Rendezvous* (all 1977), *The Wild Geese* (1978), *Game for Vultures, Ravagers,* and *Your Ticket Is No Longer Valid* (1979). He has worked sporadically since then, but increasingly in eccentric character roles: *Tarzan, the Ape Man* (1981, as Bo Derek's father), *Martin's Day* (1984), and *Mack the Knife* (1989). In 1990 he made a dramatic comeback with his commanding performance in *The Field*, a dour Irish story that earned him a Best Actor Oscar nomination and made him a latter-day media darling. He followed this up with meaty character parts in *Patriot Games*

(1992, as an Irish rebel leader), *Unforgiven* (also 1992, as a dandified gunslinger), *Wrestling Ernest Hemingway* (1993), and Sam Shepard's *Silent Tongue* (1994).

HARRISON, REX (SIR). Actor. *(b. Mar. 5, 1908, Huyton, England, as Reginald Carey Harrison; d. June 2, 1990.)* Debonair, fastidious British star, in his early years a roguish leading man in sophisticated drawing-room comedies, but later a superb character actor, best remembered as Professor Henry Higgins in *My Fair Lady* (1964), an Oscar-winning reprise of the part he created on Broadway. A starstruck youngster who always wanted to be an actor, Harrison joined a repertory company while still in his teens; by 1930 he'd worked his way to the London stage. During the 1930s he made a name for himself in witty, urbane comedies, and he charmed American audiences upon hitting Broadway in 1936. Harrison broke into films shortly after scoring his initial stage success, appearing in *The Great Game, School for Scandal* (both 1930), *Get Your Man* (1934), *All at Sea* (1935), *Men Are Not Gods* (1936), *Over the Moon, School for Husbands, Storm in a Teacup* (all 1937), *The Citadel, Sidewalks of London* (both 1938), and *Ten Days in Paris* (1939), mostly in support.

Night Train to Munich (1940), a Hitchcockian thriller directed by Carol Reed, gave Harrison top billing and was the first of his films to receive significant U.S. distribution. He costarred with Wendy Hiller in the delightful adaptation of George Bernard Shaw's *Major Barbara* (1941) before taking a hiatus to serve in the R.A.F. (achieving the rank of flight lieutenant) during World War 2. Immediately after the war, in 1945, he starred in three successive hits—Noël Coward and David Lean's *Blithe Spirit, A Yank in London,* and *The Rake's Progress* (aka *Notorious Gentleman*)—and was wooed to Hollywood by 20th Century-Fox's Darryl F. Zanuck.

Harrison was initially served well by his relationship with Fox. He played the Oriental potentate in *Anna and the King of Siam* (1946, opposite Irene Dunne), a philandering colonial in *The Foxes of Harrow* (opposite Maureen O'Hara), and a suave spirit in *The Ghost and Mrs. Muir* opposite Gene Tierney (both 1947). He was then cast opposite Linda Darnell in *Unfaithfully Yours* (1948), a mordant comedy written and directed by Preston Sturges, in which he played a jealous symphony conductor who fantasizes about murdering the devoted wife he suspects of infidelity. It was one of Harrison's favorites, a brilliant comedy—though a flop in its day.

In 1948 Harrison, at that time married to actress Lilli Palmer, was implicated in the suicide of actress Carole Landis, with whom he'd had an affair. Harrison, whom the gossip columnists referred to as "Sexy Rexy," fled to England, where he filmed *Escape* (1948), and found his popularity unaffected by the scandal. After several years of stage work, he returned to movies in *The Long Dark Hall* (1951), and even returned to the States, this time with Palmer in tow, to star in the charming two-character piece *The Four Poster* (1952). (They also made a cameo appearance as themselves in 1953's *Main Street to Broadway.)* Thereafter he alternated stage appearances with British film chores and Hollywood assignments, starring in *King Richard and the Crusaders* (1954), *The Constant Husband* (1955, with Kay Kendall, whom he was to marry in 1957), *The Reluctant Debutante* (1958, again with Kendall), *Midnight Lace* (1960), *The Happy Thieves* (1962), *Cleopatra* (1963, Oscar-nominated for his turn as Julius Caesar), and *The Yellow Rolls-Royce* (1965).

After his *My Fair Lady* triumph, an elegantly middle-aged Harrison appeared in *The Agony and the Ecstasy* (1965, as Pope Julius II opposite Charlton Heston's Michelangelo), *The Honey Pot* (1967, as a modern Volpone), and *Doctor Dolittle* (also 1967, as the amiable eccentric who talks to the animals, one of his most charming portrayals). But there were fewer leading roles available to him onscreen. After completing the French farce *A Flea in Her Ear* (1968) and *Staircase* (1969, in which he took the unexpected role of Richard Burton's gay lover), he was offscreen for nearly a decade before appearing in *Crossed Swords* (1978), a *Prince and the Pauper* remake. He made three films in 1979— *The Fifth Musketeer, Ashanti,* and *A Time to Die* (the latter unreleased until 1983)—before saying goodbye to motion pictures. He appeared in one lone telefilm, *Anastasia: The Mystery of Anna* (1986), and then returned to the stage for good, working in London, on Broadway, and on tour in a series of popular stage revivals (including "My Fair Lady") right up to the time of his death from cancer. Harrison, whose six wives also included actress Rachel Roberts, was knighted in 1989. He wrote an autobiography, "Rex," in 1974; another book about the art of comedy, "A Damned Serious Business," was released posthumously in 1990.

HARROLD, KATHRYN. Actress. (b. Aug. 2, 1950, Tazewell, Va.) Coolly intelligent, attractive actress who began in experimental theater and off-Broadway plays before landing a part on the soap opera "The Doctors." She made her film debut in the silly vampire bat epic *Nightwing* (1979). She appeared in several critical failures—*The Hunter* (1980, opposite Steve McQueen), *The Pursuit of D. B. Cooper* (1981), and *Yes, Giorgio* (1982, opposite opera star Luciano Pavarotti)—as well as many interesting projects like Albert Brooks' *Modern Romance* (1981), *The Sender* (1982), *Heartbreakers* (1984), and *Into the Night* (1985). Few, however, were widely seen—except for the Arnold Schwarzenegger vehicle *Raw Deal* (1986)—and she never made the cut of A-list actresses. Harrold has had more success (relatively speaking) on TV, with a number of short-lived series like "MacGruder and Loud" (1985), "The Bronx Zoo" (1987–88), and "I'll Fly Away" (1991–93). She also played Lauren Bacall in the 1980 TV movie *Bogie*. She joined the second season of "The Larry Sanders Show" as Garry Shandling's ex-wife.

HART, WILLIAM S. Actor, director, producer. (b. Dec. 6, 1865, Newburgh, N.Y.; d. June 24, 1946.) Although he spent some time in the West in his youth, William S. Hart was primarily a New York stage actor noted for villainous roles in "Ben-Hur," "The Virginian," and "The Squaw Man" before becoming one of the movies' first great Western stars. A veteran player in the grand manner, Hart brought passion and intensity to his Westerns, and his obvious affinity for the genre helped endear him to audiences. He first saw a Western film while playing a theatrical engagement in Cleveland. He was appalled. "Here were reproductions of the old West being seriously presented to the public—in almost a burlesque manner—and they were successful," he recalled later. "I was an actor and I knew the West . . . The opportunity that I had been waiting for years to come was knocking at my door."

While in Los Angeles with a touring company of "The Trail of the Lonesome Pine," Hart looked up his old friend Thomas Ince, who was a supervising director for the New York Motion Picture Corporation. The actor persuaded Ince to give him an opportunity to make some Westerns, and he made his screen debut in the two-reeler *His Hour of Manhood* (1914). Soon after he made two features, *The Bargain* (1914) and *On the Night Stage* (1915), both released by Paramount. Hart's pictures clicked with the public, though he was an unlikely cowboy hero: nearly 50, his rugged features were more suited to the villains he played on stage. Still, he brought great authority to his screen roles. His screenwriters (including C. Gardner Sullivan, Lambert Hillyer, and J. G. Hawks) developed Hart's "good bad man" persona, which offered a more rounded characterization than the usual stalwart hero and added an intriguing dimension that enhanced the Western actor's popularity. He wrote many of his own screenplays, and even directed a number of his vehicles during the teens.

At his best, in pictures like *Hell's Hinges* (1916) and *The Toll Gate* (1920), Hart gave the screen its first classic Westerns; but at his most self-indulgent, as in *The Narrow Trail* (1917) or *Singer Jim McKee* (1924), Hart could be both tedious and self-parodying. Even at his peak, he occasionally played nonwestern roles, as in *Shark Monroe* (1918), *The Poppy Girl's Husband* (1919), and *The Whistle* (1920). Under personal contract to Ince from the time he first entered pictures, Hart finally broke free and signed with Famous Players-Lasky in 1920; but his days as the screen's favorite cowboy were numbered. He planned to retire after completing *Three Word Brand* (1921), but was lured back to the screen in 1923 for *Wild Bill Hickok*, which owed more to Hart than to history and was not well received. Neither was *Singer Jim McKee,* and Hart again left the screen, only to return the follow-ing year as an independent producer for his final film, *Tumbleweeds* (1925). Poor distribution spelled failure for the spectacular epic of the Oklahoma land rush, and Hart spent the rest of the 1920s reissuing his old films and writing books for boys, several of which were vanity publications. His 1929 autobiography, "My Life, East and West," is highly readable, but not always reliable.

Hart's final film effort was preparing a reissue of *Tumbleweeds* in 1939. The picture was cut by three reels, and Hart added a moving spoken prologue that revealed his early theatrical training. Despite his declamatory style, Hart was still able to bring a tear to the eye when he remembered his days in pictures and lamented, "Oh, the thrill of it all!" He left his Newhall, California, ranch to the people of Los Angeles County as a repayment for the loyalty of the fans who spent their dimes and nickels to see his pictures, and it has become a public park.

HARTLEY, HAL. Director, screenwriter. *(b. Nov. 3, 1959, Lindenhurst, N.Y.)* Highly original independent filmmaker whose austere, deadpan "comedies" have become a favorite with critics. Hartley studied at the State University of New York at Purchase; his graduation project *Kid* (1984) had many of the stylistic elements that surfaced in his first feature, *The Unbelievable Truth* (1988), about a romance between a teenager and an ex-con mechanic: stone-faced delivery, bursts of philosophical dialogue, and off-kilter pacing. *Trust* (1991) won several festival awards, and *Simple Men* (1992), about two brothers in search of their missing anarchist father, continued to develop his idea of love and trust between unlikely people. His latest film is *Amateur* (1994).

HARVEY, LAURENCE. Actor. *(b. Oct. 1, 1928, Yomishkis, Lithuania, as Lauruska Mischa Skikne; d. Nov. 25, 1973.)* Handsome leading man who helped dominate 1960s films about modern society and its disaffected citizens, characters that perfectly utilized the emotional aloofness he projected so well. After serving in World War 2, he enrolled in the Royal Academy of Dramatic Art and was soon acting in such films as *House of Darkness* (1949), *Ro-*

meo and Juliet (1954), and *I Am a Camera* (1955). Harvey's breakthrough role was that of ruthless social climber Joe Lampton in *Room at the Top* (1959), for which he received a Best Actor Oscar nomination. He followed it with varied roles in *Butterfield 8, Expresso Bongo, The Alamo* (all 1960, in the last-named as Col. Travis), *The Ceremony* (1963, which he also directed), and *Darling* (1965), among others. Harvey achieved his greatest success as the brainwashed assassin in *The Manchurian Candidate* (1962), a well-rounded performance that completely overshadowed those of stars Frank Sinatra and Janet Leigh. He later appeared in *A Dandy in Aspic* (1968, which he directed after Anthony Mann died during shooting), *The Magic Christian* (1969), *WUSA* (1970), and his last film, 1974's *Welcome to Arrow Beach* (aka *Tender Flesh,* which was released shortly after he died of cancer; he assisted in its editing by phone from his deathbed). Perhaps his most unusual gig: guesting on the 1970 TV show "Can You Top This?" telling Jewish dialect jokes!

HATFIELD, HURD. Actor. *(b. Dec. 7, 1918, New York City, as William H. Hatfield.)* If ever there was a one-picture star, it's Hurd Hatfield. This slender, handsome, coolly suave actor—trained in England and seasoned on the Broadway stage—was an overnight sensation in the title role of *The Picture of Dorian Gray* (1945), but never again achieved that level of notoriety or success from one of his screen assignments. In recent years he has become a first-rate character actor.
OTHER FILMS INCLUDE: 1944: *Dragon Seed* (his first film); 1946: *Diary of a Chambermaid;* 1947: *The Beginning or the End;* 1948: *Joan of Arc;* 1950: *Tarzan and the Slave Girl;* 1958: *The Left-Handed Gun;* 1961: *King of Kings* (as a handsome, cruel, aloof Pontius Pilate); 1965: *Harlow* (the Carol Lynley version, miscast as Harlow's husband Paul Bern); 1968: *The Boston Strangler;* 1985: *King David;* 1986: *Crimes of the Heart;* 1989: *Her Alibi.*

HATHAWAY, HENRY. Director. *(b. Mar. 13, 1898, Sacramento, Calif.; d. Feb. 11, 1985.)* Though he lacks the reputation of his contemporaries Ford and Hawks, Hathaway spent more than 40 years turning out quality Westerns and thrillers, many of which have attained classic status. He began as a protégé to Allan Dwan, appearing as a child actor in countless silent Westerns during the teens. In 1919 he graduated to assistant director, working with such giants as Victor Fleming and Josef Von Sternberg. (He even assisted in the filming of the chariot race for the silent *Ben-Hur.*) He began directing B Westerns at Paramount in 1932 (beginning with *Wild Horse Mesa),* moving up to the big time in 1935 with *The Lives of a Bengal Lancer,* which starred old friend Gary Cooper, and got him his only Oscar nomination as Best Director. He also made his most unusual (and atypical) film with Cooper that year, the ethereally romantic *Peter Ibbetson.* The following year, he directed the first outdoor film in full Technicolor, *The Trail of the Lonesome Pine,* and handled Mae West in *Go West, Young Man.* Other high points include the gangster drama *Johnny Apollo* (1940), the WW2 epic *A Wing and a Prayer* (1944), the influential "realistic" spy drama *The House on 92nd St.* (1945), the legendary crime thriller *Kiss of Death* (1947), the journalistic mystery *Call Northside 777* (1948), the suicide drama *Fourteen Hours* (1951, Grace Kelly's first film), the blindman mystery *23 Paces to Baker Street* (1956), the gold-rush comedy *North to Alaska* (1960), three-fifths of *How the West Was Won* (1962), and two late John Wayne hits, *The Sons of Katie Elder* (1965) and *True Grit* (1969). Oddly, his last film, *Superdude* (1974), placed him in the alien world of blaxploitation. All of them were marked by slick production, solid acting, and thorough professionalism. Actors who worked with him also vividly recall his fiery temper and disregard of social amenities on the set.
OTHER FILMS INCLUDE: 1937: *Souls at Sea;* 1938: *Spawn of the North;* 1939: *The Real Glory;* 1940: *Johnny Apollo, Brigham Young—Frontiersman;* 1942: *China Girl;* 1944: *Home in Indiana;* 1946: *The Dark Corner, 13 Rue Madeleine;* 1949: *Down to the Sea in Ships;* 1951: *Rawhide, The Desert Fox;* 1953: *Niagara;* 1954: *Prince Valiant;* 1957: *Legend of the Lost;* 1960: *Seven Thieves;* 1964: *Circus World;* 1966: *Nevada Smith;* 1968: *5 Card Stud;* 1971: *Raid on Rommel, Shootout.*

HATTON, RONDO. Actor. *(b. Apr. 29, 1894, Fla.; d. Feb. 2, 1946.)* This unfortunate man, the victim of acromegaly (a disease of the pituitary gland that stimulates growth hormones and leads to oversized, distorted bone structure), owes his admittedly limited fame as a cult figure to his rare illness, which transformed him from a good-looking youth to a grotesque adult. A former journalist who first appeared onscreen in Henry King's *Hell Harbor* (1930), shot in his native Florida, Hatton journeyed west to Hollywood and worked as an extra and bit player for many years before being cast by Universal as "the Oxford Creeper," a murderous madman, in the 1944 Sherlock Holmes opus *The Pearl of Death.* Hatton's frightening physiognomy struck a chord with horror-hungry moviegoers, and he was cast in similar roles in *Jungle Captive* (1945), *House of Horrors, The Spider Woman Strikes Back,* and *The Brute Man* (all 1946). The last-named film, an incredibly tasteless, wretched exercise, was so much of an embarrassment to Universal that the company sold it to independent studio PRC. Hatton died before it was released. Makeup artist (and lifelong horror-movie fan) Rick Baker, working on *The Rocketeer* (1991), fitted actor Tiny Ron with a Hattonesque likeness as an homage to the Creeper.

HAUER, RUTGER. Actor. *(b. Jan. 23, 1944, Breukelen, Netherlands.)* Brawny, handsome leading man whose steely blue eyes, strong jaw, and blond hair immediately telegraph his Aryan ancestry. Although he was a leading man in his early Dutch films and has starred in many English-language movies in recent years, Hauer is at his best when playing icy villains like the rogue replicant in *Blade Runner* (1982), which first drew him the attention of mainstream American audiences. He initially won international recognition as a heroic freedom fighter in Paul Verhoeven's *Soldier of Orange* (1979) and worked with the director again in *Spetters* (1980) and the English-language *Flesh + Blood* (1985). He made an impressive American debut as a terrorist pursued by New York cop Sylvester Stallone in *Nighthawks* (1981), and made his American TV debut in *Inside the Third Reich* (1982), playing Albert Speer. The

costume adventure *Ladyhawke* (1985) cast him in a classic hero mold, but he was unable to land followup roles in the same vein. Since then he's worked for the most part in action films, some of them made for TV or released direct to video: *Wanted: Dead or Alive* (1987), *The Blood of Heroes, Blind Fury* (both 1990), *Deadlock* (1991), *Split Second, Past Midnight* (both 1992), *Blind Side, Voyage* (both 1993), *Surviving the Game* and *The Beans of Egypt, Maine,* (both 1994). He made a disappointing vampire in *Buffy the Vampire Slayer* (1992). His first starring opus, a 1973 Dutch-made film for Verhoeven called *Turkish Delight,* featuring explicit sex scenes, only came to light—on video—after Hauer established himself on these shores.
OTHER FILMS INCLUDE: 1975: *The Wilby Conspiracy;* 1983: *The Osterman Weekend;* 1984: *A Breed Apart;* 1985: *Eureka;* 1986: *The Hitcher* (in one of his most chilling villainous roles); 1988: *The Legend of the Holy Drinker;* 1989: *Bloodhounds of Broadway* (curiously but effectively cast as a Damon Runyon gangster).

HAUSER, WINGS. Actor, director. *(b. Dec. 12, 1947.)* He's probably the big screen's premier psychotic—at least judging from his over-the-top performances as villains in *Vice Squad* (1982), *Tough Guys Don't Dance* (1987), and *L.A. Bounty* (1989)—but this curly-haired, dimpled, and baby-faced character actor and leading man originally achieved prominence in a steady role on the TV soap opera "The Young and the Restless" (1977–81). Hauser leaped to the pantheon of great screen psychos as a despicable, murderous pimp in *Vice Squad* (1982), and thereafter worked almost exclusively in movies. He appeared in *Uncommon Valor* (1983), *A Soldier's Story* (1984), and *Hostage* (1987), although he seldom works in mainstream films anymore. He's one of the busiest B-movie actors around, alternating between heroic and villainous roles in made-for-home-video epics such as *The Carpenter* (1988), *Street Asylum* (1989), *Bedroom Eyes II* (1990), *Frame Up* (1991), and *Frame Up II: The Cover-Up* (1992). Hauser's sympathetic leads are hard-edged characters, and he still incorporates some of his distinctive, wide-eyed nuttiness into his performances. His recurring role as a next door neighbor on TV's "Roseanne" probably earned him a bigger audience than all his films put together.

HAVER, JUNE. Actress. *(b. June 10, 1926, Rock Island, Ill., as June Stovenour.)* Bubbly blond actress who spent most of her on-screen years at 20th Century-Fox, handpicked by Darryl F. Zanuck as an addition to the studio's lineage of fair-haired musical stars (beginning with Alice Faye, who had been succeeded by Betty Grable). Haver's popularity owed mostly to her wholesome, vivacious personality; although she was a competent singer, dancer, and actress, her abilities never quite equaled her enthusiasm. She debuted as a hat-check girl in the 1943 Faye musical *The Gang's All Here,* played second lead in the 1944 rural fable *Home in Indiana,* and won top billing in *Irish Eyes Are Smiling* that year. She teamed with Grable as one of *The Dolly Sisters* (1945), and starred or costarred in *Three Little Girls in Blue, Wake Up and Dream* (both 1946), *I Wonder Who's Kissing Her Now* (1947), *Scudda Hoo! Scudda Hay!* (1948), *Oh, You Beautiful Doll, Look for the Silver Lining* (both 1949), *The Daughter of Rosie O'Grady, I'll Get By* (both 1950), *Love Nest* (1951), and *The Girl Next Door* (1953). A devout Roman Catholic, Haver retired in 1953 to become a nun, but she left the convent sometime later and married Fred MacMurray, a union that lasted until his death in 1992.

HAVOC, JUNE. Actress. *(b. Nov. 8, 1916, Seattle, Wash., as Ellen Evangeline Hovick.)* The younger sister of stripper/authoress/actress Gypsy Rose Lee, Havoc also got an early start in show business: At the age of 2, she worked in several Harold Lloyd short subjects. She went on stage shortly afterwards, prodded by an ambitious, almost tyrannical stage mother. She was a vaudeville headliner at age 5, a child bride at age 13, a model, a dancer, and an actress in stock. Well received in the 1940 Broadway production of "Pal Joey," Havoc went to Hollywood and appeared in a number of films, mostly comedies and musicals, but never achieved the fame (or the notoriety) enjoyed by her big sister, Gypsy.

FILMS INCLUDE: 1941: *Four Jacks and a Jill;* 1942: *Sing Your Worries Away, Powder Town, My Sister Eileen;* 1943: *Hello Frisco, Hello* (her best break to date, playing Alice Faye's pal), *No Time for Love;* 1944: *Timber Queen;* 1945: *Brewster's Millions;* 1947: *Gentleman's Agreement* (probably her best film work in this Oscar-winning classic); 1948: *When My Baby Smiles at Me;* 1949: *Chicago Deadline;* 1950: *Once a Thief;* 1951: *Follow the Sun;* 1956: *Three for Jamie Dawn;* 1977: *The Private Files of J. Edgar Hoover.*

HAWKE, ETHAN. Actor. *(b. Nov. 6, 1970, Austin, Texas.)* Handsome young actor who made his film debut in Joe Dante's *Explorers* (1985) but really came into his own as the shy student who stands on a desk to yell "O Captain, my Captain" to Robin Williams in *Dead Poets Society* (1989). Since then, Hawke has appeared as Ted Danson's son in *Dad* (1989), the victim of a *Mystery Date* (1991), a prospector in *White Fang* (1991), a WW2 infantry leader in *A Midnight Clear* (1992), and a rugby player marooned in the Andes in *Alive* (1993). He costarred with Jeremy Irons in *Waterland* (1992) and Albert Finney in *Rich in Love* (1993), and became something of a "Generation X" poster boy with his turns in *Reality Bites* (1994) and *Before Sunrise* (1995).

HAWKINS, JACK (SIR). Actor. *(b. Sept. 1, 1910, London; d. July 18, 1973.)* Rugged, square-jawed British actor whose innate strength and rich voice ideally suited him to play authoritarians. In films from the early 1930s, Hawkins essayed juveniles and character parts for many years, then came into his own in the 1950s. Best remembered as the Egyptian ruler in *Land of the Pharaohs* (1955), the stiff-upper-lipped Major Warden in *The Bridge on the River Kwai* (1957), an intrepid C.I.D. inspector in *Gideon of Scotland Yard* (1958), Quintus Arrius in *Ben-Hur* (1959), the former military officer turned criminal in *The League of Gentlemen* (1960), and General Allenby in *Lawrence of Arabia* (1962). Stricken with throat cancer in 1966, Hawkins had an operation that forced the removal of his larynx; gamely, he continued acting in pictures, for which his voice was dubbed by others. He was once married to actress Jessica Tandy (1932–42).

OTHER FILMS INCLUDE: 1932: *The Lodger;* 1933: *The Good Companions;* 1937: *The Frog;* 1940: *The Flying Squad;* 1948: *The Fallen Idol;* 1949: *The Small Back Room;* 1950: *The Black Rose, The Elusive Pimpernel, State Secret;* 1953: *The Cruel Sea;* 1954: *Front Page Story;* 1958: *Fortune Is a Woman;* 1962: *Five Finger Exercise;* 1963: *Rampage;* 1964: *Zulu;* 1965: *Lord Jim, Masquerade;* 1966: *The Poppy Is Also a Flower;* 1968: *Great Catherine;* 1969: *Goodbye, Mr. Chips;* 1970: *Waterloo;* 1971: *Kidnapped, Nicholas and Alexandra;* 1972: *The Ruling Class, Young Winston;* 1973: *Tales That Witness Madness, Theatre of Blood.*

HAWKS, HOWARD. Producer, director. *(b. May 30, 1896, Goshen, Ind.; d. Dec. 26, 1977.)* It would not be imprudent to label Hawks the greatest American director who is not a household name. Yet his films continue to enchant audiences everywhere and but for a very few exceptions (Ford, Welles, Hitchcock), his is the name most often cited by modern filmmakers as an influence. His visual style is clean, uncluttered, almost invisible; and unlike many directors who preferred to work in one or two genres, Hawks did them all. His best films celebrate "the group": professionals bound together by camaraderie and their work, to whom the ultimate compliment is "you're good."

Another reason Hawks' films seem so fresh is that the women are just as smart, tough, and fast-talking as the men—sometimes more so; indeed, he staged scenes with dialogue that always sounded natural and real. This was immediately apparent in his first sound film, *The Dawn Patrol* (1930), in which the actors "talked," rather than emoting in the then-normal style of early talkies, and in *Scarface* (1932), the most ferocious of that era's gangster films. Hawks defined the then-new subgenre of screwball comedy with his frenetic *Twentieth Century* (1934), which made Carole Lombard a star. Later in the decade he helmed three masterpieces with Cary Grant: the definitive screwball comedy, *Bringing Up Baby* (1938), the mail-pilot adventure *Only Angels Have Wings* (1939), and the breathless "Front Page" remake *His Girl Friday* (1940).

In 1944 he launched the film career of 19-year-old Lauren Bacall and teamed her with Humphrey Bogart in *To Have and Have Not;* when romance erupted, he quickly cast them in the even more successful *The Big Sleep* (not released till 1946). *Red River* (1948) was his first Western and first film with John Wayne; it also was the debut of young Montgomery Clift. He gave Marilyn Monroe two key early roles in *Monkey Business* (1952) and *Gentlemen Prefer Blondes* (1953, featuring her legendary "Diamonds Are a Girl's Best Friend" number), and in 1959 made what some consider his finest film, *Rio Bravo,* which encapsulated virtually all his themes and moods. (His later Westerns, 1967's *El Dorado* and 1970's *Rio Lobo,* attempted to duplicate its ambience—and success.)

In later years he became a kind of elder statesman to young directors, and received a long overdue special Oscar in 1974. Ironically, he considered himself a craftsman, preferring to make hits rather than works of art. (As a footnote, he wasn't bashful about taking credit that didn't belong to him, and his often outrageous fabrications about the making of his films have wreaked considerable havoc among film historians and scholars.) OTHER FILMS INCLUDE: 1926: *The Road to Glory;* 1927: *The Cradle Snatchers, A Girl in Every Port;* 1932: *The Crowd Roars, Tiger Shark;* 1935: *Barbary Coast;* 1936: *Ceiling Zero, The Road to Glory, Come and Get It* (codirected by William Wyler); 1941: *Sergeant York* (his only Oscar nomination), *Ball of Fire;* 1942: *Air Force;* 1949: *I Was a Male War Bride;* 1951: *The Thing* (producer and uncredited codirector); 1955: *Land of the Pharaohs;* 1962: *Hatari!;* 1964: *Man's Favorite Sport?;* 1965: *Red Line 7000.*

HAWN, GOLDIE. Actress. *(b. Nov. 21, 1945, Washington, D.C.)* Attractive, towheaded performer whose career has prospered despite early typecasting as a ditzy blonde and her subsequent appearance in a string of mediocre starring vehicles. Hawn studied drama at American University, but dropped out to crash show business. Her "break" came in the form of a job on the can-can line at the 1965 World's Fair, which led to a stint as a go-go dancer. Hawn eventually made her way to Los Angeles, where she landed a spot in the ill-fated ABC series "Good Morning World" (1967–68). Although the show was a bomb, Hawn's work was noticed by producer George Schlatter, who hired her for his comedy show starring stand-up specialists Dan Rowan and Dick Martin. "Rowan and Martin's Laugh-In" was an instant smash: Hawn's befuddled, air-headed character made her one of the show's main attractions. She made her feature-film debut as a dancer in *The One and Only, Genuine, Original Family Band* (1968), and parlayed her "Laugh-In" prominence into a plum supporting role in 1969's *Cactus Flower,* a comedy starring Walter Matthau and Ingrid Bergman, for which she won a Supporting Actress Oscar. Still playing the dizzy blonde, she appeared in *There's a Girl in My Soup* (1970), *$ (Dollars),* and *Butterflies Are Free* (both 1972), earning a "one-trick-pony" tag from Hollywood wags.

Hawn's career as a "serious" actress was launched by Steven Spielberg, who cast Hawn as a desperate mother on the run in his feature *The Sugarland Express* (1974). Since then, she has demonstrated her versatility and comedic talents in such pictures as *Shampoo* (1975), *The Duchess and the Dirtwater Fox* (1976), *Foul Play* (1978), *Private Benjamin* (1980, a career high point that made her a bankable star and earned her a Best Actress nomination), *Best Friends* (1982), *Protocol, Swing Shift* (both 1984), *Wildcats* (1986), *Overboard* (1987), and *Bird on a Wire* (1990). As one of Hollywood's reigning female stars, Hawn has developed and produced many of her own films, and has attempted to maintain a balance between comedy and drama in her choice of vehicles, but the box-office success of *HouseSitter* and *Death Becomes Her* (both 1992) and the failure of *Deceived* (1991) and *CrissCross* (1992) seem to indicate that audiences still like Goldie best in lighthearted roles. She has a son by actor Kurt Russell, her longtime companion.

HAYAKAWA, SESSUE. Actor. *(b. June 10, 1889, Chiba, Japan; d. Nov. 23, 1973.)* Veteran Japanese actor who made his mark on American audiences in silent movies from the teens, enjoying a lengthy and generally distinguished screen career, the climax of which was his Oscar-nominated portrayal of a Japanese prison-camp commander in *The Bridge on the River Kwai* (1957). Hayakawa originally

came to America in 1908 as a University of Chicago student, and later returned to this country with an acting troupe. Signed to a movie contract by pioneer producer Thomas H. Ince, he actually made his biggest impact as the villain in Cecil B. DeMille's *The Cheat* (1915), delivering an understated performance very much ahead of its time. Hayakawa worked through the silent era in a number of exotic melodramas (many of which he also produced) and made his talkie debut in *Daughter of the Dragon* (1931), a Fu Manchu thriller in which he played a heroic Chinese detective. His performance was poorly received, and he left Hollywood for Europe, where he appeared in films throughout the 1930s. In the late 1940s Hayakawa returned to Hollywood and made a new career for himself as a successful character actor in *Tokyo Joe* (1949), *Three Came Home* (1950, a high point), *House of Bamboo* (1955), *The Geisha Boy* (1958), *Green Mansions* (1959), *Swiss Family Robinson* (1960), *The Big Wave* (1962), and *The Daydreamer* (1966).

HAYDEN, STERLING. Actor. *(b. Mar. 26, 1916, Montclair, N.J., as Sterling Relyea Walter; d. May 23, 1986.)* Massive, gravel-voiced leading man known for his gruff, macho characterizations. Hayden, whose first and constant love was the sea, became a model and an actor as a young man, as a means of financing his voyages. Paramount signed him to a contract in 1940 (billing him initially as Sti*r*ling Hayden); in his first two films, *Bahama Passage* and *Virginia* (both 1941), Hayden was paired with glamorous Madeleine Carroll, whom he later married. A poor man's John Wayne (but without the Duke's range), Hayden starred in Westerns, war films, and crime thrillers throughout the 1940s and 1950s. His career faltered briefly in 1950, after giving his all-time best performance in *The Asphalt Jungle,* when it was learned he'd spent six months in the Communist party. Subpoenaed by the House Un-American Activities Committee in 1951, Hayden willingly named names in public testimony and was able to resume his career.

Although his 1950s films include some bona fide gems—*Johnny Guitar* (1954), *The Last Command* (1955, as Jim Bowie), and *The Killing* (1956) among them—

Hayden dropped out of film work in the latter part of the decade, returning to the screen in character roles, beginning with *Dr. Strangelove* (1964), in which he played the insane General Jack D. Ripper. He exhibited a greater range in his subsequent screen appearances than he'd ever shown while a top-billed star. Although Hayden's career was relatively successful, he never felt truly at home in the Hollywood machine, and he often took to the sea for peace and solitude. In 1966 he wrote an autobiography, "Wanderer."
OTHER FILMS INCLUDE: 1949: *Manhandled;* 1952: *The Star* (opposite Bette Davis), *Flat Top;* 1953: *So Big;* 1954: *Prince Valiant;* 1955: *Battle Taxi;* 1957: *The Iron Sheriff, Zero Hour* (parodied as *Airplane!);* 1969: *Hard Contract;* 1970: *Loving;* 1972: *The Godfather* (a memorable bit as a brutal, corrupt police captain shot by Al Pacino); 1973: *The Long Goodbye;* 1977: *1900;* 1978: *King of the Gypsies;* 1980: *9 to 5;* 1982: *Venom.*

HAYDN, RICHARD. Actor, director. *(b. Mar. 10, 1905; d. Apr. 25, 1985.)* Even people who don't know Richard Haydn's name know the voice of his most familiar character, a pinched, nasal sound that's been imitated in countless animated cartoons. That voice belonged to one Edwin Carp, a supposed fish expert and mimic who first appeared in London stage revues in the 1930s, and then in several Broadway equivalents—all to rave reviews. Haydn resisted putting Carp on film, and played a college student in his debut picture, *Charley's Aunt* (1941), but then agreed to play a Carp-like professor in *Ball of Fire* (1941), and the die was cast. Haydn—in this hilarious guise—was seen at his best in Ernst Lubitsch's *Cluny Brown* (1946, as Jennifer Jones' fiancé) and in the popular *Sitting Pretty* (1948, as a snoopy neighbor who becomes Clifton Webb's nemesis).

He played a variety of character parts—generally quite well—in such films as *Tonight and Every Night, And Then There Were None* (both 1945), *The Green Years* (1946, one of his best, and most serious roles, as a Scottish schoolteacher), *The Late George Apley, The Foxes of Harrow, Forever Amber* (all 1947), *The Emperor Waltz* (1948), *The Merry Widow* (1952), *Never Let Me Go* (1953), *Please Don't Eat The Daisies* (1960), *Five Weeks in a*

Balloon, and *Mutiny on the Bounty* (both 1962). His best-known film, *The Sound of Music* (1965), gave him his most "normal" and least colorful part, as the impresario friend of the Von Trapps. (His other enduring performance is a vocal one, as the voice of the caterpillar in the 1951 Disney cartoon feature *Alice in Wonderland.)*

In the late 1940s Paramount gave him the opportunity to direct, and he made three feature films: the very odd black comedy *Miss Tatlock's Millions* (1948), and the more conventional *Dear Wife* (1949) and *Mr. Music* (1950) with Bing Crosby. He took small roles in each of the films, billing himself variously as Richard Rancyd, Stanley Stayle, and Claude Curdle.

Edwin Carp surfaced in an episode of "The Dick Van Dyke Show" in the 1960s, and another Carp fan, Mel Brooks, hired Haydn to play a professor at the outset of *Young Frankenstein* (1974), which was his final film appearance.

HAYES, ALLISON. Actress. *(b. Jan. 6, 1930, as Mary Jane Hayes; d. Feb. 27, 1977.)* Haughty, buxom brunette actress (and former symphony-orchestra pianist) whose appearances in low-budget 1950s movies have made her something of a camp icon. A no-nonsense gal with a withering gaze, she frequently played "bad girls" in her films and seemed to relish doing so. Her metier was the grade-Z horror film, although she also appeared in Westerns and crime films. Most famous as the titular terror of *Attack of the 50 Ft. Woman* (1958, shrieking "Harr-rry!" as she stomps along looking for her errant husband), Hayes also appeared in *Francis Joins the Wacs* (1954, her first film), *Chicago Syndicate, Count Three and Pray* (both 1955), *Gunslinger, Mohawk, The Steel Jungle* (all 1956), *The Unearthly, The Disembodied, The Undead, Zombies of Mora Tau, Voodoo Woman* (all 1957), *The Hypnotic Eye* (1960), *The Crawling Hand* (1963), and *Tickle Me* (1965). The still-beautiful Hayes died at 47 from blood poisoning.

HAYES, GEORGE "GABBY." Actor. *(b. May 7, 1885, Wellsville, N.Y.; d. Feb. 9, 1969.)* Beloved Western-movie sidekick and prolific character actor, who was so convincing as garrulous "Gabby" that fans still have a hard time believing he was just an actor playing a part. Hayes, a former vaudevillian and stock player, broke into movies in the 1920s, winning character parts (heavies, mostly) in a number of silent films beginning with *Why Women Marry* (1923). The coming of sound didn't inhibit him at all, and for the first few years of talkies he appeared in movies as diverse as *Love Me Tonight* (1932) and *Beggars in Ermine* (1934). In the early 1930s he began playing crusty but lovable western old-timers, fostering the illusion of age by removing his false teeth and letting his beard grow. He played heavies, sidekicks, and even sheriffs in many of John Wayne's Monogram Westerns of the mid-1930s, including *The Star Packer* and *Randy Rides Alone* (both 1934).

Hired by producer Harry Sherman to appear in the first six "Hopalong Cassidy" films (beginning with *Hop-a-long Cassidy),* Hayes tried out several characters before settling into the role of "Windy Halliday," which he played until 1939, when a salary dispute sent him scurrying to Republic. Forbidden to use the "Windy" sobriquet, Hayes was renamed "Gabby" and teamed with new singing-cowboy star Roy Rogers, beginning with *Southward Ho* (1939). Gabby's best opportunity with Rogers came with *Don't Fence Me In* (1945), in which he played the "Wildcat Kelly" of Cole Porter's title tune, a reformed bandit long thought dead. Hayes made 40 Rogers Westerns between 1939 and 1947, taking time out in 1943 to perform similar chores and help launch "Wild Bill" Elliott's Republic series.

Hayes' nonseries Westerns include *The Texas Rangers* (1936), *The Plainsman* (1936), *Gold Is Where You Find It* (1938), *Man of Conquest* (1939), *Dark Command* (1940, reunited with John Wayne, with whom Hayes appeared several more times), *In Old Oklahoma* (1943), *Tall in the Saddle* (1944), *The Big Bonanza* (1945), *Badman's Territory* (1946), *Wyoming* (1947), *El Paso* (1949), and *The Cariboo Trail* (1950). Typecast as a horse-opera player, Hayes found work scarce as movie Westerns dried up in the 1950s thanks to competition from TV. He went on TV himself, hosting an early 1950s program and introducing reruns of his old oaters.

HAYES, HELEN. Actress. *(b. Oct. 10, 1900, Washington, D.C., as Helen Hayes Brown; d. Mar. 17, 1993.)* The "First Lady of the American Theater" never enjoyed much success with movie audiences, despite her prodigious talent and impeccable performances, until quite late in her career. She started acting on stage while still a small child, and made her film debut at the age of 10 in a two-reeler, *Jean and the Calico Doll,* but she only went to Hollywood, years later, because her playwright husband, Charles MacArthur, was signed to an MGM contract. She made her sound film debut in *The Sin of Madelon Claudet* (1931), playing a woman who sacrifices everything to help her illegitimate son. It was an amazing performance, for which she won a Best Actress Academy Award. With such an impressive launch, Hayes seemed a screen natural. She took well-written roles in quality films, such as *Arrowsmith* (1931), *A Farewell to Arms* (1932), *The White Sister* (1933), *What Every Woman Knows* (1934), and *Vanessa: Her Love Story* (1935). But Hayes never really clicked with moviegoers, possibly because she lacked the magnetism or the sexual spark that put over many of the era's top stars. She ultimately returned to New York (as did MacArthur) and made only a few film appearances thereafter, concentrating on her enormously successful stage career, which was highlighted by a three-year run in the play "Victoria Regina" in the 1930s. (In fact, a Broadway theater was later named in her honor; ironically, it was later torn down during a renovation of New York's theater district.)

Hayes played cameos in *Stage Door Canteen* (1943), *Main Street to Broadway* (1953), and *Third Man on the Mountain* (1959, which starred her son, James MacArthur), along with meatier roles in *My Son John* (1952) and *Anastasia* (1956). She snagged another Oscar for her scene-stealing characterization of an ingenuous stowaway in *Airport* (1970), which introduced and endeared her to a new generation. She then lent her talents to the innocuous Disney films *Herbie Rides Again* (1974), *One of Our Dinosaurs Is Missing* (1976), and *Candleshoe* (1977). She also acted in several made-for-TV movies and even played one of "The Snoop Sisters" in that 1973–74 series. Hayes wrote three volumes of memoirs, "A Gift of Joy" (1965), "On Reflection" (1969), and "My Life in Three Acts" (1990).

HAYS, ROBERT. Actor. (b. July 24, 1947, Bethesda, Md.) In the disaster-movie spoof *Airplane!* (1980) and its 1982 sequel, this likable if colorless leading man was perfectly cast as the hapless hero. His blandness, though, may explain why, by 1992, he was appearing in TV commercials for Cheez-Whiz. Hays got his big break on the TV sitcom "Angie" (1979–80) and has starred in such lighthearted fare as *Take This Job and Shove It* (1981), *Scandalous* (1984), and *Honeymoon Academy* (1990), and was well cast as the Dad in Disney's *Homeward Bound: The Incredible Journey* (1993). He has been busier of late on the small screen, where he has starred in the short-lived shows "Starman" (1986–87), "FM" (1989–90), and "Cutters" (1993).

HAYWARD, LOUIS. Actor. (b. Mar. 19, 1909, Johannesburg, South Africa, as Seafield Grant; d. Feb. 21, 1985.) Debonair British leading man (and sometimes supporting player) of Hollywood movies from the 1930s to the 1970s. Although he often played heroes in swashbucklers, Hayward never seemed wholly comfortable in the genre; manly without being rugged, he frequently affected an annoying bravado as if to underscore his virility. (Come to think of it, the boyish-looking actor had a "soft" side he tried to obscure in many of his films.) Debuting in the British-made *Self-Made Lady* (1932, which also starred future Hollywood stars Heather Angel and Henry Wilcoxon), Hayward made several more films in England before coming to America in 1935 for a Broadway debut. His first Hollywood film was *The Flame Within* (1935), a gooey Ann Harding drama in which he played a patient infatuated with his female psychiatrist. He played Denis Moore in *Anthony Adverse* (1936, a high-profile role for him) and bounced around for several years, becoming the first actor to play Leslie Charteris' "modern Robin Hood," Simon Templar, in *The Saint in New York* (1938), first of the RKO series. He got his first swashbuckler

assignment in *The Man in the Iron Mask* (1939), playing both Louis XIV and his evil twin Philippe. In *The Son of Monte Cristo* (1940), Hayward played a Zorro-type character called "The Torch," investing the role with all the derring-do any Saturday-matinee audience could ask for. Hayward served with the Marines in World War 2 for several years, winning a Bronze Star for his real-life heroism, then returned to the screen in 1945's *And Then There Were None,* the first of four screen adaptations of Agatha Christie's "Ten Little Indians." He starred in another swashbuckler, *The Return of Monte Cristo* (1946), and returned to the genre in *The Black Arrow* (1948, as Richard Shelton), *The Pirates of Capri* (1949), *The Fortunes of Captain Blood* (1950, in the title role), *The Lady and the Bandit* (1951, as Dick Turpin), and *Lady in the Iron Mask* (1952, as D'Artagnan). He was once married to actress Ida Lupino.
OTHER FILMS INCLUDE: 1937: *Midnight Intruder* (his first lead); 1940: *Dance, Girl, Dance;* 1947: *Repeat Performance* (an offbeat fantasy/mystery); 1948: *Ruthless, Walk a Crooked Mile;* 1951: *The Son of Dr. Jekyll* (in the title role); 1954: *Duffy of San Quentin;* 1966: *The Christmas Kid;* 1973: *Terror in the Wax Museum* (his last).

HAYWARD, SUSAN. Actress. (b. June 30, 1918, Brooklyn, as Edythe Marrener; d. Mar. 14, 1975.) A sexy, gutsy redhead whose personal determination to scale the heights of her chosen profession also manifested itself in many of her screen characterizations. Born into a working-class family, she studied for a career in fashion design before becoming a photographer's model. Going to Hollywood in 1937, Hayward tested unsuccessfully for the role of Scarlett O'Hara in *Gone With the Wind,* but did manage to secure extra work and bit parts at Warner Bros. in *Hollywood Hotel* (1937), *The Sisters, Girls on Probation, I Am the Law,* and *Comet Over Broadway* (all 1938).
Hayward signed a Paramount contract in 1939, making her tyro appearance for the studio in *Our Leading Citizen.* That same year's prestige production *Beau Geste* garnered her considerable publicity. Her youthful prettiness made Hayward an ideal ingenue, but early on she lobbied for more demanding roles. She played an un-

sophisticated, grasping tart in a B picture, *Among the Living* (1941), and her obvious talent didn't escape perceptive critics. But Paramount insisted on giving her secondary female leads in Cecil B. DeMille's *Reap the Wild Wind, I Married a Witch, The Forest Rangers* (all 1942), *Young and Willing* (1943), and *And Now Tomorrow* (1944). Hayward won her first leads on loan to Republic, first in an innocuous musical, *Hit Parade of 1943*, and then in the John Wayne starrer, *The Fighting Seabees* (1944). That same year, she won her best role to date, as the vile rich bitch who torments bestial ship stoker William Bendix in the film version of Eugene O'Neill's *The Hairy Ape*, a United Artists release.

At Universal, she costarred in the Technicolor Western *Canyon Passage* (1946) and, more important, in *Smash-Up: The Story of a Woman* (1947), snagging a Best Actress Oscar nomination for her portrayal of an alcoholic. At RKO she starred in a fascinating B thriller, *Deadline at Dawn* (1946) and *They Won't Believe Me* (1947), a tense film noir. As Hayward matured physically, her career kept pace. There would be no more dewy-eyed ingenues for her; instead, she frequently played indomitable women with smoldering, sometimes uncontrollable passions.

After starring in *The Lost Moment* (1947), *Tap Roots, The Saxon Charm* (both 1948), *Tulsa*, and *House of Strangers* (both 1949), Hayward earned her second Oscar nod for a tender romantic drama, *My Foolish Heart* (1950), based on a J. D. Salinger story. By now a top star, she chose her starring vehicles carefully; in 1951 alone she appeared in *I'd Climb the Highest Mountain, Rawhide, I Can Get It for You Wholesale*, and *David and Bathsheba*—as wide a range of properties as any star could ask for. Hayward then played singer Jane Froman in *With a Song in My Heart* (1952), picking up another Academy Award nomination for her earnest performance in the sometimes sappy biopic. Now at 20th Century-Fox, she spent the next few years in big-budget star vehicles such as *The Snows of Kilimanjaro, The Lusty Men* (both 1952), *The President's Lady, White Witch Doctor* (both 1953), *Demetrius and the Gladiators, Garden of Evil* (both 1954), and *Untamed* (1955) before going to MGM to tackle another demanding biopic role, as

alcoholic singer Lillian Roth in *I'll Cry Tomorrow* (also 1955). Roth provided the vocals, while Hayward supplied the histrionics; the result was a box-office smash and yet another Oscar nomination.

Hayward filmed the ill-fated *The Conqueror* (1956) and *Top Secret Affair* (1957) before assuming her most challenging role, that of prostitute and convicted murderess Barbara Graham in *I Want to Live!* (1958), a chilling drama proffering the theory that Graham had been framed. It was certainly her career high point—finally winning her an Oscar—but one on which she seemed unable to capitalize. Her subsequent starring vehicles, which included *Woman Obsessed, Thunder in the Sun* (both 1959), the comedy *The Marriage-Go-Round* (1960), *Ada*, a remake of the classic sudser *Back Street* (both 1961), *I Thank a Fool* (1962), *Stolen Hours* (1963), *Where Love Has Gone* (1964), and *The Honey Pot* (1967), were undistinguished at best. By this time, finding suitable starring roles was difficult. She replaced Judy Garland as a washed-up actress in the embarrassing *Valley of the Dolls* (1967), but found nothing else to her liking for years to follow. She did star in a pair of TV movies, *Heat of Anger* and *Say Goodbye, Maggie Cole* (both 1972). Her final theatrical film was an abysmal Western, *The Revengers* (1972), which reunited her with former leading man William Holden but wrote an unfortunate "finis" to a fine career. After her death, it was revealed that an alarming number of people who'd worked on *The Conqueror* on location in St. George, Utah, had died of cancer, as she did; the site's proximity to atomic bomb testing was certainly more than coincidental.

HAYWORTH, RITA. Actress. *(b. Oct. 17, 1918, Brooklyn, as Margarita Carmen Cansino; d. May 14, 1987.)* One of the screen's premier "love goddesses," this Latin beauty enjoyed remarkable screen success following a humble beginning and a long grooming period. Born to professional dancers, she started dancing at age 12 and was working in Hollywood nightclubs at age 17. During one such engagement, the raven-haired, slightly chubby teen was spotted by Fox executive Winfield Sheehan, who enabled her to get a contract. Billed as Rita Cansino, she played exotic Latin dancers in 1935's *Under the Pampas Moon* (her first feature), *Dante's Inferno,* and *In Caliente* (on loan to Warner Bros.), and even delivered some dialogue as an Egyptian servant in *Charlie Chan in Egypt* that same year. The following year she was cut loose from Fox (following Sheehan's departure), but a star-struck Cansino now determined to become a successful movie actress. She freelanced in B Westerns—including *Rebellion* (1936); *Old Louisiana, Trouble in Texas,* and *Hit the Saddle* (all 1937)—before marrying businessman Edward Judson, an older man who took her under his wing and helped her get a contract with Columbia.

First billed as Rita Hayworth (above the title, at that) in a modest B mystery, *The Shadow* (1937), she learned her craft the hard way, toiling in low-budget quickies, sometimes playing the lead, sometimes in support. *Criminals of the Air, The Game That Kills, Paid to Dance, Girls Can Play* (all 1937), *Who Killed Gail Preston?, Renegade Ranger* (on loan to RKO for this George O'Brien horse opera), *Juvenile Court, Convicted* (all 1938), *Homicide Bureau,* and *The Lone Wolf Spy Hunt* (both 1939) aroused little interest from either critics or audiences, but they provided valuable learning experience for the supremely dedicated Hayworth, who lost weight, raised her hairline with electrolysis, and took elocution lessons. Columbia president Harry Cohn believed in Hayworth and pressed director Howard Hawks to use her as the "other woman" in *Only Angels Have Wings* (1939), a hard-boiled adventure story about mail pilots in South America. She acquitted herself admirably, prompting Cohn to take her out of B pictures after *Blondie on a Budget* (1940).

Cohn tested Hayworth on two 1940 "nervous A" pictures, *Angels Over Broadway* and *Music in My Heart,* before loaning her out to other studios. She appeared in *Susan and God* (1940), supporting Joan Crawford and Fredric March, for MGM; played an aristocratic Spanish temptress in a Technicolor remake of *Blood and Sand* (1941) for 20th Century-Fox; and assumed the title role (having dyed her raven tresses red) in *The Strawberry Blonde* (1941) for Warner Bros. She won enthusiastic reviews for her work in these films,

which encouraged Cohn to bring her home and try her out in big-budget A vehicles. Fred Astaire, recently departed from RKO and Ginger Rogers, chose her to costar with him in *You'll Never Get Rich* (1941) and *You Were Never Lovelier* (1942), enjoyable musicals that showed a radiant Hayworth at her best. (Though her dancing was faultless, her singing voice was dubbed, as it always would be.)

Back at Fox, Hayworth—by now an established star and a national pinup favorite, thanks to a sultry negligee shot originally taken for "Life" magazine—starred in a period musical, *My Gal Sal,* and the episodic drama *Tales of Manhattan* (both 1942). That same year she divorced Judson to marry *Sal* costar Victor Mature, but the proposed nuptials never came off and Hayworth began dating Orson Welles, whom she married the following year.

Cover Girl (1944), a lavish Technicolor musical, helped boost Hayworth into stardom's top ranks, even though the next year's *Tonight and Every Night* (the story of a London music hall that never closed during the WW2 bombings) was actually a better picture. Hayworth achieved another milestone in 1945: Her famous pinup shot was attached to the atomic bomb dropped on Bikini. *Gilda* (1946), probably her best-remembered picture, reteamed her with Glenn Ford—they first worked together in a 1940 programmer, *The Lady in Question*—for a steamy, corny, campy melodrama. In that film she performed a genteel (partial) striptease while singing the torchy "Put the Blame on Mame." That number ultimately became one of the most frequently anthologized sequences in movie history.

The Technicolor musicals *Down to Earth* (1947, a semi-sequel to the nonmusical Columbia hit *Here Comes Mr. Jordan)* and *The Loves of Carmen* (1948) kept Rita's followers happy but broke no new ground. It was *The Lady From Shanghai* (1948), written, directed by, and starring Orson Welles (whom she had divorced the previous year), that really shocked moviegoers. For her role as a sultry seductress, Hayworth sheared off most of her lustrous locks and dyed what was left platinum. (This reportedly infuriated Cohn.) By this time anxious to prove herself a serious actress, Hayworth delivered a creditable performance as a femme fatale.

Her runaway romance with millionaire Moslem playboy Aly Khan—played out all over Europe—kept Hayworth off the screen for several years and engendered more than a little unfavorable publicity. She married him in 1949, had a daughter, and won a divorce in 1951. A heartbroken Hayworth, without money of her own, returned to Hollywood the following year to pick up where she'd left off at Columbia. She was immediately reteamed with Glenn Ford for *Affair in Trinidad* (1952), a mediocre attempt to fashion another *Gilda,* and the following year starred in a watered-down Biblical opus, *Salome,* and a similarly diluted version of Somerset Maugham's "Rain," *Miss Sadie Thompson* (which did feature one good musical number, "The Heat Is On"). Disturbed by her inability to regain the heights she'd reached in the mid 1940s, Hayworth clashed repeatedly with Cohn over story choices, budgets, and directors, with the result that she left Columbia again in 1953. The same year she married singer Dick Haymes, but the union was dissolved after just two years. Swallowing her pride, she returned to Columbia again to play second female lead in *Pal Joey* (1957), with Frank Sinatra and Kim Novak. Her opportunities in that film were limited, but she made the most of them, particularly in the "Bewitched, Bothered and Bewildered" number.

Hayworth gave creditable dramatic performances in *Separate Tables* (1958), *They Came to Cordura,* and *The Story on Page One* (both 1959), and more or less walked through *The Happy Thieves* (1962), *Circus World* (1964), *The Money Trap* (reunited with old friend and costar Glenn Ford), *The Poppy Is Also a Flower* (both 1966), *The Road to Salina* (1971), and *The Wrath of God* (1972) before retiring from the screen. A victim of Alzheimer's disease, she was cared for in her later years by Yasmin, her daughter by Prince Aly Khan. She was portrayed in a 1983 TV movie, *Rita Hayworth: The Love Goddess,* by Lynda Carter.

HEAD, EDITH. Costume designer. *(b. Oct. 28, 1907, Los Angeles; d. Oct. 24, 1981.)* For decades, her name was synonymous with Hollywood costumes. Edith Head also influenced American fashion for decades by dressing some of Hollywood's leading female stars, and winning a bushel of Oscars along the way. A college educated woman who taught school, she got into the movie business by answering a newspaper ad for sketch artists in 1923 figuring she would learn enough on the job to be able to teach art later on. She was hired by Paramount Pictures designer Howard Greer and stayed at the studio for 44 years.

As a member of the studio staff, and then as head designer (from 1937 on), she worked closely with such stars as Carole Lombard, Barbara Stanwyck, Olivia de Havilland, Audrey Hepburn, and Shirley MacLaine. She dressed Bette Davis as Margo Channing in *All About Eve* (1950), Gloria Swanson as Norma Desmond in *Sunset Blvd.* (1950), Elizabeth Taylor as the young socialite in *A Place in the Sun* (1951), and in the early 1950s began a long and successful collaboration with Alfred Hitchcock. (Her gold lamé gown for Grace Kelly in 1955's *To Catch a Thief* was particularly memorable, and Head later cited this as her all-time favorite assignment.) In 1967 Head moved to Universal where she continued to function at the top of her profession right through the 1970s, on films like *Sweet Charity* (1969), *Airport* (1970), and *Rooster Cogburn* (1975), and on loan-out for such prominent pictures as *Butch Cassidy and the Sundance Kid* (1969) and *The Man Who Would Be King* (1975).

Head amassed an incredible 35 Academy Award nominations, and won Oscars for *The Heiress, Samson and Delilah* (both 1949), *All About Eve, A Place in the Sun* (1951), *Roman Holiday* (1953), *Sabrina* (1954), *The Facts of Life* (1960), and *The Sting* (1973). She wrote several books, including "Dress Doctor" and "How to Dress for Success."

HEADLY, GLENNE. Actress. *(b. Mar. 13, 1955, New London, Conn.)* Although this intelligent, attractive actress has been working steadily on stage since the late 1970s and in films since 1981's *Four Friends,* it took the nondemanding role of Tess Trueheart in *Dick Tracy* (1990) to firmly fix her in the public eye. A versatile stage performer, Headly has fared best on film in light comedies, especially *Dirty Rotten*

Scoundrels (1988) in which she more than held her own opposite Michael Caine and Steve Martin. Formerly married to actor John Malkovich, with whom she appeared in *Eleni* (1985) and *Making Mr. Right* (1987). Headly adopted a New York accent for her chilling, critically acclaimed turn as a brutalized wife in *Mortal Thoughts* (1991). Her other films include *Fandango* (1985), *Nadine* (1987), *Paperhouse*, and *Stars and Bars* (both 1988), the miniseries "Lonesome Dove" (1989), two 1993 made-for-TV projects, David Lynch's *Hotel Room* and *And the Band Played On*, and *Getting Even With Dad* (1994).

HEARD, JOHN. Actor. *(b. Mar. 7, 1946, Washington, D.C.)* Personable, boyish-looking supporting player and occasional leading man, an experienced stage performer who broke into movies with a sizable part in *First Love* (1977), then starred in *Between the Lines* that same year. He proffered an interesting characterization as the obsessive ex-boyfriend of Mary Beth Hurt in *Head Over Heels* (1979) and took the male lead in *Cat People* (1982), but has been perhaps more effective in character roles, especially unctuous yuppies and sinister or obstructionist bureaucrats. Audiences may be most familiar with Heard from his supporting turns as Macaulay Culkin's father in *Home Alone* (1990) and *Home Alone 2: Lost in New York* (1992). OTHER FILMS INCLUDE: 1979: *Heart Beat;* 1981: *Cutter's Way* (another standout performance in a little-seen film); 1982: *Too Scared to Scream;* 1984: *Best Revenge, C.H.U.D., Violated;* 1985: *After Hours, Heaven Help Us, The Trip to Bountiful;* 1987: *Dear America* (voice only); 1988: *Beaches, Betrayed, Big, The Milagro Beanfield War, The Seventh Sign, The Telephone;* 1989: *One Point of View, The Package;* 1990: *Awakenings;* 1991: *The End of Innocence, Mindwalk, Deceived;* 1992: *Waterland;* 1993: *In the Line of Fire* (cameo), *Me and Veronica, The Pelican Brief.*

HECHT, BEN. Screenwriter, director, producer, playwright, novelist. *(b. Feb. 28, 1893, New York City; d. Apr. 18, 1964.)* One of the most prolific and accomplished screenwriters in Hollywood history was a man who claimed to hate Hollywood and all it stood for. But the cynical mercenary in him could not resist the lure of "easy money." Hecht was raised in Racine, Wisconsin, and as a young man moved to Chicago, where he became a reporter and, eventually, a short-story writer and novelist. He traveled in literary circles that eventually landed him in New York, where he met young movie mogul David O. Selznick; the two were to be lifelong friends and frequent collaborators (although Hecht's contributions to Selznick's films, such as his intertitles for *Gone With the Wind*, often went uncredited).

A now-famous telegram from friend and fellow scribe Herman Mankiewicz—promising Hecht that "your only competition is idiots"—summoned him to Hollywood, where he scripted Josef von Sternberg's classic gangster story, *Underworld* (1927), and won an Oscar for his work at the very first Academy Awards presentation. Hecht worked very quickly (he claimed in his autobiography that he completed most of his scripts in two weeks), and the credits piled up. His most famous work was the semiautobiographical stage comedy "The Front Page," which he wrote with frequent collaborator Charles MacArthur; it was first translated to film in 1931 and three times since, most notably as Howard Hawks' *His Girl Friday* in 1940.

Hecht and MacArthur indulged their "artistic" sides by writing, directing, and producing a handful of unusual, serious films that qualify mainly as oddities: *Crime Without Passion* (1934), *The Scoundrel* (1935, specially crafted as a starring vehicle for their friend and fellow playwright, Nöel Coward; the screenplay won an Oscar), *Once in a Blue Moon* (1935), *Soak the Rich* (1936), and *Angels Over Broadway* (1940), most of which were directed more by cinematographer Lee Garmes than by the writing duo. Although Hecht wrote scripts for just about every genre, his sharp wit and native cynicism made him a natural for the frantic screwball comedies of the 1930s and 1940s, which he helped define with *Twentieth Century* (1934).

Hecht's other screenplays and screen stories, written alone or in collaboration, include *Scarface* (1932), *Turn Back the Clock, Design for Living* (both 1933), *Viva Villa!, Upperworld* (both 1934), *Barbary Coast* (1935), *Nothing Sacred* (1937), *Gunga Din, Wuthering Heights, It's a*

Wonderful World (all 1939), *Comrade X* (1940), *Lydia* (1941), *Tales of Manhattan, The Black Swan* (both 1942), *Spellbound* (1945), *Notorious* (1946), *Kiss of Death, Ride the Pink Horse* (both 1947), *Where the Sidewalk Ends* (1950), *Monkey Business* (1952), *Ulysses* (1955), *Miracle in the Rain* (1956, adapted from his own novel), *Legend of the Lost, A Farewell to Arms* (both 1957), and *Circus World* (1964). Interestingly, two 1958 B movies were based on Hecht works: *The Fiend Who Walked the West* was adapted from *Kiss of Death*, and *Queen of Outer Space* used one of his original stories as a basis for its screenplay!

Hecht also contributed, without credit, to *Back Street* (1932), *Queen Christina* (1933), *The Hurricane* (1937), *Foreign Correspondent, The Shop Around the Corner* (both 1940), *Roxie Hart* (1942), *The Outlaw* (1943), *Lifeboat* (1944), *Gilda* (1946), *Rope* (1948), and *Roman Holiday* (1953), among others. His autobiography, "A Child of the Century," was published in 1954, and turned into a mediocre movie, *Gaily, Gaily,* in 1969 (with its hero rechristened "Ben Harvey").

HECKERLING, AMY. Director, screenwriter. *(b. May 7, 1954, New York City.)* In her up-and-down career, Heckerling has proved that a woman filmmaker is just as capable as any male of directing (a) a box office hit; (b) an insightful comedy which keenly reflects contemporary culture; (c) formulaic comedies and derivative sequels. Educated at New York University and The American Film Institute, Heckerling showed much promise with her debut feature, *Fast Times at Ridgemont High* (1982), a perceptive comic portrait of modern, suburban teenagers which featured a gallery of up-and-coming performers (including Sean Penn, Jennifer Jason Leigh, Judge Reinhold, Phoebe Cates, Forest Whitaker, James Russo, Eric Stoltz, Anthony Edwards, and Nicolas Cage). Next came a pair of major disappointments: *Johnny Dangerously* (1984), a limp gangster comedy; and *National Lampoon's European Vacation* (1985), a dreadful sequel to *National Lampoon's Vacation* (1983). Heckerling did not direct a feature for another four years, but her next credit was a box office smash, *Look Who's Talking* (1989), a clever, congenial comedy which she also scripted, featuring the voice of Bruce Willis imparting the thoughts of sperm, fetus, and infant. A sequel was rushed into production, but the formula wore distressingly thin in *Look Who's Talking Too* (1990). She coproduced, but did not direct, yet another sequel, *Look Who's Talking Now* (1993). Heckerling also was one of many directors to play cameo roles in John Landis' *Into the Night* (1985).

HEDAYA, DAN. Actor. *(b. July 24, 1940, Brooklyn.)* A virtuoso in the portrayal of slimy, disreputable characters, Hedaya was actually a junior high school teacher for many years before deciding to take up acting full time. For someone who was, presumably, an effective role model, Hedaya sports a distinctly untrustworthy look. He has appeared in *The Hunger* (1983), *Tightrope* (1984), *Running Scared* (1986), *Joe Versus the Volcano* (1990), *The Addams Family* (1991, as the family lawyer), and, most memorably, as the bleeding, vomiting husband in *Blood Simple* (1984). A prolific TV actor, Hedaya may be best known to that medium's fans as Carla Tortelli's scummy—but somehow irresistible—ex-husband on the sitcom "Cheers." Recent credits include *Rookie of the Year, Mr. Wonderful, For Love or Money* (all 1993), and *Maverick* (1994).

HEDREN, TIPPI. Actress. *(b. Jan. 19, 1931, Lafayette, Minn., as Nathalie Hedren.)* Sophisticated, icy blonde whose screen persona was molded by Alfred Hitchcock in one of his latter-day attempts to develop another Grace Kelly. Hedren worked as a fashion model while still in her teens, making her film debut in 1950's *The Petty Girl.* Hitchcock "discovered" her much later, and effectively launched her film career by giving her the lead in *The Birds* (1963), in which she replaced a pregnant Vera Miles. Hedren reportedly went through hell making that classic chiller, reportedly suffering innumerable pecks and scrapes from her avian costars. Her reward, unfortunately, was lukewarm reaction to her tyro performance. Undaunted, Hitchcock cast her opposite Sean Connery in *Marnie* (1964), a psychological thriller that presumably offered her better opportunities. Saddled with a difficult role and an enigmatic script, Hedren proved unequal to the challenge and was again critically lambasted. Charlie Chaplin gave her a supporting role in his lackluster *A Countess From Hong Kong* (1967); after that she worked less frequently.

In 1973 Hedren appeared in two offbeat films: *The Harrad Experiment,* a free-love-among-college-kids drama that featured her daughter Melanie Griffith, then 14, in a bit part, and *Mr. Kingstreet's War,* an interesting WW2-era drama in which she and screen hubby John Saxon resisted Nazis in Africa. Hedren and then-husband Noel Marshall spent much of the 1970s (and most of their money) making a film called *Roar,* based on their experiences living among wild animals in Africa; it finally debuted in 1981. Her subsequent film roles have all been minor ones in the likes of *Foxfire Light* (1986), *Deadly Spygames* (1989), and *In the Cold of the Night* (1991). In 1990 she appeared once again in a film with her daughter, but this time in support of Melanie, the star of *Pacific Heights.* She has been more visible of late on television, in made-for-TV movies including a 1994 sequel to *The Birds.*

HEFLIN, VAN. Actor. *(b. Dec. 13, 1910, Walters, Okla., as Emmett Evan Heflin, Jr.; d. July 23, 1971.)* A rugged rather than romantic leading man and character actor, Heflin enjoyed a lengthy, generally meritorious screen career that began in 1936 and ended only with his untimely death in 1971. Educated at the University of Oklahoma (and trained at the Yale School of Drama), he alternated acting and odd jobs until he landed on Broadway in the early Depression years. For his screen debut, Heflin was selected by RKO to costar with Katharine Hepburn in *A Woman Rebels* (1936); he would appear opposite her on Broadway a few years later in "The Philadelphia Story." Briefly under contract to RKO, he drew meager assignments in insignificant pictures the likes of *Annapolis Salute* and *The Outcasts of Poker Flat* (both 1937). He landed a juicy supporting role in the Warner Bros. all-star historical epic *Santa Fe Trail* (1940) just before being signed by MGM. *Johnny Eager* (1941) provided Heflin with the well-written role of Robert Taylor's alcoholic pal, and he delivered an Oscar-winning

performance that convinced MGM that he warranted grooming for stardom. Heflin's first leads for the studio were for a pair of 1942 B mysteries, *Grand Central Murder* and *Kid Glove Killer;* in the latter, which was planned as the first in a series, he played a tough-talking but cerebral forensic investigator who solved murders from his downtown laboratory.

Although Heflin failed to click as a top star—his square-cut features and rumpled appearance worked against him—he brightened many films of the 1940s, including *Presenting Lily Mars* (1943), *The Strange Love of Martha Ivers* (1946), *Green Dolphin Street* (1947), *Act of Violence* (1949, starring again for *Kid Glove Killer* director Fred Zinnemann, as a former army officer stalked by psychotic enlisted man Robert Ryan), and *Madame Bovary* (1949). He shifted easily into character work in the 1950s, most memorably complementing Alan Ladd's heroics in the classic Western *Shane* (1953) and starring in *Patterns* (1956). He worked in many action dramas, including *Battle Cry* (1955), *3:10 to Yuma* (1957), *They Came to Cordura* (1959), and *Stagecoach* (1966) but like many other Hollywood actors spent several years appearing in nondescript European productions as well.

Heflin also returned to the stage whenever he could, making a solid impression on Broadway in "A Case of Libel." (He received an Emmy nomination for the 1967 ABC TV-version of that play.) Heflin played a disaffected terrorist in *Airport* (1970), which proved to be his last film: he suffered a massive heart attack while swimming at his home in Los Angeles just a few months later.

HELLMAN, MONTE. Director, screenwriter. *(b. July 12, 1929, New York City.)* Intriguing director whose films have earned a cult following over the years. After studying drama at Stanford and film at UCLA, he directed his first film, *Beast From Haunted Cave* (1960), for producer Roger Corman and worked on other Corman productions like *Creature From the Haunted Sea* (1961) and *The Terror* (1963). Hellman went to the Phillipines to film the WW2 drama *Back Door to Hell* (1964) and *Flight to Fury* (1966) and began a collaboration with another Corman veteran, Jack Nicholson, who starred in both and wrote the screenplay for the latter. Nicholson starred in Hellman's next two projects, the enigmatic Westerns *Ride in the Whirlwind* (1965) and *The Shooting* (1967), which were filmed back-to-back in the Utah Desert for a mere $150,000. Both were extremely offbeat, stylish efforts, particularly *The Shooting* which has often been called the first "existential Western." Though they won acclaim at international festivals, the films were barely released in the U.S. *Two-Lane Blacktop* (1971), a road movie with thematic parallels to *The Shooting,* was highly touted, but Hellman's distinctively low-key, unromantic approach did not click with audiences. He maintained his uncompromising style in *Cockfighter* (1974) and *China 9, Liberty 37* (1978, both of which starred Warren Oates, a Hellman regular), but his only directorial efforts since then have been *Iguana* (1988, which he also wrote and edited) and *Silent Night, Deadly Night III—Better Watch Out!* (1989, adapted from his story). In between directing chores, Hellman edited the Corman films *The Wild Angels* (1966) and *Target: Harry* (1969), as well as *A Time for Killing* (1967) and Sam Peckinpah's *The Killer Elite* (1975). In 1992 he enjoyed his greatest success in years as executive producer of the critically acclaimed *Reservoir Dogs.*

HEMINGWAY, MARIEL. Actress. *(b. Nov. 22, 1961, Ketchum, Idaho.)* Already granted a fair measure of notoriety because of her famous grandfather (author Ernest Hemingway), the squeaky-voiced Mariel made her film debut at 14 along with older sister Margaux in the distasteful box-office flop *Lipstick* (1976). In point of fact, the film was intended to build up successful model Margaux as a movie star; instead, Mariel stole the show. She received a Supporting Oscar nomination for her work in Woody Allen's *Manhattan* (1979, playing Allen's teenage lover in an eerie precursor of the actor-director's 1992 situation), then starred in *Personal Best* (1982, as an athlete who has a lesbian experience), and *Star 80* (1983, cast as murdered "Playboy" model Dorothy Stratten, a role for which she had her breasts surgically enhanced). She got plenty of publicity for the preceding films,

but stardom resolutely avoided her, and meaningless vehicles such as *Creator* and *The Mean Season* (both 1985) did little to promote her. She fared little better in *Superman IV: The Quest for Peace* (1987), and had no more luck in escaping the debacle of *Sunset* (1988) than did stars Bruce Willis and James Garner. The appallingly stupid *Delirious* (1991), which costarred Hemingway with John Candy, finally drove her to the small screen, where she starred in the prime-time dramatic series "Civil Wars" in 1991–92. She had earlier married restaurateur Stephen Crismant; together they produced *The Suicide Club* (1987, in which Mariel starred) and planned to make *Across the River and Into the Trees* (based on grandpa Hemingway's novel). They also own a string of restaurants. In a controversial and highly publicized guest shot on TV's "Roseanne" in 1994 she and Roseanne shared a kiss.

HEMMINGS, DAVID. Actor, producer, director. *(b. Nov. 18, 1941, Surrey, England.)* Puffy-faced, tousle-haired British actor who often played characters of dubious moral strength; best remembered as the mod photographer in Michelangelo Antonioni's *Blowup* (1966), he enjoyed brief popularity as a leading man but achieved greater industry recognition as a director, then as one of the founders of the Hemdale corporation (with his manager John Daly). Highly trained in various artistic media—his paintings have been exhibited frequently—Hemmings broke into movies as a child actor and worked steadily throughout his adult years, drifting into character roles while he was still in his thirties. His directorial credits include *Running Scared* (1972), *Just a Gigolo* (1979), and *Race to the Yankee Zephyr* (1981).
OTHER FILMS INCLUDE: 1950: *Night and the City;* 1957: *Saint Joan;* 1961: *The Painted Smile;* 1962: *Play It Cool;* 1963: *Live It Up;* 1964: *The System;* 1966: *Eye of the Devil;* 1967: *Camelot;* 1968: *Barbarella, The Charge of the Light Brigade;* 1969: *The Best House in London;* 1971: *The Love Machine;* 1973: *Voices;* 1977: *Crossed Swords;* 1979: *Murder by Decree;* 1980: *Beyond Reasonable Doubt;* 1981: *The Survivor;* 1983: *Prisoners;* 1989: *The Rainbow.*

HENIE, SONJA. Actress. *(b. Apr. 8, 1912, Oslo, Norway; d. Oct. 12, 1969.)* Bright-eyed, bubbly blonde who parlayed three Olympic ice-skating championships (1928, 1932, and 1936) into a relatively brief motion-picture career. Henie wasn't any great shakes as an actress, but her natural effervescence and enchanting smile—together with her physical and athletic attributes—went a long way toward covering up thespic deficiencies. For her, 20th Century-Fox tailored vehicles with light comedy, romance, and music, surrounded her with top-rank stars, and—perhaps most important—kept her on the ice as much as possible.

During the 1940s Henie performed in many ice shows across the United States, drawing huge crowds. She retired in 1960 and died of leukemia nine years later. Her autobiography, "Wings on My Feet," was published in 1940.

FILMS INCLUDE: 1936: *One in a Million;* 1937: *Thin Ice;* 1938: *Happy Landing, My Lucky Star;* 1939: *Second Fiddle, Everything Happens at Night;* 1941: *Sun Valley Serenade;* 1942: *Iceland;* 1943: *Wintertime;* 1948: *The Countess of Monte Cristo* (after her peak period); 1958: *Hello London.*

HENREID, PAUL. Actor, director. *(b. Jan. 10, 1908, Trieste, as Paul Hernreid Ritter von Wasel-Waldingau; d. Mar. 29, 1992.)* He's the luckiest guy in movie history: As freedom fighter Victor Laszlo in *Casablanca* (1942), he came *this* close to losing Ingrid Bergman's Ilsa to Humphrey Bogart's Rick. (And he darn near lost Bette Davis in 1942's *Now, Voyager* despite that neat trick of lighting two cigarettes at once!) Henreid, a distinguished, sober leading man and supporting player, was discovered by Otto Preminger (then a stage director) in Vienna, where he first began acting. He went to England in 1935, appeared in a few films there (including 1937's *Victoria the Great,* 1939's *Goodbye, Mr. Chips,* and 1940's *Night Train to Munich* billed as Paul von Hernreid) before coming to the United States and becoming an American citizen. Early in his career Henreid almost always played an elegant, refined, continental type (which, of course, he was), but in later years he starred in a surprising number of swashbucklers and sword-and-sandal epics.

Henreid turned to directing in the 1950s, helming *For Men Only* (1952), *A Woman's Devotion* (1956), *Girls on the Loose* (1958), *Dead Ringer* (1964, with former costar Bette Davis), and *Blues for Lovers* (1966), among others, as well as countless TV episodes for such series as "Alfred Hitchcock Presents." His autobiography, "Ladies Man," was published in 1984.

OTHER FILMS INCLUDE: 1942: *Joan of Paris;* 1944: *Between Two Worlds, The Conspirators, Hollywood Canteen;* 1945: *The Spanish Main* (his first as a swashbuckling hero); 1946: *Of Human Bondage* (as Philip Carey); 1947: *Song of Love* (as Schumann); 1948: *The Scar;* 1950: *Last of the Buccaneers* (as Jean Lafitte); 1952: *Thief of Damascus;* 1953: *Siren of Bagdad;* 1955: *Pirates of Tripoli;* 1956: *Meet Me in Las Vegas;* 1957: *Ten Thousand Bedrooms;* 1959: *Never So Few;* 1962: *Four Horsemen of the Apocalypse;* 1969: *The Madwoman of Chaillot;* 1977: *Exorcist II: The Heretic.*

HENRIKSEN, LANCE. Actor. *(b. May 5, 1940, New York City.)* Gaunt-looking character actor who has appeared in a variety of villainous and sympathetic roles. He had his first major part as an FBI agent in *Dog Day Afternoon* (1975), and later appeared in *Close Encounters of the Third Kind* (1977), *Damien—Omen II* (1978), and *Prince of the City* (1981) before he gained attention as Mercury astronaut Wally Schirra in *The Right Stuff* (1983). Director James Cameron used him in his first film, *Piranha II: The Spawning* (1981), and then gave him better parts in *The Terminator* (1984) and, in his flashiest role to date, as the android Bishop in the sci-fi hit *Aliens* (1986), which propelled him into the fantasy-film world (and away from better parts in mainstream movies): the cult vampire film *Near Dark* (1987), *Pumpkinhead* (1988, in the lead), *Hit List* (also 1988, as the villain), *The Horror Show* (in the lead), *Survival Quest* (in the lead), *Johnny Handsome* (all 1989), *The Pit and the Pendulum* (as Torquemada), *Stone Cold* (both 1991), and the thrillers *Jennifer 8* (1992), *Hard Target, Man's Best Friend, Excessive Force* (all 1993), and *No Escape* (1994). Many of Henriksen's films have gone straight to video, but his presence invariably puts them a notch above the norm for exploitation schlock.

HENRY, BUCK. Actor, writer, director. (b. Dec. 9, 1930, New York City.) Meek-looking, bespectacled funnyman whose diminutive stature and diffident manner mask an often diabolical talent. He came to national attention as a writer/performer on the ground-breaking TV satire "That Was the Week That Was" (1964–65) and, with Mel Brooks, created the classic sitcom "Get Smart" (1965–70). He shared an Oscar nomination for his second screenplay, *The Graduate* (1967, in which he also had a cameo as a hotel desk clerk), and has been busy ever since acting in such films as *Catch-22* (1970, which he also wrote), *Taking Off* (1971), *The Man Who Fell to Earth* (1976), *Gloria* (1980), *Eating Raoul* (1982), *Aria* (1988), *Defending Your Life* (1991), and *Grumpy Old Men* (1993). He also wrote *The Owl and the Pussycat* (1970, adaptation), *What's Up, Doc?* (1971, adaptation), *The Day of the Dolphin* (1973), and *Protocol* (1984). In 1978 he coproduced and codirected *Heaven Can Wait* with Warren Beatty, earning an Oscar nomination for the latter, and graduated to his first solo directing effort with *First Family* (which he also wrote) in 1980. In 1992 he had a self-deprecating cameo role in *The Player,* hilariously pitching "The Graduate, Part Two" to producer Tim Robbins. In 1993 he turned up in Robert Altman's *Short Cuts* and in 1994, *Even Cowgirls Get the Blues.*

HEPBURN, AUDREY. Actress. (b. May 4, 1929, Brussels, as Edna Hepburn-Ruston; d. Jan. 20, 1993.) When thinking of this dark, almost luminously beautiful actress, especially as a young woman, the words "waiflike" and "gamine" frequently spring to mind. It's true that Hepburn's large, hypnotic eyes, slender figure, and distinctive voice marked her as a true original in an era when Marilyn Monroe was everyone's favorite pinup, but physical attributes don't explain her appeal. Winsome, delicate almost to fragility, she brought to her performances an effortless charm perhaps best described as ethereal. A former ballet dancer, Hepburn broke into movies in 1948, playing bits in several European and English productions, most notably a walk-on in the opening scene of *The Lavender Hill Mob* (1951). In 1953, she came to Hollywood to star as the princess on the run in *Roman Holiday;* she subsequently won an Oscar for the role, confirming her newfound stardom.

Hepburn opted to work at a leisurely pace, seeking a variety of roles; these include a chauffeur's daughter in *Sabrina* (1954, which brought her another Oscar nomination), Natasha in *War and Peace* (1956), a Greenwich Village intellectual in *Funny Face* (1957, in which she sang and danced with Fred Astaire), a Parisian romantic in *Love in the Afternoon* (also 1957), a South American "bird woman" in *Green Mansions* (1959, one of her best remembered—if least successful films), the lead role in *The Nun's Story* (1959, another Academy Award nomination), a half-Indian in *The Unforgiven* (1960), the blithe Holly Golightly in *Breakfast at Tiffany's* (1961, which snagged her yet another Oscar nod), a newly widowed target in *Charade* (1963), Eliza Doolittle in *My Fair Lady* (1964), a bickering wife in the delicious *Two for the Road* (1967). It was she who asked Henry Mancini to compose the (memorable) score for that movie, as he had for several of her best films; it was also she who fought to keep "Moon River" from being cut from *Breakfast at Tiffany's.* She introduced that Oscar-winning Mancini–Johnny Mercer song in the film, in her own pleasing voice, but when she starred in *My Fair Lady,* it was decided that she had to be dubbed!

Hepburn earned her final Oscar nomination playing a terrorized blind woman in *Wait Until Dark* (1967), which was produced by her longtime husband Mel Ferrer (who also acted with her in *War and Peace* and directed her in *Green Mansions*). Soon after, she divorced him, and began to devote herself to a variety of causes, notably world hunger. She became a tireless supporter of UNICEF and traveled the world raising funds and calling attention to the plight of needy children. More or less retired, she was lured back to the camera occasionally—as an aging Maid Marian opposite Sean Connery in *Robin and Marian* (1976), another damsel in distress in *Bloodline* (1979), an elegant jewel thief in the made-for-TV *Love Among Thieves* (1987), or as an angel in *Always* (1989)—but seemed content to stay busy with more important things than movies. She appeared with her son Sean Ferrer in Peter Bogdanovich's *They All Laughed* (1981). Just months after her death, he appeared on stage to accept her posthumous Jean Hersholt Humanitarian Award at the 1993 Oscar ceremony.

HEPBURN, KATHARINE. Actress. *(b. May 12, 1907, Hartford, Conn.)* She was branded "box-office poison" by the nation's exhibitors in 1938, but Katharine Hepburn has come to be regarded as a national treasure. One of the most frequently honored screen actresses (with eight Academy nominations *and* four Oscars to her credit), Hepburn came to films in *A Bill of Divorcement* (1932), as John Barrymore's daughter, following a sometimes tempestuous career on stage in amateur theatricals, college shows, stock, and finally on Broadway. Her unusual looks and manner—and her unique New England voice—put off some moviegoers at first, but her endearing performance as a naive, impulsive young actress trying to crash Broadway, in 1933's *Morning Glory,* won her her first Academy Award. Hepburn proved her versatility in such pictures as *Little Women* (1933), *The Little Minister* (1934), *Alice Adams* (1935, for which she received an Oscar nomination), *Mary of Scotland* (1936), and the wonderful *Stage Door* (1937, an interesting companion piece to *Morning Glory).* But for every success in her early Hollywood career, there was also a major misfire—including such all-time oddities as *Christopher Strong* (1933, in which she played an aviatrix) and *Sylvia Scarlett* (1935, in which she disguised herself as a boy).

By the time she made the classic screwball comedy *Bringing Up Baby* (1938, for which the understandably nervous actress took comedy "pointers" from veteran screen funnyman Walter Catlett) and the equally delightful comedy-drama *Holiday* (also 1938), Hepburn's film career was on the skids. (Although it was that same year that Walt Disney immortalized her in cartoon form, as a haughty Little Bo-Peep in his animated short subject *Mother Goose Goes Hollywood.)* She returned to Broadway to star as spoiled socialite Tracy Lord in Philip Barry's "The Philadelphia Story," forsaking a huge salary for a percentage of profits and title to the screen rights. Her successful gamble paid off, and led to an equally triumphant return to Hollywood in the 1940 film version, which earned her another Oscar nomina-

tion. She was nominated again for her next film, *Woman of the Year* (1942) which cast her as an opinionated newspaper columnist opposite Spencer Tracy (as a down-to-earth sportswriter). It was a match made in movie heaven; the two would star in eight subsequent films over the next 25 years. (They also commenced an offscreen relationship that lasted until his death.)

Some of the early Tracy-Hepburn collaborations were heavy dramas such as *Keeper of the Flame* (1942) and *The Sea of Grass* (1947). Dramatic fireworks flew as well in *State of the Union* (1948), but the team is best remembered for its humorous skirmishes in the battle of the sexes with *Without Love* (1945), *Adam's Rib* (1949), *Pat and Mike* (1952), and *Desk Set* (1957). While Hepburn's work in the 1930s and 1940s receives the most attention today, many of the star's peak achievements were realized in the 1950s and 1960s. She picked up Oscar nominations for her work in *The African Queen* (1951, opposite Humphrey Bogart, as a missionary whose personality she patterned after Eleanor Roosevelt), *Summertime* (1955), *The Rainmaker* (1956), *Suddenly, Last Summer* (1959, as Elizabeth Taylor's shrewish, sinister aunt), and *Long Day's Journey Into Night* (1962). Offscreen for five years, she returned to costar with Tracy in *Guess Who's Coming to Dinner* (1967), which proved to be his final film; it won her a second Oscar. Hepburn received her third gold statuette the following year for her work in the period drama *The Lion in Winter,* as Eleanor of Aquitaine, which showed the aging actress in full command of her inestimable talent. She followed this triumph by making her Broadway musical debut as couturier Coco Chanel in "Coco." Other films around this time include *The Madwoman of Chaillot* (1969), *The Trojan Women* (1972), and *A Delicate Balance* (1973).

A much-anticipated pairing of Hepburn with John Wayne yielded disappointing results, as *Rooster Cogburn* (1975) turned out to be a watered-down retread of *The African Queen.* But her teaming with another screen giant, Henry Fonda, in *On Golden Pond* (1981), brought her a fourth Best Actress Academy Award, and proved to be her finest latter-day film. Hepburn's TV work has largely been confined to long-form dramas. She received Emmy nominations for Tennessee Williams' "The Glass Menagerie" (1973), and "The Corn Is Green" (1979), directed by her longtime friend and collaborator, George Cukor. She won an Emmy for "Love Among the Ruins" (1975), also directed by Cukor and costarring Laurence Olivier. Since that time she has starred in several "star-vehicle" TV movies, including *Laura Lansing Slept Here* (1988), *The Man Upstairs* (1992), and *This Can't Be Love* (1994). Her 1991 autobiography, "Me," was a best-seller, as was her more specific 1987 memoir, "The Making of *The African Queen,* or How I Went to Africa with Bogart, Bacall and Huston and Almost Lost My Mind." After years away from the big screen, Hepburn was coaxed back to do *Love Affair* (1994); she provided that film's highlight, as Warren Beatty's aunt.

HERBERT, HUGH. Actor. *(b. Aug. 10, 1885, Binghamton, New York; d. Mar. 12, 1952.)* This wacky comic actor with fluttery hands, rapid dialogue delivery, and trademark exclamation "woo-woo" (or was it really "hoo hoo hoo"?) was one of the 1930s' busiest players, appearing in dozens of movies. In the early 1930s he occasionally played serious roles (in films like 1931's *Friends and Lovers),* but soon that gave way to typecasting; a notorious scene-stealer, his zany antics added spice to *Hook, Line & Sinker* (1930), *Million Dollar Legs* (1932), *Diplomaniacs* (1933, as a Confucius-type wise man), *Bureau of Missing Persons, Footlight Parade* (both 1933), *Fashions of 1934, Wonder Bar, Fog Over Frisco, Dames* (all 1934), *Gold Diggers of 1935* (1935), *A Midsummer Night's Dream* (1935, as Snout), and *Colleen* (1936), to name a few. Having won so many laughs, Warners decided to star him in a series of B pictures, including *Marry the Girl, Sh! The Octopus,* and *That Man Is Here Again* (all 1937). In 1940 Universal fashioned similarly lightweight vehicles for him with titles like *La Conga Nights* and *Meet the Chump.* But his greatest moments came in supporting roles; he was memorable in *Hellzapoppin* (1941), *Kismet* (1944), and *The Beautiful Blonde from Bashful Bend* (1949). He also starred in a series of two-reel comedies for Columbia in the 1940s. Although Herbert wrote dozens of vaudeville sketches

and playlets, he shouldn't be confused with F. Hugh Herbert, a prolific screenwriter who was also a Warners contractee.

HERMAN, PEE-WEE. (PAUL REUBENS). Actor. *(b. Aug. 27, 1952, Peekskill, New York, as Paul Rubenfeld.)* A bizarre, infantile character with short, slick hair, a gray, too-small suit, red bow tie, and white shoes, Pee-wee Herman debuted in 1978 as a member of the Groundlings comedy troupe in Los Angeles. Stand-up comedian Reubens (as he was now billed) continued to play the character in his act, while appearing in such movies as *The Blues Brothers* (1980), *Cheech & Chong's Nice Dreams* (1981), and *Meatballs Part II* (1984). A cable-TV special called "The Pee-wee Herman Show," a goony reincarnation of 1950's kiddie shows, brought the character national prominence, which in turn led to a big-screen starring vehicle, *Pee-wee's Big Adventure* (1985) directed by Tim Burton. The film became a sleeper hit and spawned a sequel (1988's *Big Top Pee-wee)* and a successful Saturday morning TV series—which turned out to be the perfect vehicle for his blend of childlike whimsy and subversive comedy. He vanished for a while in 1991 after being caught masturbating in a Florida porno theater, but returned to the big screen in two 1992 roles: as the Penguin's father in Tim Burton's *Batman Returns,* and as a hissing vampire in *Buffy the Vampire Slayer,* an effective and amusing performance. He also provided a voice for Burton's *The Nightmare Before Christmas* (1993).

HERRMANN, BERNARD. Composer. *(b. July 29, 1911, New York City; d. Dec. 24, 1975.)* Herrmann's music is an intrinsic element of the movies on which he worked; try, for example, to imagine the *Psycho* shower scene without the shrieking strings that accompany it. (And try to imagine a horror film since that hasn't "borrowed" the idea.) A Juilliard graduate and orchestra leader at the age of 20, Herrmann first went to Hollywood to score *Citizen Kane* (1941) for his radio colleague Orson Welles. That innovative score earned him an Oscar nomination; he won an Oscar that same year for his equally impressive *All That Money Can*

Buy (aka *The Devil and Daniel Webster)* and signed again with Welles to score *The Magnificent Ambersons* (1942). His work ran the gamut from *Anna and the King of Siam* (1946, Oscar-nominated) and *The Ghost and Mrs. Muir* (1947) to the innovative, electronic *The Day the Earth Stood Still* (1951), and on through the fantasy world of *The 7th Voyage of Sinbad* (1958). But he is most closely associated with Alfred Hitchcock, for whom he wrote scores to *The Trouble With Harry* (1955), *The Man Who Knew Too Much* (1956, in which he also appears, as himself, in the Albert Hall sequence), *The Wrong Man* (1957), *Vertigo* (1958), *North by Northwest* (1959), the aforementioned *Psycho* (1960), *The Birds* (1963, which used sounds rather than conventional music), and *Marnie* (1964). They parted after a dispute over the music for *Torn Curtain* (1966). He was then hired by Hitchcock's disciple Francois Truffaut to score two of his films, *Fahrenheit 451* (1966) and *The Bride Wore Black* (1968).

A demanding, uncompromising artisan, Herrmann applied rigorous standards to every score on which he worked. Late in life, he was adopted by a younger generation of filmmakers who admired his work, including Brian De Palma, Larry Cohen, and Martin Scorsese. He died the night after conducting his score for *Taxi Driver* (1976). (Ironically, that score and the one he did that year for *Obsession* were both nominated for Academy Awards.) Scorsese subsequently used the Herrmann score for 1962's *Cape Fear* in his 1991 remake. A 1992 documentary *Music for the Movies: Bernard Herrmann,* was nominated for an Academy Award.
OTHER FILMS INCLUDE: 1944: *Jane Eyre;* 1945: *Hangover Square;* 1953: *The Snows of Kilimanjaro;* 1957: *A Hatful of Rain;* 1959: *Journey to the Center of the Earth;* 1963: *Jason and the Argonauts;* 1973: *Sisters;* 1974: *It's Alive!*

HERRMANN, EDWARD. Actor. *(b. July 31, 1943, Washington, D.C.)* This fine actor, often seen as a bureaucrat or corporate executive, hasn't gotten the big-screen opportunities he truly merits; TV gave him his best roles, as FDR in the telefilms *Eleanor and Franklin* (1976) and *Eleanor and Franklin: The White House Years* (1977), and baseball great Lou Gehrig in

A Love Affair: The Eleanor and Lou Gehrig Story (1978). He also appeared as the founder of the hospital in "St. Elsewhere." Tall, somewhat ungainly, and usually bespectacled, Herrmann might well be an unlikely leading man, but has provided able support in many movies and can always be counted upon for exemplary performances. He works frequently on stage (he won a Tony for "Mrs. Warren's Profession") and in television.
OTHER FILMS INCLUDE: 1973: *The Day of the Dolphin, The Paper Chase;* 1974: *The Great Gatsby;* 1975: *The Great Waldo Pepper;* 1978: *The Betsy, Brass Target, Take Down;* 1979: *The North Avenue Irregulars;* 1981: *Death Valley, Harry's War, Reds;* 1982: *A Little Sex, Annie* (as FDR); 1984: *Mrs. Soffel;* 1985: *Compromising Positions, The Man With One Red Shoe, The Purple Rose of Cairo;* 1987: *The Lost Boys, Overboard;* 1988: *Big Business;* 1993: *Born Yesterday, A Foreign Field.*

HERSHEY, BARBARA. Actress. *(b. Feb. 5, 1948, Hollywood, as Barbara Herzstein.)* Beautiful brunette typecast early in her career as a loving flower child, but who matured into a versatile actress who has taken on more varied roles. Hershey, who lived with actor David Carradine from 1969–75 and changed her name to Barbara Seagull (1973–75), made her first major impression on moviegoers as a promiscuous, manipulative teen in *Last Summer* (1969). She appeared in *With Six You Get Eggroll* (1968), *The Baby Maker* (1970), and *The Pursuit of Happiness* (1971) before starring in the Roger Corman production of *Boxcar Bertha* (1972), during which she showed director Martin Scorsese a novel by Nikos Kazantzakis called *The Last Temptation of Christ.* Scorsese filmed it some 16 years later, rewarding Hershey with the plum role of Mary Magdalene. During the 1980s her career took an upswing with her work in *The Stunt Man* (1980), *The Entity* (1983), *The Right Stuff* (also 1983, as the wife of test pilot Chuck Yeager), *The Natural* (1984), *Hannah and Her Sisters* (1986), *Hoosiers* (also 1986, as a mild-mannered schoolteacher), *Shy People* (as a backwoods matriarch), *Tin Men* (both 1987), *A World Apart* (1988), and *Beaches* (also 1988, as long-suffering best friend to Bette Midler) to name a few. *Shy People* and *A World Apart* earned her unprecedented back-to-back Best Actress awards at the Cannes Film Festival.

Still a beautiful woman, Hershey eschews meaningless, conventional leading-lady roles in favor of offbeat leads and colorful supporting parts. She won an Emmy playing a murderess in the TV movie *A Killing in a Small Town* (1990). Recent credits include *Tune in Tomorrow* . . . (1990), *Defenseless, Paris Trout* (both 1991), *The Public Eye* (1992), *Swing Kids, Splitting Heirs, Falling Down,* and *A Dangerous Woman* (all 1993).

HERSHOLT, JEAN. Actor. *(b. July 12, 1886, Copenhagen; d. June 2, 1956.)* Born to famous Danish performers, Hersholt entered the family profession as a young man, touring Europe before emigrating to the United States in 1914. Within a year he was acting in silent films (unhampered by his thick accent), generally playing heavies. By the 1920s he was recognized as one of the movie world's premier supporting actors, who prided himself on creating his own character makeup. His films include *Hell's Hinges* (1916), *The Four Horsemen of the Apocalypse* (1921), and *Stella Dallas* (1925); he was wondrously smarmy in von Stroheim's *Greed* (1924), wonderfully endearing in Lubitsch's *The Student Prince in Old Heidelberg* (1927). In the sound era he was prominently featured in such films as *The Sin of Madelon Claudet, Private Lives* (both 1931), *Grand Hotel, The Mask of Fu Manchu* (both 1932), *Dinner at Eight* (1933), *Men in White* (1934), *Mark of the Vampire* (1935), *One in a Million* (1936), *Sins of Man* (1936, a leading role), *Heidi* (1937, as Shirley Temple's grandfather), *Alexander's Ragtime Band* (1938), and *Mr. Moto in Danger Island* (1939). His success playing Dr. Dafoe, who delivered the Dionne Quintuplets, in *The Country Doctor* (1936) led to his being cast by RKO as Dr. Christian in a series of programmers *(Meet Dr. Christian, Courageous Dr. Christian,* and others). He also played the role on a radio show that ran for an astonishing 17 years. His final screen credit was *Run for Cover* (1955). Hersholt devoted himself to many humanitarian and charitable causes offscreen (including the construction of the Motion Picture Country Home and Hospital), inspiring the Academy of Motion Picture Arts and Sciences to establish a special Humanitarian Award in his name, presented periodically at the Oscar ceremonies since his death in 1956. His nephew is actor Leslie Nielsen.

HERZOG, WERNER. Director, screenwriter, producer. *(b. Sept. 5, 1942, Sachrang, Germany, as Werner Stipetic.)* A leading figure in the German cinema's "new wave," Herzog has stimulated considerable debate among film scholars, some of whom regard him as a poetic genius while others brand him a self-indulgent charlatan. In either case, he can't be easily dismissed. Herzog's films—the most interesting of which include *Aguirre, the Wrath of God* (1972), *The Mystery of Kaspar Hauser* (1975), *Nosferatu the Vampyre* (1978), and *Fitzcarraldo* (1982)—are often breathtaking in their visuals if diffuse in their narratives. His powerful imagery, which often incorporates impressive landscapes and natural wonders captured on film under arduous circumstances, more than compensates for his questionable development of theme. The director, who shrouds himself in a cloak of self-fashioned mythology, will probably be linked forever with actor Klaus Kinski, his frequent (and eccentric) leading man, with whom he and his family lived for a time in Munich. Herzog has appeared in several of his movies, and was the centerpiece of Les Blank's candid documentary about the trouble-plagued production of *Fitzcarraldo* called *Burden of Dreams* (1982). He was also featured in the short-subject *Werner Herzog Eats His Shoe* (1979), in which he paid off a bet to budding filmmaker Errol Morris in the manner described in the title.

OTHER FILMS INCLUDE: 1968: *Signs of Life, Even Dwarfs Started Small;* 1976: *Heart of Glass;* 1984: *Where the Green Ants Dream;* 1988: *Slave Coast, Lightning Over Braddock: A Rustbowl Fantasy;* 1989: *Hard to Be a God.*

HESTON, CHARLTON. Actor. *(b. Oct. 4, 1924, St. Helen, Mich., as Charles Carter.)*

"Charlton Heston is an axiom. By himself alone he constitutes a tragedy, and his presence in any film whatsoever suffices to create beauty." Few at the time agreed with this off-the-wall 1960 tribute to the imposing leading man by—who else—a French critic, and today's "hip" filmgoers are likely to be convulsed by it. But they're wrong too. Heston was and is an actor of absolutely undeniable presence, and was never more so than during his late-1950s/early-1960s heyday, when Hollywood needed all the presence it could get to compete with television.

Heston's earliest screen performances were seen in independently made productions of *Julius Caesar* and *Peer Gynt* in the 1940s. But neither his Hollywood debut in 1950's *Dark City* nor his subsequent leading-man assignments (in the likes of *Lucy Gallant* and *The Greatest Show on Earth)* could foretell the impact he would make as Moses in Cecil B. DeMille's spectacular *The Ten Commandments* (1956), which started him on a long string of historical parts, including the title role in William Wyler's 1959 *Ben-Hur,* for which he won a Best Actor Oscar.

Heston went on to play the title role in Anthony Mann's excellent wide-screen epic *El Cid* (1961), and portrayed Michelangelo in *The Agony and the Ecstasy* (1965). He also worked in a number of Westerns, including Peckinpah's *Major Dundee* (1965) and *Will Penny* (1968, one of Heston's personal favorites). In 1968 he played an astronaut trapped on a simian-run Earth in *Planet of the Apes,* reprising the role in its first sequel, *Beneath the Planet of the Apes* (1970). The brief sci-fi vogue of those years also saw him in *The Last Man on Earth* remake, *The Omega Man* (1971), and the eco-cannibal thriller *Soylent Green* (1973).

Heston was a near-constant presence in 1970s disaster films, including the notorious *Earthquake* (1974). While he turned up less and less on the big screen in the 1980s, he could be seen more and more—ironically enough—on TV, both as a spokesperson for the many conservative issues he espouses and in many made-for-cable period pieces, including remakes of *A Man for All Seasons* (1988, which he also directed) and *Treasure Island* (1990). In 1991 he went rather against type, portraying distinctly un-rugged detective Sherlock Holmes in the made-for-cable

The Crucifer of Blood. He was directed in this, and several other recent productions, by his son Fraser. He published a diary, "The Actor's Life," in 1978.

OTHER FILMS INCLUDE: 1953: *Pony Express;* 1954: *The Naked Jungle;* 1955: *The Far Horizons* (as Bill Clark of Lewis and Clark); 1958: *The Buccaneer* (as Andrew Jackson), *The Big Country;* 1965: *The War Lord;* 1966: *Khartoum;* 1969: *Number One;* 1970: *Julius Caesar, The Hawaiians;* 1972: *Call of the Wild;* 1973: *Antony and Cleopatra* (also directed and adapted); 1974: *Airport 1975, The Three Musketeers* (as Cardinal Richelieu); 1975: *The Four Musketeers;* 1976: *The Last Hard Men, Midway, Two-Minute Warning;* 1978: *Crossed Swords;* 1982: *Mother Lode* (also directed); 1990: *Almost an Angel* (a cameo, as God), *Little Kidnappers* (made for TV); 1992: *Solar Crisis;* 1993: *Tombstone, Wayne's World 2* (as the "Good Actor"); 1994: *True Lies;* 1995: *In the Mouth of Madness.*

HICKEY, WILLIAM. Actor. *(b. Sept. 19, 1928, Brooklyn, New York.)* Wizened character actor with an unmistakable sing-song, raspy delivery, who finally earned screen fame—and an Oscar nomination—for his supporting performance as Don Corrado Prizzi in John Huston's black comedy *Prizzi's Honor* (1985). Hickey has been a respected New York acting teacher since the early 1950s; his students have included Barbra Streisand, Steve McQueen, George Segal, Sandy Dennis, and Christine Lahti. When Hickey and Jack Nicholson met on the *Prizzi* set, Nicholson revealed he had audited two of Hickey's classes before leaving for Hollywood. Hickey's response: "How did it work out?" He made his film debut in *A Hatful of Rain* (1957) and in-between numerous stage productions, he had small roles in *The Producers, The Boston Strangler* (both 1968), *A New Leaf* (1971), *Happy Birthday, Wanda June* (1971, in a performance that reminded many of Jerry Lewis in his heyday), *Mikey and Nicky* (1976), and John Huston's *Wise Blood* (1979). Since *Prizzi,* he has been featured in *The Name of the Rose* (1986), *Bright Lights, Big City* (1988), *Da, National Lampoon's Christmas Vacation* (both 1989), *Sea of Love* (1989, as Al Pacino's father), *My Blue Heaven,* and *Tales From the Darkside: The Movie* (both 1990). He also contributed a vocal performance, as a mad scientist, to the animated *The Nightmare Before Christmas* (1993).

HICKS, CATHERINE. Actress. *(b. Aug. 6, 1951, Scottsdale, Ariz.)* An attractive soap-opera veteran, Hicks seemed a sure bet for stardom after being Emmy-nominated playing the blond bombshell in the made-for-TV *Marilyn: The Untold Story* (1980). The following year she starred in her first feature, *Death Valley* (1981), which began a maddeningly unrewarding screen career. Hicks has given solid performances in such films as *Garbo Talks, The Razor's Edge* (both 1984), *Fever Pitch* (1985), *Peggy Sue Got Married, Star Trek IV: The Voyage Home* (both 1986), *Like Father, Like Son* (1987), and *She's Out of Control* (1989), but the meaty leading roles and flashy supporting parts always go to other actresses. The surprise success of *Child's Play* (1988), in which she played a single mom who inadvertently buys her son a demonically possessed doll, failed to give her career the real jolt it needs.

HILL, GEORGE ROY. Director. *(b. Dec. 20, 1922, Minneapolis.)* Veteran director who began in TV's "Golden Age" and went on to make some of the most popular American films of the last three decades. After studying music at Yale and literature at Trinity College in Dublin (and serving as a Marine pilot in World War 2 and the Korean conflict) Hill began a career in acting. In the early 1950s he started directing for television, and later performed similar chores for stage productions. His first films were reverent adaptations of plays he had directed on Broadway: Tennessee Williams' *Period of Adjustment* (1962) and Lillian Hellman's *Toys in the Attic* (1963). It was not until *The World of Henry Orient* (1964), a delightful comedy starring Peter Sellers, that Hill showed his flair for directing actors in breezy situations, a trademark in many of his later films, notably *Butch Cassidy and the Sundance Kid* (1969), a hip revisionist Western that made a superstar of Robert Redford (and earned Hill a Best Director Oscar nomination), and the multi-Oscar-winning con-artist comedy *The Sting* (1973), which reunited Redford and Paul Newman, and won Hill a Best

Director Academy Award. He also adapted to the screen two difficult, reality-bending books: Kurt Vonnegut, Jr.'s *Slaughterhouse-Five* (1972), and John Irving's *The World According to Garp* (1982). His other films have run the gamut from epic sagas to political thrillers: *Hawaii* (1966), *Thoroughly Modern Millie* (1967), *The Great Waldo Pepper* (1975, with Redford), *Slap Shot* (1977, with Newman), *A Little Romance* (1979), *The Little Drummer Girl* (1984), and *Funny Farm* (1989).

HILL, TERENCE. Actor. *(b. Mar. 29, 1941, Venice, Italy, as Mario Girotti.)* This popular blond leading man of Italian cinema—of Italian and German descent—began appearing in films while still in his teens (beginning with 1951's *Vacanze col gangster)*, often using his given name. He worked steadily for more than 10 years before being seen by American audiences in *The Wonders of Aladdin* (1961), *Seven Seas to Calais* (1962), and *The Leopard* (1963), among others. Later on, rechristened Terence Hill, he made the comic spaghetti Westerns *They Call Me Trinity* (1971) and *Trinity Is STILL My Name!* (1972) for which he is best known, costarring with burly Bud Spencer, his frequent on-screen partner. Hill's other movies include *God Forgives, I Don't* (1967) and *My Name Is Nobody* (1973). His first American feature film, the Jonathan Kaplan comedy *Mr. Billion* (1977), failed to translate his European success to the States; a 1980 effort titled *Super Fuzz* performed reasonably well on the drive-in circuit. In 1994 he reteamed with Bud Spencer for *Troublemakers,* which he also directed.

HILL, WALTER. Director, screenwriter. *(b. Jan. 10, 1942, Long Beach, Calif.)* Solid writer-director of mostly mainstream action films, but with a few cult items under his belt. If Hill has any stylistic predilection, it's for extremely fast, graphic, violent action that literally explodes on-screen. He started as a screenwriter, penning Sam Peckinpah's *The Getaway, Hickey & Boggs* (both 1972), *The Mackintosh Man, The Thief Who Came to Dinner* (both 1973), and *The Drowning Pool* (1976). He wrote and, as a tyro, directed

Hard Times (1975), a Depression-era story set in New Orleans, which starred Charles Bronson as a bare-knuckled street fighter. Perhaps his best, and most personal film, is *The Warriors* (1979), an almost dreamlike look at street gangs in New York City. *The Long Riders* (1980), Hill's first attempt at a Western, didn't reveal any particular affinity for that genre, but *48 HRS.* (1982, which he also cowrote) was a loud, fast, tough urban drama that introduced Eddie Murphy to the big screen and was spectacularly successful, indicating that Hill had found his metier. His subsequent directorial outings— including *Extreme Prejudice* (1987), *Red Heat* (1988), and the sequel *Another 48 HRS.* (1990)—haven't been nearly as effective or as financially rewarding to their distributors. He returned to the Western form for a large-scale 1993 production, *Geronimo,* and cowrote the screenplay for the 1994 remake of *The Getaway.* He is also coexecutive producer of the TV series "Tales From the Crypt" (1989–   ).
OTHER FILMS INCLUDE: 1978: *The Driver;* 1979: *Alien* (producer only); 1981: *Southern Comfort;* 1984: *Streets of Fire;* 1985: *Brewster's Millions;* 1986: *Aliens* (producer and cowriter), *Crossroads;* 1989: *Johnny Handsome;* 1992: *Trespass* (directing only).

HILLER, ARTHUR. Director. *(b. Nov. 22, 1923, Alberta, Canada.)* Former psych major and law student who abandoned his academic pursuits to take up directing in TV and movies. After a prolific career in episodic TV, Hiller moved on to feature films and proved to be a journeyman who can rise to the occasion with a strong script in hand. He picked up his one Oscar nomination for the smash 1970 weepie *Love Story.* He has also served as president of the Directors Guild of America and The Academy of Motion Picture Arts and Sciences.
OTHER FILMS INCLUDE: 1957: *The Careless Years;* 1963: *Miracle of the White Stallions;* 1964: *The Americanization of Emily;* 1966: *Penelope;* 1967: *Tobruk;* 1970: *The Out-of-Towners;* 1971: *The Hospital* (one of his best, owing mainly to a superior script by Paddy Chayefsky), *Plaza Suite;* 1972: *Man of La Mancha;* 1975: *The Man in the Glass Booth;* 1976: *Silver Streak* (which launched the Gene Wilder-Richard Pryor team and was one of Hiller's most successful films),

W. C. Fields and Me; 1979: *The In-Laws;* 1982: *Making Love;* 1983: *Romantic Comedy;* 1984: *The Lonely Guy, Teachers;* 1987: *Outrageous Fortune;* 1989: *See No Evil, Hear No Evil* (another Wilder-Pryor vehicle); 1990: *Taking Care of Business;* 1992: *The Babe;* 1993: *Married to It.*

HILLER, WENDY (DAME). Actress. *(b. Aug. 15, 1912, Cheshire, England.)* Primarily a stage actress, Wendy Hiller has brightened the screen with some of its most memorable performances, beginning with her inspired Eliza Doolittle in Shaw's *Pygmalion* (1938, opposite Leslie Howard), which earned her an Academy Award nomination. A handsome (if not beautiful) young woman with obvious poise and intelligence, she was particularly striking as Shaw's *Major Barbara* (1941), a wealthy young British lady who joins the Salvation Army. As her stage career flourished, Hiller made few films, but always impressed audiences when she did—even if the films themselves were less than memorable. She won a Best Supporting Actress Oscar for her portrayal of a lonely innkeeper in the all-star drama *Separate Tables* (1958), and was nominated for her costarring turn as Alice More in Fred Zinnemann's acclaimed *A Man for All Seasons* (1966). She has also starred in productions of *Witness for the Prosecution* (1982) and *The Importance of Being Earnest* (1985) for British TV.
OTHER FILMS INCLUDE: 1945: *I Know Where I'm Going!* (in a rare and delightful romantic lead); 1951: *Outcast of the Islands;* 1957: *How to Murder a Rich Uncle;* 1960: *Sons and Lovers;* 1963: *Toys in the Attic;* 1970: *David Copperfield* (as Mrs. Micawber); 1974: *Murder on the Orient Express;* 1976: *Voyage of the Damned;* 1978: *The Cat and the Canary* (as Lawyer Crosby, a role previously played by men); 1980: *The Elephant Man;* 1986: *The Death of the Heart;* 1987: *The Lonely Passion of Judith Hearne.*

HINDS, SAMUEL S. Actor. *(b. Apr. 4, 1875, Brooklyn; d. Oct. 13, 1948.)* Most recognizable as James Stewart's father in *It's a Wonderful Life* (1946), this Harvard graduate and practicing lawyer, long involved in amateur theatrics, only turned to acting as a career after suffering severe financial setbacks in the 1929 crash. Almost always played authority figures, sometimes kindly, sometimes taciturn and inflexible. Hinds appeared in *Little Women* (1933), *Men in White* (1934), *The Raven, She* (both 1935), *The Road Back* (1937), *Stage Door* (1937, as Katharine Hepburn's father), *Young Dr. Kildare* (1938, as the *senior* Dr. Kildare, a role he repeated in two more pictures), *Test Pilot, You Can't Take It With You* (both 1938), *Destry Rides Again* (1939, cast against type as a crooked judge), *Shepherd of the Hills, Buck Privates* (both 1941), *The Spoilers, Pittsburgh* (both 1942), *Son of Dracula* (1943), *Cobra Woman* (1944), *Lady on a Train* (1945), *The Egg and I* (1947), and *The Boy With Green Hair* (1948), among many others; he made more than 150 films altogether. He was also one of the founders and guiding lights of the renowned Pasadena Playhouse.

HINES, GREGORY. Actor, dancer. *(b. Feb. 14, 1946, New York City.)* Sleepy-eyed, silky-smooth black performer who has almost single-handedly kept the art of big-screen tap dancing alive. He's also a capable dramatic actor who has shown he can command attention as a leading man. With his brother Maurice he became part of a successful show-business act called Hines, Hines and Dad, and developed his show-business savvy at a tender age. Also a skilled choreographer, Hines was a staple in New York clubs and on Broadway, most memorably in "Sophisticated Ladies" (when he took the show on the road, Maurice replaced him on Broadway). He got his first film role, as a Roman slave in Mel Brooks' *History of the World—Part 1* (1981), as a last-minute replacement for an ailing Richard Pryor, and made a convincing if unorthodox medical examiner later that year in *Wolfen.* In *The Cotton Club* (1984), Hines made his screen dancing debut as a thinly disguised Nicholas Brother (Maurice played his sibling). He used his dancing shoes again, opposite ballet star Mikhail Baryshnikov, in *White Nights* (1985), and *Tap* (1989), as an ex-con trying to stay straight. His nonmusical characterizations include an unwilling gunrunner in *Deal of the Century* (1983), a wise-cracking cop (partnered with Billy Crystal) in *Running Scared* (1986), a non-wise-cracking cop in *Eve of Destruction,* and a fast-talking con artist in *A Rage in*

Harlem (both 1991). In 1994 he appeared in *Renaissance Man.* In 1992 he won a Tony Award for the Broadway musical "Jelly's Last Jam."

HINGLE, PAT. Actor. *(b. July 19, 1923, Denver, Colo., as Martin Patterson Hingle.)* Veteran character actor whose career on stage, TV, and in movies spans four decades. After joining the Actors' Studio in 1952, Hingle made his film debut in *On the Waterfront* (1954), and for years alternated between movies and the theater. A burly, steely-eyed bruiser who often affects a raspy snarl, Hingle has excelled in the portrayal of heavies, lawmen, and authority figures, such as Warren Beatty's domineering father in *Splendor in the Grass* (1961), the judge in *Hang 'em High* (1968), Sally Field's antiunion father in *Norma Rae* (1979), and Police Commissioner Gordon in *Batman* (1989) and its 1992 and 1995 sequels. He's also appeared to good advantage in *The Gauntlet* (1977), *Sudden Impact* (1983), *The Falcon and the Snowman* (1985), and, memorably, in *The Grifters* (1990, contributing a frightening cameo as Anjelica Huston's sadistic boss, Bobo). In 1994, he appeared in Paul Hogan's *Lightning Jack.* Additionally, Hingle is a veteran of episodic TV, where he's made dozens (if not hundreds) of appearances over the last 35 years. The 1992 cable-TV movie *Citizen Cohn* gave him the opportunity to play J. Edgar Hoover. In another made-for-TV movie, *Simple Justice* (1993), he played Chief Justice Earl Warren.

HIRSCH, JUDD. Actor. *(b. Mar. 15, 1935, New York City.)* With a prominent nose and ethnic mien, Hirsch might seem an unlikely candidate for stardom, but he has toplined several TV series in between successful Broadway runs in such plays as "Talley's Folly," and the Herb Gardner plays "I'm Not Rappaport," and "Conversations With My Father," both of which earned him Tony Awards. He was cabbie Alex Rieger in the popular sitcom "Taxi" (1978–83, winning two Emmys) and also starred in "Delvecchio" (1976–77) and "Dear John" (1988–91). He's also done some fine work in movies, especially as the sympathetic shrink in *Ordinary People* (1980, earning an Oscar nomination), the understanding cop in *Without a Trace* (1983), and as the former 1960s radical in *Running on Empty* (1988). Other credits include *King of the Gypsies* (1978, his debut), *Teachers* (1984), and *The Goodbye People* (also 1984, written and directed by Herb Gardner).

HITCHCOCK, ALFRED. Director, producer. (b. Aug. 13, 1899, Leytonstone, England; d. Apr. 28, 1980.) Perhaps only one other filmmaker—Walt Disney—lived to see his name become synonymous with a certain type of screen entertainment: In Hitchcock's case, it was stylish, sophisticated suspense, laced with humor and romance. Moreover, his bald pate, pear-shaped body, and lugubrious drawl made him as recognizable as any star he ever directed. Educated by Jesuits, the young Hitchcock developed a flair for things mechanical, and first went to work for a telegraph company. He later took up art, applying his talents to print advertisements. Hitchcock broke into the British film industry in 1920 as a title-card illustrator, working his way up to art director, assistant director, editor, writer, and finally director. His first hit was the thriller *The Lodger* (1926), by which time many of his now-familiar cinematic trademarks were already apparent, including his ritual cameo appearance. He mastered the new medium of talking pictures with seeming effortlessness in *Blackmail* (1929) and proved that the presence of sound was no reason not to continue to tell stories with visual panache. (Speaking of things visual, 1930's all-star talkie revue *Elstree Calling* gave Hitchcock his only opportunity to direct a pie-throwing scene—with Anna May Wong, of all people.) He reached the top of his game with such outstanding films as *The Man Who Knew Too Much* (1934), *The 39 Steps* (1935), *Sabotage* (1936), and *The Lady Vanishes* (1938), all of which placed ordinary people—with whom audiences could readily identify—in life-or-death situations, often being chased by the authorities as well as the villains.

Hitchcock succumbed to the lure of Hollywood in 1939; his first film there, the romantic thriller *Rebecca* (1940), won the Best Picture Oscar and cemented his standing. He continued to masterly manipulate audiences' emotions in such classics as *Foreign Correspondent* (1940), *Suspicion* (1941), *Shadow of a Doubt* (1943, reportedly his personal favorite among his films), *Lifeboat* (1944), *Spellbound* (1945), and *Notorious* (1946). During this period, as he immersed himself in the slickness of Hollywood filmmaking, he continued to draw from a seemingly inexhaustible cinematic bag of tricks, using his mechanical and electrical knowledge to create memorable little effects and images (such as the illuminated glass of milk carried upstairs by Cary Grant in *Suspicion).* His first color movie, *Rope* (1948), was an experiment—not altogether successful—in shooting an entire film in one seemingly continuous shot.

In the 1950s Hitchcock set himself new challenges and created a gallery of unique and memorable films, including the psychological cat-and-mouse thriller *Strangers on a Train* (1951), the 3-D opus *Dial M for Murder* (1954), the visually challenging *Rear Window* (1954), the elegant and witty *To Catch a Thief* (1955), the incomparably droll black comedy *The Trouble With Harry* (1955), the remake of his own *The Man Who Knew Too Much* (1956, with its bravura climax in London's Albert Hall), and the low-key, documentary-style *The Wrong Man* (1957). In 1955 he agreed to host (and occasionally direct) a weekly TV anthology series, "Alfred Hitchcock Presents," a diversion that lasted a full ten years. His droll commentary (written by James Allardice) and distinctive greeting ("Good eeeevening") made him more famous than ever. The TV years also saw him directing four of his greatest films in a row: the incredibly complex and adult thriller *Vertigo* (1958), the witty and exciting *North by Northwest* (1959, with its audacious set-pieces in a desolate cornfield and atop Mount Rushmore), the starkly frightening, very black *Psycho* (1960, which he made quickly and inexpensively with his TV crew), and that masterpiece of manipulation and control, *The Birds* (1963). Hitchcock brought out the best in his stars (including James Stewart, Cary Grant, and the ultimate "Hitchcock blonde," Grace Kelly) and inspired composer Bernard Herrmann to do some of his finest work on his films.

Hitchcock's work past this point became uneven. *Marnie* (1964) was ahead of its time. *Torn Curtain* (1966) had star power but little else. *Topaz* (1969) told an intriguing tale, but the lack of recognizable stars made audiences feel aloof. *Frenzy* (1972) saw the director back in form—in peak form, to be precise, pulling some new visual tricks out of his bottomless bag, and playing violence against humor as only he could. (Hitchcock always hosted his own coming attractions trailers; for the British-made film, his first in more than 30 years, he appeared on-screen floating in the Thames River!) *Family Plot* (1976) tipped the scales too far toward comedy, and was only a middling success. Hitchcock continued to develop properties for future production, but failing health curtailed those plans. In 1979 he received the American Film Institute Life Achievement Award; he died the following year.

Astoundingly, the man considered by many the finest director who ever lived never won an Oscar, though he did receive the Irving Thalberg Award in 1967, and a long-running mystery magazine bears his name. His influence on a younger generation of filmmakers is impossible to overstate; virtually every thriller that comes along is described as "Hitchcockian," though few manage to live up to that description. As if that weren't enough, the director almost literally returned from the grave in 1985, when NBC revived "Alfred Hitchcock Presents": the episodes were new, but Hitch (now colorized) was still introducing them!

HOBSON, VALERIE. Actress. *(b. Apr. 14, 1917, Larne, Ireland.)* While still in her teens, this beautiful brunette—an army officer's daughter—accepted a contract with Universal, where she starred in *Bride of Frankenstein* (as Henry Frankenstein's wife), *Werewolf of London, The Great Impersonation,* and *Chinatown Squad* (all in 1935). She'd debuted in the British-made 1933 drama *Eyes of Fate.* Not happy with parts that mostly called for her to scream and faint, Hobson returned to England where, now a seasoned movie actress, she won leading roles enabling her to display her considerable charm and talent. Her films in this period included *Drums, This Man Is News* (both 1938), *Q Planes* and *The Spy in Black* (both 1939). Hobson hit

her peak during the post-WW2 period with mature, carefully realized performances in *Great Expectations* (1946, as Estella), *Blanche Fury* (1947), *Kind Hearts and Coronets, The Rocking Horse Winner* (both 1949), *The Promoter* (1951), *Tonight at 8:30* (1952), and *Lovers, Happy Lovers* (1954). Shortly afterward, her marriage to producer Anthony Havelock-Allan collapsed; upon divorcing him, she married politician John Profumo (a key figure in the British government's 1963 sex scandal) and retired from the screen.

HODIAK, JOHN. Actor. *(b. Apr. 16, 1914, Pittsburgh; d. Oct. 19, 1955.)* Handsome, square-jawed but generally wooden leading man, one of several second-string stars who achieved top-billing during and immediately after World War 2. A former car salesman whose smooth voice enabled him to act on radio, Hodiak (who was 4-F during the war) was signed by MGM in 1943. He played unimportant roles in *A Stranger in Town, Swing Shift Maisie,* and *I Dood It* (all 1943) before getting an opportunity (via loan-out) to play the male lead in Hitchcock's *Lifeboat* (1944), a prestigious assignment in which he didn't disappoint. After that he got better parts in better pictures, including *A Bell for Adano* (1945), *The Harvey Girls, Somewhere in the Night* (both 1946, the latter an absorbing *noir* in which he played an amnesiac with a sinister past), *Desert Fury* (1947, in which, although the ostensible star, he played second fiddle to supporting players Burt Lancaster and Mary Astor), *Homecoming, Command Decision* (both 1948), and *Battleground* (1949, another WW2 drama, his last good starring role). Hodiak's popularity began to wane thereafter, and the quality of his films dropped precipitously, as witness *The Miniver Story, Lady Without a Passport* (both 1950), *The People Against O'Hara* (1951), *Battle Zone* (1952), *Conquest of Cochise* (1953), *Dragonfly Squadron* (1954), *Trial* (1955), and *On the Threshold of Space* (1956). A longtime sufferer from hypertension, he died of a heart attack. He was once married to Anne Baxter, and their daughter Katrina Hodiak has acted too.

HOFFMAN, DUSTIN. Actor. *(b. Aug. 8, 1937, Los Angeles.)* Only in the 1960s, with Hollywood conventions being stood on their heads along with societal mores, could this physically unprepossessing actor have made it as a leading man; in a previous era Hoffman would probably have plied his trade as a character actor rather than a powerful megastar. Although he shot his first movie, *Madigan's Million,* in 1966 (released in 1968), Hoffman first impressed 1960s audiences in *The Graduate* (1967, earning his first Academy Award nomination), playing a disaffected, uncertain young man who drifts into a sexual affair with a woman in his parents' circle, only to fall in love with her daughter. The film's droll humor, relatively frank sexuality, satirical view of the upper middle class, and observation of a "troubled" younger generation made it a surprise smash.

The bashful, nasal Hoffman soon proved himself capable of submerging himself in any role. His performance as street hustler Ratso Rizzo in 1969's *Midnight Cowboy* (another Oscar-nominated turn) was uncannily convincing. As an Old West rogue in 1970's *Little Big Man,* Hoffman's scenes as a 121-year-old man show him radiating that age through layers of latex makeup. During the 1970s he consistently knocked out critics and audiences in a variety of roles, playing a doomed Devil's Island prisoner in *Papillon* (1973), hounded comedian Lenny Bruce in *Lenny* (1974, again Oscar-nominated), and Watergate journalist Carl Bernstein in *All the President's Men* (1976). Often described as taking "Method" techniques to the point of absurdity, he once kept himself awake for days to look more tired for a scene in 1976's *Marathon Man.*

Constantly looking for challenges, Hoffman played an ex-con in *Straight Time* (1978) and earned some of the best reviews of his career (and some of his worst for 1979's *Agatha*). He then took a much warmer role, becoming a modern Everyman in *Kramer vs. Kramer* (1979) as a careerist man whose wife walks out on him, leaving him to raise their son—and reorder the priorities in his life. The performance earned him an Academy Award. Several years later he took another sharp turn, tackling a role that some people thought unplayable: a failed actor who disguises as a woman and achieves great success on TV. The film was *Tootsie* (1982), an enormous hit which earned Hoffman an Oscar nomination and convinced whatever naysayers were left that there was nothing he couldn't do.

Mixing stage and screen work in the 1980s, he created a new interpretation of the Willy Loman character in a 1984 revival of Arthur Miller's "Death of a Salesman." (He recreated the performance on television a year later and won an Emmy Award in the process.) In 1987 he teamed with pal Warren Beatty for the megabomb *Ishtar;* the two were very funny as hapless songwriter/performers, but the film wasn't; both stars attributed its failure to lack of youth appeal, rather than the fact that it was a lousy movie. To ameliorate this perceived problem, Hoffman teamed with handsome young superstar Tom Cruise for his next film, *Rain Man* (1988), limning the character of an autistic savant with skill and integrity and earning another Best Actor Oscar in the process. In 1989 he was cast, rather improbably, as Sean Connery's son (and Matthew Broderick's father) in *Family Business.* Then in Beatty's own stab at the youth market, *Dick Tracy* (1990), Hoffman contributed a brief but funny cameo as the petty crook Mumbles. The year 1991 saw him cast as two legendary bad guys: gangster Dutch Schultz in *Billy Bathgate* and Captain Hook in . . . *Hook* (a performance he based, in part, on William F. Buckley, with some Terry-Thomas thrown in). In 1992 he put a new slant on Ratso Rizzo as the title character in *Hero,* then played a heroic army medical researcher in *Outbreak* (1995).

HOGAN, PAUL. Actor, producer, screenwriter, director. *(b. Oct. 8, 1939, Lightning Ridge, Australia.)* "We'll put another shrimp on the barbie," said the engagingly laid-back Hogan in his U.S. commercials for Australian tourism—and the oft-played TV spots made him a star in the States! So much so that his modest comedy vehicle *"Crocodile" Dundee* (1986), about an Aussie fish-out-of-water who journeys to New York City, became a runaway success (having already conquered Australia and the rest of the world); it even earned him an Oscar nomination for Best Original Screenplay. The handsome if weatherbeaten Hogan, a laborer-turned-comedian in his native Australia, hasn't been able to grab another brass ring since *Dundee,* although he tried with *"Crocodile" Dundee II* (1988, which he cowrote) and *Almost an Angel* (1990, which he wrote and executive produced). His earlier films include the made-for-Australian-TV *Anzacs* (1985), in which he acted, and *The Humpty Dumpty Man* (1989), which he wrote and directed. Hogan is married to his *Dundee* and *Angel* leading lady Linda Kozlowski. In 1993 Hogan lobbied his fellow Aussies to raise financing for his latest film by selling shares in the production. The film, *Lightning Jack,* which he cowrote, appeared in 1994.

HOLBROOK, HAL. Actor. *(b. Feb. 17, 1925, Cleveland, Ohio.)* A veteran of stage, screen, and television, Holbrook is probably best remembered for his portrayal of Mark Twain, which he has been performing as a one-man stage show on and off since 1954; he earned a Tony Award for its 1966 Broadway run. He made his film debut in *The Group* (1966) and has since appeared in many different films, often as an authority figure or a deceptively sinister villain. In addition to numerous stage performances, Holbrook has been seen in many TV productions, including the 1970–71 series "The Senator" (part of "The Bold Ones"), which earned him one of five Emmy Awards; the landmark TV movie *That Certain Summer* (1972), in which he played a homosexual father; and later, the sitcom "Evening Shade" (1990–94) as Burt Reynolds' father-in-law. He is also in demand as a narrator. Holbrook is married to actress Dixie Carter, with whom he occasionally appeared on her hit series "Designing Women."
OTHER FILMS INCLUDE: 1968: *Wild in the Streets;* 1970: *The Great White Hope;* 1973: *Magnum Force;* 1976: *Midway, All the President's Men* (as Deep Throat); 1977: *Julia* (as Lillian Hellman's friend Alan Campbell); 1978: *Capricorn One;* 1980: *The Kidnapping of the President;* 1983: *The Star Chamber;* 1987: *Wall Street;* 1989: *Fletch Lives;* 1993: *The Firm.*

HOLDEN, WILLIAM. Actor. *(b. Apr. 17, 1918, O'Fallon, Ill., as William F. Beedle, Jr.; d. Nov. 16, 1981.)* There are very few "over-night" stars in Hollywood history; their creation is a convention generally reserved for the movies themselves. But William Holden beat the odds by achieving instant stardom with his first leading role, that of the wholesome young prizefighter in *Golden Boy* (1939). He'd originally taken up acting as a lark while a student at Pasadena Junior College, but was spotted in a school play by a Paramount representative. The handsome, earnest young Holden had bits in *Prison Farm* (1938) and *Million Dollar Legs* (1939) before being chosen out of 65 candidates (including John Garfield) to play sensitive Joe Bonaparte, the violinist-turned-boxer in the Columbia production *Golden Boy.* His inexperience made filming difficult, and after two weeks Columbia president Harry Cohn was ready to fire him—but costar Barbara Stanwyck, who had great faith in Holden, persuaded the executive to relent. Although the film took some liberties with the Clifford Odets play, Holden's performance was singled out for near-unanimous praise. (The actor remained forever grateful to Stanwyck for "pulling him through" that picture.)

Although Holden supported George Raft in the Warner Bros. melodrama *Invisible Stripes* (also 1939), he was soon very much in demand as a clean-cut leading man. His early films didn't always show him to best advantage, but Holden built a fan following on the strength of well-received appearances in *Our Town, Arizona* (both 1940), *I Wanted Wings, Texas* (both 1941), *The Remarkable Andrew, Meet the Stewarts, The Fleet's In* (all 1942), and *Young and Willing* (1943). He served with the Army during World War 2, achieving the rank of lieutenant, and returned to the screen in 1947, first with a cameo in *Variety Girl,* then with a leading role as an aviator in *Blaze of Noon.*

Still youthfully handsome, Holden worked in comedies, dramas, thrillers, and Westerns with equal facility, appearing in *Dear Ruth* (1947), *Apartment for Peggy, The Man From Colorado, Rachel and the Stranger* (all 1948), *Miss Grant Takes Richmond, Streets of Laredo,* and *Dear Wife* (all 1949).

But Holden's maturity—built in part on his wartime experiences—came to the fore in *The Dark Side* (1948), in which he played an escaped killer, and reached fruition in Billy Wilder's sardonic black comedy, *Sunset Blvd.* (1950, regarded by many as his finest performance), as the hack screenwriter who milks his unhealthy relationship with washed-up movie star Gloria Swanson. His unqualified success in these characterizations (he was Oscar-nominated for *Sunset Blvd.*) presaged many later portrayals of cynical, world-weary opportunists. Wilder exploited that aspect of Holden's talent in his 1953 prisoner-of-war drama *Stalag 17,* which won the star his only Academy Award for his finely limned characterization of a smooth-talking con man who may or may not be informing on his fellow prisoners.

Unfortunately, Holden was a double victim of the studio system. His long-term contract was shared by Columbia and Paramount, which not only underpaid him, but forced him into potboilers unworthy of his talent and popularity. Good movies like *Born Yesterday* (1950), in which he played the tutor hired by gangster Broderick Crawford to give Judy Holliday "class," were counterbalanced by strictly standard time-fillers like *Submarine Command* (1951) and *Forever Female* (1953). Other 1950s' assignments included *Union Station* (1950), *Force of Arms* (1951), *Boots Malone, The Turning Point* (both 1952), *The Moon Is Blue,* and *Escape From Fort Bravo* (both 1953). His luck improved in mid-decade, with a string of fine films: *Executive Suite* (which reunited him with Stanwyck), *The Bridges at Toko-Ri, Sabrina, The Country Girl* (all 1954), *Love Is a Many Splendored Thing* (1955), and *Picnic* (also 1955, which included the smoldering dance scene with Kim Novak that Holden was so nervous about he had to film it dead drunk!). Many of these films were among the top grossers of their day, solidifying Holden's star standing during the transitional decade of the 1950s, which saw many big names of the 1930s and 1940s pass from the scene. He became one of Hollywood's most popular and potent leading men.

After making *Toward the Unknown* and *The Proud and Profane* (both 1956), Holden negotiated a ground-breaking contract with Columbia to star in David Lean's blockbuster *The Bridge on the River Kwai* (1957), which made him a part-owner of the film; the film was, quite rightly, an enormous success, and the deal he made paid him handsomely for years to come. *The Key* (1958), *The Horse Soldiers* (1959), and *The World of Suzie Wong* (1960) were to follow.

Holden loved traveling; he accepted some film assignments for the opportunity to go to exotic locations, and journeyed to other regions of the world on his own. (He even owned a country club in Kenya, where he spent much of his time in later years.) In fact, his other activities probably accounted for the perceptible decline in the quality of his performances during the 1960s; he seemed tired and disinterested as the decade wore on: *The Counterfeit Traitor, Satan Never Sleeps, The Lion* (all 1962), *Paris—When It Sizzles, The 7th Dawn* (both 1964), *Alvarez Kelly* (1966), *Casino Royale* (1967, in a cameo), *The Devil's Brigade* (1968), and *The Christmas Tree* (1969).

Sam Peckinpah's blood-soaked Western, *The Wild Bunch* (1969), took advantage of Holden's increasingly apparent weariness; as one of the aging outlaws who plans to retire after staging a final haul, he turned in one of his best performances in years. *Wild Rovers* (1971), *The Revengers* (1972), and *Breezy* (1973, directed by Clint Eastwood) didn't amount to much, but Holden enjoyed considerable success in the TV-movie *The Blue Knight* (1973, earning an Emmy Award for his performance), *The Towering Inferno* (1974), and, especially, *Network* (1976). The latter film, a brilliant black comedy written by Paddy Chayefsky and directed by Sidney Lumet, offered him one last really impressive star turn (for which he secured his final Oscar nomination), as the jaded TV executive at first indifferent to, then finally repulsed by, the disgraceful practices of his peers.

Holden's final few films included *Damien—Omen II* (1978), *Fedora* (also 1978, for Billy Wilder), *Ashanti* (1979), *When Time Ran Out . . .* (1980), and Blake Edwards' black comedy about Hollywood, *S.O.B.* (1981, a fitting follow-up for the man who'd starred in *Sunset Blvd.*). Shortly after completing the last-named movie, he slipped and fell, cutting his head open, and bled to death. Holden was married to actress Brenda Marshall from 1941 to 1971. Bob Thomas' melancholy biography, "Golden Boy," revealed that the handsome, self-assured actor so admired by men and women alike onscreen was in fact a man fraught with insecurity who essentially drank himself to an early grave.

HOLLAND, AGNIESZKA. Director, screenwriter. *(b. Nov. 28, 1948, Warsaw, Poland.)* Internationally acclaimed filmmaker whose harshly realistic but sensitively handled dramas—many based on real-life events—have won her a growing audience in the United States. She studied filmmaking in Prague during the late 1960s (her professors included Milos Forman and Ivan Passer) and remained there even after Soviet troops invaded Czechoslovakia. She was arrested and jailed in 1970 after months of police harassment and interrogation, and eventually returned to Poland, where she worked in film, TV, and theater. After codirecting her first feature, *Screen Tests* (1977), she helmed the low-budget films *Provincial Actors* (1979), *Fever* (1980), and *A Woman Alone* (1981). She also began a fruitful relationship with famed Polish director Andrzej Wajda, writing the screenplay for *Without Anesthesia* (1979) and cowriting *A Love in Germany* (1984). After martial law was declared in Poland, she moved to Paris.

Holland received a Best Foreign Film Oscar nomination for *Angry Harvest* (1985), about a Polish farmer's relationship with a Jewish woman who escapes a train going to a death camp. She then became involved in two American movie projects, writing the screenplay for *Anna* (1987) and cowriting and directing *To Kill a Priest* (1988), based on the murder of the activist Polish priest Jerzy Popieluszko. Holland got raves for *Europa, Europa* (1991), the devastating true story of Solomon Perel, a German-Jewish boy who concealed his identity even while part of the Nazi Youth. Although Germany refused to submit it for a Best Foreign Film Oscar, Holland was nominated for her screenplay. *Olivier, Olivier* (1992), again based on a real event, is about a French family whose son reappears after missing for six years; it continues to examine her frequent theme of hidden identities and the depths of cultural biases. She then tackled a mainstream project, for executive producer Francis Ford Coppola, directing a handsome remake of *The Secret Garden* (1993). She was also credited with additional screenwriting on the French-made *Blue* (1993). Holland's career is still blossoming and one senses that in years to come she may earn a place in the pantheon of international filmmakers.

HOLLIDAY, JUDY. Actress. *(b. June 21, 1922, New York City, as Judith Tuvim; d. June 7, 1965.)* Luminously talented actress best known for two famous "dumb blonde" characterizations: Doris Attinger in *Adam's Rib* (1949) and Billie Dawn in *Born Yesterday* (1950, reprising her star-making Broadway performance and winning an Oscar for it). Holliday was a onetime switchboard operator who performed in New York cabarets before signing with 20th Century-Fox in 1944. She was released after being assigned small roles in three of that year's pictures—*Greenwich Village, Something for the Boys, Winged Victory*—and returned to New York and found stardom on stage. A brilliant comedienne with an effervescent personality, she appeared to good advantage in a handful of films after *Born Yesterday,* although never again attaining the same heights. *The Marrying Kind* (1952), *It Should Happen to You, Phffft!* (both 1954), *The Solid Gold Cadillac, Full of Life* (both 1956), and *Bells Are Ringing* (1960) rounded out Holliday's Hollywood career, and she succumbed to cancer at age 43.

HOLM, CELESTE. Actress. *(b. Apr. 29, 1919, New York City.)* Intelligent, sophisticated, attractive actress (mostly in supporting roles) who came to films in 1946 after a decade-long stage career, during which time she originated the role of Ado Annie in the original Broadway production of "Oklahoma!" A well-educated woman who as a young girl had taken ballet and drama lessons, she brought her natural smarts to a variety of movie roles in comedies, musicals, and melodramas. She was particularly adept at characterizations calling for sharp delivery of tart dialogue—which kept her in supporting rather than starring roles. Holm debuted onscreen in *Three Little Girls in Blue* (1946), and won a Best Supporting Actress Oscar for her third film, Elia Kazan's anti-Semitism treatise *Gentleman's Agreement* (1947). Within just a few more years she had snagged two more nominations, first for *Come to the Stable* (1949), then for *All About Eve* (1950, as the perceptive wife of a playwright in this classic drama starring Bette Davis). Holm continued to do stage work and appeared on TV shows and made-fors through the 1990s.

OTHER FILMS INCLUDE: 1948: *Road House, The Snake Pit;* 1949: *Chicken Every Sunday, A Letter to Three Wives* (an off-screen voiceover); 1950: *Champagne for Caesar;* 1955: *The Tender Trap;* 1956: *High Society* (singing with Frank Sinatra); 1961: *Bachelor Flat;* 1967: *Doctor, You've Got to Be Kidding;* 1973: *Tom Sawyer* (as Aunt Polly); 1977: *The Private Files of J. Edgar Hoover;* 1987: *3 Men and a Baby* (as Ted Danson's mother).

HOLM, IAN. Actor. *(b. Sept. 12, 1931, Essex, England.)* Phenomenally talented British actor who has appeared in a myriad of chameleonlike film roles since his memorable Oscar-nominated performance as running coach Sam Mussabini in *Chariots of Fire* (1981). Holm studied at the Royal Academy of Dramatic Art and spent 14 seasons with the Royal Shakespeare Company (touring with Laurence Olivier in the 1957 production of "Titus Andronicus") before coming to the New York stage. After winning a Tony on Broadway for "The Homecoming," he made his film debut in *The Fixer* (1968), then won a British Oscar for *The Bofors Gun* (1968). He has been memorable in the film adaptation of *The Homecoming* (1973, reprising his stage role), *Alien* (1979, as the android Ash), *Time Bandits* (1981, as Napoleon), *Greystoke: The Legend of Tarzan, Lord of the Apes* (1984), *Dreamchild* (as Reverend Charles Dodgson), *Brazil, Wetherby* (all 1985), *Another Woman* (1988), and *Naked Lunch* (1991), as well as two very different Shakespearean adaptations: Kenneth Branagh's revisionist *Henry V* (1989, as Fluellen) and Franco Zeffirelli's *Hamlet* (1990, as Polonius). In 1993, he appeared in *The Hour of the Pig,* and in 1994, *Mary Shelley's Frankenstein,* for Branagh.

HOLT, TIM. Actor. *(b. Feb. 5, 1918, Beverly Hills, as Charles John Holt, Jr.; d. Feb. 15, 1973.)* Tim Holt was a popular second-generation cowboy star (his father Jack had been one of Paramount's top silent-era horse-opera heroes) who had the distinction of also costarring in two great non-Western films: *The Magnificent Ambersons* and *The Treasure of the Sierra Madre.* He got his first film experience in *The Vanishing Pioneer* (1928), playing dad Jack's character as a boy. As a handsome, curly-haired young man Tim appeared in 1937's *History Is Made at Night* and *Stella Dallas* before donning six-guns and spurs to support Harry Carey in *The Law West of Tombstone* and George O'Brien in *The Renegade Ranger* (both 1938); he also did well in the small role of a young cavalry officer in *Stagecoach* (1939). So, when O'Brien (RKO's top cowhand) left his studio in 1940, Tim took over his series of low-budget Westerns, beginning with *Wagon Train* (1940). He gathered a following over the next few years, but went into the service in 1943 and was offscreen for three years. (Tim had also played supporting roles in the 1939 Ginger Rogers starrer *5th Ave. Girl,* Orson Welles' 1942 saga *The Magnificent Ambersons,* and a 1943 "sleeper" called *Hitler's Children.)*

Upon returning to Hollywood, he was cast by John Ford as one of the Earp brothers in *My Darling Clementine,* and by John Huston as Humphrey Bogart's partner in *The Treasure of the Sierra Madre* (both 1946, although *Treasure* wasn't released until 1948). Tim once again assumed his position as RKO's resident B-Western star (a post that, in his absence, had been briefly held by Robert Mitchum) with several adaptations of Zane Grey stories: *Thunder Mountain, Wild Horse Mesa* (a remake of the silent version in which his dad had starred), and *Under the Tonto Rim* (all 1947). Still youthful-looking, he had been matured by the war, and was more grim, more thoughtful on-screen than he'd ever been before. He made another two dozen or so Westerns—which were among the best in the field—between 1948 and 1952.

Holt worked in TV, and starred in only a few more films, none of them particularly good: *The Monster That Challenged the World* (1957), *The Yesterday Machine* (1963), and *This Stuff'll Kill Ya!* (1971). He drifted into the business world, and was at the time of his death the manager of an Oklahoma radio station. Tim's sister Jennifer also acted in movie Westerns, playing leading lady to many top screen cowboys in the 1940s.

HOMOLKA, OSCAR. Actor. *(b. Aug. 12, 1898, Vienna; d. Jan. 27, 1978.)* With his menacing features, bushy eyebrows, guttural accent, and brutish demeanor, Homolka made an ideal screen heavy—particularly in the years following World War 2, when Iron Curtain types were much in demand. A disciple of Max Reinhardt, he spent many years in Austrian and German theater before leaving Europe when Hitler took power. His early English-language film successes included strong supporting roles in Hitchcock's *Sabotage* (1936) and *Ebb Tide* (1937), in which he made his American screen debut. Homolka, in spite of his physical appearance, sometimes essayed comedic roles, generally with success. He was Oscar-nominated for his portrayal of Uncle Chris in *I Remember Mama* (1948), and is also memorable in *Seven Sinners, Comrade X* (both 1940), *Ball of Fire* (1941), *Mission to Moscow* (1943), *Anna Lucasta* (1949), *The White Tower* (1950), *Prisoner of War* (1954), *The Seven Year Itch* (1955), *War and Peace* (1956), *A Farewell to Arms* (1957), *Mr. Sardonicus* (1961, as the title character's sinister servant), *Boys' Night Out, The Wonderful World of the Brothers Grimm* (both 1962), *The Long Ships* (1964), a pair of Harry Palmer spy thrillers, *Funeral in Berlin* (1966) and *Billion Dollar Brain* (1967), *Song of Norway* (1970), and *The Tamarind Seed* (1974).

HOOPER, TOBE. Director. *(b. Jan. 25, 1943, Austin, Tex.)* After knocking around as a teacher and documentary maker for several years, Hooper galvanized horror fans around the world with his 1974 independent production, *The Texas Chainsaw Massacre,* now enshrined by cultists as one of the forerunners of the "splatter" subgenre. While not nearly as gory as its title suggests, *Massacre* is a genuinely terrifying film made even more unsettling by its twisted but undeniably hilarious black comedy. Hooper followed that with the entertaining but not nearly as resonant *Eaten Alive* (1976). The disappointing *Funhouse* (1981), which boasted an intriguing premise but ended up sinking to the teen-body-count-clichés of that era, had many *Texas Chainsaw* fans wondering what had happened to their idol. Steven Spielberg enlisted Hooper to direct the effective haunted-house shocker *Poltergeist* (1982); there is much speculation, though, that Spielberg himself, displeased with Hooper's approach, overrode the director on many points and diluted some strong sequences.

Hooper's career trajectory is all downhill from there; the high point of his 1985 vampires-from-outer-space story, *Lifeforce,* is the sight of French beauty Mathilda May strolling through London stark naked. His remake of the low-budget cult classic *Invaders From Mars* (1986) was, to put it charitably, ill advised. And 1986's desperate *The Texas Chainsaw Massacre 2* is best completely forgotten. *Spontaneous Combustion* (1990) was released directly to video. Hooper, one of many youngish directors influenced by old horror movies and early TV shows, has demonstrated that, once past the trademark gore and shock scenes with which he loads his pictures, there's less to his directorial style than meets the eye. In 1994 he directed *Tobe Hooper's Night Terrors;* he also directed a Billy Idol music video, "Dancing With Myself" (1983).

HOPE, BOB. Actor; producer. *(b. May 29, 1903, Eltham, England, as Leslie Townes Hope.)* What can anyone say about the man who may be the most popular entertainer in the history of Western civilization? Having conquered every conceivable medium, he approaches the twenty-first century with characteristic energy and enthusiasm, although age has slowed him up somewhat in recent years. He began his show-business life as a vaudeville comedian, and his machine-gun delivery of jokes quickly earned him the nickname "Rapid Robert." Hope worked his way to Broadway by the early 1930s, and made numerous comedy shorts in New York studios through mid-decade, including a generally mediocre series for Warner-Vitaphone. A radio regular, he was starring on "The Pepsodent Show" by 1938; that same year he made his feature-film debut in Paramount's *The Big Broadcast of 1938,* in which he and Shirley Ross sang the wistful "Thanks for the Memory," which became (and remains) his signature tune. Paramount knew it had a hot property, and kept Hope busy in such light fare as *College Swing, Thanks for the Memory* (both 1938), *Some Like It Hot* (no relation to the Tony Curtis–Jack Lemmon–Marilyn Monroe film), and *Never Say Die* (both 1939) before dusting off and retailoring the old barnstorming thriller *The Cat and the Canary* (1939) for him. In that film, playing a wisecracking ham actor whose scaredy-cat antics and topical references delighted movie audiences, Hope delivered what could be called his prototypical performance, delineating a screen persona that served him well for more than 30 years.

Cat's success led to another chiller, *The Ghost Breakers* (1940), which reunited him with *Cat* costar Paulette Goddard. That same year he joined forces with crooner Bing Crosby and sarong-clad siren Dorothy Lamour in *Road to Singapore*, a modest program picture that became a sleeper hit, due in no small way to Hope's easy rapport with Crosby and their breezy, often ad-libbed repartee. Over the next two decades they found themselves on the respective roads to … *Zanzibar* (1941), … *Morocco* (1942), … *Utopia* (1945), … *Rio* (1947), … *Bali* (1952), and … *Hong Kong* (1962), each outing screwier than the last. Hope and Crosby also made frequent cameos in each other's solo starring films, and carried on a genial bantering "feud" for years.

Other Hope hits during the 1940s include *Caught in the Draft, Louisiana Purchase, Nothing But the Truth* (all 1941), *My Favorite Blonde* (1942), *Let's Face It, They Got Me Covered* (both 1943), *The Princess and the Pirate* (1944, the first of many period pictures brightened by Hope's anachronistic, contemporary references), *Monsieur Beaucaire* (1946), *My Favorite Brunette* (1947), and a blockbuster Western spoof, *The Paleface* (1948), which introduced an Oscar-winning song ("Buttons and Bows") and spawned a sequel, *Son of Paleface*, in 1952.

Hope made his first TV special for NBC in 1950, beginning an uninterrupted, four-decade-plus run on that network. His film work during the 1950s, while still entertaining, wasn't quite up to his 1940s output, although he did broaden his appeal by taking occasional dramatic roles. *Fancy Pants* (1950, the first of several comedies that paired him with Lucille Ball), *The Lemon Drop Kid, My Favorite Spy* (both 1951), *Here Come the Girls* (1953), *The Seven Little Foys* (1955, a straight role as vaudevillian Eddie Foy, Sr.), *That Certain Feeling, The Iron Petticoat* (both 1956), *Beau James* (1957, another dramatic role, as scapegrace New York mayor Jimmy Walker), *Paris Holiday* (1958), *Alias Jesse James* (1959), *The Facts of Life* (1960), *Bachelor in Paradise* (1961), *Critic's Choice,* and *Call Me Bwana* (both 1963) all have elements to recommend them, even if they are inferior to Hope's 1940s vehicles.

As he grew older (and devoted more of his life to TV work and entertaining U.S. troops in the Far East), the quality of his starring films deteriorated rapidly, resulting in such lame comedies as *A Global Affair* (1964), *I'll Take Sweden* (1965), *Boy, Did I Get a Wrong Number!* (1966), *Eight on the Lam* (1967), *The Private Navy of Sergeant O'Farrell* (1968), *How to Commit Marriage* (1969, opposite fellow TV icon Jackie Gleason), and *Cancel My Reservation* (1972, mercifully his final starring feature). He did contribute a very Hope-like cameo to the Chevy Chase–Dan Aykroyd comedy *Spies Like Us* (1985). He spent many years as the host of the annual Academy Awards ceremonies ("Or as it's known at my house, Passover," he once quipped, though in fact he did receive four honorary Oscars). Hope has written (or, at least, is credited with writing) several humorous memoirs, including "I Never Left Home," "Have Tux—Will Travel," "I Owe Russia $1200," "Don't Shoot, It's Only Me," and "The Last Christmas Show." His wife, Dolores, sometimes appears with him on his TV specials, and his granddaughter, Leslie, has acted in a few films, including *It Takes Two, Talk Radio* (both 1988), and *Men at Work* (1990).

HOPKINS, ANTHONY (SIR). Actor. *(b. Dec. 31, 1937, Port Talbot, South Wales.)* After a brilliant career on stage and film, Anthony Hopkins finally received wide public recognition—and genuine movie stardom—in the unlikely but compelling role of cannibalistic killer Hannibal Lecter in *The Silence of the Lambs* (1991), and capped it off with an Academy Award as Best Actor. Although his quiet, placid expression and naturally calm voice evoke typical English reserve, in his best work Hopkins often violently overturns those preconceptions of him. True, he was completely effective playing the kind, decent doctor in *The Elephant Man* (1980), but in fact he was much more effective playing the unhinged ventriloquist in *Magic* (1978) and, of course, Lecter in *Lambs*. His performance in the latter is the sort that fixes itself in viewers' minds forever; it's fortunate for Hopkins that he did it later in his career than Anthony Perkins did Norman Bates.

Trained at the Cardiff College of Drama, Hopkins enjoyed extensive stage work before beginning his film career, essaying supporting roles in a series of distinguished films, including *The Lion in Winter* (1968) and *Hamlet* (1969). His screen output during the 1970s was largely impressive, and he appeared in many made-for-TV movies—an uncommon career path for classically trained British actors. Beginning with *Magic* (1978) he showed a penchant for eccentric roles, and while he didn't exactly stumble through the 1980s, his good work in small films—such as *84 Charing Cross Road* and *The Good Father* (both 1987)—often went unnoticed, while his better-than-they-deserved performances in such tripe as *A Change of Seasons* (1980) and the TV miniseries "Hollywood Wives" got more public attention. Not that he didn't get plum parts: he won Emmy Awards for *The Lindbergh Kidnapping Case* (1976), in which he played Bruno Hauptmann, and *The Bunker* (1981), as Hitler. In 1984 Hopkins played the domineering Captain Bligh in *The Bounty*, a much-heralded remake that fizzled at box offices. Much in demand after *Lambs*, he appeared in *Freejack*, *Howards End* (in a brilliant performance), *Bram Stoker's Dracula* (as vampire hunter Dr. Van Helsing) and *Chaplin* (as a book editor), all in 1992 and was Oscar-nominated again for *The Remains of the Day* (1993). Trivia fans take note: He looped several of Laurence Olivier's lines for a scene in the restored version of *Spartacus*.

OTHER FILMS INCLUDE: 1969: *The Looking Glass War;* 1971: *When Eight Bells Toll;* 1972: *Young Winston;* 1973: *A Doll's House;* 1974: *The Girl From Petrovka, Juggernaut, All Creatures Great and Small* (made for TV); 1976: *Dark Victory, Victory at Entebbe* (both made for TV); 1977: *Audrey Rose, A Bridge Too Far;* 1978: *International Velvet;* 1981: *Peter and Paul* (as Paul; made for TV); 1982: *The Hunchback of Notre Dame* (made for TV); 1985: *Mussolini: The Decline and Fall of*

Il Duce (made for TV); 1988: *The Tenth Man* (made for TV), *A Chorus of Disapproval;* 1990: *Desperate Hours;* 1992: *The Efficiency Expert;* 1993: *Shadowlands;* 1994: *Legends of the Fall, The Road to Wellville;* 1995: *The Innocent.*

HOPKINS, BO. Actor. (b. Feb. 2, 1942, Greenwood, S.C.) Sandy-haired, rangy, drawling character actor and occasional lead who made his film debut as Crazy Lee in Sam Peckinpah's *The Wild Bunch* (1969). Peckinpah also used Hopkins in *The Getaway* (1972) and *The Killer Elite* (1975); in between the actor appeared in many low-budget feature films, made-for-TV movies and TV series, (including "Doc Elliot," 1973–74; "Dynasty," the first season, 1981–82; "The Rockford Files," 1978–79 season) along with high-profile features like *Monte Walsh* (1970), *The Culpepper Cattle Co.* (1972), *American Graffiti, White Lightning* (both 1973), *The Day of the Locust* (1975), *Midnight Express* (1978), and *More American Graffiti* (1979). Still active in action cheapies such as *Big Bad John* (1989), almost always playing rednecks. In 1993 he landed one of the best parts of his career, as a somewhat cantankerous westerner who befriends a young man—never suspecting "he" is really a woman—in *The Ballad of Little Jo*. His rich, shaded performance confirmed that Hopkins is worthy of better material than he's been handed in recent years.

HOPKINS, MIRIAM. Actress. (b. Oct. 18, 1902, Bainbridge, Ga.; d. Oct. 9, 1972.) A brittle, fascinating performer, Miriam Hopkins projected great talent but little warmth from the screen. Still, her best performances from the 1930s hold up exceptionally well. A chorus girl from 1921, she went legit in the mid 1920s and developed a reputation as a solid Broadway actress. In the Hollywood rush to sign theater stars for the talkies, Hopkins contracted with Paramount in 1930. Her first picture was the deadly dull *Fast and Loose*, but it was followed by a nearly unbroken string of first-rate films. In Ernst Lubitsch's *The Smiling Lieutenant* (1931), Claudette Colbert showed Hopkins how to "Jazz Up Your Lingerie" to win the heart of Maurice Chevalier. Hopkins played a reluctant live-in girlfriend to Fredric March's *Dr. Jekyll and Mr. Hyde* (1932) in the Rouben Mamoulian classic; her uninhibited sensuality as Ivy wasn't lost on audiences any more than it was on Hyde. She played a delectable jewel thief in Lubitsch's *Trouble in Paradise* (also 1932), the apex of a free-love romantic triangle in *Design for Living,* and a not-so-reluctant kidnap victim in *The Story of Temple Drake* (both 1933), based on William Faulkner's "Sanctuary."

Hopkins was ideally cast in the title role of Mamoulian's *Becky Sharp* (1935), playing Thackeray's selfish heroine in the first full Technicolor feature and getting Oscar-nominated in the bargain, and then moved to Samuel Goldwyn Productions, where after *Barbary Coast* (1935) and the outstanding *These Three* (1936), her career began to falter. By the time Hopkins arrived at Warner Bros. in 1939 she was reduced to playing second fiddle to Bette Davis in *The Old Maid* (1939) and *Old Acquaintance* (1943), and for publicity purposes the studio spread tales of great rivalry between the two ladies. (The climactic scene in the latter film, in which Davis shakes the living daylights out of her costar, was gleefully anticipated by audiences.)

The Lady With Red Hair (1940) offered a vehicle for Hopkins alone, but the biopic of actress Mrs. Leslie Carter did little to spark audience enthusiasm. She seemed ill at ease as a saloon gal matching wits with Errol Flynn in *Virginia City* (1940). Hopkins retreated to the theater in the mid 1940s, but came back to the screen periodically as a character actress, notably in William Wyler's *The Heiress* (1949) and *The Children's Hour* (1962), the latter based on Lillian Hellman's lesbian-themed play, and a sentimental remake for Hopkins, who had starred in Wyler's soft-peddled *These Three*. Her final film appearance on-screen was in *The Chase* (1966), a multi-star monument to thick-sliced method acting. *The Comeback* offered her one final starring screen role in 1969, but the well-worn tale of an aging star was never released.

HOPPER, DENNIS. Actor, director. *(b. May 17, 1936, Dodge City, Kans.)* "Don't you f—in' look at me!" With those words, Dennis Hopper, whose mainstream career had floundered throughout the 1970s and early 1980s, was reborn as the apotheosis of middle-American menace. The movie was David Lynch's celebrated 1986 thriller *Blue Velvet,* and while his terrifying performance as villain Frank Booth did perhaps lead to a few too many subsequent psycho roles, it announced the full-fledged comeback of an artist whose full talents were often ill-utilized (by both himself and others) the first time around. As a young man in the 1950s, he played a series of minor roles, twice in movies featuring James Dean (1955's *Rebel Without a Cause* and 1956's *Giant),* a friend Hopper regarded as a mentor. Graduating to supporting roles and guest-star slots in TV dramas in the 1960s, the method actor was soon pegged as "difficult." He began working in Roger Corman productions; in 1967 he appeared in Corman's acid spectacular *The Trip.*

Offscreen Hopper was an active part of the pop art explosion of the era, both as a savvy and appreciative collector and a photographic chronicler of the "scene"; recent books and exhibitions of his pictures show him to be a fine photographer who had some fascinating subjects to work with. In 1969 he directed, cowrote, and starred in *Easy Rider,* the ultimate counterculture movie that was a box-office and critical sensation. (The script was Oscar-nominated.) Flush with its success, he went on to direct the daring, self-reflexive, and willful *The Last Movie* (1971), the crushing failure of which alienated him from the Hollywood establishment. His screen appearances from that point on were varied and desultory; by his account, he was wandering in a morass of drugs and drink throughout the 1970s. He seemed totally spaced-out in Francis Coppola's 1979 *Apocalypse Now,* but he was capable of doing some solid work in that state, as witness his affecting, layered performance in Wim Wenders' *The American Friend* (1977).

After spending the early 1980s getting himself cleaned up, he auditioned for *Blue Velvet* by telephoning Lynch and telling him "I am Frank Booth." He has worked steadily since, both as actor (playing a wide variety of roles, including an Oscar-nominated turn as a town drunk in 1986's *Hoosiers* and a burned-out ex-hippie in 1990's *Flashback)* and a director (showing a solid command of mainstream moviemaking in 1988's *Colors,* and an arresting command of visual style and a wry appreciation of noir irony in the genuinely erotic thriller *The Hot Spot* [1990]). More recently Hopper won kudos for his superb starring turn in *Paris Trout* (1991) and had the distinction of being the most normal character to appear on screen in *True Romance* (1993), as Christian Slater's father. OTHER FILMS INCLUDE: 1955: *I Died a Thousand Times;* 1957: *Gunfight at the O.K. Corral, Sayonara;* 1958: *From Hell to Texas;* 1963: *Night Tide;* 1965: *The Sons of Katie Elder;* 1967: *Cool Hand Luke, The Glory Stompers;* 1968: *Hang 'em High;* 1969: *True Grit;* 1973: *Kid Blue;* 1976: *Tracks;* 1980: *Out of the Blue* (also directed); 1983: *The Osterman Weekend;* 1983: *Rumble Fish;* 1985: *My Science Project;* 1986: *The Texas Chainsaw Massacre 2;* 1987: *O.C. & Stiggs, Black Widow, The Pick-up Artist, River's Edge, Straight to Hell;* 1989: *Backtrack* (also directed); 1990: *Chattahoochee;* 1992: *Nails* (made for TV); 1993: *Boiling Point, Super Mario Bros., Red Rock West;* 1994: *Chasers* (as director; also had cameo), *Speed* (acting only); 1995: *Search and Destroy, Waterworld.*

HORNER, JAMES. Composer. *(b. Aug. 14, 1953, Los Angeles.)* One of today's most prolific film composers, Horner studied at London's Royal College of Music and later USC. He was teaching at UCLA when he was asked to score a film for the American Film Institute. More AFI films followed before Horner went to work for Roger Corman's New World Pictures and scored low-budget features like *The Lady in Red* (1979), *Battle Beyond the Stars* and *Humanoids From the Deep* (both 1980). This led to bigger films like *The Pursuit of D. B. Cooper* and *The Hand* (both 1981), several made-for-TV movies and then *Star Trek II: The Wrath of Khan* (1982), which proved his ability to write "big" orchestral scores in the classic Hollywood tradition.

That, and his musical versatility, have kept him busy nonstop ever since on films both big and small, including *48HRS* (1982), *The Dresser, Uncommon Valor* (both 1983), *Star Trek III: The Search for Spock, The Stone Boy* (both 1984), *Cocoon, Commando* (both 1985), *The Name of the Rose* (1986), **batteries not included* (1987), *Cocoon: The Return* (1988), *Dad, Honey, I Shrunk the Kids, In Country* (all

1989), *I Love You to Death* (1990), and *Once Around* (1991). Other credits include *Sneakers, Patriot Games* (both 1992), *Searching for Bobby Fischer, Bopha!,* and *The Man Without A Face* (all 1993). He was Oscar-nominated for the scores of *Aliens* (1986) and *Field of Dreams* (1989), as well as the song "Somewhere Out There" from the animated *An American Tail* (1986). He won a Grammy for Best Instrumental Composition for *Glory* (1989), which, like many of his scores, integrated choral work into the orchestration.

HORTON, EDWARD EVERETT. Actor. *(b. Mar. 18, 1886, Brooklyn, N.Y.; d. Sept. 29, 1970.)* Expert in the delineation of high-strung, easily exasperated characters, Horton enjoyed a long and generally prestigious film career, amassing more than 150 credits. He was no matinee idol but nonetheless played quite a few leads, dating back to the silent era's *Ruggles of Red Gap* (1923), *Beggar on Horseback* (1925), *La Boheme* (1926), and *The Whole Town's Talking* (1926), among others. Blessed with impeccable comic timing, and skillful at delivering brittle dialogue, he was much in demand when talkies arrived, sometimes as the leading man's confidant, sometimes as an excitable fussbudget. He even had the lead in the first all-talking mystery movie, *The Terror* (1928). He's fondly remembered for his work in three Fred Astaire–Ginger Rogers musicals, *The Gay Divorcee* (1934), *Top Hat* (1935), and *Shall We Dance* (1937), and a handful of Lubitsch comedies: *Trouble in Paradise* (1932), *Design for Living* (1933), *The Merry Widow* (1934), and *Bluebeard's Eighth Wife* (1938). As late as 1937 he still got top billing in *The Man in the Mirror* and *Wild Money,* both comedies of the "worm turns" school. He also appeared to good advantage in *The Front Page* (1931), *Alice in Wonderland* (1933, as The Mad Hatter), *The Devil Is a Woman* (1935), *The Singing Kid* (1936, in which he warbles with Allen Jenkins), *Lost Horizon* (1937, as the prissy schoolteacher), *Holiday* (1938, repeating the role he played in the 1930 film), *Here Comes Mr. Jordan* (1941, as a heavenly messenger who fouls up), *Arsenic and Old Lace* (1944), *Down to Earth* (1947, repeating

his role from *Here Comes Mr. Jordan),
The Story of Mankind* (1957), *Pocketful of
Miracles* (1961), *Sex and the Single Girl*
(1964, as a publisher of girlie magazines), The Perils of Pauline (1967), and
Cold Turkey (1971). As an octogenarian,
he was still working regularly on-screen,
and as the narrator of "Fractured Fairy
Tales" on the Bullwinkle cartoon show.
Once, the show's coproducer and head
writer, Bill Scott, asked Horton the secret of his longevity. "Well, Bill, I'll tell
you," he replied. "Right now I'm on my
way to my mother's birthday party." A
street in Encino, California, bears his
name.

HOSKINS, BOB. Actor. *(b. Oct. 26,
1942, Bury St. Edmunds, England.)* Balding,
stocky supporting player and character
lead whose pugnacious manner and Cockney accent make him instantly distinctive.
Hoskins worked only sporadically in the
1970s, beginning with *The National
Health* (1973). He was notable as the
porno king in *Inserts* (1976) and as the
doomed salesman in the original British
TV version of Dennis Potter's "Pennies
From Heaven" (1979). His breakthrough
role was that of the mob boss whose
world crumbles around him in *The Long
Good Friday* (1980), though it temporarily
typed him as a gangster. Hoskins made
American audiences sit up and take notice
of his performance as Owney Madden in
The Cotton Club (1984), and won Best
Actor honors at Cannes as well as an Oscar nomination as the put-upon hood in
Mona Lisa (1986). He was, however,
smart enough to vary his roles, and turned
in splendid work as the cloying screenwriter in *Sweet Liberty* (1986), the pathetic suitor in *The Lonely Passion of Judith Hearne,* a priest in *A Prayer for the
Dying* (both 1987), a bigoted L.A. cop in
Heart Condition, a nurturing shoe salesman in *Mermaids* (both 1990), an eccentric private eye in *Shattered,* and a grizzled Mr. Smee opposite Dustin Hoffman
in *Hook* (both 1991). In 1988 he starred in
the smash hit *Who Framed Roger Rabbit,*
and made his writing/directing debut on
The Raggedy Rawney. Other credits include the TV movie *Mussolini: The Decline
and Fall of Il Duce* (1985, as Mussolini),
Passed Away (1992), *Super Mario Bros.*

(1993), and *World War II: When Lions
Roared* (1994, telefilm, as Churchill).

HOUSEMAN, JOHN. Actor, producer.
*(b. Sept. 11, 1902, Bucharest, as Jacques
Haussman; d. Oct. 31, 1988.)* At 71, when
most people have already retired, this distinguished, stentorian-voiced author/
producer/director/teacher suddenly found
himself an Academy Award winner, and
embarked on a brand new career as a star-
billed character actor. It was just one more
surprise in a life full of them. He
cofounded the Mercury Theatre with
Orson Welles, with whom he worked
closely on both stage and in radio. (The
pair quarreled and split during production
of *Citizen Kane,* which is why Houseman's name is missing from the credits.)
He returned to New York and the stage,
but returned to Hollywood after World
War 2 as the producer of such intelligent
films as *The Blue Dahlia* (1946), *Letter
From an Unknown Woman, They Live By
Night* (both 1948), *On Dangerous Ground*
(1951), *The Bad and the Beautiful* (1952),
Julius Caesar (1953), *Executive Suite*
(1954), *Lust for Life* (1956), *Two Weeks in
Another Town* (1962), and *This Property
Is Condemned* (1966).

Houseman debuted onscreen in a 1957
British film called *Ill Met by Moonlight,*
but his bit was cut from the American release version; more noticeable was a small
role as an admiral in *Seven Days in May*
(1964). It was director and former student
James Bridges who cast him as the brilliant but terrifying Harvard law professor
Charles Kingsfield in *The Paper Chase*
(1973), a performance that won him a
Best Supporting Actor Oscar and changed
his life. Houseman immediately plunged
into his new career, playing similarly imperious (though not always noble) types in
such films as *Rollerball, Three Days of
the Condor* (both 1975), *The Cheap
Detective* (1978, parodying Sydney
Greenstreet), *The Fog* (1980), *Ghost Story*
(1981), *Bright Lights, Big City* (1988, for
James Bridges) and Woody Allen's *Another Woman* (1988), as well as continuing the role of Kingsfield on the "Paper
Chase" TV series (1978–79;1983–86).

He worked extensively in TV during the
1980s, on "Silver Spoons," in such movies and miniseries as *Fear on Trial, The*

French Atlantic Affair, Gideon's Trumpet, and "The Winds of War," and in dozens of commercials, adding, "They make money the old-fashioned way—they *earn* it!" to the vernacular. Houseman continued to work right up to the end, completing cameos in *Scrooged* and *The Naked Gun* weeks before his death. His autobiography spanned several volumes ("Run-Through," "Front & Center," "Final Dress"), and a theater in New York bears his name. He really did earn it.

HOWARD, JOHN. Actor. *(b. Apr. 14, 1913, Cleveland, as John R. Cox, Jr.)* Good-looking, personable leading man in B pictures and supporting player in numerous A's. As a Paramount contractee the handsome, exuberant Howard toiled in some of that studio's programmers—including *Four Hours to Kill* (1935), *Thirteen Hours by Air,* and *Border Flight* (both 1936)—before getting a shot to star in *Bulldog Drummond Comes Back* (1937), although he lost top billing to John Barrymore, as Drummond's friend Col. Nielsen. Howard interpreted the title character in six more films, ending with 1939's *Bulldog Drummond's Bride.* He was ideally cast as Ronald Colman's impetuous younger brother in Frank Capra's *Lost Horizon* (1937), and gave one of his best performances as Katharine Hepburn's wealthy, straitlaced fiancé in *The Philadelphia Story* (1940). But Howard's subsequent starrers were B's—including *The Invisible Woman* (also 1940, with Barrymore), *Texas Rangers Ride Again* (1941), *The Undying Monster,* and *Isle of Missing Men* (both 1942). He went into the service during World War 2 and became a real-life hero, winning the Navy Cross and France's Croix de Guerre. Unfortunately, his starring career never really got back on track. Howard also worked in many TV series episodes during the 1950s, 1960s, and 1970s and starred in several series: "Public Prosecutor" (1947–48), "Dr. Hudson's Secret Journal" (1955–57), and "The Adventures of the Sea Hawk" (1958).
OTHER FILMS INCLUDE: 1935: *Annapolis Farewell;* 1936: *Soak the Rich, Valiant Is the Word for Carrie;* 1948: *I, Jane Doe;* 1949: *The Fighting Kentuckian;* 1950: *Radar Secret Service;* 1952: *Models Inc.;* 1954: *The High and the Mighty* (a standout performance); 1957: *Unknown Terror;* 1966: *Destination Inner Space;* 1970: *The Sky Bike;* 1972: *Buck and the Preacher;* 1975: *Capone.*

HOWARD, LESLIE. Actor, director, producer. *(b. Apr. 24, 1893, London, as Leslie Stainer; d. June 2, 1943.)* Many moviegoers remember this blond, British-born (of Hungarian ancestry) leading man for his supporting role as Ashley Wilkes in *Gone With the Wind* (1939), but his cinematic legacy includes quite a number of fine starring performances as well. Slender and handsome, he generally played urbane, intuitive, introspective, and soft-spoken characters, but was equally effective in livelier roles—even in farce. A WW1 veteran who took up acting after being mustered out of service with shell shock, he made his feature-film debut in *The Happy Warrior* (1917) and took roles in a few other British-made silent movies. But he honed his ability with frequent stints on the London stage and eventually made it to Broadway, becoming a top stage star.

Howard's first talkie, *Outward Bound* (1930), established him as an able leading man for movies, and he spent the rest of the decade bouncing back and forth between the U.S. and England. Oscar-nominated for his leading roles in *Berkeley Square* (1933, a delicate romantic fantasy) and *Pygmalion* (1938, as Professor Henry Higgins, in this Shaw adaptation he codirected with Anthony Asquith), Howard also impressed in *Of Human Bondage* (1934, opposite Bette Davis, as tragic protagonist Philip Carey), *The Scarlet Pimpernel* (1935, as the Zorro-like title character), *The Petrified Forest* (1936, reprising his acclaimed Broadway characterization and, incidentally, insisting that the film's producers cast his stage nemesis, Humphrey Bogart), *Romeo and Juliet* (also 1936, as Romeo to Norma Shearer's Juliet), the romantic *Intermezzo* (1939, which he also coproduced), and *Pimpernel Smith* (1941, a *Scarlet Pimpernel* updating that he also produced and directed). Howard returned to his native England after World War 2 began, and was shot down by Nazi fighter planes while flying from Portugal in 1943. His son is actor Ronald Howard, who played Sherlock Holmes on television.
OTHER FILMS INCLUDE: 1931: *Never the Twain Shall Meet, A Free Soul, Five and Ten, Devotion;* 1932: *Service for Ladies, Smilin'*

Through, The Animal Kingdom; 1933: Secrets, Captured; 1934: The Lady Is Willing, British Agent; 1937: It's Love I'm After, Stand-In; 1941: 49th Parallel; 1942: Spitfire (which he also produced and directed).

HOWARD, RON. Director, actor, producer, screenwriter. *(b. Mar. 1, 1954, Duncan, Okla.)* Since directing his first film for low-budget king Roger Corman, this red-headed, freckle-faced former child actor has become one of today's most popular mainstream directors. For years he played the precocious Opie on TV's classic "The Andy Griffith Show" (1960–68) and later essayed the role of milk-fed nice-guy Richie Cunningham on the nostalgic "Happy Days" (1974–80). He made his film debut at age five in the Yul Brynner adventure *The Journey* (1959) and subsequently became one of the 1960s' most recognizable juvenile stars. (Who could forget him, lisp and all, in 1962's *The Music Man*?) *Grand Theft Auto* (1977), a car-chase flick aimed primarily at drive-ins, was his first stab at feature directing, though its routine contents offered no hint of the savvy work to follow.

Howard has gone on to direct extremely popular mainstream movies, including *Night Shift* (1982), *Splash* (1984), *Cocoon* (1985), and *Parenthood* (1989), often in collaboration with writers Lowell Ganz and Babaloo Mandel. At their best, these films are smart, straightforward, and self-assured. Even his lesser films are entertaining; if anything, they suffer from formulaic scripts, not a lack of filmmaking knowhow: *Gung Ho* (1986), *Willow* (1988), *Backdraft* (1991), and *Far and Away* (1992). His latest films are *The Paper* (1994) and *Apollo 13* (1995). Other acting credits include *Door-to-Door Maniac* (1961), *The Courtship of Eddie's Father* (1963), *Village of the Giants* (1965), *The Wild Country, Happy Mother's Day, Love George, American Graffiti* (all 1973), *Eat My Dust,* and *The Shootist* (both 1976). His parents are actors Rance and Jean Howard; brother Clint also is an actor, who turns up in everything Ron directs.

HOWARD, TREVOR. Actor. *(b. Sept. 29, 1916, Cliftonville, England; d. Jan. 7, 1988.)* Prolific British actor who effortlessly jumped from starring to supporting roles, playing heroes and heavies alike, from the 1940s to the 1960s, taking character parts exclusively in the years just prior to his death. Howard studied at the Royal Academy of Dramatic Art and acted on the London stage for several years before World War 2 interrupted his career; he served with the Royal Artillery until being wounded and honorably discharged. Returning to acting, he entered films with *The Way Ahead* (1944) and delighted audiences on both sides of the Atlantic with his intense yet underplayed turn as one of the lovers in David Lean's *Brief Encounter* (1945). Howard, pleasant looking but hardly a matinee idol, developed into a fine screen performer with an unobtrusive style, and worked in English- and American-made movies. He was memorable in *The Third Man* (1949, as the tight-lipped police major), *Sons and Lovers* (1960, earning an Oscar nomination as the drunken Walter Morel in this D. H. Lawrence adaptation), *Mutiny on the Bounty* (1962, as Captain Bligh), *The Charge of the Light Brigade* (1968, as Lord Cardigan), *Mary, Queen of Scots* (1971, as Lord Burleigh), *Pope Joan* (1972, as Pope Leo), *Ludwig* (1973, as Richard Wagner), and *A Doll's House* (also 1973, with Jane Fonda; as Dr. Rank). Sadly, many of the actor's later films were unworthy of his talent, and in his 1980s films the ruddy-faced, brown-haired Howard frequently appeared to be in poor health.

OTHER FILMS INCLUDE: 1946: *Green for Danger, I See a Dark Stranger;* 1947: *They Made Me a Fugitive;* 1949: *The Golden Salamander;* 1951: *The Clouded Yellow, Lady Godiva Rides Again, Outcast of the Islands;* 1953: *The Gift Horse, The Heart of the Matter;* 1956: *The Cockleshell Heroes, Around the World in Eighty Days, Run for the Sun;* 1957: *Interpol;* 1958: *The Key, The Roots of Heaven;* 1960: *Moment of Danger;* 1962: *The Lion;* 1964: *Father Goose, Man in the Middle;* 1965: *Saboteur: Code Name Morituri, Von Ryan's Express, Operation Crossbow;* 1966: *The Liquidator, The Poppy Is Also a Flower;* 1967: *The Long Duel, Pretty Polly;* 1969: *Battle of Britain;* 1970: *Ryan's Daughter;* 1971: *Kidnapped;* 1973: *Persecution;* 1974: *11 Harrowhouse;* 1975: *Conduct Unbecoming, Hennessy, Whispering Death;* 1976: *Aces High, The Bawdy Adventures of Tom Jones, Eliza Fraser;* 1977: *The Last Remake of Beau*

Geste, Slavers; 1978: *Superman;* 1979: *Hurricane, Meteor;* 1980: *Windwalker;* 1982: *The Missionary, Gandhi;* 1984: *Sword of the Valiant;* 1985: *Time After Time;* 1986: *Foreign Body;* 1988: *White Mischief, The Dawning, The Unholy.*

HOWE, JAMES WONG. Cinematographer, director. *(b. Aug. 28, 1899, Canton, China, as Wong Tung Jim; d. July 12, 1976.)* One of the pioneering cameramen of American cinema, Howe had an incredibly extensive and prolific career, extending from 1917 (when one of his jobs was slate boy for director Cecil B. De Mille) to 1975 (when he was Oscar-nominated for *Funny Lady).* In between he was one of the earliest masters of deep focus photography, earning the nickname "Low Key Howe" for his distinctive lighting style. He was also known for doing quality work with high efficiency, bringing a distinguished look to even quickie assignments (of which the first *Thin Man* movie in 1934 was one). His work could be spooky and atmospheric too, as demonstrated in *Chandu the Magician* (1932) and *Mark of the Vampire* (1935). He photographed *Kings Row* (1942) in stunning fashion, aided by brilliant art director William Cameron Menzies, with whom Howe had worked on *Chandu.* He staged a now-famous tracking shot of eye-popping length for *The Prisoner of Zenda* (1937) and donned roller skates to put himself into the prizefight action of *Body and Soul* (1947). Howe won Oscars for his work on 1955's *The Rose Tattoo* and 1963's *Hud;* his work on the unsettling 1966 thriller *Seconds* was black-and-white cinematography at its finest. One of his few forays in directing was the 1954 feature *Go, Man, Go!,* the story of the Harlem Globetrotters basketball team. Howe's work remained innovative and contemporary right to the end.
OTHER FILMS INCLUDE: 1923: *To the Last Man;* 1924: *Peter Pan;* 1925: *The King on Main Street;* 1926: *Mantrap;* 1928: *Laugh, Clown, Laugh;* 1931: *The Criminal Code;* 1934: *Manhattan Melodrama;* 1937: *Fire Over England;* 1938: *Algiers* (Oscar-nominated); 1940: *Abe Lincoln in Illinois;* 1942: *Yankee Doodle Dandy;* 1943: *Air Force* (Oscar-nominated, as co-cinematographer), *The North Star* (Oscar-nominated); 1948: *Mr. Blandings Builds His Dream House;* 1955: *Pic-*nic; 1958: *The Old Man and the Sea* (Oscar-nominated); 1968: *The Heart Is a Lonely Hunter;* 1970: *The Molly Maguires.*

HOWELL, C. THOMAS. Actor. *(b. Dec. 7, 1966, Van Nuys, Calif.)* The son of stuntman Chris Howell, C. Thomas originally was interested in joining the rodeo circuit. He was named All-Around Cowboy by the California Junior Rodeo Association from 1978 to 1980 and even stunt doubled for young actors. That all changed with his debut (billed as Tom) as one of the neighborhood kids who helps *E.T. The Extraterrestrial* (1982) and his acclaimed performance as Pony Boy in Francis Ford Coppola's *The Outsiders* (1983). Bigger roles followed in *Grandview, U.S.A.* and the Russian invasion fantasy *Red Dawn* (both 1984), and then starring roles which boosted him to teen-idol status in *Secret Admirer* (1985), *The Hitcher,* and *Soul Man* (both 1986), in which he played a white student who masquerades as a black student for a scholarship. His work since then has been confined to such little-seen projects as *A Tiger's Tale* (1987), the ludicrous Zeffirelli-directed *Young Toscanini* (1987, opposite Elizabeth Taylor), *The Return of the Musketeers* (1989), *Side Out* (1990), *Nickel & Dime* (1992), and *That Night* (1993). He also played a featured role in *Gettysburg* (1993). Formerly married to Rae Dawn Chong, with whom he starred in *Soul Man* and *Far Out Man* (1990), a Chong family project.

HUBLEY, JOHN. Animator, director. *(b. May 21, 1914, Marinette, Wisc.; d. Feb. 21, 1977.)* An art director at the Walt Disney studio during its peak period of creativity (during production of *Snow White and the Seven Dwarfs, Pinocchio, Fantasia, Dumbo,* and *Bambi),* Hubley was active in the bitter Disney strike of 1941, and wound up moving with a number of his colleagues to the Columbia/Screen Gems studio. After a short time there, Hubley and some of his cohorts found themselves making training films for the Army's First Motion Picture Unit during World War 2. Many of them moonlighted on a campaign film for President Roosevelt called *Hell Bent for Election* (which Chuck Jones directed) that was executed in a bold, modern graphic style. Several people who'd worked on the film then formed an official partnership called United Productions of America (UPA), and Hubley joined them for an even bolder film called *Brotherhood of Man,* a plea for tolerance designed to help union organizers in the South.

UPA then landed a contract with Columbia Pictures for theatrical cartoons, and Hubley directed a pair of modern-style films with The Fox and Crow, *Robin Hoodlum* (1948, nominated for an Oscar) and *The Magic Fluke* (1949), before launching the studio's first (and most successful) cartoon series, featuring the near-sighted Mister Magoo. *Ragtime Bear* (1949) introduced the cantankerous character, whom Hubley directed again in *Spellbound Hound* (1950) and *Fuddy Duddy Buddy* (1951). By this time, UPA was winning critical notice for their innovative approach to animated cartoons. Blending modern-art graphics with often innovative, nonformulaic content, UPA broke down one barrier after another. Among Hubley's other personal triumphs: *Rooty Toot Toot* (1952), a stylish rendering of "Frankie and Johnny" that won an Academy Award, and some clever, beautifully designed linking sequences for the live-action feature *The Four Poster* (1952).

Unfortunately, the witch-hunt politics of the era forced Hubley to leave UPA and set out on his own. An independently backed animated production of the Broadway musical *Finian's Rainbow* lost its financing in midstream, but Hubley found financial salvation in the production of TV commercials, and artistic satisfaction by making at least one "personal" animated short every year, in collaboration with his wife, the former Faith Elliott. These highly individual, graphically advanced films—which reflected the Hubleys' love for jazz through the participation of such musicians as Dizzy Gillespie, Benny Carter, and Quincy Jones—won countless honors, including Academy Awards for *Moonbird* (1959), *The Hole* (1962), and *Herb Alpert and the Tijuana Brass Double Feature* (1966). Oscar nominations came their way for *Windy Day* (1968), *Of Men and Demons* (1970), and *Voyage to Next* (1974). Hubley's final film was a half-hour special that brought the *Doonesbury* comic strip to television,

in 1977. (Although made for television, it was nominated for an Academy Award.)

Since John's death, Faith Hubley has continued to make original and challenging films, along with her daughters Georgia and Emily and son Mark, all of whom provided charming and wonderful soundtracks for their parents' earlier films when they were unknowingly tape-recorded while at play.

HUDSON, ERNIE. Actor. *(b. Dec. 17, 1945, Benton Harbor, Mich.)* Skilled black actor known to the world as Winston Zeddemore, one of the ectoplasm-chasers in *Ghostbusters* (1984) and its 1989 sequel. Before this, Hudson appeared in the films *Leadbelly* (1976), *The Main Event* (1979), and *The Jazz Singer* (1980). After the success of *Ghostbusters,* he was featured as the Black Muslim prisoner in *Weeds* (1987) and won kudos for his work as the retarded, heroic handyman in *The Hand That Rocks the Cradle* (1992), a sensitive performance that deserved a better film to showcase it. Recent credits include the TV miniseries "Wild Palms" (1993) and *Sugar Hill, The Crow, Airheads, The Cowboy Way, No Escape* (all 1994), and *Congo* (1995).

HUDSON, HUGH. Director. *(b. Aug. 25, 1936, London.)* TV commercial helmer turned moviemaker whose first feature, *Chariots of Fire* (1981), about two runners in the 1924 Olympics, won an Oscar for Best Picture and earned him a Best Director nomination. His subsequent efforts include the stately *Greystoke: The Legend of Tarzan, Lord of the Apes* (1984), the colossal misfire *Revolution* (1985), and the underrated, small-scale youth drama *Lost Angels* (1989).

HUDSON, ROCHELLE. Actress. *(b. Mar. 6, 1914, Oklahoma City; d. Jan. 17, 1972.)* Wholesomely pretty brunette who worked throughout the 1930s and early 1940s as an ingenue both in A and B pictures (mostly the latter), projecting great warmth and personality. In her earliest films Hudson mostly played wide-eyed innocents, although she quickly grew into more worldly characterizations. Her first picture was *Laugh and Get Rich* (1930),

and her first leading role was that of a female Tarzan in *Savage Girl* (1932). She
appeared a number of times with Will
Rogers, often as his daughter: *Mr. Skitch*
(1933), *Doctor Bull, Judge Priest* (both
1934), and *Life Begins at Forty* (1935),
but is perhaps best remembered as Claudette Colbert's daughter in 1934's *Imitation of Life,* and an ideally cast Cosette in
the 1935 *Les Miserables.* In 1942 she accompanied her then-husband, a Naval reserve officer, to Central America, where
she worked for Naval Intelligence! Hudson returned to picture work in 1947, but
appeared only sporadically on-screen
thereafter, owing to domestic strife and
nagging health problems.
OTHER FILMS INCLUDE: 1932: *Hell's
Highway;* 1933: *Wild Boys of the Road, She
Done Him Wrong;* 1935: *Curly Top* (with
Shirley Temple); 1936: *Everybody's Old Man;*
1937: *Born Reckless;* 1938: *Mr. Moto Takes a
Chance;* 1939: *Missing Daughters;* 1940: *Island of Doomed Men;* 1941: *Meet Boston
Blackie;* 1942: *Queen of Broadway;* 1948: *The
Devil's Cargo;* 1955: *Rebel Without a Cause*
(as Natalie Wood's mother); 1964: *Strait-
Jacket;* 1967: *Return From the Past.*

HUDSON, ROCK. Actor. *(b. Nov. 17,
1925, Winnetka, Ill., as Roy Scherer, Jr.; d. Oct.
2, 1985.)* He cut an imposing figure on the
big screen: Tall, brawny, boyishly handsome, with wavy dark hair and a dazzling
smile, Rock Hudson was one of the last
major stars developed under the studio
system. And make no mistake about it: he
was wholly a studio creation. A former
mail carrier, mechanic, and truck driver,
he determined to break into films on the
strength of his looks alone and, after getting a bit role in Warner Bros.' *Fighter
Squadron* (1948), won a berth at
Universal-International. He was given lessons in acting, elocution, riding, fencing,
and singing; his teeth were capped and he
learned how to hit the "marks" placed on
movie sets by cameramen to ensure critical focusing. He posed for hundreds of
publicity photos, which were already appearing in fan magazines before he'd appeared in his first U-I film, *Undertow*
(1949).

Owing to his total lack of acting experience, Hudson was brought along slowly,
playing bits and supporting roles in *One
Way Street, Winchester '73, Peggy, The*
Desert Hawk (all 1950), *The Fat Man, Air
Cadet, Tomahawk, Iron Man, Bright Victory* (all 1951), *Bend of the River,* and
Here Come the Nelsons (both 1952) before getting his first lead, opposite Yvonne
De Carlo in *Scarlet Angel* (1952), a modestly budgeted Western. After taking a
few more supporting roles, he starred in
several mundane actioners—including *The
Golden Blade, Back to God's Country*
(both 1953), and *Taza, Son of Cochise*
(1954)—before winning his star-making
role, that of a drunken playboy who becomes a respected surgeon after unintentionally blinding costar Jane Wyman in an
auto accident, in a remake of the 1935 hit
Magnificent Obsession (1954). He received his best reviews to date, and the
picture, like its predecessor, was an enormous box-office success.

Hudson continued to star in big-budget
Universal-International films, alternating
action pictures with glossy soap operas
throughout the decade: *Bengal Brigade*
(also 1954), *Captain Lightfoot, One Desire, All That Heaven Allows* (all 1955),
*Never Say Goodbye, Battle Hymn, Written
on the Wind, Four Girls in Town* (all
1956), *The Tarnished Angels* (1957), *Twilight for the Gods* (1958), and *This Earth
Is Mine* (1959). He got the best U-I had to
offer, but his best roles during this period
were those he got while on loan. George
Stevens cast him as maverick oilman Bick
Benedict, a performance for which he received his only Oscar nomination, in
George Stevens' massive adaptation of
Edna Ferber's *Giant* (1956, which paired
him with Elizabeth Taylor, who would become a lifelong friend), and David O.
Selznick selected him to play an Army
ambulance driver opposite Jennifer Jones
in Ernest Hemingway's WW1 saga *A
Farewell to Arms* (1957).

Back at Universal, Hudson entered a
new phase of his career when he made
Pillow Talk (1959) with Doris Day; a
lively, fast-paced sex comedy, it demonstrated his adeptness with lighthearted,
witty, and ever-so-slightly naughty material, and set the pattern for several spin-
offs, also costarring Day. By now at the
zenith of his personal popularity, Hudson
spent most of the next decade at Universal, starring in *The Last Sunset, Come
September, Lover, Come Back* (all 1961),
The Spiral Road (1962), *A Gathering of
Eagles* (1963), *Man's Favorite Sport?*

(1964, directed by Howard Hawks, and a particular favorite of movie-comedy aficionados), *Send Me No Flowers* (also 1964), *A Very Special Favor* (1965), *Blindfold* (1966), and *Tobruk* (1967), among others. His infrequent forays off the Universal lot included starring stints in *Seconds* (1966), a gripping (and decidedly nonglamorous) psychological thriller directed by John Frankenheimer, and one of Hudson's all-time best films; *Ice Station Zebra* (1968), a Cold War suspense drama set in the frozen Arctic; *A Fine Pair* (1969), a dismal comedy-thriller that could have been called "A Fine Mess"; and *The Undefeated* (also 1969), a Civil War Western in which Hudson costarred with John Wayne.

The 1970s saw both the demise of the studio system and a gradual diminishing of Hudson's box-office potency, and even while appearing in *Darling Lili* (a 1970 fiasco in which he supported Julie Andrews), *Hornets' Nest* (also 1970), *Pretty Maids All in a Row* (1971, a clever black comedy), *Showdown* (1973), *Embryo* (1976), *Avalanche* (1978), *The Mirror Crack'd* (1980, costarring him with three of his contemporaries—Elizabeth Taylor, Tony Curtis, and Kim Novak), and *The Ambassador* (1984), he lavished much of his energy on the small screen, where he top-lined the popular TV series "McMillan and Wife" (1971–77), made a handful of telefilms, and guest-starred on the hugely popular "Dynasty" (1984–85). Appearing in the latter series, Hudson seemed tired and gaunt—and he was. By that time he was already fighting the AIDS virus, a struggle he lost in 1985. But before he died, Hudson courageously went public with details of the disease and how he caught it: Rock Hudson, the romantic idol of millions, had been a closet homosexual; his earlier marriage had been a union of convenience.

HUGHES, BARNARD. Actor. *(b. July 16, 1915, Bedford Falls, N.Y.)* Currently the screen's most accomplished delineator of crusty-but-lovable old men, this white-haired character actor has been delighting audiences for decades on stage, TV, and in movies. His more memorable film roles include the homosexual conventioneer Towny in *Midnight Cowboy* (1969), the foul-mouthed general in *Where's Poppa?* (1970), a murderous wacko in *The Hospital* (1971), the judge in *Oh, God!* (1977), Goldie Hawn's father in *Best Friends,* a computer scientist in *Tron* (both 1982), a soda-guzzling grandfather in *The Lost Boys* (1987), and a cranky small-town medic in *Doc Hollywood* (1991). On TV, he won an Emmy as a senile judge on "Lou Grant," and starred in such sitcoms as "Doc," (1975–76) "Mr. Merlin," (1981–82) "The Cavanaughs," (1986–89) and "Blossom" (1991–   ). He won a Tony Award playing a meddlesome Irish father in "Da," and recreated the role in the 1988 film. Most recently he appeared in *Sister Act 2: Back in the Habit* (1993).

HUGHES, JOHN. Screenwriter, producer, director. *(b. Feb. 18, 1950, Chicago.)* A former writer for "National Lampoon" magazine, this fabulously successful filmmaker, arguably the most facile chronicler of the baby boom zeitgeist, has tapped into middle-class suburban life and sensibilities with considerable skill. He made his name in Hollywood as screenwriter of *National Lampoon's Class Reunion* (1982), *National Lampoon's Vacation,* and *Mr. Mom* (both 1983), the success of which earned him a chance to direct, from his own script, *Sixteen Candles* (1984), starring Molly Ringwald. This breakthrough film tapped into a teenage audience as few others ever managed to do, articulating adolescent angst with insight and humor. His next, more serious effort, *The Breakfast Club* (1985), also dealt with teenagers' feelings of self-doubt, and served as a springboard for a whole generation of Brat Pack stars. *Weird Science* (1985) went way off-course, but *Pretty in Pink* (1986, again with Ringwald) and *Ferris Bueller's Day Off* (also 1986) reaffirmed Hughes' uncanny knack for communicating with 1980s adolescents.

Hughes then moved into adult territory with *Planes, Trains & Automobiles* (1987) and the twenty-something comedy-drama *She's Having a Baby* (1988), before reverting to kid stuff in *Uncle Buck* (1989) and *Curly Sue* (1991). These later films veer between cogent observation, puerile jokes, and heavy-handed sentimentality, but audiences seem to respond even if critics don't. (John Candy, the star of *Planes* and *Uncle Buck,* became Hughes' good-luck charm, appearing, sometimes without billing, in many of the producer's films, often in hilarious cameo roles.)

Beginning with *Pretty in Pink*, the prolific Hughes started assigning some of his scripts to other directors, retaining control as executive producer. Since then, most of his scripts have been directed by others, including Howard Deutch (*Pretty in Pink, Some Kind of Wonderful, The Great Outdoors*), Jeremiah S. Chechik (*National Lampoon's Christmas Vacation*), Brian Gordon (*Career Opportunities*), Peter Faiman (*Dutch*), and Chris Columbus, who with Hughes turned *Home Alone* (1990) and *Home Alone 2: Lost in New York* (1992) into a virtual cottage industry. Hughes then patterned *Dennis the Menace* (1993) after his winning *Home Alone* formula, letting Nick Castle direct the slapstick comedy. In 1994 Hughes wrote and coproduced *Baby's Day Out*.

HUGHES, WENDY. Actress. *(b. July 29, 1950, Melbourne, Australia.)* Like fellow countrywoman Judy Davis, Hughes has established herself as an actress of seemingly limitless range, though she has not enjoyed her colleague's international success. After studying at Australia's National Institute of Dramatic Arts, she acted with The Melbourne Theatre Company for two years and made early films like *Petersen* (1974), *Sidecar Racers* (1975), and *High Rolling* (1977). Phillip Noyce's *Newsfront* (1978) gave her a breakthrough role as a tough film editor, and she followed with a string of memorable performances: as an upper-class woman involved with a Greek journalist in *Kostas*, Judy Davis' aunt in *My Brilliant Career* (both 1979), a shy, 30-year-old virgin embarking on a relationship in *Lonely Hearts* (1981), a rich woman battling for custody of her sister's nephew in *Careful, He Might Hear You* (1983), and a wife who leaves her husband in *My First Wife* (1984). This brilliant actress, who can appear either plain or beautiful, moved to Hollywood to costar with Peter Falk in the comedy *Happy New Year* (1987), which wasted her talent—and barely got released. It was a portent of things to come; she never caught on with American producers, though she continues to work in both the U.S. and Australia. She was featured in the TV miniseries "Amerika" (1987) and "A Woman Named Jackie" (1991, as Jacqueline Kennedy's mother). OTHER FILMS INCLUDE: 1987: *Echoes of Paradise, Warm Nights on a Slow Moving Train;* 1989: *The Heist* (made-for-cable); 1992: *Wild Orchid 2: Two Shades of Blue;* 1994: *Princess Caraboo.*

HULCE, TOM. Actor. *(b. Dec. 6, 1953, Plymouth, Mich.)* Best known for his engaging but unorthodox portrayal of hedonistic, cackling composer Wolfgang Amadeus Mozart in Milos Forman's hit film *Amadeus* (1984, a performance for which he was Oscar-nominated), Tom Hulce is one of those chameleonlike actors who can walk down the street unrecognized. Minus the powdered wig, he has played such diverse characters as a cartoonist in the stupefyingly awful *Slamdance* (1987), a retarded garbage man in the critically acclaimed *Dominick and Eugene* (1988), and a degenerate gambler in *Parenthood* (1989). Hulce—who studied at the North Carolina School of the Arts—made his film debut in *September 30, 1955* (1978), but first attracted attention as the only "normal" frat boy in *National Lampoon's Animal House* (also 1978). A boyish, sensitive type, Hulce has also appeared in *Those Lips, Those Eyes* (1980), *Echo Park* (1986), *Black Rainbow* (1989), and *The Inner Circle* (1991). He acted in theatrical productions of "Equus" (which marked his Broadway debut), "Julius Caesar," "Candide," "The Sea Gull," and "A Few Good Men." Known to his colleagues for his thorough preparation for his acting roles, Hulce made his directorial stage debut with the play "Sleep Around Town." In 1993 he had one of his best film roles in years, as the self-consciously slimy lawyer in *Fearless* (1993). In 1994 he appeared in *Mary Shelley's Frankenstein.*

HULL, HENRY. Actor. *(b. Oct. 3, 1890, Louisville, Ky.; d. Mar. 8, 1977.)* The son of a theater critic, Hull initially pursued an engineering career before succumbing to the lure of the footlights, as an actor and playwright. Shortly after making his Broadway debut in 1916 he acted in his first movie, but concentrated on theater work until 1934, when he went to Hollywood to star in *Great Expectations* and then take the title role in *Werewolf of London*

(1935), and became involved in film work. Tall and slender, and possessing a rich, cultured voice, he played a wide variety of supporting roles over the next 30 years, periodically returning to the stage. (His greatest triumph was his interpretation of Jeeter Lester in the original production of "Tobacco Road.")

OTHER FILMS INCLUDE: 1938: *Three Comrades, Boys Town;* 1939: *Stanley and Livingstone, Jesse James* (as The Major, a part he repeated in the following year's *The Return of Frank James);* 1941: *High Sierra;* 1944: *Lifeboat* (one of his best roles); 1947: *Mourning Becomes Electra;* 1948: *Portrait of Jennie;* 1949: *The Fountainhead, The Great Gatsby;* 1958: *The Buccaneer;* 1961: *Master of the World;* 1966: *The Chase;* 1967: *A Covenant With Death.*

HUNT, HELEN. Actress. *(b. June 15, 1963, Los Angeles.)* She made her acting debut, in the TV movie "Pioneer Woman," at the age of nine—she is the daughter of famed theater director and acting coach Gordon Hunt. Since then, Hunt has appeared in numerous TV projects, plays, and films but this versatile and appealing young actress has just come into her own in the 1990s. She appeared in *Girls Just Want to Have Fun* (1985), played Kathleen Turner's daughter in *Peggy Sue Got Married* (1986) and Matthew Broderick's love interest in *Project X* (1987) and has also appeared in *Miles From Home* (1988), *Next of Kin* (1989), the low-budget sci-fi films *Trancers* (1985) and *Trancers II* (1991), and the direct-to-video comedy *Only You* (1991). Overdue for a break on the big screen, Hunt gave excellent performances as a married woman having an affair with a paraplegic writer in *The Waterdance* (1992) and as an aging Billy Crystal's youthful talent agent in *Mr. Saturday Night* (also 1992). After years of appearances in episodic TV and made-for-TV movies, she finally attained stardom in the winning sitcom "Mad About You" (1992–) opposite Paul Reiser.

HUNT, LINDA. Actress. *(b. Apr. 2, 1945, Morristown, N.J.)* This tiny, homuncular supporting player won an Oscar for playing a man in *The Year of Living Dangerously* (1983), one of her earliest films. (And certainly her best to date, incidentally.) The problem with accomplishing such a feat: How does one top it? If that's impossible, it's no fault of Hunt's; she's been highly effective—albeit used mainly for novelty value—in such films as *Popeye* (1980), *Dune* (1984), *Silverado* (1985), and *Kindergarten Cop* (1990). Other credits include *The Bostonians* (1984) and *Eleni* (1985). She raised eyebrows with a superb characterization of Alice B. Toklas in *Waiting for the Moon* (1987), an otherwise ponderous and uninteresting film. She recently played the Lotte Lenya–inspired villainess in *If Looks Could Kill* (1991). Other recent credits include *Rain Without Thunder, Twenty Bucks, Younger and Younger* (1993); *Ready to Wear/Prêt-à-Porter* (1994), and *Pocahontas* (1995, voice only); she also starred in the short-lived science-fiction TV series "Space Rangers" (1992).

HUNT, MARSHA. Actress. *(b. Oct. 17, 1917, Chicago, as Marcia Virginia Hunt.)* Pretty (sometimes radiantly so), slender actress with big, expressive eyes and one of the warmest smiles ever to flash across the screen. She never quite caught the brass ring of stardom, despite possessing the requisite talent and charm. A former Powers model, she was signed by Paramount, and made an effective debut in *The Virginia Judge* (1935). Hunt played demure, virginal ingenues in most of her 1930s pictures, including *The Accusing Finger* (1936), *Murder Goes to College, Born to the West* (both 1937), *Come On Leathernecks* (1938), and *Star Reporter* (1939). She only appeared in a couple of A's for Paramount: *College Holiday* (1936) and *Easy Living* (1937).

Hunt was signed by MGM in 1939, and that studio should have provided her with the Big Break, but instead she found herself running in place again: leads in unimportant (if well-made) programmers, character parts in big pictures. (They did give her a few opportunities to sing, which she did quite well.) Her films for MGM include *The Hardys Ride High* (1939), *Pride and Prejudice* (1940), *Blossoms in the Dust* (1941), *The Affairs of Martha* (her first top-billed appearance at Metro), *Kid Glove Killer, Seven Sweethearts* (all 1942), *Cry Havoc, Thousands Cheer, The Human Comedy* (all 1943),

Music for Millions (1944), *A Letter for Evie,* and *The Valley of Decision* (both 1945).

She began freelancing after World War 2, landing leads in some interesting but minor films, including *Carnegie Hall* (1947), *The Inside Story, Raw Deal* (both 1948), *Jigsaw, Take One False Step,* and *Mary Ryan, Detective* (all 1949). She was a lovely mother to Bobby Driscoll in *The Happy Time* (1952), which was released around the time she was blacklisted after testifying before the House Un-American Activities Committee (she'd always been, and continues to be, an activist in liberal causes). Hunt got some minor parts in cheesy late 1950s films and abandoned movies around 1960, but returned to the screen several times in later years, playing Timothy Bottoms' mother in *Johnny Got His Gun* (1971, written by fellow blacklist victim Dalton Trumbo) and in a small role in *Rich and Famous* (1981). She has also appeared on many TV series in guest shots. The honorary mayor of Sherman Oaks, California, since 1980, Hunt remains active (and even appeared in an episode of "Star Trek: The Next Generation"). In 1993 she produced a visual autobiography, "The Way We Wore," emphasizing changes in fashions over the years.

HUNTER, HOLLY. Actress. *(b. Feb. 2, 1958, Conyers, Ga.)* Diminutive actress whose versatility is her trump card; she can be pixieish or heartbreakingly intense. Hunter was educated at Pittsburgh's Carnegie Mellon Institute before acting in films, and made an inauspicious screen debut in *The Burning* (1981), a dismal slasher film. She worked in several TV movies and in the Goldie Hawn starrer *Swing Shift* (1984) before attracting attention as the lovesick, maternal police officer Ed in *Raising Arizona* (1987). She had an even meatier role as the self-driven TV news producer that same year in James Brooks' *Broadcast News.* Her richly detailed characterization of a successful workaholic earned her an Oscar nomination for Best Actress. Since then, Hunter has continually demonstrated her ability to command the screen in leading roles. She was Richard Dreyfuss' star-crossed lover in Steven Spielberg's *Always,* and recreated her stage role as a plucky small-town girl who aspires to greatness in *Miss Fire-*

cracker (both 1989). She reteamed with *Always* star Richard Dreyfuss as a plain-Jane type who's swept off her feet by a fast-talking salesman in *Once Around* (1991). But everyone's got a skeleton in his or her cinematic closet, and Hunter's is *Animal Behavior* (1989), an alleged "comedy" that is truly mindboggling in its awfulness. She has appeared in a handful of notable TV movies, including *Crazy in Love* (1992) and won Emmys for her memorable performances in *Roe vs. Wade* (1989) and *The Positively True Adventures of the Alleged Texas Cheerleader-Murdering Mom* (1993), and followed that triumph with two completely variant movie roles: as Gary Busey's sexpot secretary in *The Firm,* and as the repressed, mute 19th-century immigrant woman in Jane Campion's *The Piano* (both also 1993). This remarkable performance won her a Best Actress award at the Cannes Film Festival, but it was her two-movie parlay that won her twin Oscar nominations, and an Oscar for *The Piano.*

HUNTER, JEFFREY. Actor. *(b. Nov. 25, 1925, New Orleans, as Henry Herman McKinnies; d. May 27, 1969.)* He belongs to that small fraternity of actors who've played Jesus Christ on the screen (in 1961's *King of Kings),* and while he may or may not have been the movies' most convincing Son of God, he was surely the prettiest. This boyish, blue-eyed actor, almost absurdly handsome, probably couldn't have held his own with Olivier, but his screen persona combined virility and sensitivity in a way atypical of most Hollywood leading men. A former radio actor and summer-stock player, he was contracted by 20th Century-Fox (where his early career paralleled that of another handsome juvenile, Robert Wagner) in 1951. Among Hunter's early films were *Call Me Mister, Take Care of My Little Girl* (both 1951), *Red Skies of Montana, Belles on Their Toes* (both 1952), *Princess of the Nile* (1954), *White Feather,* and *Seven Angry Men* (both 1955).

On loan to Warners, Hunter played the excitable young man who trailed along with John Wayne in his quest for kidnapped Natalie Wood in John Ford's *The Searchers* (1956), and more than held his own in his scenes with the Duke. (Ford used Hunter again in 1958's *The Last*

Hurrah and 1960's *Sergeant Rutledge.)* Back at Fox, he and fellow pretty-boy Bob Wagner appeared together in *A Kiss Before Dying* (1956), an underrated thriller. *In Love and War* (1958), *Hell to Eternity* (1960), and *The Longest Day* (1962) saw Hunter in good form, but his career took an unexplained downturn after the worldwide success of *King of Kings*. He spent several years working in minor European films before returning stateside to assume the role of Captain Christopher Pike in the abortive 1965 pilot for the "Star Trek" TV series (although the Hunter pilot did air, worked into a two-part episode called "The Menagerie"). Roles in *A Guide for the Married Man* (1967), *Custer of the West,* and *The Private Navy of Sgt. O'Farrell* (both 1968) followed, none of which did anything to improve Hunter's standing. He died after surgery following a bad fall. He was once married to actress Barbara Rush.

HUNTER, KIM. Actress. *(b. Nov. 12, 1922, Detroit, as Janet Cole.)* She put up with a lot of grief from Marlon Brando in *A Streetcar Named Desire* (1951)—being the "Stella" for whom he was shouting—but it paid off with an Academy Award for Best Supporting Actress. Unfortunately, however, it was the high point of her movie career, partially because she was blacklisted for several years during the McCarthy era. On stage from age 17, the Actors' Studio student made an impressive screen debut as the fresh-faced ingenue of *The Seventh Victim* (1943), a creepy low-budget thriller from producer Val Lewton. She played a similar role in another stylish B, *When Strangers Marry* (1944, directed by William Castle and costarring Robert Mitchum, then on his way up stardom's ladder), and was cast by Michael Powell and Emeric Pressburger in their brilliant fantasy, *Stairway to Heaven* (1946).

Hunter returned to Broadway in 1947, where she created the part of Stella Kowalski in the original stage production of "Streetcar," and didn't make any more movies until reprising that role for the screen in 1951. She remains active on stage and television today.
OTHER FILMS INCLUDE: 1952: *Anything Can Happen, Deadline U.S.A.;* 1956: *Storm Center;* 1957: *The Young Stranger;* 1958: *Money, Women and Guns;* 1964: *Lilith;* 1968:

Planet of the Apes (smothered beneath monkey makeup, as the sympathetic simian scientist she played in 1970's *Beneath the Planet of the Apes* and 1971's *Escape From the Planet of the Apes); 1968: The Swimmer;* 1986: *The Kindred.*

HUNTER, ROSS. Producer, actor. *(b. May 6, 1916, Cleveland.)* Former schoolteacher and actor who, after becoming a movie producer in the early 1950s, turned out a string of mainstream Hollywood hits. As a Columbia contract player in the mid 1940s, he acted in *Louisiana Hayride* (1944), *A Guy, a Gal, and a Pal* (1945), and *Hit the Hay* (1946), among others, before returning to the classroom for a number of years. As a producer at Universal-International, his typical ingredients were big stars, lavish production values, lush musical scores, and plenty of schmaltz. His films, many of them remakes of classic movies, very much reflect his nostalgia for and affinity with old-time Hollywood.
FILMS (AS PRODUCER) INCLUDE: 1954: *Magnificent Obsession;* 1955: *The Spoilers, All That Heaven Allows;* 1957: *Tammy and the Bachelor, My Man Godfrey;* 1959: *Imitation of Life, Pillow Talk* (which kicked off the Doris Day-Rock Hudson cycle); 1960: *Midnight Lace;* 1961: *Back Street, Flower Drum Song;* 1963: *The Thrill of It All;* 1964: *The Chalk Garden;* 1965: *The Art of Love;* 1966: *Madame X;* 1967: *Thoroughly Modern Millie;* 1970: *Airport* (a huge success that launched the 1970s' disaster-film vogue); 1973: *Lost Horizon.*

HUNTER, TAB. Actor. *(b. July 1, 1931, New York City, as Arthur Gelien.)* Despite having no formal acting training whatsoever, this blond boy-next-door type became one of the 1950s' biggest teen idols due to extensive exposure on film, TV, and Broadway. His earliest movies include such films as *The Lawless* (1950) and *Gun Belt* (1953), with leads in *The Girl He Left Behind* and *The Burning Hills* (both 1956) soon following. His career hit its peak in 1958, when he starred opposite Gwen Verdon in the baseball musical *Damn Yankees* (1958). "The Tab Hunter Show," a sitcom in which he played a cartoonist, lasted from September 1960 to September 1961. While his 1970s filmic output was

meager, in 1981 he returned to the big screen with a vengeance, savagely parodying his squeaky-clean image in John Waters' cult hit *Polyester* (1981), as Todd Tomorrow, a coke-snorting art-house drive-in owner. He rejoined costar Divine in *Lust in the Dust* (1985).
OTHER FILMS INCLUDE: 1965: *The Loved One;* 1972: *The Life and Times of Judge Roy Bean;* 1982: *Grease 2;* 1989: *Out of the Dark.*

HUPPERT, ISABELLE. Actress. *(b. Mar. 16, 1955, Paris.)* Her rather plain looks belie an almost shockingly smoldering sensuality, exhibited in such films as *Loulou* (1980), in which she plays a woman content to have a purely physical affair with loutish Gerard Depardieu, and *Sincerely, Charlotte* (1987), in which she was cast against type as a flat-out vamp. Huppert made her screen debut at age 16 in *Faustine* (1971, aka *Growing Up)* and has since become an extremely seasoned and compelling actress (on stage and TV in France, as well as on film). In 1978 she won the Cannes Film Festival's Best Actress award for her chilling portrayal of the murderous *Violette Noziere.* Unfortunately, her first major American-made film, Michael Cimino's doomed *Heaven's Gate* (1980), flopped horribly and set back her bid for U.S. stardom. She did appear to good effect in *The Bedroom Window* (1987), lending some distinction to that middling thriller. In 1988 she starred in Claude Chabrol's devastating *The Story of Women,* about a housewife who becomes an abortionist in WW2 France.
OTHER FILMS INCLUDE: 1972: *Cesar and Rosalie;* 1975: *Rosebud;* 1977: *The Lacemaker;* 1980: *Every Man for Himself;* 1981: *Coup de Torchon;* 1983: *Entre Nous;* 1991: *Madame Bovary;* 1993: *Love After Love;* 1994: *Amateur.*

HURT, JOHN. Actor. *(b. Jan. 22, 1940, Derbyshire, England.)* After giving up his training as a painter at London's St. Martin's School for Art, John Hurt made his London stage debut in 1962 as Knocker White in "Infanticide in the House of Fred Ginger," a performance that ensured his continuance of a career before the footlights. (The gifted young thespian went on to perform with the Royal Shakespeare Company and over the years, he appeared in numerous productions with them.) Hurt also made his film debut in 1962 with a role in *The Wild and the Willing.* International recognition followed his vibrant performance in Fred Zinnemann's 1966 classic, *A Man for All Seasons,* which won six Oscars. Hurt, a quiet, somewhat sinister looking fellow who's never as effective as when he's limning characters who dwell in their dark sides, alternated movie work with stage stints.
Hurt's films include *Before Winter Comes, Sinful Davey* (both 1969), *10 Rillington Place* (1970), *The Pied Piper* (1972), *The Ghoul* (1975), *Spectre* (1977), *The Naked Civil Servant* (1978; TV movie as Quentin Crisp), *Midnight Express* (1978, in an Oscar-nominated turn), *Alien* (1979), *Heaven's Gate* (1980), *The Elephant Man* (1980, again Oscar-nominated for his demanding role, rendered unrecognizable under heavy makeup, but still enormously affecting), *History of the World—Part I* (1981, as Jesus), *Partners* (1982), *The Osterman Weekend* (1983), *The Hit, 1984* (both 1984), *Jake Speed* (1986), *From the Hip* (1987, singlehandedly making the film tolerable with his highly controlled performance as an arrogant murder suspect), *Vincent* (also 1987, as the voice of Vincent van Gogh), *Spaceballs* (also 1987, in a parody of his *Alien* role), *Aria, White Mischief* (both 1988, memorable in the latter as a dissipated Englishman in Africa), *Scandal* (1989, his best part in years, as social gadfly Stephen Ward, who becomes involved with British call girls Christine Keeler and Mandy Rice-Davies), *The Field, Frankenstein Unbound* (both 1990), *King Ralph* (1991), *Great Moments in Aviation* (1993) and *Even Cowgirls Get the Blues* (1994).

HURT, MARY BETH. Actress. *(b. Sept. 26, 1948, Marshalltown, Iowa.)* This pretty, diminutive, highly acclaimed stage performer—like many of her theater-seasoned contemporaries—hasn't had the greatest opportunities presented to her in film, but has nonetheless impressed with a string of capable portrayals. Debuting in Woody Allen's dour *Interiors* (1978), Hurt first raised eyebrows as Helen, the loving but wandering wife, in *The World According to Garp* (1982). She's held her own in movies of otherwise dubious merit, such as *D.A.R.Y.L.* (1985), *Parents,* and *Slaves of New York* (both 1989). Hurt enjoyed one of her best screen opportunities as a spurned wife in 1991's *Defenseless.* Divorced from actor William Hurt, she is now married to screenwriter-director Paul Schrader. Her other films include *Head Over Heels/Chilly Scenes of Winter* (1979) and *Compromising Positions* (1985). She was seen on TV in the comedy "Tattinger's" (aka "Nick and Hillary") from 1988–89 and "Working It Out" (1990). Recent credits include *My Boyfriend's Back, The Age of Innocence, Six Degrees of Separation,* and *Shimmer* (all 1993).

HURT, WILLIAM. Actor. *(b. Mar. 20, 1950, Washington, D.C.)* This handsome, cerebral, WASPy-looking actor has amassed an amazingly diverse gallery of performances, and is perhaps the most talented of the generation of actors that came to prominence during the 1980s. After studying theology in London and Boston (and acting at Juilliard), he performed in many stage productions and made his film debut as the intense, obsessed scientist in *Altered States* (1980). Movie audiences found him more accessible as the mild-mannered janitor in the thriller *Eyewitness* (1981), which led to two star-making leading roles for writer-director Lawrence Kasdan: the manipulated Southern lawyer in *Body Heat* (also 1981) and the impotent drug dealer in *The Big Chill* (1983).

Hurt established himself as an actor unafraid to assume totally different personas from film to film, and cemented that reputation as an imprisoned homosexual in *Kiss of the Spider Woman* (1985), winning a Best Actor Oscar (as well as honors at the Cannes Film Festival) for his chores. He also snared Oscar nominations as a teacher of deaf students in *Children of a Lesser God* (1986, opposite Marlee Matlin) and as a not-so-bright TV anchorman in *Broadcast News* (1987). He has continued to choose surprising and challenging roles, among them a Russian police inspector in *Gorky Park* (1983), the melancholy travel-book author in *The Accidental Tourist* (1988, directed by Kasdan), a comic would-be assassin in Kasdan's *I Love You to Death* (1990), Mia Farrow's wealthy and aloof husband in Woody Allen's *Alice* (also 1990, a wonderfully knowing performance in essenti-

ally a cameo role), a wisecracking, irreverent medico who is humanized by his own illness in *The Doctor* (1991), and the world traveler working on a machine to benefit blind people in *Until the End of the World* (also 1991). Hurt frequently returns to the stage; other film credits include *The Plague* (1992), *Mr. Wonderful* (1993), *Trial by Jury* (1994), and *Smoke* (1995).

HUSSEY, OLIVIA. Actress. *(b. Apr. 17, 1951, Buenos Aires.)* This dark-haired beauty made a stunning Juliet in Franco Zeffirelli's *Romeo and Juliet* (1968), and although her performance wasn't exactly sob-inducing, she scored at least a *few* points for being the only actress in screen history to play the part while in the proper age range. Hussey, who'd already appeared in TV shows and other movies (beginning with 1965's *The Battle of the Villa Fiorita),* became a "name" from the worldwide exposure as Juliet, but wasn't able to parlay that fame into stardom. She appeared in mostly undistinguished movies, including *All the Right Noises* (1969), *The Summertime Killer* (1971), *Lost Horizon* (1973), *Black Christmas* (1974), *The Cat and the Canary, Death on the Nile* (both 1978), *The Man With Bogart's Face,* and *Virus* (both 1980), before abandoning the big screen to do TV work here and abroad. Hussey's recent comeback attempt hasn't gotten very far to date; 1987's *Distortions* and 1990's *The Undeclared War* went right to videotape. *Psycho IV: The Beginning* (also 1990), in which she played the mother of Norman Bates, was produced for cable TV.

HUSTON, ANJELICA. Actress. *(b. July 8, 1951, Los Angeles.)* This striking, dark-haired actress made an inauspicious film debut in 1969's *A Walk With Love and Death,* directed by her famous father, John Huston, and played in two other films that same year—*Sinful Davey* (also directed by her dad) and *Hamlet*—before vanishing from the screen for many years and appearing only sporadically for many years after that. She surprised everybody—critics, audiences, movie-industry types—with her sly performance in 1985's brilliant black comedy *Prizzi's Honor* (again, directed by her father), which won her a Best Supporting Actress Oscar. Since then she's limned many fine characters in a string of meritorious movies with varying box-office success. She earned additional Academy Award nominations as Ron Silver's long-lost wife in *Enemies, A Love Story* (1989) and as John Cusack's amoral mom in *The Grifters* (1990).

Huston was perfectly cast as the sinister but svelte Morticia Addams in *The Addams Family* (1991) and its 1993 sequel, *Addams Family Values*. She teamed up with Jack Nicholson for *The Crossing Guard* (1995). As if to prove she could play women of a non-exotic nature as well, she starred in the outstanding 1993 miniseries "Family Pictures," following a woman's life over several decades through her relationship with her husband and children. In truth, Huston has little to prove; she has become one of the screen's finest, most original actresses.

OTHER FILMS INCLUDE: 1976: *Swashbuckler, The Last Tycoon;* 1981: *The Postman Always Rings Twice* (starring her longtime flame and *Prizzi's* costar Jack Nicholson); 1982: *Frances;* 1984: *The Ice Pirates, This Is Spinal Tap;* 1987: *Gardens of Stone, The Dead* (the latter John Huston's final directorial effort); 1988: *Mr. North* (directed by half-brother Danny Huston); 1989: *Crimes and Misdemeanors* (as the murdered mistress); 1990: *The Witches;* 1992: *The Player* (in a cameo); 1993: *Manhattan Murder Mystery, And the Band Played On* (made-for-TV); 1995: *The Perez Family.*

HUSTON, JOHN. Director, screenwriter, actor. (b. Aug. 5, 1906, Nevada, Mo.; d. Aug. 28, 1987.) A restless man with seemingly boundless energy but diffuse ambitions, John Huston made his mark on movie history as a writer and director, with many enduring screen classics and an almost equal number of flops to his credit. Born into a family of actors (his father was the distinguished Walter Huston), he performed on stage with his parents at the age of three. A sickly child, Huston eventually achieved physical fitness and even took up boxing in his teens. Tiring of that, he flirted with an acting career and married his high-school sweetheart, only to abandon both for the promise of adventure in the Cavalry. He wrote his first play, "Frankie and Johnny," in 1928. With the help of his father, John was given a Universal screenwriting contract in 1932. He contributed dialogue to two of his father's films, *A House Divided* and *Law and Order,* as well as *Murders in the Rue Morgue* (all 1932), before leaving the studio abruptly to go to Europe. Virtually penniless, he wandered around London and Paris for months before returning to America, where he briefly edited a magazine and dabbled in acting once again.

In 1938 Huston, by now remarried and over 30 years old, decided to "settle down" and apply himself to a career. He resumed writing for the screen, landing a Warner Bros. contract in 1938. After contributing to scripts for *Jezebel* (1938), *Juarez* (1939), *Dr. Ehrlich's Magic Bullet* (1940, for which he secured his first Academy Award nomination), and *High Sierra* (1941), Huston lobbied studio executives for a property to direct. He was given Dashiell Hammett's private-eye novel, "The Maltese Falcon," a studio-owned property that had already been filmed twice in the last decade. Huston crafted a taut, no-nonsense screenplay that was more faithful to the novel than the previous two adaptations, and eagerly accepted *High Sierra* star Humphrey Bogart as his leading man (after George Raft turned the part down). His father, still enjoying tremendous popularity, took a brief cameo for good luck. *The Maltese Falcon* (1941), a surprise hit, became the definitive private-eye picture, catapulting Bogart to major stardom, earning Huston another Oscar nod for the script, and cementing his status as a top director.

After writing *Sergeant York* (also 1941), which netted Huston his third Academy Award nomination, and directing the Bogart vehicle *Across the Pacific* and the domestic drama *In This Our Life* (both 1942), Huston went into the Signal Corps and turned out the wartime documentaries *Report from the Aleutians* (1943), *The Battle of San Pietro,* and *Let There Be Light* (both 1945), which were among the finest produced during World War 2. (The latter, a straightforward study of psychological problems in the military, was banned and went unseen until the 1970s.) He saw action on both the Pacific and European fronts, and attained the rank of major.

Back in Hollywood after the conflict, he made uncredited contributions to the screenplays of *The Killers* and *The Stranger* (both 1946) before resuming his career at Warner Bros. He initially tackled

B. Traven's dense novel *The Treasure of the Sierra Madre*, for which he recruited Bogart, his father Walter, and RKO cowboy star Tim Holt. Filmed in 1946 but unreleased until 1948, the screen version of their ill-fated odyssey in search of gold in Mexico won Huston Oscars both for his direction and his screenplay (and won Walter a Best Supporting Actor statuette). John also contributed an amusing cameo near the beginning of the picture. His other Warners films of the period, *Three Strangers* (1946, for which he wrote the script), *Key Largo* (1948, also with Bogart), and *We Were Strangers* (1949), were somewhat less successful, artistically if not commercially.

Huston moved to MGM, where he was immediately assigned to direct the Biblical spectacle *Quo Vadis?*, a project for which he had no enthusiasm whatsoever. He persuaded studio head Louis B. Mayer to release him from that obligation, and then produced, wrote, and directed *The Asphalt Jungle* (1950), a gritty urban crime drama that earned him more Oscar nominations and, ultimately, became a much-imitated classic of the film noir genre. Huston's next MGM film, *The Red Badge of Courage* (1951), faithfully adapted from Stephen Crane's harrowing Civil War novel, flopped miserably upon initial release but has since come to be recognized as one of Huston's best films. (He always despaired that it was taken from him and recut, however. The saga of its making, and unmaking, was recounted in Lillian Ross' classic 1952 book *Picture*.) He collaborated with prominent film critic (and faithful Huston booster) James Agee on the script for *The African Queen* (1951), which teamed Humphrey Bogart and Katharine Hepburn for unusually felicitous results. The film's critical and commercial success restored Huston's reputation and, once again, resulted in Oscar nods for his and Agee's screenplay and his direction; it also earned Bogey his only Academy Award.

Moulin Rouge (1952), a lush, colorful biography of the artist Toulouse-Lautrec starring Jose Ferrer, also netted Huston a Best Director nomination and was well received. But the director's subsequent efforts were erratic (possibly reflecting tumultuous changes in his personal life during the period). *Beat the Devil* (1954), filmed in Italy, was something of an in-

joke for Huston and Humphrey Bogart, with a spoofy, *Maltese Falcon*-esque script by the director and Truman Capote. It took him three years to get *Moby Dick* (1956) on screens, and Huston's moody treatment of the Melville story seemed inaccessible to many. After that, the quality and success of Huston's output varied considerably: *Heaven Knows, Mr. Allison* (1957) gave him another Oscar nomination (for his script), but *The Barbarian and the Geisha, The Roots of Heaven* (both 1958), *The Unforgiven* (1960), *Freud* (1962), *The List of Adrian Messenger* (1963), *The Night of the Iguana* (1964), *The Bible* (1966), *Reflections in a Golden Eye* (1967), *Casino Royale* (also 1967, codirected with several others), *Sinful Davey, A Walk With Love and Death* (both 1969, and both featuring his teenaged daughter Anjelica), and *The Kremlin Letter* (1970) showed a progressive and precipitous decline. Only *The Misfits* (1961) seemed up to Huston's earlier works—and even this film has achieved greater stature in the years since its initial release.

Huston began his screen acting career in 1963, earning an Oscar nod for his first supporting role, in *The Cardinal*. He also appeared in his own *Adrian Messenger, The Bible* (as Noah), *Casino Royale*, and *A Walk With Love and Death* (1969), and worked for other directors in *Candy* (1968), *De Sade* (1969), *Myra Breckinridge* (1970), *The Deserter* (1971), *Battle for the Planet of the Apes* (1973), *Chinatown* (1974, a standout as the film's heavy), *Breakout, The Wind and the Lion* (both 1975), *Sherlock Holmes in New York* (1976 telefilm), *The Great Battle* (1978), *The Visitor* (1979), *Winter Kills* (1979, as a Joseph P. Kennedy prototype), *Lovesick* (1983), and *Momo* (1986).

Huston directed and took a cameo role in *The Life and Times of Judge Roy Bean* (1972), a muddled revisionist Western, and the forgettable *The Mackintosh Man* (1973). *Fat City* (1972), a gritty story about a washed-up boxer, helped rehabilitate his directorial reputation, and *The Man Who Would Be King* (1975), a Kipling adventure story Huston originally hoped to film in the 1950s with Bogart and Clark Gable, restored him to critical favor with an Oscar nomination. *Wise Blood* (1979) showed the aging director more than equal to the task of adapting

Flannery O'Connor's Southern Gothic. But these were small, personal films; his more mainstream studio films *Phobia* (1980), *Victory* (1981), and *Annie* (1982, his only musical) were unmitigated disasters. What's more, Huston's health was failing. But he rebounded—physically and artistically—for a trio of films as mature and provocative as any he'd ever made, all of them adapted from unusual (even "difficult") novels: *Under the Volcano* (1984), *Prizzi's Honor* (1985), a black comedy about Mafia assassins that got Huston his final Oscar nod (and won daughter Anjelica an Oscar for Best Supporting Actress), and *The Dead* (1987), a James Joyce story adapted by his son Tony (and which also featured Anjelica). (He also directed a special film commemorating America's Bicentennial, *Independence,* in 1976.) At the time of his death Huston was handling preproduction chores and preparing the story for *Mr. North* (1988), which was ultimately directed by his son Danny. His role in the film was assumed by Robert Mitchum.

Huston, who was as colorful as any character he depicted on film, wrote an autobiography, "An Open Book," in 1980. Screenwriter Peter Viertel's fictionalized chronicle of Huston directing *The African Queen,* "White Hunter, Black Heart," published in 1953, became a film in 1990, with Clint Eastwood doing a pretty fair imitation of the director. Huston is also the only person to direct both a parent and a child to Oscar-winning performances. In fact, the Huston family is the only one in the Academy annals with three generations of Oscar winners. He was once married to actress Evelyn Keyes.

HUSTON, WALTER. Actor. *(b. Apr. 6, 1884, Toronto, as Walter Houghston; d. Apr. 7, 1950.)* A powerful, compelling performer who became the talkie era's first successful character lead, Huston's reputation—as one of America's finest actors—seems to grow with each passing year. A veteran of vaudeville and stock, Huston became a leading star on Broadway during the 1920s in such plays as "Mr. Pitt" and "Desire Under the Elms." He made his film debut in *Gentlemen of the Press* (1929, shot in Paramount's Astoria, New York, studio while he was appearing on Broadway) and made a strong impression as the reluctant villain Trampas, opposite Gary Cooper in *The Virginian* (both 1929). The following year he played the title role in D. W. Griffith's production *Abraham Lincoln.*

Hollywood kept Huston busy over the next few years, in such early talkie classics as *The Criminal Code* (1931), *American Madness, Law and Order* (as a thinly disguised Wyatt Earp in a Western parable—cowritten by his son John—with resonance to Prohibition-era gangsterism), *Rain* (all 1932), and *Gabriel Over the White House* (1933, one of his most fascinating roles, as a corrupt president transfigured by an unexplained heavenly influence). He also appeared in *Star Witness, The Ruling Voice* (both 1931), *Kongo, Night Court, Beast of the City* (all 1932), *Hell Below, The Prizefighter and the Lady, Ann Vickers, Storm at Daybreak* (all 1933), *Keep 'Em Rolling* (1934), *Transatlantic Tunnel* (1935), and *Rhodes of Africa* (1936), among others.

Huston scored his greatest personal triumph in both stage and screen adaptations of Sinclair Lewis's *Dodsworth,* playing the retired industrialist who sheds his nagging, unfaithful wife for true love with an American expatriate in Europe. Huston received a 1936 Oscar nomination for his solid, intelligent work in that film, although he more or less abandoned movies for the next few years (except for supporting turns in 1938's *Of Human Hearts* and 1939's *The Light That Failed*). He earned another Academy Award nomination for his canny performance as "Mr. Scratch" in *All That Money Can Buy* (1941), the screen adaptation of Stephen Vincent Benet's "The Devil and Daniel Webster," scored a triumph on Broadway in "Knickerbocker Holiday" (singing "September Song"), and played a bit in his son John Huston's directorial debut, *The Maltese Falcon* (1941, as the mortally wounded ship captain who brings Bogart the Falcon).

The role of George M. Cohan's father in *Yankee Doodle Dandy* (1942) brought Huston his first Academy nomination for Best Supporting Actor. He appeared in John Ford's propagandistic *December 7th* (1942), Howard Hughes's oft-delayed *The Outlaw* (filmed in 1941), played in the Russian-themed *Mission to Moscow* and *The North Star* (both 1943), and was misguidedly cast as an Asian in *Dragon Seed*

(1944). (Many thought of him as a quintessentially American actor.) *And Then
There Were None* (1945), based on a novel
by Agatha Christie, gave Huston a delicious supporting role as a drunken doctor
who may also be a murderer. Huston was
among the all-star cast in David O.
Selznick's epic Technicolor Western, *Duel
in the Sun* (1946), and finally won an Oscar for his rich supporting role in son
John's *The Treasure of the Sierra Madre*
(1948), as the crusty, cackling old desert
rat who leads Humphrey Bogart and Tim
Holt to a gold deposit. It was an unqualified triumph for both Hustons. He remained active—and prominent—in such
movies as *Summer Holiday* (1948), *The
Great Sinner* (1949), and *The Furies*
(1950), the last-named completed shortly
before his death.

HUTTON, BETTY. Actress. *(b. Feb. 26,
1921, Battle Creek, Mich., as Betty Jane
Thornburg.)* Irrepressible blond bombshell
of many 1940s musicomedies and fanciful
biopics, a bright-eyed bundle of energy
who for a time was one of the screen's
most popular and best-paid performers. A
former big-band singer, she made her film
debut in a 1939 musical short starring
Vincent Lopez and his orchestra. (She also
was leading lady to song-and-dance man
Hal LeRoy in some of his Brooklyn-
filmed Vitaphone short subjects.) Hutton's
first feature film, *The Fleet's In* (1942),
saw her backing up Dorothy Lamour and
registering strongly with an exuberant
comic performance and a memorable novelty number. *Star Spangled Rhythm* (also
1942), an all-star farrago, saw her in the
nominal female lead and effectively
launched her as a top-liner. Paramount's
resident "genius," writer-director Preston
Sturges, gave Hutton her best role, that of
small-town girl Trudy Kockenlocker,
whose unexpected pregnancy (without
benefit of clergy) produces quintuplets in
The Miracle of Morgan's Creek (1944), a
hilarious wartime comedy that cheerfully
thumbed its nose at the prohibitive Production Code.

Hutton played legendary nightclub
queen Texas Guinan in *Incendiary Blonde*
(1945) and silent-screen star Pearl White
in *The Perils of Pauline* (1947), but both
characterizations hewed closely to her
well-established persona. MGM borrowed

her from Paramount to replace ailing star
Judy Garland in the big-budget production
of Irving Berlin's Broadway smash *Annie
Get Your Gun* (1950), a well-remembered
musical built around Wild-West shooting
star Annie Oakley. Two years later she
surprised movie audiences with her athletic feats in *The Greatest Show on Earth*
(1952), a colorful, Oscar-winning drama
of circus life directed by Cecil B.
DeMille. The always tempestuous Hutton,
who had taken to flexing her star muscles
in bitter disputes with Paramount management, walked out on her contract after finishing *Somebody Loves Me* (1952, a biopic of vaudeville great Blossom Seeley),
effectively ruining her screen career. She
made only one more film, the dismal
Spring Reunion (1957), before retiring
from the screen. In the 1970s she was discovered, broke and forgotten, doing menial labor at a New England rectory of
Catholic clergymen. Subsequent rumors of
a comeback were ill founded. Her sister
Marion was a successful big-band singer.
OTHER FILMS INCLUDE: 1943: *Happy Go
Lucky, Let's Face It;* 1944: *And the Angels
Sing, Here Comes the Waves;* 1945: *Duffy's
Tavern, The Stork Club;* 1946: *Cross My
Heart;* 1947: *Dream Girl;* 1949: *Red, Hot and
Blue;* 1950: *Let's Dance;* 1951: *Sailor Beware.*

HUTTON, JIM. Actor. *(b. Mar. 31, 1934,
Binghamton, N.Y.; d. June 2, 1979.)* This gangly, boyish leading man was discovered
by director Douglas Sirk, who saw him
performing in Germany while the young
actor was stationed there with the U.S.
Army. Equally capable in both action and
comic fare, but especially winning in the
latter, Hutton appeared in Sirk's *A Time to
Love and a Time to Die* (1958, his first
film), *Where the Boys Are* (1960, his first
hit), *The Horizontal Lieutenant* (1962),
*Major Dundee, The Hallelujah Trail,
Never Too Late* (all 1965), *Walk, Don't
Run* (1966), *The Green Berets* (1968),
Hellfighters (1969), and *The Psychic
Killer* (1975). In the latter part of his regrettably brief career, Hutton found his
services most in demand on the small
screen; he was especially winning as the
likable, absent-minded supersleuth Ellery
Queen in the TV series of the same name
(1975–76). Sadly, he didn't live to see his
son Timothy win his Oscar in 1981.

HUTTON, LAUREN. Actress. *(b. November 17, 1943, Charleston, S.C., as Mary Hutton.)* At one time this top model graced the cover of more magazines than any other American personality. Easily recognizable by her husky, purring voice and gap-toothed smile, the willowy Hutton apprenticed in TV commercials before making her film debut in the football comedy *Paper Lion* (1968). Her acting successes never matched her modeling successes, and although she made other fairly substantial appearances in *Little Fauss and Big Halsy* (1970), *Gator* (1976), and *Welcome to L.A.* (1977), among others, Hutton never really clicked as a movie star. Aside from a choice role as the distaff lead in *American Gigolo* (1980), her subsequent films—including *Viva Knievel!* (1977), *Zorro, the Gay Blade* (1981), *Once Bitten* (1985), and *Malone* (1987)—were even less commercially and artistically rewarding. She is no stranger to TV, having appeared in both "Paper Dolls" (1984) and "Falcon Crest" (1987), and in numerous telepix. In 1993, at age 50, Hutton, attractive as ever, enjoyed a modeling comeback, appearing on leading magazine covers and in advertisements.

HUTTON, TIMOTHY. Actor. *(b. Aug. 16, 1960, Malibu, Calif.)* This sensitive young leading man, who in the early years of his career specialized in portraying "difficult" characters, grabbed immediate attention and won a Best Supporting Actor Oscar as the troubled son of Donald Sutherland and Mary Tyler Moore in the multi-Oscar-winning family drama *Ordinary People* (1980). He made his film debut at the age of five in the Bud Yorkin comedy *Never Too Late* (1965), which costarred his father, the late actor Jim Hutton, but began his screen career in earnest with a string of TV movies in the late 1970s including the highly acclaimed *Friendly Fire* (1979). Hutton has given several exceptional performances, to name two, as the son of a couple based on convicted spies Julius and Ethel Rosenberg in Sidney Lumet's *Daniel* (1983), and as an inexperienced assistant D.A. who goes head-to-head with a corrupt cop in Lumet's *Q&A* (1990). Formerly married to actress Debra Winger, he has, for the most part, stayed away from blatantly commercial fare. He also directed the music videos "Drive" by

The Cars and "Not Enough Love" by Don Henley.
OTHER FILMS INCLUDE: 1981: *Taps;* 1984: *Iceman;* 1985: *Turk 182! The Falcon and the Snowman;* 1987: *Made in Heaven;* 1988: *Everybody's All-American, A Time of Destiny;* 1990: *Torrents of Spring;* 1993: *The Dark Half, The Temp, Zelda* (TV movie, as F. Scott Fitzgerald); 1995: *French Kiss.*

HYAMS, PETER. Director, screenwriter, producer, cinematographer, editor. *(b. July 26, 1943, New York City.)* Solid director and writer with a track record of very commercial, if not particularly inspired, movies, Hyams studied art and music at Hunter College, worked as a CBS newscaster, covered Vietnam as a war correspondent, and later taught filmmaking. He wrote and produced his first film in 1971: *T.R. Baskin,* which starred Candice Bergen, and then directed the well-received TV movies *Rolling Man* (1972) and *Goodnight My Love* (1973). This earned him his first feature assignment as director *and* writer, *Busting* (1974), with Elliott Gould and Robert Blake as street cops. He directed *Our Time* (1974) and *Peeper* (1975), as well as writing and directing the enjoyable Mars cover-up thriller, *Capricorn One* (1978), the soapy *Hanover Street* (1979), *Outland* (1981, often referred to as *"High Noon* in outer space"), *The Star Chamber* (1983), and his most ambitious—and daunting—project, *2010* (1984), a literal-minded sequel to Kubrick's classic film *2001: A Space Odyssey* which was, nonetheless, very well done. Since then, Hyams has relegated himself to slick entertainments like the buddy cop comedy *Running Scared* (1986) and *The Presidio* (1988), neither of which he wrote, and the remake of *Narrow Margin* (1990). *Stay Tuned* (1992), a TV satire which he directed but did not write, was a notable flop. Hyams then returned to sci-fi territory for the Jean-Claude Van Damme vehicle *Timecop* (1994), and directed Van Damme's next vehicle, *Sudden Death* (1995). Hyams also cowrote the screenplay for *Telefon* (1977) and executive-produced the silly kid comedy *The Monster Squad* (1987). Unique among contemporary directors, he often edits his films, and also serves as his own cinematographer; he has photographed all of his films since *2010.*

HYDE-WHITE, WILFRID. Actor. *(b. May 12, 1903, Bourton, England; d. May 6, 1991.)* Slender, droll, veddy-veddy British character actor recognizable by his sly expressions, devilishly twinkling eyes, and wry dialogue delivery. Hyde-White was a born supporting player (if such a thing exists), but he did enact at least one interesting lead role, American detective Philo Vance, in the English-made *The Scarab Murder Case* (1936, a lost film). Perhaps he is best remembered as Colonel Pickering in the movie version of *My Fair Lady* (1964). He delighted audiences for years, although by the mid 1970s he'd slowed up considerably, and his performance in *The Toy* (1982), one of his last films, bordered on catatonia. He appeared in two TV series, "The Associates" (1979) and the second season of "Buck Rogers in the 25th Century" (1980–81). His son Alex Hyde-White is also an actor with such films as *Indiana Jones and the Last Crusade* (1989) and *Pretty Woman* (1990) to his credit. He starred in *Biggles: Adventures in Time* (1986) and was one of the *Fantastic Four* (1994).

OTHER FILMS INCLUDE: 1936: *Rembrandt;* 1937: *Elephant Boy;* 1946: *Night Boat to Dublin;* 1948: *The Winslow Boy;* 1949: *The Third Man, The Man on the Eiffel Tower;* 1951: *The Browning Version, Outcast of the Islands;* 1953: *Man With a Million;* 1954: *The Story of Gilbert and Sullivan;* 1957: *Tarzan and the Lost Safari;* 1960: *Let's Make Love;* 1962: *Crooks Anonymous, In Search of the Castaways;* 1966: *Ten Little Indians, Chamber of Horrors;* 1969: *Gaily, Gaily, The Magic Christian;* 1970: *Skullduggery;* 1971: *Fragment of Fear;* 1978: *The Cat and the Canary;* 1980: *Oh God! Book II.*

HYER, MARTHA. Actress. *(b. Aug. 10, 1924, Fort Worth, Tex.)* It would be easy (if somewhat unkind) to say that Martha Hyer made more of an impression on Hollywood as the wife of powerful producer Hal Wallis than she ever did as a second-string leading lady and supporting player. But it wouldn't be entirely true: While no Garbo, she did deliver some fine performances, including an Oscar-nominated turn in *Some Came Running* (1958). A Pasadena Playhouse alumna, she made her screen debut in *The Locket* (1946, as an extra in a party scene), apprenticed in B-Westerns as leading lady to Tim Holt in *Thunder Mountain* (1947), *Gun Smugglers* (1948), and *The Rustlers* (1949); and played support in *Woman on the Beach* (1947), *The Judge Steps Out, The Clay Pigeon* (both 1949), and other RKO B's. Hyer developed quite a skill for playing coldhearted society women and outright bitches, but she adeptly essayed sympathetic characters when the opportunities presented themselves.

She reportedly was the actual (uncredited) screenwriter of her husband's production *Rooster Cogburn* (1975). Her autobiography, "Finding My Way," was published in 1990.

OTHER FILMS INCLUDE: 1951: *Geisha Girl;* 1953: *So Big, Abbott and Costello Go to Mars;* 1954: *Lucky Me, Sabrina;* 1955: *Francis in the Navy;* 1956: *Battle Hymn;* 1957: *My Man Godfrey;* 1958: *Houseboat;* 1960: *Desire in the Dust;* 1961: *The Last Time I Saw Archie;* 1963: *The Man From the Diners' Club;* 1964: *The Carpetbaggers;* 1965: *The Sons of Katie Elder;* 1966: *The Chase;* 1967: *The Happening;* 1968: *House of 1,000 Dolls;* 1969: *Once You Kiss a Stranger;* 1971: *The Tyrant.*

INGRAM, REX. Actor. *(b. Oct. 20, 1895, Cairo, Ill.; d. Sept. 19, 1969.)* Not to be confused with the silent film director, this Ingram was an imposing black actor—a possessor of a medical degree, and a member of Phi Beta Kappa—who appeared in movies as early as 1918 (playing a native in the original *Tarzan of the Apes*). He also reportedly appeared in small roles in Cecil B. DeMille's silents *The Ten Commandments* (1923) and *The King of Kings* (1927). A powerfully built man with a thundering voice, Ingram avoided conventional stereotype parts, and cut an imposing figure as De Lawd in *The Green Pastures* (1936, in which he also played Adam and Hezdrel). Among his best parts were the slave Jim in *Huckleberry Finn* (1939), the towering genie in *The Thief of Bagdad* (1940), and the Ethiopian soldier in *Sahara* (1943). He also appeared in *A Thousand and One Nights* (1945, again as a genie), *Moonrise* (1948), *Tarzan's Hidden Jungle* (1955), *God's Little Acre, Anna Lucasta* (both 1958), *Elmer Gantry* (1960), *Your Cheatin' Heart* (1964), *Hurry Sundown* (1967), and *Journey to Shiloh* (1968). A great talent, who also appeared on stage, Ingram never got the opportunities—or, in truth, the recognition—he deserved.

IRELAND, JOHN. Actor. *(b. Jan. 30, 1914, Vancouver; d. Mar. 21, 1992.)* Slender, sinister-looking character actor and occasional leading man, best represented in roles (usually villains) that called upon him to display cynicism and cruelty. Ireland was Oscar-nominated for his turn as a hard-boiled lackey to corrupt politico Broderick Crawford in *All the King's Men* (1949), although he seems to have been remembered primarily for his portrayals of heavies in high-profile horse operas, including *My Darling Clementine* (1946), *Red River* (1948, which also featured Joanne Dru, his wife from 1949–56 and a frequent costar), and *Gunfight at the O.K. Corral* (1957). A former swimming star (!) who began acting on the New York stage and even played in Shakespearean dramas, he was far less effective in starring vehicles, of which *Hurricane Smith* (1952) is most representative. In 1953 he coproduced and codirected an offbeat Western (in 3-D, no less) called *Outlaw Territory,* also known as *Hannah Lee;* Ireland costarred with Dru. The astonishingly prolific Ireland worked incessantly throughout his career, although far too often in cheesy American independents and foreign-made quickies. In 1961 he starred in the syndicated TV series "The Cheaters," and later costarred in the 1965–66 season of "Rawhide," and the short-lived "Cassie & Co." (1982). In 1988 he replaced Lorne Greene as the father figure in the TV movie *Bonanza: The Next Generation,* a pilot for a proposed series.
OTHER FILMS INCLUDE: 1945: *A Walk in the Sun* (his first); 1947: *Railroaded, The Gangster;* 1948: *Raw Deal, Joan of Arc;* 1949: *I Shot Jesse James, Roughshod, The Doolins of Oklahoma;* 1950: *The Return of Jesse James;* 1951: *Vengeance Valley, The Scarf, Little Big Horn;* 1953: *The 49th Man, Combat Squad;* 1954: *Security Risk, The Fast and the Furious, The Steel Cage;* 1957: *Queen Bee, Hell's Horizon;* 1956: *Gunslinger;* 1958: *Party Girl;* 1960: *Spartacus;* 1961: *Wild in the Country;* 1963: *55 Days at Peking, The Ceremony;* 1964: *The Fall of the Roman Empire;* 1965: *I Saw What You Did;* 1968: *Arizona Bushwhackers;* 1970: *The Adventurers;* 1972: *Escape to the Sun;* 1974: *The House of the Seven Corpses, Welcome to Arrow Beach;* 1975: *Farewell, My Lovely;* 1977: *Satan's Cheerleaders;* 1979: *The Shape of Things to Come;* 1980: *Guyana: Cult of the Damned;* 1982: *The Incubus;* 1983: *Martin's Day,* 1986: *Thunder Run;* 1988: *Messenger of Death;* 1989: *Sundown: The Vampire in Retreat;* 1991: *Waxwork II: Lost in Time.*

IRONS, JEREMY. Actor. *(b. Sept. 19, 1948, Cowes, Isle of Wight, England.)* Gaunt-faced British actor with a definite upper-crust bearing, Irons' greatest triumphs have been in delineating the darker side of such types. Trained at the venerable Bristol Old Vic Theatre School, he came to the attention of American viewers via the TV miniseries "Brideshead Revisited" (1981), a sprawling depiction of Evelyn Waugh's novel in which he played witness-to-aristocratic-decadence Charles Ryder. He acted opposite Meryl Streep in the lavish but only partly successful *The French Lieutenant's Woman* (1981) and showed his versatility by going wildly against type—with most successful results—in Jerzy Skolimowski's *Moonlighting* (1982), in which he played a Polish laborer stranded in England during his home country's political strife. At this juncture, the public started to catch up with what film buffs and critics had known for years: Irons is one of the best actors alive. Irons' best roles have been his most recent ones: He depicted the slow mental breakdown of twin gynecologists in David Cronenberg's very chilly thriller *Dead Ringers* (1988) and delivered an ironic, witty, and self-aware performance as accused wife murderer Klaus von Bulow in *Reversal of Fortune* (1990), which won him a Best Actor Academy Award. (He also won a Tony Award on Broadway for "The Real Thing," in which he costarred with *Reversal*'s Glenn Close.) Since then, he's starred in *Kafka* (1991), Louis Malle's *Damage, Waterland* (both 1992), *M. Butterfly,* and *The House of the Spirits* (both 1993). He provided the delightfully sinister voice of Scar in *The Lion King* (1994, paying homage to his own Klaus von Bulow by intoning the line, "You have no idea") and proved a worthy foe to Bruce Willis in *Die Hard With a Vengeance* (1995). He also directed Carly Simon's music video "Tired by Being Blonde."

OTHER FILMS INCLUDE: 1983: *The Wild Duck, Betrayal;* 1984: *Swann in Love;* 1986: *The Mission;* 1988: *A Chorus of Disapproval.*

IRVING, AMY. Actress. *(b. Sept. 10, 1953, Palo Alto, Calif.)* This girlishly beautiful actress, with captivating blue eyes, launched a starring career in the late 1970s that never quite came to fruition. If anything, she's fared better on Broadway in a number of well-received performances, though she's impressed moviegoers with her work in such films as *Carrie* (1976, as a semi-sympathetic coed), *The Fury* (1978), *Voices* (1979, as a deaf woman), *The Competition* (1980, as a concert pianist), *Honeysuckle Rose* (also 1980), and *Micki + Maude* (1984). She was Oscar-nominated for her supporting role in Barbra Streisand's *Yentl* (1983), but got her best opportunities some years later in *Crossing Delancey* (1988, as a slightly eccentric New York bookseller) and *A Show of Force* (1990, as a TV reporter investigating political corruption in Puerto Rico). Two of her most vivid performances were unseen by audiences: as the singing voice of sexy Jessica Rabbit in *Who Framed Roger Rabbit* (1988) and as a not dissimilar character in *An American Tail: Fievel Goes West* (1991). Irving's parents are actress Priscilla Pointer and acting teacher Jules Irving. She worked with her mother in 1987's *Rumpelstiltskin,* which was directed by her brother David Irving. She was married for several years to director Steven Spielberg.

ITAMI, JUZO. Director, screenwriter, actor. *(b. May 15, 1933, Kyoto, Japan.)* Unique filmmaker whose pointed, unusually paced comedies about modern Japanese mores have brought him international recognition. The son of Japanese film director Mansaku Itami (who was famous for his Samurai films), Juzo has been a boxer, a band organizer, an essayist, a talk-show host, and an actor in American and Japanese films, including *55 Days at Peking* (1963), *Lord Jim* (1965), *The Family Game* (1984), and *The Makioka Sisters* (1985). He made his directorial debut with *The Funeral* (1984), a black comedy about a family that must hold a Buddhist funeral for their brothel-owning father. Next came the "noodle Western" *Tampopo*

(1986), about a young widow who learns the secrets of cooking noodles from a Shane-like truck driver. *A Taxing Woman* (1987) and *A Taxing Woman's Return* (1988) followed the adventures of a female tax inspector who doggedly chases tax evaders, and continued Itami's comic exploration of the darker elements of a seemingly complacent Japanese society. Nobuko Miyamoto, Itami's wife, has starred—memorably—in all of his films.

IVES, BURL. Actor, singer. *(b. June 14, 1909, Hunt, Ill., as Burle Icle Ivanhoe; d. Apr. 14, 1995.)* Who, having seen him, could ever forget this massive, bearded actor as Big Daddy in *Cat on a Hot Tin Roof* (1958), bellowing "Ah smell th' powahful odah of *mendacity!*" It was a career highlight for this former football player and professional balladeer, who broke into films strumming a guitar and singing folk songs in that incomparable voice of his (which sold millions of records). That same year, 1958, he won an Oscar playing another patriarch, the ranch owner in *The Big Country.* Amazingly, it took years for movie producers to discover that Ives was a good actor, too. Ives also loaned his mellifluous voice to numerous documentaries and animated features.
OTHER FILMS INCLUDE: 1946: *Smoky;* 1948: *Green Grass of Wyoming, Station West;* 1949: *So Dear to My Heart* (introducing "Lavender Blue"); 1950: *Sierra;* 1955: *East of Eden;* 1956: *The Power and the Prize;* 1958: *Desire Under the Elms;* 1960: *Our Man in Havana, Let No Man Write My Epitaph;* 1963: *Summer Magic;* 1964: *The Brass Bottle, Ensign Pulver;* 1970: *The McMasters;* 1976: *Baker's Hawk;* 1979: *Just You and Me, Kid, Heidi;* 1981: *Earthbound;* 1982: *White Dog;* 1985: *Uphill All the Way;* 1988: *Two-Moon Junction.*

IVEY, JUDITH. Actress. *(b. Sept. 4, 1951, El Paso, Tex.)* Versatile, two-time Tony Award-winning actress (for "Steaming" and "Hurlyburly"), who has made a gradual transition to character parts on-screen. A lively redhead with an extremely winning personality, she appeared as Gene Wilder's jealous wife in *The Woman in Red* and Steve Martin's girlfriend in *The Lonely Guy* (both 1984), but made her first really strong impression as Susan Sarandon's sharp-tongued friend in *Compromising Positions* (1985). She has also appeared in *Brighton Beach Memoirs* (1986), *Hello Again, Sister, Sister* (both 1987), *In Country* (1989), *Everybody Wins, Love Hurts* (both 1990), *Alice* (also 1990, in a cameo), but continues to devote much of her time to stage work. She starred in the short-lived TV sitcom "Down Home" and joined the cast of "Designing Women" in its 1992–93 season, playing a filthy-rich widow.

JACKSON, GLENDA. Actress. *(b. May 9, 1936, Cheshire, England.)* An exceptionally talented leading lady who specializes in intelligent, strong-willed characters, Jackson belongs to that select sorority of top screen actresses who achieved stardom by virtue of expert performances and force of personality rather than physical attributes. Like many actresses of her day, Jackson left school at a young age to try her hand at the theater; years of waitressing and other menial jobs followed. She was discovered by director Peter Brook in 1964, who cast her in his stage play "Marat/Sade (Persecution and Assassination of Jean-Paul Marat as Performed by the Inmates of the Asylum of Charenton Under the Direction of the Marquis de Sade)" as the assassin Charlotte Corday, a role she reprised in the 1966 film version, garnering some good notices. (She'd made her film debut in 1963's *This Sporting Life.)*

A favorite of British director Ken Russell, Jackson won her first Best Actress Oscar for her sparkling stint in his D. H. Lawrence adaptation *Women in Love* (1969). She subsequently appeared in Russell's *The Boy Friend* (in a very amusing cameo), *The Music Lovers* (both 1971), *Salome's Last Dance* (1988), and *The Rainbow* (1989, as the mother of the character she played in *Women in Love).* In her peak period, the 1970s, Jackson was Oscar-nominated for her performances in *Sunday, Bloody Sunday* (1971), the romantic comedy *A Touch of Class* (1973, for which she won her second Academy Award), and *Hedda* (1975). Frequently seen in period productions such as *The Incredible Sarah* (1976, as legendary actress Sarah Bernhardt), she is equally at home in contemporary dramas and comedies like *The Romantic Englishwoman*

(1975). In 1971 she won an Emmy Award for her dazzling performance in the British miniseries "Elizabeth R," which aired in the U.S. on "Masterpiece Theatre." She has made occasional television appearances since then, in such high-profile TV movies as *The Patricia Neal Story* (1981) and *A Murder of Quality* (1991).

In 1990 she mounted an unsuccessful campaign to run for Parliament, as a member of the Labour Party; she ran again in 1992 and won. The political world's gain is our loss.

OTHER FILMS INCLUDE: 1974: *The Maids;* 1977: *Nasty Habits;* 1978: *House Calls, Stevie;* 1979: *Lost and Found* (reteamed with George Segal from *A Touch of Class);* 1980: *Hopscotch;* 1981: *The Return of the Soldier;* 1985: *Turtle Diary;* 1987: *Beyond Therapy;* 1990: *King of the Wind.*

JACKSON, SAMUEL L. Actor. *(b. Dec. 21, 1948, Atlanta.)* After years of small parts in films like *Coming to America* (1987), *Sea of Love* (1989), and *GoodFellas* (1990), Jackson broke through as the crack addict Gator in Spike Lee's *Jungle Fever* (1991), a performance so good that the 1991 Cannes Film Festival judges created a Supporting Actor award in order to honor him. A graduate of Morehouse College, Jackson has extensive stage experience—he originated the roles of Boy Willie and Wolf in the premieres of August Wilson's "The Piano Lesson" and "Two Trains Running"—and has worked with Spike Lee in *School Daze* (1988), *Do the Right Thing* (1989, as Senor Love Daddy), and *Mo' Better Blues* (1990). He has been featured in *Patriot Games, White Sands, Jumpin at the Boneyard* (all 1992), and in 1993 graduated to starring parts in *Amos & Andrew* and *National Lampoon's Loaded Weapon 1* (unfortunately, a pair of less than sterling vehicles). He had more supporting roles in *Menace II Society, Jurassic Park, True Romance* (all 1993), and *The New Age* (1994, terrific as a telemarketer), before he blew audiences away—and earned a supporting Oscar nomination—as the philosophical hit man Jules in *Pulp Fiction* (1994). The tireless Jackson followed with *Losing Isaiah* (opposite his wife, La Tanya Richardson), *Kiss of Death,* and *Die Hard With a Vengeance* (all 1995).

JACOBI, DEREK. Actor. *(b. Oct. 22, 1938, Leytonstone, London.)* Brilliant English stage actor who has made occasional screen appearances. He studied at Cambridge and trained at the Birmingham Repertory Company until Laurence Olivier saw him perform and eventually invited him to join the National Theatre Company. Jacobi performed in a myriad of roles and was featured in the Olivier-produced films of *Othello* (1965, as Cassio) and *Three Sisters* (1970, released here in 1974). He has also been featured in *The Day of the Jackal* (1973), *The Odessa File* (1974), *The Medusa Touch* (1978), *The Human Factor* (1979), *Enigma* (1982), *Little Dorrit* (1988), and the Kenneth Branagh films *Henry V* (1989, as the Chorus) and *Dead Again* (1991, in an amusingly flashy part). Jacobi won a Tony Award for his role as Benedick in "Much Ado About Nothing," and may be best known in this country for his stunning TV work in the BBC series "I, Claudius" and as Hitler in "Inside the Third Reich."

JACOBI, LOU. Actor. *(b. Dec. 28, 1913, Toronto.)* "You cut the turkey?" Lou Jacobi asks incredulously in *Avalon* (1990), "you cut the turkey??!!" It's hard to think of anyone more ideal for the role of the aging, crotchety Jewish uncle in Barry Levinson's highly personal film. This jowly, balding character actor has built a successful acting career around the portrayal of sad sacks, henpecked husbands, and cranky old Jews. His show-biz career began in Canadian theater; he went to London in the mid 1950s, and secured a key role in Carol Reed's *A Kid for Two Farthings* (1955). Here in the States, Jacobi has found work in dozens of films, stage plays, and TV shows. His important film work includes roles in *The Diary of Anne Frank* (1959), *Irma la Douce* (1963), *Little Murders* (1971), as an unlikely cross-dresser in Woody Allen's *Everything You Always Wanted to Know About Sex (But Were Afraid to Ask)* (1972), *Next Stop, Greenwich Village* (1976), *Roseland* (1977), and *My Favorite Year* (1982). In 1976 he starred as a Russian patriarch in the short-lived TV sitcom "Ivan the Terrible."

JAECKEL, RICHARD. Actor. *(b. Oct. 10, 1926, Long Beach, N.Y.)* You name it, this character actor's played it. Short but solidly built, with light-colored, usually close-cropped hair and a boyish face (well, during most of his career, anyway), Jaeckel's portrayed good guys, bad guys, cops, soldiers, astronauts, gangsters, juvenile delinquents, and Western heavies. He broke into pictures while working as a delivery boy in the mailroom of 20th Century-Fox, where he made his film debut in *Guadalcanal Diary* (1943). He belongs to the legions of competent, sometimes exemplary actors who've peopled motion pictures in secondary roles for decades. (He's hard to forget as the youthful hotshot who tries to draw on Gregory Peck in 1950's *The Gunfighter,* even though the scene is brief.) Jaeckel's films include *Battleground, Sands of Iwo Jima* (both 1949), *Come Back, Little Sheba* (1952, as Terry Moore's boyfriend), *3:10 to Yuma* (1957), *Platinum High School* (1960), *Town Without Pity* (1961, a standout as one of the soldier-rapists), *Once Before I Die* (1965), *The Dirty Dozen* (1967), *The Green Slime* (1969), *Pat Garrett and Billy the Kid* (1973), *Grizzly* (1976), *The Dark* (1979), *Cold River* (1982), *Starman* (1984), *Black Moon Rising* (1986), and *Delta Force 2* (1990). He was nominated for a Best Supporting Actor Oscar for his role in Paul Newman's *Sometimes a Great Notion* (1971). He's never been far from a camera; in the early 1990s he was costarring in the "Baywatch" TV series.

JAFFE, SAM. Actor. *(b. Mar. 8, 1891, New York City; d. Mar. 24, 1984.)* A slight, frail-looking man with wispy hair and large eyes, Jaffe didn't work all that much in Hollywood, but many of his character parts are among the most memorable in movie history. Originally a math teacher from the Bronx, he started acting in 1915 with the Washington Square Players, later moved to Broadway, and then to Hollywood, making his screen debut as the mad Grand Duke Peter in *The Scarlet Empress* (1934). He played the benevolent High Lama in *Lost Horizon* (1937), and achieved cinematic immortality as the native water boy (he was then 46), in *Gunga Din* (1939). Jaffe earned an Oscar nomination for his turn as the criminal master-

mind in *The Asphalt Jungle* (1950), and worked frequently in TV, where he was well known as Dr. Zorba on the "Ben Casey" series (1961–65).
OTHER FILMS INCLUDE: 1934: *We Live Again;* 1943: *Stage Door Canteen* (cameo); 1946: *13 Rue Madeleine;* 1947: *Gentleman's Agreement;* 1948: *The Accused;* 1949: *Rope of Sand;* 1951: *Under the Gun, The Day the Earth Stood Still;* 1958: *The Barbarian and the Geisha;* 1959: *Ben-Hur;* 1967: *A Guide for the Married Man* (cameo); 1968: *Guns for San Sebastian;* 1969: *The Great Bank Robbery;* 1970: *The Dunwich Horror;* 1971: *Bedknobs and Broomsticks.*

JAGGER, DEAN. Actor. *(b. Nov. 7, 1903, Lima, Ohio; d. Feb. 5, 1991.)* In his thirties a wavy-haired, handsome, likable leading-man type, Jagger never quite reached the mark, and spent the bulk of his screen career playing second leads and character parts. By the early 1950s he was a bald supporting player who always proffered intelligent characterizations and delivered smooth performances. Jagger, who began his show-biz career in vaudeville during the early 1920s, won a Best Supporting Actor Oscar for his work in the drama *Twelve O'Clock High* (1949). He also essayed the title role in *Brigham Young—Frontiersman* (1940), a well-remembered effort. Jagger's few leads include a 1935 Zane Grey Western for Paramount, *Wanderer of the Wasteland,* a 1936 Poverty Row thriller, *Revolt of the Zombies* (1936), and *When Strangers Marry,* an unheralded little B thriller of surprising quality, costarring Jagger with Kim Hunter and Robert Mitchum and directed by William Castle. He also played the high school principal on the TV series "Mr. Novak" (1963–64).
OTHER FILMS INCLUDE: 1929: *The Woman From Hell;* 1934: *You Belong to Me, College Rhythm;* 1935: *Wings in the Dark, Home on the Range, People Will Talk;* 1941: *Western Union, The Men in Her Life;* 1942: *Valley of the Sun;* 1943: *The North Star;* 1945: *A Yank in London;* 1946: *Sister Kenny;* 1947: *Pursued;* 1949: *C-Man;* 1950: *Dark City;* 1951: *Rawhide;* 1952: *My Son John;* 1953: *The Robe;* 1954: *Executive Suite, White Christmas;* 1955: *Bad Day at Black Rock;* 1956: *The Great Man, X the Unknown;* 1958: *King Creole;* 1959: *The Nun's Story;* 1960: *Elmer Gantry;* 1961: *The Honeymoon Ma-*

chine; 1962: Billy Rose's *Jumbo;* 1968: *Firecreek, Day of the Evil Gun;* 1968: *Smith!;* 1970: *The Kremlin Letter;* 1971: *Vanishing Point;* 1975: *So Sad About Gloria;* 1978: *Game of Death;* 1980: *Alligator.*

JAGLOM, HENRY. Director, screenwriter, actor, producer. *(b. Jan. 26, 1941, London.)* Independent filmmaker in the John Cassavetes mold, who has created a very personal, highly eclectic body of work outside of the studio system. He began as an actor in plays and summer stock and landed roles on TV sitcoms before producer Bert Schneider gave him a job as an editorial consultant on *Easy Rider* (1969). Schneider then produced *A Safe Place* (1971), Jaglom's first film as writer and director that starred Tuesday Weld as a woman lost in her own fantasy world. Jaglom cajoled Orson Welles into playing a supporting role in the film, which led to a long relationship between the two. The movie was Jaglom's last studio-backed venture. With independent financing, he has produced a formidable body of work since then, all highly personal films in which he often stars with real-life friends, lovers, and wives. Jaglom's films are typically rambling, amusing, observational, and seemingly improvisational.
OTHER FILMS INCLUDE: 1976: *Tracks* (with Dennis Hopper as a burned-out Vietnam vet); 1980: *Sitting Ducks;* 1983: *Can She Bake a Cherry Pie?;* 1985: *Always;* 1987: *Someone to Love* (which featured Orson Welles in his last screen appearance); 1989: *New Year's Day;* 1990: *Eating;* 1992: *Venice/Venice;* 1994: *Babyfever.*

JANNINGS, EMIL. Actor. *(b. July 23, 1884, Rorschach, Switzerland, as Theodor Friedrich Emil Janenz; d. Jan. 3, 1950.)* At one time a major star of the international screen, this imposing, Oscar-winning actor spent the WW2 years in Germany, where he made numerous pro-Nazi films, virtually guaranteeing his exile by moviemakers after the Allied victory. A bearlike man whose stern features made him most effective as rigid authoritarians (most often unsympathetic), Jannings became a professional actor while still in his teens, making a name for himself as a member of the distinguished Max Reinhardt company in Berlin in the years before World War 1. Although he made his film debut in 1914's *Arme Eva,* Jannings got mostly unrewarding parts until the end of the decade, when he began playing prominent historical figures in elaborate German and Italian films, including *Madame DuBarry* (1919, as Louis XV), *Anne Boleyn* (1920, as Henry VIII), *Peter the Great* (1921, in the title role), and *Quo Vadis?* (1924, as Nero).

During this period Jannings also essayed many great characters from legend and literature, including Dimitri Karamazov in *The Brothers Karamazov* (1920), *Othello* (1922), and *Faust* (1926, as Mephistopheles). These roles, along with his star turns in two classics—Murnau's *The Last Laugh* (1924, as the proud doorman at a posh hotel who is suddenly demoted and subsequently humiliated) and Dupont's *Variety* (1925)—eventually brought Jannings to the attention of American filmmakers. He came to Hollywood in 1927, signing a Paramount contract and winning the first Best Actor Oscar ever awarded for his work in *The Way of All Flesh* (1927) and *The Last Command* (1928, as a refugee Russian general working as an extra in Hollywood costume dramas), his first two American films.

Jannings made several more silents in Hollywood before the talkie revolution, of which the thickly accented actor was an early casualty. But he scored an amazing triumph back in Germany, playing a pompous college professor enraptured by nightclub singer Marlene Dietrich in Josef von Sternberg's *The Blue Angel* (1930, which was produced in both German- and English-language versions). After Hitler's rise to power in 1933, an enthusiastic Jannings eagerly accepted an offer from propaganda minister Goebbels to appear in pro-German, anti-Semitic movies. He appeared in a number of such films throughout the 1930s and early 1940s, and was named "Artist of the State" by Goebbels in 1941. Illness forced Jannings to abandon work on *Where Is Mr. Belling?* (1945), and when Hitler's regime was destroyed shortly thereafter, Jannings found himself persona non grata with the international filmmaking community. He never made another film, and died from cancer five years later.

JANSSEN, DAVID. Actor. *(b. Mar. 27, 1930, Naponee, Nebr., as David Mayer; d. Feb. 13, 1980.)* Most people remember this dark, perpetually grimacing, gravelly voiced actor as the star of numerous TV shows from the 1950s through the 1970s, but few recall that he had a fairly substantial film career as well. Janssen, who claimed to have appeared in many WW2 films as a child actor, can be traced back to *It's a Pleasure* (1945). His distinctive tendency to underplay—which manifested itself in assorted mumblings, pained expressions, and sleepy body language—is less apparent in the movies in which he appeared as a young man. His early career includes the films *Francis Goes to West Point, Bonzo Goes to College* (both 1952), *The Private War of Major Benson, Cult of the Cobra, All That Heaven Allows* (all 1955), *Away All Boats, Toy Tiger, The Girl He Left Behind* (all 1956), *Lafayette Escadrille* (1958), *Hell to Eternity* (1960), and *Dondi* (1961). He played a tough, taciturn private eye in *Twenty Plus Two* (1961), which more or less solidified the persona he'd established on TV as Richard Diamond.

King of the Roaring Twenties (1961), *My Six Loves* (1963), *Warning Shot* (1967), *The Green Berets, The Shoes of the Fisherman* (both 1968), *Marooned* (1969), *Macho Callahan* (1971), *Once Is Not Enough, The Swiss Conspiracy* (both 1975), *Two Minute Warning* (1976), *Golden Rendezvous* (1978), and *Inchon* (1982) kept Janssen on big screens, but by then he was firmly established as a TV star, and people are reluctant to pay for what they can see for free in their living rooms. Janssen's TV series were "Richard Diamond, Private Detective" (1957–59), "The Fugitive" (1963–67), "O'Hara, U.S. Treasury" (1971–72), and "Harry O" (1974–76).

JARMAN, DEREK. Director, screenwriter. *(b. Jan. 31, 1942, Northwood, London; d. Feb. 19, 1994.)* Uniquely idiosyncratic filmmaker noted for his bold experimental form, pointed social criticism, and explorations of homosexuality. Jarman studied painting in the 1960s and then worked as a production designer first in theater and then on the Ken Russell films *The Devils* (1971) and *Savage Messiah* (1972). After trying his hand at super-8mm short films, he made his feature debut, *Sebastiane* (1976, which he codirected and wrote), and got considerable attention for *Jubilee* (1978), a stinging critical essay which had Queen Elizabeth I observing the decay of future England. Following a dizzying reworking of Shakespeare's *The Tempest* (1979), Jarman worked on a number of short films until *Caravaggio* (1986), a handsome-looking, intentionally anachronistic account of the Italian painter which examines his art and sexuality. Three highly impressionistic films followed— *The Last of England* (1987), *War Requiem* (1988), and *The Garden* (1990)—and then *Edward II* (1991), a harsh, graphic modernization of Christopher Marlowe's play about the downfall of Britain's openly gay king, with strong parallels to the current climate of homophobia. Jarman's work remained challenging with a typically unusual "biography" of the philosopher *Wittgenstein* (1993), *Blue* (also 1993), which in Warholian fashion displayed a cobalt blue screen for 76 minutes as Jarman and others discussed many issues, including his own (losing) battle with AIDS, and *Glitterbug* (1994). Jarman also contributed the "Louise" segment to the omnibus opera film *Aria* (1988).

JARMUSCH, JIM. Director, screenwriter. *(b. Jan. 22, 1953, Akron, Ohio.)* Highly original independent filmmaker who has carved out a niche all his own; Pauline Kael called it the "low-key minimalist comedy about American anomie." Jarmusch studied filmmaking at New York University; his final student project, *Permanent Vacation* (1980), was seen overseas and greeted with acclaim. His next feature, *Stranger Than Paradise* (1984), was expanded from a 30-minute short made two years earlier and followed the marginally comic adventures of a young man, his best friend, and his cousin from Budapest. The film received the Camera d'Or prize at Cannes and was named Best Picture of the year by the National Society of Film Critics. It established Jarmusch's cool, measured style, which looks at America through the eyes of people from foreign lands. *Down by Law* (1986) featured Italian comic Roberto Benigni as the outsider, and *Mystery Train* (1989) offered a trio of stories about foreigners staying in a Memphis hotel. *Night*

on Earth (1991), a five-part story set in five taxis in major cities around the world, is probably his most accessible film to date. In 1993 he won the Palme d'Or at Cannes for his short film *Coffee and Cigarettes (Somewhere in California),* which featured Tom Waits and Iggy Pop, and directed the Waits video "It's All Right With Me."

JARRE, MAURICE. Composer. *(b. Sept. 13, 1924, Lyons, France.)* Internationally famous composer whose work has graced small films as well as some of the greatest epics ever made. After a stint as musical director of the Theatre National Populaire in Paris, he wrote his first film music for French director George Franju in 1952. Jarre composed the scores for such major films as *The Longest Day* (1962), *The Collector* (1965), *Topaz, The Damned* (both 1969), *The Man Who Would Be King* (1975), *The Spy Who Loved Me* (1977), *The Tin Drum* (1979), *The Year of Living Dangerously* (1983), *Fatal Attraction* (1987), *Dead Poets Society, Enemies, A Love Story* (both 1989), and *Fearless* (1993). He was Oscar-nominated for *Sundays and Cybele* (1962), *The Life and Times of Judge Roy Bean* (1972, for the song "Marmalade, Molasses and Honey"), *Mohammad, Messenger of God* (1977), *Witness* (1985), *Gorillas in the Mist* (1988), and *Ghost* (1990). He won Academy Awards recognizing the beautiful music he wrote for the David Lean films *Lawrence of Arabia* (1962), *Doctor Zhivago* (1965), and *A Passage to India* (1984). In fact, his "Lara's Theme" from *Zhivago* became an international hit record. His son Kevin Jarre is a screenwriter with such films as *Glory* (1989) and *Tombstone* (1993) to his credit.

JENKINS, ALLEN. Actor. *(b. Apr. 9, 1900, New York City, as Al McConegal; d. July 20, 1974.)* A charter member of Warners' stock company of the 1930s, Jenkins made his film debut in *Blessed Event* (1932), recreating his stage characterization of a half-witted triggerman. His pronounced New York accent, dour appearance, and coarse manner insured him plenty of work in Warners' urban melodramas and gangster films. He was a convincing tough guy, but he played comic sidekicks with equal gusto. His numerous credits include *Three on a Match* (1932), *I Am a Fugitive from a Chain Gang* (1932), *The Mayor of Hell, The Mind Reader, 42nd Street* (all 1933), *Jimmy the Gent* (1934), *The Case of the Curious Bride* (1935, a Perry Mason mystery, as "Spudsy" Drake, based on the novels' Paul Drake character), *The Singing Kid* (1936, in which he sings with Edward Everett Horton), *Three Men on a Horse* (1936), *Dead End* (1937), *A Slight Case of Murder* (1938), *Destry Rides Again* (1939), *Brother Orchid, Tin Pan Alley* (both 1940), *Ball of Fire* (1939), *The Falcon Takes Over* (1942, one of several films in RKO's Falcon series, supporting George Sanders), *Lady on a Train* (1945), *The Senator Was Indiscreet* (1947), *Pillow Talk* (1959), *It's a Mad Mad Mad Mad World* (1963). Jenkins worked consistently, in films and TV, right up until he died in 1974. He was a regular on the 1956–60 TV series "Hey Jeannie." His last film was Billy Wilder's remake of *The Front Page* (1974).

JEWELL, ISABEL. Actress. *(b. July 14, 1909, Shoshoni, Wyo.; d. Apr. 5, 1972.)* In an uncanny example of life imitating art, the petite and pretty Jewell achieved Broadway success in 1930 by assuming a key role on the opening night of "Up Pops the Devil" after only three hours of rehearsal. Winning raves for her pivotal supporting part in "Blessed Event," she was brought to Hollywood by Warners to repeat her role in the 1932 film version. Jewell seldom played leads; although an attractive woman, her brassy voice and hardbitten manner predisposed studios to cast her as a hard-boiled dame. In her most memorable outing, Jewell played a tubercular prostitute in Frank Capra's *Lost Horizon* (1937). She was also impressive in *Counsellor-at-Law* (1933), *A Tale of Two Cities* (1935, as the doomed woman in the final scene), *Ceiling Zero* (1935), *Marked Woman* (1937), *Gone With the Wind* (1939, as Emmy Slattery, who gets a fistful of dirt hurled in her face by Scarlett O'Hara), *Northwest Passage* (1940), *High Sierra* (1941), *The Leopard Man* (1943), *Born to Kill* (1947), *Unfaithfully Yours, The Snake Pit* (both 1948), among many others. Beset by personal problems, she worked with less frequency throughout the

1940s and 1950s, and died in poverty in 1972.

JEWISON, NORMAN. Director, producer. *(b. July 21, 1926, Toronto.)* Solid, workmanlike director with occasional flashes of brilliance, Jewison's stock-in-trade is his ability to coax superlative performances from his actors while advancing his narratives in a clean, direct fashion. Like other directors of his generation, Jewison first worked in TV, writing, directing, and even acting in the medium. (He produced and directed many high-profile TV variety specials in the 1950s and 1960s, and was onetime executive producer of the legendary "Judy Garland Show" in 1963–64.) His first feature film was *Forty Pounds of Trouble* (1963). Jewison directed several films for producer Ross Hunter (including 1963's *The Thrill of It All* and 1965's *The Art of Love)* before making his reputation with three consecutive winners: *The Cincinnati Kid* (1965), a Steve McQueen card-playing drama; *The Russians Are Coming! The Russians Are Coming!* (1966), a hysterical comedy of cold-war paranoia; and, best of all, *In the Heat of the Night* (1967, that year's Oscar winner for Best Picture), a satisfying mystery in which the whodunit plot provided a backdrop for the racially charged confrontations between black detective Sidney Poitier and redneck cop Rod Steiger. *Russians* was nominated for Best Picture, but *Heat* actually won five Oscars—although none for the director.

In *The Thomas Crown Affair* (1968) Jewison played with flamboyant visual imagery; in the misfired *Gaily, Gaily* (1969) he attempted a period piece; and the rousing *Fiddler on the Roof* (1971) vibrantly brought the Broadway musical to film, netting him another Oscar nod. Several of his recent films have been adaptations of stage plays, which he has "opened up" with considerable skill, as in *A Soldier's Story* (1984, Best Picture Oscar nomination). *Moonstruck* (1987, nominated for Best Picture and Director), a screen original by playwright John Patrick Shanley, had the literacy and "feel" of a good play. Jewison has also produced films for other directors, and helped launch the directing career of his editor, Hal Ashby, with *The Landlord* (1970).

OTHER FILMS INCLUDE: 1973: *Jesus Christ*

Superstar; 1975: *Rollerball;* 1979: *... And Justice for All;* 1982: *Best Friends;* 1985: *Agnes of God;* 1989: *In Country;* 1991: *Other People's Money;* 1994: *Only You.*

JHABVALA, RUTH PRAWER. Screenwriter, novelist. *(b. May 7, 1927, Cologne, Germany.)* Acclaimed screenwriter who is best known as part of the filmmaking triumvirate that includes director James Ivory and producer Ismail Merchant. Jhabvala and her family fled Germany in 1939 and emigrated to England; she moved to India in the early 1950s with her husband and began to write novels about life there which brought her international attention. She wrote her first screenplay for Merchant-Ivory in 1963, *The Householder,* based on her novel; it launched a collaboration that has lasted more than thirty years, comprising original works, adaptations of classics, contemporary tales, and costume pictures, including *Shakespeare Wallah* (1965), *The Guru* (1969), *Bombay Talkie* (1970), *Autobiography of a Princess* (1975), *Roseland* (1977), *The Europeans* (1979), *Jane Austen in Manhattan* (1980), *Quartet* (1981), *Heat and Dust* (1983, from her own novel), *The Bostonians* (1984), *Mr. & Mrs. Bridge* (1990), *The Remains of the Day* (1993, Oscar-nominated), and *Jefferson in Paris* (1995). She won Academy Awards for her adaptations of E. M. Forster's *A Room With a View* (1985) and *Howards End* (1992, the team's masterpiece); both are perfect examples of Jhabvala's consummate skill at intelligently and literately constructing scenarios for the screen. She also adapted *Madame Sousatzka* (1988) with director John Schlesinger.

JOFFÉ, ROLAND. Director, screenwriter, producer. *(b. Nov. 17, 1945, London.)* A veteran of the British theater (he was one of the founders of the Young Vic) and television (where he did both dramatic and documentary work), Joffé made a remarkable feature debut with *The Killing Fields* (1984), a harrowingly realistic account of reporter Sidney Schanberg's time in Cambodia, which won three Academy Awards and earned Joffé a Best Director nomination. He confirmed his talent for dazzling imagery in *The Mission* (1986), a visually spectacular but dramatically uneven story of Jesuit priests in 18th-century Brazil, which nonetheless earned top honors at the Cannes Film festival and scored Joffé another Best Director nomination. He has since directed *Fat Man and Little Boy* (1989, which he also cowrote), about the Manhattan Project, and *City of Joy* (1992), with Patrick Swayze as an American surgeon living in Calcutta. No doubt itching to get away from more serious-minded subjects, he coproduced the video game knockoff *Super Mario Bros.* (1993).

JOHNS, GLYNIS. Actress. *(b. Oct. 5, 1923, Durban, South Africa.)* Blessed with a uniquely appealing voice, this bright-eyed actress (the daughter of character actor Mervyn Johns) brought her sparkling personality and considerable allure to many high-spirited characters in British movies of the 1940s and 1950s, and spent some profitable time in Hollywood as well. Beginning as a teenager, she had solid supporting roles in such entertaining films as *49th Parallel* (1941), *Adventures of Tartu* (1943), and *Vacation From Marriage* (1945), and enjoyed her first real success, as a mermaid, in *Miranda* (1948). Johns received an Oscar nomination for *The Sundowners* (1960, in which her father also appeared), but chances are she is best known as the musical suffragette and mother Mrs. Banks in *Mary Poppins* (1964). In 1994 she appeared in *The Ref.* She also carved a niche for herself in Broadway history by introducing the song "Send in the Clowns" in Stephen Sondheim's *A Little Night Music,* for which she won a Tony Award. She has specialized in comedic supporting roles for most of her U.S. career and starred in a 1963 TV sitcom, "Glynis."
OTHER FILMS INCLUDE: 1938: *Murder in the Family;* 1947: *Frieda;* 1950: *State Secret;* 1951: *Appointment With Venus, The Magic Box;* 1953: *Rob Roy;* 1954: *The Weak and the Wicked;* 1956: *Around the World in Eighty Days, The Court Jester* (one of her best Hollywood outings); 1959: *Shake Hands With the Devil;* 1962: *The Cabinet of Caligari, The Chapman Report;* 1963: *Papa's Delicate Condition;* 1968: *Don't Just Stand There;* 1973: *Under Milk Wood, The Vault of Horror;* 1988: *Zelly and Me;* 1994: *The Ref.*

JOHNSON, BEN. Actor. *(b. June 13, 1920, Pawnee, Okla.)* Former rodeo star Johnson broke into the movie business in 1940, first as a horse wrangler and later as a double for cowboy star Wild Bill Elliott. After years of stuntwork, he was "discovered" by director John Ford, who may have seen another John Wayne in the tall, good-looking, slow-drawling Oklahoman. Johnson eased into acting with supporting roles in *She Wore a Yellow Ribbon, Mighty Joe Young* (both 1949), and *Rio Grande* (1950), and Ford starred him with Harry Carey, Jr., in *Wagon Master* (1950), but the likable Johnson just didn't seem to be star material. He returned to character parts, mostly in Westerns (including *Shane, One-Eyed Jacks,* and *Hang 'em High),* and matured into a fine, if limited, actor. (He never forsook his roots; in 1953 he was the World's Champion Steer Roper.) He was a favorite of director Sam Peckinpah, and appeared in his *Major Dundee* (1965), *The Wild Bunch* (1969), *Junior Bonner,* and *The Getaway* (both 1972). Johnson's career took a major leap forward when he won an Oscar for his performance as Sam the Lion, the theater owner in *The Last Picture Show* (1971). He subsequently appeared in *Dillinger* (1973, as Melvin Purvis), *The Sugarland Express* (1974), *Bite the Bullet* (1975), *Breakheart Pass* (1976), *The Town That Dreaded Sundown* (1977), *The Swarm* (1978), *Tex* (1982), *Red Dawn* (1984), *My Heroes Have Always Been Cowboys* (1991), and *Radio Flyer* (1992), among others. More recently, he appeared in *Angels in the Outfield* (1994) and *Outlaws* (1995). Johnson's weather-beaten features make him an icon for any filmmaker chronicling the American West—past or present.

JOHNSON, DON. Actor. *(b. Dec. 15, 1950, Flatt Creek, Mo.)* One of those 15-years-in-the-making overnight successes, this ruggedly handsome, dirty-blond heartthrob burst onto the cinema scene in 1970 playing the title role in the hippie drama *The Magic Garden of Stanley Sweetheart,* which he followed with parts in the rock Western *Zachariah* (1971), the sex-clinic romp *The Harrad Experiment* (1973), *Return to Macon County* (which also starred then-unknown Nick Nolte), and the cult sci-fi film *A Boy*

and His Dog (both 1975). His career in eclipse for nearly a decade, Johnson re-emerged on TV in 1984 as the hip, unshaven, pastel-clad star of "Miami Vice." The show's success revitalized his big-screen career, and his recent feature-film work has been commendably diverse. He's played a Vietnam vet in *Cease Fire* (1985), a midlife crisis case in *Sweet Hearts Dance* (1988), a weary cop in *Dead Bang* (1989), a lecherous drifter in *The Hot Spot* (1990), a would-be bank robber in *Harley Davidson & the Marlboro Man* (1991) and a suave, sexy murder suspect in *Guilty as Sin* (1993). Johnson met actress Melanie Griffith when she was 14 and they both worked in *The Harrad Experiment;* they were married three years later, subsequently divorced, and then remarried in 1989. In recent years they've costarred in the moving drama *Paradise* (1991) and a remake of the comedy *Born Yesterday* (1993), in which they were both well cast. In fact, he has delivered consistently strong, credible performances, but his box-office batting average has been poor; none of his starring vehicles has been a financial success.

JOHNSON, NUNNALLY. Screenwriter, producer, director. *(b. Dec. 5, 1897, Columbus, Ga.; d. Mar. 25, 1977.)* This prolific screenwriter began his writing career as a reporter and gained entry into Hollywood as a short-story writer (one of his stories was adapted for *Rough House Rosie,* a 1927 Clara Bow film). After a brief, unrewarding stint at Paramount in 1933, he signed with Darryl F. Zanuck's 20th Century Pictures, cranking out literate screenplays for *House of Rothschild, Bulldog Drummond Strikes Back* (both 1934), *Thanks a Million,* and *The Man Who Broke the Bank at Monte Carlo* (1935) before Zanuck merged his fledgling company with Fox Film to become 20th Century-Fox in 1936. Johnson settled in for a long run with Zanuck, scripting both *The Prisoner of Shark Island* (1936) and the exceptional *The Grapes of Wrath* (1940, an Oscar-nominated adaptation of John Steinbeck's best-selling novel) for director John Ford, and serving as writer and associate producer on many 20th Century-Fox A films of the 1930s, 1940s, and 1950s, including *Jesse James, Rose of Washington Square* (both 1939), *Chad Hanna* (1940), *Tobacco*

Road (1941), *Roxie Hart* (1942), *The Pied Piper* (1942), *The Moon Is Down, Holy Matrimony* (both 1943, the latter earning an Oscar nomination), *Keys of the Kingdom* (1944), *Everybody Does It* (1949), *Three Came Home, The Mudlark* (both 1950), *The Desert Fox* (1951), *We're Not Married* (1952), and *How to Marry a Millionaire* (1953).

Johnson took a mid 1940s sabbatical from Fox to help fund International Pictures, for which he wrote and produced *The Woman in the Window* (1944, directed by Fritz Lang), *The Dark Mirror* (1946), and *Mr. Peabody and the Mermaid* (1948). The company, which was managed by fellow Fox alumnus William Goetz, was subsequently sold to Universal; Goetz went along for the ride. Johnson finally picked up the megaphone in 1953, but never achieved the success as a director he enjoyed as a writer-producer. Some of the few films he directed dealt with the troubled lives of contemporary characters: *Black Widow* (1954) found theatrical producer Van Heflin suspected of murdering a young woman with whom he'd been unfairly accused of having an affair; *The Man in the Gray Flannel Suit* (1956) focused on the malaise of the successful executive; and *The Three Faces of Eve* (1957), based on a true story, dealt with people afflicted with multiple personalities. Other directing credits include *Night People* (1954), *How to Be Very, Very Popular* (1955), *Oh Men! Oh Women!* (1957), *The Man Who Understood Women* (1959), and *The Angel Wore Red* (1960).

Johnson's later screenplays—still for Fox—include *Flaming Star* (1960) and *Mr. Hobbs Takes a Vacation* (1962). In 1964 he collaborated with his daughter Nora on the screen adaptation of her comic novel *The World of Henry Orient*, with delightful results. His last screen credit was for cowriting the gritty war picture *The Dirty Dozen* (1967). A volume of his letters was published in 1981. He was once married to *Grapes of Wrath* costar Dorris Bowdon.

JOHNSON, VAN. Actor. *(b. Aug. 25, 1916, Newport, R.I., as Charles Van Johnson.)* Blue-eyed, carrot-topped, freckle-faced leading man who zoomed to screen prominence at MGM during the WW2 years, when many top stars were in uniform.

(Johnson was exempted from military service due to a serious injury he'd suffered earlier in a car crash.) A New England Yankee of Swedish descent, Johnson was a chorus boy on the New York stage before making the trek westward in 1940. He was visible in RKO's *Too Many Girls* (1940, in the ensemble) and Warner Bros.' *Murder in the Big House* (1942) before landing his Metro contract. He made his debut for the studio in *The War Against Mrs. Hadley* (also 1942), taking a small supporting role. Johnson's career got an unexpected boost when he was assigned the juvenile lead in *Dr. Gillespie's New Assistant* (also 1942), replacing Lew Ayres in what had been the Dr. Kildare series, now a showcase for longtime Metro contractee Lionel Barrymore. The brawny but boyish Johnson soon became a fan favorite (albeit mostly with bobbysoxers), supporting Greer Garson in *Madame Curie*, Mickey Rooney in *The Human Comedy*, and Spencer Tracy in *A Guy Named Joe* (all 1943) before finally winning top billing in *Two Girls and a Sailor* (1944).

Johnson spent most of the next 15 years at MGM. He frequently appeared in the studio's all-star films and starred in many minor efforts, but his best films— including 1948's *State of the Union* and *Command Decision,* for example—saw the likable redhead in meaty supporting parts. As a wisecracking best friend (in 1954's *Brigadoon*) or a sharp-tongued lieutenant (in that same year's *The Caine Mutiny*) he fared better than in most of his less demanding, and less inspired, starring films. Like many other Hollywood stars of the 1940s and 1950s, Johnson found himself little in demand after the studio system self-destructed. During the 1970s and early 1980s he was a frequent guest on TV series and sitcoms, especially "The Love Boat," that Elephant's Graveyard of Golden-Age Hollywood stars.

OTHER FILMS INCLUDE: 1942: *Somewhere I'll Find You;* 1943: *Pilot #5;* 1944: *Between Two Women* (another *Kildare* entry), *The White Cliffs of Dover, Thirty Seconds Over Tokyo;* 1945: *Weekend at the Waldorf, Thrill of a Romance;* 1946: *Till the Clouds Roll By, Ziegfeld Follies, Easy to Wed;* 1947: *High Barbaree, The Romance of Rosy Ridge;* 1949: *Battleground* (in the leading role, and one of his best films), *In the Good Old Summertime;* 1950: *Grounds for Marriage, The Big Hangover;* 1951: *Too Young to Kiss, Go for Broke;*

1952: *Washington Story, Plymouth Adventure;*
1953: *Easy to Love;* 1954: *The Siege at Red
River, The Last Time I Saw Paris;* 1955: *The
End of the Affair;* 1956: *23 Paces to Baker
Street* (playing a blind playwright in this off-
beat crime thriller), *The Bottom of the Bottle,
Miracle in the Rain;* 1957: *Kelly and Me;*
1958: *The Last Blitzkrieg;* 1963: *Wives and
Lovers;* 1967: *Divorce American Style;* 1968:
Yours, Mine and Ours; 1970: *Eagles Over Lon-
don;* 1980: *The Kidnapping of the President;*
1985: *The Purple Rose of Cairo;* 1988: *Killer
Crocodile;* 1990: *Fuga dal Paradiso.*

JOLSON, AL. Singer, actor. *(b. May 26,
1886, St. Petersburg, Russia, as Asa Yoelson;
d. Oct. 23, 1950.)* This remarkable entertainer had already enjoyed a long and
profitable career on the stage when he
ushered in the talking-picture era, saying,
"You ain't heard nothin' yet" in *The Jazz
Singer* (1927). The son of a cantor, Jolson
first sang before audiences in his father's
synagogue. The lure of show business led
him first to join a circus, then to work in
vaudeville, and later to conquer Broadway
and become a top-selling recording star.
Although he'd been hired to make his
movie debut in *Mammy's Boy,* which was
to have been directed by the legendary
D. W. Griffith, the 1923 project was aborted and Jolson didn't appear on-screen until 1926, when he warbled a couple of
songs in a short, *Plantation Act,* using the
just-perfected Vitaphone sound process.
When fellow entertainer George Jessel
turned down a starring role in *The Jazz
Singer,* Jolson (whose own life story bore
an uncanny resemblance to that of the
leading character) eagerly accepted the
challenge. *The Jazz Singer,* often credited
as the first "talkie," was in fact a silent
picture with several musical interludes,
during which Jolson spoke a few lines of
dialogue. The film's great success
prompted Warner Bros., owners of the
Vitaphone process, to contract Jolson for
several more movies, which hewed fairly
closely to *The Jazz Singer*'s winning formula: *The Singing Fool* (1928), *Say It
With Songs* (1929), and *Mammy* (1930).
Big Boy (also 1930) replicated a 1925
Jolson stage vehicle, with the star in the
unlikely role of a stable boy, and in blackface throughout the picture!
Undeniably a forceful personality, and a
great entertainer, Jolson was not a very

good actor, and audiences were soon sated
with his repetitious musicals (and the
whole early-talkie musical genre, in fact).
He left the screen for several years, and
returned in his most adventurous film, the
charming and offbeat Depression fable,
Hallelujah, I'm a Bum (1933), which offered songs and rhyming dialogue by
Rodgers and Hart. It was not a great success.
Back at Warners, Jolson starred in *Wonder Bar* (1934, as "Al Wonder"), *Go Into
Your Dance* (1935, his only screen appearance with then-wife Ruby Keeler, a bigger
screen star at that point than he was), and
The Singing Kid (1936, which even included a number poking fun at his
"Mammy" songs) to progressively diminishing returns; the relative failure of *Kid*
effectively ended his starring career in
movies. He costarred in *Swanee River*
(1939), a Stephen Foster biography, and
played himself (or a reasonable facsimile
thereof) in *Rose of Washington Square*
(1939, a thinly disguised, unauthorized biopic of Fanny Brice), *Hollywood Cavalcade* (1939, recreating a *Jazz Singer* sequence), and *Rhapsody in Blue* (1945,
playing himself in this George Gershwin
biopic).
When Columbia Pictures decided to film
The Jolson Story in 1945, the "World's
Greatest Entertainer" (as he was by then
known) suffered the indignity of a screen
test to determine if he could play himself!
(It seemed unlikely to Columbia prexy
Harry Cohn that the 59-year-old Jolson
could convincingly appear as the much
younger man of his early stage triumphs.)
Studio contractee Larry Parks was chosen
to play the role, lip-synching to Jolson's
prerecorded vocals. Although it was not
known to moviegoers at the time, Jolson
himself did appear in some long shots,
doing his inimitable dance steps. The
1946 film was a sensational success, and
Jolson enjoyed one of the most spectacular comebacks in show-business history.
Never really away (as he worked steadily
on radio), he nevertheless found himself a
headliner again—on top of the heap, and
loving it. He repeated vocal chores for a
sequel, *Jolson Sings Again* (1949), and
died soon after returning from Korea,
where he had entertained U.S. troops.
Jolson was married to actress-dancer
Keeler from 1928 to 1940.

JONES, ALLAN. Actor; singer. *(b. Oct. 14, 1908, Old Forge, Pa.; d. June 27, 1992.)* Buoyant, wavy-haired, good-looking leading man of Hollywood musicals, a coal miner's son who escaped the mines by earning scholarships to study music in New York and Paris. Noticed by Hollywood talent scouts after performing on the stage, Jones was signed by MGM in 1935, first appearing in the Jean Harlow musical *Reckless,* then singing "A Pretty Girl is Like a Melody" off-camera for Dennis Morgan in *The Great Ziegfeld* (1936). He held his own as juvenile lead with The Marx Brothers in *A Night at the Opera* (1935) and *A Day at the Races* (1937). But it was as Gaylord Ravenal, the charming but irresponsible cad in *Show Boat* (1936), that Jones made his mark on movie-musical history, singing the songs of Jerome Kern and Oscar Hammerstein as though they had been written for him alone. In *The Firefly* (1937), opposite Jeanette MacDonald, he sang Friml's "Donkey Serenade," which became his theme song (he repeated it on-screen in 1943's *Crazy House).* After leaving MGM Jones went to work for Paramount (in such mediocre fare as 1939's *The Great Victor Herbert)* and Universal, where most of his vehicles (excepting 1940's *The Boys From Syracuse* and *One Night in the Tropics)* were undistinguished B pictures. After laboring in the likes of *Moonlight in Havana, True to the Army* (both 1942), *You're a Lucky Fellow, Mr. Smith* (1943), *The Singing Sheriff* (1944), and *Honeymoon Ahead* (1945), Jones returned to the stage and nightclubs. He was singing, beautifully, right into the 1990s. Once married to actress Irene Hervey; their son is singer Jack Jones.

JONES, BUCK. Actor. *(b. Dec. 4, 1889, Vincennes, Ind., as Charles Frederick Gebhart; d. Nov. 30, 1942.)* Buck Jones was one of the most beloved stars in movie history—with fans and colleagues alike. Ruggedly handsome, solidly built, a man's man in every way, his unswerving embodiment of fair play made him the idol of millions of kids. A former Cavalryman who saw action in Mexico, Jones, then known as Gebhart, worked the rodeo circuit and toured with circuses and Wild-West shows before coming to Hollywood as a wrangler, extra, and stuntman. In 1917 he

started working at the Fox studio, and within three years was given his first chance to carry a picture, *The Last Straw* (1920). He showed an affinity for performing from the first, though he could never be mistaken for a trained actor. Although he worked predominantly in Westerns, Jones (as he was by now known) also starred in two exceptional pictures, *Just Pals* (1920, directed by John Ford) and *Lazybones* (1925, directed by Frank Borzage), rural dramas that called upon him to display a wider range of emotions, including humor and pathos, than was demanded by his unpretentious oaters. Good as he was, though, Jones stayed pretty much within the Western genre, nearly equaling Tom Mix in popularity during the 1920s.

In 1928, flush with his own success, Jones broke with Fox and tried producing his own talkie film, *The Big Hop,* which flopped badly and tarnished his reputation within the industry. He began making low-budget horse operas for Columbia release in 1930, and such above-average Bs as *The Deadline* (1931), *White Eagle* (1932), and *The Thrill Hunter* (1933) helped him regain his standing. He joined Universal in 1934 and over the next three years he made 22 features and four serials there, alternating sober stories such as *Stone of Silver Creek, The Ivory-Handled Gun* (both 1935), and *Empty Saddles,* with lighthearted romps the likes of *Ride 'Em Cowboy* (both 1936) and *Law for Tombstone* (1937). Escalating costs and studio infighting eventually drove him back to Columbia, where a poor 1937–38 series injured his marketability. A couple of lean years followed, during which he played a prizefighter in a 1939 drama, *Unmarried,* and—heresy!—a crooked marshal in the 1940 Chester Morris starrer *Wagons Westward.*

In 1941, however, his old friend and Fox producer Scott Dunlap brought Jones to Monogram, where he was teamed with Tim McCoy and Raymond Hatton for the "Rough Riders" series. With scripts that made Jones the dominant member of the trio, such films as *Arizona Bound* (1941), *Forbidden Trails,* and *Ghost Town Law* (both 1942) proved extremely popular, and put Jones back at the top of the horse-opera heap. Sadly, *Dawn on the Great Divide* (1942, with Rex Bell replacing McCoy) proved to be Jones' last film.

While stopping at Boston's famous Coconut Grove on Nov. 28, 1942, he was caught in the devastating fire that killed more than 300 people. Having struggled to save many customers that night, at the expense of his own life, he was hailed as a real-life hero.

JONES, CAROLYN. Actress. *(b. Apr. 28, 1929, Amarillo, Tex.; d. Aug. 3, 1983.)* Jones' unique look—a beautiful face with a vaguely sinister cast—made her a natural to play Morticia Addams, the slinky matriarch of the TV series "The Addams Family" (1964–66), and the generation that grew up watching those shows is probably unaware that she was also an Oscar-nominated actress. She was already a stage performer of considerable experience when she made her film debut at age 23 in *The Turning Point* (1952). Jones played her share of floozies and adulterous wives throughout the decade, but snared her Academy Award nomination for a delightful supporting turn as a philosophical nymphomaniac in *The Bachelor Party* (1957). Her movie career petered out in the early 1960s and she turned to TV, making only a few feature-film appearances after the "Addams Family" series. She was once married to actor-turned-producer Aaron Spelling.
OTHER FILMS INCLUDE: 1952: *Road to Bali;* 1953: *House of Wax, The Big Heat;* 1954: *Desiree;* 1955: *The Seven Year Itch, The Tender Trap;* 1956: *Invasion of the Body Snatchers, The Man Who Knew Too Much, The Opposite Sex;* 1958: *Marjorie Morningstar, King Creole;* 1959: *Career;* 1962: *Sail a Crooked Ship, How the West Was Won;* 1969: *Color Me Dead;* 1977: *Eaten Alive.*

JONES, CHUCK. Animation director, producer. *(b. Sept. 1, 1912, Spokane, Wash., as Charles M. Jones.)* One of the grand masters of animated cartoons, Jones can get laughs out of his characters' tiniest gestures: a wriggle of Bugs Bunny's eyebrows, a snap of Daffy Duck's bill. Those nuances are among his trademarks, and though he worked for years in the Warner Bros. "house style," his cartoons were always distinctively his own.
Graduating from the animator's chair to the director's in the late 1930s, Jones at first was intrigued with size and proportion, and made many films about little characters—from Joe Glow the Firefly to Sniffles the mouse to Porky's Ant. He made many fine cartoons, including *The Dover Boys, The Rabbit of Seville,* but reached his peak in the 1950s, collaborating mostly with writer Michael Maltese. Their cartoons struck an amazing balance between visual slapstick and verbal wit, as in *Rabbit Seasoning* (1952), *Bully for Bugs,* and *Duck Dodgers in the 24½th Century* (both 1953). In *Duck Amuck* (1953) they deconstructed the cartoon itself; in *What's Opera, Doc?* (1957) they squished Wagner's Ring Cycle into seven minutes of stylized nonsense; and in *One Froggy Evening* (1955) they created a timely and timeless parable about greed and exploitation. They also set themselves the formidable task of creating a series of cartoons with a fixed set of rules when they made the Road Runner/Coyote series, and managed to find endless (and hilarious) variations on their own formula. Pepe LePew was also a Jones/Maltese creation.
When the Warner Bros. cartoon department expired, Jones cowrote (with his wife Dorothy) a feature for UPA, *Gay Purr-ee* (1963), then joined the reconstituted MGM cartoon department, where he directed and supervised a new series of Tom and Jerry shorts, adapted an award-winning book into an Oscar-winning short film, *The Dot and the Line* (1965), and codirected the live-action/animated feature *The Phantom Tollbooth* (1969). Jones spent the balance of his career creating high-quality half-hour TV specials, including such perennials as *How the Grinch Stole Christmas.* Widely celebrated in recent years at film festivals and special programs around the world, Jones has lent advice to various filmmakers and even made cameo appearances in the films of his fan Joe Dante (who featured him in 1984's *Gremlins*—and named a high school after him in the plot; he also had Jones direct funny closing credits for 1990's *Gremlins 2*). Jones produced an animated segment for the 1992 live-action feature *Stay Tuned* which—not surprisingly—was the best thing about the movie. In 1994 he launched a new series of theatrical shorts—for Warner Bros. His autobiography, "Chuck Amuck," was published in 1989.

JONES, DEAN. Actor. *(b. Jan. 25, 1935, Morgan County, Ala.)* Amiable, lightweight leading man best known for his string of starring roles in Walt Disney films. A former blues singer, he made his film debut in *Gaby*, and appeared in *Somebody Up There Likes Me, Tea and Sympathy* (all 1956), *Designing Woman, Jailhouse Rock* (both 1957), *Imitation General* (1958), *Never So Few* (1959), *Under the Yum Yum Tree* (1963), *The New Interns* (1964), and *Two on a Guillotine* (1965) before becoming house lead for the Disney studio, where he generally played second fiddle to clever animals or cars that drove themselves. His movies for Walt include *That Darn Cat* (1965), *The Ugly Dachshund* (1966), *Monkeys, Go Home!* (1967), *Blackbeard's Ghost, The Horse in the Gray Flannel Suit* (both 1968), *The Love Bug* (1969), *$1,000,000 Duck* (1971), *Snowball Express* (1972), *The Shaggy D.A.* (1976), and *Herbie Goes to Monte Carlo* (1977). (His reputation won him a similar vehicle away from Disney, *Mr. Superinvisible*, in 1973.) In 1971 he created the leading role in Stephen Sondheim's Broadway musical *Company*, which at that point was an impressive departure for the actor. In 1978 Jones played convicted Watergate trickster Charles Colson in *Born Again*, and claimed to have been spiritually renewed himself; he subsequently dropped out of show business to work in Christian organizations. Returning to acting on TV, he landed a major film role again in 1991's *Other People's Money*, and delivered a solid performance. He was then cast, amusingly against type, as an evil veterinarian in the family comedy *Beethoven* (1992). His autobiography, "Under Running Laughter," was published in 1982.

JONES, JAMES EARL. Actor. *(b. Jan. 17, 1931, Arkabutla, Miss.)* This distinguished actor's booming voice and imposing presence command instant attention. He was a dominant force on Broadway throughout the 1960s and 1970s, giving Tony-winning performances as boxer Jack Johnson in "The Great White Hope" (a role that also won him an Oscar nomination when he filmed it in 1970) and, more recently, "Fences." His first feature-film appearance was a small but notable role as a member of Slim Pickens' flight crew in *Dr. Strangelove* (1964). Other early credits include *The Comedians* (1967) and *End of the Road* (1970). After *Hope*, his movie offers increased; Jones played the first black president in *The Man* (1972), a cheerful garbageman in *Claudine* (1974), a baseball veteran in *The Bingo Long Traveling All Stars & Motor Kings* (1976), a jolly pirate in *Swashbuckler* (1976), the monstrous Thulsa Doom in *Conan the Barbarian* (1982), a downtrodden coal miner in *Matewan* (1987), an African king in *Coming to America* (1988), a reclusive author in *Field of Dreams* (1989), and a high-ranking naval officer in *The Hunt for Red October* (1990). Although often cast in serious, even somber parts, he has shown equal facility with lighter material—from *The Last Remake of Beau Geste* (1977) to *The Meteor Man* (1993). In some recent films, however, he has unfortunately been used as something of a self-caricature (as symbols of authority in 1992's *Sneakers* and 1993's *Sommersby*). Other credits include *Patriot Games* (1992, repeating his role from *The Hunt for Red October*), *The Sandlot, Excessive Force* (both 1993), *Clean Slate, Clear and Present Danger* (both 1994), *The Lion King* (also 1994, as the voice of Mufasa), and *Jefferson in Paris* (1995).

His TV work includes playing author Alex Haley in "Roots: The Next Generation," a short-lived police show, "Paris," and, in his Emmy-winning role as an ex-con, "Gabriel's Fire." But it's that incredible voice that will remain his calling card: Millions of kids know it as the asthmatic rasp of Darth Vader in *Star Wars* (1977), *The Empire Strikes Back* (1980), and *Return of the Jedi* (1983), and millions hear it every half hour: "This . . . is CNN." His father, Robert Earl Jones, is also an actor. His autobiography, "Voices and Silences," was published in 1993.

JONES, JEFFREY. Actor. *(b. Sept. 28, 1947, Buffalo, N.Y.)* Comic patsies aren't easy to come by these days, but Jones admirably fills the bill, as he demonstrated early in his film career, playing the suspicious, pratfalling high-school principal in the teen comedy *Ferris Bueller's Day Off* (1986). This fair-haired, hawk-nosed character player first impressed moviegoers as the supercilious, music-loving Emperor

Joseph II in *Amadeus* (1984), and has consistently delivered fine performances in comedies, dramas, and fantasies, including the notorious box-office bomb *Howard the Duck* (1986), *The Hanoi Hilton* (1987), *Beetlejuice, Without a Clue* (both 1988), *Valmont* (1989), and *The Hunt for Red October* (1990). Recent credits include *Mom and Dad Save the World, Out on a Limb, Stay Tuned* (all 1992), and *Ed Wood* (1994, as Criswell). He also starred in the TV fantasy sitcom "The People Next Door" (1989).

JONES, JENNIFER. Actress. *(b. Mar. 2, 1919, Tulsa, Okla., as Phylis Isley.)* For a brief period she was one of Hollywood's brightest stars, thanks to careful grooming and career guidance from top producer David O. Selznick, to whom she was married for many years. Born to vaudeville performers with whom she performed as a child, the dark-haired, soulful Phylis Isley always wanted to be an actress. She studied at New York's American Academy of Dramatic Arts (where she met and married Robert Walker, himself an aspiring actor) before winning a six-month contract from Republic Pictures; her father, by this time, owned a prominent theater chain upon which Republic depended, so studio brass proved more than willing to give his daughter a tryout. She assumed ingenue chores in 1939's *New Frontier,* a B Western starring John Wayne, and *Dick Tracy's G-Men,* a popular serial, before being dropped summarily.

David Selznick spotted Phylis Isley in Hollywood shortly thereafter and reasoned that he could mold her, Pygmalion-like, into a star. He signed her to a personal contract, changed her name to Jennifer Jones, and saw to it that she was the recipient of intensive training as well as a big publicity buildup. Selznick canvassed the Hollywood studios for the right property in which to feature his discovery, and found it in *The Song of Bernadette* (1943), a 20th Century-Fox spectacular that cast her as a young French girl who claims to have seen the Virgin Mary in a vision. Jones won a well-deserved Oscar for her first big role, and Selznick rushed her into his own production, *Since You Went Away* (1944), a wartime domestic drama for which she was Oscar-nominated. She impressed moviegoers with her warm, touch-

ing portrayal of an average American girl coping with home-front hardships. Amazingly, Jones earned Academy Award nods for her next two performances as well, first as a fragile amnesiac in *Love Letters* (1945), then as a tempestuous half-breed in Selznick's elephantine, sexy Western, *Duel in the Sun* (1946). By this time she had blossomed into a beautiful, sensitive actress.

Jones, whose relationship with Selznick had become personal as well as professional, divorced Walker and married the producer in 1949. Although he produced fewer films as the years went on, he still guided her career closely—and sent voluminous memos to producers and directors who hired her. She contributed consistently fine performances in the likes of *Cluny Brown* (1946), *Portrait of Jennie* (1948), *Madame Bovary* (1949), *The Wild Heart* (1950, aka *Gone to Earth), Carrie* (1952), *Love Is a Many Splendored Thing* (snagging another Oscar nomination for her work in this 1955 soaper), *Good Morning, Miss Dove* (also 1955), *The Man in the Gray Flannel Suit* (1956), *The Barretts of Wimpole Street, A Farewell to Arms* (Selznick's swan song as producer, both 1957), and *Tender Is the Night* (1961).

After Selznick died in 1965, Jones seemed to lose interest in her career, appearing in just three more films—*The Idol* (1966), *Cult of the Damned* (1969), and *The Towering Inferno* (1974)—before retiring altogether. She remarried, to businessman-philanthropist Norton Simon, and has stayed out of the limelight. Her son Robert Walker, Jr., is also an actor (and the very image of his father).

JONES, L. Q. Actor. *(b. Aug. 19, 1927, as Justice Ellis McQueen.)* In 1955, a blond, gaunt actor named Justus McQueen played a soldier called L. Q. Jones in *Battle Cry.* He liked the name so much he took it for his own, and for the next quarter-century was indispensable as a scurvy bad guy, often in Westerns, including *The Naked and the Dead, Buchanan Rides Alone* (both 1958), *Hang 'Em High* (1968), *The Hunting Party* (1971), and *White Line Fever* (1975), reaching his peak as a member of the Sam Peckinpah repertory company in *Ride the High Country* (1962), *Major Dundee* (1965),

The Wild Bunch (1969), *The Ballad of Cable Hogue* (1970), memorably teamed with Strother Martin in the latter two movies, and *Pat Garrett and Billy the Kid* (1973). Jones could play comedy, too, and did so in the likes of *Operation Mad Ball* (1957) and *Mother, Jugs & Speed* (1976). Later credits include *Timerider* and *Lone Wolf McQuade* (both 1983). He also produced several small genre films, most notably *The Brotherhood of Satan* (1971) and *A Boy and His Dog* (1975, which he also directed). On TV, he had regular roles on two classic Westerns, "Cheyenne" and "The Virginian." Inactive in recent years, though he turned up as a scummy guide in *River of Death* (1989), and in *Lightning Jack* (1994) and *Casino* (1995).

JONES, QUINCY. Composer. *(b. Mar. 14, 1935, Chicago.)* Although better known today as Michael Jackson's producer, Jones has had a distinguished career as composer, arranger, and bandleader, extending back to the early 1950s. His jazz background, acquired at the Berklee School of Music in Boston, resulted in a sophisticated body of work that has netted six Academy Award nominations. The first major picture to feature his music was Sidney Lumet's *The Pawnbroker* (1965), which was followed by *In Cold Blood* (1967), for which his score was Oscar-nominated. He later received other nominations for scoring *The Wiz* (1978) and *The Color Purple* (1985, as well as one song), and got nods for Best Song in *Banning* (1967) and *For Love of Ivy* (1968). He also provided music scores for animated shorts and features by John and Faith Hubley, including *Eggs* and *Of Men and Demons* (both 1970). Jones, who was for many years married to actress Peggy Lipton and later had a child with actress Nastassja Kinski, is the winner of numerous Grammy awards for his work on both sides of the recording-studio wall. Other films sporting his music include *The Slender Thread* (1965), *Walk, Don't Run* (1966), *In the Heat of the Night* (1967), *Cactus Flower* (1969), *Come Back, Charleston Blue*, *The Getaway* (both 1972), *Mother, Jugs & Speed* (1976), and *The Slugger's Wife* (1985). In recent years Jones has become a show business entrepreneur, with many irons in the fire; he in fact coproduced *The Color Purple*. In 1990 he was the subject of a feature-length documentary, *Listen Up: The Lives of Quincy Jones.* In 1995, Jones received the Academy's Jean Hersholt Humanitarian Award.

JONES, SHIRLEY. Actress, singer. *(b. Mar. 31, 1934, Smithton, Pa.)* The archetypal "girl next door"—pretty, wholesome, vivacious—stunned critics and moviegoers alike with her deft performance as a prostitute in *Elmer Gantry* (1960), winning a Best Supporting Actress Oscar for that portrayal. It was the high point in a screen career that began with starring roles in two classic Rodgers and Hammerstein musicals: *Oklahoma!* (1955) and *Carousel* (1956), both of which demonstrated that Jones had a voice as lovely as her face. *April Love* (1957), *Never Steal Anything Small* (1959), and *Two Rode Together* (1961) all featured Jones but didn't tax her abilities. She found an ideal vehicle for her talent in *The Music Man* (1962), Meredith Willson's delightful turn-of-the-century musical, playing the prim and proper Marian the Librarian. Her subsequent films—including *The Courtship of Eddie's Father* (1963), *Bedtime Story* (1964, for which she tried to ditch her "image" by going brunette), *The Secret of My Success* (1965), *The Happy Ending* (1969), *The Cheyenne Social Club* (1970), *Beyond the Poseidon Adventure* (1979) and *Tank* (1984) among them—have not been of particular importance. But it would be a mistake to remember her only for "The Partridge Family" (1970–74) and her innumerable other TV appearances. She is married to onetime actor, latter-day talent agent Marty Ingels.

JONES, TOMMY LEE. Actor. *(b. Sept. 15, 1946, San Saba, Tex.)* Dark, pockmarked, but handsome in a sinister way, Jones attended Harvard University (where his roommate was future Vice President Al Gore), studying English Literature, and graduating cum laude. He made his feature-film debut in a small part in *Love Story* (1970). He worked throughout the 1970s, usually in supporting roles, making critics and audiences sit up and notice him late in the decade, following performances in *Jackson County Jail* (1976, a showy costarring part), *Eyes of Laura Mars*, *The*

Betsy (both 1978), and *Coal Miner's Daughter* (1980, another prime showcase, as Sissy Spacek's husband). Jones scored heavily as convicted murderer Gary Gilmore in a TV adaptation of *The Executioner's Song* (1982, which won him an Emmy Award), which set a pattern for his career to come; he's repeatedly earned greater attention for his character parts and heavies than for his periodic leading-man roles. He gave an outstanding performance as Texas Ranger-turned-cowboy Woodrow Call in the highly acclaimed TV miniseries "Lonesome Dove" (1989), and was memorable as a down-at-the-heels private eye in HBO's erotic thriller *Gotham* (1988). He earned an Oscar nomination for his vivid portrayal of colorful New Orleans businessman Clay Shaw in *JFK* (1991), and enjoyed a scenery-chewing heavy assignment in the 1992 action thriller *Under Siege*. Busier than ever, he won an Oscar in the smash hit *The Fugitive* (1993) as the Javert-like federal marshal on Harrison Ford's trail, then rejoined Oliver Stone for *Heaven and Earth* (1993) and *Natural Born Killers* (1994). He also appeared in *Blue Sky* (1994, filmed in 1990; his tenderest role), *Blown Away, The Client, Cobb* (all 1994), and *Batman Forever* (1995, as Two-Face), and even found time to direct, cowrite, and star in the made-for-cable movie *The Good Old Boys* (also 1995).
OTHER FILMS INCLUDE: 1983: *Nate and Hayes;* 1986: *Black Moon Rising;* 1987: *The Big Town;* 1988: *Stormy Monday;* 1989: *The Package;* 1990: *Fire Birds* (an especially good part as an aging fighter pilot); 1993: *House of Cards.*

JORDAN, NEIL. Director, screenwriter. *(b. Feb. 25, 1950, Sligo County, Ireland.)* Original, highly personal filmmaker whom critic David Denby described as having "perhaps the most poetically eloquent temperament in the English-speaking language." Jordan began his career as a writer, with two novels and a collection of stories to his credit, and made his first venture into film as a script consultant on John Boorman's *Excalibur* (1981). His debut film as writer and director was *Angel* (1982, released in the U.S. as *Danny Boy*), a thriller set in Northern Ireland, but he captured more attention with *The Company of Wolves* (1984), a

dark, adult retelling of "Little Red Riding Hood" that earned awards for Best Film and Best Director from the London Critics Circle. International acclaim greeted *Mona Lisa* (1986), the story of a small-time hood who falls for a black call girl; critics were impressed by Jordan's ability to combine elements of violence and a noir atmosphere into a story that was ultimately romantic at heart. Jordan's first ventures for American studios, *High Spirits* (1988) and *We're No Angels* (1989), were unsatisfying for the filmmaker—and moviegoers—and the former film, something of a disaster, was taken from him during the editing process. He returned to Ireland to make the fantasy-themed *The Miracle* (1991) and received his finest notices (and a Best Screenplay Oscar) for *The Crying Game* (1992), a superb romantic thriller that continued and deepened the themes of forbidden sexual desire and the price of love first explored in *Mona Lisa*. He leaped back into the high-profile Hollywood arena with a big-budget adaptation of *Interview With the Vampire* (1994). He also directed a Kirsty MacColl music video, "Miss Otis Regrets," and The Pogles' "Just One of Those Things."

JORDAN, RICHARD. Actor. *(b. July 19, 1938, New York City; d. Aug. 30, 1993.)* Edgily handsome, Harvard-educated supporting player often seen in villainous parts. He debuted in *Lawman* (1970), and worked steadily thereafter, earning audience awareness in such TV productions as "Captains and the Kings" (1976) and *Les Misérables* (1978), which offered heroic roles usually denied him by movie producers. Primarily a stage actor, Jordan had scores of Broadway and off-Broadway credits (not to mention eight years with the New York Shakespeare Festival) and was also a respected theater director. His final, prominent screen performance, as Brig. General Lewis Armistead in *Gettysburg* (1993), was shown after his untimely death from cancer. He had begun filming *The Fugitive* when illness forced him to leave the production; Jeroen Krabbe took over his part. Jordan was married to actress Blair Brown.
OTHER FILMS INCLUDE: 1972: *Chato's Land;* 1973: *The Friends of Eddie Coyle;* 1975: *Rooster Cogburn;* 1976: *Logan's Run;* 1978: *Interiors;* 1979: *Old Boyfriends;* 1980: *Raise*

the Titanic!; 1984: *Dune;* 1985: *The Mean Season;* 1986: *The Men's Club;* 1986: *Solarbabies;* 1987: *The Secret of My Success;* 1990: *The Hunt for Red October;* 1991: *Heaven Is a Playground, All Shook Up, Nameless.*

JORY, VICTOR. Actor. *(b. Nov. 23, 1902, Dawson City, Alaska; d. Feb. 11, 1982.)* Durable character actor with mesmerizing dark eyes, hawk nose, and menacing manner. Jory toured with several theater troupes and appeared on Broadway before making his film debut in 1932. He initially played romantic leads in *The Devil's in Love* (1932), *Sailor's Luck* (1933, in an insanely funny performance as Baron Bartolo, the lecherous, over-the-top villain who at one point hosts a marathon dance contest), *My Woman* (also 1933), and *I Believed in You* (1934), but a natural ambiguity in his performances suggested he was better cast in unsympathetic parts. Jory made a memorable Oberon in *A Midsummer Night's Dream* (1935), but alternated leads in B pictures and serials (1940's *The Shadow* and *The Green Archer*) with heavies in A pictures (1938's *Adventures of Tom Sawyer,* as Injun Joe, 1939's *Dodge City,* and *Gone With the Wind,* in which he's Tara's overseer, Jonas Wilkerson). Other films include *State Fair* (1933), *Meet Nero Wolfe* (1936), *Man of Conquest* (1939, as Col. William Travis), *Each Dawn I Die* (1939), *Charlie Chan in Rio* (1941), *South of St. Louis* (1949), *The Miracle Worker* (1962, as Helen Keller's father), *Cheyenne Autumn* (1964, as a stoic Indian), *Jigsaw* (1968), *Flap* (1970), and *Papillon* (1973). He appeared in dozens of Westerns, but his personal favorite film was *The Fugitive Kind* (1959), in which he supported Marlon Brando and Joanne Woodward. Jory made more than 150 films, all told, and dozens of TV episodes; he also wrote two plays.

JOSEPHSON, ERLAND. Actor. *(b. June 15, 1923, Stockholm.)* Renowned as one of the chief members of the great Ingmar Bergman's "repertory company," Josephson has appeared in eight of the director's films, starting with *It Rains on Our Love* (1946) and continuing with *Brink of Life* (1958), *Hour of the Wolf* (1968), *The Passion of Anna* (1969), *Cries*

and Whispers (1972), *Face to Face* (1976), *Autumn Sonata* (1978), *Fanny and Alexander* (1983), and probably most memorably, *Scenes From a Marriage* (1973, as Liv Ullmann's husband). He played an opera company executive in *Meeting Venus* (1991), a slight change from his onetime real-life position as head of Sweden's Royal Dramatic Theatre for nine years during the 1960s and 1970s.
OTHER FILMS INCLUDE: 1981: *Montenegro;* 1988: *Hanussen, The Unbearable Lightness of Being;* 1991: *Prospero's Books, The Ox;* 1995: *Ulysses' Gaze.*

JOSLYN, ALLYN. Actor. *(b. July 21, 1901, Milford, Pa.; d. Jan. 21, 1981.)* Already well established on stage and in dramatic radio before making his film debut in *They Won't Forget* (1937), Joslyn in Hollywood never matched the success he achieved on Broadway. He was a fine actor capable of playing widely varying roles, but movie producers often cast him as a supercilious society type. His films include *Only Angels Have Wings* (1939), *The Great McGinty, No Time for Comedy* (both 1940), *I Wake Up Screaming* (1941), *My Sister Eileen* (1942), *Heaven Can Wait* (1943), *The Horn Blows at Midnight* (1945, as one of the "fallen" angels), *Junior Miss* (1945), *It Shouldn't Happen to a Dog* (1946, a rare leading role), *Moonrise* (1948), *Harriet Craig* (1950), *As Young As You Feel* (1951), *Titanic* (1953, as a cowardly passenger), *The Fastest Gun Alive* (1956), *Nightmare in the Sun* (1965), and *The Brothers O'Toole* (1973). Active on TV, he costarred in the 1962–63 series "McKeever and the Colonel."

JOST, JON. Director, screenwriter, producer, cinematographer, editor, composer. *(b. May 16, 1943, Chicago.)* Over the course of three decades, Jost has carved for himself an estimable career as a director of films which are fiercely independent, and which focus on provocative contemporary themes while offering a singular cinematic sensibility. The facts of his early adult life portend the course of his career, and define his political and social esthetic: He was expelled from college in 1963, at which time he began making 16mm films; he was imprisoned as a draft resister during the Vietnam era; he helped establish

JOURDAN, LOUIS 452

the Chicago branch of Newsreel, a New Left movie production and distribution organization.

Jost's short and feature-length films are as idiosyncratic as their titles, from *Speaking Directly (some American notes)* (1973) through *Plain Talk & Common Sense (uncommon senses)* and *Rembrandt Laughing* (both 1988). They explore such topics as the legacy of Vietnam, the manner in which men and women relate, consumerism in American society, and friction between the classes. Jost's works are most personal when examining the inability of the individual to communicate meaningfully in an increasingly alienating world. That world may be urban: in *All the Vermeers in New York* (1990) he spotlights the obvious and subtle ways in which people exploit one another, while scrutinizing the duplicitous connection between art and commerce. Or it may be rural: in *The Bed You Sleep In* (1993), the last of a trilogy following *Last Chants for a Slow Dance* (1977) and *Sure Fire* (1990), he tells a story of economic and familial upheaval in a small Oregon town. Jost is not so much interested in storyline as in creating a mood which reflects his viewpoint. Stylistically, his films are loaded with lingering, artfully designed shots, extemporized dialogue, and long stretches where there is no dialogue.

JOURDAN, LOUIS. Actor. *(b. June 19, 1919, Marseilles, as Louis Gendre.)* Handsome, suave, but emotionally restrained actor whose Gallic charm endeared him to American audiences (particularly female), although the repetitive sameness of his film roles eventually eroded his star status and forced him into character work. A French film star who made his screen debut in 1939's *Le Corsaire,* Jourdan joined the French Underground during World War 2. After the war he came to Hollywood at the behest of David O. Selznick, and made his American film debut in the lackluster Hitchcock drama *The Paradine Case* (1948). He had a better opportunity as the musician doggedly coveted by Joan Fontaine in *Letter From an Unknown Woman* (also 1948), a starring role that effectively launched his Hollywood career. He appeared in *Madame Bovary* (1949), *Bird of Paradise* (1951), *The Happy Time* (1952, a tailor-made role

as a gay, irrepressible French-Canadian charmer), *Decameron Nights* (1953, in which he played four parts), *Three Coins in the Fountain* (1954), *The Swan* (1956), *Gigi* (1958, as the debonair Frenchman who falls for courtesan-in-training Leslie Caron), *Can-Can* (1960), *The V.I.P.s* (1963), *Made in Paris* (1966), *The Count of Monte Cristo* (1975 telefilm), and *Silver Bears* (1978) among others. Although he remained a remarkably handsome man in his 50s, Jourdan moved into character work, becoming a dependable heavy, especially in 1982's *Swamp Thing* and its 1989 sequel, and the 1983 James Bond thriller *Octopussy.* In 1978 he played an elegantly effective Dracula in a well-received British television production.

JULIA, RAUL. Actor. *(b. Mar. 4, 1940, San Juan, Puerto Rico; d. Oct. 24, 1994.)* Droopy-eyed, dark, and suavely handsome, this extremely versatile actor was one of the most respected stage performers of his generation. His Broadway credits range from "Two Gentlemen of Verona" and "Threepenny Opera" to "Charley's Aunt" and the Fellini-inspired musical "Nine." His earliest film credits date back to 1971 *(Been Down So Long It Looks Like Up to Me),* but he never achieved superstar status in the movies despite some strong roles, particularly as a political prisoner in *Kiss of the Spider Woman* (1985) and a Salvadoran priest in the 1989 sleeper *Romero.* He provided strong support in a number of A productions that didn't live up to their pedigree, including the Jane Fonda starrer *The Morning After* (1986) and the Kurt Russell/Mel Gibson/Michelle Pfeiffer romantic thriller *Tequila Sunrise* (1988). As brilliant defense lawyer Sandy Stern in *Presumed Innocent* (1990), Julia whisked the movie out from under star Harrison Ford, whose dour character was no match for the flamboyant attorney. Although taller and less jowly than artist Charles Addams' conception of the character, he played Gomez Addams in 1991's big-screen comedy *The Addams Family,* a hit that revealed his flair for wacky comedy. He and Anjelica Huston repeated their roles in the sequel, *Addams Family Values* (1993). One of Julia's most memorable roles—as Brazilian environmentalist and

trade unionist Chico Mendes—was in the made-for-cable movie *The Burning Season* (1994), aired shortly before his death from a stroke.
OTHER FILMS INCLUDE: 1971: *The Panic in Needle Park;* 1978: *Eyes of Laura Mars;* 1982: *The Escape Artist, Tempest, One From the Heart;* 1988: *Moon Over Parador;* 1989: *Mack the Knife;* 1990: *Frankenstein Unbound, The Rookie;* 1992: *The Plague;* 1994: *Street Fighter* (released posthumously).

JURADO, KATY. Actress. *(b. Jan. 16, 1927, Guadalajara, Mexico, as Maria Cristina Jurado Garcia.)* Smoldering, sensual, fiery-eyed Mexican actress who was a movie star in her own country for nearly a decade before appearing as second female lead in Budd Boetticher's *Bullfighter and the Lady* (1951), launching a lengthy but spotty American film career. Jurado got her best opportunities in *High Noon* (1952, her passion effectively contrasted with Grace Kelly's patrician reserve), *Broken Lance* (1954, in an Oscar-nominated supporting role), and *One-Eyed Jacks* (1961, directed by and starring Marlon Brando). Once married to Ernest Borgnine.
OTHER FILMS INCLUDE: 1953: *San Antone;* 1955: *Trial;* 1956: *Trapeze;* 1958: *The Badlanders;* 1962: *Barabbas;* 1966: *Smoky;* 1968: *Stay Away, Joe;* 1973: *Pat Garrett and Billy the Kid;* 1978: *The Children of Sanchez;* 1984: *Under the Volcano.*

JURGENS, CURT. Actor. *(b. Dec. 13, 1912, Munich; d. June 18, 1982.)* Tall, solidly built, fair-haired German actor with piercing blue eyes, a former journalist who took up acting in the early 1930s and made his film debut in 1935's *The Royal Waltz.* Devilishly handsome in his youth, Jurgens became a Continental stage and screen star, although he was taken out of circulation during World War 2 by Nazi propaganda minister Goebbels and interned in a concentration camp as "politically undesirable" to the Third Reich. Jurgens started appearing in English-language movies during the 1950s, and became a familiar face to moviegoers on both sides of the Atlantic. A notorious hedonist who married five times (including once to actress Eva Bartok), he could be

counted upon to provide dependable performances in the weakest of movies.
OTHER FILMS INCLUDE: 1953: *The Last Waltz;* 1954: *Orient Express;* 1955: *Heroes and Sinners;* 1956: *... And God Created Woman;* 1957: *Michael Strogoff* (in the title role), *The Enemy Below;* 1958: *The Inn of the Sixth Happiness;* 1959: *The Blue Angel;* 1960: *I Aim at the Stars* (as rocket scientist Wernher von Braun); 1962: *The Longest Day;* 1963: *The Threepenny Opera, Miracle of the White Stallions;* 1965: *Lord Jim;* 1969: *The Assassination Bureau, Battle of Britain;* 1971: *The Mephisto Waltz, Nicholas and Alexandra;* 1973: *Vault of Horror;* 1977: *The Spy Who Loved Me;* 1979: *Just a Gigolo, Goldengirl;* 1980: *Checkpoint Charlie;* 1981: *Daisy Chain.*

KAHN, MADELINE. Actress. *(b. Sept. 29, 1942, Boston.)* This vibrant comic actress originally trained to sing opera, and appeared in cabaret revues before winning acting jobs, first on stage, then in films beginning with the hilarious Swedish-dialect short *The Dove/Die Duva* (1968). Peter Bogdanovich cast her as Ryan O'Neal's uptight fiancée for a hilarious feature debut in *What's Up, Doc?* (1972), and also steered her Oscar-nominated performance in *Paper Moon* (1973). Kahn's giddy charm was best exploited by director Mel Brooks in three 1970s comedies: *Blazing Saddles* (1974, as Dietrich-styled temptress Lily von Shtupp, which earned her an Oscar nomination), *Young Frankenstein* (1974, hilarious as the Monster's bride), and *High Anxiety* (1977, as a Hitchcockian heroine). Pigeonholed as a comedienne, she has also played more restrained characters such as Molly Ringwald's mother in *Betsy's Wedding* (1990). A 1983–84 attempt to make her TV's new Lucy, in a series called "Oh Madeline," failed badly. She has spent more time on stage in recent years, and won a 1993 Best Actress Tony Award for her work in Wendy Wasserstein's "The Sisters Rosensweig."
OTHER FILMS INCLUDE: 1975: *The Adventure of Sherlock Holmes' Smarter Brother* (with fellow Brooks ensemble member Gene Wilder), *At Long Last Love* (Bogdanovich's ill-fated homage to 1930s musicals, which at least gave her the opportunity to sing Cole Porter on-screen); 1978: *The Cheap Detective;* 1979: *The Muppet Movie;*

1980: *The First Family, Simon, Wholly Moses;* 1981: *History of the World—Part I;* 1983: *Yellowbeard;* 1984: *City Heat, Slapstick of Another Kind;* 1985: *Clue;* 1986: *An American Tail* (contributing a voice to this animated fable), *My Little Pony* (another cartoon feature); 1994: *Mixed Nuts.*

KANE, CAROL. Actress. *(b. June 18, 1952, Cleveland.)* One of the most distinctive and dependable actresses working in movies today, this tiny, waiflike woman with frizzy red (sometimes blond) hair sports an indescribable voice that seems to originate in another galaxy. Her first screen appearance, in *Is This Trip Really Necessary?* (1970), didn't attract much attention, but Kane accumulated several small but choice parts thereafter that boosted her stock with movie producers: the goofy girlfriend in *Carnal Knowledge* (1971), the pathetic whore in *The Last Detail* (1973), and one of the hostage bank tellers in *Dog Day Afternoon* (1975). Her role as a Jewish bride in *Hester Street* (1975) brought her an Oscar nomination and greater prominence. She played Woody Allen's first wife in *Annie Hall,* Gene Wilder's Valentino-struck wife in *The World's Greatest Lover* (both 1977), and the terrorized baby-sitter in *When a Stranger Calls* (1979). A well-received guest shot on the TV sitcom "Taxi" as Simka, a babble-speaking immigrant, led to her joining the series' cast (eventually marrying Andy Kaufman's character, Latka) and earning her two Emmy Awards, in 1982 and 1983. Since then, she has kept busy with supporting parts in such films as *Racing With the Moon* (1984), *Jumpin' Jack Flash* (1986), *The Princess Bride, Ishtar* (both 1987), and *Scrooged* (1988), as well as three showier roles in 1990: *Flashback, The Lemon Sisters,* and *My Blue Heaven;* she was also hilarious as the Southern-fried soap-opera writer in the short-lived sitcom "All Is Forgiven" (1986). Recent credits include the made-for-TV sequel *When a Stranger Calls Back, Addams Family Values* (both 1993) and *Even Cowgirls Get the Blues* (1994).

KANIN, GARSON. Screenwriter, director, playwright, novelist. *(b. Nov. 24, 1912, Rochester, N.Y.)* Kanin was in the midst of a splendid Broadway career when Hollywood beckoned and he earned a reputation as Tinseltown's newest "wonder boy." Initially he worked as a director (beginning with a low-budget 1938 sleeper, *A Man to Remember,* recognized as one of the best B pictures ever made) and was responsible for such sparkling comedies as *The Great Man Votes, Bachelor Mother* (both 1939), *My Favorite Wife* (1940, started by Leo McCarey), and *Tom, Dick and Harry* (1941), as well as the wrenching drama *They Knew What They Wanted* (1940). During World War 2 he mainly toiled for the war effort, producing and directing documentaries for the Office of Emergency Management. He married actress/writer Ruth Gordon in 1942, and together they collaborated on the scripts for *A Double Life* (1947), directed by George Cukor, and *Adam's Rib* (1949) and *Pat and Mike* (1952), two of the best Tracy/Hepburn vehicles, also directed by Cukor. All three screenplays were nominated for Academy Awards.

In 1950 Kanin's hit stage play, *Born Yesterday,* was brought to the screen, also directed by Cukor; it was a smash hit and made a screen star of Judy Holliday, who'd been showcased in *Adam's Rib.* Kanin and Gordon subsequently wrote two more movies for her: *The Marrying Kind* (1952) and *It Should Happen to You* (1954). Kanin returned to film directing in 1969 with two dreadful, "with-it" comedies, *Some Kind of Nut* and *Where It's At.* Since that time he has concentrated on writing books and plays, penning a memoir about Tracy and Hepburn, and several volumes of Hollywood lore, among other works. His book "Movieola" was adapted into three separate made-for-TV movies in 1980.

KAPLAN, JONATHAN. Director. *(b. Nov. 25, 1947, Paris.)* A graduate of the Roger Corman school of B-moviemaking during the 1970s, Kaplan has gone on to make many critically acclaimed and successful films. Formerly a child actor (he debuted at the age of 11 in Elia Kazan's Broadway production of "The Dark at the Top of the Stairs"), Kaplan was a film major at New York University (where Martin Scorsese was one of his professors) and directed an award-winning short film. Scorsese recommended him to Corman, who hired him to make *Night Call Nurses*

(1972) and *The Slams* (1973). He then gained popular recognition with the trucker movie *White Line Fever* (1975). Critical attention followed with *Over the Edge* (1979), a story of alienated teens in a suburban town (which featured Matt Dillon in his first screen role), and *Heart Like a Wheel* (1983), which starred Bonnie Bedelia as real-life drag racer Shirley Muldowney. After *Project X* (1987), Kaplan achieved great success with *The Accused* (1988), which won Jodie Foster her first Best Actress Oscar as a woman who is gang raped. Since then, Kaplan has made *Immediate Family* (1989), the popular thriller *Unlawful Entry* (1992), and the interracial romance *Love Field* (also 1992), and *Bad Girls* (1994). The director's father, Sol Kaplan, provided the music score for *Over the Edge.* He also directed the Rod Stewart music video "Infatuation."

KARINA, ANNA. Actress. *(b. Sept. 22, 1940, Copenhagen, as Hanna Karin Blarke Bayer.)* Once the darling of New Wave filmmakers (especially Jean-Luc Godard, her first husband, who starred her in many of his films), this slender, stylish actress appeared to best advantage in roles exploiting her innate, good-natured mischievousness. Although she has appeared in a few English-language movies, she's primarily a Continental star. The sensitive, intelligent Karina wrote, directed, and starred in 1973's *Vivre Ensemble,* but thereafter chose to remain in front of the camera.
OTHER FILMS INCLUDE: 1960: *Le Petit Soldat, A Woman Is a Woman;* 1962: *Cleo From 5 to 7, Scheherazade;* 1963: *My Life to Live;* 1964: *Band of Outsiders, La Ronde;* 1965: *Alphaville* (a cult favorite and one of her best-known films on this side of the Atlantic), *Pierrot le Fou, The Nun;* 1966: *Made in U.S.A.;* 1968: *Before Winter Comes;* 1969: *Justine;* 1972: *The Salzburg Connection;* 1978: *Bread and Chocolate, Chaussette Surprise;* 1983: *L'Ami de Vincent;* 1987: *Last Song* (which she also wrote); 1988: *The Abyss;* 1990: *Man, Der Ville Vaere Skyldig.*

KARLOFF, BORIS. Actor. *(b. Nov. 23, 1887, Dulwich, England, as William Henry Pratt; d. Feb. 2, 1969.)* Hollywood's most successful boogeyman, a gaunt, bow-legged actor whose menacing mien scared the bejesus out of several generations of film fans, was in fact one of the movie colony's most popular citizens, and by all accounts a gentle, sensitive, highly cultured man. The scion of a family of British diplomats, he eschewed foreign-service work in favor of acting, emigrating to Canada and eventually touring with small companies all over North America. He made his screen debut as an extra in *The Dumb Girl of Portici* (1916), but didn't approach film work in earnest until 1919, when he appeared in the Douglas Fairbanks starrer *His Majesty, the American.*

By now billed as Boris Karloff, he played supporting roles—mostly heavies—in dozens of minor features and serials throughout the 1920s, including *The Hope Diamond Mystery* (1921), *Nan of the North* (1922), *Dynamite Dan* (1924), *Lady Robin Hood* (1925), *Eagle of the Sea* (1926), *Tarzan and the Golden Lion* (1927), *King of the Kongo* (1929), and *The Fatal Warning* (1929). He appeared in a few A movies, too, including 1926's *Old Ironsides* and 1927's *Two Arabian Knights.* Although Karloff spoke in soft, cultured tones, he affected a harsh, guttural voice in his early sound films, which included *The Unholy Night* (1929), *The Sea Bat* (1930), *Public Defender, Smart Money, Business and Pleasure,* and *The Mad Genius* (all 1931).

Karloff, who had resigned himself to working as a character actor, was more than happy to assume a role originally offered to *Dracula* star Bela Lugosi, who refused it on the ground that he would be unrecognizable under heavy makeup in a part with no dialogue. So Karloff played the lumbering monster in *Frankenstein* (1931), a physically demanding assignment that made him a star. Makeup artist Jack Pierce and director James Whale helped him flesh out the characterization, which enabled him to steal the picture from top-billed Colin Clive.

Karloff spent the next several years alternating horror films with more prestigious major-studio productions. He scared moviegoers witless with his starring turns in *The Old Dark House, The Mummy, The Mask of Fu Manchu* (all 1932), *The Ghoul* (1933), *Bride of Frankenstein, The Black Room* (both 1935), and *The Walking Dead* (1936), in addition to three films that teamed him with his partner-in-menace

Lugosi: *The Black Cat* (1934), *The Raven* (1935), and *The Invisible Ray* (1936). He also took colorful supporting roles, playing a sleazy reporter in *Five Star Final* (1931), a gangster in *Scarface* (1932), an anti-Semitic nobleman in *House of Rothschild,* a religious fanatic in *The Lost Patrol* (both 1934), a kindly inventor in *Night Key,* and a suspicious opera singer in *Charlie Chan at the Opera* (both 1937).

As the horror cycle waned in the late 1930s, Karloff found himself mired in undistinguished B films, including *West of Shanghai* (1937), *The Invisible Menace* (1938), and *British Intelligence* (1940). He starred as a low-rent Charlie Chan in several "Mr. Wong" mysteries for Monogram, the best of which was *The Mystery of Mr. Wong* (1939). Back at Universal, he played the Frankenstein monster for a third and final time in *Son of Frankenstein,* and then supported Basil Rathbone in an elaborate costume drama with horrific overtones, *Tower of London* (both 1939).

By now typecast as a movie menace, Karloff worked during the 1940s almost exclusively in B horror films and thrillers, including *The Man With Nine Lives* (1939), *Before I Hang, You'll Find Out* (a horror spoof that teamed him with Lugosi and Peter Lorre), *The Ape* (all 1940), *The Devil Commands* (1941), *The Boogie Man Will Get You* (1942), *The Climax* (a cut above his usual 1940s' vehicles), *House of Frankenstein* (both 1944, this time as mad scientist rather than monster), and *Dick Tracy Meets Gruesome* (1947). The "murder man" (as he was sometimes billed) spoofed his screen persona in the 1941 stage production of "Arsenic and Old Lace," enjoying a lengthy Broadway run as that play's menacing madman (but, unfortunately, missing out on repeating the role in the movie). He was well served by RKO producer Val Lewton, whose stylish, low-budget chillers ranked head and shoulders above the usual run of horror films; his assignments in Lewton's *The Body Snatcher* (1945, which again teamed him with Lugosi), *Isle of the Dead* (also 1945), and *Bedlam* (1946) were among his most memorable of the decade.

Karloff got a few nice supporting roles in A films of the immediate post WW2 era, including *The Secret Life of Walter Mitty* (1947), *Unconquered* (1948, as an Indian), and *Tap Roots* (1949), but by the 1950s he was working almost exclusively in dreary, low-budget horrors (in both senses of that word) that traded on the success of his earlier films. *Abbott and Costello Meet the Killer, Boris Karloff* (1949), *The Strange Door* (1951), *The Black Castle* (1952), *Abbott and Costello Meet Dr. Jekyll and Mr. Hyde* (1953), *Voodoo Island* (1957), *The Haunted Strangler,* and *Frankenstein–1970* (both 1958) saw an aging Karloff going through the motions with obvious professionalism but little enthusiasm.

He fared better on Broadway during the 1950s, playing Captain Hook opposite Jean Arthur as Peter Pan, costarring with Julie Harris in "The Lark," and participating in a number of live TV plays as well. He starred in the filmed TV series "Colonel March of Scotland Yard" (1957–58), and hosted "Thriller" (1960–62) in addition to guesting in dozens of dramatic series, anthologies, sitcoms, and variety shows throughout the 1950s and 1960s.

Producer Roger Corman used Karloff in several of his colorful, all-star horror films and spoofs of the 1960s, including *The Raven, The Terror* (both 1963, built entirely around an unfulfilled three-day commitment Karloff owed Corman), and *The Comedy of Terrors* (1964). Bravely, the aging master subjected himself to the indignities of *Bikini Beach* (1964) and *The Ghost in the Invisible Bikini* (1966), in addition to a quartet of Mexican-made horror cheapies, all of which were released posthumously. Karloff's swan song was *Targets* (1968), a modestly budgeted thriller directed by Peter Bogdanovich, which had the star playing an elderly horror-film actor. It was an offbeat role that Karloff obviously relished, and he delivered his best performance in years. Since the early 1960s he'd been afflicted with respiratory problems, and frequently retired to a wheelchair and an oxygen mask between scenes. He died in 1969, still a much beloved screen star.

KARLSON, PHIL. Director. *(b. July 2, 1908, Chicago, as Philip Karlstein; d. Dec. 12, 1985.)* While lacking the passionate, near-visionary intensity of a Samuel Fuller, Karlson showed himself an unflinching action director of more-than-average gifts in a handful of gritty B pictures in the 1950s. He received his training as an assistant director and second-unit director, then started directing at Monogram, one of the Poverty Row schlock outfits, helming low-budget series films featuring Charlie Chan, the Shadow, and The Bowery Boys. Looking at *Kansas City Confidential, Scandal Sheet* (both 1952), and especially the breakneck-paced *The Phenix City Story* (1955), one gets the impression that Karlson could have been a *noir* master; but much of his other output plays like the ordinary hackwork it frequently was. 1973's *Walking Tall* was, like *Phenix,* based on the true story of one man cleaning up a corrupt town; its Southern setting, redneck hero, and rather indifferent attitude toward due process made the film quite controversial and occasioned a mini-Karlson revival (he had directed the hideous *Willard* sequel, *Ben,* only a year before). This did not translate into more work, however; he directed only one subsequent film, 1975's *Framed,* which also featured *Walking Tall* star Joe Don Baker. OTHER FILMS INCLUDE: 1944: *G. I. Honeymoon;* 1945: *The Shanghai Cobra;* 1946: *Behind the Mask, Bowery Bombshell, Dark Alibi, Live Wires, Swing Parade of 1946;* 1947: *Black Gold, Kilroy Was Here;* 1949: *The Big Cat, Ladies of the Chorus;* 1951: *Lorna Doone, The Mask of the Avenger, The Texas Rangers;* 1952: *Assignment Paris, The Brigand;* 1953: *99 River Street;* 1954: *They Rode West;* 1955: *Five Against the House, Hell's Island, Tight Spot;* 1957: *The Brothers Rico;* 1960: *Hell to Eternity, Key Witness;* 1961: *The Young Doctors;* 1962: *Kid Galahad;* 1966: *The Silencers;* 1968: *The Wrecking Crew.*

KASDAN, LAWRENCE. Director, screenwriter, producer. (b. Jan. 14, 1949, Miami.) This former ad-agency copywriter directed and/or wrote some of the 1980s' most popular films, showing an unusual facility with thematic elements and characterizations gleaned from pop-culture artifacts (especially old movies) and the baby-boomer zeitgeist. Many of his films' virtues, however, are strictly superficial; for example, his first attempt at a Western, *Silverado* (1985), corralled most of that genre's obvious trappings with no apparent understanding of how to use them. Kasdan broke into films working for George Lucas, cowriting *The Empire Strikes Back* (1980) and scripting *Raiders of the Lost Ark* (1981) solo. The phenomenal reception accorded those pictures earned him a shot at writing and directing

his own film, *Body Heat* (also 1981), a successful synthesis of old film noirs which helped make a star of Kathleen Turner and earned Kasdan an instant following. *The Big Chill* (1983), which he also produced in addition to cowriting and directing, romanticized 1960s countercultursts surviving the Reagan era (something done more effectively by independent filmmaker John Sayles in *Return of the Secaucus 7,* as some savvy critics pointed out), and earned Kasdan an Academy Award nomination for Best Screenplay (with Barbara Benedek).

Kasdan's greatest strength is his diversity; he's tackled a variety of movie genres, albeit not with total success. His finely detailed adaptation of Anne Tyler's novel *The Accidental Tourist* (1988) resembles none of his other films, in content or approach, but may be his best. It netted the cowriter-director-producer Oscar nods for Best Picture and Best Screenplay. *I Love You to Death* (1990) was a labored, fitfully funny black comedy, and *Grand Canyon* (1991) tried too hard to be meaningful at the expense of providing real entertainment. The director and his wife Meg shared an Oscar nomination for its screenplay. In 1992 Kevin Costner dusted off an old screenplay of Kasdan's (originally intended for Steve McQueen) and hit box-office pay dirt with *The Bodyguard;* Kasdan coproduced. He returned to the Western with Costner in *Wyatt Earp* (1994), which he also cowrote, then directed *French Kiss* (1995). Kasdan, whose other screenplay credits include *Continental Divide* (1981) and *Return of the Jedi* (1983), produced *Cross My Heart* (1987) and executive produced *Immediate Family* (1989) and *Jumpin at the Boneyard* (1992). He appeared in a small role, as did many contemporary directors, in John Landis' *Into the Night* (1985).

KAUFMAN, GEORGE S. Playwright, screenwriter, director. (b. Nov. 14, 1889, Pittsburgh; d. June 2, 1961.) One of the sharpest wits in the convocation of New York literary types known as the Algonquin Round Table, Kaufman steadily resisted the siren call of Hollywood in the 1930s (making only two exceptions, contributing story only to 1933's Eddie Cantor vehicle *Roman Scandals* and coscripting 1935's *A Night at the Opera* for old acquaintances The Marx Brothers), even as his colleagues like Dorothy Parker and S. J. Perelman flocked there to write film scripts for big bucks. (One Hollywood siren this notorious womanizer did heed, however, was star Mary Astor, whose diary praising Kaufman's sexual stamina was a hot item during Astor's bitter 1936 divorce.) Unlike many of his contemporaries, Kaufman didn't really need the money; his stage plays (often written in collaboration with Moss Hart or others, and frequently staged by Kaufman) were enormous critical and popular Broadway successes. Many of them were adapted (and diluted) for Hollywood use, including two Marx Brothers vehicles, *The Cocoanuts* (1929) and *Animal Crackers* (1930), the trenchant Hollywood satire *Once in a Lifetime* (1932), *You Can't Take It With You* (1938), and *The Man Who Came to Dinner* (1941). In 1947 he directed his first and only picture, *The Senator Was Indiscreet*, starring William Powell. While the very funny comedy was well received, Kaufman was uncomfortable with the technical aspects of filmmaking and hightailed it back to the stage immediately.

KAUFMAN, PHILIP. Director, screenwriter. (b. Oct. 23, 1936, Chicago.) Gifted, iconoclastic filmmaker whose work includes thrillers, Westerns, and adaptations of seemingly unadaptable books. His first film, *Goldstein* (1965), was made on a shoestring budget and won the Prix de la Nouvelle Critique award at the Cannes Film Festival. After making the comicbook satire *Fearless Frank* (1967), which featured Jon Voight in his film debut, Kaufman went on to write and direct *The Great Northfield, Minnesota Raid* (1972) and *The White Dawn* (1974), which established his reputation as an original and intelligent filmmaker. His subsequent films include the remake of *Invasion of the Body Snatchers* (1978), *The Wanderers* (1979), the striking and impressionistic view of teenage life in the Bronx, circa 1963, the unwieldy but richly detailed adaptation of Tom Wolfe's space-age saga *The Right Stuff* (1983), and his masterpiece, a stunning adaptation of Milan Kundera's *The Unbearable Lightness of Being* (1988, Oscar-nominated for Best Screenplay). His *Henry & June* (1990), based on the relationship between author Henry Miller and

Anais Nin, earns a historical footnote as the film that resulted in the creation of the NC-17 rating. It also confirmed Kaufman as one of the few American directors to openly embrace erotic subjects in films. Ironically, this individualistic writer-director also wrote the mainstream Western *The Outlaw—Josey Wales* (1976, which he was originally supposed to direct), and the story for the hugely popular, mass-appeal Saturday-matinee homage *Raiders of the Lost Ark* (1981). His most recent film was an adaptation of Michael Crichton's controversial *Rising Sun* (1993), which he cowrote and directed.

KAVNER, JULIE. Actress. (b. Sept. 7, 1951, Burbank, Calif.) Kavner's distinctive voice, described by one writer as "creaking like a gate hinge in need of oiling," gives the impression of a veteran New Yorker, but in fact Kavner was born and raised in southern California. She made her professional acting debut as Valerie Harper's kid sister on the popular TV sitcom "Rhoda" (1974–78), winning an Emmy for her work, but after the show's demise she fell out of the public eye. (Her movie debut, in 1981's *National Lampoon Goes to the Movies*, went unseen when that film was shelved.) Then Woody Allen gave her a juicy part in *Hannah and Her Sisters* (1986), and she became part of his repertory company, blossoming in *Radio Days* (1987) and winning Woody onscreen, in *New York Stories* (1989). She also appeared in smaller roles for him in *Alice* (1990) and *Shadows and Fog* (1992). Her other credits include *Bad Medicine* (1985), *Surrender* (1987), *Awakenings* (1990, a warm performance as doctor Robin Williams' faithful nurse), and her first starring role, *This Is My Life* (1992, playing a hard-working single mom who finds fulfillment as a standup comic). She displayed her versatility in a variety of roles on "The Tracey Ullman Show" (1987–90) and is the voice of cartoon mother Marge Simpson on "The Simpsons" (1990—), which began as a segment on the Ullman series. Recent credits include *I'll Do Anything* (1994).

KAYE, DANNY. Actor. (b. Jan. 18, 1913, New York City, as David Kaminski; d. Mar. 3, 1987.) Though in his later years he was known primarily for his work with UNICEF, this pixieish, red-haired entertainer had been convulsing both kids and their parents his entire life with his energetic clowning and his ingenious patter songs. Like most of his generation of performers, he worked his way up through vaudeville, nightclubs, and even the borscht belt. Beginning in 1937, he appeared in two-reel comedies for Educational Pictures *(Dime a Dance, Getting an Eyeful, Cupid Takes a Holiday)*, but they did not showcase him to best advantage. Kaye's real break came when he hit Broadway in 1939's "Straw Hat Revue," where he met his future wife, Sylvia Fine, who wrote the trip-hammer song parodies that became his trademark. He later appeared in other shows, including "Lady in the Dark," in which his showcase number, "Tchaikovsky," rocketed him to stardom, and brought him to the attention of producer Samuel Goldwyn, who guaranteed him an astonishing $150,000 per film.

Kaye made his feature debut in *Up in Arms* (1944), a reworking of the old Eddie Cantor vehicle *Whoopee!*, which made room for two patter routines, "Melody in F" and "The Theatre Lobby Number," and cast him as a likable nebbish. Goldwyn's instincts proved correct, and the instantly successful Kaye continued in a similar vein with *Wonder Man* (1945, the first of three films to cast him in dual roles), *The Kid From Brooklyn* (1946, a remake of Harold Lloyd's *The Milky Way)*, *The Secret Life of Walter Mitty* (1947, in perhaps his best-known role), and *A Song Is Born* (1948). He then freelanced in *The Inspector General* (1949) and *On the Riviera* (1950, another dual role), before returning to Goldwyn to play the title role in the musical biopic *Hans Christian Andersen* (1952). He then moved over to Paramount, where he produced his own vehicles, with the writing-directing team of Norman Panama and Melvin Frank. They turned out to be his all-time best: *Knock on Wood* (1954), in which he plays a ventriloquist caught up in international intrigue, and *The Court Jester* (1956), an uproarious swashbuckler parody which includes the unforgettable "vessel with the pestle" wordplay routine. (Panama and Frank also wrote the maudlin screenplay for 1954's smash hit *White Christmas,* in which Kaye served as a last-minute replacement for Donald O'Connor.)

His later vehicles were an uneven lot, including the circus-themed *Merry Andrew,* the whimsical *Me and the Colonel* (1958), the dramatic musical *The Five Pennies* (1959, which did give him a great special-material duet with Louis Armstrong), and the sprightly *On the Double* (1961), which returned him to surefire material with a dual role. Following the slapsticky *The Man from the Diner's Club* (1963), Kaye starred for four years (1963–67) in a one-hour variety series on CBS; both he and the series won Emmys the first season. His only other screen role of note was that of the Ragpicker in *The Madwoman of Chaillot* (1969). He starred on Broadway in "Two by Two" (as Noah), and was featured in a number of television specials (including a "Pinocchio" that cast him as Geppetto). He was effectively cast as a concentration camp survivor in the powerful TV movie *Skokie* (1981), and toward the end of his life made a memorable appearance as a wacky dentist on "The Cosby Show." Most of his time in later years was spent conducting symphony orchestras in fund-raising concerts.

KAZAN, ELIA. Director, screenwriter, producer, actor. *(b. Sept. 7, 1909, Constantinople, as Elia Kazanjoglou.)* A truly pioneering Hollywood director, Elia Kazan in the late 1940s and early 1950s helped blaze trails into the largely uncharted territories of social consciousness and cinematic naturalism, turning out some of the era's most memorable movies and influencing subsequent generations of filmmakers. Born to Greek parents who came to America when he was a small child, Kazan fell under the spell of the theater as a young man, acting in New York's avant-garde Group Theatre troupe and eventually becoming a director whose Broadway triumphs included the original productions of "The Skin of Our Teeth," "All My Sons," "A Streetcar Named Desire," and "Death of a Salesman."

Kazan, whose first brush with the movie industry consisted of assisting documentarian Ralph Steiner in the mid 1930s and acting in two Warner Bros. films, *City for Conquest* (1940) and *Blues in the Night* (1941), was courted by 20th Century-Fox's Darryl F. Zanuck, who signed him to a contract in 1944. From the first, directing *A Tree Grows in Brooklyn*

(1945), Kazan evinced an ability to coax great performances from his actors; star James Dunn and child actress Peggy Ann Garner both won Oscars for their turns in this lovely, evocative film. *Boomerang!* (1947), part-murder mystery, part-courtroom drama, also featured superb performances and presented a subtle but definite comment on political corruption. *Gentleman's Agreement* (also 1947), starring Gregory Peck, was a full-blown treatise on anti-Semitism that won Oscars for Kazan, supporting actress Celeste Holm, and as Best Picture. Seen today, the picture seems rather tame and obvious, but it was considered a real breakthrough back in 1947. Kazan took on race relations in *Pinky* (1949), the story of a light-skinned black woman (improbably played by Jeanne Crain) who passes for white; it too was thought very daring at the time but has lost much of its impact in the intervening years. In retrospect, Kazan considered his first "real" film to be *Panic in the Streets* (1950), a solid thriller about efforts to contain a burgeoning epidemic which was shot entirely on the streets of New Orleans.

A *Streetcar Named Desire* (1951) not only earned Kazan another Oscar nod for Best Director, it made a full-fledged screen star of Marlon Brando, leading exponent of the "Method" acting technique taught at Lee Strasberg's Actors' Studio, which was cofounded by Kazan. The Tennessee Williams play, which Kazan had directed on Broadway, was strong stuff to moviegoers of 1951, but it ushered in an era of similarly ambitious and unusual stage-to-screen translations. Brando continued his association with the director most successfully, first in *Viva Zapata!* (1952, which, like *Streetcar,* netted him a Best Actor nomination) and then in the classic *On the Waterfront* (1954), which took eight Academy Awards, including Best Picture, Best Director, and Best Actor. Budd Schulberg's hard-hitting exposé of the longshoremen's unions was ideal fodder for Kazan's mastery of heightened realism. (It came, ironically, on the heels of the director's still-infamous decision to testify and name names before the House Un-American Activities Committee.) He went abroad to make *Man on a Tightrope* (1953), the story of a circus troupe's escape from behind the Iron Curtain.

Kazan picked up yet another nomination for *East of Eden* (1955), in which he did

for newcomer James Dean what he'd done for Brando a few years earlier. Viewers today are still riveted by the rawness of emotions the director managed to capture in this powerful Steinbeck story of a family in conflict. By this time, he had fully mastered the cinematic technique (critics of his earlier pictures suggested that they were too much like filmed stage plays), and was producing his own pictures. The wildly provocative *Baby Doll* (1956), *A Face in the Crowd* (1957), *Wild River* (1960), and *Splendor in the Grass* (1961) all bore Kazan's stamp of quality, but didn't quite match his earlier successes. *America, America* (1963), based on the experiences of Kazan's own uncle, movingly captured the turn-of-the-century immigrant experience and snagged Oscar nominations for Best Picture, Best Director, and Best Screenplay (which Kazan himself had written). It also ended his most fertile creative period.

Since then, Kazan has directed only three films—*The Arrangement* (1969, based on his own novel), the little-seen *The Visitors* (1972), and *The Last Tycoon* (1976, a highly anticipated but ultimately disappointing F. Scott Fitzgerald adaptation)— and has abandoned the theater altogether. Kazan was married to actresses Molly Day Thatcher and Barbara Loden. His autobiography, "A Life," was published in 1988. His son, Nicholas Kazan, is a screenwriter who was Oscar-nominated for *Reversal of Fortune* (1990) and made his directing debut with *Dream Lover* (1994).

KEACH, STACY. Actor. *(b. June 2, 1941, Savannah, Ga.; as Walter Stacy Keach, Jr.)* This rugged, handsome leading man was once touted as a leading contender for major screen stardom but like many others similarly hyped, he found TV to be his true metier, achieving fame and recognition as Mickey Spillane's archetypal private-eye Mike Hammer. Part of a show-business family (his brother James is an actor and producer; his father was a drama teacher and dialogue coach), Keach started acting on stage at an early age. He came to prominence on stage in the 1960s, and entered films in 1968, landing a solid supporting role in *The Heart Is a Lonely Hunter.* He appeared in many counterculture-driven films of the early 1970s, including *End of the Road, Brewster*

McCloud (both 1970), *Doc* (1971, a disastrous revisionist Western), and John Huston's *Fat City* (1972) among them. He contributed a funny cameo to Huston's *The Life and Times of Judge Roy Bean* (also 1972). Keach was also effective as an L.A. cop in *The New Centurions* (1972) and in the title role of the theatrical adaptation *Luther* (1974). But his big-screen career was spotty from there on. He was chilling as an easygoing homicidal sheriff in *The Killer Inside Me* (1976), a stunning adaptation of a Jim Thompson novel that went virtually unnoticed until its later release on video. He struggled through the awful *Slave of the Cannibal God* and Cheech and Chong's *Up in Smoke* (both 1978). He also appeared in *Cheech & Chong's Nice Dreams* (1981).

Two pet projects failed at the box office: the fraternal Western *The Long Riders* (1980, in which he appeared with brother James, and which he also cowrote and helped produce), and *That Championship Season* (1982, the long-delayed screen version of the Broadway play about the bittersweet reunion of a championship basketball squad 25 years after its triumph). Eventually, Keach drifted into TV work. He played Mike Hammer for several years, with an interruption when he served time in a British prison after being convicted on a drug charge. His later film credits include *Class of 1999* (1990) and *False Identity* (1990). Keach has also appeared in many made-for-TV movies and remains active on stage.

KEATON, BUSTER. Actor, director, screenwriter. *(b. Oct. 4, 1895, Piqua, Kans., as Joseph Francis Keaton; d. Feb. 1, 1966.)* The silent screen's "Great Stone Face," and arguably its greatest comic player, Buster Keaton possessed a prodigious talent that, fortunately, was properly utilized as much as it was abused—which, owing to the comedian's personal demons, was frequently. On stage from infancy in his family's knockabout vaudeville act, he came to films in 1917 after visiting the New York studio where Roscoe "Fatty" Arbuckle was making two-reelers for producer Joseph M. Schenck. Keaton made his film debut supporting Arbuckle in *The Butcher Boy* (1917), and over the next two years appeared with the rotund comic in more than a dozen shorts.

When the Arbuckle company moved to California, Keaton followed, and when "Fatty" signed with Paramount in 1920, Schenck turned his Comique Studio over to Keaton. The short, slender, sad-faced performer initially produced *The High Sign* (1920), but it was held up for release; audiences first saw *One Week,* a bizarre tale of newlyweds trying to assemble a prefabricated house kit that has been sabotaged by the hero's rival. He turned out nearly 20 two-reelers in three years (taking time out to star in a partially successful, if conventional, feature for Metro called *The Saphead* in 1920). *The Boat* (1921), *Cops* (1922), and *The Balloonatic* (1923) set the pattern for Keaton films to come, each one full of inventive gags and surreal imagery.

Unlike his greatest competitor, Charlie Chaplin (who used the camera merely to record his brilliant performances), Keaton immersed himself in the medium of film, learning by experimentation how to use the mechanics of cinema to enhance his comedies. Schenck, for his part, gave Keaton free rein in making the films, and even though the comedian often collaborated with directors Eddie Cline and Mal St. Clair, he was largely responsible for guiding his own work.

Buster graduated to features in 1923 with *The Three Ages,* a sendup of the DeMille historical flashback genre. *Our Hospitality* (also 1923) combined the visual appeal of a lovingly recreated early steam train with a strong dramatic story about a family feud. *Sherlock, Jr.* (1924) was a wild gag comedy about a projectionist who dreamed himself onto the theater screen; it delineated, in sharp relief, both his fascination with things mechanical and his remarkable grasp of motion-picture grammar and artifice. *The Navigator* (also 1924) found Buster on an abandoned ocean liner adrift with only a single companion, and *Seven Chances* (1925) climaxed with a tremendous chase showing Keaton pursued by hundreds of jilted brides (and an avalanche of rocks and boulders). *Go West* (also 1925) and *Battling Butler* (1926) were weak efforts, but *The General* (also 1926), a picturesque retelling of a Civil War railroad raid, showed the star at his best in a meticulously constructed comedy that also reflected his almost fetishistic penchant for historical accuracy. Although *The General* fared poorly with audiences of the day, it is generally considered Keaton's greatest work. *Steamboat Bill, Jr.* (1927) was another top-notch comedy, and featured as its highlight an hysterical and, at the same time, terrifying tornado sequence. By comparison, *College* (1927) seemed a minor effort, even though it too was packed with laughs.

In 1928 Joe Schenck sold Keaton's contract to MGM, which was headed by his brother Nicholas Schenck. The star's first MGM vehicle, *The Cameraman* (1928), was up to his very best work, but increasing interference (by a studio that was accustomed to having its stars follow orders, not create their own movies) and Keaton's own losing battle with alcoholism contributed to a steady decline thereafter. *Spite Marriage* (1929) had many fine moments, and the star's first talkie, *Free and Easy* (1930), showed promise. But *Doughboys* (also 1930) was dismal, and in *Parlor, Bedroom, and Bath* (1931), Keaton—the ostensible star—was relegated to comic relief. By the time of *What! No Beer?* (1933), he was forced to team with Jimmy Durante, as the studio had lost faith in his ability to carry a picture alone. Keaton completed seven talkies for Metro, all pale imitations of his silent work, but all moneymakers.

Finally fired for embarrassing alcohol-related escapades, Keaton could find employment only in low-budget two-reel shorts, first with Educational Pictures and then, late in the decade, for Columbia. (He also traveled abroad in 1935 to appear in two interesting but unsatisfying comedies, the English-made *An Old Spanish Custom* and the French-made *Le Roi des Champs-Elysées.)* Although there were flashes of the old Keaton brilliance in such shorts as *Allez Oop* (1934) and *Grand Slam Opera* (1936), generally these three-day wonders only served to diminish Keaton's earlier achievements.

By the late 1930s and early 1940s Keaton was reduced to playing bit parts (most notably as himself in 1939's *Hollywood Cavalcade)* and working as a screenwriter. He supplied gags for *The Jones Family in Hollywood* (1939), directed by his old friend Mal St. Clair. Returning to MGM in virtual anonymity during the 1940s, he did the same on several Red Skelton comedies, and served as a comedy troubleshooter at the studio. He had occasional roles in features (1940's *Li'l Abner,* 1943's *Forever and a Day,*

1944's *San Diego, I Love You),* and even though most of them were minor, he brought to each a flash of Keatonesque invention that proved his mind was still fertile. He also appeared as one of the "waxworks" in an all-too-brief cameo in *Sunset Blvd.* (1950), and did a much-anticipated but sadly unsatisfying star turn with Charlie Chaplin in *Limelight* (1952).

Television, however, provided both a new vehicle of employment, and a chance to regain lost ground. He starred in his own live half-hour series in Los Angeles, and then filmed another series of half-hours that were later edited into an ersatz feature titled *The Misadventures of Buster Keaton* (1950) for foreign release. TV commercials, series guest shots, theater appearances in a revival of "Merton of the Movies," and cameos in feature films kept Keaton before the public. *The Buster Keaton Story* (1957), starring Donald O'Connor, was a typically white-washed and ill-conceived screen biopic, but the fee paid to Buster enabled him to buy a comfortable house in which he lived out his years.

In the 1960s, a rediscovered Keaton found himself in ever-increasing demand. Canadian filmmaker Gerald Potterton directed him in a silent-film-style short, *The Railrodder* (1965), while another crew chronicled the production in a poignant documentary called *Buster Keaton Rides Again.* He appeared in Stanley Kramer's all-star *It's a Mad Mad Mad Mad World* (though his best scenes wound up on the cutting-room floor), and a series of Beach Party movies (1965's *Beach Blanket Bingo* and *How to Stuff a Wild Bikini,* to name two), in which he was allowed to devise his own sight gags. Director Richard Lester hired him, in spite of failing health, to appear in *A Funny Thing Happened on the Way to the Forum* (1966), and American-International Pictures (producers of the Beach Party movies) released an Italian-made comedy with Buster's name above the title, *War, Italian Style* (1967).

Had he lived, there is no question that other projects—perhaps even better ones—would have followed. A posthumous biography, "Keaton," by Rudi Blesh received Keaton's full cooperation and became the life story the comedian himself should have written. (His official autobiography, 1960's "My Wonderful World of Slapstick," was ghostwritten.) In 1959 Keaton received a special Oscar "for his unique talents which brought immortal comedies to the screen."

KEATON, DIANE. Actress. *(b. Jan. 5, 1946, Los Angeles, as Diane Hall.)* This gawky but attractive actress achieved her stardom by creating a most unlikely screen persona: a stuttering, often clumsy bundle of Me Generation eccentricities and urban neuroses. That screen character (elements of which still surface occasionally in her work) seems to owe a great deal to Keaton's former companion and mentor, Woody Allen. They met when she was cast opposite him in his Broadway comedy "Play It Again, Sam." She subsequently costarred in the 1972 movie version of the show, and continued as Woody's leading lady in *Sleeper* (1973), *Love and Death* (1975), *Manhattan* (1979), and, most notably, *Annie Hall* (1977), for which she won the Best Actress Oscar. (She also starred in his first dramatic film, 1978's *Interiors.)*

Keaton began her show-business career in summer stock, eventually landing an understudy job on Broadway in the musical "Hair," in which she starred for most of 1968. She first became a familiar face on TV commercials, and made her film debut in *Lovers and Other Strangers* (1970). She then managed to hold her own among the powerhouse cast of Francis Ford Coppola's *The Godfather* (1972), playing the wife of Mafia family scion Al Pacino, a role she reprised in the 1974 and 1990 sequels. Her quirky side got plenty of exposure in the Allen films and such trifles as *I Will, I Will . . . For Now* (1976) and *Harry and Walter Go to New York* (1976), but she proved her dramatic abilities in *Looking for Mr. Goodbar* (1977), playing a sexually repressed Catholic schoolteacher whose later promiscuity leads to tragedy.

After appearing in *Shoot the Moon* (1982), the emotional domestic drama, Keaton costarred with then-lover Warren Beatty in his ambitious but financially unsuccessful Russian Revolution epic, *Reds* (also 1981 and Oscar-nominated as Best Actress), then took a brief sabbatical. Her return to the screen, in *Mrs. Soffel* (1984), was largely unheralded, and the mediocre box-office performance of *The Little Drummer Girl* (1984) failed to appreciably check her career's apparent decline.

Crimes of the Heart (1986), an adaptation of Beth Henley's Pulitzer Prize-winning play about Southern sisters, forced her to compete for screen time with Jessica Lange and Sissy Spacek but proved to be a more satisfactory vehicle for her than previous outings. She cameoed as a nightclub singer in Woody Allen's *Radio Days* before starring in *Baby Boom* (both 1987) as a fast-track corporate shark whose life changes dramatically after she "inherits" a baby. The film was a popular success that restored the luster to Keaton's tarnished star, and reminded audiences of her considerable comic prowess. Unfortunately, her follow-up films—including *The Good Mother* (1988) and *The Lemon Sisters* (1990)—didn't sustain that momentum. In 1991 she fared better in the hit comedy *Father of the Bride,* which saw her playing Steve Martin's wife in a placid, decorative manner most unusual for her. The following year she was well cast opposite Ed Harris in the political-themed romantic comedy *Running Mates* (1992, made for TV). She provided a canine voice-over for 1993's *Look Who's Talking Now,* and played the title role in a 1994 TV movie, *Amelia Earhart.* She first tried her hand behind-the-camera with an oddball quasi-documentary, *Heaven* (1987), and then piloted the well-received cable-TV drama *Wildflower* (1991). She directed an episode of "Twin Peaks," and earned an Emmy nomination as Best Director for an After School Special, "The Girl With the Crazy Brother" (1990).

KEATON, MICHAEL. Actor. *(b. Sept. 9, 1951, Pittsburgh, as Michael Douglas.)* All Hollywood—if not the *rest* of the civilized world—was positively agog when it was announced that this mischievous, physically unprepossessing comic actor would be playing comic-book crimebuster Batman in a big-budget motion picture. That reaction was topped by the one experienced after the film's premiere, which demonstrated that he'd pulled it off with aplomb. Keaton, a former speech major at Kent State University and nightclub comedian, landed a costarring role (with Jim Belushi) in a 1979 sitcom, "Working Stiffs," that died after just three weeks. He first startled moviedom with his side-splitting debut in *Night Shift* (1982), which he stole effortlessly from its ostensible lead, Henry Winkler. ("Is this a great country or *what?"*) *Mr. Mom* (1983) gave him his first solo starring hit. His film career thereafter was spotty: Although he won star status, he didn't always choose his projects wisely. *Johnny Dangerously* (1984), *Gung Ho, Touch and Go* (both 1986), and *The Squeeze* (1987) demonstrated that he had talent to spare, but his engaging personality alone couldn't compensate for uneven scripts or lackluster direction.

Beetlejuice (1988), Tim Burton's hugely successful comedy, cast Keaton as a gravel-voiced ghost and put him in outlandish makeup. Apparently liberated by his bizarre appearance, he gave his loosest, funniest performance to date and in so doing bolstered his sagging reputation. He played a substance abuser in *Clean and Sober* (also 1988), proving that he could carry a serious drama. Then Burton hired him to play the title role in *Batman* (1989). Aided by a molded costume that added size and muscle to his slight frame, Keaton managed to convince audiences that he *was* the Caped Crusader. Moreover, Burton had him play Bruce Wayne as a brooding neurotic, which added an interesting dimension to a flat character. The movie became one of the all-time biggest box-office grossers and spawned a much-anticipated if not-quite-as-successful sequel, *Batman Returns,* in 1992.

After playing a mental patient in *The Dream Team* (1989), a fitfully funny comedy, Keaton went villainous in *Pacific Heights* (1990), portraying a ruthless, scheming tenant. He was a New York policeman in *One Good Cop* (1991), an uneasy mixture of urban toughness and cloying sentimentality that fizzled at the box office. In 1993 he played the scuzzy Dogberry, with an accent of indeterminate origin, in Kenneth Branagh's production of Shakespeare's *Much Ado About Nothing,* then returned to safer ground as an expectant father in the tearjerker *My Life.* Keaton followed with *The Paper* and *Speechless* (both 1994).

KEEL, HOWARD. Actor, singer. *(b. Apr. 13, 1917, Gillespie, Ill., as Harry Clifford Leek.)* Towering, solidly built, robust screen performer with gleaming smile and booming baritone, the movie musical's Great White Hope during the 1950s, the genre's declining years. An untrained natural talent who worked as a singing waiter and for an aircraft manufacturer before turning to the stage, Keel made his film debut in England (1948's *The Small Voice,* aka *Hideout)* while touring with a production of "Oklahoma!" Back in the United States, his dynamic performance opposite Betty Hutton in *Annie Get Your Gun* (1950) launched him as a Hollywood leading man. Keel subsequently starred in a slew of musicals, many of them remakes; his best role was that of riverboat gambler Gaylord Ravenal in the 1951 version of *Show Boat.* He also appeared in *Pagan Love Song* (1950), the TV-cowboy satire *Callaway Went Thataway* (1951), *Desperate Search, Lovely to Look At* (both 1952), *Calamity Jane* (as Wild Bill Hickok), *Kiss Me, Kate* (both 1953), *Deep in My Heart, Rose Marie,* the jubilant *Seven Brides for Seven Brothers* (all 1954), *Kismet,* and *Jupiter's Darling* (both 1955).

When the studios phased out lavish movie musicals, Keel took a variety of leading roles (he was Saint Peter in 1959's *The Big Fisherman)* in mostly undistinguished dramas, Westerns, and action films, among them *Armored Command* (1961), *The Day of the Triffids* (1963, a modest sci-fi film now well regarded), *The Man From Button Willow* (1965, a voice in this animated feature), *Waco* (1966), *The War Wagon* (1967, as a wisecracking Indian, supporting John Wayne and Kirk Douglas), and *Arizona Bushwackers* (1968). During the 1970s he toured on stage with his *Seven Brides* costar Jane Powell. In 1981, a silvery-haired, distinguished Keel assumed the role of Clayton Farlow on the TV soap "Dallas," which he played for the remainder of the run. The renewed recognition this series brought him enabled Keel to play concert dates and record a new album.

KEELER, RUBY. Dancer, actress. *(b. Aug. 25, 1909, Halifax, Nova Scotia; d. Feb. 28, 1993.)* Her singing was adequate if not particularly lilting, her dancing was energetic if not particularly graceful, and her acting . . . well, never mind. Suffice it to say that Ruby Keeler owed her Hollywood success, brief as it was, to being in the right place at the right time: at the Warner Bros. studio, when director Busby

Berkeley was staging his most inventive and best-remembered musical extravaganzas. Keeler, a Canadian-born chorus girl who hoofed in Broadway shows for several years before marrying entertainer Al Jolson in 1928, made her screen debut at her husband's home studio. As Peggy Sawyer, the bashful dancer plucked from the chorus line to replace ailing star Bebe Daniels in the Broadway musical depicted in *42nd Street* (1933), Keeler delivered an earnest, unskilled but somehow endearing performance and, like her screen character, worked her way into the hearts of her audiences.

Backed by solid production values, good scores, accomplished casts (including crooner Dick Powell, with whom she was most frequently teamed), and patient directors, Keeler clumped her way through some of the decade's most popular musicomedies: *Gold Diggers of 1933, Footlight Parade* (also 1933, in which she got to dance with movie tough-guy James Cagney), *Dames, Flirtation Walk* (both 1934), *Go Into Your Dance* (her only screen appearance with Jolson), *Shipmates Forever* (both 1935), *Colleen* (1936, her personal favorite among her films, and one of her best), and *Ready, Willing and Able* (1937, in which she danced on giant typewriter keys). When Jolson left Warners in 1937, he insisted Keeler come with him. Consequently, her career came to a screeching halt. Aside from a guest shot in *Mother Carey's Chickens* (1938) for RKO and a final starring role in Columbia's *Sweetheart of the Campus* (1941), she never appeared in pictures again. She divorced Jolson in 1940, then married a real-estate man and, essentially, retired. But the lure of the footlights pulled her back, first to guest shots on TV programs, then to Broadway, in a 1970 revival of "No, No, Nanette," directed by none other than Busby Berkeley, and fueled by the popularity (and newly defined "camp" status) of her old films. She made cameo appearances in *They Shoot Horses, Don't They* (1969, later cut from the film) and *The Phynx* (1970, which was never released).

KEITEL, HARVEY. Actor. *(b. May 13, 1941, Brooklyn, N.Y.)* Intense, quintessentially "New Yawk" actor who made his first big impression standing in for direc-

tor Martin Scorsese in Scorsese's highly autobiographical breakthrough feature *Mean Streets* (1973). He had also played a Scorsese surrogate in the director's earlier *Who's That Knocking at My Door?* (1968), his first film. Italian Catholic Scorsese has commented: "I found him very much like me, even though he's a Polish Jew from Brooklyn." Keitel studied at the Actors' Studio and worked in summer stock and rep theaters for 10 years before breaking into films. When his work for Scorsese threatened to typecast him in tough, contemporary, urban roles, he took some parts that legitimately stretched him, and others that seemed way out of left field. While his turn as a violent-good-old-boy in Scorsese's *Alice Doesn't Live Here Anymore* (1974) was convincing, Keitel seemed to be struggling as an Austrian detective in 1980's *Bad Timing: A Sensual Obsession.* (Oddly enough, he played almost exactly the same role—thankfully minus the imitation-Freud accent—in 1991's *Mortal Thoughts.)*

Aside from character and second leads in a wide variety of American pictures, he has done extensive work overseas, starring in Ridley Scott's *The Duellists* (1977), Bertrand Tavernier's *Deathwatch* (1980), and *La Nuit de Varennes* (1982), among others. His performance as a Brooklyn-accented Method Judas in Scorsese's controversial *The Last Temptation of Christ* (1988) provoked almost as many arguments as the movie itself.

The year 1991 brought Keitel breakthrough recognition, after more than twenty years in movies. Key supporting roles in *Thelma & Louise* and *Mortal Thoughts* (as detectives in both films) and an Oscar-nominated turn as gangster Mickey Cohen in *Bugsy* comprised an impressive parlay. (Interestingly, he had played Bugsy Siegel in a 1974 TV movie, *The Virginia Hill Story.*) Making no distinction between starring or supporting roles, Keitel continues to work steadily in projects that command his interest. He gave powerful lead performances as a thief in the gritty *Reservoir Dogs* (which he also coproduced) and, especially, as a corrupt cop looking for redemption in Abel Ferrara's *Bad Lieutenant* (both 1992) then etched memorable supporting turns as an assassin in *Point of No Return,* and a racist cop in *Rising Sun* (both 1993). Most recently, he costarred in Jane Cam-

pion's acclaimed *The Piano* (1993), as an unusually romantic and vulnerable character (and performed in the nude, as he had in *Bad Lieutenant,* with an apparent nonchalance rare in actors), and Ferrara's *Dangerous Game* (1993), as a movie director, opposite Madonna. In 1994 Keitel's versatility was showcased in *Monkey Trouble, Pulp Fiction* (a comic variation on his *Point of No Return* role as a "cleaner"), and *Imaginary Crimes.* He followed with *Smoke* and *Clockers* (both 1995). Sometimes frighteningly intense, and often associated with the dark side of humanity, Keitel may not be a star in the conventional sense of the term, but a growing number of filmmakers have come to rely on him. And Keitel always delivers.
OTHER FILMS INCLUDE: 1976: *Mother, Jugs & Speed, Taxi Driver, Buffalo Bill and the Indians;* 1977: *Welcome to L.A.;* 1978: *Fingers, Blue Collar;* 1982: *The Border;* 1983: *Exposed;* 1984: *Falling in Love;* 1986: *The Men's Club, Wise Guys;* 1987: *The Pickup Artist;* 1989: *The January Man;* 1990: *The Two Jakes;* 1992: *Sister Act;* 1995: *Ulysses' Gaze.*

KEITH, BRIAN. Actor. *(b. Nov. 14, 1921, Bayonne, N.J.)* Though this gruff, burly, sandy-haired actor is probably still best known for his television work—particularly as the star of "Family Affair" (1966–71)—he is a superlative character actor with more than 100 films to his credit. The scion of a theatrical family (whose father, Robert, became a prominent character actor in films and television) Keith began his acting career after serving in the Marines as an aerial gunner during World War 2 (though he did make his film debut as a cherub in 1924's *The Pied Piper of Malone).* He acted in many live television productions and had his first major film role in *Arrowhead* (1953). He has appeared in *Storm Center* (1956), *The Parent Trap* (1961, a rare romantic comedy lead), *The Russians Are Coming! The Russians Are Coming!* (1966), *Nickelodeon* (1976), *Hooper* (1978), *Sharky's Machine* (1981), and *Young Guns* (1988), among many others. He was particularly memorable in *Reflections in a Golden Eye* (1967), *Gaily, Gaily* (1969), the TV movie *The Silent Lovers* (1980, as director Mauritz Stiller), and especially *The Wind and the Lion* (1975, as Teddy Roosevelt).

His other TV series include "The Westerner" (1960), "Archer" (1975), "Hardcastle and McCormick" (1983–86), and the sitcom "Walter and Emily" (1991).

KEITH, DAVID. Actor. *(b. May 8, 1954, Knoxville, Tenn.)* This likable actor, who affects an "aw, shucks" attitude both on- and offscreen (and resembles actor Kurt Russell), snared a key supporting role as Richard Gere's suicidal boot-camp buddy in *An Officer and a Gentleman* (1982) and was tagged a comer. Keith showed leading-man appeal in his first starring role, as a cadet in *The Lords of Discipline* (1983), but somehow missed his grab at the brass ring of stardom. He has directed two films: *The Curse* (1987), a cheap horror film, and *The Further Adventures of Tennessee Buck* (1988), an uneven but entertaining Indiana Jones spoof in which he also starred. Keith's best performance in recent years, however, was as the psycho pursuing Cathy Moriarty in *White of the Eye* (1987). In the early 1990s he was appearing in a sitcom, "Flesh 'n Blood."
OTHER FILMS INCLUDE: 1979: *The Great Santini;* 1980: *Brubaker;* 1990: *The Two Jakes;* 1994: *Major League II.*

KELLAWAY, CECIL. Actor. *(b. Aug. 22, 1893, Capetown, South Africa; d. Feb. 28, 1973.)* Pudgy, soft-spoken, and kindly, this popular stage and screen actor generally played benevolent characters. He made quite a few films in Australia during the 1930s, but first attracted American audiences in *Wuthering Heights* (1939), and was particularly busy as a Paramount contract player in the 1940s. Kellaway delivered a fine performance as Lana Turner's doomed husband in *The Postman Always Rings Twice* (1946), although his character was considerably altered from that in James Cain's book. Kellaway was nominated twice for Best Supporting Actor Oscars: in 1948 for *The Luck of the Irish* (playing a leprechaun) and in 1967 for *Guess Who's Coming to Dinner* (playing a priest). He appeared in more than 100 films altogether, including *Intermezzo* (1939), *The House of the Seven Gables, The Mummy's Hand, The Letter* (all 1940), *I Married a Witch* (1942), *Forever and a Day* (1943), *Mrs. Parkington* (1944), *Kitty* (1946, as Thomas Gainsborough), *Uncon-*

quered (1947), *Joan of Arc, Portrait of Jennie* (both 1948), *Harvey* (1950), *The Prodigal* (1955), *The Proud Rebel* (1958), *The Cardinal* (1963), *Hush . . . Hush, Sweet Charlotte* (1965), and *Getting Straight* (1970), his final film.

KELLERMAN, SALLY. Actress. (b. June 2, 1938, Long Beach, Calif.) To many moviegoers, she'll always be remembered as "Hot Lips" Houlihan, the uptight, sexually repressed but desirable Army nurse in Robert Altman's *MASH* (1970). By that time, the tall, husky-voiced blonde with the wry, wide-mouthed smile had been toiling in bit parts for more than a decade, from the exploitative *Reform School Girls* (1957) to the mainstream *The Boston Strangler* (1968). Her turn as "Hot Lips" earned Kellerman an Oscar nomination for Best Supporting Actress and made her, if not a major star, a popular and always welcome screen personality. She appeared in Altman's *Brewster McCloud* (1970), *The Last of the Red Hot Lovers* (1972), the ill-fated *Lost Horizon* (1973, in which she sang—and came off better than most of her costars), *Slither* (also 1973), *Rafferty and the Gold Dust Twins* (1975), *The Big Bus* (1976), *Welcome to L.A.* (1977), *A Little Romance* (1979), *Foxes, Serial,* and *Loving Couples* (all 1980), among others, before taking a hiatus from movie work. She returned to the screen in the mid 1980s, playing a college professor who falls for Rodney Dangerfield in *Back to School,* Julie Andrews' flaky neighbor in *That's Life!* (both 1986), a dead porno star who coaches a lovesick lad in *Meatballs III* (1987), and the distaff half of *Boris and Natasha* (1992), the long-unreleased live-action "comedy" based on characters from the old "Rocky and Bullwinkle" cartoon show. During that period she most frequently appeared in movies packaged and/or produced by her husband, Jonathan Krane. Kellerman's sensual voice is often heard behind major TV commercials, and in a well-received cabaret act. She also provided voices for the animated features *The Mouse and His Child* (1977) and *Happily Ever After* (1990). Other credits include Percy Adlon's *Younger and Younger* (1993) and Altman's *Ready to Wear/Prêt-à-Porter* (1994).

KELLY, GENE. Dancer, actor, director, choreographer. (b. Aug. 23, 1912, Pittsburgh.) The enduring image of this handsome, robust performer gaily dancing to and crooning "Singin' in the Rain" (in the classic 1952 film of the same name), one of the most frequently repeated sequences in movie history, shouldn't obscure the other impressive achievements in his lengthy, generally distinguished career. A dancer since childhood, Kelly studied economics at Penn State and the University of Pittsburgh, but had the misfortune of graduating during the Depression and was forced to take menial jobs to support himself. At one time a dancing teacher, he finally parlayed his natural ability into a chorus-boy assignment on the Broadway stage. In 1940 he won the leading role in Rodgers and Hart's "Pal Joey," which catapulted him to stardom. During this period he also choreographed several hit plays, including the 1941 production of "Best Foot Forward."

It was probably inevitable that Kelly should wind up in Hollywood, where the film musical had produced some of the screen's most popular players. Kelly's good looks, brawny physique, and vigorous, athletic dancing style set him apart from most male dancers, and while he lacked Fred Astaire's stylish elegance, he more than made up for it with his own ebullience and winning personality. Paired with Judy Garland in *For Me and My Gal* (1942), he got off to a fine start, making a hit with audiences and eliciting favorable reviews. Kelly spent most of his film career at MGM, home of the fabled Arthur Freed unit, which produced Hollywood's finest musicals. *DuBarry Was a Lady, Pilot #5, The Cross of Lorraine,* and *Thousands Cheer* (all 1943) gave Kelly prominent exposure and allowed the MGM publicity machine to build upon his initial success. In 1944 the studio loaned him to Columbia for *Cover Girl* (opposite Rita Hayworth) and to Universal for *Christmas Holiday* (opposite Deanna Durbin in a downbeat musical drama); being paired with those company's top musical stars added luster to his own career, and in *Cover Girl* he helped design his first bravura solo specialty, the ingenious double-exposure number "Alter Ego." He returned to Metro a top draw, and started exercising more control over his work on-screen. In *Anchors Aweigh*

(1945) he and choreographic partner Stanley Donen.concocted a brilliant and innovative dance sequence with the animated Jerry the Mouse. (The musical also earned Kelly a Best Actor Oscar nomination, and marked the first of three screen teamings with Frank Sinatra, whom he taught to dance.) *Ziegfeld Follies* (1946) teamed him with Fred Astaire for the amusing "Babbitt and the Bromide" number. *Words and Music* (1948), a dubious biography of songwriters Rodgers and Hart, enabled him to make a guest appearance performing an impressive rendition of Rodgers' "Slaughter on 10th Avenue" ballet. *The Pirate* (1948) teamed him with Judy Garland in a particularly exuberant musical, and *The Three Musketeers* (also 1948) allowed Kelly, as D'Artagnan, to use his graceful body movements in a nonmusical swashbuckler. *Take Me Out to the Ball Game* (1949), a modestly entertaining baseball musical, gave Kelly and Donen screen credit for contributing the picture's storyline. Only *Living in a Big Way* (1947), a notorious flop about postwar reacclimation, marred Kelly's late 1940s winning streak.

Kelly and Donen earned their director's stripes with *On the Town* (1949), the wonderful Betty Comden–Adolph Green–Leonard Bernstein musical about sailors on leave in New York, New York, in which Kelly also starred. Among its other distinctions was the fact that this musical left the confines of a Hollywood studio and filmed its exteriors on location. After making *Summer Stock* (1950) with former costar Judy Garland, Kelly took a dramatic role in that year's *Black Hand,* which cast the dark-haired performer as an Italian-American crimebuster.

Although directed by Vincente Minnelli, *An American in Paris* (1951) bore Kelly's mark just as strongly. (He is a lifelong Francophile.) His singing and dancing were never better showcased, and the lengthy Gershwin ballet that climaxes the film is one of the highpoints of Kelly's career. It earned him a special Academy Award that year. He took a supporting part in an all-star, picaresque drama, *It's a Big Country* (also 1951) before joining forces with Donen for *Singin' in the Rain* (1952), arguably the finest movie musical of all time, and a delightful spoof of Hollywood's chaotic transition from silent films to sound. Supported by Donald O'Connor

and Debbie Reynolds, Kelly the Actor turned in one of his best performances, while Kelly the Dancer/Choreographer provided inventive terpsichore and Kelly the Codirector contributed dynamic staging. With this one film he reached the apogee of his career.

Kelly went dramatic again in *The Devil Makes Three* (1952), and then had to face the fact that MGM was scaling back on the production of lavish musicals. Lerner and Loewe's *Brigadoon* (1954), directed by Minnelli, was supposed to have been filmed in Scotland, but budget cutbacks kept it on a soundstage instead. Although quite entertaining it was not the film Kelly had hoped for. He persuaded MGM to let him make *Invitation to the Dance* (1957, but filmed years earlier), but this earnest, ambitious episodic dance musical was not a great success artistically or financially. *Les Girls* (also 1957) was Kelly's last starring musical, a pleasant soufflé with Cole Porter songs and George Cukor direction. (Kelly did make an amusing cameo as Yves Montand's dancing coach in 1960's *Let's Make Love,* and appeared in Jacques Demy's French-made homage to the Hollywood musical, *The Young Girls of Rochefort,* in 1968, though his singing voice was—incredibly—dubbed in the French-language version. But his singing and dancing, for the most part, was confined to television from the 1960s on.)

Acting had never been Kelly's strongest suit, but he was tailor-made for the part of a charming heel in *Marjorie Morningstar* (1958). He was less ideal in the role of a cynical reporter, inspired by H. L. Mencken, in *Inherit the Wind* (1960). By this time Kelly was content to spend most of his time behind the camera. He directed *The Happy Road* (1957, in which he also starred), *The Tunnel of Love* (1958), Jackie Gleason's pantomime vehicle *Gigot* (1962), a 1965 telefilm remake of *Woman of the Year,* the all-star comedy *A Guide for the Married Man* (1967), the overstuffed musical *Hello, Dolly!* (1969), and *The Cheyenne Social Club* (1970).

Kelly appeared, both in old film clips and newly shot footage, in MGM's musical compilation film, *That's Entertainment!* (1974). He agreed to direct new sequences (which teamed him with *Ziegfeld Follies* dancing partner Fred Astaire) for the 1976 sequel and also appeared as one of the "hosts" of the second sequel, *That's*

Entertainment! III (1994). He made subsequent screen appearances in *Viva Knievel!* (1977), *Xanadu* (1980), *Reporters* (1981), and *That's Dancing!* (1985). Kelly was married to actress Betsy Blair from 1941 to 1957.

KELLY, GRACE. Actress. *(b. Nov. 12, 1928, Philadelphia; d. Sept. 14, 1982.)* Generally, beautiful young ladies only marry handsome princes in Walt Disney cartoons, but this blond, patrician model turned actress did just that, turning her back on a soaring movie career in the process. Cool and sophisticated, hers was not an easily accessible beauty, and she constantly struggled to keep from seeming aloof on screen. Born into one of Philadelphia's leading families, she turned to acting professionally upon leaving school. (Her uncle was popular playwright George Kelly.) After landing a small role in *Fourteen Hours* (1951), Kelly achieved recognition for her performance as the Quaker wife of Gary Cooper in *High Noon* (1952).

Propelled to "overnight" stardom, she was paired with many of Hollywood's top leading men: Clark Gable, William Holden, Bing Crosby, Ray Milland, James Stewart, and Cary Grant. She more than held her own, not only with her breathtaking beauty, but with growing confidence as an actress. She was swept off her feet by Gable in *Mogambo* (1953, earning an Oscar nomination as Best Supporting Actress), then won an Academy Award as the plain, long-suffering wife of alcoholic Bing Crosby in *The Country Girl* (1954). Going directly from one film to the next, she appeared in *Green Fire* and *The Bridges at Toko-Ri* (both 1954) as well as a trio of Alfred Hitchcock films over two years' time. Her cool elegance made her the ideal Hitchcock blonde in *Dial M for Murder, Rear Window* (both 1954), and the delicious *To Catch a Thief* (1955).

It was while filming the latter on the French Riviera that she met and fell in love with Prince Rainier of Monaco, and after completing two films in 1956—the sleek musical *High Society* (in which she recreated Katharine Hepburn's *Philadelphia Story* role as Tracy Lord and sang "True Love" with Crosby) and *The Swan*

(a story about a young woman betrothed to a prince!)—she left Hollywood to become Princess Grace. (MGM even released a Technicolor film of their wedding ceremony.) She never acted again, though she received comeback offers on a regular basis. She sat on the board of 20th Century-Fox for several years, and occasionally lent her presence to documentaries like *The Children of Theatre Street* (a 1977 film about the Kirov Ballet School). Cheryl Ladd portrayed her in a 1983 TV movie. Her death in an auto accident stunned the world and ended what had truly seemed a fairy-tale life.

KENDALL, KAY. Actress. *(b. May 21, 1926, Hull, England, as Justine McCarthy; d. Sept. 6, 1959.)* Delightful, energetic redhead whose beauty, grace, and charm were matched only by her flawless comedy timing and bubbly screen persona. Born into a family of show folk, she was a chorus girl at age 13, a music-hall performer at 16, and a motion-picture actress at 18 (beginning with 1944's *Fiddlers Three).* She alternated film roles with stage work (her early screen credits include 1944's *Champagne Charlie,* 1946's *London Town,* 1950's *Dance Hall,* 1951's *Happy Go Lovely,* and 1952's *Curtain Up),* making her first real impression as one of the competitive roadster racers in the hit British comedy *Genevieve* (1953). Kendall brightened a number of English films over the next few years (especially 1954's *Doctor in the House),* always leaving one with the impression that she deserved better material than she was getting. (Other credits include *The Constant Husband* and *Fast and Loose* of 1954 and *Quentin Durward* and *Simon and Laura* of 1955.) She made her American screen debut as one of the showgirls involved with Gene Kelly in *Les Girls* (1957), charming stateside audiences. She then costarred in *The Reluctant Debutante* (1958) with husband Rex Harrison (they would have made a wonderful British Nick and Nora Charles), and played Yul Brynner's wife in the mediocre *Once More, With Feeling* (1960), which, sadly, was her last film. Kendall died of leukemia just before the picture's release, robbing the screen of a great talent.

KENNEDY, ARTHUR. Actor. *(b. Feb. 17, 1914, Worcester, Mass., as John Arthur Kennedy; d. Jan. 5, 1990.)* A versatile character actor and occasional lead, the sandy-haired, pleasant-looking Kennedy alternated between stage and screen, winning a Tony as the troubled young Biff in Arthur Miller's "Death of a Salesman," and earning five Academy Award nominations during his long and generally distinguished screen career. Kennedy, reportedly discovered by James Cagney while acting on stage in Los Angeles, first hit movie screens playing Cagney's artistic kid brother in *City for Conquest* (1940). He then spent several years as a Warner Bros. contract player, popping up in *Bad Men of Missouri, High Sierra, Highway West* (his first lead), *They Died With Their Boots On* (all 1941), *Desperate Journey* (1942), *Air Force* (1943), and *Devotion* (1946), among others. Physically, Kennedy wasn't the he-man type, but he played tough, cynical characters with authority, and worked both sides of the law (filmically speaking) with equal facility.

The late 1940s and 1950s saw him turn out an impressive body of work, including *Boomerang!* (1947), *Champion* (1949, picking up his first Oscar nomination in support of Kirk Douglas), *The Glass Menagerie* (1950), *Bright Victory* (1951, in an Oscar-nominated lead as a blind veteran adjusting to civilian life), *Bend of the River* (a memorable heavy part, opposite James Stewart), *The Lusty Men, Rancho Notorious* (all 1952), *The Desperate Hours, The Man From Laramie, The Naked Dawn, Trial* (all 1955, the last providing him another Academy Award nod), *Peyton Place* (1957, another Oscar nomination, as Lucas Cross), *Some Came Running* (1958, yet another unsuccessful shot at the Oscar, in support of Frank Sinatra), *A Summer Place* (1959), and *Elmer Gantry* (1960).

Like so many of his Hollywood generation, Kennedy increasingly found himself working abroad during the 1960s and 1970s, and he was finally reduced to the ignominy of *Emmanuelle on Taboo Island* (1977). Not that there weren't some solid English-language roles for him during that period: *Barabbas, Lawrence of Arabia* (both 1962, a small but solid role as the reporter), *Cheyenne Autumn* (1964), *Joy in the Morning* (1965), *Fantastic Voyage, Nevada Smith* (both 1966), *Anzio!* (1968),

and *Hail, Hero!* (1969, as young Michael Douglas' father), to name a few. Kennedy left the screen in 1979, returning a decade later to take one of the leads in a modest, homespun drama, *Signs of Life* (1989), chronicling the predicament of workers in a boat-building business abruptly thrown out of work. All things considered, it provided a graceful, even charming "finis" for Kennedy's career; he died shortly after its release.

KENNEDY, BURT. Writer, producer, director. *(b. Sept. 3, 1922, Muskegon, Mich.)* Amiable filmmaker who specializes in light-hearted Westerns. The son of vaudevillians, he got his show-biz start in the late 1940s as a radio writer, then turned to screenwriting in the 1950s, penning several of the famous Budd Boetticher/Randolph Scott Westerns that attracted critical attention in France: *Seven Men From Now* (1956), *The Tall T* (1957), *Ride Lonesome* (1959), and *Comanche Station* (1960). After an inauspicious directorial debut—*The Canadians* (1961)—he moved to TV and wrote and directed episodes of "Combat!" He returned to the big screen with *Mail Order Bride* in 1964, and followed it with such comic hits as *The Rounders* (1965) and *The War Wagon* (1967), as well as such grim fare as *The Money Trap* (1966) and *Welcome to Hard Times* (1967). He had a sleeper hit in *Support Your Local Sheriff!* in 1969, and followed it with *Dirty Dingus Magee* (1970) and *Support Your Local Gunfighter* (1971), as well as the bizarre Raquel Welch oater *Hannie Caulder* (1972) and an intriguing adaptation of Jim Thompson's *The Killer Inside Me* (1974). Since that time Kennedy's work has mostly been for the small screen, but in 1991 he piloted the Hulk Hogan formula comedy *Suburban Commando* (1991). He also cowrote the screenplay for Clint Eastwood's *White Hunter, Black Heart* (1990).

KENNEDY, EDGAR. Actor. *(b. Apr. 26, 1890, Monterey, Calif.; d. Nov. 9, 1948.)* One of the screen's finest comic actors, and the master of the "slow burn," Kennedy inaugurated his movie career in 1914, working for Mack Sennett; he was reportedly one of the original Keystone Kops. In the

1920s he defected to the camp of rival producer Hal Roach, supporting Laurel and Hardy in such classics as *Two Tars* (1928) and *Perfect Day* (1929), and directing them (as E. Livingston Kennedy) in *From Soup to Nuts* and *You're Darn Tootin'* (both 1928). He supported the Our Gang kids in *Moan and Groan Inc., Shivering Shakespeare* (both 1929), *The First Seven Years, When the Wind Blows* (both 1930), and other Roach stars, occasionally starring in films of his own (like 1929's hilarious *A Pair of Tights*). By 1931, Kennedy had launched his own starring series of two-reel comedies for RKO (initially titled *Mr. Average Man*), in which he played a henpecked husband perpetually exasperated by his scatterbrained wife and obstreperous in-laws, giving him ample opportunities to do the slow burn. The series amassed 103 entries between 1931 and 1948. Kennedy also played supporting roles in features, often cast as a dumb detective. *Little Orphan Annie* (1932, as Daddy Warbucks), *Duck Soup* (1933, as the lemonade vendor), *Professional Sweetheart* (1933), *Tillie and Gus, Twentieth Century* (both 1934), *San Francisco* (1936), *Mad Holiday, Super Sleuth, Hollywood Hotel* (all 1937), *A Star Is Born* (1937, as Janet Gaynor's landlord), *The Black Doll* (1938), *It's a Wonderful World* (1939), *In Old California* (1942), *Air Raid Wardens* (1943, reunited with Laurel and Hardy), *The Falcon Strikes Back* (1943), *It Happened Tomorrow* (1944), and *Captain Tugboat Annie* (1945) are just a few of the full-length films in which he appeared. Late in his career, Kennedy got two of his best parts in successive pictures directed by Preston Sturges: *Mad Wednesday* (1947, as an "artistic" bartender) and *Unfaithfully Yours* (1948, as a music-loving detective). He died shortly afterward, still a popular player and very much in demand. His last role was as Doris Day's uncle in *My Dream Is Yours* (1949).

KENNEDY, GEORGE. Actor. *(b. Feb. 18, 1925, New York City.)* As the no-nonsense, cigar-chomping troubleshooter Joe Patrone in *Airport* (1970) and its three sequels, this beefy, fair-haired supporting actor chewed scenery as well as stogies and stole most of the scenes he was in. The role wasn't much of a stretch for Kennedy—he'd made a career of playing loutish heavies and sympathetic "big lug" characters—but it solidified his following and won him flashier roles. The son of show-biz parents, Kennedy first appeared on stage at age two and later moved into radio. After a 16-year stint in the Army, he decided on acting as a full-time career. Debuting on film in *The Little Shepherd of Kingdom Come* in 1961, he worked steadily thereafter in the likes of *Lonely Are the Brave* (1962), *The Man from the Diner's Club, Charade* (both 1963), *Strait-Jacket, McHale's Navy* (both 1964), *In Harm's Way* (1965), *The Dirty Dozen* (1967), and *Cool Hand Luke* (also 1967), in which he played the prisoner Dragline (earning an Oscar for Best Supporting Actor in the bargain). In the 1970s he appeared in *Earthquake* (1974), *The Eiger Sanction* (1975), and *Death on the Nile* (1978), to name a few, and hit the airwaves as star of "Sarge" (1971–72) and "The Blue Knight" (1976). During the 1980s Kennedy continued to appear regularly on-screen, but in less memorable movies, of which *Bolero* (1984), *Radioactive Dreams* (1986), and *Nightmare at Noon* (1988) are, sadly, all too representative. He gently spoofed his own straightforward screen image as Leslie Nielsen's police squad colleague in the comedy hits *The Naked Gun* (1988), *The Naked Gun 2½: The Smell of Fear* (1991), and *The Naked Gun 33⅓: The Final Insult* (1994). OTHER FILMS INCLUDE: 1965: *Hush . . . Hush, Sweet Charlotte, The Sons of Katie Elder;* 1966: *The Flight of the Phoenix;* 1968: *The Boston Strangler;* 1969: *Gaily, Gaily;* 1973: *Lost Horizon;* 1974: *Thunderbolt and Lightfoot;* 1981: *Modern Romance* (a very funny cameo as himself); 1986: *The Delta Force.*

KENSIT, PATSY. Actress. *(b. Mar. 4, 1968, Hounslow, London.)* Striking blond British actress who began her acting career at the age of four, as the daughter of Mia Farrow and Bruce Dern in *The Great Gatsby* (1974). She appeared in *The Blue Bird* (1976), *Hanover Street* (1979), as well as many British TV and stage productions but made her first big splash as singing star Crepe Suzette in the stylish *Absolute Beginners* (1986). She went on to appear in *A Chorus of Disapproval* (1988), *Lethal Weapon II* (1990), and achieved her greatest critical success as an outspoken young woman in *Twenty-One*

(1991). The stardom that was predicted after the *Lethal Weapon* exposure hasn't materialized, but Kensit has kept busy in both television and theatrical films including *Blame It on the Bellboy, Blue Tornado, Timebomb* (all 1991), *The Turn of the Screw* (1992), *Bitter Harvest,* and *Full Eclipse* (both 1993, the latter made for TV). She came full circle in her career by playing Mia Farrow in the TV miniseries "Love and Betrayal: The Mia Farrow Story" (1995).

KERR, DEBORAH. Actress. *(b. Sept. 30, 1921, Helensburgh, Scotland, as Deborah Jane Kerr-Trimmer.)* Perhaps the screen epitome of ladylike British reserve, this beautiful star was Oscar-nominated a whopping six times in 12 years—and never once won. Yet few film performers have accumulated as many meritorious movies to their credit. A former ballet dancer who also acted on stage before making her screen debut opposite Rex Harrison and Wendy Hiller in Shaw's *Major Barbara* (1941), Kerr achieved stardom early in her career. British director Michael Powell gave the actress one of her best roles, that of a Catholic nun trying to run a mission school in the Himalayas, in *Black Narcissus* (1946), and it brought her to the attention of MGM, which signed her up immediately. (The promotion for her first Hollywood movie instructed Americans thusly: "Deborah Kerr—rhymes with Star!")

Although her dominant screen "image" is that of an elegant, refined and possibly reserved British woman, Kerr played a wide variety of roles, and went decidedly against type as the American adulteress in *From Here to Eternity* (1953), in which she shared a famous smooch in the surf with Burt Lancaster.

She was a charming—if unusual—match for Clark Gable in *The Hucksters* (1947, her Hollywood debut), a plucky heroine in *King Solomon's Mines* (1950), a credible Lygia in *Quo Vadis?* (1951), an effective Portia in *Julius Caesar* (1953), an utterly unflappable Anna in *The King and I* (1956, with Marni Nixon providing her singing voice), an elegantly witty woman who shares a shipboard romance with Cary Grant in *An Affair to Remember* (1957), a shipwrecked nun forced to contend with the scruffy marine Robert Mitchum in *Heaven Knows, Mr. Allison* (1957), the real-life Sheilah Graham, in love with F. Scott Fitzgerald in *Beloved Infidel* (1959), a governess haunted by her surroundings in *The Innocents* (1961), to name just a few. She never gave a bad performance.

She was Oscar-nominated for *Edward, My Son* (1949), *From Here to Eternity* (1953), *The King and I* (1956), *Heaven Knows, Mr. Allison* (1957), *Separate Tables* (1958), and *The Sundowners* (1960).

She has lived for many years in Switzerland with her husband, author Peter Viertel, occasionally agreeing to make a TV movie or miniseries. In 1994 she received an honorary Academy Award.

OTHER FILMS INCLUDE: 1943: *The Life and Death of Colonel Blimp;* 1945: *Vacation From Marriage;* 1946: *The Adventuress (aka I See a Dark Stranger);* 1947: *If Winter Comes;* 1950: *Please Believe Me, King Solomon's Mines;* 1952: *The Prisoner of Zenda;* 1953: *Young Bess, Dream Wife;* 1955: *The End of the Affair;* 1956: *The Proud and the Profane, Tea and Sympathy;* 1958: *Bonjour Tristesse;* 1959: *The Journey, Count Your Blessings;* 1960: *The Grass Is Greener;* 1961: *The Naked Edge;* 1964: *The Chalk Garden, The Night of the Iguana;* 1967: *Eye of the Devil, Casino Royale;* 1968: *Prudence and the Pill;* 1969: *The Gypsy Moths, The Arrangement;* 1982: *Witness for the Prosecution* (telefilm); 1985: *The Assam Garden;* 1986: *Hold the Dream* (telefilm).

KERR, JOHN. Actor. *(b. Nov. 15, 1931, New York City.)* Based on his well-received leading role as the sensitive student having an affair with his teacher in *Tea and Sympathy* (1956, a characterization he had created on Broadway three years earlier), this quiet, delicately handsome actor should have been a screen sensation. But, aside from his costarring role as the ill-fated Lt. Cable in *South Pacific* (1958), Kerr's movie career amounted to little. A Harvard graduate and onetime stage star, he also appeared in the films *The Cobweb* (1955), *Gaby* (1956), *The Vintage* (1957), *Girl of the Night, The Crowded Sky* (both 1960), *The Pit and the Pendulum,* and *Seven Women From Hell* (both 1961). Kerr made sporadic appearances in TV as well before retiring to practice law. He has occasionally accepted minor roles since then, as in *The Silent Partner* (1978).

KERSHNER, IRVIN. Director. *(b. Apr. 29, 1923, Philadelphia.)* Though best known for his action-adventure sagas, Kershner's finest films are personal stories that focus on outsiders trying to cope with the demands of modern living. After work in advertising, Kershner made documentaries for the U.S. Information Service and worked for three years on the TV documentary series "Confidential File." He made his film debut with the Roger Corman production *Stakeout on Dope Street* (1958), followed it with *The Young Captives* (1959), and later gained recognition for *The Hoodlum Priest* (1961), which starred Don Murray as a cleric dealing with juvenile delinquents. His next films dealt similarly and compassionately with outsiders: *A Face in the Rain* (1963), with Rory Calhoun as an American spy hiding out in Italy, *The Luck of Ginger Coffey* (1964), with Robert Shaw as an Irish misfit who moves to Montreal, and *A Fine Madness* (1966), with Sean Connery as a nonconformist poet. After the entertaining comedy *The Flim Flam Man* (1967) with George C. Scott, Kershner directed *Loving* (1970), a little-known but perceptive account of suburban problems. He worked in different genres through the 1970s with varying degrees of success: *Up the Sandbox* (1972), *S*P*Y*S* (1974), *The Return of a Man Called Horse* (1976), and *Eyes of Laura Mars* (1978). Kershner achieved his greatest popular success with *The Empire Strikes Back* (1980), the second installment of the Star Wars series that many critics felt surpassed the original. Since then, he has directed the "unofficial" James Bond film *Never Say Never Again* (1983), the TV movie *Traveling Man* (1989), the ultra-violent *Robocop 2* (1990), and the premiere episode of Steven Spielberg's ambitious TV series "SeaQuest DSV" (1993). He also appeared in a small role in Martin Scorsese's *The Last Temptation of Christ* (1988).

KEYES, EVELYN. Actress. *(b. Nov. 20, 1919, Port Arthur, Tex.)* Although she's best remembered for her turn as Suellen O'Hara in *Gone With the Wind* (1939), this feline blonde enjoyed a brief period of popularity while under contract to Columbia Pictures, where she played leading lady to Robert Montgomery in *Here Comes Mr. Jordan* (1941) and to Larry Parks in *The Jolson Story* (1946), two of the studio's biggest 1940s hits. A former nightclub dancer who wangled bit parts at Paramount (beginning with 1937's *Artists and Models*) before appearing in *Wind,* Keyes signed with Columbia in 1940, apprenticing in a "Wild Bill" Elliott horse opera (*Beyond the Sacramento*) and a Boris Karloff thriller (*Before I Hang*) before making a third B, *The Face Behind the Mask* (1941), in which, cast as a blind girl who falls in love with disfigured gangster Peter Lorre, she delivered an earnest, genuinely touching performance that won her a shot at the big time.

Unfortunately, many of Keyes' vehicles were routine, and while her performances were consistently good, they couldn't lift the films themselves out of programmer class. She appeared in *Ladies in Retirement* (1941), *Flight Lieutenant, Dangerous Blondes* (both 1943), *Nine Girls, Strange Affair* (both 1944), *A Thousand and One Nights* (1945), *The Thrill of Brazil* (1946), *Johnny O'Clock* (1947), *Enchantment, The Mating of Millie* (both 1948), *Mrs. Mike, Mr. Soft Touch* (both 1949), and *The Killer That Stalked New York* (1950) before scouting around for roles outside Columbia. Joseph Losey's *The Prowler* (1951) was a good choice, but Keyes lost more ground (thanks to the likes of 1951's *Smuggler's Island* and *Iron Man,* 1952's *One Big Affair,* 1953's *99 River Street,* and 1954's *Hell's Half Acre*), finally taking a small supporting role in *The Seven Year Itch* (1955) before retiring. (Although she did take small roles in 1972's *Across 110th Street,* 1987's *Return to Salem's Lot,* and 1989's *Wicked Stepmother.*)

By all accounts, Keyes' performances *off*screen were more interesting than her movie exploits. Her first husband shot himself after their divorce. She then married director Charles Vidor, leaving him after two years for director John Huston, to whom she was married for four turbulent years. In the mid 1950s she lived with producer Mike Todd, and took a cameo in his *Around the World in Eighty Days* (1956). In 1957 she wed bandleader Artie Shaw. Much of her stormy private life was chronicled in her 1977 autobiography, "Scarlett O'Hara's Younger Sister."

KIBBEE, GUY. Actor. *(b. Mar. 6, 1882, El Paso, Tex.; d. May 24, 1956.)* Ruddy-faced, bald, bulbous character actor in films of the 1930s and 1940s, and one of the busiest members of the Warners stock company. A former riverboat performer and stage actor, Kibbee crashed pictures in 1931 and appeared in dozens of Warners films, often as an ignorant, obnoxious boob. He played a know-nothing political hack in *The Dark Horse* (1932), a lecherous producer in *42nd Street* (1933), a crafty but slovenly detective in the starring role of *While the Patient Slept* (1935), and the list goes on and on: *Blonde Crazy* (1931), *Union Depot, Central Park* (both 1932), *Gold Diggers of 1933, Footlight Parade, The Silk Express, The Life of Jimmy Dolan* (all 1933), *Wonder Bar* (1934), and *Captain Blood* (1935). The seemingly tailor-made part of *Babbitt* (1934) was trivialized when Warners virtually ignored Sinclair Lewis' novel and turned the character into a typical Kibbee buffoon. After leaving Warners, Kibbee appeared in *Captain January* (1936, as Shirley Temple's guardian), *Babes in Arms, Mr. Smith Goes to Washington* (both 1939), *Our Town* (1940), *It Started With Eve* (1941), *Girl Crazy* (1943), *The Horn Blows at Midnight* (1945), *Fort Apache,* and *3 Godfathers* (both 1948), among others. He also starred in RKO's *Scattergood Baines* series in the early 1940s. Offscreen he was one of Hollywood's most avid golfers.

KIDDER, MARGOT. Actress. *(b. Oct. 17, 1948, Yellowknife, Northwest Territories, Canada.)* Sharp-featured brunette actress whose husky voice and energetic manner made her one of the 1970s' most interesting leading ladies. After making her first screen appearance in *Gaily, Gaily* (1969), a limp newspaper story based on Ben Hecht's memoirs, Kidder showed real personality in the wacky *Quackser Fortune Has a Cousin in the Bronx* (1970). She toiled on the TV-movie assembly line for a couple of years before making audiences sit up and take notice of her with an accomplished, eerie interpretation of separated Siamese twins in Brian De Palma's *Sisters* (1973). In 1975, after starring in the quirky, minor *92 in the Shade,* written by her future husband Thomas McGuane, Kidder played leads in the mainstream movies *The Great Waldo Pepper* and *The Reincarnation of Peter Proud* (in which, donning heavy makeup, she played a middle-aged murderess). She turned her attentions to directing that same year, helming the noncommercial film *And Again.*

Kidder was a delightfully spunky yet vulnerable Lois Lane in *Superman* (1978), a role she repeated in the three sequels (1980, 1983, 1987). Nothing she's done since—with the exception of *The Amityville Horror* (1979)—has attained any real degree of success: *Willie and Phil* (1980), *Heartaches, Miss Right* (both 1981), *Trenchcoat* (1983), *Little Treasure* (1985), *The Canadian Conspiracy* (1986), *Mob Story* (1989), *The White Room* (1990), among them. Kidder raised some hackles during the U.S. intervention in Kuwait, when she ridiculed the press and the military for not seeing the larger consequences of their actions. In 1990 she was injured while driving a car for a cable-TV series episode in Canada, was fired, and filed suit against the producers. In 1994 she made a cameo appearance in *Maverick.* Kidder was married to director Philippe de Broca and actor John Heard.

KIDMAN, NICOLE. Actress. *(b. June 20, 1967, Hawaii.)* Born in Hawaii and raised in Australia, she studied dance and drama from childhood and made her film debut in *Bush Christmas* (1983) at the age of 14. Her performance in the 1985 Australian miniseries "Vietnam" made her a star in that country and won her several awards. Other credits include *BMX Bandits* (1983), *Wills and Burke: The Untold Story* (1985), *Windrider* (1986, as a rock star), *Emerald City* (1989), and the miniseries "Five Mile Creek" (1985) and "Bangkok Hilton" (1990). Her performance as a snooty upperclasswoman in *Flirting* (1990) was duly noted when American moviegoers got to see the film in 1992. This tall, strawberry-blond actress garnered excellent notices for her first major film role, as the terrorized but resourceful wife adrift with a homicidal maniac in the Australian sailing thriller *Dead Calm* (1989). She came to America for *Days of*

Thunder (1990), in which she was conveniently cast as a doctor for leading man Tom Cruise. The highly touted racing saga failed to live up to expectations, but off-screen Kidman won the heart of costar Cruise, whom she subsequently married. Since then, she has played Dutch Schultz's moll in *Billy Bathgate* (1991), an Irish immigrant in *Far and Away* (1992, reteamed with Cruise), an American spouse (who's a psychopath in reality), in the overheated *Malice,* and an expectant mother in the tearjerker *My Life* (both 1993). In 1995, Kidman starred in *Batman Forever* and *To Die For.*

KILEY, RICHARD. Actor. *(b. Mar. 31, 1922, Chicago.)* Astonishingly prolific player on stage (winning a Tony for his performance as Don Quixote in the musical "Man of La Mancha") and in TV drama (winning Emmys for "The Thorn Birds" and "A Year in the Life" among his dozens of small-screen assignments) whose film career has been spotty. Kiley, a former radio actor whose rich, booming voice has served him especially well in the theater, made his movie debut in *The Mob* (1951), and followed it with a string of crime thrillers and urban dramas, including *The Sniper* (1952), *Pickup on South Street* (1953), *Blackboard Jungle,* and *The Phenix City Story* (both 1955). *Spanish Affair* (1958) gave him an interesting leading part, as an American architect traveling in Iberia. *The Little Prince* (1974) gave him his only opportunity to star in a screen musical, as The Pilot in this middling adaptation of the Saint-Exupéry children's classic. His best latter-day screen role was that of Diane Keaton's impossibly strict Catholic father in *Looking for Mr. Goodbar* (1977). Aside from a supporting part in *Endless Love* (1981), Kiley's work since then has been confined to the stage and television. With one notable exception: He provided the voice of the tour guide in the 1993 megahit *Jurassic Park.*

KILMER, VAL. Actor. *(b. Dec. 31, 1959, Los Angeles.)* In the 1984 comedy *Top Secret!,* this young Juilliard-trained actor starred as a hip-swinging, Elvis-like rock 'n' roll spy. It took seven years (and several starring films) for him to attain real stardom as self-destructive rock singer Jim Morrison in Oliver Stone's *The Doors* (1991). Kilmer's physical and vocal resemblance to the late Morrison was remarkable; Stone also used Kilmer's own singing on the film's soundtrack. Kilmer's wife is actress Joanne Whalley-Kilmer, with whom he appeared in the Ron Howard fantasy *Willow* (1988) and the noirish *Kill Me Again* (1989). His other screen turns include the lead in the youth comedy *Real Genius* (1985) and a standout performance as Tom Cruise's cocky nemesis in *Top Gun* (1986). In 1993 he costarred in *The Real McCoy,* appeared as the spirit of Elvis Presley in *True Romance* (though his face was never seen), and turned in a scene-stealing performance as Doc Holliday in *Tombstone* (1993). He then took over the role of the Caped Crusader from Michael Keaton in *Batman Forever* (1995).

KING, ALAN. Actor. *(b. Dec. 26, 1927, Brooklyn, N.Y., as Irwin Alan Kniberg.)* Famed stand-up comedian who has proven himself a formidable actor in a number of comedic and dramatic roles. In his teens, he began performing comedy in the Catskills and gradually moved to cabarets, then opened for such performers as Judy Garland and Lena Horne. King's film career began in the 1950s with small parts in films like *Miracle in the Rain* (1956) and *The Helen Morgan Story* (1957), and he costarred with a young Sean Connery in *Operation Snafu* (1961). After years of TV and nightclub success, he returned to films when Sidney Lumet called on him to appear in *Bye Bye Braverman* (1968) and *The Anderson Tapes* (1972). Since his acclaimed starring performance as a harried business tycoon in Lumet's *Just Tell Me What You Want* (1980), King has been busier than ever, with solid supporting roles in *Author! Author!, I, the Jury* (both 1982), *Lovesick* (1983), *Cat's Eye* (1985), *Memories of Me* (1988, actually more of a costar turn as Billy Crystal's father), *Enemies, A Love Story* (1989, as Rabbi Lembeck), *The Bonfire of the Vanities* (1990, getting one of the best scenes in this bad movie), and *Night and the City* (1992, as a mobster cum fight promoter). He displays his storytelling skills in the documentary *Funny* (1989). King has also written three books and produced several stage plays and movies, including *Cattle*

Annie and Little Britches (1980) and *Wolfen* (1981).

KING, HENRY. Director. *(b. June 24, 1888, Christiansburg, Va.; d. June 29, 1982.)* Skillful, commercially successful director whose list of credits includes many of the most highly respected and popular movies of the 1920s, 1930s, 1940s, and beyond. A Southern boy who acted in small stock companies and burlesque before breaking into the "flickers" in 1912, he began directing as well in 1915. By 1920 he'd quit acting to stay behind the camera; the following year he directed Richard Barthelmess (his partner in Inspiration Films) in *Tol'able David,* his first major success. His evocative handling of the nostalgic story set in rural America presaged a fascination with that aspect of American history and culture, to which he would return continually throughout his career.

King's high-profile silent films, most of them commercial hits, included *The White Sister* (1923), *Romola* (1924), *Stella Dallas* (1925), *The Winning of Barbara Worth* (1926), *The Magic Flame* (1927), and *The Woman Disputed* (1928). His first talkie was *Hell Harbor* (1930), which was shot largely on location in Florida. He spent most of the sound era under contract to Fox, turning out some of the studio's best-remembered films: *Lightnin'* (1930), *Over the Hill* (1931), *State Fair* (1933), *Marie Galante* (1934), *Way Down East* (1935), *Ramona, Lloyd's of London* (both 1936), *Seventh Heaven* (1937), *In Old Chicago, Alexander's Ragtime Band* (both 1938), *Jesse James, Stanley and Livingstone* (both 1939), *Chad Hanna, Little Old New York* (both 1940), *A Yank in the RAF* (1941), *The Black Swan* (1942), *The Song of Bernadette* (1943, for which he received an Academy Award nomination), *Wilson* (1944, Oscar-nominated again), *A Bell for Adano* (1945), *Margie* (1946), *Captain From Castile* (1947), *Prince of Foxes, Twelve O'Clock High* (both 1949), *The Gunfighter* (1950), *I'd Climb the Highest Mountain* (1951), *The Snows of Kilimanjaro* (1952), *King of the Khyber Rifles* (1953), *Love Is a Many Splendored Thing* (1955), *Carousel* (1956), *The Sun Also Rises* (1957), *This Earth Is Mine* (1959), and *Tender Is the Night* (1962). Never an individualist, or a visual stylist, King was one of those craftsmen who thrived under the studio system, and made an impressive number of good, solid films. He was still active in his 90s, mentally and physically, still piloting planes as he had for most of his life.

KINGSLEY, BEN. Actor. *(b. Dec. 31, 1943, Yorkshire, England, as Krishna Bhanji.)* Prodigiously talented British leading man of Indian descent. Kingsley was born to an Indian physician and English fashion model, and as a young man gravitated toward the theater. He honed a subtle acting style in numerous Shakespearean productions, but his film debut, in *Fear Is the Key* (1972), was disappointing by comparison. One year later he had a small part as a Pakistani taxi company owner in Mike Leigh's *Hard Labour.* Kingsley was content to remain on stage until winning the title role in Sir Richard Attenborough's epic *Gandhi* (1982). His subtle, heartfelt performance as the pacifist leader not only brought international fame, but a Best Actor Academy Award in his first major leading role. Kingsley has since appeared in many "smaller" pictures, including several written by Harold Pinter. Among them are *Betrayal* (1983), *Turtle Diary, Harem* (both 1985), *Testimony, Maurice* (both 1987), *Pascali's Island, Without a Clue* (a rare stab at comedy, playing a brilliant Dr. Watson to Michael Caine's inept Sherlock Holmes, both 1988), *Slipstream* (1989), *The Children* (1990), and *Bugsy* (1991, in an Oscar-nominated turn as gangster Meyer Lansky). Since then he has turned up in a number of films, in an impressive variety of character parts: as the voice of Freddie in the animated *Freddie as F.R.O.7,* the onetime student radical in *Sneakers* (both 1992), the timid but honest Vice President of the United States in *Dave,* the quietly determined chess master in *Searching for Bobby Fischer,* the title character's Jewish accountant (and conscience) in *Schindler's List* (all 1993), and the accused torturer in *Death and the Maiden* (1994). He also starred in the 1989 TV movie *Murderers Among Us: The Simon Wiesenthal Story,* as the fabled Nazi-hunter.

KINSKI, KLAUS. Actor. *(b. Oct. 8, 1926, Sopot, Poland, as Nikolaus Nakszynski; d.*

Nov. 25, 1991.) **Born** into poverty, this army veteran spent some time in sanitariums before catching the acting bug and appearing on the Berlin stage. An irascible-looking actor with pale skin, intense eyes, thick lips, and a seemingly stone-chiseled visage, Kinski subsequently starred in numerous European-made (or localed) movies, including such notable ones as *A Time to Love and a Time to Die* (1958), *The Counterfeit Traitor* (1962), *Doctor Zhivago* (1965), *For a Few Dollars More* (1966), *Grand Slam* (1968), but gained international fame for his collaborations with German director Werner Herzog: *Aguirre: The Wrath of God* (1972), *Woyzeck* (1978), *Nosferatu the Vampyre* (1979), and *Fitzcarraldo* (1982, replacing the more conventionally cast Jason Robards as an Irish-born dreamer). Kinski also played in many cheap thrillers and horror movies throughout the 1960s and 1970s, most memorably the ultraviolent *Jack the Ripper* (1976). Fiercely pragmatic, he is said to have turned down a role in *Raiders of the Lost Ark* for one in *Venom* (1982) because the money was better. In later years he alternated appearances in ambitious A pictures (1981's Billy Wilder comedy *Buddy Buddy,* 1984's *The Little Drummer Girl*) with stints in worthless genre flicks (1986's *Crawlspace*). He is the father of actress Nastassja Kinski. His autobiography was published in America in 1989, but was soon withdrawn for legal reasons.

KINSKI, NASTASSJA (or NASTAS-SIA). Actress. *(b. Jan. 24, 1960, Berlin.)* The daughter of actor Klaus Kinski, this slender, pouty brunette made a bid for stardom in the early 1980s after receiving considerable attention in the title role of *Tess* (1979), directed by Roman Polanski. But aside from a few noteworthy leads—in *Cat People* (1982), *Unfaithfully Yours* and *Paris, Texas* (both 1984)— she failed to get the meaty roles that would have sustained her as a box-office draw. She's better known for her well-publicized offscreen antics, and for a striking poster in which she posed with a snake wrapped around her! She has one child with composer/producer Quincy Jones.
OTHER FILMS INCLUDE: 1975: *False Move, To the Devil, a Daughter;* 1982: *One*

From the Heart; 1983: *Exposed;* 1984: *The Hotel New Hampshire, Maria's Lovers;* 1985: *Harem, Revolution;* 1988: *Silent Night;* 1989: *Torrents of Spring;* 1990: *The Secret, Night Sun;* 1991: *The Insulted and the Injured;* 1993: *Faraway, So Close!;* 1994: *Terminal Velocity.*

KIRBY, BRUNO. Actor. *(b. Apr. 28, 1949, New York City.)* Widely acclaimed as the womanizing sporting-goods salesman in *City Slickers* (1991), this youthful-looking, high-voiced supporting player currently enjoys greater popularity—and name recognition—than at any other time during his two-decade-old career. Often cast as a cranky straight man or quintessential New York character, Kirby first appealed to audiences while a regular on the 1972 TV sitcom "The Super." The show was created by Rob Reiner, who would later cast Kirby for a hilarious cameo (as the limo driver) in his directorial debut, *This Is Spinal Tap* (1984), and later still for a large role in his *When Harry Met Sally . . .* (1989). After costarring in the sexual-freedom drama *The Harrad Experiment* (1973, which also featured Don Johnson), Kirby landed a plum role as the young Clemenza, opposite Robert De Niro's young Corleone, in Francis Coppola's *The Godfather, Part II* (1974). *Where the Buffalo Roam* (1980) found him playing a thinly disguised "Rolling Stone" editor Jann Wenner to Bill Murray's gonzo journalist Hunter S. Thompson. Kirby's other memorable roles include the uptight Army radio-station honcho in Barry Levinson's *Good Morning, Vietnam* (1987) who knows in his heart that he's funny, and mobster Marlon Brando's gofer in *The Freshman* (1990). In some of his earlier roles, he was credited as B. Kirby, Jr. His father is actor Bruce Kirby.
OTHER FILMS INCLUDE: 1977: *Between the Lines;* 1981: *Modern Romance;* 1984: *Birdy;* 1985: *Flesh + Blood;* 1989: *We're No Angels;* 1993: *Mr. Wonderful;* 1994: *Golden Gate.*

KIRKLAND, SALLY. Actress. *(b. Oct. 31, 1944, New York City.)* This hyperkinetic blond actress with the crooked smile and penchant for provocative wardrobe, a former Andy Warhol confrere and disciple of Lee Strasberg (who taught at the Actors' Studio), got her 15 minutes of fame as the Academy Award-nominated star of *Anna* (1987), in which she played a failed Czech actress struggling in New York. Long before that, she'd won supporting roles in a number of high-profile films—including *The Sting, The Way We Were* (both 1973), *A Star Is Born* (1976), and *Private Benjamin* (1980), *The Incredible Shrinking Woman* (1981)—and a slew of unsuccessful movies, many of them exploitative, low-budget, avant-garde turkeys, such as *Coming Apart, Futz* (both 1969), *The Young Nurses* (1973), *Big Bad Mama* (1974), *Pipe Dreams* (1976), *Talking Walls* (1982), and *Love Letters* (1983). Despite her personal success in *Anna* (a fine performance), Kirkland was unable to land decent follow-up roles in major movies; she starred instead in a string of minor films, some of which went straight to videotape: *White Hot* (1988), *Best of the Best, Cold Feet* (both 1989), *Paint It Black, Two Evil Eyes, Revenge* (all 1990, the last a high-profile film that bombed), and *In the Heat of Passion* (1992, a semipornographic "erotic thriller"). She fared much better on TV, winning juicy supporting roles in a number of made-for-TV movies and appearing in several episodes of "Roseanne." Kirkland, probably the only Academy Award nominee who was a regular habitué of "The Joe Franklin Show," also had a bit role in Oliver Stone's *JFK* (1991). In 1992, she acted in and coexecutive produced *Paper Hearts*.

KLINE, KEVIN. Actor. *(b. Oct. 24, 1947, St. Louis.)* This bright, boyish, exuberant actor is one of the 1990s' most versatile leading men, being equally facile in comedic and dramatic roles. After graduating from Indiana University, aspiring actor Kevin Kline entered Juilliard, where he studied with Harold Guskin. He made his stage debut in 1970, in the off-Broadway "Wars of Roses," and went on to appear with the New York Shakespeare Festival for their 1970 season. Kline was a founding member of John Houseman's The Acting Company, with whom he made his Broadway debut in 1972. Years of stage work were capped in 1978, when the talented Kline won a Tony (Outstanding Featured Actor in a Musical) for his performance in "On the Twentieth Century."

He picked up another two years later for his role in "The Pirates of Penzance." After years of success both on and off Broadway (as well as in TV soap operas), the magnetic stage actor finally made his film debut opposite Meryl Streep in *Sophie's Choice* (1982). He reprised his "Penzance" stage role for the 1983 film adaptation, and also appeared in such popular films as *The Big Chill* (1983) and the eighties-style Western *Silverado* (1985), both directed by Lawrence Kasdan.

Interesting turns in *Violets Are Blue* (1986) and *Cry Freedom* (1987) showed Kline maturing as a screen talent but otherwise added little to his portfolio. In 1988, however, Kline stunned moviegoers with a hysterical comedic performance as an oafish thug in *A Fish Called Wanda,* and won himself an Oscar in so doing. *The January Man* (1989), a muddled, uneven thriller, was a temporary setback, and Kline's performance as an oversexed but good-hearted pizza man in Kasdan's *I Love You to Death* (1990) raised lots of chuckles but little box-office coin. His breezy, offhand acting style more suited to comedy, Kline scored a personal triumph as a ham actor returning to daytime TV in *Soapdish* (1991), but the film was just so-so. *Grand Canyon* (1991) reunited Kline with Kasdan yet again for a downbeat look at contemporary life in Los Angeles. In 1992, he was reunited with *January Man* costar Mary Elizabeth Mastrantonio for the muddled thriller *Consenting Adults.* Having essayed theatrical, larger-than-life characters before, he was ideally cast as silent film star Douglas Fairbanks, Sr., in *Chaplin* (1992). His irresistible performance as a down-to-earth guy who impersonates the President of the United States in *Dave* in 1993 had critics and magazine writers proclaiming this his "breakthrough" to bona fide movie stardom. Kline, however, seems content alternating film work with the stage, and is Associate Producer with the New York Shakespeare Festival. He is married to actress Phoebe Cates, who made an unbilled appearance with him in *I Love You to Death.* In 1994 he appeared with Cates in *Princess Caraboo,* then starred in *French Kiss* (1995). He narrated *George Balanchine's The Nutcracker* (1993).

KLUGMAN, JACK. Actor. (b. Apr. 27, 1922, Philadelphia.) Trained at New York's American Theatre Wing, this late-coming character actor made his film debut at age 34 in the crime programmer *Timetable* (1956). Klugman was active in the "golden age" of live TV drama during the 1950s, and worked extensively on stage; he even sang in the original Broadway cast of "Gypsy." He attained small-screen stardom in 1970 as the slovenly sportswriter Oscar Madison in the TV version of Neil Simon's "The Odd Couple," which enjoyed a five-year run. It also earned him two Emmy Awards. (Klugman and Randall reunited for a TV movie, *The Odd Couple,* in 1993.) Later he enjoyed more success as a crime-solving medical examiner on TV's "Quincy" (1976–83). His film roles have been few and far between, but he was memorable in *12 Angry Men* (1957), *Cry Terror* (1958), *Days of Wine and Roses* (1962), *Act One* (1963), *The Detective* (1968), *Goodbye, Columbus* (1969), *Who Says I Can't Ride a Rainbow?* (1971), and *Two Minute Warning* (1976). Klugman has been battling throat cancer and his once impassioned, cantankerous growl has been replaced with a feeble—but still audible—rasp.

KNIGHT, SHIRLEY. Actress. (b. July 5, 1937, Goessel, Kans.) An expert at playing disturbed modern women, Knight trained at the Pasadena Playhouse before making her film debut in *Five Gates to Hell* (1959). Still a relative newcomer to film, she astounded viewers with her accomplished performances in *The Dark at the Top of the Stairs* (1960) and *Sweet Bird of Youth* (1962), both of which earned her Best Supporting Actress Oscar nominations. She turned her attentions to Broadway in the mid 1960s, then moved to Britain for several years, appearing in films only sporadically, as in *Juggernaut* (1974) and *Endless Love* (1981). Knight was memorable in *The Group* (1966), *Petulia* (1968), and especially *The Rain People* (1969), a probing proto-feminist road film written and directed by a young Francis Ford Coppola. Other credits include *Beyond the Poseidon Adventure* (1979) and *The Sender* (1982). She appeared in a 1958 Western TV series, "Buckskin," and has become very active in television in recent years, winning a 1988 Emmy for her recurring role as Mel Harris' mother on "thirtysomething."

KNOTTS, DON. Actor. (b. July 21, 1924, Morgantown, W. Va.) What does an actor do when he earns Emmy after Emmy playing a high-strung, overenthusiastic sheriff's deputy on a long-running TV comedy hit? If he's Don Knotts, he brings variations of that same character to the big screen in a succession of juvenile comedy features. This skinny, bug-eyed comic performer, adept at playing hypertense, frequently unnerved types, is a former ventriloquist who made his way to radio and the stage. He made his film debut opposite Andy Griffith in *No Time for Sergeants* (1958), in a memorable role he'd played previously on Broadway. He followed Griffith to series TV, finding fame as small-town deputy Barney Fife on "The Andy Griffith Show" (1960–65), the role that earned him five Emmy awards. This fame led to his unlikely positioning as a movie star, in such broad (often kiddie-oriented) comedy vehicles as *The Incredible Mr. Limpet* (1964, in which his character was transformed into an animated cartoon fish), *The Ghost and Mr. Chicken* (1966), *The Reluctant Astronaut* (1967), *The Shakiest Gun in the West* (1968, a remake of Bob Hope's *The Paleface*), the misfired "adult" comedy *The Love God?* (1969), and *How to Frame a Figg* (1971). He then became part of an unofficial comic repertory company at Disney, costarring in *No Deposit, No Return* (1976), *Herbie Goes to Monte Carlo* (1977), and *Hot Lead and Cold Feet* (1978), and, teamed with Tim Conway, in *The Apple Dumpling Gang* (1975), *Gus* (1976), and *The Apple Dumpling Gang Rides Again* (1979). He and Conway also costarred in some non-Disney comedies, *The Prize Fighter* (1979) and *The Private Eyes* (1980). In addition to hosting his own eponymous TV variety show from 1970–71, Knotts enjoyed a long run as an irascible landlord on "Three's Company" (1979–84).

KNOWLES, PATRIC. Actor. (b. Nov. 11, 1911, Horsforth, England, as Reginald Lawrence Knowles.) More than a supporting player but something less than a full-fledged star, this suave, handsome, wavy-haired Britisher essayed leads in B films and took character parts in A's. He worked in a number of films in his native country (beginning with 1932's *Men of Tomorrow*) before coming to Hollywood in 1936, when he impressed American audiences as Errol Flynn's younger brother in *The Charge of the Light Brigade.* He stayed at Warner Bros. for several years, starring as detective Lance O'Leary in *The Patient in Room 18* and playing Will Scarlett in *The Adventures of Robin Hood* (both 1938), as well as appearing in *It's Love I'm After* (1937), *Four's a Crowd,* and *The Sisters* (both 1938). After freelancing for a couple more years (logging stints in 1939's *Another Thin Man,* 1940's *A Bill of Divorcement,* and 1941's *How Green Was My Valley,* among others), Knowles signed with Universal, where he became the resident leading man in that studio's mysteries and horror films. Occasionally he got a starring role, as in *The Strange Case of Dr. Rx* (1942), but he mostly played second fiddle to the monsters and maniac killers: *The Wolf Man* (1941), *The Mystery of Marie Roget* (1942), *Frankenstein Meets the Wolf Man* (1943), and so on. After his Universal contract expired, Knowles freelanced, playing supporting roles until the mid 1970s.

OTHER FILMS INCLUDE: 1943: *Hit the Ice, Crazy House;* 1944: *Pardon My Rhythm;* 1945: *Kitty;* 1946: *Of Human Bondage, Monsieur Beaucaire;* 1948: *Dream Girl;* 1950: *Three Came Home;* 1952: *Tarzan's Savage Fury;* 1953: *Flame of Calcutta;* 1954: *Khyber Patrol;* 1957: *Band of Angels;* 1958: *Auntie Mame;* 1967: *The Way West;* 1970: *Chisum;* 1973: *Arnold.*

KNOX, ALEXANDER. Actor, screenwriter. *(b. Jan. 16, 1907, Strathroy, Ontario; d. Apr. 25, 1995.)* In 1944, Knox was chosen by Darryl F. Zanuck to play the title role in one of the year's most prestigious and expensive productions: *Wilson,* a biography of the American president. For his sturdy performance, he earned an Academy Award nomination; *Variety* even dubbed him a "new-born star." However, Knox lacked the looks and personality to allow him to continue playing lead roles in Hollywood, and *Wilson* remained his only shot at major stardom.

Knox began his career on the stage in Boston, then settled in England during the 1930s and appeared in such films as *The Phantom Strikes* (1938) and *The Four Feathers* (1939), before returning to America. His Hollywood debut was promising, as the intellectual Humphrey Van Weyden opposite Edward G. Robinson in *The Sea Wolf* (1941). He continued to play major parts in such films as *This Above All* (1942), *The Commandos Strike at Dawn* (1943), *None Shall Escape* (1944), and in the wake of *Wilson,* the costarring part opposite Irene Dunne in *Over 21* (1945). He also cowrote two films in which he appeared, *Sister Kenny* (1946) and *The Judge Steps Out* (1949, in the starring role).

After playing Ingrid Bergman's husband in Rossellini's *Europa '51* (1951), filmed in Italy, he resettled in England. He later appeared as figures of authority in such international productions as *The Vikings* (1958), *The Longest Day* (1962, as Gen. Bedell Smith), *Khartoum* (1966), *How I Won the War* (1967), and *Nicholas and Alexandra* (1971). Two of Knox's 1960s roles may be seen as fusions of his most famous part: in *Accident* (1967) he played a college provost, and in the James Bond adventure *You Only Live Twice* (1967) he was the President of the United States. Knox also penned a pair of adventure novels, "Night of the White Bear" and "Totem Dream."

OTHER FILMS INCLUDE: 1949: *Tokyo Joe;* 1951: *I'd Climb the Highest Mountain;* 1954: *The Divided Heart;* 1955: *The Night My Number Came Up;* 1956: *Reach for the Sky;* 1958: *Chase a Crooked Shadow, Intent to Kill, The Two-Headed Spy;* 1960: *Oscar Wilde, Crack in the Mirror, These Are the Damned;* 1963: *In the Cool of the Day;* 1964: *Woman of Straw;* 1968: *Villa Rides, Shalako;* 1969: *Fraulein Doktor;* 1971: *Puppet on a Chain;* 1983: *Gorky Park;* 1985: *Joshua Then and Now.*

KOPPLE, BARBARA. Director. *(b. July 30, 1946, Bear Mountain, N.Y.)* Social-minded documentary filmmaker who learned much of her craft with the *cinema verité* practitioners Albert and David Maysles, whom she assisted on several projects after graduating from Northeastern University. She made her first film, *People's Tribunal* (1971, not released), about the prison riots at Attica, but gained fame—and a Best Documentary Oscar—for *Harlan County, U.S.A.* (1977), a sympathetic look at a Kentucky mine workers strike. Kopple devoted years to that project, and lived with the workers themselves. After work on the concert-film documentary *No Nukes* (1980), she directed *Keeping On* (1981), a fictional film about textile workers for PBS' "American Playhouse," and later won another Best Documentary Oscar for *American Dream* (1989), which focused on the labor strike at Hormel's meat plant in Austin, Minnesota. Her other projects include *Hurricane Irene* (1987, a high-definition video of a peace festival), *Civil Rights: The Struggle Continues* (1989), *Out of Darkness: The Mine Workers Story* (1990, about the history of the United Mine Workers of America), *Beyond JFK: The Question of Conspiracy* (1992) and the acclaimed *Fallen Champ: The Untold Story of Mike Tyson* (1993), a rare prime-time network TV documentary that pulled no punches.

KORDA, ALEXANDER (SIR). Producer, director. (b. Sept. 16, 1893, Pusztaturpaszto, Hungary; d. Jan. 23, 1956.) Of Korda, film composer Miklos Rozsa once wrote, "Had he been born under different circumstances, [he] would have become, beyond doubt, a Prime Minister, the President of General Motors, or of a republic. He was born to lead—and a born diplomat, who could handle people with dazzling skill. He used his perfect manners, natural charm, and superior intelligence to train them as an animal-trainer shapes wild beasts."

One of the seminal figures in British film history, Korda helped to change that nation's motion picture industry by making a product that could effectively compete overseas and still have a flavor all its own. Growing up in Hungary, he wrote for several publications—and film magazines—before falling into directing. He took to it easily and with enthusiasm, directing over twenty films in Hungary and more in Vienna and Germany. He then came to America and worked for First National and Fox on films like *The Private Life of Helen of Troy* (1927), *Love and the Devil* (1929), and *The Princess and the Plumber* (1930), but he disliked the Hollywood arena and fled to France, where he made the colorful provincial satire *Marius* (1931), among others. He ev-

entually settled in England in 1931 where he first worked on films for the British branch of Paramount and then started his own company, London Films, one year later. The first films made there—like the comedy *Wedding Rehearsal* (1932), *Men of Tomorrow, Strange Evidence,* and *Cash* (all 1933)—did not create much of a stir, but *The Private Life of Henry VIII* (also 1933) changed all of that.

Korda had trouble getting anybody to back the low-budget production, or even to show the film when it was completed, but this grand, entertaining (if not terribly accurate) slice of history turned out to be an international hit and a turning point in British films. It was nominated for an American Academy Award as Best Picture, and Charles Laughton won an Oscar for his indelible performance as the monarch. *Henry VIII* marked the emergence of Britain as a force in the film world. The film's success also made Korda a major player: He was offered a distribution deal with United Artists for future films, and established his own studio at Denham in 1935. His growing responsibilities as head of London Films forced him to gradually hand directorial control of individual pictures to others (notably his brother Zoltan). Of the remaining films he helmed, *Rembrandt* (1936), with Charles Laughton as the Dutch painter, is probably his finest work.

He remained a central figure as a producer, first repeating the successful formula of *Henry VIII* with *The Private Life of Don Juan* and *Catherine the Great* (both 1934) and then branching out on a series of memorable projects: the rousing costume epic *The Scarlet Pimpernel* (1935), the stunning adaptation of H. G. Wells' *Things to Come* (1936), the historical drama *Fire Over England,* the documentary-like *Elephant Boy* (both 1937), the superb defense of imperialism *The Four Feathers* (1939), and the classic fantasy *The Thief of Bagdad* (1940). All reflected Korda's desire for superb craftsmanship and performances that would rival any American film and subject matter that represented British ideals at their best. (His adopted homeland returned the favor by knighting him in 1942.) They also introduced a whole new galaxy of talent to movies, including such longtime collaborators as cinematographer Georges Perinal, writers Lajos Biro and Arthur

Wimperis, and stars like Laughton, Robert Donat, Sabu, Merle Oberon, Vivien Leigh, and Leslie Howard. During this remarkably productive period, however, London Films was heavily in debt and Korda was forced to give up Denham Studios in 1938. One of his major expenses was an ambitious production of Robert Graves' *I, Claudius* which began filming in 1937 under the direction of Josef von Sternberg, with Charles Laughton in the lead. The production was jinxed from the start, and later had to be abandoned. (It later became the subject of a fascinating documentary, *The Epic That Never Was.)*

Korda returned to America to direct *That Hamilton Woman* (1941) and reactivated London Films a few years later, merging it with the British branch of MGM. This resulted in only one film—*Perfect Strangers* (1945, which he directed)—before Korda went independent again; he acquired an interest in British Lion Film Corporation, a distribution source for several years (until its financial collapse), and spent the rest of his life using his charm and energy to find different backers and distributors for his projects. After *An Ideal Husband* (1947, his last film as director), Korda served as a producer and later executive producer on films that covered a wide variety of subjects, including *Mine Own Executioner* (1947), *Anna Karenina, The Fallen Idol* (both 1948), *The Third Man* (1949), *Tales of Hoffman, Cry, the Beloved Country* (both 1951), *Breaking the Sound Barrier* (1952), *The Captain's Paradise* (1953), *Hobson's Choice* (1954), *Summertime* and *Richard III* (both 1955). Until his death in 1956, Korda was still planning projects; his last feature was *Smiley* (1956). Korda was married to actresses Maria Corda and Merle Oberon, whose respective careers he launched and nurtured. His nephew Michael, a successful publishing executive and author, wrote a chronicle of his father and uncles, "Charmed Lives: A Family Romance" in 1979.

Korda's brother Zoltan, who had a penchant for African-themed projects, had begun working with him in Hungary and continued his collaboration at London Films directing such films as *Sanders of the River* (1935), *Elephant Boy* (collaborating with Robert Flaherty), *The Four Feathers,* and *Jungle Book* (1942), as well as *Sahara* (1943), *The Macomber Affair*

(1947), and *Cry, the Beloved Country.* Another brother, Vincent Korda, a brilliant production designer, first teamed with Alexander in France on *Marius* and showed his mettle on *Henry VIII,* recreating elaborate Tudor sets on a minimal budget and stage space. When larger budgets were allotted, he showed his imaginative genius on films as diverse as *Things to Come, Rembrandt, The Four Feathers,* and *The Third Man.* He was Oscar-nominated for *That Hamilton Woman, The Jungle Book,* and won for the marvelous *The Thief of Bagdad.*

KORNGOLD, ERICH WOLFGANG. Composer. *(b. May 29, 1897, Brno, Czechoslovakia; d. Nov. 29, 1957.)* Along with fellow Europeans Max Steiner and Franz Waxman, Korngold elevated the status of film music from incidental accompaniment to a new art form. A successful composer on the Continent and protégé of impresario Max Reinhardt before emigrating to the United States, Korngold was a child prodigy who began composing at age 13. Reinhardt brought him to Hollywood when the director made his ambitious film version of *A Midsummer Night's Dream* (1935). Korngold's beautiful adaptation of Mendelssohn's music themes so impressed Warner Bros. that the studio hired him to score *Captain Blood* (1935) and *Anthony Adverse* (1936, which won Korngold his first Oscar). He returned to Austria to stage an opera, but a postponement brought him back to Hollywood to work on *The Adventures of Robin Hood;* while there he learned his home had been seized by invading Nazis, and was forced to remain. Ironically, he felt he was the wrong choice to score a swashbuckler, but *Robin Hood* turned out to be one of his finest scores, majestic and beautiful, ringing with memorable themes. It won him his second Oscar, and led to him scoring yet another great Errol Flynn adventure yarn, *The Sea Hawk* (1940). Many Korngold aficionados consider *Kings Row* (1942) to be his greatest work. Other scores include *Juarez, The Private Lives of Elizabeth and Essex* (both 1939), *The Sea Wolf* (1941), *The Constant Nymph* (1943), *Devotion, Deception, Of Human Bondage* (all 1946), *Escape Me Never* (1947), and *Magic Fire* (1956, his last). He worked in all areas of musical composition, never limiting himself to film scores alone; his operas, symphonies, chamber music, and concertos are still performed today.

KORSMO, CHARLIE. Actor. (b. July 20, 1978, Minneapolis.) As the streetwise ragamuffin Junior in *Dick Tracy* (1990), this relaxed, natural kid actor constantly blurted a familiar refrain—"When do we eat?"—that, along with his vigorous performance, endeared him to movie audiences. He entered show business after watching a TV-show taping and convincing his mother that he could do that, too; soon after he was appearing in commercials. Korsmo made a memorable film debut opposite Jessica Lange in *Men Don't Leave* (1990), and in 1991 played the sons of Richard Dreyfuss (in *What About Bob?*), William Hurt (in *The Doctor*), and Robin Williams (in *Hook*).

KORTY, JOHN. Director, screenwriter, editor, photographer. (b. July 22, 1936, Lafayette, Ind.) Principled filmmaker who has worked both outside and within the mainstream, attempting to find projects that support his humanistic beliefs. He started making amateur films during the early 1950s, went on to create animated TV commercials, and received an Oscar nomination for the antismoking short *Breaking the Habit* (1964). He wrote, directed, edited, and photographed his first feature *Crazy Quilt* (1966), a ragged, funny comedy about the sexes for less than $100,000; both it and his follow-up feature, *Funnyman* (1967), with Peter Bonerz as a comedian in search of meaning in his life, won Korty a critical following. Since then he has directed such Hollywood features as *Riverrun* (1970), *Silence* (1974), *Alex and the Gypsy* (1976), and the *Love Story* sequel, *Oliver's Story* (1978), none of them remarkable or particularly successful. But for TV, he piloted such noteworthy films as *Class of '63* (1973), *Farewell to Manzanar* (1976), and the classic *The Autobiography of Miss Jane Pittman* (1974), which won him a Best Director Emmy. In 1977 his affecting documentary *Who Are the DeBolts? . . . And Where Did They Get 19 Kids?* won an Academy Award. Since then, he has mainly directed TV movies like *A Christmas Without Snow* (1980) and *The Ewok Adventure*

(1984), produced by his Bay Area colleague George Lucas, who also executive-produced Korty's delightful (but little-seen) cutout-animation feature *Twice Upon a Time* (1983).

KOSTER, HENRY. Director. (b. May 1, 1905, Berlin, as Hermann Kosterlitz; d. Sept. 21, 1988.) Blessed with a light touch (and good taste), this former painter turned to scriptwriting in Berlin in the 1920s, and became a director in the early days of sound. Forced to flee from Nazism in 1932, he made films in Austria and France before emigrating to the U.S. with his friend, producer Joseph Pasternak. The two set up shop at Universal and proved their mettle with a modest film called *Three Smart Girls* (1936), which made a star of Deanna Durbin. That and subsequent Durbin vehicles like *One Hundred Men and a Girl* (1937), *Three Smart Girls Grow Up* (1939), *Spring Parade* (1940), and *It Started With Eve* (1941)—sunny, amusing, full of schmaltz and great character actors—helped save the studio from bankruptcy. Koster followed Pasternak to MGM in the 1940s, then set off on his own and continued to make polished, entertaining films through the 1960s. Among his best: *The Bishop's Wife* (1947, which earned him an Oscar nomination), *Harvey* (1950), *My Cousin Rachel* (1952), and *Good Morning, Miss Dove* (1955). Darryl F. Zanuck also entrusted Koster with directing his ambitious production of *The Robe* (1953), the first film released in CinemaScope.
OTHER FILMS INCLUDE: 1938: *The Rage of Paris;* 1944: *Music for Millions;* 1947: *The Unfinished Dance;* 1948: *The Luck of the Irish;* 1949: *Come to the Stable, The Inspector General;* 1950: *Wabash Avenue, My Blue Heaven;* 1951: *No Highway in the Sky;* 1952: *Stars and Stripes Forever;* 1954: *Desiree;* 1955: *The Virgin Queen;* 1956: *D-Day the Sixth of June;* 1957: *My Man Godfrey;* 1959: *The Naked Maja;* 1960: *The Story of Ruth;* 1961: *Flower Drum Song;* 1962: *Mr. Hobbs Takes a Vacation;* 1963: *Take Her, She's Mine;* 1965: *Dear Brigitte;* 1966: *The Singing Nun.*

KOTCHEFF, TED. Director. (b. Apr. 7, 1931, Toronto.) Talented director who began his career in Canadian television, then moved to England where he won acclaim as a director for the BBC as well as for

many stage productions. He made his feature debut with *Tiara Tahiti* (1962), a mild
satire on the class struggle, and followed
with *Life at the Top* (1965, a sequel to the
far superior *Room at the Top)* and *Two
Gentlemen Sharing* (1969). *Outback*
(1971) drew attention for its depiction of a
descent into barbarism, but it was *The Apprenticeship of Duddy Kravitz* (1974) that
brought Kotcheff international attention.
Based on a novel by Mordecai Richler (a
frequent Kotcheff collaborator), this
tough, funny look at a Jewish boy (played
by Richard Dreyfuss) trying to make it in
1940s Montreal was a major critical and
commercial success. Kotcheff subsequently became a comedy specialist in
Hollywood's eyes, and directed *Fun With
Dick and Jane* (1977), *Who Is Killing the
Great Chefs of Europe?* (1978), *Switching
Channels* (1988, a remake of *His Girl Friday),* and *Weekend at Bernie's* (1989), as
well as the fine drama *Split Image* (1982),
the action film *Uncommon Valor* (1983),
Winter People (1989), and the no-brainer
Folks! (1992). Though he is better known
for the raucous football comedy *North
Dallas Forty* (1979) and for introducing
Sylvester Stallone's John Rambo to the
world in *First Blood* (1982), one of
Kotcheff's best movies is also one of his
most personal, the small, quirky *Joshua
Then and Now* (1985), like *Duddy Kravitz*
a Richler adaptation set in Canada, with
James Woods as a writer and Alan Arkin
as his gangster father.

KOTTO, YAPHET. Actor. *(b. Nov. 15,
1937, New York City.)* When this physically
imposing, authoritative black actor is on
the screen, it's hard not to watch his every
move. He's forceful and dynamic, and
usually gets roles that allow him to display those attributes. He comes from a
New York stage background, having
played on Broadway in "The Great White
Hope." Kotto made his big-screen debut
in 1964's *Nothing But a Man,* and has appeared in dozens of movies since. He's
best remembered for his turns in the 1973
James Bond entry *Live and Let Die* and in
1979's *Alien* (suffering a grisly fate). He
is a regular on TV's "Homicide: Life on
the Streets" (1993–), and appeared in the
television movie of Arthur Miller's *The
American Clock* (1993).
OTHER FILMS INCLUDE: 1968: *The*

Thomas Crown Affair; 1970: *The Liberation of
L. B. Jones;* 1972: *Bone;* 1975: *Report to the
Commissioner;* 1976: *Drum;* 1978: *Blue Collar;* 1980: *Brubaker;* 1983: *The Star Chamber;*
1985: *Warning Sign;* 1987: *The Running Man*
(one of his best roles); 1988: *Midnight Run;*
1991: *Freddy's Dead: The Final Nightmare;*
1993: *Almost Blue, Extreme Justice.*

KOVACS, ERNIE. Actor. *(b. Jan. 23,
1919, Trenton, N.J.; d. Jan. 12, 1962.)* One of
the great innovators in the TV medium,
Kovacs wasn't nearly as well served by
the cinema, where his multifarious talents
were pretty much ignored and what work
he did get was mainly as a character actor.
As that, though, he was able to make
something of an impression, especially in
the witchcraft comedy *Bell, Book and
Candle* (1958) and in a role as a somewhat menacing Cuban in *Our Man in Havana* (1960). Kovacs' other films include
Operation Mad Ball (1957, his first),
North to Alaska (1960), and *Sail a
Crooked Ship* (1961). His best work,
though, was seen on the small screen; his
TV series combined his offbeat humor
with pioneering special effects in a way
that was practically surrealistic. A car
crash took his life at the height of his career. He was married to actress-singer
Edie Adams.

KOVACS, LASZLO. Cinematographer.
(b. May 14, 1933, Hungary.) Top-rank cinematographer who learned his craft at the
Academy of Theater and Film Art in Budapest. Kovacs came to America shortly
after the Soviet crackdown on his native
land in 1956; he and fellow cinematographer Vilmos Zsigmond, a school chum,
shot thousands of feet of film during the
October crisis and smuggled it out to
the West, but by the time they screened
the footage, the world media was uninter-
ested. A series of menial jobs in upstate
New York followed, and the two expatriates drove to Hollywood in 1958. Kovacs
found work on no-budget cheapies such as
The Time Travelers (1964, his first as
camera operator) and *Hell's Angels on
Wheels* (1967). His lensing of *Easy Rider*
(1969) brought his work to the attention
of the major studios. He was a favorite
collaborator of director Peter Bogdanovich, for whom he shot *What's Up, Doc?*

(1972), *Paper Moon* (1973), *At Long Last Love* (1975), and *Nickelodeon* (1976). Although never nominated for an Oscar, he's one of the most respected directors of photography in the business, having lensed such classics as *Five Easy Pieces* (1970) and elements of *Close Encounters of the Third Kind* (1977). His malleable photographic style makes Kovacs a workable choice for any type of movie. His other films include *Alex in Wonderland* (1970), *Shampoo* (1975), *New York, New York* (1977), *Inside Moves* (1980), *The Legend of the Lone Ranger* (1981), *Frances* (1982), *Ghostbusters* (1984), *Legal Eagles* (1986), *Say Anything . . .* (1989), and *Deception* (1993).

KRABBE, JEROEN. Actor. *(b. Dec. 5, 1944, Amsterdam, Netherlands.)* This tall, pleasant-looking, and capable Dutch lead made his initial splash in three films directed by fellow countryman Paul Verhoeven: *Soldier of Orange* (1979), *Spetters* (1980) and, most notably, as the tortured writer in the kinky thriller *The Fourth Man* (1979). He soon found himself cast in numerous American and international productions, including *Jumpin' Jack Flash, No Mercy* (both 1986), *The Living Daylights* (1987), *A World Apart* (1988), *Scandal,* and *The Punisher* (both 1989), often in a villainous capacity. He was especially memorable as Amy Irving's egotistical would-be suitor in *Crossing Delancey* (1988), and played a similarly irritating violinist in Barbra Streisand's *The Prince of Tides* (1991). In 1993 he had a particularly successful parlay, as Harrison Ford's doctor "friend" in the smash hit *The Fugitive,* and as the young Depression-era protagonist's ever-optimistic father in *King of the Hill.* He also appeared in the independent feature *For a Lost Soldier* (1993), *Immortal Beloved,* and *Farinelli* (both 1994). His name, by the way, is pronounced Yeh-roon Kra-bay.

KRAMER, STANLEY. Producer, director. *(b. Sept. 23, 1913, New York City.)* Although unfashionable with latter-day film critics who find some of his "message movies" to be simplistic, Stanley Kramer can take credit for producing (and later directing) some of Hollywood's boldest, most so-

cially conscious movies—at a time when much of the industry was reverting to formula and cowering in the wake of the Communist witch-hunts. Moreover, his projects consistently attracted the top talent working on both sides of the cameras in Hollywood. Making his pictures independently gave Kramer freedom from studio interference, and he produced a run of powerful films, among them the gritty boxing drama *Champion;* a study of Army racism, *Home of the Brave* (both 1949); a drama of paralyzed war veterans, *The Men* (1950, Marlon Brando's first film); a notable adaptation of Arthur Miller's play *Death of a Salesman* (1951); and the anti-McCarthy Western, *High Noon* (1952). He then signed with Columbia, where he produced the first "biker" film, *The Wild One,* and *The Caine Mutiny* (both 1954), as well as a Dr. Seuss musical fantasy, *The 5,000 Fingers of Dr. T.* (1953), a notorious flop in its day but now a cult classic. Kramer finally began directing with, oddly, a glossy soap opera, *Not as a Stranger* (1955).

After helming a large-scale actioner, *The Pride and the Passion* (1957), he returned to social commentary, attacking racism in *The Defiant Ones* (1958, Oscar-nominated for Best Picture and Best Director), nuclear proliferation in *On the Beach* (1959), creationism in *Inherit the Wind* (1960), and Nazi war criminals in *Judgment at Nuremberg* (1961, Oscar-nominated for Best Picture and Director). Challenged to make something "a little less serious," he vowed to make the "comedy to end all comedies," and almost pulled it off with the elephantine, overproduced, all-star blockbuster *It's a Mad Mad Mad Mad World* (1963), still his most popular film. After a lavish adaptation of *Ship of Fools* (1965), Kramer made *Guess Who's Coming to Dinner* (1967, Oscar-nominated for Best Picture and Director), which dealt head-on with interracial marriage. His later films, including *The Secret of Santa Vittoria* (1969), *R.P.M.* (1970), *Bless the Beasts and Children* (1971), the underrated *Oklahoma Crude* (1973), and *The Domino Principle* (1977), were not successful, to say the least. *The Runner Stumbles* (1979), a particularly aloof and unconvincing thriller, was dismissed by critics and audiences alike, making it a dismal swan song to Kramer's career. In 1980 he retired and moved to Seattle, where he taught and wrote a newspaper column; a decade later he was back in Hollywood, planning new film projects.

KRASNA, NORMAN. Screenwriter, director, producer. *(b. Nov. 7, 1909, Queens, N.Y.; d. Nov. 1, 1984.)* Savvy scribe who did just about everything show folk can do with typewriters—and then some. A student at New York University, Columbia University, and Brooklyn Law School, Krasna wrote news stories, promotional copy, play reviews, movie reviews, short stories, novels, plays, treatments for movies and, finally, movie scripts. He was most successful at comedy, although the melodramas *Four Hours to Kill* (1935, from his play "Small Miracles"), *Fury* (1936, Oscar-nominated for Best Story), and *You and Me* (1938) were among his best 1930s works. Krasna was also nominated for his work on *The Richest Girl in the World* (1934) and *The Devil and Miss Jones* (1941), and he won the gold statuette for scripting *Princess O'Rourke* (1943, which he also directed), a popular wartime comedy; together, those three films typified Krasna's fondness for social comedy, and his interest in class distinction. Krasna became a producer with *The Big City* (1937, adapted from one of his stories). He contributed stories and/or scripts to *Hollywood Speaks* (1932), *Hands Across the Table* (1935), *Wife vs. Secretary* (1936), *The King and the Chorus Girl* (1937), *Bachelor Mother* (1939), *It's a Date* (1940), *It Started with Eve* (1941), *Bride by Mistake, Practically Yours* (both 1944), *The Big Hangover* (1950), *White Christmas* (1954), *The Ambassador's Daughter* (1956), *Indiscreet* (1958), *Who Was That Lady?, Let's Make Love* (both 1960), *My Geisha* (1962), and *Sunday in New York* (1963), among others. He also cowrote the stage play "Time for Elizabeth" with his longtime friend Groucho Marx.

KRIGE, ALICE. Actress. *(b. June 28, 1955, Upington, South Africa.)* After giving up psychology for acting, the delicate-featured Krige moved to London and went to work on stage and in TV, making a reputation for herself as a gifted, genuine performer. She made her film debut as the actress who flirted with Ben Cross in the Oscar-winning *Chariots of Fire* (1981), a colorful role that attracted attention. Krige has since appeared in *Ghost Story* (1981), *King David* (1985, as Bathsheba), *Barfly* (1987), *See You in the Morning* (1989), and, impressively, as the mysterious cat-like creature seeking virgin blood in *Sleepwalkers* (1992). In 1993 she appeared in the made-for-cable movie *Ladykillers.*

KRISTEL, SYLVIA. Actress. *(b. Sept. 28, 1952, Utrecht, Netherlands.)* Striking brunette beauty whose uninhibited performances in the Emmanuelle soft-core porn films (*Emmanuelle, Emmanuelle—Joys of a Woman, Goodbye Emmanuelle,* et al.) of the 1970s and 1980s brought her international fame and belied her Calvinist upbringing. Kristel isn't likely to win any Oscars, but in those roles that allow her to release her sexual energy (which is to say, most of them) she becomes almost compulsively watchable, because she seems to be having such a good time! Kristel was cast in art-house fare by the likes of Alain Robbe-Grillet, Claude Chabrol, and Fons Rademakers, whose *Because of the Cats* (1972) was her first feature film. Her casting in subsequent English-language pictures, including *The Fifth Musketeer, The Concorde—Airport '79* (both 1979), *Private Lessons, The Nude Bomb* (both 1980), *Lady Chatterley's Lover* (1981), *Mata Hari, Red Heat* (both 1985), and *Dracula's Widow* (1988), was intended to capitalize on her Emmanuelle-generated notoriety, and to that end featured liberal doses of nudity. Nevertheless, they were mostly duds.

KRISTOFFERSON, KRIS. Actor, singer, songwriter. *(b. June 22, 1936, Brownsville, Tex.)* It's unfortunate when bad movies happen to a good actor, and even more so when those movies are the first that pop into your head when he comes to mind. Such is the case with this tall, lanky (usually bearded) leading man. A Rhodes Scholar at Oxford University, Kristofferson has had a varied career that includes a stint in the Army and a spell as an English Literature teacher. In the 1960s he became a successful country-and-Western music star (he frequently contributes songs to his and others' films) and, trading on that reputation, he made his big-screen debut in Dennis Hopper's *The Last Movie* (1971).

Kristofferson gave a series of craggy, effective performances in the 1970s, most notably as the outlaw Billy in Sam Peckinpah's *Pat Garrett and Billy the Kid* (1973) and as the understanding rancher who comforts recent widow Ellen Burstyn in Martin Scorsese's *Alice Doesn't Live Here Anymore* (1974). He fared better than costar Barbra Streisand (with critics anyway) in the 1976 remake of a *A Star Is Born*, playing a doomed rock star, then survived Michael Cimino's notoriously sprawling Western epic *Heaven's Gate* (1980). But nothing, apparently, could completely squelch his appeal as a tough, cool loner with heart. He teamed with fellow country-music superstar Willie Nelson in 1984's *Songwriter* (which earned him an Oscar nomination for Original Song Score). The generally laid-back Kristofferson has a likeable screen presence that has helped him overcome more than his share of bad movies.

OTHER FILMS INCLUDE: 1972: *Cisco Pike;* 1973: *Blume in Love;* 1974: *Bring Me the Head of Alfredo Garcia;* 1976: *The Sailor Who Fell From Grace With the Sea;* 1977: *Semi-Tough;* 1978: *Convoy;* 1981: *Rollover;* 1985: *Trouble in Mind;* 1986: *Stagecoach* (a remake for TV); 1988: *Big Top Pee-wee;* 1989: *Millennium;* 1989: *Welcome Home;* 1990: *A Pair of Aces* (made for TV); 1991: *Another Pair of Aces* (made for TV).

KRUGER, OTTO. Actor. *(b. Sept 6, 1885, Toledo, Ohio; d. Sept. 6, 1974.)* This prominent matinee idol of the 1920s theater never attained the same stature in Hollywood, but he certainly contributed many superb performances in movies of the 1930s, 1940s, 1950s, and 1960s. Kruger, a slightly built man with smooth manner and cruel smile, specialized in urbane heavies (he played crooked lawyers and businessmen with particular gusto, and even portrayed Nazis in several films). He made one silent, 1923's *Under the Red Robe*, but didn't take up movie work in earnest until 1933. In one of his first films, *Ever in My Heart* (1933), he costarred with Barbara Stanwyck and was tagged a "comer," but he settled into character work shortly thereafter (although he was acceptable as the nominal hero of

1936's *Dracula's Daughter*). A series of minor strokes finally forced Kruger to retire in the mid 1960s, and he died on his 89th birthday.

OTHER FILMS INCLUDE: 1933: *Turn Back the Clock;* 1934: *Gallant Lady, Crime Doctor, Men in White, Treasure Island;* 1936: *Lady of Secrets;* 1937: *They Won't Forget;* 1939: *Another Thin Man;* 1940: *Dr. Ehrlich's Magic Bullet;* 1942: *Saboteur;* 1943: *Hitler's Children, Tarzan's Desert Mystery;* 1944: *Murder, My Sweet;* 1945: *Wonder Man;* 1946: *Duel in the Sun;* 1951: *Valentino;* 1952: *High Noon* (as the judge who leaves town); 1954: *Magnificent Obsession, Black Widow;* 1959: *Cash McCall;* 1964: *Sex and the Single Girl.*

KUBRICK, STANLEY. Director, writer, producer. *(b. July 26, 1928, Bronx, N.Y.)* Few directors have inspired as much controversy as this unpredictable artist and innovative craftsman, whose output spans many film genres. The Bronx-born Kubrick first became interested in directing via photography, his teenage hobby. After making a couple of documentary shorts, he got together financing for a short feature, 1953's *Fear and Desire*, which he wrote, produced, edited, and photographed as well. After *Killer's Kiss* (1955), Kubrick's first real film of note was the dark caper picture *The Killing* (1956). Featuring a quintessential film noir cast (including Sterling Hayden and Elisha Cook, Jr.), this exciting, unusually structured picture was well received by critics. His next picture was the powerful, antiwar *Paths of Glory* (1957), a moving, well-written, and beautifully acted film that raised eyebrows. That film's star, Kirk Douglas, was impressed enough by Kubrick to place him in the director's chair for 1960's literate costume epic *Spartacus* (which Douglas executive-produced), replacing Anthony Mann. Director and star clashed mightily during production, and the experience was so unpleasant for Kubrick that he forsook Hollywood altogether and moved to London, where he has been based ever since. His first project there was an intermittently successful screen version of Nabokov's then-still-red-hot novel *Lolita* (1962). Far better was 1964's *Dr. Strangelove, or: How I Learned to Stop Worrying and Love the Bomb*, with its crackerjack cast (Peter Sellers in three roles, an over-the-top

George C. Scott, a chilling Sterling Hayden) and razor-sharp screenplay, which had broad fun with everyone's worst nuclear doomsday fantasies. It earned Oscar nominations for Best Picture, Best Direction, and Best Screenplay (by Kubrick, Terry Southern, and Peter George).

Kubrick spent four years working on what would be, for many, the definitive sci-fi film: *2001: A Space Odyssey* (1968; nominated for Best Direction and Screenplay, it earned Kubrick a Visual Effects Oscar). Diffuse and slowly paced, it acquired nearly as many detractors as admirers, and still divides viewers who come upon it today in theaters or on video. Much the same type of reaction was accorded the cynical, savagely violent *A Clockwork Orange* (1971), which featured Malcolm McDowell as Alex, a Beethoven-loving thug who leads his vicious pack of "droogs" through a bleak, futuristic London. It also earned Kubrick nominations for Picture, Director and Screenplay. Kubrick's next film was the considerably gentler and more picturesque (though equally pessimistic) *Barry Lyndon* (1975), adapted from a novel by 19th-century writer William Thackeray. Too slow and deliberate for some viewers, it mesmerized others, and was particularly notable for its visual style, which was an attempt to capture the look of the period by using only natural light; he even developed, with his longtime cinematographer John Alcott, the ability to shoot by candlelight. Again, it scored nominations for Picture, Director and Screenplay. Around this period Kubrick's reputation as a relentless, near-obsessive perfectionist began to get a good deal of play in the press; while the number of years between post-1960 projects was something of a tip-off, reports that *Lyndon* required 300 days just to shoot sent many reeling. Similar reports came from the set of 1980's *The Shining;* one story had Kubrick asking elderly actor Scatman Crothers for 75 takes of slamming a car door.

While fluid tracking camera movements have always been a hallmark of Kubrick's visual style, they reached their apotheosis in *The Shining,* wherein the camera glides through the hallways of a deserted resort hotel and later, in the film's terrifying climactic chase, around the walls of a snow-covered hedge maze. Kubrick's Vietnam war film *Full Metal Jacket* (1987), is an even more bitter picture than *Paths of Glory,* less a depiction of history than a blatant disavowal of the human race from an increasingly reclusive artist. In 1993 Kubrick began working in earnest (and under his usual shroud of secrecy) on a futuristic, special effects–oriented story called *AI* (for artificial intelligence).

KUROSAWA, AKIRA. Director, screenwriter. (b. Mar. 23, 1910, Tokyo.) One of the undisputed giants of cinema, this magnificent artist boasts a career of a half-century's duration, encompassing almost every genre, from flat-out, shameless action films to historical epics to humanistic dramas to sheer flights of fancy. Highly trained in Western literature, art, and tradition, Kurosawa was unable to earn a living as a painter, so he applied for a job as an assistant director at a film studio in 1936 and served his apprenticeship with Kajiro Yamamoto. He worked on screenplays during this time and eventually made his directing debut with *Sugata Sanshiro/Judo Saga* (1943), a film in the jidai-geki tradition. During the war, his films like *The Most Beautiful* (1944, a study of factory workers), the sequel *Judo Saga II* and *The Men Who Tread on the Tiger's Tail* (both 1945) were carefully monitored by the Japanese government; the latter film was banned by the U.S. Army's General Headquarters. Afterward, he turned to more "acceptable" fare such as *No Regrets for Our Youth* (1946), based on a true-life incident involving a professor with Communist sympathies.

Kurosawa has called *Drunken Angel* (1948) his first real film, made without interference. The story of a doctor and a young gangster, it marked Kurosawa's first collaboration with Toshiro Mifune, the actor who would go on to appear in many of his greatest films. He made *Stray Dog* (1949, with Mifune as a policeman searching for a thief who stole his gun) and *Scandal* (1950, an attack on the press) but gained international fame for *Rashomon* (1950), a classic study of the relativity of truth, with four different views of a rape and a murder in 9th-century Kyoto. The film not only established Kurosawa as a world-class filmmaker, but became the first Japanese film to be widely shown in the West, opening the door for other directors ranging from Ozu to Mizoguchi. *The Idiot* (1951) was an uneven but fascinating adaptation of the Dostoyevsky novel, but *Ikiru* (1952), the story of a dying civil servant who tries to find significance in his life, is perhaps Kurosawa's most personal and beautiful work; it has often been compared to the classic humanist films of the Italian neo-realists.

Kurosawa's appreciation of Western values and philosophy—as well as filmmaking—contributed to his own cinematic development, which depended a great deal on heroic protagonists who follow a rigid ethical code while battling against hostile forces. His heroes are Japanese equivalents of our own private eyes, cowboys, and tough cops. *Stray Dog* drew on Hollywood thrillers of the 1940s for atmosphere and visual touches. In another cultural crossover, Kurosawa transferred Dashiell Hammett's double-cross classic "Red Harvest" to feudal Japan in *Yojimbo* (1961), a violent, satiric twist on Western conventions, with Mifune as a samurai who hires himself out to a town's rival factions. (Kurosawa continued the exploits of Mifune's samurai in the 1962 sequel *Sanjuro.*) *The Hidden Fortress* (1958) similarly fused classic Western and Japanese elements. *Throne of Blood* (1957) was a startlingly kinetic reinterpretation of "Macbeth" set in medieval Japan; *The Bad Sleep Well* (1960) a modern variation on "Hamlet," which dealt with corruption and big business. *High and Low* (1963), a kidnapping thriller, was based on an Ed McBain novel.

At the same time, Kurosawa's approach to storytelling—within recognizable genres—had a profound influence on filmmakers in Europe and America. His best-known film, *The Seven Samurai* (1954), one of the most exhilarating action films ever made, provided the blueprint for the American Western *The Magnificent Seven* (1960). *Yojimbo* was used as source material for Sergio Leone's first "spaghetti Western," *A Fistful of Dollars* (1964). And *The Hidden Fortress* was a definite (and acknowledged) influence on George Lucas when he was concocting *Star Wars* (1977).

After the medical drama *Red Beard* (1965), Kurosawa signed to direct part of 20th Century-Fox's Pearl Harbor epic *Tora! Tora! Tora!* (1970) but problems over communication and artistic control led to his resignation; rumors that he was mentally unfit seriously hurt his career. He could not get backing for his own projects until Japanese directors Keisuke Kinoshita, Masaki Kobayashi, and Kon Ichikawa joined as coproducers on 1970's *Dodes'ka-den,* an interesting look at life in a Tokyo slum which was Kurosawa's first color film. It was also his first financial failure, and this, combined with health problems, led Kurosawa to attempt suicide. He recovered and lived to enjoy a kind of artistic renaissance (although he never entirely regained his financial footing in Japan). He directed the Russian-produced *Dersu Uzala* (1975), which took two years to film in Siberia and won the Academy Award for Best Foreign Film. Acolytes Francis Ford Coppola and George Lucas bankrolled his 1980 epic *Kagemusha,* a spectacular return to the samurai film. French cofinancing enabled him to make *Ran* (1985), an awesome retelling of "King Lear" that showed Kurosawa had lost none of his wizardry at staging battle sequences, nor his ability to portray the humanity of his characters even in the midst of chaos. The film earned Kurosawa his only Academy Award nomination as Best Director. Steven Spielberg presented *Akira Kurosawa's Dreams* (1990), the director's visually sumptuous, but dramatically uneven rendering of his nighttime fantasies, which included among its cast members Martin Scorsese, as van Gogh. *Rhapsody in August* (1991) featured American star Richard Gere in a controversial look back at the American bombing of Nagasaki, from the point of view of a contemporary Japanese family. Still active in his 80s, Kurosawa's latest film in *Madadayo (Not Yet).* An artist who was not always appreciated in his native country, where his outlook was considered too Western for local tastes, Kurosawa nevertheless attained worldwide acclaim and admiration. In 1989 he was presented with an honorary Academy Award "for accomplishments that have inspired, delighted, enriched, and entertained audiences and influenced filmmakers throughout the world." He published his memoir, "Something Like an Autobiography," in 1982.

KURTZ, SWOOSIE. Actress. *(b. Sept. 6, 1944, Omaha, Nebr.)* Named after her father's WW2 air force plane, which got its monicker from a Kay Kyser song ("Half swan, half goose, Alexander is a swoose"), this two-time Tony Award-winning stage actress has a flair for eccentric characters which she's brought successfully to her screen work in a variety of supporting roles. Bright and unconventionally attractive, sometimes simpering, sometimes sharp-tongued, Kurtz has stolen many a scene with her uniformly meritorious performances in *First Love* (her first film), *Slap Shot* (both 1977), *Oliver's Story* (1978), *The World According to Garp* (1982, outstanding as a hooker), *Against All Odds* (1984), *Bright Lights, Big City, Dangerous Liaisons* (somewhat ill at ease in a costume picture), *Vice Versa* (all 1988), *A Shock to the System* (another outstanding turn in this black comedy), *Stanley and Iris* (both 1990), and especially as "the laziest woman in the world" in *True Stories* (1986). She starred in the TV series "Love, Sidney" (1981–83) and "Sisters" (1991–). In 1993 she starred in two of the year's most prominent made-for-cable movies, *The Positively True Adventures of the Alleged Texas Cheerleader-Murdering Mom* and *And the Band Played On.*

KWAN, NANCY. Actress. *(b. May 19, 1939, Hong Kong.)* Seductively beautiful Eurasian actress whose starring performances in her first two films, *The World of Suzie Wong* (1960) and *Flower Drum Song* (1961), seemed to presage a substantial film career that never quite materialized. A former dancer who actually trained for the British Royal Ballet, Kwan worked fairly steadily in movies, but never again reached the plateau she'd attained early on. Kwan also appeared in episodic TV and some made-fors. By the early 1990s she was hawking cosmetics on TV "infomercials."
OTHER FILMS INCLUDE: 1962: *Main Attraction;* 1964: *Honeymoon Hotel, Fate Is the Hunter;* 1965: *The Wild Affair;* 1966: *Lt. Robin Crusoe, USN, Arrivederci, Baby;* 1968: *Nobody's Perfect;* 1969: *The Wrecking Crew;* 1970: *The McMasters;* 1973: *Wonder Women;* 1976: *Project: Kill;* 1978: *Devil Cat;*

1981: *Angkor: Cambodia Express;* 1983: *Walking the Edge;* 1989: *Cold Dog Soup.*

LA CAVA, GREGORY. Director. *(b. Mar. 10, 1892, Towanda, Pa.; d. Mar. 1, 1952.)* This former cartoonist and animator (who once worked with Woody Woodpecker creator Walter Lantz) graduated to directing in 1922, making his debut behind the megaphone with several comedy shorts, one of which was expanded into the feature *His Nibs,* starring Chic Sale. La Cava earned a reputation as a facile comedy director with his modestly budgeted but highly successful Paramount silents starring W. C. Fields, Richard Dix, and Bebe Daniels, among others; these include *Womanhandled* (1925), *So's Your Old Man* (1926), *Running Wild* (1927), and *Feel My Pulse* (1928). He adapted readily to sound, and while he broadened his directorial horizons to include dramas—such as *The Age of Consent, Symphony of Six Million* (both 1932), *Gabriel Over the White House* (1933, a fascinating, politically themed dramatic fantasy that is perhaps his most underrated film), *Gallant Lady* (1934), and *Private Worlds* (1935)—he continued to turn out topnotch comedies. One of these, the delightfully madcap *My Man Godfrey* (1936, starring William Powell and Carole Lombard), earned La Cava an Academy Award nomination and is probably his most enduring laughfest. The director was also nominated for *Stage Door* (1937, starring Katharine Hepburn, Adolphe Menjou, and Ginger Rogers), a letter-perfect adaptation of the Edna Ferber–George S. Kaufman play. His visual style was simple and unobtrusive, but his great strength lay in his ability to coax great performances from his casts. La Cava's output inexplicably dwindled after 1942. La Cava also produced several of his films, and frequently collaborated on their scripts.
OTHER FILMS INCLUDE: 1932: *The Half-Naked Truth;* 1934: *Affairs of Cellini;* 1935: *She Married Her Boss;* 1939: *5th Ave. Girl;* 1940: *The Primrose Path;* 1941: *Unfinished Business;* 1942: *Lady in a Jam;* 1947: *Living in a Big Way* (one of his few flops).

LADD, ALAN. Actor. *(b. Sept. 3, 1913, Hot Springs, Ark.; d. Nov. 7, 1964.)* To casual observers, the young Alan Ladd might have seemed an unlikely bet for screen stardom: He was short (five feet, five inches), his admittedly handsome face almost never changed expression, and he had a laconic manner that seemed to border on the catatonic. And yet, at the time of his starring debut in *This Gun for Hire* (1942), Ladd was hailed as one of Hollywood's hottest new stars—a pronouncement borne out by the enthusiastic reception afforded him by moviegoers.

Ladd at an early age moved to California with his family. As a young man he held a number of menial jobs, and spent two years toiling as a grip on the Warner Bros. lot. He began acting in the early 1930s, taking small roles in local theatrical productions, radio shows, and movies. By 1940 he had graduated to featured roles and onscreen billing, albeit mostly in low-budget B movies for independent studios like Republic and PRC. He appeared briefly (as a reporter) in Orson Welles' *Citizen Kane* (1941). He even sang with Rita Rio and Her All-Girl Orchestra in a "soundie" short, *I Look at You* (1941).

Ladd's career was guided by his agent, former actress Sue Carol, who also became his wife in 1942. That year she was instrumental in getting him cast as the cold-blooded killer in Paramount's screen adaptation of Graham Greene's "A Gun for Sale." Ladd's cool manner and deep voice made him ideally suited for tough-guy parts, although his diminutive stature presented casting and production problems: His costars were often forced to walk in shallow trenches alongside him, so as not to tower over him. And Ladd sometimes stood on planks or fruit boxes to make love to tall leading ladies.

Throughout the 1940s Ladd maintained his position in the top rank of Hollywood stars, appearing in Westerns, war dramas, and crime films. He frequently teamed with sultry Veronica Lake (most effectively in *Gun*, 1942's *The Glass Key*, and 1946's *The Blue Dahlia*), partly because their onscreen chemistry was good, and partly because she was shorter than he was. Just as Ladd's star began to wane, he was cast for the leading role in George Stevens' production of *Shane* (1953), a critical and commercial success that revitalized his career. As middle age approached, however, Ladd apparently realized that his days as a two-fisted leading man were numbered. Shortly after his fiftieth birthday, he was found dead of an overdose of sedatives and alcohol, an apparent suicide. Ironically, in his last film, an adaptation of Harold Robbins' *The Carpetbaggers*, Ladd had been cast as an aging, washed-up movie star. His son David Ladd had a brief career as a juvenile actor in films like *The Big Land* (1957, with his father) and on his own in the lead roles of *A Dog of Flanders* (1959) and *Misty* (1961). He continued working, with diminishing success, into adulthood. His other son, Alan Ladd, Jr., became a successful movie producer and studio executive.

OTHER FILMS INCLUDE: 1932: *Once in a Lifetime, Tom Brown of Culver* (in bits); 1936: *Pigskin Parade;* 1937: *Last Train From Madrid, Hold 'Em Navy;* 1938: *The Goldwyn Follies;* 1939: *Rulers of the Sea;* 1940: *The Light of Western Stars, The Green Hornet, Captain Caution;* 1941: *Paper Bullets, The Reluctant Dragon;* 1942: *Joan of Paris, Lucky Jordan, Star Spangled Rhythm* (in a cameo); 1943: *China;* 1944: *And Now Tomorrow;* 1945: *Salty O'Rourke;* 1946: *O.S.S., Two Years Before the Mast;* 1947: *Calcutta, Wild Harvest, Variety Girl, My Favorite Brunette* (cameos in the latter two); 1948: *Saigon, Beyond Glory, Whispering Smith* (his first starring Western); 1949: *The Great Gatsby, Chicago Deadline;* 1950: *Captain Carey, U.S.A., Branded;* 1951: *Red Mountain;* 1952: *The Iron Mistress;* 1953: *Thunder in the East;* 1954: *The Black Knight, Hell Below Zero, Drum Beat;* 1955: *The McConnell Story, Hell on Frisco Bay;* 1956: *Santiago;* 1957: *Boy on a Dolphin;* 1958: *The Deep Six, The Proud Rebel;* 1959: *The Man in the Net;* 1960: *Guns of the Timberland, All the Young Men, One Foot in Hell;* 1961: *Duel of Champions;* 1962: *13 West Street.*

LADD, DIANE. Actress. *(b. Nov. 29, 1939, Meridian, Miss., as Rose Diane Ladner.)* Feisty character actress with a flair for eccentric Southern ladies, best known for her Oscar-nominated turn as the tart-tongued waitress Flo in *Alice Doesn't Live Here Anymore* (1974). She has really come into her own (onscreen) in recent years, with meatier roles, and higher billing. In 1990 she costarred with her daughter Laura Dern in David Lynch's bizarre *Wild at Heart*, playing her maniacally possessive mother; it earned her a second Oscar nomination. Then, in 1991, she and

Laura became the first mother and daughter ever to earn simultaneous Oscar nominations, in *Rambling Rose,* Laura taking the more flamboyant leading part this time, with Diane playing an independent-thinking Southern woman. Ladd's first husband was actor Bruce Dern.
OTHER FILMS INCLUDE: 1961: *Something Wild;* 1966: *The Wild Angels* (with Dern); 1969: *The Reivers;* 1970: *Macho Callahan, Rebel Rousers;* 1973: *White Lightning;* 1974: *Chinatown;* 1976: *Embryo;* 1981: *All Night Long;* 1983: *Something Wicked This Way Comes;* 1987: *Black Widow;* 1988: *Plain Clothes;* 1989: *National Lampoon's Christmas Vacation;* 1991: *A Kiss Before Dying;* 1992: *Hold Me Thrill Me Kiss Me;* 1993: *The Cemetery Club, Father Hood, Carnosaur.*

LAHR, BERT. Actor. *(b. Aug. 13, 1895, New York City; d. Dec. 4, 1967.)* His place in cinema history is secure as a result of his unforgettable performance as the Cowardly Lion in *The Wizard of Oz* (1939), but in fact this veteran of burlesque, vaudeville, and legitimate theater didn't have nearly as extensive a film career as many of his contemporaries who also worked in Hollywood. Lahr, who was funny and funny *looking,* specialized in broad clowning; the word "subtle" had no place in his lexicon. (This may have been why he never became a true movie success.) In the 1930s he also appeared in a handful of two-reel comedy shorts for Educational Pictures (*Henry the Ache, No More West, Off the Horses*). His son John wrote his biography, "Notes on a Cowardly Lion" (1975).
OTHER FILMS INCLUDE: 1931: *Flying High* (his first); 1933: *Mr. Broadway;* 1937: *Merry Go Round of 1938, Love and Hisses;* 1938: *Josette, Just Around the Corner;* 1939: *Zaza;* 1942: *Sing Your Worries Away, Ship Ahoy;* 1949: *Always Leave Them Laughing;* 1951: *Mr. Universe;* 1954: *Rose Marie* (a standout role as a comic Mountie); 1955: *The Second Greatest Sex;* 1968: *The Night They Raided Minsky's* (back in his real milieu, fittingly, for his last film, though he died before production was completed.).

LAHTI, CHRISTINE. Actress. *(b. Apr. 4, 1950, Birmingham, Mich.)* The failure of this tall, intelligent, red-haired actress to reach the Hollywood actress A-list remains one of the great mysteries of the 20th century. A drama major at the University of Michigan, Lahti worked extensively on stage before making a stunning film debut as an attorney in ... *And Justice for All* (1979), more than holding her own opposite Al Pacino. Lahti was equally impressive as a doctor in *Whose Life Is It Anyway?* (1981), but somehow failed to click with audiences. After show-stealing best-pal roles in *Swing Shift* (1984, an Oscar-nominated performance) and *Just Between Friends* (1986), she graduated to offbeat leads in a pair of 1987 art films, *Stacking* and *Housekeeping,* followed by a magnificent performance as the wife-and-mother-in-hiding in *Running on Empty* (1988). Her considerable range, as well as her apparent affinity for colorful characters, hasn't limited Lahti to conventional leading-lady parts—but that one role, that one great script, continues to elude her. A long dry spell has included *Gross Anatomy* (1989), *Funny About Love* (1990), and *The Doctor* (1991). In the wake of 1991's popular *Thelma & Louise,* Lahti costarred in the female road movie *Leaving Normal* (1992). Married to director Thomas Schlamme, for whom she did a gag cameo in *Miss Firecracker* (1989), and who directed her in the well-received made-for-TV movie *Crazy From the Heart* (1991). Other prominent TV movie credits include *Amerika* (1987), *No Place Like Home* (1989), and *The Good Fight* (1992).

LAKE, ARTHUR. Actor. *(b. Apr. 17, 1905, Corbin, Ky. as Arthur Silverlake; d. Jan. 9, 1987.)* Although he had appeared in a couple dozen movies by 1938, once this boyish, high-voiced actor assumed the role of perpetually perplexed suburban husband Dagwood Bumstead in that year's *Blondie,* his fate was sealed; audiences forevermore would associate him with that character, which he played in 28 films from 1938–50 (and also on radio and TV). Lake, the son of show people, was playing vaudeville as a small child, and made his film debut in 1917's *Jack and the Beanstalk.* He worked steadily throughout the 1920s and 1930s, occasionally in leads (most notably 1928's *Harold Teen,* another comic-strip character) but mostly in comedic supporting roles. The success of *Blondie* (which also

typed leading lady Penny Singleton) was both a blessing and a curse to Lake, who rarely played anyone but Dagwood thereafter. (At least 1941's *Blondie Goes Latin* gave Singleton and Lake a rare opportunity to display their musical talents.) Lake's sister Florence also had a long film career, and played Edgar Kennedy's wife in his long-running comedy short-subject series.
OTHER FILMS INCLUDE: 1926: *Skinner's Dress Suit;* 1928: *The Air Circus;* 1929: *On With the Show, Tanned Legs;* 1930: *She's My Weakness;* 1931: *Indiscreet;* 1934: *The Silver Streak;* 1937: *Topper;* 1938: *There Goes My Heart;* 1948: *16 Fathoms Deep.*

LAKE, VERONICA. Actress. *(b. Nov. 14, 1919, Brooklyn, N.Y., as Constance Frances Ockelman; d. July 7, 1973.)* The petite, sultry blonde with the low, husky voice and "peek-a-boo" hairstyle (long, wavy tresses hanging down over one side of her face) zoomed to stardom in the early 1940s, was a top screen attraction (and favorite pinup girl of GIs) during the WW2 years, and virtually disappeared by decade's end. She entered films in 1939 under the name of Constance Keane, snagging bits in that year's *All Women Have Secrets, Sorority House,* and *Dancing Co-Ed,* and 1940's *Forty Little Mothers* and *As Young As You Feel.* The following year, under contract to Paramount and rechristened Veronica Lake, she played the second female lead in *I Wanted Wings* and all but stole the film out from under the noses of leading men Ray Milland and William Holden.

Lake got her big break when Paramount's resident genius, writer-director Preston Sturges, chose her to star opposite Joel McCrea in *Sullivan's Travels* (also 1941), a brilliant comedy-drama in which she played a failed Hollywood hopeful taken under the wing of big-time director McCrea. The film's success assured Lake's own, and when the diminutive blonde was costarred with short leading man Alan Ladd in *This Gun for Hire* (1942)—a taut thriller from Graham Greene's story—a screen team was born. She delivered an effective performance in Rene Clair's clever *I Married a Witch.* Then Ladd and Lake were rushed into *The Glass Key* (also 1942), a modestly budgeted remake of a Dashiell Hammett

crime drama, the success of which guaranteed promising futures for them both.

She and her hairstyle were so popular that Billy Wilder made a joke about them in his comedy *The Major and the Minor* (1942), while Lake herself participated in a gag song, "A Sweater, A Sarong and a Peekaboo Bang" with Paulette Goddard and Dorothy Lamour in Paramount's *Star Spangled Rhythm* (also 1942).

And yet, Lake's career never took off the way Ladd's did. She starred and cameoed in a string of films for Paramount, including *So Proudly We Hail!* (1943), *The Hour Before the Dawn* (1944), *Bring on the Girls, Out of This World, Duffy's Tavern, Hold That Blonde, Miss Susie Slagle's* (all 1945), *The Blue Dahlia* (1946, a Raymond Chandler–written thriller that reunited her with Ladd), *Variety Girl* (1947), *Saigon, The Sainted Sisters,* and *Isn't It Romantic?* (all 1948), but never enjoyed the critical enthusiasm she'd engendered in her early appearances. (It almost seemed as if her allure disappeared when she was forced to remove the peekaboo bangs; that occurred when wartime defense plants complained that women who'd imitated her hairstyle were at risk of getting their hair caught in machinery!) Her performances ranged from inspired to lackluster; she did some of her best work in the 1947 Western *Ramrod,* reteamed with Joel McCrea and directed by then-husband Andre de Toth.

Lake starred in *Slattery's Hurricane* (1949, for de Toth) and *Stronghold* (1951) before vanishing from the screen. Her marriage to de Toth dissolved in 1952 along with her career; she filed bankruptcy petitions and subsequently disappeared. In later years she made headlines several times by being arrested for drunkenness and disorderly conduct. By the early 1960s she'd been reduced to working as a cocktail waitress in the lounge of a downtown New York hotel. She eventually returned to acting, winning roles in minor stage productions and two low-budget films, the Canadian-made *Footsteps in the Snow* (1966) and *Flesh Feast* (1970), an execrable horror cheapie. She wrote a 1971 autobiography, "Veronica."

LAMARR, HEDY. Actress. *(b. Nov. 9, 1913, Vienna, as Hedwig Eva Maria Kiesler.)* One of the most beautiful actresses ever to grace the screen, she entered the film business in her native Austria, initially working as a script girl before making her acting debut in 1930's *Geld auf der Strasse*, billed as Hedy Kiesler. She created an international sensation with her role in Gustav Machaty's *Extase* (1933, released in the U.S. as *Ecstasy*), which called for her to appear completely nude and simulate orgasm. The resulting furor drove her from the screen, and her Austrian husband made a feeble attempt to buy the film and withdraw it from circulation.

She came to America in 1938, and was immediately signed by producer Walter Wanger, who cast her opposite Charles Boyer in his exotic melodrama *Algiers* later that year. Billed as Hedy Lamarr, the dark, radiant beauty displayed a figure much streamlined from that on view in *Ecstasy*, and while her acting ability was plainly more limited than her command of the English language, she made an impressive Hollywood debut.

MGM signed the glamorous beauty in 1939, occasionally giving her suitably exotic roles—as in *Lady of the Tropics* (1939) and *White Cargo* (1942, which saw her steaming up movie screens everywhere as the seductive, sarong-clad Tondelayo)—but frequently putting her in mainstream films, opposite the studio's biggest stars, that often strained her meager talents to the utmost. Her MGM films include *I Take This Woman, Boom Town, Comrade X* (all 1940), *Come Live With Me, Ziegfeld Girl* (all 1941), *H.M. Pulham, Esq.* (also 1941, and probably her best performance, as an independent-thinking career woman), *Tortilla Flat, Crossroads* (both 1942), *The Heavenly Body* (1943), *Her Highness and the Bellboy* (1945, one of her more charming efforts), and, after she'd been freelancing for several years, *A Lady Without Passport* (1950). Her other films, which most often cast her as an enigmatic femme fatale, include *The Conspirators, Experiment Perilous* (both 1944), *The Strange Woman* (1946), *Dishonored Lady* (1947), *Let's Live a Little* (1948), *Samson and Delilah* (1949, as the notorious Old Testament temptress, one of her best roles), *Copper Canyon* (1950), *My Favorite Spy* (1951), *The Love of Three Queens* (1953), *The Story of Mankind*, and *The Female Animal* (both 1957). Lamarr, who made headlines in 1965 when arrested for shoplifting (she was later exonerated), was married six times; her husbands included screenwriter Gene Markey and actor John Loder. Her "autobiography," "Ecstasy and Me," was published in 1966; she later sued her ghostwriters for allegedly misrepresenting her story.

LAMAS, FERNANDO. Actor. *(b. Jan. 9, 1915, Buenos Aires; d. Oct. 8, 1982.)* As one of MGM's resident Latin Lovers during the 1950s, Lamas got all the parts for which Ricardo Montalban was unavailable. Or was it vice versa? In any event, he was already a screen star in Argentina (since 1942) when Metro brought him to Hollywood in 1951. A supporting role in *Rich, Young and Pretty* marked his American screen debut, and his costarring turn with Lana Turner in the 1952 remake of *The Merry Widow* established him as a popular leading man. The following year the athletic star was cast opposite Esther Williams in *Dangerous When Wet*, which led to an off-screen romance and marriage. Lamas' arched eyebrows and tight-lipped mouth suggested a hint of cruelty that producers didn't properly exploit; he should have played more heavies.

Lamas starred in and directed two feature films *The Magic Fountain* (1961) and *The Violent Ones* (1967), and wielded the megaphone on many TV series episodes. Billy Crystal's Fernando ("You look *mah*velous") was inspired by Lamas, who was a popular talk-show guest in his later years. He was also married to actress Arlene Dahl; their son is actor Lorenzo Lamas who is probably best known for his TV series "Falcon Crest" and "Renegade" and a series of direct-to-video action films.

OTHER FILMS INCLUDE: 1951: *The Law and the Lady;* 1953: *The Girl Who Had Everything, Sangaree, The Diamond Queen;* 1954: *Jivaro, Rose Marie;* 1955: *The Girl Rush;* 1960: *The Lost World;* 1967: *Valley of Mystery, Kill a Dragon;* 1969: *100 Rifles;* 1978: *The Cheap Detective.*

LAMBERT, CHRISTOPHER. Actor. *(b. Mar. 29, 1957, New York City.)* Tall, sullen-faced leading man who came to prominence in the mid 1980s with his starring role in *Greystoke: The Legend of Tarzan,*

Lord of the Apes (1984). Lambert was raised in Switzerland and studied at the Paris Conservatoire before making his screen debut in *Le Bar du Telephone* (1980). Fittingly, it is in France (and Europe) that Lambert has enjoyed his greatest success, billed there as "Christophe." In the wake of his science-fiction films *Highlander* (1986), and its 1991 and 1994 sequels, Lambert starred in the futuristic *Fortress* (1993), which was a hit overseas before it reached the U.S. He was married to actress Diane Lane, with whom he costarred in *Priceless Beauty* (1988) and *Knight Moves* (1993).

OTHER FILMS INCLUDE: 1980: *Legitimate Violence;* 1984: *Love Songs;* 1985: *Subway;* 1986: *I Love You;* 1987: *The Sicilian;* 1994: *Gunmen;* 1995: *The Hunted, Mortal Kombat.*

LAMOUR, DOROTHY. Actress. *(b. Dec. 10, 1914, New Orleans, as Mary Leta Dorothy Slaton.)* The erstwhile "sarong girl" of 1930s-vintage Hollywood exotica such as *The Jungle Princess* (1936), *The Hurricane* (1937), *Her Jungle Love* (1938), and others, Lamour enjoyed a lengthy screen career, during which time she was one of the movie industry's most popular stars, both on- and offscreen. While she always seemed most at home in lighthearted musicals and comedies (such as the "Road" pictures in which she costarred with Bing Crosby and Bob Hope), Lamour occasionally delivered skillful, heartfelt performances in dramatic pictures as well.

Named "Miss New Orleans" in 1931, Lamour entered show business as a big-band vocalist. She made her screen debut, in fact, in a Vitaphone big-band short subject. Signed by Paramount in 1936, she made her feature debut in *College Holiday* that year, playing a bit part, but it was her chance casting in the title role of *Jungle Princess* (also 1936) that changed the course of her career and made her a star. When director John Ford cast her and Jon Hall as the juvenile lovers in his South Seas spectacular *The Hurricane* (1937) her future was assured—and her screen image, with long dark tresses and a sarong, was cemented forever. Paramount kept her busy throughout the rest of the decade in *Swing High, Swing Low, Last Train From Madrid, Thrill of a Lifetime* (all 1937), *The Big Broadcast of 1938, Her Jungle Love, Spawn of the North,*

Tropic Holiday (all 1938), *St. Louis Blues, Man About Town,* and *Disputed Passage* (all 1939).

Oddly enough, Lamour got her best dramatic opportunities on loan to 20th Century-Fox for a brace of big-budget 1940 productions: the crime drama *Johnny Apollo,* which costarred her with Tyrone Power, and the circus story *Chad Hanna,* pairing her with Henry Fonda. Later that year, back at Paramount, she was cast in another South Seas role, this time opposite Crosby and Hope, in a modest programmer titled *Road to Singapore.* The surprise success of that buoyant comedy launched one of moviedom's most popular (and profitable) series, which reunited the starring triumverate on the *Road to Zanzibar* (1941), *Road to Morocco* (1942), *Road to Utopia* (1945), *Road to Rio* (1947), *Road to Bali* (1952), and, much later, *The Road to Hong Kong* (1962). Lamour made an engaging straight woman for the duo, and got to introduce some popular songs along the way (including "Personality," in *Road to Utopia*). Lamour and Hope also worked together in *Caught in the Draft* (1941), *They Got Me Covered* (1943), and *My Favorite Brunette* (1947), and she became a mainstay of his later TV specials, whenever he'd gather former leading ladies around him.

When movie work dwindled in the 1950s, Lamour turned to nightclubs and the stage, and toured successfully in "Hello, Dolly!" Her autobiography, "My Side of the Road," was published in 1980.

OTHER FILMS INCLUDE: 1941: *Aloma of the South Seas;* 1942: *The Fleet's In, Beyond the Blue Horizon;* 1943: *Dixie, Riding High;* 1944: *And the Angels Sing, Rainbow Island;* 1945: *A Medal for Benny, Duffy's Tavern, Masquerade in Mexico;* 1947: *Wild Harvest, Variety Girl;* 1948: *On Our Merry Way, Lulu Belle, The Girl From Manhattan;* 1949: *The Lucky Stiff;* 1951: *Here Comes the Groom* (making an unbilled cameo appearance in this Bing Crosby vehicle); 1952: *The Greatest Show on Earth* (playing a supporting role in this Cecil B. DeMille circus spectacular); 1963: *Donovan's Reef;* 1964: *Pajama Party;* 1976: *Won Ton Ton, the Dog Who Saved Hollywood;* 1987: *Creepshow 2.*

LANCASTER, BURT. Actor; producer, director; writer. *(b. Nov. 2, 1913, New York City; d. Oct. 20, 1994.)* In a postwar era that considered movie swashbuckling passé, Burt Lancaster kept the torch burning—even though he was equally at home in Westerns, crime thrillers, comedies, and serious drama—and approached his costume actioners with the nimble athleticism and Fairbanksian flamboyance of a born acrobat. In fact, he was, having worked in circuses at an early age with boyhood chum (and occasional supporting player) Nick Cravat. Though he initially professed disdain for acting, Lancaster tried out for and landed a part in a Broadway play; it was a failure, but he got good notices personally and landed an agent, Harold Hecht, who brought him to the attention of movie producer Mark Hellinger. Cast as the mysterious "Swede" in *The Killers* (1946), Lancaster was an instant success, and the next year starred or costarred in *Desert Fury, Brute Force,* and *I Walk Alone* (the latter his first with longtime pal Kirk Douglas).

Lancaster turned to drama with *All My Sons* (1948), and more than held his own with veteran movie star Edward G. Robinson. The thrillers *Sorry, Wrong Number, Kiss the Blood Off My Hands* (both 1948), *Criss Cross,* and *Rope of Sand* (both 1949) all solidified his reputation as a grim, two-fisted lead in crime stories, but rather than risk further typecasting Lancaster produced and starred in *The Flame and the Arrow* (1950), a rousing swashbuckler that reunited him with old pal Cravat (playing his mute sidekick) and dazzled audiences with the star's athletic ability. *The Crimson Pirate* (1952) also saw Lancaster and Cravat performing amazing feats of derring-do, and was even more successful at the box office. *Mister 880* (1950), *Jim Thorpe, All-American* (in which he was miscast as the Native American champion athlete), and *Ten Tall Men* (both 1951) found Lancaster running in place, but he took major strides forward with solid dramatic roles in *Come Back, Little Sheba* (1952, as a drunken, brooding ex-doctor) and *From Here to Eternity* (1953, playing a tough Army sergeant in pre-WW2 Pearl Harbor, sharing an iconographic beachside love scene with Deborah Kerr). An Oscar nomination for the latter performance lent additional prestige to Lancaster's career, and he and agent Hecht formed their own production company to develop star vehicles for him. *Apache, Vera Cruz* (both 1954), and *The*

Kentuckian (1955, which he starred in and also directed) were successful if hardly challenging.

But Lancaster continued to push himself, taking a variety of parts in *The Rose Tattoo* (also 1955), *Trapeze, The Rainmaker* (both 1956), *Gunfight at the O.K. Corral* (1957, playing Wyatt Earp to Kirk Douglas' Doc Holliday), *Sweet Smell of Success* (also 1957, a standout as steely columnist J. J. Hunsecker), *Run Silent, Run Deep, Separate Tables* (both 1958), *The Devil's Disciple* (1959, again with Douglas), and *The Unforgiven* (1960). He enjoyed one of his greatest successes as Sinclair Lewis' *Elmer Gantry* (also 1960), winning a Best Actor Oscar, a Golden Globe, and the New York Film Critics Award for his portrayal of the fire-and-brimstone evangelist and con artist.

The 1960s found him involved in more prestige projects, including *The Young Savages, Judgment at Nuremberg* (both 1961), *Birdman of Alcatraz* (1962, in the title role, once again Oscar-nominated for his work), Luchino Visconti's *The Leopard* (1963), *Seven Days in May* (1964), *The Train, The Hallelujah Trail* (both 1965), *The Professionals* (1966), *The Swimmer, The Scalphunters* (both 1968), *The Gypsy Moths* (1969), and *Airport* (1970). Nearing 60, Lancaster eased into character roles, notably in a trio of offbeat Westerns: *Valdez Is Coming* (1970), *Lawman* (1971), and *Ulzana's Raid* (1972). Others in this period include *Executive Action* (1973), *The Midnight Man* (1974, which he cowrote, coproduced, and codirected with Roland Kibbee), *Moses* (1975, in the title role, cut down from a TV miniseries), *Buffalo Bill and the Indians* (1976, as Bill Cody), *Twilight's Last Gleaming* (1977), *Go Tell the Spartans* (1978), and *Zulu Dawn* (1979).

Able to pick and choose, Lancaster consistently went for the offbeat and the challenging—from Bertolucci's sprawling *1900* (1977) to Louis Malle's *Atlantic City* (1980), which gave him his greatest latter-day success, as a small-time hood who misses "the old days" of that seaside resort. This superlative performance earned him a passel of awards, including an Oscar nomination.

He suffered a heart attack during production of *Cattle Annie and Little Britches* (1980), but was able to complete his work on this underappreciated film. Lancaster then appeared in the ultimate "sleeper," Bill Forsyth's endearing *Local Hero* (1983), as an eccentric industrialist. He went on to work with Sam Peckinpah on *The Osterman Weekend* (1983), with Kirk Douglas in the very silly *Tough Guys* (1986), as a retired general called back to action in the TV movie *On Wings of Eagles* (1986), in the sentimental *Rocket Gibraltar* (1988) as a dying patriarch, and in *Field of Dreams* (1989), as a kindly doctor who still cherishes his bygone experience as a ballplayer. By this time Lancaster wasn't so much an actor as an icon; his very presence lent distinction to every film. Shortly after completing the prestigious TV movie *Separate but Equal* (1990), as Thurgood Marshall's adversary, John W. Davis, he suffered a massive stroke and did not work after that.

LANCHESTER, ELSA. Actress. *(b. Oct. 8, 1902, Lewisham, England, as Elizabeth Sullivan; d. Dec. 26, 1986.)* She hissed her way into screen immortality (and had the movies' most memorable Bad Hair Day) as the titular temptress in *Bride of Frankenstein* (1935), her American film debut. Lanchester—who also played authoress Mary Shelley in that monster-movie milestone—delighted moviegoers on both sides of the Atlantic with her eccentric, sometimes impish characterizations. Trained as a dancer by Isadora Duncan, she turned to acting while still in her teens, and made her film debut in a 1924 short subject, *The Scarlet Woman*. Lanchester, a dedicated nonconformist, married actor Charles Laughton in 1929, an unconventional union that lasted until his death in 1962. Her supporting roles in *The Private Life of Henry VIII* (1933, as Anne of Cleves) and *The Private Life of Don Juan* (1934) brought Lanchester to the attention of director James Whale, who cast her in *Bride* and launched her Hollywood career. She was Oscar-nominated for her performances in *Come to the Stable* (1949, as a dotty artist) and *Witness for the Prosecution* (1957, as Laughton's exasperated nurse). Lanchester infused many of her screen characterizations with an almost childlike playfulness. She wrote an early volume of memoirs, "Charles and Me," in 1939, and an autobiography, "Elsa Lanchester Herself" in 1983.

OTHER FILMS INCLUDE: 1935: *David Copperfield* (as Clickett); 1936: *Rembrandt* (costarring with Laughton), *The Ghost Goes West;* 1942: *Tales of Manhattan, Son of Fury;* 1943: *Forever and a Day, Lassie Come Home;* 1946: *The Spiral Staircase, The Razor's Edge;* 1947: *The Bishop's Wife;* 1948: *The Big Clock;* 1949: *The Inspector General;* 1952: *Les Miserables;* 1955: *The Glass Slipper;* 1958: *Bell, Book and Candle;* 1964: *Mary Poppins, Pajama Party;* 1965: *That Darn Cat;* 1968: *Blackbeard's Ghost;* 1971: *Willard;* 1973: *Terror in the Wax Museum;* 1976: *Murder by Death* (delightful as Miss Marbles); 1980: *Die Laughing.*

LANDAU, MARTIN. Actor. *(b. June 20, 1931, Brooklyn, N.Y.)* A star of both big and small screens, this brooding, stone-faced actor worked for a time as a cartoonist for the New York *Daily News.* After attending New York City's famed Actors' Studio, where he counted James Dean among his close friends, Landau landed major supporting roles in such movies as *North by Northwest* (1959, as James Mason's henchman who stalks Cary Grant) and *Cleopatra* (1963, as Rufio). He found fame as a costar of TV's "Mission: Impossible" (1966–69) and "Space: 1999" (1975–77), both of which teamed him with real-life spouse Barbara Bain, whom he has since divorced. From the late 1970s through the mid 1980s Landau worked mainly as an acting teacher, while onscreen he was mired in low-budget genre films (including 1980's *Without Warning,* a career low), until a juicy supporting role as Jeff Bridges' unlikely partner Abe Karatz in *Tucker: The Man and His Dream* (1988) earned him an Oscar nomination and renewed attention. Woody Allen gave him a prime leading part as an amoral married man who has his mistress killed in *Crimes and Misdemeanors* (1989), which merited another Oscar nomination. But this being show business, Landau continued to appear in cheapies such as *Firehead* (1991), as well as *Mistress* (1992, as a has-been producer), *Sliver* (1993), and *Intersection* (1994). Then Tim Burton thought of Landau for another perfect part: that of aging Bela Lugosi in his offbeat biopic *Ed Wood* (1994). Landau's performance was nothing short of astonishing, and it finally earned him a Supporting Actor Oscar. He followed with *City Hall* (1995).

LANDI, ELISSA. Actress. *(b. Dec. 6, 1904, Venice, as Elizabeth Marie Christine Kuehnelt; d. Oct. 21, 1948.)* Aristocratic beauty whose motion picture work constituted only part of an active and creative life. Reportedly a descendant of Austria's Emperor Franz Josef, she received a world-class education and became a published writer. Landi's dignified bearing and cultured voice served her well on the London stage. She made her film debut in *London* (1926), and appeared in other British-made films. After starring in "A Farewell to Arms" on Broadway, she was signed to a Fox contract in 1931, and rushed into a slew of program melodramas: *Body and Soul, Always Goodbye, Wicked,* and *The Yellow Ticket* in that year alone. Cecil B. DeMille cast Landi as the virginal heroine of his Roman Empire epic *The Sign of the Cross* (1932), but most of the critical attention went to Claudette Colbert in the flashier role of a pagan temptress. At Fox, she was lavishly promoted but assigned to mediocre films such as *I Loved You Wednesday* and *The Warrior's Husband* (both 1933). She fared better as Ronald Colman's leading lady in *The Masquerader* (1933), in the Continentally flavored comedy *By Candlelight* (1934), and as Mercedes to Robert Donat's Edmund Dantes in *The Count of Monte Cristo* (1934). Landi was signed by MGM in 1936, but her talents were squandered in *After the Thin Man* (1936), *Mad Holiday,* and *The Thirteenth Chair* (both 1937). She returned to the stage, and continued writing, appearing in only one more picture—the low-budget *Corregidor* (1943)—before succumbing to cancer in 1948.

LANDIS, CAROLE. Actress. *(b. Jan. 1, 1919, Fairchild, Wis., as Frances Lillian Mary Ridste; d. Aug. 3, 1948.)* This beautiful blonde from the Midwest was a teenage beauty-contest winner who came to Hollywood in 1937 after having worked as a waitress, usherette, and dancer. She played bits in many Warner Bros. films over the next two years, particularly those directed by Busby Berkeley, with whom she was reportedly involved romantically. After

playing the ingenue in a 1939 Republic serial, *Daredevils of the Red Circle,* Landis pursued starring roles more aggressively. Independent producer Hal Roach cast her for the female lead in *One Million B.C.* (1940), and featured her in three subsequent features.

Landis was signed by 20th Century-Fox in 1941, where she appeared in many lavish productions, sometimes as second female lead. One film, *Four Jills in a Jeep* (1944), was based on her experiences as a USO entertainer during World War 2. She was fairly popular with film fans, but her career never really took off. By 1946, having been dropped by Fox, she was playing leads in B pictures. Worse yet, her personal life was in a shambles: She had had four unsuccessful marriages, and a torrid affair with Rex Harrison (at that time married to Lilli Palmer) which ended when Landis, not yet 30 and still breathtakingly beautiful, committed suicide.

OTHER FILMS INCLUDE: 1937: *A Star Is Born, A Day at the Races;* 1938: *Over the Wall, Four's a Crowd;* 1939: *Three Texas Steers* (a B Western starring John Wayne, himself on the threshold of major stardom); 1940: *Turnabout, Mystery Sea Raider;* 1941: *Road Show, Topper Returns, Moon Over Miami, I Wake Up Screaming, Cadet Girl, Dance Hall;* 1942: *It Happened in Flatbush, My Gal Sal, Orchestra Wives, Manila Calling;* 1943: *Wintertime;* 1944: *Secret Command;* 1945: *Having Wonderful Crime;* 1946: *Behind Green Lights, It Shouldn't Happen to a Dog, A Scandal in Paris;* 1947: *Out of the Blue;* 1948: *The Brass Monkey, The Noose.*

LANDIS, JOHN. Director, screenwriter, producer, actor. *(b. Aug. 3, 1950, Chicago.)* Specialist in loud, lavish, expensively mounted comedies starring some of the country's biggest talents. A former stuntman, he has a predilection for slapstick, as displayed in his debut directing effort, the shaggy gorilla B-movie parody *Schlock* (1971), which he also wrote and acted in. The picture also contains many film buff in-jokes—a trend that would also inform his later films. The success of two of his early comedy efforts, *The Kentucky Fried Movie* (1977, also actor) and *National Lampoon's Animal House* (1978), led to his taking the helm of the large-scale *The Blues Brothers* (1980, which he also cowrote), an anarchic affair that tried to get laughs from crashing cars. *An American Werewolf in London* (1981), on which he also served as scripter, is probably his most personal and critically acclaimed film. Two comedies he made with Eddie Murphy were also two of his biggest hits, *Trading Places* (1983) and *Coming to America* (1988). Landis has also worked in music videos, most notably directing Michael Jackson's super-expensive "Thriller" and "Black or White." His other directing efforts include *Into the Night* (also actor), *Spies Like Us* (both 1985), *¡Three Amigos!* (1986), *Oscar* (1991), and *Innocent Blood* (1992). He directed Murphy again in *Beverly Hills Cop III* (1994). He also had a hand in the tragic *Twilight Zone—The Movie* (1983), as the director of the framing story and the segment of the anthology in which three actors, including Vic Morrow, were killed in a helicopter crash during filming.

As an actor, Landis has appeared in small or cameo roles in such films as *Battle for the Planet of the Apes* (1973), *Death Race 2000* (1975), *1941* (1979), *Spontaneous Combustion* (1989), and *Darkman* (1990).

LANE, CHARLES. *(b. Jan. 26, 1905, San Francisco, as Charles Levison.)* This sharp-featured character actor is one of the most familiar faces in film, with hundreds of movies and TV episodes to his credit—though he is one of those ubiquitous players whose name is known to only a few. A graduate of the fabled Pasadena Playhouse, he made his film debut in 1931 and hasn't stopped working since. One of his best parts was that of producer Max Jacobs—or is it Mandelbaum?—in *Twentieth Century* (1934) with John Barrymore. Frank Capra liked him and used him in virtually all his films, most notably as the tax collector in *You Can't Take It With You* (1938). Having appeared as one of the racetrack gamblers in *Broadway Bill* (1934) he recreated the role in Capra's remake, *Riding High* (1950). His numerous other credits include *42nd St.* (1933), *Mr. Deeds Goes to Town* (1936), *In Old Chicago* (1938), *The Cat and the Canary, Mr. Smith Goes to Washington* (both 1939), *Ball of Fire* (1941), *Arsenic and Old Lace* (1944), *It's a Wonderful Life* (1946), *Teacher's Pet* (1958, one of his best parts as a member of Clark Gable's

newspaper editorial board), *The Gnome-Mobile* (1967), *The Little Dragons* (1980), *Murphy's Romance* (1985, playing an 89-year-old man), and the miniseries "The Winds of War" (1983) and "War and Remembrance" (1988) as Admiral Standley. He also had recurring roles in the TV series "Dennis the Menace" (1959–63), "Petticoat Junction" (1963–70), "Karen" (1975), and "Soap"' (1980).

LANE, DIANE. Actress. *(b. Jan. 22, 1963, New York City.)* When this precociously beautiful teenager was selected to costar with Laurence Olivier in *A Little Romance* (1979) she landed on the cover of "Time" magazine. Her winning performance in that paean to puppy love launched a career that endured through adolescence and has flowered in adulthood. Good parts in *Cattle Annie and Little Britches* and *Touched by Love* (both 1980) alternated with run-of-the-mill projects like *Six Pack* (1981) and *Ladies and Gentlemen, The Fabulous Stains* (1982). She was sullen in a trio of Francis Coppola films—*The Outsiders, Rumble Fish* (both 1983), and *The Cotton Club* (1984)—but as the decade progressed she began to take on increasingly offbeat and challenging parts. She was a rock star in *Streets of Fire* (1984), a stripper in *The Big Town*, and a psycho's victim in *Lady Beware* (both 1987). She brought warmth and a wry sense of humor to her part as a hooker in the outstanding TV miniseries "Lonesome Dove" (1989). Recent credits include *Vital Signs* (1990), *Chaplin* (1992, as Paulette Goddard), the deadpan lead in the undernourished black comedy *My New Gun* (also 1992), *Indian Summer* (1993, as a young widow who blossoms during a summer camp reunion), *Wild Bill* (as Savannah Moore), and *Judge Dredd* (both 1995). Lane returned to TV in the 1994 miniseries "Oldest Living Confederate Widow Tells All" and a 1995 production of *A Streetcar Named Desire* (as Stella). She was married to actor Christopher Lambert, with whom she has costarred in *Priceless Beauty* (1988, as a genie who emerges from a lamp) and *Knight Moves* (1993).

LANG, FRITZ. Director. *(b. Dec. 5, 1890, Vienna; d. Aug. 2, 1976.)* Fritz Lang's vision of the world, as expressed in many of his brilliant films, was a dark and hostile one. To him, man was often little more than a puppet in a malevolent universe determined by chaos, degradation, and violence. And the imagery he used, especially in his German films, reflected that worldview: bold, expressionistic, shadowy, sinister. A former painter who drifted into movie work after being mustered out of the Austrian army during World War 1, he wrote scenarios for German-made melodramas and surrealistic serials. Lang first directed in 1919 and, with his third effort, *Die Spinnen (The Spiders),* a colorful two-part adventure film, achieved considerable notoriety.

Having enjoyed great popular success, Lang went on to achieve critical favor as well with *Der müde Tod* (U.S. title, *Destiny)* in 1921, which marked his first collaboration with screenwriter Thea von Harbou, who became his wife in 1924. An allegorical tale of love and death, it was the first of many ambitious films they would make together. *Dr. Mabuse: der Spieler* (1922), like *The Spiders* a two-part film, saw the earliest successful depiction of Lang's now-familiar nightmare world. Set against the backdrop of a decadent postwar Berlin, it starred Rudolf Klein-Rogge as a master criminal ultimately driven insane by the vision of his former victims. (Klein-Rogge was a Lang favorite who starred in several of the director's other German films, and reprised his famous role in 1933's *The Testament of Dr. Mabuse.*).

Die Nibelungen (1924) required two feature-length parts *(Siegfried* and *Kriemhild's Revenge)* to dramatize the ancient legend better known through Wagner's "Ring Cycle" operas. Lang's next film galvanized audiences worldwide, and remains his best-known work: *Metropolis* (1926), a stunning look at a futuristic city and society, which took two years to devise and produce. Although the story is simplistic, its images of faceless workers dwarfed by machines—turned *into* machines in order to serve the master race—remain powerful and unique after all these years.

He returned to familiar territory with *Spies* (1928), and made another science-fiction film, *Woman in the Moon* (1929), before fashioning a full-blown masterpiece, *M* (1931). The story of a

child molester and murderer who is hunted down and tried by the criminal element of his own city, it brilliantly integrated sound and picture, and showcased Peter Lorre's remarkable performance in a film of tremendous suspense and heightened drama.

When Lang's anti-Nazi sentiments became too apparent in *The Testament of Dr. Mabuse* (1933), he ran afoul of Joseph Goebbels and even his own wife, who divorced him. By 1934 Lang was in Paris, directing *Liliom* (1934), before emigrating to America with a one-picture contract from MGM. Lang's Hollywood debut was the still-impressive mob violence drama *Fury* (1936). He went on to make a pair of interesting films about society's outcasts, *You Only Live Once* (1937) and *You and Me* (1938).

Firmly established in Hollywood, he enjoyed a prolific if varied career through the mid 1950s, excelling at crime melodramas like *Man Hunt* (1941), *Ministry of Fear, The Woman in the Window* (both 1944), *Scarlet Street* (1945), *The Blue Gardenia, The Big Heat* (both 1953), *Human Desire* (1954), *While the City Sleeps,* and *Beyond a Reasonable Doubt* (both 1956). If none of them approached the brilliance of his great German films, they were certainly good entertainment and clearly the work of a master craftsman. He even tried his hand at Westerns (1940's *The Return of Frank James,* 1941's *Western Union,* 1952's *Rancho Notorious).* Whether or not Lang could have risen above the level of pulp fiction to the status of an Alfred Hitchcock is matter for speculation; it could be that his fiery personality (which did not endear him to actors) got in the way. Finally tiring of Hollywood and studio pressures, he went back to Germany—where, in his twilight years, he returned to the melodramatic stories and characters he created years earlier: *The Tiger of Eschnapur* and *The Indian Tomb* (a 1958 two-parter) recalled a 1921 serial Lang and von Harbou had written for director Joe May. (It was edited into the 1962 feature *Journey to the Lost City.)* And his final film, *The Thousand Eyes of Dr. Mabuse* (1960), took the director back to the character upon which his reputation was originally founded. In 1963 he appeared as himself in Jean-Luc Godard's *Contempt.*

OTHER FILMS INCLUDE: 1943: *Hangmen*

Also Die; 1946: *Cloak and Dagger;* 1948: *Secret Beyond the Door;* 1950: *The House by the River, American Guerilla in the Philippines;* 1952: *Clash by Night;* 1955: *Moonfleet.*

LANGDON, HARRY. Actor; director. *(b. June 15, 1884, Council Bluffs, Iowa; d. Dec. 22, 1944.)* In his prime, during the mid 1920s, silent-screen comedian Harry Langdon rated right up there with Chaplin, Keaton, and Harold Lloyd. But his decline was both rapid and precipitous, and he is currently regarded with much less respect than he probably deserves. Part of that, of course, is due to the fact that his unique comic persona has not weathered the years well. Somewhat short and shapeless, with baby face and blank stare, Langdon comes across as infantile rather than innocent.

A peripatetic youth who was at various times a barber and a cartoonist before entering show business, Langdon toured with circuses, minstrel shows, burlesque and vaudeville troupes for more than 20 years before entering pictures in 1924. Signed by pioneering comedy producer Mack Sennett, he worked tirelessly to refine the wide-eyed, ingenuous naif he'd first played in pantomime before live audiences. On-screen he was the butt of every joke, the dupe of every sharper, and the victim of every bully, yet he persevered. Director Harry Edwards and gag writer Frank Capra came along and helped shape Langdon's comic persona in a string of successful two-reel comedies including *The Luck of the Foolish, All Night Long* (both 1924), *Saturday Afternoon,* and *Soldier Man* (both 1926). Out-growing the Sennett shorts, he graduated to features in 1926, and his first three full-length films—*The Strong Man, Tramp, Tramp, Tramp* (both 1926), and *Long Pants* (1927)—were undoubtedly his best. (Not coincidentally, Capra wrote the first and directed the last two.)

Langdon, by this time puffed up with his own success and confident that he alone knew best, abandoned Edwards and Capra to write and direct his own vehicles. But those films were neither good nor successful, and by 1929 he was back in two-reelers, this time on the payroll of comedy producer Hal Roach. He stubbornly clung to his silent-era characterization, which was revealed to be painfully ineffectual in talking pictures.

He never again starred in a feature-length movie, although he contributed memorable supporting performances to such films as *Hallelujah, I'm a Bum* (1933, as hobo Al Jolson's socialistic pal) and *Zenobia* (1939, teamed with Oliver Hardy while Stan Laurel was feuding with Roach over his new contract). He continued to star in two-reelers, first for Educational and then for Columbia, throughout the 1930s. He returned to the Hal Roach studio as a gag writer, appeared occasionally on-screen in a supporting role, and even provided caricatures for the main title of a Laurel & Hardy film.

By the mid 1940s, a tired-looking, dissipated Langdon was forced to share his Columbia short-subject series with Swedish dialectician El Brendel, and was further reduced to bit parts in low-budget turkeys produced by Monogram and PRC. OTHER FILMS INCLUDE: 1927: *Three's a Crowd;* 1928: *The Chaser, Heart Trouble;* 1930: *A Soldier's Plaything;* 1933: *My Weakness;* 1935: *Atlantic Adventure;* 1938: *He Loved an Actress, There Goes My Heart;* 1941: *All-American Co-Ed, Road Show, Double Trouble;* 1943: *Spotlight Scandals;* 1944: *Block Busters, Hot Rhythm;* 1945: *Swingin' on a Rainbow.*

LANGE, HOPE. Actress. *(b. Nov. 28, 1931, Redding Ridge, Conn.)* Attractive, reserved blond actress who made quite a splash with her first two pictures: *Bus Stop* (1956, in the supporting role of Emma) and *Peyton Place* (1957, which earned her an Oscar nomination for her performance as Selena Cross). Born to show people, she was already a 12-year veteran of the Broadway stage by the time she'd first appeared on-screen. She played leads and supporting roles in many other films, including *The Young Lions* (1958), *The Best of Everything* (1959), *Wild in the Country, Pocketful of Miracles* (both 1961), *Love Is a Ball* (1963), and *Jigsaw* (1968), but failed to catch fire with the public and remained a second-tier star. She starred in the TV series "The Ghost and Mrs. Muir" (1968–70) and "The New Dick Van Dyke Show" (1971–74), achieving more recognition for her small-screen work than she had for her movie roles. She had a small but memorable part in

Death Wish (1974), playing Charles Bronson's brutalized wife. Lange returned to the stage in the late 1970s and has made infrequent film appearances since, including *The Prodigal* (1983), *A Nightmare on Elm Street Part 2: Freddy's Revenge* (1985), *Blue Velvet* (1986, in the latter as Laura Dern's mother), *Tune In Tomorrow . . .* (1990), and *Just Cause* (1995). She was once married to actor Don Murray, her *Bus Stop* costar, and later wed director Alan Pakula.

LANGE, JESSICA. Actress. *(b. Apr. 20, 1949, Cloquet, Minn.)* Versatile leading lady whose beauty, intensity, and professionalism have made her one of the most important actresses in Hollywood. She overcame a disastrous film debut which made her something of a joke by dint of rigorous training and unceasing effort. Lange's early years had a nomadic quality; by her own count, her traveling salesman father moved the family some 18 times while she was growing up. Although she won a scholarship to the University of Minnesota to study art, she dropped out to travel extensively, studying mime and drama in Paris and eventually working in New York as a model and waitress. In her highly publicized first film, the ghastly 1976 remake of *King Kong,* Lange gamely (and futilely) tackled the Fay Wray role. The ensuing debacle nearly ended her career before it started; both the picture and her performance were trashed by critics, and she languished in obscurity for three years before making another picture. In the interim she took acting lessons and made connections; in 1979 her friend Bob Fosse cast her as the angel of death in his autobiographical *All That Jazz.* As a result of that movie's critical and popular acclaim (and her ideal casting), Lange's stock rose considerably.

Lange took on a supporting role in *How to Beat the High Co$t of Living* (1980) before being cast as Cora, the lusty waitress in Bob Rafelson's sexually charged remake of *The Postman Always Rings Twice* (1981, opposite Jack Nicholson), in which she shocked moviegoers not only with her raw, animal sensuality, but also with an electric performance. She reached her career high-water mark in 1982, first with a tour de force as the tragic actress Frances Farmer in *Frances* (for which she

was Oscar-nominated), then as an engaging leading lady in the smash hit *Tootsie* (for which she *won* an Oscar). By this time established as one of the screen's premier actresses, Lange copped subsequent Oscar nominations, for her work in *Country* (1984), *Sweet Dreams* (1985, as Patsy Cline), and *Music Box* (1989). She was also memorable in *Crimes of the Heart* (1986), *Everybody's All-American* (1988, outstanding in that underrated film), *Far North* (1988), *Men Don't Leave* (1990), and Martin Scorsese's powerhouse *Cape Fear* (1991). Lange and *Fear* costar Robert De Niro reteamed for a 1992 remake of *Night and the City,* a Scorsese-like urban melodrama that just missed. That same year she made her TV movie debut in the well-received *O Pioneers!* and her Broadway bow opposite Alec Baldwin in "A Streetcar Named Desire," which she recreated for a 1995 television production. Lange earned a Best Actress Oscar for her powerful, complex performance as an Army officer's troubled wife in *Blue Sky* (1994, filmed in 1990); she followed with the child custody drama *Losing Isaiah* and *Rob Roy* (both 1995). Adamantly clinging to her single status, Lange has a daughter by dancer Mikhail Baryshnikov and two children by playwright Sam Shepard, with whom she's costarred several times, and who directed her in *Far North.*

LANGELLA, FRANK. Actor. *(b. Jan. 1, 1940, Bayonne, N.J.)* Dark, exotic leading man with broad stage experience who never fared as well on film; neither his looks, nor his aloof demeanor, were suited to conventional leading-man roles, though he did star in the 1979 production of *Dracula.* (A part he played to perfection on stage, in *Dangerous Liaisons,* went on film to John Malkovich instead.) He has found more opportunity in recent years as a character actor, particularly in villainous parts. He debuted on-screen with a juicy role as Carrie Snodgress' lover in *Diary of a Mad Housewife,* and followed that with *The Twelve Chairs* (both 1970), *The Wrath of God* (1972), *The Mark of Zorro* (1974, playing the title role in this made-for-TV movie), *Those Lips, Those Eyes* (1980, very entertaining as a down-on-his-luck actor romancing local lasses in a small town), *Sphinx* (1981), *The Men's Club*

(1986), *Masters of the Universe, And God Created Woman* (both 1987), *True Identity* (1991), and *1492: Conquest of Paradise* (1992). Even when Hollywood offered a perfect part, as Dracula, he was forced to subvert the lusty, tongue-in-cheek characterization that had won him such acclaim on Broadway, in favor of a more serious (and conventional) approach. In 1993 he snared two plum supporting roles, as Madonna's humiliated former lover in *Body of Evidence,* and as the power-hungry Chief of Staff in the White House comedy *Dave.* He appeared next in *Brainscan* (1993), *Bad Company,* and *Cutthroat Island* (both 1995).

LANGFORD, FRANCES. Singer, actress. *(b. Apr. 4, 1914, Lakeland, Fla.)* Nobody's ever accused Langford of being a great actress, but few could resist her crooning "I'm in the Mood for Love" (in her debut film, 1935's *Every Night at Eight*). As a slender, dark-haired vocalist—already popular on radio—she seemed ill at ease before the cameras in her tyro appearance, but subsequently sang "Broadway Rhythm" and "You Are My Lucky Star" with great assurance in *Broadway Melody of 1936.* After a few years, Langford filled out, dyed her hair blond, and relaxed considerably before the camera, becoming a capable, pleasing performer. She played leads and supporting parts in a number of fluffy Hollywood musicomedies over the next decade or so, including *Palm Springs, Born to Dance* (both 1936), *The Hit Parade, Hollywood Hotel* (both 1937), *All-American Co-Ed* (1941), *Yankee Doodle Dandy* (1942, belting out "Over There" with James Cagney), *This Is the Army, Follow the Band, Never a Dull Moment* (all 1943), *Dixie Jamboree* (1944), *Radio Stars on Parade* (1945), and *Beat the Band* (1947). She even appeared in a Western, *Deputy Marshal* (1949), costarring with then-husband Jon Hall. She endeared herself to thousands of servicemen during World War 2, tirelessly entertaining them and boosting morale as part of Bob Hope's traveling troupe. (She was also a featured performer on his radio show.) Langford played herself in her last film to date, *The Glenn Miller Story* (1954).

LANSBURY, ANGELA. Actress. *(b. Oct. 16, 1925, London.)* So what if she's won four Tonys? So what if she's been in movies for half a century? To millions of Americans, this tweedy, plum-voiced actress is "Murder, She Wrote" author and amateur sleuth Jessica Fletcher, and that's just fine with them, thank you very much. But Lansbury has enjoyed a distinctive career on stage and film, with a much wider range than her "Murder" fans may realize. She had acting ambitions while still a young girl in London, but she fled to New York when the blitz started and worked as a salesgirl while studying drama there. When Hollywood beckoned, Lansbury went eagerly, earning an Oscar nomination for her debut as a sinister maid in *Gaslight* (1944) and snaring a contract at MGM.

She also did fine work in *National Velvet* (1944), *The Picture of Dorian Gray* (1945, winning another Oscar nomination for the wide-eyed waif who sings "The Little Yellow Bird"; her mother, Moyna MacGill, also appeared in the film), *Till the Clouds Roll By* (1946, singing "How D'ya Like to Spoon With Me?"), *The Harvey Girls* (1946, another musical, in which she menaced Judy Garland), *State of the Union* (1948, as the would-be power broker who tries to manipulate Spencer Tracy's presidential candidacy), *The Three Musketeers* (also 1948, as Queen Anne), and *Samson and Delilah* (1949, as Hedy Lamarr's older sister—though she was obviously younger). Still a young woman, Lansbury was typed early on in parts calling for iron-willed, domineering, and treacherous she-cats. During the 1950s she concentrated on stage work, but appeared in the likes of *The Court Jester* (1956), *The Long Hot Summer* (1958), *The Dark at the Top of the Stairs* (1960), and even played Elvis Presley's mother in *Blue Hawaii* (1961).

Lansbury's blood-chilling, Academy Award-nominated performance as a politician's monstrous wife in *The Manchurian Candidate* (1962) is considered by many to be her finest. Other notable Lansbury turns can be seen in *The World of Henry Orient* (1964), *Mister Buddwing* (1966), *Something for Everyone* (1970), *Bedknobs and Broomsticks* (1971, as an amateur witch in this Disney musical), *Death on the Nile* (1978), *The Pirates of Penzance*

(1983), and *The Company of Wolves* (1984). In 1980 she warmed up for "Murder, She Wrote" by playing Agatha Christie's spinster sleuth, Miss Marple, in *The Mirror Crack'd*. She's won Tony awards for "Mame," "Dear World," "Gypsy," and "Sweeney Todd." Lansbury has also starred in TV movies and miniseries, including *Little Gloria . . . Happy At Last* (1982), *Lace* (1984), *The Shell Seekers* (1989), and *Mrs. 'Arris Goes to Paris* (1992). And she endeared herself to younger fans as the voice of Mrs. Potts in Disney's animated *Beauty and the Beast* (1991). Married to producer Peter Shaw; their son, Anthony, often directs his mother in "Murder, She Wrote." Her first husband was actor Richard Cromwell.

LANTZ, WALTER. Producer, animation director. *(b. Apr. 27, 1899, as Walter B. Lantza; d. Mar. 22, 1994.)* One of the most successful—and durable—animation producers of all time, Lantz learned resourcefulness and resiliency early on. His mother died giving birth to his younger brother, and his father was an invalid, so Walter shouldered family responsibilities right from the start. At the age of 15 he got a job as an office boy in the art department of William Randolph Hearst's "New York American" newspaper, and took art courses at night. One year later, his boss recommended him for a job at Hearst's new animation studio. By the age of 18 he was a full-fledged animator, drawing such Hearst characters as Happy Hooligan, Krazy Kat, and the Katzenjammer Kids.

After the Hearst studio closed, Lantz worked for the Barre/Bower Studio, and then signed with John R. Bray, where he became studio manager and developed his own cartoon series, notably "Dinky Doodles," a variation on Max Fleischer's "Out of the Inkwell" series in which Lantz appeared on camera along with his animated stars. In 1927, Bray shut down his studio, and Lantz moved to Hollywood, where he worked for several years as a gagman for Mack Sennett. After a similar stint for Hal Roach, he found himself at Universal, working on the Andy Gump comedies, and came to meet the studio's founder and president, Carl Laemmle, who gave him the opportunity to launch a cartoon department right on the lot.

Lantz inherited the character of Oswald the Lucky Rabbit, whose cartoons had been distributed by Universal up to that point (made first by Walt Disney, and then by a splinter group of Disney animators working for M. J. Winkler). With a formidable schedule of 26 films a year, Lantz took in veteran animator Bill Nolan as his partner to split the directing chores. But first, they completed an unusual assignment: an introductory sequence for Universal's multimillion-dollar musical, *The King of Jazz* (1930), with Paul Whiteman. Their jaunty musical number featured the voice of Whiteman vocalist Bing Crosby, and was the first animated cartoon to be made in two-color Technicolor.

Lantz's output was steady but unspectacular through the 1930s, though such talents as Tex Avery and Preston Blair were among his animators. In 1935 he and Nolan parted company, and a year later Lantz set up his own production entity with Universal as his distributor. He introduced other characters in the late 1930s, but the first to really catch on was Andy Panda, who debuted in *Life Begins for Andy Panda* (1939). A year later, Andy was bothered by a grotesque-looking woodpecker in *Knock Knock* (1940) and Lantz's biggest star was born: Woody Woodpecker. Woody fit right in with the brash, often violent characters of the 1940s, and though his looks, voice, and manner changed over the years, he was Lantz's bread-and-butter for decades to come. Among his best cartoons: *The Barber of Seville, Ski for Two* (both 1944), *Woody the Giant Killer* (1947), *Termites From Mars* (1952). His theme song was even nominated for an Academy Award in 1948. Mel Blanc originally provided Woody's voice; then gagman Ben Hardaway took over, though his speaking voice was sped up for the final effect. In the early 1950s, Walter's wife Grace Stafford assumed the job and was the voice of Woody the rest of her life.

Lantz left Universal briefly in the late 1940s, and suffered financial reverses that caused him to close down for more than a year. In 1950 he re-signed with Universal, and continued producing a regular slate of cartoons for them through 1972, by which time most of his colleagues had given up on theatrical short subjects. Woody remained his leading star to the very end, along with penguin Chilly Willy and, in later years, The Beary Family.

Talented animators and directors passed through Lantz's studio over the years, including Shamus Culhane, Grim Natwick, Dick Lundy, Jack Hannah, and for a brief time in the 1950s, Tex Avery, but it was usually a way station. Lantz's typical output was serviceable but uninspired. He followed Walt Disney's lead and hosted "The Woody Woodpecker Show" on TV in the late 1950s, showing his young viewers how cartoons were made in fascinating weekly installments. He received an honorary Academy Award at the 1979 ceremonies, for "bringing joy and laughter to every part of the world through his unique animated motion pictures."

LANZA, MARIO. Singer, actor. *(b. Jan. 31, 1921, Philadelphia, as Alfred Arnold Coccozza; d. Oct. 7, 1959.)* Lanza was a high school dropout who worked in his family's grocery business, but his voice—a commanding tenor—could not be ignored. Upon auditioning for conductor Serge Koussevitzky in 1942, he earned a music scholarship, performed at the Berkshire Summer Music Festival and toured in concert. After service in World War 2, Lanza signed a contract with MGM and starred in four films which successfully exploited his powerful voice and rugged good looks. In his first two he was teamed with Kathryn Grayson: *That Midnight Kiss* (1949), in which he performed songs both popular (Jerome Kern's "They Didn't Believe Me") and operatic ("Celeste Aida," Donizetti's "Una furtiva lacrima" and "Mama mia che vo sape," from "Cavalleria Rusticana"); and *The Toast of New Orleans* (1950), singing various opera works (including the drinking song from "La Traviata") and popular songs ("Be My Love"), and dueting with Grayson in a brief segment from "Madame Butterfly." His other MGM credits were *The Great Caruso* (1951, in the title role, a natural fit) and *Because You're Mine* (1952). However, his stardom was short-lived, owing to his extreme sense of self-importance, troubles with alcohol and barbiturates, and his ballooning weight. Lanza was slated to star in *The Student Prince* (1954)—indeed, his voice is heard on the soundtrack—but the role of Prince Karl went to Edmund Purdom. Lanza's weight problems cost him the part. Lanza was to play in only three more films: *Serenade* (1956), and two features filmed in Italy, *The Seven Hills of Rome* (1958) and *For the First Time* (1959). While in Rome, he undertook a rigorous diet, which helped to contribute to his death— from a heart attack—at age 38.

LAPAGLIA, ANTHONY. Actor. *(b. Jan. 31, 1959, Adelaide, Australia.)* This brooding, intense actor has played such convincing New Yorkers (mostly Italian ones, we hardly need add) that it's hard to believe he was actually born in Australia. After moving to the U.S. and working as a teacher and at several other odd jobs, LaPaglia took to the stage, quickly learning his craft and landing small roles on TV as well (most notably in a 1988 telepic, *Frank Nitti: The Enforcer*). He made his feature-film debut in a small part in *Slaves of New York* (1989), then went on to quietly steal *Betsy's Wedding* (1990) as polite mobster Stevie Dee. LaPaglia, a surprisingly natural screen presence, has since been seen to good advantage in *He Said, She Said, One Good Cop,* and especially, the picaresque New York saga *29th Street* (all 1991). The good notices he got for the latter film may have prompted his casting in two 1992 mainstream genre efforts: *Whispers in the Dark* (as a badgering cop who hounds Annabella Sciorra—a terrific performance) and *Innocent Blood* (in the male lead, again as a cop). He played another cop—for humorous effect—in *So I Married an Axe Murderer* (1993). He switched gears to play a slimy New Orleans hit man in *The Client,* an excon in *Mixed Nuts* (both 1994), and another hit man in *Bulletproof Heart* (1995).

LARUE, JACK. Actor. *(b. May 3, 1902, New York City, as Gaspare Biondolillo; d. Jan. 11, 1984.)* Swarthy, slick-haired, dark-eyed character actor, one of the screen's most recognizable heavies. Although he most frequently played gangsters in pin-striped suits, LaRue plied his villainous trade in period pictures as well, including Westerns (1933's *To the Last Man* and 1943's *Wild Horse Stampede*) and swashbucklers (1940's *The Sea Hawk* and 1945's *The Spanish Main*). Possibly his most memorable gangster characterization was that of Trigger, the sadistic rapist of Miriam Hopkins in *The Story of Temple Drake*

(1933), the first screen adaptation of William Faulkner's "Sanctuary."
OTHER FILMS INCLUDE: 1932: *The Mouthpiece, A Farewell to Arms;* 1933: *Christopher Strong, The Woman Accused, The Kennel Murder Case;* 1935: *Special Agent;* 1936: *Strike Me Pink;* 1937: *Captains Courageous, Trapped by G-Men;* 1939: *Big Town Czar;* 1941: *Footsteps in the Dark, Paper Bullets;* 1943: *Never a Dull Moment;* 1944: *Dangerous Passage;* 1945: *Road to Utopia, Cornered;* 1946: *Murder in the Music Hall; My Favorite Brunette;* 1950: *For Heaven's Sake;* 1963: *Forty Pounds of Trouble;* 1964: *Robin and the Seven Hoods.*

LA RUE, "LASH." Actor. *(b. June 15, 1917, Michigan, as Alfred La Rue.)* With his jet-black outfit, rakishly tilted Stetson, and frequently flashing whip, this sinister-looking Western hero enjoyed a brief success in the late 1940s, making innumerable personal appearances and licensing his character to comic books to help promote his minuscule-budgeted horse operas. As Al La Rue, he played bits in several early and mid 1940s features and serials, finally getting a meaty role in a Universal chapterplay, *The Master Key* (1945). Then he played a ruthless killer who sacrifices his life to right some wrongs at the end of *Song of Old Wyoming* (1945), stealing the film from its ostensible star, Eddie Dean. La Rue played second banana to Dean in several other PRC Westerns before being given his own series in 1947, accompanied by veteran sidekick Al "Fuzzy" St. John. La Rue, who briefly starred in a 15-minute TV show in the early 1950s, drifted out of the picture business. Arrested several times on charges of vagrancy, drunkenness, and possession of drugs, the oft-married La Rue (10 times by his own count) also appeared in the nonpornographic scenes of an X-rated film, *Hard on the Trail,* in 1972. He became a preacher in later years, and is a popular guest at Western-film festivals.
OTHER FILMS INCLUDE: 1947: *Cheyenne Takes Over;* 1948: *Border Feud, The Fighting Vigilantes;* 1949: *Son of Billy the Kid, Dead Man's Gold;* 1950: *King of the Bullwhip;* 1951: *Frontier Phantom.*

LASKY, JESSE L. Producer, production executive. *(b. Sept. 13, 1880, San Francisco;* *d. Jan. 13, 1958.)* One of Hollywood's true visionaries, Lasky—like many of the entrepreneurial spirits who helped build the motion-picture industry—had a varied background (as reporter, musician, bandleader, and promoter) before forming the Jesse L. Lasky Feature Play Company with brother-in-law Samuel Goldfish (later Goldwyn) and Cecil B. DeMille in 1913. Their first film, an adaptation of *The Squaw Man* (1914), was mostly shot in and around Hollywood, California. Its success spurred Lasky and DeMille to further heights; in 1916 Lasky merged with budding mogul Adolph Zukor and his Famous Players production company. That union eventually metamorphosed into Paramount Pictures, an organization in which Lasky had considerable power—until being forced out by Zukor in 1932. He went to Fox as an independent producer, and his 1933 projects for that studio have become landmark films: the time-travel fantasy *Berkeley Square,* the Preston Sturges–written *The Power and the Glory,* and the whimsical romance *Zoo in Budapest.*

Lasky, rare among Hollywood's old-time moguls, had a genuine respect for and tolerance of the creative process; he therefore enjoyed more cordial relations with his writers, directors, and stars than most bosses. He produced *The Gay Deception* (1935), *Sergeant York* (1941), *The Adventures of Mark Twain* (1944), *Rhapsody in Blue* (1945), *Without Reservations* (1946), and *The Miracle of the Bells* (1948), among others. Lasky, who was also once partner to Mary Pickford, got into trouble with the IRS in the late 1950s and wangled a production job at Paramount, but died before his first project went before the cameras. His autobiography, "I Blow My Own Horn," was published in 1957. His son, Jesse Jr., became one of Cecil B. DeMille's staff writers and later authored several books on Hollywood history.

LAUGHLIN, TOM. Actor, director, producer, screenwriter. *(b. Aug. 10, 1931, Minneapolis.)* The creator of the 1970s phenomenon *Billy Jack* got his start playing youths in such films as *Tea and Sympathy* (1956) and *Gidget* (1959). By the age of 34, Laughlin had become an independent filmmaker—writing, producing, directing, editing, and starring in *The Young Sinner* (1965). His character Billy Jack, a taciturn half-breed and antiestablishment loner who seemed to espouse peace through violence, made his first appearance in Laughlin's *Born Losers* (1967), a biker epic released by American International Pictures. The follow-up, *Billy Jack* (1971), which cost $800,000 to produce, earned tens of millions, making it one of the most profitable films up to that time. A sequel, *The Trial of Billy Jack* (1974), grossed $22 million in 30 days, but *Billy Jack Goes to Washington* (1977), a heavy-handed reworking of *Mr. Smith Goes to Washington,* showed the Billy Jack character played out and was barely released at all. Laughlin's non–Billy Jack 1975 flop *The Master Gunfighter,* all attitude and no substance, showed him to be a ham-handed filmmaker whose success was as much a matter of timing as anything else. Out of the public eye for many years, Laughlin (who employed the pseudonyms Lloyd E. James and T. C. Frank) in 1992 announced he was interested in running for president.

LAUGHTON, CHARLES. Actor. (b. July 1, 1899, Scarborough, England; d. Dec. 15, 1962.) It would be easy to think that as distinctive looking a performer as Laughton—roly-poly, fish-faced, with thick, blubbery lips and sleepy eyes—would be typed based on his physical appearance and play the same kinds of parts throughout his career. But this hugely talented English actor refused to be pigeonholed, either in his native England or later in Hollywood—and, as a result, left behind a wide gallery of portrayals, many of which rank among the movies' most colorful. A former hotel clerk who enrolled in Britain's prestigious Royal Academy of Dramatic Art after World War 1, Laughton made his professional stage debut in London's West End in 1926. He made several silent comedy shorts in 1928, and it was during production of these that he met Elsa Lanchester, whom he married in 1929. Coming to America in 1931 with the play "Payment Deferred," in which he played an unlikely murderer, Laughton eventually went to Hollywood to star in MGM's screen adaptation (released 1932).

Within a very short time Laughton had appeared in *The Old Dark House, The Sign of the Cross* (both 1932, in the latter

as a pouty Nero), and *The Island of Lost Souls* (1932, as the evil Dr. Moreau). He also had a memorable cameo appearance in a vignette in Paramount's all-star *If I Had a Million* (1932), as the man who gives his boss the razzberry. Laughton was subsequently counted on to bring a patina of real English class to the literary adaptations MGM essayed in the early to mid 1930s. Of course, he brought a lot more than just that, delivering bravura performances as Captain Bligh in *Mutiny on the Bounty* (an Oscar-nominated turn), and Javert in *Les Miserables,* both made in 1935. (He was replaced, however, in the role of Micawber in *David Copperfield,* by W. C. Fields.) He also showed off his comic skills as a deferential British butler transplanted to the American West in *Ruggles of Red Gap* (1935). His recitation of the Gettysburg Address was particularly memorable.

Laughton bounced back and forth between Britain and America during the 1930s, working in two memorable movies directed by Alexander Korda: *The Private Life of Henry VIII* (1933, for which he won a Best Actor Oscar) and *Rembrandt* (1936). He showed his lighter side, as a street entertainer or "busker," in *Sidewalks of London* (1938, original British title, *St. Martin's Lane*). Back in Hollywood, his poignant turn as Quasimodo in 1939's *The Hunchback of Notre Dame*—smothered as he was under heavy makeup—won Laughton more critical acclaim. He worked steadily in Hollywood during World War 2, being especially memorable in *The Canterville Ghost* (1944) and *Captain Kidd* (1945). He wasn't always successful at restraining his urge to chew the scenery, but he was capable of subtle, understated performances when he had good scripts and good directors. He was very effective in *The Big Clock* (1948), a thriller that casts him as a publishing magnate with a horrible secret, played French detective hero Maigret in *The Man on the Eiffel Tower* (1950), and tackled Henry VIII again in *Young Bess* (1953).

In 1955 Laughton directed his only film, the strange and beautiful *Night of the Hunter,* written by James Agee and starring Robert Mitchum and Lillian Gish. Although well received (it's considered a minor classic today), this thriller did not lead to any more directing assignments and Laughton continued acting; his last

few films feature some of his best characterizations, including an eccentric lawyer in *Witness for the Prosecution* (1957, Oscar-nominated) and a corrupt Roman senator in *Spartacus* (1960). His last film was *Advise and Consent* (1962).
OTHER FILMS INCLUDE: 1933: *White Woman;* 1938: *The Beachcomber;* 1939: *Jamaica Inn;* 1940: *They Knew What They Wanted;* 1941: *It Started With Eve;* 1942: *Stand By for Action, Tales of Manhattan, The Tuttles of Tahiti;* 1943: *Forever and a Day, The Man From Down Under, This Land Is Mine;* 1944: *The Suspect;* 1946: *Because of Him;* 1947: *The Paradine Case;* 1948: *Arch of Triumph;* 1949: *The Bribe;* 1951: *The Blue Veil, The Strange Door;* 1952: *Abbott and Costello Meet Captain Kidd, O. Henry's Full House;* 1953: *Salome;* 1954: *Hobson's Choice.*

LAUNDER AND GILLIAT. Directors, screenwriters, producers. (**Frank Launder**—b. Jan. 1906, Hitchin, England. **Sidney Gilliat**—b. Feb. 15, 1908, Edgeley, England; d. May 31, 1994.) One of the most creative teams in movie history. Both prolific during the 1930s, writing a variety of screenplays for films noteworthy and otherwise, they worked together on *Seven Sinners* (1936), Hitchcock's *The Lady Vanishes* (1938, in which they introduced the two twits, played by Naunton Wayne and Basil Radford, who also appeared in later films), *Night Train to Munich* (1940), and other successful British films before becoming producers and directors as well. *Millions Like Us* (1943), an effective wartime morale booster, was their first joint venture as writer-producer-directors. They teamed again on *The Rake's Progress* (1945), then decided to pursue their own projects under the umbrella of a partnership.

Although they both suffused their screenplays with wit and irony, Gilliat leaned more toward mystery and melodrama. His writing credits include *Jamaica Inn* (1939, for Hitchcock), *The Girl in the News* (1940), *Kipps* (1941), and *Waterloo Road* (1944). His directing credits (all of which he wrote, some in partnership with Launder) include the superb *Green for Danger* (1946), *State Secret* (1950), *The Story of Gilbert and Sullivan* (1953), *The Constant Husband* (1954), *Left, Right and Centre* (1959), *Only Two Can Play* (1961), and *Endless Night* (1972). Launder preferred straight dramas, costume pictures, and comedies. He was most successful with the "St. Trinian's" comedies about a wacky girls' school: *The Belles of St. Trinian's* (1954), *Blue Murder at St. Trinian's* (1957), *The Pure Hell of St. Trinian's* (1960), and *The Great St. Trinian's Train Robbery* (1966, codirected with Gilliat). Although they had separate films and production chores to their credits, Launder and Gilliat each had input in the other's work. Launder also directed (and wrote, some in partnership with Gilliat) *I See a Dark Stranger* (1946, aka *The Adventuress*), *Captain Boycott* (1947), *The Blue Lagoon* (1949), *The Happiest Days of Your Life* (1950), and *Folly to Be Wise* (1952).

LAUREL AND HARDY. Actors. (**Stan Laurel**—b. June 16, 1890, Ulverston, England, as Arthur Stanley Jefferson; d. Feb. 23, 1965. **Oliver Hardy**—b. Jan. 18, 1892, Harlem, Ga.; d. Aug. 7, 1957.) There had been fat-and-skinny teams before; it was an obvious "visual pun" during the silent-film era. But when Laurel and Hardy began developing their onscreen relationship, it yielded something more. With the coming of sound, their unexpected voices—one British, one Southern—added to the uniqueness of the partnership. Perhaps the most amazing thing about them is that they seemed absolutely, positively real—and yet "Stan" and "Ollie" were about as far removed from the real-life Laurel and Hardy as one could imagine. They were great comic actors, playing two beautifully crafted roles.

Stan Laurel had been raised in English music halls. He made his first trip to America as part of the Fred Karno musical-comedy troupe, which also included Charlie Chaplin. Laurel decided to stay in the U.S., and toured in vaudeville, landing an occasional movie job. (In one of them, the 1917 short subject *Lucky Dog,* he shared a scene with a screen heavy played by Oliver Hardy!) Many of Stan's solo films survive, and show him to be an able comedy performer, but there is nothing memorable about his screen personality. Hal Roach felt his biggest problem was in having blue eyes, which photographed as "dead eyes" to the insensitive film stock of that period. Laurel worked on and off for Roach, but by 1926 was employed there primarily as a gag writer and sometime director.

Oliver Hardy's boyhood soprano voice gave him his first entree to show business, but he might not have thought of a film career had not the Lubin film company located itself in Jacksonville, Florida, in the early teens. Hardy, who'd been running a movie theater in Georgia, decided to try his luck in pictures—and didn't have far to go for that effort. His girth made him a "natural" in silent comedies, and after working with the Lubin troupe for several years he moved to Hollywood, and found steady employment in the comedy shorts of Billy West (a Chaplin imitator), Larry Semon, and others. By the mid 1920s, he too was working as an all-purpose comic at the Hal Roach studio.

There are many variations on how Laurel and Hardy came together, and who first realized their screen potential. But there is no question that within one year of their first dual appearance, they were being touted as a new comedy team . . . and within that first year they made a handful of classic films. They suited one another, and what's more, they were guided by some of the great comedy minds at the Hal Roach studio. The tit-for-tat destruction technique, Oliver Hardy's long, slow-burn "takes," Stan's blank look, Ollie's fastidious gestures, all came about in this creative comic atmosphere. Silent comedy gems like *Putting Pants on Philip, The Battle of the Century* (both 1927, the latter with its apocalyptic pie fight), *From Soup to Nuts, Two Tars* (both 1928), and *Big Business* (1929) were the result.

By the time sound came along, Laurel and Hardy understood their characters, and they took to talkies with relative ease. *Men O'War, Perfect Day,* and *The Hoose-Gow* (all 1929, made just months after their talking debut) bear that out. Their international success demanded that they appear in feature films as well as shorts, and Hal Roach obliged with such vehicles as *Pardon Us* (1931), *Pack Up Your Troubles* (1932), their first comic operetta *The Devil's Brother/Fra Diavolo, Sons of the Desert* (both 1933, the latter often called their best feature), the delightful *Babes in Toyland* (aka *March of the Wooden Soldiers,* 1934), *Bonnie Scotland* (1935), *The Bohemian Girl, Our Relations* (both 1936; in the latter they play their own twins),

Way Out West (1937, another candidate for their best feature), *Swiss Miss, Block-Heads* (both 1938), *A Chump at Oxford* (the only film in which Stan changes character), and *Saps at Sea* (both 1940).

Still, many believe that their best work was done in the short-subject format—short and sweet. Their 1932 three-reeler *The Music Box* (in which they try to deliver a piano up an enormous flight of steps) won an Academy Award, and is perfection itself. Other great shorts include *Brats* (in which they play their own children), *Hog Wild* (both 1930), *Chickens Come Home* (1931), *Helpmates, County Hospital, Their First Mistake, Towed in a Hole* (all 1932), *Me and My Pal, Busy Bodies* (both 1933), *Going Bye Bye,* and *Them Thar Hills* (both 1934).

The team had been split by contractual problems with Hal Roach (which is why Hardy made *Zenobia* for Roach in 1939 without Stan), but retrenched when 20th Century-Fox expressed interest in them. Unfortunately, the features they made there in the 1940s were second-rate at best, with even the pleasant ones (like 1941's *Great Guns* and 1943's *Jitterbugs*) a pale imitation of their best work. The same was true of other features they made at MGM (1943's *Air Raid Wardens,* 1944's *Nothing but Trouble*). And then, astonishingly, there was no further interest in Laurel and Hardy in Hollywood. They toured English music halls with great success and made one last film together, *Utopia* (aka *Atoll K,* 1952), in France. But no one in Hollywood wanted to put these beloved clowns on camera.

With the TV revival of their films in the 1950s, Hal Roach, Jr., expressed interest in starring them anew, but illness interfered. At least they knew in their final years how much they were loved by millions and millions of fans.

LAURIE, PIPER. Actress. *(b. Jan. 22, 1932, Detroit, as Rosetta Jacobs.)* Pert, pretty, generally appealing ingenue who, under contract to Universal in the 1950s, appeared in innumerable swashbucklers, costume dramas, and sword-and-sandal epics, often costarred with Tony Curtis. Rarely given an opportunity to display her abundant talent, Laurie got her first really meaty role in *The Hustler* (1961), playing Paul Newman's girlfriend

and earning an Oscar nomination in the process. But, having just married, she abruptly retired and was absent from the screen for 15 years. She returned with a vengeance as Sissy Spacek's domineering, fanatical mother in *Carrie* (1976), picking up another Academy Award nomination, and launching a new screen career as a major character actress. She's had a handful of meaty supporting roles since then, and even played young Mel Gibson's love interest in the Australian-made *Tim* (1979). She got a third Oscar nod for her supporting role as Marlee Matlin's mother in *Children of a Lesser God* (1986), and won an Emmy for that same year's TV movie *Promise,* with James Garner and James Woods. Laurie appeared as a shrewish, scheming villainess in David Lynch's TV series "Twin Peaks" (1990–91), and in "Traps" (1994).
OTHER FILMS INCLUDE: 1950: *Louisa* (her first), *The Milkman;* 1951: *The Prince Who Was a Thief, Francis Goes to the Races;* 1952: *Has Anybody Seen My Gal?, Son of Ali Baba;* 1953: *The Mississippi Gambler, The Golden Blade;* 1954: *Dangerous Mission, Johnny Dark, Dawn at Socorro;* 1955: *Ain't Misbehavin';* 1957: *Until They Sail;* 1977: *Ruby;* 1985: *Return to Oz;* 1987: *Distortions;* 1988: *Appointment With Death, Tiger Warsaw;* 1989: *Dream a Little Dream;* 1991: *Other People's Money;* 1993: *Rich in Love, Wrestling Ernest Hemingway.*

LAUTER, ED. Actor. *(b. Oct. 30, 1940, Long Beach, N.Y.)* Balding, stringy, mean-looking character player in mainstream movies since the 1970s, probably best known as the sadistic Captain Knauer from the prison/football film *The Longest Yard* (1974). Lauter occasionally essays sympathetic roles, but he's much more effective as a heavy, flashing his squinty, withering gaze and snarling dialogue at hapless opponents. His recent films include *Gleaming the Cube, Fat Man and Little Boy* (both 1989), and *The Rocketeer* (1991). He's also a familiar face on TV in telefilms and miniseries.
OTHER FILMS INCLUDE: 1972: *The New Centurions;* 1973: *Lolly Madonna XXX;* 1976: *King Kong, Breakheart Pass, Family Plot;* 1977: *The White Buffalo;* 1978: *Magic;* 1981: *Death Hunt, Eureka;* 1983: *Cujo;* 1985: *Girls Just Want to Have Fun, Nickel Mountain;* 1986: *Raw Deal;* 1987: *Revenge of the Nerds*

II: Nerds in Paradise; 1992: *School Ties;* 1993: *Extreme Justice.*

LAW, JOHN PHILLIP. Actor. *(b. Sept. 7, 1937, Hollywood.)* A native of the world's movie capital, this six-foot-four, blond and blue-eyed actor debuted in *The Magnificent Yankee* (1950), but spent most of the first decade of his film career abroad in Italian-made productions. Law was "introduced" in *The Russians Are Coming! The Russians Are Coming!* (1966), in which he had a key role as a Russian sailor. Written off by critics as just a good-looking hunk, he subsequently appeared in *Hurry Sundown* (1967), *Barbarella* (1968), *The Hawaiians* (1970), *The Last Movie, The Love Machine* (both 1971), *The Golden Voyage of Sinbad* (1974, in the title role) and a horde of international productions, many of them routine action flicks. By the late 1980s he had been reduced to such grade-Z fare as *Night Train to Terror* and *Alienator* (both 1990). But—he keeps working.

LAWFORD, PETER. Actor. *(b. Sept. 7, 1923, London; d. Dec. 24, 1984.)* Perhaps better remembered for his offscreen jet-setting than for his performances, this handsome, debonair actor made most of his best movies at MGM, where he was a longtime contract player. Lawford, the privileged scion of a distinguished family, made his film debut at the age of eight in the British-made *Poor Old Bill* (1931), and worked in his first American film, *Lord Jeff,* in 1938. Signed by MGM in 1942, he was usually cast as charming, mild-mannered, innocuous young Brits. Never a great actor, Lawford was reliably good, and occasionally had a chance to shine. (He acquitted himself admirably in the 1947 musical *Good News,* especially in the delightful special-material song "The French Lesson," with June Allyson.)
He enjoyed the company of Washington's exclusive social set, thanks to his 1954–66 marriage to Patricia Kennedy, and was a visible member of Frank Sinatra's high-living "Rat Pack," with whom he appeared in *Ocean's Eleven* (1960) and *Sergeants 3* (1962). He later costarred with fellow Rat Packer Sammy Davis, Jr., in *Salt and Pepper* (1968) and *One More Time* (1970), two astoundingly

bad comedy-thrillers, which Lawford also produced. Lawford also starred in the TV series "Dear Phoebe" (1954–55), "The Thin Man" (1957–59, as Nick Charles), and had a regular role in "The Doris Day Show" (1971–72). OTHER FILMS INCLUDE: 1942: *Mrs. Miniver, Random Harvest;* 1943: *Girl Crazy, Above Suspicion, Sahara;* 1944: *The White Cliffs of Dover, The Canterville Ghost, Mrs. Parkington;* 1945: *The Picture of Dorian Gray, Son of Lassie;* 1946: *Cluny Brown;* 1947: *It Happened in Brooklyn;* 1948: *Easter Parade, Julia Misbehaves;* 1949: *Little Women, The Red Danube;* 1951: *Royal Wedding;* 1952: *Just This Once;* 1953: *Rogue's March;* 1954: *It Should Happen to You;* 1959: *Never So Few;* 1960: *Exodus;* 1962: *Advise and Consent, The Longest Day;* 1964: *Dead Ringer;* 1965: *Harlow;* 1966: *The Oscar;* 1968: *Skidoo;* 1969: *Buona Sera, Mrs. Campbell, The April Fools;* 1972: *They Only Kill Their Masters;* 1974: *That's Entertainment!* (as one of the host/presenters); 1975: *Rosebud;* 1979: *Angels' Brigade;* 1981: *Body and Soul;* 1983: *Where Is Parsifal?*

LAWRENCE, MARC. Actor. *(b. Feb. 17, 1910, New York City, as Max Goldsmith.)* Dark-haired, swarthy, pockmarked actor, a venerable heavy in Hollywood films of the 1930s, 1940s, and 1950s, but subsequently a supporting player who has played skid-row derelicts, desert rats, and a variety of foreign-born characters. Lawrence, a former stage performer who made his movie debut in 1933's *White Woman,* affected a curious speech pattern that, along with his sinister appearance, made him an immediately identifiable screen menace. (Perhaps his biggest change of pace was his touching performance as a mute simpleton in 1941's *The Shepherd of the Hills.*) Lawrence was perhaps the only character actor of the 1930s and 1940s still being cast in similar gangsterish roles in the 1980s and 1990s, in such films as *The Big Easy* (1987) and *Ruby* (1992). He has also directed several low-budget films, beginning with the John Derek–Ursula Andress starrer *Nightmare in the Sun* (1964, which he also coproduced and cowrote). In 1991 he published his autobiography, "Long Time No See: Confessions of a Hollywood Gangster." OTHER FILMS INCLUDE: 1935: *Dr. Socrates;* 1936: *Road Gang;* 1937: *The Shadow, Charlie Chan on Broadway, San*

Quentin; 1938: *Convicted, The Spider's Web* (serial), *I Am the Law;* 1939: *Homicide Bureau, Dust Be My Destiny;* 1940: *Johnny Apollo, The Great Profile;* 1941: *The Monster and the Girl, Hold That Ghost;* 1942: *This Gun for Hire;* 1943: *The Ox-Bow Incident;* 1944: *Tampico, Rainbow Island;* 1945: *Dillinger;* 1946: *The Virginian, Cloak and Dagger;* 1947: *Unconquered, Captain From Castile;* 1948: *I Walk Alone, Key Largo;* 1950: *Black Hand, The Asphalt Jungle;* 1951: *My Favorite Spy;* 1958: *Kill Her Gently;* 1963: *Johnny Cool;* 1968: *Custer of the West;* 1970: *The Kremlin Letter;* 1974: *The Man With the Golden Gun;* 1976: *Marathon Man;* 1977: *A Piece of the Action;* 1978: *Foul Play;* 1992: *Newsies.*

LEACHMAN, CLORIS. Actress. *(b. Apr. 30, 1926, Des Moines, Iowa.)* This former Miss America runner-up, oddly enough, is perhaps best remembered (in film, at least) as the hideously ugly Frau Blucher in Mel Brooks' *Young Frankenstein* (1974), a comic gem of a performance. In fact, Leachman played an even more unappealing character in Brooks' 1977 Hitchcock parody *High Anxiety* (and a worse one yet in his 1981 *History of the World—Part 1*). She was genuinely sexy in her debut film, the crazed film noir *Kiss Me Deadly* (1955); her small but showy role wasn't enough to catapult her to prominence, however. She worked mainly in television, but started getting good parts in the late 1960s and early 1970s, in films like *Butch Cassidy and the Sundance Kid* (1969) and *Lovers and Other Strangers* (1970).

She won a Best Supporting Actress Academy Award as a housewife who has an affair with a younger man in 1971's *The Last Picture Show* (she also showed up in that movie's 1990 sequel, *Texasville*), and won the affection of exploitation movie fans for her over-the-top portrayal of a rampaging female criminal in the Jonathan Demme–directed *Crazy Mama* (1975). Her handful of other films include *Dillinger* (1973), *Daisy Miller* (1974), *The North Avenue Irregulars* (1979), *Herbie Goes Bananas* (1980), *Prancer* (1989), *Love Hurts* (1990), and *My Boyfriend's Back* (1993). Leachman's real claim to fame is her television work, on "The Mary Tyler Moore Show" (1970–77) and its spinoff "Phyllis" (1975–77), and in a variety of made-for-TV movies. She has six Emmy Awards to her credit. She returned to the big screen as Granny in the feature version of TV's Beverly Hillbillies (1993), playing—quite engagingly—the part originated by Irene Ryan. In 1994 she toured on stage as Grandma Moses.

LEAN, DAVID (SIR). Director, screenwriter, producer. (b. Mar. 25, 1908, Croydon, England; d. Apr. 16, 1991.) Distinguished British filmmaker of impeccable taste, not nearly as prolific as his contemporaries but a much better craftsman than most. He was noted for the care he lavished upon his films, particularly in evoking time and place and in extracting perfect performances from his casts. Lean entered the film industry in the late 1920s, at first working as a clapper boy for cameramen, later graduating to the cutting room (editing 1938's *Pygmalion,* 1941's *49th Parallel,* and 1942's *One of Our Aircraft Is Missing,* among others), finally wielding the megaphone (with Noël Coward) on *In Which We Serve* (1942). The film that cemented his reputation—and cinched his first Oscar nomination—was *Brief Encounter* (1945), the lyrical, romantic story of a housewife (Celia Johnson) tempted to have an affair with a doctor (Trevor Howard).

Lean's two Dickens adaptations, *Great Expectations* (1946) and *Oliver Twist* (1948), are very likely the definitive screen translations of those endearing works; the former netted Lean his second Academy Award nomination for Best Director. The ever-meticulous director chose his subsequent projects—three of which starred his second wife, actress Ann Todd—carefully and bestowed upon them his customary attention to period detail, mood, and characterization. *Summertime* (1955), which starred Katharine Hepburn as an American spinster in Venice, earned Lean another Oscar nomination.

The Bridge on the River Kwai (1957), his magnum opus up to that time, finally won Lean the Oscar, one of seven the picture received. A commercial as well as critical success, it launched the director on a series of big-budget epics, including *Lawrence of Arabia* (1962), his spectacular biopic of the enigmatic WW1 hero T. E. Lawrence (played by Peter O'Toole), and *Doctor Zhivago* (1965), one of the screen's classic romances. He won another Oscar for the former and secured another nomination for the latter. He was also nominated for directing, adapting, and editing *A Passage to India* (1984), a sumptuous adaptation of E. M. Forster's novel. He devoted a year of preparation to *The Bounty* in the early 1980s, only to see it made by other hands; he and frequent collaborator Robert Bolt then spent years preparing Joseph Conrad's *Nostromo* for the screen. Lean died shortly before filming was to begin.
OTHER FILMS INCLUDE: 1944: *This Happy Breed;* 1945: *Blithe Spirit;* 1949: *The Passionate Friends, Madeleine;* 1952: *Breaking the Sound Barrier;* 1954: *Hobson's Choice.*

LÉAUD, JEAN-PIERRE. Actor. (b. May 5, 1944, Paris.) Sad-faced French actor who will always be remembered as Antoine Doinel, the hero of a series of films directed by François Truffaut. The son of writer and assistant director Pierre Léaud and actress Jacqueline Pierreux, Léaud was a maladjusted youth and had been expelled from half a dozen boarding schools by the time he was 13. He read in a newspaper about the search for a "young type" to star in a film and won the lead in Truffaut's first feature, the semiautobiographical *The Four Hundred Blows* (1959). The film was an international success, and Léaud became one of the most identifiable faces of the French New Wave. Truffaut called on him for a series of subsequent films that followed the Antoine Doinel character from young love to marriage to fatherhood, through infidelity, various jobs, and divorce: *Love at Twenty* (1962, part of a multiepisode film), *Stolen Kisses* (1968), *Bed and Board* (1970), and *Love on the Run* (1979). The character grew to be more than Truffaut's alter-ego, to accommodate Léaud's introspective personality; Truffaut once wrote, "Jean-Pierre interests me precisely because of his anachronism and his romanticism: he is a nineteenth-century man."

Léaud starred in other non-Antoine roles for Truffaut, such as *Two English Girls* (1971) and *Day for Night* (1973), and Truffaut even dedicated *The Wild Child* (1969) to him. He also worked extensively for Jean-Luc Godard in many of his pop-revolutionary films of the 1960s, like *Pierrot le fou* (1965), *Made in USA, Masculine-Feminine* (both 1966), *La*

Chinoise, and *Weekend* (both 1967). Léaud was memorable in Jean Eustache's *The Mother and the Whore* (1973) and in Bertolucci's controversial *Last Tango in Paris* (1973, as Maria Schneider's filmmaker boyfriend). He has continued to act in films like Godard's *Detective* (1985), *With All Hands* (1986), *36 Fillette* (1988), and *I Hired a Contract Killer* (1990).

LEDERER, FRANCIS. Actor. *(b. Nov. 6, 1899, Prague, as Frantisek Lederer.)* Highly trained, skillful actor and former European matinee idol whose American film career got off to a promising start but never developed along anticipated lines. A darkly handsome Continental type whose soothing voice and heavy accent lent allure to his screen characters, Lederer supported American silent-screen actress Louise Brooks in the German-made *Pandora's Box* (1928), and made a number of German, French, and British films (usually billed as Franz Lederer) before coming to America in 1932. A well-received Broadway debut led RKO to sign Lederer, who was cast as an Eskimo in his first Hollywood film, *Man of Two Worlds* (1934). He then had a star-building role, as a newcomer to our shores, opposite Ginger Rogers in the charming *Romance in Manhattan* (also 1934), but neither that nor *One Rainy Afternoon* (1936) managed to make him a bona fide star. He segued into second leads, quite successfully, in films like *Midnight* and *Confessions of a Nazi Spy* (both 1939) and kept busy for years to come. He even played Dracula once, in 1958's *The Return of Dracula.*

Lederer retired to pursue a career in real estate and participate in a number of civic, artistic, and charitable institutions. In his 80s he was still active in The American National Theatre and Academy, over which he presided for years. By buying much of what is now Canoga Park, California, he became independently wealthy. OTHER FILMS INCLUDE: 1934: *The Pursuit of Happiness;* 1935: *The Gay Deception;* 1938: *The Lone Wolf in Paris* (improbably cast as debonair American jewel thief Michael Lanyard); 1940: *The Man I Married;* 1944: *The Bridge of San Luis Rey, Voice in the Wind* (a gloomy little PRC melodrama which has acquired a cult reputation); 1946: *Diary of a Chambermaid;* 1948: *Million Dollar Weekend;* 1950: *A Woman of Distinction, Captain Carey U.S.A.;* 1956: *The Ambassador's Daughter;* 1959: *Terror Is a Man.*

LEE, ANNA. Actress. *(b. Jan. 2, 1913, Ightham, England, as Joanna Winnifrith.)* Wholesomely pretty, petite, blond ingenue of British films of the 1930s, then a supporting player and occasional leading lady in Hollywood movies from the 1940s on. Bright-eyed and energetic (and, occasionally, a bit saucy), Lee made her screen debut in *Ebb Tide* (1932), supported musical star Jessie Matthews in *First a Girl* (1935), and was a delightful leading lady in *The Man Who Changed His Mind* (1936), *King Solomon's Mines* (1937), *Young Man's Fancy,* and *Return to Yesterday* (both 1939, and directed by then-husband Robert Stevenson). In Hollywood from 1940, she was a demure supporting player in *Seven Sinners,* but scored heavily as the widowed daughter-in-law of the Welsh coal-mining family in John Ford's *How Green Was My Valley* (1941). She was the pretty nurse for whom John Wayne and John Carroll competed in *Flying Tigers* (1942), and performed leading-lady chores in other WW2-themed dramas such as *The Commandos Strike at Dawn* (1942) and *Hangmen Also Die* (1943). After costarring with Boris Karloff in the period melodrama *Bedlam* (1946), Lee found herself more or less confined to supporting roles—many of them for Ford. Lee has also appeared in many made-for-TV movies and has played Lila Quartermaine on the soap opera "General Hospital" since 1978. She was also married to author Robert Nathan. Her daughter, Venetia Stevenson, was an actress who then moved into film and television production. A son, known professionally as Jeffrey Byron, is an actor. OTHER FILMS INCLUDE: 1947: *The Ghost and Mrs. Muir;* 1948: *Fort Apache;* 1952: *Boots Malone;* 1958: *Gideon of Scotland Yard, The Last Hurrah;* 1959: *The Horse Soldiers;* 1961: *Two Rode Together;* 1962: *The Man Who Shot Liberty Valance, Jack the Giant Killer, What Ever Happened to Baby Jane?;* 1964: *The Unsinkable Molly Brown;* 1965: *The Sound of Music;* 1966: *7 Women;* 1967: *In Like Flint;* 1968: *Star!;* 1981: *Scruples* (made for TV); 1984: *Clash.*

LEE, BRUCE. Actor. *(b. Nov. 27, 1940, San Francisco; d. July 20, 1973.)* Martial-arts expert of Chinese descent and virtual deity to a legion of enthusiasts the world over. A philosophy major who graduated from the University of Washington, Lee entered show business in the mid 1960s, achieving recognition as Kato, devoted sidekick to "The Green Hornet" in the 1966 TV series designed to capitalize on the wild popularity of the "Batman" show. He supervised the martial-arts stunts in *The Wrecking Crew* and *Marlowe* (both 1969), also appearing in the latter, before starring in his own action vehicles *Fists of Fury* (1972), *Enter the Dragon, The Chinese Connection,* and *Return of the Dragon* (all 1973). His acting was negligible, but his athletic skills seemed almost superhuman, and he practically defined the fledgling martial-arts movie genre. The circumstances surrounding Lee's death just one year after his starring debut were somewhat mysterious (he was only 32), and helped transform him into a cult figure. Three "Green Hornet" episodes were edited into a feature to capitalize on his popularity *(Kato and the Green Hornet,* 1974), and a 1979 release, *Game of Death,* was cobbled together from old outtakes and stock footage. (The 1978 release *The Silent Flute* was based on a story he had written with James Coburn.) Perhaps the ultimate testament to his enduring stardom was a Hong Kong picture called *The Clones of Bruce Lee* (1977), in which three karate experts, Bruce Li, Bruce Le, and Bruce Lei battled it out for the right to assume the master's throne. Actor Jason Scott Lee (no relation) starred in a 1993 screen biography, *Dragon: The Bruce Lee Story.* Son Brandon Lee launched his own film career in the 1990s, but died in a tragic accident during production of *The Crow* in 1993.

LEE, CHRISTOPHER. Actor. *(b. May 27, 1922, London.)* "Peter Cushing and I have made so many horror films," Lee once said, "that people think we live in a cave together." He was kidding, of course, but there's no doubt that this towering, sharp-featured actor has enjoyed his most memorable screen roles opposite the suave, aristocratic Cushing in such stylish Hammer Films chillers as *Curse of Frankenstein* (1957, as the monster), *Horror of*

Dracula (1958, as the vampiric Count, the first of many appearances in that role), *The Mummy* (1959, in the title role), *The Gorgon* (1964), *Dracula A.D. 1972,* and *The Satanic Rites of Dracula* (1974), not to mention such other spine-tinglers as *The Hound of the Baskervilles* (1959, as Sir Henry Baskerville), *Dr. Terror's House of Horrors* (1965), *The Skull* (1965), *The House That Dripped Blood, Scream and Scream Again* (both 1970), *The Creeping Flesh* (1972), and *House of the Long Shadows* (1982, teamed with fellow horror veterans Vincent Price and John Carradine).

Lee has, however, done some films on his own—dozens of them, to be exact. His early movies include *Hamlet* (1948), *Captain Horatio Hornblower* (1951), *The Crimson Pirate, Moulin Rouge* (both 1952), and *Storm Over the Nile* (1956). He played Dracula *sans* Cushing in many films, among them *Dracula—Prince of Darkness* (1965), *Dracula Has Risen From the Grave* (1968), *Taste the Blood of Dracula* (1969), *The Scars of Dracula,* the German-made *Count Dracula* (both 1970), and the 1976 spoof *Dracula and Son.* He's essayed the classic "yellow peril," Fu Manchu, in five films—*Face of . . .* (1965), *Brides of . . .* (1966), *Vengeance of . . .* (1967), *Blood of . . .* (1968), and *Castle of . . .* (1969). And he's the only man to play both Sherlock Holmes (in the 1964 German-made *Sherlock Holmes and the Deadly Necklace* and a British-made miniseries that yielded the 1991 feature films *Incident at Victoria Falls* and *Sherlock Holmes and the Leading Lady)* and brother Mycroft (in 1970's *The Private Life of Sherlock Holmes).*

Among the other titles that stand out on Lee's lengthy roster are *Taste of Fear* (1961), *Rasputin—The Mad Monk* (1965, the title role), *The Devil's Bride* (1967), *Julius Caesar* (1970), *Hannie Caulder* (1972), *The Wicker Man* (1973), *The Three Musketeers* (1974 and sequels in 1975 and 1989, as Rochefort), *The Man With the Golden Gun* (also 1974), *Airport '77* (1977), *Return From Witch Mountain,* and *The Silent Flute* (both 1978). He has also demonstrated a flair for comedy, playing a Nazi officer in *1941* (1979), a cycle-riding guru in *Serial* (1980), and a genetic scientist in *Gremlins 2: The New Batch* (1990). Like John Carradine, to whose career Lee's own bears a striking similarity, he is an actor of the bravura school who's not averse to self-parody. (In 1983's spoofy *The Return of Captain Invincible* he even sang. And he turned up as a host one week on TV's "Saturday Night Live.") Since the 1980s Lee has also been active in made-for-TV productions.

LEE, SPIKE. Director, screenwriter, actor, producer. *(b. Mar. 20, 1957, Atlanta, Ga., as Shelton Jackson Lee.)* Activist filmmaker who single-handedly brought about a resurgence in Afro-American cinema. Lee grew up in Brooklyn, the son of a jazz musician (Bill Lee, who scored many of his son's films) and a schoolteacher. He attended Morehouse College and the New York University film school, where his student short, *Joe's Bed-Stuy Barbershop: We Cut Heads* garnered sufficient acclaim to enable Lee to beg and borrow financing for his first feature, *She's Gotta Have It* (1986), in which he also costarred. This shoestring independent production won worldwide acclaim, and spawned Lee's popular "Mars Blackmon" character, who showed up in Nike TV commercials. Lee's second feature, *School Daze* (1988), was partially financed by Columbia; despite lukewarm public reaction, the film was a modest commercial success, and was important as one of the first major-studio motion pictures over which a black filmmaker was given complete control. It also raised eyebrows in the black community for its examination of black cultural divisions and its apparent stereotyping.

Lee's next film, *Do the Right Thing* (1989), aroused even more attention. A story about racial tension on a hot summer's day in Brooklyn, it featured a provocative climax, in which a street riot started over the accidental killing of a neighborhood youth. *Do the Right Thing* sparked a tremendous amount of debate and discussion, but also established Lee as a filmmaker of genuine distinction and originality. It earned an Oscar nomination for Best Screenplay.

Seeking a change of pace, Lee then wrote and directed *Mo' Better Blues* (1990), the story of an egocentric jazz musician. (A basically apolitical film, it nonetheless sparked some controversy over two characters—nightclub owners— depicted as Jewish stereotypes.) *Jungle Fever* (1991) put Lee front and center once more, garnering major media attention for its examination of an interracial love affair. (Having made no mention of drugs in *Do the Right Thing,* and been chastised for the "omission," Lee shoehorned a drug-abuse subplot into *Jungle Fever,* which some felt diluted the impact of his main storyline.)

Lee then tackled his most ambitious film, a biography of black leader *Malcolm X* (1992) starring Denzel Washington. Building on the foundation of an existing script by Arnold Perl, and a twenty-year-old documentary Perl had made with producer Marvin Worth (who executive produced this film), Lee developed a sprawling, intelligent, and surprisingly even-handed portrait of the fiery historical figure. With impending cost overruns, Lee called on major black show business personalities to help fund completion of his film. The result, running more than three hours, was (according to one critic) the shortest movie of 1992, and certainly one of the most arresting.

His next project, considerably smaller in scale, was *Crooklyn* (1994), a family portrait set, like so many of his films, in Brooklyn, New York. He returned to grittier subject matter with the urban crime drama *Clockers* (1995). Lee has also executive-produced *Drop Squad* (1994), *New Jersey Drive,* and *Tales From the Hood* (both 1995).

Lee usually reserves an interesting supporting role in each of his movies for himself—often as the main character's sidekick or best friend.

LEGRAND, MICHEL. Composer. *(b. Feb. 24, 1932, Paris.)* Esteemed composer who studied at the Paris Conservatory at the age of eleven and later became a well-known singer, pianist, songwriter, and conductor in the jazz and pop music field. He began writing film scores in the early 1950s and gained fame for his work with directors like Agnes Varda (*Cleo From 5 to 7,* 1961), Jean-Luc Godard (*A Woman Is a Woman,* 1961; *My Life to Live,* 1962; *Band of Outsiders,* 1964), and especially Jacques Demy, with whom he collaborated on *Lola* (1961), *Bay of Angels* (1962), and the unforgettable musical *The Umbrellas of Cherbourg* (1964), which earned him Oscar nominations for Best

Score and the song "I Will Wait For You." Since then, Legrand has composed scores for numerous international and American projects, including *Ice Station Zebra* (1968), *A Doll's House* (1973), *The Three Musketeers* (1974), *The Other Side of Midnight, Semi-Tough* (both 1977), *Atlantic City, Melvin and Howard* (both 1980), *Never Say Never Again* (1983), *Switching Channels* (1988), and the Demy films *The Young Girls of Rochefort* (1968), *Donkey Skin* (1971), *Lady Oscar* (1979), *Parking* (1985), and *Three Places for the 26th* (1988). He was Oscar-nominated for songs from *Rochefort, The Thomas Crown Affair* (1968, "The Windmills of Your Mind"), *Pieces of Dreams* (1970), and *Best Friends* (1982) and won twice: for Best Original Score, with *The Summer of '42* (1971); and Best Original Song Score, with the Barbra Streisand psuedo-musical *Yentl* (1983). His theme for the TV movie *Brian's Song* (1970) became extremely popular.

LEIBMAN, RON. Actor. *(b. Oct. 11, 1937, New York City.)* Integrity, both in and out of character, clearly means something to Leibman, who once took his name off the prints and advertising of a movie he *starred* in! (The movie was 1980's *Up the Academy.*) This explosive, wild-eyed character lead shuttles from stage to screen to TV with ease, and is one of the few contemporary actors who can chew up scenery mercilessly and get away with it. His peak movie activity was in the 1970s and early 1980s, playing such colorful roles as the perpetual mugging victim in *Where's Poppa?* (1970), the hilariously obsessive getaway driver in *The Hot Rock* and a lunatic killer in *Slaughterhouse-Five* (both 1972), one-half of *The Super Cops* (1974), the Jewish labor organizer in *Norma Rae* (1979), a military academy sergeant in *Up the Academy* (in truth not really that awful), a Mexican governor in *Zorro, the Gay Blade* (1981), and Dolly Parton's sleazy manager in *Rhinestone* (1984). His TV roles include his Emmy-winning convict turned unorthodox attorney on "Kaz" (1978–79) and a comically swinish cop on "Pacific Station" (1991). Previously married to Linda Lavin, he is now married to Jessica Walter, with whom he often costars, most notably on Broadway in Neil

Simon's "Rumors." In 1993 he won a Tony Award for his virtuoso performance as Roy Cohn in the Pulitzer Prize–winning play "Angels in America."

LEIGH, JANET. Actress. *(b. July 6, 1927, Merced, Calif., as Jeanette Helen Morrison.)* Millions of female moviegoers swore they'd never step into a shower again after seeing this pretty, curvaceous blond actress hacked to death in Alfred Hitchcock's *Psycho* (1960). The performance earned Leigh an Oscar nomination, and it remains the career high point of a talented actress who survived the studio system to appear in some of the most noteworthy films of the 1950s and 1960s. She was initially signed to MGM after being spotted by Norma Shearer while still in her teens (debuting in 1947's *The Romance of Rosy Ridge*), but only a handful of her films there were memorable, notably *Little Women* (1949), the baseball fantasy *Angels in the Outfield* (1951), and the psycho-Western *The Naked Spur* (1953).

In 1951 Leigh married Universal contract player Tony Curtis, and they were celebrated as Hollywood's Perfect Young Couple, appearing together in *Houdini* (1953), *The Black Shield of Falworth* (1954), *The Perfect Furlough,* and *The Vikings* (both 1958). She played the luscious younger sib in the musical *My Sister Eileen* (1955), a Russian flier in the campy *Jet Pilot* (1957), a newlywed kidnapped by drug dealers in Orson Welles' *Touch of Evil* (1958), and long-suffering girlfriends in two wildly different films, *The Manchurian Candidate* (1962) and *Bye Bye Birdie* (1963, in which she performed an energetic dance routine). Leigh was more active on TV than in features from the late 1960s on, as an attractive, mature lead or in strong secondary roles. She costarred with daughter Jamie Lee Curtis in *The Fog* (1980). In 1984 she published an autobiography, "There Really Was a Hollywood" and her memoir of the filming of *Psycho* appeared in 1995. OTHER FILMS INCLUDE: 1947: *If Winter Comes;* 1949: *Holiday Affair, That Forsyte Woman;* 1951: *Two Tickets to Broadway;* 1952: *Scaramouche;* 1953: *Walking My Baby Back Home;* 1954: *Living It Up;* 1955: *Pete Kelly's Blues;* 1960: *Who Was That Lady?;* 1963: *Wives and Lovers;* 1966: *An American*

Dream, Harper, Three on a Couch; 1972: *One Is a Lonely Number;* 1979: *Boardwalk.*

LEIGH, JENNIFER JASON. Actress. *(b. Feb. 5, 1962, Los Angeles, as Jennifer Jason Leigh Morrow.)* From her early interpretation of the inexperienced high-schooler whose naiveté leads to an abortion in Amy Heckerling's *Fast Times at Ridgemont High* (1982), this affecting, vulnerable, blond leading lady has developed into a fine actress whose performances are often the outstanding feature of her films. The daughter of actor Vic Morrow, Leigh received raves for her portrayal of a young undercover narcotics cop who gets in too deep in *Rush* (1991), having previously startled audiences with her honest, uninhibited turns as the fatalistic young hooker in *Last Exit to Brooklyn* (1989) and a devoted girlfriend in *Miami Blues* (1990). Christopher Guest's Hollywood satire *The Big Picture* (1989) showcased her little-used comedic talents, in the role of a free-spirited performance artist. Judging from the remainder of her oeuvre, it's safe to say she often rises above mediocre material. *Single White Female* (1992) gave her a particularly juicy role as a psychopathic killer drawn to roommate Bridget Fonda. (Ironically, her worst performance to date was in 1991's *Backdraft,* in which she attempted to play—just once—a "normal" character.) In Robert Altman's *Short Cuts* (1993) she played a woman who turns men on as a telephone-sex operator while feeding and diapering her baby. In the Coen brothers' *The Hudsucker Proxy* (1994) she affected a vintage Katharine Hepburn accent and attitude, with delightful comic results. Alan Rudolph then cast her as celebrated writer and wit Dorothy Parker in *Mrs. Parker and the Vicious Circle* (1994). She followed with *Dolores Claiborne* (1995). OTHER FILMS INCLUDE: 1981: *Eyes of a Stranger* (her debut, in which she played a blind rape victim); 1983: *Easy Money;* 1985: *Flesh + Blood;* 1986: *The Hitcher, The Men's Club;* 1987: *Sister, Sister;* 1988: *Heart of Midnight;* 1991: *Crooked Hearts.*

LEIGH, MIKE. Director, screenwriter. *(b. Feb. 20, 1943, Salford, Lancashire, England.)* Provocative and highly original filmmaker whose kitchen-sink films capture working-class English life better than anyone of his generation. Leigh develops a script by collaborating with his actors (including his wife, the extraordinary, chameleonlike Alison Steadman) in an improvisational atmosphere; then he sets the dialogue and it remains intact. Concerned with the everyday lot of ordinary people, as well as the eccentrics of the world, Leigh has created works that are individual and yet, of a piece. With the exception of his feature debut, *Bleak Moments* (1971), his first decade's output was made for television and barely seen outside of England, except for a handful of film festivals. Fortunately, such rich, seriocomic works as *Hard Labour* (1973), *Nuts in May* (1976), *Abigail's Party* (1977), *Grown Ups* (1980), *Meantime* (1983), *Four Days in July* (1985), and *The Short & Curlies* (1990) are now available on video. With the theatrical release of his anti-Thatcher comedy *High Hopes* (1988) and the skewed family portrait *Life Is Sweet* (1991), a growing number of Americans joined the ranks of his admirers. Although Leigh's works are resolutely unpredictable, the disturbing *Naked* (1993) was certainly his most unusual film to date; it won him a Best Director award at the Cannes Film Festival. Active in theater as well as film, Leigh is still midstream in an exceptional career.

LEIGH, VIVIEN. Actress. *(b. Nov. 5, 1913, Darjeeling, India, as Vivian Mary Hartley; d. July 8, 1967.)* Her place in movie history secured by her near-legendary, Oscar-winning star turn as the tempestuous Scarlett O'Hara in David O. Selznick's *Gone With the Wind* (1939), this beautiful English actress contributed a number of memorable performances in movies, nearly all of which have been regrettably overshadowed by her supreme achievement. The convent-educated Leigh made her film debut in a 1934 British film, *Things Are Looking Up,* and toiled in a handful of undistinguished quickies before being cast in *Fire Over England* (1937) opposite Laurence Olivier, with whom she fell in love almost immediately. They continued their courtship while co-starring in *21 Days Together* (1938), a middling drama based on a John Galsworthy story. Both married, they kept up their well-publicized romance for several years; finally granted divorces by their respective spouses, they married in 1940.

Having appeared in such British films as *Dark Journey, Storm in a Teacup* (both 1937) and *Sidewalks of London,* aka *St. Martin's Lane* (1938, charming as a girl whom Charles Laughton teaches to be a "busker," or street entertainer), Leigh made her first impression on American movie audiences in the British-filmed *A Yank at Oxford* (1938), which starred MGM matinee idol Robert Taylor. Producer Selznick, then at wit's end after searching futilely for a Scarlett to appear in *Gone With the Wind,* already in production, was introduced to the actress, who had accompanied Olivier to Hollywood (where he was filming *Wuthering Heights*). He was immediately smitten with her exquisite beauty; the rest was history.

Leigh's success as Scarlett won her the coveted female lead in MGM's moving remake of *Waterloo Bridge* (1940), a starcrossed romance that reunited her with Robert Taylor. She was paired with Olivier for *That Hamilton Woman* (1941), a lavish costume drama depicting the scandalous love affair between Britain's Admiral Lord Nelson and Lady Emma Hamilton (it was, reportedly, Winston Churchill's favorite film), before taking a five-year sabbatical from the screen. She returned to play the fabled Egyptian seductress in *Caesar and Cleopatra* (1946), and took the title role in *Anna Karenina* (1948), a turgid remake of the Tolstoy classic.

Leigh's riveting performance as the emotionally fragile Blanche du Bois in the 1951 film adaptation of Tennessee Williams' *A Streetcar Named Desire* won her a second Oscar. But her own emotional travails and precarious health (physically delicate, she was a longtime tuberculosis sufferer) kept her off the screen for years at a time. Her last films were *The Deep Blue Sea* (1955), *The Roman Spring of Mrs. Stone* (1961), and *Ship of Fools* (1965)—in all of which, it should be stated, she gave superb performances. Leigh succumbed to tuberculosis, which by the 1960s had faded her beauty. She had divorced Olivier in 1960.

LEISEN, MITCHELL. Director. *(b. Oct. 6, 1899, Menominee, Mich.; d. Oct. 28,*

1972.) Visually oriented director, a former artist and architect before entering the movie business in 1919 as a designer of sets and costumes. In the silent era Leisen worked for such directors as Allan Dwan, Ernst Lubitsch, and Raoul Walsh, but it was his association with Cecil B. DeMille—for whom he served as art director on *The King of Kings* (1927), *The Godless Girl* (1929), *Dynamite* (also 1929, for which he was Oscar-nominated for Interior Decoration), *Madam Satan* (1930), and *The Sign of the Cross* (1932), among others—that won him the opportunity to direct at Paramount, where he spent the bulk of his career.

Befitting his training, background, and prior experience, Leisen concentrated on boosting the eye appeal of his films and was not a favorite of such writers as Billy Wilder and Preston Sturges, whose scripts he directed. But it's hard to conceive how anyone could improve upon such sleek and tasteful productions as *Easy Living* (1937, a screwball comedy written by Sturges), *Midnight* (1939, a sophisticated comedy/romance written by Wilder and Charles Brackett), *Remember the Night* (1940, a heartwarming, sentimental romance by Sturges), or *Hold Back the Dawn* (1941, a deeply felt soap opera saga by Wilder and Brackett), without question four of Leisen's finest films.

Leisen thrived at Paramount in an era of tastefulness, and turned out such first-rate films as *Death Takes a Holiday* (1934), *Hands Across the Table* (1935), *Arise, My Love* (1940), *Take a Letter, Darling* (1942), *To Each His Own* (1946), and *The Mating Season* (1951). As the studio system collapsed, so did his career. He wound up directing television episodes, mostly for stars and producers he'd known in better days. One of his best: the 1959 "Twilight Zone" show called "The Sixteen-Millimeter Shrine," with Ida Lupino as an aging movie star. Leisen appeared as himself, directing *I Wanted Wings* (1941), in a scene for *Hold Back the Dawn.*

OTHER FILMS INCLUDE: 1933: *Cradle Song, The Eagle and the Hawk* (both as co-director); 1934: *Murder at the Vanities;* 1936: *The Big Broadcast of 1937, Thirteen Hours by Air;* 1937: *Swing High, Swing Low;* 1938: *The Big Broadcast of 1938, Artists and Models Abroad;* 1942: *The Lady Is Willing;* 1943: *No Time for Love;* 1944: *Lady in the*

Dark, Frenchman's Creek, Practically Yours;
1945: *Masquerade in Mexico* (a remake of
Midnight); 1947: *Golden Earrings;* 1948:
Dream Girl; 1949: *Song of Surrender;* 1950:
Captain Carey U.S.A.; 1951: *Young Man With
Ideas;* 1953: *Tonight We Sing;* 1955: *Bedev-
illed;* 1957: *The Girl Most Likely.*

LELOUCH, CLAUDE. Director, screenwriter, cinematographer, producer. *(b.
Oct. 30, 1937, Paris.)* Highly sentimental
French director whose gauzily shot romances have endeared him to many
moviegoers (if not many critics). He won
a prize at Cannes' Amateur Film Festival
for his short *La Mal du siècle* at age 13,
and worked on shorts and TV commercials before making his first feature, *The
Right of Man* (1960), financed by his own
family. Several unsuccessful features followed before Lelouch struck gold with *A
Man and a Woman* (1966), a glossy story
about race-car driver Jean-Louis Trintignant and script girl Anouk Aimée, both
widowed, who fall in love. The film won
the Palme D'Or at Cannes as well as Oscars for Best Foreign Language Film and
Best Original Screenplay (by Lelouch and
Pierre Uytterhoeven). His follow-up, *Live
for Life* (1967), about a news reporter who
leaves his wife and has an affair with a
fashion model, was another success and
was nominated for Best Foreign Language
Film. Lelouch tried to tackle capital punishment in *Life Love Death* (1969) and
made a pseudo-gangster film, *The Crook*
(1971, also known as *Simon the Swiss*),
but was more comfortable with romances
involving beautiful people and equally
beautiful places, like *Love Is a Funny
Thing* (1969), *Happy New Year* (1973,
later remade in America in 1987), *And
Now My Love* (1975, Oscar-nominated for
Best Screenplay), and *Another Man, Another Chance* (1977), a near-remake of *A
Man and a Woman* set in the Far West in
the 1870s. Critics continually took him to
task for his superficial stories and characters and fashion magazine approach to
directing. (Tom Milne once noted, "When
in doubt, Lelouch's motto seems to be,
use a colour filter or insert lyrical shots of
dogs and horses; when in real doubt, use
both.") But Lelouch continued unabated,
with *Bolero* (1981), *Edith and Marcel*
(1983), a sequel to his biggest hit, *A Man
and a Woman: Twenty Years Later* (1986)

with Aimée and Trintignant, and *Bandits*
(1987, aka *Attention Bandits*), a typically
lighthearted romantic comedy about jewel
thieves. Lelouch also contributed to *Far
From Vietnam* (1967) and directed "The
Losers" segment of the omnibus Olympics
film *Visions of Eight* (1973). His latest
film is 1993's *Tout Ca . . . Pour Ca! (All
That . . . For This?!)*

LE MAT, PAUL. Actor. *(b. Sept. 22, 1952,
Rahway, N.J.)* Thick, stoic leading man who
enjoyed low-key success as affable Every-
men in a series of 1970s movies, including *American Graffiti* (1973), *Aloha,
Bobby and Rose* (1975), and Jonathan
Demme's *Citizen's Band* (aka *Handle with
Care,* 1977). His most notable performance was as Melvin Dummar, a small-
town man who claimed to be heir to
Howard Hughes' fortune, in Demme's
Melvin and Howard (1980), and he starred
in *Strange Invaders* (1983). In 1984 he
costarred as an abusive husband murdered
by his wife (Farrah Fawcett) in the TV
movie *The Burning Bed.* He has since appeared mostly in horror fare such as *Puppetmaster* (1989) and *Grave Secrets* (1990).

LEMMON, JACK. Actor. *(b. Feb. 8, 1925,
Boston, as John Uhler Lemmon III.)* This actor
makes what he does look easy; perhaps
that's why he's sometimes taken for
granted. Look again, and you see forty
years of stardom, an unusually high degree
of quality films, a daunting range of parts,
and (especially in recent years) a bent for
the challenging and unpredictable. The
Harvard-educated actor demonstrated his
ability early on, more than holding his
own among Henry Fonda, James Cagney,
and William Powell in *Mister Roberts*
(1955), and even winning a Best Supporting Actor Oscar for his comic turn as
the scheming Ensign Pulver. He was nominated for his leading roles in two Billy
Wilder classics, *Some Like It Hot* (1959,
in drag with Tony Curtis) and *The Apartment* (1960, as a sniveling toadie to
amoral executives), and again for his harrowing turn as an alcoholic in *Days
of Wine and Roses* (1962) for Blake
Edwards.
  The essential Lemmon, however, is the
hapless victim of fate, constantly victimized by life's vicissitudes through no fault

of his own. He most skillfully delineated that comic persona in his vehicles of the 1960s and early 1970s, and was felicitously teamed with hangdog-faced Walter Matthau in several of those films, most notably *The Fortune Cookie* (1966, another Billy Wilder gem) and *The Odd Couple* (1968, from the pen of playwright Neil Simon). He continued to work with Wilder, in a too-little-seen midlife crisis comedy, *Avanti!* (1972), as Hildy Johnson (opposite Matthau as Walter Burns) in the 1974 remake of *The Front Page,* and with Matthau again in *Buddy, Buddy* (1981). Matthau and Lemmon reteamed in 1993 for the surprise hit *Grumpy Old Men* (as feuding neighbors).

In 1973, however, he won an Oscar for a dramatic role, as a beleagured dress manufacturer in *Save the Tiger,* and in recent years some of his finest work has flown in the face of his lighthearted image. He was Oscar-nominated for *The China Syndrome* (1979, as a nuclear plant executive who refuses to participate in an accident coverup), *Tribute* (1980, recreating his Broadway performance as a dying playwright who wants to reconcile with his son), and *Missing* (1982, as an American businessman searching for his activist son in a Latin American country).

At a time when other actors might play it safe, Lemmon, in his 50s and 60s, took more risks than ever—and also took his time between films, waiting for good scripts instead of settling for junk. He headlined an impressive Broadway production of Eugene O'Neill's *Long Day's Journey Into Night* (which was later telecast), took an intriguing cameo part in Oliver Stone's *JFK* (1991), and got some of the best reviews of his career for a powerhouse performance in *Glengarry Glen Ross* (1992). He made a fleeting appearance in Robert Altman's *The Player* (1992, playing the piano) and then contributed a poignant vignette to Altman's *Short Cuts* (1993) as Bruce Davison's long-estranged father.

Lemmon directed his friend Matthau in *Kotch* (1971), his only fling behind the camera. In Blake Edwards' *That's Life!* (1986) he appeared on screen with his actress wife, Felicia Farr (who played a fortune teller) and his actor son, Chris Lemmon (who played . . . his son). Lemmon received the American Film Institute Life Achievement Award in 1988,

but, as a lifelong pianist (and a good one), one of his most satisfying achievements was contributing a song to his 1957 movie *Fire Down Below.*

OTHER FILMS INCLUDE: 1954: *It Should Happen to You, Phffft!;* 1955: *Three for the Show, My Sister Eileen;* 1956: *You Can't Run Away From It;* 1957: *Fire Down Below, Operation Mad Ball;* 1958: *Cowboy, Bell, Book and Candle;* 1959: *It Happened to Jane;* 1960: *The Wackiest Ship in the Army, Pepe* (a cameo); 1962: *The Notorious Landlady;* 1963: *Irma La Douce, Under the Yum Yum Tree;* 1964: *Good Neighbor Sam;* 1965: *How to Murder Your Wife, The Great Race;* 1967: *Luv;* 1969: *The April Fools;* 1970: *The Out-of-Towners;* 1972: *The War Between Men and Women;* 1975: *The Prisoner of Second Avenue;* 1976: *The Entertainer* (telefilm), *Alex and the Gypsy;* 1979: *Airport '77;* 1984: *Mass Appeal;* 1985: *Macaroni;* 1987: *Long Day's Journey Into Night* (telefilm); 1989: *Dad;* 1992: *For Richer, For Poorer,* (telefilm); 1993: *A Life in the Theater* (telefilm).

LEONARD, ROBERT SEAN. Actor. *(b. Feb. 28, 1969, Westwood, N.J.)* Talented young actor who, after small roles in *The Manhattan Project* (1986) and *My Best Friend Is a Vampire* (1988), scored a major success as Neil Perry, the sensitive student driven to suicide in *Dead Poets Society* (1989). A stage veteran since the age of 12, Leonard has worked on Broadway in "Brighton Beach Memoirs" and "Breaking the Code" and received a Tony nomination for his work as Eugene Marchbanks in a revival of "Candida." He has also appeared in *Mr. & Mrs. Bridge* (1990), *Married to It* (1993), as Claudio in Kenneth Branagh's version of *Much Ado About Nothing* (1993), as a jazz enthusiast fighting the rise of Nazism in *Swing Kids* (1993), and as Daniel Day-Lewis' son in *The Age of Innocence* (also 1993). In 1994 he costarred in *There Goes My Baby.*

LEONARD, SHELDON. Actor, producer, director. *(b. Feb. 22, 1907, New York City, as Sheldon Leonard Bershad.)* One of the archetypal movie gangsters, this swarthy, wavy-haired actor—whose mouth seemed permanently curled in a sneer—portrayed heavies of the dese-dem-dose type for years before achieving enormous success as a producer and director of TV shows. Leonard, who plied his villainous trade in both comedic and dramatic films, seldom appeared onscreen in anything other than a pin-stripe suit and snap-brim fedora. He was equally effective on radio, where he was a busy character actor and a regular on "The Jack Benny Show," among others.

Leonard, whose entertainment-industry fame really derives from his work behind the cameras, produced the TV series "The Danny Thomas Show" (1953–64, on which he was also a semiregular), "The Andy Griffith Show" (1960–68), "The Dick Van Dyke Show" (1961–66), "I Spy" (1965–68), and "My World and Welcome to It" (1969–70). Still enough of a ham to step in front of the camera, he made occasional guest appearances on TV shows through the 1980s (including one with Bill Cosby, whose TV career he launched on "I Spy"). In 1975 he starred in a short-lived sitcom, "Big Eddie."

OTHER FILMS INCLUDE: 1939: *Another Thin Man;* 1941: *Tall, Dark and Handsome, Private Nurse* (in the male lead, as the ex-racketeer father of young Ann Todd), *Buy Me That Town, Rise and Shine, Weekend in Havana;* 1942: *Street of Chance* (memorably and effectively cast against type), *Tortilla Flat* (as a Latino character), *Lucky Jordan;* 1943: *Hit the Ice;* 1944: *To Have and Have Not, The Falcon in Hollywood;* 1945: *Why Girls Leave Home* (another lead); 1946: *Some where in the Night, It's a Wonderful Life* (as Nick), *Decoy;* 1947: *Sinbad the Sailor, The Gangster;* 1949: *Take One False Step;* 1951: *Come Fill the Cup;* 1952: *Stop, You're Killing Me;* 1955: *Guys and Dolls* (as Damon Runyon gambler Harry the Horse); 1961: *Pocketful of Miracles;* 1978: *The Brink's Job* (as FBI chief J. Edgar Hoover!).

LEONE, SERGIO. Writer, producer, director. *(b. Jan. 3, 1921, Rome, Italy; d. Apr. 30, 1989.)* One-of-a-kind filmmaker whose movies could truly be termed "operatic." The son of silent-film director Vincenzo Leone, he apprenticed in film production in the late 1940s, gradually rising to screenwriting and second unit direction, and finally making his feature directorial debut with *The Colossus of Rhodes* (1960). After some other sword-and-sandal fare, he single-handedly invented the "spaghetti Western" with his stark, stylized remake of *Yojimbo,* starring an American TV cowboy, Clint Eastwood. *A Fistful of Dollars* (1964; U.S. release 1967) made both of them international screen sensations (as well as composer Ennio Morricone, whose striking theme became a kind of Leone signature). They reunited for the sequels *For a Few Dollars More* (1966; U.S. release 1967) and *The Good, the Bad, and the Ugly* (1966), which became his biggest hit.

Leone then went on to create his "ultimate Western," the lengthy *Once Upon a Time in the West* (1968), which boasted Bernardo Bertolucci among its writers, and featured Henry Fonda as a heartless gunman. While these films toyed light-heartedly with genre conventions, they also embodied Leone's own convictions, which include a distrust of the capitalist entrepreneurs who, as he feels, exploited the pioneers, and a bleak nihilism that, although hitting a responsive note with 1960s moviegoers, was out of touch with the general optimism that characterized American-made Westerns.

After making a lighter Western, *Duck, You Sucker* (1972), Leone was relatively inactive, occasionally producing films directed by others. Then he brought forth his magnum opus, the nearly four-hour Jewish crime saga *Once Upon a Time in America* (1984), which incorporated many of his signature themes and stylistic devices. The film was drastically cut for its U.S. release, then restored after being critically praised. Leone died while in preparation for another massive epic, this one about the Russian Revolution.

LERNER, MICHAEL. Actor. *(b. June 22, 1941, Brooklyn, N.Y.)* Lerner's delicious Oscar-nominated performance as fictional movie mogul Jack Lipnick in *Barton Fink* (1991) was informed by considerable prior experience: He had portrayed real-life moguls Jack Warner and Harry Cohn, respectively, in the TV movies *Moviola: This Year's Blonde* (1980) and *Rita Hayworth: The Love Goddess* (1983). A late-blooming actor with extensive stage experience, the pudgy Lerner has also appeared in *Alex in Wonderland* (1970), *The Candidate* (1972), *Outlaw Blues* (1977), *The Postman Always Rings Twice* (1981), *Eight Men Out* (1988, as notorious gambler Arnold Rothstein), *Harlem Nights*

(1989), *Newsies* (1992), *Amos & Andrew* (1993), and *Blank Check* (1994). He plays the kinds of characters who always seem to be sweating.

LEROY, MERVYN. Director, producer, writer, actor. *(b. Oct. 15, 1900, San Francisco; d. Sept. 13, 1987.)* Prolific, mainstream Hollywood filmmaker who, while lacking the stylistic individualism that stamped the works of his more talented brethren, had an intuitive, almost uncanny grasp of what constituted successful screen entertainment. As a youngster he sang on stage and impersonated Charlie Chaplin to impressed audiences. Drifting south from San Francisco, he played bit parts in "Broncho Billy" Anderson's short Westerns before landing a lab job through the courtesy of his cousin, producer Jesse Lasky. LeRoy toiled in many odd jobs around the Famous Players-Lasky studio, performing in the films *Double Speed* (1920), *The Ghost Breaker* (1922), and *Broadway After Dark* (1924), among others.

He moved to First National and took up comedy writing, contributing gags and titles to *Sally* (1925), *Irene, Ella Cinders* (both 1926), and *Orchids and Ermine* (1927), among others. That same year, the ambitious and aggressive LeRoy wangled a directorial assignment, on *No Place to Go,* and ingratiated himself with the studio brass, which included the brothers Warner, who'd recently purchased the company and merged it with their own. He helmed several light, breezy jazz-age concoctions—including *Harold Teen* (1928), *Little Johnny Jones* (1929), and *Show Girl in Hollywood* (1930)—before scoring his first major success with the seminal gangster thriller *Little Caesar* (also 1930). He alternated musicals and comedies with grimmer fare throughout the remainder of his Warner Bros.–First National tenure, and his list of directorial credits is, in the main, impressive: *Broad-Minded, Five Star Final* (both 1931), *Two Seconds, Three on a Match, I Am a Fugitive From a Chain Gang* (all 1932), *Hard to Handle, The World Changes, Gold Diggers of 1933* (all 1933), *Heat Lightning, Hi, Nellie!* (both 1934), *Page Miss Glory, Oil for the Lamps of China* (both 1935), *Anthony Adverse* (1936), and *They Won't Forget* (1937) are among his better efforts.

He never claimed to be a social activist, but films like *I Am a Fugitive* and *They Won't Forget* were hard-hitting exposés just the same, and LeRoy was extremely skillful in putting across their messages.

LeRoy left Warners in 1938 and signed with MGM as a producer, overseeing *The Wizard of Oz* and The Marx Brothers' *At the Circus* (both 1939), among others, before returning to directing with the 1940 remake of *Waterloo Bridge.* LeRoy's subsequent Metro films, all of them glossy, well-produced products in the studio's established tradition, include *Blossoms in the Dust, Johnny Eager* (both 1941), *Random Harvest* (1942; Oscar-nominated for Best Director), *Madame Curie* (1943), *Thirty Seconds Over Tokyo* (1944), *Homecoming* (1948), *Little Women, Any Number Can Play,* and *East Side, West Side* (all 1949).

After taking over the epic *Quo Vadis?* (1951) from John Huston, LeRoy shifted his attention to musicals, helming *Lovely to Look At, Million Dollar Mermaid* (both 1952), *Latin Lovers* (1953), and *Rose Marie* (1954) in his typically invisible style. He then returned to Warners, replacing John Ford on *Mister Roberts* (1955), and subsequently directing *The Bad Seed* (1956), *No Time for Sergeants* (1958), *The FBI Story* (1959), *Gypsy* (1962), and *Mary, Mary* (1963). He went to other studios to make *The Devil at Four O'Clock, A Majority of One* (both 1961), and his final film, *Moment to Moment* (1966). One of Hollywood's authentic elder statesmen (and biggest boosters) in later years, LeRoy tried to soft-pedal the hard edge he brought to his 1930s Warners films and claimed that all he'd ever done was try to please an audience. LeRoy retired (save for some uncredited help on 1968's *The Green Berets*) and wrote his autobiography, "Take One," in 1974.

LESLIE, JOAN. Actress. *(b. Jan. 26, 1925, Detroit, as Joan Agnes Theresa Brodel.)* Wholesome, pretty girl-next-door type who flourished at Warner Bros. during the early 1940s, particularly as the virginal girl who melts Humphrey Bogart's cold, cold heart in *High Sierra* (1941), the sweetheart of Gary Cooper in *Sergeant York* (also 1941) and of James Cagney in *Yankee Doodle Dandy* (1943). She even sang and danced with Fred Astaire in RKO's *The Sky's the Limit* (also 1943)—and celebrated her 18th birthday on the set! Leslie was a trouper from age three who'd done a song-and-dance act with her sisters, and had also been a child model. She had more spunk than others who essayed the same kind of parts in films, and consequently was more entertaining to watch. She first appeared on screen under her own name, playing bits in the likes of *Camille* (1937), *Love Affair* (1939), *Star Dust, Susan and God,* and *Foreign Correspondent* (all 1940). As Joan Leslie, she joined Warners in 1941 and had six good years; she was more even featured in a short-subject called *Alice in Movieland* (1940) that paralleled her own Cinderella-like success story. Other films for the studio include *The Wagons Roll at Night* (1941), *The Male Animal, The Hard Way* (both 1942), This Is the Army, Thank Your Lucky Stars (both 1943), *Hollywood Canteen* (1944), *Where Do We Go From Here?* (for 20th Century-Fox), *Rhapsody in Blue, Too Young to Know* (all 1945), *Cinderella Jones, Janie Gets Married,* and *Two Guys From Milwaukee* (all 1946).

A battle with Warner Bros. over her long-term contract ended her tenure there and made it hard for her to find work at the other major studios. She got one meaty part in the independently produced *Repeat Performance* (1947), and then landed at Republic Pictures, where prestige was scarce but some meaty roles came her way. During her bland period at Warners it's unlikely she would have starred in something called *The Woman They Almost Lynched* (1953). Other later films include *Born to Be Bad* (1950), *Hellgate* (1952), *Flight Nurse, Jubilee Trail* (both 1954) and *The Revolt of Mamie Stover* (1956). Happily married since 1950, she retired in the mid 1950s to raise a family, but has worked in commercials and occasional TV episodes in recent years, and had a small part in a TV movie remake of *Repeat Performance* called *Turn Back the Clock* (1989).

LESTER, MARK. Actor. *(b. July 11, 1958, Oxford, England.)* As the pathetic, tousled-haired little waif who tremulously asked, "Please, sir, can I have some more?" in *Oliver!* (1968), this British child star charmed his way into the hearts of international movie audiences. He was, by that time, already a seasoned veteran, having appeared on British TV and in films from the age of six (beginning with 1964's *The Counterfeit Constable*). The extraordinarily successful musical version of Dickens' "Oliver Twist" established him, briefly, as a star. Lester's screen appeal didn't survive puberty.
OTHER FILMS INCLUDE: 1966: *Fahrenheit 451;* 1967: *Our Mother's House;* 1969: *Run Wild, Run Free;* 1971: *Eyewitness, Melody, Black Beauty, Who Slew Auntie Roo?* (his best year); 1973: *Scalawag;* 1978: *Crossed Swords* (aka *The Prince and the Pauper*).

LESTER, RICHARD. Director. *(b. Jan. 19, 1932, Philadelphia.)* American expatriate whose British films of the Swinging Sixties not only helped to define that puzzling era but marked a startling departure from conventional moviemaking technique. His use of multiple cameras (including handheld ones) and jarring editorial technique won him the approbation of the New Wave's cinematic cognoscenti while irritating the hell out of traditionalists. A former vocalist who broke into TV as a stagehand and worked his way up to a director (at age 20!), Lester left the U.S. for Europe in 1954 and settled in Britain two years later. Picking up more work as a TV director, Lester collaborated with Peter Sellers on a hilarious Oscar-nominated comedy short, *The Running, Jumping and Standing Still Film* (1959), which introduced his work to theatrical audiences.

After directing *It's Trad, Dad!* (1962) and *The Mouse on the Moon* (1963), Lester hit commercial paydirt with two wacky—and wildly popular—comedies starring The Beatles, *A Hard Day's Night* (1964) and *Help!* (1965). *The Knack, and How To Get It* (also 1965), adapted from a popular play, cemented Lester's reputation as a chronicler of the "mod" decade. After tackling the zany burlesque *A Funny Thing Happened on the Way to the Forum* (1966), he returned to more contemporary subjects in *How I Won the War* (1967), *Petulia* (1968, one of his most acclaimed, by critics if not the public) and *The Bed-Sitting Room* (1969).

Curiously, with the end of the 1960s Lester's passion for "hip" subjects seemed to dissipate; since then he has occupied himself mostly with period pieces, many of them big-budget international productions. His later films include the smash hit *The Three Musketeers, Juggernaut* (both 1974), *The Four Musketeers, Royal Flash* (both 1975), *The Ritz* (1976, a prominent exception, taking place in a gay bathhouse!), *Robin and Marian* (also 1976), *Butch and Sundance: The Early Days, Cuba* (both 1979), *Superman II* (1980), *Superman III* (1983), *Finders Keepers* (1984), and *The Return of the Musketeers* (1989). In 1991, he reunited with former Beatle Paul McCartney to film the documentary concert feature *Get Back.*

LEVENE, SAM. Actor. *(b. Aug. 28, 1907, New York City; d. Dec. 17, 1980.)* This pugnacious, bulldog-faced actor with the coiled-spring temperament came to Hollywood in 1936, hired by Warner Bros. to reprise his highly praised stage role in the film version of *Three Men on a Horse* (1936). It marked the beginning of a lengthy career for this volatile, distinctly urban character actor, who played Runyonesque hoods, exasperated businessmen, and hard-boiled cops with equal panache.

Alas, he was denied the opportunity of repeating his greatest stage role, that of Nathan Detroit in the musical hit "Guys and Dolls," on film; recast in a different light, the part went to Frank Sinatra.
OTHER FILMS INCLUDE: 1936: *After the Thin Man;* 1938: *The Shopworn Angel, The Mad Miss Manton;* 1939: *Golden Boy;* 1941: *Shadow of the Thin Man;* 1942: *Grand Central Murder, The Big Street;* 1943: *Action in the North Atlantic, I Dood It, Gung Ho!;* 1944: *The Purple Heart;* 1946: *The Killers;* 1947: *Boomerang!, Brute Force, Crossfire;* 1948: *The Babe Ruth Story;* 1950: *Guilty Bystander;* 1953: *Three Sailors and a Girl;* 1956: *The Opposite Sex;* 1957: *Sweet Smell of Success, Designing Woman, A Farewell to Arms;* 1963: *Act One;* 1969: *A Dream of Kings;* 1971: *Such Good Friends;* 1977: *Demon (God Told Me To);* 1979: *Last Embrace, ... And Justice for All.*

LEVINE, JOSEPH E. Producer. *(b. Sept. 9, 1905, Boston; d. July 21, 1987.)* One of the last of the old-fashioned movie moguls, Levine followed a career path not unlike that of Carl Laemmle, the founder of Universal Pictures. Levine left the clothing business to become an exhibitor, and then discovered he could make more money distributing pictures. Since he didn't have the money or influence to buck the major Hollywood studios, Levine started importing foreign pictures for U.S. distribution, including the well-regarded *Open City* (1945) and *The Bicycle Thief* (1947). In the post-WW2 era, Levine kept a canny eye on the drive-in market, and imported innumerable sword-and-sandal epics (including 1959's *Hercules* and its 1960 sequel, *Hercules Unchained*) and 1956's *Godzilla, King of the Monsters,* to which he added scenes with American star Raymond Burr). Based on the popularity of Italian imports, Levine's Embassy Pictures actually helped bankroll *Two Women* (1961), *Boccaccio '70* (1962), and Fellini's *8½* (1963), among others. As an independent powerhouse with a rock-solid distribution network, he was finally able to crack the domestic market with self-produced films including *The Carpetbaggers* (1964), *Harlow* (1965), *Nevada Smith* (1966), *The Graduate* (1967), *The Lion in Winter* (1968), *The Adventurers* (1970), *Carnal Knowledge* (1971), *The Day of the Dolphin* (1973), *Paper Tiger* (1975), *A Bridge Too Far* (1977), *Magic* (1978), and *Tattoo* (1981). He sold his original company, Embassy Pictures, to the Avco company in the late 1960s, but remained a producer until his retirement in the 1980s. In 1962 he was the subject of a documentary profile by the Maysles brothers called *Showman.*

LEVINSON, BARRY. Director, writer, producer. *(b. Apr. 6, 1942, Baltimore.)* Talented writer-director who has managed to balance commercial success with a desire to tell personal stories, many of them drawn from his life growing up in Baltimore. Levinson broke into show business as a writer and performer, partnered for a time with Valerie Curtin. He won two Emmy Awards while a staff writer on "The Carol Burnett Show" in the 1970s, and got his first screen credit for writing *The Internecine Project* (1974). He then joined Mel Brooks' platoon of writers for *Silent Movie* (1976) and *High Anxiety* (1977, also contributing a hilarious cameo as a lunatic bellhop); he returned to the fold, briefly, to do another cameo in Brooks' *History of the World—Part 1* (1981). Levinson and Curtin earned an

Oscar nomination for the screenplay of ... *And Justice for All* (1979) and later collaborated on *Best Friends* (1982), which, perhaps not coincidentally, was the story of male-female screenwriting partners. Levinson took solo writing credit for the well-received *Inside Moves* (1980).

His first directorial effort, *Diner* (1982, which he also wrote), was an autobiographical look back at 1950s Baltimore, and a group of buddies who hang around a diner and try to deal with life—and the specter of marriage. The film's distributor was ready to shelve the picture, thinking it had no box-office potential whatsoever, but a New York opening changed all that. *Diner* became a critical hit, a modest success, and earned Levinson another Best Screenplay Oscar nomination (as well as helping to launch the careers of Mickey Rourke, Kevin Bacon, Daniel Stern, Steve Guttenberg, and Ellen Barkin). After directing *The Natural* (1984) and *Young Sherlock Holmes* (1985), Levinson returned to home turf as writer-director of *Tin Men* (1987), the second of his Baltimore pictures, set in 1963 and depicting the lives of rival aluminum-siding salesmen (Richard Dreyfuss and Danny DeVito) who—not so incidentally—tend to hang out in a diner.

Levinson's stock as a director rose considerably with his piloting of *Good Morning, Vietnam* (1987, which solidified Robin Williams' status as a movie star) and *Rain Man* (1988), a critical and commercial smash which earned him an Academy Award as Best Director. All of this earned Levinson the clout to return to Baltimore one more time for his most ambitious "personal" film (as writer and director), the multigenerational family saga *Avalon* (1990). A deeply felt, meticulously crafted film, it failed to find a large audience, but did earn Levinson another Oscar nomination for Best Screenplay. Levinson then coproduced and directed *Bugsy* (1991), the stylish saga of gangster Benjamin Siegel starring Warren Beatty; it was a box-office hit, and that got him a Best Director nomination. He then turned to another pet project: a long-unproduced screenplay (cowritten with Valerie Curtin) called *Toys* (1992), which starred Robin Williams as a gentle toymaker whose peaceful beliefs are threatened by a warmongering uncle who takes over the family business. Heavy-handed and abysmally

bad, it proved that some personal projects are best left in the proverbial trunk. The next year Levinson won an Emmy for directing the pilot of a cutting-edge cop show he helped create, "Homicide: Life on the Streets" (1993–). He returned to the big screen with the misfire *Jimmy Hollywood,* followed by the mainstream hit *Disclosure* (both 1994).

LEWIS, GEOFFREY. Actor. *(b. Jan. 1, 1935, San Diego.)* Edgy character actor best known for his eccentric portrayals in many of Clint Eastwood's movies, including *High Plains Drifter* (1973), *Thunderbolt and Lightfoot* (1974), *Every Which Way But Loose* (1978), *Bronco Billy* (1980), and *Pink Cadillac* (1989). Lewis has had brief runs on the TV series "Flo" (1980–81) and "Gun Shy" (1983), and appeared in numerous TV movies, along with such films as *Smile, The Wind and the Lion* (both 1975), *Heaven's Gate* (1980), *Lust in the Dust* (1985), *Fletch Lives* (1989), *The Lawnmower Man* (1992), *Only the Strong, The Man Without a Face* (both 1993), and *Maverick* (1994). Lewis is part of the three-member performance group Celestial Navigations, which weaves new age music together with Lewis' original stories. He is also the father of actress Juliette Lewis.

LEWIS, HERSCHELL GORDON. Director. *(b. June 15, 1926, Pittsburgh.)* Now revered as "the Godfather of Gore," this affable advertising executive (with a Ph.D in English literature) worked on industrial films in the late 1950s before teaming up with producer David Friedman to grind out several "nudie-cuties" before inventing the gore movie in 1963. *Blood Feast* made little sense, featured wildly inept actors and was, technically speaking, barely competent. But its graphic display of blood-and-guts (using butcher-shop rejects) offered moviegoers something the major studios wouldn't deliver. *2,000 Maniacs* (1964), in which a Confederate town is resurrected in the modern South to treat some visiting Yankees with special "hospitality," lifted its premise from *Brigadoon,* revealing Lewis' sly sense of humor. After making a dozen or so followups—including *The Gruesome Twosome* (1968) and *The Wizard of Gore*

(1971)—Lewis left the movie business in the early 1970s and became a direct-mail consultant; he has since written and marketed several books on advertising. Lewis enjoys his reputation as the progenitor of the "splatter" movie, although he doesn't take it too seriously. When told that the French film journal "Cahiers du Cinema" considered him a "subject for further research," Lewis quipped, "That's what they say about cancer!"

LEWIS, JERRY. Actor, director, producer, screenwriter. *(b. Mar. 16, 1926, Newark, N.J., as Joseph Levitch.)* It's impossible to overstate the impact with which Jerry Lewis and partner Dean Martin burst onto the show business scene in the late 1940s and early 1950s. They were, to put it mildly, a phenomenon. No mere straight-man-and-cutup duo, they convulsed audiences in nightclubs, theaters, and on television by fooling around—in a uniquely manic way. Signed by producer Hal Wallis in 1949, they made their debut as comedy relief in *My Friend Irma,* and appeared in the sequel, *My Friend Irma Goes West* (1950) as well. After that, they took a back seat to no one. Unfortunately, their movie vehicles boxed the team into conventional formats, with Jerry as an overgrown juvenile and Dean as his perpetual friend/nemesis who would burst into song. Many of the films were very funny indeed, but they seldom captured the lunacy of a live Martin and Lewis performance.

What they did do was showcase Lewis' great comic gifts. His silly appearance in drag in *At War with the Army* (1950), his prizefighting routine in *Sailor Beware* (1951), his comic conducting of a chorus in both *Sailor Beware* and *You're Never Too Young* (1955), his comic-book dreams in *Artists and Models* (also 1955), his imitations of moviegoers around the world in the prologue of *Hollywood or Bust* (1956) were Jerry in top form. The team fared particularly well in remakes of solid movie vehicles of the past: *You're Never Too Young* was a retread of *The Major and the Minor,* and *Living It Up* (1954), one of their best, was a remake of *Nothing Sacred.* Lewis' desire to do something more than mug was evident early on, in the pathos of *That's My Boy* (1951) and *The Stooge* (1953, a show-biz saga about

a team's volatile relationship that had at least a few parallels to the Martin and Lewis saga).

Martin and Lewis stayed together—through occasional rifts—for ten years, then split. Jerry's first solo film, *The Delicate Delinquent* (1957), proved he could succeed on his own, maintaining the same basic character he'd played all along. Hit after hit followed: *The Sad Sack* (1957), *Rock-a-Bye Baby, The Geisha Boy* (both 1958), *Don't Give Up the Ship* (1959). His films were guaranteed moneymakers for Paramount, so when, in 1960, there was no Jerry Lewis film in the pipeline for Christmastime release, he determined to make a movie by himself in barely a month's time. The result was *The Bellboy* (1960), a series of blackout gags filmed in and around the Fontainbleau Hotel in Miami, Florida. It marked Lewis' first time as director and cowriter as well as star, and changed the course of his career.

Thereafter he alternated between self-made films and star vehicles directed by others (usually his mentor, former cartoon director Frank Tashlin). The French critics—and public—came to revere Lewis during this period, and hailed *The Nutty Professor* (1963), a comic Jekyll and Hyde story, as his masterpiece. Less charitable viewers came to feel that Jerry's own films were suffering from an ever-increasing dose of ego—and fewer laughs—than before. By the end of the 1960s, the magic spell was broken, and Lewis movies were no longer box-office gold.

Having dabbled in television before (with Dean on "The Colgate Comedy Hour" and their own "Dean Martin & Jerry Lewis Show," and in variety specials of his own), he now made history with an unprecedented live, two-hour Saturday night talk-and-variety program in 1963. Lewis originally wanted to direct the show himself from a console at his desk, but was talked out of it at the last minute. His ego could not be contained on the air, however, and the show was a colossal fiasco. Audience exposure to the "real" Jerry Lewis may have played a part in their disillusionment with "That Kid" (as he called himself) onscreen, and the erosion of his box-office potency.

After the excruciating *Which Way to the Front?* (1970) he was off-screen for more than a decade, though he did direct his friend Sammy Davis, Jr., in the buddy comedy *One More Time* (1970) with Peter Lawford. Lewis remained in the public eye on a somewhat conventional variety show ("The Jerry Lewis Show," 1967–69) and on his hugely successful annual telethon benefiting the Muscular Dystrophy Association.

The 1980s saw a Jerry Lewis renaissance, however. He made some new movies, including the one-man-show *Hardly Working* (1981) and the hardly released *Cracking Up* (1983, aka *Smorgasbord*). Then he performed brilliantly for Martin Scorsese as a somber TV talk-show host idolized and victimized by an obsessed fan (Robert De Niro) in *The King of Comedy* (1983). This led to prominent TV guest shots and offers to play semi-dramatic parts, including a multi-episode story on TV's "Wiseguy" (1988–89), in which he did himself proud as a self-made garment center mogul. He played himself in an amusing cameo for Billy Crystal's *Mr. Saturday Night* (1992), and gave impressive "straight" performances in *Arizona Dream* (1995, filmed in 1991) and *Funny Bones* (1995). He then made his Broadway debut in a revival of "Damn Yankees" (as the Devil). He also produced a series of cable-TV specials culled from his library of TV kinescopes, which reminded people just how funny he could be.

OTHER FILMS INCLUDE: 1952: *Road to Bali* (cameo with Dean Martin), *Jumping Jacks;* 1953: *Scared Stiff, The Caddy, Money from Home;* 1954: *Three Ring Circus;* 1956: *Pardners;* 1959: *Li'l Abner* (cameo); 1960: *Don't Give Up the Ship, Visit to a Small Planet, Raymie* (singing title song only), *CinderFella;* 1961: *The Ladies Man* (also produced, directed, wrote), *The Errand Boy* (also produced, directed, wrote); 1962: *It's Only Money;* 1963: *It's a Mad Mad Mad Mad World* (cameo), *Who's Minding the Store?;* 1964: *The Patsy* (also directed, wrote), *The Disorderly Orderly;* 1965: *The Family Jewels* (also produced, directed, wrote), *Boeing, Boeing;* 1966: *Three on a Couch* (also produced, directed, wrote); 1968: *Don't Raise the Bridge, Lower the River;* 1969: *Hook, Line & Sinker* (also produced); 1972: *The Day the Clown Cried* (unreleased); 1984: *Slapstick of Another Kind;* 1987: *Fight for Life* (telefilm); 1989: *Cookie.*

LEWIS, JOSEPH H. Director. *(b. Apr. 6, 1900, New York City.)* Stylish director of low-budget genre films whose facility with unusual camera angles and canny sense of mise-en-scène distinguished his output and made him one of the darlings of auteurist critics who "discovered" him in the late 1960s. Lewis, a former assistant cameraman, took to the cutting room in the early 1930s, eventually becoming editorial supervisor for Mascot and its successor, Republic Pictures. He codirected a 1937 Grand National potboiler, *Navy Spy,* then moved on to B Westerns, first at Universal, then Columbia (where he directed Bill Elliott in 1940's *The Man From Tumbleweeds* and Charles Starrett in 1940's *Blazing Six-Shooters,* among others).

He launched the East Side Kids series at Monogram, directing such early entries as *Boys of the City, That Gang of Mine* (both 1940), and *Pride of the Bowery* (1941) before returning to Universal for Johnny Mack Brown Westerns and a lame horror opus, *The Mad Doctor of Market Street* (1942).

Lewis landed at Columbia in 1945 where, after directing two stylish, intelligent low-budget thrillers—*My Name Is Julia Ross* (1945, reworked in 1987 as *Dead of Winter*) and *So Dark the Night* (1946)—he staged the musical numbers for *The Jolson Story* (1946), his first A picture. He subsequently handled *The Swordsman* (1948, a swashbuckler starring Larry Parks), *The Return of October* (1948, a horse story starring Terry Moore), and *The Undercover Man* (1949, a crime drama starring Glenn Ford) for Columbia; while several notches above the type of films he'd previously turned out, Lewis seemed destined to remain in the minor leagues.

Gun Crazy (1949), Lewis' best film, was a gritty, occasionally startling crime drama with a Bonnie-and-Clyde theme. One amazing, ten-minute-long shot brought the audience right into the getaway car as the young criminals robbed a bank (Lewis had previously done a similar one-shot sequence for *Secrets of a Co-Ed* in 1942). This minor gem should have propelled him to the first ranks of filmmakers . . . but it didn't.

Lewis' subsequent films—*A Lady Without Passport* (1950), *Retreat, Hell!, Desperate Search* (both 1952), *Cry of the*

Hunted (1953), *The Big Combo, A Law-less Street* (both 1955), *Seventh Cavalry* (1956), *The Halliday Brand* (1957), and *Terror in a Texas Town* (1958)—reflect the careful craftsmanship of a talented journeyman.

LEWIS, JULIETTE. Actress. *(b. June 21, 1973, Los Angeles.)* Fast-rising actress who earned raves—and a Supporting Oscar nomination—as the teenager who flirts dangerously with psycho Max Cady (Robert De Niro) in the thriller *Cape Fear* (1991). The daughter of character actor Geoffrey Lewis, Juliette,'who was legally emancipated at 14, dropped out of high school to concentrate on her acting and appeared in *National Lampoon's Christmas Vacation* (1989, as Chevy Chase's daughter) and *Crooked Hearts* (1991) before the success of *Cape Fear.* She replaced Emily Lloyd in mid-production as the college student who attracts and intrigues professor Woody Allen in *Husbands and Wives* (1992), and has also starred in *That Night* (1993), *Kalifornia* (1993, opposite then boyfriend Brad Pitt), *What's Eating Gilbert Grape* (1993), *Romeo Is Bleeding, Natural Born Killers,* and *Mixed Nuts* (all 1994).

LEWTON, VAL. Producer, screenwriter, writer. *(b. May 7, 1904, Yalta, Russia, as Vladimir Ivan Leventon; d. Mar. 14, 1951.)* Lewton serves as a textbook example of the producer as auteur. He closely supervised production of the low-budget features he produced at RKO during the 1940s: films which bear as much of his personal taste and influence as that of their directors. Lewton came to the United States at age seven, and was raised by his mother and his aunt, Alla Nazimova. Prior to commencing his film career in the early 1930s (as an MGM publicist and assistant to David O. Selznick), he studied journalism at Columbia University and authored eighteen works of nonfiction, fiction, and poetry; in his writing, he occasionally worked under the pseudonyms Carlos Keith and Cosmo Forbes. One of his novels, "No Bed of Her Own," was filmed by Wesley Ruggles as *No Man of Her Own* (1933); one of his more notable assignments for Selznick was writing some scenes for (and directing crowd scenes in) *A Tale of Two Cities* (1935).

Lewton hit his creative stride when he was given control of a special RKO production unit and made a series of sophisticated, visually arresting horror classics with deceptively lurid titles. You won't find any oversized apes or haunted houses in these films; they were designed as exercises in the psychological aspects of horror. Working with directors Robert Wise, Jacques Tourneur, and Mark Robson, Lewton effectively utilized creative camerawork, light and shadow, and sound effects to concoct an eerie, atmospheric effect, and the films remain as frightening today as when first released. His best were among the first he produced: *Cat People* (1942), Lewton's most famous film, in which a girl is convinced that she will turn into a panther; *I Walked With a Zombie* (1943), a paraphrase of *Jane Eyre* about a nurse in the West Indies who discovers the walking dead; *The Seventh Victim* (1943), a chronicle of devil worship in Greenwich Village; and *The Curse of the Cat People* (1944), the story of a lonely little girl who conjures up a make-believe playmate. Other Lewton films covered a variety of subjects: a series of murders in *The Leopard Man* (1943); a ship captain's insanity in *The Ghost Ship* (1943), a French village under siege in *Mademoiselle Fifi* (1944); and teens in wartime in *Youth Runs Wild* (1944). His final three RKO films starred Boris Karloff: *The Body Snatcher* (1945, which Lewton also scripted), *Isle of the Dead* (1945), set on a Greek island clouded by superstition; and *Bedlam* (1946, which Lewton also scripted), set in an insane asylum and inspired by "The Rake's Progress," William Hogarth's series of sardonic paintings.

Lewton never again had the opportunities he had enjoyed at RKO. His final films were forgettable studio product: *My Own True Love* (1949), another romance, made at MGM; and *Apache Drums* (1951), a Western, made at Universal. He died of a heart attack at age 46, just prior to signing on with Stanley Kramer as an associate producer.

LINDFORS, VIVECA. Actress. *(b. Dec. 29, 1920, Uppsala, Sweden, as Elsa Viveca Torstensdotter Lindfors.)* Striking, dark-haired actress who came to Holly-

wood in 1947 already a film veteran of several years' experience in her native country. A graduate of Stockholm's Royal Dramatic Theater and an experienced stage performer, she signed with Warner Bros. in 1948 and made her American screen debut in that year's *To the Victor.* Lindfors, like many actresses of her training and ability, seldom got challenging roles in Hollywood, but worked consistently and could always be counted upon for fine performances. Once married to director Don Siegel, with whom she had a son (who later took his stepfather's surname), actor Kristoffer Tabori. Lindfors also worked frequently in TV and on the stage, notably in a 1973 one-woman show, "I Am a Woman." In 1990 she received an Emmy award for a guest appearance on the dramatic series "Life Goes On."
OTHER FILMS INCLUDE: 1948: *Adventures of Don Juan;* 1950: *Backfire, Dark City, No Sad Songs for Me;* 1951: *Gypsy Fury;* 1952: *The Raiders;* 1955: *Run for Cover, Moonfleet;* 1958: *I Accuse!;* 1960: *The Story of Ruth;* 1961: *King of Kings;* 1962: *These Are the Damned;* 1965: *Brainstorm;* 1969: *Coming Apart;* 1973: *The Way We Were;* 1977: *Welcome to L.A.;* 1978: *Girlfriends, A Wedding;* 1979: *Voices;* 1981: *The Hand;* 1982: *Creepshow;* 1985: *The Sure Thing;* 1987: *Lady Beware;* 1988: *Going Undercover;* 1989: *Forced March;* 1990: *The Exorcist III;* 1991: *Zandalee;* 1994: *Stargate.*

LINDSAY, MARGARET. Actress. *(b. Sept. 19, 1910, Dubuque, Iowa, as Margaret Kies; d. May 9, 1981.)* She got her big break, in Fox's 1933 adaptation of Noël Coward's *Cavalcade,* by convincing a casting director that she was British—when, in reality, the Iowa-born actress had spent only a few months on the London stage and had come to Fox directly from the set of a Tom Mix Western! Lindsay, a graduate of the American Academy of Dramatic Arts, held her own in *Cavalcade* among the seasoned all-British players. Signed by Warner Bros. later that year, the attractive, raven-haired actress became one of the studio's workhorses, appearing in three dozen films between 1933 and 1940. She bounced between A and B pictures, playing leads in some and supporting roles in others, and working with such top leading men as Paul Muni, James Cagney, William Powell, Errol Flynn, and even the up-and-coming

Humphrey Bogart. The only thing she lacked was star quality. She later costarred in seven Ellery Queen mysteries for Columbia between 1940 and 1942. By 1947, looking tired and overweight, Lindsay had segued into supporting roles, retiring after *Tammy and the Doctor* (1963).
OTHER FILMS INCLUDE: 1932: *Once in a Lifetime, Okay America!;* 1933: *Baby Face, Christopher Strong, Voltaire, Lady Killer;* 1934: *Fog Over Frisco, The Dragon Murder Case;* 1935: *Bordertown, "G"-Men, The Case of the Curious Bride;* 1936: *Public Enemy's Wife;* 1937: *Slim, Green Light;* 1938: *Jezebel, Gold Is Where You Find It;* 1939: *Hell's Kitchen;* 1940: *British Intelligence, Ellery Queen, Master Detective* (first in the series, playing Ellery's gal Friday, Nikki Porter); 1942: *The Spoilers;* 1943: *Crime Doctor;* 1944: *Alaska;* 1945: *Scarlet Street, Club Havana;* 1947: *Seven Keys to Baldpate, Cass Timberlane;* 1948: *B. F.'s Daughter;* 1956: *The Bottom of the Bottle;* 1958: *The Restless Years;* 1960: *Please Don't Eat the Daisies.*

LIOTTA, RAY. Actor. *(b. Dec. 18, 1955, Union, N.J.)* Dark-haired, heavy-browed lead and supporting actor who began on TV in the soap "Another World" and on a TV version of *Casablanca* (1983). In 1983, he also landed a bit part in the trashy Pia Zadora sudser *The Lonely Lady.* He made his initial big-screen impact as Melanie Griffith's maniacal ex in Jonathan Demme's quirky road comedy *Something Wild* (1986), followed by a sensitive, deeply felt performance as a caretaking brother in *Dominick and Eugene* (1988) and an attention-grabbing role as Shoeless Joe Jackson in *Field of Dreams* (1989). He then got the plum part of gangster turned canary Henry Hill in Martin Scorsese's underworld saga *GoodFellas* (1990). Recent credits include *Unlawful Entry* and *Article 99* (both 1992). He went to Australia to film *No Escape* (1994) and appeared in *Corrina, Corrina* (also 1994).

LITHGOW, JOHN. Actor. *(b. Oct. 19, 1945, Rochester, N.Y.)* "The Wall Street Journal" once called Lithgow "the film character actor of his generation." Indeed, he has created an extraordinary gallery of villains, nice guys, and genuine flakes. Lithgow grew up around theater people— his father ran a theater in New Jersey and produced Shakespeare festivals in Ohio—and studied at Harvard, as well as at the London Academy of Music and Dramatic Arts on a Fulbright scholarship. After performing with the Royal Court Theatre and the Royal Shakespeare Company, he moved back to New York and won a Tony for his Broadway debut in "The Changing Room." He subsequently appeared in many other Broadway and off-Broadway plays, in addition to directing for regional companies. He made his film debut, as a bad guy, in *Dealing: or The Berkeley-to-Boston Forty-Brick Lost-Bag Blues* (1972) and followed with supporting roles in *Obsession* (1976, another baddie, his first for Brian DePalma), *The Big Fix* (1978), *All That Jazz, Rich Kids* (both 1979) and *Blow Out* (1981, another wild-eyed villain for DePalma). He then captured the attention of critics and moviegoers alike with his remarkable performance as transexual Roberta Muldoon in *The World According to Garp* (1982), which earned him an Oscar nomination as Best Supporting Actor.

Lithgow went on to prove that he could take on practically any kind of role: a terrified airline passenger in *Twilight Zone—The Movie* (1983), Debra Winger's painfully shy lover in *Terms of Endearment* (1983, another Oscar nomination), the insane, electricity-eating Dr. Lizardo in *The Adventures of Buckaroo Banzai Across the Eighth Dimension* (1984), a dance-hating minister in *Footloose* (1984), and a spacebound scientist in *2010* (1984). Lithgow has had his share of movie misfires—*Santa Claus* (1985), *The Manhattan Project* (1986), *Harry and the Hendersons* (1987), *Distant Thunder* (1988), *Out Cold* (1989), and *Memphis Belle* (1990)—but most recently has come to the fore again playing over-the-top villains, in *Ricochet* (1991), Brian De Palma's *Raising Cain* (1992), and the smash hit *Cliffhanger* (1993). Lithgow has continued to work on stage between films, in a revival of "Requiem for a Heavyweight" and the acclaimed "M. Butterfly." He has also appeared in numerous TV movies like *The Day After* and *A Resting Place* and earned an Emmy for an episode of "Amazing Stories." A father of three, Lithgow also entertains for children and released a videotape: "John Lithgow's Kid-Size Concert." Other credits include *The Pelican Brief* (1993), *Princess Caraboo, World War II: When Lions Roared* (1994 telefilm, as F.D.R.), and *Silent Fall* (also 1994).

LITTLEFIELD, LUCIEN. Actor. *(b. Aug. 16, 1895, San Antonio; d. June 4, 1960.)* This bald, bland-looking character actor started playing old men in his 20s, during the silent-film era, and remained active long enough to grow into those parts. His appearance and nervous manner made him particularly well suited for Milquetoast roles, but from time to time he played mad scientists, western sidekicks, crooked lawyers, and even suave villains. Well remembered as the scraggly settler in William S. Hart's *Tumbleweeds* (1925), the grotesque-looking "doctor" in *The Cat and the Canary* (1927), and Mary Pickford's aging father in *My Best Girl* (1927), he went on to an equally prolific career in talkies, starring in his own series of homespun situation-comedy shorts for Warner Bros. and being featured as a bogus doctor in Laurel and Hardy's *Sons of the Desert* (1933), Ginger Rogers' father in *Chance at Heaven* (1933), W. C. Fields' officious boss in *The Man on the Flying Trapeze* (1935), and in a long-running stint as a self-important schoolteacher in the Henry Aldrich series of the 1940s.

OTHER FILMS INCLUDE: 1921: *The Sheik;* 1930: *Tom Sawyer;* 1932: *If I Had a Million;* 1935: *Ruggles of Red Gap;* 1936: *Rose Marie;* 1937: *Wells Fargo;* 1938: *The Gladiator;* 1941: *The Little Foxes;* 1945: *Scared Stiff;* 1954: *Casanova's Big Night;* 1957: *Bop Girl.*

LITVAK, ANATOLE. Director, producer, screenwriter. *(b. May 21, 1902, Kiev, Russia, as Mikhail Anatol Litwak; d. Dec. 15, 1974.)* Litvak was a competent craftsman whose credits are sprinkled with outstanding, commercially successful features. As a teenager, he worked at an avant-garde theater in Petrograd, and studied acting at a drama school. Eventually he found a job as an assistant director at the Nordkino studio, where he directed his debut feature, *Tatiana* (1925). That same year, he resettled in Germany. Litvak assisted G. W. Pabst as an editor on *The Joyless Street* (1925), but did not direct his second feature until 1930, when he signed with the UFA studio. Upon Hitler's rise to power, Litvak (who was Jewish) fled first to England, where he directed one film, *Sleeping Car* (1933), and then to France. One of the features he made there, *Mayerling* (1936), a historical romance starring Charles Boyer and Danielle Darrieux, earned him international acclaim and an offer from Hollywood.

Litvak's American debut was at RKO: *The Woman I Love* (1937), a remake of his French film *L'Équipage* (1935), about two men in love with the same woman. During a long stint at Warner Bros. he specialized in high drama, though his first assignment was the Robert Sherwood comedy about Russian emigrés, *Tovarich* (1937). He also directed Warners' landmark anti-Nazi drama, *Confessions of a Nazi Spy* (1939). Other films of this period were *The Sisters*, *The Amazing Dr. Clitterhouse* (both 1938), *Castle on the Hudson, City for Conquest, All This, and Heaven Too* (all 1940), *Out of the Fog, Blues in the Night* (both 1941), and, on loan to Fox, *This Above All* (1942). Upon America's entry into WW2, Litvak joined the U.S. Army, worked with Frank Capra on the "Why We Fight" series, and was placed in charge of all combat photography during the Normandy invasion. Easily his most popular postwar films were *Sorry, Wrong Number* (1948) and the groundbreaking mental health drama *The Snake Pit* (also 1948). Also noteworthy were *Decision Before Dawn* (1951), an exceptional spy thriller, and *Anastasia* (1956), the story of Russian court intrigue, as well as a television remake of *Mayerling* (1957) with Audrey Hepburn and Mel Ferrer. Litvak's later films include *The Journey* (1959), *Goodbye Again* (1961), *Five Miles to Midnight* (1962), *Night of the Generals* (1967), and *The Lady in the Car With Glasses and a Gun* (1970).

LIVESEY, ROGER. Actor. (b. June 25, 1906, Barry, South Wales; d. Feb. 5, 1976.) Stocky, genial British supporting player and character lead with a most distinctive voice, equally effective in good-natured best friend and blustery, thick-lipped roles. He came from an acting family; his father Sam and brothers Jack and Barry all appeared on stage and screen during lengthy careers. His best screen work was done for director Michael Powell and screenwriter Emeric Pressburger: first in the title role of *The Life and Death of Colonel Blimp* (1943, playing a staunch, somewhat thickheaded officer followed over a period of several decades), then in the quirky romantic comedy *I Know Where I'm Going!* (1945) and the wartime fantasy *Stairway to Heaven* (originally titled *A Matter of Life and Death;* 1946), in which he played the surgeon/advocate.
OTHER FILMS INCLUDE: 1921: *The Four Feathers;* 1931: *East Lynne on the Western Front;* 1935: *Lorna Doone;* 1936: *Rembrandt;* 1938: *Drums;* 1940: *Girl in the News;* 1949: *If This Be Sin;* 1953: *The Master of Ballantrae;* 1960: *The League of Gentlemen, The Entertainer;* 1964: *Of Human Bondage;* 1965: *The Amorous Adventures of Moll Flanders;* 1969: *Hamlet.*

LIVINGSTON, ROBERT. Actor. (b. Dec. 9, 1908, Quincy, Ill., as Robert E. Randall; d. Mar. 7, 1988.) This handsome, wavy-haired leading man at one time played both Zorro (in 1936's *The Bold Caballero*) and The Lone Ranger (in a 1939 serial, *The Lone Ranger Rides Again*). A former journalist, Livingston drifted into acting in the late 1920s, first appearing in one of Universal's "Collegians" shorts. He was signed by MGM in 1934, and worked in many shorts and features—including *Mutiny on the Bounty* (1935) and *Three Godfathers* (1936)—and was being groomed for stardom, but lost the male lead opposite Greta Garbo in *Camille* (1937) to his friend Robert Taylor. On a dare, he answered an ad from Republic, then scouting for actors to play "The Three Mesquiteers" in a new Western series. He won the part of Stony Brooke, the hotheaded member of the trio, and played it in 30 B Westerns from 1936 to 1941 (with occasional sabbaticals during which he starred in "civilian" pictures). He left Republic to play "The Lone Rider" (a Lone Ranger knockoff) in six poorly made PRC Westerns of 1942–43, then returned to his home studio and teamed with pert Ruth Terry in *Pistol Packin' Mama* (1943), *Goodnight Sweetheart* (1944), and *Tell It to a Star* (1945). By decade's end he was playing heavies in such cheapies as *The Feathered Serpent* (1948, an anemic Charlie Chan mystery) and *Riders in the Sky* (1949).

Livingston worked steadily into the mid 1950s, in B Westerns and on TV, before retiring. He was coaxed back in front of the camera by independent producer Sam Sherman, who starred him in *The Naughty Stewardesses, Girls for Rent* (both 1974), and *Blazing Stewardesses* (1975, his last film). The failure of Livingston—a talented, personable leading man—to achieve greater success is one of moviedom's great mysteries. Livingston's brother Addison was also a cowboy star, billed as Jack Randall.

LLOYD, CHRISTOPHER. Actor. *(b. Oct. 22, 1938, Stamford, Conn.)* This tall, odd-looking supporting actor has forged a successful screen career as the preeminent delineator of eccentric and, occasionally, dangerous characters. Lloyd made an unnerving screen debut as one of the mental patients in *One Flew Over the Cuckoo's Nest* (1975), and over the next several years played small, weird parts in such films as *Goin' South* (1978), *The Onion Field, The Lady in Red* (both 1979, in the latter as a gangster named "Frogface"), and *The Black Marble* (1980). His icy villainy was the only notable element in the otherwise execrable *The Legend of the Lone Ranger* (1981). But a one-shot appearance on the TV sitcom "Taxi" as a freaked-out druggie led to a regular role (1979–83), two Emmys, and bona fide stardom as the burned-out Reverend Jim. Bigger movie roles followed, including a Nazi in *To Be or Not to Be* (1983), an escaped lunatic in *The Adventures of Buckaroo Banzai,* and even a Klingon in *Star Trek III: The Search for Spock* (both 1984). In 1985, he scored as the wigged-out Doc Brown in *Back to the Future*—a sympathetic role he repeated in 1989 and 1990 sequels, even getting the girl (Mary Steenburgen) in the latter. (He has continued to play the part on a Saturday morning TV series offshoot, and shot special footage for the multimedia "Back to the Future" ride for the Universal theme parks.) Cast more to type, he has also appeared as the shady Professor Plum in *Clue* (1985), a toy-train-obsessed doctor in *Track 29,* a corrupt gambler in *Eight Men Out,* the evil Judge Doom in *Who Framed Roger Rabbit* (all 1988), and an escaped mental patient in *The Dream Team* (1989). In 1991 he finally reached a sort-of milestone by playing a nice, normal guy in *Suburban Commando* . . . but immediately followed it as ooky Uncle Fester in *The*

Addams Family. In 1992 he won an Emmy for a guest appearance as a drama teacher cum drifter on the TV series "Avonlea." Recent movies include *T-Bone and Weasel* (1992, made for cable), *Dennis the Menace, Twenty Bucks, Addams Family Values* (all 1993), *Angels in the Outfield, Camp Nowhere* (both 1994), and the short "interactive" film *Mr. Payback* (1995).

LLOYD, EMILY. Actress. *(b. Sept. 29, 1970, London.)* This cute, spunky young lead made a commanding debut as a shamelessly sexual teenager in David Leland's British drama *Wish You Were Here* (1987). Two years later she successfully dropped her English accent for two American films—as a Kentuckian in Norman Jewison's post-Vietnam drama *In Country* and as a mobster's daughter in Susan Seidelman's *Cookie* (both 1989). Her films, which also include the British-made *Chicago Joe and the Showgirl* (1990), have yet to meet with the commercial success her talents deserve. She "went American" again for director Robert Redford in *A River Runs Through It* (1992).

LLOYD, FRANK. Director. *(b. Feb. 2, 1888, Glasgow; d. Aug. 10, 1960.)* The son of a U.K. music-hall star, Lloyd himself hit the boards while still a teenager. Touring with a stock company in 1913, he came to America and decided to stay. He entered films in 1914 as an actor and began directing a year later, turning out dozens of films, among them popular adaptations of *A Tale of Two Cities* (1917), *Riders of the Purple Sage, Les Miserables* (both 1918), *Madame X* (1920), *Oliver Twist* (1922), and *Black Oxen* (1924). He won his first Oscar for *The Divine Lady* (1929), a lavish costume drama starring Corinne Griffith, and his first film to utilize sound (albeit music and sound effects only).

An accomplished if prosaic journeyman, Lloyd adapted readily to talkie filmmaking and helmed many prestige productions in the 1930s, among them the Oscar-winning Best Picture *Mutiny on the Bounty* (1935), *Under Two Flags* (1936), *Wells Fargo* (1937), and *If I Were King* (1938). Although he had an all-but-invisible directorial "style," Lloyd was adept at drawing together top talent on both sides of the camera, and bringing out the best in his people. This skill was never more apparent than in *Cavalcade* (1933), another Best Picture winner, for which he won his second Best Director Oscar; an elaborate recreation of early 20th-century England, based on a Noël Coward stage hit, it amazed even native-born Brits with its painstaking attention to detail.

Also active as a producer, Lloyd oversaw several films at Universal, including *The Spoilers, Invisible Agent,* and Hitchcock's *Saboteur* (all 1942). He directed James Cagney in the 1945 drama of pre–Pearl Harbor intrigue in Japan, *Blood on the Sun,* but was less active in the years to follow. Lloyd's last film was *The Last Command* (1955), an overlong Trucolor account of the battle of the Alamo, for which the action scenes (which won Lloyd much praise) were actually directed by B-Western veteran William Witney.

LLOYD, HAROLD. Actor, producer. *(b. Apr. 20, 1893, Burchard, Nebr.; d. Mar. 8, 1971.)* Harold Lloyd was often dismissed as a comedian without heart who was more interested in building gags than in exploring the human condition. The sight of Lloyd dangling from the arms of a skyscraper clock in *Safety Last* (1923) cemented the star's reputation as "the king of daredevil comedy," one that he never really shook. But there was more to Lloyd than thrill-based humor, and his boy next door underdog character has proven as durable as any of those of his comedy colleagues from the silent era. As revivals of his films continually prove, Lloyd's films are virtually audience-proof, even after all these years.

After moving to San Diego as a boy, Lloyd began his movie apprenticeship in 1912 as an extra for the Edison Company. By 1913 he was in Hollywood, where he struck up a friendship with fellow extra Hal Roach. Roach inherited $3,000 in 1915 and set himself up as a producer, hiring Lloyd as his lead comedian. After some initial disappointments, they developed the character of "Lonesome Luke" in rough and tumble shorts like *Just Nuts* (1915) and *Stop! Luke! Listen!* (1917). The character was a barely disguised imitation of Chaplin's tramp, and despite his

success, Lloyd chafed at being a second-string derivative.

In 1917 he created the "glasses" character—a normal boy without eccentric makeup whose identifying signature was a simple pair of horn-rimmed glasses. The spectacles gave Lloyd vulnerability, and the character evolved into a shy, lovelorn youth perpetually struggling to win the big game, land the right job, impress the beautiful girl. His unflagging exuberance and optimism encapsulated the American spirit in the heady days after World War 1 and the Roaring Twenties, although neither Lloyd nor Roach attached such a lofty interpretation to the character's success with audiences.

While posing for publicity photos in 1920, Lloyd was injured when a prop bomb turned out to be real; he lost both thumb and forefinger on his right hand and was temporarily blinded. Though his eyesight returned and his face was unmarred, he took to wearing a nearly unnoticeable prosthetic device and flesh-colored glove on-screen, and carried on performing his hair-raising stunts. Lloyd adapted his short-comedy style into feature-length films beginning with *A Sailor-Made Man* (1921). His breakthrough film came the following year with *Grandma's Boy,* a heartfelt parody of Charles Ray's 1915 drama *The Coward.* In 1923, after making *Why Worry?,* one of his best films, Lloyd married his leading lady, Mildred Davis, and left Roach to become his own producer. *Girl Shy* (1924), *The Freshman* (1925), *For Heaven's Sake* (1926), and *The Kid Brother* (1927) were well constructed, hilarious, and beautifully photographed, making him the most popular screen comedian of the 1920s.

Lloyd's success continued into the sound era with *Welcome Danger* (1929) and *Feet First* (1931), but *Movie Crazy* (1932), although one of his best talkies, was a box-office disappointment. Feeling the need for change, Lloyd experimented with a different kind of comedy in *The Cat's Paw* (1934), and put himself in the hands of a strong comedy director, Leo McCarey, for *The Milky Way* (1936), but it was evident that newer, fresher screen comics were dominating the screen. *Professor Beware* (1938) marked a further erosion in his popularity, and while Lloyd never officially retired he drifted out of filmmaking. In the early 1940s he was briefly a producer for RKO, and in 1947 writer-director Preston Sturges persuaded him to take the lead in *The Sin of Harold Diddlebock*, which explored what might have happened to that go-getting Lloyd character of the 1920s; it even opened with footage from Harold's 1925 hit, *The Freshman*. A troubled production that distressed Lloyd, it was finally released in truncated form as *Mad Wednesday* in 1950, and did nothing to revive his career. In 1962 Lloyd prepared a compilation film called *Harold Lloyd's World of Comedy*, which sparked a revival of interest in his work. He talked of mounting a major reissue of his earlier films, but seemed content to do personal appearances with the movies at college campuses and film festivals. He published an autobiography, "An American Comedy," in 1928; it was later reissued. In 1992 his granddaughter Suzanne Lloyd Hayes published "3-D Hollywood," a collection of the comedian's 3-D photography.

LLOYD, NORMAN. Actor, director, producer. *(b. Nov. 8, 1914, Jersey City, N.J.)* This distinguished, mellifluous-voiced actor is probably best known as Dr. Auschlander from the TV series "St. Elsewhere" (1982–88) but he has amassed an impressive body of work in virtually every medium. He began in theater, acting with such groups as The Mercury Theatre, run by John Houseman and Orson Welles, before Alfred Hitchcock selected him to portray the villainous Fry, who dangles from the Statue of Liberty in *Saboteur* (1942). He worked again with Hitchcock in *Spellbound* (1945) and later served as associate producer on the TV anthology "Alfred Hitchcock Presents" (1957–62), for which he also directed a number of episodes. Lloyd also served as a production associate with Jean Renoir (*The Southerner*, 1945) and Charlie Chaplin (*Limelight*, 1952) and was very busy as a character actor from the mid-1940s to the early 1950s, appearing in *The Unseen, A Walk in the Sun* (both 1945), *The Green Years* (1946), *The Beginning or the End* (1947), *No Minor Vices* (1948), *Calamity Jane and Sam Bass, Scene of the Crime, Reign of Terror* (all 1949), *The Flame and the Arrow, Buccaneer's Girl* (both 1950), *He Ran All the Way*, and *The Light Touch* (both 1951). He spent most of his time af-

ter that acting and directing for TV and the stage, although he had supporting roles in *Audrey Rose* (1977), *FM* (1978), and *The Nude Bomb* (1980) and recently made memorable contributions to *Dead Poets Society* (1989, as the stern headmaster) and *The Age of Innocence* (1993). His Directors Guild of America oral history was published as "Stages" in 1990.

LOACH, KEN. Director, screenwriter. *(b. June 17, 1936, Warwickshire, England.)* Politically active, humane filmmaker known for his examinations of class conflict, who studied law at Oxford before training as an actor and then as a director with the BBC. He and producer Tony Garrett, who shared similar views regarding the potential impact of TV for social change, worked on several TV films—notably *Up the Junction* (1965) and *Cathy Come Home* (1966)—which were made in a very stark, realistic style. *Poor Cow* (1967), Loach's feature debut about a teenage girl's troubled life, was directed in similar documentary-type fashion, but *Kes* (1969), about a young boy and his trained falcon, offered at least the glimmer of hope in a grim look at the stifling impact of an unfeeling class system. After *Family Life* (1971), which powerfully portrayed a young woman's mental deterioration, Loach worked mostly in TV, and resurfaced for *Black Jack* (1980), an adaptation of a children's novel. He returned to examinations of social inequities with *The Gamekeeper* (1980) and *Looks and Smiles* (1981) and changed pace with *Singing the Blues in Red/Fatherland* (1986), about an artist exiled to West Berlin. *Hidden Agenda* (1990) was an exciting, trenchant political thriller that was outspoken about British involvement in Ireland. *Riff-Raff* (1991) was a rare stab at comedy which had to be subtitled in U.S. release because the accents and dialects of its cast were so thick! *Raining Stones* (1993) and *Ladybird, Ladybird* (1994) show that Loach has lost none of his bite or socially conscious energy.

LOCKE, SONDRA. Actress, director. *(b. May 28, 1947, Shelbyville, Tenn.)* Slim, blonde waiflike leading lady whose debut movie role, 1968's *The Heart Is a Lonely Hunter*, earned her an Oscar nomination for Best Supporting Actress. Subsequent films include *Cover Me Babe* (1970), *Willard* (1971), and *A Reflection of Fear* (1973). She later starred opposite then-boyfriend Clint Eastwood in a half-dozen of his vehicles, including *The Outlaw Josey Wales* (1976), *The Gauntlet* (1977), *Every Which Way but Loose* (1978), *Any Which Way You Can, Bronco Billy* (both 1980, the latter probably their best collaboration), and *Sudden Impact* (1983). In 1986, she turned her focus to directing with the poorly received *Ratboy.* Her next effort, the 1990 cop-thriller *Impulse*, fared just slightly better.

LOCKHART, GENE. Actor. *(b. July 18, 1891, Ontario; d. Apr. 1, 1957.)* He was one of the screen's most versatile character actors, capable of making audiences laugh while playing a cheerful cherub in one film, and making them hiss while playing a conniving weasel in the next. Puffy-faced and jowly, this stage veteran portrayed gentility and brutality with equal skill and relish. He debuted on-screen in *Smilin' Through* (1922), but didn't actively pursue movie roles until 1935. Among some of his more memorable characterizations: the doddering suitor Lushin in *Crime and Punishment* (1935), the sniveling informant Regis in *Algiers* (1938, an Oscar-nominated performance), the unfortunate Bob Cratchit in *A Christmas Carol* (also 1938), corrupt sheriff "Pinky" Hartwell in *His Girl Friday,* Stephen Douglas in *Abe Lincoln in Illinois* (both 1940), and the revolutionary Molotov in *Mission to Moscow* (1943).

Lockhart's wife Kathleen was also an accomplished actress and appeared in many films; although several years older than Gene, she outlived him by 20 years. Their daughter June (*b. June 25, 1925*), who debuted with her parents in *A Christmas Carol* (1938), appeared in a number of 1940s films—including *Sergeant York* (1941), *Meet Me in St. Louis* (1944), *She-Wolf of London* (1946, in the title role), and *T-Men* (1947)—before becoming a small-screen star in the TV series "Lassie" (1958–64) and "Lost in Space" (1965–68), among others. June's daughter Anne carried on the family tradition, appearing in several low-budget movies and telefilms throughout the 1970s and 1980s. OTHER FILMS INCLUDE: 1935: *Star of*

Midnight; 1936: *The Garden Murder Case, The Devil Is a Sissy;* 1937: *Make Way for Tomorrow;* 1938: *Blondie, Sweethearts;* 1939: *The Story of Alexander Graham Bell, Tell No Tales, Blackmail;* 1940: *Edison the Man, A Dispatch From Reuters;* 1941: *Meet John Doe, The Sea Wolf, Billy the Kid, The Devil and Daniel Webster* (aka *All That Money Can Buy);* 1942: *They Died With Their Boots On;* 1943: *Hangmen Also Die, Northern Pursuit, The Desert Song;* 1944: *Going My Way;* 1945: *The House on 92nd Street, Leave Her to Heaven;* 1947: *Miracle on 34th Street, The Foxes of Harrow;* 1948: *Apartment for Peggy, Joan of Arc;* 1949: *Madame Bovary, The Inspector General;* 1950: *Riding High;* 1951: *I'd Climb the Highest Mountain;* 1952: *A Girl in Every Port, The Hoodlum Empire;* 1953: *Androcles and the Lion;* 1956: *Carousel, The Man in the Gray Flannel Suit;* 1957: *Jeanne Eagels* (his last).

LOCKWOOD, MARGARET. Actress. *(b. Sept. 15, 1916, Karachi, as Margaret Day; d. July 15, 1990.)* Flashing-eyed, dark-haired British beauty who was successful as a screen ingenue in the 1930s and early 1940s, but found her real metier in the portrayal of wicked, mysterious females in costume dramas made later in the decade. Already an experienced stage actress when she made her film debut in 1934's *Lorna Doone,* Lockwood adapted readily to the new medium. She appeared in *Midshipman Easy* (1935), *The Amateur Gentleman* (1936), *Dr. Syn* (1937), *Bank Holiday* (1938), and several other British-made films before achieving international recognition as the plucky heroine of Alfred Hitchcock's *The Lady Vanishes* (1938). She went to Hollywood in 1939, but her two American films—*Susannah of the Mounties* and *Rulers of the Sea*—didn't set the town on fire, and she returned to England. She gave a first-rate performance in Carol Reed's coal-mining drama, *The Stars Look Down,* and was an ideal leading lady in the Hitchcockian *Night Train to Munich* (both 1940).

Lockwood starred in a number of unimportant British films during the war years, then suddenly made an amazing about-face and took a deliciously malevolent starring role as *The Wicked Lady* (1945), a scheming vixen who teams with highwayman James Mason in that costume melodrama. It was a rousing success that revi-

talized her career, and she continued to star in period pictures. Lockwood retired from films fairly early, sensing that her starring career was drawing to a close. She did, however, return to the screen as Cinderella's wicked stepmother in *The Slipper and the Rose* (1977). Her autobiography, "Lucky Star," was published in 1955.
OTHER FILMS INCLUDE: 1946: *Bedelia;* 1947: *Hungry Hill, Jassy, Bad Sister;* 1949: *Cardboard Cavalier* (playing Nell Gwyn); 1950: *Highly Dangerous;* 1952: *Trent's Last Case* (still very attractive in modern dress, but mired in an unconvincing mystery); 1954: *Trouble in the Glen;* 1955: *Cast a Dark Shadow.*

LODER, JOHN. Actor. *(b. Jan. 3, 1898, London, as John Lowe; d. Dec. 9, 1988.)* The epitome of British reserve, this stolid, square-jawed actor appeared in dozens of British- and American-made films of the 1930s and 1940s, yet rarely gave a performance that could be described as memorable. Loder, the son of a British general, won a commission in Her Majesty's Service himself, and was a prisoner of war during World War 1. He took a job as an extra in the 1926 German-made *Madame Wants No Children* (which also featured a young Marlene Dietrich), and decided to pursue an acting career. By 1929 he was in Hollywood, working in silent and early talkie films, including *Sunset Pass* (1929), *The Seas Beneath* (1931), and a Thelma Todd/ZaSu Pitts comedy short, "Let's Do Things." Back in the U.K., Loder carved out a niche for himself as the ramrod-stiff (but dependable) leading man (or juvenile lead) of *Java Head, Lorna Doone* (both 1934), *The Man Who Lived Again, Sabotage* (both 1936), *Dr. Syn, Non-Stop New York* (both 1937), and *Murder Will Out* (1939). Returning to Hollywood, he found himself stuck in character roles and occasional leads in nondescript B pictures.

He worked in *Tin Pan Alley* (1940), *How Green Was My Valley* (1941), *Now, Voyager, Gentleman Jim* (both 1942), *The Gorilla Man, The Mysterious Doctor, Murder on the Waterfront* (all 1943), *Passage to Marseille,* and *The Hairy Ape* (both 1944), among others, before getting three juicy lead roles in succession: a sympathetic lover in *Jealousy,* an actor turned maniac killer in *The Brighton*

Strangler (both 1945), and a shipwrecked sportsman in *A Game of Death* (1946, a remake of *The Most Dangerous Game*). He appeared onscreen sporadically thereafter, in *The Wife of Monte Cristo* (1946), *Dishonored Lady* (1947, supporting then-wife Hedy Lamarr), *The Story of Esther Costello* (1957, back in England), and *Gideon of Scotland Yard* (1958) before retiring. He later moved to Argentina with his fifth wife.

LOGAN, JOSHUA. Director. *(b. Oct. 5, 1908, Texarkana, Tex.; d. July 12, 1988.)* Renowned theater director who also forged a successful, though limited, film career. While studying at Princeton, he helped form the University Players, a stock company whose members included James Stewart, Henry Fonda, and Margaret Sullavan. Logan studied with the great teacher Konstantin Stanislavsky in Moscow, and later began his Broadway career, directing such classic productions as "Annie Get Your Gun," "John Loves Mary," "Mister Roberts," "South Pacific" and "Fanny" (the last three of which he also cowrote). He had already worked in Hollywood, during the 1930s, as a dialogue director on the Charles Boyer films *The Garden of Allah* (1936) and *History Is Made at Night* (1937) and codirected the melodrama *I Met My Love Again* in 1938. After his numerous stage successes, Logan resumed his career with *Picnic* (1955), an excellent adaptation of the William Inge play, which won kudos from critics and earned him an Oscar nomination for Best Director. Logan had similar success with *Bus Stop* (1956, which gave Marilyn Monroe one of her best roles) and scored another Best Director nomination for *Sayonara* (1957), a popular romantic story with Marlon Brando falling in love with a Japanese entertainer during the Korean War. He did a surprisingly flat job in bringing *South Pacific* to the screen in 1958, and *Tall Story* (1960) did little more than introduce audiences to Jane Fonda. By the time of the lavishly mounted *Fanny* (1961), Logan had fallen out of critical favor: *Ensign Pulver* (1964), a sequel to *Mister Roberts,* was a dud, and his next projects, *Camelot* (1967) and *Paint Your Wagon* (1969), were overproduced, joyless musical adaptations that showed little spark or ingenuity (although *Wagon* did feature the novelty of Lee Marvin and Clint Eastwood singing). Though he made no further films, Logan continued to remain active in the theater and even served as a production consultant on a live TV production of "Mister Roberts" in 1984. He wrote an autobiography, "Josh" (1976), and also "Movie Stars, People, and Me" (1978).

LOGGIA, ROBERT. Actor. *(b. Jan. 3, 1930, Staten Island, N.Y.)* As an occasional leading man in the 1950s and 1960s, this tough, leathery actor often seemed wooden and unconvincing. As a gruff but lovable supporting player in the 1980s and 1990s, he's come into his own. An alumnus of the prestigious Actors' Studio, Loggia made his screen debut in *Somebody Up There Likes Me* (1956), and won a starring role in the bleak sci-fi saga *The Lost Missile* (1958). He achieved greater success on TV, first in 1959 as the "unkillable" lawman Elfego Baca on "Walt Disney Presents," then in 1965 as a supercool cat burglar turned crime-fighter on "T.H.E. Cat." Loggia's better feature roles include *Che* (1969), *The Ninth Configuration* (1980), *S.O.B.* (1981), *An Officer and a Gentleman* (1982), *Psycho II* (1983), as well as three Pink Panther movies, and he was memorably nasty in *Scarface* (1983) and *Prizzi's Honor* (1985). His Oscar-nominated role as the foul-mouthed investigator in *Jagged Edge* (1985) finally boosted him to the top rank of character actors, and he even nabbed such comedy roles as the boozy priest in *That's Life!* (1986) and the kindly toy magnate in *Big* (1988). His performance in the miniseries "Favorite Son" led to a spinoff series, "Mancuso, FBI" (1989–90). He later starred in the Norman Lear sitcom "Sunday Dinner," and continued his comic ways in such features as *Opportunity Knocks* (1990), *The Marrying Man*, and *Necessary Roughness* (both 1991). Loggia played a mobster turned vampire in the black comedy *Innocent Blood* (1992). In 1994 he appeared in *I Love Trouble*.

LOLLOBRIGIDA, GINA. Actress. *(b. July 4, 1927, Subiaco, Italy.)* When Americans got their first look at "La Lollo" in the late 1940s, she was proclaimed the best thing to come from Italy since spaghetti. She held that distinction until being eclipsed by Sophia Loren (a younger bombshell and better actress) in the late 1950s. Lollobrigida, a graduate of the Rome Academy of Fine Arts well versed in painting and sculpture, never became a professional artist but, instead, inspired artists—first as a model, then as a much-photographed beauty-contest winner. Within a few years of her film debut in *Aquila Nera* (1946) the earthy, voluptuous Lollobrigida had become one of the Italian film industry's top stars. Originally slated for an American film debut in 1949, she lost the opportunity due to a contract foul-up with Howard Hughes. Ironically, her first "Hollywood" film was John Huston's *Beat the Devil* (1954), which was largely shot in Italy. When she finally got to Hollywood, she was seen as just another sex symbol, and she was shunted from one witless picture to another. Lollobrigida returned to Europe, and retired from the screen in the early 1970s to market cosmetics and fashions. She also put some of her artistic training to use as a professional photographer. She made a couple of appearances in European-made TV dramas in the mid 1980s, still looking beautiful.

OTHER FILMS INCLUDE: 1948: *I Pagliacci;* 1950: *The White Line;* 1951: *Fan-Fan the Tulip, The Young Caruso;* 1952: *The Unfaithful;* 1954: *Crossed Swords, Woman of Rome;* 1955: *Beautiful but Dangerous;* 1956: *Trapeze;* 1957: *The Hunchback of Notre Dame* (as Esmeralda to Anthony Quinn's Quasimodo); 1958: *Fast and Sexy;* 1959: *Solomon and Sheba* (as the Queen of Sheba), *Never So Few;* 1961: *Come September;* 1964: *Woman of Straw;* 1965: *Strange Bedfellows;* 1966: *Hotel Paradiso;* 1968: *The Private Navy of Sgt. O'Farrell;* 1969: *Buona Sera, Mrs. Campbell;* 1972: *King Queen Knave;* 1975: *The Lonely Woman.*

LOM, HERBERT. Actor. *(b. Jan. 9, 1917, Prague, as Herbert Charles Schluderpacheru.)* Polished Czechoslovakian actor who has logged screen time in romantic leads and sinister supporting roles alike, and who played the title role in the 1962 remake of *The Phantom of the Opera*, but is best known as the twitching, mugging, scene-stealing Sûreté inspector in the "Pink Panther" films: *A Shot in the Dark* (1964),

The Return of the Pink Panther (1975), *The Pink Panther Strikes Again* (1976), *Revenge of the Pink Panther* (1978), *Trail of the Pink Panther* (1982), *Curse of the Pink Panther* (1983), and ten years later, *Son of the Pink Panther* (1993). At one time considered a British counterpart to Charles Boyer (whom he resembled), Lom didn't get as many starring assignments as he rated, but makes a lasting impression in character parts, from the surly mountain climber in Disney's *Third Man on the Mountain* (1959) to a pirate chieftain in *Spartacus* (1960) to Christopher Walken's sympathetic doctor in *The Dead Zone* (1983). He has also played Napoleon twice—in 1942's *The Young Mr. Pitt* and 1956's *War and Peace.*
OTHER FILMS INCLUDE: 1945: *The Seventh Veil;* 1950: *Night and the City;* 1953: *The Paris Express;* 1955: *The Ladykillers;* 1957: *Fire Down Below;* 1959: *The Big Fisherman;* 1961: *Mysterious Island* (as Captain Nemo); 1961: *El Cid;* 1966: *Gambit;* 1968: *Villa Rides;* 1970: *The Secret of Dorian Gray;* 1970: *Count Dracula;* 1971: *Murders in the Rue Morgue;* 1973: *And Now the Screaming Starts!;* 1975: *Ten Little Indians;* 1979: *The Lady Vanishes;* 1980: *Hopscotch;* 1985: *King Solomon's Mines;* 1987: *Skeleton Coast;* 1989: *Ten Little Indians* (again!); 1991: *The Pope Must Die(t).*

LOMBARD, CAROLE. Actress. *(b. Oct. 6, 1908, Fort Wayne, Ind., as Jane Alice Peters; d. Jan. 19, 1942.)* The epitome of the screwball heroine, this saucy, fast-talking blonde was Hollywood's top comedy actress of the 1930s and subsequently became an icon to a later generation of wannabes, despite a relatively slim body of work. She broke into film in the silent era, first appearing onscreen as a child in *A Perfect Crime* (1921). Throughout the 1920s she toiled in low-budget melodramas, Westerns, and Mack Sennett slapstick comedies. Although Lombard's voice was fine for talkies, she made little impact on audiences during the early sound years, mired as she was in lackluster vehicles and roles that repressed her natural warmth and exuberance. She attracted some attention opposite then-husband William Powell in *Ladies' Man* and *Man of the World* (both 1931), husband-to-be Clark Gable in *No Man of Her Own* (1932), Cary Grant and Fredric

March in *The Eagle and the Hawk* (1933), and George Raft in *Bolero* (1934).
Once home studio Paramount loaned her out for *Twentieth Century* (1934), Lombard found her true metier; cast as a mercurial actress, and goaded mercilessly by director Howard Hawks and costar John Barrymore, she responded with a fiery, sometimes over-the-top performance that made the film—and her—a smash, virtually inventing screwball comedy in the process. Now established as a comedienne—and a star—she carried such films as *Hands Across the Table* (1935), *The Princess Comes Across, Love Before Breakfast* (both 1936), and two screwball comedy milestones, *My Man Godfrey* (1936, in which she was Oscar-nominated for her superb performance as a dizzy heiress, opposite real-life ex-husband William Powell), and *Nothing Sacred* (1937, as naive Hazel Flagg, who's knocked cold in one famous scene by wiseguy reporter Fredric March). *True Confession* (1937) was another tailor-made vehicle, which cast her opposite frequent (and highly compatible) costar Fred MacMurray.
Very few leading ladies in Hollywood were capable of being sexy and funny at the same time, but Lombard did it with ease, and her rapid-fire dialogue delivery and wry double takes set a standard rarely matched by subsequent screen actresses. She brought the same conviction and unaffected approach to dramatic roles in *Swing High, Swing Low* (1937), *Made for Each Other, In Name Only* (both 1939), *Vigil in the Night,* and *They Knew What They Wanted* (both 1940), before returning to screwball with *Mr. and Mrs. Smith* (1941), directed by Alfred Hitchcock, of all people; she insisted on directing him in his inevitable cameo appearance, riding him as ruthlessly as he had her. (This event was chronicled in the RKO short subject *Picture People.*) The landmark black comedy *To Be or Not to Be* (1942), an Ernst Lubitsch–directed story set in Nazi-occupied Poland, proved to be her last film; before its release, she was killed in a plane crash while on a War Bond tour, leaving husband Clark Gable and millions of fans desolate. Many have hoped to replace her; none have succeeded (least of all Jill Clayburgh, who played her in an inept 1976 biopic, *Gable and Lombard).*

LONE, JOHN. Actor. *(b. Oct. 13, 1952, Hong Kong.)* Lone's own background is as interesting as any of the startlingly varied characters he has played. His parents separated before he was born, and at the age of ten Lone was sent to Hong Kong's Peking Opera, an enclosed society that rigorously teaches the traditions of classical Chinese theater. He left the troupe and came to the United States, sponsored by an American family doing business in Hong Kong. He earned praise for his stage work in New York and made a remarkable film debut as the thawed-out Neanderthal in Fred Schepisi's *Iceman* (1984). He was the best thing in *Year of the Dragon* (1985) and gained international fame as the title character of Bernardo Bertolucci's Oscar-winning epic *The Last Emperor* (1987). He also appeared in the Australian-made *Echoes of Paradise* (also 1987), Alan Rudolph's *The Moderns* (1988), and *Shadow of China* (1990), and was the mysterious Beijing opera diva in David Cronenberg's flat adaptation of *M. Butterfly* (1993). Most recently, Lone played the evil Shiwan Khan in *The Shadow* (1994).

LONG, SHELLEY. Actress. *(b. Aug. 23, 1949, Fort Wayne, Ind.)* This savvy comic actress established herself in feature films, became a star on TV, then returned to movies with decidedly mixed results.

She worked in TV, both as producer and performer, before joining Chicago's Second City comedy troupe. Her first film was *A Small Circle of Friends* (1980), followed by one of the female leads in *Caveman* (1981). Long's performance as the cheerful hooker in *Night Shift* (1982) led to her casting as snooty barmaid Diane Chambers in "Cheers" (1982–87), a tailor-made role that brought her stardom and an Emmy. (Around that same time, she made *Losin' It,* a small-scale comedy released in 1983, in which she starred opposite an up-and-comer named Tom Cruise.) She was equally effective as a screenwriter in *Irreconcilable Differences* (1984), which encouraged her to leave her hit sitcom in 1987 to concentrate on features. Long did excellent work in such lightweight fare as *The Money Pit* (1986), *Hello Again* (1987), and *Outrageous Fortune* (also 1987, felicitously teamed with Bette Midler), but increasingly poor career choices (1989's *Troop Beverly Hills,* 1990's *Don't Tell Her It's Me)* and poorer scripts have derailed her express train to stardom—temporarily, at least. In 1992 she starred opposite fellow TV star Corbin Bernsen in *Frozen Assets.* She launched another starring sitcom "Good Advice" (1993–94) before playing Carol Brady in *The Brady Bunch Movie* (1995).

LOREN, SOPHIA. Actress. *(b. Sept. 20, 1934, Rome, as Sofia Scicolone.)* To many she's best remembered as the voluptuous, jet-haired siren of many 1960s Italian sex comedies, but this international star is a talented actress as well (the first performer to win an Oscar for a performance given entirely in a foreign language, as a woman raped by two soldiers in 1961's *Two Women).* Born into poverty, she nursed ambitions of becoming an actress at a very early age, and as soon as her budding physical attributes would allow, she entered beauty contests as a stepping-stone to that end. (She also appeared as an extra in *Quo Vadis?,* filmed in 1949 but not released until 1951.) In fact, Loren first encountered her mentor (and future husband), Italian producer Carlo Ponti, when he helped judge a contest in which she was entered. He sensed star potential in the ambitious teenager, and signed her to a contract. She played a bit in the 1950 Federico Fellini film *Variety Lights,* which launched her screen career in earnest. Loren's earthy sensuality made her an immediate screen favorite, and she achieved leading-lady status at the age of 19 in *Aida* (1953, playing the title role, though dubbed by diva Renata Tebaldi). Her other films of the period included *Attila, The Gold of Naples, Two Nights with Cleopatra* (all 1954), *Too Bad She's Bad* (1955), and *Lucky to Be a Woman* (1956).

As an established Italian star whose films got play dates in the U.S., Loren attracted the attention of American producers, who used her in Hollywood-financed productions shot abroad, including *Boy on a Dolphin* (which produced a much-published shot of a dripping wet Sophia), *Legend of the Lost,* and *The Pride and the Passion* (all 1957), all of which teamed her with major stars: Cary Grant, John Wayne, Frank Sinatra, Alan Ladd. She exerted an undeniable fascination, although American moviegoers were more impressed with her striking appearance than her thespic abilities. Indeed, when Loren made the inevitable pilgrimage to Hollywood, she was the recipient of a typical "glamour" buildup that detracted from her natural, earthy appeal and threatened to make her just another Tinseltown love goddess. She starred in *Desire Under the Elms, The Key, Houseboat* (all 1958), *The Black Orchid, That Kind of Woman* (both 1959), *Heller in Pink Tights,* and *A Breath of Scandal* (both 1960), among others, before returning to Italy for *Two Women,* pretty much remaining there for many years, though continuing to appear in international productions, among them *El Cid* (1961), *The Condemned of Altona* (1962), *The Fall of the Roman Empire* (1964), *Lady L* (1965), *Arabesque* (1966), and Charlie Chaplin's *A Countess From Hong Kong* (1967).

In her home country, Loren was entering her peak period, starring in bawdy Italian fare—often opposite Marcello Mastroianni and directed by Vittorio De Sica—such as *Boccaccio '70* (1962), *Yesterday, Today, and Tomorrow,* and *Marriage Italian-Style* (both 1964, and Oscar-nominated for the latter performance). She worked sporadically in the 1970s, most notably in *Mortadella* (aka *Lady Liberty*), the unfortunate *Man of La Mancha* (both 1972), *The Cassandra Crossing* (1977), *Brass Target* (1978), and *Firepower* (1979). Amid these mostly forgettable productions, *A Special Day* (1977) easily stood out, as it reunited her with Mastroianni, in a serious film directed by Ettore Scola. Loren has since moved to the U.S. and starred in a handful of TV movies and miniseries, including *Aurora* (1984, in which her son Edouardo Ponti made his acting debut), *Courage* (1986), Mario Puzo's *The Fortunate Pilgrim* (1988), and an Italian television remake of *Two Women* (1989). Having written an autobiography, "Sophia: Living and Loving," in 1979, she starred in a television adaptation, *Sophia Loren: Her Own Story,* the following year. She teamed up with Mastroianni again for Robert Altman's *Ready to Wear/Prêt-à-Porter* (1994). In 1991 she received a second, special Academy Award for the whole of her distinguished career.

LORRE, PETER. Actor. *(b. June 26, 1904, Rozsahegy, Hungary, as Ladislav*

Loewenstein; d. Mar. 23, 1964.) Few screen actors have ever had as powerful a first film as Peter Lorre's *M* (1931), made in Germany by Fritz Lang. He is positively mesmerizing as the pathetic child murderer, delivering an unforgettable performance that made him an internationally recognized personality if not a major star. He was a peculiar little man, almost gnomelike, with moon face, bulging eyes, and gapped teeth, and as good a character actor as ever worked in Hollywood. He fled Germany in the early 1930s, appearing in both British and American films, including two directed by Alfred Hitchcock: *The Man Who Knew Too Much* (1934) and *Secret Agent* (1936).

With his florid portrayal of a mad doctor in the Grand Guignol–like *Mad Love* (1935), Lorre took Hollywood—then in the midst of its first talkie horror cycle—by storm. That same year he played Raskolnikov in von Sternberg's uneven *Crime and Punishment*—and he was off and running. At 20th Century-Fox, Lorre was cast as Japanese sleuth Mr. Moto in eight B films made from 1937 to 1939, of which *Thank You, Mr. Moto* (1937) was the best. He also had memorable roles in bottom-of-the-bill pictures, some of which were little gems: 1940's *The Stranger on the Third Floor,* for example, was an excellent short thriller with more than a touch of German Expressionism in its visual style. But Lorre's real breakthrough with American audiences came with his oily performance as sinister but fastidious Joel Cairo in John Huston's adaptation of *The Maltese Falcon* (1941). (He shared other memorable moments with *Falcon* star Humphrey Bogart in 1942's *Casablanca.)*

Lorre and *Falcon* menace Sydney Greenstreet were seen as a great screen team, and they subsequently appeared together in several films such as 1944's *The Mask of Dimitrios* and 1946's *The Verdict* and *Three Strangers.* (He became, during this period, arguably the most mimicked and caricatured actor in movies.) As his career in character roles progressed, he began to show his comic talents more, sending up his sinister persona in the likes of *Arsenic and Old Lace* (1944) and *My Favorite Brunette* (1947). And he was a droll delight in Huston's parodic *Beat the Devil* (1954). In 1951 he returned to Germany to write, direct, and act in the rarely seen but highly regarded *Die Verlorene (The Lost One)*, a drama of betrayal set in World War 2. Lorre aged poorly during the 1950s; he grew puffy and tired-looking, and he seemed increasingly to be walking through films such as *Congo Crossing* (1956) and *The Big Circus* (1959). A frequent television guest star (whose credits ranged from a live dramatic production of Ian Fleming's "Casino Royale" in 1954 to a famous "Alfred Hitchcock Presents" episode opposite Steve McQueen), he rounded out his film career teamed with Boris Karloff and Vincent Price in both *The Raven* (1963) and *The Comedy of Terrors* (1964), in which he was very funny indeed. In fact, his performance as the half-man, half-raven endeared Lorre to a whole new generation of fans.

OTHER FILMS INCLUDE: 1937: *Lancer Spy;* 1941: *The Face Behind the Mask;* 1942: *The Boogie Man Will Get You;* 1943: *Background to Danger;* 1944: *Passage to Marseille;* 1945: *Confidential Agent;* 1946: *Black Angel, The Beast With Five Fingers;* 1948: *Casbah;* 1954: *20,000 Leagues Under the Sea;* 1956: *Around the World in Eighty Days;* 1957: *Silk Stockings;* 1961: *Voyage to the Bottom of the Sea;* 1964: *The Patsy* (his last).

LOSEY, JOSEPH. Director, producer. *(b. Jan. 14, 1909, La Crosse, Wisc., as Joseph Walton Losey III; d. June 22, 1984.)* To a generation of film buffs coming of age in the 1960s and 1970s, Joseph Losey appeared to be a very British moviemaker. During these years he resided in England, often working in collaboration with playwright-screenwriter Harold Pinter, and his films featured a distinctly European sensibility. However, he was born not in Leeds, Lancashire, or Liverpool, but in La Crosse, Wisconsin, the heart of Middle America. After studying medicine at Dartmouth and English literature at Harvard, he came to New York and eventually became involved in New Deal theater projects; his concern with using film as a tool for social analysis may be linked to his early theatrical work. Losey also began an artistic collaboration with Bertolt Brecht; in 1947, he directed Charles Laughton on stage in Brecht's "Galileo," which he was to film in 1973.

Losey had started making short films for the Rockefeller Foundation in 1938. In Hollywood, he managed to imbue mainstream movies with provocative social considerations, as in his debut, *The Boy With Green Hair* (1948), about a war orphan who is ostracized after his hair turns the title color, and *The Lawless* (1950), recounting the plight of Chicano fruit pickers in Southern California. (He even remade Fritz Lang's classic *M,* in 1951.) The political climate of the times was destined to affect Losey's life and career. Screenwriter Leo Townsend, while testifying before the House Un-American Activities Committee, was the first to publicly name Losey and his wife, Louise, as Communist Party members. In order to avoid a subpoena to testify before HUAC, he fled to England in 1951, and was summarily blacklisted. He spent the next decade directing mostly forgettable features, usually under pseudonyms, among them *Stranger on the Prowl* (1953, also known as *Encounter;* as "Andrea Forzano"), *The Sleeping Tiger* (1954; as "Victor Hanbury") and *Finger of Guilt* (1956, also known as *The Intimate Stranger;* as "Joseph Walton"). Losey came into his own with *The Servant* (1963), a symbolic psychological drama focusing on the complex involvement between a young, upper-class man and his manservant. He further explored interpersonal relationships and the inability of the individual to transcend class differences and communicate meaningfully in *King and Country* (1964), *Accident* (1967), *The Go-Between* (1971, one of his best, and one of his most successful), *The Romantic Englishwoman* (1975), *Mr. Klein* (1976), and *The Trout* (1982). Even as the blacklist faded, Losey chose not to return to America. While thematically in tune with his previous work, Losey's final feature, *Steaming* (1985), based on Nell Dunn's play in which various women interact in a Turkish bath, was an artistically disappointing end to an otherwise arresting career. Tom Milne edited the volume "Losey on Losey," which was published in 1968.

OTHER FILMS INCLUDE: 1951: *The Prowler, The Big Night* (also cowrote); 1956: *Time Without Pity;* 1959: *Chance Meeting* (aka *Blind Date*); 1960: *The Concrete Jungle;* 1962: *These Are the Damned* (aka *The Damned*), *Eva;* 1966: *Modesty Blaise;* 1968: *Secret Ceremony, Boom!;* 1970: *Figures in a Landscape;* 1972: *The Assassination of*

Trotsky; 1973: *Galileo, A Doll's House* (Jane Fonda version); 1979: *Don Giovanni.*

LOUISE, ANITA. Actress. *(b. Jan. 9, 1915, New York City, as Anita Louise Fremalt; d. Apr. 25, 1970.)* Radiantly beautiful actress whose talent, sadly, didn't match her looks. A pretty but gangly youngster, Louise acted in many silent movies, from 1924's *The Sixth Commandment* to 1929's *Square Shoulders* (the first film in which she was billed as Anita Louise). As a teenager, she found herself typed as wide-eyed innocents and virginal younger sisters in the likes of *The Floradora Girl* (1930), *Everything's Rosie* (1931), *The Phantom of Crestwood* (1932), *Our Betters* (1933), and *Judge Priest* (1934) before landing a solid "grown-up" role as Marie Antoinette in *Madame Du Barry* (1934). She was a lovely Titania in Warner Bros.' all-star version of *A Midsummer Night's Dream* (1935), and thereafter played ingenues and secondary female leads in *The Story of Louis Pasteur, Anthony Adverse* (both 1936), *Green Light, That Certain Woman, Tovarich* (all 1937), *Marie Antoinette* (on loan to MGM, but not in the title role), *The Sisters,* and *Going Places* (all 1938). Louise freelanced thereafter, but never became a top-ranked star (even though she regularly placed high on lists of Hollywood's most beautiful women). She turned her attention to TV in the 1950s, starring in the "My Friend Flicka" series (1956–57) and guesting on many shows.
OTHER FILMS INCLUDE: 1939: *The Little Princess, The Gorilla;* 1940: *Glamour for Sale, The Villain Still Pursued Her;* 1941: *Harmon of Michigan;* 1943: *Dangerous Blondes;* 1944: *Nine Girls* (one of her best roles as the bitchy sorority sister murdered early in the film); 1945: *The Fighting Guardsman;* 1946: *The Bandit of Sherwood Forest, The Devil's Mask;* 1947: *Bulldog Drummond at Bay;* 1952: *Retreat, Hell!*

LOUISE, TINA. Actress. *(b. Feb. 11, 1934, New York City, as Tina Blacker.)* To baby boomers she'll always be Ginger, the sexy movie star shipwrecked on TV's "Gilligan's Island"; that's a status this curvaceous redhead couldn't quite attain in real life. A former model and singer who studied at the famed Actors' Studio, she appeared on Broadway in "Li'l Abner." Her role as the lusty Griselda in *God's Little Acre* (1958) portended great things for Louise, but her subsequent films—including *The Hangman* (1959), *The Warrior Empress* (1960), *Armored Command* (1961), *For Those Who Think Young* (1964), and *The Wrecking Crew* (1968)—saw her in roles that were merely decorative. Her turn in *The Stepford Wives* (1975) prompted whispers that a comeback was in order, but it didn't materialize. She worked mostly on episodic TV and in made-fors throughout the 1970s and early 1980s, although she appeared on the big screen as recently as 1992 in *Johnny Suede.*

LOVE, MONTAGU(E). Actor. *(b. Mar. 15, 1877, Portsmouth, England; d. May 17, 1943.)* Stolid British actor remembered as one of the screen's most despicable villains. A former newspaper illustrator, he took up acting shortly after the turn of the century and came to America with a touring company. In films since 1915, Love's perfidy reached great heights in the 1920s: He crossed swords with Barrymore in *Don Juan* (1926), matched wits with Valentino in *Son of the Sheik* (1926), and lusted after Lillian Gish in *The Wind* (1928). In the sound era he played stuffy officials, inflexible bankers, corrupt politicians—in short, his villainy was less flamboyant, though he became a mainstay of costume pictures. He even got to play sympathetic roles. His last film, *Devotion,* was made in 1943 but wasn't released until 1946, three years after his death.
OTHER FILMS INCLUDE: 1929: *Bulldog Drummond;* 1931: *Alexander Hamilton* (as Thomas Jefferson); 1935: *The Crusades, Clive of India;* 1937: *The Prisoner of Zenda, The Prince and the Pauper* (as Henry VIII); 1938: *The Adventures of Robin Hood* (as The Archbishop); 1939: *Gunga Din* (as the stern commander); 1940: *The Sea Hawk* (as King Philip II), *The Mark of Zorro;* 1942: *The Remarkable Andrew* (as George Washington); 1943: *The Constant Nymph.*

LOVEJOY, FRANK. Actor. *(b. Mar. 28, 1914, Bronx, N.Y.; d. Oct. 2, 1962.)* Rough-hewn, taciturn supporting player and occasional leading man who came to the screen in the late 1940s after acting on the stage and in dramatic radio for many years. A dependable player singularly lacking in charisma, Lovejoy was effective in Everyman roles and played his share of unlucky slobs caught up in intrigues not of their own making. He also played several dogface soldiers in WW2 stories.

Lovejoy, a good private-eye type, played detectives in the TV series "Man Against Crime" (1956) and "Meet McGraw" (1957–58). In retrospect, one can see that his real metier was radio, where he did outstanding work for many years in both supporting and starring roles.

OTHER FILMS INCLUDE: 1948: *Black Bart;* 1949: *Home of the Brave;* 1950: *In a Lonely Place, Breakthrough;* 1951: *I Was a Communist for the FBI* (one of his few leads), *Try and Get Me, Force of Arms;* 1952: *Retreat, Hell!;* 1953: *She's Back on Broadway, House of Wax* (as the nominal hero in this 3-D horror film), *The Hitch-Hiker, The Charge at Feather River;* 1954: *Beachhead;* 1955: *Strategic Air Command, The Americano, Finger Man, The Crooked Web, Shack Out on 101;* 1957: *Three Brave Men;* 1958: *Cole Younger, Gunfighter.*

LOVITZ, JON. Actor. *(b. July 21, 1957, Tarzana, Calif.)* "Saturday Night Live" veteran whose delivery has been described as "an almost melodic mix of pomposity and self-doubt," Lovitz has evolved into a successful character actor on-screen. He began with small roles in *Last Resort* (1985), *Jumpin' Jack Flash, ¡Three Amigos!* (both 1986), *Big,* and *My Stepmother Is an Alien* (both 1988), then nearly walked away with the comedy hit *A League of Their Own* (1992) in his relatively brief screen time as crabby baseball scout Ernie "Cappy" Capadino (a role he repeated in the 1993 pilot for a TV-series spinoff of the movie). He had his first leading role in the inane *Mom and Dad Save the World* (1992). He also added his own comic energy to the 1987 animated feature *The Brave Little Toaster,* as the voice of an obnoxious radio, and provided the voice of Chula the tarantula in *An American Tail: Fievel Goes West* (1991). Recent credits include *National Lampoon's Loaded Weapon I* (1993), *City Slickers 2: The Legend of Curly's Gold* (1994), and TV's animated "The Critic."

LOWE, EDMUND. Actor. *(b. Mar. 3, 1892, San Jose, Calif.; d. Apr. 21, 1971.)* As often as this slick-haired, mustached leading man appeared in debonair screen roles, it must be pointed out that his star-making portrayal was that of the wise-cracking, womanizing roughneck Sergeant Quirt (opposite Victor McLaglen's Captain Flagg) in the landmark antiwar film, *What Price Glory?* (1926). It was a characterization Lowe repeated many times; although the original character names were eventually dropped, Lowe and McLaglen continued their screen scrapping for more than a decade in *The Cock-Eyed World* (1929), *Women of All Nations* (1931), *Guilty as Hell* (1932), *No More Women* (1934), *Under Pressure, The Great Hotel Murder* (both 1935), and, unfortunately, in *Call Out the Marines* (1942). Lowe, who'd been a schoolteacher before joining a Los Angeles stock company, made his first film, *The Spreading Dawn,* in 1917, and appeared in more than a dozen undistinguished silents before *What Price Glory?* When not trading barbs with McLaglen, he affected a smooth, debonair screen personality; no actor spent more time in "dinner clothes" than he. (Although he did don Cavalry garb to match wits with bandito Warner Baxter in 1929's *In Old Arizona* and 1931's *The Cisco Kid.)* As the top-hatted, silk-caped prestidigitator of *The Spider* (1931), his appearance inspired the look of the comic-strip character Mandrake the Magician. He also played radio's favorite illusionist in *Chandu the Magician* (1932).

But it was for his successful string of whodunits that Lowe was best known. He solved murders in *Bombay Mail* (1934), *Mr. Dynamite* (as the dapper T. N. Thompson in a Dashiell Hammett story), *Grand Exit* (both 1935), *The Garden Murder Case* (as Philo Vance), *Seven Sinners, Mad Holiday* (all 1936), *Under Cover of Night* (as dilettante detective Chris Cross), *Murder on Diamond Row* (both 1937, in the latter as Scotland Yard's Inspector Barrabal), and *Honeymoon Deferred* (1940) to name a few. By the 1940s, the rapidly graying Lowe seemed tired and bored; his starring vehicles were strictly B pictures, and not particularly good ones at that. He accepted supporting roles in *Good Sam* (1948), *The Wings of Eagles* (1957), *The Last Hurrah* (1958), and *Heller in Pink Tights* (1960) before retiring.

He and McLaglen appeared together one last time, cameo-style, in *Around the World in Eighty Days* (1956). Lowe played the "Front Page Detective" in a 1951–53 TV series. He was married to actress Lilyan Tashman, who died in 1935. OTHER FILMS INCLUDE: 1930: *Born Reckless;* 1931: *Transatlantic;* 1932: *Attorney for the Defense;* 1933: *Dinner at Eight;* 1935: *The Great Impersonation* (in a dual role); 1937: *Every Day's a Holiday* (opposite Mae West); 1945: *Dillinger, The Enchanted Forest.*

LOWE, ROB. Actor. *(b. Mar. 17, 1964, Charlottesville, Va.)* Initially dismissed as an unctuous pretty-boy pinup, this young leading man and former Brat Packer later redeemed himself with a string of capable performances. He started acting on TV in the late 1970s, working steadily right up to being cast in *Class* and Francis Coppola's *The Outsiders* (both 1983), a film that launched the careers of several young actors. He won star positioning in the mid 1980s, headlining *Oxford Blues* (1984), and costarring in *The Hotel New Hampshire* (1984), the Brat Pack ensemble piece *St. Elmo's Fire* (1985), *About Last Night . . .* , and *Youngblood* (both 1986).

Eager to broaden his range, Lowe played a slow-witted youth in *Square Dance* (1987) and a scheming ladykiller in *Masquerade* (1988). The young actor made headlines in 1989 when explicit private videotapes of him carousing with an underage girl at the time he was attending the Democratic National Convention in Atlanta were made public. While not a career-enhancing incident by any means, he did survive the notoriety; if anything, it lent some credibility to his later performances as a menacing stranger in *Bad Influence* (1990) and slimy show-biz types in *The Dark Backward* (1991) and *Wayne's World* (1992). He also took a costarring role in a television production of "Suddenly, Last Summer" in 1992 and costarred in the 1994 miniseries of Stephen King's "The Stand." His brother Chad Lowe is also an actor who has appeared in such films as *Nobody's Perfect* (1990) and *Highway to Hell* (1991) and won a 1993 Emmy Award playing a young man with AIDS on the TV series "Life Goes On."

LOY, MYRNA. Actress. *(b. Aug. 2, 1905, Raidersburg, Mont., as Myrna Williams; d. Dec. 15, 1993.)* Loy's enduring popularity as Nora Charles, the wryly wisecracking wife of urbane detective Nick Charles (William Powell) in MGM's "Thin Man" series, not only overshadowed the other fine work she did in a long film career, but also, perhaps more fortunately, the dozens of campy, exotic characterizations she essayed in her salad days, with varying degrees of success. Born to an influential Montana cattle baron (who died when she was 12), a young, lissome Loy danced in chorus lines until 1925, when she made her screen debut—as a chorus girl—in the backstage drama *Pretty Ladies.*

She soon graduated to meatier roles, many of them sinister vamps of various nationalities. Loy's auburn hair photographed dark, and the combination of her striking features—sleepy blue eyes, prominent, upturned nose, pursed lips, and strong chin—gave her an exotic allure interpreted most frequently by filmmakers as being Oriental in nature. She worked steadily throughout the late silent era, mostly for Warner Bros., appearing in *Ben-Hur, Don Juan, Cave Man, Across the Pacific* (all 1926), *The Girl From Chicago, Bitter Apples* (both 1927), *A Girl in Every Port, The Crimson City, Midnight Taxi* (all 1928), and *Noah's Ark* (1929), among many others. She even had a supporting role in the historic *The Jazz Singer* (1927), albeit confined to the silent footage.

Loy's weak, reedy voice made her transition to talkies a difficult one, but she eventually mastered the technique of projecting her voice for the movie microphones. Many of her early sound-film characterizations were Oriental or Mexican vamps, as in *The Black Watch, The Desert Song* (both 1929), *The Bad Man* (1930), *Under a Texas Moon, Rogue of the Rio Grande* (both 1931), *The Mask of Fu Manchu,* and *13 Women* (both 1932). But she also broadened her repertoire with "occidental" characterizations (more than a few of which, come to think of it, were vampish in nature) in *Cameo Kirby* (1930), *Arrowsmith, A Connecticut Yankee* (both 1931, in the latter as Morgan le Fay), *The Wet Parade, Love Me Tonight, The Animal Kingdom, Vanity Fair* (all 1932), *Topaze, The Barbarian,* and *The Prizefighter and the Lady* (all 1933).

Loy's witty, winning performance in *Penthouse* (also 1933), a stylish mystery melodrama written by Frances Goodrich and Albert Hackett and directed by W. S. Van Dyke, convinced MGM to costar her in *The Thin Man* (1934), a sophisticated Dashiell Hammett mystery being prepared by the same creative team. She displayed remarkable chemistry with debonair leading man William Powell, and the final film delighted everyone who saw it. Moreover, it marked Loy's ascent to stardom's upper echelon after years of trouping on the periphery. (In 1937 she was crowned Queen of Hollywood by columnist Ed Sullivan; at the same time Clark Gable was declared King.)

As one of MGM's top stars (and the recipient of an unsubtle but very effective publicity buildup), she appeared in a dizzying succession of box-office hits and while she was dubbed "the perfect wife," she in fact played a variety of roles: *Men in White, Manhattan Melodrama* (opposite Powell and Clark Gable), *Evelyn Prentice* (all 1934), *Wings in the Dark, Whipsaw* (both 1935), *After the Thin Man, The Great Ziegfeld* (with Powell again, Loy somewhat miscast as stage star Billie Burke), *Wife vs. Secretary, Libeled Lady* (all 1936), *Parnell, Double Wedding, Man-Proof* (all 1937), *Test Pilot, Too Hot to Handle* (both 1938), *Another Thin Man, Lucky Night* (both 1939), *Third Finger, Left Hand, I Love You Again* (both 1940), *Shadow of the Thin Man,* and *Love Crazy* (both 1941, both costarring her with Powell).

After America's entrance into World War 2 following the attack on Pearl Harbor, Loy took a hiatus from movie work for the duration (returning to the screen just once, for 1944's *The Thin Man Goes Home*), devoting herself to Red Cross activities and war bond fundraising. She resumed movie acting full-time in 1946, as popular as ever, and starred in some major movie hits, but by the 1950s she was more involved in politics than in acting, and worked only sporadically from that time on.

Loy's post-WW2 films include William Wyler's moving and brilliant *The Best Years of Our Lives* (1946), *Song of the Thin Man* (the last in the series), *The Bachelor and the Bobby-Soxer* (both 1947), *Mr. Blandings Builds His Dream House* (1948, one of her best comic performances), *The Red Pony* (1949), *Cheaper by the Dozen* (1950), *Belles on Their Toes* (1952), *The Ambassador's Daughter* (1956), *Lonelyhearts* (1958), *From the Terrace* (1960), *The April Fools* (1969), *Airport 1975* (1974), *The End* (1978, as Burt Reynolds' mother), and *Just Tell Me What You Want* (1980, as Alan King's long-suffering secretary). She also appeared in several telefilms and made her Broadway debut in a 1973 revival of "The Women." Her four husbands included screenwriter Gene Markey. Her autobiography, "Myrna Loy: Being and Becoming," was published in 1987. In 1991 she was awarded an honorary Academy Award "for a lifetime's worth of indelible performances."

LUBITSCH, ERNST. Director, producer. *(b. Jan. 28, 1892, Berlin; d. Nov. 30, 1947.)* Noted for the distinctive, if ill-defined, "Lubitsch touch," which depended mostly on his sly, continental/sophisticated treatment of sexuality and nose-thumbing at contemporary mores (then daring terrain for a filmmaker), this brilliant director had a gift that others tried to imitate but seldom achieved. Lubitsch had turned his back on his father's business to enter the theater, and by 1911 he was a member of Max Reinhardt's Deutches Theater. His first film work came in 1912 as an actor. In the late teens Lubitsch turned to directing, and turned out whimsical entertainments like *Die Austerprinzessin* (The Oyster Princess), *Rausch* (Intoxication), and *Die Puppe* (The Puppet) (all 1919), but he made his international reputation with a series of large-scale spectacles starring Pola Negri. *Carmen* (1918, released in the U.S. in 1921 as *Gypsy Blood*), *Madame Dubarry* (aka *Deception,* 1919), which costarred Emil Jannings, and a film version of Reinhardt's famed pantomime *Sumurun* (aka *One Arabian Night,* 1920), in which Lubitsch made his final acting appearance, brought the director to the attention of silent star Mary Pickford, who imported him to Hollywood in 1923 to work with her.

While critics were pleased with their collaboration, audiences found Pickford's role as the Spanish street singer in *Rosita* to be an unacceptable departure from her established screen persona. Dissatisfied with the film, Pickford allowed Lubitsch to sign with Warner Bros., where he established his reputation for sophisticated comedy with such stylish and delightful films as *The Marriage Circle* (1924), *Lady Windermere's Fan* (1925), and *So This Is Paris* (1926). Lubitsch went to MGM to make *The Student Prince in Old Heidelberg* (1927), an outstanding film but a costly failure; like many of his subsequent films, it won critical praise and appealed to discerning urban patrons, but never won a broad constituency among American moviegoers. Within the ranks of filmmakers, Lubitsch was revered, not only for his mastery of the medium as a whole, but for his ability to coax effervescent performances out of his cast (often by acting out the parts for them, scene by scene), and for his ability to convey a sexual sparkle even in the face of Hollywood's moral watchdogs.

In 1928 Lubitsch joined Paramount to reunite with Emil Jannings on a lavish drama, *The Patriot;* the return to spectacle gave Lubitsch's career a shot in the arm, and earned him his first Academy Award nomination. Then, sound arrived in Hollywood, and Lubitsch thrived. With his first talkie, *The Love Parade* (1929) starring Maurice Chevalier and Jeanette MacDonald, Lubitsch hit his stride as a maker of worldly musical comedies (and got himself another Oscar nomination). *Monte Carlo* (1930), *The Smiling Lieutenant* (1931), and *One Hour With You* (1932, codirected by George Cukor) followed, each a delight. But whether with music, as in MGM's opulent *The Merry Widow* (1934), or without, as in Paramount's delicious *Trouble in Paradise* (1932, probably his best film) and *Design for Living* (1933) Lubitsch continued to specialize in comedy. He made only one other dramatic film, *Broken Lullaby* (aka *The Man I Killed,* 1932), a moving antiwar tale starring Nancy Carroll and Phillips Holmes.

In 1935 Lubitsch was made head of production for Paramount, but he gave up the job in 1936 to return to directing with *Angel* (1937), a Marlene Dietrich vehicle. After the disappointing *Bluebeard's Eighth Wife* (1938, written by Billy Wilder and Charles Brackett), Lubitsch returned to MGM to make two of his best films, *Ninotchka* (1939, a Wilder–Brackett–Walter Reisch script), in which Greta Garbo laughed, and *The Shop Around the Corner* (1940), with James Stewart and Margaret Sullavan as a pair of secret admirers. He went independent to direct *That Uncertain Feeling* (1941, a remake of his 1925 film *Kiss Me Again*), and the dark anti-Nazi comedy *To Be or Not to Be* (1942), starring Jack Benny and Carole Lombard.

Lubitsch spent the balance of his career at 20th Century-Fox, but a heart condition curtailed his activity. After directing the delightful *Heaven Can Wait* (1943, which merited his third Oscar nomination), starring Don Ameche, Lubitsch was forced to let Otto Preminger take over *A Royal Scandal* (1945). He returned to the megaphone for *Cluny Brown* (1946), but Preminger again stepped in on *That Lady in Ermine* (1948) after Lubitsch's death. Many tried but few succeeded in duplicating the Lubitsch touch. At the director's funeral, a distraught Billy Wilder said, "No more Lubitsch," to which fellow filmmaker William Wyler replied, "Worse than that. No more Lubitsch pictures."

LUCAS, GEORGE. Director, producer, screenwriter. *(b. May 14, 1944, Modesto, Calif.)* Despite the fact that he has directed only a handful of films, George Lucas' name looms large in the motion picture industry. The staggering success of his films enabled him to become his own mogul, overseeing both moviemaking projects and technical developments that have made him Hollywood's foremost futurist. A child of the TV generation, Lucas studied film at the University of Southern California (where one of his teachers was Jerry Lewis). He had already made several short subjects when he won an internship at Warner Bros., where he met Francis Ford Coppola, who was making *Finian's Rainbow* there. Coppola took him on as an assistant, and allowed him to make a cinema-verité documentary about his next production, *The Rain People,* which Lucas called *Filmmaker* (1968). Coppola then persuaded the studio to finance an expansion of Lucas' student film into the feature-length *THX-1138* (1971), an intelligent if somewhat nihilistic sci-fi yarn. The film's poor box-office performance persuaded Lucas to direct his energies toward a project with mainstream appeal. Coppola's willingness to serve as executive producer persuaded Universal to finance Lucas' *American Graffiti* (1973), a semiautobiographical coming-of-age story set in 1962 that took off like a rocket and became one of the decade's biggest hits, launching a number of young actors on the road to stardom. It also earned the young filmmaker dual Oscar nominations, as director and coscreenwriter.

Over the next few years Lucas developed his next project, another sci-fi outing, but with a very different sensibility. *Star Wars* (1977) synthesized elements of hokey old space operas and serials Lucas had enjoyed as a kid, and even borrowed from Akira Kurosawa's 1958 adventure *The Hidden Fortress,* but had a pop-culture feeling all its own. As with *Graffiti,* the studio that backed this project had no faith in it whatsoever, and it came as a total surprise that *Star Wars* became a megahit—no, more of a *phenomenon.* It earned more than $400 million dollars, and in fact helped usher in the era of the blockbuster hit (for better or worse). It spun off a mini-industry of its own, and saw its characters become part of contemporary lore. (Lucas also received Oscar nominations for writing and directing the picture.) What's more, the film inspired Lucas to establish his own full-time special effects company, Industrial Light and Magic (ILM), which would create dazzling new illusions for the *Star Wars* sequels, *The Empire Strikes Back* (1980) and *Return of the Jedi* (1983). With the clout his earnings gave him, he saw no need to work in Hollywood, and built his own filmmaking "empire"—actually a ranch named after his character Luke Skywalker—on his home turf in Northern California to house Lucas Film Ltd.

He also decided to relinquish the director's chair and escape from that nerve-wracking job. He and another Bay Area filmmaker, Philip Kaufman, created the character of archeologist/adventurer Indiana Jones (inspired, again, by old-time Saturday matinee serials), and persuaded Steven Spielberg to direct *Raiders of the Lost Ark* (1981), which Lucas also coexecutive produced. This gave him yet another film in the All-Time Top-Grossing Hits roster, and led to a pair of sequels, *Indiana Jones and the Temple of Doom* (1984) and *Indiana Jones and The Last Crusade* (1989). Lucas later brought his character to television in the lavishly produced, award-winning (but, sadly, little-

seen) series "The Young Indiana Jones Chronicles" (1992–).

Lucas was also responsible for executive producing such other films as *More American Graffiti* (1979), *Body Heat* (1981, for which he took no screen credit), *Twice Upon a Time* (1983), *Mishima* (1985), the notorious flop *Howard the Duck* (1986), *Labyrinth* (1986), *The Land Before Time, Tucker: The Man and His Dream* (for Coppola), *Willow* (all 1988), and *Radioland Murders* (1994, from a story he had written years earlier). He also executive produced and wrote the screenplay for the 3-D Disneyland attraction *Captain EO* (1986), which Francis Coppola directed. In addition to LucasFilm Ltd. and Industrial Light and Magic, Lucas also developed the THX Sound System, which sought to improve the quality of sound in movie theaters. In 1992 he was given the prestigious Irving Thalberg Award by the Academy of Motion Picture Arts and Sciences. As for his millions of fans, Lucas has promised them a new series of *Star Wars* adventures to come.

LUGOSI, BELA. Actor. *(b. Oct. 20, 1882, Lugos, Hungary, as Bela Blasko; d. Aug. 16, 1956.)* The man who will always be known as Dracula actually had a long and distinguished acting career (mostly on stage) before donning cape and fangs in Hollywood. In 1901, after studying at the Budapest Academy of Theatrical Arts, this banker's son made his stage debut as a featured juvenile. Tall, aristocratic, and handsome in a vaguely sinister way (with piercing eyes and a cruel mouth), he spent the next two decades building a reputation as one of Hungary's great matinee idols, and made his first film—*A Leopard*—in 1917. Political turmoil in his homeland drove Lugosi to Germany in 1919; he appeared in several films there, including a 1920 adaptation of *Dr. Jekyll and Mr. Hyde* and a 1922 filmization of *The Last of the Mohicans.*

Emigrating to America shortly thereafter, Lugosi toiled in stage melodramas and routine programmers (such as 1923's *The Silent Command* and 1925's *The Midnight Girl*) before assuming the title role in the 1927 Broadway production of "Dracula," which he also essayed for two years on the road. The thick, almost impenetrable accent that hampered him in most roles actually proved to be an asset when he played Bram Stoker's Transylvanian vampire. Film rights to the play were sold to Universal, which announced that Lon Chaney would play the title role. But Chaney's untimely death from cancer in 1930 prompted producer-director Tod Browning to cast Lugosi instead. *Dracula* (1931) launched Universal's long-running cycle of horror movies and made its star a household name overnight.

Unfortunately, the movie's success also doomed Lugosi to a lifetime of boogeyman roles in vehicles of steadily diminishing quality. After refusing to play the Monster in *Frankenstein* (1931, the role taken by Boris Karloff), he played his first mad doctor in *Murders in the Rue Morgue,* a voodoo master in *White Zombie* (delivering a wonderfully florid, over-the-top performance), and a priest of the Black Arts in *Chandu the Magician* in 1932 alone. But the next year he was already working for Poverty Row producers, getting top billing in Mascot's *The Whispering Shadow* and Majestic's *The Death Kiss,* but winning only supporting roles in major-studio productions such as *The Island of Lost Souls* and *International House* (all 1933). Independent producer Sol Lesser gave Lugosi a bona fide hero role as the star of *The Return of Chandu,* a 1934 serial also released in feature-length version. That same year he returned to Universal for *The Black Cat* (1934), the first (and best) of several chillers that teamed him with Karloff, whose career eclipsed Lugosi's almost from the start.

Lugosi's typecasting and his failure to master the nuances of the English language certainly hampered his American film career, but he also proved to be his own worst enemy, taking leads in the most abysmal mini-budget schlockers for whatever money producers were willing to pay. A colorful character role, that of Ygor, the mad shepherd in *Son of Frankenstein* (1939), briefly restored Lugosi to prominence, and he appeared to good advantage in that year's *Ninotchka* (starring Greta Garbo), but he alternated strong supporting roles in Universal's *Black Friday* (1940), *The Wolf Man* (1941), and *The Ghost of Frankenstein* (1942, again as Ygor) with negligible turns in low-budget Monogram melodramas produced by schlockmeister Sam Katzman, who teamed Lugosi most ignobly with the East Side Kids in *Spooks Run Wild* (1941) and *Ghosts on the Loose* (1942).

In 1943 Lugosi, by this time in no position to be choosy about his roles, agreed to play the Frankenstein monster—a part he had previously eschewed on the grounds it offered him no dialogue and would submerge him beneath heavy makeup—in *Frankenstein Meets the Wolf Man.* He played a Dracula-like character in *The Return of the Vampire* that same year, and made the most of a small role (again opposite Karloff) in Val Lewton's literate, effective version of *The Body Snatcher* (1945). Lugosi then plunged into the depths of Poverty Row hell, a descent checked only briefly with his wonderfully deadpan turn as Dracula in *Abbott and Costello Meet Frankenstein* (1948), the last good picture he made. By the 1950s the pickings were slimmer than ever; he submitted to demeaning personal appearance tours, and even starred in a self-named comedy-chiller, *Bela Lugosi Meets a Brooklyn Gorilla* (1952). An addiction to morphine finally got the best of him and in 1955 he checked himself into a rehab hospital for treatment. His last screen appearance was undertaken for fan/producer Edward D. Wood in *Plan 9 From Outer Space* (filmed 1956 but released 1959); he died during production and his scenes were completed by a stand-in. Lugosi was buried in the cape he always wore as Dracula. He was portrayed by Martin Landau in *Ed Wood* (1994).

OTHER FILMS INCLUDE: 1929: *The Thirteenth Chair;* 1931: *The Black Camel;* 1933: *Night of Terror, The Devil's in Love;* 1934: *The Gift of Gab* (cameo with Karloff); 1935: *The Mysterious Mr. Wong, Murder by Television, Mark of the Vampire, The Raven* (with Karloff, playing a Poe-inspired surgeon); 1936: *The Invisible Ray* (again with Karloff), *Shadow of Chinatown;* 1937: *S.O.S. Coast Guard;* 1939: *Dark Eyes of London* (aka *The Human Monster*), *The Phantom Creeps;* 1940: *You'll Find Out* (with Karloff and Peter Lorre); 1941: *The Devil Bat, The Invisible Ghost;* 1942: *Black Dragons, The Corpse Vanishes, Bowery at Midnight;* 1943: *The Ape Man;* 1944: *Voodoo Man, Return of the Ape Man, One Body Too Many;* 1945: *Zombies on Broadway;* 1946: *Genius at Work;* 1947: *Scared to Death;* 1952: *Old Mother Riley Meets the Vampire;* 1953: *Glen or Glenda?*

(his first for Ed Wood); 1955: *Bride of the Monster;* 1956: *The Black Sleep.*

LUKE, KEYE. Actor. *(b. June 18, 1904, Canton, China; d. Jan. 12, 1991.)* Forever identified as detective Charlie Chan's lively, Americanized Number One Son, Lee, Luke was a talented actor who played many other roles. He moved to America while still a boy, and studied art at Washington University. Hired as a poster artist by Fox West Coast Theatres (for whom he created artwork which appeared at Grauman's Chinese), Luke occasionally acted as technical adviser on films with Oriental backgrounds, and was eventually cast in a small part in *The Painted Veil* (1934) with Greta Garbo. He debuted as Lee Chan in *Charlie Chan in Paris* (1934), and subsequently appeared in eight more 1930s entries with "honorable father" Warner Oland. (Luke returned to the role in 1948, appearing in the last two Charlie Chan features, *The Feathered Serpent* and *Sky Dragon,* opposite Roland Winters.) He played Lee Chan again in *Mr. Moto's Gamble* (1938), a Peter Lorre starrer written as a Chan film but revamped when Oland died suddenly. Luke also appeared as Kato, faithful valet and chauffeur of crime-busting newspaper publisher Britt Reid, in the serials *The Green Hornet* and *The Green Hornet Strikes Again* (both 1940). And he played Charlie Chan ripoff James Lee Wong (a part vacated by Boris Karloff, no less) in the low-budget *Phantom of Chinatown* (also 1940).

Luke had meaty supporting roles in *Oil for the Lamps of China* (1935), *The Good Earth* (1937), *Barricade* (1939), *Mr. and Mrs. North* (1941), and *Across the Pacific* (1942) before becoming a regular in MGM's "Dr. Gillespie" series, an offshoot of the "Dr. Kildare" films, beginning with *Dr. Gillespie's New Assistant* (1942). He also appeared in the serials *Adventures of Smilin' Jack* (1943), *Secret Agent X-9* (1945), and *Lost City of the Jungle* (1946) in addition to the features *Dragon Seed* (1944) and *Between Two Women* (1945). His film assignments dwindled in the post-WW2 years, but he was seen to good advantage in *Sleep My Love* (1948), *Hell's Half Acre* (1954), *Love Is a Many Splendored Thing* (1955), *The Yangtse Incident* (1957), *Nobody's Perfect* (1968), *The Ha-*

waiians (1970), *The Amsterdam Kill* (1977), and notably in *Gremlins* (1984, as the keeper of the Mogwai, a role he repeated in the 1990 sequel). He appeared on Broadway in "Flower Drum Song" in the late 1950s, but inexplicably, wasn't cast in the film.

Luke also played Master Po, wise instructor to David Carradine in the TV series "Kung Fu" (1972–75), and did the voice of Charlie Chan for a TV cartoon series, "The Amazing Chan and the Chan Clan" (1972–74). His final screen role was one of his best in years, as the mysterious Chinatown herbalist who ministers to Mia Farrow in Woody Allen's *Alice* (1990).

LUMET, SIDNEY. Director, producer, writer. *(b. June 25, 1924, Philadelphia.)* Long regarded as an actor's director, this New York–based filmmaker has handled a wide variety of movies with finesse and class. In his teens, he acted in Yiddish theater and on Broadway (in, among others, the classic "Dead End"), before moving behind the camera during TV's Golden Age, directing many live dramas for CBS in the 1950s. Henry Fonda gave him the opportunity to direct his first feature film, the classic jury drama *12 Angry Men* (1957; Oscar-nominated for Best Picture and Director), which in fact was based on a TV play. He continued with such all-star theatrical adaptations as Tennessee Williams' *The Fugitive Kind* (1960), Eugene O'Neill's *Long Day's Journey Into Night,* and Arthur Miller's *A View From the Bridge* (both 1962). Next came the cold war nightmare *Fail-Safe* (1964), and his horrifying study of a New York Jew (Rod Steiger) haunted by the Holocaust, *The Pawnbroker* (1965). Lumet then hit a slump, only regaining his footing with a slick caper film, *The Anderson Tapes* (1971), and an extraordinarily intense study of police brutality, *The Offence* (1973). Then, his career reenergized, Lumet turned out a splendid run of critical and commercial successes: the police corruption drama *Serpico* (1973), the all-star whodunit *Murder on the Orient Express* (1974), the darkly comic bank robbery epic *Dog Day Afternoon* (1975; Oscar-nominated for Best Picture and Director), and Paddy Chayefsky's landmark (and amazingly prophetic) TV satire, *Network* (1976, again Oscar-nominated for Best Picture and Director).

Among his subsequent films are the elephantine musical *The Wiz* (1978); a bitchy sex comedy, *Just Tell Me What You Want* (1980); the mammoth police drama *Prince of the City* (1981, Oscar-nominated for the screenplay, which he cowrote); the riveting courtroom thriller *The Verdict* (1982; Oscar-nominated for Best Picture and Director); a thinly veiled look at the Rosenberg case, *Daniel* (1983); a romantic whodunit, *The Morning After* (1986, his first film shot in Hollywood); a heart-breaking drama about 1960s activists, *Running on Empty* (1988); and a corrosive portrait of a bigoted cop, *Q&A* (1990, which he also wrote). Lumet's films are generally intelligent and marked by a clean, unobtrusive directing style, but his signature is the caliber of performance he elicits from his actors (who speak of him—and his theater-based rehearsal process—in the most glowing terms). His 1995 book, "Making Movies," is a fascinating, nuts-and-bolts look at how films are made today.

OTHER FILMS INCLUDE: 1958: *Stage Struck;* 1959: *That Kind of Woman;* 1965: *The Hill;* 1966: *The Group;* 1967: *The Deadly Affair;* 1968: *Bye Bye Braverman, The Seagull;* 1969: *The Appointment;* 1970: *Last of the Mobile Hot-Shots;* 1972: *Child's Play;* 1974: *Lovin' Molly;* 1977: *Equus;* 1982: *Deathtrap;* 1984: *Garbo Talks;* 1986: *Power;* 1989: *Family Business;* 1992: *A Stranger Among Us;* 1993: *Guilty as Sin.*

LUNDGREN, DOLPH. Actor. *(b. Nov. 3, 1959, Stockholm.)* Former disco doorman and bodybuilder, this imposing but wooden action star first appeared on-screen in 1985's *A View to a Kill* (which also starred his then-girlfriend Grace Jones) and *Rocky IV* (as Sylvester Stallone's Soviet opponent). A Fulbright scholar at MIT, Lundgren is also a championship kickboxer, a skill he has used in starring vehicles *Masters of the Universe* (1987), *Red Scorpion, The Punisher* (both 1989), *I Come in Peace* (1990), and *Showdown in Little Tokyo* (1991). In 1992 he costarred with fellow muscle-star Jean-Claude Van Damme in *Universal Soldier.*

LUNDIGAN, WILLIAM. Actor. *(b. June 12, 1914, Syracuse, N.Y.; d. Dec. 20, 1975.)* Handsome but colorless supporting player and occasional leading man (especially in the 1950s) who attained prominence with small-screen audiences as a series star, host, and commercial pitchman. Lundigan, a former radio announcer (a skill he put to good use in one of his earliest films, 1938's *Danger on the Air*), broke into movies in 1937 as a Universal contract player. He appeared in *Armored Car* (1937), *The Black Doll* (1938), *Three Smart Girls Grow Up* (1939), and several others before signing with Warner Bros., where he played support in big pictures—such as *Dodge City, The Old Maid* (both 1939), *The Fighting 69th, The Sea Hawk,* and *Santa Fe Trail* (all 1940)—and leads in small ones, such as *The Case of the Black Parrot* and *A Shot in the Dark* (both 1941). Lundigan subsequently worked for MGM, RKO, and Fox, achieving some status at the latter studio as leading man to Susan Hayward, Jeanne Crain, and June Haver. On TV he hosted "Climax" (1954–58, hawking Chryslers during each episode), "Shower of Stars" (1956–57), and "Men Into Space" (1959–60).

OTHER FILMS INCLUDE: 1943: *Salute to the Marines;* 1947: *Dishonored Lady, The Fabulous Dorseys;* 1949: *Follow Me Quietly, Pinky;* 1950: *I'll Get By;* 1951: *I'd Climb the Highest Mountain* (one of his best roles, as a rural minister), *Love Nest, The House on Telegraph Hill;* 1953: *Down Among the Sheltering Palms;* 1954: *Riders to the Stars;* 1962: *The Underwater City;* 1967: *The Way West;* 1968: *Where Angels Go, Trouble Follows.*

LUPINO, IDA. Actress, director. *(b. Feb. 4, 1914 [also listed as 1918], London; d. Aug. 3, 1995.)* The daughter of famed British comedian Stanley Lupino, she broke into films with a supporting role in *Her First Affaire* (1933), then toiled in several minor British films before coming to America later that year. Under contract to Paramount she made her American debut as a Hollywoodized platinum blond in *Search for Beauty* (1934). Very petite and fragile-looking, she typically portrayed conventional ingenues during her first few years on these shores, appearing in *Ready for Love, Come On Marines!* (both 1934), *Paris in Spring, Peter Ibbetson, Smart Girl* (all 1935), *Anything Goes, The Gay*

Desperado, One Rainy Afternoon, Yours for the Asking (all 1936), *Sea Devils, Fight for Your Lady, Artists and Models, Let's Get Married* (all 1937), *The Lone Wolf Spy Hunt,* and *The Adventures of Sherlock Holmes* (both 1939).

Lupino played a selfish, fiery-tempered Cockney in *The Light That Failed* (1939), all but stealing the film from star Ronald Colman with her florid performance. It showed a side of the demure British actress heretofore unseen by movie audiences, and following that turn she played increasingly harsh, hard-boiled characters. Never a top star, Lupino nonetheless had her own niche in Hollywood, and scored her biggest personal successes during the 1940s, especially at Warner Bros., in films like *They Drive by Night* (1940, climaxed by a great mad scene), *High Sierra, The Sea Wolf, Out of the Fog* (all 1941), *Moontide, The Hard Way, Life Begins at 8:30* (all 1942), *Forever and a Day, Thank Your Lucky Stars* (both 1943), *In Our Time, Hollywood Canteen* (both 1944), *Pillow to Post* (1945), *Devotion* (1946), *The Man I Love, Deep Valley, Escape Me Never* (all 1947), *Road House* (1948, in which she sings—as best she can—the ballad "Again"), and *Lust for Gold* (1949).

Beginning in 1949 with *Not Wanted* (on which she worked uncredited), Lupino took up directing; although the silent era had seen many women directors, there were precious few working behind the camera in the post-WW2 years. She showed surprising aptitude for the job, and even managed to tackle contemporary social problems in some of her modestly budgeted pictures: *Outrage* (dealing with rape), *Never Fear* (both 1950), *Hard, Fast and Beautiful* (1951), *The Bigamist* (1953, in which she played support, the only time she directed herself), *The Hitch-Hiker* (also 1953, and arguably her best), and years later, *The Trouble With Angels* (1966).

Lupino acted sporadically in 1950s films, among them *Woman in Hiding* (1950), *On Dangerous Ground* (1951, a showy role as a blind woman in peril), *Beware My Lovely* (1952), *Jennifer* (1953), *Private Hell 36* (1954, which Lupino produced and cowrote), *Women's Prison* (as a vicious superintendent of the title institution), *The Big Knife* (both 1955), *While the City Sleeps, Strange Intruder* (both 1956). She devoted increasing amounts of time and energy to television, where she worked on both sides of the camera, as a regular on "Four Star Playhouse" (1952–56) and "Mr. Adams and Eve" (1957–58, with then-husband Howard Duff), and as director for "Have Gun, Will Travel," "The Donna Reed Show," "Mr. Novak," "Dr. Kildare," and other series of the 1950s and 1960s.

She made a few token appearances in big-screen films of the 1970s, including *Deadhead Miles, Junior Bonner* (both 1972), *The Devil's Rain* (1975), *Food of the Gods* (1976), and *My Boys Are Good Boys* (1978) before retiring altogether. Lupino was married to actors Louis Hayward (1938–45) and Howard Duff (1951–68).

LYNCH, DAVID. Director, writer, actor. *(b. Jan. 20, 1946, Missoula, Mont.)* America's premier avant-garde director (and, thanks to "Twin Peaks," now something of a cultural icon) was an Eagle Scout in his teens, not unlike the squeaky-clean protagonists—usually played by Kyle MacLachlan—that are thrust into bizarre situations in his films. He went to art school and was trained as a painter but began showing an interest in films there, making several shorts that were utilized in art installations he constructed. His first feature, the surrealistic, bleak, and often unsettlingly hilarious *Eraserhead,* took about five years to complete. Released as a "midnight movie" in 1978, it quickly achieved cult status. Mel Brooks enlisted Lynch to direct his company's production of *The Elephant Man* (1980), which was based on the actual case history of the horribly disfigured individual called by that name in Victorian England, rather than the then-popular Broadway play of the same name. Like *Eraserhead,* this Lynch movie was shot in black-and-white and boasted a distinctive visual style. It earned eight Oscar nominations, including Best Picture, Best Director, and Best Screenplay, which Lynch also co-wrote.

Lynch's first color feature was the box-office disaster *Dune* (1984), which was certainly unlike any sci-fi epic ever made; while Lynch clearly had little interest in the story (adapted from Frank Herbert's long-revered novel), he seemed to enjoy bringing mutated art-deco designs into deep space, and the movie contains some genuinely perverse bits of business bearing his queasy stamp. It has been reported that he only accepted producer Dino de Laurentiis' *Dune* assignment in return for carte blanche on his next project, the 1986 erotic thriller *Blue Velvet*. While not a box-office smash, it was one of the most talked-about films of the 1980s, and many of its images—villain Dennis Hopper ingesting a mysterious substance via gas mask, warring insects swarming beneath an "ordinary" suburban lawn—have gained cinematic notoriety. The film also netted Lynch his second Oscar nomination for Best Director.

Lynch's next foray was, surprisingly enough, into television; his 1990 series, "Twin Peaks," a twisted prime-time soap about the dark secrets in a seemingly placid town in the Pacific Northwest, was the darling of critics if not audiences. Initially daring and innovative, the show eventually got silly and in-jokey, losing most of its initially rabid supporters rather quickly. Lynch's 1990 film *Wild at Heart*, the director's discursive, fantasy-laden road movie, won the Palme d'Or at Cannes but wildly divided viewers in the States, many of whom felt the director had descended into self-parody. In 1992 he brought to theater screens *Twin Peaks: Fire Walk With Me* a prequel to the TV pilot that reunited many of the show's cast members. He also executive produced and directed "On the Air" (1992) and "Hotel Room" (1993) for TV. Lynch appeared as an actor in the little-seen feature *Zelly and Me* (1988), took a small role as an FBI chief in "Twin Peaks" and *Fire Walk With Me*. He also directed Chris Issak's music video "Wicked Game." His daughter Jennifer Chambers Lynch made a notorious debut as writer-director with the much-discussed *Boxing Helena* (1993).

LYNCH, KELLY. Actress. *(b. Jan. 31, 1959, Minneapolis.)* Leggy ex-model turned sexy leading lady. Memorable—in fact, unforgettable—as Matt Dillon's unrepentant drug-addict girlfriend in *Drugstore Cowboy* (1989), she's also had supporting roles in *Bright Lights, Big City* (1988), *Cocktail* (1988), *Road House* (1989), and *Desperate Hours* (1990). Thought to be on the verge of stardom more than once,

her films have ranged from John Hughes' cutesy *Curly Sue* (1991) to *Three of Hearts* (1993), in which she played a woman who loses her female lover. In 1994 she appeared in *The Beans of Egypt, Maine.*

LYNE, ADRIAN. Director. *(b. Mar. 4, 1941, Peterborough, England.)* Commercially minded director who, along with fellow Brits Alan Parker and Ridley Scott, graduated to filmmaking from the world of TV commercials. Lyne's first feature, the modest teen picture *Foxes* (1980), established him as a visual stylist. He helmed the hugely successful *Flashdance* (1983), a preposterous feel-good story about a sexy steelworker who lives in a loft and spends her off-hours dancing. By then an easily bankable director, Lyne was given carte blanche to pick his next project, which turned out to be the exploitative *Nine ½ Weeks* (1986), which again emphasized style over substance. Lyne hit pay dirt (and earned an Oscar nomination) for *Fatal Attraction* (1987), a highly charged sexual thriller starring Michael Douglas and Glenn Close, but not without a detour along the way: after preview audiences rejected its clever finale, the studio pressured Lyne to reshoot a more crowd-pleasing ending. (He later showed the original denouement and discussed its evolution on a special video release of the picture, admitting that the studio was right.)

In 1990 he directed the downbeat *Jacob's Ladder,* but bounced back to the top of the box-office heap with *Indecent Proposal* (1993), which like *Fatal Attraction* managed to strike a responsive chord with the mass moviegoing audience. Like all of Lyne's films, even at its dumbest it remained good-looking and watchable.

LYNLEY, CAROL. Actress. *(b. Feb. 13, 1942, New York City.)* As the adorable young daughter in *The Light in the Forest* (1958) and the troubled teen faced with unwanted pregnancy in *Blue Denim* (1959), this fresh-faced, blue-eyed blond seemed to be destined for major stardom. A sensation as a teen model, Lynley delivered meritorious if not technically sophisticated performances in her early films, which ran the gamut from *Hound-Dog*

Man (1960) to *Return to Peyton Place* (1961). She did appear in some fine movies as a young adult (such as 1963's *The Cardinal* and 1964's *Shock Treatment*), and even played legendary sex goddess Jean Harlow in a forgettable 1965 biopic, but the likes of *The Maltese Bippy* (1969), *Norwood* (1970), and *Beware the Blob!* (1972) drove her to the small screen, where she guested in many series and costarred in a number of made-fors, including the well-received vampire story, *The Night Stalker* (1971). The 1980s saw her much less active, although she surprised her old fans by doing a brief topless scene in the straight-to-video thriller *Blackout* (1988).

OTHER FILMS INCLUDE: 1963: *The Stripper, Under the Yum Yum Tree;* 1965: *Bunny Lake Is Missing;* 1968: *Danger Route;* 1969: *Once You Kiss a Stranger;* 1972: *The Poseidon Adventure;* 1975: *The Four Deuces;* 1977: *Bad Georgia Road;* 1978: *The Cat and the Canary* (in the female lead); 1979: *The Shape of Things to Come;* 1982: *Vigilante;* 1987: *Dark Tower;* 1991: *Spirits.*

LYNN, DIANA. Actress. *(b. Oct. 7, 1926, Los Angeles, as Dolores Loehr; d. Dec. 18, 1971.)* A child prodigy who made her film debut playing the piano in *They Shall Have Music* (1939), the button-cute Dolly Loehr was on the Paramount lot as accompanist to soprano Susanna Foster, singing in *There's Magic in Music* (1941), when someone decided the pert pianist might have possibilities as a screen personality. The studio changed her name to Diana Lynn and gave her acting lessons; oddly, the powers-that-be chose to ignore her musical abilities. She played a succession of smart-mouthed kid sisters and best friends, beginning with *The Major and the Minor* (1942), in which she fared surprisingly well in her scenes with old pro Ginger Rogers. Under Preston Sturges' direction, Lynn really sparkled as Betty Hutton's sassy sister in *The Miracle of Morgan's Creek,* and played Gail Russell's bosom pal in *Our Hearts Were Young and Gay* (both 1944) and *Our Hearts Were Growing Up* (1945).

Lynn, a pretty teenager who melted boyish hearts, matured into a beautiful woman, but the fire she'd displayed in her earlier films seemed to have burned out by the time she was playing leads. Even in

My Friend Irma (1949) and *My Friend Irma Goes West* (1950), although Marie Wilson was obviously the focus of attention, Lynn seemed curiously subdued. Her later films included the notorious *Bedtime for Bonzo, The People Against O'Hara* (both 1951), *Meet Me at the Fair* (1953), *Track of the Cat* (1954), *The Kentuckian* (1955), and *The Company of Killers* (1970). She also worked extensively in TV.

LYON, SUE. Actress. *(b. July 10, 1946, Davenport, Iowa.)* She was only 13 and a total "unknown" when cast as the angel-faced nymphet who was the underaged object of James Mason's affections in Stanley Kubrick's controversial *Lolita* (1962), but her performance raised moviegoers' pulses and, to coin a phrase, a star was born. The resulting publicity made the pretty blond starlet a hot item in Hollywood, and she played another young temptress in *The Night of the Iguana* (1964), this time attempting to seduce Richard Burton. Supporting roles in *7 Women* (1966), *The Flim Flam Man* (1967), *Evel Knievel* (1972) and the horror/sci-fi films *Crash!, End of the World* (both 1977), and *Alligator* (1980) suggest that her appeal, like her adolescence, was short-lived.

MACCHIO, RALPH. Actor. *(b. Nov. 4, 1962, Huntington, N.Y.)* Before he shot to worldwide fame as the young star of *The Karate Kid* (1984) and its 1986 and 1989 sequels, this dark, lanky juvenile performer appeared on TV in commercials and series episodes. His first TV role of any note was as Jeremy, the troubled nephew, on the popular family drama "Eight Is Enough" (1980). That same year he starred in his first movie, the alleged comedy *Up the Academy.* His other movies include *The Outsiders* (1983), *Teachers* (1984), *Crossroads* (1986), and *Distant Thunder* (1988). *Up the Academy* director Robert Downey cast Macchio as a foul-mouthed con man in the amusing farce *Too Much Sun* (1991), but with his still-youthful appearance and manner, he has found it difficult to progress to more "serious" parts on-screen. In 1992 he costarred in *My Cousin Vinny,* and in 1994, *Naked In New York.* He made an impressive Broadway debut opposite Robert DeNiro in the play "Cuba and His Teddy Bear" in 1986.

MACDONALD, JEANETTE. Actress, singer. *(b. June 18, 1901, Philadelphia; d. Jan. 14, 1965.)* This musical star may not have been the biggest box-office draw of all time, but she still has an international fan club, and a devoted following, indicative of the impact she made on-screen. She was a Broadway chorus girl in the early 1920s, but was soon picked to play leads in operettas and musical comedies. Given a screen test at Paramount's New York studio in 1929, she was chosen by director Ernst Lubitsch to costar with French singing sensation Maurice Chevalier in *The Love Parade,* the success of which made her one of the most popular female stars of the early talkie era. Pretty and vivacious (but, oddly, without much sex appeal), MacDonald's saucy characterizations in her early films for Lubitsch are quite at odds with the image she later presented as a star at MGM.

She starred in *The Vagabond King,* Lubitsch's *Monte Carlo, Let's Go Native, Lottery Bride, Oh for a Man!* (all 1930), *Don't Bet on Women, Annabelle's Affairs* (both 1931), Lubitsch's *One Hour With You, Love Me Tonight* (both 1932, reteamed with Chevalier in two of her best screen outings), *The Cat and the Fiddle,* and *The Merry Widow* (both 1934, the latter marking her final film with Chevalier and director Lubitsch) before her first fateful teaming with Nelson Eddy.

The movie operetta had enjoyed some popularity in the early talkie years, but the form was largely moribund in 1935 when MGM paired MacDonald with blondined singing star Eddy in *Naughty Marietta,* a Victor Herbert concoction that scored surprisingly well with audiences then sated by a surfeit of backstage musicals. MacDonald and Eddy suited each other perfectly on-screen, and their chaste romantic relationship won them a big fan following. MGM reteamed them seven times—for *Rose Marie* (1936), *Maytime* (1937), *The Girl of the Golden West, Sweethearts* (both 1938), *New Moon, Bitter Sweet* (both 1940), and the ill-fitting modern-day musical *I Married an Angel* (1942)—before the studio decided it had milked the winning format for every last

drop. (She had also appeared in *San Francisco,* a hugely successful 1936 drama costarring Clark Gable and Spencer Tracy, in which she warbled the title tune that became the Bay City's unofficial theme song.) After completing *Cairo* (1942), a strained musicomedy spoof of spy films, she was released by MGM. She took a cameo in *Follow the Boys* (1944) and played supporting roles in *Three Daring Daughters* (1948) and *The Sun Comes Up* (1949) before retiring from the screen altogether. MacDonald sang frequently on stage and in concert for years thereafter, but was eventually sidelined with a heart ailment, which contributed to her passing. She was survived by actor Gene Raymond, whom she'd married in 1937. They costarred in the sentimental drama *Smilin' Through* (1941).

MACDOWELL, ANDIE. Actress. *(b. Apr. 21, 1958, South Carolina, as Rose Anderson MacDowell.)* This ex-model first made waves in a series of saucy Calvin Klein TV commercials, which led to her casting in *Greystoke: The Legend of Tarzan, Lord of the Apes* (1984), but the producers decided that her Southern accent was too noticeable, and asked Glenn Close to dub all her lines after the fact. She was mere decoration in *St. Elmo's Fire* (1985), and her film career seemed over, until her eye-opening performance as the dissatisfied wife in Steven Soderbergh's *sex, lies, and videotape* (1989) revealed an actress worth watching. That film propelled her, overnight, to the ranks of leading ladies, in such pictures as *Green Card* (1990), *The Object of Beauty, Hudson Hawk* (both 1991), *Groundhog Day, Short Cuts,* and *Deception* (all 1993), *Four Weddings and a Funeral,* and *Bad Girls* (both 1994). At her best, MacDowell is able to project intelligence along with sex appeal.

MACGRAW, ALI. Actress. *(b. Apr. 1, 1938, Pound Ridge, N.Y.)* "Love means never having to say you're sorry," went the early 1970s pop homily that originated with the phenomenally popular *Love Story* (1970). But along with that catchy little phrase we also got Ali MacGraw, whose star shone briefly but brightly. This dark-haired, olive-skinned beauty, an art-history student at Wellesley before joining "Harper's Bazaar" in 1960 as a photographer's assistant, found working in front of the camera much more rewarding; her exotic features and inviting smile soon made her a top fashion model. A bit role in a 1968 thriller, *A Lovely Way to Die,* didn't exactly set the screen on fire, but MacGraw's film career ratcheted up a notch the following year with *Goodbye, Columbus,* and she won surprisingly good notices for her portrayal of a spoiled, immature suburban girl headed for marriage. *Love Story,* an unabashed three-handkerchief weepie that cast MacGraw as a college student whose tragic illness disrupts her rapturous romance, catapulted her to international stardom and earned her an Oscar nomination for Best Actress.

MacGraw played opposite future husband Steve McQueen in *The Getaway* (1972), a gritty thriller directed by Sam Peckinpah, before bowing out of the Hollywood scene; although she ostensibly retired to devote time to her marriage, MacGraw has revealed that she was plagued by serious personal problems as well. She returned to the screen in 1978's *Convoy,* a lackluster trucker opus also directed by Peckinpah, and followed that with *Players* (1979), a dreadful misfire in which she portrayed a kept woman. *Just Tell Me What You Want* (1980) gave MacGraw an opportunity to display a hitherto unsuspected flair for comedy, playing the mistress of obnoxious tycoon Alan King. Her work in two well-received TV miniseries, "China Rose" and "The Winds of War," kept her in the public eye, but her big-screen career fizzled again. In 1991 she resurfaced, this time as spokesperson for a line of cosmetics, and as the author of a candid memoir, "Moving Pictures." MacGraw's son Josh Evans is also an actor.

MACLACHLAN, KYLE. Actor. *(b. Feb. 22, 1959, Yakima, Wash.)* If coffee and cherry pie are back in fashion, credit (or blame) this jut-jawed, steely-eyed actor, who played the oddball FBI agent Dale Cooper in the much-talked-about-but-little-watched TV series "Twin Peaks," the media sensation of 1990. (Sharp-eyed viewers may have recognized the character as a variation on the alien cop he played in the 1987 sci-fi thriller *The Hid-*

den.) "Peaks" was just another chapter in the saga of the amiable, assured MacLachlan as on-screen alter ego of director David Lynch, who first cast him as the messianic Paul Atreides in *Dune* (1984), and then as the small-town innocent caught up in the horrors of *Blue Velvet* (1986). He also played a goofy editor in *Don't Tell Her It's Me* (1990) and keyboardist Ray Manzarek in *The Doors* (1991). MacLachlan reprised his Dale Cooper characterization in the 1992 "Peaks" prequel, *Twin Peaks: Fire Walk With Me.* A low-key romantic drama, *Rich in Love* (1993), gave MacLachlan his warmest, most endearing role to date, as a young historian in a Southern coastal town. He then costarred in a remake of Kafka's *The Trial* (1993), *The Flintstones* (1994), and *Showgirls* (1995). MacLachlan made his debut behind the camera directing an episode of cable TV's "Tales From the Crypt" (also 1993).

MACLAINE, SHIRLEY. Actress. *(b. Apr. 24, 1934, Richmond, Va., as Shirley MacLean Beatty.)* In a distinctly Hollywoodian success story, this long-legged dancer was literally plucked from a chorus line to replace star Carol Haney in a Broadway performance of "The Pajama Game" in 1954, immediately establishing herself as a star. A gamin-like MacLaine—with freshly short-cut auburn hair, bright eyes, and open face—made her film debut in Alfred Hitchcock's black comedy *The Trouble With Harry* (1955) and followed it immediately with a saucy secondary lead in the Dean Martin–Jerry Lewis vehicle *Artists and Models* (also 1955).

Subsequent turns in *Around the World in Eighty Days* (1956, as an Indian princess!), *Hot Spell,* and *The Sheepman* (both 1958) brought MacLaine additional recognition. She then embarked on a starring career that included *Some Came Running* (also 1958, earning her first Oscar nomination), *Ask Any Girl, Career* (both 1959), *Ocean's Eleven* (1960), *Can-Can* (also 1960, a welcome opportunity to see her dance on-screen), Billy Wilder's seriocomic *The Apartment* (1960, a career standout that netted her another Oscar nod), *All in a Night's Work, Two Loves* (both 1961), *My Geisha, Two for the Seesaw* (both 1962), *Irma La Douce* (1963, snagging another Academy Award nomination for this comedy that reunited her with director Billy Wilder and costar Jack Lemmon from *The Apartment*), and *What a Way to Go!* (1964, which included one old-fashioned Hollywood musical production number with MacLaine and Gene Kelly). Although her screen characters most frequently displayed sunny, naive personalities during these years (in what she has called her "doormat" period), MacLaine occasionally tackled more demanding roles, such as a lesbian schoolteacher in *The Children's Hour* (1962), opposite Audrey Hepburn.

The stupefyingly awful *John Goldfarb, Please Come Home* (1965)—an alleged comedy set in the Middle East—would have decimated a lesser career, but MacLaine bounced back with top-billed turns in *The Yellow Rolls-Royce* (1964), *Gambit* (1966), *Woman Times Seven* (1967, in seven different parts), the underrated *The Bliss of Mrs. Blossom* (1968), and *Sweet Charity* (1969), the latter a dynamic musical directed by Bob Fosse that showed the former chorus girl still able to kick up her heels with gusto.

MacLaine tackled more ambitious and unusual parts in *Two Mules for Sister Sara* (1970, opposite Clint Eastwood), *Desperate Characters* (1971), and *The Possession of Joel Delaney* (1972). She left the screen voluntarily for several years, during which time she completed a documentary about China, *The Other Half of the Sky* (1974), and pursued other interests, some of them spiritual. An older MacLaine took a costarring role in *The Turning Point* (1977), getting yet another Oscar nomination for her performance as a Midwestern housewife who reflects on her former life as a ballet dancer. She followed that with costarring assignments in the cult hit *Being There* (1979) and *Loving Couples* (1980), before hitting paydirt as Debra Winger's self-centered, possessive mother in *Terms of Endearment* (1983), for which she finally won a Best Actress Academy Award.

MacLaine starred in a handful of well-received TV musical specials, and has taken her act around the world, in theaters and nightclubs. In recent years she has chosen her roles carefully, looking for colorful character roles and succeeding admirably. She was charming as the piano teacher in *Madame Sousatzka* (1988), hilarious as the sharp-tongued Southern har-

ridan in *Steel Magnolias* (1989), and wryly humorous as Meryl Streep's showbiz mother in *Postcards From the Edge* and an eccentric great-aunt in *Waiting for the Light* (both 1990). More recently she has costarred in *Used People* (1992, not completely convincing as a Jewish woman romanced by Marcello Mastroianni), *Wrestling Ernest Hemingway* (1993), and *Guarding Tess* (1994). MacLaine's brother is actor-producer-director Warren Beatty; her daughter Sachi Parker is also an actress. She has written a series of bestselling books, starting with her autobiography, 1970's "Don't Fall Off the Mountain," and going on in successive volumes to explore her inner self. "Out on a Limb" (1983) revealed her experience with reincarnation; MacLaine subsequently played herself in a 1987 TV miniseries based on the book. (Revealing a sense of humor about her involvement with such phenomena, she made a cameo appearance as herself in Albert Brooks' 1991 comedy *Defending Your Life*.)

MACLANE, BARTON. Actor. *(b. Dec. 25, 1902, Columbia, S.C.; d. Jan. 1, 1969.)* Bulky, doughy-faced supporting actor and occasional leading man, a veteran of nearly 200 films, who usually portrayed coarse, vulgar men of limited intelligence (on either side of the law). MacLane was educated at Wesleyan and planned to become a writer before taking up acting. After early walk-on appearances in the 1920s, and supporting roles in a pair of 1933 Zane Grey Westerns, MacLane spent most of his time at Warners, where he played gangsters, cops, and pugs, as well as marginally sympathetic leads in *Man of Iron* (1935), *Bengal Tiger* (1936), and *Draegerman Courage* (1937), among others. As two-fisted police detective Steve MacBride, he played second fiddle to brash reporter Glenda Farrell in the *Torchy Blane* series from 1936 to 1939. He also starred on TV's "The Outlaws" (1961–62) and appeared as General Peterson on the popular "I Dream of Jeannie" series from 1965 to 1969.

OTHER FILMS INCLUDE: 1936: *Bullets or Ballots*; 1937: *San Quentin*; 1939: *Big Town Czar*; 1941: *The Maltese Falcon* (as the cynical police detective); 1945: *The Spanish Main*; 1948: *The Treasure of the Sierra Madre*; 1952: *The Half-Breed*; 1954: *The*

Glenn Miller Story; 1961: *Pocketful of Miracles;* 1965: *Town Tamer.*

MACMURRAY, FRED. Actor. *(b. Aug. 30, 1908, Kankakee, Ill.; d. Nov. 5, 1991.)* Throughout his long screen career, Fred MacMurray was such a dependable light comedian that audiences tended to forget he was also a fine dramatic actor. The onetime saxophone player toured the country with various bands in the 1920s and early 1930s, and even did some extra work in silents while playing an extended engagement in Los Angeles. With the California Collegians, MacMurray played in the Broadway musical "Roberta," and attracted the attention of Paramount scouts, who convinced him to try his hand at screen work. His first few roles generated little notice, but in *The Gilded Lily* and *Alice Adams* (both 1935, on loan to RKO), MacMurray held his own opposite Claudette Colbert and Katharine Hepburn, and managed to become a star.

Tall, wavy-haired, and virile, he made an able leading man, and conveyed an easygoing sensibility and self-effacing charm that immediately endeared him to audiences. MacMurray costarred with Henry Fonda and Sylvia Sidney for director Henry Hathaway in the first all-outdoor Technicolor drama, *Trail of the Lonesome Pine,* for King Vidor in *The Texas Rangers* (both 1936), and for Frank Lloyd in *Maid of Salem* (1937), but his most frequent director in the 1930s and early 1940s was Mitchell Leisen, who had a fine light touch in such MacMurray pictures as *Hands Across the Table* (1935), *The Princess Comes Across* (1936, in which he got to sing), *Swing High, Swing Low,* and *True Confession* (both 1937), all of which paired him with the delectable Carole Lombard.

His early 1940s vehicles, such as *New York Town* (1941), *Take a Letter, Darling, The Forest Rangers* (both 1942), and *No Time for Love* (1943) were pleasant if unspectacular, and his box-office appeal began to slip. In a daring move, Billy Wilder tapped MacMurray to play crooked insurance man Walter Neff in *Double Indemnity* (1944), and extracted one of the star's best performances ever; amazingly, the picture, script, direction, music score, and actress Barbara Stanwyck all received Oscar nominations while MacMurray's superb hard-boiled performance was overlooked. He again played an insurance salesman in *Murder, He Says* (1945), a wacky black comedy about a group of murderous inbred hillbillies.

MacMurray continued to move with ease from comedy to drama to musicals in such popular films as *Captain Eddie* (as ace aviator Eddie Rickenbacker), *Where Do We Go From Here?* (costarring with future wife June Haver, both 1945), *The Egg and I* (1947, paired with Claudette Colbert, another of his frequent costars), *The Miracle of the Bells* (1948), *The Caine Mutiny* (1954, another plum role as a heel), and *The Rains of Ranchipur* (1955). As his box-office power declined again, MacMurray retreated to the refuge of aging leading men—the Western. *At Gunpoint* (1955), *Quantez* (1957), *Day of the Badman* (1958), and *Good Day for a Hanging* (1959) kept MacMurray on the big screen though, as he later admitted, "I never felt at one with the horse."

His career started to turn around again in 1959, when he made the first of many popular comedies for Walt Disney, *The Shaggy Dog.* The following year his brilliant portrayal of a slimy businessman in Billy Wilder's *The Apartment* offered a final dramatic triumph just as he settled into kiddie films for Disney and a 12-year run as the star of TV's "My Three Sons." Thereafter his movie roles, with the exception of *The Swarm* (1978) for Irwin Allen, were limited to the Disney studio; these included turns in the hugely popular *The Absent Minded Professor* (1961), *Son of Flubber* (a 1963 sequel), *Follow Me, Boys* (1966), *The Happiest Millionaire* (1967, another musical role), and *Charley and the Angel* (1973).

Long taken for granted, MacMurray proved to be one of the most durable and popular stars in Hollywood history. He also has the distinction of having served (unknowingly) as the model for comic-book artist C. C. Beck's Captain Marvel! MacMurray was married from 1954 to screen actress June Haver.

MACNICOL, PETER. Actor. *(b. Apr. 10, 1954, Dallas.)* Boyish-looking actor who made a big splash on film in the early 1980s, with leading roles in the fantasy *Dragonslayer* (1981) and in Alan J. Pakula's acclaimed adaptation of *Sophie's*

Choice (1982) as the young writer Stingo. After that, MacNicol concentrated on stage work and did not return to the screen until the tepid actioner *Heat* (1987). He has since appeared in *Hard Promises* (1991), *Housesitter* (1992) and, most memorably, as the indecipherable art restorer Janosz in *Ghostbusters II* (1989). More recently he costarred in *Addams Family Values* (1993) and has had running parts in the TV series "The Powers That Be" (1992) and "Chicago Hope" (1994–).

MACRAE, GORDON. Actor. *(b. Mar. 12, 1921, East Orange, N.J.; d. Jan. 24, 1986.)* Good-looking leading man, with booming baritone and an easy smile, of late 1940s and 1950s musicals, a casualty of the genre's meltdown toward the end of the latter decade. A former band singer and nightclub performer, blessed with a glorious voice, MacRae went to Hollywood in 1948 under contract to Warner Bros., which promoted him—with some success—as a clean-cut leading man somewhat in the image of aging studio songster Dennis Morgan. He reached his personal peak as the star of *Oklahoma!* (1955, as the carefree Curly) and *Carousel* (1956, as carnival barker Billy Bigelow, a part he won after Frank Sinatra dropped out of production), but only made two more films before returning to the stage and nightclubs.

His daughters, Meredith and Heather MacRae, acted in films and TV shows during the 1960s and 1970s; former wife, Sheila ("The Jackie Gleason Show") wrote a 1992 autobiography that contained some harrowing revelations about him. OTHER FILMS INCLUDE: 1948: *The Big Punch;* 1949: *Look for the Silver Lining;* 1950: *The Daughter of Rosie O'Grady, Return of the Frontiersman* (a straight action role), *Tea for Two, West Point Story;* 1951: *On Moonlight Bay;* 1952: *About Face;* 1953: *By the Light of the Silvery Moon, The Desert Song, Three Sailors and a Girl;* 1956: *The Best Things in Life Are Free* (as Buddy De Sylva of the songwriting team De Sylva, Brown, and Henderson); 1979: *The Pilot* (in a small supporting role).

MACREADY, GEORGE. Actor. *(b. Aug. 29, 1909, Providence, R.I.; d. July 2, 1973.)* Tall, slender, urbane actor with dis-

tinctive scar on his right cheek. Who could forget him as Rita Hayworth's hissworthy husband in *Gilda* (1946)? Or as the cold-blooded French general who decimates his own battalion in *Paths of Glory* (1957)? Macready specialized in villains, both debonair and psychotic; the sound of his deep, husky voice alone was enough to send chills down the spines of movie audiences. He was an experienced stage actor who came to Hollywood in 1942, under contract to Columbia; he made his film debut in *The Commandos Strike at Dawn* (1942) and then bounced between A and B productions. A TV generation came to know him as the patriarch of "Peyton Place" (1965–68).
OTHER FILMS INCLUDE: 1945: *I Love a Mystery, My Name Is Julia Ross;* 1947: *Down to Earth;* 1948: *The Black Arrow* (one of several swashbucklers), *The Big Clock* (memorable as Charles Laughton's toady); 1949: *Knock on Any Door;* 1951: *Detective Story;* 1953: *Julius Caesar;* 1956: *A Kiss Before Dying;* 1964: *Seven Days in May;* 1965: *The Great Race* (uncharacteristically involved in the huge pie fight); 1970: *Tora! Tora! Tora!* (as Cordell Hull), *Count Yorga, Vampire.*

MADIGAN, AMY. Actress. *(b. Sept. 11, 1950, Chicago.)* Intense blond actress whose fresh-scrubbed appearance and diminutive stature can't mask her feisty, nononsense attitude. After stage and TV work and a stint as a rock singer, she first impressed moviegoers as a prisoner who gives birth in *Love Child* (1982). Subsequent roles included a soldier of fortune (originally written for a man) in *Streets of Fire* (1984), the adulterous neighbor in *Places in the Heart* (also 1984), and the embittered daughter in *Twice in a Lifetime* (1985), which earned her an Oscar nomination. Other films include *Love Letters* (1983), *Nowhere to Hide* (1987), and *The Prince of Pennsylvania* (1988). She had a banner year in 1989, playing the strong-willed, supportive wife of Kevin Costner in *Field of Dreams* (1989), the tenacious attorney in the TV movie *Roe vs. Wade* (1989), which won her an Emmy nomination and a Golden Globe, and John Candy's girlfriend in *Uncle Buck.* In 1993 she appeared in *The Dark Half.* Not an actress for whom projects are developed, Madigan remains a dependable, enjoyable performer whose presence invariably inflates a movie's net worth. Active on stage, she played Stella in the 1992 Broadway revival of *A Streetcar Named Desire.* Married to Ed Harris, with whom she costarred in *Places in the Heart* and *Alamo Bay* (1985).

contributes songs to her and others' movies (including Sean Penn's 1986 vehicle *At Close Range).*
OTHER FILMS INCLUDE: 1985: *Vision Quest;* 1989: *Bloodhounds of Broadway;* 1992: *Shadows and Fog.*

MADONNA. Actress, singer, songwriter. *(b. Aug. 16, 1959, Bay City, Mich., as Madonna Louise Veronica Ciccone.)* It's little wonder that the best-reviewed film starring this mega-successful pop diva is the candid musical documentary *Truth or Dare* (1991). Recording artists often have a difficult time translating their appeal to the big screen, and only occasionally demonstrate the ability to command an entire motion picture. Madonna commands the screen in *Truth or Dare,* but can't seem to deliver a competent performance elsewhere. Early in her career, in *Desperately Seeking Susan* (1985), this platinum-blond siren found a hip romantic comedy tailormade for her tough and sexy "downtown" persona. But despite her attempts to reincarnate the image of Marilyn Monroe (which she has frequently played up in her music videos), she has not yet mastered the art of screwball comedy, as evidenced by her work in the execrable *Shanghai Surprise* (1986), which costarred thenhusband Sean Penn, and *Who's That Girl?* (1987).

Madonna seems to fare best when she's not required to carry a movie, as was the case when she played femme fatale Breathless Mahoney in *Dick Tracy* (1990); she also had a highly publicized fling with director and star, Warren Beatty. Her work in *A League of Their Own* (1992), which starred Tom Hanks and Geena Davis, was also relaxed and amusing. But *Body of Evidence* (1993), which cast her as a sexaddicted femme fatale, put the burden of its patently ridiculous (and undernourished) script on her slender shoulders, which weren't quite up to the challenge; it was a classically bad movie that enjoyed little box-office success despite all the attendent publicity. Later that same year she costarred with Harvey Keitel in Abel Ferrara's *Dangerous Game* (1993).

In 1985 she unsuccessfully tried to block the video release of *A Certain Sacrifice,* a tawdry, ultra-low-budget film (and her debut), which she made as a desperate newcomer to New York. She occasionally

MADSEN, VIRGINIA. Actress. *(b. Sept. 11, 1963, Winnetka, Ill.)* Blond, strikingly beautiful young lead, whose debut, in 1983's *Class,* had her exposing one breast in a comic melee. (She got to wear clothes, at least, for her supporting role in the following year's *Dune.)* Her subsequent output has been extremely variable, from good parts in *Electric Dreams* (1984), *Creator* (1985), and *Candyman* (1992) to forgettable leads in *Fire With Fire* (1986), *Slamdance, Zombie High* (both 1987), *Hot to Trot* (1988), and *Highlander II: The Quickening* (1991). Despite some strong (and often uninhibited) performances, particularly as the devious and insatiable Southern belle in Dennis Hopper's *The Hot Spot* (1990), the popular success her talent hints at has yet to materialize. She has fared better in some high-profile made-for-TV movies, including *The Hearst and Davies Affair* (1985, as Marion Davies), *Long Gone* (1987), *Third Degree Burn* (1989), *Ironclads* (1991), and *A Murderous Affair: The Carolyn Warmus Story* (1992). She was married briefly to director Danny Huston, in whose films *Mr. North* (1988) and *Becoming Colette* (1992) she had juicy supporting roles. Her brother is actor Michael Madsen, featured as Susan Sarandon's boyfriend in *Thelma & Louise* (1991), as well as in *Reservoir Dogs* (1992), *Free Willy, Money for Nothing* (both 1993), *Wyatt Earp,* and *The Getaway* (both 1994).

MAGNANI, ANNA. Actress. *(b. Mar. 7, 1908, Alexandria, Egypt; d. Sept. 26, 1973.)* Legendary, powerful star of international films whom Andrew Sarris wrote "can tear a dramatic scene to tatters and in the next instant turn on a brilliant comedy style." She was born illegitimate and in poverty, raised by her maternal grandmother and educated in a convent. She studied at Rome's Accademia d'Arte Drammatica and at the same time, sang at nightclubs and performed in variety shows and then dramatic stock companies. She made her film debut with a bit part in *Scampolo* (1927), then later had a starring role in *La Cieca di Sorrento/The Blind Woman of Sorrento* (1934). After her marriage to director Goffredo Alessandrini (which was later annulled) she appeared mostly in supporting roles in films like *Cavalleria* (1936), *La Fuggitiva,* and *Teresa Venerdi* (both 1941). It was her performance as a pregnant widow shot by Germans in Roberto Rossellini's neorealist classic *Roma, Citta Aperta/Open City* (1945) that made the world take notice; the film was ignored by Italian critics but hailed abroad. Magnani's raw, emotional performance and unglamorous looks made her a star. She subsequently won the Best Actress Award at the Venice Film Festival as a woman who rallies tenement dwellers in *L'Onorevole Angelina* (1947), and starred in Rossellini's *Amore* (1948), which originally consisted of the monologue *La Voce Umana* and the controversial *Il Miracolo/The Miracle,* in which Magnani beautifully played a peasant woman who believes her unborn child is Christ. She was also memorable as an actress in Renoir's *The Golden Coach* (1952), a role he tailored for her.

In Hollywood, she starred in *The Rose Tattoo* (1955) as Serafina Delle Rose, a part Tennessee Williams had originally written with her in mind for the Broadway stage, which she was unable to accept at the time. She won the Best Actress Oscar for her performance, but subsequent roles were less rewarding. She received another Oscar nomination as a mail-order bride in *Wild Is the Wind* (1957, opposite Anthony Quinn) and appeared in *The Fugitive Kind* (1959), Pasolini's *Mamma Rosa* (1962), *The Secret of Santa Vittoria* (1969) and, briefly, in *Fellini's Roma* (1972), as herself. She died at 65. There was a tremendous public gathering at her funeral; for many she was, as Pauline Kael noted, "The actress who has come to be the embodiment of human experience, the most 'real' of actresses."

MAHONEY, JOCK. Actor, stuntman. *(b. Feb. 17, 1919, Chicago, as Jacques O'Mahoney; d. Dec. 14, 1989.)* One of the greatest stuntmen who ever lived, this tall, rangy athlete made a name for himself doubling such stars as Gregory Peck and Errol Flynn (making the famous staircase leap for Flynn in 1948's *The Adventures of Don Juan).* Along the way, the handsome Mahoney started taking small parts in films, including some Three Stooges Western short subjects (1947's *Out West;* 1950's *Punchy Cowpunchers),* billed as Jacques, then Jock O'Mahoney. He was instrumental in the success of the "Durango Kid" Westerns for Columbia; every time leading man Charles Starrett put on his mask, it was really Mahoney doing all the action. Eventually, Starrett encouraged him to play roles in the films as well, and on more than one occasion, Mahoney (as a villain) engaged in a fight scene with himself (doubling Starrett). He starred in two Columbia serials, *Cody of the Pony Express* (1950) and *Roar of the Iron Horse* (1951), saving producers the expense of hiring a stunt double. Then he starred in the popular action-packed early TV Western series "The Range Rider" (1951–53). Mahoney worked in other films, but gained more name recognition as the star of the TV series "Yancy Derringer" (1958–59). He made an excellent villain in *Tarzan the Magnificent* (1960) and in fact stole the movie from star Gordon Scott. Two years later he was cast as the jungle king in *Tarzan Goes to India* (1962), but he fell ill during filming of the exciting *Tarzan's Three Challenges* (1963), which is all too apparent from his dramatic weight loss in the course of the story. Mahoney never fully recovered, and eased into character parts and TV guest shots. Married to Maggie Field, he was the stepfather of Sally Field and performed a stunt (going off a bridge in a wheelchair) in Burt Reynolds' *The End* (1978), in which she costarred. In *Hooper* (also 1978), another Reynolds film about wild and woolly stuntmen, Field's father was played by Brian Keith, and named Jocko in tribute to Mahoney.

MAHONEY, JOHN. Actor. *(b. June 20, 1940, Manchester, England.)* One of the most solidly American character players on-screen, Mahoney is actually British! He determined to lose his accent when he moved here in the 1950s, and succeeded. Although the soft-spoken, white-haired Mahoney only took up acting as he approached middle age, following a career in medical journalism, he has achieved a critical and commercial success many performers never attain. He spent his showbiz salad days on stage, winning a Tony for his performance as the sad-sack songwriter in "The House of Blue Leaves." After small roles in *Code of Silence* (1985) and *Streets of Gold* (1986), Mahoney raised eyebrows in a brace of 1987 movies, first as one of the aluminum-siding hustlers in *Tin Men,* next as the biased judge in *Suspect,* and then as Olympia Dukakis' hapless suitor in *Moonstruck.* This parlay propelled him to the front ranks of working character actors. He was a deceptively benign white supremacist in *Betrayed,* a weary coach in *Eight Men Out* (both 1988), a kindly father with a secret in *Say Anything . . .* (1989), and a CIA creep in *The Russia House* (1990). In 1991 he was seen to advantage in *Barton Fink,* as a Faulkneresque screenwriter, and stood out among a distinguished cast in the unsuccessful *Article 99* (1992). Other films include *In the Line of Fire, Striking Distance* (both 1993), and *The Hudsucker Proxy* (1994). He has also been active in TV movies, including *Dinner at Eight* (1989, opposite Lauren Bacall), *The Image* (1990, opposite Albert Finney), and David Mamet's *The Water Engine* (1992), and costars in the TV sitcom "Frasier" (1993–   ).

MAIN, MARJORIE. Actress. *(b. Feb. 24, 1890, Acton, Ind., as Mary Tomlinson; d. Apr. 10, 1975.)* Probably best known as feisty Ma Kettle, this versatile actress also sparked a number of other, bigger films with her boisterous manner and memorably scratchy voice. She logged nearly 100 film appearances in all during a 20-year screen career. Her breakthrough role was that of the weary, sad, and impoverished mother of gangster Humphrey Bogart in *Dead End* (1937); it was a characterization she repeated, with little variation but astonishing consistency, in at least a half-dozen other movies, including *Boy of the Streets* (1937) and *The Angels Wash Their Faces* (1939). She appeared in more than 20 movies—including *The Women* (1939), *Honky Tonk* (1941), *Johnny Come Lately* (1943, as Gas House Mary), *Meet Me in St. Louis* (1944, as the housekeeper), *Murder, He Says* (1945), and *The Harvey*

Girls (1946)—before her tyro appearance as Ma Kettle in *The Egg and I* (1947), which earned her an Oscar nomination and led to the popular 1950s series costarring Percy Kilbride. She was well matched with Wallace Beery in *Barnacle Bill* (1941), *Jackass Mail* (1942), *Bad Bascomb* (1946), and *Big Jack* (1949), and was cast opposite James Whitmore in *Mrs. O'Malley and Mr. Malone* (1950), in an attempt to launch a series that never came to be. She even sang with Bert Lahr in *Rose Marie* (1954). Main retired in 1957, shortly after completing the ninth and final Kettle film, *The Kettles on Old Macdonald's Farm.*
OTHER FILMS INCLUDE: 1931: *A House Divided;* 1934: *Crime Without Passion;* 1939: *Another Thin Man;* 1940: *Dark Command;* 1947: *The Wistful Widow of Wagon Gap;* 1950: *Summer Stock;* 1952: *The Belle of New York;* 1954: *The Long, Long Trailer;* 1956: *Friendly Persuasion.*

MAKO. Actor. *(b. Dec. 10, 1933, Kobe, Japan, as Makoto Iwamatsu.)* Talented Japanese actor who came to the U.S. in the late 1940s and studied architecture before becoming interested in theater and acting. He debuted in a small role in *Never So Few* (1959), earned a Supporting Actor Oscar nomination for his role as the engine room attendant (and boxing champion) in *The Sand Pebbles* (1966), and has also appeared in *The Private Navy of Sgt. O'Farrell* (1968), *The Great Bank Robbery* (1969), *The Hawaiians* (1970), *The Island at the Top of the World* (1974), *The Killer Elite* (1975), *Conan the Barbarian* (1982), *Testament* (1983), *Conan the Destroyer* (1984), *Tucker: The Man and His Dream* (1988), *Pacific Heights, Taking Care of Business* (both 1990), *Rising Sun,* and *RoboCop 3* (both 1993). He holds a black belt in karate and has appeared in such action films as *The Big Brawl* (1980), *Armed Response* (1986), *Silent Assassins* (1988), and *The Perfect Weapon* (1991). In addition to numerous TV credits, Mako also earned a Tony nomination for his work in the Stephen Sondheim musical "Pacific Overtures" (1976) and has been involved in L.A.'s theater group East West Players, which he cofounded in the mid 1960s.

MALDEN, KARL. Actor. *(b. Mar. 22, 1914, Chicago, as Karl Mladen Sekulovich.)* It just wasn't in the cards for this craggy-faced, bulbous-nosed actor to become a matinee idol, but he's done pretty well for himself as a supporting player, limning a string of memorable characters in presti-gious films made during the past five de-cades. He won a Best Supporting Actor Academy Award for his characterization of Mitch in *A Streetcar Named Desire* (1951, reprising his role from the Broad-way production) and was nominated for his turn as Father Barry in *On the Water-front* (1954). A commanding screen pres-ence, Malden enriches every film in which he appears, and invariably brings his in-nate dignity to every role he tackles. He starred in the 1972–77 TV series "Streets of San Francisco" and was for many years a commercial pitchman for American Ex-press ("Don't leave home without it!"). In recent years he has been active in made-for-TV movies, many of which he's car-ried almost singlehandedly; in 1985 he won an Emmy for his performance in *Fa-tal Vision.* Malden has also served as pres-ident of the Academy of Motion Picture Arts and Sciences.
OTHER FILMS INCLUDE: 1940: *They Knew What They Wanted* (his first); 1944: *Winged Victory;* 1946: *13 Rue Madeleine;* 1947: *Kiss of Death, Boomerang!;* 1950: *The Gunfighter, Halls of Montezuma, Where the Sidewalk Ends;* 1952: *The Sellout, Operation Secret, Ruby Gentry;* 1953: *I Confess, Take the High Ground;* 1954: *Phantom of the Rue Morgue;* 1956: *Baby Doll* (as husband of the child bride, another standout role); 1957: *Bomb-ers B-52, Time Limit* (as director, not actor); 1959: *The Hanging Tree;* 1960: *The Great Im-postor, Pollyanna;* 1961: *One-Eyed Jacks;* 1962: *All Fall Down, Birdman of Alcatraz, Gypsy, How the West Was Won;* 1964: *Chey-enne Autumn;* 1965: *The Cincinnati Kid;* 1966: *Murderers' Row, Nevada Smith;* 1967: *Billion Dollar Brain, Hotel;* 1968: *Blue, Hot Millions;* 1970: *Patton* (another fine role, as Omar Bradley); 1971: *The Cat o' Nine Tails, Wild Rovers;* 1973: *Summertime Killer;* 1979: *Be-yond the Poseidon Adventure, Meteor;* 1980: *Skag* (telefilm which became a short-lived TV series); 1981: *Miracle on Ice* (telefilm, as coach of the U.S. Olympic hockey team); 1983: *The Sting II;* 1986: *Billy Galvin;* 1987: *Nuts* (as Barbra Streisand's father); 1991: *Absolute Strangers* (telefilm).

MALICK, TERRENCE. Producer, direc-tor, screenwriter. *(b. Nov. 30, 1943, Ottawa, Ill.)* As Greta Garbo learned, elusiveness and inactivity can feed a legend; so it is that Terrence Malick has become one of the most intriguing figures in recent film history, as much for his long sabbatical as for his striking movie work. The son of an oil company executive, Malick was educa-ted at Harvard and Oxford University and taught philosophy at MIT before attending the American Film Institute. He cowrote the screenplay for *Deadhead Miles* (1972), an offbeat allegory that sat on the shelf for years before ever being screened, and wrote the modern Western *Pocket Money* (also 1972) before producing, writ-ing, and directing *Badlands* (1973), a lyr-ical story of alienation loosely based on the Starkweather–Fugate killings of the late 1950s. Critics hailed the film as one of the finest debuts by an American direc-tor and were equally enthusiastic about his next film, the moving and stunningly pho-tographed *Days of Heaven* (1978), which won Malick the Best Director award at Cannes. His inactivity (and low profile) since then has made him the cinematic eq-uivalent of J. D. Salinger, but Malick apparently has several projects—including a remake of James Jones' "The Thin Red Line"—in the works at this writing.

MALKOVICH, JOHN. Actor. *(b. Dec. 9, 1953, Benton, Ill.)* Intense, serious actor and unlikely leading man who came to Holly-wood from an exceptional career in the theater. Malkovich was one of the original founders of Chicago's Steppenwolf Thea-ter Company, where he directed and per-formed in some of America's most vital noncommercial stage productions. He made a couple of TV movies in the early 1980s, but continued to concentrate on stage work. His first film role, that of an American photographer in *The Killing Fields* (1984), showed Malkovich to be just as effective before the camera as he was behind the footlights. He snagged his first Oscar nomination for Best Supporting Actor playing Sally Field's blind, cantan-kerous boarder in *Places in the Heart* (1984). Though he has tried his hand at comedy (*Making Mr. Right*, 1987), Malkovich excels at limning aloof, amoral, generally unsympathetic charac-ters such as the black marketeer in *Empire* *of the Sun* (1987), the Vicomte de Valmont in *Dangerous Liaisons* (1988), the bored intellectual in *The Sheltering Sky* (1990), and the desperate, materialistic yuppie in *The Object of Beauty* (1991). His other films include *Eleni* (1985), *The Glass Menagerie* (1987), *Miles From Home* (1988), and *Queens Logic* (1991). In 1992 he played the brutish, simple-minded Lennie in *Of Mice and Men,* directed by and costarring Steppenwolf colleague Gary Sinise, and appeared to thoroughly enjoy himself in a supporting role as a badgering prosecutor in the muddled thriller *Jennifer 8* that same year. Following that, he earned an Oscar nomination in the plum role of a wily would-be assassin opposite Clint Eastwood in *In the Line of Fire* (1993), his biggest hit in years. He then played Kurtz in Nicolas Roeg's TV production *Heart of Darkness* (1994).

MALLE, LOUIS. Director, screenwriter. *(b. Oct. 30, 1932, Thumeries, France.)* One of France's most acclaimed directors, Malle rose to prominence during the New Wave and has maintained a remarkably consistent critical and popular consensus, with an extraordinary variety of films. The scion of a wealthy industrial family, Malle studied political science at the Sorbonne, but, against his parents' wishes, turned to film studies at the Institut des Hautes Études Cinématographiques. He served as an assistant to explorer Jacques Cousteau, with whom he codirected the Oscar-winning documentary *The Silent World* (1956), then made short films on his own, and assisted Robert Bresson on *A Man Escaped* (1956) before writing and directing his first feature, *Frantic* (1957), starring a young Jeanne Moreau. Malle's next film, *The Lovers* (1958), caused a scandal with its beautifully photographed and highly sensual depiction of a bored wife's extramarital affair. It firmly established Malle's reputation, and made Moreau a star. Varied projects followed: the frenetic comedy *Zazie dans le Metro* (1960), *A Very Private Affair* (1962, with Brigitte Bardot playing a spoiled movie star), and *The Fire Within* (1963), a powerful look at the last days of a writer before he kills himself. Following the wild, raucous *Viva Maria!* (1965, costarring Bardot and Moreau) and the period piece *The Thief of Paris*

(1967), Malle claimed he was tired of "actors, studios, fiction, and Paris" and headed for India where he made *Calcutta* and *Phantom India* (both 1969), outstanding documentaries which revealed the beauty, complexity, and misery of the country.

At a time when directors' individual styles were valued above all, Malle's eagerness to embrace different subjects may have worked against his critical reputation. Unlike fellow countrymen Truffaut, Godard, and Resnais, however, Malle maintained an audience while continuing to grow as an artist. He returned to fictional films with one of his most daring efforts, *Murmur of the Heart* (1971), a charming, intelligent exploration of adolescence and bourgeois contentment, which raised eyebrows over its depiction of an incestuous relationship between a mother and son. (It nevertheless earned Malle an Oscar nomination for Best Original Screenplay.) Even better—though just as controversial—was *Lacombe, Lucien* (1974), a shattering study of French collaboration during World War 2, which was nominated for a Best Foreign Language Film Oscar. After *Black Moon* (1975), an awkward attempt at fantasy, Malle made his American film debut with *Pretty Baby* (1978), an elegant but bloodless tale of a photographer and a twelve-year-old prostitute (Brooke Shields). Then came *Atlantic City* (1980), a sleeper about an aging gangster and a younger woman; it was a magical fusion of American themes and European tone, and it earned Malle an Oscar nomination as Best Director. His next film, *My Dinner With Andre* (1981), could have been merely a stunt, depicting friends talking over dinner for almost two hours, but it took on a life of its own, as a bold comment on artistic temperaments—and an audacious cinematic coup.

Two negligible American films followed—*Crackers* (1984) and *Alamo Bay* (1985)—before Malle returned to France to make the devastating, autobiographical *Au Revoir, Les Enfants* (1987, Oscar-nominated for Best Screenplay and Best Foreign Language Film). A powerful vignette from Malle's childhood in wartime France, it was a subject he wanted to tackle earlier—but couldn't face. *May Fools* (1990) was a leisurely essay on complacency in light of the events of May 1968. In stark contrast, the English-language *Damage* (1992) returned to the theme of adultery and caused a flap over scenes that had to be trimmed in the U.S. to avoid an NC-17 rating. In typical idiosyncratic fashion, Malle next made *Vanya on 42nd Street* (1994), a bold, challenging, and deliberately small-scale adaptation of "Uncle Vanya." He also directed the documentaries *Humain, trop humain* (1972) and *Place de la Republique* (1973) and contributed the "William Wilson" episode to 1968's *Spirits of the Dead.* He has been married to actress Candice Bergen since 1980 and made an appearance—as himself—on a 1994 episode of her long-running sitcom "Murphy Brown."

MALONE, DOROTHY. Actress. *(b. Jan. 30, 1925, Chicago, as Dorothy Eloise Maloney.)* This former child model got her "big break" when she was signed to an RKO contract at 18, after being spotted in a college play by a talent scout. Initially billed under her real name, she changed her cognomen to Malone when she went to Warners in 1945. At that studio she essayed many supporting roles (including a well-remembered small one as a bookstore clerk questioned by Humphrey Bogart in 1946's *The Big Sleep*) and worked her way up to ingenue status. Malone appeared in many Westerns, thrillers, and melodramas before lighting up the big screen as the nymphomaniacal sister of playboy Robert Stack in Douglas Sirk's torrid *Written on the Wind* (1956), winning an Oscar for her performance. Unfortunately, getting that gold statuette didn't immediately translate into better roles, and although she did land a few more good ones (as James Cagney's emotionally disturbed first wife in 1957's Lon Chaney biopic, *Man of a Thousand Faces,* and as the tragic Diana Barrymore in 1958's *Too Much, Too Soon*), Malone soon languished in unrewarding assignments. She is perhaps best remembered for her leading role in the TV soap opera "Peyton Place" (1964–69). Her first husband was actor Jacques Bergerac.

OTHER FILMS INCLUDE: 1943: *The Falcon and the Co-Eds* (her first); 1945: *Too Young to Know;* 1946: *Night and Day;* 1948: *One Sunday Afternoon;* 1949: *Colorado Territory, Flaxy Martin, South of St. Louis;* 1950: *The Killer That Stalked New York, Mrs. O'Malley and Mr. Malone;* 1951: *Saddle Legion;* 1952:

The Bushwackers; 1953: *Jack Slade, Law and Order, Scared Stiff;* 1954: *Loophole, Young at Heart;* 1955: *Artists and Models, Battle Cry, Tall Man Riding;* 1956: *Tension at Table Rock;* 1957: *Tip on a Dead Jockey;* 1958: *The Tarnished Angels;* 1960: *The Last Voyage;* 1961: *The Last Sunset;* 1963: *Beach Party;* 1975: *Abduction;* 1976: *The November Plan;* 1977: *Golden Rendezvous;* 1979: *Good Luck, Miss Wyckoff, Winter Kills;* 1980: *The Day Time Ended;* 1983: *The Being;* 1986: *Rest in Pieces;* 1992: *Basic Instinct* (a surprise cameo).

MAMET, DAVID. Screenwriter, director, playwright. *(b. Nov. 30, 1947, Chicago.)* This Pulitzer Prize–winning playwright has devoted an increasing amount of time and energy to film scripts and filmmaking. While his films rarely capture the profane, highly theatrical dialogue that distinguishes his stage work ("Mametspeak"), his intelligence and sense of irony often come through undiluted. His first screenplay was the 1981 adaptation of James M. Cain's *The Postman Always Rings Twice.* The following year he earned an Academy Award nomination for *The Verdict* (1982). He returned to films for *The Untouchables* (1987), a pet project set in his home town of Chicago, and then took on the more lighthearted remake *We're No Angels* (1989). In 1987 Mamet made an impressive directing debut with *House of Games* (from his own script), a story of con artists which starred his then-wife, Lindsay Crouse, and a host of longtime stage associates, including his acting alter ego, Joe Mantegna. Mantegna also starred in Mamet's subsequent directing efforts *Things Change* (1988, an ironic, low-key comedy costarring Don Ameche) and *Homicide* (1991, an intriguing if not fully realized urban drama). Mamet adapted his Pulitzer Prize-winning play for the film *Glengarry Glen Ross* (1992), adding one dynamic character (played by Alec Baldwin) who didn't appear in the play, and wrote the screenplay for *Hoffa* (also 1992). In 1994, he adapted and directed his play *Oleanna,* and adapted *Vanya on 42nd Street* from "Uncle Vanya." Mamet's play "A Life in the Theater" became a cable-TV movie in 1993; his earlier play "Sexual Perversity in Chicago" was adapted, and diluted, as the film *About Last Night . . .* in 1986. He appeared as one of Debra Winger's poker-playing pals in *Black Widow* (1987).

MAMOULIAN, ROUBEN. Director. *(b. Oct. 8, 1897, Tiflis, Russia; d. Dec. 8, 1987.)* A tireless experimenter whose innate taste and intelligence enabled him to succeed where less talented directors had failed, Mamoulian directed only 16 movies but left an indelible mark on film history. He grew up in Russia and studied law at the University of Moscow, but indulged his passion for the theater by taking acting classes at night. Mamoulian became a director and staged well-received productions in London and New York, culminating in his hugely successful 1926 Broadway play "Porgy," which featured an all-black cast. On the strength of that success, he was signed by Paramount to direct its backstage drama *Applause* (1929), filmed in its Astoria, Long Island studio.

Mamoulian chafed under the restrictive methods of early-sound filmmaking, and by a process of trial and error obtained adequate recordings with multiple microphones, thereby freeing his cameras and restoring the visual mobility cinematographers had achieved in the silent era. His subsequent films—*City Streets* (1931), *Dr. Jekyll and Mr. Hyde,* and the incomparable *Love Me Tonight* (both 1932)—saw Mamoulian refining his cinematic technique while continuing to experiment with subjective camera work and the melding of picture and sound. His *Becky Sharp* (1935), the first feature film made with the newly perfected three-strip Technicolor process, utilized its bright hues for dramatic rather than merely pictorial effect.

A born maverick whose independence repeatedly clashed with major-studio assembly-line methods of operation, Mamoulian seldom got the opportunity to indulge his penchant for perfectionism, and was fired from nearly as many films as he made (including *Laura, Porgy and Bess,* and *Cleopatra).* Other Hollywood technicians caught up to him in the late 1930s and early 1940s, and Mamoulian seemed less an innovator in his later films. He returned frequently to the stage (achieving great success as the original director of "Oklahoma!") and in later years turned to writing. But he maintained his passion for cinema, and right up until the time he died was a frequent and outspoken commentator on the form.

OTHER FILMS INCLUDE: 1933: *Queen Christina, Song of Songs;* 1934: *We Live Again;* 1936: *The Gay Desperado;* 1937: *High, Wide and Handsome;* 1939: *Golden Boy;* 1940: *The Mark of Zorro;* 1941: *Blood and Sand;* 1942: *Rings on Her Fingers;* 1948: *Summer Holiday;* 1957: *Silk Stockings* (his last, a musical remake of *Ninotchka).*

MANCINI, HENRY. Composer. *(b. Apr. 16, 1924, Cleveland, as Enrico Nicola Mancini; d. June 14, 1994.)* Astoundingly prolific composer whose music was heard in scores of films and TV shows, Mancini enjoyed great popularity as a conductor/arranger/songwriter while maintaining an equally high profile behind the scenes in the movie world. Schooled at Juilliard, he worked as a pianist and arranger with several big bands before going into movie work. He learned the ropes of film music in the waning days of the studio system at Universal, where he was a staff arranger/composer. (He even wrote music cues for the newsreel!) He earned his first Academy Award nomination for his second credited film assignment, *The Glenn Miller Story* (1954). Mancini, who popularized jazz themes on TV's "Peter Gunn" and "Mr. Lucky" in the late 1950s, also helped put soundtracks—and even instrumental selections from soundtracks—onto the record charts (as in his popular score for *Hatari!),* and had a string of title tunes that became major hits, including a pair of Oscar nominees, "Charade" and "Dear Heart," and two Oscar winners, "Days of Wine and Roses" and "Moon River" (from *Breakfast at Tiffany's).* Mancini also won Oscars for scoring *Breakfast at Tiffany's* (1962) and *Victor/Victoria* (1982). Other nominations came his way for songs in, and/or scores of, *Bachelor in Paradise* (1961), *The Pink Panther* (1964), *The Great Race* (1965), *Darling Lili* (1970), *Sunflower* (also 1970; original Italian title *I Girasoli), Sometimes a Great Notion* (1971), *The Pink Panther Strikes Again* (1976), *10* (1979), and *That's Life!* (1986). The composer often cited the score for *Two for the Road* (1967) as his personal favorite (which it remains for many fans as well), but his most enduring work is undoubtedly the theme from *The Pink Panther,* which was not only an instrumental hit in 1964 but has continued to be used for the character's subsequent cartoons as well as feature films right up through 1993's *Son of the Pink Panther.* Mancini's collaboration with producer-director Blake Edwards, which began with TV's "Peter Gunn" in 1958 and continued to the 1990s, was one of the longest and most fruitful in movie (and television) history. Mancini published his autobiography, "Did They Mention the Music?" in 1989.

MANKIEWICZ, HERMAN J. Screen-writer, critic, journalist. *(b. Nov. 7, 1897, New York City; d. Mar. 5, 1953.)* The older brother of writer-producer-director Joseph L. Mankiewicz, this cynical scribe has earned cinematic immortality as the coscreenwriter of Orson Welles' *Citizen Kane* (1941), even though cineastes still argue over the extent of his contributions to that classic film. Educated at New York's Columbia University and the University of Berlin, Mankiewicz became drama critic for "The New York Times" and "The New Yorker" magazine in the early 1920s, after spending several years as a reporter. Lured by the promise of easy money in Hollywood, where clever writers were very much in demand, Mankiewicz abandoned his job (and his spot at the prestigious Algonquin Round Table) to move west and write silent-movie titles and continuities for *The Road to Mandalay* (1926), *Fashions for Women, A Gentleman of Paris* (both 1927), *Gentlemen Prefer Blondes, The Last Command, Abie's Irish Rose* (all 1928), and many others. (He urged his friend Ben Hecht to come west, wiring him: "Millions are to be grabbed out here and your only competition is idiots. Don't let this get around.") The coming of sound didn't faze Mankiewicz one bit; on the contrary, his extensive knowledge of the theater and the mechanics of dialogue writing made him invaluable to Hollywood producers, and his rapier-like wit enabled him to grind out snappy dialogue with machine-like regularity. He wrote, cowrote, or added dialogue to *The Man I Love, Thunderbolt* (both 1929), *The Vagabond King, Honey, Ladies Love Brutes, The Royal Family of Broadway* (all 1930), *Ladies' Man* (1931), *Girl Crazy, The Lost Squadron* (both 1932), *Dinner at Eight, Another Language, Duck Soup* (all 1933),

Stamboul Quest, Escapade (both 1934), *After Office Hours* (1935), *My Dear Miss Aldrich* (1937), and *It's a Wonderful World* (1939).

Actually, Mankiewicz's career was on the wane by the time he hooked up with Orson Welles; years of high living, heavy drinking, and reckless gambling had impoverished him both financially and spiritually. Nonetheless, as a once-frequent guest at William Randolph Hearst's enormous California pleasure palace, he was the ideal person to help Welles craft his inflammatory portrait of a Hearst-like publishing magnate. He and Welles (who shared screenplay credit) won Academy Awards for their script; Mankiewicz was subsequently nominated for cowriting *The Pride of the Yankees* (1942), the biopic of baseball great Lou Gehrig.

Mankiewicz's output gradually diminished, both in quantity and quality. *Stand by for Action* (1942), *Christmas Holiday* (1944), *The Enchanted Cottage, The Spanish Main* (both 1945), *Fighting Father Dunne* (1948), *A Woman's Secret* (1949), and *The Pride of St. Louis* (1952) were hardly worthy of this exceptional talent. He died virtually penniless. His son Donald is a novelist and occasional screenwriter himself.

MANKIEWICZ, JOSEPH L. Writer, producer, director. *(b. Feb. 11, 1909, Wilkes-Barre, Pa.; d. Feb. 5, 1993.)* One of America's wittiest and most urbane filmmakers, Mankiewicz managed to please both critics and audiences with a wide variety of films, marked by an extraordinary degree of intelligence and sophistication. After working in Berlin, first as a reporter and then as a titles translator of German silent films intended for American distribution, he followed his older brother Herman to Hollywood in the late 1920s. He wrote (or cowrote) many top films, ranging from wacky comedies such as *Million Dollar Legs* (1932) and *Diplomaniacs* (1933) to tear-jerking melodramas such as *Skippy* (1931), and from the big-budget gloss of *Manhattan Melodrama* to the gritty realism of *Our Daily Bread* (both 1934). In 1936, he began producing as well with the powerful lynch mob drama *Fury,* which was followed over the next decade by such superior films as *The Shopworn Angel* (1938), *The Philadelphia Story* (1940),

Woman of the Year (1942), and *Keys of the Kingdom* (1944).

Mankiewicz finally ascended to the director's chair in 1946 with the period melodrama *Dragonwyck,* and scored another hit the following year with *The Ghost and Mrs. Muir.* He pulled a still unequaled double hat trick by winning writing and directing Oscars in 1949 for the superb *A Letter to Three Wives,* and then again the very next year for *All About Eve,* the bitchy backstage comedy-drama starring Bette Davis, still his most famous and revered film. Other noteworthy pictures include the racial drama *No Way Out* (1950, Sidney Poitier's first film), an offbeat and cerebral romance, *People Will Talk* (1951), the espionage tale *5 Fingers* (1952, which netted him an Oscar nomination), a moody adaptation of *Julius Caesar* (1953), a mordant look at filmmaking, *The Barefoot Contessa* (1954), the smash musical comedy *Guys and Dolls* (1955), Tennessee Williams' *Suddenly, Last Summer* (1959), the gargantuan *Cleopatra* (1963, which he took over in mid-production), a modern-day "Volpone" called *The Honey Pot* (1967), a cynical comic Western, *There Was a Crooked Man . . .* (1970), and a bravura filming of the hit mystery play *Sleuth* (1972, for which he earned his final Oscar nomination). Even his lesser films are marked by literate dialogue and fine performances; his best films are as good as any ever made. His son, Tom Mankiewicz, is himself a writer/director whose films include the 1987 *Dragnet.*

MANN, ANTHONY. Director. *(b. June 30, 1906, San Diego, as Emil Anton Bundsmann; d. Apr. 29, 1967.)* Celebrated for his often innovative visual style and idiosyncratic approach to character, Mann is probably best known for the Westerns he directed starring James Stewart: *Winchester '73* (1950), *Bend of the River* (1952), *The Naked Spur* (1953), *The Far Country,* and *The Man From Laramie* (both 1955). (He also directed Stewart in 1954's *The Glenn Miller Story.)* Mann's Westerns boast lean, taut narratives driven by the violent, often vengeful actions of desperate men; Stewart has seldom been as hardbitten on screen as he appears in this director's films. Good as they are, Mann's Westerns represent only part of his work. In the 1940s, working for RKO, Republic, and Eagle-Lion, Mann (often working in tandem with cinematographer John Alton) crafted a series of low- to medium-budgeted film noir thrillers that are among the best of that influential subgenre: *Desperate, T-Men* (both 1947), *He Walked by Night, Raw Deal* (both 1948), and *Follow Me Quietly* (1949). In the early 1960s Mann distinguished himself by directing two of the most intelligent, least bombastic historical epics of that era, *El Cid* (1961) and *The Fall of the Roman Empire* (1964), both of which are often cited as examples of wide-screen cinema at its best. (Mann was originally assigned to direct 1960's *Spartacus,* but executive producer/star Kirk Douglas replaced him with Stanley Kubrick.)

At first a New York stage actor and then a director, Mann initially worked for producer David O. Selznick as an assistant director upon moving to Hollywood. He first wielded the megaphone solo on *Dr. Broadway* (1942), an entertaining if unimportant Paramount programmer. Respected as a journeyman in his day, Mann became something of a cult figure with the emergence of the *auteur* school of film criticism and scholarship, and he is still very popular in France. Mann died during the shooting of 1968's *A Dandy in Aspic;* the film's star, Laurence Harvey, took over the directorial chores.

MANN, DANIEL. Director. *(b. Aug. 8, 1912, New York City; d. Nov. 21, 1991.)* Although many of his films reveal their stage origins (and the director's own background as a Broadway director), Mann worked exceptionally well with his actors, and shepherded some great properties to the screen with taste and skill. His first directorial effort, *Come Back Little Sheba* (1952, which he'd also helmed on Broadway), was distinguished by unusually fine performances; Shirley Booth's won her an Oscar. Mann also guided Anna Magnani (in 1955's *The Rose Tattoo*) and Elizabeth Taylor (in 1960's *Butterfield 8*) in Academy Award-winning star turns. Ironically, as his cinematic sense developed, the quality of the scripts given him declined sharply.
OTHER FILMS INCLUDE: 1954: *About Mrs. Leslie;* 1955: *I'll Cry Tomorrow* (with Susan Hayward delivering one of her best per-

formances as singer Lillian Roth); 1956: *The Teahouse of the August Moon;* 1958: *Hot Spell;* 1959: *The Last Angry Man;* 1961: *Ada;* 1962: *Five Finger Exercise;* 1963: *Who's Been Sleeping in My Bed?;* 1966: *Judith, Our Man Flint;* 1968: *For Love of Ivy;* 1969: *A Dream of Kings;* 1971: *Willard;* 1972: *The Revengers;* 1973: *Interval;* 1974: *Lost in the Stars;* 1975: *Journey Into Fear;* 1978: *Matilda;* 1980: *The Incredible Mr. Chadwick.*

MANN, DELBERT. Director. *(b. Jan. 30, 1920, Lawrence, Kans.)* One of the most prolific directors from TV's "Golden Age," Mann made his feature debut adapting one of the dramas he had already handled on the small screen: Paddy Chayefsky's *Marty* (1955). Though now somewhat dated, this sensitive story of a lonely Bronx butcher ushered in an era of naturalism in American films and won four Academy Awards, including one for Mann's direction. He helmed two more Chayefsky properties—*The Bachelor Party* (1957) and *The Middle of the Night* (1959)—as well as the adaptations of *Desire Under the Elms, Separate Tables* (both 1958), and *The Dark at the Top of the Stairs* (1960), firmly establishing himself in Hollywood and leaving live television behind. After the biopic *The Outsider* (1961), Mann proved he could handle lighter material with the Doris Day vehicles *Lover Come Back* (1961) and *That Touch of Mink* (1962) as well as romances (*Dear Heart,* 1964) and adventures (*The Pink Jungle,* 1968). By the 1970s he found more intelligent and satisfying assignments—ironically enough—in television, and piloted many impressive TV movies, including *Jane Eyre* (1971), *A Girl Named Sooner* (1975), *All Quiet on the Western Front* (1979), and a live version of "The Member of the Wedding" in 1982.
OTHER FILMS INCLUDE: 1963: *A Gathering of Eagles;* 1964: *Quick Before It Melts;* 1966: *Mister Buddwing;* 1967: *Fitzwilly;* 1970: *David Copperfield* (telefilm); 1971: *Kidnapped;* 1977: *Birch Interval;* 1981: *Night Crossing;* 1983: *Bronte.*

MANN, MICHAEL. Director, producer, screenwriter. *(b. Feb. 5, 1943, Chicago.)* Director who has brought an impressive visual flair to TV and several feature films.

After graduate work at the London Film School, he directed documentaries, commercials, and a short film, *Juanpuri* (1970), which won the Jury Prize at Cannes. Back in the United States, he worked as a writer on several TV dramas before receiving acclaim (and a cowriting Emmy) for the TV movie *The Jericho Mile* (1979), which he also directed. Mann made his feature debut as writer and director of *Thief* (1981), a stylish look at a professional thief (played by James Caan), and followed with the murky WW2 drama *The Keep* (1983). He returned to TV as executive producer of "Miami Vice" (1984–89), a slick cop series that redefined the way TV looked and sounded. He brought some of that same "high style" to his next feature, *Manhunter* (1986), a gripping thriller that was a precursor to Jonathan Demme's *The Silence of the Lambs,* based on a Thomas Harris novel. After producing the TV series "Crime Story," Mann cowrote and directed *The Last of the Mohicans* (1992), a beautifully detailed adaptation of James Fenimore Cooper's novel that, in true Mann fashion, became a visceral epic. He also executive-produced *The Band of the Hand* (1986).

MANSFIELD, JAYNE. Actress. *(b. Apr. 19, 1933, Bryn Mawr, Pa., as Vera Jayne Palmer; d. June 29, 1967.)* She was often called "the poor man's Marilyn Monroe." Yet Jayne Mansfield was a larger-than-life figure who, even today, continues to hold a Monroe-like fascination for people (though obviously in far smaller numbers). Mansfield studied acting in college and reportedly took her chosen profession very seriously, but her squeaky voice, eye-popping figure, and limited range made her tough to cast. In fact, it was a Monroe parody that first brought her fame, in the Broadway comedy "Will Success Spoil Rock Hunter?" She had small roles in *Illegal, Pete Kelly's Blues, Hell on Frisco Bay* (all 1955), and *The Female Jungle* (1956) before director Frank Tashlin, who had a cartoonist's eye for outsized women, cast her as a gangster's moll in *The Girl Can't Help It* (also 1956). It was an instant smash, and they collaborated again the following year for the film version of *Rock Hunter;* these two pictures are still considered her best, mostly because Tashlin was able to cunningly turn her limited gifts into assets. (Mansfield's then-husband Mickey Hargitay played a small role in *Hunter.*) Her subsequent roles, in the likes of *Kiss Them for Me, The Wayward Bus* (both 1957), *The Sheriff of Fractured Jaw* (1959), *Too Hot to Handle* (1960), *The George Raft Story* (1961), and *It Happened in Athens* (1962), were mostly decorative if not frankly self-parodying.

By the early 1960s she was pretty much washed up, and finished her movie career in low-budget stinkers—some of them made in Europe—including *Promises, Promises* (1963), *Panic Button, Dog Eat Dog* (both 1964), *The Fat Spy* (1965), *Las Vegas Hillbillys* (1966), and *Single Room Furnished* (directed by then-husband Matt Cimber and released posthumously in 1968). She did at least have a funny guest shot in *A Guide for the Married Man* (1967). During this bleak period she kept her flame burning with a series of layouts in "Playboy" magazine and appearances in numerous TV shows. Her untimely, tragic death—in a gruesome auto accident—completed the Monroe parallel, and today she's remembered largely as an emblem of America before the Sexual Revolution—in which she played a small but ingratiating role. Her daughter Mariska Hargitay is an actress who has appeared on television and in such films as *Ghoulies* (1985) and *Bank Robber* (1993).

MANTEGNA, JOE. Actor. *(b. Nov. 13, 1947, Chicago.)* Dynamic, dark character lead who gained fame on the New York stage as a member of David Mamet's "Chicago Mafia," a brilliant collaboration that resulted in several plays and three films to date, not the least of which was "Glengarry Glen Ross," for which he won a Tony as the real-estate sales whiz Ricky Roma. Mantegna's debut film, *Towing,* did nothing for his career, but he got good notices as the dentist lothario whose murder kicks off *Compromising Positions* (1985). After such small roles as a studio head in *¡Three Amigos!,* a shady contractor in *The Money Pit* (both 1986), and a prosecutor in *Suspect* (1987), he starred in two much-praised but little-seen Mamet-directed features: *House of Games* (also 1987), as an ultra-professional scam artist, and *Things Change* (1988), as a small-time hood who baby-sits a Mob fall guy,

Don Ameche. He had the lead in Francis Coppola's production of *Wait Until Spring, Bandini* (1989) but the film sat on the shelf for two years before a desultory release on video. More visibly, he played Mia Farrow's lover in *Alice,* a hot-tempered gangster in *The Godfather, Part III* (both 1990), and a Jewish cop in turmoil in Mamet's *Homicide* (1991). *Bugsy* (1991) offered Mantegna a supporting role in a high-profile film, but he was miscast as George Raft, and ill-served by the underwritten part. Recent films include *Queens Logic* (1991), David Mamet's made-for-TV *The Water Engine* (1992), *Body of Evidence, Family Prayers, Searching for Bobby Fischer* (all 1993), *Airheads,* and *Baby's Day Out* (both 1994).

MARAIS, JEAN. Actor. *(b. Dec. 11, 1913, Cherbourg, France, as Jean Alfred Villain-Marais.)* Blond, Aryan-looking French actor probably best remembered for his starring roles in two classic films directed by his close friend Jean Cocteau: *Beauty and the Beast* (1946, playing the Beast and the prince) and *Orpheus* (1950, in the title role). In movies since 1933, Marais initially coasted on his striking good looks and breezy personality, but developed into a dependable actor—especially in swashbucklers and romantic dramas—as he matured. His films include *Carmen* (1945), *The Count of Monte Cristo* (1955, as Edmund Dantes), *The Testament of Orpheus* (1960, in the title role), *The Iron Mask* (1962, as D'Artagnan), and *Fantomas* (1964). Marais is still popular in his native country, warmly remembered as Americans would regard Errol Flynn or Douglas Fairbanks.

MARCH, FREDRIC. Actor. *(b. Aug. 31, 1897, Racine, Wis., as Frederick Ernest McIntyre Bickel; d. Apr. 14, 1975.)* One of the finest actors who ever worked onscreen, Fredric March resisted typecasting by the studios—and, in fact, refused long-term contracts—hand-picking his roles with incredible success. The result was an exemplary film career. Bitten by the acting bug while studying economics in college, he participated in campus dramatics but followed through on his original plans and, after graduating, went to New York to work at the National City Bank. A brush with death (necessitating an emergency appendectomy) shocked him into abandoning the financial world in favor of an acting career. After working in bit roles for several years (during which time he also worked as an extra in New York-made films, beginning with 1921's *The Devil*), he won his first Broadway lead in 1926. While touring with the Theatre Guild's first repertory troupe (accompanied by his new wife, actress Florence Eldridge), March landed a Paramount Pictures contract. He appeared in a number of early talkies—among them *The Dummy, The Wild Party, The Studio Murder Mystery, Jealousy* (all 1929), *Sarah and Son, Paramount on Parade, True to the Navy, Manslaughter,* and *Laughter* (all 1930)—before achieving his first major success, repeating a role he'd performed on stage, broadly mimicking John Barrymore in the film adaptation of *The Royal Family of Broadway* (1930), and earning his first Oscar nomination in the process.

Following several routine assignments in 1931, March lobbied for and won the dual role in Rouben Mamoulian's production of *Dr. Jekyll and Mr. Hyde* (released 1932), resulting in his best screen outing to date, which won him a Best Actor Academy Award. Today, his Mr. Hyde seems very much over the top, with March slobbering over his grotesque makeup and chewing whatever scenery hasn't been nailed down. Nonetheless, his phenomenal success in the part made him one of Hollywood's hottest tickets.

Still a relatively young man, March had the leading man's classic good looks, which served him well in *Merrily We Go to Hell* (1932), *The Sign of the Cross* (also 1932, memorable in this Cecil B. DeMille spectacular as a Roman officer won over to Christianity), *Tonight Is Ours, The Eagle and the Hawk* (both 1933), *Design for Living* (also 1933, particularly engaging in this sophisticated Noël Coward comedy), *Death Takes a Holiday* (another well-remembered role, as the Grim Reaper himself), *Good Dame, Affairs of Cellini* (in the title role), *The Barretts of Wimpole Street* (as Robert Browning), *We Live Again* (all 1934), *Les Miserables* (as the persecuted Jean Valjean), *Anna Karenina, The Dark Angel* (all 1935), *Anthony Adverse* (in the title role), and *The Road to Glory* (both 1936).

Two David O. Selznick productions in 1937, both filmed in the then-novel three-strip Technicolor process, showed March to particularly good advantage: In *A Star Is Born,* he was Oscar-nominated for the role of Norman Maine, a washed-up movie star whose career fades as his young wife's soars. In *Nothing Sacred,* he played the conniving reporter who makes a media celebrity of Carole Lombard, who's mistakenly thought to be dying. Those roles, along with his starring stints as Jean Lafitte in DeMille's *The Buccaneer* and a debonair detective in Tay Garnett's *Trade Winds* (both 1938), elevated March to a lofty pinnacle reached by few other stars in the Hollywood of the 1930s.

March took fewer film assignments in the 1940s. *Susan and God, Victory* (both 1940), *So Ends Our Night, One Foot in Heaven, Bedtime Story* (all 1941), *I Married a Witch* (1942), *The Adventures of Mark Twain,* and *Tomorrow the World* (both 1944) were, for the most part, worthy vehicles for the star, but none of them achieved the success of his best films of the preceding decade. A notable exception: the Academy Award-winning classic *The Best Years of Our Lives* (1946, a Goldwyn film directed by William Wyler), a nearly perfect production from every standpoint, offered March a strong role as a returning WW2 veteran; he won his second Oscar for the performance.

By this time March was working on Broadway as often as his schedule allowed, and after the war he chose his screen roles with even greater care. He starred in *Another Part of the Forest, An Act of Murder* (both 1948, in the latter with Eldridge), *Christopher Columbus* (1949, in the title role), *Death of a Salesman* (1951, as Arthur Miller's tired, tragic Willy Loman, for which he was Oscar-nominated), *It's a Big Country* (1952), *Man on a Tightrope* (1953), *Executive Suite* (1954), *The Bridges at Toko-Ri* (1954), *The Desperate Hours* (1955, effective as the put-upon paterfamilias), *Alexander the Great, The Man in the Gray Flannel Suit* (both 1956), and the touching *Middle of the Night* (1959).

Inherit the Wind (1960), Stanley Kramer's riveting filmization of the Jerome Lawrence-Robert E. Lee play about the Scopes "monkey trial," gave March his flashiest latter-day character part, that of the fiery orator based on William Jennings Bryan (opposite Spencer

Tracy, whose character was modeled after Clarence Darrow), and marked his last screen appearance with Eldridge, who played his faithful wife. His final films included *The Young Doctors* (1961), *The Condemned of Altona* (1962), *Seven Days in May* (1964, properly authoritative as a U.S. president), *Hombre* (1967), . . . *tick . . . tick . . . tick . . .* (1969), and *The Iceman Cometh* (1973, his last). Throughout the years he also lent his name, and talent, to worthy causes, and, with his wife, was a liberal activist in the Democratic party.

MARSHALL, E. G. Actor. *(b. June 18, 1910, Owatonna, Minn., as Everett G. Marshall.)* Authoritative character actor who enjoyed a lengthy stage career during the 1930s and 1940s while making occasional, minor appearances in such films as *The House on 92nd St.* (1945), *13 Rue Madeleine* (1946), and *Call Northside 777* (1948). Two of his best screen roles came in the 1950s, when he gave finely tuned performances as an aging bookkeeper/hypochondriac in *The Bachelor Party* (1957) and an unruffled stockbroker serving on a jury in *12 Angry Men* (1957). Marshall could be depended upon to play characters of authority: Lieutenant Commander Challee in *The Caine Mutiny* (1954), The Governor in *Broken Lance* (1954) and Governor Claiborne in *The Buccaneer* (1958). He gave workmanlike performances as a cop in *Pushover* (1954), a doctor in *The Left Hand of God* (1955), a lawyer in *Man on Fire* (1957), and a state's attorney in *Compulsion* (1959). Woody Allen gave him his best latter-day screen role as a wealthy man who leaves his disturbed wife for a more vivacious companion in *Interiors* (1978). He was then cast—credibly, as always—as the President of the United States in *Superman II* (1980). Other films include *Tora! Tora! Tora!* (1970), *Creepshow* (1982), *National Lampoon's Christmas Vacation* (1989), and *Consenting Adults* (1992).

Marshall earned his greatest fame for his work in hundreds of live 1950s television dramas, and for his starring role in "The Defenders" (1961–65), one of the rare socially conscious TV series of the period; he earned two Emmy Awards playing veteran attorney Lawrence Preston. He later starred in "The New Doctors" segment of "The Bold Ones" (1969–73). His voice is well known for his narration of countless documentaries, and his face is likewise familiar as a ubiquitous TV host/narrator. At age 84, Marshall appeared as an American tourist determined to pilfer a priceless Russian antiquity in *Russian Holiday* (1993), then joined the cast of TVs "Chicago Hope" (1994–).

MARSHALL, GARRY. Director, screenwriter, producer, actor. *(b. Nov. 13, 1934, Bronx, N.Y.)* Enormously popular television writer and producer who later duplicated his success on the big screen. Educated at Northwestern, Marshall began writing jokes for comedians like Joey Bishop and Phil Foster, then wrote for "The Tonight Show" in the Jack Paar era. He moved to Hollywood in 1961 and teamed up with writer Jerry Belson to write more than one hundred episodes for sitcoms like "The Dick Van Dyke Show," "The Danny Thomas Show," and "The Lucy Show" before producing the TV adaptation of Neil Simon's "The Odd Couple" (1970–75). Marshall went on to create and produce the hits "Happy Days" (1974–84), "Laverne and Shirley" (1976–83, starring his sister Penny Marshall), and "Mork and Mindy" (1978–82).

Marshall and Belson had already cowritten and coproduced the films *How Sweet It Is* (1968) and *The Grasshopper* (1970), but it wasn't until a decade later that Marshall left television behind to direct the feature *Young Doctors in Love* (1982), a silly spoof of daytime soaps. He proved himself a filmmaker with *The Flamingo Kid* (1984), which gave Matt Dillon one of his best roles as a working-class Brooklyn boy seduced by 1963 country club life. He followed it with the seriocomic *Nothing in Common* (1986), the formula comedy *Overboard* (1987), and the soap opera *Beaches* (1988), before scoring a box-office bull's-eye with *Pretty Woman* (1990), a modern day "Pygmalion" with businessman Richard Gere "buying" hooker Julia Roberts. The film rocketed Roberts to stardom. Many critics cite the moving *Frankie and Johnny* (1991) as Marshall's best film to date; his latest project is *Exit to Eden* (1994), based on the Anne Rice novel. Marshall, a glib raconteur, is also a good comic actor, and has appeared in several films, including

Psych-Out (1968), *Lost in America* (1985, unforgettable as a Vegas casino owner), *Soapdish* (1991), and two films directed by his sister, *Jumpin' Jack Flash* (1986) and *A League of Their Own* (1992). He has also had a funny recurring role as demented network president Stan Lansing on the sitcom "Murphy Brown" (1994–).

MARSHALL, GEORGE. Director. (*b. Dec. 29, 1891, Chicago; d. Feb. 17, 1975.*) Prolific journeyman director of mainstream Hollywood fare. As an extra at Universal in the pre-WW1 years, he observed and absorbed every aspect of filmmaking, and started directing Westerns (beginning with *Love's Lariat*) in 1916. Marshall served with the military during the war, then returned to his chosen profession, beginning an uninterrupted 50-year run as a director. He had a special affinity for comedy, as evidenced by his successful films starring Laurel and Hardy, W. C. Fields, Bob Hope, Jerry Lewis, and others, but was equally facile in every genre.

Among his best films: *Destry Rides Again* (1939), proof that even a supposedly "uninspired" director could thrive amidst the studio system and turn out a genuinely great movie, and *Murder, He Says* (1945), an engagingly wacky comedy starring Fred MacMurray that, according to Marshall, was largely made up from day to day while the film was in production!

Glenn Ford insisted on having Marshall direct his 1971–72 TV series, "Cade's County." Marshall also occasionally appeared on-camera, as the villain in Laurel and Hardy's *Pack Up Your Troubles* (1932), as himself in *Variety Girl* (1947), and in a character part in *The Crazy World of Julius Vrooder* (1974).
OTHER FILMS INCLUDE: 1919: *The Adventures of Ruth* (a Ruth Roland serial); 1921: *After Your Own Heart;* 1923: *Haunted Valley;* 1934: *She Learned About Sailors;* 1935: *In Old Kentucky, Show Them No Mercy;* 1936: *A Message to Garcia;* 1937: *Nancy Steele Is Missing;* 1938: *The Goldwyn Follies, Hold That Co-ed;* 1939: *You Can't Cheat an Honest Man;* 1940: *The Ghost Breakers;* 1941: *Pot o' Gold, Texas;* 1942: *Valley of the Sun, Star Spangled Rhythm;* 1943: *Riding High;* 1944: *And the Angels Sing;* 1945: *Incendiary Blonde;* 1946: *The Blue Dahlia, Monsieur Beaucaire;* 1947: *The Perils of Pauline;* 1948: *Tap Roots;* 1949: *My Friend Irma;* 1950: *Fancy Pants, Never a Dull Moment;* 1953: *Scared Stiff, Houdini;* 1955: *Destry* (remaking his 1939 film, but not very effectively); 1957: *The Sad Sack;* 1958: *The Sheepman, Imitation General;* 1959: *The Mating Game;* 1960: *The Gazebo;* 1962: *How The West Was Won* (as codirector); 1963: *Papa's Delicate Condition;* 1964: *Advance to the Rear;* 1967: *Eight on the Lam;* 1969: *Hook, Line and Sinker.*

MARSHALL, HERBERT. Actor. (*b. May 23, 1890, London; d. Jan. 22, 1966.*) Urbane British leading man and, later, distinguished character actor, most often seen in elegant, refined characterizations but occasionally utilized in sophisticated comedy roles (e.g., as the suave jewel thief in 1932's *Trouble in Paradise* and the priggish lawyer in 1935's *The Good Fairy*, two of his best). Marshall, who was drawn to the theater after spending several years as an accountant, appeared on the London stage before entering His Majesty's Army during World War 1. He lost a leg in the conflict, but replaced it with a prosthetic limb and continued his acting career without making the loss apparent.

Marshall made his screen debut in the British-made *Mumsie* (1927), but attracted more attention opposite stage star Jeanne Eagels in the American-made 1929 adaptation of Somerset Maugham's *The Letter.* Tall and handsome, with a round face and slicked-back hair, he used his cultivated voice to great effect, becoming a popular romantic lead in early talkies. Marshall subsequently worked with distinction over the balance of a lengthy career. His five wives included actresses Edna Best (1928–40) and Boots Mallory (1946–58).
OTHER FILMS INCLUDE: 1932: *Blonde Venus;* 1934: *Four Frightened People;* 1935: *The Dark Angel;* 1936: *Till We Meet Again;* 1937: *Angel;* 1938: *Mad About Music;* 1940: *A Bill of Divorcement, Foreign Correspondent, The Letter* (a remake of his 1929 success); 1941: *The Little Foxes;* 1942: *The Moon and Sixpence;* 1943: *Forever and a Day;* 1945: *The Enchanted Cottage;* 1946: *The Razor's Edge, Duel in the Sun;* 1949: *The Secret Garden;* 1952: *Angel Face;* 1955: *The Virgin Queen;* 1958: *Stage Struck, The Fly;* 1960: *Midnight Lace;* 1963: *The List of Adrian Messenger.*

MARSHALL, PENNY. Director, actress. *(b. Oct. 15, 1942, Bronx, N.Y.)* Still seen daily—in most parts of the civilized world, anyway—on syndicated reruns of the sitcom "Laverne and Shirley," in which she starred from 1976–83. Marshall first attracted notice in a recurring role on "The Odd Couple" (1973–75), which like "Laverne" was produced by her brother Garry. Today she is recognized as a talented director of highly commercial mainstream movies, including *Big* (1988), *Awakenings* (1990), *A League of Their Own* (1992), and *Renaissance Man* (1994). As an actress she appeared in the movies *The Savage Seven, How Sweet It Is* (both 1968), *1941* (1979), *Movers and Shakers* (1985), *The Hard Way* (1991), and *Hocus Pocus* (1993). Her feature-film directorial debut, *Jumpin' Jack Flash* (1986), is best forgotten; she has since vindicated herself with more successful offerings. Once married to actor/director Rob Reiner (with whom she starred in the 1979 TV movie *More Than Friends*, which he wrote about their early courtship), she has used daughter Tracy Reiner in some of her films. She also found parts for her brother in *Jumpin' Jack Flash* and *A League of Their Own*.

MARTIN, DEAN. Actor, singer. *(b. June 7, 1917, Steubenville, Ohio, as Dino Crocetti.)* During the time that this tall, wavy-haired singing star was teamed with comedian Jerry Lewis, he made a genuinely engaging screen personality, equally adept with songs and wisecracks. After the team's acrimonious split in 1956, his career continued to flourish through nightclub engagements, record sales, TV shows, and occasional movie roles. Increasingly, though, his sleepy-eyed characterizations became tiresome, and by the late 1960s it seemed as though he was caricaturing himself. Although Martin was capable of delivering first-rate performances—as he proved in *Some Came Running* (1958), *Rio Bravo* (1959), *Kiss Me, Stupid* (1964), *The Sons of Katie Elder* (1965), and *Airport* (1970)—he more often gave the impression of one bored with his work, eager to finish a scene and pour himself a dry martini. He latched on to the "secret agent" craze of the swinging sixties with his campy "Matt Helm" movies: *The Silencers, Murderers Row* (both 1966), *The Am-*

bushers (1967), and *The Wrecking Crew* (1968). His TV variety series, "The Dean Martin Show," enjoyed a long run, from 1965 to 1974.
OTHER FILMS INCLUDE: 1949: *My Friend Irma;* 1950: *At War With the Army, My Friend Irma Goes West;* 1951: *Sailor Beware, That's My Boy;* 1953: *Scared Stiff;* 1955: *Artists and Models;* 1956: *Pardners, Hollywood or Bust;* 1957: *Ten Thousand Bedrooms* (his first without Lewis); 1958: *The Young Lions;* 1960: *Bells Are Ringing, Who Was That Lady?, Ocean's Eleven* (with his "Rat Pack," Frank Sinatra, Sammy Davis, Jr., Peter Lawford, and Joey Bishop); 1961: *Ada, All in a Night's Work;* 1962: *Sergeants 3, Who's Got the Action?;* 1963: *4 for Texas, Toys in the Attic;* 1964: *Robin and the Seven Hoods, What a Way to Go!;* 1966: *Texas Across the River;* 1968: *5 Card Stud, How to Save a Marriage and Ruin Your Life, Bandolero;* 1971: *something big;* 1975: *Mr. Ricco;* 1980: *Cannonball Run;* 1984: *Cannonball Run II.*

MARTIN, MARY. Actress. *(b. Dec. 1, 1913, Weatherford, Tex.; d. Nov. 3, 1990.)* Vibrant Broadway musical star whose failure to attain Hollywood stardom commensurate with her stage status was one of filmdom's great mysteries. A Texas gal (who never *quite* lost her accent) educated in Tennessee, Martin taught dance for a while before forming her own troupe in the mid 1930s. She made her film debut—as a dance teacher—in *The Rage of Paris* (1938), but shortly thereafter left Hollywood for New York, where she became the toast of Broadway after appearing in Cole Porter's "Leave It to Me," in which she performed a genteel (partial) striptease while cooing "My Heart Belongs to Daddy." Signed by Paramount in 1939, Martin appeared in that year's *The Great Victor Herbert, Love Thy Neighbor* (1940, getting between feuding Jack Benny and Fred Allen), *New York Town, Kiss the Boys Goodbye, Birth of the Blues* (all 1941), *Star Spangled Rhythm* (1942), *True to Life,* and *Happy Go Lucky* (both 1943), all with negligible box-office impact. Dissatisfied with her lot in Hollywood, Martin returned to the stage (although she consented to perform a watered-down version of "Daddy" for the 1946 Cole Porter biopic, *Night and Day*). She played herself in a small role for *Main Street to Broadway* (1953), but otherwise confined herself to the stage, where she achieved amazing success (in, among others, "South Pacific," "Peter Pan," "The Sound of Music," and "I Do, I Do"), and TV, where her broadcast version of "Peter Pan" was a hardy perennial. She was the mother of actor Larry Hagman.

MARTIN, STEVE. Actor, screenwriter. (b. Aug. 14, 1945, Waco, Tex.) It's difficult to reconcile the Steve Martin of today—a top-rated film star who alternates between situational comedy and light drama—with the "wild and crazy guy" whose absurdist stand-up comedy and TV work paralyzed 1970s audiences. The Martin who attempted to fill Spencer Tracy's old shoes in a 1991 remake of *Father of the Bride* is the same performer who convulsed us by shouting, "Well, excuuuuuse me!" more than a decade ago. In the 1960s, before his stand-up career, Martin was an Emmy-winning writer for "The Smothers Brothers Comedy Hour" TV show. This artistic philosophy student became one of the 1970s' most popular comedians, alternating stints on "The Tonight Show" and "Saturday Night Live" with sellout concert appearances and hit records.

The unfortunate musical pastiche *Sgt. Pepper's Lonely Hearts Club Band* (1978) provided Martin with his first film role, enacting the Beatles song "Maxwell's Silver Hammer." He subsequently cowrote his first "proper" film, *The Jerk* (1979), a starring vehicle that visualized situations he described in some stand-up routines, and the first of his several collaborations with Carl Reiner. Around this time he directed himself in a funny short subject called *The Absent-Minded Waiter* which wound up earning an Oscar nomination. Back then he was compared to Jerry Lewis, but Martin made his loftier screen ambitions plain by taking the lead in the daring but ill-fated film adaptation of Dennis Potter's mordant BBC series *Pennies From Heaven* (1981). He fared better in *Dead Men Don't Wear Plaid* (1982), a private-eye spoof and technical tour de force that had him interacting with long-deceased screen legends like Bogart and Alan Ladd via intercut footage from vintage thrillers.

Martin was an egotistical brain surgeon nearly done in by vamp Kathleen Turner in *The Man With Two Brains* (1983). But

he achieved a turning-point the following year in *All of Me* (1984), a clever comedy in which he had to act as if Lily Tomlin controlled half of his body! This skillful performance won him critical praise, a handful of awards, and genuine respect as a comic *actor.* (It was also on that film that he met his future wife, Victoria Tennant.) Since then he has expanded his range, reining in his surrealistic comedic style to assume "straight" roles that rely on kinder and gentler humor. He was most affecting as a latter-day Cyrano de Bergerac in *Roxanne* (1987), which he wrote and helped produce. He made a believable if befuddled father in *Parenthood* (1989), and invaded Woody Allen territory with *L.A. Story* (1991), writing and starring in that quirky California counterpart to Allen's *Manhattan.* In addition to *Story* and the aforementioned *Father of the Bride,* 1991 saw the release of Lawrence Kasdan's *Grand Canyon,* in which Martin took a basically non-comedic part as a disaffected movie producer.

No longer the "wild and crazy guy" of comic TV sketches, he made his New York stage debut in a celebrated production of "Waiting for Godot" in 1988 directed by Mike Nichols. He then took a *Leap of Faith* (1992) on screen, playing a phony evangelist; he was, as usual, entertaining to watch, but not entirely convincing. In 1993 he added a new credential to his resume, writing a play, "Picasso at the Lapine Agile."

OTHER FILMS INCLUDE: 1984: *The Lonely Guy;* 1985: *Movers and Shakers;* 1986: *¡Three Amigos!, Little Shop of Horrors* (as the pain-inflicting dentist); 1987: *Planes, Trains & Automobiles;* 1988: *Dirty Rotten Scoundrels;* 1990: *My Blue Heaven;* 1993: *And the Band Played On* (made-for-TV); 1994: *A Simple Twist of Fate* (also wrote), *Mixed Nuts.*

MARTIN, STROTHER. Actor. (b. Mar. 26, 1919, Kokomo, Ind.; d. Aug. 1, 1980.) White-haired, moon-faced supporting player whose uniquely whiny, nasal voice kept him busy for three decades playing "prairie scum" in numerous Westerns, especially those of Ford and Peckinpah during the 1950s and 1960s. He'll always be remembered as the actor who immortalized the now-familiar line, "What we have here is failure to commu-

nicate," playing an ice-hearted chain-gang boss in *Cool Hand Luke* (1967).
OTHER FILMS INCLUDE: 1950: *The Asphalt Jungle;* 1955: *The Big Knife;* 1956: *Attack!;* 1959: *The Horse Soldiers;* 1962: *The Man Who Shot Liberty Valance;* 1963: *McLintock!;* 1965: *Shenandoah;* 1966: *Harper;* 1969: *Butch Cassidy and the Sundance Kid, The Wild Bunch;* 1970: *The Ballad of Cable Hogue;* 1972: *Hannie Caulder;* 1975: *Hard Times;* 1977: *Slap Shot* (in a side-splitting performance as the frantic hockey-team owner); 1978: *The End.*

MARVIN, LEE. Actor. *(b. Feb. 19, 1924, New York City; d. Aug. 29, 1987.)* Rugged actor who, like many tough-looking leading men, started his movie career as a heavy, then graduated to heroic roles when he became a star. Marvin, a WW2 veteran, took up acting in the late 1940s following an unfulfilling stint as a plumber. Initially appearing in summer stock and off-Broadway productions, he graduated to the Great White Way in 1951. That same year, he broke into movies with a bit part in *You're in the Navy Now,* and two years later achieved recognition as the psychopathic gang leader who hurled scalding coffee in his girlfriend's face in *The Big Heat* (1953). Marvin also played a rival gangleader in *The Wild One* (1954), a nasty townsman in *Bad Day at Black Rock,* a burned-out jazzman in *Pete Kelly's Blues* (both 1955), and Western baddies in *Gun Fury, The Stranger Wore a Gun* (both in 1953), *Seven Men From Now* (1956), and *The Comancheros* (1961). After starring for three seasons on the TV cop show "M Squad" (1957–60), he reached his apex as a big-screen bad guy playing the whip-cracking terror of John Ford's *The Man Who Shot Liberty Valance* (1962), which starred John Wayne and James Stewart.

Following the lighthearted *Donovan's Reef* (1963, again for Ford), Marvin returned to form as the contract killer who guns down crime boss Ronald Reagan (in his last film) in *The Killers* (1964). He followed that with a memorable turn as a washed-up ball player in *Ship of Fools* (1965). Next came the Western spoof *Cat Ballou* (also 1965); Marvin's dual role as a drunken gunslinger and a tin-nosed desperado won him an Oscar and elevated him to leading-man status. He maintained

it by heading up two all-star action blockbusters, *The Professionals* (1966) and *The Dirty Dozen* (1967), and for the next 20 years gave solid performances in such varied films as the quirky thriller *Point Blank* (1967), the two-man war movie *Hell in the Pacific* (1968), the big-budget musical *Paint Your Wagon* (1969), the elegiac Western *Monte Walsh* (1970), the satiric gangster opus *Prime Cut* (1972), the allegorical train adventure *Emperor of The North* (1973), the comic Western *Great Scout and Cathouse Thursday* (1976), and Sam Fuller's autobiographical war film, *The Big Red One* (1980), which gave him one of his all-time best parts as an indomitable sergeant in the infantry. Later films include *Death Hunt* (1980), *Gorky Park* (1983), *The Delta Force* (1986), and a TV movie sequel *The Dirty Dozen: The Next Mission* (1985). Perhaps his most underrated work was his performance as Hickey in the 1973 film adaptation of Eugene O'Neill's *The Iceman Cometh.* Marvin also left a legacy of quite a different sort: his longtime companion, Michelle Triola, successfully sued him for support after their breakup, bringing the word "palimony" into the American lexicon.

THE MARX BROTHERS. Actors. *(**Groucho**—b. Oct. 2, 1890, New York City, as Julius; d. Aug. 19, 1977. **Harpo**—b. Nov. 21, 1888, New York City, as Adolph/ Arthur; d. Sept. 28, 1964. **Chico**—b. Mar. 26, 1886, New York City, as Leonard; d. Oct. 11, 1961. **Zeppo**—b. Feb. 25, 1901, New York City, as Herbert; d. Nov. 30, 1979.)* One of the most colorful comedy teams of all time is happily also one of the most popular, despite having made only a dozen films together. Their anarchic style, honed during years of stage work and complemented by absurdist screenwriting, made the Marxes unique among screen comedians of the 1930s, although it must be said that most of their early films, highly regarded today, were indifferently received by Depression-era audiences. The brothers were encouraged by their mother Minnie, the daughter of vaudevillians, to take music lessons while still young boys. She also steered them into a show-business career, first in musical acts and later in bona fide stage productions in which they established their distinctive personae. Groucho was the fast-talking wisenheimer,

Harpo the skirt-chasing mute, Chico (pronounced "Chick-o," by the way) the Italian-accented scam artist, and Zeppo the handsome straight man.

In 1925 they conquered Broadway with "The Cocoanuts," and four years later were signed by Paramount to recreate their mayhem on film. The movie version, shot in New York's Astoria studio during the day while the brothers were engaged in performing "Animal Crackers" at night on stage, was reasonably successful, and was followed by a film adaptation of "Crackers" in 1930, also produced in New York. The Marxes then left for Hollywood and made three original films that purists consider their best: *Monkey Business* (1931), *Horse Feathers* (1932), and *Duck Soup* (1933), a unique blend of political satire and pure nonsense made at a time when Hitler was rising to power. It was not a hit, and the brothers (minus Zeppo), now considered a liability by their home studio Paramount, accepted an offer to work at MGM, where producer Irving Thalberg suspected he could utilize their talents to better advantage in more lavish, and better-crafted, films. He hired such writers as George S. Kaufman, and sent the brothers on the road to try out their new "scripts" before live audiences until the material (and the timing) were airtight. Although the Marxes' madcap comedy was diluted by liberal splashes of music and romance, *A Night at the Opera* (1935) and *A Day at the Races* (1937) turned out to be terrific movies and their most successful at the box office. After Thalberg's death in 1937 and the brothers' reassignment to other producers, the quality of their vehicles slipped. After filming *Room Service* (which had been a successful stage farce, the screen adaptation of which was reworked to accommodate their personae) while on loan to RKO in 1938, the Marxes ended their MGM stay with the less successful *At the Circus* (1939), *Go West* (1940), and *The Big Store* (1941).

The team split up as the brothers pursued individual interests in and out of show business. They later reunited for *A Night in Casablanca* (1946); all three appeared in *Love Happy* (1949), but Groucho only briefly, and they were in separate segments of *The Story of Mankind* (1957). Groucho made a few films on his own, such as *Copacabana* (1947), *Double Dynamite* (1951), and *Skidoo* (1968), and had a lengthy career in radio, ultimately leading to the sort-of game show "You Bet Your Life" in 1947, which moved to TV in 1950 for 11 years (and decades more in reruns). Groucho lived long enough to see the team rediscovered and adored anew, even performing a one-man show near the end of his life and receiving a special Oscar in 1973.

MASINA, GIULIETTA. Actress. *(b. Feb. 22, 1920, San Giorgio di Piano, Italy; d. Mar. 23, 1994.)* Described by "The New York Times" as "film's eternal waif," Masina is best known for the plucky, indomitable performances she gave in the films of her husband, Federico Fellini. She acted with a drama group at the University of Rome and later met Fellini when she performed in a radio program he wrote about a young married couple. (They married soon after this.) She made her film debut with a small part in *Paisan* (1946, cowritten by Fellini) and won kudos for her work in *Without Pity* (1948; original Italian title *Senza pietà*) and later had featured roles in Fellini's first films, *Variety Lights* (1950) and *The White Sheik* (1951). But it was *La Strada* (1954) that won her international acclaim for her touching performance as Gelsomina, the much-abused assistant to strongman Anthony Quinn. She was even better as the ever-hopeful prostitute in *Nights of Cabiria* (1957, recreating a role she originated in *The White Sheik*), and evoked comparisons to Chaplin and Garbo. She brought similar enchanting qualities to three more of her husband's films—*Il Bidone* (*The Swindlers,* 1955), *Juliet of the Spirits* (1965), and *Ginger and Fred* (1986)—but had too few opportunities to display her talent elsewhere. Her other films include *Europa '51* (1951), *Fortunella* (1958), *Bluebeard* (1962; original French title *Landru*), *The Madwoman of Chaillot* (1969), and *Frau Holle* (1985).

MASON, JAMES. Actor. *(b. May 15, 1909, Huddersfield, England; d. July 27, 1984.)* Born to a well-to-do British merchant, Mason studied architecture at Cambridge before deciding on an acting career, which began with bit roles at the Old Vic and Dublin's Gate Company players. Debuting on-screen in *Late Extra,* a 1935 "quota quickie" (the term for England's home-grown B pictures), he carved out a niche for himself as a charismatic heavy with more than a touch of sadism in his demeanor. Seen in *Blind Man's Bluff* (1936), *Fire Over England, The Mill on the Floss* (both 1937), *The Return of the Scarlet Pimpernel* (1938), *I Met a Murderer* (1939), *This Man Is Dangerous* (1941), and *The Night Has Eyes* (1942), among others, he made his mark on British audiences. He was a handsome but sadistic villain in *The Man in Gray* (1943), and a memorably nasty mentor to Ann Todd in *The Seventh Veil* (1945); both films were big hits.

Mason's saturnine countenance and rich voice, tinged with sardonic cruelty, made him an ideal menace, but somewhere inside him a leading man was trying to claw his way out. Two high-profile British movies, *The Wicked Lady* (1945) and *Odd Man Out* (1947, possibly his best role), brought Mason to the attention of international audiences. In the latter film, cast as an Irish rebel leader pursued by British authorities and directed by Carol Reed, Mason proved he could carry a film on his own shoulders. After starring in a quasi-sympathetic role, as a doctor driven to murder to avenge his lover's death in *The Upturned Glass* (also 1947), he came to Hollywood, making his American film debut in Max Ophuls' *Caught* (1949).

Mason's Hollywood films generally showcased him in more refined roles; when he essayed heavies, it was with more urbane charm than he had exhibited on his home soil. He played Flaubert in *Madame Bovary* (1949), Rupert of Hentzau in *The Prisoner of Zenda* (1952), Brutus in *Julius Caesar* (1953), and Captain Nemo in *20,000 Leagues Under the Sea* (1954), to name a few. And his icy demeanor served him well in *The Desert Fox* (1951) and *The Desert Rats* (1953), cast in both as German Field Marshal Rommel! The lavish Technicolor remake of *A Star Is Born* (1954) found Mason in the role played by Fredric March in the 1937 original, that of washed-up movie star Norman Maine; he earned his first Academy Award nomination for his poignant interpretation of the part.

An intelligent man, Mason tried taking a hand in filmmaking early on, producing several of his own pictures (including 1952's *Lady Possessed,* which he also wrote, 1956's *Bigger Than Life,* one of the first Hollywood movies to deal with the danger of drugs, 1962's *Hero's Island,* and 1969's *Age of Consent).*

In later years Mason took colorful supporting roles and character leads. He menaced Cary Grant in Hitchcock's peerless *North by Northwest* (1959), was obsessed with nymphet Sue Lyon in *Lolita* (1962, playing Humbert Humbert), and pursued Lynn Redgrave in *Georgy Girl* (1966), in spite of their age differences, earning another Oscar nod in the bargain. Like many of his contemporaries, Mason worked in foreign-language productions that generally wasted his abilities, but he continued to win memorable roles in English and Hollywood movies as well. He played the eternally patient Mr. Jordan in *Heaven Can Wait* (1978), a charmingly bumbling Dr. Watson in *Murder by Decree* (1979), and, best of all, a brilliant but ruthless trial lawyer (described by supporting character Jack Warden as "the Prince of f—king Darkness") in *The Verdict* (1982), a performance for which he picked up his last Oscar nomination. Toward the end of his life, he agreed to appear in conjunction with the restoration of 1954's *A Star Is Born,* a film he never particularly liked. But the adulation he received for his moving performance—especially as reconstituted—brought him great satisfaction. *The Shooting Party* (1984), a perceptive look at class structure with Mason as the host of a weekend in the country, featured the actor in a part—and a performance—worthy of being his swan song.

OTHER FILMS INCLUDE: 1949: *East Side, West Side;* 1951: *Pandora and the Flying Dutchman;* 1952: *5 Fingers, Face to Face;* 1953: *The Story of Three Loves, Botany Bay, The Man Between;* 1954: *Prince Valiant;* 1956: *Forever Darling;* 1957: *Island in the Sun;* 1958: *Cry Terror, The Decks Ran Red;* 1959: *Journey to the Center of the Earth;* 1960: *A Touch of Larceny, The Green Carnation, The Marriage-Go-Round;* 1962: *Escape From Zahrain, Tiara Tahiti;* 1964: *The Fall of the Roman Empire, The Pumpkin Eater;* 1965: *Lord Jim;* 1966: *Genghis Khan;* 1967: *The Deadly Affair;* 1968: *Cop Out;* 1970: *Spring and Port Wine;* 1971: *Cold Sweat;* 1973: *The Last of Sheila, The Mackintosh Man;* 1974: *11 Harrowhouse;* 1976: *Voyage of the Damned;* 1977: *Cross of Iron;* 1978: *The Boys From*

Brazil, The Water Babies; 1979: Bloodline, The Passage; 1982: Evil Under the Sun; 1983: Yellowbeard.

MASON, MARSHA. Actress. *(b. Apr. 3, 1942, St. Louis.)* During the 1970s this fresh-faced leading lady—equally facile in comedy and drama—was one of the screen's brightest stars, but her filmic output diminished during the following decade, and the early 1990s saw her playing mother parts in support. Mason, a former ballet student and prolific stage performer in the 1960s and 1970s, was Oscar-nominated for her lively performances in *Cinderella Liberty* (1973, as a hooker with a heart of gold in her first attention-grabbing role), *The Goodbye Girl* (1977), *Chapter Two* (1979), and *Only When I Laugh* (1981), the last three written by Neil Simon, her then-husband. *(Chapter Two* was, in fact, a fictionalized version of their courtship.) She has also appeared in several TV movies, most notably the well-received 1982 drama *Lois Gibbs and the Love Canal* and the 1989 remake of *Dinner at Eight.* In 1991 she starred in the short-lived sitcom "Sibs."
OTHER FILMS INCLUDE: 1966: *Hot Rod Hullabaloo;* 1973: *Blume in Love;* 1977: *Audrey Rose;* 1978: *The Cheap Detective* (another Simon script); 1979: *Promises in the Dark;* 1983: *Max Dugan Returns* (also written by Simon); 1986: *Heartbreak Ridge;* 1990: *Stella;* 1991: *Drop Dead Fred;* 1994: *I Love Trouble.*

MASSEY, RAYMOND. Actor. *(b. Aug. 30, 1896, Toronto; d. July 29, 1983.)* Tall, gaunt, taciturn character actor and occasional lead, best known for his stage and screen turns in the title role of *Abe Lincoln in Illinois* (1940), written for him by playwright Robert E. Sherwood. This Oxford-educated Canadian began his acting career on the British stage in the early 1920s, taking bit parts in the films *International Spy* and *High Treason* (both 1929) before getting the plum role of Sherlock Holmes in *The Speckled Band* (1931). He hopped the Atlantic several times during the 1930s, appearing in such Hollywood films as *The Old Dark House* (1932), *The Prisoner of Zenda* (as Black Michael), and *The Hurricane* (both 1937, a particular meanie in the latter), and such dis-

tinguished British films as *The Scarlet Pimpernel* (1935), *Things to Come* (1936), *Fire Over England* (1937), and *Drums* (1938).

After getting an Oscar nomination for *Abe Lincoln in Illinois,* Massey might have gone on to sympathetic character leads, as Edward Arnold had done, but he showed a preference for villainy, playing wide-eyed zealots and sadistic Nazis with equal relish. His 1940s films include *Santa Fe Trail* (as the fanatical abolitionist John Brown), *49th Parallel, Dangerously They Live* (all 1941), *Desperate Journey, Reap the Wild Wind* (both 1942), *Action in the North Atlantic* (1943), *Arsenic and Old Lace* (a memorably deadpan comic performance as villainous Jonathan Brewster, a character inspired by the screen persona of Boris Karloff, who played the part on Broadway), *The Woman in the Window* (both 1944), *Hotel Berlin, God Is My Co-Pilot* (both 1945), *Stairway to Heaven* (1946), *Possessed, Mourning Becomes Electra* (both 1947), *The Fountainhead, Chain Lightning,* and *Roseanna McCoy* (all 1949).

Massey, who worked on stage between picture assignments, maintained a considerable screen presence during the 1950s and early 1960s, turning up in *Dallas, Barricade* (both 1950), *Sugarfoot, Come Fill the Cup, David and Bathsheba* (all 1951, in the latter as the prophet Nathan), *Carson City* (1952), *The Desert Song* (1953), *Battle Cry, Seven Angry Men* (again as John Brown), *Prince of Players, East of Eden* (all 1955), *Omar Khayyam* (1957), *The Naked and the Dead* (1958), *The Great Impostor* (1960), *The Fiercest Heart* (1961), *How the West Was Won* (1962, as Lincoln again). After that he appeared on the big screen only once more, in the sprawling Western *Mackenna's Gold* (1969).

Television kept Massey busy during the late 1950s, 1960s, and early 1970s. He starred in the series "I Spy" (1956–57), and played firm but good-hearted Doctor Gillespie to Richard Chamberlain's "Dr. Kildare" (1961–66). He also appeared in several anthology shows, dramatic specials, and other series. Massey's son Daniel and daughter Anna have followed in the family footsteps, distinguishing themselves as fine talents, although neither has been particularly active in films. (Daniel *did* get an Oscar nomination for his performance as Noel Coward in 1968's *Star!*) Massey wrote two volumes of autobiography, "When I Was Young" (1976) and "A Hundred Different Lives" (1979).

MASTERSON, MARY STUART. Actress. *(b. June 28, 1966, New York City.)* The daughter of actress Carlin Glynn and writer-actor-director Peter Masterson, this spirited performer made her film debut at age 7 as her real-life father's daughter in the chiller *The Stepford Wives* (1975). Masterson resumed film work in earnest during the mid-1980s, and has offered thoughtful, endearing support in *Heaven Help Us* (1985), *Chances Are, Immediate Family* (both 1989, particularly effective in the latter as a young surrogate mother), and in *Fried Green Tomatoes* (1991), which gave her an outstanding showcase part as a feisty, free-spirited soul. She was especially appealing as the tomboyish drummer in *Some Kind of Wonderful* (1987). Her other films include *At Close Range* (1986), *Gardens of Stone* (1987, with both real-life parents), *Mr. North* (1988), and *Funny About Love* (1990). A talented young actress, she could be one of the 1990s' brightest stars. Recent films include *Married To It, Benny & Joon, Mad at the Moon* (all 1993), *Bad Girls* and *Radioland Murders* (both 1994). Her father has directed the films *The Trip to Bountiful* (1985), *Full Moon in Blue Water* (1988), and *Convicts* (1991).

MASTRANTONIO, MARY ELIZABETH. Actress. *(b. Nov. 17, 1958, Oak Park, Ill.)* Attractive actress most suited at playing strong-willed, intelligent, and contentious leads, she was a formidable adversary for Paul Newman in Scorsese's *The Color of Money* (1986; an Oscar-nominated performance), Ed Harris in James Cameron's *The Abyss* (1989), and Gene Hackman in Michael Apted's *Class Action* (1991). She first appeared on-screen as the strong-willed sister of gangster Tony Montana (Al Pacino) in Brian De Palma's 1983 remake of *Scarface,* and while she has appeared in several mediocre productions—including *Slamdance* (1987) and *The January Man* (1989)—she's always acquitted herself well. Her established screen persona stood her in good stead for her role as the new,

middlingly "politically correct" Maid Marian in 1991's *Robin Hood: Prince of Thieves.* She is married to *January Man* director Pat O'Connor. Still active on stage, her recent films include *Consenting Adults* (1992).

MASTROIANNI, MARCELLO. Actor. *(b. Sept. 28, 1923, Fontana Liri, Italy.)* One of the world's most admired screen actors, Mastroianni has remained an international star for more than three decades, with his cool, sophisticated, self-mocking style and sad, soulful eyes (which say more than any dialogue possibly could). He began his career as a bookkeeper for a film company, then joined a theatrical group (making his stage debut opposite Giulietta Masina) and was brought to the attention of Luchino Visconti. Mastroianni performed with the director's company for the next ten years and during that time also made many films, starting with a small role in an Italian-made adaptation of *Les Misérables* (1947). He appeared in many mediocre offerings—*Atto d'accusa* (1950), *L' Eterna Catena* (1951) and *Lulu* (1952), to name a few—but gained recognition and genuine fame for his leading role in *Chronicle of Poor Lovers* (1954). He became a major star in Italy with Visconti's *White Nights* (1957) and the caper film *Big Deal on Madonna Street* (1958), and then came to international prominence as the self-searching columnist in Federico Fellini's landmark *La Dolce Vita* (1960).

That film expertly utilized Mastroianni's extraordinary ability to project a quizzical, almost opaque reticence—as did Antonioni's *La Notte* (1961)—but Mastroianni went on to display a remarkable range: as the impotent husband in *Bell' Antonio* (1960), the Sicilian count who tries to murder his wife in *Divorce—Italian Style* (1962, an Oscar-nominated performance), a professor who helps factory workers unionize in *The Organizer* (1963) and, perhaps most memorably, as the creatively stymied director Guido in Fellini's masterpiece, *8½* (1963). His reputation overseas was now as strong as in his native country. Mastroianni worked nonstop, in films both good and bad: the delightful Vittorio De Sica comedies *Yesterday, Today and Tomorrow* and *Marriage Italian-Style* (both 1964, opposite frequent costar Sophia Loren), the fine adaptation of Camus's *The Stranger* (1967), the middling caper *Diamonds for Breakfast* (1968), the awful *A Place for Lovers* (1969, opposite Faye Dunaway), John Boorman's odd class drama *Leo the Last* (1970), and Ettore Scola's dark comedy *The Pizza Triangle* (1970, which earned him the Best Actor Award at Cannes).

By this time, Mastroianni's subtle mastery of acting was as reliable as his effortless charm, and though he often chose projects unworthy of his talent, he could still amaze: as the disillusioned aristocrat in the Taviani brothers' *Allonsanfan* (1974), a homosexual radio announcer in *A Special Day* (1977, again Oscar-nominated), the dissipated Casanova in *La Nuit de Varennes* (1982), a former cabaret dancer in Fellini's *Ginger and Fred* (1986), and a wealthy but unfulfilled Italian in *Dark Eyes* (1987, another Oscar nomination and a second Cannes Award). Though his English is halting at best, he has made a handful of English-language movies, including *Macaroni* (1985, opposite Jack Lemmon), the American-made *Used People* (1992, opposite Shirley MacLaine), and *Ready to Wear/Prêt-à-Porter* (1994), in which he was reunited with Loren.

Mastroianni has made as many headlines for his off-screen behavior as for his stellar performances, and is well known for affairs with leading ladies like Faye Dunaway and Catherine Deneuve (with whom he has a child) though he has been married to the same woman since 1950. He has made light of his various dalliances as well as his own image as a sex symbol. In interviews, he is self-deprecating about his abilities as an actor, once noting, "I'm shamelessly lucky. I've loved beautiful women. I've acted for 39 years. And so far, nobody has shot me." OTHER FILMS INCLUDE: 1955: *Too Bad She's Bad;* 1958: *Where the Hot Wind Blows!;* 1962: *A Very Private Affair;* 1965: *Casanova '70, The 10th Victim;* 1966: *Shoot Loud, Louder ... I Don't Understand;* 1971: *It Only Happens to Others, The Priest's Wife;* 1973: *What?;* 1977: *We All Loved Each Other So Much* (cameo as himself); 1979: *Blood Feud;* 1981: *City of Women* (for Fellini); 1983: *Gabriela;* 1987: *Intervista* (for Fellini).

MASUR, RICHARD. Actor, director. *(b. Nov. 20, 1948, New York City.)* Masur is one of those reliable character actors whose face, if not name, is familiar to most moviegoers. Masur studied theater at New York University and appeared on the New York stage before breaking into movies and television in the 1970s. He made his first impact on the small screen, with recurring roles on the sitcoms "Rhoda" (1974–78), "One Day at a Time" (1975–76), and "Hot L Baltimore" (1975).

His familiarity as a sympathetic actor on TV didn't keep him from landing other kinds of parts in films, however; one of his best early roles is in *Who'll Stop the Rain* (1978), cast as a ruthless hitman lusting after a cache of heroin. He also played a friendly photographer who coerces teen runaways into posing for pornographic pictures in the notorious made-for-TV movie *Fallen Angel* (1981). Since then he's been a Princeton recruiter in *Risky Business* (1983), a manipulative political flack in *Under Fire* (also 1983), Kurt Russell's newspaper editor in *The Mean Season* (1985), Jack Nicholson's lawyer and friend in *Heartburn* (1986), a corrupted lawman in *Rent-a-Cop* (1988), a fisherman who might be a killer in *Shoot to Kill* (also 1988), and an overaged hippie in *Flashback* (1990). He also appeared in *My Girl* (1991) and the 1994 sequel. In 1986 he made his debut behind the camera, directing a short subject, *Love Struck,* that earned an Academy Award nomination. OTHER FILMS INCLUDE: 1977: *Semi-Tough;* 1979: *Hanover Street;* 1982: *The Thing;* 1987: *The Believers;* 1988: *Walker;* 1993: *The Man Without a Face, And the Band Played On* (made for TV); 1995: *Forget Paris.*

MATHESON, TIM. Actor. *(b. Dec. 31, 1947, Glendale, Calif.)* Who would have expected the voice of kid cartoon hero Jonny Quest to grow up to play Otter, the oversexed fraternity brother, in *National Lampoon's Animal House* (1978)? Probably not "Father Knows Best" 's Robert Young, who starred in one of Matheson's earliest professional gigs, the TV series "Window on Main Street" (1961–62). Now usually cast as smarmy but likable romantics, Matheson somehow failed to parlay his extensive screen experience (dating back to 1967's *Divorce American Style*) into mainstream, leading-man status. He turned

instead to producing with the Rutger Hauer comic actioner *Blind Fury* (1990) and briefly co-owned "The National Lampoon" magazine. He continues to do much TV work and recently starred in the 1991 sitcom "Charlie Hoover." He is also active in made-for-TV movies.
OTHER FILMS INCLUDE: 1968: *Yours, Mine and Ours;* 1973: *Magnum Force;* 1982: *A Little Sex;* 1983: *To Be or Not to Be;* 1984: *Up the Creek, Impulse;* 1985: *Fletch;* 1989: *Speed Zone!;* 1991: *Drop Dead Fred.*

MATLIN, MARLEE. Actress. *(b. Aug. 24, 1965, Morton Grove, Ill.)* This striking, petite actress with brown hair and hazel eyes made a big splash in her film debut as a deaf woman who has isolated herself from the hearing world in *Children of a Lesser God* (1986). The performance won her an Academy Award and made her an overnight star.

Matlin developed roseola at the age of eighteen months, which left her completely deaf in her right ear, and 80 percent deaf in her left ear. As a child she developed an interest in performing, and played in a stage version of "The Wizard of Oz" (as Dorothy) at the age of eight. She continued to act in plays at the Children's Theatre of the Deaf in Des Plaines, Illinois, throughout her childhood.

Her first adult role was a supporting one in Mark Medoff's play "Children of a Lesser God." Director Randa Haines saw her and cast her in the lead for the film adaptation, opposite William Hurt as the teacher who brings her out of her shell. (The two became a couple offscreen as well.) Unfortunately, there were few worthy roles to follow for Matlin. She appeared in the historical satire *Walker* (1988), had a bit part in *The Linguini Incident* and a cameo in *The Player* (both 1992), but it wasn't until 1993 that another lead role was fashioned for her, in the tepid thriller *Hear No Evil.* She has fared better on television, in guest shots on such shows as "Moonlighting" and "Seinfeld," in the TV movie *Bridge to Silence* (1989), with Lee Remick, and in her own series "Reasonable Doubts" (1991–93), costarring Mark Harmon, in which she played a tough assistant D.A. who happens to be hearing-impaired.

MATTHAU, WALTER. Actor. *(b. Oct. 1, 1920, New York City, as Walter Matuschanskavasky.)* Peerless, beloved character actor whose hangdog features, shambling gait, and low-and-inside delivery have delighted audiences since 1955. The son of poor immigrants, Matthau first acted on stage while still a youngster, playing bits for pocket change in one of New York's Yiddish theaters. He didn't seriously take up performing until after World War 2. Matthau honed his craft in theaters, large and small, and on TV, much of which originated from New York in the 1950s.

He spent his first decade on-screen mostly in straight roles, often as villains or cynical Greek choruses, in such films as *The Kentuckian* (1955, his debut), *Bigger Than Life* (1956), *A Face in the Crowd* (1957), *King Creole* (1958), *Gangster Story* (1960, which he also directed), *Lonely Are the Brave* (1962), and *Fail-Safe* (1964). In his true metier, comedy, Matthau essayed audience-grabbing parts in *Onionhead* (1958), *Charade* (1963), and *Goodbye Charlie* (1964) before his Oscar-winning role as the ambulance-chasing "Whiplash Willie" opposite Jack Lemmon in Billy Wilder's *The Fortune Cookie* (1966) solidified his position as a top screen funnyman.

Matthau maintained his stardom with such solid turns as Neil Simon's quintessential slob Oscar Madison in *The Odd Couple* (1968, recreating his Tony Award–winning Broadway role and reunited with Jack Lemmon), Horace Vandergelder in *Hello, Dolly!* (1969), a cranky old-timer in *Kotch* (1971, Oscar-nominated and directed by Lemmon), unscrupulous newspaper editor Walter Burns in Billy Wilder's remake of *The Front Page* (1974, again with Lemmon), a sardonic Transit Authority inspector in *The Taking of Pelham One Two Three* (1974), a cantankerous old vaudevillian in Neil Simon's *The Sunshine Boys* (1975, Oscar-nominated), a boozy pool cleaner redeemed by his coaching of a Little League team in *The Bad News Bears* (1976), a skirt-chasing doctor who meets his match (Glenda Jackson) in *House Calls* (1978), a renegade CIA operative in *Hopscotch* (1980, reteamed with Jackson), and a liberal Supreme Court justice in *First Monday in October* (1981).

Matthau is most effective when he underplays, though often he's been allowed (or perhaps encouraged) to indulge in overheated scenery chewing. He's also been pigeonholed as a comic actor when in fact he's turned in fine dramatic work in such thrillers as *Charley Varrick* (1973) and *The Laughing Policeman* (1974).

He's been somewhat choosy in recent years, and hasn't worked as much, though he toplined Roman Polanski's much-maligned *Pirates* (1986), took an intriguing cameo in Oliver Stone's *JFK* (1991), and agreed to participate in the slapstick indignities of *Dennis the Menace* (1993) as poor Mr. Wilson. He rounded out that year by rejoining his friend and colleague Jack Lemmon in *Grumpy Old Men,* then made a delightful Albert Einstein in the romantic comedy *I.Q.* (1994). He has appeared in a select number of TV movies, including the Emmy-winning *The Incident* (1990, as a small-town lawyer embroiled in a controversial case), as well as a pair of sequels, and *Mrs. Lambert Remembers Love* (1991), in which he was directed by his son Charles Matthau.

OTHER FILMS INCLUDE: 1957: *Slaughter on Tenth Avenue;* 1958: *Ride a Crooked Trail, Voice in the Mirror;* 1960: *Strangers When We Meet;* 1962: *Who's Got the Action?;* 1963: *Island of Love;* 1964: *Ensign Pulver;* 1965: *Mirage;* 1967: *A Guide for the Married Man;* 1968: *The Secret Life of an American Wife;* 1969: *Cactus Flower;* 1971: *A New Leaf, Plaza Suite;* 1972: *Pete 'n' Tillie;* 1974: *Earthquake* (a cameo under his real name); 1978: *California Suite, Casey's Shadow;* 1980: *Little Miss Marker* (also executive produced); 1981: *Buddy Buddy* (with Lemmon, for Wilder); 1982: *I Ought to Be in Pictures;* 1983: *The Survivors;* 1985: *Movers and Shakers;* 1988: *The Couch Trip.*

MATTHEWS, JESSIE. Actress, singer, dancer. (b. Mar. 11, 1907, London; d. Aug. 20, 1981.) Forgotten by all but the most rabid film buffs, this British actress was her country's top film star during the 1930s, and the first to develop a following in America. Born into an impoverished Soho family, she escaped the slums by performing, breaking into a chorus line at the age of 16. That same year, 1923, she made her movie debut in *The Beloved Vagabond.* She toured with the famed Andre Charlot troupe before becoming a stage sensation on her own, especially in the Rodgers and Hart show "Evergreen."

Matthews appeared in a few minor talkies, including *Out of the Blue* (1931), *There Goes the Bride,* and *The Midshipmaid* (both 1932) before being taken under the wing of director Victor Saville.

It was Saville who saw to it that Matthews—a saucer-eyed girl with an upturned nose, weak chin, and prominent teeth (but a great figure)—was properly photographed. He also forced her to hone her limited acting skills, and concentrate on projecting her personality. As a result, their films together, including *The Good Companions, Friday the Thirteenth* (both 1933), *Evergreen* (1934, based on her stage success), *First a Girl* (1935), and *It's Love Again* (1936), were not only exceptional star vehicles, but among the finest films exported by Britain; several of them opened in New York's prestigious Radio City Music Hall. While Matthews' singing and dancing were certainly commendable, it was the buoyant persona that really put over her filmusicals. She was billed, with Hollywood-inspired hyperbole, as "The Dancing Divinity."

When Saville left Matthews' home studio, Gaumont-British, the direction of her vehicles was turned over to her husband (and former costar) Sonnie Hale, who lacked his predecessor's light touch and technical virtuosity. *Head Over Heels, Gangway* (both 1937), and *Sailing Along* (1938) all had their moments, but failed to please audiences as had the Saville pictures. After *Climbing High* (1938), a nonmusical outing, Jessie left the movies. She made an abortive comeback attempt with *Candles at Nine* (1944), a low-budget, old-dark-house thriller that was poorly conceived. Her foundering marriage to Hale collapsed that same year, intensifying her emotional problems, which had disrupted her work several times over the preceding decade.

Matthews appeared in a 1947 short subject, *Life Is Nothing Without Music,* but didn't appear in a feature film until 1958, when she took a supporting role as the title character's mother in *tom thumb.* She spent more than 20 years costarring in a popular BBC radio soap opera, and made her final screen appearance in *The Hound of the Baskervilles* (1977). She wrote an autobiography, "Over My Shoulder" (the title of her best-remembered song from *Evergreen*), in 1974.

MATURE, VICTOR. Actor. *(b. Jan. 29, 1915, Louisville, Ky.)* Look up the word "beefcake" in your slang dictionary and, chances are, you'll find a picture of this brawny, dark, wavy-haired leading man. Extroverted and gregarious by nature, he seldom had a chance to use those traits on-screen. Born to immigrant parents, he took up acting as a young man, making his way to California and the Pasadena Playhouse before being signed to a contract by producer Hal Roach. Mature made an inauspicious debut, opposite veteran Joan Bennett, in *The Housekeeper's Daughter* (1939), but the following year he delighted feminine filmgoers as the muscular, fur-clad caveman in *One Million B.C.* He finished his Roach tenure with *Captain Caution,* then appeared in *No, No, Nanette* (both 1940) and *The Shanghai Gesture* (1941) before signing with 20th Century-Fox.

Mature, who at that time was romantically linked with Fox star Betty Grable, appeared opposite her in three Fox films—*I Wake Up Screaming* (1941, a rare dramatic vehicle for Grable, and a clever, suspenseful noir-like thriller), *Song of the Islands,* and *Footlight Serenade* (both 1942); they made a striking and compatible couple on-screen. He also starred opposite Rita Hayworth in *My Gal Sal* (also 1942), a colorful period musical that cast him as songwriter Paul Dresser. After being loaned to RKO for *Seven Days' Leave* (also 1942), Mature went into the service for the duration of World War 2.

Director John Ford cast him as tubercular dentist Doc Holliday in *My Darling Clementine* (1946), opposite Henry Fonda as Wyatt Earp. Although it played fast and loose with the facts (such as killing off Holliday in the shootout at the O.K. Corral, even though he actually lived for several years afterward), the film was a big hit and got Mature's career back on track. (It also marked the first time critics took him seriously.) The top-billed star of *Kiss of Death* (1947), he saw supporting player Richard Widmark steal the film with his portrayal of a cold-blooded killer. Undeterred, Mature worked steadily over the next 13 years, essaying hard-boiled characterizations in Westerns, crime dramas, Biblical spectaculars, and costume dramas—even musical comedy and farce. Often kidded for his beefy looks and stolid demeanor on-screen, he was actually a very capable performer.

Off the big screen for many years, Mature made an amusing comeback in 1966, playing a vain former movie star in the Italian-made caper comedy, *After the Fox,* which starred Peter Sellers. A genuinely enjoyable spoof, it showed Mature capable of laughing at his own screen image. He subsequently appeared, briefly, in *Head* (1968, in which the miniaturized Monkees cavort on his scalp!), *Every Little Crook and Nanny* (1972), *Won Ton Ton, the Dog Who Saved Hollywood* (1976), and *Firepower* (1979). Content playing golf in his retirement, Mature was coaxed in front of the cameras one more time, for a TV remake of *Samson and Delilah* (1984) in which he played the strongman's father.

OTHER FILMS INCLUDE: 1948: *Fury at Furnace Creek, Cry of the City;* 1949: *Easy Living, Samson and Delilah* (cast as the Biblical strongman seduced by torrid temptress Hedy Lamarr in this Cecil B. DeMille spectacular); 1950: *Wabash Avenue* (reunited with Grable), *Stella;* 1952: *The Las Vegas Story, Androcles and the Lion, Something for the Birds, Million Dollar Mermaid;* 1953: *Affair With a Stranger, The Robe* (in a solid performance as Demetrius that was overshadowed by newcomer Richard Burton); 1954: *Betrayed, The Egyptian, Demetrius and the Gladiators* (a sequel to *The Robe*); 1955: *Chief Crazy Horse, Violent Saturday, The Last Frontier;* 1956: *Safari, The Sharkfighters;* 1957: *Zarak, Pickup Alley, The Long Haul;* 1958: *China Doll, Tank Force;* 1959: *Escort West, The Bandit of Zhobe, The Big Circus, Timbuktu;* 1960: *Hannibal.*

MAY, ELAINE. Director, screenwriter, actress. *(b. Apr. 21, 1932, Philadelphia, as Elaine Berlin.)* This improvisational comedienne found stardom teamed with Mike Nichols in the 1960s, when they graduated from Chicago's Second City to headline in nightclubs, TV, recordings, and in their own Broadway show. After an amicable split she took acting roles in *Enter Laughing* and *Luv* (both 1967) before making her debut as writer, director, and star with *A New Leaf* (1971), in which she played the ultimate nebbish, victimized by greedy Walter Matthau. Although the film was taken from her and reedited, it nevertheless established her own comedic voice. It also set a pattern for her highly erratic screen career. In 1971 she had her name removed from the screenplay of Otto Preminger's *Such Good Friends*. She enjoyed her only mainstream success the following year with *The Heartbreak Kid* (1972, from a Neil Simon script) in which she directed her daughter, Jeannie Berlin. Stories of the years she spent tinkering with *Mikey and Nicky* are legend; when this quirky comedy, starring John Cassavetes and Peter Falk, was finally released in 1976, it was barely seen. She took a supporting role in *California Suite* (1978), and then shared an Oscar nomination for her contribution to the screenplay of Warren Beatty's *Heaven Can Wait* (1978), establishing a relationship with the star and filmmaker that would lead to the legendary turkey *Ishtar* (1987, which May wrote and directed), another film whose production history was infinitely more interesting than the movie itself. In 1990 she returned to performing, costarring with Marlo Thomas in the small-scale comedy *In the Spirit*, with daughter Berlin in the cast. May has also worked without credit as a script doctor on a number of films, most notably *Tootsie* (1982).

MAYNARD, KEN. Actor. *(b. July 21, 1895, Vevey, Ind.; d. Mar. 23, 1973.)* One of the flamboyant, flashily dressed cowboy stars who rose to screen prominence during the 1920s in the wake of Tom Mix's success, this slick-haired, square-jawed son of the sage for a time enjoyed a popularity second only to Mix himself. Maynard, a former Ringling Brothers rider and rodeo champion, never mastered even the rudiments of screen acting; nonetheless, he projected a daredevil personality that endeared him to youthful moviegoers for more than two decades. He entered films in 1923, appearing in several cheapies before being cast as Paul Revere in the Marion Davies historical epic *Janice Meredith* in 1924. He achieved stardom in a series of superior Westerns for First National, among them *Senor Daredevil, The Unknown Cavalier* (1926), *The Red Raiders* (1927), *The Phantom City* (1928), and *Cheyenne* (1929).

Maynard went to Universal for a 1929–30 series of sound Westerns—including *Lucky Larkin, Mountain Justice,* and *Song of the Saddle*—but was dropped

when the studio inexplicably suspended horse-opera production. At this point, Maynard fell in with "Poverty Row" producers; his early independent oaters, including *Dynamite Ranch* (1932), *Tombstone Canyon,* and *The Phantom Thunderbolt* (both 1933), were actually quite good. He returned to Universal in 1933, making eight fairly lavish Westerns there—including *King of the Arena, The Strawberry Roan, Wheels of Destiny,* and *Gun Justice*—before leaving the studio in 1934 following a series of battles with Carl Laemmle, Jr. In 1934 he also made a well-received serial, *Mystery Mountain,* and a medium-budget feature, *In Old Santa Fe,* for Nat Levine's Mascot Pictures. Fledgling cowboy star Gene Autry (who, in later years, cited Maynard as his greatest influence) got his first screen exposure playing bits in both productions. Maynard's subsequent vehicles were uniformly weak, and the star's obvious lethargy (and rapidly expanding waistline) contributed to a rapid decline in popularity.

In 1943 Maynard, who once made several thousand dollars per picture, accepted $5,000 to costar in "The Trail Blazers," six abysmally cheap horse operas with Hoot Gibson, also on hard times. *Harmony Trail* (1944) was Maynard's last starring Western; he returned to the screen just once, taking a cameo role in *Bigfoot* (1970), a ludicrous monster movie. Sadly, Maynard lived out his last years in an alcoholic stupor, locking himself in a tiny trailer for weeks at a time. His brother Kermit, who doubled Ken in the 1930s and was himself a cowboy star (albeit briefly), worked well into the 1950s in bit parts and was actively involved in the Screen Actors Guild for many years.

MAYSLES BROTHERS, THE. Directors. *(Albert Maysles—b. Nov. 26, 1926, Brookline, Mass. David Maysles—b. Jan. 10, 1932, Boston; d. Jan. 3, 1987.)* Often credited with inventing the documentary style known as "direct cinema," the Maysles created a body of work based on the random energy of life and, as Albert noted, "a conviction that it's a noble thing to record reality without controlling it." After teaching psychology at Boston University, Albert went to Russia and made *Psychiatry in Russia* (1955), a short about mental hospitals there which was later shown on public TV. He and David then collaborated on *Youth of Poland* (1957) before joining the documentary team of Robert Drew and Richard Leacock, with whom they worked on *Primary* (1960). This behind-the-scenes look at the 1960 Democratic primary in Wisconsin between John F. Kennedy and Hubert Humphrey presaged many technical, aural, and "storytelling" breakthroughs in documentary film.

The Maysles went on to codirect a series of celebrity portraits, including *Showman* (1962, about producer Joseph Levine), *What's Happening! The Beatles in the U.S.A.* (1964; later reedited and released on video as *The Beatles! The First U.S. Visit*), *Meet Marlon Brando* (1965), and *A Visit With Truman Capote* (1966). Then came *Salesman* (1968), a feature-length study of four door-to-door Bible salesmen, which became a classic in its unblinking depiction of their lives. *Gimme Shelter* (1970), a spellbinding (and disturbing) record of the Rolling Stones performance at Altamont, eschewed the rules of "direct cinema" with the Maysles themselves appearing on camera as the Stones watched and reacted to footage of the infamous murder which took place at the concert. In doing so, the film raised many serious questions about the nature, validity, and responsibility of the documentary form.

Since then, the Maysles have explored a variety of subjects in *Christo's Valley Curtain* (1974, Oscar-nominated for Best Documentary Short), *Grey Gardens* (1976, a bizarre, feature-length "visit" with the eccentric aunt and cousin of Jackie Kennedy), and *Mohammed and Larry* (1980, about boxers Ali and Holmes). After David's death, Albert continued working with longtime collaborators like Susan Froemke, Deborah Dickson, and Charlotte Zwerin on projects ranging from the Emmy-winning *Horowitz Plays Mozart* (1987) and *Abortion: Desperate Choices* (1992) to the ultra-commercial *Sports Illustrated: Swimsuit '92* (also 1992).

MAYO, VIRGINIA. Actress. (b. Nov. 30, 1920, St. Louis, as Virginia Jones.) Beautiful blonde with peaches-and-cream complexion, frequently seen in Technicolor productions of the 1940s and 1950s. Entering show business as a chorus girl, Mayo crashed the movies in the same capacity, dancing in the likes of *Follies Girl, Sweet Rosie O'Grady,* and *Hello Frisco, Hello* (all 1943). She was then signed by producer Samuel Goldwyn, who featured her as a decorative "Goldwyn Girl" in Danny Kaye's *Up in Arms* (1944) before promoting her to the female lead in Bob Hope's *The Princess and the Pirate* that same year.

Mayo held her own opposite the ski-nosed comic, and the hit comedy launched her starring career with a bang. Goldwyn teamed her with Danny Kaye in *Wonder Man* (1945), *The Kid From Brooklyn* (1946), *The Secret Life of Walter Mitty* (1947), and *A Song Is Born* (1948), and gave her a solid supporting role as Dana Andrews' fickle wife in William Wyler's Oscar-winning *The Best Years of Our Lives* (also 1946).

Warner Bros. wooed Mayo away from Goldwyn in 1948 and, beginning with that year's *Smart Girls Don't Talk,* starred her in a wider variety of vehicles, including Westerns, swashbucklers, and crime dramas in addition to comedies and musicals. Her films for the studio include *Flaxy Martin, Colorado Territory, The Girl From Jones Beach, Always Leave Them Laughing* (all 1949), *The Flame and the Arrow, West Point Story* (both 1950), *Painting the Clouds With Sunshine, Captain Horatio Hornblower* (both 1951), *She's Working Her Way Through College, The Iron Mistress* (both 1952), *She's Back on Broadway, South Sea Woman* (both 1953), the very silly *King Richard and the Crusaders* (1954), *The Silver Chalice* (also 1954, opposite a debuting Paul Newman), *The Big Land, The Story of Mankind* (both 1957), and *Fort Dobbs* (1958). Although she retained her looks as she approached middle age, Mayo worked less frequently as the studio system, of which she was a creation, gradually dissolved. Unlike many of her contemporaries, Mayo eschewed television work. She was married to actor Michael O'Shea from 1947 to 1973, when he passed away.

OTHER FILMS INCLUDE: 1953: *Devil's Canyon;* 1955: *Pearl of the South Pacific;* 1956: *The Proud Ones;* 1957: *The Tall Stranger;* 1966: *Castle of Evil;* 1967: *Fort Utah;* 1969: *The Haunted;* 1976: *Won Ton Ton, the Dog Who Saved Hollywood, The Glass Cage;* 1977: *French Quarter;* 1990: *Evil Spirits.*

MAZURKI, MIKE. Actor. (b. Dec. 25, 1909, Tarnopol, Austria, as Mikhail Mazurwski; d. Dec. 9, 1990.) This massively built, craggy-featured ex-wrestler was both ideally cast and remarkably effective as the dull-witted thug Moose Malloy ("I want you should find my Velma") in the classic 1944 whodunit, *Murder, My Sweet*. It was the high point of his lengthy (if somewhat one-note) acting career. Mazurki often played dumbbell hoods, but he also inherited Victor McLaglen's place in John Ford's stock company, and appeared in many costume dramas and swashbucklers as well. He had enough of a sense of humor to kid his own tough-guy image in many feature-film and TV appearances, including a 1986 Rod Stewart music video.
OTHER FILMS INCLUDE: 1941: *The Shanghai Gesture;* 1943: *Behind the Rising Sun;* 1945: *The Spanish Main, Dick Tracy* (notable as "Splitface"); 1947: *Nightmare Alley* (memorable as a murderous carnival strongman), *Sinbad the Sailor, Unconquered;* 1949: *Samson and Delilah;* 1950: *Night and the City;* 1951: *My Favorite Spy;* 1954: *The Egyptian;* 1955: *Blood Alley, Kismet;* 1958: *The Buccaneer;* 1959: *Some Like It Hot;* 1961: *Pocketful of Miracles;* 1963: *Donovan's Reef, It's a Mad Mad Mad Mad Mad World;* 1964: *Cheyenne Autumn;* 1966: *7 Women;* 1967: *The Adventures of Bullwhip Griffin;* 1975: *The Wild McCullochs;* 1976: *Challenge to Be Free* (playing the lead in this kiddie adventure film, made in 1972); 1987: *Amazon Women on the Moon;* 1990: *Dick Tracy*.

MAZURSKY, PAUL. Producer, director, screenwriter, actor. (b. Apr. 25, 1930, Brooklyn, N.Y.) While other filmmakers may grab more headlines, Mazursky has built up a body of work that proves him to be one of our most gifted social observers. He caught the acting bug at a young age, and after appearing in college and off-Broadway productions, he made his screen debut in *Fear and Desire* (1953), for a first-time director named Stanley Kubrick. Mazursky later appeared as a juvenile delinquent in *The Blackboard Jungle* (1955), but to make ends meet, he worked as a waiter and a stand-up comic. Eventually he moved to L.A. where he and partner Larry Tucker wrote for "The Danny Kaye Show" and helped create the pilot for "The Monkees." Their first

script, *I Love You, Alice B. Toklas,* was filmed in 1968, with Peter Sellers as a lawyer who gets turned on to hippiedom. Mazursky made his directorial debut with *Bob & Carol & Ted & Alice* (1969), a look at late sixties lifestyles—L.A.-style encounter groups, wife-swapping, etc.—that became a much-talked-about hit, and netted an Oscar nomination for Mazursky's and Tucker's screenplay.
Their next collaboration, *Alex in Wonderland* (1970) was a seriocomic self-examination inspired by Fellini's *8½;* Mazursky even talked Fellini himself into making a cameo appearance in the picture. It was a box office flop, but Mazursky rebounded with a series of funny, touching comedies marked by a loose, almost European tone that eschewed formula in favor of characters and themes: *Blume in Love* (1973), a study of marriage and romance; *Harry and Tonto* (1974), with Art Carney in an Oscar-winning performance as a modern-day Lear who travels the country with his cat, visiting his grown children; and *Next Stop, Greenwich Village* (1976), an autobiographical look at Mazursky's Village days in the 1950s. *An Unmarried Woman* (1978), probably his best film, follows a woman picking up the pieces after her husband leaves her; it earned Oscar nominations for Best Picture, Best Screenplay and Jill Clayburgh's marvelous lead performance. Following *Willie and Phil* (1980, inspired by Truffaut's *Jules and Jim*) and *Tempest* (1982, a paraphrase of Shakespeare's play), Mazursky gave Robin Williams one of his best early roles in *Moscow on the Hudson* (1984) and resuscitated the careers of Richard Dreyfuss and Bette Midler in the enormously popular rags-to-riches story *Down and Out in Beverly Hills,* inspired by Renoir's *Boudu Saved From Drowning.* Mazursky and Dreyfuss teamed up again for the silly *Moon Over Parador* (1988) before Mazursky brought one of his pet projects to the screen, *Enemies, A Love Story* (1989, Oscar-nominated for his and Roger L. Simon's screenplay), a beautiful adaptation of Isaac Bashevis Singer's novel about a Jewish man who is haunted by the Holocaust. Mazursky followed with two misfires: the meandering *Scenes From a Mall* (1991, which boasted the inspired casting of Woody Allen and Bette Midler as husband and wife) and the labored Hol-

lywood satire *The Pickle* (1993). Since then, he has directed *Faithful* (1995). Still an actor at heart, Mazursky has appeared in many of his own films, most memorably in *Alex in Wonderland* (as a movie producer), *Blume in Love* (as George Segal's law partner), and *Moon Over Parador* (as, yes, Richard Dreyfuss' mother). He has also taken supporting roles in *A Star Is Born* (1976, as Kris Kristofferson's record producer), *A Man, a Woman and a Bank* (1979), *Punchline* (1988, as a joke salesman), *Scenes From the Class Struggle in Beverly Hills* (1989), *Man Trouble* (1992), *Carlito's Way* (1993, as a weary judge in the opening scene), *Love Affair* (1994), and *Miami Rhapsody* (1995). Mazursky also executive produced *Taking Care of Business* (1991), a comedy written by his daughter Jill.

McBRIDE, JIM. Director, screenwriter. (b. Sept. 26, 1941, New York City.) A product of New York University's film program, McBride made a splash with his debut feature, *David Holzman's Diary* (1968), and it remains his calling card after all these years. A stylistic outgrowth of the French New Wave and cinema-verité filmmaking, *Diary* is an inventive, quick-witted satire of self-reverential movie-making and the underground film world. It tells the story of a young filmmaker who venerates cinema-as-truth and begins shooting a visual diary. Made for just $2,500, the film remains a minor classic. His subsequent films—*My Girlfriend's Wedding* (1969), *Glen and Randa* (1971), and *Hot Times* (1974)—generated little interest. Then in the 1980s McBride went mainstream, directing an audacious but unsuccessful remake of Godard's French New Wave classic *Breathless* (1983) with Richard Gere, the atmospheric (and unabashedly sexy) New Orleans–based thriller *The Big Easy* (1987), and the Jerry Lee Lewis bio/musical *Great Balls of Fire!* (1989). (Trivia buffs will recall that Richard Gere's character in *Breathless* is addicted to Jerry Lee Lewis music.) McBride, who has scripted most of his films, has also appeared on camera in *Hot Times* and the Jonathan Demme thriller *Last Embrace* (1979). His latest credit as writer-director is *Uncovered* (1993).

McCAMBRIDGE, MERCEDES. Actress. (b. Mar. 17, 1918, Joliet, Ill., as Carlotta Mercedes Agnes McCambridge.) Versatile and prolific stage and radio actress (a regular on, among others, the well-remembered "I Love a Mystery" series) who established a formidable screen presence in her handful of films. She won an Oscar for her screen debut as Broderick Crawford's hard-boiled secretary/lover in *All the King's Men* (1949), but may be even better remembered as the icy villainess who locked horns with Joan Crawford in the role-reversal Western *Johnny Guitar* (1954) and Rock Hudson's strong-willed sister in *Giant* (1956, for which she was Oscar-nominated). Her most notorious movie performance was given offscreen, as the guttural voice of the possessed Linda Blair in *The Exorcist* (1973). She was married at one time to director Fletcher Markle. Still active on stage, she published her autobiography, "The Quality of Mercy," in 1981.
OTHER FILMS INCLUDE: 1950: *The Scarf;* 1951: *Inside Straight, Lightning Strikes Twice;* 1957: *A Farewell to Arms;* 1958: *Touch of Evil;* 1959: *Suddenly, Last Summer;* 1960: *Cimarron;* 1961: *Angel Baby;* 1968: *The Counterfeit Killer;* 1977: *Thieves;* 1979: *The Concorde—Airport '79;* 1980: *Echoes.*

McCAREY, LEO. Director, producer, screenwriter. (b. Oct. 3, 1898, Los Angeles; d. July 5, 1969.) One of the most inspired comedy directors who ever worked in Hollywood broke into the business as an assistant director to Tod Browning in 1920, but honed his skills at the Hal Roach studio for the rest of that decade. Hired by Roach in 1923, McCarey initially wrote gags for Our Gang and other studio stars, then produced and directed shorts—including a string of inventive and hilarious two-reelers with the underrated Charley Chase. He was then instrumental in teaming, and establishing the comic foundation for, Stan Laurel and Oliver Hardy, though his only official credits appear as director of the 1929 shorts *We Faw Down, Liberty,* and *Wrong Again.* By that time he was, in fact, vice-president of production for the entire studio.
In the sound era McCarey ventured into feature-film directing, and after some tentative early efforts he got the knack. He subsequently worked with many of the

greatest comedic talents in movies, including Eddie Cantor (1932's *The Kid From Spain*), The Marx Brothers (1933's *Duck Soup*), W. C. Fields (1934's *Six of a Kind*), Mae West (1934's *Belle of the Nineties*), and Harold Lloyd (1936's *The Milky Way*), to name a few. He won his first Best Director Oscar for his inspired handling of *The Awful Truth* (1937, with Cary Grant and Irene Dunne), one of the best screwball comedies. (Set to direct that duo again in *My Favorite Wife*, he was sidetracked midway through production by a near-fatal auto accident; Garson Kanin completed the picture.)

More than just a gag man, McCarey developed a fine storytelling sense. He also had a flair for sentimental stories, as proved by the wrenching portrait of old age, *Make Way for Tomorrow* (1937), the touching romance *Love Affair* (1939), and *Going My Way* (1944, for which he won his second Best Director Oscar, and snagged another for his screenplay). His post-WW 2 output, generally less impressive, included *The Bells of St. Mary's* (1945, the equally successful sequel to *Going My Way*, which earned him another Oscar nomination), *Good Sam* (1948), *An Affair to Remember* (1957, a middling remake of his own *Love Affair*), *Rally 'Round the Flag, Boys!* (1958), and *Satan Never Sleeps* (1962). A fierce anti-Communist, McCarey was involved in many internecine squabbles with fellow filmmakers during the HUAC days. In 1952 he wrote and directed *My Son John*, a hysterical portrait of one American family's struggle against the influence of the Red Menace. It actually earned him an Academy Award nomination for Best Screenplay.

McCARTHY, ANDREW. Actor. (b. Nov. 29, 1962, Westfield, N.J.) Perpetually youthful actor who made his debut in *Class* (1983) and became associated (briefly) with the so-called Brat Pack of that decade. Never charismatic enough to attain stardom, he gave low-key performances in such films as *St. Elmo's Fire, Heaven Help Us* (both 1985), *Pretty in Pink* (1986, as Molly Ringwald's unattainable heartthrob), *Mannequin* (1987), and *Less Than Zero* (1987, as the rich, jaded college grad). In 1989 he gave an uncharacteristically lively comedy performance in the silly *Weekend at Bernie's*, which led to a 1993 sequel. He also won dramatic roles in an impressive variety of films including *Waiting for the Moon* (1987), *Fresh Horses, Kansas* (both 1988), Claude Chabrol's *Quiet Days in Clichy* (1990), *Year of the Gun* (1991), *Only You* (1992), and *The Joy Luck Club* (1993).

McCARTHY, KEVIN. Actor. (b. Feb. 15, 1914, Seattle.) To many moviegoers, he'll always be the frantic fugitive, pursued by pod people from outer space, who dashes onto a busy highway screaming, "They're here! They're here!" That's the climax of the sci-fi classic *Invasion of the Body Snatchers* (1956), and it's such a memorable moment that McCarthy has in recent years been hired on other films to spoof his own performance. (He even made a cameo in the 1978 remake, along with the original film's director, Don Siegel.) But his career extends far beyond that. A stage player from Washington, McCarthy earned a Supporting Actor Oscar nomination for his first film in 1951: *Death of a Salesman*, in which he appeared as elder son Biff (a role he played on the London stage). Over the next 10 years he alternated leads in small movies (such as 1956's *Nightmare*) with supporting roles in larger movies (such as 1961's *The Misfits*, in which he's Marilyn Monroe's husband, and 1964's *The Best Man*). In recent years, director Joe Dante, an inveterate fan, has cast McCarthy in colorful roles in a number of his films, including *The Howling* (1981), *Twilight Zone—The Movie* (1983), *Innerspace* (1987), and *Matinee* (1993). He can still be seen both in large-scale theatrical films and made-for-video cheapies, though he takes greater pride, no doubt, in his long-running stage vehicle "Give 'Em Hell, Harry!" (as Harry Truman). His sister was author Mary McCarthy.
OTHER FILMS INCLUDE: 1968: *The Hell With Heroes;* 1972: *Kansas City Bomber;* 1976: *Buffalo Bill and the Indians;* 1980: *Hero At Large, Those Lips, Those Eyes;* 1989: *Fast Food, UHF;* 1991: *Eve of Destruction;* 1992: *The Distinguished Gentleman;* 1995: *Just Cause.*

McCOY, TIM. Actor. (b. Apr. 10, 1891, Saginaw, Mich.; d. Jan. 29, 1978.) In his prime, this cowboy star cut an impressive figure: Ramrod straight, with pale, piercing blue eyes and firmly set jaw, he wore an all-black outfit, topped with a high-crowned white Stetson hat and a flowing white neckerchief. Infatuated with the West from boyhood, he moved to Wyoming after college and immersed himself in Indian lore and language. He served with the Army in World War 1 and was discharged with the rank of colonel. Back in Wyoming, he was made an Indian agent; when director James Cruze needed Indian extras for his 1923 epic *The Covered Wagon,* Tim supplied them and acted as go-between. Paramount saw star potential in McCoy, and gave him a key role in *The Thundering Herd* (1925). But it was MGM that signed him, and in the late 1920s he appeared in more than a dozen Westerns and historical adventure pictures, most notably *Winners of the Wilderness* (1927), a Revolutionary War tale that costarred up-and-coming Joan Crawford.

In 1930, Tim went to Universal and starred in the first all-talking serial, *The Indians Are Coming.* Columbia contracted him for a series of B Westerns in 1931, and during his four-year tenure at the studio McCoy honed his screen persona. Essentially humorless on-screen (and seemingly ill at ease in his infrequent romantic scenes), McCoy stared down any villains he couldn't outshoot—which was practically never; he had the fastest draw of any Hollywood cowboy (six film frames, according to his editors, or one-quarter of a second). Economical but carefully made horse operas such as *Texas Cyclone* (1931), *Cornered* (1932), *Rusty Rides Alone* (1933), *The Prescott Kid* (1934), *The Law Beyond the Range,* and *Revenge Rider* (both 1935) cemented McCoy's reputation as a top Western star. He apparently took a hand in writing *The End of the Trail* (1932), an impassioned indictment of the white man's mistreatment of the Indian.

McCoy left Columbia in 1935 to make Westerns for minor studios such as Puritan, Victory, Monogram, and PRC. By 1941, he was sharing top billing with Buck Jones in Monogram's "Rough Riders" series, which included *Arizona Bound* (1941), *Below the Border,* and *West of the Law* (both 1942, the last of the series). McCoy, who liked Jones personally, felt producer Scott Dunlap was steering the

series Buck's way, and resigned. He served with the armed forces during World War 2, and afterward returned to his Wyoming ranch. He hosted a TV series on western lore during the 1950s, and was coaxed into taking bit roles in *Around the World in Eighty Days* (1956), *Run of the Arrow* (1957), and *Requiem for a Gunfighter* (1965, his last film).

McCREA, JOEL. Actor. *(b. Nov. 5, 1905, Los Angeles; d. Oct. 20, 1990.)* Like many natives of southern California, McCrea more or less drifted into movies because they were there. He did extra work while attending Pomona State College (and can be seen in such late silent films as Marion Davies' *The Fair Co-ed);* a growing interest in acting led him into collegiate theatrics and community playhouses. Cecil B. DeMille gave McCrea his first featured role (as a young playboy) in *Dynamite* (1929), the director's first talkie. Tall, lithe, and handsome—but not in a matinee-idol way—McCrea was an immediate success, and bounced back and forth between supporting roles and leads for the next several years, appearing in drawing-room dramas, comedies, and adventure films, including *Lightnin', Silver Horde* (both 1930), *Once a Sinner, Kept Husbands, Born to Love, Girls About Town* (all 1931), *Business and Pleasure, Rockabye,* and *The Sport Parade* (all 1932).

Three RKO films in 1932 cemented McCrea's reputation. *Bird of Paradise* teamed him with exotic Delores Del Rio in a dreamy, audience-pleasing South Seas romance (which gave female moviegoers ample opportunity to coo over his physique); *The Most Dangerous Game* pitted him against Russian hunter Leslie Banks in a robust adaptation of Richard Connell's classic short story; and *The Lost Squadron,* ostensibly a Richard Dix vehicle, gave him a plum role as a daredevil pilot. McCrea starred opposite RKO's top female star, Irene Dunne, in a tepid 1933 drama, *The Silver Cord.* During production of that film he first met actress Frances Dee, whom he would marry within the year.

McCrea became one of the 1930s' most dependable leading men, although, oddly enough, during that decade he seldom essayed the rugged, virile characterization for which he is so fondly remembered. He fared particularly well in films produced by Samuel Goldwyn, including *Barbary Coast* (1935, as a young prospector smitten by gambler Miriam Hopkins), *Splendor* (also 1935, again paired with Hopkins), *These Three* (1936, as the doctor in love with schoolteacher Merle Oberon), *Come and Get It* (also 1936, as the idealistic son of rugged lumber king Edward Arnold), and *Dead End* (1937, as the impoverished, would-be architect in a New York slum). These movies, more than most others McCrea made during the 1930s, solidified his box-office standing.

Wells Fargo (1937) reunited McCrea and Dee on-screen, and was the first bona fide Western he made; overblown but oddly unexciting, it now seems a lackluster initiation into the genre for which McCrea is best remembered. DeMille's *Union Pacific* (1939) had more hair on its chest, so to speak, and added to McCrea's standing as an action star. His vigorous turn as the all-American reporter in Hitchcock's *Foreign Correspondent* (1940) was equally well received.

McCrea claimed that he was never anyone's first choice for a part; in fact, Hitchcock had wanted Gary Cooper for *Foreign Correspondent*. But writer-director Preston Sturges liked McCrea and sought him out specifically in the early 1940s; they made a felicitous team. *Sullivan's Travels* (1941) cast him as a pretentious movie director who, while researching conditions in America for a forthcoming socially conscious epic, finds himself behind the eight ball and learns that making people laugh is a noble profession. By turns hilariously funny and relentlessly grim, *Sullivan's Travels* demonstrated that McCrea, in addition to his obvious dramatic talents, could do a pratfall with the best of 'em. *The Palm Beach Story* (1942) teamed him with Claudette Colbert, but Sturges gave most of the funniest material to Colbert and supporting player Rudy Vallee. *The Great Moment* (1944), an odd mixture of comedy and drama, starred McCrea as the dentist who invented anesthesia. The offbeat film, removed from Sturges' control, was recut to little avail by Paramount executives and poorly received.

The More the Merrier (1943) proved McCrea could be funny for other directors as well: George Stevens paired him with Jean Arthur in a cute story of WW 2 domestic travails that showed both stars to great advantage. Immediately after completing that film, McCrea went to 20th Century-Fox to star as *Buffalo Bill* (1944), a handsomely made biopic that was a huge box-office success. Most of McCrea's subsequent films were Westerns. Even the gentle (and underrated) *Stars in My Crown* (1950), in which he plays a minister, was set in the American West. In 1962, after several years offscreen, McCrea agreed to costar with Randolph Scott in an elegiac Western to be directed by a young Sam Peckinpah: *Ride the High Country* (1962) turned out to be a minor classic and one of McCrea's all-time best.

McCrea also dabbled in television, as a regular on "Four Star Playhouse" (1952–53) and as the star of "Wichita Town" (1959–60). (He even headlined a Western series on radio: "Tales of Texas Rangers.") He invested wisely in real estate and livestock, and listed his occupation as "Rancher" on his tax returns, claiming his movie acting was just an avocation. He was still married to Dee when he died in 1990, making theirs one of Hollywood's longest unions. Their son Jody briefly pursued an acting career in the 1960s.

OTHER FILMS INCLUDE: 1946: *The Virginian* (the fourth version of Owen Wister's popular novel); 1947: *Ramrod*; 1948: *Four Faces West* (with Dee); 1949: *South of St. Louis, Colorado Territory* (the latter a Western reworking of *High Sierra*); 1950: *The Outriders, Saddle Tramp, Frenchie*; 1951: *Cattle Drive*; 1952: *Shoot First*; 1953: *Lone Hand*; 1954: *Border River, Black Horse Canyon*; 1955: *Wichita* (as Wyatt Earp), *Stranger on Horseback*; 1956: *The First Texan* (as Sam Houston); 1957: *The Oklahoman, Trooper Hook, The Tall Stranger*; 1958: *Cattle Empire, Fort Massacre*; 1959: *Gunfight at Dodge City* (as Bat Masterson); 1970: *Cry Blood, Apache*; 1976: *Mustang Country*.

McDANIEL, HATTIE. Actress. (b. June 10, 1895, Wichita, Kans.; d. Oct. 26, 1952.) The first black actress to win an Academy Award—for her performance as Mammy in *Gone With the Wind* (1939)—this preacher's daughter appeared in dozens of movies. Though generally cast as a servant, her commanding presence made every moment on-screen count. McDaniel's intimidating bulk, moon face, and throaty chuckle created memorable scenes in *Judge Priest* (1934, in which she trades vocal choruses with Will Rogers), *Alice Adams* (1935, in which she all but ruins a dinner party), *The Little Colonel* (1935), *Show Boat* (1936, in which she sings "Ah Suits Me"), *Libeled Lady* (1936), *Saratoga, Nothing Sacred* (both 1937), *Carefree* (1938), *The Male Animal, In This Our Life* (both 1942), *Johnny Come Lately* (1943), *Since You Went Away* (1944), *Song of the South* (1946), and *Mr. Blandings Builds His Dream House* (1948), among others. She's also Buckwheat's mother in a number of Our Gang comedies. She was one of several actresses to star as "Beulah" on radio and TV.

McDONNELL, MARY. Actress. *(b. Apr. 28, 1952, Wilkes-Barre, Pa.)* After years of accomplished performances on the New York stage, McDonnell made a vivid impression on movie audiences—and received an Oscar nomination as Supporting Actress—as Stands With a Fist, the white woman living with Indians in Kevin Costner's Oscar-winning *Dances With Wolves* (1990). Before this, she had appeared in plays ranging from Sam Shepard's "Buried Child" to "Still Life" (for which she won an Obie), appeared briefly in *Garbo Talks* (1984), and had featured roles in John Sayles' *Matewan* (1987) and the action film *Tiger Warsaw* (1988, opposite Patrick Swayze). Since the success of *Dances With Wolves,* McDonnell has played Kevin Kline's wife in *Grand Canyon* (1991) and Robert Redford's onetime girlfriend in *Sneakers* (1992). She had her first starring role in John Sayles' *Passion Fish* (1992), playing an acid-tongued actress who's confined to a wheelchair after a crippling accident; it was, at last, a part she could sink her teeth into, and her riveting performance earned her a Best Actress Oscar nomination. She has also appeared in the TV movie *Arthur Miller's The American Clock* (1993) and *Blue Chips* (1994).

McDORMAND, FRANCES. Actress. *(b. June 23, 1957, Ill.)* Toothy, persuasive actress with a chameleonlike ability to disappear into her roles. She instantly attracted notice in her movie debut as the faithless wife in the Coen brothers' *Blood Simple* (1984), and rejoined the sibling filmmakers for cameos as a wacky neighbor in *Raising Arizona* (1987) and a secretary in *Miller's Crossing* (1990). McDormand's Oscar nomination for a heartfelt performance as a woman reluctantly testifying against her Klansman husband in *Mississippi Burning* (1988) led to steady work, including her appearances as a human rights activist in *Hidden Agenda,* a shell-shock victim's wife in *Chattahoochee,* a perplexed yet resourceful leading lady in *Darkman* (all 1990), and a late-blooming lesbian shoe clerk in *The Butcher's Wife* (1991). On TV, she played a cocaine-snorting assistant D.A. in several episodes of "Hill Street Blues," and a non-wacky neighbor on "Leg Work" (1987). Recent credits include *Passed Away* (1992) and Robert Altman's *Short Cuts* (1993).

McDOWALL, RODDY. Actor. *(b. Sept. 17, 1928, London.)* One of the few child stars who was actually more successful as an adult, this genteel, reliable actor loves Hollywood as much as it does him, and has even spun off a second career as a celebrity photographer. He appeared in numerous British films of the late 1930s before coming to Hollywood to play the pivotal role of a Welsh coal miner's youngest son in John Ford's *How Green Was My Valley* (1941). His endearing and unaffected performance made him an instant star and he went on to appear in such natural "boy" films as *My Friend Flicka, Lassie Come Home* (both 1943), and *Thunderhead—Son of Flicka* (1945), as well as such "adult" fare as *Man Hunt* (1941), *Son of Fury* (1942), *The White Cliffs of Dover, Keys of the Kingdom* (both 1944), *Hangover Square* (1945), and the Orson Welles version of *Macbeth* (1948, as Malcolm).

In 1948, McDowall began coproducing as well as appearing in a series of low-budget films for Monogram, including *Kidnapped* (1948), *Black Midnight* (1949), and *Killer Shark* (1950). Away from movies most of the next decade, he kept busy on stage and television, and in 1960 won an Emmy for a TV drama called "Not Without Honor," and a Tony for his supporting role in the Broadway play "The Fighting Cock." (He also costarred in the original production of Lerner and Loewe's

"Camelot," as Mordred.) McDowall returned to films in such high-profile pictures as *The Subterraneans, Midnight Lace* (both 1960), *The Longest Day* (1962), *Cleopatra* (1963, as Octavius), *Shock Treatment* (1964), *The Greatest Story Ever Told, The Loved One, Inside Daisy Clover, That Darn Cat* (all 1965), *Lord Love a Duck* (1966), and in the starring role of Disney's *The Adventures of Bullwhip Griffin* (1967). Then came what may be his best-known adult roles (though, ironically, unrecognizable in heavy makeup), as a sympathetic simian in *Planet of the Apes* (1968), as well as three of the four sequels—*Escape From . . .* (1971), *Conquest of . . .* (1972), and *Battle for . . .* (1973)—and the subsequent TV series. He also costarred in a superior shocker, *The Legend of Hell House* (1973).

McDowall won the admiration of a new generation of fans in two 1980s horror movies, playing horror-movie-host-turned-vampire-hunter Peter Vincent in *Fright Night* (1985 and its 1989 sequel).

In the 1980s he was hired by MGM to look for properties worth remaking, but wound up executive producing a brand-new story instead, the Goldie Hawn vehicle *Overboard* (1987), in which he took a small role as well. Today McDowall is also busy in made-fors and episodic TV, and is well known as a photographer: He has had four volumes of his celebrity photos published under the title "Double Exposure."

OTHER FILMS INCLUDE: 1968: *5 Card Stud;* 1971: *Bedknobs and Broomsticks;* 1972: *The Poseidon Adventure, The Life and Times of Judge Roy Bean;* 1975: *Funny Lady;* 1976: *Embryo;* 1978: *Rabbit Test;* 1979: *Scavenger Hunt;* 1982: *Evil Under the Sun, Class of 1984;* 1987: *Dead of Winter.*

McDOWELL, MALCOLM. Actor. *(b. June 15, 1943, Leeds, England.)* Best known as the rebellious protagonist of Lindsay Anderson's trilogy of films indicting British traditions and institutions, McDowell was a popular actor during the 1970s, and continues to work in showy character roles. He began his professional life serving drinks in a pub; acting classes offered relief from his working-class existence, and eventually he secured work as an extra with the Royal Shakespeare Company. McDowell made his screen debut in *Poor Cow* (1967). Two years later, Anderson's *if. . . .* (1969) cast him as a sensitive boy hiding behind cocksure arrogance. His performance caught the attention of Stanley Kubrick, who cast McDowell as the lead in *A Clockwork Orange* (1971). Unfortunately, despite winning great acclaim for his role as the urbane leader of a gang of futuristic toughs, the film may have done for McDowell what Hitchcock's *Psycho* did for Anthony Perkins: create a characterization so indelible that the public had a hard time separating actor from character. Fortunately, good parts did come his way, both on stage and screen. He rejoined Lindsay Anderson for the ambitious *O Lucky Man!* (1973) and *Britannia Hospital* (1982), and starred in *Royal Flash* (1975). He costarred in *Voyage of the Damned* (1976), and made an auspicious Hollywood-movie debut as a charming H. G. Wells in *Time After Time* (1979). That popular movie also introduced him to Mary Steenburgen, whom he subsequently married; they divorced some years later. (They costarred in a 1987 London stage revival of "Holiday" directed by Lindsay Anderson, and McDowell played a small part, as famed editor Maxwell Perkins, in her 1983 movie *Cross Creek.*)

For some reason, McDowell drifted into villainous parts in the 1980s—none more notorious than the title character in *Caligula* (1980)—and has seldom been able to break out of that mold since then, appearing in too many low-budget time-wasters, though he did have a good time spoofing Mick Jagger in the rock comedy *Get Crazy* (1983), and had a telling cameo in Robert Altman's *The Player* (1992).

OTHER FILMS INCLUDE: 1970: *Long Ago, Tomorrow;* 1982: *Cat People;* 1983: *Blue Thunder;* 1988: *Sunset;* 1989: *The Caller;* 1990: *Disturbed, Jezebel's Kiss, Moon 44;* 1993: *Bopha!, Chain of Desire;* 1994: *Milk Money, Star Trek: Generations.*

McGAVIN, DARREN. Actor. *(b. May 7, 1922, Spokane, Washington.)* Veteran actor of stage, screen, and television who has played villains, blustery types, or comic roles with equal skill. A student of New York's Neighborhood Playhouse and Actors' Studio, McGavin was in films as early as 1946's *Fear,* but he really came into his own in 1955 with supporting parts in Otto Preminger's *The Court-Martial of*

Billy Mitchell, David Lean's *Summertime,* and especially Preminger's *The Man With the Golden Arm,* in which he played the dope peddler, Louie. He had one of his most memorable roles as the hysterically befuddled father in *A Christmas Story* (1983). McGavin is also well known for his numerous TV credits, beginning with "Crime Photographer" (1951–52, replacing Richard Carlyle) and including title roles in "Mike Hammer" (1958), "The Outsider" (1968–69), and the fondly remembered "The Night Stalker" (1974–75) as reporter Carl Kolchak, based on the TV movies *The Night Stalker* (1971) and *The Night Strangler* (1972). He won a 1990 Emmy for his recurring role on "Murphy Brown" as Murphy's father, and directed the 1973 feature *Happy Mother's Day, Love George.*
OTHER FILMS INCLUDE: 1957: *Beau James, The Delicate Delinquent;* 1964: *Bullet for a Badman;* 1965: *The Great Sioux Massacre;* 1968: *Mission Mars;* 1971: *Mrs. Pollifax—Spy;* 1976: *No Deposit, No Return;* 1977: *Airport '77;* 1978: *Hot Lead and Cold Feet;* 1980: *Hangar 18;* 1984: *The Natural* (curiously unbilled as bookie/gambler Gus Sands); 1985: *Turk 182!;* 1986: *Raw Deal;* 1987: *From the Hip;* 1988: *Dead Heat;* 1991: *Blood and Concrete.*

McGILLIS, KELLY. Actress. *(b. July 9, 1957, Newport Beach, Calif.)* Based on her first two movie roles, the beautiful McGillis should have scaled heights she failed to reach, and her career to date seems to fall into the category of "promise unfulfilled." The Juilliard-trained actress first appeared on-screen as Tom Conti's love interest in *Reuben, Reuben* (1983), a critical if not commercial success. Based on her work in that film, Australian director Peter Weir cast her as a young Amish widow in *Witness* (1985), and she brought quiet charm to a well-written part. Costarring with Harrison Ford made McGillis a top Hollywood prospect, and she landed the coveted part of flyboy Tom Cruise's leading lady in the jet opera *Top Gun* (1986), a box-office blockbuster but an artistic pariah. Since then, McGillis' output has been uneven: Her angelic role in *Made in Heaven* (1987) and her damsel-in-distress turn in *The House on Carroll Street* (1988) certainly didn't advance her career. A meaty

role, as the prosecutor of Jodie Foster's rapists in *The Accused* (1988), didn't help, either; Foster got most of the best notices—and an Academy Award. *Winter People* (1989) was barely seen and *Cat Chaser* (1990) went direct to video. Then *The Babe* (1992) flopped at the box office, though McGillis' warm performance as the second Mrs. Babe Ruth scored her some long-overdue points. Hoping to shape a better vehicle for herself, she coproduced and starred in the made-for-TV *Grand Isle* (1992).

McGOVERN, ELIZABETH. Actress. *(b. July 18, 1961, Evanston, Ill.)* This fresh-faced actress made an impressive screen debut as a teenager who reaches out to troubled youth Timothy Hutton in *Ordinary People* (1980). Stardom seemed to be in the offing, and she earned an Oscar nomination the following year as the notorious Victorian-era trollop Evelyn Nesbit in *Ragtime* (1981), then was paired with Dudley Moore in the romantic comedy *Lovesick* (1983) and Sean Penn in *Racing With the Moon* (1984), and had a plum part in Sergio Leone's sprawling *Once Upon a Time in America* (also 1984). But none of these were smash hits, to say the least, and McGovern's growing fondness for "interesting" parts and films—rather than mainstream success—steered her in a different direction than might have been anticipated. Aside from *The Bedroom Window* (1987) and *She's Having a Baby* (1988), McGovern has eschewed conventional Hollywood offerings to work on stage, and pursue offbeat film projects, often in supporting roles. She was a scene-stealer in *The Handmaid's Tale* (1990) and had a showy part as a prostitute in *King of the Hill* (1993). There's no telling what may yet lay in store for this talented actress.
OTHER FILMS INCLUDE: 1986: *Native Son;* 1989: *Johnny Handsome, Tune in Tomorrow . . .* (cameo); 1990: *A Shock to the System;* 1993: *Me and Veronica;* 1994: *The Favor* (filmed in 1991).

McGRAW, CHARLES. Actor. *(b. May 10, 1914, New York City; d. July 30, 1980.)* Tough-as-nails leading man with granite-carved face, steely eyes, and gravelly voice, best known for his portrayals of cops and crooks in a string of low-budget,

noirish thrillers including *The Threat* (1949), *Armored Car Robbery* (1950), *Road Block* (1951), and, best of all, *The Narrow Margin* (1952). McGraw's outward grit and cynicism seemed to mask an essential world-weariness and fatalism that made him an ideal film noir protagonist. In later years he played stern authoritarians. On TV he played The Falcon in a 1955 series, "The Adventures of Falcon," and inherited Humphrey Bogart's role as Rick in a short-lived "Casablanca" series that was part of the omnibus program "Warner Bros. Presents" in 1955–56.
OTHER FILMS INCLUDE: 1943: *The Moon Is Down;* 1946: *The Killers;* 1948: *Blood on the Moon;* 1949: *The Black Book, Border Incident;* 1951: *His Kind of Woman;* 1954: *Loophole, The Bridges at Toko-Ri;* 1957: *Slaughter on Tenth Avenue;* 1958: *The Defiant Ones;* 1960: *Spartacus, Cimarron;* 1963: *The Birds, It's a Mad Mad Mad Mad World;* 1965: *Nightmare in Chicago;.* 1967: *In Cold Blood;* 1968: *Hang 'em High;* 1969: *Tell Them Willie Boy Is Here;* 1971: *Johnny Got His Gun;* 1976: *The Killer Inside Me;* 1977: *Twilight's Last Gleaming.*

McGUIRE, DOROTHY. Actress. *(b. June 14, 1918, Omaha, Nebr.)* A sensation in her first movie, *Claudia* (1943, as the childlike wife of Robert Young, reprising her starring role from the original Broadway production), this wholesomely pretty, soft-spoken actress moved too quickly into mother roles, befitting her warm, appealing screen persona, but continued to deliver fine performances in well-regarded movies of the 1940s, 1950s, and 1960s. After first appearing on stage in regional theater, McGuire came to New York and made her Broadway debut understudying for Martha Scott in the 1938 production of "Our Town." Memorable as the patient mother in *A Tree Grows in Brooklyn* (1945) and the mute servant in *The Spiral Staircase* (1946), McGuire picked up a Best Actress Oscar nomination for her work in *Gentleman's Agreement* (1947). Some of her later successes include *Three Coins in the Fountain* (1954), *Friendly Persuasion* (1956, one of her best mother parts, as the Quaker wife of Gary Cooper), and a trio of Walt Disney favorites, *Old Yeller* (1957), *Swiss Family Robinson* (1960), and *Summer Magic* (1963). In 1965 she was cast in the ultimate

mother part, as the Virgin Mary in *The Greatest Story Ever Told* (1965). McGuire still works in episodic TV and made-for-TV movies.
OTHER FILMS INCLUDE: 1945: *The Enchanted Cottage;* 1946: *Claudia and David, Till the End of Time;* 1950: *Mister 880;* 1951: *Callaway Went Thataway;* 1952: *Invitation;* 1955: *Trial;* 1959: *A Summer Place;* 1960: *The Dark at the Top of the Stairs;* 1961: *Susan Slade;* 1971: *Flight of the Doves;* 1973: *Jonathan Livingston Seagull* (voice only).

McHUGH, FRANK. Actor. *(b. May 23, 1898, Homestead, Pa.; d. Sept. 11, 1981.)* Amiable Irish character actor (and charter member of Hollywood's "Irish mafia," along with such pals as James Cagney and Pat O'Brien) who often used his trademark laugh—soft, high-pitched, and mocking—to punctuate his scenes. McHugh was the son of troupers and learned his trade on the road under his family's tutelage. He played in vaudeville for the Orpheum and Keith circuits before being signed by Warners in 1930 and becoming part of the studio's ever-present stock company. His 150 films include *The Dawn Patrol* (1930), *The Front Page* (1931), *One Way Passage* (1932), *Mystery of the Wax Museum, Lilly Turner, Footlight Parade* (all 1933), *Return of the Terror* (1934, as the nominal male lead), *Gold Diggers of 1935, A Midsummer Night's Dream* (both 1935), *Stage Struck* (1936), *Three Men on a Horse* (1936, in the starring role as the mild-mannered odds-maker), *Boy Meets Girl* (1938), *The Roaring Twenties, The Fighting 69th* (both 1939), *City for Conquest* (1940), *All Through the Night* (1942), *Going My Way* (1944), *State Fair* (1945), *Mighty Joe Young* (1949), *My Son John* (1952), *A Lion Is in the Streets* (1953), *There's No Business Like Show Business* (1954), *The Last Hurrah* (1958), and *Easy Come, Easy Go* (1967). He was a regular on TV's "The Bing Crosby Show" in 1964–65. His lookalike brother Matt was also an actor.

McKEAN, MICHAEL. Actor, writer. *(b. Oct. 17, 1947, New York City.)* Talented actor who is responsible for two of pop culture's more memorable icons—Lenny from TV's "Laverne and Shirley" and rhythm guitarist David St. Hubbins of the

mock rock group Spinal Tap, introduced
in Rob Reiner's *This Is Spinal Tap* (1984).
McKean began his career as a member of
the comedy group Credibility Gap with
future Spinal Tap member Harry Shearer
and David L. Lander. The three became
writers on "Laverne and Shirley," and
McKean and Lander soon gained fame
onscreen as the strange greaser duo Lenny
and Squiggy. McKean appeared with Lander in *Used Cars* (1980), then starred—
playing it straight—in the soap opera
spoof *Young Doctors in Love* (1982,
directed by "Laverne" producer Garry
Marshall). Since the cult success of *Spinal
Tap*, McKean has appeared in *D.A.R.Y.L.*,
Clue (both 1985), *Light of Day, Planes,
Trains & Automobiles* (both 1987), *Short
Circuit 2* (1988), *Earth Girls Are Easy*
(1989), *Flashback* (1990), *Memoirs of an
Invisible Man, Man Trouble* (both 1992),
Coneheads (1993), *Airheads, Radioland
Murders* (both 1994), and *The Brady
Bunch Movie* (1995). He also cowrote and
acted in the Hollywood satire *The Big
Picture* (1989, directed by fellow Tap
member Christopher Guest). He starred in
Billy Crystal's excellent made-for-cable
series "Sessions" (1992) and appears on
the TV comedy "Dream On." In 1994, he
joined the cast of TV's "Saturday Night
Live."

McKEE, LONETTE. Actress. *(b. July 22,
1956, Detroit.)* When McKee debuted in
Sparkle (1976), film critic Pauline Kael
noted that she was "so sexy that she lays
waste to the movie." She demonstrated
her terrific vocal skills in that movie, as
well as in *The Cotton Club* (1984) and
'Round Midnight (1986, as a sort of Billie
Holiday), and has appeared in *Which Way
Is Up?* (1977), *Cuba* (1979), *Brewster's
Millions* (1985), *Gardens of Stone* (1987),
Jungle Fever (1991), and *Malcolm X*
(1992, as Malcolm's mother). A respected
stage actress, McKee was Tony-nominated
for her work in a revival of "Show Boat"
and starred in the one-woman show "Lady
Day at Emerson's Bar and Grill," a tribute
to Billie Holiday.

McKELLEN, IAN (SIR). Actor. *(b. May
25, 1939, Bolton, England.)* Brilliant Shakespearean actor who has made occasional
forays into the film world, starting with

roles in 1969's *The Promise, Alfred the
Great,* and *Thank You All Very Much.*
McKellen studied English literature at
Cambridge University and acted in 21 un-
dergraduate theatrical productions before
performing in repertory companies and
eventually gaining a reputation for his
bold, emotionally powerful portrayals of
characters ranging from Richard II to Napoleon to Hamlet. His film career resumed
with 1981's *Priest of Love* (as D. H. Lawrence), *The Keep* (1983), *Plenty, Zina*
(both 1985), and probably his most notable role, as Cabinet Minister John
Profumo in *Scandal* (1989). Recently,
McKellen has been very busy with projects big and small like *The Ballad of Little Jo* (1993, in an uncharacteristic Western frontier setting), *Last Action Hero*
(also 1993, as Death), *Six Degrees of Separation* (also 1993), and *The Shadow*
(1994). A fervent gay rights spokesman,
McKellen also played San Francisco gay
activist Bill Kraus in the 1993 TV movie
And the Band Played On. His numerous
stage credits include the world premiere of
"Bent," "Amadeus" (for which he won a
1981 Tony), and his celebrated one-man
show "Ian McKellen Acting Shakespeare."
He was knighted in 1991.

McKERN, LEO. Actor. *(b. Mar. 16,
1920, Sydney, as Reginald McKern.)* This
portly, bulbous-nosed character actor has
put his stamp on a wide variety of roles,
but it took TV's "Rumpole of the Bailey"
to make him truly well known. After
fighting in New Guinea during World War
2, McKern traveled to England where he
began his theatrical career at London's
Old Vic. He made his screen debut in
Murder in the Cathedral (1952), and had
substantial roles in *A Tale of Two Cities*
(1958), *The Mouse That Roared* (1959),
Scent of Mystery (1960), *Mr. Topaze, The
Day the Earth Caught Fire* (1962), and
Doctor in Distress (1963), among others,
but was especially notable as a bungling
train robber in Disney's *The Horse Without a Head* (1963), a menace to The
Beatles in *Help!* (1965), and Cromwell,
the persecutor of Sir Thomas More in *A
Man for All Seasons* (1966).

McKern played half the title role in
David Lean's *Ryan's Daughter* (1970),
archfiend Professor Moriarty in the spoof
The Adventure of Sherlock Holmes'

Smarter Brother (1975), an archeologist with apocalyptic secrets in *The Omen* (1976), and a comic con man opposite Jodie Foster in Disney's *Candleshoe* (1977). He also appeared in *The Blue Lagoon* (1980), *The French Lieutenant's Woman* (1981), and *Ladyhawke* (1985), as well as Laurence Olivier's television production of "King Lear" (1984), in which he played Gloucester.

Indeed, it was television that brought McKern some measure of personal fame when he began playing John Mortimer's irascible British barrister Horace P. Rumpole in the 1980s. (The on-again, off-again British series was broadcast in the U.S. on PBS.) McKern's performance as the claret-swilling Tennyson-quoting trial lawyer was irresistible. Recent film projects include a return to his native Australia for a rare starring role in *Travelling North* (1987) and a costarring role with Alec Guinness in *Monsignor Quixote* (1989).

McLAGLEN, ANDREW V. Director. *(b. July 28, 1920, London.)* The son of actor Victor McLaglen, he grew up around movie people and, early on, developed an affinity for the business. Briefly involved in production of industrial films, he entered Hollywood filmmaking in the late 1940s, initially working as an assistant director (on such films as *The Quiet Man,* which costarred his father and gave him the opportunity to work with John Ford). McLaglen made his solo directorial debut with *Gun the Man Down* (1956), and worked steadily throughout the late 1950s, the 1960s, and the 1970s before slowing up somewhat. He specialized in Westerns and adventure films—especially those of his father's frequent costar John Wayne—and, while lacking any specific visual "trademark," turned out consistently entertaining and commercial movies. He also became a prolific TV director, helming episodes of "Perry Mason," "Rawhide," and "Have Gun—Will Travel," among others. He was the principal director of "Gunsmoke" during its first years on the air.

OTHER FILMS INCLUDE: 1956: *Man in the Vault;* 1957: *The Abductors* (starring his dad); 1960: *Freckles;* 1961: *The Little Shepherd of Kingdom Come;* 1963: *McLintock!;* 1965: *Shenandoah;* 1966: *The Rare Breed;* 1967: *The Way West;* 1968: *Bandolero!, The Devil's Brigade;* 1969: *The Undefeated;* 1970: *Chisum;* 1971: *Fools' Parade, One More Train to Rob, something big;* 1973: *Cahill—United States Marshal;* 1975: *Mitchell;* 1976: *The Last Hard Men;* 1978: *The Wild Geese;* 1980: *The Sea Wolves, ffolkes;* 1984: *Sahara;* 1989: *Return to the River Kwai;* 1991: *Eye of the Widow.*

McLAGLEN, VICTOR. Actor. *(b. Dec. 10, 1886, Tunbridge Wells, England; d. Nov. 7, 1959.)* Once described, aptly, as "a British-born Wallace Beery," this hulking supporting player and character lead brought a similar gruff charm to his movie roles, often winning audience sympathy in unsympathetic characterizations. A clergyman's son, McLaglen took up prospecting and boxing before unleashing his extroverted personality in stage and music-hall performances. After debuting on-screen in *The Call of the Road* (1920), McLaglen labored in several other British films before emigrating to America; he made his tyro screen appearance here in *The Beloved Brute* (1924).

Typically cast as a two-fisted man of action—on either side of the law—McLaglen brightened *The Unholy Three, The Fighting Heart* (both 1925), *Men of Steel,* and *Beau Geste* (both 1926) before assuming the role of hard-bitten Captain Flagg in *What Price Glory?* (also 1926, directed by Raoul Walsh), the antiwar smash adapted from a hit Broadway play. Movie audiences seemed less interested in the film's pacifistic sentiments than in the gregarious, ribald byplay between Flagg and his sergeant, Quirt (played by Edmund Lowe). McLaglen and Lowe reprised their characterizations in *The Cock-Eyed World* (1929) and *Women of All Nations* (1931), then went on to embellish them, without the Quirt or Flagg cognomen, in the similarly boisterous *Guilty as Hell* (1932), *Hot Pepper* (1933), *No More Women* (1934), *Under Pressure,* and *The Great Hotel Mystery* (both 1935).

McLaglen made his talkie debut in John Ford's *The Black Watch* (1929) and went on to appear in *Devil With Women* (1930), *Dishonored* (opposite Marlene Dietrich), *Not Exactly Gentlemen* (both 1931, the latter a remake of Ford's *Three Bad Men),* *While Paris Sleeps, Devil's Lottery, The Gay Caballero* (all 1932, in the last taking

5tt6t

second billing to George O'Brien in this B-plus Western), *Laughing at Life* (1933, his only foray to Poverty Row), *Murder at the Vanities,* and *The Captain Hates the Sea* (both 1934), before being reunited with Ford for two of his best starring vehicles: *The Lost Patrol* (1934), in which he played the commander of a small British detail stranded in the Arabian desert, and *The Informer* (1935), a remake of Liam O'Flaherty's story of the Irish Rebellion that cast McLaglen as dull-witted turncoat Gypo Nolan. He won the Best Actor Oscar for his portrayal of the dazed behemoth; legend has it that Ford encouraged him to drink before filming his scenes, and used the resultant mental fog to best advantage.

McLaglen finished out the 1930s in a variety of roles, many of them secondary leads, most of them in melodramas or spectacular adventure films, including *Professional Soldier* (1935), *Klondike Annie* (opposite Mae West), *Under Two Flags, The Magnificent Brute* (all 1936), *Sea Devils, Nancy Steel Is Missing, This Is My Affair, Wee Willie Winkie* (all 1937, the last fortuitously paired with Shirley Temple, again for director Ford), *The Devil's Party, We're Going to Be Rich* (both 1938), *Pacific Liner, Let Freedom Ring, Captain Fury, Ex-Champ, Full Confession,* and *Rio* (all 1939). He concluded the decade in grand fashion, playing the dashing Sergeant MacChesney (an archetypal McLaglen part) in George Stevens' *Gunga Din* (1939), one of the screen's greatest adventure films.

McLaglen did most of his 1940s work in films of steadily diminishing quality, such as *Broadway Limited* (1941), *Call Out the Marines* (the last of his starring vehicles with Lowe, but a pale shadow of their earlier successes), *China Girl* (both 1942), *Tampico, Roger Touhy, Gangster* (both 1944), *Rough, Tough and Ready* (1945), *Whistle Stop* (1946), *Calendar Girl,* and *The Michigan Kid* (both 1947). Ford gave McLaglen juicy supporting parts in his Cavalry trilogy—*Fort Apache* (1948), *She Wore a Yellow Ribbon* (1949), and *Rio Grande* (1950)—before awarding the burly Englishman his last formidable role, that of Maureen O'Hara's bullying brother in *The Quiet Man* (1952, for which he earned a Best Supporting Actor Academy Award nomination).

After appearing in *Fair Wind to Java*

(1953), *Prince Valiant* (1954), *Many Rivers to Cross, City of Shadows, Bengazi, Lady Godiva* (all 1955), *Around the World in Eighty Days* (1956, cameoing with Lowe), and *The Abductors* (1957), an increasingly ill McLaglen called it quits. He died of a heart attack two years later. His son Andrew is a director; while working his way up the ladder in Hollywood, he served as an assistant director on *The Quiet Man.* He later directed his father in *The Abductors.*

McMILLAN, KENNETH. Actor. *(b. July 2, 1932, Brooklyn, N.Y.; d. Jan. 8, 1989.)* Burly, brusque, raspy-voiced, quintessentially New York character actor most effectively cast as a blue-collar working stiff. His significant characterizations include a harried police officer in *The Taking of Pelham One Two Three* (1974), a tough Irish cop in *True Confessions,* a villainous fire chief in *Ragtime,* a compassionate judge in *Whose Life Is It Anyway?* (all 1981), the slobbering Baron Harkonnen in *Dune,* a boozy father in *Reckless* (both 1984), and a venal high-roller in *Cat's Eye* (1985). Other key films include *Serpico* (1973), *Bloodbrothers* (1978), *Carny* (1980), *Eyewitness* (1981), *The Pope of Greenwich Village, Protocol* (both 1984), and *Runaway Train* (1985). McMillan died just before his final film, *Three Fugitives,* was released in 1989. On TV, he played sheriff Bull Conner in "King," the frightened police constable of "Salem's Lot," a New York police commissioner on the short-lived series "Our Family Honor," and the blustery customer Jack Doyle on "Rhoda."

McQUEEN, STEVE. Actor. *(b. Mar. 24, 1930, Slater, Mo., as Terrence Steven McQueen; d. Nov. 7, 1980.)* One of the first "cool" movie stars, a true icon of the Beatles generation, McQueen drew upon his own background as a reform-school graduate, ex-Marine, and drifter to craft his persona: a brooding, taciturn, fatalistic loner who relied on his own instincts and considerable physical attributes in coping with a hostile environment. After studying at New York's Actors' Studio and making a successful Broadway debut in "A Hatful of Rain," McQueen broke into films with a bit part in *Somebody Up There Likes*

Me (1956). He first played a lead in *The Blob* (1958), earnestly enacting his role in this cult favorite as though it had been written by Shakespeare. That same year he created the character of bounty hunter Josh Randall in the TV series "Wanted: Dead or Alive" (1958–60), which further boosted his popularity.

McQueen played one of the hired gunfighters in *The Magnificent Seven* (1960), and appeared in *The Honeymoon Machine* (1961), *Hell Is for Heroes,* and *The War Lover* (both 1962) before making a strong impression on moviegoers as the daring P.O.W. who attempted to flee his Nazi captors on a motorcycle in *The Great Escape* (1963). McQueen, whose offscreen passion was racing, did most of his own stunts in the memorable chase sequence. He subsequently starred in *Soldier in the Rain, Love With the Proper Stranger* (both 1963), *Baby The Rain Must Fall, The Cincinnati Kid* (both 1965), *Nevada Smith* (a "prequel" to Harold Robbins' *The Carpetbaggers), The Sand Pebbles* (both 1966, Oscar-nominated for his work in the latter), and *The Thomas Crown Affair* (1968) before thrilling moviegoers with another mind-boggling chase sequence, this time in a car flying up and down the hilly streets of San Francisco in *Bullitt* (also 1968), one of his most successful films.

By now at the peak of his popularity, McQueen occasionally eschewed straight action films in favor of character-driven stories such as *The Reivers* (1969), *Junior Bonner* (1972), and *Papillon* (1973)—all of them first-rate. He also participated in Bruce Brown's documentary on his favorite hobby, motorcycling, *On Any Sunday* (1971). Then he gave action fans what they craved in *Le Mans* (1971), *The Getaway* (1972, costarred with Ali MacGraw, whom he later married), and *The Towering Inferno* (1974). Beset by a variety of personal demons, McQueen was offscreen for several years; when he returned, it was in almost unrecognizable form, under a mane of hair and full beard in a "pet project" rendition of Ibsen's *An Enemy of the People* (1977) that was seen by few of his fans. Several years later he unexpectedly turned up in a pair of mainstream movies, the Western *Tom Horn* and a contemporary bounty hunter story, *The Hunter* (both 1980). He died later that year of a heart attack following a cancer operation.

McTIERNAN, JOHN. Director. *(b. Jan. 8, 1951, Albany, N.Y.) Nomads* (1986), a little-seen sci-fi opus, marked the inauspicious directorial debut of McTiernan, a former film student and director of TV commercials who has gone on to become one of Hollywood's leading "money" moviemakers. A visually oriented craftsman who relies more on fluid camera work and tight cutting than on fluid performances and tight scripts, he specializes in big-budget, spectacular action-adventure fare such as *Predator* (1987), *Die Hard* (1988), and *The Hunt for Red October* (1989). Without the trappings of technowizardry, *Medicine Man* (1992) seemed to find McTiernan adrift. *Last Action Hero* (1993) put him back in his element, but the overblown production, stupefying budget, and lack of cohesive storyline made it an inviting target for critical potshots. McTiernan returned to familiar ground for *Die Hard With a Vengeance* (1995). He served as executive producer of *Flight of the Intruder* (1991).

MEDAK, PETER. Director. *(b. Dec. 23, 1937, Budapest.)* Versatile director whose films have covered a wide range of genres and subject matter. Medak trained at the London-based Associated British Picture Cooperation, then moved to Hollywood where he worked as an associate producer on TV series like "Wagon Train" and "The Alfred Hitchcock Hour" before directing his first film, *Negatives* (1968). Medak expertly handled the difficult black comedy *A Day in the Death of Joe Egg* and scored a major success with *The Ruling Class* (both 1972), a biting satire of England's upper class that featured a brilliant performance by Peter O'Toole as a lord who thinks he is Jesus Christ and Jack the Ripper. Subsequent films were hit-and-miss: *The Odd Job* (1978), the ghost story *The Changeling* (1979), and the farce *Zorro, the Gay Blade* (1981). Following the disastrous *The Men's Club* (1986), Medak returned to England to make two powerful films concerning real-life events: *The Krays* (1990), about two brothers who ruled London's underworld during the 1960s, and *Let Him Have It* (1991), the story of a young man who was sentenced to death for a murder he did not commit. These films have shown an energized and focused talent worthy of more grade-A material. Recent credits include *Romeo Is Bleeding* and *Pontiac Moon* (both 1994).

MEEK, DONALD. Actor. *(b. July 14, 1880, Glasgow; d. Nov. 18, 1946.)* One of the most aptly named actors in Hollywood history, this diminutive, prematurely bald character actor excelled in depicting nervous, excitable little men who spoke with quivering voices. Meek had extensive stage experience but concentrated on movie work after 1933, amassing more than one hundred screen credits. His parts were usually small, but he made an eccentric and enjoyable sidekick to Walter Pidgeon in MGM's short-lived *Nick Carter* series in 1939–40.
OTHER FILMS INCLUDE: 1929: *The Hole in the Wall;* 1935: *The Informer, The Whole Town's Talking, Top Hat, Barbary Coast, China Seas, Captain Blood;* 1938: *The Adventures of Tom Sawyer, You Can't Take It With You;* 1939: *Young Mr. Lincoln, Stagecoach* (in one of his meatiest roles), *Hollywood Cavalcade, Jesse James;* 1940: *My Little Chickadee, The Return of Frank James;* 1942: *Keeper of the Flame;* 1945: *State Fair;* 1947: *Magic Town* (released one year after his death).

MEEKER, RALPH. Actor. *(b. Nov. 21, 1920, Minneapolis, as Ralph Rathgeber; d. Aug. 5, 1988.)* He made a convincingly tough Mike Hammer in Robert Aldrich's delirious thriller *Kiss Me Deadly* (1955), and he won leads in several other 1950s films, but this dour, sluggish actor didn't have what it took to be a movie star. He *was* a solid supporting player whose delineations of blustery, cowardly characters revealed a more prodigious talent than was suggested in his infrequent starring turns. Meeker worked on the stage during the 1940s and 1950s (succeeding Marlon Brando in the Broadway production of "A Streetcar Named Desire"), and made his film debut in *Teresa,* followed by *Shadow in the Sky* (both 1951). Under Stanley Kubrick's direction, he turned in what may be the finest performance of his career as one of the doomed WW 1 soldiers in *Paths of Glory* (1957). He was a prolific TV performer as well.
OTHER FILMS INCLUDE: 1952: *Glory Alley;* 1953: *The Naked Spur;* 1955: *Big House U.S.A., Desert Sands;* 1956: *A Woman's Devo-*

tion; 1957: *Run of the Arrow;* 1961: *Something Wild* (a provocative leading role as a kidnapper and rapist); 1963: *Wall of Noise;* 1967: *The Dirty Dozen, The St. Valentine's Day Massacre, Gentle Giant;* 1968: *The Detective;* 1969: *The Devil's Eight;* 1970: *I Walk the Line;* 1972: *The Anderson Tapes, The Happiness Cage;* 1975: *Brannigan;* 1976: *Food of the Gods;* 1979: *Winter Kills;* 1980: *Without Warning.*

MÉLIÈS, GEORGES. Director. *(b. Dec. 8, 1861, Paris; d. Jan. 21, 1938.)* Remember the rocket ship hitting The Man in the Moon in the eye? That's the most famous of Georges Méliès's many innovative special effects, which made him the father of *cinéma fantastique.* His primitive trick films, created in the early years of this century, still have the power to charm and astonish. The son of a boot manufacturer, he was inspired to show and make movies after seeing an exhibition of the Lumière brothers' Cinématographe in 1895. As a theater owner, it occurred to him that with film he could create spectacles that weren't possible to mount on the stage. Building much of his own equipment (the Lumières wouldn't sell him theirs) and eventually an entire studio, Méliès made hundreds of short films in the late 1890s and early 1900s; his special effects began with the most rudimentary (i.e., making actors disappear in midshot) and went on to combine innovative film wizardry with standard theatrical gimmicks like trap doors.
Some of Méliès's discoveries were accidental; the jamming of a camera and its subsequent recovery in the middle of a single shot revealed the possibilities of time-lapse cinematography to the director. Shorts like *A Trip to the Moon,* the multiscene *Adventures of Robinson Crusoe* (both 1902) and literally hundreds of others pioneered narrative cinema . . . but by 1911 he was finished in motion picture production. The burgeoning industry regarded Méliès as a purveyor of novelty, and nothing more. After going bankrupt in the early 1920s, he eventually ran a toy concession stand in Montparnasse. Méliès was given his due in 1931, when he received a French Legion of Honor medal for his contribution to the growth of what was by then acknowledged as an art form. The French government also gave him a

free apartment where he spent his final years.

MENGES, CHRIS. Cinematographer, director. (b. Sept. 15, 1940, Kingston, England.) Outstanding cinematographer who initially worked on documentaries in Africa, Southeast Asia, and the Amazon jungles. In the early 1970s, he remained in Burma for a year and a half to shoot film on the drug trade there, and had a price put on his head by the local government. His feature-film career began with Ken Loach's *Poor Cow* (1967) and *Kes* (1970), and Stephen Frears' first feature, *Gumshoe* (1971). He subsequently found major assignments on *Local Hero* (1983), *Comfort and Joy* (1984), and two films for director Roland Joffé—*The Killing Fields* (1984) and *The Mission* (1986)—that won him Oscars for cinematography. He photographed four other films for Ken Loach—*Black Jack* (1979), *The Gamekeeper* (1980), *Looks and Smiles* (1981), and *Fatherland* (1986)—as well as *Marie* (1985) and *Shy People* (1987). Menges made his own directorial debut in 1988 with the critically acclaimed apartheid story *A World Apart,* and followed with the mainstream Goldie Hawn movie *CrissCross* (1992).

MENJOU, ADOLPHE. Actor. (b. Feb. 18, 1890, Pittsburgh; d. Oct. 29, 1963.) He was known as the best-dressed man in Hollywood; yet for all his elegance, Adolphe Menjou made his strongest impression when he played against type. A Cornell graduate and trained engineer, Menjou was attracted to acting in 1916, first in vaudeville and later on the stage. He made his film debut in *The Blue Envelope Mystery* (1916) and, following service in World War 1 and a period of stage work, he clicked on-screen as Rudolph Valentino's friend in *The Sheik* and King Louis XIII in Douglas Fairbanks' *The Three Musketeers* (both 1921). In 1923 he was tapped by Charles Chaplin for the lead in *A Woman of Paris,* which solidified his image as an impeccably dressed man of the world, and through the 1920s he made a string of popular films including *The Marriage Circle* (1924, for Ernst Lubitsch), *The Sorrows of Satan* (1925, as a dapper Devil) for D. W. Griffith, and *A Gentleman of Paris* (1927) for Chaplin's former codirector Harry D'Arrast.

Menjou's starring career faltered with the arrival of sound, but he scored big as a world-weary army officer supporting Gary Cooper in *Morocco* (1930), and even received an Oscar nomination as rough-and-tumble newspaper editor Walter Burns in *The Front Page* (1931). Through the 1930s Menjou seemed to alternate between playing urbane producers and hard-drinking low-lifes. *Morning Glory* (1933), *Stage Door,* and *A Star Is Born* (both 1937), among others, were in the former category; while *Little Miss Marker* (1934) and *Golden Boy* (1939) were in the latter. He played a thinly disguised John Barrymore in the delightful 1936 musicomedy *Sing, Baby, Sing,* delivering one of his finest (and funniest) performances, and put that same flamboyance to work in *Roxie Hart* (1942), as Ginger Rogers' courtroom defender.

He continued to give vital performances in such film as *The Hucksters* (1947), and *State of the Union* (1948), but his most *notorious* performance came before the House Committee on Un-American Activities, where he took a smug, hard-line, anticommunist stance, and pointed an accusing finger at a number of his Hollywood colleagues. In Anthony Mann's taut Civil War thriller *The Tall Target* (1951), Menjou was a traitorous Union officer, and the following year he was surprisingly realistic (and almost unrecognizable, without his mustache) as a police detective in *The Sniper.* Good roles were scarce for the aging Menjou that decade, but Stanley Kubrick gave him a memorable part in *Paths of Glory* (1957) as a hypocritical WW 1 French officer. Menjou made his final big-screen appearance as a curmudgeon in Walt Disney's *Pollyanna* (1960). He hosted the syndicated TV anthology "Favorite Story" in 1953. His autobiography, "It Took Nine Tailors," was published in 1947.

MENZIES, WILLIAM CAMERON. Designer, director. (b. July 29, 1896, New Haven, Conn.; d. Mar. 5, 1957.) Hailing from the silent era, when visuals determined a picture's impact, Menzies revolutionized the craft of art direction in Hollywood, becoming the first man billed as "production designer" and in some cases playing a bigger part in the design of a film than its director. His 1924 collaboration with Douglas Fairbanks on *The Thief of Bagdad* led to a career that has yet to be equaled. Menzies' visual style is characterized by a three-dimensional sensibility, and his input extended to costume design and special effects, as well as set design and construction. Silent films that bore his distinctive stamp include *The Eagle* (1925), *The Bat, Son of the Sheik* (both 1926), *The Beloved Rogue* (1927), *Sadie Thompson* (1928), and *Lady of the Pavements* (1929). The first year that Academy Awards were given, he was presented one for Interior Decoration, for *The Dove* and *The Tempest* (both 1928); he was subsequently nominated for Douglas Fairbanks' *The Iron Mask* and *Bulldog Drummond* (both 1929). In 1930 producer Joseph M. Schenck enabled him to direct a series of early talkie short subjects pictorializing great works of music, including *Zampa, The Wizard's Apprentice,* and *Hungarian Rhapsody.* They offered Menzies his first opportunity to craft his own films (mostly on leftover sets from *The Beloved Rogue, Tempest,* et al). Several years later he began directing features (teamed with various codirectors) including the stylish *The Spider* (1931) and *Chandu the Magician* (1932). His best, and best-remembered, film as director was the British-made *Things to Come* (1936), an art director's dream, but Menzies returned to production work in the late 1930s and did some of his finest work in the decade to follow.

He was given an honorary Academy Award for his landmark work on *Gone With the Wind* (1939) and also made distinctive visual contributions to *The Adventures of Tom Sawyer* (1938), Alfred Hitchcock's *Foreign Correspondent* (1940, featuring, among other showpieces, a unique airplane), and *For Whom the Bell Tolls* (1943). He returned to directing in earnest in the 1950s, showing an odd taste in material, including *Drums in the Deep South,* the anti-Communist *The Whip Hand* (1951), his fondly remembered science fiction outing *Invaders from Mars* (1953, a visual treat), and the extremely strange gothic yarn *The Maze* (1953) which was shot in 3-D. He also worked as art director on all of those projects, and added producing to his résumé with *The Black Book* (1949) and *Around the World in Eighty Days* (1956), on which he served as associate producer.

MERCHANT AND IVORY. Producer-director team. *(Ismail Merchant*—b. Dec. 25, 1936, Bombay. *James Ivory*—b. June 7, 1928, Berkeley, Calif.) One of the most enduring partnerships in film history, this producer and director have become something of a brand name in the field of literate cinema. To some critics, they are merely purveyors of safe, respectable "Masterpiece Theatre"–type fare; to many moviegoers, however, their names are an almost iron-clad guarantee of intelligent and thought-provoking entertainment. Merchant, educated in Bombay and New York (where he studied business administration), made his first mark on the film world directing and coproducing an Oscar-nominated short, *The Creation of Woman* (1961). Ivory studied film at USC and won acclaim for the short documentaries *Venice: Theme and Variation* (1957) and *The Sword and the Flute* (1959). Impressed by the latter work, New York's Asia Society commissioned Ivory to make a documentary about Delhi. While shooting the film in India, Ivory met Merchant and in 1961, they formed Merchant–Ivory Productions with the goal of making English-language films in India for international release; Ivory directed while Merchant sought funding from numerous sources.

Their first project was *The Householder* (1963), based on the novel by Ruth Prawer Jhabvala. (She also wrote the screenplay, beginning a thirty-year collaboration with Merchant–Ivory during which time she has written almost all of their films.) *Shakespeare Wallah* (1965), a sly, compassionate story of a traveling English theater group in India, was a critical and commercial success and established the themes of culture clash and obsolete traditions that would resurface in most Merchant–Ivory projects. More Indian-themed films followed—*The Guru* (1969), *Bombay Talkie* (1970), and *Adventures of a Brown Man in Search of Civilization* (1970, a documentary about writer Nirad Chaudhari)—before the team explored new territory (unsuccessfully) with the allegory *Savages* (1972) and *The Wild Party* (1975), a story of 1920s Hollywood which was drastically recut by its distributor. (Ivory later made his version available.) The team returned to familiar turf for *Autobiography of a Princess* (1975), a one-hour made-for-TV exploration of feudal India, featuring James Mason. They then guided a superb ensemble cast through *Roseland* (1977), a trilogy of stories set in the fabled New York dance hall.

Following *Hullabaloo Over Georgie and Bonnie's Pictures* (a 1978 telefilm), Merchant and Ivory made their first stab at bringing a major literary work to the screen, with a handsome adaptation of Henry James' *The Europeans* (1979). Next came *Jane Austen in Manhattan* (1980), *Quartet* (1981, from Jean Rhys' novel), *Heat and Dust* (1983, adapted by Jhabvala from her novel), and *The Bostonians* (1984, Henry James again), all carefully made, intelligently wrought (and low-budget) affairs which found a loyal, if limited, audience. *A Room With a View* (1985), a romantic and surprisingly lively adaptation of the E. M. Forster novel, won the best reviews of the team's career. It also scored a huge popular success, playing in areas that had never seen Merchant–Ivory films before, and won three Academy Awards (for Best Screenplay, Art Direction, and Costumes), as well as nominations for Best Picture, Best Director, and Best Supporting Actor (Denholm Elliott).

E. M. Forster was tapped again for *Maurice* (1987), followed by a disastrous adaptation of Tama Janowitz's *Slaves of New York* (1989, one of their few excursions into the modern era) and *Mr. & Mrs. Bridge* (1990), notable for the casting of Paul Newman and Joanne Woodward as a long-married Kansas City couple. Just when it seemed that Merchant–Ivory was slipping back into providing entertainment for a specialized demographic, they presented their crowning achievement, *Howards End* (1992), a magnificent rendering of Forster's novel of class conflict. The team's attention to performance, period detail, and storytelling—combined with flawless casting of world-class actors—created a masterpiece. It also won three Oscars (Best Actress Emma Thompson, Screenplay, and Art Direction), as well as Best Picture and Director nominations. They reteamed Emma Thompson and Anthony Hopkins in their next adaptation, *The Remains of the Day* (1993, Oscar-nominated again), another meticulous pe-

riod piece set in pre-WW2 England, then followed with *Jefferson in Paris* (1995). Merchant, who directed the TV film *Mahatma and the Mad Boy* (1974) and the documentary *The Courtesans of Bombay* (1983), made his feature directorial debut with *In Custody* (1993).

MERCOURI, MELINA. Actress. *(b. Oct. 18, 1923, Athens; d. Mar. 6, 1994.)* Spirited Greek beauty who enjoyed her greatest success (and earned a Best Actress Oscar nomination) as a good-natured prostitute in the comedy *Never on Sunday* (1960), directed by and featuring her husband, expatriate American director Jules Dassin. Her earthy charm and flamboyant acting style ensured her domination of any scene she was in. While her presence distinguished and enlivened the likes of *Topkapi* (1964), *Gaily, Gaily* (1969), and *Once Is Not Enough* (1975), Mercouri's own story is more compelling than almost any movie she was in: In 1967 she was expelled from her own country by its repressive junta government, and on returning to her homeland she entered politics. In 1977 she won a seat in Greece's parliament, running on the Socialist party ticket. Her film career then took a backseat to politics; in 1978 she appeared in Dassin's overwrought modern Medea story, *A Dream of Passion*, which also starred American actress Ellen Burstyn. Dassin also directed her in *He Who Must Die* (1957), *Where the Hot Wind Blows!* (1958), *Phaedra* (1962), *Topkapi, 10:30 P.M. Summer* (1966), and *Promise at Dawn* (1970). Her other credits include *The Victors* (1963), *Nasty Habits* (1976), and *Not by Coincidence* (1983).

MEREDITH, BURGESS. Actor, director. *(b. Nov. 16, 1907, Cleveland.)* A veteran of stage and film whose numerous accomplishments in dramatic roles will, alas, probably be forever overshadowed by his portrayal of "The Penguin" on the 1960s TV series "Batman" (and the 1966 theatrical feature of the same name). After toiling in many odd jobs during the 1920s, Meredith joined Eva LeGallienne's Student Repertory Group and became a prominent Broadway actor in the 1930s. He made his film debut in Maxwell Anderson's *Winterset* (1936), recreating his own acclaimed stage performance, and followed with memorable work in *Of Mice and Men* (as George), *Idiots Delight* (both 1939), *Second Chorus* (1940, with wife-to-be Paulette Goddard), *Tom, Dick and Harry* (1941), *The Story of G.I. Joe* (1945, as fabled war correspondent Ernie Pyle), *Diary of a Chambermaid* (1946, with Goddard, which he also produced and wrote), *Mine Own Executioner* (1947), and *On Our Merry Way* (1948, which he also coproduced).

Meredith, whose lively countenance and intensity of performance compensated for his "shortcomings" as a Hollywood leading man (i.e., his lack of matinee-idol looks), enjoyed two early starring roles in the B melodramas *San Francisco Docks* (1940) and *Street of Chance* (1942, as an amnesiac murder suspect in an early exercise in film noir based on a Cornell Woolrich novel). He directed and performed in *The Man on the Eiffel Tower* (1949), a fascinating, seldom-seen thriller based on one of the popular "Maigret" novels by Georges Simenon. Meredith's film roles thinned out during the 1950s after he was considered an unfriendly witness during the McCarthy era, but he continued to do stage work (winning a Tony for directing "The Thurber Carnival"), returned to films in Otto Preminger's *Advise and Consent* (1962) and *The Cardinal* (1963), and thereafter never let up.

He snared Best Supporting Actor Oscar nominations for *The Day of the Locust* (1975) and for his most popular latter-day characterization, that of the trainer Mickey in the first *Rocky* (1976), a role he repeated in the 1979, 1982, and 1990 sequels. He has appeared in scores of TV shows (winning an Emmy for his performance in 1977's *Tail Gunner Joe*) and has lent his distinctive voice to innumerable commercials, documentaries, and feature films (including, memorably, 1969's *The Reivers*). He published his autobiography, "So Far, So Good," in 1994.

OTHER FILMS INCLUDE: 1938: *Spring Madness;* 1940: *Castle on the Hudson;* 1941: *That Uncertain Feeling;* 1946: *Magnificent Doll* (as President James Madison); 1957: *Joe Butterfly;* 1966: *Madame X, A Big Hand for the Little Lady;* 1967: *Hurry Sundown;* 1970: *There Was a Crooked Man;* 1975: *92 in the Shade;* 1978: *Foul Play, Magic;* 1981: *True Confessions;* 1987: *King Lear;* 1988: *Full Moon in Blue Water;* 1990: *State of Grace;* 1993: *Grumpy Old Men;* 1995: *Tall Tale.*

MERKEL, UNA. Actress. *(b. Dec. 10, 1903, Covington, Ky.; d. Jan. 2, 1986.)* She usually played the leading lady's tart-tongued best friend, delivering wisecracks in a southern drawl oozing sarcasm. Merkel, a onetime stand-in for Lillian Gish (whom, with her sweet, round face and pale blue eyes, she strongly resembled), appeared in several silent films, worked on the Broadway stage, and returned to film work at the dawn of the talkie era. In 1930 she played Ann Rutledge in D. W. Griffith's *Abraham Lincoln* and a whimpering ingenue in a Roland West thriller, *The Bat Whispers.* But she found more opportunities in supporting roles, beginning with *The Maltese Falcon* (1931), in which she played the loyal secretary Effie to Ricardo Cortez's Sam Spade. Her most fertile period was the 1930s, during which time she appeared in innumerable comedies and musicals (and, occasionally, in serious dramas). Merkel's films during this decade include *Red-Headed Woman* (1932), *Whistling in the Dark, 42nd Street, Reunion in Vienna, Bombshell* (all 1933), *Bulldog Drummond Strikes Back, The Cat's Paw* (as leading lady to Harold Lloyd), *The Merry Widow, Evelyn Prentice* (all 1934), *Broadway Melody of 1936, Baby Face Harrington, It's in the Air* (all 1935), *Riffraff, Born to Dance* (both 1936), *Don't Tell the Wife, Saratoga, True Confession* (all 1937), *Some Like It Hot, On Borrowed Time* (both 1939), and *Destry Rides Again* (also 1939, as a frontier frau who engages saloon-singer Marlene Dietrich in a memorable catfight).

Her screen career took a downward turn in the 1940s; no longer an A-list costar, she even made some cheap two-reel comedies for Columbia in 1944, one *(To Heir Is Human)* paired with Harry Langdon. She moved to New York and worked on the stage instead, with some distinction (winning a Tony Award in 1956 for *The Ponder Heart*), before returning to movies in earnest in the late 1950s. One of her best latter-day roles was as Geraldine Page's mother in *Summer and Smoke* (1961), which earned her an Oscar nomination as Best Supporting Actress.

OTHER FILMS INCLUDE: 1940: *The Bank*

Dick (as W. C. Fields' daughter); 1941: *Road to Zanzibar, Cracked Nuts;* 1942: *The Mad Doctor of Market Street;* 1943: *This Is the Army;* 1947: *It's a Joke, Son;* 1948: *The Bride Goes Wild;* 1950: *Kill the Umpire, My Blue Heaven;* 1951: *Golden Girl;* 1952: *The Merry Widow;* 1953: *I Love Melvin;* 1956: *Bundle of Joy;* 1958: *The Girl Most Likely;* 1959: *The Mating Game;* 1961: *The Parent Trap;* 1964: *A Tiger Walks;* 1966: *Spinout.*

MERMAN, ETHEL. Actress, singer. *(b. Jan. 16, 1909, Queens, N.Y., as Ethel Zimmerman; d. Feb. 15, 1984.)* The star of such legendary Broadway hits as "Annie Get Your Gun" and "Gypsy," this brassy brunette singer and veteran stage performer with the high-decibel voice and dynamic presence never scored as well on-screen as she did on-stage. As an attractive younger woman, Merman cut a pleasing figure in such musicals as *Follow the Leader* (1930), *The Big Broadcast* (1932), *We're Not Dressing, Kid Millions, Shoot the Works* (all 1934), *The Big Broadcast of 1936* (1935), *Anything Goes* (1936, reprising her stage role of Reno Sweeney in this much-altered version of Cole Porter's smash show), *Strike Me Pink* (also 1936), *Happy Landing, Straight, Place and Show,* and *Alexander's Ragtime Band* (all 1938, the latter a standout for Merman, who got to sing a slew of Irving Berlin hits). She left Hollywood in the late 1930s and, except for a bit in the all-star *Stage Door Canteen* (1943), didn't return until the 1950s. Her later films include *Call Me Madam* (1953, reprising her Tony Award–winning Broadway role as Perle Mesta), *There's No Business Like Show Business* (1954), *It's a Mad Mad Mad Mad World* (1963, in a broad comic turn), *The Art of Love* (1965), *Won Ton Ton, the Dog Who Saved Hollywood* (1976), and *Airplane!* (1980, a hilarious cameo as Lt. Hurwitz, whose war injury has him believing he's Ethel Merman). She contributed her incomparable voice to the animated features *Journey Back to Oz* (1974) and TV's "Rudolph and Frosty's Christmas in July" (1979). Merman was briefly married to actor Ernest Borgnine.

MERRILL, GARY. Actor. *(b. Aug. 2, 1915, Hartford, Conn.; d. Mar. 5, 1990.)* Margo Channing's boyfriend: that's how Gary Merrill will always be remembered. An intelligent-looking leading man, he achieved movie immortality as the director and paramour of the fading Broadway star played by Bette Davis in the classic backstage comedy/drama *All About Eve* (1950). Then he and Davis (who was seven years his senior) got married in real life. They appeared together in 1952's *Another Man's Poison* and *Phone Call From a Stranger,* but Merrill's solo screen career never took off. His best non-Davis film is *Twelve O'Clock High* (1949); others include *Winged Victory* (1944), *Where the Sidewalk Ends* (1950), *The Frogmen* (1951), *The Savage Eye* (1960), *The Pleasure of His Company, Mysterious Island* (both 1961), *Around the World Under the Sea* (1966), the Elvis Presley vehicle *Clambake* (1967) and *Huckleberry Finn* (1974, as the violent Pap). He and Davis divorced in 1960, after a stormy marriage. Merrill left film to enter politics in 1968, running unsuccessfully for a seat in Maine's legislature. He continued to work on stage, and occasionally on film (in 1977's *Thieves),* but he kept busiest in later years doing voice-overs for scores of radio and TV commercials. In 1988 he published a memoir titled, inevitably, "Bette, Rita and the Rest of My Life."

METCALF, LAURIE. Actress. *(b. June 16, 1955, Edwardsville, Ill.)* Best known for her three-time Emmy-winning role as Roseanne's sister Jackie on "Roseanne" (1988–), Metcalf has made a number of film appearances in varied character roles. She began her acting career as one of the original members of Chicago's famed Steppenwolf Theatre, opposite such alumni as John Malkovich, Gary Sinise, and Glenne Headly. After critical acclaim in the New York production of "Balm in Gilead," she made her film debut as Rosanna Arquette's sister-in-law in the sleeper *Desperately Seeking Susan* (1985). She has since appeared in *Making Mr. Right* (1987, opposite Malkovich and Headly), *Miles From Home* (1988, directed by Sinise), *Uncle Buck* (1989), *Internal Affairs* (1990), *JFK* (1991, as Assistant D.A. Suzie Cox), *Mistress* (1992) as Robert Wuhl's neglected wife, *A Dangerous Woman* (1993), and *Blink* (1994).

METZGER, RADLEY. Director. *(b. Jan. 21, 1929, New York City.)* Renowned as a stylish director of soft-core erotica in the late 1960s and early 1970s, Metzger is a lifelong movie buff who worked as an assistant director immediately upon graduating college. He first attracted attention by importing and distributing *I, a Woman* (1966), a Scandinavian sex film that was enormously successful. His visually sumptuous soft-core films, which include *Therese and Isabelle* (1968) and *Camille 2000* (1969), were mostly shot in Europe. Metzger turned to hard-core (under the pseudonym Henry Paris) in the 1970s, distinguishing such films as *The Private Afternoons of Pamela Mann* (1975) and *The Opening of Misty Beethoven* (1976) with a competence rarely seen in that genre. In 1978 he directed a relatively distinguished international cast (including Wendy Hiller, Edward Fox, Olivia Hussey, Honor Blackman, Daniel Massey, and Carol Lynley) in the fourth screen version of *The Cat and the Canary.*

MEYER, NICHOLAS. Director, screenwriter. *(b. Dec. 24, 1945, New York City.)* This former Hollywood publicist has become a successful Hollywood scripter and director, known primarily for his work on some *Star Trek* films. His first movie success came when his screenplay based on his novel *The Seven Percent Solution* (1976), which teamed up Sherlock Holmes and Sigmund Freud, was nominated for an Academy Award. He wrote the script for and directed *Time After Time* (1979), which similarly featured two larger-than-life characters, H. G. Wells and Jack the Ripper. Meyer subsequently was tapped to direct *Star Trek II: The Wrath of Khan* (1982) and *Star Trek VI: The Undiscovered Country* (1991, which he also cowrote), and co-write *Star Trek IV: The Voyage Home* (1986). In 1983 he rocked television with a startling, and much-discussed, vision of a post–nuclear war world, *The Day After.* (He also cowrote, but did not direct, the 1975 TV movie *The Night That Panicked America,* about Orson Welles' legendary "War of the Worlds" radio broadcast.) While all of these films have been hands-down successes, his non-sci-fi efforts have not fared as well: *Volunteers* (1985) was a lame comedy about the Peace Corps, and

The Deceivers (1988) and *Company Business* (1991) were poorly received. More recently he cowrote *Sommersby* (1993).

MEYER, RUSS. Director. *(b. Mar. 21, 1923, San Leandro, Calif.)* The acknowledged pioneer of the sexploitation film began shooting home movies as a teenager, using a camera given him by his mother. He was a combat photographer stationed in Europe during World War 2, an experience he claims molded his outlook and personality. Upon returning to the States, Meyer photographed industrial films, girlie-magazine layouts, and occasionally worked on Hollywood productions, such as *Guys and Dolls* (1955) and *Giant* (1956). He directed a "nudie-cutie," *The Immoral Mr. Teas* (1959), which dispensed with the usual conventions of nudist films and served up a ribald storyline and amazingly endowed women. The overwhelming success of *Teas* started Meyer on a prolific career in sexploitation films, with titles like *Lorna* (1964), *Faster Pussycat! Kill! Kill!* (1966), *Cherry, Harry and Raquel* (1969), *Supervixens* (1974), *Up!* (1976), and *Beneath the Valley of the Ultravixens* (1979), all characterized by a frenetic editing style, a predilection for big-breasted women, and liberal doses of rough violence.

The critical and commercial success of *Vixen* (1968) caught the attention of 20th Century-Fox execs, who signed Meyer to direct *Beyond the Valley of the Dolls* (1970, his biggest success, written by Roger Ebert) and his "straightest" project, *The Seven Minutes* (1971, a flop adapted from an Irving Wallace novel). Meyer's experiences with Fox soured the iconoclastic filmmaker on major studios, and he resumed the independent production and distribution of his own movies. The demise of the drive-in market and the emphasis on hard-core pornography (which Meyer always eschewed) effectively ended his directorial career, though he continues to promote and sell his product on video. He appeared as himself in a spoofy sequence of *Amazon Women on the Moon* (1987).

MIDDLETON, CHARLES. Actor. *(b. Oct. 3, 1879, Elizabethtown, Ky.; d. Apr. 22,*

1949.) Venerable screen heavy with a rich, theatrical voice who achieved screen immortality as Ming the Merciless, Buster Crabbe's nemesis in the serials *Flash Gordon* (1936), *Flash Gordon's Trip to Mars* (1938), and *Flash Gordon Conquers the Universe* (1940). Extremely thin, with a deeply lined, cruel face, Middleton worked in carnivals, circuses, in vaudeville, and on stage before entering movies in 1928. Few character actors surpassed him when it came to meting out death and destruction with such obvious glee— though he occasionally played sympathetic roles, and even sang one line in the courtroom scene of *Duck Soup* (1933). Middleton appeared in *Safe in Hell* (1931, one of his juiciest parts), *Pack Up Your Troubles, Mystery Ranch* (both 1932), *The Miracle Rider* (1935), *Hop-a-long Cassidy* (1935, as Hoppy's boss Buck Peters), *Show Boat* (1936), *Dick Tracy Returns* (1938, as the villainous Pa Stark), *Daredevils of the Red Circle* (1939, as the criminal mastermind known only by his prison number, 39–0–13), *Jesse James* (1939), *The Grapes of Wrath* (1940), *Abe Lincoln in Illinois* (1940, as Tom Lincoln), *Belle Starr* (1941), and *Strangler of the Swamp* (1946), to name a few. In the 1934 short subject boosting FDR's National Recovery Act, *The Road Is Open Again,* he played Abraham Lincoln—quite well.

MIDLER, BETTE. Actress, singer, producer. *(b. Dec. 1, 1945, Honolulu.)* Not many superstars get their show-biz starts entertaining in gay bathhouses, but Bette Midler is not your average superstar. Short, busty, and totally uninhibited on stage, her brassy demeanor, passion for old songs and older jokes, and self-mocking devotion to the muse of comedy make her a refreshing change in an era when most divas take themselves so-o-o seriously. Her legendary concerts are preserved in several cable specials and albums, as well as the 1980 feature *Divine Madness!* (She earned two Emmys, one for a performance on "The Tonight Show," the program that introduced her to a national audience, and another for a 1978 variety special. She was also awarded a special Tony Award in 1974.) After some extra work (in films like *Hawaii,* largely filmed in her home state) and a role in a 1970s cheapie retitled *The Di-*

vine Mr. J, she hit the big time with her first major role, playing a thinly disguised Janis Joplin in *The Rose* (1979), and earned a Best Actress Oscar nomination for her performance. She then crashed in the aptly titled *Jinxed!* (1982); her feuds with costar Ken Wahl and director Don Siegel garnered more ink than the film itself.

Midler would seem to have been finished in movies, though she did film a very funny music video, "Beast of Burden," with Mick Jagger (in which they each got a pie in the face). Then in 1986 Paul Mazursky cast her as an uptight Beverly Hills matron in *Down and Out in Beverly Hills,* and she scored a hit. The Disney studio then kept her busy in such popular comedies as *Ruthless People* (also 1986), *Outrageous Fortune* (1987), and *Big Business* (1988); that same year, she provided a voice for the animated *Oliver & Company* and starred in the soapy *Beaches,* which she produced, and which earned her a Grammy for the song "Wind Beneath My Wings." She wasn't as lucky with *Stella,* a treacly 1990 remake of *Stella Dallas.* Her teaming with Woody Allen in *Scenes From a Mall* (1991) was more inspired than the film itself. She produced and starred in the ambitious, lavish musical drama *For the Boys* (also 1991), which failed at the box office but did give Midler some residual satisfaction when her performance was nominated for an Academy Award. In 1993 she starred as a witch in the uninspired comedy *Hocus Pocus,* and then took the plum role of Mama Rose in a TV production of the Broadway musical "Gypsy."

MIFUNE, TOSHIRO. Actor. *(b. Apr. 1, 1920, Tsingtao, China.)* Mifune is perhaps the screen's ultimate warrior, if only because he's portrayed that type in infinite variety. He has been brash and reckless in *The Seven Samurai* (1954), stoic and droll in *Yojimbo* (1961) and its sequel *Sanjuro* (1962), paranoid and irrational in *Throne of Blood* (1957), and swashbucklingly heroic in *The Hidden Fortress* (1958). All of the preceding films were directed by Akira Kurosawa, who is responsible for shaping Mifune's rugged, imposing screen persona. He scored an early triumph in Kurosawa's *Rashomon* (1950), playing a medieval outlaw, but he's also portrayed a

number of contemporary characters including detectives and businessmen. Mifune had originally planned a film career behind the camera as a cinematographer, but wound up before the lens in 1946's *Shin Baka Jidai;* he first worked with Kurosawa in 1948's *Drunken Angel.* He made one attempt at directing in 1963, *Goju Man-nin no Isan,* which was a failure; his production company now makes films for TV. Mifune's forceful personality, projected through baleful expressions and dynamic physical presence, won him international recognition and led to many roles in American productions, including *Grand Prix* (1966), *Hell in the Pacific* (1968, in a two-man tour de force opposite Lee Marvin), Kurosawa fan Steven Spielberg's *1941* (1979), and the TV miniseries "Shogun" (1980). Less active during the past decade, Mifune recently appeared in *Shogun Mayeda* (1990).
OTHER FILMS INCLUDE: 1952: *The Life of Oharu;* 1962: *High and Low;* 1965: *Red Beard;* 1975: *Paper Tiger;* 1976: *Midway;* 1979: *Winter Kills;* 1982: *The Challenge;* 1993: *Shadow of the Wolf.*

MILES, SARAH. Actress. *(b. Dec. 31, 1941, Ingatestone, Essex, England.)* This British stage actress has contributed some striking characterizations in films, but her screen appearances have been sporadic at best. Initially the darling of "New Wave" devotees for her turns in Joseph Losey's *The Servant* (1963) and Michelangelo Antonioni's *Blow Up* (1966), Miles endeared herself to American audiences with her Academy Award-nominated performance in *Ryan's Daughter* (1970). Her torrid sex scenes with Kris Kristofferson in *The Sailor Who Fell From Grace With the Sea* (1976) aroused censorial ire and made the tabloids. Since the mid 1980s Miles has been seen in character roles, most effectively in *Steaming* (1985), *Hope and Glory* (superb as the matriarch of a British family during the WW2 blitz), and *White Mischief* (1988, as a depraved hedonist living in Africa during the 1940s). Miles married writer-director Robert Bolt in 1967, divorced him in 1976, then remarried him in 1988.
OTHER FILMS INCLUDE: 1963: *The Ceremony;* 1965: *Those Magnificent Men in Their Flying Machines;* 1972: *Lady Caroline Lamb* (directed by her husband); 1973: *The Man*

Who Loved Cat Dancing, The Hireling; 1978: *The Big Sleep;* 1981: *Priest of Love;* 1982: *Venom;* 1983: *Loving Walter;* 1984: *Ordeal by Innocence;* 1993: *The Silent Touch.*

MILES, SYLVIA. Actress. *(b. September 9, 1932, New York City.)* Blowsy character actress of the stage and screen, Miles first attracted major notice as Jon Voight's one-night stand in *Midnight Cowboy* (1969), which earned her an Oscar nomination. She picked up another nomination for *Farewell, My Lovely* (1975), but has only appeared occasionally in films over the years. Her most recent films have cast her as an archetypal Jewish yenta, most successfully in *Wall Street* (1987), *Crossing Delancey* (1988), and *She-Devil* (1989).
OTHER FILMS INCLUDE: 1960: *Murder, Inc.;* 1971: *The Last Movie;* 1972: *Heat;* 1975: *92 in the Shade;* 1982: *Evil Under the Sun;* 1987: *Critical Condition;* 1988: *Spike of Bensonhurst.*

MILES, VERA. Actress. *(b. Aug. 23, 1929, Boise City, Okla., as Vera Ralston.)* How many actresses can claim to have been favorites of Alfred Hitchcock, John Ford, and Walt Disney? The appealing actress with all-American looks got her Hollywood break via a beauty-contest win, earned a minor part in *Two Tickets to Broadway* (1951), posed for cheesecake photos, and married her leading man from *Tarzan's Hidden Jungle* (1955), Gordon Scott (they later split). Then John Ford cast her as Jeffrey Hunter's spirited love interest in *The Searchers* (1956), and her career took a dramatic turn. A year later, she showed tremendous skill and range as Henry Fonda's beleaguered wife in Hitchcock's *The Wrong Man* (1957). Pregnancy cost her the lead in *Vertigo,* but Hitchcock did cast her as Janet Leigh's sister in *Psycho* (1960), which made her the one who discovered the truth about Norman Bates' mother. Following another stint for Ford in 1962's *The Man Who Shot Liberty Valance,* she got her first parts at the Disney studio, in *A Tiger Walks* (1964) and *Those Calloways* (1965, a particularly good role), which led to a long string of Disney commitments into the 1970s. Better parts came her way in episodic TV than on-screen from that time on. In 1983 she reprised her most famous role in *Psycho II,*

vociferously protesting the proposed parole of killer Norman Bates (played, as in the original, by Anthony Perkins).
OTHER FILMS INCLUDE: 1953: *The Charge at Feather River;* 1955: *Wichita;* 1956: *Autumn Leaves, 23 Paces to Baker Street;* 1957: *Beau James;* 1959: *The FBI Story, A Touch of Larceny;* 1960: *5 Branded Women;* 1961: *Back Street;* 1966: *Follow Me, Boys!;* 1967: *Gentle Giant;* 1968: *The Hellfighters, The Hanged Man* (telefilm); 1973: *One Little Indian;* 1974: *The Castaway Cowboy;* 1977: *Twilight's Last Gleaming;* 1978: *Run for the Roses;* 1985: *Into the Night.*

MILESTONE, LEWIS. Director. *(b. Sept. 30, 1895, Odessa, Russia; d. Sept. 25, 1980.)* Upon emigrating to the United States from Russia in the years just prior to World War 1, Milestone held a number of odd jobs before enlisting in the U.S. Signal Corps, where he worked as an assistant director on Army training films during the war. After the conflict he went to Hollywood, eventually securing work as a cutter, and later as an assistant director. Dilettante movie producer Howard Hughes promoted Milestone to director, and one of his early efforts, *Two Arabian Knights* (1928), won him an Oscar in the first Academy Award ceremony that next year. In 1928 he also helmed *The Racket,* a seminal gangster film, and later helped Hughes direct scenes for his WW1 aviation saga *Hell's Angels* (for which he never received credit).

Milestone won his second Academy Award for *All Quiet on the Western Front* (1930), a brilliant screen adaptation of the antiwar novel by Erich Maria Remarque. *All Quiet* mesmerized audiences upon initial release, and made a star of young leading man Lew Ayres. Interestingly, for someone who made such a compelling case for pacifism, Milestone was oddly drawn to the war-film genre, and returned to it repeatedly throughout his career. Milestone's next, *The Front Page* (1931), brought the Ben Hecht–Charles MacArthur play to the screen with all its rat-a-tat energy intact. Far more fluid than many early talkies, it still compares favorably with its later (and slicker) remakes, and demonstrates Milestone's penchant for visual flamboyance. It earned him another Oscar nomination.

Rain (1932), which starred Joan Craw-

ford as Somerset Maugham's Sadie Thompson, was similarly innovative, as was the offbeat musical *Hallelujah, I'm a Bum* (1933), but after those films Milestone seemed to settle into a rut; *The Captain Hates the Sea* (1934), *Paris in the Spring* (1935), and *Anything Goes* (1936) were pleasant but routine. *The General Died at Dawn* (1936, an exotic adventure starring Gary Cooper), however, showed him in peak form and proved that, when provided with good scripts, he could rise to the occasion. Subsequent efforts such as *Of Mice and Men* (1939), *The Purple Heart* (1944), *A Walk in the Sun* (1945), and *The Red Pony* (1949) bore out this conclusion.

At his best, Milestone was a skilled craftsman who fully understood both the technical and aesthetic tricks of his trade, and utilized them well. At his worst, he was a journeyman who seemed content to just get his movie in the camera with the least amount of fuss or bother. He worked extensively in television from the mid 1950s.
OTHER FILMS INCLUDE: 1939: *Night of Nights;* 1940: *Lucky Partners;* 1941: *My Life With Caroline;* 1943: *Edge of Darkness, The North Star;* 1946: *The Strange Love of Martha Ivers;* 1948: *No Minor Vices, Arch of Triumph;* 1950: *Halls of Montezuma;* 1952: *Kangaroo, Les Miserables;* 1953: *Melba;* 1954: *They Who Dare;* 1955: *The Widow;* 1959: *Pork Chop Hill;* 1960: *Ocean's Eleven;* 1962: *Mutiny on the Bounty* (replacing Carol Reed).

MILIUS, JOHN. Director, screenwriter, producer. *(b. Apr. 11, 1944, St. Louis.)* This distinctive filmmaker has been called "Mr. Macho," "General Milius," the "George Patton of film directors" and the "Herman Goering of film directors" because of his high-octane movies populated by characters whose political leanings would not win them positions in Bill Clinton's cabinet. Rejected by the Army because of chronic asthma, Milius went to the USC film school and made a prize-winning short, "Marcello, I'm So Bored," a satire of Italian art-house films. He went on to become a prolific screenwriter starting with *The Devil's Eight* (1969), *Evel Knievel* (1972), *The Life and Times of Judge Roy Bean, Jeremiah Johnson* (both 1972), and the second "Dirty Harry" movie, *Magnum Force* (1973, cowritten with Michael Cimino). *Dillinger* (1973), his directorial debut, was a violent, romanticized look at the famous gangster, but *The Wind and the Lion* (1975), a rousing modern epic, showed Milius' growth as a director and his concern with myths, codes of honor, and individual choice. *Big Wednesday* (1978) lovingly evoked Milius' own days of California surfing, and *Apocalypse Now* (1979), an adaptation of Joseph Conrad's "Heart of Darkness" which Milius had begun years earlier for Francis Ford Coppola, earned him an Adapted Screenplay Oscar nomination with Coppola. His next films as writer and director featured a variety of heroes who willingly embraced violence to serve their purposes: *Conan the Barbarian* (1982, cowritten with Oliver Stone), the teens turned guerilla fighters in *Red Dawn* (1984), the army deserter turned rebel leader in *Farewell to the King* (1989), and the Vietnam bombardiers in *Flight of the Intruder* (1991). His most recent screenwriting credits: *Geronimo* (1993, story and coscenarist) and *Clear and Present Danger* (1994, coscenarist). Milius also executive produced *Hardcore* (1979) and *Used Cars* (1980), produced *Uncommon Valor* (1983), and did uncredited rewrite work on the original *Dirty Harry* (1971). He also wrote the TV movie *Melvin Purvis—G-Man* (1974) and the great scene in *Jaws* (1975) with Robert Shaw describing the sinking of the *Indianapolis*.

MILLAND, RAY. Actor; director. (b. Jan. 3, 1905, Neath, Wales, as Reginald Truscott-Jones; d. Mar. 10, 1986.) From a callow juvenile to a respected leading man to a competent director to a distinguished character actor, this urbane, mellow-voiced Welshman spanned the Hollywood scene for more than half a century. He broke into films in England in 1929's *The Plaything,* and that same year had a bit in the seldom-seen first version of Liam O'Flaherty's *The Informer.* He came to Hollywood in 1931, and worked steadily in small roles, usually of the martini-sipping variety, for years; among the more familiar titles are *Bachelor Father, Blonde Crazy* (both 1931), *Polly of the Circus, The Man Who Played God, Payment Deferred* (all 1932), *Bolero, We're Not Dressing, Charlie Chan in London* (all 1934), *The Gilded Lily, Four Hours to Kill, The Glass Key* (all 1935), *The Return of Sophie Lang,* and *The Big Broadcast of 1937* (both 1936). That same year, he scored a hit in *The Jungle Princess,* which also brought stardom to sarong-clad newcomer Dorothy Lamour.

Finally, the handsome young actor was being given a chance to show some personality, as he moved toward leading roles in such entertaining fare as *Three Smart Girls* (1936), *Easy Living* (1937), *Her Jungle Love, Men With Wings* (both 1938), and *Hotel Imperial* (1939). By this time firmly ensconced at Paramount, he entered his peak period as the youngest Geste brother in *Beau Geste* (also 1939), and continued as a full-fledged leading man in such popular fare as *The Doctor Takes a Wife, Untamed* (both 1940), and *I Wanted Wings* (1941). In *Arise, My Love* (1940), opposite frequent costar Claudette Colbert, he showed a range few had suspected before. *The Major and the Minor* (1942) showed just how skilled a farceur he had become. First-rate films like *The Uninvited* and *Ministry of Fear* (both 1944) proved that he could carry a film— and engage an audience to follow him through an interesting story. After plowing through some Cecil B. DeMille silliness in *Reap the Wild Wind* (1942) and locking horns with career-driven Ginger Rogers in *Lady in the Dark* (1944) it seemed there was nothing he couldn't do within the domain of an all-purpose leading man. But no one suspected he was capable of a performance like the one he gave for Billy Wilder in *The Lost Weekend* (1945). Milland won the Oscar, and an overwhelming dose of respect, for his portrayal of an alcoholic writer who can't live without his booze, and reaches rock-bottom when he suffers the d.t.'s in a hospital ward. It was a daring film for anyone to make; for Milland, it was an unqualified triumph. Alas, there were few films to come that were quite as potent, and fewer roles still that tested his mettle as that one did.

He kept busy for the next decade, starring in such varied films as *Kitty* (also 1945), *California* (1946), *Golden Earrings* (1947), *The Big Clock* (1948, a film noir masterpiece that ranks among the handful of his best), *Alias Nick Beal* (as Satan himself), the delightful baseball fantasy *It*

Happens Every Spring (both 1949), *A Life
of Her Own, Copper Canyon* (both 1950),
Rhubarb (1951), *The Thief* (a bizarre film
done completely without dialogue), *Some-
thing to Live For* (both 1952), *Let's Do It
Again* (1953), Alfred Hitchcock's *Dial M
for Murder* (1954), and *The Girl in the
Red Velvet Swing* (1955, as Stanford
White). He also worked frequently on TV,
including a two-season sitcom, "Meet Mr.
McNutley" (later "The Ray Milland
Show").

In 1956 Milland made *Lisbon,* the first
of four features he directed as well as
starred in. After performing in and directing *The Safecracker* (1958), Milland concentrated on TV directing, in addition to
starring in another series, this time as a
private eye named "Markham" (1959–60).
In 1962 he returned to features with *Panic
in Year Zero!* (which he also directed),
and two by Roger Corman: *Premature
Burial* (as a rather advanced college student!) and *X—the Man with X-Ray Eyes*
(1963, title role). After a few years of relative inactivity, including his last directorial feature, the British-made *Hostile Witness* (1968), he returned to TV and kept
busy in a variety of TV movies, among
them *Daughter of the Mind* (1969) and
Company of Killers (1970).

In 1970 Milland made a comeback of
sorts as Ryan O'Neal's snooty father in
the blockbuster *Love Story,* a role he repeated in the 1978 sequel, *Oliver's Story.*
Though he kept busy in the 1970s, it was
often in schlock like *The Thing With Two
Heads* (1972), *Terror in the Wax Museum*
(1973), and *Survival Run* (1980), or in international productions in need of a cheap
marquee name, such as *Gold* (1974), *The
Swiss Conspiracy* (1975), and *Blackout*
(1978). He costarred in Disney's *Escape
to Witch Mountain* (1975), then in 1976
played Duncan Calderwood on TV's
"Rich Man, Poor Man," had a good part
in *The Last Tycoon,* and published his autobiography, "Wide-Eyed in Babylon." He
worked in one final film, the Spanish-
made *The Sea Serpent* (1986), before declining health put an end to a lengthy and
generally satisfying career.

MILLER, ANN. Actress, dancer, singer. *(b.
Apr. 12, 1919, Chireno, Tex., as Lucille Ann
Collier.)* Raven-tressed dancer whose gor-
geous gams flashed in a number of Holly-

wood musicals during the 1940s and
1950s. In her childhood a professional
dancer, Miller entered movies as a bit
player in 1934, making her debut in that
year's *Anne of Green Gables* and also appearing in *The Good Fairy* (1935) and
Devil on Horseback (1936) before signing
with RKO in 1937. She won billing (and
a full-screen close-up) as one of the *New
Faces of 1937,* and gamely tried to keep
up with the accomplished cast of *Stage
Door* later that year. She stayed at RKO
for the next three years, toiling in *The Life
of the Party* (1937), *Radio City Revels,
Room Service* (manhandled by the Marx
Brothers), *Having Wonderful Time* (1938),
and *Too Many Girls* (1940). She was
loaned to Columbia for a supporting role
as one of the madcap family members in
Frank Capra's Oscar-winning version of
the Kaufman and Hart play *You Can't
Take It With You* (also 1938).

Moving to Republic, she won her first
lead in the Gene Autry musical-Western
hit *Melody Ranch* (1940), and followed it
with a turn in *Hit Parade of 1941.* Miller's vigorous tap-dancing style, even at
this early point in her career, far out-
stripped her acting ability, and when Columbia signed her the following year, it
kept her hoofing in a string of low- and
medium-budget musicomedies. *Time Out
for Rhythm, Go West, Young Lady* (both
1941), *Reveille With Beverly, What's
Buzzin', Cousin?* (both 1943), *Jam Session, Hey, Rookie, Carolina Blues* (all
1944), *Eve Knew Her Apples, Eadie Was
a Lady* (both 1945), and *The Thrill of Brazil* (1946) put scant demands on her ability to emote, and just as well.

By the time Miller reached MGM, home
of the most lavish movie musicals, she
was too old and too brassy to play ingenues, so she played secondary leads, some
of them manipulative, temperamental
dames. But the inventive style of the
MGM musicals offered Miller frequent
opportunities to strut her stuff in flashy,
brilliantly choreographed dance routines,
and she never disappointed. *The Kissing
Bandit, Easter Parade* (both 1948, in the
latter paired with Fred Astaire), *On the
Town* (1949), *Watch the Birdie* (1950),
Texas Carnival, Two Tickets to Broadway
(both 1951), *Lovely to Look At* (1952),
Kiss Me, Kate (1953, her all-time best),
Small Town Girl (also 1953, with a spectacular Busby Berkeley featured number),

Hit the Deck (1955), *The Opposite Sex,* and *The Great American Pastime* (both 1956) rounded out Miller's MGM career. Aside from a cameo in *Won Ton Ton, the Dog Who Saved Hollywood* (1976) and a stint as one of the "hosts" of *That's Entertainment! III* (1994), she's never returned to the big screen, but has worked frequently on television, appearing in variety shows, series episodes, and even commercials (tapping atop a giant soup can in an early 1970s ad). In the 1980s she enjoyed tremendous success on Broadway (and in a lengthy tour) opposite Mickey Rooney in the burlesque musical pastiche "Sugar Babies." She published an autobiography, "Miller's High Life" in 1972, and went on to express her belief in the occult in "Tapping into the Force" (1990).

MILLER, DICK. Actor. *(b. Dec. 25, 1928, Bronx, N.Y.)* Craggy-faced character actor best remembered for a variety of roles in low-budget drive-in fodder produced during the 1950s and 1960s. He debuted in Roger Corman's *Apache Woman* (1955), playing both a cowboy and an Indian (audiences weren't supposed to notice), and subsequently appeared in *It Conquered the World* (1956), *Rock All Night* (1957), *The Little Shop of Horrors* (1960), and *The Terror* (1963), to name just a few. Miller's finest hour was as the wimpy busboy who makes sculptures from corpses in *A Bucket of Blood* (1959). A cult favorite of baby-boomer filmmakers like Jonathan Kaplan and Allan Arkush, Miller has worked in dozens of films made during the last 20 years, often snagging plum cameo roles in major productions, such as *Heart Like a Wheel* (1983), *The Terminator* (1984), and *After Hours* (1985). Director Joe Dante has showcased Miller in his *Hollywood Boulevard* (1976, as a sleazy agent), *The Howling* (1981, as a wisecracking book dealer), *Amazon Women on the Moon* (1987, as a hapless ventriloquist) and, most memorably, as the jittery Mr. Futterman in *Gremlins* (1984) and *Gremlins 2: The New Batch* (1990). Miller had recurring roles on the TV series "Fame" (1985–87) and "The Flash" (1990).

MILLER, GEORGE. Director, screenwriter. *(b. Mar. 3, 1945, Brisbane, Australia.)* Now renowned as a world-class action director, Miller was actually in his final year of studies at medical school when a one-minute film he and his twin brother made won first prize in a student competition. He later met future partner Byron Kennedy at a film workshop and they collaborated on an award-winning short film before making their first feature, *Mad Max* (1979), a futuristic thriller about a cop out for revenge. The film became the most successful Australian film up to that date, and the sequel, *Mad Max 2* (1981, retitled *The Road Warrior* outside of Australia), was a critical and popular smash internationally, making Mel Gibson a star and establishing Miller as an expert director of action films. Miller went on to direct "Nightmare at 20,000 Feet," the best segment of the omnibus *Twilight Zone— The Movie* (1983), as well as *Mad Max Beyond Thunderdome* (1985), the third of the popular series, before coming to America to make *The Witches of Eastwick* (1987), a very broad, entertaining adaptation of John Updike's novel. It was apparently an unhappy experience for the director, who immediately returned to his native country. Miller has also produced Australian productions, such as *The Year My Voice Broke* (1987), *Dead Calm* (1989), and *Flirting* (1990). In 1992 he returned to Hollywood filmmaking with the unblinking drama of parents facing their son's unfathomable affliction in *Lorenzo's Oil* (1992), which earned him an Oscar nomination for cowriting the screenplay. (Clearly, Miller's medical background drew him to the story and made him an ideal filmmaker to communicate this difficult material.) He is sometimes confused with another Australian director with the same name, who directed such films as *The Man From Snowy River* (1982).

MILLER, PENELOPE ANN. Actress. *(b. Jan. 13, 1964, Los Angeles.)* This winsome, wholesome young actress has the dubious distinction of having given Pee-wee Herman his first screen kiss (in 1988's *Big Top Pee-wee*), but has gone on to costar with such formidable actors as Marlon Brando, Robert De Niro, and Al Pacino. Miller made her film debut in *Adventures in Babysitting* (1987), but first attracted notice reprising her Broadway performance in Neil Simon's *Biloxi Blues*

(1988). Other films quickly followed, including *Miles from Home* (1988), *Dead-Bang* (1989), *Downtown,* and *Kindergarten Cop* (both 1990). She was a slyly funny daughter to comic Mafioso Brando in *The Freshman* (1990) and a warm friend to Robert De Niro in *Awakenings* (also 1990). She was miscast as Danny De Vito's adversary in *Other People's Money* (1991), and was marking time in the leading roles of two 1992 releases, *Year of the Comet* and *The Gun in Betty Lou's Handbag.* Her appearance as Charlie Chaplin's leading lady Edna Purviance in *Chaplin* that same year promised more, but was far too brief to make any impact. Then in 1993 she won the most ambitious role of her career, as Al Pacino's girlfriend (a topless dancer, no less) in *Carlito's Way;* the character caused Miller to stretch more than she ever had on-screen before, and leave behind some of the "nice-girl" blandness of her earlier work. In 1994 she won the role of Margo Lane, girlfriend to Lamont Cranston, aka *The Shadow.* Her father is actor-director Mark Miller, best remembered as the leading man on the TV sitcom "Please Don't Eat the Daisies."

MILLS, HAYLEY. Actress. *(b. Apr. 18, 1946, London.)* In the 1960s, Mills (daughter of actor John Mills and playwright-novelist Mary Hayley Bell, and younger sister of actress Juliet Mills) was one of the world's top child stars. She proved herself a more than capable dramatic performer at the age of twelve in her debut film, *Tiger Bay* (1959), costarring with her father. For her performance as a terrorized girl who witnesses a murder and is abducted by the killer, Mills earned an acting prize at the Berlin Film Festival and a five-year contract with Walt Disney. Her first Disney production was *Pollyanna* (1960), a remake of the Eleanor H. Porter novel which Mary Pickford had filmed forty years earlier. Playing the ever-cheerful and optimistic title character, Mills earned a special Academy Award: a miniature statuette for giving "the most outstanding juvenile performance during 1960." Following *Pollyanna,* Disney cast her in a series of highly popular family-oriented films: *The Parent Trap* (1961, cast as twins), *In Search of the Castaways* (1962), *Summer Magic* (1963), and *That Darn Cat* (1965). She also took a pair of

challenging dramatic roles away from the Disney studio: *Whistle Down the Wind* (1961, based on a work by her mother), in the role of a fifteen-year-old who mistakes a murderer for Jesus Christ, and *The Chalk Garden* (1964), playing a sixteen-year-old who lives in a fantasy world and attempts to unearth the mystery of her new governess. She costarred as a mischievous nun-in-training in *The Trouble With Angels* (1966), and worked with her father once more in *A Matter of Innocence* (1967), aka *Pretty Polly,* but the mystique of her innocence was irrevocably tarnished when she played a nude scene in *The Family Way* (1966), an otherwise innocuous comedy. She made headlines when she engaged in a highly publicized affair with that film's director, Roy Boulting, who was more than thirty years her senior; they wed in 1971, and later divorced. She made occasional, mostly forgettable films in the 1970s, including *Take a Girl Like You* (1970), *Endless Night* (1971), and *The Kingfisher Caper* (1975). Long out of the limelight, Mills returned to familiar turf to star in a trio of movies made for cable television's The Disney Channel: *Parent Trap II* (1986); *Parent Trap III* (1989); and *Parent Trap Hawaiian Honeymoon* (1989), as well as the more dramatic *Back Home* (1990).

MILLS, JOHN (SIR). Actor. *(b. Feb. 22, 1908, North Elmham, England.)* Unprepossessing and slight of stature, Mills played mild-mannered but iron-willed leads early in his career, instead of callow juveniles. He built on this foundation to become one of England's most reliable and enormously popular stars. A teacher's son, he gravitated to the stage as a youth, and was already an accomplished song-and-dance man in his early 20s (a skill he put to good use in an early starring vehicle, 1937's *Four Dark Hours,* aka *The Green Cockatoo).*

Mills' early films included *The Midshipmaid* (1932), *Those Were the Days* (1934), *Tudor Rose* (1936), and *O.H.M.S.* (1937). His role as the grown Peter Colley in the successful U.S.-Britain coproduction *Goodbye, Mr. Chips* (1939) introduced him to American filmgoers. A medical discharge forced him out of World War 2, but he contributed to morale by fighting the war on-screen, playing authoritative characters in such popular and important films as Noël Coward's *In Which We Serve* (1942, his first encounter with codirector David Lean), *We Dive at Dawn* (1943), and *This Happy Breed* (1944, again for Coward and Lean).

Lean's *Great Expectations* (1946) gave Mills one of his greatest parts, as Pip, the former orphan who becomes a gentleman of means, in this superb rendering of Dickens' novel. It propelled Mills into a string of solid films, including *The October Man, So Well Remembered* (both 1947), *Scott of the Antarctic* (1948), *The History of Mr. Polly* (1949), *The Rocking Horse Winner* (also 1949, a particularly memorable performance), *Morning Departure* (1950), *Mr. Denning Drives North* (1951), *The Long Memory* (1952), *Hobson's Choice* (1954, again for David Lean), *The End of the Affair* (1955), *Escapade* (1955), *War and Peace* (1956, excellent as a Russian peasant), *Town on Trial* (1957), *I Was Monty's Double* (1958), and *Tunes of Glory* (1960), which saw him in top form as a callous army colonel who's about to crack up.

In 1959 Mills acted opposite daughter Hayley in *Tiger Bay,* and was upstaged by the precocious child, who was immediately signed by Walt Disney and brought to America. (John also worked for Disney, as the head of the *Swiss Family Robinson* in 1960.) Father and daughter worked together again in *The Chalk Garden* (1964), *The Truth About Spring* (1965), and *The Family Way* (1966).

The 1960s saw Mills evolve from leading man to character actor, with seeming ease, in films like *The Singer Not the Song* (1961), *Tiara Tahiti* (1962), *King Rat* (1965), *The Wrong Box* (1966, a very funny comic outing), *Africa—Texas Style!, Chuka* (both 1967), *Lady Hamilton* (1968), *Oh! What a Lovely War,* and *Run Wild, Run Free* (both 1969). Submerged beneath heavy makeup, Mills portrayed a village idiot in *Ryan's Daughter* (1970) for David Lean, and won a Best Supporting Actor Oscar for a performance that was uncharacteristically overstated. Since then Mills has chosen to keep as busy as possible, taking supporting (and even cameo) roles in films of extremely variable quality: *Lady Caroline Lamb* (1972), *Oklahoma Crude* (1973), *The Human Factor* (1975), *Dirty Knight's Work* (1976), *The Big Sleep, The Thirty-Nine Steps* (both 1978), *Zulu Dawn* (1979), *Gandhi* (1982, one of his best latter-day appearances), *Sherlock Holmes and the Masks of Death* (1984 telefilm, as an aging Dr. Watson), *Sahara* (also 1984), *Who's That Girl?* (1987), and *The Last Straw* (1991). In 1993 he played the Blind Man in the cable-TV remake of *Frankenstein.* He also directed *Gypsy Girl* (1966), his sole effort behind the camera, which starred Hayley. Mills' other daughter, Juliet, is also an actress; she made her film debut as an infant in his *In Which We Serve,* and also played with him in *So Well Remembered, The October Man, The History of Mr. Polly,* and *The Last Straw.* She did a few minor ingenue parts in the early 1960s, then achieved greater success in television, especially as the star of the sitcom "Nanny and the Professor." Her only major starring film was Billy Wilder's *Avanti!* (1972).

MIMIEUX, YVETTE. Actress. (b. Jan. 8, 1942, Los Angeles.) This beautiful blonde first became known to moviegoers as an appealing ingenue in such early 1960s films as *The Time Machine* (her first), *Where the Boys Are* (both 1960), *Light in the Piazza* (one of her best parts), *Four Horsemen of the Apocalypse, The Wonderful World of the Brothers Grimm,* and *Diamond Head* (all 1962). Her surprisingly skilled performance as Dean Martin's childlike bride in *Toys in the Attic* (1963) engendered favorable critical comments, but Mimieux's subsequent films found her taking undemanding roles in mediocre movies, including *Joy in the Morning* (1965), *The Caper of the Golden Bulls, Monkeys, Go Home!* (both 1967), *Dark of the Sun, Three in the Attic* (both 1968), *The Picasso Summer* (1969), *The Delta Factor* (1970), *Skyjacked* (1972), *The Neptune Factor* (1973), *Journey Into Fear* (1975), *Jackson County Jail* (1976, a sleazy melodrama that saw Mimieux victimized in a graphic, brutal rape scene), *Outside Chance* (1978), *The Black Hole* (1979, an ambitious but only partially successful sci-fi film produced by Disney), and *Circle of Power* (1983). She worked extensively in TV during the 1970s and 1980s, starring in a slew of made-fors (one of which, 1974's *Hit Lady,* she also wrote) and even doing episodic work. Her *Obsessive Love* (1984, which she also cowrote and coproduced) convincingly depicted an older woman/younger man romance. Mimieux was once married to director Stanley Donen.

MINEO, SAL. Actor, director. *(b. Jan. 10, 1939, Bronx, N.Y., as Salvatore Mineo; d. Feb. 12, 1976.)* Back in the mid 1950s, Mineo was one of the most talented and exciting adolescent actors working in Hollywood. He earned his acting stripes on Broadway, appearing first in "The Rose Tattoo" (1951) and then in "The King and I" (1952), taking over the role of Yul Brynner's son. He effortlessly made the transition to the screen, appearing in *Six Bridges to Cross* and *The Private War of Major Benson* (both 1955) before earning celluloid immortality opposite James Dean and Natalie Wood in the teen angst classic *Rebel Without a Cause* (1955). For his role as the soulful, abandoned Plato, he earned a Best Supporting Actor Academy Award nomination. Mineo went on to play variations of the role in such films as *Crime in the Streets* (1956), *Dino* (1957), and *The Young Don't Cry* (1957). He was also featured in *Somebody Up There Likes Me, Rock, Pretty Baby,* and *Giant* (all 1956). He starred in Walt Disney's *Tonka* (1958, as a Sioux brave), *A Private's Affair* (1959), *The Gene Krupa Story* (1959, in the title role), and received another Oscar nomination for his last important role, the young Holocaust survivor Don Landau in *Exodus* (1960). Mineo was just another face among the all-star casts in *The Longest Day* (1962) and *The Greatest Story Ever Told* (1965), but John Ford gave him a good part in *Cheyenne Autumn* (1964) playing an Indian named Red Shirt. In 1969, he directed "Fortune and Men's Eyes," a drama of homosexuality behind bars, on the Los Angeles and Broadway stages. By this time he was finding it tougher and tougher to find good parts; his later films include *Who Killed Teddy Bear?* (1965), *80 Steps to Jonah, Krakatoa, East of Java* (both 1969), and *Escape From the Planet of the Apes* (1971). He was stabbed to death outside his Hollywood apartment in 1976; his murderer was never found.

MINNELLI, LIZA. Actress, singer. *(b. Mar. 12, 1946, Los Angeles.)* Rather than languish forever in the shadow of her supremely talented parents (Judy Garland and Vincente Minnelli)—as has been the fate of some talented offspring of megastars—this bright-eyed bundle of energy has forged her own career with strength and determination. And if she doesn't immediately come to mind as a movie star, don't forget that she won an Oscar for her portrayal of Sally Bowles in *Cabaret* (1972) and was nominated for her heart-tugging performance in *The Sterile Cuckoo* (1969) as well. Liza made her film debut as a toddler in her mom's starring vehicle *In the Good Old Summertime* (1949), and at 18 began establishing herself as a talented singer and dancer in nightclubs and on stage. Her (relative) failure to attain true movie-star status derives from some of the feeble properties in which she's appeared. Minnelli has picked up an impressive array of awards in her career: three Tonys (one for "Flora, the Red Menace," one for "The Act," and a special citation), one Emmy (for the TV special "Liza With a Z"), and the aforementioned Oscar.
OTHER FILMS INCLUDE: 1968: *Charlie Bubbles;* 1970: *Tell Me That You Love Me, Junie Moon;* 1974: *That's Entertainment!;* 1975: *Lucky Lady;* 1976: *A Matter of Time* (the last film directed by her father, and a bomb); 1977: *New York, New York;* 1981: *Arthur* (her biggest screen success post-*Cabaret);* 1984: *The Muppets Take Manhattan;* 1985: *That's Dancing!, A Time to Live* (made for TV); 1988: *Arthur 2: On the Rocks, Rent-a-Cop;* 1991: *Stepping Out.*

MINNELLI, VINCENTE. Director. *(b. Feb. 28, 1910, Chicago; d. July 25, 1986.)* This onetime art director (he worked in that capacity at New York's Radio City Music Hall before becoming a Broadway director) is remembered as one of American cinema's most distinctive and creative visual stylists. His lavish use of color and, in the 1950s, widescreen, was praised by French critics who deemed him a master of "mise-en-scène." A generation of younger American filmmakers, including Martin Scorsese (whose 1977 *New York, New York,* starring Vincente and Judy Garland's daughter Liza Minnelli, contains many touches in homage to Minnelli) has cited him as an influence. His best-known screen work was done in the musical genre, where he also worked as a stage director before going to Hollywood. He started out as a troubleshooter/jack-of-all-trades at MGM, contributing ideas to a number of different films before "flying solo" as a director.

Beginning with the all-black *Cabin in the Sky* (1943), Minnelli helmed a series of increasingly innovative musicals for MGM, including the exquisite *Meet Me in St. Louis* (1944), on which he first worked with Garland (they were married from 1945 to 1951), *An American in Paris* (1951, featuring Gene Kelly and an extended ballet sequence), and 1953's splendid *The Band Wagon*, with Fred Astaire and Cyd Charisse. Other Minnelli/MGM musicals include *Brigadoon* (1954), *Gigi* (1958), and *Bells Are Ringing* (1960). Two of his musicals had the distinction of winning Oscars as Best Picture (*An American in Paris*, for which he was nominated as Best Director, and *Gigi*, for which he won his only Academy Award). The same sense of style and visual finesse he brought to musical films served such emotional dramas as *Madame Bovary* (1949), *Tea and Sympathy* (1956), *Some Came Running* (1958), and *Home From the Hill* (1960), as well.

His behind-the-scenes-of-moviemaking soap operas, *The Bad and the Beautiful* (1952) and *Two Weeks in Another Town* (1962) are highwater marks in the Hollywood-on-Hollywood genre, while *Lust for Life* (1956) remains one of the finest films ever made about the passion of a great artist—in this case, Vincent van Gogh. Minnelli also exhibited a flair for light comedy, directing the popular 1950 Spencer Tracy–Elizabeth Taylor starrer, *Father of the Bride*, its 1951 sequel, *Father's Little Dividend*, plus *Designing Woman* (1957) and *The Reluctant Debutante* (1958). He even steered Lucille Ball and Desi Arnaz through the slapstick antics of *The Long, Long Trailer* (1954). It almost didn't matter what kind of film he tackled; any Minnelli movie had taste and style. In 1976 he came out of retirement to direct daughter Liza and Ingrid Bergman in *A Matter of Time;* the result was deemed a botch, and Minnelli denounced the studio-edited cut of the film, which was his last. His 1974 autobiography was titled "I Remember It Well."

OTHER FILMS INCLUDE: 1943: *I Dood It;* 1945: *The Clock, Yolanda and the Thief;* 1946: *Ziegfeld Follies, Undercurrent;* 1948: *The Pirate;* 1953: *The Story of Three Loves;* 1955: *The Cobweb, Kismet;* 1962: *Four Horsemen of the Apocalypse;* 1963: *The Courtship of Eddie's Father;* 1964: *Goodbye, Charlie;* 1965: *The Sandpiper;* 1970: *On a Clear Day You Can See Forever.*

MIRANDA, CARMEN. Singer, dancer, actress. *(b. Feb. 9, 1909, Lisbon, Portugal, as Maria da Cuhna; d. Aug. 5, 1955.)* The vivacious "Brazilian Bombshell," immediately identifiable by her bare-midriff costumes and elaborate, fruit-covered headwear, delighted American movie audiences with her energetic singing and dancing, and with her endless, often hysterical malapropisms. A Brazilian star whose fame extended to South American radio, records, and films (beginning with 1933's *A Voz do Carnaval),* she played Broadway and New York nightclubs before being signed by 20th Century-Fox in 1940, when Hollywood adopted the government's "good neighbor" policy—primarily to help sell films in South America to offset the WW 2-related loss of European markets.

She made a smashing debut in *Down Argentine Way* (1940), appearing with her own Brazilian band (in Technicolor segments photographed in New York and later edited—seamlessly—into the picture), and from that moment on she was a star, becoming a fixture in Fox musicals during the war years.

She was less in demand as the decade waned, and was stuck in a one-note mode, to Hollywood's way of thinking. Only *Copacabana* (1947) offered any challenge, allowing her to play a dual role. Her last screen appearance was a guest shot with Martin and Lewis in *Scared Stiff* (1953).

She died of a heart attack, after performing a dance number on a Jimmy Durante TV show.

OTHER FILMS INCLUDE: 1941: *That Night in Rio, Weekend in Havana;* 1942: *Springtime in the Rockies;* 1943: *The Gang's All Here* (singing her signature tune, "The Lady in the Tutti Frutti Hat"); 1944: *Four Jills in a Jeep, Greenwich Village;* 1945: *Doll Face;* 1946: *If I'm Lucky;* 1948: *A Date With Judy;* 1950: *Nancy Goes to Rio.*

MIRREN, HELEN. Actress. *(b. July 26, 1945, Chiswick, London.)* Commanding British actress who has proven her versatility and range in a series of consistently challenging parts. She began her career on stage with Britain's National Youth Theatre and later, the Royal Shakespeare Company, winning acclaim for performances in plays like "Troilus and Cressida" and "Hamlet." She made her film debut as Hermia in Peter Hall's version of *A Midsummer Night's Dream* (1968), and alternated between theater and movies from then on, costarring in *Age of Consent* (1969), *Savage Messiah* (1972), *O Lucky Man!* (1973), *Hussy,* and *Caligula* (both 1980) before eliciting raves for her turn as gangster Bob Hoskins' mistress in *The Long Good Friday* (1981). Mirren went on to give impressive performances in *Excalibur* (1981, as Morgana) and *2010* (1984, as a Russian cosmonaut), and won a Cannes Best Actress Award for her portrayal of an Irish widow in *Cal* (1984). Other films include *White Nights* (1985, again as a Russian), *The Mosquito Coast* (1986), *Pascali's Island* (1988), and the highly controversial *The Cook, The Thief, His Wife & Her Lover* (1989). More recently, she starred in *The Comfort of Strangers* (1991), the adaptation of *Where Angels Fear to Tread* (also 1991, as Lilia), *Dr. Bethune, The Hawk* (both 1993), and most notably, as "Mrs. King" in *The Madness of King George* (1994), for which she received a Supporting Actress Oscar nomination. She also starred as a tough police inspector in the acclaimed British TV miniseries "Prime Suspect" (1992–). Many actresses are described as "fearless," but the word really applies to Mirren, who can—and will—do anything that befits her character—and who is drawn to unusual, provocative parts. She has lived for many years with producer-director Taylor Hackford.

MITCHELL, CAMERON. Actor. *(b. Nov. 4, 1918, Dallastown, Pa.; d. July 6, 1994.)* Rugged, multipurpose actor whose Broadway credits go back to "Jeremiah," in 1939. He debuted on screen in 1945's *What Next, Corporal Hargrove?* and made a handful of films for MGM, including *They Were Expendable* (also 1945), *Homecoming,* and *Command Decision* (both 1948) before returning to Broadway to originate the part of Happy, one of Willy Loman's sons, in the landmark 1949 production of Arthur Miller's "Death of a Salesman." He recreated the role on film in 1951—yet, that same year, Mitchell starred in the low-budget sci-fi movie *Flight to Mars,* a portent of things to come. He proved an all-purpose leading man in such A-list 1950s fare as *How to Marry a Millionaire* (1953), *Desiree* (1954), *Love Me or Leave Me, Strange Lady in Town, The Tall Men, House of Bamboo* (all 1955), and *Carousel* (1956). Two of his best films were *Monkey on My Back* (1957), as drug-addicted fighter Barney Ross, and *No Down Payment* (also 1957), as an ambitious war veteran.

By the early 1960s, he was relegated to such foreign-made, sword-and-sandal epics as *The Last of the Vikings* (1960), *Erik the Conqueror* (1961), and *Caesar the Conqueror* (1963). Leading roles in *Blood and Black Lace* (1964) *Man-Eater of Hydra* (1967), and *Rebel Rousers* (1970, top-billed over Jack Nicholson, Bruce Dern, and Diane Ladd) were sandwiched between supporting roles in such Hollywood fare as *Hombre* (1967), *Buck and the Preacher* (1972), and *The Midnight Man* (1974). His later credits included such low-grade fare as *The Toolbox Murders* (1978), *Blood Link* (1983), *Kill-Point* (1984), *The Tomb* (1985), *Hollywood Cop* (1987), *Deadly Prey* and *Nightforce* (both 1987). Mitchell starred in a trio of television series, the most successful of which was "High Chaparral" (1967–71), cast as Buck Cannon; the others were "The Beachcomber" (1960–61) and "Swiss Family Robinson" (1975–76).

MITCHELL, THOMAS. Actor. *(b. July 11, 1892, Elizabeth, N.J.; d. Dec. 17, 1962.)* During his screen tenure, this remarkable actor essayed a series of memorable roles that, collectively, comprise a body of work rivaled by few other supporting players. Mitchell's list of credits reads like a roster of Hollywood's most famous movies. He nearly always *looked* the same—fleshy and rumpled, with unruly hair and burning eyes—but his performances varied greatly in range, though they were consistent in their intensity. He worked as a reporter, and eventually wrote some plays before settling on the other side of the footlights. He first attracted serious critical attention as the cocky embezzler in *Lost Horizon* (1937), and then appeared in a dazzling array of films during 1939: *Only Angels Have Wings, Mr. Smith Goes to Washington, Gone With the Wind* (as Scarlett O'Hara's father), *The Hunchback of Notre Dame,* and *Stagecoach,* for which he won an Oscar playing a drunken, fatalistic doctor. Contemporary moviegoers might know him more immediately for his portrayal of James Stewart's ne'er-do-well Uncle Billy in *It's a Wonderful Life* (1946). He was playing Daniel Webster in *The Devil and Daniel Webster* (1941) when a runaway horse cart sidelined him, and forced the producers to reshoot all his footage with Edward Arnold.

OTHER FILMS INCLUDE: 1936: *Craig's Wife, Theodora Goes Wild;* 1937: *Make Way for Tomorrow, The Hurricane* (another Oscar-nominated performance); 1938: *Trade Winds;* 1940: *Our Town* (as Dr. Gibbs), *The Long Voyage Home, Angels Over Broadway, Swiss Family Robinson;* 1942: *This Above All, Tales of Manhattan;* 1943: *The Outlaw;* 1944: *Wilson, The Sullivans;* 1949: *Alias Nick Beal;* 1952: *High Noon* (as the mayor); 1954: *Destry;* 1956: *While the City Sleeps;* 1961: *Pocketful of Miracles.*

MITCHUM, ROBERT. Actor. *(b. Aug. 6, 1917, Bridgeport, Conn.)* An underrated performer for much of his lengthy career, Robert Mitchum in recent years has finally earned the respect that should have been paid him years ago—although, ironically, most of his recent screen work has shown the aging lion guilty of the apathetic listlessness of which he was accused in earlier days. Tall and broad chested, with sleepy eyes, Mitchum always moved with languid, catlike grace and delivered his dialogue in deep voice with careful deliberation, a mode of acting that didn't always endear him to critics. But more often than not, something was *seething* beneath that placid, casual exterior. There was *always* more to Mitchum than the obvious, whether benign or malignant. And that quality has kept him in stardom's top rank for many years.

As a youth Mitchum wandered around the country, sometimes taking odd jobs, sometimes traveling aimlessly like a hobo. The itinerant finally settled down in 1940, marrying his high-school sweetheart and taking a job in a southern California airplane factory. Bitten by the acting bug, he joined a local theater group and drifted into movie work in 1943. He played heavies (and one sympathetic secondary character) in several Hopalong Cassidy Westerns that year, including *Bar 20, Hoppy Serves a Writ, Border Patrol,* and *Colt Comrades.* Mitchum crashed other studios and took small roles in war films and horse operas, including *Beyond the Last Frontier, The Lone Star Trail, Corvette K-225, Gung Ho!, The Leather Burners, Doughboys in Ireland, Aerial Gunner, Cry Havoc, The Human Comedy,* and *Minesweeper*—all in 1943! That year he also supported Laurel and Hardy in *The Dancing Masters,* the first of his relatively few comedies.

RKO signed Mitchum in 1944 and gave him his big break, replacing cowboy star Tim Holt (who'd gone into wartime service) in two Zane Grey B Westerns, *Nevada* (1944) and *West of the Pecos* (1945). No great shakes as pictures, they did at least provide Mitchum with his first starring roles. He also made a cheapie thriller for Monogram, *When Strangers Marry* (1944), which elicited surprisingly favorable reviews, all of which directed attention to Mitchum's fine performance as a supposedly sympathetic character who turned out to be the heavy. That same year, his well-received supporting turn as Lt. Walker in *The Story of G.I. Joe* (1945) earned him an Oscar nomination. (After playing so many soldiers, he was finally drafted in 1945, but spent only a few months in the service before the war ended.)

By now a recognizable figure, Mitchum was loaned to MGM for *Undercurrent* (1946) and *Desire Me,* and to Warner Bros. for *Pursued* (both 1947). But his home studio, RKO, gave him a big buildup with good parts in high-profile films such as *Till the End of Time, The Locket* (both 1946), *Crossfire, Out of the Past* (both 1947, the latter being the archetypal film noir and a cornerstone in the building of Mitchum's tough-guy screen persona), *Rachel and the Stranger* (1948, in which he took third billing behind Loretta Young and William Holden), and *Blood on the Moon* (also 1948, a moody, atmospheric Western).

A well-publicized (and apparently trumped-up) 1948 arrest for marijuana possession convinced Mitchum that his career was over but, amazingly enough, the public took it in stride; perhaps such behavior wasn't very much out of character for this quietly menacing tough guy. After loaning him to Republic for the first-rate Steinbeck adaptation *The Red Pony* (1949), RKO kept Mitchum busy in a string of gritty melodramas and action films (and at least one lighthearted romance, 1949's *Holiday Affair*), including *The Big Steal* (1949), *Where Danger Lives* (1950), *The Racket* (cast as a hard-as-nails police captain in one of his best vehicles during this period), *My Forbidden Past, His Kind of Woman* (all 1951), *Macao, One Minute to Zero, Angel Face* (all 1952), *The Lusty Men* (also 1952, excellent as a lonely but independent rodeo cowboy), and *Second Chance* (1953). *She Couldn't Say No* (1954), an alleged comedy starring Jean Simmons, cast Mitchum as a small-town doctor in one of his few duds; it ended his decade-long association with RKO, then only a few years from corporate extinction.

At 20th Century-Fox, Mitchum starred in two routine but enjoyable adventure films, *White Witch Doctor* (1953, opposite Susan Hayward) and *River of No Return* (1954, opposite Marilyn Monroe). Then he got a career plum: the actor was sublimely menacing as a psychotic religious fanatic (with LOVE and HATE tattooed on his knuckles!) who plots to murder two children in *The Night of the Hunter* (1955), an atmospheric, almost hallucinogenic allegory brilliantly directed by actor Charles Laughton. It remains one of his all-time best films—and performances.

Among the highlights of Mitchum's subsequent career: *Heaven Knows, Mr. Allison* (1957), in which he played a Marine trapped with nun Deborah Kerr (a favorite and frequent costar) on a Japanese-infested island during World War 2; *Thunder Road* (1958), a low-budget, high-octane moonshining opus that saw Mitchum's son Jim playing his dad's brother (and which gave Mitchum a hit record in the title tune!); *Cape Fear* (1962), a taut thriller in which he delivered a truly blood-curdling performance as a slimy ex-convict who menaces lawyer Gregory Peck and his family; *El Dorado* (1967), which teamed him with John Wayne in Howard Hawks' loose remake of his own *Rio Bravo;* and David Lean's *Ryan's Daughter* (1970), which proved that he could play completely against type—here, as a quiet Irish schoolteacher.

By 1975, Mitchum's personal popularity and box-office potency had eroded, but he had a surprise hit in that year's *Farewell, My Lovely,* which cast him as Raymond Chandler's world-weary private eye Philip Marlowe. Although he was too old (and too paunchy) for the part, Mitchum acquitted himself nicely in the carefully made, faithfully adapted period piece. (He played Marlowe again in a 1978 remake of *The Big Sleep,* an updated misfire set and shot in England.)

Since then Mitchum has kept himself busy in a succession of theatrical movies, telefilms, and miniseries of varying quality. He even played William Randolph Hearst in a TV movie (1985's *The Hearst and Davies Affair);* his last starring vehicle for the big screen was *The Ambassador* (1984). A games-player in interviews, he professes indifference about his craft, but the evidence reveals otherwise. It's also clear that in spite of many mediocre films in recent years, he's still capable of delivering the goods when inspired by first-rate material (and/or a good director), as witness *The Friends of Eddie Coyle* (1973), *The Yakuza* (1975), and *Mr. North* (1988).

Mitchum, who had always eschewed TV series work, starred in the short-lived series "A Family for Joe" (1990), about which commitment he later claimed to have been deceived. He was also much praised for his work in the starring role of the miniseries "The Winds of War" (1983) and its sequel "War and Remembrance" (1988–89). Sons Jim and Christopher followed in the family footsteps, although without the old man's success. He gave a witty, knowing performance as a police lieutenant in Martin Scorsese's remake of *Cape Fear* (1991), and returned to the Western genre as narrator in *Tombstone* (1993). He also appeared in *Midnight Ride* (1993).

OTHER FILMS INCLUDE: 1955: *Not as a Stranger, Man With the Gun;* 1956: *Foreign Intrigue, Bandido;* 1957: *Fire Down Below, The Enemy Below;* 1958: *The Hunters;* 1959: *The Angry Hills;* 1960: *Home From the Hill, The Night Fighters, The Sundowners, The Grass Is Greener;* 1961: *The Last Time I Saw Archie;* 1962: *The Longest Day, Two for the Seesaw;* 1963: *The List of Adrian Messenger, Rampage;* 1964: *Man in the Middle, What a Way to Go!;* 1965: *Mister Moses;* 1968: *Anzio, Villa Rides, 5 Card Stud, Secret Ceremony;* 1969: *Young Billy Young, The Good Guys and the*

Bad Guys; 1972: *The Wrath of God;* 1976: *Midway, The Last Tycoon;* 1977: *The Amsterdam Kill;* 1978: *Matilda, Breakthrough;* 1980: *Nightkill;* 1981: *Agency;* 1982: *That Championship Season;* 1984: *Maria's Lovers;* 1988: *Scrooged;* 1989: *Jake Spanner, Private Eye* (a telefilm); 1993: *Woman of Desire.*

MIX, TOM. Actor. *(b. Jan. 6, 1880, Mix Run, Pa.; d. Oct. 12, 1940.)* Arguably the most important cowboy star who ever rode the cinema range—judging both by his popularity with silent-era moviegoers and his influence on the Western genre and its subsequent practitioners—Tom Mix was truly a larger-than-life figure. Reportedly a military-school graduate, a hero of both the Spanish-American War and the Boxer Rebellion, and a two-gun deputy marshal (in fact, he was none of these), he really had been a champion rodeo star and, briefly, a Texas Ranger. Hired by the Selig Company in 1910 to wrangle cattle for that studio's *Ranch Life in the Great Southwest,* Mix promoted a supporting role for himself, thereby launching a screen career that encompassed more than 100 short subjects and dozens of feature-length Westerns. His early features included an unauthorized version of Zane Grey's *The Light of Western Stars,* recut and retitled *The Heart of Texas Ryan* (1917) after Grey threatened legal action.

Joining the Fox Film Corporation in 1917, Mix initially starred in shorts that were loaded with action and were frequently comedic rather than melodramatic in content. An expert rider, marksman, and athlete, he did virtually all his own stunts. Mix was also a born showman who eschewed realism in favor of a fanciful, circus-like approach to Western-movie production. While not a trained actor, Mix succeeded in films when more talented performers failed because he cultivated an image for himself early on and seldom deviated from its presentation; whatever character name he was given, Tom Mix always played Tom Mix (a tack adopted by subsequent cowboy stars). *The Untamed,* a 1920 adaptation of a popular Max Brand novel, not only propelled Mix into the top rank of screen stars but established many of the conventions used in B Westerns thereafter. The next decade saw a dizzying succession of Mix vehicles

maintaining an amazing level of quality, including *Sky High* (1921), *Soft Boiled* (1923), *North of Hudson Bay* (also 1923, directed by John Ford), *The Best Bad Man* (1925), and *The Great K&A Train Robbery* (1926). Many of his greatest hits—such as *The Lone Star Ranger* (1923), *Riders of the Purple Sage, The Rainbow Trail* (both 1925), and *The Last Trail* (1927)—were adaptations *(legitimate* ones) of best-selling Zane Grey novels. His flashy outfits, sneered at by working cowboys, were nonetheless copied slavishly by the prairie poseurs who emulated him at every Hollywood studio. And his screen persona—that of a clean-living, sportsmanlike, good-natured cowpoke of almost superhuman ability—provided a blueprint for the characterization of every sagebrush star who followed.

During his peak years, the 1920s, Mix was pulling down $7,500 a week, making him one of moviedom's top-paid performers. But his exorbitant salary, combined with a 1927–28 slump in the market for Westerns, finally did him in at Fox, and he finished out the silent era in a brief series of lackluster oaters for the FBO studio controlled by Joseph Kennedy. Mix returned to the screen, talking, in a 1932–33 series of nine films released by Universal. The first two entries, *Destry Rides Again* (with no resemblance to the 1939 James Stewart version) and *Rider of Death Valley,* were among his best pictures, but the aging cowboy great was ill at 'ease before the microphone, and no longer agile enough to perform the breathtaking stunts that had enlivened his best silent efforts. He retired from films after 1933's *Rustlers' Roundup,* returning briefly in 1935's *The Miracle Rider,* a cheap Mascot serial in which he was extensively doubled. Mix often toured with circuses during the 1930s, and his name (and legend) provided the basis for a long-running radio show that began in 1933 and ended in 1950—10 years after the star met his death when his speeding roadster flipped over careening around a bend in an Arizona highway. He was portrayed by Bruce Willis(!) in *Sunset* (1988).

MIZOGUCHI, KENJI. Director, actor. *(b. May 16, 1898, Tokyo; d. Aug. 24, 1956.)* As a youth, Kenji Mizoguchi (growing up in desperate poverty) was a witness to the selling of his older sister as a geisha and his father's brutalization of his sister and mother, both of which had a penetrating effect on his worldview. It is no surprise, then, that once he reached his artistic maturity, Mizoguchi's chief thematic concern was the role—and particularly, the exploitation—of women in society. The abuse of second-class members of Japanese society had its roots in the nation's tradition; as such, many of his films reflect upon the social and sexual mores of feudal Japan. Mizoguchi began his film career as an actor, commenced directing in 1922, and ended up making over 80 features. Stylistically, his best films are noted for their expert use of shadow and light, graceful camera movement, and long takes. His initial artistic achievements, *Osaka Elegy* and *Sisters of the Gion* (both 1936), examine the plight of women in a male-oriented prewar society. *Osaka Elegy* is the story of a telephone operator whose life is left in shambles after being seduced by her boss; *Sisters of Gion* (which Mizoguchi remade in 1953 as *Gion Bayashi*) details the conflict between a tradition-bound geisha and her younger, more progressive-minded sister. During World War 2, Mizoguchi temporarily abandoned his emphasis on women to spotlight his country's militarism: the two-part *The Loyal 47 Ronin* (1941–42) is an epic about the legendary, historical figures who, as an act of honor, committed mass suicide. In the postwar years, his films remained concerned with Japanese history, but from a more critical and humanistic perspective as they depicted the manner in which women were victimized by a corrupt class system. *The Life of Oharu* (1952) was the first of many masterpieces. The film's heroine is a wealthy, respected woman who is seduced by a servant, and ends up a prostitute. The two main characters in *Ugetsu* (1953) are men: ambitious peasants, one craving wealth and the other wishing to become a samurai. In the course of the scenario the former abandons his wife, who is summarily murdered; the latter's mate is raped and becomes a prostitute. In *Sansho the Bailiff* (1954), a provincial governor's family is forced into exile, with the wife becoming a prostitute and the children finding themselves in a labor camp. *Chikamatsu Monogatari* (1954; U.S. title, *The Crucified Lovers*) tells of a forbidden affair between a merchant's spouse and her servant. In *Princess Yang Kwei Fei* (1955; original Japanese title, *Yokihi*)—set in China rather than Japan—an emperor falls for a beautiful servant. *Street of Shame* (1956), Mizoguchi's last film, is an examination of the lives of various prostitutes toiling at Dreamland, a present-day Tokyo brothel. Its point: the manner in which women are treated in Japan had changed little over the centuries.

MODINE, MATTHEW. Actor. *(b. Mar. 22, 1959, Loma Linda, Calif.)* Good-looking, mild-mannered "boy next door" type whose varied performances have transcended his youthful appearance and generally placid screen persona. Raised in Utah, Modine spent his teenage years in San Diego, and paid the rent in his early adult years by digging ditches, grinding valves, and working on cars. Studying acting with Stella Adler later paid off, when the tall, boyish actor landed his first role in John Sayles' *Baby, It's You* (1983), playing a high-school kid. Costarring parts in *Private School,* Robert Altman's *Streamers* (both 1983) and *The Hotel New Hampshire* (1984) followed, but it took a brilliant starring performance in *Birdy* (1984), as a traumatized Vietnam vet who thinks he's a bird, to make critics and audiences sit up and take notice. He starred in the youth-oriented *Vision Quest* (1985), then took the lead in Stanley Kubrick's challenging *Full Metal Jacket* (1987) and the actors' showcase *Orphans* (1987). His winning turn as an FBI agent in *Married to the Mob* (1988), with Michelle Pfeiffer, showed that Modine could handle lighter material, as well. Since then he's starred in *Gross Anatomy* (1989), *Memphis Belle, Pacific Heights* (both 1990), *Wind* (1992), *Equinox,* Robert Altman's *Short Cuts* (as a sexually distant doctor), the made-for-TV *And the Band Played On* (all 1993), *The Browning Version* (1994), *Bye Bye, Love, Fluke,* and *Cutthroat Island* (all 1995).

MOFFAT, DONALD. Actor. *(b. Dec. 26, 1930, Plymouth, England.)* Tall, imposing stage and screen actor who has been appearing with greater frequency on the big screen over the last several years. Equally adept at comic or dramatic roles, he is often cast as an authority figure. Among his credits: *Rachel, Rachel* (1968), *Earthquake* (1974), *H.E.A.L.T.H.* (1979), *Popeye* (1980), *The Thing* (1982), *Alamo Bay* (1985), *The Best of Times* (1986), *Music Box* (1989), *Class Action* (1991), *HouseSitter* (1992) and *Clear and Present Danger* (1994). He has done three films for director Philip Kaufman: *The Great Northfield, Minnesota Raid* (1972), *The Unbearable Lightness of Being* (1988, as Daniel Day-Lewis' superior in the Czech hospital), and, most memorably, *The Right Stuff* (1983), in a broad caricature of President Lyndon B. Johnson. Moffat has also logged frequent appearances on TV.

MOLINA, ALFRED. Actor. *(b. May 24, 1953, London.)* Molina is one of those rare, chameleonlike performers who disappears into every part he plays. This large, ungainly-looking character actor performed in a two-man comedy act and worked with the Royal Shakespeare Company before making his film debut as the treacherous guide who almost gets the golden idol from Indiana Jones at the beginning of *Raiders of the Lost Ark* (1981). Alternating among films, theater, and TV since then, Molina appeared in *Meantime* (1983), *Water, Eleni,* and *Ladyhawke* (all 1985) before commanding attention for his quiet, charming, and credible performance as the Russian sailor on leave in *Letter to Brezhnev* (also 1985). Two years later he played the showier part of playwright Joe Orton's lover Kenneth Halliwell in *Prick Up Your Ears* (1987) and won rave reviews. Following *Manifesto* (1988) and *Drowning in the Shallow End* (1989), he was Sally Field's Iranian-born husband who is transformed from a loving spouse to a threatening tyrant in *Not Without My Daughter* (1991), and then got one of his most sympathetic parts in *Enchanted April* (1992), as the stuffed-shirt Briton who mellows in the Italian sun. He proved to be a perfect Western heavy in *Maverick* (1994) and was equally convincing as a Cuban emigré in *The Perez Family* (1995).

MONROE, MARILYN. Actress. *(b. June 1, 1926, Los Angeles, as Norma Jean Mortenson; d. Aug. 5, 1962.)* Probably no other movie star—certainly no female one—has had her life as documented, discussed, and dissected.

Her unhappy childhood has been well reported, as has her early work as a pinup model and her eventual signing by 20th Century-Fox. She was barely visible in *Scudda Hoo! Scudda Hay!* (1948), *Ladies of the Chorus* (1949), and *A Ticket to Tomahawk* (1950), but had a memorable bit opposite Groucho Marx in *Love Happy* (1949). She first turned heads with minor but well-crafted supporting roles (as mistresses) in two 1950 classics, *All About Eve* and *The Asphalt Jungle.*

It's difficult to pinpoint, at this late date, just who it was that first spotted the quiet blonde and saw in her a latent star quality that eluded others. (Certainly there are many who *claimed* to have recognized her talent.) In any event, her buildup began with better parts in *Love Nest, Let's Make It Legal* (both 1951), *Clash by Night, We're Not Married,* and *Monkey Business* (all 1952). Though used most frequently as a sex object, it was clear that she had a sense of comedy and a magnetic screen presence. Her first leading role, as a psychotic baby-sitter in a 1952 programmer, *Don't Bother to Knock,* identified Monroe as an emerging talent. She became a full-fledged star in 1953, shining as the murderous wife in *Niagara,* the husband-hunting, not-so-dumb blonde in *How to Marry a Millionaire,* and the delightfully scheming showgirl Lorelei Lee in *Gentlemen Prefer Blondes* (performing the classic "Diamonds Are a Girl's Best Friend"). She showed some real fire in the Western *River of No Return* (1954), and resumed singing-and-dancing chores in *There's No Business Like Show Business* that same year. Billy Wilder's *The Seven Year Itch* (1955), a funny if mildly salacious comedy featuring Monroe as the lust object of bored husband Tom Ewell, included the classic scene in which the blond bombshell stands over a subway grating and has her skirt billowed by the breeze of a passing train. Her genuine sex appeal, wholesome yet somehow unattainable, made her a natural love goddess. (Her marriage to baseball hero Joe DiMaggio in 1954 completed the larger-than-life image.)

Monroe, knowing that her star was on the ascent but keenly aware of her thespic limitations, studied with the New York guru of the Actors' Studio, Lee Strasberg, and subsequently gave a powerful performance as a hapless entertainer in *Bus Stop* (1956), and she took a flyer as producer of the unsuccessful *The Prince and the Showgirl* (1957), which teamed her with Laurence Olivier (who also directed)—and revealed no chemistry between the two. Wilder cast her as ukelele-strumming band singer Sugar Kane in his energetic 1920s farce *Some Like It Hot* (1959) and, in spite of well-publicized on-the-set tension, again got a delicious comic performance from her. Monroe, wracked by personal problems, insecurity, and self-induced health problems, only completed two more films: *Let's Make Love* (1960), an entertaining if unsubstantial movie costarring Yves Montand, and *The Misfits* (1961), a thoughtful and powerful drama written for her by her then-husband Arthur Miller and directed by John Huston (who'd cast her eleven years earlier in *The Asphalt Jungle*). Again, there was more written about the film's troubled production than about the picture itself—it was said to have brought on costar Clark Gable's fatal heart attack—but it served Monroe well, with a substantial part that indicated her still-untapped potential.

Her behavior became more and more erratic, and she was fired from Fox's 1962 *Something's Got to Give* (which was revamped and filmed the next year as *Move Over, Darling* with Doris Day). Soon after she was found dead, from an "accidental overdose" of pills, though her alleged affairs with both John and Robert Kennedy have brought out foul-play conspiracists by the carload. In 1963 Fox released a compilation feature, *Marilyn,* and a list of books and articles written about her would itself fill a book. Her tragic death—and troubled life—have inspired authors, songwriters, pop psychologists, and fervent fans, some of whom weren't alive during her heyday in the 1950s. She has also been portrayed—literally and symbolically—in a number of features and TV movies, most notably by Catherine Hicks in *Marilyn: The Untold Story* (1980, made for TV) and Theresa Russell in *Insignificance* (1985). It is obvious, however, that Monroe's many portrayers, and pretenders, can only hint at the natural charisma and sex appeal she projected.

MONTALBAN, RICARDO. Actor. *(b. Nov. 25, 1920, Mexico City.)* For several years this tall, dark, and handsome Mexican matinee idol vied with Fernando Lamas for the position of MGM's resident "Latin lover" (we're still not sure who won). A stage-trained actor who appeared on Broadway, in Mexican films (beginning in 1942), and even in some U.S.-made "soundies" (including *He's a Latin from Staten Island*) before signing with Metro in 1948, Montalban was a charming leading man, often in musicals, but was even more effective when he made the transition to character parts, particularly in *Sayonara* (1957, as a famous Kabuki actor) and *Cheyenne Autumn* (1964, as the Indian Little Wolf). He again played a Native American—this time a chief of the Sioux tribe—in the TV miniseries "How the West Was Won" (1976) and earned an Emmy for his performance. In 1982 the *Star Trek* team remembered his forceful performance in an episode of the series ("Space Seed") that aired fifteen years earlier, and fashioned *Star Trek II: The Wrath of Khan* around that character's villainy. All of this was obscured by the actor's great success as ringleader of the popular "Fantasy Island" TV series (1978–84), in which he played the ubiquitous Mr. Roarke. He has remained active in episodic TV, telefilms, and even commercials (in which he memorably sold cars outfitted in "rich Corinthian leather"). He published his autobiography, "Reflection: A Life in Two Worlds," in 1980.

OTHER FILMS INCLUDE: 1947: *Fiesta;* 1948: *On an Island with You, The Kissing Bandit;* 1949: *Neptune's Daughter, Border Incident, Battleground;* 1950: *Mystery Street, Right Cross, Two Weeks With Love;* 1951: *Across the Wide Missouri;* 1953: *Sombrero, Latin Lovers;* 1954: *The Saracen Blade;* 1956: *Three for Jamie Dawn;* 1960: *Let No Man Write My Epitaph;* 1966: *The Money Trap, Madame X, The Singing Nun;* 1968: *Sol Madrid, Blue;* 1969: *Sweet Charity;* 1971: *Escape from the Planet of the Apes;* 1972: *Conquest of the Planet of the Apes;* 1973: *The Train Robbers;* 1976: *Joe Panther;* 1984: *Cannonball Run II;* 1988: *The Naked Gun.*

MONTAND, YVES. Actor. *(b. Oct. 13, 1921, Florence, as Ivo Livi; d. Nov. 9, 1991.)* Italian-born singing star and actor of international renown whose world-weary appearance and cynical manner made him an oddly personable if not overly charismatic, leading man. Montand's family moved to France to escape Mussolini's evil influence. As a boy, he quit school and took a number of menial jobs. He was "discovered" singing in a small night spot by Edith Piaf, who offered him guidance and gave him a part in her 1946 movie *Star Without Light.* Montand made several unimportant films before attaining international stardom as one of the truck drivers carrying nitroglycerin in Henri-Georges Clouzot's classic thriller *The Wages of Fear* (1952). He subsequently starred in *Heroes and Sinners* (1955) and—with his wife Simone Signoret—in a French adaptation of Arthur Miller's *The Crucible* (1956), among others, before coming to America, first with a one-man show on Broadway and then as a leading man in Hollywood. He got to sing in his debut film, *Let's Make Love* (1960), which introduced him to American moviegoers in a high-profile teaming with Marilyn Monroe. He then worked in both English-language and continental films, including *Sanctuary, Goodbye Again* (both 1961), *My Geisha* (1962, *Grand Prix, Is Paris Burning?* (both 1966), and the musical *On a Clear Day You Can See Forever* (1970). A political activist himself, Montand's most fruitful collaboration was with radical filmmaker Costa Gavras, beginning with *The Sleeping Car Murder* (1965) and continuing with *Z* (1969), *The Confession* (1970), and *State of Siege* (1973). Other key films include Claude Lelouch's *Live for Life* (1967), Jean-Luc Godard's *Tout va bien* (1972), *César and Rosalie* (also 1972), and *Vincent, François, Paul and the Others* (1974). Toward the end of his life Montand delivered a stunning character performance as a greedy, scheming farmer in Claude Berri's two-part saga *Jean de Florette* and *Manon of the Spring* (1986). He remained a major star in his homeland to his dying day. His last film was *IP5* (1992).

MONTEZ, MARIA. Actress. *(b. June 6, 1918, Barahona, Dominican Republic, as Maria Africa Vidal de Santo Silas; d. Sept. 7, 1951.)* Exotic leading lady best remembered for a string of Technicolor escapist adventures she made in the 1940s opposite Jon Hall. A sensual, curvaceous bru-

nette whose thick accent couldn't conceal her obvious lack of ability, she was the daughter of the Dominican Republic's Spanish consul, and enjoyed a brief career as a photographic model before being signed to a movie contract by Universal. After "testing" the newly rechristened Montez in cheapie Westerns and B films—including *Boss of Bullion City* (1940), *Raiders of the Desert, The Invisible Woman, Moonlight in Hawaii* (all 1941), *The Mystery of Marie Roget,* and *Bombay Clipper* (both 1942)—the studio gave her a break.

Montez was assigned to Walter Wanger's lavish (and downright silly) Technicolor fantasy *Arabian Nights* (1942), cast as the fabled dancing girl Scheherazade, and given second billing (beneath Jon Hall). Although her acting was hopeless, she bewitched moviegoers in the mood for opulent escapism. The film was a big hit, and Universal reteamed the stars in *White Savage* (1943), *Ali Baba and the Forty Thieves, Cobra Woman, Gypsy Wildcat* (all 1944), and *Sudan* (1945, which saw Hall demoted to third billing behind Montez and Universal contractee Turhan Bey). The films all hewed to a simple formula based on the adroit blending of action, romance, low comedy, and high camp (before that term worked its way into the pop-culture lexicon). While Montez never really mastered the art of screen acting, she settled comfortably into the siren roles routinely written for her.

When the Hall-Montez cycle finally played itself out, she starred in several more (mostly minor) features for Universal, including *Tangier* (1946), *The Exile,* and *Pirates of Monterey* (both 1947), before being dropped. After making *Siren of Atlantis* (1948) Montez and her husband, French actor Jean-Pierre Aumont, went to Europe, where she top-lined a few forgettable Italian and French actioners before suffering a fatal heart attack while taking an unusually hot bath. Her daughter Tina Aumont is also an actress.

MONTGOMERY, GEORGE. Actor. *(b. Aug. 29, 1916, Brady, Mont., as George Montgomery Letz.)* This brawny, virile leading man, best remembered for his numerous Westerns, was a true son of the west, born into a large Montana family. He studied interior decorating at the University of Montana and engaged in collegiate athletics as well. Drifting to Hollywood in search of movie work, he settled at Republic Pictures, where he played bits and performed stunts in such low-budget Westerns as *The Singing Vagabond* (1935, his first film), and Gene Autry's *Springtime in the Rockies* (1937), and *Gold Mine in the Sky* (1938). Billed as George Letz, he won his first sizable movie role as one of five "suspects" who could have been under the mask in *The Lone Ranger* (also 1938), Republic's million-dollar serial.

After more supporting roles at Republic, Letz was signed by 20th Century-Fox. Initially slotted in B-plus horse operas—including *The Cisco Kid and the Lady* (1940, in support), *The Last of the Duanes,* and *Riders of the Purple Sage* (both 1941)—and now billed as George Montgomery, he was groomed for stardom. He appeared in a raft of high-grade programmers and A pictures, including *Cadet Girl* (1941), *Orchestra Wives, Ten Gentlemen From West Point, China Girl, Roxie Hart* (all 1942), and *Coney Island* (1943, opposite Fox's top draw, Betty Grable).

Montgomery had done well at Fox, but he left Hollywood to serve in the military during World War 2, and upon returning found himself mired in medium-budgeted, cookie-cutter Westerns (with one notable exception: he played Raymond Chandler's private eye Philip Marlowe in 1947's *The Brasher Doubloon).* To his credit, Montgomery matured into a capable, engaging performer, and even produced and directed some of his own films in the 1960s. But he became better known in the Hollywood community as a world-class furniture maker; he even supplemented his acting income by constructing sets and props for Columbia films, beginning in the late 1940s.

For many years married to singer Dinah Shore, he also starred in the TV series "Cimarron City" (1958–59). His 1981 book "The Years of George Montgomery" chronicles the actor's life and works, including his furniture-making, housebuilding, painting, and Western sculptures. In recent years he has presented a bronze of John Wayne to an annual recipient of his Hollywood Westerner Hall of Fame Award.

OTHER FILMS INCLUDE: 1948: *Lulu Belle, Belle Starr's Daughter;* 1950: *Dakota Lil, Davy Crockett, Indian Scout;* 1951: *The Sword of Monte Cristo, The Texas Rangers;* 1952: *Cripple Creek, The Pathfinder;* 1954: *Battle of Rogue River, Masterson of Kansas;* 1955: *Robber's Roost;* 1956: *Canyon River;* 1957: *Last of the Badmen;* 1958: *Toughest Gun in Tombstone;* 1959: *Watusi;* 1961: *The Steel Claw* (his first directorial effort); 1962: *Samar;* 1964: *From Hell to Borneo;* 1965: *Battle of the Bulge;* 1967: *Hostile Guns;* 1970: *Ride the Tiger;* 1986: *Wild Wind;* 1988: *Ransom in Blood.*

MONTGOMERY, ROBERT. Actor, director. (b. May 21, 1904, Beacon, N.Y., as Henry Montgomery, Jr.; d. Sept. 27, 1981.) As one of the youthful stage actors who migrated from Broadway to Hollywood at the dawn of the talkie era, this archetypal tall, dark, and handsome juvenile first endeared himself to moviegoers as an engaging leading man (sometimes affecting a British accent) in sophisticated comedies and drawing-room dramas; he later proved himself capable of much more. Born into a prominent family but rendered penniless after the death of his father and the failure of the family business, Montgomery worked in several odd jobs before his creative side asserted itself; he first tried writing (unsuccessfully), and switched to acting in the mid 1920s, eventually reaching Broadway and attracting favorable attention from reviewers.

Signed in 1929 by MGM, the studio that most assiduously courted stage talent, Montgomery made his screen debut opposite Greta Garbo in *The Single Standard* that year. He had sizable roles in *So This Is College, Untamed, Three Live Ghosts* (all 1929), *Their Own Desire, Free and Easy* (supporting Buster Keaton), and *The Divorcee,* before scoring his first triumph in the studio's all-star prison drama, *The Big House* (all 1930). That wildly successful film, along with *Private Lives* (1931, opposite frequent costar Norma Shearer in an elegant adaptation of the witty Noël Coward play), tagged Montgomery as a "comer."

He subsequently starred or costarred in countless Metro movies, generally cast as an upper-class sophisticate, including *Strangers May Kiss, Inspiration, Shipmates, Man in Possession* (all 1931), *Lovers Courageous, But the Flesh Is Weak, Letty Lynton, Blondie of the Follies,*

Faithless (all 1932), *Hell Below, Made on Broadway, Night Flight, Another Language* (all 1933), *Riptide, Forsaking All Others* (both 1934), *Vanessa, Her Love Story, Biography of a Bachelor Girl, No More Ladies* (all 1935), *Petticoat Fever, Piccadilly Jim* (both 1936), and *The Last of Mrs. Cheyney* (1937).

There were infrequent but welcome exceptions to the routine: In 1934 alone, he played an escaped convict on a cross-country bus trip in *Fugitive Lovers,* an amiable gangster on the lam in *Hideout,* and, best of all, a debonair Raffles-type cracksman trying to clear himself of murder in *The Mystery of Mr. X.* But Montgomery really shattered his image (over the objections of MGM boss Louis B. Mayer) by playing a psychotic killer in *Night Must Fall* (1937, based on a play written by Emlyn Williams for himself), startling both critics and audiences with his eye-opening performance, and earning a Best Actor Oscar nomination to boot.

Loaned to Warner Bros. for *Ever Since Eve* (also 1937), which turned out to be Marion Davies' last film (and a turkey besides), Montgomery returned to MGM and starred in several unmemorable if enjoyable pictures—including *Live, Love and Learn* (1937), *The First 100 Years, Yellow Jack, Three Loves Has Nancy* (all 1938), *Fast and Loose* (1939), and *Haunted Honeymoon* (1940, playing Dorothy Sayers' Lord Peter Wimsey in this MGM-financed, British-made mystery-comedy)—before stepping out of character again to play an American gangster who inherits a British estate in *The Earl of Chicago* (1940). He played another tough guy of the dese-dem-dose school, in a lighter vein, on loan to Columbia in *Here Comes Mr. Jordan* (1941). As the late prizefighter given a second chance at life, Montgomery delighted moviegoers in this wonderful fantasy and snagged his second Academy Award nomination. That same year, at RKO, he costarred opposite Carole Lombard in Alfred Hitchcock's *Mr. and Mrs. Smith,* one of the director's few (and, sadly, unsuccessful) forays into screen comedy.

Montgomery went into the Naval Reserve in 1941, and when war broke out served with distinction, first as a PT-boat commander in the Pacific, and later on board a destroyer in the European theater, where he participated in the D-Day invasion. Toward the end of the war he returned to the screen in *They Were Expendable* (1945), a moving story of, amazingly enough, PT-boat operations in the Pacific. Owing to his extensive experience, Montgomery was enlisted by director John Ford to help out behind the camera, and his good work enabled him to press MGM to let him direct a feature by himself. *Lady in the Lake* (1946), based on one of Raymond Chandler's Philip Marlowe mysteries, was built around the stylistic but thematically faithful conceit of showing the lead character's movements subjectively, with the camera acting as his eyes. The experiment came off as a gimmick, nothing more, but it marked Montgomery as a budding filmmaker with imagination.

Upon leaving MGM in 1947, Montgomery promoted another star-director parlay for himself, this time at Universal, where he made *Ride the Pink Horse,* a noirish thriller based on a Dorothy B. Hughes novel (but considerably reworked, to make the leading character more sympathetic for movie audiences). After acting in *The Saxon Charm, June Bride* (both 1948), and *Once More My Darling* (1949), Montgomery starred and directed in one final crime story, the British-made *Eye Witness* (1950), before leaving movies behind. (He returned to the screen only once more, playing a cameo in 1960's *The Gallant Hours,* a WW 2 drama starring James Cagney as Admiral "Bull" Halsey, which Montgomery produced and directed.) In 1955 he earned a Tony award for directing the Broadway production of "The Desperate Hours." He hosted and appeared in the TV anthology series "Robert Montgomery Presents" (1950–57); his daughter Elizabeth, best known as the lovable witch from the TV series "Bewitched," was a regular on her dad's show during the 1953–54 season.

Although Montgomery was a four-term president of the Screen Actors Guild, in the late 1930s he exposed organized-labor fraud in Hollywood amid much publicity. A political conservative, he organized the Hollywood Republican Committee to help elect Thomas Dewey and, more successfully, Dwight D. Eisenhower, to whom he became the first Media Consultant to the White House. He also took a vigorous anti-Communist stance and cooperated with the House Un-American Activities

Committee. In later years he wrote a book decrying the mediocrity of television programming.

MONTY PYTHON'S FLYING CIR-CUS. Actors, screenwriters. (*Graham Chapman*—b. Jan. 8, 1941, Leicester, England; d. Oct. 4, 1989. *John Cleese*—b. Oct. 27, 1939, Weston-super-Mare, England. *Terry Gilliam*—also director, animator—b. Nov. 22, 1940, Minneapolis. *Eric Idle*—b. Mar. 23, 1942, South Shields, England. *Terry Jones*—also director—b. Feb. 1, 1942, Colwyn Bay, North Wales. *Michael Palin*—b. May 5, 1943, Sheffield, England.)

This inspired, revolutionary group of anarchic satirists are probably second only to The Marx Brothers as the best-known comedic collective of this century. The five U.K.-born members of the group were all TV writers (Cleese, Idle, and Chapman wrote for David Frost, whom they later frequently lampooned) before concocting their own show in the late 1960s, in which they acted mainly because they thought no one else would. Gilliam had met Cleese when the latter toured the United States in another comedy troupe; finding that Gilliam had moved to England to work as a cartoonist, Cleese recruited him to do the bizarre cutout animation for the show. Their first feature-film foray, *And Now for Something Completely Different* (1972, directed by their regular series helmer Ian McNaughton), consisting of refilmed sketches from their show, was met by blank indifference and befuddlement by an American public that had never heard of them. But the troupe became a cult item when episodes of the series began airing in the United States shortly thereafter; around that time a couple of Python record albums also became must-owns among collegiate cognoscenti and others in the know. By the time their second film, the medieval sendup *Monty Python and the Holy Grail* (1975, codirected by Jones and Gilliam), opened in the States, America—or a particularly demented portion thereof—was ready for them.

The troupe's TV series ended in the mid-1970s—tall "silly walks" master Cleese had actually departed before its last season, to work on his own hysterical series "Fawlty Towers"—but Python's worldwide popularity reunited the group for two more proper film projects, both controversial. *Life of Brian* (1979, directed by Jones), a religious satire that targeted the corruption of Christ's message rather than Christ himself, was widely condemned by many who thought it sacrilegious. The ultra-bleak *Monty Python's The Meaning of Life* (1983, directed by Jones) was an hysterical compendium of bad taste and extremely pointed, bitter satire.

In the meantime, all the members of the troupe were pursuing their own individual projects. In 1977, Gilliam directed his first solo feature, the Middle Ages fantasy *Jabberwocky;* he then helmed the sleeper hit *Time Bandits* (1981) and wrangled with studio heads over his futuristic satire *Brazil* (1985; which earned him an Oscar nomination for co-writing the screenplay). His spectacular, big-budget *The Adventures of Baron Munchausen* (1989) fizzled, but Gilliam came back with a 1991 surprise hit, *The Fisher King,* a more optimistic (and for Gilliam, conventional) project starring Robin Williams and Jeff Bridges. Idle acted in and cowrote a funny produced-for-TV Beatles sendup, *All You Need Is Cash* (1978, aka *The Rutles),* and has acted in numerous comedies, including *National Lampoon's European Vacation* (1985, as a Brit with a truly stiff upper lip), Gilliam's *Baron Munchausen,* the minor hit *Nuns on the Run* (1990), and the terrible *Mom and Dad Save the World* (1992). He also cowrote and executive produced *Splitting Heirs* (1993). Palin and Jones stayed in projects closer to England, together concocting a veddy British series called "Ripping Yarns." Jones directed but did not act in the prostitution-tweaking comedy *Personal Services* (1987) and wrote, appeared in, and helmed the flop comedy *Erik the Viking* (with Tim Robbins and Cleese; based on a children's book by Jones, who's an acknowledged expert on the period of history in which it's set) in 1989. Jones also directed an episode of TV's short-lived "The Young Indiana Jones Chronicles." Palin wrote and coproduced a starring vehicle for himself, *The Missionary* (1982), but has mostly stuck to acting, as in *A Private Function* (1985), and was memorable as the stuttering fish-fancier in the Cleese-written hit comedy *A Fish Called Wanda* in 1988. He then embarked on a pair of madly ambitious TV projects, "Around the World in 80 Days" (1990) and "Pole to Pole"

(1993) in which he documented his far-flung travels. He also cowrote and starred in *American Friends* (1991). Chapman's last project before he died in 1989 was the failed pirate parody *Yellowbeard* (1983), which he cowrote.

Cleese is the most visible Python member, appearing in many films and TV ads on both sides of the Atlantic, including *The Great Muppet Caper* (1981), *Privates on Parade* (1982), *Silverado* (1985, incongruously cast in a Western), *Clockwise* (1986), and the aforementioned *Wanda* (which earned Cleese an Oscar nomination for Best Screenplay). He won a 1987 Emmy for his appearance in an episode of "Cheers," and provided a villainous voice for *An American Tail: Fievel Goes West* (1991). He then took a supporting role in Eric Idle's *Splitting Heirs* (1993). Cleese also runs a company that makes unusual, comic-oriented training films for executives. There has been a good deal of cross-pollination in the solo projects of the Python individuals, but the death of Chapman effectively ruled out the possibility of any full-scale reunion of the troupe.

MOORE, COLLEEN. Actress. *(b. Aug. 19, 1900, Port Huron, Mich., as Kathleen Morrison; d. Jan. 25, 1988.)* One of the silent screen's most popular stars, she started out a conventional ingenue but during the 1920s achieved great success as the archetypal flapper. The convent-educated Moore broke into movies through the intervention of famed director D. W. Griffith (reportedly to repay one of Moore's relatives for his help in facilitating release of *The Birth of a Nation* and *Intolerance).* She did not, however, work as an extra in *Intolerance,* as some sources insist; her debut was the 1917 *Bad Boy.* Moore subsequently appeared in Westerns and rural melodramas, including *A Hoosier Romance* (1918), *The Busher, The Cyclone* (both 1919, opposite cowboy star Tom Mix), *The Devil's Claim* (1920), *The Sky Pilot, His Nibs* (both 1921), *The Wallflower* (1922), and *Slippy McGee* (1923).

By 1924 it was easy to see where her career was headed by the titles of her latest films: *Flaming Youth, Flirting With Love, The Perfect Flapper.* Moore showed boundless energy in these jazz-baby vehi-

cles, and her popularity swelled accordingly. Girls across America rushed to have their hair bobbed like hers. She graduated to bigger, more important pictures such as *So Big* (1925, based on the Edna Ferber novel), *Sally* (1925) and *Irene* (1926), both based on hit Broadway shows, and *Ella Cinders* (1926, adapted from a popular comic strip). She was best in bouncy comedies such as *Naughty But Nice* and *Orchids and Ermine,* but occasionally applied herself to meatier fare such as *Twinkletoes* (all 1927, the latter a melodrama) and *Lilac Time* (1928, a WW 1 drama that costarred young Gary Cooper).

In 1929, after the mad rush to talking pictures had begun, Moore left the screen. She returned in 1933, playing Spencer Tracy's wife in *The Power and the Glory,* an ambitious but unsuccessful film that effectively scotched her comeback effort. The following year she costarred with Douglas Fairbanks, Jr., in *Success at Any Price,* and played Hester Prynne in a Poverty Row production of *The Scarlet Letter.* Her talent was intact, but apparently her time had passed. Upon retiring from the screen, Moore applied herself to other interests. At one time one of Hollywood's top-paid female stars, she invested her money in the stock market, and did well enough to write a book, "How Women Can Make Money in the Stock Market." She also collected miniatures, and assembled an Olympic-class dollhouse, which now resides at the Chicago Museum of Science and Industry. In 1968 she wrote her autobiography, "Silent Star," and, right up until she died, enthusiastically discussed her career on TV shows and in personal appearances at film festivals, often in tandem with her longtime friend King Vidor.

MOORE, DEMI. Actress. *(b. Nov. 11, 1962, Roswell, N.M., as Demi Guynes.)* Beautiful, husky-voiced brunette who has struggled to escape her identification with the 1980s' Brat Pack of young screen actors. An alumna of the popular TV soap opera "General Hospital" (1981–83), Moore debuted on the big screen in 1981's *Choices.* Roles in *Parasite* and *Young Doctors in Love* (both 1982, in the latter doing a gag cameo as her "General Hospital" character) did nothing to advance her career, and she was almost invisible as Michael Caine's daughter in *Blame It on Rio* (1984). She finally got parts that commanded attention in *No Small Affair* (1984), *St. Elmo's Fire* (1985), *About Last Night . . .,* and *One Crazy Summer* (both 1986), but aside from her voice, there seemed nothing exceptional about her. She won top billing in a supernatural thriller, *The Seventh Sign* (1988), and then managed to hold her own with more accomplished costars Robert De Niro and Sean Penn in *We're No Angels* (1989), prompting speculation—in some quarters, anyway—that hers was a talent worth developing.

Ghost (1990) paired her with Patrick Swayze, and gave her ample opportunity to emote. The film's enormous box-office success boosted Moore's stock in Hollywood and, to her credit, she gambled her newly bolstered popularity on *Mortal Thoughts* (1991), a small-scale, downbeat melodrama which she coproduced and costarred in (with husband Bruce Willis). As a working-class woman implicated in murder, Moore took on her biggest acting challenge—with impressive results. The all-star, lamebrain comedy *Nothing But Trouble* (1991) was a career setback if ever there was one, and *The Butcher's Wife* (1991), a full-fledged Moore vehicle, tried hard—perhaps too hard—to be a whimsical, low-key romantic comedy. (She affected a Southern accent and went blond for the picture.) That same year she raised eyebrows by posing nude on the cover of "Vanity Fair" while heavy with child, beginning something of a "tradition." (The following year she posed nude, covered in paint to simulate a man's business suit.) Moore gave a spirited performance as a Navy lawyer in *A Few Good Men* (1992) opposite Tom Cruise, then did the best she could amid the silliness of *Indecent Proposal* (1993) as the devoted wife who sleeps with Robert Redford in order to earn a million bucks. She scored as a voracious high-tech executive in the thriller *Disclosure* (1994), then tackled the demanding role of Hester Prynne in *The Scarlet Letter* (1995).

MOORE, DUDLEY. Actor, composer. *(b. Apr. 19, 1935, Essex, England.)* Puckish comedic performer who entered movies following a successful career writing and performing in British satirical revues.

Born club-footed and stunted of growth as a child, Moore, like many laughmakers, embraced comedy as a form of escapism. He studied music while at Oxford, where he met Peter Cook, Jonathan Miller, and Alan Bennett; in the early 1960s they formed "Beyond the Fringe," a comedy troupe best described as a precursor to Monty Python's Flying Circus. Moore and Cook later teamed for several two-man shows, eventually reaching the screen in *The Wrong Box* (1966), *Bedazzled* (1967), *The Bed-Sitting Room* (1969), and the dreadful *The Hound of the Baskervilles* (1977). He made his solo starring debut in the little-seen *30 Is a Dangerous Age, Cynthia* (1968), costarring Suzy Kendall, to whom he was briefly married. It took him ten years to win another major movie role, but after getting most of the laughs in *Foul Play* (1978), he was chosen to replace George Segal as leading man in Blake Edwards' mid-life-crisis comedy *10* (1979). Moore's performance as a middle-aged, would-be Romeo struck a chord with moviegoers, and he became the 1980s' unlikeliest movie star.

Arthur (1981) cast Moore as a spoiled, perpetually tipsy millionaire who somehow falls in love with working-class Liza Minnelli. Moore earned a Best Actor Oscar nomination for his funny, freewheeling portrayal, but none of his subsequent films—including *Six Weeks* (1982), *Lovesick, Romantic Comedy* (both 1983), *Unfaithfully Yours, Best Defense, Micki + Maude* (all 1984), *Like Father, Like Son* (1987), *Arthur 2: On the Rocks* (1988), and *Crazy People* (1990)—have attained the same degree of success, critically or commercially. In 1993 he starred in a short-lived TV sitcom, "Dudley." In addition to his acting talents, Moore is an accomplished pianist who also composed the scores for such films as *Bedazzled* (1967), *Inadmissible Evidence* (1968), *Staircase* (1969), and *Six Weeks*.

MOORE, MARY TYLER. Actress, producer. *(b. Dec. 29, 1937, Brooklyn, N.Y.)* Leggy, brunette actress/dancer who is America's undisputed Sweetheart of Sitcoms, owing to lengthy stints on "The Dick Van Dyke Show" (1961–66) and "The Mary Tyler Moore Show" (1970–77), which earned her five Emmy awards. Like her contemporary Carol Burnett, though, Moore has never enjoyed a noteworthy movie career. She was excellent as Julie Andrews' pal in *Thoroughly Modern Millie* (1967), spirited as the leading lady of such fluff as *What's So Bad About Feeling Good?* and *Don't Just Stand There* (both 1968), but unconvincing as a nun opposite Elvis Presley in *Change of Habit* (1969). She showed real dramatic ability, however, as the frigid mother in *Ordinary People* (1980; earning a Best Actress Oscar nomination), as the mother of a dying girl in *Six Weeks* (1982), and as the distraught wife in *Just Between Friends* (1986). She may ultimately be best remembered as the producer, along with ex-husband Grant Tinker, of many memorable TV series, including "Lou Grant," "Hill Street Blues," "St. Elsewhere," "The Bob Newhart Show," and "WKRP in Cincinnati." She also produced the theatrical feature *A Little Sex* (1982). Her best acting opportunities have come in such well-received TV movies as *Heartsounds* (1984), *Finnegan Begin Again* (1985), *Gore Vidal's Lincoln* (1988, as Mary Todd Lincoln), and *Stolen Babies* (1993, an Emmy winner as the stern-faced head of an illegal adoption ring).

MOORE, ROGER. Actor. *(b. Oct. 14, 1927, London.)* It's unlikely that this likeable, urbane, devilishly handsome British leading man would rate a berth in this book had he not succeeded Sean Connery as secret agent James Bond. Although he studied at London's Royal Academy of Dramatic Art, Moore got his first film exposure in Hollywood, and was groomed as a leading man in the waning days of the studio system at MGM, appearing in such major films as *The Last Time I Saw Paris* (1954), *Interrupted Melody, The King's Thief* (both 1955), and *Diane* (1956), before switching his attention to television. He starred in the TV series "Ivanhoe" (1958), "The Alaskans" (1959–60), "Maverick" (1960–61, as cousin Beau), and "The Saint" (1967–69). He first played Agent 007 in *Live and Let Die* (1973), and essayed the role in six more series entries: *The Man With the Golden Gun* (1974), *The Spy Who Loved Me* (1977), *Moonraker* (1979), *For Your Eyes Only* (1981), *Octopussy* (1983), and *A View to a Kill*

(1985). As the Bond films degenerated into elaborate, live-action cartoons, Moore's boyish insouciance became less spontaneous and eventually grew tiresome. He played the title role in a 1976 made-for-TV movie, *Sherlock Holmes in New York*, but has had few worthwhile big-screen opportunities since retiring from the role of 007.
OTHER FILMS INCLUDE: 1961: *The Sins of Rachel Cade;* 1974: *Gold;* 1976: *Shout at the Devil;* 1978: *The Wild Geese;* 1979: *Escape to Athena;* 1980: *ffolkes, Sunday Lovers;* 1981: *The Cannonball Run;* 1985: *The Naked Face;* 1989: *Bullseye!;* 1990: *Fire, Ice and Dynamite;* 1992: *Bed and Breakfast.*

MOORE, TERRY. Actress. *(b. Jan. 7, 1929, Los Angeles, as Helen Koford.)* By the time she got her first "adult" role, as the young woman whose simian sidekick was *Mighty Joe Young* (1949), the pretty, petite Moore was already a well-seasoned screen player, having been in films since 1940, variously billed as Helen Koford, Judy Ford, and Jan Ford. The former child model played fresh-faced ingenues in *The Return of October* (1948), *The Great Rupert* (1950), and *The Barefoot Mailman* (1951) before being Oscar-nominated for her supporting role in *Come Back, Little Sheba* (1952). Prone to overacting and overexuberance, Moore never again delivered as winning a performance, although she worked in some reasonably good movies: *Man on a Tightrope, Beneath the 12 Mile Reef, King of the Khyber Rifles* (all 1953), *Shack Out on 101, Daddy Long Legs* (both 1955), *Between Heaven and Hell* (1956), and *Peyton Place* (1957), among others. Once linked to Howard Hughes, she later claimed to have secretly married the billionaire, a claim honored in 1984 by the Hughes estate, which paid her an undisclosed settlement.

She acted less frequently on-screen in the 1960s and 1970s, appearing in *Platinum High School* (1960), *Black Spurs, Town Tamer* (both 1965), *Waco* (1966), *A Man Called Dagger* (1968), *Daredevil* (1972), and *Death Dimension* (1977). Her mid-1980s "comeback"—kicked off by a 1984 "Playboy" pictorial—amounted to little, netting her supporting roles in cheap comedies and actioners such as *Hellhole* (1985), *W.A.R.* (1986), *Beverly Hills Brats*

(1989, which she cowrote and coproduced), and *Father's Day* (1989).

MOORE, VICTOR. Actor. *(b. Feb. 24, 1876, Hammonton, N.J.; d. July 23, 1962.)* On film, this beloved comic actor specialized in portraying the ineffectual milquetoast characters he had developed years before in vaudeville and on stage. His physical appearance—a large, balding head, bulbous rear end and short limbs—and nervous manner made him a natural funnyman, a role in life he was happy to play. Moore appeared in silent films as early as 1915 (for Cecil B. DeMille, of all people, in *Chimmie Fadden* and *Chimmie Fadden Out West*), but generated the bulk of his screen output in the mid 1930s and 1940s. At RKO he and Helen Broderick supported Fred Astaire and Ginger Rogers in *Swing Time* (1936); they worked so well together that RKO teamed them in several programmers including *We're on the Jury* and *The Life of the Party* (both 1937). Moving to Paramount, he gave an outstanding dramatic performance in the timeless tearjerker *Make Way for Tomorrow* (1937), as an elderly parent shunted aside by his family. He went on to brighten many musical comedies, including *Louisiana Purchase* (1941), *Star Spangled Rhythm* (1942, as the Paramount studio guard), *True to Life* (1943), and *Duffy's Tavern* (1945). He also appeared in *Ziegfeld Follies* (1946, enacting "Pay the Two Dollars"), *We're Not Married* (1952, as the befuddled justice of the peace), and *The Seven Year Itch* (1955). And once, he lent his voice to a Warner Bros. cartoon *(Ain't That Ducky,* 1945) as a hunter chasing Daffy Duck.

MOOREHEAD, AGNES. Actress. *(b. Dec. 6, 1906, Clinton, Mass.; d. Apr. 30, 1974.)* One of Hollywood's premier character actresses, she played puritanical matrons, neurotic spinsters, possessive mothers, even comical secretaries. A highly educated woman who taught speech and drama for several years, Moorehead started working in dramatic radio during the 1930s, often impersonating Eleanor Roosevelt on "The March of Time." Orson Welles recruited her for his Mercury Theater, and later invited her to join him in Hollywood for *Citizen Kane*

(1941), in which she played the title character's mother. She was superb as a spinster in Welles' *The Magnificent Ambersons* (1942), picking up the first of four Oscar nominations for her performance (the others were for 1944's *Mrs. Parkington*, 1948's *Johnny Belinda*, and 1965's *Hush . . . Hush, Sweet Charlotte).* Continuing to work on radio between picture assignments, Moorehead starred in the classic *Sorry, Wrong Number,* but was passed up in favor of Barbara Stanwyck when it was adapted for the screen. Active on television, she's familiar to babyboomers as Endora, the "mother witch" on "Bewitched" (1964–72).
OTHER FILMS INCLUDE: 1942: *Journey Into Fear;* 1944: *Since You Went Away, Jane Eyre* (with Welles); 1945: *Her Highness and the Bellboy;* 1948: *Summer Holiday, The Woman in White;* 1950: *Caged;* 1951: *Show Boat;* 1954: *Magnificent Obsession;* 1955: *All That Heaven Allows;* 1957: *The Story of Mankind* (as Queen Elizabeth I); 1959: *The Bat* (as the spinster detective); 1960: *Pollyanna;* 1962: *How the West Was Won;* 1966: *The Singing Nun;* 1972: *Dear, Dead Delilah* (in the title role); 1973: *Charlotte's Web* (voice only).

MORANIS, RICK. Actor. *(b. Apr. 18, 1954, Toronto.)* A graduate of Canada's famed Second City comedy troupe, this slight, nebbishy performer harkened back to the days of Fred MacMurray playing an absent-minded professor in the Disney comic fantasy hits *Honey, I Shrunk the Kids* (1989) and *Honey, I Blew Up the Kid* (1992). Older baby boomers still recall him as one of the brain-dead, beer-swilling McKenzie Brothers (first seen in a series of TV skits) in *Strange Brew* (1983), which Moranis cowrote and codirected with "SCTV" colleague Dave Thomas. He's also been seen in *Ghostbusters* (as another nerd), *Streets of Fire, The Wild Life* (all 1984), *Brewster's Millions* (1985), *Club Paradise, Little Shop of Horrors* (as Seymour Krellboin), *Head Office* (all 1986), *Spaceballs* (1987, as a nerdy Darth Vader type), *Ghostbusters II* (1989, with one hilarious speech), *Parenthood* (also 1989, as a straitlaced, yuppie papa), *My Blue Heaven* (1990, as a nervous FBI agent), *L.A. Story* (1991), and *Splitting Heirs* (1993). Quietly, without the usual Hollywood fanfare, Moranis has carved himself a niche as a major comedy star. He was cast—ideally, it seemed to many—as Barney Rubble in the live-action feature version of the cartoon show, *The Flintstones* (1994).

MORE, KENNETH. Actor. *(b. Sept. 20, 1914, Gerrard's Cross, England; d. July 12, 1982.)* Personable, good-looking British leading man and supporting player equally comfortable in comedic and dramatic roles. Bitten by the acting bug in the mid 1930s (after working as a fur trapper and engineer's assistant), More logged screen time in several films, beginning with 1935's *Look Up and Laugh,* before interrupting his career to serve with His Majesty's Navy during World War 2. After years of playing in support, More landed costarring parts in two smash hits: the carrace comedy *Genevieve* (1953) and the hilarious *Doctor in the House* (1954). Their successes made him an "overnight" film star at age 40.

He quickly became one of England's most popular leading men, following his comedy successes with solid dramatic performances in films like *The Deep Blue Sea* (1955), *A Night to Remember* (1958), and *Sink the Bismarck!* (1960). He took more lighthearted leads in *The Admirable Crichton* (1957), *The Sheriff of Fractured Jaw* (1959), and a remake of Hitchcock's *The 39 Steps* (1959). By the mid 1960s, his starring career was waning in films, and he spent more time on stage and television, returning to movies mainly in all-star ensembles such as *Oh! What a Lovely War* (as Kaiser Wilhelm!) and *Battle of Britain* (both 1969). He appeared as The Ghost of Christmas Present in the 1970 musical *Scrooge* and made a charming chamberlain in the Cinderella musical *The Slipper and the Rose* (1976). He gave one of his most endearing performances in the landmark BBC series "The Forsyte Saga." More's autobiography, "More or Less," was published in 1978.

OTHER FILMS INCLUDE: 1948: *Scott of the Antarctic;* 1950: *Chance of a Lifetime, The Clouded Yellow;* 1951: *The Galloping Major, No Highway in the Sky;* 1952: *Brandy for the Parson, The Yellow Balloon;* 1953: *The Adventures of Sadie, Never Let Me Go;* 1954: *Raising a Riot;* 1956: *Reach for the Sky;* 1958: *Next to No Time;* 1959: *Flame Over India;* 1960: *Man in the Moon;* 1961: *Loss of Inno-* *cence;* 1962: *The Longest Day;* 1963: *The Comedy Man;* 1968: *Dark of the Sun;* 1978: *Leopard in the Snow, Where Time Began;* 1979: *Unidentified Flying Oddball.*

MOREAU, JEANNE. Actress. *(b. Jan. 23, 1928, Paris.)* A near-flawless embodiment of cinematic sensuality, Moreau's physical beauty, sensitivity, and charm made her instantly successful following an almost-simultaneous film and stage debut in 1948. She first impressed American audiences in two 1958 films directed by Louis Malle: *Elevator to the Gallows* (aka *Frantic)* and *The Lovers,* both successes on the art-house circuit. Moreau's appeal made her the thinking man's Brigitte Bardot; her intelligent, sensual persona was perfectly in keeping with the new freedom in films of the 1960s. Very much in demand, she starred for Michelangelo Antonioni in *La Notte* (1961), for Joseph Losey in *Eva* (1962), for Orson Welles in *The Trial* (1963) and *Chimes at Midnight* (1966), for Luis Buñuel in *Diary of a Chambermaid* (1964). Moreau's most memorable movies, however, may have been those she did for François Truffaut, including *Jules and Jim* (1961, arguably her greatest role, as the center of a classy, three-sided bohemian relationship) and *The Bride Wore Black* (1968, as the woman who coolly seeks revenge for the death of her husband on their wedding day).

During the 1970s Moreau acted in a handful of American films (including the melancholy 1970 Western *Monte Walsh* and 1976's *The Last Tycoon*), tried her hand at directing (first with the well-received features *Lumière* in 1976 and *L'Adolescente* in 1979, and then with a 1984 documentary on Lillian Gish), and even briefly married an American director, William Friedkin (a union long since dissolved). She is still sought after by the world's foremost filmmakers, and has taken a number of glorified cameo roles, in movies ranging from Bertrand Blier's *Going Places* (1974) to Luc Besson's *La Femme Nikita* (1990). She had an especially robust part, as a flamboyant family friend, in the British production *The Summer House* (1993). She adds a distinction to every film in which she appears. Moreau has no peer in projecting worldly womanliness.

OTHER FILMS INCLUDE: 1959: *The Four*

Hundred Blows, Les Liaisons Dangereuses;
1960: *5 Branded Women;* 1961: *A Woman Is
a Woman;* 1963: *Bay of Angels, The Fire
Within, The Victors;* 1964: *Banana Peel;* 1965:
The Train, Viva Maria! (teamed with Brigitte
Bardot); 1968: *The Immortal Story* (made for
TV), *Great Catherine;* 1970: *Alex in Wonderland* (as herself); 1977: *Mr. Klein;* 1982:
Querelle, La Truite; 1991: *Until the End of the
World.*

MORELAND, MANTAN. Actor. *(b.
Sept. 3, 1901, Monroe, La.; d. Sept. 28,
1973.)* There won't be any Mantan
Moreland retrospectives anytime soon, but
even the most Politically Correct would
have to concede that this chunky, pop-
eyed black actor had absolutely impeccable comedy timing, and a hoarse, quicksilver voice that could wring big laughs out
of the lamest material (which he often
got). He was one of the best of a long line
of comic relief "Negroes," usually superstitious, easily frightened, generally lazy
sidekicks (purportedly it was he who
coined the phrase, "Feets, do yo' stuff!"),
reaching the peak of this form in 15 Charlie Chan mysteries made between 1944
and 1949, playing Birmingham Brown,
the very reluctant chauffeur ("Murder's all
right, Mr. Chan, but you wholesales it!").
He was also a star in black-cast films, including such oaters as *Harlem on the
Prairie* and *Two-Gun Man From Harlem*
(both 1938), eventually meriting his name
in the title: *Mantan Messes Up* and
Mantan Runs for Mayor (both 1946). He
teamed with Frankie Darro in several B
comedies, and even popped up in some
early rock cheapies, such as *Rockin' the
Blues* (1955) and *Rock 'n' Roll Jamboree*
(1957). He appeared in some major films
(though not in major roles), most notably
It Started With Eve (1941), *The Palm
Beach Story, Tarzan's New York Adventure*
(both 1942), *Cabin in the Sky* (1943), *See
Here, Private Hargrove* (1944), and in his
later years, *Enter Laughing* (1967), *Spider
Baby* (1968), and *Watermelon Man*
(1970). Though modern audiences may
wince at what he had to do, there is no denying he did it fabulously.

MORENO, RITA. Actress, dancer, singer.
*(b. Dec. 11, 1931, Humacao, Puerto Rico, as
Rosita Dolores Alverio.)* This charismatic little firecracker exploded onto movie
screens as the tempestuous Anita in *West
Side Story* (1961), delivering a dynamic
performance for which she won a Best
Supporting Actress Academy Award. It
was the shining moment in an extensive
screen career: Moreno debuted on film at
the age of 14 in *A Medal for Benny*
(1945), and played supporting roles (usually fiery Latins) in nearly two dozen
movies during the 1950s. Among the best:
a small but noticeable role as starlet Zelda
Zanders in *Singin' in the Rain* (1952) and
a plummier part as Tuptim in *The King
and I* (1956).

Since *West Side Story,* her film output
has been sporadic, but she's had memorable supporting roles in *Marlowe* (1969, as
a stripper), *Carnal Knowledge* (1971, as a
worldly hooker who services Jack
Nicholson), and *The Ritz* (1976, in which
she recreated her hilarious Broadway performance as the spectacularly untalented
bathhouse entertainer Googie Gomez).
The versatile Moreno was also a charter
cast member of the 1970s landmark children's TV show "The Electric Company."
(In fact, a spinoff recording earned her a
Grammy Award to go along with her Oscar, her Tony for "The Ritz," and two
Emmys, for guest shots on "The Rockford
Files" and "The Muppet Show.") In 1990
the ever-energetic performer released a
very successful exercise video. Still active
on television, Moreno's prodigious talent
has only barely been tapped; it seems
there's nothing she can't do, and do well.
OTHER FILMS INCLUDE: 1950: *The Toast
of New Orleans, Pagan Love Song;* 1953:
Latin Lovers; 1954: *Jivaro, The Yellow Tomahawk;* 1955: *Untamed;* 1956: *The Vagabond
King;* 1957: *The Deerslayer;* 1960: *This Rebel
Breed;* 1961: *Summer and Smoke;* 1963: *Cry
of Battle;* 1969: *The Night of the Following
Day;* 1978: *The Boss' Son;* 1981: *The Four
Seasons;* 1992: *Life in the Food Chain.*

MORGAN, DENNIS. Actor, singer. *(b.
Dec. 30, 1910, Prentice, Wis., as Stanley
Morner; d. Sept. 7, 1994.)* Handsome Irish
leading man whose twinkling eyes, toothy
grin, husky physique, and rich baritone
sent feminine film fans' hearts aflutter in
the late 1930s, 1940s, and 1950s. A background in radio and local theater served
young Stanley Morner well when he arrived in Hollywood in 1935: He almost

immediately landed a strong supporting role in *I Conquer the Sea*. Billed first as Morner, then as Richard Stanley, he sang specialty numbers in *Suzy* and *The Great Ziegfeld* (both 1936, inexplicably dubbed in the latter by Allan Jones), and played bits in *Navy Blue and Gold* (1937), *Men With Wings, King of Alcatraz* (both 1938), and others.

He was then signed by Warner Bros., which changed his name to Dennis Morgan, gave him leads in B pictures (1939's *Waterfront* and *The Return of Dr. X,* 1940's *River's End)*, and supporting parts and secondary leads in A's (1940's *The Fighting 69th,* 1941's *Affectionately Yours,* 1942's *Captains of the Clouds, In This Our Life,* 1943's *Thank Your Lucky Stars)* before elevating him to top billing, beginning with *The Desert Song* (1943). He'd previously demonstrated star ability on loan to RKO for *Kitty Foyle* (1940), in which he played the rich-kid love interest of Ginger Rogers. Morgan was teamed with character actor Jack Carson, in a Warners attempt to duplicate the success of Paramount's Bob Hope-Bing Crosby pictures, beginning with *Two Guys From Milwaukee* (1946); they also appeared together in *The Time, the Place, and the Girl* (1946), *Two Guys From Texas* (1948), and *It's a Great Feeling* (1949), among others.

He was unexpectedly good in *One Sunday Afternoon* (1948), a remake of *The Strawberry Blonde,* and sometimes starred in straight dramas and Westerns, including *Perfect Strangers* (1950, again with Rogers), *This Woman Is Dangerous, Cattle Town* (both 1952), *The Nebraskan* (1953), *The Gun That Won the West, Pearl of the South Pacific* (both 1955), and *Uranium Boom* (1956). Like many other Hollywood veterans, he was lured in front of the camera to appear in the excruciating *Won Ton Ton, the Dog Who Saved Hollywood* (1976). Morgan also starred in a 1959 TV series, "21 Beacon Street."

MORGAN, FRANK. Actor. *(b. June 1, 1890, New York City, as Francis Phillip Wupperman; d. Sept. 18, 1949.)* Beloved character actor of Hollywood's Golden Age, for many years a fixture at MGM, where he essayed the title role in 1939's *The Wizard of Oz* ("Pay no attention to the

man behind that curtain!"), his most fondly remembered film. Born into a large family, he followed his elder brother Ralph into the theatrical world and made his Broadway debut in 1914. Morgan appeared in a number of silent films, beginning with *The Suspect* (1916), but didn't really make his mark until the beginning of the sound era. He quickly fell into characterizations of blustery, addle-brained but generally sympathetic middle-aged men, and played them throughout the remainder of his career. When the occasion demanded, however, he could be sophisticated (as the Mayor of New York in 1933's *Hallelujah, I'm a Bum*), roguish (as the philandering husband in 1935's *Enchanted April*), imposing (as the shop owner of 1940's classic *The Shop Around the Corner*), or heartbreakingly sympathetic (as the professor/father in 1940's *The Mortal Storm* or the drunken telephone operator in 1943's *The Human Comedy*). He was nominated for two Academy Awards: for *Affairs of Cellini* (1934, as the cuckolded Duke of Florence), and *Tortilla Flat* (1942, as the simple Latino dog-lover). He was one of a handful of well-known character actors who reportedly was given a "lifetime contract" at MGM; the studio occasionally starred him in his own (mostly) grade-B vehicles, such as *Hullabaloo* (1940), *The Vanishing Virginian* (1942), and *The Cockeyed Miracle* (1946). His final film, *Key to the City* (1950, with fellow Metro workhorse Clark Gable), was released after his death. OTHER FILMS INCLUDE: 1917: *Raffles the Amateur Cracksman;* 1924: *Manhandled;* 1930: *Laughter;* 1932: *Secrets of the French Police* (playing a dapper Surete inspector!), *The Half-Naked Truth;* 1933: *Reunion in Vienna, The Kiss Before the Mirror, Bombshell, Broadway to Hollywood;* 1934: *The Cat and the Fiddle, A Lost Lady;* 1935: *The Good Fairy, Escapade, Naughty Marietta;* 1936: *The Great Ziegfeld, Dimples, Dancing Pirate;* 1937: *The Last of Mrs. Cheyney, The Emperor's Candlesticks, Saratoga, Rosalie;* 1938: *Port of Seven Seas, Sweethearts;* 1939: *Balalaika;* 1940: *Broadway Melody of 1940, Boom Town;* 1941: *Honky Tonk;* 1942: *White Cargo;* 1944: *The White Cliffs of Dover;* 1945: *Yolanda and the Thief;* 1946: *Courage of Lassie;* 1947: *Green Dolphin Street;* 1948: *Summer Holiday, The Three Musketeers;* 1949: *The Stratton Story, Any Number Can Play.*

MORGAN, HARRY (HENRY). Actor.
*(b. Apr. 10, 1915, Detroit, as Harry Brats-
burg.)* Originally billed as Henry Morgan,
this agile, prolific character actor changed
his name to "Harry" to avoid confusion
with the radio comedian and quiz-show
panelist. He has enjoyed a fifty-year career in films and television by being an
everyman, equally effective playing characters who are wisecracking (the soda jerk
in 1942's *Orchestra Wives*), brutal (the
bodyguard thug in 1948's *The Big Clock*),
obtuse (the next door neighbor in 1948's
All My Sons) or authoritative (the Scopes
Monkey Trial judge in 1960's *Inherit the
Wind*). However, he is best known for his
roles in an astonishing array of television
series, both dramatic and comedic: "December Bride" (1954–59, as Pete Porter)
and its spinoff "Pete and Gladys"
(1960–62), "The Richard Boone Show"
(1963–64), "Kentucky Jones" (1964–65),
"Dragnet" (1967–70, as Officer Bill
Gannon), "The D.A." (1971–72), "Hec
Ramsey" (1972–74, also starring Boone),
"M*A*S*H" (1975–83, as Col. Sherman
T. Potter, for which he won an Emmy in
1980) and its spinoff "AfterMASH"
(1984–85), and "Blacke's Magic" (1986).
In retrospect, one of his most entertaining
screen roles is in *Dark City* (1950), in
which he and Jack Webb, his later "Dragnet" costar, are respectively cast as a
former pug and punk who are forever antagonists. Morgan got to play Bill Gannon
again in the 1987 remake of *Dragnet,* as
the head of the L.A.P.D.
OTHER FILMS INCLUDE: 1942: *To the
Shores of Tripoli;* 1945: *A Bell for Adano, State
Fair;* 1946: *Dragonwyck;* 1947: *The Gangster;*
1948: *Yellow Sky;* 1949: *Madame Bovary;*
1951: *The Well, The Blue Veil;* 1952: *My Six
Convicts, What Price Glory?;* 1953: *Torch Song;*
1954: *The Glenn Miller Story;* 1955: *Not as a
Stranger;* 1956: *The Teahouse of the August
Moon;* 1962: *How the West Was Won;* 1966:
Frankie and Johnny; 1969: *Support Your Local
Sheriff!;* 1971: *Support Your Local Gunfighter;*
1973: *Charley and the Angel* (as the Angel);
1975: *The Apple Dumpling Gang;* 1976: *The
Shootist;* 1979: *The Apple Dumpling Gang
Rides Again.*

MORGAN, RALPH. Actor. *(b. July 6,
1882, New York City, as Ralph Wupperman;
d. June 11, 1956.)* Brother of Frank, Ralph
enjoyed an equally lengthy if not as distinguished screen career; he toiled more
frequently in Poverty Row productions
and missed out on the colorful roles Frank
usually got. Film buffs revere Ralph for
his numerous appearances as the least-
likely suspect who is revealed as a maniacal killer in 1930s whodunits.
OTHER FILMS INCLUDE: 1932: *Strange
Interlude* (one of his best parts), Rasputin
and the Empress; 1933: *Trick for Trick* (a rare
lead), *Dr. Bull, The Power and the Glory, The
Kennel Murder Case;* 1934: *Stand Up and
Cheer, The Last Gentleman;* 1935: *Little Men,
Star of Midnight, Magnificent Obsession;*
1937: *The Life of Emile Zola, Mannequin;*
1939: *Man of Conquest;* 1941: *Dick Tracy vs.
Crime, Inc.* (as a master criminal who has
perfected an invisibility device), *The Mad
Doctor;* 1943: *Hitler's Madman;* 1944: *The
Monster Maker;* 1947: *Song of the Thin Man.*

MORIARTY, CATHY. Actress. *(b. Nov. 29,
1960, Bronx, N.Y.)* Martin Scorsese
counted on the fact that this young, striking blonde had no acting training when
he cast her to play prizefighter Jake
LaMotta's ravishing and much-abused
wife, Vikki, in *Raging Bull* (1980). He
wanted a fresh, unsullied natural performer who wouldn't be thrown by the
improvisations of star Robert De Niro.
And he was right: Moriarty's casual,
seemingly effortless performance got her
tagged an up-and-comer and won her an
Oscar nomination for Best Supporting
Actress. But bad luck dogged her:
Neighbors (1981), a John Belushi-Dan
Aykroyd vehicle in which she played a
suburban seductress, laid an egg at the
box office after being trounced by critics. Plagued by bad advice, Moriarty
dropped out of sight for several years,
making a low-key return to the screen in
the curious thriller *White of the Eye*
(1987). More recently she has landed
better parts in such higher-profile films
as *Soapdish* (1991, as a predatory,
transsexual soap opera star) and *Matinee*
(1993, as flamboyant producer John
Goodman's wry leading lady and companion), both of which revealed a disarming sense of humor. Other credits include *Burndown* (1989), *Kindergarten
Cop* (1990), *The Gun in Betty Lou's
Handbag* (1992), *Me and the Kid* (1993),
Forget Paris, and *Casper* (both 1995).

She also owns a fashionable pizzeria in Beverly Hills.

MORIARTY, MICHAEL. Actor. *(b. Apr. 5, 1941, Detroit.)* Wide-eyed, baby-faced character actor and occasional leading man with a diverse array of skilled performances to his credit. He uses his delicate, high-pitched voice very skillfully, effectively registering menace on those infrequent occasions he essays villainous roles. A graduate of the London Academy of Music and Dramatic Arts, Moriarty acted in the New York Shakespeare Festival at 22, and subsequently appeared in many stage productions and TV shows, winning a Tony in 1974 (for "Find Your Way Home") and Emmys in 1974 (for his role in *The Glass Menagerie)* and 1978 (for his chilling work as a Nazi in the miniseries "Holocaust"). His early screen work includes memorable turns in two 1973 films, *Bang the Drum Slowly* (as the baseball pitcher who befriends and protects simple-minded Robert De Niro) and *The Last Detail* (as Jack Nicholson's duty officer), and a lead in *Report to the Commissioner* (1975). Although he worked steadily, Moriarty seldom played leads until the 1980s, when he starred in *Q* (1982) for filmmaker Larry Cohen (who also cast him in 1985's *The Stuff* and 1987's *It's Alive III: Island of the Alive).* Other films include *Hickey & Boggs* (1972), *Who'll Stop the Rain* (1978), *Pale Rider* (1985), *Blood Link* (also 1985, as twin brothers), *Troll* (1986), *The Hanoi Hilton, Dark Tower* (both 1987), and *Full Fathom Five* (1990). More people may know him from his costarring role in the TV series "Law and Order" (1990–94) than from his starring films. He is also an accomplished jazz pianist and singer.

MORISON, PATRICIA. Actress. *(b. Mar. 19, 1914, New York City, as Eileen Patricia Morison.)* Dark-haired, slightly sulky-looking actress with piercing blue eyes, a talented performer whose Hollywood accomplishments never matched her stage success as the lead in "Kiss Me Kate" (1948). Born to a playwright-actor and a talent agent (what a combination!), she studied dancing and fashion design as a young girl, only to abandon those pursuits in favor of acting. Already a Broadway regular by 1933, she signed with Paramount, making her film debut in *Persons in Hiding* (1939), a low-budget, thinly disguised version of the Bonnie and Clyde story. Over the next 10 years, Morison accepted thankless roles, many of them leads, in unimportant pictures, displaying considerable talent but getting nowhere in her quest for meaty parts in prestige productions. Aside from her supporting role as George Sand in the Liszt biography *Song Without End* (1960), Morison eschewed film work for the remainder of her career.
OTHER FILMS INCLUDE: 1939: *The Magnificent Fraud;* 1940: *Untamed, Rangers of Fortune;* 1941: *Romance of the Rio Grande, One Night in Lisbon;* 1942: *Beyond the Blue Horizon, A Night in New Orleans;* 1943: *Hitler's Madman, The Fallen Sparrow* (a decent part in a good movie, for once), *Calling Dr. Death, The Song of Bernadette* (wasted in a small role); 1945: *Lady on a Train;* 1946: *Dressed to Kill;* 1947: *Tarzan and the Huntress* (as a villainess), *Queen of the Amazon, Song of the Thin Man;* 1948: *The Prince of Thieves.*

MORITA, NORIYUKI "PAT." Actor. *(b. June 28, 1933, Berkeley, Calif.)* Talented Japanese-American actor who gained fame and a Supporting Actor Oscar nomination for his performance as the wise karate master, Mr. Miyagi, in *The Karate Kid* (1984), a role he repeated in parts II (1986), III (1989), and IV, aka *The Next Karate Kid* (1994). After a long bout with spinal tuberculosis and years in a Japanese internment camp during World War 2, Morita worked as a computer programmer but gave up the job to become a stand-up comic. Billed as "the hip Nip," he played nightclubs and TV variety shows, and made appearances in *Thoroughly Modern Millie* (1967), *Cancel My Reservation* (1972), and *Midway* (1976). His first major break was playing restaurant proprietor Arnold on two seasons of the popular "Happy Days" sitcom (1975–76 and 1982–83); he also starred in his own short-lived comedy, "Mr. T. and Tina" (1976). He began billing himself as Noriyuki for *The Karate Kid,* but the promise of film stardom proved elusive. His other film credits include *Savannah Smiles* (1982), *Jimmy the Kid* (1983), *Slapstick (of Another Kind)* (1984), the straight-to-video *Collision Course* (1987, costarring Jay Leno), *Do or Die* (1991), *Honeymoon in Vegas* (1992), and *Even Cowgirls Get the Blues* (1994). He starred in and wrote the screenplay for the WW2 romance *Captive Hearts* (1987) and had his own TV detective series, "Ohara" (1987–88).

MORLEY, ROBERT. Actor. *(b. May 25, 1908, Semley, England; d. June 3, 1992.)* Jovial British supporting player, recognizable by his ungainly bulk, bushy eyebrows, thick lips, and double chin, especially noted for his portrayals of eccentric comedic characters. Already a 10-year veteran of the London stage when he made his film debut in the Hollywood-made *Marie Antoinette* (1938, as the simple-minded Louis XVI), Morley got an Oscar nomination his first time out of the gate. A consistently delightful actor, he was particularly effective when cast as a pompous windbag, though he was actually quite versatile (very effective as Katharine Hepburn's missionary brother in 1951's *The African Queen*, for instance). Among his best parts: the self-serving director of a repertory troupe in *Curtain Up* (1952), Oscar Hammerstein in *Melba*, W. S. Gilbert in *The Story of Gilbert and Sullivan* (both 1953), Sydney Greenstreet reincarnated (more or less) in *Beat the Devil* (1954), King George III in *Beau Brummel* (also 1954), the title role in *Oscar Wilde* (1960, a part he played on stage as well), an obnoxious critic who meets a grisly end in *Theatre of Blood* (1973), and the world's preeminent gourmet in *Who Is Killing the Great Chefs of Europe?* (1978). He was also a successful author, playwright, and TV pundit and guest; in later years he was most recognizable to Americans from his long-running series of commercials for British Airways.
OTHER FILMS INCLUDE: 1941: *Major Barbara*; 1945: *A Yank in London*; 1949: *The Small Back Room*; 1956: *Around the World in Eighty Days*; 1958: *Law and Disorder*; 1959: *The Battle of the Sexes*; 1962: *The Road to Hong Kong*; 1963: *Murder at the Gallop, The Old Dark House*; 1964: *Of Human Bondage*; 1965: *A Study in Terror, Life at the Top, The Loved One*; 1966: *The Alphabet Murders*; 1968: *Hot Millions*; 1970: *Cromwell*; 1971: *When Eight Bells Toll*; 1976: *The Blue Bird*; 1981: *The Great Muppet Caper*; 1983: *High

Road to China*; 1984: *The Trouble With Spies* (released 1987); 1988: *Little Dorrit*; 1990: *Istanbul.*

MORRICONE, ENNIO. Composer. *(b. Oct. 11, 1928, Rome.)* It is hard to imagine what impact Sergio Leone's "spaghetti Westerns" of the 1960s would have had without the stylized and unforgettable music provided by this composer. Besides working on all of Leone's films—most notably *A Fistful of Dollars* (1964), *For a Few Dollars More, The Good, the Bad, and the Ugly* (both 1966), *Once Upon a Time in the West* (1969), and *Once Upon a Time in America* (1984)—Morricone has more than 300 other scores to his credit. His distinctive, highly innovative work has graced countless international films by such directors as Pontecorvo (1965's *Battle of Algiers* and 1969's *Queimada/Burn!*), Petri (1970's *Investigation of a Citizen Above Suspicion*), Pasolini (1970's *The Decameron*), Bertolucci (1977's *1900*), the Taviani brothers (1984's *Kaos* and 1987's *Good Morning, Babylon*), and Polanski (1988's *Frantic*). His scores for *Days of Heaven* (1978), *The Mission* (1986), *The Untouchables* (1987), and *Bugsy* (1991) have been Oscar-nominated, and recordings of such scores as *The Bird With the Crystal Plumage* (1969) and *Cinema Paradiso* (1991) are prized by film music aficionados.
OTHER FILMS INCLUDE: 1964: *Before the Revolution*; 1967: *China Is Near*; 1968: *Teorema*; 1969: *The Sicilian Clan*; 1970: *Two Mules for Sister Sara*; 1971: *The Red Tent, The Cat o' Nine Tails, The Canterbury Tales*; 1972: *Four Flies on Grey Velvet, Duck, You Sucker*; 1974: *My Name Is Nobody, Allonsanfan*; 1975: *The Human Factor, Salo, or the 120 Days of Sodom*; 1979: *Luna*; 1982: *White Dog, The Thing*; 1989: *Casualties of War*; 1990: *Everybody's Fine, Tie Me Up! Tie Me Down!*; 1993: *In the Line of Fire.*

MORRIS, CHESTER. Actor. *(b. Feb. 16, 1901, New York City, as John Chester Morris; d. Sept. 11, 1970.)* To many he'll always be remembered as Boston Blackie, the retired safecracker and amateur detective in 13 well-remembered B movies of the 1940s. But this compactly built, tight-lipped actor with the patent-leather hair was a potential first-rank star at the outset of the talkie era. Morris, who'd been on stage since his teens (and made his film debut in 1917's *An Amateur Orphan)*, starred in the only three talkies made by eccentric, autocratic director Roland West: *Alibi* (for which he was Oscar-nominated), *The Bat Whispers* (both 1930), and *Corsair* (1931). At MGM, he costarred with Wallace Beery in the seminal prison picture, *The Big House* (1930), a huge success that cemented his reputation, and played leads in many 1930s' productions, big and small, including *Red-Headed Woman, The Miracle Man* (both 1932), *Blondie Johnson, King for a Night* (both 1933), *The Gay Bride* (1934), *Princess O'Hara, Public Hero No. 1* (both 1935), *3 Godfathers, Frankie and Johnny* (both 1936), *Devil's Playground, I Promise to Pay* (both 1937), *Law of the Underworld, Sky Giant* (both 1938), *Blind Alley, Five Came Back* (both 1939, the latter a classic of the B picture), *Wagons Westward,* and *Girl From God's Country* (both 1940).

In 1941 Morris inaugurated his popular series with *Meet Boston Blackie;* that same year he signed with independent producers William Pine and William Thomas (the "Dollar Bills") to make a series of low-budget actioners for Paramount release. These included *No Hands on the Clock* (1941), *I Live on Danger* (1942), *Tornado* (1943), and *Double Exposure* (1944). Between the Pine-Thomas epics and the Boston Blackie series (which ended with 1949's *Boston Blackie's Chinese Venture)* and his radio and stage work, Morris was one of the 1940s' busiest actors. But typecasting hurt him, and he found picture work scarce during the 1950s, *Unchained* (1955) and *The She Creature* (1957) being the best he could get. (Morris did appear in some hit stage shows, including "Detective Story.") Shortly after making a "comeback" appearance in *The Great White Hope* (1970), Morris was found dead, the victim of a drug overdose.

MORRIS, ERROL. Director. *(b. Feb. 5, 1948, Hewlett, N.Y.)* Morris' fame as a documentarian of odd human behavior gained national attention with the extraordinary *The Thin Blue Line* (1988), detailing the wrongful arrest and conviction of Randall Dale Adams, who was accused of killing a Dallas policeman. The film was so convincing that it resulted in a new trial for Adams and his eventual release from prison. Morris, who actually worked as a private eye for two years, was a philosophy student at U.C. Berkeley when filmmaker Werner Herzog encouraged him to make his first film, the well-received documentary *Gates of Heaven* (1978), about California pet cemeteries. (In fact, Herzog said he'd eat his shoe if Morris completed the film; his fulfillment of the bet was chronicled by Les Blank in the 1979 short *Werner Herzog Eats His Shoe.)* His follow-up feature was *Vernon, Florida* (1981, about the elderly people in that small town). After *The Thin Blue Line* he directed *A Brief History of Time* (1992), about the wheelchair-bound scientific genius Stephen W. Hawking. Morris' lone attempt at fictional filmmaking to date, *The Dark Wind* (1991) did not receive theatrical release, and went straight to video.

MORRIS, WAYNE. Actor. *(b. Feb. 17, 1914, Los Angeles, as Bert de Wayne Morris; d. Sept. 14, 1959.)* This blond-haired hulk with the kind, open face first impressed moviegoers as the good-natured bellhop-turned-prizefighter in *Kid Galahad* (1937), and went on to become a dependable leading man in program pictures for Warner Bros. Morris, who grew up a stone's throw from Hollywood and apprenticed at the Pasadena Playhouse before signing with Warners in 1936, starred or costarred in *The Kid Comes Back* (1937), *Men Are Such Fools, Brother Rat, Valley of the Giants* (all 1938), *The Kid From Kokomo, The Return of Dr. X* (both 1939), *Ladies Must Live, The Quarterback* (both 1940), *Bad Men of Missouri, I Wanted Wings,* and *The Smiling Ghost* (all 1941) before serving with the Navy during World War 2. As a combat aviator he flew dozens of missions, shot down seven enemy aircraft, and was awarded a slew of medals, including four Distinguished Flying Crosses.

After the war, heavier and tougher, Morris resumed his career playing rugged, two-fisted heroes in Westerns and crime dramas. He appeared in *The Voice of the Turtle* (1947), *The Big Punch* (1948), *John Loves Mary, The Younger Brothers, The House Across the Street, Task Force* (all 1949), *The Tougher They Come*

(1950), *Sierra Passage,* and *The Big Gusher* (1951) before agreeing to star in a series of cheapie Westerns for Monogram (by then calling itself Allied Artists). *Desert Pursuit* (1952), *Star of Texas, The Fighting Lawman* (both 1953), and *Two Guns and a Badge* (1954, the last B series Western) showed Morris looking tired and bored. He made only a few more films—one of them being Stanley Kubrick's powerful antiwar drama *Paths of Glory* (1957) before dying of a heart attack.

MORRISSEY, PAUL. Director. *(b. Feb. 23, 1938, New York City.)* After a stint in the Army, and following jobs as varied as insurance clerk and social worker, Morrissey served as production assistant and cameraman on many of Pop Art guru Andy Warhol's experimental films. He then began producing and directing Warhol films, many of which featured the artist's name in their titles. In *Flesh* (1968), *Blue Movie* (1969), *Andy Warhol's Women* (1971), *Heat* (1972), *Andy Warhol's Frankenstein* and *Andy Warhol's Dracula* (both 1974), he imparted rudimentary coherence and a semblance of narrative structure, tempering his mentor's trademark avant-garde excesses. He left the Warhol camp in the mid-1970s to direct more personal projects, including the barely released Peter Cook and Dudley Moore *The Hound of the Baskervilles* (1977). His pictures have yet to cross over from the art house to the multiplex, though *Spike of Bensonhurst* (1988) came close. He's appeared as an actor in *Rich and Famous* (1981) and *Resident Alien* (1990), and in the Warhol documentary *Superstar* (1990).

MORROW, VIC. Actor. *(b. Feb. 14, 1932, Bronx, N.Y.; d. July 23, 1982.)* Perpetually scowling (or so it seemed) supporting player and, later, leading man of films and TV, unfortunately remembered as much for the grisly manner in which he died as for the films he made. Morrow had some limited stage experience before making his movie debut as a bullying high school student in *Blackboard Jungle* (1955); the vicious, chip-on-his-shoulder characterization he affected in that role carried over to many of his subsequent parts. He turned

up in *Tribute to a Bad Man* (1956), *Men in War* (1957), *God's Little Acre* (1958), *Cimarron* (1960), *Portrait of a Mobster* (in the lead, playing Dutch Schultz), and *Posse From Hell* (both 1961) before assuming the costarring role of hard-bitten Sergeant Chip Saunders in the "Combat!" TV series (1962–67). In 1966 he cowrote, coproduced, and directed a film adaptation of Jean Genet's *Deathwatch* which starred Leonard Nimoy. Morrow's later film assignments include *Dirty Mary Crazy Larry* (1974), *The Bad News Bears* (1976), *Funeral for an Assassin* (1977), *The Evictors* (1979, which he also directed), *Humanoids From the Deep* (1980), and *Bronx Warriors* (1982). He also appeared in a number of made-for-TV movies and miniseries, among them *The Glass House* (1972) and "Captains and the Kings" (1976), and costarred in the short-lived series "B.A.D. Cats" (1980). While filming a pyrotechnically complex stunt sequence for *Twilight Zone—The Movie* (released 1983), Morrow and two child actors were accidentally killed when an out-of-control helicopter crashed. His daughter is actress Jennifer Jason Leigh.

MORTON, JOE. Actor. *(b. Oct. 18, 1947, Brooklyn, N.Y.)* Versatile black actor with stage, television, and ever-increasing film credits. After a Broadway debut in "Hair" and years of experience in musicals (he was nominated for a Tony Award for "Raisin") and theater classics, he made his first big movie impression as the mute alien in John Sayles' *The Brother From Another Planet* (1984). He has since appeared to good effect playing a wide variety of roles in *Trouble in Mind* (1985), *Crossroads* (1986), *The Good Mother* (1988), *Tap* (1989), *Terminator 2: Judgment Day* (1991), *City of Hope* (also 1991, another choice role written for him by Sayles), *Of Mice and Men, Forever Young* (both 1992), *The Inkwell, Speed* (both 1994), and *The Walking Dead* (1995). He starred on the TV series "Equal Justice" (1990–91) and "Under One Roof" (1995–).

MOSTEL, ZERO. Actor. *(b. Feb. 28, 1915, Brooklyn, N.Y., as Samuel Joel Mostel; d. Sept. 8, 1977.)* Rotund, flamboyant charac-

ter actor who, early in his screen career, played sinister heavies but was far more enjoyable in comedic roles, especially those that allowed him to display the gleeful amorality that enlivened his best performances, in *A Funny Thing Happened on the Way to the Forum* (1966) and *The Producers* (1968). A City College of New York graduate, and a talented artist (who apparently preferred painting to performing), Mostel began in show business as a stand-up comic. It was his nightclub success that led to his movie debut in the MGM musical *DuBarry Was a Lady* (1943). He was memorable as Jack Palance's sniveling toadie in *Panic in the Streets* (1950), and was busy playing other colorful characters at 20th Century-Fox when he was called before the House Un-American Activities Committee. Although he denied affiliation with the Communist party, he was blacklisted just the same, and barely managed to make a living until he made a comeback on stage in Eugene Ionesco's "Rhinoceros," for which he won a Tony Award. He earned a second Tony for "A Funny Thing" and a third for his rich performance as Tevye in the musical smash "Fiddler on the Roof." In his last live-action film, *The Front* (1976), he played boisterous comedian Hecky Brown, a victim of the blacklist, not unlike himself. His son Josh is also an actor with a vast number of stage, television and movie credits, including *Jesus Christ, Superstar* (1973), *Harry and Tonto* (1974), *Sophie's Choice* (1982), *Star 80* (1983), *The Brother From Another Planet* (1984), *Stoogemania* (1985, in the starring role), *The Money Pit* (1986), *Radio Days, Matewan, Wall Street* (all 1987), and *City Slickers* (1991).
OTHER FILMS INCLUDE: 1951: *The Enforcer, Mr. Belvedere Rings the Bell;* 1952: *The Model and the Marriage Broker;* 1969: *The Great Bank Robbery;* 1970: *The Angel Levine;* 1972: *The Hot Rock;* 1975: *Journey Into Fear;* 1978: *Watership Down* (voice only).

MOWBRAY, ALAN. Actor. *(b. Aug. 18, 1896, London; d. Mar. 26, 1969.)* Dignified-looking British character actor equally proficient at dramatic and comedic roles. With numerous stage plays to his credit before going to Hollywood in 1931, Mowbray delivered consistently entertaining performances—especially when play-ing eccentric, egotistical windbags. He's best remembered for comedies like *My Man Godfrey* (1936), *Topper, On the Avenue, Hollywood Hotel* (all 1937), *Merrily We Live* (1938), *Never Say Die* (1939), *The Devil with Hitler* (1942, as The Devil), and *Tell It to a Star* (1945), but is also well featured in *Becky Sharp* (1935), *Mary of Scotland* (1936), and other serious films. An incorrigible mugger, he and Donald MacBride traded double-takes in two RKO Bs, *Curtain Call* (1940) and *Footlight Fever* (1941), his only starring assignments, and Mowbray went on to play an itinerant ham actor in two John Ford films, *My Darling Clementine* (1946) and *Wagon Master* (1950). Mowbray also played several historical figures on screen: George Washington in *Alexander Hamilton* (1931), Metternich in *House of Rothschild* (1934), and Sir William Hamilton in *That Hamilton Woman* (1941), to name a few. He had a bit part in 1932's *Sherlock Holmes,* and went on to appear in two other Holmes movies: as Inspector Lestrade in *A Study in Scarlet* (1933) and the villainous Col. Sebastian Moran in *Terror By Night* (1946). In 1953 he starred as a charming con man in the TV comedy series "Colonel Humphrey Flack," and continued working on stage and television into the 1960s.

MUELLER-STAHL, ARMIN. Actor. *(b. Dec. 17, 1920, Tilsit, East Prussia.)* One of Germany's leading actors, now becoming a familiar face in American films. An interesting face, at that: strong but gentle, with plenty of character and sensitivity. Once a highly successful film and stage actor in East Germany, he was blacklisted by the government and emigrated to West Germany in 1980. Finding ample work in that country's film industry, he appeared in such films as Rainer Werner Fassbinder's *Lola* (1981) and *Veronika Voss* (1982), Andrzej Wajda's *A Love in Germany* (1984), *Angry Harvest* and *Colonel Redl* (both 1985). After making an impressive American film debut as Jessica Lange's father in *Music Box* (1989), Stahl was featured as the lead in *Midnight Cop* (1989), and subsequently took a number of strong character parts in *Kafka, Night on Earth* (both 1991), *The Power of One* (1992), *Utz, The House of the Spirits* (both 1993), and *A Pyromaniac's Love*

Story (1995), and had a starring role in *The Last Good Time* (also 1995). He's probably best known for his touching portrayal of the kindly Jewish patriarch in *Avalon* (1990).

MULLIGAN, ROBERT. Director. *(b. Aug. 23, 1925, Bronx, N.Y.)* Mulligan had considered becoming a priest before joining the Navy and later entering the entertainment world through television. He rose from messenger boy to a director on "Suspense" (helming more than one hundred episodes) as well as productions like "Billy Budd," "A Tale of Two Cities," and "The Moon and Sixpence," for which he won an Emmy. Mulligan made an impressive film debut with *Fear Strikes Out* (1957), a complex account of baseball player Jimmy Piersall that marked the director's first collaboration with producer Alan J. Pakula. He handled the Tony Curtis vehicles *The Great Impostor* and *The Rat Race* (both 1960) and the Rock Hudson comedy *Come September* (1961) before reteaming with Pakula on the superb adaptation of Harper Lee's *To Kill a Mockingbird* (1962), which earned Gregory Peck a Best Actor Oscar and netted Mulligan a nomination as Best Director. Five more Mulligan–Pakula projects followed: *Love With the Proper Stranger* (1963), *Baby The Rain Must Fall, Inside Daisy Clover* (both 1965), *Up the Down Staircase* (1967), and *The Stalking Moon* (1969). All deal with troubled personal relationships and the stresses of life and, especially in *Baby* and *Staircase,* are marked by Mulligan's great sensitivity to his subject matter and his persuasive handling of actors.

After Pakula went on to pursue his own directing career, Mulligan made the underrated *The Pursuit of Happiness* (1971) and had a tremendous hit with *Summer of '42* (also 1971), a sentimental but affecting story of a teenager's brief romance with a war bride. *The Other* (1972) was a highly effective adaptation of Thomas Tryon's supernatural novel, but few of Mulligan's films since then—*The Nickel Ride* (1975), *Same Time, Next Year, Bloodbrothers* (both 1978), *Kiss Me Goodbye* (1982), and *Clara's Heart* (1988)—have generated much excitement. He was back on firm ground with the coming-of-age story *The Man in the Moon* (1991), one of his best

films in years but one that was seen by virtually no one.

MUNI, PAUL. Actor. *(b. Sept. 22, 1895, Lemberg, Austria-Hungary, as Muni Weisenfreund; d. Aug. 25, 1967.)* Paul Muni was the sort of "great actor" whose theatricality impressed some moviegoers and left others cold. Time has not been kind to some of his performances, but his best film work still carries weight and emotional power. The son of actors, he came to the United States in 1902, and later took up his own career in the Yiddish theater. In 1926 he landed on Broadway in "We Americans," and scored well enough to be signed by Fox at the dawn of the sound era. His starring turn in *The Valiant* (1929), based on a hoary vaudeville playlet about a death-row convict with a self-sacrificing streak of nobility, earned Muni an Oscar nomination. *Seven Faces* (also 1929) offered him a tour de force with its seven roles.

After returning to Broadway to star in "Counsellor-at-Law" (for which he won stellar reviews), Muni became a true film star with the release of the Howard Hughes production of *Scarface* (1932), directed by Howard Hawks. It was a frank and brutal portrait of a Capone-like mobster, and Muni was extremely effective in the title role. *I Am a Fugitive From a Chain Gang* (1932) brought him his second Oscar nomination, for his chillingly believable performance as the unwitting criminal accomplice whose life is forever changed when he's nabbed by the police. Pleased with the results, Warner Bros. signed him to a long-term contract, and while he's best remembered today for the historical biographies he made there, he was equally good in a series of contemporary films he made at the studio: *The World Changes* (1933), *Hi, Nellie* (1934, one of his few films with comic elements), *Bordertown,* and *Black Fury* (both 1935).

Muni finally won an Oscar for his work in *The Story of Louis Pasteur* (1936), the first of his major biopics, and then was loaned to MGM where the combination of skillful makeup and brilliant acting turned him into a Chinese peasant in *The Good Earth* (1937). He triumphed again in *The Life of Emile Zola* (1937), which earned him another Oscar nomination (and took the prize as Best Picture). *Juarez* (1939), the story of the Mexican leader, was somewhat less successful, but added another characterization to Muni's ever-growing gallery. After playing a gentle (and naive) British physician in *We Are Not Alone* (1939) he left Warners to freelance.

He kept busy during the first half of the 1940s, in *Hudson's Bay* (1940, as a boisterous French Canadian), the wartime saga *The Commandos Strike at Dawn* (1942), *Stage Door Canteen* (1943, a cameo as himself), *Counter-Attack* (1945), *A Song to Remember* (also 1945, in which he gave a scenery-chewing performance as Chopin's mentor), and *Angel on My Shoulder* (1946, an enjoyable fantasy). Then he abandoned Hollywood and moviemaking, which he'd never particularly enjoyed, and returned to the stage. (There was one foray into film in 1953, when he starred in the Italian-made *Stranger on the Prowl* for director Joseph Losey.)

In 1955 he scored a personal triumph (and won a Tony award) playing the Clarence Darrow–inspired character in "Inherit the Wind" on Broadway (the part Spencer Tracy took in the later film version). While he dabbled in television, he made just one more movie: *The Last Angry Man* (1959), a tailor-made script about an aging Jewish doctor. It earned Muni his fifth and final Academy Award nomination. Although his bravura style of acting may not be fashionable today, Muni's best performances still hold up. His film career is also notable for having existed almost entirely on the strength of prestige, and the sheer power of his work—not on personal popularity.

MURCH, WALTER. Editor, sound designer, director, screenwriter. *(b. July 12, 1943, New York City.)* Peter Cowie wrote that Murch "marshals sound with the infinite subtlety of a major composer." A graduate of USC Film School, Murch first worked on Francis Ford Coppola's *The Rain People* (1969), then did the sound for USC classmate George Lucas' *THX-1138* (1971), as well as cowriting the film's screenplay. He did the sound montage and recording for Lucas' *American Graffiti* (1973) and earned an Oscar nomination for his sound work on Coppola's *The Conversation* (1974), a film whose suc-

cess depends so much on its aural qualities. (Coppola, busy with chores on *The Godfather Part II,* also entrusted Murch with much of the creative decision-making in the film's editing process.) He has since edited or co-edited *Julia* (1977, Oscar-nominated), *Apocalypse Now* (1979, Oscar-nominated), *The Unbearable Lightness of Being* (1988), *Ghost* (1990), *The Godfather Part III* (also 1990, Oscar-nominated) and won an Oscar for the stunning and innovative sound design of *Apocalypse Now*. He also directed and cowrote *Return to Oz* (1985), a dour and unsuccessful sequel to the 1939 classic.

MURNAU, F. W. Director. *(b. Dec. 28, 1888, Bielefeld, Westphalia, as Friedrich Wilhelm Plumpe; d. Mar. 11, 1931.)* One of the greatest film directors of the silent era, as influential and essential an artist as any number of his better-known and more prolific contemporaries. Many of his early, German-made films are lost, but at least three of the surviving ones are regarded as cinematic milestones: 1922's *Nosferatu,* a still-chilling (and unauthorized) adaptation of "Dracula" that was long suppressed by the widow of the novel's author, Bram Stoker; *The Last Laugh* (1924), a bitterly ironic chronicle of a proud doorman's decline; and *Faust* (1926), an elaborate, atmospheric adaptation of Goethe's work. All these films reveled in visual invention: *Nosferatu*'s expressionist lighting and camera angles and use of fast motion remain audaciously stunning; *The Last Laugh*'s tracking camera broke with the too-often static compositions of the day, telling its story without words, relying solely on images; and *Faust*'s sweep, grandeur, and imaginative visual design.

Murnau's German successes attracted the attention of Hollywood, where technical innovation flourished and studio heads studied German expressionist cinema; his first film there, the classic *Sunrise* (1927), starring Janet Gaynor and George O'Brien, was a big success and won several Academy Awards at the first Oscar ceremony. *Four Devils* (1928) and *City Girl* (1930, which was reworked as a talkie) followed, similarly innovative but not as well received. A disenchanted Murnau broke off his five-film contract with Fox Film after completing only three pictures. He traveled to the South Seas to make *Tabu* (1931), initially a collaboration with documentarian Robert Flaherty. But the combination of the two strong-willed artists was a case of too many cooks, and Flaherty abandoned the project. Murnau's finished film, made under trying and often impossible circumstances, was nonetheless a work of great beauty, as moving in its own way as *The Last Laugh.* Having survived the rigors of making *Tabu,* Murnau then saw it censored on initial release for the partial nudity of the native girls portrayed therein. It was to prove the embattled director's final film; he died in a car accident in southern California the year of its release.

MURPHY, AUDIE. Actor. *(b. June 20, 1924, Kingston, Tex.; d. May 28, 1971.)* Seeing this slight, boyish actor on-screen in any of his many Westerns, you'd be hard pressed to recognize him as the most highly decorated American serviceman in World War 2: 24 citations in all, including the Congressional Medal of Honor. The poor son of Texas sharecroppers, he found himself in glamorous Hollywood in 1948, making his film debut in an Alan Ladd starrer, *Beyond Glory.* Murphy gave a sincere performance as a belligerent delinquent in *Bad Boy* (1949), and something about the natural, untrained actor appealed to Universal-International's casting directors, who starred him in a series of budget Westerns, many of them shot in Technicolor, beginning with *The Kid from Texas* (1950), in which he played Billy the Kid. *Sierra, Kansas Raiders* (both 1950), *The Cimarron Kid, Duel at Silver Creek* (both 1952), *Gunsmoke, Tumbleweed* (both 1953), *Ride Clear of Diablo, Drums Across the River* (both 1954), and *Destry* (1955) followed, all of them tailored to Murphy's personality and limited acting ability. (His efforts at smoldering hatred or grim determination usually looked like adolescent petulance.)

In 1951 MGM borrowed Murphy from Universal to star in John Huston's adaptation of Stephen Crane's classic Civil War story, *The Red Badge of Courage,* in which the young star was effectively cast as a young Union soldier who flees under fire. Murphy played himself in *To Hell and Back* (1955), based on his best-selling autobiography, and its success boosted

him, for a short time at least, into better movies: *Walk the Proud Land* (1956), *The Guns of Fort Petticoat, Night Passage* (both 1957), *The Quiet American* (1958), *No Name on the Bullet* (1959), *The Unforgiven* (1960, supporting Burt Lancaster). By the early 1960s he was back in budget Westerns such as *Six Black Horses* (1962), *Showdown* (1963), *Apache Rifles* (1964), *Arizona Raiders* (1965), and *40 Guns to Apache Pass* (1966).

Victimized by bad investments (he declared bankruptcy in 1968) and personal problems, some relating to war-inflicted trauma, Murphy left moviemaking for a few years. He died in a plane crash shortly after completing what he hoped would be his comeback picture, *A Time for Dying* (1971), in which he played Jesse James. Murphy was briefly married to *Sierra* costar, Wanda Hendrix.

MURPHY, EDDIE. Actor, director, screenwriter, producer. *(b. Apr. 3, 1961, Hempstead, N.Y.)* By the time he was 19, this quick-witted, sharp-tongued black comedian had achieved stardom as the standout cast member on "Saturday Night Live" (1981–84). Having distinguished himself in TV and nightclubs (where he'd done stand-up comedy since age 16), Murphy's next step was motion pictures. His first break came when a last-minute change of plans caused producers to offer him a costarring part with Nick Nolte in *48HRS.* (1982). A hastily rewritten script drew on his already familiar smartass personality from television and proved a perfect showcase. He had more of a chance to act in *Trading Places* (1983), opposite Dan Aykroyd, which confirmed that the earlier film had been no fluke: Murphy was a bona fide movie star. After an overpromoted cameo in the dismal *Best Defense* (1984), the comedian hit pay dirt with his first solo starring vehicle, *Beverly Hills Cop* (1984), which originally had been written for Sylvester Stallone.

Murphy has taken control of his career since then. In the enjoyable *Coming to America* (1988) he augmented his starring role with some very funny cameos (in heavy makeup and costuming)—as an elderly Jewish man, a loquacious barber, and a lounge lizard entertainer. In *Harlem Nights* (1989) he managed to billboard his name five times in the opening credits (as presenter, executive producer, director, writer, and star)—but failed to provide a coherent or compelling script for himself and a stellar cast, including his hero Richard Pryor. His sequels have been a mixed blessing: *Beverly Hills Cop II* (1987) was a terrible film, but a huge hit; the equally dismal *Another 48HRS.* (1990) was far from a flop, as well, on the strength of Murphy's potent name. He has pleased both critics and fans most often returning to familiar comic territory, in *Boomerang, The Distinguished Gentleman* (both 1992), and the inevitable *Beverly Hills Cop III* (1994).

OTHER FILMS INCLUDE: 1986: *The Golden Child;* 1987: *Eddie Murphy Raw.*

MURPHY, GEORGE. Actor, dancer. *(b. July 4, 1902, New Haven, Conn.; d. May 3, 1992.)* Reliable, pleasant-looking hoofer-turned-actor, a self-made man whose real-life accomplishments rival (if not over-shadow) his screen successes. A college dropout who toiled in a wide variety of physical jobs, he started dancing for a living in the mid 1920s, creating a nightclub act with his wife-to-be. Murphy became a well-known dancer in New York, and found employment on Broadway in revues and musical comedies. He went to Hollywood to play the juvenile lead in the Eddie Cantor starrer *Kid Millions* (1934), and stayed to sing and dance his way through *After the Dance* (1935), *Top of the Town, You're a Sweetheart* (both 1937), *Hold That Co-ed* (1938), *Public Deb No. 1, Little Nellie Kelly* (both 1940), *A Girl, A Guy, and a Gob, Rise and Shine* (both 1941), *For Me and My Gal* (1942), *Show Business,* and *Step Lively* (both 1944), among others. In *Little Miss Broadway* (1938) he danced with Shirley Temple; in *Broadway Melody of 1940* he teamed with Fred Astaire. And in *This Is the Army* (1943) he played the show-biz father of Ronald Reagan, who in real life would follow him into California politics.

The easygoing Murphy, a screen natural with limited range but considerable personality, occasionally essayed roles in straight comedies, dramas, and crime films, including *Jealousy* (1934), *Public Menace* (1935), *London by Night* (1937), *Risky Business* (1939), *Ringside Maisie* (1941), *The Navy Comes Through* (1942), *Having Wonderful Crime* (1945), *The*

Arnelo Affair (1947), *Big City* (1948), *Border Incident, Battleground* (both 1949), *It's a Big Country, Walk East on Beacon,* and *Talk About a Stranger* (all 1952). A born activist, Murphy served as president of the Screen Actors Guild during the 1940s, helped found the Hollywood Republican Committee in 1947, and acted as public-relations spokesman for MGM, Desilu, and Technicolor before making a successful Senate bid in 1964. His bout with throat cancer cost Murphy a second term. His autobiography, "Say—Didn't You Used to Be George Murphy?," was published in 1970. In 1950 he received a special Oscar for his p.r. work relating to the film industry.

MURPHY, MICHAEL. Actor. *(b. May 5, 1938, Los Angeles.)* This tall, slim, pleasant-looking actor (and former high-school teacher) had a lock on white-bread, guilt-ridden urban males during his years of peak productivity on-screen. He reached the high point of this particular art as Jill Clayburgh's adulterous husband in Paul Mazursky's *An Unmarried Woman* (1978) and as Woody Allen's morally ambiguous best friend in *Manhattan* (1979). His early film appearances, for director Robert Altman, include *Countdown* (1968), *That Cold Day in the Park* (1969), *MASH, Brewster McCloud* (both 1970), *McCabe and Mrs. Miller* (1971), and *Nashville* (1975). He's also been featured in *The Legend of Lylah Clare* (1968), *Count Yorga, Vampire* (1970), *What's Up, Doc?* (1972), *The Front* (1976), *The Year of Living Dangerously* (1983), *Cloak & Dagger* (1984), *Salvador* (1986), *Shocker* (1989), *Batman Returns* (1992, as the Mayor), and *Clean Slate* (1994). Murphy has also been active in television, with such prominent TV movies as *The Autobiography of Miss Jane Pittman* (1974) and Robert Altman's *The Caine Mutiny Court-Martial* (1988) to his credit, and running parts in two series, "Two Marriages" (1983–84) and "Hard Copy" (1987). Often described as being Kennedy-like, he was cast as a presidential candidate in "Tanner '88," a satirical cable-TV series created by Robert Altman and Garry Trudeau.

MURRAY, BILL. Actor. *(b. Sept. 21, 1950, Chicago.)* Another "Saturday Night

Live" alumnus who graduated to the big screen, the bedraggled, pockmarked Murray brings an insouciant charm to his movie roles—that is, when he isn't saddled with puerile material, which has been known to happen. He broke into show business, along with older brother Brian Doyle-Murray, as a member of Chicago's "Second City" comedy troupe and landed a spot on "SNL" in 1977. Murray made a sort-of screen debut providing one of the voices for *Shame of the Jungle,* a 1975 animated spoof of Tarzan films, but got his big break as the sly summer camp counselor in the Canadian-made *Meatballs* (1979), directed by Ivan Reitman, with whom he's collaborated several times since.

Murray and Reitman made the most of that smart aleck characterization in the country-club farce *Caddyshack* (1980) and the service comedy *Stripes* (1981, teamed with writer-performer Harold Ramis), then struck box office gold with *Ghostbusters* (1984, in which Murray and Ramis were joined by Dan Aykroyd). From the start, Murray was also intrigued by other kinds of film projects, however. He played fabled "gonzo" journalist Hunter S. Thompson in *Where the Buffalo Roam* (1980), reportedly ad-libbed his supporting role opposite Dustin Hoffman in *Tootsie* (1982), and used his box office clout to star in (and cowrite) a serious, and ambitious, remake of W. Somerset Maugham's story of a man's quest for inner peace, *The Razor's Edge* (1984), which failed to please many critics or moviegoers.

Murray contributed a hilarious cameo as the pain-addicted dental patient in *Little Shop of Horrors* (1986), starred in a too mean-spirited *Scrooged* (1988), and sailed through *Ghostbusters II* (1989) before taking his first turn behind the camera, as cowriter and codirector of the very funny (if low-key) caper comedy *Quick Change* (1990). Since then he's had some of his best screen opportunities, as the insufferably ingratiating hypochondriac in *What About Bob?* (1991), in a surprisingly serious part as a gangster who wants to be accepted as a stand-up comic in *Mad Dog and Glory* (1993), as a cocky TV weatherman who's doomed to relive the same day over and over again in the clever *Groundhog Day* (also 1993), and as a member of fringe filmmaker Ed Wood Jr.'s bizarre coterie in *Ed Wood* (1994).

Murray's brother Brian Doyle-Murray— stockier and older-looking than his sibling—has become a familiar character actor in television and films, including a number of Bill's, including *Caddyshack, The Razor's Edge,* and *Groundhog Day.*

MURRAY, DON. Actor, director. (b. July 31, 1929, Hollywood.) Best remembered for his wonderful, Oscar-nominated performance as the naïve cowboy who romances Marilyn Monroe in *Bus Stop* (1956), Murray was no hick in real life. A graduate of the American Academy of Dramatic Arts, he was also a conscientious objector who refused to serve in the Korean War. After a solid start on Broadway, and the great success of *Bus Stop,* he seemed headed for a long career as a leading man, in major films like *A Hatful of Rain, The Bachelor Party* (both 1957), and *Shake Hands With the Devil* (1959). But it turned out he was primarily interested in moviemaking as a form of community service; in 1961 he coproduced, cowrote (under the name of Don Deer), and starred in *The Hoodlum Priest,* the story of a priest's attempts to reform juvenile delinquents. He went on to play the Rev. Norman Vincent Peale in 1964's *One Man's Way,* and in 1972 made his directorial debut with *The Cross and the Switchblade,* another priests-and-delinquents tale, starring Pat Boone and Erik Estrada. In 1977 he directed *Damien,* the story of the famous priest who treated lepers. Other acting credits, major and minor, include *Advise and Consent* (1962), *Baby The Rain Must Fall* (1965), *Sweet Love, Bitter* (1967), *Happy Birthday, Wanda June* (1971), *Deadly Hero* (1976), *Peggy Sue Got Married* (1986), *Made in Heaven* (1987) and *Ghosts Can't Do It* (1990), along with a two-year stint on the nighttime soap opera "Knots Landing" (1979–81). In 1961 he married actress Hope Lange; they divorced that same year.

MUSE, CLARENCE. Actor. (b. Oct. 7, 1889, Baltimore; d. Oct. 13, 1979.) A highly educated man who held a law degree, Muse had an unusually long and varied career, appearing in dozens of films from 1929 to 1972. Muse's deep voice and soulful expressions often lifted his performances above his stereotypical assignments. He occasionally got substantial, well-written roles in major films—and when he didn't, wrote the parts himself. He cowrote the script (and songs) for the Bobby Breen vehicle *Way Down South* (1939), and wrote himself a starring vehicle, *Broken Strings* (1940), that was aimed at all-black audiences. (He was also featured in a 1932 *Hollywood on Parade* short subject performing his musical tone poem "Congo.") He debuted in a costarring part in the all-black *Hearts in Dixie* (1929), and went on to appear in *Huckleberry Finn* (1931, as Jim), *White Zombie* (1932), *Broadway Bill* (1934, a role he repeated in the 1950 remake *Riding High*), *Show Boat* (1936), *Tales of Manhattan, The Black Swan* (both 1942), *Shadow of a Doubt* (1943), *An Act of Murder* (1948), *Porgy and Bess* (1959), *Buck and the Preacher* (1972), *Car Wash* (1976), and *The Black Stallion* (1979). He was one of the first inductees in the Black Filmmakers' Hall of Fame, in 1973.

NAGEL, CONRAD. Actor. *(b. Mar. 16, 1897, Keokuk, Iowa; d. Feb. 24, 1970.)* Stoic leading man of silent and early talkie films, with wavy blond hair and matinee-idol features. Nagel already had years of stage experience under his belt when he debuted on-screen in a 1918 version of *Little Women,* and he worked tirelessly in films throughout the 1920s, including *Saturday Night* (1922), *Tess of the D'Urbervilles, Three Weeks* (both 1924), *Pretty Ladies, Lights of Old Broadway* (both 1925), *The Exquisite Sinner* (1926), *London After Midnight* (1927, supporting Lon Chaney), *The Michigan Kid, The Mysterious Lady* (opposite Greta Garbo), *Glorious Betsy* (all 1928), and *The Kiss* (1929, again with Garbo). The coming of sound didn't bother the stage-seasoned Nagel one whit, and his authoritative baritone perfectly matched his serious countenance. He starred or costarred in *Dynamite* (also 1929), *The Divorcee, One Romantic Night, Free Love* (all 1930), *East Lynne, Son of India, Pagan Lady* (all 1931), *Hell Divers, Kongo, Fast Life* (all 1932), *Ann Vickers, The Constant Woman* (both 1933), and *Dangerous Corner* (1934). His active participation in the mid 1930s founding of the Screen Actors Guild infuriated the Hollywood hierarchy, especially MGM's Louis B. Mayer, and he

was tacitly blacklisted by the major studios for many years.

Nagel starred as FBI agent Alan O'Connor in an inexpensive four-film series for Grand National, beginning with *Yellow Cargo* (1936) and ending with *Navy Spy* (1937); these cheapies gave Nagel his last leading roles in American films. He even tried his hand at directing at Grand National, with *Love Takes Flight* (1937), but found his steadiest work in Hollywood in the medium of radio, where he hosted and directed "The Silver Theatre" (which featured many movie personalities) from 1937 to 1942. He then moved to New York, and was active on Broadway, as well as radio and, in later years, live television. Nagel made occasional film appearances over the years in character parts, among them *The Adventures of Rusty* (1945), *The Vicious Circle* (1948), *All That Heaven Allows* (1955), *Hidden Fear* (1957), *Stranger in My Arms,* and *The Man Who Understood Women* (both 1959). A cofounder and former president of the Academy of Motion Picture Arts and Sciences, he received a special Oscar plaque in 1939 for his efforts on behalf of the Motion Picture Relief Fund. In later years he ran an acting school.

NAISH, J. CARROL. Actor. *(b. Jan. 21, 1900, New York City; d. Jan. 24, 1973.)* Prolific character actor whose swarthy complexion, dark eyes, and wavy black hair belied his Irish ancestry. A talented dialectician, Naish played virtually every ethnic type in movies, including blacks and Orientals—but almost never an Irishman! He was an aggressive scene stealer who often infuriated his fellow performers, but none denied his ability. Naish snared Oscar nominations for his vivid portrayals of an Italian prisoner of war in *Sahara* (1943) and a poor Mexican father in *A Medal for Benny* (1945). He played a hissable Japanese villain in the *Batman* serial (1943), and a lovelorn hunchback in *House of Frankenstein* (1944). He twice played Sitting Bull, in the musical *Annie Get Your Gun* (1950) and in *Sitting Bull* (1954), while working the other side of the street as Gen. Sheridan in *Rio Grande* (1950) and Gen. Santa Ana in *The Last Command* (1955). Naish played Oriental detective Charlie Chan in a 1957 TV series; he'd earlier starred on the radio and

TV comedy series "Life with Luigi," and was later very funny as a savvy Indian chief in 1960–61's "Guestward Ho!"
OTHER FILMS INCLUDE: 1932: *The Hatchet Man, The Kid From Spain, Tiger Shark;* 1935: *Captain Blood, The Lives of a Bengal Lancer, Black Fury;* 1936: *Anthony Adverse, The Charge of the Light Brigade, Ramona;* 1937: *Think Fast, Mr. Moto;* 1938: *King of Alcatraz, Her Jungle Love;* 1939: *King of Chinatown, Beau Geste;* 1940: *Typhoon, Down Argentine Way;* 1941: *That Night in Rio, Blood and Sand, The Corsican Brothers;* 1942: *Dr. Broadway, The Pied Piper, Tales of Manhattan;* 1943: *Behind the Rising Sun, Gung Ho!, Calling Dr. Death;* 1944: *The Monster Maker, Jungle Woman, Dragon Seed;* 1945: *The Southerner;* 1946: *Humoresque, The Beast With Five Fingers;* 1947: *The Fugitive;* 1948: *Joan of Arc;* 1949: *The Midnight Kiss;* 1950: *The Black Hand, Rio Grande;* 1951: *Across the Wide Missouri;* 1952: *Clash by Night;* 1955: *New York Confidential, Hit the Deck, Violent Saturday;* 1957: *The Young Don't Cry;* 1971: *Dracula vs. Frankenstein.*

NAPIER, CHARLES. Actor. *(b. Apr. 12, 1936, Scottsville, Ky.)* After service in the Army and experience on the stage and TV, this rugged-looking character actor got his film career rolling with a series of films by sexploitation guru Russ Meyer: *Cherry, Harry & Raquel* (1969), *Beyond the Valley of the Dolls* (1970), *The Seven Minutes* (1971), and *Super Vixens* (1974). Napier eventually went on to more prestigious efforts and is probably best known for his frequent performances for director Jonathan Demme, starting with *Handle With Care* (1977, as the bigamist trucker Chrome Angel), and including *Last Embrace* (1979), *Melvin and Howard* (1980), *Swing Shift* (1984), *Something Wild* (1986), *Married to the Mob* (1988, as Michelle Pfeiffer's hairdresser), *The Silence of the Lambs* (1991, as one of the cops who's attacked by Anthony Hopkins), and *Philadelphia* (1993, as the Judge). He has also appeared in *The Blues Brothers* (1980), *Rambo: First Blood Part II* (1985, as Marshal Murdock), *Miami Blues,* and *The Grifters* (both 1990), and has maintained a presence in low-budget movies, with roles in films like *Thunder and Lightning* (1977), *Deep Space* (1987, starring as an alien-chasing cop), *The Night Stalker* (1987, starring as a serial killer–chasing cop), *Hit List* (1989), and *Center of the Web* (1992).

NATWICK, MILDRED. Actress. *(b. June 19, 1908, Baltimore; d. Oct. 25, 1994.)* Talented character actress whose presence was always welcome, an Academy Award nominee for her portrayal of Jane Fonda's jittery mother in *Barefoot in the Park* (1967). A Bryn Mawr graduate, she went into acting after finishing college and made her Broadway debut in 1932. Natwick first appeared on screen in *The Long Voyage Home* (1940), directed by John Ford, who hired her frequently. She always looked older than she was, and was playing spinsters while still in her thirties.
OTHER FILMS INCLUDE: 1945: *Yolanda and the Thief;* 1947: *The Late George Apley;* 1948: *The Kissing Bandit, 3 Godfathers;* 1949: *She Wore a Yellow Ribbon;* 1950: *Cheaper by the Dozen;* 1952: *The Quiet Man, Against All Flags;* 1955: *The Trouble With Harry;* 1956: *The Court Jester;* 1957: *Tammy and the Bachelor;* 1969: *If It's Tuesday, This Must Be Belgium;* 1974: *Daisy Miller;* 1975: *At Long Last Love;* 1988: *Dangerous Liaisons.*

NEAL, PATRICIA. Actress. *(b. Jan. 20, 1926, Packard, Ky.)* Strong dramatic actress whose real-life experiences rivaled any of her superb screen performances. After studying speech and drama at Northwestern University, she understudied on Broadway in "Voice of the Turtle" and won a Tony Award for Lillian Hellman's "Another Part of the Forest." This led to numerous offers from Hollywood, and she debuted opposite Ronald Reagan in *John Loves Mary* (1949). Neal's role in *The Fountainhead* (1949) resulted in a long, and much publicized, affair with the film's married star, Gary Cooper. Neal continued to work in films like *The Breaking Point* (1950), *The Day the Earth Stood Still,* and *Operation Pacific* (both 1951), but suffered a nervous breakdown after ending the affair with Cooper. After recovering, she married writer Roald Dahl in 1953, and returned to American films as the woman who discovers the dangerous hayseed Lonesome Rhodes in *A Face in the Crowd* (1957).
Her career peaked with a searing, Oscar-winning performance as Alma, the house-

keeper in *Hud* (1963), but during the 1960s Neal sustained great personal tragedy: her youngest child, Theo, was hit by a cab and her daughter Olivia died from measles at the age of seven. She had finished *In Harm's Way* (1965) and had begun work on *7 Women* when she suffered a series of paralyzing strokes. Neal went through years of rehabilitation and made a triumphant comeback as the mother of a returning war veteran in *The Subject Was Roses* (1968), earning another Best Actress nomination. Since then, she has appeared sporadically in films like *The Night Digger* (1971), *Baxter* (1972), *The Passage* (1979), and *Ghost Story* (1981), and in several TV movies, *Tail Gunner Joe* (1977), *All Quiet on the Western Front* (1979), and most notably *The Homecoming—A Christmas Story* (1971), the forerunner of "The Waltons." Her autobiography "As I Am" (published in 1988) details her relationships with Cooper and Dahl; she was divorced from Dahl in 1983. Glenda Jackson played her in the TV movie *The Patricia Neal Story* (1981).
OTHER FILMS INCLUDE: 1949: *The Hasty Heart;* 1950: *Bright Leaf, Three Secrets;* 1952: *Diplomatic Courier, Washington Story;* 1961: *Breakfast at Tiffany's;* 1973: *Happy Mother's Day—Love George.*

NEESON, LIAM. Actor. *(b. June 7, 1952, Ballymena, Northern Ireland.)* This tall, earthy, stage-trained lead made his film debut in a small role in John Boorman's *Excalibur* (1981), and appeared in *The Bounty* (1984) and *The Mission* (1986) before becoming familiar to U.S. audiences as the deaf murder suspect in *Suspect* (1987), the obnoxious horror-film director in the Dirty Harry entry *The Dead Pool,* and the accused child molester in *The Good Mother* (both 1988). After an unsuccessful stab at a Southern twang as Patrick Swayze's brooding brother in *Next of Kin* (1989), he impressively masked his Irish accent in his first lead in an American film, as the scientist turned masked avenger in Sam Raimi's *Darkman* (1990). Gaining in prominence with each successive role—and impressively busy—he has also starred in *Crossing the Line* (1991), *Shining Through, Under Suspicion,* Woody Allen's *Husbands and Wives* (all 1992), *Leap of Faith* (also

1992, miscast as a sheriff), *Ethan Frome, Deception* (both 1993), and in a galvanizing Oscar-nominated performance as opportunist turned humanitarian Oskar Schindler in *Schindler's List* (also 1993). That same year, he received a Tony Award nomination for a Broadway revival of "Anna Christie" and later married his co-star, Natasha Richardson. He starred again with Richardson in *Nell* (1994), then played *Rob Roy* (1995).

NEGULESCO, JEAN. Director, screenwriter. *(b. Feb. 26, 1900, Cariova, Romania; d. July 18, 1993.)* Negulesco was a painter who lived in Paris during the 1920s and a lifelong art collector and connoisseur. He became a set designer for films, and brought an innate sense of taste and style to the movies he later directed. A jack-of-all-trades in his earliest years in Hollywood, he wrote stories, worked as an "associate director," and even shot second unit for Frank Borzage's *A Farewell to Arms* in 1932. He graduated to directing at Warner Bros., where he made some fifty short subjects, including dozens of big-band one-reelers in the early 1940s, as well as the Cinderella-in-Hollywood fable *Alice in Movieland* (1940) with Joan Leslie.
Negulesco's first feature credit was *Singapore Woman* (1941), a forgettable remake of Bette Davis' *Dangerous* (1935), but his career as feature director wasn't cemented until 1944, when he made *The Mask of Dimitrios* and *The Conspirators.* He proved he could handle suspense, as in *Three Strangers,* lush romanticism, in *Nobody Lives Forever* and *Humoresque* (all 1946), hard-boiled drama, in *Road House* (1948), as well as understatement, which added distinction to such diverse (and excellent) films as *Johnny Belinda* (also 1948, Oscar-nominated), *Three Came Home,* and *The Mudlark* (both 1950). Other interesting credits include *Under My Skin* (1950) and *Phone Call From a Stranger* (1952). He spent most of the 1950s at 20th Century-Fox, and enjoyed great success with *O. Henry's Full House* (1952, "The Last Leaf" episode), *Titanic, How to Marry a Millionaire* (both 1953), *Three Coins in the Fountain, Woman's World* (both 1954), *Daddy Long Legs, The Rains of Ranchipur* (both 1955), *Boy on a Dolphin* (1957), *The Gift of Love, A Certain Smile* (both 1958), *Count Your Bless-*

ings, and *The Best of Everything* (both 1959). They were the very definition of the term "glossy." Later credits include *Jessica* (1962), *The Pleasure Seekers* (1964), *Hello-Goodbye,* and *The Invincible Six* (both 1970). He spent his later years traveling, painting, and working on his autobiography, "Things I Did and Things I Think I Did," which was published in 1984. In 1973 he acted in a French-language film, *Un Officier de Police sans Importance.*

NEILL, SAM. Actor. *(b. Sept. 14, 1947, Northern Ireland, as Nigel Neill.)* This Irish-born actor, raised in New Zealand, broke into Australian films just around the time that country's movie industry was going into its renaissance, and he impressed theatergoers as a virile yet sensitive leading man. Neill made his debut in *Ashes* (1975), but first attracted attention as the male lead in Gillian Armstrong's turn-of-the-century drama, *My Brilliant Career* (1979). Since then he has alternated between Australian-made movies and international productions, flirting with stardom at several junctures. He supported Meryl Streep in Fred Schepisi's production of *Plenty* (1985), then costarred with her in the same director's *A Cry in the Dark* (1988), the harrowing tale of an Australian couple accused of murdering their own child; in the rush to praise Streep's brilliant work, Neill's equally compelling and controlled performance as her agonized husband was somewhat taken for granted. The truth is, he's *always* good. He's had prominent showcases on American TV in the high-profile miniseries "Kane and Abel" (1985) and "Amerika" (1987) and the telefilm *One Against the Wind* (1991, opposite Judy Davis), and costarring roles in such mainstream movies as *Dead Calm* (1989) and *The Hunt for Red October* (1990), but nothing could top his parlay in 1993, starring in the biggest hit movie of all time, *Jurassic Park,* and the critical hit of the year, Jane Campion's *The Piano,* as Holly Hunter's sexually repressed husband. If Neill is still not quite "star material," there is no question of his status among the best, and most versatile, actors working today.
OTHER FILMS INCLUDE: 1977: *Sleeping Dogs;* 1981: *The Final Conflict* (as Damien); 1982: *Enigma;* 1983: *The Country Girls;* 1985:

For Love Alone; 1986: *The Good Wife;* 1991: *Until the End of the World;* 1992: *Memoirs of an Invisible Man;* 1994: *Sirens;* 1995: *In the Mouth of Madness.*

NELLIGAN, KATE. Actress. *(b. Mar. 16, 1951, London, Ontario.)* Excellent stage-trained actress who, after several false starts, has finally gained notice for her film work. She left Canada at 18 to study at London's Central School of Speech and Drama and gradually won acclaim for a variety of stage and television roles. She made her film debut in *The Romantic Englishwoman* (1975) and appeared in *Dracula* (1979, as Lucy), *Mr. Patman* (1980), and *Eye of the Needle* (1981), in which she was excellent as a lonely woman who becomes romantically involved with a Nazi spy. Nelligan moved to L.A. and starred in 1983's *Without a Trace* but had better luck on Broadway (earning Tony nominations for "Plenty," "A Moon for the Misbegotten," "Serious Money," and "Spoils of War") and appeared only sporadically in features, most notably *Eleni* (1985). There had been a certain coldness to her screen characters, but in 1991 she dazzled moviegoers and critics alike with an unexpected performance blending comic knowhow and a poignant believability as a sexually active, tough-talking New York waitress in *Frankie and Johnny;* it was followed months later by a bravura turn as Nick Nolte's iron-willed mother in *The Prince of Tides,* which earned her an Oscar nomination. She has since appeared in a number of TV movies as well as *Fatal Instinct* (1993) and *Wolf* (1994).

NELSON, CRAIG T. Actor. *(b. Apr. 4, 1946, Spokane, Wash.)* This strapping American Everyman endeared himself to movie audiences as the besieged patriarch in *Poltergeist* (1982), his first substantial film role. A former radio performer and stand-up comic whose pals included writer-director Barry Levinson (his film debut was the Levinson-scripted ... *And Justice for All* in 1979), Nelson became a familiar face. He played a football coach in the working-class teen drama *All the Right Moves* (1983) and quickly settled into supporting character roles in A productions such as *Silkwood* (1983) and *The*

Killing Fields (1984). In 1986 he reprised his star-making role in the sequel *Poltergeist II: The Other Side.* Nelson played an over-the-top villain in 1988's trashy slugfest *Action Jackson,* proving that he could chew scenery with the best of 'em. The quality of his films declined sharply—1989's *Troop Beverly Hills* and *Turner and Hooch* are two prime examples—and he turned to TV work. He starred in the short-lived series "Call to Glory" (1984–85) and then won an Emmy playing the lead in the popular sitcom "Coach" (1989–). He's also been active in made-for-TV movies and miniseries, one of which (*Ride With the Wind,* 1994) he executive produced and wrote. In the 1991 telefilm *The Josephine Baker Story* he was cast as columnist Walter Winchell.

NELSON, JUDD. Actor. *(b. Nov. 28, 1959, Portland, Maine.)* This dark-haired former Brat Packer flares his nostrils and glowers better than any of his youthful contemporaries, but he's probably the least appealing performer in the whole bunch. Part of that might be due to the roles he's played—obnoxious, troubled wiseacres—in the likes of *The Breakfast Club* and *St. Elmo's Fire* (both 1985). Nelson got his first bona fide lead in the appalling *Blue City* (1986), a seedy, coarse thriller set in Florida. He "reformed," briefly, to play a hotshot lawyer in *From the Hip* (1987), and chillingly portrayed a serial killer in the otherwise negligible *Relentless* (1989). In 1991 he was effectively cast as a streetwise cop in *New Jack City.* OTHER FILMS INCLUDE: 1984: *Making the Grade;* 1985: *Fandango;* 1986: *Transformers—The Movie* (voice only); 1987: "Billionaire Boys Club" (miniseries); 1989: *Never on Tuesday;* 1991: *The Dark Backward;* 1993: *Primary Motive, Every Breath* (also cowrote).

NERO, FRANCO. Actor. *(b. Nov. 23, 1941, Parma, Italy.)* Strikingly handsome international film star whose smooth features, wavy dark hair, and light blue eyes made him a particular favorite of female filmgoers. Hampered by a poor grasp of English language and pronunciation, Nero hasn't won much acceptance on this side of the Atlantic, although he is fondly remembered as Sir Lancelot in the 1967 film version of *Camelot,* in which he costarred with longtime flame Vanessa Redgrave (who bore him a child).
OTHER FILMS INCLUDE: 1966: *The Bible;* 1968: *Texas, Addio;* 1970: *The Mercenary, The Virgin and the Gypsy;* 1972: *Pope Joan;* 1973: *Don't Turn the Other Cheek;* 1977: *Submission;* 1978: *Force 10 From Navarone;* 1980: *The Man With Bogart's Face;* 1981: *The Salamander;* 1982: *Querelle;* 1983: *Wagner;* 1986: *Sweet Country;* 1988: *Silent Night;* 1990: *Die Hard 2.*

NEWELL, MIKE. Director. *(b. Mar. 28, 1942, England.)* British TV director who has become a prominent feature filmmaker on both sides of the Atlantic. After studying at Cambridge, Newell worked at Granada Television for several years before directing TV movies. His first feature was *The Man in the Iron Mask* (1977, aired in the United States as a TV movie), and followed with the negligible horror film *The Awakening* (1980), *Bad Blood* (1981), and the miniseries "Blood Feud" (1983) about Jimmy Hoffa and Robert Kennedy. But Newell's reputation was cemented by *Dance With a Stranger* (1985), a tough examination of his country's mores, which starred Miranda Richardson as Ruth Ellis, the last woman to be executed in Britain. *The Good Father* (1987) was a trenchant account of Thatcher-induced gloom, but was followed by the Capraesque nuclear war fantasy *Amazing Grace and Chuck* (1987) and the lovely, sunny comedy of spiritual rebirth *Enchanted April* (1992, made for the BBC but released theatrically in the United States). Most recently, Newell directed the dour Irish fable *Into the West* (1993), with Gabriel Byrne, and the hit romantic comedy *Four Weddings and a Funeral* (1994).

NEWMAN, ALFRED. Composer. *(b. Mar. 17, 1901, New Haven; d. Feb. 17, 1970.)* Arguably the most important musical craftsman who ever worked in Hollywood, Newman was associated with more than two hundred films during his 40-year career. He scored every conceivable type of film, and as longtime head of the music department at 20th Century-Fox supervised many other scores as well. A child prodigy, he was giving piano concerts at the age of seven, and was working on

Broadway as a conductor when Samuel Goldwyn lured him to Hollywood in 1930. One of his first compositions was the haunting theme for the Depression-era cityscape *Street Scene* (1931). This vivid piece of music became synonymous with Hollywood depictions of New York City, and was reused countless times in the decades ahead. (Newman conducted a performance in stereophonic sound with the 20th Century-Fox orchestra as an overture to *How to Marry a Millionaire* in 1953). He composed another oft-used standard for Douglas Fairbanks' *Mr. Robinson Crusoe* (1932) which gained fame when it was reused in *The Hurricane* (1937) and given the title "Moon of Manikoora."

Newman won nine Academy Awards— for *Alexander's Ragtime Band* (1938), *Tin Pan Alley* (1940), *The Song of Bernadette* (1943), *Mother Wore Tights* (1947), *With a Song in My Heart* (1952), *Call Me Madam* (1953), *Love Is a Many Splendored Thing* (1955), *The King and I* (1956), and *Camelot* (1967, adaptation only)—and was nominated 36 other times! As so often happens, film-music buffs would argue (rather persuasively) that some of Newman's best scores were those that didn't win Oscars—like *Wuthering Heights* (1939), *How Green Was My Valley* (1941), and *All About Eve* (1950). His brother Lionel was a composer, conductor, and later musical director at Fox; brother Emil also composed scores at Fox in the 1940s before freelancing in the 1950s and 1960s. Alfred's sons David and Thomas are successful film composers in their own right. David's credits include *Throw Momma From the Train* (1987), *The War of the Roses* (1989), and *The Freshman* (1990); Thomas received Oscar nominations for 1994's *The Shawshank Redemption* and *Little Women*. Alfred's and Lionel's nephew Randy Newman, a successful pop composer/performer, has written some notable film scores, including *Ragtime* (1981), *The Natural* (1984), *Parenthood* (1989), and *The Paper* (1994).
OTHER FILMS INCLUDE: 1931: *Arrowsmith;* 1933: *The Bower;* 1934: *Our Daily Bread;* 1935: *Les Miserables, Call of the Wild;* 1936: *Dodsworth;* 1937: *The Prisoner of Zenda;* 1939: *The Hunchback of Notre Dame, The Rains Came;* 1940: *The Mark of Zorro;* 1941: *Ball of Fire;* 1942: *The Black Swan;* 1944: *Keys of the Kingdom;* 1946: *Centennial Summer;* 1948: *The Snake Pit;* 1952: *The Prisoner of Zenda;* 1956: *Anastasia;* 1959: *The Diary of Anne Frank;* 1962: *How the West Was Won;* 1965: *The Greatest Story Ever Told;* 1970: *Airport.*

NEWMAN, PAUL. Actor, director. *(b. Jan. 26, 1925, Cleveland, Ohio.)* Yes, kids, that handsome, middle-aged man whose face you see on spaghetti sauce and salad dressing containers used to make your mothers swoon. In fact, he's an essential figure in film history, a bridge between the larger-than-life stars of Hollywood's Golden Age and the more down-to-earth, realistic actors who have dominated movies since the mid 1960s. With his magnetic blue eyes, gentle humor, and malleable persona, Paul Newman had—and still has—genuine star charisma . . . but his tenure at the Method-oriented Actors' Studio and his propensity for playing outsider types set him apart from the traditional movie leading man. Newman debuted on Broadway in 1953 in William Inge's "Picnic," and almost instantly turned heads at the Hollywood studios; after a false start with his debut in the ludicrous Biblical saga *The Silver Chalice* (1954), Newman scored as tough, star-crossed boxer Rocky Graziano in *Somebody Up There Likes Me* (1956) and his film career was off and running.

Newman and second wife Joanne Woodward were paired in a number of films *(The Long Hot Summer, From the Terrace, Rally 'Round the Flag, Boys!, Paris Blues, A New Kind of Love)* that only boosted his appeal. He hit his stride with an Oscar-nominated performance as Brick in 1958's *Cat on a Hot Tin Roof,* and achieved further career milestones (and two more Oscar nods) as pool shark Eddie Felson in *The Hustler* (1961) and as an ambitious heel in *Hud* (1963). He was outstanding as the chain-gang prisoner in 1967's *Cool Hand Luke* (another Academy Award-nominated portrayal) and, of course, as a likable outlaw in the classic *Butch Cassidy and the Sundance Kid* (1969; he was also one of the film's executive producers) in which he first teamed with Robert Redford. In 1969 he got to combine his avid, real-life interest in auto racing with a film assignment in *Winning* (which costarred Woodward). He turned to directing with 1968's *Rachel, Rachel,* the first of several first-rate films he would make with his wife as star. In the 1970s he alternated between quirky Robert Altman films and brash Hollywood disaster epics, but scored solidly, reteamed with Redford, in the delightful con-artist comedy *The Sting* (1973). In the 1980s, with traces of world-weariness etched in his still-handsome face and a hint of raspiness in his voice, Newman left the matinee-idol persona behind for good. He was effective as an unfairly maligned businessman in *Absence of Malice* (1981) and startlingly powerful as a whiskey-soaked lawyer in *The Verdict* (1982); he was Oscar-nominated for both roles (nominations five and six, respectively). Never having won an Oscar, Newman was finally presented with an honorary award for the body of his work in 1985 (and for his "personal integrity and dedication to his craft"). Ironically, he won a bona fide Academy Award the very next year, when he reprised the role of pool hustler Eddie Felson—brilliantly—in Martin Scorsese's *The Color of Money* (1986).

No contemporary screen idol has ever aged more gracefully, but Newman refused to fall back on his looks, or his "persona," and continued to seek out challenges both as actor and director. In the latter guise he directed Woodward in a 1980 TV movie of the Broadway play "The Shadow Box," and 1987 remake of Tennessee Williams' *The Glass Menagerie,* and costarred with her in James Ivory's ironic *Mr. & Mrs. Bridge* (1990). He played wildly colorful, eccentric Louisiana governor Earl Long in *Blaze* (1989) and Gen. Leslie R. Groves, the military leader in charge of The Manhattan Project, in *Fat Man and Little Boy* (1989).

The 1980s also saw him launch the manufacture and marketing of "Newman's Own" spaghetti sauce, salad dressing, and microwave popcorn, the proceeds from which benefit various children's charities. The politically conscious Newman continues to be outspoken on important issues, alternating screen work with labors for various liberal causes (and the drug treatment center named for his son Scott, who died in 1978 from an overdose of liquor and tranquilizers). Newman and Woodward shared Kennedy Center honors in 1992, but unlike many honorees they have not yet retired; far from it. In 1994 he

starred for the Coen brothers in *The Hudsucker Proxy* and earned his eighth Best Actor nomination for his portrayal of an amiable small-town loser in Robert Benton's *Nobody's Fool.* He works only when a script inspires him, which allows audiences to place a certain stock in any movie he chooses to make.

OTHER FILMS INCLUDE: 1958: *The Left-Handed Gun;* 1959: *The Young Philadelphians;* 1960: *Exodus;* 1962: *Sweet Bird of Youth, Hemingway's Adventures of a Young Man;* 1963: *The Prize;* 1964: *What a Way to Go!, The Outrage;* 1965: *Lady L.;* 1966: *Harper, Torn Curtain;* 1967: *Hombre;* 1968: *The Secret War of Harry Frigg;* 1970: *WUSA* (with Woodward; also coproduced); 1971: *They Might Be Giants* (coproduced only); 1972: *The Effect of Gamma Rays on Man-in-the-Moon Marigolds* (produced and directed only), *The Life and Times of Judge Roy Bean* (also coexecutive produced); 1973: *The Mackintosh Man;* 1974: *The Towering Inferno;* 1976: *The Drowning Pool, Silent Movie* (cameo as himself), *Buffalo Bill and the Indians;* 1977: *Slap Shot;* 1979: *Quintet;* 1980: *When Time Ran Out ...;* 1981: *Fort Apache, The Bronx;* 1984: *Harry and Son* (with Woodward; also directed, cowrote, and coproduced).

NEWMAR, JULIE. Actress. *(b. Aug. 16, 1935, Los Angeles, as Julie Newmeyer.)* Statuesque beauty who was a decorative asset in several movies during the 1950s and 1960s. She first appeared in *The Band Wagon* (1953) in "The Girl Hunt" ballet number, then was featured as one of the dancing *Seven Brides for Seven Brothers* (1954). She returned to Broadway and appeared in "Li'l Abner" as Stupefyin' Jones, a part she reprised in the 1959 movie. She also won a Tony Award for "The Marriage-Go-Round" and got to repeat that role in the 1960 film. The remainder of her film assignments were mediocre, however: *The Rookie* (1960), *For Love or Money* (1963), *Mackenna's Gold* and *The Maltese Bippy* (both 1969), to name a few. She was a delightful "Catwoman" on the "Batman" TV show, and that's the one role for which she's best remembered (though diehard TV buffs may also recall her in "My Living Doll," a 1964–65 sitcom starring Bob Cummings). She's been less effective as an aging sex kitten in *Deep Space* (1987),

Ghosts Can't Do It (1990), and *Oblivion* (1994).

NEWTON, ROBERT. Actor. *(b. June 1, 1905, Shaftesbury, England; d. Mar. 25, 1956.)* To several generations of moviegoers, he *was* Long John Silver. This dark, physically imposing British actor had a distinctive voice and malleable features, which enabled him to play a wide variety of roles. Not a conventional leading man, Newton nonetheless dominated many of the films in which he appeared. Moreover, he consistently rated among Britain's top box-office draws, a rare achievement for any character actor. He's memorable in *Fire Over England* (1937), *The Beachcomber* (1938), *Jamaica Inn* (1939), *Haunted Honeymoon* (1940), *Major Barbara* (1941), *Henry V* (1945), *Odd Man Out* (1947), *Oliver Twist* (1948, as Bill Sykes), *Tom Brown's School Days* (1951), *Les Miserables* (1952, as Javert), *The High and the Mighty* (1954), and *Around the World in 80 Days* (1956, as Inspector Fix). Newton's robust performance as Long John Silver in Walt Disney's *Treasure Island* (1950) created a mini-career for the actor, who repeated the part in *Long John Silver* (1954) and a TV series; he also played a variation on the character in *Blackbeard the Pirate* (1952).

NGOR, HAING S. (DR.) Actor. *(b. Mar. 22, 1950, Samrong Young, Cambodia.)* Ngor was an obstetrician and gynecologist in Phnom Penh when the Khmer Rouge took over. He spent four years as a slave laborer and lost most of his family before the Vietnamese came to power. He escaped to Thailand and eventually to the U.S., where he continued his medical career. A casting director spotted him at a Cambodian wedding and, with no formal acting experience, he got the part of journalist Dith Pran in 1984's harrowing *The Killing Fields* and won a Best Supporting Actor Oscar for his heart-rending performance. Since then, he has occasionally appeared in films like *The Iron Triangle* (1989), *Vietnam, Texas* (1990), and *Ambition* (1991), and TV movies like *In Love and War* (1987) and *Last Flight Out* (1990). Most recently he appeared in *My Life* (1993, as a mystical healer) and as the heroine's father in the third film of Ol-

iver Stone's "Vietnam Trilogy," *Heaven and Earth* (1993). He devotes much of his time to helping Southeast Asian refugees. His autobiography, "Haing Ngor: A Cambodian Odyssey" (1988), is a painfully honest account of his life.

THE NICHOLAS BROTHERS. Dancers. *(Fayard—b. Oct. 20, 1914. Harold—b. Mar. 27, 1924.)* Fans who admired Michael Jackson's dancing and body movements in the 1980s and 1990s might do well to take a look at what Harold and Fayard Nicholas were doing in the 1930s and 1940s. The most celebrated of the era's specialty "flash acts," their eye-popping blend of acrobatics, leaps, splits, and tapping left audiences gasping. Though they appeared in shorts, *The Big Broadcast of 1936* (1935) and black-cast films while still in their early teens, they hit their stride working in numerous Fox musicals in the early 1940s, among them *Down Argentine Way, Tin Pan Alley* (both 1940), *The Great American Broadcast* (1941), *Sun Valley Serenade* (also 1941, in which they introduced "Chattanooga Choo Choo"), and *Orchestra Wives* (1942). In most of these, their race limited them to marginal roles (e.g., railroad porters) in order to shoehorn their routines into the pictures; in the all-black *Stormy Weather* (1943), they merely sprang out of the audience near the end to join the number in progress. They're probably best known for "Be a Clown," which they performed with Gene Kelly in *The Pirate* (1948). They remained active on stage and in clubs, though lately Harold has been soloing in such shows as "Sophisticated Ladies," which he also choreographed, and in such films as *Tap* (1989), *The Five Heartbeats* (1991), and *Funny Bones* (1995). In 1992 they participated in a documentary about their careers.

NICHOLS, DUDLEY. Screenwriter, director. *(b. Apr. 6, 1895, Wapakeneta, Ohio; d. Jan. 4, 1960.)* Highly regarded screenwriter of the 1930s and 1940s, Nichols was a former New York newspaperman who went to Hollywood at the dawn of the talkie era. He was a frequent collaborator with director John Ford, winning an Academy Award for writing *The Informer* (1935) and eventually writing the screenplay for Ford's *Stagecoach* (1939), the landmark film that elevated the Western to the status of respected genre. Also for Ford, he penned two films starring Will Rogers, *Judge Priest* (1934) and *Steamboat 'Round the Bend* (1935), the adventure yarns *The Lost Patrol* (1934) and *The Hurricane* (1937), the historical *Mary of Scotland*, the Irish-themed *The Plough and the Stars* (both 1936), and the symbol-laden *The Fugitive* (1947).

In 1940 he was nominated for an Oscar for writing the adaptation of Eugene O'Neill's *The Long Voyage Home* for Ford.

He also received Oscar nominations for his scripts for *Air Force* (1943, for Howard Hawks) and *The Tin Star* (1957, for Anthony Mann). Nichols produced and directed three interesting films, *Government Girls* (1943), *Sister Kenny* (1946), and *Mourning Becomes Electra* (1947, from the Eugene O'Neill play), but his career behind the megaphone never really took off. He also wrote original stories and/or screenplays for *Born Reckless, A Devil With Women* (both 1930), *Not Exactly Gentlemen, The Seas Beneath* (both 1931), *This Sporting Age* (1932), *The Man Who Dared*, and *Robber's Roost* (both 1933). Nichols wrote two popular hits of 1938, Astaire and Rogers' *Carefree* and the screwball comedy classic *Bringing Up Baby*. For director Fritz Lang, he wrote the political thriller *Man Hunt* (1941) and the murder-guilt drama *Scarlet Street* (1945). Diversity certainly proved to be Nichols' long suit as seen in his scripts for *The Arizonian* and *The Crusades* (both 1935), *The Toast of New York* (1937), *For Whom The Bell Tolls* (1943), *It Happened Tomorrow* (1944), Agatha Christie's *And Then There Were None* (1945), *The Bells of St. Mary's* (1945), the racially controversial *Pinky* (1949), *Rawhide* (1951), *The Big Sky* (1952), *Prince Valiant* (1954), *Run for the Sun* (1956), *The Hangman* (1959), and *Heller in Pink Tights* (1960). In all, an extraordinary range of subjects befitting a former Gotham newspaperman.

NICHOLS, MIKE. Director, producer. *(b. Nov. 6, 1931, Berlin, as Michael Igor Peschkowsky.)* Born to Russian Jews who emigrated to the United States just before the outbreak of World War 2, Nichols worked diligently to educate himself, taking several odd jobs while attending the University of Chicago. Bitten by the acting bug, he came to New York and briefly studied with Lee Strasberg. Back in Chicago, he helped form a landmark comedy troupe (Second City) and, with partner Elaine May, evolved a clever nightclub act. Nichols and May toured for several years, had their own show on Broadway, and played on TV variety shows before splitting up in 1961. He took up directing, and staged several successful Broadway comedies, including "Barefoot in the Park" and "The Odd Couple."

Nichols made a highly acclaimed film directorial debut with his 1966 adaptation of another well-known theatrical property, *Who's Afraid of Virginia Woolf?* Starring Richard Burton and Elizabeth Taylor, it brought a frank, gritty realism to the screen and earned Nichols an Academy Award nomination. His next film, *The Graduate* (1967), broke ground in a number of ways: by giving voice to disaffected youth of the late 1960s, by treating seduction and adultery with humor, by using a contemporary song score (by Simon and Garfunkel) to set and amplify the film's tone, and by starring an unconventional-looking leading man (Dustin Hoffman). It was enormously successful and influential, earning Nichols an Academy Award, and a "golden boy" reputation which he dispelled, somewhat, by taking on riskier and more offbeat projects in the years that followed.

The Joseph Heller adaptation *Catch-22* (1970) was highly anticipated, but proved a disappointment to most viewers. *Carnal Knowledge* (1971) turned heads with its startlingly frank examination of sexual mores, attitudes, and behavior. The failure of *The Day of the Dolphin* (1973) and the only moderate success of the farcical *The Fortune* (1975) made Nichols a lot choosier about his film projects, and he spent most of the next decade working with great success on Broadway (where he won six Tony awards) and directing an occasional television special. He also served as coexecutive producer of the highly regarded TV series "Family" (1976–80). Nichols' films since the 1980s are no longer groundbreakers—they blend into the mainstream—but they are marked by intelligence, top-quality craftsmanship, and high-caliber talent on both sides of the camera.

OTHER FILMS INCLUDE: 1980: *Gilda Live;* 1983: *Silkwood* (for which he was Oscar-nominated); 1986: *Heartburn;* 1988: *Biloxi Blues, Working Girl* (another Oscar nod); 1990: *Postcards from the Edge;* 1991: *Regarding Henry;* 1993: *The Remains of the Day* (co-executive producer only); 1994: *Wolf.*

NICHOLSON, JACK. Actor, director, writer, producer. *(b. Apr. 22, 1937, Neptune, N.J.)* Not many actors could have risen from a bit in the three-day *The Little Shop of Horrors* (1960) to the lead in the multimillion-dollar epic *Hoffa* (1992); fewer still are sufficiently comfortable with their stardom to continue to take small but challenging roles, but this paunchy, balding actor with what "Time" magazine once called a "shark's grin" has always been a consummate professional, albeit an incredibly well-paid one, as well as one of the few contemporary stars whom *anybody* can do an impression of.

Nicholson got his movie start with legendary cheapie producer Roger Corman, who cast him in the title role of *Cry Baby Killer* (1958). He played small roles for the next few years; in addition to playing a masochistic dental patient in *Little Shop,* he costarred as Peter Lorre's moron son in *The Raven* (1963), and hung around to play the lead in *The Terror,* filmed shortly thereafter on the same sets and starring Boris Karloff. Nicholson got his first screenplay credit that same year, co-writing the virtually unknown *Thunder Island.* After a period of relative inactivity, he resurfaced by producing, writing, and costarring in a trio of low-budget Monte Hellman films: a pair of existential Westerns, *Ride in the Whirlwind* (1965), and *The Shooting* (1967), and *Flight to Fury* (1966), a tropical adventure.

Nicholson played a filling-station attendant named "Poet" in *Hell's Angels on Wheels* (1967), a pony-tailed rocker in *Psych-Out,* wrote the script for Corman's LSD epic *The Trip,* and co wrote, coproduced (with Bob Rafelson), and briefly appeared in the cult favorite *Head* (all 1968). He stepped in to replace Rip Torn at the last minute and played a boozy Southern lawyer in another biker film . . . but this one, *Easy Rider* (1969), changed his life. The unexpected, phenomenal success of this counterculture road film (and

his riveting performance as a drop-out lawyer) made Nicholson a demi-star, especially to the Beatles-generation audiences who comprised the bulk of the moviegoing public in those years. (It also earned him his first Oscar nomination.) His role in Vincente Minnelli's *On a Clear Day You Can See Forever* (1970) was cut down to nothing, but Nicholson's vibrant portrayal of an angry, disaffected ex-musician in *Five Easy Pieces* (also 1970) proved to be a star-making turn, thanks in large part to his memorable "chicken salad sandwich" tirade; it also brought him a second Oscar nomination, in the Best Actor category. His sublimely cynical sexual politician in *Carnal Knowledge* (1971) cemented his reputation as the star of a new generation. His followups, *A Safe Place* (1971) and *The King of Marvin Gardens* (1972), didn't endear him to the moviegoing mainstream, but reaffirmed his status as an individualist who sought out challenging and contemporary material. He then cowrote, coproduced, and directed the X-rated coming-of-age drama *Drive, He Said* (1972).

Nicholson hit his stride with starring roles in *The Last Detail* (1973, Oscar-nominated again as a career sailor on m.p. duty), *Chinatown* (1974, Oscar-nominated as detective Jake Gittes), and *One Flew Over the Cuckoo's Nest* (1975, winning his first Oscar as the not-so-crazy, rebellious asylum patient Randall Patrick McMurphy). In his Academy Award acceptance speech, the sly Nicholson thanked film pioneer Mary Pickford—who'd just made an appearance on the show—"for being the first actor to get a percentage of her pictures."

Now a full-fledged star, Nicholson took chances that few others would dare, playing a goofy sidekick to Warren Beatty in the farcical *The Fortune,* leaving Hollywood to work for Michelangelo Antonioni in the inscrutable *The Passenger,* taking a singing role in *Tommy* (all 1975), and a supporting part in *The Last Tycoon* (1976). His subsequent starring films were a mixed bag, however: *The Missouri Breaks* (1976, a disappointing "summit meeting" with Marlon Brando), *Goin' South* (1978, a quixotic comedy which he directed), *The Shining* (1980, an over-the-top tour de force in which he went crazy for nearly two hours, under Stanley Kubrick's direction), *The Postman Always*

Rings Twice (1981, a seamy and steamy remake of the James M. Cain classic), and *The Border* (1982, a muddled drama about illegal aliens).

The actor's choices grew cannier at this time. He was surprisingly effective as playwright Eugene O'Neill in Warren Beatty's sprawling *Reds* (1981, earning a Best Supporting Actor Oscar nomination), and charming as the comically dissolute former astronaut who laconically romances Shirley MacLaine in *Terms of Endearment* (1983), which won him a Best Supporting Actor Academy Award. John Huston gave him one key piece of direction to play a dimwitted hit-man in *Prizzi's Honor* (1985)—"Remember, he's *dumb*"—and the result was one of his all-time best performances, opposite Kathleen Turner and his longtime girlfriend Anjelica Huston. He chalked up another Oscar nomination, then played a thinly disguised version of journalist Carl Bernstein in *Heartburn* (1986), creating an unforgettable Nicholson moment by bursting into song (the "Soliloquy" from *Carousel!*).

He was devilishly well cast as Satan in modern-day guise in *The Witches of Eastwick,* which allowed him to "let go" in a furiously funny climax, then played a heartbreaking man on the skids in *Ironweed,* which earned him another Oscar nomination (both 1987). He rounded out 1987 with a very funny, deadpan cameo appearance as an imperious network anchorman in *Broadcast News.* By now something of an icon—as actor, movie star, and power broker—he accepted a whopping salary (and percentage) to play The Joker in *Batman* (1989), and chewed the scenery to his heart's content (and his fans'). In 1990 he realized a longtime ambition to make a sequel to *Chinatown,* directing and starring in the disappointing *The Two Jakes.*

After some time off, he appeared in three movies in succession in 1992: the dreadful comedy *Man Trouble* (which reunited him with director Bob Rafelson), the smash hit *A Few Good Men* (which gave him a plum, Oscar-nominated supporting role as a Machiavellian Marine officer), and the ambitious biography *Hoffa* (in which his galvanizing performance—in very convincing makeup—had to carry a diffuse and unsatisfying script). He then reteamed with director Mike Nichols to try something completely different—a werewolf movie, namely *Wolf* (1994). In 1994 he received the American Film Institute Life Achievement Award, reaffirming his unique status as a counterculture hero who has managed to function extraordinarily well in the movie mainstream. His next film was *The Crossing Guard* (1995).

NIELSEN, LESLIE. Actor. *(b. Feb. 11, 1926, Regina, Saskatchewan.)* He's a good, solid actor who spent 30 years in movies and on TV playing good, solid roles before achieving significant success in, of all things, lowbrow comedy. The Canadian-born actor, a nephew of character actor Jean Hersholt, was a radio announcer and d.j. before turning to acting. He played a stolid spaceship commander in *Forbidden Planet* (1956), Debbie Reynolds' love interest in *Tammy and the Bachelor* (1957), the Revolutionary War hero "Swamp Fox" on "Walt Disney Presents" (on TV, 1959–61), a Howard Hughes prototype in *Harlow* (1965), a movie studio chief on "Bracken's World" (also TV, 1970), the ill-fated captain in *The Poseidon Adventure* (1972), a drug kingpin in *Viva Knievel!* (1977), and more cops, doctors, and attorneys than you could shake a nightstick/stethoscope/law book at. Among his "straight" credits: *The Vagabond King, The Opposite Sex* (both 1956), *Rosie!* (1967), *Counterpoint, Dayton's Devils* (both 1968), *How to Commit Marriage* (1969), *The Amsterdam Kill* (1977). That all changed in 1980, when he was one of several good, solid actors hired to send up their images in the hit spoof *Airplane!* He enjoyed it so much that he signed on to play bumbling cop Frank Drebin in the cult TV series "Police Squad!" and in the features *The Naked Gun* (1988), *The Naked Gun 2½: The Smell of Fear* (1991), and *The Naked Gun 33⅓: The Final Insult* (1994), which followed. He also starred in a short-lived sitcom, "Shaping Up" (1984), played an Ivy League snot in *Soul Man* (1986), a goofy exorcist in *Repossessed* (1990), a decidedly pragmatic Santa Claus in *All I Want for Christmas* (1991), and a bad guy in the silly *Surf Ninjas* (1993). Occasionally he even goes back to serious roles, as in *Wrong Is Right, Creepshow* (both 1982), and most notably as the sleazy john Barbra Streisand kills in *Nuts* (1987). But it's his mastery of deadpan farce that brought him belated, unexpected stardom in his 60s.

NIMOY, LEONARD. Actor; director. *(b. Mar. 26, 1931, Boston.)* This gaunt, saturnine, deep-voiced actor has earned popculture immortality—whether he likes it or not—as the unemotional half-Vulcan Mr. Spock on the original "Star Trek" TV series, a role he has played for a quarter-century. Initially an actor trained in the theater (a venue he continues to visit), Nimoy first worked on the big screen doing bits in such classics as *Francis Goes to West Point* (1953), *Them!* (1954), and *The Brain Eaters* (1958), the most notorious—and prescient—being an alien invader in the serial *Zombies of the Stratosphere* (1952). He coproduced and starred in a film adaptation of Genet's *Deathwatch* in 1966, just before he was cast in "Star Trek," which ran on network TV until 1969. After "Trek" was canceled, he was a regular on "Mission: Impossible" (1972–74) and hosted the reality series "In Search of . . ." (1976–82), while doing occasional features such as *Catlow* (1971) and *Invasion of the Body Snatchers* (1978). In 1979 he glued on the pointy ears again for *Star Trek: The Motion Picture,* and killed off his breadwinning character (temporarily) in 1982's *Star Trek II: The Wrath of Khan.* Nimoy made his feature directorial debut in 1984 with *Star Trek III: The Search for Spock,* and repeated the chore (as well as cowriting the story) for the fourth chapter, *The Voyage Home,* in 1986. He then went on to direct other features, including *3 Men and a Baby* (1987), *The Good Mother* (1988), *Funny About Love* (1990), and *Holy Matrimony* (1994), and added "executive producer" to his résumé with the sixth *Trek* feature, *The Undiscovered Country,* in 1991, which he also cowrote. Nimoy has also appeared in a number of TV movies and miniseries, notably as Golda Meir's first husband in "A Woman Called Golda" (1982) and starred as concentration camp survivor Mel Mermelstein in *Never Forget* (1991), which he also produced.

NIVEN, DAVID. Actor. *(b. Mar. 1, 1909, Kirriemuir, Scotland, as James David Graham Niven; d. July 29, 1983.)* One of many dapper, urbane actors who emigrated to Hollywood from the United Kingdom, this wavy-haired charmer with the pencil mustache enjoyed a lengthy film career, alternating starring roles with second leads and finely drawn character parts. Born into a family of professional soldiers (he himself attended military school and served briefly in the infantry), Niven bounced around Europe quite a bit—in jobs of dubious merit and legality—before taking up acting and making his film debut in 1932's *There Goes the Bride.* He got to Hollywood in 1935, initially doing extra work (in 1935's *Mutiny on the Bounty* and *Barbary Coast,* among others) but becoming a dependable supporting player in short order. Niven made a delightfully dotty Bertie Wooster in Fox's forgotten "Jeeves" films of 1936–37, and a suave *Raffles* in 1940.

Blood will tell, and Niven was back in military uniform at the outbreak of World War 2, serving with the British commandos and attaining the rank of colonel. After the war he frequently commuted between the United States and England to appear in films, and increasingly took supporting roles in comedies, in which his mischievous wit and marvelous timing were put to good use. Niven won an Oscar for a memorable dramatic role, as the fraudulent major in *Separate Tables* (1958). He also worked frequently on TV, cofounding the Four Star Production company and starring in the series "The David Niven Show" (1959) and "The Rogues" (1964–65). Niven also authored two volumes of memoirs, "The Moon's a Balloon" (1971) and "Bring on the Empty Horses" (1975), as well as a 1951 novel, "Round the Rugged Rocks." In his final film, *Curse of the Pink Panther* (1983), the ailing actor's voice was dubbed by mimic Rich Little.

OTHER FILMS INCLUDE: 1935: *Splendor;* 1936: *Rose Marie, Thank You, Jeeves, Dodsworth, The Charge of the Light Brigade;* 1937: *The Prisoner of Zenda, Dinner at the Ritz;* 1938: *Bluebeard's Eighth Wife, Four Men and a Prayer, The Dawn Patrol;* 1939: *Wuthering Heights, The Real Glory, Eternally Yours;* 1942: *Spitfire;* 1946: *Stairway to Heaven;* 1947: *The Bishop's Wife;* 1948: *Enchantment;* 1949: *A Kiss in the Dark, A Kiss for Corliss;* 1950: *The Elusive Pimpernel, The Toast of New Orleans;* 1951: *Soldiers Three,*

Happy Go Lovely; 1952: The Lady Says No; 1953: The Moon Is Blue; 1954: Tonight's the Night; 1955: Court Martial, The King's Thief; 1956: Around the World in Eighty Days; 1957: Oh, Men! Oh, Women!, The Little Hut, My Man Godfrey; 1958: Bonjour Tristesse; 1959: Ask Any Girl; 1960: Please Don't Eat the Daisies; 1961: The Guns of Navarone, The Best of Enemies; 1963: 55 Days at Peking; 1964: The Pink Panther, Bedtime Story; 1965: Lady L; 1966: Where the Spies Are; 1967: Casino Royale, Eye of the Devil; 1968: Prudence and the Pill, The Impossible Years; 1969: Before Winter Comes; 1971: The Statue; 1974: Old Dracula; 1975: Paper Tiger; 1976: Murder by Death; 1977: Candleshoe; 1978: Death on the Nile; 1979: Escape to Athena; 1980: Rough Cut, The Sea Wolves; 1982: Trail of the Pink Panther, Better Late Than Never.

NOIRET, PHILIPPE. Actor. (b. Oct. 1, 1931, Lille, France.) Often called the greatest French star character actor of his generation, Noiret and his marvelous hangdog expression have been seen in dramas and comedies to equal advantage. He began acting on the stage and worked in everything from nightclub cabaret to classic theater, making his film debut in Agnes Varda's feature La Pointe Courte (1956). Since then, he has worked with Louis Malle (1960's Zazie dans le Metro), Alfred Hitchcock (1969's Topaz), George Cukor (1969's Justine), and Philippe de Broca (1977's Tendre Poulet/Dear Detective), but is best known for his long collaboration with director Bertrand Tavernier, for whom he has acted in L'Horloger de Saint-Paul/The Clockmaker (1974), Que La Fete commence!/Let Joy Reign Supreme (1975), Le Juge et l'Assassin/The Judge and the Assassin (1976), A Week's Vacation (1980), Coup de Torchon/Clean Slate (1981), Round Midnight (1986), and Life and Nothing But (1989). Noiret achieved possibly his greatest latter-day success as the crusty but warmhearted projectionist in Giuseppe Tornatore's Cinema Paradiso (1988), a charming, emotional film that won the Best Foreign Film Oscar.
OTHER FILMS INCLUDE: 1969: The Assassination Bureau; 1973: Night Flight From Moscow, The Grande Bouffe; 1978: Who Is Killing the Great Chefs of Europe?; 1987: Masques; 1989: The Return of the Musketeers; 1991:

Uranus; 1993: Especially on Sunday; 1995: The Postman.

NOLAN, LLOYD. Actor. (b. Aug. 11, 1902, San Francisco; d. Sept. 27, 1985.) We're still not sure why someone raised and educated in northern California would speak with such a distinctive Bronx accent—but then, this dependable character lead spent half a century confounding both critics who predicted major stardom for him, and audiences who took him for granted even while looking forward to seeing him on-screen. Nolan, who started acting on stage in 1927, most often played contemporary American types. This handsome, easygoing actor found a welcome home in such vintage crime films as "G"-Men (1935), Exclusive, King of Gamblers (both 1937), Dangerous to Know, King of Alcatraz (both 1938), Johnny Apollo (1940), Blues in the Night (1941), The House on 92nd St. (1945), Lady in the Lake (1946), and The Street With No Name (1948), as well as in comedies such as Every Day's a Holiday (1938), Buy Me That Town (1941), and The Lemon Drop Kid (1951).
Nolan occasionally climbed into the saddle, as in The Texas Rangers (1936) and Wells Fargo (1937), but won more fans as the dapper detective Michael Shayne in seven Fox films from 1940–42. His presence brightened Guadalcanal Diary (1943), A Tree Grows in Brooklyn (1945), Easy Living (1949), Island in the Sky (1953), A Hatful of Rain, Peyton Place (both 1957), Circus World (1964), Never Too Late (1965), Ice Station Zebra (1968), Airport (1970), Earthquake (1974), and Hannah and Her Sisters (1986, released after his death). He's also remembered as the crabby Dr. Chegley on the TV series "Julia" (1968–71), as well as for his long run of commercials for denture cream. Other TV roles include a guest shot as Bugs Moran on "The Untouchables," the title role in "Martin Kane, Private Eye" (1951 only), and his Emmy-winning performance as Capt. Queeg in a live "The Caine Mutiny Court Martial" (1955).

NOLTE, NICK. Actor. (b. Feb. 8, 1941, Omaha, Nebr.) This blond, beefy leading man's Oscar nomination for The Prince of

Tides (1991) seems to have finally awakened movie-watchers (both in and outside the movie industry) to an appreciation of his remarkable talent. After appearing in a number of TV movies, Nolte made a less-than-auspicious feature debut (opposite a still-struggling Don Johnson) in *Return to Macon County* (1975), then returned to the small screen the next year to star as the shiftless Tom Jordache in the blockbuster miniseries "Rich Man, Poor Man." It won him an Emmy nomination and made him a star, which led to an immediate big-screen assignment as leading man of *The Deep* (1977). He then surprised experts by taking tricky roles in difficult films: the Vietnam drug runner in *Who'll Stop the Rain* (1978), an aging footballer in *North Dallas Forty* (1979), Jack Kerouac's companion Neal Cassady in *Heart Beat* (1980), and a marine biologist in *Cannery Row* (1982).

After costarring with Eddie Murphy in the smash action-comedy *48HRS.*, Nolte returned to his offbeat ways, playing a photographer on the front lines in *Under Fire* (1983), one of the eponymous *Teachers* (1984), a soft-hearted hit man (opposite Katharine Hepburn) in *Grace Quigley* (1985, aka *The Ultimate Solution of Grace Quigley*), a "filthy bum" in *Down and Out in Beverly Hills* (1986), a Texas lawman in *Extreme Prejudice*, a convict playwright in *Weeds* (both 1987), an army deserter who fashions himself into a South Sea god in *Farewell to the King,* an obsessed artist in the Martin Scorsese segment of *New York Stories,* a holdup man just freed from prison in the comic *Three Fugitives* (all 1989), a beleaguered private eye in *Everybody Wins,* a bigoted cop in *Q&A,* and Eddie Murphy's nemesis in the boring sequel *Another 48HRS* (all 1990).

Nolte hit pay dirt in 1991, first in Martin Scorsese's *Cape Fear,* in a layered performance as a not so happily married lawyer stalked by a crazed Robert De Niro, and then in *The Prince of Tides,* as a man who keeps a lifetime of harrowing memories bottled up inside. He followed this parlay with the equally impressive *Lorenzo's Oil* (1992), adopting an Italian accent to play Susan Sarandon's husband, who joins her in a determined search for the root of their son's illness. His 1994 credits include *Blue Chips,* James L. Brooks' near-musical *I'll Do Anything,* and *I Love Trouble;* he was then cast by

Merchant and Ivory as Thomas Jefferson for their *Jefferson in Paris* (1995). Nolte is an actor who continues to grow, confounding the early detractors who dismissed him as a blond beefcake type. His strength and charisma have made him, at the same time, a movie star of the first order.

NORRIS, CHUCK. Actor. *(b. Mar. 1, 1939, Ryan, Okla., as Carlos Ray Norris.)* In his numerous, seemingly interchangeable potboilers, this sandy-blond, mustached (and often bearded) karate-champ-turned-action-star doesn't say much. But then, he doesn't have to—his feet do most of the talking. Since making his film debut in *The Wrecking Crew* (1968), and appearing opposite Bruce Lee in *Return of the Dragon* (1973), Norris has displayed his soft-spoken, high-kicking persona in a string of violent actioners, many of them made for the Cannon studio. When his *Rambo*-like vehicle *Missing in Action* (1984) was successful, he followed Sylvester Stallone's lead by making two more, *Missing in Action 2—The Beginning* (1985) and *Braddock: Missing in Action III* (1988). Norris got his only taste of critical acceptance with the urban cop movie *Code of Silence* (1985), which reportedly had been written as a Clint Eastwood "Dirty Harry" vehicle. Threatened by an eroding audience (and a number of young Turks invading the action arena), Norris took a meaner, more bloodthirsty turn in *Hitman* (1991), then did a complete turnaround in 1993's *Sidekicks,* playing to a juvenile audience as himself, coaching a young fan. That same year he made his TV debut with a telefilm that launched the series "Walker, Texas Ranger" (1993–). Norris' brother Aaron has directed him in most of his recent films. Chuck's son Mike is also an actor who appeared in *Delta Force 3* (1991).
OTHER FILMS INCLUDE: 1973: *Slaughter in San Francisco;* 1978: *Good Guys Wear Black* (his first starrer); 1979: *A Force of One;* 1980: *The Octagon;* 1981: *An Eye for an Eye;* 1982: *Silent Rage;* 1983: *Lone Wolf McQuade;* 1986: *Firewalker, The Delta Force;* 1988: *Hero and the Terror;* 1993: *Hellbound.*

NORTH, ALEX. Composer. *(b. Dec. 4, 1910, Chester, Pa.; d. Sept. 8, 1991.)* In

1986, North received a special Academy Award for his lifetime achievement in film music—the only composer to be so honored. It's a measure of the respect his colleagues have always had for his challenging, often innovative work. The highly learned, skilled North studied at the Curtis Institute, Juilliard, and the Moscow Conservatory, and composed scores for documentaries during World War 2. After writing scores for Broadway musicals, he composed the highly influential music for *A Streetcar Named Desire* (1951), which incorporated jazz for the first time in a major Hollywood score. John Huston valued North as a collaborator and worked with him on *The Misfits* (1961), *Wise Blood* (1979), *Under the Volcano* (1984), *Prizzi's Honor* (1985), and *The Dead* (1987). The composer's work has run the gamut of musical styles (though he's done more than his share of "big" scores), and he amassed fourteen Academy Award nominations, for *Streetcar, Death of a Salesman* (also 1951), *Viva Zapata!* (1952), *The Rose Tattoo* (1955), *The Rainmaker* (1956), *Spartacus* (1960), *Cleopatra* (1963), *The Agony and the Ecstasy* (1965), *Who's Afraid of Virginia Woolf?* (1966), *The Shoes of the Fisherman* (1968), *Shanks* (1974), *Bite the Bullet* (1975), *Dragonslayer* (1981), and *Under the Volcano*. When Maurice Jarre's score for *Ghost* was nominated in 1990, there were some who felt the citation should have been shared by North, whose haunting song "Unchained Melody" (originally written for the 1955 film *Unchained*, and nominated as Best Song that year) permeated the film.

North's work remained challenging and contemporary right through the 1970s and 1980s. He won an Emmy for scoring the miniseries "Rich Man, Poor Man" (1976) and contributed a particularly potent score to *Carny* (1980). Other credits range from *The Long Hot Summer* (1958) to *Good Morning, Vietnam* (1987).

NORTH, SHEREE. Actress. *(b. Jan. 17, 1933, Hollywood, as Dawn Bethel.)* You'd never know from her sexy dancing in 1955's *How to Be Very, Very Popular* that North was the mother of a five-year-old child at the time. A lifelong show-biz professional, she first attracted attention in the 1953 Broadway production of "Hazel Flagg," and reprised her show-stopping dance in the 1954 film adaptation, *Living It Up,* which starred Dean Martin and Jerry Lewis. The shapely blonde was then considered the brightest of the would-be Marilyn Monroes, but her studio, 20th Century-Fox (after casting her in films like *How to Be Very, Very Popular, The Lieutenant Wore Skirts, The Best Things in Life Are Free,* and *No Down Payment*), decided to build up Jayne Mansfield instead. North polished her acting talent in stock and on episodic TV, and by the time she returned to the big screen in the late 1960s, she offered a different image, playing a succession of worldly-wise, sometimes tarnished women in often meaty supporting roles. She gave affecting performances in the 1968 detective thriller *Madigan,* 1973's *Charley Varrick,* and 1976's *The Shootist* (all for director Don Siegel, who also cast her in 1977's *Telefon*).

Other credits include *The Trouble With Girls, The Gypsy Moths* (both 1969), *Lawman, The Organization* (1971), *The Outfit* (1974), *Breakout* (1975), and *Maniac Cop* (1988, a good part as a crippled, embittered policewoman). During the 1974–75 season she appeared as Edward Asner's girlfriend on "The Mary Tyler Moore Show," and costarred in the TV series "Big Eddie" (1975), "I'm a Big Girl Now" (1980–81), and "Our Family Honor" (1985–86). North rates this special footnote in film history: Her show-stopping hoofing for the "Shake, Rattle, and Roll" number in *How to Be Very, Very Popular* was advertised as "the first rock 'n' roll dance on the screen"! She also played Kramer's mother on a 1995 episode of "Seinfeld" and revealed his real name, Cosmo.

NORTON, JACK. Actor. *(b. Sept. 2, 1889, Brooklyn, N.Y.; d. Oct. 15, 1958.)* Norton was Hollywood's perennial drunk, a dapper supporting player with a high forehead and pencil mustache. This former vaudeville trouper originally developed his inebriate characterization for skits in Broadway's Ziegfeld Follies and Earl Carroll's Vanities, later reprising it in other plays. He went to Hollywood in 1934 and, in nearly 25 years on-screen, scarcely drew a sober breath. It's worth noting that off-screen Norton was a teetotaler. He appeared in dozens of two-reel comedies.

FILMS INCLUDE: 1934: *Cockeyed Cavaliers;* 1937: *Marked Woman;* 1940: *The Bank Dick;* 1942: *The Palm Beach Story* (as a member of the Ale and Quail Club); 1944: *Ghost Catchers* (as a drunken *ghost), Hail the Conquering Hero;* 1946: *Blue Skies;* 1950: *Mad Wednesday.*

NOVAK, KIM. Actress. *(b. Feb. 13, 1933, Chicago, as Marilyn Pauline Novak.)* Classical Hollywood sex goddess, blond and buxom, who owed her initial success to her physical allure, but developed into a capable (and at times first-rate) actress. The daughter of a Slavic railway worker, Novak made an inauspicious entry into show business, touring the country as "Miss Deepfreeze" and pitching refrigerators. She also modeled and, as a clotheshorse in the Jane Russell starrer *The French Line* (1954), was spotted by Columbia prexy Harry Cohn, then looking for a sexy star to replace the "difficult" Rita Hayworth. (Cohn's failure to sign Marilyn Monroe some time earlier may well have been the impetus behind his massive effort to groom the husky-voiced blonde for stardom.) She made her Columbia debut in *Phffft!* (1954), and played a femme fatale that same year in *Pushover.* Despite her (initially) limited talents, Novak became a box-office attraction; she worked hard and delivered credible performances in the likes of *The Man With the Golden Arm, Picnic* (both 1955), *Jeanne Eagels,* and *Pal Joey* (both 1957), among others. By that time she was Hollywood's #1 draw, and her extracurricular relationships with Sammy Davis, Jr., Cary Grant, and Frank Sinatra filled newspaper gossip pages.

In 1958 Novak appeared in her two most enduring pictures, both costarring James Stewart: Alfred Hitchcock's obsessive, sinister *Vertigo* (in a "dual" role as Stewart's suicidal girlfriend and as a lookalike molded in the dead woman's image) and Richard Quine's *Bell, Book and Candle* (as a fetching witch). She acquitted herself well in 1960's soap opera *Strangers When We Meet,* two 1962 comedies, *Boys' Night Out* and *The Notorious Landlady,* and tried, valiantly but unsuccessfully, to do justice to the role of the vulgar waitress in the 1964 remake of Somerset Maugham's *Of Human Bondage.* She showed a cunning sense of humor in Billy Wilder's notorious *Kiss Me, Stupid* (1964), and essayed a "female Tom Jones" in *The Amorous Adventures of Moll Flanders* (1965). Personal problems and changing audience tastes sent her career into a tailspin later in the decade, and her highly touted comeback feature, *The Legend of Lylah Clare* (1968), failed to generate much enthusiasm. She has worked in film infrequently since then, appearing in *The Great Bank Robbery* (1969), *Tales That Witness Madness* (1973), *White Buffalo* (1977), *Just a Gigolo* (1979), *The Mirror Crack'd* (1980, still glamorous playing a bitchy actress), and, in a pair of interesting character parts, in *The Children* (1990) and *Liebestraum* (1991). She has made occasional TV appearances over the years, starring as an aging showgirl in *The Third Girl From the Left* (1973), toplining an "Alfred Hitchcock Presents" revival in the 1980s, and joining the regular cast of "Falcon Crest" for its 1986–87 season. She was married at one time to actor Richard Johnson.

NOYCE, PHILLIP. Director, screenwriter. *(b. Apr. 29, 1950, Griffith, New South Wales, Australia.)* Talented Australian filmmaker who began making short films as a teenager and directed documentaries for Film Australia. After his debut feature, *Backroads* (1977), Noyce scored a commercial and critical success with *Newsfront* (1978), a salute to the movie newsreel industry that won Australian awards for Best Film, Director, and Screenplay. He directed *Heatwave* (1983) with Judy Davis, *Echoes of Paradise* (1987; original Australian title *Shadows of the Peacock),* and worked on two miniseries for Australian TV that were coproduced by fellow Aussie George Miller. Miller also produced the film that brought Noyce his greatest acclaim in the United States—the skillful three-character thriller *Dead Calm* (1989). Noyce first worked in the United States on the TV series "The Hitchhiker" and directed his first American feature, *Blind Fury,* in 1989. His greatest commercial success to date has been the Tom Clancy spy thriller *Patriot Games* (1992), which confirmed his abilities as a director of suspense and action. He followed it with *Sliver* (1993) and another Clancy adaptation, *Clear and Present Danger* (1994).

NYKVIST, SVEN. Cinematographer, di-
rector. *(b. Dec. 3, 1922, Moheda, Sweden.)*
Much-admired Swedish cinematographer
inextricably linked with brilliant director
Ingmar Bergman, for whom he lensed
Sawdust and Tinsel (1953), *The Virgin
Spring* (1959), *Through a Glass, Darkly*
(1962), *The Silence* (1963), *All These
Women* (1964), *Persona* (1966), *Shame,
Hour of the Wolf* (both 1968), *The Passion
of Anna* (1969), *The Touch* (1971), *Scenes
From a Marriage* (1973), *The Magic Flute*
(1975), *Face to Face* (1976), *The Serpent's Egg, Autumn Sonata* (both 1978),
From the Life of the Marionettes (1980),
and *After the Rehearsal* (1984), as well as
Cries and Whispers (1972) and *Fanny and
Alexander* (1983), both of which won him
Academy Awards. He also received a
nomination for his work on *The Unbearable Lightness of Being* (1988). Known as
a meticulous artist who does his own
lighting and operates the camera himself,
Nykvist for many years eschewed the use
of color but finally embraced it in the mid
1960s, mastering soft-lighting techniques
that gave him the muted-hues look that is
his trademark. (Reviewing *Scenes From a
Marriage,* John Simon wrote, "[Nykvist]
tames colors as a lion tamer does his royal
beasts: now keeping them harmless pussy-
cats, now urging them to display regal
powers.") He has also worked for Louis
Malle (*Black Moon,* 1975; *Pretty Baby,*
1978), Roman Polanski (*The Tenant,*
1976) and Ingmar Bergman's biggest fan,
Woody Allen (*Another Woman,* 1988;
Crimes and Misdemeanors, 1989; "Oedipus Wrecks" from *New York Stories,*
1989), among others. His American credits include *King of the Gypsies* (1978),
Starting Over, Hurricane (both 1979), *Willie and Phil* (1980), *The Postman Always
Rings Twice* (1981), *Cannery Row* (1982),
Agnes of God (1985), *Chaplin* (1992),
Sleepless in Seattle (1993), and *With Honors* (1994). He tried his hand at directing
just a few times, most notably in 1991
when he piloted Bergman regulars Liv
Ullmann, Max von Sydow, and Erland
Josephson in *The Ox.*

OAKIE, JACK. Actor. *(b. Nov. 12, 1903,
Sedalia, Mo., as Lewis Delaney Offield; d.
Jan. 23, 1978.)* This jovial, moon-faced
performer was one of the screen's most
expert second bananas (and a notorious
scene-stealer), although he occasionally
starred in films as well. After spending his
early years in Oklahoma (from which he
took his stage name), Oakie moved to
New York, where he worked as a Wall
Street clerk before entering show business
in the early 1920s. A passable song-and-
dance man and talented comic actor, he
was signed by Paramount with the coming
of sound, and appeared in dozens of films
there, sometimes in starring roles but often as the leading man's best friend. Titles
include *The Fleet's In* (1928), *Fast Company* (playing an egotistical ballplayer in
this Ring Lardner story), *The Wild Party,
Close Harmony* (all 1929), *The Sap From
Syracuse* (1930), *Million Dollar Legs, If I
Had a Million* (both 1932), *The Eagle and
the Hawk, Alice in Wonderland* (as Twee-
dledum), *College Humor* (all 1933), *College Rhythm* (1934), and *The Texas Rangers* (1936). He played leads in *Sitting
Pretty* (1933), *Murder at the Vanities*
(1934), and *The Big Broadcast of 1936*
(1935), among others.

At RKO he top-lined the first screen version of *Hit the Deck* (1930). On loan to
Universal, Oakie gave an uncharacteristically low-key (and extremely successful)
performance as the dull-witted cohort of a
pair of con artists in 1932's *Once in a
Lifetime,* a hilarious adaptation of the
Kaufman-Ferber play satirizing Hollywood. At Fox, he had prime costarring
roles opposite Spencer Tracy in *Looking
for Trouble* (1934), Clark Gable in *Call of
the Wild,* and Warner Baxter in *King of
Burlesque* (both 1935).

In 1937 Oakie moved to RKO, where he
costarred in *That Girl From Paris* (1936),
Hitting a New High, and *The Toast of New
York,* and headlined such program pictures
as *Super Sleuth* (all 1937), *The Affairs of
Annabel* (which launched the starring ca-
reer of Lucille Ball), *Annabel Takes a
Tour,* and *Radio City Revels* (all 1938).

By this time Oakie was positively rotund, and his screen persona—brash, egotistical, and frequently obnoxious—
dominated his offscreen personality as
well. He abruptly left RKO for a long
"vacation" in 1938, effectively killing his
starring career. But Oakie made a startling
comeback as Napoloni, the hilariously
bombastic Mussolini-styled despot in
Charlie Chaplin's *The Great Dictator*
(1940); the performance earned him an
Oscar nomination.

Oakie's career then enjoyed a second wind at 20th Century-Fox, where he was second banana in a parade of popular musical comedies, including *Young People* (as Shirley Temple's vaudevillian father), *Tin Pan Alley* (both 1940), *The Great American Broadcast* (1941), *Song of the Islands* (1942), *Hello Frisco, Hello* (1943, reprising his *King of Burlesque* characterization in this Technicolored retread), *It Happened Tomorrow,* and *Sweet and Lowdown* (both 1944). He starred in *Rise and Shine* (1941) as a dumb football player kidnapped by gangsters.

After top-lining a couple of mediocre Universal musicals, *On Stage, Everybody* and *That's the Spirit* (both 1945), Oakie found his career in irreversible decline, and appeared in only a few more films—in progressively smaller roles—including *Northwest Stampede, When My Baby Smiles at Me* (both 1948), *Thieves' Highway* (1949), and *Last of the Buccaneers* (1950). Oakie worked sporadically during the 1950s and 1960s, on TV and in such features as *Around the World in 80 Days* (1956), *The Rat Race* (1960), and *Lover Come Back* (1961), but increasing deafness finally forced him out of the business. He continued to be a familiar face in Hollywood right up until his death. His widow, actress Victoria Horne, published his memoirs, "Jack Oakie's Double Takes," in 1980.

OATES, WARREN. Actor. *(b. July 5, 1928, Depoy, Tex.; d. Apr. 3, 1982.)* It's sadly typical that this actor wasn't really appreciated until it was almost too late. With his beady eyes, snaggled teeth, and raspy voice, he was a natural villain in Westerns and thrillers for nearly 25 years—but he only came into his own toward the end of his career. Directors Sam Peckinpah, Burt Kennedy, and Monte Hellman used him time and again, knowing he would always come through with accomplished performances, and he was memorably slimy in such oaters as *Yellowstone Kelly* (1959), *Ride the High Country* (1962), *Mail Order Bride* (1964), *Major Dundee* (1965), *The Shooting, Welcome to Hard Times* (both 1967), *The Wild Bunch* (1969), *There Was a Crooked Man . . .* (1970), and *The Hired Hand* (1971). He did, however, play a white hat in *Return of the Seven* (1966), and was hilarious as

the goofy deputy in *In The Heat of the Night* (1967).

Thereafter Oates demonstrated his versatility in such diverse roles as a motorist in the existential *Two-Lane Blacktop* (1971), a vintage detective in *Chandler* (1972), the notorious gangster in *Dillinger,* Muff Potter in *Tom Sawyer,* a dogged insurance investigator in *The Thief Who Came to Dinner* (all 1973), a burnt-out musician in *Bring Me the Head of Alfredo Garcia,* an Alaskan fur trapper in *The White Dawn,* the ill-fated father in *Badlands* (all 1974), a Florida fishing boat captain in *92 in the Shade* (1975), a moonshiner in *Dixie Dynamite* (1976), one of the heist artists of *The Brink's Job* (1978), a comically tough drill sergeant in *Stripes* (1981), a boxing coach in *Tough Enough* (1982), and a no-nonsense police officer in the posthumously released *Blue Thunder* (1983).

His TV work included a regular role in the rodeo drama "Stoney Burke" (1962–63), Rooster Cogburn in a remake of *True Grit* (1978), the father in the miniseries "East of Eden" (1981), and a preacher in "The Blue and the Gray" (1982). But perhaps his most unusual role was in Hellman's *Cockfighter* (1974), in which his character didn't speak until the very end of the movie. In 1993 he was celebrated in a documentary film, *Warren Oates: Across the Border.*

OBERON, MERLE. Actress. *(b. Feb. 19, 1911, Tasmania, as Estelle Merle O'Brien Thompson; d. Nov. 23, 1979.)* Exotically beautiful, raven-haired actress of regal bearing who has the distinction of having been "owned" jointly by top producers on both sides of the Atlantic, enabling her to achieve stardom simultaneously on two continents during the 1930s. After being raised and educated in India, Oberon went to London in the late 1920s and broke into the British film industry as an extra, first appearing in *The Three Passions* (1929). She played several bit roles before being discovered by producer Alexander Korda, for whom she took a small part in *Service for Ladies* (1932). Korda groomed her for stardom and thrust her into lavish costume dramas, including *The Private Life of Henry VIII* (1933, as Anne Boleyn), *The Private Life of Don Juan* (1934), and *The Scarlet Pimpernel* (1935), opposite

Charles Laughton, Douglas Fairbanks, and Leslie Howard respectively.

In 1935 Korda sold "shares" in Oberon's contract to Hollywood producer Samuel Goldwyn, who immediately put her in his lavish WW1 drama, *The Dark Angel* (1935), for which she was Oscar-nominated. For the next several years she bounced from Hollywood to London and back again, appearing in prestige productions for both employers (Korda was something more to her; they were married in 1939, but divorced in 1945), such as *These Three* (1936), *Over the Moon* (1937), *The Divorce of Lady X, The Cowboy and the Lady* (both 1938), *Wuthering Heights* (1939, as a radiantly beautiful Cathy, to Olivier's Heathcliff in the best movie version of Brontë's classic romance, probably her best-remembered film), and *Lydia* (1941).

Although Oberon could deliver strikingly effective performances (especially for Goldwyn's directorial ace, William Wyler), she remained a cool, aloof screen personality, and her career began to suffer in the 1940s. At first, in *'Til We Meet Again* (1940), *That Uncertain Feeling* (1941, for director Ernst Lubitsch), and *The Lodger* (1944), Oberon's star turns were satisfactory, but by the time of *A Night in Paradise* (1946), *Night Song* (1947), and *Pardon My French* (1951), her exotic appeal had largely dissipated. (She did appear in a couple of good films late in the decade, such as the 1948 thriller *Berlin Express,* photographed by her then-husband Lucien Ballard, who did most of her mid-1940s movies.) As her looks faded, Oberon made fewer screen appearances; *Of Love and Desire* (1963) was an embarrassing soaper, but *Hotel* (1967) did at least offer a decent costarring part. (She also played herself in 1966's *The Oscar.*)

She actually produced a lackluster "comeback" vehicle, the May–December romance *Interval* (1973), but it was indifferently received and effectively ended Oberon's long career. Alexander Korda's nephew Michael fictionalized her life story—including the dark secret that she was "half-caste"—in his novel "Queenie," which became a TV miniseries with Mia Sara in the leading role.

One of Oberon's more interesting credits is a film that was never finished: Josef von Sternberg's ill-fated *I, Claudius* (1937), which costarred her with Charles Laughton. Her near-fatal car crash later that year took Oberon out of circulation and was given as the reason for shutting down production.

O'BRIEN, EDMOND. Actor. *(b. Sept. 10, 1915, New York City; d. May 9, 1985.)* The beefy, frantic, average Joe spending his last 24 hours trying to find out who administered a fatal dose of slow-acting poison to him—that's how O'Brien is best remembered, as the lead in the inventive film noir thriller *D.O.A.* (1950). A screen veteran whose movie appearances date back to 1938's *Prison Break,* O'Brien played leads in 1940s B pictures such as *Parachute Battalion* (1941) and *Powder Town* (1942), and graduated to gritty thrillers such as *The Killers* (1946) and *The Web* (1948). As he gained weight, though, producers passed him by for starring roles and he became one of the most interesting character players of the 1950s and 1960s. O'Brien was at his best in modern urban roles, such as the seedy press agent in 1954's *The Barefoot Contessa* (which earned him a Best Supporting Actor Oscar). He also excelled at broad comedy, witness his turn as a weight-sensitive gangster in 1956's *The Girl Can't Help It.* He kept a high profile in solid supporting roles in *Birdman of Alcatraz, The Man Who Shot Liberty Valance* (both 1962), *Seven Days in May* (1964, for which he picked up another Oscar nomination), and *The Wild Bunch* (1969). Having starred on radio in the title role of "Yours Truly, Johnny Dollar" (one of several actors to play that part), he went on to topline such TV series as "Johnny Midnight" (1960), "Sam Benedict" (1962–63), and "The Long Hot Summer" (1965–66), and appear in numerous series episodes and telefilms, but his latter-day feature films were unmemorable. His last movie was 1980's *Dream No Evil.* O'Brien, who died of Alzheimer's disease, was formerly married to actresses Nancy Kelly and Olga San Juan. His daughter (with San Juan), Maria O'Brien, is an actress who had a juicy part in *Smile* (1975).

OTHER FILMS INCLUDE: 1939: *The Hunchback of Notre Dame;* 1943: *The Amazing Mrs. Holliday;* 1944: *Winged Victory;* 1947: *A Double Life;* 1948: *Another Part of* the Forest, An Act of Murder, Fighter Squadron; 1949: White Heat; 1950: 711 Ocean Drive, The Admiral Was a Lady; 1951: Silver City; 1952: The Denver and the Rio Grande, The Turning Point; 1953: Man in the Dark, Julius Caesar (as Casca); 1954: Shield for Murder (which he codirected), Pete Kelly's Blues; 1956: 1984, The Rack; 1957: The Big Land; 1958: Sing Boy Sing; 1959: Up Periscope; 1960: The Last Voyage, The Great Impostor; 1961: Man-Trap (which he directed and coproduced); 1962: The Longest Day; 1964: Rio Conchos; 1965: Sylvia, Synanon; 1972: They Only Kill Their Masters; 1974: Lucky Luciano.

O'BRIEN, GEORGE. Actor. (b. Apr. 19, 1900, San Francisco; d. Sept. 23, 1985.) This handsome, barrel-chested, good-natured Irishman starred in several classic silent movies, but spent much of his sound-era career in medium- and low-budget horse operas, at least partially by choice. The son of San Francisco's popular chief of police, O'Brien used parental pull to wangle a supporting role in Moran of the Lady Letty, a 1922 Rudolph Valentino vehicle shot on location in the Bay City. Infatuated with moviemaking, he went to Hollywood as an assistant cameraman for the Fox studio, and was later chosen by director John Ford to play the youthful leading man in his epic Western, The Iron Horse (1924), the success of which won O'Brien overnight stardom. Self-confident and extroverted, he took to acting like a duck to water, and rapidly became one of Fox's top personalities, achieving his best results in Ford's Three Bad Men (1926, another epic Western), F. W. Murnau's silent masterpiece Sunrise (1927, in which the happy-go-lucky O'Brien surprised viewers with a skillful, serious performance), and Noah's Ark (1929), made at Warner Bros.

O'Brien easily made the transition to talkies, appearing for old pal Ford in Salute (1929, as a West Point cadet) and Seas Beneath (1931, as a WW1 sub commander). But during the 1930s this gregarious, athletic star spent most of his time on horseback, starring in a series of well-produced Westerns, many of them adaptations of Zane Grey novels, including The Lone Star Ranger (1930), Riders of the Purple Sage (1931), The Rainbow Trail, Mystery Ranch (both 1932), Robbers' Roost, The Last Trail (both 1933), The Dude Ranger

(1934), When a Man's a Man (a Harold Bell Wright story considered by Western aficionados to be among O'Brien's best), and Thunder Mountain (both 1935).

At RKO, he eschewed Westerns at first in favor of outdoor action pictures, including Daniel Boone (1936), Park Avenue Logger, and Windjammer (both 1937), but in 1938 he began another Western series, strictly in the Saturday-matinee groove but among the best of the breed. These films included The Renegade Ranger (1939, costarring Rita Hayworth), Marshal of Mesa City (also 1939), Bullet Code, and Triple Justice (both 1940). He enlisted in the Navy before Pearl Harbor, the second of four stints (he also served during World War 1, the Korean War, and the early days of the Vietnam War), and didn't appear on-screen again until 1947, when he took a supporting role in the Warner Bros. musical My Wild Irish Rose. He worked again with Ford in Fort Apache (1948) and She Wore a Yellow Ribbon (1949, playing second fiddle to John Wayne, who'd been a bit player in Salute). O'Brien made one more starring Western, Gold Raiders (1951, playing straight man for The Three Stooges!), and had a bit part in Ford's Cheyenne Autumn (1964) before retiring from the screen. He married actress and Purple Sage costar Marguerite Churchill in 1933; they were divorced in 1948.

O'BRIEN, MARGARET. Actress. (b. Jan. 15, 1937, Los Angeles, as Angela Maxine O'Brien.) As a pigtailed waif with expressive brown eyes, this child star proved capable of delivering more naturalistic performances than most movie moppets, and for a few brief years was a genuine screen favorite. O'Brien, a model at age three, made her screen debut in Babes on Broadway (1941, billed as Maxine O'Brien), but first struck moviegoers as a diminutive scene-stealer in Journey for Margaret (1942). She subsequently appeared in Dr. Gillespie's Criminal Case (1943) and Lost Angel (1944) and was featured in MGM's all-star Technicolor musical Thousands Cheer (also 1943). But it was the role of "Tootie" Smith, irrepressible kid sister to Judy Garland in the lavish period piece Meet Me in St. Louis (1944), that cemented O'Brien's reputation; her duet with Garland, "Under the Bamboo Tree" is a particular charmer. Indeed, she received an Oscar as Outstanding Child Actress of 1944. She dominated *The Canterville Ghost* (1944), *Our Vines Have Tender Grapes* (1945), *Three Wise Fools,* and *Bad Bascomb* (both 1946), overshadowing old pros like Edward G. Robinson, Edward Arnold, and Wallace Beery. *The Secret Garden* and *Little Women* (both 1949) showed a rapidly maturing O'Brien to good advantage, but as she entered adolescence her appeal waned mysteriously.

Her First Romance (1951), a plodding, saccharine story in which O'Brien received her first screen kiss, was intended to launch a new phase of her career, but it had the opposite effect. Aside from a limp horse racing drama, *Glory* (1956), O'Brien never starred again in a big-screen movie, and several later comeback attempts fizzled, though she still works in films and TV in supporting roles.

OTHER FILMS INCLUDE: 1943: *You, John Jones* (a memorable WW2 propaganda short), *Madame Curie;* 1944: *Jane Eyre, Music for Millions;* 1948: *Tenth Avenue Angel, The Big City;* 1960: *Heller in Pink Tights;* 1971: *Diabolical Wedding;* 1981: *Amy.*

O'BRIEN, PAT. Actor. *(b. Nov. 11, 1899, Milwaukee, as William Joseph Patrick O'Brien; d. Oct. 15, 1983.)* A kingpin of Hollywood's "Irish Mafia," this gregarious, stocky performer often portrayed sons of Erin on-screen; possibly no other leading man of the 1930s and 1940s played as many cops, servicemen, or priests. Arguably the fastest-talking actor of his day (only Lee Tracy could deliver dialogue at the same rat-a-tat-tat pace), O'Brien generally played sympathetic characters, but he also occasionally limned smooth-talking con men. A boyhood chum of Spencer Tracy, with whom he attended school and joined the Navy during World War 1, O'Brien was also bitten by the acting bug and played vaudeville (for a time as a hoofer) before making his mark on the Broadway stage in the late 1920s.

Some sources list O'Brien as appearing in films as far back as 1919, but since there was another leading man named Pat O'Brien in films of that era, those reports remain unconfirmed. He made his first big impression as cynical, hard-boiled (and yes, fast-talking) reporter Hildy Johnson in Lewis Milestone's 1931 adaptation of *The Front Page,* a hit play by Ben Hecht and Charles MacArthur. Then he freelanced for a couple of years—appearing in such films as *Honor Among Lovers, Flying High* (both 1931), *The Final Edition, Hell's House, American Madness* (as the juvenile lead in this Frank Capra Depression drama), *Air Mail* (for director John Ford), *Virtue* (all 1932), and *The World Gone Mad* (1933)—before settling down at Warner Bros., his home for the next seven years.

O'Brien starred in quite a few Warners films, although he took supporting roles and costarring assignments just as often. He was most felicitously teamed with James Cagney (offscreen a close friend), usually playing a responsible authority figure to Cagney's cocky, rebellious ladies' man. They worked together in *Here Comes the Navy* (1934), *Devil Dogs of the Air, The Irish in Us* (both 1935), *Ceiling Zero* (1936), *Boy Meets Girl* (1938, as Hollywood screenwriters!), *Angels With Dirty Faces* (also 1938, their best film together, with Cagney a gangster and O'Brien a priest), *The Fighting 69th,* and *Torrid Zone* (both 1940).

Unlike Cagney, who was constantly at loggerheads with Warner brass over choice of vehicles and salary increases, O'Brien was a team player who accepted his assignments, generally, without protest. His other films for the studio include *College Coach, Bureau of Missing Persons* (both 1933), *Twenty Million Sweethearts, I Sell Anything, I've Got Your Number, Flirtation Walk* (all 1934), *In Caliente, Oil for the Lamps of China, Page Miss Glory, Stars Over Broadway* (all 1935), *Public Enemy's Wife, China Clipper* (both 1936), *Slim* (with Henry Fonda), *The Great O'Malley, Submarine D-1* (all 1937), *The Cowboy From Brooklyn, Garden of the Moon* (both 1938), *The Kid From Kokomo, Indianapolis Speedway* (both 1939), *'Til We Meet Again, Flowing Gold,* and the film for which he's best remembered, *Knute Rockne, All American* (all 1940), in which he convincingly played the famous Notre Dame football coach who urged his players to win the Big Game for the "Gipper," Ronald Reagan. For the rest of his life, O'Brien willingly repeated his famous locker-room pep talk at dinners and various public functions.

O'Brien left Warners in 1940 to

freelance. He played leads more often than not, although he occasionally took secondary roles, as in *Broadway* (1942, as a tough cop) and *His Butler's Sister* (1943, monitoring the relationship between Deanna Durbin and Franchot Tone). He got his best roles at RKO, playing a sharp lawyer drawn into murder in *Having Wonderful Crime,* a supposedly dead husband who poses as a ghost to keep his wife honest in *Man Alive* (both 1945), an iron-willed oilfield troubleshooter in *Riffraff* (1947), an iron-willed priest in *Fighting Father Dunne,* and an understanding soul who befriends *The Boy With Green Hair* (both 1948).

O'Brien costarred with boyhood pal Spencer Tracy in *The People Against O'Hara* (1951), a middling courtroom drama that promised more than it delivered. He worked less frequently thereafter, appearing in *Criminal Lawyer* (1951), *Okinawa* (1952), *Jubilee Trail, Ring of Fear* (both 1954), *Kill Me Tomorrow* (1957), *The Last Hurrah* (1958, a fine latter-day performance in this all-star drama of political shenanigans, for director John Ford), *Some Like It Hot* (1959, little more than a cameo), *Town Tamer* (1965), *The Over-the-Hill Gang* (a 1969 telefilm), *Billy Jack Goes to Washington* (1977), *The End* (1978, teamed with Myrna Loy as Burt Reynolds' parents), and *Ragtime* (1981, which also featured his old crony Cagney).

On TV, O'Brien starred in a short-lived sitcom, "Harrigan and Son" (1960–61), guested on numerous series and anthology shows, and brightened talk shows with colorful anecdotes about Hollywood. His autobiography, "The Wind at My Back," was published in 1964.

O'BRIEN, WILLIS H. Special Effects Designer. *(b. Mar. 2, 1886, Oakland, Calif.; d. Nov. 8, 1962.)* Special effects wizard best known to the world as the man who created King Kong. O'Brien was a sculptor and cartoonist for the San Francisco "Daily News" before he first dabbled in the medium of film during the 'teens. His work caught the attention of the Edison company, for whom he produced several short subjects with a prehistoric theme. (Titles include *The Dinosaur and the Missing Link, RFD 10,000 B.C.,* and *Prehistoric Poultry.*) His method of animating small rubber figures, carefully molded over metal skeletons with movable joints, by moving them a fraction of an inch for each frame of film exposed, became the standard process of live-action animation. In 1918 he made his most ambitious film yet, *The Ghost of Slumber Mountain,* paving the way for *The Lost World* (1925), a major Hollywood feature which told of a search for prehistoric creatures. O'Brien's dinosaurs were his most realistic yet, and still impress today, even in the wake of *Jurassic Park.* Still, Obie (as he was known) kept experimenting. When producer Merian C. Cooper saw his work, he hired O'Brien to animate King Kong (which, up to that point, was to have been shot with an actor in a gorilla suit). The extraordinary success of *King Kong* (1933) spawned an immediate sequel, *The Son of Kong* (also 1933), and made O'Brien a hero to several generations of fantasy filmmakers to come. O'Brien won his only Oscar for his effects in *Mighty Joe Young* (1949), another giant-monkey movie, on which his protégé (and successor) Ray Harryhausen worked. O'Brien worked on other giant-monster movies (including 1957's *The Black Scorpion,* his last) before dying in 1962. Today, O'Brien would be kingpin of his own studio, but even in the wake of *King Kong* he had trouble launching other film projects, and many promising ideas languished on studio drawing boards for decades to follow. One of the RKO staff with whom he'd worked in the 1930s, Linwood Dunn, gave O'Brien his final employment, doing stop-motion figures for *It's a Mad Mad Mad Mad World* (1963).

O'CONNOR, CARROLL. Actor. *(b. Aug. 25, 1925, Bronx, N.Y.)* His long-running gig as TV's loudmouth bigot Archie Bunker quite justifiably earned him pop-culture immortality—but if he were judged only by his work in movies, this beefy, growling actor wouldn't score very high. O'Connor, a New York native who studied at Dublin's University College, began his acting career in Ireland, returning to the U. S. to make his Broadway debut in 1958. He made his film debut in 1961's *A Fever in the Blood,* and landed supporting roles in such other films as *Lonely Are the Brave* (1962), *Cleopatra* (1963), *In Harm's Way* (1965), *Hawaii*

(1966), *Warning Shot* (1967), *For Love of Ivy, The Devil's Brigade* (both 1968), *Death of a Gunfighter, Marlowe* (both 1969), and *Doctors' Wives* (1971). O'Connor has played nasty heavies and gruff, boorish characters more often than not. He played cigar-chomping military men in *What Did You Do in the War, Daddy?* (1966) and *Kelly's Heroes* (1970), a sleazy mobster in *Point Blank* (1967), and in one of his best movies, played a New Yorker who becomes an auxiliary cop (with pal Ernest Borgnine) in the underrated *Law and Disorder* (1974). He has worked almost exclusively on television since then, not only in the TV series "All in the Family" (1971–79), which earned him four Emmy awards, and its spinoff "Archie Bunker's Place" (1979–83), but in the late 1980s and 1990s as the star (and co-executive producer) of "In the Heat of the Night" (1988–95), for which he won an Emmy in 1989.

O'CONNOR, DONALD. Actor, dancer. *(b. Aug. 28, 1925, Chicago.)* A great all-around talent who seldom got movie vehicles worthy of his abilities, Donald O'Connor is best remembered for his exuberant performance as Gene Kelly's pal Cosmo Brown in the 1952 MGM musical *Singin' in the Rain,* and secondarily for his six on-screen gabfests with Francis the Talking Mule. His long career dates back to the fading days of vaudeville in the late 1920s and early 1930s, when he was part of a family act. At age 12 O'Connor made his film debut with his siblings in a not-too-memorable programmer entitled *Melody for Two* (1937). The following year he was signed by Paramount to costar with Bing Crosby and Fred MacMurray in a featured role in *Sing, You Sinners* (1938), and he appeared in a handful of pictures at the studio, including *Tom Sawyer, Detective* (1938, playing Huckleberry Finn) and *Beau Geste* (1939, playing Gary Cooper as a boy).

O'Connor left the screen to return to what was left of vaudeville, but returned to Hollywood in 1942 and signed with Universal to star in their budget-minded youth musicals. *What's Cookin', Get Hep to Love* (both 1942), and *Strictly in the Groove* (1943) were typical of the forgettable fluff in which the always-brash and energetic O'Connor starred during World War 2 (often paired with the equally energetic Peggy Ryan), and his postwar films, including *Are You With It?* and *Feudin', Fussin' and A-Fightin'* (both 1948), were little better.

Francis (1949), a potboiler about an Army private who finds he is the only person who can carry on a conversation with an otherwise taciturn mule, proved to be a big hit with kids and led to five sequels with O'Connor (and one final entry with Mickey Rooney). His other starring vehicles, like *The Milkman* (1950), and *Double Crossbones* (1951) were invariably modest efforts, but after the success of *Singin' in the Rain* (1952, with its showstopping "Make 'Em Laugh" number), MGM did fashion a starring vehicle for him, the enjoyable *I Love Melvin* (1953), and he went on to better costarring parts in *Call Me Madam* (1953, with Ethel Merman at 20th Century-Fox), *There's No Business Like Show Business* (1954, with Merman and Marilyn Monroe, also at Fox), and *Anything Goes* (1956, with Bing Crosby and Mitzi Gaynor, back at Paramount). He was given the full star treatment in Paramount's highly fictionalized version of *The Buster Keaton Story* (1957), but the movie flopped badly, and he made only a handful of films thereafter.

On TV O'Connor was one of the rotating hosts of "The Colgate Comedy Hour." (He was nominated for an Emmy as the Outstanding Personality of 1952, but lost out to Bishop Fulton J. Sheen.) He *did* win an Emmy the following year, and starred in three different incarnations of "The Donald O'Connor Show" for NBC in 1951 and 1954–55. In 1968 he hosted a short-lived talk show. Since leaving the screen, O'Connor has devoted considerable energy to the composition of concert music, and has also appeared extensively as a nightclub performer, teamed for years with Sidney Miller, and more recently with his *Singin' in the Rain* costar Debbie Reynolds. He did a cameo as a vaudevillian in *Ragtime* (1981), and has appeared as Captain Andy in a popular touring stage revival of "Show Boat." In 1992 he was chosen to play Robin Williams' dreamy-eyed toy-manufacturer father in *Toys,* and the following year released his own exercise-oriented videocassette, "Let's Tap."

O'HARA, CATHERINE. Actress. *(b. Mar. 4, 1954, Toronto.)* Vivacious, blond comedienne who was one of the mainstays of "SCTV," notably as the self-centered entertainer Lola Heatherton, who always told her audience, "I want to bear all your children!" O'Hara, a talented mimic blessed with superb comic timing and a flair for spontaneity, moved to features in the mid 1980s but to date has been cast in roles that really haven't drawn on her abilities. She was a hysterically vengeful barmaid in *After Hours* (1985), a gossipy friend in *Heartburn* (1986), and one of the in-laws in *Betsy's Wedding* (1990), for example—roles that could've been handled easily by any number of actresses. She did, however, get to cut loose as the arriviste yuppie who knocks off a mean version of "Banana Boat Song" in *Beetlejuice* (1988), and enjoyed a banner year in 1990, appearing as a romantic lead in *Little Vegas,* as Macaulay Culkin's frantic mom in the hugely successful *Home Alone* (and its 1992 sequel), and under plenty of makeup as a grotesque distaff criminal in *Dick Tracy.* More recently she provided the voices of Sally and Shock in Tim Burton's *The Nightmare Before Christmas* (1993), played Allie Earp in *Wyatt Earp,* and appeared in *A Simple Twist of Fate* with Steve Martin (both 1994), and *Tall Tale* (1995, as Calamity Jane).

O'HARA, MAUREEN. Actress. *(b. Aug. 17, 1920, Millwall, Ireland, as Maureen FitzSimons.)* By far the prettiest colleen who ever came to Hollywood from the Emerald Isle, this spirited actress played a wide variety of roles in films of the 1940s, 1950s, and 1960s, appearing to best advantage in those directed by John Ford. Red-haired and green-eyed, with a lovely complexion, sunny smile, and eye-catching figure, she looked positively stunning in Technicolor. In her teens an ingenue with Dublin's Abbey Players, O'Hara made her screen debut in the British-made *Kicking the Moon Around* (1938). Shortly thereafter she appeared opposite Charles Laughton in *Jamaica Inn* (1939), a stodgy Victorian costumer directed by Alfred Hitchcock. Laughton urged O'Hara to seek her fame in Hollywood, and she came to America later that year, playing Esmerelda to his Quasimodo

in RKO's lavish production, *The Hunchback of Notre Dame.* Subsequent roles in *A Bill of Divorcement, Dance, Girl, Dance* (both 1940), and *They Met in Argentina* (1941) did little to enhance her reputation, but after John Ford cast her in the female lead of *How Green Was My Valley* (also 1941), the moving, Oscar-winning picture about a Welsh coal-mining family, her career took off.

O'Hara bounced back and forth between RKO and 20th Century-Fox throughout the 1940s, starring in *To the Shores of Tripoli, Ten Gentlemen From West Point, The Black Swan,* (all 1942, the last-named her first in Technicolor), *The Immortal Sergeant, This Land Is Mine, The Fallen Sparrow* (all 1943), *Buffalo Bill* (1944), *The Spanish Main* (1945), *Sentimental Journey, Do You Love Me?* (both 1946), *Sinbad the Sailor, The Homestretch, The Foxes of Harrow,* the classic *Miracle on 34th Street* (all 1947), *Sitting Pretty* (1948), *The Forbidden Street, A Woman's Secret,* and *Father Was a Fullback* (all 1949). She then appeared in several actioners for Universal: *Bagdad* (1949), *Comanche Territory* (1950), and *Flame of Araby* (1951).

John Ford approached O'Hara about starring in his labor-of-love project, *The Quiet Man,* in the mid 1940s; she even took pages of script down in shorthand for the director during jaunts on his yacht. But the film wasn't made until the early 1950s, and not until Ford, O'Hara, and John Wayne agreed to make a Western first (to satisfy Republic Pictures' chief Herbert J. Yates): 1950's *Rio Grande.* The chemistry between Wayne and O'Hara was unmistakable, and they reached their peak in *The Quiet Man* (1952), as the American boxer and the high-spirited Irish lass he wants to marry.

Always at her most fetching in period garb, O'Hara matched blades with male antagonists in two 1952 swashbucklers, *Against All Flags* (opposite Errol Flynn) and *At Sword's Point* (opposite Cornel Wilde). She made several minor films before being called again by Ford, this time to costar in his West Point story, *The Long Gray Line* (1955). This same year she played *Lady Godiva,* making the famous bareback horse ride demurely covered by long tresses. She was reunited with Wayne and Ford on *The Wings of Eagles* (1957), the story of Naval commander and screen-writer Frank "Spig" Wead.

O'Hara was off the screen for several years but returned, just as beautiful as ever, in *Our Man in Havana* (1960). By now playing mother parts, she appeared in *The Parent Trap* (1961, one of her favorites), *Mr. Hobbs Takes a Vacation* (1962), and *Spencer's Mountain* (1963), before re-uniting with Wayne for the boisterous Western comedy *McLintock!* (also 1963). She subsequently made *The Battle of the Villa Fiorita* (1965), *The Rare Breed* (1966), *How Do I Love Thee?* (1970), and *Big Jake* (1971, her last with Wayne) before abandoning the screen altogether. She made occasional appearances on TV over the years, even singing on a number of variety shows, and costarred in the 1973 remake of *The Red Pony*. At that point, she left show business behind for the better part of two decades, before being wooed by writer-director Chris Columbus to play John Candy's irrepressible, obstinate mother in *Only the Lonely* (1991), a forceful performance that might have yielded an Oscar nomination if the film had been more widely seen. Her daughter, Bronwyn FitzSimons, pursued an acting career at one time, as did her brothers, James Lilburn and Charles FitzSimons (the latter becoming a producer instead).

O'HERLIHY, DAN. Actor. *(b. May 1, 1919, Wexford, Ireland.)* A handsome leading man with more artistic ambitions than most, O'Herlihy first appeared in British director Carol Reed's 1947 *Odd Man Out,* and then made his American screen debut opposite Orson Welles in the odd, moody, Welles-directed *Macbeth* (1948). Stardom never came, but he won an Oscar nomination for his rich performance in Luis Buñuel's *The Adventures of Robinson Crusoe* (1952), a career high point. Active in TV on both sides of the Atlantic, O'Herlihy had a plum role (along with other Irish and Irish-American actors) in John Huston's directorial swan song, *The Dead* (1987), and in 1991 turned up in David Lynch's surreal prime-time TV series, "Twin Peaks." Contemporary moviegoers might know him best as the CEO of Omni Consumer Products in *RoboCop* (1987) and *RoboCop 2* (1990). In recent years O'Herlihy has been active with California Artists Radio Theatre.

OTHER FILMS INCLUDE: 1948: *Kidnapped;* 1951: *The Desert Fox, Soldiers Three, The Blue Veil;* 1952: *Actors and Sin, At Sword's Point, Invasion U.S.A.;* 1954: *The Black Shield of Falworth;* 1955: *The Virgin Queen;* 1959: *Imitation of Life;* 1962: *The Cabinet of Caligari* (in the leading role); 1964: *Fail-Safe;* 1969: *The Big Cube;* 1977: *MacArthur* (as President Franklin Roosevelt); 1983: *Halloween III: Season of the Witch;* 1984: *The Last Starfighter.*

O'KEEFE, DENNIS. Actor. *(b. Mar. 29, 1908, Fort Madison, Iowa, as Edward Vance Flanagan; d. Aug. 31, 1968.)* A handsome, good-natured juvenile lead, later a rugged star of mysteries and actioners, O'Keefe was born to Irish vaudevillians touring the United States. Young "Bud" Flanagan (nicknamed for a famous British music-hall comedian) joined the family's act while still a toddler. He later wrote skits for the stage, and reportedly contributed gags for some of Hal Roach's "Our Gang" comedies before making the rounds as an extra, appearing in *Cimarron* (1931), *Scarface, I Am a Fugitive from a Chain Gang* (both 1932), *Gold Diggers of 1933* (1933), *Wonder Bar* (1934), *Dante's Inferno, Top Hat* (both 1935), *San Francisco,* and *The Plainsman* (both 1936), among countless others—never receiving screen billing.

Signed by MGM in 1937 and rechristened Dennis O'Keefe, he supported Wallace Beery in *The Bad Man of Brimstone* and played other character parts before winning the lead in *Burn 'Em Up O'Connor* (1939), a B melodrama about auto racing that made him a minor-league star. Shortly afterward, O'Keefe left Metro to freelance, mostly in low or moderately budgeted features such as *La Conga Nights* (1940), *Mr. District Attorney* (1941, as P. Cadwallader Jones), *The Affairs of Jimmy Valentine* (1942), and *Hi Diddle Diddle* (1943), which took advantage of his facility with sharp dialogue and physical comedy (he did a mean double-take). He was delightful as a wisecracking, reluctantly heroic cab driver (in the Bob Hope manner) in the more polished *Topper Returns* (1941).

O'Keefe took dramatic roles as well, shining in *The Leopard Man* (1943, a stylish B horror film), *The Fighting Seabees* (1944, competing with John Wayne for Susan Hayward's attentions), and *The*

Story of Dr. Wassell (1944). But he continued to star in farcical comedies such as
*Up in Mabel's Room, Abroad With Two
Yanks* (both 1944), *Brewster's Millions,*
and *Getting Gertie's Garter* (both 1945).
In the late 1940s, a mature, slightly
weatherbeaten O'Keefe top-lined several gritty crime melodramas—including
1947's *T-Men* and 1948's *Raw Deal* and
Walk a Crooked Mile—modifying his
screen persona in the bargain.

He also tried his hand at directing, with
such films as *Angela* (1955, in which he
also starred), and headlined his own short-
lived TV sitcom, "The Dennis O'Keefe
Show," in 1959. O'Keefe married Hungarian actress Steffi Duna in 1940, after
costarring with her in an undistinguished
Republic programmer, *The Girl From Havana,* earlier that year.

OTHER FILMS INCLUDE: 1950: *The Eagle
and the Hawk;* 1951: *Passage West;* 1953:
The Lady Wants Mink; 1954: *Drums of Tahiti;*
1955: *Las Vegas Shakedown, Chicago Syndicate;* 1956: *Inside Detroit;* 1961: *All Hands on
Deck;* 1965: *The Naked Flame* (his last).

O'KEEFE, MICHAEL. Actor. *(b. Apr. 24,
1955, Paulland, N.J.)* Before making movies, this affable young leading man studied at the American Academy of Dramatic
Arts and cofounded the Colonnade Theatre Lab. He made his feature-film debut in
1978 in the submarine adventure *Gray
Lady Down,* and received an Oscar nomination as Best Supporting Actor for
his performance as Robert Duvall's browbeaten son in *The Great Santini* (1979).
O'Keefe gave a sensitive, carefully textured performance, easily keeping pace
with the experienced, accomplished
Duvall; critics recognized his achievement
and predicted big things for him. This artistic success led to a commercial one,
when O'Keefe starred the next year in the
hit comedy *Caddyshack* (1980). His career
has since fluctuated between leads and
second leads in mostly lousy films, such
as *Nate and Hayes* (1983), *Finders Keepers* (1984), *The Slugger's Wife* (1985), and
The Whoopee Boys (1986), though he was
excellent as a brainwash victim in *Split
Image* (1982) and moving in the Jack
Nicholson starrer *Ironweed* (1987). In
1990, he starred in the short-lived though
critically acclaimed TV crime show "Against the Law." He has also worked on

and off Broadway, in such plays as
"Streamers" and "Mass Appeal." More recently he appeared in a recurring role on
the popular TV sitcom "Roseanne," and
costarred in *Me and Veronica* (1993). He
is married to recording star Bonnie Raitt.

OLAND, WARNER. Actor. *(b. Oct. 3,
1880, Umea, Sweden, as Werner Ohlund; d.
Aug. 5, 1938.)* The screen's most prolific
Caucasian delineator of Asian characters,
this Swedish actor earned immortality as
Earl Derr Biggers' famous Hawaiian-
Chinese detective, Charlie Chan. Oland,
who moved to America at the age of 10,
had already enjoyed a successful career in
the theater—as actor, set designer, and
translator of Strindberg plays—before
breaking into films in the teens. Stocky
and sinister-looking, he most frequently
played heavies, early on in the serials *Pa-
tria, The Fatal Ring* (both 1917), *The
Lightning Raider* (1919, donning Oriental
makeup for the first time as Pearl White's
nemesis Wu Fang), *The Third Eye* (1920),
and *Hurricane Hutch* (1921), then later in
Douglas Fairbanks' *Don Q, Son of Zorro,
Riders of the Purple Sage* (both 1925),
Don Juan (1926), and *Old San Francisco*
(1927), among others. He had a sympathetic role (but no audible dialogue) as Al
Jolson's cantor father in *The Jazz Singer*
(1927), then made his mark in the early
sound era as Sax Rohmer's evil genius in
The Mysterious Dr. Fu Manchu (1929),
The Return of Dr. Fu Manchu (1930), and
Daughter of the Dragon (1931, which
killed off the character, much to Rohmer's
chagrin). He also played the malevolent
doctor in a gag cameo for *Paramount on
Parade* (1930).

Although Oland plied his villainous
trade, in and out of Oriental makeup, in
several more talkies—including *Drums of
Jeopardy* (1931), *Shanghai Express*
(1932), *Bulldog Drummond Strikes Back*
(1934), *Werewolf of London* (1935)—
it was as Biggers' mild-mannered, apho-
rism-spouting detective that he attained international stardom. The Chan character
had been interpreted on screen three times
before, and Oland's first effort, *Charlie
Chan Carries On* (1931), wasn't expected
to launch a series. But its popularity led
first to a Biggers-written sequel, *The
Black Camel* (1931), and then a slew of
lower-budgeted entries: *Charlie Chan's*

Chance (1932), *Charlie Chan's Greatest Case* (1933), *Charlie Chan's Courage, Charlie Chan in London* (both 1934), *Charlie Chan in Paris, Charlie Chan in Egypt, Charlie Chan in Shanghai* (all 1935), *Charlie Chan's Secret, Charlie Chan at the Circus, Charlie Chan at the Race Track, Charlie Chan at the Opera* (all 1936), *Charlie Chan at the Olympics, Charlie Chan on Broadway* (both 1937), and *Charlie Chan at Monte Carlo* (1938). Criticized in recent years for his pidgin-English dialogue, Oland was defended by costar Keye Luke, who explained that the intelligent actor (who spent much time studying Chinese culture) approached his role as that of a Chinese mandarin who had to think in one language, then speak in another.

When Oland, a heavy drinker with a history of health problems, took ill in 1938, *Charlie Chan at the Ringside* was revamped—slightly—to become *Mr. Moto's Gamble,* starring Peter Lorre as another Oriental detective. Oland died shortly thereafter from bronchial pneumonia.

OLDMAN, GARY. Actor. *(b. Mar. 21, 1958, South London.)* Sid Vicious. Lee Harvey Oswald. Dracula. There's no one this young British actor can't play—convincingly. After making a shattering impression on the British stage, he galvanized film audiences as doomed, frantic punk rocker Sid Vicious in 1986's *Sid and Nancy.* It was a performance so harrowingly good that it didn't seem to be a performance at all, but reality itself. (His earlier credits include Mike Leigh's 1983 telefilm *Meantime.*) The auburn-haired, pockmarked Oldman then transformed himself into the far more articulate but equally tormented gay British playwright Joe Orton in *Prick Up Your Ears* (1987). After an enigmatic turn in Nicolas Roeg's inaccessible *Track 29* (1988), Oldman played an American lawyer in 1989's *Criminal Law* (losing his British accent completely), an institutionalized Korean War vet in the little-seen *Chattahoochee,* and the easily addled Rosencrantz in Tom Stoppard's *Rosencrantz and Guildenstern Are Dead* (both 1990). After an intense performance in the crime drama *State of Grace* and an appearance in *Heading Home* (both also 1990),

Oldman went on to play Lee Harvey Oswald in the mosaic of flashbacks in Oliver Stone's controversial *JFK* (1991), which was likely seen by more American moviegoers than all his other films combined! How do you follow a part like that? By assuming the title role in Francis Ford Coppola's highly eroticized version of *Bram Stoker's Dracula* (1992), of course, decked out in elaborate period costumes, smothered in heavy makeup, and sporting a thick, almost impenetrable accent. Since then he's appeared in *True Romance* (1993, with a mane of dreadlocks, as a Chicago drug dealer), *Romeo Is Bleeding, The Professional, Immortal Beloved* (all 1994, in the last named as Beethoven), *Murder in the First,* and *The Scarlet Letter* (both 1995, in the latter as Arthur Dimmesdale). He was married to actress Uma Thurman.

OLIN, LENA. Actress. *(b. Mar. 22, 1955, Stockholm.)* Dark beauty who got middlebrow audiences in the U. S. all hot and bothered playing the sensualist Sabina in Philip Kaufman's film of Milan Kundera's novel *The Unbearable Lightness of Being* (1988). She enjoyed much prestige in Sweden prior to that, appearing frequently on stage (she is a member of Stockholm's Royal Dramatic Theater) and in a number of films, including *The Adventures of Picasso* (1978) and two Ingmar Bergman films, *Fanny and Alexander* (1983) and *After the Rehearsal* (1984). Olin played another free spirit in 1989's *Enemies, a Love Story,* which earned her a Best Supporting Actress Oscar nomination. Small wonder: Few actresses today radiate the earthy sexuality Olin projects with apparent effortlessness. In 1990 she was paired with Robert Redford in the *Casablanca*-meets-Castro flop *Havana,* hindering her chances to become better known to mainstream American moviegoers. She's also known for *not* getting some highly touted roles: Much was made of her potential casting as Maria in *The Bonfire of the Vanities* (1990); Olin lost out to Melanie Griffith. And she lost the part of Catwoman in *Batman Returns* (1992) to Michelle Pfeiffer. She has, however, costarred with Richard Gere in *Mr. Jones* (1993) and appeared in *Romeo Is Bleeding* (1994, her most outrageous and flamboyant performance to date, as a terrorist-assassin).

OLIVIER, LAURENCE (LORD). Actor, director, producer. *(b. May 22, 1907, Dorking, England; d. July 11, 1989.)* The man commonly referred to as the greatest actor of the century never thought of himself as much of a screen actor, but "just another player," as screenwriter William Goldman reported. A clergyman's son—with no interest in inheriting the family business—Olivier began acting in his teens (making his stage debut at 15, playing Kate [!] in "The Taming of the Shrew"), and was encouraged to study at London's Central School of Speech Training and Dramatic Arts. From there, he joined the Birmingham Repertory Company and debuted on Broadway in 1929. The dark, handsome performer enjoyed stage successes in both New York and London, including the very successful "Journey's End" and "Private Lives," but he also had many failures, and real respectability eluded him. Moreover, Olivier's performances in his first American films, *Friends and Lovers* and *The Yellow Ticket* (both 1931), were indifferently received, and he lost the male lead in *Queen Christina* (1933), which would have costarred him with Greta Garbo.

Back in England, Olivier won notoriety in John Gielgud's production of "Romeo and Juliet" (in which they swapped the roles of Romeo and Mercutio), and then as a very modernized, Freudian-influenced Hamlet. Throughout the remainder of the 1930s, he became one of England's leading stage actors and established a romantic screen persona in *Fire Over England* (1937), *The Divorce of Lady X* (1938), and *Q Planes* (1939). He returned to Hollywood with Vivien Leigh (whom he'd met when they costarred in *Fire Over England*). She was hired to star as Scarlett O'Hara, while he played Heathcliff in Samuel Goldwyn's lavish production of *Wuthering Heights* (1939, directed by William Wyler); his brooding, intense performance—the credit for which Olivier always gave to director Wyler—brought the vibrant Englishman his first Oscar nomination and international acclaim besides. Olivier became known for his amazing prowess at exposing characters' inner selves with his meticulous exploitation of external details: accents, physical

impairments, and makeup. (Upon learning that his *Marathon Man* costar Dustin Hoffman had stayed awake for two days to look properly exhausted in one scene, he told the younger actor, "You should try acting, my boy. It's much easier.")

Olivier cemented his Hollywood reputation with skillful performances in Hitchcock's *Rebecca* (Oscar-nominated) and *Pride and Prejudice* (both 1940), and scored with moviegoers across the Atlantic as the male star of *That Hamilton Woman*, opposite Leigh, and then in the all-star war yarn *49th Parallel* (both 1941). After World War 2 began, Olivier asked William Wyler to direct him in a film version of Shakespeare's "Henry V," but Wyler turned him down and suggested Olivier direct it himself. He did, and the resulting 1945 film was hailed as a milestone: the first serious and successful translation of Shakespeare to the screen. It won Olivier a special Oscar in recognition of outstanding achievement (and a Best Actor nomination). Just a few years later he topped himself, directing and starring in an ambitious, moody adaptation of *Hamlet* (1948) that won four Oscars, including one for Best Picture and one for him as Best Actor. He is the only performer in Oscar history to direct himself in an Academy Award-winning performance.

Olivier's stage work took precedence during the 1950s and 1960s, during which time he directed himself in only two other films: the spellbinding *Richard III* (1955, Oscar-nominated) and *The Prince and the Showgirl* (1957, which teamed him with Marilyn Monroe). He played a few roles for other directors, notably appearing in Wyler's *Carrie* (1952), which many critics consider one of his best performances. His portrayal of seedy vaudevillian Archie Rice in *The Entertainer* (1960, Oscar-nominated, recreating his acclaimed stage role) began his transition into character parts, and led to supporting roles in *Spartacus* (1960, as Crassus), *Khartoum* (1966, as the Mahdi), *Oh! What a Lovely War* (1969), and *Nicholas and Alexandra* (1971), although he still astonished audiences in leading roles like the title part in *Othello* (1965) and the cuckolded mystery writer in *Sleuth* (1972, earning more Oscar nominations for the last two).

Film critic Pauline Kael once rhapsodized: "Every time we single out the feature that makes Olivier a marvel—his lion eyes or the voice and the way it seizes on a phrase—he alters it or casts it off in some new role, and is greater than ever." In the 1970s Olivier accepted parts in a number of commercial films, bringing artistic authority—if a dubious mastery of dialects—to films like *Marathon Man* (1976, again Oscar-nominated), *The Boys From Brazil* (for which he was Oscar-nominated), and *The Betsy* (both 1978), and hamming delightfully in concoctions like *A Little Romance* (1979). His health grew worse, but he continued to work and was grateful to the movie industry for giving him a chance to do so.

Some critics took Olivier to task for appearing in negligible films such as *The Jazz Singer* (1980), *Inchon* (1982, as General MacArthur!), and *The Jigsaw Man* (1984), but dissenting critic Richard Schickel commented, "To those of us who believe that the best kind of heroism is to be found in the relentless practice of one's profession . . . he now became a genuinely heroic figure." (Olivier explained, quite candidly, that he was trying to earn enough money to provide for his young family.) He made occasional forays into television, winning five Emmy Awards; he was particularly active in later years, with acclaimed productions of "Long Day's Journey Into Night" (1972) and "Cat on a Hot Tin Roof" (1976), the TV movies *Love Among the Ruins* (1975, opposite Katharine Hepburn), *Mr. Halpern and Mr. Johnson* (1983, opposite Jackie Gleason), and *The Ebony Tower* (1984), and the miniseries "Brideshead Revisited" (1981), and "Lost Empires" (1986). Olivier's last great performance was, appropriately enough, King Lear in a 1983 TV production that won him the last of his Emmy Awards and was considered a fitting valediction. Olivier was married to actresses Jill Esmond, Vivien Leigh (1940–60), and Joan Plowright (1961 until his death). He was knighted in 1947, and took a seat in the House of Lords in 1971. His autobiography, "Confessions of an Actor," was published in 1984.
OTHER FILMS INCLUDE: 1930: *Too Many Crooks;* 1932: *Westward Passage;* 1933: *Perfect Understanding;* 1935: *Moscow Nights* (aka *I Stand Condemned*); 1936: *As You Like It;* 1938: *21 Days Together* (with Leigh); 1943: *The Demi-Paradise;* 1951: *The Magic Box* (cameo); 1953: *The Beggar's Opera;*

1959: *The Devil's Disciple;* 1962: *Term of Trial;* 1965: *Bunny Lake Is Missing;* 1968: *The Shoes of the Fisherman;* 1969: *Battle of Britain;* 1970: *David Copperfield* (telefilm), *Three Sisters* (also directed); 1972: *Lady Caroline Lamb;* 1976: *The Seven Percent Solution* (as Prof. Moriarty); 1977: *A Bridge Too Far;* 1979: *Dracula* (as Dr. Van Helsing); 1981: *Clash of the Titans* (as Zeus); 1983: *Wagner;* 1984: *The Bounty;* 1985: *Wild Geese II;* 1988: *War Requiem.*

OLMI, ERMANNO. Director, screenwriter, cinematographer, editor. *(b. July 24, 1931, Bergamo, Italy.)* Extraordinary Italian filmmaker whose gentle, unforced and humanistic approach to his characters and themes has resulted in a body of often breathtaking work. After World War 2, Olmi worked as a clerk at the Edison-Volta electric plant and made some forty documentary films about the facility. With some funding from Edison, he was allowed to make his first feature film, *Time Stood Still* (1959), about an older man and a boy guarding an unfinished dam, and the relationship that develops between them. Next came *Il Posto* (1961, released in the U.S. as *The Sound of Trumpets*), a masterpiece about a young boy from a poor family who comes to the big city (Milan) to work as a clerk for a large company, and *The Fiancés* (1963), which follows an engaged couple who are separated when he must take a job away from her for 18 months. For many critics, these three films established Olmi as the "heir" to Italy's original neorealist movement with their depictions of the lower classes and use of nonprofessional actors. Olmi's refusal to caricature or condescend and his obvious affection for the characters and their environment made him difficult to pigeonhole, however. David Thomson wrote, "His near-mystical tenderness for people is more impressive than De Sica's sentiment, and the most intriguing element in his films seems closer to the abstracting eye of an Antonioni." *And There Came a Man* (1964), starring Rod Steiger as Pope John XXIII, was Olmi's first and last intentionally commercial effort. *One Fine Day* (1969) dealt with a troubled middle-class character, and *The Scavengers* (1970) was a variation on *Time Stood Still.* *During the Summer* (1971), about a poor wanderer and his world of noble illusions, found Olmi in a lighthearted mood, but his study of a distant bourgeois family in *The Circumstance* (1974) was done sincerely and soberly. He won the Palme D'Or at Cannes for *The Tree of Wooden Clogs* (1978), a beautiful, episodic look at several peasant families in 19th-century Lombardy, but did not make another film until 1983's *Cammina Cammina,* a whimsical reworking of the journey of the Magi. Since then, he has made *Long Live the Lady!* (1987) a satire of bourgeois society, *The Legend of the Holy Drinker* (1988) with Rutger Hauer, and *Down the River* (1992). Olmi's quiet, unobtrusive style has probably worked against his recognition by a larger audience, but he still has his champions. John Simon once compared his films to those of the similarly empathetic Jan Troell, by noting "they make you love not only them but also the man who made them."

OLMOS, EDWARD JAMES. Actor. *(b. Feb. 24, 1947, Los Angeles.)* Hypnotic, pockmarked Latino actor known as much for his integrity, and commitment to meaningful films, as for his acting ability. His first screen credit was 1975's *aloha, bobby and rose,* but he first came to attention as the "stage manager" El Pachuco in the musical "Zoot Suit," a role he reprised in the 1981 film version. That same year, he had his first substantial screen role as the construction worker who may or may not be a werewolf in *Wolfen.* After playing the sinister, origami-obsessed cop in *Blade Runner* (1982), he starred in *The Ballad of Gregorio Cortez* (also 1982), which he also coproduced. It was so important a project to Olmos that he actually ran it in an L.A. theater free of charge to encourage attendance. In 1984 he signed to play the enigmatic, unsmiling Lt. Castillo on "Miami Vice," and it brought him an Emmy and small-screen stardom. His performance as math teacher Jaime Escalante in *Stand and Deliver* (1987) earned him an Oscar nomination and vindicated his dedication to films that matter. He has since played a concentration camp prisoner in *Triumph of the Spirit* (1989), a baseball scout in *Talent for the Game* (1991), and produced, directed, and starred in the anti-gang drama *American Me* (1992). Recent credits include the TV miniseries "Menendez: A Killing in Bev-

erly Hills" (1994), *My Family/Mi Familia* and *Roosters* (both 1995).

OLSEN AND JOHNSON. Actors. *(Ole Olsen—b. Nov. 6, 1892, Wabash, Ind., as John Sigvard Olsen; d. Jan. 26, 1963. Chic Johnson—b. Mar. 5, 1891, Chicago, as Harold Ogden Johnson; d. Feb. 28, 1962.)* These madcap stage comics brought their unique brand of lunacy to the screen with uneven results, although their best films— *Hellzapoppin* (1941), *Crazy House* (1943), and *Ghost Catchers* (1944)—amply define their peculiar appeal. The chubby Johnson, a onetime saloon pianist whose trademark was a high-pitched laugh, teamed with the lanky Olsen in 1914; their freewheeling comic style, perfected during years of vaudeville engagements, reached its fruition in "Hellzapoppin," a wacky revue that ran on Broadway for nearly three years (1938–41). Olsen and Johnson jammed the show with a rapid-fire succession of blackouts, novelty numbers, and elaborate sight gags (many of which revolved around cast members planted in the audience).

In their first films, Warner Bros. musicomedies *Oh Sailor Behave!* (1930) and *Fifty Million Frenchmen* (1931), O&J were cast in conventional comic-relief roles, their hyperkinetic brand of humor effectively muted. A starring vehicle, *Gold Dust Gertie* (also 1931), was little better, and the team returned to the stage. Two Republic starrers, *Country Gentlemen* (1936) and *All Over Town* (1937), were no great improvement. But Universal's 1941 *Hellzapoppin,* while trying too hard to graft a plot onto O&J's lunatic revue, generally succeeded in translating their anarchic comedy to the screen, even to including many of the Broadway show's original gags. The follow-ups *Crazy House* (1943), and *Ghost Catchers* (1944) offered surfeits of zany humor, but the team's final film, *See My Lawyer* (1945), was a tepid affair that showed Universal incapable of sustaining the cyclonic pace and surrealistic bent of the earlier entries. The team lived out its career on stage, and occasionally on TV.

ONDRICEK, MIROSLAV. Cinematographer. *(b. Nov. 4, 1934, Prague.)* This talented cinematographer learned his craft at the Barrandov Studio Training School and commenced his career in 1962, at the time of the Czech New Wave. He photographed Milos Forman's debut feature, *Konkurs* (1962, *Competition*), and went on to shoot some of Czechoslovakia's most significant films, including Ivan Passer's *Intimate Lighting* (1965) and Forman's *Loves of a Blonde* (also 1965) and *The Firemen's Ball* (1967). At the time of the Soviet invasion of his homeland in 1968, Ondricek went to work in England and began an association with Lindsay Anderson on *if . . .* (1968). He then moved to America, where he continued his work with fellow émigré Forman on *Taking Off* (1971). Other important credits include George Roy Hill's *Slaughterhouse-Five* (1972), Anderson's *O Lucky Man!* (1973), Forman's *Hair* (1979) and *Ragtime* (1981, earning his first Oscar nomination), Hill's *The World According to Garp* (1982), Mike Nichols' *Silkwood* (1983), Forman's *Amadeus* (1984, another Oscar nomination) and *Valmont* (1989), and Penny Marshall's *Awakenings* (1990) and *A League of Their Own* (1992). For a change of pace, he agreed to photograph *Distant Harmony* (1987), a documentary record of Luciano Pavarotti's tour of China. For the most part, Ondricek may be defined by the films he has worked on, and the filmmakers he has worked for: serious, artistic, often political, and always humanistic. According to Milos Forman, "He has his own opinion, his own eyes, and they are strictly his own; yet he always tries to harmonize them with mine."

O'NEAL, RYAN. Actor. *(b. Apr. 20, 1941, Los Angeles, as Patrick Ryan O'Neal.)* Boyish, sandy-haired, good-looking actor who gained fame as one of the stars of TV's prime-time soap opera "Peyton Place" (1964–69), then boosted his stock with an Oscar-nominated performance in the drippy romance *Love Story* (1970). Nothing he's done since has equaled that success, but he proved an amiable screen presence in such comedies as Peter Bogdanovich's *What's Up, Doc?* (1972, doing his best to match Cary Grant's exasperation from the film's inspiration/source, *Bringing Up Baby)* and *Paper Moon* (1973, in which he was upstaged by his own daughter Tatum), and acquitted himself admirably in Stanley Kubrick's

meticulous period piece *Barry Lyndon* (1975). His career has had more downs than ups, but he proved he'd lost none of his skill as a light comedian in 1981's *So Fine,* 1984's *Irreconcilable Differences,* and 1989's *Chances Are.* He also had the distinction of being directed by Norman Mailer in his very odd *Tough Guys Don't Dance* (1987). In 1992 he costarred with Katharine Hepburn in the telefilm *The Man Upstairs.* Formerly married to actresses Joanna Moore and Leigh Taylor-Young, O'Neal has lived for many years with Farrah Fawcett, with whom he costarred in a short-lived sitcom, "Good Sports" (1991), and the acclaimed dramatic TV movie *Small Sacrifices* (1989). OTHER FILMS INCLUDE: 1969: *The Big Bounce;* 1971: *Wild Rovers;* 1973: *The Thief Who Came to Dinner;* 1976: *Nickelodeon;* 1977: *A Bridge Too Far;* 1978: *The Driver, Oliver's Story* (a *Love Story* sequel); 1979: *The Main Event;* 1981: *Green Ice;* 1982: *Partners;* 1985: *Fever Pitch.*

O'NEAL, TATUM. Actress. *(b. Nov. 5, 1963, Los Angeles.)* At ten years of age, this actress made history with her film debut as the tough-talking, cigarette-smoking orphan in *Paper Moon* (1973), opposite her real-life father, Ryan O'Neal. She stole the movie from him and won an Academy Award for her performance— the youngest performer ever to do so. For a while, she was Hollywood's hot child actor, with hand-tailored roles in the baseball comedy *The Bad News Bears* and *Nickelodeon* (both 1976) and the horse-racing drama *International Velvet* (1978), but efforts at more mature parts in 1980's *Little Darlings* (paired with Kristy McNichol) and *Circle of Two* (in which she appeared topless as a student in love with a 60-year-old artist played by Richard Burton) were coolly received. After the wretched *Certain Fury* (1985), she retired from acting to marry tennis player John McEnroe and raise a family. (They have since broken up.) O'Neal made a TV movie, *15 and Getting Straight* (1989), returned to the big screen in the 1991 independent feature *Little Noises,* and starred in the title role of the TV movie *Woman on the Run: The Lawrencia Bembenek Story* (1993).

O'NEILL, JENNIFER. Actress. *(b. Feb. 20, 1948, Rio de Janeiro.)* What red-blooded American male, having seen this winsome brunette as the young war widow in *Summer of '42* (1971), can honestly say she didn't make his heart beat a little faster? That appearance remains the high point in a generally mundane career. Born to affluent parents and raised in New York and Connecticut, O'Neill pursued a modeling career before breaking into movies with a bit in *For Love of Ivy* (1968). She won the female lead in the John Wayne starrer *Rio Lobo* (1970), but still had a lot to learn about acting (director Howard Hawks later referred to her as "a damn fool"). Otto Preminger had better luck directing her in his black comedy *Such Good Friends* (1971), by which time the surprise success of *Summer of '42* had catapulted her to stardom. But O'Neill's leading roles in *The Carey Treatment* (1972), *Lady Ice* (1973), *The Reincarnation of Peter Proud,* and *Whiffs* (both 1975) asked little of her other than to look beautiful. Her sporadic career since then has included Luchino Visconti's *The Innocent* (1976, in which she was surprisingly effective), *Caravans* (1978), *A Force of One, Steel* (both 1979), *Cloud Dancer* (1980), *Scanners* (1981), *I Love N.Y.* (1987), *Committed* (1988), *The Raven* (1990), and *Love Is Like That* (1992). Still a model and cosmetics spokesperson, she is more familiar from her TV work (including two series, 1983's "Bare Essence" and 1984–85's "Cover-Up") than any movies she's made in recent memory. She's also remained in the headlines, with marital problems (she's been wed six times) and a self-inflicted (accidental) gunshot wound.

OPHULS, MARCEL. Director. *(b. Nov. 1, 1927, Frankfurt, Germany.)* The son of famed director Max Ophuls, Marcel spent his adolescent years in Hollywood, where his father worked on major studio productions. Bitten himself by the movie bug, the young Ophuls returned to Europe and made his directorial debut with one segment of *Love at Twenty* (1962), followed by the light comedy *Banana Peel* (1964), starring Jeanne Moreau and Jean-Paul Belmondo. Conventional narrative motion pictures didn't interest him as much as documentary film making, and in the late 1960s he hurled himself into *The Sorrow and the Pity,* a 4½-hour exposé of French complacency and collaboration during World War 2. The film, which took Ophuls more than three years to complete, was finally released in 1970 and established him as a world-class documentarian. The following year he explored the ongoing conflicts in Ireland in *A Sense of Loss* (1972). His next film, *The Memory of Justice* (1976), an examination of the Nuremberg trials and their aftermath, French intervention in Algeria, and American involvement in Vietnam, was such a draining experience that he abandoned filmmaking for several years to write, teach, and lecture. Eventually he relented, and in 1987 completed *Hotel Terminus: The Life and Times of Klaus Barbie,* an Oscar-winning documentary about a notorious Nazi war criminal. His latest film is *The Troubles We've Seen: A History of Journalism in Wartime* (1994).

OPHULS, MAX. Director, writer. *(b. May 6, 1902, Saarbrucken, Germany, as Max Oppenheimer; d. Mar. 26, 1957.)* One of cinema's great stylists, Ophuls became an actor in his teens, but gravitated to directing and staged scores of plays in Germany and Austria in the 1920s. After making his first films in Germany in the early 1930s, including the touching *Libelei* (1933), the Jewish Ophuls fled his native country, and spent the next decade globe-hopping, making films along the way in France, Italy, and Holland, before settling in America in the early 1940s. After several aborted projects (including Howard Hughes' *Vendetta,* which he began) he finally got a job directing Douglas Fairbanks, Jr., in the swashbuckling adventure *The Exile* (1947), under the name Max Ophuls, which he used on his subsequent American productions. His Hollywood career reached its peak with the lushly romantic *Letter From an Unknown Woman* (1948), but he proved his mettle as an interpreter of darker subject matter with *Caught* and *The Reckless Moment* (both 1949). His fondness for sophisticated camera movement made him the butt of many derisive stories, but also defined his unmistakable visual style. He returned to France in the 1950s where he created his masterpieces—wise, witty, elegant, and intriguing films in which style and content were married in joyful harmony: *La Ronde*

(1950, Oscar-nominated for Best Screenplay), *Le Plaisir* (1951, Oscar-nominated for his art direction), *The Earrings of Madame de . . .* (1953), and *Lola Montes* (1955). He cowrote them all, and left his mark not only on cinema but on a number of future directors who have admitted their debt to this master. As Andrew Sarris wrote, "In the final analysis, Ophuls is, like all great directors, inimitable, and if all the dollies and cranes in the world snap to attention when his name is mentioned, it is because he gave camera movement its finest hours in the history of the cinema." His son is Marcel Ophuls.

O'QUINN, TERRY. Actor. (b. July 15, 1952, Newbury, Mich.) He was the outwardly gentle but actually maniacal master of the house in Joseph Ruben's chilling *The Stepfather* (1987), giving an unpredictable, beautifully modulated performance. O'Quinn, who seemed to materialize from thin air (but who actually had appeared in such films as 1984's *Mrs. Soffel*, 1985's *Mischief* and *Silver Bullet*, 1986's *SpaceCamp* and *Black Widow* among others), also did yeoman service in *The Stepfather*'s unsubtle (and far less effective) 1989 sequel. Subsequent assignments include *Young Guns* (1988), and starring roles in the dreary erotic thriller *The Forgotten One*, the science-run-amok chiller *Pin* (both 1989), and the Australian drama *Prisoners of the Sun* (1990), as well as supporting work in the ludicrous actioner *Blind Fury* (1990). O'Quinn played the young Howard Hughes, to whom he bears a surprising resemblance, in *The Rocketeer* (1991), and appeared in *The Cutting Edge* (1992).

ORBACH, JERRY. Actor. (b. Oct. 20, 1935, Bronx, N.Y.) A Tony Award–winning veteran of the New York musical theater ("The Fantasticks," "42nd Street"), this quintessentially Noo Yawk character actor made his film debut in 1958's *Cop Hater* and later became a staple on episodic television. Usually cast as double-dealers, gangsters, or cops, he offered memorable support in 1981's *Prince of the City*, 1986's *F/X*, and 1989's *Crimes and Misdemeanors*. He took the leading role in a movie just once, in the adaptation of Jimmy Breslin's *The Gang That Couldn't*

Shoot Straight (1971). He has since costarred in several TV series, including "The Law and Harry McGraw" (1987–88, a spinoff from "Murder, She Wrote") and "Law and Order" (1993–), in which he replaced Paul Sorvino.
OTHER FILMS INCLUDE: 1961: *Mad Dog Coll;* 1965: *John Goldfarb, Please Come Home;* 1977: *The Sentinel;* 1985: *Brewster's Millions;* 1987: *Dirty Dancing* (as Jennifer Grey's father), *Someone to Watch Over Me;* 1989: *Last Exit to Brooklyn;* 1992: *Mr. Saturday Night, Universal Soldier.*

O'SHEA, MILO. Actor. (b. June 2, 1926, Dublin.) With his twinkling dark eyes, bushy black eyebrows, and mischievous grin, this short, stocky Irish character actor is an infrequently used but always effective screen player. An alumnus of Dublin's Abbey Players, he turned to film work in the 1960s, and enjoyed his greatest screen success as multifaceted, sympathetic Leopold Bloom in director Joseph Strick's ambitious film adaptation of James Joyce's *Ulysses* (1967). In 1968 he played Friar Lawrence in *Romeo and Juliet* and the villainous Duran Duran in the sci-fi parody *Barbarella*. He was memorably smarmy in *Theatre of Blood* (1973), but was wasted in mindless 1970s fodder such as *Percy's Progress, Digby—The Biggest Dog in the World* (both 1974), and *Arabian Adventure* (1979). Milking the choice role of a corrupt judge in *The Verdict* (1982), he stole scenes right out from under pros Paul Newman and James Mason. He was Father Donnelly in the film within a film of Woody Allen's *The Purple Rose of Cairo* (1985), and had good (if sometimes too brief) supporting roles in *The Dream Team* (1989), *Opportunity Knocks* (1990), *Only the Lonely* (1991), *The Playboys* (1992), and the TV miniseries "Murder in the Heartland" (1993).

O'SULLIVAN, MAUREEN. Actress. (b. May 17, 1911, Boyle, Ireland.) This adorable Irish colleen was discovered by American director Frank Borzage at a Dublin horse show shortly after coming out of a convent school, and starred for him in the John McCormack vehicle *Song o' My Heart* (1930). A few years later she was signed by MGM, where she spent the bulk of her screen career playing virginal inge-

nues, and had substantial secondary roles in such classics as *David Copperfield, Anna Karenina* (both 1935) and *Pride and Prejudice* (1940), not to mention The Marx Brothers' *A Day at the Races* (1937). She is best remembered, however, as Jane, the mate of jungle lord Tarzan, a role she first played with Johnny Weissmuller in *Tarzan, the Ape Man* (1932) and then reprised five more times, evolving in terms of costume (from pre–Production Code scanties to a modified Mother Hubbard) and role (becoming stepmother to Boy). She left the screen for several years in 1942 to raise a family with her husband, director John Farrow. O'Sullivan returned to films as Ray Milland's wife in Farrow's taut thriller *The Big Clock* (1948), and landed some more interesting parts in the 1950s. She was also a cohost of the "Today" show on television in 1963. Infrequently seen on the big screen over the last three decades, she has taken a few colorful supporting roles, most notably in *Hannah and Her Sisters* (1986), a Woody Allen film that costarred her daughter Mia Farrow.
OTHER FILMS INCLUDE: 1930: *Just Imagine;* 1932: *Skyscraper Souls, Payment Deferred, Strange Interlude;* 1933: *Tugboat Annie, Stage Mother;* 1934: *Tarzan and His Mate, Hide-Out, The Barretts of Wimpole Street;* 1935: *Cardinal Richelieu;* 1936: *Tarzan Escapes, The Devil-Doll;* 1937: *The Emperor's Candlesticks;* 1938: *A Yank at Oxford, Port of Seven Seas, The Crowd Roars;* 1939: *Tarzan Finds a Son, Let Us Live;* 1941: *Tarzan's Secret Treasure;* 1942: *Tarzan's New York Adventure;* 1950: *Where Danger Lives;* 1952: *Bonzo Goes to College;* 1953: *All I Desire;* 1954: *Duffy of San Quentin, The Steel Cage;* 1957: *The Tall T;* 1965: *Never Too Late;* 1970: *The Phynx* (cameo; never released); 1985: *Too Scared to Scream;* 1986: *Peggy Sue Got Married;* 1987: *Stranded;* 1992: *The Habitation of Dragons* (telefilm).

O'TOOLE, ANNETTE. Actress. *(b. Apr. 1, 1953, Houston.)* Sparkling, intelligent, red-haired actress, singer and dancer whose talents haven't always been used to best advantage. The wholesomely attractive O'Toole seems tailor-made for perky, girl-next-door types, but is also capable of much more. Debuting in the 1973 TV movie *The Girl Most Likely to . . . ,* O'Toole first drew attention to herself as one of the conniving beauty pageant contestants in *Smile* (1975), and she was briefly typecast as The Loyal Girlfriend in *One on One* (1977), *King of the Gypsies* (1978), and *48HRS.* (1982). More diverse roles finally followed: She escaped feline Nastassia Kinski in *Cat People* (1982), played Lana Lang in *Superman III* (1983), suffered through The Date From Hell (with Martin Short) in *Cross My Heart* (1987), and was one of a bigamist's unsuspecting wives in *Love at Large* (1990). She also impressed in many small-screen telefilms throughout the 1970s and 1980s, most memorably in *The War Between the Tates* (1977, as a student involved with her professor) and *Stand By Your Man* (1981, as Tammy Wynette). She started off the 1990s by starring in the latest remake of the venerable drama *A Girl of the Limberlost* (1990). Her many other TV movie and miniseries credits include *The Entertainer* (1975), "Stephen King's 'It' " (1990), and *Danielle Steel's Jewels* (1992).

O'TOOLE, PETER. Actor. *(b. Aug. 2, 1932, Connemara, Ireland.)* Slender, blond, blue-eyed Irish actor who brings passion and intensity to his screen characters, more than a few of whom have been wild-eyed visionaries. A graduate of London's Royal Academy of Dramatic Art and an acclaimed Shakespearean actor, O'Toole debuted on film in *The Savage Innocents* (1959), but shot to stardom in the title role of *Lawrence of Arabia* (1962), earning an Academy Award nomination to boot. It's possible he'll always be associated with the role of T. E. Lawrence (though, ironically, he was a secondary choice, replacing Albert Finney); his intensely credible portrayal of this desert dreamer is one of the most dynamic in movie history. He's had no trouble moving on, however, to other larger-than-life roles, and has in fact earned another six Oscar nominations for playing King Henry II in both *Becket* (1964, opposite Richard Burton) and *The Lion in Winter* (1968, opposite Katharine Hepburn), the shy schoolteacher in the musical *Goodbye, Mr. Chips* (1969), a wacked-out British lord who thinks he's Jesus Christ in *The Ruling Class* (1972), maniacal movie director Eli Cross (inspired, O'Toole said, by David Lean) in *The Stunt Man* (1980), and washed-up,

Errol Flynn–ish movie swashbuckler Alan Swann in the sweetly comic *My Favorite Year* (1982), With it all, O'Toole has yet to win an Academy Award! An admitted alcoholic, O'Toole squandered his fame (and, some say, his talent) on many projects clearly beneath his abilities. Nonetheless, he remains a compulsively watchable actor whose presence brings color (and some measure of respectability) to any film or TV project in which he appears. In 1985 he lent his voice to a series of animated features about Sherlock Holmes. Among his television ventures: the miniseries "Masada" (1981), a 1983 remake of *Svengali* with Jodie Foster, a 1984 remake of *Kim, Crossing to Freedom* (1990), and *The Dark Angel* (1992). In 1992 he published his first volume of memoirs, "Loitering With Intent," which was greeted with rave reviews.
OTHER FILMS INCLUDE: 1960: *Kidnapped, The Day They Robbed the Bank of England;* 1965: *Lord Jim, What's New, Pussycat?;* 1966: *How to Steal a Million, The Bible;* 1967: *Night of the Generals, Casino Royale* (just a cameo); 1968: *Great Catherine;* 1969: *Brotherly Love;* 1971: *Murphy's War;* 1972: *Man of La Mancha;* 1973: *Under Milk Wood;* 1975: *Rosebud;* 1976: *Man Friday;* 1978: *Power Play;* 1979: *Zulu Dawn;* 1980: *Caligula;* 1984: *Supergirl;* 1985: *Creator;* 1986: *Club Paradise;* 1987: *The Last Emperor;* 1988: *High Spirits;* 1990: *Wings of Fame;* 1991: *King Ralph;* 1993: *The Seventh Coin.*

OWEN, REGINALD. Actor. *(b. Aug. 5, 1887, Wheathampton, England; d. Nov. 5, 1972.)* One of the busiest character actors in Hollywood (who occasionally won leading roles), Owen continued working long after most of his colleagues had retired—or passed on. He studied at Sir Herbert Tree's Academy of Dramatic Arts in England, and made his professional debut at the age of 18. Owen first appeared on Broadway in 1924, and made his film debut in *The Letter* (1929). His Hollywood career flourished in the 1930s; notable roles included Sherlock Holmes in *A Study in Scarlet* (1933, following an appearance as Doctor Watson in the 1932 Fox production of *Sherlock Holmes,* starring Clive Brook), the snarling villain in *Call of the Wild,* Stryver in *A Tale of Two Cities* (both 1935), Talleyrand in *Conquest* (1937), Scrooge in *A Christmas Carol*

(1938), and Louis XV in three films: *Voltaire* (1933), *Madame Du Barry* (1934), and *Monsieur Beaucaire* (1946). A longtime member of the MGM roster, he also appeared in *Queen Christina* (1933), *Rose Marie, The Great Ziegfeld* (both 1936), *The Earl of Chicago* (1940), *A Woman's Face, Tarzan's Secret Treasure* (both 1941), *Woman of the Year, Mrs. Miniver, Random Harvest* (all 1942), *Madame Curie* (1943), *The Canterville Ghost, National Velvet* (both 1944), *The Pirate, The Three Musketeers* (both 1948), *The Miniver Story* (1950), and many others. In later years, Owen played in *Mary Poppins* (1964, as Admiral Boom) and *Rosie!* (1967).

OZ, FRANK. Director, puppeteer, actor. *(b. May 24, 1944, Hereford, England.)* The man who has given life to such beloved Muppet characters as Miss Piggy, Fozzie Bear, Bert (on "Sesame Street"), Cookie Monster, Grover, and Animal has become a film director of note, with a number of popular comedies to his credit. Oz moved to California with his parents in the 1950s and began staging puppet shows when he was 12. He joined Jim Henson's staff of puppeteers seven years later and gradually became Henson's closest collaborator, on the landmark children's TV show "Sesame Street," "The Muppet Show," and the subsequent Muppet features *The Muppet Movie* (1979), *The Great Muppet Caper* (1981), *Sesame Street Presents Follow That Bird* (1985), and *The Muppet Christmas Carol* (1992), in which he performed his familiar characters. Oz codirected the fantasy film *The Dark Crystal* (1983) with Henson and then soloed on the third Muppet movie, *The Muppets Take Manhattan* (1984). Ready to branch out beyond Muppetdom, he brought a keen eye (and sense of humor) to the stylized musical remake of *Little Shop of Horrors* (1986), which proved his mettle as a filmmaker. Since then he has directed the more conventional comedies *Dirty Rotten Scoundrels* (1988), *What About Bob?* (1991), and *HouseSitter* (1992). (He was the original director of 1990's *Mermaids,* but was replaced after filming began.) Oz has also taken cameo roles in a trio of John Landis movies: *The Blues Brothers* (1980), *An American Werewolf in London* (1981), and *Trading Places* (1983), but his most notable "performance" was as the Muppet-like Jedi master Yoda in *The Empire Strikes Back* (1980) and *Return of the Jedi* (1983).

OZU, YASUJIRO. Director, screenwriter. *(b. Dec. 15, 1903, Tokyo; d. Dec. 11, 1963.)* Celebrated as one of the world's greatest filmmakers, Ozu was renowned for his strict, highly personal visual style and considered the most "Japanese" of all directors. Interested in film at an early age, Ozu rejected his schooling and began work as an assistant cameraman to Tadamoto Okuba in 1923, at Shochiko Studios. He directed his first film, *The Sword of Penitence,* in 1927, and made 21 more films over the next four years. His early work like *Days of Youth* (1929) and *I Flunked, But . . .* (1930) dealt with comical student situations and crooks, and reflected Ozu's keen interest in American films of the 1920s; by the time of *Tokyo Chorus* (1931), about a married student who gets kicked out of college, he began to develop his own style. Ozu won the first of three consecutive film awards for *I Was Born, But . . .* (1932), the story of two boys who learn their father is not the important man that they thought, and eventually resign themselves to accepting life's compromises.

Ozu dealt primarily with the dynamics of middle-class Japanese family life and the subtle tensions between the generations. He planned his camera shots meticulously and focused almost entirely on compositions; he never used pans, fades in or out, and employed virtually no dollies or tracking shots. Chishu Ryu, who acted in many of Ozu's films, said, "By the time he had finished writing a script . . . he had already made up every image in every shot, so that he never changed the scenario after we went on the set." Ozu's most famous shot—taken from the eye level of a person seated on a tatami, a Japanese floor mat—became symbolic of a Japanese person's "viewpoint."

After *What Did the Lady Forget?* (1937), Ozu was drafted and worked on propaganda films in Singapore. When he returned, Ozu made *The Record of a Tenement Gentleman* (1947) and *A Hen in the Wind* (1948), both of which deal with the effects of the war on Japanese families. His next film, *Late Spring* (1949), re-united Ozu with his early collaborator Kogo Nada; they worked on each of Ozu's next 13 films. *Late Spring* also marked the beginning of wider distribution for Ozu's films; he achieved his greatest success during the 1950s with films like *The Flavor of Green Tea Over Rice* (1952), *Early Spring* (1956), *Floating Weeds* (1959), and his last film, *An Autumn Afternoon* (1962). *Tokyo Story* (1953), about an elderly couple who visit their uncaring children, is considered by many critics to be one of his greatest achievements. All of these later films found Ozu's style firmly entrenched and even more focused; in his last films the camera never moves at all. From his minimalist approach, Ozu was able to fully and eloquently examine the intricacies of his culture and become, as Stanley Kauffmann noted, "A lyric poet whose lyrics swell quietly into the epic."

PABST, G. W. Director. *(b. Aug. 27, 1885, Raudnitz, Bohemia, as Georg Wilhelm Pabst; d. May 29, 1967.)* One of the prime architects of modern cinema, Pabst began in Viennese theater in 1904, after entering the Academy of Decorative Arts. He was coaxed into filmmaking by the German film pioneer Carl Froelich, who gave him a break as an assistant director. Pabst began his own directorial career in 1923 with *The Treasure,* a film that expanded cinematic language by expressive use of mise-en-scène (the details of the frame's setting). Pabst refused throughout his career to be pigeonholed into any one genre or style, and each picture brought with it another advancement. In *The Joyless Street* (1925), he did extensive location shooting and pioneered the cinema-verité style; in *Secrets of a Soul* (1926) he used distorted lenses and special effects for dream sequences.

In 1928 Pabst directed his best-known work, *Pandora's Box,* which starred expatriate American film star Louise Brooks. Its surprisingly blatant sexual content (including a lesbian scene) aroused critical ire in some quarters; as a result, the picture met with a generally hostile reaction, although modern audiences have recognized it for the masterpiece that it is. Pabst's follow-up with Brooks, *Diary of a Lost Girl* (1929), mined the same vein but with a tad less success. *The White Hell of*

Pitz Palu (1929), one of the German mountain-climbing films so popular in the 1920s and 1930s, was strong enough to be released here by Universal. He also filmed adaptations of *The Threepenny Opera* (in 1931) and *Don Quixote* (1933). His only Hollywood film, *A Modern Hero* (1934), starring Richard Barthelmess, flopped badly, and Pabst returned to Germany, where he stayed throughout World War 2. In 1947 he directed *The Trial,* a treatise on anti-Semitism that would have gotten him shot by a firing squad just a few years before. His last film was 1956's *Durch die Walder, duch di Auen,* completed shortly before he suffered a stroke.

PACINO, AL. Actor. *(b. Apr. 25, 1940, New York City.)* He first galvanized movie audiences as quiet Mafia scion Michael Corleone in Francis Coppola's 1972 *The Godfather* (for which he was Oscar-nominated). He returned to the character twice more, playing it in *The Godfather, Part II* (1974, nominated again) as a steely, paranoid, implacably heartless don, and then in *The Godfather, Part III* (1990) as an aging, infirm, and tragic figure. For these three films, if for nothing else, Pacino will always be remembered. Debuting on film in 1969's *Me, Natalie* (the same year he won a Tony Award for Broadway's "Does a Tiger Wear a Necktie?"), Pacino brought unique integrity to many roles, from a sexually confused would-be bank robber in *Dog Day Afternoon* (1975) to an incorruptible maverick cop in *Serpico* (1973). He had a way of commanding the screen, whether as a junkie in *The Panic in Needle Park* (1971) or a quiet drifter in *Scarecrow* (1973). He virtually defined screen intensity, and brought it with him even to projects that were unworthy, like *Bobby Deerfield* (1977) and a controversial look at the gay netherworld, *Cruising* (1980). He fared better as an idealistic lawyer in ... *And Justice For All* (1979, earning another Oscar nomination) and was quite likable in the critically savaged comedy *Author! Author!* (1982). His explosive performance as Cuban drug kingpin Tony Montana in Brian De Palma's *Scarface* (1983, a latter-day cult favorite) was followed by a deadly costume drama, *Revolution* (1985), in which his Colonial Noo Yawk accent prompted widespread derision.

Pacino took a layoff from Hollywood, going back to his first love, the stage, and working for a long time (as both actor and producer) on an independent film adaptation of British playwright Heathcote Williams' *The Local Stigmatic.* His excellent work as a hard-drinking, emotionally disconnected detective in 1989's *Sea of Love* heralded a triumphant return to the screen, and his hammy, often improvised antics under heavy makeup in Warren Beatty's 1990 *Dick Tracy* revealed a heretofore unseen comedic talent (and netted him a Supporting Actor Oscar nomination). In 1991 he reteamed with *Scarface* costar Michelle Pfeiffer in *Frankie and Johnny,* in his warmest and most appealing screen role in years. The following year he had an unbeatable parlay, as shark-like real estate salesman Ricky Roma in *Glengarry Glen Ross,* which earned him a Best Supporting Actor Oscar nomination, and in a bravura turn as the blind, blustery former lieutenant colonel in *Scent of a Woman,* which won him a Best Actor Oscar, at last. His stardom reconfirmed, Pacino has kept busy both on stage (in such unexpected projects as "Richard III" and "Salome") and screen, where he reteamed with Brian De Palma for another riveting performance in *Carlito's Way* (1993), as a streetwise Puerto Rican ex-con trying to go straight. In 1995, he played a corrupt New York mayor in *City Hall.* In the wake of *The Local Stigmatic,* he has been working on a documentary about Shakespeare.

PAGE, GERALDINE. Actress. *(b. Nov. 22, 1924, Kirksville, Mo.; d. June 13, 1987.)* More a fixture of the New York stage than the Hollywood screen, the Method-tinged performances of this highly acclaimed actress also won her eight Academy Award nominations; she finally won a Best Actress Oscar for her touching, seemingly effortless performance in *The Trip to Bountiful* (1986). It was the swan song for an actress whose carefully wrought delineations of fragile, neurotic, and eccentric characters were her stock in trade. In her first movie, *Hondo* (1953), Page played a frontier widow opposite the imposing John Wayne, and more than held her own, winning her first Oscar nomination. In 1961 she reprised her well-remembered stage role in the screen version of Tennessee

Williams' *Summer and Smoke,* and followed that with an equally memorable
turn as a washed-up, aging actress opposite Paul Newman's opportunistic gigolo
in the highly watered-down movie of Williams' *Sweet Bird of Youth* (1962). Her
Oscar bids for both performances came to
naught, as did a subsequent nomination
for Woody Allen's *Interiors* (1978). In
later years she worked in *The Pope of
Greenwich Village* (1984, delivering a
standout, Oscar-nominated performance as
a chain-smoking harridan), *White Nights,
The Bride* (both 1985), *My Little Girl,* and
Native Son (both 1986). She won two
Emmy Awards, for a pair of acclaimed
TV movies, Truman Capote's *A Christmas
Memory* (1967) and *The Thanksgiving Visitor* (1969). Page was married to stage and
screen actor Rip Torn.
OTHER FILMS INCLUDE: 1963: *Toys in the
Attic;* 1964: *Dear Heart;* 1966: *The Three Sis-
ters;* 1967: *You're a Big Boy Now* (Oscar-
nominated); 1969: *Trilogy, Whatever Hap-
pened to Aunt Alice?;* 1971: *The Beguiled;*
1972: *J.W. Coop, Pete 'n' Tillie* (Oscar-
nominated); 1975: *The Day of the Locust* (as
an Aimee Semple McPherson type); 1977:
Nasty Habits, The Rescuers (as the voice of
Madame Medusa); 1981: *Harry's War,
Honky Tonk Freeway;* 1982: *I'm Dancing as
Fast as I Can.*

PAGET, DEBRA. Actress. *(b. Aug. 19,
1933, Denver, as Debralee Griffin.)* Auburn-
haired beauty blessed with a demurely
pretty face and a curvaceous figure, who
(perhaps unconsciously) infused many of
her screen characterizations with both virginal innocence and seductive passion.
Signed at age 15 to a long-term contract
by 20th Century-Fox, Paget made her debut in *Cry of the City* (1948). She appeared in Westerns, swashbucklers, and
Biblical dramas throughout the 1950s,
making her biggest impressions as an Indian squaw in *Broken Arrow* (1950) and a
South Seas beauty in *Bird of Paradise*
(1951). Her other films include *House of
Strangers, It Happens Every Spring* (both
1949), *Stars and Stripes Forever, Fourteen Hours* (both 1951), *Belles on Their
Toes* (1952), *Les Miserables* (also 1952,
somewhat out of her depth as Cosette),
*Prince Valiant, Demetrius and the Gladia-
tors* (both 1954), *White Feather* (1955),
The Ten Commandments (1956), *Love Me*

Tender (also 1956, opposite Elvis Presley
in his first film), *Omar Khayyam* (1957),
and *From the Earth to the Moon* (1958).
  In 1958 she went to Germany to star for
Fritz Lang in his back-to-back productions
The Tiger of Eschnapur (1958) and *The
Indian Tomb* (1959), edited together and
released here as *Journey to the Lost City*
(1959). These exotic adventures saw Paget
effectively cast as an Indian temple
dancer, whose seductive wrigglings were
the highlights of the films. She also
starred in *Cleopatra's Daughter* (1960)
while overseas. Back in America, Paget
found her star on the wane and, after appearing in the horror films *The Most Dangerous Man Alive* (1961), *Tales of Terror*
(1962), and *The Haunted Palace* (1963),
retired from the screen. Still heart-
stoppingly gorgeous, she frequently turns
up at Hollywood social events. Paget was
once married—for all of three weeks—to
director Budd Boetticher.

PAKULA, ALAN J. Director, screenwriter, producer. *(b. Apr. 7, 1928, New York
City.)* Intelligent, craftsmanlike director
who began as an assistant in the cartoon
department at Warner Bros., before becoming an apprentice at MGM and eventually a producer at Paramount. Pakula's
first film as a producer was the Jimmy
Piersall story *Fear Strikes Out* (1957); it
launched a successful collaboration with
director Robert Mulligan which led to *To
Kill a Mockingbird* (1962), *Love With the
Proper Stranger* (1963), *Baby the Rain
Must Fall, Inside Daisy Clover* (both
1965), *Up the Down Staircase* (1967), and
The Stalking Moon (1969). These all dealt
with modern social problems and complex
interpersonal relationships, themes evident
in Pakula's debut film as a director, *The
Sterile Cuckoo* (1969), which starred Liza
Minnelli as an odd college girl coping
with her first love. Next came *Klute*
(1971), an acclaimed thriller with Jane
Fonda in a stunning, Oscar-winning performance as a threatened call girl. The
film established Pakula's quietly probing
visual style as well as his sure hand with
actors, and also marked the first of what
critics would later call his "paranoia
trilogy." The second—after *Love and
Pain (and the Whole Damn Thing)*
(1972)—was the chilling *The Parallax
View* (1974), with reporter Warren Beatty

investigating a senator's assassination. The bookend was *All the President's Men* (1976), a superb retelling of the Watergate scandal with Robert Redford (whose company helped produce the film) and Dustin Hoffman as "Woodstein," the team of Bob Woodward and Carl Bernstein, who broke the story. The film won four Oscars and earned Pakula a Best Director nomination. He followed with the beautiful, lethargic *Comes a Horseman* (1978) and gave Burt Reynolds one of his best roles, as a divorcee in the romantic comedy *Starting Over* (1979). His next, *Rollover* (1981), was a rare dud.

He directed (and earned an Oscar nomination for adapting) the gripping and emotional *Sophie's Choice* (1982), which won Meryl Streep a Best Actress Oscar, but *Dream Lover* (1986) was a misfire and the fine *Orphans* (1987) was seen by no one. After *See You in the Morning* (1989, a semi-autobiographical love story), Pakula returned to the halls of labyrinthian intrigue, directing and adapting (with Frank Pierson) Scott Turow's best-selling court drama *Presumed Innocent* (1990). The unsuccessful thriller *Consenting Adults* (1992) led him again into the legal arena, this time adapting and directing *The Pelican Brief* (1993), a well-crafted thriller, and his biggest box-office success in years—aided in no small way by the casting of Julia Roberts in the leading role.

PAL, GEORGE. Producer, director, animator. (b. Feb. 1, 1908, Ceglad, Hungary; d. May 2, 1980.) Fans of imaginative movies from all periods owe this popular innovator a great debt of gratitude—and many fantasy filmmakers of the Lucas-Spielberg generation have acknowledged that debt. Pal originally worked as a production designer for Germany's massive UFA studios before moving to Holland and making advertising shorts for the Philips company using stop-motion animation. He relocated to England, and then to Hollywood in 1940, where he developed his famous "Puppetoons": clever, often bizarre, short subjects best described as three-dimensional cartoons. Among the best: *Jasper in a Jam, Tubby the Tuba, John Henry and the Inky-Poo, A Date with Duke.* Many of the shorts were nominated for Oscars, and Pal received a special Academy Award for his pioneering work

in this field in 1943. He forsook the series to devote his energies to live-action films, mostly fantasies and science fiction that utilized state-of-the-art special effects. Those effects won him five more Oscars, first as a producer, then as producer-director, for *Destination Moon* (1950), *When Worlds Collide* (1951), *War of the Worlds* (1953), *tom thumb* (1958), and *The Time Machine* (1960). Pal even used his Puppetoons technique (and his original animators) for sequences of *tom thumb* and *The Wonderful World of the Brothers Grimm* (1962). *7 Faces of Dr. Lao* (1964) was not a great hit in its day, but has acquired a following among fantasy fans.

As audience tastes for the fanciful dissolved in the turbulence of the late 1960s, Pal worked less; his last theatrical sci-fi production was the tense 1968 suspenser *The Power.* In 1975 he cowrote and produced *Doc Savage: The Man of Bronze,* based on an old pulp-magazine hero who was a forerunner of Indiana Jones. In 1986 he was the subject of a feature-length documentary, *The Fantasy Film World of George Pal.*

OTHER FILMS INCLUDE: 1948: *The Great Rupert* (producer); 1953: *Houdini* (producer); 1954: *The Naked Jungle* (producer); 1955: *Conquest of Space* (producer); 1961: *Atlantis, the Lost Continent* (producer and director).

PALANCE, JACK. Actor. (b. Feb. 18, 1919, Lattimer, Pa., as Walter Jack Palahnuik.) After more than 40 years in pictures, Jack Palance finally won a Best Supporting Actor Oscar for *City Slickers* (1991), playing a tough, wheezy, old cowboy with rapidly hardening arteries. As he accepted his award, he felt compelled to demonstrate that his physical condition in the film had nothing to do with the actual state of his health, and he demonstrated his physical prowess by doing a set of one-arm push-ups. Palance's rugged face, which took many beatings in the boxing ring, was disfigured during World War 2. Plastic surgeons repaired the obvious damage but left him with a distinctive, somewhat menacing look. He became an actor after the war and had several stage roles before coming to the movies.

In his first film (billed as Walter Jack Palance), Elia Kazan's tingling *Panic in the*

Streets (1950), the actor made a definite impression, as a plague-carrying fugitive hunted by military physician Richard Widmark. Following *Halls of Montezuma* (1950), he got to menace Joan Crawford in *Sudden Fear* (1952) and was nominated for a Best Supporting Actor Oscar. He received a second nomination for his unforgettable portrayal of a pathological gunfighter in *Shane* (1953), and won an Emmy for Best Actor as the prizefighter in "Requiem for a Heavyweight" on CBS' "Playhouse 90" (1956). His other films during this fertile period include *The Silver Chalice* (1954), *The Big Knife, I Died a Thousand Times* (both 1955), *Attack!* (1956, playing a "hero" of sorts), *The Lonely Man* (1957), and *The Man Inside* (1958).

Inexplicably, by the early 1960s, Palance was toiling in a seemingly endless string of marginal films, including *Sword of the Conquerer, The Mongols* (both 1961), and *Warriors Five* (1962). (A happy exception was 1963's *Contempt*, for director Jean-Luc Godard.) In 1963–64 Palance played the part of Johnny Slate in the ABC series "The Greatest Show on Earth." *The Professionals* (1966) brought Palance back to the attention of American filmmakers; he landed a meaty role in *The Desperados*, and played Fidel Castro in *Che!* (both 1969).

Palance was in demand during the last gasp of the Western through the early 1970s in pictures like *The McMasters, Monte Walsh* (both 1970), and *Oklahoma Crude* (1973), but he was again forced into the international arena to remain active, churning out an alarming number of foreign-language turkeys. Palance has also occasionally ventured into the realm of "art" movies with the dreadful Warhol factory tedium of *Cocaine Cowboys* (1979) and the German-made *Bagdad Cafe* (1988), in which he played a "dropout" artist living at a remote cafe in the American southwest. *Batman* (1989) brought him back to the Big Time with a vengeance, casting him as a sleazy crime king; then *City Slickers* offered him a role with humor and heart, a perfect invitation for Oscar voters to respond not only to a performance but to a career. More recently, he appeared in *Solar Crisis* (1992), *Cops and Robbersons* (1994, playing straight to Chevy Chase), and *City Slickers 2: The Legend of Curly's Gold* (1994, as his deceased character's twin

brother) and participated in a number of TV documentaries.

PALLETTE, EUGENE. Actor. *(b. July 8, 1889, Winfield, Kans.; d. Sept. 3, 1954.)* This rotund, moon-faced, ex-streetcar conductor was one of filmdom's most popular supporting players. Born to theatrical parents, he trouped as a child and made his film debut in a 1910 short subject. Not yet corpulent, Pallette won leads in silent movies, and was featured in D. W. Griffith's *Intolerance* (1916). He also played Aramis in Doug Fairbanks' *The Three Musketeers* (1921). During the sound era, Pallette was easily recognizable by his deep, froggy voice and stout figure. He's memorably funny as pragmatic patriarchs in both *My Man Godfrey* (1936) and *The Lady Eve* (1941), and effective as Friar Tuck in *The Adventures of Robin Hood* (1938).

OTHER FILMS INCLUDE: 1929: *The Virginian;* 1932: *Shanghai Express;* 1933: *The Kennel Murder Case* (as Sergeant Heath, a role he repeated in several Philo Vance mysteries); 1935: *Bordertown* (as Bette Davis' boorish husband), *Steamboat 'Round the Bend;* 1936: *The Ghost Goes West, Stowaway;* 1937: *Topper, One Hundred Men and a Girl;* 1939: *Mr. Smith Goes to Washington;* 1940: *The Mark of Zorro;* 1942: *The Male Animal, Tales of Manhattan;* 1943: *It Ain't Hay, Heaven Can Wait, The Gang's All Here;* 1944: *Step Lively;* 1946: *Suspense.*

PALMER, LILLI. Actress. *(b. May 24, 1914, Posen, Germany as Lillie Marie Pieser; d. Jan. 27, 1986.)* The gracious, beautiful Palmer was a stage and screen fixture in Europe during the 1930s (appearing in British films, including Hitchcock's *Secret Agent,* in 1936), as she bounced from country to country fleeing the Nazi threat of her homeland. In the mid-1940s she arrived in Hollywood with then-husband Rex Harrison, and was transformed into an instant leading lady, in such films as Fritz Lang's 1946 *Cloak and Dagger* and the 1947 melodrama *Body and Soul* with John Garfield. Her best Hollywood film was *The Four Poster* (1952), in which she costarred with Harrison; in it was the key to her subsequent international success—a growing worldliness, and sense of humor. Returning to Europe in the 1950s, she cemented her reputation as a top international star, and from that time, she alternated between continental and American-made films, including *Maedchen in Uniform* (1958), *But Not for Me* (1959), *The Pleasure of His Company* (1961), *The Counterfeit Traitor, Adorable Julia* (both 1962), *Operation Crossbow* (1965), *Oedipus the King* (1968), *De Sade* (1969), *The Boys From Brazil* (1978), and her last, *The Holcroft Covenant* (1985). Her witty 1975 autobiography, "Change Lobsters and Dance," was a best seller.

PANGBORN, FRANKLIN. Actor. *(b. Jan. 23, 1893, Newark, N.J.; d. July 20, 1958.)* Slender, dapper character actor best known for his portrayals of prissy, exasperated hotel managers, clerks, tailors, and professional men in countless films of the 1930s and 1940s. A veteran of the New York stage (where he played Messala in a revival of "Ben-Hur"), Pangborn entered movies in 1926, and played heroes and leading men before talkies typecast him in comic parts. Among his notable appearances: *Cockeyed Cavaliers* (1934, as a singing town crier), *My Man Godfrey* (1936, as the chairman of the scavenger hunt), W. C. Fields' *The Bank Dick* (1940, as J. Pinkerton Snoopington) and *Never Give a Sucker an Even Break* (1941, as the movie studio chief), and a series of Preston Sturges comedies: *Christmas in July* (1940), *Sullivan's Travels* (1941), *The Palm Beach Story* (1942), *Hail the Conquering Hero, The Great Moment* (both 1944), and *Mad Wednesday* (1947). He was a thorough professional who could always be counted on for a slick performance, even in minor quickies. He also starred in short subjects for Mack Sennett, and appeared in many other two-reel comedies. In 1957 he was hired to be announcer/sidekick to Jack Paar on TV's "Tonight Show," but the job was short-lived.

OTHER FILMS INCLUDE: 1926: *Exit Smiling;* 1927: *Getting Gertie's Garter;* 1933: *International House, Design for Living, Flying Down to Rio;* 1936: *Mr. Deeds Goes to Town;* 1937: *The Mandarin Mystery, A Star Is Born, Easy Living, Stage Door;* 1938: *Rebecca of Sunnybrook Farm, Vivacious Lady, Mad About Music;* 1942: *Now, Voyager;* 1943: *Crazy House;* 1945: *The Horn Blows at Midnight;* 1949: *My Dream Is Yours;* 1957: *Oh, Men! Oh, Women!, The Story of Mankind* (his last).

PAPAS, IRENE. Actress. *(b. Mar. 9, 1926, Chiliomodion, Greece.)* Regal international star who began performing as a singer and dancer in variety shows, becoming one of Greece's leading actresses by her early 20s. Renowned for her work in classic tragedy roles, she is best known to American audiences for her work in *The Guns of Navarone* (1961), *Zorba the Greek* (1964), *The Brotherhood* (1968), *Anne of the Thousand Days, Z, A Dream of Kings* (all 1969), *Mohammad, Messenger of God* (1977), *Eboli, Bloodline* (both 1979), *Lion of the Desert* (1981), *Erendira* (1984), *Into the Night* (1985), *High Season* (1987), and *Island* (1989). She has frequently worked with director Michael Cacoyannis on stage and film productions, including *Electra* (1962), *The Trojan Women* (1972), and *Iphigenia* (1977). Recent credits include *Up, Down and Sideways* (1993) and *Homecoming* (1994).

PARE, MICHAEL. Actor. *(b. Oct. 9, 1959, Brooklyn, N.Y.)* Tough-talking and -looking lead who got his start on the small screen as a regular on the first season of the popular TV comedy-adventure series "The Greatest American Hero" (1981). He made his big-screen debut two years later as the enigmatic rock singer in *Eddie and the Cruisers,* reprising the role for a less-successful 1989 sequel. Despite starring roles in two 1984 efforts, *The Philadelphia Experiment* and Walter Hill's *Streets of Fire,* he failed to join the ranks of big-screen action heroes. Recently he's carved out a niche for himself as the star of modestly budgeted straight-to-video actioners, including *Moon 44* (1990) and *Killing Streets* (1991). Recent credits include *Into the Sun* (1992).

PARKER, ELEANOR. Actress. *(b. June 26, 1922, Cedarville, Ohio.)* Striking redhead whose many outstanding performances (three of them Oscar-nominated) inexplicably failed to secure true and lasting stardom for her; even today, she remains unfairly unappreciated by movie buffs. Bitten by the acting bug while in her teens, Parker apprenticed in local theater and in stock before heading to Hollywood. She was seen at the Pasadena Playhouse and signed by Warner Bros. in 1941, making her tyro film appearance in the Errol Flynn starrer *They Died With Their Boots On*. Parker toiled in low-budget programmers such as *Buses Roar* (1942), *The Mysterious Doctor* (1943), and *Crime By Night* (1944) before being given a shot at a "prestige" lead in *Between Two Worlds* (1944, opposite John Garfield). She brightened *Hollywood Canteen* (also 1944) and *Pride of the Marines* (1945, again with Garfield) before taking the role of slatternly waitress Mildred Rogers in *Of Human Bondage* (1946), a highly touted but middling remake of the 1934 Bette Davis-Leslie Howard success; its mediocre reception hampered her ascent to first-tier stardom.

Parker, whose good looks and silky voice may have partially obscured her versatility, starred or costarred in *Never Say Goodbye* (1946), *Escape Me Never*, *The Voice of the Turtle* (both 1947), *The Woman in White* (1948, in a dual role), and *Chain Lightning* (1950) before earning her first Oscar nomination for her chilling portrayal of a first-time prison inmate who rapidly hardens in *Caged* (1950). She got another Oscar nod as the neglected wife of hard-boiled cop Kirk Douglas in *Detective Story* (1951).

By this time Parker had left Warners; she starred in *Scaramouche* and *Above and Beyond* (both 1952) for MGM, and appeared opposite Charlton Heston in Paramount's *The Naked Jungle* (1954). She snagged her third Academy Award nomination for her starring role in *Interrupted Melody* (1955), the inspiring story of polio-stricken opera star Marjorie Lawrence (although she was dubbed by singer Eileen Farrell). Parker continued to contribute fine performances—in *The Man With the Golden Arm* (1955), *The King and Four Queens* (1956), *A Hole in the Head* (1959), *Return to Peyton Place* (1961), *Madison Avenue* (1962), *The Sound of Music* (1965), and *An American Dream* (1966), among others—but seemed unable to achieve a stable position in the rapidly changing Hollywood hierarchy. She started working in TV, first as the unflappable gal Friday to a seldom-seen studio head in "Bracken's World" (1969–71), then in a slew of TV movies, including *Vanished* (1970), *Home for the Holidays* (1972), and the pilot film *Fantasy Island* (1977). Despite prominent billing, she barely appeared in *Sunburn* (1979), her last theatrical feature to date.

PARKER, SARAH JESSICA. Actress. *(b. Mar. 25, 1965, Nelsonville, Ohio.)* As a child, the versatile Parker danced with the Cincinnati Ballet, sang with the Metropolitan Opera, appeared in her first TV show (at age 8), and took over the role of "Annie" on Broadway for two years. She made her film debut in *Rich Kids* (1979) and started gathering fans with her work on the intelligent teen sitcom "Square Pegs" (1982–83). Supporting roles followed in *Footloose*, *Firstborn* (both 1984), *Girls Just Want to Have Fun* (1985), and *Flight of the Navigator* (1986), before she returned to TV in the critically acclaimed series "A Year in the Life" (1987–88). In 1990 she joined the cast of another short-lived series, "Equal Justice," then, finally, won a really good role, as the Venice Beach babe SanDeE* in *L.A. Story* (1991) with Steve Martin. She has since appeared as the object of James Caan's and Nicolas Cage's affections in *Honeymoon in Vegas* (1992), a reborn witch in *Hocus Pocus* (1993), a river patrol cop in *Striking Distance* (also 1993), a 1950s starlet in *Ed Wood* (1994), and a fiancée with second thoughts about marriage in *Miami Rhapsody* (1995).

PARKS, GORDON. Director, screenwriter. *(b. Nov. 30, 1912, Fort Scott, Kans.)* A highly influential figure in black cinema, Parks had a number of jobs before he became interested in photography. He worked for the Farm Security Administration during World War 2 and later became a staff photographer for "Life" magazine, a position he held for some twenty years. In 1969, Parks became the first black director to helm a major studio film when he directed, wrote, and composed the score for *The Learning Tree* (1969), a beautifully realized adaptation of his autobiographical novel about growing up in Kansas. His next film, *Shaft* (1971), starred Richard Roundtree as the unflappable detective John Shaft; tough, sexy and violent, it was a sleeper hit with black and white audiences alike, and provided a black hero at a time when there were few to be found onscreen. Parks then directed the sequel *Shaft's Big Score!* (1972), the comedy-drama *The Super Cops* (1974), and the fine (but little-seen) musical biography *Leadbelly* (1976). After spending some years on nonfilm projects, Parks returned to directing with the American Playhouse production *The Odyssey of Solomon Northrup* (1984) and *Moments Without Proper Names* (1986, from his own book). He has written a number of books, and was a founder of "Essence" magazine. His son Gordon Parks, Jr. (who died in 1979), worked as a cameraman on *The Learning Tree* and directed three films, including *Superfly* (1972).

PARKS, LARRY. Actor. *(b. Dec. 13, 1914, Olathe, Kans., as Samuel Lawrence Parks; d. Apr. 13, 1975.)* It's unlikely that this dark, wavy-haired actor would be remembered at all if he hadn't played Al Jolson in a pair of popular biopics. Educated at the University of Illinois, he labored for several years in stock companies and local theater before being signed by Columbia Pictures in 1941. He bounced back and forth between B movies—including *Honolulu Lu* (his first), *Harvard Here I Come* (both 1941), *Alias Boston Blackie, Blondie Goes to College, The Boogie Man Will Get You* (all 1942), *The Deerslayer, Power of the Press* (both 1943), *Hey, Rookie* and *She's a Sweetheart* (both 1944)—and supporting roles in A pictures, including *You Were Never Lovelier* (1942), *Destroyer, Reveille With Beverly* (both 1943), and *Counter-Attack* (1945).

When Columbia decided not to use Al Jolson himself to star in his big-budget Columbia biopic, Parks tried out for the role and won; he then put in countless hours to make his lip-synching of Jolson's voice tracks believable. *The Jolson Story* (1946) was a smash hit; it made Parks a star and earned him an Oscar nomination. But Columbia didn't quite know what to do with him: He costarred with Rita Hayworth in a Technicolored musical fantasy, *Down to Earth* (1947), and swashbuckled through *The Swordsman* (1947) and *The Gallant Blade* (1948). But it was plain that he was no Gable or Cooper or Flynn, and it took the successful sequel *Jolson Sings Again* (1949) to keep Parks in the limelight.

On loan to MGM, he costarred with Elizabeth Taylor in *Love Is Better Than Ever* (1951), and then made headlines by admitting his past affiliation with the Communist Party to the House Un-American Activities Committee. Although he wasn't "officially" blacklisted, Parks was dropped by Columbia and generally ignored by Hollywood. He made only two more screen appearances, in *Tiger by the Tail* (1955) and *Freud* (1962), before giving up his acting career. Parks was married to actress Betty Garrett; a chronic heart problem led to his untimely death.

PARKS, MICHAEL. Actor. *(b. Apr. 4, 1938, Corona, Calif.)* Handsome, brooding lead (and, more recently, lead heavy) of minor action films, very much in the James Dean mold, best known for his starring stint in the 1969–70 TV series "Then Came Bronson." Parks made his film debut as the star of the arty road movie *The Wild Seed* (1965), and the following year played Adam in John Huston's abysmal *The Bible* (1966)—not exactly a great career-booster. Other starring films from this period include *Bus Riley's Back in Town* (1965), *The Idol* (1966), and *The Happening* (1967). He went into professional eclipse in the years immediately following "Bronson," and appearances in sundry low-budget vehicles, like *Sidewinder 1, The Private Files of J. Edgar Hoover* (both 1977), and *The Evictors* (1979), failed to advance his career. Parks did experience an upturn in 1990 when he appeared as an enigmatic bad guy on David Lynch's cult TV series "Twin Peaks." In the 1991 shoot 'em up *The Hitman*, Parks played the villain to Chuck Norris' hero. He also appeared in *Over the Line* (1994).

PARSONS, ESTELLE. Actress. *(b. Jan. 20, 1927, Marblehead, Mass.)* Edgy character actress best suited to playing shrill neurotics and wild-eyed fanatics. A former TV writer and producer who once worked on the "Today" show, Parsons took up acting in the late 1950s and, after spending several years in stock, off-Broadway, and Broadway productions, moved into film work with a part in *Ladybug, Ladybug* (1963). She's at her best in her Academy Award–winning portrayal of wigged-out Blanche Barrow in *Bonnie and Clyde*

(1967), and as a religious zealot in *Rachel, Rachel* (1968), which earned her another Oscar nomination. Still active on stage, Parsons has made a major impression in recent years playing Roseanne's annoying mother on the hit sitcom "Roseanne" (1988–).
OTHER FILMS INCLUDE: 1969: *Don't Drink the Water;* 1970: *I Never Sang for My Father, I Walk the Line, Watermelon Man;* 1973: *Two People;* 1974: *For Pete's Sake;* 1975: *Foreplay;* 1989: *The Lemon Sisters;* 1990: *Dick Tracy;* 1992: *A Private Matter* (telefilm); 1993: *Arthur Miller's "The American Clock"* (telefilm).

PARTON, DOLLY. Actress, singer, songwriter. *(b. Jan. 19, 1946, Sevierville, Tenn.)* The diminutive, blond, busty, and bewigged Parton turned from country music to acting in 1980, landing a role in that year's office comedy, *9 to 5,* and proving to be a natural. (She also composed the music and earned an Oscar nomination for the catchy title song.) Already an ultrasuccessful country star, this popular tabloid figure subsequently displayed her winning personality (and her cartoonish curves) in the mediocre films *The Best Little Whorehouse in Texas* (1982) and *Rhinestone* (1984). She held her own among top female stars Sally Field, Shirley MacLaine, Daryl Hannah, and Julia Roberts in *Steel Magnolias* (1989), and dispensed down-home advice over the radio as a phony psychiatrist in *Straight Talk* (1992), a Cinderella story that featured Parton's most relaxed performance, wasted on a sappy script. She took on an unusually dramatic part in a TV movie, *Wild Texas Wind* (1991), and appeared in a cameo as herself in *The Beverly Hillbillies* (1993). Her theme park, "Dollywood," is a success, and she's a partner (with Hollywood mogul Sandy Gallin) in what has quickly become a formidable movie-making entity, Sandollar Productions.

PASOLINI, PIER PAOLO. Director, screenwriter, poet, novelist. *(b. Mar. 5, 1922, Bologna, Italy; d. Nov. 2, 1975.)* This prolific, multitalented artist remains one of the most provocative figures in cinema history. A politically radical homosexual whose perspective on life was equally influenced by Karl Marx and the Catholic Church, his oeuvre defies classification. Pasolini's first film, *Accatone* (1961, on which Bernardo Bertolucci served as assistant director), adapted from his novel "A Violent Life," was a neorealist look at Rome's dark underbelly, but subsequent works took different approaches to different subject matter. On the one hand, there's the gently poetic parable *Hawks and Sparrows* (1966), and the confounding but haunting allegory *Teorema* (1968); on the other, there are the lush, erotically charged adaptations of *The Decameron* (1970), *The Canterbury Tales* (1971), and *Arabian Nights* (1974). He also fashioned a visually arresting adaptation of *Oedipus* (1967) which was filmed in Morocco. And finally, there's the horrible brutality of *Salo—The 120 Days of Sodom* (1975), in which de Sade meets Mussolini, so to speak, with results that still leave hardened shock-cinema aficionados' jaws dropping. That controversial picture overshadowed what had been Pasolini's most famous to date, *The Gospel According to St. Matthew* (1966, in which Christ was played—quite convincingly—by a Marxist truck driver, and the Virgin Mary by Pasolini's own mother), an almost documentary-like adaptation of that work which won lavish praise, even from the Church itself. He also directed one segment of the omnibus feature *RoGoPag* (1962).
Pasolini was murdered in 1975 under circumstances that many find suspect; though reportedly bludgeoned to death and run over by a youth to whom he'd made sexual advances, some friends (including Bertolucci) believe he was assassinated for political reasons.

PASSER, IVAN. Director, screenwriter. *(b. July 10, 1933, Prague.)* Noted Czech "New Wave" director who has had critical, if not commercial, success in the United States. He worked as a bricklayer, a steelworker, and a construction worker before gaining admission to the Prague Film School, FAMA, and went on to cowrite screenplays for fellow countryman Milos Forman. Passer achieved solo success with the short film *A Boring Afternoon* (1964) and the critically acclaimed feature *Intimate Lighting* (1965), a story of friends, both professional musicians, who are reunited after a long absence. The film brought Passer to the attention of American audiences and in 1968, when the Russians invaded Czechoslovakia, he moved to the U.S. and started a new career. His first films were *Born to Win* (1971), which featured George Segal in one of his best performances, as a junkie, and *Law and Disorder* (1974), a modest, well-observed seriocomedy about middle-aged New Yorkers who become auxiliary cops. Both were noted for their humanity and the attention to the details of the characters' environments. Passer's next films, *Crime and Passion* (1976) and *Silver Bears* (1978), were not well received, but *Cutter's Way* (1981, originally released as *Cutter and Bone*), a gripping story about a crippled Vietnam vet and his best friend, was championed by critics, and remains one of his best works. Since then, he has directed *Creator* (1985), *Haunted Summer* (1988), and the ambitious and well-received made-for-cable movie *Stalin* (1992) with Robert Duvall in the title role.

PATINKIN, MANDY. Actor, singer. *(b. Nov. 20, 1947, Chicago.)* Prodigiously talented and versatile stage performer whose movie appearances haven't been quite as impressive as his Broadway vehicles. The Juilliard-trained Patinkin electrified audiences as Che Guevara in the Broadway musical "Evita," for which he won a Tony Award, and made his film debut in *The Big Fix* (1978). He's had a few juicy parts, among them ones in *Ragtime* (1981), as the silhouette artist who becomes a pioneering moviemaker, *Yentl* (1983), as Barbra Streisand's lusty friend, a rabbinical student, *The Princess Bride* (1987), as a swashbuckling hero of the old school, *Alien Nation* (1988), unrecognizable under elaborate makeup as a sympathetic alien cop partnered with James Caan, *The House on Carroll Street* (1988), as a venal Sen. Joseph McCarthy type, and *The Music of Chance* (1993), as the existential hero of this low-key parable, a man who throws in his lot with smarmy James Spader. Warren Beatty's *Dick Tracy* (1990) is the only film to date to take advantage of Patinkin's musical talent, allowing him to sing some of Stephen Sondheim's songs as Madonna's accompanist, 88 Keys. Patinkin has carved a concert career for himself, with a one-man

show, "Dress Casual," and remains a headliner on stage, but has yet to enjoy a similar impact in movies. Most recently, he joined the cast of TV's "Chicago Hope" (1994–).
OTHER FILMS INCLUDE: 1979: *French Postcards, Last Embrace;* 1980: *Night of the Juggler;* 1983: *Daniel;* 1985: *Maxie;* 1991: *Impromptu, True Colors.*

PATRIC, JASON. Actor. *(b. June 17, 1966, New York City, as Jason Patrick Miller.)* This dark-haired, brooding, seemingly humorless performer made his initial splash as a teenager who tangles with a pack of rock 'n' roll vampires in *The Lost Boys* (1987), and later earned high marks for his portrayal of the slow-witted, menacing drifter in the modern-day film noir *After Dark, My Sweet* (1990). The son of actor/playwright Jason Miller (and grandson of Jackie Gleason), Patric made headlines in 1991 when he was romantically linked with actress Julia Roberts. Late that year, he got generally favorable notices as a drug-addicted undercover cop in the gritty thriller *Rush.* Other credits include *Solarbabies* (1986), *The Beast* (1988), *Frankenstein Unbound* (1990, as Lord Byron), and *Geronimo: An American Legend* (1993, in the leading role opposite Wes Studi). An intense actor with enormous potential, Patric is definitely one to watch in the 1990s.

PAXTON, BILL. Actor. *(b. May 17, 1955, Fort Worth, Tex.)* Energetic actor who has appeared in a number of movies both major and minor, who after 10 years onscreen gained recognition for his performance as Sheriff Dale "Hurricane" Dixon in the "sleeper" *One False Move* (1992). Paxton began as a set dresser on several B movies (starting with Roger Corman's *Big Bad Mama*), then studied acting and earned roles in the low-budget *Mortuary* (1981) and *Night Warning* (1982). He then scored parts in such grade-A fare as *The Lords of Discipline* (1983), *Streets of Fire,* and *The Terminator* (both 1984), and received critical notice as the obnoxious brother in *Weird Science* (1985), and as the hysterical soldier Hudson in *Aliens* (1986). Paxton was featured in the vampire film *Near Dark* (1987), as well as *Pass the Ammo* (1988), *Next of Kin*

(1989), *Predator 2, Navy SEALS* (both 1990), *The Dark Backward* (1991), *Trespass* (1992), *Boxing Helena, Indian Summer, Tombstone* (all 1993), *True Lies, Monolith* (both 1994), and *Apollo 13* (1995). He also directed the video for the cult song "Fish Heads."

PAYNE, JOHN. Actor. *(b. May 23, 1912, Roanoke, Va.; d. Dec. 6, 1989.)* Virile, handsome leading man who resisted pigeonholing and handled starring roles in musicals, comedies, dramas, and action pictures with equal aplomb. Musically trained from childhood (his mother was an opera soprano), Payne sang professionally during the mid 1930s before making his film debut in a supporting role in William Wyler's *Dodsworth* (1936, billed as John Howard Payne). That same year he won his first lead (and sang a cute song, "Twinkle Twinkle Little Star"), in *Hats Off,* a would-be musical spectacular pecuniously produced by Grand National. Very much at ease in front of the camera, even at this early stage in his career, Payne was a breezy, engaging juvenile lead in *Fair Warning* (1937), a forgotten B whodunit made at 20th Century-Fox.

He signed with Warner Bros. shortly thereafter, appearing in such unmemorable fare as *Garden of the Moon* (1938, his only A picture for the studio), *Wings of the Navy, Indianapolis Speedway* (both 1939), *King of the Lumberjacks,* and *Tear-Gas Squad* (both 1940) before hopping over to Fox. Although he was occasionally assigned leading roles in "straight" pictures (such as 1940's *Star Dust,* his first for the studio, 1941's lovely *Remember the Day,* 1942's *To the Shores of Tripoli*), Payne spent most of his Fox tenure costarring with the studio's top musical stars—Alice Faye, Betty Grable, and Sonja Henie—in lavish tunefests, many of them shot in Technicolor, including *Tin Pan Alley* (1940), *The Great American Broadcast, Week-end in Havana, Sun Valley Serenade* (all 1941), *Iceland, Springtime in the Rockies* (both 1942), *Hello Frisco, Hello* (1943), and *The Dolly Sisters* (1945).

Given costarring roles (albeit good ones) in *The Razor's Edge* (1946) and *Miracle on 34th Street* (1947), Payne saw his opportunities limited at Fox, and left the studio to freelance, finding most of his work in Westerns, crime dramas, and action films. He did his best work in a series of hard-boiled B pictures directed by Phil Karlson: *Kansas City Confidential* (1952), *99 River Street* (1953), and *Hell's Island* (1955, which he helped to write, without credit). He was most uncharacteristic in *The Boss* (1956), as a post-WW1 urban crimelord.

He turned to TV, playing gunfighter Vint Bonner on the series "Restless Gun" (1957–59), and was off the big screen until 1968, when he was seen in *Gift of the Nile* and *They Ran for Their Lives* (the latter shot in 1965, and directed by Payne himself under a pseudonym).

In 1973 Payne was reunited with Alice Faye in a touring revival of the old college musical "Good News." The actor, who died from congestive heart failure, was once married to actresses Anne Shirley and Gloria De Haven. Julie, his daughter by Shirley, is also an actress.
OTHER FILMS INCLUDE: 1948: *The Saxon Charm, Larceny;* 1949: *El Paso, Captain China;* 1950: *The Eagle and the Hawk, Tripoli;* 1951: *Passage West, Crosswinds;* 1952: *Caribbean, The Blazing Forest;* 1953: *The Vanquished, Raiders of the Seven Seas;* 1954: *Rails Into Laramie, Silver Lode;* 1955: *Santa Fe Passage, The Road to Denver;* 1956: *Slightly Scarlet, Rebel in Town, Hold Back the Night;* 1957: *Bailout at 43,000, Hidden Fear.*

PEARCE, RICHARD. Director. *(b. Jan. 25, 1943, San Diego.)* Talented director whose best films examine the struggles of rural living. A graduate of Yale, Pearce first got involved in filmmaking as an assistant on D. A. Pennebaker's documentary *Dont Look Back* (1967). He later directed his own documentary *Campamento* (1970), about the Socialist revolution in Chile, and photographed the Oscar-winning documentaries *Woodstock, Interviews With My Lai Veterans* (both also 1970), and *Marjoe* (1972), in addition to working as cinematographer and associate producer on the Oscar-winning *Hearts and Minds* (1974). He directed several well-received TV movies and then made his commercial feature debut with *Heartland* (1979), an acclaimed drama about frontier life in Wyoming, circa 1910. He followed *Threshold* (1981), about the first artificial heart transplant, with *Country* (1984), which starred Jessica Lange as a farm mother fighting government foreclosure on her land. *No Mercy* (1986) was an atypical move into florid melodrama, but Pearce then directed the powerful (and too-little-seen) Civil Rights story *The Long Walk Home* (1990). His latest film, *Leap of Faith* (1992), had a misfired lead performance by Steve Martin (as a traveling evangelist) and more than a few story problems, but benefited greatly from Pearce's keen eye for detail, and feeling for atmosphere in his Kansas setting. Pearce also directed the TV movie *The Final Days* (1989), which chronicled Richard Nixon's Watergate years.

PECK, GREGORY. Actor. *(b. Apr. 5, 1916, La Jolla, Calif., as Eldred Gregory Peck.)* Whether or not it's something he deliberately cultivated, Gregory Peck has attained in his screen persona an almost spiritual nobility, rooted in his earnest, sober portrayals of earnest, sober men. The quiet strength and dignity with which the tall, exceedingly handsome Peck invests many of his characters has made his occasional forays into villainy—and comedy—all the more surprising, and effective.

Although he once planned on being a doctor, and even studied medicine at the University of California at Berkeley, Peck was lured to the stage as a young man, leaving his native California for an uncertain existence as an actor in New York. His 1942 Broadway debut, in "The Morning Star," was very well received, and after spending another year or so on stage he returned to California, this time to appear in RKO's *Days of Glory* (1944), playing a Russian partisan fighting the Nazis. But it was his next role, as a Roman Catholic priest in *Keys of the Kingdom* (also 1944) that really launched him to stardom, and earned him his first Academy Award nomination. High-profile parts followed: a mentally disturbed patient of psychiatrist Ingrid Bergman in Hitchcock's *Spellbound* (1945), an understanding father in *The Yearling* (1946, again nominated for an Oscar), and the lusty Lewt McCanles in David O. Selznick's *Duel in the Sun* (also 1946), a patently ridiculous, overheated Western.

After completing the excellent (and underrated) adaptation of Hemingway's *The Macomber Affair,* Peck took on a daring role, that of the courageous reporter uncovering anti-Semitism in Elia Kazan's *Gentleman's Agreement* (both 1947), snagging his third Oscar nomination for this multi-award-winning film. He played a lawyer in love with his dangerous client in *The Paradine Case* (1948, for Hitchcock), an Air Corps colonel on the verge of a crackup in *Twelve O'Clock High* (1949, earning yet another Oscar nod for this first-rate film), a weary, fatalistic hired killer in *The Gunfighter* (1950, one of his finest roles, and one for which he *should* have gotten Oscar recognition), the title role in *Captain Horatio Hornblower,* the Hebrew monarch in *David and Bathsheba* (both 1951), a Hemingway protagonist in *The Snows of Kilimanjaro* (1952), a reporter in love in the charming *Roman Holiday* (1953), and a disaffected ad executive in the quintessentially 1950s drama of Madison Avenue angst, *The Man in the Gray Flannel Suit* (1956), among others.

Peck's robust performance as the tormented Captain Ahab in *Moby Dick* (1956) brought to the fore a quality previously hinted at in *Spellbound* and *Twelve O'Clock High,* that of a strong-willed man driven to madness by internal demons. He went on to star in the delightful comedy *Designing Woman* (1957, opposite Lauren Bacall), *The Big Country, The Bravados* (both 1958), *Pork Chop Hill* (a pet project which he also produced), *Beloved Infidel* (as F. Scott Fitzgerald), *On the Beach* (all 1959), *The Guns of Navarone* (1961), and *Cape Fear* (1962), which he produced, and in which he allowed Robert Mitchum to take the flashier, more memorable part. That same year he produced and starred in the film for which he is most celebrated, *To Kill a Mockingbird,* in which he plays a lawyer who defends a black man against a rape charge in the South. He won his only Oscar for his moving portrayal of Atticus Finch, the hero of Harper Lee's best-selling novel.

Peck's subsequent films include *How the West Was Won* (1962), *Captain Newman, M.D.* (1963), *Behold a Pale Horse* (1964), *Mirage* (1965, a Hitchcockian thriller in which he plays an amnesiac), *Arabesque* (1966, an espionage drama teaming him with Sophia Loren), *The Stalking Moon* (1968), *Mackenna's Gold, The Chairman, Marooned* (all 1969), *I Walk the Line* (1970), *Shootout* (1971), *Billy Two Hats* (1974), *The Omen* (1976, a hit horror film), *MacArthur* (1977, in the title role as the famed general), *The Boys From Brazil* (1978, badly cast as Nazi scientist Josef Mengele in this silly thriller), and *The Sea Wolves* (1980).

Peck found little to attract him in the 1980s. However, having been described more than once as Lincolnesque, he finally got the chance to play the Great Emancipator in the TV miniseries "The Blue and the Gray" (1982). He took a supporting role as the president of the United States in the innocuous fable *Amazing Grace and Chuck* (1987), and then replaced an ailing Burt Lancaster in the plum role of curmudgeonly Ambrose Bierce, would-be romantic, in *Old Gringo* (1989); it was one of his best latter-day performances. He petitioned filmmaker Norman Jewison to cast him in the tailor-made part of a principled factory owner in *Other People's Money* (1991, which was perhaps *too* tailor-made—too pat), and took an amusing cameo as a Southern lawyer in Martin Scorsese's remake of *Cape Fear* (1991). In 1993 he produced a made-for-TV adaptation of an off-Broadway play that offered ideal parts for himself, Lauren Bacall, and daughter Cecilia Peck: *The Portrait*. His son Tony Peck has also begun to carve a reputation for himself as a young leading man.

Very much an activist, Peck supports many charitable and political causes. He has been a chairman of the American Cancer Society and of the American Film Institute, and served as president of the Academy of Motion Picture Arts and Sciences from 1967 to 1970. In 1989 he received the AFI's Life Achievement Award.

PECKINPAH, SAM. Director, writer. (b. Feb. 21, 1925, Fresno, Calif.; d. Dec. 28, 1984.) One of Hollywood's great mavericks, this outstanding filmmaker had a life as colorful and turbulent as any of his movies; his battles with studio heads have achieved a legendary status. He began as a protégé to action-movie director Don Siegel, often working uncredited on scripts (and even acting: he played the meter reader in 1956's *Invasion of the Body Snatchers*). In the late 1950s he wrote and directed numerous episodes of TV Westerns, one of which, "The Westerner" (1960), he created, produced, and directed. It lasted just three months.

Peckinpah made his feature directorial debut in 1961 with a modest oater, *The Deadly Companions,* followed the next year by the extraordinary, elegiac Western *Ride the High Country,* which starred Randolph Scott and Joel McCrea. In 1965, he saw *Major Dundee* butchered by its studio—the first of many such incidents—followed immediately by his quick firing from *The Cincinnati Kid.* More or less persona non grata, he worked sporadically in TV over the next few years, returning to the big screen in 1968 as coscripter (with Robert Towne) of *Villa Rides.* He won the opportunity to direct a large-scale Western again, but *The Wild Bunch* (1969) wasn't quite like any Western that preceded it. Teamed with a simpatico cinematographer (Lucien Ballard), a solid Oscar-nominated script (which he wrote with Walon Green and Roy N. Sickner), and a strong cast (including William Holden, Ernest Borgnine, Robert Ryan, and "regulars" Warren Oates, Ben Johnson, L. Q. Jones, Bo Hopkins, and Strother Martin), Peckinpah emphasized what has come to be called "balletic violence," lingering in slow-motion on scenes of then-startling blood-letting. The film was hailed in some circles, reviled in others, and it made Peckinpah a much publicized *enfant terrible* in Hollywood.

He went West again for the kinder, gentler *The Ballad of Cable Hogue* (1970) before making waves with the controversially violent everyman melodrama *Straw Dogs* (1971), then turned around and confounded his critics with another relaxed, sweet-natured film, *Junior Bonner* (1972), starring Steve McQueen as an aging rodeo star. McQueen then paired with Ali MacGraw in Peckinpah's biggest box-office hit, *The Getaway* (1972), a slick, sexually charged, typically violent piece of entertainment. He never enjoyed that level of success again. *Pat Garrett and Billy the Kid* (1973) was mutilated by MGM, but it was championed by many critics; Peckinpah's version remained unseen until 1988. His subsequent output was erratic; no one would name *Bring Me the Head of Alfredo Garcia* (1974), *The Killer Elite* (1975), *Cross of Iron* (1977), *Convoy* (1978), or *The Osterman Weekend* (1983) among his finest work, but his films remained distinctively his just the same. (In 1978 he was persuaded to act by Monte Hellman in his *China 9, Liberty 37.*) His last directing assignments were a pair of Julian Lennon music videos, "Too Late for Goodbyes" and "Valotte." A wild, tempestuous, hard-living man, Peckinpah alternately seduced and outraged his friends and coworkers. His talent was admired by everyone except, perhaps, the producers and studio heads for whom he worked. He was the subject of a television documentary, *Sam Peckinpah: Man of Iron* (1993).

PENDLETON, AUSTIN. Actor. *(b. Mar. 27, 1940, Warren, Ohio.)* To look at this ferretlike actor—who's so often cast as comic nebbishes—you wouldn't guess that in his "other life" he's a respected stage director and performer. In fact, he was nominated for a Tony Award for directing Elizabeth Taylor in a Broadway revival of "The Little Foxes" in 1981. On screen, he's best remembered as the wealthy musical patron in *What's Up, Doc?* (1972) and the pathetic killer Earl Williams in Billy Wilder's remake of *The Front Page* (1974). He also added comic grace notes to such films as *Skidoo* (1968), *Catch-22* (1970), *The Thief Who Came to Dinner* (1973), *Starting Over, The Muppet Movie* (both 1979), *Simon* (1980), and *Short Circuit* (1986). He waxed more serious as the lonely Mr. Gadbury in *Mr. & Mrs. Bridge* (1990) and the lawyer in *The Ballad of the Sad Cafe* (1991). He played another attorney, this time back in a comedic vein, in *My Cousin Vinny* (1992). Other recent credits include *True Identity* (1991), *Four Eyes and Six-Guns* (1992, made for TV), *Mr. Nanny, My Boyfriend's Back* (both 1993), and *Guarding Tess* (1994).

PENDLETON, NAT. Actor. *(b. Aug. 8, 1895, Davenport, Iowa; d. Oct. 11, 1967.)* A world-class grappler when wrestling was still a legitimate sport, Pendleton represented the U.S. Olympic team in 1920, and four years later became world champion. He entered films the same year in *The Hoosier Schoolmaster* (in a scene calling upon his mat ability), and played in subsequent silent pictures as an athlete or simple-minded heavy. Pendleton soon became adroit at portraying amiable if dullwitted oafs (frequently sporting Brooklyn accents), and acted as a comic foil for the Marx Brothers, Abbott and Costello, and other screen funnymen, developing a likable screen presence—and expert comedic knowhow. He's on view in *The Last of the Duanes, The Big Pond* (both 1930), *Taxi, The Sign of the Cross, Horse Feathers* (all 1932), *Lady for a Day* (1933, one of his best), *The Thin Man* (1934, as Detective Guild, a role he repeated in 1939's *Another Thin Man*), *Manhattan Melodrama* (also 1934), *The Great Ziegfeld* (1936, as Sandor the strongman, Ziegfeld's first star), *Gangway* (1937), *On Borrowed Time, At the Circus* (both 1939), *Northwest Passage* (1940), *Buck Privates* (1941), *Swing Fever* (1944), *Buck Privates Come Home* (1947, reprising his role from the original), *Death Valley* (1949), and in eight *Dr. Kildare/Dr. Gillespie* films of the late 1930s, as ambulance driver Joe Wayman. He had the lead in *Top Sergeant Mulligan* (1941), and wrote a screen vehicle for himself, *Deception* (1933), in which, not surprisingly, he played a wrestler.

PENN, ARTHUR. Director. *(b. Sept. 27, 1922, Philadelphia.)* An often remarkable director, whose best films deal provocatively and intelligently with the role of the outsider and the destructive power of myth in American culture. Involved in acting at a young age, Penn joined a military stage troupe during World War 2 and later taught acting before finding work in television. He began as a floor manager for NBC's "Colgate Comedy Hour" and eventually directed productions of "Philco Playhouse" and "Playhouse 90," as well as Broadway plays like "Two for the Seesaw" (1958) and "The Miracle Worker" (1959), for which he won a Tony Award. Penn's first film, produced by long-time friend Fred Coe, was *The Left-Handed Gun* (1958), a bold, quirky retelling of the Billy the Kid legend (from Gore Vidal's TV play), which was seen by few in this country but won great acclaim in Europe. In 1962, he piloted the screen version of *The Miracle Worker,* a powerful, emotionally overwhelming (and surprisingly unsentimental) drama that won Oscars for actresses Anne Bancroft and Patty Duke and earned Penn a nomination as Best Director. He had less success with the artsy, existential thriller *Mickey One* (1965) and *The Chase* (1966), an overheated all-star Southern gothic piece, which was notable for production squabbles between Penn, screenwriter Lillian Hellman, and producer Sam Spiegel.

Bonnie and Clyde (1967), however, caused a hailstorm of controversy and became a milestone in American film. An episodic treatment of the Depression-era outlaws, the film mixed humor, drama, social commentary, pathos, and unprecedented screen violence to redress and redefine America's mythic past. Penn achieved a startling physicality in setting and performance; the film won two Oscars and Penn earned another Best Director nomination. He was also nominated for the sad, gentle look at hippie life *Alice's Restaurant* (1969) and had another critical and commercial hit with *Little Big Man* (1970), a sprawling, picaresque adaptation of the Thomas Berger novel, with a revisionist depiction of classic Western heroes and themes.

Night Moves (1975) was an exceptional, underrated update of the private eye genre, but *The Missouri Breaks* (1976), another attempt at debunking the Western, was a failure, despite the potent combination of Jack Nicholson and Marlon Brando in the lead roles. *Four Friends* (1981), an emotional look at a group of friends in the sixties, made few waves and neither did subsequent attempts at more "commercial" fare, *Target* (1985) and *Dead of Night* (1987). His latest film, *Penn & Teller Get Killed* (1989), was a return to idiosyncratic form, but again, virtually no one saw it. Penn has remained active in theater throughout the years, and also directed the segment on pole vaulters for the omnibus Olympics film *Visions of Eight* (1973). His brother is famed photographer Irving Penn.

PENN, SEAN. Actor. *(b. Aug. 17, 1960, Burbank, Calif.)* Intense, brooding actor, known as much for his off-camera exploits as for his diverse and sometimes searing performances. He first caught audiences' attention as a young military cadet in *Taps* (1981) and (in a hilarious turn) as the ultimate surfer dude, Jeff Spicoli, who uttered the immortal line, "Hey bud, let's party!" right into the pop-culture lexicon in *Fast Times at Ridgemont High* (1982). Born to a show-business family, Penn was active in local theater while in his teens; he apprenticed at Los Angeles'

Group Repertory Theater and worked as assistant to actor/director Pat Hingle. His work on Broadway in "Heartland" led to his first movie. Penn graduated to leading roles in *Bad Boys* (1983), *Racing With the Moon* (1984), *The Falcon and the Snowman* (1985, as real-life spy Daulton Lee, who sold CIA secrets to the Russian KGB), *At Close Range* (1987, as the son of sociopathic Christopher Walken), *Colors* (1988, improbably cast as a cop by director Dennis Hopper), *We're No Angels* (1989, as a comic convict, mugging alongside Robert De Niro), and *Casualties of War* (also 1989, as a brutal sergeant in Vietnam), giving totally different nuances and shadings to each performance. He was briefly married to pop icon Madonna, with whom he costarred in the abysmal *Shanghai Surprise* (1986) and then lived with actress Robin Wright, whom he met while making *State of Grace* (1991) and with whom he had two children. Penn turned his energies behind the camera to direct *The Indian Runner* (1991), an impressive drama about two brothers trying to cope in the wake of the Vietnam War. Offscreen for several years (excepting a brief appearance in the 1992 Oscar-nominated short-subject *Cruise Control*), he startled moviegoers by altering his appearance—shaving back his hairline, frizzing his hair, wearing wire-rim glasses—to play Al Pacino's sleazy lawyer in *Carlito's Way* (1993). Penn went behind the scenes once more for *The Crossing Guard* (1995), which he wrote, directed, and coproduced. He also directed the Lyle Lovett music video "North Dakota."

Unfortunately, his enormous talent has been overshadowed in the public eye by his headline-making outbursts of temper, often aimed at members of the paparazzi. He is the son of director Leo Penn and actress Eileen Ryan; his brother Christopher is also an actor *(Footloose, Short Cuts)*.

PENNEBAKER, D. A. Documentary filmmaker. *(b. July 15, 1925, Evanston, Ill., as Don Alan Pennebaker.)* Influential documentary filmmaker who made several shorts and the hour-long *Opening in Moscow* (1959, about the opening of the American Exhibition) before joining Drew Associates, a group that included such notable names as Richard Leacock and Albert Maysles. It was Leacock and Pennebaker who invented the portable 16mm synchronized sound camera that could be positioned on a person's shoulder, an important step in defining the style of filmmaking known as "direct cinema." After such pioneering political works as *Primary* (1960, about the Democratic Presidential Primary in Wisconsin) and *Crisis* (1963, about the desegregation of the University of Alabama), Pennebaker left Drew and collaborated with Leacock on two music-oriented documentaries: *Dont Look Back* (1967) and *Monterey Pop* (1969). The first, a behind-the-scenes look at Bob Dylan's 1965 tour of England, was an energetic, probing mix of backstage scenes, performances, and ironic views of Dylan; the second, a record of 1967's Monterey Pop Festival, is considered the first "concert" film. Both films tapped into the youth audience's interest in music and did amazing business for documentaries.

Pennebaker tackled music again in the hour-long film *Company* (1970, chronicling the recording of the cast album for this Stephen Sondheim show), *Keep on Rockin'* (1972), *Elliott Carter* (1980), *Ziggy Stardust and the Spiders From Mars* (1983, filmed in 1973), and *Depeche Mode 101* (1989). He also worked on *The Energy War* (1979), a look at President Carter's struggle to deregulate natural gas that was produced for PBS, *Rockaby* (1983), which documented the rehearsal and performance of the Samuel Beckett play, and *The War Room* (1993), a fascinating, Oscar-nominated fly-on-the-wall view of Bill Clinton's 1992 Presidential campaign. Since 1977, Pennebaker has worked with cameraperson-turned-filmmaker Chris Hegedus, whom he married in 1982.

PEPPARD, GEORGE. Actor. *(b. Oct. 1, 1928, Detroit; d. May 8, 1994.)* A fair-haired, blue-eyed, handsome leading man who was groomed for stardom in the waning years of the studio system, Peppard started as a radio performer and stock player, and studied at New York's Actors' Studio while working on Broadway and in TV. A role in *The Strange One* (1957) gave Peppard a serviceable screen debut, and after good parts in *Pork Chop Hill* (1959) and *Home From the Hill* (1960), he was signed to star opposite Audrey Hepburn in the popular *Breakfast at Tiffany's* (1961).

Established as a leading man, Peppard subsequently played tough guys, though he was buried in the large, prestigious casts of *How the West Was Won* (1962) and *The Victors* (1963). He was the charismatic lead—a thinly disguised Howard Hughes—in the overblown Harold Robbins saga *The Carpetbaggers* (1964, with Elizabeth Ashley as one of his wives, a role she played offscreen as well). The remainder of Peppard's films were mostly actioners, Westerns, or thrillers.

Peppard spent much of the 1970s and 1980s on TV, where he starred in many unmemorable TV movies but achieved greater success in the series "Banacek" (1972–74), "Doctors Hospital" (1975–76), and, as the tongue-in-cheek, cigar-chomping star of "The A-Team" (1983–87). In 1978 he wrote, directed, produced, and starred in a heart-tugging vehicle, *Five Days From Home.*

OTHER FILMS INCLUDE: 1960: *The Subterraneans;* 1965: *Operation Crossbow, The Third Day;* 1966: *The Blue Max;* 1967: *Tobruk, Rough Night in Jericho;* 1968: *P.J., What's So Bad About Feeling Good?;* 1969: *House of Cards, Pendulum;* 1970: *The Executioner, Cannon for Cordoba;* 1971: *One More Train to Rob;* 1972: *The Groundstar Conspiracy;* 1974: *Newman's Law;* 1977: *Damnation Alley;* 1980: *Battle Beyond the Stars;* 1981: *Helicopter, Race for the Yankee Zephyr;* 1982: *Target Eagle;* 1989: *Silence Like Glass;* 1990: *Night of the Fox* (telefilm).

PEREZ, ROSIE. Actress. *(b. Sept. 6, 1964, Brooklyn, N.Y.)* Dynamic, sassy, fast-rising actress who made a memorable screen debut as Spike Lee's girlfriend Tina in 1989's *Do the Right Thing.* (She also danced under the film's opening credits to the song "Fight the Power.") She went on to costar in Jim Jarmusch's *Night on Earth* (1991), *White Men Can't Jump* (1992, terrific as Woody Harrelson's girlfriend whose dream is to appear on TV's "Jeopardy"), and *Untamed Heart* (1993), and was impressive as an airplane-crash survivor coping with the death of her baby in *Fearless* (also 1993), which earned her an Oscar nomination. Perez has choreographed many music videos and earned Emmy nominations for her choreography on TV's "In Living Color." More recently, she played Nicolas Cage's wannabe society wife in *It Could Happen to You* (1994).

PERKINS, ANTHONY. Actor, director. *(b. April 4, 1932, New York City; d. Sept. 12, 1992.)* Despite numerous film and stage credits, Perkins will forever be remembered as creepy Norman Bates, the blood-curdling killer in Alfred Hitchcock's classic *Psycho* (1960). The son of actor Osgood Perkins, he debuted in *The Actress* (1953), and received an Oscar nomination as Gary Cooper's pacifist son in *Friendly Persuasion* (1956). This dark, slender, quiet performer played many sensitive youths, and was extremely effective as mentally disturbed baseball player Jimmy Piersall in *Fear Strikes Out* (1957) and as one of the doomed Australians in *On the Beach* (1959). He was Jane Fonda's first screen leading man, in *Tall Story* (1960). After *Psycho,* Perkins tackled a number of unusual roles, including the accused Josef K in Orson Welles' version of Kafka's *The Trial* (1963), the arsonist in *Pretty Poison* (1968), and the troubled chaplain in *Catch-22* (1970). With his Norman Bates still in audiences' minds, he played other psychotics in such films as *Mahogany* (1975), *Crimes of Passion* (1984), and the Jekyll-and-Hyde inspired *Edge of Sanity* (1989). Still youthful-looking in middle age, Perkins reprised his most famous role in *Psycho II* (1983), *Psycho III* (1986, which he also directed), and *Psycho IV* (1990, made for TV). He also directed the black comedy *Lucky Stiff* (1988). Perkins did formidable work on stage in "Greenwillow" (a musical), "Look Homeward, Angel," and "Equus," and cowrote *The Last of Sheila* (1973) with his friend, composer Stephen Sondheim. When he died of AIDS in 1992, he left behind quotes from *Casablanca,* including the observation that the problems of a few people don't amount to a hill of beans in this crazy world. His son, Osgood, is also an actor.
OTHER FILMS INCLUDE: 1957: *The Tin Star;* 1958: *The Matchmaker, Desire Under the Elms;* 1959: *Green Mansions;* 1961: *Goodbye Again;* 1962: *Phaedra;* 1967: *The Champagne Murders;* 1970: *WUSA;* 1972: *The Life and Times of Judge Roy Bean, Play It As It Lays;* 1974: *Lovin' Molly, Murder on the Orient Express;* 1978: *Remember My Name;* 1979: *Winter Kills, The Black Hole;* 1980: *ffolkes.*

PERKINS, ELIZABETH. Actress. *(b. Nov. 18, 1960, Queens, N.Y.)* Pretty, gifted actress who could become a major star in the 1990s, although that doesn't seem to be her primary motivation. Perkins raised eyebrows in her film debut, playing the cynical, acerbic girlfriend of Demi Moore in *About Last Night . . .* (1986), the mediocre adaptation of David Mamet's play "Sexual Perversity in Chicago." She has since accepted some "conventional" leading-lady assignments—costarring with Judd Nelson in *From the Hip* (1987) and, most notably, playing the love interest of man-boy Tom Hanks in *Big* (1988)—but is drawn to sometimes quirky characters, even if it means taking smaller supporting parts. *Sweet Hearts Dance* (1988) saw her in a secondary female role as the girlfriend of Jeff Daniels, while *Avalon* (1990) saw her tackling (very effectively) her first "domestic" role. She played a ditzy private eye in *Love at Large* (1990) and a volatile TV commentator paired with obnoxious Kevin Bacon in *He Said, She Said* (1991). Later that year, Perkins appeared in *The Doctor* as a young cancer patient who has lost her hair from chemotherapy; it was a showy turn that eclipsed the starring performances of William Hurt and Christine Lahti. But Perkins really sparkled in the little-seen *Enid Is Sleeping* (1990, retitled *Over Her Dead Body* for video release), an uneven but occasionally brilliant black comedy in which she apparently kills—accidentally, of course—her hated sister, who's been having an affair with her husband. (She later had a child with the film's director, Maurice Phillips.) Recent credits include *Indian Summer* (1993, another good young-character part) and her highest-profile role in years, that of Wilma Flintstone in *The Flintstones* (1994). Later in 1994, she took the Maureen O'Hara role in the remake of *Miracle on 34th Street.*

PERRINE, VALERIE. Actress. *(b. Sept. 3, 1944, Galveston, Tex.)* What a difference an era makes. Had Perrine, with her pneumatic dimensions, button-cute face, and high-pitched lisping voice, come along in the 1950s, she might have been promoted as an MM-type sex symbol. (She did work as a topless showgirl in Las Vegas.) But emerging in the early 1970s with some post-counterculture appeal on her side, Perrine made an impressive screen debut slyly parodying sex-bomb types, as porn queen Montana Wildhack, the object of hero Billy Pilgrim's fantasies, in the film adaptation of Kurt Vonnegut's time-tripping satire *Slaughterhouse-Five* (1972). Subsequent films revealed her to be a sensitive actress who always tried to reveal the person behind the erotic appeal; she won Best Actress honors at the Cannes Film Festival and was nominated for a Best Actress Oscar for her frank, accomplished performance as comedian Lenny Bruce's stripper wife in 1974's *Lenny.* She had good parts in a handful of other films including *W. C. Fields and Me* (1976, in half the title role, as Fields' lover Carlotta Monti) and *The Electric Horseman* (1979), but in *Superman* (1978) and its 1980 sequel she succumbed to playing the kind of ditzy bimbo role (as Lex Luthor's buxom companion) she'd managed to avoid earlier in her career. Her nadir was reached in the hideous disco extravaganza *Can't Stop the Music* (1980). 1982's *The Border,* in which she held her own with Jack Nicholson, was a brief return to form. Recent films, including *Maid to Order* (1987), *Bright Angel,* and *Hit Man* (both 1991), have wasted her talents, although she did land a solid part in the 1989 TV remake of *Sweet Bird of Youth,* and a good character role as Dennis Hopper's ex-girlfriend in *Boiling Point* (1993).

PERRY, FRANK. Director, writer. *(b. Aug. 21, 1930, New York City.)* Perry's directorial debut, *David and Lisa* (1962), instantly propelled him into the front rank of film-makers, a status he was unable to maintain. An independently produced drama about two emotionally disturbed teenagers, it earned Perry a Best Director Oscar nomination and pegged him as a director who could depict problems affecting people in modern society. He went on to film the cautionary nuclear-war story *Ladybug, Ladybug* (1963), *The Swimmer* (1968, a dense, almost impenetrable view of suburbia featuring excellent performances), *Last Summer* (1969), *Diary of a Mad Housewife* (1970), the revisionist Western *Doc* (1971), the modern Western

Rancho Deluxe (1975), *Mommie Dearest* (1981, the unintentionally campy Joan Crawford biopic), *Monsignor* (1982), *Compromising Positions* (1985), and the Shelley Long comedy vehicle *Hello Again* (1987). His TV work includes *A Christmas Memory* (1966), one of the best adaptations of Truman Capote's work, and *Dummy* (1979). He also directed the pilot film of "Skag" (1980) with Karl Malden. Perry's wife Eleanor (who died in 1981) wrote or cowrote the scripts for his pictures until their divorce in 1970—which ended his most fertile filmmaking period. Recently, however, he made *On the Bridge* (1992), a very personal documentary of his own bout with cancer.

PESCI, JOE. Actor. *(b. Feb. 9, 1943, Newark, N.J.)* Alternately hilarious and horrifying as the loud-mouthed, vicious mobster in *GoodFellas* (1990), Pesci snagged a well-deserved Academy Award for that finely tuned characterization—one of many he's delivered over the years. No one has achieved greater success playing comical urban types and sinister criminals in recent years, though Pesci's range is broader than his frequent typecasting might indicate. His first appearance on film was an incidental one, as a guitarist with Joey Dee and the Starliters in *Hey, Let's Twist!* (1961). Impressed by Pesci's performance in the obscure, low-budget crime film *Death Collector* (1975), director Martin Scorsese first cast the pugnacious actor as Robert De Niro's boorish brother-in-law in the Jake LaMotta biopic *Raging Bull* (1980); Pesci was rewarded with a Best Supporting Actor nomination for his stunning portrayal. He had strong supporting roles in *I'm Dancing as Fast as I Can* (1982) and *Easy Money* (1983, very funny as Rodney Dangerfield's best friend) before he worked again with De Niro in Sergio Leone's period gangster epic, *Once Upon a Time in America* (1984). The following year he popped up on TV in "Half-Nelson" (1985), a short-lived sitcom about a pint-sized private investigator, but left the silver screen for a couple of years, resurfacing as cartoonishly shrill police informant Leo Getz in *Lethal Weapon 2* (1989) and in a small role in Alan Alda's *Betsy's Wedding* (1990).

Following his stunning work in

GoodFellas, Pesci turned comic again as one of the bungling burglars in the smash hit *Home Alone* (1990), then headlined his first starring vehicle, *The Super* (also 1991), an unfortunate comedy misfire. Those who would write him off as a one-note actor sat up and took notice of his riveting perfomrnace (in makeup and toupee) as hyperkinetic conspirator David Ferrie in *JFK* (also 1991). In 1992 he found a pair of strong starring vehicles, the fish-out-of-water comedy *My Cousin Vinny* and the 1940s period piece *The Public Eye* (as a streetwise photographer inspired by the real-life Weegee), reprised the role of Leo Getz in *Lethal Weapon 3,* then suffered more abuse at the hands of Macaulay Culkin in *Home Alone 2: Lost in New York.* He made a cameo appearance for Robert De Niro in the latter's debut film as director, *A Bronx Tale* (1993), then starred in a pair of films *(With Honors* and *Jimmy Hollywood,* both 1994) whose commercial and critical failure had some questioning Pesci's ability to "carry" a movie. He then teamed up with Scorsese and De Niro for *Casino* (1995). On television, the actor has guest-starred on "Tales from the Crypt," in an amusing dual role (as a guy who adopts two identities) and as real-estate tycoon "Ronald Grump" in a "Sesame Street" 25th-Anniversary prime-time special.

PETERS, BERNADETTE. Actress, singer, dancer. *(b. Feb. 28, 1948, Queens, N.Y., as Bernadette Lazzara.)* Kewpie-doll cutie whose centerfold figure, bee-stung lips, and high-pitched voice have made her one of the brightest comic players on stage and screen, while making her difficult to cast in "serious" dramatic roles. Peters achieved her first success in the off-Broadway show "Dames at Sea," a 1967 spoof of 1930s movie musicals, which capitalized on her physical attributes as well as her prodigious musical talents. She has subsequently done her best work on Broadway, in such Stephen Sondheim shows as "Sunday in the Park With George" and "Into the Woods" and Neil Simon's "The Goodbye Girl." She won a Tony in 1985 for her tour de force in "Song and Dance."

Always at her best in period vehicles, Peters made her film debut in *Ace Eli and Rodger of the Skies,* a 1973 flop about 1920s stunt flyers. Supporting parts in *The Longest Yard* (1974) and *Vigilante Force* (1976) followed; then Mel Brooks' *Silent Movie* (1976) offered her a juicy role as a comic femme fatale. Her film career since then has been spotty: *W. C. Fields and Me* (1976), *The Jerk* (1979), *Heartbeeps* (1981, as a female robot), *Annie* (1982), *David* (1988 telefilm), *Pink Cadillac* (1989, a costarring part with Clint Eastwood, but a distressingly stupid one), and *Slaves of New York* (also 1989, miscast as a hapless hat designer). Woody Allen gave her a key supporting role in *Alice* (1990), and she contributed a lively performance to the 19th-century romp *Impromptu* (1991). Her best showcase to date remains *Pennies From Heaven* (1981), in which she was heart-tuggingly convincing as a prim schoolteacher who falls for 1930s sheet-music salesman Steve Martin. The lavish musical numbers also gave her ample opportunity to show moviegoers why Broadway audiences have appreciated her for years. In 1976–77 she starred with Richard Crenna in the short-lived TV sitcom "All's Fair."

PETERS, BROCK. Actor, producer. *(b. July 2, 1927, New York City.)* Veteran black actor of stage, screen, and TV, probably best remembered as Tom Robinson, the man accused of raping a white woman in the classic *To Kill a Mockingbird* (1962). After years of stage performances in the 1940s and 1950s, Peters made his film debut as the snarling Sgt. Brown in *Carmen Jones* (1954) and played the vicious Crown in *Porgy and Bess* (1959). His critically lauded work in *Mockingbird* led to more varied roles in such films as *The L-Shaped Room* (1963), *Major Dundee,* *The Pawnbroker* (both 1965), and *The Incident* (1967). He has also appeared in *P.J.* (1968), *The McMasters* (1970, a rare starring role), *Slaughter's Big Rip-Off, Soylent Green* (both 1973), *Two Minute Warning,* (1976), *Star Trek IV: The Voyage Home* (1986, as Admiral Cartwright), and *Star Trek VI: The Undiscovered Country* (1991, reprising the same part). In 1992 he played the part of Dr. Chausible in an all-black production of *The Importance of Being Earnest.* The American Film Theatre production of *Lost in the Stars* (1974) enabled him to recreate his stage performance as Reverend Stephen Kumalo, one of his all-time best roles. Peters also coproduced the family comedy *Five on the Black Hand Side* (1973) and has been involved in numerous theater organizations.

PETERS, JEAN. Actress. *(b. Oct. 15, 1926, Canton, Ohio, as Elizabeth Jean Peters.)* Although this dark-haired beauty won star status with her first screen appearance—opposite Tyrone Power in *Captain From Castile* (1947)—Peters won more notoriety as the wife of eccentric tycoon Howard Hughes, whom she secretly married in 1957. She initially went to Hollywood after competing in the Miss Ohio State beauty contest, and 20th Century-Fox signed her immediately. For the next several years Peters played sexy spitfires, often in period dramas and Westerns. She retired from the screen upon marrying Hughes, but resumed her career on TV after their 1971 divorce.
OTHER FILMS INCLUDE: 1948: *Deep Waters;* 1949: *It Happens Every Spring;* 1950: *Love That Brute;* 1951: *Take Care of My Little Girl,* As *Young As You Feel, Anne of the Indies;* 1952: *Viva Zapata!, Wait 'Til the Sun Shines, Nellie, O. Henry's Full House, Lure of the Wilderness;* 1953: *Niagara* (stolen from her by fellow Fox contractee Marilyn Monroe), *Pickup on South Street, Blueprint for Murder, Vicki;* 1954: *Three Coins in the Fountain, Apache, Broken Lance;* 1955: *A Man Called Peter.*

PETERSEN, WILLIAM (L.). Actor. *(b. Feb. 21, 1953, Chicago.)* Major stardom has eluded this handsome, capable actor who began acting while attending Idaho State University on a football scholarship. He spent a year honing his craft in Spain as a Shakespearean student, and returned to Chicago to pursue a career on the stage. He played Stanley Kowalski in "A Streetcar Named Desire" at the Stratford Festival in Ontario, Canada, which led to his being cast in his first film, *To Live and Die in L.A.* (1985), as an impetuous, intense Secret Service agent on the trail of a counterfeiter. Other starring roles followed: a stressed-out ex-FBI agent sniffing out a serial killer, with help from Hannibal Lecter, in *Manhunter* (1986); a reckless confirmed bachelor and minor league player/manager in *Long Gone*

(1987, made for TV); an artist attempting to return to his roots in *Keep the Change* (1992, made for TV). These were mixed with second leads and supporting parts in *Amazing Grace and Chuck* (1987), *Cousins* (1989, as a womanizing husband), and *Young Guns II* (1990, as Pat Garrett). He produced and starred in *Hard Promises* (1991) as a man who attempts to disrupt his ex-wife's wedding. He continues to take part in productions of the Remains Theater, a Chicago-based troupe which he and a number of other performers organized in 1979. Recent credits include *Passed Away* (1992), *Curacao* (1993 telefilm), and the miniseries "Return to Lonesome Dove" (also 1993).

PETERSEN, WOLFGANG. Director, screenwriter. *(b. Mar. 14, 1941, Emden, Germany.)* Acclaimed German filmmaker who trained as a director for the stage and later television before making his feature debut with *One of Us Two* (1973). Following *The Consequence* (1977, a controversial film about homosexuality) and *Black and White Like Day and Night* (1978), Petersen wrote and directed *Das Boot* (1982), a tense and extraordinarily mounted drama set aboard a U-boat in the Atlantic during World War 2. The film, hailed for its claustrophobic detail, was an international hit and earned Petersen Oscar nominations for Best Director and Best Screenplay. He followed with the children's fantasy *The NeverEnding Story* (1984) and an elaborate, if plodding, science fiction tale, *Enemy Mine* (1985). After years of looking for a suitable project, he wrote and directed *Shattered* (1991), a complex Hitchcockian thriller based on Richard Neely's "The Plastic Nightmare," which was not popular with critics or audiences. He enjoyed his greatest commercial success with *In the Line of Fire* (1993), an unusually intelligent action-thriller, starring Clint Eastwood and enhanced no end by Petersen's expert craftsmanship. He then directed *Outbreak* (1995).

PFEIFFER, MICHELLE. Actress. *(b. Apr. 29, 1958, Santa Ana, Calif.)* It's doubtful that anyone would have chosen the California blonde from *Grease 2* to become one of the movies' biggest stars and leading actresses. The preternaturally beautiful Pfeiffer, with haunting green eyes and silken blond hair, had her looks held against her during her struggle to be taken seriously. Her career began with appearances in short-lived TV comedies like "Delta House," and such films as *The Hollywood Knights, Falling in Love Again* (both 1980), and *Charlie Chan and the Curse of the Dragon Queen* (1981). Landing the female lead in *Grease 2* (1982) should have been a plum, but the film was a flop, she was dull, and few moviegoers took notice. She had little to do but look beautiful as the wife of drug dealer Tony Montana (played by Al Pacino) in 1983's ultraviolent remake of *Scarface.* But gradually, her parts—and her performances— got better: in *Ladyhawke* and *Into the Night* (both 1985), and especially in *Sweet Liberty* (1986), delivering a multilayered, amusing performance as an eccentric actress. She then held her own alongside Cher, Susan Sarandon, and Jack Nicholson in 1987's *The Witches of Eastwick,* but really blossomed in Jonathan Demme's lively comedy *Married to the Mob* (1988), in a knowing and appealing performance as a mobster's young widow. Later that year she won over most remaining skeptics in the period drama *Dangerous Liaisons* (1988) for which she earned her first Oscar nomination, as Best Supporting Actress.

Pfeiffer cemented her newly fortified stardom with her sultry portrayal of a call girl turned torch songstress in *The Fabulous Baker Boys* (earning another Oscar nomination), and caused a sensation with her sexy rendition of "Makin' Whoopee" atop Jeff Bridges' piano. She was now a world-class star. She adopted a Russian accent for 1990's *The Russia House,* and deglamorized herself for a moving performance opposite Al Pacino in 1991's *Frankie and Johnny,* playing a lonely waitress terrified of human contact. When Annette Bening became pregnant, Pfeiffer inherited her most flamboyant role to date: Catwoman in *Batman Returns* (1992). Later that year she top lined Jonathan Kaplan's moving drama *Love Field,* and scored her third Oscar nomination.

In 1993 she was cast by Martin Scorsese as the slightly scandalous young woman who overwhelms Daniel Day-Lewis in the 1870s period piece *The Age of Innocence,* then reunited with Jack Nicholson for the contemporary werewolf saga *Wolf* (1994).

PHILLIPS, LOU DIAMOND. Actor. *(b. Feb. 17, 1962, Philippines, as Lou Upchurch.)* Before making a name for himself as the ill-fated teenage rock star Ritchie Valens in *La Bamba* (1987), this striking, almond-eyed actor cowrote and starred in the little-known *Trespasses* (1983). Good movies have been few and far between for this earnest young performer (who's part Cherokee, part Hawaiian, part Chinese, part Spanish and part Scotch-Irish!), but he never seems to stop working. Highlights include *Stand and Deliver* (1988, as a gang leader inspired by a great teacher), *Young Guns* (1988), *Young Guns II* (1990), and *A Show of Force* (1990, a Puerto Rico–based political thriller which gave him one of his best roles). He continued to work on both sides of the camera, as associate producer and star of *Dakota* (1988), screenwriter and star of *Ambition* (1991), and director and star of *Sioux City* (1994). Other films include *Disorganized Crime, Renegades* (both 1989), *Extreme Justice* (a telefilm) and *Shadow of the Wolf* (both 1993). He also starred in Errol Morris' unreleased *The Dark Wind* (made in 1991).

PHOENIX, RIVER. Actor. *(b. Aug. 23, 1971, Madras, Oreg.; d. Nov. 1, 1993.)* Startlingly mature, gifted young actor who made a major impact on screen before drugs ended his life at the age of 23. His all-American looks and pensive manner made him appealing to teenage fans, but his dedication to the craft of acting set him apart from other youthful heartthrobs. Born to unconventional parents (who named their other children Leaf, Rainbow, Summer, and Liberty), he landed his first steady job as a cast member in the short-lived TV series "Seven Brides for Seven Brothers" (1982–83), and had a notable part in the telefilm *Surviving* (1985). He made his big-screen debut in *Explorers* (1985), but it was his role as Wil Wheaton's pal from the wrong side of the tracks in *Stand by Me* (1986) that established him as a comer. He had a meaty part as Harrison Ford's son in *The Mosquito Coast* (1986), and then earned an

Oscar nomination for his heartrending performance as the son of radicals-on-the-run Judd Hirsch and Christine Lahti in *Running on Empty* (1988). His other films include *Little Nikita, A Night in the Life of Jimmy Reardon* (both also 1988), *Indiana Jones and the Last Crusade* (1989, as young Indy), and *I Love You to Death* (1990). He gave knockout performances in a pair of 1991 movies, *Dogfight* (as a Vietnam-bound Marine) and *My Own Private Idaho* (as a narcoleptic male hustler). He had costarring roles in *Sneakers* (1992), *The Thing Called Love* (1993), and Sam Shepard's *Silent Tongue* (1994). He was in production on a movie called *Dark Blood* and was scheduled to begin production on *Interview With the Vampire* (both 1994) when he collapsed from a drug overdose and died.

PICCOLI, MICHEL. Actor. (b. Dec. 27, 1925, Paris, as Jacques Daniel Michel Piccoli.) One of Europe's most elegant and distinguished leading men of stage and screen, Piccoli began his film career in 1945, at first playing support and then graduating to leading roles by the 1960s. A kind of Everyman figure, he has worked with practically every great modern director in the medium, including Jean-Luc Godard (1963's *Contempt,* 1982's *Passion*), Costa-Gavras (1965's *The Sleeping Car Murder,* 1966's *Shock Troops*), Louis Malle (1980's *Atlantic City,* 1989's *May Fools*), Claude Chabrol (1972's *Ten Days Wonder* and *Wedding in Blood*), Alfred Hitchcock (1969's *Topaz*), and Luis Buñuel (1967's *Belle de jour,* 1969's *The Milky Way,* 1972's *The Discreet Charm of the Bourgeoisie,* 1974's *The Phantom of Liberty*). He won the Best Actor prize at Cannes for his performance in Marco Bellocchio's *Leap Into the Void* (1979), and has also appeared in Rene Clement's *Is Paris Burning?* (1966), Alain Resnais's *La Guerre est Finie* (1966), *The Grande Bouffe* (1973), and *Vincent, Francois, Paul and the Others* (1974). He even sang, for director Jacques Demy, in the musical *The Young Girls of Rochefort* (1968). More recently, he appeared in *Martha and I* (1992).

PICKENS, SLIM. Actor. (b. June 29, 1919, Kingsberg, Calif., as Louis Bert Lindley, Jr.; d. Nov. 20, 1983.) Former rodeo clown who broke into movies—Westerns, naturally—in 1950, debuting in *Rocky Mountain,* an Errol Flynn vehicle. A big, rangy man with a weak chin and perpetually perplexed expression, Pickens acted as sidekick to cowboy star Rex Allen in several low-budget Republic horse operas of the early 1950s, including *Colorado Sundown* (1952) and *The Old Overland Trail* (1953). He graduated to major Westerns and became something of a fixture in films like *The Last Command* (1955), *The Sheepman* (1958), *One-Eyed Jacks* (1961), *Major Dundee* (1965), *Stagecoach* (1966), *Will Penny* (1968), *The Ballad of Cable Hogue* (1970), *The Getaway, The Cowboys* (both 1972), *Pat Garrett and Billy the Kid* (1973), and even *Blazing Saddles* (1974—"I work for Mel Brooks!"), among others. Pickens may be best remembered, however, as Major T. J. "King" Kong, the whooping maniac who rides an A-bomb in *Dr. Strangelove* (1964). He continued to work throughout the late 1970s, although in increasingly poor health. Later films include *Rancho Deluxe, The Apple Dumpling Gang* (both 1975), *The White Buffalo* (1977), *Beyond the Poseidon Adventure, 1941* (both 1979), *Honeysuckle Rose, Tom Horn* (both 1980), and *The Howling* (1981). He also made a slew of cheapie movies in later years, and was a regular on TV's "Custer: The Legend of Custer" (1967), "B.J. and the Bear" (1979–81), and "Filthy Rich" (1982).

PICKFORD, MARY. Actress, producer. (b. Apr. 8, 1893, Toronto, as Gladys Smith; d. May 29, 1979.) She was known as "America's Sweetheart" (though born in Canada), but Mary Pickford was capable of much more than she generally showed in her crowd-pleasing film appearances as a ringlet-haired youngster. In fact, she was a capable dramatic actress and an astute businesswoman as well: She produced many of her own pictures, negotiated some of the toughest, most lucrative starring contracts in silent-film history, was one of the founders of United Artists, and helped establish the Motion Picture Relief Fund. And as the wife of actor Douglas Fairbanks, and coproprietor of their "Pickfair" estate, she was one of the leaders of Hollywood's social set.

Her career started early; following the death of her father, Pickford was on stage from age five as "Baby Gladys Smith." In 1907, while in New York working for impresario David Belasco in the play "The Warrens of Virginia," she allowed Belasco to convince her to change her name, and Gladys Smith became Mary Pickford. She entered films with the Biograph Company in 1909, initially working with director D. W. Griffith. The next year she jumped to the IMP Company for triple her Biograph salary; it was obvious that "the girl with the golden curls" sold movie tickets. The Majestic Company captured Pickford in 1911 for the princely sum of $225 a week, but she returned to Biograph the following year to make some of her best early films, including *The New York Hat, The Old Actor,* and *The Informer.*

She signed with Adolph Zukor's Famous Players Film Company in 1914, and scored a big hit with that year's *Tess of the Storm Country,* which she remade in 1922. For Famous Players Mary played a variety of roles, including an East Indian in *Less Than the Dust,* a Japanese in *Madame Butterfly* (both 1915), and a Scottish lass in *Pride of the Clan* (1917), but she made her strongest impression playing young girls just coming of age in charming entertainments like *Rags* (1915), *Poor Little Rich Girl, Rebecca of Sunnybrook Farm* (both 1917), and *M'liss* (1918). Occasionally she attempted more demanding material such as *Stella Maris* (1918), in which she played a dual role, but the public balked at such attempts, and she inevitably returned to the characterization that made her famous.

Pickford's salary grew exponentially throughout the teens, and in 1918 she left Famous Players-Lasky. In 1919 she joined with Douglas Fairbanks, D. W. Griffith, and Charles Chaplin to form United Artists. Her first picture for the new company was *Pollyanna* (1920). It was a hit, but *Suds* (1920) and *The Love Light* (1921) were both offbeat and somewhat disappointing. Pickford took a page from Doug Fairbanks' book and started producing pictures on a grander scale, beginning with *Little Lord Fauntleroy* (1921), in which she played both mother and son. She imported Ernst Lubitsch from Germany to make *Rosita* (1923), which proved to be a success d'estime and a box office letdown, and she fol-

lowed it with a dull and bloated production of *Dorothy Vernon of Haddon Hall* (1924).

In her final three silent films, the scrappy *Little Annie Rooney* (1925), the plucky and melodramatic *Sparrows* (1926), and the romantic comedy *My Best Girl* (1927, which costarred her future husband, Charles "Buddy" Rogers), Mary gave audiences what they wanted to see—and in the process, produced three of her very best starring vehicles. And while she won an Oscar playing a Southern belle in her first talkie, *Coquette* (1929), that performance seems highly mannered and ineffective today (unlike much of her earlier work, which holds up extremely well). Married to Douglas Fairbanks since 1920 (after a first marriage to actor Owen Moore ended in divorce), Pickford appeared with her equally famous husband in only one picture, the 1929 talkie *The Taming of the Shrew* (although she reportedly stood in for Fairbanks' *Black Pirate* costar Billie Dove for the final screen kiss in that 1926 picture, and also played a cameo in Doug's 1927 production, *The Gaucho).* Despite her stage training and experience, though, Mary only mouthed her lines in *Shrew,* while black singer-actress Freita Shaw spoke the dialogue into an offstage microphone.

Pickford starred in two more pictures before retiring from screen acting, *Kiki* (1931) and *Secrets* (1933). A projected live-action/animation production of *Alice in Wonderland* for Walt Disney never came to fruition. Throughout the 1930s she was active in radio, and also produced several pictures with her former boss Jesse Lasky. In 1936 she divorced Doug Fairbanks and married her *My Best Girl* costar, Charles "Buddy" Rogers. Pickford campaigned heavily for the lead role in *I Remember Mama* (1948), but lost out to Irene Dunne. In 1953 she and Chaplin sold their interests in United Artists, and as the years passed she became increasingly reclusive. Her final public appearance was a taped acceptance of a special Oscar in 1975. Her 1955 autobiography is titled "Sunshine and Shadow."

PIDGEON, WALTER. Actor. *(b. Sept. 23, 1897, East St. John, New Brunswick, Canada; d. Sept. 25, 1984.)* In his physical prime a tall, handsome man with a deep, rich voice, Pidgeon never attained real stardom, despite his obvious ability. It may have been that he was just too solemn and stolid; even in his earliest sound films he was playing supporting roles, mostly "other man" parts with a stiff-upper-lip bent. While Pidgeon's essential sobriety proved an asset in later years, there's little doubt that it kept him from achieving greater success.

He went into the theater after training at the New England Conservatory of Music in Boston, using his booming baritone to good advantage in several stage musicals. Hollywood beckoned, but Pidgeon was assigned largely decorative roles without ever getting a star-making part, in *Mannequin* (1925), *Old Loves and New, The Outsider, Marriage License?* (all 1926), *The Thirteenth Juror, The Gorilla, The Girl From Rio* (all 1927), *Turn Back the Hours, Gateway to the Moon,* and *Clothes Make the Woman* (all 1928), among others.

The coming of sound should have provided more opportunity for the stage-voiced Pidgeon, but although he sang in several early-talkie musicals, he was never considered for top-billed roles. He worked sporadically throughout the early and mid 1930s, appearing in *Bride of the Regiment, Viennese Nights, Sweet Kitty Bellairs, Going Wild* (all 1930), *Kiss Me Again, The Hot Heiress* (both 1931), *Rockabye* (1932), *The Kiss Before the Mirror* (1933), *Journal of a Crime* (1934), *Fatal Lady, Big Brown Eyes, Girl Overboard* (all 1936), *She's Dangerous,* and *A Girl With Ideas* (both 1937, the latter giving him a funny part as a smooth-talking, unscrupulous newspaper publisher).

In 1937 Pidgeon became an MGM contract player, and though he continued to play supporting roles and other-man types—in *Saratoga* (1937), *Man-Proof, The Girl of the Golden West, The Shopworn Angel, Too Hot to Handle* (all 1938), *Society Lawyer, Stronger Than Desire* (both 1939)—the studio did at least attempt to make him a star, although he was badly miscast as wisecracking private detective Nick Carter in a trio of good B thrillers, *Nick Carter, Private Detective* (1939), *Sky Murder,* and *Phantom Raiders* (both 1940). He did better on loan to Fox in 1941, taking top billing in John Ford's

How Green Was My Valley, a story of Welsh coal miners, and Fritz Lang's *Man Hunt,* a taut thriller about a big-game hunter whose attempt to assassinate Hitler goes awry. Both pictures, well received by critics and public alike, boded well for Pidgeon's ascent to stardom.

Indeed, MGM seemed inclined to give him better assignments, beginning with *Blossoms in the Dust* (also 1941), his first picture opposite Greer Garson. Their collaboration continued with the wartime hit *Mrs. Miniver* (1942), which, being a starring vehicle for Garson, gave her the lion's share of showy scenes but allowed Pidgeon plenty of good moments too—and earned him an Oscar nomination for Best Actor. They made an intriguing screen team—mature and dignified, neither one particularly lively or spontaneous—and appeared together several more times, in *Madame Curie* (1943, for which he was again Oscar-nominated), *Mrs. Parkington* (1944), *Julia Misbehaves* (1948, a change-of-pace comedy with slapstick scenes), *That Forsyte Woman* (1949), the sequel *The Miniver Story* (1950), and *Scandal at Scourie* (1953).

Pidgeon remained at MGM through 1956, mainly working in support, but always getting solid, dramatically rewarding roles. (He did star in 1951's *Calling Bulldog Drummond,* poorly cast and too old for the part.) His other Metro films include *White Cargo* (1942), *The Youngest Profession* (1943, a cameo as himself), *Weekend at the Waldorf* (1945), *Holiday in Mexico* (1946), *Cass Timberlane* (1947), *Command Decision* (1948, featuring one of his best portrayals), *Red Danube* (1949), *Soldiers Three* (1951), *The Sellout* (1952, very good as a newspaper publisher who knuckles under to a corrupt sheriff), *Million Dollar Mermaid, The Bad and the Beautiful* (both also 1952), *Dream Wife* (1953), *Executive Suite, Men of the Fighting Lady, The Last Time I Saw Paris* (all 1954), *Hit the Deck* (1955), and *The Rack* (1956). One of his most enduring successes, the science fiction classic *Forbidden Planet* (also 1956, based on Shakespeare's "The Tempest"), cast him as Dr. Morbius, the erudite scientist on the planet Altair-4.

Pidgeon took up stage work for several years, returning to the big screen in *Voyage to the Bottom of the Sea* (1961, playing the commander of a futuristic submarine), *Advise and Consent* (1962, a solid part in this all-star tale of Washington wheeling and dealing), and *Big Red* (also 1962, an outdoor canine yarn for Disney).

He retired in 1977, still wanting to work and still sought for supporting roles, but unwilling to abandon a lifetime of professionalism: he was no longer steady on his feet, and wouldn't think of holding up a production. He died some years later following a series of strokes.
OTHER FILMS INCLUDE: 1967: *Warning Shot, Two Colonels;* 1968: *Funny Girl* (as Florenz Ziegfeld); 1969: *The Vatican Affair;* 1970: *The Mask of Sheba* (telefilm); 1972: *Skyjacked;* 1973: *The Neptune Factor;* 1976: *Won Ton Ton, the Dog Who Saved Hollywood, Two Minute Warning, The Lindbergh Kidnapping Case (telefilm);* 1978: *Sextette.*

PINTER, HAROLD. Writer, director. *(b. Oct. 10, 1930, London.)* One of the most influential playwrights of the modern era, Pinter originally trained as an actor, performing on radio and with a touring company. He won critical acclaim with his first plays, "The Birthday Party" and "The Caretaker," and established the sparse, cryptic style that was to characterize his work. He adapted many of his plays for the screen, including *The Guest* (1964, based on "The Caretaker"), *The Birthday Party* (1968), and *The Homecoming* (1973) and wrote many successful screenplay adaptations of works other than his own, including *The Pumpkin Eater* (1964) and *The Last Tycoon* (1976). He enjoyed a long and rich collaboration with director Joseph Losey, adapting *The Servant* (1963), *Accident* (1967), and *The Go-Between* (1971), and was nominated for Academy Awards for the screenplays of *The French Lieutenant's Woman* (1981) and *Betrayal* (1983, based on his own play). He also directed the film version of Simon Gray's *Butley* in 1974. More recent screenplays include *Turtle Diary* (1985), *The Handmaid's Tale, Reunion* (both 1990), *The Comfort of Strangers* (1991) and *The Trial* (1994). Pinter was married to actress Vivien Merchant, who appeared in many of his plays and was featured in the film versions of *Accident* and *The Homecoming.* He also appeared onscreen briefly as a bookstore customer in *Turtle Diary.*

PITT, BRAD. Actor. *(b. Dec. 18, 1963, Shawnee, Okla.)* Since his scene-stealing performance as J.D., the hitchhiking thief who teaches Geena Davis about the joys of sex and robbing convenience stores in *Thelma & Louise* (1991), Pitt has become one of the hottest young actors in Hollywood. His earlier credits include such low-budget films as *Cutting Class, Happy Together* (both 1989), and *Across the Tracks* (1991) as well as TV roles on "Dallas" and "Another World." In 1992 he was the human cop in the animated *Cool World,* starred in *Johnny Suede,* and received critical acclaim for his performance as the wild Paul MacLean in Robert Redford's *A River Runs Through It.* Since then he has appeared in the Oscar-nominated short *Contact* (1992), *Kalifornia* (1993, opposite then-girlfriend Juliette Lewis), *True Romance* (1993, in an amusing cameo), *The Favor* (1994, filmed in 1991), *Interview With the Vampire, Legends of the Fall* (both 1994), and *Seven* (1995).

PITT, INGRID. Actress. *(b. Nov. 21, 1945, Poland, as Ingoushka Petrov.)* This busty, exotic-looking actress decorated several British horror films in the early 1970s, including *The Vampire Lovers* (1970, as a lesbian bloodsucker), *The House That Dripped Blood* (1971), *Countess Dracula* (1972), and *The Wicker Man* (1973), accounting for her limited but clearly defined status as a cult figure. Perhaps more talented than she was able to display onscreen, Pitt frequently appeared in characterizations that traded mostly on her physical attributes. Other appearances include *Where Eagles Dare* (1969), *The Final Option* (1982), *Hanna's War* (1988), and the British TV miniseries "Smiley's People."

PITTS, ZASU. Actress. *(b. Jan. 3, 1898, Parsons, Kansas; d. June 7, 1963.)* This well-known supporting player—named, per a family compromise, after both her father's sisters, Eliza and Susan—was discovered for movies by Mary Pickford, who gave her small parts in *A Little Princess* and

Rebecca of Sunnybrook Farm (both 1917). She stood out in vivid dramatic roles for Erich von Stroheim in *Greed* (1924, as the gold-crazy Trina) and *The Wedding March* (1928, as the pitiful bride), but in the sound era was known almost exclusively as a comedienne. (In fact, her scenes as a distraught mother in 1930's *All Quiet on the Western Front* were refilmed with actress Beryl Mercer, because preview audiences reportedly couldn't accept her in a dramatic part.) A plaintive voice and fluttery hands became her trademarks, and in her most prolific period—the early 1930s—she was costarring in both a series of Hal Roach short subjects (with Thelma Todd) and a series of medium-budget Universal features (with Slim Summerville) while continuing to play supporting roles in movies such as *Monte Carlo* (1930), *Blondie of the Follies, Roar of the Dragon, Once in a Lifetime, Make Me a Star* (all 1932), *Mr. Skitch* (1933, as Will Rogers' wife), *The Meanest Gal in Town, Dames* (both 1934), *Mrs. Wiggs of the Cabbage Patch* (1934, in the leading role), *Ruggles of Red Gap* (1935), *Broadway Limited* (1941), and *Miss Polly* (1941, reunited with Slim Summerville) among others. She also played spinster sleuth Hildegarde Withers in two 1936 RKO programmers, *The Plot Thickens* and *Forty Naughty Girls.* As film roles grew scarce, she took to the stage, and worked occasionally in television, winning a sidekick spot on "Oh Susanna/The Gale Storm Show" from 1956 to 1960. Later credits include *Life With Father* (1947), *Francis* (1949), *Teenage Millionaire* (1961), and her last film, *It's a Mad Mad Mad Mad World* (1963). She authored the book "Candy Hits by ZaSu Pitts."

PLEASENCE, DONALD. Actor. *(b. Oct. 15, 1919, Nottinghamshire, England; d. Feb. 2, 1995.)* Often cited as the busiest actor in the world, there seemed to be no part this bald, big-eyed, creepy-looking little Englishman wouldn't take. Among his many horror films, Pleasence is best known as the tormented psychiatrist who, Ahab-like, relentlessly pursues psychotic killer Michael Meyers in the *Halloween* movies (1978–89). Pleasence, whose first movie was *The Beachcomber* (1954), is instantly recognizable to even the most casual film watcher. He was especially prolific during the 1960s and 1970s; he appeared as James Bond arch-villain Blofeld in *You Only Live Twice* (1967), got smothered by a blood cell in the miniaturization fantasy *Fantastic Voyage*, and appeared in drag in Roman Polanski's bizarre *Cul-de-Sac* (both 1966). Pleasence also played memorable but less flamboyant roles, including a touching turn as a near-blind forger in the WW2 drama *The Great Escape* (1963). More recently, he was among the star-studded supporting players in Woody Allen's pretentious *Shadows and Fog* (1992). All told, he appeared in well over 100 films (as many as 25 in one year), though many of them are worthless pieces of junk—and in some, his was the only recognizable name in the cast.

OTHER FILMS INCLUDE: 1959: *Look Back in Anger;* 1964: *The Guest;* 1965: *The Greatest Story Ever Told;* 1968: *Will Penny;* 1969: *The Madwoman of Chaillot;* 1971: *THX-1138;* 1972: *Wedding in White, The Pied Piper;* 1975: *Escape to Witch Mountain, Hearts of the West;* 1976: *The Last Tycoon;* 1977: *The Eagle Has Landed, Telefon;* 1978: *Sgt. Pepper's Lonely Hearts Club Band;* 1979: *Dracula;* 1981: *Escape From New York;* 1993: *The Hour of the Pig;* 1994: *Femme Fatale.*

PLESHETTE, SUZANNE. Actress. *(b. Jan. 31, 1937, New York City.)* This dark, husky-voiced actress broke into films with a supporting role in Jerry Lewis' *The Geisha Boy* (1958), and then signed a long-term contract with Warner Bros., which groomed her for stardom. She teamed with Troy Donahue (to whom she was briefly married) in the romantic comedy *Rome Adventure* (1962), but won her first really memorable part on loan-out as the sympathetic schoolteacher who meets a grisly end in Hitchcock's *The Birds* (1963). She showed maturing talent in *Youngblood Hawke, A Distant Trumpet* (both 1964, with Donahue), *A Rage to Live* (1965), *Mister Buddwing,* and *Nevada Smith* (both 1966), but her career veered toward comedy in such films as the Disney outings *The Ugly Dachshund* (1966), *The Adventures of Bullwhip Griffin* (1967), and *Blackbeard's Ghost* (1968), plus *If It's Tuesday, This Must Be Belgium* (1969), and *Support Your Local Gunfighter* (1971). Her comic skills reached fruition when she was cast as Bob

Newhart's wife on "The Bob Newhart Show" (1972–78). She's only appeared in a handful of theatrical features since then, among them Disney's *The Shaggy D.A.* (1976), and the lackluster *Hot Stuff* (1979) and *Oh, God! Book II* (1980). More's the pity; she's a winning performer whose talents have been infrequently used by Hollywood. She has snagged a number of good parts in TV movies, however, including the title role in *Leona Helmsley: The Queen of Mean* (1990).

PLIMPTON, MARTHA. Actress. *(b. Nov. 16, 1970, New York City.)* Surely, when casting directors of major films need to find "The Rebellious Teenage Daughter," their first choice must be this tomboyish supporting actress. She has consistently essayed such roles with skill and passion far beyond her years. She first appeared in *Rollover* (1981), and made a strong impression in both *The River Rat* (1984) and *The Goonies* (1985). Plimpton's best screen outings include *The Mosquito Coast* (1986), *Shy People* (1987), *Running on Empty, Another Woman* (both 1988), *Parenthood* (1989), and *Stanley & Iris* (1990). Making the transition to more mature parts, she starred in *Samantha* (1992), and appeared in *Chantilly Lace* (a telefilm), *Inside Monkey Zetterland, Josh and S.A.M.* (all 1993), *My Life's in Turnaround, The Beans of Egypt, Maine,* and *Mrs. Parker and the Vicious Circle* (all 1994). Her parents are actors Keith Carradine and Shelley Plimpton.

PLOWRIGHT, JOAN. Actress. *(b. Oct. 28, 1929, Brigg, England.)* Long considered one of Britain's finest stage actresses, it wasn't until the 1980s that Plowright came into her own as a character actress in films. She trained at the Old Vic Theatre School and made her stage debut in 1951, later appearing in such groundbreaking productions as John Osborne's "The Entertainer" and Ionesco's "Rhinoceros." She received acclaim for her title roles in "Major Barbara" and "Saint Joan" and won a Tony for her Broadway performance in "A Taste of Honey." She made her film debut in *Moby Dick* (1956), but received more attention when she recreated her stage role in the film adaptation of *The Entertainer* (1960), playing the

daughter of Laurence Olivier, whom she later married in real life. While raising a family, she worked only sporadically, in films like *Three Sisters* (1970, directed by Olivier) and *Equus* (1977). Her output increased in the 1980s: *Brimstone and Treacle, Britannia Hospital* (both 1982), *Wagner* (1983), and *Revolution* (1985). She was excellent in starring roles in *Drowning by Numbers* (1987) and *The Dressmaker* (1988), then demonstrated her extraordinary range (and ability with accents) in the American films *I Love You To Death* (1990, as Tracey Ullman's Yugoslavian mom) and *Avalon* (1990, as Aidan Quinn's Jewish mom). She was wonderful as an uptight Victorian widow in *Enchanted April* (1992, Oscar-nominated), costarred in the TV movie *Stalin* (1992), and, incredibly, played Mrs. Wilson in John Hughes' adaptation of *Dennis the Menace* (1993). She costarred in *The Summer House* (also 1993) and appeared in *Widows' Peak* (1994). She was married to Olivier from 1961 until his death in 1989; in 1993's *Last Action Hero* she made a cameo appearance as a schoolteacher gamely trying to interest her pupils in Shakespeare by showing them a film clip of his 1948 *Hamlet.*

PLUMMER, CHRISTOPHER. Actor. *(b. Dec. 13, 1927, Toronto, as Arthur Plummer.)* Handsome, award-winning Shakespearean-trained actor who will probably forever be remembered as Baron Von Trapp from *The Sound of Music* (1965), a film he reportedly referred to as "The Sound of Mucus." A veteran of the Montreal stage, Plummer is adept at both comedy and drama, and is particularly effective in sinister roles, such as the Israeli diplomat in *Eyewitness* (1981), and the head of covert intelligence in *Dreamscape* (1984). Plummer made his film debut in *Wind Across the Everglades* (1958), and was memorable in *Stage Struck* (also 1958), *The Fall of the Roman Empire* (1964), *Inside Daisy Clover* (1965), *Oedipus the King* (1968), *Royal Hunt of the Sun* (1969), *The Man Who Would Be King* (1975, as Rudyard Kipling), *The Return of the Pink Panther, Conduct Unbecoming* (both also 1975), *The Silent Partner* (1978), *Murder by Decree* (1979, as Sherlock Holmes), and *Somewhere in Time* (1980).

The 1980s saw him playing heavies and appearing in many lackluster films, including a few that went straight to video. But the decade also saw him tackling more lighthearted parts, displaying a hitherto unsuspected comedic facility. His films in this period include *Ordeal by Innocence* (1984), *The Boy in Blue* (1985), *An American Tail* (1986, voice only), *The Boss' Wife* (also 1986), *Dragnet, I Love N.Y., Souvenir* (all 1987), *Stage Fright* (1988), *Mind Field* (1990), *Where the Heart Is* (also 1990, all but unrecognizable playing a filthy bum), *The Dispossessed, Firehead, Red-Blooded American Girl* (all also 1990), *Star Trek VI: The Undiscovered Country* (1991, as a Shakespeare-quoting Klingon opposite William Shatner, who had understudied for Plummer on stage in Canada), *Malcolm X* (1992, in a cameo as a prison priest), *Liar's Edge* (1993), *Wolf* (1994), and *Dolores Claiborne* (1995). Plummer continues to divide his time among film, stage, and TV work. (He won a 1974 Tony Award for the Broadway musical "Cyrano," and a 1977 Emmy Award for the TV miniseries "The Moneychangers.") His daughter (by former wife Tammy Grimes) is actress Amanda Plummer *(Daniel, The Fisher King).*

POITIER, SIDNEY. Actor, director. *(b. Feb. 20, 1924, Miami, Fla.)* Talented, passionate actor whose pioneering screen work in the 1950s and 1960s paved the way for countless other black performers. Born in Miami, Poitier was raised in the Bahamas by tomato growers, living in poverty and completing only a few years of formal education. Making his way back to his birthplace as a teenager, he labored in several menial jobs before entering the Army. Afterward, he joined the American Negro Theater, eventually finding his way to New York and appearing on Broadway in "Anna Lucasta" (1948). He first appeared on the big screen in *No Way Out* (1950), in a plum role as a hospital intern who locks horns with racist punk Richard Widmark, and went on to costar with veteran black actor Canada Lee in *Cry, the Beloved Country* (1951), which was filmed on location in South Africa. His subsequent films were a mixed bag, but he made a vivid impression as a rebellious student in *Blackboard Jungle* (1955), and

did excellent work as a good-hearted dock worker in *Edge of the City* (1957). In 1958 he received his first Oscar nomination, for his portrayal of an escaped convict in *The Defiant Ones*. With that film he became Hollywood's first black leading man—and star. A string of hits followed, including *Porgy and Bess* (1959), *All the Young Men* (1960), *A Raisin in the Sun, Paris Blues* (both 1961), *Pressure Point* (1962), and *Lilies of the Field* (1963); this last picture brought Poitier his only Oscar to date.

Throughout the rest of the decade, Poitier served as a symbol of black progress during the civil rights era. In 1967, his peak year, Poitier starred in three box-office smashes: *Guess Who's Coming to Dinner,* as the handsome suitor who forces in-laws Spencer Tracy and Katharine Hepburn to reconsider their attitudes toward blacks; *To Sir With Love,* as a teacher in a tough London school who wins the respect of his working-class students; and *In the Heat of the Night,* as police detective Virgil Tibbs, opposite Rod Steiger (playing a redneck Southern cop). *Night's* success spawned two sequels, *They Call Me MISTER Tibbs!* (1970) and *The Organization* (1971). With this formidable parlay of films, Poitier became a top box-office attraction, breaking further ground and opening more doors. In 1968 he wrote the story for (and starred in) another pioneering effort, a black romantic comedy, *For Love of Ivy,* then made his directing debut with *Buck and the Preacher* (1972), in which he also starred, alongside longtime friend Harry Belafonte. He then starred in and directed a trio of broad (and extremely popular) all-black comedies, *Uptown Saturday Night* (1974), *Let's Do It Again* (1975), and *A Piece of the Action* (1977). It was a giant leap from the "serious" Poitier vehicles of the sixties.

Poitier all but abandoned screen acting in the 1980s to concentrate on directing, guiding Gene Wilder and Richard Pryor in *Stir Crazy* (1980), then Wilder and his wife Gilda Radner in *Hanky Panky* (1982), and a bunch of break-dancing kids in *Fast Forward* (1985). Poitier essayed another tough-cop characterization in *Shoot to Kill* (1988), and played an FBI agent in *Little Nikita* that same year. In 1990 he returned to the field of movie farce to direct Bill Cosby in the dreadful

Ghost Dad, then found his best role in years, as future Supreme Court justice Thurgood Marshall in the made-for-TV movie *Separate but Equal* (1991). The following year he received the American Film Institute Life Achievement Award, and was back onscreen with Robert Redford in *Sneakers* (1992).

His autobiography, "This Life," was published in 1980. It is impossible to overstate the influence Poitier had on blacks and whites in the 1950s and 1960s, as both role model and image-maker. He has never betrayed that trust.

OTHER FILMS INCLUDE: 1952: *Red Ball Express;* 1954: *Go, Man, Go!;* 1956: *Goodbye, My Lady;* 1957: *Something of Value, Band of Angels, The Mark of the Hawk;* 1959: *Virgin Island;* 1964: *The Long Ships;* 1965: *The Greatest Story Ever Told* (cameo), *The Bedford Incident, A Patch of Blue, The Slender Thread;* 1966: *Duel at Diablo;* 1969: *The Lost Man;* 1972: *Brother John;* 1973: *A Warm December* (also directed); 1975: *The Wilby Conspiracy.*

POLANSKI, ROMAN. Director, screenwriter, actor. (b. Aug. 18, 1933, Paris.) The themes of disaffection and victimization repeatedly recur in the films of this talented, tormented director, undoubtedly owing to the unique circumstances of his life. Born to Jewish parents in Paris, where he now makes his home, Polanski and his parents moved back to Poland when he was three. Without parents during World War 2 (his mother died in a concentration camp), he spent his childhood wandering through occupied Poland and was often victimized by sadistic German soldiers who would shoot at him for the sheer pleasure of watching him scamper to avoid being hit. After the war Polanski was reunited with his father and began his schooling. He began acting while in his teens; in the 1950s he entered the Lodz Film School, where he made his famous short film *Two Men and a Wardrobe* (1959), which won several international awards. His first feature, *Knife in the Water* (1962), was a tense, claustrophobic erotic thriller indifferently received in his own country but recognized as a masterwork in the West. It was even nominated for an Academy Award as Best Foreign Language Film.

Seeking better opportunities, Polanski moved to England where he made *Repulsion* (1965), a chilly thriller about a sexually repressed young beauty (Catherine Deneuve) who's driven to murder by the sexual attentions of men. He followed that film with the weird *Cul-de-Sac* (1966), starring Deneuve's sister, Françoise Dorleac. *Dance of the Vampires* (1967), a funny and clever horror comedy, was re-edited by its American distributors and retitled *The Fearless Vampire Killers;* Polanski asked to have his name taken off the U.S. version. Courted by Hollywood, he came to America to adapt and direct *Rosemary's Baby* (1968, Oscar-nominated for Adapted Screenplay), the blood-chilling story of devil worship in urban America that established him as a master of the sophisticated latter-day thriller.

In 1969 tragedy struck his life again when his wife, Sharon Tate (who'd appeared with her husband in *Fearless Vampire Killers*), and a number of the couple's friends, were slaughtered by the Manson family at Polanski's Los Angeles home. His subsequent films (most uncomfortably his 1971 *Macbeth,* which contained scenes of violence reminiscent of the crime that took his wife's life, and the 1973 black comedy *What?,* in which he also appeared) seemed to be stained by the tragedy, but 1974's period detective thriller, *Chinatown* (in which Polanski played a knife-wielding hood), benefitted from the pessimistic fatalism Polanski brought to it (along with, it must be added, much humor and atmosphere). It was one of the most successful films of that decade and earned Polanski a Best Director Oscar nomination.

Polanski directed and starred in the black comedy *The Tenant* (1976), playing the same sort of tormented character portrayed by others in his earlier films. He was embroiled in a scandal over having sex with an underage model in 1977; rather than face the charges, he chose to flee the country. Working abroad, he made *Tess,* a sumptuous and evocative adaptation of Thomas Hardy's "Tess of the D'Urbervilles" (which he says was Sharon Tate's favorite book) in 1979, which earned Polanski another Best Director nomination. He has also done some stage direction in his native Poland, directed the spectacularly unsuccessful *Pirates* (1986), and made a decent but unspectacular mainstream thriller, *Frantic,* in 1988. In

1992 he produced, directed, and cowrote the delirious sex melodrama *Bitter Moon,* then directed a tense adaptation of the play *Death and the Maiden* (1994). He also acted opposite Gerard Depardieu in the French drama *A Pure Formality* (1994).

POLLACK, SYDNEY. Director, actor, producer. (b. July 1, 1934, Lafayette, Ind.) This talented, intelligent director is also a first-rate actor; perhaps that's why he communicates so well with his stars. Pollack studied with Sanford Meisner at New York's Neighborhood Playhouse, and briefly served as one of its acting coaches, before embarking on his own career on stage and television. While acting in the 1962 movie *War Hunt* he became friendly with Robert Redford, who was making his screen debut. When Pollack decided to move behind the camera, Redford was eager to work with him. They have since collaborated on seven films: *This Property Is Condemned* (1966), *Jeremiah Johnson* (1972), *The Way We Were* (1973), *Three Days of the Condor* (1975), *The Electric Horseman* (1979), *Out of Africa* (1985), and *Havana* (1990). *Out of Africa,* in fact, won Pollack his first Academy Award as Best Director.

Pollack was also nominated for the wrenching Depression-era drama *They Shoot Horses, Don't They?* (1969) and the crackerjack comedy *Tootsie* (1982), which forced him back in front of the camera when Dustin Hoffman insisted that Pollack play his agent in the movie, which he did, delightfully. In 1992 he appeared in *The Player,* contributed the funniest scene to *Death Becomes Her,* as Meryl Streep's addled doctor, and delivered a superb seriocomic performance as Judy Davis' errant husband in Woody Allen's *Husbands and Wives.*

In recent years Pollack has devoted more time to producing than directing, numbering among his credits (as producer or executive producer) *Honeysuckle Rose* (1980), *Songwriter* (1984), *Bright Lights, Big City* (1988), *Major League, The Fabulous Baker Boys* (both 1989), *Presumed Innocent, White Palace* (both 1990), *Dead Again, King Ralph* (both 1991), *Searching for Bobby Fischer,* and *Flesh and Bone* (both 1993). He also executive produced the high-profile cable TV series "Fallen

Angels" in 1993, then returned to the director's chair for *The Firm* (1993) and *Sabrina* (1995).
OTHER FILMS INCLUDE: 1965: *The Slender Thread;* 1968: *The Scalphunters;* 1969: *Castle Keep;* 1975: *The Yakuza;* 1977: *Bobby Deerfield;* 1981: *Absence of Malice.*

POLLARD, MICHAEL J. Actor. (b. May 30, 1939, Pacific, N.J., as Michael J. Pollack.) This homuncular, elfin character actor studied at New York City's Actors' Studio and appeared as a semi-regular on the "Dobie Gillis" TV series in 1959 before making his feature debut in *Hemingway's Adventures of a Young Man* (1962). He worked in *The Stripper* (1963), *The Wild Angels* (1966), and *Enter Laughing* (1967) before being cast as filling-station attendant turned outlaw C. W. Moss in *Bonnie and Clyde* (1967), a role for which he was Oscar-nominated. Inexplicably popular, though he never seemed to be playing anyone other than himself, Pollard subsequently appeared in several movies, including *Hannibal Brooks* (1969), *Little Fauss and Big Halsy* (1970), *Dirty Little Billy* (1972, the lead), *Between the Lines* (1977), *Melvin and Howard* (1980), and *America* (1982), but took long vacations from the screen. By the late 1980s, though, he began working more frequently, playing virtually the same offbeat, imbecilic character in both A pictures (1987's *Roxanne,* 1988's *Scrooged*) and B's (1989's *Night Visitor,* 1991's *The Art of Dying,* 1992's *Split Second*). He reunited with Warren Beatty in *Dick Tracy* (1990) playing phone tapper Bug Bailey, and appeared in *Enid Is Sleeping, I Come in Peace* (both 1990), and *Arizona Dream* (1995, filmed in 1991).

POWELL, DICK. Actor, singer. (b. Nov. 14, 1904, Mountain View, Ark.; d. Jan. 2, 1963.) The amiable, boyish, perpetually energetic crooner of 1930s musicals was one of the screen's most popular attractions, but nobody took him very seriously until he did a complete about-face, becoming one of moviedom's top tough guys in the 1940s. A former singer and bandleader, and a popular theater m.c., Powell won a Warner Bros. contract in 1932, making his film debut (playing a bandleading singer) in that year's *Blessed Event.* He made a lasting impression as the wide-eyed juvenile lead opposite hoofer Ruby Keeler in a string of backstage musicals including *42nd Street, Footlight Parade, Gold Diggers of 1933* (all 1933), *Dames, Flirtation Walk* (both 1934), *Shipmates Forever* (1935), and *Colleen* (1936). He made musicals without Keeler, as well: *Twenty Million Sweethearts, Wonder Bar* (both 1934), *Gold Diggers of 1935, Page Miss Glory, Broadway Gondolier* (all 1935), *Stage Struck* (1936), *Gold Diggers of 1937, The Singing Marine, Varsity Show, Hollywood Hotel* (all 1937), and *The Cowboy From Brooklyn* (1938), among them. (He also crooned amiably in two Fox musicals for former Warners honcho Darryl Zanuck, 1935's *Thanks a Million* and 1937's *On the Avenue*.)

From his earliest years at Warners, though, Powell chafed at the insipid characters he was forced to play in those musicals. From time to time the studio let him appear in nonmusical films such as *College Coach, Convention City* (both 1933), and *A Midsummer Night's Dream* (1935), but he was most valuable to Warners as a singing star, and studio brass never let him forget it.

Powell left Warners after completing *Naughty but Nice* (1939), and landed the lead in *Christmas in July* (1940), a straight comedy by writer-director Preston Sturges, then at the beginning of his short but sensational filmmaking career. While he did a creditable job, Powell still found himself in demand for his vocal prowess, and starred in *In the Navy* (1941, with Abbott and Costello), *Star Spangled Rhythm* (1942), *Happy Go Lucky, True to Life,* and *Riding High* (all 1943) before tackling another "straight" part, in the whimsical fantasy *It Happened Tomorrow* (1944), directed by Rene Clair.

Seeking a total break from his clean-cut image, Powell campaigned vigorously to play Raymond Chandler's private eye Philip Marlowe in *Murder, My Sweet* (1944), RKO's film adaptation of "Farewell, My Lovely" (which the studio had previously used as the basis for a 1942 "Falcon" stanza). He won the part and did a terrific job in the role, striking just the right balance between world-weary cynicism and principled two-fistedness. Overnight he became one of the screen's premier tough guys, starring in hard-hitting film noirs and actioners such as *Cornered*

(1945), *Johnny O'Clock* (1947), *To the Ends of the Earth, Pitfall, Stations West, Rogue's Regiment* (all 1948), *Right Cross* (1950), *Cry Danger,* and *The Tall Target* (1951). He also tackled an offbeat role in *You Never Can Tell* (1951), playing a murdered dog who is reincarnated as a man to find his killer (!), and was excellent as a screenwriter in *The Bad and the Beautiful* (1952). In a lighter vein he did *Mrs. Mike* (1949), *The Reformer and the Redhead* (1950), *Callaway Went Thataway* (1951), and *Susan Slept Here* (1954) ... but never crooned a note.

Powell turned his attentions behind the camera during the 1950s, directing *Split Second* (1953), *The Conqueror* (1956), *You Can't Run Away From It* (also 1956, starring his wife June Allyson), *The Enemy Below* (1957), and *The Hunters* (1958). (Directing *The Conqueror* on location in Utah, near an atomic testing site, may have hastened his death; like a startling number of others involved with that film, he succumbed to cancer.) Powell was one of the founders of Four Star Television; he hosted (and occasionally acted in) "Four Star Playhouse" (1952–56), "Dick Powell's Zane Grey Theatre" (1956–62), and "The Dick Powell Show" (1961–63), as well as supervising a number of other shows produced by the company. He's been credited with boosting many budding careers, including those of Sam Peckinpah and Aaron Spelling, during the late 1950s and early 1960s. He also made an amusing, unbilled cameo appearance in an episode of Four Star's sitcom "Ensign O'Toole," auditioning for a talent show by singing one of his 1930s songs—and being turned away! He was married to actresses Joan Blondell and June Allyson; his son by Allyson, Richard Jr., played him in the 1930s-set Hollywood drama *The Day of the Locust* (1975).

POWELL, ELEANOR. Dancer, actress. (b. Nov. 21, 1912, Springfield, Mass.; d. Feb. 11, 1982.) Leggy, fresh-faced dancing star of the 1930s and 1940s whose sunny smile and exuberant hoofing endeared her to movie audiences who were perfectly willing to overlook her limitations as an actress. A dancer from childhood, Powell brought her graceful, athletic style to Broadway when she was just 17, performing in various revues and musical comedies. She had already been dubbed "the world's greatest tap dancer" (although, for once, the hyperbole may have been justified) when she came to Hollywood to do a specialty number in *George White's 1935 Scandals.* Immediately thereafter she was signed by MGM—which, with minimal changes in her makeup and comportment, groomed her for stardom.

Well received in *Broadway Melody of 1936* (and carefully supported with comedy from Jack Benny and singing from Frances Langford), Powell delighted Depression-era moviegoers with her boundless energy and optimism. She was equally well showcased in *Born to Dance* (1936), *Rosalie* (1937), *Broadway Melody of 1938,* and *Honolulu* (1939), although Powell's increasingly huge production numbers—each one more "spectacular" than the last—got to be a bit silly. In *Broadway Melody of 1940* Powell had the chance to dance with Fred Astaire—without gimmicks or elephantine sets—and the results were exhilarating.

It became increasingly apparent, however, that a Powell "vehicle" needed to lean on others to carry the storylines, as in *Lady Be Good* (1941), which gave her top billing but really belonged to Robert Young and Ann Sothern, playing songwriters, and *Ship Ahoy* (1942), and *I Dood It* (1943), both of which spotlighted Red Skelton. Powell parted company with Metro after doing a specialty number in *Thousands Cheer* (1943). She danced in a giant pinball machine in *Sensations of 1945,* but otherwise this "comeback" picture was a disappointment, and Powell retired from the screen to concentrate on her marriage to actor Glenn Ford, whom she'd wed in 1943. (They were divorced in 1959.) She returned to MGM just once, in 1950, to guest star in the Esther Williams vehicle *Duchess of Idaho.* Powell continued to perform, mostly on stage and in nightclubs, for many years, maintaining her supple figure and girlishly pretty looks well into middle age. In later years she became profoundly interested in religion, and was actually ordained a minister of the Unity Church.

POWELL, JANE. Actress, singer. *(b. Apr. 1, 1929, Portland, Oreg., as Suzanne Burce.)* Pretty, peppy blond singing star of MGM musicals of the late 1940s and 1950s, who played dewy-eyed, lovestruck adolescents until she was well into her 20s. A coloratura soprano who sang on radio while still a preteen, she made her first film, *Song of the Open Road* (1944), at age 15. MGM debuted her in 1946's *Holiday in Mexico,* in which her bubbly personality (and voice) recalled that of Deanna Durbin, who'd risen to stardom in similar vehicles for Universal. Powell was one of the *Three Daring Daughters* and sailed on the *Luxury Liner* before moving up to costar billing in *A Date With Judy* (all 1948). *Nancy Goes to Rio* (1950) was actually a remake of Durbin's *It's a Date,* and served very well as a vehicle for Powell.

Her biggest break came accidentally, when she replaced June Allyson (who'd become pregnant) and Judy Garland (who'd taken ill) in *Royal Wedding* (1951). The dances had already been choreographed for (and rehearsed by) the other actresses, but Powell did her best, and really shone as the Brooklynese tough-girl in the comic showpiece "How Could You Believe Me When I Said I Love You When You Know I've Been a Liar All My Life?"

In 1954 she reached her pinnacle onscreen, as the indomitable young woman who impulsively marries Howard Keel in *Seven Brides for Seven Brothers.* No other musical ever gave her the opportunity to play such a rounded, mature, and appealing character. Her other films: *Rich, Young and Pretty* (1951), *Small Town Girl* (1953), *Three Sailors and a Girl* (also 1953, on loan to Warners), *Athena, Deep in My Heart* (both 1954), *Hit the Deck* (1955), and *The Girl Most Likely* (1957). Not yet 30 but having already milked her screen persona for all it was worth, Powell quit after doing *The Female Animal* and the uncharacteristic *Enchanted Island* (as a South Sea island princess!) in 1958.

Still a young and vibrant woman, Powell kept performing on TV, in nightclubs, and on the stage (touring for several years with her *Seven Brides* costar Howard Keel). She starred on Broadway in the revival of "Irene," replacing Debbie Reynolds in 1973. Her fifth and current husband is former child actor Dick Moore. Most recently she appeared as Alan Thicke's mother on the TV sitcom "Growing Pains." Her autobiography,

"The Girl Next Door ... And How She Grew," was published in 1988.

POWELL, MICHAEL. Director, screenwriter, producer. *(b. Sept. 30, 1905, Kent, England; d. Feb. 19, 1990.)* Next to Alfred Hitchcock (for whom he once worked as an assistant), Powell may be the most talented and important film director to come out of the English cinema. Initially hired to work with director Rex Ingram in his Nice, France, studio at the age of 20, he learned the business from top to bottom and earned his solo directorial spurs on a number of "quota quickies"—England's answer to Hollywood B films—in the mid 1930s. *The Edge of the World* (1937), the story of Scottish fishermen struggling against the elements, brought Powell the respect and freedom he deserved to make more important films. He achieved his best results in partnership with screenwriter/codirector Emeric Pressburger, with whom he first worked on *The Spy in Black* (1939). As "The Archers," they jointly wrote, planned, and directed a string of memorable films, though they are difficult to categorize and even more difficult to describe: intelligent, unpredictable, embracing a heightened sense of reality (and often mysticism) that no one else has ever duplicated.

The Life and Death of Colonel Blimp (1943), a sentimental, multigenerational saga, was surely the most unusual film to emerge from wartime England, where jingoism and fellowship were the norm. *I Know Where I'm Going!* (1945) played its modest love story against a Scottish seacoast backdrop, and drew on the writer/directors' fondness for British eccentricities. *A Matter of Life and Death* (1946, released in the U.S. as *Stairway to Heaven*) again flew against convention by injecting a dose of fantasy into a timely and serious story of a pilot recovering from the emotional stress of war duty. *Black Narcissus* (1946) brought forbidden emotions to the story of a young nun swept up in the exoticism—and remoteness—of the Himalayas. *The Red Shoes* (1948) juxtaposed art and life in a tragic tale of a ballerina and her two masters.

In these, and other, films Powell and Pressburger marched to their own drum, creating films that were like no others on earth. They also took the medium of Technicolor away from Hollywood garishness and toward a new, creative application that was nothing short of breathtaking.

After splitting up the team in 1956, Powell gradually wound down, a process no doubt hastened by the vicious critical reception accorded *Peeping Tom* (1960), his pioneering and controversial psychosexual thriller. Now seen as a brilliant film—and a precursor to the post-modern horror films of the 1970s and 1980s—*Peeping Tom* virtually stopped Powell's career dead. His visual technique, particularly his bold use of color and composition, has inspired many younger directors, including Martin Scorsese, Ken Russell, and Nicolas Roeg. In the last years of his life, Powell and Scorsese became soulmates, and Powell married Scorsese's longtime film editor Thelma Schoonmaker. His autobiography, "A Life in Movies," was published in 1987.

OTHER FILMS INCLUDE: 1940: *The Thief of Bagdad* (codirected), *Blackout;* 1941: *49th Parallel;* 1942: *One of Our Aircraft Is Missing* (his first cowritten and codirected with Pressburger; Oscar-nominated for screenplay); 1944: *A Canterbury Tale;* 1949: *The Small Back Room;* 1950: *The Wild Heart* (aka *Gone to Earth), The Elusive Pimpernel;* 1951: *Tales of Hoffman;* 1957: *Pursuit of the Graf Spee, Night Ambush* (aka *Ill Met by Moonlight);* 1960: *The Queen's Guards;* 1969: *Age of Consent;* 1978: *Return to the Edge of the World.*

POWELL, WILLIAM. Actor. *(b. July 29, 1892, Pittsburgh; d. Mar. 5, 1984.)* It is impossible to write about this popular star without using the words "suave" or "debonair": both call him to mind better than any others in the dictionary. Certainly few other stars could match the casual cynicism and insouciance with which he invested so many of his characters (especially in the talkie era), and his essential urbanity made even the unsympathetic ones seem palatable. (He must also be saluted for his limitless, and seemingly effortless, capacity to drink scotch and make wry faces.)

Powell developed and polished his smooth manner on the Broadway stage during the teens, and he was already a veteran by the time he first appeared onscreen, in John Barrymore's 1922 version of *Sherlock Holmes* (*not* as Dr. Watson, as some sources report, but as a minor character). For the remainder of the silent era, he distinguished himself by playing heavies, some charming and sophisticated, others snarling and brutish. He appeared in *When Knighthood Was in Flower* (1922), *The Bright Shawl* (1923), *Romola* (1924), *Too Many Kisses* (1925), *Beau Geste* (1926, as the untrustworthy Boldini), *The Great Gatsby* (also 1926, as George Wilson), *Nevada* (1927, playing a Western heavy in this Zane Grey story starring Gary Cooper), and *Senorita* (also 1927), before being assigned the plum role of the cruel movie director who torments Emil Jannings in *The Last Command* (1928). (Although the picture boosted Powell's stock with Paramount, he refused to renew his contract unless studio brass promised him he'd never again have to work with its director, Josef von Sternberg.)

Powell toiled in a few more silents—including the 1929 version of *The Four Feathers*—before making his talkie debut in *Interference.* But it was his characterization of gentleman detective Philo Vance in *The Canary Murder Case* (1929, started as a silent but finished as a talkie) that finally elevated Powell to stardom. He reprised the role in *The Greene Murder Case* (also 1929), *The Benson Murder Case,* in a short comedy skit for *Paramount on Parade* (both 1930), and, under his later contract to Warner Bros., in the best of the bunch, *The Kennel Murder Case* (1933).

After starring in a string of mediocre movies, including one, *Ladies' Man* (1931), which paired him with his then-wife, Carole Lombard, Powell left Paramount for Warner Bros., which immediately put him into better pictures, all in 1932: *High Pressure* and *Lawyer Man* were crackling melodramas with elements of comedy, in the best Warner Bros. style; *Jewel Robbery* was a Lubitsch-like romantic comedy that showed him and Kay Francis at their best; and *One Way Passage* reunited Powell and Francis for a classic shipboard romance about a captured killer and a woman who's dying. By the time Powell left Warners in 1934 he was a top box-office draw.

At that time a movie actor couldn't do much better than MGM, the studio with "more stars than there are in the heavens." Powell began his 13-year tenure there

with *Manhattan Melodrama* (1934), which pitted him, a crusading district attorney, against boyhood pal Clark Gable, now a vicious gangster. Also featured in the successful film was Myrna Loy, with whom Powell was teamed later that year for what was to be a low-budget mystery, an adaptation of Dashiell Hammett's *The Thin Man,* directed by W. S. Van Dyke. Powell and Loy were born to play the witty, lighthearted, cocktail-sipping sleuths Nick and Nora Charles, and audiences loved them in those roles. The performance earned Powell his first Oscar nomination.

Powell and Loy were reunited for the first time in *Evelyn Prentice* (1934). *Reckless* (1935) costarred Powell with platinum blond superstar Jean Harlow, to whom he was engaged at the time of her tragic death in 1937. In 1936 Powell and Loy made the first of five sequels, *After the Thin Man,* then costarred in *The Great Ziegfeld,* in which she played Billie Burke to his Flo Ziegfeld, and *Libeled Lady,* which also featured Harlow and Spencer Tracy. All three were big hits, with *Ziegfeld* winning the Best Picture Academy Award.

During this period Powell, at the peak of his popularity, was loaned out several times. RKO starred him in two pretty good attempts to replicate *The Thin Man's* success: *Star of Midnight* (1935, with Ginger Rogers) and *The Ex-Mrs. Bradford* (1936, with Jean Arthur, his costar in Paramount's 1929 Philo Vance mystery, *The Greene Murder Case).* Universal paired him with ex-wife Carole Lombard, whom he'd divorced in 1933, in the classic screwball comedy *My Man Godfrey* (1936), which saw Powell in one of his most endearing roles (and netted him an Oscar nomination), as the educated tramp who becomes butler to a madcap Park Avenue family.

Back at MGM, Powell starred in *The Last of Mrs. Cheyney, The Emperor's Candlesticks,* and *Double Wedding* (all 1937, the last-named with Loy) before tragedy struck: Harlow's sudden death sent him into an emotional tailspin. His depression and a serious health problem kept him off the screen for more than a year. MGM reintroduced him to the public in *Another Thin Man* (1939) and he made his next three films with Loy as well: *I Love You Again* (1940), *Shadow of the*

Thin Man, and *Love Crazy* (both 1941).
Powell's subsequent starring vehicles,
even the Thin Man sequels, weren't terribly good, and after completing a run of
pictures that included *Crossroads* (1942),
*The Heavenly Body, The Thin Man Goes
Home* (both 1944), *Ziegfeld Follies* (1946,
in a cameo as the great showman), *The
Hoodlum Saint* (also 1946), and *Song of
the Thin Man* (1947), he left Metro to
freelance.

An aging Powell realized he couldn't
continue to play cocktail-swizzling urban-
ites forever, and undertook a wider variety
of roles, including the eccentric, red-
headed paterfamilias in the smash hit *Life
With Father* (1947, snaring his third Best
Actor Oscar nomination), a rakish politico
in *The Senator Was Indiscreet* (also 1947),
and a befuddled fisherman in *Mr. Peabody
and the Mermaid* (1948). Following
Dancing in the Dark and *Take One False
Step* (both 1949), he went back to MGM
for a cameo in the all-star *It's a Big Country* (1951), then played Elizabeth Taylor's
father in *The Girl Who Had Everything*
(1953). That same year he provided able
support to Betty Grable, Marilyn Monroe,
and Lauren Bacall in *How to Marry a
Millionaire.* His last role was that of the
worldly wise doctor in *Mister Roberts*
(1955), a good part (and a good film) to
round out a career.

Powell retired to Palm Springs, perfectly
content to while away his remaining years
with his young wife "Mousie," former
MGM starlet Diana Lewis, whom he'd
married in 1940. He was frequently offered "comeback" roles but declined them
all (although, according to some reports, a
few sorely tempted him).

POWER, TYRONE. Actor. *(b. May 5,
1913, Cincinnati; d. Nov. 15, 1958.)* In his
prime, as a 20th Century-Fox star of the
1930s and early 1940s, this dark-haired,
almost devilishly handsome star made
millions of female hearts flutter every
time he appeared on the big screen. He
even had that effect on some of his distaff
costars: Alice Faye once said kissing
Power "was like dying and going to
Heaven." And while he could hardly be
considered one of filmdom's finest actors,
Power got better as he got older, maturing
into an able performer who could have ac-

complished even more had he not died so
young.

The son of silent-movie actor Tyrone
Power (who died in 1931 shortly after
completing his only talkie, *The Big Trail*),
he resolved at an early age to follow in his
father's footsteps, acting on stage while
still in his teens and making his movie debut as a cadet in *Tom Brown of Culver*
(1932). He played bits in a few other films,
including *Flirtation Walk* (1934), before
being offered a contract by Darryl F.
Zanuck's 20th Century-Fox. Power was
assigned featured roles in *Girls' Dormitory, Ladies in Love* (both 1936), and
Lloyd's of London (also 1936, as the
grown-up character played as a youth by
top-billed Freddie Bartholomew) before
winning top billing in *Love Is News*
(1937), an insipid comedy-romance that
costarred Loretta Young. That same year
they appeared together in two other films,
Cafe Metropole and *Second Honeymoon.*

In Old Chicago (1938), Henry King's
epic of the Windy City at the time of the
1871 fire, had been planned for Clark Gable and Jean Harlow, who would have
been loaned to Zanuck by MGM in exchange for the services of Shirley Temple,
intended to star in *The Wizard of Oz.*
Harlow's sudden, tragic death scotched
the deal, and Zanuck, to preserve his investment in the project, ordered director
Henry King to cast the picture "in house."
King selected Power and Alice Faye, with
Zanuck's blessing (and, some say, his
urging). The picture was a huge success,
making Power a bona fide star at last. He,
Faye, and costar Don Ameche were reunited for King's *Alexander's Ragtime
Band* later that year; it was an even bigger
hit. Power and Faye did it one more time,
in *Rose of Washington Square* (1939), a
barely disguised version of entertainer
Fanny Brice's ill-fated marriage to gambler Nicky Arnstein; it too was a smash,
despite Power's limning of a basically unsympathetic character.

Loaned to MGM for *Marie Antoinette*
(1938), in which he starred opposite
Norma Shearer, Power spent the next sev-
eral years at Fox, racking up hit after hit:
Suez (1938), *Jesse James, The Rains
Came, Second Fiddle, Day-Time Wife* (all
1939), *Johnny Apollo, Brigham Young—
Frontiersman* (both 1940), *The Return of
Frank James* (1940, in a flashback of his
death scene from the 1939 picture), *The*

Mark of Zorro (also 1940, a superb re-make of the Douglas Fairbanks swash-buckler with a dashing Power wielding his rapier with great aplomb), *Blood and Sand* (1941, another remake, this time of a bull-fighting saga that originally starred Rudolph Valentino), *A Yank in the RAF* (also 1941, his only picture with top Fox star Betty Grable), *Son of Fury, This Above All, The Black Swan* (all 1942), and *Crash Dive* (1943).

Power then entered the armed services and remained there until the end of World War 2, distinguishing himself in action. He returned from the conflict a changed man, his once-boyish face sporting notice-able lines and a grim cast. Picking up at Fox where he'd left off, Power starred in the film version of Somerset Maugham's *The Razor's Edge* (1946), his own experi-ence lending credibility to his perfor-mance as the weary protagonist seeking truth and goodness. He played an outright rotter in *Nightmare Alley* (1947), one of his best parts, as a manipulative mind-reader at a successful carnival. *Captain From Castile* (also 1947), a sober adven-ture film, was one of his biggest successes of the postwar period. The remainder of his Fox films, however, were a mixed bag. Still a compelling figure on-screen, the star seemed increasingly tired and listless (although some of that was written into his characters): *The Luck of the Irish, That Wonderful Urge* (both 1948), *Prince of Foxes* (1949), *The Black Rose, An Ameri-can Guerilla in the Philippines* (both 1950), *Rawhide, I'll Never Forget You* (both 1951), *Diplomatic Courier, Pony Soldier* (both 1952), and *King of the Khyber Rifles* (1953).

Director John Ford pressed him into ser-vice for his West Point story, *The Long Gray Line* (1955), and he played the fa-mous pianist in *The Eddy Duchin Story* (1956). His last year on-screen, 1957, saw the release of three fine films, better than most he'd made that decade. *Abandon Ship!* was a taut drama about luxury-liner passengers set adrift in a small lifeboat. *The Sun Also Rises,* adapted from Ernest Hemingway's classic "lost generation" novel, featured a perfectly cast Power as Jake Barnes, the story's tragic protagonist. And he contributed a tour de force in his characterization of the murder suspect in Billy Wilder's *Witness for the Prosecu-tion,* adapted from Agatha Christie's short

story and play. Increasingly tired and nervous, drinking heavily and not taking care of himself, Power went overseas to shoot the Biblical epic *Solomon and Sheba,* but died of a heart attack while on location; his scenes were reshot with Yul Brynner in the role. Power's three wives included actresses Annabella (1939–48) and Linda Christian (1949–55); his daugh-ter by Christian, Taryn, was an actress during the 1970s. Tyrone Power, Jr., has also made a stab at movies, with such films as *Cocoon* (1985) and *Shag* (1989) to his credit.

PREMINGER, OTTO. Director, pro-ducer. (b. Dec. 5, 1906, Vienna, Austria; d. Apr. 23, 1986.) This bald dictatorial direc-tor of Austrian birth almost out–von Stroheimed von Stroheim in capitalizing on a forbidding public image. A former law student and onetime assistant to Ger-man stage director Max Reinhardt, Preminger directed a couple of German films before coming to America to stage plays on Broadway. He was spotted as a potential film director and signed by 20th Century-Fox. In Hollywood he almost im-mediately clashed with studio chief Darryl Zanuck; after directing two minor pic-tures, *Under Your Spell* (1936) and *Danger—Love at Work* (1937), he balked at what he felt to be a waste of time and energy. Suspended from directing, the imposing-looking Preminger turned to act-ing; after the outbreak of World War 2 he was much in demand to play Nazis, which he did quite well (in spite of being born Jewish) in *The Pied Piper* (1942), *Margin for Error,* and *They Got Me Covered* (both 1943). Finally given another chance at directing—taking over an unfinished film from Rouben Mamoulian—Preminger dis-tinguished himself with the 1944 thriller *Laura,* starring Gene Tierney and Dana Andrews; the movie was a big hit, and he was nominated for a Best Director Oscar. He went on to helm a number of prestige studio productions, including *Centennial Summer* (1946), *Forever Amber* (1947), *Where the Sidewalk Ends* (1950), and *An-gel Face* (1953).

Preminger turned independent producer in 1953, working outside the studio sys-tem for most of the remainder of his ca-reer, and consistently attracting major talent for his projects. His first was the disarmingly benign romantic comedy *The Moon Is Blue,* which caused great controversy at the time for its then-saucy dialogue, replete with words like "mistress" and "virgin." That year he briefly returned to acting, doing the Nazi bit again in Billy Wilder's cynical P.O.W. drama *Stalag 17.* Preminger's own films ran an amazing gamut of subjects and treatments, from the all-black musicals *Carmen Jones* (1954) and *Porgy and Bess* (1959) to *The Man With the Golden Arm* (1955), a harrowing portrait of drug addiction starring Frank Sinatra, and *Saint Joan* (1957), the Bernard Shaw version of Joan of Arc, which introduced newcomer Jean Seberg. In subsequent years Preminger made increasingly bigger, more ambitious projects, like the sizzling courtroom melodrama *Anatomy of a Murder* (1959), the sprawling historical drama *Exodus* (1960), the lengthy Senate spectacular *Advise and Consent* (1962), the all-star war picture *In Harm's Way* (1965), and the sensational Southern racial melodrama *Hurry Sundown* (1967).

A competent technician revered by cultish critics but dismissed by mainstream types, Preminger found himself adrift in the late 1960s, helming the legendary LSD-themed bomb *Skidoo* (1968), bouncing back with the sensitive drama *Tell Me That You Love Me, Junie Moon* (1970), and the outrageous *Such Good Friends* (1971). His last film was *The Human Factor* (1979), an adaptation of a Graham Greene novel. A popular talk-show guest during the 1970s and 1980s, witty and articulate, he never ducked an issue—except regarding details of his life and career. "Preminger: An Autobiography" was published in 1977.

OTHER FILMS INCLUDE: 1944: *In the Meantime, Darling;* 1945: *A Royal Scandal* (codirected with Ernst Lubitsch), *Fallen Angel;* 1947: *Daisy Kenyon;* 1949: *The Fan, Whirlpool;* 1951: *The 13th Letter;* 1954: *River of No Return;* 1955: *The Court-Martial of Billy Mitchell;* 1958: *Bonjour Tristesse;* 1963: *The Cardinal* (Oscar-nominated as Best Director); 1965: *Bunny Lake Is Missing;* 1975: *Rosebud.*

PRESLEY, ELVIS. Singer; actor. *(b. Jan. 8, 1935, Tupelo, Miss.; d. Aug. 16, 1977.)* The King of Rock 'n' Roll scored big in his initial screen outings, revealing early on a

genuine charisma; later he even learned to act. After a creditable debut in a supporting role in *Love Me Tender* (1956, renamed at the last minute to capitalize on that hit song, which had been released just prior to the movie), he went on to star in *Loving You* (1957) and the film many consider his best, *Jailhouse Rock* (1957). These films depicted a snarling Elvis, not the kind of boy a girl would bring home to Mother. He seemed to get better with each new film, and was given some solid properties like *King Creole* (1958) and *Flaming Star* (1960, in which he played a half-breed Indian).

After his celebrated Army hitch, however, Elvis' pictures became more bland and standardized. *Blue Hawaii* (1961), *Viva Las Vegas,* and *Roustabout* (both 1964) were fun, but the formula soon wore thin, and the scores produced fewer Presley hits. Col. Tom Parker, who guided Presley's career, had no interest in the quality of his movie vehicles; he just counted the money and made sure Elvis kept working. Producers like Hal Wallis and Sam Katzman had no incentive to make better Presley movies when the potboilers they were turning out kept turning a profit. By the time someone realized it was important to give Elvis' screen career a shot of adrenalin, audiences weren't interested, and mediocre films like *Charro!* and *Change of Habit* (both 1969) couldn't turn things around. The entertainer fared much better in a pair of whitewashed cinéma verité–style performance documentaries, *Elvis: That's the Way It Is* (1970) and *Elvis on Tour* (1972).

Barbra Streisand approached Presley to play the Norman Maine role in her rock remake of *A Star Is Born* (1976), which could have changed the course of his career—and offered him his greatest challenge—but Colonel Tom nixed the idea. Presley died of a heart attack at his Tennessee mansion, Graceland; his death at the age of 42 was brought on, apparently, by years of dependence on amphetamine drugs. He has been portrayed in a number of films and TV movies, most notably John Carpenter's telefilm *Elvis* (1979), in which he was played by Kurt Russell, who as a child had appeared with Presley in *It Happened at the World's Fair* (1963). He has also been the subject of many documentaries, including the theatrically released hybrid film *This Is Elvis*

(1981), which combined actual Presley footage with reenactments of incidents in his life.

OTHER FILMS INCLUDE: 1960: *G.I. Blues;* 1961: *Wild in the Country;* 1962: *Follow That Dream, Kid Galahad, Girls! Girls! Girls!;* 1963: *Fun in Acapulco;* 1964: *Kissin' Cousins;* 1965: *Girl Happy, Tickle Me, Harum Scarum;* 1966: *Frankie and Johnny, Paradise, Hawaiian Style, Spinout;* 1967: *Easy Come, Easy Go, Double Trouble, Clambake;* 1968: *Stay Away, Joe, Speedway, Live a Little, Love a Little;* 1969: *The Trouble With Girls.*

PRESTON, KELLY. Actress. *(b. Oct. 13, 1962, Honolulu.)* This sexy blonde actress has shown comic flair in a handful of films, notably *Secret Admirer, Mischief* (both 1985), and *Only You* (1992) and was well cast as an alluring witch in *Spellbinder* (1988), but she has spent most of her time in potboilers. She finally got a break, playing Arnold Schwarzenegger's love interest in *Twins* (1988), but it didn't lead to better parts, or better films. *The Experts* (1989) was deemed so bad by its studio that it didn't receive theatrical release at all, but it did serve to introduce Preston to John Travolta, who married her. Her other credits include *Christine* (1983), *52 Pick-Up, SpaceCamp* (both 1986), *Love at Stake* (1987), *Run* (1990, as a brunette), *Arthur Miller's "The American Clock"* (1993 telefilm), and *Love Is a Gun* (1994).

PRESTON, ROBERT. Actor. *(b. June 8, 1918, Newton Highlands, Mass., as Robert Meservey; d. Mar. 21, 1987.)* He's the guy who had trouble, right there in River City, in *The Music Man* (1962), his most memorable starring vehicle. But in fact the virile, ebullient Preston had been a fixture in movies since the late 1930s, often playing secondary leads and heavies, though even his unsympathetic characters possessed a certain ration of charm and warmth. He was barely 20 years old when a Paramount talent scout spotted him at the Pasadena Playhouse, and before the year was out he had joined the studio's roster of contract players. First appearing in B pictures such as 1938's *Illegal Traffic* and *King of Alcatraz,* he quickly graduated to supporting roles in A productions such as 1939's *Union Pacific* and *Beau Geste.*

Preston finally won costar billing as the male lead in *Typhoon* (1940), after which he switched effortlessly from leads to character parts, sometimes getting the girl, sometimes not. He played larger-than-life parts for Cecil B. DeMille, for whom he'd worked on *Union Pacific,* in *Northwest Mounted Police* (1940) and *Reap the Wild Wind* (1942), and later in the decade had meaty costarring roles in *The Macomber Affair* (1947), *Whispering Smith* (1948; he had one of his best parts in this Alan Ladd Western), and *Blood on the Moon* (1948; another superior characterization of a Western heavy). He eschewed big-screen roles for much of the 1950s, concentrating on stage work. In 1958 he scored an astounding triumph on Broadway as the star of "The Music Man," Meredith Willson's paean to rural America of the early 20th century, which earned him the first of two Tony Awards. (He earned his second costarring with Mary Martin in the musical "I Do! I Do!" in 1966.) He reprised the role for Warner Bros.' 1962 film adaptation of *The Music Man,* pleasantly surprising moviegoers who heretofore had seen him mostly in Westerns, war pictures, and melodramas. After completing *Island of Love* (a comedy) and *All the Way Home* (a drama) in 1963, Preston left the screen again, this time for nearly a decade. His film work thereafter was scattershot, although he enjoyed colorful character parts in *Semi-Tough* (1977), *S.O.B.* (1981), and *Victor/Victoria* (1982, earning a Best Supporting Actor Oscar nomination as the gay mentor of cabaret star Julie Andrews in this stylish Blake Edwards farce).

Preston took a brief fling in TV during the early 1950s, starring in "Man Against Crime" (1951) and "Anywhere, USA" (1952), but did most of his work in that medium during the late 1970s and 1980s, as one of the stars of the 1979 miniseries "The Chisholms," and in the telefilms *My Father's House* (1975), *September Gun* (1983), *Finnegan Begin Again* (1985), and *Outrage!* (1986), among others.

OTHER FILMS INCLUDE: 1939: *Disbarred;* 1940: *Moon Over Burma;* 1941: *The Lady From Cheyenne, Parachute Battalion, New York Town, The Night of January 16th;* 1942: *Star Spangled Rhythm, This Gun for Hire, Wake Island;* 1943: *Night Plane from Chungking;* 1947: *Wild Harvest, Variety Girl;* 1949: *Tulsa, The Lady Gambles;* 1950: *The Sun-*

downers; 1951: *When I Grow Up, Best of the Badmen, Cloudburst;* 1952: *Face to Face;* 1956: *The Last Frontier;* 1960: *The Dark at the Top of the Stairs;* 1962: *How the West Was Won;* 1972: *Junior Bonner, Child's Play;* 1974: *Mame;* 1984: *The Last Starfighter.*

PRICE, VINCENT. Actor. *(b. May 27, 1911, St. Louis, Mo., d. Oct. 25, 1993.)* It's odd that this well-educated, urbane, velvet-voiced actor found his greatest success—for at least one generation, anyway—as the King of the Horror Movie. A Yale graduate with a master's degree in theater arts from the University of London, he began a stage career in England, then returned to the U.S. in the mid 1930s, appearing on Broadway in "Victoria Regina" opposite Helen Hayes. Price went to Hollywood in 1938, debuting in *Service De Luxe,* an ill-fated attempt to make him a conventional romantic leading man. Many of his early films were costume dramas—*The Private Lives of Elizabeth and Essex* (1939), *The House of the Seven Gables* (1940), *The Song of Bernadette* (1943)—but he also showed a flair for unusual characters, notably in *Tower of London* (1939) and *The Invisible Man Returns* (1940).

Price built a solid reputation in the 1940s as a utility player at 20th Century-Fox, where he appeared in *Brigham Young—Frontiersman* (1940, as the founder of the Mormon church, Joseph Smith), *Hudson's Bay* (1940), *The Song of Bernadette, The Eve of St. Mark, Wilson, Keys of the Kingdom, Laura* (all 1944, the last a personal favorite of his), *A Royal Scandal, Leave Her to Heaven* (both 1945), and *Dragonwyck* (1946), among others. His distinctive half-sneering smile, sly manner, and sinister chuckle marked him as a suave screen menace; even in sympathetic roles he seldom seemed wholly trustworthy. He was a perfect Richelieu in *The Three Musketeers* (1948), a hilariously distraught soap tycoon in *Champagne for Caesar* (1950), and the cunning land-grabber called *The Baron of Arizona* (also 1950). In 1953, he starred in what remains his most popular film, the 3-D smash *House of Wax,* in which he played a mad sculptor who uses molten wax to make statues of corpses!

After *The Ten Commandments, While the City Sleeps* (both 1956), and *The Story of Mankind* (1957) the siren call of terror beckoned, and in rapid order came *The Fly, House on Haunted Hill* (both 1958), *The Bat, The Tingler,* and *Return of the Fly* (all 1959). In 1960, he signed with Roger Corman for *House of Usher,* and over the next five years became the principal screen interpreter of Poe in six more Corman adaptations, including *The Pit and the Pendulum* (1961), the farcical *The Raven* (1963), *The Masque of the Red Death* (1964), and *Tomb of Ligeia* (1965). Price continued to mine a livelihood from the dead, so to speak, in such chillers as the new version of *Tower of London* (1962, this time in the starring role), another spoof, *The Comedy of Terrors* (1964), *The Conqueror Worm* (1968), *Madhouse* (1974), and a trio of black comedies: *The Abominable Dr. Phibes* (1971), *Dr. Phibes Rises Again* (1972), and *Theatre of Blood* (1973); in the latter, as a Shakespearean ham who literally slays the critics, Price can be seen at his very best.

With the passing of years, good parts became fewer; Price often appeared on television and even spoofed his "image" in TV commercials. When asked why he agreed to appear in some of the terrible films he made, he explained without apology that as an actor, it was his job to act. He also used the money to support his passion for art, often turning in "per diem" money on location, and downgrading travel accommodations, to buy paintings. (Price wrote several books on art, and several more on his other great passion, food.)

His indelible identification with the macabre had its benefits: in the 1980s he was selected to host the PBS anthology series "Mystery," and was asked to recite a poem as a part of Michael Jackson's widely seen music video "Thriller" (1982). He also inspired a young filmmaker named Tim Burton to make a stop-motion animation short (with partner Rich Heinricks) called *Vincent* (1982), about a boy obsessed with Vincent Price. Price was so pleased with the project that he agreed to narrate the film. Toward the end of his life he had a handful of good parts: as the speaking and singing voice of cartoon villain Ratigan in the Disney studio's *The Great Mouse Detective* (1986), as an elegant Russian count in *The Whales of August* (1987), and as the kindly inventor who brings the title character to life in Tim Burton's *Edward Scissorhands* (1990). He was visibly frail in that film, but rose to the occasion, a thorough professional to the end. Price's final appearance was in the cable-TV movie *The Heart of Justice* (1993).

PROCHNOW, JURGEN. Actor. *(b. June 10, 1941, Berlin.)* His acting career began when he joined an amateur theater company at age 14, but this powerful performer first stunned international movie audiences as the dedicated submarine commander in Wolfgang Petersen's tense WW2 drama *Das Boot* (1981). Prochnow worked frequently in repertory theater and on television before making his film debut in *Zoff* (1971), and followed it with appearances in *The Brutalization of Franz Blum* (1974), *The Lost Honor of Katharina Blum* (1975), and *The Consequence* (1977, also directed by Petersen). His commanding presence made Prochnow an effective heavy in such American films as *Beverly Hills Cop II* (1987) and *The Seventh Sign* (1988), though he played the sympathetic Duke Leto in David Lynch's *Dune* (1984). Prochnow has also appeared in *The Keep* (1983), *A Dry White Season* (1989), *The Fourth War,* and *The Man Inside* (both 1990). He costarred in the TV miniseries "Danielle Steel's Jewels" (1992) and "The Fire Next Time" (1993); other recent credits include *Twin Peaks: Fire Walk With Me* (1992), *Body of Evidence* (1993), *In the Mouth of Madness,* and *Judge Dredd* (both 1995).

PROSKY, ROBERT. Actor. *(b. Dec. 13, 1930, Philadelphia.)* Gruff, bearlike character actor with broad stage experience who started appearing in movies at a relatively late age, but has more than made up for it, playing such colorful roles as a criminal mastermind in *Thief* (1981), a Vatican bigwig in *Monsignor* (1982), a European priest in *The Keep,* a military academy officer in *The Lords of Discipline* (both 1983), a shady gambler in *The Natural* (1984), a Russian acting teacher in *Outrageous Fortune* (1987), a friendly Mafia don in *Things Change* (1988), and a thinly disguised Grandpa Munster TV personality in *Gremlins 2 The New Batch* (1990). He has also worked extensively in

the theater (notably as a Russian diplomat in "A Walk in the Woods" on Broadway), and is probably best known as the crusty Sgt. Jablonski on "Hill Street Blues" (1984–87). Recent credits include *Hoffa* (1992), *Last Action Hero* (as the projectionist), *Rudy,* and *Mrs. Doubtfire* (all 1993).

PRYCE, JONATHAN. Actor. *(b. June 1, 1947, Holywell, North Wales.)* Subtle, incisive actor who can play Casper Milquetoast types and sinister villains alike. A stage veteran, Pryce studied at London's Royal Academy of Dramatic Art and acted with the Royal Shakespeare Company in such productions as "Measure for Measure" and "Antony and Cleopatra." His early film credits include *Voyage of the Damned* (1976), *Loophole* (1980), *The Ploughman's Lunch* (1983), and *Something Wicked This Way Comes* (also 1983, as Mr. Dark), but it was his performance as the timid clerk Sam Lowry in Terry Gilliam's nightmare comedy *Brazil* (1985) that made him a movie "name." He has since appeared in some very negligible comedies like *Haunted Honeymoon, Jumpin' Jack Flash* (both 1986), and *Consuming Passions* (1988), in addition to Gilliam's *The Adventures of Baron Munchausen* and *The Rachel Papers* (both 1989). Pryce was memorable as Al Pacino's potential client in *Glengarry Glen Ross* (1992), Monsieur Rivière in *The Age of Innocence* (1993), and especially as the ice-like Henry Kravis in the TV movie *Barbarians at the Gate* (1993). He won the Best Actor award at Cannes for *Carrington* (1995). On Broadway, he won Tony Awards for "Comedians" (1977) and "Miss Saigon" (1990), the latter causing a furor from Actors' Equity over objections to a white man playing a Eurasian part.

PRYOR, RICHARD. Actor, screenwriter, director. *(b. Dec. 1, 1940, Peoria, Ill.)* A groundbreaking standup comic who became a major screen personality, Pryor's personal life has been more dramatic than anything a screenwriter could concoct. After dropping out of school, Pryor (who claimed to have grown up in a brothel) served a two-year hitch in the Army, then started working in nightclubs, eventually making a name for himself. Variety and talk-show appearances on TV led to occasional movie work (in 1967's *The Busy Body,* 1968's *Wild in the Streets,* and 1971's *Dynamite Chicken*) and a prominent supporting role with Diana Ross in *Lady Sings the Blues* (1972). He also worked as one of the writers of Mel Brooks' classic comedy spoof *Blazing Saddles* (1974).

As censorship barriers began to fall, Pryor came into his own; his profane but sharp-eyed observations about American life and the black experience made him hugely popular. An unexpurgated film record of a 1979 performance was released as *Richard Pryor—Live in Concert,* which showcases the comedian at his very best. (Subsequent concert movies, glitzier to be sure, were not quite as good: 1982's *Richard Pryor Live on the Sunset Strip* and 1983's *Richard Pryor Here and Now.*)

Meanwhile, Hollywood was trying to find a way to capitalize on this formidable talent. Television was not ready for Pryor; his NBC comedy series was canceled after just a handful of shows in 1977. He seemed to fare best in supporting roles, as in *Car Wash, The Bingo Long Traveling All-Stars & Motor Kings* (both 1976), *The Wiz,* and *Blue Collar* (both 1978), though even in that capacity he was often let down by bad material, as in *California Suite* (1978, teamed with Bill Cosby), *In God We Trust* (1980, as God), and *Wholly Moses* (also 1980). His starring films were a very mixed bag: *Which Way Is Up?, Greased Lightning* (both 1977), *Bustin' Loose* (1981), *Some Kind of Hero, The Toy* (both 1982), *Superman III* (1983), and *Brewster's Millions* (1985). At their best, they gave Pryor a stage for some moments of high comedy; at their worst, they straitjacketed him into a Hollywood formula that suppressed his comic instincts.

One of Pryor's best opportunities came in the romantic comedy thriller *Silver Streak* (1976), in which he supported the film's star, Gene Wilder. Their scenes together were so good, and their chemistry so obvious, that they were reteamed (under Sidney Poitier's direction) for a costarring comedy, *Stir Crazy* (1980), which was an even bigger hit. (Unfortunately, their reteamings a decade later, in 1989's *See No Evil, Hear No Evil* and 1991's *Another You* were pathetically poor.)

Pryor's career came to a temporary halt at the start of the 1980s; while preparing a highly volatile cocaine mixture called freebase, he lit himself on fire, suffering third-degree burns over half his body. (He was about to start filming Mel Brooks' *History of the World—Part I,* and was replaced at the last minute by Gregory Hines.) The comedian made an amazing recovery, and reflected on his tumultuous life in the autobiographical comedy-drama *Jo Jo Dancer, Your Life Is Calling* (1986), which he cowrote, produced, and directed. His subsequent films—*Critical Condition* (1987), the bland but amusing *Moving* (1988), and the Eddie Murphy fiasco *Harlem Nights* (1989)—were unable to restore the luster to his once red-hot movie career. Failing health (he is a victim of multiple sclerosis) made it difficult for him to get through his last film with Gene Wilder in 1991, but he managed somehow; it just seemed a shame to expend that effort for a movie that (like so many others before it) failed to make the most of his unique comic gift.

By 1992, Pryor seemed to be headed for retirement. In addition to accolades for his screen work, Pryor has won several Grammy awards for his comedy recordings.

PULLMAN, BILL. Actor. *(b. Dec. 17, 1953, Delhi, N.Y.)* Until 1995, movie buffs had come to think of this actor as the Ralph Bellamy of the 1990s: he never got the girl! This impression was driven home by his 1993 output: *Sommersby* (a serious part, and a forceful performance, as Jodie Foster's suitor), *Sleepless in Seattle* (a comic turn as Meg Ryan's wimpy fiancé), and *Malice* (in which he has the girl—at first—then loses her to Alec Baldwin). After years of stage work, Pullman made a big impression in his film debut in *Ruthless People* (1986) as Earl, the so-called stupidest person on the face of the Earth. He went on to play Lone Starr in Mel Brooks' sci-fi parody *Spaceballs* (1987), and then changed venues as the anthropologist in the horror-thriller *The Serpent and the Rainbow* (1988). Since then, Pullman has been featured in *The Accidental Tourist* (1988), *Cold Feet* (1989), *Sibling Rivalry* (1990), *Liebestraum* (1991), *Newsies, A League of Their Own* (as Geena Davis' husband) and *Singles* (all

1992), *The Favor,* and *Wyatt Earp* (both 1994). His career shifted into high gear with *The Last Seduction* (also 1994), *Casper* and, especially, *While You Were Sleeping* (both 1995), in which he finally does get the girl.

QUAID, DENNIS. Actor. *(b. Apr. 9, 1954, Houston.)* With boyish good looks, an easy manner, and a lopsided grin, Dennis Quaid should have been an instant candidate for stardom. But this son of a Houston electrician worked as an amusement-park clown and a singing waiter before making his film debut in *September 30, 1955* (1978). Quaid toiled in many movies—including *I Never Promised You a Rose Garden* (1977), *Seniors* (1978), *Breaking Away* (1979), *Gorp* (1980), *The Long Riders* (1980, a Western in which he appeared with brother Randy), *All Night Long, Caveman, The Night the Lights Went Out in Georgia* (all 1981), *Tough Enough* (1982) and *Jaws 3-D* (1983) —before hitting pay dirt as astronaut Gordon Cooper in *The Right Stuff* (1983), which elevated him to leading-man status. His dimpled smile and insouciant manner have accounted for his success at least as much as his acting ability, which is considerable. He met his wife, Meg Ryan, while costarring with her in *Innerspace* (1987); they were reteamed in *D.O.A.* (1988). His other starring vehicles include *Dreamscape* (1984), *Enemy Mine* (1985), *The Big Easy* (1987, one of his best parts, as a stylish New Orleans homicide detective), *Suspect* (also 1987), the underrated *Everybody's All-American* (1988), *Great Balls of Fire!* (1989, in which he played rocker Jerry Lee Lewis), and *Come See the Paradise* (1990). He also had a brief but memorable bit part in *Postcards From the Edge* (1990), playing a cocky Tinseltown type who beds a vulnerable Meryl Streep but gets a hilarious comeuppance. More recently, he's starred in *Wilder Napalm, Undercover Blues, Flesh and Bone* (all 1993, in the last with Ryan), and *Wyatt Earp* (1994, as Doc Holliday). Also a musician, Quaid performs with his band, "The Eclectics," whenever his schedule allows.

QUAID, RANDY. Actor. *(b. Oct. 1, 1950, Houston.)* His ungainly bulk and jowly, hangdog countenance rule out this fine actor for the conventional leading-man assignments such as those given his younger brother Dennis, but Randy has done pretty well for himself as a supporting player and offbeat character lead. Director Peter Bogdanovich more or less discovered him as a drama student and featured him in several of his early films: *Targets* (1968), *The Last Picture Show* (1971), *What's Up, Doc?* (1972), and *Paper Moon* (1973). He earned an Oscar nomination for his role as a hapless sailor in *The Last Detail* (1973), and over the years has landed a series of multifaceted roles that attest to his versatility: Chevy Chase's addlebrained relative in *National Lampoon's Vacation* (1983) and *National Lampoon's Christmas Vacation* (1989), Lennie to Robert Blake's George in a TV remake of *Of Mice and Men* (1981), Mitch in a distinguished TV version of *A Streetcar Named Desire* (1984), President Lyndon Johnson (an inspired piece of casting) in *LBJ: The Early Years* (1987, telefilm), and the Frankenstein monster in a cable TV version of *Frankenstein* (1993). He also spent one season on TV's "Saturday Night Live" (1985–86). He's appeared with brother Dennis on stage in Sam Shepard's play "True West," and on film in *The Long Riders* (1980) with several other sets of acting brothers. He also starred in his own TV sitcom, "Davis Rules" (1990–92).
OTHER FILMS INCLUDE: 1974: *The Apprenticeship of Duddy Kravitz;* 1975: *Breakout;* 1976: *The Missouri Breaks, Bound for Glory;* 1977: *The Choirboys;* 1978: *Midnight Express;* 1980: *Foxes, Guyana Tragedy: The Story of Jim Jones* (telefilm); 1981: *Heartbeeps;* 1984: *The Wild Life;* 1985: *The Slugger's Wife, Fool for Love;* 1986: *The Wraith, Sweet Country;* 1987: *No Man's Land, Dear America* (voice only); 1988: *Caddyshack II, Moving;* 1989: *Parents, Out Cold, Bloodhounds of Broadway;* 1990: *Days of Thunder, Quick Change, Texasville;* 1993: *Freaked, "Murder in the Heartland"* (miniseries); 1994: *Major League II, The Paper.*

QUAYLE, ANTHONY (SIR). Actor. *(b. Sept. 7, 1913, Ainsdale, England; d. Oct. 20, 1989.)* Ruddy-faced, distinguished British stage actor, a graduate of the Royal Academy of Dramatic Art, who in his big-screen assignments specialized in authoritative characters both sympathetic and

unsympathetic—he was the King who was not amused by court jester Woody Allen in 1972's *Everything You Always Wanted to Know About Sex (But Were Afraid to Ask)*. An Old Vic regular who served with the Royal Artillery during World War 2, Quayle had small roles in the films *I Stand Condemned* (1935) and *Pygmalion* (1938), but primarily confined himself to acting and directing for the stage until 1948, when he played Marcellus in Laurence Olivier's film adaptation of *Hamlet*. He earned an Academy Award nomination for his portrayal of Cardinal Wolsey in *Anne of the Thousand Days* (1969). He also wrote two books, "Eight Hours From England" and "On Such a Night." Quayle was knighted in 1985. Trivia buffs take note: He appeared in *two* films that pitted fictional detective Sherlock Holmes against real-life killer Jack the Ripper—*A Study in Terror* (1965) and *Murder by Decree* (1979).
OTHER FILMS INCLUDE: 1948: *Saraband for Dead Lovers;* 1956: *The Wrong Man;* 1959: *Tarzan's Greatest Adventure;* 1961: *The Guns of Navarone;* 1962: *Lawrence of Arabia;* 1964: *The Fall of the Roman Empire;* 1965: *Operation Crossbow;* 1966: *The Poppy Is Also a Flower;* 1969: *Before Winter Comes, Mackenna's Gold;* 1974: *The Tamarind Seed;* 1977: *The Eagle Has Landed;* 1978: *The Chosen;* 1988: *Buster, Silent Night;* 1990: *King of the Wind.*

QUINLAN, KATHLEEN. Actress. *(b. Nov. 19, 1954, Pasadena, Calif.)* This stately, beautiful brunette brings a poetic appeal to all her roles, no matter how mundane— and she's had more than her share of mundane roles. A veteran of 1970s TV shows and made-fors (her first feature was 1972's *One Is a Lonely Number* and she had a small part in *American Graffiti* the following year), she won her first lead in *Lifeguard* (1976), and then earned great acclaim for her skillful performance as a teenaged schizophrenic in *I Never Promised You a Rose Garden* (1977). Big things were predicted for her, but *The Promise* (1979), *The Runner Stumbles* (1979), *Sunday Lovers* (1980), *Hanky Panky* (1982), and *Independence Day* (1983) squandered her abilities. Excellent as a compassionate, repressed schoolteacher thrust into a bizarre environment in Joe Dante's segment of 1983's *Twilight Zone—The Movie*, Quinlan spent much of the decade toiling in made-for-TV movies, surfacing occasionally in lackluster feature films. By 1988 she was playing supporting roles, backing up Bruce Willis in *Sunset* and Whoopi Goldberg in *Clara's Heart*. In 1991 she came back with a vengeance, in a plum role as a journalist who initiates rock star Jim Morrison into the dark arts in Oliver Stone's *The Doors*. Quinlan's shot at stardom may have come and gone, but it's certainly not too late for her to be offered the solid parts she deserves. She was most recently featured in *Apollo 13* (1995).

QUINN, AIDAN. Actor. *(b. Mar. 8, 1959, Chicago.)* Handsome, sensitive leading man with pale blue eyes, introduced to moviegoers as a James Dean wannabe in his debut film, *Reckless* (1984). He made more of an impression the following year as the nominal male lead in *Desperately Seeking Susan* (1985) and won critical kudos as an AIDS victim in the landmark telefilm *An Early Frost* (also 1985), which made it clear that this was an actor worth watching. Born to Irish immigrant parents in Chicago, his family moved back and forth from the U.S. to Ireland during his youth, and only after holding a variety of odd jobs did Quinn decide to focus on acting. He amassed some stage experience in Chicago and New York, and has matured into one of the screen's most interesting and intelligent young actors. His other credits include *The Mission* (1986), *Stakeout* (1987), *Crusoe* (1988, in the title role), *The Handmaid's Tale, The Lemon Sisters, Avalon* (all 1990, in the last as a young Jewish patriarch), *At Play in the Fields of the Lord* (1991), *The Playboys* (1992, which brought him back to Ireland), *A Private Matter* (1992, telefilm, opposite Sissy Spacek), *Benny & Joon* (1993), *Blink, Legends of the Fall,* and *Mary Shelley's Frankenstein* (all 1994).

QUINN, ANTHONY. Actor. *(b. Apr. 21, 1915, Chihuahua, Mexico.)* Dynamic, prolific character actor and occasional leading man who, during the course of his nearly 60 years in motion pictures, has played nearly every exotic ethnic type imaginable at least once. For much of his screen career an effective, quietly persuasive performer, Quinn in recent years has taken to overacting and has sometimes exercised poor judgment in accepting roles. Born to an Irish father and Mexican mother, Quinn enjoyed a brief career as a prizefighter before entering movies in 1936.

He had small roles in *Parole, Sworn Enemy,* and *Night Waitress* (all 1936) before signing with Paramount, for which he appeared exclusively until 1940, mostly playing gangsters and Indians. Quinn's Paramount films include *The Plainsman* (1936, directed by Cecil B. DeMille, who became Quinn's father-in-law the following year), *Waikiki Wedding, The Last Train From Madrid, Daughter of Shanghai* (all 1937), *The Buccaneer* (also for DeMille), *Dangerous to Know, Tip-Off Girls, Bulldog Drummond in Africa, King of Alcatraz* (all 1938), *King of Chinatown, Television Spy,* DeMille's *Union Pacific* (all 1939), *Parole Fixer, The Ghost Breakers,* and *Road to Singapore* (all 1940).

During the war years Quinn worked mostly at Warner Bros. and 20th Century-Fox, although he did return to Paramount for a hilarious deadpan turn as an Arab sheik in the Crosby-Hope vehicle *Road to Morocco* (1942). Still a character player, he was assigned increasingly important and showy roles in bigger, more expensive pictures, including *City for Conquest* (1940), *Blood and Sand, Manpower* (both 1941), *They Died With Their Boots On* (also 1941, as Chief Crazy Horse), *The Black Swan, Larceny, Inc.* (both 1942), *The Ox-Bow Incident, Guadalcanal Diary* (both 1943), *Buffalo Bill, Roger Touhy, Gangster, Irish Eyes are Smiling* (all 1944), *Where Do We Go From Here?* and *Back to Bataan* (both 1945, superb in the latter as a Filipino guerilla, costarring with John Wayne).

Quinn and his wife Katherine, DeMille's adopted daughter and a talented actress in her own right, starred together in *Black Gold* (1947), a low-budget sleeper released by Allied Artists. Playing a proud but kindly Indian who discovers oil on his property and allows a Chinese refugee to race his prize thoroughbred, Quinn delivered a warm, heartfelt performance that ranks among his best. He subsequently appeared in *Sinbad the Sailor, Tycoon* (both 1947), *The Brave Bulls* (1951, marvelous in this bullfighting story), *Against All Flags,* and *The Brigand* before winning his first Academy Award as the brother of a Mexican revolutionary (played by Marlon Brando) in *Viva Zapata!* (all 1952). (He also replaced Brando in the original Broadway production of "A Streetcar Named Desire.")

Quinn's career picked up following his Oscar win; he got better roles and worked almost nonstop throughout the remainder of the decade. High spots include *La Strada* (1954, the classic Fellini film and Best Foreign Film Oscar-winner, in which he played a brutish, simple-minded strongman who tours with acrobat Richard Basehart), *Ulysses* (1955, as Antinous), *Lust for Life* (1956, playing artist Paul Gauguin, a performance for which he won his second Best Supporting Actor Oscar), and *The Hunchback of Notre Dame* (1957, playing the hunchbacked Quasimodo to Gina Lollobrigida's Esmeralda). His other 1950s films include *Mask of the Avenger* (1951), *The World in His Arms* (1952), *Seminole, City Beneath the Sea, Ride, Vaquero!, Blowing Wild* (all 1953), *The Long Wait* (1954), *The Magnificent Matador, Seven Cities of Gold* (all 1955), *The Wild Party* (1956), *The River's Edge, Wild Is the Wind* (both 1957, Oscar-nominated for his work in the latter), *Hot Spell* (1958), *Warlock,* and *Last Train From Gun Hill* (both 1959). His father-in-law gave Quinn a shot at directing with the 1958 remake of *The Buccaneer,* a critical and commercial disappointment.

In 1959 he chalked up a memorable portrayal as a stoic Eskimo in *The Savage Innocents.* By now his once slender, swarthy face had become craggy, and he'd put on quite a bit of weight. That stood him in good stead for his role as the former prizefighter humiliated by his work as a "professional" wrestler in *Requiem for a Heavyweight* (1962). That same year he contributed a vibrant performance as an amoral Bedouin chieftain (who is "a river to my people") in David Lean's *Lawrence of Arabia.* In 1964 he secured another Academy Award nomination, this time for his starring role in *Zorba the Greek,* the story of an earthy Greek peasant he helped produce (and a role to which he returned a quarter-century later on Broadway). He again played a robust Greek character in *A Dream of Kings* (1969), a low-key drama set in Chicago's Greek community.

In 1965 he divorced Katherine DeMille, by whom he'd had three children.

The 1970s saw the beginning of a decline for Quinn, who increasingly took roles in poor American-made pictures and poorer foreign ones. Moreover, his burgeoning tendency to overact was not curbed by most of his directors. He has remained a compelling on-screen figure, however, even in his latter-day films.
OTHER FILMS INCLUDE: 1960: *Heller in Pink Tights;* 1961: *The Guns of Navarone;* 1962: *Barabbas* (in the title role); 1964: *Behold a Pale Horse;* 1965: *A High Wind in Jamaica, Marco the Magnificent;* 1966: *Lost Command;* 1967: *The 25th Hour, The Happening;* 1968: *Guns for San Sebastian, The Shoes of the Fisherman* (in the last-named as a Russian-born Pope); 1969: *The Secret of Santa Vittoria;* 1970: *Flap, R.P.M., A Walk in the Spring Rain;* 1971: *Arruza;* 1972: *Across 110th Street;* 1973: *Deaf Smith and Johnny Ears, The Don Is Dead;* 1974: *The Destructors;* 1977: *Mohammad, Messenger of God;* 1978: *Caravans, The Children of Sanchez, The Greek Tycoon* (in the latter as an Onassis-type billionaire); 1979: *The Passage;* 1981: *Lion of the Desert, The Salamander;* 1982: *Valentino/1919;* 1985: *Ingrid;* 1988: "Onassis: The Richest Man in the World" (miniseries); 1989: *Stradivari;* 1990: *Revenge, Ghosts Can't Do It* (opposite Bo Derek, a career low point); 1991: *A Star for Two* (opposite Lauren Bacall), *Mobsters, Jungle Fever, Only the Lonely* (wooing Maureen O'Hara); 1993: *Last Action Hero;* 1994: *This Can't Be Love* (telefilm, opposite Katharine Hepburn).

RADNER, GILDA. Actress. *(b. June 28, 1946, Detroit, Mich.; d. May 20, 1989.)* One of the original "Not Ready for Prime Time Players" of TV's "Saturday Night Live," this talented comedic actress studied drama at the University of Michigan before dropping out and moving to Toronto, where she made her stage debut in a 1972 production of "Godspell." A stint with the Second City comedy troupe ripened her comic skills and led to her casting on "SNL," where she created a gallery of funny and eccentric characters and won an Emmy Award for the 1977-78 season. Unlike her male colleagues she never had major movies fashioned for her talents (though 1980's *Gilda Live* captured her one-woman Broadway show). She met husband Gene Wilder when they were teamed in *Hanky Panky* (1982) and they subsequently appeared together in *The*

Woman in Red (1984) and *Haunted Honeymoon* (1986). Shortly thereafter, Radner was diagnosed as having ovarian cancer, to which she succumbed in 1989, just before the publication of her autobiography "It's Always Something."
OTHER FILMS INCLUDE: 1979: *Mr. Mike's Mondo Video;* 1980: *First Family;* 1982: *It Came From Hollywood* (as one of the on-camera hosts); 1985: *Movers and Shakers.*

RAFELSON, BOB. Director, screenwriter, producer. *(b. Feb. 21, 1933, New York City.)* Maverick director whose early explorations of contemporary culture had a profound effect on American filmmaking in the seventies. The nephew of veteran screenwriter Samson Raphaelson, he worked as a rodeo rider, served on an ocean liner, and played jazz before studying philosophy at college. He went on to radio work and eventually adapted stage plays for television. He and friends Bert Schneider and Steve Blauner formed the production company BBS; in 1966 he and Schneider "created" the musical group The Monkees, and won an Emmy for "The Monkees" comedy TV series. Rafelson made his feature debut directing The Monkees in *Head* (1968), a wild, surreal hodgepodge of music and parody which is a fun time capsule of late sixties fads. Given this start, Rafelson's next film *Five Easy Pieces* (1970) was astonishing: a lyrical, adult study of identity and confusion, with Jack Nicholson as an oil-rig worker alienated from his girlfriend, his job, and his elitist family. Critics were dazzled by the film's intelligent, elliptical, European-influenced tone, and Rafelson received Oscar nominations for Best Picture and Screenplay, written with Adrian Joyce (Carole Eastman).
The King of Marvin Gardens (1972), a bleak, underrated spin on the American dream, starred Nicholson again, this time as a passive man who is sucked into his brother Bruce Dern's visions of success. It did not fare well with the public or critics (although it is highly regarded today). *Stay Hungry* (1976), a quirky story about body-building, featured a young Arnold Schwarzenegger, but didn't find an audience. Rafelson was slated to direct the prison film *Brubaker* (1980) but was fired by producer/star Robert Redford. He went on to direct a grim remake of *The Postman*

Always Rings Twice (1981) with Nicholson and Jessica Lange. It was six years before Rafelson tackled another feature; the psychological thriller *Black Widow* (1987) was one of his most conventional (and popular) films. He followed it three years later with an idiosyncratic—but invigoratingly original—epic story, *Mountains of the Moon* (1990), about explorer Sir Richard Burton. Unfortunately, his next film—a much anticipated reunion with Nicholson and *Five Easy Pieces* writer Carole Eastman—turned out to be a dog: *Man Trouble* (1992). Rafelson also directed the Lionel Richie music video "All Night Long." Given the long gestation period between films, it's hard to predict when we'll see another Rafelson picture, but it certainly won't be a cookie-cutter copy of someone else's work.

RAFFIN, DEBORAH. Actress, producer. *(b. Mar. 13, 1953, Los Angeles.)* This virginally pretty actress, the daughter of 1940s starlet Trudy Marshall, was a fashion model before making her screen debut in *40 Carats* (1973) as Liv Ullmann's daughter. A seeming vapidness kept her from full-fledged stardom, although she initially appeared in such mainstream Hollywood fare as *The Dove* (1974) and *Once Is Not Enough* (1975). She found meatier material in the likes of *Demon* (1976, aka *God Told Me To), The Sentinel, Maniac* (both 1977), but only came into her own in the 1980s as a leading lady in TV miniseries such as "Lace II" (1985), Sidney Sheldon's "Windmills of the Gods" (1988), and particularly James Clavell's "Noble House" (1988), which won her a major following in Asia. Other credits include *Death Wish 3* (1986), "Night of the Fox" (1990 miniseries), Sidney Sheldon's "The Sands of Time" (1992), and *Morning Glory* (1993). She and husband Michael Viner have also produced a number of telefilms, an outgrowth of their hugely successful books-on-tape company, Dove Audio.

RAFT, GEORGE. Actor. *(b. Sept. 26, 1895, New York City; d. Nov. 24, 1980.)* He became an overnight screen sensation playing a small-time, coin-flipping gangster in *Scarface* (1932), but movie buffs know Raft better as the guy who turned down many of the choicest roles in Hollywood. Born and raised in New York's "Hell's Kitchen," Raft tried prizefighting before becoming a dancer on Broadway and in Prohibition-era nightclubs, where he got to know some of the biggest racketeers in the city. In movies from 1929 (beginning with *Queen of the Night Clubs*), he seemed at first a lounge-lizard type, with his aloof manner, slick hair, impeccable tailoring, and dispassionate monotone voice. But he almost immediately slid into gangster portrayals, most of which had the ring of truth. *Quick Millions, Hush Money,* and *Palmy Days* (all 1931) saw him on the wrong side of the law; then came the star-making *Scarface.*

Paramount tried to rehabilitate Raft's image by casting him sympathetically wherever possible—as a *tough* guy but a *right* guy—in films like *Night After Night, Dancers in the Dark, If I Had a Million* (all 1932), *Pick-up* (1933), *All of Me, Limehouse Blues* (both 1934), and *Stolen Harmony* (1935). He played a dancer in *Bolero* (1934) and *Rumba* (1935), but professional dancers Veloz and Yolanda actually did the ballroom steps for him and costar Carole Lombard. In *Every Night at Eight* (1935, with Alice Faye), he was an egotistical bandleader.

Raft had only one, seemingly insurmountable obstacle to attaining top-rank stardom: He couldn't act. That actually helped him in one of his best starring vehicles, Dashiell Hammett's *The Glass Key* (1935). His enigmatic character is suspected of playing on both sides of a mob turf war, and it's impossible to tell just who he's favoring. But after several more tries, including *She Couldn't Take It* (also 1935), *Souls at Sea* (1937), and *You and Me* (1938), Paramount abandoned its attempt to make Raft a big star.

He continued playing tough guys in such films as *Each Dawn I Die, I Stole a Million* (both 1939), *Invisible Stripes, They Drive by Night, House Across the Bay* (all 1940), and *Manpower* (1941). He turned down the role of "Mad Dog" Earle in *High Sierra,* reportedly because he didn't want to die on-screen, and nixed Sam Spade in *The Maltese Falcon* because it seemed to him a lowly B picture. The two films combined made Humphrey Bogart a major star.

Raft exploited his own somewhat shady mob connections in *Broadway* (1942) by playing a whitewashed version of himself.

He then played himself—literally—in the wartime morale booster *Stage Door Canteen* (1943) and an entertainer in *Follow the Boys* (1944). But most of his 1940s films cast him as cookie-cutter hard-boiled characters: *Background to Danger* (1943), *Johnny Angel* (1945), *Nocturne, Mr. Ace, Whistle Stop* (all 1946), *Intrigue* (1947), *Race Street* (1948), *Dangerous Profession, Outpost in Morocco, Red Light,* and *Johnny Allegro* (all 1949). He at least had an offbeat role in the comedy-drama *Christmas Eve* (1947).

Raft experienced a run of bad luck in the 1950s, on-screen and off. His self-owned syndicated TV series, "I Am the Law," was a costly flop. He had troubles with the Internal Revenue Service. And he looked bored with such humdrum vehicles as *Lucky Nick Cain* (1951), *Loan Shark* (1952), *I'll Get You, The Man From Cairo* (both 1953), and *A Bullet for Joey* (1955). *Black Widow* (1954) was a welcome change; he did a cameo in *Around the World in Eighty Days* (1956), and did a deadpan gangster turn for Billy Wilder in *Some Like It Hot* (1959). By now his starring days were over; he continued to appear in small roles playing on his old tough-guy image, in such films as *Ocean's Eleven* (1960), *The Ladies' Man* (1961), *For Those Who Think Young, The Patsy* (both 1964), *Casino Royale* (1967), *The Silent Treasure* (1968), *Hammersmith Is Out, Deadhead Miles* (both 1972), *Sextette* (1978, reunited with Mae West, who looked nearly as ghastly as he did), and *The Man With Bogart's Face* (1980).

Raft, a married man whose wife refused to divorce him, was involved with many women, most notably Betty Grable, with whom he carried on an extraordinarily public courtship in the early 1940s. During his later period of financial duress, he sold movie rights to his life, which was filmed as *The George Raft Story* (1961), with Ray Danton in the title role. More recently, Raft was played on-screen by Joe Mantegna in Barry Levinson's *Bugsy* (1991). An authorized biography, "George Raft," was published in 1974.

RAIMI, SAM. Director, screenwriter, producer, actor. *(b. Oct. 23, 1959, Royal Oak, Mich.)* As one of today's most refreshing, invigorating directors, Raimi boasts a distinctive visual style characterized by acrobatic camerawork, rapid steadicam shots, and a violent physicality whose only analogues are found in slam-bang comic books and Three Stooges shorts. Raimi began shooting films at the tender age of eight with an 8mm film camera, and in his late teens financed his first feature, *The Evil Dead* (1983), with investments from local businesspeople and doctors. The over-the-top horror film became a hit at the 1983 Cannes Film Festival and had a very successful theatrical and video life. After he misstepped with the cartoonish action comedy *Crimewave* (1985), Raimi rebounded with *Evil Dead 2* (1987), a technically proficient sequel to his first film. Winning a reputation as one of the most visually inventive cult directors, he was finally tapped for his first major-studio assignment, cowriting and directing the action fantasy *Darkman* (1990), which successfully melded elements of *The Phantom of the Opera* and any number of comic-book superheroes. He followed it with *Army of Darkness* (1993, the third in the *Evil Dead* series, which he also cowrote) and the Western *The Quick and the Dead* (1995). He coexecutive-produced John Woo's American debut film, *Hard Target* (1993), cowrote *The Hudsucker Proxy* with his friends Joel and Ethan Coen and shot second-unit for it as well, and coproduced *TimeCop* (both 1994). He has also worked as an actor in *Spies Like Us* (1985, one of many gag cameos by directors), *Thou Shalt Not Kill ... Except* (1987), *Maniac Cop* (1988), *Intruder* (1989), *Innocent Blood* (1992), *Journey to the Center of the Earth* (1993 telefilm), and most prominently in *Indian Summer* (also 1993), in an amusing role as the camp flunky.

RAINER, LUISE. Actress. *(b. Jan. 12, 1910, Vienna.)* Once this delicate, dark-haired Austrian actress had won two consecutive Oscars—for her turns as showgirl Anna Held in the lavish biography *The Great Ziegfeld* (1936) and a patient Chinese wife in the distinguished adaptation of Pearl Buck's *The Good Earth* (1937)—the remainder of her career was anticlimactic. Plagued with personal problems, and unwilling to be "molded" by Hollywood, she turned on her heels and never looked back. On stage from childhood in her native country, Rainer worked with the great Max Reinhardt and appeared in a handful of German films before coming to Hollywood in 1935. She signed with MGM, which immediately put her in *Escapade,* and then boosted her into bigger roles. Following *The Good Earth,* Rainer was seen in *The Emperor's Candlesticks, Big City* (both 1937), *The Toy Wife, The Great Waltz,* and *Dramatic School* (all 1938)—most of them casting her in similar parts calling for a naive, almost schoolgirlish charm. Married to the brilliant but troubled playwright Clifford Odets at the time, she forsook her career in Hollywood, and made only one more film, *Hostages* (1943, a grim story of wartime Czech resistance), before retiring from the screen. She returned to Hollywood in the 1980s, was feted and interviewed, appeared in a 1983 episode of "The Love Boat" (in a dual role, no less) and made a TV movie in Switzerland, *A Dancer* (1988).

RAINS, CLAUDE. Actor. *(b. Nov. 10, 1889, London, as William Claude Rains; d. May 30, 1967.)* He made a startling screen debut, given top billing in a highly touted Hollywood production helmed by a prestigious director . . . yet he didn't appear on-screen until just a few seconds before the final fade-out. The film was James Whale's *The Invisible Man* (1933), and Rains spent most of its footage either with his face swathed in surgical bandages or as a disembodied voice hurling invective at various cast members. A stage actor since his childhood in Britain, Rains first came to the United States in 1914, and from the mid 1920s on worked in New York Theatre Guild productions. Short and not particularly handsome, Rains nonetheless had a charismatic stage presence and a distinctive voice (the most important qualification for his *Invisible Man* role).

Universal tried to make Rains another Karloff by starring him in two melodramas, *The Man Who Reclaimed His Head* (1934) and *The Mystery of Edwin Drood* (1935). But Rains drifted into character roles instead, which afforded him more interesting opportunities. His all-time worst performance came in 1939's *They Made Me a Criminal,* which miscast him as a Dick Tracy–like detective; interestingly enough, a memo printed in the 1980s re-

vealed that Rains begged Warner Bros. not to make him play the part! By the 1940s he had joined the rarefied league of secondary actors who were virtually stars themselves. He earned four Academy Award nominations for Best Supporting Actor: as the corrupt Senator in *Mr. Smith Goes to Washington* (1939), the delightfully dapper, amoral police captain in *Casablanca* (1942), the faithful stockbroker husband of Bette Davis in *Mr. Skeffington* (1944, actually a costarring part), and Ingrid Bergman's self-centered husband and Nazi spy in *Notorious* (1946, directed by Alfred Hitchcock).

The Rains gallery includes many other finely limned character portraits as well, such as Napoleon in *Hearts Divided* (1936), a self-serving Southern lawyer in *They Won't Forget* (1937), the treacherous Prince John in *The Adventures of Robin Hood* (1938), Napoleon III in *Juarez* (1939), a peripatetic pater in *Four Daughters* (1938) and its sequels *Daughters Courageous* (1939) and *Four Mothers* (1941), a Heavenly administrator in *Here Comes Mr. Jordan* (1941, in the title role), a small-town doctor in *Kings Row* (1942), Bette Davis' understanding psychiatrist in *Now, Voyager* (1942), a murderous musician in *Phantom of the Opera* (1943, the title role), Julius Caesar in *Caesar and Cleopatra* (1946), the intrepid Professor Challenger in *The Lost World* (1960), and King Herod the Great in *The Greatest Story Ever Told* (1965). In his best screen roles, Rains fairly bristled with sardonic malevolence. He was as distinctive in his final films as he was in his first. See his delicious performance as a diplomat, with eyebrows perpetually raised, in *Lawrence of Arabia* (1962).

OTHER FILMS INCLUDE: 1935: *The Last Outpost;* 1936: *Anthony Adverse* (the first of his many Warner Bros. films); 1937: *The Prince and the Pauper;* 1938: *Gold Is Where You Find It;* 1940: *Saturday's Children, The Lady With Red Hair* (as famed stage actor/impresario David Belasco), *The Sea Hawk;* 1941: *The Wolf Man;* 1942: *Moontide;* 1944: *Passage to Marseille;* 1945: *This Love of Ours;* 1946: *Angel on My Shoulder, Deception;* 1947: *The Unsuspected;* 1949: *One Woman's Story;* 1950: *The White Tower;* 1951: *Sealed Cargo;* 1953: *Paris Express;* 1956: *Lisbon;* 1959: *This Earth Is Mine;* 1961: *Battle of the Worlds;* 1963: *Twilight of Honor.*

RALSTON, VERA HRUBA. Actress. *(b. July 12, 1919, Prague, as Vera Helena Hruba.)* Few Hollywood personalities have been the butt of as many cruel jokes as this skating star, who was the latter-day "queen" of Republic Pictures (and, according to some, one of the reasons for its demise in the 1950s). An Olympic athlete who competed with Sonja Henie in the 1936 games, she came to America to escape World War 2 and was hired by Republic to appear in *Ice Capades* (1941) and *Ice Capades Revue* (1942). Republic president Herbert J. Yates, infatuated with the Slavic skater, signed her to a longterm contract and groomed her for stardom. With the addition of the surname "Ralston," she assumed leading-lady responsibilities in *The Lady and the Monster* (1944), followed by the wartime drama *Storm Over Lisbon* and the iceskating musical *Lake Placid Serenade* (both 1944). Ralston's thick accent and lack of training made her a target of critics from the first.

A defiant Yates insisted on pushing ahead, teaming her with the studio's top star, John Wayne, in *Dakota* (1945), then thrusting her into countless Westerns, thrillers, and costume dramas, on which he lavished huge (for Republic, at least) amounts of money. Ralston eventually became a passable actress, but she lacked warmth (or, perhaps, the ability to project it) and never won public acceptance. Yates virtually forced exhibitors to play her pictures by threatening to withhold other, more popular Republic products; his obstinacy, it is said, helped break the studio (in actuality, Republic's demise was more complex than that).

Ralston, who never appeared on-screen after Republic folded, married Yates in 1952 and stayed with him until he died. OTHER FILMS INCLUDE: 1946: *Plainsman and the Lady, Murder in the Music Hall;* 1947: *Wyoming, The Flame;* 1948: *Angel of the Amazon;* 1949: *The Fighting Kentuckian* (also starring Wayne, who reportedly threatened to leave the studio if forced to work with Ralston again); 1951: *Belle Le Grand;* 1952: *Hoodlum Empire;* 1953: *Fair Wind to Java* (as a dark-haired, exotic islander in one of her better pictures); 1954: *The Jubilee Trail;* 1956: *Accused of Murder;* 1958: *The Man Who Died Twice* (her last).

RAMPLING, CHARLOTTE. Actress. *(b. Feb. 5, 1946, Sturmer, England.)* Offbeat roles have served this striking actress well, but none so much as the concentration camp survivor of *The Night Porter* (1974), improbably reunited with the SS guard who raped and tortured her throughout her captivity. Graphic and uncompromising, the film unnerved many moviegoers, and marked another departure from the conventional by the slender, coolly attractive Rampling. She'd first impressed viewers with her supporting role as Lynn Redgrave's roommate in the 1966 hit *Georgy Girl,* and achieved some notoriety three years later for her performance in Luchino Visconti's *The Damned* (1969), chillingly believable in that tale of moral and spiritual decadence. Her turn in *The Night Porter* fixed her in moviegoers' minds as an actress unafraid to bare herself—emotionally and spiritually as well as physically—in daring characterizations. She costarred with Sean Connery in the sci-fi film *Zardoz* (1974), and appeared opposite Robert Mitchum (playing detective Philip Marlowe) in *Farewell, My Lovely* (1975), perfectly cast as an exotic, enigmatic femme fatale. Woody Allen had her play a mentally disturbed actress in his bleak *Stardust Memories* (1980). In *The Verdict* (1982), she portrayed a mercenary temptress hired to spy on lawyer Paul Newman; in *Angel Heart* (1987), she was an occult expert queried by private eye Mickey Rourke, who later finds her dead body sans heart. But Rampling's strangest film is certainly *Max, My Love* (1986), in which she takes a chimpanzee for a lover.

RANDALL, TONY. Actor. *(b. Feb. 26, 1920, Tulsa, Okla., as Leonard Rosenberg.)* When he won a long overdue Emmy for his portrayal of Felix Unger on "The Odd Couple" (1970–75) after the show had been canceled, Randall quipped: "I'm so happy I won. Now if I only had a job." He needn't have been worried. An actor who's built a career on playing best friends and fussbudgets (usually simultaneously), this crisp, impeccable comedy star has been a favorite to stage, screen, radio, and TV audiences for four decades. Randall made his feature-film debut in *Oh, Men! Oh, Women!* (1957), quickly followed by his best comedy vehicle, reprising his Broadway role as a hapless ad executive caught up in the rat race in *Will Success Spoil Rock Hunter?* (1957). In 1959 he played the fussy best friend (what did we tell you?) in the Doris Day/Rock Hudson smash romantic comedy *Pillow Talk,* and performed the same task for them in *Lover Come Back* (1961) and *Send Me No Flowers* (1964). That same year, he had his most unusual screen role—actually, *roles*—in the fantasy *7 Faces of Dr. Lao,* submerged under clever makeups and sporting elaborate accents.

Randall has also been effective in *The Mating Game* (1959), *Let's Make Love* (1960), *The Brass Bottle* (1964), *Fluffy* (1965), *Hello Down There* (1969), *Everything You Always Wanted to Know About Sex (But Were Afraid to Ask)* (1972), *Scavenger Hunt* (1979), *Foolin' Around* (1980), *The King of Comedy* (1983, as himself), and *Gremlins 2 The New Batch* (1990, as the voice of the Brain Gremlin). Randall's most enjoyable change-of-pace role was his turn as the comically pompous but brilliant detective Hercule Poirot in an Agatha Christie whodunit, *The Alphabet Murders* (1966). Frank Tashlin, who directed that film as well as *Rock Hunter,* said that directing him was like playing a Stradivarius. In the late 1980s he founded the National Actors Theatre in New York, a longtime dream finally brought to fruition.

RATHBONE, BASIL. Actor. (b. June 13, 1892, Johannesburg, South Africa, as Philip St. John Basil Rathbone; d. July 21, 1967.) To many devoted fans, Basil Rathbone was *born* to play Sir Arthur Conan Doyle's famous detective, Sherlock Holmes—a role he essayed in 14 films (15 if you count his delightful cameo in 1943's *Crazy House*) and hundreds of radio broadcasts, and a character he came to detest. His high forehead, penetrating eyes, prominent nose, cruel mouth, and firm chin gave him an uncanny resemblance to the Holmes illustrated in books and magazines, although those same saturnine features—along with his cool voice, aloof manner, and general aspect of quiet menace—ideally suited him to play ruthless villains, which he did with great aplomb.

Born in South Africa but educated in England, he took up acting there and was appearing on stage—often in Shakespear-ean roles—during the 1920s, when he first dabbled in film work (including 1921's *Innocent* and 1923's *School for Scandal*). Toward the end of the decade he moved to America, and made his talkie film debut in *The Last of Mrs. Cheyney* (1929). That same year, he played his first movie detective, amateur sleuth Philo Vance, in MGM's stodgy but faithful adaptation of *The Bishop Murder Case.*

Rathbone spent several years in Hollywood before really catching on with American moviegoers. His stints in *The Flirting Widow* (1930), *A Woman Commands* (1932), and *One Precious Year* (1933), to name a few, aroused scant attention. That all changed in 1935, a busy year in which his credits included fine villainous parts in *Captain Blood* (the first of his swashbucklers opposite Errol Flynn), *A Tale of Two Cities* (as the Marquis de St. Evremonde), *David Copperfield* (as Mr. Murdstone), *Anna Karenina* (as Garbo's cruel husband Karenin), and *The Last Days of Pompeii.*

Rathbone earned a Best Supporting Actor Oscar nomination for his performance as Tybalt in *Romeo and Juliet* (1936), and went on to costar in *The Garden of Allah* (also 1936), *Tovarich, Love From a Stranger* (a particularly chilling characterization as Ann Harding's menacing mate), *Confession, Make a Wish* (all 1937), *The Adventures of Robin Hood* (one of his all-time best roles, as Sir Guy of Gisbourne), *The Adventures of Marco Polo, The Dawn Patrol* (both 1938), *If I Were King* (also 1938, delivering a delightful, Oscar-nominated performance as the eccentric King Louis XI), *Son of Frankenstein* (in the title role), *Tower of London* (at his cunning, malevolent best as Richard III), *The Sun Never Sets* (all 1939), *Rhythm on the River* (1940), *The Mark of Zorro* (also 1940, particularly memorable as the cold-blooded, ruthless villain), *The Mad Doctor, The Black Cat, Paris Calling, International Lady* (all 1941), *Crossroads,* and *Fingers at the Window* (both 1942).

In 1939, 20th Century-Fox cast Rathbone as Sherlock Holmes in a screen adaptation of *The Hound of the Baskervilles* (the fourth, as a matter of fact). The handsome production was a big success, and spawned a sequel, *The Adventures of Sherlock Holmes.* When Universal undertook to update the Holmes stories in 1942,

Rathbone and Nigel Bruce (who'd played Dr. Watson in both Fox features) were signed to reprise their popular roles in a dozen Universal Bs: *Sherlock Holmes and the Voice of Terror, Sherlock Holmes and the Secret Weapon* (both 1942), *Sherlock Holmes in Washington, Sherlock Holmes Faces Death* (both 1943), *Sherlock Holmes and the Spider Woman, The Scarlet Claw* (the best in the series), *The Pearl of Death* (all 1944), *The House of Fear, Pursuit to Algiers, The Woman in Green* (all 1945), *Terror By Night*, and *Dressed to Kill* (both 1946).

Rathbone feared—rightly so, as it happened—that typecasting as Holmes would ruin his film career. During the series' run he had secured juicy roles in a few big-budget pictures—including *Above Suspicion* (1943), *Frenchman's Creek*, and *Bathing Beauty* (both 1944)—but found work scarce after finishing the last Holmes opus, and never again had a truly great part on-screen. His best opportunities came when he was called upon to spoof his earlier screen villainy, in Bob Hope's *Casanova's Big Night* (1954) and more memorably in Danny Kaye's *The Court Jester* (1956). He also appeared in *We're No Angels* (1955), *The Black Sleep* (1956), *The Last Hurrah* (1958), *Pontius Pilate, The Magic Sword, Tales of Terror* (all 1962), and *The Comedy of Terrors* (1964). Rathbone's last pictures were the uniformly worthless *Queen of Blood, Voyage to a Prehistoric Planet* (both 1966), *The Ghost in the Invisible Bikini*, and *Hillbillys in a Haunted House* (1967).

Rathbone was active in radio and TV as well, playing Sherlock Holmes on radio from 1939 to 1946, and appearing in the TV series "Your Lucky Clue" (1952) and "Dunninger" (1953) as well as guest-starring on dozens of anthology shows, variety programs, and dramatic series through the 1950s and 1960s. He played Holmes on TV at least once, in a 1950 episode of "NBC Showcase." He also narrated the memorable Walt Disney version of "The Wind in the Willows" which was half of the 1949 animated feature film *The Adventures of Ichabod and Mr. Toad*. Rathbone's wife Ouida was widely regarded for her lavish parties, which for many years were de rigueur for the Hollywood social set.

RATOFF, GREGORY. Actor, director, producer. *(b. Apr. 20, 1897, St. Petersburg, Russia; d. Dec. 14, 1960.)* A man who led an unusual double life in Hollywood as actor and director, this Russian emigré's American show-business career began with a stretch as one of New York's Yiddish Players troupe. He graduated to Broadway, producing and directing as well as acting prior to his 1932 film debut in *Symphony of Six Million*. Ratoff specialized in comedic, eccentric character roles; he frequently played producers and agents (often named "Max") as in *What Price Hollywood?* (1932), *Once in a Lifetime* (also 1932, as the movie mogul who "turned down the Vitaphone"), and most memorably in *All About Eve* (1950). Other films include *Secrets of The French Police* (1932, as an international spy/hypnotist/killer!), *Remember Last Night?, King of Burlesque* (both 1935), *Sing, Baby, Sing, Under Two Flags* (both 1936), *Sally, Irene and Mary* (1938), *The Great Profile* (1940), *The Sun Also Rises* (1957), and *The Big Gamble* (1961), his last.

His best-known films as a director are the lovely romance *Intermezzo* (1939) and the first-rate swashbuckler *The Corsican Brothers* (1941). His many other credits behind the camera include *Sins of Man* (1936), *Lancer Spy* (1937), *Barricade, Hotel for Women, Rose of Washington Square, Wife, Husband and Friend* (all 1939), *The Men in Her Life* (1941), *Footlight Serenade* (1942), *The Heat's On, Something to Shout About* (both 1943), *Song of Russia* (1944), *Paris Underground, Where Do We Go From Here?* (both 1945), *Carnival in Costa Rica, Moss Rose* (both 1947), *Black Magic* (1949), *Taxi* (1953), *Abdulla the Great* (1955, also acted), and the Robert Morley version of *Oscar Wilde* (1960).

RAY, ALDO. Actor. *(b. Sept. 25, 1926, Pen Argyl, Pa., as Aldo DaRe; d. Mar. 27, 1991.)* Archetypal 1950s screen tough guy, with a distinctively high-pitched gravel voice, former Navy frogman Ray had no acting experience at all when he won a bit part in *Saturday's Hero* (1951), and then found himself in demand. He displayed a disarming vulnerability as a man on the verge of divorce in *The Marrying Kind*, a thick-witted sports figure in *Pat and Mike* (both 1952), and a sympathetic Marine in *Battle Cry* (1955). His subsequent roles got tougher and tougher: He was positively brutal as a Korean war dogface in *Men in War* (1956), a white-trash drunk in *God's Little Acre* (1958), and another hard-boiled soldier in *The Naked and the Dead* (1958). By the time Ray appeared as a drill sergeant in John Wayne's *The Green Berets* (1968), his image was completely fixed. Hit with financial troubles and long since reduced to rock-bottom exploitation movies such as *Stud Brown* (1975) and *The Bad Bunch* (1976), Ray in 1982 consented to appear in a hard-core porno film, *Sweet Sexy Savage* (he did not, however, appear in any sex scenes). He contracted throat cancer in the late 1980s and had to keep working in order to raise money to combat it, taking roles in low-budget thrillers and horror pictures. He succumbed to the illness in 1991, shortly after completing his scenes for *The Shooters.* Ray's son, Eric DaRe, played vicious wife-beater Leo Johnson in the TV series "Twin Peaks" in 1990–91.

RAY, NICHOLAS. Director. *(b. Aug. 7, 1911, Galesville, Wis., as Raymond Nicholas Kienzle; d. June 16, 1979.)* This director's best Hollywood films were invested with an emotional urgency and psychological acuity that influenced both the directors of the French New Wave and the more personally oriented American and European directors of the present day. His best-known picture, *Rebel Without a Cause* (1955, which earned him an Oscar nomination for Best Story), features his signature protagonist: the soul-shattered, alienated man unable to make the rest of the world understand his anguish. The director realized his most painful and trenchant treatment of this character in 1950's *In a Lonely Place,* which starred Humphrey Bogart and Ray's onetime wife Gloria Grahame. Bogart played a misanthropic Hollywood screenwriter suspected of murder; Ray, while canny enough to develop the plot along formula whodunit lines, also exploited the character's profound alienation.

Before starting his directorial career, Ray worked or studied with some American cultural giants, including architect Frank Lloyd Wright and theater directors Elia Kazan and John Houseman. It was Houseman who gave Ray his first shot be-

hind the megaphone, on the poignant 1949 film noir *They Live by Night.* It was immediately apparent that he not only had great sensitivity but a great visual style as well, which was enhanced when he got to work in color and widescreen in the 1950s (see *Rebel Without a Cause,* in particular). He made some of the decade's most unusual films, within the studio system: *Johnny Guitar* (1954) is the kinkiest role-reversal Western of all time, leading to a memorable shootout between Joan Crawford and Mercedes McCambridge. *Bigger Than Life* (1956) was one of the first Hollywood films to deal with drug addiction. His later films grew more ambitious, in a variety of ways: *The Savage Innocents* (1959, which he also wrote) depicted Eskimo culture, while *King of Kings* (1961) chronicled the life of Christ.

In 1976, while teaching film at New York University, he and his students made the highly personal *You Can't Go Home Again.* In 1980 his friend German director Wim Wenders (who had cast Ray in a small part for his 1977 film *The American Friend*) released *Lightning Over Water* (1980), an often painful documentary chronicling Ray's life and his death from cancer.

OTHER FILMS INCLUDE: 1949: *Knock on Any Door, A Woman's Secret;* 1950: *Born to Be Bad;* 1951: *On Dangerous Ground, Flying Leathernecks;* 1952: *The Lusty Men;* 1954: *Run for Cover;* 1956: *Hot Blood;* 1957: *The True Story of Jesse James, Bitter Victory* (also wrote); 1958: *Party Girl, Wind Across the Everglades;* 1963: *55 Days at Peking;* 1964: *Circus World* (story only).

RAY, SATYAJIT. Director, screenwriter. *(b. May 2, 1921, Calcutta; d. Apr. 23, 1992.)* India's preeminent filmmaker, and one of the cinema's true masters, Ray was born into a prominent Calcutta family and benefitted from an extensive education both in business science and the arts and humanities. For many years a layout artist in a British-owned advertising agency, he illustrated books on the side; one of these, "Pather Panchali," so moved him that he resolved to make it into a movie. Without any prior filmmaking experience, but reportedly inspired by De Sica's *The Bicycle Thief,* he decided to shoot the movie on location, using his friends as actors and crew, and financing the project with his own money. He ran out of funds before completing the film, but the Bengal government—at the behest of New York's Museum of Modern Art, to which news of Ray's work had spread—arranged for a necessary completion loan.

Pather Panchali (1955) was shown to wildly appreciative audiences at the 1956 Cannes Film Festival. A grippingly realistic, unrelenting study of Apu, a young boy living with his impoverished family in a Bengal village, it overwhelmed audiences with its visual beauty and thematic simplicity, and immediately won Ray a spot in the cinematic pantheon. The film also drew serious international attention to the Indian film industry, known heretofore for its mass-produced formula pictures. Two sequels filled out what would come to be known as "The Apu Trilogy": *Aparajito* (1956) follows Apu's education and gradual estrangement from his mother and village, and in *The World of Apu* (1959), the boy is now a man (played by Soumitra Chatterjee, one of Ray's favorite players) contending with marriage and a child of his own. David Shipman wrote that "the Apu films are to cinema what Proust is to literature: they are simply richer and more universal than most films ever made."

Between the Apu films, Ray made the lovely fable *The Philosopher's Stone* (1957) and *Jalsaghar* (1958), and later, *Devi* (1960), a film about religious fanaticism which revealed his concern with the clash of cultures and ideologies in his country. After the omnibus *Three Daughters* (1961), Ray examined spiritual awakening and the constrictions of tradition in works like *Kanchenjungha* (1962), *Manangar* (1963, aka *The Great City*), *Charulata* (1964), and *Days and Nights in the Forest* (1969), and scored a big success with *The Adventures of Goopy and Bagha* (1968), a colorful adventure adapted from a folktale by his own grandfather. Ray's style in the first four is slow, stately, and oblique, with changes in character linked to their surroundings and the mystic forces of nature. But by the time of 1970's *The Adversary,* Ray had begun to deal more directly with social and political problems in modern India, and his tone, though still full of his usual compassion and insight, became infused with irony and anger. Such works include *Company Limited* (1971), a sharp portrait of moral compromise; *Distant Thunder*

(1973), a powerful look at a 1943 Bengali village in the midst of famine; *The Middleman* (1975), in which moral compromise becomes a key to survival; and *The Chess Players* (1977), in which contrasting British and Indian values are reflected in two Indian noblemen who play chess while their country crumbles.

Ray found time to make the lighthearted adventures *The Golden Fortress* (1974) and a sequel *The Elephant God* (1978) as well as *The Kingdom of Diamonds* (1980), which brought back Goopy and Bagha. He suffered two heart attacks after making *The Home and the World* (1984) and returned five years later with *An Enemy of the People* (1989), an adaptation of Ibsen's play set in a Bengal town. One of his last films, *Branches of the Tree* (1990), is a masterly, elegiac look at the changing tide of moral values in modern India. In 1992, Ray received a Lifetime Achievement Oscar for his enormous contributions to cinema; he accepted the award from a sickbed, and died less than one month later.

RAYE, MARTHA. Actress. *(b. Aug. 27, 1916, Butte, Mont., as Margaret Teresa O'Reed; d. Oct. 19, 1994.)* She was one of the few female clowns in movies; a sort of distaff Joe E. Brown, with a cavernous mouth and a vigorous, energetic screen personality. She was also a first-rate singer, though given little credit for that talent. Born into a vaudeville family, she was part of the act as a small child and sang with dance bands as a teenager; her first film, in fact, was a band short subject. Signed by Paramount, she made her feature debut in *Rhythm on the Range*, a 1936 Bing Crosby vehicle, from which emerged her screen persona: a buxom, boisterous, usually man-crazy second banana who belted out novelty numbers and performed physical comedy with equal aplomb. Her other Paramount films include *The Big Broadcast of 1937, College Holiday* (both 1936), *Waikiki Wedding, Artists & Models, Double or Nothing* (all 1937), *College Swing, The Big Broadcast of 1938* (as W. C. Fields' daughter!), *Tropic Holiday* (all 1938), *Give Me a Sailor* (also 1938, a rare starring role), *Never Say Die,* and *$1,000 a Touchdown* (both 1939).

Raye continued playing the same types

in *The Boys From Syracuse* (1940), *Navy Blues, Hellzapoppin* (both 1941), *Keep 'Em Flying* (also 1941, playing twins opposite Abbott and Costello), *Pin Up Girl* (1944), and *Four Jills in a Jeep* (also 1944, playing herself in a fictionalized account of her experiences entertaining troops during World War 2 with three actress cohorts). Charlie Chaplin gave her a plum role in his black comedy *Monsieur Verdoux* (1947), and she was hilarious as an intended victim apparently impervious to the wife-killer's murderous attempts. She took her high-decibel style to nightclubs, theaters, and TV (headlining "The Martha Raye Show" from 1954 to 1956), while continuing to entertain American soldiers during the Korean and Vietnam wars. In 1962 she had her last great showcase on screen, cast opposite Jimmy Durante as the second leads in the splashy circus musical comedy *Billy Rose's Jumbo.* (Years later she joined the all-star cast of *The Concorde—Airport '79.*) In 1969 she became the first female recipient of the Jean Hersholt Humanitarian Award. The oft-married Raye made headlines in 1991 when allegations surfaced concerning her current husband's mishandling of her affairs. She later filed suit against Bette Midler, claiming that *For the Boys* (1991) was based on her experiences— and her attempt to turn them into a motion picture.

RAYMOND, GENE. Actor. *(b. Aug. 13, 1908, New York City, as Raymond Guion.)* This husky, blond actor, handsome almost to the point of being pretty, enjoyed his greatest popularity during the 1930s, when he was a dependable leading man and occasional supporting player; he also proved to have a pleasant singing voice. A child performer and Broadway veteran at the age of 12, Raymond broke into movies with a role in *Personal Maid* (1931); soon he was working steadily. Among his credits: *Ladies of the Big House* (1931), *If I Had a Million* (1932), *Red Dust* (also 1932, as Mary Astor's husband and Clark Gable's nemesis), and a notable trio of 1933 releases, *Ex-Lady* (as Bette Davis' husband), *Zoo in Budapest* (a whimsical, offbeat romance costarring Loretta Young), and *Flying Down to Rio* (a charming, escapist musical even better re-

membered for the initial teaming of Fred Astaire and Ginger Rogers).

Raymond continued to freelance, starring in *Sadie McKee* (opposite Joan Crawford), *Transatlantic Merry-Go-Round* (both 1934), *Behold My Wife, The Woman in Red* (both 1935), and a series of amiable grade-B musicals for RKO that teamed him with Ann Sothern, including *Hooray for Love* (1935), *Love on a Bet* (1936), *There Goes My Girl,* and *She's Got Everything* (both 1937). *Smilin' Through* (1941) cast him opposite real-life wife Jeanette MacDonald, and *Mr. and Mrs. Smith* (also 1941) cast him as "the other man" in this Alfred Hitchcock-directed comedy with Carole Lombard and Robert Montgomery.

Raymond also starred in, produced, and directed *Million Dollar Weekend* (1948), a fair mystery that flopped at the box office. Widowed by MacDonald in 1965, Raymond remains active in Hollywood society.

OTHER FILMS INCLUDE: 1946: *The Locket;* 1948: *Assigned to Danger;* 1955: *Hit the Deck;* 1957: *Plunder Road;* 1964: *The Best Man, I'd Rather Be Rich;* 1970: *Gun Riders* (as narrator).

REA, STEPHEN. Actor. *(b. Oct. 31, 1943, Belfast, Ireland.)* After years of acting in the Irish and British theater and a decade's worth of film roles, Rea received stardom—and a Best Actor Oscar nomination—for his subtle, complex performance as Fergus, the reluctant IRA volunteer in Neil Jordan's *The Crying Game* (1992). Rea trained at the Abbey Theatre School and divided his time in the 1970s and 1980s between fringe theater, major stage productions, TV, and films; he has also starred in or directed all of the productions of the Field Day Theatre, a group he and playwright Brian Friel formed in 1980. Rea made his film debut in Neil Jordan's *Angel* (1982, released in the United States as *Danny Boy*), a sort of precursor to *The Crying Game,* starring as a saxophone player who gets involved in gangland violence. Rea also appeared in Jordan's *The Company of Wolves* (1984), *The Doctor and the Devils* (1985), *Loose Connections* (1988), and Mike Leigh's *Life Is Sweet* (1991). He got a chance to show his lighter side in the comedy of manners *Bad Behaviour* (1993), and also starred in

Angie, Princess Caraboo, Interview With the Vampire, and *Ready to Wear/Prêt-à-Porter* (all 1994).

REAGAN, RONALD. Actor. *(b. Feb. 6, 1911, Tampico, Ill.)* Handsome, wavy-haired, broad-shouldered leading man who enjoyed a modest, two-decade-long screen career before moving on to other fields of endeavor, at which he achieved some little success. A gregarious youth and overachiever, Reagan graduated Eureka College and went into sportscasting on local radio, eventually becoming the regular announcer for the Chicago Cubs games. Then known as "Dutch" Reagan, he eventually wound up working for NBC. In 1937 he went to Hollywood where, as a contract player for Warner Bros., he was groomed for stardom, playing leads in B pictures and supporting roles in A's. He had a pleasant screen presence, and was by no means as bad an actor as his detractors would have one believe. Nor was he strictly, as the press would have it, "a B-movie actor."

Reagan debuted in *Love Is on the Air* (1937, in the male lead), and appeared in such Warners studio fare as *Hollywood Hotel* (1937), *Accidents Will Happen, The Cowboy From Brooklyn, Boy Meets Girl, Brother Rat, Going Places* (all 1938), *Dark Victory* (as one of Bette Davis' suitors), *Naughty but Nice, Hell's Kitchen, The Angels Wash Their Faces* (all 1939), *Brother Rat and a Baby, An Angel from Texas, Knute Rockne, All American* (as Notre Dame football star George Gipp, aka "the Gipper," a nickname that stuck to Reagan), *Tugboat Annie Sails Again* (all 1940), *Santa Fe Trail* (also 1940, as George Armstrong Custer), *Million Dollar Baby, Nine Lives Are Not Enough,* and *International Squadron* (all 1941). He also starred as Treasury Department G-man "Brass" Bancroft in four entertaining B's, *Secret Service of the Air, Code of the Secret Service* (both 1939), *Smashing the Money Ring,* and *Murder in the Air* (both 1940). On his one loan-out, to MGM for *The Bad Man* (1941), Lionel Barrymore ran over his feet with his wheelchair.

Kings Row (1942), Warners' elaborately mounted adaptation of Henry Bellamann's best-selling melodrama about small-town America, gave Reagan his most challenging (and best remembered) role, as happy-go-lucky Drake McHugh—who, upon reviving from an operation that amputated his legs, looks at himself under the bedclothes and cries, "Where's the rest of me?" After completing *Juke Girl, Desperate Journey* (both 1942), and *This Is the Army* (1943, with George Murphy as his father), he went into the Army Air Corps (although bad eyesight kept him from seeing combat) and made numerous training films.

Reagan returned from military service to resume his career, which failed to regain the momentum it had achieved following his well-received performance in *Kings Row.* Warners put him in some good films, including *The Voice of the Turtle* (1947), *The Hasty Heart* (1949), and *Storm Warning* (1951, a hard-hitting film about contemporary Ku Klux Klan activities), but as a freelance he found himself mostly in low-budget adventure films, Westerns, and witless comedies. His postwar films include *That Hagen Girl* (opposite Shirley Temple), *Stallion Road* (both 1947), *John Loves Mary, Night Unto Night, The Girl From Jones Beach* (all 1949), *Louisa* (1950), *Hong Kong* (1951), *Bedtime for Bonzo* (also 1951, upstaged by a monkey), *She's Working Her Way Through College* (1952), *The Winning Team* (also 1952, as baseball pitcher Grover Cleveland Alexander), *Tropic Zone, Law and Order* (both 1953), *Prisoner of War, Cattle Queen of Montana* (1954), *Tennessee's Partner* (1955), and *Hellcats of the Navy* (1957, with his wife Nancy Davis).

Reagan's flagging screen career prompted him to seek TV work as early as 1950. In addition to guesting on dozens of anthology shows and series, he was a regular on "The Orchid Award" (1953–54), hosted and occasionally starred in "General Electric Theatre" (1954–61), and hosted "Death Valley Days" (1964–66).

Reagan displayed an affinity for politics as early as 1947, when he was elected president of the Screen Actors Guild, serving in that capacity for five years (and returning to the post again in 1959). A onetime liberal turned staunch conservative who supported Barry Goldwater for president in 1964 (the year he made his last movie appearance, in *The Killers,* which was originally intended for TV but released theatrically instead), he became governor of California in 1966, holding that position for eight years. He lost the

1976 Republican primary to Gerald Ford but won his party's candidacy in 1980 and was subsequently elected president in 1980 and 1984, proving during his two terms that he was a much better actor than anyone had suspected.

Reagan's first wife was actress Jane Wyman, another Warners contractee; they were married from 1940 to 1948 and had two children, Michael and Maureen. He married Nancy Davis in 1952; their son Ron was a dancer and, latterly, talk-show host, while daughter Patti became a novelist.

REDFORD, ROBERT. Actor, director, producer. *(b. Aug. 18, 1937, Santa Monica, Calif., as Charles Robert Redford.)* This blond, square-jawed leading man combined good looks with genuine intelligence and unmistakable charisma to become one of the 1970s' true superstars. Certainly he owed much of his popularity to the female filmgoers who flocked to see him in the likes of *The Way We Were* (1973) and *The Great Gatsby* (1974), but Redford's appeal—like that of most great movie stars—cuts across gender lines. As a youth he won a baseball scholarship to the University of Colorado but dropped out to go to Europe; upon returning to the States, he settled in New York and took up acting. He scored in the original Broadway production of Neil Simon's "Barefoot in the Park," did a lot of television, and made his film debut in *War Hunt* (1962), a minor antiwar drama.

He started winning bigger—and better— parts in films like *Inside Daisy Clover* (1965), *This Property Is Condemned,* and *The Chase* (both 1966), but he took a giant step toward stardom in the movie version of *Barefoot in the Park* (1967, opposite Jane Fonda) and nailed it with his irresistible performance opposite Paul Newman in *Butch Cassidy and the Sundance Kid* (1969). It immediately became apparent that Redford was not one to trade on his "pretty-boy" looks and charisma, as he sought out challenging and intelligent film projects, from *Downhill Racer* and *Tell Them Willie Boy Is Here* (both 1969) to *The Candidate* (1972), a film that in fact exploited his looks in a mordant satire of modern-day political campaigns.

That film seemed to launch Redford on a winning streak. In 1973 he reteamed with Paul Newman for the con-artist comedy *The Sting* (for which he earned his first Oscar nomination) and struck box-office gold opposite Barbra Streisand in *The Way We Were.* He produced and starred as "Washington Post" journalist Bob Woodward in *All the President's Men* (1976), which enabled him to combine his political interests with mainstream moviemaking. In 1980 he moved behind the camera to make his directing debut with *Ordinary People,* a highly charged domestic drama, and won an Academy Award for his efforts.

That film marked a watershed in his career, as he became choosier about acting assignments, and devoted more time to political causes, environmentalism, and the establishment of The Sundance Institute in Utah, a year-round workshop for burgeoning filmmakers. He took occasional movie leads—as in *The Natural* (1984), *Out of Africa* (1985), and *Legal Eagles* (1986)—but he clearly put his starring career on the back burner. In 1988 he directed his second feature, *The Milagro Beanfield War.* After four years offscreen Redford made a starring "comeback" in *Havana* (1990), a romantic drama with *Casablanca* pretensions, but it was a costly flop, in spite of good personal reviews. It was one of his few outright failures with longtime collaborator Sydney Pollack, who worked with him as an actor in *War Hunt* (1962) and directed him in *This Property Is Condemned, Jeremiah Johnson* (1972), *The Way We Were, Three Days of the Condor* (1975), *The Electric Horseman* (1979), and *Out of Africa.*

In 1992 he made a conscious decision to put his career back in high gear, and enjoyed great success on every front. *Sneakers* proved he had lost none of his star power (or his light comedy touch); *A River Runs Through It* revealed his strengths as a director; and *Incident at Oglala,* which he executive-produced and narrated, reaffirmed his social commitment. Then in 1993 he defined charisma (and box-office clout) as the sexy millionaire who offers Demi Moore a million dollars to sleep with him, in the smash hit *Indecent Proposal.* He earned Oscar nominations for directing and coproducing the intelligent, superbly crafted *Quiz Show* (1994).

OTHER FILMS INCLUDE: 1965: *Situation Hopeless—But Not Serious;* 1970: *Little Fauss and Big Halsy;* 1972: *The Hot Rock;* 1975: *The Great Waldo Pepper;* 1977: *A Bridge Too Far;* 1980: *Brubaker.*

REDGRAVE, LYNN. Actress. *(b. Mar. 8, 1943, London.)* Already a veteran of stage, screen, and television when she earned an Academy Award nomination as the good-natured ugly duckling in *Georgy Girl* (1966), this engaging actress never again got a comparably good role in movies. The daughter of actor Michael Redgrave and younger sister of actress Vanessa, Lynn was on the plump side when she began her movie career but later slimmed down and became a svelte leading lady with a cheeky sense of humor.

She worked on Broadway and television, and was a longtime spokeswoman for Weight Watchers foods. With no Hollywood offers at hand, she accepted the role of notorious madam Xavier Hollander in the low-budget opus *The Happy Hooker* (1975), and played it for all it was worth—complete with accent. In 1979 she starred in the TV sitcom "House Calls," but said she was fired two years later for wanting to breast-feed her baby on the set. Redgrave sued, and later claimed that as a result of the brouhaha, she was blacklisted in Hollywood; indeed, no roles—decent or otherwise—seemed to come her way. In 1989 she had one of her best screen opportunities, as a jaded London hostess in *Getting It Right.* In 1991 she costarred with her sister Vanessa in a television remake of *Whatever Happened to Baby Jane?* Then in 1993 she enjoyed a triumphant Broadway success with an autobiographical one-woman show, "Shakespeare for My Father."

OTHER FILMS INCLUDE: 1963: *Tom Jones* (her first); 1967: *The Deadly Affair;* 1970: *Last of the Mobile Hot-Shots;* 1972: *Every Little Crook and Nanny, Everything You Always Wanted to Know About Sex (But Were Afraid to Ask);* 1973: *The National Health;* 1976: *The Big Bus;* 1980: *Sunday Lovers;* 1987: *Morgan Stewart's Coming Home* (probably the worst film of her career); 1989: *Midnight.*

REDGRAVE, MICHAEL (SIR). Actor. *(b. Mar. 20, 1908, Bristol, England; d. Mar. 21, 1985.)* Tall, slender, distinguished-looking British leading man and, later, character actor. The son of silent-film star Roy Redgrave, and a Cambridge man who briefly taught school before going into acting, he made his stage debut in 1934 and first delighted moviegoers as the amiably eccentric musician/hero in Alfred Hitchcock's stylish comedy-thriller *The Lady Vanishes* (1938). In addition to starring in three early Carol Reed films— *Climbing High, The Stars Look Down* (both 1939), and *Kipps* (1941)—he aroused audience attention with his skillful turns as a lighthouse-keeper in *Thunder Rock* (1942) and a demented ventriloquist whose dummy comes to life in an episode of the incomparable thriller *Dead of Night* (1945).

Redgrave came to America in 1947, costarring with Rosalind Russell in the heavy, mind-numbing, Dudley Nichols-directed screen adaptation of Eugene O'Neill's *Mourning Becomes Electra.* Originally released at 173 minutes, the edited version seen today seems unusually talky and ponderous, yet Redgrave's performance—for which he was Oscar-nominated—still impresses. He also starred in Fritz Lang's *Secret Beyond the Door* (1948) before returning to England.

The early 1950s gave Redgrave two excellent roles: the repressed schoolteacher in *The Browning Version* (1951) and the madcap Ernest Worthing in *The Importance of Being Earnest* (1952). He also played the cruelly manipulative inquisitor in *1984* (1956), and was truly harrowing as an alcoholic father in *Time Without Pity* (also 1956).

Redgrave, knighted in 1959, also produced and directed numerous plays, wrote three books—"The Actor's Ways and Means" (1955), "Mask or Face" (1958), and "The Mountebank Tale" (1959)—and sired actresses Lynn and Vanessa, and actor Corin. He was married to actress Rachel Kempson. He published his autobiography, "In My Mind's I," in 1983.

OTHER FILMS INCLUDE: 1942: *Lady in Distress;* 1945: *The Way to the Stars;* 1946: *The Captive Heart;* 1947: *The Man Within;* 1951: *The Magic Box;* 1954: *The Green Scarf, The Sea Shall Not Have Them, The Dam Busters;* 1955: *The Night My Number Came Up, Mr. Arkadin;* 1958: *The Quiet American, Law and Disorder, Behind the Mask* (in the last-named with daughter Vanessa); 1959: *Shake Hands With the Devil, The Wreck of the Mary Deare;* 1961: *No, My Darling Daughter!, The Innocents;* 1962: *The Loneliness of the*

Long Distance Runner; 1963: *Uncle Vanya;* 1964: *Young Cassidy;* 1965: *The Hill, The Heroes of Telemark;* 1967: *The 25th Hour, Heidi* (telefilm), *Assignment K;* 1969: *Oh! What a Lovely War, Battle of Britain, Goodbye, Mr. Chips;* 1970: *Goodbye Gemini;* 1971: *The Go-Between, Nicholas and Alexandra.*

REDGRAVE, VANESSA. Actress. *(b. Jan. 30, 1937, London.)* Gifted actress whose significant dramatic achievements are matched only by her profound sense of artistic and political daring. Born into a distinguished theatrical family (her father was the actor Sir Michael Redgrave, and her sister is actress Lynn), young Vanessa trained for the stage at the Central School of Speech and Drama in London. In her first major theatrical role, "A Touch of the Sun" (1958), she played the daughter of a school headmaster (played by her own father). She made her screen debut that year in *Behind the Mask.* In 1959 she became a member of the Stratford-Upon-Avon Theater Company, where she worked with some of the most distinguished talents of the British stage, including her future husband, director Tony Richardson. After successfully negotiating Shakespearean roles, Redgrave easily moved into film work, winning her first international notices for her role in Michelangelo Antonioni's landmark *Blowup* (1966). The same year, she played Anne Boleyn in *A Man for All Seasons,* and was nominated for her first Best Actress Oscar for her work in *Morgan!* She was a lovely and charming Guinevere in *Camelot* (1967), but subsequently eschewed conventional parts and became noted for her uncompromsing approach to difficult and even controversial roles.

Redgrave was again Oscar-nominated for her performance as famed dancer Isadora Duncan in 1968's *Isadora,* aroused the ire of the Vatican for her portrayal as a sexually delirious Mother Superior in Ken Russell's scandalous *The Devils* (1971), and captured yet another nomination for her superbly nuanced portrayal as *Mary, Queen of Scots* (1971). In 1978 Redgrave won an Academy Award for her haunting work in the title role of *Julia,* as the woman who inspires writer Lillian Hellman (played by Jane Fonda). Making her acceptance speech, she managed to alienate much of the Hol-lywood establishment by lambasting "Zionist hoodlums" and using the Oscar ceremony as a bully pulpit to trumpet her support for the Palestinian cause. As a result, there was some protest when she agreed to star as a Jewish concentration camp survivor in the TV movie *Playing for Time* (1980).

She has never backed down from her often volatile opinions, and has lost films, TV, and stage work as a result. Nonetheless, she made memorable appearances in *Agatha* (1979, as mystery writer Agatha Christie), Merchant and Ivory's *The Bostonians* (1984, for which she was Oscar-nominated), *Prick Up Your Ears* (1987, as playwright Joe Orton's agent), and the Merchant-Ivory masterpiece *Howards End* (1992, Oscar-nominated for her heartbreaking performance as the owner of the estate named in the title). She has done some of her best work in high-profile television films such as *Playing for Time* (for which she won an Emmy), *Second Serve* (1986, as transsexual tennis star Renee Richards), Charlton Heston's remake of *A Man for All Seasons* (1988, this time as Alice More), and a remake of *Whatever Happened to Baby Jane?* (1991) that paired her, for the first time, with sister Lynn. She is the mother of actresses Natasha and Joely Richardson. Her autobiography was published in 1994.

OTHER FILMS INCLUDE: 1968: *The Sea Gull, The Charge of the Light Brigade;* 1969: *Oh! What a Lovely War;* 1972: *The Trojan Women;* 1974: *Murder on the Orient Express;* 1976: *The Seven Percent Solution;* 1979: *Yanks;* 1983: *Wagner;* 1985: *Steaming, Wetherby;* 1988: *Consuming Passions;* 1990: *Romeo-Juliet;* 1991: *The Ballad of the Sad Cafe;* 1993: *Great Moments in Aviation;* 1995: *Little Odessa, A Month by the Lake.*

REED, CAROL (SIR). Director, producer. *(b. Dec. 30, 1906, London; d. Apr. 25, 1976.)* The director of so many distinguished films actually began his career in movies as assistant to the decidedly undistinguished (but at the time wildly popular) thriller author Edgar Wallace. Having worked with the writer on his stage productions, Reed aided Wallace in a shortlived plan for Wallace to adapt his own works to the screen. He won his own directorial wings in 1935 on *Midshipman Easy.* His output in that decade included

Climbing High (1938), a pedestrian vehicle for British superstar Jessie Matthews, and the superb The Stars Look Down (1939), about the entry of coal miner's son Michael Redgrave into politics. He began the 1940s auspiciously, artfully helming a Hitchcockian thriller, Night Train to Munich (starring Rex Harrison and Margaret Lockwood, and written by Lady Vanishes scripters Sidney Gilliatt and Frank Launder) and Kipps (1941), the charming H. G. Wells story of a shopkeeper who inherits money and attempts to crash British society.

During World War 2 Reed worked on propaganda features, including an Oscar-winning collaboration with American director Garson Kanin, The True Glory (1945), a documentary assembled from front-line footage shot by Allied cameramen. His first postwar feature was the absorbing drama of the Irish resistance, Odd Man Out (1947), a well-received film, starring James Mason, that led to Reed's five-film stint with producer Alexander Korda. The resulting movies were among his finest, and included two for which he was Oscar-nominated as Best Director: The Fallen Idol (1948), a haunting child's-eye view of adult relations, and The Third Man (1949), the famous Orson Welles–Joseph Cotten thriller focusing on postwar intrigue in divided Vienna. Both films were based on stories by Graham Greene, who also penned Our Man in Havana (1960), another of the director's successes.

Reed helmed the moody circus triangle Trapeze (1956, with Burt Lancaster, Tony Curtis, and Gina Lollobrigida), a Hollywood-packaged drama shot in Europe. The 1960s saw him working on several epics, including the notorious remake of Mutiny on the Bounty (1962) starring Marlon Brando, from which he was fired (and replaced by Lewis Milestone), and The Agony and the Ecstasy (1965), starring Charlton Heston as Michelangelo painting the Sistine Chapel. Reed won a Best Director Academy Award for Oliver! (1968), the elaborate musical retelling of Dickens' "Oliver Twist." His last film was Follow Me (1972, known as The Public Eye in the United States), an unsuccessful romantic pairing of Mia Farrow and Fiddler on the Roof star Topol. His nephew is British star Oliver Reed, who played Bill Sykes in Oliver!

OTHER FILMS INCLUDE: 1937: Talk of the Devil, Bank Holiday; 1939: A Girl Must Live; 1940: The Girl in the News; 1942: The Young Mr. Pitt; 1944: The Way Ahead; 1951: Outcast of the Islands; 1953: The Man Between; 1954: A Kid for Two Farthings; 1958: The Key; 1963: The Running Man; 1970: Flap.

REED, DONNA. Actress. (b. Jan. 27, 1921, Denison, Iowa, as Donna Belle Mullenger; d. Jan. 14, 1986.) She was the perfect wife, the all-American embodiment of feminine appeal, in Frank Capra's enduring classic It's a Wonderful Life (1946). But her wholesome appeal was rarely put to good use; MGM signed the farm-raised campus queen in 1941, and made her a utility player in the likes of Babes on Broadway (her debut), Shadow of the Thin Man (both 1941), The Courtship of Andy Hardy, Calling Dr. Gillespie (both 1942), The Human Comedy (1943), and numerous others. Her role as Navy nurse (and John Wayne's love interest) in John Ford's They Were Expendable (1945) gave her more shading and nuance, and showed what she was capable of. She finally broke the mold in 1953's From Here to Eternity, playing Alma, a prostitute (though not referred to as such, given Hollywood's censorship restrictions); the performance earned her a Best Supporting Actress Oscar. But it was back to the kitchen for her most successful venture, "The Donna Reed Show," a long-running sitcom (1958–66), produced by her husband, Tony Owen. Her movie career basically finished, she appeared in a few TV movies and on the series "Dallas" during the 1984–85 season.

OTHER FILMS INCLUDE: 1941: The Get-Away; 1942: Eyes in the Night; 1945: See Here, Private Hargrove, The Picture of Dorian Gray; 1947: Green Dolphin Street; 1951: Saturday's Hero; 1953: Trouble Along the Way, The Caddy; 1954: The Last Time I Saw Paris; 1955: The Far Horizons, The Benny Goodman Story.

REED, OLIVER. Actor. (b. Feb. 13, 1938, London.) Oliver Reed first raised eyebrows in the title role of Curse of the Werewolf, a 1961 Hammer horror film—but this dark, sullen leading man wasn't about to be typecast in cheesy genre films. His talent earned him better roles in better films like These Are the Damned (1963),

I'll Never Forget What's 'is Name, The Jokers (both 1967), *Hannibal Brooks* (1969) and, especially, as brutish Bill Sykes in the multi-Oscar-winning *Oliver!* (1968, directed by his uncle, Carol Reed). Ken Russell cast him as one of the principals in his groundbreaking 1969 hit *Women in Love,* which startled audiences with the sight of Reed and costar Alan Bates wrestling in the nude. He appeared in Russell's hysterical, excessive *The Devils* (1971), and achieved popularity starring in high-profile adventure flicks like Richard Lester's *The Three Musketeers* (1974, as Athos) and its sequel, *The Four Musketeers* (1975). He gave singing a try in Russell's has-to-be-seen-to-be-believed lensing of The Who's rock opera *Tommy* (1975), with results almost as jaw-dropping as the movie itself. Increasingly he took to working in genre films, such as *Maniac* (1977), *The Brood* (1979), *Venom* (1981), *Spasms* (1982), *Dragonard,* and *Gor* (both 1987).

Nicolas Roeg's *Castaway* (1987) gave Reed a temporary respite from the junk parade, casting him as a middle-aged romantic who hires a "wife" (Amanda Donohoe) to accompany him to an uninhabited desert island. Often described as a hard-drinking, temperamental, difficult type, both his girth and his never-entirely-quashed tendency to chew scenery have swelled over the years, and both can be viewed in abundance in the low-budget horror films he's taken to appearing in recently, including the distasteful 1988 *The House of Usher.*
OTHER FILMS INCLUDE: 1960: *The Angry Silence, The League of Gentlemen;* 1975: *Ten Little Indians;* 1978: *Crossed Swords;* 1980: *Dr. Heckle and Mr. Hype;* 1989: *The Adventures of Baron Munchausen* (as Vulcan), *The Return of the Musketeers;* 1993: "*Return to Lonesome Dove*" (miniseries).

REED, PAMELA. Actress. *(b. Apr. 2, 1949, Tacoma, Wash.)* She's been cast as a long-suffering wife or girlfriend once too often, as in *Melvin and Howard* (1980), *The Right Stuff* (1983), *The Goodbye People* (1984), *The Best of Times* (1986), and *Cadillac Man* (1990), but Pamela Reed consistently enlivens the films in which she appears, and it's not impossible that she'll yet scale greater heights. This fresh-faced actress, who first elicited attention as Belle Starr in *The Long Riders* (1980),

had good supporting parts in *Eyewitness* (1981) and *The Clan of the Cave Bear* (1986), and virtually stole *Kindergarten Cop* (1990) with her hilarious impersonation of Arnold Schwarzenegger's "sister." And her deadpan delivery of some clever lines in *Passed Away* (1992) confirms the belief that comedy may well be her metier. On TV Reed has played the feisty campaign manager on "Tanner '88," the beleaguered maid on "Grand" (both 1990), and costarred in "Family Album" (1993). She worked with Arnold again in *Junior* (1994).

REEVE, CHRISTOPHER. Actor. *(b. Sept. 25, 1952, New York City.)* He's become synonymous with Superman—but he's yet to make a dent with moviegoers in any other role. The Juilliard-trained stage actor played the part so winningly in 1978's *Superman* it made him an overnight star. (He'd already made one brief screen appearance in 1978's *Gray Lady Down.*) He returned for *Superman II, III,* and *IV* and meanwhile tried to carve a career away from the Man of Steel, but met with mixed results in such films as *Somewhere in Time* (1980), *Deathtrap,* and *Monsignor* (both 1982). He took a risk with the gritty *Street Smart* (1987), playing an opportunistic reporter drawn into a seedy world of pimps and prostitutes, but was outshone by supporting cast members, including Kathy Baker and Morgan Freeman. He used his leverage with the Superman producers to make *Superman IV: The Quest for Peace* (1987) more socially relevant than earlier entries, and helped concoct the simplistic script. He's fairly active in miniseries and made-for-TV movies, as well as on stage; he's found his greatest success in farcical roles that make fun of his somewhat stolid demeanor, as in *Switching Channels* (1988, in "the Ralph Bellamy part") and *Noises Off* (1992).
OTHER FILMS INCLUDE: 1984: *The Bostonians;* 1985: *The Aviator;* 1993: *The Sea Wolf* (telefilm), *The Remains of the Day, Morning Glory;* 1995: *Village of the Damned.*

REEVES, KEANU. Actor. *(b. Sept. 2, 1964, Beirut.)* Gangly, vacant-looking young actor who has proven himself a skilled screen performer in a surprising variety of roles, beginning in 1986 (with *Youngblood)*, from the dumb-but-goodhearted in gonzo teen comedies *Bill & Ted's Excellent Adventure* (1989) and *Bill & Ted's Bogus Journey* (1991), to the appealing-but-venal in the extremely off-beat *My Own Private Idaho* (1991). He seems to have been born to play troubled modern teens, as he has in *River's Edge* (1987), *The Prince of Pennsylvania, The Night Before,* and the high-school suicide tale *Permanent Record* (all 1988). But he's been equally impressive in the costume drama *Dangerous Liaisons* (1988) and the offbeat early-1950s comedy *Tune in Tomorrow* . . . (1990). He can play straight (as in 1989's *Parenthood*) or for laughs (as in 1990's *I Love You to Death*).

He's come face-to-face with the Prince of Darkness in *Bram Stoker's Dracula* (1992), tackled Shakespeare in Kenneth Branagh's *Much Ado About Nothing* (1993), and played Prince Siddhartha for Bernardo Bertolucci in *Little Buddha* (1994). (He also contributed a cameo to his friend—and *Bill & Ted* costar—Alex Winter's 1993 film *Freaked*.) Other recent credits include *Even Cowgirls Get the Blues* and *Speed* (both 1994). Not everyone has accepted this youthful actor in his "classical" parts, but his earnestness has won many converts.

REINER, CARL. Actor, writer, producer, director. (b. Mar. 20, 1923, Bronx, N.Y.) A veritable Renaissance man of comedy, this genial one-man band has been an integral cog in American humor for four decades. He came to fame in the 1950s as a writer/performer on "Your Show of Shows" and "Caesar's Hour," winning two Emmys supporting the show's star, Sid Caesar. In 1961 he created (and often wrote) "The Dick Van Dyke Show," on which he also played tyrannical variety show host Alan Brady; he won five Emmys for the show, three for writing and two for producing. He broke into screenwriting with two popular Norman Jewison comedies, *The Thrill of It All* (1963, also playing a funny cameo) and *The Art of Love* (1965); Jewison then gave him a starring role in *The Russians Are Coming! The Russians Are Coming!* (1966). That same year, he published the autobiographical "Enter Laughing," and made his directorial debut in 1967 with its screen adaptation. He reunited with Dick Van Dyke for the bitter-

sweet depiction of early Hollywood, *The Comic* (1969, which he cowrote) and then directed the cult comedy *Where's Poppa?* (1970). A period of inactivity ended with *Oh, God!* (1977) and a spate of films that led stand-up comic Steve Martin to screen stardom: *The Jerk* (1979), *Dead Men Don't Wear Plaid* (1982), *The Man With Two Brains* (1983), all of which he also cowrote, and *All of Me* (1984). Other films include *The One and Only* (1978), *Summer Rental* (1985), *Summer School* (1987), *Bert Rigby, You're a Fool* (1989, which he also wrote), *Sibling Rivalry* (1990), and *Fatal Instinct* (1993). His acting credits over the years include *The Gazebo* (1959), *Gidget Goes Hawaiian* (1961, as Gidget's father), *It's a Mad Mad Mad Mad World* (1963), *A Guide for the Married Man* (1967), *Generation* (1969), *The End* (1978), along with amusing cameos in many of his own movies. He also appeared many times on television (and in a series of hilarious record albums) as straight man to Mel Brooks' 2000-Year-Old Man. Reiner's sons Rob and Lucas have followed him into acting and directing.

REINER, ROB. Director, producer, actor. (b. Mar. 6, 1945, New York City.) As an actor, Rob Reiner cut his teeth in films directed by his father Carl, including *Enter Laughing* (1967) and *Where's Poppa?* (1970). Then he costarred in one of television's landmark shows, the sharp-tongued sitcom "All in the Family" (1971–78). Cast as the liberal son-in-law of bigoted Archie Bunker (who referred to him as "Meathead") he found his niche in TV history, and won two Emmy Awards. His attempts to create his own followup series were nowhere near as successful, but he did cowrite and coproduce a pair of TV movies, in which he also starred, *More Than Friends* (1979, with then-wife Penny Marshall) and *Million Dollar Infield* (1982). He also appeared in such features as *Halls of Anger* (1970), *Summertree* (1971), and *Fire Sale* (1977). He scored his first hit behind the camera as the director and cowriter of the mock rock documentary, *This Is Spinal Tap* (1984); he also appeared onscreen as director Marty DeBergi. With one foot in the director's door, he followed up with *The Sure Thing* (1985) and then caught the brass ring with

Stephen King's ode to adolescence, *Stand by Me* (1986). Since then he's become one of Hollywood's most bankable directors, with such varied mainstream movies as *The Princess Bride* (1987), *When Harry Met Sally . . .* (1989), *Misery* (1990), *A Few Good Men* (1992), and *North* (1994). As a principal in Castle Rock Productions, he has also had a hand in producing films and TV series, often in partnership with longtime friends like Billy Crystal. He occasionally takes an acting part, and makes the most of it, as he did in *Throw Momma From the Train* (1987, directed by Crystal), *Postcards From the Edge* (1990), *The Spirit of 76* (1990, directed by his brother Lucas), *Sleepless in Seattle* (1993), Woody Allen's *Bullets Over Broadway* (1994), and *Bye Bye, Love* (1995).

REINHOLD, JUDGE. Actor. *(b. May 21, 1957, Wilmington, Del.)* As the clear-headed high-school senior Brad in *Fast Times at Ridgemont High* (1982), this likable, lanky blond comedic actor established a goofy but endearing persona that has made him one of today's most recognizable screen presences. He was equally effective as a second (or was it third?) banana in *Beverly Hills Cop* (1984, plus the 1987 sequel) and *Ruthless People* (1986), but less effective in his own starring vehicles *Head Office, Off Beat* (both 1986), and *Vice Versa* (1988), in which his minimalistic style reached an extreme. He was best served in recent years by the made-for-TV Western comedy *Four Eyes and Six-Guns* (1992). In 1994 he joined Eddie Murphy for a third time in *Beverly Hills Cop 3.*
OTHER FILMS INCLUDE: 1981: *Stripes;* 1982: *Pandemonium;* 1983: *The Lords of Discipline;* 1984: *Gremlins, Roadhouse 66;* 1988: *A Soldier's Tale* (in a small role); 1989: *Rosalie Goes Shopping;* 1990: *Daddy's Dyin' . . . Who's Got the Will?;* 1991: *Zandalee;* 1993: *Near Misses, Bank Robber.*

REISZ, KAREL. Director, producer, critic, essayist. *(b. July 21, 1926, Ostrava, Czechoslovakia.)* Czech-born filmmaker who lived in England from age 12, narrowly avoiding the Nazi scourge that overtook his native land, and developed a fascination with film in the early 1950s, writing numerous essays on the medium, and a seminal book on film esthetics, "The Technique of Film Editing." Along with fellow theorists Lindsay Anderson and Tony Richardson, he was a prime proponent of British Free Cinema. He and Richardson codirected a 1955 short, *Momma Don't Allow,* and in 1959 Reisz soloed on the well-received documentary *We Are the Lambeth Boys.* He made an impressive feature directing debut with *Saturday Night and Sunday Morning* (1960), a highly acclaimed look at British working-class life. Reisz's output has been sporadic since then (although he's kept busy making commercials and working for British television), but it includes the remake of *Night Must Fall* (1964), the cult favorite *Morgan! A Suitable Case for Treatment* (1966), and the biographical drama *Isadora* (1968). He also produced *This Sporting Life* (1963) for Lindsay Anderson. His American films have been similarly varied in nature: *The Gambler* (1974), *Who'll Stop the Rain* (1978), *The French Lieutenant's Woman* (1981), *Sweet Dreams* (1985), and *Everybody Wins* (1990). He is married to actress Betsy Blair.

REITMAN, IVAN. Director, producer, composer. *(b. Oct. 26, 1946, Czechoslovakia.)* Canadian-raised filmmaker who began his show-biz career as a stage and TV producer, but is now a top producer/director of commercially successful mainstream films, mostly comedies. Reitman directed *Foxy Lady* (1971) and *Cannibal Girls* (1972), two modest Canadian films, before assuming the role of producer on director David Cronenberg's first mainstream horror films, *They Came From Within* (1975) and *Rabid* (1977, starring ex-porn diva Marilyn Chambers). With close links to the Canadian- and Chicago-based "Second City" troupes, he embarked upon a group of comedies. He produced the hugely successful *National Lampoon's Animal House* (1978), which helped launch John Belushi as a major screen presence, then directed *Meatballs* (1979), which made a box-office star of Bill Murray, and *Stripes* (1981) which starred Murray, writer/performer Harold Ramis, and John Candy. *Ghostbusters* (1984) really hit pay dirt, teaming Dan Aykroyd, Murray, and Ramis in a blockbuster comedy that demanded a 1989 sequel.

Since then Reitman has directed (and produced) a series of major-league Hollywood films: *Legal Eagles* (1986, a rare flop), *Twins* (1988, Arnold Schwarzenegger's first hit comedy), *Kindergarten Cop* (1990), *Dave* (1993), and *Junior* (1994). He has also produced or executive produced *Big Shots* (1987), *Casual Sex?* (1988), *Beethoven* (1992), and *Beethoven's 2nd* (1993).

REMICK, LEE. Actress. *(b. Dec. 14, 1935, Quincy, Mass.; d. July 2, 1991.)* Versatile, stunningly beautiful actress with wavy blond hair and pale blue eyes, whose screen appeal stemmed from a prim, patrician bearing that barely concealed her sensuality. Remick was born in a Boston suburb and taken to New York by her divorced mother at the age of seven. She acted as a student at Barnard College and the Actors' Studio, making it to Broadway in 1953 with "Be Your Age." At the tender age of 21, she made her film debut in Elia Kazan's *A Face in the Crowd* (released 1957), playing a drum majorette who becomes involved with TV personality Lonesome Rhodes (Andy Griffith). This led to a series of starring parts in high-visibility pictures, which included *The Long Hot Summer* (1958, as Orson Welles' daughter-in-law), *Anatomy of a Murder* (1959, as a kittenish rape victim who makes things difficult for attorney James Stewart), *Sanctuary* (1961, as a curiously willing rape victim in this notorious William Faulkner tale), *Experiment in Terror* (1962, as a psycho's frightened prey) and *Days of Wine and Roses* (also 1962). In the latter, she gave a dazzling performance as an alcoholic, earning an Oscar nomination as Best Actress. Rather than pigeonhole herself, she diversified, returning to the stage and appearing in numerous TV productions in between screen assignments in *The Wheeler Dealers* (1963), *Baby the Rain Must Fall* (1965, as the wife of ex-con Steve McQueen), *The Hallelujah Trail* (also 1965, as a temperance evangelist), *No Way to Treat a Lady* (1968), *The Detective* (also 1968, as Frank Sinatra's oversexed wife), *Sometimes a Great Notion* (1971), and *A Delicate Balance* (1973). Throughout the 1970s she lived in London, but

found time to film *The Omen* (1976, as the unwitting mother of the Antichrist), *The Medusa Touch* (1978), *The Europeans* (1979), *The Competition*, and *Tribute* (both 1980). Remick became increasingly active in television, starring in such high-profile telefilms as *The Blue Knight* (1973), *Hustling* (1975), *Ike* (1979, as General Eisenhower's wartime driver and lover), *The Women's Room* (1980), *Haywire* (also 1980, as troubled actress Margaret Sullavan) *The Letter* (1982, in the role played onscreen earlier by Jeanne Eagels and Bette Davis), "Mistral's Daughter" (1984 miniseries), "Nutcracker: Money, Madness, Murder" (1987 miniseries), *Bridge to Silence* (1989), and the delightful British-made miniseries "Jennie: Lady Randolph Churchill" (1974), in which she played Jennie Churchill.

RENOIR, JEAN. Director, screenwriter, actor. *(b. Sept. 15, 1894, Paris; d. Feb. 12, 1979.)* This filmmaker is universally regarded as one of the greatest artists the medium has ever known. Unique in outlook, individual in treatment, he had an uncanny appreciation of what was true and honest in cinema. Several of his pictures—notably *Grand Illusion* and *Rules of the Game*—repeatedly turn up on lists of the greatest movies ever made. The son of painter Auguste Renoir, he began directing in the 1920s, financing some of his films by selling some of his late father's works. Renoir's first films—*Une Vie sans joie/Catherine* (1924, written but not directed by Renoir), *La Fille de l'eau* (1925), and *Nana* (1926)—starred then-wife Catherine Hessling (his father's model in later years). The last mentioned, an adaptation of Zola's novel "Nana," was a costly failure and Renoir had to become a director for hire on *Marquitta* (1927) before he could make *The Little Match Girl* (1928) and *Tire-au-Flance* (also 1928), an army comedy which featured Michel Simon, who would become the filmmaker's favorite actor. Following more purely commercial assignments, Renoir made his first sound film, *On purge Bébé* (1931) and then his first great film, *La Chienne* (also 1931), with Simon as a timid cashier who is drawn into murder. *La Nuit du Carrefour* (1932) starred Renoir's older brother Pierre as Inspector Maigret and *Boudu Saved From Drowning* (also 1932) featured Simon in a brilliant performance as a tramp who is saved from suicide and proceeds to wreak havoc on his savior's life. (Renoir admirer Paul Mazursky remade it, decades later, as *Down and Out in Beverly Hills.*)

David Thomson wrote that "Renoir's greatness lies in his repeated desire to take risks, to make new sorts of film, to be experimental" and that "during the 1930s there is not an adventure in natural light, camera movement, depth of focus, real location, the blending of interior and exterior that Renoir did not make." He adapted *Madame Bovary* (1934), used real locations and nonprofessional actors in *Toni* (1935), and turned to politics with the working-class studies *The Crime of Monsieur Lange* and *The People of France* (both 1936). *Grand Illusion* (1937), a magnificent study of three French POWs and the commandant who runs the prison camp, has frequently been called the greatest antiwar film ever made, although its insights into loyalty, class, and humanity transcend any labels. It was Renoir's first international success and it remains his best-known work. Following *La Marseillaise* and *La Bête humaine* (both 1938), Renoir made *Rules of the Game* (1939), often cited as one of the greatest works in the history of cinema. Set at a country house party (with Renoir himself in a central role), this magesterial examination of class divisions and manners was a commercial failure when it was originally released. The film was severely edited, then banned, and only restored to its original length years later.

After an aborted attempt at directing an Italian-French production, Renoir came to the United States and made films for 20th Century-Fox, beginning with *Swamp Water* (1941), a thriller set in the Okefenokee area of Georgia. The films that followed—*This Land Is Mine* (1943), *Diary of a Chambermaid* (1946), and *The Woman on the Beach* (1947)—saw Renoir basically marking time. Only *The Southerner* (1945), a beautifully told story of struggling sharecroppers, came close to embodying the style of his early French films. (It also earned him an Oscar nomination as Best Director.) Renoir went to India to make *The River* (1951, in color), an adaptation of Rumer Godden's novel about an English family in Bengal, that showed the director's lyrical eye had not been dulled by his time spent in the U.S. Next came the sublime *The Golden Coach* (1953), starring Anna Magnani, and finally a return to France for *Only the French Can/French Can-Can* (1955), a gorgeous homage to the Moulin Rouge, which was a tremendous success. He followed with the lightweight *Paris Does Strange Things* (1956), a stunningly shot *Picnic on the Grass* (1959), and *The Testament of Dr. Cordelier* (also 1959), a loose reworking of "Dr. Jekyll and Mr. Hyde" for TV. *The Elusive Corporal* (1962) found Renoir back in the territory of *Grand Illusion,* with Frenchmen trying to escape from a Nazi prison camp. Following the short *La Direction d'acteur par Jean Renoir* (1968), he directed his last film, *The Little Theatre of Jean Renoir* (1971), a slight but charming collection of sketches (originally made for TV) that reaffirmed the humanity at the core of his art. His autobiography, "My Life and My Films," was published in 1974; a year later, he received an honorary Academy Award for his incalculable effect on films. As Thomson put it, "He is the greatest of directors; he justifies cinema."

RESNAIS, ALAIN. Director, screenwriter, editor, cinematographer. *(b. June 3, 1922, Vannes, France.)* Influential French New Wave director whose infatuation with cinema dates back to his youth. At age fourteen, he made his first amateur 8mm film; he went on to study at the Institut des Hautes Études Cinématographiques in Paris. Resnais's professional career began in the immediate postwar era when he made a series of short films, a number of which dealt with artists and art-related subjects: *Van Gogh* (1948), which won an Academy Award, *Gauguin* and *Guernica* (both 1950). During this period, he also shot and edited films for other directors. His documentary featurettes *Night and Fog* (1955), a chilling, landmark examination of German concentration camps, and *Le Chant du Styrene* (1958), a poetic look at a plastics factory (in widescreen, no less), demonstrated that he was ready for more ambitious projects. Resnais's first 35mm feature, *Hiroshima, mon amour* (1959)—in 1946, he made a 16mm feature, *Ouvert pour cause d'inventaire*—dealt with the nature of history and

memory, and deviated from traditional no-
tions of narrative time as it recounted a
fleeting liaison between a French actress
and Japanese architect. Its sexual candor
and provocative ideas, wedded to a dazzlingly sophisticated visual style, made
Hiroshima, Mon Amour the New Wave's
The Birth of a Nation, and it deservedly
won the Cannes Film Festival International Critics Prize. Resnais's follow-up
was *Last Year at Marienbad* (1961), in
which a man encounters a woman at a resort, where they may or may not have previously met (and had an affair). The film,
which further examined the nature of
memory, was an elliptical, clever bit of
cinematic conjuring that even today pro-
vokes widely divergent responses.

Resnais's directorial output since then
has been spotty—he has made barely a
dozen films—but his highly personal approach has always been in evidence. The
political realities of 20th-century Europe,
along with a continued concern with time
and remembrance, were dealt with in
Muriel (1963) and *La Guerre est finie*
(1966), a portrait of a weary, aging Leftist
which is arguably Resnais's richest film
emotionally. *Stavisky* (1974), the biography of a Russian-Jewish swindler in
1930s France, was sparkling and intellectually engaging, showing Resnais at his
peak. *Providence* (1977) was his first
English-language effort, a stylish but
muddled misfire about a dying novelist.
Resnais was back in top form with *Mon
oncle d'Amerique* (1980), in which he fo-
cuses on the intertwining connection
among three individuals and, in so doing,
scrutinizes human relations via the theories of the French research biologist Henri
Laborit. He was equally compelling in
Life Is a Bed of Roses (1983), his last important film to date, in which he continued
to experiment with narrative structure by
contrasting the stories of a wealthy count
who constructs a "temple of happiness"
during the 1920s and a symposium on al-
ternative education at that site in the present day. Since *Life Is a Bed of Roses,*
Resnais's films have been far less engaging: *L'Amour à Mort* (1984), *Melo* (1986),
about a love triangle, *I Want to Go Home*
(1989), scripted by cartoonist/playwright
Jules Feiffer and starring playwright-
lyricist Adolph Green (which for some
reason was never released in the U.S.),
and most recently, a matched pair of

films, *Smoking* and *No Smoking* (1993).
He also directed *Gershwin* (1992), a one-
hour video tribute to George Gershwin,
whose music he had featured in *I Want to
Go Home.* Resnais has worked in collaboration with some of the top writers and in-
tellectuals of his time, including Marguerite Duras, Alain Robbe-Grillet, Jean
Gruault, Jorge Semprun and Jean Cayrol.

REY, FERNANDO. Actor. *(b. Sept. 20,
1917, La Coruna, Spain, as Fernando Casado
Arambillet; d. Mar. 9, 1994.)* Once described
as "probably the most believable man of
the world in contemporary movies," this
elegant Spanish actor's witty, urbane performances have graced scores of international films. He studied at Madrid's
School of Architecture before joining his
father, a Republican Army officer, in battle during the Spanish Civil War. After the
war, Rey found work as a movie extra and
then became noted for dubbing the voices
of stars like Tyrone Power and Laurence
Olivier into Spanish, before establishing
his own reputation on camera. He is probably best known to American audiences as
the elusive drug kingpin "Frog One" in
the Oscar-winning thriller *The French
Connection* (1971) and its less-successful
sequel, *French Connection II* (1975). He
did some of his finest work for Luis
Buñuel, starring in four of the director's
striking films: *Viridiana* (1961), *Tristana*
(1970), *The Discreet Charm of the Bourgeoisie* (1972), and *That Obscure Object
of Desire* (1977). Rey, who also appeared
in Orson Welles' *Chimes at Midnight*
(1966, as Worcester), Lina Wertmuller's
Seven Beauties, and *Voyage of the
Damned* (both 1976), won the Best Actor
Award at Cannes for his role as a writer in
Elisa, My Love (1977).
OTHER FILMS INCLUDE: 1954: *The Siege;*
1963: *The Ceremony;* 1968: *The Immortal
Story, Villa Rides;* 1969: *Guns of the Magnificent Seven;* 1973: *Antony and Cleopatra;*
1976: *A Matter of Time;* 1979: *Quintet;*
1980: *Caboblanco;* 1982: *Monsignor;* 1984:
The Hit; 1986: *Saving Grace;* 1988: *Moon
Over Parador;* 1992: *1492: Conquest of Par-
adise.*

REYNOLDS, BURT. Actor, director. *(b.
Feb. 11, 1936, Waycross, Ga.)* Popular star
of 1970s and early 1980s films who, in

various phases of his career, has played stone-faced, macho types and cocky, smart-mouthed good ol' boys with equal ease. Part Cherokee Indian, he grew up near Palm Beach, Florida, and was a college football star with Florida State University before being sidelined first by a knee injury and then by a serious car accident. Reynolds quit college to become an actor and made his way to New York, where he toiled in menial jobs between infrequent stage stints. Spotted in a revival of "Mister Roberts," he won a contract with Universal and came to Hollywood.

Initially costarring in the TV series "Riverboat" (1959–60), Reynolds made his feature-film debut in *Angel Baby* (1961). For the next 10 or so years he bounced between TV and features, appearing as a regular on "Gunsmoke" (1962–65) and starring in two cop shows, "Hawk" (1966) and "Dan August" (1970–71), in addition to working in the films *Armored Command* (1961), *Operation C.I.A.* (1965), *Navajo Joe* (1966), *Sam Whiskey, 100 Rifles, Impasse, Shark!* (all 1969), and *Skullduggery* (1970). His dark, brooding countenance and tight-lipped acting style frequently got him cast as full-blooded Indians or half-breeds.

In 1972 Reynolds decided his career needed shaking up. He posed for a "nude" centerfold shot in "Cosmopolitan" magazine, which was considered to be the height of good sportsmanship in that era of burgeoning feminism. His easy charm and self-deprecating wit also made him a popular guest on the TV talk-show circuit. And he sought out roles with comedic aspects, such as *Fuzz* and *Everything You Always Wanted to Know About Sex (But Were Afraid to Ask)* (both 1972). But it was his hard-bitten turn as the weekend warrior in *Deliverance* (also 1972) that firmly, and finally, established Reynolds as a top box-office draw—and an actor of some skill.

White Lightning (1973) was the first Reynolds vehicle to exploit his good-ol'-boy appeal, and involve him with car chases, gorgeous girls, lamebrain comedy, fast action, moonshine, and menace. *W.W. and the Dixie Dancekings* (1975), *Gator* (1976, which he also directed), and his collaborations with old friend and stunt specialist/director Hal Needham, *Smokey and the Bandit* (1977), *Smokey and the Bandit II* (1980), *The Cannonball Run*

(1981), *Stroker Ace* (with future wife Loni Anderson), *Cannonball Run II,* and *Smokey and the Bandit 3* (all 1983) saw Reynolds tapping into his prime market, the drive-in circuits and rural neighborhood houses.

He top lined other types of films as well: *Shamus, The Man Who Loved Cat Dancing* (both 1973), the gritty prison football yarn *The Longest Yard* (1974), the musical misfire *At Long Last Love,* the Prohibition-era comedy *Lucky Lady* (both 1975), and the silent-movie-era saga *Nickelodeon* (1976).

Reynolds hit his stride in the late 1970s with a string of highly entertaining films that were enjoyed by audiences and critics alike: *Semi-Tough* (1977, as a football star), *The End* (1978, a sharp black comedy that he also directed), *Hooper* (also 1978, an exuberant comedy about stuntmen), and *Starting Over* (1979, as a divorced man trying to regain his footing). In interviews he spoke of his "game plan" to alternate sophisticated fare like *Starting Over* with more yahoo comedies, but his luck soon ran out as the quality of his vehicles, from both ends of the spectrum, slipped—and with it, his box-office potency.

Films like *Rough Cut* (1980), *Paternity* (1981), *Sharky's Machine* (also 1981, which he also directed), *Best Friends, The Best Little Whorehouse in Texas* (both 1982), *The Man Who Loved Women* (1983), *City Heat* (1984), and *Stick* (1985, which he also directed) saw a downward spiral abetted by more than one bad-luck production involving a change of director, extensive reshooting, etc.

By this time, a noticeably gaunt Reynolds looked and sounded so weak that rumors began to spread that he had AIDS. It wasn't true, but he did battle a debilitating illness that kept him out of the public eye for more than a year. Unfortunately, his "comeback" vehicles *Heat, Malone* (both 1987), and *Rent-a-Cop* (1988) were uniformly poor. He did his best work in *Switching Channels* (1988), in the Cary Grant role from *His Girl Friday,* but it too failed to score at the box office. Reynolds then essayed his first character role, as an aging safecracker in the Bill Forsyth film *Breaking In* (1989), and turned in an excellent job. (That same year he voiced the lead character in the animated feature *All Dogs Go to Heaven,* with then-wife Loni

Anderson as his animated leading lady.) Ironically, Reynolds' celebrity remained intact during this period; he just couldn't seem to land a hit movie, or draw an audience.

Television finally came to the rescue. He starred in the short-lived series "B.L. Stryker" (1988–90) and then hit pay dirt with an easygoing sitcom, "Evening Shade" (1990–94), that reunited him with many favorite costars and colleagues (and won him an Emmy). This led in turn to a new starring vehicle, *Cop and a Half* (1993).

Since 1978 he has owned and operated a dinner theater in Jupiter, Florida, frequently directing as well as starring in shows there, and persuading Hollywood pals to do the same. Formerly married to actresses Judy Carne and Loni Anderson.

REYNOLDS, DEBBIE. Actress. *(b. Apr. 1, 1932, El Paso, Tex., as Mary Frances Reynolds.)* Spunky, sassy, and charming, Debbie Reynolds' discovery was a Cinderella story come true. As a child her family moved to Burbank, California, and when she was crowned Miss Burbank in 1948, Warner Bros. took notice and signed the teenager to a film contract. She made her film debut in *June Bride* (1948), and following *The Daughter of Rosie O'Grady,* Reynolds moved to MGM, where she made her mark as the pert songstress of *Three Little Words* (playing Helen Kane, who dubbed her vocalizing of "I Wanna Be Loved by You"). She nearly stole *Two Weeks With Love* (1950) out from under star Jane Powell with her peppy production number, "Abba Dabba Honeymoon" with Carleton Carpenter.

With 1952 came *Singin' in the Rain,* her best opportunity to date. As the chorus girl who lends her voice to a silent-film star in the early days of talkies, Reynolds held her own with costars (and more accomplished troupers) Gene Kelly and Donald O'Connor, keeping pace with them in a spirited presentation of "Good Morning." It was a star-making turn for Reynolds, who subsequently played in lighthearted musicals and comedies such as *I Love Melvin, The Affairs of Dobie Gillis* (both 1953), *Athena* (1954), and *The Tender Trap* (1955), as well as Paddy Chayefsky's *The Catered Affair* (1956). Then she married handsome singing star

Eddie Fisher, and their "perfect" coupling was celebrated in the movie *Bundle of Joy* (1956). (The union abruptly ended in divorce when Fisher left Reynolds to marry Elizabeth Taylor in 1959.)

The rural romance *Tammy and the Bachelor* (1957) not only gave Reynolds an ideal romantic vehicle of her own, but also produced a Top 10 hit for her with the title song "Tammy." *This Happy Feeling* (1958), *It Started With a Kiss, The Mating Game, The Gazebo, Say One for Me* (all 1959), *The Rat Race* (1960), *The Pleasure of His Company, The Second Time Around* (both 1961), *How the West Was Won* (1962), *Mary, Mary,* and *My Six Loves* (1963) were by and large popular choices for the perky actress, but her choicest role was that of *The Unsinkable Molly Brown* (1964), the musical biography of a rambunctious, larger-than-life figure, for which she was Oscar-nominated. The triumph of *Molly Brown* had little lasting impact on her screen career, though. The movie musical was all but dead in Hollywood, and finding suitable starring vehicles was difficult.

The much-maligned *The Singing Nun* (1966) was only slightly better than its bad reviews would indicate, and the intelligent comedy *Divorce American Style* (1967), while it had its moments (casting her against type, like costar Dick Van Dyke), did little to bolster the star's sagging box-office appeal. Other 1960s vehicles like *Goodbye Charlie* (1964) and *How Sweet It Is!* (1968) are better forgotten. What's more, her TV sitcom "The Debbie Reynolds Show" lasted just one season (1969–70). In *What's the Matter With Helen?* (1971), Reynolds did well as a character in the Baby Jane/Norma Desmond groove. In 1973 she was the principal voice in the animated *Charlotte's Web* (1973) and was the youngest "host" of *That's Entertainment!* (1974). She is also one of the onscreen "hosts" of *That's Entertainment! III* (1994). When her screen career slowed down, Reynolds became a popular stage and nightclub entertainer (emphasizing her gift for mimicry), and has been a Las Vegas mainstay for decades. She received a Tony nomination for her 1973 revival of "Irene" on Broadway, and has toured with "The Unsinkable Molly Brown." On TV she's starred in *Sadie and Son,* a movie/pilot for a proposed series that cast her as a Jewish-momma cop! But sadly, a proposed TV vehicle that would pair her with daughter Carrie Fisher has yet to materialize. (In 1993 she did take a small but notable part as Tommy Lee Jones' mother in Oliver Stone's *Heaven and Earth.*) Years ago, Reynolds began acquiring movie costumes and memorabilia, hoping they would become part of a Hollywood museum; finally, in 1993, she acquired a hotel in Las Vegas to house the collection.

RICHARDSON, MIRANDA. Actress. *(b. Mar. 3, 1958, Lancashire, England.)* Talented British actress who made a phenomenal screen debut as Ruth Ellis, the last woman to be executed in England, in Mike Newell's *Dance With a Stranger* (1985). A student of the Old Vic Drama School, Richardson appeared in many theatrical and TV productions, and has worked in such films as *The Innocent* (1985), *Underworld* (1986), *Empire of the Sun* (1987), and *The Fool* (1990). But in 1992, she dazzled critics and audiences alike in three successive roles that demonstrated her extraordinary versatility: as the depressed London housewife in *Enchanted April* (again with director Newell, in a sunnier mood), as the wife of a philandering Parliament minister in Louis Malle's *Damage* (for which she was Oscar-nominated), and as a cold-blooded IRA terrorist in Neil Jordan's *The Crying Game*. Recent credits include *Century* (1993), the made-for-cable movie *Fatherland,* and an emotional turn as T. S. Eliot's disturbed wife in *Tom & Viv* (both 1994), which earned her a Best Actress Oscar nomination. The future for this gifted performer is limitless.

RICHARDSON, NATASHA. Actress. *(b. May 11, 1963, London.)* Richardson has established herself as one of the finest actresses of her generation. The talent is all hers, but bloodlines must count for something: her parents are Vanessa Redgrave and the late Tony Richardson. Described by a "New York Times" writer as having "a profile of exquisite purity and a seductively husky voice that caresses you with metal filings and honey," Richardson studied at England's Central School of Speech and Drama and made her first big splash on stage as Nina in "The Seagull," first opposite Samantha Eggar and then her mother. Her film debut as Mary Shelley in Ken Russell's bizarre *Gothic* (1986) was singled out as one of the film's few redeeming features. She followed with *A Month in the Country* (1987), then starred in the title role of Paul Schrader's dour *Patty Hearst* (1988), giving a powerful performance despite limp writing. Richardson won applause for two more odd projects: the adaptation of Margaret Atwood's *The Handmaid's Tale* (1990) and Schrader's bizarre *The Comfort of Strangers* (1991); her first comedy, *The Favor, The Watch, and the Very Big Fish* (also 1991) was seen by few. Since then, she earned a Tony nomination for her Broadway debut in "Anna Christie," a role she also played to acclaim in London. It remains for filmmakers to find roles worthy of her considerable talent. She's appeared in several TV movies, including *Heading Home* (1990), and in 1994 costarred in *Widows' Peak*. She is married to actor Liam Neeson, with whom she starred in *Nell* (1994).

RICHARDSON, RALPH (SIR). Actor. *(b. Dec. 19, 1902, Cheltenham, England; d. Oct. 10, 1983.)* If you should come across the 1939 film *Clouds Over Europe* (aka *Q Planes*), and the bowler-hatted, umbrella-brandishing, impudent British secret agent should seem familiar . . . well, it's *not* Patrick Macnee of "The Avengers" (though he acknowledged borrowing the character) but this outstanding, tweedy actor. Richardson came out of the Old Vic to become one of England's stage royalty, alongside Guinness, Olivier, and his dear friend John Gielgud. He preferred to work in the theater, but made enough movies to leave us generous cinematic samples of his genius.

Richardson's early roles, all done in England, tended toward eccentric characters; good an actor as he was, it wasn't too much of a stretch: He was something of an eccentric himself, and was dashing about England on a motorcycle well into his 70s. He starred in some films, but just as easily slid into secondary roles—no sacrifice, since he often stole the scenes he was in. Among his better-known early films are *The Ghoul* (1933), *Bulldog Jack* (1935), *Things to Come, The Man Who Could Work Miracles* (both 1936), *The Divorce of Lady X* (1938), *The Citadel*

(1938, one of his best, as Robert Donat's stalwart friend), and *The Four Feathers* (1939, probably his best leading role, as the military "coward" who must prove himself).

In the late 1940s and early 1950s he appeared in a string of startlingly good films: *Anna Karenina, The Fallen Idol* (both 1948), *The Heiress* (1949, his first Hollywood film, which earned him an Oscar nomination as Olivia de Havilland's steely father), *Outcast of the Islands* (1951), and *Breaking the Sound Barrier* (1952). In 1953 he made his only stab at directing with the first-rate thriller *Home at Seven* (aka *Murder on Monday*), in which he also starred. He went on to appear in Olivier's *Richard III* (1955, as Buckingham), *Our Man in Havana,* and *Oscar Wilde* (both 1960).

Beginning with *Exodus* in 1960, Richardson increasingly turned up in "international" productions, among them *The 300 Spartans, Long Day's Journey Into Night* (both 1962), *Woman of Straw* (1964), *Doctor Zhivago* (1965), *The Wrong Box, Khartoum* (both 1966), *The Bed-Sitting Room, Midas Run, Oh! What a Lovely War, Battle of Britain* (all 1969), *Eagle in a Cage, Who Slew Auntie Roo?* (both 1971), *Tales From the Crypt, Lady Caroline Lamb, Alice's Adventures in Wonderland* (all 1972, in the last named as the Caterpillar), *A Doll's House, O Lucky Man!* (both 1973), *Rollerball* (1975), *Dragonslayer, Time Bandits* (both 1981), *Wagner* (1983) and *Give My Regards to Broad Street* (1984). Throughout this time he remained active on the stage in both London and New York, and worked several times with his contemporary John Gielgud. His final film, *Greystoke: The Legend of Tarzan* (1984), in which he played the apeman's grandfather, Lord Greystoke, was released posthumously, and earned him a second Academy Award nomination.

RICHARDSON, TONY. Director. *(b. June 5, 1928, Shipley, Yorkshire, England, as Cecil Antonio Richardson; d. Nov. 14, 1991.)* Stylish, influential stage and film director who spearheaded Britain's "New Wave" of filmmaking in the late 1950s and early 1960s. Educated at Oxford's Wadham College, Richardson trained at the BBC and helped found the English Stage Com-

pany, whose express goal was to revitalize English theater. John Osborne's reflective play "Look Back in Anger" (1956) was a pivotal point in contemporary drama— giving birth to the "angry young man"— and Richardson, its director, was suddenly in demand. Following a short film, *Momma Don't Allow* (1955, codirected with fellow "Free Cinema" colleague Karel Reisz), Richardson, Osborne, and Harry Saltzman formed Woodfall Films; their first two projects were adaptations of Osborne plays Richardson had already directed onstage: *Look Back in Anger* (1959) and *The Entertainer* (1960). Though essentially stagebound, they successfully injected "kitchen sink" realism into British films and were notable for the searing lead performances by Richard Burton and Laurence Olivier, respectively. Richardson produced Karel Reisz's first feature, the influential *Saturday Night and Sunday Morning* (1960), and directed two more grimy portraits of the working-class, the poignant *A Taste of Honey* (1961) and the trenchant *The Loneliness of the Long Distance Runner* (1962), which showed his increasing interest and skill as a visual director. His gifts exploded in *Tom Jones* (1963), a ribald comic romp that augmented the satire of Henry Fielding's novel for an overwhelming number of bright, funny, and deliriously inventive gags. The film was a surprise hit and earned Academy Awards for Best Picture, Osborne's screenplay, and Richardson's direction.

He took on America in the very black comedy *The Loved One* (1965), but *The Sailor From Gibraltar* (1967) was a pretentious mess, and *The Charge of the Light Brigade* (1968), despite its stunning craftsmanship and stellar cast, was considered a disappointment. His next films were a mixed lot: Nabokov's *Laughter in the Dark* (1969), *Hamlet* (also 1969, an adaptation of Richardson's staging with Nicol Williamson), the odd outlaw yarn *Ned Kelly* (1970), a flat adaptation of *A Delicate Balance* (1973), and Henry Fielding's bawdy *Joseph Andrews* (1977), an unsuccessful attempt to recapture the *Tom Jones* magic. Moving to America, Richardson directed *The Border* (1982) and made a typically idiosyncratic version of John Irving's *The Hotel New Hampshire* (1984). He also directed the TV movie *Penalty Phase* (1986), the miniseries "Shadow on the Sun" (1988), and *The Phantom of the Opera* (1991, with Charles Dance in the title role). His last film, *Blue Sky* (1994), was completed in 1990, before his death from complications of AIDS. He was married at one time to Vanessa Redgrave; their children Natasha and Joely are also actresses. His autobiography, "The Long Distance Runner," was published posthumously in 1993.

RICKLES, DON. Actor. *(b. May 8, 1926, New York City.)* Bald, bellicose comedian whose decades as "The Merchant of Venom" have obscured the fact that he is a trained actor who attended the American Academy of Dramatic Arts. He has had supporting roles in films as far-ranging as *Run Silent, Run Deep* (1958), *The Rat Race* (1960), *Enter Laughing* (1967), and *Keaton's Cop* (1980), as well as in numerous TV shows. He brightened several "Beach Party" epics in the 1960s, including *Muscle Beach Party, Bikini Beach* (both 1964), and *Beach Blanket Bingo* (1965). In *Kelly's Heroes* (1970), he successfully combined dramatic and comedic elements in his best performance, as the crafty supply sergeant who suggests making a deal with Nazi soldiers. More active on TV than in films, with several failed series and a slew of talk- and variety-show appearances, he got his first chunky movie role in years in John Landis' vampiric *Innocent Blood* (1992).

RICKMAN, ALAN. Actor. *(b. Feb. 21, 1946, London.)* This classically trained actor's hawklike facial features, ready sneer, and cultured voice have made him a natural in roles calling for suave villainy, notably the terrorist-bandit leader in *Die Hard* (1988, the role that introduced him to most American moviegoers), the ruthless land baron in *Quigley Down Under* (1990), and the Sheriff of Nottingham in *Robin Hood: Prince of Thieves* (1991). But Rickman, a versatile performer, is capable of much more: He was personally amusing in the otherwise dull *The January Man* (1989) as a wacky sidekick to unconventional cop Kevin Kline, and charming in *Truly, Madly, Deeply* (1991) as a ghostly musician. He also had an amusing role in Tim Robbins' political satire *Bob Roberts* (1992). The actor first

gained acclaim (and a Tony nomination) on Broadway in a transplant of the British stage production "Les Liaisons Dangercuses." His most recent screen credits are *Mesmer* (1994, in the title role) and *An Awfully Big Adventure* (1995).

RIEFENSTAHL, LENI. Director, actress, photographer. *(b. Aug. 22, 1902, Berlin.)* She directed one of the most accomplished and notorious propaganda films of all time, 1935's *Triumph of the Will*. The movie "documented"—in fact it prettified and pumped up—the Sixth Nazi Party Congress in Nuremberg; it starred, of course, Adolf Hitler, who was portrayed as the savior of Germany. Riefenstahl, a onetime ballet dancer and actress (whose best-remembered film was 1929's *The White Hell of Pitz Palu*), got the assignment because Hitler was impressed by her 1932 directorial effort, the suitably German-Romantic and "stirring" *The Blue Light*. Riefenstahl then went on to direct *Olympia* (1936), a depiction of the Berlin Olympic games in which the Fuhrer benignly oversees the magnificent Aryan athletes competing for honors. Both films are brilliantly shot and edited, absolute textbook examples of creative filmmaking; of course, some argue that being so effective and so technically proficient only makes them more insidious. After World War 2, Riefenstahl declared that her work was mere documentary, and many testified to her naiveté at the time, claiming she really didn't know what kind of people she was dealing with. She was nonetheless made to spend four years in a French detention camp after the war as punishment for her Nazi-glorifying activities. Unable to get financing for any features, she worked as a still photographer in Africa during the 1960s and won great acclaim for her work, although some were not convinced she had changed. In 1992 she published her autobiography, "Leni Riefenstahl: A Memoir," and was the subject of a documentary, *The Wonderful, Horrible Life of Leni Riefenstahl* (1993).

RIEGERT, PETER. Actor. *(b. Apr. 11, 1947, New York City.)* This youthful character actor (and occasional lead) is an alumnus of the War Babies improvisational comedy troupe. He made his big-screen debut as one of the debauched frat brothers in *National Lampoon's Animal House* (1978). Since then, he has scored as an oil-company yuppie businessman in *Local Hero* (1983), the earnest pickle vendor in *Crossing Delancey* (1988), and a cigar-chomping majordomo to gangster Sylvester Stallone in the farcical *Oscar* (1991). In 1993 he had key roles in two of the most watched TV movies of the year: *Barbarians at the Gate* (as the overreaching financial dealmaker), and *Gypsy* (as Bette Midler's long-suffering agent and perennial fiancé).

OTHER FILMS INCLUDE: 1979: *Americathon, Head Over Heels;* 1982: *National Lampoon Goes to the Movies* (never theatrically released); 1984: *City Girl;* 1987: *The Stranger, A Man in Love;* 1989: *That's Adequate;* 1990: *A Shock to the System;* 1991: *The Object of Beauty;* 1992: *Passed Away;* 1994: *The Mask.*

RIGG, DIANA (DAME). Actress. *(b. July 20, 1938, Doncaster, England.)* Stylish, intelligent British actress who made her biggest impact on American audiences as the seductive, leather-clad Mrs. Peel in the 1960s TV thriller "The Avengers." Rigg, another highly trained Shakespearean trouper who found fame and fortune in mass-market entertainments unworthy of her talent, hasn't made many films—but there are some good ones among the few. She was a charming Helena in *A Midsummer Night's Dream* (1968), Portia in *Julius Caesar* (1970), George C. Scott's paramour in *The Hospital* (1971), and coconspirator with murderous actor Vincent Price in *Theatre of Blood* (1973). She also played the first Mrs. James Bond (albeit not for long, as the plot would have it) in *On Her Majesty's Secret Service* (1969), the hapless George Lazenby's only turn as the suave secret agent. Other credits include *The Assassination Bureau* (1969), *A Little Night Music* (1978), and *The Great Muppet Caper* (1981). In recent years her film appearances have been mainly limited to all-star-cast murder mysteries such as *Evil Under the Sun* and *Witness for the Prosecution* (both 1982). A 1994 Tony award winner for "Medea," Rigg also hosts the PBS anthology series "Mystery!" In 1983 she edited a book of the most outrageous critical pans in theater history called "No Turn Unstoned."

RINGWALD, MOLLY. Actress. *(b. Feb. 18, 1968, Sacramento, Calif.)* Pouty redhead who endeared herself to movie audiences in several "Brat Pack" films written by John Hughes: *Sixteen Candles* (1984), *The Breakfast Club* (1985), and *Pretty in Pink* (1986). Ringwald has shown real ability and forthrightness, beginning with her debut performance in *Tempest* (1982), and continuing right on through *Betsy's Wedding* (1990). Hughes wrote the part that, to date, has best suited her: the lower-class daughter of Harry Dean Stanton who simultaneously anticipates and dreads her date with one of her better-heeled classmates in *Pretty in Pink.* She made the cover of "Time" magazine, and was emblematic of a new generation on screen; then her career fizzled. Bad choices and bad luck seem to have conspired against this once promising young talent. Her most recent credits have been telefilms and miniseries, including Stephen King's "The Stand" (1994). She's the daughter of blind jazz musician Bob Ringwald, with whom she was performing while still a preschooler.

OTHER FILMS INCLUDE: 1982: *P.K. and the Kid* (released 1987); 1983: *Spacehunter: Adventures in the Forbidden Zone;* 1987: *King Lear, The Pick-up Artist;* 1988: *For Keeps, Fresh Horses;* 1989: *Strike It Rich.*

RISKIN, ROBERT. Screenwriter, playwright. *(b. Mar. 30, 1897, New York City; d. Sept. 20, 1955.)* In recent years this prolific screen scribe has gotten the belated recognition he so manifestly deserves for his contributions to the much beloved social comedy/dramas directed by Frank Capra. A highly skilled dramatist whose first play was produced when he was still a teenager, Riskin came to Hollywood in 1931 when Harry Cohn's Columbia Pictures bought screen rights to several of his plays, two of which—*Illicit* and *The Miracle Woman*—made it to the screen that year as starring vehicles for Barbara Stanwyck. Riskin cowrote a snappy comedy that Capra directed, *Platinum Blonde* (1931), then penned *Men Are Like That, Men in Her Life* (both 1931), and *The Big Timer* (1932)—routine programmers all—before beginning his collaboration with Capra, Columbia's directorial ace, in earnest by writing the original story for *American Madness* (1932).

Although he continued to script other Columbia films, Riskin is best known for his string of top screenplays for Capra: Three of them, *Lady for a Day* (1933), *Mr. Deeds Goes to Town* (1936), and *You Can't Take It With You* (1938), earned him Academy Award nominations. He won the Oscar for *It Happened One Night* (which, as Capra's greatest success to that point, swept the 1934 awards). He also wrote the director's *Broadway Bill* (1934, which was remade in 1950 as *Riding High*), *Lost Horizon* (1937), and *Meet John Doe* (1941), and produced or helped produce several Capra movies as well.

Riskin, whose innate sense of commercial dramatic structure, plot, and characterization enabled him to write director-proof scripts, eventually chafed under Capra's repeated assertions that he was the principal creative talent behind his pictures. (A possibly apocryphal story has an outraged Riskin storming into Capra's office, hurling a sheaf of blank paper on the director's desk, and shouting, "There! Let's see you give *that* 'the Capra Touch'!") He also contributed screen stories and scripts for *Night Club Lady* (1932), *Ann Carver's Profession* (1933), *Carnival, The Whole Town's Talking* (both 1935), *The Thin Man Goes Home* (1944), and *Mister 880* (1950). He wrote and produced *Magic Town* (1947), which almost seemed like a Capra film—with Jimmy Stewart, no less, in the lead—but it was not well received, leading to the obvious conclusion that he and Capra needed *each other*. He also tried his hand at directing, but only once: on the 1937 Grace Moore musical *When You're in Love* (which he also wrote). In 1950 he suffered a stroke that made it impossible for him to work again; ironically, he received an Oscar nomination for the following year's Bing Crosby vehicle *Here Comes the Groom*, a story he'd sold to Paramount that wound up being directed by Capra. Riskin was married to actress Fay Wray.

RITCHIE, MICHAEL. Director, producer. *(b. Nov. 28, 1938, Waukesha, Wis.)* Intelligent director whose best films examine the foibles of American life in a style that James Monaco describes as a "remarkable fusion of identifiable realism and commentative irony." He studied at Harvard and staged the first production of Arthur Kopit's "Oh Dad, Poor Dad, Mama's Hung You in the Closet and I'm Feelin' So Sad" before working in TV as an assistant producer on "Omnibus" and a director on series like "The Man From U.N.C.L.E.," "Dr. Kildare," and "The Big Valley" in the 1960s. His first feature, *Downhill Racer* (1969), starred Robert Redford as a self-absorbed Olympic skier, and was notable for its almost documentary-like execution. This style was fundamental to *The Candidate* (1972), a darkly humorous look at the election campaign of a young senatorial candidate (also played by Redford) that is arguably his finest film.

Ritchie's work on the mob comedy *Prime Cut* (1972) was severely edited and reworked before its release, but his next film, *Smile* (1975), wittily explored the hollowness of the American dream through the goings-on at a teenage beauty pageant. (Ritchie also helped write some of the songs featured in the film.) The director enjoyed great success with *The Bad News Bears* (1976) and *Semi-Tough* (1977), both stories about the competition, ruthlessness, and silliness involved in nonprofessional and professional sports. Unfortunately, most of his work since then has been blandly commercial, with little of the edge that marked his best films. The year 1993 *did* see a belated return to his old form with the cable-TV version (following by several months a network effort) of a notorious story, *The Positively True Adventures of the Alleged Texas Cheerleader-Murdering Mom*. The film used the media hoopla over sensational news events as part of its "docudrama," which starred Holly Hunter. Ritchie made a cameo appearance as a night watchman in John Landis' *Innocent Blood* (1992).

OTHER FILMS INCLUDE: 1979: *An Almost Perfect Affair;* 1980: the Bette Midler concert film *Divine Madness, The Island;* 1983: *The Survivors;* 1985: *Fletch;* 1986: *Wildcats, The Golden Child;* 1988: *The Couch Trip;* 1989: *Fletch Lives;* 1992: *Diggstown;* 1993: *Cool Runnings* (story only); 1994: *Cops and Robbersons.*

RITT, MARTIN. Director. *(b. Mar. 2, 1920, New York City; d. Dec. 8, 1990.)* Talented director whose work usually focused on weighty moral themes and their impact on everyday people. Ritt originally thought to pursue an athletic career, and prepared for it at a college in North Carolina before changing his mind and returning to New York. Ritt was all set to study law at St. John's before he met Elia Kazan, who convinced him to try his hand at the theater. Ritt's athletic background came in handy here; his first job was to teach Luther Adler how to box for his role in Clifford Odets' "Golden Boy" in 1937. Ritt soon proved himself an able actor and director, and after his hitch in the Army during World War 2 (where he also directed and acted), became a visible talent in TV productions. Unfortunately, he got caught up in the McCarthy hysteria in the early 1950s, and in 1951 he was blacklisted because of prior involvement with the Communist Party.

Unable to find work in television anymore, Ritt began teaching at the Actor's Workshop, where some of his students included Paul Newman, Rod Steiger, and Lee Remick. Especially adept at extracting top performances from his casts, Ritt directed the successful Broadway show "A Very Special Baby" in 1956, which led to a call from Hollywood. His first movie, *Edge of the City* (1957), showed an uncanny (for a newcomer) grasp of screen directorial technique. Ritt never became a visual stylist, however; his concerns were content and performance, and indeed, he steered three actors to Academy Awards: Patricia Neal and Melvyn Douglas in *Hud* (1963), and Sally Field in *Norma Rae* (1979). (Ironically, he was nominated for an Oscar just once, for *Hud*.) Ritt enjoyed a long association with screenwriters Irving Ravetch and Harriet Frank, Jr., with whom he worked for several decades. He was occasionally coaxed in front of the camera, and gave creditable performances in *End of the Game* (1976) and *The Slugger's Wife* (1985). In 1976 Ritt exacted some revenge for his blacklisted days by directing *The Front*, a fictionalized tale of the HUAC terror.

OTHER FILMS INCLUDE: 1957: *No Down Payment;* 1958: *The Long Hot Summer;* 1959: *The Sound and the Fury, The Black Orchid;* 1960: *5 Branded Women;* 1961: *Paris Blues;* 1962: *Hemingway's Adventures of a Young Man;* 1964: *The Outrage;* 1965: *The Spy Who Came in From the Cold;* 1968: *The Brotherhood;* 1970: *The Great White Hope, The Molly Maguires;* 1972: *Sounder, Pete 'n' Tillie;* 1974: *Conrack;* 1978: *Casey's Shadow;* 1981: *Back Roads;* 1983: *Cross Creek;* 1985: *Murphy's Romance;* 1987: *Nuts;* 1990: *Stanley & Iris.*

RITTER, TEX. Actor; singer. *(b. Jan. 12, 1905, Murvaul, Tex., as Woodward Maurice Ritter; d. Jan. 2, 1974.)* If you've seen *High Noon* (1952), you've heard Tex Ritter: He performs the film's Oscar-winning theme song, "Do Not Forsake Me, Oh My Darlin'." But that was only one accomplishment in a lengthy show-business career. Steeped in Texas history and tradition, he quit law school to take up singing on radio and the stage, performing authentic cowboy ditties and folk songs (even on Broadway, in "Green Grow the Lilacs"). Following the huge success of singing cowboy Gene Autry, producer Ed Finney signed Ritter to star in similar low-budget horse operas, first for Grand National Pictures and then for Monogram. Beginning with *Song of the Gringo* (1936), Ritter yipped and yodeled his way through 32 cheapie Westerns distinguished mostly by his penchant for authentic sagebrush songs.

Lanky, drawling, not particularly handsome, Ritter nonetheless seemed (and, in fact, was) more of a real Westerner than the other cowboy crooners, and for a time his popularity rivaled Autry's. But his solo starring career ended with *The Pioneers* in 1941. He then supported "Wild Bill" Elliott in 1941–42 (beginning with *King of Dodge City*), and Johnny Mack Brown from 1942–44. The latter (including *The Lone Star Trail,* which featured young Robert Mitchum as one of the heavies, and *Oklahoma Raiders,* a solo starrer) were among his best Westerns. His *worst* were the eight "Texas Rangers" films he made for bottom-barrel PRC Pictures in 1944–45; after those, he hung up his spurs, and concentrated instead on recordings and personal engagements (although he had cameos in 1955's *Apache Ambush* and 1967's *What Am I Bid?).* A popular performer right up until the day he died, Ritter headlined Nashville's "Grand Ole Opry," hosted a popular syndicated TV show, "Tex Ritter's Ranch Party," and was elected to both the Cowboy Hall of Fame and the Country Music Hall of Fame. (He was not elected to the U.S. Senate, however, when he ran for office in Tennessee in 1970.) He married one of his Monogram leading ladies, Dorothy Fay, in 1941; their son John is the well-known TV star who won an Emmy for the sitcom "Three's Company" (1977–84) and has remained a prolific television performer but has not fared as well in his starring movies, including *Hero at Large* (1980), *They All Laughed* (1981), *Skin Deep* (1989), *Problem Child* (1990), *Problem Child 2* (1991), and *Noises Off* (1992).

RITTER, THELMA. Actress. *(b. Feb. 14, 1905, Brooklyn, N.Y.; d. Feb. 5, 1969.)* Distinguished supporting actress with a flair for cynical, sharp-tongued characters. She played plain—and plainspeaking—women, with sensitivity as well as superb comic knowhow, and came as close to being beloved (by audiences and critics alike) as any actress of her time.

Ritter, a native New Yorker, attended the American Academy of Dramatic Arts prior to working on the Broadway stage. She made a memorable film debut in *Miracle on 34th Street* (1947), playing a bit part as an outspoken mother in Macy's, and was signed to a Fox contract on the strength of that performance. Ritter evolved into a "character lead" whose colorful (but never superficial) performances added starch and substance to every film. She earned six Academy Award nominations, for her performances in *All About Eve* (1950, as Margo Channing's salty helpmate), *The Mating Season* (1951), *With a Song in My Heart* (1952), *Pickup on South Street* (1953), *Pillow Talk* (1959), and *Birdman of Alcatraz* (1962)—though she never won. (She *did* win a Tony Award in 1958 for the Broadway musical "New Girl in Town.") She was also memorable in *A Letter to Three Wives* (1949), *The Model and The Marriage Broker* (1951), *Titanic* (1953), *Rear Window* (1954), *Daddy Long Legs* (1955), *A Hole in the Head* (1959), *The Misfits* (1961), *How the West Was Won* (1962), and *Move Over, Darling* (1963). Her last film was *What's So Bad About Feeling Good?* (1968).

THE RITZ BROTHERS. Actors, singers, dancers. *(Al—b. Aug. 27, 1901, Newark, N.J., as Al Joachim; d. Dec. 22, 1965.* **Jimmy**—*b. Oct. 5, 1903, Newark, N.J.; d. Nov. 17, 1985.* **Harry**—*b. May 22, 1906,*

Newark, N.J.; d. Mar. 29, 1986.) Almost nobody is ambivalent about The Ritz Brothers: You either love them or you hate them. Their broad, bombastic, ethnic-based comic *schtick* made them headliners—and although film seldom captured them at their best, their brightest moments still shine. Al, the eldest brother, did extra work in a 1918 film and dabbled in vaudeville before teaming with his siblings in 1925. Before long they were featured in Broadway revues, and in 1934, the Ritzes made their film debut in a lackluster comedy short, *Hotel Anchovy.*

20th Century-Fox's Darryl F. Zanuck saw the brothers in a nightclub (their true metier) and signed them immediately. Their musical comedy gifts (and particularly their precision dance routines) suited show-biz-based musical comedies to a T, and they played themselves (in support of stars Alice Faye and Sonja Henie) in *Sing, Baby, Sing, One in a Million* (both 1936), *On the Avenue,* and *You Can't Have Everything* (both 1937). Harry, "the one in the middle" (as immortalized in one of their songs), got most of the laughs with his outrageous mugging, which inspired Danny Kaye, Jerry Lewis, Sid Caesar, Mel Brooks, and a host of later comedians. A proposed sequel to Fox's musical hit *Pigskin Parade* became the Ritzes' first starring vehicle, the moderately successful *Life Begins in College* (1937). But studio scribes found it difficult to give the Brothers good enough material to carry whole films and, with the exception of an inspired musical-comedy version of *The Three Musketeers* (1939), their other Fox starrers were routine.

The Ritzes then jumped ship, landing at Universal; their first film for that studio, *Argentine Nights* (1940), teamed the boys with the Andrews Sisters for satisfactory results, but *Behind the Eight Ball* (1942), *Hi'ya, Chum,* and *Never a Dull Moment* (both 1943) failed to live up to the opener's level of quality. Abandoning the screen for nightclub and stage work, the Ritzes worked together until Al's death in 1965. Harry and Jimmy subsequently appeared in the B-Western parody *Blazing Stewardesses* (1975), reprising many of their famous routines and gamely attempting one of their precision dance numbers. They also had cameos in *Won Ton Ton, the Dog Who Saved Hollywood* (1976), and Harry appeared solo in a cute cameo for avid Ritz Brothers fan Mel Brooks in *Silent Movie* that same year.

ROACH, HAL. Producer. *(b. Jan. 14, 1892, Elmira, N.Y.; d. Nov. 2, 1992.)* Although Mack Sennett was known as The King of Comedy, Hal Roach eclipsed him in the 1920s, and reigned as Hollywood's leading producer of comedy films through the early 1940s. And while most of Sennett's films are viewed (if viewed at all) as quaint artifacts of their time, Roach's work has survived, and continues to entertain millions of people today.

Roach came to Hollywood in 1912, having prospected for gold in Alaska, skinned mules in Arizona, and pursued a variety of occupations. He found work as an extra in those rough-and-ready days, and became friendly with a fellow extra (and would-be actor) named Harold Lloyd. When Roach formed his own movie company in 1914, with some money he'd inherited, he hired Lloyd to be his first star; Roach worked behind the camera as the company's chief director. Their *Lonesome Luke* series was modestly successful, but when Lloyd moved on to a more distinctive character, playing an all-American boy, the films became even more popular. By the end of the decade, Lloyd was a leading comedy star, and Roach was a major producer/director.

In the 1920s, Roach hired others to direct the films for him, and he became more of a producer and studio chief. It was his idea to form Our Gang in 1921 (the first film was released in 1922), and it was his friendship with Will Rogers that brought the beloved humorist to his studio for a series of comedy shorts in 1923–24. Charley Chase, originally hired as a director, became one of the studio's top comedy stars by the mid 1920s, and several years later, two journeyman players named Stan Laurel and Oliver Hardy were felicitously teamed to bring the Roach studio its greatest success of all. Top talent behind the camera included directors Leo McCarey and James Parrott (Charley Chase's brother), and cameraman George Stevens, who got his first chance to direct at Roach's in the early 1930s. (His opportunity came when Roach, who was directing a short himself, got bored and/or eager to get to the racetrack; he simply let Stevens take over. It was not a unique occasion.)

Chase, Our Gang, and Laurel and Hardy all made a smooth transition to sound in 1929, and enjoyed even greater popularity in the 1930s. (A talkie comeback for silent-comedy star Harry Langdon at the Roach studio was short-lived, though Langdon returned there in the late 1930s as a staff writer and supporting player.) Roach bowed to economic pressure to put Laurel and Hardy into feature films beginning in 1931, but still believed in shorts. He launched other series in the 1930s, including Thelma Todd and ZaSu Pitts (then Thelma Todd and Patsy Kelly), The Boy Friends, and The Taxi Boys. But by the middle of that decade, the popularity of the double feature meant the short subject's days were numbered. Roach let stars like Charley Chase go (after a failed attempt to star him in a feature film), and sold Our Gang lock, stock, and barrel to his distributor, MGM. Laurel and Hardy remained, though contract squabbles—and Stan's insistence on producing his own films—made their relationship with Roach a prickly one.

In the late 1930s Roach expanded his feature-film slate, and began producing a variety of films. The most successful was *Topper* (1937), which yielded two sequels; the most prestigious was *Of Mice and Men* (1939), which made no money. Other features included *There Goes My Heart* (1938), *Captain Fury* (1939), and *One Million B.C.* (1940). (For *One Million B.C.* Roach engaged down-on-his-luck D. W. Griffith, but stories conflict over whether he actually expected the veteran filmmaker to direct his movie or not. In any case, after participating in some screen tests, he had no further contact with the project.) In the early 1940s Roach developed "Streamliners," a compromise between short-subject and feature-length films, and produced a series of comedy featurettes, including a Brooklyn taxi-driver series with William Bendix, a hayseed series with Noah Beery, Jr., and Jimmie Rogers (Will's son), and an Army series with William Tracy and Joe Sawyer. They were mostly awful, but Roach always claimed they made money.

While Roach served during World War 2, his studio was commandeered as Fort Roach, for the production of war-related films. At war's end, Roach returned to Hollywood and tried to relaunch his featurettes—including an Our Gang knockoff, *In Curley* (1946), and *Who Killed Doc Robbin* (1948)—but they laid a giant egg. Roach decided to retire, and in 1955 sold his studio and its assets to his son Hal Roach, Jr. The younger Roach had turned the studio into a beehive of TV film activity in the early 1950s, but bad business practices led to complete bankruptcy within just a few years. The elder Roach was forced to come out of retirement to save his studio—and his life's savings.

In later years he enjoyed spinning tales of his colorful career, and receiving the accolades of comedy fans around the world. Roach, given an honorary Academy Award in 1984, outlived his fellow moguls and most of his stars, and was a valuable link to Hollywood's earliest days. To the very end he had movie and TV ideas he was eager to sell.

ROBARDS, JASON (JR.). Actor. *(b. July 22, 1922, Chicago.)* Gruff, raspy-voiced supporting player and character lead, one of the finest working in film today. The son of actor and silent-screen star Jason Robards, he served in the Navy during World War 2 (surviving the attack on Pearl Harbor), and studied at the American Academy of Dramatic Arts before scoring a spectacular triumph in the 1956 Broadway production of Eugene O'Neill's "The Iceman Cometh." After winning the prestigious New York Drama Critics Award for his turn in "Long Day's Journey Into Night" the following year, Robards became a bona fide stage star (and cemented an indelible association with the works of O'Neill). He won a Tony award in 1959 for "The Disenchanted." His success in films hasn't been quite as stunning, possibly because he has remained, with few exceptions, in character roles, often registering best playing real-life figures.

Robards made his movie debut in *The Journey* (1959), then didn't appear on-screen for another two years, resurfacing in *By Love Possessed* (1961). His portrayal of F. Scott Fitzgerald protagonist Dick Diver in *Tender Is the Night* (1962) earned Robards considerable praise, as did his reprise of the Jamie Tyrone role for

that year's film adaptation of *Long Day's Journey Into Night,* and his turn as playwright George S. Kaufman in *Act One* (1963).

He had a rare starring role in *A Thousand Clowns* (1965), recreating his Broadway triumph as the irrepressible (and irresponsible) misfit and surrogate father to an adoring nephew. He then played gangster Al Capone in *The St. Valentine's Day Massacre* and Western gunslinger Doc Holliday in *Hour of the Gun* (both 1967). His parts in the late 1960s and early 1970s ran the gamut from a divorce lawyer in *Divorce American Style* (1967) to a burlesque performer in *The Night They Raided Minsky's* (1968), from a gunman in the super–spaghetti Western *Once Upon a Time in the West* (1968) to a wartime general in *Tora! Tora! Tora!* (1970), from Brutus in *Julius Caesar* (1971) to a Western dreamer in Sam Peckinpah's *The Ballad of Cable Hogue* (1970, the starring role). He rejoined Peckinpah to play New Mexico governor (and "Ben-Hur" author) Lew Wallace in *Pat Garrett and Billy the Kid* (1973). Other credits during this period include *Isadora* (1968), *Johnny Got His Gun* (1971), and *The War Between Men and Women* (1972). Then in the late 1970s he won back-to-back Oscars, playing "Washington Post" editor Ben Bradlee in the Watergate thriller *All the President's Men* (1976) and following it with a skillful, sharply delineated turn as novelist Dashiell Hammett (to whom, with his unruly white hair and mustache, he bore a surprising resemblance) in the Lillian Hellman memoir *Julia* (1977). He was subsequently nominated (but did not win) for his purposely eccentric characterization of tycoon Howard Hughes in *Melvin and Howard* (1980).

Robards, who juggles TV work and stage appearances with his movie assignments, made relatively few films in the 1980s, among them *Raise the Titanic!* (1980), *The Legend of the Lone Ranger* (1981), *Something Wicked This Way Comes, Max Dugan Returns* (both 1983), *Square Dance* (1987), *Bright Lights, Big City, The Good Mother* (both 1988), *Dream a Little Dream, Black Rainbow, Reunion,* and *Parenthood* (all 1989, the last offering his best part in years, as Steve Martin's crotchety father). He was the original, well-cast star of Werner Herzog's problem-plagued *Fitzcarraldo*

(1982), but was replaced by Klaus Kinski; he can be seen in Les Blank's revealing documentary on the making of that film, *Burden of Dreams*. He has since appeared on the big screen in *Quick Change* (1990, delightful as a world-weary New York cop) and *Storyville* (1992). Beginning with *A Christmas to Remember* (1978), he turned some of his energies to TV movies and miniseries, which have included *Haywire* (1980, as show-biz agent Leland Hayward), *The Day After* (1983), *The Long Hot Summer* (1985), *Laguna Heat* (1987), *Inherit the Wind* (1988, for which he won an Emmy), *Mark Twain and Me* (1991, unrecognizable under heavy makeup as the fabled author), and *Heidi* (1993). Recent credits include *The Adventures of Huck Finn, Philadelphia* (both 1993), *The Paper, The Trial,* and *Little Big League* (all 1994). Formerly married to Lauren Bacall; their son Sam Robards has launched an acting career of his own, with roles in such films as *Tempest* (1982) and *The Ballad of Little Jo* (1993).

ROBBINS, TIM. Actor, director, screenwriter. *(b. Oct. 16, 1958, West Covina, Calif.)* Subtle, incisive actor whom director Robert Altman says "has qualities that could make him the next Orson Welles." Robbins grew up in Greenwich Village (his father is actor and folksinger Gil Robbins of The Highwaymen) and was surrounded by politics and theater at a young age. After two years at the State University of New York, he returned to California and studied theater at UCLA. He cofounded a theater company called the Actors' Gang, which became known for its innovative, avant-garde productions and attracted members like John Cusack. (Robbins is still very active with the group.) During this time, he took small roles in films like *No Small Affair* (1984), *Fraternity Vacation* (1985), and *The Sure Thing* (1985), and was featured in the disastrous *Howard the Duck* (1986). Following a role in *Top Gun* (1986), Robbins gained his first critical attention as the civil rights worker Harry in *Five Corners* (1988), and then scored a popular success as Ebby "Nuke" LaLoosh, the wild rookie pitcher in *Bull Durham* (1988). He followed with two comedy flops, *Tapeheads* (1989, opposite Cusack), and *Erik the Viking* (1989), but received strong reviews for his roles in

Miss Firecracker (1989), *Cadillac Man* (1990), and especially *Jacob's Ladder* (1990), in the leading role, as a hallucinating Vietnam vet. Robbins really came into his own with back-to-back films in 1992: first, as unscrupulous studio executive Griffin Mill in Robert Altman's acid Hollywood comedy *The Player* (1992), a dead-on performance that earned him the Best Actor Award at Cannes. Next came *Bob Roberts* (1992), a pet project Robbins wrote and directed (inspired by a short film he made in 1986 for TV's "Saturday Night Live"), in which he starred as a manipulative, ultraconservative, folk-singing senatorial candidate. (Robbins also wrote the film's songs with his brother.) Both films showcased Robbins' keen intelligence and the ability, as Bill Zehme wrote, "to be at once contemptible and attractive—the rarest of gifts" (though he was able to sacrifice those qualities to play a likable dummy in the Coen brothers' *The Hudsucker Proxy* in 1994). He reunited with Altman for *Short Cuts* (1993) and *Ready to Wear/Prêt-à-Porter* (1994), and starred in the prison drama *The Shawshank Redemption* and the romantic comedy *I.Q.* (both 1994). Robbins and actress Susan Sarandon met during the filming of *Bull Durham,* and have been together ever since; they have two children.

ROBERTS, ERIC. Actor. *(b. Apr. 18, 1956, Biloxi, Miss.)* This accomplished, offbeat actor began appearing in stage productions by the age of 5. After studying at both the London Academy of Dramatic Art and the American Academy of Dramatic Arts, he made his film debut in *King of the Gypsies* (1978), and stardom was predicted for him. Roberts turned out to be choosy, however, and was drawn to dark, offbeat characters, such as those in *Raggedy Man* (1981) and *Miss Lonelyhearts* (1983). He got his best opportunities in *Star 80* (also 1983), as the psychotic husband of doomed Playmate, Dorothy Stratten, and *The Pope of Greenwich Village* (1984), as Mickey Rourke's screw-up cousin. These showy performances were followed by *The Coca-Cola Kid* (1985) and *Runaway Train* (1985), which earned him an Oscar nomination as Best Supporting Actor. His choices thereafter were erratic at best, as were his performances. The darkly handsome Roberts has turned out to be more effective in antihero and villainous parts in recent years—as in *Final Analysis* (1992). Other credits include *Nobody's Fool* (1986), *To Heal a Nation* (1988 telefilm, as the Vietnam vet who championed a Washington, D.C., memorial), *Best of the Best* (1989), *Rude Awakening* (also 1989, a rare comedy performance), *Blood Red* (1990), *The Ambulance* (1991), *Best of the Best 2* (1993), "Free Fall" (miniseries), *Love Is a Gun,* and *The Specialist* (all 1994). His superstar sister Julia made her acting debut in his starring vehicle *Blood Red.*

ROBERTS, JULIA. Actress. *(b. Oct. 28, 1967, Smyrna, Ga.)* It would seem unlikely that an actress could become "America's Sweetheart" by playing a hooker, but it was the role of an implausibly winsome, adorable prostitute in *Pretty Woman* (1990) that secured that title—and superstardom—for the charming, leggy Roberts. The younger sister of actor Eric Roberts, the brown-eyed, beaming, coltish Julia first demonstrated her appeal in the 1988 girls-coming-of-age comedy *Mystic Pizza.* (Her first film, *Blood Red,* which starred brother Eric, was made in 1987 but not released until 1990, after she'd become a "name.") She had a costarring role in *Satisfaction* (1988, later known as *Girls of Summer*), and then won a meaty part in the ensemble comedy-cum-tearjerker *Steel Magnolias* (1989), enchanting audiences (and earning an Oscar nomination) as Sally Field's fragile daughter. She then costarred in *Flatliners* (1990). But it was *Pretty Woman* that made Roberts, overnight, the hottest property in show business and an omnipresent magazine cover girl. (It also earned her another Oscar nomination.) The success of the mediocre *Sleeping With the Enemy* (1991) persuaded Hollywood that her name alone guaranteed box-office success—which the dismal showing for *Dying Young* (1991) dispelled. She made headline news by announcing, then canceling, her wedding to actor Kiefer Sutherland (she married musician Lyle Lovett in 1993), and wound up in Steven Spielberg's *Hook* (1991) playing Tinkerbell. After a self-imposed hiatus from work, and a retreat from tabloid headlines, during which she appeared in only one film

(a cameo in Robert Altman's *The Player* in 1992), she made a return to major-league stardom in *The Pelican Brief* (1993), followed by *I Love Trouble, Ready to Wear/Prêt-à-Porter* (both 1994), and *Mary Reilly* (1995). She seems to have weathered her personal storms, and retained her star status (earning up to that time the most money ever paid to an actress—some eight million dollars per film) despite two years away from movies.

ROBERTS, RACHEL. Actress. *(b. Sept. 20, 1927, Carmarthen, Wales; d. Nov. 27, 1980.)* Distinctive-looking, charismatic stage actress who made periodic forays into motion pictures, best known for her Oscar-nominated rendering of a frustrated widow in *This Sporting Life* (1963). She was also memorable as the raucous housewife in *Saturday Night and Sunday Morning* (1960), which got her more or less typecast in similar roles. Roberts was married to actor Rex Harrison from 1962 to 1971; her volume of memoirs, "No Bells on Sunday," describes the gradual dissolution of their relationship and his desertion of her. A heavy drinker, she committed suicide by poisoning herself. OTHER FILMS INCLUDE: 1953: *The Limping Man;* 1954: *The Weak and the Wicked;* 1957: *The Good Companions;* 1960: *Our Man in Havana;* 1968: *A Flea in Her Ear;* 1971: *Doctors' Wives, Wild Rovers;* 1973: *O Lucky Man!;* 1974: *Murder on the Orient Express;* 1975: *Picnic at Hanging Rock;* 1978: *Foul Play;* 1979: *Yanks;* 1981: *Charlie Chan and the Curse of the Dragon Queen.*

ROBERTS, TONY. Actor. *(b. Oct. 22, 1939, New York City.)* If he had done nothing else, Tony Roberts would rate a place in film-history tomes for his six stints in Woody Allen movies; as it happens, this tall, curly-haired, reliable actor/singer has in the course of a lengthy career run the gamut from Broadway musicals to horror movies. Allen uses him well, usually as The Best Friend (as in 1977's *Annie Hall*). His others with Woody: *Play It Again, Sam* (1972, repeating the role he'd played with Allen on Broadway), *Stardust Memories* (1980), *A Midsummer Night's Sex Comedy* (1982), *Hannah and Her Sisters* (1986), and *Radio Days* (1987). Roberts also shines as fast-talking white-collar types, notably in *Serpico* (1973), *The Taking of Pelham One Two Three* (1974), *Just Tell Me What You Want* (1980), and *Switch* (1991). He stooged for a water fowl in Disney's *$1,000,000 Duck,* starred in Neil Simon's *Star Spangled Girl* (both 1971) and made a reasonably credible hero in *Amityville 3-D* (1983). Other films include *Key Exchange* (1985), *18 Again!* (1988), and *Arthur Miller's The American Clock* (1993 telefilm). None of his numerous TV series lasted very long; far and away the best was the lighthearted "Rosetti and Ryan" (1977), about a pair of wiseacre attorneys. His father is veteran radio and TV announcer Kenneth Roberts who also appeared in *Radio Days* and *Bullets Over Broadway* (1994).

ROBERTSON, CLIFF. Actor. *(b. Sept. 9, 1925, La Jolla, Calif.)* A competent, personable leading man, Robertson had too few standout opportunities in films, but those moments were memorable: as PT-boat commander and future President John F. Kennedy in *PT 109* (1963, for which he was reportedly handpicked by JFK himself), a McCarthyesque Presidential candidate in *The Best Man* (1964), and the mild-mannered retarded person given supernormal intelligence in *Charly* (1968, which won him an Oscar). A former sailor, Robertson turned to the stage in the 1950s, and made his film debut in *Picnic* (1955), playing the wealthy boyfriend of Kim Novak. He also found steady work on TV, particularly in the "golden age" of live TV drama; he starred in the Saturday morning series "Rod Brown of the Rocket Rangers" (1953–54), guested on many TV anthology shows, and created the role of the alcoholic husband in "Days of Wine and Roses" (1958) played on film by Jack Lemmon. (In later years he made other high-profile TV appearances, won an Emmy for a "Chrysler Theater" episode in 1965, and even spent a season on "Falcon Crest" in the 1983–84 season.)

Robertson's most ambitious undertaking was *J. W. Coop* (1972), an engrossing drama following the career of a would-be rodeo star, which he wrote, produced, and directed in addition to starring. (A second effort as star/director/writer, *The Pilot,* was made in 1979 but barely released.) In recent years he has done some particularly fine character work, in films like *Wild Hearts Can't Be Broken* (1991, as a poor man's 20th-century Buffalo Bill Cody). He was married to actress Dina Merrill from 1966–89.

Robertson made headlines as the victim of check-forging studio head David Begelman, who put the actor's name on checks he cashed himself; when Robertson blew the whistle on the popular producer, he found himself ostracized in Hollywood. He was for years the TV spokesman for AT&T.

OTHER FILMS INCLUDE: 1956: *Autumn Leaves;* 1957: *The Girl Most Likely;* 1958: *The Naked and the Dead;* 1959: *Gidget;* 1961: *Underworld U.S.A., The Big Show;* 1962: *The Interns;* 1964: *Sunday in New York;* 1965: *Love Has Many Faces, Masquerade;* 1967: *The Honey Pot;* 1968: *The Devil's Brigade;* 1970: *Too Late the Hero;* 1972: *The Great Northfield, Minnesota Raid;* 1973: *Ace Eli and Rodger of the Skies;* 1975: *Three Days of the Condor;* 1976: *Midway, Obsession;* 1977: *Fraternity Row;* 1983: *Brainstorm, Class, Star 80* (as "Playboy" publisher Hugh Hefner); 1985: *Shaker Run;* 1987: *Malone;* 1992: *Wind;* 1994: *Renaissance Man.*

ROBESON, PAUL. Actor, singer. *(b. Apr. 9, 1898, Princeton, N.J.; d. Jan. 23, 1976.)* Robeson was one of the few true Renaissance men of the 20th century: a scholar, athlete, political activist, and performer. He could dominate a stage or concert hall with his resonant, melodic baritone, but because of his outspokenness against racism and his political activism, he encountered challenges throughout his lifetime. The son of a schoolteacher and former slave who became a Protestant minister, Robeson earned a scholarship to Rutgers College, becoming the third black ever to attend the school. In 1917, he was the first black Walter Camp All-American football player; he won varsity letters in basketball, baseball, and track, and was awarded a Phi Beta Kappa key. While attending Columbia University Law School, he performed in an amateur stage production, and in 1921 made his professional debut in the theater. He apprenticed with the famous Provincetown Players, where he was cast in Eugene O'Neill's "All God's Chillun Got Wings" and "The Emperor Jones."

He made his screen debut in *Body and Soul* (1924), directed by Oscar Micheaux;

it was the only time in his career that he would be directed by a black filmmaker. He first performed the role of Joe the Riverman in "Show Boat" in London in 1928, a role he was to recreate on film some years later. In 1933 he starred in the movie version of *The Emperor Jones,* playing Brutus Jones, the Pullman porter/convict turned island ruler. Although the film was made outside the Hollywood mainstream, it was nevertheless a milestone, with a white actor (Dudley Digges) supporting Robeson in his leading role. In 1936 he sang his thrilling rendition of "Old Man River" in the Hollywood production of *Show Boat.*

Robeson's remaining film opportunities came in England, where he felt he could escape stereotyping and find better parts. However, while he avoided having to "shuffle along," his characters consistently remained in the shadows of the Great White Hunter in *Sanders of the River* (1935), *Song of Freedom* (1936), in the tailor-made role of a dock worker turned concert singer who is heir to an African tribal throne, *Big Fella* (1937), *Jericho* (1937, aka *Dark Sands*), in which he sang "Shortnin' Bread," *King Solomon's Mines* (1938), as an exiled tribal chief, and *Proud Valley* (1940). Robeson was consistently good; the same could not be said for the movies. In 1942 he returned to Hollywood to act in a segment of the multi-episode *Tales of Manhattan.* It would be his final film appearance. Robeson's politics were to become his undoing. He defied the House Committee on Un-American Activities; the State Department revoked his passport. In 1958, a Supreme Court ruling reinstated the passport, and he performed in concert until illness forced him to retire. In 1958 Robeson published his autobiography, "Here I Stand."

ROBINSON, BRUCE. Director, screenwriter. *(b. May 2, 1946, Broadstairs, Kent, England.)* Formally trained as an actor at London's Central School of Speech and Drama, Robinson appeared in such films as Zeffirelli's *Romeo and Juliet* (1968, as Benvolio), *The Music Lovers* (1971), and *The Story of Adele H* (1975) before turning full-time to writing. His first produced script was the acclaimed *The Killing Fields* (1984), which earned him a Best Screenplay Oscar nomination. This wrenching, fact-based drama of Cambodia in the 1970s earned him the chance to direct, but for his debut film he made a 180-degree turn: *Withnail and I* (1987) was a low-key ensemble comedy from his own autobiographical screenplay about two unemployed actors in 1969 London. It won critical praise and a small but fervent following. Robinson followed up with the bizarre satire *How to Get Ahead in Advertising,* and cowrote the screenplay for *Fat Man and Little Boy* (both 1989). Then he switched gears again to write and direct a slick mainstream thriller, *Jennifer 8* (1992).

ROBINSON, EDWARD G. Actor. *(b. Dec. 12, 1893, Bucharest, Rumania, as Emmanuel Goldenberg; d. Feb. 26, 1973.)* "Mother of mercy," gasps the mortally wounded gangster, "is this the end of Rico?" With those words, the talkies' first antihero, the protagonist of *Little Caesar* (1930), died—granting screen immortality to the actor playing that part. Short and squat, with his pudgy face, broad mouth, and nasal voice, Edward G. Robinson shot to stardom overnight and, while hardly a matinee idol, became a popular leading man at his home studio, Warners, where he toiled for more than a decade. As a youthful immigrant he considered becoming a rabbi, but his love of the theater drew him instead to the American Academy of Dramatic Arts, and then to a stage career.

Robinson first acted on-screen in *The Bright Shawl,* a 1923 silent, but made his mark on movie audiences in 1929's *The Hole in the Wall,* opposite Claudette Colbert. *Little Caesar* not only cast Robinson in the role with which he was forever identified, it in fact launched the hugely successful line of crime films produced during the early 1930s. He maintained his stardom for decades with such varied roles as a conscience-stricken tabloid editor in *Five Star Final* (1931), a Chinese executioner in *The Hatchet Man* (1932), a Colorado empire-builder (patterned after real-life Horace Tabor) in *Silver Dollar* (1932), a comically reformed gangster in *Little Giant* (1933) and *A Slight Case of Murder* (1938), a murderous actor in *The Man With Two Faces* (1934), a dance-hall boss in *Barbary*

Coast (1935), a boxing manager in *Kid Galahad* (1937), the inventor of a cure for syphillis in *Dr. Ehrlich's Magic Bullet* (1940), the crazed captain of *The Sea Wolf* (1941), a wily insurance investigator in *Double Indemnity*, a hapless professor in *The Woman in the Window* (both 1944), a Nazi-hunter in *The Stranger* (1946), a gangster in *Key Largo* (1948), a father harboring a terrible secret in Arthur Miller's *All My Sons* (1948), a ruthless banker in *House of Strangers* (1949), a TV researcher in *The Glass Web* (1953), a cattle baron in *The Violent Men* (1955), a turncoat Jew in *The Ten Commandments* (1956), a tyrannical movie director in *Two Weeks in Another Town* (1962), a legendary poker player in *The Cincinnati Kid* (1965), and an aging survivor in the futuristic *Soylent Green* (1973, his last film).

The quality of Robinson's performances seldom faltered; dynamic and aggressive though he frequently was, especially in his 1930s films, he also showed tenderness and sensitivity when the role demanded. Although beset with personal problems (including blacklisting during the witch-hunt days) in later years, Robinson worked steadily right up until his death from cancer in 1973. Astoundingly, he was never even nominated for an Oscar, but was given an honorary Academy Award that was presented posthumously. His autobiography, "All My Yesterdays," was also published after his death in 1973.

OTHER FILMS INCLUDE: 1930: *East Is West, The Widow From Chicago;* 1931: *Smart Money* (his only pairing with fellow "gangster" James Cagney); 1932: *Two Seconds, Tiger Shark;* 1933: *I Loved a Woman;* 1934: *Dark Hazard;* 1935: *The Whole Town's Talking;* 1936: *Bullets or Ballots;* 1937: *Thunder in the City, The Last Gangster;* 1938: *The Amazing Dr. Clitterhouse, I Am the Law;* 1939: *Confessions of a Nazi Spy, Blackmail;* 1940: *Brother Orchid, A Dispatch From Reuters;* 1941: *Manpower, Unholy Partners;* 1942: *Larceny, Inc., Tales of Manhattan;* 1943: *Destroyer, Flesh and Fantasy;* 1944: *Tampico, Mr. Winkle Goes to War;* 1945: *Our Vines Have Tender Grapes, Scarlet Street;* 1947: *The Red House;* 1948: *The Night Has a Thousand Eyes;* 1952: *Actors and Sin;* 1953: *Vice Squad, Big Leaguer;* 1954: *Black Tuesday;* 1955: *Tight Spot, A Bullet for Joey, Illegal, Hell on Frisco Bay;* 1956: *Nightmare;* 1959: *A Hole in the Head;* 1960: *Seven Thieves;* 1962: *My Geisha;* 1963: *A Boy Ten Feet Tall, The Prize;* 1964:

Good Neighbor Sam, Robin and the Seven Hoods (cameo), *The Outrage, Cheyenne Autumn;* 1967: *Grand Slam;* 1968: *The Biggest Bundle of Them All, Never a Dull Moment;* 1969: *Mackenna's Gold;* 1970: *Song of Norway, The Old Man Who Cried Wolf* (telefilm).

ROBINSON, PHIL ALDEN. Director, screenwriter. *(b. Mar. 1, 1950, Long Beach, N.Y.)* After working in radio and TV news, Robinson made scores of industrial films and broke into the entertainment industry by writing two episodes of the TV drama "Trapper John, M.D." His first screenplays were produced in 1984: the delightful Steve Martin body-switch comedy *All of Me* and the heavy-handed Sylvester Stallone–Dolly Parton comedy *Rhinestone* (which Stallone rewrote). Alden won the chance to direct his own screenplay *In the Mood* (1987), a slight but funny story of the real-life "Woo Woo Kid" that showed signs of cleverness and originality. Then he struck gold with the baseball fantasy *Field of Dreams* (1989), an adaptation of W. P. Kinsella's "Shoeless Joe." The film touched a deep emotional chord in audiences and earned Oscar nominations for Best Picture and for Robinson's screenplay. It was a tough act to follow and Robinson took several years before committing to his next project: *Sneakers* (1992), a sort of *Three Days of the Condor* Lite, with Robert Redford as the leader of a misfit-laden security team.

ROBSON, FLORA (DAME). Actress. *(b. Mar. 28, 1902, Brighton, England; d. July 7, 1984.)* Distinguished British stage actress—a decorated graduate of the Royal Academy of Dramatic Art—whose career spanned nearly 60 years, on screen since the mid 1930s, usually in character roles calling for strength and determination. Her portrayal of Queen Elizabeth I in *Fire Over England* (1937) was typically superlative; in fact, when she moved to Hollywood she was asked to play that role again in Errol Flynn's period swashbuckler *The Sea Hawk* (1940). She won other good roles during her brief tenure in tinseltown, including Paul Muni's domineering wife in *We Are Not Alone* (1939), the housekeeper in *Wuthering Heights* (also 1939), and Ingrid Bergman's fiercely protective servant in *Saratoga Trunk*

(1945), which earned her an Oscar nomination. She brought distinction to every film in which she appeared.
OTHER FILMS INCLUDE: 1931: *A Gentleman of Paris;* 1933: *One Precious Year;* 1934: *Catherine the Great;* 1940: *Invisible Stripes;* 1941: *Bahama Passage;* 1945: *Great Day;* 1946: *Caesar and Cleopatra, Holiday Camp, Black Narcissus;* 1948: *Saraband for Dead Lovers;* 1952: *The Frightened Bride;* 1953: *The Malta Story;* 1954: *Romeo and Juliet;* 1957: *No Time For Tears;* 1963: *Murder at the Gallop, 55 Days at Peking;* 1964: *Guns at Batasi;* 1965: *The Epic That Never Was* (with scenes from the unfinished 1937 production of *I, Claudius*), *Young Cassidy;* 1966: *7 Women;* 1967: *Eye of the Devil, The Shuttered Room;* 1970: *Fragment of Fear;* 1972: *Alice's Adventures in Wonderland* (as the Queen of Hearts); 1978: *Dominique;* 1981: *Clash of the Titans.*

ROBSON, MARK. Director. *(b. Dec. 4, 1913, Montreal; d. June 20, 1978.)* Like many directors who began their careers with modestly budgeted B movies, Robson worked especially well on a small canvas; some of his most memorable pictures were made before the advent of television. He started as a prop boy and began editing in the mid 1930s at RKO. Robson assisted Robert Wise in cutting Orson Welles' *Citizen Kane* (1941) and *The Magnificent Ambersons* (1942). Like Wise, he was taken under the wing of B-unit producer Val Lewton, for whom he edited, then directed, some of the intelligent, haunting, low-budget horror films in which Lewton specialized. Among these were *The Ghost Ship, The Seventh Victim* (both 1943), *Isle of the Dead* (1945), and *Bedlam* (1946), the latter two starring Boris Karloff. He also directed Lewton's non-horror outing *Youth Runs Wild* (1944).

Robson's breakthrough picture was *Champion,* a gritty, uncompromising, and surprisingly realistic 1949 boxing drama starring Kirk Douglas. That same year he directed *Home of the Brave,* a somber, hard-hitting look at racial bigotry among American soldiers during World War 2. He also helmed *Roughshod* (1949), *Edge of Doom, My Foolish Heart* (both 1950), *I Want You, Bright Victory* (both 1951), *Return to Paradise* (1953), *Hell Below Zero,* the excellent *The Bridges at Toko-Ri* (both 1954), *Prize of Gold,* and *Trial* (both

1955). *The Harder They Fall* (1956) brought Robson back to the boxing ring—with another contemporary story (by Budd Schulberg)—and another chance to score a knockout. By now a successful mainstream director, Robson continued to turn out big-budget, star-laden, commercial films, many of which were quite good—but few, if any, seemed as interesting as his Lewton output.

Among Robson's later pictures were *Peyton Place* (1957, for which he was Oscar-nominated), *The Little Hut* (also 1957), *The Inn of the Sixth Happiness* (1958, for which he earned another Oscar nod), *From the Terrace* (1960), *Lisa* (1962, producer only), *The Prize, Nine Hours to Rama* (both 1963), *Von Ryan's Express* (1965), *Lost Command* (1966), the trashy *Valley of the Dolls* (1967), *Daddy's Gone A-Hunting* (1969, a particularly sleazy thriller unworthy of a Val Lewton disciple), the small-scale Kurt Vonnegut adaptation *Happy Birthday, Wanda June* (1971), and the formulaic disaster film *Earthquake* (1974). The star of his final film, *Avalanche Express* (1979), Robert Shaw, died before the film was completed (forcing most of his dialogue to be dubbed by an impersonator); then Robson succumbed as well. The finished product was poorly received, making it an unfortunate swan song to a lengthy and interesting career.

ROC, PATRICIA. Actress. *(b. June 7, 1918, London, as Felicia Riese.)* One of Britain's top female stars of the mid 1940s and 1950s, this beautiful honey-blond actress spent several years playing insipid ingenues before winning better roles in Gainsborough films, beginning with *The Wicked Lady* (1945), in which she appeared with top star Margaret Lockwood. Roc made her screen debut in a trio of Edgar Wallace thrillers, *The Gaunt Stranger* (1938), *The Mind of Mr. Reeder,* and *The Missing People* (both 1939), costarred in *The Rebel Son* (also 1939), then moved on to bigger and better films. *Madonna of the Seven Moons* (1944), introduced Roc to American audiences, and she visited Hollywood to take a small supporting part in *Canyon Passage* (1946)—hardly a fitting role for the glamorous Brit. Aside from a small role in *The Man on the Eiffel Tower* (1949), Roc confined her movie work to

British and European productions and, although still beautiful as she passed 40, drifted out of the film business.
OTHER FILMS INCLUDE: 1943: *Millions Like Us;* 1944: *Love Story;* 1947: *The Brothers, So Well Remembered, Jassy, Holiday Camp;* 1948: *One Night With You;* 1949: *The Perfect Woman;* 1951: *Circle of Danger;* 1954: *Cartouche;* 1957: *The Hypnotist;* 1960: *Bluebeard's Ten Honeymoons.*

ROEG, NICOLAS. Director, cinematographer. *(b. Aug. 15, 1928, London.)* This director invests his films with both a heightened visual and heightened erotic sense, often at the expense of coherent storytelling. He entered the film business in the late 1940s, first as a dubber, then as a camera operator, and finally a full-fledged director of photography. Some of his major credits as cinematographer include Roger Corman's *The Masque of the Red Death* (1964), *Fahrenheit 451* (1966), *Far From the Madding Crowd* (1967), and *Petulia* (1968). Roeg also shot second-unit footage for *Lawrence of Arabia* (1962). He codirected and photographed *Performance* (1970, with scripter Donald Cammell), a weird switched-identities tale, which was Mick Jagger's fiction-feature debut. He then directed (and shot) the striking Australian wilderness saga *Walkabout* (1971), which marked him as a filmmaker with a very personal vision. The love scene between Donald Sutherland and Julie Christie in Roeg's dour 1973 thriller *Don't Look Now* set a new standard for on-screen sexual frankness and is still eye-opening today. He found a niche in the "cult" pantheon by directing rock star David Bowie in the peculiar, paranoid science-fiction drama *The Man Who Fell to Earth* in 1976. His more recent films have been erratic, to say the least, but several of them—including *Bad Timing: A Sensual Obsession* (1980), *Eureka* (made in 1981, barely released in 1985), *Insignificance* (1985), and *Track 29* (1988)—have served as showcases for Roeg's wife, the gifted and uninhibited actress Theresa Russell. Other films include *Castaway* (1987), a segment of *Aria* (1988), *Sweet Bird of Youth* (1989 telefilm with Elizabeth Taylor), *The Witches* (a 1990 treat on which Roeg collaborated with executive producer Jim Henson), and *Heart of Darkness* (1994, telefilm). He also directed an episode of TV's "The Young Indiana Jones Chronicles."

ROEMER, MICHAEL. Director, screenwriter, producer. *(b. Jan. 1, 1928, Berlin.)* This earnest, talented filmmaker saw his two major fiction features revived to great acclaim in the early 1990s, more than 20 years after they were made: *Nothing But a Man* (1964) and *The Plot Against Harry* (1969). Roemer came to the United States in 1945 and attended Harvard University, where he made a feature-length film, *A Touch of the Times.* Upon graduation he went to work for Louis de Rochemont, and worked on numerous documentaries, as well as *Cinerama Holiday* and *Windjammer.* He produced and directed countless documentary films after that, mostly for public TV, before collaborating with Harvard classmate Robert M. Young on *Nothing But a Man,* a powerful, personal look at blacks in the South. Their next project, the TV documentary *Faces of Israel* (1967), was nominated for an Emmy. In 1969 Roemer wrote and directed *The Plot Against Harry,* working again with Young as coproducer and cinematographer. When production was completed, there was no interest from distributors, and for lack of money the film was shelved until 1990—when it debuted at the New York Film Festival and went on to become a critical and commercial sleeper. Since *Harry,* Roemer has produced and directed *Dying* (1976), a PBS documentary, and written and directed the fictional films *Pilgrim, Farewell* (1982), and *Haunted* (1983). Since 1966 he has taught film at Yale University.

ROGERS, CHARLES "BUDDY." Actor. *(b. Aug. 13, 1904, Olathe, Kans.)* This energetic, affable star of the late silent and early talkie years often appears in reference books as only a footnote to biographical sketches of his wife, Mary Pickford, whom he married in 1936 (and with whom he costarred in the delightful 1927 comedy *My Best Girl*). A University of Kansas graduate and accomplished musician (his signature tune, as a bandleader, was "Twelfth Street Rag," a few bars of which he played on nearly every instrument), the boyishly handsome Rogers was signed by Paramount in 1926 and groomed as a screen actor. He appeared with W. C. Fields in *So's Your Old Man* that same year, and then with "It" Girl Clara Bow in *Get Your Man* and the Academy Award-winning aviation epic *Wings* in 1927. Rogers' performance in the latter, as an Army Air Corps pilot in World War 1, remains his best remembered.

"America's Boy Friend" was no Barrymore, but he was well suited to lightweight musicals and comedies like *Close Harmony* (1929), *Follow Thru, Paramount on Parade, Safety in Numbers* (all 1930), *The Road to Reno* (1931), *Take a Chance* (1933), *Dance Band* (a British attempt to emulate Hollywood musicals), *Old Man Rhythm* (both 1935), and *This Way Please* (1937). He then played straight man to Lupe Velez in several 1941–42 entries in the slapstick "Mexican Spitfire" series. (Reviving his band, he also appeared in several Soundies shorts with vocalist Marvel—later Marilyn—Maxwell.) After the war, he supported Fred MacMurray and Madeleine Carroll in *An Innocent Affair* (1948), an outmoded sex comedy, and then was offscreen for a decade (working instead on radio and TV), inexplicably returning to take a small role in *The Parson and the Outlaw* (1957), a minor Billy the Kid Western. Rogers remained devoted to Pickford until her death in 1979. Still dapper, this silver-haired philanthropist was given the Jean Hersholt Humanitarian Award at the 1986 Academy Award ceremony.

ROGERS, GINGER. Actress. (b. July 16, 1911, Independence, Mo., as Virginia McMath; d. Apr. 25, 1995.) To remember her only as the beautiful, vivacious dancing partner of Fred Astaire in their classic 1930s musicals is to do Ginger Rogers a great disfavor: She was a much better actress than most Hollywood wags gave her credit for, even before her Oscar win for *Kitty Foyle* (1940). Rogers was a performer from childhood, the product of an aggressive stage mother. She danced professionally in vaudeville while still in her teens, married to partner Jack Pepper at the age of 17. Her first film was *Campus Sweethearts* (1929), a short subject starring Rudy Vallee; she made several mini-musicals in New York while performing in the Gershwin stage smash "Girl Crazy," in which she had the second female lead. Paramount, at that time operating a stu-

dio in Astoria, Queens, gave Rogers a break in feature films, slotting her in the Claudette Colbert starrer *Young Man of Manhattan* (1930). She appeared in a few more minor films for the studio before going in 1931 to Hollywood, where she worked as leading lady in a slew of program pictures including *The Tip Off, Suicide Fleet* (both 1931), *Carnival Boat, The Tenderfoot, Hat Check Girl, You Said a Mouthful, The Thirteenth Guest* (all 1932), *A Shriek in the Night, Broadway Bad, Don't Bet on Love, Sitting Pretty* (introducing the song "Did You Ever See a Dream Walking?"), and *Chance at Heaven* (all 1933). Unlike many attractive young women in Hollywood, Rogers seldom played dewy-eyed ingenues; her characters were nearly always wisecracking, worldly dames who knew their apples.

The year 1933 provided Ginger with her best breaks to date. First, she won star billing for the first time at a major studio in RKO's *Professional Sweetheart.* Second, she won plum supporting roles in two Warner Bros. musicals, *42nd Street* (as monocled "Anytime Annie") and *Gold Diggers of 1933* (introducing the song "We're in the Money"—and singing one chorus in pig latin). Third, she was teamed with dancer Fred Astaire for the first time in *Flying Down to Rio,* also for RKO, in which they danced to the lilting strains of the "Carioca."

RKO put Rogers under contract in 1934 (after she'd finished *Twenty Million Sweethearts* for Warners), developing a starring vehicle for her and Astaire. *The Gay Divorcee* sported songs by Cole Porter (including "Night and Day") and gave the Astaire-Rogers team plenty of opportunity to strut their stuff. The picture's overwhelming success kept the pair together in a series of delightful, lavishly mounted musicals, all of which featured songs by the country's top tunesmiths (Porter, Irving Berlin, Jerome Kern, the Gershwins) and provided escapist entertainment for Depression-battered moviegoers. Rogers and Astaire were an incomparably well-matched team; as perceptive critics noticed, they seemed to make love through their dance routines, and their smart comic performances as on-again, off-again lovers were a treat. Rogers also made sure she always had one prime solo song in each film. Audiences loved *Top Hat, Roberta* (both 1935), *Swing Time,*

Follow the Fleet (both 1936), *Shall We Dance?* (1937), *Carefree* (1938), and the more serious *The Story of Vernon & Irene Castle* (1939).

Although RKO allowed her to make films without Astaire—including *Romance in Manhattan* (1934), *Star of Midnight* (1935, opposite William Powell in this imitation *Thin Man*), *In Person* (1936), *Stage Door* (1937, in which she provided a lively and engaging counterpart to top-billed Katharine Hepburn), *Vivacious Lady, Having Wonderful Time* (both 1938), and *Bachelor Mother* (1939)—she felt she'd never blossom on her own without shedding her demanding dancing partner. For his part, Astaire had had enough of Rogers and the RKO musicals, and was more than willing to leave for greener pastures elsewhere.

After starring in two relatively minor films, *Lucky Partners* and *The Primrose Path,* Rogers hit pay dirt by letting her blond hair go naturally dark and forgoing glamour-girl treatment to play the feisty, independent working girl in *Kitty Foyle* (all 1940), pleasantly surprising critics and audiences with her warm, impassioned performance. She won a Best Actress Academy Award, and solidified her position as RKO's top star.

Tom, Dick and Harry (1941) gave her a delightful romantic comedy vehicle. The following year, off the RKO lot, Rogers shined in *Roxie Hart* (playing a gum-chomping, wisecracking publicity hound) and *The Major and the Minor* (as another high-spirited, self-reliant working girl, who disguises herself as a 12-year-old to save on train fare). By contrast, her RKO vehicles of the period, including *Once Upon a Honeymoon* (1942) and *Tender Comrade* (1943), seemed weak. Paramount's overproduced, Technicolor *Lady in the Dark,* though, gave Rogers her first real flop, being the tale (based on a Moss Hart play—but shorn of most of its Kurt Weill–Ira Gershwin songs) of a "boss lady" who undergoes psychoanalysis.

Rogers' star never again shone as brightly, even though she still retained the power to hold and satisfy audiences. *Weekend at the Waldorf* (1945), *Heartbeat, Magnificent Doll* (both 1946, miscast in the latter as Dolley Madison), *It Had to Be You* (1947), *The Barkleys of Broadway* (1949, reteamed one last time with Astaire, this time at MGM), *Perfect*

Strangers (1950), the highly dramatic *Storm Warning,* and *The Groom Wore Spurs* (both 1951) saw a gradual diminution in her popularity. She made something of a comeback with three 1952 comedies—*We're Not Married, Dreamboat* (playing a silent-screen star, a part for which she seemed too young), and *Monkey Business*—but she couldn't compete with a newer, younger group of stars such as *Monkey Business*'s Marilyn Monroe.

Rogers gave tolerably good performances in *Forever Female* (1953), *Black Widow* (1954, as a temperamental actress), *Tight Spot* (1955), and *The First Traveling Saleslady* (1956), but found decent starring vehicles fewer and far between, and after *Teenage Rebel* (also 1956) and *Oh, Men! Oh, Women!* (1957), she returned to the stage and nightclubs. (Some years later, she played a madam opposite Ray Milland in 1964's mercifully unreleased *The Confession/aka Quick, Let's Get Married/aka Seven Different Ways,* and was Carol Lynley's mother in 1965's *Harlow.*)

She remained a star, however, as she proved when she took over the leading role in the Broadway smash "Hello, Dolly!" in 1965, and played the title role in the 1969 London production of "Mame." Professionally inactive in her later years, she was confined to a wheelchair but still made myriad personal appearances, especially to promote her 1991 autobiography, "Ginger: My Story." (A 1942 juvenile novel, "Ginger Rogers and the Riddle of the Scarlet Cloak," was written by her mother Lela, who also worked for years as a talent scout and nurturer at RKO, and caused considerable ripples as a Communist witch-hunter in the 1950s.) Rogers was married to actors Lew Ayres (1934–41), Jacques Bergerac (1953–57), and William Marshall (1961–62).

ROGERS, MIMI. Actress. *(b. Jan. 27, 1956, Coral Gables, Fla.)* It's ironic, and not a little unfair, that this attractive actress with the crooked smile drew more attention for her brief marriage to young superstar Tom Cruise than for any of her film appearances. She cut a stylish figure, albeit one of very little substantive appeal, in several 1980s films, beginning with *Blue Skies Again* (1983). She costarred in the short-lived TV series "Paper Dolls" (1984), and played Michael Keaton's wife in the popular comedy *Gung Ho* (1986). She was the smoldering socialite who tempted working-class cop Tom Berenger in 1987's *Someone to Watch Over Me,* Christopher Reeve's girlfriend in that same year's *Street Smart,* the unknowing object of a voyeur's desire in *Hider in the House,* a decadent aristocrat in *The Mighty Quinn* (both 1989), an imperiled housewife in *Desperate Hours* (1990), and a hip photojournalist in *The Doors* (1991). Rogers' previous involvement with the Scientology movement gave her something on which to draw for her work in *The Rapture,* a controversial examination of religious fundamentalism that was one of 1991's top cocktail-party-argument movies. Her supporting role in the muddled thriller *White Sands* (1992) was drastically cut prior to the film's release. Little by little, she ekes out favorable reviews for her work; she may soon be recognized as a serious actress and not just the ex-Mrs. Cruise. Recent credits include *Far From Home: The Adventures of Yellow Dog* and *Bulletproof Heart* (both 1995).

ROGERS, ROY. Actor, singer. *(b. Nov. 5, 1912, Duck Run, Ohio, as Leonard Slye.)* The "King of the Cowboys," a star of more than 90 feature-length Westerns and more than 100 half-hour TV shows, remains one of the most beloved figures in show business. A shy, unassuming man whose self-deprecating humor makes him even more appealing in person, Rogers was one of the few cowboy heroes who "crossed over" into mainstream Hollywood: His pictures played major-circuit theaters and he was among the movie industry's top-grossing stars for several years. Born into humble surroundings, he left Ohio in 1929 for California, where he worked as a transient fruit picker before forming a musical group, "The Rocky Mountaineers," with several friends. Evolving into "The Sons of the Pioneers," the group sang Western songs on radio and, beginning in 1935, in films—the Thelma Todd/Patsy Kelly short *Slightly Static,* and a feature called *The Old Homestead.* In 1936, billed as Dick Weston, he appeared with the Sons in *The Old Corral,* one of Gene Autry's musical Westerns, which put the newly formed Republic Pictures on the Hollywood map.

When Autry went on strike for more money in 1938, Republic held auditions for a replacement, and Weston—rechristened Roy Rogers—got the job. His first starring film, *Under Western Stars* (1938), was an instant smash, and an eye-opener to the Republic brass; although Autry was quick to compromise with studio management, Rogers was retained to star in a competing series. He made eight Westerns per season, playing historical figures in *Billy the Kid Returns* (1938), *Young Buffalo Bill, Young Bill Hickok* (both 1940), and *Jesse James at Bay* (1941), among others. He rode a magnificent palomino stallion initially named Golden Cloud (who'd carried Olivia de Havilland in *The Adventures of Robin Hood)* but renamed Trigger for Roy's films, and was usually accompanied by grizzled sidekick George "Gabby" Hayes.

After Autry went into the Army in 1942, the studio bought hit tunes and promoted bigger budgets for Rogers' vehicles, beginning with *Heart of the Golden West* (1942). Now backed up by his old friends, the Sons of the Pioneers, and given top production backing, Roy became the screen's top Western star and won the "King of the Cowboys" title. Roy's status was confirmed by a guest appearance (with Trigger) in the all-star Warner Bros. feature *Hollywood Canteen* (1944), and in the Walt Disney feature *Melody Time* (1948), in which he and the Sons of the Pioneers sang and told the story (animated by Disney) of "Pecos Bill." In the mid 1940s, the Rogers films eschewed traditional Western plot lines and action sequences in favor of elaborate musical presentations, reflecting Republic president Herbert Yates' infatuation with the Broadway production of "Oklahoma!"; *The Cowboy and the Senorita* (1944) first teamed Rogers with Dale Evans, then a feisty blonde who often played a "city gal" initially at odds with Roy. She appeared in many of his top 1940s pictures, including *Lights of Old Santa Fe* (also 1944), *Don't Fence Me In* (one of Roy's highest-grossing, and best-remembered, series Westerns), *Along the Navajo Trail* (both 1945), *My Pal Trigger,* and *Roll On, Texas Moon* (both 1946). Roy, a widower, married Dale in 1947.

By the late 1940s, a new production

team had invigorated the series with color photography, more adult plot lines, and an almost sadistic emphasis on violent action. The Sons of the Pioneers left, and were replaced by Foy Willing's Riders of the Purple Sage. When Gabby Hayes departed in 1947, a succession of sidekicks—including Andy Devine, Gordon Jones, and Pinky Lee—provided comedy relief. Roy's last Republic Western, *Pals of the Golden West,* was released in 1951, and, aside from costarring with Bob Hope in *Son of Paleface* (1952)—and making a gag cameo in the comedian's *Alias Jesse James* (1959)—he confined most of his energies to his long-running TV show (1951–57), personal appearances, and recording career. Roy appeared in a modern-dress Western, *Mackintosh and T.J.,* in 1975; it was a pleasant but decidedly unexciting "comeback" for the King of the Cowboys. Roy also lent his name to a chain of fast-food restaurants, eventually bought by the Marriott Corporation, and made frequent personal appearances at the openings. Open-heart surgery and other health problems curtailed his workload in the 1980s, but in 1987 he and Dale taped a series of reminiscences to introduce their old movies for cable TV, and in 1991 he was prevailed upon to record a new album, called "Tribute," which served as a valedictory for his career. He and Dale regularly welcome visitors to their homey museum in Victorville, California. Their joint autobiography, "The Story of Roy Rogers and Dale Evans: Happy Trails," was published in 1979.

ROGERS, WILL. Actor, writer, producer. *(b. Nov. 4, 1879, Oologah, Okla.; d. Aug. 15, 1935.)* "An actor is a fella that just has a little more monkey in him." Thus spake one of the greatest of all American humorists, and while he always spoke self-deprecatingly of his work on-screen, he was in fact "a natural," with more charisma—and honesty as a performer—than many a trained actor of his generation. No wonder he became a major box-office star. Born in the then-wild Oklahoma Territory (before it was a state!), Rogers got his show-biz start at the turn of the century, working as a trick roper in rodeos, circuses, wild-West shows, and, eventually, vaudeville and Broadway. By 1915 he was working in a Ziegfeld revue,

and moved up to the legendary Follies the next year, where his pithy comments on man's foibles, delivered in a folksy drawl and punctuated by rope tricks, convulsed the elite New York audiences.

In 1918 Rogers made his film debut in a Samuel Goldwyn (then still Sam Goldfish) production, *Laughing Bill Hyde,* shot in New Jersey. It was successful enough for Goldwyn to offer Rogers a contract; he starred in 13 features over the next three years, among them the delightful *Jubilo* (1919), *Honest Hutch* (1920), and the uproarious Shakespeare-inspired *Doubling for Romeo* (1921). Rogers' screen persona, an extension of his own personality, registered surprisingly well with moviegoers in spite of their inability to hear him. His unique brand of humor came through just the same. After the Goldwyn contract expired, he went out on his own, producing, writing, and starring in his own two-reelers, but the venture was catastrophic: only three shorts were actually produced, the last one was never released, and their failure put him deeply in debt.

Rogers signed with Hal Roach in 1923 and spent the next two years starring in what became some of his best known shorts, including a pair of broadly funny Hollywood spoofs, *Uncensored Movies* (1923) and *Big Moments From Little Pictures* (1924), as well as a guest appearance in an Our Gang comedy, *Jubilo, Jr.* (also 1924). In 1927 he made a series of one-reel humorous travelogues for Pathé, but it took the coming of sound to give Rogers the screen showcase he deserved. In 1929 he inked a deal with Fox to star in talking pictures, as well as "help out" with the writing.

Rogers' first talkie, *They Had to See Paris* (1929), was an immediate hit; the star showed himself to be completely at ease before the microphone, unlike many other silent stars. His gentle, folksy humor was perfect for talking pictures, and his directors (and costars) learned to give him the freedom to make up his own dialogue even while the cameras were running. He proceeded in the same pleasant vein with such easygoing comedies as *So This Is London* (1930), *A Connecticut Yankee* (a Rogersian update of Mark Twain), *Ambassador Bill* (both 1931), *Down to Earth* (1932), *State Fair, Doctor Bull* (his first film for director John Ford), and *Mr. Skitch* (all 1933). Though the plots changed, Rogers did not; these were star vehicles in the truest sense, and audiences loved them. By 1934 he was the top box-office draw in the country, according to a "Motion Picture Herald" exhibitors poll. That year he starred in such hits as the bucolic *David Harum* and Ford's wonderful *Judge Priest* (perhaps his best film), as well as cowriting the story for *Stand Up and Cheer* (in which he did not appear). In 1935 Rogers really hit his stride in *The County Chairman, Life Begins at Forty,* and *Doubting Thomas,* a winning streak ended by his tragic death in an airplane crash. His last two films, *Steamboat 'Round the Bend* (directed by Ford) and *In Old Kentucky,* were released posthumously that year.

His eagle-eyed observations about American life are still widely quoted. Actors from James Whitmore and Keith Carradine (on stage) to his son Will Rogers, Jr. (in 1952's *The Story of Will Rogers*), have tried to recapture his personality. And his writings, including a 1927 autobiography, "There's Not a Bathing Suit in Russia," are still read and enjoyed. His name also graces several state parks in Los Angeles, a turnpike in Oklahoma, and the well-known medical research institute in White Plains, New York. But Will Rogers is underappreciated as a movie star; fortunately, the films exist and await that happy rediscovery.

ROHMER, ERIC. Director, screenwriter. (*b. Apr. 4, 1920, Nancy, France.*) Highly intellectual writer-director and former film critic/historian—in 1957 he cowrote a book on Hitchcock with fellow enthusiast and director-to-be Claude Chabrol—whose dialogue-heavy, deceptively simple cinematic parables and proverbs on love and morality among the young French bourgeoisie actually represent some of the most astute and philosophically trenchant filmmaking ever. He makes his films as portions of cycles—Six Moral Tales, Comedies and Proverbs, Tales of the Four Seasons—although each work functions as a self-contained whole. In his work as a critic during the 1950s he teamed with Jean-Luc Godard and Jacques Rivette, so while considerably older than many of his New Wave contemporaries, his early films were bracketed in that category. Since finding his niche in the 1960s with the in-

ternationally acclaimed *My Night at Maud's* (1969, Oscar-nominated for Best Screenplay), he has been making his little films as regularly as he can, to the delight of his fans and confused resignation of his detractors, whose feelings about his films are summed up in a line of dialogue uttered by Gene Hackman's character in *Night Moves* (1975) apropos Rohmer: "I saw one of his films once; it was like watching paint dry." For aficionados, however, the pleasures (both sensual and cerebral) of watching *Claire's Knee* (1971), *Chloe in the Afternoon* (1972), *The Aviator's Wife* (1981), *Pauline at the Beach* (1983), or *Boyfriends and Girlfriends* (1987) are unique and indescribable. His movies are unlike those of any other filmmaker in the world.

OTHER FILMS INCLUDE: 1962: *La Boulangère de Monceau;* 1963: *La Carrière de Suzanne;* 1967: *La Collectioneuse;* 1976: *The Marquise of O;* 1978: *Perceval;* 1982: *Le Beau Mariage;* 1984: *Nights of the Full Moon;* 1986: *Summer, Four Adventures of Reinette and Mirabelle;* 1989: *A Tale of Springtime;* 1992: *A Tale of Winter;* 1993: *The Tree, The Mayor, and The Mediathèque.*

ROMAN, RUTH. Actress. (*b. Dec. 22, 1924, Boston.*) Although this coldly beautiful, full-figured actress won the title role in a 1945 serial, *Jungle Queen* (in which she played a mythical white goddess fighting Nazis in Africa!), she spent several more years playing supporting parts before achieving stardom. Roman, who studied at Boston's prestigious Bishop Lee Dramatic School, had bits in *Stage Door Canteen* (1943) and *Since You Went Away* (1944) prior to her cliffhanger experience, and accepted other small roles until she won her first feature-film lead as the title character in *Belle Starr's Daughter* (1948), a so-so horse opera. She had featured roles in *Champion, The Window, Beyond the Forest,* and *Always Leave Them Laughing* (all 1949) before getting another lead in the Randolph Scott Western *Colt .45* (1950).

That same year, Roman joined Eleanor Parker and Patricia Neal in *Three Secrets,* which cast them as anxious mothers waiting to learn whether or not their children have survived a plane crash. Her fine performance in that film won her a costarring part in King Vidor's *Lightning Strikes*

Twice (1951). Then Alfred Hitchcock starred Roman in his taut thriller *Strangers on a Train* (also 1951). Roman fared best in film noir, especially on those infrequent occasions when she was cast as a cynical, world-weary, hardbitten femme fatale. She worked on screen less in the 1960s, and by the 1970s was appearing primarily in episodic TV ("Knots Landing," for example) and made-fors.
OTHER FILMS INCLUDE: 1952: *Mara Maru, Young Man With Ideas;* 1953: *Blowing Wild;* 1954: *The Shanghai Story, Down Three Dark Streets, Tanganyika;* 1955: *The Far Country;* 1956: *Joe Macbeth, The Bottom of the Bottle;* 1957: *Five Steps to Danger;* 1961: *Look in Any Window;* 1965: *Love Has Many Faces;* 1973: *The Killing Kind;* 1974: *Dead of Night, Impulse;* 1977: *Day of the Animals;* 1980: *Echoes;* 1983: *Silent Sentence.*

ROMERO, CESAR. Actor. *(b. Feb. 15, 1907, New York City; d. Jan. 1, 1994.)* Suave, handsome, dark-haired Latin, whose grandfather was Jose Martí, the liberator of Cuba. Romero broke into show business as a professional dancer, and later turned to acting. He came to Hollywood in 1934 and was seldom idle for the next sixty years, though he never became a full-fledged star—a curse, he felt, of being thought of as a "Latin lover." In fact, he was a very capable and surprisingly versatile actor. He played a suspect in *The Thin Man* (1934), one of Marlene Dietrich's luckless lovers in *The Devil Is a Woman* (1935), a tough-as-nails gangster in *Show Them No Mercy!* (1935), an Afghan leader confronted by Shirley Temple in *Wee Willie Winkie* (1937), Doc Halliday (*sic*) in *Frontier Marshal* (1939), and the Cisco Kid in a half-dozen B movies made in 1940–41 at his home studio, 20th Century-Fox.

He was a staple in Fox musicals of the 1940s, and even got to dance with Betty Grable in *Springtime in the Rockies* (1942). In 1947 he got one of his all-time best roles, as the Spanish conqueror Cortés in *Captain From Castile* (1947), then showed a flair for knockabout slapstick as an oafish acrobat in *Julia Misbehaves* (1948). But by the 1950s, with the studios slowing down, his career slid. There were still occasional plums, like the Vegas gangster he played in *Ocean's Eleven* (1960), and the comic villains he

essayed in a handful of Disney comedies, including *Now You See Him, Now You Don't* (1972) and *The Strongest Man in the World* (1975). By then Romero had become a familiar face on TV, where he enjoyed latter-day fame in the unlikely role of The Joker on "Batman" (1966–68) and in the 1966 feature, *Batman,* it inspired. Having starred in his own short-lived series, "Passport to Danger" (1954–55), he joined the cast of the hit show "Falcon Crest" in 1985 (at the age of 78) as Jane Wyman's love interest, and stayed for two seasons. He remained active, performing and hosting vintage films on cable TV, to the very end of his life.
OTHER FILMS INCLUDE: 1935: *The Good Fairy, Cardinal Richelieu, Diamond Jim;* 1936: *Public Enemy's Wife, 15 Maiden Lane;* 1937: *Dangerously Yours;* 1938: *Happy Landing, My Lucky Star;* 1939: *The Little Princess, Charlie Chan at Treasure Island, The Cisco Kid and the Lady;* 1940: *Viva Cisco Kid, Lucky Cisco Kid;* 1941: *Weekend in Havana, The Great American Broadcast;* 1942: *Orchestra Wives, Tales of Manhattan;* 1943: *Coney Island;* 1948: *That Lady in Ermine;* 1949: *The Beautiful Blonde From Bashful Bend;* 1951: *The Lost Continent, FBI Girl;* 1952: *The Jungle;* 1954: *Vera Cruz;* 1955: *The Americano;* 1956: *Around the World in Eighty Days;* 1957: *The Story of Mankind;* 1963: *The Castillian, Donovan's Reef;* 1964: *A House Is Not a Home;* 1965: *Marriage on the Rocks;* 1968: *Skidoo, Hot Millions, Madigan's Million;* 1969: *Midas Run, Crooks and Coronets;* 1970: *The Computer Wore Tennis Shoes;* 1973: *The Spectre of Edgar Allan Poe;* 1976: *Won Ton Ton, the Dog Who Saved Hollywood;* 1985: *Lust in the Dust;* 1988: *Mortuary Academy;* 1989: *Street Law;* 1990: *Simple Justice.*

ROMERO, GEORGE A. Director, screenwriter, producer, editor. *(b. Feb. 4, 1940, New York City.)* Innovative director who—for better or worse—helped usher in the modern horror film. Interested in movies as a child, Romero made 8mm shorts and his first "feature," *The Man From the Meteor,* in 1954. (During production he was arrested by security guards for throwing a burning dummy off a rooftop.) After college, he and his friends formed The Latent Image, a production company that made very creative TV commercials and industrial shorts, and eventually secured enough money for a "real" film, *Night of the Living Dead* (1968). This grainy black-and-white chiller about flesh-eating zombies became a cult hit and its lean, graphic, no-nonsense approach to horror influenced many future practitioners of the genre. Romero didn't have as much success with *There's Always Vanilla* (1972), *Hungry Wives* (1973), or *Code Name: Trixie* (1973, about a plague which hits a small town; aka *The Crazies*), so he produced a series of hour-long sports documentaries called "The Winners" before directing *Martin* (1978), a clever and supremely gory tale of a teen who believes he is a vampire.

Rather than move to Hollywood, or even New York, Romero decided to remain in Pittsburgh, and continued to make features there away from the movie mainstream, often drawing on local talent—including actors from prestigious Carnegie-Mellon University. *Dawn of the Dead* (1979), a sequel to *Night of the Living Dead* (and possibly Romero's best film), mixed horror, satire and even social commentary as zombies attack four people trapped in a shopping mall. *Knightriders* (1981) followed a troupe of bikers living under Arthurian codes and was an amusing, effective change of pace for the filmmaker. It was an early credit for actor Ed Harris, in the leading role, and featured as its chief villain Tom Savini, who'd established himself as a master makeup artist on Romero's horror pictures. The filmmaker returned to familiar turf for *Creepshow* (1982, his first collaboration with horrormeister Stephen King), *Day of the Dead* (1985, the third and weakest of the trilogy), the interesting *Monkey Shines: An Experiment in Fear* (1988), and "The Facts in the Case of Mr. Valdemar" segment of *Two Evil Eyes* (1990). In 1984 he introduced the long-running TV anthology series "Tales From the Darkside," and served as executive producer. Romero scripted 1987's *Creepshow 2*, and executive-produced the 1990 remake of *Night of the Living Dead*, directed by longtime collaborator Tom Savini; it only proved how good the original was. Most recently, he returned to King territory, adapting and directing the author's *The Dark Half* (1993).

ROOKER, MICHAEL. Actor. *(b. Apr. 6, 1955, Jasper, Ala.)* Large, soft-spoken, quietly powerful actor whose frightening performance in the cult film *Henry: Portrait of a Serial Killer* (1986) earned him widespread acclaim when it was finally released in 1990. Rooker's accomplished performance accounted for much of the underground success of the gritty low-budget opus. By that time, he'd also been seen in *Light of Day* (1987) and *Rent-a-Cop* (1988), prior to landing juicier parts as Black Sox player Chick Gandil in *Eight Men Out,* a KKK member in *Mississippi Burning* (both 1988), and a psychopathic husband in *Sea of Love* (1989). He has since played several "good guys," in *Music Box* (1989), *Days of Thunder* (1990), and *JFK* (1991, as one of Jim Garrison's assistants). In 1993 he costarred in *The Dark Half, Cliffhanger* (as Sylvester Stallone's friend-turned-foe), and *Tombstone.*

ROONEY, MICKEY. Actor. *(b. Sept. 23, 1920, Brooklyn, N.Y., as Joe Yule, Jr.)* This diminutive dynamo, the son of veteran vaudevillians, began performing just about the time he could stand on a stage. He learned to sing, dance, play the piano and drums, and troupe with all the aplomb (and, it must be said, swagger) of much older, more experienced thespians. By 1927 he had not only made his feature-film debut—playing a cigar-smoking midget in *Orchids and Ermine*—but was starring in a series of two-reel comedies based on the "Toonerville Trolley" comic strip. Wearing ragged clothes and a tattered, oversized derby hat, he played "Mickey 'Himself' McGuire" in dozens of shorts from 1927 to 1934.

During those years he occasionally took small roles in feature films such as *Beast of the City, My Pal the King* (playing a boy monarch rescued from palace plotters by cowboy star Tom Mix!), *Fast Companions* (all 1932), *Broadway to Hollywood, The Life of Jimmy Dolan, The World Changes, The Big Cage* (all 1933), *The Lost Jungle, Manhattan Melodrama, Hide-Out, Upper World, Death on the Diamond,* and *Blind Date* (all 1934).

In 1935 Mickey Rooney (as he was now billed, having legally changed his name in 1932) played the mischievous Puck in Warner Bros.' lavish adaptation of Shakespeare's *A Midsummer Night's Dream,* as well as taking roles in *Ah, Wilderness, Reckless,* and *Riffraff* for MGM, which signed him that year to a long-term contract. He appeared in *The Devil Is a Sissy* (1936) and *Captains Courageous* (1937) before taking the role of young Andy Hardy, an energetic teenager, in *A Family Affair* (also 1937). The surprise success of that modestly budgeted picture spurred Metro to turn the Hardy family's adventures into a series, and Rooney's ever-increasing participation in the stories quickly boosted him to top-billed status, as a survey of the titles indicates: *You're Only Young Once, Judge Hardy's Children, Love Finds Andy Hardy, Out West With The Hardys* (all 1938), *The Hardys Ride High, Judge Hardy and Son, Andy Hardy Gets Spring Fever* (all 1939), *Andy Hardy Meets Debutante* (1940), *Life Begins for Andy Hardy, Andy Hardy's Private Secretary* (both 1941), *The Courtship of Andy Hardy, Andy Hardy's Double Life* (both 1942), *Andy Hardy's Blonde Trouble* (1944), and *Love Laughs at Andy Hardy* (1946). Each series entry put Andy in a seemingly inextricable predicament, from which he usually escaped with the help of his dad, the Judge (played by Lewis Stone, taking over from Lionel Barrymore after the series opener).

As it turned out, though, Rooney didn't need the Andy Hardy movies to make him a star. MGM kept him busy in a dizzying series of films designed to show off his versatility. *Boys Town* (1938), the fictional account of the institution founded by one Father Flanagan (played by Spencer Tracy), cast Rooney as Whitey Marsh, a troubled youth who disrupts the boys' community but reforms by the final, tearful fadeout. (The stars reunited in 1941 for a sequel, *Men of Boys Town.*) Rooney and Judy Garland, who'd first costarred in *Love Finds Andy Hardy,* were teamed in the "barnyard" musicals *Babes in Arms* (1939, for which, amazingly, he was Oscar-nominated), *Strike Up the Band* (1940), *Babes on Broadway* (1941), and *Girl Crazy* (1943), the last-named their best picture together, adapted from the hit stage show with most of the original Gershwin numbers intact. Some measure of Rooney's impact is indicated by the fact that the Academy voted him an honorary Oscar in 1938—for "significant contribution in bringing to the screen the

spirit and personification of youth, and . . . setting a high standard of ability and achievement."

In 1939 Rooney became America's top box-office draw, unseating former title holder Shirley Temple. He demonstrated his ability to master demanding dramatic roles in *Young Tom Edison* (1940, playing the famed inventor as a boy), and two of his all-time best, *The Human Comedy* (1943, picking up his second Oscar nomination), and *National Velvet* (1944, with young Elizabeth Taylor). In later years, *Velvet* director Clarence Brown—who'd worked with every top MGM star in his long career—named Rooney the finest actor he'd ever directed!

When he returned from wartime service, Rooney found it hard to regain his footing. The precociousness of his youth, which had become the cockiness of his adolescence, still manifested itself in his screen persona, but in a mature man was seen as obnoxiousness. He starred in a musical version of *Ah, Wilderness* called *Summer Holiday* (1948) and had top billing in *Words and Music* (1948), playing Lorenz Hart in MGM's sappy biography of the Rodgers & Hart songwriting team, but he left the studio shortly thereafter, and it was the last prestige production, with one or two exceptions, in which he appeared for many years.

Rooney's subsequent films were a mixed bag at best, including *Killer McCoy* (1947), *The Big Wheel* (1949), *He's a Cockeyed Wonder* (1950), *The Strip* (1951), *Sound Off* (1952), *A Slight Case of Larceny* (1953), *The Bridges at Toko-Ri* (1954, a notable standout), *The Twinkle in God's Eye* (1955), *Francis in the Haunted House* (1956, taking over for Donald O'Connor in the last of the talking mule series), *Baby Face Nelson* (1957), *Andy Hardy Comes Home* (1958, a depressingly poor Hardy family reunion), *The Last Mile* (1959, with Rooney snarling and growling like a pit bull in the role of Killer Mears, which had boosted Spencer Tracy to stage stardom years before), *Platinum High School* (1960), *King of the Roaring Twenties, Everything's Ducky* (both 1961), *Breakfast at Tiffany's* (also 1961, with Rooney in comedy relief as an Oriental character!), *The Secret Invasion* (1964), *How to Stuff a Wild Bikini* (1965), *Ambush Bay* (1966), *The Extraordinary Seaman, Skidoo* (both 1969), and *The*

Comic (also 1969, as Dick Van Dyke's silent-film comedy sidekick).

But just when one might have been tempted to write off Rooney, he'd turn up in something like *The Bold and the Brave* (1956), playing an American dogface fighting in Italy during World War 2 (and once again nominated for an Academy Award), or *Requiem for a Heavyweight* (1962), supplying a skillful, touching performance as the pathetic cohort of washed-up fighter Anthony Quinn. Or in *It's a Mad Mad Mad Mad World* (1963), funnier in a few scenes than he'd been in a dozen previous "comedies."

Rooney gave his all in *Pulp* (1972), *Rachel's Man* (1975), *The Domino Principle, Pete's Dragon* (both 1977), and *The Magic of Lassie* (1978), and finally found another part worthy of his talent, as a horse trainer in *The Black Stallion* (1979). The role was filled with resonance from his earlier equestrian saga, *National Velvet,* and his touching performance earned him another Oscar nomination. Late in the decade he was signed, along with former MGM contractee Ann Miller, to star in an old-fashioned burlesque revue, "Sugar Babies," which turned out to be a surprise hit in which he toured all across the country and played for a lengthy run on Broadway.

His subsequent film work has been spotty, although he distinguished himself (and won a well-deserved Emmy) playing a retarded man in the 1981 telefilm *Bill,* and its 1983 sequel *Bill: On His Own.* In 1983 he was honored again by the Academy of Motion Picture Arts and Sciences with an honorary Oscar, a tangible reminder of the fact that in spite of his roller-coaster career, and the tendency of critics, audiences, and his Hollywood peers to take him for granted, he has always been an exceptional actor. In recent years he's provided voices for such animated features as *The Fox and the Hound* (1981), *The Care Bears Movie* (1985), and *Little Nemo: Adventures in Slumberland* (1992). Recent feature appearances include *Erik the Viking* (1989), *My Heroes Have Always Been Cowboys, Silent Night, Deadly Night 5: The Toymaker* (both 1991) and the Western *Outlaws* (1995, which he also wrote). He also served as a "host" of *That's Entertainment! III* (1994). Long active on TV, with numerous guest shots and a pair of short-lived starring sit-coms (1954's "Hey Mulligan/The Mickey Rooney Show," and 1964's "Mickey") to his credit, he has most recently costarred in the cable-TV series "The Adventures of the Black Stallion." Rooney's eight wives (!) have included actresses Ava Gardner (1942–43) and Martha Vickers (1949–51). He has written two autobiographies, "i.e.," (1965) and "Life Is Too Short" (1991).

ROSENBERG, STUART. Director. *(b. Aug. 11, 1927, New York City.)* Solid director who was originally a teacher before becoming a film editor for a television commercial company. He graduated to directing and helmed countless episodes of series like "Naked City," "Philco Playhouse," "The Untouchables," "Alfred Hitchcock Presents," and "The Defenders," for which he won an Emmy. During this time, Rosenberg codirected (with Burt Balaban) *Murder, Inc.* (1960) and soloed on *Question 7* (1961), but he made his career with *Cool Hand Luke* (1967), a tough, funny updating of prison camp films, with a classic lead performance by Paul Newman. He had less success with the romantic comedy *The April Fools* (1969) and *Move* (1970), or the subsequent Newman vehicles *WUSA* (1970), *Pocket Money* (1972), and *The Drowning Pool* (1976, which brought back the title character of 1966's *Harper).* The all-star *Voyage of the Damned* (1976) was indifferently received, while the Charles Bronson vehicle *Love and Bullets* (1979) and the popular *The Amityville Horror* (also 1979) were little more than exercises in formula. *Brubaker* (1980), a return to the prison genre, showed Rosenberg could execute a routine story with skill and *The Pope of Greenwich Village* (1984) had atmosphere and a rich gallery of character performances. He had his name removed from *Let's Get Harry* (1986). His most recent film was *My Heroes Have Always Been Cowboys* (1991).

ROSS, DIANA. Actress, singer. *(b. Mar. 26, 1944, Detroit.)* The long-reigning diva of popular music is better known as a singer than an actress, but she has been reasonably successful as the latter, in spite of her painfully shy temperament and a larger-than-life persona. As a young girl, Ross sang in the choir of her local Baptist church, and after high school, she and friends Florence Ballard and Mary Wilson auditioned for Berry Gordy at Motown records. After a ditty called "Where Did Our Love Go" became a monster hit, Diana Ross and the Supremes were on their way to becoming one of America's biggest acts. In 1970, Diana went solo, and under Gordy's guidance began a film career. For her debut film she tackled the challenging role of Billie Holiday in *Lady Sings the Blues* (1972), and though the film was flawed, she delivered a stirring performance that earned her an Academy Award nomination. Subsequent vehicles *Mahogany* (1975) and *The Wiz* (1978) were lackluster, effectively dashing Ross' hopes for enduring big-screen stardom. In 1994 she starred in the TV movie *Out of Darkness*.

ROSS, HERBERT. Director. *(b. May 13, 1927, New York City.)* Successful director of middle-of-the-road commercial fare, especially light comedies and dance pictures. Ross began as a dancer and choreographer, working for the American Ballet Theater while in his 20s. He began choreographing Hollywood films in the mid 1950s, including *Carmen Jones* (1954), *The Young Ones* (1961), *Dr. Dolittle* (1967), and *Funny Girl* (1968). The following year saw Ross' debut as film director with a musical version of *Goodbye, Mr. Chips;* since then he has directed an average of a picture per year. His *The Turning Point* and *The Goodbye Girl* were both among the biggest hits of 1977; the former earned Oscar nominations for Best Picture and Best Director, and the latter (which was also nominated for Best Picture) was the second of a series of successful collaborations with writer Neil Simon, for whom Ross has also directed the film versions of *The Sunshine Boys* (1975), *California Suite* (1978), *I Ought to Be in Pictures* (1982), and the screen original *Max Dugan Returns* (1983). OTHER FILMS INCLUDE: 1972: *Play It Again, Sam* (based on a Woody Allen play, with Woody in the lead); 1981: *Pennies From Heaven;* 1984: *Footloose, Protocol;* 1987: *Dancers;* 1988: *The Secret of My Success;* 1989: *Steel Magnolias;* 1990: *My Blue Heaven;* 1991: *True Colors;* 1995: *Boys on the Side.*

ROSS, KATHARINE. Actress. *(b. Jan. 29, 1942, Los Angeles.)* If there was no other credit in her filmography, Ross would forever be remembered for her role as Elaine Robinson, the object of Benjamin Braddock's romantic obsession in *The Graduate* (1967). Her look was just right for this role: cool and pretty, detached but not so much so that only the Campus Jock could win her. This performance earned a Best Supporting Actress Oscar nomination and thrust her into the spotlight. She'd already appeared in *Shenandoah, The Singing Nun* (both 1965), and *Mister Buddwing* (1966), and was window dressing in John Wayne's action saga *Hellfighters* (1969). She then played third fiddle to Paul Newman and Robert Redford in *Butch Cassidy and the Sundance Kid* (also 1969), and Robert Blake's girlfriend in *Tell Them Willie Boy Is Here* (also 1969), but her budding stardom diminished during the 1970s. Among her credits: *Fools* (1970), *Get to Know Your Rabbit* (1972), *The Stepford Wives* (1975), *Voyage of the Damned* (1976), *The Swarm, The Betsy* (both 1978), *The Final Countdown* (1980), *Wrong Is Right* (1982), and *Red-Headed Stranger* (1986). Her career took an upturn at the time of her marriage to actor Sam Elliott; they have appeared together in *The Legacy* (1979), *Murder in Texas* (1981, TV movie), *Louis L'Amour's "The Shadow Riders"* (1982, made for TV), and *Travis McGee* (1983, made for TV), and produced the telefilm adaptation of Louis L'Amour's *Conagher* (1991) in which they starred.

ROSSELLINI, ISABELLA. Actress, model. *(b. June 18, 1952, Rome.)* Beautiful daughter of Ingrid Bergman (whom she closely resembles) and director Roberto Rossellini who turned to acting in the midst of a long, successful modeling career and now wears both hats with ease. She initially worked as a TV journalist in Europe; her first movie appearance, opposite her mother in Vincente Minnelli's little-seen *A Matter of Time* (1976), was more or less a lark. American audiences next saw her in 1985's *White Nights*, in which she appeared with then-lover, ballet dancer Mikhail Baryshnikov. Rossellini took a gamble on her modeling future—she was earning millions of dollars as the primary model in all Lancôme cosmetics advertising—by appearing in a distinctly unglamorous, explicit, even unpleasant role in David Lynch's *Blue Velvet* (1986). (The director and actress were companions for a few years thereafter, and appeared together in the 1988 feature *Zelly and Me*.) She has almost consistently chosen roles in non-mainstream pictures, an exception being *Cousins* (1989), a Hollywood remake of the French comedy *Cousin, Cousine*. Her other films include *Siesta, Tough Guys Don't Dance* (both 1987), and Lynch's *Wild at Heart* (1990)—all of which indicate a decidedly iconoclastic attitude toward stardom. She took a colorful supporting role in *Death Becomes Her* (1992), then gave her best performance to date as Jeff Bridges' wife in *Fearless* (1993), and appeared in *Wyatt Earp* (1994). She was briefly married to director Martin Scorsese.

ROSSELLINI, ROBERTO. Director. *(b. May 8, 1906, Rome; d. June 4, 1977.)* The Italian director who pioneered that country's school of neorealist cinema, he is still best remembered for his early, low-budget, shaky-camera works dealing with life in a country torn by war. An architect's son who began making shorts in 1938, Rossellini actually directed a few features sponsored by Italy's Fascist government during World War 2. In 1945, he created an international sensation with the wrenching, frank *Open City*. Shot almost entirely on location in real houses, apartments, and exteriors, its distinctly primitive look, combined with its moving storyline and a sterling performance by Anna Magnani, heralded a new era in filmmaking. Rossellini subsequently made *Paisan* (1946) and *Germany Year Zero* (1947) in this vein, but began moving toward a more polished, almost Romanticist style. He met Hollywood star Ingrid Bergman in the late 1940s after she wrote him a fan letter; they fell in love and had a child, and the resultant scandal (Bergman was married at the time) led to her virtual banishment from Hollywood. Together the two made several films (1949's *Stromboli* is the best known) highly regarded by cineastes but virtually unknown to mass audiences. They eventually married and had twins, one of whom is model/actress Isabella Rossellini.

Their marriage broke up when Rossellini took up with (and impregnated) an Indian screenwriter in 1957.

The year 1959 brought the director's first popular success in some time: *General Della Rovere,* another WW2 story, this one starring fellow director Vittorio De Sica. In the 1960s Rossellini made several period pieces shot in a peculiarly rigorous style, including 1966's *The Rise of Louis XIV.* Thought incredibly ponderous by many, these films also have their admirers. Rossellini also contributed a scenario to a Godard film, 1962's *Les Carabiniers.* He continued working up until his death, making historical films for Italian TV.

ROTA, NINO. Composer. *(b. Dec. 31, 1911, Milan; d. Apr. 10, 1979.)* World-renowned composer, best remembered for his fruitful, 25-year collaboration with director Federico Fellini, Rota's music became as much a part of those films as Fellini's images, producing a magical combination of sights and sounds. While his scores for *La Strada* (1954), *8½* (1963), and *Amarcord* (1974) are especially well known, Rota also composed the music for *The White Sheik* (1951), *I Vitelloni* (1953), *Il Bidone* (1955; American title, *The Swindle), Nights of Cabiria* (1957), *La Dolce Vita* (1960), *Boccaccio '70* (1962), *Juliet of the Spirits* (1965), *Spirits of the Dead* (1968, one segment only), *Fellini Satyricon* (1970), *The Clowns* (1971), *Fellini's Roma* (1972), *Fellini's Casanova* (1976), and *Orchestra Rehearsal* (1979). Rota also worked several times for directors Luchino Visconti (1960's *Rocco and His Brothers,* 1963's *The Leopard)* and Franco Zeffirelli (1967's *The Taming of the Shrew,* 1968's *Romeo and Juliet),* and wrote the scores for *Obsession* (1949), *War and Peace* (1956), *Love and Anarchy* (1973) and *Death on the Nile* (1978). His Oscar nomination for *The Godfather*'s haunting music score in 1972 was withdrawn, because it was discovered that Rota had taken the film's love theme from an older score, for an obscure 1958 Italian picture. He later shared an Oscar with Carmine Coppola for *The Godfather, Part II* (1974). Undoubtedly Rota's best-known work is "The Love Theme From Romeo and Juliet," which (with lyrics added) became a tremendous popular success.

ROTH, TIM. Actor. *(b. May 14, 1961, London.)* Another dazzling addition to a roster of chameleonlike British actors, Roth has quickly established his ability to disappear into almost any kind of role (and dialect). Originally interested in studying sculpture, he chose acting instead and gained notice in public theater and British TV movies, including *Meantime* by Mike Leigh and *Made in Britain* by David Leland. Roth's performance as the young hood Myron in *The Hit* (1984) won him the "Standard" newspaper's award for Best Newcomer; he went on to appear in *A World Apart* (1988), *The Cook, The Thief, His Wife & Her Lover* (1989) and made vivid impressions as the hapless Guildenstern in *Rosencrantz and Guildenstern Are Dead* (1990) and, especially, as the artist van Gogh in Robert Altman's powerful (and little-seen) *Vincent & Theo* (1990). He has become familiar to American audiences as the bleeding Mr. Orange in *Reservoir Dogs* (1992), the bored appliance salesman Nick in *Bodies, Rest & Motion* (1993), and a truly chilling Charles Starkweather (with expert Midwestern drawl) in the TV miniseries "Murder in the Heartland" (1993). Recent credits include *Heart of Darkness* (1994, telefilm), *Pulp Fiction* (also 1994, as Pumpkin), *Little Odessa,* and *Rob Roy* (both 1995).

ROUNDTREE, RICHARD. Actor. *(b. Sept. 7, 1942, New Rochelle, N.Y.)* As black private eye John Shaft in the gritty crime drama *Shaft* (1971), this college-dropout-turned-model became the first icon of blaxploitation filmmaking in the 1970s. He was cool, romantic, and ultratough, and the runaway success of that film led to two sequels—*Shaft's Big Score!* (1972) and *Shaft in Africa* (1973)—and a short-lived TV series (1973–74) in which he also starred. Before this "instant" success, Roundtree had been a member of New York City's respected Negro Ensemble Company stage troupe, first appearing on film in a bit part in Allen Funt's *What Do You Say to a Naked Lady?* (1970). Winning plum roles in *Embassy* (1972), *Earthquake* (1974), *Man Friday* (1976),

Escape to Athena (1979), *An Eye for an Eye* (1981), *Q* (1982), *Killpoint* (1984), and *City Heat* (1984), it was obvious his career was not limited to black superguy parts. Currently he collects paychecks for working in numerous low-budget action flicks and thrillers, such as *Party Line* (1988), *The Banker, Crack House* (both 1989), and *A Time to Die* (1991), usually essaying the role of a no-nonsense police chief.

ROURKE, MICKEY. Actor. *(b. Sept. 16, 1953, Schenectady, N.Y.)* Rugged, sullen-looking leading man with the cynical, fatalistic mien of a James M. Cain protagonist. A former boxer who has since returned to his original avocation, Rourke burst onto movie screens with two attention-grabbing performances: that of the ruthless arsonist in *Body Heat* (1981) and the hapless hairdresser in *Diner* (1982). Promoted to stardom in *The Pope of Greenwich Village* (1984) and *Year of the Dragon* (1985), Rourke seemed to have the anti-hero charisma to carry a film. Then his choice of films veered from the offbeat (the erotic *Nine ½ Weeks* in 1986, the too-little-seen *Barfly* in 1987) to the genuinely odd (1987's *Angel Heart,* 1989's *Johnny Handsome*) to the utterly worthless (1990's *Wild Orchid,* 1991's *Harley Davidson & The Marlboro Man*). Combined with press accounts of his erratic behavior, and his increasingly unkempt appearance, the momentum he'd gathered in the mid 1980s eroded quickly. Rourke returned to boxing between now sporadic film assignments.
OTHER FILMS INCLUDE: 1979: *1941;* 1980: *Fade to Black, Heaven's Gate;* 1983: *Rumble Fish;* 1987: *A Prayer for the Dying;* 1988: *Homeboy;* 1990: *Desperate Hours;* 1992: *White Sands;* 1993: *The Last Outlaw* (telefilm).

ROWLANDS, GENA. Actress. *(b. June 19, 1934, Cambria, Wis.)* An actress who never quite reached the ranks of stardom but who has given some extremely moving and capable performances, especially in the films written and directed by her late husband, John Cassavetes. After achieving success on Broadway in the late 1950s, Rowlands went to Hollywood and starred in such films as *The High Cost of Loving*

(1958), *Lonely Are the Brave, The Spiral Road* (both 1962), and *A Child Is Waiting* (1963, an early "mainstream" movie directed by Cassavetes). She also worked in *Tony Rome* (1967), *Two Minute Warning* (1976), and *The Brink's Job* (1978). But it was her later work in Cassavetes' films— including *Faces* (1968), *Minnie and Moskowitz* (1971), *Opening Night* (1977), and *Love Streams* (1984)—that attracted critics and audiences to this strong, attractive actress and her raw, no-holds-barred performances. Rowlands' work as a woman suffering a nervous breakdown in *A Woman Under the Influence* (1974) and an ex-mobster's girlfriend in *Gloria* (1980) earned her Best Actress Oscar nominations. She continues to work sporadically in films such as *Tempest* (1982, acting with Cassavetes in this Paul Mazursky film), *Light of Day* (1987, as Michael J. Fox's mother), *Another Woman* (1988, a leading role for writer-director Woody Allen), *Once Around* and *Night on Earth* (both 1991), and has given several acclaimed performances on TV, winning Emmys for *The Betty Ford Story* (1987) and *Face of a Stranger* (1991). Her most recent telefilm is *Parallel Lives* (1994). Her son, Nick Cassavetes, is also an actor.

ROZSA, MIKLOS. Composer. *(b. Apr. 18, 1907, Budapest; d. July 27, 1995.)* One of the all-time great film composers, Rozsa has a résumé that reads like a checklist of Hollywood classics. His career began in Leipzig in the 1930s; from there he studied in Paris and went on to London to work with Alexander Korda. The two collaborated on *The Thief of Bagdad* (1940), which brought the composer to Hollywood and earned him an Academy Award nomination, the first of many. (Among the others: 1941's *Lydia* and *Sundown*, 1942's *Jungle Book*, 1943's *The Woman of the Town*, 1945's *A Song to Remember*, 1946's *The Killers*, 1951's *Quo Vadis?*, 1952's *Ivanhoe*, and 1953's *Julius Caesar*.) Rozsa stayed on to begin a career that spanned four decades. His scores were noted for full-bodied orchestrations in the European Romantic tradition; as a result, he was much in demand both for small, intense melodramas such as *Double Indemnity* (1944) and *The Lost Weekend* (1945), both of which rated Oscar nominations, and for epics such as *King of Kings* and *El Cid*

(both 1961, the latter an Oscar nominee for Best Score and Song). In fact, he scored nearly every single type of film there is. Rozsa won three Academy Awards for best original score: *Spellbound* (1945, which made pioneering use of the theremin, an electronic instrument), *A Double Life* (1947), and *Ben-Hur* (1959). Less active in the 1980s; his last full score was written for *Dead Men Don't Wear Plaid* (1982).
OTHER FILMS INCLUDE: 1937: *Knight Without Armor;* 1941: *That Hamilton Woman;* 1943: *Five Graves to Cairo, Sahara;* 1946: *The Strange Love of Martha Ivers;* 1947: *Brute Force, The Macomber Affair;* 1949: *Madame Bovary, Criss Cross, Adam's Rib;* 1950: *The Asphalt Jungle;* 1952: *Plymouth Adventure;* 1953: *Knights of the Round Table;* 1956: *Lust for Life;* 1959: *The World, The Flesh, and the Devil;* 1963: *Sodom and Gomorrah, The V.I.P.s;* 1970: *The Private Life of Sherlock Holmes;* 1977: *Providence;* 1979: *Fedora, Time After Time, Last Embrace;* 1981: *Eye of the Needle.*

RUBEN, JOSEPH. Director. *(b. May 10, 1950, Briarcliff Manor, N.Y.)* Ruben has taken the skill and economy he used in years of directing B-grade youth-oriented fodder to produce many impressive thrillers. He began modestly, writing and directing *The Sister-in-Law* (1974), which starred a young John Savage, and then *The Pom-Pom Girls* (1976), a teen comedy that gained a cult following of sorts. Following three more youth pictures, *Joyride* (1977), *Our Winning Season* (1978), and *Gorp* (1980), Ruben gained attention for his imaginative handling of *Dreamscape* (1984), a sci-fi tale about a man who can enter people's dreams. He won critics over with a sleeper hit, *The Stepfather* (1987), a tense, well-crafted tale of a psychopath who marries widows and kills them. Ruben next directed *True Believer* (1989), which starred James Woods in a flamboyant performance as a once-radical lawyer, and finally achieved box-office success with *Sleeping With the Enemy* (1991), starring Julia Roberts; ironically, it's his least suspenseful thriller. Since then he's directed *The Good Son* (1993).

RUBINEK, SAUL. Actor. *(b. July 2, 1948, Wolfrathausen, Germany.)* Skilled actor who has risen to prominence in a number of (mostly comic) supporting roles. Rubinek was born in a German refugee camp, but grew up in Canada, where as a young man he became interested in acting. He was a founding member of the Toronto Free Theatre, and amassed numerous stage and TV credits in both Canada and the United States before making his film debut in *Agency* (1981). Rubinek won a Genie Award for his work in *Ticket to Heaven* (1981) as the best friend of a man who is brainwashed by a cult. He subsequently starred in the New York-set comedy *Soup for One* (1982), but has since worked mostly in supporting roles. His U.S. credits include *Young Doctors in Love* (1982), *Against All Odds* (1984), *Wall Street* (1987), and *The Bonfire of the Vanities* (1990). Rubinek was memorable as the egotistical movie director in *Sweet Liberty* (1986) and as the dime-store novelist W. W. Beauchamp in Clint Eastwood's *Unforgiven* (1992), but received particular acclaim for his starring performance as an Orthodox Jewish rabbi in the provocative Canadian film *The Quarrel* (1992). Recent credits include *Undercover Blues, True Romance,* the TV movie *And the Band Played On* (all 1993), *Death Wish V, I Love Trouble,* and *Getting Even With Dad* (all 1994).

RUDOLPH, ALAN. Director, screenwriter. *(b. Dec. 18, 1943, Los Angeles.)* Important independent filmmaker whose eccentric tastes have not endeared him to the filmgoing masses. His first feature, *Premonition* (1972), was barely released, and he found work as an assistant director on several of Robert Altman's films; he ultimately cowrote the screenplay for Altman's *Buffalo Bill and the Indians* (1976), a bizarre revisionist Western. Altman in turn produced Rudolph's first two major directorial efforts, *Welcome to L.A.* (1977) and *Remember My Name* (1978), which featured actors from former Altman projects, and dealt with troubled people in very individualistic ways. After directing the studio-originated films *Roadie* (1980) and *Endangered Species* (1982), Rudolph won raves for *Choose Me* (1984), and the dreamlike, *noir*-ish way it examined modern relationships. (He also directed the documentary account of Timothy Leary and G. Gordon Liddy's

face-off, *Return Engagement,* in 1983.) He has since written and directed *Trouble in Mind* (1985), *The Moderns* (1988), and *Love at Large* (1990), all immediately identifiable as Rudolph projects from their look and feel, as well as the more mainstream *Songwriter* (1984) and the particularly disappointing *Made in Heaven* (1987). Rudolph achieved his first successful compromise between a distinctively personal project and a studio "property" in his direction of the dark-themed *Mortal Thoughts* (1991). He can be seen in Altman's *The Player* (1992), pitching a political film that is described as *Ghost* meets *The Manchurian Candidate.* In 1994 he cowrote and directed *Mrs. Parker and the Vicious Circle,* and has expressed a desire to adapt the offbeat comic-strip panel "The Far Side."

RUEHL, MERCEDES. Actress. *(b. Feb. 28, 1948, Queens, N.Y.)* Moviegoers sat up and took notice of the blowsy, foulmouthed, gun-wielding wife of Mafia boss Dean Stockwell in *Married to the Mob* (1988), then wondered where she came from. In fact, by that time the actress had already appeared in several movies and won an Obie for her performance in Christopher Durang's "The Marriage of Bette and Boo." She also wowed theatergoers in the stage production of "Other People's Money." The bronze, raw-boned Ruehl usually plays streetwise, tarttongued *Noo Yaw*kers; she has muted her distinct accent on occasion but seldom needs to. Debuting in *The Warriors* (1979), Ruehl went on to appear in *Four Friends* (1981), *Heartburn* (1986), *84 Charing Cross Road, Leader of the Band, Radio Days, The Secret of My Success* (all 1987), and *Big* (1988, as Tom Hanks' mom). Established as an exciting new player in the wake of *Mob*'s surprising success, she won better roles in *Slaves of New York* (1989), *Crazy People* (1990, as a sympathetic psychotherapist), and *Another You* (1991, as foil to Gene Wilder and Richard Pryor, she was the best thing about that turkey). Real recognition came with the release of *The Fisher King* (1991): Her strong—but never strident— performance as Jeff Bridges' longsuffering girlfriend won her a welldeserved Oscar—and stardom. *Lost in Yonkers* (1993) saw her reprising her Tony

Award-winning stage role as the crazy sister in the film version of Neil Simon's hit play, while that summer's *Last Action Hero*, an Arnold Schwarzenegger vehicle, took her in a completely different direction.

RUGGLES, CHARLIE. Actor. *(b. Feb. 8, 1886, Los Angeles; d. Dec. 23, 1970.)* During his 65-year career in show business, the prolific Ruggles worked in more than 100 movies as well as appearing on Broadway and in stock, radio, and TV. Slightly built, with mischievous eyes, Ruggles had impeccable comic timing and matchless dialogue delivery, which made him a natural for sophisticated comedies of the early sound era. He was a favorite of Ernst Lubitsch, who used him expertly in *The Smiling Lieutenant* (1931), *Love Me Tonight, Trouble in Paradise,* and *One Hour With You* (all 1932). He also appeared in *Charley's Aunt* (1930, in the title role), *If I Had a Million* (1932, as the Milquetoast who goes berserk in a china shop), *This Is the Night* (1932, as the admitted nonathlete who "used to jump at conclusions"), and *Bringing Up Baby* (1938), to name a few. Ruggles played henpecked husbands (especially in an early 1930s series of domestic comedies in which he costarred with Mary Boland), browbeaten businessmen, eccentric fathers, and wisecracking playboys with equal facility. Ruggles, whose brother Wesley was a top director in the 1920s and 1930s, starred in a pioneering TV situation comedy, *The Ruggles* (1949–52), and worked steadily in film and TV through the 1960s. Baby-boomers might remember his voice from the "Aesop and Son" segment on "The Bullwinkle Show." Less active in films during the 1950s, he went to Broadway and won a Tony Award for his performance in "The Pleasure of His Company," then recreated the part in the 1961 film, which spurred a new period of activity. He appeared in *The Parent Trap* (1961, the first of many Disney films), *Son of Flubber, Papa's Delicate Condition* (both 1963), *I'd Rather Be Rich* (1964), *The Ugly Dachshund* (1966), and *Follow Me, Boys!* (also 1966), his last. OTHER FILMS INCLUDE: 1933: *Alice in Wonderland* (as the March Hare), *Murders in the Zoo;* 1934: *Six of a Kind;* 1935: *Ruggles of Red Gap* (as the yahoo who wins Charles

Laughton in a poker game); 1936: *Anything Goes;* 1937: *Exclusive;* 1940: *No Time for Comedy, The Invisible Woman;* 1941: *The Parson of Panamint* (in the lead); 1942: *Friendly Enemies;* 1944: *Our Hearts Were Young and Gay;* 1947: *It Happened on 5th Avenue* (his personal favorite); 1949: *Look for the Silver Lining.*

RUMANN, SIG. Actor. *(b. Oct. 11, 1884, Hamburg, as Siegfried Rumann; d. Feb. 14, 1967.)* Burly German character actor often used as a comic menace, pompous Prussian, or dull-witted Nazi in films of the 1930s and 1940s; he continued playing Viennese doctors and colorful mid-European types into the 1960s. (During World War 2 he shortened his name to "Ruman.") Rumann acted in German-language plays staged in New York during the 1920s, graduating to Broadway roles after his "discovery" by the New York critics. As a movie actor, he's probably best remembered as a blustery foil for the Marx Brothers in *A Night at the Opera* (1935), *A Day at the Races* (1937), and *A Night in Casablanca* (1946), though he also had a memorable showcase as one of the errant Russian emissaries tracked by Greta Garbo in *Ninotchka* (1939). Lubitsch used him again in *To Be or Not to Be* (1942), and Lubitsch colleague and admirer Billy Wilder cast him in *Stalag 17* (1953, as Schulz) and *The Fortune Cookie* (1966), his final film. He was an improbable menace to Bob Livingston as Zorro in *The Bold Caballero* (1936), and also appeared in *Marie Galante* (1934), *On the Avenue, Nothing Sacred* (both 1937), *Only Angels Have Wings, Confessions of a Nazi Spy* (both 1939), *The Song of Bernadette* (1943), *Tarzan Triumphs* (1943), *The Hitler Gang* (1944), *White Christmas* (1954), *Living It Up* (also 1954, repeating his part from *Nothing Sacred* in this remake), *The Wings of Eagles* (1957), *The Errand Boy* (1961), and *The Last of the Secret Agents?* (1966).

RUSH, RICHARD. Director, writer. *(b. Apr. 15, 1929, New York City.)* Like some of today's most prominent filmmakers, Rush cut his directorial teeth on low-budget exploitation films such as *Too Soon to Love* (1960), and cult classics such as *Hell's Angels on Wheels* (1967) and *Psych-Out*

(1968), which all featured a pre-*Easy Rider* Jack Nicholson. Other early credits include *Of Love and Desire* (1963), *The Fickle Finger of Fate, Thunder Alley* (both 1967), *A Man Called Dagger* (1968), and *The Savage Seven* (also 1968). He moved on to more commercial pictures with *Getting Straight* (1970) and *Freebie and the Bean* (1974), then startled critics with *The Stunt Man* (1980), a metaphysical "reel vs. real" comedy-drama about filmmaking that took years to get released (during which time Rush suffered a heart attack) and ultimately earned him Oscar nominations for Best Director and Best Adapted Screenplay. But there was no encore to that triumphant film, and Rush's career languished in the 1980s. He cowrote *Air America* (1990), which he initiated and was originally supposed to direct. In 1994 he returned to the director's chair, at long last, for *Color of Night,* with Bruce Willis in the lead.

RUSSELL, GAIL. Actress. *(b. Sept. 21, 1924, Chicago; d. Aug. 26, 1961.)* An ethereal beauty whose personal demons kept her from attaining the screen success once predicted for her, Gail Russell was spotted by Paramount talent scouts shortly after graduating from high school. Finding the prospect of screen stardom appealing, the introverted girl submitted to the arduous process of grooming and training, and made her film debut in *Henry Aldrich Gets Glamour* (1943), proving that, as was suspected, the camera "loved" her. Russell's supporting role as the fragile object of spectral persecution in *The Uninvited* (1944) elicited rave reviews; a 1945 follow-up, *The Unseen,* failed to duplicate the previous film's success, but earned additional kudos for Russell. Nonetheless, she suffered dreadfully from stage fright and other insecurities, and became progressively more difficult to handle.

Russell was seen to good advantage in *Our Hearts Were Young and Gay* (1944, and its 1946 sequel, *Our Hearts Were Growing Up,* teamed with fellow contractee Diana Lynn), *Salty O'Rourke, Duffy's Tavern* (both 1945), *The Bachelor's Daughters* (1946), and *Variety Girl* (1947) before jumping to Republic, where she gave her best-remembered performance as the strong-willed Quaker girl who

reforms outlaw John Wayne in *Angel and the Badman* (1947). She then costarred with Dane Clark in *Moonrise* (1948), a muddled psychological melodrama directed by Frank Borzage, and was reteamed with Wayne (whose interest in her reportedly extended beyond the soundstage) in *Wake of the Red Witch* later that year. *The Night Has a Thousand Eyes* (also 1948), another supernatural thriller, gave Russell a plum role—but it was her last. Films like *Song of India, El Paso, The Great Dan Patch, Captain China* (all 1949), *The Lawless* (1950), and *Air Cadet* (1951) kept her in the public eye, but accomplished little else. She was offscreen for five years, during which time her marriage to actor Guy Madison collapsed, before costarring opposite Randolph Scott in an above-average Western, *Seven Men From Now* (1956), directed by Budd Boetticher. *The Tattered Dress* (1957) and *No Place to Land* (1958) saw Russell reduced to secondary roles, and although she wasn't yet 40 years old, she looked much older—and sadder. In 1961 she top-lined *The Silent Call,* which was a bomb. Russell's dead body was found later that year in her apartment, surrounded by liquor bottles.

RUSSELL, JANE. Actress. *(b. June 21, 1921, Bemidji, Minn., as Ernestine Jane Geraldine Russell.)* A soft-spoken brunette with come-hither eyes and a 38-inch bust, Jane Russell was just what aviator/inventor/movie producer Howard Hughes envisioned as the leading lady for his production of *The Outlaw,* a retelling of the Billy the Kid saga. Hughes lavished great attention on its production and direction (personally designing, as part of his official duties, a special brassiere to accentuate Russell's figure—though the actress says she never wore it). Shot during 1940, the overheated horse opera was first tradeshown in 1943, briefly released in 1946, and not widely distributed until 1950, by which time Russell had already achieved notoriety, if not stardom.

Only 19 years old when she was hired by Hughes, Russell was the recipient of an extraordinary publicity campaign that kept her in the public eye (via an unending series of cheesecake pinups distributed to soldiers, magazine covers, rotogravure layouts, and personal appearances) for years while Hughes noodled with his super-epic. A major stockholder in RKO, he arranged for her to star in that studio's *Young Widow,* a 1946 soap opera in which her inexperience showed all too readily. Loaned to Paramount two years later, she was much better in *The Paleface* opposite Bob Hope. Little by little, the public began to take a shine to this young woman, who painstakingly learned her craft in a succession of mostly mediocre RKO musicals and melodramas, including *His Kind of Woman, Double Dynamite* (both 1951), *The Las Vegas Story, Macao, Montana Belle* (all 1952), *The French Line* (1954, causing a sensation for its scenes of her performing a vibrant dance number in a brief costume—in 3-D, no less), and *Underwater!* (1955).

Paramount borrowed her back for the enjoyable *Son of Paleface* (also 1952), and gave her a surprise cameo in that year's Crosby-Hope opus *Road to Bali.* Russell then went to 20th Century-Fox, where she costarred with Marilyn Monroe in *Gentlemen Prefer Blondes* (1953), delivering a wry comic performance that went largely unnoticed—a shame, since it's her best work on-screen. (She subsequently starred in a 1955 followup, *Gentlemen Marry Brunettes,* sans Monroe.) *Foxfire,* The Tall Men (both 1955), *Hot Blood, The Revolt of Mamie Stover* (both 1956), and *The Fuzzy Pink Nightgown* (1957) rounded out her starring career.

Russell devoted much greater energy to WAIF, a national adoption organization she founded, and to a successful nightclub career, than to maintaining her movie stardom. After years offscreen, she took character parts and cameos in *Fate Is the Hunter* (1964), *Johnny Reno, Waco* (both 1966), *Born Losers* (1967), *Darker Than Amber* (1970), and *The Jackass Trail* (1981). She wound up a TV commercial spokeswoman for Playtex bras in the 1980s, pitching products designed for "us full-figured gals."

As a youngster she'd taken drama classes, including a semester with famed Russian actress Maria Ouspenskaya. In her 1985 autobiography, "Jane Russell: My Life and My Detours," the star recalled, "Years later (Ouspenskaya) was watching me at a television rehearsal. When I came off the stage to say hello, she said to me in her marvelous Russian accent, 'You know, Jen, you could be a very good acktress, but you haff no henergy.' No energy. It's true. I've watched myself too often on the screen and I seemed to be moving in slow motion."

RUSSELL, KEN. Writer, producer, director. *(b. July 3, 1927, Southampton, England.)* Truly the Bad Boy of British cinema, his failures are often more interesting than most directors' successes. His penchant for the bizarre and excessive announced itself early in his career with his series of biographies for the BBC on Debussy and Isadora Duncan. Russell began directing features in 1963 with *French Dressing,* and later helmed the spy thriller *Billion Dollar Brain* (1967, perhaps his most conventional movie, ever). It was his third film, a sexually graphic but (for him) quite restrained adaption of D. H. Lawrence's *Women in Love* (1969) that brought him an Oscar nomination and international acclaim. It also gave him the freedom to throw off the leash with such outlandish pseudo-biographies as *The Music Lovers* (1971), *Savage Messiah* (1972), *Mahler* (1974), *Liztomania* (1975), and *Valentino* (1977), and to demonstrate an odd sort of versatility in 1971 by moving from the X-rated *The Devils* to the G-rated *The Boy Friend,* which he turned into an homage to 1930s movie musicals.

In 1975 he turned his attention to The Who's rock opera *Tommy* and gave the project his personal spin; one scene with Ann-Margaret must be seen to be believed. Russell had a mainstream American hit in 1980's *Altered States,* but then returned to small budgets and more personal projects with such flamboyant fare as *Crimes of Passion* (1984), *Gothic* (1986), *Salome's Last Dance,* and the cult horror-comedy *The Lair of the White Worm* (both 1988). He revisited Lawrence for a straightforward adaptation of *The Rainbow* (1989), followed by the unusually gritty *Whore* (1991). His performance as the tea-pouring secret agent in *The Russia House* (1990) was a welcome bit of comedy relief. In 1991 he directed Richard Dreyfuss in the TV movie *Prisoner of Honor.* He also tried out a music video, making "Nikita" for Elton John. Frequently vulgar, always outrageous, he's nonetheless a master stylist. He published an autobiography, "Altered States," in 1992, and a broad-ranging collection of film critiques, "The Lion Roars," in 1994.

RUSSELL, KURT. Actor. *(b. Mar. 17, 1951, Springfield, Mass.)* This onetime child star was really aiming for a career in pro baseball, until an injury scotched those plans. He first came to attention in the starring role of the 1963 TV series "The Travels of Jamie McPheeters," and had a small part that same year with Elvis Presley in *It Happened at the World's Fair*. Then a key role as a troubled youth in the Walt Disney picture *Follow Me, Boys!* (1966) led to a studio contract, and after costarring in *The Horse in the Gray Flannel Suit* and *The One and Only, Genuine, Original Family Band* (both 1968) he was featured in a string of silly comedies, including *The Computer Wore Tennis Shoes* (1970), *The Barefoot Executive* (1971), *Charley and the Angel* (1973), *Superdad* (1974), and *The Strongest Man in the World* (1975). After a career hiatus, the title role in John Carpenter's hugely popular 1979 made-for-TV biopic *Elvis* launched Russell as an adult star—and broke the clean-cut Disney image. He was hilarious as a sleazy salesman in *Used Cars* (1980), and became a favorite of Carpenter, who cast the now-rugged, handsome actor in stolid, laconic (and often tongue-in-cheek) leads in *Escape From New York* (1981), *The Thing* (1982), and *Big Trouble in Little China* (1986). Russell emerged as a mainstream movie star in *Silkwood* (1983), with Meryl Streep, and *Swing Shift* (1984), which teamed him for the first time with off-screen companion Goldie Hawn. Unable to ignite a box-office hit singlehanded, he has proved instead to have staying power, in such high-profile films as *The Mean Season* (1985), *The Best of Times* (1986, with Robin Williams), *Overboard* (1987, also with Hawn), *Tequila Sunrise* (1988), *Winter People* (1989), *Tango & Cash* (1989, teamed with Sylvester Stallone), and *Backdraft* (1991). Since then he's starred in *Unlawful Entry, Captain Ron* (both 1992), *Tombstone* (1993, as Wyatt Earp), and *Stargate* (1994).

RUSSELL, ROSALIND. Actress. *(b. June 4, 1908, Waterbury, Conn.; d. Nov. 28, 1976.)* Though Carole Lombard is generally remembered as the queen of screwball, Roz could match her wisecrack for wisecrack, sneer for sneer. This brunette actress began her screen career in serious roles—as upper-class ladies—in *Evelyn Prentice, The President Vanishes* (both 1934), *Craig's Wife* (1936, a prime early showcase in the title role), *Night Must Fall* (1937), and *The Citadel* (1938), though traces of the comedienne-to-be were clearly visible in such adventures as *China Seas* (1935) and *Under Two Flags* (1936). In her first big comedy part, as a wisecracking scribe in *Four's a Crowd* (1938), Russell instantly crystallized her tart comic style, which she exercised in similar (and even better) turns as the gossipy "pal" in *The Women* (1939), and as fast-talking reporter Hildy Johnson in the superb *His Girl Friday* (1940, opposite Cary Grant), considered by many to be her two best screen outings.

Russell had memorable parts in *No Time for Comedy* (also 1940), *Design for Scandal* (1941), *My Sister Eileen* (1942, a role she later recreated in the Broadway musical "Wonderful Town," and one that earned her an Academy Award nomination), and *Roughly Speaking* (1945). In the 1950s she shined as the spinster schoolteacher in *Picnic* (1955), and then won the role for which she's best remembered, *Auntie Mame* (1958), that larger-than-life lady who steered her to another Oscar nomination. In 1962 she landed another great role, as Mama Rose in the adaptation of the Broadway musical *Gypsy;* she gave a terrific performance, though there were inevitable comparisons to her Broadway predecessor Ethel Merman (especially since Russell was dubbed in some of her songs). She also occasionally returned to drama, as in *Sister Kenny* (1946, getting another Oscar nod), *Mourning Becomes Electra* (1947, as Lavinia, snagging yet another Oscar nomination), *A Majority of One* (1961), and *Five Finger Exercise* (1962).

Russell's last few films were pretty pale, but she still gave her best, whether playing a nun in *The Trouble With Angels* (1966) and *Where Angels Go . . . Trouble Follows* (1968), or the maternal *Mrs. Pollifax—Spy* (1971, a film she scripted, produced by husband Frederic Brisson). She played a pair of wealthy widows, a comic one in *Rosie!* (1967), and an endangered one in the TV movie *The Crooked*

Hearts, her last performance. In 1972 she was the recipient of the Academy's Jean Hersholt Humanitarian Award for her contributions to charity. The title of her 1977 autobiography, "Life Is a Banquet," came from a famous line of Auntie Mame's.
OTHER FILMS INCLUDE: 1934: *Forsaking All Others;* 1935: *The Casino Murder Case, The Night Is Young, Reckless;* 1936: *Trouble for Two;* 1937: *Live, Love and Learn;* 1938: *Man-Proof;* 1939: *Fast and Loose;* 1940: *Hired Wife;* 1941: *The Feminine Touch, This Thing Called Love;* 1942: *Take a Letter, Darling;* 1943: *Flight for Freedom, What a Woman!* 1945: *She Wouldn't Say Yes;* 1949: *Tell It to the Judge;* 1950: *A Woman of Distinction;* 1952: *Never Wave at a WAC;* 1955: *The Girl Rush;* 1967: *Oh Dad, Poor Dad, Mama's Hung You in the Closet and I'm Feeling So Sad.*

RUSSELL, THERESA. Actress. *(b. Mar. 20, 1957, San Diego, Calif., as Theresa Paup.)* Something of a sex symbol for the art-house crowd, this alluring actress has given some memorably daring and provocative performances, particularly in films by her husband, director Nicolas Roeg. Discovered by a photographer when she was twelve, Russell modeled and eventually dropped out of high school to study at the Lee Strasberg Theatre Institute. She made her film debut in Elia Kazan's *The Last Tycoon* (1976, as Robert Mitchum's daughter) and held her own opposite Dustin Hoffman in *Straight Time* (1978). It was her powerful, sexually frank work as a woman involved with a psychiatrist in *Bad Timing: A Sensual Obsession* (1980) that established her as a major actress, unafraid to take chances with risky material. The film was also her first for Roeg; they fell in love (he is nearly thirty years older) and married several years later. She went on to work with him in *Eureka* (1981, released in 1985), a segment of the omnibus film *Aria* (1988), *Track 29* (also 1988) and *Cold Heaven* (1992) and was striking as a very Marilyn Monroe–like actress in *Insignificance* (1985). Russell's attempts at more "commercial" ventures have been sporadic and largely unsuccessful (1989's *Physical Evidence* is probably a nadir) but she was the best thing in the critically lambasted remake of *The Razor's Edge* (1984) and she scored a popular success as the seductive

killer who intrigues Debra Winger in *Black Widow* (1987). She also made a high-profile television appearance as Maureen Dean in the miniseries "Blind Ambition" (1979). She was terrific as an undercover narc in *Impulse* (1990) and did her best to make something out of the title role in *Whore* (1991). Russell also narrated 1994's *Being Human.*

RUTHERFORD, MARGARET (DAME). Actress. *(b. May 11, 1892, London; d. May 22, 1972.)* Delightful British character actress who elevated the interpretation of sassy spinsters and dotty dowagers to a high art in her movie appearances. A former speech teacher who studied acting at the Old Vic and began her stage career in 1925, Rutherford entered films as an already dumpy, frumpy middle-aged woman in *Dusty Ermine* (1936). In no time at all, she mastered the technique of screen acting and was a champion scene-stealer by the time she got the plum role of the eccentric medium, Madame Arcati, in *Blithe Spirit* (1945). Rutherford could always be counted upon for a deft comedy performance, and she was ideally cast as Agatha Christie's spinster sleuth, Miss Marple, in four 1960s whodunits: *Murder, She Said* (1961), *Murder at the Gallop* (1963), *Murder Ahoy,* and *Murder Most Foul* (both 1964). She won an Oscar for her supporting role in *The V.I.P.s* (1963).
OTHER FILMS INCLUDE: 1940: *Quiet Wedding;* 1943: *The Yellow Canary;* 1946: *Meet Me at Dawn;* 1948: *Miranda;* 1949: *Passport to Pimlico;* 1950: *The Happiest Days of Your Life;* 1951: *The Magic Box;* 1952: *Miss Robin Hood, The Importance of Being Earnest;* 1953: *Innocents in Paris;* 1954: *Aunt Clara;* 1955: *An Alligator Named Daisy;* 1957: *The Smallest Show on Earth;* 1959: *I'm All Right Jack;* 1961: *On the Double;* 1963: *The Mouse on the Moon;* 1966: *The Alphabet Murders, Chimes at Midnight* (aka *Falstaff);* 1967: *A Countess From Hong Kong, The Wacky World of Mother Goose* (voice only); 1969: *Arabella.*

RYAN, MEG. Actress. *(b. Nov. 19, 1961, Fairfield, Conn.)* Perky blond actress, with twinkly blue eyes and a broad smile, who has endeared herself to audiences in a handful of hit movies. She made her screen debut as Candice Bergen's daughter in *Rich and Famous* (1981), and appeared as a regular on the daytime drama "As the World Turns" and the short-lived prime-time series "Wild Side" (1985) while amassing a handful of other film credits (1983's *Amityville 3-D*, 1986's *Armed and Dangerous*). Her climb toward stardom began with a solid supporting role in *Top Gun* (1986, as the wife of flyer Anthony Edwards) and continued with *Innerspace* (1987), *D.O.A., Promised Land,* and *The Presidio* (all 1988). But it was her engaging performance opposite Billy Crystal in the romantic comedy *When Harry Met Sally . . .* (1989) that put her over the top; her "fake orgasm" scene became an instant classic. She's had other successes, both comedic and dramatic (notably as Jim Morrison's drugged-out girlfriend in 1991's *The Doors),* but audiences seem to like her best in romantic comedy, as was reaffirmed by the enormous success of *Sleepless in Seattle* (1993, opposite Tom Hanks, with whom she starred in 1990's *Joe Versus the Volcano),* which again gave her a tailor-made role. In 1991 she married longtime boyfriend Dennis Quaid, whom she met on *Innerspace* and with whom she appeared in *D.O.A.* and the downbeat drama *Flesh and Bone* (1993). She's also starred in *Prelude to a Kiss* (1992), *When a Man Loves a Woman* (1994, in a bravura performance as an alcoholic), *I.Q.* (also 1994), and *French Kiss* (1995).

RYAN, ROBERT. Actor. *(b. Nov. 11, 1909, Chicago; d. July 11, 1973.)* He was unforgettable as the protagonist of *The Set-Up* (1949), a washed-up prizefighter debating whether or not to take a dive during a much-awaited bout. His acting was superb, and his scenes in the ring bespoke a familiarity with boxing that few actors could fake. And with good reason: As a college student at Chicago's Loyola and Dartmouth, he held the national collegiate boxing title for four years. After graduating, and working in a variety of odd jobs, Ryan studied drama at the Max Reinhardt Theatrical Workshop in Hollywood. His ring prowess enabled him to secure a part in *Golden Gloves* (1940), and his movie career was off and running; two years later, he was under contract to RKO. Although he appeared in some films during the war—*The Sky's the Limit*

(1943) and *Marine Raiders* (1944) among them—Ryan didn't achieve any real screen success until 1947, when he snared an Academy Award nomination for his portrayal of an anti-Semitic killer in *Crossfire.* In the following two years he appeared in such first-rate films as *Return of the Bad Men, The Boy With Green Hair* (both 1948), *Caught* (1949), and *Act of Violence* (also 1949, as a revenge-bent psychotic who stalks Van Heflin).

Craggy, gruff, and virile, Ryan played both heavies and heroes throughout his career, working in Westerns, war stories, and crime dramas. He was a psychopath in *Beware, My Lovely* (1952), a memorable menace in *The Naked Spur* (1953) and *Bad Day at Black Rock* (1955), a rugged adversary of *The Dirty Dozen* (1967), and the lawman who stalked William Holden and *The Wild Bunch* (1969). He was never a star in the Clark Gable sense of the word, but his name carried weight, and his presence counted in both main and secondary roles that ran the gamut from John the Baptist in *King of Kings* (1961) to Ike Clanton in *Hour of the Gun* (1967). He was not a "showy" actor, but his work was distinguished by emotional honesty, whatever the role.

OTHER FILMS INCLUDE: 1940: *Northwest Mounted Police, Queen of the Mob, Texas Rangers Ride Again;* 1941: *The Feminine Touch;* 1943: *Bombardier, Behind the Rising Sun, The Iron Major, Gangway for Tomorrow;* 1944: *Tender Comrade, Marine Raiders;* 1947: *Trail Street, The Woman on the Beach;* 1948: *Berlin Express;* 1950: *I Married a Communist* (aka *Woman on Pier 13), The Secret Fury, Born to Be Bad;* 1951: *Best of the Badmen, Flying Leathernecks, The Racket, On Dangerous Ground;* 1952: *Clash by Night, Horizons West;* 1953: *City Beneath the Sea, Inferno;* 1954: *About Mrs. Leslie, Her Twelve Men;* 1955: *Escape to Burma, House of Bamboo, The Tall Men;* 1956: *The Proud Ones, Back From Eternity;* 1957: *Men in War;* 1958: *God's Little Acre, Lonelyhearts;* 1959: *Odds Against Tomorrow, Day of the Outlaw;* 1960: *Ice Palace;* 1961: *The Canadians;* 1962: *Billy Budd, The Longest Day;* 1965: *The Crooked Road, Battle of the Bulge;* 1966: *The Dirty Game, The Professionals;* 1967: *The Busy Body, A Minute to Pray, a Second to Die;* 1968: *Custer of the West;* 1970: *Captain Nemo and the Underwater City;* 1971: *The Love Machine, Lawman;* 1972: *And Hope to*

Die; 1973: *Lolly Madonna XXX, The Iceman Cometh, Executive Action;* 1974: *The Outfit.*

RYDELL, MARK. Director, producer, actor. *(b. Mar. 23, 1934, New York City.)* A former jazz musician (who studied at Juilliard) and actor (who made his film debut alongside John Cassavetes and Sal Mineo in 1957's *Crime in the Streets),* Rydell won critical kudos for his first directorial effort, *The Fox* (1968), and has enjoyed considerable success ever since. The picaresque Faulkner story *The Reivers* (1969) remains one of his best films, and *Cinderella Liberty* (1973) told its offbeat love story with refreshing candor and credibility. *The Rose* (1979) was the first film to tap Bette Midler's dramatic potential, and *On Golden Pond* (1981) meshed the talents of its formidable cast (Henry Fonda, Katharine Hepburn, Jane Fonda) with great skill, creating a hit that earned Rydell an Oscar nomination. He moved in front of the camera to play vicious gangster Marty Augustine for Robert Altman in *The Long Goodbye* (1973), and has been persuaded to act again from time to time, as in *Punchline* (1988) and *Havana* (1990). Rydell's other films as director include *The Cowboys* (1972), *Harry and Walter Go to New York* (1976), *The River* (1984), *For the Boys* (1991), and *Intersection* (1994).

RYDER, WINONA. Actress. *(b. Oct. 29, 1971, Winona, Minn.)* Raven-haired, mesmerizing young actress of considerable talent and range. The daughter of confirmed counterculture types (her godfather is Dr. Timothy Leary) who grew up on a California commune, Ryder performed on stage in small theaters as a preteen. Her fair skin, contrasted with dark, soulful eyes, made her a natural for sensitive teen types in *Lucas* (1986) and *Square Dance* (1987), but she really scored as the black-garbed, death-obsessed daughter in *Beetlejuice* (1988), a high-profile hit comedy that opened doors for her. She was convincing as the child-bride cousin of Jerry Lee Lewis in *Great Balls of Fire!,* a high-school conspirator in *Heathers* (both 1989), a small-town weirdo in *Welcome Home, Roxy Carmichael,* the long-suffering daughter of Cher in *Mermaids,* and the sensitive blond girlfriend of *Edward*

Scissorhands (all 1990). That nonstop work schedule caused her to bow out of *The Godfather, Part III,* but her career picked up with the female lead in Francis Coppola's *Bram Stoker's Dracula* (1992), a project she brought to the director's attention. Martin Scorsese then chose her to play the deceptively docile fiancée in *The Age of Innocence* (1993), for which she earned a Supporting Oscar nomination. She followed with *The House of the Spirits* (also 1993), then starred in *Reality Bites* and earned a Best Actress nomination for her enchanting work as Jo March in *Little Women* (both 1994), a pet project of hers.

SABU. Actor. *(b. Jan. 24, 1924, Myrsore, India, as Saby Dastagir; d. Dec. 2, 1963.)* As a dusky, impish native boy (which he was), this natural performer proved a revelation in his first picture, Robert Flaherty's documentary-style *Elephant Boy* (1937), which chronicled the search for a mythical elephant herd. Reportedly plucked from a maharajah's stables, Sabu subsequently made two other English films, *Drums* (1938) and *The Thief of Bagdad* (1940, in the title role), spectacular Technicolored adventures both, for producer Alexander Korda. Impetuous and daring, he made a lovable Mowgli in the 1942 adaptation of Kipling's *Jungle Book* before settling at Universal, where he supported Jon Hall and Maria Montez in a series of lavish Technicolor adventures with exotic settings: *Arabian Nights* (1942), *White Savage* (1943), and *Cobra Woman* (1944). He served with distinction during the latter years of World War 2, and returned to Hollywood as a highly decorated war hero. But the wartime vogue for escapist fantasies had passed, and after contributing a fine performance as a native prince to *Black Narcissus* (1946), a remarkable drama of nuns in the Himalayas, Sabu found himself mired in a succession of progressively poorer films, including *Tangier* (1946, with Montez), *The End of the River* (1947), *Man-Eater of Kumaon* (1948), *Song of India* (1949), *Savage Drums* (1951), *Hello Elephant* (1952), *Jaguar* (1956), *Sabu and the Magic Ring* (1957), *Rampage* (1963), and *A Tiger Walks* (1964). His untimely death was caused by a heart attack.

SAGEBRECHT, MARIANNE. Actress.
(b. Aug. 27, 1945, Starnberg, Bavaria.) German actress whose short, rotund physique
and undeniable talent made her a refreshingly different international star. Her tyro
film performance as a lovestruck morti-
cian in *Sugarbaby* (1984, a part written
specifically for her by director Percy
Adlon) proved to be a revelation, and deservedly won raves. Sagebrecht followed
it with two more leading roles for Adlon,
in *Bagdad Cafe* (1988) and *Rosalie Goes
Shopping* (1989). Her work in these similarly lauded films brought her to the attention of American filmmakers, in *Moon
Over Parador* (1988) and *The War of the
Roses* (1989). But Hollywood didn't give
her the opportunities that Adlon did, and
she drifted into undistinguished character
work until *Martha and I* (1992, for which
she won the Best Actress award at the
Venice Film Festival). Recent credits include *The Milky Life, Dust Devils: The
Final Cut* (both 1993), and *Erotique*
(1994).

SAINT, EVA MARIE. Actress. *(b. July 4,
1924, Newark, N.J.)* Luminous blond leading lady groomed for stardom in the
1950s, only to find few vehicles worthy of
her talents. Saint studied acting at Bowling Green University, and later found
work in both radio and TV drama. For her
first film role, that of Marlon Brando's
tenement love interest in *On the Waterfront* (1954), she won an Oscar for Best
Supporting Actress. She was extremely effective in *A Hatful of Rain* (1957), a startlingly frank drama of drug addiction.
Alfred Hitchcock cast her opposite Cary
Grant in *North by Northwest* (1959, a deliciously romantic performance), and Otto
Preminger costarred her with Paul
Newman in *Exodus* (1960), but her splendid work in those two classics didn't keep
her star from fading. A younger generation may know her only as Cybill Shepherd's mother on the "Moonlighting" TV
show. She won an Emmy in 1990 for the
miniseries "People Like Us," and has also
appeared in a number of undistinguished
made-for-TV movies.
OTHER FILMS INCLUDE: 1956: *That Certain Feeling;* 1957: *Raintree County;* 1962: *All
Fall Down;* 1964: *36 Hours;* 1965: *The Sandpiper;* 1966: *The Russians Are Coming! The
Russians Are Coming!, Grand Prix;* 1969: *The*
Stalking Moon; 1970: *Loving;* 1972: *Cancel
My Reservation;* 1986: *Nothing in Common.*

SAKALL, S. Z. ("CUDDLES"). Actor.
*(b. Feb. 2, 1884, Budapest, as B. Eugene
Gero Szakall; d. Feb. 12, 1955.)* This jowly,
bespectacled,   roly-poly   supporting
player—a veteran of German films and
stage productions—fled from Germany in
1939 in the wake of Hitler's war overtures. (He'd appeared onscreen as early as
1916, and worked in German, Hungarian,
and British movies before coming to the
U.S.) He learned his first Hollywood roles
phonetically, but it was his manner and his
appearance that endeared him to
audiences—almost immediately—playing
(usually) lovable uncles, shopkeepers,
waiters, etc. He became a ubiquitous
presence in lighthearted movies of the
1940s and early 1950s, including *It's a
Date, Spring Parade* (both 1940), *That
Night in Rio, The Devil and Miss Jones,
Ball of Fire* (all 1941), *Seven Sweethearts,
Yankee Doodle Dandy* (both 1942), *Casablanca* (1942, as Carl the waiter), *Thank
Your Lucky Stars, The Human Comedy*
(both 1943), *Christmas in Connecticut,
The Dolly Sisters, San Antonio, Wonder
Man* (all 1945), *Two Guys from Milwaukee, Never Say Goodbye* (both 1946), *Ro-
mance on the High Seas* (1948), *My
Dream Is Yours, In the Good Old Sum-
mertime, Oh, You Beautiful Doll* (all
1949), *The Daughter of Rosie O'Grady,
Montana, Tea for Two* (all 1950), *Lullaby
of Broadway* (1951), *Small Town Girl*
(1953), and *The Student Prince* (1954), his
last. His autobiography, "The Story of
Cuddles (My Life Under the Emperor
Francis Joseph, Adolf Hitler and the
Warner Brothers)," was published in 1953.

SALT, WALDO. Screenwriter. *(b. Oct. 18,
1914, Chicago; d. Mar. 7, 1987.)* Before he
was blacklisted in 1951 by the House Un-
American Activities Committee for refusing to testify, Waldo Salt had achieved
some success in Hollywood writing such
froth as *The Shopworn Angel* (1938), *The
Wild Man of Borneo* (1941), *Mr. Winkle
Goes to War* (1944), and the swashbuckling *The Flame and the Arrow* (1950).
When he resumed his work in the early
1960s his work took on a darker, more
cynical character.

His brilliant, despairing adaptation of James L. Herlihy's novel *Midnight Cowboy* (1969) won him an Oscar. In 1973, he cowrote with Norman Wexler the screenplay for *Serpico,* an unflinching look at rampant corruption within the New York Police Department. Adapted from Peter Maas' novel, *Serpico* was a landmark of profane, gritty, realistic hard-core screenwriting and earned an Oscar nomination. Salt brought Nathaniel West's *The Day of the Locust* (1975) to the screen with its bleak, depressing, and fascinating look at the seamy underside of Hollywood intact. And in 1978, he shared screenplay credit for the post–Vietnam War saga *Coming Home.* One of the first films to deal with the wretched return Vietnam veterans received after the war, the film brought him another Oscar. His daughter is actress Jennifer Salt.

SANDERS, GEORGE. Actor. *(b. July 3, 1906, St. Petersburg, Russia; d. Apr. 25, 1972.)* Equally successful at limning debonair leading men and ruthless cads, this long-faced, soft-spoken Britisher was actually born in Russia, to an English family that moved back home when the Russian Revolution began. Sanders resolved to succeed in business but, dissatisfied with his forays into the tobacco and textile markets, he took up acting in the early 1930s. He made his film debut in *Life, Love and Laughter* (1934), and toiled in several more undistinguished British films before coming to Hollywood two years later. Under contract to 20th Century-Fox, he played Tyrone Power's rival in *Lloyd's of London* (1936), a WW1 undercover agent in *Lancer Spy* (1937), and one of the heroic brothers in *Four Men and a Prayer* (1938), among many others.

A suave, urbane performer who oozed cynicism from every pore, Sanders excelled in the portrayal of smooth, rakish heavies, as in *Allegheny Uprising* (1939), *The Son of Monte Cristo* (1940), and *Quiet Please, Murder* (1942). His first starring opportunity came when he took over from Louis Hayward the characterization of Simon Templar, a modern Robin Hood nicknamed "The Saint," in a handful of extremely popular RKO B thrillers, beginning with *The Saint Strikes Back* and followed by *The Saint in London* (both 1939), *The Saint Takes Over* (1940), *The*

Saint's Double Trouble (also 1940, in which he played a dual role), and *The Saint in Palm Springs* (1941). RKO then starred Sanders in a paraphrase of the "Saint" series as "The Falcon" in several more programmers beginning with 1941's *The Gay Falcon.* (He left the series in 1942's *The Falcon's Brother,* succeeded onscreen by his real-life brother Tom Conway.)

Sanders also found time to play often juicy supporting roles in A pictures, including Hitchcock's *Foreign Correspondent* and *Rebecca* (both 1940), *The Black Swan* (1942), *The Lodger* (1944), *Hangover Square, The Strange Affair of Uncle Harry* (both 1945), *Forever Amber, The Ghost and Mrs. Muir* (both 1947), and *Samson and Delilah* (1949). Dilettante director Albert Lewin was especially fond of Sanders, and gave him three of his best parts: the lead in *The Moon and Sixpence* (1942, playing an artist based on Paul Gauguin), the decadent Lord Henry Wotton in *The Picture of Dorian Gray* (1945), and another richly textured starring role as a womanizing rogue in *The Private Affairs of Bel Ami* (1947).

For his portrayal of a character he was *born* to play, Sanders won a Best Supporting Actor Oscar as Addison DeWitt, the acid-tongued Broadway critic in *All About Eve* (1950). Over the next 20 years Sanders never seemed to be out of work, but many of his projects were substandard. Among the better films: *Ivanhoe* (1952), *Call Me Madam* (1953, which revealed his excellent singing voice), *Moonfleet* (1955), *While the City Sleeps* (1956), *From the Earth to the Moon* (1958), *Bluebeard's Ten Honeymoons* (1960), *A Shot in the Dark* (1964), *The Quiller Memorandum* (1966), and *The Kremlin Letter* (1970, in which he appears in drag). In his last film, *Psychomania* (1972), he appeared particularly listless. Ironically, his most enduring work may turn out to be his vocal performance as the villainous tiger Shere Khan in Walt Disney's animated feature *The Jungle Book* (1967).

Sanders was married at various times to Zsa Zsa Gabor, her sister Magda, and actress Benita Hume. His 1960 autobiography, "Memoirs of a Professional Cad," revealed its author to possess a brilliant but restless mind. Sanders committed suicide by taking an overdose of sleeping pills, leaving behind a note that read, in part, "Dear World: I am leaving because I am bored."

OTHER FILMS INCLUDE: 1936: *The Man Who Could Work Miracles;* 1937: *Love Is News, Slave Ship;* 1939: *Mr. Moto's Last Warning, Confessions of a Nazi Spy, Nurse Edith Cavell;* 1940: *Green Hell, The House of the Seven Gables;* 1941: *Rage in Heaven, Bitter Sweet, Man Hunt, Sundown;* 1942: *Son of Fury, Her Cardboard Lover, Tales of Manhattan;* 1943: *Appointment in Berlin, Paris After Dark, They Came to Blow Up America, This Land Is Mine, Action in Arabia;* 1944: *Summer Storm;* 1946: *The Strange Woman, Thieves' Holiday;* 1947: *Lured;* 1949: *The Fan;* 1951: *I Can Get It for You Wholesale, The Light Touch;* 1952: *Assignment—Paris;* 1954: *Witness to Murder, King Richard and the Crusaders;* 1955: *The Scarlet Coat, The King's Thief;* 1956: *Never Say Goodbye, That Certain Feeling, Death of a Scoundrel;* 1957: *The Seventh Sin;* 1959: *That Kind of Woman, A Touch of Larceny, Solomon and Sheba;* 1960: *The Last Voyage, Village of the Damned;* 1961: *Five Golden Hours, Call Me Genius;* 1962: *In Search of the Castaways;* 1965: *The Amorous Adventures of Moll Flanders;* 1967: *Warning Shot, Good Times;* 1969: *The Best House in London.*

SANDS, JULIAN. Actor. *(b. Jan. 15, 1958, Yorkshire, England.)* Handsome British actor whose first major role cast him opposite Anthony Hopkins in the British TV miniseries "A Married Man" (1981). He had a one-line part in *Privates on Parade* (1982), but film audiences first noticed him as photographer Jon Swain in *The Killing Fields* (1984). After playing supporting roles in *Oxford Blues* (1984) and *The Doctor and the Devils* (1985), Sands won kudos from critics worldwide for his portrayal of George Emerson in the Merchant–Ivory adaptation of *A Room With a View* (1985). He has since appeared in a number of unusual films, including *Gothic* (1986), *Siesta* (1987), *Vibes* (1988), *Arachnophobia* (1990), *Impromptu* (as Franz Liszt), and *Naked Lunch* (both 1991). Recent credits include *Warlock* (1991), and its 1993 sequel *Warlock: The Armageddon,* the TV movies *Crazy in Love* and *Grand Isle* (both 1992), *Tale of a Vampire, Boxing Helena* (both 1993), and *Black Water* (1994).

SAN GIACOMO, LAURA. Actress. *(b. Nov. 14, 1961, Orange, N.J.)* This dark, seductive brunette—earthy and sensual—created a stir in her first important film role, as an amoral barmaid sleeping with her sister's husband in the breakthrough independent film *sex, lies, and videotape* (1989). Subsequent roles in big-budget Hollywood productions have not been as distinctive, although she showed spunky charm opposite Tom Selleck in the Australian Western *Quigley Down Under,* and played Julia Roberts' wisecracking best friend in *Pretty Woman* (both 1990). A graduate of Carnegie-Mellon University, this well-trained stage actress needs the right roles to showcase her not-inconsiderable talents, but she was badly cast as a sophisticated femme fatale in *Under Suspicion* (1992). Other credits include *Vital Signs* (1990), *Once Around* (1991), *The Other Woman* (1992), the Stephen King miniseries "The Stand" (1994), and *Nina Takes a Lover* (1995).

SARANDON, SUSAN. Actress. *(b. Oct. 4, 1946, New York City, as Susan Abigail Tomalin.)* From her early film output, one would never have guessed that Susan Sarandon would emerge as a major female star in the 1980s—or that, in her 40s, she would stand as the very definition of a mature, modern, liberated, sexual woman on screen. She debuted as the defiant hippie daughter in 1970's *Joe,* and kept busy throughout the seventies in a mixed bag of movies, including *Lady Liberty* (1971), *Lovin' Molly, The Front Page* (both 1974), *The Great Waldo Pepper* (1975), *One Summer Love* (1976; aka *Dragonfly), The Other Side of Midnight* (1977), *King of the Gypsies* (1978), and *Something Short of Paradise* (1979). She played a virginal ingenue in the decade's ultimate cult movie, *The Rocky Horror Picture Show* (1975), spending much of her screen time clad only in a bra and slip. The following year she coproduced and appeared in *The Great Smokey Roadblock* (1976). But it wasn't until 1978 that she had a really substantial part, in Louis Malle's controversial look at turn-of-the-century prostitution, *Pretty Baby.* Moviegoers were impressed, and so was Malle, who cast her again as a weary working woman in his brilliant *Atlantic City* (1980), which earned Sarandon her first Oscar nomination.

A constant screen presence in the 1980s, she gave consistently strong performances in such films as *Loving Couples* (1980), *Tempest* (1982), *The Hunger* (1983, as a vampire), *The Buddy System* (1984), *Compromising Positions* (1985), *The Witches of Eastwick* (1987), *Sweet Hearts Dance* (1988), *The January Man,* and *A Dry White Season* (both 1989). She won her best notices, however, for her performance as a seductive, middle-aged baseball groupie in the baseball comedy *Bull Durham* (1988), then took the lead as a sexy waitress who falls in love with a younger man in *White Palace* (1990). But nothing compared to the stir that was raised when she and Geena Davis starred in the role-reversal road movie *Thelma & Louise* (1991); she and Davis were ideally matched in this liberated "buddy" movie, and it earned them both Academy Award nominations. She was Oscar-nominated again for her intense dramatic performance as the mother of a boy with a baffling—and heartbreaking—disease in *Lorenzo's Oil* (1992). Other credits include *Light Sleeper* (1992), *Little Women, Safe Passage,* and *The Client* (all 1994, the last-named earning her a fourth Best Actress nomination). She also contributed a funny cameo (as a newscaster) to Tim Robbins' satiric *Bob Roberts* (1992). Formerly married to actor Chris Sarandon (himself Oscar-nominated for *Dog Day Afternoon,* and memorable in *Fright Night* and *The Princess Bride),* she met Robbins on the set of *Bull Durham* and has since had two children with him.

SARRAZIN, MICHAEL. Actor. *(b. May 22, 1940, Quebec City.)* As a youthful, open-faced supporting player and leading man in films of the late 1960s and 1970s, this slender, dark-haired actor seemed to be poised on the brink of stardom. Sarrazin trained at New York's Actors' Studio and worked on the stage before breaking into films with a supporting role in the undistinguished *Gunfight in Abilene* (1967). After appearing in *The Flim Flam Man* (also 1967, with George C. Scott) and *Journey to Shiloh* (1968), he connected with youthful audiences in the 1968 surfing saga *The Sweet Ride* which costarred longtime girlfriend Jacqueline Bisset. Sub-

stantial roles in *They Shoot Horses, Don't They?, Eye of the Cat, A Man Called Gannon* (all 1969), *In Search of Gregory* (1970), *The Pursuit of Happiness, Sometimes a Great Notion* (both 1971), *The Groundstar Conspiracy* (1972), and *Harry in Your Pocket* (1973) followed, some of which found him in rites-of-passage characterizations. He played a sensitive, tormented Monster in *Frankenstein: The True Story* (1973), an above-average TV movie that got theatrical release in Europe, and was overshadowed by costar Barbra Streisand in the comedy *For Pete's Sake* (1974).

Starring roles in *The Reincarnation of Peter Proud* (1975), *The Gumball Rally, Scaramouche* (both 1976), *Caravans* (1978), *The Seduction,* and *Fighting Back* (both 1982) gave way to supporting roles in *The Train Killer* (1983), *Joshua Then and Now* (1985), *Keeping Track, Captive Hearts, Mascara* (all 1987), *Malarek* (1989), and *Lena's Holiday* (1990), among others. In recent years he's taken many unsympathetic roles, including white-collar criminals.

SAVAGE, JOHN. Actor. *(b. Aug. 25, 1949, Long Island, N.Y.)* Quiet, intense, and delicately handsome, Savage was the least flamboyant of the three buddies who went to Vietnam in *The Deer Hunter* (1978), and his subsequent career certainly hasn't been as distinctive as costars Robert De Niro and Christopher Walken. An earnest performer, with a solid stage background (he graduated from the American Academy of Dramatic Arts), his emotional coolness kept him from achieving stardom. Early credits include *Bad Company* (1972), *The Killing Kind, Steelyard Blues* (both 1973), and *The Sister-in-Law* (1974). He was brilliant as a cop emotionally shattered by the death of a partner in 1979's *The Onion Field,* and quite moving as a man, crippled in a suicide attempt, who finds hope and redemption among other disabled people in *Inside Moves* (1980). His career has seesawed from prestige films like *Hair* (1979) *Cattle Annie and Little Britches* (1980), *The Amateur* (1982), *Maria's Lovers* (1984), and *Salvador* (1986) to time-wasters like *Soldier's Revenge* (1984), *The Beat* (1987), and *Caribe* (1988). More recently he's been seen in better pictures again, but in dispiritingly small roles; his parts in *Do the Right Thing* (1989) and *The Godfather, Part III* (1990) are little more than cameos. Other recent credits include such obscure films as *Hunting* (1990), *Primary Motive* (1992), and *My Forgotten Man* (1993), as well as Sean Penn's production of *The Crossing Guard* (1995).

Town Called Hell, Pretty Maids All in a Row, Clay Pigeon; 1972: Sonny and Jed, Pancho Villa, Horror Express; 1975: Lisa and the Devil (aka The House of Exorcism); 1978: Capricorn One; 1979: Beyond the Poseidon Adventure, The Muppet Movie, Escape to Athena, The Border; 1984: Cannonball Run II; 1993: Mind Twister.

SAVALAS, TELLY. Actor. *(b. Jan. 21, 1925, Garden City, N.Y., as Aristotle Savalas; d. Jan. 21, 1994.)* This hard-boiled character actor (and TV's most popular chrome dome) didn't begin his show-business career as an actor. Rather, he enjoyed stints as a casting assistant and senior news director at WABC in New York before turning to acting in his mid 30s. A recipient of a Purple Heart for his service in World War 2, Savalas made his TV debut in 1959 and his big-screen bow two years later in John Frankenheimer's *The Young Savages*. In 1962 he copped a Best Supporting Actor Oscar nomination as Feto Gomez, a prisoner on solitary row in Frankenheimer's *Birdman of Alcatraz*. Memorable performances followed in such pictures as *The Dirty Dozen* (1967) and *Kelly's Heroes* (1970). He also impressed as James Bond nemesis Blofeld in *On Her Majesty's Secret Service* (1969), an exotic villain role for which his bald head and prominent facial features made him a natural. A frequent guest-star on episodic TV, Savalas found stardom as the lollipop-sucking New York police lieutenant Theo Kojak ("Who loves ya, baby?") in a highly rated TV movie, *The Marcus-Nelson Murders* (1973), which spun off the hit series "Kojak" (1973–78). He earned an Emmy during the first season of the show (which also featured his brother George). Savalas later starred in a pair of Kojak TV movies in 1985 and 1987 before unsuccessfully relaunching the series (as part of the "ABC Saturday Mystery Movie") in the 1989–90 season.
OTHER FILMS INCLUDE: *1961: Mad Dog Coll; 1962: The Interns, Cape Fear; 1963: The Man From the Diner's Club, Johnny Cool; 1964: The New Interns; 1965: The Greatest Story Ever Told (as Pontius Pilate), Genghis Khan, Battle of the Bulge, The Slender Thread; 1966: Beau Geste (as Dagineau); 1968: The Scalphunters, Sol Madrid, Buona Sera, Mrs. Campbell; 1969: The Assassination Bureau, Mackenna's Gold; 1970: The Family; 1971: A*

SAXON, JOHN. Actor. *(b. Aug. 5, 1935, Brooklyn, N.Y., as Carmen Orrico.)* Swarthy, serious ex-model who broke into films during the 1950s, playing brooding, rebellious youths in low-budget epics such as *Running Wild* (1955, his first) and *Rock, Pretty Baby* (1956). Saxon, who studied acting under Stella Adler, seldom broke out of B movies, although he graduated to leads with 1959's *Cry Tough.* He enjoyed a brief flourish in mainstream, big-budget feature films such as *The Reluctant Debutante, This Happy Feeling* (both 1958), *The Big Fisherman* (1959), *The Unforgiven, Portrait in Black* (both 1960), *Mr. Hobbs Takes a Vacation* (1962), *The Cardinal* (1963), and *The Appaloosa* (1966) before returning to the B-movie netherworld of *For Singles Only* (1968) and *Death of a Gunfighter* (1969). He occasionally won costarring parts in high-profile films, including *Joe Kidd* (1972), *Enter the Dragon* (1973), *The Electric Horseman* (1979), *Battle Beyond the Stars* (1980), and *A Nightmare on Elm Street* (1984), as well as Richard Brooks' *Wrong Is Right* (1982) and *Fever Pitch* (1985). Showcase roles in prestige pictures eluded him, though; his later credits include the likes of *The Bees* (1978), *Blood Beach, The Glove* (both 1981), *The Big Score* (1983), and *My Mom's a Werewolf* (1989). Saxon appeared on the TV series "The Bold Ones" (1969–72) and "Falcon Crest" (guest starring in many episodes throughout the 1980s). He remains active in low-budget, primarily direct-to-video feature films.

SAYLES, JOHN. Writer, director, actor. *(b. Sept. 28, 1950, Schenectady, N.Y.)* The paradigm of the independent American filmmaker, specializing in moving, intelligent ensemble films about small people dealing with large problems. Originally (and still) a novelist and short-story writer, he quixotically broke into films writing genre scripts, at first for Roger Corman; typically, they stood out for their humor and cockeyed viewpoints. The money he earned from *Piranha* (1978), *The Lady in Red* (1979), *Alligator, Battle Beyond the Stars* (both 1980), and *The Howling* (1981) helped to finance his first film, *Return of the Secaucus Seven* (1980), which he also edited and acted in; a critical success, and the obvious inspiration for *The Big Chill,* it was made at a reported cost of $40,000! (Sayles cannily designed that film to be a small-scale project, choosing a contemporary setting—thus, no need for costumes, placing the action in and around a rambling house—thus, no need for sets, with youthful characters—so he could cast young actor friends in the leading roles.) His next film, *Lianna* (1983), took an intelligent and empathic look at an unhappily married housewife who falls in love with another woman; like all his best work, it had not one false note. (Sayles' ear for dialogue is uncanny.) The off-center romance *Baby, It's You* (also 1983) and the low-key science-fiction comedy *The Brother From Another Planet* (1984) enlarged Sayles' small but hardy legion of admirers. Sayles continued to finance his own films by writing *The Challenge* (1982, cowriter), *Enormous Changes at the Last Minute* (1983, cowriter; he also acted), the telefilm *Unnatural Causes, The Clan of the Cave Bear* (both 1986), *Wild Thing* (1987), *Breaking In* (1989), and the made-for-TV *Shannon's Deal* (also 1989), which launched a (sadly) short-lived series in the 1990–91 season. He also directed several music videos for fellow New Jersey resident Bruce Springsteen (whose music was heard in *Baby, It's You):* "I'm on Fire," "Glory Days," and "Born in the U.S.A."

His next films—a pair of period pieces—were bigger in scale and for a literary-trained director unusually rich in visual detail: *Matewan* (1987), based on a tragic coal miners' strike, and photographed by the great Haskell Wexler, and *Eight Men Out* (1988), which documented the Chicago "Black Sox" scandal of 1919. (Sayles also kept a journal while filming *Matewan,* and published it as "Making Pictures.") Despite good reviews, and the occasional presence of "name" actors, his movies have remained "specialized" products, well outside the Hollywood mainstream. Sayles has never succumbed to pressure to make more commercial prod-

uct, however. He calls on many of the same talented actors from one film to the next, and almost always writes a meaty supporting part for himself, as he did in the sprawling urban political drama *City of Hope* (1991).

In 1992 Sayles got his first Academy Award nomination, for the biting, often witty screenplay of *Passion Fish* (1992), which also earned an Oscar nomination for its star, Mary McDonnell, playing a self-centered soap opera actress who's paralyzed in an accident. His latest project is an Irish tale—unlike anything he's tackled before—called *The Secret of Roan Inish* (1995). But then, he's also written a mainstream script for a remake of *The Mummy.*

A convincing and naturalistic actor, Sayles has also played small supporting roles in other directors' films, including *The Howling* (1981), *Hard Choices* (1986), *Little Vegas* (1990), *Straight Talk* (1992), *Malcolm X* (1992, as a CIA operative), *My Life's in Turnaround* and *Matinee* (both 1993).

SCACCHI, GRETA. Actress. *(b. Feb. 18, 1960, Milan.)* It would be unfair (not to say ungentlemanly) to suggest that moviegoers—primarily male ones—follow the career of this ravishing blonde because she so often removes her clothes, but the statistics are undeniable. Nonetheless, Scacchi is a talented performer who has tackled a wide variety of roles in her relatively brief starring career; no pallid ingenues for this actress. First noticed in flashback segments of *Heat and Dust* (1983), she scored as the secretary in *The Coca-Cola Kid* (1985), a silent-film actress (who even gets a pie in the face) in *Good Morning, Babylon* and as an actress in love with her costar in *A Man in Love* (both 1987). Scacchi has played sensual femmes fatale in *White Mischief* (also 1987) and *Presumed Innocent* (1990). She has a child by Vincent D'Onofrio, with whom she appeared in *Fires Within* (1991) and *Desire* (1993). Other credits include *Shattered* (also 1991), *The Player* (1992), and *The Browning Version* (1994).

OTHER FILMS INCLUDE: 1983: *Dr. Fischer of Geneva* (telefilm); 1985: *Defence of the Realm;* 1986: "Lost Empires" (miniseries), *Burke and Wills;* 1988: *Fear and Love, Waterfront;* 1995: *Jefferson in Paris.*

SCARWID, DIANA. Actress. *(b. Aug. 27, 1955, Savannah, Ga.)* An Oscar nomination seemed to promise great things for this skilled and appealing actress—but her career has never blossomed as it should have. A seasoned stage performer, with a solid academic background, she debuted onscreen in *Pretty Baby* (1978), and received a Best Supporting Actress Oscar nomination for her work as John Savage's girlfriend in 1980's *Inside Moves* prior to being abused as Christina Crawford in *Mommie Dearest* (1981). She played Cher's dour lesbian lover in 1983's *Silkwood*, and a suicidal nun in the excessive *Psycho III* (1986). Scarwid was among the unfortunates who labored in the ill-fated, long-unreleased comic-strip adaptation *Brenda Starr* (1992). She deserves better. OTHER FILMS INCLUDE: 1980: *Honeysuckle Rose,* 1983: *Strange Invaders, Rumble Fish;* 1986: *Extremities, The Ladies Club;* 1987: *Heat;* 1993: *Simple Justice* (telefilm).

SCHAFFNER, FRANKLIN J. Director. *(b. May 30, 1920, Tokyo; d. July 2, 1989.)* One of the best of TV's "Golden Age" directors, Schaffner brought intelligence and visual sweep to many of his films. The son of American missionaries, Schaffner began his directing career on TV's "March of Time," then worked at CBS News before moving on to live drama. He won Emmys for "Twelve Angry Men" (1954), "The Caine Mutiny Court-Martial" (1955), and "The Defenders" (a filmed series in 1961–62), and a special award for Jacqueline Kennedy's "Tour of the White House" (1962). Schaffner's first feature, *The Stripper* (1963), was a minor debut but he made a big impression with *The Best Man* (1964), a biting (and completely convincing) political drama adapted from Gore Vidal's play. Schaffner hit his stride with the enormously popular *Planet of the Apes* (1968), a wholly credible and entertaining sci-fi film that revealed the director's eye for dramatic wide-screen composition. His next film, *Patton* (1970), is one of the screen's great biographies, maintaining enormous sweep while never losing sight of its subject (brilliantly portrayed by George C. Scott); the film won seven Oscars, including one for Schaffner as Best Director. *Nicholas and Alexandra* (1971) and *Papillon* (1973) were handsomely produced and executed,

but they were not received as well as his previous hits. His subsequent output was mostly disappointing.
OTHER FILMS INCLUDE: 1965: *The War Lord;* 1967: *The Double Man;* 1977: *Islands in the Stream;* 1978: *The Boys From Brazil;* 1982: *Yes, Giorgio;* 1987: *Lionheart;* 1989: *Welcome Home.*

SCHEIDER, ROY. Actor. *(b. Nov. 10, 1935, Orange, N.J.)* If you need someone to help you do away with a great white shark, here's your man. This rugged, versatile actor with the weatherbeaten face is equally effective in lead and character roles. Scheider originally envisioned an athletic career as a teenager, playing amateur baseball and entering the New Jersey Diamond Gloves boxing competition. He changed his mind while in college, and he studied drama at both Rutgers and William and Mary. After three years in the Air Force, Scheider began taking theater seriously, appearing with the New York Shakespeare Festival and winning an Obie award in 1968 for his performance in "Stephen D." Scheider's screen career began inauspiciously with a role in *Curse of the Living Corpse* (1963, billed as Roy R. Sheider [*sic*]). Other parts followed in *Paper Lion* (1968), *Stiletto* (1969), *Loving, Puzzle of a Downfall Child* (both 1970). Then in 1971 he hit pay dirt with supporting parts in two pictures, *Klute* and *The French Connection.* The latter was one of the year's biggest hits, and Scheider earned an Oscar nomination as second banana to Gene Hackman's "Popeye" Doyle. He spent two years in France, returning to Hollywood to star in the *French Connection*-inspired *The Seven-Ups* (1973), again as a police detective.
In 1975, Scheider starred in *Jaws,* which would eventually become the highest grossing film of all time (since surpassed), playing—naturally—a police chief in a small seaside community terrorized by a great white shark. He accepted a supporting role in *Marathon Man* (1976), appearing with Dustin Hoffman and Laurence Olivier, but was back in the top slot in *Sorcerer* (1977), *Jaws 2* (1978), and *Last Embrace* (1979). Determined to break the tough-cop mold, Scheider starred in 1979's *All That Jazz,* a flamboyant, semiautobiographical look at the life (and death) of choreographer/director Bob

Fosse. This eye-opening performance landed Scheider another Oscar nomination. He again proved to be a perfect Everyman in the underrated science fiction saga *2010* (1984), but for reasons that are difficult to understand, his career floundered. There were high-profile misfires like *Still of the Night* (1982) and *Blue Thunder* (1983), long absences from the screen, and forgettable films like *The Men's Club* (1986), *52 Pick-Up* (1986), *Cohen and Tate, Listen to Me, Night Game* (all 1989), and *The Fourth War* (1990). He also narrated *Mishima* (1985). By the 1990s he was turning up—if at all—in costarring parts, as in *The Russia House* (1990) and *Naked Lunch* (1991). In 1993 he regained the rank of star on Steven Spielberg's ambitious sci-fi television series "seaQuest DSV." He costarred in *Romeo Is Bleeding* (1994).

SCHELL, MARIA. Actress. *(b. Jan. 5, 1926, as Margarete Schell, Vienna.)* The older sister of Academy Award–winning actor Maximilian Schell and daughter of poet-playwright Ferdinand Hermann Schell and actress Margarethe Noe, Schell made a splash on the international film scene in the mid 1950s in a series of exceptional, critically acclaimed performances. Billed as Gritli Schell, she made her screen debut in 1942, at age sixteen, and appeared in various German and British films during the late 1940s and early 1950s. Her role in Helmut Kautner's antiwar drama, *The Last Bridge* (1954), earned her the Cannes Film Festival Best Actress prize. She gave a striking performance as a German doctor who is humanized after being captured by Yugoslav partisans in World War 2. This was followed by a Venice Film Festival citation for her work in René Clément's *Gervaise* (1956, based on a work by Zola), playing a downtrodden washerwoman in 1850s Montmartre. Schell also offered notable performances in Visconti's *White Nights* (1957, based on a Dostoyevski story), as a desperate woman awaiting the return of her lover; and in Alexander Astruc's *End of Desire* (1958, based on a short story by De Maupassant), as a wife saddled with an unfaithful husband. In the late 1950s, she even appeared in several American films, including Dostoyevski's *The Brothers Karamazov* (1958, as Grushenka), *The*

Hanging Tree (1959, opposite Gary Cooper), and *Cimarron* (1960), the remake of Edna Ferber's frontier saga. In 1963, she retired from movies, but came back five years later and has since appeared in various supporting and character roles in films as diverse as *Night of the Blood Monster* (1971), *Voyage of the Damned* (1976), *Just a Gigolo* (1979), *Superman* (1978), *Christmas Lilies of the Field* (1979, made for TV), "Inside the Third Reich" (1982, miniseries, as Albert Speer's mother), and *Samson and Delilah* (1984, made for TV).

SCHELL, MAXIMILIAN. Actor, director, producer, screenwriter. *(b. Dec. 8, 1930, Vienna.)* Dark, handsome, and intelligent leading man who, never content to play the matinee idol, undertook a variety of ambitious projects instead, on both sides of the camera. He made his American screen debut in the all-star WW2 melodrama *The Young Lions* (1958). In 1961 he tackled the difficult role of the defense attorney in the sprawling war-crimes epic *Judgment at Nuremberg,* for which he won a Best Actor Oscar. While he continued to appear in such crowd-pleasers as the caper flick *Topkapi* (1964) and the wartime thriller *Counterpoint* (1968), Schell explored other aspects of filmmaking, producing an adaptation of Kafka's *The Castle* in 1968 and writing, producing, and directing a film of Turgenev's *First Love* in 1970. 1974's *The Pedestrian,* which Schell wrote, produced, directed, and starred in, was nominated for a Best Foreign Language Film Oscar. During the 1970s he seemed to appear in just about every picture made that had anything to do with World War 2, from the Eichmann-based drama *The Man in the Glass Booth* (1975; Oscar nomination) to the epic adventure *A Bridge Too Far* to the battlefield gorefest *Cross of Iron* to the personal-heroism tale *Julia* (all 1977; Oscar nomination for the last-named). In 1984 he made *Marlene,* a fascinating documentary on the legendary Dietrich, with whom he'd costarred in *Nuremberg*—but at the last minute, the actress refused to appear on camera. Schell turned this to his advantage, using only his audio interviews with her to create an artistic, elegiac film. In 1990 he played a small, wonderfully comic part in the gangster-movie parody

The Freshman. Then in 1992 he played Lenin in the acclaimed TV movie *Stalin*. In 1993 he directed and costarred in the family-oriented telefilm *Candles in the Dark*. His sister is actress Maria Schell; they costarred in *The Odessa File* (1974). OTHER FILMS INCLUDE: 1962: *Five Finger Exercise, The Reluctant Saint;* 1965: *Return From the Ashes;* 1967: *The Deadly Affair;* 1969: *Krakatoa, East of Java;* 1972: *Pope Joan;* 1976: *St. Ives;* 1979: *Players, Avalanche Express, The Black Hole;* 1981: *The Chosen;* 1985: *The Assisi Underground;* 1989: *The Rose Garden;* 1993: *A Far Off Place;* 1995: *Little Odessa.*

SCHEPISI, FRED. Director, screenwriter, producer. (b. Dec. 26, 1929, Melbourne.) One of the most talented directors to have emerged from Australia's "New Wave" of the 1970s, Schepisi began in the advertising world, rising from messenger boy to head of the The Film House, a production firm known for its innovative commercials and documentaries. His first solo project was the half-hour "The Priest" for the four-part *Libido* (1973), but he established his reputation as a director with *The Devil's Playground* (1976), a semi-autobiographical look at a young boy in a Catholic seminary, and *The Chant of Jimmy Blacksmith* (1979), an unflinching story about a half-caste Aborigine who goes on a killing spree. The near-cult status of *Jimmy Blacksmith* soon earned Schepisi a ticket to America.

He did preparation work on *Raggedy Man* (1981) but made his U.S. debut instead with the moody Western *Barbarosa* (1982), which won acclaim for its original treatment of Western myths and its striking use of widescreen (a hallmark of Schepisi's work), also readily apparent in the unsung *Iceman* (1984) and *Plenty* (1985), a fine adaptation of David Hare's play. Schepisi scored a popular hit with *Roxanne* (1987), then returned to Australia to make *A Cry in the Dark* (1988), the gripping true-life story of the media frenzy that surrounded Lindy Chamberlain, who was accused of killing her child. It featured stunning performances from Meryl Streep and Sam Neill and won Best Film and Director honors from the Australian Film Institute. Since then he has directed *The Russia House* (1990), *Mr. Baseball* (1992), *Six Degrees of Separa-*

tion (1993, another fine stage-to-screen transformation), and *I.Q.* (1994).

SCHILDKRAUT, JOSEPH. Actor. (b. Mar. 22, 1895, Vienna; d. Jan. 21, 1964.) Dignified character actor from a famous acting family, best remembered for his suave villainy but equally convincing in sympathetic roles. Schildkraut first visited America in 1910 with his father, the esteemed Rudolph, and returned a decade later to settle here, having made some films in Germany and Austria. Soon a Broadway leading man, he made a major impression on film in D. W. Griffith's *Orphans of the Storm* (1922) and became a star in two Cecil B. DeMille films, *Road to Yesterday* (1925) and *The King of Kings* (1927, as Judas). He played Gaylord Ravenal in the first, silent movie version of *Show Boat* (1929), and made the transition to talkies with little difficulty; years of stage work had dulled his Austrian accent and sharpened his diction. He did two more DeMille spectaculars, *Cleopatra* (1934) and *The Crusades* (1935), before playing Captain Dreyfus in *The Life of Emile Zola* (1937), for which he won a Best Supporting Actor Academy Award. He appeared in swashbucklers (1939's *The Three Musketeers* and *The Man in the Iron Mask),* Westerns (1946's *The Plainsman and the Lady),* and biblical epics (1965's *The Greatest Story Ever Told,* his cinematic swan song). One of his most unforgettable latter-day roles was that of the father, Otto Frank, in *The Diary of Anne Frank* (1959). Other films include *Viva Villa!* (1934), *The Garden of Allah* (1936), *Marie Antoinette* (1938), *The Rains Came* (1939), *The Shop Around the Corner* (1940), *Flame of the Barbary Coast* (1945), and *Monsieur Beaucaire* (1946). His autobiography, "My Father and I," was published in 1959.

SCHLESINGER, JOHN. Director. (b. Feb. 16, 1926, London.) Celebrated director whose early experiences helming stage productions and TV documentaries prepared him for the rigors of the filmmaking process. A lifelong movie buff (and amateur filmmaker since the age of 11), he served with the Royal Engineers during World War 2 and joined the Oxford University Dramatic Society upon resuming his education after the conflict's end. During the 1950s he worked in several entertainment mediums, acting in films, radio, and TV in addition to directing documentaries for the BBC. Schlesinger's first feature film, a 1961 documentary on London's Waterloo Station titled *Terminus,* won him a British Academy Award and launched his movie career in earnest.

His debut feature was the well-received *A Kind of Loving* (1962, starring a young Alan Bates), followed by the equally successful *Billy Liar* (1963, which featured Tom Courtenay and, in her first leading role, Julie Christie). Schlesinger's reputation was cemented by his third feature, *Darling* (1965), a satire on "mod" London that made a star of Julie Christie, and earned three Oscars, plus a nomination for Best Director. *Far From the Madding Crowd* (1967), a sumptuous adaptation of the Thomas Hardy novel, was not as well received (although it has many champions today). Schlesinger then made an impressive American debut with the superb *Midnight Cowboy* (1969), which in spite of an X rating won the Oscar as Best Picture that year, and another Oscar for Schlesinger as Best Director. Like all of the director's best work, it is marked by exceptional performances and a keen sense of observation. Back in England he scored again with the piercing adult drama *Sunday, Bloody Sunday* (1971), which earned him a third Oscar nomination.

Since that time Schlesinger has wandered from the Hollywood mainstream to British stage and television drama, with varying degrees of success. Two of his best (and best-received) works have been BBC feature-length films: *An Englishman Abroad* (1983) and *A Question of Attribution* (1991), both written by Alan Bennett. His other films include the Marathon segment of the Olympics feature *Visions of Eight* (1973), the harrowing Hollywood fable *The Day of the Locust* (1975), the solid thriller *Marathon Man* (1976), *Yanks* (1979), the unfortunate *Honky Tonk Freeway* (1981), *The Falcon and the Snowman* (1985), the surprisingly graphic horror tale *The Believers* (1987), *Madame Sousatzka* (1988, which he also cowrote), *Pacific Heights* (1990), and *The Innocent* (1995).

SCHNEIDER, ROMY. Actress. *(b. Sept. 23, 1938, Vienna, as Rosemarie Albach-*

Retty; d. May 29, 1982.) As a pretty, wholesome teenager, this Austrian-born actress achieved European stardom by portraying youthful royalty. Born into a distinguished theatrical family (her mother Magda Schneider was a great star of stage and screen), she played Britain's Queen Victoria in *The Story of Vickie* (1954) and Austria's Princess Elizabeth in *Sissi* (1956, and 1957 and 1958 sequels). Director Luchino Visconti gave her a more mature, substantive role in his segment of *Boccaccio '70* (1962), and she appeared in Orson Welles' adaptation of Kafka's *The Trial* the next year, effectively launching her "adult" career. The beautiful, multilingual Schneider chalked up a string of prominent parts in international productions such as *The Victors, The Cardinal* (both also 1963), *Good Neighbor Sam* (1964), *What's New, Pussycat?* (1965), *Triple Cross* (1967), *Otley, The Swimming Pool* (both 1969), and *The Things of Life* (1970).

Her pivotal role in *Cesar and Rosalie* (1972), as one-third of a long-running ménage à trois, marked the beginning of a new phase in Schneider's career, marked by daring portrayals (in which she proved willing to bare body and soul) of emotionally complex characters. She won the French Cesar Award twice, for 1976's *L'Important c'est aimer* and 1978's *Une Histoire Simple.* Schneider took her own life.

OTHER FILMS INCLUDE: 1958: *Maedchen in Uniform;* 1972: *The Assassination of Trotsky;* 1973: *Ludwig* (once again cast as Austria's Elizabeth, now an Empress); 1974: *Love at the Top;* 1975: *Innocents With Dirty Hands, The Old Gun;* 1979: *A Woman at Her Window, Mado, Bloodline, Clair de Femme;* 1980: *Deathwatch;* 1981: *Fantasma d'Amore;* 1982: *La Passante.*

SCHRADER, PAUL. Writer, director. *(b. July 22, 1946, Grand Rapids, Mich.)* Cerebral writer/director whose wildly uneven career has given post-Vietnam Hollywood some of its most celebrated pictures, as well as a few provocative flops. Schrader was raised as a strict Calvinist in Grand Rapids, a repressive environment to which he would return for the inspiration of his 1979 film, *Hardcore.* Upon graduation from a local college, he studied for his master's degree at UCLA. His writings on film, first for the "LA Weekly Press" and then "Cinema" magazine, were widely admired, and in 1972, he published a still-influential book of essays entitled "The Transcendental Style in Film: Ozu, Bresson, Dreyer." Schrader tried his hand at original screenplays, but didn't sell one until 1975: A Japanese crime picture called *The Yakuza* (cowritten with Robert Towne). Although the movie flopped, it brought Schrader to the attention of a new generation of filmmakers, steeped in film-school theories and armed with studio backing.

In 1976 Schrader penned the Hitchcockian *Obsession* for Brian De Palma, and the grim modern-day urban parable *Taxi Driver* for Martin Scorsese. Together they won him great acclaim and earned him an opportunity to direct one of his own screenplays, *Blue Collar* (1978), a gritty, quasi-Marxist look at exploited auto workers. His subsequent forays into the movie mainstream have met with middling success, as witness *American Gigolo* (1980, also wrote), *Cat People* (1982), the very intriguing *Mishima* (1985, cowritten with his brother Leonard), *Light of Day* (1987, also wrote), *Patty Hearst* (1988), *The Comfort of Strangers* (1991), and *Light Sleeper* (1992, also wrote). Schrader has managed to maintain both his independence and his singular (if downbeat) vision throughout.

His screenplays for other directors are more impressive, overall, including the underrated *The Mosquito Coast* (1986) and two key films for Scorsese, *Raging Bull* (1980, cowritten with Mardik Martin) and *The Last Temptation of Christ* (1988).

SCHROEDER, BARBET. Director, screenwriter, producer. *(b. Apr. 26, 1941, Tehran.)* Acclaimed international filmmaker who has had increasing commercial success in the U.S. since the late 1980s. He studied philosophy at the Sorbonne and wrote criticism for the famous film journal "Cahiers du Cinéma" before he assisted Jean-Luc Godard on *Les Carabiniers* (1963, in which he also had a small part) and Eric Rohmer on the short *La Boulangère de Monceau*, in which he also starred. In 1964, Schroeder established his own production company, Les Films du Losange, to produce the early feature films of Rohmer, and after the success of *My Night at Maud's* (1969) and *Claire's*

Knee (1971), the company produced the works of such diverse directors as Jacques Rivette (1974's *Celine and Julie Go Boating),* Wim Wenders (1977's *The American Friend),* and Rainer Werner Fassbinder (1976's *Chinese Roulette).* Schroeder cowrote and directed his first feature, *More* (1969), a story about a man who gets involved with love and heroin, which became a hit in Europe. He next directed *Le Vallée* (1972), about a group of people searching for paradise, the fascinating documentary *General Idi Amin Dada* (1974), and the controversial *Maîtresse* (1976), which starred Bulle Ogier as a professional dominatrix and Gerard Depardieu as her off-hours lover. After the documentary *Koko, the Talking Gorilla* (1978), Schroeder came to the U.S. and worked with cult writer Charles Bukowski on a project that eventually became *Barfly* (1987). Schroeder fought hard to secure financing for the film (and actually threatened to cut off one of his fingers with a Black & Decker jigsaw in a lawyer's office to ensure the necessary release papers) and the result was a critical success. He later garnered an Oscar nomination for his direction of *Reversal of Fortune* (1990), a darkly humorous take on the Claus von Bulow case which won Jeremy Irons a Best Actor Oscar, and achieved his greatest commercial success with the slick psychological thriller *Single White Female* (1992). Schroeder followed with a remake of the noir classic *Kiss of Death* (1995).

SCHWARZENEGGER, ARNOLD. Actor. *(b. July 30, 1947, Graz, Austria.)* He had a name you couldn't pronounce, an accent you couldn't cut, and a body out of a Frank Frazetta painting, yet this world-champion bodybuilder defied all the naysayers to become the undisputed Biggest Movie Star in the World, as well as a restaurateur, political activist, and leading spokesman for physical fitness. The product of a difficult childhood, he turned to weight training as both an escape and a self-esteem booster. Coming to America to make his fortune, Schwarzenegger landed the title role in the low-budget, barely released *Hercules in New York* (aka *Hercules Goes Bananas,* 1970), billed as Arnold Strong. The movie revealed two things: his impressively sculptured body, and the fact that he couldn't act (let alone speak English). Schwarzenegger's less-than-spectacular film debut sent him back to the weight room, and he concentrated on bodybuilding for some time thereafter, winning seven Mr. Olympia titles—a record only recently beaten—and earning the nickname "the Austrian Oak."

Writers George Butler and Charles Gaines featured him prominently in their book *Pumping Iron,* a comprehensive examination of bodybuilding; he then made a considerable impact in the 1977 film of the same name, and was much talked about. He'd been cast as a bodybuilder (what else?) in the comedy *Stay Hungry* (1976, starring Jeff Bridges and Sally Field). His performance was, in the main, kindly reviewed, but Schwarzenegger still didn't actively pursue a screen career until accepting the role of the impeccably costumed Handsome Stranger in a cartoonish Western, *The Villain* (1979). He realized that he'd milked bodybuilding and decided to tackle a new career.

Schwarzenegger threw himself wholeheartedly into acting, beginning with roles in *Scavenger Hunt* (1979) and the TV movie *The Jayne Mansfield Story* (1980, earnestly but ineptly playing Mansfield's muscleman husband, Mickey Hargitay), then graduating to the title role of 1982's sword-and-sorcery blockbuster *Conan the Barbarian,* and its 1984 sequel, *Conan the Destroyer.* Later in 1984 he starred in *The Terminator,* a sci-fi actioner that cast him as an unstoppable killer robot from the future; its success made him a superstar and gave him a signature line—"I'll be back!"—that he managed to work into many subsequent films for a knowing laugh. In fact, Schwarzenegger's sense of humor (even about himself) set him apart from the other pumped-up action stars of the 1980s. He played a Conan-like barbarian in *Red Sonja* (1985), and then churned out a string of blood-and-wisecracks blockbusters including *Commando* (also 1985), *Raw Deal* (1986), *Predator, The Running Man* (both 1987), and *Red Heat* (1988). He turned to silly comedy for real in *Twins* (also 1988, costarring with Danny DeVito), proving he could make cash registers jingle without killing dozens of adversaries in every reel. Since then he's alternated between "serious" action films like *Total Recall* (1990) and *Terminator 2: Judgment Day* (1991), which have been hugely successful, and "lighter"

fare like *Kindergarten Cop* (1990), a modest hit, and the overblown, tongue-in-cheek *Last Action Hero* (1993), a colossal fiasco that had the media clucking that even the mighty Arnold could fail. In 1994 he reteamed with *Terminator*'s James Cameron for the smash hit *True Lies,* then starred as a pregnant man in *Junior.*

Though he does not officially produce his films, Schwarzenegger pretty much calls all the shots, right down to planning publicity, and he has dabbled in directing for TV (an episode of "Tales From the Crypt" and the 1992 remake of *Christmas in Connecticut*) as a possible prelude to big-screen helming. In 1990 he was named chairman of the President's Council on Physical Fitness, and his lengthy association with Republican politics sparked rumors that he might someday run for office. Ironically, he is married to TV journalist Maria Shriver, one of the (Democratic) Kennedy clan.

SCHYGULLA, HANNA. Actress. *(b. Dec. 25, 1943, Kattowitz, Germany.)* A coolly beautiful, somewhat enigmatic blond actress, Schygulla achieved international recognition in the films of Rainer Werner Fassbinder, turning in many unforgettable performances, including the lead in the widely celebrated *The Marriage of Maria Braun* (1978). Most of her films haven't been distributed here, although Schygulla herself came to these shores in the mid 1980s. Her career has not fared as well since Fassbinder's demise, as demonstrated by the parts she's played in the likes of *Sheer Madness* (1985), *Storm in Venice, The Delta Force* (both 1986), *Casanova* (1987), and *Abraham's Gold* (1989). She has been seen to good advantage in *Forever, Lulu* (1987) and, almost unrecognizable in heavy makeup, in *Dead Again* (1991). Other Fassbinder credits include *Love Is Colder Than Death* (1969), *The Merchant of Four Seasons* (1971), *Wild Game* (1972), *The Bitter Tears of Petra Von Kant* (1973), *Effi Briest* (1974), *The Third Generation* (1979), *Berlin Alexanderplatz* (1980), and *Lili Marleen* (1981). She also worked for Volker Schlondorff in *Circle of Deceit* (1981), Jean-Luc Godard in *Passion* (1982), Ettore Scola in *La Nuit de Varennes*

(1982), and Andrzej Wajda in *A Love in Germany* (1984).

SCIORRA, ANNABELLA. Actress. *(b. Mar. 24, 1964, New York City.)* This pretty, dark-haired young actress first attracted attention as a worrisome young bride-to-be in the mordantly funny independent film *True Love* (1989). Her winning performance and warm personality catapulted her into major studio projects, albeit in ordinary supporting roles. She was Tim Robbins' wife in *Cadillac Man* (1990), precipitating that film's comedic carnage. She played Richard Gere's wife in *Internal Affairs* (1990) and James Woods' girlfriend in *The Hard Way* (1991), then snagged a starring role as the Italian-American woman from Brooklyn who falls in love with Wesley Snipes in Spike Lee's controversial *Jungle Fever* (1991), a high-profile film that put her on magazine covers, and heralded her arrival as an actress to watch. Since then she's appeared in the surprise hit *The Hand That Rocks the Cradle, Whispers in the Dark* (both 1992), *The Night We Never Met, Mr. Wonderful* (both 1993), and *Romeo Is Bleeding* (1994).

SCOFIELD, PAUL. Actor. *(b. Jan. 21, 1922, Hurstpierpoint, England.)* If this commanding and distinguished British stage actor had made only *A Man for All Seasons* (1966, featuring an Oscar-winning portrayal of Sir Thomas More), he'd still rate a berth in this book. (He created the role on stage and won a Tony award playing it on Broadway.) As it happens, he's contributed several other great performances to movies, although he clearly prefers stage to screen. Scofield, whose vaguely ascetic appearance and gentle manner bespeaks quiet intelligence and emotional honesty, made his film debut in *That Lady* (1955), and has also appeared in *Carve Her Name With Pride* (1958), *The Train* (1965), *Tell Me Lies* (1967), *King Lear* (1971, in the title role), *Bartleby* (1972), *Scorpio, A Delicate Balance* (both 1973), *19/19* (1985), *The Conspiracy* (1986), *When the Whales Came, Henry V* (both 1989, in the latter as the French King), *Hamlet* (1990, as The Ghost), and *Utz* (1993). He's also made occasional television appearances; he won

an Emmy in 1969 for a production of "Male of the Species," and starred in the acclaimed 1988 TV movie *The Attic: The Hiding of Anne Frank*. In 1994 he took the role of Mark Van Doren in *Quiz Show,* and earned a Supporting Oscar nomination. Most recently, he appeared in a "Masterpiece Theatre" version of "Martin Chuzzlewit" (1995).

SCOLA, ETTORE. Director, screenwriter. *(b. May 10, 1931, Trevico, Italy.)* One of the Italian cinema's most provocative writer-directors, Scola has successfully carried the mantle of two of his illustrious predecessors, Vittorio De Sica and Roberto Rossellini. Scola studied law at the University of Jurisprudence in Rome, but his love of creative writing, storytelling, and the cinema was to take precedence over a legal career. He broke into the film industry in 1954, and for the next decade wrote comedy scripts (including 1962's *The Easy Life* and 1964's *The Magnificent Cuckold*). He made his directorial debut with *Let's Talk About Women* (1964), a sex comedy, and followed it with such films as *The Devil in Love* (1966) and *The Pizza Triangle* (1970), but didn't hit his stride until the mid 1970s. Scola's finest films are bittersweet affairs which mix Italian and European politics and history, with the key addition of male bonding and, occasionally, sex. As in the postwar films of De Sica and Rossellini, they explore the manner in which the individual survives within a hostile, uncaring society. Scola's concern for the individual may seem ironic in that he has been a member of the Italian Communist Party; however, his finest work is driven by his humanism and concern for his characters' plight and fate, rather than any political ideology.

His best film, *We All Loved Each Other So Much* (1974), tells the story of a trio of WW2 resistance fighters who become friends, and who, despite their class and personal differences, share a collective optimism that is dampened in the postwar years. Filmed in assorted cinematic styles, it is also an homage to three decades of Italian filmmaking in general and Vittorio De Sica in particular. Scola's interest in the downtrodden is never more evident than in *Down and Dirty* (1976), in which he depicts the humiliating effects of impoverishment on a group of people residing in a

Rome shantytown. In *A Special Day* (1977), set in Rome in May 1938, Scola tells the story of a neglected housewife and an anti-Fascist homosexual, characters who are on the fringes of the society in which they live. As Mussolini welcomes Hitler to the city, they share a brief, compassionate encounter. *The Terrace* (1980) is thematically linked to *We All Loved Each Other So Much* as a portrait of middle-aged men who have lost their creativity and verve and are disillusioned by their lives. *La Nuit de Varennes* (1982) is an allegorical tale set during the French Revolution, with the various characters (including Casanova and Thomas Paine) responding to the political turbulence of the times while getting on with their lives. *Le Bal* (1982), a stylized musical, is set in a Parisian ballroom and has no spoken dialogue; it is made up of vignettes depicting the political and cultural changes in France between 1936 and 1982. *The Family* (1987), the filmmaker's most autobiographical film (and the best of his most recent efforts), chronicles the situation of an extended family over five generations, amid political and societal upheaval. Scola has repeatedly worked with Italy's most renowned postwar actors: Marcello Mastroianni, Nino Manfredi, and Vittorio Gassman.

SCORSESE, MARTIN. Director, actor, writer, producer. *(b. Nov. 17, 1942, Flushing (Queens), N.Y.)* The man often referred to as America's best movie director, as well as one of the cinema's most dedicated preservationists, grew up in Manhattan's Little Italy, and his experiences there inform most of his early work. Although at one point he entered a seminary, hoping to become a priest, moviemaking proved a stronger calling. In the early 1960s he was in the film studies program at New York University, where he eventually became an instructor. He first attracted notice in the film community with his provocative short subjects *What's a Nice Girl Like You Doing in a Place Like This?* (1963), *It's Not Just You, Murray!* (1964), and *The Big Shave* (1967), the latter two winning berths at the New York Film Festival. In 1968 he attempted his first feature film, *Who's That Knocking at My Door?* (with Harvey Keitel), then agreed to work as an assistant director and editor on the groundbreaking musical documentary

Woodstock (1970). He served as supervising editor on *Medicine Ball Caravan* (1971) and *Unholy Rollers* (1972); then producer Roger Corman hired him to direct *Boxcar Bertha* (1972). Scorsese managed to imbue the low-budget actioner with several personal touches (including a crucifixion scene that is reprised almost shot for shot in 1988's *The Last Temptation of Christ*) even while meeting Corman's sex and violence quotas. After getting berated by friend John Cassavetes for spending "a year of your life making a piece of s——" he decided to direct a film that mattered to him. The result was the powerful *Mean Streets* (1973), a Little Italy slice of life in which the extremely confused protagonist (Harvey Keitel) tries to take care of too many people, with disastrous results. The film marked the first collaboration between Scorsese and an electrifying young actor named Robert De Niro, and it brought them both widespread acclaim. (Even after achieving some degree of mainstream success, Scorsese continued making highly personal documentaries like *Italianamerican* in 1974, a film about his parents, and *American Boy: A Profile of Steven Prince,* in 1978.)

Although his next film, *Alice Doesn't Live Here Anymore* (1974), was a critical and commercial hit, it took 1976's widely misunderstood *Taxi Driver* to bring Scorsese into his own. This nightmare vision of New York and a disturbed loner's self-appointed mission in the urban jungle generated a lot of controversy, and unfortunately provided some fuel for real-life disturbed loner John Hinckley, Jr., who maintained his 1981 attempt on President Reagan's life was inspired by an obsession with *Taxi Driver* actress Jodie Foster. 1977's big-budget musical, *New York, New York,* with visuals inspired by Vincente Minnelli (his daughter Liza was one of the film's stars) and histrionics inspired by the Lee Strasberg school, was a bit of a misfire, but showed Scorsese's deeply felt love for old Hollywood movies from which uninformed viewers saw his films as such radical departures. In fact, Scorsese builds on cinematic tradition as much as he subverts it, and will in any given interview name dozens of formative influences from Hollywood and elsewhere.

The Last Waltz (1978), chronicling an all-star send-off to the influential rock group The Band, is arguably the finest concert movie ever made, thanks to Scorsese's mapping out camera movements in advance of the show itself and editing with great musical sense. *Raging Bull* (1980), now acclaimed by critics as the decade's greatest movie, was a black-and-white powerhouse that saw Robert De Niro undergo an amazing physical transformation to play middleweight champion Jake LaMotta in both his prime and in older, bloated form (production had to halt for several months in order for De Niro to put on the necessary weight). The film's amazing boxing sequences, overall visual style, and overwhelming dramatic impact made this story of a seemingly irredeemable brute an unforgettable film. It earned eight Oscar nominations, including Best Picture and Director, and won for Best Actor and Best Editing; it was bested by the much more genteel *Ordinary People*. The 1980s also saw Scorsese experiment with quirky, very black comedy—the amazing, unsettling terror-of-celebrity picture *The King of Comedy* (1983) and the nightmare date movie *After Hours* (1985)—and conventional Hollywood forms—*The Color of Money* (1986), a kinetic sequel to *The Hustler* starring Paul Newman and Tom Cruise.

Scorsese's final film of the decade, *The Last Temptation of Christ* (1988), was his most controversial. Adapted from Greek author Nikos Kazantzakis' novel, it represented Scorsese's sincere, reverent attempt to humanize Christ—and was almost shut down by protests from Fundamentalist Christians (most of whom hadn't even seen the movie) on release. It still managed to earn Scorsese a Best Director nomination. (Scorsese had tried to make the picture earlier in the decade, but backing studio Paramount, fearing Fundamentalist backlash, canceled the production right before shooting was scheduled to start.) Scorsese didn't let the controversy keep him out of action; in 1989 he contributed the best episode to the three-part anthology film *New York Stories* (which also featured work from Woody Allen and Francis Ford Coppola). 1990's *Good-Fellas* (Oscar-nominated for Best Picture, Director, and Screenplay, which Scorsese cowrote), a dizzying, exhilarating, frightening look at the everyday life of a Mafia "wiseguy," won wide acclaim and also reunited Scorsese and De Niro for the sixth

time. They continued the collaboration with the 1991 remake of *Cape Fear,* another attempt for Scorsese (perpetually a Hollywood outsider) to crack the mainstream. Even with Steven Spielberg as executive producer, the film managed to reflect Scorsese's darker vision, and emerged a curious hybrid of conventional 1990s horror/thriller and brooding psychological melodrama. Then in 1993 he turned to wholly unexpected source material, Edith Wharton's novel of sexual repression in the late 1800s, *The Age of Innocence,* a flawed but stunningly realized evocation of an era and its social mores. (Scorsese received an Oscar nomination as cowriter.) He teamed up again with De Niro—their eighth time—for *Casino* (1995).

Scorsese has also directed Michael Jackson's music video "Bad" (1987), and Robbie Robertson's "Somewhere Down the Crazy River" (1988), as well as two Giorgio Armani commercials and an episode of Steven Spielberg's "Amazing Stories" called "Mirror Mirror." He produced *The Grifters* (1990), coproduced *Mad Dog and Glory* (1993) and *Clockers* (1995), and executive produced *Naked in New York* (1994). He has lent his name and prestige to a number of American theatrical releases of both contemporary and classic films, and even interviewed one of his mentors, director Michael Powell, for the laserdisc release of *Black Narcissus.*

The director has also worked in front of the camera, contributing cameos to a number of his own movies (most notably *Taxi Driver* as a psycho passenger) and working as an actor in such films as *Round Midnight* (1986), *Akira Kurosawa's Dreams* (1990, as Vincent van Gogh), *Guilty by Suspicion* (1991), and *Quiz Show* (1994). Most of his movies involve extended family participation, not only with longtime collaborators like actors De Niro, Harvey Keitel, and Joe Pesci, screenwriters Paul Schrader, Mardik Martin and Jay Cocks, editor Thelma Schoonmaker, and cinematographer Michael Ballhaus, but in his frequent casting of his parents in actual roles. Mrs. Scorsese had a particularly memorable scene as Joe Pesci's mother in *GoodFellas.* Scorsese was formerly married to actress Isabella Rossellini and producer Barbara De Fina.

SCOTT, CAMPBELL. Actor. *(b. July 19, 1962, South Salem, N.Y.)* The second son of George C. Scott and Colleen Dewhurst, Campbell Scott has begun to carve out an impressive acting career for himself. After appearing in many Broadway and off-Broadway productions, Scott made his film debut in *Five Corners* (1988), then drew raves for his performance in *Longtime Companion* (1990) as Willy, a homosexual who watches his friends ravaged by AIDS. He had roles in *The Sheltering Sky* (1990), *Dead Again* (1991), and his first lead, as a dying recluse in *Dying Young* (1991, opposite Julia Roberts). *Singles* (1992) provided his most lighthearted (and likable) showcase to date; it was followed by *Mrs. Parker and the Vicious Circle* (also 1994), in which he played Robert Benchley, and *The Innocent* (1995).

SCOTT, GEORGE C. Actor. *(b. Oct. 18, 1927, Wise, Va.)* An actor's actor, George C. Scott has carved a solid reputation as a charismatic screen performer, although the body of his work is not nearly as imposing as memory would have us believe. Coming to the theater after service in the Marines, Scott became a familiar figure on stage and TV in New York in the late 1950s. His first film was *The Hanging Tree* (1959), a Gary Cooper Western, in which he showed promise as a supporting player. In fact, he received a Best Supporting Actor nomination for his role as the prosecuting attorney in his second picture, Otto Preminger's *Anatomy of a Murder* (also 1959).

During that period Scott was riding high on Broadway in plays like "Comes a Day" and "The Andersonville Trial," and making prominent guest appearances on television as well. He earned another Oscar nomination for his supporting performance in *The Hustler* (1961), then costarred in *The List of Adrian Messenger* (1963), *Dr. Strangelove* (1964, a memorable turn as the gung ho Gen. Buck Turgidson), *The Yellow Rolls-Royce* (also 1964), *The Bible* (1966, as Abraham), and *Not With My Wife You Don't!* (also 1966). He also received critical acclaim for his starring role in the New York-based TV series "East Side, West Side," which lasted just one season, 1963–64.

He starred in *The Flim Flam Man* (1967), as a roguish con artist, and *Petulia*

(1968), as a recently divorced doctor, before taking on the role for which he's best remembered, the eccentric but brilliant General George S. Patton in *Patton* (1970). His galvanizing performance in this sweeping and intelligent biopic won him an Academy Award, but ever since *The Hustler* he'd openly disdained acting honors, and true to form, refused to accept the Oscar—the first actor ever to do so. Undeterred by this rebuff, Academy voters nominated him again the following year for his electrifying performance in Paddy Chayefsky's black comedy *The Hospital* (1971). That same year he played a delightfully deranged man who thinks he is Sherlock Holmes in *They Might Be Giants.* He also starred in a TV production of Arthur Miller's "The Price," for which he won an Emmy—which, naturally, he refused.

This was Scott's busiest and most fruitful period. He starred in *The New Centurions* (1972), *Oklahoma Crude* (a rare and welcome chance to play comedy), *The Day of the Dolphin* (both 1973), *Bank Shot* (1974, another comedy), *The Hindenburg* (1975), *Islands in the Stream* (1977), *Crossed Swords,* the Hollywood parody *Movie Movie* (both 1978), and *The Changeling* (1979). He was particularly effective in *Hardcore* (also 1979), as a middle-aged, midwestern Calvinist drawn into the seedy world of urban decay while searching for his runaway daughter. He also directed two films in which he starred with his wife Trish Van Devere, *Rage* (1972) and *The Savage Is Loose* (1974), but neither was especially well received. Since the early 1980s, Scott has assumed roles in feature films only infrequently, with *The Formula* (1980), *Taps* (1981), *Firestarter* (1984), and *The Exorcist III* (1990) as his only significant efforts, but he has continued to be a busy TV actor in specials and long-form dramas like *Oliver Twist* (1982), *A Christmas Carol* (1984, winning special kudos for his performance as Scrooge), "Mussolini: The Untold Story" (1985), *The Murders in the Rue Morgue* (1986), and *The Ryan White Story* (1989). Scott reprised his Oscar-winning role for the small screen in *The Last Days of Patton* (1986), but failed to repeat the success of his earlier effort. His eventual decision to star in a TV sitcom, "Mr. President" (1987), seemed a sorry indication of how few good roles remained for him.

Recent credits include a villainous voice characterization in Disney's animated feature *The Rescuers Down Under* (1990), glorified cameo roles in *Malice* and *Rudy* (both 1993), and the lead in the telefilm *Curacao* (1993) and the TV series "Traps" (1994). His son Campbell Scott, from a marriage to actress Colleen Dewhurst, is also an actor.

SCOTT, LIZABETH. Actress. *(b. Sept. 29, 1922, Scranton, Pa., as Emma Matzo.)* She slithered onto movie screens, this smoldering blonde with the husky voice, in the mid 1940s, making a name for herself in the era's burgeoning film noir genre, playing tarnished, world-weary pseudo-heroines, cruel and cynical femmes fatales, and—occasionally—susceptible innocents pursued by dangerous men. A former model and veteran of stage and stock, Scott was discovered by producer Hal Wallis and assigned a leading role in her first film, *You Came Along* (1945). She supported Barbara Stanwyck and debuting Kirk Douglas in *The Strange Love of Martha Ivers* (1946), but came into her own in *Dead Reckoning* (1947, opposite Humphrey Bogart in a Bacall-like role), *Desert Fury, I Walk Alone* (two 1947 films teaming her with Burt Lancaster), *The Pitfall* (1948), *Too Late for Tears, Easy Living* (both 1949, excellent in the latter as a grasping wife but nearly overshadowed by Lucille Ball as a sympathetic secretary), *Paid in Full, Dark City* (both 1950), *The Company She Keeps* (1951), *The Racket* (also 1951, memorable as gangster Robert Ryan's moll), *Stolen Face* (1952), *Scared Stiff* (1953, an attractive foil for Dean Martin and Jerry Lewis in this haunted-house comedy), and *Bad for Each Other* (1953), among others. She played the shrewd publicist who promoted small-town boy Elvis Presley into a singing star in *Loving You* (1957), her last film for mentor Wallis, which also signaled the virtual end of her career. Aside from a lead in *Pulp* (1972), an interesting throwback that played on her appeal as a *noir* icon, Scott has taken no other film roles.

SCOTT, MARTHA. Actress. *(b. Sept. 22, 1914, Jamesport, Mo.)* This talented actress, a stage performer who captivated jaded Broadway theatergoers with her sensitive portrayal of Emily Webb in the original production of Thornton Wilder's "Our Town," fared reasonably well onscreen, impressing movie audiences with her natural warmth and sincerity instead of affecting the glamour-girl artificiality that was de rigueur in the 1940s. She reprised her stage characterization in the 1940 film adaptation of *Our Town* (her screen debut), earning an Academy Award nomination. Scott, a product of the American heartland, drew upon her own environment and life experience for her roles in *Cheers for Miss Bishop* (1941, as a small-town spinster schoolteacher who devotes her entire life to her pupils) and *One Foot in Heaven* (also 1941, as the faithful wife of preacher Fredric March).

After taking a cameo in *Stage Door Canteen* and costarring with John Wayne in an oil-field actioner, *In Old Oklahoma* (both 1943), she left the screen for several years, returning in the British-made *So Well Remembered* (1947), uncharacteristically harsh as the blindly ambitious wife of newspaper editor John Mills. *Strange Bargain* (1949) starred Scott as the wife of a bookkeeper (Jeffrey Lynn), falsely accused of murder; interestingly, they reprised the roles in a sequel that aired as an episode of the TV series "Murder, She Wrote" in 1987. Long active in theater, she has spearheaded stage troupes with such colleagues as Henry Fonda, and remained active in television as well, appearing occasionally on the 1970s "The Bob Newhart Show" as Bob's mom. She is married to musician and composer Mel Powell.

OTHER FILMS INCLUDE: 1940: *The Howards of Virginia;* 1943: *Hi Diddle Diddle;* 1951: *When I Grow Up;* 1955: *The Desperate Hours;* 1956: *The Ten Commandments;* 1957: *Sayonara;* 1959: *Ben-Hur* (as Miriam); 1974: *Airport 1975;* 1977: *The Turning Point;* 1988: *Doin' Time on Planet Earth.*

SCOTT, RANDOLPH. Actor, producer. *(b. Jan. 23, 1903, Orange County, Va., as Randolph Crane; d. Mar. 3, 1987.)* Few stars—even the legendary John Wayne—have been so closely identified with one genre as Randolph Scott was with the Western. Tall, ruggedly handsome, with blond (or light brown) hair and piercing blue eyes, he typifies the Hollywood cowboy star for many film buffs, having managed to bend the genre's clichés to his own purposes, especially in the modestly budgeted, often gritty Westerns he coproduced and starred in during the 1950s. A graduate of the University of North Carolina and Georgia Tech, where he studied engineering, Scott developed a love for the stage that took him west. He had been acting with the Pasadena Playhouse troupe when a chance meeting with millionaire and dilettante filmmaker Howard Hughes got him an introduction at Fox, where he made his debut in *The Far Call* (1929).

Scott's mellow voice, Southern accent and all, was well suited to talkies, and he took supporting roles in *Women Men Marry, Sky Bride* (both 1931), and *A Successful Calumity* (1932) before signing with Paramount. He played easygoing romantic leads in such programmers as *Hot Saturday, Hello Everybody!* (both 1932), *Murders in the Zoo, Supernatural, Cocktail Hour,* and *Broken Dreams* (all 1933), and assumed starring roles in the studio's extensive series of B Westerns based on Zane Grey novels. Scott went through the familiar horse-opera paces in *Wild Horse Mesa* (1932), *Heritage of the Desert, To the Last Man, Man of the Forest, The Thundering Herd, Sunset Pass* (all 1933), *Wagon Wheels, The Last Roundup* (both 1934), *Home on the Range,* and *Rocky Mountain Mystery* (both 1935).

At RKO, he costarred with Fred Astaire and Ginger Rogers in *Roberta* (1935) and *Follow the Fleet* (1936), uttering the word "swell" more times than anyone could count, and played intrepid adventurer Leo Vincey in Merian C. Cooper's lavish remake of *She* (1935), the H. Rider Haggard adventure classic. These appearances, as well as his starring turn as Hawkeye in Edward Small's production of *The Last of the Mohicans* (also 1936), took Scott out of B Westerns and elevated him to real stardom.

Scott worked opposite Mae West in *Go West, Young Man* (also 1936), Irene Dunne in *High, Wide and Handsome* (1937, an overblown Jerome Kern-Oscar Hammerstein period musical), and Shirley Temple in *Rebecca of Sunnybrook Farm* (1938) and *Susannah of the Mounties* (1939). He supported Tyrone Power and Henry Fonda in *Jesse James* (1939), and starred in the seldom-revived *Frontier Marshal* (also 1939) as Wyatt Earp. Still

most popular in Westerns, albeit more spectacular ones—such as *Virginia City, When the Daltons Rode* (both 1940), *Western Union,* and *Belle Starr* (both 1941). Scott also played military men in *Coast Guard* (1939), *To the Shores of Tripoli* (1942), *Bombardier, Corvette K-225,* and *Gung Ho!* (all 1943). He was amusingly cast as a stolid hunk with Irene Dunne in *My Favorite Wife* (1940), then teamed with John Wayne and Marlene Dietrich for two 1942 action dramas, *The Spoilers* and *Pittsburgh;* he played a heel in the first and a nice guy in the second—but didn't get Dietrich in either.

After an ill-advised stint in a lame swashbuckler, *Captain Kidd* (1945), and his turn in a delightful comedy-mystery, *Home, Sweet Homicide* (1946), Scott returned to the range for the remainder of his career, in vehicles that, at first, seemed interchangeable: *Abilene Town, Badman's Territory* (both 1946), *Trail Street, Gunfighters* (both 1947), *Albuquerque, Coroner Creek, Return of the Badmen* (all 1948), *The Walking Hills, Canadian Pacific, The Doolins of Oklahoma* (all 1949), *The Nevadan, Colt .45, Cariboo Trail* (all 1950), *Sugarfoot, Santa Fe,* and *Fort Worth* (all 1951).

Beginning with *Man in the Saddle* (1951), Scott worked almost exclusively in Westerns produced by his own company, Ranown, in which he was partnered with veteran producer Harry Joe Brown. Throughout the 1950s, this team produced many of the finest medium-budgeted Westerns ever made. Scott was still in top physical condition, but his face had become weary and weatherbeaten; this physical aspect, combined with his deliberate characterizations of soft-spoken, fatalistic, yet supremely self-reliant protagonists (the word "hero" doesn't apply to all his characters during this period), brought a new dimension to Scott's performances that, sadly, has been much ignored until recent years. *Carson City, Hangman's Knot* (both 1952), *Man Behind the Gun, The Stranger Wore a Gun, Thunder Over the Plains* (all 1953), *Riding Shotgun, The Bounty Hunter* (both 1954), *Ten Wanted Men, Rage at Dawn, Tall Man Riding, A Lawless Street* (all 1955), *Seven Men From Now, Seventh Cavalry* (both 1956), *The Tall T, Shootout at Medicine Bend, Decision at Sundown* (all 1957), *Buchanan Rides Alone* (1958), *Ride Lonesome, West-*

bound (both 1959), and *Comanche Station*
(1960) are astonishingly consistent in
quality, more "adult" than most Westerns
but still up to par in the action quotient
expected by the genre's devotees. The best
of the lot were written by Burt Kennedy
and directed by Budd Boetticher.

Scott's final film was, arguably, one of
his greatest: *Ride the High Country* (1962,
directed by Sam Peckinpah) teamed him
with old friend and fellow horse-opera favorite Joel McCrea in a touching, elegiac
tale of aged gunfighters, now on opposite
sides of the law, reunited in one last adventure. For Scott, approaching 60, it was
an altogether fitting vehicle with which to
end his screen career. An immensely
wealthy man (whom coworkers remember
reading "The Wall Street Journal" between scenes) thanks to his investments in
real estate, oil development, and the stock
market, Scott lived out the remainder of
his days in peaceful retirement.

SCOTT, RIDLEY. Director. *(b. Nov. 30,
1937, Northumberland, England.)* Successful
British director whose artistic signature is
an elaborate visual style, developed
through years of experience as set designer and director of TV commercials.
Scott studied art and film at the Royal
College of Art in London before landing
work as a set designer for the BBC. In the
mid 1960s he began directing BBC TV
shows, but soon left to pursue a freelance
career, helming hundreds of commercials
before his first feature in 1977, *The
Duellists.* This pet project was critically
noted as a sumptuous visual feast, and although it appealed primarily to a small
cult following, it was enough to earn the
director a shot at helming the graphic sci-
fi/horror film *Alien* in 1979. It was an exceptionally good vehicle to display Scott's
visual talents, albeit to the exclusion of
plot and character development. The same
charges were leveled against the director
and his next picture, the elaborate *Blade
Runner* (1982), in which he created a
bleak, futuristic Los Angeles that served
as the inspiration for a generation of
cyberpunk literature, music, and art. This
science fiction opus has built a devoted
following over the years, even though
Scott complained that his original vision
was subverted by studio tampering. (In
1993 he finally got the opportunity to re-

lease a "director's cut" of the picture,
which won even stronger reviews than it
received a decade earlier.) Another elaborate fantasy saga, *Legend* (1985), fizzled
badly. For his next film, Scott moved to
entirely different turf, but the first-rate romantic thriller *Someone to Watch Over Me*
(1987) failed to find much of an audience.
Black Rain (1989), a cop thriller set in Japan, reinforced his reputation as a visual
stylist with its recurring images of neon
and smoke. Continually accused of favoring style over content and character,
Scott then piloted *Thelma & Louise*
(1991), a feminist take on the buddy-
movie genre whose title characters were
the talk of the country the summer it was
released. The film also earned him his
first Oscar nomination as Best Director.
Since then he has directed the lumbering
saga of Christopher Columbus, *1492:
Conquest of Paradise* (1992) and produced the remake of *The Browning Version* (1994).

SCOTT, ZACHARY. Actor. *(b. Feb. 24,
1914, Austin, Tex.; d. Oct. 3, 1965.)* The appearance of this slender, shifty-eyed,
moustachioed performer almost invariably
signaled the perpetration of expert screen
villainy in films of the 1940s and 1950s.
A restless youth who dropped out of college and sailed to England, where he initially took up acting, Scott eventually
made his way to Broadway and enjoyed
some success there. He was signed by
Warner Bros. in 1944, making his tyro
screen appearance that year in *The Mask
of Dimitrios* (playing the enigmatic title
character). He was loaned to producer-
director Jean Renoir to play a tenacious
sharecropper in *The Southerner* (1945,
taking the starring role refused by Joel
McCrea), and was extremely effective in a
heroic part. Back at Warners, though, he
mostly played smooth, ruthless heavies—
like Joan Crawford's indolent husband in
Mildred Pierce (1945).

By the mid 1950s, Scott's career had
slumped, and he spent the last decade of
his life in second-rate movies. A theater
center in his hometown of Austin, Texas,
bears his name, and there are two chairs
endowed by his family at the University
of Texas–Austin Theater Department.
OTHER FILMS INCLUDE: 1945: *Danger
Signal;* 1946: *Her Kind of Man;* 1947: *The*

Unfaithful, Stallion Road, Cass Timberlaine;
1948: *Ruthless* (starring as an ambitious heel
for director Edgar G. Ulmer), *Whiplash;*
1949: *Flaxy Martin, South of St. Louis, Flamingo Road;* 1950: *Guilty Bystander* (starring
as seedy detective Max Thursday in this
modest but effective *noir), Colt .45, Born to
Be Bad, Pretty Baby;* 1951: *Lightning Strikes
Twice, Let's Make It Legal;* 1952: *Wings of
Danger;* 1953: *Appointment in Honduras;*
1955: *Flame of the Islands;* 1956: *Bandido;*
1960: *Man in the Shadow, The Young One* (a
Mexican film directed by Luis Buñuel);
1962: *It's Only Money.*

SEAGAL, STEVEN. Actor, writer. *(b.
Apr. 10, 1951, Detroit.)* It's easy to recognize this scowling martial arts star by his
squinty eyes, trademark ponytail, and re-
ceding hairline. Reportedly a self-made
aikido champ in Japan, Seagal returned to
America to teach martial arts to the rich
and famous. One of his pupils was powerful agent Michael Ovitz, who, perhaps to
test a theory that he could make anyone a
movie star, engineered a deal for the unknown to coproduce, cowrite, and star in
Above the Law (1988). Its success has led
to other formulaic action vehicles with
three-word titles: *Hard to Kill, Marked for
Death* (both 1990), *Out for Justice* (1991).
In his early pictures he invariably played a
cop "with an attitude" who had to go a little over the line of accepted police proce-
dure in order to "take out the garbage."
Under Siege (1992), a surprise hit that extended beyond his core audience, cast him
as a former Navy SEAL turned aircraft-
carrier cook. Its great success enabled
him to direct as well as star in *On Deadly
Ground* (1994). Seagal, who gives ego-
drenched interviews, enjoys making
cryptic references to his shadowy past,
indicating a former association with the
CIA which investigative journalists have
questioned. He was married to actress/
model Kelly LeBrock.

SEBERG, JEAN. Actress. *(b. Nov. 13,
1938, Marshalltown, Iowa; d. Sept. 8, 1979.)*
It should have been a great American success story: Small-town girl wins the leading role in a major motion picture and
rockets to overnight stardom. Anyway,
part of it's true. Seberg was an Iowa University student who longed to be a movie

star, tried out for and won the lead (beating out a reported 18,000 applicants) in
Otto Preminger's *Saint Joan* (1957). The
attendant publicity was voluminous, but
the picture flopped. She got a more colorful, and disturbing, role as the manipulative teenage temptress in Preminger's
Bonjour Tristesse (1958), and followed
that with a lead in Jean-Luc Godard's
seminal New Wave picture, *Breathless*
(1959). Petite and pert, the elfin Seberg
projected definite star quality, but the
public—at least, the *American* public—
wasn't buying. She remained in Europe
and enjoyed a moderately successful film
career there, including two films with
Claude Chabrol, *La Ligne de démarcation*
(1966) and *The Road to Corinth* (1967),
returning to the U.S. during the late
1960s. Back in Paris, Seberg, who was
married to director François Moreuil and
novelist-cum-filmmaker Romain Gary,
was found dead under mysterious circumstances. It was later suggested that the unstable, emotionally fragile characters she
sometimes played (most effectively in
1964's *Lilith)* might have reflected more
of the offscreen Seberg than audiences
could have suspected.
OTHER FILMS INCLUDE: 1959: *The Mouse
That Roared;* 1960: *Let No Man Write My
Epitaph;* 1962: *Playtime;* 1966: *A Fine Madness, Moment to Moment;* 1969: *Paint Your
Wagon, Pendulum;* 1970: *Airport, Macho
Callahan;* 1976: *The Wild Duck.*

SEGAL, GEORGE. Actor. *(b. Feb. 13,
1934, Great Neck, N.Y.)* Like it or not,
many moviegoers will always remember
George Segal as the repressed attorney
whose senile mom (played by Ruth Gordon) pulls down his pants and kisses his
tushie in *Where's Poppa?* (1970). This amiable, wavy-haired leading man is equally
at home in drama and comedy, although
he's more often seen in the latter. Originally a stage actor and musician (he plays
a mean banjo), Segal appeared in several
nondescript films in the early 1960s before raising eyebrows in 1965 as a distraught newlywed in *Ship of Fools* and as
a P.O.W. in *King Rat.* He followed with
top performances as Nick in *Who's Afraid
of Virginia Woolf?* (1966, for which he
was Oscar-nominated), a Cagneyesque
gangster in *The St. Valentine's Day Massacre* (1967), perplexed police detective

Mo Brummel in *No Way to Treat a Lady* (1968), a bookworm in *The Owl and the Pussycat* (1970), and in a pair of impressive dramatic performances, a man laying waste to his marriage in *Loving* (1970) and a hairdresser turned junkie in *Born to Win* (1971). He was an inept burglar in *The Hot Rock* (1972), a comically unfaithful husband in *A Touch of Class,* a midlife crisis victim in *Blume in Love* (both 1973), a suburbanite-turned-bank-robber in *Fun With Dick and Jane* (1977), and a faux gourmet in *Who Is Killing the Great Chefs of Europe?* (1978). Segal was so appealing that too often he was asked to carry a film on his charm alone, especially in the 1970s. His *Maltese Falcon* spoof, *The Black Bird* (1975), was a major disappointment, while *Lost and Found* (1979) reunited him with *Touch of Class* costar Glenda Jackson with no discernible sparks. He was relatively inactive in the 1980s, but bounced back as the sleazy father of Kirstie Alley's baby in *Look Who's Talking* (1989, and in the 1993 sequel *Look Who's Talking Now*), and as the left-wing comedy writer in *For the Boys* (1991), as well as the long-suffering insurance investigator in the short-lived TV series "Murphy's Law" (1988–89).
OTHER FILMS INCLUDE: 1961: *The Young Doctors;* 1963: *Act One;* 1964: *Invitation to a Gunfighter;* 1966: *Lost Command, The Quiller Memorandum;* 1968: *Bye Bye Braverman, The Girl Who Couldn't Say No;* 1969: *The Southern Star, The Bridge at Remagen;* 1974: *The Terminal Man, California Split;* 1975: *Russian Roulette;* 1976: *The Duchess and the Dirtwater Fox;* 1977: *Rollercoaster;* 1980: *The Last Married Couple in America;* 1981: *Carbon Copy;* 1985: *Stick;* 1989: *All's Fair.*

cluding *Myra Breckinridge* (1970), *The Seven Minutes* (1971), *Daughters of Satan* (1972), *Terminal Island* (1973), *Midway* (1976), and *Coma* (1978), Selleck spent much of the 1970s in episodic TV and telefilms, among which the Louis L'Amour Western sagas *The Sacketts* (1979) and *The Shadow Riders* (1982) showed him off to best advantage.

After winning fame (and an Emmy) as private detective Thomas Magnum on TV, Selleck renewed his bid for big-screen stardom—having had to turn down Steven Spielberg's offer to play Indiana Jones because of his series schedule—with three duds in a row: *High Road to China* (1983, as a 1930s aviator), *Lassiter* (1984, as a 1940s cat-burglar), and the futuristic cop thriller *Runaway* (also 1984). As one of the carefree bachelors in *3 Men and a Baby* (1987), Selleck finally got a bona fide box office hit. But *Her Alibi* and *An Innocent Man* (both 1989) moved him back to square one.

The inevitable sequel, *3 Men and a Little Lady* (1990), scored Selleck another hit, but that year's *Quigley Down Under,* an offbeat "Western" set in Australia, was the biggest disappointment of all: a first-rate film with a first-rate performance from Selleck that barely found an audience (until its release on video). The actor took plenty of lumps in three 1992 releases: *Folks!,* in which he's terrorized (and brutalized) by parents Don Ameche and Anne Jackson, *Christopher Columbus—The Discovery,* in which he was miscast as King Ferdinand (!), and the pleasant but routine *Mr. Baseball,* as an American ballplayer "exiled" to a Japanese team.

SELLECK, TOM. Actor. *(b. Jan. 29, 1945, Detroit.)* True, enduring big-screen stardom still eludes this likable leading man who seems to have everything going for him: ruggedly handsome features, a massive frame, obvious athletic ability, and genuine charm. But the strong identification with a particular TV role—as the lighthearted "Magnum, P.I." (1980–88)—and an unfortunate choice of movie vehicles (trying, perhaps too hard, to be as different from the Magnum character as possible) have worked against him. A former model who played handsome hunks in most of his early films, in-

SELLERS, PETER. Actor. *(b. Sept. 8, 1925, Southsea, England, as Richard Henry Sellers; d. July 24, 1980.)* Notwithstanding the devilishly assured grin that he flashed in candid photographs, Peter Sellers was an extremely ordinary-looking fellow. What was *extraordinary* about him was his ability to mold those plain features into any number of comedic countenances, a talent that enabled him to create many memorable characters in the movies in which he appeared. Spending his late teens in the RAF as part of a camp entertainment troupe, the talented young Sellers worked with legendary British comic

Spike Milligan on the BBC's popular "The Goon Show." With an uncanny gift for mimicry, he became a prolific voice dubber (and reportedly looped some lines for Humphrey Bogart in 1954's *Beat the Devil*), then started to work on-screen as well, notably in *The Ladykillers* (1955, with Alec Guinness), *Your Past Is Showing* (1957, in multiple roles; original British title, *The Naked Truth*), *The Smallest Show on Earth* (1957, as a befuddled old movie projectionist), and *tom thumb* (1958, teamed with Terry-Thomas for some buffoonish villainy). In 1959 he won the British equivalent of the Oscar for his performance as a labor leader in *I'm All Right Jack*, starred in Richard Lester's very funny short-subject *The Running, Jumping, and Standing-Still Film*, then showed off his versatility by playing three roles in the hilarious satire *The Mouse That Roared*. Multiple role-playing is an honored tradition among British comic actors, and Sellers apotheosized that tradition while simultaneously bringing it up to date on the big screen. His one-role-only turns of the early 1960s are rather colorless compared with his multifaceted Clare Quilty in Stanley Kubrick's *Lolita* (1962). The director was reportedly so taken with Sellers' abilities that he kept expanding the movie's scenario to accommodate them, and he subsequently had Sellers play a milquetoast U.S. president, a pragmatic British soldier, and a mutant German scientist in *Dr. Strangelove or: How I Learned to Stop Worrying and Love the Bomb* (1964, an Oscar-nominated performance).

After Kubrick, the director with whom Sellers fared best was Blake Edwards, for whom he played the indefatigably inept French detective Inspector Clouseau in the Pink Panther series (beginning with 1964's *The Pink Panther* and encompassing six films featuring Sellers, the last of which, 1982's *Trail of the Pink Panther*, Edwards assembled out of previously unseen footage). He was also memorable as a luckless Indian actor in Edwards' slapstick gagfest *The Party* (1968). When not in Edwards' movies, Sellers spent the late 1960s and early 1970s in faux-hip films of varying success, including *What's New, Pussycat?* (1965) and the James Bond spoof *Casino Royale* (1967). In 1979 he fulfilled a longtime ambition by playing Chauncey Gardener, a human tab-

ula rasa, in the film adaptation of Jerzy Kosinski's novel *Being There;* the role won Sellers a great deal of acclaim from critics and audiences alike, and an Oscar nomination. It was a welcome return to form for Sellers, who'd been squandering his talent of late in a string of (mostly) awful films on both sides of the Atlantic. Unfortunately, this turned out to be something of a last hurrah; long troubled by a weakened heart, he died the following year. Married four times, Sellers was once wed to actress Britt Ekland, with whom he worked in *The Bobo* (1967).

OTHER FILMS INCLUDE: 1960: *The Millionairess;* 1961: *Mr. Topaze;* 1962: *Waltz of the Toreadors, The Wrong Arm of the Law;* 1963: *Heavens Above!;* 1964: *A Shot in the Dark, The World of Henry Orient;* 1966: *After the Fox;* 1968: *I Love You, Alice B. Toklas;* 1969: *The Magic Christian;* 1970: *Hoffman, There's a Girl in My Soup;* 1972: *Alice's Adventures in Wonderland, Where Does It Hurt?;* 1973: *The Blockhouse, Ghost in the Noonday Sun, The Optimists;* 1974: *The Great McGonagall* (as Queen Victoria); 1975: *Undercovers Hero, The Return of the Pink Panther;* 1976: *The Pink Panther Strikes Again, Murder by Death* (as a Charlie Chan type); 1978: *Revenge of the Pink Panther;* 1979: *The Prisoner of Zenda;* 1980: *The Fiendish Plot of Dr. Fu Manchu.*

SENNETT, MACK. Producer, director. (b. Jan. 17, 1880, Danville, Quebec, as Michael Sinnott; d. Nov. 5, 1960.) The man whose name became synonymous with slapstick comedy in the silent-film era came from the humblest of beginnings. In fact, it was his background—as a rough-hewn "have-not"—that formed his style of knockabout comedy. An aspiring singer, he moved to New York and landed occasional jobs on the stage before going to work at the Biograph film company in 1908 and ingratiating himself with D. W. Griffith to the point where Griffith allowed (and encouraged) him to direct some films himself.

Backing from two dubious men, Kessel and Bauman, put Sennett in business for himself in 1912, and shortly thereafter he moved to California, with star comedian Ford Sterling, leading man Fred Mace, and girlfriend (and leading lady) Mabel Normand in tow. The newly formed Keystone company cranked out one-reel comedies at a steady clip, relying on stock situations (a stroll in the park, a jealous husband or wife, and so on), outsized behavior (kicking a rival in the pants was de rigueur), and natural locations, rather than carefully worked-out scripts. The saga of Sennett and his crew building a film around the real-life draining of a Los Angeles lake is absolutely true; the resulting comedy, *A Muddy Romance* (1913), features "production value" (and a level of comic messiness) that the penny-pinching producer never could have afforded otherwise.

Sennett's lifelong disdain for policemen found an ideal outlet in the phenomenally clumsy Keystone Kops, whose ranks included such performers as Edgar Kennedy, Mack Swain, and Slim Summerville. His weakness for pretty women inspired the scantily clad Mack Sennett Bathing Beauties, who never did much onscreen but got him lots of free publicity in newspapers and magazines. His studio became a magnet for an incredible-looking gallery of performers from the worlds of circus, music halls, and vaudeville—as well as a training ground for an entire generation of writers and directors who cut their teeth at this comedy factory, where resourcefulness was king. Among the graduates: Frank Capra, Malcolm St. Clair, Roy Del Ruth, Lloyd Bacon, William Beaudine, Erle C. Kenton, Eddie Cline, and Del Lord.

As early as 1914 Sennett experimented with a feature-length comedy. *Tillie's Punctured Romance* headlined the great stage star Marie Dressler (who had been kind to Sennett when he was starting out in show business), Mabel Normand, and Sennett's greatest discovery, Charlie Chaplin. But features were never his strong suit, though he made some good ones with Mabel Normand (1918's *Mickey*, 1921's *Molly O'*, 1923's *Suzanna* and *The Extra Girl*), Louise Fazenda (1920's *Down on the Farm*), and Ben Turpin (1921's *A Small Town Idol*, 1923's *The Shriek of Araby*).

Sennett's talent roster was astonishing, but so was his inability to keep that talent under his roof. Charlie Chaplin, his greatest discovery, moved on after just one year. So did Roscoe "Fatty" Arbuckle, Wallace Beery, Gloria Swanson, Charley Chase, Raymond Griffith, Harry Langdon, and Carole Lombard. Mabel Normand, the love of his life, left more than once, but came back to Sennett in the 1920s when her (innocent) involvement in the William Desmond Taylor murder scandal made her too "hot" for other studios to handle.

Sennett's own star dimmed with each passing year, though he continued to find talented (if workmanlike) comic performers, gagmen, and directors to fill out a yearly schedule of short subjects. By the sound era, Sennett's product was definitely grade-B material, though he continued to seek out and find new talent, including lighthearted crooner Bing Crosby, the inimitable W. C. Fields, who made four classic short subjects for Sennett in the early 1930s, and young comedienne Joan Davis, whom he directed in his final short subject, *Way Up Thar* (1935). Hal Roach had long since eclipsed Sennett as the uncrowned King of Comedy in Hollywood; Roach's talkie films were modern, well made, and extremely popular, while Sennett's looked cheap and tired by comparison. In 1935 Sennett was out of business; he went home to Canada, virtually penniless, but returned to Hollywood in the late 1930s, and became a living anachronism, a tangible reminder of the industry's pioneering days (which weren't so very distant). In 1937 he received an honorary Academy Award, and two years later his story was told, in fictional form, in *Hollywood Cavalcade*, with Don Ameche as the Sennett-esque character. He made guest appearances in films from time to time, playing himself (as in 1949's *Down Memory Lane* and 1955's *Abbott and Costello Meet the Keystone Cops*), but there was no call for his services. He wrote an entertaining, if fanciful, autobiography, "King of Comedy," in 1954. His name still evokes the freewheeling era of silent comedy filmmaking. He was portrayed by Dan Aykroyd in the 1992 biographical film *Chaplin*.

SEYMOUR, JANE. Actress. *(b. Feb. 15, 1951, Hillingdon, England, as Joyce Frankenberger.)* This beautiful British brunette may be a miniseries actress nonpareil, but she's yet to prove her viability as a compelling big-screen draw. In fact, she seems to have all but abandoned theatrical feature films. After debuting in Richard Attenborough's cumbersome, episodic *Oh! What a Lovely War* (1969), she took supporting roles in *The Only Way* (1970) and

Young Winston (1972), then won the female lead in *Frankenstein: The True Story*, a 1973 telefilm that got theatrical distribution in Europe. That same year American audiences noticed her as the fetching albeit strictly decorative heroine of *Live and Let Die*, the first James Bond adventure to star Roger Moore as 007. She donned eye-catching Arabian togs for *Sinbad and the Eye of the Tiger* (1977) and played second fiddle to Benji in *Oh, Heavenly Dog!* (1980) before starring opposite Christopher Reeve in a fantasy-laden tearjerker, *Somewhere in Time* (also 1980), an (inexplicably) fondly remembered film. Since the 1984 flop *Lassiter* (with Tom Selleck) she's appeared only a few times on the big screen (most notably, if that's the word, in 1986's *Head Office*). On TV, however, she's starred in innumerable well-received telefilms and miniseries, including *The Four Feathers* (1977), *The Pirate*, the feature version of *Battlestar: Galactica* (both 1979), "East of Eden" (1981), *The Phantom of the Opera* (1982), *The Scarlet Pimpernel* (1983), *The Sun Also Rises* (1984), *The Woman He Loved* (1988), and *Angel of Death* (1990). Her series "Dr. Quinn, Medicine Woman" debuted in 1993.

SHARIF, OMAR. Actor. *(b. Apr. 10, 1932, Alexandria, Egypt, as Michael Shalhoub.)* International film star whose exotic looks and soft-spoken manner made him something of a sex symbol for years, but also typecast him later in his career. Sharif studied mathematics and physics and worked in his family's lumber business before landing a part in an Egyptian film, beginning a career that would make him his country's top movie star. It was the part of T. E. Lawrence's friend Ali in David Lean's epic *Lawrence of Arabia* (1962) that won him worldwide fame and snagged him an Oscar nomination for Best Supporting Actor. He followed with Lean's *Doctor Zhivago* (1965, at his most charismatic in the title role), *More Than a Miracle* (1967), *Funny Girl* (1968, as the wayward husband of Fanny Brice, played by Barbra Streisand), *Mayerling* (1969), and *Che!* (also 1969, in the title role), but his romantic appeal had waned by the 1970s and after starring performances in *The Last Valley* (1971), *The Tamarind Seed*, and *Juggernaut* (both 1974), his

film appearances dwindled to supporting roles in such films as *The Pink Panther Strikes Again* (1976), and *Green Ice* (1981). (In 1984's *Top Secret!* he revealed a disarming willingness to poke fun at himself and play broad comedy.) He has worked in TV, appearing in telefilms and miniseries. Sharif is also known worldwide as an expert at bridge, a game he took up on the set of his first movie, after running out of between-scenes reading matter; he is the author of "Omar Sharif's Life in Bridge."
OTHER FILMS INCLUDE: 1953: *The Struggle in the Valley;* 1954: *Devil of the Desert;* 1955: *Land of Peace;* 1957: *Goha;* 1959: *Struggle on the Nile;* 1960: *The Agony of Love;* 1964: *Behold a Pale Horse, The Fall of the Roman Empire;* 1965: *Genghis Khan;* 1966: *The Poppy Is Also a Flower;* 1967: *The Night of the Generals;* 1969: *The Appointment, Mackenna's Gold;* 1971: *The Horsemen;* 1974: *The Mysterious Island of Captain Nemo;* 1975: *Funny Lady* (reprising his role as Nicky Arnstein); 1976: *Crime and Passion;* 1979: *Ashanti, Bloodline;* 1980: *The Baltimore Bullet, Oh, Heavenly Dog!;* 1992: *Mrs. 'Arris Goes to Paris* (telefilm).

SHARKEY, RAY. Actor. *(b. Nov. 14, 1952, Brooklyn, N.Y.; d. June 11, 1993.)* This slight, thin, intense actor guested on numerous TV series, such as "Kojak" and "Barney Miller" and "Police Story," often as greasy hoods, and first appeared on the big screen in 1976's *Trackdown.* After working in *Paradise Alley* and *Who'll Stop the Rain* (both 1978) he won plum roles in *Heart Beat* (1980, as a character patterned after Allen Ginsberg) and *Willie and Phil* (also 1980, as one corner of the love triangle involving Michael Ontkean and Margot Kidder). But it was his performance in the title role of *The Idolmaker* (also 1980), as a rock 'n' roll promoter, that made people predict major stardom for Sharkey. But the 1980s were a rocky decade for the actor, with creditable movies (1982's *Some Kind of Hero*) giving way to utter junk (1984's *Body Rock,* 1985's *Hellhole*). He returned to the mainstream in supporting roles in *No Mercy* and *Wise Guys* (both 1986), and on the TV series "Wiseguy" (1987–88 season). He continued to work in such films as *Scenes From the Class Struggle in Beverly Hills, Wired* (both 1989), *Dead On* (1991), and *Zebrahead* (1992), but by now it was no secret that he had a major problem with drugs that had dogged him throughout the 1980s. In 1992, he was arrested in Canada on drug-possession charges. Sharkey, a talented actor with too few films to prove his worth, died of AIDS.

SHATNER, WILLIAM. Actor. *(b. Mar. 22, 1931, Montreal.)* When Shatner was cast to play Captain James Kirk in the "Star Trek" TV show, his small-screen immortality was assured (even though no one knew it at the time). The solidly built, handsome actor had previously worked on Broadway and in live TV before making his movie debut as Alexei in *The Brothers Karamazov* (1958). Shatner alternated film appearances with episodic TV work; his other early features include *Judgment at Nuremberg* (1961), *The Outrage* (1964), and leading roles in *The Explosive Generation* and the barely seen *The Intruder* (both 1961), in which he delivered a mature, spine-chilling performance as a racist Southern agitator for director Roger Corman. The immediate post-"Trek" years brought Shatner few opportunities from the major studios, and by the mid 1970s he was toiling in *Big Bad Mama* (1974), *The Devil's Rain* (1975), *Kingdom of the Spiders* (1977), and *The Kidnapping of the President* (1980). Beginning with 1979's *Star Trek—The Motion Picture*, Shatner returned to the role he made famous on TV, and has appeared in the five big-budget sequels (even directing 1989's *Star Trek V: The Final Frontier).* He's shown an ability to spoof himself in *Airplane II: The Sequel* (1982) and *National Lampoon's Loaded Weapon I* (1993), but he's played it straight in his post-"Trek" TV series, "Barbary Coast" (1975–76), "T.J. Hooker" (1982–87), and "Rescue 911" (1989–   ). He published "Star Trek Memories" in 1993; and has written a series of science fiction novels called "Tekwar" which were adapted for TV in 1994. He costarred in the seventh Star Trek movie, *Star Trek Generations* (1994).

SHAVER, HELEN. Actress. *(b. Feb. 24, 1952, Ontario.)* Only 25 years old when tapped to play one of the praiseworthy subjects in 1978's *In Praise of Older Women* (for which she received glowing reviews), this striking actress hasn't been blessed with many similarly showy roles (though she was in one certified hit, 1979's *The Amityville Horror).* Other films include *Shoot* (1976), *Outrageous!, Starship Invasions, Who Has Seen the Wind* (all 1977), *High-Ballin'* (1978), *Harry Tracy, Desperado* (1982), *The Osterman Weekend* (1983), *The Land Before Time* (1988, voice only), and *Innocent Victim* (1989). Writer-producer Larry Gelbart cast her opposite Beau Bridges in his prestigious TV series "United States" (1980), but it met an early demise. (So did her solo dramatic series "Jessica Novak" in 1981.) Occasionally a good part, like that of a repressed teacher who discovers her true sexuality in *Desert Hearts* (1985), or a long-suffering, compassionate cohort to Paul Newman in *The Color of Money* (1986), has come along. But Shaver's been handed more than her share of colorless or thankless parts, including those in the comedy bomb *Best Defense* (1984) and the grisly horror vehicle *The Believers* (1987). Recently seen in *Dr. Bethune* (1989), *Zebrahead* (1992), *That Night,* and *Morning Glory* (both 1993) as well as a variety of TV movies.

SHAW, ROBERT. Actor, playwright, novelist. *(b. Aug. 9, 1927, Westhoughton, England; d. Aug. 27, 1978.)* Many American moviegoers best remember this burly Brit as Quint, the fatalistic, Ahab-like shark hunter in *Jaws* (1975), and while that was certainly a colorful characterization, it was just one of many he created over a quarter-century. The son of an alcoholic doctor, attracted to the dramatic arts at an early age, Shaw studied at England's Royal Academy of Dramatic Art before making his stage debut with a Shakespearean company in 1949. He had a small bit in *The Lavender Hill Mob* (1951), but first elicited attention in *The Dam Busters* (1954), and won a juvenile following as the star of the 1950s TV series "The Buccaneers." He subsequently appeared in *A Hill in Korea* (1956), and *Sea Fury* (1958), before chilling audiences as the blondined assassin trained to annihilate James Bond in *From Russia With Love* (both 1963). He starred with real-life wife Mary Ure in a low-key domestic drama, *The Luck of Ginger Coffey* (1964), worked opposite Donald Pleasence and Alan Bates in Harold Pinter's *The Guest* (also 1964; British title *The Caretaker*, like the original play), and costarred with Henry Fonda in the elaborate WW2 saga, *Battle of the Bulge* (1965), before winning the key supporting role of Henry VIII in the Academy Award-winning *A Man for All Seasons* (1966, an Oscar-nominated performance). Gruff, forceful, and charismatic, Shaw proved himself capable of playing good-natured slobs and heartless villains with equal facility.

He was improbably cast in the title role of *Custer of the West*, and also appeared in *The Birthday Party* (both 1968), *Royal Hunt of the Sun* (1969), *Battle of Britain*, *Figures in a Landscape* (both 1970), *A Town Called Hell* (1971), *Young Winston* (1972, as Lord Randolph Churchill), *A Reflection of Fear*, and *The Hireling* (both 1973) before bolstering his commerciality in a string of high-profile Hollywood films including *The Sting* (1973, playing the "mark" of Paul Newman and Robert Redford), *The Taking of Pelham One Two Three* (1974), *Diamonds, Jaws* (both 1975), *Robin and Marian* (1976, as the Sheriff of Nottingham), *Swashbuckler* (also 1976), *The Deep*, and *Black Sunday* (both 1977). *Force 10 From Navarone* (1978) and *Avalanche Express* (1979) were released posthumously, following Shaw's death from a heart attack. One of his novels, "The Hiding Place," served as the basis for the Alec Guinness–Robert Redford film *Situation Hopeless—But Not Serious* (1965). His play "The Man in the Glass Booth," dealing with Nazi war crimes, was filmed in 1975, but Shaw (who'd also starred in this arresting drama on stage) was displeased and demanded his credit be removed from the picture.

SHAWN, WALLACE. Actor, playwright, screenwriter. *(b. Nov. 12, 1943, New York City.)* Short, frazzle-haired character actor with blubbery lower lip and distinctive lisp, who frequently plays nervous, untrustworthy characters (usually for laughs). He's also a talented writer with several plays to his credit, as well as the script for *My Dinner With Andre* (1981), a partially autobiographical film he penned with costar Andre Gregory. The son of longtime "New Yorker" editor William Shawn, he made his stage debut in 1977 in a self-translated production of Machia-

velli's "The Mandrake," and broke into films two years later with supporting roles in Bob Fosse's *All That Jazz* and Woody Allen's *Manhattan*.
OTHER FILMS INCLUDE: 1979: *Starting Over;* 1980: *Atlantic City, Simon;* 1982: *The First Time, A Little Sex;* 1983: *Deal of the Century, Lovesick;* 1984: *The Bostonians, Crackers, The Hotel New Hampshire, Micki + Maude;* 1985: *Heaven Help Us;* 1986: *Head Office;* 1987: *The Bedroom Window, Nice Girls Don't Explode, Prick Up Your Ears, Radio Days, The Princess Bride* (a wonderful role as an unlikely fairy-tale villain); 1988: *The Moderns;* 1989: *Scenes From the Class Struggle in Beverly Hills, She's Out of Control, We're No Angels;* 1992: *Shadows and Fog, Mom and Dad Save the World;* 1993: *Unbecoming Age, The Cemetery Club, The Meteor Man.*

SHEARER, MOIRA. Actress, dancer. *(b. Jan. 26, 1926, Dunfermline, Scotland, as Moira King.)* She only made a handful of films, but no one who's ever seen her as the tragic ballerina of *The Red Shoes* (1948) will ever forget the beautiful, delicate Moira Shearer. A real-life ballerina who was an international star at age 16, this radiant redhead delivered an exquisite performance under the direction of Powell and Pressburger, who also starred her in their *Tales of Hoffman* (1951), a less successful but equally intriguing production. She also costarred in *The Story of Three Loves* (1953). Shearer's fiery hair made her an ideal subject for *The Man Who Loved Redheads* (1955), a charming comedy that proved she didn't have to dance to be an eminently watchable screen performer. Powell used her again in his controversial, disturbing thriller *Peeping Tom* (1960), the creepy story of a photographer who records his models' death throes; it has since been cited as having influenced many directors of contemporary horror films. Shearer contributed a lovely ballet sequence, built around Rostand's "Cyrano," to *Black Tights* (1960); shortly thereafter she married British novelist Ludovic Kennedy and retired from acting (although she did return to the stage during the 1970s).

SHEARER, NORMA. Actress. *(b. Aug. 10, 1900, Montreal, as Edith Norma Shearer; d. June 12, 1983.)* It would be easy (and more than a little cruel) to assert that Norma Shearer kept her job by marrying the boss. But MGM production chief Irving Thalberg couldn't have maintained Shearer's star status indefinitely if she hadn't been able to deliver the goods—and she did, time after time, in the vehicles he lovingly produced for her. A former child model who began her screen career in 1920's *The Flapper,* she was signed by Thalberg in 1923 after making a strong impression in *Lucretia Lombard.* He brought her to Metro (where he had recently set up shop after a stint at Universal) and groomed her for stardom, seeing that she got the best makeup, the smartest gowns, and the ablest cinematographers on the lot. (She had unconventional beauty and charm, but also had a pair of oddly focused eyes that had to be photographed just right.)

Shearer appeared in *He Who Gets Slapped* (1924), *Pretty Ladies, Tower of Lies* (both 1925), *The Devil's Circus, Upstage* (both 1926), Ernst Lubitsch's delightful *The Student Prince in Old Heidelberg* (1927), *A Lady of Chance,* and *The Latest From Paris* (both 1928), among other silent films. Thalberg married her in 1927, from which time she got preferential treatment, including first choice of hot properties bought for or developed by MGM. She made her talkie debut in *The Last of Mrs. Cheyney* (1929), and followed it up later that year with two better films, *The Trial of Mary Dugan* and *Their Own Desire* (for which she was Oscar-nominated).

Shearer won an Oscar for her starring performance in *The Divorcee* (1930), playing a tolerant young society wife who finally tires of her husband's indiscretions and decides to match them with her own. She snagged another nomination for her turn as the spoiled lawyer's daughter who falls for exonerated racketeer Clark Gable in *A Free Soul* (1931). That same year she appeared with frequent costar Robert Montgomery in the delightfully witty adaptation of Noël Coward's *Private Lives.* Thalberg guided Shearer's career choices, making sure she got the most sophisticated and elegant female parts MGM had to offer; he even took to buying established stage properties, such as *Strange Interlude* and *Smilin' Through* (both 1932), specifically for her.

The Barretts of Wimpole Street (1934), a literate, tasteful screen adaptation of the 19th-century romance between Elizabeth Barrett and Robert Browning, featured another Oscar-nominated Shearer performance, as did *Romeo and Juliet* (1936, opposite Leslie Howard) for which Shearer, who tried valiantly in the role, was far too old to be totally convincing.

Thalberg's untimely death in 1936 devastated Shearer, who nonetheless went ahead with the filming of *Marie Antoinette* (1938), the last project he had developed for her. She earned yet another nod from the Academy. In blond wig for her role in *Idiot's Delight* (1939), again opposite Clark Gable, she was annoyingly mannered and, for the first time, seemed ill at ease. *The Women* (1939) gave her a more down-to-earth characterization, which she carried off admirably. But her career was nearly over; after finishing *Escape* (1940), and a pair of duds, *Her Cardboard Lover* and *We Were Dancing* (both 1942), she retired from the screen. Left very well off by Thalberg, Shearer remarried happily and lived in contentment until mental problems plagued her in her final years. Her last contributions to movies were in the guise of talent scout: she spotted Janet Leigh's picture while vacationing at a ski resort and arranged for an MGM screen test in the late 1940s; then, in the 1950s, she spotted handsome garment center executive Robert Evans alongside a swimming pool, thought he bore a strong resemblance to her late husband, and suggested him to play Thalberg in the Lon Chaney biopic *Man of a Thousand Faces,* launching Evans' short-lived acting career. Her brother Douglas was MGM's Sound Department head for decades, winning 12 Oscars for achievement on individual pictures and developing many technical innovations now considered commonplace.

SHEEDY, ALLY. Actress. *(b. June 13, 1962, New York City.)* A Brat Packer made good, this spunky, attractive actress debuted as Sean Penn's girlfriend in *Bad Boys* (1983), was paired with Matthew Broderick in the hit *WarGames* that same year, and won major attention as the morbid nonconformist in *The Breakfast Club* (1985), before doing postgraduate work in the brat-pack-faces-life saga *St. Elmo's Fire* (1985). But her unpredictably uneven performances—ranging from vacuous Valley-speak renditions in *Short Circuit* and *Blue City* (both 1986) to endearing comic turns in *Maid to Order* (1987) and *Betsy's Wedding* (1990)—have kept critics on guard. The precocious Sheedy wrote a children's book at age 12 and published a more recent collection of confessional poetry. Other credits include *Oxford Blues* (1984), *Twice in a Lifetime* (1985), *Heart of Dixie* (1989), *Only the Lonely* (1991), *Home Alone 2: Lost in New York* (1992, a cameo) *Chantilly Lace* (1993 telefilm), *The Pickle* (1993, a cameo), and *Man's Best Friend* (also 1993).

SHEEN, CHARLIE. Actor. *(b. Sept. 3, 1965, Los Angeles, as Carlos Estevez.)* This dark-haired, broodingly handsome leading man has achieved a level of stardom that has eclipsed both his father, Martin Sheen, and his brother, Emilio Estevez. He seems to have escaped the stigma of Brat Packdom and earned a reputation as a solid talent. He made his youthful screen debut in the telefilm *The Execution of Private Slovik* (1974), which starred his dad (and also appeared in 1979's *Apocalypse Now* with his father) before launching his career in earnest with supporting roles in *Red Dawn* (1984) and *The Boys Next Door* (1985). His portrayal of a thoughtful high-school jock in *Lucas* opened some eyes, as did an amusing cameo in *Ferris Bueller's Day Off* (both 1986); he won star billing in *The Wraith* that same year, just before the release of Oliver Stone's harrowing Vietnam saga, *Platoon* (both also 1986), which cast him as a young soldier introduced to the horrors of war. Its surprise commercial success established Sheen as a young star on the rise.

His films since then—a mixed bag—include the youth saga *Three for the Road,* the cop drama *No Man's Land* (both 1987), *Wall Street* (1987, a prime part as an unprincipled yuppie aligned with ruthless tycoon Michael Douglas), *Young Guns* (1988, a successful Brat Pack Western with brother Emilio), *Eight Men Out* (1988, the first of two back-to-back baseball films), *Major League, Courage Mountain, Backtrack* (all 1989), *Navy SEALS* (1990), *Men at Work* (also 1990, an alleged comedy about garbagemen written and directed by his brother), *The Rookie* (1990, as Clint Eastwood's young

partner), *Cadence* (directed by his father), and *Hot Shots!* (both 1991), a silly but funny movie parody that led to a sequel, *Hot Shots! Part Deux* (1993). He also took a cameo in his brother's parody film *National Lampoon's Loaded Weapon I* (1993), and starred in *The Three Musketeers* (1993, as Aramis), *Deadfall, Major League II, Terminal Velocity,* and *The Chase* (all 1994).

SHEEN, MARTIN. Actor. *(b. Aug. 3, 1940, Dayton, Ohio, as Ramon Estevez.)* This earnest actor was hailed on Broadway in "The Subject Was Roses"; Sheen got to recreate his performance in the 1968 movie with costars Patricia Neal and Jack Albertson, but it wasn't until 1973 that he landed another comparably good movie role, as the disaffected killer in Terrence Malick's *Badlands.* Later that decade he won his most memorable part, as the Army man sent up-river to find (and assassinate) renegade officer Marlon Brando in Francis Ford Coppola's *Apocalypse Now* (1979). Sheen suffered a heart attack during the strenuous (and seemingly endless) filming in the Philippines, and later discussed the travail in the probing documentary *Hearts of Darkness: A Filmmaker's Apocalypse* (1991). With the distance of time, he was even able to poke fun at himself and the role in a gag appearance in his son Charlie's parody movie *Hot Shots! Part Deux* (1993).

A respected actor—if not quite a star—Sheen has had a sporadic screen career; among his better films are *Gandhi* (1982), *The Dead Zone* (1983, cast against type as a slimy politician), and *Da* (1988, which he also executive produced). Television has offered him far greater opportunities: as the convicted deserter in *The Execution of Private Slovik* (1974), as President John F. Kennedy in the miniseries "Kennedy" (1983), and as JFK's brother Robert in *The Missiles of October* (1974), to name just a few. In fact, he's been a prolific small-screen actor since 1961, and continues to appear in telefilms and miniseries, especially those that push his politically conscious buttons. (Sheen is an indefatigable activist for liberal causes who has been arrested many times at protest marches and sit-ins.)

His sons Emilio and Carlos (the latter better known as Charlie Sheen) and daughter Renee are also actors. Martin has appeared in Charlie's *Wall Street* (1987) and directed him in *Cadence* (1991), in which they both starred; Charlie's brother Ramon Estevez was also featured in the cast.

OTHER FILMS INCLUDE: 1967: *The Incident*; 1970: *Catch-22*; 1971: *No Drums, No Bugles*; 1972: *Rage, Pickup on 101*; 1976: *The Little Girl Who Lives Down the Lane*; 1977: *The Cassandra Crossing*; 1980: *The Final Countdown, Loophole*; 1982: *Enigma, That Championship Season*; 1983: *Man, Woman and Child*; 1984: *Firestarter*; 1985: *Broken Rainbow* (voice only); 1987: *The Believers, Siesta*; 1988: *Judgment in Berlin* (also executive-produced); 1989: *Beverly Hills Brats, Cold Front*; 1991: *The Maid, JFK* (voice only); 1992: *The Water Engine* (telefilm); 1993: *Hear No Evil, Gettysburg* (as Robert E. Lee).

SHEPARD, SAM. Actor, screenwriter, director, playwright. *(b. Nov. 5, 1943, Ft. Sheridan, Ill., as S. S. Rogers.)* While his rugged good looks, sinewy frame, and pleasant drawl seem to make this actor an all-American hero in the Gary Cooper mold, Shepard's background renders him something more than that. He is also a highly regarded playwright who won the Pulitzer Prize for his 1979 play "Buried Child." He was one of the writers on *Zabriskie Point* (1970), and later won critical acclaim for his original screenplay *Paris, Texas* (1984). As an actor, he made his film debut in Bob Dylan's pretentious *Renaldo and Clara* (1978), but turned heads in a series of considerably more interesting pictures to follow, most of which cast him as the "strong, silent type": *Days of Heaven* (1978), *Resurrection* (1980), *Raggedy Man* (1981), *Frances* (1982, his first with longtime partner Jessica Lange), and especially *The Right Stuff* (1983), for which he earned an Oscar nomination playing fabled test pilot Chuck Yeager. He reteamed with Lange in *Country* (1984) and *Crimes of the Heart* (1986), and played the lead in Robert Altman's adaptation of his play *Fool for Love* (1985). People who remembered him performing his rock 'n' roll play "Cowboy Mouth" with cowriter Patti Smith may have had a hard time reconciling that image of Shepard with the genial leading man opposite Diane Keaton in *Baby Boom* (1987) or

Dolly Parton in *Steel Magnolias* (1989), or the quiet but determined police detectives he played in *Defenseless* (1991) and *Thunderheart* (1992), but the actor/writer has had no problem wearing more than one hat comfortably. He was also well cast in *Bright Angel* (1991), in Volker Schlondorff's provocative *Voyager* (1991, as the title character) and as the self-destructive law professor (and Julia Roberts' lover) in *The Pelican Brief* (1993). Shepard made an inauspicious directing debut with *Far North* (1988, starring Lange) and more recently tackled a Western, *Silent Tongue* (1994).

SHEPHERD, CYBILL. Actress. *(b. Feb. 18, 1950, Memphis, Tenn.)* Beautiful, patrician blond actress who, after a career as a model (beginning in her teens) was spotted on a magazine cover by director Peter Bogdanovich and cast as the town tease in his landmark film, *The Last Picture Show* (1971). She found another ideal role the following year, as the "ultimate shiksa" in *The Heartbreak Kid* (1972), but Bogdanovich's infatuation with her caused him to star her in movies that were beyond her reach—the costume drama *Daisy Miller* (1974) and the elephantine musical *At Long Last Love* (1975)—which nearly spelled an end to both their careers. She acquitted herself well in Martin Scorsese's *Taxi Driver* (1976), but after a series of flops, including *Special Delivery* (1976), *Silver Bears* (1978), and an embarrassing remake of Hitchcock's *The Lady Vanishes* (1979), she left show business and moved back to Tennessee. In 1983 she tested for and won the leading role in a short-lived Western TV series, "The Yellow Rose," revealing a worldliness she'd never projected before onscreen. On the strength of that work, she was signed for the lead in the lighthearted comedy-mystery series "Moonlighting" (1985–89), her best vehicle to date. She's appeared since then in a handful of theatrical films, including the underrated romantic comedy *Chances Are* (1989), *Texasville* (1990, a sequel to *The Last Picture Show*), *Alice* (1990), and *Married to It* (1993), but has fared better on TV, where she's starred in such telefilms as *Memphis* (1992), which she also cowrote and executive-produced, and the aptly named sitcom "Cybill" (1995–).

SHERIDAN, ANN. Actress. *(b. Feb. 21, 1915, Denton, Tex., as Clara Lou Sheridan; d. Jan. 21, 1967.)* An irresistibly likable actress, Ann Sheridan was promoted to stardom as "The 'Oomph' Girl," which might have made good copy for fan-magazine scribes but didn't help her get the kind of parts she deserved. A former beauty-contest winner who came to Hollywood in Paramount's 1933 "search for beauty," she made her film debut in a 1934 film of the same name. Billed under her real name, she played bits in *Come On, Marines, The Lemon Drop Kid, Ladies Should Listen, Murder at the Vanities, Bolero, Shoot the Works, Kiss and Make Up, College Rhythm* (all 1934), *Rumba, Enter Madame,* and *Home on the Range* (all 1935) before finally landing her first leading role, billed as Ann Sheridan, in *Rocky Mountain Mystery* (1935), a Western-set whodunit.

Paramount kept her busy throughout 1935, but mostly in supporting roles. After appearing in *Behold My Wife, The Glass Key, Mississippi, Car 99,* and *The Crusades,* she left the studio, working in a Poverty Row Western quickie, *The Red Blood of Courage,* before winding up at Warner Bros. She had supporting roles in *Black Legion* and *Sing Me a Love Song* (both 1936), and became a leading lady in *The Great O'Malley* (1937), which starred Pat O'Brien and Humphrey Bogart.

Warners put Sheridan into a succession of mostly B pictures such as *Footloose Heiress, San Quentin* (both 1937), *The Cowboy From Brooklyn, She Loved a Fireman, Little Miss Thoroughbred,* and *Broadway Musketeers* (all 1938). Then director Michael Curtiz gave her the role of a strong-minded slum girl in his gangster drama *Angels With Dirty Faces* (also 1938), the success of which earned Sheridan better roles in bigger pictures: She was loaned out for *Winter Carnival* (1939), and made a strong impression in *They Made Me a Criminal, Dodge City* (both 1939), *Torrid Zone* (showing she had a way with a wisecrack), *It All Came True* ("selling" a couple of popular songs with verve and style), *Castle on the Hudson, City for Conquest,* the crackling *They Drive by Night (all* 1940!), *Navy Blues, Honeymoon for Three* (both 1941), and *The Man Who Came to Dinner* (also 1941, displaying a flair for farce as a haughty actress in this Kaufman and Hart gem).

Sheridan delivered her best performance up to that time (and possibly the best of her career) as Randy Monoghan, the loyal small-town girl of *Kings Row* (1942), Warners' elaborate adaptation of Henry Bellamann's best-selling novel. She won excellent reviews in the role, and Warners responded by putting her in other big-budget films, including *Juke Girl, George Washington Slept Here* (both also 1942), *Thank Your Lucky Stars, Edge of Darkness* (both 1943), *The Doughgirls, Shine On, Harvest Moon* (both 1944), *One More Tomorrow* (1946), *Nora Prentiss, The Unfaithful* (both 1947), and *Silver River* (1948). She left the studio after making an unbilled guest appearance in *The Treasure of the Sierra Madre* (also 1948). As a freelance player, the always-appealing Sheridan starred or costarred in *Good Sam* (1948), *I Was a Male War Bride* (1949), *Stella, Woman on the Run* (both 1950), *Steel Town, Just Across the Street* (both 1952), the charming *Take Me to Town, Appointment in Honduras* (both 1953), the underrated *Come Next Spring, The Opposite Sex* (both 1956), and *Woman and the Hunter* (1957). She worked several years in stock before turning to TV, where she starred in the daytime soap opera "Another World" (1965–66) and the sitcom "Pistols and Petticoats" (1966–67) before dying from cancer. Her first two husbands were actors Edward Norris (1936–39) and George Brent (1942–43).

SHERIDAN, JIM. Director, screenwriter, producer. *(b. Feb. 6, 1949, Dublin.)* Successful stage director and playwright who won kudos for his first film, *My Left Foot* (1989), the rousing story of artist-writer Christy Brown, which earned Oscars for stars Daniel Day-Lewis and Brenda Fricker, and nominations for Best Picture, Director, and Screenplay. For several years, Sheridan was artistic director of Dublin's fringe theater the Project Arts Center. He left for New York in 1982 (after controversy over a play called "The Gay Sweat Shop"), took over the New York Irish Arts Center and studied filmmaking at New York University. After *My Left Foot,* Sheridan directed and adapted *The Field* (1990, from John B. Keane's play), a drama of Greek-tragedy proportions, wrote the dour Irish fable *Into the West* (1993) and teamed up again with Day-Lewis for *In the Name of the Father* (1993), the intense, true-life story of a wrongly imprisoned man. Sheridan won Oscar nominations for Best Director, Screenplay (as cowriter), and Best Picture (as producer).

SHERMAN, VINCENT. Director, screenwriter, actor. *(b. July 16, 1906, Vienna, Ga.)* One of the stalwart stable of directors at Warner Bros., Sherman flourished under the studio system, successfully steering such stars as Bette Davis, Errol Flynn, John Garfield, and Joan Crawford. He started out as an actor himself, and is memorable as the young anarchist who explodes at John Barrymore in *Counselor-at-Law* (1933), a part he'd also played on Broadway. He drifted away from acting after several years and became a screenwriter, then director under contract to Warners, where his films included *The Return of Dr. X* (1939), *Saturday's Children, The Man Who Talked Too Much* (both 1940), *Flight From Destiny, Underground* (both 1941), *All Through the Night, The Hard Way* (both 1942), *Old Acquaintance* (1943), *In Our Time, Mr. Skeffington* (both 1944), *Pillow to Post* (1945), *Janie Gets Married* (1946), *Nora Prentiss, The Unfaithful* (both 1947), *The Adventures of Don Juan* (1949), *The Hasty Heart, The Damned Don't Cry, Harriet Craig, Backfire* (all 1950), *Goodbye, My Fancy* (1951), *Lone Star,* and *Affair in Trinidad* (both 1952). His feature output dwindled in the 1950s, as he busied himself on television; he also made one feature in Italy. His later films (including several for Warners) include *The Garment Jungle* (1957), *The Naked Earth* (1958), *The Young Philadelphians* (1959), *Ice Palace* (1960), *A Fever in the Blood* (1961), *The Second Time Around* (1961) and *Cervantes* (1967; aka *The Young Rebel).* Sherman remained active in series television right through the 1970s, and even produced and directed a pilot for a series starring Shirley Temple that never sold.

SHIELDS, BROOKE. Actress. *(b. May 31, 1965, New York City.)* Former child model (since the age of 1) "discovered" for movies by director Louis Malle, who cast her as a barely pubescent prostitute in his *Pretty Baby* (1978). Although Malle (and Shields' zealous stage mother, Teri Shields) claimed that Brooke's nude scenes were handled tastefully, a naked 13-year-old was a bit daunting for many fundamentalist and anti-pornography groups, who caused much commotion and generated free publicity with their protests. Shields (whose first movie had actually been 1977's *Alice, Sweet Alice)* worked feverishly over the next couple of years, appearing in *King of the Gypsies, Tilt* (both 1978), *Wanda Nevada, Just You and Me, Kid* (both 1979), *Endless Love* (1981) and, most visibly, in the execrable *The Blue Lagoon* (1980), a tale of two young children, stranded on a desert island, who discover love and sex (without parental guidance).

Although she was by that time one of the biggest celebrities in America, Shields took a four-year sabbatical from pictures to attend Princeton. Her subsequent films have been, for the most part, ghastly, and while Shields is a lovely young woman who tries very hard, she's never become much of an actress. Other credits include *Sahara* (1984), *The Muppets Take Manhattan* (1984, cameo), *Wet Gold* (1984 telefilm), *Speed Zone!* (1989, cameo), *Backstreet Dreams* (1990), and *Brenda Starr* (1992, filmed in 1986).

SHIRE, TALIA. Actress. *(b. Apr. 25, 1946, Jamaica, N.Y., as Talia Rose Coppola.)* Small, dark, mousy actress best known for two continuing characterizations: the faithful wife of prizefighter Sylvester Stallone in the "Rocky" series, and the volatile daughter of Mafioso Marlon Brando in the *Godfather* series directed by her brother, Francis Ford Coppola. After making her screen debut in *Gas-s-s-s* (1970), Talia (who married composer David Shire and took his surname) played Connie Corleone in *The Godfather* (1972) and *The Godfather, Part II* (1974), snagging an Oscar nomination for the latter interpretation of the character. She picked up a second nomination for her first turn as Adrian in *Rocky* (1976). Both characters matured over the course of their respective series. After five films—*Rocky* (1976), *Rocky II* (1979), *Rocky III* (1982), *Rocky IV* (1985), *Rocky V* (1990)—Rocky's wife doesn't suffer in silence anymore, and Connie Corleone took an active role in "family" business in *The*

Godfather, Part III (1990). Her other films include *Old Boyfriends, Prophecy* (both 1979), *Windows* (1980), *Rad* (1986), *New York Stories* (1989, in the Coppola segment), *Bed and Breakfast* (1992), *Chantilly Lace* (1993, telefilm), *Deadfall* (also 1993), and *Parallel Lives* (1994, telefilm). She also coproduced *Lionheart* (1987).

SHIRLEY, ANNE. Actress. *(b. Apr. 17, 1918, New York City, as Dawn Eveleen Paris; d. July 4, 1993.)* This appealing, wholesomely pretty actress was on stage at the age of fourteen months, with a "stage mother" promoting her budding career as an actress and child model. She won her first film role at the age of five, billed as Dawn O'Day, and worked steadily through childhood, in everything from Tom Mix's *Riders of the Purple Sage* (1925) to some of Walt Disney's *Alice* comedies in which she cavorted against a cartoon backdrop. In the early 1930s she had featured roles in such films as *So Big, Three on a Match* (both 1932), and *Rasputin and the Empress* (also 1932, as young Anastasia). Then in 1934 she was ideally cast as Anne Shirley, the plucky heroine of *Anne of Green Gables,* and thereafter took the Lucy Maude Montgomery character's name as her own. As a winsome teenager, she won more prominent roles in such films as *Steamboat 'Round the Bend* (1935), *Make Way for a Lady* (1936), and *Stella Dallas* (1937), for which she won an Oscar nomination playing Barbara Stanwyck's daughter. RKO put her under contract, but wasted her talent in a good many mediocre films, but she shone in *Mother Carey's Chickens, A Man to Remember* (both 1938), *Vigil in the Night,* the *Green Gables* sequel *Anne of Windy Poplars* (both 1940), and *The Devil and Daniel Webster* (1941; aka *All That Money Can Buy).* Among her films as leading lady: *The Mayor of 44th Street, The Powers Girl* (both 1942), *Lady Bodyguard, Government Girl* (1943), and *Music in Manhattan* (1944). Ironically, her most unusual role was also her last, as Claire Trevor's stepdaughter in *Murder, My Sweet* (1944), after which she retired, having worked from the time she was in a cradle. Married first to actor John Payne, she then wed RKO producer Adrian Scott, and after their divorce in 1949 married screenwriter Charles Lederer; they re-mained together until his death in 1976. Her daughter by Payne is actress Julie Payne.

SHORT, MARTIN. Actor. *(b. Mar. 26, 1950, Hamilton, Canada.)* The man who gave the world Ed Grimley and Jackie Rogers, Jr., has yet to achieve in his big-screen work the prominence he enjoyed as one of TV's brightest lights. The tightly wound comedic performer, whose expressive face and body enable him to change himself, chameleonlike, into any one of a dozen characters, is a native-born Canadian who initially wowed audiences as one of the "SCTV" comedy troupe. Short's self-created original characters, spot-on impersonations of real-life personalities (from Jerry Lewis to Katharine Hepburn), improvisational skills, and flair for physical comedy won him a berth on "Saturday Night Live" (1984–85 season) before director John Landis paired him with Steve Martin and Chevy Chase in the cowboy-hero spoof *¡Three Amigos!* (1986). (He'd already debuted on-screen in 1979's *Lost and Found.)* Short was a nebbishy, reluctant hero in *Innerspace* (1987), then toplined his first romantic comedy, *Cross My Heart* (also 1987). The farcical *Three Fugitives* (1989) was a misfire, as was the pratfall-laden *Pure Luck* (1991, in which he played the world's unluckiest man), and *Captain Ron* (1992), in which he played it straight and Kurt Russell went for the laughs! Short's supporting roles, however, have been hilarious, indicating that this may be his ideal movie niche. He was uproarious as a wigged-out Hollywood agent in *The Big Picture* (1989) and as a flamboyant wedding planner with an impenetrable accent in *Father of the Bride* (1991). He provided a voice for *We're Back! A Dinosaur's Story* (1993) and played a ten-year-old boy in *Clifford* (1994). His Ultimate Nerd character from TV skits was also featured in the animated TV series "The Completely Mental Misadventures of Ed Grimley" (1988–89).

SHUE, ELISABETH. Actress. *(b. June 10, 1963, Wilmington, Del.)* If her hyperkinetic lip-synching of "And Then He Kissed Me," performed under the opening credits of *Adventures in Babysitting* (1987), is the most memorable thing this wholesome, girl-next-door-pretty blonde has yet contributed to the screen, it's hardly her fault. Her effective supporting turns in *The Marrying Man* and *Soapdish* (both 1991) suggest she has a barely tapped reservoir of comedic skill. To date she's taken a backseat to many of her male costars: She was Ralph Macchio's romantic interest in *The Karate Kid* (1984), Tom Cruise's in *Cocktail* (1988), and Michael J. Fox's in *Back to the Future Part II* (1989) and *Part III* (1990). Even more embarrassingly, she was up-staged by a lust-crazed chimp in *Link* (1986)! Other credits include *Heart and Souls* and *Twenty Bucks* (both 1993).

SHYER, CHARLES and MEYERS, NANCY. Director-producer team, cowriters. *(Shyer—b. Oct. 11, 1941, Los Angeles. Meyers—b. Dec. 8, 1949, Philadelphia.)* This husband-and-wife team has enjoyed great popular success with a series of smart contemporary comedies. Shyer was born into the film industry, attended UCLA, and worked behind the scenes as an assistant director and production manager before focusing on writing. He enjoyed his first success on television, where he became head writer on the terrific "The Odd Couple" series in the 1970s. He then shared screenplay credit on the smash hit *Smokey and the Bandit* (1977), Jack Nicholson's *Goin' South* (1978), and *House Calls* (also 1978). When he met Meyers she was working as a story editor for producer Ray Stark and had just made a connection with fellow American University alumna Goldie Hawn. Together with Harvey Miller they wrote *Private Benjamin* (1980) as a vehicle for Hawn; it earned them an Oscar nomination, and its box-office success enabled them to make a deal to write, direct, and produce *Irreconcilable Differences* (1984), which featured Ryan O'Neal as a young man who—like Shyer—is a diehard old-movie buff who winds up making films himself. Since then they've continued to share writing chores, with Shyer directing and Meyers producing *Baby Boom* (1987, and its short-lived TV series spinoff), *Father of the Bride* (1991), *I Love Trouble* (1994), and a *Father of the Bride* sequel. They

also wrote but did not direct or produce *Once Upon a Crime* (1992).

SIDARIS, ANDREW ("Andy" W.) Director, producer, writer. *(b. Feb. 20, 1932, Chicago.)* While not a "woman's director" in the same vein as George Cukor, few filmmakers today are better than Sidaris when it comes to getting half-nude bimbos to say a line like "Let's hit the jacuzzi!" with real meaning. Sidaris specializes in making bikini-packed "t&a" adventure films on exotic locales; they're not pornographic, just titillating, and they've found a substantial audience, mostly on video. Casting centerfolds in leading roles became a Sidaris trademark in *Malibu Express* (1985), *Hard Ticket to Hawaii* (1987), and *Picasso Trigger* (1989), which included a record seven former "Playboy" Playmates. Other Sidaris titles (produced for the most part by his wife Arlene) include *Stacey* (1973), *Seven* (1979), *Savage Beach* (1989), *Do or Die* (1991), *Hard Hunted* (1992), and *Fit to Kill* (1993).

Sidaris spent more than 20 years as a top director at ABC Sports, winning numerous Emmys along the way. He also did episodic TV, and staged the hilarious football sequence in Robert Altman's *MASH* (1970).

SIDNEY, GEORGE. Director, producer. *(b. Oct. 4, 1916, New York City.)* Born to a show business family, this onetime child actor joined MGM in the early 1930s and apprenticed in a variety of jobs. He graduated from directing screen tests to filming short subjects (including Our Gang) and won Oscars for *Quicker 'n a Wink* (1940, a Pete Smith short) and *Of Pups and Puzzles* (1941, part of "John Nesbitt's Passing Parade"). He made his feature debut with *Free and Easy* (1941) and soon became a musical specialist, directing *Bathing Beauty* (1944), *Anchors Aweigh* (1945), *The Harvey Girls* (1946), *Annie Get Your Gun* (1950), and his two best, *Show Boat* (1951) and *Kiss Me Kate* (1953). He left MGM in 1956 to produce and direct at Columbia, amassing an impressive track record before retiring in the late 1960s to pursue other interests.

OTHER FILMS INCLUDE: 1943: *Thousands Cheer;* 1948: *The Three Musketeers;* 1950: *Key to the City;* 1952: *Scaramouche;* 1953:

Young Bess; 1956: *Jeanne Eagels;* 1957: *Pal Joey;* 1960: *Who Was That Lady?,* Pepe; 1961: *Bye Bye Birdie;* 1963: *Viva Las Vegas;* 1964: *The Swinger;* 1968: *Half a Sixpence.*

SIDNEY, SYLVIA. Actress. *(b. Aug. 8, 1910, Bronx, N.Y., as Sophia Kosow.)* Petite and pretty, with round face, plaintive eyes and melancholy demeanor, she played more lower-class working girls than any other actress in Hollywood during the Depression. Among her vivid portraits: Roberta Alden in *An American Tragedy,* Rose Maurrant in *Street Scene* (both 1931), the title role in *Jennie Gerhardt* (1933), and Drina in *Dead End* (1937). Looking back at that period, she has said, "I was paid by the tear." Enrolling in the New York-based Theatre Guild School while still in her teens, she made her stage debut in 1926 and broke into movies three years later in the courtroom drama *Thru Different Eyes* (1929).

Sidney made most of her 1930s films—including *City Streets, Confessions of a Co-Ed* (both 1931), *Madame Butterfly, Ladies of the Big House, The Miracle Man, Merrily We Go to Hell* (all 1932), *Pick-up* (1933), *Good Dame, Thirty Day Princess, Behold My Wife* (all 1934), *Accent on Youth, Mary Burns, Fugitive* (both 1935), *Trail of the Lonesome Pine, A Woman Alone* (both 1936), and . . . *One Third of a Nation* (1939)—at Paramount, where her longtime benefactor (and lover) was executive B. P. Schulberg. She journeyed to England to make *Sabotage* for Alfred Hitchcock in 1936, and worked for Fritz Lang three times, as the fatalistic heroines in *Fury* (1936), *You Only Live Once* (1937), and *You and Me* (1938).

Although she occasionally tackled other types of parts (including the mountain girl in *Lonesome Pine* and a dual role in the lighthearted *Princess),* Sidney came to resent her typecasting and left movies for the stage, making only one film—*The Wagons Roll at Night* (1941)—during the WW2 years. A comeback attempt, beginning with *Blood on the Sun* (1945), and continuing with *The Searching Wind, Mr. Ace* (both 1946), and *Love From a Stranger* (1947), failed to reestablish her with moviegoers. After another five-year absence from the screen, she played Fantine in the 1952 movie adaptation of *Les Miserables,* beginning a second career as a character actress of great distinction. Since then she's been seen to good advantage in *Violent Saturday* (1955), *Behind the High Wall* (1956), *Summer Wishes, Winter Dreams* (1973, in an Oscar-nominated performance as Joanne Woodward's mother), *Demon* (1977, aka *God Told Me To), I Never Promised You a Rose Garden* (1977), *Damien—Omen II* (1978), *Hammett* (1982), *Finnegan Begin Again* (1985, a made-for-cable telefilm), *Beetlejuice* (1988, very funny as a businesslike case worker from the netherworld), *The Exorcist III* (1990), and as Jessica Tandy's best friend in *Used People* (1992).

Sidney's many TV credits include the highly praised AIDS drama *An Early Frost* (1985), in which she was Aidan Quinn's grandmother. She was married to editor-publisher Bennett Cerf and actor-teacher Luther Adler.

SIEGEL, DON. Director, producer. *(b. Oct. 26, 1912, Chicago; d. Apr. 20, 1991.)* One of the darlings of France's *auteur*-minded cineastes of the 1960s, this director was both stylish and innovative, although making a specialty of straightforward action films inhibited praise from stateside critics, who tended to dismiss him as a journeyman craftsman of potboilers. Educated at Cambridge, and trained in acting at London's Royal Academy of Dramatic Art, Siegel turned to film work in the early 1930s following an unimpressive period as a performer. He began as an editor at Warner Bros., specializing in unusual montage sequences that graced such films as *Blues in the Night* (1941) and *Casablanca* (1942).

Siegel graduated to directing with two 1945 shorts, *Star in the Night* and *Hitler Lives?;* he hit the jackpot when both won Oscars. That led to his first features: a clever locked-room mystery, *The Verdict* (1946), and a soap opera, *Night Unto Night* (1949, starring his then-wife Viveca Lindfors). Siegel left Warners and spent the next two decades piloting mostly minor-league films in a spare, straightforward style that made the most of his material (and meager budgets), among them *The Big Steal* (1949), *China Venture* (1953), *Private Hell 36, Riot in Cell Block 11* (both 1954), *Crime in the Streets* (1956), *Baby Face Nelson* (1957), *The Lineup* (1958), *Flaming Star* (1960, with one of Elvis Presley's best performances), and *Hell Is for Heroes* (1962). Siegel's best-remembered film of this period is the sci-fi classic *Invasion of the Body Snatchers* (1956), which in spite of two remakes no one has yet surpassed for understated eeriness. (Siegel took an amusing cameo as a cab driver in Philip Kaufman's 1978 retread.)

The director wound up at Universal in the mid 1960s, and made a handful of exceptionally good "little" films for television, including *The Killers* (1964, which was so good it was released theatrically), *The Hanged Man* (also 1964), and *Stranger on the Run* (1967). This led to theatrical assignments like the crime drama *Madigan* and the Clint Eastwood vehicle *Coogan's Bluff* (both 1968). The latter was not only a hit but a congenial experience for star and director; Siegel and Eastwood subsequently collaborated on four more films, *Two Mules for Sister Sara* (1970), their mutual favorite, the daring and unusual *The Beguiled* (1971), the smash hit *Dirty Harry* (1971), and *Escape From Alcatraz* (1979). When Eastwood decided to try directing, he asked Siegel to act (as a bartender) in his debut feature, *Play Misty for Me* (1971).

Siegel continued to ply his craft in such films as *Death of a Gunfighter* (1969, which he took over from Robert Totten and refused to take credit for), the crackerjack caper yarn *Charley Varrick* (1973), *The Black Windmill* (1974), John Wayne's valedictory film, *The Shootist* (1976), and the ingenious thriller *Telefon* (1977). Siegel's last two films, *Rough Cut* (1980) and *Jinxed!* (1982), were plagued by production problems and he decided to retire. He was feted at film festivals around the world, where his work was hailed for its startling directness, its refusal to pander to convention, and its brilliant camerawork and editing. His autobiography, "A Siegel Film," was published posthumously in 1993, with a foreword by his friend and protégé Clint Eastwood.

SIEMASZKO, CASEY. Actor. *(b. Mar. 17, 1961, Chicago.)* Siemaszko began his acting career in a Polish community theater before graduating from Chicago's Goodman School of Drama and making his film debut in the Chicago-filmed comedy *Class* (1983). He went on to play sup-

porting roles in *Back to the Future, Secret Admirer* (both 1985), *Stand By Me* (1986), and *Gardens of Stone* (1987) before winning his first lead as the terrorized high school student in *Three O'Clock High* (1987). He has also appeared in *Biloxi Blues,* the youth Western *Young Guns* (both 1988), and *Back to the Future Part II* (1989), as well as a pair of lesser titles released direct to video, *The Big Slice* (1990) and *Near Misses* (1991). He was particularly memorable as Burt Reynolds' partner in crime in *Breaking In* (1989) and as Curley in *Of Mice and Men* (1992). Recent credits include *My Life's in Turnaround* (1993). His sister Nina Siemaszko is also an actress who has appeared in such films as *Bed and Breakfast, Wild Orchid 2: Two Shades of Blue* (both 1992), and *Airheads* (1994), and played Mia Farrow in the TV miniseries "Sinatra" (1992).

SIGNORET, SIMONE. Actress. *(b. Mar. 25, 1921, Wiesbaden, Germany, as Simone Kaminker; d. Sept. 30, 1985.)* The thinking man's sex symbol for most of the 1950s, slinky, almond-eyed Signoret wowed viewers in the delicious romantic comedy *La Ronde* (1950), as the mistress in the tricky French thriller *Diabolique* (1955), and the spurned girlfriend in the crackling British drama *Room at the Top* (1959, for which she won a Best Actress Oscar). She married French superstar Yves Montand in 1951, and the celebrated couple socialized with the era's French intellectual elite (including Jean Paul Sartre, who adapted Arthur Miller's *The Crucible* for a 1957 film starring the two). In the late 1950s, Americans marveled at Signoret's nonchalant "European" attitude toward her husband's affair with American sex symbol Marilyn Monroe (the couple remained married till Signoret's death). As Signoret fleshed out in the 1960s, she welcomed mature roles, such as the celebrated one she had in *Ship of Fools* (1965, Oscar-nominated). In 1967 she appeared in *Games,* Curtis Harrington's chilly American homage to *Diabolique.* By the 1970s her looks had dissipated; Signoret philosophically turned it to her advantage, taking the role of a weary madam who looks after the children of hookers in the international hit *Madame Rosa* (1977). Her 1978 autobiog-

raphy, "Nostalgia Isn't What It Used to Be," was extremely well received. She continued working in French films through 1983.
OTHER FILMS INCLUDE: 1948: *Against the Wind;* 1953: *Thérèse Raquin;* 1956: *Evil Eden;* 1962: *Term of Trial;* 1963: *The Day and the Hour;* 1965: *The Sleeping Car Murder* (with Montand); 1966: *Is Paris Burning?;* 1967: *The Deadly Affair;* 1968: *The Sea Gull;* 1970: *The Confession* (with Montand); 1971: *Le Chat;* 1979: *L'Adolescente;* 1981: *I Sent a Letter to My Love;* 1982: *L'Etoile du nord.*

SILVER, JOAN MICKLIN. Director, screenwriter. *(b. May 24, 1935, Omaha, Nebr.)* Notable director who began writing scripts for educational film companies before cowriting the screenplay for the Vietnam-wives movie *Limbo* (1972) and making her directing debut with *Hester Street* (1975), a lovely, evocative story about Jewish immigrants in turn-of-the-century New York. Silver's husband released the film himself, and it earned critical acclaim and even some commercial success. She followed with the excellent *Between the Lines* (1977, about an underground newspaper) and the quirky *Head Over Heels* (1979, reissued as *Chilly Scenes of Winter),* but did not direct again until *Crossing Delancey* (1988), a charming opposites-attract love story, which remains her most popular film to date. She has since directed two distressingly formulaic pictures, *Loverboy* (1989), and *Big Girls Don't Cry . . . They Get Even* (1992). She also directed the charming TV movies *Bernice Bobs Her Hair* (1976) and *Finnegan Begin Again* (1985).

SILVER, RON. Actor. *(b. July 2, 1946, New York City.)* Dynamic, versatile character lead who was once a busy sitcom actor, notably on "Rhoda" (1976–78) and his own short-lived series, "Baker's Dozen" (1982). After an inauspicious screen debut in *Tunnelvision* (1976), Silver scored with hilarious supporting roles in *Best Friends* (1982) as a yuppie Hollywood executive, and *Lovesick* (1983) as an Al Pacino-like actor. The following year he had the lead in *Garbo Talks,* but found greater success on Broadway, where he won a Tony Award starring in David Mamet's "Speed-the-Plow" (1988). More

film roles followed: the leading role of a Jewish immigrant wearily juggling three women in *Enemies, A Love Story* (1989, one of his best), a blacklisted writer in *Fellow Traveler* (1989), a dapper serial killer in *Blue Steel,* and his spot-on impersonation of attorney Alan Dershowitz in *Reversal of Fortune* (both 1990). His other credits include *Semi-Tough* (1977), *The Entity, Silent Rage* (both 1982), *The Goodbye People, Oh, God! You Devil* (both 1984), *Mr. Saturday Night* (1992), *Married to It* (1993), and *Timecop* (1994). He also has many television credits, and played Jerry Lewis' estranged son in a memorable multi-episode story on "Wiseguy" (1988–89 season). In 1993 he directed the TV movie *Lifepod,* in which he also appeared. Silver, a highly visible member of the arts community, is also a forceful and outspoken advocate of liberal causes.

SILVERMAN, JONATHAN. Actor. *(b. Aug. 5, 1966, Los Angeles.)* Genial young lead who came to prominence playing Neil Simon's alter ego, Eugene Jerome, in *Brighton Beach Memoirs* (1986). Silverman had played the part on Broadway and subsequently appeared in Simon's followup plays, "Biloxi Blues" and "Broadway Bound," recreating his part in the TV-movie adaptation of the latter. Silverman debuted onscreen in *Girls Just Want to Have Fun* (1985) and has appeared in *Caddyshack II, Stealing Home* (both 1988), *Class Action* (1991), *Breaking the Rules, Death Becomes Her* and the telefilm *For Richer, For Poorer* (all 1992), although he is probably best known as the hapless insurance executive who—along with Andrew McCarthy—must contend with a corpse in *Weekend at Bernie's* (1989) and the inevitable *Weekend at Bernie's II* (1993). Silverman was a regular on the TV sitcom "Gimme a Break!" from 1984 to 1986.

SILVERS, PHIL. Actor. *(b. May 11, 1912, Brooklyn, N.Y.; d. Nov. 1, 1985.)* The ingratiating fraud with a pearly smile, a slap on the back, and a "glad-ta-see-ya" was in the American tradition of lovable con men like the real-life P. T. Barnum and the reel-life W. C. Fields. The title song from Phil Silvers' 1951 Broadway hit "Top Banana," which in part declared, "If you wanna be the Top Banana, you gotta start from the bottom of the bunch," might have been the star's personal anthem. Starting as a child in vaudeville, by 1934 Silvers was toiling in Minsky's Burlesque. The ritualistic humor of the classic burlesque routines offered first-class training in comic performance and timing. Eventually, he was brought to Hollywood. (He used to tell a hilarious story about being contracted by MGM, which didn't know what to do with him; at one point, they had him test for the role of a vicar in *Pride and Prejudice!*) So indecisive were studio heads about his place in the scheme of things that within one year's time he had the costarring role with Jimmy Durante in one film (*You're in the Army Now*, 1941) and a nearly unnoticeable bit part in another at the same studio (*All Through the Night*, 1942). He landed small, but often funny, roles in such films as *Hit Parade of 1941* (1940), *Lady Be Good, Tom, Dick and Harry* (both 1941), *Roxie Hart, My Gal Sal, Footlight Serenade* (all 1942), *Coney Island*, and *A Lady Takes a Chance* (both 1943). Gradually, the size (if not the quality) of his parts increased; he got one of his best opportunities alongside Rita Hayworth and Gene Kelly in *Cover Girl* (1944). Other films include *Something for the Boys, Four Jills in a Jeep* (both 1944), *Diamond Horseshoe, A Thousand and One Nights, Don Juan Quilligan* (all 1945), *If I'm Lucky* (1946), *Summer Stock* (1950), and *Lucky Me* (1954).

Even Silvers' first forays into television were not great successes. Ironically, "Top Banana," the Broadway show he headlined, was about a burlesque comic who became a TV star; it was filmed, in an odd stagebound manner, in 1953. Silvers finally came into his own as Master Sergeant Ernie Bilko, con man extraordinaire, in Nat Hiken's "You'll Never Get Rich" (1954–59, aka "The Phil Silvers Show"). The series was a gem, and Silvers was brilliant in the role he was born to play; it earned him two Emmy Awards and made him, finally, a star. Later TV efforts were simply also-rans, but he occasionally found opportunities on-screen, most of them Bilko-esque, in such films as *It's a Mad Mad Mad Mad World* (1963), *A Funny Thing Happened on the Way to the Forum* (1966), *A Guide for the Married Man* (1967), *Buona Sera, Mrs. Campbell* (1968), and *The Boatniks* (1970). A stroke

left him with slightly slurred speech and made it hard to enjoy him in *The Strongest Man in the World* (1975), *Won Ton Ton, the Dog Who Saved Hollywood* (1976), *The Chicken Chronicles* (1977), and *The Cheap Detective* (1978). His daughter Cathy Silvers was an actress on the TV sitcom "Happy Days." His 1973 autobiography is titled "This Laugh Is on Me."

SIM, ALASTAIR. Actor. *(b. Oct. 9, 1900, Edinburgh; d. Aug. 19, 1976.)* If he'd never played any character other than Scrooge in the 1951 *A Christmas Carol* (surely the definitive screen version of that oft-filmed Dickens tale), this lanky, pop-eyed, rubber-faced character actor would rate a spot in this book. A former elocution teacher (not surprising, considering the precision of that deliciously rich voice), Sim worked on stage in Britain during the 1930s before appearing in his first film, *The Case of Gabriel Perry,* in 1935. Very busy on-screen from that time on, most often in supporting, comedic roles, he stole scenes right and left, in films like *Gangway, The Squeaker* (both 1937), *Sailing Along, Alf's Button Afloat, This Man Is News* (all 1938), *Inspector Hornleigh,* and *Inspector Hornleigh on Holiday* (both 1939, as a comic sidekick to the leading character). He achieved star status in the postwar period; *Green for Danger* (1946), one of the classiest whodunits ever made, starred Sim as Inspector Cockrill, a saucy detective who very nearly bungles a murder investigation. He played a frazzled headmaster of a prep school in *The Happiest Days of Your Life,* Jane Wyman's father in Hitchcock's *Stage Fright* (both 1950), a girl's school headmistress (!) *and* her brother in *The Belles of St. Trinian's* (1954, and a 1957 sequel, *Blue Murder at St. Trinian's),* another detective, albeit one with a strange secret, in *An Inspector Calls* (1954), and a laughable clergyman in *The Ruling Class* (1972), among many others. He remained active on stage throughout his life.

OTHER FILMS INCLUDE: 1941: *Cottage to Let;* 1944: *Waterloo Road;* 1947: *Hue and Cry;* 1951: *Laughter in Paradise;* 1952: *Folly to Be Wise;* 1953: *Innocents in Paris;* 1956: *Wee Geordie;* 1958: *The Doctor's Dilemma;* 1959: *Left, Right and Centre;* 1960: *School for Scoundrels, The Millionairess;* 1961: *The Anat-*

omist; 1975: Royal Flash; 1977: The Littlest Horse Thieves.

SIMMONS, JEAN. Actress. *(b. Jan. 31, 1929, London.)* The precipitous and somewhat curious decline of this demure beauty's career—in the 1960s, when she was at the peak of her talents and still alluring—was a blow to her admirers on both sides of the Atlantic. A teenaged dance student plucked from her school to play Margaret Lockwood's precocious sister in *Give Us the Moon* (1944), the winsome, dark-haired Simmons instantly enchanted British audiences. She remained in films and made a name for herself in such major British productions as *Caesar and Cleopatra* (1946), *Great Expectations* (also 1946, as the spoiled, selfish Estella), *Black Narcissus* (also 1946, as a sultry native beauty), *Hamlet* (1948, playing Ophelia to Laurence Olivier's great Dane and earning a Best Supporting Actress Oscar nomination), *The Blue Lagoon* (1949), and *So Long at the Fair* (1950), among others.

Simmons married screen star Stewart Granger in 1950 and went with him to Hollywood, where she signed first with Howard Hughes and then with 20th Century-Fox. In short order she was toplining such major films as *Androcles and the Lion* (1952), *Angel Face, Affair With a Stranger, The Actress* (playing a young Ruth Gordon), *Young Bess* (as Queen Elizabeth I), *The Robe* (all 1953), *The Egyptian, Demetrius and the Gladiators, Desiree* (all 1954), *Guys and Dolls* (1955, in one of her best-remembered roles, as Sarah Brown, costarring with Frank Sinatra and Marlon Brando), *Hilda Crane* (1956), *Until They Sail* (1957), *The Big Country* (1958), and *This Earth Is Mine* (1959).

Simmons divorced Granger in 1960, and almost immediately married writer-director Richard Brooks, who cast her as Sister Sharon opposite Burt Lancaster in *Elmer Gantry* (1960), a memorable adaptation of the Sinclair Lewis novel. That same year she costarred with Kirk Douglas in Stanley Kubrick's *Spartacus* and played a would-be home-wrecker opposite Cary Grant in *The Grass Is Greener.* Off the screen for a few years, she captivated moviegoers with a brilliant performance as the mother in *All the Way Home* (1963), a literate, tasteful adaptation of

James Agee's "A Death in the Family." After that, however, she found quality projects somewhat harder to come by. *Life at the Top* (1965), *Mister Buddwing* (1966), *Divorce American Style, Rough Night in Jericho* (both 1967), *The Happy Ending* (1969, a Richard Brooks film for which she was again Oscar-nominated, this time as Best Actress), *Say Hello to Yesterday* (1971), *Mr. Sycamore* (1974), and *Dominique* (1978) comprise a motley list of credits for such a fine talent. She has remained visible on television, in such TV movies as *Valley of the Dolls* (1981) and *Perry Mason: The Case of the Lost Love* (1987), and in a miniseries of "Great Expectations" (1989) in which she played Miss Havisham! Simmons also appeared in the short-lived revival of the gothic soap opera "Dark Shadows" (1991). A feature-film "comeback" in 1988, consisting of roles in *Going Undercover* and *The Dawning,* only pointed to an appalling paucity of suitable roles for this still-entrancing actress.

SIMON, NEIL. Screenwriter, playwright. *(b. July 4, 1927, Bronx, N.Y.)* Prolific middle-brow playwright whose plays have been popular successes both on stage and in their screen adaptations. Simon cut his comedy teeth in one of the most famous laugh factories of all time, writing for Sid Caesar (along with such colleagues as Woody Allen, Mel Brooks, and Carl Reiner, among others) on the TV series "Your Show of Shows" and "Caesar's Hour" in the 1950s. (In 1993 he drew on those experiences for a hit Broadway play, "Laughter on the 23rd Floor.") Adept at creating colorful characters and fashioning clever dialogue, Simon harbored ambitions of Broadway fame and fortune. He achieved that goal with his first play, 1961's "Come Blow Your Horn," which was adapted for the screen two years later. In 1963 he followed it with another hit, "Barefoot in the Park," which was filmed in 1967. In 1966 he wrote the book for the Broadway musical success "Sweet Charity," which was adapted as a movie in 1969.

The almost impossibly prolific Simon churned out plays at the rate of two or more a year. Few had depth, but they offered some of the biggest laugh-lines in Broadway history. Among his plays that were adapted for the screen: *The Odd Couple* (1968, Oscar-nominated for Screenplay and later spun off into a TV series), *Star Spangled Girl, Plaza Suite* (both 1971), *Last of the Red Hot Lovers* (1972), *The Sunshine Boys* (1975, Oscar-nominated), *California Suite* (1978, Oscar-nominated), and *I Ought to Be in Pictures* (1982). His ambitious comedy-drama "The Gingerbread Lady" was transformed into the film *Only When I Laugh* (1981). A series of autobiographical plays showed a more thoughtful Simon. These too became films: *Chapter Two* (1979), *Brighton Beach Memoirs* (1986), *Biloxi Blues* (1988); the made-for-TV *Broadway Bound* (1992), and *Lost in Yonkers* (1993). (The height of verisimilitude was reached in *Chapter Two,* the story of widower Simon's meeting with, and courting of, his second wife, when the part was played by the actual woman in question, actress Marsha Mason.)

All along, Simon kept busy writing screen originals as well: *After the Fox* (1966), *The Out-of-Towners* (1970), *The Heartbreak Kid* (1972, based on a Bruce Jay Friedman story), the detective parody *Murder by Death* (1976), the sweetly sentimental *The Goodbye Girl* (1977, also Oscar-nominated; in 1993 it became a Broadway musical), *The Cheap Detective* (1978), the 1930s-type screwball farce *Seems Like Old Times* (1980), *Max Dugan Returns* (1983), *The Lonely Guy* (1984, adaptation only), *The Slugger's Wife* (1985), and *The Marrying Man* (1991). His well-publicized feud with the stars of the last film, and unhappiness at his treatment by producers, led him to declare it his last screenplay (though he did later adapt *Lost in Yonkers).* A man of the theater, where a playwright's word is law, he finds Hollywood increasingly frustrating.

SIMON, SIMONE. Actress. *(b. Apr. 23, 1911, Bethune, France.)* Although film buffs remember this French actress as Irena Dubrovna, the feline beauty of Jacques Tourneur's stylish low-budget horror film *Cat People* (1942), it should be noted that Simon, a top screen star in her native country, came to Hollywood amid much hoopla and predictions that she would become one of Tinseltown's brightest stars. With modeling experience behind her, the beautiful Simon made her

film debut in 1931. Darryl F. Zanuck imported her to 20th Century-Fox in 1936; her debut, in the routine programmer *Girls' Dormitory* (1936), showed her to have the prettiest pout in the movie capital, but put little demand on her acting ability (which was hampered somewhat by her limited grasp of the English language). She played the Janet Gaynor role in a sappy 1937 remake of the silent classic *Seventh Heaven,* opposite a badly miscast James Stewart. Her other Fox films, including *Ladies in Love* (1936), *Love and Hisses* (1937), and *Josette* (1938), were cookie-cutter products of no particular merit.

Disenchanted with Hollywood in general and Fox in particular, she returned to France, where her luminous performance in Jean Renoir's *La Bête humaine* (1938) reestablished her as an international star. World War 2 drove her back to America, where she appeared as the Devil's temptress in *All That Money Can Buy* (1941, aka *The Devil and Daniel Webster)* before accepting producer Val Lewton's offer to star in *Cat People,* a literate, tasteful exercise in terror that called upon her in ways that her more expensive Fox pictures never did. She reprised her Irena characterization in a limited way for *The Curse of the Cat People* (1944) and starred in Lewton's *Mademoiselle Fifi* (also 1944).

Simon remained in Hollywood until the end of the war, languishing in undistinguished B pictures such as *Tahiti Honey* (1943) and *Johnny Doesn't Live Here Anymore* (1944) for such outfits as Republic and Monogram. Back in France following the conflict, she made a handful of films, including Max Ophuls' witty and charming *La Ronde* (1950) and *Le Plaisir* (1951) before retiring in 1956.

SINATRA, FRANK. Singer, actor, producer, director. *(b. Dec. 12, 1915, Hoboken, N.J.)* "Ol' Blue Eyes," the prodigiously talented and equally controversial king of American popular song, created almost as much excitement on the big screen as he did behind a microphone. An untrained, instinctive actor, he developed into a powerful screen performer; a lifelong maverick, he sought constant challenge when he could have easily coasted. Sinatra made his first film appearances as a vocalist with the Tommy Dorsey Band in 1941's

Las Vegas Nights. Just two years later a role was written especially for him in *Higher and Higher,* in which he more or less played himself. (He went on to become the most caricatured star of the decade, in animated cartoons that depicted the impossibly skinny vocalist making female bobbysoxers swoon—see Warner Bros.' *Swooner Crooner* or MGM's *Little Tinker* for evidence.) Sinatra's star rose steadily throughout the decade as he played light, likable roles in a series of musical comedies, including *Anchors Aweigh* (1945, well teamed with Gene Kelly), *It Happened in Brooklyn* (1947), *The Kissing Bandit* (1948), *Take Me Out to the Ball Game* (1949) and *On the Town* (1949), that displayed a winning personality—and even the ability to hoof (thanks to coaching from his frequent costar and friend Gene Kelly). He also helped cement his public image as a fighter for the underdog by starring in a dramatic short (with music) about tolerance called *The House I Live In* (1945), which won him a special Academy Award, and was shown by schools and civic groups for years to come.

When Sinatra's vocal cords hemorrhaged in 1952, he was dropped by talent agency MCA and had to beg to be cast in a nonsinging role—originally intended for Eli Wallach—in the wartime drama *From Here to Eternity* (1953). His impressive performance as the pathetic, luckless soldier Maggio earned him an Oscar—and made him the comeback story of the decade. Now a hot ticket in Hollywood, he tackled a number of ambitious roles, including a would-be presidential assassin in *Suddenly* (1954) and a junkie trying to put his life right in Otto Preminger's *The Man With the Golden Arm* (1955, Oscar nomination). He reasserted himself musically in *Guys and Dolls* (1955) *High Society* (1956), and *Pal Joey* (1957), but continued to look for dramatic punch—and found it in Vincente Minnelli's colorful adaptation of James Jones' melodrama *Some Came Running* (1958, as Jones' alter ego). He and the film's costar Dean Martin (another singer-turned-actor) became leaders of a Vegas-loving, high-rolling "Rat Pack" of entertainers, which appeared in a handful of lively if forgettable films, of which *Ocean's Eleven* (1960) and *Robin and the Seven Hoods* (1964,

with elder statesman Bing Crosby joining in) have undeniable time-capsule value.

Sinatra was eager to star in the 1962 Cold War paranoia thriller *The Manchurian Candidate,* which got made only after Richard Condon's controversial novel was endorsed by Sinatra's friend President John F. Kennedy. He limned his own version of the hard-boiled, wisecracking movie private eye in *Tony Rome* (1967) and its sequel, *Lady in Cement* (1968, opposite Raquel Welch). Sinatra announced his retirement in 1971, one year after making the peculiar comic Western *Dirty Dingus Magee;* he returned to singing after a brief hiatus, but didn't make a screen comeback until 1980, when he returned to the genre he was drawn to in the late 1960s—the urban crime drama. But *The First Deadly Sin* was a disappointment, as was the similarly themed movie for TV, *Contract on Cherry Street* (1977).

Sinatra has lived his life in the headlines, with two of his four marriages to actresses (Ava Gardner and Mia Farrow). In 1992, with his blessing, daughter Tina Sinatra produced a TV miniseries based on his eventful life; Philip Casnoff starred in "Sinatra," but the vocal tracks were the originals by the one and only.

OTHER FILMS INCLUDE: 1942: *Ship Ahoy;* 1943: *Reveille With Beverly;* 1944: *Step Lively;* 1946: *Till the Clouds Roll By;* 1948: *The Miracle of the Bells;* 1951: *Meet Danny Wilson, Double Dynamite;* 1955: *Not as a Stranger, The Tender Trap;* 1956: *Johnny Concho;* 1957: *The Pride and the Passion, The Joker Is Wild;* 1958: *Kings Go Forth;* 1959: *A Hole in the Head, Never So Few;* 1960: *Can-Can, Pepe* (cameo); 1961: *The Devil at 4 O'Clock;* 1962: *Sergeants 3* (also produced); 1963: *Come Blow Your Horn, The List of Adrian Messenger* (cameo), *4 for Texas;* 1965: *None but the Brave* (also directed), *Marriage on the Rocks, Von Ryan's Express;* 1966: *The Oscar* (cameo), *Cast a Giant Shadow* (cameo), *Assault on a Queen;* 1967: *The Naked Runner;* 1968: *The Detective;* 1974: *That's Entertainment!* (host); 1984: *Cannonball Run II* (cameo).

SINGLETON, JOHN. Director, screenwriter. (b. Jan. 6, 1968, Los Angeles.) After winning several awards at USC's Filmic Writing Program, Singleton exploded onto the scene with his first film, *Boyz N the Hood* (1991), a tough, intelligent, plainspeaking look at friends in gang-ridden South Central L. A. that earned him Oscar nominations for Best Original Screenplay and Best Director, becoming the first African-American (and the youngest filmmaker ever) to do so. It was a tough act to follow, and critics (perhaps unfairly) took him to task when his second film, the ambitious *Poetic Justice* (1993, starring Janet Jackson), wasn't as good. He also directed the Michael Jackson music video "Remember the Time." He followed with the highly charged campus drama *Higher Learning* (1995).

SINISE, GARY. Actor, director. *(b. Mar. 17, 1955, Chicago.)* A founder of Chicago's famed Steppenwolf Theatre Company, Sinise has begun an impressive film career on both sides of the camera. He made his directing debut with the downbeat rural drama *Miles From Home* (1988, which featured Steppenwolf members John Malkovich and Laurie Metcalf) and appeared as Mother in the acclaimed war drama *A Midnight Clear* (1992), before tackling his most ambitious film project to date: directing and starring in a remake of *Of Mice and Men* (1992) as George, opposite John Malkovich's Lennie (which they'd both performed on stage). He rounded out that busy year costarring with Danny DeVito in *Jack the Bear* (released 1993), then scored a Supporting Oscar nomination as the embittered, legless Army lieutenant in *Forrest Gump* (1994). Sinise also starred in the TV miniseries "The Stand" (1994) and had a small role in *The Quick and the Dead* (1995, as Sharon Stone's father).

SIODMAK, ROBERT. Director. *(b. Aug. 8, 1900, Memphis, Tenn.; d. Mar. 10, 1973.)* Renowned director of handsome, stylish mystery and suspense films, an early exponent of Hollywood film noir. Born in the United States but raised in Germany, Siodmak entered the film industry there during the 1920s, when the bold expressionistic style popularized by Wiene and Murnau still dominated the country's output. He codirected *Menschen am Sonntag* (1929, aka *People on Sunday),* a sort of "docudrama" on which many future Hollywood filmmakers worked, including Edgar G. Ulmer (his codirector), Fred

Zinnemann, Billy Wilder, and Siodmak's brother Curt. Siodmak, of Jewish extraction, fled Germany shortly after Hitler rose to power; he directed a number of French films, none of them particularly memorable, before emigrating to Hollywood in 1939.

Initially assigned to B pictures such as *West Point Widow* (1941), *Fly by Night* (1942), and *Son of Dracula* (1943), Siodmak was eventually entrusted with bigger projects at Universal. In 1944 he directed the downbeat Deanna Durbin vehicle *Christmas Holiday,* a flop; *Cobra Woman,* a campy Jon Hall-Maria Montez romp; and *Phantom Lady,* a particularly skillful mystery based on a Cornell Woolrich novel now regarded as one of the seminal *noir* movies. *The Strange Case of Uncle Harry* (1945), *The Spiral Staircase,* and *The Dark Mirror,* good as they were, just warmed up Siodmak for *The Killers* (all 1946), a careful and effective expansion of Ernest Hemingway's classic short story, starring Burt Lancaster and Ava Gardner, which earned the director an Academy Award nomination.

Siodmak turned out taut, efficient crime dramas one by one: *Cry of the City* (1948), *Criss. Cross, The File on Thelma Jordon* (both 1949), *Deported* (1950), and *The Whistle at Eaton Falls* (1952) among them. He even tackled swashbucklers, helming the much-admired Burt Lancaster vehicle *The Crimson Pirate* (1952) with élan. After completing that film he returned to Europe, where he directed mostly mediocre films until 1969. His brother Curt, who also migrated to the United States, had a lengthy screenwriting career and wrote the oft-filmed novel "Donovan's Brain."

SIRK, DOUGLAS. Director. *(b. Apr. 26, 1900, Hamburg, Germany, as Claus Detlev Sierk; d. Jan. 16, 1987.)* When this German director landed in Hollywood in the late 1930s, having fled his native Germany in opposition to the Third Reich, he changed his name to appease prewar jingoists. He had been a top stage director, and then a film director for UFA, before deciding that Germany under Hitler was not for him. It's not surprising that his first film here was the rabidly anti-Nazi *Hitler's Madman* (1943). Sirk's subsequent career was marked by his controlled, visually lush direction of florid melodramas, many of them in wide screen and in color. The best of these—including *Magnificent Obsession* (1954), *All that Heaven Allows* (1955), *Written on the Wind* (1956), *The Tarnished Angels* (1958) and *Imitation of Life* (1959)—are distinguished by distancing techniques that some critics contend are consciously Brechtian. While the films might well collapse under such intellectual baggage, it is well known that Sirk was a cultivated, aesthetically advanced man who brought more to such projects than they might have "deserved." He was championed by many of the critics-turned-directors of the French New Wave, and German director Rainer Werner Fassbinder frequently cited him as a major influence, and even worked with Sirk when the aged director returned to Germany in the 1970s to teach film. It's undeniable that many of his films were strictly formulaic potboilers, and some literal-minded film scholars are baffled at the continued interest in Sirk's soap operas.

OTHER FILMS INCLUDE: 1946: *A Scandal in Paris;* 1947: *Lured;* 1948: *Sleep My Love;* 1949: *Slightly French, Shockproof;* 1950: *Mystery Submarine;* 1951: *The First Legion, Thunder on the Hill, The Lady Pays Off, Weekend With Father;* 1952: *No Room for the Groom, Has Anybody Seen My Gal?;* 1953: *Meet Me at the Fair, Take Me to Town, All I Desire;* 1954: *Taza, Son of Cochise, Sign of the Pagan;* 1955: *Captain Lightfoot;* 1956: *There's Always Tomorrow;* 1957: *Battle Hymn, Interlude;* 1958: *A Time to Love and a Time to Die.*

SKELTON, RED. Actor, comedian. *(b. July 18, 1913, Vincennes, Ind., as Richard Bernard Skelton.)* Rubber-faced, carrot-topped clown fondly remembered as the star of a long-running (1951–71) TV showcase, but also a supporting player and top-billed comedy star in movies of the 1930s, 1940s, and early 1950s. The son of a circus clown raised in poverty, he quit school while still a young boy and trouped in circuses, carnivals, burlesque houses, and vaudeville theaters. He also worked on radio before making his film debut at RKO in a Ginger Rogers vehicle, *Having Wonderful Time* (1938).

Billed as Richard Skelton, he performed some of his own set pieces—such as a demonstration of how different people walk up and down stairs. He performed

more of his own material in a pair of Warner Bros. short subjects, *Seeing Red* and *The Broadway Buckaroo.* When MGM signed him in 1940, it was to use him as comedy relief, as in *Flight Command* (1940) and two of the Dr. Kildare films, in which he played an ambulance driver. But with *Whistling in the Dark* (1941) he proved he could carry a comedy vehicle by himself, and his movie career took off. Having played a radio sleuth called "The Fox" in his first starring vehicle, he repeated the role in a pair of enjoyable sequels, *Whistling in Dixie* (1942) and *Whistling in Brooklyn* (1943).

Buster Keaton, then down on his luck and working as a comedy script doctor at MGM, took Skelton in tow and coached him for such films as *I Dood It* (1943, based on Keaton's *Spite Marriage*), *A Southern Yankee* (1948), *The Yellow Cab Man* (1950), and *Watch the Birdie* (1950, based on Keaton's *The Cameraman*). Unfortunately, MGM never understood slapstick comedy, and wouldn't let Keaton and Skelton create their own "little" films. Instead, Red was featured in heavy-handed remakes of classic properties like *Merton of the Movies* and *The Show-Off* (both 1947) and grafted onto big musicals like *Lady Be Good* (1941), *Ship Ahoy, Panama Hattie* (both 1942), *DuBarry Was a Lady* (1943, opposite Lucille Ball), *Bathing Beauty* (1944), *Neptune's Daughter* (1949), *Three Little Words* (1950, playing Bert Kalmar to Fred Astaire's Harry Ruby), *Texas Carnival* (1951), and *Lovely to Look At* (1952). He had many good moments in these tuneful films, but they weren't "his" movies. At least in *Ziegfeld Follies* (1946) he had committed to film his all-time best solo routine, the uproarious "Guzzler's Gin." He also scored a hit on loan-out to Columbia for *The Fuller Brush Man* (1948).

His film career started to peter out in the 1950s, as his television career was on the ascent. MGM tried him in more subdued situation comedies like *Half a Hero* (1953), and even cast him in a straight dramatic role. *The Clown* (also 1953) was a not-bad remake of the classic tearjerker *The Champ*, with Skelton going from pathos to melodrama as a washed-up entertainer who's idolized by his son. He made his last starring film in 1957, *Public Pigeon No. One.* Occupied with television and nightclubs, Skelton's remaining film appearances were guest-star bits in *Around the World in Eighty Days* (1956), *Ocean's Eleven* (1960), and *Those Magnificent Men in Their Flying Machines* (1965), which featured him in a very funny pantomime prologue.

SKERRITT, TOM. Actor. *(b. Aug. 25, 1933, Detroit.)* Talented, personable character actor and occasional lead, whose noteworthy performances have graced many big-screen films and TV shows, including the highly acclaimed "Picket Fences" (1992–), which won him an Emmy Award. He can be seen in movies dating back to *War Hunt* (1962, which was also Robert Redford's first film), but didn't make much of an impression on audiences until he played the drawling Army-surgeon buddy of Donald Sutherland and Elliott Gould in *MASH* (1970). Skerritt has several times played the husband of strong female protagonists in movies such as *The Turning Point* (1977, as Shirley MacLaine's spouse) and *Steel Magnolias* (1989, as Sally Field's), and was memorable as the beleaguered space captain in *Alien* (1979) and as Viper, the commanding officer in *Top Gun* (1986). He also had a recurring role on one season of "Cheers" (1987–88) as Kirstie Alley's boss.
OTHER FILMS INCLUDE: 1964: *One Man's Way;* 1965: *Those Calloways;* 1971: *Wild Rovers;* 1972: *Fuzz;* 1974: *Big Bad Mama, Thieves Like Us;* 1975: *The Devil's Rain;* 1978: *Cheech & Chong's Up in Smoke;* 1979: *Ice Castles;* 1981: *Silence of the North, A Dangerous Summer;* 1982: *Fighting Back;* 1983: *The Dead Zone;* 1986: *Opposing Force, SpaceCamp, Wisdom;* 1987: *The Big Town, Maid to Order;* 1988: *Poltergeist III;* 1989: *Big Man on Campus;* 1990: *The Rookie;* 1993: *Knight Moves.*

SKYE, IONE. Actress. *(b. Sept. 4, 1971, London, as Ione Skye Leitch.)* An earthy, sensitive, and promising young actress, notable as John Cusack's headstrong girlfriend in *Say Anything . . .* (1989), Skye seems poised on the threshold of real screen stardom. The daughter of popular folksinger Donovan, she made her movie debut as one of the wayward youths in Tim Hunter's *River's Edge* (1987). She then costarred in the short-lived TV series "Covington Cross" (1992). Brother Donovan Leitch is also an actor.
OTHER FILMS INCLUDE: 1987: *Stranded;* 1988: *A Night in the Life of Jimmy Reardon;* 1989: *The Rachel Papers;* 1991: *Mindwalk;* 1992: *Gas, Food Lodging, Guncrazy, Wayne's World* (bit part).

SLATER, CHRISTIAN. Actor. *(b. Aug. 18, 1969, New York City.)* Much has been made of handsome young Slater's uncanny mimicry of Jack Nicholson in several of his movie performances. The observation is relevant, but not especially important: Slater has a commanding, charismatic presence all his own. The son of a casting agent (who says he was first spotted on the New York TV institution "The Joe Franklin Show"), he debuted in *The Legend of Billie Jean* (1985), and appeared in such other films as *The Name of the Rose, Twisted* (both 1986), *Tucker: The Man and His Dream* (1988), *Gleaming the Cube,* and *The Wizard* (both 1989), but he made his first real impact as the sardonic, murderous (and Nicholson-esque) highschooler in *Heathers* (1989). The next year he collected good reviews for *Pump Up the Volume* (1990), starring as a pirate radio deejay who touches the lives of the local misunderstood youth. In much the same way, he quickly became something of a teen idol in real life. He appeared in *Tales From the Darkside: The Movie,* joined the cast of *Young Guns II* (both also 1990), costarred as Lucky Luciano in the urban "young-guns" saga *Mobsters,* and added youth appeal to *Robin Hood: Prince of Thieves* (both 1991), as Will Scarlett. (He also did a cameo in *Star Trek VI: The Undiscovered Country* in 1991.) His first solo starring vehicle, *Kuffs* (1992), was a dog, but he fared considerably better in *Untamed Heart* and *True Romance* (both 1993); recent credits include *Jimmy Hollywood, Interview With the Vampire* (both 1994), and *Murder in the First* (1995).

SLATER, HELEN. Actress. *(b. Dec. 15, 1963, New York City.)* Attractive blond actress whose anticipated big break, the title role in 1984's *Supergirl,* broke the producers' hearts (and wallets) when it flopped miserably, establishing Slater's name but not her talent. She has managed to prevail, though, turning in credible and endearing performances as a modern martyr in *The Legend of Billie Jean* (1985), a comic would-be kidnapper in *Ruthless People* (1986), Michael J. Fox's yuppie girlfriend in *The Secret of My Success* (1987), an accidental thief in *Sticky Fingers* (1988), and a bashful trail rider (and token female) in *City Slickers* (1991). Recent credits include a pair of 1993 telefilms, *12:01* and *Chantilly Lace*, its 1994 followup *Parallel Lives*, and *Lassie* (also 1994).

SLEZAK, WALTER. Actor. *(b. May 3, 1902, Vienna; d. Apr. 22, 1983.)* The son of Metropolitan Opera star Leo Slezak, Walter entered show business by chance after meeting director Michael Curtiz, who cast him for a part in his silent German epic, *Sodom and Gomorrah* (1922). The former bank clerk continued acting in films and on stage, becoming a Broadway stalwart in the 1930s. A strong, handsome man in his youth, he gained weight rapidly as middle age approached, pegging him as a character actor; as it happened, he could play villains or teddy bears with equal élan. He made his American film debut as the Nazi baron in *Once Upon a Honeymoon* (1942), but made an equally strong impression as a buffoonish villain in Bob Hope's *The Princess and the Pirate* (1944). Slezak appears in *The Fallen Sparrow* (1943), *Lifeboat* (1944, a key performance), *Cornered* (1945), *Sinbad the Sailor* (1947), *The Pirate* (1948), *The Inspector General* (1949), *Bedtime for Bonzo, People Will Talk* (both 1951), *Call Me Madam* (1953), *The Miracle* (1959), *The Wonderful World of the Brothers Grimm* (1962), *Emil and the Detectives* (1964), and *Treasure Island* (1972), to name a few. In 1955 he won a Tony for his role in the Broadway production of "Fanny," and went on to sing at the Metropolitan Opera. His autobiography, "What Time's the Next Swan?" was published in 1962. His daughter Erika has gained fame as a star on TV soaps.

SLOANE, EVERETT. Actor. *(b. Oct. 1, 1909, New York City; d. Aug. 6, 1965.)* After more than a decade as a stage performer and radio actor (one of the medium's finest, appearing on an estimated 15,000 broadcasts), Sloane went to Hollywood with Orson Welles' Mercury Theater group and made his movie debut in *Citizen Kane* (1941), playing the excitable Mr. Bernstein. An extremely capable and talented supporting player, Sloane also appeared with Welles in *Journey Into Fear* (1942), *The Lady From Shanghai* (1948, as Rita Hayworth's husband), and *Prince of Foxes* (1949). Perhaps his best part was in *Patterns* (1956), in which he recreated his performance from the Rod Serling teleplay as a ruthlessly pragmatic business executive. He was active on television, and provided the voice of Dick Tracy for a series of early 1960s TV cartoons.
OTHER FILMS INCLUDE: 1950: *The Men;* 1951: *The Enforcer, The Blue Veil, The Desert Fox;* 1955: *The Big Knife;* 1956: *Somebody Up There Likes Me, Lust for Life;* 1958: *Marjorie Morningstar;* 1960: *Home From the Hill;* 1964: *The Patsy, The Disorderly Orderly* (his final screen appearance).

SLOCOMBE, DOUGLAS. Cinematographer. *(b. Feb. 10, 1913, London.)* Veteran lenser who began his film career as a WW2 newsreel cameraman and is adept at photographing period pieces, stark dramas, action-adventures, and even musicals. He joined Britain's Ealing Studios as director of photography in 1948 and stayed there for 17 years, working on many classic comedies including *Kind Hearts and Coronets* (1949), *The Lavender Hill Mob,* and *The Man in the White Suit* (both 1951). Slocombe has since adapted his talents to many projects calling for multivaried visual styles, including *Freud* (1962), *The Servant* (1963), *The Fearless Vampire Killers* (1967), *The Lion in Winter* (1968), *Jesus Christ Superstar* (1973), *The Great Gatsby* (1974), *Rollerball* (1975), *Indiana Jones and the Temple of Doom* (1984), and *Indiana Jones and the Last Crusade* (1989). Slocombe received Oscar nominations for his lensing of *Travels With My Aunt* (1972), *Julia* (1977), and *Raiders of the Lost Ark* (1981)—all period pictures, it should be noted.

SMITH, ALEXIS. Actress. *(b. June 8, 1921, Penticton, British Columbia, as Gladys Smith; d. June 9, 1993.)* Reliable, ravishing redhead best remembered for her long tenure at Warner Bros., though she found more fulfilling work later. Bitten by the acting bug while in her teens, Smith briefly worked in Canadian summer stock before heading south to Los Angeles where, spotted in a local stage production, she inked a contract with Warners before reaching her twentieth birthday.

She started out with a supporting role in *The Lady With Red Hair* (1940) and was kept busy throughout 1941 in the likes of *Affectionately Yours, Singapore Woman, She Couldn't Say No,* and *Flight From Destiny.* She won the female lead in an A picture that same year *(Dive Bomber),* and a year later was working opposite Errol Flynn in *Gentleman Jim* (1942). She was set from that point on, though Warners alternated leading-lady parts with those of the "other woman," at which she excelled. Her Warners films include *Thank Your Lucky Stars, The Constant Nymph* (both 1943), *The Adventures of Mark Twain* (as Twain's wife), *Hollywood Canteen, The Doughgirls* (all 1944), *The Horn Blows at Midnight, Conflict, Rhapsody in Blue, San Antonio* (all 1945), *Night and Day* (as the wife of songwriter Cole Porter), *Of Human Bondage* (both 1946), *Stallion Road, The Two Mrs. Carrolls* (both 1947), *The Woman in White, The Decision of Christopher Blake, Whiplash* (all 1948), *South of St. Louis* (1949), *Any Number Can Play* (also 1949, on loan to MGM), and *Montana* (1950).

Her favorite experience was playing the other woman for Frank Capra in *Here Comes the Groom* (1951), and indeed, she seemed looser, more natural than in almost any of her previous films. But such opportunities were rare; her freelance credits include *Undercover Girl* (1950), *The Turning Point* (1952), *Split Second* (1953), *The Sleeping Tiger* (1954), *The Eternal Sea* (1955), *Beau James* (1957), *This Happy Feeling* (1958), and *The Young Philadelphians* (1959), her last for many years.

In 1971 Smith astonished fans when she kicked up her heels (literally) as the vivacious and seemingly ageless singing star in Stephen Sondheim's Broadway musical "Follies" (for which she won a Tony Award.) It led to new offers for films, TV appearances, and stage work. Her later movies include *Once Is Not Enough* (1975), *The Little Girl Who Lives Down the Lane* (1976), *Casey's Shadow* (1978), *The Trout* (1982), and *Tough Guys* (1986).

Smith was a regular on the nighttime soaps "Dallas" (1984) and "Hothouse" (1988). She was married to actor Craig Stevens, whom she met when both were under contract to Warner Bros., from 1944 till her death. Her last film, *The Age of Innocence* (1993), in which she played an influential New York society matron, was released posthumously.

SMITH, C. AUBREY (SIR). Actor. *(b. July 21, 1863, London; d. Dec. 20, 1948.)* The man who saved the British empire a dozen times (on film), and recreated his battlefield triumphs with pineapple and walnuts in *The Four Feathers* (1939), was Hollywood's idea of the archetypal English aristocrat. One of the screen's most recognizable character actors, this tall, powerfully built Britisher—with his dignified bearing, square jaw, and bushy eyebrows—appeared in dozens of films throughout the 1930s and 1940s. A world-class cricket player who toured with championship teams, Smith began acting in the 1890s and made his American stage debut before the turn of the century. After settling in Hollywood in 1930, he started playing British diplomats, soldiers, noblemen and, occasionally, mere gentlemen of leisure in a string of prestigious productions including *Trader Horn* (1930), *The Bachelor Father* (1931, in the title role), *Tarzan, the Ape Man* (1932, as the father of "Jane"), *Love Me Tonight, Trouble in Paradise* (both 1932), *Morning Glory* (1933, as a "grand old actor" who befriends Katharine Hepburn), *Bombshell, Queen Christina* (both 1933), *Bulldog Drummond Strikes Back, Cleopatra, The Scarlet Empress* (all 1934), *The Lives of a Bengal Lancer, China Seas, Clive of India* (all 1935), *Little Lord Fauntleroy, Lloyd's of London, The Garden of Allah* (all 1936), *Romeo and Juliet* (1936, as Lord Capulet), *The Hurricane, Wee Willie Winkie, The Prisoner of Zenda* (all 1937), *Kidnapped* (1938), *Rebecca, Waterloo Bridge* (both 1940), *Dr. Jekyll and Mr. Hyde* (1941), *Madame Curie* (1943), *The White Cliffs of Dover, The Adventures of Mark Twain* (all 1944), *And Then There Were None* (1945), *Cluny Brown* (1946), and *Little Women* (1949, his last film). Smith also played the Duke of Wellington several times, most notably in *House of Rothschild* (1934). He was considered the dean of Hollywood's British colony—especially on the cricket field.

SMITH, CHARLES MARTIN. Actor, director. *(b. Oct. 30, 1953, Los Angeles.)* Probably best remembered as Terry the Toad in George Lucas' *American Graffiti* (1973), Smith has appeared in a number of films, usually as shy, repressed individuals who are ultimately roused into action. He debuted in *The Culpepper Cattle Company* and followed in *Fuzz* (both 1972), *Pat Garrett and Billy the Kid* (1973), *Rafferty and the Gold Dust Twins* (1975), *No Deposit, No Return* (1976), and later *The Buddy Holly Story* (1978, as bass player Ray Bobb), the sequel *More American Graffiti* (1979), and *Herbie Goes Bananas* (1980). A born character actor, Smith won a once-in-a-lifetime leading role in the little-known *Never Cry Wolf* (1983), doing an excellent job as a scientist studying the behavior of wolves in the Arctic. He then returned to supporting roles in films like *Starman* (1984) and *The Untouchables* (1987, as federal tax accountant Oscar Wallace) before branching out into directing. Smith made his feature directing debut with *Trick or Treat* (1986), followed by the live-action "Rocky and Bullwinkle" spin-off *Boris and Natasha* (1989, released 1992) and *Fifty/Fifty* (1992). (He also appeared in all three films.) Other acting credits include *The Experts* (1989), *The Hot Spot* (1990), and *And the Band Played On* (1993 telefilm).

SMITH, DICK. Makeup artist. *(b. June 26, 1922, Larchmont, N.Y.)* One of the deans of movie makeup, Smith began his career in television in the 1940s, becoming head of NBC's makeup department and achieving fame for work on such productions as "Alice in Wonderland," "Cyrano de Bergerac," "The Moon and Sixpence" (with Laurence Olivier) and "Victoria Regina" (1957, for which he "aged" young Claire Bloom in minutes for the live production). Smith left NBC in 1959 and did his first film work on *Requiem for a Heavyweight* (1962), followed by *The World of Henry Orient* (1964) and *Midnight Cowboy* (1969), all made in New York. He gained true fame, however, for the extraordinary makeup on *Little Big Man* (1970), in which he transformed Dustin Hoffman into 121-year-old Jack Crabbe, and pioneered the use of multiple overlapping appliances (instead of a single mask) and foam latex eyelids, which added natural realism and allowed an actor more freedom to move. Smith went on to create the makeup for Marlon Brando's aging Don Corleone in *The Godfather* (1972) and the astounding "special effects makeup" for Linda Blair in *The Exorcist* (1973), which included a full body dummy with a swiveling head, and hoses that allowed the dummy to "vomit." He also invented the mutated body suits for William Hurt and Blair Brown to wear in *Altered States* (1980), as well as the network of air "bladders" which created the appearance of undulations in Hurt's arm and chest.

Smith's other films include *The Godfather, Part II* (1974), *The Sunshine Boys* (1975), *Taxi Driver* (1976), *Ghost Story* (1981), and *Amadeus* (1984), for which he shared an Academy Award (with Paul Le-Blanc). More recently, he earned another nomination for *Dad* (1989), and designed the wizardly makeup for *Death Becomes Her* (1992). Smith won an Emmy for designing Hal Holbrook's makeup for 1967's TV production "Mark Twain, Tonight!" and later turned the actor into Abraham Lincoln for the 1985 miniseries "North and South." Many younger artists have emulated Smith—with varying degrees of success, particularly in the art of aging an actor. Smith has said, "The goal of all of us makeup artists is to try to make whatever we do *not* look like makeup . . . there's the magician's trick."

SMITH, KURTWOOD. Actor. *(b. July 3, 1942, San Francisco.)* Short, feral-looking actor with a knack for playing slimy villains. Smith broke into films as a deadly CIA agent in *Flashpoint* (1984), and went on to play a drug czar in *Robocop* (1987), a shady government lawyer in *True Believer* (1989), an unforgiving father who drives his son to commit suicide in *Dead Poets Society* (1989), a Mafia chief in *Quick Change* (1990), and a paranoid citizen in Woody Allen's *Shadows and Fog* (1992). He also starred in the well-received short subject *12:01* (1990). He has occasionally been seen as a good guy too, notably under heavy makeup as the

Federation President in *Star Trek VI: The Undiscovered Country* (1991). Other credits include *Rambo III* (1988), *Heart of Dixie* (1989), *Oscar* (1991), *Boxing Helena, Fortress,* and *The Crush* (all 1993). He was a series regular on "The Renegades" (1983) and "The New Adventures of Beans Baxter" (1987–88).

SMITH, LANE. Actor. *(b. Apr. 29, 1936, Memphis, Tenn.)* Versatile character actor, adept at playing charming but slithery types, who has finally been getting roles of larger prominence. He studied at the Actors Studio (along with Al Pacino and Dustin Hoffman) and did numerous stage productions before branching out with small parts in *Network* (1976), *Blue Collar* (1978), *Honeysuckle Rose* (1980), *Prince of the City* (1981), and *Frances* (1982). Larger parts followed in *Places in the Heart* (1984, as the banker trying to repossess Sally Field's property), *Red Dawn* (1984), *Weeds* (1987, as Nick Nolte's cellmate), *Prison* (1988, a starring role as a state penitentiary warden), and *Air America* (1990). In recent years he's become very recognizable, as Joe Pesci's opposing counsel in *My Cousin Vinny* (1992), a crooked congressman in *The Distinguished Gentleman* (1992), a hockey coach in *The Mighty Ducks* (1992), and a hapless father in *Son-in-Law* (1993). Smith is familiar to TV audiences from stints on the short-lived "Good Sports" (1991) and "Good and Evil" (also 1991) and "Lois & Clark: The New Adventures of Superman" (1993–), as "Daily Planet" editor Perry White. He is probably best remembered for his superb performance as Richard Nixon in the TV movie *The Final Days* (1989). His stage credits include the original production of "Glengarry Glen Ross" and some 600 performances as McMurphy in a revival of "One Flew Over the Cuckoo's Nest."

SMITH, MAGGIE (DAME). Actress. *(b. Dec. 28, 1934, Ilford, England.)* One of Britain's acting treasures, Smith has scored innumerable triumphs on the stage (both in England and on Broadway) as well as on the screen. Trained at the Oxford Playhouse School, she made her stage debut in 1952 and her first film, *Nowhere to Go,* in 1958. American moviegoers first noticed

her in *The V.I.P.s* (1963), and her brilliant turn as Desdemona in Olivier's 1965 movie adaptation of *Othello* earned Smith an Oscar nod for Best Supporting Actress. Appearances in *The Pumpkin Eater* (1964), *Young Cassidy* (1965), *The Honey Pot* (1967), *Hot Millions* (1968), and *Oh! What a Lovely War* (1969) didn't do much to boost her stock with American audiences, but her dynamic, Oscar-winning performance as an eccentric schoolmistress in *The Prime of Miss Jean Brodie* (1969) finally established her here as a star. She snared another Best Actress nomination for her picaresque portrayal in *Travels With My Aunt* (1972), starred in *Love and Pain (and the Whole Damn Thing)* (also 1972), and won her second Oscar playing, oddly enough, an actress who's nominated for an Oscar—and loses—in the funniest episode of Neil Simon's *California Suite* (1978). She worked for Merchant and Ivory in *Quartet* (1981) and then snagged another Oscar nomination for her impeccable work in their *Room With a View* (1985).

Smith, whose range is seemingly limitless, appeared in many mainstream commercial films, often playing comedic characters. She made a charming Nora Charles-type female detective in *Murder by Death* (1976), played suspects in the all-star Agatha Christie whodunits *Death on the Nile* (1978) and *Evil Under the Sun* (1982), and managed to make her presence felt in the special effects–laden fantasy *Clash of the Titans* (1981), as Thetis. She starred opposite Monty Python alumnus Michael Palin in *The Missionary* (1982) and *A Private Function* (1985), hilarious in the latter film as a social-climbing shrew. *The Lonely Passion of Judith Hearne* (1987) gave her a plum role as a lonely Irish woman struggling in humble surroundings. She charmingly played an elderly Wendy in *Hook* (1991), Steven Spielberg's "Peter Pan" saga. She then costarred in a bona fide hit, *Sister Act* (1992, as the unamused Mother Superior), the all-star TV remake of *Suddenly, Last Summer* (also 1992), *The Secret Garden,* and *Sister Act 2: Back in the Habit* (both 1993). In 1989 Smith was knighted by the British Crown, as a token of appreciation and respect for her prodigious dramatic accomplishments.

SMITH, WILLIAM. Actor. *(b. May 24, 1932, Columbia, Mo.)* The brawny, rough-hewn Smith had already labored in many films and TV shows before becoming a familiar face as the villainous Falconetti on the miniseries "Rich Man, Poor Man" (1976). In fact, his appearances in countless low-budget actioners—sometimes as the star—made him one of the screen's most prolific character players in the last three decades. He enjoyed some recognition as one of the stars of the "Laredo" TV series (1965–67), but was especially active on the silver screen during the biker-flick craze of the late 1960s and early 1970s. In less than a year, he appeared in three such epics as *Run Angel Run* (1969), *The Losers,* and *C.C. and Company* (both 1970). He was top-billed as an intrepid federal agent in the campy *Invasion of the Bee Girls* (1973), a cult favorite that remains his best starring vehicle. Throughout the 1970s and 1980s he hopscotched from A movies to B movies, from *The Frisco Kid* (1979) and *Any Which Way You Can* (1980) to *Hell Comes to Frogtown* (1987) and *Maniac Cop* (1988). His latest feature—a major one, at that—is *Maverick* (1994).

SMITHEE, ALLEN (aka ALAN). Director, producer. *(b. Dec. 18, 1940, Teaneck, N.J.)* Notorious director who made his debut on *Death of a Gunfighter* (1967) when he replaced the original directors Don Siegel and Robert Totten. Little is known about Smithee, except for his amazing ability to show up on projects when Directors Guild of America members wish to remove their names from the onscreen and advertising credits. Smithee followed with *Fade-In* (1968, replacing Jud Taylor) and several TV movies including *City in Fear, Fun and Games* (both 1980), and *Moonlight* (1982). Although associated with directing, he occasionally has taken producer credit, as on the failed slasher-comedy *Student Bodies* (1981, filling in for Michael Ritchie). He later made the medical comedy *Stitches* (1985), *Let's Get Harry* (1986, replacing Stuart Rosenberg), and had a banner year in 1987, with *Morgan Stewart's Coming Home* (replacing Paul Aaron), *Riviera,* and *Ghost Fever* (replacing Lee Madden). He seems to have been the only director willing to take credit for *The Shrimp on the Barbie*

(1990), and most recently, he was named director of the TV movie *The Birds II: Land's End* (1994) and took credit for an expanded TV version of *Dune* (1984), which was organized under protest from its original director, David Lynch. Smithee has no set future projects, but one never knows when he will strike next.

SMITS, JIMMY. Actor. *(b. July 9, 1955, Brooklyn, N.Y.)* Tall, smoldering, Latino actor who first melted feminine hearts (and won an Emmy) as the passionate attorney Victor Sifuentes on "L.A. Law" (1986–91). Movie stardom has been a little slower in coming to this Cornell-educated performer—his role as the fiery Mexican revolutionary in *Old Gringo* (1989) might have done it if anyone had seen the picture—but Smits has been noteworthy as a corrupt cop in *Running Scared* (1986), a voodoo victim in *The Believers* (1987), a paternal doctor in *Vital Signs* (1990), and a Cuban freedom fighter in *Fires Within* (1991). His performance as Ellen Barkin's befuddled best friend in *Switch* (1991) proved he could handle comedy as well. Recent credits include the Stephen King miniseries "The Tommyknockers" (1993), the TV movie *The Cisco Kid* (1994), in the title role, and *My Family/Mi Familia* (1995).

SNIPES, WESLEY. Actor. *(b. July 31, 1962, South Bronx, N.Y.)* This commanding and versatile actor got his first big break not in a feature film or TV series, but in a music video: he was the gang leader who threatened Michael Jackson in his enormously popular video "Bad" (1987). He'd already appeared in supporting roles in *Wildcats* (1986) and *Streets of Gold* (1986); after the video exposure, he made strong impressions in the baseball comedy *Major League* (1989), Abel Ferrara's *King of New York* (1990), and Spike Lee's *Mo' Better Blues* (1990). But Snipes really came into his own in 1991, in a pair of sharply contrasting performances: first as a vicious but stylish druglord in the melodramatic *New Jack City,* then as a middle-class architect who becomes romantically involved with a white woman in Spike Lee's *Jungle Fever.* The two-picture parlay made him a star. Snipes cemented his lead status as a basketball hustler in the popular comedy *White Men Can't Jump* (1992, opposite *Wildcats* costar Woody Harrelson), then gave one of his best performances as a paraplegic in *The Waterdance* (1992). He toplined his first action film in 1993, *Passenger 57,* and played a credible cop in the film-noirish *Boiling Point* (1993), then costarred in the high-profile thriller *Rising Sun* (1993) with Sean Connery. He bleached his hair to play a larger-than-life, futuristic villain opposite Sylvester Stallone in *Demolition Man* (1993), then returned to the streets of Harlem for the starring vehicle *Sugar Hill* (1994). He starred in yet another action opus, *Drop Zone* (1994), then played a drag queen in *To Wong Foo, Thanks for Everything, Julie Newmar* (1995).

SNODGRESS, CARRIE. Actress. *(b. Oct. 27, 1946, Barrington, Ill.)* Intelligent, subtle actress who left a blossoming career in the early 1970s to concentrate on her relationship with rock star Neil Young. Snodgress studied theater at the Goodman School of Northern Illinois University, which eventually landed her roles in local Chicago theater. She graduated to TV before making her big-screen debut in *Diary of a Mad Housewife* (1970), which earned her an Oscar nomination. Her role as the "good" wife driven to distraction and adultery by an overbearing husband was right in step with the then-emerging Women's Liberation movement. Snodgress followed *Housewife* with *Rabbit, Run* later the same year, and then left the big screen until 1978, when she accepted a role in Brian De Palma's *The Fury.* Since then she has appeared, without much fanfare, in a number of films, playing a stalwart frontier wife in Clint Eastwood's *Pale Rider* (1985) and a psychopathic villainess who's stalked by Charles Bronson in *Murphy's Law* (1986), among others. Other credits include *Homework* (1982), *A Night in Heaven* (1983), *Blueberry Hill* (1988), *The Chill Factor* (1989), *Across the Tracks* (1991), *The Ballad of Little Jo* (1993), *8 Seconds,* and *Blue Sky* (both 1994).

SODERBERGH, STEVEN. Director, screenwriter. *(b. Jan. 14, 1963, Atlanta.)* Talented filmmaker who burst onto the scene with his first feature, *sex, lies and videotape* (1989), a much-talked-about examination of modern morals and sexual attitudes that earned him the Palme d'Or at Cannes and an Original Screenplay Oscar nomination. Before this, Soderbergh had worked at a video production house and gained attention for a Grammy-nominated concert film he directed for the rock group Yes. Following the extraordinary critical success of *sex . . .* (a tough, if not impossible, act to follow), Soderbergh directed *Kafka* (1991), an intriguing blend of different thematic elements from Kafka's stories that received mixed notices. He then adapted and directed *King of the Hill* (1993), a brilliantly evocative film based on A. E. Hotchner's memoir about growing up in the Depression, and directed but did not write *The Underneath* (1995), a stylish, low-key film noir based on the 1949 movie *Criss Cross.*

SOMMER, ELKE. Actress. *(b. Nov. 5, 1940, Berlin, as Elke Schletz.)* Platinum-blond, pouty, German-born sexpot star of numerous films made on both sides of the Atlantic during the 1960s, 1970s, and 1980s, noted—fairly or unfairly—more for her anatomical attributes than her histrionic ability. An intelligent, educated woman (she speaks seven languages) and a talented artist who has had several exhibitions of her paintings, Sommer got into show business via modeling and starred in several German- and Italian-made movies before getting noticed by American audiences in the all-star WW2 drama *The Victors* (1963). In recent years she has worked often on stage. Sommer was for many years married to Hollywood writer Joe Hyams.
OTHER FILMS INCLUDE: 1963: *The Prize;* 1964: *A Shot in the Dark;* 1965: *The Art of Love;* 1966: *The Money Trap, The Oscar, Boy, Did I Get a Wrong Number!, Deadlier Than the Male, Venetian Affair;* 1968: *The Wicked Dreams of Paula Schultz, The Invincible Six;* 1969: *The Wrecking Crew;* 1971: *Percy, Zeppelin;* 1972: *Baron Blood;* 1975: *Ten Little Indians, House of Exorcism* (aka *Lisa and the Devil);* 1977: *The Swiss Conspiracy;* 1979: *The Prisoner of Zenda, The Double McGuffin;* 1985: *Lily in Love;* 1986: *Death Stone;* 1988: *Left for Dead;* 1991: *Army.*

SOMMER, JOSEF. Actor. *(b. June 26, 1934, Griefswald, Germany, as Maximilian Josef Sommer.)* Solid, dependable character actor who attended Carnegie-Mellon University and had extensive stage experience (including a wide range of classical and Shakespearean roles) before making his screen debut as district attorney Rothko in *Dirty Harry* (1971). A brilliant stage actor, he's rarely had parts of great substance or shading on film, but he has been featured in a number of prominent movies, in often notable parts. He was the congressional committee chairman in *The Front* (1976), then appeared in *Close Encounters of the Third Kind* (1977), *Absence of Malice* (as investigative reporter Sally Field's editor), *Rollover,* and *Reds* (all 1981), and *Hanky Panky* (1982). He also narrated *Sophie's Choice* (1982). As the years passed, the quality and scope of his roles grew, and his name inched upward in the credits. He was a therapy patient/murder victim (as well as Meryl Streep's lover) in *Still of the Night* (also 1982), Kathleen Quinlan's father in *Independence Day,* a labor union executive in *Silkwood* (both 1983), a scientist in *Iceman* (1984), one of Gene Hackman's ex-CIA cronies in *Target* (1985), third-billed as narcotics cop Harrison Ford's immediate superior in *Witness* (also 1985), a corrupt judge in *Chances Are,* top-billed in a potboiler, *Dracula's Widow* (both 1989), and part of the all-star ensemble in Woody Allen's *Shadows and Fog* (1992). He has also appeared in a number of made-for-TV movies, including *Brotherly Love* (1985), *Yuri Nosenko, KGB* (1986), *Bridge to Silence* (1989), and *Hostages* (1993).

SONDERGAARD, GALE. Actress. *(b. Feb. 15, 1899, Litchfield, Minn., as Edith Holm Sondergaard; d. Aug. 14, 1985.)* Dark, exotic-looking, coldly attractive supporting player adept at portraying sinister, manipulative women. Educated at the University of Minnesota (where her father was a professor), Sondergaard joined a stock company shortly after graduating and worked her way to New York, where she signed with the prestigious Theatre Guild. When she went to Hollywood in 1936, it was at the side of her husband, director Herbert Biberman, rather than at the behest of casting agents. Nonetheless, after being spotted by producer-director

Mervyn LeRoy, she was signed to the key role of the scheming Faith in *Anthony Adverse* (1936)—and won the first Best Supporting Actress Oscar for her performance. LeRoy initially cast her as the Wicked Witch in *The Wizard of Oz,* but after some tests they both agreed she was not right for the role.

She was pretty much typecast as a villainess but still found a striking variety of parts in such major films as *Maid of Salem* (1937), *The Life of Emile Zola* (1937, a sympathetic role as Mme. Dreyfus), *Juarez* (1939, as Countess Eugenie), *The Cat and the Canary* (1939, the first of several encounters with Bob Hope), *The Blue Bird* (as the catlike villainess opposite Shirley Temple), *The Mark of Zorro, The Letter* (all 1940), *Sherlock Holmes and the Spider Woman* (1944, matching wits with Basil Rathbone), *Anna and the King of Siam* (an Oscar-nominated performance as Lady Thiang), *The Time of Their Lives* (as a Mrs. Danvers–type housekeeper, playing straight to Abbott and Costello), and *The Spider Woman Strikes Back* (all 1946, the last-mentioned a cheapie trading on her role in the Sherlock Holmes film).

Blacklisted with her husband following the House Un-American Activities Committee hearings, Sondergaard's last Hollywood film was *East Side, West Side* (1949, for her friend Mervyn LeRoy). She returned to television in the 1960s, and worked occasionally thereafter in such films as *Slaves* (1969, directed by Biberman), *The Return of a Man Called Horse* (1976), and *Echoes* (1983).
OTHER FILMS INCLUDE: 1937: *Seventh Heaven;* 1939: *Never Say Die;* 1941: *The Black Cat;* 1942: *Paris Calling, My Favorite Blonde;* 1943: *Isle of Forgotten Sins;* 1944: *The Invisible Man's Revenge, Christmas Holiday, The Climax;* 1946: *A Night in Paradise;* 1947: *Road to Rio.*

SONNENFELD, BARRY. Director, cinematographer. *(b. Apr. 1, 1953, New York City.)* Stylish, visually distinctive cameraman who has made a successful splash as a director. He graduated from New York University's Graduate Institute of Film and Television in 1978 and worked on corporate films and documentaries—including the Oscar-nominated *In Our Water* (1982)—before making his film debut shooting Joel and Ethan Coen's acclaimed film-noirish thriller *Blood Simple* (1984). This collaboration continued on *Raising Arizona* (1987) and *Miller's Crossing* (1990) and showcased Sonnenfeld's versatility with lurid colors, burnished images, and dazzling, fast-tracking camera movements (dubbed the "wacky-cam" by the Coens). He filmed *Compromising Positions* (1985), *Throw Momma From the Train* (1987, Danny DeVito's directing debut, full of Coen-like camera moves), *Big* (1988), *When Harry Met Sally . . .* (1989), and *Misery* (1990) before directing his first feature, the box-office hit *The Addams Family* (1991). He has since directed (the inevitable) *Addams Family Values* and the Michael J. Fox romantic comedy *For Love or Money* (both 1993).

SORVINO, PAUL. Actor. *(b. Apr. 13, 1939, Brooklyn, N.Y.)* Beefy, imposing character actor who's been a fixture on the big screen and on TV, in roles both jovial and sinister. He's at his best playing tough, urban characters, and was excellent as a mob capo in Martin Scorsese's 1990 gangster picture *GoodFellas.* That same year, he was barely recognizable under a ton of makeup in Warren Beatty's *Dick Tracy* (1990, as Lips Manlis); Sorvino also acted for Beatty in *Reds* (1981). His other films include *Where's Poppa?* (1970, his debut), *The Panic in Needle Park, Made for Each Other* (both 1971), *A Touch of Class, The Day of the Dolphin* (both 1973), *The Gambler* (1974), *I Will, I Will . . . For Now* (1976), *Oh, God!* (1977), *Bloodbrothers* (1978), *Lost and Found* (1979), *Cruising* (1980), *I, the Jury* (1982), *That Championship Season* (1982, reprising his stage role), *Turk 182!, The Stuff* (both 1985), *A Fine Mess* (1986), and *The Rocketeer* (1991), along with the starring role in the unforgettable *Vasectomy: A Delicate Matter* (1986). In 1991 he took over for George Dzundza in the crime series "Law and Order," for one year, then filled in for an ailing Raymond Burr in a 1993 "Perry Mason" TV movie. That same year he appeared unbilled as an underworld kingpin in *The Firm.*

SOTHERN, ANN. Actress. *(b. Jan. 22, 1909, Valley City, N.D., as Harriette Lake.)* Best known for her wisecracking-blonde characterizations, this likable star occasionally showed her mettle in dramatic roles, too. A highly trained vocalist who aspired to a stage career, she entered films, as Harriet Lake, with bit parts in *Broadway Nights* (1927), *The Show of Shows* (1929), *Doughboys,* and *Hold Everything* (both 1930) before actually getting a Broadway break. She returned to Hollywood under contract to Columbia, billed as Ann Sothern in *Let's Fall in Love* (1934), in which she introduced the title tune.

Columbia put her in insignificant pictures such as *The Party's Over, Blind Date* (both 1934), *Eight Bells, Grand Exit* (both 1935), *You May Be Next,* and *Don't Gamble With Love* (both 1936). She fared better on loan to Samuel Goldwyn for Eddie Cantor's *Kid Millions* (1934), and at 20th Century in *Folies Bergère* (1935, opposite Maurice Chevalier). Under contract to RKO she was teamed with Gene Raymond in a number of grade-B musicals, including *Hooray for Love* (1935) and *Walking on Air* (1936), and was a fine foil for comic Jack Oakie in *Super Sleuth* (1937).

After freelancing in such films as *Danger—Love at Work* (1937), *Trade Winds* (1938), and *Hotel for Women* (1939), Sothern signed with MGM. She starred in an unpretentious B called *Maisie* (1939), playing a brassy showgirl with a heart of gold. The film's unexpected success triggered a series, and while none of the follow-ups were as good as the opener, they were popular with audiences: *Congo Maisie, Gold Rush Maisie* (both 1940), *Maisie Was a Lady, Ringside Maisie* (both 1941), *Maisie Gets Her Man* (1942), *Swing Shift Maisie* (1943), *Maisie Goes to Reno* (1944), *Up Goes Maisie* (1946), and *Undercover Maisie* (1947). She also played the part in an MGM-produced radio series.

Sothern starred in two major MGM musicals, *Lady Be Good* (1941, in which she sang the Oscar-winning tune "The Last Time I Saw Paris") and *Panama Hattie* (1942), and was among the all-star ensemble cast of the wartime drama *Cry Havoc* (1943). But Metro never really made room for her at the top; she left the studio after playing the second female lead in *Words and Music* (1948). She made *April Showers* (1948) at Warners, and then won one of her all-time best parts, as one of the spouses (married to Kirk Douglas) in *A Letter to Three Wives* (1949). She spent most of the 1950s on TV, starring in the popular sitcoms "Private Secretary" (1953–57) and "The Ann Sothern Show" (1958–61). (Later, she was the voice of "My Mother, the Car," a memorably titled 1965–66 series.)

In the 1960s, an overweight Sothern returned to feature-film work in blowsy character parts, including *Lady in a Cage, The Best Man* (both 1964), *Sylvia* (1965), *Chubasco* (1968), *The Killing Kind* (1973, never released), *Golden Needles* (1974), *Crazy Mama* (1975), *The Manitou* (1978), and *The Little Dragons* (1980). In 1985 she had a bit in the TV remake of *A Letter to Three Wives,* and then earned an Oscar nomination as the ebullient New England neighbor of Bette Davis and Lillian Gish in *The Whales of August* (1987). She was disappointed when it didn't lead to more offers. Sothern was married to actor Robert Sterling (1943–49); daughter Tisha Sterling is an actress who played her mom as a young woman in *Whales.*

SPACEK, SISSY. Actress. *(b. Dec. 25, 1949, Quitman, Tex., as Mary Elizabeth Spacek.)* This small, freckle-faced, all-American-girl type defied conventional casting-director wisdom to become one of the screen's biggest stars of the 1970s and 1980s—something that, in Hollywood's glamour-conscious Golden Age, probably wouldn't have happened. Originally interested in a career as a singer, Spacek sang at Greenwich Village coffee houses, did background vocals for commercials and even recorded a song, "John, You Went Too Far This Time" (under the name Rainbo). She turned to acting, studied at the Lee Strasberg Theatrical Institute, and soon landed her first movie role (not counting her work as an extra in Andy Warhol's 1971 *Trash)* in Michael Ritchie's *Prime Cut* (1972). Spacek, who's never shaken her Texas accent, raised eyebrows as the teenage companion to the mass murderer played by Martin Sheen in *Badlands* (1973); it was also on that film that she met her future husband, art director Jack Fisk. She starred in the little-seen *Ginger in the Morning* (1973), won critical notice—and public attention—in the highly rated TV movie *Katherine* (1975),

then shot to stardom playing the telekinetic teen in the Stephen King shocker *Carrie* (1976), which earned her an Oscar nomination. (She'd first met the film's director, Brian De Palma, while working as a set decorator on his 1974 film *Phantom of the Paradise.)* Not the easiest actress to cast, she nevertheless found interesting, often challenging roles in such films as *Welcome to L.A.* (1977), Robert Altman's *3 Women* (also 1977), the telefilm *Verna: USO Girl* (1978), and *Heart Beat* (1979, as Jack Kerouac's soulmate Carolyn Cassady). Then she snagged a perfect part in a mainstream hit, playing country music star Loretta Lynn in *Coal Miner's Daughter* (1980), for which she did her own singing. The performance earned her an Academy Award.

Her husband directed her in *Raggedy Man* (1981); then she won Oscar nominations for *Missing* (1982, as the young wife of a missing American in Latin America) and *The River* (1984, as a farm mother). She was effective as the true-life heroine *Marie* (1985), and after tackling downbeat drama in *'Night Mother* and romance in *Violets Are Blue . . .* (both 1986), she earned another Oscar nomination for her uncharacteristic (and quite funny) performance as the ditziest of three eccentric Southern sisters in *Crimes of the Heart* (also 1986). Since then she's focused more on raising a family than maintaining a starring career; her sporadic credits include *The Long Walk Home* (1990), *JFK* (1991, as Kevin Costner's wife), *Hard Promises* (also 1991), *A Private Matter* (1992, telefilm), *Trading Mom* (1994), and *A Place for Annie* (also 1994, telefilm).

SPADER, JAMES. Actor. *(b. Feb. 7, 1960, Buzzards Bay, Mass.)* For a time the screen's premier delineator of devious, unprincipled yuppies and WASPs from Hell, this talented young actor could become one of the 1990s' most formidable leading men. Spader, the son of teachers, dropped out of prep school in the 11th grade to pursue an acting career in New York. His feature film debut, in *Endless Love* (1981), was followed by turns in exploitation pictures such as *Tuff Turf* (1985) and *The New Kids* (1985), and TV work including a stint as Robert Mitchum's son in *A Killer in the Family* (1983). Spader's unctuous "charm" enlivened *Pretty in Pink* (1986), *Mannequin, Baby Boom,*

Less Than Zero (delivering that film's best performance as a yuppie drug dealer), and *Wall Street* (all 1987). He starred in *Jack's Back* (1988, as a possible modern-day Jack the Ripper) and *The Rachel Papers* (1989), but he really hit his stride as the sexually troubled young man in *sex, lies, and videotape* (also 1989), for which he won the Best Actor award at the 1989 Cannes Film Festival.

Spader's reputation cemented, he starred in *Bad Influence* (1990), playing a gullible young businessman opposite manipulative psycho Rob Lowe (in what would earlier have been a Spaderesque turn) and *White Palace* (also 1990), as a callow preppie who falls for earthy waitress Susan Sarandon. In other words, he was still playing yuppies, albeit sympathetic ones. *True Colors* (1991) saw him pitted against former friend and law-school classmate John Cusack, and in *Storyville* (1992) he played a young politician entwined in a web of deceit. Recent credits include *Bob Roberts* (also 1992, in a hilarious cameo as a newscaster), the oddball, existential *The Music of Chance* (1993), the werewolf saga *Wolf* (as another scummy yuppie), *Stargate,* and *Dream Lover* (all 1994). Spader is a great fan of Charles Laughton, and has said he aspires to great roles like his in the years ahead.

SPHEERIS, PENELOPE. Director, screenwriter, producer. *(b. Dec. 2, 1945, Algiers, La.)* Spheeris produced Albert Brooks' short films during the first season of TV's "Saturday Night Live," as well as his first film, *Real Life* (1979), before making her own directorial debut with *The Decline of Western Civilization* (1981), an acclaimed documentary of L.A.'s punk rock scene in the late seventies. She followed with a number of extremely violent fiction films about disenchanted youth, including *The Wild Side* (1983, aka *Suburbia), The Boys Next Door* (1985), and *Dudes* (1988), and another documentary, *The Decline of Western Civilization Part II: The Metal Years* (also 1988). Her affinity for rock and roll culture made her a most excellent choice as director of *Wayne's World* (1992), the feature-length spinoff of the "Saturday Night Live" Mike Myers–Dana Carvey sketch which became a monster hit. She then tackled another TV transformation, directing and coproducing a clumsily un-

funny screen version of *The Beverly Hillbillies* (1993). Steven Spielberg subsequently hired her to direct a feature-length update of *The Little Rascals* (1994). Spheeris also worked as a story editor on TV's "Roseanne," helped create the TV action spoof "Danger Theatre," and wrote the odd "Lord of the Flies" modernization, *Summer Camp Nightmare* (1987).

SPIELBERG, STEVEN. Director, producer. *(b. Dec. 18, 1947, Cincinnati.)* Probably the most commercially influential director of all time, with a handful of his films listed among the top 10 biggest moneymakers of all time, Spielberg at his best combines a childlike sense of wonder with the expert craftsman's sure-handed manipulation of the medium's most effective and evocative image-making techniques. A moviemaker since boyhood, he launched his professional career at Universal, where he was signed to a seven-year contract at the age of twenty-one. His skill was immediately apparent in a showy segment of the episodic TV movie *Night Gallery* (1969) in which Joan Crawford played a blind woman who receives an eye transplant. He attracted particular notice for a TV "movie of the week," *Duel* (1971), a study in suspense featuring Dennis Weaver and a menacing diesel truck. His other TV movies include *Something Evil* (1972) and *Savage* (1973). His first theatrical feature, *The Sugarland Express* (1974), was a slickly made "road" story that marked him as a comer. Nightmarish production problems on the big-budget, highly anticipated *Jaws* (1975) almost detoured his rise to prominence; he was nearly replaced at one point, and was still making last-minute changes on the eve of its release. The minute the public saw it, however, all tongue-wagging ceased; it was a gut-wrenching thriller of the highest order, and its extraordinary success made Spielberg an "overnight" sensation.

Close Encounters of the Third Kind (1977) was an epic of a different sort, a mammoth sci-fi story that earned the director his first Academy Award nomination. (His dissatisfaction with the film, and its muddled midsection, caused him to reedit the picture and reissue it in 1980 as "The Special Edition.") His next film was also epic in scope, but it was a comedy;

unfortunately, *1941* (1979) had more production values than actual laughs, and was
Spielberg's first failure. He then teamed
up with George Lucas, his contemporary
and fellow wunderkind, to create a large-
scale action adventure that would synthe-
size the best elements of old cliffhanger
serials. Lucas produced and Spielberg
directed *Raiders of the Lost Ark* (1981), a
massive hit that earned him a second Oscar nomination, and inspired a pair of sequels (which Spielberg also directed), *Indiana Jones and the Temple of Doom*
(1984) and *Indiana Jones and The Last
Crusade* (1989).

E.T. The Extra-Terrestrial (1982) saw
Spielberg at the height of his creative
powers, celebrating the nurturing environment of the nuclear family while offering
the comforting notion of a benign, almost
messianic visitor from another planet,
whose magical powers give life to the
most primal fantasies of a child's imagination. Few other films in history can approach the mythic strength of this masterwork, which became the highest-grossing
film ever made (till that time). Again
Spielberg was nominated for an Oscar but
neither he nor his wildly popular movie
were winners.

After contributing one segment (the saccharine "Kick the Can") to *Twilight
Zone—The Movie* (1983), he set his sights
on a more "adult" project, an adaptation
of Alice Walker's controversial novel
about a young black woman's odyssey to
womanhood and self-recognition, *The
Color Purple* (1985). Hailed in many
quarters, it was also attacked by some
who felt Spielberg presented this material
exactly as he had *E.T.,* with swooping
camera-crane movements, lush music
swells, and too much sugar. The same
charges were leveled—more widely—at
Empire of the Sun (1987), a serious and
(again) epic-length saga of a boy's experiences in war-torn China, based on J. G.
Ballard's autobiographical novel. No one
questioned Spielberg's craftsmanship or
his storytelling drive, but it seemed that
style and substance weren't merging com-
patibly. Nevertheless, at the 1987 Oscar
ceremony he was presented the prestigious
Irving G. Thalberg Award.

The filmmaker then decided to remake a
boyhood favorite, the sentimental romantic fantasy *A Guy Named Joe* (1943) as
Always (1989), but here again he seemed

to be off his mark. A much anticipated
followup to Peter Pan called *Hook* (1991)
was a commercial success, but to some
observers showed Spielberg at his whimsical worst, lavishing his enormous skills on
a film that was hollow at its center.

Then came 1993. First, Spielberg presented the world with *Jurassic Park,* an
eye-popping dinosaur yarn that followed
formulaic story guidelines, but set audiences afire with its unprecedented special
effects—and scenes of characters in jeopardy. It quickly became the biggest moneymaking movie of all time. While editing
that film he was busy in Krakow filming a
much more personal project, one which
had a ten-year gestation period: *Schindler's List,* the powerful true-life story of a
man who became the savior of more than
one thousand Jews in wartime Poland.
The director, an assimilated American
Jew, had never dealt with his ethnicity on
film before, and critics, who never thought
him capable of anything so dark or
wrenching, were floored by the results.
Filmed in black and white, with a deliberate lack of "Hollywood" gloss, it earned
Spielberg the greatest accolades of his career, and his long-coveted pair of Academy Awards for both Best Director and
Best Picture.

From the moment he achieved success,
Spielberg was eager to have a hand in
movies he wouldn't be able to direct personally. He coproduced and cowrote the
screenplay for *Poltergeist* (1982), which
reportedly he also helped direct. Under the
Amblin banner, he became an executive
producer on a variety of films, including *I
Wanna Hold Your Hand* (1978), *Used
Cars* (1980), *Continental Divide* (1981),
Twilight Zone—The Movie (1983), *Gremlins* (1984), *Back to the Future, The Goonies* (from Spielberg's story), *Young Sherlock Holmes* (all 1985), *The Money Pit*
(1986), **batteries not included, Innerspace* (both 1987), *Back to the Future
Part II, Dad* (both 1989), *Back to the Fu-
ture Part III, Joe Versus the Volcano,
Arachnophobia, Gremlins 2 The New
Batch* (all 1990), *The Flintstones* (1994, as
"Steven Spielrock"), and *Casper* (1995).

A rabid animation fan, Spielberg also
produced the cartoon features *An American Tail* (1986), *The Land Before Time*
(1988), the combination live-action/
animation feature *Who Framed Roger
Rabbit* (1988), and from his own

Amblimation studio, *An American Tail:
Fievel Goes West* (1991) and *We're Back!
A Dinosaur's Story* (1993). He also executive produced several animated TV series,
"Tiny Toon Adventures" (1990–), "Family Dog" (1993), and "Animaniacs"
(1993–). Spielberg's most ambitious TV
venture was a big-budget anthology series,
"Amazing Stories" (1985–87) which attracted major talent on both sides of the
camera (including Spielberg himself, who
directed a special hour-long episode, "The
Mission," starring Kevin Costner), but
was generally a disappointment. He also
executive produced a series of TV movies
by major playwrights under the "Screen-
works" umbrella, beginning with David
Mamet's *The Water Engine* (1992), a telefilm about the Civil War called *Class of
'61* (1993), and the family-oriented, futuristic underwater series "seaQuest DSV"
(1993–). Spielberg has also made cameo
appearances in *The Blues Brothers* (1980)
and *Gremlins* (1984).

In 1995, Spielberg made worldwide
headlines by joining forces with high-
profile executives David Geffen and Jeffrey Katzenberg to form DreamWorks
SKG, an instant multimedia empire.

STACK, ROBERT. Actor. *(b. Jan. 13,
1919, Los Angeles.)* Growing up in Hollywood, handsome, wavy-haired Robert
Stack was a part of the movie colony before he ever set foot on a sound stage:
many actors and executives (including
Clark Gable and Carole Lombard) rented
horses from his family for riding and
hunting expeditions. His contacts—along
with his good looks and friendly
manner—landed Stack in *First Love*
(1939), in which he gave maturing child
star Deanna Durbin her first "adult"
screen kiss. It was followed by *The Mortal Storm* (1940), *Nice Girl?* (1941, again
with Durbin), Ernst Lubitsch's *To Be or
Not to Be* (in which he keeps walking out
on Jack Benny's Hamlet soliloquy), *Eagle
Squadron* (both 1942), and some Westerns
for Universal before World War 2 put the
brakes on his career. After the war he had
some difficulty reestablishing himself in
Hollywood, and seemed more distant and
taciturn.

Stack starred or costarred in *Fighter
Squadron, Miss Tatlock's Millions, A Date
With Judy* (all 1948), and a number of

early 1950s films, including *Bullfighter
and the Lady* (1951) and the first 3-D feature, *Bwana Devil* (1953), before scoring
his best-remembered screen roles in *The
High and the Mighty* (1954) and *Written
on the Wind* (1956, for which he received
a Best Supporting Actor Oscar nomination). However, it was on television where
Stack was to make his most lasting impression, playing G-Man Eliot Ness in the
Prohibition-era dramatic series "The Untouchables" (1959–63), which earned him
an Emmy in its first season. But his tight-
lipped, stone-faced characterization pigeonholed him, and it took years to break
the association with Ness.

Most of Stack's theatrical film work in
the 1960s and 1970s was in Europe, but
he remained a potent attraction on TV, and
was one of the revolving stars of "The
Name of the Game" (1968–72). By the
time of *1941* (1979) he was even willing
to play with his own deadpan screen persona, showing the character of Gen.
Stilwell crying at Disney's *Dumbo;* the
following year he threw all caution to the
wind with a hilarious self-parody in *Airplane!* (1980). In 1991 he made peace
with his former albatross and starred in
the TV movie *The Return of Eliot Ness.*
Since 1988 he has been the host of TV's
"Unsolved Mysteries."

OTHER FILMS INCLUDE: 1953: *Sabre Jet;*
1954: *The Iron Glove;* 1955: *House of Bamboo, Good Morning, Miss Dove;* 1956: *Great
Day in the Morning;* 1958: *The Tarnished Angels, The Gift of Love;* 1959: *John Paul Jones*
(in the title role); 1960: *The Last Voyage;*
1963: *The Caretakers;* 1983: *Uncommon
Valor;* 1988: *Caddyshack II;* 1990: *Joe Versus
the Volcano.*

STALLONE, SYLVESTER. Actor, director, writer. *(b. July 6, 1946, New York
City.)* He was just a bit player for the first
five years of his movie career, playing
leather-jacketed greasers or small-time
hoods, before breaking into the star ranks
with *Rocky* (1976), the feel-good story of
a two-bit boxer who gets a once-in-a-
lifetime title shot and makes good. In a
way, it was also Stallone's once-in-a-
lifetime shot; it remains one of the most
enjoyable movies he's ever done. A drama
student at the University of Miami, he returned to his hometown to crash the stage,
appearing in a few off-Broadway produc-

tions and a porno film (since retitled *The Italian Stallion)* before making his "legitimate" screen debut as a subway thug who menaces Woody Allen in *Bananas* (1971).

The heavy-lidded Stallone worked in *The Lord's of Flatbush* (1974, to which he contributed some dialogue), *The Prisoner of Second Avenue, Capone, Death Race 2000, Farewell, My Lovely* (all 1975), and *Cannonball* (1976) before taking his biggest gamble to date. Thinking himself doomed to a lifetime of stereotypical supporting roles, he wrote *Rocky* with himself in mind, selling the property for little money (but a share of the profits) with the proviso that he play the lead. The low-budget sleeper won a Best Picture Academy Award, earned Stallone Oscar nominations both for his script and his acting, and made him an overnight star. Flush with success, in 1978 he cowrote and starred in *F.I.S.T.,* an epic story about union organizing, and the picaresque comedy-drama *Paradise Alley*, an urban drama about three brothers, which he also directed. Neither of these was very successful, and Stallone penned, directed, and starred in *Rocky II* (1979) to recapture lost ground.

The problem was, audiences didn't seem to want to see him as anyone but Rocky. Neither *Nighthawks* (1981, a solid urban thriller) nor *Victory* (also 1981, a misfired actioner with a soccer theme) drew the expected crowds, but the surprise success of *First Blood* (1982) gave Stallone another icon-like character that audiences cottoned to: taciturn tough guy and Vietnam vet John Rambo. *Rambo: First Blood Part II* (1985) and *Rambo III* (1988) were denigrated by most critics, but scored big at the box office.

Stallone's subsequent films have been hit-or-miss propositions, both artistically and commercially. *Staying Alive* (1983, a sequel to *Saturday Night Fever* that he cowrote and directed but did not star in), *Rhinestone* (1984), *Cobra* (1986, costarring then-wife Brigitte Nielsen), *Over the Top* (1987), and *Lock Up* (1989) can most charitably be described as mistakes. Typically Stallone has followed these unsuccessful experiments with returns to the *Rocky* saga (sequels in 1979, 1982, 1985, and 1990), which, amazingly, have all paid off handsomely.

In recent years he's shown a willingness to kid his own macho image, as witness the lighthearted *Tango & Cash* (1989, as a bespectacled, yuppified federal agent), the old-fashioned farce *Oscar* (1991, as a Prohibition-era gangster trying to go straight), and the broadly comic *Stop! or My Mom Will Shoot* (1992, as a cop tormented by his loud-mouthed mother). His summer 1993 release, *Cliffhanger,* brought him back to straightforward action fare—and big-time box-office success. He followed it with the futuristic *Demolition Man* (1993) and the action vehicles *The Specialist* (1994) and *Judge Dredd* (1995).

STAMP, TERENCE. Actor. *(b. July 23, 1939, Stepney, East London.)* As a pale, almost beautiful young man, Stamp seemed born to play Herman Melville's angelic hero in 1962's *Billy Budd* (even if he had to bleach his hair blond to do it). This debut performance earned him an Oscar nomination. His haunting looks also enabled Stamp to infuse otherworldly qualities into such characters as the unbalanced kidnapper in 1965's *The Collector.* In fact, his face achieved a near-iconic status among film fans of that era, in such diverse films as *Modesty Blaise* (1966), *Far From the Madding Crowd, Poor Cow* (both 1967), the Fellini segment of *Spirits of the Dead, Blue,* Pasolini's *Teorema* (all 1968), and *The Mind of Mr. Soames* (1970). Stamp's film appearances in the 1970s were sporadic; near the end of the decade, looking cooler and more distinguished, he popped up in villainous character roles, most visibly as one of a trio of Kryptonian criminals in *Superman* (1978) and *Superman II* (1980). After costarring in the sly British black comedy *The Hit* (1984) he appeared in a handful of mainstream American films, including *Legal Eagles* (1986), *The Sicilian, Wall Street* (both 1987, the latter an effective turn as a financier), *Alien Nation* (1988), the Brat-Pack Western *Young Guns* (also 1988), and *The Real McCoy* (1993), and won great acclaim for his portrayal of a stoic transsexual performer in *The Adventures of Priscilla, Queen of the Desert* (1994).

STANDER, LIONEL. Actor. *(b. Jan. 11, 1908, New York City; d. Nov. 30, 1994.)* Wavy-haired, gravel-voiced actor best remembered for his comedic supporting roles. More or less stumbling into show business upon graduating from high school, Stander made his stage debut at 19 and worked several years both on stage and in radio. His first films were Warner Bros./Vitaphone short subjects filmed in Brooklyn (with such stars as Roscoe "Fatty" Arbuckle) in the early 1930s. After making a favorable impression in *The Scoundrel* (1935), a Hecht-MacArthur film shot in New York, Stander went to Hollywood, where he quickly became a popular supporting player in *Soak the Rich, The Milky Way, Mr. Deeds Goes to Town* (all 1936), *Meet Nero Wolfe* (1936, as sidekick Archie Goodwin), *A Star Is Born* (1937, as the acid-tongued press agent), *The League of Frightened Men* (1937, the second and last Nero Wolfe movie), *The Last Gangster* (1937), *Professor Beware* (1938), *What a Life* (1939), *Guadalcanal Diary* (1943), *The Kid From Brooklyn* (1946, repeating his role in this remake of *The Milky Way*), *Spectre of the Rose* (1946), *Mad Wednesday* (1947, aka *The Sin of Harold Diddlebock*) and *Unfaithfully Yours* (1948), before being blacklisted following a volatile session before the House Un-American Activities Committee. He returned to the screen in 1965, taking up more or less where he left off, playing comic hoods. Later credits include *The Loved One* (1965), *Cul-De-Sac* (1966), *Once Upon a Time in the West* (1968), *The Gang That Couldn't Shoot Straight* (1971), *Pulp* (1972), *The Black Bird* (1975), *New York, New York* (1977), *1941* (1979), *Wicked Stepmother, Cookie* (both 1989), and numerous Italian-made productions of the 1970s. Stander's career got a boost when he was cast as the valet Max in the long-running "Hart to Hart" TV show (1979–84) and its 1993 reunion movie, *Hart to Hart Returns*. Stander's final film was *The Last Good Time* (1995).

STANTON, HARRY DEAN. Actor. *(b. July 14, 1926, West Irvine, Ky.)* Stanton is the screen's quintessential disaffected outsider, a status he has enjoyed for many years, and which he brilliantly reaffirmed in his first starring role, a near-catatonic drifter who eventually comes to terms with the life he left behind in Wim Wenders' *Paris, Texas* (1984). Easily recognizable by his gaunt, weatherbeaten, haunted face, Stanton can be spotted in lit-erally dozens of bit parts or supporting roles in movies beginning with *Revolt at Fort Laramie* (1957). His better-known films of the 1960s and 1970s include *Cool Hand Luke* (1967), *Pat Garrett and Billy the Kid* (1973), *The Godfather, Part II* (1974), *Farewell, My Lovely* (1975), *Wise Blood,* and *Alien* (both 1979). His performance as an eccentric auto repossessor in the cult favorite *Repo Man* (1984) endeared him to young, hipper audiences; he also became something of a spiritual godfather to such younger actors as Emilio Estevez and Sean Penn. In the wake of *Paris, Texas* he won sympathetic roles in *One Magic Christmas* (1985) as an angel (!), *Pretty in Pink* (1986), as a sensitive, working-class dad, and *Mr. North* (1988), as a jaunty Irish member of the hired-help brigade in Newport, R.I. He also delivered a harrowing performance as the Apostle Paul in Martin Scorsese's controversial *The Last Temptation of Christ* (also 1988). Stanton appeared in supporting roles in *The Fourth War* and *Wild at Heart* (both 1990); he occasionally plays leads in low-budget independent films such as *Twister* (1988). He had a small but creepy part in *Twin Peaks: Fire Walk With Me* (1992).

OTHER FILMS INCLUDE: 1958: *The Proud Rebel;* 1959: *Pork Chop Hill;* 1962: *Hero's Island;* 1963: *The Man From the Diner's Club;* 1965: *Ride in the Whirlwind;* 1967: *The Hostage;* 1971: *Two-Lane Blacktop;* 1973: *Dillinger;* 1974: *Cockfighter;* 1975: *Rancho Deluxe, 92 in the Shade;* 1976: *The Missouri Breaks;* 1978: *Straight Time;* 1980: *Private Benjamin;* 1981: *Escape From New York;* 1982: *One From the Heart;* 1983: *Christine;* 1984: *Red Dawn;* 1985: *Fool for Love;* 1992: *Man Trouble;* 1993: *Hostages* (telefilm).

STANWYCK, BARBARA. Actress. *(b. July 16, 1907, Brooklyn, N.Y., as Ruby Stevens; d. Jan. 20, 1990.)* In the period during which she established her reputation as a dependable leading lady, Stanwyck specialized in hard-edged, brittle characters who were often revealed to have hearts of gold, but who also displayed the actress' trademark independence and determination. Many of her tart-tongued, working-class heroines resembled those played by Joan Crawford in the 1930s, but Stanwyck managed to invest most of them with a winning vulnerability and other appealing traits that Crawford was less successful in portraying.

Her early years themselves seem like the stuff of a 1932 Warner Bros. programmer: Born Ruby Stevens, she was orphaned at a young age and raised by an older sister (a chorus girl) who occasionally left her to board with family friends. She quit school at age 13 and, after working in several menial jobs, wangled a spot in a chorus line. Intent on becoming an actress, she worked hard and eventually landed straight parts, finally winning the female lead in a popular Broadway melodrama, "The Noose." Stanwyck made her film debut (playing a dancer) in *Broadway Nights* (1927), but returned to the Great White Way for more stage successes. In 1928 she married vaudeville and stage star Frank Fay, with whom she went to Hollywood. Other early films include *The Locked Door* and *Mexicali Rose* (both 1929).

Stanwyck quickly developed a reputation as a dedicated, hard-working professional and came into her own under the direction of Frank Capra, in *Ladies of Leisure* (1930), *The Miracle Woman* (1931), *Forbidden* (1932), and most important, *The Bitter Tea of General Yen* (1933), his bald-faced bid for an Academy Award and respectability. Stanwyck also spent time at Warner Bros., where her hard-boiled screen persona was developed in tough little programmers such as *Night Nurse* (1931), *Ladies They Talk About,* and *Baby Face* (both 1933, at her best in the latter, as an experience-hardened woman who sleeps her way to the top of the business world). Other films from the first half of the thirties include *Illicit, Ten Cents a Dance* (both 1931), *Shopworn, So Big, The Purchase Price* (all 1932), *Ever in My Heart* (1933), *A Lost Lady, Gambling Lady* (both 1934), *The Secret Bride, Woman in Red,* and *Red Salute* (all 1935).

In 1935 Stanwyck freed herself from the shackles of marriage by divorcing Fay, who had deeply resented her success as his own career dwindled to nothingness. She also left Warners to freelance, immediately snagging the title role in George Stevens' *Annie Oakley* (1935). She costarred with handsome Robert Taylor in *His Brother's Wife* (1936); their partnership extended beyond the screen, and they were married in 1939. After taking leads in *A Message to Garcia, Banjo on My Knees, The Plough and the Stars* (all 1936), and *Internes Can't Take Money* (1937, the first movie to feature the "Dr. Kildare" character, played here by Joel McCrea), she assumed the title role in *Stella Dallas* (also 1937), King Vidor's definitive version of the well-known weepie about mother love and sacrifice. Stanwyck earned her first Oscar nomination for her heart-rending performance, and entered the peak of her career. (Not that she didn't still make potboilers, as witness 1936's *The Bride Walks Out,* 1937's *That Is My Affair,* with Taylor, and *Breakfast for Two,* 1938's *Always Goodbye* and *The Mad Miss Manton.*)

Cecil B. DeMille starred her in his Western epic *Union Pacific* (1939), and she helped newcomer William Holden make a memorable debut in *Golden Boy* that same year. She was alternately tough and funny as a convicted shoplifter in Mitchell Leisen's *Remember the Night* (1940), written by Preston Sturges, who, as writer-director, gave her a memorable role as a predatory card shark who sinks her teeth into girl-shy millionaire Henry Fonda in *The Lady Eve* (1941), a screwball-comedy classic just as funny today as it was a half-century ago. Later that year she played a sassy stripteaser opposite Gary Cooper in *Ball of Fire,* another terrific comedy (which got her an Oscar nod), and was reunited with Cooper and Frank Capra for *Meet John Doe,* in a tailor-made role.

Back in tights for *Lady of Burlesque* (1943), a ribald adaptation of Gypsy Rose Lee's best-selling mystery "The G-String Murders," Stanwyck next sported blond tresses as the treacherous temptress in Billy Wilder's *Double Indemnity* (1944), picking up her third Academy Award nomination. As the seductive schemer who cons morally lax insurance salesman Fred MacMurray into committing murder for her, she delivered what many believe to be her finest screen performance.

In the late 1940s Stanwyck's vehicles began to slip—at first almost imperceptibly, but by decade's end rather precipitously. A notable exception was *Sorry, Wrong Number* (1948), a taut thriller for which, as the intended victim of a murder plot she has overheard on the telephone, she got her fourth and final Oscar nomination. But *Christmas in Connecticut* (1945), *The Bride Wore Boots* (1946), *The Strange*

Love of Martha Ivers (1946), *The Two Mrs. Carrolls, Cry Wolf, The Other Love* (all 1947), *B.F.'s Daughter* (1948), *The Lady Gambles, East Side, West Side,* and *The File on Thelma Jordon* (all 1949), even though they all had elements to recommend them, were on the whole not up to her earlier 1940s films.

The 1950s brought Stanwyck some interesting roles—notably in *The Furies* (1950), *The Man With a Cloak* (1951), *Clash by Night* (1952), *Executive Suite* (1954), and *The Maverick Queen* (1956)—but they were the exception to more standard fare like *All I Desire, Titanic, Blowing Wild, Jeopardy, The Moonlighter* (all 1953), *Cattle Queen of Montana, Witness to Murder* (both 1954), *Escape to Burma, The Violent Men* (both 1955), *These Wilder Years, There's Always Tomorrow* (both 1956), *Forty Guns, Trooper Hook* (both 1957), and *Walk on the Wild Side* (1962).

She made only a few films in the 1960s—including 1964's *Roustabout* (with Elvis Presley) and *The Night Walker* (which reunited her with Robert Taylor, whom she'd divorced in 1952)—but achieved small-screen fame (and an Emmy) as the silvery-haired, indomitable frontier matriarch in "The Big Valley" (1965–69). Stanwyck was coaxed out of privacy to appear in the 1983 miniseries "The Thorn Birds" (for which she won an Emmy) and the spinoff series "Dynasty II: The Colbys" (1985–86). In 1982 she received an honorary Academy Award.

STAPLETON, MAUREEN. Actress. *(b. June 21, 1925, Troy, N.Y.)* Outstanding character actress who has excelled in dramatic and comedic roles on stage, screen, and television. Enamored of theater and movies from childhood (and a lifelong, passionate fan of Joel McCrea), she went to New York immediately after high school and studied at the Herbert Berghof Acting School before making her Broadway debut in Burgess Meredith's 1946 production of "The Playboy of the Western World." She went on to win a Tony Award for her performance as Serafina in Tennessee Williams' "The Rose Tattoo" (1951) and appeared in numerous stage productions, including Williams' "Twenty-Seven Wagons Full of Cotton" and "Orpheus Descending," Lillian Hellman's "Toys in

the Attic," and Neil Simon's "The Gingerbread Lady" (for which she won a second Tony, in 1971).

Stapleton received a Supporting Actress Oscar nomination for her very first film role in *Lonelyhearts* (1958) and earned nominations for *Airport* (1970) and Woody Allen's first "serious" film, *Interiors* (1978). She took home an Oscar for her portrayal of a no-nonsense Emma Goldman in Warren Beatty's epic *Reds* (1981), and was also excellent in *The Fugitive Kind* (1959, adapted from "Orpheus Descending") and *A View From the Bridge* (1962) and gave a delightful comic performance in Neil Simon's *Plaza Suite* (1971), which she had also played on Broadway. Stapleton has also starred in many TV movies and plays, earning an Emmy for *Among the Paths to Eden* (1967) and nominations for *Queen of the Stardust Ballroom* (1975), *The Gathering* (1977), and *Miss Rose White* (1992).
OTHER FILMS INCLUDE: 1979: *Lost and Found;* 1981: *The Fan;* 1984: *Johnny Dangerously;* 1985: *Cocoon;* 1986: *The Money Pit, Heartburn;* 1987: *Made in Heaven, Nuts, Sweet Lorraine* (in the leading role, as the owner of a Catskills hotel); 1992: *Passed Away;* 1994: *Trading Mom;* 1995: *The Last Good Time.*

STARRETT, CHARLES. Actor. *(b. Mar. 28, 1903, Athol, Mass.; d. Mar. 22, 1986.)* Scion of a wealthy Yankee family (founders of the Starrett Tool & Die Works) and a Dartmouth football star, this tall, handsome, self-assured young man first appeared on-screen as an extra in *The Quarterback* (1926), partially filmed at his alma mater. Starrett was expected to help run the family business upon graduating but elected to take up acting instead. He spent several years on stage before landing a contract with Paramount in 1930, appearing opposite Carole Lombard in *Fast and Loose* and Fredric March in *The Royal Family of Broadway.* He played the juvenile lead in MGM's *The Mask of Fu Manchu* (1932), but didn't win top billing until he left the major studios for Poverty Row. Starrett starred in *Jungle Bride* (1933), *Sons of Steel* (1934), *A Shot in the Dark,* and *Murder on the Campus* (both 1935) before signing with Columbia to appear in Westerns, replacing the recently departed Tim McCoy. *Gallant Defender*

(1935) was the first of more than 100 horse operas he made for Columbia between 1935 and 1952.

Although the earlier oaters—including *The Cowboy Star* (1936), *Outlaws of the Prairie* (1938), *Texas Stagecoach* (1940), and *Bad Men of the Hills* (1942)—are by far the better films, it's the post-1945 films in which he played the masked, Robin Hood-like "Durango Kid" for which Starrett is best remembered. From *Return of the Durango Kid* (1945) to *The Kid From Broken Gun* (1952)—a 64-picture run—the Starrett series thrived in a declining market for B Westerns, and the star himself enjoyed a personal popularity equaled by few other cowboy heroes. Always better than his material, Starrett redeemed the films with his professionalism, never once allowing condescension to slip into his performances. He retired from the screen following the "Durango" run, and continued to receive fan mail—despite the fact that most of his Westerns never played on TV.

STEELE, BARBARA. Actress. *(b. Dec. 29, 1937, England.)* The mother of all scream queens, at least to the postwar generation of horror-film fans, Steele owes to her exotic good looks and hypnotic screen presence her standing as something of a fetish object for a particularly intense segment of the cognoscenti. Her dual role as an evil, undead witch and virginal princess in Mario Bava's splendid *Black Sunday* (1961) set up her madonna/whore credentials quite convincingly, after which a handful of Italian horror directors lined up to see who got to chain Steele to a wall next. Ricardo Freda's *The Horrible Dr. Hichcock* (1962) is often cited as the exemplary "appreciation" of Steele. The actress also worked with Fellini (in a supporting role in *8½*, 1963) and German director Volker Schlondorff *(Young Torless,* 1966). She took time off from acting after her second marriage, and came back in *Caged Heat* (1974), playing a sadistic, crippled women's-prison warden who performs a dream striptease. Steele played small parts in both *Pretty Baby* and *Piranha* (both 1978) before going behind the scenes to work with TV producer Dan Curtis; she was one of the producers of his epic miniseries "War and Remembrance" (1989; she had a cameo in it as well) and worked in his short-lived revival of the horror soap opera "Dark Shadows" in 1991.

OTHER FILMS INCLUDE: 1958: *Bachelor of Hearts* (her first); 1961: *The Pit and the Pendulum;* 1963: *Castle of Blood;* 1965: *Revenge of the Blood Beast;* 1968: *The Crimson Cult;* 1975: *They Came From Within;* 1977: *I Never Promised You a Rose Garden;* 1980: *Silent Scream.*

STEELE, BOB. Actor. *(b. Jan. 23, 1906, Pendleton, Oreg., as Robert North Bradbury, Jr.; d. Dec. 21, 1988.)* This short, muscular, curly-haired actor was a well-liked horse-opera hero for nearly 20 years before turning to character work and achieving considerable success in smaller, showier roles. He debuted on film in the short-subject series, "The Adventures of Bill and Bob," directed by his father (prolific B-Western filmmaker Robert N. Bradbury) and costarring his brother Bill (who later provided the on-screen warbling lip-synched by John Wayne as "Singin' Sandy" in the Bradbury-directed *Riders of Destiny* [1933]). He became Bob Steele for a series of FBO Westerns beginning with 1927's *The Mojave Kid.* A riding whirlwind and scrappy screen fighter who convincingly bested adversaries twice his size, Steele remained popular throughout the 1930s in a series of cookie-cutter Westerns for a number of independent studios. (He's best represented by the World Wides, including 1932's *Son of Oklahoma* and *The Man from Hell's Edges,* and Republics, including 1936's *Desert Phantom* and 1937's *Arizona Gunfighter.)*

Steele took his first shot at "mainstream" movie character work in 1939's *Of Mice and Men,* and surprised critics and audiences alike with his skillful performance as the sadistic Curley. He played "Tucson Smith" in 20 "Three Mesquiteers" Westerns for Republic, beginning in 1940 with *Under Texas Skies* and ending with the last series entry, *Santa Fe Scouts,* in 1943. He also appeared in eight 1940 PRC oaters as Billy the Kid. A short stint as one of Monogram's "Trail Blazers" (Ken Maynard and Hoot Gibson were the others) proved unrewarding, and Steele again took up character work in such movies as *The Big Sleep* (1946, as the killer Canino), *Killer McCoy* (1947), *South of St. Louis* (1949), *The Enforcer* (1951), *The Steel Jungle* (1956), *Rio*

Bravo (1959), *The Comancheros* (1961), *Taggart* (1964), *Requiem for a Gunfighter* (1965), *Hang 'Em High* (1968), *Rio Lobo* (1970), and *something big* (1971). Never known for his comic ability, Steele was surprisingly effective as the slightly senile Trooper Duffy in the TV series "F Troop" (1965–67).

STEENBURGEN, MARY. Actress. (b. Feb. 8, 1953, Newport, Ark.) Most of the women she plays on screen are soft-spoken and gentle; a few have been a wee bit ditzy. But she's equally capable of endowing her characters with fiery passion and indomitable resolve. In short, Mary Steenburgen is an extraordinarily versatile and appealing actress. After a lengthy stint at New York's Neighborhood Playhouse, Steenburgen made her film debut in *Goin' South* (1978), a pleasantly zany Western starring and directed by Jack Nicholson. She played a modern-day career woman confronted by time-traveling H. G. Wells in the fanciful *Time After Time* (1979), and married costar Malcolm McDowell in real life. (They later divorced.) But it was her disarming performance as the slightly daffy wife of hapless Howard Hughes heir Melvin Dummar (played by Paul LeMat) in *Melvin and Howard* (1980) that cemented her stardom—and won her an Oscar for Best Supporting Actress.

Steenburgen essayed a proper but strong-willed mother in the turn-of-the-century *Ragtime* (1981), appeared again in period costume for Woody Allen's *A Midsummer Night's Sex Comedy* (1982), and yet again as real-life author Marjorie Kinnan Rawlings in the leisurely paced but eminently satisfying drama *Cross Creek* (1983). *Romantic Comedy* (also 1983) paired her with Dudley Moore in a wafer-thin script. She top lined the Disney-produced family film *One Magic Christmas* (1985, in another "mom" role), and did her best to carry *Dead of Winter* (1987), an intriguing (and uncredited) ripoff of a 1945 B mystery titled *My Name Is Julia Ross*.

End of the Line (also 1987), which Steenburgen executive produced and acted in, was a potentially interesting but ultimately sappy, Capraesque exercise. She starred as the woman who hid Otto Frank and his family in the well-received TV movie *The Attic: The Hiding of Anne Frank* (1988). She had a wistful cameo playing Lillian Gish as a young woman in *The Whales of August* in 1987, but was prominent as the former beauty-contest winner in *Miss Firecracker* and as Steve Martin's infinitely patient wife in the hit comedy *Parenthood,* two 1989 efforts. In 1990, playing a teacher in the Wild West of *Back to the Future Part III,* she provided love interest for series regular Christopher Lloyd. Later that year she narrated *The Long Walk Home,* a drama of changing times in the segregated South of the 1950s. She got a chance to exercise her vocal cords—with considerable skill, we might add—in *The Butcher's Wife* (1991), making the most of her supporting role as an introverted woman who finally yields to her desire to sing in public. Recent credits include *What's Eating Gilbert Grape* (1993), *Philadelphia* (also 1993, as the attorney opposing victim Tom Hanks), *Clifford, It Runs in the Family,* and *Pontiac Moon* (all 1994). Steenburgen remains one of the screen's most compulsively watchable actresses.

STEIGER, ROD. Actor. (b. Apr. 14, 1925, Westhampton, N.Y.) Beefy, round-faced Method actor whose trademark is a coiled-spring intensity. This New York stage veteran (who quit high school to join the Navy during World War 2) made an impression in the early days of live television in such plays as Paddy Chayefsky's "Marty" (1953), and loomed large in films of the 1950s and 1960s, often walking a fine line between bravura work and outright overacting. Among his more notable performances: Marlon Brando's older brother, who shoulda looked out for him, in *On the Waterfront* (1954, his first Oscar nomination), "pore Jud" in *Oklahoma!* (1955), the venal movie studio mogul in *The Big Knife* (also 1955), a heartless boxing promoter in *The Harder They Fall* (1956), an Irish-brogued adoptive Sioux Indian in *Run of the Arrow* (1957), the title character in *Al Capone* (1959), a sympathetic psychiatrist in *The Mark* (1961), Komarovsky in *Doctor Zhivago* (1965), and the haunted concentration-camp survivor in *The Pawnbroker* (1965), which earned him another Oscar nomination.

He finally won an Academy Award playing a gum-chewing, redneck Southern sheriff opposite Sidney Poitier in *In the Heat of the Night* (1967), invaded Alec Guinness territory playing a murderer with a penchant for disguises in the black comedy *No Way to Treat a Lady* (1968), and starred as the tattooed protagonist of *The Illustrated Man* (1969), opposite then-wife Claire Bloom. Good parts grew scarce in the 1970s, and health problems also caused his career to suffer. He made a comeback of sorts in *W. C. Fields and Me* (1976), giving a remarkably potent performance as the famous comedian, managing to stop short of nightclub imitation but still conveying his trademark voice and mannerisms. Steiger thought this film would win him another Oscar, and rekindle his stardom; sad to say, it did not. Since that time he's continued to work in a variety of projects, not all of them worthy. Among the better ones: *F.I.S.T.* (1978), *The Chosen* (1981), and the minor-league black comedy *Guilty as Charged* (1992).

OTHER FILMS INCLUDE: 1951: *Teresa* (his first); 1955: *The Court-Martial of Billy Mitchell;* 1956: *Jubal, Back From Eternity;* 1957: *The Unholy Wife;* 1958: *Cry Terror;* 1960: *Seven Thieves;* 1962: *13 West Street, Convicts Four, The Longest Day;* 1965: *The Loved One;* 1969: *Three Into Two Won't Go;* 1971: *Waterloo* (as Napoleon), *Happy Birthday, Wanda June;* 1972: *Duck, You Sucker, The Heroes;* 1973: *Lolly Madonna XXX;* 1974: *Lucky Luciano;* 1975: *Hennessy;* 1976: *Dirty Hands;* 1977: *Portrait of a Hitman;* 1979: *Love and Bullets, The Amityville Horror;* 1980: *Cattle Annie and Little Britches;* 1981: *Lion of the Desert;* 1985: *The Naked Face;* 1987: *The Kindred;* 1989: *The January Man;* 1990: *Men of Respect;* 1991: *The Ballad of the Sad Cafe;* 1992: *The Player* (a cameo), "Sinatra" (miniseries, as Sam Giancana); 1994: *Black Water, The Specialist.*

STEINER, MAX. Composer. *(b. May 10, 1888, Vienna, as Maximilian Raoul Steiner; d. Dec. 28, 1971.)* One of the greatest composers ever to score motion pictures, Max Steiner was also among the most prolific, with some 250 feature films to his credit (although the only music in some of his early talkies was that heard under the opening credits). A child prodigy who studied with Gustav Mahler, Steiner emigrated to America in 1914, working as conductor and orchestrator on many

Broadway musicals before coming to Hollywood in 1929, shortly after the arrival of sound. Working first for RKO and then, for the bulk of his career, at Warner Bros., Steiner developed a lusty, fully orchestrated type of movie music that made up in dynamism and visceral impact what it lacked in subtlety.

An Oscar winner for the scores of *The Informer* (1935), *Now, Voyager* (1942, which produced the hit song "Wrong"), and *Since You Went Away* (1944), Steiner was also nominated for his work on *The Gay Divorcee, The Lost Patrol* (both 1934), *The Charge of the Light Brigade, The Garden of Allah* (both 1936), *The Life of Emile Zola* (1937), *Dark Victory* (1939), *Gone With the Wind* (also 1939, considered by many aficionados to be his finest score), *The Letter* (1940), *Sergeant York* (1941), *Casablanca* (1942, in which he wanted to replace "As Time Goes By" with a song of his own), *The Adventures of Mark Twain* (1944), *Rhapsody in Blue* (1945, adroitly blending with his own music some themes and motifs written by this biopic's subject, George Gershwin), *Night and Day* (1946, doing the same in this Cole Porter biography), *Life With Father, My Wild Irish Rose* (both 1947), *Beyond the Forest* (1949), *The Flame and the Arrow* (1950), *The Jazz Singer, The Miracle of Our Lady of Fatima* (both 1952), *The Caine Mutiny* (1954), and *Battle Cry* (1955).

Oddly, the Academy failed to recognize some of his greatest scores, such as those composed for RKO's *Symphony of Six Million* (1932) and *King Kong* (1933, portions of which were being used in RKO movies years later), and those for Warners' *Dodge City* (1939), *They Died With Their Boots On* (1941), *The Beast With Five Fingers* (1946), *Johnny Belinda, The Treasure of the Sierra Madre* (both 1948), *Springfield Rifle* (1952), and *The Searchers* (1956). In his later years at Warners, a desperately overworked Steiner reportedly drafted fellow Music Department composer William Lava on a regular basis to write music for which Steiner took credit. Even so, he produced a staggering amount of remarkably high-quality work in the course of a long and distinguished career.

STERLING, JAN. Actress. *(b. Apr. 3, 1923, New York City, as Jane Sterling*

Adriance.) This icy blonde certainly looked like the hard-boiled dames she often played in movies of the 1950s, and she played them well, being Oscar-nominated for one such portrayal in *The High and the Mighty* (1954). Born into a well-to-do New York family, she studied at exclusive private schools and trained for the theater in England. Sterling, already a 10-year stage veteran when she made her film debut in *Tycoon* (1947, billed as Jane Adrian), took roles in *Johnny Belinda* (1948), *Caged, Mystery Street* (both 1950), and *Appointment With Danger,* before getting the assignment to play a cynical opportunist in Billy Wilder's *The Big Carnival* (both 1951), the film that established her as a comer. She occasionally played comedy (as in 1951's *Rhubarb),* but is widely recognized for her peroxided floozies. Since moving to London she has retired happily into private life. She was married to actors Jack Merivale and Paul Douglas.

OTHER FILMS INCLUDE: 1951: *The Mating Season;* 1952: *Flesh and Fury;* 1953: *Pony Express, Split Second;* 1954: *The Human Jungle;* 1955: *Man With the Gun, Women's Prison, Female on the Beach;* 1956: *1984, The Harder They Fall;* 1957: *Slaughter on Tenth Avenue;* 1958: *The Female Animal, High School Confidential!;* 1961: *Love in a Goldfish Bowl;* 1967: *The Incident;* 1969: *The Minx;* 1981: *First Monday in October;* 1982: *Dangerous Company.*

STERN, DANIEL. Actor. *(b. Aug. 28, 1957, Bethesda, Md.)* The 1990s could be Daniel Stern's decade, judging from his high-profile appearances in the megahits *Home Alone* (1990, as one of the bumbling burglars trounced by young Macaulay Culkin) and *City Slickers* (1991, as a depressed, ineffectual grocery-store manager regenerated during a cattle drive). The likable Stern may not be leading-man material but rates high on the list of able supporting players of the baby-boom generation. Debuting as one of the young friends in the sleeper hit *Breaking Away* (1979), Stern enjoyed his first real success in *Diner* (1982), giving a particularly layered, complex performance as the sole married man in a group of 1950s-era buddies. He has labored in several mediocre films (such as the silly 1984 horror flick *C.H.U.D,* for example), alternating

with prestige productions such as Woody Allen's *Hannah and Her Sisters* (1986). Other credits for this prolific actor include *Starting Over* (1979), *It's My Turn, One-Trick Pony, A Small Circle of Friends, Stardust Memories* (all 1980), *Honky Tonk Freeway* (1981), *I'm Dancing as Fast as I Can* (1982), *Get Crazy, Blue Thunder* (both 1983), the Tim Burton short *Frankenweenie* (1984), *Key Exchange* (1985), *The Boss' Wife* (1986), *Born in East L.A.* (1987), *The Milagro Beanfield War* (1988), *Leviathan, Little Monsters* (both 1989), *My Blue Heaven,* and *Coupe de Ville* (both 1990). He reprised his familiar role of the hapless burglar Marv in *Home Alone 2: Lost in New York* (1992). Stern also provided the narration for the those-were-the-days sitcom "The Wonder Years" (1988–93) and directed episodes of the popular show, as a warmup to directing his first feature, the amiable *Rookie of the Year* (1993, in which he also played a broadly comic supporting role). In 1994 he rejoined Billy Crystal in *City Slickers II: The Legend of Curly's Gold.*

STEVENS, GEORGE. Director, producer. *(b. Dec. 18, 1904, Oakland, Calif.; d. Mar. 8, 1975.)* Meticulous Hollywood director whose well-known penchant for perfectionism kept him from amassing as large a body of work as most other Golden Age directors. But, like his contemporary and fellow perfectionist William Wyler, Stevens enjoyed uncommon success with his creations, several of which—*Swing Time, Gunga Din,* and *Shane,* for example—are now regarded as the archetypal examples of their respective genres. The son of performers (his father George and uncle Landers were familiar faces in films of the silent and early-talkie eras), he broke into the film industry as a cameraman, shooting many great comedies at the Hal Roach studio during the 1920s, including such Laurel and Hardy classics as *Two Tars* (1928), *Liberty,* and *Big Business* (both 1929). Roach allowed Stevens to helm a series of two-reelers, "The Boy Friends," and the young director plied his trade in other short subjects made for Universal and RKO before making his tyro feature film, *The Cohens and Kellys in Hollywood,* in 1933.

His grounding in slapstick comedy shorts served him well as he directed

Wheeler and Woolsey in *Kentucky Kernels* (1934) and *The Nitwits* (1935), and he continued to work with such Hal Roach colleagues as comic actor Grady Sutton and screenwriter Fred Guiol for years to come.

The turning point in his career came when he directed Katharine Hepburn in Booth Tarkington's slice of Americana, *Alice Adams* (1935). It showed that Stevens was capable of something more than sight-gag comedy. He went on to great success with *Annie Oakley* (1935), the Fred Astaire–Ginger Rogers gem *Swing Time* (1936), the Astaire-without-Rogers musical *A Damsel in Distress* (1937), the Rogers comedy vehicle *Vivacious Lady* (1938), and the rousing action-adventure yarn *Gunga Din* (1939), a troubled project that turned out to be a smash hit—and one of Stevens' all-time best. Desiring greater control over his work, he became his own producer as well.

As Stevens' reputation grew more substantial, so did his films: the quietly dramatic *Vigil in the Night* (1940), the romantic tearjerker *Penny Serenade* (1941), and the comedies *Woman of the Year*, *The Talk of the Town* (both 1942), and *The More the Merrier* (1943, which earned him his first Oscar nomination) were marked not only by superior scripts and performances, but by an overriding intelligence. When Stevens returned from active duty in World War 2, which included photographing the liberation of the concentration camp at Dachau, his films took on even greater weight. The lovely *I Remember Mama* (1948) was the last Stevens film with any comedic elements. He worked slowly but steadily on his subsequent films, assembling them with the detailed precision of a watchmaker, routinely demanding reshoots and recuts to perfect the pacing of his scenes or capture just the right nuance of performance. He also became a fan of the slow dissolve, which he mastered in *A Place in the Sun* (1951). He won an Oscar for that film, and was nominated for the stately Western *Shane* (1953), and the heartrending *The Diary of Anne Frank* (1959); he won his second Academy Award for directing the sprawling, larger-than-life Edna Ferber saga *Giant* (1956). Stevens' last major project was the ambitious but overproduced *The Greatest Story Ever Told* (1965). He recruited Elizabeth Taylor (whom he'd directed twice before) and Stevens fan Warren Beatty to star in his final film, *The Only Game in Town* (1970), a project so forgettable that it wasn't even mentioned in his son's loving documentary tribute, *George Stevens: A Filmmaker's Journey* (1984). George Stevens, Jr., who started out as an assistant on his father's last films, went on to run the film division of the U.S. Information Agency, before embarking on a successful career as a television producer/director. He also served as president of the American Film Institute.

OTHER FILMS INCLUDE: 1933: *The Cohens and the Kellys in Hollywood;* 1934: *Bachelor Bait;* 1935: *Laddie;* 1952: *Something to Live For.*

STEVENS, INGER. Actress. *(b. Oct. 18, 1934, Stockholm, as Inger Stensland; d. Apr. 30, 1970.)* The seeming epitome of good cheer and healthy sexuality, this Swedish beauty masked her myriad sorrows, illnesses, and insecurities from the camera, showing great promise in her relatively few films, but heading inexorably toward a tragic end. When her parents divorced, young Inger accompanied her father to the United States, successfully muting her accent. She ran away from home at age 16, working as a stripper and chorus girl while studying at New York's Actors' Studio. She toiled in commercials, TV shows, and off-Broadway plays before getting her big break as the second female lead in *Man on Fire* (1957), starring Bing Crosby, with whom she had an affair. She was impressive as a terrified wife in *Cry Terror* (1958), had a juicy supporting role in *The Buccaneer* that same year, and played the only woman left on Earth in the apocalyptic *The World, the Flesh, and the Devil* (1959). Even greater recognition came her way as the star of the wholesome TV series "The Farmer's Daughter" (1963–67); she made only one film, *The New Interns* (1964), during that stint. Stevens, who'd attempted suicide in 1962, was frequently despondent, enduring many fractious affairs with married men, some of them prominent Hollywood figures. She contributed skillful performances to *A Guide for the Married Man, A Time for Killing* (both 1967), *Madigan, 5 Card Stud, Hang 'Em High* (all 1968), *House of Cards* and especially *A Dream* *of Kings* (both 1969) before killing herself with an overdose of sleeping pills.

STEVENS, STELLA. Actress. *(b. Oct. 1, 1936, Hot Coffee, Mo., as Estelle Egglestone.)* Someday they'll erect a statue of Stella Stevens somewhere, and its base will read, "Beautiful Women Can Also Be Funny." Unfortunately, this bright-eyed, voluptuous blonde was only fitfully given a chance to exercise her comedy chops, and never achieved the stardom she so richly merited. A former "Playboy" Playmate, she had her first noteworthy screen role as the deep-breathing Appassionata Von Climax in *Li'l Abner* (1959). She cavorted with Elvis Presley in *Girls! Girls! Girls!* (1962) and was also terrific as a faux drummer in *The Courtship of Eddie's Father,* Jerry Lewis' love object in *The Nutty Professor* (both 1963), a rebel spy in *Advance to the Rear* (1964), and a world-class klutz in *The Silencers* (1966). She also gave convincing dramatic performances as a would-be jazz singer in *Too Late Blues* (1962) and a pathetic junkie in *Synanon* (1965). She also appeared in *The Secret of My Success* (1965), *How to Save a Marriage (And Ruin Your Life), Where Angels Go . . . Trouble Follows* (both 1968), and *The Mad Room* (1969). Her most acclaimed role was probably that of the prostitute who tames Jason Robards in *The Ballad of Cable Hogue* (1970).

Ever conscious of her physical appeal, something she never shied away from exploiting, Stevens brought earthy charm and easygoing good humor to many of her screen characterizations, something not always achieved by highly trained actors. Other roles of note include the long-suffering wife in *The Poseidon Adventure* (1972), a woman who marries a corpse in *Arnold* (1973), the campy villainess The Dragon Lady in *Cleopatra Jones and the Casino of Gold* (1975), and a silent-screen actress in *Nickelodeon* (1976). In recent years, she has worked sporadically, mainly in exploitation fare like *Chained Heat* (1983). On TV, she came out of a coma to romance "Ben Casey," and ran a bordello in "Flamingo Road." Her son, Andrew, began as a promising TV actor, including a regular role on "Dallas," but has become a familiar leading man in and director of numerous low-budget genre films that invariably premiere on videocassette. In fact, he costarred with and directed his mom in *The Terror Within II* (1992).

STEWART, JAMES. Actor. *(b. May 20, 1908, Indiana, Pa.)* One of America's most beloved actors, Stewart today is less movie star than cultural icon, a gracefully aged embodiment of values and traditions our nation holds dear, as we are continually reminded by endless broadcasts of his best-remembered film, *It's a Wonderful Life.* The tall, gangly, soft-spoken youth who endeared himself to moviegoers by virtue of his appealing diffidence, boyish earnestness, and innate kindness is the Stewart most film lovers cherish, although he certainly proved that he was much more, especially in his films of the 1950s and 1960s.

In his youth Stewart aspired to be an architect, and he applied himself to that goal during his stay at Princeton, but in 1932 fellow classmate Joshua Logan convinced him to join the newly formed University Players group in Massachusetts, where he first met Henry Fonda (who was to become a lifelong friend) and Margaret Sullavan, among others. Stewart was already a Broadway veteran when Hollywood beckoned in 1935. He made his film debut in a short subject, *Important News,* and then appeared in his first feature film, *The Murder Man,* later that year (as a reporter named Shorty). Contracted to MGM, he was assigned supporting roles in *Wife vs. Secretary, Small Town Girl, The Gorgeous Hussy, Rose Marie,* and *After the Thin Man* (all 1936, memorably if unconvincingly cast in the last-named as a maniacal killer!). On loan to Universal, he played the male lead in a glossy soap opera, *Next Time We Love* (also 1936), opposite old friend Margaret Sullavan, who'd specifically requested him.

Back at his home studio, Stewart finally got a lead in *Speed,* an entertaining but unimportant B, and *Born to Dance* (both 1936), in which he romanced Eleanor Powell and even warbled (tentatively) Cole Porter's "Easy to Love." From then on, his rise to stardom was steady if not meteoric, helped along by well-received stints in *Seventh Heaven* (20th Century-Fox's tepid remake of a silent classic), *The Last Gangster, Navy Blue and Gold* (all 1937), *Of Human Hearts, Vivacious Lady* (on loan to RKO, opposite Ginger

Rogers), *The Shopworn Angel* (again opposite Sullavan), and *You Can't Take It With You* (all 1938), that year's Academy Award winner for Best Picture. In the last-named film, third-billed behind Jean Arthur and Lionel Barrymore, Stewart began his fruitful association with director Frank Capra, who saw in Stewart's shy, stammering, sincere screen character the ideal incarnation of his American Everyman.

Capra played on that persona by casting Stewart as the idealistic young senator in *Mr. Smith Goes to Washington* (1939), a box-office blockbuster that earned the actor his first Academy Award nomination. He followed it up that same year with a well-remembered turn as the seemingly gun-shy sheriff in *Destry Rides Again* (opposite Marlene Dietrich), then the first-rate soaper *Made for Each Other* (opposite Carole Lombard), the screwball comedy-mystery *It's a Wonderful World* (opposite Claudette Colbert), and two more collaborations with Margaret Sullavan (1940's *The Shop Around the Corner*, a charming, gentle romance directed by Ernst Lubitsch, and 1940's *The Mortal Storm*, a Frank Borzage-directed drama of Nazi Germany) before winning an Oscar for his surprising portrayal of a fast-talking reporter who falls for Katharine Hepburn in *The Philadelphia Story* (also 1940).

Stewart's next new films—1941's *Come Live With Me, Pot o' Gold,* and *Ziegfeld Girl*—weren't nearly as impressive as their immediate predecessors, and it's interesting to speculate what might have happened to his career if World War 2 hadn't intervened. Stewart enlisted in the Army Air Corps as a private and worked his way up to colonel, flying in more than 1,000 missions over enemy territory and winning both the Air Medal and the Distinguished Flying Cross. (Stewart remained in the Air Force Reserves after the war, and had attained the rank of brigadier general by the time he retired in 1968.)

He returned to Hollywood in 1946, teaming up once again with Frank Capra for *It's a Wonderful Life.* As George Bailey, the small-town dreamer who reaches rock bottom—the literal depths of despair—before learning how many lives he's touched, Stewart delivered what may be his best performance, and picked up another Oscar nomination. No longer the

gawky, stammering youth, he tried a wide variety of roles over the next several decades, adapting himself to the more naturalistic screen style of the post-WW2 era. He played a crusading reporter in *Call Northside 777,* an intellectual detective (of sorts) in *Rope* (both 1948, the latter a fascinating if ultimately unsuccessful thriller directed by Alfred Hitchcock, who generally used Stewart's talents wisely), a disabled ballplayer in *The Stratton Story* (1949), and an ex-Cavalry officer in *Broken Arrow* (1950).

Stewart adopted a lighter, breezier tone for his portrayal of kindly, eccentric Elwood P. Dowd, a man befriended (so he says) by a six-foot-tall white rabbit in *Harvey* (1950). He'd had plenty of practice in the role, having played it for a brief time on Broadway; he snagged another, much deserved Academy Award nomination for his delightful performance. But then it was on to sterner stuff. The 1950s saw Stewart in several extremely tough Westerns, occasionally showing a harshness hitherto unsuspected by his fans. *Winchester '73* and the aforementioned *Broken Arrow* (both 1950) kicked off the cycle, which really went into high gear when Stewart negotiated an unprecedented contract with Universal that would entitle him to a cut of his films' profits. His most frequent collaborator behind the camera was director Anthony Mann, with whom he did *Bend of the River* (1952), *Thunder Bay* (1953), *The Naked Spur* (also 1953, but made for MGM; probably the best of the bunch), *The Far Country* (1955), and *The Man From Laramie* (also 1955, for Columbia).

Stewart didn't confine his efforts to Westerns in this decade. He had a memorable role as a mercy-killing doctor who hides with a circus in Cecil B. DeMille's *The Greatest Show on Earth* (1952, his face always hidden beneath clown makeup), and worked for Hitchcock in three of the director's best 1950s films: *Rear Window* (1954, playing a wheelchair-bound voyeur who spots a murder through the window of an adjoining building), *The Man Who Knew Too Much* (1956, as the husband of Doris Day in this updated remake of Hitch's 1934 thriller), and, perhaps best of all, *Vertigo* (1958, giving an edgy performance as a fearful detective obsessed by *two* Kim Novaks). He also played the famous swing-era bandleader in *The Glenn Miller Story* (1954), and finished out the decade with a masterful turn as a cagey country lawyer for the defense in a sensational trial in *Anatomy of a Murder* (1959), a characterization for which he was again Oscar-nominated.

Stewart made the best of his starring roles in two John Ford Westerns, *Two Rode Together* (1961, as a cynical lawman) and *The Man Who Shot Liberty Valance* (1962, as a tenderfoot lawyer aided by gunman John Wayne), but increasingly, as the 1960s progressed, he fell back on his well-established persona to carry him through uninspired, undistinguished films such as *Mr. Hobbs Takes a Vacation* (1962), *Take Her, She's Mine* (1963), *Cheyenne Autumn* (1964, one of Ford's more uneven films, an overlong, episodic drama with Stewart superfluous as Wyatt Earp), *Shenandoah* (1965), *The Rare Breed* (1966), *Firecreek* (1968), *Bandolero!* (1968), and, in the 1970s, *The Cheyenne Social Club* (1970), *Fools' Parade* (1971), *Airport '77* (1977), *The Big Sleep,* and *The Magic of Lassie* (both 1978). Two meritorious exceptions: *Flight of the Phoenix* (1966), which starred him as a pilot struggling to save his passengers after a crash in the Arabian desert, and *The Shootist* (1976), which gave him a small but juicy supporting role as the doctor who tells aging gunfighter John Wayne that he's terminally ill.

Active in radio (with a fine 1950s series, "The Six Shooter," to his credit), Stewart was a longtime TV holdout, though he did appear in a 1962 episode of the "Alcoa Premiere" anthology series, "Flashing Spikes," directed by John Ford. His attempts to find a suitable starring TV series in the 1970s were ill-fated however; neither "The Jimmy Stewart Show" (1971–72) nor "Hawkins (on Murder)" (1973–74) lasted very long. In 1983 he costarred with Bette Davis in a mediocre made-for-cable movie, *Right of Way.* Since then he has appeared in several Hollywood-themed documentaries, done considerable voiceover work (including a delightful turn as Wylie Burp, an aged sheriff, in the 1991 animated film *An American Tail: Fievel Goes West),* become a favorite talk-show guest on TV, and authored a bestselling collection of poems.

OTHER FILMS INCLUDE: 1939: *Ice Follies of 1939;* 1940: *No Time for Comedy;* 1947: *Magic Town;* 1948: *On Our Merry Way* (one segment, with Henry Fonda), *You Gotta Stay Happy;* 1950: *The Jackpot;* 1952: *Carbine Williams;* 1955: *Strategic Air Command;* 1957: *Night Passage;* 1958: *Bell, Book and Candle;* 1959: *The FBI Story;* 1960: *The Mountain Road;* 1962: *How the West Was Won;* 1965: *Dear Brigitte;* 1974: *That's Entertainment!* (as a host).

ST. JOHN, JILL. Actress. *(b. Aug. 19, 1940, Los Angeles, as Jill Oppenheim.)* This sultry redhead used to boast of her high IQ on TV talk shows, but her brains didn't take her far beyond decorative parts in often-forgettable films. Debuting in *Summer Love* (1957), she appeared in major productions such as *Holiday for Lovers* (1959), *The Lost World* (1960), *The Roman Spring of Mrs. Stone* (1961), *Tender Is the Night* (1962), and *Come Blow Your Horn* (1963) early in her career. St. John is usually remembered, though, in goofy comedies the likes of *Who's Minding the Store?, Who's Been Sleeping in My Bed?* (both 1963), and *Honeymoon Hotel* (1964), as well as unintentional comedies like *The Oscar* (1966). Other credits include *Banning* and *Eight on the Lam* (both 1967). She fared best as a Bond girl—a spunky one, at that—in *Diamonds Are Forever* (1971). After making such TV movies as *The Concrete Jungle* in the early 1980s, St. John more or less abandoned the profession. Once married to singer Jack Jones and linked romantically with Henry Kissinger, St. John wed longtime friend Robert Wagner in 1990 and launched a new career as a TV chef, with cookbooks now bearing her byline.

STOCKWELL, DEAN. Actor. *(b. Mar. 5, 1935, North Hollywood.)* This remarkable performer has had three distinct careers. He first appeared in films as a child actor, reestablished himself in his 20s, and, after experiencing some personal problems, bounced back as a middle-aged character player, which has brought him his greatest success and popularity. The son of Broadway performers (his father Harry sang the voice of the Prince in Walt Disney's *Snow White and the Seven Dwarfs),* the earnest, bright-eyed Stockwell appeared in such films as *Anchors Aweigh* (1945), *Gentleman's Agreement* (1947), *The Boy With*

Green Hair (1948, a memorable starring role in this fable about social outcasts), *Down to the Sea in Ships, The Secret Garden* (both 1949), *The Happy Years,* and *Kim* (both 1950), proving to be a skilled and appealing performer.

Stockwell left Hollywood when he was about 16 and traveled across the country, working at odd jobs. He returned to acting when he hit New York, eliciting raves as one of the college-boy killers in the Broadway production of "Compulsion," a role he repeated in the 1959 film (which won him and his costars an award at the Cannes Film Festival). He solidified his reputation with a mature, sensitive performance as a troubled youth in *Sons and Lovers* (1960), and received a second Cannes ensemble award for his role as Eugene O'Neill's alter ego in *Long Day's Journey Into Night* (1962). But then, Stockwell dropped out of acting again.

Later, he took occasional parts in the likes of *The Last Movie* (1971), and *Tracks* (1976), both with his friend Dennis Hopper. In the 1980s he made a spectacular comeback with sizable supporting roles in *Dune, Paris, Texas* (both 1984), *Blue Velvet* (1986, a flamboyant and memorable performance), *Gardens of Stone* (1987), and a stunning cameo as Howard Hughes in *Tucker: The Man and His Dream* (1988). This culminated in an Oscar nomination for his droll comic turn as a mob boss in *Married to the Mob* (1988), and led to his being cast as the holographic observer Al on the TV series "Quantum Leap" (1989–93). He also appeared in *Limit Up* (1989) and in an amusing role as a desperate screenwriter's agent in Robert Altman's *The Player* (1992). His brother Guy was also an actor, whose limited achievements included starring in a 1966 remake of *Beau Geste.*

OTHER FILMS INCLUDE: 1945: *The Valley of Decision;* 1946: *The Green Years, Home Sweet Homicide, The Mighty McGurk;* 1947: *The Arnelo Affair, The Romance of Rosy Ridge, Song of the Thin Man* (as Nick Charles, Jr.); 1948: *Deep Waters;* 1950: *Stars in My Crown;* 1951: *Cattle Drive;* 1957: *The Careless Years, Gun for a Coward;* 1965: *Rapture;* 1968: *Psych-Out;* 1970: *The Dunwich Horror;* 1972: *The Loners;* 1973: *The Werewolf of Washington;* 1975: *Win, Place or Steal;* 1982: *Alsino and the Condor, Human Highway, Wrong Is Right;* 1985: *The Legend of Billie Jean, To Live and Die in L.A.;* 1987: *Beverly*

Hills Cop II, The Time Guardian; 1988: *The Blue Iguana;* 1989: *Backtrack.*

STOLTZ, ERIC. Actor, producer. *(b. Sept. 30, 1961, American Samoa.)* This talented, red-haired, soft-spoken actor, who debuted as a surfer dude in *Fast Times at Ridgemont High* (1982), was poised for stardom as the lead character in *Back to the Future* (1985), but after filming began he was replaced by Michael J. Fox (apparently the producers' first choice, who was initially unavailable). He rebounded with an empathetic performance as the disfigured teen in *Mask* (1985), but since his real face was never seen, his success in this part didn't lead to audience recognition. He followed in a myriad of projects, including *The New Kids* (1985), *Some Kind of Wonderful, Lionheart* (both 1987), *Haunted Summer* (1988, as Percy Bysshe Shelley), *The Fly II, Say Anything . . .* (both 1989) and *Memphis Belle* (1990). His powerful work as a paraplegic in *The Waterdance* (1992) signaled a new chapter in his career, and he has since become an invaluable player, usually in supporting roles, and often in small, quirky independent films, two of which he starred in and coproduced, *Bodies, Rest & Motion* (1993, with his real-life companion Bridget Fonda) and *Sleep With Me* (1994). In 1994, his range was amply demonstrated in *Naked in New York, Killing Zoe, Pulp Fiction,* and *Little Women.* Most recently he was featured in *Rob Roy* and *Fluke* (both 1995). On stage, Stoltz received a 1989 Tony nomination for an acclaimed revival of "Our Town."

STONE, GEORGE E. Actor. *(b. May 23, 1903, Lodz, Poland; d. May 26, 1967.)* Diminutive character actor who worked in vaudeville and on stage prior to his 1916 film debut. Stone appeared in movies periodically throughout the 1920s, scoring his first major success with an "adult" role in *Seventh Heaven* (1927), as The Sewer Rat. As talkies were ushered in, Stone frequently played small-time hoods—many of them squealers and cowards—and later achieved recognition as The Runt, comical stooge to Chester Morris' Boston Blackie in a dozen Columbia B films of the 1940s, beginning with *Confessions of Boston Blackie* (1941). His best latter-day films—

like *The Man With the Golden Arm, Guys and Dolls* (both 1955), *Some Like It Hot* (1959), and *Pocketful of Miracles* (1961)—played on his familiar screen persona as a street tough. His face was also familiar to TV viewers from his regular appearances as a bailiff on the "Perry Mason" series (1957–66).

OTHER FILMS INCLUDE: 1928: *The Racket;* 1930: *Little Caesar;* 1931: *The Front Page, Cimarron, Five Star Final;* 1933: *42nd Street;* 1934: *Viva Villa!;* 1936: *Bullets or Ballots;* 1938: *Mr. Moto's Gamble;* 1940: *Northwest Mounted Police;* 1941; *The Face Behind the Mask, Alias Jimmy Valentine;* 1946: *Suspense;* 1952: *Bloodhounds of Broadway.*

STONE, LEWIS. Actor. *(b. Nov. 15, 1879, Worcester, Mass.; d. Sept. 12, 1953.)* The much beloved Judge Hardy of MGM's "Andy Hardy" series ("Andrew, let's you and I have a man-to-man talk . . .") was a mainstay at the Culver City studio, where he was said to have had a lifetime contract. Ramrod stiff, authoritarian, stern, gentlemanly, softspoken—Stone was all of these on-screen. A Broadway star in the pre-WW1 years, Stone made his movie debut in *The Man Who Found Out* (1915), served in the cavalry during the Great War (which possibly accounts for his rigid bearing), and returned to acting afterward, with increasing emphasis on his motion-picture career. He played the dual role of king and pretender in the 1922 version of *The Prisoner of Zenda,* and made an elegant villain in that year's *Scaramouche.* He helped scientist Wallace Beery (a future comrade at MGM) bring great dinosaurs to London in *The Lost World* (1925, as "Sir John Roxton—Sportsman"), and counseled Greta Garbo in *A Woman of Affairs* (1928). That same year he earned an Oscar nomination for his performance as a Russian Count who engineers his Czar's death in *The Patriot.*

Talkies didn't panic Stone, with his strong, stage-trained voice; he relished the coming of sound, although his advanced age and white hair more or less limited him to supporting roles and character leads. He appeared in *The Big House* (1930), *The Secret Six, The Sin of Madelon Claudet* (both 1931), *The Mask of Fu Manchu* (as the intrepid Sir Nayland Smith), *Mata Hari, Grand Hotel* (in which he spoke the fatalistic final line of dialogue), *Red-Headed Woman* (all 1932), *The White Sister* (1933), *Queen Christina* (also 1933, the last of his films with Garbo), *Treasure Island* (1934, as Captain Smollett), *David Copperfield* (as Mr. Wickfield), *China Seas* (both 1935), *Suzy* (1936), and *The Thirteenth Chair* (1937).

In 1938, he inherited the role of Carvel's Judge James Hardy from Lionel Barrymore, who'd essayed it in the previous year's *A Family Affair.* Stone made the role his own, appearing as the kindly Judge in *You're Only Young Once* and 13 subsequent films, ending with *Love Laughs at Andy Hardy* (1946). His later credits include *Three Wise Fools* (1946), *State of the Union* (1948), *Any Number Can Play* (1949), *Stars in My Crown* (1950), *Scaramouche* (1952, but not in the role he played in 1922, naturally), *The Prisoner of Zenda* (also 1952, ditto), and *All the Brothers Were Valiant* (1953). He remained active—at MGM—right up until his death.

STONE, OLIVER. Writer, producer, director. *(b. Sept. 15, 1946, New York City.)* Described by one critic as his generation's Samuel Fuller, this controversial filmmaker blends a flamboyant, in-your-face style with passionate, issue-oriented storytelling, often about people caught up in the turbulent 1960s. After serving in Vietnam, he attended film school at New York University. His first feature (excluding an early documentary) was *Seizure* (1974), a muddled Canadian shocker with a cast full of cult favorites. Stone won an Oscar for his screenplay of *Midnight Express* (1978), ostensibly based on the true story of American Billy Hayes' incarceration in a Turkish prison; like many subsequent Stone movies, this one embellished the truth with fanciful fiction. The Oscar earned him a shot at directing a major-studio movie, *The Hand* (1981), but its failure gave him a temporary career setback.

Stone concentrated on screenwriting for a while—*Conan the Barbarian* (1982), *Scarface* (1983), *Year of the Dragon* (1985), *8 Million Ways to Die* (1986)—before directing his first "personal" film, the highly charged, low-budget political drama *Salvador* (1986), which starred James Woods as real-life journalist Richard Boyle (who cowrote the Oscar-nominated screenplay with Stone). Later in 1986, he followed with *Platoon,* a harrowing look at a young man's tour of duty in Vietnam, which Stone had tried to make for more than a decade. The film was hailed as the first true look at the war from the "grunt's" point of view; it also became (surprisingly) a big commercial success and earned four Oscars, including Best Picture and Best Director. Next came *Wall Street* (1987), a ham-fisted but very entertaining study of power and corruption that gave America the catch phrase "greed is good," and *Talk Radio* (1988), an adaptation of Eric Bogosian's stage show about an obnoxious radio personality.

Stone returned to the subject of Vietnam—and won a second Best Director Oscar—for the emotionally wrenching *Born on the Fourth of July* (1989), which gave Tom Cruise his most demanding role as Nam veteran (and antiwar activist) Ron Kovic. By this time in his career, Stone had reached an enviable position, making highly personal films about important subjects that were also commercially accessible. Some critics, however, began to accuse him of being mired in the sixties, and *The Doors* (1991), a flashy profile of rock star Jim Morrison, did little to dispel that perception. *JFK* (also 1991) gained instant notoriety for its examination of Jim Garrison and the various conspiracy theories surrounding the assassination of John F. Kennedy. A masterful cinematic achievement, it earned Stone Oscar nominations as Best Director and cowriter of the screenplay. (Stone later poked fun at his own perceived "conspiracy" mentality with a funny cameo in the 1993 movie *Dave.)* In 1993, Stone made *Heaven and Earth,* the third of his "Vietnam trilogy," which addressed the lack of strong female characters in his previous films. This one chronicled the real-life odyssey of Le Ly Hayslip, from Southeast Asia to the U.S. He made a sharp turn with his next project, the dark comedy *Natural Born Killers* (1994). Stone has also produced or coproduced such films as *Reversal of Fortune, Blue Steel* (both 1990), *Iron Maze* (1991), *South Central, Zebrahead* (both 1992), *The Joy Luck Club* (1993), *The New Age* (1994), and the 1993 miniseries "Wild Palms."

STONE, SHARON. Actress. *(b. Mar. 10, 1958, Meadville, Pa.)* The role of the manipulative, bisexual murder suspect in *Basic Instinct* (1992), which other more established actresses turned down, finally brought Stone the recognition she's been after for years. Through luck, talent, or a combination of both, this impossibly pretty blonde managed to not get lost in the shuffle of other impossibly pretty blondes in Hollywood. The former model and musician made her film debut in a fleeting appearance at the beginning of Woody Allen's *Stardust Memories* (1980), but got her first good part in *Irreconcilable Differences* (1984), in a funny supporting role as a temperamental actress. She became a full-fledged leading lady in the campy action-adventure films *King Solomon's Mines* (1985) and *Allan Quatermain and the Lost City of Gold* (1987). *Action Jackson* (1988) and *Total Recall* (1990) boosted her name value and, in the latter film especially, fostered the belief that perhaps she could act after all. 1991, which found her playing secondary female lead in *He Said, She Said* and costarring as a daring photojournalist in the John Frankenheimer thriller *Year of the Gun,* also saw Stone making her starring debut as a tormented young woman in the psychological thriller *Scissors.* Her attention-grabbing sexuality in *Basic Instinct* made her an "overnight" hot property in Hollywood, but her first major solo starring vehicle, the mediocre *Sliver* (1993), didn't live up to its hype—or its box-office forecast. Stone consoled herself by racking up other high-profile projects for 1994, including *Intersection,* opposite Richard Gere, and *The Specialist,* opposite Sylvester Stallone. She coproduced and donned Western duds for *The Quick and the Dead,* then teamed up with Martin Scorsese and Robert De Niro for *Casino* (both 1995).

OTHER FILMS INCLUDE: 1981: *Deadly Blessing, Bolero;* 1987: *Cold Steel, Police Academy 4: Citizens on Patrol;* 1988: *Above the Law;* 1989: *Blood and Sand;* 1992: *Diary of a Hitman.*

STOPPARD, TOM. Writer, director. *(b. July 3, 1937, Zlin, Czechoslovakia, as Thomas Straussler.)* Esteemed British playwright who has written teleplays and many screenplays for a wide and eclectic group of world-class directors. Stoppard is renowned for his use of language and word-play, and three of his stage works— "Rosencrantz and Guildenstern Are Dead," "Travesties," and "The Real Thing"—won Tony Awards for Best Play. He wrote the screenplays for Joseph Losey's *The Romantic Englishwoman* (1975), Rainer Werner Fassbinder's *Despair* (1979), Otto Preminger's *The Human Factor* (1979), Steven Spielberg's *Empire of the Sun* (1987), Fred Schepisi's *The Russia House* (1990), and Robert Benton's *Billy Bathgate* (1991). Stoppard was Oscar-nominated for cowriting Terry Gilliam's futuristic nightmare comedy *Brazil* (1985). In 1990 he made his directing debut with the screen adaptation of his own *Rosencrantz,* which proved that a work so much about language works better on stage than on film.

STORARO, VITTORIO. Cinematographer. *(b. June 24, 1940, Rome.)* Fittingly, Storaro was the son of a projectionist, who encouraged the boy to formally study photography at the age of 11. At 18 he was one of the youngest students ever admitted to the national Italian film school; at 21 he was already an assistant cameraman. Noted for his expressive lighting techniques, Storaro made a name for himself working with Bernardo Bertolucci on *The Spider's Stratagem, The Conformist* (both 1970), *Last Tango in Paris* (1973), *1900* (1977), *Luna* (1979), *The Sheltering Sky* (1990), and *Little Buddha* (1994). His first "Hollywood" picture was *Apocalypse Now* (1979, actually shot on location in the Philippines), which won him the first of his three Oscars for Best Cinematography; the others were for *Reds* (1981) and *The Last Emperor* (1987, again for Bertolucci). Both Francis Coppola and Warren Beatty have continued to use Storaro on later films, among them *Tucker: The Man and His Dream* (1988) and *Dick Tracy* (1990, Oscar-nominated). His camerawork was singled out as the most notable achievement in *One From the Heart* (1982) and *Ladyhawke* (1985). He also photographed the notorious *Ishtar* (1987).

STORM, GALE. Actress. *(b. Apr. 5, 1922, Bloomington, Tex., as Josephine Owaissa Cottle.)* As a button-cute leading lady in grade

B musicals of the 1940s, this Hollywood-named ingenue showed promise that remained unfulfilled until she got her own TV series. Still in high school when she won a "Gateway to Hollywood" radio contest presented by producer Jesse Lasky, she came to Tinseltown upon graduating, and had her name changed, per "Gateway" custom. At RKO she had bit parts in *Tom Brown's School Days* and *One Crowded Night* (both 1940), before moving to Republic, where she costarred in several Westerns—including two with Roy Rogers, 1941's *Red River Valley* and *Jesse James at Bay.* She wound up at lowly Monogram, where she achieved stardom of sorts in the likes of *Nearly 18, Smart Alecks* (both 1942), *Rhythm Parade, Revenge of the Zombies, Where Are Your Children?* (all 1943), *Forever Yours* (1944), *G.I. Honeymoon, Sunbonnet Sue* (both 1945), and *Swing Parade of 1946,* among others, giving her all to these low-rent vehicles.

She appeared in unimportant Westerns and crime dramas before landing her own hit TV show, "My Little Margie" (1952–56) and "The Gale Storm Show," retitled "Oh, Susannah" (1956–60). She also had a modest recording career during this period. Her autobiography, "I Ain't Down Yet" was published in 1981. She is married to fellow "Gateway" alumnus Lee Bonnell.

STOWE, MADELEINE. Actress. *(b. Aug. 18, 1958, Eagle Rock, Calif.)* Beautiful, dark-haired actress who has finally begun to come into her own. Stowe worked as a volunteer at a Beverly Hills theater and eventually got involved in acting herself, performing in various stage and television productions. She won her first significant parts in made-for-TV movies, including a 1978 rendition of *The Deerslayer* (in the part of Hetty Hutter) and *The Nativity* (also 1978), in which she had the lead. Perhaps it was her inexperience that kept her from moving further ahead. She starred in a 1986 feature, *Tropical Snow,* that sat on the shelf for three years before getting desultory release. Stowe finally won a big-screen berth as the leading lady in *Stakeout* (1987, opposite Richard Dreyfuss), and then appeared in a string of commercial and critical duds: the lame comedy *Worth Winning* (1989), the highly touted *Chinatown* sequel, *The Two Jakes* (1990), the Kevin Costner vehicle *Revenge* (also 1990), and the pretentious *Closet Land* (1991). Stowe redeemed herself as Cora in the exhilarating *The Last of the Mohicans* (1992) and gave a startling performance as a wife who willingly hangs on to her cheating husband in Robert Altman's dark mosaic *Short Cuts* (1993). In 1994, she played a blind woman who "sees" a murder in *Blink*, a Wild West prostitute in *Bad Girls,* and starred opposite Ed Harris in *China Moon* (actually completed in 1992). She is married to actor Brian Benben, with whom she worked on TV's "The Gangster Chronicles: An American Story" (1981).

STRAIGHT, BEATRICE. Actress. *(b. Aug. 2, 1918, Old Westbury, N.Y.)* As far as moviegoers were concerned, she came from out of nowhere, this mature redhead with the pale blue eyes, to startle them with her heartfelt performance as William Holden's faithful wife, devastated by his infidelity, in *Network* (1976). Though small, the part won her a Best Supporting Actress Academy Award and established her name. In fact, she had been acting for years, on stage (where she won a 1953 Tony Award for "The Crucible") and television, and in such films as *Phone Call From a Stranger* (1952), *Patterns* (1956), and *The Nun's Story* (1959). After *Network* she was offered thankless roles in trashy movies, including *Bloodline, The Promise* (both 1979), *The Formula* (1980), *Endless Love* (1981), and *Two of a Kind* (1983). The one exception was *Poltergeist* (1982), in which she convincingly played a paranormal investigator overwhelmed by malevolent spirits in the home of leading players Craig T. Nelson and JoBeth Williams. Later credits include the 1985 miniseries "Robert Kennedy and His Times" and the 1986 political drama *Power,* directed by *Network*'s Sidney Lumet. She was married to actor Peter Cookson.

STRANGE, GLENN. Actor. *(b. Aug. 16, 1899, Weed, N. Mex.; d. Sept. 20, 1973.)* This craggy-faced, mustached actor, a prolific heavy who menaced virtually every major cowboy star in more than 200 Westerns, was himself a cowboy before launching a singing career in the late 1920s, performing western songs on the radio. Strange got into movies in 1934, at first singing, then playing unbilled bits in cheapie horse operas. He worked his way up to featured billing and, occasionally, played sidekicks (in 1937's *The Land Beyond the Law,* for one). Although Strange worked primarily in Westerns, he earned his niche in movie history by being cast as the Frankenstein monster in *House of Frankenstein* (1944), *House of Dracula* (1945), and *Abbott and Costello Meet Frankenstein* (1948). He can also be seen in *Red River* (1948), *The Red Badge of Courage* (1951), *The Lawless Breed* (1952), and *Quantrill's Raiders* (1958), to name a few. In 1962 Strange joined the "Gunsmoke" TV show as Sam the bartender where he worked until his death.

STRASBERG, SUSAN. Actress. *(b. May 22, 1938, New York City.)* As the daughter of noted acting teacher Lee Strasberg, big things were expected of Susan Strasberg when she launched her own career in the mid-1950s. Indeed, the attractive brunette won praise for her 1955 turn in Broadway's "The Diary of Anne Frank" and her early movies, including *Picnic* (1955) and *Stage Struck* (1958). She could be winsome, coy, and youthfully exuberant; she also displayed soulfulness and fragility. But, as with many ingenues of her era, Strasberg fell victim to the 1960s, and soon found herself playing parts in entertaining but trivial relics of the time like *The Trip* (1967), *Psych-Out*, and *Chubasco* (both 1968, the latter with then-husband Christopher Jones). By 1978 she was starring in *The Manitou,* playing a woman tormented by a malignant Indian spirit, and playing a not-so-very-mature matron in *In Praise of Older Women,* and there have been few worthwhile films on her résumé. She has written an autobiography, "Bittersweet" (1980), and a memoir of her friend and onetime roommate Marilyn Monroe. Father Lee (born 1901, died 1982) waited until he was 73 to make his film debut and earned an Oscar nomination playing a Jewish mobster based on Meyer Lansky in *The Godfather, Part II* (1974). He also appeared in *Going in Style* (1979), a poignant tale of geriatric bank robbers.
OTHER FILMS INCLUDE: 1955: *The Cobweb* (her debut); 1962: *Hemingway's Adven-*

*tures of a Young Man; 1968: The Brother-
hood; 1977: Rollercoaster; 1986: The Delta
Force; 1989: The Runnin' Kind; 1990:
Schweitzer.*

STRATHAIRN, DAVID. Actor. *(b. Jan. 26,
1949, San Francisco.)* The year 1992 provided the gifted Strathairn with three plum
supporting roles that made critics and audiences take notice: the sympathetic pro-
motions man Ira Lowenstein in *A League
of Their Own,* the blind sound expert
Whistler in *Sneakers,* and Rennie, the Cajun swamp guide in *Passion Fish.* A graduate of Williams College and the Ringling
Brothers Clown College, Strathairn has
been in numerous stage productions as
well as in the films *Lovesick, Enormous
Changes at the Last Minute, Silkwood* (all
1983), *Iceman* (1984), *At Close Range*
(1987), *Dominick and Eugene* (1988), and
Memphis Belle (1990). Most notably, he
has also appeared in six films written and
directed by John Sayles, starting with his
screen debut in *Return of the Secaucus 7*
(1980), and including *The Brother From
Another Planet* (1984), *Matewan* (1987, as
Chief of Police Sid Hatfield), *Eight Men
Out* (1988, as pitcher Eddie Cicotte), and
City of Hope (1991, in a flamboyant role
as a street crazy). As other filmmakers
have come to appreciate his talent—and
versatility—he's become more sought-
after. Recent credits include *The Firm* (as
Tom Cruise's brother), *Lost in Yonkers,
Arthur Miller's "The American Clock"*
(telefilm), *A Dangerous Woman* (all
1993), *The River Wild* (1994), *Losing Isaiah,* and *Dolores Claiborne* (both 1995).

STRAUSS, ROBERT. Actor. *(b. Nov. 8,
1913, New York City; d. Feb. 20, 1975.)* A
seemingly ubiquitous presence in films of
the 1950s, this beefy character actor
drifted from one menial job to another before turning to dramatics. He worked on
the stage for several years before breaking
into movies in 1952. Typically played
gruff characters—sometimes comic, sometimes menacing—and essayed quite a few
gangster roles as well. He won an Oscar
nomination for his portrayal of Animal in
Stalag 17 (1953), a role he had originated
on Broadway. He also appeared in *Sailor
Beware* (1951), *Jumping Jacks* (1952),
The Bridges at Toko-Ri (1954), *The Seven*

Year Itch (1955), *The Man With the
Golden Arm* (1955), *Attack!* (1956), *Li'l
Abner* (1959, as Romeo Scragg), *The
George Raft Story* (1961), *The Thrill of It
All* (1963), *The Family Jewels,* the Carol
Lynley *Harlow* (both 1965), and *Fort
Utah* (1967), to name a few, in addition to
many TV shows in the 1960s and 1970s.
He was incapacitated during the final
years of his life, from a paralytic stroke.

STREEP, MERYL. Actress. *(b. June 22,
1949, Summit, N.J.)* Arguably the best actress working in American films today,
this brilliant performer has mastered to an
almost uncanny degree the skill of trans-
forming herself into whatever character
she portrays. She has accomplished this at
the expense of establishing a clearly defined star persona, but her chameleonlike
ability makes her the envy of her contemporaries. Setting her sights while just a
schoolgirl, Streep studied theater arts at
Vassar, Dartmouth, and Yale, appearing in
an astounding number of productions
(more than 40, according to some esti-
mates) during her college and graduate
school years. She descended upon the
New York theatrical community like a
whirlwind, first in off-Broadway shows
(including those of legendary producer Joe
Papp) and then on the Great White Way
itself.

Streep made her screen debut in *Julia*
(1977), taking a showy supporting role in
that Jane Fonda starrer, and made a strong
impression the same year in the TV movie
The Deadliest Season and the highly rated
miniseries "Holocaust" (1978, for which
she won an Emmy). She then took the
nominal female lead in *The Deer Hunter*
(also 1978), picking up the first of nine
Academy Award nominations. In 1979 she
appeared in three films—*The Seduction of
Joe Tynan* (her first "light" part, as a
smart Southern belle), *Manhattan,* and
Kramer vs. Kramer (winning her first Oscar, for Best Supporting Actress, as Dustin
Hoffman's troubled spouse)—firmly establishing herself with moviegoers. Her
rise to fame was nothing short of meteoric.

One stunning performance followed another. Streep seldom appeared in heavy
makeup, yet she looked different in each
picture—and sounded different, too, going
to great pains to master foreign accents

and regional dialects. She won a second Oscar, now as Best Actress, for her portrayal of a Polish woman who survives Nazi persecution during World War 2 in *Sophie's Choice* (1982), and was nominated for her turns in *The French Lieutenant's Woman* (1981, appearing as both an actress and the Victorian character she plays), *Silkwood* (1983, her first working-class character, a doomed factory employee), *Out of Africa* (1985, as Danish author Karen Blixen), *Ironweed* (1987, as Jack Nicholson's boozing partner and fellow vagrant), *A Cry in the Dark* (1988, as an Australian woman accused of murdering her own baby), and *Postcards From the Edge* (1990, as the weary actress overshadowed by her overbearing mother).

Ironically, Streep's majestic talent and versatility began to be seen as a liability. Journalists started complaining about her aloofness onscreen, the lack of warmth in her characters; writers even started making cracks about her penchant for dialects. So the actress began looking for ways to expand both her horizons—and her audience appeal. Her attempt to play a "normal" character opposite her male chameleon counterpart, Robert De Niro, in *Falling in Love* (1984) was sunk by a dull script. But her broad, comic turn as a narcissistic romance novelist in *She-Devil* (1989) took critics and moviegoers by surprise, and her gutsy vocalizing at the end of *Postcards From the Edge* revealed a strong, trained singing voice. (She was set at one point to play the title role in a film version of the musical "Evita" that sadly fell apart.)

Since then, a more "humanized" Streep has played genteel comedy with Albert Brooks in *Defending Your Life* (1991) and over-the-top farce opposite Goldie Hawn in *Death Becomes Her* (1992). In 1994 she tackled her first action film, *The River Wild,* then starred opposite Clint Eastwood in *The Bridges of Madison County* (1995). Because Meryl Streep can do anything, and do it well, the only question is, what will she do next?

OTHER FILMS INCLUDE: 1982: *Still of the Night;* 1985: *Plenty;* 1986: *Heartburn;* 1993: *The House of the Spirits.*

STREISAND, BARBRA. Actress, singer, producer, director. *(b. Apr. 24, 1942, Brooklyn, N.Y.)* If America can be said to have a Queen of Show Business, then Streisand surely fills the bill. Absolutely uncompromising in her determination to excel in whatever she attempts, this performer/producer/director has fought every step of the way for respect in an industry that doles it out sparingly to women. A cabaret singer and recording artist who burst onto Broadway in 1962's "I Can Get It for You Wholesale," Streisand wowed audiences with her seemingly boundless energy and astonishing vocal range. She subsequently won a Tony nomination for her characterization of show-biz legend Fanny Brice in "Funny Girl," and taped a number of TV specials (one of which, 1965's "My Name Is Barbra," won her an Emmy) before starring in the movie adaptation of *Funny Girl* (1968), which earned her a Best Actress Oscar (in a rare tie, with Katharine Hepburn for *The Lion in Winter*).

Hello, Dolly! (1969) and *On a Clear Day You Can See Forever* (1970) followed, and despite their shortcomings, Streisand joined the firmament of great movie-musical stars. The genre was on the wane, though, and she elected to broaden her range in nonmusical vehicles. She scored as a comically crude hooker in *The Owl and the Pussycat* (also 1970) and as the madcap heroine of *What's Up, Doc?* (1972). *Up the Sandbox* (also 1972) gave her a more serious role. She was then paired with 1970s dreamboat Robert Redford in the romantic *The Way We Were* (1973, Oscar-nominated), a smash hit she followed with the feeble comedy *For Pete's Sake* (1974) and a surprisingly lame sequel, *Funny Lady* (1975).

With then-boyfriend Jon Peters, Streisand turned producer; her 1976 remake of *A Star Is Born* earned her a Best Song Oscar with Paul Williams for "Evergreen," but irritated some observers who felt she lost objectivity as both producer and star. She slipped further with a pair of flop comedies, *The Main Event* (1979) and the underrated *All Night Long* (1981); in the latter she hurriedly replaced Lisa Eichhorn in midproduction, taking her only supporting role to date. Since then, her output has been meager, but she has revealed, from movie to movie, an increasingly impressive grasp of the filmmaking process. She donned the director's cap (as well as men's clothing) for the ambitious musical *Yentl* (1983; she also produced and cowrote), played a psychotic hooker in *Nuts* (1987), and directed, produced, and costarred in *The Prince of Tides* (1991), enduring critical snipes along the way, but earning a growing degree of respect as well for her accomplishments. Divorced from Elliott Gould, by whom she has a son, Jason; he appeared as her offspring in *Tides*.

STRODE, WOODY. Actor. *(b. July 28, 1914, Los Angeles; d. Dec. 31, 1994.)* Sturdy, bald-headed African-American actor who, because of the time in which he was most active in movies, was limited in the breadth and scope of his roles. With Jackie Robinson and Kenny Washington (who went on to play supporting roles in movies, mostly during the 1940s), Strode was a football star at UCLA. In 1946, Strode and Washington became the first blacks to play in the National Football League. He went on to star for the Calgary Stampeders in the Canadian Football League, and in the 1950s became a professional wrestler. Strode made his screen debut in a small role in *Sundown* (1941), but became more active in movies a decade later, in roles which required little more than his striking presence: *Androcles and the Lion* (1952, costumed as a lion!), *Caribbean* (also 1952), *City Beneath the Sea* (1953), *The Ten Commandments* (1956, playing two roles, the King of Ethiopia and a slave), *The Buccaneer, Tarzan's Fight for Life* (both 1958), and *Pork Chop Hill* (1959). Strode is best remembered for *Spartacus* (1960), in which he makes a brief but riveting appearance as a gladiator who battles Kirk Douglas to the death. John Ford gave him his most interesting part, the title role in *Sergeant Rutledge* (1960), as a proud, heroic member of the black Ninth Cavalry who's falsely accused of rape and murder. A long-time personal friend of Ford, Strode also appeared in *Two Rode Together* (1962, as Stone Calf, a determined Indian warrior wedded to an abducted Spanish aristocrat), *The Man Who Shot Liberty Valance* (1962, as Pompey, John Wayne's right-hand man), and *7 Women* (1966, as a Chinese warrior). He also starred in *Black Jesus* (1968), as a character based on the African leader Patrice Lumumba, and had a prominent supporting part in Sergio Leone's *Once Upon a Time in the West* (1968). In 1990, Strode (who enjoyed a

forty-plus-year marriage to an authentic Hawaiian princess) published his autobiography, "Goal Dust."
OTHER FILMS INCLUDE: 1963: *Tarzan's Three Challenges;* 1969: *Che!;* 1977: *Kingdom of the Spiders;* 1980: *Cuba Crossing;* 1983: *The Violent Breed, Jungle Warriors, The Final Executioner;* 1984: *Angkor: Cambodia Express, The Cotton Club;* 1989: *The Bronx Executioner;* 1993: *Posse;* 1995: *The Quick and the Dead.*

STUART, GLORIA. Actress. *(b. July 14, 1910, Santa Monica, Calif.)* This beautiful blonde appeared in dozens of films during the 1930s but never quite achieved stardom. As a young woman, she worked as a newspaper reporter to pay for her acting lessons; Stuart was performing at the Pasadena Playhouse when she was signed by Universal in 1932. She got off to a good start, costarring for directors James Whale (in 1932's *The Old Dark House* and 1933's *The Invisible Man* and *The Kiss Before the Mirror)* and John Ford (1932's *Air Mail),* but she failed to live up to the studio's expectations for her and was dropped in 1934. (She fared better on loan-out, in RKO's *Sweepings* and Samuel Goldwyn's *Roman Scandals* with Eddie Cantor, in 1933.) Her failure to click is puzzling: few screen ingenues of the 1930s could match her in looks, poise, charm, or ability.

Stuart appeared in Warner Bros.' *Here Comes the Navy* (1934, with James Cagney and Pat O'Brien) and *Gold Diggers of 1935* among others, before signing with 20th Century-Fox in 1936. She made an auspicious debut for that studio, playing the wife of Dr. Mudd (the surgeon who treated John Wilkes Booth) in the Ford-directed *The Prisoner of Shark Island,* and supported Shirley Temple in that year's *Poor Little Rich Girl* (both 1936), the first of several pictures that teamed her with fellow contract player Michael Whalen. They appeared together in *The Lady Escapes* (1937), *Change of Heart, Island in the Sky,* and *Time Out for Murder* (all 1938), well-made programmers that entertained audiences but did little to advance their careers. Stuart, in fact, never got a big-budget vehicle to herself while at Fox; instead, she supported Victor McLaglen and Freddie Bartholomew in *Professional Soldier* (1936), The Ritz

Brothers in *Life Begins in College* (1937) and *The Three Musketeers* (1939), and Temple again in *Rebecca of Sunnybrook Farm* (1938). In 1938 she served on the Board of Directors of the Screen Actors Guild, but left the screen in 1939 when her Fox contract expired.

Stuart went back to the stage, touring all over the country. She only made a few films after that, the most notable being *The Whistler* (1944, directed by William Castle). In 1946 she left show business, content to raise a family and pursue other interests. Since then she's become an accomplished artist, and has occasionally returned to acting, appearing in the 1975 telefilm *The Legend of Lizzie Borden* and on the big screen in *My Favorite Year* (1982, as the matron who dances with Peter O'Toole), *Mass Appeal* (1984), and *Wildcats* (1986). Stuart was for many years married to drama critic and occasional screenwriter Arthur Sheekman, whom she met on the set of *Roman Scandals*.

STURGES, JOHN. Director, producer. (b. Jan. 3, 1910, Oak Park, Ill.; d. Aug. 18, 1992.) The dean of big-budget action movies made during the 1950s and 1960s has almost no reputation today, despite having directed many films that remain hugely popular. He began as an editor in 1932, and first wielded the megaphone during World War 2, making documentaries and training films for the Army Air Corps. Sturges' mainstream directorial career began in 1946 with *The Man Who Dared,* the first of many grade-B programmers he helmed before winning bigger and better projects at MGM, including *Right Cross, The Magnificent Yankee* (both 1950), *Kind Lady, The People Against O'Hara* (both 1951), *It's a Big Country* (also 1951, as codirector), *The Girl in White* (1952), *Jeopardy, Fast Company,* and *Escape From Fort Bravo* (all 1953). He then showed how the widescreen CinemaScope format could be used imaginatively by placing Spencer Tracy all alone against a vast desert panorama in the suspense classic *Bad Day at Black Rock* (1955, for which he received a Best Director Oscar nomination). He also steered the Sinatra "Rat Pack" through *Sergeants 3* (1962).

Sturges helmed two Western block-busters, *Gunfight at the O.K. Corral* (1957) and *The Magnificent Seven* (1960), reteamed with Tracy when he replaced Fred Zinnemann as director of *The Old Man and the Sea* (1958), and made the all-star war epic *Never So Few* (1959). His 1960s output included two in Cinerama—the comic Western *The Hallelujah Trail* (1965) and the cold war thriller *Ice Station Zebra* (1968)—the soap operas *By Love Possessed* (1961) and *A Girl Named Tamiko* (1962); a chillingly prophetic nail-biter, *The Satan Bug* (1965); an *O.K. Corral* sequel, *Hour of the Gun* (1967), and the astronaut suspenser *Marooned* (1969). The decade also saw the release of his all-time biggest hit, the legendary POW adventure *The Great Escape* (1963).

After directing Clint Eastwood in *Joe Kidd* (1972), Charles Bronson in *Chino* (1973), John Wayne in *McQ* (1974), and an all-star cast in *The Eagle Has Landed* (1977), Sturges retired, leaving Hollywood to a younger generation of filmmakers who scarcely know his name. His style was clean and uncluttered; he generally eschewed fancy camera tricks, but his compositions were invariably effective and evocative. Moreover, he seldom failed to extract skillful performances from his actors.

STURGES, PRESTON. Director, screenwriter, playwright. (b. Aug. 29, 1898, Chicago, as Edmond Preston Biden; d. Aug. 6, 1959.) His career is the stuff of legend. Like a supernova, Sturges burst into prominence with dazzling brightness, but burned out after a few short years, leaving a trail of frustration behind along with a handful of brilliant movies. The son of a free-spirited, self-styled *artiste* (whose circle included legendary dancer Isadora Duncan), he traveled through Europe with his mother, and was educated in a variety of institutions both here and abroad. As a young man, he managed the New York branch of a cosmetics company his mother had started, but a life-threatening emergency appendectomy instilled in him a keen awareness of his own mortality and a burning desire to accomplish things of which heretofore he only dreamed. He summarily quit the business world to become a playwright.

Sturges' first effort went nowhere, but

his second, "Strictly Dishonorable," became a hit on Broadway and was purchased for the movies. He saw the 1931
film adaptation, liked it, and resolved to
make his own way to Hollywood. After a
brief stint at Universal, his screenplay
The Power and the Glory, purchased by
Jesse L. Lasky for production by Fox,
became the talk of the industry—both for
its unusual narrative structure and for
Sturges' unusually close collaboration
with director William K. Howard.

Although 1933's *Power* (the story of a
ruthless industrialist said to have been an
influence on Orson Welles' *Citizen Kane)*
didn't exactly set any box-office records,
it established Sturges as a formidable talent. Witty, urbane, shaped by his cultured
continental upbringing, Sturges also possessed a discerning ear for American
speech patterns and colloquialisms. He
was particularly adept at adapting European material for American sensibilities.
Over the next several years he penned
some remarkable scripts, either alone or in
collaboration, including *Thirty Day Princess, We Live Again* (both 1934), *Diamond Jim, The Good Fairy* (both 1935),
Next Time We Love (1936, uncredited),
Hotel Haywire, Easy Living (both 1937),
Port of Seven Seas, If I Were King (both
1938), *Never Say Die* (1939), and the
lovely *Remember the Night* (1940).

Increasingly, Sturges chafed at having to
relinquish his scripts to directors who, he
felt, never did them justice. In 1940, he finally persuaded Paramount to let him direct one of his own screenplays by selling
them the script for one dollar, and tackling
a modestly budgeted production. *The
Great McGinty,* a political satire, was a
sleeper hit. Sturges followed it with
Christmas in July (also 1940), reworked
from one of his unsold plays; this modest
comedy, starring Dick Powell and Ellen
Drew, also elicited fine reviews and did
good business.

After Sturges won a Best Screenplay Oscar for *McGinty,* Paramount opted to let
him bring in an A picture with big stars.
The Lady Eve (1941) starred Henry Fonda
and Barbara Stanwyck, and featured the
incongruous but effective blend of sophisticated, sometimes ribald dialogue and uproarious slapstick that became a Sturges
trademark. He had his third straight hit.
Sullivan's Travels (also 1941, starring Joel
McCrea and Veronica Lake) was next, and

it represented a radical departure: in the
early reels a bona fide comedy, it shifted
gears halfway through and suddenly
turned starkly serious. This ambitious
story of a disenchanted movie director
who wants to make "important" movies is
one of the most unusual ever to emerge
from Hollywood. Whatever misgivings
Paramount had were assuaged by the critics, who began using the word "genius" to
describe Sturges.

The Palm Beach Story (1942), a screwball comedy teaming McCrea with
Claudette Colbert, convulsed moviegoers
with laughter. *The Miracle of Morgan's
Creek* and *Hail the Conquering Hero*
(both 1944, both nominated for Best
Screenplay Oscars), arguably his best
films, followed in rapid succession, delighting audiences and wowing reviewers,
who wondered in print if Sturges was only
one man. But by the time those films were
in theaters, Sturges had left Paramount.
He was bitter over the treatment the studio
had given his seriocomic story about the
man who invented anesthesia, *The Great
Moment* (made in 1942, not released until
1944). The studio was beginning to chafe
at the independence and perceived arrogance of its resident genius. Neither party
realized at the time what a disaster
Sturges' departure would be. Paramount
lost an almost consistent hit-maker;
Sturges lost a comfortable home base
where he did his best work.

Sturges entered into a star-crossed partnership with millionaire filmmaker Howard Hughes. Only one film resulted: *The
Sin of Harold Diddlebock* (1947), a clever
comeback vehicle for silent-screen comedy star Harold Lloyd. But Hughes never
liked the film, and shelved it until 1950,
when, considerably recut, it was released
as *Mad Wednesday.* Sturges also worked
on *Vendetta,* a similarly troubled pet property of Hughes.

Sturges moved next to 20th Century-
Fox, where an enthusiastic Darryl F.
Zanuck proclaimed that the screen's master of comedy would find a happy home
(and a profitable one; his deal made him
one of the highest-paid men in the United
States). *Unfaithfully Yours* (1948) starred
Rex Harrison as a violently jealous conductor who fantasizes about murdering the
wife (Linda Darnell) he mistakenly believes unfaithful to him. It was received
with mixed reviews and indifferent audi-

ence reaction; only in later years was its black comedy truly appreciated. *The Beautiful Blonde From Bashful Bend* (1949), a Western farce starring the studio's top star, Betty Grable, was an unabashed flop that sunk Sturges at Fox.

Astonishingly, just a few years after reigning as Hollywood's "wonder boy" of comedy, Sturges was out of work. Unable to save a dime, he was broke, as well. He wound up in Europe, nearly penniless, with his third wife and infant son. He wangled a job adapting and directing *The French, They Are a Funny Race* (1956) with British star Jack Buchanan. A misfire, it effectively ended his directing career. He worked here and there, mostly for old friends who felt sorry for him, doctoring scripts that didn't need the help. He died in New York, where he was negotiating new projects for the stage and TV. His widow and sons worked to keep his name alive, and managed to get his autobiography (which he'd dictated and nearly completed just before his death) published in 1990, and to mount a well-received New York production of his unproduced play "A Cup of Coffee," which was the genesis of *Christmas in July*.

SULLAVAN, MARGARET. Actress. *(b. May 16, 1911, Norfolk, Va., as Margaret Brooke; d. Jan. 1, 1960.)* Luminous, huskyvoiced, petite charmer who made her reputation in high-profile soap operas of the 1930s. She went to exclusive girls' schools in the Northeast, studying the dramatic arts and making her acting debut with the Cape Cod-based University Players (which at that time also included James Stewart and Henry Fonda, whom she married in 1931). She screen-tested with Fonda for MGM, but it was director John M. Stahl who signed her to star in *Only Yesterday* (1933), one of his innumerable, glossy weepies for Universal. The winsomely soulful Sullavan became a screen favorite in *Little Man, What Now?* (1934), the charming comedy *The Good Fairy, So Red the Rose* (both 1935), *The Moon's Our Home* (1936, her only film with Fonda, from whom she was already divorced), *Next Time We Love* (also 1936, her first film with James Stewart), *The Shining Hour* (1938), *The Shopworn Angel* (also 1938, with Stewart), the moving *Three Comrades* (also 1938, earning an

Academy Award nomination for this performance), *The Shop Around the Corner* (1940, a beguiling, gentle comedy, directed by Ernst Lubitsch, that paired her again with Stewart), *The Mortal Storm* (also 1940, also with Stewart), *Appointment for Love, So Ends Our Night, Back Street* (all 1941), and the wartime drama *Cry Havoc* (1943).

The onscreen epitome of grace and charm, Sullavan offscreen was tempestuous and self-destructive. More attracted to stage work than movies, she hit the boards as frequently as possible, but when her theatrical career floundered she took to drink. Her last film was *No Sad Songs for Me* (1950). Sullavan divorced Fonda in 1933, then married director William Wyler during production of *The Good Fairy* in 1935. That union too was short-lived. She then married producer-agent Leland Hayward. She gradually became deaf during the last years of her life, and committed suicide with an overdose of pills at age 49. Her daughter by Hayward, Brooke, wrote a harrowing memoir of the family's life, "Haywire." It became a TV movie in 1980, with Lee Remick portraying Sullavan.

SULLIVAN, BARRY. Actor. *(b. Aug. 29, 1912, New York City, as Patrick Barry; d. June 6, 1994.)* Tall, dark leading man with a menacing cast to his features, a veteran of innumerable crime dramas and Westerns. A college graduate who, in the depths of the Depression, worked as a theater usher before turning to the stage, Sullivan had his first film experience in some New York–made short subjects, like *Dime a Dance* (1937), with such fellow up-and-comers as Danny Kaye, June Allyson, and Imogene Coca. He made his Hollywood debut in a strong supporting part in the Harry Sherman Western *The Woman of the Town* (1943). He labored at Paramount throughout the 1940s, and was occasionally loaned out to other studios. Grim and relentless (on-screen, anyway), Sullivan convincingly depicted a variety of hard-boiled, cynical characters—on both sides of the law, both in lead roles and in support—during his career, which included a lengthy stint at MGM. Among his better roles: Tom Buchanan in *The Great Gatsby* (1949), the movie director betrayed by ruthless careerist Kirk Douglas in *The Bad and the Beautiful* (1952), and the title role in *Wolf Larsen* (1958) as Jack London's insane sea captain. He also worked extensively in TV beginning in the mid 1950s.

Sullivan played a Western lawman in the 1960–62 TV series "The Tall Man," and was a regular on several other shows in addition to guest-starring in countless series episodes and telefilms.
OTHER FILMS INCLUDE: 1944: *Lady in the Dark, Rainbow Island;* 1945: *Getting Gertie's Garter, Duffy's Tavern;* 1946: *Two Years Before the Mast, Suspense;* 1947: *The Gangster;* 1948: *Smart Woman;* 1950: *A Life of Her Own, Nancy Goes to Rio, Grounds for Marriage;* 1951: *Three Guys Named Mike, Inside Straight, Payment on Demand, I Was a Communist for the FBI;* 1953: *Cry of the Hunted, Jeopardy, China Venture;* 1954: *The Miami Story, Loophole;* 1955: *Strategic Air Command, Queen Bee;* 1956: *The Maverick Queen;* 1957: *Dragoon Wells Massacre, Forty Guns;* 1958: *Another Time, Another Place;* 1960: *Seven Ways From Sundown, The Purple Gang;* 1962: *Light in the Piazza;* 1963: *A Gathering of Eagles;* 1965: *My Blood Runs Cold, Harlow* (Carol Lynley version); 1966: *An American Dream;* 1969: *Night Gallery* (telefilm), *Tell Them Willie Boy Is Here;* 1973: *Pat Garrett and Billy the Kid* (cut from original release prints but restored for cable and video versions); 1974: *Earthquake;* 1976: *Survival;* 1977: *Oh, God!;* 1978: *Caravans.*

SULLIVAN, FRANCIS L. Actor. *(b. Jan. 6, 1903, London; d. Nov. 19, 1956.)* Heavyset, sinister-looking English character actor whose extensive stage experience included everything from Shakespeare to Shaw before he turned to film work. An expert at playing larger-than-life characters (pun intended), Sullivan seldom lacked for work, and made a vivid impression in most of his movies. First appeared on-screen in *The Missing Rembrandt* (1932), a British-made Sherlock Holmes mystery. In Hollywood, Sullivan was cast in a brace of Dickens' adaptations: *Great Expectations* (1934, playing "Jaggers," a role he reprised in the classic 1946 British film version directed by David Lean) and *The Mystery of Edwin Drood* (1935). Returning to his homeland, Sullivan was featured in *Drums* (1938), *The Citadel* (1938), *The Four Just Men* (1939, as one of the heroes), *Pimpernel Smith* (1941), *Caesar and Cleopatra* (1946), *Oliver*

Twist (as Mr. Bumble), *Joan of Arc, The Winslow Boy* (all 1948), *Night and the City* (1950), and many others. Back in Hollywood during the 1950s he made *My Favorite Spy* (1951), and finished his screen career in crummy American movies like *Drums of Tahiti* (1954), in most of which he played bilious Sydney Greenstreet types. His last film was *The Prodigal* (1955).

SURTEES, ROBERT L. Cinematographer. *(b. Aug. 9, 1906, Covington, Ky.; d. Jan. 5, 1985.)* One of this country's great cinematographers, Surtees went to Hollywood in 1927 and became an apprentice to such top cameramen as Gregg Toland and Joseph Ruttenberg. He spent 20 years at MGM, lensing both black-and-white and color films with equal expertise. Surtees won Oscars for his cinematography on *King Solomon's Mines* (1950), *The Bad and the Beautiful* (1952), and *Ben-Hur* (1959). He also received nominations for *Thirty Seconds Over Tokyo* (1944, shared with Harold Rosson), *Quo Vadis?* (1951), *Oklahoma!* (1955), *Mutiny on the Bounty* (1962), *Doctor Dolittle, The Graduate* (both 1967), *The Last Picture Show, Summer of '42* (both 1971), *The Sting* (1973), *The Hindenburg* (1975), *A Star Is Born* (1976), and *The Turning Point* (1977). Surtees was one of the few cameramen from the studio system who adapted (with apparent ease) to contemporary filmmaking standards in the 1960s and 1970s. His son Bruce Surtees is also a highly respected cinematographer and a favorite of Clint Eastwood, having served as director of photography on *Play Misty for Me* (1971), *The Outlaw Josey Wales* (1976), *Escape From Alcatraz* (1979), *Sudden Impact* (1984), and *Pale Rider* (1985), and was Oscar-nominated for his work on *Lenny* (1974).

SUTHERLAND, DONALD. Actor. *(b. July 17, 1934, St. John, New Brunswick.)* Tall, lanky, and unusual looking to say the least, Sutherland took full advantage of the antiglamour backlash that swept Hollywood in the late 1960s and early 1970s. Which is not to say that his success was merely a matter of being in the right place at the right time; Sutherland is an extremely gifted, albeit occasionally eccentric performer. After studying at the London Academy of Music and Dramatic Arts in the late 1950s, he knocked around Europe playing small roles (usually creepy types) in horror films and thrillers; he got a career boost as one of the second-tier Army misfits in the U.S./U.K. co-production *The Dirty Dozen* (1967). It was in a radically different war movie that he stunned American audiences: Robert Altman's groundbreaking *MASH* (1970), in which he originated the role of icono-clastic surgeon Hawkeye Pierce. Immedi-ately catapulted to stardom, the actor mixed mainstream successes with risky, sometimes politically volatile ventures; he costarred with Jane Fonda not only in the popular thriller *Klute* (1971), but also in the incendiary anti-Vietnam war film *F.T.A.* (1972, which he also coproduced, cowrote, and codirected). Another daring move found Sutherland and Julie Christie enacting one of the most graphic love scenes depicted in a nonpornographic film in Nicolas Roeg's *Don't Look Now* (1973). Unlike many other stars, Sutherland wasn't afraid to play unattractive, even downright repulsive characters; his depic-tions of crazed brutishness in 1975's *The Day of the Locust* and 1977's *1900* are un-forgettable if sometimes excessive.

The 1970s was really Sutherland's de-cade; while he got the occasional juicy role in the 1980s (as the father in 1980's *Ordinary People* and a Nazi spy in 1981's *Eye of the Needle*), in recent years he's lent star power to smaller productions in supporting roles or been reduced to play-ing the heavy in films of varying pedigree—as in *Lock Up* (1989) and *Backdraft* (1991). Sutherland's breathless turn in *JFK* (1991), playing an ex-soldier-turned-informant, was a pivotal scene in that controversial movie. His son is actor Kiefer Sutherland.

OTHER FILMS INCLUDE: 1964: *Castle of the Living Dead;* 1965: *Dr. Terror's House of Horrors, The Bedford Incident, Die! Die! My Darling!;* 1968: *Sebastian, Interlude, Oedipus the King, The Split, Joanna;* 1970: *Start the Revolution Without Me, Kelly's Heroes, Alex in Wonderland, Act of the Heart;* 1971: *Little Murders, Johnny Got His Gun;* 1973: *Steelyard Blues, Lady Ice, Alien Thunder;* 1974: *S*P*Y*S;* 1976: *End of the Game, Fellini's Casanova;* 1977: *The Eagle Has Landed, The Kentucky Fried Movie* (as the Clumsy Waiter), *The Disappearance, Bethune;* 1978: *National Lampoon's Animal House, Invasion of the Body Snatchers, Blood Relatives;* 1979: *The Great Train Robbery, Murder by Decree, A Man, a Woman and a Bank;* 1980: *Bear Is-land, Nothing Personal;* 1981: *Gas, Threshold;* 1983: *Max Dugan Returns;* 1984: *Crackers, Ordeal by Innocence;* 1985: *Heaven Help Us, Revolution;* 1987: *Wolf at the Door* (as Gauguin), *The Rosary Murders, The Trouble With Spies;* 1988: *Apprentice to Murder;* 1989: *Lost Angels, A Dry White Season;* 1991: *Eminent Domain;* 1992: *The Railway Station Man* (telefilm), *Buffy The Vampire Slayer;* 1993: *Shadow of the Wolf, Benefit of the Doubt, Six Degrees of Separation, Younger and Younger;* 1994: *Disclosure;* 1995: *Out-break.*

SUTHERLAND, KIEFER. Actor. *(b. Dec. 21, 1966, London.)* The spitting image of his father, Donald Sutherland, this young, square-faced actor seems due for major success in the 1990s. He handles starring roles and supporting parts equally well, and to date he's avoided typecasting. First appearing on-screen in *Max Dugan Returns* (1983, a bit part with his father) and 1984's *The Bay Boy,* he was widely noticed as the adolescent tough in *Stand By Me* (1986). In 1987, a creepy turn as a young vampire in *The Lost Boys* cemented his burgeoning-star status. More ensemble films with hot young actors followed, in-cluding *Young Guns* (1988), its 1990 se-quel, and *Flatliners* (also 1990), which costarred Julia Roberts, to whom he was briefly engaged; the last-minute cancella-tion of their planned Hollywood wedding was headline fodder for months. Since then Sutherland has, like his father, shown a willingness to try almost any kind of part, from comic (a straitlaced FBI agent trying to deal with flaky fugitive Dennis Hopper in 1990's *Flashback)* to creepy (a venal, by-the-book Marine who's been in-volved in foul play in 1992's *A Few Good Men).* He was an effective and empathic lead in the American version of *The Van-ishing* and a lively Athos in *The Three Musketeers* (both 1993). That same year, he made a credible directing debut on the telefilm *Last Light,* in which he also starred, as a convicted killer sentenced to death. Clearly, the sky's the limit for this talented young man.

OTHER FILMS INCLUDE: 1986: *At Close Range, Crazy Moon;* 1987: *The Killing Time, Promised Land, 1969;* 1988: *Bright Lights, Big*

City; 1989: *Renegades;* 1990: *Chicago Joe and the Showgirl, The Nutcracker Prince* (voice only); 1992: *Article 99, Twin Peaks: Fire Walk With Me;* 1994: *The Cowboy Way.*

SVENSON, BO. Actor. *(b. Feb. 13, 1942, Goteborg, Sweden.)* This blond, muscular ex-Marine and UCLA student landed his first major acting role in the TV series "Here Come the Brides" (1968–70), playing a character named (appropriately enough) Big Swede. Since then he's most often been cast, for big-screen and small-screen parts alike, as athletes, lawmen and, occasionally, dim-witted heavies. Svenson first impressed movie audiences as basketball star Jack Twyman in *Maurie* (1973), delivering a solid performance in a downbeat, unsuccessful film. In 1975 he inherited from Joe Don Baker the role of real-life, head-busting Tennessee Sheriff Buford Pusser in *Part 2, Walking Tall,* a role he reprised in not only the feature film *Final Chapter—Walking Tall* (1977), but also a 1981 TV series. His other major films include *North Dallas Forty* (1979), *The Delta Force,* and *Heartbreak Ridge* (also 1986). Svenson has toiled in more than his share of junky movies like 1978's *Inglorious Bastards* (costarring ex-jock Fred Williamson, with whom he frequently appears), *Curse II: The Bite* (1988), *Beyond the Door III* (1991), and *Savage Land* (1994). He deserves better.

SWANSON, GLORIA. Actress. *(b. Mar. 27, 1899, Chicago, as Gloria Swenson; d. Apr. 4, 1983.)* It is ironic (and perhaps unfortunate) that Gloria Swanson will forever be identified with her portrayal of aging movie queen Norma Desmond in *Sunset Blvd.,* because it obscures the fact that she first captured the hearts of movie audiences as a superb light comedienne. An Army brat, Swanson found extra work at Chicago's Essanay Film Mfg. Co. in 1913. While there, she met and married Wallace Beery and came with him to Hollywood in 1915. Under contract to Mack Sennett's Triangle-Keystone studio, Swanson became leading lady to diminutive comedian Bobby Vernon in two-reelers such as *The Danger Girl* (1916) and *Teddy at the Throttle* (1917). She hated rough-and-tumble slapstick, so when Sennett joined Paramount Swanson

jumped at a chance to return to Triangle as a dramatic star. She registered well in films like *Shifting Sands* (1918), but Triangle was on its last legs and her films suffered from shoddy production and poor distribution. Cecil B. DeMille noticed one of her Sennett-Paramount shorts, and offered a contract when Triangle let her go.

DeMille's *Don't Change Your Husband* and especially *Male and Female* (1919) established Swanson as a star, and she became closely associated with the director in the public mind. After their sixth picture, *The Affairs of Anatol* (1921), Paramount broke up the team to maximize box-office potential. Although she continued to make an occasional drama, such as *Beyond the Rocks* (1922) with Rudolph Valentino, Swanson made her strongest impression in working-girl fantasies like Allan Dwan's delightful *Manhandled* (1924, in which she first performed her Charlie Chaplin imitation) and the equally delectable *Fine Manners* (1926). In 1925 she went to France to star in *Madame Sans Gene,* and returned to Hollywood on the arm of her third husband, the Marquis Henri de la Falaise de Coudray. She shortly left Paramount and set up shop as an independent producer for United Artists. *The Love of Sunya* (1927) was a well-mounted weepie that, unfortunately, laid an egg.

Swanson received her first Oscar nomination and regained her box-office stature with *Sadie Thompson* (1928), a rollicking, sexy adaptation of Somerset Maugham's "Rain," costarring and directed by Raoul Walsh. Her third independent production was the ill-fated *Queen Kelly* (1928), directed by Erich von Stroheim in his best costs-and-schedule-be-damned style. After finally pulling the plug, Swanson pieced together a version for European release, but the silent film was a dead loss in the U.S., where sound films were becoming increasingly popular. She sang as well as emoted in her first talkie, *The Trespasser* (1929), introducing the popular song "Love, Your Magic Spell Is Everywhere," and earning a second Best Actress nomination, but *What a Widow!* (1930), *Indiscreet* (another musical), and *Tonight or Never* (both 1931) proved that her career had reached the point of diminishing returns.

Swanson went to England for *Perfect Understanding* (1933), which met the fate of most British pictures with American audiences of the time: it flopped. Back in Hollywood, she made the Teutonic operetta *Music in the Air* (1934), with script by Billy Wilder and direction by Joe May, both refugees from the Third Reich. It, too, was given a tepid reception. Swanson was off the screen until 1941 when she made the enjoyable *The Father Takes a Wife* with Adolphe Menjou at RKO. It did nothing to revive her screen career. Nor, for that matter, did *Sunset Blvd.* (1950). Despite receiving a third Oscar nomination for the performance of a lifetime—as a character too many people, especially in retrospect, are willing to believe was just like her—there was no encore. *Three for Bedroom C* (1952) was a dog, *Nero's Mistress* (1956) an Italian-French nonentity, *Airport '75* (1974) an all-star farrago in which she played herself. (She also starred in a campy telefilm, *Killer Bees,* in 1974.) In the 1960s Swanson toured in a play called "Reprise," and starred on Broadway in "Butterflies Are Free" in 1971, but her screen magic never really projected across the footlights. Her 1980 autobiography is titled "Swanson on Swanson."

SWAYZE, PATRICK. Actor. *(b. Aug. 18, 1954, Houston, Tex.)* If one movie can "make" a career, 1987's *Dirty Dancing* is a perfect example. Overnight, it turned journeyman beefcake actor Swayze into a star—and a female heartthrob. He'd been in movies since 1979 (*Skatetown, U.S.A.*) and had appeared in a variety of prominent TV and film projects (including Coppola's 1983 *The Outsiders,* 1984's *Red Dawn* and *Grandview, U.S.A.,* the lead in the 1985 miniseries "North and South," and 1986's *Youngblood*), but none had lifted him to stardom—until he "got physical" with Jennifer Grey in *Dirty Dancing,* which also called on his solid terpsichorean background (he's trained in ballet and tap, and danced extensively on stage). After this runaway sleeper, Hollywood fashioned a number of "vehicles" built solely around his name and intensely physical presence—*Tiger Warsaw* (1988), *Next of Kin,* and *Road House* (both 1989)—with middling results. Winning the lead in the enormously popular, romantically charged *Ghost* (1990) opposite Demi Moore gave his career a second

boost of adrenaline. His limited acting range makes it difficult to predict where his career will go from here. Other films include *Point Break* (1991), the very ambitious *City of Joy* (1992), *Father Hood* (1993), *Tall Tale* (as Pecos Bill), and *To Wong Foo, Thanks for Everything, Julie Newmar* (both 1995). Swayze is married to actress Lisa Niemi, with whom he was teamed in the mediocre actioner *Steel Dawn* (1987).

SWINTON, TILDA. Actress. *(b. Nov. 15, 1960, England.)* Striking, translucent-skinned actress whose ethereal beauty has been a major asset on a number of very unusual projects. Educated at Cambridge, Swinton has acted with the Royal Shakespeare Company and appeared in the films *Friendship's Death* (1987) and *Play Me Something* (1989) but is best known (relatively speaking) for her work in the Derek Jarman films *Caravaggio* (1986), his segment in *Aria* (1988), *The Last of England* (1987), *War Requiem* (1988), *The Garden* (1990), and *Edward II* (1992), for which she won the Venice Film Festival's Best Actress Award as the cold, repressed Queen Isabella. She had a major triumph as the title character in *Orlando* (1993), a dazzling adaptation of Virginia Woolf's novel about an English aristocrat whose life spans four centuries—and two genders! She also worked in Jarman's *Blue* (voice only) and *Wittgenstein* (both also 1993).

SYLBERT, RICHARD. Production designer. *(b. Apr. 16, 1928, Brooklyn, N.Y.)* Unparalleled production designer who has influenced a generation of filmmakers. Trained as a painter, he began his career in television and eventually worked with the legendary William Cameron Menzies before serving as art director on such films as *Crowded Paradise* and *Patterns* (both 1956). He went on to work with such luminaries as Elia Kazan (*Baby Doll,* 1956; *A Face in the Crowd,* 1957; *Splendor in the Grass,* 1961), Sidney Lumet (*The Fugitive Kind,* 1959; *Long Day's Journey Into Night,* 1962; *The Pawnbroker,* 1965), and Mike Nichols (*The Graduate,* 1967; *Catch-22,* 1970; *Carnal Knowledge,* 1971; *The Fortune,* 1975). He won Academy Awards for his work on Nichols' first film, *Who's Afraid of Virginia Woolf?* (1966) and for the amazing six-color stylized sets of *Dick Tracy* (1990), and received additional nominations for *Chinatown* (1974), *Shampoo* (1975), *Reds* (1981), and *The Cotton Club* (1984).

Peter Biskind noted that one of Sylbert's strengths is to "boil down a script into one or two visual metaphors that express the essence of the movie, and then use them to structure the film's look." In *Chinatown,* all the buildings are white to reflect heat and parallel the story's plot about drought; in *Shampoo,* Sylbert created constant images of latticework and mirrors to capture the fake, pleasure-filled world of Beverly Hills. In the mid 1970s, Sylbert became head of production at Paramount and approved films ranging from *The Bad News Bears* (1976) to *Looking for Mr. Goodbar* (1977) before leaving to resume his designing career. His other credits include *Murder, Inc.* (1960), *The Manchurian Candidate* (1962), *All the Way Home* (1963), *Grand Prix* (1966), *Rosemary's Baby* (1968), *Fat City, The Heartbreak Kid* (both 1972), *Frances* (1982), *Shoot to Kill, Tequila Sunrise* (both 1988), *Bonfire of the Vanities* (1990), *Deception,* and *Carlito's Way* (both 1993). His brother Paul is also an art director and won an Oscar for *Heaven Can Wait* (1978).

TALBOT, LYLE. Actor. (b. Feb. 8, 1902, Pittsburgh, as Lisle Henderson.) This remarkably prolific actor, an occasional leading man in the 1930s but more often a secondary lead or character player, got into show business as a teenage magician. Once he switched to acting, Talbot traveled with various repertory companies before settling in Memphis to establish his own, The Talbot Players. He entered films as a Warner Bros. contract player in the dawn of the talkie era; over the next five years he appeared opposite Bette Davis and other up-and-coming stars in dozens of films like *Three on a Match* (1932), *20,000 Years in Sing Sing, Ladies They Talk About, The Life of Jimmy Dolan* (all 1933), *Mandalay, Fog Over Frisco, Heat Lightning, Murder in the Clouds* (all 1934, starring in the last-named as a daredevil aviator), *The Case of the Lucky Legs, Page Miss Glory, Oil for the Lamps of China* (1935), *Red Hot Tires* (also 1935, in the lead), and *The Singing Kid* (1936).

Talbot was frequently loaned to other studios during his Warners tenure (most notably with fellow Warner Bros. contractee Ginger Rogers for the 1932 Monogram mystery *The Thirteenth Guest*). He started freelancing in 1937, and initially played leads in low-budget melodramas including *Three Legionnaires* (1937) and *What Price Vengeance?* (1938) but, rapidly gaining weight, settled into character roles—many of them heavies—after *They Raid by Night* (1942). Talbot starred once more, in a 1946 Columbia serial, *Chick Carter, Detective.* In fact, he worked frequently in cliffhangers, playing Commissioner Gordon in *Batman and Robin* (1949) and villainous Lex Luthor opposing Man of Steel Kirk Alyn in *Atom Man vs. Superman* (1950).

Although his last feature film was *Sunrise at Campobello* (1960), Talbot continued to work in TV right up through the 1980s, and is best known to baby boomers as Ozzie Nelson's pal in the long-running "Adventures of Ozzie and Harriet." He has the distinction of having worked with the notorious filmmaker Edward Wood, Jr., in several of his awful movies, including *Glen or Glenda?* (1953) and *Plan 9 From Outer Space* (1959).

TAMBLYN, RUSS. Actor. (b. Dec. 30, 1934, Los Angeles.) This exuberant, boyish actor began appearing in movies in his early teens—*The Boy With Green Hair* (1948), *Samson and Delilah, Gun Crazy* (both 1949), and *Father of the Bride* (1950) among them, billed as Rusty then—but he is best known for his remarkable, acrobatic dancing in such films as *Seven Brides for Seven Brothers* (1954), *Hit the Deck* (1955), *tom thumb* (1958, in the title role), *West Side Story* (1961, his standout role), and *The Wonderful World of the Brothers Grimm* (1962). He was also nominated for a Best Supporting Actor Oscar for *Peyton Place* (1957), and was memorable in *How the West Was Won* (1962) and *The Haunting* (1963). Offscreen for several years in the 1960s, Tamblyn starred in the brutal biker flick *Satan's Sadists* (1970), a film that led to his sporadic casting in other dubious projects throughout the 1970s and 1980s (including 1971's classically awful *Dracula vs. Frankenstein,* a low point). He appeared in Dennis Hopper's *The Last*

Movie (1971), and with his contemporary Dean Stockwell in 1975's *Win, Place or Steal*. His career was revived yet again when he assumed a role in the acclaimed David Lynch TV series "Twin Peaks" in 1990. Recent credits include *Running Mates* (1992 telefilm) and *Cabin Boy* (1994), as Chocki, the half-man, half-shark.

TAMIROFF, AKIM. Actor. *(b. Oct. 29, 1899, Baku, Russia; d. Sept. 17, 1972.)* Bombastic, colorful character actor (classically trained at the Moscow Art Theatre) who, despite a thick Russian accent, played a wide variety of ethnic characters onscreen. In Hollywood from the early 1930s, he started with unbilled bits and worked his way up to major supporting roles in *The Lives of a Bengal Lancer* (1935), *The General Died at Dawn* (1936, as the title character, which earned him an Oscar nomination), *The Soldier and the Lady* (1937), *The Buccaneer* (1938), *Union Pacific* (1939, with the unlikely Western cognomen "Fiesta"), *Northwest Mounted Police* (1940), *The Corsican Brothers* (1941), *Tortilla Flat* (1942), *Five Graves to Cairo* (1943), *For Whom the Bell Tolls* (1943, an Oscar-nominated performance as the partisan Pablo who will "no prowoke"), *The Bridge of San Luis Rey* (1944), *My Girl Tisa* (1948), and *Black Magic* (1949), to name a few. At his home studio, Paramount, Tamiroff won leading roles in a number of modest but well-made programmers, including *The Great Gambini* (1937), *Dangerous to Know* (1938), *Ride a Crooked Mile* (1938), *King of Chinatown, Disputed Passage* (both 1939), *The Magnificent Fraud* (also 1939, in multiple roles), and a remake of Emil Jannings' *The Way of All Flesh* (1940). He occasionally turned his talents to comedy, with surprisingly good results; director Preston Sturges cast him as The Boss, a crooked politico, in *The Great McGinty* (1940); he repeated the characterization in a cameo for Sturges' *The Miracle of Morgan's Creek* (1944). Tamiroff traveled throughout Europe during the 1950s and 1960s, appearing in movies made in several different countries and languages. His most memorable American film during those years was Orson Welles' *Touch of Evil* (1958); he also appeared in Welles' *Mr. Arkadin*

(1955) and *The Trial* (1963), and costarred as Sancho Panza in the actor-director's unfinished *Don Quixote* (circa 1955). Later credits include *Ocean's Eleven* (1960), *Topkapi* (1964), *Alphaville* (1965), and *After the Fox* (1966); Tamiroff worked consistently right up until he died in 1972, although in later years he frequently appeared in shoddy productions far beneath his talent.

TANDY, JESSICA. Actress. *(b. June 7, 1909, London; d. Sept. 11, 1994.)* After a brilliant acting career spanning some 65 years, Tandy found latter-day movie stardom in big-budget, major-studio releases and intimate dramas alike. At a young age she determined to be an actress, and first appeared on the London stage in 1927, playing, among others, Katherine opposite Laurence Olivier's Henry V and Cordelia opposite John Gielgud's King Lear. She also worked in British films. Following her first marriage to actor Jack Hawkins, she moved to New York and met actor Hume Cronyn, who became her second husband and frequent partner on stage and screen. She made her American film debut in *The Seventh Cross* (1944), and appeared in *The Valley of Decision* (1945), *The Green Years* (1946, as Cronyn's daughter!), and *Forever Amber* (1947). After her legendary, Tony-winning performance as Blanche DuBois in the original Broadway production of Tennessee Williams' "A Streetcar Named Desire," she concentrated on the stage and only appeared sporadically in films such as *The Light in the Forest* (1958) and *The Birds* (1963).

The beginning of the 1980s saw a resurgence in her film career, with character roles in *The World According to Garp, Best Friends, Still of the Night* (all 1982), and *The Bostonians* (1984), and the hit film *Cocoon* (1985), opposite Cronyn, with whom she reteamed for **batteries not included* (1987) and *Cocoon: The Return* (1988). She and Cronyn had been working together more and more, on stage and television, to continued acclaim (notably in 1987's *Foxfire*, which won her an Emmy Award recreating her Tony-winning Broadway role), but it was her colorful performance in *Driving Miss Daisy* (1989), as an aging, stubborn Southern matron, that made her a bona fide Hollywood star, and earned her a Best Actress Oscar. She subsequently earned a Supporting Actress nomination for her work in the grass-roots hit *Fried Green Tomatoes* (1991), and costarred in *The Story Lady* (1991 telefilm, with daughter Tandy Cronyn), *Used People* (1992, as Shirley MacLaine's Jewish mother), *To Dance With the White Dog* (1993 telefilm, with Cronyn), *Nobody's Fool* (1994), and *Camilla* (also 1994, with Cronyn).

OTHER FILMS INCLUDE: 1932: *Indiscretions of Eve;* 1938: *Murder in the Family;* 1946: *Dragonwyck;* 1947: *A Woman's Vengeance;* 1950: *September Affair;* 1951: *The Desert Fox;* 1962: *Hemingway's Adventures of a Young Man;* 1974: *Butley;* 1981: *Honky Tonk Freeway;* 1988: *The House on Carroll Street.*

TANNER, ALAIN. Director, screenwriter, producer. *(b. Dec. 6, 1929, Geneva.)* Unique, quirky filmmaker who, along with his friend and fellow countryman Claude Goretta, helped bring international attention to the Swiss film industry. Tanner took a degree in economics at Geneva's Calvin College but became interested in film instead. He went to Britain and worked for the British Film Institute and BBC-TV, then made shorts in France before returning to Switzerland and making documentaries for Swiss TV. His first feature, *Charles Dead or Alive* (1969), examined a middle-aged man who leaves his business and family and moves in with a young couple; *The Salamander* (1971, cowritten with John Berger) follows a journalist and a novelist as they try unlocking the secret of a working-class woman accused of shooting her uncle. Both films revealed the influence of the French New Wave on Tanner's sensibilities, and his ability to juggle bold visual schemes, left-wing polemics, and sympathy for his characters living on the fringes of society. After *Return From Africa* (1972) and the heavy *The Middle of the World* (1974), Tanner received some of his best reviews for *Jonah Who Will Be 25 in the Year 2000* (1976, again cowritten with Berger), a light-hearted political comedy about eight individuals coming to terms with their ideals and changes since the political climate of 1968. *Messidor* (1978) is a vivid precursor of *Thelma & Louise,*

with two bored women taking to the road and becoming wanted criminals. Tanner's films since then have continued to examine outcasts, their disillusionments and rationalizations, albeit more bleakly than before, particularly *In the White City* (1983), *No Man's Land* (1985) and *A Flame in My Heart* (1987). His later films include *The Phantom Valley* (1987), *The Woman of Rose Hill* (1989), and *The Man Who Lost His Shadow* (1992).

TARANTINO, QUENTIN. Director, screenwriter, actor. *(b. Mar. 27, 1963, Knoxville, Tenn.)* Former video store clerk whose debut, the complex heist film *Reservoir Dogs* (1992), became an immediate cult hit and established Tarantino as a talent to watch. Two of his early screenplays were subsequently brought to the screen by other directors—*True Romance* (1993, Tony Scott) and *Natural Born Killers* (1994, Oliver Stone)—and showcased Tarantino's penchant for quirky dialogue, mangy characters, and graphic, almost casual violence (although *Killers* was extensively rewritten and Tarantino received only a story credit). Nothing, however, prepared critics or the public for *Pulp Fiction* (1994), a brutal, profane, and sensationally entertaining piece that dazzled with a bizarre narrative structure and knowing salutes to pop culture. It became a surprise popular hit, won the Palme d'Or at Cannes, and earned Tarantino a Best Director Oscar nomination and an Original Screenplay Oscar (cowriting with Roger Avary, whose film *Killing Zoe* was executive-produced by Tarantino). Tarantino, who had originally studied acting, has appeared in both of his own films, as well as *Sleep With Me* (1994) and *Destiny Turns on the Radio* (1995). He even spoofed *Pulp Fiction* on an episode of his friend Margaret Cho's TV sitcom "All-American Girl" and directed an episode of the medical drama "E.R."

TARKOVSKY, ANDREI. Director, screenwriter. *(b. Apr. 4, 1932, Laovrazhe, Ivanova, USSR; d. Dec. 29, 1986.)* Tarkovsky is one of the bards of the Soviet cinema: a filmmaker whose works are intensely intimate, occasionally controversial, always beautiful to behold. He is at his most compelling when examining the individual's search for his soul, the lack of true spirituality in contemporary society, and the inability of mankind to adequately respond to the demands of a rapidly evolving technology. Tarkovsky was educated at the Institute of Oriental Languages and the All-Union State Cinematography Institute, where he directed a prize-winning short subject, *Katok i skrypka* (1960, *The Steamroller and the Violin*). He earned international acclaim with his first feature, *My Name Is Ivan* (1962), a drama about a 12-year-old boy who becomes a partisan after his family is slaughtered by German soldiers during World War 2. Ingmar Bergman described the film, which earned Tarkovsky the top prize at the Venice Film Festival, as "like a miracle. I felt encouraged and stimulated: someone was expressing what I had always wanted to say without knowing how. . . . [The film] captures life as a reflection, life as a dream." Tarkovsky's next film was his most controversial: *Andrei Rublev* (1966), a historical drama about the famed 15th-century icon painter, which won the International Critics Award at the Cannes Film Festival. The film examines the role and responsibility of the artist in society; as it does not depict the artist as a "worker" who simply reflects the politics of the state, *Andrei Rublev* was suppressed by the Soviet authorities and not released until 1971. Next, Tarkovsky earned the Cannes Film Festival Special Jury Prize for *Solaris* (1972), the USSR's answer to Kubrick's *2001: A Space Odyssey* (1968), the story of an astronaut who travels to an orbiting space station. *Zerkalo* (1976, American title, *The Mirror*), Tarkovsky's most autobiographical work, is a collage of images and dream sequences relating to his childhood, parents and adult life. *Stalker* (1979) is the story of an odyssey to a prohibited area hidden within a police state. In *Nostalgia* (1983), Tarkovsky's first film made outside the USSR, a weary academic finds more than he bargained for upon coming to Tuscany to research the life of a 17th-century composer. *The Sacrifice* (1986), his final feature, explores the impact of an impending nuclear attack on a group living on a remote island; in it, Tarkovsky used an unedited ten-minute take.

TASHLIN, FRANK. Director, writer, animator. *(b. Feb. 19, 1913, Weehawken, N.J.;*

d. May 5, 1972.) Tashlin occupies a very special place in Hollywood history: he is the only major cartoon director to switch to live-action features—making them look like cartoons, to boot. His outlandish comic style first flourished at Warner Bros.' cartoon shop in the mid 1930s, where, alongside Tex Avery, he pioneered fast cutting, bizarre angles, and inside jokes; his best shorts include *Porky's Romance, Speaking of the Weather* (both 1937), *Porky Pig's Feat, Scrap Happy Daffy* (both 1943), *Plane Daffy* (1944), and *Unruly Hare* (1945). (Between Warner stints, he worked briefly for Disney and the Columbia cartoon studio.) He finally succeeded in his desire to move to features by writing the story for *Delightfully Dangerous* (1945) and scripts for *Variety Girl* (1947), *The Fuller Brush Man, The Paleface* (both 1948), The Marx Brothers' *Love Happy* (1949), *Miss Grant Takes Richmond* (also 1949), *The Fuller Brush Girl,* and *Kill the Umpire* (both 1950), all of them marked by outrageous, cartoon-style sight gags that caused one production manager to complain that the script should have been drawn instead of filmed.

Tashlin finally made it to the director's chair in 1952 with a mild family comedy, *The First Time,* but immediately followed it with one of his (and Bob Hope's) finest efforts, *Son of Paleface* (1952). In 1956 Tashlin wrote, produced, and directed that living cartoon character, Jayne Mansfield, in the seminal *The Girl Can't Help It,* and they reteamed the next year for the even better *Will Success Spoil Rock Hunter?,* with his favorite actor, Tony Randall. In 1955, he drew on his years as a cartoonist to fashion one of Martin and Lewis' best films, *Artists and Models;* it would be the first of eight with Lewis, who proved a receptive receptacle for his unique comic ideas (Lewis in turn repeatedly called Tashlin his "mentor") in such hits as *Hollywood or Bust* (1956), *The Geisha Boy, Rock-a-Bye Baby* (both 1958), *Cinderfella* (1960), *It's Only Money* (1962), *Who's Minding the Store?* (1963), and *The Disorderly Orderly* (1964). His later work included *The Man From the Diner's Club* (1963) and Agatha Christie's *The Alphabet Murders* (1966), which could have been considered a change of pace but for the casting of Tony Randall as Hercule Poirot. Though long revered in Europe, it was not until the Warner cartoons were rediscovered that the whole of Tashlin's career finally came to be appreciated in the U.S. OTHER FILMS INCLUDE: (as writer or cowriter) 1945: *Delightfully Dangerous;* 1947: *Variety Girl;* 1948: *One Touch of Venus;* 1950: *The Good Humor Man;* (as director) 1953: *Marry Me Again* (also wrote); 1954: *Susan Slept Here;* 1956: *The Lieutenant Wore Skirts* (also wrote); 1959: *Say One for Me;* 1961: *Bachelor Flat* (also wrote); 1966: *The Glass Bottom Boat;* 1967: *Caprice* (also wrote); 1968; *The Private Navy of Sgt. O'Farrell* (also wrote).

TATI, JACQUES. Actor, director, producer, screenwriter. *(b. Oct. 9, 1908, Le Pecq, France, as Jacques Tatischeff; d. Nov. 5, 1982.)* There aren't too many filmmaking legends whose entire output can be counted on the fingers of both hands, but this towering, graceful, pipe-puffing auteur, a comedic genius often compared with Buster Keaton, achieved his reputation on the basis of six feature films. His theme, his style, his mise-en-scène, all suggested the eternal struggle between Man and Machine; his was a kind of intricate slapstick in which characters found themselves at the mercy of progress, and his affinity for silent-screen comedy was mirrored in his own nearly total abstinence from dialogue (though his uses of natural sound and comic sound effects were nonpareil).

Tati honed his comic skills in French music halls, eventually appearing in several short subjects in the 1930s and 1940s, some of which he also wrote and directed. In his first feature, *Jour de Fete* (1949), Tati played a village postman obsessed with modernizing his already-simple job. Four years later, in *Mr. Hulot's Holiday* (1953), he introduced the umbrella-toting, raincoat-clad Everyman for whom nothing—even a seaside vacation—goes right. It was an international smash, and Hulot became Tati's screen alter ego for much of the remainder of his career. The film also earned Tati his first Oscar nomination—for Best Screenplay!

In *Mon Oncle* (1958), Tati's first color film, Hulot is victimized by an automated house in which—you guessed—everything goes wrong. (It won the Oscar for Best Foreign Film.) He spent years working on *Playtime* (1967), shot on 70mm

film, which pitted Hulot and a group of tourists against the high-tech vagaries of modern Paris, with an extended climax at the opening of a chi-chi restaurant where—that's right—everything goes wrong. Critics hailed it a masterpiece, but it was not a financial success, and a devastated Tati only made two more (small) films before retiring: *Traffic* (1972), with Hulot traveling to a modern auto show, and *Parade* (1974), a quasi-documentary showcasing French cabaret acts, with Tati recreating some of his old music-hall routines. He also made a gag cameo appearance as Hulot in Truffaut's *Stolen Kisses* (1968). Not unlike Keaton, Tati was totally devoted to his comic muse, and suffered when he moved too far ahead of his audience. It's lamentable that he left behind so few films, but any five minutes of any of them is sufficient to restore his spirit.

TAVERNIER, BERTRAND. Director, screenwriter. *(b. Apr. 25, 1941, Lyons, France.)* Intelligent and versatile writer-director who has impressed international audiences with his work in various genres. Like so many French filmmakers, he started as a critic (contributing to "Cahiers du Cinéma") and wrote extensively on American films. He worked as a publicist and then an assistant director. His first feature film, *The Clockmaker* (1973), based on a Georges Simenon novel, won international prizes and established him as a major talent. It also marked the beginning of a long and fruitful collaboration with actor Philippe Noiret, who has gotten some of his best opportunities in Tavernier's beautifully crafted films. He followed this world-class debut with *The Judge and the Assassin, Let Joy Reign Supreme* (both 1975), *Spoiled Children* (1977), *Deathwatch* (1980), a sci-fi commentary on media voyeurism starring American actors Harvey Keitel and Harry Dean Stanton, *A Week's Vacation* (1980), and *Coup de Torchon* (1981, also known as *Clean Slate),* a superb adaptation of a Jim Thompson novel that Tavernier moved from America to a French colony in Africa. In 1983 he made a documentary, *Mississippi Blues,* about the American South, then earned international acclaim for his sensitive and exquisite *A Sunday in the Country* (1984). Two years later he adapted the true story of a French fan's attempt to watch over doomed jazz pianist Bud Powell into the moody and expressive *Round Midnight* (1986), in which real-life tenor sax great Dexter Gordon played the musician. Tavernier then made the medieval saga *Beatrice* (1988) with a surprising score by jazz bassist Ron Carter. His recent triumphs include the moving war drama *Life and Nothing But* (1989) and *Daddy Nostalgie* (1990), which marked actor Dirk Bogarde's return to the screen after a long absence. Other credits include *L627* (1992), *D'Artagnan's Daughter* (1994), and *L'Appat* (1995).

TAVIANI, PAOLO and VITTORIO. Directors, screenwriters. (*Vittorio*—b. Sept. 20, 1929. *Paolo*—b. Nov. 8, 1931, San Miniato, Pisa, Italy.) Each of the Tavianis' films is like a chapter in a book, a part of a greater whole. They are all in some way intensely autobiographical, and focus on such universal themes as violence and injustice perpetrated upon the innocent, often in time of war; the manner in which money or power can corrupt; the absolute importance of justice and liberty both to the individual and all of humanity; and the manner in which the individual responds to, and triumphs over, his surroundings. Additionally, they are concerned with the manner in which folklore and religion delineate people's lives and place in history. The intensely political and humanistic nature of their work may be traced to the influence of their father, a lawyer who was harassed by the authorities for his antifascist beliefs. Both brothers attended the University of Pisa, with Vittorio focusing on law and Paolo studying liberal arts. However, their love of cinema overrode any other career considerations. While in their early twenties, they collaborated with Cesare Zavattini on a documentary short, *San Miniato, July 1944* (1954), which recounts a Nazi bloodbath in their hometown; they were later to retell the story as a feature, *The Night of the Shooting Stars* (1982), a story of the idiocy of war that manages to transcend its setting to become a hopeful reflection of humanity. The Tavianis' first two features, *Un Uomo da bruciare* (1962, *A Man for Burning)* and *I Fuorilegge del Matrimonio* (1963), were codirected with Valentino Orsini, better known as a resistance fighter. In the

neorealist style, they employed nonprofessional actors and natural lighting, but abandoned this style when it did not jibe with their artistic aims. While going on to direct other features—for example, *Allonsanfan* (1974; the title is an Italian phonetic rendering of the first two words of the "Marseillaise"), the tale of a 19th-century Italian nobleman's involvement with revolutionary politics—they hit their stride with *Padre Padrone* (1977, *Father Master)*, the fact-based account of a solitary, illiterate Sardinian peasant, treated as a virtual slave by his tradition-bound father, who grows up to become a respected man of letters. The film was the first to earn two top Cannes Film Festival awards: the Golden Palm and International Critics Prize. Other Taviani films are *Kaos* (1984), an adaptation of various folkloric Pirandello stories; *Good Morning, Babylon* (1987), their first film in English, the story of two Italian brothers who come to America and end up working as set designers for D. W. Griffith; *Night Sun* (1990), based on Tolstoi's "Father Sergius," about an idealistic young man's attempt to find solitude in a world rife with temptation; and *Fiorile* (1993), based on a story told the filmmakers by their mother, chronicling a family's history beginning with the manner in which it dishonestly came into wealth during the Napoleonic era.

TAYLOR, DUB. Actor. (b. Feb. 26, 1907, Richmond, Va., as Walter Clarence Taylor, Jr.; d. Oct. 3, 1994.) Veteran character actor who was famed for his thick Southern drawl and squat, grizzled appearance. His film career began with an audition for director Frank Capra, who was casting the nutty family in *You Can't Take It With You* (1938). Capra later described him as "a merry oaf wearing a perpetual infectious grin as big as a sunburst." Taylor played "Dinah" on the xylophone, and Capra cast him on the spot as Ann Miller's husband—keeping the xylophone as part of his "business." Capra also gave Taylor parts in *Mr. Smith Goes to Washington* (1939), *Riding High* (1950), and *A Hole in the Head* (1959), but Taylor is most closely associated with Westerns. He was a familiar face in B's of the 1940s and 1950s, as a sidekick to the likes of Charles Starrett, Bill Elliott (with whom he earned his nickname Cannonball), Russell Hayden, and Jimmy Wakely, but graduated to character parts in A Westerns in later years: *How the West Was Won* (1962), *Major Dundee* (1965), *Bandolero!* (1968), *The Undefeated* (1969), *The Wild Bunch* (1969), and *A Man Called Horse* (1970). His other films include *No Time for Sergeants* (1958), *Sweet Bird of Youth* (1962), *Thunderbolt and Lightfoot* (1974), and *Gator* (1976). He was particularly memorable in *Bonnie and Clyde* (1967) as Ivan Moss, father of C. W. Moss (Michael J. Pollard). In recent years, still spry, he had become an icon for those trying to capture the look and feel of vintage Westerns, and appeared in that guise in *Back to the Future Part III* (1990), *My Heroes Have Always Been Cowboys* (1991), and *Maverick* (1994). He also played the colorful grandfather of John Mellencamp in the latter's debut feature as director and star, *Falling From Grace* (1992). Taylor was a regular on "Casey Jones" (1957–58), "Please Don't Eat the Daisies" (1965–66), and the syndicated reincarnation of "Hee Haw" (1985–). He was a semi-regular on "Little House on the Prairie," and a frequent guest star on "Gunsmoke," which featured his son, the Western artist and actor Buck Taylor, as a regular cast member.

TAYLOR, ELIZABETH. Actress. (b. Feb. 27, 1932, London.) Without question one of the most beautiful women to ever grace the screen, and a much better actress than she has generally been given credit for. Her stormy personal life has overshadowed a substantial career, during the course of which she won two Oscars and was nominated for three more. Born to American parents living in London, Elizabeth took dancing lessons as a little tyke, and even performed before the Royal Family with her class. The Taylors returned to America just before the outbreak of World War 2, settling in Beverly Hills. A strikingly beautiful, graceful child, with raven hair and violet eyes, she broke into movies at the age of 10, teamed with Carl "Alfalfa" Switzer in a Universal B, *There's One Born Every Minute* (1942). At MGM, Taylor appeared with Roddy McDowall (who was to become a lifelong friend) in *Lassie Come Home* (1943), but made a greater impression opposite Mickey Rooney in *National Velvet* (1944), as a young girl determined to enter her horse in the Grand National Steeplechase race. Her earnest, irresistible performance paved the way to stardom. Loaned to Fox for *Jane Eyre* (1944), she came back to Metro for *The White Cliffs of Dover* (1944), *Courage of Lassie* (1946), *Cynthia, Life With Father* (both 1947), *A Date With Judy, Julia Misbehaves* (both 1948), and *Little Women* (1949) before winning her first "adult" role, as Robert Taylor's wife in *Conspirator* (also 1949), which she followed with *The Big Hangover* (1950). She had miraculously bypassed the "awkward" adolescent phase, going from pretty girl to beautiful woman without the usual coltish stage.

She was adorable as the excitable daughter of Spencer Tracy and Joan Bennett in *Father of the Bride* (1950) and *Father's Little Dividend* (1951). Also in 1951, on loan to Paramount, she played the society girl who inflames working-class Montgomery Clift in *A Place in the Sun,* George Stevens' remake of *An American Tragedy.* It marked the first time that Taylor was taken seriously by the critics—and, she has said, the first time she ever thought of herself as an actress. Back at Metro, she was positively radiant in period garb for *Ivanhoe* (1952), positively wasted in the musical *Love Is Better Than Ever* (also 1952), and positively bewitching in *The Girl Who Had Everything* (1953), *Beau Brummel, The Last Time I Saw Paris,* and *Rhapsody* (all 1954). (She was decorative in Paramount's *Elephant Walk* that same year, replacing an ailing Vivien Leigh.)

George Stevens again gave Taylor a memorable screen assignment as the indomitable wife of oil tycoon Rock Hudson in *Giant* (1956), an epic story for which she received favorable reviews. By now a real stunner, whose voluptuous curves perfectly complemented her flawless features, Taylor had developed her instinct for bonding with the camera lens, an intangible ability reserved for only a special few performers. As if by magic, she delivered three consecutive Oscar-nominated performances, in *Raintree County* (1957, as unstable Southern belle Susanna Drake), *Cat on a Hot Tin Roof* (1958, as the fiery Maggie the Cat), and *Suddenly, Last Summer* (1959, as the haunted Catherine), the last two films based on Tennessee Williams plays, and more demanding than anything she'd done before.

Taylor's offscreen life, which up to this point had included marriages to hotel heir Nicky Hilton, actor Michael Wilding, producer Mike Todd (reportedly her happiest union, curtailed by his untimely death), and singer Eddie Fisher, made nearly as many show-biz columns as her screen work. Persistent health problems (and an emergency tracheotomy) sapped her energy and nearly led to her death. Amid all that turmoil, she won her first Academy Award for the disaffected call girl she played in *Butterfield 8* (1960). Absent from the screen for several years, she resurfaced in *Cleopatra* (1963), one of the most publicized movies ever, and at that time the most expensive movie ever made. Its lengthy production schedule had taken its toll on both the Taylor–Fisher marriage (an on-set romance with leading man Richard Burton didn't help) and on Taylor herself, whose performance was uneven at best.

Taylor was divorced in 1964 and immediately wed Burton. As the most famous married couple in the world, they commanded unprecedented salaries to costar on-screen, though only a few of their films were really good. *The V.I.P.s* (1963), *The Sandpiper* (1965), *The Taming of the Shrew, The Comedians, Dr. Faustus* (all 1967), *Boom!* (1968), *Under Milk Wood* (1973), *Hammersmith Is Out* (1972), and the TV movie *Divorce His—Divorce Hers* (1973) all take a backseat to *Who's Afraid of Virginia Woolf?* (1966), for which Taylor won her second Oscar as Burton's blowsy, foul-mouthed wife. It was a brave and electrifying performance for a "glamor queen" to give—and it remains one of her very best. (She and Burton divorced in 1974.)

She also starred in *Reflections in a Golden Eye* (1967), *Secret Ceremony* (1968), *The Only Game in Town* (1970), *X Y and Zee* (1972), *Ash Wednesday, The Driver's Seat* (1973), and *Night Watch* (1974). The Taylor of this period was bloated and weary looking, and frequently delivered lethargic performances. Guest-star appearances in *That's Entertainment!* (1974), *The Blue Bird,* the prestige TV movie *Victory at Entebbe* (both 1976), *Winter Kills* (1979), and a major role in *A Little Night Music* (1978) singing "Send

in the Clowns," were duly noted without much enthusiasm, but her performance as an aging movie star in Agatha Christie's *The Mirror Crack'd* (1980) at least gave her something fun to do.

She has also starred in several made-for-TV movies, including *Return Engagement* (1978), *Between Friends* (1983, perhaps her best, well matched with costar Carol Burnett), *Malice in Wonderland* (1985, as famed gossip columnist Louella Parsons), *There Must Be a Pony* (1986), *Poker Alice* (1987), and *Sweet Bird of Youth* (1989). At decade's end she costarred with C. Thomas Howell in Franco Zeffirelli's unreleased *Young Toscanini*. In her later movies, Taylor's work has ranged from vital to vapid; clearly, a good script and a good director are necessary to coax from Taylor the kind of performance she's capable of giving.

Over the years Taylor's personal life has continued to make fodder for the press. She briefly remarried Burton in 1976, then wed Virginia Senator John Warner, then Larry Fortensky, a man some 20 years her junior, whom she met while in a rehab center getting treatment for substance abuse. She is an indefatigable crusader for continued and expansive AIDS research and care funding, and says her acting career is behind her. (Nevertheless, she was coaxed into appearing in 1994's *The Flintstones*—of all things—as Pearl Slaghoople, Fred's mother-in-law, and gave a deliciously funny performance.) Her efforts on behalf of AIDS sufferers was rewarded with the prestigious Jean Hersholt Humanitarian Award at the 1993 Academy Awards ceremony. That same year she received the American Film Institute Life Achievement Award. An "informal memoir," "Elizabeth Taylor by Elizabeth Taylor," was published in 1965.

TAYLOR, ROBERT. Actor. *(b. Aug. 5, 1911, Filley, Nebr., as Spangler Arlington Brugh; d. June 8, 1969.)* At one time billed "The Man With the Perfect Profile," this handsome, wavy-haired leading man for a time rivaled Clark Gable as the screen's top romantic lead. A music major in Nebraska's Doane College, he came to California in the early 1930s and enlisted in Pomona College, where he studied medicine before taking up acting. After making his film debut with a bit in Fox's *Handy Andy,* Taylor won an MGM contract and was groomed for stardom. He first starred in short subjects for the company (including *Buried Loot,* the first of MGM's long-running "Crime Does Not Pay" series), then graduated to B features such as *Society Doctor, Times Square Lady, West Point of the Air,* and *Murder in the Fleet* (all 1935).

Taylor got his big break, oddly enough, at Universal, where he was loaned to appear opposite Irene Dunne in John Stahl's elaborate weepie, *Magnificent Obsession* (also 1935). As the callow playboy whose recklessness causes Dunne's blindness, and who devotes the rest of his life to medicine in amends, Taylor won the hearts of countless female fans. (His acting still left something to be desired, and the addition of white to his temples for aging couldn't disguise his youthful handsomeness.)

Back at Metro, Taylor made a few more minor pictures before being rewarded with leading roles in bigger and better films. He starred opposite Eleanor Powell in *Broadway Melody of 1936,* and the already-legendary Greta Garbo in *Camille* (1937), a little stiff as her young lover Armand, but once again sending feminine hearts a-flutter. MGM subsequently kept him busy in three or four movies a year, giving his vehicles top production mounting (even when they didn't deserve it). Every now and again he was given roles to which, frankly, he couldn't do justice, but he impressed his producers and directors with his willingness to work hard. His Metro films of this period included *The Gorgeous Hussy, Small Town Girl* (both 1936), *Personal Property, Broadway Melody of 1938,* (both 1937), *The Crowd Roars, Three Comrades, A Yank at Oxford* (all 1938), *Lucky Night, Stand Up and Fight* (both 1939), *Escape,* and *Flight Command* (both 1940). On loan to 20th Century-Fox for *This Is My Affair* (1937), a turn-of-the-century drama, he fell in love with costar Barbara Stanwyck; they were married two years later.

Taylor costarred with Vivien Leigh, then fresh from her triumph in *Gone With the Wind,* in a high-grade soap opera, *Waterloo Bridge* (1940), which gave him another boost up stardom's ladder. He starred in *Billy the Kid, Johnny Eager, When Ladies Meet* (all 1941), *Her Cardboard Lover, Stand by for Action* (both 1942), *Bataan,* and *Song of Russia* (both 1943) before going into the Navy, serving for a time as a flight instructor for the Air Transport division, directing many training films, and narrating the documentary *The Fighting Lady* (1944).

After the war Taylor, like many of his contemporaries, adapted to tougher kinds of pictures, flirting with film noir thrillers, increasingly hard-boiled Westerns, nail-biting suspensers, and even costume epics and Biblical spectacles, including *Undercurrent* (1946), *High Wall* (1947), *Ambush, The Bribe,* (both 1949), *Conspirator* (also 1949, in an uncharacteristically sinister role opposite Elizabeth Taylor), *Devil's Doorway* (1950), *Quo Vadis?, Westward the Women* (both 1951), *Above and Beyond, Ivanhoe* (both 1952), *All the Brothers Were Valiant, Knights of the Round Table, Ride, Vaquero!* (all 1953), *Rogue Cop, Valley of the Kings* (both 1954), *Many Rivers to Cross, Quentin Durward* (both 1955), *D-Day the Sixth of June, The Last Hunt, The Power and the Prize* (all 1956), *Tip on a Dead Jockey* (1957), *The Law and Jake Wade, Party Girl, Saddle the Wind* (all 1958), *The Hangman,* and *Killers of Kilimanjaro* (both 1959).

After a quarter-century run as a star, Taylor decided it was time to give TV a try, and took the part of police detective Matt Holbrook in "The Detectives" (1959–62), a tough, violent series. His subsequent theatrical films, including *Cattle King* and *Miracle of the White Stallions* (1963), *A House Is Not a Home* (1964), *The Night Walker* (also 1964, with Stanwyck, whom he'd divorced in 1951), *Johnny Tiger* (1966), *Return of the Gunfighter* (1967 telefilm), *The Glass Sphinx* (also 1967), and *Where Angels Go . . . Trouble Follows* (1968), were mostly undistinguished. He died from lung cancer in 1969. Taylor's second wife, and widow, was actress Ursula Thiess.

TAYLOR, ROD. Actor. *(b. Jan. 11, 1929, Sydney, Australia.)* Rugged Australian actor, a mid-1950s emigré to Hollywood, who played supporting roles for several years before coming into his own as a charming, virile leading man, mostly in action pictures. In his starring debut, as the Time Traveler in George Pal's *The Time Machine* (1960), Taylor proved himself more than capable of carrying a picture; high-profile performances in 1963's *The Birds* (for Alfred Hitchcock), *The V.I.P.s* (with Elizabeth Taylor and Richard Burton), and *Sunday in New York* (displaying surprising aptitude for comedy in this sex romp) reinforced his star status. He also provided the voice of "leading dog" Pongo in Walt Disney's animated *One Hundred and One Dalmatians* (1961). A top box-office attraction during the 1960s and early 1970s, his career petered out, for no discernible reason, and his most recent work has been on TV.

His first TV series, the delightful "Hong Kong" (1960–61), remains his best; others since have all failed: "Bearcats" (1971), "The Oregon Trail" (1977), "Masquerade" (1983–84), and "Outlaws" (1986–87). In 1993 he and Alan Young appeared in a documentary about *The Time Machine* and recreated their characters for an epilogue to this much-loved film.

OTHER FILMS INCLUDE: 1954: *Long John Silver* (Australian-made); 1955: *The Virgin Queen* (his first Hollywood film, billed as Rodney Taylor); 1956: *Giant, The Catered Affair;* 1957: *Raintree County;* 1958: *Separate Tables;* 1959: *Ask Any Girl;* 1963: *A Gathering of Eagles;* 1964: *36 Hours, Fate Is the Hunter;* 1965: *Young Cassidy* (one of his most ambitious—and successful—performances, as a character based on Sean O'Casey), *Do Not Disturb;* 1966: *The Glass Bottom Boat, The Liquidator;* 1967: *Hotel, Chuka;* 1968: *Dark of the Sun, The Hell With Heroes;* 1970: *Zabriskie Point, Darker Than Amber* (as John D. MacDonald's detective Travis McGee); 1973: *The Train Robbers* (sharing the spotlight with John Wayne), *Deadly Trackers, Trader Horn;* 1977: *The Picture Show Man* (making a glorified cameo—as an American!—in this Australian film about the early days of that country's movie exhibition); 1978: *An Eye for an Eye;* 1982: *On the Run;* 1985: *Marbella.*

TEMPLE, SHIRLEY. Actress. (*b. Apr. 23, 1928, Santa Monica, Calif.*) The golden curls, dimpled cheeks, and twinkling eyes have long since become inconographic, yet it's almost impossible to overstate the near-magical ability of this child to bring 1930s audiences out of their Depression-induced gloom. In film after film, she overcame all obstacles with boundless energy and optimism. It's no accident that

she was America's top box-office draw from 1935 to 1938.

She was little more than three years old when she made her film debut in *War Babies* (1932), one of the "Baby Burlesks" short-subject series. Temple played toddlers in a number of feature films, including *Red-Haired Alibi* (1932), *To the Last Man, Out All Night* (both 1933), *Carolina, Now I'll Tell,* and *Change of Heart* (all 1934), but a featured number in the Depression-busting musical *Stand Up and Cheer* (also 1934), "Baby Take a Bow," allowed her to steal the show. She won costarring parts in Paramount's *Now and Forever* and *Little Miss Marker* (also 1934) before being signed to an exclusive Fox contract. Fox capitalized on her growing fame by starring her in *Baby Take a Bow* and *Bright Eyes* that same year; she even won a special Academy Award for her "outstanding contribution to screen entertainment" in 1934.

Fox placed her in hit after hit, backing her up with top directors, songwriters, and contract players from the studio ranks; she made terpsichorean history when she tap-danced with the great Bill "Bojangles" Robinson. But there was no question what the main attraction was in a Temple picture: Shirley herself, and her thousand-watt personality. In many cases her vehicles were remakes of popular children's stories or earlier films with other child stars, as a perusal of the titles will show: *The Little Colonel, Our Little Girl, Curly Top, The Littlest Rebel* (all 1935), *Captain January, Poor Little Rich Girl, Dimples, Stowaway* (all 1936), *Wee Willie Winkie, Heidi* (both 1937), *Rebecca of Sunnybrook Farm, Little Miss Broadway, Just Around the Corner* (all 1938), *The Little Princess, Susannah of the Mounties* (both 1939), and *Young People* (1940). Studio chief Darryl F. Zanuck refused to loan her to MGM to star in *The Wizard of Oz,* but after its great success, he decided to compete with his own lavish fantasy, *The Blue Bird* (1940). Then Shirley Temple did the unthinkable: She grew up.

Once she hit adolescence, Temple lost the special appeal that had made her a star. *Kathleen* (1941) and *Miss Annie Rooney* (1942) demonstrated how difficult it was to fashion vehicles for the "aging" youngster, but she performed admirably in ensemble, as proved by her performances in *Since You Went Away, I'll Be Seeing*

You (both 1944), *The Bachelor and the Bobby-Soxer* (1947), and *Fort Apache* (1948, as an ingenue in this John Ford-directed cavalry story, opposite then-husband John Agar).

She retired from the screen after a flurry of activity in 1949 and divorced Agar the same year. Her last contact with show business came in the late 1950s when she hosted (and frequently starred in) the TV anthology programs "Shirley Temple's Storybook" (1958–59) and "Shirley Temple Theatre" (1960–61). As Shirley Temple Black she has been active in politics for a quarter-century now, serving as ambassador to Ghana and Czechoslovakia and holding other government-related positions at home. In all her pursuits, she benefits from the fact that, decades after her retirement, she remains one of the most famous women in the world. Her autobiography, "Child Star," was published in 1988.

OTHER FILMS INCLUDE: 1945: *Kiss and Tell;* 1947: *Honeymoon, That Hagen Girl;* 1949: *Mr. Belvedere Goes to College, Adventure in Baltimore, The Story of Seabiscuit, A Kiss for Corliss.*

TERRY-THOMAS. Actor. *(b. July 14, 1911, London, as Thomas Terry Hoar Stevens; d. Jan. 8, 1990.)* Gap-toothed comic actor whose exaggerated screen persona reinforced the sterotypical view of British upper-class twits held by American moviegoers. He frequently played scheming heavies or hapless aristocrats of the "have a cocktail, old boy" school, and was always a delight. A dress extra in 1930s British films—in *It's Love Again* (1936), among others—Terry-Thomas became a popular stand-up comic in the late 1940s, and revitalized his screen career during the next decade, eventually going to Hollywood.

His activity was curtailed when he contracted Parkinson's disease in 1971; its debilitating effects worsened year by year, and drained his finances. Toward the end of his life his plight was publicized and both fans and colleagues came to his aid. His autobiography, "Filling the Gap," was published in 1959.

OTHER FILMS INCLUDE: 1948: *A Date With a Dream;* 1949: *Helter Skelter;* 1956: *Private's Progress;* 1957: *The Green Man, Blue Murder at St. Trinian's, Your Past Is Showing,*

The Brothers in Law; 1958: *tom thumb* (teamed with Peter Sellers), *Too Many Crooks;* 1959: *Man in a Cocked Hat, I'm All Right Jack;* 1960: *School for Scoundrels, Make Mine Mink;* 1961: *Bachelor Flat;* 1962: *Operation Snatch, The Wonderful World of the Brothers Grimm;* 1963: *The Mouse on the Moon, It's a Mad Mad Mad Mad World;* 1964: *Strange Bedfellows;* 1965: *How to Murder Your Wife, Those Magnificent Men in Their Flying Machines;* 1966: *Don't Look Now, Munster, Go Home;* 1967: *The Perils of Pauline, Bang, Bang, You're Dead, A Guide for the Married Man;* 1968: *Where Were You When the Lights Went Out?, Don't Raise the Bridge, Lower the River;* 1969: *Those Daring Young Men in Their Jaunty Jalopies;* 1971: *The Abominable Dr. Phibes;* 1972: *Dr. Phibes Rises Again;* 1973: *Robin Hood* (as the voice of Sir Hiss); 1976: *The Bawdy Adventures of Tom Jones;* 1977: *The Last Remake of Beau Geste, The Hound of the Baskervilles;* 1981: *Happy Birthday, Harry!*

THALBERG, IRVING G. Production executive, producer. *(b. May 30, 1899, Brooklyn, N.Y.; d. Sept. 14, 1936.)* Fabled "boy wonder" production head at Metro-Goldwyn-Mayer who, in the decade prior to his untimely death from pneumonia at age 37, was the guiding force behind many of the studio's top films. Thalberg demanded the highest quality in every facet of his films, while becoming a champion of the assembly line aspect of film production. He was a sickly child, and his early life was marred by a series of ailments. Upon completing high school, he was employed by Universal Pictures' New York office, where he worked as personal secretary to legendary studio founder Carl Laemmle. Thalberg was bright and persistent, and by age 21 was executive in charge of production at Universal City, the studio's California production site. He quickly established his tenacity as he battled with Erich von Stroheim over the length of *Foolish Wives* (1922), and controlled every aspect of the production of *The Hunchback of Notre Dame* (1923). In 1923, he left Universal for Louis B. Mayer Productions, which shortly thereafter linked up with Metro Pictures to become Metro-Goldwyn-Mayer. (Ironically, Thalberg found himself pitted against von Stroheim once again, editing down his massive cut of *Greed* in

1924 and ousting him from *The Merry Widow* the following year.)

The Big Parade (1925) was Thalberg's first major triumph at MGM. Until 1932, when he suffered a major heart attack, he supervised every important studio production, and combined careful preproduction groundwork with prerelease sneak previews which measured audience response. MGM became the crème de la crème of the Hollywood dream factories. Thalberg's wife, Norma Shearer, became one of the studio's major stars; a good actress, she won the most important roles and productions (often inciting jealousy among other female stars), even when they weren't ideally suited to her. Upon his illness, Louis B. Mayer, who had come to resent Thalberg's power and success, replaced him with David O. Selznick and Walter Wanger. When he returned to work in 1933, it was as one of the studio's unit producers. Nonetheless, he helped develop some of MGM's most prestigious ventures, including *Mutiny on the Bounty* (1935), *China Seas* (1935), *A Night at the Opera* (1935), *San Francisco* (1936), and *Romeo and Juliet* (1936). Thalberg died during the preproduction of *A Day at the Races* (1937). Production in Hollywood ground to a halt for his funeral. When *The Good Earth* was released posthumously in 1937 it became the first Thalberg production to feature his name on screen, a practice he had scrupulously avoided during his lifetime. A year after his demise, the Academy of Motion Picture Arts and Sciences established the Irving G. Thalberg Memorial Award, presented to a producer whose work exhibits "the most consistent high level of production achievement." "The Last Tycoon," F. Scott Fitzgerald's last novel, was inspired by Thalberg; it was filmed in 1976. Robert Evans played the real Thalberg in the Lon Chaney biography *Man of a Thousand Faces* (1957).

THOMPSON, EMMA. Actress. *(b. Apr. 15, 1959, London.)* Extraordinarily gifted and appealing actress who catapulted to stardom with her brilliant, Oscar-winning performance as Margaret Schlegel in the Merchant-Ivory adaptation of *Howards End* (1992). Thompson began acting at Cambridge University with the comedy troupe Footlights, and after experience on television with fellow troupe members Stephen Fry and Hugh Laurie, she starred in her first stage musical, "Me and My Girl," opposite Robert Lindsay. She won a British Academy Award for her work on the BBC series "Tutti Frutti" and "Fortunes of War" and became friends with her "Fortunes" costar, Kenneth Branagh, who cast her as Katherine of France in his Oscar-winning adaptation of Shakespeare's *Henry V* (1989). Branagh and Thompson were married after the film's release and since then, she has starred in many of his films: in the dual role of a present-day Californian and a forties European woman in *Dead Again* (1991), in a deliciously funny performance as a nerdy, neurotic cat lover in *Peter's Friends* (1992), and most memorably, as Beatrice opposite Branagh's Benedick in the rousing *Much Ado About Nothing* (1993). They starred, as well, in a BBC production of *Look Back in Anger* (1993). Thompson has also appeared in *The Tall Guy* (1990) and *Impromptu* (1991), and was featured in a memorable episode of television's "Cheers." She reteamed with her *Howards End* costar Anthony Hopkins in the Merchant-Ivory film *The Remains of the Day* (1993), and played a lawyer defending an accused IRA terrorist in *In the Name of the Father* (1993), earning Oscar nominations for both performances. She made an unbilled cameo as Gerard Depardieu's girlfriend in *My Father the Hero,* and teamed with her least likely costar, Arnold Schwarzenegger, in *Junior* (both 1994) before taking the title role in *Carrington* (1995).

THOMPSON, FRED DALTON. Actor. *(b. Aug. 19, 1942, Laurenceburg, Tenn.)* A practicing lawyer in Washington and Nashville for more than 25 years, Thompson's first appearance before a camera was in 1973—as House Minority Counsel during the Watergate hearings. His first "reel" performance came when he was asked to play himself in *Marie* (1985), which retold the true story of a Tennessee woman who challenged a corrupt governor. Critics said Thompson stole the movie from costars Sissy Spacek and Jeff Daniels, and since then he has become one of the busiest character actors around—while still continuing his law practice. Usually seen as an authority figure (and at six foot five, it's easy to see why). In 1994 he won a seat in the Senate, representing his home state of Tennessee. OTHER FILMS INCLUDE: 1987: *No Way Out;* 1988: *Feds;* 1989: *Fat Man and Little Boy;* 1990: *Days of Thunder, The Hunt for Red October, Die Hard 2;* 1991: *Flight of the Intruder, Class Action, Cape Fear, Necessary Roughness, Curly Sue;* 1992: *Aces: Iron Eagle III, Keep the Change* (telefilm), *Thunderheart;* 1993: *Born Yesterday, Barbarians at the Gate* (telefilm), *In the Line of Fire;* 1994: *Baby's Day Out.*

THOMPSON, LEA. Actress. *(b. May 31, 1961, Rochester, Minn.)* Appealing, all-American actress who was first noticed in a series of Burger King TV commercials. She first appeared on screen as Tom Cruise's girlfriend in *All the Right Moves* (1983). She played cute cheerleader types in *Jaws 3-D* (also 1983), *Going Undercover, The Wild Life, Red Dawn* (all 1984), and *SpaceCamp* (1986), but assumed more challenging roles as well: She donned heavy makeup to play the middle-aged mother of Michael J. Fox in *Back to the Future* (1985, reprising the role with less screen time in the 1989 and 1990 sequels), walked a fine line portraying a potentially unsympathetic character in the teen-angst exercise *Some Kind of Wonderful* (1987), played the youngish aunt of Lukas Haas in the WW2-era *The Wizard of Loneliness* (1988), and tackled topical comedy with a racy edge in *Casual Sex?* (also 1988). Recent credits include *Nightbreaker* (1989 telefilm), *Article 99* (1992), *Dennis the Menace* (1993, as Dennis' mom), *Stolen Babies* (a high-profile 1993 telefilm) and *The Beverly Hillbillies* (also 1993, as a femme fatale with a fake French accent). In time, she may even live down *Howard the Duck* (1986).

THE THREE STOOGES. Actors, eye-pokers. *(Moe Howard —b. June 19, 1897, Brooklyn, as Moses Horwitz; d. May 4, 1975. Larry Fine—b. Oct. 5, 1902, Philadelphia, as Louis Feinberg; d. Jan. 24, 1975. Jerome "Curly" Howard—b. Oct. 22, 1903, Brooklyn, as Jerome Lester Horwitz; d. Jan. 18, 1952. Samuel "Shemp" Howard—b. Mar. 17, 1895, Brooklyn, as Samuel Horwitz; d. Nov. 23, 1955. Joe Besser—b. Aug. 12, 1907; d. Mar. 1, 1988. Joe DeRita—b. July 12, 1909, as Joseph Wardell; d. July 3,*

1993.) It's no exaggeration to say that The Three Stooges are more popular today than they were in their heyday. Generations raised on their antics (televised daily) know them better than Chaplin, Laurel and Hardy, or The Marx Brothers—and for them, The Stooges are the kings of slapstick comedy.

They began in vaudeville as sidekicks to comedian Ted Healy; his "Racketeers" were Moe, Larry, Shemp, and a man named Fred Sanborn. (This is the group that made its film debut in the 1930 feature *Soup to Nuts.*) Soon after, Fred and Shemp left (the latter to embark on a solo career as a character comedian), and were replaced by Curly and a straight-woman, Bonny Bonnell. Under contract to MGM, they appeared in such features as *Meet the Baron* (1933), *Dancing Lady* (also 1933, with Joan Crawford), *Fugitive Lovers* and *Hollywood Party* (both 1934), as well as a handful of musical short subjects. (In 1933's *Plane Nuts* they recreate their hilarious vaudeville act.)

The three male "stooges" then struck off on their own and signed with Columbia for a series of two-reel comedies—a commitment that would last a full quarter-century, from 1934 to 1959. (The first year their two-reeler *Men in Black* even earned an Academy Award nomination!) With Moe assuming Healy's role as the aggressor, they quickly convulsed audiences with their slapping, poking, punching, and tweaking, as well as plenty of elaborate slapstick set pieces and outlandish verbal gags. The most reliable format was to present them on the job as anything from plumbers to doctors, and let them screw things up almost immediately. They even satirized Hitler in *You Natzy Spy* (1940) and *I'll Never Heil Again* (1941). Other memorable efforts include *Three Little Pigskins* (1934, costarring a young Lucille Ball), *Hoi Polloi* (1935), *Violent Is the Word for Curly* (1938), *In the Sweet Pie and Pie, An Ache in Every Stake, Dutiful But Dumb* (all 1941), and *Micro-Phonies* (1945).

The trio appeared in an occasional feature film (1938's *Start Cheering,* 1941's *Time Out for Rhythm,* 1946's *Swing Parade of 1946),* but shorts were their bread and butter. In 1946, Curly suffered a stroke and retired; his brother Shemp returned to fill out the trio, and they kept turning out two-reelers into the TV era.

They even made two in 3-D, *Spooks* and *Pardon My Backfire* (both 1953). When Shemp died in 1955, use of doubles and stock footage kept the shorts afloat, until veteran comedian Joe Besser was hired to join the act for a last burst of comedy shorts in the late 1950s.

The act was on the verge of quitting when Columbia sold all those shorts to TV, and almost overnight a new generation discovered 25 years of great comedy. The Stooges returned to the studio for a feature, *Have Rocket, Will Travel* (1959), with a new "third stooge," Joe DeRita, nicknamed Curly Joe. They made extensive personal appearances, launched a line of merchandise and comic books, and made new comedy feature films aimed at kids: *The Three Stooges Meet Hercules, The Three Stooges in Orbit* (both 1962), and *The Outlaws Is Coming* (1965), as well as a series of live-action wraparounds for a series of animated cartoons, after which they more or less retired. The veteran comedians lived long enough to see their work lionized by yet another generation—and celebrated by film buffs as well. Though criticized for their violence (which was extreme), and reviled by many women (for understandable reasons), they have become comedy icons in the latter part of the 20th century. And they did so with no pretensions except working hard to make people laugh.

THURMAN, UMA. Actress. *(b. Apr. 29, 1970, Boston.)* Her placid face bears the wide eyes and full lips of a classic vamp. These (and other) physical attributes, combined with an air of youthful sophistication, make Thurman the thinking filmgoer's dream date. She made her film debut in *Kiss Daddy Goodnight* (1987), but neither it nor *Johnny Be Good* (1988), a sub–John Hughes–type teen comedy, held much promise for this model and cover girl. *Dangerous Liaisons* (also 1988), however, changed people's perception of Thurman, and her erotically charged performance won her critical praise. *Henry & June* (1990) gave her a leading role as Henry Miller's wife in the controversial (but little-seen) film based on Anaïs Nin's diaries; another 1990 film, John Boorman's *Where the Heart Is,* also failed to win much of an audience. But Thurman acquitted herself nicely in those

parts, and in subsequent roles as well: Kim Basinger's emotionally disturbed sister in *Final Analysis* (1992), a blind woman stalked by a serial killer in *Jennifer 8* (also 1992), the unwilling pawn of gangster Bill Murray who falls in love with Robert De Niro in *Mad Dog and Glory* (1993), and the leading characters in the long-awaited *Even Cowgirls Get the Blues* (1994) and *Pulp Fiction* (also 1994, for which she received an Oscar nomination). She was formerly married to actor Gary Oldman.

TIERNEY, GENE. Actress. *(b. Nov. 20, 1920, Brooklyn, N.Y.; d. Oct. 6, 1991.)* Can anybody remember this dark-haired, radiantly beautiful 1940s star without hearing the haunting strains of David Raksin's theme for *Laura* (1944), her most famous film? Tierney, who was better known for her beauty than her talent, was the daughter of a wealthy stockbroker, and started acting on stage in the late 1930s. A supporting role in the Broadway production of "The Male Animal" in 1940 brought Tierney to the attention of 20th Century-Fox; she was signed and received a rapid star buildup in such pictures as *The Return of Frank James, Hudson's Bay* (all 1940), and *Tobacco Road,* receiving star billing with *Belle Starr* (both 1941). She was loaned to director Josef von Sternberg for *The Shanghai Gesture* (also 1941), but was woefully miscast as an exotic dragon lady; at her home studio, her projects were carefully tailored to her talents.

Tierney was at her best in such films as Ernst Lubitsch's *Heaven Can Wait* (1943), the aforementioned *Laura* (1944), and the memorable *The Ghost and Mrs. Muir* (1947, opposite Rex Harrison); she earned an Oscar nomination for her persuasive performance as a venal woman who "just loves too much" in *Leave Her to Heaven* (1945), one of several films to capture her beauty with the full force of Technicolor. Other films include *Sundown* (1941), *China Girl, Thunder Birds, Rings on Her Fingers, Son of Fury* (all 1942), *A Bell for Adano* (1945, as a blonde), *Dragonwyck, The Razor's Edge* (both 1946), *That Wonderful Urge* (1948), *Whirlpool* (1949), *Night and the City, Where the Sidewalk Ends* (both 1950), *On the Riviera, The Mating Season* (both 1951), *Plymouth Adventure* (1952), *Never Let Me Go* (1953),

Black Widow, The Egyptian (both 1954), and *The Left Hand of God* (1955), among others.

From 1941 to 1952 Tierney was married to designer Oleg Cassini, and as her career began to falter in the mid 1950s, her love affair with Aly Kahn was the main focus of press attention. She suffered a nervous breakdown, and was hospitalized for two extended periods. She remarried in 1960 and returned to the screen in *Advise and Consent* (1962), directed by Otto Preminger, who had helmed *Laura*. She appeared in *Toys in the Attic* (1963) and *The Pleasure Seekers* (1964) before going into semiretirement. Her final film work was in the 1980 miniseries "Scruples." The tragic story of how an innocent kiss from a female fan, who had German measles, caused her to give birth to a retarded child was dramatized, without citing Tierney, years later in the mystery film *The Mirror Crack'd* (1980). Her autobiography "Self Portrait" was published in 1979.

TIERNEY, LAWRENCE. Actor. (b. Mar. 15, 1919, Brooklyn, N.Y.) One of the screen's preeminent tough guys during the 1940s, Tierney played the same role off-screen as well; as a result, his colorful real-life exploits got the attention most of his pictures—routine grade-B melodramas, for the most part—never did. As a massive, square-jawed, grim-visaged leading man, Tierney cut an imposing figure on-screen; at RKO he landed supporting roles in such films as *The Ghost Ship* (1943) and *The Falcon Out West* (1944) before achieving stardom as the vicious gangster in *Dillinger* (1945), on loan to independent producers Maurice and Frank King. Knowing a good thing when they saw it, RKO took pains to keep him playing two-fisted characters—on both sides of the law. His starring vehicles included *San Quentin, Step by Step* (both 1946), *The Devil Thumbs a Ride, Born to Kill* (both 1947), *Bodyguard* (1948), and *Kill or Be Killed* (1950).

In between headlines and brushes with the law, Tierney slipped to supporting roles in big-budget pictures and occasional leads in grade-Z thrillers. In the 1980s Tierney, by now bald and rotund, made a rather remarkable comeback in a series of colorful character parts in films and TV (with a recurring part on "Hill Street

Blues"). His younger brother was actor Scott Brady.

OTHER FILMS INCLUDE: 1952: *The Greatest Show on Earth;* 1954: *The Steel Cage;* 1956: *Female Jungle;* 1963: *A Child Is Waiting;* 1968: *Custer of the West;* 1971: *Such Good Friends, Andy Warhol's Bad;* 1981: *Arthur;* 1981: *Midnight* (a lead of sorts, playing a brutal, corrupt cop); 1985: *Prizzi's Honor;* 1986: *Murphy's Law;* 1987: *Tough Guys Don't Dance* (as Ryan O'Neal's father); 1989: *The Horror Show;* 1992: *The Runestone, Reservoir Dogs.*

TILLY, MEG. Actress. (b. Feb. 14, 1960, Long Beach, Calif.) Sweet-faced, soft-spoken actress who brings an ethereal quality to her characters, particularly the dreamy young nun in *Agnes of God* (1985, for which she was Oscar-nominated) and the enigmatic *Girl in a Swing* (1989). The Canadian-raised Tilly, a former dancer permanently sidelined by a back injury, first impressed moviegoers as the girlfriend of the dead Kevin Costner in *The Big Chill* (1983). She's also been seen in *Fame* (1980, as one of the dance students), *Tex* (1982), *Psycho II, One Dark Night* (both 1983), *Impulse* (1984), *Off Beat* (1986), *Masquerade* (1988), *Valmont* (1989, Milos Forman's version of *Dangerous Liaisons,* as the young wife), *The Two Jakes* (1990), *Leaving Normal* (1992), *Body Snatchers,* and *Sleep With Me* (both 1994). Meg's older sister Jennifer (b. Sept. 16, 1958) is also an actress; she has played mostly airheaded bimbos in such films as *Moving Violations* (1985), *The Fabulous Baker Boys* (1989), *Made in America* (1993), and *The Getaway* (1994), and received an Oscar nomination as an airheaded bimbo with artistic pretensions in Woody Allen's *Bullets Over Broadway* (1994).

TIOMKIN, DIMITRI. Composer. (b. May 10, 1899, St. Petersburg, Russia; d. Nov. 11, 1979.) One of the most prolific composers in Hollywood, Tiomkin was also one of the most respected, and one of the few—along with Max Steiner and Franz Waxman—who brought a level of Continental sophistication to American film music. Educated at the St. Petersburg Conservatory, Tiomkin was a successful pianist and conductor in his homeland,

and is generally credited for bringing the music of George Gershwin to European audiences. In 1925 he emigrated to the U.S., and never looked back, becoming an American citizen in 1937. By then, he was already a flourishing screen composer, having created memorable music for *Mad Love* (1935) and Frank Capra's *Lost Horizon* (1937). The latter won him the first of a remarkable 23 Oscar nominations. He and Capra had a falling-out over the director's displeasure with Tiomkin's dark, brooding score for *It's a Wonderful Life* (1946); the complete, original work wasn't heard until a restoration and recording was made in the late 1980s. Highlights from Tiomkin's work include his Oscar-winning scores for *High Noon* (1952, which also won him a Best Song Oscar for "Do Not Forsake Me, Oh My Darlin' "); *The High and the Mighty* (1954), and *The Old Man and the Sea* (1958). The great success of the song from *High Noon* caused producers to hire Tiomkin and lyricist Ned Washington, hoping they could work the same magic on *their* pictures. Some of the songs were quite successful, like the theme from *The High and the Mighty;* others never caught on. Still, Tiomkin's résumé is formidable, including Oscar nominations for *Lost Horizon* (1937), *Mr. Smith Goes to Washington* (1939), *The Corsican Brothers* (1941), *The Moon and Sixpence* (1942), *The Bridge of San Luis Rey* (1944), *Champion* (1949), *Giant* (1956), the song "Thee I Love" from *Friendly Persuasion* (1956), the title song from *Wild Is the Wind* (1957), the song "Strange Are the Ways of Love" from *The Young Land* (1959), *The Alamo* (1960) and the song "The Green Leaves of Summer" from the same film, *The Guns of Navarone* (1961), the title song from *Town Without Pity* (1961), *55 Days at Peking* (1963), the song "So Little Time," from *The Fall of the Roman Empire* (1964), and best adaptation of *Tchaikovsky* (1971, which he also produced). He published his autobiography, "Please Don't Hate Me," in 1959.

TODD, ANN. Actress. *(b. Jan. 24, 1909, Hartford, England.)* Beautiful, icy British blonde who was for some years one of the U.K.'s most popular stars, largely as a result of her superb performance as an emotionally disturbed pianist in *The Seventh*

Veil (1945). Earlier, during the 1930s, she'd been seen in *The Ghost Train* (1931), *The Return of Bulldog Drummond* (1934), *Things to Come* (1936), *The Squeaker* (1937, aka *Murder on Diamond Row), South Riding, Action for Slander* (both 1938), and *Poison Pen* (1939), among others, taking routine ingenue roles. She made a big impression on director David Lean, starring in his *The Passionate Friends, Madeleine* (both 1949), and *Breaking the Sound Barrier* (1952), marrying him in 1949 (they divorced in 1957). Turning to the stage, she joined the Old Vic company and played Shakespeare, which movies had never given her the chance to do. Todd's narrative-film output diminished greatly in the mid 1950s, partially because she began producing and directing travel films and documentaries. Her autobiography, "The Eighth Veil," was published in 1980.

OTHER FILMS INCLUDE: 1946: *Daybreak;* 1948: *The Paradine Case* (her only Hollywood venture); 1948: *So Evil My Love;* 1954: *The Green Scarf;* 1956: *Time Without Pity;* 1961: *Scream of Fear;* 1962: *The Son of Captain Blood;* 1964: *Ninety Degrees in the Shade;* 1971: *Beware the Brethren;* 1979: *The Human Factor;* 1985: *The McGuffin.*

TODD, RICHARD. Actor. *(b. June 11, 1919, Dublin, as Richard Andrew Palethorpe-Todd.)* Dark-haired Irish actor, a moderately popular leading man who suggested passionate intensity in many of the characters he played (even the stiff-necked ones). An accomplished stage player from the 1930s, Todd interrupted his career to serve his country during World War 2, then returned to the theater, and broke into films in 1949. He riveted audiences that same year with his Oscar-nominated portrayal of a proud, terminally ill Scottish soldier in *The Hasty Heart.* Todd worked in both American and English films throughout the next decade, including three British-made costume films for Walt Disney in which he played the leads: *The Story of Robin Hood and His Merrie Men* (1952), *The Sword and the Rose* (1953), and *Rob Roy, the Highland Rogue* (1954). He alternated leading roles with supporting turns, but never again attained the summit he'd reached at the outset of his film career. He returned to the theater, his first love, as frequently as his schedule would permit, and by the late 1960s seemed to be quite indifferent in his choice of screen parts.

OTHER FILMS INCLUDE: 1949: *Interrupted Journey;* 1950: *Stage Fright;* 1951: *Lightning Strikes Twice;* 1953: *The Assassin;* 1955: *The Dam Busters, A Man Called Peter, The Virgin Queen* (as Sir Walter Raleigh), *Marie Antoinette;* 1956: *D-Day, the Sixth of June;* 1957: *Saint Joan;* 1958: *Chase a Crooked Shadow, Intent to Kill;* 1960: *Never Let Go;* 1961: *Why Bother to Knock;* 1962: *The Longest Day;* 1965: *Operation Crossbow;* 1967: *The Love-Ins;* 1969: *Subterfuge;* 1970: *Dorian Gray;* 1972: *Asylum;* 1977: *Number One of the Secret Service;* 1978: *The Big Sleep;* 1983: *House of the Long Shadows.*

TODD, THELMA. Actress. *(b. July 29, 1905, Lawrence, Mass.; d. Dec. 18, 1935.)* It's sad that this actress is known more for her mysterious death than for any of her accomplishments in life. In point of fact, Thelma Todd was a delightful comedienne as well as a great beauty. Winner of a beauty contest in Massachusetts, she was signed by a Paramount talent scout and brought to Hollywood with such other young hopefuls as Buddy Rogers, all of whom were featured in the silent *God Gave Me Twenty Cents* (1926). Typed as a conventional ingenue for several years, even appearing as a Western leading lady opposite Gary Cooper in *Nevada* (1927), Thelma finally found her niche with the coming of sound, when she was signed by comedy producer Hal Roach to act as leading lady to Laurel and Hardy, Charley Chase, and Harry Langdon. She had no qualms about being spritzed with seltzer, and her natural charm made her a perfect vis-à-vis for these comedy stars. In 1931 Roach decided to pair her with fluttery comedienne ZaSu Pitts in their own starring series; alas, the two stars were always better than their material, which was also true when wisecracking Patsy Kelly took ZaSu's place in 1933.

By then, Thelma was also appearing regularly in features, usually as a comedy foil—to Joe E. Brown in *Broadminded* (1931) and *Son of a Sailor* (1933), to The Marx Brothers in *Monkey Business* (1931) and *Horse Feathers,* to Buster Keaton and Jimmy Durante in *Speak Easily* (both 1932), to Laurel and Hardy in *Fra Diavolo/The Devil's Brother* (1933), to

Wheeler and Woolsey in *Hips, Hips, Hooray* and *Cockeyed Cavaliers* (both 1934) among others. Her boyfriend Roland West starred her in the dramatic feature *Corsair* (1931) for which she used the stage name Alison Loyd, but good parts proved few and far between. She was effective as detective Miles Archer's widow in the 1931 *Maltese Falcon,* but she soon became typecast as a vampish "other woman" in such movies as *Call Her Savage* (1932, engaging in a catfight with Clara Bow), *Sitting Pretty, Counsellor-at-Law* (both 1933), *Palooka, Bottoms Up* (both 1934), and *Two for Tonight* (1935). She got her meatiest starring part opposite Stanley Lupino in a British-made feature, *You Made Me Love You* (1933).

Well liked by colleagues, Thelma liked to party, and it was after a late-night soiree that she met her untimely end. Her body was found slumped over the steering wheel of her car, in a locked garage, where she apparently died of carbon monoxide poisoning. Speculation continues as to the cause of the tragedy. One fanciful book says she was murdered on orders of her alleged boyfriend, gangster Lucky Luciano. Other accounts by knowledgeable survivors of the period said that Roland West locked her in the garage to keep her from going out again, or to punish her, and the resulting death was accidental. Either way, a beautiful screen presence became one of Hollywood's unsolved mysteries.

TOLAND, GREGG. Cinematographer. *(b. May 29, 1904, Charleston, Ill.; d. Sept. 28, 1948.)* The convention-shattering camera work and "look" of Gregg Toland's cinematography on *Citizen Kane* (1941) is not so surprising when you consider Toland's previous films. Just a year earlier, John Ford's *The Grapes of Wrath* (1940) had haunted the screen with its stark silhouettes and expressionistic faces along the road from the Okie Dustbowl to California. Likewise for Ford's even more stylized *The Long Voyage Home* that same year. Before that, Toland gave Sam Goldwyn and William Wyler's *Wuthering Heights* (1939) a wild and stormy look that befitted Olivier's Heathcliff and won an Oscar. When he heard that "boy wonder" Welles was going to make his first film, he introduced himself to Welles and volunteered to join him on the Great Adventure.

Toland had started as a camera assistant in the silent-film era, working his way up the ladder; his arrival as director of photography coincided with the coming of sound. It was then that producer Samuel Goldwyn put him under contract. Goldwyn wanted everything about his films to be "the best," and he recognized in Toland a man who shared his passion for quality. Indeed, the Goldwyn films of the 1930s and 1940s have a unique sheen to them that has everything to do with Toland's presence behind the camera.

Toland had finished Howard Hawks' *Ball of Fire* and William Wyler's *The Little Foxes* (both 1941) when Pearl Harbor gave Lt. Toland the chance to collaborate again with Lt. John Ford on the Oscar-winning war documentary *December 7th* (1942).

After VE-Day, he teamed again with Wyler and Fredric March (whom Toland had photographed years earlier in the 1935 *Les Miserables*) in the beloved postwar classic *The Best Years of Our Lives* (1946) again using the deep-focus photography he had pioneered.

Toland would work but three more years, felled prematurely by a heart attack at age 44. By way of tribute, Welles later told Peter Bogdanovich why—as Ford had done on *The Long Voyage Home*—he gave Toland credit on the same title card as himself on *Citizen Kane:* "Up till then, cameramen were listed with about eight other names. Nobody those days—only the stars, the director, the producer—got separate cards. Gregg deserved it, didn't he?"
OTHER FILMS INCLUDE: 1929: *Bulldog Drummond*; 1930: *Raffles, Whoopee!*; 1931: *Palmy Days*; 1932: *The Kid From Spain*; 1933: *Roman Scandals*; 1935: *Mad Love, The Dark Angel*; 1936: *These Three, The Road To Glory*; 1937: *History Is Made at Night, Dead End*; 1939: *The Cowboy and the Lady, Kidnapped, Intermezzo*; 1940: *The Westerner*; 1943: *The Outlaw*; 1946: *Song of the South* (live-action sequences only), *The Kid From Brooklyn*; 1947: *The Bishop's Wife*; 1948: *A Song Is Born*.

TOLER, SIDNEY. Actor. (b. Apr. 28, 1874, Warrensburg, Mo.; d. Feb. 12, 1947.) Although he was nearly 65 years old when he accepted the part of Chinese-Hawaiian detective Charlie Chan in 1938, this versatile performer—a stage veteran from the turn of the century—continued to essay the role for the next nine years. As a sleepy-eyed, jowly, heavyset character actor, Toler entered films in 1929, taking a wide variety of supporting roles in such films as *Strictly Dishonorable* (1931), *Speak Easily, Tom Brown of Culver, Blonde Venus* (all 1932), *King of the Jungle, The Narrow Corner* (both 1933), *Upperworld* (1934, very effective as an obsessive cop), *Call of the Wild* (1935), *The Gorgeous Hussy* (as Daniel Webster), *Three Godfathers, Our Relations* (all 1936), *That Certain Woman* (1937), *The Mysterious Rider* (as a knife-throwing Western sidekick!), and *If I Were King* (both 1938), before being signed by 20th Century-Fox to play Chan after the death of series star Warner Oland.

Toler had only to add slight makeup and speak in a monotone to adapt himself to the role, which he first assumed in *Charlie Chan in Honolulu* (1938), a lackluster series entry. He subsequently starred in *Charlie Chan at Treasure Island* (1939, considered by many to be the series' best), *Charlie Chan in Reno, Charlie Chan in City in Darkness* (also 1939), *Charlie Chan in Panama, Charlie Chan's Murder Cruise, Charlie Chan at the Wax Museum, Murder Over New York* (all 1940), *Charlie Chan in Rio, Dead Men Tell* (both 1941), and *Castle in the Desert* (1942) before Fox sold rights to the character to Monogram. The Monogram Chans, low-budget productions without the sturdy scripts and strong supporting casts of the Fox stanzas, relied heavily on Toler's facility in the character (and the antics of his chauffeur-sidekick Mantan Moreland) to carry them. *Charlie Chan in the Secret Service, Black Magic, The Chinese Cat* (all 1944), *The Jade Mask, The Scarlet Clue, The Shanghai Cobra, The Red Dragon* (all 1945), *Shadows Over Chinatown, Dark Alibi, Dangerous Money* (all 1946), and *The Trap* (1947) showed a steady decline in the series, and Toler walked through his last few entries with no apparent enthusiasm. (After he died the character was given to Roland Winters, whose series entries were uniformly dismal.) Virtually typecast (and apparently content) as Chan, Toler appeared outside the role only a handful of times after 1938, in *Heritage of the Desert* (1939), *The Adventures of*

Smilin' Jack (again in Oriental makeup), *White Savage,* and *Isle of Forgotten Sins* (all 1943) among them.

TOLKAN, JAMES. Actor. *(b. June 20, 1931, Calumet, Mich.)* Solid, reliable character actor who's played cops, thugs, army officers, and district attorneys. After attending college on a football scholarship and doing a tour of duty in the Navy, Tolkan moved to New York, where he studied with Stella Adler and then Lee Strasberg, at the Actors' Studio. He replaced Robert Duvall in the Broadway productions of "A View From the Bridge" and "Wait Until Dark" in the 1960s, and continued to work on stage even after establishing himself in films, notably in David Mamet's Broadway hit "Glengarry Glen Ross" in 1984. Tolkan made his film debut in a small role in *Stiletto* (1969); among his screen credits are *They Might Be Giants* (1971), *The Friends of Eddie Coyle* (1973), *Love and Death* (1975, as Napoleon), *The Amityville Horror* (1979), and *Wolfen* (1981). He became even more active in movies during the 1980s, winning a showy part as a hard-nosed district attorney in Sidney Lumet's *Prince of the City* (1981). It was followed by *Author! Author!, Hanky Panky* (both 1982), *WarGames* (1983), *Iceman, The River* (both 1984), *Turk 182!* (1985), *Opportunity Knocks* (1990), and *Dick Tracy* (1990, as Numbers). He was conspicuously featured in a pair of mid-1980s box office champs: *Back to the Future* (1985, as the sour high school principal, replaying the role in the 1989 and 1990 sequels) and *Top Gun* (1986, as a naval officer). He's also turned up in such grade-B fare as *Ministry of Vengeance* (1989), *True Blood* (1989), and *Hangfire* (1991). He is a frequent presence on television, appearing as a regular on "Mary" (1985–86, as Lester Mintz), "Sunset Beat" (1990), and in a long list of series and made-for-TV movies.

TOMEI, MARISA. Actress. *(b. Dec. 4, 1964, Brooklyn, N.Y.)* Joe Pesci may have received top billing in the comedy *My Cousin Vinny* (1992), but it was Tomei who stole the film as his wisecracking, Brooklynese girlfriend Mona Lisa Vito and received a Supporting Actress Oscar in the process. A veteran of theatrical productions on both coasts, Tomei made her film debut with a bit part in *The Flamingo Kid* (1984), and had her first notable role on TV, as Lisa Bonet's roommate in the first season of "A Different World" (1987–88). She showed comic flair as Sylvester Stallone's daughter in *Oscar* (1991) and since *My Cousin Vinny,* has appeared in Richard Attenborough's *Chaplin* (1992, in an underwritten part as silent-screen comedienne Mabel Normand). She won raves for her passionate performance as a waitress head over heels in love with Christian Slater in *Untamed Heart* (1993). Recent credits include *Equinox* (also 1993), *The Paper, Only You* (both 1994), and *The Perez Family* (1995).

TOMLIN, LILY. Actress. *(b. Sept. 1, 1939, Detroit, as Mary Jean Tomlin.)* Versatile actress and comedienne whose successes in television, nightclubs, and the theater have yet to find a corollary in motion pictures, despite her impressive screen debut. Tomlin was actually a pre-med student before taking up performing. She was a regular on the popular "Rowan and Martin's Laugh-In" TV comedy series from 1970 to 1973, creating several daffy characters whom she portrayed on a successful record album and in nightclubs. Tomlin made a widely praised Hollywood debut as the mother of a hearing-impaired child in Robert Altman's epic *Nashville* (1975), which earned her an Oscar nomination for Best Supporting Actress. Not a conventional leading lady, Tomlin has had a hard time finding appropriate screen vehicles. She's had her share of successes including *The Late Show* (1977), the smash hit *9 to 5* (1980), *All of Me* (1984, in which she was overshadowed by Steve Martin), and *Big Business* (1988, well teamed with Bette Midler). *The Incredible Shrinking Woman* (1981) was a major disappointment, however, and the jaw-dropping *Moment by Moment* (1978), in which she starred with John Travolta, has made many lists of all-time worst movies. She also collaborated with Jane Wagner on two Tony award-winning Broadway shows, "Appearing Nitely" (1977) and "The Search for Signs of Inteligent Life in the Universe" (1986, which was filmed in 1991). Tomlin allowed documentary filmmakers Nicholas Broomfield and Joan Churchill to chronicle the preparation of the latter show in their feature-length film *Lily Tomlin* (1986). In 1993 she gave one of the warmer performances in Robert Altman's *Short Cuts* (opposite Tom Waits), played Miss Jane in *The Beverly Hillbillies,* and appeared in the prestige telefilm *And the Band Played On.* In 1994 she produced two animated specials based on Edith Ann, the little-girl character she introduced on "Laugh-In."

TONE, FRANCHOT. Actor, director, producer. *(b. Feb. 27, 1905, Niagara Falls, N.Y., as Stanislaus Franchot Tone; d. Sept. 18, 1968.)* Suave leading man who initially achieved prominence in the 1930s but never really broke through to the A-list, and evolved into a character actor. Born into a well-to-do family, Tone was educated at Cornell University, where he was president of the Dramatic Club. Forsaking the family business to take up acting, he toiled in stock for several years before reaching Broadway. In 1932 Tone came to Hollywood to appear in Paramount's *The Wiser Sex;* he didn't last very long at that studio but *did* manage to make a hit with MGM, which put him under contract and kept him busy through much of the decade.

Often cast as wealthy playboys, Tone appeared in seven Metro films during 1933 alone: *Bombshell* (he was the one who wanted to run barefoot through Jean Harlow's hair), *Today We Live, Gabriel Over the White House, Midnight Mary, Stage Mother, Dancing Lady* (romancing Joan Crawford), and *The Stranger's Return.* 1934 was similarly busy for him, with appearances in *Moulin Rouge, Sadie McKee, The World Moves On, The Girl From Missouri, Straight Is the Way,* and *Gentlemen Are Born.* He got two good parts in 1935: He was Oscar-nominated as midshipman Byam in MGM's spectacular *Mutiny on the Bounty,* supporting Clark Gable and Charles Laughton, and backed up Gary Cooper as the insouciant Lieutenant Fortesque in *The Lives of a Bengal Lancer.* That same year he played opposite a rip-roaring Bette Davis in her Oscar-winning melodrama *Dangerous.*

Tone also appeared in *The Gorgeous Hussy, Suzy* (both 1936), *Quality Street, They Gave Him a Gun* (both 1937), *Three Comrades* (1938, with Roberts Taylor and Young in this poignant tale of post-WW1 Germany coscripted by F. Scott Fitzgerald), and *Fast and Furious* (1939, as bookseller-turned-detective Joel Sloane). In the 1940s it seemed as if he was doomed to play nothing but The Other Man in love triangles, but there were occasional bright spots: *Trail of the Vigilantes* (1940), *Nice Girl?* (1941), *Five Graves to Cairo* (1943, as a secret agent trying to extract war secrets from Nazi Field Marshal Rommel in this marvelous thriller directed and cowritten by Billy Wilder; arguably Tone's best 1940s film), *Pilot #5, His Butler's Sister* (both also 1943), *Phantom Lady* (1944, another fine performance in a first-rate suspense film), *Honeymoon* (1947), *I Love Trouble* (1948, as private eye Stuart Bailey, the character played by Efrem Zimbalist, Jr., on the TV series "77 Sunset Strip"), *Every Girl Should Be Married* (also 1948), *The Man on the Eiffel Tower* (1949, as a suspected murderer in this Inspector Maigret thriller starring Charles Laughton and directed by Burgess Meredith), *Jigsaw* (also 1949), *Without Honor* (1950), and *Here Comes the Groom* (1951).

Tone's screen career had pretty much petered out, so he moved over to TV and kept busy for most of the decade in the era's numerous dramatic anthology shows. He also returned to the stage. In 1958 he coproduced, codirected, and starred in *Uncle Vanya,* an unsuccessful comeback vehicle. He more or less retired, emerging only to play character roles in *Advise and Consent* (1962, as the President), *In Harm's Way, Mickey One* (both 1965), and *The High Commissioner* (aka *Nobody Runs Forever,* 1968). He costarred with Vince Edwards, replacing Sam Jaffe, in the 1965–66 season of the "Ben Casey" TV series. Tone was married four times, all to actresses: Joan Crawford (1935–39), Jean Wallace (1941–48), Barbara Payton (1951–52), and Dolores Dorn (1956–59). A barroom brawl he had with actor Tom Neal over Payton made headlines in 1952.

TOPOL. Actor. *(b. Sept. 9, 1935, Tel Aviv, as Chaim Topol.)* This burly, boisterous performer has worked more in theater than in film, and is remembered principally for his lively performance as Tevye in the hit film version of *Fiddler on the Roof*

(1971). He received an Academy Award nomination for his work in the film, which brought him instant and enduring recognition (20 years later he was still playing the part on stage). Pre-*Fiddler* credits include *Sallah* (1965, Israeli-made), *Cast a Giant Shadow* (1966), *Before Winter Comes,* and *A Talent for Loving* (both 1969). His subsequent attempt to convince as a romantic lead in 1972's *The Public Eye* fell flat, but he did take the lead in *Galileo* (1973). Most of his movie roles since have been broad portrayals in big productions such as *Flash Gordon* (1980, as Doctor Zarkov) and the James Bond picture *For Your Eyes Only* (1981).

TORN, RIP. Actor. *(b. Feb. 6, 1931, Temple, Tex., as Elmore Rual Torn, Jr.)* Sporting one of the great monikers in Hollywood history (who, having seen it in 1969, could ever forget a theater marquee with the words, *"Coming Apart . . . Rip Torn"*?), this dynamic, chameleonlike character actor has enjoyed a lengthy career in motion pictures. As an ambitious young man, anticipating eventual success as an actor in Hollywood, Torn took employment in a variety of odd jobs during the mid 1950s before landing work on TV and in films (he made his film debut in 1956's *Baby Doll*). Intent on honing his skills, Torn moved to New York City shortly thereafter, where he studied at the Actors' Studio and appeared in many stage productions there. (Although he had the starring male role in "Sweet Bird of Youth" on Broadway, he lost out to Paul Newman for the 1962 movie, and played Tom Finley, Jr., instead; then, in the 1989 made-for-TV remake, he took the part of Boss Finley, Tom's father.) In movies, he has been often seen as twangy Southerners and dyspeptic authority figures (he also played Judas in 1961's *King of Kings*) and on TV he effectively played former President Richard Nixon in "Blind Ambition" (1977). Torn has frequently taken challenging leads in non-mainstream fare, such as *Tropic of Cancer* (1970, as Henry Miller), *Payday* (1973, his meatiest leading role on film, as a country singer), *Heartland* (1979, as a dour Scottish rancher in early 20th-century Wyoming), *Jinxed!* (1982, which some critics said he stole—in spite of playing a character who's dead through most of the proceed-

ings), and *Cross Creek* (1983), which earned him an Oscar nomination as Best Supporting Actor for his performance as a backwoodsman. He also earned a niche in pop culture history as the man who quit the film *Easy Rider,* paving the way for Jack Nicholson's star-making role as a dropout lawyer. Torn has leapfrogged between B movies (1989's *Hit List*), mainstream features (1991's *Defending Your Life*), and independent productions (1992's *Beautiful Dreamers*, as Walt Whitman). He made an inauspicious directing debut with the dreadful Whoopi Goldberg thriller *The Telephone* (1988). Torn achieved comic perfection with his wickedly funny portrayal of a TV producer on "The Larry Sanders Show" (1992–). He has twice been married to actresses: Ann Wedgeworth and Geraldine Page. His cousin is Sissy Spacek.

OTHER FILMS INCLUDE: 1957: *A Face in the Crowd;* 1959: *Pork Chop Hill;* 1965: *The Cincinnati Kid;* 1967: *You're a Big Boy Now;* 1976: *The Man Who Fell to Earth;* 1977: *Birch Interval, The Private Files of J. Edgar Hoover;* 1978: *Coma;* 1979: *The Seduction of Joe Tynan;* 1980: *One-Trick Pony, First Family;* 1982: *Airplane II: The Sequel, The Beastmaster;* 1984: *City Heat, Songwriter;* 1985: *Summer Rental;* 1987: *Nadine, Extreme Prejudice;* 1992: *Dead Ahead: The Exxon Valdez Story* (telefilm), *T-Bone and Weasel* (telefilm); 1993: *RoboCop 3.*

TOWNE, ROBERT. Screenwriter, director, producer. *(b. Nov. 23, 1934, Los Angeles.)* One of the most highly regarded screenwriters of the 1970s, Towne, like so many of his film contemporaries, got his Hollywood break from exploitation director Roger Corman. During the 1960s he acted in a handful of Corman cheapies and wrote several, including *The Last Woman on Earth* (1960, also acting under the name Edward Wain) and the Poe adaptation *The Tomb of Ligeia* (1965). Towne's reputation grew, among Hollywood insiders, when it became known that he'd written key scenes in *Bonnie and Clyde* (1967) and *The Godfather* (1972), among others, without official credit. Then he had three exceptional scripts produced in three consecutive years: *The Last Detail* (1973), *Chinatown* (1974), and *Shampoo* (1975, cowritten with Warren Beatty). All three scripts were Oscar-nominated, with

Chinatown taking the prize. (It's often cited by screenwriting teachers, as a perfect contemporary screenplay.) Towne spent the following years trying to get directing projects off the ground while also working as a "script doctor," doing uncredited work on *Marathon Man* and *The Missouri Breaks* (both 1976). His tyro directorial effort, *Personal Best* (1982), the story of a lesbian relationship between track runners and the project to which Towne had devoted so many years, underwhelmed most critics and was a box-office failure. An even greater disappointment, perhaps, was seeing *Greystoke: The Legend of Tarzan, Lord of the Apes* (1984) taken away from him after eight years' work (and the promise that he would get to direct). When he saw the finished product, he removed his name and substituted, as screenwriter, P. H. Vazak, who later earned an Oscar nomination. Vazak, it turned out, was the name of his sheepdog. His second stab at directing, *Tequila Sunrise* (1988), did somewhat better thanks to its considerable star power (Mel Gibson, Michelle Pfeiffer, Kurt Russell). In 1990 Towne lent his writing services to blockbuster producers Don Simpson and Jerry Bruckheimer for their flat stock-car saga *Days of Thunder;* he also revived several *Chinatown* characters for that year's sequel, *The Two Jakes,* which Jack Nicholson directed. He also took acting roles in *Drive, He Said* (1971, directed by Nicholson) and *The Pick-up Artist* (1987, produced by Beatty). Towne's other credits include *The Yakuza* (1975, cowriter) and *The Bedroom Window* (1987, executive producer only). His most recent screenwriting credit was yet another collaboration with Warren Beatty, *Love Affair* (1994).

TOWNSEND, ROBERT. Actor, writer, director. *(b. Feb. 6, 1957, Chicago.)* This comedian turned filmmaker studied acting at Illinois State University, and graduated to comedy work via the famous Second City troupe in Chicago. His first screen appearance was a minor role in Paul Mazursky's *Willie and Phil* (1980), but he languished in obscurity for another four years until making a (minor) splash in a skillful, memorable performance in *A Soldier's Story* (1984). Disillusioned by the lack of substantial roles for black actors, Town-

send set about to create some. With the assistance of friends and associates, funded by an assortment of credit cards, Townsend raised enough capital to direct his first feature, *Hollywood Shuffle* (1987), in which he played an underemployed actor forced to take demeaning part-time jobs to feed himself until the next (exploitative) role comes along. Townsend's spoof was a surprise success, and by the end of the year he had signed with Eddie Murphy to direct a film version of Murphy's stand-up act, *Eddie Murphy Raw.* Since then, Townsend has divided his time between films and television, with only modest success. He cowrote, directed, and starred in *The Five Heartbeats* (1991), a pleasant but clichéd story of a 1950s r&b group, and did triple-duty again on *The Meteor Man* (1993), a superhero spoof that also fizzled at the box office. Townsend's upbeat attitude puts him in sharp contrast to other contemporary black filmmakers, but his films have not (yet) found a substantial audience. He also created and starred in the short-lived comedy series "Townsend Television" (1993). His other acting credits include *Odd Jobs, Streets of Fire* (both 1984), *American Flyers* (1985), *Ratboy* (1986), and *The Mighty Quinn* (1989).

TRACY, LEE. Actor. *(b. Apr. 4, 1898, Atlanta, as William Lee Tracy; d. Oct. 18, 1968.)* How's this for a guaranteed career-killer: get drunk and urinate on a passing military parade in a foreign country. That's just what Tracy did in Mexico while filming *Viva Villa!* in 1934, creating a minor international incident that not only got him fired from the picture, but severely damaged the career of this enormously talented actor. With his rat-a-tat dialogue delivery, expressive gestures, and a devilish twinkle in his eyes, Tracy could've been one of the most popular character actors of all time, instead of merely a film-buff favorite. He was a popular Broadway star throughout the 1920s, creating the role of Hildy Johnson in the original stage production of "The Front Page." Soon after, talkies were invented and Hollywood beckoned (though Pat O'Brien played Hildy in the 1931 movie). Tracy ran up a string of remarkable performances as reporters, press agents, and con artists in such snappy movies as *Doctor X, Love Is* *a Racket, The Strange Love of Molly Louvain, Night Mayor, The Half-Naked Truth* (all 1932), *Dinner at Eight, The Nuisance, Advice to the Lovelorn, Bombshell* (all 1933), and *The Lemon Drop Kid* (1934); he also played a naive congressman in *Washington Merry-Go-Round* (1932) and a small-town businessman who goes back in time in *Turn Back the Clock* (1933).

When work became harder to get, Tracy found employment in such RKO programmers as *Behind the Headlines, Criminal Lawyer* (both 1937), *Crashing Hollywood* (1938), *The Spellbinder* (1939), and *Millionaires in Prison* (1940). After World War 2, he retired—though he worked briefly in early TV (including one season of "Martin Kane, Private Eye"). He returned to the big screen just once, to recreate his Broadway role as the Trumanesque president in *The Best Man* (1964, earning an Oscar nomination). But his archetypal performance can be seen in *Blessed Event* (1932), in which he plays a Walter Winchell–like columnist who raises the art of gossip to hilariously uncharted depths.

TRACY, SPENCER. Actor. *(b. Apr. 5, 1900, Milwaukee; d. June 10, 1967.)* It is one thing for a movie star to earn the adulation of the public. It is another thing to win the praise of the critics. It is still another thing to win the respect and admiration of one's peers, who actually know a thing or two about acting. Spencer Tracy was one of the very few in Hollywood history who won over all three groups. Stocky, round-faced, and not particularly handsome, he nonetheless radiated that peculiar charisma that drew every pair of eyes to his corner of the screen. He could deliver dynamic performances to match any ever filmed, but he could (and usually did) accomplish just as much in a quiet, understated way, mesmerizing audiences with simple gestures, expressions, and body language. The result—invariably— was complete credibility. He made every line of dialogue ring true.

A former Jesuit prep-school student who once intended to become a priest, Tracy joined the Navy in the waning days of World War 1, and upon being mustered out enrolled in Northwestern Military Academy and Wisconsin's Ripon College;

in the latter school he took up dramatics, and determined to become an actor. He entered New York's American Academy of Dramatic Arts and studied diligently, even landing a few small roles in Broadway productions. Mostly, though, he supported himself by working in odd jobs. Tracy eventually penetrated New York's community of stock actors, took more Broadway assignments, and finally won a leading role, as a convicted killer on Death Row, in "The Last Mile."

Although Tracy tested the celluloid waters with roles in some New York-filmed short subjects, including 1930's "Taxi Talks" and "Hard Guy," he confided to his wife Louise that, as a decidedly unhandsome character, he had no future in movies. But director John Ford, who'd seen him in "The Last Mile," had Fox sign Tracy to star in a prison yarn he was filming, *Up the River* (1930, which also featured New York stage actor Humphrey Bogart). Tracy's skillful performance, coupled with his "Last Mile" fame, kept him confined to gangster and tough-guy roles for his first several years in Hollywood. He was already a better actor than many of the leading men out there (having mastered early the technique of underemoting for the camera), but studio brass insisted on casting him as a thick-ear type in the likes of *Quick Millions, Six-Cylinder Love, Goldie* (all 1931), *Sky Devils, Disorderly Conduct, Young America, Society Girl, The Painted Woman,* the delightful *Me and My Gal,* and *She Wanted a Millionaire* (all 1932), among others.

An increasingly truculent Tracy, loaned to Warners for yet another prison picture (1933's *20,000 Years in Sing Sing),* took to drinking heavily and grousing loudly. Fox loaned him to Columbia to star opposite Loretta Young (with whom Tracy was once romantically linked) in Frank Borzage's Depression romance, *Man's Castle* (1933), and did offer him some better roles, as the itinerant sign painter in *Face in the Sky* (also 1933), for example. Producer Jesse L. Lasky even selected him to star in his prestigious, innovative drama, *The Power and the Glory* (also 1933), playing the ruthless industrialist with a tragic personal life. The literate, handsome production (written by Preston Sturges) was not a box-office success, and Tracy finished out his Fox contract in mostly undistinguished fare, including *The*

Mad Game, Shanghai Madness (also 1933), *The Show-Off, Bottoms Up, Now I'll Tell, Marie Galante* (all 1934), and *It's a Small World* (1935). (Two of his better outings during this period were 1934's jaunty *Looking for Trouble* and 1935's *Dante's Inferno.*)

MGM's wonder boy, production head Irving Thalberg, thought Tracy would make an ideal secondary lead and character actor, and signed him in 1935 to a long-term contract. That year, after getting top billing in a nondescript B, *The Murder Man,* Tracy took the number two spot supporting Metro stars Myrna Loy (in *Whipsaw*) and Jean Harlow (in *Riffraff*), as well as borrowed Paramount star Sylvia Sidney (in 1936's *Fury,* a Fritz Lang drama in which Tracy made his best impression to date for MGM). He supported Clark Gable and Jeanette MacDonald in *San Francisco* (and was Oscar-nominated for his work as a priest), and William Powell, Myrna Loy, and Jean Harlow in *Libeled Lady* (both 1936) before being cast as the Portuguese fisherman Manuel, in support of child star Freddie Bartholomew, in Victor Fleming's letter-perfect adaptation of Kipling's *Captains Courageous* (1937), a characterization that won him his first Academy Award.

Tracy's next few assignments—in *They Gave Him a Gun, The Big City, Mannequin* (all 1937), and *Test Pilot* (1938, again in support of Gable and Loy)—weren't particularly demanding, nor were the films particularly great. But *Boys Town* (also 1938) offered him the plum role of a real-life hero, Nebraska's famous Father Flanagan, whose private community for wayward boys had made headlines. Tracy superbly limned the priest as tough but tender, and won a second Academy Award for his portrayal. (He reprised the role in a 1941 sequel, *Men of Boys Town.*)

Loaned to 20th Century-Fox for *Stanley and Livingstone* (1939, in which he played the former, uttering the immortal line "Dr. Livingstone, I presume."), Tracy returned to Metro first to support Gable and Claudette Colbert in *Boom Town,* but then appeared in several top-notch starring vehicles: *Edison, the Man,* the rugged *Northwest Passage, I Take This Woman* (all 1940), and *Dr. Jekyll and Mr. Hyde* (1941). In 1942 Tracy was teamed for the first time with Katharine Hepburn, who

had made a surprising comeback—after being labeled "box-office poison" by exhibitors—in Metro's *The Philadelphia Story. Woman of the Year* (1942) was a delightful comedy directed by George Stevens that showed them playing out the battle of the sexes with élan; it was a routine they would evolve together periodically onscreen over the next quarter-century. An offscreen romance began as well, although Tracy—a devout Catholic—refused to divorce his wife, even though they lived apart for decades.

Tracy, by this time a top star at MGM, worked throughout the 1940s: *Keeper of the Flame* (with Hepburn), *Tortilla Flat* (both 1942), *A Guy Named Joe* (1943), *The Seventh Cross, Thirty Seconds Over Tokyo* (both 1944), *Without Love* (1945, with Hepburn), *Cass Timberlane, Sea of Grass* (both 1947, the latter with Hepburn), *Edward, My Son.* He always seemed at his best with Hepburn, and most of their films were unusually intelligent. In *State of the Union* (1948, based on the hit Broadway play), he's an industrialist who tries to maintain his integrity while running for President; Hepburn is his wife, who loses faith in him when he seems to be swallowed by the political machine (and its power broker, played by Angela Lansbury). In *Adam's Rib* (1949, written especially for them by their friends Ruth Gordon and Garson Kanin, and directed by another close friend, George Cukor) they're a liberated married couple, both successful as lawyers, who lock horns when they represent opposing sides in a love-triangle shooting.

Acting didn't come easily for Tracy, a tormented man who would disappear on binges for days, even weeks at a time. Still, he managed to rein himself in often enough to work on a steady basis, and toplined such 1950s vehicles as *The People Against O'Hara* (1951), *Plymouth Adventure* (1952), *The Actress* (1953, as the father of a budding actress, an autobiographical story by Ruth Gordon), *Broken Lance* (1954), and *The Mountain* (1956). He gave one of his most endearing performances in *Father of the Bride* (1950), as the hapless (but doting) dad of Elizabeth Taylor, and earned another Oscar nomination; he and his costars fared equally well in a sequel, *Father's Little Dividend* (1951).

He snagged another Oscar nod as the

grizzled, one-armed veteran who exposes a Western town's dirty little secret in *Bad Day at Black Rock* (1955), and yet another for his tour de force as an aging fisherman battling the elements in Hemingway's *The Old Man and the Sea* (1958). He found other good opportunities in the 1950s: opposite Hepburn again in *Pat and Mike* (1952) and *Desk Set* (1957), and reunited with director John Ford and an all-star cast in the sentimental *The Last Hurrah* (1958), which offered him a tailor-made role as an old-time politico.

By this time Tracy was white-haired and craggy-faced, his natural contrariness and irascibility gradually seeping into his performances. *Inherit the Wind* (1960), based on the real-life "monkey trial" of 1925, cast him as a fictionalized Clarence Darrow, a characterization that garnered him yet another Academy Award nod. He repeated the feat with his turn as the U.S. judge presiding over Nazi war criminals' trials in *Judgment at Nuremberg* (1961). But he couldn't save *The Devil at 4 O'Clock* (1961, playing a priest for the last time), and had little to do as the nominal straight man to a cast of scene-stealing comics in *It's a Mad Mad Mad Mad World* (1963). He also narrated the epic western *How the West Was Won* in 1962.

Increasingly ill, Tracy returned to the screen just once more, at the behest of his friend, producer Stanley Kramer, to costar with his beloved Hepburn one last time in *Guess Who's Coming to Dinner* (1967). An occasionally syrupy but well-intentioned and well-made plea for racial tolerance, it provided a fitting swan song for this great actor, who delivered a lengthy, moving speech in the final reel. Desperately ill during production, Tracy summoned up his last ounce of strength to finish the picture; he died just a few weeks after shooting was completed. He received a posthumous Best Actor Academy Award nomination—his ninth—for his performance.

TRAVIS, NANCY. Actress. *(b. Sept. 21, 1961, Astoria, Queens, N.Y.)* After years of supporting and mainly decorative roles, this actress has begun to establish herself as a talent to watch. She made her film debut as the English mom who skips town in *3 Men and a Baby* (1987), and went on to a variety of parts in *Eight Men Out,*

Married to the Mob (both 1988), *Loose Cannons, Air America,* and the sequel *3 Men and a Little Lady* (all 1990). Early in 1990, Travis got considerable attention for her work as Andy Garcia's wife in *Internal Affairs;* she added spice to the ensemble cast of *Passed Away* (1992), and landed an unusually showy part as the mentally unbalanced Joan Barry in *Chaplin* (also 1992). She won the female lead (a demanding part) in *The Vanishing* (1993) and showed her comic skill opposite Mike Myers in *So I Married an Axe Murderer* (also 1993), but neither enjoyed the box-office success that might boost her stock as a genuine star. In 1994 she costarred in *Greedy* and lent her voice to TV's animated "Duckman." A stage veteran, Travis appeared in the Broadway production of "I'm Not Rappaport" and is one of the founders of Naked Angels, an off-Broadway theater company.

TRAVOLTA, JOHN. Actor. *(b. Feb. 18, 1954, Englewood, N.J.)* This good-humored hunk burst onto the scene as teen heartthrob Vinnie Barbarino of TV's "Welcome Back, Kotter" (1975–79). Travolta, a high-school dropout (from an acting family) who acted in summer stock before touring in "Grease" and on Broadway in the Andrews Sisters' "Over Here!" all but stole the sitcom from nominal star Gabe Kaplan with his characterization of a dull-witted high-school wise guy. His beaming smile, cleft chin, and wavy dark hair—not to mention his insouciant manner and casual sensuality—made him a favorite of adolescent girls (and, ostensibly, male underachievers as well), and he stayed close to the character in some of his early movies: *Carrie* (1976), *Grease* (1978, based on the Broadway musical), and, in a more serious vein, *Saturday Night Fever* (1977), which earned him an Oscar nomination as the white-suited disco hustler. But that triumph was also (it turns out) Travolta's career peak. *Moment by Moment* (1978) was an unmitigated fiasco. *Urban Cowboy* (1980) was a fine film, but not the hit its studio expected.

Brian De Palma's *Blow Out* (1981) marked the beginning of Travolta's lengthy eclipse, and *Staying Alive* (1983), a follow-up to *Saturday Night Fever,* was a transparent—and ill-fated—attempt to replicate the original's success. *Two of a*

Kind (also 1983) reunited him with *Grease* costar Olivia Newton-John in an embarrassing comedy-fantasy flop. Travolta, who'd always been an engaging personality if not a particularly skillful actor, was positively ludicrous as an investigative reporter in *Perfect* (1985, written and directed by *Urban Cowboy*'s James Bridges), and its indifferent reception sent him into a self-imposed exile for several years.

His first comeback effort, *The Experts* (1989), barely got released, but *Look Who's Talking* (also 1989), which cast him as a garrulous but good-hearted cabbie who helps Kirstie Alley raise her illegitimate child, surprised everyone and became one of the year's top hits. He returned to TV to appear in a Robert Altman production of "The Dumbwaiter" (1987), then appeared in *Chains of Gold* (also 1987, which went direct to video), *Look Who's Talking Too, Shout* (both 1991), and *Look Who's Talking Now* (1993). Just when Hollywood had written Travolta off, he made a spectacular comeback as hit man Vincent Vega in *Pulp Fiction* (1994) and earned a Best Actor Oscar nomination. He followed with *Get Shorty* (1995). Travolta was once involved with actress Diana Hyland, with whom he appeared in the 1976 TV movie *The Boy in the Plastic Bubble*. In 1989 he married Kelly Preston, his costar in *The Experts*.

TREVOR, CLAIRE. Actress. *(b. Mar. 8, 1909, New York City, as Claire Wemlinger.)* Every casting director in Hollywood must have felt the same way about this hard-boiled blonde, who played every conceivable type of "bad girl," from hooker to gun moll to showgirl to saloon girl. She was good at it, too, judging from the Oscar she won for her turn as Edward G. Robinson's floozy in *Key Largo* (1948) and the nominations she earned for similar roles in *Dead End* (1937) and *The High and the Mighty* (1954). A native New Yorker who studied at the American Academy of Dramatic Arts before attempting a stage career, she got her first experience before the cameras acting in Vitaphone short subjects shot in Brooklyn.

Trevor came to Hollywood under contract to Fox. "The first thing I was told," she remembered, "was 'Don't fall in love with your leading man.' Of course, that's just what I did." The leading man was brawny Western star George O'Brien, and her first two films were his *Life in the Raw* and *The Last Trail* (both 1933). For the next five years she worked exclusively at Fox, except for 1937 loan-outs to Samuel Goldwyn for *Dead End* and Paramount for *King of Gamblers*. Trevor's films of this period, which include *Jimmy and Sally* (1933), *Hold That Girl, Baby Take a Bow* (both 1934), *Dante's Inferno, Spring Tonic, Navy Wife, Black Sheep* (all 1935), *Human Cargo, To Mary—With Love, Career Woman* (all 1936), *One Mile From Heaven, Time Out for Romance, Second Honeymoon, Big Town Girl* (all 1937), *Walking Down Broadway,* and *Five of a Kind* (both 1938), were mostly program pictures, but she at least got to play some bona fide ingenue roles. She also played a female detective in *15 Maiden Lane* (1936), getting a bullet in the belly for her trouble!

She freelanced from 1938 on, appearing in that year's *The Amazing Dr. Clitterhouse* and *Valley of the Giants* before accepting the role of a sympathetic prostitute in John Ford's classic *Stagecoach* (1939), opposite John Wayne (but getting top billing). They reteamed in *Allegheny Uprising* (also 1939) and *Dark Command* (1940), but her parts were much more conventional.

Trevor continued to get star billing for another few years, toplining such pictures as *Texas* (1941), *Streets of Chance* (1942, a superb B, with one of her best performances), *The Woman of the Town* (1943), and *Murder, My Sweet* (1944, a crackerjack Raymond Chandler mystery, opposite Dick Powell). But early on, she accepted secondary and character parts as well, and switched between leads and support for many years to come; her Oscar for *Key Largo* was in the Best Supporting Actress category. She was especially good as a young tennis star's domineering mother in Ida Lupino's *Hard, Fast and Beautiful* (1951). Only semi-retired, she continued to take parts when the occasion suited her. In 1982 she played Sally Field's mother in *Kiss Me Goodbye,* and in the 1987 TV movie *Breaking Home Ties* she was a delight as an aged schoolteacher.

OTHER FILMS INCLUDE: 1941: *Honky Tonk*; 1942: *The Adventures of Martin Eden, Crossroads*; 1943: *The Desperadoes, Good Luck, Mr. Yates*; 1945: *Johnny Angel*; 1946:

Crack-Up; 1947: Born to Kill; 1948: Raw Deal, The Velvet Touch, The Babe Ruth Story; 1949: The Lucky Stiff; 1950: Borderline; 1951: Best of the Bad Men; 1952: Hoodlum Empire, Stop, You're Killing Me; 1953: The Stranger Wore a Gun; 1955: Man Without a Star, Lucy Gallant; 1956: The Mountain; 1958: Marjorie Morningstar; 1962: Two Weeks in Another Town; 1963: The Stripper; 1965: How to Murder Your Wife; 1967: The Capetown Affair.

TRINTIGNANT, JEAN-LOUIS. Actor. *(b. Dec. 11, 1930, Fiolenc, France.)* His impassive face radiates French sangfroid, but Trintignant has also been more than convincing in passionately romantic roles. It was in one of the latter that he made his biggest impression on American audiences, playing a race-car driver intimately involved with Anouk Aimée in the 1966 art-house classic *A Man and a Woman* (a decade before he'd been seen in 1956's ... *And God Created Woman*, but most U.S. viewers were too engrossed in debuting sex goddess Brigitte Bardot to pay Trintignant much notice). His other outstanding performances include a hilariously deadpan turn in Alain Robbe-Grillet's delirious *Trans-Europ-Express* (1967); a convincing portrayal of a romantically torn clerk in Eric Rohmer's *My Night at Maud's* (1969); and a terrifying portrait of an individual seduced by fascism in Bernardo Bertolucci's *The Conformist* (1971). Trintignant also played the determined investigator in the 1969 political thriller *Z.* He worked steadily throughout the 1980s, somewhat less impressively, in such vehicles as *Confidentially Yours* (1983), *Under Fire* (1983), *A Man and a Woman: 20 Years Later* (1986), and *Bunker Palace Hotel* (1989), but had one of his best roles in years as a bitter, reclusive judge in *Red* (1994). Trintignant was once married to actress Stephane Audran. His wife, Nadine, is a director, and his daughter, Marie, is an actress.
OTHER FILMS INCLUDE: 1959: *Dangerous Liaisons 1960;* 1963: *The Easy Life;* 1965: *The Sleeping Car Murder;* 1966: *Is Paris Burning?;* 1968: *Les Biches;* 1972: *And Hope to Die;* 1973: *The Outside Man;* 1974: *Les Violins du bal;* 1985: *Rendez-vous.*

TROELL, JAN. Director, writer, editor, cinematographer. *(b. July 23, 1931, Limhamn, Skane, Sweden.)* Swedish director, famous for his understated rhythms and for writing, directing, editing, and shooting his own films. A former schoolteacher, Troell made short films, then worked as a cameraman for Bo Widerberg before making his feature debut with the coming-of-age story *Here's Your Life* (1966). After *Who Saw Him Die?* (1968), he made his best-known works, *The Emigrants* (1971, which earned Oscar nominations for Best Picture, Director, and Screenplay) and its sequel, *The New Land* (1972), which together presented a sweeping account of Swedish immigrants coming to America in the 1840s, based on Vilhelm Moberg's novel "Unto a Good Land." The films were hailed collectively as the Swedish equivalent of *Gone With the Wind* and were notable for Troell's direct and humane treatment of his characters' plight. They also won him American film assignments, but *Zandy's Bride* (1974) and *Hurricane* (1979) were decidedly lesser efforts. *The Flight of the Eagle* (1982) returned to Swedish history with a story of the failed 1897 North Pole expedition undertaken by S. A. Andree. Since then, Troell has made *Sagolandet* (1986) and *Il Capitano* (1991).

TRUFFAUT, FRANÇOIS. Director, screenwriter, producer, actor. *(b. Feb. 6, 1932, Paris; d. Oct. 21, 1984.)* Influential filmmaker who was at the forefront of Europe's New Wave movement of the late 1950s. A lifelong movie buff whose initial contact with the industry was as a critic and historian for André Bazin's influential magazine "Cahiers du Cinéma," Truffaut laid down the groundwork for the "auteur" theory—that the director is the primary creator of a film—in a 1954 article that inspired a generation of European filmmakers. He began making short films around that time, and also worked as assistant to director Roberto Rossellini for a time before finishing his debut feature, *The 400 Blows,* in 1959. A semiautobiographical story, it focused on the difficult adolescence of one Antoine Doinel, who was played by Jean-Pierre Leaud, and earned the writer-director an Oscar nomination for his screenplay. (Throughout his career, Truffaut kept coming back to Doinel, who aged into adulthood over a 20-year period and was always played by

Leaud. This autobiographical strain of the director's work includes one segment of the episodic 1962 film *Love at Twenty,* 1968's *Stolen Kisses,* 1970's *Bed and Board,* and 1979's *Love on the Run.*)

The commercial and critical success of *The 400 Blows* established Truffaut's international reputation. His follow-up, *Shoot the Piano Player* (1960), reflected a more complex sensibility, influenced by American B movies but tempered by mischievous wit and technical virtuosity. *Jules and Jim* (1961, based on Henri-Pierre Roche's book), arguably Truffaut's best film, follows the ever-changing relationship among three friends—Jeanne Moreau, Oskar Werner, and Henri Serre—before and after World War 1. An extraordinarily playful and evocative work, it is, as Stanley Kauffmann noted, "one of the moments when the history of the film suddenly grows."

The 400 Blows and *Jules and Jim* established Truffaut's debt to Renoir, but *Shoot the Piano Player* and many others that followed revealed his darker, more ironic side. *The Soft Skin* (1964), *Mississippi Mermaid* (1969), *Such a Gorgeous Kid Like Me* (1973), *Confidentially Yours* (1983, his last film) and, especially, *The Bride Wore Black* (1968), showed his fondness for American thrillers, in particular the amoral tone of Alfred Hitchcock, a particular favorite whom Truffaut interviewed at length for the landmark critical tome *Hitchcock-Truffaut* (1967). Truffaut tried his hand at science-fiction with an intriguing, though curiously detached, adaptation of *Fahrenheit 451* (1967) and made a number of intriguing, if not entirely successful, period dramas: *The Wild Child* (1970), about a late 18th-century scientist who tries to civilize a wild boy found in the woods; *The Story of Adele H* (1975), with Isabelle Adjani, unforgettable as the daughter of Victor Hugo; *The Green Room* (1978), with Truffaut in the lead role as a death-obsessed journalist; and *The Last Metro* (1980), about a French theatrical troupe dealing with Nazi occupation. He also perceptively examined the pains of romantic entanglements in the comedy *The Man Who Loved Women* (1977) and the sensitive *The Woman Next Door* (1981).

Some critics complained that Truffaut's later films did not match the explosive quality of his early work, but Joseph McBride noted, "If the sweeping camerawork, breathless cutting and joie de vivre of Truffaut's early work seemed less evident as his career progressed, the lessening of those qualities was balanced by a more rigorous approach to narrative, a masterful sobriety of style and an even more profound richness of emotion." Some of his later triumphs include the exquisite ménage à trois *Two English Girls* (1972), also based on a Roche novel and almost on a par with *Jules and Jim,* and the charming and insightful children's story *Small Change* (1976). He enjoyed one of his greatest latter-day successes with *Day for Night* (1973), a delightful, episodic salute to the highs and lows of filmmaking, conveyed with the ease and apparent effortlessness that characterized so much of Truffaut's work. (It won an Oscar for Best Foreign Film and earned Truffaut nominations for Best Director and for cowriting the screenplay.) Such ease behind the camera was occasionally proven in front of it as well, with his performances as the scientist in *The Wild Child,* the supremely patient director in *Day for Night,* a small role as an officer in *The Story of Adele H,* and the lead in *The Green Room.* He also took the role of the French scientist Lacombe in Steven Spielberg's *Close Encounters of the Third Kind* (1977) to learn what it was like to work for another director.

At the time of his death (from a brain tumor) Truffaut was planning to direct *The Little Thief;* his associate Claude Miller ultimately made the film, from Truffaut's script. His longtime assistant and frequent collaborator Suzanne Schiffman also embarked on her own directing career after his death. His early film criticism has been anthologized, as has a volume of his letters.

TRUMBO, DALTON. Screenwriter. *(b. Dec. 9, 1905, Montrose, Colo.; d. Sept 10, 1976.)* One member of the infamous "Hollywood Ten" who was blacklisted for his leftist views and spent years writing in anonymity, Trumbo began as a newspaper reporter and editor and gained fame with his pacifist novel "Johnny Got His Gun." He became a screenwriter in 1935 and wrote a number of program pictures at RKO, including such well-received B's as *A Man to Remember* (1938, on which

Garson Kanin made his directing debut), the suspenseful *Five Came Back* (1939), and the theatrical comedy *Curtain Call* (1940). He graduated to A pictures with his Oscar-nominated screenplay for *Kitty Foyle* (1940), which earned Ginger Rogers an Oscar. His subsequent screenplays include *The Remarkable Andrew* (1942), *A Guy Named Joe* (1943), *Thirty Seconds Over Tokyo* (1944), and *Our Vines Have Tender Grapes* (1945). His screenplay for the stiff-upper-lip, let's-all-sacrifice wartime romance *Tender Comrade* (1943) was later cited as evidence of Communist infiltration in Hollywood. After a term of imprisonment for refusing to name names before the House Un-American Activities Committee, Trumbo was blacklisted by Hollywood. He moved to Mexico, where he wrote many screenplays under various pseudonyms; it was a source of industry embarrassment when his screenplay for *The Brave One* (1956), supposedly written by "Robert Rich," won an Oscar. He became the first blacklisted writer to return to the industry, thanks to Kirk Douglas and Otto Preminger, who openly credited him for his work on their respective productions of *Spartacus* and *Exodus* (both 1960). He remained active writing such films as *The Last Sunset* (1961), *Lonely Are the Brave* (1962), *The Sandpiper* (1965), *Hawaii* (1966, cowriter), *The Fixer* (1968), *The Horsemen* (1971), *Executive Action* and *Papillon* (both 1973), and even directed his own adaptation of *Johnny Got His Gun* in 1971. In March 1992 Trumbo received belated, posthumous credit for his original story for *Roman Holiday* (1953), which had won an Oscar for his "front," Ian McLellan Hunter.

TRUMBULL, DOUGLAS. Special effects designer, director. *(b. Apr. 8, 1942, Los Angeles.)* Renowned special effects creator, who began as a background illustrator on Navy, Air Force, and NASA films and gained fame for his revolutionary work on Stanley Kubrick's classic *2001: A Space Odyssey* (1968). One of the film's special photographic effects supervisors, Trumbull designed the "slit-scan" machine which created the astounding light show that Keir Dullea experiences. He directed the fine ecological/science fiction film *Silent Running* (1971), but subsequent projects

fell through and he returned to special effects work on *Close Encounters of the Third Kind* (1977), *Star Trek—The Motion Picture* (1979), and *Blade Runner* (1982), each of which earned him Oscar nominations. His last directorial job was *Brainstorm* (1983), which gained more publicity for Natalie Wood's death than anything else. Always an innovator, Trumbull developed Showscan (a format using 70mm film stock projected at 60 frames per second for super clarity) and hoped to open a number of specialized theaters around the U.S. to exhibit films made in that process. It never came to pass. He has since formed Berkshire Motion Picture Corporation, whose Berkshire Ride Film subsidiary creates movie rides, most notably, the amazing Back to the Future attraction at Universal Studios, and a trio of presentations at Las Vegas' Luxor Hotel.

TUCKER, FORREST. Actor. *(b. Feb. 12, 1919, Plainfield, Ind.; d. Oct. 25, 1986.)* The crafty Sergeant O'Rourke of "F Troop" (1965–67) began his acting career on a lark, coaxed into trying out for films while vacationing in California in 1940. He made his debut in William Wyler's *The Westerner,* supporting Gary Cooper and Walter Brennan, and toiled as a contract player in many Columbia films (mostly Bs) of the early and mid 1940s. Tucker, a huge, solidly built man with wavy blond hair and inviting blue eyes, often played nasty, brutal heavies in Westerns and action films. (His most memorable: the Marine with a chip on his shoulder who squares off with John Wayne in 1949's *Sands of Iwo Jima,* made for his longtime home studio, Republic.) His extroverted personality lent itself to broad comedic characterizations, but he seldom displayed that aspect of his talent until being signed to star in the TV comedy series. Also in many telefilms of the 1970s and early 1980s, he was reteamed with "F Troop" partner Larry Storch for the Saturday morning kids' series "The Ghost Busters" (1975–76).

OTHER FILMS INCLUDE: 1940: *The Howards of Virginia;* 1941: *Emergency Landing* (his first lead, on loan to PRC); 1942: *Boston Blackie Goes Hollywood, My Sister Eileen, Counter-Espionage;* 1946: *Never Say Goodbye, The Yearling;* 1947: *Gunfighters;* 1948: *Coroner Creek, The Plunderers;* 1951:

Fighting Coast Guard, The Wild Blue Yonder; 1952: *Hoodlum Empire, Bugles in the Afternoon, Montana Belle;* 1953: *Pony Express;* 1954: *Jubilee Trail;* 1955: *The Vanishing American;* 1956: *The Quiet Gun;* 1957: *The Abominable Snowman, Three Violent People, The Deerslayer;* 1958: *The Crawling Eye, The Cosmic Monster, Auntie Mame;* 1959: *Counterplot;* 1966: *Don't Worry, We'll Think of a Title;* 1968: *The Night They Raided Minsky's;* 1970: *Chisum;* 1972: *Cancel My Reservation;* 1975: *The Wild McCullochs;* 1977: *Final Chapter—Walking Tall;* 1985: *Thunder Run, Bridge Across Time* (telefilm).

TURNER, KATHLEEN. Actress. (b. June 19, 1954, Springfield, Mo.) After making a stunning feature-film debut as the sultry schemer in *Body Heat* (1981), this sensual, throaty-voiced leading lady earned a reputation for willingness to try virtually anything on-screen. A University of Maryland graduate and former gymnast (a skill she used in *The War of the Roses,* by the way), Turner began acting in the 1970s and enjoyed a stint on the daytime soap "The Doctors" before her *Body Heat* breakthrough. She confounded expectations by next appearing as a *comic* femme fatale in a goofy farce, *The Man With Two Brains* (1983), and in 1984 she continued expanding her screen persona as an environmentalist in *A Breed Apart,* and a woman who moonlights as a hooker (named China Blue) by night in Ken Russell's *Crimes of Passion* (1984). But it was the sleeper hit *Romancing the Stone* (also 1984) that cemented her stardom with mainstream moviegoers; as a mousy romance novelist who "lives" one of her own stories, she won a legion of fans. She followed it with a bravura turn as a Mafia hit lady, opposite Jack Nicholson, in *Prizzi's Honor* (1985), reteamed with Michael Douglas for a *Stone* sequel, *The Jewel of the Nile* (1985), then earned an Oscar nomination playing a time-traveling housewife in *Peggy Sue Got Married* (1986). She went on to play a woman living out two lives in *Julia and Julia* (1987), a feisty TV anchorwoman in *Switching Channels* (1988), the seductive voice of Jessica Rabbit in *Who Framed Roger Rabbit* (also 1988, followed by two subsequent short cartoons), and William Hurt's frigid wife in *The Accidental Tourist* (1988). She again reteamed with Mi-

chael Douglas as their *Romancing the Stone* costar Danny DeVito moved behind the camera for the very black divorce comedy *The War of the Roses* (1989), then came a cropper as the solo lead of the poorly made adaptation of Sara Paretsky's Chicago private eye story *V.I. Warshawski* (1991). She electrified Broadway as Maggie in the 1989 revival of "Cat on a Hot Tin Roof," but her return to films in 1993 was less salutary for her career: *House of Cards* and *Undercover Blues* were both seen as failures. Her most recent credits: *Naked in New York* and John Waters' *Serial Mom* (both 1994).

TURNER, LANA. Actress. (b. Feb. 8, 1921, Wallace, Idaho, as Julia Jean Mildred Frances Turner; d. June 29, 1995.) According to Hollywood legend Lana Turner was discovered sipping a soda at Schwab's drugstore while playing hooky. Like many legends, the story is untrue: Turner was actually spotted at the counter of Currie's Ice Cream Parlor across the street from Hollywood High School. After the death of her father in a robbery, her mother brought Julia Jean Turner to California, first to San Francisco and later to Los Angeles. After her discovery, the newly renamed Lana Turner made her film debut in a bit for *A Star Is Born* (1937). That same year she made an indelible impression on moviegoers as the overripe, sweater-clad schoolgirl whose murder sets into motion the plot of *They Won't Forget.* By the following year she was under contract to MGM and gaining experience in such studio fare as *Dramatic School, Rich Man, Poor Girl, Love Finds Andy Hardy* (all 1938), *These Glamour Girls, Dancing Co-Ed,* and *Calling Dr. Kildare* (all 1939).

Turner became a bona fide star in a quartet of major 1941 movies: *Ziegfeld Girl, Dr. Jekyll and Mr. Hyde* (as the "good" girl), *Honky Tonk* (opposite Clark Gable, at the peak of his popularity), and *Johnny Eager* (opposite Robert Taylor). Her "sweater girl" image also made her a favorite of our boys in uniform. Turner came into her own after the war in steamy melodramas such as *The Postman Always Rings Twice* (1946, a tough but oddly glamorous version of a gritty James M. Cain novel) and *Cass Timberlane* (1947), but she was still often called upon to add star appeal without having to carry a picture. She played Milady de Winter in *The Three Musketeers* (1948) and a highly emotional movie star in MGM's ensemble epic supposedly dissecting Hollywood life, *The Bad and the Beautiful* (1952); but she was badly miscast as *The Merry Widow* (also 1952). She was highly decorative, but little else, in a 1955 sword-and-sandal sizzler, *The Prodigal,* which showed that she could still muster the oomph, but did little to maintain her star standing. After 20 years in films, Turner got her biggest break with *Peyton Place* (1957), receiving an Oscar nomination for her work as a worried mother in the once scandalous tale of sex and passion in a New England town. She then became mired in a succession of three-hankie pictures the likes of *Imitation of Life* (1959), *By Love Possessed* (1961), and the oft-filmed soap opera *Madame X* (1966). Her name still had enough drawing power to fuel a few low-budget potboilers such as *The Big Cube* (1969), but *Bittersweet Love* (1976), was hopelessly out of touch with then-current audience tastes.

Turner's TV appearances include a starring role in Harold Robbins' continuing saga, "The Survivors," a 1969–70 series; she also put in the obligatory stint on "Love Boat" and appeared briefly in the serial "Falcon Crest" (1982–83). Throughout her career, Turner enjoyed (if that's the word) a reputation based at least as much on her stormy private life as on her screen work. At one time or another she was married to bandleader Artie Shaw, millionaire Bob Topping, and screen Tarzan Lex Barker, among others. Her longtime boyfriend, mobster Johnny Stompanato, was stabbed to death by Turner's daughter Cheryl Crane in 1958, a tale that was retold in highly fictionalized form in Woody Allen's *September* (1987). She published her autobiography, "Lana: The Lady, The Legend, The Truth" in 1982.

OTHER FILMS INCLUDE: 1937: *The Great Garrick;* 1938: *The Adventures of Marco Polo;* 1940: *Two Girls on Broadway, We Who Are Young;* 1942: *Somewhere I'll Find You;* 1943: *Slightly Dangerous;* 1944: *Marriage Is a Private Affair;* 1945: *Keep Your Powder Dry, Weekend at the Waldorf;* 1947: *Green Dolphin Street;* 1948: *Homecoming;* 1950: *A Life of Her Own;* 1951: *Mr. Imperium;* 1953: *Latin Lovers;* 1954: *Betrayed, The Flame and the Flesh;* 1955: *The Rains of Ranchipur, The Sea Chase;* 1956: *Diane;* 1958: *The Lady Takes a Flyer, Another Time, Another Place;* 1960: *Portrait in Black;* 1961: *Bachelor in Paradise;* 1962: *Who's Got the Action?;* 1965: *Love Has Many Faces;* 1974: *Persecution;* 1980: *Witches' Brew.*

TURTURRO, JOHN. Actor. *(b. Feb. 28, 1957, Brooklyn, N.Y.)* Frizzy-haired, nervous-looking, viscerally unappealing actor (with considerable stage experience, including training at the prestigious Yale Drama School) played a series of eccentric bits, in 1980's *Raging Bull* and throughout the decade in *Exterminator II, The Flamingo Kid* (both 1984), *Desperately Seeking Susan, To Live and Die in L.A.* (both 1985), *The Color of Money, Gung Ho, Hannah and Her Sisters, Off Beat* (all 1986) and *The Sicilian* (1987). He finally caught the attention of critics—and audiences—with his ultra-creepy portrayal of a neighborhood nut fixated on Jodie Foster in the urban comedy/drama *Five Corners* (1987). Since that time he's become a favorite of director Spike Lee and producer-director siblings Ethan and Joel Coen, who've cast him in a total of six films between them. His portrayals of extremely unsavory Jewish characters in Lee's *Mo' Better Blues* and the Coens' *Miller's Crossing* (1990), and of a thickheaded Italian racist in *Do the Right Thing* (1989) were controversial, but most of the flak was directed at the filmmakers rather than the actor. He appeared in Dennis Hopper's *Backtrack* (1989) and a pair of contemporary gangster films, *State of Grace* (1990) and *Men of Respect* (1991), and *Barton Fink* (also 1991; he had starring roles in the last two). That same year he proved he could play sympathetic characters just as well, giving a touching performance as a befuddled but good-hearted spurned boyfriend in Lee's interracial romance-cum-polemic *Jungle Fever* (also 1991). In 1992 he played a Groucho Marx–like character in *Brain Donors,* a game try at reinventing The Marx Brothers, then tackled his most personal project to date: *Mac,* a blue-collar slice-of-life story which he cowrote (based on his father's life), starred in, and directed. His most recent credits include *Fearless* (1993), *Being Human* (1994), *Quiz Show* (also 1994, terrific as Herb Stempel), *Search and Destroy,* and *Clockers* (both 1995). His brother, Nick, is also an actor, who stars on the TV drama "NYPD Blue" (1993–).

TUSHINGHAM, RITA. Actress. *(b. March 14, 1940, Liverpool.)* Doe-eyed actress who hit her stride during the early 1960s, while in her early twenties, but was unable to sustain a career which began with such immense promise. Tushingham first acted in plays presented at a hometown convent, and trained at the Liverpool Playhouse; she made her stage debut in 1960 and screen debut in Shelagh Delaney's *A Taste of Honey* (1961). Cast as Jo, a working-class innocent impregnated by a black sailor and looked after by a homosexual friend, she offered a keenly observed performance and walked off with the British Academy Award for Most Promising Newcomer and shared a Cannes Film Festival prize. Unfortunately, Tushingham never had another role which so successfully exploited her look and talent. She followed up *A Taste of Honey* with a starring part in *The Leather Boys* (1963), playing a flaky teen who marries too young. She was typecast as a country lass new to the Big City in *Girl With Green Eyes* (1964), *The Knack, and How to Get It* (1965), and the slapstick comedy *Smashing Time* (1967). Tushingham still was enough of a name to be offered a key role in a prestige international production, *Doctor Zhivago* (1965), cast as a girl who is believed to be the offspring of Omar Sharif and Julie Christie. But clearly, no one quite knew what to do with her, and her screen roles diminished in quantity and quality. By the mid 1980s, she was playing aging caricatures of her early roles in films like *A Judgment in Stone* (1986, aka *The Housekeeper*), an obscure chiller with Rita cast as an uneducated, repressed, ultimately deranged spinster.

TYLER, TOM. Actor. *(b. Aug. 9, 1903, Port Henry, N.Y., as Vincent Markowski; d. May 1, 1954.)* Anyone who's seen *Stagecoach* remembers him as Luke Plummer, the slit-eyed, granite-jawed outlaw who, shot by John Wayne in a climactic gunfight, staggers into a saloon with a sneer on his face before collapsing on the floor (a bit he repeated, with some exaggeration, in the 1945 Errol Flynn starrer *San Antonio*). But to others he's best known as the indomitable hero of countless B Westerns and serials. The former champion weight-lifter started in films as an extra, then became the star of low-budget Westerns such as *Let's Go Gallagher* (1925) and *The Cherokee Kid* (1927). Rechristened Tom Tyler, he ranked high among filmdom's second-echelon cowboy heroes, and easily made the transition to sound. In addition to his 40-odd oaters for indie studios Syndicate, Monogram, Freuler, Reliable, and Victory—most of which were bottom-barrel in every respect—Tyler also starred in many serials, including *Phantom of the West* (1930), *Battling with Buffalo Bill* (1931, in the title role), *Adventures of Captain Marvel* (1941, as the first comic-book superhero to make it to live-action movies), and *The Phantom* (1943).

Tyler played "Stony Brooke" in 12 of Republic's "Three Mesquiteers" Westerns, including *Gauchos of El Dorado* (1941), *The Phantom Plainsmen* (1942), and *Santa Fe Scouts* (1943); he'd also appeared in the first Mesquiteers movie, *Powdersmoke Range* (1935), as a villainous gunfighter. When his starring career began to wane in the late 1930s, Tyler accepted character roles: he was a commanding officer during the evacuation of Atlanta in *Gone With the Wind* (1939), and also appeared in *Brother Orchid* (1940), *The Talk of the Town* (1942), *Badman's Territory* (1946), *Blood on the Moon* (1948), *She Wore a Yellow Ribbon* (1949), and *Cow Country* (1953). Tyler fell victim to rheumatoid arthritis in the early 1950s; its devastating effect distorted his facial features so that he was nearly unrecognizable in his last few film appearances and it eventually crippled him.

TYSON, CICELY. Actress. *(b. Dec. 19, 1933, New York City.)* Majestic African-American actress with extraordinary range. Born in Harlem to Caribbean parents, Tyson toiled in a number of menial jobs before finding success as a model. She moved into acting in the late 1950s, and was noticed in several off-Broadway productions. (She also had a bit part in 1959's *Odds Against Tomorrow.*) A regular part as the secretary on the 1963–64 TV series "East Side/West Side" won Tyson audience recognition, and she played the female lead in the pretentious black drama, *A Man Called Adam* (1966), opposite Sammy Davis, Jr. Other early credits include *The Comedians* (1967) and *The Heart Is a Lonely Hunter* (1968). Tyson's breakthrough role was that of a sharecropper's wife in *Sounder* (1972); this earned her a Best Actress Oscar nomination. She followed that with a stunning starring performance in the TV drama *The Autobiography of Miss Jane Pittman* (1974), which won her an Emmy, portraying a fictional 110-year-old slave who traces her life from the Civil War through the beginning of the Civil Rights movement. In fact, her best opportunities have come on television, not on the big screen, in such miniseries and TV movies as "Roots" (1977), "King" (1978, as Coretta Scott King), *The Marva Collins Story* (1981), *When No One Would Listen* (1992), and "Oldest Living Confederate Widow Tells All" (1994). Her feature credits include *The River Niger* (1975), *The Blue Bird* (1976), *A Hero Ain't Nothin' But a Sandwich* (1978), *The Concorde—Airport '79* (1979), and *Bustin' Loose* (1981). She returned to movies in a supporting role in *Fried Green Tomatoes* (1992).

ULLMAN, TRACEY. Actress, singer. *(b. Dec. 30, 1959, Slough, England.)* This versatile comedienne and actress happily buries her own personality—and features—to create diverse characters in films and television. After receiving a scholarship to theatrical school at the age of twelve, she toured as a dancer and singer, eventually making a name for herself on stage and especially on television. Her TV popularity led to her film debut, opposite Paul McCartney in *Give My Regards to Broad Street* (1984). Meanwhile, she scored four top-ten hits on the British pop charts, leading to the American hit single "They Don't Know." Fans who thought of her mostly as a singer and comedienne were then dazzled by her performance as Meryl Streep's eccentric friend in *Plenty* (1985). She moved to America and starred in "The Tracey Ullman Show" (1987–90), playing a multitude of characters every week (and winning an Emmy in the process). She also appeared in *Jumping Jack Flash* (1986), had the lead—with a flawless American accent—in *I Love You to Death* (1990), and has costarred in *Robin Hood: Men in Tights* (1993, as a haggish witch), *I'll Do Anything,* Woody Allen's *Bullets Over Broadway,* and Robert Altman's *Ready to Wear/Prêt-à-Porter* (all 1994). She continues to star in cable TV

specials that feature her talents as a chameleonlike comedienne.

ULLMANN, LIV. Actress. *(b. Dec. 16, 1939, Tokyo.)* This serene-looking, classically beautiful, Norwegian actress was already well established on stage before making her film debut in Ingmar Bergman's *Persona* (1966), which depicted the melding of two women's personalities. Bergman cast Ullmann partially for her resemblance to costar Bibi Andersson, a Bergman regular. Ullmann, extremely effective in the film and well received by audiences, soon became the director's top actress as well as his mate; together they plumbed the depths of Bergmanesque angst in a series of impressive and original films, including *Hour of the Wolf* (1968), *The Passion of Anna* (1969), *Cries and Whispers* (1972), *The Serpent's Egg,* and *Autumn Sonata* (both 1978, in the last-mentioned opposite another Bergman, namely Ingrid). She gave particularly startling performances for Bergman as an apolitical woman drawn into the horrors of war in *Shame* (1968), a wife who learns her husband is having an affair in *Scenes From a Marriage* (1973), and—maybe most remarkable of all—a psychiatrist who has a nervous breakdown in *Face to Face* (1976), a portrayal which earned her an Oscar nomination and moved John Simon to rhapsodize: "It is not just sublime acting: it is a piece of great, invaluable daring." Ullmann also proved her mettle away from Bergman, with magnificent work as the Swedish peasant who adapts to 19th-century life in the U.S. in Jan Troell's *The Emigrants* (1971, also Oscar-nominated) and *The New Land* (1972).

Her career in America has not been as distinguished; she attempted comedy with uneven results in *40 Carats* and starred in the embarrassing musical remake of *Lost Horizon* (both 1973). Her roles in the 1980s were little-seen turns in international coproductions, although her performances in them have all been topflight. 1987's *Gaby: A True Story,* detailing the struggles of a cerebral palsy victim, received critical kudos and became a sleeper hit on cable TV a couple of years after its release. Ullmann then decided to try her hand at directing, and received excellent notices for her debut film, *Sofie*

(1992). She has also written two books of memoirs, "Changing" (1977) and "Choices" (1984).
OTHER FILMS INCLUDE: 1970: *The Night Visitor;* 1971: *Cold Sweat;* 1972: *Pope Joan;* 1974: *Zandy's Bride, The Abdication;* 1975: *Leonor;* 1977: *A Bridge Too Far;* 1980: *Richard's Things;* 1983: *The Wild Duck;* 1984: *The Bay Boy, Dangerous Moves;* 1989: *The Rose Garden;* 1991: *Mindwalk;* 1994: *Zorn.*

ULMER, EDGAR G. Director. *(b. Sept. 17, 1904, Vienna; d. Sept. 30, 1972.)* Remarkably resourceful B-movie director whose works often transcended their budgetary and artistic limitations. Ulmer started out in Austria and then Germany as a set designer, visiting the U.S. on several occasions with theater impresario Max Reinhardt and director F. W. Murnau. In 1929 he worked with Robert Siodmak on the celebrated German documentary *People on Sunday,* and two years later left permanently for Hollywood, where he worked first as a set decorator, and then as a director. He ground out several independently made features (including a B Western, 1933's *Thunder Over Texas,* which he directed as John Warner) before being assigned to *The Black Cat,* a 1934 Universal horror film—one of the studio's best, in fact—starring Boris Karloff and Bela Lugosi. Ulmer, an eccentric and iconoclast, refused to become part of the studio machine, and was banished to Poverty Row, directing for small, independent studios, including much work on Yiddish and Ukrainian projects. Ironically, these nonmainstream environments allowed Ulmer an artistic freedom he would probably have been denied working for the bigger studios, and his films came to be characterized by a visual style steeped in his German Expressionist background.

He was the resident "auteur" at lowly PRC during the 1940s, and while most of his output there defies analysis, he did at least create one bona fide cult classic, the minimalist *noir* thriller *Detour* (1946), reportedly shot in three days with a tiny cast and crew. He also made a modern-day "Hamlet" called *Strange Illusion* (1945). His work was "rediscovered" by French film theorists of the 1950s and 1960s who, as was their wont, found hidden merit even in his lesser films. He is still re-

garded as an interesting if minor figure in Hollywood annals.
OTHER FILMS INCLUDE: 1937: *Damaged Lives, Green Fields;* 1939: *Cossacks in Exile, Moon Over Harlem;* 1942: *Tomorrow We Live;* 1943: *Girls in Chains, Jive Junction;* 1944: *Bluebeard;* 1945: *Club Havana;* 1946: *Her Sister's Secret, The Strange Woman, The Wife of Monte Cristo;* 1947: *Carnegie Hall;* 1948: *Ruthless;* 1949: *The Pirates of Capri;* 1951: *St. Benny the Dip, The Man From Planet X;* 1952: *Babes in Bagdad;* 1955: *Murder Is My Beat, The Naked Dawn;* 1957: *Daughter of Dr. Jekyll;* 1960: *Hannibal, The Amazing Transparent Man, Beyond the Time Barrier;* 1966: *The Cavern.*

USTINOV, PETER (SIR). Actor, director, screenwriter, playwright. *(b. Apr. 16, 1921, London.)* Portly British character actor, a master dialectician and entertaining raconteur who shines in comedic roles but rates kudos for his dramatic performances as well. Ustinov was, in his own way, the U.K.'s Wellesian "boy wonder": He began acting at 17, sold his first screenplay (for *The True Glory*) at 24, and directed his first film *(School for Secrets)* at 25. Ustinov excels in characterizations of vain, selfish, petulant characters. He earned an Oscar nomination for his supporting role in *Quo Vadis?* (1951, as Nero), and won Academy Awards for outstanding supporting turns in *Spartacus* (1960) and *Topkapi* (1964). Ustinov startled even his admirers with the superb *Billy Budd* (1962), which he wrote, produced, directed, and acted in. In later years he was well received as pompous Belgian detective Hercule Poirot in the Agatha Christie whodunits *Death on the Nile* (1978), *Evil Under the Sun* (1982), and *Appointment With Death* (1988). He had one of his best screen roles in years as the sympathetic doctor in *Lorenzo's Oil* (1992). He has also provided voices for such animated features as Disney's *Robin Hood* (1973), *The Mouse and His Child* (1977), and *Grendel, Grendel, Grendel* (1980). He won Emmy Awards in 1957, for an "Omnibus" drama on Samuel Johnson; 1966, for his performance as Socrates in "Barefoot in Athens," and 1970, for "A Storm in Summer." His 1977 volume of memoirs is titled "Dear Me."
OTHER FILMS INCLUDE: 1942: *One of Our Aircraft Is Missing;* 1944: *The Way Ahead*

(acted, cowrote); 1948: *Vice Versa* (produced, wrote and directed); 1949: *Private Angelo* (wrote, codirected); 1951: *Hotel Sahara, The Magic Box* (cameo), *Le Plaisir* (narration); 1954: *Beau Brummel, The Egyptian;* 1955: *Lola Montes, We're No Angels;* 1960: *The Sundowners;* 1961: *Romanoff and Juliet* (which he also adapted from his own play, produced, and directed); 1965: *John Goldfarb, Please Come Home, Lady L;* 1967: *The Comedians;* 1968: *Blackbeard's Ghost, Hot Millions* (also cowrote; Oscar nominated for screenplay); 1969: *Viva Max!;* 1972: *Hammersmith Is Out;* 1976: *One of Our Dinosaurs Is Missing, Logan's Run;* 1977: *The Last Remake of Beau Geste;* 1979: *Ashanti;* 1981: *The Great Muppet Caper, Charlie Chan and the Curse of the Dragon Queen* (as Chan); 1987: *Memed My Hawk* (wrote, directed, starred); 1989: *The French Revolution.*

VACCARO, BRENDA. Actress. *(b. Nov. 18, 1939, Brooklyn, N.Y.)* Sparkling, husky-voiced Broadway star who has been less well served by Hollywood, even though she got good notices right from the start, in her first significant film role, playing one of Jon Voight's customers in *Midnight Cowboy* (1969). She's at her best in wisecracking comic turns such as Deborah Raffin's man-chasing pal in *Once Is Not Enough* (1975, for which she got an Oscar nomination), but too often she's cast as shrieking harridans, as in *Zorro, the Gay Blade* (1981), *Water* (1985), and *Cookie* (1989). She did fine work in relatively routine roles in such pictures as *Where It's At* (1969), *I Love My . . . Wife* (1970), *Summertree* (1971), and *Capricorn One* (1978), and even survived a slasher film, *The House by the Lake* (1977). She also achieved the distinction of doing both an "Airport" movie (the 1977 edition) and an "Airplane" spoof (the 1982 sequel). Other credits include *Fast Charlie, The Moonbeam Rider* (1979), *Supergirl* (1984), *Heart of Midnight* (1988), *Ten Little Indians* (1989), *The Masque of the Red Death* (1992). A prolific TV player in made-fors (such as 1971's *Honor Thy Father)* and series ("Sara," 1976; "Dear Detective," 1979), she won an Emmy for a 1976 special called "The Shape of Things."

VADIM, ROGER. Director, screenwriter, actor. *(b. Jan. 26, 1928, Paris, as Roger Vadim Plemiannikov.)* New Wave director at least as well known for his romantic liaisons with his female stars as for the films in which he directed them. A former stage actor and journalist, he burst upon the international cinema scene with the sexually charged *And God Created Woman* (1956), which catapulted his then-wife Brigitte Bardot to worldwide fame. His subsequent successes include *Clair de lune* (1958, with Bardot), *Dangerous Liaisons* (1960, with Jeanne Moreau), the "Pride" segment of *The Seven Deadly Sins, Warriors Rest* (both 1962, the latter with Bardot), *Vice and Virtue* (1963, with Catherine Deneuve), and *Circle of Love* (1964), with Jane Fonda. He enjoyed international notoriety when he directed second wife Fonda in the sexy sci-fi comic strip adaptation *Barbarella* (1968); they later collaborated on one segment of *Spirits of the Dead* (also 1968). He made an effective Hollywood debut with the sexy black comedy *Pretty Maids All in a Row* (1971), but it was to be his only American film of note. Later films include *Don Juan '73* (1973), *Charlotte* (1974, aka *La Jeune Fille assassinée), Hot Touch* (1982), *Surprise Party* (1983), and a lackluster 1987 remake of *And God Created Woman* with Rebecca De Mornay in the Bardot role. He also took small acting roles in *Rich and Famous* (1981) and *Into the Night* (1985). In addition to wives Bardot and Fonda, Vadim has been romantically linked with actresses Catherine Deneuve (who bore him a son, Christian, also an actor) and Marie-Christine Barrault. He wrote a 1975 autobiography, "Memoirs of the Devil," and a 1987 memoir modestly titled "Bardot, Deneuve, Fonda: My Life With the Three Most Beautiful Women in the World."

VALENTINO, RUDOLPH. Actor. *(b. May 6, 1895, Castellaneta, Italy; d. Aug. 23, 1926.)* For all the excitement Rudolph Valentino generated, his starring career spanned barely six years, and for two of those years he was off the screen altogether. He came to America in 1913, and worked as a landscape gardener, dishwasher, waiter, gigolo, and petty criminal before establishing a minor career as a ballroom dancer. He was befriended by

Alla Nazimova, and toured with her on stage. Arriving in Hollywood in 1917, Valentino quickly became known to casting directors as a reliable "oily Latin villain" type. He appeared in such films as *A Society Sensation* (1918), *The Delicious Little Devil, A Rogue's Romance, Virtuous Sinners* (all 1919), and gained some notice in *Eyes of Youth* (1919) with Clara Kimball Young, and in *Once to Every Woman* (1920), supporting Dorothy Phillips. Screenwriter June Mathis brought Valentino to the attention of Metro director Rex Ingram, who cast him as Julio in *The Four Horsemen of the Apocalypse* (1921). Based on a popular novel by Vicente Blasco Ibanez, *Horsemen* was a hit, and featured a memorable scene of Valentino dancing the tango. The actor quickly scored again with Ingram's *The Conquering Power* (1921), and in a self-consciously arty version of *Camille* (also 1921) with Nazimova in the leading role.

Metro was unwilling or unable to capitalize on their new star's popularity, and Valentino signed with Paramount. The first film under his new contract was *The Sheik* (1921), based on a lurid "rape fantasy" by British author Edith M. Hull; it was little more than a routine program picture but it created a sensation just the same. Just as the female "vamp" was an icon in the teens, the male "sheik" became an archetype in the 1920s. Valentino transcended the type, however: He was a decent actor and he brought a great deal of charm and humor to his roles.

Married briefly to actress Jean Acker in 1920, Valentino's second wife was a home-grown girl with artistic pretensions who called herself Natasha Rambova. She was appalled by what she perceived to be the crass exploitation of Valentino's talent in *Moran of the Lady Letty, Beyond the Rocks,* which costarred Gloria Swanson, and *The Young Rajah* (all 1922), but she conveniently ignored Paramount's attempt to duplicate the success of *The Four Horsemen* with another adaptation of an Ibanez novel, *Blood and Sand* (also 1922). Rambova took charge of his career and became such a nuisance that Paramount barred her from the Valentino sets. The couple quit in protest, and went on an extended personal appearance tour. When he returned in 1924, Natacha became art director on a bloated adaptation of Booth Tarkington's *Monsieur Beaucaire,* but the couple split up soon after. He also starred in *A Sainted Devil* (1924).

Valentino went on to make *Cobra* (1925) for Paramount release, then signed with United Artists to make *The Eagle* (1925) and *Son of the Sheik* (1926). Both vehicles took advantage of Valentino's humor and swashbuckling athleticism as well as his bedside manner. Shortly before the New York release of *Son of the Sheik,* Valentino was admitted to the hospital with a perforated ulcer. He developed peritonitis and died at age 31. The mad public frenzy surrounding his funeral helped further the Valentino legend, and it was June Mathis who quietly paid to have Valentino's body shipped to Hollywood and interred in her family crypt. (Mathis herself died the following year.) The annual visit of a "woman in black" to Valentino's grave has always been good for a couple of columns or a brief TV news segment, and keeps the Valentino name—and mystique—alive for a public that is probably unfamiliar with his actual films.

VAN CLEEF, LEE. Actor. (b. Jan. 9, 1925, Somerville, N.J.; d. Dec. 14, 1989.) With his steely, squinty eyes, pencil mustache, and coiled-spring body language, the lean, mean Van Cleef was an archetypal Western and action-picture villain, making dozens of movies beginning with 1952's *High Noon.* He worked in all kinds of films, primarily Westerns and crime dramas, including *Untamed Frontier, Kansas City Confidential, The Lawless Breed* (all 1952), *Arena* (1953), *Rails Into Laramie* (1954), *Tribute to a Bad Man* (1956), *Gunfight at the O.K. Corral* (1957), *The Young Lions* (1958), *The Man Who Shot Liberty Valance,* and *How the West Was Won* (both 1962). Always cast in supporting roles in these pictures, he graduated to lead villain opposite Clint Eastwood in two Sergio Leone-directed "spaghetti Westerns," *For a Few Dollars More* (1965) and *The Good, the Bad, and the Ugly* (1967). Van Cleef's popularity in those pictures made him a bona-fide star in Europe during the late 1960s and early 1970s, and he made several other pictures there, including *Death Rides a Horse* (1967), *The Big Gundown* (1968), *Sabata, Barquero, El Condor* (all 1970), *Captain Apache, Return of Sabata* (1971), *The*

Magnificent Seven Ride! (1972), *Mean Frank and Crazy Tony* (1973), *Take a Hard Ride* (1975), *The Stranger and the Gunfighter, Crime Boss* (both 1976), and *The Rip-Off* (1978). He continued to work, less actively, in the U.S. as well, snaring an occasional mainstream movie like *The Octagon* (1980, with Chuck Norris) and *Escape From New York* (1981). He costarred in a short-lived martial arts TV series, "The Masters" (1984). His final films were mostly grade-Z product such as *Jungle Raiders* (1984), *Code Name: Wild Geese, Armed Response* (both 1986), and *Thieves of Fortune* (1990). In his last years he parodied his villain image for a series of snack-food TV commercials.

VAN DAMME, JEAN-CLAUDE. Actor. *(b. Oct. 18, 1960, Brussels, Belgium.)* Former karate champion who, like predecessors Bruce Lee and Chuck Norris, stars in action pictures highlighting his martial-arts skills. He has bounced around the various subcategories of the chop-socky genre, working in a sci-fi vehicle (1989's *Cyborg*), a spy thriller (1988's *Black Eagle*), and a gladiator-for-hire drama (1991's *Lionheart*). His thick-as-Heinz accent, wooden line readings, and noticeable lack of humor and irony mark him as one of the World's Worst Actors—he played twins in *Double Impact* (1991) and was twice as unconvincing as usual—but this handsome performer tries hard and, unlike fellow horrible actor/martial-arts star Steven Seagal, projects a certain modesty that could almost be mistaken for Gallic charm. (But, of course, it can't be Gallic charm—the guy's Belgian!) Recent credits include *Universal Soldier* (1992), *Nowhere to Run,* a cameo in *Last Action Hero,* John Woo's American debut picture *Hard Target* (all 1993), and *Timecop* (1994).

VAN DEVERE, TRISH. Actress. *(b. March 9, 1945, Englewood Cliffs, N.J., as Patricia Dressel.)* This skilled, attractive actress was one of the 1970s' hot prospects for stardom, but after making a few interesting films her career stalled and never really got going again. She was billed as Patricia Van Devere in a small but solid supporting turn in *The Landlord,* became Trish in *Where's Poppa?* (both 1970, in the latter as George Segal's frustrated girlfriend), and won good notices for her leading role in the divorced-singles drama *One Is a Lonely Number* (1972). Her marriage to much-older actor George C. Scott led to several onscreen collaborations, including *The Last Run* (1971), *The Day of the Dolphin* (1973), the disastrous Scott-directed, desert-island incest drama *The Savage Is Loose* (1974), the likable parody *Movie, Movie* (1978), and *The Changeling* (1979). A well-respected stage actress, she appeared primarily in cheap movies during the 1980s, including such stinkers as *The Hearse* (1980), *Hollywood Vice Squad* (1986), and *Messenger of Death* (1988) which teamed her with Charles Bronson. She got major billing, but minor screen time, in a 1993 TV movie with Scott, *Curacao.*

VAN DOREN, MAMIE. Actress. *(b. Feb. 6, 1931, Rowena, S.D., as Joan Lucille Olander).* Platinum-blond bombshell often referred to as the poor man's Lana Turner. Van Doren, a former dance-band singer whose first movie was *Jet Pilot* (filmed in 1950 but unreleased until 1957), is best remembered for a series of showy roles in cheap 1950s melodramas that emphasized her physical endowments rather than her somewhat meager dramatic abilities. *Untamed Youth, The Girl in Black Stockings* (both 1957), *High School Confidential!* (1958), *The Beat Generation, Guns, Girls and Gangsters, Girls Town, Born Reckless, The Big Operator* (all 1959), *The Private Lives of Adam and Eve, College Confidential,* and *Sex Kittens Go to College* (1960) were just a few of those epics. (She did have a good role in 1958's *Teacher's Pet,* an A film starring Clark Gable.) She also appeared in the unforgettable *The Navy vs. the Night Monsters* (1966). Van Doren dropped out of Hollywood altogether in the late 1960s, concentrating on a jet-set life-style in the company of celebrities and athletes, particularly (then) quarterback Joe Namath. She made a brief comeback in the 1980s, appearing in *Boarding School* (1986) to no discernible advantage. As one of the few surviving sex symbols of that era, she's become something of a pop culture queen in recent years, hosting B-movie festivals, making personal appearances, and the like. (She even turned up, as herself, on an episode of "L.A. Law.") Her autobiography, "Playing the Field," was published in 1987. She was married at one time to bandleader Ray Anthony, who appeared with her in *High School Confidential!* and *Girls Town.*

VAN DYKE, DICK. Actor. *(b. Dec. 13, 1925, West Plains, Mo.)* Lanky, likable comic actor best known as the pratfall-prone TV writer Rob Petrie in the beloved sitcom "The Dick Van Dyke Show," (1961–66), which earned him three Emmy awards. He'd already starred in the musical *Bye Bye Birdie* (1963, recreating his Broadway role), the timeless Disney classic *Mary Poppins* (1964, as Bert the chimney sweep, sidewalk artist and one-man band), and *What a Way to Go!* (1964, as one of Shirley MacLaine's many husbands). After the demise of his TV series, however, he repeatedly failed to find movie vehicles worthy of his enormous talent. *Divorce American Style* (1967) was an intelligent comedy in which he and Debbie Reynolds were cast against type, *Chitty Chitty Bang Bang* (1968) was a mediocre musical fantasy with Disney aspirations, and *The Comic* (1969) was a sincere but unsuccessful attempt to fashion a portrait of a self-destructive silent-screen clown. Most of the others weren't even up to that level: *The Art of Love* (1965), *Lt. Robin Crusoe, USN* (1966, for Disney), *Fitzwilly* (1967), *Never a Dull Moment* (1968, for Disney), and *Some Kind of a Nut* (1969). *Cold Turkey* (1971) was a biting satire that stood out from the crowd. Van Dyke seemed to have a hard time finding his footing again even on television, with two failed series and a season with Carol Burnett; admitting that he was an alcoholic, he played such a character in the TV movie *The Morning After* (1974). He also starred as a priest accused of murder in the failed feature *The Runner Stumbles* (1979). In 1990 Warren Beatty cast him against type as a crooked D.A. in *Dick Tracy,* and in 1992 he launched a series of TV movies as a doctor/sleuth that became the weekly series "Diagnosis Murder" in 1993. His brother Jerry is also a comic actor; his son Barry costars with him on his newest TV series.

VAN DYKE, W. S. Director. *(b. Mar. 21, 1889, San Diego, as Woodbridge Strong Van Dyke II; d. Feb. 5, 1943.)* Back when the studio system reigned in Hollywood, "One Take Woody" Van Dyke was (from the viewpoint of the studio head, at least) the ideal movie director. While he had no special style of his own, he was a proficient craftsman who could, on the orders of his superiors at Metro-Goldwyn-Mayer, get a film—any film—in on time and under budget. Van Dyke started out as a child actor in vaudeville. He entered the movies as an assistant director, working with D. W. Griffith on *Intolerance* (1916). He honed his craft during the late teens and the twenties directing dozens of action serials and now-forgotten features, especially Westerns, and came into his own upon taking over for his codirector, Robert Flaherty, on *White Shadow of the South Seas* (1928). (The rugged Van Dyke later directed the problem-plagued *Trader Horn* in Africa in 1930, and another naturalistic, documentary-style feature, *Eskimo,* in 1933.)

Van Dyke could direct everything and anything, and did, during his long tenure at MGM: Westerns, musicals, mysteries, epics, jungle dramas, urban melodramas, and costume pictures. Van Dyke earned two Best Director Academy Award nominations, for *The Thin Man* (1934) and *San Francisco* (1936). Four of his films (1931's *Trader Horn, The Thin Man,* 1935's *Naughty Marietta, San Francisco)* won Best Picture nominations; and he guided his share of actors (William Powell, Spencer Tracy, Norma Shearer, Robert Morley) to Oscar nominations or wins.

OTHER FILMS INCLUDE: 1927: *Winners of the Wilderness, California, Wyoming;* 1931: *The Cuban Love Song;* 1932: *Tarzan, the Ape Man;* 1933: *Penthouse, The Prizefighter and the Lady;* 1934: *Manhattan Melodrama, Forsaking All Others;* 1935: *Naughty Marietta, Rose Marie;* 1936: *The Devil Is a Sissy, After the Thin Man;* 1937: *Personal Property, They Gave Him a Gun, Rosalie;* 1938: *Marie Antoinette, Sweethearts;* 1939: *It's a Wonderful World, Andy Hardy Gets Spring Fever, Another Thin Man;* 1940: *I Take This Woman, Bitter Sweet;* 1941: *Rage in Heaven, Shadow of the Thin Man, Dr. Kildare's Victory;* 1942: *I Married an Angel, Cairo, Journey for Margaret.*

VAN EYCK, PETER. Actor. *(b. July 16, 1913, Steinwehr, Germany, as Gotz von Eick; d. July 15, 1969.)* The very epitome of the Teutonic-Terror type, Van Eyck started playing Nazis on-screen in 1943—the year he became an American citizen. A former musician who'd left his native land when Hitler came to power in the early 1930s, he was familiar to American moviegoers throughout the war years, and then afterward to international audiences in a plethora of films made on both sides of the Atlantic. Van Eyck was most effective (even when not playing Nazis) as cold-blooded, impassive heavies. Among his more notable performances: as one of the drivers of the nitro-filled trucks in *The Wages of Fear* (1952), the reincarnated villain in Fritz Lang's remake of his own 1932 classic *The Thousand Eyes of Dr. Mabuse* (1960), and in the leading role of *The Brain* (1965), a surprisingly good remake of *Donovan's Brain.*
OTHER FILMS INCLUDE: 1943: *The Moon Is Down, Edge of Darkness, Action in the North Atlantic, Five Graves to Cairo;* 1944: *Address Unknown, The Hitler Gang;* 1949: *Hello, Fraulein;* 1951: *The Desert Fox;* 1954: *Night People;* 1955: *Tarzan's Hidden Jungle, Mr. Arkadin;* 1956: *Attack!, Run for the Sun;* 1959: *Sweetheart of the Gods;* 1961: *World in My Pocket;* 1965: *The Spy Who Came in From the Cold;* 1967: *Assignment to Kill;* 1968: *Shalako;* 1969: *Code Name, Red Roses.*

VAN FLEET, JO. Actress. *(b. Dec. 30, 1919, Oakland, Calif.)* Already a prominent, award-winning character player on Broadway, this plain-featured actress startled moviegoers in her 1955 film debut, playing James Dean's madam-mother in Elia Kazan's adaptation of John Steinbeck's novel *East of Eden,* a performance that won her a Best Supporting Actress Oscar. Her subsequent film work was spotty, but she always appeared to good advantage, especially when cast as abrasive, coarse women such as the drunken mistress of Kirk Douglas' Doc Holliday in *Gunfight at the O.K. Corral* (1957).
OTHER FILMS INCLUDE: 1955: *The Rose Tattoo, I'll Cry Tomorrow;* 1956: *The King and Four Queens;* 1958: *The Sea Wall;* 1960: *Wild River;* 1967: *Cool Hand Luke* (as Arletta); 1968: *I Love You, Alice B. Toklas;* 1969: *80 Steps to Jonah;* 1971: *The Gang That Couldn't Shoot Straight;* 1976: *The Tenant.*

VAN PEEBLES, MARIO. Actor, director. *(b. Jan. 15, 1957, Mexico City.)* Melvin Van Peebles once told his son that Hollywood wasn't predominantly black or predominantly white: it was predominantly green. With that in mind, young Mario got a B.A. in economics from Columbia University, and then got a job with a film investment firm, before pursuing a career in the more glamorous end of show business. He'd actually made his screen debut in the opening scene of his father's 1971 feature *Sweet Sweetback's Baadasssss Song,* but now, considerably more mature, he earned parts in such films as *Heartbreak Ridge* (1986, for which he won an NAACP Image Award), and *Jaws The Revenge* (1987), and such TV movies as *Children of the Night* (1985) and *Blue Bayou* (1990).
He got his first chance to direct on his own starring series, "Sonny Spoon" (1988), and went on to direct episodes of "Wiseguy," "21 Jump Street," and others, including an after-school special, "Malcolm Takes a Shot," in which he also appeared.
In 1990 he collaborated with his father on a poorly received comedy feature, *Identity Crisis* (serving as writer, unofficial codirector, and coproducer), but it was 1991's *New Jack City* that really launched Mario's career behind the camera. This hyperkinetic, melodramatic antidrug movie certainly won Van Peebles notice as a novice director; he followed it with the black-themed Western *Posse* (1993), in which he also starred, then directed his father's script *Panther* (1995). In 1994 he starred in *Gunmen* and appeared in *Highlander 3.*

VAN PEEBLES, MELVIN. Director, writer, composer, actor. *(b. Aug. 21, 1932, Chicago.)* Something more than a one-picture wonder, something less than the major filmmaker he promised to be at one time, Van Peebles has had a career that can certainly be described as broadranging. After all, he has written a Broadway musical ("Ain't Supposed to Die a Natural Death") as well as a guide to commodities trading!

While living in France, Van Peebles made his feature-film debut as the director, writer, and composer of *The Story of a Three Day Pass* (1967), which generated sufficient interest to snare him a "mainstream" directing job, on the satirical comedy *Watermelon Man* (1970). But it was his self-financed, self-distributed *Sweet Sweetback's Baadasssss Song* (1971), a potent slice of black street life, that cemented his reputation, and makes him to this day a figure for study in the field of African-American filmmaking. Unfortunately, his output since then has been erratic and largely undistinguished. *Don't Play Us Cheap* (1973) was an adaptation of his Broadway play; *Greased Lightning* (1977) was a disappointing studio scriptwriting assignment. *Identity Crisis* (1990), a comic farce made in collaboration with his son Mario, was an out-and-out embarrassment. The elder Van Peebles has also appeared as an actor in *America* (1982), *Jaws The Revenge* (1987, with his son), *O.C. & Stiggs* (also 1987), and *Posse* (1993, with Mario). In 1995, Mario directed Melvin's screenplay *Panther*, about the Black Panther Party.

VAN SANT, GUS. Director, writer. (b. July 24, 1952, Louisville, Ky.) Experimental filmmaker who has established himself as one of the most influential voices in independent films. After a stint making commercials for an ad agency in New York, Van Sant moved to Portland, made numerous short films and a small independent feature, *Alice in Hollywood*. His film *Mala Noche* (1986) gained much critical praise; his follow-up feature, *Drugstore Cowboy* (1989), a credible, low-key tale of drug addicts on the run, won Best Picture and Director citations from the National Society of Film Critics. Van Sant's *My Own Private Idaho* (1991), about a pair of male hustlers (Keanu Reeves and River Phoenix), confirmed his status as an important chronicler of society's fringe dwellers. After breaking off from a much-anticipated Hollywood project about San Francisco city supervisor Harvey Milk, Van Sant directed a disappointing adaptation of Tom Robbins' *Even Cowgirls Get the Blues* (1994), then followed with the dark comedy *To Die For* (1995). He also directed a Red Hot Chili Peppers music video.

VARDA, AGNES. Director, screenwriter. (b. May 30, 1928, Brussels.) Innovative, pioneering talent who began her career as the official photographer of Jean Vilar's Théâtre National Populaire. With virtually no knowledge of filmmaking, she wrote and directed *La Pointe courte* (1954), a low-budget feature that contrasted a young couple's marital problems with the struggles of fishermen and their families in a Mediterranean village. The film's narrative structure was a precursor to stylistic devices later used by France's New Wave directors, and Francois Truffaut wrote, at the time, "It is difficult to form a judgment of a film in which the true and the false, the true-false and the false-true are intermingled according to barely perceived rules." Varda made several short films (including two commissioned by the French National Tourist Office) before her next features, *Cleo From 5 to 7* (1962, told in "real time" as a singer awaits a cancer diagnosis) and the odd love triangle *Le Bonheur* (1965). Some critics complained about the surfeit of visual elegance in both, but they confirmed her as a filmmaker to watch. She followed *The Creatures* (1966) with two documentaries made in the U.S.—*Uncle Yanko* and *The Black Panthers* (both 1968)—and after the bizarrely experimental *Lions Love* (1969), came back strongly with *One Sings, the Other Doesn't* (1977), a feminist-tinged study of two very different women friends. Varda concentrated on documentaries for the next several years before resurfacing with *Vagabond* (1985), one of her best, a powerful, near-documentary-style look at events leading to the death of a young drifter. Since then, she has made *Jane B. by Agnes V.* (1987, with actress Jane Birkin) and *Kung Fu Master!* (1987, cowritten with Birkin), about the relationship between a grown woman and a young boy. Varda was married to filmmaker Jacques Demy from 1962 until his death in 1990; she paid tribute to him in the lovely *Jacquot de Nantes* (1991, aka *Jacquot*), which filters his life through the films he made.

VARSI, DIANE. Actress. (b. Feb. 23, 1938, San Mateo, Calif.; d. Nov. 19, 1992.)

The striking Varsi didn't need Hollywood stardom to complicate her life; by age 21 she had already been married twice. The product of a broken home, she went from one menial job to another, and had barely enrolled in acting school when she was discovered and cast in a star-making role as Lana Turner's daughter in the big-budget soap opera *Peyton Place* (1957). Varsi's heartfelt performance earned her an Academy Award nomination, and she became a valuable property to home studio 20th Century-Fox. She was excellent in *From Hell to Texas, Ten North Frederick* (both 1958), and *Compulsion* (1959), but broke her contract in 1959 to "retire." When she sought film work in the late 1960s, she was spurned by most of the town. Independent filmmakers didn't care, though; former costar Don Murrary gave her a supporting role in *Sweet Love, Bitter* (1967), and she appeared in such exploitation fare as *Wild in the Streets, Killers Three* (both 1968), and *Bloody Mama* (1970). Varsi's subsequent film appearances were sporadic, generally in low-budget or offbeat projects, including 1971's antiwar drama *Johnny Got His Gun* and 1977's well-received *I Never Promised You a Rose Garden*.

VEIDT, CONRAD. Actor. *(b. Jan. 22, 1893, Potsdam, Germany; d. Apr. 3, 1943.)* You may remember him as Major Strasser, the charming but ruthless Nazi officer in *Casablanca* (1942) . . . or perhaps as Jaffar, the sinister sorcerer in *The Thief of Bagdad* (1940) . . . or maybe as Cesare, the stiffly stalking somnambulist in *The Cabinet of Dr. Caligari* (1919), his most frequently revived silent film. Whatever the role, this slender, saturnine German with the piercing eyes and cruel mouth was sure to make an indelible impression. A protégé of famed theatrical impresario Max Reinhardt, Veidt made his stage debut in 1913 and began appearing in Germany's unique, expressionistic silent films in 1917. He played a variety of roles, ranging from Chopin to Dr. Jekyll and Mr. Hyde to King Richard to Lucifer himself before achieving international fame as the star of *The Student of Prague* (1926).

In 1927 Veidt went to Hollywood, where American directors were beginning to dabble in German Expressionism, and

contributed a delightfully eccentric performance as King Louis XI to *The Beloved Rogue* (1927). He remained to star in Universal's *The Man Who Laughs* (1928, playing the grotesquely disfigured protagonist of that Germanic drama) and *The Last Performance* (1929) before returning to Germany. He starred in *Congress Dances* (1931), *Rasputin* (1932), *Jew Suss* (1933), and *The Legend of William Tell* (1934), among others, then fled to England with his Jewish wife to escape Nazi persecution. Veidt continued to work in film, both in England and France, appearing in *The Passing of the Third Floor Back* (1935), *King of the Damned* (1936), *Dark Journey, Under the Red Robe* (both 1937), and *The Spy in Black* (1939), to name a few, before sailing to America again in 1940. Ironically, Hollywood cast him mostly as Nazis for the rest of his career.

OTHER FILMS INCLUDE: 1940: *Contraband, Escape;* 1941: *A Woman's Face, Whistling in the Dark;* 1942: *Nazi Agent* (top-billed in a dual role), *All Through the Night;* 1943: *Above Suspicion.*

VELEZ, LUPE. Actress. *(b. July 18, 1908, San Luis Potosi, Mexico, as Maria Guadalupe Velez de Villalobos; d. Dec. 14, 1944.)* The tempestuous "Mexican Spitfire" lived her role onscreen and off; her high-octane personality made the petite Latin beauty a familiar figure in Hollywood's social circle, especially during her 1933–38 marriage to screen Tarzan Johnny Weissmuller. The convent-educated Velez danced on stage in her native country and in Hollywood nightclubs before making her screen debut in a 1927 Laurel and Hardy short, *Sailors, Beware!* That same year Douglas Fairbanks cast her as his leading lady in *The Gaucho,* and her film career was off and running. She nearly always played the same part, that of a hot-tempered, passionate woman used to getting her own way, in such films as *Stand and Deliver* (1928), *Wolf Song* (1929), *Lady of the Pavements* (1929, directed by D. W. Griffith), *Hell Harbor* (1930), *The Cuban Love Song, Resurrection* (both 1931), *The Squaw Man* (also 1931, in a surprisingly subdued and effective performance), *The Half-Naked Truth, Kongo* (both 1932), *Hot Pepper* (1933), *Palooka, Strictly Dynamite* (both 1934), and *Hollywood Party* (also 1934, reunited with Laurel and Hardy). She went to England to star in *Gypsy Melody* (1936) and *Mad About Money* (1938, aka *He Loved an Actress).*

Sound didn't faze Velez one little bit; she sang passably well, and mangled the English language in a hundred ways, freely mixing Spanish invective into her mercurial outbursts. In 1939 she first played Carmelita, a fiery Mexican entertainer "adopted" by advertising executive Donald Woods, in a modest slapstick programmer titled *The Girl From Mexico,* the unexpected success of which prompted RKO to spin off a series. There were seven more "Mexican Spitfire" movies made between 1940 and 1943, with titles like *Mexican Spitfire's Baby* (1941) and *Mexican Spitfire Sees a Ghost* (1942); the scripts were astonishingly redundant, but Velez's bubbly personality (and the antics of costar Leon Errol) kept them alive. Over at Columbia she continued in character for *Redhead From Manhattan* (1943), and made her last screen appearance in a 1944 version of *Nana.* In that year, despondent over the latest in a long string of failed romances since her divorce from Weissmuller, Velez committed suicide by taking an overdose of sleeping pills.

VERHOEVEN, PAUL. Director. *(b. July 18, 1938, Amsterdam.)* This helmer of violent, big-budget crowd pleasers got his filmmaking start as a documentarian for the Royal Dutch Navy. After working for Dutch television he took his first feature assignment, *Business Is Business* (1971). His second film, the sexy *Turkish Delight* (1973), starred fellow countryman and frequent collaborator Rutger Hauer, who also top-lined *Keetje Tippel* (1975). Verhoeven's initial stateside exposure—with the release here of the war saga *Soldier of Orange* (1979), the sexually frank *Spetters* (1980), and the erotic thriller *The Fourth Man* (also 1979)—won him contracts to direct films in America. His next three films were all ultraviolent fantasies: *Flesh + Blood* (1985), *RoboCop* (1987), and *Total Recall* (1990). Rowdy, overblown, and satirical, these three pictures confirmed Verhoeven's talent as a creator of muscular, fast-moving films. But the box-office success of *Basic Instinct* (1992), a gritty, sexually explicit thriller (following two other major hits), allowed Verhoeven the freedom to pick and choose his next projects. His next was *Showgirls* (1995).

VIDOR, KING. Director, producer, screenwriter, actor. *(b. Feb. 8, 1894, Galveston, Tex.; d. Nov. 1, 1982.)* Although mention of his name doesn't ring the same bells that "Ford," "Hawks," or "Hitchcock" does, his is nonetheless one of Hollywood's most distinguished careers, spanning nearly half a century and encompassing a formidable number of great films, genuine classics, and intensely personal projects that he managed to get made in the midst of the studio system. Born into a well-to-do family, he was obsessed with moving pictures at an early age and even worked in the neighborhood nickelodeon. Vidor actually broke into filmmaking in his native Texas, shooting news events and later selling the footage to newsreel companies. He came to Hollywood in 1915 with his actress wife Florence, and proceeded to write, direct, and even star in a handful of short comedies.

In 1919 he graduated to feature films, writing and directing such pictures as *The Turn in the Road, The Other Half,* and *Poor Relations,* the latter two starring his wife. The next year they made two more films together, *The Jack-Knife Man* and *The Family Honor.* In 1921 he directed his lifelong friend Colleen Moore in *The Sky Pilot* and the following year directed legendary stage actress Laurette Taylor in an adaptation of her stage success *Peg o' My Heart* (1922). By this time Florence was well established as a picture personality, and shortly thereafter the couple formed Florence Vidor Productions, for which King made 1922's *The Real Adventure, Dusk to Dawn,* and *Conquering the Woman.* They dissolved their professional partnership shortly afterward, and were soon divorced as well. Vidor moved to Metro, where he directed *Three Wise Fools* (the first of several pictures with next-wife-to-be Eleanor Boardman), *The Woman of Bronze* (both 1923), *Wild Oranges, Happiness, Wine of Youth* (all 1924), and *Proud Flesh* (1925).

The turning point in Vidor's career came with his production of *The Big Parade* (1925), one of the highest-grossing of all silent films and an unforgettable antiwar masterpiece that still enthralls audiences today. His achievement in blending scenes of prewar domestic tranquility, the camaraderie of service life, and the horror of battle ranks among the supreme achievements of the early American cinema. Hailed as one of the screen's master craftsmen, Vidor teamed *Big Parade*'s John Gilbert with Lillian Gish for a handsome but unexciting version of *La Bohème* (1926), and directed Gilbert again in *Bardelys the Magnificent* that same year. Then he used his clout to make the decidedly uncommercial drama *The Crowd* (1928), a fable about the loneliness and isolation of individuals living and working in the big city. Simple and affecting, it earned Vidor his first Oscar nomination. That same year he helmed two delightful and utterly unpretentious comedies starring Marion Davies (in fact, the best films she ever made), *Show People* (an affectionate Hollywood fable) and *The Patsy.*

Vidor's first talkie was another unusual and "personal" project: the all-black musical drama, *Hallelujah* (1929, for which he snagged another Academy Award nomination). With naturalistic use of sound (some of it post-dubbed), it showed Vidor in full command of his medium. He directed Marion Davies again in *Not So Dumb* (1930), then made an epic Western, *Billy the Kid* (1930), in the short-lived 70mm Grandeur format, and followed with such handsome, thoughtful entertainments as *The Champ* (earning another Oscar nod), *Street Scene* (both 1931, skillfully adapting an Elmer Rice play to the screen), *Bird of Paradise, Cynara* (both 1932), and *The Stranger's Return* (1933, a charming, underrated film almost totally forgotten today). Then Vidor hit upon an idea that was too radical for the studios: *Our Daily Bread* (1934), a Depression-era landmark extolling the virtues of communal, back-to-the-soil living. So determined was he to make this film (in the midst of the Depression) that he found independent financing—a most unusual move for a commercially successful director-producer.

After slogging through *The Wedding Night* (1935), a turgid and unsuccessful Anna Sten vehicle, and *So Red the Rose* (1935), Vidor bounced back with *The Texas Rangers* (1936), the best-known version of the classic weepie *Stella Dallas* (1937), *The Citadel* (1938, a superb, British-made drama that scored him another Oscar nomination), the epic *Northwest Passage, Comrade X* (both 1940), and the remarkably intelligent and mature social comedy *H. M. Pulham, Esq.* (1941). (He also shot a few days' footage for 1939's *The Wizard of Oz.*) His next "pet project," *An American Romance* (1944), was an epic saga about an immigrant steelworker and his rise to power; after MGM cut a huge chunk out of the picture, Vidor left the studio in a huff. David O. Selznick talked him into helming his elephantine super-Western, *Duel in the Sun* (1946), which turned out extremely well from a production standpoint, although its lurid pulp-story plot brought the picture a fair amount of well-deserved derision. He directed a segment of *On Our Merry Way* (1948), then closed out the decade at Warner Bros., where he directed two memorable 1949 pictures, *The Fountainhead,* from Ayn Rand's novel, and *Beyond the Forest,* a Bette Davis vehicle that has since become something of a camp classic.

Vidor's output dwindled in the 1950s, although he still turned out some interesting and notable films, including *Lightning Strikes Twice* (1951), *Japanese War Bride, Ruby Gentry* (both 1952), *Man Without a Star* (1955), *War and Peace* (1956, a sprawling adaptation of Tolstoy that landed him yet another Academy Award nomination), and *Solomon and Sheba* (1959). He also made occasional cameo appearances, and even had a sizable screen role in *Love and Money* (1980). In 1953 Vidor wrote his autobiography, "A Tree Is a Tree," and a quarter-century later penned "King Vidor on Filmmaking," but never got around to finishing a book on the long-unsolved death of silent-era director William Desmond Taylor, based on his personal investigation of the case. (His research became the foundation of Sidney Kirkpatrick's "A Cast of Killers.") Vidor, who never won an Oscar in competition, got a special one in 1979 in recognition of his extraordinary body of work. His career is one of the most distinctive (and impressive) in the history of American cinema.

VIGO, JEAN. Director. *(b. Apr. 26, 1905, Paris, as Jean Bonaventure de Vigo; d. Oct. 26, 1934.)* Though he only completed three short films and one feature in his life, Vigo had an extraordinary effect on motion pictures. The son of a French anarchist known as Miguel Almereyda, Vigo's childhood was an unhappy one: plagued by respiratory problems, he lived in different hospitals, sanitoriums, and boarding schools. After studying at the Sorbonne, he worked with the French cameraman Leonce-Henry Burel and eventually bought his own movie camera. His first film, *À propos de Nice* (1930), a "documentary" about a Riviera resort, savagely juxtaposes images of the idle rich with the poor of Nice. *Taris, champion de natation* (1931), ostensibly a profile of a swimmer, becomes a study of rhythm and cinematic effects. Vigo's next work, *Zero for Conduct* (1933), a chronicle of revolution at a French boarding school, redressed all of his personal grievances from childhood. Banned until 1945, the film is real, surreal, and magical in its depiction of the children's world; it had a profound impact on many of France's later New Wave directors, as well as Lindsay Anderson, who borrowed the film's central premise for his feature-film *if . . .* (1968). *L'Atalante* (1934) was Vigo's only full-length feature. A beautiful, sensuous story of love lost and found, it was severely recut by distributors upon release and restored only years later. It now stands as a masterpiece of his sadly brief career: sad, harsh, lyrical, hopeful.

VINCENT, JAN-MICHAEL. Actor. *(b. July 15, 1944, Ventura, Calif.)* Handsome, athletic blond actor who often played the youthful apprentice to experienced men of action, from contract killers (1972's *The Mechanic*, in which his mentor was Charles Bronson) to stuntmen (1978's *Hooper*, as the protégé of a veteran stuntman played by Burt Reynolds). Vincent, who debuted in *Journey to Shiloh* (1968), also played leads in modestly budgeted, unimportant but generally popular films (mostly actioners) such as *Buster and Billie* (1974), *White Line Fever* (1975), *Baby Blue Marine* (1976), and *Damnation Alley* (1977). Other credits include *The Undefeated* (1969), *Tributes* (1970, telefilm), *Going Home* (1971), *The World's Greatest Athlete* (1973), *Bite the Bullet* (1975), *Vigilante Force* (1976), *Shadow of the Hawk* (1976), *Big Wednesday* (1978), and *Defiance* (1980). Although he fared well in the 1980s miniseries "The Winds of War" and the

TV series "Airwolf" (1984–88) Vincent was unable to translate those successes into prestigious big-screen projects, and by the end of the decade (and into the 1990s) he was appearing in threadbare B pictures, many of which bypassed theatrical release and went straight to home video. Vincent, who displayed some charisma in his younger days, gave somnambulistic performances in the likes of *The Haunting Fear, Alienator* (both 1990), *Raw Nerve,* and *Xtro II* (both 1991).

VISCONTI, LUCHINO. Director. *(b. Nov. 2, 1906, Milan; d. Mar. 17, 1976.)* One of the primary forces in the rebuilding of the Italian cinema after World War 2, Visconti was an enigmatic and influential figure. Born a count into one of Italy's most aristocratic families, the young Visconti lived a carefree life, cultivating a taste for opera and the theater. At the age of 30, he befriended Jean Renoir and followed him to Paris, working as a costume designer and assistant director. Here he also became influenced by Marxist ideology and, despite his family background, became an avid leftist and anti-fascist throughout the remainder of his life. In 1940 he returned to Italy to make films of his own, but his first feature, *Ossessione* (1942), came under fire from Mussolini's government. An unauthorized reworking of James M. Cain's "The Postman Always Rings Twice," the film angered authorities with its gritty representation of everyday life, and was severely censored.

After codirecting a documentary, *Giorni di Gloria* (1945), Visconti made his second feature, *La Terra trema* (1947), a story of class exploitation in a small Sicilian fishing village. Along with Rossellini's *Open City* and *Paisan* and De Sica's *Shoeshine* and *The Bicycle Thief, La Terra trema* officially inaugurated the Italian neorealist movement. Notable for their use of nonprofessional actors and naturalistic settings, these films provided a sharp contrast to the ornate, studio-produced escapist fare officially sanctioned by the (now deposed) fascist regime. Visconti's subsequent films were deeply personal, and almost operatic in structure. His most prominent themes were class exploitation and the manner in which the upper classes responded to a changing, tumultuous world; moral decay within families of all classes;

and male (and occasionally female) self-delusion. In *Bellissima* (1951), he told the story of a movie-crazed stage mother obsessed with attaining stardom for her untalented young daughter. *Senso* (1954), set in Austrian-occupied Venice in 1866, when Italian partisans were scheming to repossess their land, detailed the relationship between an Austrian officer and his married Italian mistress. Here Visconti united the realism of his earlier works with the romanticism that was to categorize his later films. *White Nights* (1957), a further example of his break with neorealism, told of a shy young man who falls for a woman awaiting the reappearance of her lost love. He returned to neorealism one last time in the superb *Rocco and His Brothers* (1960), a gritty, tragic tale of Southern Italian peasants who relocate to Milan in search of economic stability.

The Leopard (1963), one of Visconti's all-time classics (with American star Burt Lancaster effectively cast in the leading role), was set in the same time period as *Senso*. It dealt with an aristocratic Sicilian family responding to the death of its class and the rise of the bourgeoisie. The finale, a lengthy banquet sequence, remains one of film history's great set pieces. *Sandra* (1965) centered on an upper-crust woman's incestuous involvement with her brother (as well as her awareness that her mother had doubled-crossed her father, a Jew, during World War 2). After directing an excellent adaptation of Camus's *The Stranger* (1967) with Marcello Mastroianni, Visconti further explored the rise of Naziism in *The Damned* (1969), his most celebrated film, a pitiless look at the disintegration of a German industrialist family under the Hitler regime. Again he gathered an international cast (headed by Dirk Bogarde); the film won Visconti his sole Academy Award nomination, for best screenplay. In *Death in Venice* (1971), the filmmaker as never before focused on the theme of male vanity in telling of an aging homosexual's search for beauty and purity, in the person of a good-looking young boy. *Ludwig* (1973), another tale of decadent, declining European society, spotlighting the "mad" king of Bavaria, was seen as heavy-handed, and *Conversation Piece* (1975, with Burt Lancaster) was a talky tale of an aging intellectual, but Visconti was back in form for what would be his final film, *The Innocent*

(1976), a melodrama about an aristocrat, married to a beautiful woman, who nonetheless feels compelled to take a lover. To the end, Visconti remained an individualistic—and inspired—filmmaker.

VITTI, MONICA. Actress, director, screenwriter. *(b. Nov. 3, 1931, Rome, as Maria Louisa Ceciarelli.)* Stunning, sensuous actress best remembered for starring in a trio of features directed by Michelangelo Antonioni in the early 1960s: *L'Avventura* (1960), in a star-making role as a woman who becomes involved with the lover of a friend who has mysteriously disappeared; *L'Eclisse* (1962, American title: *Eclipse*), playing a translator who breaks up with her man of the moment and commences a dispassionate affair with a stockbroker; and *Red Desert* (1964), as an alienated woman trapped in a modern urban landscape. Vitti also took a secondary role in Antonioni's *La Notte* (1961), the story of a decaying marriage. All four films are studies of isolation and moral decay in a hopelessly bourgeois contemporary society. Vitti is perfectly cast: in her three starring roles, she is at once intense, distant, and believably troubled. As a teen, Vitti acted in amateur plays and studied at Italy's National Academy of Dramatic Arts. Her first film was *Ridere Ridere Ridere* (1955); prior to her casting in *L'Avventura*, she had appeared in various plays directed by Antonioni. In the mid 1960s, she went mod in her English-language debut, playing the female heroine in *Modesty Blaise* (1966), a British-made James Bond clone. Vitti has since appeared in dozens of mostly Italian-made features, few of which earned international theatrical distribution. In *An Almost Perfect Affair* (1979), her first English-language film since *Modesty Blaise,* she gave a fine performance as a producer's wife who becomes romantically involved with a young filmmaker. Vitti has lately turned to directing and screenwriting herself, with *Scandalo segreto* (1989, *Secret Scandal).*

VOIGHT, JON. Actor. *(b. Dec. 29, 1938, Yonkers, N.Y.)* This blond, blue-eyed, perpetually boyish-looking leading man—whose breakthrough role, in 1969's *Midnight Cowboy,* was that of a male prostitute—helped define the "sensitive" man for American movie audiences of the 1970s and 1980s. Voight, the son of a Czechoslovakian-American golf pro, embraced the dramatic arts while still a teenager, and worked his way from high-school stages to Broadway while still in his 20s. His first film, a superhero satire titled *Fearless Frank*, was made in 1965 but wasn't widely released until 1969, after his big splash (and Oscar nomination) as hick hustler Joe Buck in *Cowboy*. Other early films include *Hour of the Gun* (1967) and *Out of It* (1969). Voight went on to appear in several "antiestablishment" films, including Mike Nichols' clumsy adaptation of *Catch-22* and *The Revolutionary* (both 1970). He was also part of a superb ensemble cast in the harrowing thriller *Deliverance* (1972), which is still one of his best-remembered films.

Voight made a few pictures of varying quality—including *The All-American Boy* (1973), *Conrack, The Odessa File* (both 1974), and *End of the Game* (1976)—over the next few years, before finding another truly great part: that of a quadriplegic Vietnam War vet in *Coming Home* (1978), opposite Jane Fonda. His moving performance won him a Best Actor Academy Award, but again, it was difficult to find other parts of commensurate quality. He starred in a soppy remake of *The Champ* (1979), and in Hal Ashby's troubled production of *Lookin' to Get Out* (1982, which Voight cowrote and coproduced) before producing the sentimental *Table for Five* (1983), in which he played a widower suddenly forced to raise his children singlehandedly.

His over-the-top performance in the action/allegory *Runaway Train* (1985, from a story by Akira Kurosawa) was atypical, to say the least, but earned him a third Oscar nomination. He followed it with *Desert Bloom* (1986). Voight underwent a spiritual reawakening near the end of the 1980s, often exhorting puzzled interviewers of the need for man's transcendence of evil, while trying to get intellectually related film projects off the ground. *Eternity*, a 1990 film he wrote and acted in, has not been widely seen, but sheds some light on his current worldview: it deals with a TV reporter, trying to uncover government corruption and falling for a model who's a tool of the very forces he's trying to expose. He has also been seen in the TV movies *Chernobyl: The Final Warning* (1991), *The Last of His Tribe* (1992), *Rainbow Warrior* (1993), the miniseries "Return to Lonesome Dove" (1993), taking over Tommy Lee Jones' part as Woodrow Call, and *The Tin Soldier* (1995), which he also directed.

VON STERNBERG, JOSEF. Director, producer, writer, cinematographer. *(b. May 29, 1894, Vienna, as Jonas Sternberg; d. Dec. 22, 1979.)* Though best remembered today for the products of his almost Svengali-like relationship with actress Marlene Dietrich, this outstanding filmmaker developed an extraordinary style, with innovative use of lighting and decor, and managed to put a personal stamp on every film he made. He was one of many European filmmakers who emigrated to Hollywood in the silent era; unlike most of the others, though, he had not worked in Europe first. Von Sternberg served in the U.S. Signal Corps during World War 1, and afterward worked as an assistant director, making his directorial debut with an experimental drama, *The Salvation Hunters* (1925). Three more films followed, including a never-released Chaplin vehicle for Edna Purviance, *A Woman of the Sea* (1926). He then went to Paramount to rewrite and reshoot much of *Children of Divorce* (1927), the success of which kept him at that studio for the most productive period of his career.

Von Sternberg's first "signed" film was the seminal *Underworld* (also 1927), which laid the groundwork for the classic gangster dramas of the 1930s. Next came *The Last Command* (starring Emil Jannings in an Oscar-winning performance), *The Dragnet, Docks of New York* (all 1928), and *The Case of Lena Smith* (1929), all of which demonstrated his ability to bring a continental visual sensibility to uniquely American subject matter. In 1929 he made *Thunderbolt* in both silent and sound versions, mastering the new technology with little apparent difficulty.

The following year Jannings convinced von Sternberg to return with him to Germany and direct *The Blue Angel* (1930), which featured the bulky actor as a middle-aged professor obsessed with a music-hall chanteuse. Though Jannings was the star, and the property clearly developed around his character, it was

Marlene Dietrich, as the saucy Lola-Lola, who captivated audiences—and von Sternberg as well. He shot both German- and English-language versions of the film, the success of which brought him back to Paramount with Dietrich in tow. They embarked upon a personal and professional relationship that lasted five years and produced six more films: *Morocco* (1930), which earned von Sternberg his first Oscar nomination), *Dishonored* (1931, for which he also wrote the story and accompanying music), *Shanghai Express* (earning him another Oscar nod), *Blonde Venus* (both 1932), *The Scarlet Empress* (1934, for which he also composed some music), and *The Devil Is a Woman* (1935, which he helped photograph). With their sweeping, expressionistic visuals, exotic and sometimes risque narratives, and Dietrich's ambiguous, enigmatic sensuality, the von Sternberg Paramounts of this period were movie milestones, though not always appreciated in their day.

Von Sternberg, whose Paramount credits also included an unsuccessful attempt to film Dreiser's *An American Tragedy* (1931), left the studio in 1935 and, not unlike fellow studio prodigy Preston Sturges a decade later, his career went quickly downhill. He directed a modestly budgeted version of *Crime and Punishment* (1935) and *The King Steps Out* (1936), a Grace Moore musical, for Columbia, and then tackled the immense, ill-fated *I, Claudius* for British producer Alexander Korda. After six weeks, during which time he faced innumerable problems and got little usable footage, the production was shut down and never finished (though surviving footage made a fascinating BBC documentary, *The Epic That Never Was,* decades later). After an abortive stint at MGM that resulted in only one completed film, *Sergeant Madden* (1939), von Sternberg obtained independent financing for his last really good film, *The Shanghai Gesture* (1941, which he cowrote).

He worked fitfully thereafter, helming the Howard Hughes production *Jet Pilot,* which was filmed in 1950 but shelved for seven years and ill-advisedly "updated" with newly shot footage. After another Hughes production, *Macao* (1950, released 1952), on which he was replaced by Nicholas Ray, von Sternberg made one final film, *The Saga of Anatahan* (1952), which was financed by a Japanese pro-

ducer and used an entirely Japanese cast. He also wrote, narrated, and photographed the picture, which was not widely seen in the United States until years after he'd finished it. Thereafter von Sternberg retired and became an elder statesman of cinema, appearing at film festivals and colleges (he taught a course at UCLA), writing his memoirs (1965's "Fun in a Chinese Laundry"), and remaining inscrutable and irascible to the end.

VON STROHEIM, ERICH. Director, actor, screenwriter. *(b. Sept. 22, 1885, Vienna, as Erich Oswald Stroheim; d. May 12, 1957.)* Bald-pated, monocled, Teutonic terror frequently billed as "the man you love to hate," the skillful delineator of stern, autocratic Prussian and Nazi officers, but also a brilliant (if wildly extravagant) director whose *Greed* (1924) still ranks among the greatest achievements in cinema history. Variously described as a scion of Prussian nobility and a high-ranking career Army officer (he only served briefly, although he retained a fascination for all things military), he was in fact the supervisor of his father's straw-hat factory in Vienna before emigrating to America several years before World War 1. Von Stroheim entered the movie business in 1914 as a bit player, adviser on military costume and customs, and finally an assistant director; he spent some time with pioneering director D. W. Griffith, reportedly acting in *The Birth of a Nation* (1915) and *Intolerance* (1916), among others. His unmistakable ancestry made him an ideal villain in many propagandistic films made when America entered the war, including *Sylvia of the Secret Service* (1917), and three 1918 releases, *Hearts of the World* (a Griffith film on which he also served as technical adviser), *The Hun Within,* and *The Heart of Humanity* (in which he hurled a baby out a window!).

With horrible-Hun types out of fashion after war's end, von Stroheim (as he was by now billed) turned to directing at Universal, first with *Blind Husbands* (1919), based on his own short story. It, as well as his subsequent films *The Devil's Passkey* (1920) and *Foolish Wives* (1922), concentrated on overtly if not explicitly sexual themes, with more than a hint of depravity for those clever enough to spot it. But von Stroheim wasn't just interested in making exploitative melodramas; his films were rich in characterization and detail, and he lavished attention on sets, costumes, props, and makeup. Too much so, in fact: He constantly bickered with Universal management about cost overruns on his pictures. (One well-known and perhaps apocryphal story had him ordering embroidery of authentic *underwear* for his soldier extras to wear, on the grounds that they would know exactly how their real-life counterparts felt!)

Von Stroheim's extravagance extended to the amount of film he exposed, forcing Universal to cut *Foolish Wives* by nearly a third. An enormously successful film, it barely recouped its costs. Universal production head Irving Thalberg, finally fed up with von Stroheim's continued intransigence, removed him from *Merry-Go-Round* (1923), which was finished by Rupert Julian. Unrepentant, he began production on what would become his one true masterpiece, *Greed,* for the newly merged Metro and Goldwyn studios. Based on a novel of the naturalist school written by Frank Norris, *Greed* provided von Stroheim ample opportunities to explore the human frailties he so loved delineating on the screen. Shot on location in San Francisco and Death Valley, the picture ran to 42 reels (about seven hours) and went way over budget.

Even von Stroheim realized that there was no way the new company could exhibit a seven-hour film. He reluctantly cut it to four hours, and another director, Rex Ingram, shaved it by another hour. Metro-Goldwyn finally cut it to 10 reels (little over 100 minutes) and released it to mixed reviews. Nonetheless, no one disputed von Stroheim's artistry and filmmaking expertise, and in 1925 MGM (now joined by Louis B. Mayer) assigned him to direct a silent version of the Lehar operetta *The Merry Widow.* Predictably, von Stroheim all but threw out the libretto and stuffed the picture with scenes of debauchery and perversion. It was his swan song at MGM. He then cowrote, directed, and starred in *The Wedding March* (1928, for independent producer Pat Powers), the story of a roguish Viennese prince who agrees to marry into a wealthy family to help his own, only to fall in love with a beautiful but impoverished girl (Fay Wray). A stunning and emotional film, it too ran much longer than its distributor,

Paramount, could bear; Americans saw only the first half of the story. (The second half, *The Honeymoon,* was released separately in Europe.)

Von Stroheim's last silent film was another disaster. Gloria Swanson produced and starred in *Queen Kelly* (1928), the story of a convent girl swept off her feet by a roguish prince (they were, if you hadn't noticed by now, von Stroheim fixtures) and whisked away to Africa. His trademark scenes of decadence were much in evidence, but Swanson fired him halfway through shooting, after he'd already spent some $600,000. The film was quickly and choppily finished, released tentatively in some overseas markets, then shelved forever (or so it seemed; a restored version with still photographs printed into the film was prepared in the 1980s).

Still adamant about maintaining his work methods, von Stroheim began a Fox talkie, *Walking Down Broadway,* in 1932. Once again, the plug was pulled when he ran over schedule and over budget. Much of his completed footage sat on the studio shelf for a year, then was interpolated into newly shot material and released in 1933 as *Hello Sister.*

Von Stroheim never again directed a film, but stayed in the industry as a character actor—on occasion a darn good one. In the talkie era he appeared in *The Great Gabbo* (1929, as a ventriloquist!), *Three Faces East* (1930, one of his best, as an elegant spy), *Friends and Lovers* (1931), *The Lost Squadron* (1932, as a dictatorial movie director), *Crimson Romance, The Fugitive Road* (both 1934), and *The Crime of Dr. Crespi* (1935) before returning to Europe, where he made many films, including one timeless gem: Jean Renoir's *Grand Illusion* (1937), in which he unforgettably portrayed a cultured German commandant overseeing Allied prisoners during World War 1.

Back in America to escape the Nazi juggernaut of death and devastation, von Stroheim played supporting parts in *I Was an Adventuress* (1940), *So Ends Our Night* (1941), *The North Star* (1943), *Five Graves to Cairo* (also 1943, as Field Marshal Rommel in this excellent Billy Wilder film), *Storm Over Lisbon, Armored Attack, 32 Rue de Montmartre, The Lady and the Monster* (all 1944), *Scotland Yard Investigator, The Great Flamarion* (both

1945), and *The Mask of Dijon* (1946). After the war's end he went back to Europe
for good, returning to Hollywood only
once more, to appear (most effectively) as
Gloria Swanson's devoted servant in Billy
Wilder's *Sunset Blvd.* (1950, Oscar-
nominated). He worked in a handful of
European-made films and collaborated on
several screenplays before his death in
1957. Though reduced to a caricature in
many of his Hollywood films, and scorned
for his indulgences as a director, he was
awarded the Legion of Honor in France
shortly before his death. His sons both
pursued careers behind the scenes in Hollywood.

VON SYDOW, MAX. Actor, director. *(b.
Apr. 10, 1929, Lund, Sweden, as Carl Adolf
von Sydow.)* Lean-faced, sandy-haired,
pencil-thin actor who made his name with
America's art-house crowd playing tormented protagonists in a number of director Ingmar Bergman's best-known features, including *The Seventh Seal* (1957),
in which he played chess with the hooded
figure of Death. He was cast as Christ in
George Stevens' biblical epic *The Greatest Story Ever Told* (1965) and has enjoyed international star status ever since.
Von Sydow, a classically trained actor
who studied at Stockholm's Royal Dramatic Theater School, won his first film
role in *Bara en Mor* (1949), but spent the
first half of the 1950s perfecting his craft
on stage. He appeared in a number of
Bergman films in the late 1950s and
1960s, including *Wild Strawberries*
(1957), *The Magician, Brink of Life* (both
1958), *The Virgin Spring* (1959), *Through
a Glass, Darkly* (1962), *Hour of the Wolf,
Shame* (both 1968), *The Passion of Anna*
(1969), and *The Touch* (1971). As von
Sydow's stock rose with international producers, he was enlisted to appear in many
American and English-language films, including *The Quiller Memorandum, Hawaii* (both 1966), *Steppenwolf* (1974),
Three Days of the Condor (1975), and
Hurricane (1979). He starred in Jan
Troell's epic two-part story *The Emigrants*
(1971) and *The New Land* (1972), and in
1973 made a vivid impression as frail Father Merrin, the title character in *The Exorcist.* (He also appeared in *Exorcist II:
The Heretic,* in 1977.) Von Sydow is one
of those actors of whom it can be said that

he always, always maintains his own dignity in a film, regardless of how silly the
production or the story may be (see
1980's *Flash Gordon,* in which he plays
Ming the Merciless). He worked almost
constantly on a wide variety of projects
during the 1980s, from high, wrenching
drama like *Pelle the Conqueror* (1988, for
which he earned his only Oscar nomination) to the hallucinatory comedy *Strange
Brew* (1983, which he appeared to enjoy
more than a "distinguished actor" might
be expected to; costar Dave Thomas even
imitates his voice in one scene, uncannily
well). In 1988 he made his directing debut
with *Katinka.* Recent films include Wim
Wenders' *Until the End of the World*
(1991) and *The Best Intentions* (1992, as
Ingmar Bergman's grandfather). He can
also be heard doing voice-overs on a
number of American TV commercials. In
1993 he played The Devil in the Stephen
King saga *Needful Things,* making him
the only actor in memory who's played
Lucifer, an exorcist, and Jesus Christ.
OTHER FILMS INCLUDE: 1976: *Voyage of
the Damned, Foxtrot;* 1977: *March or Die;*
1978: *Brass Target;* 1981: *Victory;* 1982:
Conan the Barbarian; 1983: *Never Say Never
Again;* 1984: *Dreamscape, Dune;* 1986: *Duet
for One, Hannah and Her Sisters;* 1987: *Wolf
at the Door* (as Strindberg); 1990: *Awakenings;* 1991: *The Ox* (for Sven Nykvist), *A Kiss
Before Dying;* 1993: *The Silent Touch;* 1995:
Judge Dredd.

WAGNER, ROBERT. Actor. *(b. Feb. 10,
1930, Detroit.)* Robert Wagner made a successful transition from callow youth in
movies to suave leading man in television,
although he has always relied more on
charm than Method. Under contract to
20th Century-Fox at the age of 20, Wagner made his debut in *The Happy Years*
(1950), and for several years was con-
signed to supporting roles in pictures like
Halls of Montezuma (1950), *Let's Make It
Legal* (1951), *With a Song in My Heart,
What Price Glory?* (both 1952), and *Beneath the 12 Mile Reef* (1953). He played
the page-boyed *Prince Valiant* in a 1954
screen adaptation, and was outstanding as
the cold-blooded college-boy killer in *A
Kiss Before Dying* (1956), the performance that convinced studio executives
that he could carry a feature film.
Wagner starred in *Between Heaven and*

Hell (1956), *The True Story of Jesse James, Stopover Tokyo* (both 1957), *The Hunters* (1958), and other Fox films in addition to appearing in multi-star vehicles such as *All the Fine Young Cannibals* (1960), *Sail a Crooked Ship,* and *The Longest Day* (both 1962). No longer top-billed, the still-youthful Wagner also appeared in *The Pink Panther* (1964), *Harper* (1966), *Banning* (1967), *The Biggest Bundle of Them All* (1968), *Winning* (1969, playing a cad who steals Joanne Woodward from Paul Newman), *The Towering Inferno* (1974), *Midway* (1976), and *The Concorde: Airport '79* (1979), among others. Wagner took center stage on TV in "It Takes a Thief" (1968–69), "Switch" (1975–78), and "Hart to Hart" (1979–84) a long-running success built entirely around the chemistry of Wagner and co-star Stefanie Powers.

Wagner was married twice to actress Natalie Wood; they appeared together in *All the Fine Young Cannibals,* and in 1976 costarred with Laurence Olivier in a well-received TV production of "Cat on a Hot Tin Roof." In recent years Wagner has become a staple of TV miniseries and made-fors, including remakes of *Indiscreet* (1988) and *This Gun for Hire* (1991) and revivals of "Hart to Hart." Some time after Wood's death Wagner wed actress and longtime friend Jill St. John. His daughter, Katie Wagner, is a TV personality.
OTHER FILMS INCLUDE: 1951: *The Frogmen;* 1952: *Stars and Stripes Forever;* 1953: *Titanic;* 1954: *Broken Lance;* 1955: *White Feather;* 1956: *The Mountain;* 1958: *In Love and War;* 1959: *Say One for Me;* 1962: *The War Lover;* 1963: *The Condemned of Altona;* 1982: *Trail of the Pink Panther;* 1983: *Curse of the Pink Panther;* 1983: *I Am the Cheese;* 1991: *Delirious;* 1992: *The Player* (cameo); 1993: *Dragon: The Bruce Lee Story.*

WAHL, KEN. Actor. *(b. Feb. 14, 1956, Chicago.)* With his impressively chiseled face, offhand smile, and athletic build, Wahl has an abundance of what can only be called jock appeal: He looks more like a pro-football quarterback than an actor. Nonetheless, he's a fairly competent performer, as he demonstrated playing an undercover cop in the popular TV series "Wiseguy" (1987–90). Small roles in *The Buddy Holly Story* (1978) and *The Champ* (1979) led to Wahl's starring debut as one

of the Bronx high-school toughs in the peculiar gang comedy/drama *The Wanderers* (1979). In 1981's *Fort Apache, The Bronx,* Wahl supported Paul Newman and Ed Asner, and held his own in their scenes together. With leads in the action-adventure *Race to the Yankee Zephyr* (1981), *The Soldier,* the ill-fated Bette Midler comedy *Jinxed!* (both 1982), and *Purple Hearts* (1984), it seemed as if stardom was on tap, but that never came to pass (except on TV). Since then he's appeared in *The Omega Syndrome* (1987), *The Taking of Beverly Hills* (1991, as a football quarterback), and *The Favor* (1994).

WAITS, TOM. Singer, songwriter, actor. *(b. Dec. 7, 1949, Pomona, Calif.)* Innovative growly-voiced singer and composer who has scored as an actor in a number of eclectic roles. He started his music career while working as a doorman and living in his car, before cutting his first album, "Closing Time," in 1973. He made his film debut in Sylvester Stallone's *Paradise Alley* (1978) and was nominated for a Best Original Song Score Oscar for Francis Ford Coppola's *One From the Heart* (1982). He has subsequently appeared in Coppola's *The Outsiders, Rumble Fish* (both 1983), *The Cotton Club* (1984), and *Bram Stoker's Dracula* (1992, surprisingly effective as the mad Renfield), and has also given impressive performances in *On the Yard* (1979), *Down by Law* (1986), *Candy Mountain, Ironweed* (both 1987), *Cold Feet, Mystery Train* (both 1989, voice only in the latter), *The Fisher King, At Play in the Fields of the Lord, Queens Logic* (all 1991), and *Short Cuts* (1993). Waits' songs have been featured in many films and he was lionized in *Big Time* (1988), which combined footage of him in concert and in a series of vignettes playing various characters.

WAJDA, ANDRZEJ. Director, screenwriter. *(b. Mar. 6, 1926, Suwalki, Poland.)* One of Eastern Europe's—and the world's—most important directors, Wajda has chronicled the political and social changes of his native Poland with sensitivity, passion, and a refusal to pull punches. Wajda joined the Polish resistance as a teenager during World War 2, then studied painting, and eventually went to Poland's State Film School at Lodz. He served as an assistant to veteran Polish director Aleksander Ford before making his first film, *A Generation* (1954), about the Polish resistance. This was followed by *Kanal* (1956) and *Ashes and Diamonds* (1958), which comprised a remarkable trilogy about the effects of the war on Poland, and gained Wajda international acclaim. It also made a star out of actor Zbigniew Cybulski, the "Polish James Dean," who died in 1967 and became the focus of Wajda's later film *Everything for Sale* (1968). *Ashes and Diamonds* also brought the director his first clash with the Polish government, which delayed public release of the film because it depicted the assassination of a Communist District Secretary.

Wajda continued to cast a critical eye on the futility of war in *Lotna* (1959), and on contemporary youth in *The Innocent Sorcerers* (1960, also delayed by government authorities and given limited distribution). Following an adaptation of the Russian novel *Siberian Lady Macbeth* (1962), Wajda examined the waste of battle in historical films like *Ashes* (1965), *Gates of Paradise* (1967, about the Children's Crusade of 1212), and *Landscape After Battle* (1970), set in a camp for Poles released from a concentration camp. He also directed many TV movies and stage plays—mostly by foreign writers—during the 1960s and 1970s, including an internationally lauded production of "The Possessed," which he staged at Yale in 1974.

During the 1970s, Wajda brought a number of Poland's most notable literary works to the screen, including *The Birch Wood* (1970), *The Wedding* (1972), *Land of Promise* (1975), and *The Young Ladies of Wilko* (1979). He also directed the inimitable John Gielgud in *The Orchestra Conductor* (1980). He gained his greatest fame with the films *Man of Marble* (1976) and *Man of Iron* (1981), an epic examination of the clash between the individual and the state in postwar Poland that Wajda had wanted to make for years. *Man of Marble* deals with a young female filmmaker's efforts to trace the life of a discredited worker hero from the 1950s; *Man of Iron* finds the filmmaker married to the worker's son and follows the birth of Poland's Solidarity movement. *Man of Iron* won the Golden Palm Award at Cannes and was nominated for a Foreign Language Film Oscar, but because of the government crackdown, Wajda went to France to make his next film, *Danton* (1982), which starred Gerard Depardieu in the title role and paralleled the political situations in Wajda's homeland.

During the next years, Wajda dealt with the restrictive measures of his government—including the dissolving of his own film group, Studio X, in 1983—and continued to make films like *A Love in Germany* (1984) and *The Possessed* (1987) before the ultimate political turnaround of the Eastern Bloc countries. By 1989, Wajda had been elected as the Solidarity candidate to the Polish Parliament.

OTHER FILMS INCLUDE: 1962: *Love at Twenty* (one segment only); 1969: *Hunting Flies*; 1978: *Without Anesthesia* (aka *Rough Treatment*); 1990: *Dr. Korczak.*

WALBROOK, ANTON. Actor. *(b. Nov. 19, 1900, Vienna, as Adolf Anton Wilhelm Wohlbruck; d. Aug. 9, 1967.)* It is difficult to conjure up the memory of this distinguished-looking Austrian actor without seeing Lermontov, the tyrannical ballet impresario obsessed by his ballerina in Powell and Pressburger's *The Red Shoes* (1948), one of the screen's unforgettable masterpieces. Walbrook's stern, chiseled countenance made him a natural to play suave continentals, some of whom barely concealed latent cruelty or lust; even his sympathetic characters often seemed cold and aloof. Born into a family of circus clowns, he broke with long-standing tradition and left the sawdust behind to act on the stage. He played bits in a few silent films during the 1920s, but came into his own during the 1930s with starring roles in *Viktor und Viktoria, Waltz Time in Vienna* (both 1933), *Maskerade* (1934, aka *Masquerade in Vienna*), and *The Student of Prague* (1935), among others. In 1936 he played Jules Verne's Michael Strogoff in a lavish, multinational production purchased for American release by RKO's Pandro Berman, who brought Walbrook to Hollywood to reshoot dialogue sequences with an English-speaking cast. The final product, seamlessly assembled, was released as *The Soldier and the Lady* (1937); it is a seldom-seen, underappreciated film.

Walbrook, eschewing his native country to avoid the increasing Nazi menace, settled in England, where he played Prince Albert to Anna Neagle's Queen Victoria in *Victoria the Great* (1937) and *Sixty Glorious Years* (1938). By this time his command of the English language was considerable, and he was extremely effective as the husband in *Gaslight* (1940), a concert pianist in *Dangerous Moonlight* (1941, which introduced the "Warsaw Concerto"), a German-speaking Canadian settler in *49th Parallel* (1941, aka *The Invaders),* Roger Livesey's adversary in *The Life and Times of Colonel Blimp* (1943), and a Czech resistance leader in *The Man From Morocco* (1944). In the years following his *Red Shoes* triumph, Walbrook appeared in Max Ophuls' *La Ronde* (1950, as the master of ceremonies) and *Lola Montes* (1955, as the King of Bavaria), as well as *Vienna Waltzes* (1951), *On Trial* (1953), *Saint Joan* (1957), and *I Accuse!* (1958).

WALKEN, CHRISTOPHER. Actor. *(b. Mar. 31, 1943, Queens, N.Y.)* "I am the malevolent WASP," he described himself to one journalist. To director Paul Schrader, who was lighting him from below for one shot in 1991's *The Comfort of Strangers,* he said, "I don't need to be made to look evil. I can do that on my own." And indeed, many of Walken's most compelling screen turns have been as evil characters, or tragic victims haunted by unnameable terrors. He played one such role in *The Deer Hunter* (1978), which shocked audiences, won him a Supporting Actor Oscar, and made him a recognizable player. (The stage-seasoned Walken, who started as a chorus boy in New York, had been working in films for years, winning memorable bits in 1972's *The Anderson Tapes* and 1977's *Annie Hall,* particularly effective in the latter as Diane Keaton's creepy brother.) He has appeared in a variety of films since, most effectively as quietly menacing characters, but occasionally surprising audiences as he did in *Pennies From Heaven* (1981), contributing a show-stopping dance routine. He was chilling as the telepathic lead in *The Dead Zone* (1983), and as a purely evil father initiating his son into a life of crime in the underrated *At Close Range* (1986). He also had a campy turn playing a James Bond villain in *A View to a Kill* (1985). Walken exhibited a seldom-seen comic

ability as an eccentric drill sergeant in *Biloxi Blues* (1988), but was back in form as an icy mobster/philanthropist in the hyperviolent *King of New York* (1990). Younger viewers accustomed to seeing him in villainous parts may have been surprised by his warm portrayals opposite Glenn Close in the acclaimed TV dramas *Sarah, Plain and Tall* (1991) and its sequel, *Skylark* (1993). Feature-film casting directors still seem to favor malevolent roles for him, however: he was the flamboyant Max Shreck in *Batman Returns* (1992), a mobster who interrogates Dennis Hopper in *True Romance* (1993), Tia Carrere's self-centered record producer in *Wayne's World 2* (also 1993), and a vampire in *The Addiction* (1995).

OTHER FILMS INCLUDE: 1972: *The Happiness Cage;* 1976: *Next Stop, Greenwich Village;* 1977: *Roseland, The Sentinel;* 1979: *Last Embrace;* 1980: *The Dogs of War, Heaven's Gate;* 1983: *Brainstorm;* 1988: *Homeboy, The Milagro Beanfield War;* 1989: *Communion;* 1991: *McBain;* 1992: *Mistress;* 1994: *Pulp Fiction* (unforgettable delivering a monologue about the history of a very special watch); 1995: *Search and Destroy.*

WALKER, ROBERT. Actor. *(b. Oct. 13, 1918, Salt Lake City; d. Aug. 27, 1951.)* Spine-chillingly brilliant as the softspoken psychopath in Alfred Hitchcock's *Strangers on a Train* (1951), this boyishly handsome, sensitive performer may have brought more of himself to the role than anyone could have suspected. The disturbed product of a broken home, a victim of lifelong anxiety attacks, Walker eventually lost control of his battered psyche, self-aborted his once promising career, and died at a tragically young age. In 1938 he studied acting at New York's American Academy of Dramatic Arts, where he met and fell in love with aspiring actress Phyllis Isley. They went to Hollywood together the following year; she landed minor ingenue roles at Republic, he played bits at MGM. Returning east to take jobs in radio, the Walkers had two sons before coming back to Hollywood in 1943, Phyllis under contract to David O. Selznick, Robert to MGM. He played supporting roles in 1943's *Bataan* and *Madame Curie* before winning the lead in *See Here, Private Hargrove* (1944), a mildly amusing look at army life as seen by an open, mild-mannered boy-next-door. Selznick teamed him with his wife, by now renamed Jennifer Jones (and from whom he was by this time estranged), in *Since You Went Away* that same year, and he was very touching, in a homespun way, as a sincere soldier.

MGM, by now keenly attuned to Walker's youthful appeal, featured him in *Thirty Seconds Over Tokyo* (1944), then costarred him with Hedy Lamarr in *Her Highness and the Bellboy* and Judy Garland in that charmer *The Clock* (both 1945), as well as a Hargrove sequel, *What Next, Corporal Hargrove?* (1945). But the Walkers were divorced that year (thanks in large measure to Selznick's influence on and feelings for Jennifer), and Robert never really got over it. He played songwriter Jerome Kern in *Till the Clouds Roll By* (1946), and also starred or costarred in *The Sailor Takes a Wife* (also 1946), *The Sea of Grass, The Beginning or the End* (both 1947), *Song of Love* (also 1947, as Johannes Brahms), and *One Touch of Venus* (1948) before being institutionalized for more than a year with a severe nervous breakdown.

Walker played in several minor films (including a 1951 Western, *Vengeance Valley,* cast as a slimy villain) before tackling *Strangers* with Hitchcock, who harnessed his natural edginess and released it sparingly, enabling the troubled young star to deliver his finest performance. Walker died suddenly while working on *My Son John* (1952); outtakes and close-ups from *Strangers* were edited in to help cover his absence. Ironically, his portrayal of a suspected Communist was among his very best. His lookalike son Robert Walker, Jr., is an actor who had a brief fling with stardom in the 1960s.

WALLACH, ELI. Actor. *(b. Dec. 7, 1915, Brooklyn, N.Y.)* Rumpled, harsh-voiced supporting player with a flair for untrustworthy, menacing characters. Trained at the Neighborhood Playhouse, he served in World War 2, and then made his Broadway debut in 1945; within a few years he was regarded as one of the leading lights of the New York stage, earning a Tony Award for "The Rose Tattoo" in 1951. A confirmed Method actor, he has no compunctions about going "over the top," and can be either forceful or hammy (depend-

ing, in part, on the role). He made a memorable film debut in Elia Kazan's *Baby Doll* (1956) and has become a prolific supporting player in the years since, though he's never stopped working on stage, often in tandem with his wife, Anne Jackson. He has also been active on TV, doing commercial voice-overs and acting in made-for-TV movies and miniseries; he won an Emmy for the 1966 telefeature *The Poppy Is Also a Flower.* Wallach had his best screen moments in *The Magnificent Seven* (1960, as the Mexican bandito), *The Misfits* (1961, as the truck driver who makes a play for Marilyn Monroe), and *The Good, the Bad and the Ugly* (1966, as another Mexican, this time a gunfighter). He chewed plenty of candy (and some of the scenery) as the treacherous Mafia don with a sweet tooth in *The Godfather, Part III* (1990).

OTHER FILMS INCLUDE: 1958: *The Lineup;* 1960: *Seven Thieves;* 1962: *Hemingway's Adventures of a Young Man, How the West Was Won;* 1963: *Act One, The Victors;* 1964: *The Moon-Spinners;* 1965: *Genghis Khan, Lord Jim;* 1966: *How to Steal a Million;* 1967: *The Tiger Makes Out* (with Jackson, in the lead); 1968: *A Lovely Way to Die;* 1969: *Mackenna's Gold;* 1970: *The Angel Levine;* 1971: *Romance of a Horse Thief;* 1973: *Cinderella Liberty;* 1974: *Crazy Joe;* 1977: *The Deep, Nasty Habits;* 1978: *Movie Movie, Girlfriends;* 1979: *Winter Kills;* 1981: *The Salamander;* 1984: *Sam's Son;* 1986: *Tough Guys;* 1987: *Nuts;* 1988: *Funny;* 1992: *Mistress, Night and the City.*

WALSH, J. T. Actor. *(b. Sept. 28, 1943, San Francisco.)* Tall, impassive, WASPish character actor who shot to fame on Broadway for his memorable turn as one of the corrupt realtors in David Mamet's "Glengarry Glen Ross." Since moving over to feature films, Walsh has been incredibly prolific, playing almost nothing but quietly sinister white-collar sleazeballs in such films as *Power* (his first), *Hannah and Her Sisters* (both 1986), *Tin Men* (1987), *Tequila Sunrise* (1988), *The Big Picture* (1989, as a smarmy movie executive), *The Grifters* (1990), *Narrow Margin* (also 1990, in which he was surprisingly sympathetic and vulnerable), *Backdraft* and *Defenseless* (both 1991), as well as Mamet's *House of Games* (1987) and *Things Change* (1988). He also limned an obnoxious Army officer in *Good Morn-*

ing, Vietnam (1987), reporter Bob Woodward in *Wired* (1989), and a relatively conscientious police officer in *Iron Maze* (1991). Ironically, by the time "Glengarry" finally began filming in 1991, Kevin Spacey had won the part Walsh made famous on stage. But 1992 saw him in fine form, as union leader Frank Fitzsimmons in *Hoffa* and as a Marine officer who discovers he has a conscience in *A Few Good Men*. Recent credits include *National Lampoon's Loaded Weapon I*, the telefilm *Arthur Miller's "The American Clock," Needful Things, Red Rock West, Morning Glory, Sniper* (all 1993), *Blue Chips, The Last Seduction* (both 1994), and *Outbreak* (1995, unbilled).

WALSH, M. EMMET. Actor. *(b. Mar. 22, 1935, Ogdensburg, N. Y., as Michael Emmet Walsh.)* This ruddy, pot-bellied character player—usually cast as rednecks, corrupt cops, or both—made an indelible impression on jaded moviegoers as the hard-to-kill detective in *Blood Simple* (1984). His frequent and skillful portrayals of Southerners belie the fact that he's a New York native, and testifies to the skill and conviction he brings to showy supporting roles. Educated at the American Academy of Dramatic Arts, he made his motion-picture debut in *Midnight Cowboy* (1969), and excluding a couple of detours to TV—"The Sandy Duncan Show" (1972) and "Unsub" (1989)—has become one of the busiest supporting actors in Hollywood.
OTHER FILMS INCLUDE: 1969: *Alice's Restaurant;* 1970: *Little Big Man;* 1972: *What's Up, Doc?;* 1973: *Serpico;* 1975: *At Long Last Love;* 1976: *Mikey and Nicky, Nickelodeon;* 1977: *Slap Shot;* 1978: *Straight Time;* 1979: *The Jerk;* 1980: *Brubaker, Ordinary People;* 1981: *Reds;* 1982: *Blade Runner, Fast-Walking;* 1983: *Silkwood;* 1984: *The Pope of Greenwich Village;* 1985: *Fletch;* 1986: *Back to School, The Best of Times;* 1987: *Raising Arizona, Harry and the Hendersons;* 1988: *Clean and Sober, The Milagro Beanfield War;* 1989: *The Mighty Quinn;* 1990: *Narrow Margin;* 1992: *White Sands;* 1993: *The Music of Chance, Wilder Napalm.*

WALSH, RAOUL. Director, actor. *(b. Mar. 11, 1887, New York City; d. Dec. 31, 1980.)* Raoul Walsh was a storyteller who never let the truth get in the way of a good tale. After various odd jobs and adventures he found work in the theater as an actor, notably in a touring company of Thomas Dixon's "The Clansman." His first film work was with D. W. Griffith as an actor and assistant director. He codirected and starred in *The Life of General Villa* (1914), which in later years led the filmmaker to spin yarns about his association with the Mexican bandit/hero; in fact Walsh never left Los Angeles while the film was in production. He played John Wilkes Booth in Griffith's *The Birth of a Nation* (1915), and in the wake of its success he signed with the Fox Film Corporation. His early films there, as director, included *The Regeneration* (1915, a stunning drama of tenement life) and the Theda Bara version of *Carmen* (also 1915). He also steered the career of his then-wife, Griffith discovery Miriam Cooper. (Tragically, most of Walsh's early films no longer survive, denying modern-day film historians the chance to assess his work in this period. *Regeneration* is so good—rivaling Griffith in many ways—one can only imagine what his other work from the teens and early twenties might have been like.)

In 1924 Walsh piloted Douglas Fairbanks' *The Thief of Bagdad,* the artistic and commercial success of which made him a major Hollywood director. But Walsh proved to be a director without a "vision," only as good as his material—and often unable to improve it. His biggest silent success was an adaptation of the stage hit *What Price Glory?* (1926). Walsh wore three hats on *Sadie Thompson* (1928), writing, directing, and costarring with Gloria Swanson; his exuberant performance caused Fox to sign him to direct and star in the first outdoor talkie, *In Old Arizona* (1929), but a freak auto accident cost him an eye and finished his acting career for good. (Warner Baxter replaced him on-screen and went on to win an Oscar for his performance.)

Walsh's notable talkies included *The Cock-Eyed World* (1929, the sequel to *What Price Glory?*), the epic-scale Western *The Big Trail* (1930), *Yellow Ticket* (1931), *Me and My Gal* (1932), *Wild Girl* (also 1932, a Western made in the manner of a late 19th-century stage melodrama), and *The Bowery* (1933, a loving look at New York in the Gay Nineties). *Klondike*

Annie (1936, with Mae West) also showed great feeling for fin de siècle saloon life, and *The Strawberry Blonde* (1941) and *Gentleman Jim* (1942) were similarly effective in portraying that bygone era. Other 1930s titles include *Going Hollywood* (1933), *Every Night at Eight* (1935), *Artists & Models* (1937), and *College Swing* (1938). Walsh hit his stride at Warner Bros. in the late 1930s and early 1940s, finding his true metier in that studio's rugged action pictures and crime dramas, including *The Roaring Twenties* (1939) *They Drive by Night* (1940), *They Died With Their Boots On, Manpower,* and *High Sierra* (all 1941). On loan to Republic, he directed their large-scale Western drama *Dark Command* (1940), about Quantrill's Raiders.

Routine assignments in the 1940s were occasionally sparked by the likes of the much-maligned *The Horn Blows at Midnight* (1945), *Pursued* (1947), and the gangster psycho-drama *White Heat* (1949). (He also remade *High Sierra* in 1949, as *Colorado Territory.*) Walsh continued making films, mostly Westerns and actioners, into the mid 1960s, including *Captain Horatio Hornblower* (1951), *Blackbeard the Pirate* (1952), *The Tall Men* (1955), *The King and Four Queens* (1956), and *Marines, Let's Go* (1961); his final film was the modest cavalry epic *A Distant Trumpet* (1964).

Walsh's 1974 autobiography, "Each Man in His Time," must be regarded as highly entertaining fiction with an occasional nod at the truth. His brother, George Walsh, was a popular star in the teens and 1920s, whose career went into decline when he was replaced by Ramon Novarro in the 1926 *Ben-Hur;* sadly, nearly all of his films have been lost to the inevitable decomposition that ravages old celluloid.

WALSTON, RAY. Actor. *(b. Nov. 22, 1917, New Orleans.)* Seasoned character actor active in theater, films, and television. Walston debuted on the stage in Houston in 1938, and gained major stardom in New York beginning in the mid 1940s, in such plays as "Summer and Smoke" and "The Rat Race," and the musicals "Me and Juliet" and "House of Flowers." He won a Tony Award playing Mr. Applegate, the Devil, in the musical hit "Damn Yankees" (1956), and recreated

the part onscreen in 1958; that same year he played seabee Luthur Billis in the movie version of another Broadway smash, *South Pacific* (1958), which he'd performed on stage in the road company and in London. (He returned to musicals one more time, in 1969's large-scale production of *Paint Your Wagon,* as Mad Jack Duncan.) Billy Wilder gave him one of his best film roles, as a trysting insurance executive in *The Apartment* (1960), and when a heart attack felled Peter Sellers during filming of *Kiss Me, Stupid* (1964), Wilder called on Walston to replace him as the desperate songwriter; it was his only starring role in a long film career. He had debuted onscreen in *Kiss Them for Me* (1957), and went on to appear in *Convicts Four* (1962), *Who's Minding the Store? Wives and Lovers* (both 1963), *Caprice* (1967), *The Sting* (1973), *Silver Streak* (1976), *Popeye* (1980, as Poopdeck Pappy), and *Fast Times at Ridgemont High* (1982, as the punctilious schoolteacher). He's also appeared in his fair share of junk, including *The Happy Hooker Goes to Washington* (1977), *Private School* (1983), *Galaxy of Terror* (1981), *Blood Salvage* (1990), and *Ski Patrol* (1990), a streak that was broken by his casting as Candy in *Of Mice and Men* (1992). Walston starred in TV's "My Favorite Martian" (1963–66) and was featured in "Stop Susan Williams," a part of the "Cliffhangers" series (1979), and "Fast Times" (1986), recreating his screen role from *Fast Times at Ridgemont High.* Most recently he appeared in the recurring role of a judge on the critically acclaimed series "Picket Fences" (1992–).

WALTER, JESSICA. Actress. *(b. Jan. 31, 1940, Brooklyn, N.Y.)* Dark-haired, attractive supporting actress equally at home in comedic or dramatic roles. In her most meritorious feature-film outing, she was the psychopathic fan who terrorized disc jockey Clint Eastwood in the proto–*Fatal Attraction* thriller *Play Misty for Me* (1971). Walter began working onscreen in the 1960s, appearing in such films as *Lilith* (1964), *Grand Prix* (1966), Sidney Lumet's high-class soap opera *The Group* (also 1966), his New York-intellectual comedy/drama *Bye Bye Braverman* (1968), and *Number One* (1969). From the 1970s to the present she has done extensive TV work; rare 1980s big-screen appearances included a turn in Garry Marshall's *The Flamingo Kid* (1984) and a guest bit in the hip comedy *Tapeheads* (1989). She is married to actor Ron Leibman. Recent credits include *Ghost in the Machine* (1993) and *PCU* (1994).

WALTER, TRACEY. Actor. *(b. Nov. 25, 1942, Jersey City, N.J.)* Uniquely grubby, cultish character actor who is a favorite of many of today's top directors and stars. With his distinctive face and penchant for eccentric characterizations, he's the modern equivalent of old-time Hollywood supporting players who prompted moviegoers to say, "Look, there's what's-his-name." He has worked with Woody Allen (1977's *Annie Hall),* Jack Nicholson (1978's *Goin' South* and 1990's *The Two Jakes),* Francis Ford Coppola (1983's *Rumble Fish),* Paul Schrader (1978's *Blue Collar* and 1979's *Hardcore),* Tim Burton (1989's *Batman),* and Jonathan Demme (1986's *Something Wild,* 1988's *Married to the Mob,* and 1991's *The Silence of the Lambs).* He had a significant role in *Raggedy Man* (1981), and memorable bits in *Pacific Heights* (1990), as an exterminator, and *City Slickers* (1991), playing a drunken chuck-wagon driver. He may be most fondly remembered as Miller, the philosopher of *Repo Man* (1984), who spoke that cult film's oft-quoted line, "The more you drive, the less intelligent you are." In 1993 Jonathan Demme gave him one of the his most "normal" parts, as a librarian in *Philadelphia.*

WALTERS, JULIE. Actress. *(b. Feb. 22, 1950, Birmingham, England.)* Plucky British actress, originally trained as a nurse, who made a sensational debut as the working-class heroine in *Educating Rita* (1983, recreating a part she had played on the stage) and earned a Best Actress Oscar nomination in the process. Walters went on to star in *Unfair Exchanges* (1984), the very funny farce *Car Trouble* and *She'll Be Wearing Pink Pyjamas* (both 1985) and had one of her best roles as real-life London madam Cynthia Payne in *Personal Services* (1987). She costarred opposite Phil Collins in *Buster* (1988), but most of her recent opportunities have been in character parts, such as *Prick Up Your Ears*

(1987, as Joe Orton's mother), *Mack the Knife* (1989, as Mrs. Peachum), *Stepping Out* (1991, as one of Liza Minnelli's tapdance students), and *The Summer House* (1993, as a dowdy English mum).

WALTHALL, HENRY B. Actor. *(b. Mar. 16, 1878, Shelby City, Ala.; d. June 17, 1936.)* He has earned his place in screen history as "the Little Colonel," the protagonist of D. W. Griffith's groundbreaking feature film *The Birth of a Nation* (1915)—in which, playing the Confederate officer disgusted with Reconstruction-era carpetbaggers, he mobilizes the Ku Klux Klan as an army of vigilantes! Walthall, himself a chivalrous Southerner, studied law as a young man before being bitten by the acting bug. Eventually becoming a well-known stage star, he entered motion pictures in 1909 as part of Griffith's stock company at Biograph. Over the next several years he trouped in dozens of short films for the director, gradually evolving a restrained, naturalistic style of acting far removed from the period's exaggerated pantomime and more in keeping with his quiet, gentle nature. Walthall appeared in Griffith's first feature film, *Judith of Bethulia* (1914), an impressive achievement in its day but only a warm-up for *Birth.*

Walthall left Griffith after *Birth of a Nation*'s spectacular reception, taking a wide variety of roles: in 1915, for example, he played Edgar Allan Poe (to whom the slight, sensitive actor bore some resemblance) in *The Raven,* and in 1919 he played the daring "Lone Wolf" in *False Faces.* He was assigned character parts in most of his 1920s films, which included *The Long Chance* (1922), *The Unknown Purple* (1923), *The Bowery Bishop* (1924), *The Plastic Age* (1925), *Road to Mandalay, The Scarlet Letter* (both 1926), *Wings, London After Midnight* (both 1927), and *The Bridge of San Luis Rey* (1928). The stage-trained Walthall adapted readily to talkies, working for major studios and independents alike, essaying colorful character roles in both A and B pictures. He was reunited with Griffith in *Abraham Lincoln* (1930) and played a washed-up matinee idol in *Police Court* (1932), the closest thing to a starring vehicle he had in the 1930s. He had occasional roles of merit, as in *A Tale of Two Cities* (1935);

fittingly, one of his last films was a Civil War drama, *Hearts in Bondage* (1936).

WANAMAKER, SAM. Actor, director, producer. *(b. June 14, 1919, Chicago, as Samuel Watenmaker; d. Dec. 18, 1993.)* Wanamaker had just broken into movies when the communist witchhunt changed his life. Before attending Drake University, he made his stage debut at age 17 at Chicago's Goodman Theatre, and went on to be cast in numerous stock, roadshow, and Broadway productions. Wanamaker debuted onscreen in *My Girl Tisa* (1948) as a turn-of-the-century immigrant and aspiring lawyer; "Variety" noted that he was "a young talent with a personality that builds." Expecting to be blacklisted because of his leftist politics, he settled in England, where he made his next movies, *Give Us This Day* (1949), top-billed as a struggling, ill-fated bricklayer, and *Mr. Denning Drives North* (1951), featured as a congenial but misguided patent attorney.

Active as a stage director, he reappeared in international film productions in the 1960s, including *The Concrete Jungle* (1962, second-billed, as a thief), *Taras Bulba* (1962), *Man in the Middle* (1964), *The Spy Who Came In From the Cold, Those Magnificent Men in Their Flying Machines* (both 1965), *The Day the Fish Came Out* (1967), *Warning Shot* (1967, back in the U.S.), and *Danger Route* (1968). His role in *My Girl Tisa* was bookended by his casting as a disbarred lawyer fleeing Nazi Germany in *Voyage of the Damned* (1976); he then played Moses Weiss in the acclaimed television miniseries "Holocaust" (1978). In the 1980s, welcome again in Hollywood, Wanamaker settled into roles as establishment pillars and flashy, self-assured professionals: *The Competition, Private Benjamin* (both 1980), *Irreconcilable Differences* (1984), *The Aviator* (1985), *Baby Boom, Superman IV: The Quest for Peace* (both 1987), *Judgment in Berlin* (1988), *Pure Luck* (1991), and the blacklist drama *Guilty by Suspicion* (1991, cast as a villainous attorney). He also directed a handful of (mostly unmemorable) films, including *The File of the Golden Goose* (1969), *The Executioner* (1970), *Catlow* (1971), *Sinbad and the Eye of the Tiger* (1977), and *My Kidnapper, My Love* (1980, made for TV). Perhaps his best was *The Killing of Randy Webster* (1981, made for TV), the fact-based account of a father's search for his son's murderer. He also starred in the short-lived TV series "Berrengers" (1985). He devoted much of his life to restoration of Shakespeare's Globe Theatre, which, ironically, reached fruition shortly after his death.

WANG, WAYNE. Director, screenwriter, producer. *(b. Jan. 12, 1949, Hong Kong.)* Named after John Wayne by his American-movie-loving father, Wang studied film and television at California's College of Arts and Crafts and returned home to work in those fields. Creatively frustrated, he settled in San Francisco and through grants from the AFI and NEA, he directed, produced, cowrote, and edited his first feature, *Chan Is Missing* (1982), on the absurdly low budget of $22,000. This film and *Dim Sum: a little bit of heart* (1984), which focused on the relationship between a Chinese mother and her American-born daughter, offered unique, wry looks at Chinese-Americans and their environment, and established Wang's reputation. His next film, *Slamdance* (1987), was an overstylized melodrama, but he returned to form with *Eat a Bowl of Tea* (1989), a pointed comedy about newlyweds in 1949 Chinatown, and *Life Is Cheap . . . but Toilet Paper Is Expensive* (1990), a highly experimental, graphic film that was released with no rating because of objections to some bloody scenes. Recently, Wang directed and coproduced *The Joy Luck Club* (1993) based on Amy Tan's celebrated novel of the generational conflicts between four Chinese-American women and their mothers (which *Dim Sum* anticipates). He followed with the independent feature *Smoke* (1995). Wang is married to actress Cora Niao, who has appeared in *Dim Sum, Eat a Bowl of Tea* and *Life Is Cheap . . .*

WARD, DAVID S. Director, screenwriter. *(b. Oct. 24, 1947, Providence, R.I.)* Talented filmmaker who won a Best Original Screenplay Oscar for the classic con movie *The Sting* (1973), one of that film's seven Oscars. Educated at USC and UCLA, Ward worked as an assistant editor at an educational film company and wrote the anarchic comedy *Steelyard Blues* while in grad school. The script was filmed in 1973 with Jane Fonda and Donald Sutherland and produced by Michael and Julia Phillips, who tapped Ward again as a writer when they went on to produce *The Sting.* Ward directed and adapted John Steinbeck's *Cannery Row* (1982), then scored a success with the baseball comedy *Major League* (1989). He went on to write and direct *King Ralph* (1991) and tackled the sports world again in *The Program* (1993) with James Caan as a college football coach. He contributed to the script of *Saving Grace* (1986) and cowrote the adaptation of *The Milagro Beanfield War* (1988, with John Nichols). Ward also wrote *The Sting II* (1983), an unfortunate dud, and directed (but did not write) *Major League II* (1994). He was Oscar-nominated as cowriter of *Sleepless in Seattle* (1993).

WARD, FRED. Actor. *(b. Dec. 30, 1942, San Diego, Calif.)* This gruff, likable performer usually looks as though he just stepped out of a boxing ring, but that hasn't hindered his success as a character lead and supporting player. In fact, Ward has become one of the screen's most dependable actors. An alumnus of New York's Herbert Berghof Studio, he knocked around filmdom for several years before landing a plum role—as partner to Clint Eastwood—in *Escape From Alcatraz* (1979). He first won critical attention for his portrayal of doomed astronaut Gus Grissom in Philip Kaufman's *The Right Stuff* (1983); two years later, Hollywood tried to turn him into an action lead with *Remo Williams: The Adventure Begins* (1985), but it didn't take.

Ward had a banner year in 1990, first as Florida cop Hoke Moseley—divested of his gun, badge, and most humiliatingly, his dentures—in the thriller *Miami Blues* (which he coproduced), and then as raw, Brooklyn-born writer Henry Miller in the controversial *Henry & June,* directed by old mentor Kaufman. He was chillingly effective as a murderous Native American in *Thunderheart* (1992), and equally good as the garrulous studio security chief in Robert Altman's *The Player* (1992).
OTHER FILMS INCLUDE: 1980: *Carny, UFOria;* 1981: *Southern Comfort;* 1983: *Timerider, Silkwood, Uncommon Valor;* 1984: *Swing Shift;* 1985: *Secret Admirer;* 1988: *Big Business, Off Limits, The Prince of Pennsylvania;*

1989: *Backtrack;* 1990: *Tremors;* 1992: *Four Eyes and Six-Guns* (telefilm); 1993: *Short Cuts;* 1994: *The Naked Gun 33⅓: The Final Insult, Two Small Bodies.*

WARD, RACHEL. Actress. *(b. Sept. 12, 1957, London.)* Stunningly beautiful brunette with seductively husky voice, initially seen in standard parts but latterly in some interesting, offbeat roles. A former model, she appeared in two schlocky horror films, *Night School* and *The Final Terror,* before attracting attention as the high-class hooker in *Sharky's Machine* (all 1981). She played an admirably deadpan femme fatale in Steve Martin's private-eye spoof *Dead Men Don't Wear Plaid* (1982), then tackled a similar part in earnest for *Against All Odds* (1984), a reworking of the classic *noir* thriller *Out of the Past.*

Ward was off the big screen for several years, but impressed the few moviegoers who saw her in *The Good Wife* (1986), playing the insulated, bored spouse of Bryan Brown (her real-life hubby, with whom she also costarred in the popular 1983 miniseries, "The Thorn Birds"). That same year she provided a little light and heat in the otherwise tepid *Hotel Colonial.* Ward showed surprising aptitude for black comedy as the patient wife of wacky Richard E. Grant in *How to Get Ahead in Advertising* (1989), and appeared at her sultriest as the treacherous temptress in *After Dark, My Sweet* (1990), an updated *noir* from the pen of Jim Thompson. Recent credits include *Terror Eyes* (1991), *Christopher Columbus—The Discovery* (1992, as Queen Isabella), *Wide Sargasso Sea* (1993), and a number of TV movies, including *Double Jeopardy* and *Black Magic* (both 1992).

WARDEN, JACK. Actor. *(b. Sept. 18, 1920, Newark, N.J.)* One of Hollywood's premier "utility players" since the 1950s, this ruddy, red-haired performer is in style and spirit akin to the "old dependable" character actors of the past. His recognizability hasn't hampered his ability to tackle any kind of part, serious or comic. A former boxer and stage actor, he made his first movie mark in 1957 as the sports-obsessed juror in *12 Angry Men,* a lonely attendee at *The Bachelor Party,* and a brutal dock boss in *Edge of the City.*

Some of Warden's other colorful roles include a submarine officer in *Run Silent, Run Deep* (1958), a snooty Bostonian who gets roughed up in *Donovan's Reef* (1963), a relentless sheriff in *Billy Two Hats* (1974), the cuckolded husband in *Shampoo* (1975, an Oscar-nominated performance), "Washington Post" editor Harry Rosenfeld in *All the President's Men* (1976), the cranky football coach in *Heaven Can Wait* (1978, another Oscar-nominated turn), a loony, gun-toting judge in . . . *And Justice for All,* the President in *Being There* (both 1979), twin auto salesmen in *Used Cars* (1980), a smarmy garment-district mogul in *So Fine* (1981), Paul Newman's Jiminy Cricket in *The Verdict* (1982), an easygoing pawnbroker in *Crackers* (1984), and oily discount store owner Big Ben in the two *Problem Child* comedies (1990 and 1991).

Warden's notable TV-movie stints include his Emmy-winning performance as football coach George Halas in *Brian's Song* (1970), an Israeli official in *Raid on Entebbe* (1977), terminally ill author Cornelius Ryan in *A Private Battle* (1980), and Mark Twain in *Helen Keller—The Miracle Continues* (1984). Among his numerous TV series are "Mr. Peepers" (1952–55), "N.Y.P.D." (1967–69), "Jigsaw John" (1976), "The Bad News Bears" (1979–80), and the delightful "Crazy Like a Fox" (1984–86).

OTHER FILMS INCLUDE: 1952: *Red Ball Express;* 1958: *Darby's Rangers;* 1959: *The Sound and the Fury, That Kind of Woman;* 1960: *Wake Me When It's Over;* 1962: *Escape From Zahrain;* 1966: *Blindfold;* 1968: *Bye Bye Braverman;* 1971: *The Sporting Club, Summertree, Who Is Harry Kellerman and Why Is He Saying Those Terrible Things About Me?;* 1973: *The Man Who Loved Cat Dancing;* 1974: *The Apprenticeship of Duddy Kravitz;* 1977: *The White Buffalo;* 1978: *Death on the Nile;* 1979: *Beyond the Poseidon Adventure, The Champ, Dreamer;* 1981: *Carbon Copy, The Great Muppet Caper, So Fine;* 1985: *The Aviator;* 1987: *September;* 1988: *The Presidio;* 1990: *Everybody Wins;* 1992: *Passed Away, Night and the City, Toys;* 1993: *Guilty as Sin;* 1994: *Bullets Over Broadway;* 1995: *While You Were Sleeping.*

WARHOL, ANDY. Director, producer. *(b. Aug. 8, 1928, Pittsburgh, as Andrew Warhola; d. Feb. 22, 1987.)* Famed pop artist who brought the same glacial, deadpan style that characterized much of his painting to a series of underground films. Warhol translated the visual technique he had first used as a commercial artist into a style which celebrated and mocked the commonplace, mass-marketed objects of American culture, from Campbell's soup cans to iconic images of Marilyn Monroe. He became interested in film in 1963, and applied a similar unblinking approach to such works as *Eat* (1963), in which artist Robert Indiana spends almost an hour eating a mushroom, *Kiss* (1963), in which couples kiss, *Sleep* (1963), a fixed-camera shot of a man sleeping for eight hours, and *Empire* (1964), a stationary shot of the Empire State Building recorded from sunrise to sunset. Avant-garde enthusiasts found such films an intriguing challenge to mainstream products and "Film Culture" magazine saluted Warhol for "taking cinema back to its origins, to the days of Lumière, for a rejuvenation and a cleansing."

As Warhol's celebrity increased, he attracted an assortment of hangers-on to the "Factory" in New York City—where his films and paintings were created—and began to feature them in his films, often turning his cameras on and letting them ramble. Such people—Edie Sedgwick, Viva, Ultra Violet, Brigid Polk, and Ingrid Superstar—became superstars of the underground scene and their "performances" onscreen blurred the boundaries between acting, exhibition, and mere voyeuristic probing. A variety of features resulted: *Harlot* (1964), Warhol's first sound film, *Beauty #2* (1965), with Sedgwick and a man on a bed talking, *The Life of Juanita Castro* (1965), a parody of B Westerns with transvestites, and *Vinyl* (1965), which featured Gerard Malanga dancing with chains as Sedgwick watched. These were warm-ups for *Chelsea Girls* (1966), an epic of three and a half hours with two reels of film projected side-by-side simultaneously, that features many of Warhol's "regulars" ad-libbing. A major event of the underground movement, *Chelsea Girls* was popular enough for its grosses to make it into the pages of "Variety." Warhol's subsequent films had rudimentary plots, like *Lonesome Cowboys* (1967), a campy Western with Viva as a ranch owner, but after he was shot by Valerie Solanis in 1968 (she had appeared in his

1967 *I, a Man)*, he relinquished direct control of films to colleagues like Paul Morrissey, who directed more commercial-minded features like *Flesh* (1968), *Trash* (1970), *Heat* (1972), *Andy Warhol's Dracula,* and *Andy Warhol's Frankenstein* (both 1974, and all five starring Joe Dallesandro). Warhol himself directed a music video for The Cars, "Hello Again." Many critics hailed Warhol's contribution; others considered his entire output a total waste of time. David Thomson noted his achievement was "to so simplify filmmaking that we reappraise what happens when we watch people." Whether Warhol himself was putting us on is unclear, but perhaps that too was the point. In an interview, Joseph Gelmis asked him, "Why did you make a movie like *Sleep* about a guy who sleeps for eight hours?" and "Your films are just a way of taking up time?" Warhol's responses: "This person I knew slept a lot" and "Yeah." He was the subject of a posthumous documentary by Chuck Workman, *Superstar: The Life and Times of Andy Warhol* (1991).

WARNER, DAVID. Actor. *(b. July 29, 1941, Manchester, England.)* Trained at the Royal Academy of Dramatic Art, Warner made his film debut as Albert Finney's younger brother in *Tom Jones* (1963), but really made an impact three years later as the eccentric, Marx-spouting, gorilla-infatuated title character in *Morgan!* (1966). It was a characterization that embraced and crystallized many of the sixties counterculture attitudes and, sadly, most later roles did not provide similar opportunities for Warner to show his range. He was memorable as a nervous National Serviceman in *The Bofors Gun* (1968), the slow-witted villager whom Dustin Hoffman protects in *Straw Dogs* (1971), a cool, ruthless Jack the Ripper in *Time After Time* (1979), and got to show comic flair as The Evil Genius in *Time Bandits* (1981) and a mad scientist in *The Man With Two Brains* (1983). His numerous TV credits include the miniseries "Holocaust" (1977–78), "Masada" (1981, for which he won an Emmy), "Marco Polo" (1982), and an excellent adaptation of *A Christmas Carol* (1984).
OTHER FILMS INCLUDE: 1967: *The Deadly Affair;* 1968: *The Fixer, The Sea Gull;* 1970: *The Ballad of Cable Hogue;* 1973: *A Doll's*

House (Jane Fonda version); 1976: *The Omen;* 1977: *Cross of Iron, Providence;* 1978: *Silver Bears;* 1981: *The French Lieutenant's Woman;* 1982: *Tron;* 1984: *The Company of Wolves;* 1988: *Mr. North;* 1989: *Star Trek V: The Final Frontier;* 1991: *Teenage Mutant Ninja Turtles II: The Secret of the Ooze, Star Trek VI: The Undiscovered Country;* 1992: *Drive;* 1993: *The Lost World.*

WARNER, H. B. Actor. *(b. Oct. 26, 1876, London, as Henry Byron Warner; d. Dec. 21, 1958.)* Born into a distinguished theatrical family, Warner briefly considered a career in medicine but eventually followed in his father's footsteps, touring England and America in some of the period's finest stage dramas. He made his film debut in 1914 and played leads throughout the silent era, most notably as Jesus Christ in Cecil B. DeMille's *The King of Kings* (1927). He also starred in *Sorrell and Son* (1927) and repeated the role in a 1934 remake. Tall and slender, with a cultured voice, he adapted easily to talkies. Well into middle age, Warner accepted character roles in *Five Star Final* (1931), *Tom Brown of Culver* (1932), *A Tale of Two Cities* (1935), *Mr. Deeds Goes to Town* (1936), *Lost Horizon* (1937, as the gentle Chang, a role for which he was Oscar-nominated), *You Can't Take It With You* (1938), *Mr. Smith Goes to Washington, The Rains Came* (both 1939), *All That Money Can Buy/The Devil and Daniel Webster, The Corsican Brothers, Topper Returns* (all 1941), *Hitler's Children* (1943), *It's a Wonderful Life* (1946, as the drunken pharmacist), *Sunset Blvd.* (1950, playing himself, as one of the "waxworks," along with former leading lady Anna Q. Nilsson), *Here Comes the Groom* (1951), and *The Ten Commandments* (1956, as Amminadab), among others. He also played Colonel Nielsen in several of Paramount's *Bulldog Drummond* films of the late 1930s.

WARREN, LESLEY ANN. Actress. *(b. Aug. 16, 1946, New York City.)* Comely, versatile actress who plays emotionally fragile women, tough-minded careerists, hardworking single moms, and downright wacky ladies with equal verve and skill. She made her first show-biz splash right out of her teens, playing the lead in a

1966 TV musical production of Rodgers and Hammerstein's "Cinderella." Walt Disney saw her and signed the wholesome, fresh-faced Warren to play a supporting role in *The Happiest Millionaire* (1967), the last film he personally supervised. She also appeared in the Disney studio's *The One and Only, Genuine, Original Family Band* (1968) before taking "adult" roles in the TV series "Mission: Impossible" (1970–71) and a slew of made-for-TV movies, as well as the low-budget *Pickup on 101* (1972). She worked extensively in TV movies and miniseries throughout the rest of the decade, most notably *The Legend of Valentino* (1975), *Portrait of a Stripper* (1979), and "Beulah Land" (1980).

Blake Edwards gave Warren a juicy part on the big screen in *Victor/Victoria* (1982), competing with Julie Andrews for the attentions of James Garner; she showed a real flair for broad comedy, and was Oscar-nominated for her uninhibited supporting performance. There haven't been many follow-ups of the same caliber, though she fared well in *Choose Me, Songwriter* (both 1984), and *Baja Oklahoma* (1988), in which she starred as a Texas barmaid who wants to be a songwriter. Mel Brooks gave her a good showcase in his otherwise forgettable *Life Stinks* (1991) as a homeless woman teetering on the edge of sanity. She remains active on television, and starred in *Willing to Kill: The Texas Cheerleader Story* (1992); in 1994 she costarred in the theatrical feature *Color of Night*.
OTHER FILMS INCLUDE: 1976: *Harry and Walter Go to New York;* 1981: *Race to the Yankee Zephyr;* 1983: *A Night in Heaven;* 1985: *Clue;* 1987: *Burglar, Cop;* 1990: *Worth Winning;* 1992: *Pure Country.*

WARRICK, RUTH. Actress. (b. June 29, 1915, St. Joseph, Mo.) Charming actress who began her career as a radio singer and made an indelible film debut as Emily Norton Kane, the first wife of *Citizen Kane* (1941). Warrick worked with Orson Welles again on *Journey Into Fear* (1942), as Joseph Cotten's wife, and had other good parts in *The Corsican Brothers, Obliging Young Lady* (both 1941), *Petticoat Larceny* (1943), *The Iron Major* (1943, as the devoted wife of Pat O'Brien), *Mr. Winkle Goes to War* (1944, as the flus-

tered wife of Edward G. Robinson), *China Sky* (1945), *Perilous Holiday* (1946), *Song of the South* (1946, as Bobby Driscoll's mother), and *Driftwood* (1947, in which she was top-billed). By the late 1940s, she had settled into supporting and other-woman roles: *Swell Guy, Daisy Kenyon* (both 1947), *Arch of Triumph* (1948), *The Great Dan Patch* (1949), and *Let's Dance* (1950). That same year, she played an alcoholic in *One Too Many*, an exploitation film which played roadshow engagements. From then on, her film roles were rare. She found a new home on television soap operas "Guiding Light" and "As the World Turns" in the 1950s, and went on to play Ellie Banks on the sitcom "Father of the Bride" (1961–62) and Hannah Cord on the nighttime soap "Peyton Place" (1964–67). She won enduring fame as the longtime star of "All My Children" (1970–), cast as Phoebe Tyler, and published her autobiography, "The Confessions of Phoebe Tyler," in 1980.

WASHINGTON, DENZEL. Actor. (b. Dec. 28, 1954, Mt. Vernon, N.Y.) Director Ed Zwick—who directed Washington's Oscar-winning performance in *Glory* (1989)—said of this charismatic black actor, "Whatever that mysterious electrochemical process is that makes the camera love someone, he has more of it than any one person should." It is this presence that has made Washington one of the most exciting actors onscreen. After studying theater at Fordham and San Francisco's American Conservatory Theatre, he performed on stage in New York, appeared in the TV movie *Flesh and Blood* (1979), and made his film debut in the "title" role of the negligible comedy *Carbon Copy* (1981). He caught TV audiences' attention as Dr. Chandler on the outstanding dramatic series "St. Elsewhere" (1982–88) and made a vivid impression in *A Soldier's Story* (1984), repeating his Obie Award–winning stage role. He earned his first Academy Award nomination for his portrayal of Steven Biko in *Cry Freedom* (1987), and won the Supporting Actor Oscar two years later for his rich performance as a malcontented Negro soldier in *Glory*. He also appeared in the short subject *Reunion* and *For Queen and Country* (both 1988). Washington has made an easy transition from supporting actor to leading man with roles that have proven his range and versatility: a Caribbean police chief in *The Mighty Quinn* (1989), a dead spirit inhabiting a cop's body in *Heart Condition,* a self-absorbed trumpet player in *Mo' Better Blues* (both 1990), a street cop pitted against a slimy bad guy in *Ricochet* (1991), a carpet cleaner involved in an interracial romance in *Mississippi Masala* (1992), and especially the famous black activist in *Malcolm X* (1992, for which he was Oscar-nominated), whom he had previously played on stage in "When the Chickens Came Home to Roost." In 1993 he tackled Shakespeare with Kenneth Branagh in the exhilarating *Much Ado About Nothing,* played a homophobic lawyer who agrees to take the case of an AIDS victim in *Philadelphia,* and starred with Julia Roberts in the John Grisham thriller *The Pelican Brief*—as impressive a parlay as any actor could claim in the 1990s. He almost matched it in 1995 with *Crimson Tide, Devil in a Blue Dress,* and *Virtuosity.*

WATERS, JOHN. Director, screenwriter, producer. *(b. Apr. 22, 1946, Baltimore.)* This darling of the midnight-movie set has a somewhat skewed (some say deranged) worldview. Many cineastes are hard pressed to find merit in his work, but there's no denying that he's turned out some of the most original, offbeat films of the post-Vietnam era. Waters was born and raised in an upper-middle-class part of Baltimore (where most of his films have been set and where he still lives), and began making amateur movies while in his teens. He gathered together interested friends and neighbors to form his own stock company, the undisputed star of which was Harris Glenn Milstead, a former high-school chum and 300-pound cross-dresser who billed himself as Divine.

Waters' early films—including *Mondo Trasho* (1970) and *Multiple Maniacs* (1971)—initially didn't get much exposure outside of Baltimore, but the bizarre *Pink Flamingos* (1972, reportedly made for only $10,000) was picked up by an enterprising distributor and marketed to the then-burgeoning midnight-movie market, which was peopled mostly by stoned college kids. The director's unique mix of pop-culture satire, frontal assault on what we now call "traditional family values,"

and blatant, graphic tastelessness made *Flamingos* a cult favorite. It also served as a blueprint of sorts of Waters' subsequent efforts, including *Female Trouble* (1975), *Desperate Living* (1977), and *Polyester* (1981), although the latter saw the director's trademark outrageousness toned down in broadening his market. *Hairspray* (1988) and *Cry-Baby* (1990) were clearly designed to bring his sensibilities to mainstream audiences, and jettisoned the tastelessness without losing any of Waters' manic energy or thematic conceits. His latest: *Serial Mom* (1994) with Kathleen Turner. Waters has also turned up as an actor in *Something Wild* (1986, for Jonathan Demme) and *Homer & Eddie* (1990), and has written humorous essays which have been gathered in the books "Shock Value" (1981) and "Crackpot: The Obsession of John Waters" (1986).

WATERSTON, SAM. Actor. *(b. Nov. 15, 1940, Cambridge, Mass.)* This tall, slender character actor and occasional lead, educated at the Sorbonne in Paris, was an accomplished New York stage performer before appearing on screen in a number of inconsequential pictures in the late 1960s (beginning with 1967's *Fitzwilly)* and the early 1970s, including Merchant and Ivory's *Savages* (1972). His portrayal of Nick Carraway in the undistinguished *The Great Gatsby* (1974) opened some eyes, but his screen career remained stuck in low gear, in such films as *Rancho Deluxe* (1975, a cult favorite), *Journey Into Fear* (also 1975), Dandy, the All-American Girl (1976), *Capricorn One* (1978), *Sweet William* (1979), *Hopscotch,* and the notorious *Heaven's Gate* (both 1980). His career continued to flourish on stage; then in 1984 he gave a subtle, heartfelt performance as journalist Sidney Schanberg in *The Killing Fields* (1984) and earned an Oscar nomination as Best Actor. Woody Allen adopted him as one of his informal stock company and cast him in *Interiors* (1978), *Hannah and Her Sisters* (1986, unbilled), *September* (1987), and *Crimes and Misdemeanors* (1989), in which he played the rabbi who is losing his sight. He's been highly visible in prestige TV productions such as *The Glass Menagerie* (1973, with Katharine Hepburn), *Finnegan Begin Again* (1985), the miniseries "Gore Vidal's Lincoln" (1988, in a part he reprised in a 1993 Broadway revival of "Abe Lincoln in Illinois"), and the highly acclaimed dramas "I'll Fly Away" (1991–93) and "Law and Order" (1994–). Recent film credits include *Serial Mom* (1994).

WATKIN, DAVID. Cinematographer. *(b. Mar. 23, 1925, Margate, England.)* Veteran British cameraman who began in documentary films in 1955, then became director of photography on the Richard Lester films *The Knack, and How to Get It* and *Help!* (both 1965). He continued to work on such Lester films as *How I Won the War* (1967), *The Bed-Sitting Room* (1969), *The Three Musketeers* (1974), *Robin and Marian* (1976), and *Cuba* (1979), and also shot prestigious movies including *Marat/Sade* (1966), *The Charge of the Light Brigade* (1968), *Catch-22* (1970), *The Boy Friend, The Devils* (both 1971), *The Homecoming* (1973), *Joseph Andrews* (1977), *Chariots of Fire* (1981), *Yentl* (1983), *The Hotel New Hampshire* (1984), *Moonstruck* (1987), *Hamlet* (1990), *Used People* (1992) and *This Boy's Life* (1993). Watkin won an Oscar for his stunning photography on *Out of Africa* (1985).

WAXMAN, FRANZ. Composer. *(b. Dec. 24, 1906, Konigshutte, Germany, as Franz Wachsmann; d. Feb. 24, 1967.)* Astonishingly prolific composer of movie music whose American career spanned some 30 years and included nearly 200 movies. A proponent of the heavily orchestrated, romantic type of score, Waxman won Academy Awards for *Sunset Blvd.* (1950) and *A Place in the Sun* (1951), and was nominated for *The Young in Heart* (1938), *Rebecca* (1940), *Dr. Jekyll and Mr. Hyde, Suspicion* (both 1941), *The Silver Chalice* (1954), *The Nun's Story* (1959), and *Taras Bulba* (1962). Waxman, who studied at the Dresden Music Academy and the Berlin Music Conservatory, started composing film music for Germany's UFA studio in 1930; anti-Semitic pressures at the dawn of the Nazi era drove him out of the country and, eventually, to America. He set up shop at Universal, where his music for *Bride of Frankenstein, Diamond Jim, Remember Last Night? Magnificent Obsession* (all 1935), and *Sutter's Gold* (1936) was reused for years to come. (The

music for the creation scene in *Bride* remains a towering achievement, even after some sixty years.)

Waxman moved to MGM in 1936 and stayed there for seven years, contributing scores to *Captains Courageous* (1937), *A Christmas Carol* (1938), *On Borrowed Time* (1939), *The Philadelphia Story* (1940), *Honky Tonk* (1941), and *Woman of the Year* (1942), among many others. In 1943 he went to Warners, scoring *Air Force* (1943), *Mr. Skeffington* (1944), *Pride of the Marines* (1945), *Humoresque* (1946), and *Dark Passage* (1947), to name just a few. He freelanced for a time before signing up at Fox, where he composed scores for *Demetrius and the Gladiators, Prince Valiant* (both 1954), and *Peyton Place* (1957). Waxman also contributed memorable music to *Rear Window* (1954), *Run Silent, Run Deep* (1958), *Cimarron* (1960), and *Hemingway's Adventures of a Young Man* (1962).

WAYNE, DAVID. Actor. *(b. Jan. 30, 1914, Traverse City, Mich., as Wayne McKeehan; d. Feb. 9, 1995.)* Puckish, multipurpose actor adept at playing comedy and drama. Wayne debuted on the stage in 1936, and came to Broadway two years later. He won fame in the original productions of "Finian's Rainbow" (1947, as Og the leprechaun, winning a Tony Award), "Mister Roberts" (1948, as Ensign Pulver) and "The Teahouse of the August Moon" (1954, as Sakini, earning his second Tony). His Broadway stardom led to a busy decade in front of the movie camera, beginning with *Portrait of Jennie* (1948) and *Adam's Rib* (1949, as the songwriter neighbor who flirts with Katharine Hepburn). He went on to play a wide variety of roles: the child killer in Joseph Losey's remake of Fritz Lang's *M* (1951); Bill Mauldin's Joe (of Willie and Joe fame), a humorous WW2 G.I. in *Up Front* (1951); a rich man paired romantically with Marilyn Monroe in *How to Marry a Millionaire* (1953); impresario Sol Hurok in *Tonight We Sing* (1953); a married midwesterner intrigued by New York swinger Frank Sinatra's lifestyle in *The Tender Trap* (1955); and a determined television producer in *The Last Angry Man* (1959). He was also featured in *Wait 'Til the Sun Shines, Nellie* (1952, a leading role), *We're Not Married* (1952, married to

Marilyn Monroe), *With a Song in My Heart* (1952), *The Three Faces of Eve* and *The Sad Sack* (both 1957).

Wayne's screen career petered out in the 1960s. Later films include *The Andromeda Strain* (1971) and *The Apple Dumpling Gang* (1975); easily his best latter-day roles were Bensinger, the inept, poetry-writing journalist, in Billy Wilder's remake of *The Front Page* (1974); and the world's oldest train conductor in the little-seen farce *Finders Keepers* (1984). His television series credits include "Norby" (1955, in the starring role), "The Good Life" (1971), "The Adventures of Ellery Queen" (1975–76, as Inspector Richard Queen with Jim Hutton as his son, Ellery), "Dallas" (1978 only, as Willard "Digger" Barnes), and "House Calls" (1979–82). He was also memorable in "Escape Clause," a 1959 episode of "The Twilight Zone" (written by Rod Serling) in which he makes a deal with the Devil; and several episodes of "Batman," as the Mad Hatter.

WAYNE, JOHN. Actor, producer, director. (b. May 26, 1907, Winterset, Iowa, as Marion Michael Morrison; d. June 11, 1979.) He has come to represent the archetypal American of our country's formative period: honest, direct, decisive, solitary, and reverent; one whose faith in his own ability enables him to take action when it's needed, and whose belief in justice spurs him to right wrongs when they're discovered. John Wayne, nicknamed "Duke," played that character—or variations on it—in almost every movie he made, and it became so much a part of him that most people couldn't separate the real Wayne from his screen persona.

Duke Morrison was a USC football player who often worked, as did many Southern California college students, for filmmakers as extras and/or grips. He can be spotted in several late 1920s silents, including *Brown of Harvard* (1926), *The Drop Kick, Mother Macree* (both 1927), *Hangman's House,* and *Four Sons* (both 1928). Several of those were directed by John Ford, who gave Duke and his football pal Wardell Bond bit parts in his 1929 talkie *Salute.* Ford also recommended he be tested for the lead in Fox's upcoming Western epic *The Big Trail,* to be directed by Raoul Walsh.

Duke won the role, and his name was changed to John Wayne. Making the rugged frontier drama *The Big Trail* (1930) was an arduous experience for everybody, especially novice stars Wayne and Marguerite Churchill. It was also a flop at the box office, prompting Fox to drop him after he did a few minor programmers. He took bits wherever he could, supporting Western stars Buck Jones (in 1931's *Range Feud*) and Tim McCoy (1931's *Texas Cyclone* and 1932's *Two Fisted Law),* and starring in three cheap but action-packed serials, *The Shadow of the Eagle, The Hurricane Express* (both 1932), and *The Three Musketeers* (1933).

By the time those serials hit theaters, Duke had already landed a contract with Warner Bros., where he starred in six low-budget Westerns, and got bit parts in such A-level features as *The Life of Jimmy Dolan, Central Airport, College Coach,* and *Baby Face* (all 1933). Out in the cold again, he won the lead in a Poverty Row quickie, *His Private Secretary,* then spent the next two years starring in B Westerns for Monogram Pictures. (The first, 1933's *Riders of Destiny,* cast him as "Singin' Sandy," although his warbling was dubbed by the son of director Robert N. Bradbury.)

He spent the rest of the 1930s headlining Westerns and grade-B action features, first for Republic and then for Universal. He returned to Republic in 1938 to replace Bob Livingston as Stony Burke in eight entries of the long-running "Three Mesquiteers" series, including *Pals of the Saddle, Overland Stage Raiders* (both 1938), *The Night Riders, Wyoming Outlaw,* and *New Frontier* (all 1939). Between "Mesquiteer" shoots, Wayne was called by his old friend John Ford to test for the leading role of the Ringo Kid in his groundbreaking "adult" Western *Stagecoach* (1939). After a decade in front of the camera, this film made him an "overnight" star. He remained eternally grateful to Ford.

He continued to work out his contract at Republic, starring in B-plus vehicles at the studio, but he was also in demand, for the first time, as a leading man in Hollywood. He paired off with Marlene Dietrich and Randolph Scott in both *The Spoilers* and *Pittsburgh,* shared starring honors with Ray Milland and Paulette Goddard in Cecil B. DeMille's *Reap the Wild Wind* (all 1942), romanced Joan Crawford in *Reunion in France* (also 1942), Jean Arthur in *A Lady Takes a Chance* (1943), and Claudette Colbert in *Without Reservations* (1946), and forged a lifelong association with war movies by starring in *Flying Tigers* (1942), *The Fighting Seabees* (1944), *Back to Bataan,* and John Ford's *They Were Expendable* (both 1945). (Ironically, he was exempted from military service in real life because of an ear infection developed during underwater shooting on *Reap the Wild Wind.)*

In 1948 Duke starred in Howard Hawks' *Red River,* delivering an eye-opening performance as an unforgiving cattle baron who squares off against his adopted son (Montgomery Clift). For the first time, critics sat up and took notice. He continued to do impressive work in Ford's *3 Godfathers* and *Fort Apache* (both 1948), the first of the director's cavalry trilogy. Then in 1949 Ford gave him one of his best roles, in *She Wore a Yellow Ribbon,* as aged Capt. Nathan Brittles, who's slated to retire just as an Indian war is looming. Mustached and bespectacled, Wayne convinced audiences that his bones creaked every time he moved. That same year he made war-movie history as the tough-as-nails Marine drill instructor (who has a heart, after all) in *Sands of Iwo Jima* (1949), which earned him his first Academy Award nomination. Ford and Wayne made one more Cavalry film, *Rio Grande* (1950), as a payback to Republic boss Herbert J. Yates; by turning out this surefire box-office film, they earned the right to make Ford's pet project, *The Quiet Man.*

Wayne first encountered Maureen O'Hara onscreen in *Rio Grande,* and it was immediately clear that they had a special chemistry. They reunited in *The Quiet Man* (1952), a charming, romanticized view of Ireland as seen by an American. It was one of Wayne's most endearing performances, and one of the first that allowed audiences to enjoy his lighter side.

When Wayne brought Ford to Republic, the star secured a promise from Yates to let him film the story of the Alamo, a longtime dream. Yates later reneged, and Wayne never worked on a Republic film again. Wayne formed his own production company, Batjac (the name of the shipping company in 1948's *Wake of the Red Witch),* to develop projects both for him

and for other stars. Having produced Budd Boetticher's *Bullfighter and the Lady* (1951) at Republic, he hired the director again for the Randolph Scott Western *Seven Men From Now* (1956). He also put strapping James Arness under personal contract, and recommended him to CBS for the lead in the "Gunsmoke" TV series, even introducing the first episode on-camera.

Wayne coproduced and starred in *Big Jim McLain* (1952), *Island in the Sky, Hondo* (both 1953), *The High and the Mighty* (1954), *Blood Alley* (1955), and *Legend of the Lost* (1957). He worked again with Ford on what many consider to be the finest of their collaborations, *The Searchers* (1956), with Duke as an avenging angel in pursuit of Indians who've murdered his family and kidnapped his niece. The two friends also teamed for *The Wings of Eagles* (1957), which cast Wayne as Navy aviator-turned-screenwriter "Spig" Wead, and *The Horse Soldiers* (1959), a Civil War story.

Often accused of simply "playing himself" onscreen, Wayne tried to stretch in the 1950s, but his choices were ill advised, to say the least, and both *The Conqueror* (1956, in which he played Genghis Khan) and *The Barbarian and the Geisha* (1958, in which he played 19th-century American ambassador Townsend Harris) were major fiascos. In the years to follow he stuck to the tried-and-true, and who can blame him? Audiences lined up to see a "John Wayne movie" and he gave them what they wanted.

His last "personal" projects, which he directed and starred in, were the sprawling, extravagant super-production *The Alamo* (1960), in which he played Davy Crockett, and *The Green Berets* (1968), which reinforced his real-life image as a Hawk during the Vietnam era. These aside, Wayne continued working with Howard Hawks, in *Rio Bravo* (1959), the terrific African adventure *Hatari!* (1962), the *Rio Bravo* paraphrase *El Dorado* (1967), and *Rio Lobo* (1970), and John Ford in *The Man Who Shot Liberty Valance,* one segment of *How the West Was Won* (both 1962, in the latter as Gen. William Tecumseh Sherman), and *Donovan's Reef* (1963). His son Michael took the producer's reins on *McLintock!* (1963), directed by onetime Ford assistant Andrew McLaglen, which reunited Wayne with Maureen O'Hara. He repeatedly surrounded himself with such friends and colleagues in his remaining films, giving such otherwise uninspired Westerns as *The Sons of Katie Elder* (1965), *The War Wagon* (1967), *Chisum* (1970), *Big Jake* (1971), *The Train Robbers*, and *Cahill—United States Marshal* (both 1973) a welcome feeling of continuity for his fans.

True Grit (1969) gave him his first character role in years, as a boozy, one-eyed, over-the-hill lawman, and it won him his only Academy Award. He reprised the character in *Rooster Cogburn* (1975), a mediocre film distinguished by his genial performance opposite Katharine Hepburn, in an "odd couple" teaming meant to kindle thoughts of *The African Queen*. In later years Wayne appeared in a few non-Western movies, even trying his hand at a more contemporary cop story (à la Clint Eastwood): *McQ* (1974) was pretty embarrassing, but *Brannigan* (1975) at least had the novelty of putting brawny American Wayne in a London setting. *The Shootist* (1976) was a fitting valedictory to his career. The story of an aging gunfighter who learns he's dying of cancer, it featured a thoughtful, mature lead performance that suggested Wayne knew all too well the parallels between himself and his character. His last public appearance, at the 1979 Oscar ceremony, was itself an act of courage for the cancer-ridden star, who died just a few months later. His eldest son Michael produced many of his father's later films; another son, Patrick Wayne, had small parts in a number of his films and went on to a modest career as leading man in movies and television. A much younger son from a later marriage, John Ethan Wayne, launched an acting career of his own in the 1980s.

OTHER FILMS INCLUDE: 1929: *Words and Music*; 1930: *Men Without Women, Rough Romance, Cheer Up and Smile*; 1931: *Girls Demand Excitement, Three Girls Lost, Men Are Like That, Maker of Men*; 1932: *Lady and Gent, Ride 'em Cowboy, The Big Stampede, Haunted Gold*; 1933: *The Telegraph Trail, Somewhere in Sonora, The Man From Monterey, Sagebrush Trail*; 1934: *The Lucky Texan, West of the Divide, Blue Steel, The Man From Utah, Randy Rides Alone, The Star Packer, The Trail Beyond, The Lawless Frontier, 'Neath Arizona Skies*; 1935: *Texas Terror, Rainbow Valley, The Desert Trail, The Dawn Rider, Paradise Canyon, Westward Ho, The New Frontier,* *The Lawless Range*; 1936: *The Oregon Trail, The Lawless Nineties, King of the Pecos, The Lonely Trail, Winds of the Wasteland, The Sea Spoilers, Conflict*; 1937: *California Straight Ahead, I Cover the War, Idol of the Crowds, Adventure's End, Born to the West* (aka *Hell Town*); 1938: *Santa Fe Stampede, Red River Range*; 1939: *Three Texas Steers, Allegheny Uprising*; 1940: *Dark Command, Three Faces West, Seven Sinners*; 1941: *A Man Betrayed* (aka *Wheel of Fortune*), *Lady From Louisiana, Shepherd of the Hills*; 1942: *Lady for a Night, In Old California*; 1943: *In Old Oklahoma* (aka *War of the Wildcats*); 1944: *Tall in the Saddle*; 1945: *Flame of the Barbary Coast, Dakota*; 1947: *Angel and the Badman, Tycoon*; 1949: *The Fighting Kentuckian*; 1951: *Operation Pacific, Flying Leathernecks*; 1953: *Trouble Along the Way*; 1955: *The Sea Chase*; 1957: *Jet Pilot*; 1958: *I Married a Woman* (cameo); 1960: *North to Alaska*; 1961: *The Comancheros*; 1962: *The Longest Day*; 1964: *Circus World*; 1965: *The Greatest Story Ever Told* (cameo), *In Harm's Way*; 1966: *Cast a Giant Shadow* (cameo); 1969: *Hellfighters, The Undefeated*; 1972: *The Cowboys, Cancel My Reservation* (cameo).

WEATHERS, CARL. Actor. *(b. Jan. 14, 1948, New Orleans.)* As heavyweight champion Apollo Creed in *Rocky* (1976), this muscular ex-grid star matched Sylvester Stallone with his clever turn as a boxer with a mouth (and ego) reminiscent of prime Muhammad Ali. His character mellowed in three sequels, becoming a friend to Rocky and, finally, the fall guy killed by a seemingly unstoppable Soviet boxer in *Rocky IV* (1985). Weathers, whose first films were the blaxploitation epics *Bucktown* and *Friday Foster* (both 1975), also appeared in *Close Encounters of the Third Kind, Semi-Tough* (both 1977), *Force 10 From Navarone* (1978), *Death Hunt* (1981), and had a solid supporting role in the Schwarzenegger action vehicle *Predator* (1987). His first starring vehicle, *Action Jackson* (1988), gave Weathers a character intended to be a durable black action hero, but it was indifferently received. In the early 1990s Weathers starred in the syndicated TV action series "Street Justice" and briefly substituted for Howard E. Rollins on the series "In the Heat of the Night."

WEAVER, SIGOURNEY. Actress. (b. Oct. 8, 1949, New York City, as Susan Weaver.) Most moviegoers will probably remember this striking, patrician leading lady for her characterization of Ripley, the besieged protagonist of the *Alien* movies, but she's shown herself to be capable of much more than blasting slimy monsters into atoms. Born in New York to an affluent family (her father is broadcasting executive Sylvester "Pat" Weaver; her uncle was comedian Doodles Weaver), Sigourney, who adopted her name from a character in F. Scott Fitzgerald's "The Great Gatsby," attended Yale Drama School and worked on stage before landing a lead in *Madman* (1976) and a bit in *Annie Hall* (1977, as Woody's date at the end of the film). Her role as the tough astronaut in Ridley Scott's *Alien* (1979) made Weaver a recognizable screen player. Having graduated to starring parts, Weaver appeared as a reporter in both *Eyewitness* (1981, opposite William Hurt) and *The Year of Living Dangerously* (1983, opposite Mel Gibson). Those films bolstered her standing as a compelling lead, but the immense success of *Ghostbusters* (1984), in which she played a comically possessed New Yorker romanced by Bill Murray, did more for her career.

She played an intelligent hooker in *Half Moon Street* (1986), and reprised her Ripley characterization—even tougher and more commanding than before—in *Aliens* (1986, and earned her first Oscar nomination) before pulling off the nifty trick of snagging two Oscar nominations—Best Supporting Actress for her comic turn as the bitchy businesswoman in *Working Girl*, and Best Actress for her portrayal of the devoted anthropologist in *Gorillas in the Mist*—in 1988. She appeared in the lightweight *Ghostbusters II* (1989), and returned to Ripley (with a shaved head!) in *Aliens³* (1992). She then costarred with Kevin Kline in *Dave* (1993) as an aloof First Lady who falls in love with the President's "double" and took on the demanding role of a former torture victim who confronts her tormentor in *Death and the Maiden* (1994).

WEBB, CLIFTON. Actor. (b. Nov. 19, 1891, Indianapolis, as Webb Parmallee Hollenbeck; d. Oct. 13, 1966.) As an extremely precocious and prodigiously talented child, Clifton Webb may well have exhibited many of the traits that he later portrayed in others, especially the prissy, effete snobs he limned so well. Three such characterizations—acid-tongued columnist Waldo Lydecker in *Laura* (1944), Elliott Templeton in *The Razor's Edge* (1946), and unlikely baby-sitter Mr. Belvedere in *Sitting Pretty* (1948)—earned him Academy Award nominations. Webb, a trained actor and dancer at age 10, quit grade school to study the arts, and actually sang with the Boston Opera Company when he was 17. He danced professionally, acted on stage in London and on Broadway, and became a leading musical comedy star. He had roles in several silent films, beginning with *Polly With a Past* (1920), but his movie career began in earnest with the smash hit *Laura* (cast by director Otto Preminger despite the misgivings of studio chief Darryl Zanuck, who thought him too effeminate). Webb seldom strayed very far from his patented characterization, but refined it continually.

OTHER FILMS INCLUDE: 1925: *New Toys;* 1946: *The Dark Corner;* 1949: *Mr. Belvedere Goes to College;* 1950: *Cheaper by the Dozen* (as efficiency expert Frank Gilbreth), *For Heaven's Sake;* 1951: *Elopement, Mr. Belvedere Rings the Bell;* 1952: *Dreamboat* (as a silent-movie actor turned college professor!), *Stars and Stripes Forever* (as John Philip Sousa); 1953: *Mister Scoutmaster, Titanic;* 1954: *Three Coins in the Fountain, Woman's World;* 1955: *The Man Who Never Was;* 1957: *Boy on a Dolphin;* 1959: *The Remarkable Mr. Pennypacker, Holiday for Lovers;* 1962: *Satan Never Sleeps.*

WEBB, JACK. Actor, producer, director. (b. Apr. 2, 1920, Santa Monica, Calif.; d. Dec. 23, 1982.) Although most people remember his clipped speech, manners, and haircut, Webb had a fairly solid career in movies and radio before assuming the role of police detective Joe Friday ("Just the facts, ma'am . . .") on the "Dragnet" radio and TV series and in two feature films. He had a much broader range as an actor than the Friday characterization would indicate. (He also had a sense of humor, as indicated by the colorful characters who populated the early "Dragnet" shows.) After spending several of the post-WW2 years as a radio announcer and actor, Webb reached the big screen in 1948's *He*

Walked by Night and had notable appearances in two 1950 classics—as a wisecracking paraplegic in *The Men,* and a good-time Charley in *Sunset Blvd.* He also appeared in *Dark City* (1950), doing scenes with his later "Dragnet" costar Harry Morgan, *Halls of Montezuma* (also 1950), *Appointment With Danger,* and *You're in the Navy Now* (both 1951).

After "Dragnet" moved from radio to TV (1951–59), he formed his own production company, Mark VII (whose hammer-and-chisel logo was much parodied), and subsequently produced, directed, and starred in a series of wildly varied pictures: a feature version of *Dragnet* (1954); a downbeat study of 1920s jazzmen, *Pete Kelly's Blues* (1955, based on his earlier radio show); a vivid, memorable portrait of a hard-bitten Marine sergeant, *The D.I.* (1957); a heavy-handed newspaper drama, *-30-* (1959); and an easygoing Army comedy, *The Last Time I Saw Archie* (1961). He also hosted and (without credit) supervised the classic anti-Commie short-subject "Red Nightmare." Thereafter he returned to TV, first as a production executive, then as producer, star, and director of a revived "Dragnet" (1967–70), and finally as the creator and producer of the hit shows "Adam-12" (1968–75) and "Emergency" (1972–77). Both as producer and director, Webb insisted on a deadpan, emotionless acting style from his players, along with deliberately banal dialogue—which, he felt, added verisimilitude to the proceedings. However stilted his work seems today, it's certainly distinctive and readily identifiable. And though Webb's movie work may remain secondary, it nevertheless deserves reappraisal.

WEIR, PETER. Director, writer. *(b. Aug. 8, 1944, Sydney, Australia.)* Stylish Australian director who has made a successful transition from serious dramatic work to mainstream entertainment. Weir studied art and law at Sydney University before taking on a series of minor TV jobs. Working on his own, he learned camera and editing techniques and, by 1974, he had helmed his first internationally distributed picture, a low-budget horror film laced with black comedy called *The Cars That Ate Paris.* The unlikely commercial success of that film led to an even more unlikely follow-up, *Picnic at Hanging Rock* (1975). This pseudo-mystic tale (based on a true story) of private-school girls who mysteriously disappear in the Australian outback not only established Weir as a bold new talent, but was the first film to explore the director's favorite theme, that of clashing cultures. The prim, repressed young schoolgirls are carefully contrasted with the untamed nature of Hanging Rock; this juxtaposition of "civilization" versus the unknowable is the hallmark of virtually all of the director's work. (It should be noted that Weir took time out to make a black comedy for Australian TV, *The Plumber,* in 1980.)

Other Weir films that play up this theme include *The Last Wave* (1977), in which a barrister becomes involved with Aboriginal apocalypse mythology; *Gallipoli* (1981), in which rural Australian boys are caught up in the slaughter of WW1 Turkey; *The Year of Living Dangerously* (1983), which has two Western journalists falling in love while a third-world capital collapses around them; *Witness* (1985, his first American film), which brought big-city detective Harrison Ford into the unfamiliar culture of Pennsylvania's Amish country, and *The Mosquito Coast* (1986), which saw Ford try to establish "civilization" in a remote jungle. Weir enjoyed great commercial success with *Dead Poets Society* (1989), and earned his second Oscar nomination (the first was for *Witness);* the following year he was nominated for a Best Screenplay Oscar for his more commercially contrived comedy *Green Card* (1990). His next film didn't appear until 1993, but it was worth the wait: *Fearless* was one of his strongest in years, an arresting study of a man who survives an airplane crash, and finds his life irrevocably changed by the experience.

WEISSMULLER, JOHNNY. Actor. *(b. June 2, 1904, Windber, Pa., as Peter John Weissmuller; d. Jan. 20, 1984.)* Casting the leading role in *Tarzan, the Ape Man* (1932), MGM director W. S. Van Dyke dismissed Charles Bickford (not young enough), Johnny Mack Brown (not tall enough), Clark Gable (not muscular enough), and countless other studio contractees before choosing Olympic swimming champ Weissmuller, whose motion picture experience had been limited to a brief appearance in *Glorifying the*

American Girl (1929). But he looked great in a loincloth, and acting experience didn't count for much with dialogue like "Umgawa!" MGM's lavish production was a spectacular hit, making Weissmuller an overnight star and prompting a long string of sequels: *Tarzan and His Mate* (1934), *Tarzan Escapes* (1936), *Tarzan Finds a Son!* (1939), *Tarzan's Secret Treasure* (1941), and *Tarzan's New York Adventure* (1942), all of which teamed the former University of Chicago student with petite Maureen O'Sullivan.

Diminishing returns—and the increasing unhappiness of O'Sullivan—led MGM to sell its character rights to independent producer Sol Lesser, who distributed his films through RKO. Lesser started off well with *Tarzan Triumphs* (1943), a topical story pitting the Ape Man against invading Nazis (sans Jane). It was followed by *Tarzan's Desert Mystery* (1943), *Tarzan and the Amazons* (1945), and *Tarzan and the Leopard Woman* (1946), but an aging, thickening Weissmuller, weaker scripts, and smaller budgets took their toll on the popular series by the time of *Tarzan and the Huntress* (1947). After completing *Tarzan and the Mermaids* (1948), Weissmuller hung up his loincloth for good.

Cheapie producer Sam Katzman, operating on the theory that you can take the boy out of the jungle but you can't take the jungle out of the boy, offered Weissmuller the leading role in his new "Jungle Jim" series, based on a well-liked comic strip, for Columbia. Weissmuller, told he could keep his clothes on, agreed. *Jungle Jim* (1948) launched the series adequately, but succeeding stanzas saw already-skimpy budgets reduced and increasing reliance on stock footage. Later entries included *The Lost Tribe* (1949), *Mark of the Gorilla*, *Pygmy Island* (both 1950), *Jungle Manhunt* (1951), *Voodoo Tiger* (1952), and *Cannibal Attack* (1954). After seven years and 15 films, the series went out with a whimper; by this time Katzman had stopped licensing the "Jungle Jim" character and had Weissmuller playing himself. After *Devil Goddess* (1955), the star left Africa behind—for a few years, anyway. He was back as Jungle Jim on a 1958 TV series. Weissmuller made his last screen appearance playing himself (accompanied by Maureen O'Sullivan) in *The Phynx* (1970), but the film was shelved and never saw the light of day. In the nearly 25 years that constituted his starring career, he only made two "civilian" pictures: *Stage Door Canteen* (1943, as himself) and *Swamp Fire* (1946), a drama of the bayous that pitted him against fellow Olympic swimming star (and former Tarzan) Buster Crabbe.

WELCH, RAQUEL. Actress. *(b. Sept. 5, 1940, Chicago, as Raquel Tejada.)* In the mid and late 1960s she was positively ubiquitous, wearing a furry animal-skin bikini on a best-selling poster, but for all her exposure, Raquel Welch wasn't able to maintain a long-term big-screen career. A perennial beauty-contest winner who took ballet lessons and studied drama, she broke into films in 1964 with bits in *A House Is Not a Home* and Elvis Presley's *Roustabout;* the following year she appeared briefly in *A Swingin' Summer.* She supplemented her meager income by modeling, using her sensuous, high-cheekboned face and spectacular figure to help pay the rent. In 1964 she became the "billboard girl" on TV's "Hollywood Palace."

Divorced from high-school sweetheart James Welch, in 1965 she married former child actor and press agent Patrick Curtis, who charted a course for her career. She appeared in many European magazines, and landed a role in the Italian-made *Shoot Loud, Louder . . . I Don't Understand* (1966) that led to a contract with 20th Century-Fox. *Fantastic Voyage* (also 1966) gave her a costarring part in a hit movie, while the British-made prehistoric saga *One Million Years B.C.* (also 1966) was promoted with a popular poster that made her a household figure, as well as name.

She followed up with *Fathom* (1967), *Bedazzled* (also 1967, as "Lust"), *The Biggest Bundle of Them All, Bandolero!* (both 1968), *Lady in Cement* (also 1968, opposite Frank Sinatra), *Flareup, 100 Rifles,* and *The Magic Christian* (all 1969). Welch proved to have screen presence, and a sense of humor, but moviegoers were interested in her skin-tight costumes and bikinis, not her acting range.

Myra Breckinridge (1970) teamed Raquel with Mae West, the sex symbol of an earlier era, in a horrendous misfire. *Hannie Caulder* and *Kansas City Bomber* (both 1972) followed, but her starring days were numbered. She fared best in ensemble films like *The Last of Sheila* (1973) and the send-up swashbucklers *The Three Musketeers* (1974) and *The Four Musketeers* (1975), which exploited the novelty of having her poke fun at herself. Other films include *Bluebeard, Fuzz* (both 1972), *The Wild Party* (1975), *Mother, Jugs & Speed* (1976), and *Crossed Swords* (1978).

In the 1980s she launched a cabaret act, and even made it to Broadway, taking over the lead in the musical "Woman of the Year." Her most prized personal project was the TV movie *The Legend of Walks Far Woman*, in which she played an Indian woman at various stages of her life; filmed in 1979, it didn't air until 1982. Since then she has starred in other telefilms—1987's *Right to Die* and 1988's *Scandal in a Small Town* and *Trouble in Paradise*—and found a more positive way of exploiting her still-impressive figure with a series of best-selling exercise videotapes and accompanying fitness books. She played herself in *The Naked Gun 33⅓: The Final Insult* (1994). Her daughter Tahnee Welch, also an actress, appeared in the all-star hit *Cocoon* (1985) and its 1988 sequel.

WELD, TUESDAY. Actress. *(b. Aug. 27, 1943, New York City, as Susan Weld.)* Beautiful, girlish blond actress whose tempestuous early years contrasted with her success as a child model. She'd already become a staple of gossip columns—suffering a nervous breakdown, alcoholism, and attempting suicide—by the time she reached high school! Little of this came through onscreen, at least in the early years of her career. On TV she was a persuasively unattainable Thalia Menninger on "Dobie Gillis" (1959–60), and a virginal, blue-eyed innocent in her first Hollywood movies. She also played against that image, most effectively in *Pretty Poison* (1968), as a seductive high schooler who mesmerizes Anthony Perkins. Absent from the big screen for several years during the 1970s, Weld returned to the spotlight playing Diane Keaton's sister in *Looking for Mr. Goodbar* (1977), for which she received a Best Supporting Actress Oscar nomination. Her appearances have been sporadic since then, including, most unexpectedly, the lead in a TV remake of the tear-stained soap opera

Madame X (1981). In 1993 she turned up, considerably heavier, as Robert Duvall's emotionally dependent wife in *Falling Down*. Formerly married to Dudley Moore, she later wed violinist Pinchas Zuckerman.

OTHER FILMS INCLUDE: 1958: *Rally 'Round the Flag, Boys!;* 1959: *The Five Pennies;* 1960: *High Time, Because They're Young, The Private Lives of Adam and Eve, Sex Kittens Go to College;* 1961: *Bachelor Flat, Return to Peyton Place, Wild in the Country;* 1963: *Soldier in the Rain;* 1965: *I'll Take Sweden, The Cincinnati Kid;* 1966: *Lord Love a Duck;* 1970: *I Walk the Line;* 1971: *A Safe Place;* 1972: *Play It As It Lays;* 1978: *Who'll Stop the Rain;* 1980: *Serial;* 1981: *Thief;* 1982: *Author! Author!;* 1984: *Once Upon a Time in America;* 1988: *Heartbreak Hotel.*

WELLER, PETER. Actor. *(b. June 24, 1947, Stevens Point, Wis.)* You wouldn't ordinarily think that an actor could attain stardom by portraying "a walking heap of scrap metal," but that's just what happened to Peter Weller after being cast as the quick-triggered cyborg (part robot, part human) of *RoboCop* (1987), a role he reprised in a 1990 sequel. (Working with a mime instructor, he patterned his movements after those of actor Nikolai Cherkassov in the Russian film classic *Ivan the Terrible.)* Weller, a gaunt-faced, slender actor with steely blue eyes, was an Army brat who studied at the American Academy of Dramatic Arts before acting professionally on the stage. After making his movie debut in *Butch and Sundance: The Early Days* (1979), he landed major roles in *Just Tell Me What You Want* (1980), *Shoot the Moon* (1982, as Diane Keaton's boyfriend), and *Of Unknown Origin* (1983, in which he fought a giant rat!). In 1984, he starred in the cult sci-fi opus *The Adventures of Buckaroo Banzai Across the Eighth Dimension,* and convincingly played a loutish creep in *First-Born*. His post-*RoboCop* vehicles haven't been of particularly good quality; these include *Shakedown, A Killing Affair* (both 1988), *Cat Chaser,* and *Leviathan* (both 1989). Weller did appear to good advantage in *Naked Lunch* (1991), starring as the William Burroughs surrogate. Weller is a real talent; the trick is finding roles that suit that talent. Recent credits include *Fifty/Fifty* (1992) and *The New Age*

(1994). In 1993 Weller directed and coproduced an Oscar-nominated short, *Partners.*

WELLES, ORSON. Actor, director, writer, producer. *(b. May 6, 1915, Kenosha, Wis.; d. Oct. 9, 1985.)* "People should cross themselves when they say his name," Marlene Dietrich once said. Indeed, Welles was a uniquely talented artist, but one who was doomed to spend much of his life unable to realize his ambitions. It didn't start that way: Welles was a precocious and gifted child who began acting, writing, and directing for theater in his teens. In the mid 1930s he established himself as a radio actor (on "The March of Time" and "The Shadow," among other shows) and then, with partner John Houseman, revolutionized both the radio medium and the theater with the forward-thinking productions of the Mercury Players. Their "War of the Worlds" broadcast on Halloween night of 1938 made history when it scared the bejeezus out of thousands of listeners . . . and helped plant the name of Orson Welles in the national consciousness.

Hollywood courted the "boy wonder" from New York, and RKO won his services by promising complete freedom (including the unprecedented right of "final cut" on his first feature). Welles did preliminary work on several projects, including an adaptation of Joseph Conrad's "Heart of Darkness," and a life of Christ set in the Old West, but settled instead on an ambitious pseudobiography of a publishing magnate and political kingmaker (based on William Randolph Hearst and Chicago's Robert McCormick). Welles worked with Herman J. Mankiewicz on the script, and had the great fortune of having innovative cameraman Gregg Toland volunteer to work with him on his maiden voyage. Welles would play the leading role—a tour de force in itself—and surrounded himself with members of the Mercury troupe (including Joseph Cotten, Everett Sloane, Ray Collins, and Agnes Moorehead, most of whom were making their film debuts). *Citizen Kane* (1941) rewrote the book on moviemaking in Hollywood, with bold and startling ideas about narrative storytelling, the creation of pictures and sound. (Welles worked closely with such collaborators as composer Bernard Herrmann, who'd been with him in radio, sound man James G. Stewart, and special effects man Linwood Dunn, whose optical printer helped create many of the film's most dazzling images.) Even Welles' makeup, which convincingly aged him through a period of decades, was revolutionary. Hearst's minions were extremely unhappy about the film, and tried to sabotage it in their papers; MGM's Louis B. Mayer reportedly tried to buy the negative and bury it, literally. It was never a commercial hit, but *Kane* was a critical success, and earned nine Academy Award nominations, winning one for Best Screenplay. Welles was just twenty-five years old.

For his next project he set about filming Booth Tarkington's sprawling saga of an American family—and an American era—*The Magnificent Ambersons,* which he'd already adapted for radio. This time he wouldn't star, which "freed up" the prolific Welles to appear in another RKO film, *Journey Into Fear* (sometimes shooting scenes at night after directing his own film during the day). He was urged by Nelson Rockefeller of the Office of Inter-American Affairs to go to South America and make a film there that would further understanding between our cultures, and benefit the "Good Neighbor Policy." Welles agreed, and arranged to work with editor Robert Wise on *Ambersons* just before his departure.

It was at this juncture that Welles' life and career took a disastrous turn. New management at RKO was not sympathetic to the "boy wonder," and when *Ambersons* did poorly at sneak previews, orders were given to reedit the film and shoot new scenes—without Welles' knowledge or approval. The studio also did not approve of his South American jaunt, particularly since Welles was still developing his story ideas, while bills were mounting. All at once, RKO gave the truncated *Ambersons* a desultory release, pulled the plug on his South American movie, *It's All True,* and ejected Mercury Productions from its studio headquarters. (The footage from *It's All True,* the subject of bitter fights and much speculation over the years, was finally fashioned into a feature release in 1993.) Like Erich von Stroheim twenty years earlier, Welles acquired an undeserved reputation of being a commercial failure, an irresponsible director, and a spendthrift. What's more, no studios in town were willing to give him the freedom he'd enjoyed at the outset of his RKO tenure.

He found acting jobs, in *Jane Eyre* (1944) and *Tomorrow Is Forever* (1946) but it wasn't until 1946 that he was able to direct another film, the first-rate thriller *The Stranger,* in which he starred with Loretta Young and Edward G. Robinson. He then charmed Columbia Pictures boss Harry Cohn, and made *The Lady From Shanghai* (1948) with Cohn's biggest star, Rita Hayworth (who also happened to be Mrs. Orson Welles at the time). Cohn was uncomfortable with Welles—or anyone—having as much power as he did on that film, as director, writer, and star, and there was no followup. Later that year he made a low-budget version of *Macbeth* (1948) at Republic Pictures (of all places), with many of his favorite radio-actor colleagues.

Welles relocated to Europe, where he landed one of his all-time best film roles, as the elusive Harry Lime, in Carol Reed's *The Third Man* (1949). Shortly after its completion he began filming *Othello* on location in Morocco, but had to suspend production after just a few weeks because his backers backed out. Welles immediately started taking acting jobs in Europe—in *Black Magic* and *Prince of Foxes* (both 1949) and *The Black Rose* (1950)—to help raise funds to keep his own film alive. *Othello*—filled with ingenious camerawork and a handful of vibrant performances, including Welles' own as the Moor, which compensate for its "rough edges"—was finally completed in 1952, though unseen in the U.S. until 1955. (In the 1970s Welles shot a documentary, *Filming Othello,* for German Television that's almost as interesting as the movie itself!) But his travails in getting it made were to be echoed countless times in the years ahead as he tried to float other film ventures. (While making *Othello,* he appeared as himself in a 1951 short subject called *Return to Glennascaul,* for his friends Micheal MacLiammoir—who played Iago in *Othello*—and Hilton Edwards; when released in the U.S. in 1953 it was nominated for an Academy Award.)

As always, he found acting jobs—in the British *Trent's Last Case* (1952), the Italian-made *Man, Beast and Virtue,* and the French *Royal Affairs in Versailles,* as Benjamin Franklin (both 1953), the British *Three Cases of Murder* and *Trouble in the Glen* and the French *Napoleon* (all 1954), and *Moby Dick* (1956)—but financing for his own films was another matter. With French and Spanish funding, he did direct and star in *Mr. Arkadin* (1955), one of his few fully realized projects, but even it was taken away from him in the final stages of editing.

Throughout the 1950s he wrote scripts for unrealized films, and busied himself with stage projects on both sides of the Atlantic. He also made occasional forays into television, and produced, wrote, and directed several television pilots that did not sell. After he was cast as a smarmy police detective in a small-scale Hollywood thriller, *A Touch of Evil* (1958), the film's star, Charlton Heston, suggested to Universal that Welles also direct the film. He did a quick rewrite on the script, and was hired. It was filled with visual flourishes—including a now-famous three-minute extended opening crane shot—but it was just a minor film at the time of its release, and did not result in any further directing jobs. (It was recut for release without Welles' participation, but in 1976 a print was found of his original, and that version has been in release ever since.)

From 1957 to 1960 Welles worked on a fanciful adaptation of *Don Quixote* which was never completed; a version derived from existing footage was presented posthumously in 1992. He was able to complete an adaptation of Kafka's *The Trial* (1963), a little-seen but much-praised film, *Chimes at Midnight* (1966) in which he starred as Shakespeare's Falstaff, *The Immortal Story* (1968), an hour-long adaptation of a story by Isak Dinesen, and the pseudodocumentary *F for Fake* (1974). Welles never stopped writing or planning film projects; the one that came closest to completion was a story about a Hollywood director, *The Other Side of the Wind.* Like Welles' other film endeavors, this one was made over an extended period (in this case, seven years, 1970–76), with John Huston in the starring role; it is perhaps the most frustrating of Welles' unfinished projects, because it apparently came closest to completion, with disputed ownership being the main reason it hasn't been seen. (Welles did show clips from it when he received the American Film Institute Life Achievement Award in 1975.)

Welles continued to act throughout his lifetime, sometimes in worthy roles and films like *The Long Hot Summer* (1958), *Compulsion* (1959), *Crack in the Mirror* (1960), *A Man for All Seasons* (1966), *Is Paris Burning?* (1966), *Casino Royale* (1967), *Oedipus the King* (1968), *Catch-22* (1970), *Waterloo*, Henry Jaglom's *A Safe Place* (both 1971), *Treasure Island* (1972), *Voyage of the Damned* (1976), and *It Happened One Christmas* (1977, taking Lionel Barrymore's role as Mr. Potter in this TV remake of *It's a Wonderful Life*), but more often in potboilers and outright junk, ranging from *The Tartars* (1961) to *Necromancy* (1972) and *Butterly* (1981). One novelty of Welles-watching was observing his penchant for the use of false noses and other makeup accoutrements. His last screen appearance was as himself in Jaglom's largely improvised *Someone to Love* (1987). He also narrated countless feature films, documentaries, and television shows, and made a very good living as a commercial spokesman. Although he never wrote an official autobiography, he authorized Barbara Leaming's biography "Orson Welles" (1985) and gave extensive interviews to Peter Bogdanovich which were assembled as "This Is Orson Welles" (1992).

WELLMAN, WILLIAM A. Director, producer, screenwriter. (b. Feb. 29, 1896, Brookline, Mass.; d. Dec. 9, 1975.) Prolific, workmanlike director of mainstream Hollywood fare whose output includes some remarkable films. He helped kick off the gangster movie cycle (and James Cagney's career) with *The Public Enemy* (1931), tackled Depression-era social problems in *Wild Boys of the Road* and *Heroes for Sale* (both 1933), crafted an Oscar-winning original story and screenplay for *A Star Is Born* (1937, which also earned him a nomination as Best Director), showed a flair for screwball comedy with *Nothing Sacred* (also 1937), brought verve to the old Foreign Legion standard *Beau Geste* (1939), made viewers' spines tingle with his harrowing lynch-mob tale *The Ox-Bow Incident* (1943), and saluted WW2 dogfaces with his war films *The Story of G.I. Joe* (1945) and *Battleground* (1949, Oscar nominated again). He earned

his final Oscar nomination directing the hugely popular "Grand Hotel aloft" saga *The High and the Mighty* (1954).

An adventurous youth, Wellman joined the French Foreign Legion at the outbreak of World War 1, and when America entered the conflict three years later he flew with the distinguished Lafayette Escadrille. Mustered out of the service after being seriously wounded, the highly decorated Wellman became a stunt flyer and barnstormer back in the United States. As Hollywood legend has it, he broke into movies after meeting Douglas Fairbanks when his plane made a forced landing on the actor's property. Wellman even acted in Fairbanks' *Knickerbocker Buckaroo* (1919), but quickly decided he'd rather be behind the camera. He worked his way up from prop man to assistant director to director, cutting his eyeteeth on Buck Jones' Westerns for Fox in the mid 1920s.

Wellman's *Wings* (1927), a breathtaking drama of WW1 aviators, won the first Academy Award for Best Picture and boosted the director into the front rank of Hollywood helmers. He never lost his love affair with flying, and frequently returned to aviation themes in his films. A two-fisted, no-nonsense tough guy who several times traded blows with his actors (including Spencer Tracy), Wellman earned the nickname "Wild Bill."

Wellman, who married *Wild Boys of the Road* leading lady Dorothy Coonan, wrote his memoirs, "A Short Time for Insanity," in 1974. His son, William Wellman, Jr., became an actor.

OTHER FILMS INCLUDE: 1928: *Beggars of Life*; 1929: *Chinatown Nights*; 1931: *Other Men's Women, Star Witness, Safe in Hell, Night Nurse*; 1932: *The Hatchet Man, So Big, Love Is a Racket, The Conquerors*; 1933: *Frisco Jenny, Central Airport, Lilly Turner, Midnight Mary*; 1934: *Looking for Trouble, The President Vanishes*; 1935: *Call of the Wild*; 1936: *Robin Hood of El Dorado, Small Town Girl*; 1938: *Men With Wings*; 1939: *The Light That Failed*; 1941: *Reaching for the Sun*; 1942: *Roxie Hart, The Great Man's Lady, Thunder Birds*; 1943: *Lady of Burlesque*; 1944: *Buffalo Bill*; 1946: *Gallant Journey*; 1947: *Magic Town*; 1948: *Yellow Sky*; 1950: *The Happy Years, The Next Voice You Hear*; 1951: *Westward the Women, Across the Wide Missouri, It's a Big Country* (codirected with others); 1953: *Island in the Sky*; 1954: *Track of the Cat*; 1955: *Blood Alley*; 1956:

Good-bye, My Lady; 1958: *Darby's Rangers, Lafayette Escadrille.*

WENDERS, WIM. Director. *(b. Aug. 14, 1945, Dusseldorf, Germany.)* One of the most important directors on the international scene, Wenders first came to prominence with films that focused on postwar Germany and the Americanization of its culture; the rootlessness of his characters also addresses some deeper, philosophical concerns. This was certainly true of his first, critically praised feature, *The Goalie's Anxiety at the Penalty Kick* (1971), which he followed with an adaptation of *The Scarlet Letter* (1972). His three "road movies" of the 1970s (Wenders' own production company is called Road Movies), *Alice in the Cities* (1974), *Wrong Move* (1975), and the mammoth *Kings of the Road* (1976), deal with these issues and also convey Wenders' deep love of cinema and rock and roll. *The American Friend* (1977) featured American actor Dennis Hopper along with appearances by Wenders' directorial heroes Nicholas Ray and Samuel Fuller. When Wenders finally came to the country that had intrigued him so much, things didn't go at all smoothly; his film *Hammett,* begun in 1978, was considerably altered after many conflicts with his producer, Francis Ford Coppola. It was finally released in 1983. (He drew on that harrowing experience for his 1982 movie *The State of Things,* which offered a bleak look at filmmaking.) Wenders also collaborated with Ray on a choppy film depicting Ray's final battle with cancer, *Lightning Over Water* (1980).

Wenders won worldwide acclaim for 1984's *Paris, Texas,* the story of a drifter making peace with his turbulent past, including a son he's never known; the film earned the Palme D'Or at Cannes. Wenders then returned to Germany to direct *Wings of Desire* (1988), a fable of angels hovering over Berlin; one of them falls in love with a circus acrobat and forsakes his immortal status, taking corporeal form to join her on Earth. A brilliant film that combines the fantastic appeal of Powell and Pressburger's *Stairway to Heaven* with a poetic, contemporary sensibility, *Wings* was roundly praised and earned Wenders a Best Director award at Cannes. Wenders worked on a couple of documentary projects before beginning his most ambitious production, 1991's *Until the End of the World,* a science-fiction drama shot in more than five countries and featuring an international cast led by William Hurt. In 1993 he surprised admirers by making a sequel to *Wings of Desire* called *Faraway, So Close!,* with key original cast members reprising their roles. Wenders has also made unconventional documentaries over the years, including the visual diary *Tokyo-Ga* (1985), a tribute to filmmaker Yasujiro Ozu, and *Notebook on Cities and Clothes* (1989), ostensibly a profile of Yohji Yamamoto. He directed a music video for U2 called "Night and Day."

WERNER, OSKAR. Actor, director, producer. *(b. Nov. 13, 1922, Vienna, as Oskar Josef Bschliessmayer; d. Oct 23, 1984.)* Slender, blond, soft-spoken stage director who made a handful of memorable screen appearances. At age 18, Werner joined Vienna's Burgtheater; after serving in the war, he returned to the theater, and for the next decade starred in a wide variety of productions, including "Hamlet" and "Becket," and in 1959 he established his own company, Theater Ensemble Oskar Werner. The actor's initial film credit was *Der Engel mit der Posaune* (1948). His U.S. debut came in *Decision Before Dawn* (1951), filmed in Europe, in which he played a German P.O.W. who becomes a spy for his captors. His acclaimed performance earned Werner a trip to Hollywood and a 20th Century-Fox contract, which never came to fruition. He returned to Europe, took a supporting part in Max Ophuls' *Lola Montes* (1955), and starred in *Mozart* (also 1955). Werner returned to the international spotlight in one of Truffaut's most beloved films, *Jules and Jim* (1961), playing a retiring German Jew bohemian involved in a three-cornered friendship. His next important film, *Ship of Fools* (1965), gave him his best screen role, and an Oscar nomination, as Dr. Schumann, a melancholy doctor who enjoys a brief romance with Simone Signoret aboard an ocean liner heading for Germany in 1933. Other film roles followed, including *The Spy Who Came In From the Cold* (1965, as a counterspy), Truffaut's *Fahrenheit 451* (1967, as the rebellious Montag), *The Shoes of the Fisherman* and *Interlude* (both 1968).

Werner's final screen role was reminiscent of Dr. Schumann: in *Voyage of the Damned* (1976), he plays an urbane Jew fleeing Nazi Germany on an ill-fated ship.

WERTMULLER, LINA. Director. *(b. Aug. 14, 1928, Rome, as Arcangala Felice Assunta Wertmuller von Elgg.)* Influential Italian director who caused a sensation in the 1970s. Born to an aristocratic Swiss family, Wertmuller grew up as an enfant terrible, getting thrown out of more than a dozen Catholic schools. She enrolled in the Theater Academy of Rome, performing across Europe for over a decade as an actress. Through a friend of hers, who was married to Marcello Mastroianni, Wertmuller met Federico Fellini, and worked as his assistant on the celebrated *8½* (1963). That same year she directed her own first feature, *The Lizards.* One of Wertmuller's actor-pals, Giancarlo Giannini, recommended her work to Franco Zeffirelli, and after collaborating on a successful production of Wertmuller's play *Two Plus Two Are No Longer Four* (starring Giannini), she and Giannini formed a bond comparable to the creative relationship between Robert De Niro and Martin Scorsese.

In the 1970s Wertmuller directed a string of pictures (all starring Giannini) that are still resonant and controversial, despite occasional heavy-handedness. *The Seduction of Mimi* (1972), a witty look at the link between sex and politics, won Wertmuller international attention and acclaim, and her follow-up, *Love and Anarchy,* was the hit foreign film of 1973. She had another success (sans Giannini) with *All Screwed Up* (1974). In 1975 she directed the enormously popular *Swept Away,* a sexually charged story of class and gender tension set on a desert island, and in 1976 helmed her masterpiece, *Seven Beauties,* starring Giannini as a roguish ne'er-do-well forced to survive the horrors of a Nazi concentration camp. The movie earned Wertmuller Oscar nominations for Best Screenplay and also for Best Director, the first woman in Academy history to have been nominated in that category. It was Wertmuller's artistic apogee. Amidst this fanfare, Wertmuller made her English-language debut with *A Night Full of Rain* (full title: *The End of the World in Our Usual Bed in a Night Full of Rain*); alas, this 1978 feature starring Giannini and Candice Bergen was a great disappointment, and somehow, Wertmuller never seemed to regain her momentum. *Blood Feud* (1979), *A Joke of Destiny* (1983), *A Complex Plot About Women, Softly Softly* (both 1985), *Summer Night With Greek Profile, Almond Eyes and Scent of Basil* (both 1986), *The Tenth One in Hiding, Of Crystal or Cinders, Fire or Wind, as Long as It's Love* (both 1989), *Saturday Sunday and Monday* (1990), and *Ciao, Professore* (1993) have made little impact. She's worked exclusively in her native Italy since the late 1970s, and few of her films have enjoyed extensive (if any) American release since her heyday.

WEST, MAE. Actress, screenwriter, playwright. *(b. Aug. 17, 1892, Brooklyn, N.Y.; d. Nov. 22, 1980.)* A veteran of burlesque, vaudeville, and Broadway, Mae West made her first movie when she was nearly 40, and became a sex symbol (for lack of a better term) at an age when other actresses were being considered for roles as mothers to aging adolescents. Less remembered is the fact that she wrote many of her own screen vehicles, making her one of the great comedy scenarists of her time. Her blond hair, hourglass figure, bedroom eyes, and silky-seductive voice made her a popular (if notorious) stage personality, and she attracted headlines with her 1926 play, "Sex." Police shut down the production for its alleged obscenity, but some detected the faint aroma of a publicity stunt. She wrote, directed, and starred in several other plays before signing with Paramount in 1932.

West stole her first film, *Night After Night,* from leads George Raft and Constance Cummings, and uttered the first of many quotable lines when a hatcheck girl admired her jewels, saying, "Goodness, what lovely diamonds." Mae primped and replied, "Goodness had nothing to do with it, dearie." Paramount responded by giving her the star treatment for her second picture, *She Done Him Wrong* (1933), based on her play "Diamond Lil." The film was credited with pulling Paramount out of bankruptcy, and earned an Oscar nomination for Best Picture. It was marked with the same insouciant flippancy that made Mae's stage shows so popular (typified by her saucy invitation to Cary Grant, "Come up some time an' see me"), although bluenoses noted the frequency and outrageousness of her blatantly sexual double entendres. *I'm No Angel* (1933), West's second starring vehicle, was equally popular, and was said to have fanned the flames of protest that led to adoption of the restrictive Motion Picture Production Code. In fact, though, her appeal (and her threat) was that she portrayed a woman who genuinely enjoyed sex and who could survive a "fate worse than death" without suffering the slings and arrows of outrageous fortune. Protests from the Catholic Legion of Decency only increased her popularity.

In 1935 she was the highest-paid woman in America, but she was hampered in writing new stories and scripts by the Production Code. While films like *Belle of the Nineties* (1934), *Goin' to Town* (1935), *Klondike Annie, Go West, Young Man* (both 1936) and *Every Day's a Holiday* (1937) were still fun, there was no question they lacked some of the pizzazz—and rawness—of her two pre-Code starring movies; those remain her best. In 1940 she teamed with W. C. Fields, but that momentous match-up didn't yield the comic sparks that fans hoped for. *My Little Chickadee* (1940), which West cowrote, was only a mildly funny misfire. *The Heat's On* (1943) was also a dud, and West left the screen to return to nightclubs, where she was a smash.

A 24-carat character in real life, West still thought herself as a star (and sexpot) in the 1970s. She costarred in the dreadful *Myra Breckinridge* (1970), whose failure was not her fault, and the even grimmer *Sextette* (1978, which she cowrote). She remained a newsworthy personality to the very end. Her 1959 autobiography was titled "Goodness Had Nothing to Do With It."

WESTON, JACK. Actor. *(b. Aug. 21, 1924, Cleveland, as Jack Weinstein.)* Chubby, perpetually perspiring character comedian who's invaluable as an affable stooge or goofy bad guy. A child actor in his hometown of Cleveland, and later a busy Broadway actor (with several Neil Simon plays to his credit), Weston broke into movies with 1958's *Stage Struck,* and went on to enliven such popular comedies as *Please Don't Eat the Daisies* (1960),

The Honeymoon Machine (1961), *It's Only Money* (1962), *The Incredible Mr. Limpet* (1964), *Cactus Flower* (1969), *A New Leaf* (1971), and *Fuzz* (1972). He tackled occasional serious roles along the way, in such films as *Imitation of Life* (1959), *Mirage* (1965), *The Thomas Crown Affair* (1968), and notably as one of the card players in *The Cincinnati Kid* (1965) and Alan Arkin's ill-fated henchman in *Wait Until Dark* (1967). Weston had his two best roles in 1976: In *The Ritz,* he was a schlemiel hiding from his Mafia hitman brother-in-law in a gay bathhouse; in *Gator,* he carried on a highly improbable romance with Alice Ghostley. He played Alan Alda's dentist pal in *The Four Seasons* (1981), and then continued the role in the subsequent TV series in 1984. He was seen to good effect as the owner of the Catskills resort in *Dirty Dancing,* and as the hapless agent of Warren Beatty and Dustin Hoffman in the hapless *Ishtar* (both 1987). Weston is still active on stage and television, where he had the distinction of costarring with The Marquis Chimps in "The Hathaways" (1961–62).

WEXLER, HASKELL. Cinematographer, director. *(b. Feb. 6, 1922, Chicago.)* Near-legendary cameraman—called "the most widely known and honored of today's U.S. cinematographers" by Todd McCarthy of "Variety"—who moves between Hollywood, independent, documentary, and political projects. After years of making industrial and educational films, Wexler assumed director of photography chores on the documentary-style feature *The Savage Eye* (1960), and used that as his springboard to mainstream movie work. He started with small-scale films like *The Hoodlum Priest* and *Angel Baby* (both 1961), then worked with Elia Kazan on *America, America* (1963), and Tony Richardson on *The Loved One* (1965). He directed and produced the documentary *The Bus* (1965), then won an Oscar for his black-and-white lensing of *Who's Afraid of Virginia Woolf?* (1966). Firmly ensconced in the mainstream, with credits like *In the Heat of the Night* (1967), he seized an opportunity to make a film of his own. Wexler wrote, directed, and photographed the electrifying *Medium Cool* (1969), a fictional work that integrated actual footage of the riot-torn 1968 Democratic National Convention in Chicago. It remains a landmark American film.

He was credited as Supervising Cameraman and Visual Consultant on George Lucas' *American Graffiti* (1973), and was one of the cinematographers on *One Flew Over the Cuckoo's Nest* (1975) and *Days of Heaven* (1978). Among his other feature credits: *Coming Home* (1978), *Richard Pryor Live on the Sunset Strip* (1982), *The Man Who Loved Women* (1983), and *Colors* (1988). He earned Oscar nominations for two very different period pieces, *Matewan* (1987) and *Blaze* (1989).

Always politically active, Wexler directed the Oscar-winning documentary *Interviews With My Lai Veterans* (1970), *Introduction to the Enemy* (1974, codirector), the fiction film *Latino* (1986), and was subpoenaed by a federal grand jury for the tapes and footage of *Underground* (1975), a chronicle of the Weather Underground movement. Critic John Simon, commenting on Wexler's Oscar-winning cinematography for *Bound for Glory* (1976), wrote, "The phrase 'Every frame is a work of art,' so recklessly bandied about by film reviewers, may very nearly apply here." Recent credits include *The Secret of Roan Inish* (1995).

WHALE, JAMES. Director. *(b. July 22, 1889, Dudley, England; d. May 29, 1957.)* While he is best remembered for directing some of Hollywood's most enduring horror pictures, Whale was a sensitive, artistic craftsman whose ambitions went beyond motion pictures. He'd already been a newspaper cartoonist, painter, actor, and set designer, before coming to Hollywood in 1930 to helm a screen version of the celebrated antiwar play *Journey's End*, which he'd directed on the London stage. (That same year Howard Hughes called on him to work as dialogue director on his aviation epic *Hell's Angels*.) He reused leading man Colin Clive the following year at Universal, giving him the title role in *Frankenstein* (1931). Whale followed that remarkable success with three more classics of the genre, *The Old Dark House* (1932), *The Invisible Man* (1933), and *Bride of Frankenstein* (1935), refining his visual technique and command of cinema with each picture. (Compare the simple, but effective, staging of *Frankenstein* with

the flamboyant, expressionistic rendering of *Bride* four years later.)

Whale's non-horror output isn't as well known, but encompasses many striking films, including a stark and powerful *Waterloo Bridge* (1931, much grittier than the later MGM remake), *Impatient Maiden* (1932), the highly stylized *The Kiss Before the Mirror* (1933), the romantic comedy *By Candlelight*, the veddy-British courtroom drama *One More River* (both 1934), and another exercise in stylistics, the comedy whodunit *Remember Last Night?* (1935). By this time, Whale was in love with camera movement, the more grandiose the better, and had his sets built so the camera could make sweeping moves in, around, and through them. As Universal's leading director, he won the plum assignment of directing the lavish musical *Show Boat* (1936), and did a fine job, but fell afoul of new management at the studio shortly thereafter. *The Road Back* (1937), a sequel to *All Quiet on the Western Front*, was his last major assignment there, and a disappointment. A man with an artistic temperament, and little patience for studio politics, Whale's career took a downward turn. He remained active through the end of the decade, but his days as a major, A-list director, were over. He made *The Great Garrick* (1937), *Port of Seven Seas, Sinners in Paradise, Wives Under Suspicion* (all 1938, the last-named a surprisingly good grade-B remake of his own *The Kiss Before the Mirror*), *The Man in the Iron Mask* (1939), *Green Hell* (1940), and *They Dare Not Love* (1941) before throwing in the towel. At that point, he renounced filmmaking to concentrate on painting instead (although he did make one segment for a never-released episodic feature in 1949). He drowned in his swimming pool in 1957, although the fact that it was suicide was hidden for years.

WHALLEY-KILMER, JOANNE. Actress. *(b. Aug. 25, 1964, Salford, England.)* Along with Jenny Wright and *Rocky Horror Picture Show* costar (and future nightclub hostess) Nell Campbell, this petite, sexy British actress (billed as Joanne Whalley) played one of the groupies pursuing rock star Bob Geldof in the bombastic musical *Pink Floyd—The Wall* back in 1982. From that bit she went on to more substantial roles, in films like *No Surrender* and *Dance With a Stranger* (both 1985), *The Good Father* (1987), and did excellent work as a beautiful nurse in British TV's "The Singing Detective" (1986). She played the gutsy bad girl turned good in the fantasy spectacular *Willow* (1988) and subsequently married her costar, actor Val Kilmer, with whom she also worked in 1989's little-seen thriller *Kill Me Again*. Whalley-Kilmer enjoyed a star-making role as Britain's notorious good-time girl Christine Keeler in *Scandal* (1989); if the film had been a mainstream Hollywood product, instead of an import, it might have been her ticket to stardom. Instead, she's played a thankless part in the dim-witted Mideast war drama *Navy SEALS* (1990), and a colorful character part that threatened to steal the spotlight from femme lead Greta Scacchi in *Shattered* (1991). Recent credits include David Hare's *The Secret Rapture* (1993), *A Good Man in Africa, Mother's Boys,* and *Trial by Jury* (all 1994). She also starred in the much-anticipated miniseries "Scarlett" (also 1994), stepping into Vivien Leigh's shoes as Scarlett O'Hara.

WHEELER AND WOOLSEY. Actors. *(Bert Wheeler—b. Apr. 7, 1895, Paterson, N.J.; d. Jan. 18, 1968. Robert Woolsey—b. Aug. 14, 1889; d. Oct. 31, 1938.)* A prime example of the you-either-love-'em-or-hate-'em comedy team, this lively pair have a loyal following among film buffs but remain an acquired taste for the public at large. In their outings together, Wheeler was the baby-faced naif (and nominal leading man, usually romancing leading lady Dorothy Lee), while Woolsey, with his cigar, glasses, and slicked-back hair, was the fast-talking con artist who always professed to help his pal but usually made things worse. They were veterans of vaudeville and the "Ziegfeld Follies"; in 1928 the showman teamed them as comedy relief in his Broadway musical "Rio Rita," and when the show was filmed, virtually intact by RKO in 1929, Wheeler and Woolsey made their screen debut. After two more musical comedies in a similar vein, *The Cuckoos* and *Dixiana* (both 1930), RKO thought they might be capable of carrying a film by themselves. When *Half Shot at Sunrise* (also 1930) was a success, it spurred them on to sev-

enteen more features over the next seven years, most of them gilding their simple plots with musical numbers, pretty girls, slapstick, and excruciating puns ("There's a big difference between the lions now and the lion's den"). Among their early efforts: *Hook, Line and Sinker* (1930), *Cracked Nuts, Caught Plastered, Peach O'Reno* (all 1931), *Girl Crazy, Hold 'Em Jail* (both 1932), and *So This Is Africa* (1933).

Joseph L. Mankiewicz and Henry Meyers, fresh from writing the nonsense classic *Million Dollar Legs,* penned Wheeler and Woolsey's similarly inspired *Diplomaniacs* (1933). Director Mark Sandrich, on the verge of making the classic Fred Astaire–Ginger Rogers musicals, directed two of W&W's best musical-comedies, *Hips, Hips Hooray* and *Cock-eyed Cavaliers* (both 1934). And director George Stevens, steeped in two-reel comedies and heading for feature-film renown, steered Bert and Bob through *Kentucky Kernels* (1934) and *The Nitwits* (1935). With that, the team reached its peak; their remaining films were uninspired at best: *The Rainmakers* (1935), *Silly Billies, Mummy's Boys* (both 1936), *On Again, Off Again,* and *High Flyers* (both 1937).

In 1931 each tried a solo film, Wheeler in *Too Many Cooks* and Woolsey in *Everything's Rosie,* but the experiment was not repeated. After Woolsey's untimely death, Wheeler made just a few more films (notably 1939's *Cowboy Quarterback)* before returning to Broadway and nightclubs; he later added comic relief to the TV Western "Brave Eagle" (1955–56).

WHITAKER, FOREST. Actor. *(b. July 15, 1961, Longview, Tex.)* Large, baby-faced black actor who has eluded stardom despite a number of varied leading roles. Originally planning to pursue a career in music, Whitaker debuted on-screen in *Fast Times at Ridgemont High* (1982), and followed it up with small but notable turns in *Vision Quest* (1985), *Platoon* (1986), and *Stakeout* (1987). He really came into his own with a scene-stealing performance as a hustler who out-hustles Paul Newman in *The Color of Money* (1986) and a costarring role with Robin Williams in *Good Morning, Vietnam* (1987). In 1988, actor-director Clint Eastwood gave Whitaker his chance to carry a film as jazz great Charlie Parker in the critically acclaimed (but financially unrewarding) *Bird,* for which he won a Best Actor award at the Cannes Film Festival. He has since costarred in *Johnny Handsome* (1989), *Downtown* (1990), *A Rage in Harlem* (1991), *Article 99,* and *Consenting Adults* (both 1992), all but stealing the latter film from star Kevin Kline with an understated performance as a soft-spoken insurance investigator. He was even more impressive as a kidnapped British soldier in the highly praised *The Crying Game* (also 1992). He made his directing debut in 1993 with the TV movie *Strapped,* a story of urban violence; recent acting credits include *Last Light* (1993 telefilm), *Body Snatchers, Blown Away, Jason's Lyric, Ready to Wear/Prêt-à-Porter* (all 1994), *Species,* and *Smoke* (both 1995).

WHITMAN, STUART. Actor. *(b. Feb. 1, 1926, San Francisco.)* Brawny, craggy-faced leading man, a reasonably talented actor who seems to invest effort in his characterizations commensurate with the quality of the films. After serving in the Army's Engineer Corps in the late 1940s, Whitman studied drama at Los Angeles City College before going on stage. A small part in *When Worlds Collide* (1951) launched his film career, and he took supporting roles in many 1950s films—including *The All American* (1953), *Brigadoon* (1954), *Interrupted Melody* (1955), *Seven Men From Now* (1956), *The Girl in Black Stockings* (1957), *Ten North Frederick* (1958), and *The Sound and the Fury* (1959)—before top-lining his first movie, a gritty little crime thriller called *Murder, Inc.* (1960). Whitman gave a touching, sensitive performance as a convicted sex offender who tries to rebuild his life in *The Mark* (1961), an excellent, tastefully done drama; his Oscar nomination signaled that, perhaps, a new star was on the rise. But his subsequent assignments failed to give him similarly challenging material to work with, and by the early 1970s he found himself mired in cheesy actioners.

Whitman frequently worked overseas in the 1970s and 1980s, and starred in countless made-for-TV movies, as well as the 1967–68 series "Cimarron Strip."
OTHER FILMS INCLUDE: 1961: *The Comancheros;* 1962: *Convicts Four, The Longest*

Day; 1964: *Shock Treatment, Rio Conchos;* 1965: *Sands of the Kalahari, Those Magnificent Men in Their Flying Machines;* 1966: *An American Dream;* 1970: *The Invincible Six;* 1971: *Captain Apache;* 1972: *Night of the Lepus;* 1974: *Welcome to Arrow Beach* (aka *Tender Flesh);* 1975: *Crazy Mama;* 1976: *Las Vegas Lady;* 1977: *White Buffalo, Ransom;* 1980: *Guyana: Cult of the Damned* (as the notorious Jim Jones), *Macabra;* 1981: *Butterfly;* 1983: *Flesh and Bullets;* 1985: *First Strike;* 1989: *Deadly Embrace;* 1990: *Mob Boss;* 1991: *True Colors;* 1994: *Bad Girls, Trial by Jury.*

WHITMORE, JAMES. Actor. *(b. Oct. 1, 1921, White Plains, N.Y.)* Short and stocky, with a gruff, weatherbeaten face and wry smile, James Whitmore has consistently dazzled moviegoers with expert character performances ever since he hit the screen: In fact, he earned his first Oscar nomination for his supporting role in *Battleground* (1949), his second film. A Yale graduate who participated in college dramatics before entering the Marines during World War 2, Whitmore took to the boards upon reentering civilian life, making his Broadway debut in the all-star war drama "Command Decision." He won a special Tony Award in 1948. His first movie was *Undercover Man* (1949), a modest but clever crime thriller. In 1950 he won a berth in the all-star cast of John Huston's caper film *The Asphalt Jungle,* and played his first lead—an average Joe—in *The Next Voice You Hear.* Whitmore first revealed his lighter side in the comedy-mystery *Mrs. O'Malley and Mr. Malone* (also 1950, opposite Marjorie Main); just a few years later, in *Kiss Me Kate* (1953), he played one of the comic gangsters (Keenan Wynn was the other) who admonished Howard Keel to "Brush Up Your Shakespeare." He lost his life to mutant ants in *Them!* (1954), played a tough Marine in *Battle Cry* (1955), and even impersonated a black man in *Black Like Me* (1964). He has enjoyed well-deserved success in one-man shows, first as former President Harry Truman in *Give 'Em Hell, Harry!* (1975, which, when committed to film, earned him an Oscar nomination), and later, Theodore Roosevelt (in *Bully*) and Will Rogers. He starred in several TV series—"The Law and Mr. Jones" (1960–61), "My Friend Tony"

(1969), and "Temperatures Rising" (1972–74)—and has narrated a number of documentaries. He was also the voice of the angel in *Angels in the Outfield* (1994). Whitmore is married to actress Audra Lindley; his son, James Whitmore, Jr., is also an actor/director.

OTHER FILMS INCLUDE: 1955: *Oklahoma!;* 1956: *The Eddy Duchin Story;* 1958: *The Deep Six;* 1960: *Who Was That Lady?;* 1968: *Planet of the Apes, Madigan;* 1970: *Tora! Tora! Tora!;* 1972: *Chato's Land;* 1973: *The Harrad Experiment;* 1978: *The Serpent's Egg;* 1980: *The First Deadly Sin;* 1988: *Favorite Son;* 1994: *The Shawshank Redemption.*

WHITTY, MAY (DAME). Actress. *(b. June 19, 1865, Liverpool; d. May 29, 1948.)* Best remembered as Miss Froy, the title character of Hitchcock's *The Lady Vanishes* (1938), Dame May was a darling of the London stage while still a young woman, and had already debuted on Broadway before the turn of the century. In 1918 she was named Dame Commander of the British Empire for her contributions to the war effort. Although she made her first movie (*Enoch Arden*) in 1915, Dame May didn't return to the screen until 1937, when she made *Night Must Fall* and secured a Best Supporting Actress Oscar nomination; a second nomination followed for *Mrs. Miniver* (1942). In Hollywood Whitty usually played upper-class dowagers, often with warmhearted tenderness beneath their nobility.

OTHER FILMS INCLUDE: 1937: *Conquest;* 1940: *Raffles, A Bill of Divorcement;* 1941: *Suspicion;* 1943: *Forever and a Day, The Constant Nymph, Lassie Come Home, Flesh and Fantasy, Madame Curie;* 1944: *The White Cliffs of Dover, Gaslight;* 1945: *My Name Is Julia Ross;* 1946: *Devotion;* 1947: *Green Dolphin Street;* 1948: *If Winter Comes, The Return of October* (her last).

WIDMARK, RICHARD. Actor. *(b. Dec. 26, 1914, Sunrise, Minn.)* Few screen debuts have been so memorable. As Tommy Udo, the giggling gangster and homicidal maniac who pushes a wheelchair-bound woman down a flight of stairs in *Kiss of Death* (1947), this slight, sandy-haired actor brought shudders to jaded moviegoers who thought they had seen it all. Widmark's Tommy Udo was to 1940s filmgoers what Dennis Hopper's Frank Booth (from *Blue Velvet*) was to movie fans of the 1980s: the ne plus ultra of screen villainy. Nominated for a Best Supporting Actor Academy Award for his tyro screen performance, Widmark was initially frustrated with Hollywood. He'd been a successful New York–based stage and radio actor (who later remarked that he gave up a house with a pool to move to California!); now he was being offered nothing but Tommy Udo–type roles. He took some, like the sadistic no-good who squares off against Cornel Wilde and Ida Lupino in *Road House* (1948), or the creepy bigot who goads intern Sidney Poitier in *No Way Out* (1950). But he also proved himself a capable leading man, as in the colorful *Down to the Sea in Ships* (1949), and Elia Kazan's terrific *Panic in the Streets* (1950). Still, his best characters seemed to have an edge to them, like the grifter in Samuel Fuller's flavorful *Pickup on South Street* (1953). In time, Widmark did it all, from war stories (1950's *Halls of Montezuma*) to Westerns (1948's *Yellow Sky*, 1954's *Broken Lance*) to romantic comedies (1958's *Tunnel of Love*), investing each performance with directness and honesty.

As Hollywood's studio system eroded, he produced two of his own starring films, *Time Limit* (1957) and *The Secret Ways* (1961), and after a busy decade in the 1960s (which he started off by playing Jim Bowie in *The Alamo*) he became choosier about parts in the 1970s and 1980s (though he succumbed to his share of junk, like 1978's disaster opus *The Swarm*). In 1971 he played the President of the U.S. in the highly touted telefilm *Vanished,* and later starred in a short-lived "Madigan" (1972–73) series that spun off from his successful 1968 feature. His presence in films has become a rarity in recent years, but is always welcome: he lends authority to every part he takes.

OTHER FILMS INCLUDE: 1948: *The Street With No Name;* 1949: *Slattery's Hurricane;* 1950: *Night and the City;* 1951: *The Frogmen;* 1952: *Red Skies of Montana, Don't Bother to Knock, O. Henry's Full House, My Pal Gus;* 1953: *Destination Gobi, Take the High Ground;* 1954: *Hell and High Water, Garden of Evil;* 1955: *A Prize of Gold, The Cobweb;* 1956: *Backlash, Run for the Sun, The Last Wagon;* 1957: *Saint Joan;* 1958: *The Law and Jake Wade;* 1959: *The Trap, Warlock;* 1961: *Two*

Rode Together; Judgment at Nuremberg; 1962: How the West Was Won; 1964: Flight From Ashiya, The Long Ships, Cheyenne Autumn; 1965: The Bedford Incident; 1966: Alvarez Kelly; 1967: The Way West; 1969: A Talent for Loving, Death of a Gunfighter; 1970: The Moonshine War; 1972: When the Legends Die; 1974: Murder on the Orient Express (as the murder victim); 1975: Midas Run; 1976: To the Devil—a Daughter; 1977: Twilight's Last Gleaming, The Domino Principle, Rollercoaster; 1978: Coma; 1980: Bear Island; 1982: Hanky Panky, The Final Option; 1984: Against All Odds; 1985: Blackout (telefilm); 1987: A Gathering of Old Men (telefilm); 1988: Once Upon a Texas Train (telefilm); 1989: Cold Sassy Tree (telefilm); 1991: True Colors.

WIEST, DIANNE. Actress. *(b. Mar. 28, 1948, Kansas City, Mo.)* This gifted actress enjoys a bright reputation as a New York stage performer (she won a 1983 Best Actress Obie) and director, although she's also worked in films since 1980, beginning with *It's My Turn.* Wiest's predominant screen persona is that of the put-upon mom: Whether defending Kevin Bacon's right to dance in *Footloose* (1984), coming to grips with adolescent vampires in *The Lost Boys* (1987), suffering stoically in *Bright Lights, Big City* (1988), dealing with teen pregnancy and marriage in *Parenthood* (1989, an Oscar-nominated turn) or, in an extreme case, adopting a manmade kid with razor-sharp digits in *Edward Scissorhands* (1990), Wiest is usually a tower of strength, maturity, and maternal benevolence. She's also been effective in *I'm Dancing as Fast as I Can* (1982), *Independence Day* (1983, as a beaten-down wife), and *Falling in Love* (1984). No one has tapped her versatility quite like Woody Allen, however, who's cast her as a hooker in *The Purple Rose of Cairo* (1985), an optimistic man-chaser in *Radio Days* (1987), Mia Farrow's best friend in *September* (also 1987), and most memorably, as one of Farrow's eccentric (and neurotic) siblings in *Hannah and Her Sisters* (1986), which won her an Academy Award as Best Supporting Actress. *Little Man Tate* (1991) gave her one of her meatiest parts, as a former gifted child who now tries to shape other gifted children's lives. Her talent for dithery comedy has been too little used onscreen, and had its best showcase in *Cookie* (1989), in which she played Peter Falk's sexy mistress. Recent credits include *Cops and Robbersons* and a hysterical turn as a theatrical grande dame in Woody Allen's *Bullets Over Broadway* (1994), for which she received a second Supporting Actress Oscar.

WILCOXON, HENRY. Actor, producer. *(b. Sept. 8, 1905, Dominica, West Indies, as Harry Wilcoxon; d. Mar. 6, 1984.)* Strapping, distinguished actor long associated with Cecil B. DeMille, on both sides of the camera. After stage experience in England, Wilcoxon had starring and supporting roles in a number of British films—including *The Perfect Lady* (1931), *The Flying Squad* (1932), and *Lord of the Manor* (1933)—before winning two key roles for DeMille, Marc Antony in *Cleopatra* (1934) and Richard the Lion-Hearted in *The Crusades* (1935). He never became a star, but worked steadily, often cast as characters with rank or title, as in *The Last of the Mohicans* (1936), *Souls at Sea, Dark Sands* (both 1937), *If I Were King* (1938), *That Hamilton Woman* (1941, as Capt. Hardy), *The Corsican Brothers* (1941), *Mrs. Miniver* (1942, as a vicar who reappeared in 1950's *The Miniver Story*), *A Connecticut Yankee in King Arthur's Court* (1949, as Sir Lancelot), and *Scaramouche* (1952, as the Chevalier de Chabrillaine). At the same time, Wilcoxon played roles in B films and series: *Mysterious Mr. Moto* (1938), *Prison Nurse* (1938), *Tarzan Finds a Son!* (1939), *Mystery Sea Raider* (1940), *The Lone Wolf Takes a Chance* (1941).

More significantly, he forged a relationship with DeMille, and became the producer-director's most trusted ally, an "avid shaper of ideas and craftsman of dramatic construction," as the filmmaker later put it. Beginning in 1948, he was DeMille's associate producer, but just to keep his hand in, he also appeared onscreen in *Unconquered* (1947, as Captain Steele), *Samson and Delilah* (1949, as a Philistine general), *The Greatest Show on Earth* (1952, as a detective), and *The Ten Commandments* (1956, as Pentaur). When DeMille decided to let his son-in-law Anthony Quinn direct *The Buccaneer* (1958), he chose Wilcoxon to produce the film. In later years, the still-handsome actor worked in television and in such features as *The War Lord* (1965), *F.I.S.T.* (1978), *Caddyshack,* and *The Man With Bogart's Face* (both 1980). His autobiography, "Lionheart in Hollywood," was published posthumously in 1991.

WILDE, CORNEL. Actor, director, producer. *(b. Oct. 13, 1915, New York City, as Cornelius Louis Wilde; d. Oct. 16, 1989.)* Although he certainly looked like a Latin lover, Wilde was born to Hungarian parents. A superb athlete, he won a berth on the U.S. Olympic fencing team for the 1936 games, but never competed, because a newly acquired passion for acting consumed him. A job as fencing instructor to Laurence Olivier enabled him to make contact with Warner Bros. in 1940. He played small parts in several Warners films—including *The Lady With Red Hair* (1940, his first), *Knockout, Kisses for Breakfast,* and *High Sierra* (all 1941)—before being wooed by 20th Century-Fox in 1942, making his first appearance for the studio that same year in a wartime B, *Manila Calling.*

Wilde, the archetypal "tall, dark, and handsome" leading man, was inexplicably cast as composer Frederic Chopin in *A Song to Remember* (1945, on loan to Columbia), but delivered an Academy Award-nominated performance that convinced Fox to give him bigger and better roles in *Leave Her to Heaven* (1945), *Centennial Summer* (1946), and *Forever Amber* (1947, taking the male lead in this highly touted costume drama), among others. Columbia borrowed him again, putting his athletic abilities to good use in the Arabian Nights spectacular *A Thousand and One Nights* (1945, as Aladdin) and *The Bandit of Sherwood Forest* (1946, as Robin Hood's son). Wilde made his mark in crime dramas, swashbucklers, and other adventure pictures including *Road House* (1948), *Shockproof* (1949), *Two Flags West* (1950), *At Sword's Point* (as the son of D'Artagnan), *California Conquest* (both 1952), *Treasure of the Golden Condor* (1953), *Star of India* (1954), *The Big Combo* (1955, a highly regarded film noir), *Omar Khayyam* (1957, in the title role), and *Edge of Eternity* (1959). His best 1950s role, however, was that of The Great Sebastian, the charismatic but egotistical trapeze artist who competes with Charlton Heston for Betty Hutton's affec-

tions in Cecil B. DeMille's Oscar-winning *The Greatest Show on Earth* (1952).

Wilde formed his own production company in 1955, occasionally producing and directing as well as starring in his own modestly budgeted films, most of them involving rugged action, and costarring his wife Jean Wallace: *Storm Fear* (1955), *The Devil's Hairpin* (1957), *Maracaibo* (1958), *Sword of Lancelot* (1963), *The Naked Prey* (1966, his best), *Beach Red* (1967), *No Blade of Grass* (1970), *Shark's Treasure* (1975) and *Vultures in Paradise* (1983). His presence couldn't save *The Norseman* (a 1978 starring vehicle for TV's Lee Majors) or *The Fifth Musketeer* (1979), although he contributed a lively turn as the aging D'Artagnan in the latter, calling to mind the dashing Wilde of earlier years. He completed an autobiographical film, *My Very Wilde Life,* in 1987, and died of leukemia two years later.

OTHER FILMS INCLUDE: 1942: *Life Begins at 8:30;* 1943: *Wintertime;* 1947: *The Homestretch, It Had to Be You;* 1948: *The Walls of Jericho;* 1954: *Woman's World;* 1955: *The Scarlet Coat;* 1956: *Hot Blood;* 1957: *Beyond Mombasa;* 1969: *The Comic.*

WILDER, BILLY. Writer, director, producer. *(b. June 22, 1906, Vienna, as Samuel Wilder.)* Few native-born writer-directors have studied the American psyche as perceptively—or used the language as brilliantly—as Viennese émigré Billy Wilder. He started out as a reporter in Vienna and moved to Berlin to pursue that profession, but early on he was attracted to cinema and collaborated on the script of the 1929 movie *People on Sunday* (working with such colleagues as Robert Siodmak, Edgar Ulmer, and Fred Zinnemann). He then made his living as a screenwriter and worked on a number of German films (including the 1931 success *Emil and the Detectives)* before Hitler's rise to power sent him packing. He decamped briefly in Paris, where he codirected one film, *Mauvaise Graine* (1933), then made his way to Hollywood (by way of Mexico).

It took time for Wilder to learn the English language (he never lost his accent), and longer still to land a steady job in the studios. In 1937 he sold a story to Paramount, which got his foot in the door, and the next year he found himself writing for his idol, Ernst Lubitsch. He was paired with the urbane Charles Brackett on the script of Lubitsch's *Bluebeard's Eighth Wife* (1938); when they proved to be a compatible team, Paramount kept them together and gave them a steady stream of assignments, ranging from the mundane (1939's Henry Aldrich adaptation *What a Life)* to the sublime (1939's *Midnight,* 1940's *Arise, My Love,* 1941's *Hold Back the Dawn).* They also collaborated on *Ninotchka* (1939) for Lubitsch and *Ball of Fire* (1941, a sly parody of *Snow White and the Seven Dwarfs)* for Howard Hawks and producer Samuel Goldwyn; both scripts were nominated for Oscars.

Their screenplays were consistently witty and sophisticated, but Wilder bemoaned the way they were handled by their directors, especially Mitchell Leisen. Fellow screenwriter Preston Sturges, who felt the same way, had persuaded Paramount to let him try directing his own scripts, with great success, so Wilder lobbied to do the same, and the studio agreed. The clever comedy *The Major and the Minor* (1942) was an auspicious debut, and the witty wartime drama *Five Graves to Cairo* (1943) a first-rate followup. Wilder teamed with Raymond Chandler on the film noir classic *Double Indemnity* (1944), earning writing and directing Oscar nominations, then he and Brackett (who became the team's producer) made a groundbreaking study of alcoholism, *The Lost Weekend* (1945), which won two Oscars for Wilder for Best Screenplay and Director, and two more for Best Picture and Best Actor (Ray Milland). Never a visual stylist, Wilder nevertheless created some indelible images in this film (particularly in the delirium tremens sequence), and broke with Hollywood tradition by shooting Milland on the New York streets with a hidden camera, for cinéma verité realism.

Having served the U.S. Army in Berlin during the immediate aftermath of World War 2, Wilder depicted the postwar city in an unexpectedly comic context in *A Foreign Affair* (1948, Oscar-nominated for Best Screenplay), and turned out a silly piece of froth for Bing Crosby, *The Emperor Waltz* (also 1948). He then collaborated for the last time with Brackett (and D. M. Marshman, Jr.) on the sardonic Hollywood fable *Sunset Blvd.* (1950), a brilliant black comedy about an aging, self-deluded silent film star and the desperate young writer who becomes her kept

man. MGM mogul Louis B. Mayer reportedly took Wilder to task for dramatizing the dark side of Tinseltown, but others hailed it for the masterpiece it was. It won him a Best Screenplay Oscar (with Brackett and D. M. Marshman, Jr.) and a Best Director nomination. His first solo film, *Ace in the Hole* (1951, retitled *The Big Carnival),* was the cynical story of a reporter coldbloodedly capitalizing on a tragedy. Audiences didn't warm to it, but it earned him a Best Screenplay nomination.

Wilder shrugged off that failure, and followed it with a handful of hugely successful stage adaptations: the bristling P.O.W. drama *Stalag 17* (1953, for which Wilder was Oscar-nominated), the charming romantic comedy *Sabrina* (1954), which was Oscar-nominated for Best Screenplay and Best Director, and the sexy comic fable *The Seven Year Itch* (1955, considerably "cleaned up" from its Broadway original), which marked his first encounter with Marilyn Monroe. He set himself a pair of challenges, and succeeded, dramatizing the claustrophobic flight of Charles Lindbergh in *The Spirit of St. Louis* (1957) and adapting a prototypical Agatha Christie courtoom whodunit, *Witness for the Prosecution* (also 1957, earning an Oscar nomination as Best Director). He also found a new collaborator, I.A.L. Diamond; their first joint effort was a delightful Lubitsch-inspired May-December romance, *Love in the Afternoon* (also 1957).

Wilder and Diamond then produced a pair of masterworks, the farcical gem *Some Like It Hot* (1959, Oscar nominated for Best Director and Best Screenplay), with Jack Lemmon and Tony Curtis in drag joining Marilyn Monroe in an all-girl orchestra; and the brilliant comedy-drama *The Apartment* (1960), which won Oscars for Best Picture, Best Director, and Best Screenplay. It was here that Wilder found his perfect Everyman in Jack Lemmon. Wilder returned to Berlin one more time for the brilliantly fast-paced comedy *One, Two, Three* (1961), with James Cagney, then reteamed *Apartment* stars Lemmon and Shirley MacLaine for an adaptation of the stage hit *Irma la Douce* (1963).

Not since *Ace in the Hole* had Wilder allowed his cynicism to dominate a movie as it did his next, *Kiss Me, Stupid* (1964), the story of a would-be songwriter who's so desperate to succeed that he will offer up his wife as inducement to win over a popular singer. Wilder was pilloried in the press, and offended his colleagues in Hollywood, who were outraged by this "smarmy" film; he remarked in an interview that he'd have to make a popular movie soon in order to get back on the "godfathers and pallbearers" list. He did just that with *The Fortune Cookie* (1966), an "acceptably" sardonic comedy that made a star of Walter Matthau, who won an Oscar playing Jack Lemmon's unscrupulous lawyer Whiplash Willie. (The screenplay was also nominated for an Oscar.)

The 1970s were to prove a difficult decade for Wilder. The British-made *The Private Life of Sherlock Holmes* (1970) was shorn of one entire episode before its release to tepid reviews. Critics and audiences were also indifferent to *Avanti!* (1972), a highly underrated romantic comedy with Jack Lemmon. Wilder and Diamond then aimed for the commercial bull's-eye with a colorful remake of *The Front Page* (1974) starring Lemmon and Matthau. The script stuck to the Hecht-MacArthur original for the most part, but there were many identifiable Wilder-Diamondisms as well—including an *American Graffiti*-inspired epilogue. Still, Wilder found it increasingly difficult to get projects off the ground in the "new" Hollywood, and it was four years before *Fedora* (1978) was released. An adaptation of Thomas Tryon's story of a reclusive Garbo-esque star, the project was marked (or marred) by excessive compromise—Wilder had hoped to persuade a genuine screen legend to star, but had to settle for young European actress Marthe Keller instead. He did cast William Holden in the lead, however, causing more than one observer to think of *Fedora* as an unofficial sequel to *Sunset Blvd.* Alas, it wasn't a fraction as good. He and Diamond gave it one more try, adapting the French comedy *A Pain in the A*— as a Lemmon-Matthau vehicle, *Buddy Buddy* (1981). It was not well received, to say the least, and the unkinder critics said Wilder was simply out of touch.

Wilder retired, tending to his famed art collection, gathering a roomful of awards and citations (including the Academy's Thalberg Award, lifetime honors from the Writers Guild of America and the Directors Guild of America, and the American Film Institute Life Achievement Award—

"all that's left is the Heisman Trophy," he quipped at one point), and working on his autobiography. He has remained a witty observer of the Hollywood scene, and if that industry lost patience with him in his final productive years, it has never ceased to admire the great films he made during his twenty-five-year heyday.

WILDER, GENE. Actor, director, writer. *(b. June 11, 1935, Milwaukee, Wis., as Jerry Silberman.)* One of the few modern comedy stars who can honestly be described as "gentle," this frizzy-haired, sad-eyed actor has struggled to find and hold an audience after achieving his initial fame. Wilder made his film debut as a hapless kidnap victim in *Bonnie and Clyde* (1967), then earned an Oscar nomination the next year as the "wet and hysterical" accountant Leo Bloom in *The Producers,* the first of his three films for writer-director Mel Brooks, who helped Wilder develop his comic persona. The next few years saw Wilder in a variety of films with very long titles, playing an Irish romantic in *Quackser Fortune Has a Cousin in the Bronx* (1970), a pair of mismatched French twins in *Start the Revolution Without Me* (also 1970), a cagey candymaker in *Willy Wonka and the Chocolate Factory* (1971), and a sheep-loving psychiatrist in Woody Allen's *Everything You Always Wanted to Know About Sex (But Were Afraid to Ask)* (1972). Wilder had a straight dramatic role, playing a clerk, in a deadeningly dull version of the Ionesco play *Rhinoceros* (1974, reunited with his *Producers* costar Zero Mostel), but was in fine form for Brooks in two comic hits: as the boozy gunslinger in *Blazing Saddles* (1973) and the mad doctor in *Young Frankenstein* (1974); he also earned an Oscar nomination for the latter's hilarious script, cowritten with Brooks.

After taking a cameo in *The Little Prince* (also 1974), Wilder struck out on his own, writing and directing as well as starring in *The Adventure of Sherlock Holmes' Smarter Brother* (1975), a partially successful attempt at crafting comedy in the Brooksian mold. Wilder costarred with irreverent stand-up comic Richard Pryor, making an interracial Hope-Crosby team of sorts, in the 1976 smash *Silver Streak.* Their obvious chemistry produced three follow-ups of diminishing quality: *Stir Crazy* (1980), *See No Evil, Hear No Evil* (1989), and *Another You* (1991, a real stinker in which a seriously ill Pryor was barely able to squeeze out his dialogue, much less be funny). Wilder got one of his best parts, as a rabbi in the Old West, opposite Harrison Ford in the uneven comedy adventure *The Frisco Kid* (1979). His self-written and directed vehicles, however, have been pretty disappointing: *The World's Greatest Lover* (1977), *Sunday Lovers* (1980, one melancholy segment of this episodic film), *The Woman in Red* (1984, his best solo comedy), and the dismal *Haunted Honeymoon* (1986).

He costarred in the latter two with wife Gilda Radner, whom he met when she was cast in *Hanky Panky* (1982), a Wilder vehicle originally intended to costar Pryor. They married in 1984 and enjoyed several happy years before she fell victim to cancer; Radner's long, painful struggle ended with her death in 1989, which reportedly devastated Wilder. He also starred in *Funny About Love* (1990), a tepid comedy directed by Leonard Nimoy, as well as his own TV sitcom "Something Wilder" (1994–95).

WILDING, MICHAEL. Actor. *(b. July 23, 1912, Westcliff-on-Sea, England; d. July 8, 1979.)* Popular star of 1940s British films, best known today as the second husband of Elizabeth Taylor. Wilding began his career as an artist, even working in film studios, but eventually shifted into acting. He was an extra in some early 1930s pictures, and worked as a stand-in for Douglas Fairbanks, Jr., in *Catherine the Great* (1934). Eventually he worked at his craft and appeared on the London stage. While never a great actor, Wilding was handsome and charming. Important early film roles included Ronnie Walshingham in *Kipps* (1941) and Flags in Noel Coward's *In Which We Serve* (1942). As the decade progressed, Wilding's roles increased in importance; he and Anna Neagle united to star in a series of very popular films, including *Piccadilly Incident* (1946), *The Courtneys of Curzon Street* (1947), *Spring in Park Lane* (1948), *The Lady With a Lamp* (1951), and *Maytime in Mayfair* (1952). He made two films for Hitchcock: *Under Capricorn* (1949, as an aristocrat) and *Stage Fright* (1950, playing a detective). His most im-

portant American role was in *Torch Song* (1953), as a blind pianist who falls for Joan Crawford. Wilding was second-billed in *The Glass Slipper* (1955), a Cinderella redo, playing the prince, but mostly had costarring roles from then on: *The Egyptian* (1954), *The Scarlet Coat* (1955), *The World of Suzie Wong* (1960), *The Naked Edge* (1961), and *A Girl Named Tamiko* (1962). He retired from the screen to become an agent, and accepted occasional acting roles, as in *Waterloo* (1971), *Lady Caroline Lamb* (1972), and TV's *Frankenstein: The True Story* (1973). His fourth wife was actress Margaret Leighton; he is the father of sometime actor Michael Wilding, Jr., his son by Elizabeth Taylor. His autobiography, "Apple Sauce/The Wilding Way," was published posthumously in 1982.

WILLIAM, WARREN. Actor. *(b. Dec. 2, 1895, Aitkin, Minn., as Warren Krech; d. Sept. 24, 1948.)* Often called "the poor man's John Barrymore," this slender, striking, sharp-featured leading man was most successful playing unmitigated cads, but also made his mark as Perry Mason and The Lone Wolf. Born to a newspaper publisher, he served in World War 1 and took up acting upon his return from service, studying at the American Academy of Dramatic Arts. He played in stock and made a few films on the East Coast, appearing opposite serial queen Pearl White in *Plunder* (1923), billed under his real name.

As Warren William, he was signed by Warner Bros. in 1931. He initially played supporting roles in the likes of *Expensive Women* and *Under Eighteen* (both 1931), but quickly graduated to leading-man status in a series of sharp-witted, often rowdy pre-Production Code vehicles. He brought style and authority to *Beauty and the Boss, The Mouthpiece, The Dark Horse, The Match King, Three on a Match* (all 1932), *Gold Diggers of 1933* (1933), *Employees Entrance, The Mind Reader, Goodbye Again, Bedside, Upperworld,* and *Dr. Monica* (all 1934). On loan to other studios, he made a perfect Dave the Dude for Frank Capra in the Damon Runyon story *Lady for a Day* (1933), a sympathetic leading man for Claudette Colbert in *Imitation of Life,* and an effective Julius Caesar in *Cleopatra* (both 1934).

Warners cast him as amateur detective Philo Vance (a role recently vacated by William Powell) in *The Dragon Murder Case;* then he became the screen's first Perry Mason (very different from the later TV incarnation) in *The Case of the Howling Dog.* He reprised that role in *The Case of the Lucky Legs, The Case of the Curious Bride* (both 1935), and *The Case of the Velvet Claws* (1936, which, astoundingly, married off Perry to secretary Della Street!). His other Warners films include *The Secret Bride, Living on Velvet, Don't Bet on Blondes* (all 1935), *Stage Struck,* and *Satan Met a Lady* (both 1936, the latter a heavily altered adaptation of Dashiell Hammett's "The Maltese Falcon").

William left Warners to freelance, alternating between leads and character parts. He supported Mae West in *Go West, Young Man* (1936), starred in *Wives Under Suspicion* (1938) for director James Whale, reprised his Philo Vance characterization in the zany *The Gracie Allen Murder Case* (1939), and played D'Artagnan in the swashbuckling *The Man in the Iron Mask* the same year.

In 1939 he also starred in *The Lone Wolf Spy Hunt,* as lighthearted jewel thief Michael Lanyard; it kicked off a successful Columbia series of B movies, which included *The Lone Wolf Meets a Lady, The Lone Wolf Strikes* (both 1940), *Secrets of the Lone Wolf, The Lone Wolf Takes a Chance, The Lone Wolf Keeps a Date* (all 1941), *Counter-Espionage* (1942), *One Dangerous Night,* and *Passport to Suez* (both 1943).

His other 1940s films include *Lillian Russell, Trail of the Vigilantes* (both 1940), *The Wolf Man* (1941), *Wild Bill Hickok Rides, Eyes of the Underworld* (both 1942), *Strange Illusion* (1945, an interesting Poverty Row melodrama modeled after "Hamlet"), *Fear* (1946, a quickie version of "Crime and Punishment"), and *The Private Affairs of Bel Ami* (1947), a graceful film that gave him a fine character part and allowed him to bow out in style.

WILLIAMS, BILLY DEE. Actor. *(b. Apr. 6, 1937, New York City.)* This dashingly handsome, extremely likable actor's career once held far more promise than his re-

cent Hollywood status would indicate. A child performer with considerable stage experience, he made his screen debut as a street tough in *The Last Angry Man* (1959), and started working in movies regularly throughout the 1970s in films like *The Out-of-Towners* (1970), *Hit!* (1973), and *The Take* (1974). During that decade, he stood out as the screen's leading black romantic lead, particularly in a pair of films starring pop icon Diana Ross, *Lady Sings the Blues* (1972) and *Mahogany* (1975). He was both funny and stirring in *The Bingo Long Traveling All-Stars & Motor Kings* (1976), a period saga of the Negro Baseball League, and played the title role in the biopic *Scott Joplin* (1977), originally made for TV but later released theatrically. Williams brought color to outer space in the trailblazing part of intergalactic con man and soldier of fortune Lando Calrissian, in 1980's *The Empire Strikes Back,* sequel to the megahit *Star Wars;* he reprised the role in 1983's *Return of the Jedi,* but his lack of energy and pizzazz in those plum parts may have kept him from achieving real movie stardom. (Sometimes luck plays a part, too; he was teamed with Sylvester Stallone in the first-rate crime thriller *Nighthawks* in 1981, but the picture flopped.) Tough-cop roles in the low-budgeters *Fear City* (1984) and *Number One With a Bullet* (1987) followed, as well as a starring stint in *Deadly Illusion* (also 1987), a private-eye thriller adapted for Williams from an unfilmed Mike Hammer script. Taking a smaller part in a bigger picture, he played District Attorney Harvey Dent in *Batman* (1989). Recent credits include the TV movies *The Jacksons: An American Dream* (1992, as Berry Gordy) and *Deadly Ice* (1994).

WILLIAMS, ESTHER. Actress. *(b. Aug. 8, 1923, Los Angeles.)* This lithe, leggy beauty was in the public eye early on, having become a swimming champ at age 15 and a much-photographed model at a Los Angeles department store. (A U.S. Olympics hopeful, her dreams were shattered when war in Europe canceled the planned 1940 games.) She had dropped out of college and was swimming for her supper with Billy Rose's Aquacade when she was spotted by an MGM talent scout. Immediately signed by the studio and groomed

for stardom, Williams made her movie debut—like other Metro starlets—opposite Mickey Rooney in an "Andy Hardy" film. *Bathing Beauty* (1944), a colorful exercise in wartime escapism, effectively launched her starring career; she spent the next 11 years in the water more than out of it—but made the list of Top Ten Box-Office Stars by so doing—and by offering a sunny, likable screen personality. Her starring vehicles, essentially backstage musicals tailored to incorporate her aquatic skills, sported lavish production values and top supporting casts in glorious Technicolor. When musicals faded in the 1950s, Williams tried to expand her dramatic portfolio but the public wouldn't buy her as a straight actress. Having toured with aquatic shows and headlined TV specials, she settled down with her third husband, actor Fernando Lamas (her leading man in 1953's *Dangerous When Wet*—and one of the few who could actually swim) and gradually disappeared from the limelight. After his death, she re-emerged in the public eye, making personal appearances and introducing a successful line of swimsuits modeled after the ones she wore in the 1940s and 1950s. She appeared onscreen as one of the hosts of *That's Entertainment! III* in 1994.
OTHER FILMS INCLUDE: 1942: *Andy Hardy's Double Life;* 1943: *A Guy Named Joe;* 1945: *Thrill of a Romance;* 1946: *Ziegfeld Follies, The Hoodlum Saint, Easy to Wed, Till the Clouds Roll By;* 1947: *Fiesta, This Time for Keeps;* 1948: *On an Island With You;* 1949: *Take Me Out to the Ball Game, Neptune's Daughter;* 1950: *Duchess of Idaho, Pagan Love Song;* 1951: *Callaway Went Thataway* (cameo), *Texas Carnival;* 1952: *Skirts Ahoy!, Million Dollar Mermaid;* 1953: *Easy to Love;* 1955: *Jupiter's Darling;* 1956: *The Unguarded Moment;* 1958: *Raw Wind in Eden;* 1961: *The Big Show.*

WILLIAMS, GUINN (BIG BOY). Actor. *(b. Apr. 25, 1899, Decatur, Tex.; d. June 6, 1962.)* Prolific character actor and occasional star of low-budget Westerns, this burly redhead actually was a cowboy in his youth; he also played professional baseball for a time before entering the movie business in 1919. Reportedly nicknamed "Big Boy" by Will Rogers when he worked with the comedian in *Jubilo* (1919), Williams went on to star in many cheap horse operas during the mid 1920s, but segued to solid supporting roles in major films. He's particularly memorable as Jeff, the sadistic gangster in *The Glass Key* (1935). Williams continued to appear in Westerns, of both A and B caliber, throughout the rest of his career; he played dumb cowhands and vicious heavies equally well, and even played sidekick to Roy Rogers in a handful of 1944 outings.
OTHER FILMS INCLUDE: 1929: *Noah's Ark;* 1930: *Liliom;* 1932: *You Said a Mouthful;* 1934: *Palooka;* 1935: *Private Worlds, The Littlest Rebel, Powdersmoke Range;* 1937: *A Star Is Born, You Only Live Once;* 1938: *Professor Beware;* 1939: *Dodge City, Bad Lands;* 1940: *The Fighting 69th, Santa Fe Trail* (teamed with Alan Hale); 1941: *Billy the Kid, You'll Never Get Rich;* 1944: *Nevada;* 1950: *Rocky Mountain;* 1952: *Springfield Rifle;* 1960: *The Alamo;* 1961: *The Comancheros* (his last).

WILLIAMS, JOBETH. Actress. *(b. Dec. 6, 1948, Houston.)* Williams made a show-stopping movie debut in *Kramer vs. Kramer* (1979), playing a one-night stand of Dustin Hoffman's, surprised by his young son while darting nude to the bathroom. This memorable screen moment followed years of stage work and TV soap-opera activity. Attractive, in a girl-next-door way, and energetic, she appeared in *Stir Crazy* (1980) and *Endangered Species* (1982) before landing two roles that boosted her stock in Hollywood: the terrorized mother fighting to save her children in the 1982 shocker *Poltergeist* (a role she recreated for the 1986 sequel), and the former campus radical turned housewife in the 1983 ensemble drama *The Big Chill*. Williams was one of the *Teachers* (1984, doffing her duds once again), and an adventurous housewife in *American Dreamer* (1984). She seems to have fallen in the trap of playing put-upon partners, essaying such roles in *Desert Bloom* (1986), *Memories of Me* (1988) and *Welcome Home* (1989), but snagged a deliciously funny part in *Switch* (1991), a generally brainless movie that at least showed her capable of broad comedy. TV has afforded Williams some of her finest roles: the real-life mother of a missing child in *Adam* (1983) and *Adam: His Song Continues* (1986), and real-life surrogate mother Mary Beth Whitehead in *Baby M*

(1988). Recent credits include *Me Myself and I* (1992), *Chantilly Lace, Final Appeal* (both 1993 telefilms), and *Wyatt Earp* (1994, as Bessie Earp). She received an Oscar nomination for directing the short subject *On Hope* (1994).

WILLIAMS, JOHN. Composer. *(b. Feb. 8, 1932, Floral Park, N.Y.)* It's impossible to think of *Star Wars*—or many other megahit movies—without calling to mind the stirring musical score crafted by this talented, prolific, award-winning composer. A Juilliard-trained musician who recorded several albums as a jazz pianist in the late 1950s, arranged albums for various pop stars, and worked as a studio musician (he's the one playing the piano vamp for Henry Mancini's memorable "Peter Gunn" theme), he took up scoring films and TV shows shortly thereafter. As "Johnny" Williams, he composed the memorable theme songs and musical backgrounds for "Voyage to the Bottom of the Sea" and "Lost in Space," among other 1960s TV shows. While his early scores—for *Because They're Young* (1960), *Bachelor Flat* (1962), *Gidget Goes to Rome* (1963), and *John Goldfarb, Please Come Home!* (1965), among others—weren't particularly noteworthy, Williams came into his own with *The Killers* (1964), *None But the Brave* (1965), and especially *Valley of the Dolls* (1967), for which he earned the first of many Academy Award nominations. He won an Oscar for adapting *Fiddler on the Roof* (1971), while *Goodbye, Mr. Chips, The Reivers* (both 1969), *Images, The Poseidon Adventure* (both 1972), *Cinderella Liberty* (1973), and *The Towering Inferno* (1974) all got Academy Award nods, but it was his throbbing, much-imitated score for Steven Spielberg's *Jaws* (1975) that won Williams his second Oscar and began a long and fruitful association with Spielberg which continues today.

His scores for *Star Wars* (and its sequels), *Close Encounters of the Third Kind* (1977), *Superman* (1978), and *E. T. the Extra-Terrestrial* (1982) were inexorably linked with those films' success, and their very identities (*Star Wars* and *E. T.* won Oscars). Many of his soundtrack albums became best-sellers, and Williams' name became arguably the best known in movie music history. What's more, he al-most singlehandedly returned the "big" orchestral film score to favor in the late 1970s. From 1980 to 1993 he conducted the Boston Pops Orchestra, and frequently integrated his film music into the orchestra's concerts.

OTHER FILMS INCLUDE: 1976: *Midway;* 1978: *Jaws 2;* 1979: *1941;* 1980: *Superman II, The Empire Strikes Back* (Oscar-nominated); 1981: *Raiders of the Lost Ark* (another nomination); 1983: *Jaws 3-D, Superman III, Return of the Jedi* (Oscar-nominated); 1984: *Indiana Jones and the Temple of Doom, The River* (both nominated); 1986: *SpaceCamp;* 1987: *Empire of the Sun, The Witches of Eastwick* (both Oscar-nominated); 1988: *The Accidental Tourist* (another nomination); 1989: *Always, Born on the Fourth of July, Indiana Jones and the Last Crusade* (the latter two Oscar-nominated); 1990: *Home Alone* (nominated for Best Score and Best Song, "Somewhere in My Memory," which Williams cowrote), *Presumed Innocent, Stanley & Iris;* 1991: *JFK, Hook* (the former nominated for Best Score, the latter for Best Song, cowritten by Williams); 1992: *Home Alone 2: Lost In New York;* 1993: *Jurassic Park, Schindler's List* (Oscar-winning).

WILLIAMS, ROBIN. Actor, comedian. *(b. July 21, 1952, Chicago.)* This dynamic, motor-mouthed performer, whose wicked, outrageous, free-associating humor—leavened with deadly accurate impressions of incredible variety—made him a comic sensation in the 1970s. Since then the former street performer, Juilliard acting student, and stand-up comic has worked hard to have it both ways: retaining his unique persona while growing and thriving as an actor. And, in fact, he has succeeded, securing both critical adulation and audience loyalty in the process. Williams gained a huge TV audience (and risked lifelong typecasting) playing the alien Mork in the 1978–82 sitcom "Mork and Mindy." An entrepreneurial producer put fleeting footage of Williams in his raunchy comedy-skit feature *Can I Do It . . . Til I Need Glasses?* (1977), but the performer's actual screen debut came when Robert Altman cast him as *Popeye* (1980) in an overproduced and largely unfunny live-action feature. Williams took no punches for his energetic performance, however, and accepted an even greater challenge in *The World According to Garp* (1982), George Roy Hill's outstanding adaptation of the John Irving novel. Although Williams' character was basically benign, he was decidedly not comic, and the tyro actor did an excellent job. Williams' gift for dialects was then put to good use in Paul Mazursky's *Moscow on the Hudson* (1984), in which he had to create a convincing Russian character to go along with the accent—and did.

Although Williams has appeared in his share of turkeys (1983's *The Survivors,* 1986's *Club Paradise,* 1990's *Cadillac Man,* to name a few) he has never shied away from ambitious projects. He played a difficult role beautifully in an independently produced film of Saul Bellow's novel *Seize the Day* (1986), and achieved a high level of success in roles as diverse as an irreverent Vietnam-stationed disc jockey (1987's *Good Morning, Vietnam,* for which he was Oscar-nominated) and an unorthodox prep school instructor (1989's *Dead Poets Society,* again Oscar-nominated). Having established a strong bond with audiences, who respond to his teddy-bear warmth and infectious humor, Williams can shed his comic persona completely when he wants to, as in the moving *Awakenings* (1990, as a dedicated doctor who isolates himself from the world) or the emotional roller coaster of *The Fisher King* (1991, as a mad, homeless, medieval scholar, a performance that earned him an Oscar nomination). He can disappear into a character, like the would-be jock in *The Best of Times* (1986) or the King of the Moon in Terry Gilliam's fanciful *The Adventures of Baron Munchausen* (1989). And, as a bona fide star, he can have a lark, as he did playing supporting roles in Kenneth Branagh's *Dead Again* and—as a mime teacher—in *Shakes the Clown* (both 1991).

Steven Spielberg's *Hook* (1991) offered the promising idea of casting Williams as a grownup Peter Pan who's forgotten who he is, but the result was disappointing. *Toys* (1992) was an embarrassing misfire for *Good Morning, Vietnam* director Barry Levinson. But Williams was heard at his best in a pair of animated features, *FernGully ... The Last Rainforest* (1992, as the comic relief character Batty) and Disney's megahit *Aladdin* (also 1992, as the quicksilver Genie, a part that allowed and even encouraged him to ad-lib to his heart's content). The live-action comedy

hit *Mrs. Doubtfire* (1993), which Williams produced with his wife, also enabled director Chris Columbus to take advantage of his star's gift for on-the-spot comic invention, as he played a divorced dad who disguises himself as an English nanny in order to see his kids. Williams has remained a constant presence on television, doing talk shows, guest appearances (he won a pair of Emmys for late 1980s variety specials), and cohosting the annual "Comic Relief" benefit for the homeless. Recent credits include *Being Human* (1994) and *Nine Months* (1995).

WILLIAMS, TREAT. Actor. *(b. Dec. 1, 1951, Rowayton, Conn.)* After his electrifying performance as a corrupt cop turned government informant in *Prince of the City* (1981) stardom seemed a shoo-in for this ruggedly handsome actor. It didn't happen. Williams made his screen debut in *Deadly Hero* (1976, as a cop), and followed it up with roles in *The Ritz* (as a falsetto-voiced cop) and *The Eagle Has Landed* (1977). He hit his stride in 1979, playing the leading role of a life-embracing hippie in Milos Forman's film adaptation of the counterculture stage musical *Hair,* and a thuggish, girl-crazy soldier in Steven Spielberg's *1941.* Star billing followed—in two terrible flops, *Why Would I Lie?* (1980) and *The Pursuit of D. B. Cooper* (1981), and good leading parts pretty much dried up after that. But Williams appeared to advantage in the sprawling gangster epic *Once Upon a Time in America* (1984), the provocative rape-or-seduction drama *Smooth Talk* (1985), and the turgid *The Men's Club* (1986). He hit a career low with 1988's *Dead Heat,* playing an undead, decomposing cop trying to solve his own murder. Good performances in *Heart of Dixie, Sweet Lies* (both 1989), and *Beyond the Ocean* (1990) have followed. Recent credits include the TV movies *Deadly Matrimony, The Water Engine* (both 1992), and *Parallel Lives* (1994), as well as a stint on the series "Good Advice" (1993–94) with Shelley Long.

WILLIAMSON, FRED. Actor, producer, director. *(b. Mar. 5, 1938, Gary, Ind.)* A star footballer for 10 years before taking up acting in *MASH,* and *Tell Me That You*

Love Me, Junie Moon (both 1970), Williamson has since become a prolific performer and filmmaker, riding the wave of 1970s "blaxploitation" pictures—in *Black Caesar* (1973), *Bucktown, Adios, Amigo* (both 1975, also directed), *Mean Johnny Barrows* (1976), to name just a few—and popping up in Italian-made *Road Warrior* clones such as *1990: The Bronx Warriors, Warriors of the Wasteland* (both 1983), and *The New Barbarians* (1984). His later self-directed pictures, of which *Foxtrap* (1986) is representative, tend to be amateurish vanity productions spotlighting "The Hammer," but falling far short of professional quality. Williamson, basically a humorless actor who takes himself very seriously, was the only major blaxploitation star missing from Keenen Ivory Wayans' 1988 spoof *I'm Gonna Git You Sucka.*
OTHER FILMS INCLUDE: 1972: *The Legend of Nigger Charley, Hammer* (the film that gave Williamson his nickname); 1973: *The Soul of Nigger Charley, That Man Bolt, Hell up in Harlem, Three Tough Guys;* 1974: *Crazy Joe, Three the Hard Way, Black Eye;* 1975: *Boss Nigger, Take a Hard Ride;* 1976: *No Way Back* (also directed); *Joshua* (also wrote); 1977: *Mr. Mean;* 1978: *Counterfeit Commandos;* 1980: *Fist of Fear, Touch of Death;* 1983: *Vigilante, The Big Score;* 1985: *Deadly Impact*

WILLIAMSON, NICOL. Actor. *(b. Sept. 14, 1938, Hamilton, Scotland.)* Electric stage actor who has made some memorable forays into film, beginning with *Inadmissible Evidence* (1968), a recreation of his critically hailed stage performance as the disgusted solicitor Bill Maitland. Before this, Williamson had performed with the Cambridge Arts Theatre and later the Royal Shakespeare Company in plays ranging from "Waiting for Godot" to "A Midsummer Night's Dream." Best when portraying tortured, disturbed, and angry men, Williamson scored as a drunk Irish gunner in *The Bofors Gun* (1968), a pissed-off businessman in *The Reckoning* (1969), the title role in *Hamlet* (also 1969, another role he had played on the stage), and a cocaine-addicted, psychologically unsound Sherlock Holmes in *The Seven Percent Solution* (1976). He has also shown a lighter side as Little John in *Robin and Marian* (1976), a Nazi colonel in Neil Simon's *The Cheap*

Detective (1978), one of Theresa Russell's doomed husbands in *Black Widow* (1986), and particularly, a charmingly eccentric Merlin in John Boorman's *Excalibur* (1981). His other films include *Laughter in the Dark* (1969), *The Jerusalem File* (1972), *The Wilby Conspiracy* (1975), *The Human Factor* (1979), *I'm Dancing as Fast as I Can, Venom* (both 1982), *Return to Oz* (1985), and *The Exorcist III* (1990). Williamson has also appeared on TV in the miniseries "Christopher Columbus" (1985, as King Ferdinand) and "The Last Viceroy" (1986, as Lord Mountbatten).

WILLIS, BRUCE. Actor. *(b. Mar. 19, 1955, Penn's Grove, N.J.)* Few actors have had as many ups and downs during the first decade of a career—or had to battle so many shifts in public perception. Painted by some as a Star with an Attitude, Willis has also shown himself to be a versatile actor willing to take chances. After "extra" work in *The First Deadly Sin* (1980) and *The Verdict* (1982), and a notable appearance as a wife-beating gunrunner on an episode of "Miami Vice," he became an overnight sensation (and won an Emmy) as the goofy private eye on "Moonlighting" (1985–89), opposite Cybill Shepherd. Feature-film work quickly followed, first with a pair of films for Blake Edwards: a moderately successful slapstick farce, *Blind Date* (1987), and *Sunset* (1988), a strange Hollywood whodunit set in the 1920s that miscast Willis as cowboy star Tom Mix. Just as some wags were writing Willis off as a flash in the pan, he landed himself an action film; there was skepticism that he could carry a Stallone type of part, but the role of a loner cop in *Die Hard* (1988) was tailor-made, replete with wisecracks, and the film became a tremendous hit. There was, of course, a *Die Hard 2* in 1990, and a third, *Die Hard With a Vengeance,* in 1995. The actor also starred in another smash the next year without even having to show up; he was the voice of a precocious baby in the comedy *Look Who's Talking* (1989). He also took his first serious screen role in the unsuccessful *In Country* (1989), as a shell-shocked Vietnam vet.
Willis' stock plummeted just as quickly with two mega-turkeys that cast him in arrogant roles: the writer in the misjudged

adaptation of *The Bonfire of the Vanities*
(1990) and a safecracker in the overblown
vanity production *Hudson Hawk* (1991),
for which he provided the story and the title song (!). A return to *Die Hard* territory
with *The Last Boy Scout* (1991) did only
marginally better. Meanwhile, he gave
sterling performances in supporting roles,
as an abusive husband in *Mortal Thoughts*
(1991, opposite wife Demi Moore) and a
disloyal gangster in *Billy Bathgate* (also
1991), causing some to wonder if he
wouldn't be better off *not* being a star. Recent films include *Death Becomes Her*
(1992), *The Player* (1992, as himself in a
funny cameo), *National Lampoon's
Loaded Weapon I* (1993, another gag
cameo), *Striking Distance* (also 1993),
Color of Night, and fine character roles in
Nobody's Fool and *Pulp Fiction* (all
1994).

WILLIS, GORDON. Cinematographer,
director. *(b. May 28, 1931, Queens, N.Y.)*
The warm, subdued hues that contributed
so much to the "feel" of Francis Ford
Coppola's *The Godfather* (1972) and its
1974 and 1990 sequels were the contribution of this talented cinematographer,
whose understated colors, naturalistic
lighting, and striking black-and-white
imagery make him one of the industry's
preeminent craftsmen. As a youth, he
worked in summer stock theater, both on-
stage and backstage, then served in the air
force and gained experience as a cameraman. Upon his return to civilian life, he
decided to pursue that career and spent a
number of years filming documentaries
and commercials before breaking into
mainstream movies. He photographed
such interesting 1970s pictures as *The
Landlord, Loving* (both 1970), *Klute*
(1971), *Bad Company* (1972), *The Paper
Chase* (1973), *The Parallax View* (1974),
All the President's Men (1976), and *Annie
Hall* (1977); the latter kicked off his collaboration with Woody Allen, which continued with *Interiors* (1978), *Manhattan*
(1979, in widescreen black & white), *Stardust Memories* (1980, in b & w), *A Midsummer Night's Sex Comedy* (1982),
Broadway Danny Rose (1984, b & w), and
The Purple Rose of Cairo (1985). In 1980
Willis made an ill-advised directorial debut with *Windows,* a nasty, unpleasant
thriller in which psychotic lesbian Eliza-

beth Ashley relentlessly pursued Talia
Shire. The effort was met with a hail of
well-deserved brickbats from both film
critics and gay-rights groups. Willis returned to cinematography, capturing both
moods of *Pennies From Heaven* (1981),
the Edward Hopper–esque images of the
Depression, and the thousand-kilowatt
look of 1930s movie-musical numbers. He
stretched his technical skills in Woody Allen's 1983 fantasy *Zelig,* and went on to
photograph *The Money Pit* (1986), *The
Pick-up Artist* (1987), *Bright Lights, Big
City* (1988), and *Presumed Innocent*
(1990), among others.

Long shunned by his colleagues in the
cinematography branch of the Academy of
Motion Picture Arts and Sciences, Willis
finally earned an Oscar nomination for his
brilliant work on *Zelig*—for which he deliberately made his images look as flat,
grainy, and scratchy as possible (to suit
the movie's gimmick of being a pseudodocumentary full of vintage newsreel
film). The irony was compounded when,
having been ignored for his work on the
first two multi-Oscar-winning *Godfather*
movies, he was nominated for the third
(and least impressive) of the trilogy.

WILLS, CHILL. Actor. *(b. July 18, 1903,
Seagoville, Tex.; d. Dec. 15, 1978.)* A veteran
of tent shows, stock, and vaudeville engagements throughout the Southwest, Wills
first played onscreen in 1935 as lead vocalist with the Avalon Boys, a Western-music
group he organized. Shortly after appearing
in the 1937 Laurel and Hardy comedy *Way
Out West,* Wills left the group to seek fame
and fortune as an actor. He played sidekick
to cowboy star George O'Brien in several
1939 horse operas, beginning with *Arizona
Legion,* and graduated to supporting roles
in major films such as *Boom Town* (1940),
Honky Tonk (1941), *Meet Me in St. Louis*
(1944), *Leave Her to Heaven* (1945), and
The Yearling (1946). In his youth a slender,
homely man with bobbing Adam's apple,
Wills gained weight steadily throughout the
1940s and 1950s, as his screen characters
became progressively obnoxious. He was
somewhat restrained and, consequently,
very effective in *Giant* (1956), and he
earned an Oscar nomination (then mounting an aggressive—and controversial—promotional campaign) for *The Alamo* (1960).
Wills also supplied the voice of Francis the

Talking Mule in the popular 1950s movie series. He costarred in two TV series, "Frontier Circus" (1961) and "The Rounders" (1967), a spin-off of the feature film. His last movie was *Mr. Billion* (1977).
OTHER FILMS INCLUDE: 1939: *Allegheny Uprising;* 1940: *The Westerner;* 1941: *Belle Starr;* 1942: *Tarzan's New York Adventure;* 1943: *Best Foot Forward;* 1946: *The Harvey Girls;* 1950: *Rio Grande;* 1953: *The Man From the Alamo;* 1963: *McLintock!, The Wheeler Dealers, The Cardinal;* 1965: *The Rounders;* 1970: *The Liberation of L. B. Jones;* 1973: *Pat Garrett and Billy the Kid.*

WINDSOR, MARIE. Actress. *(b. Dec. 11, 1922, Marysvale, Utah, as Emily Marie Bertelson.)* One of the best "bad girls" in movie history, this busty beauty often played cold-blooded temptresses who could drive a man crazy with passion, then cut out his heart and hand it back to him. A former Miss Utah, she broke into films as a bit player in Hal Roach's *All-American Co-Ed* (1941), and knocked around Hollywood before coming into her own as a leading lady in 1949's *Hellfire,* an above-average Republic Western. She appeared in other B-plus horse operas, including *Dakota Lil, Frenchie* (both 1950), and *Little Big Horn* (1951), before taking her best-remembered role, as the recalcitrant gangster's widow being transported to court by tough cop Charles McGraw in *The Narrow Margin* (1952). Had this taut thriller not been a lowly B (albeit one of the best ever), Windsor might have gotten more of a boost from its success. She continued working steadily, frequently playing tart-tongued trollops—as in Stanley Kubrick's *The Killing* (1956), memorably cast as Elisha Cook, Jr.'s avaricious, unfaithful wife.
Windsor also worked in many TV movies during the 1970s and 1980s, including *Wild Women* (1971) and the 1979 miniseries "Salem's Lot." Unfortunately, she never starred in a first-rate, big-budget film.
OTHER FILMS INCLUDE: 1952: *The Sniper* (another sleeper); 1953: *The Tall Texan, The City That Never Sleeps;* 1954: *Cat Women of the Moon* (a tacky sci-fi cheapie that has acquired a cult reputation among lovers of camp); 1955: *Abbott and Costello Meet the Mummy, Swamp Women;* 1957: *The Unholy Wife, The Story of Mankind* (as Napoleon's Josephine); 1958: *Island Woman;* 1960: *The*

Little Shop of Horrors; 1963: *Critics' Choice, The Day Mars Invaded Earth;* 1964: *Bedtime Story;* 1969: *The Good Guys and the Bad Guys;* 1971: *Support Your Local Gunfighter;* 1973: *Cahill—United States Marshal;* 1975: *The Apple Dumpling Gang, Hearts of the West;* 1977: *Freaky Friday;* 1983: *Lovely But Deadly.*

WINFIELD, PAUL. Actor. *(b. May 22, 1940, Los Angeles.)* This imposing black actor first came to the attention of TV audiences opposite Diahann Carroll on the sitcom "Julia" from 1968 to 1971, and he's done some of his best work on the small screen, especially as civil-rights activist Dr. Martin Luther King, Jr., in "King," a 1978 miniseries. Winfield's feature-film success has been limited to a few choice roles, notably the dignified sharecropper in *Sounder* (1972, for which he received a Best Actor Oscar nomination), but he's had plenty of movie work over the last two decades without falling into the blaxploitation quagmire. He debuted in *The Lost Man* (1969), and was visible in *R. P. M.* (1970), *Conrack, Huckleberry Finn* (both 1974), *The Greatest* (1977), *Carbon Copy* (1981), *Star Trek II: The Wrath of Khan* (1982), *Blue City* (1986), *The Serpent and the Rainbow* (1988), and *James Baldwin: The Price of the Ticket* (1989). He had a particularly thankless time going up against murderous cyborg Arnold Schwarzenegger in *The Terminator* (1984). Winfield's outstanding performance as an animal trainer trying to "break" a dog programmed to attack blacks in Samuel Fuller's *White Dog* (1982) was unseen for many years because Paramount shelved the movie, embarrassed by its subject matter. He had a good supporting role as a judge in the courtroom drama *Presumed Innocent* (1990), but his best parts in the past 15 years have mainly been on stage or in TV dramas, including the miniseries "Roots: The Next Generation" (1979), "Alex Haley's Queen" (1993), and "Scarlett" (1994).
OTHER FILMS INCLUDE: 1972: *Brother John;* 1973: *Gordon's War;* 1975: *Hustle;* 1976: *Green Eyes* (telefilm); 1977: *Damnation Alley, High Velocity, Twilight's Last Gleaming;* 1978: *A Hero Ain't Nothin' but a Sandwich;* 1984: *Mike's Murder, Go Tell It on the*

Mountain (telefilm); 1987: *Big Shots, Death Before Dishonor;* 1993: *Dennis the Menace.*

WINGER, DEBRA. Actress. *(b. May 17, 1955, Cleveland.)* This perky, throaty brunette came to acting via a route much different than those taken by most of her contemporaries. As a teenager she emigrated to Israel, where she worked for two years on a collective farm and served in the Army. Upon returning to the States, she was involved in a serious accident that left her in a coma. Partially paralyzed and blinded in one eye for several months, Winger thought long and hard about where her life was going, and decided that upon recuperating she would become an actress. She did, making several commercials before being cast as Lynda Carter's little sister Drusilla on the popular "Wonder Woman" TV series. Winger appeared in small roles in the nondescript *Slumber Party '57* (1977), *Thank God It's Friday* (1978), and *French Postcards* (1979) before beating out more than 200 hopefuls for the lead in *Urban Cowboy* (1980), which paired her with John Travolta and gave her an opportunity to demonstrate her ability. This arresting, star-making performance led to her casting as a home-grown hopeful Juliet opposite Richard Gere in *An Officer and a Gentleman* (1982), which earned her an Oscar nomination, and as Shirley MacLaine's cancer-stricken daughter in *Terms of Endearment* (1983), for which she was Oscar-nominated again. She replaced Raquel Welch in *Cannery Row* (1982), which was barely seen, and agreed to star in *Mike's Murder* for *Urban Cowboy* director James Bridges, but that muddled thriller sat on the shelf until 1984. She also participated in the extraordinary success of *E.T. The Extra-Terrestrial* (1982), but in an unusual way: her distinctive voice was among those used for the alien visitor.

Winger quickly made it known that she was not interested in playing the Hollywood game and was content to let long periods go by without making movies, rather than appear in something she didn't feel strongly about. She regretted saying yes to a blatantly commercial film, *Legal Eagles* (1986), that didn't show her to best advantage, but was back in form in the stylish thriller *Black Widow* (1986), and made the best of an underwritten role in

Costa Gavras' melodrama about white supremacists, *Betrayed* (1988). (Married for several years to actor Timothy Hutton, she made a cameo appearance, as a man, in his 1987 film *Made in Heaven.)* *Everybody Wins* (1990) had Nick Nolte as co-star, and an Arthur Miller script, but it turned out badly. Later that year she found personal fulfillment playing a hedonist in Bernardo Bertolucci's enigmatic *The Sheltering Sky* (1990). Originally announced to star in *A League of Their Own,* she backed out of the project early on, and then became uncharacteristically busy: she was terrific as Steve Martin's saucy partner in crime in *Leap of Faith* (1992), then starred in three 1993 releases: the misfired comedy *Wilder Napalm, A Dangerous Woman,* in which she brilliantly played a retarded woman, and *Shadowlands,* in which she delivered an intelligent, moving (and Oscar-nominated) performance as Joy Gresham, the American poet who fell in love with British author C. S. Lewis (Anthony Hopkins). This spurt of activity brought cheers from Winger admirers, and served as a reminder that she is one of the most gifted actresses in films. In 1995, she costarred with Billy Crystal in *Forget Paris.*

WINKLER, HENRY. Actor, director, producer. *(b. Oct. 30, 1945, New York City.)* Though only five feet six and a half inches tall, this actor created one of television's biggest characters: as the ultra-cool greaser Arthur "Fonzie" Fonzarelli on "Happy Days" (1974–84) he became a pop idol overnight. A graduate of Yale with a Masters' in Drama, he appeared in dozens of commercials before making his screen debut, prophetically enough in the youth gang picture *The Lord's of Flatbush* (1974). He had a bit part in *Crazy Joe* (also 1974) before landing the role of "The Fonz." His subsequent attempt to translate TV fame to film stardom with leading roles in *Heroes* (1977), *The One and Only* (1978), and *Night Shift* (1982, directed by his "Happy Days" costar Ron Howard) were only modestly successful. He also hosted and executive produced *Who Are the Debolts? . . . and Where Did They Get 19 Kids?* which won an Academy Award as Best Documentary of 1978. As "Happy Days" wound down, Winkler started directing his energies behind the camera. He coproduced the popular TV series "MacGyver" (1985–92) and the less successful "Mr. Sunshine" (1986), and directed the theatrical features *Memories of Me* (1988) and *Cop and a Half* (1993). He returned to acting in the TV movies *Absolute Strangers* (1991) and *The Only Way Out* (1993), and took the starring role in the sitcom "Monty" (1994) playing a right-wing talk show host.

WINNINGER, CHARLES. Actor. *(b. May 26, 1884, Athens, Wis.; d. Jan. 27, 1969.)* With show business in his blood, Winninger quit school at age nine to join the family vaudeville act. Years of stock, repertory, and legitimate stage work led to featured billing in the Ziegfeld Follies. and, in 1927, to his appearance as Cap'n Andy in the original Broadway production of "Show Boat" (a role he repeated both in stage revivals and onscreen in the 1936 movie version). Winninger made some comedy shorts in the teens and a few scattered features in the 1920s, but he returned to movies with a vengeance in 1930. He could be boisterous, cherubic, distinguished, crafty—in other words, no character role was beyond his capability. His memorable movies include *Three Smart Girls* (1936, as the father), *You're a Sweetheart, Nothing Sacred* (both 1937), *Three Smart Girls Grow Up, Babes in Arms, Destry Rides Again* (all 1939), *Little Nellie Kelly* (1940), *Ziegfeld Girl* (1941), *Hers to Hold* (1943, reprising his part from *Three Smart Girls), State Fair* (1945), *Give My Regards to Broadway* (1948), *Father Is a Bachelor* (1950), and *Raymie* (1960). John Ford chose him to star in one of his pet projects, a remake of the Will Rogers movie *Judge Priest* called *The Sun Shines Bright* (1953). He also played Charlie Farrell's father on the TV series "The Charlie Farrell Show" (1956).

WINTERS, SHELLEY. Actress. *(b. Aug. 22, 1922, St. Louis, as Shirley Schrift.)* In her heyday a sultry, svelte, blond leading lady, Shelley Winters is more firmly ensconced in memory as a blowsy, loudmouthed, colorful character type. There is a temptation to confuse the rambling, raucous talk-show guest of past years with the talented actress, so one should keep in mind that this former store clerk has won Oscars for her supporting stints in *The Di-*

ary of Anne Frank (1959) and *A Patch of Blue* (1965), and has earned nominations for *A Place in the Sun* (1951) and *The Poseidon Adventure* (1972). Winters' first film credits were decorative bit parts in such 1940s movies as *Knickerbocker Holiday* (1944) and *Tonight and Every Night* (1945). Her first big break was landing a costarring role with Ronald Colman in *A Double Life* (1947), as the mistress and unfortunate victim of the actor-gone-mad. In the aftermath of that film she was often cast as vulnerable victim types, such as Myrtle in *The Great Gatsby* (1949) and Alice Tripp in *A Place in the Sun* (1951), but she also played her share of sexpots, including the title role in *Frenchie* (1950), a reworking of *Destry Rides Again* that cast her in the Marlene Dietrich part. She was a standout in the searing Hollywood tale *The Big Knife* (1955), and the murdered mother in *The Night of the Hunter* that same year. She was memorable as the nymphet's mother in *Lolita* (1962), notorious madam Polly Adler in *A House Is Not a Home* (1964), and one of Alfie's conquests in *Alfie* (1966), but by the 1970s she was often playing caricatures, like the machine gun–toting *Bloody Mama* (1970). Paul Mazursky fleshed out potential-caricature roles for her in *Blume in Love* (1973) and *Next Stop, Greenwich Village* (1976), and she had fun (over)playing a hag in Disney's *Pete's Dragon* (1977), the Queen of the gypsies in *King of the Gypsies* (1978), and a super-agent in Blake Edwards' Hollywood saga *S.O.B.* (1981).

Busy on television when not in films (and seen in recent years in a recurring role as Roseanne's grandmother on the hit sitcom "Roseanne"), she has also taught at Lee Strasberg's Actors' Studio, and enjoyed success with her tell-all autobiographies "Shelley" (1980) and "Shelley II" (1989).

OTHER FILMS INCLUDE: 1943: *What a Woman!;* 1944: *Sailor's Holiday, She's a Soldier Too;* 1945: *A Thousand and One Nights;* 1948: *Cry of the City;* 1950: *South Sea Sinner, Winchester '73;* 1951: *The Raging Tide;* 1952: *Meet Danny Wilson, Phone Call From a Stranger;* 1954: *Executive Suite, Playgirl;* 1955: *I Am a Camera, I Died a Thousand Times;* 1960: *Let No Man Write My Epitaph;* 1961: *The Young Savages;* 1962: *The Chapman Report;* 1963: *Wives and Lovers, The Balcony;* 1965: *The Greatest Story Ever Told;* 1966: *Harper;* 1967: *Enter Laughing;* 1968: *The*

Scalphunters, Wild in the Streets; 1969: *Buona Sera, Mrs. Campbell, The Mad Room;* 1970: *How Do I Love Thee?, Flap;* 1971: *What's the Matter With Helen?, Who Slew Auntie Roo?;* 1973: *Cleopatra Jones;* 1975: *Diamonds, Journey Into Fear, That Lucky Touch;* 1979: *The Magician of Lublin, The Visitor;* 1983: *Fanny Hill, Over the Brooklyn Bridge;* 1984: *Déjà Vu, Ellie, Witchfire;* 1986: *The Delta Force;* 1989: *An Unremarkable Life;* 1991: *Touch of a Stranger, Stepping Out;* 1993: *The Pickle.*

WISE, ROBERT. Director, editor, producer. *(b. Sept. 10, 1914, Winchester, Ind.)* Dependable Hollywood veteran whose transparent cinematic style has yielded wide-ranging success. His film career began when his brother, who worked in the accounting department at RKO, got young Robert a job as an assistant editor. He eventually worked his way up to full editor, notably cutting *The Hunchback of Notre Dame* (1939), *My Favorite Wife, Dance, Girl, Dance* (both 1940), *The Devil and Daniel Webster* (1941, aka *All That Money Can Buy),* and Orson Welles' landmark *Citizen Kane* (also 1941, for which he was Oscar-nominated as Best Editor) and *The Magnificent Ambersons* (1942). Wise was given his first chance behind the camera as codirector of *The Curse of the Cat People* (1944), one of the stylish horror films produced by Val Lewton; the producer also assigned Wise to direct *The Body Snatcher* (1945). He toiled in RKO's B-picture unit until 1948, doing consistently solid work. His first boost came when he was assigned the moody Western *Blood on the Moon* (1948) and turned in a first-rate job. *The Set-Up* (1949), a prize-fight drama that took place in "real time," won Wise even more attention and was to be the turning point in his career.

In the 1950s he proved to be a master Hollywood craftsman who brought intelligence and skill to the widest possible range of material, from the landmark science-fiction tale *The Day the Earth Stood Still* (1951) to the soap opera saga *So Big* (1953) to the all-star *Executive Suite* (1954). *Somebody Up There Likes Me* (1956) proved an important acting showcase for young Paul Newman, and *I Want to Live!* (1958) gave Susan Hayward an Oscar-winning opportunity; Wise was also nominated as Best Director. He

wisely recruited choreographer Jerome Robbins to help bring *West Side Story* (1961) to the screen, and as producer-director, he won both Best Director (shared with Robbins) and Best Picture Oscars for that inventive musical. He again won dual Oscars—Best Director, Best Picture—for the beloved Rodgers and Hammerstein musical *The Sound of Music* (1965). Now typecast as a "big" moviemaker, he had difficulty finding worthy material, especially in the 1970s (although, having made the masterful modern ghost story *The Haunting* in 1963 he was a perfect choice to tackle 1977's *Audrey Rose.)* In 1973 he deliberately chose an intimate story to sink his teeth into, *Two People.* In 1986 Wise was asked to executive produce Emilio Estevez's maiden voyage as director, *Wisdom,* and three years later Wise returned to the director's chair himself, for the ill-advised urban musical *Rooftops* (1989), a film that begged unfortunate comparisons with *West Side Story.*

A past president of both the Directors Guild of America and the Academy of Motion Picture Arts and Sciences, Wise has settled comfortably into the role of Hollywood elder statesman.

OTHER FILMS INCLUDE: 1944: *Mademoiselle Fifi;* 1946: *A Game of Death, Criminal Court;* 1947: *Born to Kill;* 1948: *Mystery in Mexico;* 1950: *Three Secrets, Two Flags West;* 1951: *The House on Telegraph Hill;* 1952: *The Captive City, Something for the Birds;* 1953: *The Desert Rats, Destination Gobi;* 1955: *Helen of Troy;* 1957: *This Could Be the Night, Until They Sail;* 1958: *Run Silent, Run Deep;* 1959: *Odds Against Tomorrow;* 1966: *The Sand Pebbles;* 1968: *Star!;* 1971: *The Andromeda Strain;* 1975: *The Hindenburg;* 1979: *Star Trek—The Motion Picture.*

WISEMAN, FREDERICK. Director, editor, producer. *(b. Jan. 1, 1930, Boston.)* Acclaimed documentary filmmaker who has been called "our best and bravest observer of the grim side of contemporary existence." Educated as a lawyer at Yale, Wiseman taught at Boston College and then produced Shirley Clarke's *The Cool World* (1963), a semidocumentary look at juvenile delinquents in Harlem. After cofounding the Organization for Social and Technical Innovation in 1966, he made his first film, *Titicut Follies* (1967), photographed in the state hospital for the criminally insane in Bridgewater, Massachusetts. The film caused an uproar with state authorities there and established Wiseman's reputation as a social muckraker. His next films—the simply titled *High School* (1969), *Law and Order* (also 1969, about the Kansas City Police Dept.), *Hospital* (1970, set in New York's Metropolitan Hospital), *Juvenile Court* (1973), and *Welfare* (1975)—continued to expose the dehumanizing effects of bureaucracies in our society, using a straightforward, cinema-verité style in which the guilty usually hang themselves.

Wiseman's later films like *Sinai Field Mission* (1977), *Model* (1980), and *Store* (1983, about Neiman-Marcus) examined American society as it is reflected in consumer products and in our influence abroad, while his more recent films like *Blind, Deaf, Multi-Handicapped* (all 1987), and *Near Death* (1989) turned inward to examine physical problems and their effect on the psyche. Wiseman shoots enormous amounts of footage of his subjects and spends a great deal of time with them so they eventually forget the presence of his cameras and recorders. It is during the editing process that he finds the themes and patterns in the material. Wiseman's films use no voice-over narration or commentary and rely on the editing selection to speak for the subjects. He has written, "A documentary, by whomever made and in no matter what style, is arbitrary, biased, prejudiced, compressed, and subjective like any of its sisterly or brotherly forms." His latest work includes *High School II* (1993) and *Ballet* (1995).

WISEMAN, JOSEPH. Actor. *(b. May 15, 1918, Montreal.)* Intense, saturnine character actor best known for his performance as the title character and arch-villain of the very first James Bond film, *Dr. No* (1962). Wiseman is primarily a stage actor, with many distinguished plays to his credit; his first major screen role was in *Detective Story* (1951), recreating his scorching stage performance as a drugcrazed wiseguy who unmercifully and tragically taunts a New York City police detective. Wiseman found himself typecast as quick-tempered, mostly ethnic villains: Fernando Aguirre, a warmongering

revolutionary, in *Viva Zapata!* (1952); Genflou, a convict, in *Les Miserables* (1952); Dominic Guido, a racketeer, in *Champ for a Day* (1953); Abe Kelsey, a vengeful settler, in *The Unforgiven* (1960). After his understated performance as *Dr. No*, Wiseman continued playing heavies: Mafia bosses in both *Stiletto* (1969) and *The Valachi Papers* (1972) and the head of a counterfeit ring in *The Counterfeit Killer* (1988). And he was cast in Jewish roles: Felix Ottensteen, one of a quartet of mourners in *Bye Bye Braverman* (1968); Louis (father of Billy) Minsky in *The Night They Raided Minsky's* (1968); wealthy, emotionally distant Uncle Benjy in *The Apprenticeship of Duddy Kravitz* (1974); and Jake Weinstein in *The Betsy* (1978). He also played Colonel Haki, a role originated by Orson Welles, in the remake of *Journey Into Fear* (1975).

WITHERS, JANE. Actress. *(b. Apr. 12, 1926, Atlanta.)* The starring films of this 1930s child star are no longer widely shown, so it's difficult for those who didn't see her in theaters to realize how popular Jane Withers really was. When she debuted on screen at age 6 (in 1932's *Handle With Care),* the precocious Withers was already a veteran of vaudeville and radio. (She even provided the voice for a cartoon character, Willie Whopper, in 1933–34 for producer Ub Iwerks.) Fox signed her in 1934, after she stole scenes from Shirley Temple (!) as a bratty rival in *Bright Eyes* (1934). The studio soon launched her in her own starring series (reasoning, as studios did in those days, that a second successful child star on the lot would keep Temple in line).

In her own films, which included *Ginger, Paddy O'Day* (both 1935), *Pepper, Little Miss Nobody, Gentle Julia* (all 1936), *Wild and Woolly, The Holy Terror, Checkers* (all 1937), *Always in Trouble, Rascals, Keep Smiling,* and *Arizona Wildcat* (all 1938), among others, Withers established a most un-Templelike persona: She played quick-witted, outspoken, often mischievous brats who frequently got themselves in difficulties from which they could only be extricated by the films' nominal adult leads. Dark-haired, wide-eyed, a little pudgy, and not particularly pretty, she endeared herself to audiences with her seemingly limitless energy and impish charm.

Unfortunately, Withers outgrew her persona quickly; *Youth Will Be Served, Shooting High* (starring Gene Autry in a spoof of Western filmmaking), *The Girl From Avenue A* (all 1940), *Her First Beau, Golden Hoofs, Small Town Deb* (all 1941), *Young America,* and *The Mad Martindales* (both 1942) carried her through "that awkward age." She had a supporting role in the wartime drama *The North Star* (1943), then left the studio and appeared in only a handful of films thereafter, including *Danger Street* (1947), *Giant* (1956), and *Captain Newman, M.D.* (1963). Withers achieved small-screen recognition in the 1960s as Josephine the plumber, pitchwoman for Comet cleanser; she also dabbled in episodic TV and appeared in the 1975 telefilm *All Together Now.* Her long-range goal is to find a museum that will house her world-class (and world-famous) collection of dolls.

WOOD, EDWARD D., JR. Director, screenwriter. (b. Oct. 10, 1924, Poughkeepsie, N.Y.; d. Dec. 10, 1978.) If Academy Awards were handed out for bad movies, Edward Wood, Jr., would be the hands-down all-time Oscar champ. Furthermore, he would have been the first to be honored with a special citation for lifetime achievement. Wood's films are so uniformly, absolutely awful that they are great fun to watch, and in the years since his death he has developed into a bona fide cult personality. It should be stated, however, that Wood did not intentionally create camp classics. He sincerely meant to make good movies, and could not understand their less-than-enthusiastic reception. He made his directorial debut with the now-legendary *Glen or Glenda?* (1953, aka *I Changed My Sex, He or She,* and *I Led Two Lives).* Bela Lugosi narrates, and Wood (billed as Daniel Davis) stars as a transvestite whose fiancée is unable to comprehend his need to wear her clothes. His follow-up, *Jail Bait* (1954), is the saga of a criminal who has his face changed by plastic surgery. Lugosi stars in *Bride of the Monster* (1955) as Dr. Vornoff, desperately attempting to invent a race of superbeings; oversized Swedish wrestler Tor Johnson, a Wood regular, plays Lobo, the doctor's manservant.

Wood scripted but did not direct *The Violent Years* (1956), about a wealthy teenage girl who becomes a gangleader.

Wood then made his "masterpiece." In *Plan 9 From Outer Space* (1959), "hosted" by self-styled seer Criswell, hammy aliens attempt to overpower earth by resurrecting corpses. Bela Lugosi died after two days of filming in 1956; when Wood had enough money to finish the picture, several years later, he asked his wife's chiropractor to stand in for Lugosi, covering his face with a cape—even though the man was significantly taller than the late actor. The film is irresistibly hilarious, for all the wrong reasons. *Revenge of the Dead* (1960, aka *Night of the Ghouls)* is the story of "ghosts" invading Los Angeles and of a bogus mystic. Criswell narrates, from a coffin; Johnson reprises his role as Lobo; and Wood makes a cameo appearance as a corpse. The film went unreleased for 23 years, because Wood did not have sufficient funds to settle his account with his lab. His final directorial credit, *The Sinister Urge* (1961, aka *The Young and the Immoral),* tells of a pair of cops who expose a "smut picture" operation. Wood went on to script *Orgy of the Dead* (1965), the story of a writer and his fiancée who witness a "dance of the dead" in a cemetery, and coscript *Fugitive Girls* (1971), which follows the exploits of some women on the lam. He made a "special appearance" in the latter, playing Pop, an aging airstrip custodian. Sixteen years after Wood's death, he was the subject of a Hollywood bio, directed by Tim Burton and starring Johnny Depp; the budget for *Ed Wood* (1994) easily exceeded the combined total cost of all his films.

WOOD, ELIJAH. Actor. (b. Jan. 28, 1981, Cedar Rapids, Iowa.) Talented—and extremely busy—child actor who has amassed some impressive credits since his first acting stint in a Paula Abdul video. After small roles in *Back to the Future Part II* (1989) and *Internal Affairs* (1990), he won acclaim as a young Barry Levinson in the director/writer's personal drama *Avalon* (1990) and went on to star in *Paradise* (1991), *Radio Flyer,* and *Forever Young* (both 1992), all of which gave him roles of substance that revealed both his talent and natural appeal. He made an ideal Huckleberry in *The Adventures of Huck Finn* and squared off against child superstar Macaulay Culkin in the thriller *The Good Son* (both 1993) before starring as a young genius searching for new parents in *North* (1994).

WOOD, NATALIE. Actress. *(b. July 20, 1938, San Francisco, as Natasha Gurdin; d. Nov. 29, 1981.)* It's one of Hollywood's bitter ironies that an actress who gave the world so much pleasure, both as a child and an adult, should chiefly be remembered for the mysterious and unhappy manner in which she died. She began appearing in movies at the age of five, with a bit in *Happy Land* (1943), then reappeared a few years later with roles in *Tomorrow Is Forever* (1946) and *The Ghost and Mrs. Muir* (1947), winning the hearts of audiences that same year as the little girl who doesn't believe in Santa Claus in *Miracle on 34th Street.* She literally grew up onscreen, appearing in *Chicken Every Sunday* (1948), *Father Was a Fullback* (1949), *Never a Dull Moment* (1950), *Dear Brat* (1951), *The Star* (1952), and *The Silver Chalice* (1954), and passing into a graceful adolescence without hitting that gawky stage that so many girls suffer before attaining womanhood.

Her teenage years saw Wood in two of her best roles: as James Dean's girlfriend in *Rebel Without a Cause* (1955, for which she earned a Best Supporting Actress nomination), and as John Wayne's niece, kidnapped by Indians in *The Searchers* (1956). Wood tiptoed into adult roles in the likes of *Kings Go Forth, Marjorie Morningstar* (both 1958), *All the Fine Young Cannibals* (1960, with Robert Wagner), and *Splendor in the Grass* (1961, Oscar-nominated, and paired with young Warren Beatty). By then, she'd grown into a stunning young woman with lustrous dark hair, large eyes, and a lovely figure.

A living embodiment (and vindication) of studio-system grooming, Wood entered the peak phase of her career, starring in *West Side Story* (1961, as Maria), *Gypsy* (1962, as stripper Gypsy Rose Lee), *Love With the Proper Stranger* (1963, Oscar-nominated again), *Sex and the Single Girl* (1964, a pre-feminist comedy starring her as a "liberated" psychologist), *The Great Race, Inside Daisy Clover* (both 1965), *Penelope,* and *This Property Is Condemned* (both 1966). After costarring in the smash hit *Bob & Carol & Ted & Alice* (1969), she put her career on the back burner.

Wood made only a few more movies, including *Peeper* (1975), *The Last Married Couple in America* (1979), and *Willie and Phil* (1980, in a cameo as herself), although she enjoyed considerable success on TV, as Maggie in a small-screen adaptation of "Cat on a Hot Tin Roof" (with Robert Wagner and Laurence Olivier) and as Karen in "From Here to Eternity." Married twice to actor Robert Wagner (1957–63, and then from 1972), Wood in 1981 was working with Christopher Walken on a sci-fi thriller called *Brainstorm* when, on the Wagners' yacht, she disappeared one night. Her body washed ashore the next morning, and the circumstances of her death were never fully discovered. The unfinished *Brainstorm* languished for two years before being cobbled together and released to mixed reviews and indifferent box office. Though the film was flawed, she lent it a luminous presence.

A subsequent book by Wood's younger sister Lana, herself an actress, revealed that, in fact, Natalie's life had been filled with unhappiness and insecurity. Lana played Natalie as a child in *The Searchers* (1956), and as an adult appeared in *Diamonds Are Forever* (1971, as Plenty O'Toole), and numerous exploitation films, including *A Place Called Today* (1972), *Satan's Mistress* (1975), and *Nightmare in Badham County* (1976).

WOODARD, ALFRE. Actress. *(b. Nov. 8, 1953, Tulsa, Okla.)* Versatile black actress just beginning to achieve mainstream recognition after many years of working on stage, in TV, and, since 1978, in movies. A graduate of Boston University who took to the boards in the mid 1970s, Woodard made her film debut in Alan Rudolph's *Remember My Name* (1978), and later appeared in Robert Altman's *H.E.A.L.T.H.* (1979) before receiving an Oscar nomination for her performance in *Cross Creek* (1983), as a servant to writer Marjorie Kinnan Rawlings. She has since appeared in *Go Tell It on the Mountain* (1984), *Extremities* (1986), *Scrooged* (1988), *Miss Firecracker* (1989, a charming role in this underrated film), *Grand Canyon* (1991), and *Rich in Love* (1993). With a seemingly limitless emotional range, she has found steady work on television; she was a regular on the short-lived "Sara" (1985), won Emmys for her appearances on "Hill Street Blues" and "L.A. Law," and received an ACE award for her portrayal of Winnie Mandela in the cable TV movie *Mandela* (1987). John Sayles gave her a strong costarring role in *Passion Fish* (1992) as a woman with a troubled past who's hired to take care of a woman with a troubled present, Mary McDonnell. She's been consistently good in such other films as *The Gun in Betty Lou's Handbag* (1992), *Heart and Souls, Bopha!* (both 1993), and Spike Lee's *Crooklyn* (1994).

WOODS, HARRY. Actor. *(b. 1889, Hannibal, Mo.; d. Dec. 28, 1968.)* The dean of Western heavies, Woods traded blows and bullets with nearly every cowboy star in movie history during his 40-year screen career. The former salesman—powerfully built, with piercing eyes and a cruel smile—made an ideal villain, first in Pearl White silent serials and later in B Westerns and melodramas. Woods plied his trade in big-budget pictures also, but usually in smaller roles. He had some of his most memorable moments in *The Viking* (1929), *The Lone Rider* (1930), *When a Man's a Man* (1935), *The Plainsman* (1936), *Courage of the West* (1937), *Beau Geste* (1939), *Tall in the Saddle* (1944), *Thunder Mountain* (1947), and *Lone Star* (1952). His last film was *The Ten Commandments* (1956).

WOODS, JAMES. Actor. *(b. Apr. 18, 1947, Vernal, Utah.)* Slender, intense actor whose boring eyes, pockmarked face and curled lips added an aura of menace to many of his early characterizations—most of which, it should be noted, were psychotics and sociopaths. An MIT graduate (who majored in political science!), the intimidatingly intelligent Woods made a name for himself in character parts but, in recent years, has sought after "good guy" roles that ostensibly add luster to his star but aren't nearly as interesting as, say, his cop killer in *The Onion Field* (1979), his obsessive hoodlum in *Against All Odds* (1984), or his cold-blooded hit man in

Best Seller (1987). Oscar-nominated for his incredibly forceful performance as a scheming journalist in *Salvador* (1986), Woods has shown real versatility, bringing charm and humor to *Joshua Then and Now* (1985), over-the-top comedy to *The Hard Way* (1991), and old-fashioned charisma to his best starring vehicle, *True Believer* (1989), in which he played a 1960s radical turned "people's champion"-style lawyer. He first attracted attention on the TV miniseries "Holocaust" (1978) and has found great opportunities in that medum ever since. He won Emmy Awards for his outstanding performances in the telefilms *Promise* (1986, as James Garner's schizophrenic brother) and *My Name Is Bill W.* (1989, as the longtime drunk who cofounded Alcoholics Anonymous), and was ideally cast as notorious lawyer Roy Cohn in the cable-TV movie *Citizen Cohn* (1992).
OTHER FILMS INCLUDE: 1972: *The Visitors* (his debut), *Hickey & Boggs;* 1973: *The Way We Were;* 1974: *The Gambler;* 1975: *Distance, Night Moves;* 1976: *Alex and the Gypsy;* 1977: *The Choirboys;* 1980: *The Black Marble* (in a cameo); 1981: *Eyewitness;* 1982: *Fast-Walking, Split Image;* 1983: *Videodrome* (in the lead in this David Cronenberg-directed cult favorite); 1984: *Once Upon a Time in America;* 1985: *Cat's Eye;* 1987: *Cop;* 1988: *The Boost;* 1989: *Immediate Family;* 1992: *Straight Talk, Chaplin, Diggstown;* 1994: *The Getaway, The Specialist, Curse of the Starving Class;* 1995: *Casino.*

WOODWARD, EDWARD. Actor. *(b. June 1, 1930, Croydon, England.)* Stolid, dependable British actor usually seen in humorless roles, he became widely known to U. S. audiences playing "The Equalizer," a retired law officer who hires out to hopeless clients and crime victims on the 1985–89 TV series of the same name. He'd already established himself as a star on British television; the 1974 movie *Callan* was in fact a spinoff of a TV series with the same name (though after the success of "The Equalizer," an enterprising video company gave it a new, more saleable title in this country: *The Neutralizer*). In films since 1955 *(Where There's a Will),* he also appeared in *Becket* (1964), *The File of the Golden Goose* (1969), *Young Winston* (1972), *Stand Up Virgin Soldiers* (1977), *The Final Option* (1982),

King David (1985, an outstanding turn as King Saul), and *Mister Johnson* (1991). He does have two truly memorable movie roles to his credit: the puritanical investigator discovering a British Isle's peculiar pagan customs in the offbeat horror film *The Wicker Man* (1973), and the title role in the Australian courtroom drama *Breaker Morant* (1979).

WOODWARD, JOANNE. Actress. *(b. Feb. 27, 1930, Thomasville, Ga.)* Prodigiously talented actress whose stardom has never interfered with her personal integrity. She left the South to attend Sarah Lawrence College, and studied theater at the Actors Studio in New York. She was working on stage when she landed her first film role in *Count Three and Pray* (1955, registering solidly as a strong-willed orphan). Touted by 20th Century-Fox as an exciting new star, she played one of the sisters in *A Kiss Before Dying* (1956), a well-done adaptation of Ira Levin's thriller. From there she went to *The Three Faces of Eve* (1957), for which she won a Best Actress Oscar as a woman with multiple personalities.

Woodward first teamed with her husband, Paul Newman, in the steamy adaptation of William Faulkner's *The Long Hot Summer* (1958). Since then they have worked together frequently, costarring in *Rally 'Round the Flag, Boys!* (also 1958), *From the Terrace* (1960), *Paris Blues* (1961), *A New Kind of Love* (1963), *Winning* (1969), *WUSA* (1970), *The Drowning Pool* (1976), *Harry and Son* (1984), and one of their richest dual vehicles, *Mr. & Mrs. Bridge* (1990), for which she earned an Oscar nomination. Newman has also directed her in some of her strongest parts, including *Rachel, Rachel* (1968, which earned her an Oscar nomination as a spinster schoolteacher), *The Effect of Gamma Rays on Man-in-the-Moon Marigolds* (1972), the telefilm *The Shadow Box* (1980), and *The Glass Menagerie* (1987). She also earned an Oscar nomination for her portrayal of a frigid woman coming to terms with herself in *Summer Wishes, Winter Dreams* (1973).

Woodward, like many mature actresses, has found few worthy roles in feature films in recent years, but has been very active in high-quality made-for-TV movies, including *Sybil* (1976), in which, reversing roles from her star-making *Three Faces of Eve*, she played the psychiatrist to Sally Field, a victim of multiple personalities, *See How She Runs* (1978), for which she won an Emmy as a middle-aged housewife who decides to run in the Boston marathon, and *Do You Remember Love* (1985), the moving story of a couple coping with Alzheimer's disease, which won her another Emmy Award. In 1993 she was back on theater screens as Tom Hanks' mother in *Philadelphia;* she also narrated Martin Scorsese's *The Age of Innocence.*

OTHER FILMS INCLUDE: 1957: *No Down Payment;* 1959: *The Sound and the Fury, The Fugitive Kind;* 1963: *The Stripper* (in a starring role originally intended for Marilyn Monroe); 1965: *Signpost to Murder;* 1966: *A Big Hand for the Little Lady, A Fine Madness;* 1970: *King: A Filmed Record ... Montgomery to Memphis;* 1971: *They Might Be Giants;* 1978: *The End, A Christmas to Remember* (telefilm); 1979: *The Streets of L. A.* (telefilm); 1981: *Crisis at Central High* (telefilm); 1984: *Passions* (telefilm); 1993: *Foreign Affairs* (telefilm), *Blind Spot* (telefilm); 1994: *Breathing Lessons* (telefilm).

WOOLLEY, MONTY. Actor. *(b. Aug. 17, 1888, New York City, as Edgar Montillion Woolley; d. May 6, 1963.)* Waspish and bewhiskered, this elegant actor with the cultured voice convulsed 1941 moviegoers as bombastic, overbearing Sheridan Whiteside, the title character in Warner Bros.' hilarious adaptation of the George S. Kaufman–Moss Hart play *The Man Who Came to Dinner.* Woolley had already played Whiteside (based on well-known theater critic and radio personality Alexander Woollcott) on stage; the movie version brought his famous characterization to a much wider audience—and, basically, rendered his subsequent screen career anticlimactic. It also pretty much typecast him as glib-tongued, fastidious types. (Although, it should be noted, he picked up Oscar nominations for his starring role in 1942's *The Pied Piper* and his supporting turn in 1944's *Since You Went Away.)* No one who has seen his drunken Santa Claus in *Life Begins at Eight-Thirty* (1942) is likely to forget it. He remained enough of a star to propel an entire film—a comic treatise on enforced retirement—in 1951, *As Young As You Feel.*

Woolley, a former Yale professor and dramatics coach whose pupils included Thornton Wilder, began acting on Broadway in 1936. His close friends included songwriter Cole Porter (a Yale grad); in fact, Woolley played himself in the 1946 Porter biopic *Night and Day.*
OTHER FILMS INCLUDE: 1937: *Live, Love and Learn* (his debut), *Nothing Sacred;* 1938: *The Girl of the Golden West, Three Comrades;* 1939: *Midnight, Man About Town, Never Say Die;* 1943: *Holy Matrimony;* 1944: *Irish Eyes Are Smiling;* 1945: *Molly and Me;* 1947: *The Bishop's Wife;* 1948: *Miss Tatlock's Millions;* 1955: *Kismet.*

WORONOV, MARY. Actress. *(b. Dec. 8, 1946, Brooklyn, N.Y.)* Cult movie star/supporting player most famous for her work with director-actor Paul Bartel. Woronov's best roles are in a pair of cult classics: *Rock 'n' Roll High School* (1979), as authoritarian high school principal Miss Togar, and Bartel's *Eating Raoul* (1982), in which the pair play Mary and Paul Bland, middle-class murderers. She first surfaced as a member of Andy Warhol's Factory crowd during the 1960s, appearing in Warhol's *The 14-Year-Old Girl* and *The Chelsea Girls* (both 1966, in the latter billed as Mary Might). Her next screen roles were in such minor B films as *Sugar Cookies* (1973), *Silent Night, Bloody Night* (1974), and *Cover Girl Models* (1975). Woronov was in her element as an Amazonian bad girl named Calamity Jane in Bartel's *Death Race 2000* (also 1975), and worked in Bartel's *Cannonball* (1976), and Joe Dante and Allan Arkush's *Hollywood Boulevard* (1976), playing Mary McQueen, a jealous actress, opposite Bartel's Erich von Leppe. Since the mid 1970s, she has had smaller roles in mainstream films: *Mr. Billion* (1977), *The One and Only* (1978), *Black Widow* (1986), and *Dick Tracy* (1990). She costarred in Bartel's *Scenes From the Class Struggle in Beverly Hills* (1989) as a rich, snooty divorcee, and appeared briefly but effectively in *The Living End* (1992), playing a psychotic lesbian named Daisy. But most often, Woronov's credits have been bargain basement and bizarre: *Angel from H.E.A.T* (1982), *Hellhole* (1985), *Nomads, Chopping Mall* (replaying Mary Bland), *TerrorVision* (all 1986), *Club Fed, Rock 'n' Roll High*

School Forever (both 1991, in the latter as Dr. Vadar, another disciplinarian), *Hell-roller* (1992), and *Mortuary Academy* (also 1992, as an instructor at a school for morticians).

WRAY, FAY. Actress. *(b. Sept. 15, 1907, Alberta, Canada.)* Fay Wray will always be remembered as the shrieking, blond Beauty who "killed" the Beast in *King Kong* (1933), which is a mixed blessing. Without the classic monster movie, Wray's career might be forgotten today. On the other hand (a phrase she used as the title of her 1989 autobiography), her *Kong* notoriety overshadows her fine work in Erich von Stroheim's *The Wedding March.* Raised in Los Angeles, Wray by age 16 was working in low-budget movies. She appeared in Hal Roach comedy shorts and was leading lady to Western stars Hoot Gibson (in 1923's *The Man in the Saddle)* and Art Acord (in 1926's *Lazy Lightning),* but was largely dissatisfied with her screen work until she was signed by producer Pat Powers for *The Wedding March* in 1926.
Von Stroheim's production went over schedule and over budget, and Powers sold the picture—and Wray's contract—to Paramount. Even in its truncated form, *The Wedding March* (finally released in 1928) was a masterful film that showcased Wray's virginal beauty. Paramount's *The Street of Sin* (1927) offered Wray an opportunity to work with German star Emil Jannings and Swedish director Mauritz Stiller. She appeared in *The Legion of the Condemned* (1927) with Gary Cooper for director ·William Wellman, and also costarred in Josef von Sternberg's first talkie, *Thunderbolt* (1929).
The Four Feathers (1929) was an odd · hybrid production that combined semi-documentary footage directed by Merian C. Cooper and Ernest Schoedsack with studio footage helmed by German émigré Lothar Mendes, but it gave Wray her first opportunity to work with the team that would create *King Kong.* When she joined the cast of *Kong,* the protracted schedule allowed her to work on several other movies concurrently, especially thrillers and horror films, including a pair of Technicolor thrillers, *Doctor X* (1932) and *The Mystery of the Wax Museum, The Vampire Bat* (both 1933), and particularly

The Most Dangerous Game (1932), which was directed by Schoedsack (with actor Irving Pichel) and shot on the *Kong* jungle sets at night. Other films from this period include *Dirigible, The Unholy Garden* (both 1930), *One Sunday Afternoon,* and *The Bowery* (both 1933).

By the time *King Kong* finally reached the screen in 1933, Wray was firmly established as the talkie's first "scream queen," a persona she did her best to dispel in subsequent assignments. She acted in prestige pictures such as *Affairs of Cellini, Viva Villa!, The Richest Girl in the World,* and *The Captain Hates the Sea* (all 1934), but those films, as well as later programmers in which she toiled, did very little for her career. Divorced from screenwriter John Monk Saunders in 1939, Wray married screenwriter Robert Riskin in 1942 and retired from the screen. In the 1950s she returned to character parts in *The Cobweb, Queen Bee* (both 1955), *Rock, Pretty Baby* (1956), *Tammy and the Bachelor* (1957), and her last feature, *Dragstrip Riot* (1958). Her autobiography, "On the Other Hand" (1989) reveals that Wray had a life much more interesting than the characters she played.

WRIGHT, AMY. Actress. *(b. Apr. 15, 1950, Chicago.)* Wide-eyed, plain-looking, and placid, Wright usually impresses as the type of girl shunned by her classmates and always picked last for any team. As befitting her appearance and demeanor, she has made a specialty of playing twisted waifs. A stage veteran, she started her movie career in *Not a Pretty Picture* (1975), and went on to *The Deer Hunter, Girlfriends* (both 1978), *Breaking Away, The Amityville Horror, Heartland* (all 1979), and *Inside Moves* (1980). Wright was the perfect embodiment of a character created by Flannery O'Connor in John Huston's 1979 adaptation of *Wise Blood,* and she had an inspired bit in Woody Allen's *Stardust Memories* (1980), playing a creepy groupie. Offscreen for much of the 1980s, she resumed her movie career with a vengeance late in the decade, rounding out William Hurt's eccentric family in *The Accidental Tourist* (1988), and essaying her usual sensitive, slightly off-center characterizations in *Off Beat* (1986), *Crossing Delancey, The Telephone* (both 1988), *Miss Firecracker* (1989), *Daddy's*

Dyin' . . . Who's Got the Will?, Love Hurts (both 1990), *Deceived, Hard Promises* (both 1991), and *Where The River Flows North* (1994). She has had two children by actor Rip Torn, with whom she lives.

WRIGHT, ROBIN. Actress. *(b. Apr. 8, 1966, Dallas.)* After work as a professional model and several years as Kelly Capewell on the soap opera "Santa Barbara," Wright made an inauspicious film debut in *Hollywood Vice Squad* (1986) but really caught the public's attention as the beautiful Buttercup in *The Princess Bride* (1987). Since then, she has appeared opposite Sean Penn in *State of Grace* (1990), Jason Patric in *Denial* (1991), and Robin Williams in *Toys* (1992). A great opportunity came when Annette Bening bowed out of *The Playboys* (1992), and she was cast instead; the film boasted her best performance to date, as Tara, the strong-willed woman who has a baby out of wedlock in a rural Irish town. In real life, Wright lived with Penn for some time and had two children with him. Recent credits include *Forrest Gump* (1994, as the title character's sweetheart, Jenny), and *The Crossing Guard* (1995, directed by Penn).

WRIGHT, TERESA. Actress. *(b. Oct. 27, 1918, New York City, as Muriel Teresa Wright.)* As a quiet, gentle, sensitive ingenue, Teresa Wright made an immediate impact on Hollywood: she earned three Academy Award nominations for her first three film performances, one of which netted her the coveted Oscar. She held her own with Bette Davis in *The Little Foxes* (1941), played the devoted wife of baseball great Lou Gehrig in *Pride of the Yankees* (1942), and played Greer Garson's daughter in *Mrs. Miniver* the same year, winning the Best Supporting Actress Academy Award. Wright was top-billed in Alfred Hitchcock's *Shadow of a Doubt* (1943), playing a fresh-scrubbed teenager whose girlish admiration for charming uncle Joseph Cotten turns to terror when she discovers him to be a murderer. Wisely eschewing glamour-girl treatment and exotic roles (although that may not have been altogether of her own choosing), Wright played other wholesome young women, most notably in William Wyler's *The Best Years of Our Lives* (1946).

She matured into a fine character actress, although some of her later pictures were unworthy of her talent. She still works on stage and makes periodic forays into feature films and TV movies. She was married to writer Niven Busch and playwright Robert Anderson.
OTHER FILMS INCLUDE: 1944: *Casanova Brown;* 1947: *Pursued, The Imperfect Lady, The Trouble With Women;* 1948: *Enchantment;* 1950: *The Capture, The Men;* 1952: *Something to Live For, California Conquest, The Steel Trap;* 1953: *Count the Hours, The Actress;* 1954: *Track of the Cat;* 1956: *The Search for Bridey Murphy;* 1957: *Escapade in Japan;* 1958: *The Restless Years;* 1969: *Hail Hero!;* 1977: *Roseland;* 1980: *Somewhere in Time;* 1988: *The Good Mother.*

WUHL, ROBERT. Actor; writer. *(b. Oct. 9, 1951, Union City, N.J.)* Stand-up comedian turned actor who had his first starring role as the has-been writer in the Hollywood satire *Mistress* (1992). Before that, he made his film debut in the cheesy comedy *The Hollywood Knights* (1980, along with a young Michelle Pfeiffer) and served as story editor on the cult TV series "Police Squad!" Wuhl went on to TV guest shots and featured roles in *Good Morning, Vietnam* (1987), *Bull Durham* (1988), *Batman* (as newspaper reporter Alexander Knox), and *Blaze* (both 1989). He had a cameo in *The Bodyguard* (1992) as host of the Academy Awards, which in real life he won Emmys for cowriting in 1990 and 1991 with his friend Billy Crystal. Recent credits include *Cobb* (1994), for *Bull Durham* and *Blaze* director Ron Shelton. Wuhl made his directorial debut with *Open Season* (1995), which he also wrote and starred in.

WYATT, JANE. Actress. *(b. Aug. 12, 1911, Campgaw, N.J.)* Her latter-day success as the loving wife of Robert Young on TV's "Father Knows Best" (a characterization for which she won three Emmys during the show's six-year run) has tended to obscure this pretty, petite actress's movie career. Not that it was all that impressive, mind you: Despite her success as the flower of exotic Shangri-La in *Lost Horizon* (1937), Wyatt never achieved the prominence her obvious talent should have guaranteed. Instead she essayed largely conventional roles, dewy-eyed ingenues early in her career, patient wives later on. Born into a well-to-do family, she studied at the prestigious Barnard College before making her stage debut in 1930. Several years of stage work followed before she was signed by Universal. After 1976 she left feature films altogether, although she appeared as Mr. Spock's mom in *Star Trek IV: The Voyage Home* (1986), reprising the role she had played in one episode of the original series. Since then she has appeared frequently on TV, including several reunions of "Father Knows Best" with her longtime screen husband Robert Young.
OTHER FILMS INCLUDE: 1934: *One More River, Great Expectations;* 1936: *We're Only Human;* 1940: *The Girl From God's Country;* 1941: *Weekend for Three;* 1942: *Army Surgeon;* 1943: *Buckskin Frontier, The Kansan;* 1944: *None But the Lonely Heart* (one of her best screen outings, albeit in a supporting role); 1946: *Strange Conquest;* 1947: *Gentleman's Agreement* (another fine job in support), *Boomerang!;* 1948: *The Pitfall;* 1949: *Task Force;* 1950: *The House by the River, My Blue Heaven;* 1951: *Criminal Lawyer;* 1957: *Interlude;* 1965: *Never Too Late;* 1976: *Treasure of Matecumbe.*

WYLER, WILLIAM. Director. *(b. July 1, 1902, Mulhouse [Mülhausen], Alsace-Lorraine; d. July 27, 1981.)* One of the great directors, fondly known as "Willy," whose credits include some of the most honored and distinguished Hollywood features. Wyler studied business in Switzerland and music in Paris, but his career did not take shape until the early 1920s, when he came to the United States at the solicitation of a relative, Universal boss Carl Laemmle. He worked at the studio as a publicist, assistant director and (beginning in 1925) director of shorts and B features, mostly Westerns. First thought of as just another Laemmle relative, he soon proved himself as an able craftsman, and in the early 1930s, became one of Universal's greatest assets, directing such solid films as *The Love Trap* (1929), *Hell's Heroes* (1930), *Tom Brown of Culver* (1932), John Barrymore in the brilliant *Counsellor-at-Law* (1933, his breakthrough), and the delicious comedy *The Good Fairy* (1935, one of his few comedies, starring Margaret Sullavan, to whom he was married).

Then he was signed by Samuel Goldwyn, beginning a mutually profitable association; he remained with the producer for a decade, making such superbly crafted films as *These Three, Come and Get It* (codirected with Howard Hawks), the incomparable *Dodsworth* (all 1936), *Dead End* (1937), *Jezebel* (1938, on loan to Warner Bros.), *Wuthering Heights* (1939), *The Letter* (at Warners), *The Westerner* (both 1940), and *The Little Foxes* (1941). World War 2 was to have an incalculable impact on Wyler's life and career. Between 1942 and 1945, he served as a major in the U.S. Army Air Corps and directed a pair of documentaries, *The Memphis Belle* and the Academy Award-winning *The Fighting Lady* (both 1944). In addition, he directed two key American films which bookended the war and captured the mood of the nation as it prepared for battle and, four years later, peace. *Mrs. Miniver* (1942), an account of a middle-class English family adjusting to the war in Europe, helped condition American audiences to the stresses of life in wartime (and galvanized support for our British allies). *The Best Years of Our Lives* (1946), the story of three veterans arriving home and adjusting to civilian life, brilliantly dramatized their problems for those who had remained on the homefront. Wyler won Best Director Oscars for both films (which also won Best Picture Oscars). His postwar work (much of which he produced, as well) was substantial in both senses of the word: *The Heiress* (1949), *Detective Story* (1951), *Carrie* (1952), the charming *Roman Holiday* (1953), *The Desperate Hours* (1955), *Friendly Persuasion* (1956), *The Big Country* (1958), *The Children's Hour* (1962, a remake of *These Three*), *The Collector* (1965), *Funny Girl* (1968), and *The Liberation of L. B. Jones* (1970). Wyler earned his third Best Director Oscar for his third Best Picture: the epic drama *Ben-Hur* (1959). Wyler was famous for demanding endless takes from his actors, and his inability (or unwillingness) to articulate what exactly he wanted from them—yet the results speak for themselves. In 1965, he won the Thalberg Award for career achievement; eleven years later, he was the American Film Institute Life Achievement Award recipient. In addition to his Best Picture and Best Director Oscar wins, ten of Wyler's films earned Best Picture nominations and he won nine Best Director nominations; three dozen of his actors won Oscars or nominations. Wyler's second wife was actress Margaret Tallichet. His daughter, Catherine Wyler, produced *Directed by William Wyler* (1986), a documentary on her father's life and career, and *Memphis Belle* (1990), a fictionalized account of the famed B-17 plane's last bombing run, recorded by her father in his 1944 documentary.

WYMAN, JANE. Actress. (b. Jan. 4, 1914, St. Joseph, Mo., as Sarah Jane Fulks.) The domineering doyenne of TV's "Falcon Crest," Jane Wyman has enjoyed an extraordinarily long and varied career. She first came to Hollywood as a child as a surrogate for her ambitious mother, actress Le jerne Pichelle. However, the movie colony didn't exactly stand up and take notice, and mother and daughter returned to Missouri, where Sarah Jane attended the state university. Her entertainment career began to take off in the early 1930s when, under the name Jane Durrell, she became a radio singer. Returning to Hollywood in 1936, she landed bit parts in *My Man Godfrey* and *Cain and Mabel* before being signed by Warner Bros. to a long-term contract. Like most contract actresses, she toiled in both A and B pictures, sometimes in low-billed bits (as in the 1937 musical *Ready, Willing, and Able),* sometimes in the leading female role (as in 1939's *Torchy Plays With Dynamite,* substituting for Glenda Farrell as a demon sob-sister). She was loaned out to play the ingenue in 1938's *Wide Open Faces,* a Joe E. Brown comedy, but returned to Warners and the same old routine. Wyman played opposite her future husband, Ronald Reagan, in *Brother Rat* (1938) and its 1940 sequel.

The early 1940s found the button-cute Wyman pretty much running in place, gamely trying to invest some sparkle in dim comedies and melodramas such as *An Angel From Texas* (1940), *Honeymoon for Three, You're in the Army Now,* and *The Body Disappears* (all 1941). Wyman was loaned to Fox for *Footlight Serenade* (1942), in which she played Betty Grable's wise-cracking girlfriend—another thankless role. During this period she was always something more than a starlet and something less than a star. She finally got noticed as Ray Milland's sympathetic girlfriend in Billy Wilder's chilling drama *The Lost Weekend* (1945), and actually received an Oscar nomination as Best Actress for her turn in *The Yearling* (1946). She copped the gold statuette for her portrayal of a deaf mute in *Johnny Belinda* (1948), a touching performance that remains her career high-water mark. The Oscar win ensured that she worked with the best directors—Alfred Hitchcock on *Stage Fright* (1950), Frank Capra on *Here Comes the Groom* (1951), Michael Curtiz on *The Story of Will Rogers* (1952)—and got to work in prestige productions like *The Glass Menagerie* (1950). She sought variety in her post-*Belinda* parts, however, and starred in a few lightweight musicals, including *Just for You* (1952, with Bing Crosby) and the *Awful Truth* remake *Let's Do It Again* (1953), but it soon became clear that audiences liked her best, during this period, in soap opera–type stories. Accordingly, she starred in *The Blue Veil* (1951, Oscar-nominated), *So Big* (1953), *Magnificent Obsession* (1954, Oscar-nominated), *Lucy Gallant, All That Heaven Allows* (both 1955), and *Miracle in the Rain* (1956).

Like other now-maturing actresses, she turned to television, and took over hosting of "Fireside Theater," which soon became "Jane Wyman Theater" (1955–58); she also starred in many episodes of the anthology series, which she coproduced. Wyman returned to the big screen in *Holiday for Lovers* (1959), and as the unfeeling Aunt Polly in Walt Disney's great success *Pollyanna* (1960). Her last feature was the Bob Hope–Jackie Gleason comedy *How to Commit Marriage* (1969). In addition to her starring role on "Falcon Crest" (1981–90), Wyman toplined several made-for-TV movies.
OTHER FILMS INCLUDE: 1932: *The Kid From Spain* (bit); 1933: *Elmer the Great* (bit); 1935: *Rumba* (bit); 1936: *Anything Goes* (bit), *Stage Struck* (bit); 1940: *Brother Rat and a Baby, Tugboat Annie Sails Again;* 1942: *Larceny, Inc., My Favorite Spy;* 1943: *Princess O'Rourke;* 1944: *Make Your Own Bed, The Doughgirls, Hollywood Canteen;* 1946: *One More Tomorrow, Night and Day;* 1947: *Cheyenne, Magic Town;* 1949: *A Kiss in the Dark, It's a Great Feeling* (cameo), *The Lady Takes a Sailor;* 1951: *Three Guys Named Mike;* 1962: *Bon Voyage!;* 1971: *The Failing of*

Raymond (telefilm); 1979: *The Incredible Journey of Dr. Meg Laurel* (telefilm).

WYNN, ED. Actor. *(b. Nov. 9, 1886, Philadelphia, as Isaiah Edwin Leopold; d. June 19, 1966.)* Silly, baggy-pants comic who in later years proved himself a capable dramatic actor. At age fifteen, Wynn left home to join a touring theater company, and while still in his teens became a popular vaudeville headliner. He performed in the "Ziegfeld Follies," beginning in 1914, and directed, produced, wrote, and composed music for many of his subsequent Broadway successes, being known by then as "The Perfect Fool." During the 1930s, Wynn became a pioneering radio comedy star, as the "Texaco Fire Chief," but he was unable to translate that popularity to the screen. He had debuted in the silent *Rubber Heels* (1927), then tried out talkies in *Follow the Leader* (1930), and played off his radio success in *The Chief* (1933), but apparently his character was too broad and buffoonish for movie audiences. His career was energized by the coming of television; in 1949, he won an Emmy Award for "The Ed Wynn Show" (1949–50). He was then an alternating host of "All-Star Revue" (1951–53) and later the star of a short-lived sitcom, "The Ed Wynn Show" (1958–59). But the biggest turnabout in Wynn's career came when he took a serious role in the emotional live-TV drama "Requiem for a Heavyweight" (1956), a "Playhouse 90" scripted by Rod Serling in which Wynn appeared with his son Keenan. Wynn's performance was a revelation and led to a new career onscreen as a first-rate character actor, in *The Great Man* (1957, in which Keenan also appeared), playing a small-town radio station owner, *Marjorie Morningstar* (1958), as the title character's Uncle Samson, and *The Diary of Anne Frank* (1959), as Albert Dussell, which earned him an Oscar nomination as Best Supporting Actor. His subsequent screen credits include a pair of Jerry Lewis comedies, *Cinderfella* (1960, as Jerry's fairy godfather) and *The Patsy* (1964), *The Greatest Story Ever Told* (1965, as Old Aram), and a host of Disney movies: *The Absent Minded Professor* (1961, again with Keenan), *Babes in Toyland* (also 1961, as the Toymaker), *Son of Flubber* (1963, with Keenan), *Mary*

Poppins (1964, memorable as Mary's Uncle Albert, whose constant laughter causes him to float through the air), *Those Calloways, That Darn Cat* (both 1965), and *The Gnome-Mobile* (1967). But perhaps his most endearing Disney credit was performing the voice of the Mad Hatter in the animated *Alice in Wonderland* (1951).

WYNN, KEENAN. Actor. *(b. July 27, 1916, New York City, as Francis Xavier Wynn; d. Oct. 14, 1986.)* Gruff but likable character player, often cast as a smooth con artist or wisecracking second banana but equally effective as taciturn, sometimes brutal heavies. The son of Broadway and radio star Ed Wynn (and grandson of actor Frank Keenan), he toiled in stock and on radio before signing a long-term contract with MGM in 1942, where he remained through 1953. He played every kind of supporting role imaginable, in comedies, dramas, musicals, and melodramas. He could be broad when the occasion demanded, or subtle when allowed. Wynn felt he got his best opportunities in smaller films, such as *Kind Lady* (1951), in which he effectively underplayed the part of a brutal thug posing as a butler in Ethel Barrymore's town house. One of his best roles at MGM was among his last, as a comic gangster in *Kiss Me Kate* (1953) who (with James Whitmore) sings "Brush Up Your Shakespeare." As the studio system wound down, Wynn moved to New York and worked extensively in live television; it was then that he and his father worked together in the classic "Playhouse 90" drama "Requiem for a Heavyweight" in 1956.

Wynn remained a first-call character actor for the rest of his life, with notable performances along the way in films like *Dr. Strangelove* (1964), as Col. "Bat" Guano, *Finian's Rainbow* (1968), as the Southern bigot who suddenly turns black, and *Nashville* (1975), as the forlorn, grieving man whose disorientation is a touchstone for the overall picture.

He was a regular on the TV series "Troubleshooters" (1959–60), "Dallas" (1979–80 only, as Digger Barnes), and "Call to Glory" (1984–85), and worked in numerous telefilms and miniseries. Keenan published his autobiography, "Ed Wynn's Son," in 1959. His own son, screenwriter Tracy Keenan Wynn, continued the family show-business tradition. Tracy's brother Ned wrote a revealing book about growing up in their troubled show-business family called "We Will Always Live in Beverly Hills" (1990).

OTHER FILMS INCLUDE: 1942: *Somewhere I'll Find You* (his first), *For Me and My Gal;* 1944: *Since You Went Away, See Here, Private Hargrove;* 1945: *Without Love, The Clock, Weekend at the Waldorf;* 1946: *Easy to Wed, Ziegfeld Follies, The Thrill of Brazil;* 1947: *Song of the Thin Man, The Hucksters;* 1948: *The Three Musketeers, My Dear Secretary;* 1949: *Neptune's Daughter, That Midnight Kiss;* 1950: *Three Little Words, Annie Get Your Gun;* 1951: *Royal Wedding* (in a dual role, one American, one English), *Angels in the Outfield, Texas Carnival, It's a Big Country;* 1952: *The Belle of New York;* 1953: *All the Brothers Were Valiant;* 1955: *The Glass Slipper;* 1956: *The Man in the Gray Flannel Suit, Johnny Concho;* 1957: *The Great Man;* 1961: *The Absent Minded Professor;* 1962: *The Scarface Mob;* 1964: *The Americanization of Emily, The Patsy;* 1965: *The Great Race;* 1966: *Stagecoach;* 1967: *The War Wagon, Point Blank;* 1968: *Once Upon a Time in the West;* 1969: *Mackenna's Gold, Viva Max!;* 1970: *Loving;* 1971: *Pretty Maids All in a Row;* 1972: *Cancel My Reservation;* 1974: *Herbie Rides Again;* 1975: *The Devil's Rain;* 1976: *The Killer Inside Me, The Shaggy D.A.;* 1977: *Orca;* 1978: *Coach, Piranha;* 1980: *Just Tell Me What You Want;* 1982: *Best Friends* (as Burt Reynolds' dad).

WYNTER, DANA. Actress. *(b. June 8, 1930, London, as Dagmar Spencer-Marcus.)* Best known as Kevin McCarthy's fellow refugee from the alien "pod people" in the classic sci-fi thriller *Invasion of the Body Snatchers* (1956), this beautiful British brunette typically played refined, articulate leading ladies onscreen. Raised in South Africa, she returned to her native Britain in the early 1950s, making her film debut in *White Corridors* (1951), and playing bits in *Lady Godiva Rides Again* (also 1951), *The Crimson Pirate* (1952), and others before going to Hollywood in 1955. She certainly had beauty to spare, but something in her nature—coolness, detachment perhaps—kept her from becoming a truly engaging screen personality.

OTHER FILMS INCLUDE: 1955: *The View From Pompey's Head;* 1956: *D-Day The Sixth of June; 1957: Something of Value; 1958: Fraulein, In Love and War; 1959: Shake Hands With the Devil; 1960: Sink the Bismarck!; 1961: On the Double* (a refreshing switch to comedy-romance with Danny Kaye); *1963: The List of Adrian Messenger; 1968: If He Hollers, Let Him Go; 1970: Airport; 1973: Santee; 1975: Lovers Like Us; 1984: The Royal Romance of Charles and Diana* (telefilm).

YATES, PETER. Director, producer. *(b. July 24, 1929, Aldershot, England.)* Variety is certainly the spice of life for this British director whose films have covered an extraordinarily wide range of styles, subjects, and budgets. After graduating from the Royal Academy of Dramatic Art, Yates worked as an actor, stage manager, and director before turning to film in the 1950s as a dubbing assistant and then assistant director for Tony Richardson (on *A Taste of Honey),* Jose Quintero (on *The Roman Spring of Mrs. Stone),* and J. Lee Thompson (on *The Guns of Navarone),* all in 1961. With Richardson's encouragement, Yates worked as a stage and TV director and then made his first films, *Summer Holiday* (1963) and *One Way Pendulum* (1965). A car chase in his third feature, *Robbery* (1967), which drew on Yates' past experience as a professional racing driver, caught the attention of Steve McQueen and Yates was asked to direct the detective thriller *Bullitt* (1968). The film was highlighted by some of the greatest car chases ever put onscreen, and was a smash hit. Yates' next projects, however, were a varied lot: *John and Mary* (1969), *Murphy's War* (1971), *The Hot Rock* (1972), *The Friends of Eddie Coyle* (1973), *For Pete's Sake* (1974), *Mother, Jugs & Speed* (1976), and *The Deep* (1977). In 1979 he earned his first Oscar nomination for Best Director for the sleeper hit *Breaking Away,* a warm, irresistibly charming portrait of four young men in Bloomington, Indiana. He's continued on the commercial road ever since, earning another Oscar nomination for the delightful adaptation of the stage play *The Dresser* (1983).
OTHER FILMS INCLUDE: *1981: Eyewitness; 1982: Krull; 1985: Eleni; 1987: Suspect; 1988: The House on Carroll Street; 1989: An Innocent Man; 1992: Year of the Comet; 1993:*

Needful Things (executive producer only); *1995: Roommates.*

YORK, MICHAEL. Actor. *(b. Mar. 27, 1942, Falmer, England.)* He was a boyish, impetuous D'Artagnan in *The Three Musketeers* (1974) and *The Four Musketeers* (1975), and when a second sequel was filmed 14 years later (*Return of the Musketeers),* audiences saw that the prolific British leading man had changed very little. Particularly adept in lighthearted adventure films, York has also excelled in the portrayal of bored or dissipated aristocrats. This slim, blond actor, his almost-pretty face marred by a broken nose, began acting on the London stage while still in his teens, and as a young man joined Laurence Olivier's National Theatre in London. He first appeared onscreen in *The Mind Benders* (1962), and got his first good film role in *Accident* (1967); then Franco Zeffirelli, who'd directed him on stage, offered him key roles in *The Taming of the Shrew* (1967) and *Romeo and Juliet* (1968, as Tybalt.) A cultured, dashing young lead, he kept busy from then on, in *Alfred the Great, The Guru, Justine* (all 1969), *Something for Everyone* (1970), *Zeppelin* (1971), *Cabaret* (1972, one of his best), *England Made Me, Lost Horizon* (both 1973), *Murder on the Orient Express* (1974), *Conduct Unbecoming* (1975), *Logan's Run* (1976), "Jesus of Nazareth" (1977, a miniseries for Franco Zeffirelli in which he played John the Baptist), *The Island of Dr. Moreau, The Last Remake of Beau Geste* (both 1977), *Fedora* (1978, as himself), *The Riddle of the Sands* (1979), and *Final Assignment* (1980). His output fell off during the 1980s, both in quantity and quality; by the end of the decade he was appearing in such lesser films as *Phantom of Death* (1988) and *Midnight Cop* (1989). York enjoyed something of a renaissance in the 1990s, however, publishing an autobiography, "Accidentally on Purpose," in 1991 (which discussed the vicissitudes of an actor's life), appearing on Broadway in "Someone Who'll Watch Over Me," and in the 1993 movie *Wide Sargasso Sea.*

YORK, SUSANNAH. Actress. *(b. Jan. 9, 1941, London, England, as Susanna Yolande Fletcher.)* Beautiful blond actress who alternated conventional ingenue roles with daring performances and offbeat characterizations in controversial projects. She studied at the Royal Academy of Dramatic Art in London, and made her screen debut opposite old pros Alec Guinness and John Mills in *Tunes of Glory* (1960). She proved herself a competent screen actress with her supporting role in John Huston's *Freud* (1962), and her career gained momentum following her turn as the delicious object of Albert Finney's obsession in *Tom Jones* (1963). York raised eyebrows and attracted censorial ire for her nude lesbian scene in *The Killing of Sister George* (1968), and followed that performance with a supporting role in the harrowing *They Shoot Horses, Don't They?* (1969), for which she was Oscar-nominated as Best Supporting Actress. In 1972 she won the Best Actress award at Cannes for her role in Robert Altman's *Images* (based on a story she'd written), in which she played a disturbed author of children's books living in rural Scotland. This role had much resonance for York, as she had grown up in such a rural locale and would one day become a successful author of children's books herself.

Since the 1970s York has divided her time between small, serious pictures (*The Shout, The Silent Partner,* both 1978) and more mainstream fare, such as the *Superman* series, in which she's played Kal-El's mother (1978, 1980, and a voice only in 1987). She cowrote and appeared briefly in the modest and unmemorable *Falling in Love Again* (1980).

OTHER FILMS INCLUDE: 1965: *Sands of the Kalahari;* 1966: *A Man for All Seasons, Kaleidoscope;* 1968: *Duffy, Sebastian;* 1969: *Oh! What a Lovely War, Battle of Britain;* 1971: *Happy Birthday, Wanda June;* 1972: *X Y and Zee* (featuring another lesbian scene); 1974: *Gold;* 1975: *The Maids, Conduct Unbecoming, That Lucky Touch;* 1976: *Eliza Fraser, Sky Riders;* 1980: *The Awakening;* 1981: *Loophole;* 1983: *Yellowbeard;* 1987: *Prettykill;* 1988: *A Summer Story;* 1989: *Melancholia;* 1991: *Fate.*

YORKIN, BUD. Director, producer. *(b. Feb. 22, 1926, Washington, Pa.)* Renowned for creating some of TV's most popular situation comedies, Yorkin began his career on NBC's engineering staff in the 1950s, and worked his way to the direc-

tor's chair; he produced and directed a number of classy variety shows and won Emmys for "An Evening with Fred Astaire" (1958) and a Jack Benny Special. Yorkin founded Tandem Productions with longtime friend Norman Lear in 1959 and together they developed the groundbreaking sitcom "All in the Family" (1971–79) as well as "Maude" (1972–78), "Sanford and Son" (1972–77), and "Good Times" (1974–79). Yorkin made his feature-film directing debut with a bright adaptation of Neil Simon's first play, *Come Blow Your Horn* (1963), followed by another stage adaptation, *Never Too Late* (1965). His best film, however, was *Divorce American Style,* made in partnership with Lear, a funny and unusually perceptive examination of love and divorce. In 1985 he directed *Twice in a Lifetime,* the story of a middle-aged man who leaves his wife after many years and starts "a new life," which had more than passing resemblance to Yorkin's own experience. Yorkin executive-produced films as diverse as *Cold Turkey* (1971, directed by Lear) and *Blade Runner* (1982), and produced *Deal of the Century* (1983) and *Intersection* (1994). He is married to actress Cynthia Sikes.

OTHER FILMS INCLUDE: 1968: *Inspector Clouseau;* 1970: *Start the Revolution Without Me* (a comedy sleeper); 1973: *The Thief Who Came to Dinner;* 1988: *Arthur 2: On the Rocks;* 1990: *Love Hurts.*

YOUNG, BURT. Actor. *(b. Apr. 30, 1940, New York City.)* Squat character actor who has specialized in playing seedy roles, and is probably best remembered as Sylvester Stallone's brother-in-law, Paulie, in *Rocky* (1976, for which he earned an Oscar nomination) and the film's four sequels. He studied acting with Lee Strasberg and went on to score supporting roles in *The Gang That Couldn't Shoot Straight* (1971), *Cinderella Liberty* (1973), *Chinatown* (1974), *The Killer Elite* (1975), and *Harry and Walter Go to New York* (1976). Aside from a leading role as a trumpet player in *Uncle Joe Shannon* (1978, which he also wrote), Young has mostly played variations on cretinous archetypes in *Amityville II: The Possession, Lookin' to Get Out* (both 1982), *Once Upon a Time in America* (1984), *The Pope of Greenwich Village* (also 1984, one of his best performances, as "Bedbug Eddie"), *Back to School* (1986), *Last Exit to Brooklyn* (1989), *Betsy's Wedding* (1990), and *Excessive Force* (1993). He made an impressive Broadway debut in "Cuba and His Teddy Bear" and starred in the short-lived TV sitcom "Roomies" (1987).

YOUNG, (F. A.) FREDDIE. Cinematographer. *(b. Oct. 9, 1902, London.)* Renowned cameraman whose work has spanned more than five decades, from black-and-white productions to some of the most spectacular color epics ever filmed. At the ripe age of 15, Young began work in British films and became a cinematographer by the late 1920s. His early work includes *The Speckled Band* (1931), *Nell Gwyn* (1934), *Goodbye, Mr. Chips* (1939), and *49th Parallel* (1941), but he is more famous for the color photography of films like *Treasure Island* (1950), *Ivanhoe* (1952, Oscar-nominated), *The Inn of the Sixth Happiness* (1958), *Lord Jim* (1965), *Nicholas and Alexandra* (1971, Oscar-nominated), and collaborations on *Caesar and Cleopatra* (1946), *Mogambo* (1953), *Lust for Life* (1956), and *Invitation to the Dance* (1957). Young's greatest fame derived from his brilliant work on the David Lean epics *Lawrence of Arabia* (1962), *Doctor Zhivago* (1965), and *Ryan's Daughter* (1970), each of which earned him Oscars for Best Cinematography. His contributions to those films were integral to their success; as Stanley Kauffmann wrote in his review of *Lawrence:* "F. A. Young's camerawork is much more than the lavish photography I expected; it acts on the viewer to re-enforce the temper and tenor of the story, creating a mystique of its own through its vastness, variety, frightening grandeur." In 1993, Young received the American Society of Cinematographer's first International Award.

YOUNG, GIG. Actor. *(b. Nov. 4, 1913, St. Cloud, Minn., as Byron Elsworth Barr; d. Oct. 19, 1978.)* This debonair actor, easily identified by his sardonic onscreen manner (particularly in later years), took his professional name from the character he played in *The Gay Sisters* (1942), his first prominent movie role. As Byron Barr, he had worked at the Pasadena Playhouse be-

fore being signed by Warner Bros. in 1941; since another actor was already using that name, he adopted the Young moniker to avoid confusion. Although he initially seemed stiff, even dour, Young loosened up as he got more experience, and by the 1950s he'd become a capable actor, particularly adept at playing the wryly humorous bon vivants becoming popular in Hollywood's increasingly suggestive sex comedies. He was Oscar-nominated for performances in *Come Fill the Cup* (1951, fine dramatic work as an alcoholic) and *Teacher's Pet* (1958, a near-definitive part as the tipsy, engaging "other man"), and won the gold statuette for his splendid turn as the sleazy dance promoter in *They Shoot Horses, Don't They?* (1969). After so many years of playing the "other man" in lighthearted comedies, his potent performance made people sit up and take notice. He was equally good as the blissfully amoral father in the comedy *Lovers and Other Stangers* (1970).

He also starred in the delightful 1964–65 TV series "The Rogues." Sadly, Young failed to find happiness in his personal life: Married five times, he was thrice divorced and once widowed; he shot his last wife only a few weeks after their marriage, then turned the gun on himself. One of his other wives wrote a book about his tragic life, titled "Final Gig."

OTHER FILMS INCLUDE: 1941: *Sergeant York;* 1942: *The Male Animal;* 1943: *Air Force, Old Acquaintance;* 1947: *Escape Me Never;* 1948: *The Woman in White, The Three Musketeers, Wake of the Red Witch;* 1950: *Hunt the Man Down;* 1951: *Only the Valiant;* 1952: *Holiday for Sinners;* 1953: *The City That Never Sleeps, Arena, Torch Song;* 1954: *Young at Heart;* 1955: *The Desperate Hours;* 1957: *Desk Set;* 1958: *The Tunnel of Love;* 1959: *Ask Any Girl, The Story on Page One;* 1962: *That Touch of Mink, Kid Galahad;* 1963: *A Ticklish Affair, For Love or Money;* 1965: *Strange Bedfellows;* 1967: *The Shuttered Room;* 1974: *Bring Me the Head of Alfredo Garcia;* 1975: *The Hindenburg, The Killer Elite;* 1978: *The Game of Death.*

YOUNG, LORETTA. Actress. *(b. Jan. 6, 1913, Salt Lake City, as Gretchen Michaela Young.)* Radiantly beautiful leading lady of Hollywood's Golden Age, who kept her starring career alive with a long-running

TV series, "The Loretta Young Show" (1954–63), for which she won three Emmy Awards. Although she made her film debut at age three in *Sweet Kitty Bellairs*, Loretta—whose sisters Sally Blane and Polly Ann Young were also actresses—spent her childhood getting a convent-school education. At age 15, she decided to tackle show business head on and won a contract at First National (which merged with Warner Bros.), where she played doe-eyed ingenues for the next five years. She followed Warners production chief Darryl F. Zanuck first to his 20th Century Pictures in 1934.

She later had a dispute with Zanuck, who reportedly blackballed her. The only place she could work, at first, was Columbia Pictures, whose boss Harry Cohn didn't care about Zanuck's pronouncements. By the late 1940s she and the Fox chieftain made up and she returned to his studio for several successful films.

Never accused of being a great actress, Young did have great screen presence and that indefinable something known as star quality. In many ways, she gave livelier, more interesting performances in her "little" Warners films of the early 1930s than in her glossier star vehicles of later years—but by then, her loyal following expected a certain kind of entertainment from her and she never disappointed. She won an Academy Award for her performance as the immigrant who makes good in *The Farmer's Daughter* (1947), and was nominated again for her portrayal of a nun in *Come to the Stable* (1949). In retrospect, however, one of her most impressive films is Orson Welles' *The Stranger* (1946), in which she develops a growing wariness about her husband, played by Welles.

Young appeared with her three sisters in *The Story of Alexander Graham Bell* (1939). She was briefly married to actor Grant Withers; her second husband was producer Tom Lewis, with whom she supervised her long-running TV series.
OTHER FILMS INCLUDE: 1928: *Laugh, Clown, Laugh* (her first adult role, opposite Lon Chaney); 1929: *Forward Pass, The Show of Shows* (with sister Sally Blane); 1931: *The Devil to Pay, The Ruling Voice, Platinum Blonde* (top-billed in a Frank Capra film she did on loan to Columbia, even though the title applies to costar Jean Harlow); 1932: *The Hatchet Man, Life Begins, Play Girl, Taxi!*

(opposite James Cagney), *Week-end Marriage*; 1933: *Employees Entrance, Heroes for Sale, Grand Slam, Midnight Mary, Zoo in Budapest, The Life of Jimmy Dolan, Man's Castle*; 1934: *Caravan, House of Rothschild, Bulldog Drummond Strikes Back*; 1935: *Clive of India, Call of the Wild* (opposite Clark Gable), *The Crusades* (for director Cecil B. DeMille), *Shanghai*; 1936: *Ladies in Love, Private Number, Ramona*; 1937: *Cafe Metropole, Love Is News, Second Honeymoon, Wife, Doctor and Nurse*; 1938: *Four Men and a Prayer, Kentucky, Suez*; 1939: *Eternally Yours, Wife, Husband and Friend*; 1940: *The Doctor Takes a Wife, He Stayed for Breakfast*; 1941: *Lady From Cheyenne, Bedtime Story, The Men in Her Life*; 1942: *A Night to Remember*; 1943: *China*; 1944: *And Now Tomorrow, Ladies Courageous*; 1945: *Along Came Jones*; 1947: *The Bishop's Wife*; 1948: *The Accused, Rachel and the Stranger*; 1949: *Mother Is a Freshman*; 1950: *Key to the City*; 1951: *Cause for Alarm, Half Angel*; 1952: *Because of You, Paula*; 1953: *It Happens Every Thursday*; 1986: *Christmas Eve* (telefilm); 1989: *Lady in the Corner* (telefilm).

YOUNG, ROBERT. Actor. (b. Feb. 22, 1907, Chicago.) To many viewers, Robert Young is best known for his long-running TV series rather than for his many movies. He spent years bounding into America's living rooms as Jim Anderson, the cheerful insurance salesman in "Father Knows Best" (1954–62), then worried about our health as the kindly sawbones "Marcus Welby, M. D." (1969–76). An alumnus of the famed Pasadena Playhouse, the mild-mannered Young—whose vaguely bland handsomeness and generally placid manner made him a genial leading man but an even better secondary lead—debuted onscreen in *The Black Camel* (1931), an early Charlie Chan mystery. He was signed that same year by MGM, first appearing for the studio in *The Sin of Madelon Claudet*, opposite stage star Helen Hayes. He played support to MGM's top stars in such prestige pictures as *Tugboat Annie* and *Hell Below* (both 1933), and starred in programmers like *West Point of the Air* (1935). He was loaned to Darryl Zanuck's 20th Century Pictures to play opposite another Young, Loretta, in the lavish costume drama *House of Rothschild* (1934), and to Universal for James Whale's "Thin Man" knockoff, *Remember Last Night?* (1935).

In 1936 Young spent some time in England, starring opposite glamorous blonde Madeleine Carroll in Alfred Hitchcock's *Secret Agent* and dancing divinity Jessie Matthews in *It's Love Again,* two elaborate productions. Back in the States, though, Young slipped into the same groove: solid supporting roles in A's, cookie-cutter leads in unimportant B's. He more than held his own in *The Mortal Storm, Northwest Passage* (both 1940), and *H. M. Pulham, Esq.* (1941)—three of his very best performances—and bolstered *Joe Smith, American* and *A Journey for Margaret* (both 1942). He played the incredibly patient husband of childlike Dorothy McGuire in *Claudia* (1943), a surprise hit, and its 1946 sequel, *Claudia and David.* And he was surprisingly affecting as one of two misfits who find love in *The Enchanted Cottage* (1945, again with McGuire). His best film was *They Won't Believe Me* (1947), an intriguing *noir* that cast him as an errant husband who thinks about murdering his wife and then is arrested for the crime when she dies by accident; Young had previously essayed unsympathetic characters (infrequently), but never with the strength and assurance he displayed here. He was equally good in Elia Kazan's *Crossfire* (1947), as a police inspector.

Sitting Pretty (1948), a precursor of things to come, found Young as head of a household invaded by prissy Clifton Webb (playing the "Mr. Belvedere" character revived in the 1980s as a network sitcom). He abandoned feature films in 1954, concentrating on "Father Knows Best," for which he was Emmy-nominated four times (he won twice, in 1956 and 1957). He coproduced a fascinating if short-lived series, "Window on Main Street," in 1961; it focused on a writer who observed life from his small-town hotel room. Young won another Emmy as Marcus Welby, a characterization to which he returned in TV movies made in 1984 and 1988. Then, ostensibly retired, he was coaxed back before the cameras again for a perfect—and challenging—role, that of real-life Florida man Roswell Gilbert, who took his wife's life in order to spare her further pain, in the TV movie *Mercy or Murder?* (1987).

OTHER FILMS INCLUDE: 1932: *The Kid From Spain, Strange Interlude, The Wet Parade;* 1933: *Today We Live;* 1934: *Spitfire;* 1935: *Red Salute, The Bride Comes Home;* 1936: *The Bride Walks Out, Stowaway;* 1937: *The Bride Wore Red, The Emperor's Candlesticks, I Met Him in Paris, Navy Blue and Gold;* 1938: *Josette, Paradise for Three, Rich Man, Poor Girl, The Shining Hour, Three Comrades, The Toy Wife;* 1939: *Honolulu, Maisie;* 1940: *Dr. Kildare's Crisis;* 1941: *Western Union, Lady Be Good;* 1942: *Cairo;* 1943: *Sweet Rosie O'Grady;* 1944: *The Canterville Ghost;* 1945: *Those Endearing Young Charms;* 1946: *The Searching Wind;* 1949: *Adventure in Baltimore, That Forsyte Woman, Bride for Sale, And Baby Makes Three;* 1951: *Goodbye, My Fancy;* 1952: *The Half-Breed;* 1954: *The Secret of the Incas;* 1971: *Vanished* (telefilm); 1978: *Little Women* (telefilm).

YOUNG, ROBERT M. Director, producer, cinematographer. *(b. Nov. 22, 1924, New York City.)* Few filmmakers have straddled the worlds of independent and mainstream cinema as well—or as long—as this intelligent New York-based talent. His father was a film editor, and founded Du Art Film Laboratory. After serving in World War 2, Young studied English literature at Harvard University, and helped found the Harvard Film Society.

Hired to write, direct, and produce documentaries for NBC's prestigious "White Paper" series in the early 1960s, he and Harvard classmate Michael Roemer won a Peabody Award for "Cortile Cascino," though NBC found it too controversial to air. He and Roemer went on to cowrite and coproduce the powerful feature film *Nothing But a Man* (1964), which Roemer directed and Young photographed, the low-key comedy *The Plot Against Harry* (completed in 1969, but never shown until 1990), and *Faces of Israel* (1967), a PBS documentary.

Young's work as director includes a number of striking films dealing with "difficult" or unusual subjects: *Short Eyes* (1977), *Alambrista!* (1978, also screenplay, cinematography), *Rich Kids* (1979), *One-Trick Pony* (1980), *The Ballad of Gregorio Cortez* (1983, also screenplay), *Extremities, Saving Grace* (both 1986), *Dominick and Eugene* (1988), *Triumph of the Spirit* (1989), *Talent for the Game* (1991), and *Roosters* (1995). He also coproduced *American Me* (1992), which marked the directing debut of his longtime colleague, actor Edward James Olmos.

YOUNG, ROLAND. Actor. *(b. Nov. 11, 1887, London; d. June 5, 1953.)* He was movies' original Topper—and the sniveling Uriah Heep in *David Copperfield* (1935). He was *The Man Who Could Work Miracles* (1936), and Katharine Hepburn's Uncle Willie in *The Philadelphia Story* (1940). This architect's son was one of the screen's finest supporting players, who portrayed whimsical, suave, and eccentric characters during his long and successful career. He is probably best remembered as Thorne Smith's befuddled banker in *Topper* (1937, which earned him an Oscar nomination), *Topper Takes a Trip* (1938), and *Topper Returns* (1941). Trained at the Royal Academy of Dramatic Art, Young made his London stage debut in 1908, and his first Broadway appearance four years later. Electing to stay in America, he worked steadily in the theater, making his film debut in 1922 as Dr. Watson to John Barrymore's *Sherlock Holmes.* Young shines in *Madam Satan* (1930), *The Guardsman* (1931), *One Hour With You*, *This Is the Night* (both 1932), *His Double Life* (1933), *Ruggles of Red Gap* (1935), *King Solomon's Mines*, *Ali Baba Goes to Town* (both 1937), *The Young in Heart* (1938), *Stardust* (1940), *The Flame of New Orleans*, *Two-Faced Woman* (both 1941), *Tales of Manhattan* (1942), *Forever and a Day* (1943), *And Then There Were None* (1945), *The Great Lover* (1949), and *Let's Dance* (1950), among others. His last film was *That Man From Tangier* (1953). He also published a book of theatrical caricatures, "Actors and Others," in 1925.

YOUNG, SEAN. Actress. *(b. Nov. 20, 1959, Louisville, Ky.)* Attractive, brunette actress who receives more attention for her offscreen behavior than for her usually serviceable acting work. A former model and trained dancer, Young broke into movies with a small role in *Jane Austen in Manhattan* (1980). She was cute as an amiable MP officer in the Army comedy *Stripes* (1981) and enigmatically beautiful as a "replicant" in the 1982 sci-fi spectacular *Blade Runner.* Young's leading roles in *Young Doctors in Love* (1982) and

Baby ... Secret of the Lost Legend (1985), and appearances in *Dune* (1984) and *Wall Street* (1987, in which her part was cut back to nearly nothing) didn't do much for her career, but *No Way Out* (1987), in which she played a number of torrid love scenes opposite Kevin Costner, won her a lot of attention (not all of it wanted). In 1989 James Woods, who costarred with Young in the previous year's turgid cocaine-addiction melodrama *The Boost,* filed a harassment suit against her claiming she threatened him repeatedly after a terminated affair. Young traveled the talk-show circuit thereafter, on which various bizarre pronouncements made her a provocative guest.

Young showed herself capable of playing lighthearted, quirky comedy in *Cousins* (1989), then appeared in *Firebirds* (1990) and a pair of poorly received thrillers, *A Kiss Before Dying* and *Love Crimes,* in 1991. That same year she appeared on Joan Rivers' TV talk show in a homemade "Catwoman" costume to complain about losing that role in *Batman Returns* to Michelle Pfeiffer (although sources contended Young wasn't even considered). She joined an able comedy cast in the disastrous *Once Upon a Crime* (1992), and played a blondined femme fatale later that year in *Sketch Artist.* Recent credits include *Blue Ice* (1992), *Hold Me Thrill Me Kiss Me*, *Fatal Instinct* (both 1993), *Ace Ventura: Pet Detective*, *Even Cowgirls Get the Blues,* and *Airheads* (all 1994).

ZEFFIRELLI, FRANCO. Director. *(b. Feb. 12, 1923, Florence, Italy.)* Creator of visually ornate dramas, often based on classical sources and great music, Zeffirelli began his show business career as a theatrical designer and became an apprentice to film director Luchino Visconti in the late 1940s, working with him on such films as *La Terra trema* (1948), *Bellissima* (1951), and *Senso* (1954). Eventually Zeffirelli made his own name as a stage and opera director in London and New York. His film directing debut was the highly publicized (and handsomely mounted) production of *The Taming of the Shrew* (1967) starring Elizabeth Taylor and Richard Burton. The following year he made his best-known and best-loved film, *Romeo and Juliet* (1968), which earned him an Oscar nomination as Best Director—and a niche in film history for being the first director to cast two real teenagers to play Shakespeare's young lovers. His subsequent films have been an odd lot: *Brother Sun, Sister Moon* (1973), a poorly received biography of St. Francis, "Jesus of Nazareth" (1977 miniseries), an all-star Biblical tale produced for television, an appalling Hollywood remake of *The Champ* (1979), film version of the operas *La traviata* (1982) and *Otello* (1986), and a well-received visualization of *Hamlet* (1990) with Mel Gibson and Glenn Close. His 1988 musical biopic *Young Toscanini*, with C. Thomas Howell in the title role, was deemed unreleasable in this country. Zeffirelli remains active in the opera world, staging productions in Europe and the U.S.

ZEMECKIS, ROBERT. Director, screenwriter. (b. May 14, 1952, Chicago.) Successful director of commercial, mainstream Hollywood fare, who has helmed some of the biggest-grossing comedies of all time. Zemeckis attended the USC film school, where he met his eventual collaborator, Bob Gale. The two were lucky enough to find a supporter in Steven Spielberg, who served as executive producer for their first film, a tribute to Beatlemania called *I Wanna Hold Your Hand* (1978), which crystallized the frantic comedy style that's marked all of the duo's subsequent work. Although the film did modest business, Zemeckis and Gale impressed Spielberg enough to land them screenplay work on his overbloated flop, *1941* (1979). The pair's next picture, the underrated and savagely funny *Used Cars* (1980), attracted the attention of Michael Douglas, who signed Zemeckis to direct his 1984 comedy *Romancing the Stone.* The boffo business garnered by that picture was surpassed the next year, when Zemeckis and Gale turned out *Back to the Future,* another high-energy comedy (with souped-up special effects) that was the top-grossing film of 1985, and which earned Zemeckis and Gale an Oscar nomination for Best Screenplay. (He directed the 1989 and 1990 sequels as well; the downbeat Part 2 may have put off viewers from flocking to the delightful, Old West-set Part 3.) Zemeckis helmed the innovative live action/animated *Who Framed Roger Rabbit* (1988), a bravura technical accomplishment

that also served as an appropriate vehicle for the director's youthful enthusiasm. His similarly effects-laden *Death Becomes Her* (1992) was, however, a disappointment. He came back, however, with the tale of a simple man's journey through—and influence on—modern American history: *Forrest Gump* (1994) became one of the most popular films of all time and earned Zemeckis an Academy Award as Best Director. Between (usually exhausting) directing chores, Zemeckis has cowritten *Trespass,* executive produced *The Public Eye* (both 1992), and directed the pilot for a short-lived series he also cocreated and produced, "Johnny Bago" (1993). He has also served as one of the executive producers of the long-running cable-TV series "Tales From the Crypt" (1989–), and shared that responsibility for the 1994 feature-film version as well.

ZERBE, ANTHONY. Actor. (b. May 20, 1939, Long Beach, Calif.) This versatile supporting player, an Air Force veteran, studied at the Stella Adler Theatre Studio and appeared in regional theater and on Broadway before breaking into films in the 1960s. While he is sometimes cast as authority figures, his devilishly arched eyebrows and commanding voice have made him a natural for villainous roles, which include *Will Penny* (1968), *The Omega Man* (1971), *Who'll Stop the Rain* (1978), and *Opposing Force* (1986, which shows Zerbe at his evil best). He's also been memorable in *Cool Hand Luke* (1967), *The Laughing Policeman* (1973), *The Parallax View* (1974), *Rooster Cogburn* (1975), *The Turning Point* (1977), *The First Deadly Sin* (1980), *The Dead Zone* (1983), *Steel Dawn* (1987), *Listen to Me* (1989), and *License to Kill* (1990), to name a few. He won an Emmy for his work as Lt. K. C. Trench on the David Janssen crime series "Harry O" (1975–76), and played the boss of Pony Express recruits on the Western series "The Young Riders" (1989–92).

ZETTERLING, MAI. Actress, director. (b. May 24, 1925, Vasteras, Sweden; d. Mar. 17, 1994.) A beautiful blonde, Zetterling won her first major role at age 19, starring in *Torment* (1944), from a script by master of anxiety Ingmar Bergman. She subsequently made several films in Britain before coming a long way to America to play opposite Danny Kaye in the 1954 comedy *Knock on Wood.* While she had what it took to be groomed for stardom, she loathed Hollywood and hightailed it back to Europe immediately after finishing the picture. She performed in a number of British productions, including *Abandon Ship!* and *The Truth About Women* (both 1957), and *Only Two Can Play* (1962). In 1964 she made her directing debut with the very Swedish *Loving Couples,* a dour look at sex from the perspective of three expectant mothers. A second directorial effort, *Night Games* (1966), was based on her own novel and contained Bergmanesque scenes of characters so perverse and anxiety-ridden that their own depravity makes them vomit. (Get the idea?) In 1973 she directed "The Strongest" episode of the Olympics documentary *Visions of Eight.* In 1988 Zetterling made *Scrubbers,* a suitably bleak look at a girls' prison in England. She took up acting again in 1990, appearing that year in *The Witches* and *Hidden Agenda.*

ZIEFF, HOWARD. Director. *(b. Oct. 21, 1927, Chicago.)* Top-notch comedy director who began as a photographer in the advertising world and gained fame for helming numerous TV commercials (most notably, the Alka-Seltzer "Mama Mia, That's a Spicy Meatball" spot). Zieff made his feature directorial debut with *Slither* (1973), a very nutty chase film with James Caan, Peter Boyle, and many others chasing stolen money. Though a commercial flop, it was liked by critics, as was *Hearts of the West* (1975), a charming look at the making of B Westerns in 1930s Hollywood, which confirmed Zieff's gift for loose, subtle comedy and his genuine affection for offbeat characters. The less subtle *House Calls* (1978) was a hit, but *The Main Event* (1979), a labored reteaming of Barbra Streisand and Ryan O'Neal, was a major disappointment. *Private Benjamin* (1980) exploited Goldie Hawn's star power to the fullest, but *Unfaithfully Yours* (1984) paled beside Preston Sturges' original and *The Dream Team* (1989) missed the mark, despite a dream cast. *My Girl* (1991), the story of a spirited young girl, was a return to more gentle form for Zieff and popular enough for a 1994 sequel.

ZINNEMANN, FRED. Director. *(b. Apr. 29, 1907, Vienna.)* Genteel director who has never been popular with the auteurists, but has to his credit four Oscars and a number of classic films to assuage the pain. First intrigued with film as a young man, he worked in Germany with several other tyros (Billy Wilder, Robert Siodmak on the 1929 feature *People on Sunday),* then journeyed to Hollywood, where he found work as an extra in *All Quiet on the Western Front* (1930). Fascinated by the filmmaking process, Zinnemann apprenticed behind the cameras with documentary producer-director Robert Flaherty, and teamed with producer-writer Paul Strand to codirect a feature film, *The Wave* (1935), in Mexico with amateur actors. Back in Hollywood, he signed with MGM and directed countless shorts over the next few years, winning his first Oscar for *That Mothers Might Live* (1938). He graduated to features in 1942, turning out two crisp B mysteries, *Eyes in the Night* and *Kid Glove Killer* before getting his big break with *The Seventh Cross* (1944), a top-notch A picture starring Spencer Tracy, and his first hit.

Zinnemann's next few films included the less successful *Little Mr. Jim* and *My Brother Talks to Horses* (both 1946). He made his reputation with two superior efforts in 1949: *Act of Violence,* a taut thriller with Robert Ryan and Van Heflin, and *The Search,* a vivid drama of WW2 aftermath in Berlin filmed on location that drew on Zinnemann's skills as both documentarian and dramatist. The film marked Montgomery Clift's screen debut and earned Zinnemann his first Best Director Oscar nomination. *Teresa* (1951), like *The Search,* was a postwar love story spanning the gulf from Italy to the U.S. (He also directed *Benjy,* a fund-raising short for a Los Angeles hospital that was so moving it earned an Academy Award in 1951.) His collaboration with producer Stanley Kramer resulted in his best-known films: *The Men* (1950, which introduced Marlon Brando to moviegoers), *High Noon* (the famous "anti-Western" starring Gary Cooper, for which he snared his second Oscar nomination), *The Member of the*

Wedding (both 1952), and *From Here to Eternity* (1953, a passion-charged drama set in pre-WW2 Hawaii that won Zinnemann his first Oscar—and another for Best Picture).

Zinnemann's subsequent films—most of which he also produced—were varied in tone, yet all bore his trademark meticulousness and expert craftsmanship, whether a wide-open-spaces musical like *Oklahoma!* (1955) or a gritty little drug drama like *A Hatful of Rain* (1957). Next came *The Nun's Story* (1959, another Best Director nomination), *The Sundowners* (1960, Best Picture and Best Director nominations), *Behold a Pale Horse* (1964), and his career-climaxing *A Man for All Seasons* (1966), which won Oscars for Best Picture and Best Director. He's made only three films since, all superbly crafted: *The Day of the Jackal* (1973), *Julia* (1977, his final Best Director nomination), and *Five Days One Summer* (1982, which drew on his love of mountain climbing). He published an autobiography, "Fred Zinnemann on Cinema," in 1992.

ZSIGMOND, VILMOS. Cinematographer. *(b. June 16, 1930, Czeged, Hungary.)* Zsigmond began his career toiling in the industry's low-budget hinterlands, but was destined for A-list superstardom in the 1970s. He studied his craft at the Academy for Theater and Film Art in Budapest. Along with classmate (as well as future cinematographer) Laszlo Kovacs, he filmed footage of the 1956 Hungarian revolution, supposedly with a camera concealed in a shopping bag. Soon after, the pair left Hungary and arrived in Los Angeles, where they worked as lab technicians and still photographers and shot educational films. During the 1960s, credited as William Zsigmond, he paid his dues on various low-budget potboilers, among them *Living Between Two Worlds* (1963), *What's Up Front* (1964), *A Hot Summer Game* (1965), and *Hot Rod Action* (1969). He worked with directors James Landis on *The Sadist* (1963), *The Nasty Rabbit, Deadwood '76,* and *Rat Fink* (all 1965) and Al Adamson, on *Psycho a Go-Go!* (1965), *Five Bloody Graves* (1969), and *Horror of the Blood Monsters* (1970). Zsigmond was the cinematographer of Ib Melchior's *The Time Travelers*

(1964), on which his camera operator was Laszlo (then known as "Leslie") Kovacs; the duo shared the photography credit on a documentary, *Mondo Mod* (1967). He went solo on *The Name of the Game Is Kill* (1968), *The Monitors* (1969), and *Futz* (1969), where for the first time he was billed as Vilmos Zsigmond. His first important credit was Peter Fonda's *The Hired Hand* (1971). Since then he has worked on an all-star lineup of films directed by Scorsese, Spielberg, De Palma, Robert Altman, Michael Cimino, and Mark Rydell, among others. He is best known for his graceful camera movement and vibrant utilization of color. He has gone on to win one Academy Award, for *Close Encounters of the Third Kind* (1977), a collaboration, two nominations, for *The Deer Hunter* (1978) and *The River* (1984); and an Emmy, for *Stalin* (1992). In 1971, he competed against himself for a British Academy of Film and Television Arts' award with three of a possible four nominations (for *McCabe and Mrs. Miller, Images,* and *Deliverance);* he won the prize seven years later, for *The Deer Hunter.* Among his credits are *Red Sky at Morning* (1970); *Cinderella Liberty, The Long Goodbye, Scarecrow* (all 1973); *The Sugarland Express* (1974); *Obsession* (1976); *The Last Waltz* (1978); *The Rose, Winter Kills* (both 1979); *Blow Out* (1981); *The Border* (1982); *Table for Five* (1983); *No Small Affair* (1984); *The Witches of Eastwick* (1987); *Fat Man and Little Boy* (1989); *The Two Jakes* (1990); *Sliver* (1993); *Intersection, Maverick,* and *The Crossing Guard* (all 1994). He appeared onscreen in the documentary *Visions of Light: The Art of Cinematography* (1993), and made his directorial debut with *The Long Shadow* (1992). Zsigmond also had the bad luck to be the director of photography on a pair of Hollywood's most notorious fiascos: Cimino's *Heaven's Gate* (1980) and De Palma's *The Bonfire of the Vanities* (1990).

ZUCCO, GEORGE. Actor. *(b. Jan. 11, 1886, Manchester, England; d. May 27, 1960.)* With decades of stage experience behind him (including a long run in London's "Journey's End" and a prestigious Broadway run as Disraeli opposite Helen Hayes in "Victoria Regina"), Zucco found no trouble winning character parts in films. He appeared in almost one hundred feature films, from top-drawer productions like *Conquest* (1937), *Marie Antoinette* (1938), and *The Hunchback of Notre Dame* (1939) to the rankest schlock, like *The Mad Monster* (1942) and *Dead Men Walk* (1943, which at least gave him the novelty of a dual role). He played all sorts of characters, but is best remembered for his arch-villainy. He was a superb Prof. Moriarty in *The Adventures of Sherlock Holmes* (1939); then-critic Graham Greene said he had "an air of only having just missed the best clubs." He even played his villainy for laughs with Bob Hope in *The Cat and the Canary* (1939) and *My Favorite Blonde* (1942). Horror buffs fondly recall his work as the High Priest of Karnak in the Universal potboilers *The Mummy's Hand* (1940), *The Mummy's Tomb* (1942), and *The Mummy's Ghost* (1944). Whatever the assignment, Zucco made it count; he never gave a lackluster performance, even in the cheesiest horror movies. He may have chewed the scenery, but he never allowed condescension to creep into his portrayals.

OTHER FILMS INCLUDE: 1933: *The Good Companions;* 1936: *The Man Who Could Work Miracles, After the Thin Man;* 1937: *Saratoga, The Firefly, Rosalie;* 1938: *Suez, Charlie Chan in Honolulu;* 1939: *Arrest Bulldog Drummond;* 1940: *Arise, My Love;* 1941: *The Monster and the Girl, A Woman's Face, Ellery Queen and the Murder Ring;* 1942: *The Black Swan;* 1944: *House of Frankenstein;* 1945: *Fog Island, Sudan, Having Wonderful Crime;* 1947: *Moss Rose, Lured, Captain From Castile;* 1948: *Tarzan and the Mermaids, The Pirate, Joan of Arc;* 1949: *The Barkleys of Broadway, Madame Bovary;* 1951: *David and Bathsheba.*

ZUNIGA, DAPHNE. Actress. *(b. Oct 28, 1962, San Francisco.)* Appealing brunette whose distinctive face conveys maturity and youthful sultriness equally well. Her first parts came in *The Dorm That Dripped Blood* (1981), *The Initiation* (1983), and *VisionQuest* (1985). Then Rob Reiner cast her as the straitlaced collegiate won over by John Cusack in the better-than-average teen comedy *The Sure Thing* (1985). She's been good in her subsequent film roles, but the films themselves haven't measured up: *Modern Girls* (1986), Mel Brooks' *Spaceballs* (1987), which cast her as a Druish princess, *Last Rites* (1988), *Gross Anatomy, The Fly II,* and *Staying Together* (all 1989), the last a little-seen comedy-drama directed by Lee Grant. In 1992 she won a berth on the hit TV series "Melrose Place."